The INTERNATIONAL STANDARD BIBLE ENCYCLOPEDIA

The INTERNATIONAL STANDARD BIBLE ENCYCLOPEDIA

VOLUME ONE • A-D

GENERAL EDITOR

GEOFFREY W. BROMILEY
Church History and Doctrine

ASSOCIATE EDITORS

EVERETT F. HARRISON
New Testament

ROLAND K. HARRISON
Old Testament

WILLIAM SANFORD LASOR
Archeology

PROJECT EDITOR

EDGAR W. SMITH, JR.

FULLY REVISED • ILLUSTRATED • IN FOUR VOLUMES

WILLIAM B. EERDMANS PUBLISHING COMPANY
GRAND RAPIDS, MICHIGAN

Printed in the United States of America.

Publication History:

First published 1915; copyright 1915 by the Howard-Severance Company, Chicago. New and revised edition, edited by Melvin Grove Kyle, copyright 1929 by the Howard-Severance Company. Copyright renewed, 1956, by Wm. B. Eerdmans Publishing Company. Completely revised and reset.
Volume I: first printing, 1979
second printing, 1980

Library of Congress Cataloging in Publication Data

Main entry under title:

International standard Bible encyclopedia.

1. Bible—Dictionaries. I. Bromiley, Geoffrey William
BS440.16 1979 220.3 79-12280
ISBN 0-8028-8161-0
ISBN 0-8028-8160-2 (set)

Offset Lithography by Cushing-Malloy, Inc., Ann Arbor.
Bound at Eerdmans Printing Company, Grand Rapids.

PREFACE

The International Standard Bible Encyclopedia, popularly known as *ISBE,* has served the Church well over the past generations. Even in its revised form, however, it has naturally become dated as new work has been done in the text of Scripture and new light has been shed by continuing, and in some cases exciting, archeological discoveries. If not without some trepidation, then, the decision has been made to issue a fresh and more drastic revision of the venerable and still by no means valueless encyclopedia.

The situation in which the new edition has been prepared resembles that of the preparation of the first edition of 1915. The original preface speaks of a plethora of biblical dictionaries at that time, called forth by the remarkable advances and changes in biblical studies. The new *ISBE* comes on the scene when dictionaries again abound, and one can only repeat the words of our predecessors when they say that "it is in no spirit of rivalry . . . that the present Encyclopaedia is produced" but to fulfil what is seen to be the distinctive purpose of serving both the more advanced student and yet also "the average pastor and Bible student."

Friends of the project, and many contributors to it, will realize that this new edition has been in the making for an unusually protracted period. There are two main reasons for the delay. The first relates to the editorial team. All three of the original Associate Editors were lost to us at a formative stage in the work: Professor N. B. Stonehouse of Westminster Theological Seminary, Philadelphia, through death; Professor J. L. Kelso of Pittsburgh Theological Seminary, through sickness; and Professor J. G. S. S. Thomson of Glasgow, through the pressure of other duties. Their places have been ably filled by Professors E. F. Harrison and W. S. LaSor of Fuller Theological Seminary, Pasadena, and Professor R. K. Harrison of Wycliffe College, Toronto, but not without some unavoidable dislocation. On the managerial side, too, the death of Calvin Bulthuis, who played so large a role in the initial planning, proved to be another serious blow, and his immediate successor, John DeHoog, was able to stay with the project for only a relatively brief span. Fortunately the third project editor, Dr. E. W. Smith, has remained long enough to see the revision through to publication. The progress even at this rate would have been impossible without the diligent and intelligent contributions of Editorial Associate Allen C. Myers; Editorial Assistants Nola J. Opperwall and Dr. Ralph W. Vunderink; Illustration, Design, and Production Coordinator Joel D. Beversluis; and Typographer-Typesetter Donald M. Prus.

Changes in the scope of the revision provided the second main reason for the delay of publication. In view of the high esteem in which *ISBE* has been held, it was felt at first that the bulk of the existing material should be retained in its original format. A good deal of work was done on that premise. Increasingly it became obvious that with the pace and magnitude of biblical and archeological changes, along with the rapid shifts in the political, geographical, and social life of the Near East, more would have to be done, so that a call went out for more articles and contributors. Eventually the editors and publishers were forced to acknowledge, however reluctantly, that a thorough updating of both matter and format constituted the only logical course, so that now, although some of the most durable of the original material remains, the revision has become to all intents and purposes a new, or at least a completely reconstructed, encyclopedia. In this regard the delay has finally been an advantage, for if the work had been rapidly completed according to the original plan, much of it would already be in need of a new updating and all of it would have a decidedly old-fashioned look.

It should be emphasized that, in spite of the necessary changes, *ISBE* has by no means lost its identity. Many important features have in fact been carefully retained. To begin with, the new *ISBE* has aimed to be as consciously international as the old. If all the editors reside in North America, the General Editor and one of the Associate Editors come from Britain, and articles have been sought from scholars in many lands. As in the original *ISBE,* interdenominationalism has been practiced as well as internationalism. Coincidentally, the General Editor and three Associate Editors consist of two Anglicans and two Presbyterians, but contributors from a wide variety of churches combine to make this new edition a truly ecumenical enterprise. Along these lines, separate articles have again been included to represent different views on such matters as church polity and baptism.

Furthermore, great care has been taken to maintain what the preface of the first edition described as the attitude of "a reasonable conservatism." Freedom has naturally been allowed to individual contributors to express their views on debatable matters. At some points divergent approaches may thus be found. A hearing is also given to hypotheses and theories which cannot finally be adopted. Nevertheless, the general "attitude of mind and heart" is still one "which reverently accepts a true revelation of God in the history of Israel and in Christ." Indeed, while the high level of biblical scholarship has been retained, some of the unnecessarily mediating views of the first contributors have been eliminated, so that the new edition is, we believe, at once more scholarly and more conservative than its predecessor. This demonstrates the change from an earlier period of sharp confrontation between "criticism" and "faith" to one when the possibility grasped by the original editors has been more fully realized and "reverent criticism" is making a constructive contribution to faith.

As the first *ISBE* aimed at comprehensiveness, its successor has done the same. In this respect the original articles have served as a useful guide in both selection and execution. Some of them have, of course, been changed in length. Usually, although not uniformly, the change has taken the form of shortening to make way for the new material provided by more recent discoveries and developments. All the same, the principle has not changed. The editors have again sought the "ample and minute" treatment of "History . . ., Ethnology, Geography, Topography, Biography, Arts and Crafts, Manners and Customs," etc. which their predecessors claimed. If there has been one main innovation, it lies in the field of dogmatic history. Accounts of the main developments of thought on such central matters as Christology, election, and inspiration have been added. If more is offered here than a biblical encyclopedia strictly demands, we believe that this added feature should be of help and value to many readers.

It might be noted that, in order to maintain continuity with the past, many articles have been preserved in emended form and a few particularly significant ones have been preserved virtually unchanged. To the latter group belong especially the article on the Bible by James Orr, General Editor of the first edition, and that on inspiration by B. B. Warfield. If in Orr's article the section on the literary origin and growth of the Old and New Testaments needs revision, readers may be referred to the entries under the individual books and still profit from Orr's article, as from that of Warfield, as an evangelical statement of the early 20th century. That Orr and Warfield differed in the nuances of biblical understanding, yet did not see in this a reason for breaking evangelical unity, gives additional value to their representative articles.

Having spoken of the general continuity between the editions, we may speak more briefly of the detailed discontinuity. In one way the greatest single change is the elimination of most of the indexes. Indexes are obviously useful, but in alphabetically arranged dictionaries and encyclopedias they are obviously not essential. Their retention would have added disproportionately to the expense and price of the series. It is mainly for this reason that they have been deleted.

Of a different order, but possibly even more significant in its own way, is the adoption of the RSV instead of the ASV as the approved English rendering of the Bible. Naturally, an iron rule has not been imposed here. Variants are provided where useful and appropriate. Words from the AV or ASV which have been dropped from the RSV are still listed. It seems, however, that the RSV has now sufficiently established itself, especially in the scholarly world, to justify its general adoption.

Mention need hardly be made of the wholesale replacement of the older maps and illustrations. Even a cursory glance at the earlier editions will show the need for the radical updating which has been done.

Lesser but not unimportant changes have been made in such matters as abbreviations, pronunciations, and schemes of transliteration. The changes here are not just for the sake of change but to bring *ISBE* into line with generally accepted, although not, of course, definitively established practice in these areas. Details of the adopted schemes will be found in the pages that follow.

Superficially the old *ISBE* might seem to have been changed beyond recognition by these alterations and updatings. Readers will quickly see, however, that this is not so, for the material continuity, represented by the listings, far outweighs the formal discontinuity. The same fulness, authority, and accessibility have been sought in the new *ISBE* as in the old. Every effort has again been made to produce an encyclopedia that can meet the "exacting requirements" of teachers, students, pastors, and "all others who desire to be familiar with the Holy Scriptures." We trust that the new *ISBE* will have the same enduring value and engender the same enduring affection as the old. Above all, however, we trust that it may contribute to a better knowledge, understanding, and love of holy Scripture and thereby bring glory to God and edification to His people, thus fulfilling, in some measure at least, the service which it is our Christian privilege to render.

Pasadena, California
Trinity 1977

GEOFFREY W. BROMILEY
General Editor

Introduction

I. Purpose and Scope.–The purpose of this encyclopedia is to define, identify, and explain terms and topics that are of interest for those who study the Bible. Thus it is like the 1915 *ISBE* in combining the defining function of a dictionary with the encyclopedia's presentation of more comprehensive information, summarizing the state of knowledge about each of its topics and leading the reader to further sources of information and insight.

The entries are of several types. Every name of a person or place mentioned in the Bible has an entry here. Often a person is mentioned only once in the Bible, and the little that can be said about him or her will take only a few lines. Yet it may be helpful simply to know that a passage in question has the only mention of this person, or that the same name in another part of the Bible does refer to a different person. Other persons, however, are more frequently mentioned and have more importance in the biblical story of salvation. In such cases the articles about them are much longer, and may have to gather information from widely scattered parts of the Bible (or even from sources outside the Bible) and summarize the story of that person's life and meaning.

The same is generally true of the names of places. Some remain unidentified, while others have long been known and have been studied by archeological investigation. Some are of little importance, while others played significant roles in the story of God's redemption of His people. Generally, the length of the article reflects the relative importance. But sometimes a site receives little space because little is (yet) known about it, while a site of lesser importance may receive longer discussion because of division of scholarly opinion about it, or because archeological study of it gives us information about other sites or about passages in the Bible which do not even mention it. The article on Debir, for example, is longer than its relative importance in the Bible might warrant, because this article includes the several sides of a scholarly debate about its location and identification.

The reader will also find articles on all other terms in the Bible that have theological or ethical meaning, and on expressions that would be puzzling or unclear to the average reader. Thus *ISBE* is an exegetical tool, providing brief discussion of problem texts under the English keywords and guiding the exegete to further information in other scholarly resources.

The scope of this work also includes articles on the Bible itself, and on the transmission (e.g., text and versions), study (e.g., concordances, commentaries, Bible dictionaries), and interpretation (e.g., biblical theology) of the Bible. The sources of our knowledge about the background of the Bible have seen a steady increase as the result both of systematic pursuit of information, as in archeology, and of accidental discoveries, as of the Dead Sea Scrolls; that increase is reflected here in new articles and longer articles on the subjects that deal with the background of the Bible. This encyclopedia also goes further than others in tracing the development of some of the doctrines (e.g., about the Holy Spirit) and practices (e.g., baptism) that are based on biblical teachings.

The treatment of significant names and terms includes those from the writings of the Apocrypha. Even for those who do not accept these writings as canonical, they form an important part of the background of the New Testament, illustrating the development of some Old Testament themes and the introduction of some new ones during the intertestamental period.

Although the titles of articles on biblical terms normally follow the readings of the RSV, the distinctive readings of the AV and the NEB are included, usually as cross-reference entries to the articles that use the RSV forms. This makes the encyclopedia more readily accessible to a wider range of readers.

II. Arrangement.–Articles are arranged alphabetically, according to the following rules: In titles that have several words, the first word receives primary consideration, so that, e.g., **BAPTISM OF FIRE** precedes **BAPTISMAL REGENERATION** and **BIRTH, VIRGIN** precedes **BIRTHDAY**. All the words of the title, including articles, are alphabetized, so that **ACTS OF SOLOMON** precedes **ACTS OF THE APOSTLES**. A hyphenated word is alphabetized as a single word, so that the sequence would be **BEN-**

AMMI then **BENCH** then **BEN-DEKER,** and **BITTER WATER** before **BITTER-APPLES.** Apostrophes and commas are not considered, so that **BIRDS OF PREY** precedes **BIRDS, UNCLEAN, CITY, GOLDEN** precedes **CITY OF CHAOS,** and **AARONITES** precedes **AARON'S ROD.**

In a few cases, however, sensible presentation of material calls for exceptions to these rules. These will occur most often in the cases of articles on subjects from Old Testament perspective that precede articles on the same subject from the New Testament perspective. Thus **CANON OF THE OT** precedes **CANON OF THE NT.**

If a proper name is used for more than one person or place, the article for that name is divided accordingly, with a boldface number denoting each subject. Example:

AGAG ā'gag [Heb. *ʾ^{a}gag*].

1. The name or title of an Amalekite king mentioned by Balaam (Num. 24:7).

2. Another Amalekite king defeated by Saul but spared

If the same word is used for both a person and a place, usually the two subjects are treated in separate articles, the article on the person preceding that on the place (or object).

III. Format and Features.–The basic format has been devised to provide a maximum amount of information in compact form. Different subjects sometimes require different forms of presentation of information about them. Thus, not all of the articles have the same pattern or all of the following elements. Most of them, however, have a heading which, after the title, includes pronunciation, etymology, and variant renderings.

Sample article openings:

ABADDON ə-bad'ən [Heb. *ʾ^{a}ḇaddôn*–'(place of) destruction'; Gk. *Abaddōn*]; NEB also DESTRUCTION. In the OT, a place name for the realm of the dead. In three in-

ALABASTER [Heb. *šēš*] (Cant. 5:15); AV, NEB, MARBLE; **ALABASTER JAR** (Mt. 26:7; Mk. 14:3); **FLASK** (Lk. 7:37) [Gk. *alábastron*]; AV "alabaster box"; NEB "small bottle," "small flask." In modern mineralogy

ABIASAPH ə-bī'ə-saf, ab-i-ā'saf [Heb. *ʾ^{a}ḇîʾāsāp̄*–'my father has gathered'] (Ex. 6:24); **EBIASAPH** [Heb. *ʾeḇyāsāp̄*] (1 Ch. 6:23, 37 [MT 8, 22]; 9:19). A descendant of Kohath the son of Levi. The list in Exodus terminates

A. Title. The title of the article, usually the form of a word found in the RSV, is printed in boldface capital letters. Sometimes an article discusses several related terms. Even when these are not grouped together at the beginning of the first line, they can be easily identified by the boldface capital letters. In the second example above, the article discusses three related terms that the RSV translates as "alabaster," "alabaster jar," and "flask."

B. Pronunciation. All proper names and many uncommon English words have been provided with pronunciations. As can be seen in the first example above, the pronunciation follows the title without intervening punctuation. The reader will find the key to pronunciations inside the back cover of each volume.

It is impossible to say what is "correct" pronunciation of many biblical terms, especially of names from the Old Testament, for the forms in which they have come to us in English are the results of passage through several languages with their own distinctive patterns of pronunciation. Some of these words are used so often that certain pronunciations have become well established and familiar. In such cases, those pronunciations are given here. Often, however, uncertainty is indicated by the several forms of pronunciations that have been provided by self-pronouncing Bibles, concordances, and other dictionaries and encyclopedias. In these cases one or two of the pronunciations that seem best established have been used, with some preference given to a pronunciation that more closely resembles that of the original language. Every pronunciation provided here has been judged as acceptable by the four editors. Thus it can be used with confidence even though a definitely "correct" pronunciation may not exist.

C. Original Term. In brackets, the original Hebrew, Aramaic, or Greek terms are given in transliterated form, according to the scheme printed inside the back cover of each volume. Although the transliterations may be slightly inconvenient to the scholar, they have been used so that those who do not know the original languages of the Bible may yet have the words in some form that they can pronounce to themselves and recognize in further discussion in the article.

Cognate terms from other languages are included if they are considered helpful in understanding the meaning of the term used in the original language. A Greek term added here for a word that occurs only in the Old Testament indicates the Septuagint (LXX) translation of the Hebrew (or Aramaic) term.

The literal English meaning of a name, in single quotation marks, following a dash, is given when it is known and of interest. Thus, in the first example above, the meaning of Hebrew *ʾ^{a}ḇaddôn* is "[place of] destruction."

The Hebrew or Greek words listed in this section do not, of course, always have the same meaning as the word(s) of the article title, but are the words that are translated by these English words in certain passages. This fact is sometimes, but not always, indicated by the translation in single quotation marks.

D. Variant Renderings. Variant renderings from other English versions — especially the AV and NEB — follow the citations of original words. These renderings are usually given in lightface capital letters, but lowercase letters in double quotation marks are used if the rendering is more interpretative or based on a different understanding of the term or text in the original language. Thus the reader can see some of the other translations that have been given to a particular term.

In the first example, "NEB also DESTRUCTION"

means that the terms translated "Abaddon" in the RSV are sometimes translated "destruction" and sometimes "Abaddon" in the NEB.

The second example shows that the Hebrew term *šēš* in Cant. 5:15 is translated "marble" by both the AV and the NEB.

E. Biblical References. Unless the number of them makes it impractical, all uses of a word in the RSV are cited, either in the heading (following either the original-language term or one of the variant renderings) or in the body of the article. Even when uses of a word in the RSV are too frequent for a complete listing, every use that is likely to puzzle a Bible reader is mentioned in the article.

Variants in the chapter and verse numbering of the Hebrew Bible according to the Masoretic text are indicated by the use of "MT" in parentheses following the reference according to the English Bible. In the third example above, the bracketed notation "MT 8, 22" means that the passages mentioning Ebiasaph are 1 Ch. 6:8 and 1 Ch. 6:22 in the Hebrew Bible.

F. Definition. The preceding material is closed with a period, and is usually followed by a definition or identification unless the title word is commonly understood in English.

G. Abbreviations. As is evident from the sample headings above, the name of a book of the Bible is usually abbreviated (unless the reference is to a whole book rather than a specific passage). In order to provide information in compact form, these and many other abbreviations are used in the headings, bodies of the articles, and bibliographies. The meanings of these abbreviations are found in four groups on pages xix-xxv: General; Publications; Ancient Authors and Documents; Biblical and Extrabiblical Literature. Whenever the meaning of an abbreviation is a technical term, a cross reference to a pertinent article in this encyclopedia has been added. Thus the abbreviation J is explained as a symbol for Yahwist, and a cross reference to subsection II.D.4 of the **CRITICISM** article has been added. In the case of the abbreviation MT, the meaning has a cross reference to the article **TEXT AND MSS OF THE OT.** (The form for cross references is discussed below in section *I.*)

H. Outline. For convenience of reference, every major article has been subdivided, with divisions numbered according to the sequence ***I.***, *A.*, *1.*, *a.* Every article of more than two thousand words has a complete outline at or near its beginning. A few articles, e.g., **BAPTISM**, have major divisions that are indicated by centered titles in capitals and small capitals. As mentioned above in ***II. Arrangement***, proper names that refer to more than one person or place are designated separately by boldface arabic numbers.

I. Cross References. These have been used throughout this encyclopedia in order to lead the reader to other articles in which a particular subject, or material related to it, is discussed. A cross reference to an article is indicated by the use of capitals and small capitals for its title, often following italicized "see" or "see also."

One common kind of cross reference is in the form of a short entry whose subject is entirely subsumed under another article. This form is used especially for distinctive words of the AV or NEB that are treated under the RSV form of that word. It is also used to refer to a more comprehensive article that treats similar subjects together. Examples:

AALAR ā'a-lär. *See* IMMER **3.**

The material following the boldface number **3** in the **IMMER** article will show that Aalar is the AV form of a name used in 1 Esd. 5:36 for a person who has now been identified with the Immer of Ezra 2:59 and Neh. 7:61.

BELT. *See* GARMENTS.

This is an example of a reference to a more comprehensive article that includes several similar subjects under one title.

The other kind of cross reference occurs within or at the end of an article, to indicate that more information on a subject may be found in another article. The cross reference usually follows the term, sentence, paragraph, section, or whole article for which the other article (or part of it) is pertinent. Example:

pending on the location. The barley harvest was a well-marked season of the year (*see* AGRICULTURE III.A; HARVEST), and the barleycorn was a familiar measure of

This example, from the **BARLEY** article, shows a reference to section III.A of the **AGRICULTURE** article and to the **HARVEST** article.

ABDEEL ab'də-el [Heb. *ʿaḇdeʾēl*–'servant of God']. The father of SHELEMIAH (Jer. 36:26).

This example shows how a cross reference may be indicated by capitals and small capitals alone, without interrupting the flow of thought by use of *see* or *see also.*

The use of capitals and small capitals in this encyclopedia almost always indicates a cross reference. (The only exceptions are the titles of major divisions of a few articles, as described above in section *H. Outline.*) Of course, all biblical names and most other biblical terms are treated in this encyclopedia, but the printing of a term in capitals and small capitals indicates that the article thus designated contains information that will help the understanding of the article in which the reference is found.

J. Bibliography. Wherever it is useful, a bibliography has been provided to enable the reader to continue research beyond this encyclopedia. *ISBE* bibliographies do not aim to be exhaustive but rather to include the best and most accessible works on a given subject. The order followed in the bibliographies is usually alphabetical, but may be chronological, according to subject matter, or from the more general to the more specific. For longer bibliographies, outlines (corresponding to the outlines of their articles whenever possible) are used. A reference to a single work is indicated by the word "See" in regular type at the end of the article.

K. Authorship. Unless it has fewer than one hundred words, or is merely a compilation of information without results of scholarly research or opinion, an article has the initials and last name of its contributor(s) at the end. The full names and identifications of the contributors are found in the list on pages xi-xviii. Short articles written by the General Editor, an Associate Editor, or a member of the publisher's editorial staff are signed only with initials.

When an article from the 1915 *ISBE* has been used, in whole or in part, in this revision, the original author's name is included. In the list of contributors, an asterisk after the name indicates a contributor to the 1915 *ISBE*.

Some articles, especially those containing material from the 1915 *ISBE,* have names of two (rarely three) contributors. Where these persons made approximately equal contributions to the article, the names are on the same line, while a lesser contribution is indicated by a name placed beneath another; but the name of a contributor to the 1915 *ISBE* always appears first, regardless of the proportion of his material used in the revision of the article.

Sometimes (e.g., in **CONVERSION**) the name of an author will follow the specific section for which he was responsible, in order to distinguish his contribution from the rest of the article. The very rare editorial addition of more than several lines is enclosed in brackets, with the editor's initials at the end (e.g., in J. Orr's **BIBLE** article, IV.B.1.a).

IV. Illustrative Material. Since illustrations are so valuable as aids to understanding, a substantial amount of space in this encyclopedia has been devoted to them. Over 275 photographs and drawings have been used in the first volume alone. It was necessary to use museum photographs, perhaps familiar to some readers, for certain objects that ought to be illustrated in any work of this kind. The emphasis, however, has been on obtaining new photographs, many of them taken by scholars whose research is related to the subjects of the photographs. Each volume also has a section of color photographs, to which references are made (e.g., *see* Plate 4) in appropriate articles.

Twenty-five color maps appear at the end of the first volume. From the many maps available for the different periods and areas of the biblical world, these were selected as most fitting for a biblical reference work that is very comprehensive yet unable to present the detail that is found in a Bible atlas. After careful consideration of several possibilities, Hammond maps were chosen because they combine accuracy and awareness of current biblical scholarship with attractive and clear presentation of the topographical features. An index (pages 1001-1006) facilitates the use of these maps.

Many outline maps accompany articles on cities or areas. These have been done very simply, with a minimum of geographical features. Their purpose is to give the reader a general idea of the location of a site or area so that better use can be made of the color map section, with its topographical details and later geographical contexts.

THE PUBLISHERS

CONTRIBUTORS†

AHARONI, YOHANAN,
Late Chairman of the Department of Archaeology, Tel Aviv University, Israel.

ALLEN, GEORGE H.*
Ph.D., Editor of the *Forum Conche,* or *Fuero De Cuenca,* the Mediaeval Charter and By-laws of the City of Cuenca, Spain.

ARCHER, GLEASON L., JR.
B.A., B.D., A.M., Ph.D., LL.B., Professor of Old Testament and Semitic Languages, Trinity Evangelical Divinity School, Deerfield, Illinois.

ARMERDING, CARL EDWIN
A.B., B.D., M.A., Ph.D., Associate Professor of Old Testament, Regent College, Vancouver, British Columbia, Canada.

ARMSTRONG, WILLIAM P.*
D.D., Professor of New Testament Literature and Exegesis, Princeton Theological Seminary, Princeton, New Jersey.

ASHLEY, TIMM R.
B.A., M.A., Ph.D., Senior Pastor, Aurora Community Baptist Church, Aurora, Colorado.

AUNE, DAVID E.
B.A., M.A., M.A., Ph.D., Professor of Religion, Saint Xavier College, Chicago, Illinois.

BALCHIN, JOHN A.
M.A., B.D., Pastor, First Presbyterian Church, Papakura, New Zealand.

BANDSTRA, BARRY L.
B.A., B.D., Graduate Studies at Yale University.

BANKS, EDGAR J.*
Ph.D., Professor of Ancient History in Robert College, Constantinople, Turkey, and Field Director of the Babylonian Expedition of the University of Chicago.

BASON, ROBERT E. W.
B.A., B.D., President, Charitable Funding Services, Inc., Santa Barbara, California.

BASS, CLARENCE B.
B.A., M.A., Ph.D., Professor of Theology and Ethics, Bethel Seminary, St. Paul, Minnesota.

BEECHER, WILLIS JUDSON*
M.A., D.D., Professor of Hebrew Language and Literature, Auburn Theological Seminary, Auburn, New York.

BERRY, GEORGE RICKER*
D.D., Ph.D., Professor of Semitic Languages, Colgate University, Hamilton, New York.

BIRKEY, ARLAN J.
A.B., M.Div., Assistant Professor of Greek and Bible, Fort Wayne Bible College, Fort Wayne, Indiana.

BOWMAN, JOHN
Ph.D., Professor of Middle Eastern Studies, University of Melbourne, Australia.

BOYD, JAMES OSCAR*
Ph.D., D.D., Assistant Professor of Oriental and Old Testament Literature, Princeton Theological Seminary, Princeton, New Jersey.

BRESLICH, ARTHUR LOUIS*
B.D., Ph.D., President of Baldwin-Wallace College and Nast Theological Seminary, Berea, Ohio.

BROMILEY, GEOFFREY W.
M.A., Ph.D., Professor of Church History and Historical Theology, Fuller Theological Seminary, Pasadena, California.

BRUCE, FREDERICK FYVIE
M.A., D.D., F.B.A., Rylands Professor of Biblical Criticism and Exegesis, University of Manchester, England.

BUEHLER, WILLIAM W.
B.S., B.D., D.Th., Professor of Biblical Studies, Barrington College, Rhode Island.

BURDICK, DONALD W.
A.B., B.D., Th.M., Th.D., Professor of New Testament, Conservative Baptist Theological Seminary, Denver, Colorado.

BURKE, DAVID G.
A.B., B.D., Th.M., Ph.D., Lutheran Campus Pastor, Rutgers University, New Jersey.

BUSH, FREDERICK W.
B.A., M.Div., Th.M., M.A., Ph.D., Assistant Professor of Old Testament, Fuller Theological Seminary, Pasadena, California.

CALDECOTT, W. SHAW*
M.R.A.S., Minister of the Wesleyan Conferences of Great Britain and South Africa.

CALDER, WILLIAM M.*
M.A., LL.D., Professor of Greek and Lecturer in Christian Epigraphy in the University of Manchester, England.

†An asterisk (*) indicates a contributor to the 1915/1929 *ISBE* whose work has been retained with editorial changes.

CONTRIBUTORS

CALL, MERLIN W.
A.B., J.D., Vice-President, Tuttle & Taylor, Inc., Los Angeles, California.

CHRISTIANS, CLIFFORD G.
A.B., B.D., Th.M., M.A., Ph.D., Research Assistant Professor of Communications, University of Illinois at Urbana-Champaign.

CLEMONS, JAMES T.
A.B., B.D., Ph.D., Professor of New Testament, Wesley Theological Seminary, Washington, D.C.

CLINES, DAVID J. A.
B.A., M.A., Senior Lecturer, Department of Biblical Studies, University of Sheffield, England.

CLIPPINGER, WALTER GILLAN*
B.A., D.D., LL.D., President of Otterbein College, Westerville, Ohio.

COBERN, CAMDEN M.*
D.D., Ph.D., Professor of English Bible and Philosophy of Religion, Allegheny College, Meadville, Pennsylvania.

COHON, SAMUEL S.*
B.A., Rabbi, Zion Temple, Chicago, Illinois.

CONRAD, EDGAR W.
A.B., M.Div., Th.M., Ph.D., Teacher in Department of Religious Studies, University of Queensland, Australia.

CRANNELL, PHILIP WENDELL*
D.D., President, Kansas City Baptist Theological Seminary, Kansas City, Kansas.

CRAWFORD, ALBERT G.
B.R.E., B.D., M.A., Associate Professor of Religion and Bible, Grand Rapids Baptist College, Grand Rapids, Michigan.

DANKER, FREDERICK W.
B.D., M.Div., Ph.D., Professor, Department of Exegetical Theology and New Testament, Christ Seminary — Seminex, St. Louis, Missouri.

DAU, W. H. T.*
D.D., President of Valparaiso University, Valparaiso, Indiana.

DAVIES, T. WITTON*
B.A., D.D., Ph.D., Professor of Semitic Languages, University College at Bangor, North Wales.

DAVIES, WILLIAM WALTER*
M.A., Ph.D., Professor of Hebrew, Ohio Wesleyan University, Delaware, Ohio.

DAY, ALFRED ELY*
M.A., M.Sc., Professor of Natural Sciences, American University of Beirut.

DEBOER, WILLIS P.
A.B., Th.B., Th.D., Professor of Religion and Theology, Calvin College, Grand Rapids, Michigan.

DEERE, DERWARD W.
Th.D, Late Professor of Old Testament, Golden Gate Theological Seminary, Mill Valley, California.

DEHOOG, JOHN W.
A.B., Former Project Editor, *ISBE* Revision.

DENNISON, JAMES T., JR.
B.S., B.D., M.Div., Th.M., Pastor of Pioneer and Pleasant Grove United Presbyterian Churches, Ligonier, Pennsylvania.

DEVRIES, CARL E.
Ph.D., Former Research Associate (Associate Professor), Oriental Institute, Chicago, Illinois.

DICKIE, ARCHIBALD CAMPBELL*
M.A., F.S.A., A.R.I.B.A., Professor of Architecture, University of Manchester, England.

DICKIE, JOHN*
M.A., D.D., Principal and Professor of Systematic Theology, Knox College, Dunedin, New Zealand.

DOSKER, HENRY E.*
M.A., D.D., LL.D., Professor of Church History, Presbyterian Seminary of Kentucky, Louisville, Kentucky.

DOWNER, BENJAMIN RENO*
B.A., Th.D., Professor of Hebrew and Old Testament, Kansas City Theological Seminary, Kansas City, Kansas.

DOWNEY, GLANVILLE
A.B., Ph.D., Distinguished Professor of History and Classical Studies, Indiana University, Bloomington, Indiana.

DUGAN, ROBERT P., JR.
B.A., M.Div., Director, Office of Public Affairs of the National Association of Evangelicals, Washington, D.C.

EARLE, RALPH
A.B., B.D., M.A., Th.D., Distinguished Professor of New Testament, Emeritus, Nazarene Theological Seminary, Kansas City, Missouri.

EASTON, BURTON SCOTT*
D.D., Ph.D., Professor of the Interpretation and Literature of New Testament, General Theological Seminary, New York City.

EDWARDS, DAVID MIALL*
M.A., Ph.D., D.D., Professor of Doctrinal Theology and Philosophy of Religion, Memorial College (Congregational), Brecon, South Wales.

ELLISON, HENRY LEOPOLD
B.A., B.D., Senior Tutor, Moorlands Bible College, Dawlish, Devon, England.

EMMERSON, GRACE I.
M.A., Dip. Or. Lang., Lecturer, Department of Theology, University of Birmingham, England.

ENGELHARD, DAVID H.
A.B., B.D., M.A., Ph.D., Associate Professor of Old Testament and Academic Dean, Calvin Theological Seminary, Grand Rapids, Michigan.

ESTES, DAVID FOSTER*
M.A., D.D., Professor of New Testament Interpretation, Colgate University, Hamilton, New York.

EVANS, MORRIS O.*
D.D., Ph.D., Lecturer on English Bible and Literature, Congregational College, Bangor, North Wales.

EVANS, WILLIAM*
D.D., Ph.D., Bible Teacher, Author, and Lecturer, Pomona, California.

EVERTS, JANET MEYER
B.A., M.A., M.Div., Graduate studies at Duke University.

EWING, WILLIAM*
M.C., M.A., D.D., Minister of Grange United Free Church, Edinburgh, Scotland.

CONTRIBUTORS

FARR, F. K.*
A.M., D.D., Professor of Hebrew and Old Testament Exegesis, Lane Seminary, Cincinnati, Ohio.

FENSHAM, F. CHARLES
M.A., D.D., Ph.D., Professor of Semitic Languages and Head of Department, University of Stellenbosch, South Africa.

FINDLAY, ADAM FYFE*
M.A., D.D., Professor of Church History and Christian Ethics, United Free Church College, Aberdeen, Scotland.

FINEGAN, JACK
B.A., M.A., B.D., M.Th., Oc. theol. (=Ph.D.), Professor of New Testament and Archaeology, Pacific School of Religion, Berkeley, California.

FORRESTER, ELDRED JOHN*
B.A., D.D., Head of the Department of the Bible and Lecturer in American History, Mercer University, Macon, Georgia.

FORTUNE, A. W.*
B.D., M.A., Professor of New Testament, College of the Bible, Lexington, Kentucky.

FREE, JOSEPH P.
A.B., M.A., Ph.D., Professor of History and Archaeology, Bemidji State College, Bemidji, Minnesota.

FREEMAN, DAVID
B.A., B.D., Th.M., Ph.D., Professor Emeritus, Rhode Island Junior College, Rhode Island.

FREEDMAN, DAVID NOEL
Ph.D., Professor of Biblical Studies and Director of the Program on Studies in Religion, University of Michigan, Ann Arbor, Michigan.

FREND, W. H. C.
T.D., D.D., F.S.A., Professor of Ecclesiastical History, University of Glasgow, Scotland.

GARBER, PAUL LESLIE
Th.M., Ph.D., Professor of Bible and Religion, Emeritus, Agnes Scott College, Decatur, Georgia.

GASQUE, W. WARD
B.A., B.D., M.Th., Ph.D., Associate Professor of New Testament Studies, Regent College, Vancouver, British Columbia, Canada.

GERBERDING, G. H.*
M.A., D.D., Professor of Practical Theology, Theological Seminary of the Evangelical Lutheran Church, Maywood, Illinois.

GILL, DAVID W.
A.B., M.A., Ph.D., Project Director, New College for Advanced Christian Studies, Berkeley, California.

GREEN, NORMAN
B.A., L.Th., Assistant Curator and Head of Administration of McLaughlin Planetarium, Toronto, Ontario, Canada.

GRIDER, J. KENNETH
A.B., B.D., Th.B., M.A., M.Div., Ph.D., Professor of Theology, Nazarene Theological Seminary, Kansas City, Missouri.

GUELICH, ROBERT
B.A., M.A., S.T.B., Th.D., Professor of New Testament, Bethel Theological Seminary, St. Paul, Minnesota.

GWINN, RALPH A.
A.B., B.D., Ph.D., Professor of Religion and Philosophy, Tarkio College, Tarkio, Missouri.

HAHN, HERRICK E.
B.A., M.Div., Pastor of Bell Gardens Christian Church, Bell Gardens, California.

HAMILTON, VICTOR P.
A.B., B.D., Th.M., M.A., Ph.D., Assistant Professor of Religion, Asbury College, Wilmore, Kentucky.

HARRIS, B. F.
B.A., M.A., B.D., Ph.D., Associate Professor of History, Macquarie University, New South Wales, Australia.

HARRIS, R. LAIRD
Th.B., Th.M., Ph.D., Professor of Old Testament, Covenant Theological Seminary, St. Louis, Missouri.

HARRISON, EVERETT F.
B.A., Th.B., M.A., Ph.D., Th.D., Professor Emeritus of New Testament, Fuller Theological Seminary, Pasadena, California.

HARRISON, ROLAND K.
B.D., M.Th., Ph.D., Professor of Old Testament, Wycliffe College, Toronto, Ontario, Canada.

HARRY, JOSEPH EDWARD*
Ph.D., Professor of Greek, University of Cincinnati, Cincinnati, Ohio.

HARTLEY, JOHN E.
B.A., B.D, M.A., Ph.D., Chairman of Division of Philosophy and Religion, Azusa Pacific College, Assistant Professor of Biblical Literature, Fuller Theological Seminary, Pasadena, California.

HARVEY, DOROTHEA W.
B.A., B.D., Ph.D., Professor of Religion, Urbana College, Urbana, Ohio.

HASEL, GERHARD F.
M.A., B.D., Ph.D., Professor of Old Testament and Biblical Theology and Assistant Academic Dean, Andrews University, Berrien Springs, Michigan.

HAYDEN, ROY E.
B.A., B.D., Th.M., M.A., Ph.D., Professor of Biblical Literature, Oral Roberts University, Tulsa, Oklahoma.

HEIDEL, WILLIAM ARTHUR*
M.A., Ph.D., Research Professor of Greek Language and Literature, Wesleyan University, Middletown, Connecticut.

HEMER, COLIN J.
M.A., Ph.D., Lecturer in New Testament Studies, University of Manchester, England.

HERZOG, JOHN J.
B.A., M.A., Ph.D., Assistant Professor of Biblical and Theological Studies, Gordon College, Wenham, Massachusetts.

HEWETT, JAMES ALLEN
B.A., B.D., M.A., Ph.D., Assistant Professor of Theology, Oral Roberts University, Tulsa, Oklahoma.

HIRSCH, FRANK E.*
M.A., D.D., LL.D., President of Charles City College, Charles City, Iowa.

CONTRIBUTORS

HOEHNER, HAROLD W.
B.A., Th.M., Th.D., Ph.D., Director of Doctoral Studies, Department Chairman and Professor of New Testament Literature and Exegesis, Dallas Theological Seminary, Dallas, Texas.

HOERTH, ALFRED JOSEPH
A.B., A.M., Associate Professor of Archaeology, Wheaton College, Wheaton, Illinois.

HOLWERDA, DAVID E.
A.B., B.D., D.Th., Professor of Religion and Theology, Calvin College, Grand Rapids, Michigan.

HOVEE, GENE H.
B.A., M.Div., M.A., Ph.D., Associate Professor of Bible and Director of Student Services, Fort Wayne Bible College, Fort Wayne, Indiana.

HUGHES, ROBERT J., III
D.V.M., M.Div., Th.M., Associate Professor of Science and Chairman of Division of General Studies, Fort Wayne Bible College, Indiana.

HUNT, LESLIE
B.A., B.D., M.Th., D.D., Principal Emeritus and Professor of New Testament, Wycliffe College, Toronto, Ontario, Canada.

HUNTER, S. F.*
M.A., B.D., Professor of Knox College, Dunedin, New Zealand.

HUTCHISON, JOHN*
M.A., LL.D., Rector of the High School, Glasgow, Scotland.

ISAACS, NATHAN*
Ph.D., LL.B., S.J.D., Professor of Business Law, Harvard University.

JACOBS, HENRY E.*
D.D., LL.D., Norton Professor of Systematic Theology, Lutheran Theological Seminary, Philadelphia, Pennsylvania.

JAMME, ALBERT
S.S.L., S.T.D., D.O.R., Research Professor of Semitics, The Catholic University of America, Washington, D.C.

JOHNSTON, ELEANOR B.
B.A., Graduate Studies in Old Testament, Claremont Graduate School, Claremont, California.

JOY, ALFRED H.*
Ph.B., M.A., F.R.A.S., Astronomer and Secretary of the Mount Wilson Observatory, Pasadena, California.

JUDGE, E. A.
M.A., Professor of History, Macquarie University, New South Wales, Australia.

JUNG, KURT GERHARD
Th.D., U.S. Army Chaplain, Berlin, Germany.

KAISER, LEWIS*
Th.M., D.D., Professor of Old Testament and Life of Christ, German Department, Colgate-Rochester Divinity School, Rochester, New York.

KAISER, WALTER C., JR.
A.B., B.D., M.A., Ph.D., Department Chairman and Professor of Semitic Languages and Old Testament, Trinity Evangelical Divinity School, Deerfield, Illinois.

KAPP, JACOB W.*
M.A., D.D., General Secretary, The Brotherhood of the United Lutheran Church in America.

KERR, COLIN M.*
B.Sc., B.D., M.A., Ph.D., Professor of Political Philosophy in Scottish Churches College, Calcutta, India.

KITCHEN, KENNETH A.
B.A., Ph.D., Reader in Egyptian and Coptic Studies, University of Liverpool, England.

KNUTSON, F. BRENT
B.S., M.A., Ph.D., Associate Professor of Philosophy and Religion, University of Arkansas at Little Rock.

KYLE, MELVIN GROVE*
D.D., LL.D., President and Newburgh Professor of Biblical Theology and Biblical Archaeology, Xenia Theological Seminary, Pittsburgh, Pennsylvania.

LADD, GEORGE ELDON
Th.B., B.D., Ph.D., Senior Professor of New Testament Theology and Exegesis, Fuller Theological Seminary, Pasadena, California.

LAMBERT, J. C.*
B.D., D.D., Minister of the United Free Church of Scotland, Braeheads, Fenwick, Scotland.

LANE, WILLIAM L.
B.A., B.D., Th.M., Th.D., Professor of Religion, Western Kentucky University, Bowling Green, Kentucky.

LASOR, WILLIAM SANFORD
B.A., Th.B., Th.M., Ph.D., Th.D., Senior Professor of Old Testament, Fuller Theological Seminary, Pasadena, California.

LEWIS, ARTHUR H.
B.A., M.A., B.D., Ph.D., Professor of Old Testament, Bethel College, St. Paul, Minnesota.

LEWIS, THOMAS*
B.D., M.A., Principal of Memorial College (Congregational), Brecon, South Wales.

LIBOLT, CLAYTON G.
A.B., B.D., M.A., Graduate Studies in Old Testament at University of Michigan.

LINDSAY, JAMES*
B.Sc., M.A., D.D., F.R.S.L., F.R.S.E., F.G.S., M.R.A.S., Theological and Philosophic Author.

LINDSAY, THOMAS M.*
M.A., D.D., LL.D., Principal and Professor of Church History, United Free Church College, Glasgow, Scotland.

LOTZ, WILHELM*
D.Th., Ph.D., Professor of Theology, University of Erlangen, Germany.

LUERING, HEINRICH LUDWIG EMIL*
Ph.D., Professor of Dogmatic Theology and New Testament Greek, Martin Theological Seminary of the Methodist Episcopal Church, Frankfurt-am-Main, Germany.

MAAHS, KENNETH H.
B.A., M.Div., Th.M., Ph.D., Associate Professor of Religion, Eastern College, St. Davids, Pennsylvania.

MABEE, CHARLES
B.A., M.Div., M.A., Ph.D., Assistant Professor of Philosophy and Religion, Radford University, Radford, Virginia.

MACALISTER, ALEXANDER*
M.D., M.A., D.Sc., LL.D., F.R.S., F.S.A., Professor of Anatomy in Cambridge University, England.

MACK, EDWARD*
Ph.D., D.D., LL.D., McCormick Professor of Old Testament Interpretation, Union Theological Seminary, Richmond, Virginia.

MACLEOD, MURDO A.
M.A., Director, Christian Witness to Israel, Chislehurst, Kent, England.

MADVIG, DONALD H.
A.B., B.D., Th.M., M.A., Ph.D., Professor of Biblical Literature, Bethel Theological Seminary, St. Paul, Minnesota.

MALONY, H. NEWTON
A.B., M.Div., M.A., Ph.D., Associate Professor of Psychology, Fuller Theological Seminary, Pasadena, California.

MARE, W. HAROLD
A.B., B.D., Ph.D., Professor of New Testament, Covenant Theological Seminary, St. Louis, Missouri.

MARGOLIS, MAX L.*
Ph.D., Professor of Biblical Philology, Dropsie College, Philadelphia, Pennsylvania.

MASTERMAN, ERNEST W. G.*
M.D., F.R.C.S., F.R.G.S., Honorary Secretary of the Palestine Exploration Fund, London, England.

MAUNDER, E. WALTER*
F.R.A.S., Superintendent of the Solar Department of the Royal Observatory, Greenwich, London, England.

MCCAIG, ARCHIBALD*
B.A., LL.B., LL.D., Principal Emeritus and Theological Tutor, Spurgeon's College, London, England.

MCGLOTHIN, WILLIAM JOSEPH*
M.A., D.D., Ph.D., LL.D., President of Furman University, Greenville, South Carolina.

MCINTOSH, DUNCAN,
B.Mus., B.D., Th.M., Pastor of Geneva Road Baptist Church, Wheaton, Illinois and Adjunct Professor of Mission, Northern Baptist Theological Seminary, Lombard, Illinois.

MCKIM, DONALD K.
B.A., M.Div., Ph.D., Pastor of Friendship United Presbyterian Parish, Slippery Rock, Pennsylvania.

MCREYNOLDS, PAUL R.
A.B., M.A., Ph.D., Professor of New Testament and Greek and Vice President for Academic Affairs, Pacific Christian College, Fullerton, California.

MEYE, ROBERT P.
B.A., B.D., Th.M., D.Th., Dean and Professor of New Testament Interpretation, Fuller Theological Seminary, Pasadena, California.

MICHAELS, J. RAMSEY
Th.D., Professor of New Testament, Gordon-Conwell Theological Seminary, South Hamilton, Massachusetts.

MILLAR, JAMES*
B.D., Minister of Church of Scotland, New Cumnock, Ayrshire, Scotland.

MILLARD, ALAN R.
M.A., M.Phil., F.S.A., Rankin Senior Lecturer in Hebrew and Ancient Semitic Languages, University of Liverpool, England.

MITCHELL, TERENCE C.
M.A., Deputy Keeper, Department of Western Asiatic Antiquities, British Museum, London, England.

MÖLLER, WILHELM*
Pastor Licentiat der Theologie, Wittenberg, Germany.

MONTGOMERY, GERALD E.
B.A., B.D., Th.M., Assistant Professor of Greek, Biola College, La Mirada, California.

MORGAN, DONN F.
B.A., B.D., M.A., Ph.D., Assistant Professor of Old Testament, Church Divinity School of the Pacific, Berkeley, California.

MORRIS, LEON
M.Sc., M.Th., Ph.D., Principal of Ridley College, Melbourne, Australia.

MOSIMAN, SAMUEL K.*
Ph.D., Litt.D., President of Bluffton College, Bluffton, Ohio.

MOUNCE, ROBERT H.
B.A., B.D., Th.M., Ph.D., Dean of Arts and Humanities and Professor of Religion, Western Kentucky University, Bowling Green, Kentucky.

MOYER, JAMES C.
A.B., M.Div., M.A., Ph.D., Associate Professor of History, Southwest Missouri State University, Springfield, Missouri.

MULLINS, E. Y.*
D.D., LL.D., President of Southern Baptist Theological Seminary, Louisville, Kentucky.

MURRAY, JOHN
M.A., Th.B., Th.M., Late Professor of Systematic Theology, Westminster Theological Seminary, Philadelphia, Pennsylvania.

MYERS, ALLEN C.
B.A., M.Div., Editorial Associate, *ISBE* Revision Staff.

NICOL, THOMAS*
D.D., Professor of Divinity and Biblical Criticism, University of Aberdeen, Scotland.

NILES, DANIEL PREMAN
Ph.D., Christian Conference of Asia, Singapore.

NORMAN, JAMES GARTH GIFFORD
B.D., M.Th., Pastor of Rosyth Baptist Church, Fife, Scotland.

NUELSEN, JOHN L.*
D.D., LL.D., Bishop of Methodist Episcopal Church, Kilchberg bei Zürich, Switzerland.

OKO, ADOLPH S.*
Librarian, Hebrew Union College, Cincinnati, Ohio.

OPPERWALL, NOLA J.
A.B., M.Div., Editorial Assistant, *ISBE* Revision Staff.

OPPERWALL, RAYMOND
B.A., Th.B., Minister of Olentangy Christian Reformed Church, Columbus, Ohio.

ORR, JAMES*
M.A., D.D., Professor of Apologetics and Theology, Theological College of United Free Church, Glasgow, Scotland.

OSWALT, JOHN N.
B.A., B.D., Th.M., M.A., Ph.D., Associate Professor of Biblical Languages and Literature, Asbury Theological Seminary, Wilmore, Kentucky.

CONTRIBUTORS

PATCH, JAMES A.*
B.S., Professor of Chemistry, American University of Beirut.

PAYNE, DAVID F.
B.A., M.A., Senior Lecturer and Head of Department of Semitic Studies, The Queen's University of Belfast, Northern Ireland.

PAYNE, J. BARTON
B.A., B.D., M.A., Th.M., Ph.D., Professor and Chairman of Department of Old Testament, Covenant Theological Seminary, St. Louis, Missouri.

PECOTA, DANIEL B.
B.A., M.Div., Th.M., D.Min., Professor of Greek and Theology, Northwest College, Kirkland, Washington.

PINCHES, THEOPHILUS GOLDRIDGE*
LL.D., M.R.A.S., Lecturer in Assyrian, University College, London; Department of Egyptian and Assyrian Antiquities, British Museum, London, England.

PITTMAN, SAMUEL C.
B.A., B.D., M.A., D.Min., Associate Professor of Missions and Bible, Northwestern College, Roseville, Minnesota.

POLLARD, EDWARD BAGBY*
M.A., D.D., Ph.D., Professor of Homiletics, Crozer Theological Seminary, Chester, Pennsylvania.

PORTER, H.*
Ph.D., Professor of History and Psychology, American University of Beirut.

PRATT, DWIGHT MALLORY*
M.A., D.D., Minister, Walnut Hills Congregational Church, Cincinnati, Ohio.

PREWITT, J. FRANKLIN
B.A., B.Th., D.D., Professor of Bible and History, Western Baptist College, Salem, Oregon.

PRICE, JAMES R.
A.B., M.Div., A.M., Pastor, Faith United Methodist Church, Joliet, Illinois.

RAFFETY, WILLIAM EDWARD*
B.D., M.A., Ph.D., D.D., Professor of Religious Education, University of Redlands, Redlands, California.

RAINEY, ANSON F.
B.A., M.A., B.D., M.Th., Ph.D., Associate Professor of Ancient Near Eastern Cultures, Tel Aviv University, Israel.

RAMM, BERNARD
A.B., B.D., M.A., Ph.D., Professor of Systematic Theology, American Baptist Seminary of the West, Covina, California.

REES, THOMAS*
M.A., Ph.D., Principal and Professor of Theology, Independent College (Congregational), Bangor, North Wales.

REID, W. STANFORD
B.A., M.A., Th.B., Th.M., Ph.D., L.H.D., Professor of History, University of Guelph, Ontario, Canada.

RIBLE, ROBERT L.
S.T.B., M.A., Former Vicar, St. George's Episcopal Church, Riverside, California and Episcopal Chaplain, University of California at Riverside.

RIDDERBOS, N. H.
D.D., Professor Emeritus of Old Testament, Free University, Amsterdam, Netherlands.

ROBERTS, DAVID FRANCIS*
B.A., B.D., Minister, Fitzclarence Street Welsh Presbyterian Church, Liverpool, England.

ROBERTSON, A. T.*
M.A., D.D., LL.D., Litt.D., Professor of New Testament Interpretation, Southern Baptist Theological Seminary, Louisville, Kentucky.

ROBERTSON, JAMES*
M.A., D.D., LL.D., Professor of Hebrew and Semitic Languages, University of Glasgow, Scotland.

ROBINSON, D. W. B.
B.A., M.A., Bishop in Parramatta, New South Wales, Australia and Lecturer in New Testament, Moore Theological College and the Divinity School, University of Sydney, Australia.

ROBINSON, GEORGE L.*
M.A., Ph.D., D.D., LL.D., Professor of Biblical Literature and English Bible, Presbyterian Theological Seminary, Chicago, Illinois.

ROBINSON, WILLIAM CHILDS
A.B., M.A., B.D., Th.M., Th.D., Professor Emeritus, Columbia Theological Seminary, Decatur, Georgia.

RUTHERFURD, JOHN*
B.D., M.A., Minister, Moorpark United Free Church, Renfrew, Scotland.

SAARISALO, AAPELI A.
Th.D., Professor Emeritus of Oriental Literature, Helsinki University, Finland.

SAMPEY, JOHN RICHARD*
B.A., D.D., LL.D., Professor of Old Testament Interpretation, Southern Baptist Theological Seminary, Louisville, Kentucky.

SAYCE, ARCHIBALD HENRY*
D.D., Litt.D., LL.D., Professor of Assyriology, University of Oxford, England.

SCHODDE, GEORGE HENRY*
D.D., Ph.D., Professor in College and Theological Departments, Capital University, Columbus, Ohio.

SCHULTZ, SAMUEL J.
Th.D., Samuel Robinson Professor of Biblical Studies and Theology, Wheaton College, Wheaton, Illinois.

SEALE, MORRIS S.
B.A., Ph.D., D.D., Former Professor of Near East School of Theology, Beirut, Lebanon.

SMITH, DUANE E.
B.S., M.A., M.Th., Biblical Scholar and Lecturer; Applications Engineer, Rockwell International, Anaheim, California.

SMITH, EDGAR W., JR.
B.A., B.D., Ph.D., Project Editor, *ISBE* Revision.

SMITH, WILBUR M.
D.D., D.Litt., Late Professor of English Bible, Fuller Theological Seminary, Pasadena, California.

SOGGIN, J. ALBERTO
S.T.D., Ph.D., Professor of Old Testament, Waldensian School of Theology, Rome, Italy and Senior Lecturer of Hebrew Language and Literature, Institute for Near Eastern Studies, University of Rome, Italy.

STALKER, JAMES*
M.A., D.D., Professor of Church History, United Free Church College, Aberdeen, Scotland.

STEARNS, WALLACE NELSON*
B.D., Ph.D., Professor of Biblical History and Literature, Fargo College, Fargo, North Dakota.

STEK, JOHN H.
A.B., B.D., Th.M., Associate Professor of Old Testament, Calvin Theological Seminary, Grand Rapids, Michigan.

STEWART, ROY A.
M.A., B.D., M.Litt., Minister and Biblical Scholar, Church of Scotland (retired).

STRATTON-PORTER, GENE*
Author and Illustrator; Special Writer on Birds and Nature.

SWEET, LOUIS MATTHEWS*
M.A., S.T.D., Ph.D., Professor of Christian Theology and Apologetics, The Biblical Seminary, New York City, New York.

SWEET, RONALD F. G.
M.A., Ph.D., Associate Professor, Department of Near Eastern Studies, University of Toronto, Ontario, Canada.

THOMAS, WILLIAM HENRY GRIFFITH*
A.M., D.D., Professor of Old Testament Literature and Exegesis, Wycliffe College, Toronto, Ontario, Canada.

THOMPSON, JOHN ALEXANDER
A.B., M.Div., Th.M., Ph.D., Research Consultant, Translations Department, American Bible Society, Princeton, New Jersey.

THOMPSON, JOHN ARTHUR
B.A., B.Ed., M.Sc., M.A., Ph.D., B.D., Chairman and Senior Lecturer, Department of Middle Eastern Studies, University of Melbourne, Australia.

THOMSON, CHARLES H.*
M.A., United Free Church of Scotland Missionary to the Jews at Constantinople.

THOMSON, J. E. H.*
M.A., D.D., Missionary to the Jews in Palestine.

TOD, MARCUS NIEBUHR*
M.A., O.B.E., Fellow, Tutor, and Librarian of Oriel College, Oxford and University Reader in Greek Epigraphy, Oxford, England.

TREVER, GEORGE HENRY*
M.A., D.D., Ph.D., Professor of New Testament Exegesis and Christian Doctrine, Gammon Theological Seminary, Atlanta, Georgia.

TURNER, GEORGE A.
B.D., S.T.B., S.T.M., D.Litt., Ph.D., Professor of Biblical Literature, Asbury Theological Seminary, Wilmore, Kentucky.

UNGER, MERRILL F.
A.B., Th.M., Th.D., Ph.D., Professor Emeritus of Old Testament, Dallas Theological Seminary, Dallas, Texas.

VAN ALSTINE, GEORGE A.
B.A., B.D., Th.M., Pastor of Altadena Baptist Church, Altadena, California.

VAN BROEKHOVEN, HAROLD, JR.
B.A., M.A., M.Div., Th.M., Graduate Studies in New Testament, Boston University.

VANELDEREN, BASTIAAN
A.B., B.D., M.A., Th.D., Professor of New Testament, Calvin Theological Seminary, Grand Rapids, Michigan.

VAN PELT, J. R.*
B.A., S.T.B., Ph.D., Professor of Systematic Theology and Homiletics, Gammon Theological Seminary, Atlanta, Georgia.

VAN SELMS, ADRIANUS
D.D., Emeritus Professor of Semitic Languages, University of Pretoria, South Africa.

VERHEY, ALLEN D.
B.A., B.D., Ph.D., Assistant Professor, Department of Religion, Hope College, Holland, Michigan.

VOS, HOWARD F.
B.A., Th.M., Th.D., M.A., Ph.D., Professor of History and Archaeology, The King's College, Briarcliff Manor, New York.

WAITE, J. C. J.
B.D., Principal of South Wales Bible College, South Wales.

WALKER, W. L.*
D.D., Congregational Minister, Glasgow, Scotland.

WALLACE, RONALD STEWART
B.S., M.A., Ph.D., Professor Emeritus of Biblical Theology, Columbia Theological Seminary, Decatur, Georgia.

WALLS, ANDREW F.
M.A., B.Litt., Professor of Religious Studies, University of Aberdeen, Scotland.

WALTKE, BRUCE K.
A.B., Th.M., Th.D., Ph.D., Professor of Old Testament, Regent College, Vancouver, British Columbia, Canada.

WEAD, DAVID W.
A.B., B.Th., B.D., D.Th., Minister of Boones Creek Church of Christ, Johnson City, Tennessee.

WEDDLE, FOREST
A.B., M.S., Ph.D., Professor of Biblical Archaeology and History, Fort Wayne Bible College, Fort Wayne, Indiana.

WHEDBEE, J. WILLIAM
B.A., B.D., M.A., Ph.D., Associate Professor of Religion, Pomona College, Claremont, California.

WHITCOMB, JOHN C., JR.
B.A., B.D., Th.M., Th.D., Professor of Theology and Old Testament and Director of Postgraduate Studies, Grace Theological Seminary, Winona Lake, Indiana.

WHITE, GEORGE EDWARD*
M.A., D.D., President of Anatolia College, Salonica, Greece.

WIEAND, DAVID JOHN
A.B., M.A., B.D., Ph.D., Professor of Biblical Literature, Bethany Theological Seminary, Oak Brook, Illinois.

WIENER, HAROLD M.*
M.A., LL.B., Barrister at Law, Jerusalem.

WILSON, J. MACARTNEY*
D.D., Minister of Greyfriars Presbyterian Church, Port of Spain, Trinidad, British West Indies.

WILSON, ROBERT DICK*
M.A., Ph.D., Professor of Semitic Philology and Old Testament Introduction, Princeton, New Jersey.

WISEMAN, DONALD J.
O.B.E., M.A., D.Lit., F.B.A., F.S.A., Professor of Assyriology, University of London, England.

WOLF HORACE J.*
B.H.L., M.A., Associate Rabbi of Berith Kodish Congregation, Rochester, New York.

WOOD, A. SKEVINGTON
B.A., Ph.D., Principal of Cliff College, Derbyshire, England.

WRIGHT, GEORGE FREDERICK*
M.A., D.D., LL.D., F.G.S.A., Professor, Oberlin College, Oberlin, Ohio.

WRIGHT, J. STAFFORD
M.A., Former Principal of Tyndale Hall, Bristol and Canon Emeritus of Bristol Cathedral, Bristol, England.

WYPER, GLENN
B.A., B.D., Th.M., Pastor, Doncaster Bible Chapel, Thornhill, Ontario, Canada.

YAMAUCHI, EDWIN M.
B.A., M.A., Ph.D., Professor of History, Miami University, Oxford, Ohio.

YOUNG, FREDERICK E.
A.B., B.D., Ph.D., Dean of the Seminary and Professor of Old Testament, Central Baptist Theological Seminary, Kansas City, Kansas.

YOUNGBLOOD, RONALD F.
B.A., B.D., Ph.D., Associate Dean and Professor of Old Testament, Wheaton Graduate School, Wheaton, Illinois.

ABBREVIATIONS

GENERAL

A	Codex Alexandrinus (*See* TEXT AND MSS OF THE NT I.B)
abbr.	abbreviated, abbreviation
act.	active
Akk.	Akkadian
Amer. Tr.	J. M. P. Smith and E. J. Goodspeed, *The Complete Bible: An American Translation*
Am.Tab.	el-Amarna Letters (*See* AMARNA TABLETS)
Apoc.	Apocrypha
Apost. Const.	Apostolic Constitutions
Aq.	Aquila's Greek version of the OT (*See* SEPTUAGINT)
Arab.	Arabic
Aram.	Aramaic
art.	article
Assyr.	Assyrian
ASV	American Standard Version
AT	Altes (or Ancien) Testament
AV	Authorized (King James) Version
b.	born
B	Codex Vaticanus (*See* TEXT AND MSS OF THE NT I.B)
Bab.	Babylonian
bk.	book
Boh.	Bohairic (dialect of Coptic)
ca.	*circa,* about
Can.	Canaanite
cent., cents.	century, centuries
CG	Coptic Gnostic (*See* NAG HAMMADI LITERATURE)
ch., chs.	chapter(s)
Chald.	Chaldean, Chaldaic
col., cols.	column(s)
comm., comms.	commentary, commentaries
Copt.	Coptic
d.	died
D	Deuteronomist (*See* CRITICISM II.D.4); also Codex Bezae (*See* TEXT AND MSS OF THE NT I.B)
diss.	dissertation
DSS	Dead Sea Scrolls
E	Elohist (*See* CRITICISM II.D.4); east
E.B.	Early Bronze (Age)
ed., eds.	editor, edition, edited (by), editors, editions
Egyp.	Egyptian
E.I.	Early Iron (Age)
Einl.	*Einleitung* (Introduction)
Eng. tr.	English translation
ERV	English Revised Version (1881-1885)
esp.	especially
et al.	and others
Eth.	Ethiopic, Ethiopian
f., ff.	following
fem.	feminine
fig.	figuratively
ft.	foot, feet
gal., gals.	gallon(s)
gen.	genitive
Ger.	German
Gk.	Greek
gm.	gram(s)
H	Law of Holiness (Lev. 17–26; *See* CRITICISM II.D.5)
ha.	hectare(s)
Heb.	Hebrew
Hist.	History
Hitt.	Hittite
Hom.	Homily
impf.	imperfect (tense)
in.	inch(es)
in loc.	at/on this passage
inscr.	inscription
intrans.	intransitive
intro., intros.	introduction(s)
J	Yahwist (*See* CRITICISM II.D.4)
JB	Jerusalem Bible
K	*kethibh* (*See* TEXT AND MSS OF THE OT)
km.	kilometer(s)
l.	liter(s)
L	Lukan source (*See* GOSPELS, SYNOPTIC V)
Lat.	Latin
L.B.	Late Bronze (Age)
lit.	literally
loc. cit.	in the place cited
LXX	Septuagint
m.	meter(s)
M	Matthaean source (*See* GOSPELS, SYNOPTIC V)
masc.	masculine
M.B.	Middle Bronze (Age)
mg.	margin
mi.	mile(s)
mid.	middle voice

ABBREVIATIONS

Midr.	Midrash
Mish.	Mishna (*See* TALMUD I)
Moff.	J. Moffatt, *A New Translation of the Bible* (1926)
MS, MSS	manuscript(s)
MT	Mas(s)oretic Text (*See* TEXT AND MSS OF THE OT)
N	north
n., nn.	note(s)
NAB	New American Bible
NASB	New American Standard Bible
n.d.	no date
NEB	New English Bible
neut.	neuter
N.F.	*Neue Folge* (New Series)
NIV	New International Version
NJV	New Jewish Version
no., nos.	number(s)
N.S.	New Series
NT	New (Neues, Nouveau) Testament
Onk.	Onkelos (Targum)
op. cit.	in the work quoted
OT	Old Testament
Oxy. P.	Oxyrhynchus papyrus
p	papyrus (used only with superscript number of the papyrus)
P	Priestly Code (*See* CRITICISM II.D.5)
par.	(and) parallel passage(s)
para.	paragraph
part.	participle
pass.	passive
Pent.	Pentateuch
Pers.	Persian
Pesh.	Peshito, Peshitta (*See* VERSIONS)
pf.	perfect (tense)
Phoen.	Phoenician
pl.	plural
prob.	probably
pt., pts.	part(s)
Q	*Quelle* (*See* GOSPELS, SYNOPTIC V)
Q	*qere* (*See* TEXT AND MSS OF THE OT)
repr.	reprinted
rev.	revised (by)
RSV	Revised Standard Version
RV	Revised Version (ERV or ASV)
S	south
Sah.	Sahidic (dialect of Coptic)
Sam.	Samaritan
Sem.	Semitic
sing.	singular
sq.	square
subst.	substantive
Sum.	Sumerian
supp.	supplement(ary)
s.v.	*sub voce* (*vocibus*), under the word(s)
Symm.	Symmachus' Greek version of the OT (*See* SEPTUAGINT)
Syr.	Syriac
Talm.	Talmud
T.B.	Babylonian Talmud
Tg., Tgs.	Targum(s)
Th.	Theodotion's revision of the LXX (*See* SEPTUAGINT)
T.P.	Palestinian (Jerusalem) Talmud
TR	Textus Receptus (*See* TEXT AND MSS OF THE NT IV)
tr.	translation, translated (by)
trans.	transitive
Ugar.	Ugaritic
v., vv.	verse(s)
v.	*versus*
var.	variant
vb., vbs.	verb(s)
viz.	namely
vol., vols.	volume(s)
Vulg.	Vulgate (*See* VERSIONS)
W	west
yd., yds.	yard(s)

SYMBOLS

א	Codex Sinaiticus (*See* TEXT AND MSS OF THE NT I.B)
<	derived from (etymological)
=	is equivalent to
*	theoretical or unidentified form
§	section

PUBLICATIONS

AASOR	*Annual of the American Schools of Oriental Research*
AB	*Anchor Bible*
ADAJ	*Annual of the Department of Antiquities of Jordan*
AfO	*Archiv für Orientforschung*
AJSL	*American Journal of Semitic Languages and Literatures*
Alf.	Henry Alford, *Greek Testament* (4 vols., 1857-1861)
ANEP	J. B. Pritchard, ed., *The Ancient Near East in Pictures* (1954; 2nd ed. 1969)
ANET	J. B. Pritchard, ed., *Ancient Near Eastern Texts Relating to the Old Testament* (1950; 3rd ed. 1969)
ANT	M. R. James, *The Apocryphal New Testament* (1924; repr. 1953)
AOTS	D. W. Thomas, ed., *Archaeology and Old Testament Study* (1967)
AP	W. F. Albright, *The Archaeology of Palestine* (1949; rev. 1960)
APC	L. Morris, *Apostolic Preaching of the Cross* (3rd ed. 1965)
APOT	R. H. Charles, ed., *The Apocrypha and Pseudepigrapha of the Old Testament* (2 vols., 1913; repr. 1963)
ARAB	D. D. Luckenbill, ed., *Ancient Records of Assyria and Babylonia* (2 vols., 1926-1927)
ARI	W. F. Albright, *Archaeology and the Religion of Israel* (4th ed. 1956)
ARM	*Archives Royales de Mari* (1941–)
ATD	*Das Alte Testament Deutsch*
ATR	*Anglican Theological Review*
BA	*The Biblical Archaeologist*
BANE	G. E. Wright, ed., *The Bible and the Ancient Near East: Essays in Honor of William Foxwell Albright* (1961; repr. 1965, 1979)

BASOR — *Bulletin of the American Schools of Oriental Research*

Bauer — W. Bauer, *A Greek-English Lexicon of the New Testament*, tr. W. F. Arndt and F. W. Gingrich (1957; rev. ed. [tr. F. W. Gingrich and F. W. Danker from 5th Ger. ed.] 1979)

BC — F. J. Foakes Jackson and K. Lake, eds., *The Beginnings of Christianity* (5 vols., 1920-1933)

BDB — F. Brown, S. R. Driver, and C. A. Briggs, *Hebrew and English Lexicon of the Old Testament* (1907)

BDF — F. Blass and A. Debrunner, *A Greek Grammar of the New Testament*, tr. and rev. R. W. Funk (1961)

BDTh — *Baker's Dictionary of Theology* (1960)

BH — R. Kittel, ed., *Biblia Hebraica* (3rd ed. 1937)

BHS — K. Elliger and W. Rudolph, eds., *Biblia Hebraica Stuttgartensia* (1967-1977)

BhHW — *Biblisch-historisches Handwörterbuch* (1962–)

BHI — J. Bright, *A History of Israel* (1959; 2nd ed. 1972)

Bibl. — *Biblica*

BJRL — *Bulletin of the John Rylands Library*

BKAT — *Biblischer Kommentar, Altes Testament*

Bousset-Gressmann — W. Bousset, *Die Religion des Judentums im späthellenistischen Zeitalter*, rev. H. Gressmann (*HNT*, 21, 1926)

BZ — *Biblische Zeitschrift*

BZAW — *Beihefte zur Zeitschrift für die alttestamentliche Wissenschaft*

BZNW — *Beihefte zur Zeitschrift für die neutestamentliche Wissenschaft*

CAD — I. J. Gelb, *et al.*, eds., *Assyrian Dictionary of the Oriental Institute of the University of Chicago* (1956–)

CAH — *Cambridge Ancient History* (12 vols., rev. ed. 1962; 1970)

CBC — *Cambridge Bible Commentary on the New English Bible*

CBP — W. M. Ramsay, *Cities and Bishoprics of Phrygia* (1895-1897)

CBQ — *Catholic Biblical Quarterly*

CBSC — *Cambridge Bible for Schools and Colleges*

CCK — D. J. Wiseman, *Chronicles of Chaldaean Kings* (1956)

CD — K. Barth, *Church Dogmatics* (Eng. tr., 4 vols., 1936-1962)

CD — See Biblical and Extrabiblical Literature: Dead Sea Scrolls

CERP — A. H. M. Jones, *Cities of the Eastern Roman Provinces* (1937)

CG — P. Kahle, *The Cairo Geniza* (2nd ed. 1959)

CGT — *Cambridge Greek Testament* (20 vols., 1881-1933)

CHAL — W. L. Holladay, *A Concise Hebrew and Aramaic Lexicon of the Old Testament* (1971)

CIG — *Corpus Inscriptionum Graecarum* (1825-1859; index 1877)

CIL — *Corpus Inscriptionum Latinarum* (1862–)

ConNT — *Coniectanea Neotestamentica*

CRE — W. M. Ramsay, *The Church in the Roman Empire Before A.D. 170* (1903)

DBSup. — L. Pirot, *et al.*, eds., *Dictionnaire de la Bible: Supplement* (1928–)

DCG — J. Hastings, *Dictionary of Christ and the Gospels* (2 vols., 1906, 1908)

Deiss.LAE — G. A. Deissmann, *Light from the Ancient East* (Eng. tr., 2nd ed. 1927 [from German 4th ed.]; repr. 1978)

Dessau — H. Dessau, ed., *Inscriptiones Latinae Selectae* (3 vols., 2nd ed. 1954-1955)

DJD — *Discoveries in the Judean Desert*

DNTT — C. Brown, ed., *Dictionary of New Testament Theology* (3 vols., Eng. tr. 1975-1978)

DOTT — D. W. Thomas, ed., *Documents from Old Testament Times* (1958)

DTC — *Dictionnaire de Théologie Catholique* (15 vols., 1903-1950)

EAEHL — M. Avi-Yonah and E. Stern, eds., *Encyclopedia of Archaeological Excavations in the Holy Land* (4 vols., Eng. tr. 1975-1978)

EB — T. K. Cheyne and J. S. Black, eds., *Encyclopaedia Biblica* (4 vols., 1899)

Enc.Brit. — *Encyclopaedia Britannica*

EQ — *Evangelical Quarterly*

ERE — J. Hastings, *Encyclopaedia of Religion and Ethics* (12 vols., 1908-1926)

EtB — *Études Bibliques*

EvTh — *Evangelische Theologie*

Expos. — *The Expositor*

Expos.B. — *The Expositor's Bible* (3rd ed. 1903; rev. 1956)

Expos.G.T. — *The Expositor's Greek Testament*

Expos.T. — *Expository Times*

FRLANT — *Forschungen zur Religion und Literatur des Alten und Neuen Testaments*

FSAC — W. F. Albright, *From the Stone Age to Christianity* (2nd ed. 1957)

GAB — L. H. Grollenberg, *Atlas of the Bible* (1956)

GB — D. Baly, *Geography of the Bible* (1957; 2nd ed. 1974)

GJV — E. Schürer, *Geschichte des jüdischen Volkes im Zeitalter Jesu Christi* (3 vols., 4th ed. 1901-1909) (Converted to *HJP* when possible; but Eng. tr. not complete)

GP — F.-M. Abel, *Géographie de la Palestine* (2 vols., 2nd ed. 1933-1938)

GTTOT — J. Simons, *Geographical and Topographical Texts of the Old Testament* (1959)

HAT — *Handbuch zum Alten Testament*

HBD — M. S. Miller and J. L. Miller, eds., *Harper's Bible Dictionary* (1952; 2nd ed. 1961; 8th ed. [rev.] 1973)

HDB — J. Hastings, ed., *Dictionary of the Bible* (4 vols., 1898-1902, extra vol., 1904; rev. one-vol. ed. 1963)

HGHL — G. A. Smith, *Historical Geography of the Holy Land* (rev. ed. 1932)

HibJ — *The Hibbert Journal*

HJP — E. Schürer, *A History of the Jewish People in the Time of Jesus Christ* (Eng. tr. [of German *3rd* ed.] 1892-1901)

HJP[2] — E. Schürer, *The History of the Jewish People in the Age of Jesus Christ*, ed. G. Vermes and F. Millar (Eng. tr. and rev. 1973–)

HNT	*Handbuch zum Neuen Testament*
HNTC	*Harper's New Testament Commentaries = Black's New Testament Commentaries*
HNTT	R. H. Pfeiffer, *A History of New Testament Times with an Introduction to the Apocrypha* (1949)
HR	E. Hatch and H. A. Redpath, *Concordance to the Septuagint* (1897)
H-S	E. Hennecke and W. Schneemelcher, eds., *New Testament Apocrypha* (2 vols., Eng. tr. 1963, 1965)
HST	R. Bultmann, *History of the Synoptic Tradition* (Eng. tr., 2nd ed. 1968)
HTK	*Herders Theologischer Kommentar zum Neuen Testament*
HTR	*Harvard Theological Review*
HUCA	*Hebrew Union College Annual*
IB	*Interpreter's Bible* (12 vols., 1952-1957)
ICC	*International Critical Commentary*
IDB	*Interpreter's Dictionary of the Bible* (4 vols., 1962; Supplementary Volume, 1976)
IEJ	*Israel Exploration Journal*
ILC	J. Pedersen, *Israel: Its Life and Culture* (vols. I-II, Eng. tr. 1926; III-IV, Eng. tr. 1940)
Interp.	*Interpretation: A Journal of Bible and Theology*
IOTG	H. B. Swete, *Introduction to the Old Testament in Greek* (1902)
IP	M. Noth, *Die israelitischen Personennamen in Rahmen der gemeinsemitischen Namengebung* (1928)
ISBE	J. Orr, *et al.*, eds., *International Standard Bible Encyclopaedia* (2nd ed. 1929)
JAOS	*Journal of the American Oriental Society*
JBL	*Journal of Biblical Literature*
JBR	*Journal of Bible and Religion*
JCS	*Journal of Cuneiform Studies*
JEA	*Journal of Egyptian Archaeology*
JETS	*Journal of the Evangelical Theological Society*
Jew.Enc.	*Jewish Encyclopedia* (12 vols., 1901-1906)
JJS	*Journal of Jewish Studies*
JNES	*Journal of Near Eastern Studies*
JPOS	*Journal of the Palestinian Oriental Society*
JQR	*Jewish Quarterly Review*
JR	*Journal of Religion*
JSS	*Journal of Semitic Studies*
JTS	*Journal of Theological Studies*
KAT	E. Schrader, ed., *Die Keilinschriften und das Alte Testament* (3rd ed. 1903)
KD	K. F. Keil and F. Delitzsch, *Commentary on the Old Testament* (Eng. tr. 1864-1901; repr. 1973)
KEK	*Kritisch-exegetischer Kommentar über das Neue Testament*
KoB	L. Koehler and W. Baumgartner, *Lexicon in Veteris Testamenti Libros* (1953)
KS	A. Alt, *Kleine Schriften zur Geschichte des Volkes Israel* (3 vols., 1953-1959)
KZAT	*Kommentar zum Alten Testament*
KZNT	*Kommentar zum Neuen Testament*

ABBREVIATIONS

Lange	Lange Commentaries
LAP	J. Finegan, *Light from the Ancient Past* (1946; rev. 1959)
LBHG	Y. Aharoni, *Land of the Bible: A Historical Geography* (Eng. tr. 1967)
LCC	*Library of Christian Classics*
LCL	*Loeb Classical Library*
LSC	W. M. Ramsay, *Letters to the Seven Churches of Asia* (1905)
LSJ	H. G. Liddell, R. Scott, H. S. Jones, *Greek-English Lexicon* (9th ed. 1940)
LTJM	A. Edersheim, *Life and Times of Jesus the Messiah* (8th ed., rev., 1904; repr. 1977)
LTK	Herder, *Lexicon für Theologie und Kirche* (2nd ed. 1957–)
MM	J. M. Moulton and G. Milligan, *The Vocabulary of the Greek New Testament* (1930)
MNHK	E. R. Thiele, *The Mysterious Numbers of the Hebrew Kings* (1965 ed.)
MNTC	*Moffatt New Testament Commentary*
MPB	H. N. and A. L. Moldenke, *Plants of the Bible* (1952)
MSt	J. McClintock and J. Strong, *Cyclopaedia of Biblical, Theological and Ecclesiastical Literature* (1891)
NBC	F. Davidson, ed., *New Bible Commentary* (1953)
NBD	J. D. Douglas, ed., *New Bible Dictionary* (1962)
NHI	M. Noth, *History of Israel* (Eng. tr. 1958; 2nd ed. 1960)
NICNT	*New International Commentary on the New Testament*
NICOT	*New International Commentary on the Old Testament*
Nov.Test.	*Novum Testamentum: An International Quarterly*
NTD	*Das Neue Testament Deutsch*
NTS	*New Testament Studies*
ODCC	*Oxford Dictionary of the Christian Church* (1957; 2nd ed. 1974)
ORHI	W. O. E. Oesterley and T. H. Robinson, *History of Israel* (2 vols., 1932)
OTG	H. B. Swete, *The Old Testament in Greek According to the Septuagint* (4th ed. 1912)
OTL	*Old Testament Library*
OTMS	H. H. Rowley, ed., *The Old Testament and Modern Study* (1951)
Pauly-Wissowa	A. Pauly and G. Wissowa, eds., *Real-Encyclopädie der classischen Altertumswissenschaft*
PEF	*Palestine Exploration Fund Memoirs*
PEQ	*Palestine Exploration Quarterly*
PG	J. P. Migne, ed., *Patrologia Graeca* (162 vols., 1857-1866)
PIOT	R. H. Pfeiffer, *Introduction to the Old Testament* (1952 [1957] ed.)
PJ	*Palästinajahrbuch*
PL	J. P. Migne, ed., *Patrologia Latina* (221 vols., 1844-1864)
PSBA	*Proceedings of the Society of Biblical Archaeology*
QHJ	A. Schweitzer, *The Quest of the Historical Jesus* (1906; Eng. tr., 2nd ed. 1936)
RAC	*Reallexikon für Antike und Christentum*

RB	*Revue Biblique*
RGG	*Religion in Geschichte und Gegenwart* (5 vols., 3rd ed. 1957-1965)
RGJ	K. L. Schmidt, *Der Rahmen der Geschichte Jesu* (1919)
RHR	*Revue de l'histoire des religions*
RQ	*Revue de Qumran*
RRAM	D. Magie, *Roman Rule in Asia Minor* (2 vols., 1950)
RTWB	A. Richardson, ed., *A Theological Word Book of the Bible* (1950)
SB	H. L. Strack and P. Billerbeck, *Kommentar zum Neuen Testament aus Talmud und Midrasch* (5 vols., 1922-1961)
SBT	*Studies in Biblical Theology*
Sch.-Herz.	*The New Schaff-Herzog Encyclopedia of Religious Knowledge* (2nd ed. 1949-1952)
SE	*Studia Evangelica*
SJT	*Scottish Journal of Theology*
SPT	W. Ramsay, *St. Paul the Traveller and Roman Citizen* (1920)
SQE	K. Aland, ed., *Synopsis Quattor Evangeliorum* (2nd ed. 1964)
SSW	G. Dalman, *Sacred Sites and Ways* (1935)
ST	*Studia Theologica*
SVT	*Supplements to Vetus Testamentum*
SWP	C. R. Conder, *et al.*, eds., *Survey of Western Palestine* (9 vols., 1881-1888)
TDNT	G. Kittel and G. Friedrich, eds., *Theological Dictionary of the New Testament* (10 vols., Eng. tr. 1964-1976)
TDOT	G. J. Botterweck and H. Ringgren, eds., *Theological Dictionary of the Old Testament* (1974–)
THAT	E. Jenni and C. Westermann, eds., *Theologisches Handwörterbuch zum Alten Testament* (2 vols., 1971)
Thayer	Thayer's *Greek-English Lexicon of the New Testament*
ThHK	*Theologischer Handkommentar zum Neuen Testament mit Text und Paraphrase* (7 vols., 1928-1939; rev. 1957–)
TLZ	*Theologische Literaturzeitung*
Torch	*Torch Bible Commentaries*
TR	*Theologische Rundschau*
TU	*Texte und Untersuchungen zur Geschichte der altchristlichen Literatur*
UT	C. Gordon, *Ugaritic Textbook* (*Analecta Orientalia,* 38, 1965)
VC	*Vigiliae Christianae*
VE	*Vox Evangelica*
VT	*Vetus Testamentum*
WA	Luther's *Werke,* Weimar Ausgabe (1883–)
Wace	H. Wace, ed., *Apocrypha* (*Speaker's Commentary,* 1888)
WBA	G. E. Wright, *Biblical Archaeology* (1962)
WC	*Westminster Commentaries*
WHAB	G. E. Wright and F. V. Filson, eds., *Westminster Historical Atlas to the Bible* (1956)
WMANT	*Wissenschaftliche Monographien zum Alten und Neuen Testament*
WTJ	*Westminster Theological Journal*
ZAW	*Zeitschrift für die alttestamentliche Wissenschaft*
ZDPV	*Zeitschrift des deutschen Palästina-Vereins*
ZNW	*Zeitschrift für die neutestamentliche Wissenschaft*
ZTK	*Zeitschrift für Theologie und Kirche*

ANCIENT AUTHORS AND DOCUMENTS

Appian *Syr.*	*Syrian Wars*
Aquinas *Summa Theol.*	*Summa Theologica*
Aristotle *De an.*	*De anima* (*On the Soul*)
Eth. Nic.	*Nicomachaean Ethics*
Eth. Eud.	*Eudemaean Ethics*
Meta.	*Metaphysics*
Phys.	*Physics*
Pol.	*Politics*
Anal. post.	*Posterior Analytics*
Anal. pr.	*Prior Analytics*
Rhet.	*Rhetoric*
Poet.	*Poetics*
Augustine *Civ. Dei*	*De civitate Dei* (*The City of God*)
Conf.	*Confessiones*
De trin.	*De trinitate*
Ench.	*Enchiridion*
Ep.	*Epistulae*
Retr.	*Retractiones*
Calvin *Inst.*	*Institutes of the Christian Religion*
Chrysostom	
Hom. in Gen.	Homily on Genesis
Hom. in Heb.	Homily on Hebrews
Hom. in Jn.	Homily on John
Hom. in Mt.	Homily on Matthew
Clement of Alexandria	
Misc.	*Miscellanies* (*Stromateis*)
Paed.	*Paedagogus*
Curtius Rufus	Quintus Curtius Rufus
Digest	*See* ROMAN LAW II.G
Dio Cassius *Hist.*	*Roman History*
Hist. Epit.	Epitome of the *History*
Diodorus	Diodorus Siculus, *Library of History*
Diogenes	Diogenes Laertius, *Vitae philosophorum*
Epiphanius *Haer.*	*Adversus lxxx haereses* (*Panarion*)
Eusebius *HE*	*Historia ecclesiastica*
Onom.	*Onomasticon*
Praep. ev.	*Praeparatio evangelica*
HE	*Historia ecclesiastica* (*Church History*)
Herodotus	Herodotus *History*

Hippolytus *Ref.*	*Refutatio omnium haeresium (Philosophoumena)*
Homer *Il.*	*Iliad*
Od.	*Odyssey*
Irenaeus *Adv. haer.*	*Adversus omnes haereses*
Jerome *Ep.*	*Epistula(e)*
De vir. ill.	*De viris illustribus*
Adv. Pelag.	*Dialogi adversus Pelagianos*
Josephus *Ant.*	*Antiquities of the Jews*
BJ	*Bellum Judaicum (The Jewish War)*
CAp	*Contra Apionem*
Vita	*Life*
Justin Martyr *Apol.*	*Apologia*
Dial.	*Dialogus contra Tryphonem*
Livy *Epit.*	Epitomes of *Annals of the Roman People*
Origen *De prin.*	*De principiis*
Orosius	Orosius *Historiae*
Pliny (the Elder) *Nat. hist.*	*Naturalis historia*
Pliny (the Younger) *Ep.*	*Epistulae*
Ptolemy *Geog.*	*Geography*
Sallust	*Bellum Catilinae*
Strabo *Geog.*	*Geography*
Sulpicius Severus *Chronicorum*	*Historia sacra*
Tacitus *Ann.*	*Annals (Annales ab excessu divi Augusti)*
Hist.	*Histories*
Tertullian *Adv. Judaeos*	*Adversus Judaeos*
Adv. Marc.	*Adversus Marcionem*
Adv. Prax.	*Adversus Praxeam*
Apol.	*Apologeticum*
De orat.	*De oratione*
De praescr. haer.	*De praescriptione haereticorum*
De res.	*De resurrectione carnis*
Vergil *Aen.*	*Aeneid*

BIBLICAL AND EXTRABIBLICAL LITERATURE

OLD TESTAMENT

Gen.	Genesis
Ex.	Exodus
Lev.	Leviticus
Nu.	Numbers
Dt.	Deuteronomy
Josh.	Joshua
Jgs.	Judges
1, 2 S.	1, 2 Samuel
1, 2 K.	1, 2 Kings
1, 2 Ch.	1, 2 Chronicles
Ezr.	Ezra
Neh.	Nehemiah
Est.	Esther
Job	Job
Ps.	Psalm(s)
Prov.	Proverbs
Eccl.	Ecclesiastes
Cant.	Canticles (Song of Songs)
Isa.	Isaiah
Jer.	Jeremiah
Lam.	Lamentations
Ezk.	Ezekiel
Dnl.	Daniel
Hos.	Hosea
	Joel
Am.	Amos
Ob.	Obadiah
	Jonah
Mic.	Micah
Nah.	Nahum
Hab.	Habakkuk
Zeph.	Zephaniah
Hag.	Haggai
Zec.	Zechariah
Mal.	Malachi

NEW TESTAMENT

Mt.	Matthew
Mk.	Mark
Lk.	Luke
Jn.	John
	Acts
Rom.	Romans
1, 2 Cor.	1, 2 Corinthians
Gal.	Galatians
Eph.	Ephesians
Phil.	Philippians
Col.	Colossians
1, 2 Thess.	1, 2 Thessalonians
1, 2 Tim.	1, 2 Timothy
Tit.	Titus
Philem.	Philemon
He.	Hebrews
Jas.	James
1, 2 Pet.	1, 2 Peter
1, 2, 3 Jn.	1, 2, 3 John
	Jude
Rev.	Revelation

APOCRYPHA

1, 2 Esd.	1, 2 Esdras
Tob.	Tobit
Jth.	Judith
Ad. Est.	Additions to Esther
Wisd.	Wisdom of Solomon
Sir.	Sirach (Ecclesiasticus)
Bar.	Baruch
Ep. Jer.	Epistle (Letter) of Jeremiah
Song Three	Song of the Three Young Men
Sus.	Susanna
Bel	Bel and the Dragon
Pr. Man.	Prayer of Manasseh
1, 2 Macc.	1, 2 Maccabees

PSEUDEPIGRAPHA

Asc. Isa.	Ascension of Isaiah
Asm. M.	Assumption of Moses
2 Bar.	2 (Syriac Apocalypse of) Baruch
3 Bar.	3 (Greek Apocalypse of) Baruch
1, 2 En.	1, 2 Enoch
Jub.	Jubilees
Ps. Sol.	Psalms of Solomon
Sib. Or.	Sibylline Oracles
XII P.	Testaments of the Twelve Patriarchs
T. Reub.	Testament of Reuben
T. Sim.	Testament of Simeon
T. Levi	Testament of Levi
T. Jud.	Testament of Judah
T. Iss.	Testament of Issachar
T. Zeb.	Testament of Zebulun
T. Dan	Testament of Dan
T. Naph.	Testament of Naphtali
T. Gad	Testament of Gad
T. Ash.	Testament of Asher
T. Jos.	Testament of Joseph
T. Benj.	Testament of Benjamin

APOSTOLIC FATHERS

Barn.	Epistle of Barnabas
1 Clem.	1 Clement
2 Clem.	2 Clement
Did.	Didache
Ign.	Ignatius of Antioch
Eph.	Epistle to the Ephesians
Magn.	Epistle to the Magnesians
Trall.	Epistle to the Trallians
Rom.	Epistle to the Romans
Philad.	Epistle to the Philadelphians
Smyrn.	Epistle to the Smyrnaeans
Polyc.	Epistle to Polycarp
Polyc. Phil.	Polycarp of Smyrna, Epistle to the Philippians
M. Polyc.	Martyrdom of Polycarp
Shep. Herm.	Shepherd of Hermas
Vis.	Visions
Mand.	Mandates
Sim.	Similitudes

ABBREVIATIONS

DEAD SEA SCROLLS

Initial arabic numeral indicates cave number;
Q = Qumrân; p = pesher (commentary).

CD	Damascus Document (Zadokite Fragment)
1QapGen	Genesis Apocryphon
1QH	Thanksgiving Hymns
1QIsa[a]	First copy of Isaiah from Qumrân Cave 1
1QIsa[b]	Second copy of Isaiah
1QM	War Scroll
1QpHab	Pesher (Commentary) on Habakkuk
1QpMic	Pesher on Micah
1QpPs	Pesher on Psalms
1QS	Manual of Discipline
1Q*34*[bis]	Prayer for the Feast of Weeks (Fragment of Liturgical Prayer Scroll = 1Q Prayers)
1QDM (or 1Q*22*)	Sayings of Moses
3QInv (or 3Q*15*)	Copper (Treasure) Scroll
4QFlor	Florilegium (eschatological midrashim) from Cave 4
4QPBless	Patriarchal Blessings
4QpIsa[a, b, c, d]	Copies of Isaiah pesher from Cave 4
4QpNah	Pesher on Nahum
4QpPs37	Pesher on Ps. 37
4QSam[a, b, c]	Copies of Samuel
4QTestim	Testimonia text from Cave 4
6QD (or 6Q*15*)	Fragments of the Damascus Document

A. *See* ALEPH; WRITING.

AALAR ā'a-lär. *See* IMMER **3**.

AARON âr'ən [Heb. *'ah^{a}rôn*–meaning uncertain; Gk. *Aarōn*]. Moses' older brother, the first high priest. According to the genealogical lists he was third in descent from Levi (Ex. 6:16-20; 1 Ch. 6:1-3). However, the genealogy may be incomplete, since in Ruth 4:18-20 the Judah list has six names. He was probably a descendant rather than the immediate son of Amram and Jochebed, since Amram and his three brothers had numerous descendants within a year of the Exodus (Nu. 3:27f.). Aaron's sister Miriam was several years older, since she was set to watch the bulrush boat of the infant Moses, at whose birth Aaron was three years old (Ex. 7:7).

When Moses fled from Egypt, Aaron remained to share the hardships of his people, and possibly to render them some service; for we are told that Moses pleaded inability and God sent Aaron to aid in his mission to Pharaoh and to Israel, and that Aaron went out to meet his returning brother, as the time of deliverance drew near (Ex. 4:27). While Moses, whose great gifts lay along other lines, was slow of speech (4:10), Aaron was a ready spokesman, and became his brother's representative, being called his "mouth" (4:16) and his "prophet" (7:1). After their meeting in the wilderness the two brothers returned together to Egypt on the hazardous mission to which the Lord had called them (4:27-31). At first they appealed to their own nation, recalling the ancient promises and declaring the imminent deliverance, Aaron being the spokesman. But the heart of the people, hopeless by reason of the hard bondage and heavy with the care of material things, did not incline to them. The two brothers then at God's command made appeal directly to Pharaoh himself, Aaron still speaking for his brother (6:10-13). He also performed, at Moses' direction, the miracles commanded by God unto Moses (7:9f.). With Hur he held up Moses' hands, in order that the "rod of God might be lifted up," during the fight with Amalek (17:10, 12).

Aaron next comes into prominence when, at Sinai, he is one of the elders and representatives of his tribe to approach nearer to the mount than the people in general were allowed to do, and to see the manifested glory of God (Ex. 24:1, 9f.). A few days later, when Moses, attended by his "minister" Joshua, went up into the mountain, Aaron exercised some kind of headship over the people in his absence. Despairing of seeing again their leader, who had disappeared into the mystery of communion with the invisible God, they appealed to Aaron to prepare them more tangible gods, and to lead them back to Egypt (Ex. 32). Aaron never appears as the strong, heroic character his brother was; and here at Sinai he revealed his weaker nature, yielding to the demands of the people and permitting them to make the golden bullock. That he must have yielded reluctantly is evident from the eagerness of his tribesmen, whose leader he was, to stay and avenge the apostasy by rushing to arms at the call of Moses and slaying the idolaters (32:26-28).

Since Aaron and his sons were chosen for the official priesthood, elaborate and symbolical vestments were prepared for them (Ex. 28); and after the erection and dedication of the tabernacle, he and his sons were formally inducted into the sacred office (Lev. 8). It appears that Aaron alone was anointed with the holy oil (8:12), but his sons shared with him the duty of caring for sacrificial rites and utensils. They served in receiving and presenting the various offerings, and could enter and serve in the first chamber of the tabernacle; but Aaron alone, the high priest, the mediator of the old covenant, could enter into the holy of holies, and that only once a year, on the great Day of Atonement (16:12-14).

After Israel departed from Sinai, Aaron joined his sister Miriam in a protest against the authority of Moses (Nu. 12), which they claimed was self-assumed. For this rebellion Miriam was smitten with leprosy, but was made whole again, when, at the pleading of Aaron, Moses interceded with God for her. The sacred office of Aaron, requiring physical, moral, and ceremonial cleanness of the strictest order, seems to have made him immune from this form of punishment. Somewhat later (Nu. 16) Aaron himself, along with Moses, became the object of a revolt of his own tribe in conspiracy with leaders of Dan and Reuben. This rebellion was subdued and the authority of Moses and Aaron vindicated by the miraculous overthrow of the rebels. As they were being destroyed by the plague, Aaron, at Moses' command, rushed into their midst with the lighted censer, and the destruction was stayed. The divine will in choosing Aaron and his family to the priesthood was then fully attested by the miraculous budding of his rod, when, along with rods representing the other tribes, it was left overnight in the sanctuary (Nu. 17). *See* AARON'S ROD.

After this event Aaron does not come prominently into view until the time of his death, near the close of the wilderness period. Because of the impatience, or unbelief, of Moses and Aaron at Meribah (Nu. 20:12), the two brothers are prohibited from entering Canaan; and shortly after the last camp at Kadesh was broken, as the people journeyed eastward to the plains of Moab, Aaron died on Mt. Hor. This event is recorded in three passages: the detailed account in Nu. 20, a second incidental record in the list of stations of the wanderings in the wilderness (Nu. 33:38f.), and a third casual reference (Dt. 10:6) in an address of Moses. These are not in the least contradictory or inharmonious. The dramatic scene is fully presented in Nu. 20: Moses, Aaron, and Eleazar go up to Mt. Hor in the people's sight; Aaron is divested of his robes of office, which are formally put upon his eldest son; Aaron dies before the Lord on the mount at the age of 123, and is given burial by his two mourning relatives, who then return to the camp; when the people understand that Aaron is no more, they show both grief and love by thirty days of mourning. The passage in Nu. 33 records the event of his death just after the list of stations in the general vicinity of Mt. Hor; while Dt. 10 states from which of these stations, viz., Moserah, that remarkable funeral procession made its way to Mt. Hor.

Aaron married Elisheba, daughter of Amminadab and sister of Nahshon, prince of the tribe of Judah; and she bore him four sons: Nadab, Abihu, Eleazar, and Ithamar. The sacrilegious act and consequent judicial death of Nadab and Abihu are recorded in Lev. 10. Eleazar and Ithamar were more pious and reverent; and from them descended the long line of priests to whom was committed the ceremonial law of Israel, the succession changing from one branch to the other with certain crises in the nation. At his death Aaron was succeeded by his oldest living son, Eleazar (Nu. 20:28; Dt. 10:6).

See Plate 10. E. MACK

AARONITES âr'ən-īts [Heb. *le'aharôn*–'belonging to Aaron']. A word used in the AV only, to translate the proper name Aaron in two instances where it denotes a family and not merely a person (1 Ch. 12:27; 27:17). It is equivalent to the phrases "sons of Aaron," "house of Aaron," frequently used in the OT. According to Joshua and Chronicles the "sons of Aaron" were distinguished from the other Levites from the time of Joshua (e.g., Josh. 21:4, 10, 13; 1 Ch. 6:54).

AARON'S ROD (Nu. 17; He. 9:4). The rebellion led by Korah against the priestly authority of Aaron made it necessary for Aaron's supremacy to be stressed. Moses was instructed to take one almond rod for each tribe and one for Aaron, duly inscribed. When placed in the tabernacle, Aaron's rod was the only one to bud, blossom, and bear almonds. Thereafter it was preserved as a token of God's will (Nu. 17:10). According to the writer of Hebrews the rod was kept in the holy of holies inside the ark (He. 9:4; cf. 1 K. 8:9). R. K. H.

AB ab, ôb [Heb. and Aram. *'āḇ, 'aḇ*–'father'].

1. (a) Used of the male ancestor of a family. In a patriarchal society his authority was unquestioned (cf. 2 K. 3:27). The law commanded his children to honor him (Ex. 20:12; Dt. 5:16), and the penalty for abusing him was death (Ex. 21:15-17). He was responsible for the material and spiritual welfare of the family (Dt. 1:31; Prov. 1:8), and his offspring provided him with a sense of immortality.

(b) *Ab* often refers to a more distant ancestor such as a grandfather, and commonly to forefathers of the Israelite community (cf. Gen. 17:4). In Mk. 11:10, David was referred to in this manner (cf. Lk. 3:8; Rom. 4:1; Jas. 2:21).

(c) "Father" also described the progenitor of a class or the originator of some group, Jabal (Gen. 4:20), Jubal (4:21), Rechab (Jer. 35:6), Abraham (Rom. 4:11, 16f.) and Phinehas (1 Macc. 2:54) being thus designated. *See* BEN-.

(d) *Ab* is also a name for God, and occurred commonly as an element in personal names. By contrast, the devil also could be described as "father" (Jn. 8:44). *See* GOD, NAMES OF; ABBA; ABI.

2. The postexilic name of the fifth month of the Hebrew calendar (July/Aug.), when olives were harvested. *See* CALENDAR. R. K. H.

ABACUC ab'ə-kək [Lat. *Abacuc*] (2 Esd. 1:40, AV). *See* HABAKKUK.

ABADDON ə-bad'ən [Heb. *'aḇaddôn*–'(place of) destruction'; Gk. *Abaddōn*]; NEB also DESTRUCTION. In the OT, a place name for the realm of the dead. In three instances Abaddon is paralleled with Sheol (Job 26:6; Prov. 15:11; 27:20), while in Job 28:22 it parallels Death, and in Ps. 88:11 the grave. In Job 31:12 it is part of a metaphor of destruction.

Abaddon belongs to the realm of the mysterious. Only God understands it (Job 26:6; Prov. 15:11). It is the world of the dead in its utterly dismal, destructive, dreadful aspects, not in those more cheerful aspects which include the concept of activities. In Abaddon there are no declarations of God's lovingkindness (Ps. 88:11).

In a slight degree the OT presentations personalize Abaddon. It is a synonym for insatiableness (Prov. 27:20). It has possibilities of information mediate between those of "all living" and those of God (Job 28:22).

In the NT the word occurs once (Rev. 9:11), the personalization becoming sharp. Abaddon is here not the world of the dead, but the angel who reigns over it. The Greek equivalent of his name is given as APOLLYON.

W. J. BEECHER

ABADIAS ab-ə-dī'əs (1 Esd. 8:35, AV, NEB). *See* OBADIAH **11**.

ABAGARUS. *See* ABGAR.

ABAGTHA ə-bag'thə [Heb. *'aḇageṯā'*–perhaps 'fortunate one']. One of the seven eunuchs, or "chamberlains," of Xerxes mentioned in Est. 1:10. The name is probably of Middle Iranian origin, and is one of the many Persian marks in Esther.

See L. B. Paton, comm. on Esther (*ICC*, 1916), pp. 67f.

ABANA ab'ə-nə [Heb. *'aḇānâ*; Gk., Lat., *Abana*] (2 K. 5:12). A river mentioned along with the PHARPAR as one of the principal rivers of Damascus. The RV mg. reading "Amana" is based on the *qere* (Heb. *'amānâ*; cf. Pesh., Tg.), which may reflect an alternative in actual use, inasmuch as the interchange of *ḇ* and *m* is not without parallel (cf. Evil-merodach=Amil-marduk).

The Abana is identified with the Chrysorrhoas ("golden stream") of the Greeks, the modern Nahr Baradā (the "cold"), which rises in the Anti-Lebanon, one of its sources, the 'Ain Baradā, being near the village of Zebedani, and flows S and then SE toward Damascus. A few miles SE of ancient Abila (*see* ABILENE) the volume of the stream is more than doubled by a torrent of clear, cold water from the beautifully situated spring 'Ain Fijeh, after which it flows through a picturesque gorge till it reaches Damascus, whose many fountains and gardens it supplies liberally with water. In the neighborhood of Damascus a number of streams branch off from the parent river, and spread out like an opening fan on the surrounding plain.

The Barada, along with the streams which it feeds, loses itself in the marshes of the Meadow Lakes about 18 mi. (29 km.) E of the city. C. M. THOMSON

ABARIM ab'ə-rim [Heb. *'ᵃḇārîm*–'regions beyond']; AV also "the passages" (Jer. 22:20). A mountainous region E of the northern Dead Sea.

When the people of Abraham lived in Canaan, before they went to Egypt to sojourn, they spoke of the region E of the Jordan as "beyond Jordan." Looking across the Jordan and the Dead Sea, they designated the mountain country they saw there as "the Beyond mountains." They continued to use these geographical terms when they came out of Egypt (Nu. 27:12; 33:45-48; Dt. 32:49). We have no means of knowing the extent of the region to which they applied the name. The passages speak of the mountain country of Abarim where Moses died, including Nebo, as situated back from the river Jordan in its lowest reaches; and of the Mounds of the Abarim (*see* IYE-ABARIM) as farther SE so that the Israelites passed them when making their detour around the agricultural parts of Edom, before they crossed the Arnon. Whether the name Abarim should be applied to the parts of the eastern hill country farther N is a question on which we lack evidence.

The name Abarim occurs without the article in Jer. 22:20, where it seems to be the name of a region, on the same footing with the names Lebanon and Bashan, doubtless the region referred to in Numbers and Deuteronomy. The NEB emends Ezk. 39:11 to read this name, instead of RSV "travelers." W. J. BEECHER

ABASE [Heb. *šāpēl, šāpāl, kālam*; Aram. *šᵉpal*; Gk. *tapeinóō*] (Job 40:11; Dnl. 4:37; 2 Cor. 11:7; etc.). The word is often employed to indicate what should be done to or by him who nurtures a spirit and exhibits a demeanor contrary to the laudable humility which is a natural fruit of religion. Christ promised that self-abasement would lead to divine exaltation (Mt. 23:12; Lk. 14:11; 18:14; cf. Jas. 4:10; 1 Pet. 5:6). *See* HUMBLE; SHAME.

ABBA a'bə [Gk. *abbá*, a transliterated loanword from Aram. *'abbā'*, which represents two homonyms in Jewish Palestinian Aramaic that are identical orthographically and phonetically, but distinct morphologically; one homonym may be translated as 'the father' or 'my father,' the other as 'dada,' 'daddy.']. The common, but incorrect, morphological analysis of the Aram. *'abbā'* transliterated into Greek in Mk. 14:36; Rom. 8:15; Gal. 4:6, is that it is the emphatic state of the noun *'aḇ* ("father"). While the emphatic or determinative ending *-ā'* is a virtual Aramaic equivalent of the definite article in Hebrew, it sometimes had the force of a possessive pronoun in Jewish Palestinian Aramaic (Stevenson, § 8); consequently the context alone would determine whether *'abbā'* should be translated "the father," or "my father." Furthermore, by the time of Jesus the Aram. *'aḇ* with the first person singular pronominal suffix *-î* (*'ᵃḇî*, "my father"; cf. its use in Dnl. 5:13) had become virtually obsolete and was replaced by *'abbā'* (Dalman, pp. 191f.).

In contrast with the foregoing morphological analysis, however, comparative linguistics indicates that the Aram. *'abbā'* used by Jesus (see below) was formed in an entirely different manner. That which appears to be the Aramaic emphatic ending *-ā'* (with compensatory doubling of the final radical *b*) is in reality the reduplication of the initial syllable *'ab* in the final syllable *-bā'* characteristic of *Lallwörter* ("nursery words"). Such reduplication is a universal phenomenon in the development of the speech of children (Berry, pp. 162ff.), for which the English forms "dada/daddy," "momma/mommy" are excellent examples. The homonym *'abbā'* originated in the babbling of infants and small children in Aramaic-speaking families, and gradually achieved wider currency (cf. Jeremias, p. 58). In the colloquial speech of Jesus' time, *'abbā'* was primarily used as a term of informal intimacy and respect by children of their fathers (Jeremias, p. 60). Like the analogous Aram. *'îmmā'* ("momma") derived from the Aram. *'ēm* ("mother"), *abbā'* is a static form in Palestinian Jewish Aramaic, taking neither suffix nor inflection.

In the NT, *abbá* occurs only three times, always in the form of the compound address *abbá ho patḗr* ("abba, father"): Mk. 14:36; Rom. 8:15; Gal. 4:6. The transliteration, rather than translation, of the term *abbá* indicates that it had become a fixed liturgical expression within early Christianity, undoubtedly under the influence of Jesus' usage. Evidence from the four Gospels indicates that Jesus customarily addressed God as "Father" in all of His prayers; the sixteen examples (twenty-one including parallels) are found in every stratum of the Gospel tradition: Mark (1 time); Q (3); Luke (2); Matthew (1); John (9). (The only exception is Mk. 15:34 par. Mt. 27:46, where Jesus cries out from the cross "My God, my God" in the words of Ps. 22:1.) In Greek there are three ways in which Jesus addresses God as "Father" in prayer contexts: (1) *páter* ("father"), the Greek vocative (Mt. 11:25 par. Lk. 10:21a; Lk. 11:2; 22:42; 23:34, 46; Jn. 11:41; 12:27f.; 17:1, 5, 11, 21, 24f.); (2) *ho patḗr* ("the father"), the articular nominative used as a vocative (Mk. 14:36 [*abbá ho patḗr;* cf. Rom. 8:15; Gal. 4:6]—correct Greek form, since the second member of a compound address is always in the nominative [Robertson, p. 461]; Mt. 11:26 par. Lk. 10:21b—incorrect Greek usage, and therefore in all probability a Semitism, since the articular nominative constitutes the vocative in both Hebrew and Aramaic [Turner, p. 34]); (3) *páter mou* ("my father"), Greek vocative with first person singular possessive pronoun (Mt. 26:39, 42). This variation in expression makes it probable that the Aram. *'abbā'* was the original form of address used in each of these prayers, since the term could legitimately be translated in all of these ways (Black, p. 283).

While the OT does use the image "Father" for Yahweh, it is a comparatively marginal conception, occurring only fourteen times and usually in the sense of an absolute and irrevocable authority (*TDOT*, I, 17-19). The Judaism of the Greco-Roman era continues the reluctance to apply this image to Yahweh. However, beginning with the end of the 1st cent. A.D., the image becomes increasingly common in rabbinic literature (Dalman, pp. 186-89; SB, I, 394ff.; II, 49f.). According to Jeremias (p. 29), there is no evidence in the literature of ancient Palestinian Judaism that *'abbā'* was used as a personal address to God in prayer (cf. *TDNT,* I, 5). However, this argument from silence is so heavily qualified by Jeremias (cf. pp. 15-29) that it cannot bear the full weight he gives it (cf. Sandmel, p. 202). Nonetheless, it may be observed that *'abbā'* as a form of address to God is extremely uncommon in Jewish literature of the Greco-Roman period, doubtless because it would have appeared irreverent to address God with this familiar term. Jesus' frequent use of this term in prayer is an indirect attestation of His extraordinary claim to intimacy with God. In further contrast with the reluctance of first-century Palestinian Judaism to apply the image of "father" to God, the four Gospels preserve more than 125 instances in which Jesus refers to God as "Father" in contexts other than prayer; in all probability the Aram. *'abbā'* stands behind each of these occurrences.

Bibliography.–M. F. Berry, *Language Disorders of Children*

(1969); M. Black, *Aramaic Approach to the Gospels and Acts* (3rd ed. 1967); G. Dalman, *Words of Jesus* (1902); J. Jeremias, *Prayers of Jesus* (1967), pp. 11-65; S. V. McCasland, *JBL*, 72 (1953), 79-91; A. T. Robertson, *Grammar of the Greek NT in the Light of Historical Research* (1934); S. Sandmel, *First Christian Century in Judaism and Christianity* (1969); W. B. Stevenson, *Grammar of Palestinian Jewish Aramaic* (1924); SB; *TDNT*, I, *s.v.* ἀββᾶ (Kittel); V, *s.v.* πατήρ, esp. pp. 984f. (Schrenk); *TDOT*, I, *s.v.* "*'ābh*" (Ringgren); N. Turner, *Syntax*, Vol. III of J. H. Moulton, *Grammar of NT Greek* (1963). D. E. AUNE

ABDA ab'də [Heb. *'aḇdā'*–perhaps abbr. for 'servant of Yahweh'].

1. The father of Adoniram, King Solomon's superintendent of forced labor (1 K. 4:6).

2. A Levite mentioned in the statistical note in Neh. 11:17. This "Abda the son of Shammua" is in the partly duplicate passage in 1 Ch. 9:16 called "Obadiah the son of Shemaiah."

ABDEEL ab'də-el [Heb. *'aḇdᵉ'ēl*–'servant of God']. The father of SHELEMIAH (Jer. 36:26).

ABDI ab'dī [Heb. *'aḇdî*–prob. abbr. for 'servant of Yahweh'].

1. A Levite, father of Kishi and grandfather of King David's singer Ethan (1 Ch. 6:44 [MT 29]; cf. 15:17). This makes Abdi a contemporary of Saul the king.

2. A Levite, father of the Kish who was in service at the beginning of the reign of Hezekiah (2 Ch. 29:12). Some mistakenly identify this Abdi with **1.**

3. A man who in Ezra's time had married a foreign wife (Ezr. 10:26). He was not a Levite, but "of the sons of Elam."

ABDIAS ab-dī'əs (2 Esd. 1:39, AV). *See* OBADIAH **1.** Here in 2 Esdras it is said that Abraham, Isaac, Jacob, and the Minor Prophets shall be given as leaders to the "nation from the east" which is to overthrow Israel.

ABDIEL ab'di-əl [Heb. *'aḇdî'ēl*–'servant of God']. A Gadite who lived in Gilead or in Bashan, and whose name was reckoned in genealogies of the time of Jotham king of Judah, or of Jeroboam II king of Israel (1 Ch. 5:15-17).

ABDON ab'don [Heb. *'aḇdôn*–perhaps 'service,' 'worship'].

1. A JUDGE of Israel for eight years (Jgs. 12:13-15). He was the son of Hillel the Pirathonite, and was buried in Pirathon in the territory of Ephraim (probably to be identified with Far'âtā, about 6 mi. [10 km.] WSW of Shechem).

Abdon's numerous offspring (forty sons and thirty grandsons) indicate that he had extensive family relationships, and his possession of seventy asses points to his being a man of wealth and standing.

Abdon is the last judge in the continuous account of Jgs. 2:6-13:1. After his judgeship Israel was delivered into the hands of the Philistines for a period of forty years; then follow the stories of Samson, Micah and his Levite, the Benjaminite civil war, and the childhood of Samuel. The national history is resumed in 1 S. 4:18. Upon the death of Abdon the Philistines asserted themselves as overlords of Israel. Their policy of suppressing Israel's national consciousness resulted in their abolishing the office of judge and transferring the priesthood to Eli's house, but Eli assumed some of the judge's duties. As soon as Israel regained her independence, the office of judgeship was reestablished with Samuel as judge (1 S. 7:6; 2:27f.).

2. The son of Jehiel and his wife Maachah (1 Ch. 8:30; 9:36). Jehiel is depicted as the "father of Gibeon," perhaps the founder of the Israelite community there. This Abdon is also referred to as the brother of Ner the grandfather of King Saul.

3. One of the messengers sent by King Josiah to Huldah the prophetess (2 Ch. 34:20). In the parallel passage 2 K. 22:12 he is called ACHBOR.

4. One of the multitude of the Benjaminites who lived in Jerusalem (1 Ch. 8:23), possibly under Nehemiah's governorship, though the date is uncertain.

5. A city of the Levites in the tribe of Asher about 8 or 9 mi. (13 or 14 km.) NNE of Accho (Josh. 21:30; 1 Ch. 6:74), probably the present ruin of 'Abdeh. W. J. BEECHER

D. W. DEERE

ABED-NEGO ə-bed'nə-gō [Heb. and Aram. *'ᵃḇēḏ nᵉgô*, once Aram. *'ᵃḇēḏ nᵉgô'* (Dnl. 3:29)]. The name given in the court of Nebuchadnezzar to Azariah, one of Daniel's three companions (Dnl. 1:6f.). The name is unknown in Neo-Babylonian texts. According to many, *nego* is an intentional corruption of Nebo, the Babylonian god of wisdom, arising from the desire of the Hebrew scribes to avoid giving a heathen name to a hero of their faith. The name, according to this view, would mean "servant of Nebo." Others take it as a translation of some Babylonian name beginning with Arad, "servant." Attempts have been made to relate the second element to the Babylonian word for "morning star," a name given to the goddess Ishtar.

After he refused, along with his friends, to eat the provisions of the king's table, Abed-nego was fed and flourished upon vegetables and water. Having successfully passed his examinations and escaped the death with which the wise men of Babylon were threatened, at the request of Daniel he was appointed along with his companions over the affairs of the province of Babylon (Dnl. 2). But because he refused to bow down to the image which Nebuchadnezzar had set up, he was cast into the burning fiery furnace; and after his triumphant delivery he was caused by the king to prosper in the province of Babylon (Dnl. 3). The three friends are referred to by name in 1 Macc. 2:59, and by implication in He. 11:33f. R. D. WILSON

ABEL ā'bəl [Heb. *hāḇel*; Gk. *Abel*]. The second son of Adam and Eve (Gen. 4:1-9). His name may be derived from Akk. *aplu*, "son," and is perhaps generic in nature.

A herdsman, Abel presented to God a more acceptable sacrifice than his brother Cain, and was subsequently killed by the latter in a fit of jealousy. Why Abel's offering was more suitable is unknown, and there is no evidence that at this period animal sacrifices were deemed superior to cereal offerings. The LXX *diélēs* of Gen. 4:7 suggests that Cain's real offense was a ritual one, the offering apparently not having been presented in a proper manner. Even so, strict ceremonial regulations applied only to animal sacrifices (cf. Ex. 29:17; Lev. 8:20; Jgs. 19:29). He. 11:4, however, implies improper spiritual motivation as the real reason why the offering was rejected. Well-doing consisted not in the outward offering (Gen. 4:7) but in the right state of heart and mind.

Abel ranks as the first martyr (Mt. 23:35), whose blood cried for vengeance (Gen. 4:10; cf. Rev. 6:9f.) and produced despair, whereas that of Jesus appeals to God for man's forgiveness and brings cleansing from sin (1 Jn. 1:7). Abel's death is a prototype of Christ's death (He. 12:24). R. K. H.

ABEL ā'bəl [Heb. *'āḇēl*–'meadow']. A word used in several compound names of places. It appears by itself as the name of a city concerned in the rebellion of Sheba (2 S. 20:18), though it is there probably an abridgment of the name ABEL-BETH-MAACAH (cf. vv. 14f.). In 1 S. 6:18, where the Hebrew has "the great meadows," and the Greek "the great stone" (so RSV, NEB), the AV translates "the great stone of Abel."

ABEL-BETH-MAACAH ā'bəl-beth-mā'ə-kə [Heb. *'āḇēl bêṯ-ma'ᵃḵâ*–'meadow of the house of Maacah' (1 K. 15:20; 2 K. 15:29), also *'āḇēlâ bêṯ hamma'ᵃḵâ* (2 S. 20:15), *'āḇēlâ ûḇêṯ ma'ᵃḵâ* (v. 14)] also **ABEL OF BETH-MAACAH** (2 S. 20:14f.); AV ABEL-BETH-MAACHAH (or "of Beth-maachah"), also "Abel, and (to) Beth-maachah" (2 S. 20:14). In 2 S. 20, the city, far to the north, where Joab besieged Sheba son of Bichri; in 2 K. 15, along with Ijon and other places, a city in Naphtali captured by Tiglath-pileser king of Assyria (733 B.C.). The capture appears also in the records of Tiglath-pileser, where the city is called Abilakka. In 1 K. 15 it is mentioned with Ijon and Dan and "all the land Naphtali" as being smitten by Ben-hadad of Damascus in the time of Baasha. In the parallel account in 2 Chronicles 16:4 the cities mentioned are Ijon, Dan, and Abel-maim. Abel-maim is either another name for Abel-beth-maacah, or the name of another place in the same vicinity.

The prevailing identification of Abel-beth-maacah is with Abil, a few miles W of Dan, on a height overlooking the Jordan near its sources. The adjacent region is rich agriculturally, and the scenery and the water supply are especially fine. Abel-maim, "meadow of water," is an apt designation for it. W. J. BEECHER

ABEL-KERAMIM ā'bəl-ker'ə-mim [Heb. *'āḇēl keramîm*–'meadow of vineyards']; AV "plain of the vineyards." A city mentioned in Jgs. 11:33 along with Aroer, Minnith, and "twenty cities," in summarizing Jephthah's campaign against the Ammonites. Eusebius and Jerome speak of it as in their time a village about 7 Roman mi. from Rabbath-ammon (mod. Amman); and the site may be identified with Khirbet es-Suq, 5 mi. (8 km.) S of Amman. *GAB* suggests Na'ûr, NE of Nebo.

ABEL-MAIM ā'bəl-mā'əm [Heb. *'āḇēl mayim*–'meadow of water']. *See* ABEL-BETH-MAACAH.

ABEL-MEHOLAH ā'bəl-mə-hō'la [Heb. *'āḇēl meḥôlâ*–'meadow of dancing']. The residence of Elisha the prophet (1 K. 19:16). When Gideon and his three hundred broke their pitchers in the camp of Midian, the Midianites in their first panic fled down the valley of Jezreel and the Jordan "toward Zererah" (Jgs. 7:22). Zererah (Zeredah) is Zarethan (2 Ch. 4:17; cf. 1 K. 7:46), separated from Succoth by the clay ground where Solomon made castings for the temple. The wing of the Midianites whom Gideon pursued crossed the Jordan at Succoth (Jgs. 8:4ff.). This would indicate that Abel-meholah was thought of as a tract of country with a "border," W of the Jordan, some miles S of Beth-shean, in the territory either of Issachar or west Manasseh.

Abel-meholah is also mentioned in connection with the jurisdiction of Baana, one of Solomon's twelve commissary officers (1 K. 4:12) as below Jezreel, with Beth-shean and Zarethan in the same list.

Jerome and Eusebius speak of Abel-meholah as a tract of country and a town in the Jordan Valley, about 10 Roman mi. S of Beth-shean. At just that point the name seems to be perpetuated in that of the Wâdī Mâliḥ, and Abel-meholah is commonly located near where that wadi, or the neighboring Wâdī Helweh, comes down into the Jordan Valley. *WHAB* locates it at Tell el-Maqlûb, *GAB* at Tell Abû Sifri, both in this same general vicinity.

Presumably Adriel the Meholathite (1 S. 18:19; 2 S. 21:8) was a resident of Abel-meholah. W. J. BEECHER

ABEL-MIZRAIM ā'bəl-miz'rə-im [Heb. *'āḇēl miṣrayim*–'watercourse of Egypt']. The alternate name of Atad, E of Jordan and N of the Dead Sea, given because Joseph and his funeral party from Egypt mourned (cf. *'ēḇel*, "mourning") there over Jacob (Gen. 50:11). The reference to Atad being "beyond Jordan" may imply that the narrative standpoint was that of Transjordan; otherwise a circuitous route would have been necessary.

ABEL-SHITTIM ā'bəl-shit'im [Heb. *'āḇēl haššiṭṭîm*–'watercourse of the acacias']. This form appears in Nu. 33:49 only, the name Shittim being used elsewhere (Nu. 25:1; Josh. 2:1; 3:1; Mic. 6:5). The valley of Joel 3:18 [MT 4:18] is apparently a different location. *See* SHITTIM.

ABEZ ā'bəz (Josh. 19:20, AV). *See* EBEZ.

ABGAR ab'gär; **ABGARUS** ab-gä'rəs; **ABAGARUS** ə-bag'ər-əs [Gk. *Abgaros*]; written also AGBARUS; AUGARUS. A name common to several kings (toparchs) of Edessa, Mesopotamia. One of these, Abgar, a son of Uchomo, the seventeenth (14th?) of twenty kings, according to legend (see Eusebius *HE* i.13) sent a letter to Jesus, professing belief in His messiahship and asking Him to come and heal him from an incurable disease (leprosy?), inviting Him at the same time to take refuge from His enemies in his city, "which is enough for us both." Jesus answering the letter blessed him, because he had believed on Him without having seen Him, and promised to send one of His disciples after He had risen from the dead. The apostle Thomas sent Judas Thaddeus, one of the Seventy, who healed him.

See J. Quasten, *Patrology* (1950), I, 142f.

A. L. BRESLICH

ABHOR; ABHORRENCE; ABHORRENT [Heb. *bā'aš, gā'al, dērā'ôn, zā'am, qûṣ, šāqaṣ tā'aḇ, tā'aḇ*; Gk. *bdelýssomai*]; AV also ABOMINABLE, LOTHING (sic); NEB also SPURN (Lev. 26), LOATHE, "regard as an abomination," REPUGNANCE, DETEST, etc. Words generally indicating offense to natural, moral, or religious sensibilities. *See also* HATE; ENMITY. In the AV "abhor" also has the archaic sense "despise, treat with contempt" (e.g., 1 S. 2:17).

ABI ā'bī [Heb. *'ᵃḇî*]. The name of the mother of King Hezekiah, as given in 2 K. 18:2. It is no doubt a contraction of Abijah, found in the parallel passage 2 Ch. 29:1. The spelling in the oldest version seems to indicate that *'ᵃḇî* is not a copyist's error, but a genuine contracted form. She was the daughter of Zechariah, and the wife of Ahaz.

ABI ā'bī [Heb. *'ᵃḇî*–'father']. The first element of several Hebrew names. The Heb. *'āḇ*, "father," and *'āḥ*, "brother," are used in forming names, both at the beginning and at the end of words, e.g., Abram ("exalted one"), Joah ("Jehovah is brother"), Ahab ("father's brother"). At the beginning of a word, however, the modified forms *'ᵃḇî* and *'ᵃḥî* are the ones commonly used, e.g., Ahimelech ("king's brother") and Abimelech ("king's father").

Certain characteristics of these forms complicate the question of their use in proper names. The Heb. *'ᵃḇî* may be a nominative with an archaic ending ("father"), or in the construct state ("father-of"), or the form with the suffix ("my father"). Hence a proper name constructed with it may conceivably be either a phrase or a sentence; if it is a sentence, either of the two words may be either subject or predicate. That is to say, the name Abimelech may conceivably mean either "father of a king," or a "a king is father," or "a father is a king," or "my father is King," or "a king is my father." Moreover, the phrase "father of a king" may have as many variations of meaning as there are varieties of the grammatical genitive. Further still, it is claimed that "father" or "king" may, in a name, be a designation of a deity. Thus the intended meaning may be any one of a large number of conceivable meanings.

Earlier scholarship regarded all these names as construct phrases. For example, Abidan is "father of a judge." It explained different instances as being different varieties of the genitive construction; e.g., Abihail, "father of might," means "mighty father." The woman's name Abigail, "father of exultation," denotes one whose father is exultant. Abishai, "father of Jesse," denotes one to whom Jesse is father, and so with Abihud, "father of Judah," Abiel, "father of God," Abijah, "father of Yahweh." See the cases in detail in Gesenius' *Hebrew and Chaldee Lexicon* (1952).

More recent scholarship regards most or all of the instances as sentences. In some cases it regards the second element in a name as a verb or adjective instead of a noun; but in Hebrew the genitive construction might persist, even with the verb or adjective. In the five instances last given, the explanation "my father is exultation," "is Jesse," "is Judah," "is God," "is Yahweh," certainly gives the meaning in a more natural way than by explaining these names as construct expressions.

There is sharp conflict over the question whether we ought to regard the suffix pronoun as present in these names—whether the five instances should not rather be translated "Yahweh is father," "God is father," etc. The question is raised whether the same rule prevails when the second word is a name or a designation of deity as prevails in other cases. Should we explain one instance as meaning "my father is Jesse," and another as "God is father"? For most persons the safe method is to remember that the final decision is not yet reached, and to consider each name by itself, counting the explanation of it an open question. *See also* NAMES, PROPER.

The investigations concerning Semitic proper names, both in and out of the Bible, have interesting theological bearings. It has always been recognized that words for father and brother, when combined in proper names with Yah, Yahu, El, Baal, or other proper names of a deity, indicated some relation of the person named, or of his tribe, with the deity. It is now held, though with many differences of opinion, that in forming proper names many other words, e.g., the words for king, lord, strength, beauty, are also used as designations of deity or of some particular deity; and that the words father, brother, and the like may have the same use. To a certain extent the proper names are so many propositions in theology. It is technically possible to go very far in inferring that the people who formed such names thought of deity or of some particular deity as the father, the kinsman, the ruler, the champion, the strength, the glory of the tribe or of the individual. In particular one might infer the existence of a widely diffused doctrine of the fatherhood of God. It is doubtless superfluous to add that at present one ought to be very cautious in drawing or accepting inferences in this part of the field of human study.

See *IP*, pp. 66-75. W. J. BEECHER

ABIA; ABIAH ə-bī'ə. *See* ABIJAH.

ABI-ALBON ā-bī-al'bən [Heb. *'ᵃḇî'ᵃlᵉḇôn*; Gk. *Abiel*]. "The Arbathite," one of David's listed heroes (2 S. 23:31), called Abiel the Arbathite in 1 Ch. 11:32. Presumably he was from Beth-arabah (so NEB; cf. Josh. 15:6, 61; 18:22). Possibly Abi-albon is a textual corruption, from confusion with Shaalbon (2 S. 23:32).

ABIASAPH ə-bī'ə-saf, ab-i-ā'saf [Heb. *'ᵃḇî'āsāp*–'my father has gathered'] (Ex. 6:24); **EBIASAPH** [Heb. *'eḇyāsāp*] (1 Ch. 6:23, 37 [MT 8, 22]; 9:19). A descendant of Kohath the son of Levi. The list in Exodus terminates with Abiasaph, who is to be regarded as the contemporary of Phinehas the grandson of Aaron. The two lists in 1 Ch. 6 lead up to the prophet Samuel and the singing companies which David is said to have organized. The list in 1 Ch. 9 leads up to the Korahite porters of the time of Nehemiah. Apparently all the lists intentionally omit names, just enough being given in each to indicate the line.

W. J. BEECHER

ABIATHAR ə-bī'ə-thär, ab-i-ā'thär [Heb. *'eḇyāṯār*–'the father is preeminent']. The son of Ahimelech son of Ahitub, priest of Nob. He escaped (1 S. 22:20) Saul's slaughter of the priests there after Doeg the Edomite (21:7 [MT 8]) informed against Ahimelech (v. 2) for having given food to the fugitive David.

In 1 S. 21:2 Ahimelech is the priest par excellence of Nob (cf. 21:1; 22:11). The only mention of Abiathar in these two chapters is in 22:20, where he is the survivor who fled after David. David, feeling indirectly responsible for bringing the priests of Nob under Saul's wrath (cf. 22:22), became Abiathar's protector. Abiathar repaid this with loyal service to David throughout the latter's life.

Abiathar brought from Nob the ephod by means of which the divine will was ascertained for David (1 S. 23:2, 9f.). After David had become king and brought the ark to Jerusalem and reigned over all Israel, Zadok the son of Ahitub and Ahimelech the son of Abiathar (2 S. 8:17) are mentioned as his priests. But in eight further references (2 S. 15:24, 27, 29, 35f.; 17:15; 19:11 [MT 12]; 20:25) Zadok and Abiathar are cited as David's priests. Both were loyal to David along with their sons, Ahimaaz the son of Zadok and Jonathan the son of Abiathar, during Absalom's revolt.

In 1 K. 1:7, 19, 25, 42; 2:22, 26f., 35, Abiathar is reported to have championed Adonijah rather than Solomon for the throne in succession to David. He was subsequently dismissed by Solomon. In 1 K. 2:27 this is said to fulfil the word of Yahweh concerning Eli, Abiathar's ancestor in Shiloh. 1 K. 2:35 says that Solomon put Zadok the priest in the place of Abiathar, showing that Abiathar had been the senior priest. 1 K. 4:4, speaking of Solomon's priests, still mentions Abiathar, but after Zadok.

Despite 2 S. 8:17, there is no reason to doubt that Ahimelech had been the priest at Nob and that Abiathar, the sole survivor, was David's priest according to the books of Samuel and Kings. In any case 2 S. 8:17 (Pesh.) reads "Abiathar the son of Ahimelech." Further, Ps. 52 (title) reads ". . . A Psalm of David, when Doeg the Edomite came and told Saul and said unto him, David is come to the house of Ahimelech" (cf. 1 S. 22:9f.).

In 1 Ch. 15:11 Zadok and Abiathar are David's priests, but in 1 Ch. 18:16, following 2 S. 8:17, Zadok the son of Ahitub and A*b*imelech the son of Abiathar are his priests. Also in 1 Ch. 24:6 Zadok the priest and Ahimelech the son of Abiathar are mentioned. Abimelech and Ahimelech are one and the same (cf., e.g., the Gk. MSS A and B in 1 S. 22:16, 20; 23:6, the former reading Ahimelech, the latter Abimelech). In 1 Ch. 27:17 Zadok is mentioned as head of the Aaronite priests but Abiathar (1 Ch. 27:34) is mentioned only as one of David's advisers. However, even in two cases in 1 Chronicles Abiathar is a colleague and contemporary of Zadok.

The problem is made more difficult in that Jesus said to the Pharisees (Mk. 2:25f.): "Have you never read what David did, when he was in need and was hungry, he and those who were with him: how he entered the house of God, when Abiathar was high priest, and ate the bread of the Presence, which it is not lawful for any but the priests to eat, and also gave it to those who were with him?" To maintain the historical accuracy of this statement one might argue that Abiathar and Ab/himelech are different names for the same person, and that father and son both had the same name. But this is not very convincing. It is more likely that the reference is simply a general one, i.e., that the Abiathar who became high priest had a hand in giving the bread of the Presence to David and his men.

The following suggestion also deserves consideration. There was a long rivalry between the Abiatharite priests, descended through Eli from Aaron's younger son Ithamar, and the Zadokites, descended from his elder son Eleazar. 2 S. 8:17, if it is not a mistaken reading, removes Abiathar from being a colleague of Zadok in Jerusalem and makes him priest of another holy place — a sin in later OT times; cf. Ezk. 44:15, where only the Levitical priests, the sons of Zadok, are to serve God at the altar. The Abiatharites of Anathoth (cf. 1 K. 2:26) were not Zadokites, and were long denied all association with Jerusalem. After the Exile they were allowed one-third of the priestly courses in the second temple — more than Ezekiel would have granted.

Against this background the words of Jesus cut deep. He does not merely justify plucking ears of corn on the sabbath (Mk. 2:23). By citing the case of David, He refers to a house of God other than that at Jerusalem, which was all that the Pharisees, though anti-Sadducee, would accept. Nob had been the house of God, and the priest who served there was also high priest — something the Zadokites and Sadducees would find hard to swallow — even prior to his demotion by Solomon (cf. the precedence given to Zadok from his appearance in 2 S. 8:17).

At the same time Jesus opposed both the hyperlegalism of the Pharisees and the particularism of the Sadducees. By giving the bread of the Presence to David, Abiathar had been guilty of a serious breach of the ritual law, which was the concern of the Pharisees. But his action was right; and so, too, was that of the disciples. For the law, and with it the sabbath, was made for man; and if kept in the spirit, the details could be broken in cases of necessity. Again, Abiathar had been a true priest even at Nob, and a valid high priest at Jerusalem (which his father had not been). This carries the twofold lesson that God is not worshiped in Jerusalem alone, and that the priesthood is not confined to those of Zadokite descent. In other words, Jesus uses the incident in the manner of Haggadic midrash, i.e., with the aim of illustrating His message rather than recounting history. For this purpose it is more apt that Abiathar, the priest at Nob and later high priest at Jerusalem, should be the central figure in the story rather than his father Ahimelech; and it is imperative that he be styled high priest in spite of the mistaken, or deliberately altered, reading at 2 S. 8:17 and the derivative 1 Ch. 18:16; 24:6.

Bibliography.–*IP*, pp. 21, 33, 193; *PIOT*, pp. 356f.

J. BOWMAN

ABIB ā'bib [Heb. *'āḇîḇ*–young ear of barley or other grain; cf. Ex. 9:31; Lev. 2:14]. The first month of the Israelite year, called Nisan in Neh. 2:1; Est. 3:7, Abib in Ex. 13:4; 23:15; 34:18; Dt. 16:1. Abib is not properly a name of a month, but part of a descriptive phrase, "the month of young ears of grain." This may indicate the Israelite way of determining the new year (Ex. 12:2), the year beginning with the new moon nearest or next preceding this stage of the growth of the barley. The year thus indicated practically corresponded with the old Babylonian year, and presumably came in with Abraham. The pentateuchal laws do not introduce it, though they define it, perhaps to distinguish it from the Egyptian wandering year. *See* CALENDAR.

W. J. BEECHER

ABIDA ə-bī'də [Heb. *'^{a}ḇîḏā'*–'father of knowledge' or 'my father knows']; AV also ABIDAH (Gen. 25:4). A son of Midian and grandson of Abraham and Keturah (Gen. 25:4; 1 Ch. 1:33).

ABIDAH (Gen. 25:4, AV). *See* ABIDA.

ABIDAN ə-bī'dən [Heb. *'^{a}ḇîḏān*–'father is judge']. The son of Gideoni, and a leader (Heb. *nāśî'*) of the tribe of Benjamin (Nu. 2:22; 10:24). He was chosen to represent his tribe at the census in the wilderness of Sinai (Nu. 1:11). At the erection, anointing, and sanctification of the tabernacle, Abidan made his offering on the ninth day (Nu. 7:60, 65).

ABIDE. In the AV, "abide" is sometimes used in its now archaic sense "endure," e.g., Mal. 3:2 (Heb. *kûl*); Nah. 1:6 (*qûm*); Eccl. 1:4 (*'āmaḏ*), or "await," Acts 20:23 (Gk. *ménō*).

ABIEL ā'bi-el, ab'yel, ə-bī'əl [Heb. *'^{a}ḇî'ēl*–'my father is God' or 'God is father'].

1. A descendant of Benjamin the son of Jacob. He was the father of Kish the father of King Saul, and also, apparently, the father of Ner the father of Saul's general Abner (1 S. 9:1; 14:51).

2. One of David's mighty men (1 Ch. 11:32), called ABI-ALBON in 2 S. 23:31.

ABIEZER ab-i-ē'zər [Heb. *'^{a}ḇî'ezer*–'father of help' or 'my father is help']; **ABIEZRITE** ab-i-ez'rīt [Heb. *'^{a}ḇî hā'ezrî*].

1. Also **IEZER** ī-ē'zər [Heb. *'î'ezer*]; **IEZERITE** ī-ē'zə-rīt [Heb. *'î'ezrî*] (Nu. 26:30); AV, NEB, JEEZER; JEEZERITE. A descendant of Joseph the son of Jacob, and head of one of the families of Manasseh that settled W of the Jordan (Nu. 26:30; Josh. 17:1-6; 1 Ch. 7:14-19). As he was great-uncle to Zelophehad's daughters, who brought a case before Moses (Nu. 36), he must have been an old man at the time of the conquest. He was the son of Gilead the son of Machir in the sense of being a more remote descendant, for Machir had sons before the death of Joseph (Gen. 50:23). The Machir that possessed Gilead and Bashan because he was "a man of war" was the Manassite family of Machir, with Jair as its great general (Josh. 17:1; 13:30f.; Nu. 32:39-41; Dt. 3:12-15). To Abiezer and other sons of Gilead, territory was assigned W of the Jordan.

In later generations the name survived as that of the family to which Gideon belonged, and perhaps also of the region they occupied (Jgs. 6:34; 8:2). They are also called Abiezrites (Jgs. 6:11, 24; 8:32). The region was W of Shechem, with Ophrah as its principal city.

2. One of David's mighty men, "the Anathothite" (2 S. 23:27; 1 Ch. 11:28), who was also one of David's month-by-month captains, his month being the ninth (1 Ch. 27:12).

See *IP*, pp. 16, 18, 70, 154.

W. J. BEECHER

ABIGAIL ab'ə-gāl [Heb. *'^{a}ḇîgayil*, *'^{a}ḇîgal*, *'^{a}ḇiwgayil* (1 S. 25:18, *K*)–prob. 'my father rejoices'].

1. The wife of Nabal, a rich shepherd of southern Judea, whose home was Maon (1 S. 25:2f.). Shortly after Nabal's death she became the wife of David.

Nabal grazed his flocks in or along the Wilderness of Paran (or Maon?), where David and his men protected them from marauding tribes, so that not a sheep was lost. When Nabal was sheepshearing and feasting at Carmel (in Judea), David sent messengers requesting provisions for himself and his men. But Nabal, who was a churlish fellow, answered the messengers insultingly and sent them away empty-handed. David, angered by such mean ingratitude, gathered his four hundred warriors and set out to destroy Nabal and all he had (1 S. 25:22).

Meanwhile Abigail, a woman "of good understanding, and of a beautiful countenance" (v. 3), heard of the rebuff given the men of David by her husband; and fearing what vengeance David in his wrath might work, she gathered a considerable present of food (v. 18), and hurried to meet the approaching soldiers. Her beautiful and prudent words, as also her fair face, so won David that he desisted from his vengeful purpose and accepted her gift (vv. 32-35). When Abigail told Nabal of his narrow escape, he was stricken with fear, and died ten days afterward. Shortly after this David took Abigail to be his wife, although about the same time, probably a little before, he had also taken Ahinoam (v. 43); and these two were with him in Gath (1 S. 27:3). After David became king in Hebron, Abigail bore him his second son, Chileab (2 S. 3:3), or Daniel as he is called in 1 Ch. 3:1.

2. Also **ABIGAL** (2 S. 17:25). The sister of David and mother of Amasa, who at one time commanded David's army (1 Ch. 2:16f.; 2 S. 17:25). In the first passage she is called David's sister, along with Zeruiah; in the second she is called the "daughter of Nahash." Several explanations of this connection with Nahash have been suggested, any one of which would be sufficient to remove contradiction: (1) that Nahash was another name of Jesse, as in Isa. 14:29; (2) that Nahash was the wife of Jesse and by him mother of Abigail, which is least probable; (3) that Nahash, the father of Abigail and Zeruiah, having died, his widow became the wife of Jesse, and bore sons to him; (4) that the text of 2 S. 17:25 has been corrupted, "daughter of Nahash" having crept into the text. At all events she was the sister of David by the same mother. E. MACK

ABIHAIL ab'ə-hāl [Heb. *'ᵃḇîḥayil*–'father (i.e., cause) of strength'].

1. A Levite and the father of Zuriel, who in the wilderness was head of the house of Merari, Levi's youngest son (Nu. 3:35).

2. The wife of Abishur, a man of the tribe of Judah, in the line of Hazron and Jerahmeel (1 Ch. 2:29).

3. One of the heads of the tribe of Gad, who dwelt in Gilead of Bashan (1 Ch. 5:14).

4. Either a wife of Rehoboam king of Judah, or mother of his wife Mahalath, according to the interpretation of the text (2 Ch. 11:18). Probably the latter view is correct, since there is no conjunction in the text, and since the following verse (19) implies only one wife. If this is true, she was the wife of Jerimoth son of David, and daughter of Eliab, David's eldest brother. It is interesting to note this frequent intermarriage in the Davidic house.

5. The father of Queen Esther, who became wife of Xerxes (biblical Ahasuerus) king of Persia, after the removal of the former queen, Vashti (Est. 2:15; 9:29). He was an uncle of Mordecai.

See *IP*, pp. 15, 39f. E. MACK

ABIHU ə-bī'hū [Heb. *'ᵃḇîhû'*–'he is (my) father']. The second son of Aaron the high priest (Ex. 6:23; cf. 24:1, 9; 28:1). With his older brother Nadab he "died before the Lord," when the two "offered unholy fire" (Lev. 10:1f.). It may be inferred from the emphatic prohibition of wine or strong drink laid upon the priests immediately after this tragedy that the two brothers were going to their priestly function in an intoxicated condition (Lev. 10:8-11); *see also* UNHOLY FIRE. Their death is mentioned three times in subsequent records (Nu. 3:4; 26:61; 1 Ch. 24:2).

See *IP*, pp. 18, 70, 143.

ABIHUD ə-bī'hud [Heb. *'ᵃḇîhûḏ*–'father of majesty' or 'my father is majesty,' though some regard the second part as the proper name Judah]. The son of Bela the oldest son of Benjamin (1 Ch. 8:3).

ABIJAH ə-bī'jə [Heb. *'ᵃḇîyâ, 'ᵃḇîyāhû* (2 Ch. 13:20f.)–'my father is Yahweh' or 'Yahweh is father'; Gk. *Abia*]; AV NT ABIA (Mt. 1:7; Lk. 1:15).

1. AV, NEB, ABIAH. The seventh son of Becher son of Benjamin (1 Ch. 7:8).

2. AV, NEB, ABIAH. The second son of the prophet Samuel (1 S. 8:2; 1 Ch. 6:28 [MT 13]). With his brother he was appointed by Samuel as a judge at Beer-sheba, but both proved corrupt and were rejected by the tribal elders.

3. A descendant of Aaron, and the eighth among "the holy captains and captains of God" whom David appointed by lot in connection with the priestly courses (1 Ch. 24:10). The disasters of the 6th cent. B.C. decimated the priesthood and reduced the number of divisions to four (Ezr. 2:36-39), but it is highly probable that after the restoration twenty-four fresh priestly divisions were instituted under the old names. Zacharias the father of John the Baptist was of the division of Abijah (Lk. 1:5); it is unlikely that this refers to the Abijah of Neh. 12:4.

4. A son of Jeroboam I of Israel (1 K. 14:1-18). The narrative describes his sickness and his mother's visit to the prophet Ahijah. He is spoken of as the one member of the house of Jeroboam in whom there was "found some good thing toward Yahweh." With his death the hope of the dynasty perished.

5. AV, NEB, also ABIA (1 Ch. 3:10). The son and successor of Rehoboam king of Judah (1 Ch. 3:10; 2 Ch. 11:20–14:1). *See* the variant name ABIJAM in 1 K. 14:31; 15:1, 7f.

The statements concerning Abijah's mother are confusing. She is said to have been Micaiah the daughter of Uriel of Gibeah in 2 Ch. 13:2; in all other passages she is said to be Maacah the daughter of Absalom (1 K. 15:2, etc.). Maacah, however, is also said to be the mother of Asa, Abijah's son and successor (1 K. 15:10, 13; 2 Ch. 15:16). According to 2 S. 14:27 Absalom had but one daughter, Tamar. But these difficulties can be resolved by supposing that "daughter" of Absalom here means granddaughter. This fits the chronology better, in any case, for more than fifty years elapsed between the adolescence of Absalom and the accession of Rehoboam, whose wife Maacah was. The name Micaiah may be a variant of Maacah, but since it occurs in only the one verse it is probably a textual error. It is likely, then, that Absalom's daughter Tamar married Uriel of Gibeah, and their daughter Maacah was Rehoboam's wife and Abijah's mother. Abijah's reign was brief, and Maacah extended her influence into the reign of his son Asa, still acting as queen mother, until he deposed her because of her idolatry; it is in this sense that she is called Asa's mother. Wellhausen's conjecture that Asa was Abijah's brother, not his son, deserves consideration; the word "son" was sometimes used merely to denote a successor.

Abijah reigned *ca.* 915-913 B.C. He continued the hostilities against Israel, and the account in Chronicles deals mainly with a decisive victory gained by Abijah, in which he had 400,000 men and Jeroboam 800,000, of whom 500,000 were slain. It seems clear that these numbers are artificial, and were so intended, whatever may be the key to their meaning. At any rate, this victory enabled Abijah to occupy Bethel and the surrounding area (2 Ch. 13:19). Undoubtedly his position was strengthened by his alliance with the king of Damascus (1 K. 15:19).

His reign is condemned by the book of Kings, and Chronicles tells how he multiplied wives; yet his speech before the battle (2 Ch. 13:4-12) exhibits clear religious orthodoxy. Even if the words are those of the writer, we need not doubt that the sentiments are those of Abijah. If he was tolerant toward pagan practices, he nonetheless certainly considered himself Yahweh's appointed king (cf. v. 5).

6. The head of a priestly family in the time of Zerubbabel (Neh. 12:4, 17). An individual of the same name signed the covenant in Nehemiah's time, three-quarters of a century later (Neh. 10:7). But since the majority of the names in the list of Neh. 10:1-8 also occur in the list of Neh. 12:1-7, it is probable that clan names rather than personal names were recorded when Nehemiah's covenant was sealed.

7. (1 Ch. 2:24, RV); AV BIAH; RSV "his father"; NEB omits. In the AV and RV, the wife of Judah's grandson Hezron, to whom was traced the origin of Tekoa. It is possible, however, that the name should be revocalized to give Heb. *'āḇîhu*, "his father," in apposition to Hezron, as in the RSV. Further textual emendation of this verse makes EPHRATHAH the name of Hezron's wife.

8. The mother of King Hezekiah (2 Ch. 29:1), called ABI in 2 K. 18:2. W. J. BEECHER
D. F. PAYNE

ABIJAM ə-bī'jəm [Heb. *'aḇîyām*–'father of the sea (or west)']. The name given in Kings (1 K. 14:31; 15:1, 7f.) to the son of Rehoboam who succeeded him as king of Judah. *See* ABIJAH **5.** The name presents certain problems since the spelling varies in the MSS, with the MT of Chronicles designating him Abijah (1 Ch. 3:10; 2 Ch. 11:20–14:1). The divergence may result from a confusion in the ancient script between *h* and final *m*; from the removal of a pagan Canaanite element *yām* (the sea-deity) and the substitution of a Hebrew theophoric element (*yah*); or perhaps because he was given a throne-name (Abijah) on his accession. Mt. 1:7 presupposes Abijah as the OT reading.
R. K. H.

ABILA ab'i-lə. *See* ABILENE.

ABILENE a-bə-lē'nē [Gk. *Abilēnē*]. The tetrarchy of Lysanias at the time when John the Baptist began his ministry (Lk. 3:1). The district derived its name from Abila, its chief town, which was situated, according to the Itinerarium Antonini, 16.5 mi. (26.5 km.) from Damascus on the way to Heliopolis (Baalbek). This places it in the neighborhood of the village of Suk Wâdī Baradā (Abana), near which there are considerable ancient remains, with an inscription in Greek stating that a "freedman of Lysanias the tetrarch" made a wall and built a temple, and another in Latin recording the repair of the road "at the expense of the Abilenians." The memory of the ancient name probably survives in the Moslem legend which places the tomb of Abel in a neighboring height where there are ruins of a temple. Josephus calls this Abila *hē Lysaníou,* "the Abila of Lysanias," thus distinguishing it from other towns of the same name; and as late as the time of Ptolemy (*ca.* A.D. 170) the name of Lysanias was associated with it.

The territory of Abilene was part of the Ituraean kingdom, which was broken up when its king Lysanias was put to death by Mark Antony, *ca.* 35 B.C. The circumstances in which Abilene became a distinct tetrarchy are altogether obscure, and nothing further is known of the tetrarch Lysanias (Josephus *Ant.* xix.5.1; xx.7.1). In A.D. 37 the tetrarchy, along with other territories, was granted to Agrippa I, after whose death in A.D. 44 it was administered by procurators until 53, when Claudius conferred it, along with neighboring territories, upon Agrippa II. On Agrippa's death, toward the close of the 1st cent., his kingdom was incorporated into the province of Syria.

See also LYSANIAS. C. H. THOMSON

ABILITY. *See* ABLE; POWER.

ABIMAEL ə-bim'ə-el [Heb. *'aḇîmā'ēl*–'my father is God' or 'God is father']. The ninth of the thirteen sons of Joktan son of Eber, a descendant of Shem (Gen. 10:25-29; 1 Ch. 1:19-23). Like some of the other names in this list, the name is linguistically south Arabian, and the tribes indicated are south Arabians. W. J. BEECHER

ABIMELECH ə-bim'ə-lek [Heb. *'aḇîmeleḵ*–'father of a king' or 'my father is king'].

1. A king of Philistia and contemporary of Abraham. It is quite possible that Abimelech was the royal title rather than the personal name, since in the title of Ps. 34 we find it applied to the king of Gath, elsewhere known by his personal name Achish (1 S. 27:2f.).

Shortly after the destruction of Sodom, Abraham journeyed with his herds and flocks into the extreme southwestern country of Palestine (Gen. 20). While sojourning at Gerar, the city of Abimelech king of Philistia, he pretended that Sarah was his sister (v. 2); and Abimelech took her, intending to make her one of his wives. But God rebuked him in a dream, besides sending barrenness on the women of his household (vv. 3, 17). After Abimelech had reproved Abraham most justly for the deception, he dealt generously with him, loading him with presents and granting him the liberty of the land (vv. 14f.). When contention arose between the two men over a well that Abimelech's servants had seized, the two men made a covenant at the well, which took its name, Beer-sheba, from this covenant-making (Gen. 21:31f.). *See* ABRAHAM II, V.

2. A king of the Philistines mentioned in relation with Isaac (Gen. 26). In a time of grievous famine Isaac went down from his home, probably at Hebron, to Gerar. Fearing for his life because of his beautiful wife Rebekah, he called her his sister, just as Abraham had done with Sarah. Neither Abimelech nor any of his people took Rebekah to wife — a variation from the Abrahamic incident; but when the falsehood was detected, he upbraided Isaac for what might have happened, continuing nevertheless to treat him most graciously.

Isaac continued to dwell in the vicinity of Gerar, until contention between his herdsmen and those of Abimelech became too violent; then he moved away by stages, reopening the wells digged by his father (26:18-22). Finally, a covenant was made between Abimelech and Isaac at Beer-sheba, just as had been made between Abraham and the first Abimelech nearly a century earlier (Gen. 26:26-33). The two kings of Philistia were probably father and son.

3. The title of Ps. 34 mentions another Abimelech, who in all probability is the same as Achish king of Gath (1 S. 21:10–22:1), with whom David sought refuge when fleeing from Saul, and with whom he was dwelling at the time of the Philistine invasion of Israel, which cost Saul his kingdom and his life (1 S. 27). It appears from this that Abimelech was the royal title, and not the personal name of the Philistine kings.

4. A son of Gideon (Jgs. 9) who aspired to be king after the death of his father, and did rule three years (v. 22). He first won support of the members of his mother's family and their recommendation of himself to all Israel (vv. 3f.). He then murdered the seventy sons of his father at Ophrah, the family home in the tribe of Manasseh, Jotham the youngest son alone escaping (v. 5). After this Abimelech was made ruler by an assembly of the people at Shechem.

An insurrection broke out in Shechem, however, led by Gaal son of Ebed. Abimelech succeeded in capturing that city, and then Thebez; but while he was storming the citadel of Thebez, into which the defeated rebels had retreated, he was felled by a millstone, which a woman dropped on him from the wall (vv. 50-53). Realizing that he was mortally wounded and in order to avoid the shame of death at a woman's hand, he had his armor-bearer kill him with his sword (v. 54). His cruel treatment of the Shechemites (vv. 46-49), when they took refuge from him in their strong tower, was a just judgment for their acquiescence in his crimes (vv. 20, 57); while his own miserable death was retribution for his bloody deeds (v. 56). His shameful death is mentioned in 2 S. 11:21.

5. (1 Ch. 18:16, AV). *See* AHIMELECH **2.**

E. MACK

ABINADAB ə-bin'ə-dab [Heb. *'ᵃḇînāḏāḇ*–'father is noble'].

1. The man in whose house the men of Kiriath-jearim placed the ark after its return from the land of the Philistines. His house was either in Gibeah of Benjamin or "in the hill" (1 S. 7:1; 2 S. 6:3f.; note that Heb. *giḇ'â* means "hill," and that the place name Gibeah ordinarily has the definite article). It is natural to think that Abinadab was himself a man of Kiriath-jearim, though the account does not explicitly say so. The record is that the men of Kiriath-jearim were summoned to take charge of the ark at a time when no one else dared to have it (1 S. 6:20f.); and the implication seems to be that they had no option to refuse. Possibly this was due to their being Gibeonites, and hereditary "bondmen" of "the house of my God" (Josh. 9:17, 23). However this may be, they "sanctified" Abinadab's son Eleazar to have charge of the ark. According to the Hebrew and some of the Greek copies, the ark was in Gibeah in the middle of the reign of King Saul (1 S. 14:18).

About a century later, according to the biblical dating, David went with great pomp to Kiriath-jearim, otherwise known as Baalah or Baale-judah, to bring the ark from Kiriath-jearim, out of the house of Abinadab in the hill (or, in Gibeah), and place it in Jerusalem (1 Ch. 13; 2 S. 6). The new cart was driven by two descendants of Abinadab. There may or may not have been another Abinadab then living, the head of the house.

2. The second of the eight sons of Jesse, one of the three who were in Saul's army when Goliath gave his challenge (1 S. 16:8; 17:13; 1 Ch. 2:13).

3. One of the sons of King Saul (1 Ch. 8:33; 9:39; 10:2; 1 S. 31:2). He died in the battle of Gilboa, along with his fathers and brothers.

4. (1 K. 4:11, AV). *See* BEN-ABINADAB.

W. J. BEECHER

ABINOAM ə-bin'ō-am, ab-i-nō'am [Heb. *'ᵃḇînō'ām*–'father of pleasantness' or 'my father is pleasantness']. A man of Kadesh-naphtali, the father of Barak (Jgs. 4:6, 12; 5:1, 12).

ABIRAM ə-bī'rəm [Heb. *'ᵃḇîrām*–'exalted father' or 'my father is an exalted one'; Gk. *Abeirōn*].

1. AV Apoc. ABIRON. The son of Eliab son of Pallu son of Reuben (Nu. 26:5ff.; Dt. 11:6). In company with his brother Dathan and Korah the Levite and others, he disputed the authority of Moses and Aaron in the wilderness (Nu. 16f.; 26; Dt. 11:6; Ps. 106:17). Two hundred fifty followers of Korah perished by fire at the doorway of the tent of meeting. Dathan and Abiram refused to come to the tent of meeting, at the summons of Moses; and the earth opened where their tents were, and swallowed them with their families and their belongings. *See* KORAH.

2. The firstborn son of Hiel the Bethelite. Hiel rebuilt Jericho in the time of Ahab, and is said to have "laid its foundation at the cost of Abiram his firstborn" (1 K. 16:34, RSV; cf. Josh. 6:26). This incident acquired a new interest after discoveries were made at Gezer and Megiddo concerning foundation sacrifices offered in ancient Palestine.

One should not be too positive in making statements concerning the curse in Joshua, but the following is a possible interpretation. The curse pronounced by Joshua on the man who should rebuild Jericho was of a piece with the other details, Jericho being treated exceptionally, as a city placed under the ban. The language of Joshua's curse is capable of being translated: "Cursed be the man before the Lord who shall . . . build . . . Jericho; (who) shall lay its foundation at the cost of his firstborn, and set up its gates at the cost of his youngest." According to this interpretation the death of the builder's eldest and youngest sons is spoken of not as the penalty involved in the curse, but as an existing horrible custom, mentioned in order to give solemnity to the diction of the curse. The writer in Kings cites the language of the curse by Joshua. The context in which he mentions the affair suggests that he regards Hiel's conduct as exceptionally flagrant in its wickedness. Hiel, in defiance of the Lord, not only built the city, but in building it revived the horrible old Canaanite custom, making his firstborn son a foundation sacrifice, and his youngest son a sacrifice at the completion of the work.

W. J. BEECHER

ABIRON ə-bī'rən (Sir. 45:18, AV). *See* ABIRAM **1.**

ABISEI ab-i-sē'ī (2 Esd. 1:2, AV). *See* ABISHUA **2.**

ABISHAG ab'ə-shag, ə-bī'shag [Heb. *'ᵃḇîšag*–'father of error,' i.e., 'cause of wandering']. The woman of SHUNEM (the modern Sôlem, a village 6 mi. (10 km.) E of Megiddo in the valley of Esdraelon) who became David's nurse (1 K. 1:1-4, 15; 2:17, 21f.).

Abishag was a very beautiful virgin whose duty it was to "cherish" the king, i.e., to be his nurse, and to "lie in his bosom." This is sometimes construed as a test of the king's capacity for sexual intercourse (1 K. 1:4) as a condition for retaining the royal office, but the implication may simply be that she was keeping David warm. Either way, he appeared to receive new vigor in his last days.

After David's death Abishag was involved in the intrigues of succession, when Adonijah, the oldest living son of David, asked for her hand. This was tantamount to asking for the kingdom, for it was a rule in the ancient East that the whole of a king's harem became the personal property of his successor; though Adonijah may genuinely have loved her as well. Solomon not only refused his request, but also had Adonijah put to death, thus removing another rival to the throne.

J. A. BALCHIN

ABISHAI ab'ə-shī, ə-bī'shī [Heb. *'ᵃḇîšay*, in Chronicles *'aḇšay*–perhaps '(my) father is Jesse' (BDB) or '(my) father exists']. The eldest son of Zeruiah, David's sister, and brother of Joab and Asahel (2 S. 2:18). He was chief of the second group of three among David's "mighty men" (23:18).

He first appears with David, who was in the Wilderness of Ziph to escape Saul. When David called for a volunteer to go down into Saul's camp by night, Abishai responded, and counseled the killing of Saul when they came upon the sleeping king (1 S. 26:6-9). In the skirmish between the men of Ishbosheth and the men of David at Gibeon, in which Asahel was killed by Abner, Abishai was present (2 S. 2:18, 24). He aided Joab in the cruel and indefensible murder of Abner, in revenge for their brother Asahel (3:30). In David's campaign against the allied Ammonites and Syrians, Abishai led the attack upon the Ammonites, while Joab met the Syrians; the battle was a great victory for Israel (10:10-14).

Abishai was always faithful to David, and remained with him as he fled from Absalom. When Shimei, of the house of Saul, cursed the fleeing king, Abishai characteristically wished to kill him at once (16:8f.); and when the king returned victorious, Abishai advised the rejection of Shimei's penitence and his immediate execution (19:21). In the battle with Absalom's army at Mahanaim, Abishai led one division of David's army, Joab and Ittai commanding the other two (18:2). With Joab he put down the revolt against David by Sheba, a man of Benjamin (20:6, 10), at which Joab treacherously slew Amasa his cousin and rival, as he had likewise murdered Abner, Abishai no doubt again being party to the crime. In a battle with the Philistines late in his life, David was faint, being now an old man, and was in danger of death at the hands of the Philistine giant Ishbi-benob, when Abishai came to his rescue and killed the giant (21:17).

In the list of David's heroes (2 S. 23) Abishai's right to leadership of the "second three" is based upon his overthrowing three hundred men with his spear (v. 18). He does not appear in the struggle of Adonijah against Solomon, in which Joab was the leader, and therefore is supposed to have died before that time.

He was an impetuous, courageous man, but less cunning than his more famous brother Joab, though just as cruel and relentless toward rival or foe. David understood and feared their hardness and cruelty. Abishai's best trait was his unswerving loyalty to his kinsman David.

See *IP*, p. 34. E. MACK

ABISHALOM (1 K. 15:2, 10). *See* ABSALOM **1**.

ABISHUA ə-bish'ū-ə, ab-ə-shōō'ə [Heb. *'ᵃḇîšû(a)'*–meaning uncertain].

1. A son of Bela son of Benjamin (1 Ch. 8:4).

2. [Gk. B *Abisai,* A *Abisouai*]; AV Apoc. ABISUM, ABISEI (1 Esd. 8:2; 2 Esd. 1:2). The son of Phinehas, who was grandson to Aaron (1 Ch. 6:4f.; 50; Ezr. 7:5); an ancestor of Ezra the scribe (Apoc.).

ABISHUR ə-bī'shûr, ə-bī'shər [Heb. *'ᵃḇîšûr*–'my father is a wall']. A great-grandson of Jerahmeel and Atarah, Jerahmeel being a great-grandson of Judah. Abishur was the son of Shammai and the husband of Abihail, and the father of two sons (1 Ch. 2:28f.).

ABISUM ab'i-sum (1 Esd. 8:2, AV). *See* ABISHUA **2**.

ABITAL ab'i-tal, ə-bī'təl [Heb. *'ᵃḇîṭāl*–'father (i.e., source) of dew']. A wife of King David. In the duplicated list (2 S. 3:4; 1 Ch. 3:3) in which the sons born to David in Hebron are mentioned and numbered, the fifth is said to be Shephatiah son of Abital.

ABITUB ab'i-tub, ə-bī'tub [Heb. *'ᵃḇîṭûḇ*–'father of goodness' or 'my father is goodness']; AV AHITUB. A descendant of Benjamin and son of Shaharaim and Hushim, born in the field of Moab (1 Ch. 8:11).

ABIUD ə-bī'ud, ə-bī'əd [Gk. *Abioúd*–perhaps 'my father is majesty'; *see* ABIHUD]. In the genealogy of Jesus (Mt. 1:13 only), the son of Zerubbabel.

ABJECT (Ps. 35:15, AV). *See* CRIPPLE.

ABLE. The Gk. *dýnamai,* "have power," may refer to inherent strength, or to the absence of external obstacles, or to what may be allowable or permitted. The Gk. *ischýō,* as in Lk. 13:24; Jn. 21:6, always refers to the first of these meanings. The rendering of Gk. *hikanóō* in 2 Cor. 3:6, AV, is misleading, and has been properly changed in the RSV, "has qualified us as ministers"; cf. the AV and NEB. *See also* POWER.

See *TDNT,* II, *s.v.* δύναμαι κτλ. (Grundmann).

ABLUTION. Ceremonial washing for religious purification.

I. Biblical Terms.–The term occurs twice in the RSV (He. 6:2; 9:10), in both instances translating the Gk. *baptismós* (lit. "dipping"). It is derived from the Latin verb *abluere,* "wash off," and, as commonly used in a religious sense, it denotes a washing that is intended to yield ritual or ceremonial purity. As a religious rite or obligation it thus has nothing to do with washing for hygienic cleanness (*see* BATHE; WASH), but with the removal of ritual defilement contracted from such sources as contact with the dead (Nu. 19), bloodshed (Lev. 17), leprosy and other diseases or maladies (Lev. 13f.), childbirth (Lev. 12), copulation (Lev. 18;), and menstruating women (Lev. 15).

The requisite ablutions for removing these various kinds of uncleanness are elaborated particularly in the instructions regarding ceremonial impurity in Lev. 15–17 and Nu. 19. There the Hebrew term usually is *rāḥaṣ,* "rinse" (translated "bathe/bathing" or "wash/washing," but never "ablution"), with respect to the ceremonial cleansing of one's own person. A different term, *kāḇas* (lit. "tread, pound"), is used there for the washing of one's garments.

II. Usage in the OT and in Rabbinic Judaism.–*A. Ceremonial Importance.* Thus ablutions for ritual purity were of primary importance in the ceremonial life of Israel, especially and increasingly so in the era of rabbinic Judaism. Ablution was considered a prerequisite to approaching God, whether by means of sacrifice or prayer or merely by entering a holy place (Ex. 19:10; cf. 1 S. 16:5; Josephus *Ant.* xiv.11.5); and thus priests and Levites were known to have washed their hands, feet, clothes, and/or entire bodies in preparation for ceremonial actions (Lev. 8:6; Ex. 30:19-21; Nu. 8:21; etc.; *see also* LAVER). Cf. Ps. 26:6; Koran 5:8: "O believers, when you stand up to pray wash your faces, and your hands up to the elbows, and wipe your heads, and your feet up to the ankles" (A. J. Arberry, *Koran Interpreted* [1955], pp. 128f.); and the Ugaritic epic, *Keret* A.ii. 62-77 (*ANET*, p. 143): "Wash from hand to elbow/From [thy] fing[ers] up to the shoulder. . . ./Lift up thy hands to heaven, /Sacrifice to Bull, thy father El."

By the 1st cent. A.D. the washing of the hands before a meal had become a requirement throughout Judaism (cf. Mt. 15:2; Mk. 7:3; Lk. 11:38; *Berakoth* 53b; and *Sotah* 4b: "R. 'Awira: 'Whoever eats bread without previously washing his hands is as though he had intercourse with a harlot. . . .' R. Zerika: 'Whoever makes light of washing the hands [before and after a meal] will be uprooted from the world'" [Soncino tr. of *Babylonian Talmud* by A. Cohen (1936)]). By this time also public baths were gaining increasing acceptance through the influence of Hellenistic and Roman culture (1 Macc. 1:14; Josephus *Ant.* xvii.6.5; xviii.2.3). Herod's temple even provided a special room equipped for the ablutions and bathing of priests (*Yoma* iii.2).

B. Symbolism of Running Water. Ablutions to rectify ceremonial defilement were performed in running water (Lev. 15:13), springs (Jth. 12:7-9), rivers (2 K. 5:10-13), garden pools (2 S. 11:2-4), and in many instances required full bodily cleansing (e.g., Naaman in the Jordan [2 K. 5:10ff.], Aaron and his sons [Lev. 8:6], Bathsheba [2 S. 11:2ff.], the leprous [Lev. 14:8f.]). The symbolic character of running water made this an eminently desirable commodity for ceremonial ablutions (see Rowley, pp. 224f.), for it was understood that both the miasma of disease and the invisible stain of ritual defilement "ran off" the body with the running water. It is significant that great importance was attached to running water in early Christian baptism also.

C. Ritual vs. Ethical Purity. Ritual purity alone is the goal of these ablutions and washings (including Jewish proselyte baptism; *see* BAPTISM); they do not mediate forgiveness or ethical purity. Rabbinic Judaism envisions only purification from cultic uncleanness as their product (cf. Lev. 14:8; 15:5ff., 11; Nu. 31:23; and Mish. *Mikwaoth;* see also *TDNT,* I, 535f.). That a symbolical association with repentance was developing in late Judaism may be seen in several examples from the Pseudepigrapha: Sib. Or. 4:165ff. (Lanchester, *APOT*, II, 396), and the Life of Adam and Eve 6:1f. (Wells, *APOT*, II, 135). Jesus' response (Mt. 15:1-20 par. Mk. 7:1-23) to the inquiry of the scribes and Pharisees, "Why do your disciples not live according to the tradition of the elders, but eat with hands defiled?" (Mk. 7:5), inculcates a higher (ethical) purity that is to be sought more than ceremonial purity; for "not what goes into the mouth defiles a man, but what comes out of the mouth, this defiles a man" (Mt. 15:11).

III. NT References.–The two NT occurrences of "ablution(s)" (He. 6:2; 9:10) translate the Greek term *baptismós,* "the act of dipping or immersing" (in contrast to the specific NT term for "baptism," *báptisma*, used only for Christian baptism; see *TDNT,* I, 545). The *baptismoí* of the letter to the Hebrews represent the Levitical ablutions of the Judaic tradition (in late Judaism both the Gk. *baptízō,* "dip, immerse," and its Semitic counterpart, *ṭāḇal/ṭᵉḇal*, "dip," were already technical terms for ablutions for cleansing from ritual impurity; cf. Jth. 12:7-9; Sir. 34:25). He. 9:10 is a somewhat disdainful reference to the "various ablutions" (among other things) with which the Levitical code has to do, but which are now for the writer of Hebrews to be classed among those external rituals that have been superseded. In He. 6:2 the writer exhorts the reader to get beyond elementary doctrines, which include *baptismōn didachḗ* (RSV "instruction about ablutions"; NEB "instruction about cleansing rites"; AV "doctrine of baptisms") — i.e., teaching on the difference between Jewish (and perhaps pagan) ablutions and Christian baptism. The term *baptismós* occurs one other time in the NT — Mk. 7:4. This is a parenthetical comment that among the traditions observed by the Pharisees was that of the "washing" of cups, vessels, etc.

IV. Usage in Qumrân.–Information from such ancient historians as Josephus indicates that the Essene sect was quite meticulous about ablutions. If, as general consensus now holds, the Qumrân covenanters and the ESSENES are to be equated, the striking testimony of the numerous *miqwā'ôṯ* at Khirbet Qumrân is confirmatory. Even though most of the pools excavated there were likely to have been reservoirs, certain of the smaller ones by their very size and formation point to usage in various public ceremonies involving ablutions or ritual cleansing (see Black, pp. 95f.; Cross, pp. 67f., 85, 234; Rowley, pp. 254f.).

According to Josephus the Essene was obligated to bathe every day and to perform ablutions on various other occasions (*BJ* ii.8.5, 7, 9f.). These rites of purification by water are also mentioned in the Qumrân documents themselves. A chapter of the Damascus Document (CD 12) is devoted to the subject of purification by water. The ritual obligation of the Sons of Light to purify themselves with water after battle is mentioned in the War Scroll (1QM 14). But, as might be expected, it is the Manual of Discipline (1QS) for the community life that yields the most information. After a year's probation the novice was examined and then allowed to participate in (lit. "touch") the "purification of the Many" (1QS 6:16f.). This daily rite was conceived as foreshadowing God's own great and final lustration of the elect (1QS 4:20-22); see Vermes, pp. 45, 71ff.; Dupont-Sommer, pp. 49, 68ff.

There is also a warning against a wholly materialistic or magical conception of the ablution rites (1QS 2:25–3:9)—the covenanter had to surrender himself to the community and his will to God, lest the purificatory rites have no effect on him. While the flesh is cleansed by water, the heart is purified by the Holy Spirit (1QS 3:7-9); see Dupont-Sommer, p. 77.

It is a possibility that in combination with the daily ritual ablutions there was also a particular initiatory washing at Qumrân associated with the ceremony of entry into the "new covenant" of the community (cf. 1QS 5:8ff., esp. 13f.; and Cross, p. 234; Rowley, pp. 263f.). But this reference may indicate only the daily purificatory ablutions mentioned above.

See also CLEAN AND UNCLEAN; Plate 3.

Bibliography.–M. Black, *Scrolls and Christian Origins* (1961), pp. 91-101; F. M. Cross, Jr., *Ancient Library of Qumran and Modern Biblical Studies* (2nd ed. 1961); A. Dupont-Sommer, *Essene Writings from Qumran,* tr. G. Vermes (1961); H. C. O. Lanchester, "The Sibylline Oracles," in *APOT,* II; *TDNT,* I, *s.v.* βάπτω κτλ. (Oepke); *ANET*; H. H. Rowley, *From Moses to Qumrân* (1963), pp. 211-235, 239-279; G. Vermes, *Dead Sea Scrolls in English* (1962, repr. 1968); L. S. A. Wells, "The Books of Adam and Eve," in *APOT,* II.

D. G. BURKE

ABNER ab'nər [Heb. *'aḇnēr,* once *'ᵃḇînēr* (1 S. 14:50–'my father is a lamp' or 'my father is Ner']. The commander of the Israelite army under Saul and Ishbosheth (Eshbaal). He was either Saul's cousin (1 S. 14:50f.) or his uncle (1 Ch. 8:33; 9:39). According to 1 Ch. 27:21 Abner had a son Jaasiel.

Abner was to Saul what Joab was to David. Despite the many wars waged by Saul, we hear little of Abner during Saul's lifetime. Not even in the account of the battle of Gilboa is he mentioned. Yet both his high office and his kinship to the king must have brought the two men in close contact. On festive occasions it was the custom of Abner to sit at table by the king's side (1 S. 20:25). It was Abner who introduced the young David fresh from his triumph over Goliath to the king's court (so according to the account in 17:57). We find Abner accompanying the king in his pursuit of David (26:5ff.). Abner is rebuked by David for his negligence in keeping watch over his master (ch. 15).

Upon the death of Saul, Abner took up the cause of the young heir to the throne, Ishbosheth, whom he forthwith removed from the neighborhood of David to Mahanaim in the east Jordan country. There he proclaimed him king over all Israel. By the pool of Gibeon he and his men met Joab and the servants of David. Twelve men on each side engaged in combat, which ended disastrously for Abner, who fled. He was pursued by Asahel, Joab's brother, whom Abner slew. Though Joab and his brother Abishai sought to avenge their brother's death on the spot, a truce was effected; Abner was permitted to go his way after 360 of his men had fallen.

Joab naturally awaited his opportunity. Abner and his master soon had a quarrel over Saul's concubine Rizpah, with whom Abner was intimate. It was certainly an act of treason which Ishbosheth was bound to resent. The disgruntled general made overtures to David; he won over the tribe of Benjamin. With twenty Benjaminites he came to Hebron and arranged with the king of Judah that he would bring over to his side all Israel. He was scarcely gone when Joab learned of the affair; without the knowledge of David he recalled him to Hebron where he slew him, "for the blood of Asahel his brother."

David mourned sincerely the death of Abner. "Do you not know," he addressed his servants, "that a prince and a great man has fallen this day in Israel?" He followed the bier in person. Of the royal lament over Abner a fragment is quoted (see 2 S. 3:6-38):

"Should Abner die as a fool dieth?
Thy hands were not bound, nor thy feet put into fetters:
As a man falleth before the children of iniquity, so didst thou fall" (AV).

The death of Abner, while it can in no way be laid at the door of David, nevertheless served his purposes well. The backbone of the opposition to David was broken, and he was soon proclaimed king by all Israel.

M. L. MARGOLIS

ABODE. *See* HABITATION.

ABOLISH [Heb. *šāḇar*–'break' (Hos. 2:18); Gk. *katalýō* (Mt. 5:17), *katargéō* (Eph. 2:15; 2 Tim. 1:10), *anairéō* (He. 10:9)]; AV also BREAK, DESTROY, TAKE AWAY; NEB also BREAK, ANNUL.

In Hos. 2:18, "break" (AV, NEB) is a literal rendering of the image; RSV "abolish" is the intent. In the NT, Gk. *katalýō* in Mt. 5:17 has the meaning "repeal, annul," and is contrasted with *plēróō*, "fulfil."

By His death, Christ did away with the racial separation based on ancient ordinances and ceremonial laws (e.g., circumcision); through the cross He wrought the reconciliation, and secured that common access to the Father by which the union is maintained (Eph. 2:15).

"Our Savior Christ Jesus . . . abolished death" (2 Tim. 1:10). Men still die, "it is appointed unto men" (He. 9:27), but the fear of death as having power to terminate or affect our personal existence and our union with God, as a dreadful stepping out into the unknown and unknowable (into Sheol of the impenetrable gloom), and as introducing us to a final and irreversible judgment, has been removed. Christ has taken its sting from it (1 Cor. 15:55f.) and all its hurtful power (He. 2:14), has shown it to be under His control (Rev. 1:18), brought to light the incorruptible life beyond, and declared the ultimate destruction of death (1 Cor. 15:26; cf. Rev. 20:14). The Gk. *katargeítai* indicates that the process of destruction was then going on.

M. O. EVANS

ABOMINATION [Heb. *tô'ēḇâ*, *šeqeṣ*, vb. *šiqqēṣ*, *šiqqûṣ*, *piqqûl* (Lev. 7:18; 19:7), *zimmâ* (Jgs. 20:6); Gk. *bdélygma*]; AV also ABOMINABLE (THINGS), LEWDNESS (Jgs. 20:6); NEB also TAINTED (Lev. 7:18; 19:7), VERMIN (Lev. 11:10ff.; etc.), ABOMINABLE (THING), FILTHY OUTRAGE (Jgs. 20:6), "loathsome god(dess)" (1 K. 11:5, 7; 2 K. 23:13; etc.), DETEST (ABLE) (Prov. 3:32; 6:16; etc.), ABHORRENT, OBSCENITY, etc.

Albright (p. 176) suggests that the word *tô'ēḇâ* (Gk. *bdélygma*) probably derives from a root *w'b* which originally denoted the concept of inviolability or untouchability. This root, experiencing polar developments in the Semitic languages, came to denote either "holiness" or "abomination." The close relation between the ideas of tabu and holiness was shown in classical form by Robertson Smith (pp. 446-454). Whereas in Egyptian *w'b* means "cleanse, purify, be clean" (Erman and Grapow, I, 280), in Hebrew the derived noun means "negative tabu, abomination." The original sense of the root may be preserved partly in Arab. *wa'aba*, "keep intact." If the verbal root is *w'b*, then the Hebrew verbal form *t'b* must be considered a denominative secondarily derived from the noun *tô'ēḇâ*.

In usage *tô'ēḇâ* denotes those persons, things, or practices that offend another's sensibilities. Hence, that which is "abominable" is relative to the character, values, or culture of an individual. One displays his own character or values by that which repulses him. Accordingly, the sage opines: "to turn away from evil is an abomination to fools" (Prov. 13:19); again: "an unjust man is an abomination to the righteous, but he whose way is straight is an abomination to the wicked" (29:27). When the narrator says, "The Egyptians might not eat bread with the Hebrews, for that is an abomination to the Egyptians" (Gen. 43:32), and again, "for every shepherd is an abomination to the Egyptians" (46:34), the reader may infer that the Egyptians' sensibilities have been conditioned by their culture. In their feeling of special election and special providence the Egyptians call themselves "the people" in contrast to foreigners (see Wilson, p. 112; Herodotus ii.41; Kyle, pp. 26ff.; Ex. 8:26).

In most cases *tô'ēḇâ* has reference to that which is repugnant to Yahweh. By considering the objects and practices that repel Him one can learn much about God's character. Objects and persons that offend His sensibilities include: heathen deities such as Milcom, the "abomination of the Ammonites" (2 K. 23:13); images (Dt. 27:15) and the gold and silver belonging to them (7:25); the wages of prostitution (23:18); a false balance (Prov. 11:1); those with a perverse mind (11:20); lying lips (12:22); the sacrifice of the wicked (15:8); an arrogant man (16:5); the prayer of a lawbreaker (28:9); incense offered without regard to ethical conduct (Isa. 1:13); etc. In like manner practices associated with the pagan deity and conduct opposed to His standards repulse Him; e.g., the practice of witchcraft and kindred arts (Dt. 18:12); homosexuality and other sexual perversions (Lev. 18:22; 20:13); remarriage after divorce (Dt. 24:4); and all the "abominations" of the Canaanites (Lev. 18:26; often in Ezekiel).

In at least two passages the root *šqṣ* (also Gk. *bdélygma*) appears to be exactly synonymous with *tô'ēḇâ*. In Dt. 14:3 *tô'ēḇâ* is used to designate "unclean" animals, but in Lev. 11 *šeqeṣ* is used in the same connection; in 1 K. 11:5, Milcom is called the *šeqeṣ* of the Ammonites, but in 2 K. 23:13 he is called the *tô'ēḇâ* of the Ammonites. On the other hand, the fact that both words occur together in Ezk. 5:11; 11:18, 21 suggests there is a distinction between them. The words are synonymous in that both designate that which is repugnant; but whereas *tô'ēḇâ* denotes that which offends a person's sensibility, the root *šqṣ* is a more technical term denoting that which violates the practices of Yahweh's cult. Thus *tô'ēḇâ* is used frequently in construction with an indirect, personal object; e.g., Israel's sacrifice is repugnant to the Egyptians (Ex. 8:26 [MT 22]); the Psalmist complains that God had made him repulsive to his acquaintances (Ps. 88:9 [MT 8]); the practice of burning children is an abomination to Yahweh "which He hates" (Dt. 12:13; etc.). Probably for this reason, BDB lists Dt. 14:3 under those actions which are an abomination "to God and His people." The root *šqṣ*, on the other hand, as a technical term is used to denote animals and other things that render the Israelite "unclean." The noun *šeqeṣ* is used exclusively to designate proscribed animals (Lev. 7:21; 11:10ff.; Isa. 66:17; Ezk. 8:10). The verb *šiqqēṣ* means "contaminate" or "abominate" as Lisowsky (p. 1497) suggests. So the Israelites were not to contaminate themselves with any creeping things (Lev. 11:43), and the psalmist gives praise that God did not deprecate his affliction as uncleanness (Ps. 22:24 [MT 25]). Likewise *šiqqûṣ* designates that which is unclean and detestable according to Yahweh's religion: unclean food (Zec. 9:7), and most frequently idols and the practices associated with them (Isa. 66:17; Jer. 7:30; 13:27; etc.). Here too belongs the "abomination causing desolation" in Dnl. 11:31; 12:11, referring to the institution of a pagan altar and sacrifice in Yahweh's temple.

Piggûl is a technical term for stale flesh which has not been eaten within the prescribed time (Lev. 7:18; 19:7; Ezk. 4:14 [RSV "foul flesh"]; Isa. 65:4). Accordingly Driver would everywhere render it specifically "refuse meat" (cf. *leḥem m^{e}gō'āl,* "loathsome bread," from *gā'al,* to "loathe," Mal. 1:7). *Zimmâ* means "to plan, purpose" but is almost always used in a bad sense of "evil device," especially of unchastity.

Bibliography.–W. F. Albright, *FSAC*; A. Erman and H. Grapow, *Wörterbuch der ägyptischen Sprache*, I (1926); M. G. Kyle, *Moses and the Monuments* (1919); G. Lisowsky, *Konkordanz zum hebräischen Alten Testament* (1957); W. Robertson Smith, *Religion of the Semites* (3rd ed. 1927); J. A. Wilson, *Culture of Ancient Egypt* (1951).

B. K. WALTKE

ABOMINATION, BIRDS OF. The twenty birds listed in Lev. 11:13-19 (NEB "vermin").

I. Their Identification.–G. R. Driver, in consultation with D. L. Lack, Director of the Grey Ornithological Institute (Oxford), has provided the best study on the identification of these birds. His study presumably constituted the basis for the translation of this passage in the NEB. He established their identity by four factors: (1) a philological study of the Hebrew radicals, (2) the translations of these words in the ancient versions, (3) the description of each bird's habitat and habits in the literature, (4) the idea of "uncleanness." Significantly he also noted that they are arranged in a roughly descending scale of sizes by natural families. The chart presents his conclusions regarding the twenty birds listed in Lev. 11:13-19.

The list can be divided into three parts: (1) fifteen land birds, (2) three water birds, (3) two miscellaneous creatures. The land birds are subdivided into families in a descending scale of sizes, beginning with large birds of prey, followed by the crow tribe, the larger owls, the smaller birds of prey, and finally the smaller owls. In the second part of the list the osprey is followed by lake and river birds.

Driver suggested that few large birds of prey are named while so many owls are specified because the large ones, soaring at immense heights or swooping with sudden speed on the prey, are not easily identified, whereas the owls, flying slowly and hooting as they go, are readily noted and distinguished. Consequently generic names like *nešer* and *nēṣ* serve well enough for most of the great birds. "According to its kind" is added after four names. The *'ōrēḇ* (6) and *nēṣ* (10) are generic terms for whole classes of birds, and *'^{a}nāp̱â* (18) is possibly a general term for any number of small birds of prey hunting fish in river, lake, or sea. Why it is added after *'ayyâ* (5) is not clear. This lack of completeness should be borne in mind in connection with the twenty-one varieties listed in the parallel passage, Dt. 14:11-18.

II. Reason for Their Proscription.–The designation of these birds as an "abomination" (Heb. *šiqqēṣ*) shows that these birds are cultically obnoxious and not necessarily obnoxious to one's sensibilities. At least three reasons have been proposed for their exclusion from the cult. Martin Noth has contended that these animals and birds were "cultically unclean" because they played a part in certain foreign cults of the surrounding world as "holy animals (*Leviticus* [1965], p. 92). But advocates of this thesis have not demonstrated that all creatures associated with foreign cults were rejected by the Israelites (e.g., the bull) or that all the proscribed animals were associated with foreign cults. More probable is G. R. Driver's view that these animals and birds were rejected because they ate blood or had contact with a corpse, both of which were cultically unacceptable (cf. Lev. 7:26; 17:13f.; 21:1-4, 11; 22:4; Nu. 5:2f.; 6:6-11). All of these birds, with the exception of the last two, are birds of prey whose food consists almost entirely of carrion or flesh and which eat blood. The hoopoe and bat, which do not eat flesh in any form, are probably included because of their obnoxious habits. The hoopoe probes in filth for insects and worms, and the bat, a flying mammal, has the habit of spattering the walls of houses with ordure as it flies, has an overpowering mousey odor in its home, and is inedible.

Hebrew Name	Identification	Approximate Size	
		Total length in inches	Length of wing in inches
1. *nešer*	"griffon-vulture"	45	29
	"(golden) eagle"	34	23½
2. *peres*	"black vulture"	[45	28]
3. *'ozniyâ*	"bearded vulture"	45	31
4. *dā'â*	"(black) kite"	23	17
5. *'ayyâ*	"saker falcon"	22	15¾
	"common buzzard"	17	15
6. *'ōrēḇ*	"raven"	22	15½
	"rook"	18½	11½
7. *baṯ ya'^{a}nâ*	"eagle-owl"	18	13½
8. *taḥmās*	"short-eared owl"	14	12
9. *šāḥap̱*	"long-eared owl"	14½	12
10. *nēṣ*	"kestrel"	14	10
	"sparrow-hawk"	12½	8
11. *kôs*	"tawny owl"	16	11
12. *šālāḵ*	"fisher-owl"	?	?
13. *yanšûp̱*	"screech-owl"	13	11½
14. *tinšemeṯ*	"little owl"	[10½	7]
15. *qā'āṯ*	"scops-owl"	8	6
16. *rāḥām*	"osprey"	33	24
17. *ḥ^{a}sîḏâ*	"stork"	44	24
	"heron"	38-39	18 (½)
18. *'^{a}nāp̱â*	"cormorant"	33	13½
19. *dûḵîp̱aṯ*	"hoopoe"	12	9
20. *'^{a}ṭallēp̱*	"bat"	—	—

A third view reasons that creatures which eat carrion or flesh with blood run the risk of contagion. R. K. Harrison notes: "This categorizing is also important in view of the fact that it is unique in the annals of Near Eastern literature because its emphasis is not so much upon the avoidance of magical practices associated with certain animal species as upon the positive delineation of dietary principles intended to insure the physical well-being of the individual and the nation alike through a consistent prophylactic approach" (*Intro. to the OT* [1969], p. 603). Although the Creator undoubtedly had in mind the physical well-being of His people, this legislation emphasizes the cultic, ceremonial cleanness of the people.

See also BIRDS, UNCLEAN.

Bibliography.–G. R. Driver, *PEQ*, 87 (1955), 5-20, 129-140; A. Parmelee, *All the Birds of the Bible* (1960).

B. K. WALTKE

ABOMINATION OF DESOLATION. *See* DESOLATING SACRILEGE.

ABOUND; ABUNDANCE; ABUNDANT; ABUNDANTLY. These words are used frequently by the RSV to translate a variety of Hebrew and Greek terms. In the OT they most often represent the Hebrew noun *rōḇ*, "multitude, great quantity" (e.g., Dt. 28:47; Neh. 9:25; Ps. 37:11), the adjective *raḇ*, "numerous, much, plentiful" (e.g., Ps. 31:19; Prov. 28:20), or the hiphil of the verb *rāḇâ*, "multiply, increase" (e.g., Isa. 55:7; Ezk. 36:29f.). These cognate terms are sometimes used of Yahweh, to describe His unlimited love and covenant faithfulness. The OT authors confess that their God is "abounding in STEADFAST LOVE" (*raḇ-ḥeseḏ*, Ex. 34:6; Nu. 14:18; Neh. 9:17; Ps. 86:5, 15; 103:8; 145:8; Joel 2:13; Jonah 4:2; cf. *rōḇ ḥeseḏ*, "abundance of steadfast love," in Ps. 5:7; 69:13; 106:7, 45; Isa. 63:7; Lam. 3:32). Deutero-Isaiah (55:7) calls upon the people of Israel to repent of their wickedness and return to Yahweh, "for he will abundantly pardon" (*yarbeh lislô(a)ḥ*, lit. "multiply to pardon").

Among the other OT terms are: *hāmôn*, "riches" (Ps. 37:16; Ezk. 7:11); *śāḇa'*, "be satiated, have enough to eat" (Ps. 37:19); *yiṯrâ*, "riches, savings" (Isa. 15:7); hiphil of *yāṯar*, "make abundant" (Dt. 30:9); *ḥōsen*, "treasure" (Isa. 33:6); *dešen*, "fatness" (Jer. 31:14). In Isa. 35:2 the RSV renders "it shall blossom abundantly" for the infinitive absolute construction (*pārō[a]ḥ tiprah*) of *pāraḥ*, "blossom." In Isa. 66:11 "the abundance of her glory" is the RSV translation of the difficult *zîz kᵉḇôḏâ*. Some scholars, however, suggest "her full breast" as a better reading by relating Heb. *zîz* to Ug. *zd* (*ṯd*) and Akk. *zīzu* (J. Muilenburg, *IB*, V, 767; KoB, p. 254; *CHAL*, p. 88; cf. translations in *AB*, NEB). In Jer. 33:6 the RSV reading "abundance" is a conjectural reading for *'ᵃṯereṯ*, a hapax legomenon.

In the NT those words usually translate Gk. *perisseúō*, "be extremely rich, overflow" or "make extremely rich, cause to overflow," or one of its cognate or compound forms: *hyperperisseúō*, "be present in greater abundance" (Rom. 5:20); *perísseuma*, "fulness" (Mt. 12:34; Lk. 6:45; 2 Cor. 8:14); *perisseía*, "surplus" (Rom. 5:17; 2 Cor. 8:2); *perissós*, "profuse" (Jn. 10:10); *hyperekperissoú*, "infinitely more than" (Eph. 3:20); *perissotérōs*, "especially" (2 Cor. 2:4). Other terms are *pleonázō*, "grow, increase, multiply" (Rom. 6:1; 2 Thess. 1:3), and *hyperbolḗ*, "extraordinary number or quality" (2 Cor. 12:7).

The Scriptures repeatedly warn against putting one's trust in the abundance of material things. The psalmist advises against envy of the prosperous wicked, for they with their wealth will be destroyed, but the Lord will preserve those who put their trust in Him (Ps. 37); thus, the little that the righteous has is better than the abundance of the wicked (v. 16; cf. 4:7). Yahweh promised — and gave — to Israel an abundance of material blessings (Dt. 28:11); but He also warned that if this prosperity did not lead to service of Him it would be taken away (vv. 47ff.). This is in fact what happened to Israel, as prophesied by Ezekiel (7:11) and recounted by Ezra (Neh. 9:25ff.). Yet, Israel was promised that after she had repented of her disobedience, her fortunes would be restored and she would experience a prosperity greater than she had known before (Dt. 30:9; Isa. 66:10ff.; Jer. 31:12-14; 33:6-9; Ezk. 36:29f.).

In the NT, abundance is a characteristic of the new age of salvation begun by Jesus Christ (cf. Jn. 10:10). The Gk. *perisseúō* usually occurs in passages that speak of the fulness that is achieved in the age of salvation to a degree previously unknown, and of the growth toward a new level of maturity that is possible as this fulness is appropriated. The fulness of salvation is not manifested in the realm of material blessings but in the grace that through Jesus Christ is lavished upon the Church in the form of spiritual gifts (Rom. 5:15, 17, 20; cf. Eph. 1:3-8). Thus the Christian community is empowered to do far more than it would dare to imagine (Eph. 3:20), and the apostle Paul's constant exhortation and prayer for all the churches is that they be always advancing toward full maturity: that they grow in hope through the power of the Holy Spirit (Rom. 15:13), and in their mutual love (1 Thess. 3:12); that their love will grow increasingly in knowledge (Phil. 1:9); that they will always excel in the work of the Lord (1 Cor. 15:58) and in thanksgiving (Col. 2:7).

While the NT does not denounce material abundance, it stresses its limited value and its dangers. Jesus warned that "a man's life does not consist in the abundance of his possessions" (Lk. 12:15; cf. vv. 16ff.). Paul testified that he had learned to face both material abundance and deprivation with equanimity (Phil. 4:12). The value of material abundance lies in the opportunity it gives for generosity (2 Cor. 8:14); and to those who give generously there is the promise that "God is able to provide you with every blessing in abundance, so that you may always have enough of everything and may provide in abundance for every good work" (2 Cor. 9:8).

See also FULNESS; INCREASE; PLENTY; PROSPER, PROSPERITY; RICHES; SPIRITUAL GIFTS; WEALTH.

Bibliography.–Bauer; *TDNT*, VI, *s.v.* περισσεύω κτλ. (Hauck).

N. J. O.

ABRAHAM ā'brə-ham [Heb. *'aḇrāhām*; Gk. *Abraam*]; **ABRAM** ā'brəm [Heb. *'aḇrām*]. The great patriarch of Israel; son of Terah and father of Isaac.

I. Name
II. Career
III. Archeology and the Period of Abraham
IV. Chronology
V. Character
VI. Religious Significance

I. Name.–The shorter form Abram occurs only in Gen. 11:26–17:4, while the longer one is found elsewhere in the OT except for 1 Ch. 1:27 and Neh. 9:7. The etymology of Abram is obscure, but perhaps means "the father is exalted." It is a variant of such West Semitic names as *A-ba-ra-ma*, occurring in cuneiform texts from the 19th and 18th cents. B.C. The longer form, Abraham, is most probably a dialectical expansion of Abram, reflecting the cuneiform *A-ba-am-ra-ma* and *A-ba-am-ra-am*. In Gen. 17:5 the longer form was understood to mean "father of multitudes," and though no root *rhm* meaning "multitude" exists in Hebrew, there is a corresponding Arabic term (*ruhām*). However, the etymology of both names is far from certain.

II. Career.–Abraham was a descendant of Shem and the son of Terah, and became the ancestor of the Hebrews and other peoples (Gen. 17:5). His personal history is recorded in Gen. 11:27b–25:12, and appears to comprise one of eleven Mesopotamian tablet sources underlying the book of Genesis. This section was probably entited "Abram, Nahor, and Haran" (11:27b), and the narrative concluded with a typical Mesopotamian colophon, indicated by the phrase "these are the family histories [AV "generations"] of" in 25:12. The colophon seems to include a characteristic scribal attempt at dating in the reference to the time when Isaac lived at Beer-lahai-roi (25:11), and also appears to indicate that these family records had been at some time in the possession of Ishmael, the brother of Isaac. This material, summarized in Acts 7:2-8, stated that Abram was born in Ur of the Chaldees, where he lived with his parents and brothers, and subsequently with his wife Sarai.

After his brother Haran died, Abram moved with his wife, father, and nephew Lot to Harran, a city about 20 mi. SE of Edessa in the Balikh Valley, where Terah later died (11:26-32). Hearing God's call, Abram moved with Sarai and Lot from Harran to Shechem and Bethel before going down to Egypt to escape from a famine in Canaan. While there the pharaoh wanted to incorporate Sarai into his harem under the impression that she was Abram's sister (12:13). While Abram's statement to this effect was technically correct (cf. 20:12), and might further have reflected the Horite (Hurrian) wife-sister adoption relationship, it did not represent the whole truth.

Leaving Egypt, he returned to Bethel and subsequently parted from Lot, who chose to pasture his flocks in the fertile Jordan Valley (13:1-14). After receiving a promise from God that he would possess all the land S of the Euphrates, Abram went on to Mamre. A Mesopotamian coalition under Chedorlaomer sacked Sodom and other cities of the plain, but the attackers were themselves pursued by Abram and his Amorite allies, and defeated near Damascus (14:1-16).

Although the childless Abram had adopted his homeborn slave Eliezer as his heir, he was assured in a theophany that he would have natural offspring by the elderly Sarai, this being confirmed by a covenant (Gen. 15). In the meantime Abram had a son by Sarai's handmaid Hagar in conformity with local custom, and tensions within the household led to the latter being banished to the wilderness, only to be delivered miraculously (ch. 16). Thirteen years later God renewed His covenant promises, establishing circumcision as a sign and changing the names of Abram and Sarai to Abraham and Sarah (ch. 17). This was confirmed at Mamre by another theophany (ch. 18), despite Sarah's incredulity; and subsequently Sodom and Gomorrah were destroyed. From Mamre Abraham went through southern Canaan, staying for a time near Gerar. When Abraham planned to make a treaty to secure land rights in Beersheba, the Philistine king Abimelech desired Sarah just as the Egyptian ruler had earlier. Again Abraham pleaded the wife-sister relationship with much the same results (ch. 20). When Abraham was 100 years old Isaac was born to Sarah, and renewed tensions in the household led her to banish Hagar and Ishmael her son. This act was contrary to local custom in those days, and required a further theophany to justify the action (ch. 21).

A dramatic interlude which tested the faith of Abraham involved the near-sacrifice of Isaac (Gen. 22:1-14), after which the covenantal promises were reaffirmed. Sarah died some time later, and was buried in the cave of Machpelah, which Abraham had first to purchase from Ephron (ch. 23). In old age Abraham married Keturah, who gave birth to the ancestors of the Dedanites and Midianites. He also made certain that the son Isaac would marry within the family, the result being that Isaac later took Abraham's great-niece Rebekah as his wife (ch. 24). At an advanced age he gave gifts to the sons of his concubines and sent them home to the east, leaving Isaac as his sole heir in possession of the property. Finally Abraham died, aged 175, and was buried with Sarah in the cave of Machpelah.

"The Sacrifice of Isaac" by Rembrant van Rijn (1635), depicting Abraham's faithful obedience (Hermitage, Leningrad)

III. Archeology and the Period of Abraham.–Much of the contemporary cultural background has been illumined by archeological discoveries relating to the Middle Bronze period (*ca.* 1950-1550 B.C.) in which Abraham lived. He was apparently born at Ur somewhat after the close of the magnificent 3rd Dynasty (*ca.* 2070-1960 B.C.), and migrated early in the 19th cent. B.C. when northern Mesopotamia was under strong Amorite influence. In the Balikh Valley S of Harran sites such as Peleg, Serug, and Terah preserved the names of certain patriarchs, while Nahor occurred in the Mari texts as Nakhur, the location of some Ḫabiru.

Another contemporary Mesopotamian culture of importance for the period of Abraham was that of the Hurrians, whose capital was at Nuzi or Nuzu (Yorgan Tepe). While Nuzu texts are mostly from the 15th cent. B.C., they furnish a great deal of information about 2nd millennium B.C. Assyrian society and illumine some of the social customs underlying the Abraham narratives. Adoption was frequently represented in the Nuzu texts as a means of transferring property, although genuine adoptions by childless couples were also common (cf. Gen. 15:2). The person adopted was expected to discharge certain filial duties, and when the adopting parents died he received the estate. But if a natural son was subsequently born to the adopting parents, the adopted son had to relinquish his position as the real heir. The firstborn in the family received preferential status, including a double portion of the estate. But at Nuzu, Alalakh, and elsewhere, the father could disregard the law of primogeniture and choose a "firstborn" son from among other children in the family. The primary purpose of marriage was the procreation of children, and the marriage contracts generally obliged a wife subsequently found to be sterile to provide her husband with a concubine through whom an heir could be obtained (cf. 16:2). At Nuzu it was mandatory for the concubine and her offspring to remain as members of the household, and any attempt to expel them was treated very seriously indeed (cf. 21:11).

The places in Canaan which Abraham visited were located in a zone where annual rainfall is between 10 and 20 in., which is well suited to the requirements of the flocks of sheep which he owned. Sites such as Kadesh and Gerar seem to have been inhabited in the Middle Bronze Age, though the extent of the occupation is uncertain. Excavations at Gerar have indicated that it was most probably a fortified Egyptian outpost in the time of Abraham, while the Early Bronze period of Megiddo throws important light on the nature of contemporary Canaanite religious practices.

Hittite law has clarified some details of the sale of the Machpelah cave by Ephron, who was probably a native Canaanite rather than a Hittite as such (*see* HITTITES). Under ancient Hittite law the purchaser of an entire piece of property was legally bound to render certain feudal services of an obscure nature to the vendor. Abraham did not wish to be bound in this way, hence his concern to purchase only part of the property and thereby to avoid the prescribed feudal obligations. The mention of trees (Gen. 23:17) was in accord with the Hittite practice of listing the exact number of trees growing on property at the time of sale. References to the Philistines in the Abraham narratives are not anachronistic, as was once thought. A long series of migrations from Caphtor (Crete) to Palestine commenced in the 19th cent. B.C. Minoan and other Aegean peoples were mentioned in an eighteenth-century B.C. Mari tablet, while specimens of Middle Minoan pottery have been recovered from the seaport of Ugarit, from Hazor, and elsewhere. The term Philistine is obviously a comprehensive designation for these Aegean immigrants who in turn gave their name to their new home.

From the archeological evidence it is apparent that Abraham was the product of an advanced culture, and was typical of the upper-class patriarch of his day. His actions are set against a well-authenticated background of nonbiblical material, making him a true son of his age who bore the same name and traversed the same general territory, as well as living in the same towns as his contemporaries. He is in every sense a genuine Middle Bronze Age person, and not a retrojection of later Israelite historical thought, as used to be imagined. Consequently it is now possible to reject the "mythical theory" of Nöldeke, which saw Abraham as an ancient tribal deity; the "saga theory" of Gunkel, which envisaged Abraham as the product of cycles of sagas; and the "personification theory" of Meyer, where Abraham was thought of as personifying a tribe.

IV. Chronology.–Archeological discoveries seem to place Abraham quite readily in the early 2nd millennium B.C. The evidence for the destruction of Sodom and Gomorrah furnishes incidental proof for Abraham's sojourn in Palestine at that period. The catastrophic destruction can be correlated with the ceramic evidence from Bâb edh-Dhrâ', a festival site located about 5 mi. SE of el-Lisan, which was apparently visited periodically by the inhabitants of the cities of the plain between 2300 and 1900 B.C. Such "pilgrimages" seem to have ended with the destruction of Sodom, *ca.* 1900 B.C., showing coincidentally that Abraham was living in Palestine at this period. Attempts by H. H. Rowley and C. H. Gordon to place Abraham in the Amarna Age (15th and 14th cents. B.C.) rest upon a misunderstanding of the genealogical tables of Genesis.

V. Character.–Abraham was clearly monotheistic as contrasted with the polytheism of his precursors (cf. Josh. 24:2). He believed God to be Lord of the cosmos (Gen. 14:22; 24:3), supreme judge of mankind (15:14; 18:25), controller of nature (18:14; 19:24; 20:17), highly exalted (14:22) and eternal (21:33). Whenever God spoke to him he obeyed immediately in faith and trust (11:31; 12:1, 4; 15:7). Although from a sedentary background, he accepted the pilgrim life of the seminomad, going wherever he was guided (cf. He. 11:8f.). His faith was tested most acutely in the command to sacrifice his only son, which if implemented would have precluded the fulfillment of God's promises regarding future offspring. Abraham clearly trusted God's ability to restore the dead to life (Gen. 22:12,18; cf. He. 11:19) should circumstances warrant it. His solicitude toward strangers (18:2-8; 21:8) was matched by his ability to regulate his household along lines of morality and godliness (18:19). His love for his kin enabled him to fight successfully against numerically superior opposition (14:15), and in all he emerges from the Genesis narratives as a considerate and humane person who behaved in an especially commendable manner toward the embittered, frustrated, and childless Sarah. The deception of pharaoh and Abimelech of Gerar (12:11-13; 20:2-11) have been held to constitute flaws in Abraham's character, and while this may be true, it is also possible that the incidents have been misconstrued owing to inadequate information about the contemporary scene.

VI. Religious Significance.–Abraham was the progenitor of the Israelites who described themselves as the "seed of Abraham," and who were visible evidence of God's certain promises (Isa. 51:2; Ezk. 33:24). The "God of Abraham" was a designation of the Lord from the time of Isaac to the latest biblical period. Through faith in God, Abraham lived as a monotheist in a polytheistic society (Josh. 24:3), was chosen (Neh. 9:7), redeemed (Isa. 29:22), and blessed (Mic. 7:20). In the NT Abraham was the ancestor not merely of Israel (Acts 13:26) but of the Levitical priesthood (He. 7:5), the Messiah (Mt. 1:1), and the body of believers in Jesus Christ (Gal. 3:16, 29) as well. The oath (Lk. 1:73), divine mercy (1:54), covenant (Acts 3:25), the promise (Rom. 4:13), and the blessing (Gal. 3:14) given by free grace to Abraham are also the inheritance of his spiritual children. His faith in God's early promises became the type of faith leading to justification (Rom. 4:3), making him the "father" of Christians as believers (4:11). Abraham demonstrated his worthiness by an attitude that evidenced his righteousness (Jas. 2:21; cf. Jn. 8:39). For the author of Hebrews, Abraham's entire life under God was an outstanding illustration of faith in action (He. 11:8-19; cf. Sir. 44:19-21). As the progenitor of later Arab tribes, Abraham was also of great importance in Moslem tradition. He was one of the prophets sent by God, and apart from Moses is mentioned more frequently than anyone else in the Koran, being for Moslem as well as Jew the recipient of the divine covenant.

See MAP V.

Bibliography.–F. M. T. Bohl, *Opera Minora* (1953), pp. 26-49; N. Glueck, *Other Side of the Jordan* (1940); R. K. Harrison, *Intro. to the OT* (1969), pp. 106-112; D. J. Wiseman, *Word of God for Abraham and To-day* (1959); C. F. Pfeiffer, *Patriarchal Age* (1961), *passim.*; K. A. Kitchen, *Ancient Orient and OT* (1960), *passim.*; *AOTS*; D. J. Wiseman, ed., *People of OT Times* (1973), *passim.* R. K. HARRISON

ABRAHAM, APOCALYPSE OF. *See* PSEUDEPIGRAPHA V.B.

ABRAHAM, TESTAMENT OF. *See* PSEUDEPIGRAPHA V. C.

ABRAHAM'S BOSOM [Gk. *kólpos Abraam*]; NEB "with Abraham," "close beside him." The expression occurs in Lk. 16:22f., in the parable of the rich man and Lazarus, to denote the place of repose to which Lazarus was carried after his death. The figure is suggested by the practice of the guest at a feast reclining on the breast of his neighbor. Thus John leaned on the breast of Jesus at supper (Jn. 21:20).

The rabbis divided the state after death (SHEOL) into a place for the righteous and a place for the wicked; but it is doubtful whether the figure of Jesus quite corresponds with this idea. "Abraham's bosom" is not spoken of as in "Hades," but rather as distinguished from it (Lk. 16:23)—a place of blessedness by itself. There Abraham receives, as at a feast, the truly faithful, and admits them to closest intimacy. It may be regarded as the equivalent to the "Paradise" of Lk. 23:43.

See also HADES; PARADISE.

See *TDNT*, III, *s.v.* κόλπος (Meyer). J. ORR

ABRAM a'brəm. *See* ABRAHAM.

ABREK ā'brek [Heb. *'aḇrēk*; Gk. *kēryx*] (Gen. 41:43, RSV mg.); AV, RSV, "bow the knee"; AV mg. "tender father"; NEB "make way." A salutation of uncertain meaning which the Egyptians proclaimed before Joseph, when as grand vizier, second to Pharaoh, he appeared in his official chariot.

Explanations based on Hebrew etymology are unsatisfactory. "Bow the knee" or "kneel down," from an alleged hiphil imperative (*hāḇrēḵ* would be expected), are grammatically unsound. Others, including AV mg. "tender father" and Tg. "father of a king," are forced.

The surmises of Egyptologists are almost without number, and none is conclusive. BDB lists several (pp. 7f.), including Coptic *a-bor-k*, "prostrate thyself!"; *āprek*, "head bowed!"; *ab-rek*, "rejoice thou!"

The most satisfying parallel is Assyr. *abarakku*, "grand vizier" or "friend of a king," as suggested by F. Delitzsch; for Babylonian laws and customs were dominant in western Asia, and the Hyksos, through whom such titles would have been carried, were ruling then (M. G. Kyle, *Moses and the Monuments* [1919], p. 29). E. MACK

ABROAD. In the AV, "abroad" often has the archaic sense "outside," e.g., Gen. 15:5; 19:17; Ex. 12:46 (Heb. *ḥûṣ*). In the AV of Mk. 4:22; 6:14; Lk. 8:17 it means "manifest" (Gk. *phanerós*).

ABRON ab'rən [Gk. *Abrōna*, ℵ *Chebrōn*; Vulg. *Mambre*] (Jth. 2:24); AV ARBONAI. A wadi (RSV "brook," NEB "river") in Syria. From the description of Holofernes' march it would seem that the Abron was located between the bend of the Euphrates and the Mediterranean, in or not far from Cilicia.

ABRONAH ə-brō'nə [Heb. *'aḇrōnâ*]; AV, NEB, EBRONAH. One of the stations of Israel in the wilderness on the march from Sinai to Kadesh — the station next before that at Ezion-geber on the eastern arm of the Red Sea (Nu. 33:34f.).

ABSALOM ab'sə-lom, ab'sə-ləm.

1. [Heb. *'aḇšālôm*–'father is (or 'of') peace']; also **ABISHALOM** ə-bish'ə-ləm [Heb. *'ᵃḇîšālôm*] (1 K. 15:2, 10). David's third son by Maacah daughter of Talmai king of Geshur (a small country between Hermon and Bashan). Absalom was born at Hebron (2 S. 3:3), and moved at an early age, with the transfer of the capital, to Jerusalem, where he spent most of his life. He was a great favorite of his father and of the people as well. His charming manners, his personal beauty, his ingratiating ways, together with his love of pomp and royal pretensions, captivated the hearts of the people from the beginning. He lived in great style and drove in a magnificent chariot with fifty men running before him. Such magnificence produced the desired effect upon the hearts of the young aristocrats of the royal city (15:1ff.).

I. His Exile.–When Amnon his half-brother ravished his sister Tamar, and David shut his eyes to the grave crime and neglected to administer proper punishment, Absalom became justly enraged, yet quietly nourished his anger. After a lapse of two years he carried out a successful plan to avenge the rape of Tamar. He made a great feast for the king's sons at Baal-hazor, to which, among others, Amnon came, only to meet his death at the hands of Absalom's servants (2 S. 13:1ff.). To avoid punishment Absalom fled to the court of his maternal grandfather in Geshur, where he remained until David had relented and condoned the murderous act of his impetuous, plotting son. At the end of three years (13:38) Joab finally secured Absalom's recall to Jerusalem. It was two years later, however, before he was admitted to the royal presence (14:28).

II. Rebellion Against His Father.–Absalom, reinstated, lost no opportunity to regain lost prestige; and having made up his mind to succeed his father upon the throne, sacrificed family loyalty to political ambition. Overtly gracious and rich in promises, especially to the disgruntled and disenchanted, he found it easy enough to attract a following. His purpose was clear, namely, to alienate as many as possible from the king, and thus neutralize David's influence in the selection of a successor. Absalom fully realized that the court party, under the influence of Bathsheba, was intent upon having Solomon as the next ruler. By much flattery Absalom stole the hearts of many men in Israel (15:6).

How long a period elapsed between his return from Geshur and his open rebellion against his father David is uncertain. Most authorities regard the "forty years" of 1 S. 15:7 as an error and, following the Syriac and some editions of the LXX, suggest four as the correct reading. Whether forty or four, he obtained permission from the king to visit Hebron, the ancient capital, on pretense of fulfilling a vow he had made while at Geshur regarding his safe return to Jerusalem. With two hundred men he went to Hebron. Prior to the feast, spies had been sent throughout all the tribes of Israel to stir up the discontented and to assemble them under Absalom's flag at Hebron. Very large numbers obeyed the call, among them Ahithophel, one of David's shrewdest counselors (15:7ff.).

III. David's Flight.–Reports of the conspiracy at Hebron soon reached David, who became thoroughly frightened and lost no time in leaving Jerusalem. Under the protection of his most loyal bodyguard he fled to Gilead beyond Jordan. David was kindly received at Mahanaim, where he remained till after the death of his disloyal son. Zadok and Abiathar, two leading priests, were intent upon sharing David's fortunes and went so far as to carry the ark of the covenant with them out of Jerusalem (2 S. 15:24).

David, however, forced the priests and Levites to take it back to its place in the city and remain there as its guardians. This was a prudent stroke, for these two great priests in Jerusalem acted as intermediaries, and through their sons and some influential women kept up constant communications with David's army in Gilead (15:24ff.). Hushai, too, was sent back to Jerusalem. He feigned allegiance to Absalom, who by this time had entered the royal city and had assumed control of the government (15:32ff.). Hushai, the priests, and a few less conspicuous people performed their part well; Ahithophel's counsel, to take immediate action and advance upon the king's forces in the midst of the turmoil, was thwarted (17:1ff.). Moreover, spies constantly informed David's headquarters of Absalom's plans (17:15ff.). The delay was fatal to the rebel son. Had Absalom acted upon the shrewd counsel of Ahithophel, David's army might have been conquered at the outset.

IV. Death and Burial.–When at length Absalom's forces under the generalship of Amasa (2 S. 17:25) reached Gilead, ample time had been given to David to organize his army. There were three divisions under the efficient command of three veteran generals: Joab, Abishai, and Ittai (18:1ff.). A great battle was fought in the forests of Ephraim, where the rebel army was utterly routed. No fewer than twenty thousand were killed outright, and a still greater number, becoming entangled in the thick forest, perished that day (18:7f.). Among the latter was Absalom himself; when he fled upon his mule, his head was caught in the boughs of a great oak or terebinth, probably in a forked branch. "He was taken up between heaven and earth; and the mule that was under him went on" (18:9). Thus he was found by a soldier who at once ran to inform Joab. Without a moment's hesitation, and notwithstanding David's definite orders, Joab thrust three darts into Absalom's heart. Encouraged by the action of their general, ten of Joab's young men "compassed about and smote Absalom, and slew him" (18:15). He was buried in a great pit, close to the spot where he was killed. A great pile of stones was heaped over his body (18:17), in accordance with the custom of dishonoring rebels and great criminals (Josh. 7:26; 8:29).

V. David's Lament.–The death of Absalom was a source of great grief to his fond and aged father. David's lament at the gate of Mahanaim, though very brief, is a classic, and expresses in tender language the feelings of parents for wayward children in all ages of the world (2 S. 18:33).

Little is known of Absalom's family life, but we read in 14:27 that he had three sons and one daughter. From the language of 18:18, it is inferred that the sons died at an early age.

VI. Absalom's Tomb.–As Absalom had no son to perpetuate his memory "he reared up for himself a pillar" or a monument, in the King's Dale, which according to Josephus was two furlongs from Jerusalem (*Ant.* vii.10.3). Nothing is known with certainty about this monument. One of the several tombs on the east side of Kidron traditionally has been called Absalom's tomb; but this fine piece of masonry with its graceful cupola and Ionic pillars is probably not earlier than the Roman period.

W. W. DAVIES

2. [Gk. *Apsalōmos*]. The father of Mattathias, a captain of the Jewish army (1 Macc. 11:70; Josephus *Ant.* xiii.5.7), and of Jonathan, who was sent by Simon Maccabeus to take possession of Joppa (1 Macc. 13:11; *Ant.* xiii.6.4).

3. [Gk. *Abessalōm*]; AV ABSALON. One of two envoys of the Jews, mentioned in a letter sent by Lysias to the Jewish nation (2 Macc. 11:17).

ABSALON ab'sə-lon. *See* ABSALOM **3**.

ABSOLUTION. An ecclesiastical term, not found in the Bible, used to designate the official act described in Mt. 16:19: "Whatever you loose on earth shall be loosed in heaven," and Mt. 18:18: "Whatever you loose," etc., and interpreted by Jn. 20:23: "If you forgive the sins of any, they are forgiven" (*see* KEYS, POWER OF THE). The Roman Catholic Church regards this as the act of a properly ordained priest, by which, in the sacrament of PENANCE, he frees from sin one who has confessed and made promise of satisfaction.

Protestants regard the promise as given not to any order within the church, but to the congregation of believers, exercising its prerogative through the Christian ministry, as its ordinary executive. They differ as to whether the act be only declarative or collative. Luther regarded it as both declarative and collative, since the Word always brings that which it offers. The absolution differs from the general promise of the gospel by individualizing the promise. What the gospel, as read and preached, declares in general, the absolution applies personally.

See also FORGIVENESS. H. E. JACOBS

ABSTINENCE; ABSTAIN [Gk. *apéchomai*] (Acts 15:20, 29; 1 Thess. 4:3; 5:22; 1 Tim. 4:3; 1 Pet. 2:11); NEB also AVOID; [*mē̆ esthíōn*–'not eating'] (Rom. 14:3, 6); AV "eateth not"; NEB also "not eat." Other OT and NT terms which indicate abstinence are: Heb. *ṣûm*, *ṣôm*–"fast, fasting" (2 S. 12:16), *'ānâ*–"humble oneself" (Lev. 16:29), *kāna'*–"be humble" (1 K. 21:29), *nāzar*–"separate oneself by fasting" (Zec. 7:3), *zûr*–"be separated from" (Nu. 6:3), *lō' 'āḵal leḥem*–"not eat bread" (1 S. 28:20; cf. 2 S. 3:35), *lō' šāṯâ yayin*–"not drink wine" (Nu. 6:3), etc.; Aram. *ṭᵉwāṯ*–"fastingly," "hungrily" (Dnl. 6:18 [MT 19]); Gk. *asitía*–"without food" (Acts 27:21; cf. LXX Est. 4:16), *nēsteía, nēsteúō, nē̆stis*–"fast, fasting" (Lk. 2:37; Mk. 2:18f.; Mt. 15:32), *phylássō* (Acts 21:35). *See also* FAST.

I. Introduction
II. Fasting
   A. In the OT
   B. In the NT
III. Celibacy
IV. Second-Century Developments
V. Fasting, Prayer, and Almsgiving
VI. Function

I. Introduction.–Abstinence is the deliberate, self-imposed refusal to indulge in a specific act or acts. In prebiblical, biblical, and postbiblical periods abstinence was practiced in various ways and for a variety of purposes. Its origins cannot be determined, most theories being questionable at best, but its development as a religious practice can be traced by noting how and why it was observed by individuals and groups in different times and places. The ancient terms, as the translators show, were not always used in a strictly religious context (e.g., Mk. 8:3).

II. Fasting.–*A. In the OT.* The most common form of abstinence and the one most often referred to in the OT was fasting. The refusal to eat sometimes included or was accompanied by the refusal to drink either wine or water or both. Proscriptions regarding foods were made by law, by the decree of a religious or national leader, or by the individual. They could include all food or only certain types for periods lasting from part of a day to several weeks. In the Pentateuch only the Day of Atonement was specified as a fast binding upon all members of the community (Lev. 16:29ff.; cf. Mish. *Yoma*), although the Nazirite vow (Nu.

6:1ff.) included abstinence from wine and grapes (cf. Jer. 35). It could be taken by either a man or a woman, but a daughter or a wife could have any vow revoked by her father or husband (Nu. 30). Other community-wide fasts observed annually were added later to commemorate times of national misfortune: Nebuchadrezzar's siege of Jerusalem, its capture, its destruction, and Gedaliah's murder. These are referred to in Zec. 8:19. But they were already losing their significance during the period of the Exile. Isa. 58:3-9 complains in true prophetic fashion that the observances were often insincere, devoid of genuine repentance and the desire to do justice (cf. Joel 2:12f.). Even the external forms of all but the major fast were later abandoned.

Not all community fasts occurred annually. Frequently they were called by leaders. Fasting was often accompanied by other forms of behavior, e.g., abstaining from work (Lev. 16:29), not using a razor or touching a dead person (Nu. 6:1ff.), assembling (Nu. 29:7; Neh. 9:1), pulling the hair (Ezr. 9:3), weeping (Jgs. 20:26), mourning (2 S. 1:12), presenting various offerings (Lev. 23:27; Jgs. 20:26; Jer. 14:12), pouring water (1 S. 7:6), rending one's clothes (2 S. 1:11), putting on sackcloth (1 K. 21:27), covering oneself with ashes (Dnl. 9:3; cf. 1 Macc. 3:47f.), lying or sitting on the ground (2 S. 12:16; Est. 4:3), refusing to communicate with others (possibly 2 S. 12:16f.; cf. Mish. *Nedarim* iv-v) or to anoint oneself (2 S. 12:10), and abstaining from other pleasures (Dnl. 6:18) or sounding the shofar (Mish. *Taanith* ii). According to the book of Jonah (3:7), the king of Nineveh decreed that beasts as well as his citizens were to abstain from food and water. Later rabbinic interpretations of the Day of Atonement prohibited washing, anointing, putting on sandals, and marital intercourse, along with fasting (Mish. *Yoma* viii.l).

The old term "humbling oneself" (Lev. 23:27-29) is usually regarded as a synonym for fasting, although it may have included other acts, such as not washing or changing clothes. Later the phrase was used in poetic parallel with fasting, but may have been a separate act (cf. Ps. 35:13; 69:10; Isa. 58:3).

These self-imposed acts would last for various lengths of time. David once vowed not to eat until sundown (2 S. 3:35), and later he fasted alone for seven days in sackcloth and on the ground, until his child died (2 S. 12:16-20). Others fasted for a week following a death (1 S. 31:13). Moses and Jesus fasted forty days and nights (Ex. 34:28; Mt. 4:2). The duration of the Nazirite vow was set by the individual (Nu. 6:5), usually thirty days (Mish. *Nazir* i.3).

B. In the NT. Acts 27:9 shows that Paul and the early Christians took note of the Day of Atonement. Although we may assume that they actually observed this fast, because they observed certain Jewish feasts, there is no clear evidence for this. In the Didache (8:1) Christians were instructed not to fast on Mondays and Thursdays, when Jews customarily fasted, but on Wednesdays and Fridays.

Although Jesus Himself fasted in His ministry, He refused to give His disciples specific instructions on fasting, as both the Pharisees and John the Baptist had done (Mt. 9:14-17; Lk. 5:33-35). Like the prophets before Him, He condemned the external appearances that were designed to impress men but lacked the genuine piety that would please God (Mt. 6:16-18). But in explaining why His disciples were not to fast "while the bridegroom was with them," Jesus implied that such fasting would be appropriate later on. Thus early Christians believed they had Jesus' approval for fasting, although they did not observe the same fasts as the Jews.

Paul also insisted that whatever one's individual decision might be, whether to eat or not to eat, there should be no touch of self-righteousness involved, for either act was to be done in honor of the Lord (Rom. 14:3, 6). It was never to be a source of "boasting." The other apostles also fasted (Acts 13:2). At times the Church had to warn against certain false teachers who imposed abstinence from foods "which God created to be received with thanksgiving" (1 Tim. 4:3).

III. Celibacy.–Abstinence was not limited to food and drink among either Jews or Christians. The refusal to engage in sexual intercourse was an accepted practice in times of unusual circumstance. Uriah voluntarily refused such relations with his wife because he was still in military service (2 S. 11); and intercourse was forbidden on the Day of Atonement (Mish. *Yoma* viii.1). Lifelong CELIBACY, however, was not an accepted form of piety in normative Judaism. Marriage and having children were expected as a way of fulfilling the command to "be fruitful and multiply" (Gen. 1:28). Rather than strict abstinence, OT and rabbinic teachings generally encouraged the enjoyment of all God's gifts, but with temperance and moderation. Even the Nazirite's highly regarded abstinence was interpreted as necessitating a sin offering to cover the refusal to accept the divine gifts (Talm. *Nedarim* 10a).

Jesus' life as an unmarried person, coupled with some of His teachings about the urgency and overriding priority of the Kingdom (Mt. 19:10-12; Mk. 8:34-38) and about the future world (Mk. 12:25), has been taken by some to mean that He preferred that His followers not marry. But His overall enjoyment of life (Mt. 11:19), His presence at the wedding in Cana (Jn. 2:1-11), and His emphasis on maintaining the marriage vow (Mt. 5:31f.) put the former notion into a broader and balanced perspective.

Paul's views were influenced both by his expectation of Christ's imminent return and by the particular circumstances of those to whom he wrote. Specific statements on abstinence must be understood in terms of these two factors. He adhered to traditional Jewish ethics in condemning adultery, fornication, and relationships between homosexuals, but he went beyond Judaism in advocating that, because of the urgency of the times, Christians would do well to consider refraining from marriage. A husband and a wife were not to refuse each other, except by mutual consent, and then only for a short time (1 Cor. 7:5, 26f.), and in all cases there should be mutual respect and consideration (1 Cor. 7:2; cf. 1 Thess. 4:3). The writer of 1 Timothy warned against false teachers who "forbid marriage" (4:3), but did say that church officials were to be "married only once" (3:2; cf. Tit. 1:6). The author of the Apocalypse (Rev. 14:4) placed celibates in an honored position.

IV. Second-Century Developments.–From the Apostolic Fathers we see the development of abstinence during the second century. The "Teaching of the Apostles" turns Paul's liberal view toward meat sacrificed to idols (1 Cor. 8:1-13) into a legalism to be rigidly enforced (Did. 6). This writing also specifies that fasting was to be observed by both the person to be baptized and the baptizer (7:4). Celibacy among men and women began to be highly regarded as a Christian life-style in the Apostolic age. It was increasingly revered by Christians in the next two centuries (Ign. Polyc. 5:2; 2 Clem. 12).

The Jewish sect at Qumrân and the Gnostic Christian community at Nag Hammadi considered abstinence in one form or another quite proper, if not essential. Josephus described the Essenes as viewing pleasures as a vice and disdaining marriage (*BJ* ii.8.2). Although he and other ancient writers mention celibacy as a major teaching of the Essenes, the Qumrân community, at least at some stages, did include women and children. Both literary references and archeological evidence show that women were not forbidden there, as they were later in the monasteries.

The Gnostic Gospel of Thomas (6, 14, 27) reveals the tendency away from the traditional Jewish customs which had been embraced by most early Christians, especially prayer, fasting, almsgiving, and circumcision (cf. also Diogn. 3, 4). The Gospel of Philip shows even less awareness of or dependence on a Jewish undergirding for the essence of the Christian life.

V. Fasting, Prayer, and Almsgiving.–Fasting, prayer, and alsmgiving were three highly regarded acts of piety within Judaism which Christians quickly adopted as their own, but with modification. Although extolled separately, they were often mentioned in combination; e.g., prayer and fasting (Jgs. 20:26f.; Neh. 1:4; Lk. 5:33; Gospel of Thomas 6); fasting and almsgiving (Isa. 58:6f.; Zec. 7:3-9; Lk. 18:12), almsgiving and prayer (Tob. 12:8f.; Acts 10:31). Whenever one act stood alone in a document, scribes were prone to add one or another. This propensity accounts for several variant readings in the ancient MSS (Mt. 17:21; Mk. 9:29; cf. Peshitta, which puts fasting before prayer here). Inevitably efforts were made to put one ahead of another. 2 Clement says, "Fasting is better than prayer, but the giving of alms is better than both" (16:4). In the Didache a nondominical saying about fasting precedes the word of Jesus on prayer (8:1f.).

VI. Function.–A full appreciation of these many forms requires consideration of their functions within the given community. Although there may have been quite pragmatic reasons for their origins, they usually came into religious tradition and then into sacred writings only after they had been justified on theological grounds (but cf. 1 K. 21:9; Dnl. 6:18). The Nazirite vow to abstain from wine and grape seems to have been related to an early protest against a life tied to the soil where vines had to be tended. Such a life-style was contrary to that of the wandering shepherd. The lure of the desert, where God's people could be most faithful, continued within Israel for centuries. (Cf. the description of the Rechabites, Jer. 35:1-14 and Hos. 2:14f.)

Other reasons why various forms of abstinence were practiced in the OT were: to mark one's dedication or "separation" to the Lord (Nu. 6:1ff.), as a way of seeking the Lord, in national calamity (e.g., drought, Jer. 14:12; cf. Mish. *Taanith* i-iii; and locusts, Joel 1:14), for personal petition (1 S. 1:7), in preparation for judgment (1 S. 7:6) or divine revelation (Dnl. 9:3), or to express grief (1 Ch. 10:12), repentance (1 K. 21:27-29), fear (2 Ch. 20:3), mourning for others' sins (Ezr. 9:5; 10:6), to obtain God's favor in a plan (Est. 4:15), and on behalf of others' illness (Ps. 35:13). Some rabbis considered abstinence meritorious and desirable as a means of self-discipline. Under the eschatological spirit of the postexilic age, some believed that fasting, as part of a strict observance of the law, would move God to act dramatically in history.

Jesus' fasting was part of His temptation (Lk. 4:2), but He stressed that all religious acts were to be done only for the glory of God, not to please men (Mt. 6:16-18). According to a questionable text (cf. var. Mt. 17:21; also var. Mk. 9:29) fasting was a way of dealing with difficult demons. Abstinence in any form was justified only when observed "for the sake of the kingdom" (Mt. 19:10-12; Mk. 10:29). The early Church practiced fasting prior to appointing its officials (Acts 13:2f.; 14:23); Paul insisted that all such acts be done "in honor of the Lord" (Rom. 14:3, 6), to prevent pride and consequent dissension. The Didache urged fasting for one's persecutors (1:3; cf. Ps. 35:13). An emphasis on chastity may have developed in part to counteract charges of promiscuity against those who practiced a "love feast."

It is out of a theological context which rejected a doctrine of retribution but allowed for God's own system of rewards that specific NT statements regarding abstinence can best be appreciated. But for all of the hows and whys, Christians were constantly called to view their lives in the light of Jesus' call to self-denial (Mt. 16:24), Paul's injunction to put to death all earthly, self-oriented passions (Col. 3:5), and similar Johannine cautions (1 Jn. 2:15-17). Jesus' passion served as the final call to a life that by its essence requires sacrifice, at times, through self-imposed abstinence.

The why of abstinence, along with the how, developed among many religious groups as they sought, through centuries of varied circumstances, to give a religious dimension to their individual and community life. Most of them gave enough reflection to the matter to see the folly of relying on mere ceremony to establish a right relationship with God (Joel 2:12f.; Mt. 6:16-18). The best also saw that such outward forms functioned properly only when they led the abstainers to be more responsive to God's will and more charitable to their neighbors (Am. 8:4ff.; Zec. 7:9; Tob. 12:8f.; Talm. *Abodah Zarah* 20b; Lk. 18:9-14; Shep. Herm. Sim. 5:1; Ign. Polyc. 5).

Bibliography.–C. K. Barrett, ed., *The NT Background: Selected Documents* (1961); *TDNT*, IV, *s.v.* νῆστις (J. Behm); A.-M. Denis, *Revue des Sciences Philosophiques et Théologiques*, 47 (1963), 606-618; J. N. D. Kelly, *The Motive of Christian Asceticism* (1964); J. Lawson, *Theological and Historical Intro. to the Apostolic Fathers* (1961); E. Schweizer, *Church Order in the NT* (Eng. tr. 1961).

J. T. CLEMONS

ABUBUS ə-bōō'bus [Gk. *Aboubos*]. The father of Ptolemy, who deceitfully slew Simon Maccabeus and his sons at Dok near Jericho (1 Macc. 16:11, 15).

ABUSE [Heb. *qālôn*] (Prov. 9:7; 22:10); AV SHAME, REPROACH; NEB SNEER AT, MAKE A MOCKERY; [*'ālal*] (Jgs. 19:25; Jer. 38:19); AV also MOCK; NEB also ROUGHLY HANDLE; [Gk. *oneidismós*] (He. 10:33; 11:26; 13:13); AV REPROACH; NEB also STIGMA; [*epēreázō*] (Lk. 6:28); AV DESPITEFULLY USE; NEB TREAT (YOU) SPITEFULLY; [*blasphēméō*] (1 Pet. 4:4); AV SPEAK EVIL; NEB VILIFY; [*katalaléo*] (1 Pet. 3:16); AV SPEAK EVIL; **ABUSIVE** [Gk. *blásphēmos*] (2 Tim. 3:2); AV BLASPHEMERS.

In Proverbs the one who "corrects a scoffer" will only get himself insulted, since the scoffer is not able to profit from reproof. Abuse can come from mockery or evil speaking being directed against someone (2 Tim. 3:2); this was part of the expected experience of the early Christian community (1 Pet. 3:16; 4:4). Abusive words sometimes turn into "spiteful treatment" (Lk. 6:28), and the taunts and scorns into public spectacles of insults and persecutions (He. 10:33). The writer of Hebrews speaks of Moses' "abuse suffered for the Christ" whereby Moses identified himself with Israel's suffering and encountered the same disgrace and reproach as did Christ (He. 11:26). This "abuse of Christ" is what all Christians are called upon to suffer (He. 13:13), and has been described as "to be ill-treated to the end, and to the last breath" (Chrysostom).

The old sense of "abuse" as "to ravish" or "to defile" is retained in the story of the Levite's concubine (Jgs. 19:25).

Bibliography.–*TDNT*, V, *s.v.* ὀνειδισμός (J. Schneider); J. Moffatt, comm. on Hebrews (*ICC*, 1924); Chrysostom *Hom.* 26 *in Heb.*

D. K. MCKIM

ABYSS [Gk. *hē ábyssos*] (Lk. 8:31; Rom. 10:7); AV THE DEEP; **BOTTOMLESS PIT** [Gk. *tó phréar tēs abýssou*

(Rev. 9:1f.), *hē ábyssos* (9:11; 11:7; 17:8; 20:1, 3)]; NEB "shaft of the abyss," "abyss." According to primitive Semitic cosmogony the earth was supposed to rest on a vast body of water which was the source of all springs of water and rivers (Gen. 1:2; Dt. 8:7; Ps. 24:2; 136:6). This subterranean ocean is sometimes described as "the water under the earth" (Ex. 20:4; Dt. 5:8). According to Job 41:32 *tᵉhôm* is the home of Leviathan, in which he plows his hoary path of foam. The LXX uses *ábyssos* as a rendering of Heb. *tᵉhôm*, but never of *šᵉʾôl* (=Sheol=Hades); and probably *tᵉhôm* never meant the "abode of the dead," which was the ordinary meaning of Sheol. In Ps. 71:20 *tᵉhôm* is used figuratively, and denotes "many and sore troubles" through which the psalmist has passed (cf. Jonah 2:5).

In the NT, however, *ábyssos* means the "abode of demons." In Lk. 8:31 the demons possessing the Gerasene demoniac beg not to be sent to their place of punishment before their destined time. Mark simply says "out of the country" (5:10). In Rom. 10:7 the word is equivalent to Hades, the abode of the dead. In Revelation *ábyssos* denotes the abode of evil spirits, but not the place of final punishment; it is therefore to be distinguished from the "lake of fire and brimstone" where the beast and the false prophet are, and into which the devil is finally to be cast (19:20; 20:10).

See also CHAOS; DEEP.

See *TDNT*, *s.v.* ἄβυσσος (Jeremias). T. LEWIS

ABYSSINIA ab-ə-sin'yə, ab-ə-sin'ē-ə. *See* ETHIOPIA.

ACACIA ə-kā'shə [Heb. *šiṭṭâ*, *ʿᵃṣê-šiṭṭâ*[; AV SHITTAH TREE (Isa. 41:19), SHITTIM WOOD (Ex. 25:5, 10, 13; 26:15, 26; 27:1, 6; Dt. 10:3). Several species of tree and wood, three or four of which grow in Palestine. Most probably the OT reference is to *Acacia seyal* Delile, common in the Sinai Peninsula and parts of the Jordan Valley.

Where Shittim is used as a place name (Nu. 25:1; 33:49; Josh. 2:1; 3:1; Mic. 6:5), it probably indicates areas in which the acacias flourished. *A. seyal* and *A. tortilis* grow in the Arabian deserts. Though commonly found as shrubs, they can attain a height of 25 ft. (7.5 m.) in favorable locations. The orange-brown wood is very durable and admirably suited for the construction of tabernacle furnishings and the ark of the covenant. *A. seyal* and *A. arabica* yield gum arabic, used in pharmacy, confectionery, and making adhesives. R. K. H.

ACATAN ak'ə-tan (1 Esd. 8:38, AV). *See* HAKKATAN.

ACCAD ak'ad [Heb. *'akkaḏ*–'fortress'; Gk. *Archad*] (Gen. 10:10). One of Nimrod's cities. *See* AGADE; BABYLON.

ACCARON ak'ə-ron (1 Macc. 10:89, AV). *See* EKRON.

ACCENT, GALILEAN [Gk. *laliá*] (Mt. 26:73); AV SPEECH. A peculiarity of the speech of a Galilean person that revealed his place of residence. The normal word for speech is used in this passage to refer to peculiarities in Peter's speech that showed him to be Galilean. These marks of Galilean speech caused the servant girl to question Peter's denial that he was Jesus' disciple.

The majority of scholars still believe that Peter was speaking the Galilean form of the Aramaic language. However, recent research has shown increasing evidence for the use of the Greek language by all classes of people in the Palestine of Jesus' day.

Bibliography.–*AP*, pp. 177-203; T. Zahn, *Intro. to the NT* (Eng. tr. 1909), I, 1-48; J. N. Sevenster, *Do You Know Greek?* (Eng. tr. 1968). D. W. WEAD

ACCEPT; ACCEPTABLE; ACCEPTANCE [Heb. *lāqaḥ*, *rāṣâ*, also *nāśā'* (Gen. 4:7; 32:20; Job 42:8f.; Prov. 6:35; Eccl. 5:19), *rāwaḥ* (1 S. 26:19), *qāḇal* (Est. 4:4; Prov. 19:20), *lāmaḏ* (Isa. 29:24), *nāḵar* (Job 21:29), *yāṭaḇ* (Lev. 10:19), *bāḥar* (Prov. 21:3); Aram. *šᵉpar* (Dnl. 4:27); Gk. *déchomai, dektós*, also *apodéchomai* (Acts 24:3), *apódektos* (1 Tim. 2:3; 5:4), *apodochḗ* (1 Tim. 1:15; 4:9), *paradéchomai* (Mk. 4:20; Acts 16:21; 22:18), *prosdéchomai* (Acts 24:15; He. 10:34; 11:35), *dókimos* (2 Cor. 10:18), *pleíōn* (He. 11:4), *euprósdektos* (Rom. 15:16, 31; 2 Cor. 6:2; 8:12; 1 Pet. 2:5), *próslēpsis* (Rom. 11:15), *lambánō* (2 Cor. 11:4, 8; 3 Jn. 1:7), *euárestos* (Rom. 12:1f.; 14:18), *euaréstōs* (He. 12:28)]; AV also TAKE, RECEIVE, KNOW (Job 21:29), REGARD (Prov. 6:35), LEARN (Isa. 29:24), "own voluntary will" (Lev. 1:3; 19:5; 22:19, 29), FAVORABLE (Job 33:26); NEB also TAKE, RECEIVE, LEARN (Job 21:29), "will not buy (his forgiveness)" (Prov. 6:35), "has no more pleasure (in them)" (Jer. 14:10), "suit his words to the occasion" (Prov. 10:32), FAVOR (2 Cor. 6:2), SHOW FAVOR (Job 33:26; 42:9), APPROVE (1 Tim. 2:3; 5:4), "worship him as he would be worshipped" (He. 12:28), APPROVAL (He. 11:4).

"Accept" is used most frequently in the sense of "take" or "receive (something from someone)." A variety of objects may be accepted, e.g., money, prayers, offerings, sacrifices, testimony (Acts 22:18), and even the gospel (1 Thess. 2:13).

Very often "accept" is used in a special cultic sense, especially in the OT (*rāṣôn, rāṣâ*). Here it usually refers to God's accepting or rejecting what is offered to Him. When God accepts what is offered to Him, the man who presents the offering in effect finds favor with Him. When the people of Israel became apostate, however, their sacrifices were no longer pleasing to God (Jer. 6:20). Only when the people repent and the gentile nations join themselves to the Lord will sacrifices again be accepted by Yahweh (Isa. 56:7).

The move away from the strict cultic usage and to a more spiritualized sense is evidenced first in the Wisdom literature, where not only material sacrifices but also the thoughts (Ps. 19:14), deeds (Prov. 21:3), and prayers (Job 42:9) of the righteous man are acceptable. This sense is carried into the NT and extended to include the work and service of the Christian community (Gk. *dektós*, Phil. 4:18; 1 Pet. 2:5).

To announce the arrival of the "acceptable year of the Lord" (Lk. 4:19; cf. Isa. 61:2) and the "acceptable time" (2 Cor. 6:2) is to proclaim that the messianic era has been initiated through the ministry and work of Christ. The acceptable time is the time of fulfillment chosen by Yahweh, the time to manifest Himself incarnate. It is a time of deliverance and salvation, as in Isa. 49:8, "In a time of favor [*rāṣôn*] I have answered you, in a day of salvation I have helped you."

See also FAVOR. B. L. BANDSTRA

ACCESS. The RSV has "right of access" in Zec. 3:7 for the hiphil part. of Heb. *hālaḵ*, "walk"; the AV reads "places to walk," NEB "right to come and go." The reference is to a vision of Zechariah in which Joshua the high priest is promised access to the court of the Lord if he will obey Him.

The Gk. *prosagōgḗ* is used in the NT to indicate the acceptable way of approach to God and of admission to His favor. Jesus said, "I am the way" (Jn. 14:6). His blood is the "new and living way" (He. 10:20). Only through Him have we "access to this grace in which we stand" (Rom. 5:2); "through him we both have access in one Spirit to the Father" (Eph. 2:18); "in whom we have boldness and confidence of access through our faith in him" (3:12).

The goal of redemption is life in God, "unto the Father." The means of redemption is the cross of Christ, in whom "we have redemption through his blood" (Eph. 1:7). The agent in redemption is the Holy Spirit, "by one Spirit," "sealed with the promised Holy Spirit" (1:13). The human instrumentality is faith. The whole process of approach to God and abiding fellowship with Him is summed up in this brief sentence: access to the Father, through Christ, by the Spirit, by faith. D. M. PRATT

ACCESSORIES [Heb. *kelî*] (Nu. 3:36); AV VESSELS; NEB EQUIPMENT; [*'abôdâ*] (Nu. 4:32); AV SERVICE; NEB MAINTENANCE. Heb. *kelî* is a very general term that can refer to equipment of all sorts, receptacles for food and drink, implements for hunting, war, cultic activities, etc. In Nu. 3:36 it represents equipment connected with setting up and taking down the TABERNACLE. KD suggest "the plugs and tools." The term *'abôdâ* is likewise very general, literally meaning "service" (cf. RSV "service" in 3:36). The reference is probably to instruments and tools used in the maintenance of the tabernacle.

ACCO ak'ō [Heb. *'akkô*; Gk. *Akchō*] (Jgs. 1:31); AV ACCHO. A town on the Syrian coast a few miles N of Carmel; later known as Ptolemais (Gk. [*Akē*] *Ptolemais*); the modern 'Akka, Akko, or Acre. It is situated on a small promontory on the north side of a broad bay that lies between it and the modern town of Haifa. This bay furnishes the best anchorage for ships of any on this coast except that of St. George, at Beirut, and Alexandretta at the extreme north.

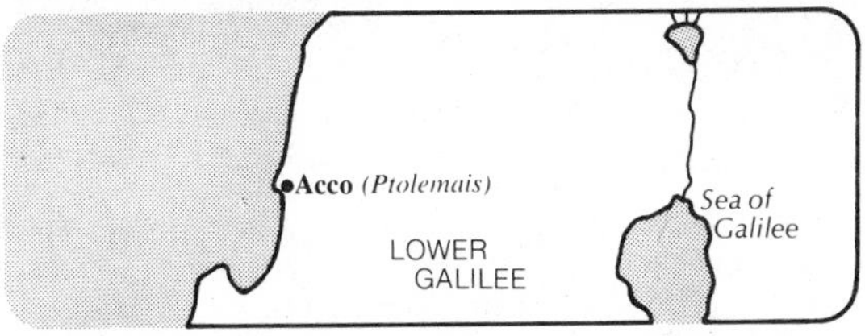

As the location commanded the approach from the sea to the rich plain of Esdraelon and also the coast route from the north, the city was regarded in ancient times as of great importance and at various periods of history was the scene of severe struggles for its possession. It fell within the bounds assigned to the Israelites, particularly to the tribe of Asher; but they were never able to take it (Josh. 19:24-31; Jgs. 1:31). It was, like Tyre and Sidon, too strong for them to attack; and it became indeed a fortress of unusual strength, so that it withstood many a siege, often baffling its assailants. In the period of the Crusades it was the most famous stronghold on the coast.

In very early times it was a place of importance, and appears in the Amarna Tablets as a possession of the Egyptian kings. Its governor wrote to his suzerain professing loyalty when the northern towns were falling away (Am. Tab. 88; 234). The Egyptian suzerainty over the coast, which was established by Thutmose III *ca.* 1480 B.C., was apparently lost in the 14th cent., as is indicated in the Amarna Tablets, but was regained under Seti I and his more famous son Ramses II in the 13th, to be lost again in the 12th when the Phoenician towns seem to have established their independence. Sidon, however, surpassed her sisters in power and exercised a sort of hegemony over the Phoenician towns, at least in the south; and Acco was included in it. But when Assyria came upon the scene Acco had to submit to this power, although it revolted whenever Assyria became weak, as appears from the mention of its subjugation by Sennacherib and by Ashurbanipal. The latter "quieted" it by a wholesale massacre and then carried into captivity the remaining inhabitants. Upon the downfall of Assyria Acco passed, together with other Phoenician towns, under the dominion of Babylon and then of Persia. We have no records of its annals during that period; but it followed the fortunes of the more important cities, Tyre and Sidon.

In the Seleucid period (312-65 B.C.) the town became of importance in the contests between the Seleucids and the Ptolemies. The latter occupied it during the struggles that succeeded the death of Alexander and made it their stronghold on the coast, changing the name to PTOLEMAIS, by which it was known in the Greco-Roman period, as we see in the accounts of the Greek and Roman writers and in Josephus, as well as in the NT (1 Macc. 5:22; 10:39; 12:48; Acts 21:7). The old name still continued locally and reasserted itself in later times. The Ptolemies held undisputed possession of Ptolemais for about 70 years; but it was wrested from them by Antiochus III of Syria in 219 B.C., and went into the permanent possession of the Seleucids after the decisive victory of Antiochus over Scopas in that year, the result of which was the expulsion of the Ptolemies from Syria, Palestine, and Phoenicia (Josephus *Ant.* xii.3.3). In the dynastic struggles of the Seleucids it fell into the hands of Alexander Bala, who there received the hand of Cleopatra, the daughter of Ptolemy Philometor, as a pledge of alliance between them (*Ant.* xiii.4.1). Tigranes king of Armenia besieged it on his invasion of Syria, but was obliged to relinquish it on the approach of the Romans toward his own dominions (*BJ* i.5.3). Under the Romans Ptolemais became a colony and a metropolis, as is known from its coins; and its importance is attested by Strabo (*Geog.* xvi.2.25).

The events that followed the conquests of the Saracens, leading to the Crusades, brought the city into great prominence. It was captured by the Crusaders A.D. 1110, and remained in their hands until 1187, when it was taken from them by Saladin and its fortifications so strengthened as to render it almost impregnable. The importance of this fortress as a key to the Holy Land was considered so great by the Crusaders that they put forth every effort during two years to recapture it, but all in vain until the arrival of Richard Coeur de Lion and Philip Augustus with reinforcements; and it was only after the most strenuous efforts on their part that the place fell into their hands. It cost them 100,000 men. The fortifications were repaired, and it was afterward committed to the charge of the knights of St. John, by whom it was held for a hundred years and renamed St. Jean d'Acre. It was finally taken by the Saracens in 1291, being the last place held by the Crusaders in Palestine.

It declined after this and fell into the hands of the Ottomans under Selim I in 1516. It remained mostly in ruins until the 18th cent., when it came into the possession of Jezzar Pasha, who usurped the authority over it and the neighboring district and became practically independent of the Sultan, defying his authority. In 1799 it was attacked by Napoleon, but was bravely and successfully defended by the Turks with the help of the English fleet. Napoleon had to abandon the siege after he had spent two months before it and gained a victory over the Turkish army at Tabor. It enjoyed a considerable degree of prosperity after this until 1831, when it was besieged by Ibrahim Pasha of Egypt, and taken, but only after a siege of more than five months in which it suffered the destruction of its walls and many of its buildings. It continued in the hands of the Egyptians until 1840, when it was restored to the Ottomans by the English,

Fortifications of the Old City of Acco, rebuilt by the eighteenth-century Turkish pashas (Consulate General of Israel in New York)

whose fleet nearly reduced it to ruins in the bombardment. It has recovered somewhat since then and is now a town of some 25,000 inhabitants. It has been surpassed, however, by Haifa as a center of commerce.

See M. Dothan, *BASOR*, 224 (Dec. 1976), 1-48.

H. PORTER

ACCOMMODATION. (1) The use or application of a Scripture reference in a sense other than the obvious and literal one intended by the author; (2) the view that a passage or verse may have more than one meaning or application; (3) the principle that God adapts His self-revelation to man.

The subject of accommodation is important because it involves the whole problem of a correct hermeneutics or mode of interpreting Scripture, because it introduces the problem of a correct balancing of the divine and human elements in Scripture, and because it involves the doctrine of the Incarnation and its purpose and nature. In all these spheres there can be a false as well as a true doctrine of accommodation, though the true doctrine is certainly not to be abandoned or neglected because of the possibility of the false.

I. Accommodated Application of Scripture Passages
II. Double Reference in Scripture
  A. Parable and Allegory
  B. Hidden Truth
  C. Prophecy and Its Fulfillment
III. Accommodation in Revelation
  A. The Problem of Revelation
  B. Accommodation in Revelation
  C. The Incarnation as Accommodation

I. Accommodated Application of Scripture Passages.–The correct understanding of any written document is a science. Indeterminate or capricious exegesis is excluded. A first and obvious principle of true interpretation is that of objective listening to the writer or speaker in terms of what he has to say and not of alien or imported considerations or concerns. The plain, literal, and original meaning always has the right-of-way. All wresting of the passage, reinterpretation in terms of a different outlook, application to a clearly divergent matter, or reading-in of meanings that are not merely new but intrinsically improbable in the light of the context is unscientific and misleading.

There are, however, two legitimate forms of accommodation in the field of exposition. First, a general truth or principle may have a valid application wider than to the localized issue of the original context. Thus, when Paul speaks of consideration for a weaker brother, we are not to take it that this applies only to the issue of idol-meats in which it is specifically enunciated. Second, a passage may well have a much wider context than the immediate one in which we initially set it, e.g., the context of the whole book, or the Testament, or ultimately the whole Bible as a unity (*see also* INTERPRETATION; QUOTATIONS IN THE NT).

II. Double Reference in Scripture.–The second point naturally leads us to the question of accommodation in the sense not merely of wider reference but of twofold meaning and application. We are not to infer from this that the Bible is full of cryptic utterances that are intrinsically ambiguous like the Delphic oracles, which may hold or acquire any meaning that we or circumstances give them. On the other hand, we are not to deny that in the light of the literary form and the larger historical and documentary context many passages may properly be given more than a single application.

A. Parable and Allegory. Thus at many points, e.g., in the story of the bramble king in Jgs. 9:7-15, or the symbolical actions of the prophets, or the parables of Our Lord, we have records in which double meaning is of the essence of the literary expression. In other words, we have descriptions of processes or events that are real and plain enough in themselves but which carry a meaning that is different and less obvious. It is true, of course, that these are not allegories in the strict sense. Nor are we to seek for hidden meanings merely because we perceive a symbolical or metaphorical form of speech. On the other hand, even the use of symbol or metaphor means that the sense transcends the literal statement; and when this is extended in a parable or in parabolic action we are brought into the sphere of an immediate but not particularly important significance, accompanied by a less immediate and often concealed meaning that demands inward perception if it is to be grasped.

B. Hidden Truths. A further point is that there is development in the unfolding and therefore in the understanding of Scripture. As the history of God's work proceeds, each part gains added significance. Similarly, as the reader considers each part in the light of all the others, and finally of the whole, implications and interconnections that could not be perceived or appreciated in isolation are brought to light.

(1) As may happen in the secular sphere, authors are sometimes seen to have spoken more wisely than perhaps they themselves knew in the isolated situation of their own time. Speaking to a specific hour in the divine history, they also speak with reference to history as a whole and to the fulness of its meaning.

(2) There is also development in the understanding and exposition of later ages. The writers speak of a history that is at every point inexhaustible in range and depth and meaning, because it is the history of God. Hence the householder may constantly bring forth from his treasure things that are new—new facets or interconnections or profundities—as well as those that are old.

(3) In view of the interrelatedness of the divine work, and therefore of its biblical attestation, each passage has a larger context as well as a narrower. The ways in which different passages fit into the wider context may vary. Nevertheless, it is only as seen in this context that their full meaning may be perceived.

C. Prophecy and Its Fulfillment. This leads us to the important truth that between the OT and the NT there is a relationship of prophecy and fulfillment, so that the OT is in fact obscure and fragmentary if taken in isolation, but finds the full sweep of its meaning when seen in the light of its NT consummation and supremely of Jesus Christ as the theme of the NT. Reference may be made to four specific points of interconnection between prophetic anticipation and historical realization in the person, life, and work of Jesus Christ.

(1) The promise made to Abraham (Gen. 12:1-3; cf. 13:14-18; 15:1-6, etc.) and later renewed to Israel (cf. Ex. 6:7; 2 S. 7; 1 Ch. 17, etc.) is seen to refer to a distant future and to find fulfillment in Jesus Christ (cf. Gal. 3, esp. v. 14).

(2) The OT sacrificial system, though not without intrinsic significance, is seen to be typical, symbolical, and predictive, fulfilled in the once-for-all offering of Jesus Christ for sin (He. 10, etc.).

(3) The Davidic kingdom is seen to be only a partial and temporary fulfillment which serves as a prophetic *locum tenens* for the true kingdom inaugurated and to be consummated in Jesus Christ the messianic King (Pss. 2, 16, 22, 110, etc.; cf. Lk. 1:69).

(4) The servant concept of the prophet (Isa. 42:1f., etc.; cf. Acts 8:32-35), while not perhaps without some local historical reference, is seen to be an anticipatory description of the character and work of Jesus Christ centered upon His vicarious death for sin (cf. esp. Isa. 53 and its use in the NT).

It is alleged by many scholars that here we have illegitimate accommodation. Three main arguments are used: that we hereby attribute to the authors a sense they neither did nor could intend to give; that in so doing we weaken their real message; and that artificial importation of this kind destroys the objectivity of true interpretation.

Against these objections, the following points are to be considered: (1) It need not be denied that an immediate and important significance does attach to each passage in its local context. (2) There is, however, a larger whole, both of the acts of God and of the record of these acts, to which the individual passages or incidents are all related. (3) If the NT message is true, Jesus Christ is the fulfillment of this work of God (He. 1:1) and therefore the unifying center of the whole history and record. (4) This is the Bible's understanding of itself when taken as the totality as we have it, and therefore a true objectivity demands that we take this factor into account in our exposition of it.

Thus there is a real promise to Abraham, which finds partial fulfillment in his own life and that of his descendants through Isaac. There is a real meaning in the sacrificial system, and this serves a useful purpose in the religious life of Israel as the people of Yahweh. There is a real Davidic kingdom realized in large measure in David himself and especially in Solomon, and continuing with varying fortunes to the tragedy of the Exile. There is a real fulfillment of sacrificial service in figures like Jeremiah or even Jeconiah, or in the righteous remnant of Israel, or even in some sense in Israel as a whole. Yet these are neither abstract concepts nor isolated phenomena. They belong to a history. Nor is this history merely that of Israel. It is that of God's dealings with Israel and in and through Israel. This history moves to a climax or consummation in which there is a concentration of all the themes upon the single figure of Jesus Christ, the true Son of Abraham and David, the true offering for sin, the true Sin-bearer who need not suffer for Himself but who willingly and obediently suffers for others. Here the whole history, and therefore each part of it, reaches its goal and thus acquires its fulness of meaning. The theme of the Bible as a whole is finally the history of Jesus Christ in its preparation, enactment, significance, and consequences. Objectivity requires rather than rejects this form of accommodation.

III. Accommodation in Revelation.–The problem answered by the divine self-revelation in Jesus Christ is threefold. First, how is man to know God at all? Second, what form will this knowledge take? Third, how can it be achieved and secured in face of the sin and the consequent spiritual ignorance and darkness of man?

A. The Problem of Revelation. As regards the first question, all human knowledge of God obviously depends upon the gracious purpose of God that there should be knowledge of Himself, and therefore upon the condescension of the divine self-revelation. This is true even in the case (now hypothetical) of unfallen man created in the divine image. As such, man might have enjoyed natural knowledge of God. But this would still be dependent upon the prior will of God to create man as he is and to give to him the knowledge appropriate to him. In other words, God is known at all only as in gracious condescension He makes Himself an object of knowledge, and not as man avails himself of a

ACCOMMODATION

capacity and right of knowledge intrinsic to his creation. We must beware of arguing in circles at this point, for God in His grace did in fact make man a fit recipient of His natural revelation. On the other hand, we do well to avoid thrusting a necessity on God, as though He were under a prior obligation to His creature to make him thus. In all circumstances, knowledge of God must involve wonder, humility, and gratitude that God has in fact chosen to make Himself knowable and known.

The formal endowment of man, willed and planned by God Himself, naturally requires the gracious adaptation of divine self-revelation. Here again we are not to think in terms of a necessity imposed on God and therefore of a problem with which He had to wrestle until He found the right solution. God Himself made man as he is in his unfallen nature, and therefore it is self-consistent with His own gracious will and purpose to meet him as he is. On the other hand, He might equally well have determined to leave man in ignorance, or to create in him a different capacity of knowledge, so far as His formal freedom is concerned. In fact, God does reveal Himself to man in accordance with the creaturely capacities with which He has endowed him. The gracious condescension of self-revelation thus fulfils itself in gracious adaptation to the limited potentialities of human knowledge. It is here that grace takes the form of accommodation.

Accommodation would have been a feature of revelation quite apart from the fall of man. Creaturely man does not have the equipment to know God with the immediacy and fulness with which God knows Himself. Many modes of apprehension, categories of thought, and forms of expression are restrictive. This does not mean that God cannot reveal Himself to man, or that any knowledge of man will necessarily be imperfect or inadequate or even distorted. It means that there is a divinely ordained limitation, and therefore that God reveals Himself in adapted or accommodated form. To take a human analogy, the teacher adapts himself and his program to the more limited capabilities of the students. Such knowledge as he imparts is correct, even though it is not all that could be given. There is accommodation to the limits of the recipients.

A new complication has arisen, however, with the fall of man, for this has brought with it the additional factor of human ignorance and error, more especially in relation to the knowledge of God. Even though God accommodates Himself, e.g., by displaying His power and wisdom in the works of His hands, sinful man fails to recognize God and substitutes a creaturely idol (Rom. 1:19ff.). Indeed, fallen man cannot have true knowledge even of himself and the creaturely world around him. It might be argued with some degree of plausibility that his very categories of thought and forms of self-expression, or at least the use he makes of them, bear marks of the distorting or damaging effects of sin. Certainly, his capacity for receiving communication is impaired. Hence a simple accommodation to the creaturely being of man is no longer enough for divine self-revelation. In consistency with His original and unabandoned purpose of grace, God's condescension must now take the form of an accommodation—not merely to the creaturely being of man but also to his sinful being.

In practice the divine self-revelation as we now have it in Holy Scripture is naturally to man as both creature and sinner. We thus have a twofold accommodation, in keeping with the twofold nature of the problem—or rather, of the divine solution to the problem. This fact gives rise to the most serious questions and difficulties in the correct understanding of the doctrine of accommodation. For example, how are we to distinguish between accommodation to man's finite nature and accommodation to his fallible and sinful nature? Is there still any possibility of the adequacy of the former alone at least for a preparatory work? Can there be the latter without an involvement of revelation itself in fallibility or sinfulness? If there is such involvement in the formal sense, e.g., in the employment of sinful and fallible men, does this necessarily imply material fallibility and sinfulness? Is not this a possibility that must be excluded from the very outset if we are truly dealing with the revelation of God?

B. Accommodation in Revelation. Although the distinction is artificial in view of the real situation of man, the adaptation to human finitude may be formally distinguished without difficulty. It simply means the divine self-expression in terms of the phenomena apprehensible to man. Thus the power and wisdom of God are declared in the material creation, and His righteousness in the human sense of right and wrong. When we come to God's special revelation, this element of accommodation continues. God is self-revealed in His acts among men. He uses the spoken or written utterances of men to declare His acts, making use of the familiar categories of human apprehension. Thus God Himself is largely described in anthropomorphic expressions. The story of His work, whether in creation or salvation, is recounted in a form that makes it generally intelligible. Where there are historical, geographical, literary, or scientific allusions, these are in a form suitable to popular presentation rather than the academic dissertation adapted only to scholars.

In itself, however, this does not give understanding; it is merely the prerequisite of understanding. The divine self-expression in terms of apprehensible objects can give rise to idolatry rather than knowledge in the case of sinners. The recounting of God's acts in historical terms can cause them either to be accepted merely as history or dismissed as legendary. For finite man is also sinful man. Hence, even in terms appropriate to finite man, the divine self-revelation must also take a form, both as act and record, that is adapted to man's inability to perceive God in general revelation. A special activity of the reconciling and revealing grace of God is needed within the sinful world. This is an activity that must be accomplished in, among, and through men who are themselves sinful. It must take such a form that the distorting veil that covers even the adapted self-expression of God is removed. In other words, God's revelation is accommodated to the situation created by the sin and fall of man.

This obviously entails a formal involvement of revelation in human fallibility and sinfulness. The divine activity takes place in the nexus of a fallen humanity. It is carried through by men who do not escape the sin and errancy of the race. Their utterances are couched in thought forms that are fashioned by and adapted to hearers whose theological and spiritual thinking is not merely incomplete but erroneous. These men themselves might make mistakes when not acting or speaking under the special direction of the Spirit of God, as Peter presumably did at Antioch. If God's history takes place within that of Israel, then the history of Israel has its place in the history of the nations. If the record of God's history is in the Bible, then the Bible can also be brought into comparison with other literary and religious documents.

This formal involvement in the human situation necessarily carries with it a material restriction. The divine history is not a history of purely supernatural action, which might astonish but could hardly redeem or reveal. The divine record does not consist in a celestial theology or science, which might impress but could hardly instruct or clarify. Israel as the chosen people is implicated in the politics of the day with all the moral dilemmas imposed by its being the politics of a fallen race. The account of God's work takes the form of a narration that even the least scientific or the most ignorant or errant of men can understand, not aiming at pedantic precision but stating things as they may be perceived by man as he is. The poetic imagery of the Bible does not derive from celestial sources, or even from an ideal humanity, but from the common heritage of observation, experience, and culture. To a large degree, we have here adaptation to man's finitude. On the other hand, an action and the record of an action of God among unfallen man would surely have differed so widely from what takes place within our fallen humanity that they would be virtually unintelligible. The special revelation of God is within a fallen as well as a finite situation.

From this formal involvement, however, we are not forced to deduce a material involvement, as many scholars contend. Limitation does not in itself mean sin or error, even when it is limitation in adaptation to a situation in which there is sin and error. Thus, in given circumstances an action may not be ideal, but it may still be right. Again, that a given narrative is put in terms that even the simplest of errant men may understand does not mean that it cannot be factually correct. A simple account may not solve all the problems of a scholar, but it may still be a true record of fact. An abbreviated story may not furnish every detail for the inquisitive, but it is not on this account to be dismissed as untrustworthy. Imagery may even reflect mythological conceptions without itself being mythological or sharing associated crudities of thought and expression. In other words, God may use forms of action and utterance accommodated to the sinful situation of man without Himself being implicated in sinfulness or error. The accommodation of revelation is not of such a nature that God contradicts His own being and therefore ceases to reveal Himself in the attempt to make communication possible. Accommodation is not abdication.

C. The Incarnation as Accommodation. This point is brought out with full clarity when we consider the climax of the divine work of reconciliation and revelation, and therefore of accommodation, in the incarnation of Jesus Christ. The divine history finally becomes the history of the incarnate Word within human history. The divine declaration of this history finally becomes the teaching of Jesus Christ and the spoken and written testimony of the apostles and their immediate associates. Again, there is here an adaptation to the finitude of the fallen creature, which entails fallibility and sin. Again, there is adaptation, which means acceptance of the form of fallibility and sin (Rom. 8:3). Again, however, we cannot say that there is material error or sinfulness either in the Word Himself or in the authentic declaration of the Word in His own teaching or the testimony raised up by Him. Jesus Christ enters the situation of sin and error. He acts and speaks within it. But He reveals in this situation the perfect righteousness of God and speaks the words of truth. He accepts the restrictions imposed by prevailing sin and ignorance, yet not in such a way as to be guilty Himself of sin and ignorance. This does not imply any diminution of His humanity; indeed, it is only in Him that we see what true humanity is. Nor does it entail any weakening of His self-identification with fallible and sinful humanity; no one goes further than Jesus either in meeting the common temptations of man or in bearing the burden of human guilt. It is the whole point of His self-identification, however, that He is the Just suffering for the unjust, the Sinless who is made sin, the One of perfect knowledge who suffers dereliction, that the unjust and sinful might be made the righteousness of God, and the ignorant might enjoy the revelation of God, in Him.

A final observation is demanded. We misunderstand the nature and purpose of accommodation if we think of it, or of the associated work of God, purely in pedagogical terms. God does not descend, or condescend, simply to make the recognition of truth easier. There is an element of truth here. Unless God acts and speaks in intelligible terms, there can be no revelation—although we should perhaps not forget that God is in fact able to raise up stones to Abraham and to give power of apprehension even where it is not obviously possible. In any case, however, we do not have here the whole truth. For God is now dealing with sinful man. This means that His revelation is at the same time reconciliation. The divine activity takes place in the human sphere, not merely that man might thereby perceive God, but that God might do for sinful man what he cannot do for himself, and that He might be revealed in this way and as this God.

Thus the accommodation of the Bible is soteriological and not merely educative. It is revelation as reconciliation and reconciliation as revelation. Again, the problem of divine knowledge is no longer just a problem of restriction. It is a problem of blindness, or of distorted and distorting vision. If accommodation to human forms is a prerequisite of the solution of this problem, it is not the solution per se. Indeed, it may carry with it a more extensive veiling. Enacted in history, God's actions are not necessarily perceived in history or accepted as history. Spoken in human categories, God's words may also be classified as human poetry or even mythology. Incarnate in the world, the Son of God can appear, to some at least, as no more than a prophet at best and an impostor at worst. The parables are not just illustrations that bring immediate clarification. The gospel can be a savor of death as well as of life. Sinful eyes can see without perceiving and sinful ears can hear without comprehending.

This hardly means that the gracious accommodation of God is useless, or that the same melancholy result is achieved as depicted in Rom. 1. For one thing the work of salvation is in fact accomplished. Furthermore, the Word of God now preached does carry light and illumination within itself. Also God Himself is present in its proclamation through the Holy Spirit poured out for the purpose. In the wisdom of God and the power of the Spirit, the accommodation of God now serves the end for which it is designed, i.e., the sifting of hearts involved in genuine relationship to God. Operating as it does on the human plane, the gospel is an intelligible declaration to all, yet not a declaration that can simply be received as an item of information to be added to the store of human knowledge. It calls for faith. Where there is no faith, there is no true understanding and the very perspicuity of the message argues for condemnation. But faith is not an impossibility. For the Holy Spirit kindles faith. Where faith is thus kindled by the Spirit, there is the fulfillment of revelation to salvation, and the graciousness of the divine condescension is seen in all its glory.

This has two important practical consequences. First, the Christian in his theological study cannot come to think of the divine accommodation merely as an educative simplification that enables him to master all mysteries apart from the Holy Spirit. Second, the Christian in his work of witness and proclamation, which is itself a kind of continued accommodation, cannot conceive of his task simply as one of making easy and persuasive, as though sinners could be won to genuine faith and knowledge by pedagogic or rhetorical or psychological techniques irrespective of the Holy Spirit. The mystery of iniquity remains. But so, too, does the mystery of the Spirit. Hence even where there is faith and knowledge, and especially where this is so, the divine revelation and the graciousness of its accommodation always demand our wonder and humility, our constant looking to God and confidence in Him, our prayer and praise.

Bibliography.–J. H. Blunt, *Dictionary of Doctrinal and Historical Theology* (rev. ed. 1892); MSt; Sch.-Herz.; *DCG*; *BDTh*; G. T. Ladd, *Doctrine of Sacred Scripture* (1883), I; Calvin *Inst. passim*; *CD*, esp. II/1 and IV/3.

L. M. SWEET
G. W. BROMILEY

ACCOMPLISH [Heb. *hāwâ*] (Jer. 39:16); [*kûn*] (2 Ch. 8:16); AV PREPARE; NEB ACHIEVE; [*kālâ*] (2 Ch. 36:22; Dnl. 11:36; 12:7; Ezr. 1:1); AV also FINISH, FULFIL; NEB DO, "come to an end," FULFIL; [*'āśâ*] (2 S. 3:9; Job 35:6; Neh. 6:16; Isa. 37:32; 46:10; 55:11); AV also DO, WROUGHT; NEB also BRING ABOUT, TOUCH, PERFORM; [*ṣālē(a)ḥ*] (2 Ch. 7:11); AV EFFECT; NEB CARRY OUT; [*qûm*] (Jer. 23:20; 30:24); AV PERFORM; NEB FULFIL, ACHIEVE; [*tāmam*] (Lam. 4:22); NEB COMPLETE; [Gk. *gínomai*] (Mt. 5:18); AV FULFIL; NEB HAPPEN; [*energéō*] (Eph. 1:11, 20); AV WORK, WROUGHT; NEB "is at work," EXERT; [*plērophoréō*] (Lk. 1:1); AV BELIEVE; NEB HAPPEN; [*plēróō*] (Lk. 9:31); NEB FULFIL; [*synteléō*] (Mk. 13:4); AV FULFIL; NEB HAPPEN; [*teleióō*] (Jn. 4:34; 5:36; 17:4; Acts 20:24); AV FINISH; NEB FINISH, COMPLETE.

The two Hebrew words used most frequently are *kālâ* and *'āśâ,* which have as primary meanings "be complete, at an end, finished" and "do, make," respectively. The term "accomplish" is used frequently with reference to the word of the Lord as it is spoken through the prophets (2 Ch. 36:22; Ezr. 1:1; Isa. 37:32; 46:10; 55:11; Jer. 23:20; 30:24; 39:16; 12:7). The ideas of completion and fulfillment are prominent in Gk. *teleióō* and *synteléō, plēróō* and *plērophoréō*.

J. R. PRICE

ACCORD; ACCORDANCE; ACCORDING. These terms come from a common Latin root (*ad-*, "to" + *cord,* "heart"), and basically denote agreement, conformity, harmony. They are used in a number of expressions:

(1) "With one accord" translates Heb. *peh 'eḥāḏ* (lit. "one mouth," Josh. 9:2; 1 K. 22:13; 2 Ch. 18:12), *lēḇ yaḥdāw* ("heart together," Ps. 83:5), *šᵉḵem 'eḥāḏ* ("shoulder to shoulder," Zeph. 3:9); Gk. *homothymadón* ("with one mind or purpose," Acts 1:14; 8:6). The phrase is always used to describe unanimous participation in a particular action.

(2) "Of one's own accord" translates Heb. *millibbî* ("from my heart," Nu. 16:28); Gk. *aph' heautoú* ("from himself," Jn. 5:19; 7:28; 8:42; 10:18; 11:51; 18:34), *authaíretos* (2 Cor. 8:17). This phrase indicates that a certain action was performed voluntarily or upon one's own authority. A similar usage is the impersonal "of its own accord" for Gk. *autómatos* ("automatically," Acts 12:10).

(3) "In accord with," "in accordance with," and "according to" translate quite a variety of OT and NT terms. All three expressions carry the meaning of "in agreement with," "in conformity with," or "in proportion to."

N. J. O.

ACCOS ak'os [Gk. *Akkōs*].

1. (1 Esd. 5:38, NEB). *See* HAKKOZ.

2. The grandfather of Eupolemus, whom Judas Maccabeus sent with others to Rome in 161 B.C., to negotiate a "league of amity and confederacy" (1 Macc. 8:17).

ACCOUNTABILITY.

I. Scriptural Principles.–The general teaching of Scripture on this subject is summarized in Rom. 14:12: "so then each one of us shall give account of himself to God." But this implies, on the one hand, the existence of a Moral Ruler of the universe, whose will is revealed, and, on the other, the possession by the creature of knowledge and free will. In Rom. 4:15 it is expressly laid down that, "where no law is, neither is there transgression"; but, lest this might seem to exclude from accountability those to whom the law of Moses was not given, it is shown that even heathen had the law to some extent revealed in conscience; so that they are "without excuse" (1:20). "For as many as have sinned without the law shall also perish without the law: and as many as have sinned under the law shall be judged by the law" (2:12). So says Paul in a passage which is one of the profoundest discussions on the subject of accountability, and with this sentiment agrees exactly the word of Our Lord on the same subject, in Lk. 12:47f.: "And that servant who knew his master's will, but did not make ready or act according to his will, shall receive a severe beating. But he who did not know, and did what deserved a beating, shall receive a light beating. Every one to whom much is given, of him will much be required; and of him to whom men commit much they will demand the more."

There is a gradual development of accountability accompanying the growth of a human being from infancy to maturity; and there is a similar development in the race, as knowledge grows from less to more. In the full light of the gospel, human beings are far more responsible than they were in earlier stages of intellectual and spiritual development; and the doom to which they will be exposed on the day of account will be heavy in proportion to their privileges.

This may seem to put too great a premium on ignorance; and a real difficulty arises when we say that the more of moral sensitiveness there is, the greater is the guilt; because, as is well known, moral sensitiveness can be lost through persistent disregard of conscience; from which it might seem to follow that the way to diminish guilt is to silence the voice of conscience. There must, however, be a difference between the responsibility of a conscience that has never been enlightened and that of one which, having once been enlightened, has lost, through neglect or recklessness, the goodness once possessed. In the practice of the law, for example, it is often claimed that a crime committed under the influence of intoxication should be condoned; yet everyone must feel how different this is from innocence, and that, before a higher tribunal, the culprit will be held to be twice guilty—first of the sin of drunkenness and then of the crime.

II. Relation to Immortality.–Wherever civilization is so advanced that there exists a code of public law, with punishments attached to transgression, there goes on a constant education in the sense of accountability; and even the heathen mind, in classical times, had advanced so far as to believe in a judgment beyond the veil, when the shades had to appear before the tribunal of Rhadamanthus, Minos, and Eacus, to have their station and degree in the underworld decided according to the deeds done in the body. How early the Hebrews had made as much progress has to be discussed in connection with the doctrine of immortality; but it is certain that, before the OT canon closed, they believed not only in a judgment after death but in resurrection, by which the sense of accountability was fastened far more firmly on the popular mind.

Long before, however, there was awakened by the sacred literature the sense of a judgment of God going on during the present life and expressing itself in everyone's condition. The history of the world was the judgment of the world; prosperity attended the steps of the good man, but retribution sooner or later struck down the wicked. It was from the difficulty of reconciling with this belief the facts of life that the skepticism of Hebrew thought arose; but by the same constraint the pious mind was pushed forward in the direction of the full doctrine of immortality.

This full doctrine came with the advent of Him who brought life and immortality to light by His gospel (2 Tim. 1:10). In the mind of Jesus not only were resurrection, judgment, and immortality unquestionable postulates, but He was brought into a special connection with accountability through His consciousness of being the Judge of mankind. In his numerous references to the Last Judgment, He developed the principles upon which the conscience will then be tried, and by which accordingly it ought now to try itself. In this connection the parable of the talents is of special significance; but it is by the grandiose picture of the scene itself, which follows in the same chapter of the First Gospel, that the mind of Christendom has been most powerfully influenced.

Reference has already been made to the discussions at the commencement of the Epistle to the Romans in which our subject finds a place. By some the apostle John has been supposed to revert to the OT notion of a judgment proceeding now in place of coming at the Last Day; but J. Weiss (*Der johanneische Lehrbegriff*, II, 9) has proved that this is a mistake.

III. Joint and Corporate Responsibility.–Up to this point we have spoken of individual accountability; but the subject becomes more complicated when we think of the joint responsibility of several or many persons. From the first the human mind has been haunted by what is called the guilt of Adam's first sin. There is a solidarity in the human race, and the inheritance of evil is too obvious to be denied even by the most optimistic. There is far from being agreement of opinion, however, as to the relation of the individual to this evil legacy; some contend fiercely against the idea that the individual can have any personal responsibility for a sin hidden in a past so distant and shadowy, while others maintain that the misery which has certainly been inherited by all can only be justified in a world governed by a God of justice if the guilt of all precedes the misery. The question enters deeply into the Pauline scheme, although at the most critical point it is much disputed what the apostle's real position is.

While joint responsibility burdens the individual conscience, it may, at the same time, be said to lighten it. Thus, in Ezk. 18 one of the most weighty ethical discussions to be found in Holy Writ is introduced with the popular proverb, "The fathers have eaten sour grapes, and the children's teeth are set on edge," which proves to be a way of saying that the responsibility of children is lightened, if not abolished, through their connection with their parents. In the same way, in our day, the sense of responsibility has diminished for many because of the control over character and destiny ascribed to heredity and environment. Even criminality is excused on the ground that many have never had a chance of virtue, and it is contended that to know everything is to forgive everything.

There can be no doubt that, as the agents of trusts and partnerships, men will allow themselves to do what they would never have thought of in private business; and in a crowd the individual sustains psychological modifications by which he is made to act very differently from his ordinary self. In the actions of nations, such as war, there is a vast and solemn responsibility somewhere; but it is often extremely difficult to locate it—whether in the leaders, the institutions, or the people. So interesting and perplexing are such problems that a morality for groups of people, as distinguished from individuals, is felt by many to be the great desideratum of ethics today.

J. STALKER

ACCOZ ak'oz (1 Esd. 5:38, AV). *See* HAKKOZ.

ACCURSED [Heb. *ḥērem*] (Dt. 7:26); AV CURSED; NEB BAN; [*qᵉlālâ*] (Dt. 21:23); NEB OFFENSIVE; [*qālal*] (Isa. 65:20); NEB DESPISED; [*'ārar*] (Ps. 119:21); AV, NEB, CURSED; [*zā'am*] (Mic. 6:10); AV ABOMINABLE; [Gk. *epáratos*] (Jn. 7:49); AV CURSED; NEB CURSE; [*anáthema*] (Rom. 9:3; 1 Cor. 16:22; Gal. 1:8f.); AV ANATHEMA (1 Cor. 16:22); NEB OUTCAST; [*katára*] (2 Pet. 2:14); AV DAMNATION; NEB CURSE; [*katáthema*] (Rev. 22:3); AV CURSE.

Canaanite idols and those who brought them into their houses were "accursed" (Dt. 7:26). This is the only verse where the RSV translates *ḥērem* as "accursed," though the AV often renders it "accursed" or "accursed thing" elsewhere, e.g., Josh. 6:17. The term *ḥērem* refers to things "devoted" (the usual RSV translation) to special use or set apart from common use. Often this means, as in Dt. 7:26, "devote to destruction"; the idols were to be burned with fire (v. 25). But sometimes *ḥērem* meant devoted to the Lord and therefore excluded from private (profane) use (Lev. 27:21, 28).

The root *qll* is twice rendered "accursed." In Dt. 21:23 the one who is hanged is under a curse of God, and in Isa. 65:20 the curse of God on the sinner results in death. In Mic. 6:10 the evils of a short bushel are denounced (*zā'am*). The most common root for curse, *'rr*, is once translated "accursed" in Ps. 119:21 where it refers to the insolent and disobedient.

In the Greek the terms *ará*, "prayer," and *aráomai*, "pray," are used as early as Homer to denote prayer for evil; thus the idea of a curse or imprecation logically follows. Such is the case with *epáratos* in Jn. 7:49, where the Pharisees consider the common people accursed for ignorance of the law. The same is true of *katára* in 2 Pet. 2:14 for those whose numerous sins have put them under a curse. The term *anáthema* originally denoted something dedicated to the deity or dedicated to destruction. It is therefore the linguistic equivalent of the Heb. *ḥērem*, which it often translates in the LXX (Dt. 7:26). Four times Paul's use of it is translated in the negative sense of accursed (Rom. 9:3, hypothetically of himself; 1 Cor. 16:22 of those who do not love the Lord; Gal. 1:8f. of those who preach a heretical gospel). Equivalent to *anáthema* is *katáthema* in Rev. 22:3 (nothing will be accursed in the New Jerusalem).

See also ANATHEMA. J. C. MOYER

ACCUSER [Heb. *šāpaṭ* (in poel part.; see BDB, p. 1048)] (Job 9:15); AV JUDGE; [Heb. *śāṭan*–'adversary'] (Ps. 71:13; 109:6, 20, 29,); AV SATAN, ADVERSARY; NEB also TRADUCER; [Gk. *katḗgoros*] (Acts 23:30, 35; 24:8; 25:16, 18; Rev. 12:10); [Gk. *antídikos*–'opponent at law'] (Mt. 5:25; Lk. 12:58); AV ADVERSARY; NEB OPPONENT, "someone (who) sues." All the terms have a legal basis, whether literal-temporal (Mt. 5:25; Acts 23–25), figurative-temporal (Ps. 109), or spiritual (Job 9:15; Rev. 12:10; cf. Zec. 3:1f.); the reference in each case is to an adversary in a law court.

In rabbinic teaching Satan was regarded as hostile to God and men, and it was a part of his work to accuse men of disloyalty and sin before God's tribunal. The classic biblical example is the book of Job (cf. 1:6ff.). *See also* SATAN.

The psalmist in Ps. 109 asked for God's intervention against his enemies who falsely accuse him. McCullough (*IB*) thinks the accusers may be fellow Hebrews; Calvin (*in loc.*) had a more universal view (*see also* PSALMS. VI).

In Mt. 5:25f. actual litigation is in view. The NEB "come to terms with him promptly" is better than the RSV, "make friends quickly."

The Gk. *katḗgoros* is used for accusers at Paul's hearing before Felix; their spokesman was Tertullus. The same word is used in Rev. 12:10 for Satan: "for the accuser of our brethren has been thrown down, who accuses them day and night before our God."

See also ADVERSARY.   J. W. D. H.

ACELDAMA ə-sel'də-mə (Acts 1:19, AV). *See* AKEL-DAMA.

ACHAEMENIANS ä-kī-men-ē'ənz. Persian kings from Cyrus II (559-530 B.C.) onward call themselves "Achaemenid" in their inscriptions, claiming descent from Achaemenes [Pers. *Hakhāmanish*–'having friendly nature'] and his son, or more distant descendant, Teispes. While these two are known only as ancestral names, Cyrus I, a son of Teispes, appears in the records of Ashurbanipal as a king tributary to Assyria *ca.* 640 B.C. His brother Ariaramnes ruled the land around Parsagadae while he held territory to the west. Cyrus' grandson, the "Great" Cyrus (II), ended this divided state, making Ariaramnes' grandson Hystaspes his governor.

Many folktales obscure the history of Cyrus' rise to power, but there is little reason to doubt the strong tradition that his mother was a Median princess. It was Media that became the first conquest of Cyrus' road to empire. The organization of the Persian empire as well as many aspects of Persian culture can be traced to Median sources, and the phrase "Medes and Persians" illustrates the close association of the two states. Persian ability to assimilate alien habits and to accommodate to the customs of other races is exemplified in Cyrus' career. Thus he was prepared to return the gods of subject peoples to their shrines, upon the capture of Babylon (Cyrus Cylinder, *ANET*, p. 316; *DOTT*, p. 93), and the Jewish treasures to Jerusalem (Ezr. 1). In imperial government distant provinces were left in the charge of native rulers, who were to a large extent autonomous. The multitude of races and cultures mingled their skills in ornamenting the king's palaces or filling his treasury. Achaemenian art, monumental sculptures, gold and silver plate, and jewelry, exhibit well the vast and varied resources of the empire.

It was upon the foundation of respect laid by Cyrus (said to have been known to the Persians as "Father") that Darius I, who succeeded Cyrus' son Cambyses, consolidated the Persian power. Darius, a descendant of Ariaramnes through Hystaspes, pacified the area from Indus to Ionia, crushing incipient rebellions, and established road systems with fast courier services between capital cities.

During the eight reigns of Darius' successors the empire suffered little diminution, although its power gradually waned, several of the rulers being men with little interest in affairs of state. Darius III, the last Achaemenian, died fleeing before Alexander in 331 B.C.

See MAP XII.   A. R. MILLARD

ACHAIA ə-kā'yə [Gk. *Achaia*]. The smallest country in the Peloponnesus, lying along the southern shore of the Corinthian Gulf, N of Arcadia and E of Elis.

The original inhabitants were Ionians; but these were crowded out later by the Achaeans, who came from the east. According to Herodotus, the Ionians founded twelve cities, many of which retain their original names to this day. These cities were on the coast and formed a confederation of smaller communities, which in the last century of the independent history of Greece attained to great importance (Achaean League). In Roman times the term Achaia (or Achaea) was used to include the whole of Greece, exclusive of Thessaly.

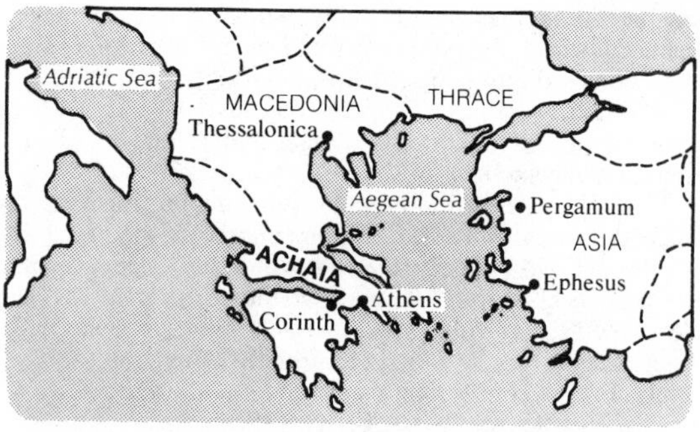

The old Achaean League was renewed in 280 B.C., but became more important in 251, when Aratus of Sicyon was chosen commander-in-chief. This great man increased the power of the League and gave it an excellent constitution, which Alexander Hamilton and James Madison consulted, adopting many of its prominent devices, when they set about framing the Constitution of the United States. In 146 B.C. Corinth was destroyed and the League broken up (see 1 Macc. 15:23); and the whole of Greece, under the name of Achaia, was transformed into a Roman province; this was divided into two separate provinces, Macedonia and Achaia, in 27 B.C.

In Acts 18:12 we are told that the Jews in Corinth made insurrection against Paul when Gallio was deputy of Achaia, and in 18:27 that Apollos was making preparations to set out for Achaia. In Rom. 16:5, AV "Achaia" should read "Asia" as in subsequent versions. In Acts 20:2 "Greece" means Achaia, but the oft-mentioned "Macedonia and Achaia" generally means the whole of Greece (Acts 19:21; Rom. 15:26; 1 Thess. 1:8). Paul commends the churches of Achaia for their liberality (2 Cor. 9:13).

Bibliography.–J. K. Anderson, *Annual of the British School at Athens*, 49 (1954), 72-92; J. A. O. Larsen, *Greek Federal States* (1968), pp. 80-89; *Roman Greece*, Vol. IV of T. Frank, ed., *Economic Survey of Ancient Rome* (1933-1940), pp. 436-496.

                    J. E. HARRY

ACHAICUS ə-kā'ə-kəs [Gk. *Akaikos*–'belonging to Achaia']. One of the leaders of the Corinthian church (to be inferred from 1 Cor. 16:15ff.) who, visiting Paul at Ephesus with Stephanas and Fortunatus, greatly relieved the apostle's anxiety for the Corinthian church (cf. 1 Cor. 5:1ff.). Paul admonishes the members of the Corinthian church to submit to their authority (cf. 1 Thess. 5:12) and to acknowledge their work (1 Cor. 16:15ff.).

ACHAN ā'kan [Heb. *'āḵān*], also **ACHAR** ā'kär [Heb. *'āḵār*–'troubler'] (1 Ch. 2:7). The descendant of Zerah the son of Judah who was put to death, in Joshua's time, for stealing some of the "devoted" spoil of the city of Jericho (Josh. 7).

The stem *'āḵan* is not used in Hebrew except in this name. The stem *'āḵar* has sufficient use to define it. It denotes trouble of the most serious kind—Jacob's trouble when his sons had brought him into blood feud with his Canaanite neighbors, or Jephthah's trouble when his vow required him to sacrifice his daughter (Gen. 34:30; Jgs. 11:35). In Prov. 11:17, 29; 15:6, 27 the word is used with intensity to describe the results of cruelty, disloyalty, greed, wickedness. The record speaks especially of Achan's conduct as the troubling of Israel (1 Ch. 2:7; Josh. 6:18; 7:24). In an outburst of temper Jonathan speaks of Saul as having troubled the land (1 S. 14:29). Elijah and Ahab accuse each other of being the troubler of Israel (1 K. 18:17f.). Achan's crime was the violation of the *ḥērem* or ban placed on Jericho, and was particularly serious because one man's guilt threatened the security of all. His execution occurred in the Valley of Achor ("trouble").

ACHAR. *See* ACHAN.

ACHAZ ā'kaz (Mt. 1:9, AV). *See* AHAZ.

ACHBOR ak'bôr [Heb. *'aḵbôr*–'mouse'].

1. The father of Baal-hanan, who was the seventh of the eight kings who reigned in Edom before there were kings in Israel (Gen. 36:38f.; 1 Ch. 1:49).

2. The son of Micaiah who went with Hilkiah the priest and other high officials, at the command of King Josiah, to consult Huldah the prophetess concerning the book that had been found (2 K. 22:12, 14). In the parallel passage 2 Ch. 34:20 he is called Abdon son of Micah (*see* ABDON **3**).

It may be presumed that this Achbor is also the man mentioned in Jer. 26:22; 36:12 as the father of Elnathan, who went to Egypt for King Jehoiakim in order to procure the extradition of Uriah the prophet, and who protested the burning of Baruch's roll. W. J. BEECHER

ACHIACHARUS a-ki-ak'ə-ras (Tobit, AV). *See* AHIKAR.

ACHIAS ə-kī'əs (2 Esd. 1:2, AV). *See* AHIJAH **3**.

ACHIM ā'kim [Gk. *Achim*]. A descendant of Zerubbabel and ancestor of Jesus, mentioned only in Mt. 1:14.

ACHIOR ā'ki-ôr [Gk. *Achiōr*]. A general of the Ammonites, who spoke on behalf of Israel before Holofernes, the Assyrian general (Jth. 5:5ff.). Holofernes ordered him bound and delivered at Bethulia to the Israelites (Jth. 6), who received him gladly and with honor. Afterward he became a proselyte and was circumcised, and he joined Israel (Jth. 14).

In Nu. 34:27 Gk. *Achiōr* is the LXX reading for Ahihud; this would assume an original Heb. *'ᵃḥî'ôr*, "brother of light."

ACHISH ā'kish [Heb. *'āḵîš*]. King of the city of Gath in the days of David. His father's name is given as Maoch (1 S. 27:2) and Maacah (1 K. 2:39).

David sought the protection of Achish when he first fled from Saul, and just after his visit to Nob (1 S. 21:10-15). Fearing rough treatment or betrayal by Achish, he feigned madness. But this made him unwelcome, whereupon he fled to the Cave of Adullam (22:1). Later in his fugitive period David returned to Gath to be hospitably received by Achish (27:1ff.), who gave him the town of Ziklag for his home. A year later, when the Philistines invaded the land of Israel, in the campaign which ended so disastrously for Saul (ch. 31), Achish wished David to participate (28:1f.); but the lords of the Philistines objected so strenuously, when they found him and his men with the forces of Achish, that Achish was compelled to send them back. Achish must have been a young man at this time, for he was still ruling forty years later at the beginning of Solomon's reign (1 K. 2:39). He is mentioned as Abimelech in the title of Ps. 34 (*see* ABIMELECH **3**). E. MACK

ACHITOB ak'ə-tob (1 Esd. 8:2; 2 Esd. 1:1, AV). *See* AHITUB **3**.

ACHMETHA ak'mə-thə (Ezr. 6:2, AV). *See* ECBATANA.

ACHOR ā'kôr [Heb. *'āḵôr*–'trouble, disturbance' (*see* ACHAN)]. The place where Achan was executed in the time of Joshua (Josh. 7:24, 26). It is always called *'ēmeq 'āḵôr*, indicating a broad, flat valley or plain with mountains on one or both sides. The location of Achor was on a higher level than the camp of Israel in the Jordan Valley, and lower than Debir, generally N of Beth-arabah and S of Debir (Josh. 7:24; 15:7).

Formerly it was identified with Wâdī Qelt, but since the discovery of the Dead Sea Scrolls it is identified with el-Buqei'ah, a plain about 4 mi. (6.5 km.) N-S on the Wâdī Qumrân, above (i.e., W of) the caves of the Scrolls. Achor is mentioned in 3QInv (3Q*15*). The term is used in a figurative sense in Isa. 65:10 and Hos. 2:15 (MT 17) to describe the messianic age or the time of restoration.

See F. M. Cross and J. T. Milik, *BASOR*, 142 (April 1956), 5-17. W. J. BEECHER
W. S. L. S.

ACHSAH ak'sə [Heb. *'aḵsâ*–'ankle-ornament']; AV also **ACHSA** (1 Ch. 2:49). The daughter of Caleb whom he gave in marriage to his younger kinsman Othniel son of Kenaz, as a reward for smiting Kiriath-sepher (Josh. 15:16ff.; Jgs. 1:12ff.). Caleb subsequently gave her some springs in the Negeb as her dowry.

ACHSHAPH ak'shaf [Heb. *'aḵšāp*–'(place of) sorcery' (?)]; NEB AKSHAPH. A city in the northern part of the territory conquered by Joshua. The king of Achshaph was a member of the coalition under Jabin and Sisera against Israel (Josh. 11:1; 12:20). In the list of conquered kings of cities, Achshaph is mentioned after Hazor and before Taanach and Megiddo, but the order does not seem to be related to geographical location (Josh. 12:7-24). It is one of the cities marking the boundaries of the tribe of Asher (Josh. 19:25). Modern scholars tend to identify it with Tell Kīsân about 6 mi. (10 km.) SE of Acre, which fits the requirements both as to antiquity and location, in the light of Egyptian inscriptional evidence (the Execration Texts, the list of towns conquered by Thutmose III at Karnak, the Amarna Tablets, and Papyrus Anastasi I).

See *GTTOT*, §§ 189f. W. S. L. S.

ACHZIB ak'zib [Heb. *'aḵzîḇ*–'lying, deceitful'].

1. A town in western Judah in the Shephelah (lowlands), mentioned with Mareshah and Keilah as one of the cities allotted to Judah (Josh. 15:44). It is probably the same as Chezib (Gen. 38:5), where Judah was at the time of the birth of his son Shelah. Mic. 1:14 has a pun on the name: "The houses of Achzib become a deception (Heb. *'aḵzāḇ*) to the kings of Israel." In 1 Ch. 4:22 the town is called Cozeba (AV Chozeba), another form of the same root, probably meaning "the deceiver." Eusebius *Onom.* 172 refers to (Gk.) *Chasbi,* near Adullam, which lends support to the identification of Achzib with Tell el-Beida, 3 mi. (5 km.) W of Adullam.

See *GTTOT*, §§ 318 C/8, 396.

2. A town in western Galilee, on the Mediterranean about 9 mi. (15 km.) N of Acre, the modern Ha-Ziv, Arab, ez-Zib. The town was assigned to Asher (Josh. 19:29), but they did not drive out the inhabitants; and Achzib, Acco, and other neighboring cities remained as Canaanite enclaves (Jgs. 1:31f.). The Assyrian king Sennacherib records the conquest of Akzibi along with Sidon, Ṣariptu (Zarephath). Akku (Acco), and other cities (701 B.C.) (Taylor Prism; cf. *ANET,* p. 287). In NT times, it was known as Ecdippa (Josephus *Ant.* v.1.22), and in the Talmud as Achzib and Chezib. In the Crusader period a walled city, known as Casal Imbert, was built on the site, serving as one of the outer fortifications of Acre (Acco). The modern town covers the ancient sites, making excavation impractical.

Bibliography.–*ARAB*, II, 119 § 239; *GP*, II, 237. W. S. L. S.

ACIPHA as'i-fə, ə-sī'fə (1 Esd. 5:31, AV). *See* HAKUPHA.

ACITHO; ACITHOH as'ə-thō (Jth. 8:1, AV). *See* AHITUB 3.

ACQUAINT; ACQUAINTANCE. Terms referring to various degrees of knowledge, but implying more or less detailed information; applied to God's omniscience (Ps. 139:3), to the grief of the Suffering Servant of the Lord (Isa. 53:3), and to the knowledge which man should have of God. The noun in the concrete, unless limited by a qualifying term, means more than one who has been known simply in passing, and implies a degree of intimacy, as may be seen in Lk. 2:44; 23:49; 2 K. 12:5. H. E. JACOBS

ACRA ak'rə. *See* JERUSALEM.

ACRABA a'krə-bə [Gk. *Egrebēl, Ekrebēl*] (Jth. 7:18); AV EKREBEL; NEB EGREBEL. A place SE of Dothan near Chusi by the brook Mochmur. It was here that several Edomite and Ammonite battalions, conjoined with the Assyrians against Israel, set up a watch to prevent the Israelites from obtaining food and water. It is probably to be identified with Akrabeh, about 25 mi. (40 km.) N of Jerusalem. K. G. JUNG

ACRABATTENE (1 Macc. 5:3, NEB). *See* AKRABATTENE.

ACRABBIM. *See* AKRABBIM, ASCENT OF.

ACRE ä'kər, ā'kər. *See* ACCO.

ACRE [Heb. *ṣemeḏ*]. This word occurs only twice in the Bible, 1 S. 14:14 and Isa. 5:10. The Hebrew word denotes a yoke of animals in the sense of a team, a span, a pair—not the literal yoke by which the team is coupled together. The phrase "ten yokes of vineyard" in Isa. 5:10, RV (AV, RSV, NEB, "acre"; Vulg. *iugerum;* LXX "yoke of oxen") seems to designate a land area that could be plowed by a team of oxen in ten days. In 1 S. 14:14 the area in which twenty Philistines were slain by Jonathan was about one-half as large as could be plowed by a team of oxen in one day.

In English the word "acre" originally denoted a field that could be plowed by an ox team in one day. A maximum acre of this kind measured 160 sq. rods. This size became the fixed standard. S. J. SCHULTZ

ACROSTIC a-kros'tik. A poem in which the initial letters of the verses are chosen with definite intent. In the OT there are various alphabetical acrostics. In Pss. 25, 34, and 145, and Prov. 31:10-31, the first verse begins with *aleph,* the second with *beth,* and so on through the Hebrew alphabet. This is also the case in Pss. 111 and 112, though here the poetical lines do not consist of two cola or clauses, so that it is the cola themselves, not the lines, that begin with successive letters of the alphabet.

In Ps. 37 and Lam. 4 not one but two lines are assigned to each letter (the first line begins with *aleph,* the third with *beth,* the fifth with *gimel,* etc.); in Lam. 1, 2, and 3 it is three lines per letter; in Ps. 119 it is eight. In Lam. 3 all three lines assigned to a letter begin with that letter, and in Ps. 119 all eight lines do. In some acrostic poems there are irregularities of alphabetical arrangement.

Concerning the question how far Pss. 9 and 10, Nah. 1, and Sir. 51:13-30 form alphabetical poems, refer to commentaries on these books. Pss. 33 and 38 and Lam. 5 have exactly the same number of poetical lines as there are alphabetical letters. It would seem that this is not accidental.

(א) אודה יהוה בכל־לבב
(ב) בסוד ישרים ועדה:
(ג) גדלים מעשי יהוה
(ד) דרושים לכל־חפציהם:
(ה) הוד־והדר פעלו
(ו) וצדקתו עמדת לעד:
(ז) זכר עשה לנפלאתיו
(ח) חנון ורחום יהוה:
(ט) טרף נתן ליראיו
(י) יזכר לעולם בריתו:
(כ) כח מעשיו הגיד לעמו
(ל) לתת להם נחלת גוים:
(מ) מעשי ידיו אמת ומשפט
(נ) נאמנים כל־פקודיו:
(ס) סמוכים לעד לעולם
(ע) עשוים באמת וישר:
(פ) פדות שלח לעמו
(צ) צוה־לעולם בריתו
(ק) קדוש ונורא שמו:
(ר) ראשית חכמה יראת יהוה
(ש) שכל טוב לכל־עשיהם
(ת) תהלתו עמדת לעד:

Psalm 111, an alphabetic acrostic. The cola begin with successive letters of the Hebrew alphabet.

Some authors suggest that in the OT there are also a few acrostics of another type. They point, for instance, to Ps. 4, in which the initial letters of the lines (including the heading) form, when read from bottom to top, the statement "unto a lamp for Zerubbabel."

The acrostic is an old form. In *ANET,* pp. 439f., is the translation of an Akkadian acrostic, the preserved exemplar of which dates from the 7th cent. B.C., but which arose in (much) earlier times.

In using the alphabetical scheme the poet perhaps provided an aid to the memory of the learner, but he also worked for a definite effect upon the listener, whose ear was trained to distinguish such linguistic niceties. Though it is more difficult to appreciate such skills today, one certainly must not underrate the alphabetical Psalms. J. Muilenburg is quite right: "What is notable about this ancient poetry is that such an artificial contrivance does not stand in the way of producing literature of a high order, in which the emotions find full expression and the language bodies forth the intensity and passion of the poet" ("A study in Hebrew rhetoric: repetition and style," in *SVT,* 1 [1953], 103). To presume that Hebrew poets let the alphabetical scheme dictate the whole course and flow of their poems is to underestimate considerably their ability. In the alphabetical poems one finds development of thought and careful construction of essential and living — not merely formal — units.

See also POETRY, HEBREW, IV, VI, VII.

Bibliography.–Comms. on Psalms, Lamentations, Nahum, Sirach; E. König, *Stilistik, Rhetorik, Poetik in Bezug auf die biblische Litteratur* (1900), pp. 357ff.; A. Deissler, *Psalm 119 (118) und seine Theologie* (1955). N. H. RIDDERBOS

ACTS, APOCRYPHAL. *See* APOCRYPHAL ACTS.

ACTS OF PILATE. *See* APOCRYPHAL GOSPELS.

ACTS OF SOLOMON, BOOK OF THE [Heb. *sēper dibrê šᵉlōmōh* (1 K. 11:41); NEB ANNALS OF SOLOMON. Probably a history based on the state documents kept by the official recorder. See 14:19, 29; 15:23, 31; 16:5, 14, 20, 27; 22:39, 45; etc.

ACTS OF THE APOSTLES. The fifth book of the NT.

I. Title
II. Text
III. Author
IV. The Book
V. Date
VI. Sources
VII. Speeches
VIII. Relation of the Acts to the Epistles
IX. Chronology of Acts
X. Historical Value
XI. Purpose
XII. Analytical Outline

I. Title.–The original title of Acts may have been "Luke to Theophilus: Book II." The title "(The) Acts of (the) Apostles" was given to it after its original close connection with the Gospel of Luke was broken, and probably at the time when it received recognition as a canonical book. The earliest occurrence of the canonical title (Gk. *Práxeis Apostólōn*) is in the anti-Marcionite prologue to Luke (*ca.* A.D. 180). A little later the Muratorian Canon, in anti-Marcionite exaggeration, titled it "The Acts of *all* the Apostles" (*acta . . . omnium apostolorum*). In the MSS the title appears in various forms, e.g., "Acts," *Práxeis* (א in the inscription); "Acts of Apostles," *Práxeis Apostólōn* (B D א in subscription); "Acts of the Apostles," *Práxeis tōn Apostólōn* (many cursives); "Acts of the Holy Apostles," *Práxeis tōn Hagíōn Apostólōn* (A E H L in subscription); "Luke the Evangelist's Acts of the Holy Apostles," *Louka euangelístou Práxeis tōn Hagíōn Apostólōn* (33 in inscription).

II. Text.–The Byzantine text of the 4th cent. and later is represented in Acts by the uncials H L P S and by the majority of the minuscules.

The text of Westcott and Hort (1881) represents what they called by the question-begging name of "Neutral" text, because, in their view, it contains none of the aberrations characteristic of the other types of text. It is, however, better to call it the Alexandrian text (after the place in which it was current) or the *beta* (β) text, after the usual symbol for its most important representative, Codex Vaticanus (B). B and א preserve this text in a very pure form, and so also, for Acts, do A and the minuscules 81 and 1175.

The main criticism of the Westcott and Hort text as a reproduction of the β text is that it follows B even where the weight of other β authorities is against B. Even so, it is near enough to the original β text to make little difference. But this is not to say whether it is as near to the text of the original NT autographs. Westcott and Hort themselves believed that it was; in their view the β text was an excellent representative of the original.

There is, however, another candidate for the honor of representing more accurately the original text. This other candidate is usually known as the Western text, because it is represented mainly by the Greco-Latin Codex Bezae (D), by the African Latin version—represented in Acts by the sixth-century MS Floriacensis (h)—and by quotations in Tertullian, Cyprian, the Latin translation of Irenaeus, and Augustine. A similar text, however, is found in the East, represented in Acts by quotations in Ephrem's commentary on that book and in an Armenian catena on Acts based mainly on Ephrem and Chrysostom, and by notes on variant readings in the Harclean Syriac version.

The text of Acts on which Ephrem's commentary (extant in Syrian and Armenian) and the Armenian catena are based is probably the otherwise lost Old Syriac version of Acts. The Harclean Syriac is a revision made in 616 by Thomas of Harkel (Heraclea) of the Philoxenian version of 508 (cf. G. Zuntz, *Ancestry of the Harklean NT* [1945]). Thomas' revision consisted mainly in bringing the Philoxenian into line with the prevalent Byzantine text, but in Acts he also gives a large number of Western readings, for the most part in marginal notes, but also in some ninety-five asterisked additions in the body of his text, with the result that, next to D, the Harclean Syriac is our most important authority for the Western text of Acts. He carried out his revision in the library of the Enaton near Alexandria, using as his standards "accurate and approved" Greek MSS, presumably of a Byzantine character, although the sources of his variant readings are not easily determined. Some of them he may have taken from earlier Syriac versions, but others he probably found in a Greek MS of a Western type. The latter is made all the more likely because most of his variant readings are cast in the same slavishly literal translation-Syriac as he used for his text. The Western MS that he probably used seems to have been similar in character to a papyrus fragment, No. 1571 in the Michigan collection (p^{38}), containing parts of Acts 18 and 19 — a fragment that belongs to the 4th cent., if not, as H. A. Sanders thinks, to the 3rd, and whose text is decidedly Western. Two other papyrus fragments of Acts may be mentioned because of their Western character: p^{48} (Società Italiana 1165), containing 23:11-16, 24-29, belonging apparently to the 3rd cent.; and p^{29} (Oxyrhynchus 1597), containing part of 26:7f., 20, belonging to the 3rd or 4th century. The presence of the Western text in Egypt in the 3rd and 4th cents., before the date of the great uncials, is very important.

As we have called the Alexandrian text the β text after B, so we may call the Western text the *delta* (δ) text, after its principal representative, Codex Bezae (D). The δ text has marked peculiarities in the Gospels (especially Luke) and in Acts. In the main it is distinguished from the β text by additions, some of which can be accounted for as scribal or editorial amplifications, while others are not so easily explained, and seem to have some primitive authority behind them.

The claims of the δ text to be regarded as the best representative of the original cannot be dismissed lightly. It has very ancient attestation, and can be traced in versions as independent of each other as the Old Latin and the Old Syriac, both of which go back to the second half of the 2nd century. It appears in patristic citations earlier than the β text does. Internally, however, the evidence for regarding it as superior to the β text is less convincing. A longer text should not invariably be regarded as later than a shorter text, but many of the δ readings that are longer than the corresponding β readings are definitely secondary in character. The many amplifications of Our Lord's name are plainly later and pious expansions; so also are phrases like "in the name of the Lord Jesus Christ" when these are absent from the β text, and references to the Spirit over and above those found in the β text. Similar, too, is the frequent harmonization of OT quotations to the LXX form. Some of the longer δ readings are of the nature of glosses. Other

ACTS OF THE APOSTLES

Agora at Ephesus, with gateway (left) built in honor of Caesar Augustus. Paul taught in the city for an extended period. (B. K. Condit)

modifications have the effect of making difficult passages in the β text read more smoothly.

In the δ text of the apostolic decree in 15:20, 29 an ethical precept is added, the negative Golden Rule, which is generally admitted to be an interpolation even by those who defend the priority of the δ text; but even if it is removed, the decree in the δ text remains purely ethical, while in the β text it is mainly concerned with food regulations. Here we have neither expansion nor abridgment, but alteration; and if we ask in which direction the alteration was likely to take place, we must remember that after A.D. 70 the relation between Jews and Gentiles in the Church was no longer the burning question that it had previously been, and the tendency would be to replace by purely ethical precepts those primitive food regulations that had been laid down to facilitate social intercourse between Jewish and gentile Christians.

Some of the δ additions are attractive, and might be accepted with greater confidence if they did not keep such questionable company. Such are: Simon the sorcerer's copious tears in 8:24; Cornelius' dispatch of a servant to meet Peter in 10:25; Peter's missionary activity on the way back from Caesarea to Jerusalem (11:2; to be taken along with the δ version of Paul's journey from Caesarea to Jerusalem in 21:17); the seven steps of 12:10; the jailer's securing the other prisoners before attending to Paul and Silas (16:30); Paul's inserting the name of Jesus in the Scripture lessons in the Corinthian synagogue (18:4); his haste to keep the feast (Passover) at Jerusalem (18:21); the hours during which he lectured at Ephesus (19:9); the Ephesian populace running into the square (19:28); the handing over of Paul to the stratopedarch (28:16). Some of these added details give the impression of local knowledge, though others have been deduced from the narrative, or even invented by the expander (though it is often difficult to see why). In 20:4 a strong case can be made out for preferring "Gaius of Doberus" (δ) to "Gaius of Derbe" (β). But the general impression is that the δ text is secondary, though its priority has been ably championed, notably by A. C. Clark. The best, most convincing work in favor of the priority of the β over the δ text is Ropes, *Text of Acts*. F. G. Kenyon (*Western Text in the Gospels and Acts* [1939]) gives his verdict against the priority of the δ text, while admitting that several of its readings contain "instances of local knowledge which give the impression of authenticity" (p. 26); and he concludes that in Acts "the editor of the 'delta' text (if we do not accept it as original) must have had access to material of good quality, such as an alternative draft by Luke, or a copy made by one of Paul's companions who felt himself at liberty to amplify the narrative from his own knowledge" (p. 31). This would explain the presence in the δ text of apparently authentic details, while leaving us free to regard as secondary the majority of the expansions in which it abounds.

Ropes suggests with some diffidence that the δ text represents a revised recension made very early in the 2nd cent., perhaps in connection with an early stage in the formation of the NT canon: "The reviser's aim was to improve the text, not to restore it, and he lived not far from the time when the New Testament canon in its nucleus was first definitely assembled. It is tempting to suggest that the

'Western' text was made when Christian books valued for their antiquity and worth were gathered and disseminated in a collection which afterwards became the New Testament, and that the two processes were parts of the same great event, perhaps at Antioch—in other words, that the 'Western' text was the original 'canonical' text (if the anachronism can be pardoned) which was later supplanted by a 'pre-canonical' text of superior age and merit" (p. ccxlv). The principal difficulty in the way of accepting this suggestion is that the δ text is more deeply tinged with Aramaisms than the β text of Acts; this fact involves a problem on which the last word has not yet been spoken (cf. Black, pp. 244ff.).

The view expressed by F. Blass and supported by T. Zahn that Luke made two editions of Acts, the δ text being the first and the β text the second, breaks down under close examination.

Even if the β text is superior to the δ text, it does not follow that the β text is equivalent to the original text. The Chester Beatty papyrus of the Gospels and Acts (p^{45}) has shown that a century before our best witnesses for the β text there existed in Egypt a text of the Gospels—or at least of Mark—similar to that which was previously known as the Caesarean text, generally resembling the β text but with some affinities to the δ text. We must take account of the possibility that there was a "Caesarean" text of Acts as well and that it may represent the original text even better than the β text. R. V. G. Tasker (*JTS*, 38 [1937], 383ff.) finds "that the text of p^{45}, the oldest Egyptian fragments of Acts preserved, is a distinctive 'non-Western' text, probably older than the texts of the great uncials and of D, and presenting the same kind of characteristics as that known as the Caesarean text of the Gospels, and that possibly it is the text used by Origen."

III. Author.–The traditional ascription of the authorship of Acts to Luke the physician can be traced back to the 2nd century. The earliest extant explicit statement to this effect comes in the anti-Marcionite prologue to the Third Gospel. This prologue begins by saying, "Luke, a physician by profession, belonged to Antioch in Syria," and after giving an account of him as author of the Third Gospel, goes on: "And afterwards the same Luke wrote the Acts of the Apostles." The Muratorian Canon ascribes the authorship of both documents to "Luke the physician." Irenaeus, Tertullian, and Clement of Alexandria toward the end of the 2nd cent., Origen in the 3rd cent., Eusebius and Jerome in the 4th cent., and other early writers add their consentient testimony.

The tradition that the author of Acts was a native of Syrian Antioch probably goes back to a still earlier date in the 2nd cent., to the time when the Western recension of the text of Acts took shape, for the Western text of Acts 11:28 opens with the words "And when we were gathered together . . ."— the scene being the church in Antioch. Possibly the same recension — or else another early one — appears actually to have named Luke in 20:13, replacing "we" by the phrase "I Luke and those who were with me" (so Ephrem, comm. *in loc.*).

This leads one to pay more careful attention to those parts of Acts in which the narrative is related in the 1st person. There are three points at which the narrative changes from the 3rd person to the 1st person plural, and the unobtrusive way in which this transition is made suggests most naturally that this is the author's way of indicating that he himself was present at the events following. The three "we" sections of Acts (so called because they are characterized by the use of that pronoun) are 16:10-17; 20:5-21; 27:1–28:16. The view that this usage indicates that the author himself was present at the events described is supported by the fact that these passages are integral to the whole narrative of Acts and exhibit the same traits of style and language as the rest of the book. A writer who used the travel diary of someone else would either have indicated the source of such important eyewitness information more plainly, or, if he worked over the language of the diary in order to assimilate it to his own style, would hardly have left the first-person forms intact.

If this is correct, the author of Acts was a traveling companion of Paul. Several of these companions are named in the extant Epistles; and of these persons Luke is one of the few not excluded for various reasons from consideration as the possible author of Acts. We have to exclude, for example, all those companions of Paul who are named in the 3rd person in the "we" passages. The narrator accompanied Paul to Rome, and in the period following their arrival there "Luke, the beloved physician" (Col. 4:14) is mentioned by Paul as one of his companions—if (as seems most probable) it was from Rome that Paul wrote to the Colossians. This does not prove that Luke was the narrator, but it is consonant with the unanimous tradition since the 2nd cent. about the authorship of Acts. Luke plays such an inconspicuous part by name in the NT that it is unlikely that the tradition of his being the author of Acts (and of the Third Gospel) would have arisen without some real foundation in fact.

The element of medical diction in the vocabulary of Acts cannot in itself be held to establish the claim that the author was a physician. W. K. Hobart's thesis is offset by H. J. Cadbury's criticisms in *Style and Literary Method of Luke*. But if we can conclude on independent grounds that the author was Luke the physician, the medical diction certainly illustrates, and perhaps even supports, that conclusion.

There is no direct statement in the critically established text of Acts to support the tradition that Luke was a native of Syrian Antioch. He does, however, show a great interest in Antioch. Apart from the account of the beginnings of the church in Antioch (chs. 11, 13), it may be of some significance that, of the seven deacons of the Jerusalem church whose names are given in 6:5, the only one whose home town is mentioned is "Nicolaus a proselyte of Antioch." If Luke was indeed an Antiochian, we may regard him as one of the Greeks of that city evangelized by the men of Cyprus and Cyrene who went there because of the persecution that followed Stephen's death (11:20). That he was a Greek, in common with Epaphras and Demas, seems plain from Col. 4:10-14, where Paul's Jewish-Christian companions at the time of writing (Aristarchus, Mark, and Jesus Justus) are mentioned separately from the others. Luke appears, in fact, to be the only gentile writer in the NT, and indeed in the whole Bible.

IV. The Book.–Luke (hereinafter designating the author by this name) sets out his purpose for writing his twofold history in the prologue that introduces the Third Gospel (Lk. 1:1-4); this should be read as his prologue not to that Gospel only but to the whole work of which the Gospel forms Book One.

It appears from the prologue that the writer himself could not claim to be an eyewitness of the events narrated in his history from the beginning, although he had access to the information such eyewitnesses could supply. He was not the first to draw up an account based on information of this kind, but he claims for his account that it rests upon thorough and accurate inquiry, and that it is arranged in a proper sequence.

The title "most excellent" (Gk. *krátistos*) by which Theophilus is addressed may mean that Theophilus was a member of the Roman equestrian order, or it may be used

ACTS OF THE APOSTLES

more loosely as a title of honor. The title is omitted when Theophilus is again addressed at the beginning of Acts (1:1), but no certain inference can be drawn from this. All that we can gather with complete certainty is that Theophilus had already received some information about the rise and progress of the Christian movement—not necessarily as a catechumen—and that Luke was concerned to see that his information was as trustworthy as possible.

Luke traces the history of Christian beginnings from the events immediately preceding the birth of Christ (7 B.C. ?) down to the end of Paul's two years' detention in Rome (A.D. 60-62). He does this in two volumes, the first carrying the story as far as the appearance of the risen Christ to His disciples in Jerusalem, the second taking up the story at that point and telling how, in accordance with the commission given to the disciples by the Lord at that time, the good news was carried stage by stage from Jerusalem to Rome. These two volumes are the longest books of the NT, the Gospel being somewhat longer than Acts. It looks as if the author in both volumes recorded as much as could be contained in a papyrus roll of normal length.

It has been suggested (e.g., by W. M. Ramsay and T. Zahn) that Luke projected a third volume, but there is no adequate evidence for this. Ramsay argued that the opening words of Acts, where the Third Gospel is referred to as the *prṓtos lógos* (lit. "first volume"), imply that a third volume was projected. This argument might have had some substance had Luke been writing in the classical Greek of an earlier date, but it is not conclusive for the Hellenistic idiom, in which *prṓtos* can mean "former" as readily as "first." Whether Ramsay is right in saying that "no one can accept the ending of *Acts* as the conclusion of a rationally conceived history" (*SPT*, pp. 351f.) is perhaps one of those questions of taste about which dispute is idle; but in point of fact many readers can and do so accept it. Luke has brought Paul to Rome, and leaves him preaching the kingdom of God in the heart of the empire, "none forbidding him." He has in fact carried out his program; and over against Ramsay's opinion we may set the note at the end of Acts in J. A. Bengel's *Gnomon* (Eng. tr., 7th ed. 1877): "The victory of the word of God: Paul at Rome, the climax of the Gospel, the end of Acts . . . It began at Jerusalem; it ends at Rome. Here, O Church, thou hast thy ground-plan; it is thine to preserve it and to guard thy deposit."

About the beginning of the 2nd cent.—quite soon, in fact, after the publication of the Fourth Gospel—the Gospel records of Matthew, Mark, Luke, and John were gathered into one collection and began to circulate as a fourfold Gospel. One consequence of this was that the first volume of Luke's history was detached from the second and attached to the other three Gospels. Possibly a minor textual adjustment was made at the end of Luke and the beginning of Acts at this time, the words "and was carried up into heaven" being added to Lk. 24:51, and "he was received up" added in Acts 1:2. But a more important result was the special place that Acts had henceforth to occupy in the NT canon.

About the time the four Gospels were brought together to form one collection, another collection was also taking shape—the collection of the Epistles of Paul. These two collections—"The Gospel" and "The Apostle," as they were called—make up the greater part of the NT. But there would be a hiatus between the two collections if it were not for Luke's second volume, which played an important part in relating the two to each other. Luke's second volume provides a general sequel to the fourfold Gospel, since it was from the beginning the proper sequel to the Third Gospel. Besides, it provides the historical background against which a great part of the Pauline corpus can be more readily understood, and — more important still — it provides clear and convincing evidence for the validity of the apostolic claims Paul makes for himself in his letters.

But the importance of Luke's second volume was further underlined as a result of the debate that was stirred up by Marcion (*ca.* A.D. 140). Marcion regarded Christ as the revealer of a completely new religion and maintained that Paul was the only apostle of Christ who preserved that religion in its purity. He drew up what he believed to be the true canon of divine scripture for this new age. Marcion's canon comprised two parts—"The Gospel" (a suitably edited recension of the Third Gospel) and "The Apostle" (a similarly edited recension of the first ten Pauline Epistles). The publication of Marcion's canon was a challenge and stimulus to the Roman church and the other churches that shared the catholic faith that Marcion rejected. They now defined with greater precision what they accepted as the canon of holy scripture. For them the NT canon did not supersede that of the OT but stood alongside it as its proper fulfillment. For them "The Gospel" comprised not one document only but four, and these four included the true form of the one that Marcion had published in a garbled edition. For them "The Apostle" comprised not ten but thirteen Pauline Epistles, and letters of other apostles as well. Linking "The Gospel" and "The Apostle" together, the second volume of Luke's history had greater importance than was ever before attached to it, for not only did it present irrefragable proof of Paul's apostleship but it presented evidence of the apostleship of the other apostles too—those whom Marcion had repudiated as false apostles and corrupters of the truth. Its "pivotal" place in the Christian canon (to use Harnack's epithet) was appreciated now as it could not have been before, and this appreciation was expressed by its being given the position between "The Gospel" and "The Apostle" which it has occupied since then. It is from this time, too, as we have said, that we find this document called the Acts of the Apostles.

This account of the origin of Acts and its role in the definition of the NT canon has not, however, been unanimously accepted. A notable challenge to it has been presented by J. Knox in *Marcion and the NT.* He argues that Marcion's Gospel was not adapted from the Third Gospel, but from an earlier Gospel writing from which the present Third Gospel also was derived; and that Marcion's Gospel resembles this earlier form more closely than the Third Gospel does. The Third Gospel as we know it, in fact, is an anti-Marcionite revision and expansion of the work that underlay Marcion's Gospel. Similarly, Knox maintains, Acts in its canonical form is an anti-Marcionite work of the 2nd century. In view of Marcion's appeal to the unique authority of Paul, it was necessary for catholic Christians not only to claim Paul for themselves in a more complete form than Marcion recognized, but to defend their recognition of the other apostles. This they did not only by acknowledging as canonical certain writings ascribed to apostles other than Paul, but in particular by appealing to a work that established their authority. The authority of Peter and John and their fellow apostles was unquestioned in the catholic Church; if Paul (as Marcion averred) really repudiated them as false apostles, then the catholic Church must repudiate Paul. If, on the other hand, Paul was not to be repudiated, it must be shown, more conclusively than Paul's letters could be made to do, that Paul had acknowledged the authority of the Twelve. There was need for an authoritative document that, without disparaging Paul's apostleship, subordinated him to the Twelve. And, says Knox, just such a book became suddenly available *ca.* A.D. 150 — a book *"of which there is not a single clear trace before this time"* (p. 119).

Linguistically, Knox would bracket Acts along with

most of the peculiarly "Lukan" parts of the Third Gospel as dating from this time; the unknown author, who has impressed his style on the whole twofold work, took the original document underlying Marcion's Gospel and worked it over in the catholic interest, and added the "second treatise," the book of Acts, which "serves the double purpose of exalting and idealizing Paul and at the same time definitely subordinating him to the leaders at Jerusalem" (p. 120).

V. Date.–One weighty argument against the view that Luke-Acts is a mid-second-century work is that the historical, geographical, and political atmosphere of Luke-Acts as a whole, and of Acts in particular, belongs to the 1st cent. and not to the 2nd. The investigations of W. M. Ramsay and A. Harnack, carried out along quite independent lines, set the first-century date on a firm foundation.

When Ramsay began his career of archeological research in Asia Minor in 1880, he did so as one who was "quite convinced" by the "ingenuity and apparent completeness of the Tübingen theory." But as he found himself increasingly brought in contact with Acts "as an authority for the topography, antiquities, and society of Asia Minor," he "gradually came to find it a useful ally in some obscure and difficult investigations" relating to the 1st century. He has left on record the impression that was made on him when he recognized that the reference to Lystra and Derbe as "cities of Lycaonia" in Acts 14:6, with the corollary that Iconium was a city of Galatian Phrygia, was (contrary to his previous belief) historically and geographically justified. He came to realize more and more that the most serious objections against accepting it in its entirety as a first-century work were the result of mistaken presuppositions (cf. *The Bearing of Recent Discovery on the Trustworthiness of the NT* [1915], pp. 16f., 35ff., *et passim*). This form of historical and archeological evidence must be allowed full weight; in fact, Acts displays an acquaintance with the persons and situations of the middle years of the 1st cent. that one would not expect in a tendentious work written in the middle of the 2nd century.

As for external evidence, there are few indubitable references to Acts in the first half of the 2nd century. After that time there is no lack of evidence. The succession of apocryphal books of "Acts" (the "Acts of John," the "Acts of Paul," etc.) appearing from *ca.* A.D. 150 on implies not only the existence of Acts as a model, but also its established recognition as authoritative. Justin Martyr (*ca.* A.D. 150) makes a fairly clear allusion to the opening paragraph of Acts (*Apol.* i.50). Earlier still, the reference in Polycarp's Epistle to the Philippians (1:2), written *ca.* A.D. 120, to Christ as the one "whom God raised up, having loosed the pangs of Hades," may be regarded with some confidence as a quotation of Acts 2:24. The account of the death of Judas Iscariot given by Polycarp's contemporary Papias has been thought (by E. J. Goodspeed and others) to be based upon the account in Acts 1:18f., but this is uncertain.

The evidence for assigning an early second-century date to the formation of the fourfold Gospel, with its implications for the first-century dating of all four documents that it incorporated, has an inevitable bearing on the date not only of Luke but of Acts. And if Goodspeed was right (as he very well may have been) in thinking that the beginning of the collection of Paul's letters toward the end of the 1st cent. was stimulated by the publication of Acts, there is a further indication in favor of a first-century date.

But even if the first-century date of Acts appears to be established, we have to consider further in which decade of the 1st cent. — i.e., in which of the last four decades of that century—the composition of the book is to be placed.

There is much in Luke-Acts, and especially in Acts, suggesting that the work was written quite soon after the last event recorded in the twofold history, the termination of Paul's two years of custody in Rome (Acts 28:30f.), the two years in question being probably A.D. 60 and 61. This at any rate provides a fixed *terminus a quo*. "From this," says Jerome, "we understand that the book was written in the same city" (*De viris illustribus* 7)—probably implying that it was completed at the end of these two years.

The following considerations may be urged in support of such an early dating:

(1) Luke shows no sign of dependence on Paul's Epistles. Yet these are so obviously a primary source of information about Paul that anyone writing an account of his career after they had begun to circulate generally among the churches could hardly have avoided making use of them. But Luke is so far from using them as a source that it becomes at times considerably difficult to reconcile his accounts of Paul's movements with theirs. E. J. Goodspeed has suggested that it was the publication of Acts that first revived an interest in Paul among the churches and (as has been noted) stimulated the collection of his Epistles. (The wider "publication" of the book did not necessarily follow immediately upon its composition.) Knox, on the other hand, aware of the difficulty presented to a second-century dating of Acts by the lack of reference to Paul's Epistles, offers a suggestion in line with his main position: that the Epistles of Paul were "under a cloud" in catholic circles because of Marcion's use of them, and "Acts undertakes to bring Paul, but *not necessarily his epistles,* into the light again. . . . Paul's only connection with church letters in the Acts of the Apostles is as *the bearer of a letter written by the Twelve*" (pp. 134f.). But there is no evidence at all that Marcion's use of Paul's Epistles reduced their prestige in the eyes of anti-Marcionites. Knox further urges that the apparent lack of knowledge of Paul's Epistles in Acts is a difficulty for any dating of Acts. But the difficulty becomes less the earlier we date Acts, and it is reduced to a minimum if we date it in the sixties of the 1st century.

(2) Luke gives no hint that Paul had died by the time he wrote his history—not even in Paul's words to the Ephesian elders in Acts 20:25 ("I know that all you . . . will see my face no more"). Paul's intention at this time was not to return to the Aegean area after his visit to Jerusalem but to evangelize Spain (cf. Rom. 15:23ff.), and that sufficiently accounts for his language here. Had Luke written after Paul's death — which may be dated in A.D. 64 or a year or two later — his knowledge of the circumstances of Paul's death would perhaps have given a definite color to some of his writing and Acts would hardly have finished on such a confident note.

(3) This last point applies not only to Paul's death but to the whole Neronian persecution in which Paul's death was traditionally an incident. The attitude to the Roman power throughout Acts makes it difficult to believe that this persecution had actually begun, or was now a matter of history. The impartiality with which the representatives of the imperial power treat the Christian missionaries in Acts reflects a situation that had completely disappeared by the end of the century. Yet it was Paul's experience of this impartial dealing that encouraged him to expect a favorable hearing before the supreme tribunal in Rome. A work written after A.D. 64 would scarcely have given its readers such an optimistic impression of the situation in Rome two or three years before that date.

(4) Another event that would have left its mark on Acts if it had already taken place was the Jewish revolt of A.D. 66 and the consequent destruction of the city and temple of Jerusalem four years later. This crisis was so epochal for both Judaism and Christianity that a clear difference in outlook can be noted between literature reflecting the

period preceding it and that reflecting the subsequent period. Brandon (pp. 208ff.) argues that the Lukan writings reflect a later phase than Mark does of the new situation that arose after A.D. 70. Furthermore, Brandon holds that Acts represents a further stage than Mark does in the process of rehabilitating Paul, and also contains "a covert polemic" against the Christianity of Alexandria, which he believes had succeeded Jerusalem "as the citadel of Jewish Christianity and of opposition to Pauline teaching." But Luke, who emphasizes Jewish opposition to the gospel throughout the cities and provinces of the empire, nowhere suggests that the "crooked generation" had met with the judgment from which Peter on the day of Pentecost urged his hearers to save themselves (Acts 2:40). In this matter, of course, the evidence of the Third Gospel must be considered as well as that of Acts, and it is in the former that many expositors have found the plainest references to the destruction of Jerusalem as having already taken place. If it were established that the canonical Gospel of Luke does in fact presuppose the events of A.D. 66-70, one might consider whether the "former treatise" to which Acts originally formed the sequel might not have been some form of "Proto-Luke" (cf. C. S. C. Williams, *Expos.T.*, 64 [1952/53], 283f.). As it is, however, the language in the Third Gospel that has been widely taken to reflect the conditions of the siege and fall of Jerusalem may well be accounted for quite differently (cf. C. H. Dodd, *Journal of Roman Studies*, 37 [1947], 47ff.).

(5) The subjects that are accorded prominent importance in Acts, and the theological outlook of the book, also tend very much to suggest a period before A.D. 70. The issue so earnestly disputed before and during the Council of Jerusalem (Acts 15) became progressively less urgent after the 60's and 70's of the 1st century. The "primitiveness" that seems to mark the theology of Acts both in substance and in expression is a less certain criterion of date, although it does confirm Luke's fidelity to his sources of information (cf. W. L. Knox, *Acts of the Apostles,* pp. 69ff.).

(6) The manner in which Acts ends is best explained if Luke stopped at that point because there was no more to relate at the time, i.e., if he wrote at the end of Paul's two years' confinement in Rome. To be sure, there is rhetorical fitness in the climactic note on which he concludes: Paul is left preaching the gospel at Rome without hindrance. But even so we should have expected some more explicit account of how the trial went (if indeed Paul's case ever came to trial), and of what happened to Paul. Even if a third volume was projected—and of this there is no evidence—we should have expected this "second treatise" to be rounded off rather differently. On the other hand the concluding note is sufficiently impressive to make us reject such a suggestion as that Acts was left unfinished because of the writer's death. All in all, no explanation of the manner of the ending seems so satisfying as that which makes Luke carry his story to the actual time of writing.

Against this argument for the early date of Acts, however, there are others that are believed to demand a date later in the century. In addition to the argument that Luke-Acts presupposes the fall of Jerusalem, E. J. Goodspeed enumerates several other reasons, but none of them seems necessarily to point to a later date than the early 60's. In any case, Goodspeed regards Paul's companion Luke as the author of Luke-Acts, and allows that much of his material was gathered earlier. Agreement on the author is more important than agreement on the date at which he completed his work. But a date toward A.D. 90 is not inevitably indicated by the points listed by Goodspeed—the literary form and features of Luke-Acts, its infancy and resurrection interest, its doctrine of the Holy Spirit, its interest in punitive miracle, the passing of the Jewish controversy, the interest in Christian hymnody, the church organization reflected, the amplified picture of glossolalia in Acts 2, the fact (as Goodspeed sees it) that Paul is dead and has attained heroic stature, "the situation presupposed by the conception of such a work—the wide success achieved by the Greek mission" (*Intro. to the NT* [1937], pp. 191ff.).

As for the last point mentioned, the Greek mission had already achieved wide success by the year 60. It is not obvious that Acts presumes that Paul is dead; and a man may very well be a hero to his friends even in his lifetime. The various interests noted by Goodspeed had adequate time for their development in the thirty years following the death and resurrection of Jesus—and the miraculous element is no exception. For, quite apart from the question whether these miracles really happened or not, that they are recorded is no argument against an early date. With regard to the "Jewish controversy," the narrative of Acts 21 indicates that one aspect of this controversy was still live enough in the author's mind; those who, following in the wake of the Tübingen scholars, view Acts as a reconciliation document, accommodating the Pauline and Petrine positions to each other, largely fail to realize that "the figure of Judaizing St. Peter is a figment of the Tübingen critics with no basis in history" (K. Lake, *Earlier Epistles of St. Paul* [1911], p. 116).

There remains one argument, which is of great weight in the opinion of some: namely, that Luke in both volumes of his history shows dependence on the *Antiquities* of Josephus, published in A.D. 93. If this were so, then Luke-Acts could not be dated earlier than that year, unless we suppose that Luke and Josephus had some contact with each other while they were compiling their respective histories.

Curiously enough, among all the points of contact between Luke's history and Josephus', the only ones where Luke is believed to have been dependent on Josephus are points in which he appears to contradict him. The alleged points of dependence in Acts are the references to Theudas (5:36) and to another insurgent of Egyptian provenance (21:38); the detailed differences between the two authors, however, make any such dependence most improbable. Another interesting point of contact between the two writers concerns the death of Herod Agrippa I (cf. Acts 12:20ff.), and in this case both writers give independently authoritative accounts. The arguments for Luke's linguistic dependence on Josephus prove on examination to lack substance. The matter may be summed up in the words of E. Schürer: "Either Luke had not read Josephus, or else he forgot all that he had read" (*Zeitschrift für wissenschaftliche Theologie,* 19 [1876], 582).

VI. Sources.–If Luke's alleged dependence on Josephus cannot be maintained, we may consider other possible sources of information that were at his disposal.

For part of the narrative of Acts, of course (that covered by the "we" sections), he required no source of information beyond his personal observation. Whether he kept a travel diary at the time, which he subsequently incorporated in his general narrative, or simply changed from the 3rd person to the 1st in the course of his writing to indicate that for certain periods he himself was present at the events described, is not certain.

Again, so close a companion of Paul as Luke appears to have been for considerable periods might be expected to have learned a good deal about Paul's life and experiences from Paul's own lips. It is difficult, however, to determine how much of the narrative can be regarded as based on Paul himself. A comparison with the autobiographical passages

ACTS OF THE APOSTLES

Ruins at Caesarea, where Paul was taken into protective custody (W. S. LaSor)

in Paul's Epistles (e.g., Gal. 1:15–2:14; 2 Cor. 11:32f.) makes it plain that they were not available to Luke as sources of information. But in the course of his travels with Paul, Luke met a number of people who were in a position to give him the information he sought as he "traced the course of all things accurately from the first"—people "who from the beginning were eyewitnesses and ministers of the word" (Lk. 1:2f.). If he was indeed a native of Antioch, he may have learned much from the founders of the church of that city; he would certainly meet Barnabas there, and possibly also Peter (cf. Gal. 2:11). One of the early leaders in that church was Manaen, foster brother of Herod Antipas (Acts 13:1); and when one considers the special interest that both parts of his history show in the Herod family, it is a reasonable supposition that he obtained some of his special knowledge about them from Manaen. At a later time (A.D. 57) Luke accompanied Paul to Palestine and met many potential informants at Jerusalem and Caesarea. He emphasizes that the man with whom he lodged at Jerusalem, Mnason by name, was "an early disciple" (Acts 21:16), or rather "an original disciple"; Mnason, a Cypriote, was probably one of the original Hellenistic members of the Jerusalem church. On one occasion at least he met James the brother of Jesus along with his fellow elders in Jerusalem.

Before this visit to Jerusalem Luke spent several days at Caesarea with Paul and his other companions, and in that connection special mention is made of Philip the evangelist, who resided in that city along with his four prophesying daughters. From Papias and other second-century writers we infer that some of these daughters were noted in their old age as authorities for persons and incidents in the early days of Christian history. It is extremely probable that Luke, at this earlier date, was indebted to them and their father for important information. Acts 6–8 in particular has on good grounds been regarded as based on Philip's knowledge.

After Paul's arrest at Jerusalem and dispatch for safe custody to Caesarea, where he remained for two years, Luke seems to have stayed near him. Even if he did not spend the whole of the two years in Caesarea itself, he does not appear to have left Palestine until he accompanied Paul on his voyage to Rome. It is, again, reasonable to suppose that during that time he gathered further information and possibly began to arrange it in written form, though we cannot go all the way with C. C. Torrey and believe that in those years he made "a collection of Semitic documents relating to the life and work of Jesus, arranged them very skilfully, and then rendered the whole into the Greek which is our Third Gospel" (*Our Translated Gospels* [1936], p. ix). But a preliminary draft of his first volume may certainly have been made during that period, based on information derived from various sources together with a digest of the teaching of Jesus, which also underlies the Gospel of Matthew.

After these two years Luke went to Rome with Paul, and there he was in Paul's company along with Mark and others about the year 60 (Col. 4:10, 14; Philem. 24). This contact with Mark has not only an important bearing on the relation between the Second and Third Gospels, but may also throw some light on a possible source of information for some of the events recorded in the earlier chapters of Acts. Whether or not Mark, having concluded his Gospel-writing at Mk. 16:8, planned a "second treatise" beginning with the resurrection appearances, as some have thought, is a matter of complete doubt; but in one way or another Mark may well have provided Luke with information about the early days of the Jerusalem church. It is noteworthy that the clearest evidence of an Aramaic substratum beneath Luke's Greek appears in the first five chapters of Acts, together with the sections recording the "Acts of Peter" (9:31–11:18; 12:1-17) and part of ch. 15. We need not suppose that all the material bearing traces of an Aramaic substratum has been derived from a single source; it is precarious, on the other hand, to use the criterion of duplicate narratives to divide the early chapters of Acts between two parallel Jerusalem sources, as Harnack did, followed by Jackson and Lake (*BC*).

Unless the sources of a writer have survived independently, or can be reconstructed to some extent by a comparison of various works that drew upon them in common, source criticism is inevitably a very speculative discipline. In Acts, therefore, the most that can be done is to point out what sources of information were probably or possibly available to Luke, and suggest that these sources did indeed bring him into touch with the course of events as he claims in his prologue. Evidently, too, he used this information in a masterly fashion as he made it serve the purpose he had in view in compiling his history of Christian beginnings.

VII. Speeches.–One feature of the tradition of Greek historical writing—a tradition that Luke seems in several respects to have inherited—was the composition of occasional speeches for appropriate occasions. Thucydides (*History of the Peloponnesian War* i.22) explains that, instead of trying to remember word by word what the various speakers had said, even when he himself had heard them, he makes them say the sort of thing that he felt the occasion demanded of them, "of course adhering as closely as possible to the general sense of what they really said." There is little doubt that Thucydides did conscientiously adhere as closely as he could to the general sense of what was really said, however much he might embellish his speeches with the tricks of contemporary rhetoric. But later historians were inclined to imitate his freedom without his historical conscience. They composed speeches freely and put them into the mouths of their characters, not with any consideration of historical probability, but as dramatic or rhetorical exercises in which they tried to show their skill in polished literary composition.

But when we look at the speeches in Acts, we are struck by the difference between them and the speeches in the works of later writers such as Josephus. Luke obviously does not attempt to reach the summit of rhetorical perfection in the speeches he reports. Some of the most un-Greek idiom in Acts appears in these speeches; and yet Luke was capable of writing excellent literary Hellenistic, as the first four verses of his Gospel prove.

That Luke did not invent the speeches recorded in his history is suggested by a comparison between the speeches

ACTS OF THE APOSTLES

in his Gospel and parallel passages in the other Synoptic Gospels, from which it must be concluded that Luke has preserved with great fidelity the source or sources from which he derived the sayings of Jesus and others. The alterations that appear in the sayings affect style and order rather than content. If this is so in reports of speeches where Luke's faithfulness to his sources can be checked, one need not suppose without good reason that he was less faithful where his sources are no longer available for comparison.

Many of the speeches reported in Acts are summaries of the primitive apostolic preaching. The outline of the gospel story that can be recovered from them is in all essentials the same outline that can be recovered from occasional references in the Pauline and other Epistles, and the same outline that appears to underlie the Gospels, particularly Mark. This suggests that these speeches—whether Peter's at Jerusalem on the day of Pentecost and at Caesarea in the house of Cornelius, or Paul's in the synagogue of Pisidian Antioch—are not mere inventions of the author but are genuine statements of the original message proclaimed both by Peter and Paul and by the other apostles as well. "When we further observe that most of the forms of the kerygma in Acts show in their language a strong Aramaic colouring, we may recognize the high probability that in these passages we are in fairly direct touch with the primitive tradition of the Jesus of history" (C. H. Dodd, *History and the Gospel* [1938], p. 73).

When we recognize the existence of this common outline of the primitive Christian message, we do away with any ground for suspecting that Luke has either made his Petrine speeches too Pauline, or his Pauline speeches too Petrine. In point of fact, Paul himself insists that, with regard to the outline of basic evangelic events, he is at one with Peter and James and the other eyewitnesses of the resurrection (1 Cor. 15:11).

The frequent use made in these speeches of quotations from the OT forms a contrast to Luke's own practice. These quotations, of course, would appeal only to audiences composed of Jews or "God-fearers"—Gentiles who attached themselves to the synagogue services. In preaching the gospel to pagans a different approach was made. The general revelation of God in creation and providence was invoked as common ground between speakers and hearers instead of the special revelation made in the election and history of Israel, and quotations from classical poets might be introduced rather than quotations from the OT. But the gospel message was the same for Jew and Gentile, whatever differences might appear in the respective methods of approach. For speeches to pagan audiences reference should be made to the expostulation of Paul and Barnabas with the indigenous population of Lystra (Acts 14:15-17) and the address of Paul to the Athenian Areopagus (17:22-31).

It is not only in evangelistic speeches that the approach is adapted to the audience. The same is true of the deliberative, apologetic, and hortatory speeches reported. For example, Paul narrates his conversion in two different contexts in Acts (22:3-21; 26:2-23), and it is instructive to mark the varying emphases according to whether he is addressing a furious Jerusalem mob or a distinguished audience in the governor's residence at Caesarea. Only one of Paul's speeches reported in Acts is delivered to a Christian audience—the address at Miletus to the elders of the Ephesian church (20:18-35); it is not surprising that this report contains more parallels with the Pauline Epistles than the rest of Acts put together.

We need not suppose that the speeches in Acts are verbatim reports in the sense that they record every word spoken on the occasions referred to. Paul, we gather, was given to long sermons, but any one of the speeches attributed to him in Acts could be delivered in its reported form in a few minutes. There is good reason, however, to hold that the speeches in Acts are at least faithful epitomes, giving the gist of the argument used by Paul and other preachers of the first Christian generation. Even in summarizing the speeches, the historian would naturally introduce more or less of his own style, but there is actually very little of Luke's own style in these reports. Taken all in all, each speech suits the speaker, the audience, and the general situation. The evidence suggests that, far from being mere inventions of the historian, the speeches in Acts are valuable and independent sources for the history and theology of primitive Christianity.

VIII. Relation of the Acts to the Epistles.–The agreement depicted in Acts between Paul on the one hand and Peter and James on the other regarding the basic principles of the gospel was seen by the Tübingen school of critics of the 19th cent. as a sure mark of the late and unhistorical character of the book. Reading the four Pauline Epistles whose genuineness they admitted (Galatians, Romans, 1 and 2 Corinthians) in the light of the Hegelian dialectical interpretation of history, with its pattern of thesis, antithesis, and synthesis, they recognized in Acts the synthesis, the latest stage, belonging to the latter half of the 2nd century. The thesis and antithesis were represented by Peter and Paul, who violently opposed one another, Paul advocating complete liberty from the Jewish law, Peter insisting on its continued observance by gentile believers as well as Jews.

Obviously, if this interpretation of history were true, Acts must be unhistorical; but in truth the picture of events in these four Pauline Epistles must be equally unhistorical. While in Gal. 1:1, 11ff. Paul insists that he received the gospel and his commission to preach it direct from the Lord, through no human mediation, in 1 Cor. 15:11 he insists that the gospel he preached had essentially the same basis as that preached by the original apostles. This is implied even in Galatians, the Epistle that seemed to those critics to lend most color to their theory. When Peter, John, and James gave Paul and Barnabas the right hand of fellowship (Gal. 2:9), there was no hint of any difference in the substance of the preaching; the only difference in question related to the respective constituencies that each group was to serve. Paul pronounces a solemn and repeated anathema on any who should preach a different gospel from that which he preached (Gal. 1:8f.), but he says nothing to imply that the Jerusalem apostles were liable to his anathema.

The picture of Peter in Galatians accords well with the one we find in Acts. According to Gal. 2:11ff., Peter's personal conviction, like Paul's, was that no distinction should be made, even socially, between Jewish and gentile believers. In Antioch, "before certain people came from James, he ate with the Gentiles; but when they came, he withdrew and separated himself"—not because he had changed his convictions, but "fearing those of the circumcision." But what had happened previously to convince Peter, the orthodox Jew, that there was nothing wrong in eating with Gentiles? We find the explanation in Acts 10, where we read how he had learned not to call common what God had cleansed. Peter's action at Antioch was a lapse, and it is evident that Paul's rebuke had its effect, for we find him maintaining true Christian liberty in Acts 15.

Besides maintaining that the writer of Acts made Peter too Pauline, the Tübingen school also insisted that he made Paul too Petrine in an attempt to reconcile the irreconcilable. The Paul who in Acts accepts the decisions of the Council of Jerusalem, circumcises Timothy, and under-

ACTS OF THE APOSTLES

takes a purificatory rite in the temple to calm those who were alarmed at rumors of his rejection of all ritual obligations—this Paul was, to them, far removed from the uncompromising controversialist of Galatians. Is the Paul of Acts really the Paul of the Epistles? In Galatians, it should be remembered, Paul was dealing in white-hot urgency with a situation that threatened the very foundations of the gospel. For the Paul of the Epistles, outward acts in themselves were neither good nor bad, except as the intention made them so.

The truly emancipated man is not in bondage to his liberty. If he wishes for certain proper purposes to perform a ritual act not sinful in itself he will do so, not as under an obligation, but freely. If meat offered to idols is set before him, and there is no risk of causing offense to others by eating it, he will eat it and give God thanks; to him an idol is nothing in the world. If expediency demands that a half-Jew be circumcised for his greater usefulness in the gospel, Paul will have him be circumcised; in such a case circumcision is simply a minor surgical operation performed for a practical purpose. But the more narrow type of mind will never grasp the difference between doing such things freely and doing them as religious obligations with a view to securing divine favor. To this type of person, Paul's behavior appears to be rank inconsistency. So it appeared to his Judaizing and other opponents in his own day; so it has appeared to many biblical critics in more recent times, who have dubbed Acts unhistorical on the ground that an apostle must not be inconsistent.

But the consistency that some expect from Paul is the "foolish consistency" that Emerson called "the hobgoblin of little minds, adored by little statesmen and philosophers and divines"; for such a consistency little minds will search the life of Paul in vain, for his was preeminently a great mind. On the great basic principles of Christianity he was uncompromising; where these were not affected he was the most adaptable of men. He circumcised Timothy, but solemnly warned the Galatian Christians against the practice. Why? Because *they* were being taught to regard it as necessary to complete their salvation, and such an attitude would bring them into bondage to rites and ceremonies, away from the liberty with which Christ had made them free. But even to them he insists that circumcision in itself is immaterial (Gal. 5:6); only when performed as a religious obligation does it carry with it the duty of obedience to all the rest of the Jewish law.

Again, one who ate meat that had been offered to an idol, and was very much aware of this fact while eating it, might violate his conscience in so doing; let him therefore refrain. But one to whom the meat was just a piece of meat like any other, and to whom the idol meant nothing at all, might eat freely, though the grace of Christ would lead him to refrain if another's conscience might be injured by his eating. Paul himself endeavored to be in Jerusalem for various festivals, and associated himself with purificatory rites; but he challenges the Galatians: "You observe days, and months, and seasons, and years" (Gal. 4:10). The difference lay in the intention; they were acting in such a way as to lose the very liberty of which Paul availed himself. Paul's real attitude to such matters is given in Rom. 14:5f.

In his attitude to the Jews, the Paul of Acts is also the Paul of the Epistles. The Paul who repeats in Romans "to the Jew first, and also to the Greek" is the Paul who in Acts visits the synagogues first, in city after city, and who in Pisidian Antioch declares to the Jews: "It was necessary that the word of God should first be spoken to you." The Paul who suffers so much from Jewish hostility in Acts is the Paul who can speak of the Jews in 1 Thess. 2:15f. as those "who both killed the Lord Jesus and the prophets, and drove out us, and please not God, and are contrary to all men, forbidding us to speak to the Gentiles that they may be saved." The Paul who in Acts refuses to stop offering the gospel to his Jewish brethren in spite of his bitter experiences at their hands is the Paul who in Rom. 9:2f. tells of his great sorrow and unceasing anguish of heart at their refusal to receive the gospel, and is willing himself to be accursed, if only his heart's desire and prayer to God for their salvation be accomplished.

The Paul who in Acts works with his hands in Corinth and Ephesus, and bids the Ephesian elders learn a lesson from him in this respect, is the Paul who in the Epistles shows the same example and teaches the same lesson to the Thessalonians and Corinthians. The Paul who in Acts can adapt himself so readily to Jew and Gentile, learned and unlearned, Areopagus and Sanhedrin, synagogue audience and city mob, Roman governor and King Agrippa, is the Paul who claims in 1 Cor. 9:19ff. that he has "become all things to all men, that by all means I might save some." The Paul who in Acts is Christ's "chosen vessel" to bear His name before the Gentiles claims in the Epistles to have been divinely set apart, even from birth, for this very purpose (Acts 9:15; Gal. 1:15f.; Rom. 1:1ff.).

Despite Luke's evident lack of knowledge of Paul's Epistles, Acts and the Epistles throw considerable light on each other. We can read several of the Epistles with greater understanding because Acts gives us some account of the founding and progress of the churches to which they were written. The references to Apollos in 1 Corinthians are better understood because of the introduction to him in Acts. A fuller picture of the gentile collection for the Jerusalem believers is available by combining the information of Acts and the Epistles.

When comparing the historical information that can be gathered from the Epistles with the narrative of Acts, we meet several difficulties—not, however, insuperable ones. If we compare the account of Paul's conversion and its sequel in Acts 9:1-30 with Paul's own narrative in Gal. 1:13-24, we find that Luke gives in greater detail what Paul passes over briefly (the actual conversion), whereas the events of the following three years and the first Jerusalem visit are given much more explicitly by Paul. Luke mentions no visit to Arabia, nor does he explain that the only apostles whom Paul saw in Jerusalem were Peter and James the Lord's brother. These details were important for Paul's argument in Galatians; Luke passes over them in general terms. The escape in the basket is related by Paul in 2 Cor. 11:32f., where he represents the danger as coming from the ethnarch of Aretas; Luke says it came from the Jews. Judging from later experiences, we need not be surprised if Paul's Jewish opponents enlisted the cooperation of non-Jews against him. Paul might well wish to draw a veil over the participation of his fellow countrymen in this hostile act.

The correspondence of Paul's Jerusalem visits in Acts and Galatians is a vexed question. That the visit of Gal. 1:18 is identical with that of Acts 9:26 is clear enough. As for the visit of Gal. 2:1, the most probable view is that it is the famine-relief visit of Acts 11:30. This purpose of the visit is hinted at in Gal. 2:10; Paul's statement (Gal. 2:2) that he went up by revelation is explained by the prophecy of Agabus in Acts 11:28. The third visit (Acts 15) is not mentioned in Galatians, and this can best be explained if this visit had not yet been paid when Galatians was written. Otherwise, it is amazing that Paul should make no mention of the apostolic decree, which would have afforded the most convincing support to his argument. It follows that Galatians must have been addressed to the south Galatian churches whose planting is recorded in Acts 13–14; in that case it would be the earliest of Paul's extant Epistles.

For the movements of Paul and his companions during the second missionary journey, there is some firsthand information in 1 Thess. 3:1-16. These data agree substantially with what we find in Acts 17:14–18:5; such differences as are there arise from the omission and addition of different details by the two authors.

From the Corinthian Epistles we can derive much information (though not so much as we should like) about the period Acts 18:18–20:3, which is passed over rapidly by Luke. It is clear from these Epistles that Paul's relations with the church at Corinth during his stay at Ephesus were marred by troubles of various kinds, of which Acts gives no hint. Timothy's visit to Macedonia in Acts 19:22 is possibly referred to in 1 Cor. 4:17; 16:10; but it probably belongs to a somewhat later period. Paul expresses his intention of following him in 1 Cor. 16:5f. His intention of wintering in Corinth may have been fulfilled in his three months' stay there (Acts 20:3). But we gather from 2 Cor. 12:14; 13:1f. that the visit of Acts 20:2f. was at least Paul's third visit to Corinth. He must therefore have paid a second visit some time previously in the course of his Ephesian ministry, probably after the writing of 1 Corinthians, the sorrowful visit implied in 2 Cor. 2:1.

There are various indications in the Corinthian Epistles that Paul's life was in peculiar danger at times during his residence in Ephesus (cf. 1 Cor. 15:30-32; 2 Cor. 1:8ff.). The only hint of danger given by Luke is the story of the riot in the theater (Acts 19:23ff.), but Paul's words seem to imply greater peril than was apparently involved in the riot. Some scholars (notably A. Deissmann, W. Michaelis, and G. S. Duncan) have argued for an Ephesian imprisonment (or more than one), during which the "Captivity Epistles" may have been written. It is not unlikely that Philippians was written at this time; in that case Phil. 2:19 must be linked with Acts 19:22; Phil. 2:24 with Acts 20:1. (Colossians, Philemon, and Ephesians are more probably to be assigned to the Roman captivity.)

Paul's statement in Acts 24:17 that he came to bring alms and offerings to his nation is illuminated by the references to the gentile collection for the Jerusalem believers (1 Cor. 16:1ff.; 2 Cor. 8:1–9:15; Rom. 15:25ff.). These references also explain why so many representatives of gentile churches accompanied Paul on his last visit to Jerusalem (cf. Acts 20:4f.); we may reasonably infer that they went as delegates bearing the contributions of their respective churches. In this, as in several other respects, the Epistles and Acts supplement and explain each other.

In short, after such a comparative survey our verdict on Acts may be pronounced in the words of F. C. Burkitt: "But when we come to test it by the Letters of Paul we find it to be historical, not fabulous: it is a real guide to us, even for the earliest period" (*Christian Beginnings* [1924], p. 144).

IX. Chronology of Acts.–The narrative of Acts covers a period of approximately thirty years. Within this period shorter time periods of approximately five years each are marked off by summary notices reporting the advance of the Christian mission (6:7; 9:31; 12:24; 16:5; 19:20; cf. C. J. Cadoux, *JTS*, 19 [1918], 333ff.). But it is not easy on the basis of information supplied by the author himself to fix the chronology of events within the wider periods. Notes of time are not altogether absent from the narrative. Especially in the "we" sections it is observable how a day-to-day record of journeys, particularly journeys by sea, is reproduced (cf. 16:10-13; 20:6–21:27; 27:1–28:17); but such notes give little assistance in the broader issues.

The ascension of Christ is dated forty days after His resurrection (1:3), and the day of Pentecost would have fallen some ten days later (2:1)—"not many days hence" (1:5). But there are no further time indications of any precision until the beginnings of the mission in Antioch, where, after Barnabas has fetched Paul from Tarsus to be his colleague, "for a whole year they were gathered together with the church" (11:26). Paul's residence at Corinth is given as "a year and six months" (18:11); his residence at Ephesus lasted for "three months" plus "the space of two years" (19:8, 10)—a total period later estimated as lasting for "the space of three years" (20:31). His custody in Caesarea lasted for the "two years" of 24:27 (there is no good reason for taking this time note to refer to the duration of Felix' governorship); and after his voyage to Italy, which included an enforced stay of three months in Malta (28:11), he was detained in Rome for a further period of two years.

To a small extent the chronology of Acts can be supplemented from time notes elsewhere in the NT. The reference in Lk. 3:1f. to the inauguration of John the Baptist's ministry "in the fifteenth year of Tiberius Caesar" (i.e., in A.D. 27/28, according to the reckoning current in the territories of the former Seleucid empire) enables us to date the incidents with which Acts commences *ca.* A.D. 30. The "three years" of Gal. 1:18 indicate the interval between Paul's conversion and his visit to Jerusalem in Acts 9:26 more precisely than do the "many days" of Acts 9:23, and the duration of that visit is stated more definitely in Gal. 1:18 ("fifteen days") than in Acts 9:26-30. The "fourteen years" of Gal. 2:1 do not help so much, because of the uncertainty about the relationship of the Jerusalem visit mentioned there to the narrative of Acts, and also because of the uncertainty whether the fourteen years are to be reckoned from Paul's conversion (like the three years of Gal. 1:18) or from the previous Jerusalem visit.

Occasionally a historical allusion in the Epistles shows that there is a gap in the record of Acts; thus we have no account in Acts of the phase of Paul's missionary campaign that brought him at least to the frontier of Illyricum, if not indeed into the province (Rom. 15:19). This must be placed in the interval between Paul's departure from Ephesus and three months' residence in Greece (Acts 20:1-3)—an interval that must have been considerably longer than the narrative of Acts would seem to suggest at first sight.

But the narrative of Acts is full of references to persons and events mentioned in extrabiblical records, which give material help in fixing chronological details. The famine that affected the Roman world, and more particularly Palestine, under Claudius (Acts 11:28) is assigned by Josephus (*Ant.* xx.5.2) to the Judean procuratorship of Tiberius Julius Alexander, i.e., between A.D. 45 and 48. "Herod the king" of Acts 12:1 was the elder Herod Agrippa, who received the royal title from the Emperor Gaius in A.D. 37 and had Judea added to his kingdom by Claudius in A.D. 41; he died in A.D. 44 (Josephus *Ant.* xix.8.2; *BJ* ii.11.6). The implication of Acts 12 is that his death took place not long after Peter's imprisonment and escape. The famine-relief visit of Barnabas and Paul from Antioch to Jerusalem (Acts 11:30; 12:25) is probably to be dated some little time after Herod Agrippa's death.

The edict of Claudius banishing Jews from Rome (Acts 18:2) cannot be dated precisely, but there are good reasons for believing Orosius to be right (even if he was right by accident) in placing it in A.D. 49. This agrees very well with a firmer piece of evidence that indicates that Paul's eighteen months in Corinth (Acts 18:11) fell between A.D. 50 and 52. According to Acts 18:12, Gallio became proconsul of Achaia during Paul's residence in Corinth. A Delphian inscription (W. Dittenberger, *Sylloge Inscriptionum Graecarum,* II [4th ed. 1960], no. 801) recording a proclamation of Claudius between January and August, A.D. 52, indicates that he entered on his proconsulship in July, A.D. 51 (or possibly, but much less probably, July, A.D. 52).

For Paul's Ephesian ministry we have no pointer of comparable precision; the most likely explanation, however, of the strange plural "there are proconsuls" in Acts 19:38 is that it reflects the interregnum in the governorship of the province of Asia which followed the assassination of Junius Silanus late in A.D. 54 (Tacitus *Ann.* xiii.2).

The authorities for the Judean procuratorships of Felix and Festus are unfortunately not so informative on points of chronology as could be wished. However, a change of coinage in the province of Judea in A.D. 59 strongly suggests a change of procurators in that year, and this change could only be the replacement of Felix by Festus (cf. Cadbury, *Book of Acts in History*, p. 10). On other grounds also A.D. 59 is a likely date for this change of procuratorship. Paul's voyage to Rome would therefore have begun in August or September of that year. The "fast" that according to Acts 27:9 was already past when the ship arrived at Fair Havens in Crete, was the Day of Atonement, which in A.D. 59 fell unusually late, on Oct. 5, when navigation would soon cease for the winter in the Mediterranean. After the winter in Malta, Paul and his party would reach Rome early in A.D. 60, and his two years' custody in Rome would run to the end of A.D. 61 or the beginning of A.D. 62.

An approximate chronology for the principal events of Acts before Paul's departure for Rome, in the light of the time indications mentioned above, can now be drawn up as follows:

A.D.	
April-May, 30	Resurrection, Ascension, Pentecost
ca. 33	Conversion of Paul
35	Paul's first postconversion visit to Jerusalem
44	Execution of James son of Zebedee; imprisonment of Peter; death of Herod Agrippa I
46	Famine in Judea; Barnabas and Paul visit Jerusalem
47-48	Barnabas and Paul evangelize Cyprus and Asia Minor
49	Council of Jerusalem
49-50	Paul and Silas visit Philippi, Thessalonica, Beroea, Athens
fall 50–spring 52	Paul in Corinth
July 51–June 52	Gallio proconsul of Achaia
fall 52–summer 55	Paul in Ephesus
summer 55–early 57	Paul in Macedonia and Greece
April, 57	Paul and his company set sail for Jerusalem
57-59	Paul in custody at Caesarea
February, 60	Paul's two years of custody in Rome begin

*X. **Historical Value.***–Unlike the other NT writers. Luke takes pains to place his story in the framework of contemporary world history. He is, for example, the only NT writer to mention a Roman emperor by name. His writing, especially in Acts, is full of references to imperial officials, provincial governors, client kings, etc. A writer who fills his pages with historical references of this kind must do it carefully to avoid inaccuracy. That Luke's casual references to first-century personages are marked by a high degree of accuracy is a further indication that he was contemporary with the events he records.

Luke does in certain obvious ways follow the example set by the great writers of history before his time. For example, Thucydides begins the second book of his *History of the Peloponnesian War* with an elaborate synchronism, in which the incident that starts his narrative proper is dated by reference to a number of dignitaries who held office at the time in the Greek world. Similarly Luke, after treating his prolegomena—the Nativity narratives—in the first two chapters of the Third Gospel, begins ch. 3 with a synchronistic note in the approved style. The preaching of John, as every Christian knew, marked the beginning of the kerygma proper; and Luke wished to fix it in its historical setting. Luke's doing this suggests that he wishes his readers to understand at the outset that this is a serious historical work.

One feature of Luke's reference to contemporary personages that has frequently excited comment is the confident ease with which he regularly gives them their proper titles. Amid the multiplicity of changing official designations in the Roman empire at that time Luke moves with sure familiarity, not so simple a matter as it would be today with ready access to convenient works of reference. Luke knew that at the time with which he deals Cyprus, Achaia, and Asia were senatorial provinces governed by proconsuls (Acts 13:7; 18:12; 19:38); that Philippi, as a Roman colony, was administered by collegiate praetors, who were attended by lictors (16:20ff., 35ff.); that Thessalonica, like other cities of Macedonia, called its chief magistrates politarchs (17:6, 8). He was acquainted with the Areopagus at Athens (17:19, 22, 34); he knew that the leading men of the cities of Asia were called Asiarchs (19:31), that Ephesus enjoyed the honorary title of *Neōkóros* ("temple warden") of Artemis (19:35) and that the town clerk (*grammateús*) occupied an important and responsible place in its municipal administration (19:35ff.). He knew that the chief official in Malta was called the *first man* (28:7).

The accuracy that Luke displays in such details as these extends also to the more general sphere of local color and atmosphere. Luke's Jerusalem, with its excitable and intolerant crowds of Jews, is in marked contrast to the busy emporium of Syrian Antioch, the former Seleucid capital, where men of different creeds and nationalities rub shoulders and have their rough corners worn away, so that we are not surprised to find the first gentile church established there, with Jews and non-Jews meeting in brotherly forbearance and fellowship. His Philippi is a Roman colony with its self-important magistrates and its citizens so proud of being Romans, so much superior to the surrounding Greeks, not to mention wandering Jews like Paul and Silas, who presumed to come among them with their outlandish teaching and stir up trouble. His Athens, with its endless disputations in the marketplace and its thirst for the latest news, is still the same Athens portrayed by classical authors, even if she has come down a little in the world since those earlier days. Stoics and Epicureans have taken the place of Socrates and Plato and Aristotle, but the chief end of man and the supreme good in life are as popular subjects for discussion as ever. Quite different is Luke's picture of Ephesus, with its temple of Artemis, one of the seven wonders of the ancient world, and so many of the citizens making their living one way or another from the cult of the great goddess; with its reputation for superstition and magic, which was so widespread in antiquity that "Ephesian writings" was a common name for magic scrolls inscribed with charms and spells. The description of the voyage to Italy in ch. 27 is so accurate in its vivid detail that it was justly described by H. J. Holtzmann as "one of the most instructive documents for our knowledge of ancient seamanship" (*Hand-Commentar zum NT* [1889], p. 421).

Luke reveals unmistakably the natural accuracy of his observant mind to such an extent that even where his statements appear to conflict with evidence from other quarters one would require very conclusive proof before deciding that Luke is wrong. In other words, judged by the standards applied to ancient narrators in general, Luke establishes his right to be regarded as a good and independent witness.

A writer may indeed have an accurate habit of mind and yet produce a work that is not uniformly accurate, because of the inequality of his sources or because he is more familiar with one field of which he treats than with another. But even in those sections of Acts where Luke relies on information received from others (dealing, e.g., with Palestinian matters), he suffers no disadvantage when compared with such an author as Josephus.

Yet, accuracy alone does not make a man a historian. An accurate narrator might be a mere chronicler, faithfully recording facts as they occurred and cramming his record with detail, without showing any appreciation of the dominating themes of his subject matter or any grasp of the chain of cause and effect in the events related. But Luke knows what he wants to do; the progress of the gospel along the road that leads to Rome is his chief theme, and the arrangement of his material is subordinated to his main purpose. The first five chapters contain scenes from the life of the infant church in Jerusalem, excellently chosen so as to give us a picture of its ups and downs, leading on to the increasing prominence of its Hellenist members, the career and martyrdom of Stephen, the consequent persecution and dispersal, the conversion of Paul, and the evangelization of the Gentiles. Thus the way is prepared for the Pauline mission, to which most of the second half of Acts is devoted.

In both his volumes, as noted, Luke confines himself within the limits of a papyrus roll of normal length. These material conditions imposed the necessity for selecting what to include and what to omit. Luke makes his selection in such a way as to promote his prime purpose; but in view of the limited space at his disposal, his repetitions are the more striking. When he gives a threefold account of Paul's conversion (chs. 9, 22, and 26), when he uses so much repetition in the story of Peter's preaching to Cornelius (ch. 10; 11:1-17; 15:7ff.), when he quotes the terms of the apostolic decree three times (15:20, 29; 21:25), it is immediately obvious that these are matters to which he attaches special importance.

Ramsay's verdict on Luke's title to be called a true historian, over and above his characteristic accuracy, is unqualified in its appreciation. Luke, he maintained, "should be placed along with the very greatest of historians" (*Bearing of Recent Discovery on the Trustworthiness of the NT* [1915], p. 222). A more modest appraisal of Luke's achievement is made by W. L. Knox: "There is no reason to doubt Luke's veracity within the limits which he sets himself; he is not a great historian or biographer by modern standards; but by the standards of his age he has given a fresh and interesting account of the vital part of Paul's missionary career, which has preserved on the whole an accurate account of the development of Christianity" (p. 61).

It is in any case unreasonable to judge an ancient author by modern standards. Knox emphasizes this himself: "It is only within the limits of what he set out to do," he says, "that Luke can fairly be criticized" (p. 56); therefore, for instance, "it is unfair to blame him for failing to mention matters about which we need information when we try to write commentaries on the Epistles to the Corinthians" (p. 61); and though we today should have liked to be told something about the progress of Christianity at Rome before Paul's arrival there, "Luke would see no point in mentioning what many of his readers knew already, while the rest could easily find out if they were curious" (p. 58).

We should certainly have been glad if Luke had given us more detailed chronological information. In the earlier part of Acts we miss such information particularly; thus commentators vary from one year to six years in their estimate of the interval that separates the ascension of Christ from the conversion of Paul. In the latter part, time notes are more frequent, and this suggests that their absence from the earlier part is due to their absence in Luke's sources of information. All ancient historians present us with chronological problems, largely because of the lack of a fixed system of reckoning dates; and this lack constitutes a limitation from the modern reader's point of view. Among other limitations mentioned by W. L. Knox is Luke's method of fitting his sources together (this, however, causes more trouble to the modern source critic than to the first-century reader for whom Luke wrote). But, while Knox disagrees with Ramsay in the matter of appraising Luke's right to be called a serious historian, he is in general agreement with him regarding Luke's honesty, trustworthiness, and success in achieving his aim in writing.

But in the opinion of certain others all this is beside the point, because Luke includes miraculous incidents in his narrative, and records them not simply (as Herodotus did) because they are good stories and worth repeating for their own sake, but because he plainly believes that they really happened. If a reader believes that miracles do not happen, then all other arguments in favor of Luke's trustworthiness must be discounted. Even if an exception must be made in favor of the miracles that he ascribes to Jesus in the first volume of his work, why should such an exception be extended to the miracles ascribed to the apostles in the second volume?

It is not enough to say that in that age all people who thought about such matters (not to mention the masses who took them for granted) believed in miracles, apart from Epicureans and Skeptics. After all, Thucydides carefully excluded miracles from his history over four hundred years before Luke, though he admitted that their absence would detract from the popularity of his work. If Thucydides did so, why not Luke? Did Luke imagine that the inclusion of miracles would promote the apologetic purpose of his work in the intelligent reading circles of Rome?

The fact is that miracles did take place in those early Christian circles. When Paul appeals to the mighty works that had been wrought among his Galatian converts (Gal. 3:5), he knows that the Galatians cannot reply that such things have never taken place. When he tells the Roman Christians that his apostolic office is confirmed by the things that Christ has accomplished through him "for the obedience of the Gentiles . . . in the power of signs and wonders" (Rom. 15:18f.), he is certainly not making a claim that he knows any eyewitness could disprove.

Furthermore, Luke is no mere swallower of the miraculous. The miracles he narrates are not miracles and nothing more: they are "signs" as well as "wonders"; they are "mighty works" giving evidence of the arrival of the new age; they are manifestations of the power of God at work among men, and an integral element in the gospel message. When the kingdom of God drew near to men in Christ, its advent was signalized by extraordinary happenings of the very kind that the prophets had foretold in that connection (cf. Lk. 7:22; 11:20). The miracle stories of Acts have the same character as those of the Gospels. Jesus is still the agent; before His departure He acted on earth, and now He acts from Heaven. It is in His name that the mighty works recorded in Acts are performed. We need think no less of Luke's historical faithfulness because he records such signs as these.

XI. Purpose.–The purpose Luke had in view is stated in the prologue to his twofold work from which we have already learned that his main concern was that Theophilus, who had already received some information about Christianity, should have a thoroughly reliable account of the relevant facts.

An examination of Luke's actual work may tell us something more about his purpose in writing. One of the most striking features that emerge from such an examination is the marked apologetic element. Luke is concerned to defend Christianity in general—and, it would appear, Paul in particular—against the accusations urged by various opponents. This he does largely by showing how responsible authorities throughout the Roman world agree that Christianity does not contravene imperial law and that those who proclaim it are innocent of any criminal action or intention. As in the "former treatise" Pontius Pilate, Roman procurator of Judea, and Herod Antipas, tetrarch of Galilee, find no substance in the charges preferred against Jesus by the Sanhedrin, so in Acts a variety of officials, gentile and Jewish, show good will toward the Christian missionaries, or admit that there is no basis for the accusations brought against them by their opponents. At Philippi the praetors have to apologize to Paul and Silas for subjecting them to illegal beating and imprisonment (Acts 16:37ff.). At Corinth the proconsul of Achaia, Gallio, decrees that the offenses with which the local Jewish community charge Paul and his companions relate to internal Jewish concerns and not to matters of which Roman law need take cognizance (18:12ff.). In Ephesus the Asiarchs, leading citizens of the province of Asia, are Paul's friends, and the town clerk declares his innocence (19:31, 37f.). In Palestine the procurators Felix and Festus find no ground for the Sanhedrin's accusation of Paul, and the Jewish client-king Herod Agrippa II and his sister Bernice agree that he has done nothing deserving imprisonment or death (24:1–26:32). In fact, the Sanhedrin is the accuser both of Jesus and of Paul (supported in Paul's case by a number of Jewish communities of the Dispersion); but the representatives of Roman law make favorable pronouncements in both cases.

When we look for an appropriate life-setting for a work that strikes the apologetic note in just this way, we might think of a time when the Sanhedrin, the chief accuser of Christianity, had discredited itself finally as it did with the outbreak of the Jewish revolt of A.D. 66. A Christian apologist at this time might well seize the opportunity to dissociate Christianity from Judaism in the public mind (cf. T. W. Manson, p. 62). The difficulty about that is that the position of Christianity in the Roman empire had already taken a turn for the worse with the events at Rome itself in A.D. 64, and the precedent established by Nero's persecution. To relate decisions of imperial officials before 64 might well appear irrelevant when everybody knew the complete reversal of those decisions that had taken place in that year. It is just possible that Luke wished to trace the course of Christianity up to the eve of the Neronian persecution to show that it was not such a shamefully criminal movement as was popularly believed. As late as 112, as well informed a Roman citizen as Tacitus could write of primitive Christianity: "The Christians got their name from one Christus, who was executed by the sentence of the procurator Pontius Pilate when Tiberius was emperor; and the pernicious superstition was checked for a short time, only to break out afresh—not only in Judaea, the home of the plague, but in Rome itself, where all the horrible and shameful things in the world collect and find a home" (*Ann.* xv.44).

Luke is not replying directly to Tacitus; but Tacitus was obviously not the first Roman to cherish this illusion about Christian beginnings. It is quite reasonable to suppose that Luke's intention was to provide intelligent Roman readers, like Theophilus, with a reliable account of the progress of Christianity before A.D. 64, to counteract the caricature that was widely held to be the truth of the matter.

If we are right in thinking that Luke wrote his history before the Neronian persecution began in 64, then we are faced with an attractive life-setting for the work. Paul, the outstanding Christian leader in the Roman world, had come to Rome early in A.D. 60, having appealed to the emperor from a provincial court. A number of people in influential quarters at Rome would know about him and his impending trial. It was important that they should be accurately informed. We need not go so far as those who have concluded that Luke's history (or at least book two) was written to supply the information required for Paul's defense before the imperial tribunal—written, in fact, to brief Theophilus, who was to act as counsel for the defense. There is too much in Acts that would be irrelevant for such a purpose, though either the book itself, or some of the notes used in its composition, may have been put in as one of the documents in the case. It is more likely that Luke seized the opportunity afforded by the circumstances of his visit to Rome to provide the intelligent reading public (or listening public) of the imperial city with an account that rebutted the common objections to Christianity by insisting on its complete and admitted innocence in the eyes of Roman law.

But Theophilus and other members of the intelligent reading public at Rome might say: Granted that Paul and other Christian messengers have been frequently not guilty of offenses against Roman law; how is it that they have been accused of such offenses so often, and how is it that there has been so much trouble and rioting wherever they have gone? On a few occasions, Luke pointed out, trouble had arisen because Christianity was felt to endanger certain financial interests, whether on a smaller scale, as with the fortune-telling slave girl's owners at Philippi (Acts 16:19), or on a larger scale, as with the guild of silversmiths at Ephesus (19:24ff.). But the chief cause of the trouble that dogged the footsteps of Paul and his companions was the opposition of the Jewish communities. This opposition is one of the secondary motifs of Acts; while the book records the progress of the gospel along the road from Jerusalem to Rome and its acceptance by pagans, it records at the same time the rejection of the gospel by the bulk of the Jewish communities of the Dispersion, until at last in Rome Paul assures the Jews of that city, in words such as he had already used in other cities, "This salvation is sent unto the Gentiles: they will also hear" (Acts 28:28).

One of the features in Acts that would have been irrelevant for exclusively apologetic purposes is Luke's interest in the Holy Spirit's activity in the Church. When he describes his "former treatise" as "concerning all that Jesus began both to do and to teach, until the day in which he was received up" (Acts 1:1f.), he probably does not use the verb "began" as a redundant auxiliary (in accordance with Aramaic idiom), but rather lays some stress on it, implying that the second volume will relate what Jesus continued to do and teach after His ascension—by His Spirit in the apostles. The second volume might therefore be entitled "The Acts of the Ascended Lord" or "The Acts of the Holy Spirit."

At the beginning of the volume the promise of the Spirit is given by Jesus (1:4, 8), and this promise is fulfilled in ch. 2 for the people of Israel and in ch. 10 for the Gentiles. The apostles proclaim their message in the power of the Spirit, a power that is manifested by supernatural signs; the converts' acceptance of the message is similarly attended by visible and audible manifestations of the

Spirit's activity. The Holy Spirit controls the whole expansion of Christianity narrated in Acts; He guides the messengers, such as Philip (8:29, 39) and Peter (10:19); He directs the Antiochian church to set Barnabas and Paul apart for the service to which He has called them (13:2); He directs them from place to place, forbidding them to preach in Asia or enter Bithynia, but giving them clear indication that they must cross the Aegean to Europe (16:6ff.); He receives prior mention as authority for the letter sent by the Jerusalem council to the churches of Syria and Cilicia (15:28, "it seemed good to the Holy Spirit, and to us"). He speaks through prophets, foretelling for example the famine in the reign of Claudius and Paul's imprisonment at Jerusalem (11:28; 21:11), just as He spoke through the prophets of OT days (1:16; 28:25). It is He primarily who appoints the elders of a church to be its superintendents (20:28). He can be lied to (5:3), tempted (5:9), and resisted (7:51). He bears witness to the truth of the gospel (5:32). The whole progress of the gospel from Jerusalem to Rome is guided by the Holy Spirit; in all the book there is nothing that is unrelated to His direction.

Luke, as we might expect, is greatly interested in the evangelization of Gentiles. This may be why, in spite of his limited space, he lays such repetitive emphasis on the story of Cornelius' conversion. The widening of the circle of those who receive the good news is marked in successive stages: while the followers of Jesus to begin with consist almost entirely of "Hebrews" (Palestine-born and Aramaic-speaking Jews), the events of the day of Pentecost bring a large accession of Hellenists (Greek-speaking Jews of the Dispersion), and these play an increasingly prominent part in the Church. It is one of these Hellenists—Philip—who takes the initiative in carrying the gospel to the schismatic Samaritans, and who later baptizes an Ethiopian. Soon afterward Peter evangelizes the semi-gentile localities of the western Palestinian coastland, and while engaged in this activity he is called to make the decisive breach with tradition and take the Christian message to the house of the gentile Cornelius at Caesarea. Not long after, a gentile mission on a wider scale is inaugurated at Antioch by Hellenistic Christians who left Jerusalem through the persecution that followed Stephen's martyrdom. The result is that the church of Antioch—the second Christian church whose inception Luke relates—is predominantly gentile from the start. And from that point onward it is mainly on the evangelization of Gentiles that Luke concentrates.

But this evangelization of Gentiles carried with it the problem of Christian liberty, in which also Luke naturally finds great interest. Were Gentiles who believed in Christ to be accepted as full members of the believing community on that ground alone, or should they be required to submit to circumcision and generally conform to the Jewish ceremonial law? It is Luke's interest in this question, and his appreciation of its importance for the expansion of Christianity, that leads him to give the Council of Jerusalem the central place that it occupies in Acts.

Luke cannot disguise that Paul is his hero. He may not have written Acts for the special purpose of establishing the reality of Paul's apostleship, but Acts does serve this purpose admirably. Yet Luke makes it plain that Paul was not the only effective apostle; in particular, a list of quite striking parallels can be drawn up between the "Acts of Peter" and the "Acts of Paul" in Luke's second volume. The parallel incidents, however, were not invented by Luke; they were selected by him, in accordance with his aim, from the mass of information at his disposal.

There is less tendency nowadays to suppose that this parallelism is a mark of the author's plan to reconcile the originally hostile Petrine and Pauline parties within the Church. It is more likely that Luke's purpose in arranging his material thus was to demonstrate either that Peter was as much an apostle as Paul or that Paul was as much an apostle as Peter. If John Knox is right in viewing Acts as a product of the anti-Marcionite reaction, then we might prefer the former of these two alternatives. But, apart from our grounds for regarding Acts as a first-century work, with the consequent implications for this question we are considering, the much greater weight that Luke lays on the "Acts of Paul" than on the "Acts of Peter" does suggest that he is more concerned with Paul's apostolic claims than with Peter's—which no Christian doubted before the time of Marcion. And even after Marcion's time, Acts was valued more for its establishment of Paul's apostleship than of Peter's, as we may see from Tertullian's remark about those heretics (presumably the Marcionites in particular) who rejected Acts and yet appealed so regularly and confidently to the authority of Paul: "You must first of all show us who this Paul was—what he was before he became an apostle, and how he became an apostle" (*De praescr. haer.* 23) — and this, of course, they found difficulty in doing without reference to Acts.

XII. Analytical Outline.

I. Birth of the Church (1:1–5:42)
  A. Introduction: Ascension of Jesus and Election of Matthias to the Apostolate (1:1-26)
  B. Day of Pentecost: Descent of the Spirit (2:1-47)
  C. A Miracle and Its Sequel: Apostles Charged Before the Sanhedrin (3:1–4:31)
  D. All Things in Common: Barnabas and Ananias (4:32–5:11)
  E. Apostles Charged Before the Sanhedrin a Second Time (5:12-42)

II. Persecution Leads to Expansion (6:1–9:31)
  A. Ministry and Martyrdom of Stephen (6:1–8:1a)
  B. Philip's Missionary Activity (8:1b-40)
  C. Conversion of Saul of Tarsus (9:1-31)

III. Acts of Peter: Gentiles Receive the Gospel (9:32–12:25)
  A. Peter in Western Palestine (9:32-43)
  B. The Gentile Cornelius Converted (10:1-48)
  C. Peter's Defense of His Action (11:1-18)
  D. Gentile-Christian Church of Antioch (11:19-30)
  E. Herod Agrippa's Attack on the Church (12:1-25)

IV. Paul's First Missionary Journey (13:1–14:28)
  A. Barnabas and Paul Called to Evangelize Farther Afield (13:1-3)
  B. Visit to Cyprus (13:4-12)
  C. Crossing to the Mainland and Preaching in Pisidian Antioch (13:13-52)
  D. Evangelization of Iconium, Lystra, and Derbe (14:1-28)

V. Council of Jerusalem (15:1-35)
  A. Judaizing Agitation at Antioch (15:1-5)
  B. Meeting of the Council (15:6-29)
  C. Apostolic Letter Received at Antioch (15:30-35)

VI. Paul's Second Missionary Journey (15:36–18:23)
  A. Separation of Barnabas and Paul (15:36-41)
  B. Paul and Silas in South Galatia (16:1-5)
  C. Crossing to Macedonia: Evangelization of Philippi (16:6-40)
  D. Thessalonica to Athens (17:1-34)
  E. Evangelization of Corinth (18:1-17)
  F. Paul's Visit to Jerusalem (18:18-23)

VII. Paul's Third Missionary Journey (18:24–21:17)
  A. Apollos at Ephesus and Corinth (18:24-28)
  B. Paul at Ephesus (19:1-41)

C. Paul's Visit to Macedonia and Greece (20:1-6)
D. Paul's Voyage to Jerusalem (20:7–21:17)

VIII. Paul's Arrest in Jerusalem and Arrival at Rome (21:18–28:31)
A. Paul in Jerusalem (21:18–23:30)
B. Paul in Caesarea: Appearances Before Felix and Festus and Defense Before Agrippa (23:31–26:32)
C. Paul's Mediterranean Voyage and Shipwreck (27:1-44)
D. Paul's Winter in Malta (28:1-10)
E. Paul in Rome (28:11-31)

See MAPS XVIII, XIX, XX.

Bibliography.–Comms. by J. V. Bartlet (*Century Bible,* 1902); O. Bauernfeind (*ThHK,* 1939); H. W. Beyer (*NTD,* 1932); E. M. Blaiklock (*Tyndale,* 1959); F. F. Bruce (Gk. text, 2nd ed. 1952; Eng. text, *NIC,* 1954); C. W. Carter and R. Earle (*Evangelical Comm.,* 1959); H. Conzelmann (*HNT,* 1963); F. J. F. Jackson (*MNTC,* 1932); E. Haenchen (*KEK,* 14th ed. 1965; Eng. tr. 1971); E. Jacquier (*EtB,* 1926); R. J. Knowling (*Expos.G.T.,* 1900); K. Lake and H. J. Cadbury (*BC,* IV [1933]); A. Loisy (1920); G. H. C. Macgregor (*IB,* IX); T. E. Page (1886); R. B. Rackham (*WC,* 1902); A. Schlatter (1902); A. Wikenhauser (2nd ed. 1951); C. S. C. Williams (*HNTC,* 1957); T. Zahn (*KZNT,* 1919-1921).

C. K. Barrett, *Luke the Historian in Recent Study* (1961); J. V. Bartlet, *Apostolic Age* (1902); M. Black, *An Aramaic Approach to the Gospels and Acts* (3rd ed. 1967); S. G. F. Brandon, *Fall of Jerusalem and the Christian Church* (2nd ed. 1957); H. J. Cadbury, *Style and Literary Method of Luke* (1920); *Making of Luke-Acts* (1927); *Book of Acts in History* (1955); G. B. Caird, *Apostolic Age* (1955); L. Cerfaux, *La Communauté apostolique* (1943); A. C. Clark, *Acts of the Apostles* (text-critical ed., 1933); H. Conzelmann, *Theology of Luke* (Eng. tr. 1960); O. Cullmann, *Early Church* (1956); M. Dibelius, *Studies in the Acts of the Apostles* (Eng. tr. 1956); E. Dobschütz, *Apostolic Age* (Eng. tr. 1909); C. H. Dodd, *Apostolic Preaching and Its Developments* (1936); J. Dupont, *Sources of Acts* (Eng. tr. 1962); *Études sur les Actes des Apôtres* (1967); B. S. Easton, *Early Christianity* (1954); W. W. Gasque, *History of the Criticism of the Acts of the Apostles* (1975); A. Harnack, *Luke the Physician* (Eng. tr. 1907); *Acts of the Apostles* (Eng. tr. 1909); *Date of the Acts and of the Synoptic Gospels* (Eng. tr. 1911); W. K. Hobart, *Medical Language of St. Luke* (1882); F. J. F. Jackson and K. Lake, eds., *BC,* I-V (1920-1933); L. E. Keck and J. L. Martyn, eds., *Studies in Luke-Acts* (1966); J. Knox, *Marcion and the NT* (1942); *Chapters in a Life of Paul* (1950); W. L. Knox, *Acts of the Apostles* (1948); T. W. Manson, *Studies in the Gospels and Epistles* (1962); A. C. McGiffert, *History of Christianity in the Apostolic Age* (1897); J. C. O'Neill, *Theology of Acts* (2nd ed. 1970); G. T. Purves, *Christianity in the Apostolic Age* (1900); *SPT*; B. Reicke, *Glaube und Leben der Urgemeinde* (1957); J. H. Ropes, *Apostolic Age in the Light of Modern Criticism* (1906); *Text of Acts* (*BC,* III [1926]); H. J. Schoeps, *Theologie und Geschichte des Judenchristentums* (1949); *Aus frühchristlicher Zeit* (1950); M. Simon, *St. Stephen and the Hellenists in the Primitive Church* (1958); J. Smith, *Voyage and Shipwreck of St. Paul* (4th ed. 1880); C. C. Torrey, *Composition and the Date of Acts* (1916); E. Trocmé, *Le "Livre des Actes" et l'histoire* (1957); J. Weiss, *Earliest Christianity* (1959); C. S. C. Williams, *Alterations to the Text of the Synoptic Gospels and Acts* (1951); S. G. Wilson, *Gentiles and the Gentile Mission in Luke-Acts* (1973); T. Zahn, *Urausgabe der Apostelgeschichte des Lucas* (1916).

F. F. BRUCE

ACUA ə-kū'ə (Esd. 5:30, AV). *See* AKKUB **3.**

ACUB ā'kub (1 Esd. 5:31, AV). *See* BAKBUK.

ACUD ā'kud (1 Esd. 5:30, NEB). *See* AKKUB **3.**

ADADAH ə-dā'də [Heb. *'aḏ'āḏâ*]; NEB ARARAH. A town in the southern part of Judah near the border of Edom (Josh. 15:22). In the LXX the passage reads (Gk.) *Arouēl,* and many scholars emend the MT to read (Heb.) *'ar'ārâ,* identifying the site as in the NEB, or as Aroer (cf. 1 S. 30:28), about 12 mi. (19 km.) SE of Beer-sheba. (Confusion of *daleth* and *resh* is often found in the OT due to the similarity of the letters, both in the old orthography and in the later "Aramaic" writing.) W. S. L. S.

ADADRIMMON ā-dad-rim'ən. *See* HADADRIMMON.

ADAH ā'də [Heb. *'āḏâ*–'adornment'].

1. One of the two wives of Lamech the descendant of Cain (Gen. 4:19f., 23); the mother of Jabal and Jubal. Josephus says that Lamech had seventy-seven sons by Ada and Zillah (*Ant.* i.2.2).

2. The Hittite wife of Esau; the daughter of Elon and mother of Eliphaz (Gen. 36:2ff.).

ADAIAH ə-dā'yə, ə-dī'ə [Heb. *'ᵃḏāyâ*–'Yahweh has adorned'].

1. Apparently the seventh of the nine sons of Shimei, presumably the same as Shema, who is the fifth of the sons of Elpaal, who is the second of the two sons of Shaharaim and Hushim (1 Ch. 8:21). Shaharaim and his descendants are listed with the descendants of Benjamin, though his relation to Benjamin is not stated.

2. A Levite; ancestor to David's singer Asaph, and a descendant of the fifth generation from Gershom (1 Ch. 6:41).

3. The father of Maaseiah, who was one of the captains of hundreds associated with Jehoiada the priest in making Joash king (2 Ch. 23:1).

4. A resident of Bozkath, and father of Jedidah the mother of King Josiah (2 K. 22:1).

5. A descendant of Judah through Perez. His great-great-grandson Maaseiah resided in Jerusalem after Nehemiah had rehabilitated the city (Neh. 11:5).

6, 7. Two men who married foreign wives in the period of Ezra (Ezr. 10:29, 39; 1 Esd. 9:30; AV Apoc. JEDEUS, NEB Apoc. JEDAEUS [Gk. *Iedaíos*]).

8. One of the priests of the latest OT times, mentioned with a partial genealogy (Neh. 11:12; 1 Ch. 9:12).

W. J. BEECHER

ADALIA ə-da'li-ə, a-də-lī'a [Heb. *'ᵃḏalyā'*–prob. Pers., meaning unknown]. One of the ten sons of Haman who were put to death by the Jews (Est. 9:8).

ADAM ad'əm [Heb. *'āḏām*; Gk. *Adam*]. The first man.

IN THE OT AND APOCRYPHA

I. Usage.–The Hebrew word occurs some 560 times in the OT with the meaning "man," "mankind." Outside Gen. 1–5 the only case where it is unquestionably a proper name is 1 Ch. 1:1. Ambiguous are Dt. 32:8; Job 31:33; Hos. 6:7. In Gen. 1 the term occurs only twice (vv. 26f.). In Gen. 2–4 it is found 26 times, and it also occurs in 5:1, 3-5. In the last four cases, and also in 4:25, it is obviously intended as a proper name; but the versions show much uncertainty in the other instances. Some exegetes alter the Masoretic pointing at 2:20; 3:17, 21, thus introducing a definite article and reading uniformly "the man" up to 4:25, where the absence of the article indicates the identity of "the man" with the Adam at the head of the genealogy in 5:1. Several conjectures have been put forth as to the root meaning of the word ("creature," "earthborn," "ruddy one," "pleasant," etc.), but some of these are highly improbable and there can be no final certainty in the matter.

II. In Genesis Stories.–The only occurrences in Gen. 1, as noted, are in vv. 26f.; and here the question has arisen whether the reference is to the creation of man, the human species, or to the creation specifically of the first man and the first woman, Adam and Eve. In favor of the first view, all the similar previous references—to the stars, plants, fish, and animals—are general. On the other hand, this proves a little too much, for they are so general that there is no mention of species. To some the mention of "male and female" would also seem to indicate the first couple, for there is no reference to a similar distinction in the case of animals, and the generic man could cover both sexes if this were merely a general reference.

In Gen. 2–3 there is perhaps some confusion between "man" and "Adam" as suitable renderings at individual points, but the narratives as a whole leave little room for doubt that the reference is always to a single man ("the man" or "Adam"), and later to a single woman. In these stories a little more light is shed on the creation of man, on his relation to the world over which he was to have dominion, and on his transgression and fall. Man is created from the dust of the earth and becomes a living creature by the breath of God. Placed in the garden to keep it, he gives names to the animals (over whom he has dominion, according to 1:27); and woman is formed from him to be his counterpart and helper. At woman's behest he eats with her of the forbidden fruit, and they are driven from the garden and condemned to toil and sorrow and eventual inevitable death. Adam becomes the father of Cain and Abel, and of Seth after the murder of Abel.

After Gen. 5 there are almost no plain references to Adam until the Apocrypha (cf. 2 Esd. 3:4-7, 10, 21, 26; 4:30; 6:54-56; 7:11, 46-48; Tob. 8:6; Wisd. 2:23f.; 9:2f.; 10:1f.; Sir. 15:14; 17:1-4; 25:24; 40:1; 49:16). Sir. 40:1 refers to the heavy yoke upon the sons of Adam, though it is by no means clear that this refers to the weight of original sin incurred by Adam's fall. The Wisdom of Solomon speaks more explicitly of death coming on men through Adam's sin, while 2 Esdras has a developed doctrine of original sin. In 4:30 we read that "a grain of evil seed was sown in Adam's heart from the beginning," and 7:48 carries the indictment: "O Adam, what have you done? for though it was you who sinned, the fall was not yours alone, but ours also who are your descendants."

III. Genre of Stories.–The meaning of the term "Adam" is closely linked with the interpretation of the Genesis stories. If it is assumed that the word bears a generic sense, one suggestion is that this is not a literal history but a very general account of the early development of the race. This may be in the form of a myth in which man and woman are personified as Adam and Eve, and general truths concerning man's origin, nature, and destiny are conveyed. Or it may be in the form of a poetic narrative of events that really happened, but not in this specific form (the *Sage* of Barth). In support of such interpretations it is pointed out that Eden is not an identifiable geographical locality even though known rivers are associated with it. In other words, an obviously imaginative element is combined with a certain factuality. The alternative is to treat the narratives as literal history in the strict sense, though here, too, a question arises as to the degree of literalness. For example, does the serpent actually use a human language and utter sounds which can be heard with the ears and which are identifiable as human speech? Or again, is there literally a tree whose fruit conveys the knowledge of good and evil? One thing that can be asserted quite firmly is that the stories are hardly intended as myth. But the nature of the factuality will always give rise to discussion.

IV. Nature of Adam–Another problem that arises is that of the nature of Adam (or man) as first created. The general consensus has been that he is perfect man in full possession of all human faculties, in perfect harmony of body and soul, and in a right relation to God, to woman, to himself, and to the natural world around him. This seems to be clearly enough suggested by the stories themselves, especially Gen. 2. In the Middle Ages, however, another view established itself. This makes of Adam a superman endowed not only with natural faculties but also with supernatural graces that secure his natural perfection. At the fall these graces are forfeited and the natural qualities, though they remain, are impaired in their operation.

More recently the philosophy of progress and an evolutionary understanding of the world have introduced a wholly different line of interpretation. At the first, Adam (or man) is at a very primitive level, hardly different from the brutes. The fall is virtually a fall upward. It is the step to self-awareness, to historical life, to ethical freedom and responsibility. In other words, the fall is the beginning of real humanity, of historical life in the true sense as compared with the prior period of hardly more than natural or animal life. It involves serious hazards, for man may obviously abuse his new power. But it is still to be regarded as a progressive step. To know good and evil carries the risk of doing evil. But it is better than to do good without knowledge. The story of the race is the story of movement from childlike or animal innocence to responsible choice, and finally, by a long process of advance, to choice of the good.

When we survey the various possibilities, it is easily seen that both the idea of supernatural endowment and that of an upward fall are fanciful, finding no real support in the narratives themselves. Conditions in Eden are idyllic, but there seems to be no suggestion that man needs an additional factor for this to be possible. On the other hand, the idea that man is virtually no more than subhuman is quite alien to the account of his creation; and the fall comes under the severest possible condemnation, not as the abuse of an upward movement, and certainly not as a Promethean attack upon God, but as a very real violation of the divine order. If the Bible can finally regard the fault as a happy one, it is only because God Himself redeems the situation by His own mighty intervention, not because it opens up a world of new possibilities for man.

V. Adam and the Race.–It may be noted that the OT does not develop any doctrine of a universal fall or of original sin. On the other hand, the very fact that Adam is a general as well as a personal name makes it impossible to dismiss the story merely as an individual or even typical account. Moreover, the condemnation is passed not just on Adam and Eve but on their successors as well. All subsequent men are involved here. This is recognized in the OT itself, for the story of one man's sin quickly becomes the story of all men's sin. Indeed, all the interpretations accept this. The deprivation of supernatural graces applies to all men, except insofar as these graces are supposedly restored in baptism. The upward step to historical awareness or ethical responsibility is one that has not been and cannot be reversed, except in a few who do not have full possession of what are now universally acknowledged to be the characteristic human capacities. The perfection of humanity has been lost, not by Adam alone, but by all his descendants, Jesus Christ apart. Even Pelagianism cannot fly wholly in the face of the fact that all men do sin, and that they do so from a very early stage. It is thus forced into the despairing hypothesis of a series of individual repetitions of Adam's sin. This means that in its own way it postulates the solidarity of Adam with the race and of the race with Adam.

The truth of the solidarity of Adam and the race is what is brought out with such force in the NT when Paul compares and contrasts the new solidarity of the race in the second Adam with the old solidarity of sin and guilt in the first (Rom. 5:12-21). G. W. BROMILEY

In the NT

The name Adam occurs nine times (in five different

passages) in the NT, though several of these are purely incidental.

I. Gospels.–In Lk. 3:38 the ancestry of Jesus Christ is traced back to "Adam, the son of God," thereby testifying to the acceptance of the OT genealogies of Genesis. This is the only place in the Gospels where Adam is actually named, though there is an allusion to him in Mt. 19:4-6 (=Mk. 10:6-8), referring to Gen. 1:27 and 2:24.

II. Epistles.–In Rom. 5:12-21 Adam is designated by Paul as the founder of the race and the cause of the introduction of sin, in order to point the comparison and contrast with Christ as the head of the new race and the cause of righteousness. The passage is the logical center of the Epistle, the central point to which everything that precedes has converged, and out of which everything that follows will flow. The great ideas of sin, death, and judgment are here shown to be involved in the connection of the human race with Adam. But over against this there is the blessed fact of union with Christ, and in this union righteousness and life.

Mankind is ranged under two heads, Adam and Christ. There are two men, two acts, and two results. In this teaching we have the spiritual and theological illustration of the great modern principle of solidarity. There is a solidarity of evil and a solidarity of good, but the latter far surpasses the former in the quality of the obedience of Christ as compared with Adam, and in the fact of the work of Christ for justification and life. The passage is thus no mere episode or illustration, but gives organic life to the entire Epistle. Although sin and death are ours in Adam, righteousness and life are ours in Christ, and these latter two are infinitely the greater (v. 11); whatever we have lost in Adam we have more than gained in Christ. As all the evils of the race sprang from one man, so all the blessings of redemption come from one Person, and there is such a connection between the Person and the race that all men can possess what the One has done.

In vv. 12-19 Paul makes a series of comparisons and contrasts between Adam and Christ; the two persons, the two works, and the two consequences. The fulness of the apostle's meaning must be carefully observed. Not only does he teach that what we have derived from the first Adam is met by what is derived from Christ, but the transcendence of the work of the latter is regarded as almost infinite in extent. "The full meaning of Paul, however, is not grasped until we perceive that the benefits received from Christ, the Second Adam, are in *inverse ratio* to the disaster entailed by the first Adam. It is the *surplusage* of this grace that in Paul's presentation is commonly overlooked" (H. C. Mabie, *Divine Reason of the Cross* [1911], p. 116).

The contrast instituted in 1 Cor. 15:22 between Adam and Christ refers to death and life, but great difficulty turns on the interpretation of the two "alls"—"As in Adam all die, so also in Christ shall all be made alive." Dods interprets it of Adam as the source of physical life that ends in death, and of Christ as the source of spiritual life that never dies: "All who are by physical derivation truly united to Adam incur the death, which by sinning he introduced into human experience; and similarly, all who by spiritual affinity are in Christ enjoy the new life which triumphs over death, and which he won" (*Expos. B.*, p. 366). So also T. C. Edwards, who does not consider that there is any real unfairness in interpreting the former "all" as more extensive than the latter, "if we bear in mind that the conditions of entrance into the one class and the other are totally different. . . . We have them in Rom. 5:5-11, where the apostle seems as if he anticipated this objection to the analogy which he instituted between Adam and Christ. Both alike are heads of humanity, but they are unlike in this (as also in other things, Rom. 5:15), that men are in Adam by nature, in Christ by faith" (comm. on 1 Corinthians [1897], p. 412). Godet considers that "perhaps this interpretation is really that which corresponds best to the apostle's view," and he shows that Gk. *zōopoieísthai*, "be made alive," is a more limited idea than *egeíresthai,* "be raised," the limitation of the subject thus naturally proceeding from the special meaning of the verb itself. "The two *pántes* (all) embrace those only to whom each of the two powers extends." But Godet favors the view of Meyer and Ellicott that "all" is to be given the same interpretation in each clause, and that the reference is to all who are to rise, whether for life or condemnation, and that this is to be "in Christ": "Christ will quicken all; all will hear His voice and will come forth from the grave, but not all to the true 'resurrection of life': see Jn. 5:29" (C. J. Ellicott, comm. on 1 Corinthians [1889], p. 301). Godet argues that "there is nothing to prevent the word 'quicken,' taken alone, from being used to denote restoration to the fulness of spiritual and bodily existence, with a view either to perdition or salvation" (comm. on 1 Corinthians [1889], p. 335). There are two serious difficulties to the latter interpretation: (1) the invariable meaning of "in Christ" as spiritual union; (2) the question whether the resurrection of the wicked really finds any place in the apostle's argument in the entire chapter.

In 1 Cor. 15:45 Paul says: "The first man Adam became a living soul. The last Adam became a life-giving spirit." The reference to Adam is from Gen. 2:7; the reference to Christ is due to what he had done and was doing in His manifestation as divine Redeemer. From results the apostle proceeds to nature. Adam was simply a living being, Christ a life-giving Being. Thus Christ is called Adam to express His headship of a race. In this verse He is called the last Adam; in v. 47 the second Adam. In the former verse the apostle deals not so much with Christ's relation to the first Adam as to the part He takes in relation to humanity, and His work on its behalf. When precisely Christ became life-giving is a matter of debate. Rom. 1:4 associates power with the resurrection as the time when Christ was constituted Son of God for the purpose of bestowing the force of divine grace. This gift of power was made available for His Church only through the ascension and the gift of the Holy Spirit at Pentecost. It is possible that the word "life-giving" may also include a reference to the resurrection of the body hereafter.

Paul uses the creation of man and woman in his argument for the subordination of woman (1 Tim. 2:13f.; cf. Gen. 2:7-25). This is no mere Jewish reasoning, but an inspired statement of the *typical* meaning of the passage in Genesis. The argument is a very similar one to that in 1 Cor. 11:8f. When the apostle states that "Adam was not beguiled," we must apparently understand it as simply based on the text in Genesis to which he refers (3:13), in which Eve, not Adam, says, "The serpent beguiled me." In Gal. 3:16 he reasons similarly from "seed" in the singular number, just as He. 7 reasons from the silence of Gen. 14 in regard to the parentage of Melchizedek. Paul does not deny that Adam was deceived, but is saying only that he was not directly deceived. His point is that Eve's facility in yielding warrants the rule as to women keeping silence.

III. Conclusions.–Reviewing the use of "Adam" in the NT, one cannot fail to observe how Paul assumes that Adam was a historical personality, and that the record in Genesis was a record of facts, that sin and death were introduced into the world and affected the entire race as the penalty for the disobedience of one ancestor. Paul evidently takes it for granted that Adam knew and was responsible for what he was doing. Again, sin and death are regarded as connected; death obtains its moral quality from sin. Paul clearly believed that physical dissolution was due to sin, and that there is some causal connection between Adam and the human race in regard to physical death. While the reference in Rom. 5 to death as coming through sin is primarily to physical death, yet physical death is the expression and sign of the deeper idea of spiritual death. The clause "for that all sinned" (v. 12) establishes a causal connection between the sin of Adam and the death of all. The need of redemption is thus made by the apostle to rest on facts. We are bound to Adam by birth, and it is open to us to become bound to Christ by faith. Thus redemption is grounded on the teaching of Scripture, and confirmed by the uncontradicted facts of history and experience. Whether, therefore, the references to Adam in the NT are purely incidental, or elaborated in theological discussion, everything is evidently based on the record in Genesis. W. H. G. THOMAS

IV. Historicity of Adam.–The viewpoint that regards the account of Adam and his fall in Gen. 2f. as mythical and not historical, as story but not history (cf. Emil Brunner, *Christian Doctrine of Creation and Redemption* [*Dogmatics*, II, Eng. tr. 1952], pp. 46-74), or according to which Adam stands for all men, so that we are all Adam and Gen. 2f. is not history but saga (cf. Barth, *CD*, IV/1, pp. 504-513; *Christ and Adam* [Eng. tr. 1956]), is not complete with the NT teaching. The following data show how the historicity of Adam and of his fall as recorded in these chapters is assumed and interwoven with the doctrine that Our Lord and His apostles enunciate.

In Mt. 19:4f.; Mk. 10:6-8 Jesus alludes to and quotes from Gen. 1:27; 2:24. The appeal to these passages in order to contrast the Mosaic permission of divorce with the original ordinance, and thereby to enforce the high ethic of marriage, would have had no practical relevance if the passages in question did not concern and presuppose human relationships analogous to those existing in the situation with which Jesus was dealing.

In 1 Cor. 15:45, 47 Adam is spoken of as the first man and is contrasted with Christ as the second man. The parallelism and contrast demand for Adam as the first man a historical identity comparable to that of Christ Himself. Otherwise the basis of comparison and contrast is lost. Adam and Christ sustain unique relations to the human race, but in order to sustain these relations there must be to both such historical character as will make those relations possible and relevant. Lk. 3:38 draws strikingly to our attention something correlative with Adam's being the first man and standing in a unique relation to the human race. The genealogy goes back no further than Adam, and while all others are said to be the son of the forefather in each case, Adam is said to be the son of God; he did not come by human generation. Furthermore, the allusion to Gen. 2:7 in 1 Cor. 15:45, 47 is unmistakable; and Lk. 3:38 is explained by Gen. 2:7.

1 Tim. 2:13 alludes to Gen. 2:7, 20-23 and assumes the temporal sequence there indicated, a sequence that presupposes historicity both before and after. The reference in 1 Tim. 2:14 to Gen. 3:1-6, 13 demonstrates the acceptance of that narrative on Paul's part.

In Rom. 5:12-19 and 1 Cor. 15:22 the reign of sin, condemnation, and death is traced to the sin of Adam, and the reign of righteousness, justification, and life to the obedience of Christ. There is both parallelism and contrast. The sin of Adam is called the transgression, trespass, and disobedience of the one man. There can be no doubt as to the identity of the trespass in Paul's view; it is that of Gen. 3:19 (cf. 2:17). And the obedience of Christ is that unto death, even the death of the cross (Phil. 2:8). The latter was discharged in time, in the arena of history. To view the parallel and contrasted disobedience of the one Adam in nonhistorical terms is to wreck the structure of Paul's thought and therefore the doctrine set forth in these passages. The consequences for the plan of redemption are apparent.

All these considerations converge to show that the conception by which Adam and the narratives of Gen. 2f. are construed as mythical or legendary and therefore not historical is wholly alien to the NT. J. MURRAY

ADAM ad'əm [Heb. *'āḏām*]. A city near the confluence of the Jordan and Jabbok rivers about 18 mi. (30 km.) N of Jericho and near the site where Israel crossed from the plains of Moab to western Palestine on the dry bed of the Jordan (Josh. 3:16).

In the area of Adam, modern Tell ed-Dâmiyeh, slides from the high limestone cliffs that border the Jordan have dammed up the river on several occasions, most recently in 1927. Such an event would cause the river to "rise up in a heap" N of Adam and drain into the Dead Sea S of Adam. D. McINTOSH

Adam (Tell ed-Dâmiyeh), where collapse of the banks may have caused damming of the Jordan, enabling Joshua and the Israelites to cross (W. S. LaSor)

ADAM, BOOKS OF. Books pretending to give the life and deeds of Adam and other OT worthies existed in abundance among the Jews and the early Christians. The Talmud speaks of a Book of Adam, which is now lost, but which probably furnished some material that appears in early Christian writings.

See APOCRYPHA; PSEUDEPIGRAPHA V.H.

M. O. EVANS

ADAMAH ad'ə-mə [Heb. *'ᵃḏāmâ*; Gk. *Adami*]. A fortified city in the territory of Naphtali, named between Chinnereth and Ramah (Josh. 19:36). The site is unknown.

ADAMANT [Heb. *šāmîr* (Ezk. 3:9; Zec. 7:12); cf. Akk. *ašmur*–'emery']. In the passages cited and in Jer. 17:1, where it is rendered "diamond" (but "adamant" in the NEB), the word *šāmîr* evidently refers to emery, a form of corundum second in hardness only to the diamond.

ADAMI ad'ə-mī, ə-dā'mī. In the AV a separate name, but in the RSV and NEB, ADAMI-NEKEB (Josh. 19:33).

ADAMI-NEKEB ad'ə-mī ne'keb [Heb. *'ᵃḏāmî hanneqeḇ*–'Adami (or 'the ground') of the pass']. A place in lower Galilee used as one of the sites to mark the border of Naphtali (Josh. 19:33). The AV, following Greek texts, reads Adami and Nekeb as separate sites; and J. Simons (*GTTOT*, § 334) follows this reading, citing the reference to *ngb* in the great city-list of Thutmose III. The Hebrew, however, seems to require a single location, and the Vulgate supports this by translating *Adami quae est Neceb,* "Adami which is Nekeb."

Adami-nekeb is probably to be located at Khirbet Dâmiyeh, about 6 mi. (10 km.) NE of Mt. Tabor, on a trail leading from Kefr Kama to Harûs (in the direction of Tiberias), in a defile or pass. J. Simons locates Adami here, and Nekeb somewhat SE toward Yavneel. *WHAB* likewise identifies Adami and Khirbet Dâmiyeh, and suggests the identification of Nekeb with el-Baṣṣah, a Bronze Age site toward the southeast.

See *GP*, II, 17, 64. W. S. L. S.

ADAR ā'där [Heb. *'^{a}ḏār*]. The Babylonian name of the twelfth month of the Hebrew CALENDAR (Feb./Mar.). It is named in Ezr. 6:15 and eight times in Esther. In order to maintain the relation of the year to the seasons it was customary to add a second Adar, as often as was needed, as an intercalary month.

ADAR ā'där (Josh. 15:3, AV). *See* ADDAR.

ADARSA ə-där'sə. *See* ADASA.

ADASA ad'ə-sə [Gk. *Adasa*]; AV ADARSA. A town N of Jerusalem where Judas Maccabeus defeated the Syrian army and killed Nicanor, a general of Demetrius (1 Macc. 7:39-50). The victory was celebrated on the 13th of Adar. The location is described as 30 furlongs (nearly 4 mi.) from Beth-horon (Josephus *Ant.* xii.10.5) and a day's journey from Gazara (1 Macc. 7:45), and is generally identified with Khirbet 'Addâseh, 1.5 mi. (2.5 km.) NW of Nebi Samwil and 3.5 mi. (5.5 km.) SSW of Ramallah.

See *GP*, II, 238. W. S. L. S.

ADBEEL ad'bə-əl [Heb. *'aḏb^e'ēl*; Akk. *Idibi'lu*]. The third of the twelve sons of Ishmael (Gen. 25:13; 1 Ch. 1:29). The name appears in Assyrian records as that of a north Arabian tribe residing somewhere SW of the Dead Sea.

ADDAN ad'an [Heb. *'addān*] (Ezr. 2:59); **ADDON** ad'on [Heb. *'addôn*] (Neh. 7:61). [Both names are connected in some way with the name of the god Addu.] A place mentioned in the list of the returning exiles (Ezr. 2:50, duplicated in Neh. 7:61). It is one of several names of Babylonian localities from which came men who were unable to declare their genealogy as Israelites.

ADDAR ad'är [Heb. *'addār*].

1. A grandson of Benjamin, sometimes counted as one of his sons (1 Ch. 8:3).

2. AV ADAR. A town on the southern border of Judah (Josh. 15:3), the same as HAZAR-ADDAR (Nu. 34:4). *See also* HEZRON.

ADDER [Heb. *peṯen* (Ps. 58:4; 91:13), *ṣip'ônî* (Prov. 23:32; Isa. 11:8; 59:5; Jer. 8:17), *ṣepa'* (Isa. 14:29)]; AV also COCKATRICE; NEB ASP, COBRA, SNAKE, VIPER. One or more kinds of poisonous snake. It is impossible to tell in any case just what species is meant, but it must be remembered that the English word adder is used very ambiguously. It is from the Anglo-Saxon *noedre,* a snake or serpent, and is the common English name for *Vipera berus* L., the common viper, which is found throughout Europe and northern Asia, though not in Bible lands; but the word adder is used also for various snakes, both poisonous and nonpoisonous, found in different parts of the world. In America, for instance, both the poisonous moccasin (*Ancistrodon*) and the harmless hog-nosed snake (*Heterodon*) are called adders.

See also ASP; SERPENT; VIPER. A. E. DAY

ADDI ad'ī [Gk. *Addi*].

1. An ancestor of Joseph the husband of Mary mother of Jesus; the fourth from Zerubbabel in the ascending genealogical series (Lk. 3:28).

2. Apparently a form of ADNA **1** used in 1 Esd. 9:31.

ADDICTED (1 Cor. 16:15, AV). The RSV has "devoted," the RV "set (themselves)," the NEB "laid (themselves) out" (Gk. *tássō*). The AV is archaic.

ADDO ad'ō (1 Esd. 6:1, AV, NEB). *See* IDDO **7.**

ADDON. *See* ADDAN.

ADDRESS; ADDRESSING [Gk. *laléō*] (Eph. 5:19; cf. 1 Cor. 3:1); AV, NEB, SPEAKING; [Heb. *'āmar* (Ezr. 10:2; Ps. 45:1); Gk. *légō* (He. 7:21; Rev. 7:13), *dialégomai* (He. 12:5), *apokrínomai* (Acts 3:12), *prosphonéō* (Lk. 23:20; Acts 22:2), *apophthéngomai* (Acts 2:14)]; AV SAY, ANSWER; NEB also "meet with words." All instances of "addressing" portray someone self-consciously confronting another person or group with words of some kind (primarily oral, but written words in Ps. 45:1; 1 Cor. 3:1). Often "addressing" is used in a compound verb phrase, following such combinations as "lifting up his voice," and "turning to him."

The single use of "addressing" (Eph. 5:19) parallels several other instances of *laléō* with the dative in contexts where the expression is further defined. *Laléō* denotes expressing oneself to someone (in contrast to remaining silent) in some form: e.g., in 1 Cor. 13:11, "expressing oneself like a child"; Rev. 13:11, "speaking in a dragon-like manner"; John 8:44, "expressing himself in a way which befits his demonic nature." Similarly the "psalms and hymns and spiritual songs" in Eph. 5:19 describe the manner in which the members of the Ephesian church were to express themselves to each other.

Paul's suggestion here about communicating with each other through music emerges from his concern that Christian exuberance be expressed in fitting ways. Instead of superficial camaraderie and aimless chatter, Paul points to the controlling Spirit as the genuine source of emotion, which results in expressions "with the heart"—not just the lips. While not ruling out spontaneous sharing (undoubtedly "spiritual songs" refer to expressions arising naturally from the Spirit), Paul recommends established psalms and hymns as well.

The breadth of the context (suggestions for practical Christianity) implies that the musical self-expressions of Eph. 5:19 are not being recommended simply as a liturgical practice. Moreover, the generality of *laléō* (no verb for "expression" is more frequently used in the NT), in contrast to the more specific "teaching and admonishing" of the parallel Col. 3:16, would indicate that Paul is advising this practice for all the types of circumstances that involved the Ephesian believers. Paul encourages Christians to express their spiritual feelings (especially victory and thanksgiving) to each other, one person singing to God in the presence of the others. (Cf. Tertullian *Apol.* 39.)

See also SPIRITUAL SONGS. On He. 12:5, *see* DISPUTE.

C. G. CHRISTIANS

ADDUS ad'əs.

1. [Gk. *Addous*]. The head of a family of "sons of Solomon's servants" who returned with Zerubbabel to

Jerusalem (1 Esd. 5:34); omitted in Ezr. 2 and Neh. 7.
2. (1 Esd. 5:38, AV). *See* JADDUS.

ADER ā'dər (1 Ch. 8:15, AV, NEB). *See* EDER **2.**

ADIABENE ā-di-a-bē'nə [Gk. *Adiabēnē*]. A state lying on the east of the Tigris, on the greater and lesser rivers Zab, in the territory of ancient Assyria. For the half-century terminating with the destruction of Jerusalem by Titus, Adiabene is especially interesting by reason of the careers of its king Izates and his mother Helena, who became Jews. They had their part in the Jewish-Roman wars, and in various ways were typical of the existing situation. (See Josephus *Ant.* xx.2-4; *BJ* ii.16.4; 19.2; v.4.2; 6.1; 11.5; vi.6.4.) Somewhat later Adiabene was absorbed into the Roman empire and became one of the six provinces which formed the larger province of Assyria, though Pliny and Ammianus sometimes call the large province by the name Adiabene.

W. J. BEECHER

ADIDA ad'ə-də [Gk. *Adida*]; OT HADID. A town of the Benjamin tribe near Lod and Ono located on a hill facing the "plain country" of Judea, rebuilt and fortified by Simon Maccabeus (1 Macc. 12:38), who later encamped here to meet the army of Trypho (1 Macc. 13:13; Josephus *Ant.* xiii.6.5). Here Aretas king of Arabia met Alexander Janneus in battle and defeated him (*Ant.* xiii.15.2). Later, Adida was fortified by Vespasian in the war against the Jews. Adida is perhaps modern el-Ḥadîtheh, located about 3 mi. (5 km.) E of Lydda (Lod).

See *GP*, II, 340f.

ADIEL ad'i-əl [Heb. *'ᵃdî'ēl*–'ornament of God'].

1. One of the "princes" of the tribe of Simeon. In the days of Hezekiah they smote the aborigines of Gedor and captured the valley (1 Ch. 4:36ff.).

2. The father of Maasai, one of the priests who dwelt in Jerusalem after the return from the Exile (1 Ch. 9:12).

3. The father of Azmaveth, who was over David's treasures (1 Ch. 27:25).

ADIN ā'dən [Heb. *'āḏîn*–'voluptuous'; Gk. *Adin, Adinos*]; NEB also ADINUS (1 Esd. 5:14). The name of a family, "the sons of Adin" (Ezr. 2:15; 8:6; Neh. 7:20; 10:16; 1 Esd. 5:14; 8:32), mentioned among the exiles who left Babylonia under Zerubbabel and Ezra to return to Jerusalem.

ADINA ad'ə-nə, ə-dī'nə [Heb. *'ᵃḏînā'*]. One of David's "mighty men," the son of Shiza the Reubenite (1 Ch. 11:42). This is in that part of the list of David's mighty men in which the Chronicler supplements the list given in 2 Samuel.

ADINO ad'ə-nō, ə-dī'nō [Heb. *'ᵃḏînô*]; RSV and NEB omit. In the AV, the senior of David's "mighty men." "Josheb-basshebeth a Tachmonite, chief of the captains; the same was Adino the Eznite, against eight hundred slain at one time" (2 S. 23:8). This very exact rendering makes it evident even to an English reader that the text is imperfect. Ginsburg (*New Massoretico-Critical Text of the Hebrew Bible* [1896]) offers a corrected form taken substantially from the parallel passage in 1 Ch. 11:11: "Jashobeam a son of a Hachmonite, chief of the captains; he lifted up his spear." This is plausible, and is very generally accepted (cf. RSV, NEB); and it eliminates the names Adino and Eznite, which do not occur elsewhere in the Bible. Some of the facts are against this. The LXX has the names Adino and Eznite. The Latin finds no proper names in the passage, but so translates the words as to presuppose the Hebrew text as we have it.

The texts concerning David's mighty men are fragmentary both in Samuel and in Chronicles. If they were more complete they would perhaps make it clear that the three seniors were comrades of David at Pas-dammim (Ephes-dammim) (1 Ch. 11:13; 1 S. 17:1), and that we have in them additional details concerning that battle. The record says that on the death of Goliath the Philistines fled and the Israelites pursued (1 S. 17:52ff.); but it is not improbable that during the retreat, portions of the Philistine force rallied, so that there was strenuous fighting.

W. J. BEECHER

ADINUS ad'ə-nus, ə-dī'nəs (1 Esd. 5:14, NEB; 9:48, AV). *See* ADIN; JAMIN **3.**

ADITHAIM ad-ə-thā'əm [Heb. *'ᵃḏîṯayim*]. A city in the Shephelah of Judah (Josh. 15:36). The site is unknown; *GAB* suggests modern el-Ḥadîtheh N of Aijalon, the same as Adida (Hadid).

ADJURATION. *See* OATH.

ADLAI ad'lī, ad'lā [Heb. *'aḏlay*; Gk. *Adli, Adai*]. The father of Shaphat, an overseer of David's herds in the lowlands (1 Ch. 27:29).

ADLON ad'lon (1 Esd. 5:34, NEB). *See* AMI; AMON **3.**

ADMAH ad'mə [Heb. *'aḏmâ*]. One of the CITIES OF THE VALLEY (Gen. 10:19; 14:2, 8; Dt. 29:23; Hos. 11:8) upon which Abraham and Lot looked from the heights of Bethel. It was destroyed with Sodom and Gomorrah. The site is unknown; *see* SIDDIM, VALLEY OF.

ADMATHA ad-ma'thə [Heb. *'aḏmāṯā'*]. One of "the seven princes of Persia and Media, who saw the king's face, and sat first in the kingdom" (Est. 1:14); cf. 2 K. 25:19; Ezr. 7:14. The LXX gives only three names.

ADMIN ad'min [Gk. *Admin*] (Lk. 3:33, RSV); AV and NEB omit. An ancestor of Jesus, omitted in some MSS (e.g., A D K Δ Ψ) but found in several early MSS (e.g., ***p***[4] ℵ B).

See also ARNI.

ADMINISTER. *See* MINISTRY.

ADMINISTRATORS [Gk. *kybérnēsis*–'steering'] (1 Cor. 12:28); AV GOVERNMENTS; NEB "those who have . . . power to guide (others)." *Kybérnēsis* may mean the gifts which qualify one to "steer" a congregation, or one who has such gifts (see *TDNT*, III, *s.v.* κυβέρνησις [Beyer]). In the LXX it translates Heb. *taḥbulôt* (Prov. 1:5; 11:14; 24:6), and is variously rendered: "counsel" or "wise counsel" by the AV; "skill" or "guidance" by the RSV; "skill" or "skilful strategy" by the NEB.

ADMIRATION. *See* MARVEL.

ADMONISH [Heb. *'ûḏ*; Gk. *noutheteō*]; AV also PROTEST (1 K. 2:42), TESTIFY (Ps. 81:8), WARN; NEB also "give solemn warning" (1 K. 2:42), "give a solemn charge" (Ps. 81:8), COUNSEL (Acts 20:31), "bring to reason" (1 Cor. 4:14), etc.; **ADMONISHING** [Gk. *nouthesía*] (Tit. 3:10); AV ADMONITION; NEB WARN; **ADMONITION** [Heb. *tôḵaḥaṯ*] (Prov. 15:5, 31f.); AV, NEB, REPROOF [*mô'ēṣôt*] (Prov. 22:20); AV COUN-

SEL; NEB WISE ADVICE. The biblical usage is that of warning or guidance given to persons through a reminder of certain principles by which they should be living (Ps. 81:8; Prov. 15:5, 31). If such counsel is heeded it will bring prosperity (cf. 1 K. 3:14), since the instruction is directed to a positive end (1 Cor. 4:14; 10:11) for the edification of the hearer. Admonition is not condemnation, and when it adduces the biblical principles for Christian living it forms a valuable element in spiritual discipline.

R. K. H.

ADNA ad'nə [Heb. *'aḏnā'*-'pleasure']. **1.** An Israelite in Ezra's time who, having married a foreign wife, divorced her. He belonged to Pahath-moab (Ezr. 10:30).
2. A priest of the family of Harum, during the high-priesthood of Joiakim son of Jethua (Neh. 12:12-15).

ADNAH ad'nə.
1. [Heb. *'aḏnāḥ*-'pleasure']. A warrior of the tribe of Manasseh, who deserted Saul and joined David's forces at Ziklag (1 Ch. 12:20f.).
2. [Heb. *'aḏnâ*]. An officer of high rank, perhaps the commander-in-chief of Jehoshaphat's army (2 Ch. 17:14).

ADONAI a-dō'nī [Heb. *'aḏōnāy*-'my sovereign']. A divine name, translated in most versions "the Lord," or "my Lord." Its vowels are found in the MT with the unpronounceable tetragrammaton *YHWH*; and when the Jewish reader came to these letters, he substituted in pronunciation the word "Adonai," rather than utter the holy name "Yahweh." But Christian translators formerly took this combination as a real word "Jehovah," the usual RV rendering. *See* GOD, NAMES OF.

ADONIBEZEK ə-dō-nī-bē'zek [Heb. *'aḏōnîḇezeq*-'lord of Bezek']. The chief of a town, Bezek, in southern Palestine, whom the tribes of Judah and Simeon overthrew. Adonibezek fled when his men were defeated, but was captured, and was punished in kind for his cruelty in cutting off the thumbs and great toes of seventy kings. He died after being brought to Jerusalem (Jgs. 1:5-7).

ADONIJAH ad-ə-nī'jə [Heb. *'aḏōnîyâ*, *'aḏōnîyāhû*-'Yahweh is my Lord']. **1.** The fourth son of David, born in Hebron, who attempted to become king (2 S. 3:4; 1 Ch. 3:2; 1 K. 1-2).
Aside from Chileab, Adonijah was the oldest living son in David's last days. During this period Adonijah built up an entourage (1 K. 1:5) and solicited the support of Abiathar the priest and Joab the army commander (1 K. 1:7; 2:22). Just before David died Adonijah made a feast for his supporters at En-rogel, doubtless expecting to conclude it with a coronation ceremony. However, Nathan and Bath-sheba secured the succession for Solomon, who was promptly anointed by Zadok the priest at Gihon, near En-rogel. Adonijah and his followers heard the noise and fled from the festal assembly, fearing an attack. Adonijah took refuge at the altar and, having assured Solomon of his loyalty, obtained a promise that he would be spared (1 K. 1:51-53). But after David died Adonijah behaved treasonably (1 K. 2:19-25), and for this was executed by Solomon.
2. A Levite sent by Jehoshaphat to teach the law in the cities of Judah (2 Ch. 17:8).
3. One of those who sealed the covenant of reform (Neh. 10:16), the Adonikam of Ezr. 2:13.

R. K. H.

ADONIKAM ad-ō-nī'kəm [Heb. *'aḏōnîqām*-'my lord has arisen']. The name of a family of returning exiles (Ezr. 2:13;

Neh. 7:18). In Neh. 10:16 the name is given as Adonijah.

ADONIRAM ad-ō-nī'rəm [Heb. *'aḏōnîrām*-'my lord is exalted'] (1 K. 4:6; 5:14); **ADORAM** ə-dôr'əm [*'aḏōrām* (2 S. 20:24; 1 K. 12:18]; **HADORAM** hə-dôr'əm [*haḏôrām*] (2 Ch. 10:18). An official in charge of forced labor under David, Solomon, and Rehoboam. He supervised 30,000 laborers drafted by Solomon. When Rehoboam alienated the northern tribes, Adoniram, who had been sent to impose forced labor upon them, was stoned to death (1 K. 12:18; 2 Ch. 10:18).

R. K. H.

ADONIS ə-dō'nis. A Syro-Phoenician vegetation deity who had a cultic center at Byblos beside the river Adonis (Nahr Ibrahim). The name occurs in Isa. 17:10 in the ERV mg. ("plantings of Adonis") and in the NEB ("gardens in honor of Adonis"). The AV, RV, and RSV have "pleasant plants."
A connection of this passage with the cult of Adonis was seen by, among others, Snijders *Oudtestamentische Studiën*, 10 [1954], 46), who compares Heb. *na'amanim* with Ugar. *n'mn* (see 2 Aqhat 6:45); in both cases the meaning is "the desirable one," which then is regarded as a reference to Adonis. See also KoB, p. 622, and references.

ADONI-ZEDEK ə-dō-nī-zē'dek [Heb. *'aḏōnîṣeḏeq*-'my Lord is righteousness (or 'Zedek')']. The king of Jerusalem at the time of the conquest of Canaan (Josh. 10:1).
When he heard of the fall of Ai and the submission of the Gibeonites, he entered into a league with four other kings to resist Joshua and Israel, and to punish Gibeon (Josh. 10:3f.), but was overthrown by Joshua in a memorable battle (vv. 12-14). Adoni-zedek and his four allies were shut up in a cave, while the battle lasted, and afterward were taken out by Joshua's order, put to death, and hanged on trees (Josh. 10:22-27).

ADOPTION; SONSHIP [Gk. *huiothesía*]. The Greek term occurs in the Bible only in Paul's Epistles (Rom. 8:15, 23; 9:4; Gal. 4:5; Eph. 1:5); for extrabiblical usage see MM, pp. 648f. The AV and RV have "adoption" throughout. The RSV has "adoption" in Rom. 8:23; Gal. 4:5, and "sonship" in Rom. 8:15; 9:4; in Eph. 1:5 the RSV reads "to be his sons." The NEB in each instance uses a phrase such as "to make us sons" or "to attain the status of sons."

I. General Legal Idea
  A. In the OT
  B. Greek
  C. Roman
II. Paul's Doctrine
  A. Liberty (Galatians)
  B. Deliverance from Debt (Romans)
III. The Christian Experience
  A. In Relation to Justification
  B. In Relation to Sanctification
  C. In Relation to Regeneration
IV. As God's Act
  A. Divine Fatherhood
  B. Its Cosmic Range

I. General Legal Idea.-The custom prevailed among Greeks, Romans, and other ancient peoples (including the Hurrians; *see* ABRAHAM III); but it does not appear in Jewish law.
A. In the OT. Three cases of adoption are mentioned: of Moses (Ex. 2:10), Genubath (1 K. 11:20), and Esther (Est. 2:7,15); but it is remarkable that they all occur outside of Palestine—in Egypt and Persia, where the practice of adoption prevailed. Likewise the idea appears in the NT only in

the Epistles of Paul, which were addressed to churches outside Palestine.

The motive and initiative of adoption always lay with the adoptive father, who thus supplied his lack of natural offspring and satisfied the claims of affection and religion, and the desire to exercise paternal authority or to perpetuate his family. The process and conditions of adoption varied with different peoples. Among oriental nations it was extended to slaves (as Moses), who thereby gained their freedom; but in Greece and Rome it was, with rare exceptions, limited to citizens.

B. Greek. In Greece a man might during his lifetime, or by will, to take effect after his death, adopt any male citizen into the privileges of his son, but with the invariable condition that the adopted son accepted the legal obligations and religious duties of a real son.

C. Roman. In Rome the unique nature of paternal authority *(patria potestas),* by which a son was held in his father's power, almost as a slave was owned by his master, gave a peculiar character to the process of adoption. For the adoption of a person free from paternal authority *(sui juris),* the process and effect were practically the same in Rome as in Greece *(adrogatio).* In a more specific sense, adoption proper *(adoptio)* was the process by which a person was transferred from his natural father's power into that of his adoptive father; and it consisted in a fictitious sale of the son, and his surrender by the natural to the adoptive father.

II. Paul's Doctrine.–As a Roman citizen the apostle would naturally know of the Roman custom; but in the cosmopolitan city of Tarsus, and again on his travels, he would become equally familiar with the corresponding customs of other nations. He employed the idea metaphorically much in the manner of Christ's parables; and, as in their case, there is danger of pressing the analogy too far in its details. It is not clear that he had any specific form of adoption in mind when illustrating his teaching by the general idea. Under this figure he teaches that God, by the manifestation of His grace in Christ, brings men into the relation of sons to Himself, and communicates to them the experience of sonship.

A. Liberty (Galatians). In Galatians Paul emphasizes especially the liberty enjoyed by those who live by faith, in contrast to the bondage under which men are held who guide their lives by legal ceremonies and ordinances, as the Galatians were prone to do (5:1). The contrast between law and faith is first set forth on the field of history, as a contrast between both the pre-Christian and the Christian economies (3:23f.), although in another passage he carries the idea of adoption back into the covenant relation of God with Israel (Rom. 9:4). But here the historical antithesis is reproduced in the contrast between men who now choose to live under law and those who live by faith.

Here three figures seem to commingle in the description of man's condition under legal bondage—that of a slave, that of a minor under guardians appointed by his father's will, and that of a Roman son under the *patria potestas* (Gal. 4:1-3). The process of liberation is first of all one of redemption or buying out (Gk. *exagorásē*) (4:5). This term in itself applies equally well to the slave who is redeemed from bondage, and the Roman son whose adoptive father buys him out of the authority of his natural father. But in the latter case the condition of the son is not materially altered by the process: he only exchanges one paternal authority for another. If Paul for a moment thought of the process in terms of ordinary Roman adoption, the resulting condition of the son he conceives in terms of the more free and gracious Greek or Jewish family life. Or he may have thought of the rarer case of adoption from conditions of slavery into the status of sonship. The redemption is only a precondition of adoption, which follows upon faith, and is accompanied by the sending of "the Spirit of his Son into our hearts, crying, Abba, Father," and then all bondage is done away (4:5-7).

B. Deliverance from Debt (Romans). In Rom. 8:12-17 the idea of obligation or debt is coupled with that of liberty. Man is thought of as at one time under the authority and power of the flesh (8:5), but when the Spirit of Christ comes to dwell in him, he is a debtor no longer to the flesh but to the Spirit (vv. 12f.), and debt or obligation to the Spirit is itself liberty. As in Galatians, man thus passes from a state of bondage into a state of sonship which is also a state of liberty. "For as many as are led by the Spirit of God, these [and these only] are sons of God" (v. 14). The spirit of adoption or sonship stands in diametrical opposition to the spirit of bondage (v. 15). And the Spirit to which we are debtors and by which we are led, at once awakens and confirms the experience of sonship within us (v. 16). In both places, Paul conveys under this figure the idea of man as passing from a state of alienation from God and of bondage under law and sin, into that relation with God of mutual confidence and love, of unity of thought and will, which should characterize the ideal family, and in which all restraint, compulsion, and fear have passed away.

III. The Christian Experience.–As a fact of Christian experience, the adoption is the recognition and affirmation by man of his sonship toward God. It follows upon faith in Christ, by which man becomes so united with Christ that His filial spirit enters into him, and takes possession of his consciousness, so that he knows and greets God as Christ does (cf. Mk. 14:36).

A. In Relation to Justification. It is an aspect of the same experience that Paul describes elsewhere, under another legal metaphor, as justification by faith. According to the latter, God declares the sinner righteous and treats him as such, admits him to the experience of forgiveness, reconciliation, and peace (Rom. 5:1). In all this the relation of father and son is undoubtedly involved, but in adoption it is emphatically expressed. It is not only that the prodigal son is welcomed home, glad to confess that he is not worthy to be called a son, and willing to be made as one of the hired servants, but he is embraced and restored to be a son as before. The point of each metaphor is, that justification is the act of a merciful judge setting the prisoner free, but adoption is the act of a generous father, taking a son to his bosom and endowing him with liberty, favor, and a heritage.

B. In Relation to Sanctification. Besides, justification is the beginning of a process which needs for its completion a progressive course of sanctification by the aid of the Holy Spirit, but adoption is coextensive with sanctification. The sons of God are those led by the Spirit of God (Rom. 8:14), and the same Spirit of God gives the experience of sonship. Sanctification describes the process of general cleansing and growth as an abstract process, but adoption includes it as a concrete relation to God, as loyalty, obedience, and fellowship with an ever loving Father.

C. In Relation to Regeneration. Some have identified adoption with regeneration, and therefore many Fathers and Roman Catholic theologians have identified it with baptismal regeneration, thereby excluding the essential fact of conscious sonship. The new birth and adoption are certainly aspects of the same totality of experience; but they belong to different systems of thought, and to identify them is to invite confusion. The new birth defines especially the origin and moral quality of the Christian experience as an abstract fact, but adoption expresses a concrete relation of man to God. Nor does Paul here raise the question of man's natural and original condition. It is pressing the analogy too far to infer from this doctrine of adoption that man is by nature not God's son. It would contradict

Paul's teaching elsewhere (e.g., Acts 17:28), and he should not be convicted of inconsistency on the application of a metaphor. He conceives man outside Christ as morally an alien and a stranger from God, and the change wrought by faith in Christ makes him morally a son and conscious of his sonship; but naturally he is always a potential son because God is always a real father.

IV. As God's Act.–Adoption as God's act is an eternal process of His gracious love, for He "foreordained us unto adoption as sons through Jesus Christ unto himself, according to the good pleasure of his will" (Eph. 1:5).

A. Divine Fatherhood. The motive and impulse of Fatherhood which result in adoption were eternally real and active in God. In some sense He had bestowed the adoption upon Israel (Rom. 9:4). "Israel is my son, my first-born" (Ex. 4:22; cf. Dt. 14:1; 32:6; Jer. 31:9; Hos. 11:1). God could not reveal Himself at all without revealing something of His Fatherhood, but the whole revelation was as yet partial and prophetic. When "God sent forth his Son" to "redeem them that were under the law," it became possible for men to receive the adoption; for to those who are willing to receive it, He sent the Spirit of the eternal Son to testify in their hearts that they are sons of God, and to give them confidence and utterance to enable them to call God their Father (Gal. 4:5f.; Rom. 8:15).

B. Its Cosmic Range. But this experience also is incomplete, and looks forward to a fuller adoption in the response, not only of man's spirit, but of the whole creation, including man's body, to the Fatherhood of God (Rom. 8:23). Every filial spirit now groans, because it finds itself imprisoned in a body subjected to vanity, but it awaits a redemption of the body, perhaps in the resurrection, or in some final consummation, when the whole material creation shall be transformed into a fitting environment for the sons of God, the creation itself delivered from the bondage of corruption into the liberty of the glory of the children of God (Rom. 8:21). Then will adoption be complete, when man's whole personality shall be in harmony with the spirit of sonship, and the whole universe favorable to its perseverance in a state of blessedness.

See also CHILDREN OF GOD.

Bibliography.–Comms. *in loc.*, esp. W. Sanday on Romans (*ICC*, 14th ed. 1913) and J. B. Lightfoot on Galatians (1900); *RTWB* (R. H. Fuller); *TDNT*, VIII, *s.v.* υἱοθεσία (Wülfing von Martitz, Schweizer).

T. REES

ADORAIM ad-ə-rā'im [Heb. *'ᵃḏôrayim*–perhaps 'a pair of knolls' or 'two hills']; **ADORA** ə-dôr'ə [Gk. *adōra*] (1 Macc. 13:20). A city of Judah that was fortified by Rehoboam (2 Ch. 11:9), identified with modern Dûrā, 5 mi. (8 km.) WSW of Hebron.

Along with MARESHAH, Adora was one of the two major cities of Idumea. There Simon Maccabeus blocked the advance of Trypho (1 Macc. 13:20), *ca.* 143-142 B.C. According to Josephus (*Ant.* xiii.9.1; *BJ* i.2.6) Adora was one of the cities captured by John Hyrcanus after the death of Antiochus VII (129 B.C.); the Jews still possessed it some fifty years later in the time of Alexander Janneus (*Ant.* xiii.15.4). Under Roman control, Adora was one of the destroyed cities that Gabinius proconsul of Syria had rebuilt in 59 B.C. (*Ant.* xiv.5.3; *BJ* i.8.4).

A battle between the forces of Esau and those of Jacob in which Esau is killed and buried at Adûrâm (Adora) is related in Jub. 38:8f.

J. W. WHEDBEE

ADORAM. A contracted form of ADONIRAM.

ADORATION [<Lat. *adorare*–(1) 'speak to,' (2) 'entreat,' (3) 'do homage, worship' < *os* (*oris*)–'mouth' (from Roman practice of kissing the hand as a token of homage?)].

I. Meaning.–Adoration is intense admiration culminating in reverence and worship, together with the outward acts and attitudes which accompany such reverence. It thus includes both the subjective sentiments, or feelings of the soul, in the presence of some superior object or person, and the appropriate physical expressions of such sentiments in outward acts of homage or of worship. In its widest sense it includes reverence to beings other than God, especially to monarchs, who in oriental countries were regarded with feelings of awe. But if finds its highest expression in religion.

Adoration is perhaps the highest type of worship, involving the reverent and rapt contemplation of the divine perfections and prerogatives, the acknowledgment of them in words of praise, together with the visible symbols and postures that express the adoring attitude of the creature in the presence of his Creator. It is the expression of the soul's mystical realization of God's presence in His transcendent greatness, holiness, and lovingkindness. As a form of prayer, adoration is to be distinguished from other forms, such as petition, thanksgiving, confession, and intercession.

II. Outward Postures.–In the OT and NT, these are similar to those which prevailed in all oriental countries, as amply illustrated by the monuments of Egypt and Assyria, and by the customs still in use among the nations of the East. The chief attitudes referred to in the Bible are the following:

A. Prostration. Among the Orientals, especially Persians, prostration (i.e., falling upon the knees, then gradually inclining the body, until the forehead touched the ground) was common as an expression of profound reverence and humility before a superior or a benefactor. It was practiced in the worship of Yahweh (Gen. 17:3; Nu. 16:45; Mt. 26:30, Jesus in Gethsemane; Rev. 1:17), and of idols (2 K. 5:18; Dnl. 3:5f.), but was by no means confined to religious exercises. It was the formal method of supplicating or doing obeisance to a superior (e.g., 1 S. 25:23f.; 2 K. 4:37; Est. 8:3; Mk. 5:22; Jn. 11:32).

B. Kneeling. A substitution for prostration was kneeling, a common attitude in worship, frequently mentioned in the OT and NT (e.g., 1 K. 8:54; Ezr. 9:5; Ps. 95:6; Isa. 45:23; Lk. 22:41, Jesus in Gethsemane; Acts 7:60; Eph. 3:14). The same attitude was sometimes adopted in paying homage to a fellow creature, as in 2 K. 1:13. "Sitting" as an attitude of prayer (only 2 S. 7:18; 1 Ch. 17:16) was probably a form of kneeling, as in Moslem worship.

C. Standing. This was the usual posture in prayer, like that of modern Jews in public worship. Abraham "stood before the Lord" when he interceded for Sodom (Gen. 18:22). Cf. 1 S. 1:26. The Pharisee in the parable "stood and prayed" (Lk. 18:11), and the hypocrites are said to "pray standing in the synagogues, and in the corners of the streets" (Mt. 6:5).

D. The Hands. These postures were accompanied by various attitudes of the hands, which were either lifted up toward heaven (Ps. 63:4; 1 Tim. 2:8) or outspread (Ex. 9:29; Ezr. 9:5; Isa. 1:15), or both (1 K. 8:54).

E. Kiss of Adoration. The heathen practice of kissing hands to the heavenly bodies as a sign of adoration is referred to in Job 31:27, and of kissing the idol in 1 K. 19:18; Hos. 13:2. The kiss of homage is mentioned in Ps. 2:12, if the text there is correct. Kissing hands to the object of adoration was customary among the Romans (Pliny *Nat. hist.* xxviii.5 [25]). The NT word for "worship" (Gk. *proskynéō*) means literally "kiss before." *See also* POSTURES.

III. Objects of Adoration.–The only adequate object of

Syrian tribute bearers kneeling in adoration before the Egyptian pharaoh. Wall painting from the tomb of Thutmose IV (1421-1413 B.C.), Thebes (Trustees of the British Museum)

adoration is the Supreme Being. He only who is the sum of all perfections can fully satisfy man's instincts of reverence, and elicit the complete homage of his soul.

A. Fellow Creatures. Yet, as already suggested, the crude beginnings of religious adoration are to be found in the respect paid to created beings regarded as possessing superior claims and powers, especially to kings and rulers. As examples we may mention the woman of Tekoa falling on her face to do obeisance to King David (2 S. 14:4), and the king's servants bowing down to do reverence to Haman (Est. 3:2). Cf. Ruth 2:10; 1 S. 20:41; 2 S. 1:2; 14:22.

B. Material Objects. On a higher plane, as involving some recognition of divinity, is the homage paid to august and mysterious objects in nature or to phenomena in the physical world which were supposed to have some divine significance. To give reverence to material objects themselves is condemned throughout the OT as idolatry. Such is the case, e.g., with the worship of "the host of heaven" (the heavenly bodies) sometimes practiced by the Hebrews (2 K. 17:16; 21:3, 5). So Job protests that he never proved false to God by kissing hands to the sun and moon in token of adoration (Job 31:26-38). The OT refers to acts of homage paid to an idol or an image, such as falling down before it (Isa. 44:15, 17, 19; Dnl. 3:7), or kissing it (1 K. 19:18; Hos. 13:2). All such practices are condemned in uncompromising terms. When, however, material things produce a reverential attitude, not to themselves, but to the deity whose presence they symbolize, then they are regarded as legitimate aids to devotion; e.g., fire as a manifestation of the divine presence is described as causing the spectator to perform acts of reverence (e.g., Ex. 3:2, 5; Lev. 9:24; 1 K. 18:38f.). In these instances, it was Yahweh Himself that was worshiped, not the fire which revealed Him. The sacred writers are moved to religious adoration by the contemplation of the glories of nature. To them, "the heavens declare the glory of God; and the firmament showeth his handiwork." (Cf. especially the "nature Psalms," 8, 19, 29, 104.)

C. Angels. On a still higher plane is the adoration practiced in the presence of supernatural agents of the divine will. When an angel of God appeared, men fell instinctively before him in reverence and awe (e.g., Gen. 18:2; 19:1; Nu. 22:31; Jgs. 13:20; Lk. 24:4f.). This was not to worship the creature instead of the Creator, for the angel was regarded not as a distinct individual having an existence and character of his own, but as a theophany, a self-manifestation of God.

D. The Deity. The highest form of adoration is that which is directed immediately to God Himself, His kingly attributes and spiritual excellencies being so apprehended by the soul that it is filled with rapture and praise, and is moved to do Him reverence. A classical instance is the vision that initiated Isaiah into the prophetic office, when he was so possessed with the sovereignty and sublimity of

God that he was filled with wonder and self-abasement (Isa. 6:1-5). In the OT, the literature of adoration reaches its high point in the Psalms (cf. esp. the group Pss. 95–100), where the ineffable majesty, power, and holiness of God are set forth in lofty strains. In the NT, adoration of the deity finds its most rapturous expression in Revelation, where the vision of God calls forth a chorus of praise addressed to the thrice-holy God (4:8-11; 7:11f.), with whom is associated the Redeemer-Lamb.

E. Jesus Christ. How far is Jesus regarded in the NT as an object of adoration, seeing that adoration is befitting only to God? During Our Lord's lifetime He was often the object of worship (Mt. 2:11; 8:2; 9:18; 14:33; 15:25; 20:20; 28:9, 17; Mk. 5:6; Jn. 9:38). Some ambiguity, however, belongs to the Gk. *proskyneín,* for while it is the usual word for "worshiping" God (e.g., Jn. 4:24), in some contexts it means no more than paying homage to a person of superior rank by kneeling or prostration, just as the unmerciful servant is said to have "fallen down and worshiped" his master the king (Mt. 8:26), and as Josephus speaks of the Jewish high priests as *proskynoúmenoi* (*BJ* iv.5.2). On the other hand it certainly implies a consciousness by those who paid this respect to Jesus, and by Jesus Himself, of a very exceptional superiority in His person; for the same homage was refused by Peter, when it was offered to him by Cornelius, on the ground that he himself also was a man (Acts 10:25f.), and even by the angel before whom John prostrated himself, on the ground that God alone was to be "worshiped" (Rev. 22:8f.). Yet Jesus never repudiated such tokens of respect.

But whatever the case during the "days of His flesh," there is no doubt that after His ascension Christ became to the Church the object of adoration as divine, and the homage paid to Him was indistinguishable in character from that paid to God. This is proved not only by isolated passages, but still more by the whole tone of the Acts and Epistles in relation to Him. This adoration reaches its highest expression in Rev. 5:9-14, where the Redeemer-Lamb who shares the throne of God is the subject of an outburst of adoring praise by the angelic hosts. In 4:8-11 the hymn of adoration is addressed to the Lord God Almighty, the Creator; here it is addressed to the Lamb on the ground of His redeeming work. In Revelation the adoration of Him "who sitteth on the throne" and that of "the Lamb" flow together into one stream of ecstatic praise (cf. 7:9-11).

D. M. EDWARDS

ADORN; ADORNMENT [Heb. *'āḏâ* (Isa. 61:10; Jer. 31:4), *yāṭaḇ* (2 K. 9:30), *ṣāpâ* (2 Ch. 3:6), *ḥēn* (Prov. 3:22), *pā'ar* (Ps. 149:4); Gk. *kósmos* (1 Pet. 3:3), *kosméō*–'order']; AV also BEAUTIFY, GARNISH, GRACE, TIRE; NEB also DRESS, ORNAMENT, CROWN, DECK, EMBELLISH, "add lustre to."

In 2 Ch. 3:6 the Heb. *ṣāpâ* means "overlay" or "plate"; the temple was overlaid or studded with precious stones for beauty. Here the LXX has Gk. *kosméō,* which is used also in Lk. 21:5 of the adornment of the temple, "with noble stones and offerings," in Mt. 23:29 of the adornment by the scribes and Pharisees of the "monuments of the righteous," and in Rev. 21:14 of the adornment with jewels of the foundations of the walls of the holy city.

The Heb. *pā'ar* in Ps. 149:4 is used for the adornment of the meek. The figurative use of *kosméō* is found in Tit. 2:10, where faithful, submissive slaves are said to "adorn the doctrine of God our Savior."

The remaining references are to adornment of the body, especially of women. On the specific forms of adornment *see* GARMENTS; JEWEL; ORNAMENT; STONES, PRECIOUS.

Both Paul and Peter give advice on how women should adorn themselves, for this was considered a vital question in the early Church. In 1 Tim. 2:9 Paul says that "women should adorn themselves modestly and sensibly in seemly apparel, not with braided hair or gold or pearls or costly attire." And Peter says, "Let not yours be the outward adornment with braiding of hair, decoration of gold, and wearing of robes" (1 Pet. 3:3).

J. W. D. H.

ADRAMMELECH ə-dram'ə-lek [Heb. *'aḏrammeleḵ*–'Ader is king' (in Assyr. usage 'Adar is prince')]. A son of Sennacherib king of Assyria—one of the two sons who slew him and escaped, indirectly leading to the accession of Esarhaddon (2 K. 19:37; Isa. 37:38). Mention of the incident is found in the Babylonian Chronicle, and traces of the name appear in the writings of Abydenus and Polyhistorus.

ADRAMMELECH AND ANAMMELECH ə-nam'əl-ek [Heb. *'aḏrammeleḵ* (see above) and *'ᵃnammeleḵ*–'Anu is king' (in Assyr. usage 'Anu is prince')]. The names given by the Israelite narrator to the god or gods imported into the Samaritan land by the men of Sepharvaim whom the king of Assyria had settled there (2 K. 17:31). In the Babylonian pantheon Anu, the god of heaven, is one of the three chief gods, and Adar, otherwise known as Ninib, is a solar god.

There are some unsolved difficulties in this passage (*see* ANAMMELECH), but at least a portion of the alleged difficulties have arisen from failure to regard the point of view of the Israelite narrator. He is writing from a time considerably later than the establishment of the institutions of which he speaks—late enough to render the phrase "unto this day" suitable (2 K. 17:34), late enough so that words and usages may have undergone modification. He is describing a mixture of religions which he evidently regards as deserving of contempt and ridicule, even apart from the falsity of the religions included in it. This mixture he describes as containing ingredients of three kinds—first, the imported religions of the imported peoples; second, the local high-place religions (e.g., v. 32); and third, the Yahweh religion of northern Israel (not that of Jerusalem). It is not likely that he thought they practiced any cult in its purity. They contaminated the religion of Yahweh by introducing Canaanite usages into it, and they are likely to have done the same with the ancestral religions which they brought with them.

The proper names may be correct as representing Palestinian usage, even if they differ somewhat from the proper Babylonian usage. The writer says that they "burnt their children in the fire to Adrammelech," but this does not necessarily prove that he thought that they brought this practice from Babylonia; his idea may be that they corrupted even their own false cult by introducing into it this horrible Canaanite rite. In considering the bearings of the evidence of the monuments on the case, considerations of this kind should not be neglected.

W. J. BEECHER

ADRAMYTTIUM ad-rə-mit'i-əm [Gk. *Adramyttion*]. An important seaport located on the northwest coast of the Roman province of Asia, at the head of the Gulf of Adramyttium, facing the island of Lesbos.

The only reference to Adramyttium in the Bible is Acts 27:2, where Paul, Luke, and Aristarchus, along with the group of prisoners in the charge of the centurion Julius, are said to have embarked on the first stage of their voyage from Caesarea to Rome in a ship from that city (Gk. *ploíō Adramyttēnṓ*). This vessel was probably one of the many small trading ships that traveled back and forth along the coast of Asia Minor. On this particular occasion it was on the homeward journey.

The plausible suggestion has been made by J. Rendel

Harris that Adramyttium was one of a number of colonies founded throughout the Mediterranean world by traders and navigators of Hadramaut, the spice-bearing area of south Arabia. The reading of the name with a rough breathing in the Vulgate (*navem Hadrumetinam*) points in this direction.

The present-day inland town of Edremit preserves the name, although the ancient location of the city is some distance away.

See J. R. Harris, *Contemporary Review,* 128 (1925), 194-202.

W. W. GASQUE

ADRIA ā'dri-ə [Gk. *Adrias*]. A body of water mentioned in the account of Paul's voyage to Rome: "as we were drifting across the sea of Adria" (Acts 27:27). Strabo, the first-century geographer, identifies the Adriatic as the Gulf of Adria and explains that the name is derived from the old Etruscan city of Atria (*Geog.* v.1.8), which was located at the mouth of the Po River. After the Syracusan colonies were developed along the coasts of Italy and Illyrica, the name gradually covered more and more, until at length it included the Ionian Sea, the Gulf of Tarentum (Servius *Aeneid* xi.540), and the Sicilian Sea (Pausanias v.25). Procopius, the Byzantine historian, located Malta on the western end of the Adriatic (*Wars* iii.14.16); and Ptolemy, a second-century geographer, stated that Crete was bounded on the west by the Adriatic, and Sicily by the same sea on the east (*Geog.* iii.4, 15). Consequently, in NT times "the Adria" designated that portion of the Mediterranean which extends from Malta to Crete.

Such a definition of the limits of that sea favors the customary identification of Malta as the island upon which Paul was shipwrecked. This broad extension of the term "Adria" finds support in Josephus' report of his experience of shipwreck, for he declares that his ship "sank in the midst of the sea of Adria" and that he was rescued subsequently by a ship from Cyrene headed for Puteoli (*Vita* 3). In medieval times, as W. M. Ramsay points out, sailors were accustomed to use the name "Adriatic" for the entire eastern portion of the Mediterranean except the Aegean Sea (*SPT,* p. 334). In modern terminology the name is restricted in application to that arm of the Mediterranean which extends about 500 mi. (800 km.) along the northeast coast of Italy.

G. H. ALLEN
D. H. MADVIG

ADRIEL ā'dri-əl [Heb. (Aram.?) *'aḏrî'ēl*–'my help is God']. The son of Barzillai the Meholathite, to whom Merab the daughter of King Saul was married when she should have been given to David (1 S. 18:19; 2 S. 21:8). Some MSS have "Michal" for "Merab" in 2 S. 21:8, a textual error easily accounted for. Adriel and Merab had five sons, whom David handed over to the blood vengeance of the men of Gibeon. The name Adriel seems to be Aramaic (see BDB, p. 727), the equivalent of the Hebrew name Azriel.

ADUEL ə-do͞o'əl [Gk. *Adouēl*]. An ancestor of Tobit (Tob. 1:1).

ADULLAM ə-dul'əm [Heb. *'^{a}ḏullām*]. The name of a city and of a cave.

1. A Canaanite royal city mentioned in Josh. 12:15; 15:35; 2 Ch. 11:7; Mic. 1:15; Neh. 11:30, the gentilic form occurring in Gen. 38:1-20. Adullam is mentioned in connection with Hormah, Arad, Libnah, Makkedah, Jarmuth, Socoh, Gath, Lachish, and Mareshah, hence is certainly to be located in the Shephelah, "down" from the Central Range (cf. Gen. 38:1). In Eusebius *Onom.* 84.23 and in the

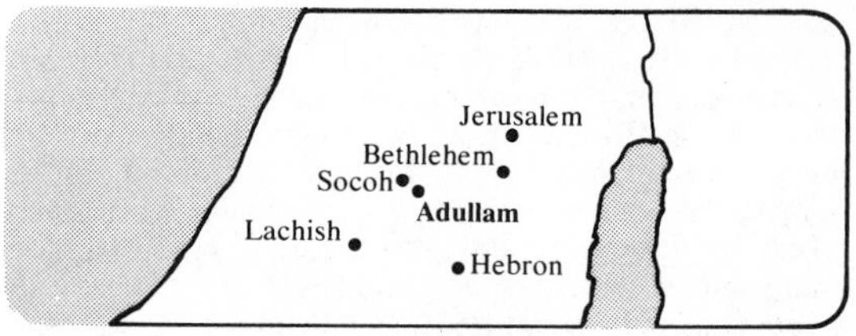

LXX of Josh. 10 Adullam is confused with Eglon, which seems to be too far W to suit the biblical descriptions.

The king of Adullam was defeated by Joshua, along with thirty others (Josh. 12:15). Adullam was one of the fourteen cities in a district of the Shephelah assigned to Judah (Josh. 15:33-36). It was one of the defense cities established by Rehoboam in Judah, possibly in anticipation of an Egyptian attack (2 Ch. 11:5-12). Along with other cities in Micah's home territory, Adullam is included in his lament (Mic. 1:10-16). Those who returned from the Exile settled in Adullam, as well as other sites in the Shephelah (Neh. 11:25-30). Judas Maccabeus withdrew to Adullam after putting the army of Gorgias to the rout (2 Macc. 12:38). Some scholars, following the suggestion of Clermont-Ganneau, believe the ancient name is preserved in the modern 'Id-el-Mâ or 'Idelmiyeh, a site with extensive ruins in Wâdī eṣ-Ṣûr at the foot of Tell esh-Sheikh Madhkûr, 7.5 mi. (12 km.) ENE of Beit-Jibrîn and about 12.5 mi. (20 km.) WSW of Bethlehem.

2. The cave of Adullam where David made his headquarters during part of the time when he was a fugitive from Saul's kingdom (1 S. 22:1; 2 S. 23:13; 1 Ch. 11:15). In the general area are numerous limestone caves, one of which may have served as David's refuge, while his followers, about four hundred in number, may have occupied other caves in the vicinity. This does not force the language of the biblical text, and it is unnecessary to look for a cave large enough to accommodate the entire number.

Because of the distance from Bethlehem, there has been some objection to the identification of the cave of Adullam with the site proposed in **1** above. Three of David's "thirty" broke through the Philistine lines to get him water from his beloved well at Bethlehem (2 S. 23:13-17; 1 Ch. 11:15-19)—which would have necessitated a round trip of about 25 miles. (It would be possible to read the text somewhat differently: David had previously expressed his desire for water from the well; the three leaders had, in the course of battle, approached Bethlehem, hence they undertook to fulfil his request—which would require a trip of something over 12 mi., certainly not unreasonable.) Accordingly, St. Chariton's cave, a few miles SE of Bethlehem, has traditionally been pointed out as the cave of Adullam. To complicate the discussion further, Josephus (*Ant.* vii.12.4) identified the "stronghold" of 2 S. 23:14=1 Ch. 11:16 as Jerusalem. There seems to be no compelling reason, however, to dissociate the location of the cave of Adullam from the location of the city of Adullam.

Bibliography.–*GP,* II, 239, 311; *GTTOT,* §§ 697f., and for a discussion of the "stronghold," §§ 757f. In § 1538 Simons tends to reject the reading Adullam in Mic. 1:15 in favor of Heb. *'aḏ-'ôlām,* "forever"; but this violates the poetic and literary structure of the passage.

W. S. LASOR

ADULLAMITE [Heb. *'^{a}ḏullāmî*]. A man of ADULLAM (**1**), used only of Judah's friend Hirah (Gen. 38:1, 12, 20).

ADULTERY. In Scripture, sexual intercourse by a married man with another than his wife, or by a married woman with another than her husband. It is distinguished from fornication, which is illicit sexual intercourse by an unmarried person.

I. Unlawful and Condemned.–Because adultery is a violation of the original divinely instituted marriage bond (Gen. 2:23f.), it is unlawful and therefore prohibited (Ex. 20:14; Lev. 18:20; 20:10; Dt. 5:18). Since the law of God is the expression of His nature, there can be no greater condemnation.

Adultery involves more than physical promiscuity. It also violates the integrity of the person, as is indicated by use of the expressions "knew his wife" and "have her" in Gen. 4:25; Mt. 14:4. The righteous in OT times viewed adultery with abhorrence. "This is an heinous crime," says Job. The stealthy way of the adulterer is marked (Job 31:11; 24:15). A warning is sounded against the flattering and beguiling ways of the adulteress (Prov. 2:16-19; ch. 7). When adultery prevails in a land so that even prophets and priests know no restraint, that land becomes like Sodom and Gomorrah (Jer. 23:10-15; 29:23).

The penalty for adultery in the OT is death (Lev. 20:10); when the method of this penalty is mentioned, it is by stoning (Dt. 22:23f.). In Ezk. 16:38-40 adultery is coupled with shedding of blood, but this does not exclude the stoning from applying to adultery itself (cf. Ezk. 23:45). The Jews in Jesus' time interpreted the law in this way (Jn. 8:5). No partiality is shown the man: both parties in the act are equally guilty.

II. Innocent or Guilty.–Where evidence of adultery was lacking and the husband was strongly suspicious, a well-defined procedure was open to him (Nu. 5:11-30). The language used in this passage gives a solemn and serious tone to the whole matter, indicating that this was not a procedure dealing with a mere whim of the husband. He was bringing his case before God. Yet the law was so concerned lest an injustice be done to the accused wife that she was given the benefit of a test. She was presented before the Lord with the waving and burning of an offering of barley, after which she was given bitter water to drink from the holy basin. This water, which caused the curse, was mingled with dust from the floor of the sanctuary and with washed-off ink of the writing containing the oath. If the woman was guilty, her belly would swell, her thigh would rot (RSV "fall away"), and she would become a "curse" and an "oath" among her people.

Trial by ordeal was practiced in the ancient Near East. In the Code of Hammurabi there is a parallel to the biblical account: "If a seignior's wife was accused by her husband, but she was not caught while lying with another man, she shall make affirmation by the god and return to her house. If the finger was pointed at the wife of a seignior because of another man, but she has not been caught while lying with the other man, she shall throw herself into the river for the sake of her husband" (*ANET*, p. 171, nos. 131f.). The following differences should be noted between the two accounts. In Hammurabi's Code the guilty might escape and the innocent suffer death. The outcome was all a matter of blind chance. And the river itself, which is characterized as a god, is the judge (*ANET,* p. 171, note 102). But the biblical record is solemn and religiously significant. The procedure was dictated by the Almighty (v. 11). There was no possible escape from the consequences of guilt, but exoneration for the innocent was certain.

III. Inward Intent.–The prohibition against marital unfaithfulness applies not only to the external act that the law alone can recognize; it also takes note of the desire of the heart. Mere external observance of the law is not the mark of OT religion. It probes deeper. From inward purity of heart proceeds the truly moral life (cf. Job 31:1, 4, 7; Prov. 6:25). This is the emphasis Jesus enunciates in Mt. 5:27f. As distinct from a mere external cleanness, to look and to lust is adultery of the heart.

IV. Change in Penalty.–As already observed, death was the penalty for adultery in the OT. This, of course, obviates the need to make any provision for divorce. However, in the teaching of Christ a man may put away his wife for reasons of adultery (Mt. 5:31f.), and so according to the NT a husband has recourse to a legitimate divorce in the case of an adulterous wife. There is here a significant change. While in the Sermon on the Mount Jesus interprets the law according to its original intent and meaning, He here indicates that as Lord He has authority to introduce a new provision. Nevertheless, it does not follow that the evil of adultery is thereby minimized. Jesus tells us that divorce never received divine sanction, and that it is, therefore, an evil. This lays upon adultery the weight of divine abhorrence and displeasure. The principle that God requires sexual fidelity in the marriage relation receives from Christ its highest vindication in the words, "I say to you: whoever divorces his wife, except for unchastity, and marries another, commits adultery" (Mt. 19:9).

See also DIVORCE.

See J. Murray, *Divorce* (1953), pp. 17-28.

D. FREEMAN

ADUMMIM ə-dum'im, **ASCENT OF** [Heb. *ma'ᵃlēh 'ᵃḏummîm*]. One of the landmarks defining the northern boundary of Judah westward from the mouth of the Jordan to Jerusalem, and the southern boundary of Benjamin eastward from Jerusalem to the mouth of the Jordan (Josh. 15:7; 18:7). The location is identified with the modern Tal'at ed-Damm ("ascent of blood"), where the ground is marked by red ochre, about 9 mi. (14.5 km.) ENE of Jerusalem.

According to Eusebius, there was a fortress at Maledomni (cf. Heb. *ma'ᵃlēh 'ᵃḏummîm*), halfway between Jericho and Jerusalem. Tradition has set the scene of the parable of the Good Samaritan (Lk. 10:30) at this place, where the road enters a narrow gorge; and the "Inn of the Good Samaritan" is shown to tourists, even though the NT never represents the story as more than a parable and does not specify any location other than "going down from Jerusalem to Jericho."

W. J. BEECHER
W. S. L. S.

ADVENT. *See* PERSON OF CHRIST; PAROUSIA; MILLENNIUM.

ADVENTURE. In the AV, an archaic word for "risk," "venture" (Dt. 28:56; Jgs. 9:17; Eccl. 5:14, RV; Acts 19:31).

ADVENTURESS [Heb. *noḵrîyâ*–'foreign woman'] (Prov. 2:16; 5:20; 6:24; 7:5; 23:27); AV STRANGER, STRANGE WOMAN; NEB LOOSE WOMAN. A woman who seeks social advancement or wealth by immoral seduction or other unscrupulous means. The word carried a sinister connotation in the OT because it was such women who had introduced immorality or the worship of alien deities into Israel (1 K. 11:1, 8). Hence the prudent were well advised to avoid all contact with such sources of temptation and moral ruin (Prov. 2:16, etc.). R. K. H.

ADVERSARY [Heb. *qûm* (part.), *qîm* (Job 22:20, perhaps corrupt), *ṣar, ṣārar, ṣûr* (part., Ex. 23:22), *śāṭān, śānē'* (Ps. 55:12), *rîḇ* (part., 1 S. 2:10), *'îš rîḇ* (Job 31:35), *ba'al mišpāṭ* (Isa. 50:8); Gk. *antídikos, antikeímenos, hypenantíos*]; AV also ENEMY, "(one who) riseth up against," "(one who) afflicteth (one's) soul," "he that hateth"; NEB also ENEMY (freq.), REBEL, INVADER, FOE, "he that stands against," "(one who) opposes," ACCUSER, "(one who) defies," "(one who) oppresses," "(one who) disputes (a) cause," OPPONENT, OPPOSITION, etc. [In Jgs. 2:3, Heb. *ṣaḏ* (AV "[thorns in your] sides") is taken by the RSV, following the Vulgate and Old Latin, as an error for *ṣar;* the NEB reads, "they will decoy you," taking *ṣaḏ* as a word for "snare," akin to Bab. and Assyr. *ṣaddu*. In Nah. 1:8 Heb. *m^eqômāh,* AV "the place thereof," is read in the RSV and NEB in the emended form *b^eqāmāyw* or *miqqāmāyw* (cf. LXX).]

The general word for a foe or enemy is Heb. *ṣar* (vb. *ṣārar*). A political adversary is meant by *śāṭān* in 1 K. 11. The *qal* participle of *qûm* designates one who "rises up" or "stands up" in opposition.

In the NT Gk. *antikeímenos* (Lk. 13:17; 21:15; 1 Cor. 16:9) means one "set over against"; *antídikos* (Lk. 18:3; 1 Pet. 5:8) is an opponent in a lawsuit or a prosecutor; *hypenantíos* (He. 10:27) is classical Greek and LXX term meaning "set over against," "contrary to."

See also ACCUSER; ENEMY; SATAN.

ADVERSITY [Heb. *ṣārâ, ṣar, ra', lahaṣ, t^elā'â*]; AV also TRAVAIL (Nu. 20:14), DISTRESS (1 K. 1:29), OPPRESSION (Job 36:15); NEB also HARDSHIPS, TROUBLES, AFFLICTION, MISFORTUNE, DISASTER, "when things go ill" (Eccl. 7:14). These words cover the whole range of misfortunes caused by enemies, poverty, sickness, etc. On the moral and ethical questions *see* AFFLICTION; EVIL.

ADVERTISE. Archaic for "advise" or "disclose" in the AV of Nu. 24:14; Ruth 4:4.

ADVICE; ADVISE; ADVISEMENT. Aside from their regular meaning these words are peculiarly employed in the AV as follows: "Advice" in 2 S. 19:43 means "request." In 1 S. 25:33, "advice" is equal to "sagacity" (RSV "discretion"). In 2 Ch. 25:17 the meaning seems to be "consult with oneself"; cf. also Jgs. 19:30. In 2 S. 24:13, "advise" means "advise oneself," i.e., "consider"; cf. also 1 Ch. 21:12; Prov. 13:10, where "well-advised" is the same as "considerate."

In 1 Ch. 12:19 "upon advisement" means "upon deliberation"; cf. 2 Macc. 14:20. A. L. BRESLICH

ADVOCATE [Gk. *paráklētos*] (1 Jn. 2:1); NEB "one to plead our cause." A designation of Jesus Christ.

The Greek word has several shades of meaning: (1) a legal advocate; (2) an intercessor; (3) a helper generally. In this passage the first and second meanings are included. Christ in heaven intercedes for Christians who sin upon earth. The next verse declares that He is the "propitiation for our sins," and it is His propitiatory work which lies at the basis of His intercession.

The same Greek word occurs also in the Gospel of John (14:16, 26; 15:26; 16:7), referring not to Christ but to the Holy Spirit, to whom Christ refers as "another paraclete" whom He will send from the Father. Here the NEB translates "Advocate," whereas the RSV has "Counselor" and the AV "Comforter."

For a full discussion of the Greek word *see* PARACLETE.

E. Y. MULLINS

ADYTUM ad'ə-təm [Lat. < Gk. *ádyton,* adj. *ádytos*–'not to be entered']. A term applied to the innermost sanctuary or chambers in ancient temples, and to secret places which were open only to priests: hence also to the holy of holies in the Jewish temple. *See* TEMPLE.

AEDIAS ā-ə-dī'əs [Gk. *Aēdeias*] (1 Esd. 9:27); RSV ELIJAH. In the AV and NEB, one of those who agreed to divorce their alien wives. The RSV takes it as a corruption of Gk. *Hēlia,* there being no Hebrew equivalent for it, and since in the parallel Ezr. 10:26 the name occurs as Elijah.

AELIA CAPITOLINA ē'lē-ə kap-ə-tō-lē'nə. The name of the new city erected by Hadrian on the site of JERUSALEM, named for his (the Aelian) clan. After the second revolt, led by Simon Bar-Cochba (A.D. 132-135), Hadrian had the portions of Jerusalem that had survived the destruction by Titus in A.D. 70 razed to the ground (much of the rubble being used to fill the Tyropoeon Valley), and Jews were forbidden under penalty of death to come within sight of the new city. Aelia Capitolina occupied approximately the site of the "Old City" (the walled city) of present-day Jerusalem.

See Ptolemy *Geography* § 15. W. S. L. S.

AENEAS ə-nē'əs [Gk. *Aineas*]. A paralytic at Lydda, who, after he "had been bedridden for eight years," was miraculously healed by Peter (Acts 9:33f.).

AENON ē'non [Gk. *Ainōn*]. A place where John was baptizing "because there was much water there" (Jn. 3:23). It was on the west side of the Jordan, John having earlier baptized on the east side (1:28; 3:26; 10:40). We may be sure it was not in Samaritan territory. Eusebius (*Onom.*) locates it 8 Roman mi. (11.8 km.) S of Scythopolis (Bethshan), for this stretch of land on the west of the Jordan was then not under Samaria but under Scythopolis. Its position is defined by nearness to SALIM. Various identifications have been suggested, the most probable being the springs near Umm el-'Amdân, which exactly suit the position indicated by Eusebius. W. EWING

AEON. *See* AGE.

AESORA ē'so-rə [Gk. *Aisōra*]; AV ESORA. A town in the borders of Samaria, mentioned in connection with Bethhoron and Jericho (Jth. 4:4), and thus evidently located in the eastern part of Samaria.

AFFECT. An archaic rendering of Gk. *zēlóō* in Gal. 4:17f., AV ("they zealously affect you, etc."; RV "zealously seek"; RSV "make much of"; NEB "are envious of") and of Gk. *kakóō* in Acts 14:2, AV ("made their minds evil affected against"; RSV and NEB "poisoned their minds against"). The AV also uses "affect" in translating Heb. *'ālal* in Lam. 3:51, "Mine eye affecteth mine heart"; the RSV renders, "my eyes cause me grief"; the NEB emends the text.

AFFECTION [Heb. *daddayim*–'breasts'] (Prov. 5:19); AV "breasts"; NEB LOVE; [Gk. *splánchna*–'bowels'] (2 Cor. 6:12; Phil. 1:8; 2:1); AV "bowels"; NEB "(your)-self," "deep yearning," "warmth of affection"; [Gk. *philóstorgos*] (Rom. 12:10); AV "kindly affectioned"; [Gk. *homeíromai*] (1 Thess. 2:8); AV, RSV, "affectionately desirous"; NEB "with yearning love"; [Gk. *philadelphía*] 2 Pet. 1:7); RSV "brotherly affection"; AV, NEB, "brotherly kindness." The Greek terms indicate the warm inner love that bound the early Christian brotherhood (in 2 Cor. 6:12 it is the possible lack of this love that is in view), and also the missionary love that Paul had for those to whom he brought the gospel (1 Thess. 2:8).

In the AV, certain archaic usages of this word occur. In Rom. 1:26; Col. 3:5 (Gk. *páthos*); and Gal. 5:24 (*páthēma*) it means "passions"; and in Col. 3:2, "set your affection on" (*phronéō*) means "think about," "set your mind on."

In Rom. 1:31, AV and NEB "without natural affection"

(*ástorgos*) is rendered in the RSV "heartless"; in 2 Tim. 3:3 the RSV has "inhuman" for the same word.

J. W. D. H.

AFFINITY. *See* MARRIAGE ALLIANCE.

AFFIRMATIVES. Hebrew does not use affirmative particles, but gives a positive reply either by repeating the word in question or by substituting the 1st person in the reply for the 2nd person in the question, or employing the formula: "You have said" or "You have rightly said." Jesus used this idiom (Gk. *sý eípas*) when answering Judas and Caiaphas (Mt. 26:25, 64).

A peculiar elegance occasionally attaches to the interpretation of the Scriptures because of their use of an affirmative and negative together, rendering the sense more emphatic. Sometimes the negative occurs first, as in Ps. 118:17: "I shall not die, but live"; sometimes the affirmative precedes, as in Isa. 38:1: "You shall die, and not live." Jn. 1:20 is made peculiarly emphatic because of the negative placed between two affirmatives: "He confessed, he did not deny, but confessed, I am not the Christ."

F. E. HIRSCH

AFFLICTION [Heb. *‘^{o}nî, makkâ, ‘ānâ, nega‘, ṣār, ṣārâ, 'āwen, ‘^{e}nîṯ, mû‘āqâ* (Ps. 66:11), *ḥ^{o}lî, laḥaṣ, ta‘^{a}lūlîm* (Isa. 66:4), *ra‘* (Ps. 34:19); Gk. *thlípsis, thlíbō*]; AV also PLAGUE, TRIBULATION, TROUBLE, SORE (2 Ch. 6:29), ENEMY (*ṣār,* Est. 7:4), DISEASE, DELUSIONS (Isa. 66:4), GRIEF (Jer. 10:19; NEB also ILL-TREATMENT, HUMILIATION, HARDSHIP, MISERY, PLAGUE, TROUBLE, SUFFERINGS, REMORSE, DISTRESS, PLIGHT, MISFORTUNE, MISCHIEF, PUNISHMENT, DISORDER, "wanton rites" (Isa. 66:4), DISASTER, etc.; in 1 S. 9:16 the RSV follows the LXX; in 2 S. 16:12 Heb. *b^{e}‘ēwnî,* "on my iniquity," is read as an error for *b^{e}‘āniyî* in the AV and RSV ("upon my affliction") and NEB ("my sufferings"), following the LXX and Vulgate.

In the OT affliction is both individual (sickness, poverty, oppression by the strong and rich, perverted justice) and national. A great place is given in the OT to affliction as a national experience, due to calamities such as war, invasion, conquest by foreign peoples, exile. These form the background of much of the prophetic writings, and largely determine their tone and character.

In the NT the chief form of affliction is that due to the fierce antagonism manifested to the religion of Jesus, resulting in persecution.

I. Sources of Affliction.–*A. God.* The Hebrew mind did not dwell on secondary causes, but attributed everything, even afflictions, directly to the great First Cause and Author of all things: "Does evil befall a city, unless the Lord has done it?" (Am. 3:6); "I form light and create darkness, I make weal and create woe [i.e., calamity], I am the Lord, who do all these things" (Isa. 45:7). Thus all things, including calamity, were referred to the divine operation. The Hebrew when afflicted did not doubt the universal sovereignty of God; yet, while assuming this sovereignty, he was sometimes tempted to accuse Him of indifference, neglect, or forgetfulness. Cf. Job *passim;* Isa. 40:27; 49:14; Ezk. 8:12; 9:9.

B. Evil Agents. Yet there are traces of a dualism which assigns a certain vague limit to God's absolute sovereignty, by referring affliction to an evil agency acting in quasi-independence of God. There could, however, never be more than a tendency in this direction, for a strict dualism was incompatible with the standpoint of Jewish monotheism.

Thus Saul's mental affliction is attributed to an "evil spirit," which is yet said to be "from the Lord" (1 S. 16:14; 18:10; 19:9); and the fall of Ahab is said by Micaiah to be due to the "lying spirit" which enticed him to his doom, in obedience to God's command (1 K. 22:20-22). In the prologue of Job, Job's calamities are ascribed to Satan; but even he receives his word of command from God, and is responsible to Him, like the other "sons of God" who surround the heavenly throne. He is thus "included in the Divine will and in the circle of Divine providence" (Schultz). After the prologue, Satan is left out of account, and Job's misfortunes are attributed directly to the divine causality. In later Judaism, the tendency to trace the origin of evil, physical and moral, to wicked spirits became more marked, probably because of the influence of Persian dualism.

In NT times, physical and mental maladies were thought to be due to the agency of evil spirits called demons, whose prince was Beelzebub or Satan (Mk. 1:23ff.; 3:22f.; 5:2ff.; Mt. 9:32f., etc.). Christ gave His assent to this belief (cf. the woman under infirmity, "whom Satan hath bound," Lk. 13:16). Paul attributed his bodily affliction to an evil angel sent by Satan (2 Cor. 12:7), though he recognized that the evil agent was subordinate to God's purpose of grace, and was the means of moral discipline (vv. 7, 9). Thus, while the evil spirits were regarded as malicious authors of physical maladies, they were not, in a strictly dualistic fashion, thought to act in complete independence; rather, they had a certain place assigned to them in the divine providence.

II. Meaning and Purpose of Affliction.–Why did God afflict men? How is suffering to be explained consistently with the goodness and justice of God? This was an acute problem which weighed heavily upon the Hebrew mind, especially in the later, more reflective, period. We can only briefly indicate the chief factors which the Scriptures contribute to the solution of the problem.

A. Punitive or Retributive. A common view in early Hebrew theology was that afflictions were the result of the divine law of retribution, by which sin was invariably followed by adequate punishment. Every misfortune was a proof of the sufferer's sinfulness. Thus Job's "friends" sought to convince him that his great sufferings were due to his sinfulness. This is generally the standpoint of the historians of Israel, who regarded national calamities as a mark of divine displeasure on account of the people's sins.

But this naive belief, though it contains an important element of truth, could not pass uncontested. The logic of facts would suffice to prove that it was inadequate to cover all cases; e.g., Jeremiah's sufferings were due not to sin, but to his faithfulness to his prophetic vocation. So the Suffering Servant in Isaiah. Job, too, in spite of his many woes, was firm in the conviction of his own integrity. To prove the inadequacy of the penal view is a main purpose of the book of Job.

A common modification of the traditional view was that the sorrows of the pious and the prosperity of the wicked were only of brief duration; in the course of time, things would adjust themselves aright (e.g., Job 20:5ff.; Ps. 73:3-20). But even granting time for the law of retribution to work itself out, experience contradicts the view that a man's fortune or misfortune is an infallible proof of his moral quality.

B. Probational. The thought is often expressed that afflictions are meant to test the character or faith of the sufferer. This idea is especially prominent in Job. God allowed Satan to test the reality of Job's piety by overwhelming him with disease and misfortunes (ch. 2). Throughout the poem Job maintains that he has stood the test (e.g., 23:10-12). Cf. Dt. 8:2, 16; Ps. 66:10f.; 17:3; Isa. 48:10; Jer. 9:7; Prov. 17:3.

C. Disciplinary and Purificatory. For those who are able to stand the test, suffering has a purificatory or disciplinary value. (1) The thought of affliction as a discipline or form of divine teaching is found in Job, especially in the speeches of Elihu, who insists that tribulation is intended as a method of instruction to save man from the pride and presumption that issue in destruction (Job 33:14-30; 36:8-10, 15). The same conception is found in Ps. 94:12; 119:67, 71.

(2) The purificatory function of trials is taught in such passages as Isa. 1:25; Zec. 13:9; Mal. 3:2f., where the process of refining metals in fire and smelting out the dross is the metaphor used.

D. Vicarious and Redemptive. The above are not fully adequate to explain the mystery of the afflictions of the godly. The profoundest contribution in the OT to a solution of the problem is the idea of the vicarious and redemptive significance of pain and sorrow. The author of Job did not touch this rich vein of thought in dealing with the afflictions of his hero. This was done by the author of the latter part of Isaiah.

The classical passage is Isa. 52:13–53:12, which deals with the woes of the oppressed and afflicted Servant of the Lord with profound spiritual insight. It makes no difference to the meaning of the afflictions whether we understand by the servant the whole Hebrew nation, or the pious section of it, or an individual member of it, and whether the speakers in ch. 53 are the Jewish nation or the heathen. The significant point here is the value and meaning ascribed to the servant's sufferings. The speakers had once believed (in accordance with the traditional view) that the servant suffered because God was angry with him and had stricken him. Now they confess that his sorrows were due, not to his own sin but to theirs (vv. 4-6, 8). His sufferings were not only vicarious (the punishment of their sin falling upon him), but redemptive in their effect (peace and health coming to them as a result of his chastisement). Moreover, it was not only redemptive, but expiatory ("his soul guilt-offering," v. 10)—a remarkable adumbration of the Christian doctrine of atonement.

E. The NT. The NT makes no new contribution to the solution of the problem, but repeats and greatly deepens the points of view already found in the OT. (1) There is a recognition throughout the NT of the law of retribution (Gal. 6:7). Yet Jesus repudiates the popular view of the invariable connection between misfortune and moral evil (Jn. 9:2f.). It is clear that He had risen above the conception of God's relation to man as merely retributive (Mt. 5:45, sunshine and rain for evil men as well as for the good). His followers would suffer tribulation even more than unbelievers, owing to the hostile reaction of the evil world, similar to that which afflicted Christ Himself (Mt. 5:10f.; 10:16-25; Jn. 15:18-20; 16:33). Similarly the Acts and the Epistles frequently refer to the sufferings of Christians (e.g., Acts 14:22; 2 Cor. 4:8-11; Col. 1:24; He. 10:32; 1 Pet. 4:13; Rev. 7:14). Hence afflictions must have some other than a merely punitive end.

(2) They are probational, affording a test by which the spurious may be separated from the genuine members of the Christian Church (Jas. 1:3,12; 1 Pet. 1:7; 4:17), and (3) a means of discipline, calculated to purify and train the character (Rom. 5:3; 2 Cor. 12:7, 9; Jas. 1:3).

(4) The idea of vicarious and redemptive suffering has a far deeper significance in the NT than in the OT, and finds concrete realization in a historical person, Jesus Christ. That which is foreshadowed in Isa. 52f. becomes in the NT a central, pervasive and creative thought. A unique place in the divine purpose is given to the passion of Christ. Yet in a sense, His followers partake of His vicarious sufferings, and "fill up . . . that which is lacking of the afflictions of Christ" (Col. 1:24; cf. Phil. 3:10; 1 Pet. 4:13). Here, surely, is a profound thought which may throw a flood of light on the deep mystery of human affliction. The cross of Christ furnishes the key to the meaning of sorrow as the greatest redemptive force in the universe.

III. Endurance of Affliction.–The Scriptures abound in words of consolation and exhortation adapted to encourage the afflicted. Two main considerations may be mentioned. (1) The thought of the beneficent sovereignty of God. "The Lord reigneth; let the earth rejoice," even though "clouds and darkness are round about him" (Ps. 97:1f.); "All things work together for good to them that love God" (Rom. 8:28, AV). Since love is on the throne of the universe, we may rest assured that all things are meant for our good. (2) The thought that tribulation is of brief duration, in comparison with the joy that shall follow (Ps. 30:5; Isa. 54:7f.; Jn. 16:22); a thought which culminates in the hope of eternal life. This hope is in the OT only beginning to dawn, and gives but a faint and flickering light, except in moments of rare exaltation and insight, when the thought of a perfect future blessedness seemed to offer a solution to the enigmas of life (Job 19:25-27; Pss. 37, 49, 73). But in the NT it is a postulate of faith, and by it the Christian is able to fortify himself in affliction, remembering that his affliction is light and momentary compared with the "far more exceeding and eternal weight of glory" which is to issue out of it (2 Cor. 4:17, AV; cf. Mt. 5:12; Rom. 8:18). Akin to this is the comfort derived from the thought of the near approach of Christ's second coming (Jas. 5:7f.).

In view of such truths as these, the Bible encourages the pious person in trouble to show the spirit of patience (Ps. 37:7; Lk. 21:19; Rom. 12:12; Jas. 1:3f.; 5:7-11; 1 Pet. 2:20), and even the spirit of positive joy in tribulation (Mt. 5:11f.; Rom. 5:3; 2 Cor. 12:10; Jas. 1:2, 12; 1 Pet. 4:13). In the NT emphasis is laid on the example of Jesus in patient endurance of suffering (Jn. 16:33; Jas. 5:7-11; 1 Pet. 2:19-23; 3:17f.). Above all, the Scriptures recommend the afflicted to take refuge in the supreme blessedness of fellowship with God, and of trust in His love, by which they may enter into a deep peace that is undisturbed by the trials and problems of life (Ps. 73, esp. vv. 23-28; Isa. 26:3f.; Jn. 14:1, 27; Phil. 4:7; etc.).

See also DISEASE. D. M. EDWARDS

AFFLUENCE [Heb. *šepa'*]; AV, NEB, ABUNDANCE. A rare word, occurring only in Dt. 33:19 and coming from a root meaning 'be abundant,' 'overflow.' Here affluence is general abundance rather than wealth as such, the reference being to the active participation of Zebulun in maritime enterprises. R. K. H.

AFOOT [Gk. *pezeúō*] (Acts 20:13, AV); RSV "by land"; NEB "by road." By walking from Troas to Assos Paul avoided the tedious voyage round Cape Lectum. (Cf. Mk. 6:33, AV, Gk. *pezḗ*.)

AFRAID. *See* FEAR.

AFRESH. In He. 6:6, the AV rendering of the prefix *ana-* in Gk. *anastauróō*, "they crucify . . . afresh." The RSV and NEB have simply "crucify," just as in classical Greek *anastauróō* has always the simple sense "crucify" (i.e., "raise *up* on a cross," *ana-* meaning merely "up"). Against this it is argued (1) that the classical writers had no occasion for the idea of crucifying anew; (2) that in many compounds *ana-* signifies both "up" and "again," as in *anablépō,* which means "recover sight" as well as "look up"; (3) that the rendering "crucify afresh" suits the context; (4) that the Greek expositors (e.g., Chrysostom) take it so without questioning (so also Bleek, Lünemann, Alford, Westcott, Bauer; cf. Vulg. *rursum crucifigentes*).

See *TDNT,* VII, *s.v.* σταυρόω (Schneider).

D. M. EDWARDS

AFRICA. The continent that forms the southern portion of the Europe-Asia-Africa land mass. It is not named in the Bible. Because North Africa is separated from the rest of the continent by the desert and the mountains of Abyssinia, except for the Nile Valley and the swampy coastlands of West Africa, very little was known of Africa in antiquity. Indeed, North Africa was part of the Mediterranean world, in many ways, and is so treated in the few biblical references. Greek and Latin writers referred to Africa as "Libya."

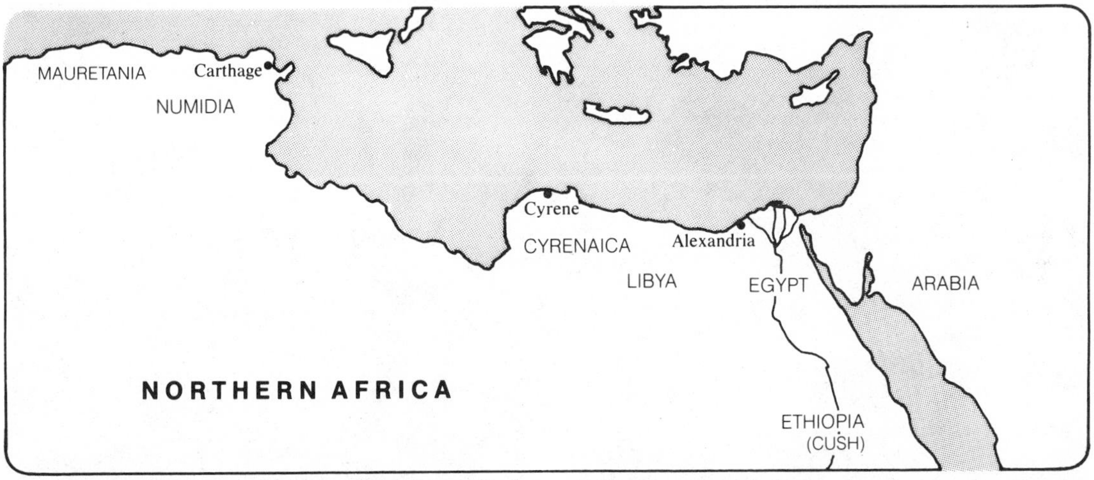

I. The People.–In the Table of Nations (Gen. 10) the "sons of Ham" are named: Cush, Egypt (or Mizraim), Put, and Canaan (10:7). Except for Canaan, whose descendants (10:15-19) occupied the eastern coastlands of the Mediterranean, these are generally located in Africa. Scholars are not in agreement concerning the location of Cush, since the Cushites in Gen. 10:7-12 are concerned with regions in Mesopotamia and in the Arabian peninsula. Cush formerly was identified as Ethiopia, due to the confusion of Ethiopia and Nubia by the Greeks; but this identification must be made with care.

Egypt is described as the father (ancestor) of Ludim, Anamim, Lehabim, Naphtuhim, Pathrusim, Casluhim, and Caphtorim (Gen. 10:13f.). All of these names are plural in form, and refer to peoples rather than individuals. The Casluhim are connected with the Philistines, and the Caphtorim are usually identified with Crete. The Lehabim are generally taken to be Libyans; and "Ludim" is sometimes amended to "Lubim," hence also Libyans. There is no agreement in attempts to identify the other "descendants" of Mizraim or Egypt.

Put is sometimes identified with the *Puṭaya* of the region adjacent to the Nile Delta; no descendants of Put are named.

It is evident that all of the peoples who can be identified as "African" are Caucasoid. There are no nations mentioned that can be identified anthropologically as Negroid. The Nubians, and for that matter the Ethiopians, while black-skinned, do not fit the anthropological description of the Negroes. (It might be mentioned at the same time that the Table of Nations does not include any peoples that can be identified in any way with the Mongolian race.) We can only conclude that the Bible limits its references to the peoples of the Eastern Mediterranean and adjacent areas; and so far as Africa is concerned, this means North Africa and the Nile Valley to Nubia.

Discussion of the origins of the Negroid, Caucasoid, and Mongoloid races does not properly belong in this article. The Bible clearly states that God created all men from a common ancestor (cf. Acts 17:26). Racial characteristics, pigmentation, etc., must therefore be results of other factors, among which are probably climate, soil, food, and

Wooden figures of Nubian bowmen carrying bows and bunches of arrows (*ca.* 2050-1800 B.C., from Siut) (Egyptian Museum, Cairo)

degrees of inbreeding. There is no biblical basis for the theory that the Negro originated because of the curse on Ham—after all, the curse, to be exact, was on Ham's son Canaan, and the Canaanites were always Caucasoid (see Gen. 9:25).

II. Language.–When we turn to the linguistic description of Africa we find similar complications. In the early days of the comparative study of language the term "Hamitic" was applied to certain African languages, a result of biblical influence. The term "Semitic" could easily be applied to the languages of most of the descendants of Shem; but the term "Japhetic" could scarcely be applied to the languages of the descendants of Japheth, and "Indo-European" became (except for most German linguistic scholars) the accepted term. It would be grossly erroneous, however, to suppose that these three terms exhaust the field of linguistic studies, and particularly to suppose that all African languages can be classified as "Hamitic." In fact, the Hamitic languages are limited to the northern part of Africa, chiefly along the Mediterranean coastal regions. We

Mosaic at Volubilis, a large Roman town in the interior of Morocco. The area became part of the Roman province of Mauretania Tingitania *ca.* A.D. 46. (B. K. Condit)

must be careful, however, not to confuse the linguistic description and the gentilic, for ancient Egyptian was partly Hamitic and partly Semitic, and the known Canaanite languages are all Semitic.

Moses married a "Cushite woman" (AV "Ethiopian," Nu. 12:1), the term probably implying a dark-skinned Egyptian, descendant of the Nubians, who were often included in and for a time ruled over Egypt (the 25th Dynasty). The Ethiopian eunuch, to whom the Spirit directed Philip the evangelist (Acts 8:26-39), was an official of the kingdom of "Ethiopia"—actually the Meroitic or Nubian kingdom, which had existed since *ca.* 750 B.C. in the Nile Valley between Aswan and Kharṭûm. Cf. F. F. Bruce, *Acts of the Apostles* (2nd ed. 1952), p. 190; *Book of the Acts* (*NIC*, 1954), pp. 186f.

See also CUSH; EGYPT; ETHIOPIA; LIBYA.

Bibliography.–E. G. Kraeling, ed., *Rand-McNally Bible Atlas* (1956), pp. 48-51 (on the Table of Nations); R. L. Beals and H. Hoijer, *Intro. to Anthropology* (2nd ed. 1959), pp. 132-197 (for a discussion of anthropological criteria of race), esp. 167-171, 184-194.

W. S. LASOR

AFTERBIRTH [Heb. *šilyâ*, Akk. *šilītu*] (Dt. 28:57). The allusion is to the consequences of disobedience to the covenant stipulations, which will result in such privation as to make a selfish cannibal of the most delicately bred and sensitive woman (cf. Lam. 2:20).

AFTERNOON. The post-noon period was described by the Heb. phrase *keḥōm hayyôm* (Gen. 18:1), "in the heat of the day," when the sun was a little past its zenith; by *lerû(a)ḥ hayyôm* (Gen. 3:8), "in the cool of the day"; and by *neṭôṯ hayyôm,* referring to the declining of day. In the orient a cooling breeze generally arises as the afternoon wanes, and it is then that much of the day's business is transacted.

AGABA ag'ə-bə.

1. (1 Esd. 5:30, AV). *See* HAGAB.

2. A fortress in Judea, mentioned by Josephus (*Ant.* xiii.16.5). It fell to Aristobulus, the son of Alexander Janneus and Alexandra, when he attempted to get control of the Judean government.

AGABUS ag'ə-bəs [Gk. *Agabos*]. A Christian prophet of Jerusalem, twice mentioned in Acts.

In Acts 11:27f., he is at Antioch foretelling "a great famine over all the world," "which," adds the historian, "came to pass in the days of Claudius." The visit of Agabus to Antioch took place in the winter of A.D. 43-44, and was the means of urging the Antiochian Christians to send relief to the brethren in Judea by the hands of Barnabas and Saul.

Two points should be noted. (1) The gift of prophecy here takes the form of prediction. The prophet's chief function was to reveal moral and spiritual truth, to "forth-tell" rather than to "foretell"; but the interpretation of God's message sometimes took the form of predicting events. (2) The phrase "over all the world" (practically synonymous with the Roman empire) must be regarded as a rhetorical exaggeration if strictly interpreted as pointing to a general and simultaneous famine. But there is ample evidence of severe periodic famines in various localities in the reign of Claudius (e.g., Suetonius *Claudius* 18; Tacitus *Ann.* xii.43), and of a great dearth in Judea under the procurators Cuspius Fadus and Tiberius Alexander, A.D. 44-48 (*Ant.* xx.2.6; 5.2), which probably reached its climax *ca.* A.D. 46.

In Acts 21:10f. we find Agabus at Caesarea warning Paul, by a vivid symbolic action (after the manner of OT prophets; cf. Jer. 13:1ff.; Ezk. 3f.), of the imprisonment and suffering he would undergo if he proceeded to Jerusalem.

In late tradition Agabus is included in lists of the seventy disciples of Christ.

D. M. EDWARDS

AGADE a-gä'dā [Akk. *a-ga-dé*]; biblical **ACCAD** a'kad [Heb. *'akkaḏ*]; elsewhere AKKAD. A principal city of Babylonia (Gen. 10:10). It was founded by Sargon of Agade (Sargon I) as his capital when he defeated Lugalzaggesi king of Uruk, ended the Sumerian domination, and established a Semite dynasty, ultimately combining Mesopotamia and portions of Syria and Asia Minor under his rule. Prior to the discoveries at Mari, his reign (and hence the founding of Agade) was dated as early as 3800 B.C.; but now Sargon's reign must be placed within the period from *ca.* 2370 to *ca.* 2150 B.C., probably (following P. van der Meer) 2242-2186.

The name Agade is found in Sargon's bilingual inscriptions, written in Sumerian as ag-gi-dé^{ki} (the ^{ki} merely indicates that the word is a place name) and in Akkadian as *a-ga-dé*^{ki}, the latter, it would seem, having been taken over from the Sumerian form of writing, since the word appears in Akkadian frequently as *ak-ka-du-ú* (with case-endings *-i* and *-a*). In Old Akkadian the form *a-ki-dí-e* (=*akide,* gen. of *akidû* or *akidi'u*) is closer to the Sumerian. Probably with the extension of kingship from the city alone to the surrounding area, the name Accad was extended in meaning to include all of northern Sumer, and was so used by Naram-Sin (2159-2123 B.C.) and Šar-kali-šarri (2122-2098 B.C.), the last kings of the dynasty of Agade.

Use of the expression "king of Sumer and Accad" (lugal Ki-en-gi Ki-uri-gè [Ki-uri, uri-gè, and just uri also occur]) is found in inscriptions of Ur-Nammu (2044-2027 B.C.), and often thereafter, even though the city Agade was destroyed by the Guti in the days of Šar-kali-šarri, and possibly never rebuilt. In the Code of Lipit-Ishtar (1864-1854 B.C.), e.g., "Sumer and Accad" (Ki-en-gi Ki-uri) occurs several times in the prologue, while Hammurabi (1724-1682) refers to "spacious Accad" (A.GA.DÉ^{KI}) and "the land of Sumer and Accad" (*su-me-ri-im u ak-ka-di-im*), using both the classical and the syllabic forms of writing the name, in the prologue to his Law Code.

The location of Agade is not positively identified, several sites in the vicinity of Babylon (notably *Tell Der*), and even Babylon itself, having been suggested as possibilities. The term "Accad" is applied to northern Babylonia, and Sumer to southern Babylonia, but the line of demarcation is uncertain.

See also BABYLON.

Bibliography.–G. A. Barton, *Royal Inscriptions of Sumer and Akkad* (1929), pp. 100-103, 136-147, 270-275; F. R. Steele, *Code of Lipit-Ishtar* (1948), pp. 10-12; G. R. Driver and J. C. Miles, *Babylonian Laws* (1955), II, 12; P. van der Meer, *Chronology of Western Asia and Egypt* (1955), Synchronistic Table 2.3.

W. S. LASOR

AGAG ā'gag [Heb. *'ᵃgāg*].

1. The name or title of an Amalekite king mentioned by Balaam (Nu. 24:7).

2. Another Amalekite king defeated by Saul but spared, along with the choicest spoil, in contravention of the divine command (1 S. 15:8f.). After rebuking Saul, Samuel himself killed Agag for all the Amalekite atrocities.

AGAGITE ā'gag-īt [Heb. *'ᵃgāgî*–'member of the house of Agag']. An opprobrious adjective applied to Haman (Est. 3:1, 10; 8:3, 5; 9:24). Jewish tradition has always credited the adversaries of the nation with membership in the house of Amalek, the hereditary foe of Israel. The

LXX has *Bougaíos* in Est. 3:1 and *Makedōn* (Macedonian) in 9:24, to signify "enemy." *See* BOUGAEAN.

AGAIN. In the AV, "bring again" may mean "bring back," as in Gen. 24:5 (Heb. *šûḇ*). Cf. "carry again" in Gen. 43:12; 2 Ch. 24:11, AV (*šûḇ*), "turn again" (Ex. 4:7), etc.

On the expression "born again" (AV, Jn. 3:3, 7; 1 Pet. 1:3, 23) *see* ANEW; REGENERATION.

AGAPE ə-gä'pē [Gk. *agápē*–(1) 'love'; (2) 'love-feast']. The brotherly common meals of the early Church.

I. In the NT.–Although the word agape was used constantly in the sense of love-feast in the postcanonical literature from the time of Ignatius onward, it is found in the NT only in Jude 12 (AV "feasts of charity"; RSV, NEB, "love-feasts"), and in 2 Pet. 2:13 according to a very doubtful reading (cf. AV "deceivings"; NEB "deceptions"; RSV "dissipation"). For the existence of the Christian common meal, however, we have abundant NT evidence.

The "breaking of bread" practiced by the primitive community in Jerusalem according to Acts 2:42, 46 must certainly be interpreted in the light of Pauline usage (1 Cor. 10:16; 11:24) as referring to the ceremonial act of the Lord's Supper. But the added clause in v. 46, "they took their food with gladness and singleness of heart," implies that a social meal was connected in some way with this ceremonial act. Paul's references to the abuses that had sprung up in the Corinthian church at the meetings for the observance of the Lord's Supper (1 Cor. 11:20-22, 33f.) make it evident that in Corinth as in Jerusalem the celebration of the rite was associated with participation in a meal of a more general character. And in one of the "we" sections of Acts (20:11) where Luke is giving personal testimony as to the manner in which the Lord's Supper was observed by Paul in a church of his own founding, we find the breaking of bread associated with and yet distinguished from an eating of food, in a manner which makes it natural to conclude that in Troas, as in Jerusalem and Corinth, Christians when they met together on the first day of the week were accustomed to partake of a common meal. That the word agape or love-feast used in Jude 12 is found early in the 2nd cent., and often afterward, as a technical expression for the religious common meals of the Church puts the meaning of Jude's reference beyond doubt.

II. Origin.–In the Jerusalem community, the common meal appears to have sprung out of the *koinōnía* or communion that characterized the first days of the Christian Church (cf. Acts 1:14; 2:1; etc.). The religious meals familiar to Jews—the Passover being the great type—would make it natural in Jerusalem to give expression to the sense of brotherhood by means of table fellowship; and the community of goods practiced by the infant Church (2:44; 4:32) would readily take the particular form of a common table at which the wants of the poor were supplied out of the abundance of the rich (6:1ff.). The presence of the agape in the Greek church of Corinth was no doubt due to the initiative of Paul, who would hand on the observances associated with the Lord's Supper just as he had received them from the earlier disciples; but participation in a social meal would commend itself very easily to men familiar with the common meals that formed a regular part of the procedure at meetings of those religious clubs and associations which were so numerous at that time throughout the Greco-Roman world.

III. Relation to the Eucharist.–In the opinion of the great majority of scholars the agape was a meal at which not only bread and wine but all kinds of viands were used, a meal which had the double purpose of satisfying hunger and thirst and giving expression to the sense of Christian brotherhood. At the end of this feast, bread and wine were taken according to the Lord's command, and after thanksgiving to God were eaten and drunk in remembrance of Christ and as a special means of communion with the Lord Himself and through Him with one another. The agape was thus related to the eucharist as Christ's last Passover to the Christian rite which He grafted upon it. It preceded and led up to the eucharist, and was quite distinct from it.

In opposition to this view it has been strongly urged by some modern critical scholars that in the apostolic age the Lord's supper was not distinguished from the agape, but that the agape itself from beginning to end was the Lord's Supper which was held in memory of Jesus. It seems fatal to such an idea, however, that while Paul makes it quite evident that bread and wine were the only elements of the memorial rite instituted by Jesus (1 Cor. 11:23-29), the abuses which had come to prevail at the social gatherings of the Corinthian church would have been impossible in the case of a meal consisting only of bread and wine (cf. vv. 21, 33f.). Moreover, unless the eucharist in the apostolic age had been discriminated from the common meal, it would be difficult to explain how at a later period the two could be found diverging from each other so completely.

IV. Separation from the Eucharist.–In the Didache (*ca.* A.D. 100) there is no sign as yet of any separation. The direction that the second eucharistic prayer should be offered "after being filled" (10:1) appears to imply that a regular meal had immediately preceded the observance of the sacrament. In the Ignatian epistles (*ca.* A.D. 110) the Lord's Supper and the agape are still found in combination (Smyrn. 8:2). It has sometimes been assumed that Pliny's letter to Trajan (*ca.* A.D. 112) proves that the separation had already taken place, for he speaks of two meetings of the Christians in Bithynia, one before the dawn at which they bound themselves by a "sacramentum" or oath to do no kind of crime, and another at a later hour when they partook of food of an ordinary and harmless character (*Ep.* x.96). But as the word "sacramentum" cannot be taken here as necessarily or even probably referring to the Lord's Supper, the evidence of this passage is of little weight.

When we come to Justin Martyr (*ca.* A.D. 150) we find that in his account of church worship he does not mention the agape at all, but speaks of the eucharist as following a service which consisted of the reading of Scripture, prayers, and exhortation (*Apol.* i.67); so by his time the separation must have taken place. Tertullian (*ca.* A.D. 200) testifies to the continued existence of the agape (*Apol.* 39), but shows clearly that in the church of the West the eucharist was no longer associated with it (*De Corona* 3). In the East the connection appears to have been longer maintained, but by and by the severance became universal; and though the agape continued for long to maintain itself as a social function of the Church, it gradually passed out of existence or was preserved only as a feast of charity for the poor.

Various influences appear to have cooperated in this direction. Trajan's enforcement of the old law against clubs may have had something to do with it (cf. Pliny, *loc. cit.*), but a stronger influence probably came from the rise of a popular suspicion that the evening meals of the Church were scenes of licentious revelry and even of crime. The actual abuses which already are attested in the apostolic age (1 Cor. 11:20ff.; Jude 12), and which would tend to multiply as the Church grew in numbers and came into closer contact with the heathen world, might suggest the advisability of separating the two observances.

The strongest influence of all, however, would come from the growth of the ceremonial and sacerdotal spirit by which Christ's simple institution was slowly turned into a mysterious priestly sacrifice. To Christ Himself it had seemed natural and fitting to institute the supper at the close of a social meal. But when this memorial supper had been transformed into a repetition of the sacrifice of Calvary by the action of the ministering priest, the ascetic idea became natural that the eucharist ought to be received fasting, and that it would be sacrilegious to link it on to the observances of an ordinary social meal.

Bibliography.–Sch.-Herz., I; J. F. Keating, *Agape and the* Eucharist (1901); B. Reicke, *Diakonie, Festfreude und Zelos* (1951), K. von Weizsäcker, *Apostolic Age,* I (Eng. tr. 1894), 52ff.; *TDNT,* I *s.v.* ἀγαπάω, ἀγάπη (Quell, Stauffer).

J. C. LAMBERT

AGAR ā'gär (Gal. 4:24f., AV). *See* HAGAR.

AGARENES ag-ə-rēnz' (Bar. 3:23, AV). *See* HAGAR.

AGATE. *See* STONES, PRECIOUS.

AGE [Heb. *'ôlām;* Gk. *aiṓn*]. Indefinitely long duration, whether backward in time, forward in time, or both.

1. God is God "from age to age" (Ps. 90:2, Heb. *mē'ôlām 'aḏ 'ôlām*; LXX, Gk. *apó toú aiṓnos héōs toú aiṓnos*), i.e., everlasting in both directions. His existence had no beginning and will have no end. The idea of eternality can be emphasized by the use of the plural *'ôlāmîm* or *aiṓnes,* or by compound expressions such as *le'ôlām wā'eḏ* (e.g., Ex. 15:18, Heb. *'eḏ* [*'aḏ*] being a synonym of *'ôlām*), "for ever and ever." In the NT Gk. *eis tón aiṓna* (lit. "to the age," but which itself can mean "forever" in appropriate contexts, such as Jn. 6:51) can be made more emphatic by the use of such forms as *eis toús aiṓnas* (lit. "to the ages," e.g., Rom. 1:25), *eis pántas toús aiṓnas* (lit. "to all the ages," Jude 25), *eis toús aiṓnas tṓn aiṓnōn* (lit. "to the ages of the ages," e.g., Gal. 1:5), or even *eis pásas tás geneás toú aiṓnos tṓn aiṓnōn* (lit. "to all the generations of the age of the ages," Eph. 3:21). God is "the king of the ages" (1 Tim. 1:17; Rev. 15:3), i.e., the eternal King.

The context alone can determine whether such expressions have the connotation of absolute eternality or simply of very long duration. The hills are "everlasting" (Heb. *giḇ'ôṯ 'ôlām,* lit. "hills of age," Dt. 33:15; Hab. 3:6), and Mt. Zion "abideth for ever" (Heb. *le'ôlām,* Ps. 125:1); but these had a beginning and will have an end. God was there before them and will continue after them (Ps. 90:2; 102:25-27). The city gates of Jerusalem are apostrophized as "everlasting doors" or rather "ancient doors" in Ps. 24:7, 9 (*piṯḥê 'ôlām*; cf. RV mg.). The "ancient high places" of Ezk. 36:2 are *bāmôṯ 'ôlām* (lit. "high places of age"). Similarly "the years of ancient times" (Ps. 77:5 [MT 6]) are literally "the years of ages" *šenôṯ 'ôlāmim*). In the NT the prophets are said to have prophesied *ap' aiṓnos,* which simply means "from of old" (Lk. 1:70; Acts 3:21). A remoter antiquity is denoted by *pró tṓn aiṓnōn*, "before the ages" (1 Cor. 2:7).

2. Toward the end of the pre-Christian era the division of the course of time into more definitely demarcated "ages" is encountered. In Zoroastrian eschatology, which exercised some influence on Jewish ideas of time in the closing centuries B.C., the world's duration of twelve thousand years was divided into four ages of three thousand years each. In 2 Esd. 6:7ff. (toward the end of the 1st cent. A.D.) one age is said to have come to an end with Isaac (or Esau); the present age runs from Jacob to the last judgment; the resurrection age follows. The last four hundred years of the present age are the days of the Messiah; at the end of them he dies, together with all mankind, and primeval silence pervades the world for seven days; then comes the resurrection.

The Qumrân community (*ca.* 130 B.C.–A.D. 70) believed itself to be living in the closing phase of the "epoch of Belial"; a new age, marked by the fulfillment of all that the prophets had foretold, would be inaugurated by the appearance of the prophet of Dt. 18:15ff. together with "the Messiahs of Aaron and Israel."

The distinction between the present age and the age to come is commonly made in the NT, but with a peculiarly Christian modification. The present age is evil (Gal. 1:4); in the age to come, which follows the resurrection and judgment, righteousness will reign (cf. 2 Pet. 3:13). Jesus differentiates between the conditions of life experienced now by "the sons of this age" (cf. Lk. 16:8), who "marry and are given in marriage," and those proper to such as "are accounted worthy to attain to that age, and the resurrection from the dead," in which marriage is unknown (Lk. 20:34-36). He speaks of "an eternal sin," which is never forgiven—"neither in this age, nor in that which is to come" (Mk. 3:29; Mt. 12:32). He tells His disciples that those who make sacrifices for His sake here and now will even in this life receive a recompense, "and in the age to come eternal life" (Mk. 10:30 par.). While "eternal life" (*zōḗ aiṓnios*) etymologically might mean simply life of indefinite or perpetual duration, it appears from its NT usage to mean more precisely "the life of the age to come," i.e., resurrection life.

In the Epistles the "present evil age" (Gal. 1:4) is dominated by "the god of this age," who blinds the minds of unbelievers (2 Cor. 4:4). The "rulers of this age" (1 Cor. 2:6, 8) are the *árchontes,* the principalities and powers, who through ignorance of God's hidden wisdom plotted the crucifixion of "the Lord of glory" and thus encompassed their own downfall (cf. Col. 2:15). From them "the wisdom of this age" derives its character (1 Cor. 2:6; cf. 3:18; 1:20). The riches of this age are perishable and transient (1 Tim. 6:17); it was through love for "this present age" that Demas forsook the company of Paul (2 Tim. 4:10). Believers are urged not to be "conformed to this age" (Rom. 12:2) but to live sober, righteous, and godly lives in "this present age" (Tit. 2:12). To do this means resisting the prevalent trend, but such resistance is possible for them because they have already come to experience "the powers of the age to come" (He. 6:5).

Here is the distinctive feature in NT teaching about the two ages. The age to come is the age of the kingdom of God. The kingdom of God has already arrived with the ministry of Jesus and has taken the field against the power of evil (Lk. 11:20; Mt. 12:28); yet Jesus bids His disciples pray for its arrival (Lk. 11:2; Mt. 6:10). In other words, through the ministry of Jesus the age to come has broken into the present age; the dead already hear the voice of the Son of God and live (Jn. 5:25); the judgment has already taken place (Jn. 3:18; 12:31); believers in Jesus receive here and now eternal life—the life of the age to come (Jn. 3:36). As participants with Christ in His death, burial, resurrection, and exaltation (Rom. 6:3ff.; Col. 2:12, 20; 3:1; Eph. 2:5f.), they belong spiritually to that age while they continue to live temporally in this age. Hence the tension to which they are constantly subject during the overlapping period between the times—the "last days" or "last hour," as this period is called in the NT. This period, in which the age to come has arrived while the present age has not yet passed away, stretches from the first advent of Christ to His parousia.

The present age will pass away finally at the *synteleía toú aiṓnos* ("the consummation of the age")—a phrase peculiar to Matthew. Then the last judgment (Mt. 13:39f., 49) and the parousia of Christ (Mt. 24:3) take place; until then the risen Christ promises His presence to His disciples on earth (Mt. 28:20). A similar phrase, *synteleía tṓn aiṓnōn* ("consummation of the ages"), appears in He. 9:26, where, however, it denotes the first inbreaking of the coming age into the present age: Christ was manifested "once at the end of the ages . . . to put away sin." So too Paul in 1 Cor. 10:11 speaks of himself and his readers as those on whom the "ends of the ages" (*télē tṓn aiṓnōn*) have come. These expressions point to the appearance of Christ as the turning point of world history (cf. Gal. 4:4).

3. Occasionally *aiṓn,* in the singular or plural, is used of the created world, as in He. 1:2; 11:3 (pl. in both places). There are antecedents for this use in the LXX, e.g., Ex. 15:18, where the Lord is described as "reigning over the world for ever and ever" (*basileúōn tón aiṓna*; cf. Wisd. 13:9; 14:6; 18:4; etc.).

4. The Gnostic use of *aiṓnes* to denote an order of spiritual beings is not found in biblical Greek. When Paul in Col. 1:26 and Eph. 3:9 speaks of the mystery of God which has been concealed "from the ages" (*apó tṓn aiṓnōn*), he means nothing more than that it has been concealed from the beginning of time until its present revelation.

Bibliography.–J. Barr, *Biblical Words for Time* (1962); O. Cullmann, *Christ and Time* (Eng. tr. 1951); G. Dalman, *Words of Jesus* (Eng. tr. 1902); G. W. H. Lampe, *Patristic Greek Lexicon* (1961), *s.v.* αἰών; J. Marsh, *Fulness of Time* (1952); C. von Orelli, *Die hebräischen Synonyma der Zeit und Ewigkeit* (1871); *TDNT*, I, *s.v.* αἰών (Sasse); N. H. Snaith, "Time in the OT," in F. F. Bruce, ed., *Promise and Fulfilment: Studies Presented to S. H. Hooke* (1964).

F. F. BRUCE

AGED. *See* OLD AGE.

AGEE ā'gē [Heb. *'āgē'*]. A Hararite, father of Shammah, one of David's three heroes (2 S. 23:11). The MT here is supported by 4QSam[a], making suggested emendations unwarranted.

AGGABA ag'ə-bə (NEB 1 Esd. 5:29). *See* HAGABAH.

AGGEUS a-gē'əs (AV 1 Esd. 6:1; 7:3; 2 Esd. 1:40). *See* HAGGAI.

AGIA ā'gē-ə [Gk. *Augia*] (1 Esd. 5:38); AV, NEB, AUGIA. The wife of Jaddus, whose sons were removed from the priesthood because their ancestors had usurped priestly functions. The name is omitted in Ezr. 2 and Neh. 7.

AGITATOR [Gk. *kinoúnta stáseis*] (Acts 24:5); AV "mover of sedition"; NEB "fomenter of discord." Both Greek words connote disquiet: *stásis* can mean "sedition," "riot," or "discord," and *kinéō* means "move" or "stir." Thus the combination indicates considerable agitation.

TERTULLUS, an orator hired to present the high priest's case against Paul, refers to him as "a pestilent fellow," "an agitator," "a ringleader." From the perspective of the established leaders in Jerusalem, Paul was a threat to the unity of Judaism and to the political status of Jews internationally. It is interesting to note that the Roman government saw the picture quite differently (cf. Acts 18:14f.; 25:18f.; 26:31).

G. A. VAN ALSTINE

AGLOW [Gk. *zéō*] (Rom. 12:11); AV FERVENT; NEB ARDOUR. The primary meaning of the underlying Greek verb is "boil, bubble up" with an extended meaning for solids of "fiery hot." It also, as today, functioned with a metaphorical sense, for example, "boil with rage" or "bubble with joy." Thus in Rom. 12:11 "be aglow with the Spirit" means that one's life should demonstrate the dynamic presence of the Holy Spirit like water boiling over a fire or metal fired to the glowing point.

See also FERVENT (Acts 18:25).

R. GUELICH

AGONE (1 S. 30:13, AV). An old past participle of the verb "go," which today has the form "ago."

AGONY [Gk. *agōnía;* Vulg. *agonia*] (Lk. 22:44); NEB "anguish of spirit." In the NT, the word used to describe the climax of the mysterious soul-conflict and unspeakable suffering of Our Lord in the garden at Gethsemane.

The term is derived from Gk. *agṓn,* "contest," and this in turn from *ágō*, "to drive or lead," as in a chariot race. Its root idea is the struggle and pain of the severest athletic contest or conflict. The wrestling of the athlete has its counterpart in the wrestling of the suffering soul of the Savior in the garden. At the beginning of this struggle He speaks of His soul being exceedingly sorrowful even unto death, and this tumult of emotion culminated in the agony. All that can be suggested by the exhausting struggles and sufferings of charioteers, runners, wrestlers, and gladiators, in Grecian and Roman amphitheaters, is summed up in the pain and death-struggle of this solitary word "agony." The word was rendered by Wyclif (1382) "maad in agonye"; Tyndale (1534) and following translators use "an agony."

The record of Jesus' suffering in Gethsemane, in the Synoptic Gospels (Mt. 26:36-46; Mk. 14:32-42; Lk. 22:39-46; and also in He. 5:7f.) indicates that it was threefold:

(1) *Physical.* The agony of His soul wrought its pain on His body, until "his sweat became as it were great drops of blood falling down upon the ground" (Lk. 22:44). He offered His prayers and supplications "with strong crying and tears" (He. 5:7). The intensity of His struggle so distressed and weakened Him that Luke says "there appeared unto him an angel from heaven, strengthening him." The threefold record of the evangelists conveys the idea of the most intense physical pain.

(2) *Mental.* The crisis of Jesus' career as Messiah and Redeemer came in Gethsemane. The moral issue of His atoning work was intelligently and voluntarily met here. The Gospels exhaust language in attempting to portray the stress and struggle of this conflict. "My soul is exceeding sorrowful even unto death." "Being in an agony he prayed more earnestly, saying, Father, if it be possible, let this cup pass away from me." The mental clearness of Christ's vision of humanity's moral guilt, and the energy of will necessary to meet the issue and take "this cup" of being the world's sin-bearer, indicate the awful sorrow and anguish of His supernatural conflict.

It is divinely significant that the word *agōnía* appears but once in all the NT. This solitary word records a solitary experience. Only One ever compassed the whole range of the world's sorrow and pain, anguish and agony. The shame of criminal arrest in the garden and of subsequent condemnation and death as a malefactor had to His innocent soul the horror of humanity's entire and ageless guilt. The mental and moral anguish of Jesus in Gethsemane interprets the meaning of Paul's description of the atonement, "Him who knew no sin he made to be sin on our behalf" (2 Cor. 5:21).

(3) *Spiritual.* The agony of Jesus was supremely within the realm of His spirit. The effect of sin in separating the human soul from God was fathomed by the suffering Savior in the fathomless mystery of His supernatural sorrow. Undoubtedly the anguish of Gethsemane surpassed the physi-

cal torture of Calvary. The whole conflict was wrought out here. Jesus' filial spirit, under the burden of the world's guilt, felt isolated from the Father. This awful, momentary seclusion from His Father's face constituted the "cup" which He prayed might pass from Him, and the "agony" of soul, experienced again on the cross, when He felt that God had forsaken Him.

No theory of the atonement can do justice to the threefold anguish of Jesus in Gethsemane and on Calvary, or to the entire trend of Scripture, that does not include the substitutionary element in His voluntary sacrifice, as stated by the prophet: "The Lord hath laid on him the iniquity of us all" (Isa. 53:6), and by His apostles: "who was delivered up for our trespasses" (Rom. 4:25), "who his own self bare our sins" (1 Pet. 2:24).

The authenticity of Lk. 22:43f. lacks full certainty inasmuch as some important ancient authorities omit it (e.g., p^{75} $\aleph^a$ A B T W, Boh., Sah., Syr.^{s}, Marcion, Clement, Origen).

In the OT, the RSV uses "agony" to translate Heb. *taḥ^{a}lu'îm* (2 Ch. 21:19, AV "diseases"), *ḥeḇel* (Isa. 13:8, AV "sorrows"), and *ḥûl* (Ezk. 30:16, AV "pain").

The AV has "agony" in 2 Macc. 3:14, 16, 21 for Gk. *agōnía* and *agōniáō,* where the RSV has "distress" and "anguish," and the NEB has "distress," "anguish," and "agony." D. M. PRATT

AGRAPHA ag'rə-fə [Gk. *ágrapha*–'unwritten (things)']. Sayings of Jesus not found in the authentic text of the canonical Gospels.

I. History of Research
II. Sources
  A. The NT
  B. Variant Readings of the NT
  C. Apocryphal Gospels
  D. Church Fathers
  E. Jewish Sources
  F. Islamic Sources
III. Development of Agrapha
IV. Possibly Authentic Agrapha
  A. From Variant Readings
  B. From Church Fathers
  C. From the Papyri
  D. From the Apocryphal Gospels and Acts
V. Other Agrapha
VI. Significance

I. History of Research.–The first comprehensive study of the agrapha was by Alfred Resch in his monumental *Agrapha.* Resch collected 361 agrapha, and believed that some of these were fragments of an "original gospel." His work was criticized by J. H. Ropes in *Die Sprüche Jesu.* The latter suggested that Resch's collection contained only fourteen valuable and thirteen possibly valuable agrapha.

Between 1897 and 1907 B. P. Grenfell and A. S. Hunt discovered at Oxyrhynchus (Behnesa) in Egypt papyri from the 2nd to the 4th cents. A.D. containing purported sayings of Jesus.

In 1945 eleven Coptic codices, one tractate, and fragments of a lost codex were discovered by accident near Nag Hammadi in upper Egypt. Among the treatises was a Gospel of Thomas, which contains 114 *logia* or sayings of Jesus, some of which are parallel to those found in the Oxyrhynchus papyri (Oxy. P. 1 = Thomas, logia 26-28, 30-33, 77; Oxy. P. 654 = Thomas, logia 1-6; Oxy. P. 655 = Thomas, logia 36-37, 39). It is possible that these papyri represent the Greek original of the Coptic Gospel of Thomas. The logia of Thomas, about half of which were unknown, constitute the most important collection of agrapha to be discovered.

The most important recent study of the agrapha is J. Jeremias, *Unknown Sayings of Jesus.* He selects eighteen sayings (including 1 Thess. 4:15ff.) which he considers "perfectly compatible with synoptic traditions, whose authenticity admits of serious consideration" (p. 42).

II. Sources.–*A. The NT.* There are in the NT apart from the Gospels a number of sayings attributed to Christ: Acts 1:4ff.; 11:16; 20:35; 1 Thess. 4:15ff. (cf. Mt. 24:30f.); and 1 Cor. 7:10 (cf. Mk. 10:11).

B. Variant Readings of the NT. Codex Bezae adds a saying on the Sabbath breaker before Lk. 6:5 (see IV.A below), and at Mt. 20:28 inserts, "But seek to increase from that which is small, and from the greater to become less" (cf. Lk. 14:8-10). It is possible to consider as agrapha later incorporated into the TR both the pericope of the woman caught in adultery (Jn. 7:53–8:11) and the longer endings of Mark (16:9-20).

C. Apocryphal Gospels. The various APOCRYPHAL GOSPELS such as the Gospels of Mary, of Peter, of the Hebrews, of the Egyptians, etc. contain numerous sayings attributed to Jesus. The overwhelming mass of materials such as those in the Protevangelium of James, the Gospel of Nicodemus, etc. are legendary and worthless. It is conceivable that a few of the logia of the Gospel of Thomas (logia 8, 77, 82) are authentic, though most of the sayings in this work betray an Encratite or Gnostic slant.

D. Church Fathers. The earliest attempt to collect the extracanonical sayings of Jesus was by Papias of Hierapolis in Phrygia. His work in five books, *An Exposition of the Oracles of the Lord* (*ca.* A.D. 130), is no longer extant, but is cited by Eusebius (*HE* iii.39). The latter recognized that Papias was quite uncritical; e.g., a saying that he attributed to Christ speaks of vines multiplying with 10,000 shoots, each having 10,000 branches, with each branch having 10,000 tendrils, etc. Other church fathers such as Justin Martyr (d. 165), Tertullian (d. after 220), and Clement of Alexandria (d. 214) have preserved possibly genuine sayings of Christ. Cf. also 2 Clem. 5:2-4.

E. Jewish Sources. The Talmud preserves but a few allusions to Jesus and his sayings. The anti-Christian polemic was later elaborated (post 9th cent. A.D.) in the Toledoth Jeshu narratives, which seek to justify Jesus' condemnation.

F. Islamic Sources. The Koran (61:6) claims that Jesus said, "I am the messenger of Allah unto you . . . bringing good tidings of a messenger who cometh after me, whose name is the Praised One [Arab. *Aḥmad,* a name cognate with Muhammad]." Islamic scholars associate this name with the Gk. *periklytós* "renowned," which they read in place of *paráklētos* in Jn. 14:26, etc. Numerous sayings are attributed to Jesus in the traditions collected by such authors as al-Ghazzali (A.D. 1058-1111). Perhaps the most noteworthy Islamic example is an Arabic inscription on a building erected by Akbar in A.D. 1601 at Fathpur-Sikri in northern India: "Jesus, on whom be peace, has said: 'This world is a bridge. Pass over it, but build not your dwelling there' " (tr. Jeremias, p. 112).

III. Development of Agrapha.–Most agrapha have been created for tendentious purposes, in some cases by the modification of canonical passages. Logion 100 of the Gospel of Thomas reads: "Give the things of Caesar to Caesar, give the things of God to God and give Me what is Mine" (tr. Guillaumont, p. 51; cf. Mk. 12:17). The infancy Gospels attempt to magnify the child Jesus by having him rebuke his teacher for ignorance. (*See* APOCRYPHAL GOSPELS II.) The purported correspondence with King Abgar of Edessa is an attempt to trace the origins of the Syrian church to the times of Jesus. To lessen the severity of the original declaration the Gospel of Peter has modified Jesus' cry from the cross to, "My power, my power, thou hast forsaken me." In order to support an ascetic denigration of marriage the Gospel of the Egyptians has the Savior saying, "I am come to undo the works of the female" (tr. H-S, I, 166-67).

IV. Possibly Authentic Agrapha.–*A. From Variant Readings.* Codex D at Lk. 6:5 inserts: "On the same day he saw a man performing a work on the Sabbath. Then said he unto him: 'Man! If thou knowest what thou doest, thou art blessed. But if thou knowest not, thou art cursed and a transgressor of the Law' " (tr. Jeremias, p. 61). In other words, Jesus warned against the thoughtless transgression of the Sabbath injunction.

B. From Church Fathers. (1) Tertullian in *De baptismo* 20 quotes Christ as saying, "No man can obtain the kingdom of heaven who has not gone through temptation" (tr. H-S, I, 89).

(2) In *Dial.* 35 Justin Martyr records that Jesus warned, "There shall be divisions and heresies" (or "dissensions and squabbles"; Gk. *schísmata kaí hairéseis*).

(3) Clement of Alexandria in *Misc.* i.24.158 records that Jesus said, "Ask for the great things, and God will add to you what is small" (tr. H-S, I, 89; cf. Mt. 6:33).

(4) Theodotus, a disciple of the Gnostic Valentinus, claimed that Christ had admonished, "Save thyself and thy soul" (tr. H-S, I, 88).

(5) The *Liber graduum*, a Syriac work which stresses asceticism as the means of attaining spiritual perfection, records the saying, "As you are found so will you be led away hence" (tr. Jeremias, p. 83).

(6) A popular statement, quoted or alluded to over fifty times in the church fathers, is "Be approved money changers [Gk. *trapezítēs*]." The idea is that we should be like the money changers who can detect counterfeit coins among the genuine (cf. 1 Thess. 5:21). Philo *De specialibus legibus* iv.77 conveys the same sense though with a different word: "And let the man who undertakes the duty of a judge, like a skillful money-changer [Gk. *arguramoibós agathós*], divide and distinguish between the natures of things, in order that confusion may not be caused by the mixing together of what is good and what is spurious." Because of this parallel, Wright believes that the saying is derivative.

C. From the Papyri. (1) Oxy. P. 840, discovered in 1905, is an amulet text in which Jesus confronts a self-righteous high priest and rebukes him as follows: "Woe to you blind that see not. Thou hast bathed thyself in water that is poured out, in which dogs and swine lie night and day and thou hast washed thyself and hast chafed thine outer skin, which prostitutes also and flute-girls anoint, bathe, chafe and rouge, in order to arouse desire in men, but within they are full of scorpions and of badness of every kind. But I and my disciples of whom thou sayest, that we have not immersed ourselves, have been immersed in the living . . . water . . . " (tr. Jeremias, p. 49).

(2) The same papyrus draws a lesson from a cunning criminal: "First, before he does wrong [?], he thinks out everything that is crafty. But be on your guard that the same thing may not happen to you as does to them. For not only among the living do evildoers receive retribution from men, but they must also endure punishment and great torment" (tr. Jeremias, pp. 104f.). The disciples are warned that they must not be like a criminal whose cleverness deludes him about his ultimate fate.

(3) In Oxy. P. 655 an admonition not to be anxious adds the promise, "He himself will give you your raiment" (tr. Jeremias, p. 97; cf. Mt. 6:25-34).

(4) In the badly damaged Oxy. P. 1224 is the following amplification of Mt. 5:44 and of Lk. 9:50: "And pray for your [ene]mies, for he who is not [against yo]u is for you. [He that] stands far off [today] will tomorrow be [near you]" (tr. Jeremias, p. 96).

D. From Apocryphal Gospels and Acts. (1) The apocryphal Acts of Peter (Actus Vercellenses), ch. 10, has Peter recalling that the Lord said, "They that are with me have not understood me" (tr. Jeremias, p. 91).

(2) The Gospel of the Nazarenes, cited by Jerome *Adv. Pelag.* iii.2, has the following amplification of the conversation about forgiving one's brother (Mt. 18:21f.) with the Lord saying to Peter, "Yea, I say unto thee, until seventy times seven. For in the prophets also, after they were anointed by the Holy Spirit, the sinful word was found" (tr. Jeremias, p. 94). The point is that if even the holy prophets were not faultless, one should be willing to forbear a fault in a brother.

(3) Origen cites the same Gospel of the Nazarenes in his commentary on Matthew 19:16-22, the story of the rich young man: "But the rich man then began to scratch his head and it pleased him not. And the Lord said to him: 'How canst thou say, "I have fulfilled the law and the prophets?" For it stands written in the law: Love thy neighbor as thyself; and behold, many of thy brethren, sons of Abraham, are begrimed with dirt and die of hunger—and thy house is full of many good things and nothing at all comes forth from it to them!' " (tr. H-S, I, 149; cf. Jas. 2:15f.; 1 Jn. 3:17). Jeremias argues that it may be an independent version, but others maintain that this is a novelistic expansion.

(4) Jerome in his commentary on Ephesians 5:4 cites a beautiful saying from the Gospel of the Hebrews: "And never be joyful save when ye look upon your brother in love" (tr. Jeremias, p. 92).

(5) The Gospel of Thomas, logion 8, has a parable which may be compared with that of the hidden treasure (Mt. 13:44) and that of the pearl of great price (Mt. 13:45f.): "And He said, 'The man is like a wise fisherman who cast his net into the sea, he drew it up from the sea full of small fish; among them he found a large (and) good fish; that wise fisherman, he threw all the small fish down into the sea; he chose the large fish without regret" (tr. Guillaumont, pp. 5, 7).

(6) The Gospel of Thomas, logion 82, contains a saying which is also known from Origen: "He who is near me is near the fire; he who is far from me is far from the kingdom!" (tr. Bruce, p. 144). Jeremias believes that a possible early allusion to this saying may be found in Ignatius' statement that he was "near to the sword, near to God" (Smyrn. 4:2).

V. Other Agrapha.–(1) An interesting but ambiguous statement is preserved both in the Gospel of Thomas, logion 77, and in Oxy. P. 1. It reads, "Lift up the stone, and there thou wilt find me; cleave the wood and I am there" (tr. Jeremias, p. 106). Jeremias believes that this is originally derived from Eccl. 10:9, "He who quarries stones is hurt by them, and he who splits logs is endangered by them," and takes this as the Lord's promise that He will be with those who are engaged in strenuous work. Doresse (*L'Évangile selon Thomas* [1959], p. 189) interprets the wood as an allusion to the cross and the stone as an allusion to the tomb. Gärtner (*Theology of the Gospel According to Thomas* [1961], pp. 144-46) and others interpret the logion as a typically Gnostic sentiment of a pantheistic Christ.

(2) The Gospel of Thomas, logion 2, reads: "Jesus said, 'Let him who seeks, not cease seeking until he finds, and when he finds, he will be troubled, and when he has been troubled, he will marvel and he will reign over the All' " (tr. Guillaumont, p. 3). The same saying is cited from the Gospel of the Hebrews by Clement of Alexandria, *Misc.* ii.9.45, and is contained in Oxy. P. 654.

(3) The Gospel of Thomas, logion 3, paralleled in Oxy. P. 654, reads: "Jesus has said: If those who lead you say to you: See, the kingdom is in heaven, then the birds will fly into the heaven in front of you. If they say to you: It is in the sea, then will the fish go before you. But the kingdom is in your inner part and it is in your outward part" (tr. H-S, I, 101; cf. Lk. 17:21).

(4) The Gospel of Thomas, logion 114, betrays a Gnostic prejudice against women: "Simon Peter said to them, 'Let Mary go out from among us, because women are not worthy of the Life.' Jesus said, 'See, I shall lead her, so that I will make her male, that she too may become a living spirit, resembling you males. For every woman who makes herself male will enter the Kingdom of Heaven' " tr. Guillaumont, p. 57). The Gnostics regarded the separation into sexes as the source of evil.

VI. Significance.–The study of the agrapha, particularly in the apocryphal Gospels, reveals the relative poverty and inferiority of the mass of the extracanonical literature, and by contrast highlights the precious value of the canonical Gospels. As Jeremias concludes, ". . . the extracanonical literature, taken as a whole, manifests a surprising poverty. The bulk of it is legendary, and bears the clear mark of forgery. Only here and there, amid a mass of worthless rubbish, do we come across a priceless jewel" (p. 120).

See also LOGIA.

Bibliography.–A. Resch, *Agrapha* (2nd ed., *TU*, NF 15/3-4, 1906; repr. 1974); J. H. Ropes, *Die Spruche Jesu* (*TU*, 14/2, 1896); *ANT*, pp. 33-37; L. E. Wright, *Alterations of the Words of Jesus As Quoted in the Literature of the Second Century* (1952); J. A. Fitzmyer, *Theological Studies*, 20 (1959), 505-560; A. Guillaumont, *et al.*, *The Gospel According to Thomas* (1959); H-S, I, 85-113; J. Jeremias, *Unknown Sayings of Jesus* (Eng. tr. 1957, 2nd ed. 1964); F. F. Bruce, *Jesus and Christian Origins Outside the NT* (1974); W. L. Lane, *JETS*, 18 (1975), 29-35.

E. M. YAMAUCHI

AGRARIAN LAWS. Laws related to landed property and cultivated land, including all laws concerning the preservation of soil, regulation of irrigation, and protection of rights concerning landed property. The only laws in the OT that can be assigned to this class are those relating to the fallow in the sabbath year and jubilee and certain laws of negligence.

The agrarian laws in the OT form a very important part of biblical institutions. In spite of the opinion that these institutions and the agrarian laws are of a late date, their antiquity must be upheld. They are linked in biblical sources to the oldest parts of legal jurisprudence.

I. Origin.–There is difference of opinion among scholars as to how earliest agriculture developed. One opinion is that agriculture was started in open fields. According to Braidwood and others, agriculture was a natural development where the need was felt. Others (e.g., Childe) see it as a revolution. Another group of scholars takes the more probable view that agricultural settlements were started near river valleys where irrigation was possible. This standpoint, advocated by Albright, has as evidence in its favor the fact that the main cultures of the ancient Near East developed in river valleys. The oldest culture in Palestine, for example, grew up around Tell es-Sulṭân (Jericho).

If one accepts Albright's explanation, the origin of agrarian laws is to be sought in the regulation of water. The need for various other stipulations developed as agriculture progressed. Thus a need was felt to protect cultivated land against negligence, such as the careless use of fire. Again, after a few years of use the ground becomes unfertile; to counteract this the fallow came into being. It must be granted that the idea of rest or leisure has a cultic value; but in the case of cultivated land, the idea of the fallow originated from practical reasons. In the OT it is, however, closely linked with religion, as will be seen below.

To grasp the background of the agrarian laws one must turn to the Egyptian and Mesopotamian cultures, because almost all evidence from early times comes from the monuments and tablets of these two cultures. No literary material is preserved of the old culture of Jericho or of any other cultures of ancient Palestine. In Egypt all of life was concentrated around the Nile and irrigation; even the calendar of the so-called Sothic year was worked out according to the annual inundation.

In Mesopotamia certain legal codices are preserved that give us a clear understanding of the legal position in a developed community. In the Code of Hammurabi there are agrarian laws concerning negligence by the owner or tenant (cf. §§ 42-44, 53, 55f.), and laws of irrigation (cf. §§ 55f.). These laws, and certain other groups of law such as those of the Hittites, form part of the background of some OT laws.

Nevertheless, it must be borne in mind that much of the legal material in the OT originated in the Israelite community, and is thus to be regarded as native to the Hebrews. In the OT legal material is closely linked with religion and with Yahweh. The idea of rest, which is not alien to the ancient Near East, forms a very important part of the religion of the OT.

II. Laws Concerning Damage to Immovable Property.–In the earliest laws of the OT punishments are prescribed for damage done to cultivated land. Ex. 22:5f. considers examples of damage to a field or vineyard, with the penalty in each case being full restitution. This kind of problem was probably encountered often in the ancient Near East, since reference to it is present in various ancient codices. The law was made to restore the financial balance.

Laws concerning damage and restitution have a broad background and can be applied to various situations. The agrarian laws of damage are thus one aspect of a general legal principle. In the OT these laws are placed under the sanction of Yahweh. From a religious standpoint they are used to create a feeling of responsibility toward a neighbor's possessions. They thus confirm the law of love for one's neighbor.

III. Sabbath Year and Jubilee.–Every seventh year, according to Ex. 23:10ff., the land was to lie fallow (cf. Lev. 25:2-7). The sabbath of the land does not mean that its natural, uncultivated increase is to be eaten by the Israelite poor; rather, the probable principle underlying this institution is that the poor must benefit from the blessed harvest of the sixth year. In spite of its close connection with religion, there is a humanitarian undertone observable in this law.

The sabbath year was primarily intended for the relief of the poor (cf. Ex. 23:11; Lev. 25:6). It is interesting to note in this connection that the widow and orphan are not mentioned. This fact led Weber to the conclusion that the poor referred to must be the propertyless able-bodied poor (cf. R. North, *Sociology of the Biblical Jubilee* [1954], p. 112).

After seven sabbath years had passed, a trumpet was to be blown throughout the land on the tenth day of the seventh month (the Day of Atonement), and the fiftieth year was to be hallowed and celebrated as a jubilee. In the passage describing this, Lev. 25:10ff., vv. 18-22 are especially problematic. In v. 21 there is an allusion to a three-year crop, but at the same time it is mentioned that they must plant and sow in the eighth year and that they should eat of the three-year crop of the sixth year until the ninth year. Some scholars have concluded from this that there should be a fallow for two years: the forty-ninth or sabbath year was followed by the fiftieth or jubilee. This is an acceptable interpretation.

IV. The Meaning of These Laws.–Various views of the meaning of these laws have been suggested. Some commentators emphasize the humanitarian vein of this legislation. The jubilee was intended to meet the economic evils that befell the poor in ancient societies. The economic climate, with frequent times of war and unfavorable seasons, was not ideal for farming, and a farmer was compelled to borrow. With the high interest he had to pay, he was soon unable to make ends meet and had to go into servitude. With the laws of the jubilee concerning restoration of land and the fallow, the danger of an overall slavery was averted. Other scholars regard the fallow in the light of the primitive Semitic conception of land. The fallow is prescribed because the land is weary, and the owner lets it rest like a beast of burden or a slave. The former view would seem to be preferable.

V. The Execution of Agrarian Laws.–Were these laws executed? Certain scholars maintain that the execution of the fallow as prescribed is impossible from an economic standpoint. Some have tried to connect it with a rotating fallow. Others seek to interpret it by appealing to another meaning of the Heb. verb *'āsap̱*, viz., "to gather to oneself." On this explanation, it was not harvesting that was forbidden, but only storing up in bins (cf. Lev. 25:20).

In spite of these problems the biblical tradition leaves no doubt that the fallow was universally prescribed. The biblical sources, however, are mute as to whether these institutions were ever carried out. The only reference to the execution of the fallow is made in 2 Ch. 36:21, but this is rather vague. In the post-OT period there is a reference to the fallow in 1 Macc. 6:49, 53.

See also GLEANING.

Bibliography.–*AP;* R. J. Braidwood, *Prehistoric Men* (1948); V. G. Childe, *New Light on the Most Ancient East* (1957); R. Clay, *The Tenure of Land in Babylonia and Assyria* (1938); A. Deimel and B. Meissner, *Reallexikon der Assyriologie,* I (1928), 18-20; P. Naster, *Muséon,* 68 (1955), 137-144; F. X. Steinmetzer, *Der alte Orient,* 19 (1919).

F. C. FENSHAM

AGREE; AGREEMENT. Especially noteworthy occurrences of these words include the following:

In Job 22:21, the RSV uses "agree" in translating the difficult Heb. *sāḵan*: "Agree with God, and be at peace." The AV reads, "Acquaint now thyself with him, and be at peace," which is supported by KoB (p. 658). The NEB renders, "Come to terms with God and you will prosper." BDB (p. 698) suggests that the meaning here is "show harmony with," which is close to the RSV understanding and compatible with the NEB. The normal root meaning of the word is "be of benefit, service, or profit"; but from the context here it would seem that reconciliation is the intended idea, as in the RSV and NEB.

The "agreement" (NEB "pact") with Sheol mentioned in Isa. 28:15, 18 is of some difficulty because Heb. *ḥōzeh* (v. 15) and *ḥāzûṯ* normally mean "seer" and "vision" respectively. The English versions follow the LXX, Vulgate, and Targum. BDB (p. 302) tries to connect the two ideas, suggesting a vision with Sheol via necromancy whereby the people are made secure, and also notes that the prophetic advice of seers was sought when treaties were made. KoB (p. 285), on the other hand, citing L. Köhler (*ZAW,* 48 [1930], 227f.), suggests emending to *ḥeseḏ* and *ḥasdeḵem,* which indicate inherent mutuality (i.e., in contrast to the acquired mutuality of the *berîṯ*); but it is questionable whether such a strong word would have been used here.

In Mt. 18:19 the word is Gk. *symphonéō,* which connotes a harmonious blending (cf. Eng. symphony). This agreement therefore is complete. Three persons are introduced: two human beings and the Father. They are in perfect agreement on the subject of purpose under consideration. It is therefore an inward unity produced by the Holy Spirit, leading the two into such an agreement with the Father. There will follow then, as a matter of course, what is promised in vv. 19f.

In Mk. 14:56 the word is *ísos* and has the thought not only that their words did not agree, but also that the testimony was not in agreement with or equal to what the law required in such a case. The idea of equality is also present at 1 Jn. 5:8 (Gk. *eis tó hén eisin).*

Other NT terms include Gk. *tó autó phronéō* ("be of one mind," 2 Cor. 13:11; Phil. 4:2) and *synkatáthesis* (2 Cor. 6:16).

J. W. KAPP N. J. O.

AGRICULTURE.

I. Development
II. Climatic Conditions and Fertility
III. Agricultural Pursuits
 A. Grain
  1. Plowing and Sowing
  2. Reaping
  3. Threshing
 B. Vineyards
 C. Olive Trees
 D. Flocks and Herds

I. Development.–Biblically the record of agricultural pursuits begins with the mandate given in the garden of Eden to "till it and keep it" (Gen. 2:15). The immediate post-Edenic situation featured both the agricultural and the pastoral way of life as represented by Cain and Abel, suggesting to some that the period represents that era known to anthropologists as the "New Stone Age Revolution" in farming and horticulture (see E. K. V. Pearce, *Who Was Adam?* [1970]). Secularly this period is best represented by the beginnings of farming in the lower Jordan valley around Jericho in the mid-8th millennium B.C. in a culture practicing irrigation-farming in a manner closely resembling that of major Mesopotamian centers. Also dating to this period or earlier are the rudimentary agricultural tools of the Natufian man of the Carmel caves, whose flint sickle and hoe blades bespeak a possibly settled farming pattern.

From Cain to the Conquest, the biblical account gives little indication that farming was important to the chosen line of Seth. Abraham, Isaac, and Jacob were herdsmen, though Lot seems to have preferred the settled life of a Jordan valley farmer (Gen. 13:10). The Israelite invasion seems to have repeated the age-old pattern of nomadic or semi-nomadic sheepherders moving into the arable land surrounding the Mediterranean littoral and taking up agricultural occupations. Apart from an occasional protest-movement (e.g., the Rechabites) the subsequent societal pattern in Israel reflected that of the stationary farming communities among whom they were settled.

It is most significant, however, that from earliest times the pattern of Israel's religious observances (cf. Ex. 23:14-16; Lev. 23) is based on an agricultural rather than a nomadic and pastoral calendar (*see* CALENDAR). The basis of society was clearly dependent on the cultivation of crops, and every major success or failure—religious, military, or economic — was tied up in some way with this fact.

II. Climatic Conditions and Fertility.–Climate varied greatly from region to region, with rainfall diminishing from a high of 45 to 60 in. (115 to 150 cm.) on the slopes in southern Lebanon to a low of less than 5 in. (13 cm.) annually in the Dead Sea rift and the Negeb below Beer-

Egyptian gardener drawing water with a counterpoised "sweep" (*shadūf*). Wall painting from the tomb of the sculptor Apuy (19th Dynasty, *ca.* 1250 B.C.) at Thebes (Metropolitan Museum of Art)

sheba. Elevation also influenced the onset and departure of the growing season, as did quality of soils. Where there was no irrigation, crops could be grown only in the season of rains, beginning with the "early rains" expected in late October-November, continuing through the period of heavy winter rains, and finishing with the much-needed "latter rains" of March and April. By mid-June much of the land had taken on the sun-burnt appearance familiar to summer tourists and nothing grew without help, though the much-valued late summer DEW provided a measure of moisture also.

Dry farming and IRRIGATION have been used successfully in many parts of Palestine from earliest times. Examples of the former may be seen from the air in observations of Nabatean water-work terracing (and its modern Israeli counterpart) in the Negeb; a particularly impressive example of the latter is still in use for distributing waters of the Wâdī Qelt in the Jericho region.

III. Agricultural Pursuits.–What knowledge we have of the subject is drawn from biblical references to methods bearing a close similarity to those of the present day, from artifacts uncovered in Palestine and surrounding countries, and from the few drawings of farming scenes on Egyptian and Mesopotamian monuments.

Four branches of agriculture were more prominent than others: the growing of grain, the care of vineyards, the orcharding of olives, and the raising of flocks. Most households owned fields and vineyards, and the richer added to these a wealth of flocks. The description of Job's wealth (Job 1) shows that he was engaged in all these pursuits. Hezekiah's riches as enumerated in 2 Ch. 32:27f. also suggest activity in each of these branches.

A. Grain. 1. Plowing and Sowing. On the plains little or no preparation for plowing was needed (*see* PLOW), but in the hilly regions the larger stones, which the tilling of the previous season had loosened and the winter's rains had washed bare, were picked out and piled into heaps on a ledge or thrown into the path, which thus became elevated above the FIELD it traversed. If grain was to be planted, the seed was scattered broadcast by the sower, either from an improvised pouch in his garment or from a jar or basket as pictured on Egyptian monuments. As soon as the seed was scattered it was plowed in, before the ever-present crows and ravens could gather it up. The path of the plow in the fields of the hilly regions was a tortuous one because of the boulders jutting out here and there and because of the ledges which frequently lay hidden just beneath the surface (the rocky places of Christ's parable). Unplowed portions of the field (such as an occasional footpath or a border) left exposed seed for the birds to eat. An additional operation, possibly to be identified with harrowing (*see* HARROW), is suggested by Isa. 28:24f.

2. Reaping. After the plowing was over, the fields were left until after the winter rains, unless an unusually severe storm of rain and hail had destroyed the young shoots (cf. Ex. 9:25), in which case a second sowing was made. In April, if the hot east winds had not scorched the grain (*see* BLAST; BLASTING) the barley began to ripen. The wheat followed from a week to six weeks later, depending upon the altitude. Toward the end of May or in the first week in

Workers reap (below) and winnow grain, while scribes register the harvest (above). From tomb of Menna, probably dating to the reign of Thutmose IV (18th Dynasty, *ca.* 1421-1413 B.C.) (Oriental Institute, University of Chicago)

Plowman guiding two-handled wooden plow pulled by two oxen. Wooden model from 6th-11th Dynasty Egypt (2350-2000 B.C.) (Trustees of the British Museum)

June, which marked the beginning of the dry season, reaping began, a task which occupied all members of the family and often meant living in the fields until harvest was over. A handful of grain was gathered by means of a sickle held in the right hand. The stalks thus gathered were then grasped by the left hand and cut off a few inches above the ground, leaving STUBBLE. The handfuls were then laid behind the reapers and were gathered up by the helpers, usually the children, and made into piles for transporting to the threshing-floor. (*See also* GLEANING.)

3. Threshing. The threshing-floors were constructed in the fields, preferably in an exposed position in order to get the full benefit of the winds. If there was danger of marauders, they were clustered together close to the village. The floor was a level, circular area 25 to 40 ft. (7½ to 12 m.) in diameter, prepared by first picking out the stones and then tamping or coating it with marly clay. A border of stones kept in the grain. The normal method of thresing seems to have been by the trampling effect of oxen or donkey hoofs as these animals were driven round the floor (Dt. 25:4), or by the use of a drag, the bottom of which was studded (2 S. 24:22). The supply of unthreshed grain was kept in the center of the floor and fed into the path of the animals. Constant turning of the partly threshed grain hastened the process of breaking all the stalks into short pieces and tearing off the husks. The mixture of chaff and grain was then winnowed by tossing it into the air so that the wind could blow away the chaff. When the chaff was gone, the grain was tossed in a wooden tray to separate from it the stones and lumps of soil which clung to the roots when the grain was reaped. The difference in weight between the stones and grain made separation by this process possible. The grain was then stored in the common store jar, usually for home use.

B. Vineyards. A clear picture of VINE culture is given in Isa. 5:1-6. The season, which began in July and extended for at least three months, provided fresh grapes for the table of rich and poor alike. Most of the harvest, however, was made into WINE. Care of the vineyards fitted well into the farmer's routine, as most of the attention required could be given when the other crops demanded no time.

C. Olive Trees. The OLIVE TREE, a plant perfectly suited to the climate of Palestine with its shallow soil, sunny summer months, and heavy dews, provided the chief source of cooking oil. Although the olive required much care in the growing and pruning stage, the harvest period was long and could be made to fit the farmer's schedule. From September to December the fruit could be picked or gathered from the ground. It was then taken to the ubiquitous oil press and converted into the oil so widely used for cooking, illumination, and anointing. As with the grapes, some olives were always kept for eating, after treatment either with salt or brine.

D. Flocks. The leaders of ancient Israel reckoned their flocks as a necessary part of their wealth. When a man's flocks were his sole possession, he often lived with them and led them in search of pasturage (Ps. 23; Mt. 18:12), but a man with other interests delegated this task to his sons (1 S. 16:11) or to hired help (Jn. 10:12) (*see* SHEEP). The flock furnished both food and raiment. The milk of camels, sheep, and goats was used fresh or made into curdled milk, butter, or cheese. More rarely the flesh of these animals was eaten. The peasant's outer coat is still made of a tawed sheepskin or woven of goats' hair or wool.

Bibliography.–E. M. Blaiklock, *Pictorial Bible Atlas* (1969), ch. 1; G. H. Dalman, *Arbeit und Sitte in Palästina,* II-IV (1932-1935);

GB; E. W. Heaton, *Everyday Life in OT Times* (1956), pp. 97-112; *MPB*; M. Noth, *The OT World* (1966), pp. 163f.; W. Walker, *All the Plants of the Bible* (1957); *WBA*, pp. 183-87.

J. A. PATCH
C. E. ARMERDING

AGRIPPA ə-grip'ə [Gk. *Agrippas*]. *See* HEROD VIII.

AGUE (Lev. 26:16, AV). *See* FEVER.

AGUR ā'gər [Heb. *'āgûr*; Akk. *agāru*; Ugar. *agr*]. A contributor of proverbs, mentioned in Prov. 30:1, otherwise unknown. (The LXX and Vulgate renderings even suggest uncertainty that this is a proper name.) The "Prayer of Agur" in Prov. 30:7-9, expressing a golden mean of practicality, is the best known part of his writing.

AH; AHA; HO. These interjections represent various words and emotional states, as follows: (1) Heb. *'ahāh*, expressing complaint (Jer. 1:6; 4:10, etc.; Ezk. 4:14). (2) *'āh*, expressing grief over Israel's coming destruction (Ezk. 21:15). (3) *he'āh*, depicting malicious delight over the misfortunes of an enemy (Ps. 35:21, 28; Ezk. 25:3, etc.). In Isa. 44:16 it expresses satisfaction, and in Job 39:25 the neighing of a horse. (4) *hôy*, expressing grief and pain (Isa. 1:4; Jer. 22:18), a threat of judgment (Isa. 10:5; 29:1), or prefacing an important announcement (55:1). (5) Gk. *ouá*, a mocking cry directed at Christ on the cross (Mk. 15:29).

AHAB ā'hab [Heb. *'aḥ'āḇ*–'the Father is my brother,' i.e., 'God is a close relative'].

1. The seventh king of Israel (*ca.* 874-852 B.C.), and son of Omri. Ahab followed a wise policy in defense, entering into alliance with Phoenicia, Judah, and even his erstwhile enemies the Arameans. On the other hand, he fell under the influence of his fanatical pagan queen Jezebel, who led him to worship Baal as Yahweh's peer, and consequently to introduce such horrors as tyranny (1 K. 21), religious persecution (18:4), and human sacrifice (16:34).

I. Ahab's Wars and Alliances.–Ahab wisely continued the alliance with the Phoenicians that his father entered into, cementing it by his own marriage with Jezebel the daughter of Ethbaal, the priest-king of Tyre. A precedent for international marriages, valuable for trade and defense, was established by King Solomon, who had married, in addition to Pharaoh's daughter, princesses of Moab, Ammon, Edom, Sidon (or Phoenicia), and the Hittites (1 K. 11:1). Ahab also arranged a marriage between the princess Athaliah and Joram, the crown prince of Judah, thus allying the two kingdoms for the first time after many years of senseless fratricidal wars. This alliance was beneficial both commercially and militarily.

There is a record of at least one effort at overseas trade undertaken jointly by Judah and Israel: a fleet was built at Ezion-geber (2 Ch. 20:35-37; 1 K. 22:48). An example of the political value of the alliance is seen in the joint military expedition to recover Ramoth-gilead from the Arameans (1 K. 22:2ff.).

For some three years before this war of reconquest, Ahab's capital had been besieged by Ben-hadad of Damascus and his thirty-two vassals (1 K. 20:1ff.). Ahab tried to buy release by rich gifts of silver and gold, but this did not satisfy Ben-hadad, who demanded the right to search the households of the king and his ministers and carry away everything dear and precious: wives and children as well as

Israelite wall at Samaria, part of Ahab's extensive building activity. These strong fortifications withstood one attack, and the city fell to the Assyrians only after a three-year siege (2 K. 17:9). (B. Van Elderen)

goods and chattels (20:5ff.). This would mean for Ahab handing over the city and all that was in it to the enemy. The king and his counselors, "the elders of the land," rejected Ben-hadad's demand and the city was attacked. But a well-timed sortie, led by the young guards attached to the military governors of the provinces, routed the enemy while Ben-hadad and his vassals were engaged in a drinking bout, and inflicted a crushing defeat.

The Arameans were again defeated the following year at Aphek, E of the Jordan, when Ben-hadad himself was taken (1 K. 20:26-34). Ahab not only spared his life but made a treaty of alliance with him. Ben-hadad promised to restore the captured Israelite cities and to set up Israelite markets in his capital of Damascus. Ahab's leniency, as subsequent history proved, cost the nation dearly. However, while this alliance lasted it produced some benefit. A coalition consisting of Damascus, Hamath, and Israel together with other smaller powers fought Shalmaneser III at Qarqar on the Orontes, putting a stop for a time to Assyrian aggression. The joint military expedition of Israel and Judah referred to above took place some three years after the truce with Ben-hadad. Struck by a stray arrow while in his chariot, Ahab died during the battle as he sat facing the enemy.

II. Ahab's Apostasy and Clash with the Prophets.–The prophets championed the causes of freedom and justice. They upheld the nomadic ideal of freedom and only reluctantly relinquished tribal sovereignty for the peace and unity that a central government under a king made possible. With their stress on the justice demanded by God, they could not but oppose a tyrant who killed and robbed people at will. Ahab's clash with Elijah concerned the king's treatment of Naboth. Ahab coveted this man's vineyard, which adjoined the palace, and Naboth refused to part with it. Jezebel, determined to get the vineyard for Ahab, suborned two rogues to say that Naboth had cursed God and the king. Naboth was taken out and stoned, and the king took possession of his vineyard. Elijah met him with these words from Yahweh:

> "'Have you killed and also taken possession? . . .' Thus saith the Lord: 'In the place where dogs licked up the blood of Naboth, shall dogs lick up your own blood!'" (1 K. 21:19).

Ahab is said to have been worse than all who preceded him. Solomon had tolerated and even patronized the worship of strange gods by his foreign wives. Jeroboam had set up two golden calves for political reasons. Ahab, however, went further: he worshiped Baal and set him up as Yahweh's peer (1 K. 16:31-33); Yahweh's prophets were massacred at Jezebel's orders, while the prophets of Baal and Asherah had all the privileges of royal pensioners and courtiers (18:4, 19). According to his own confession Ahab hated such prophets of Yahweh as Micaiah the son of Imlah (22:8). He considered the prophet Elijah to be a "troubler of Israel" (18:17). Ahab repented, it is true, when the enormity of his crime in the killing of Naboth was pointed out to him; but neither this nor the discomfiture of Baal's prophets on Mt. Carmel changed the general situation.

III. Ahab and Archeology.–Ahab is mentioned in the Monolith Inscription of Shalmaneser III (858-824 B.C.), which tells the story of the great battle Shalmaneser fought at Qarqar in 854 against an Aramean-Israelite coalition of which Hadadezer (i.e., Ben-hadad of Damascus), Irḫuleni of Hamath, and Ahab of Israel were the leading figures. Ahab alone is said to have contributed two thousand chariots and ten thousand foot soldiers. Ten lesser kings who took part made important contributions in infantry and cavalry (*ANET*, pp. 276-79). In the Moabite Stone, Mesha king of Moab tells how Omri and his son (i.e., Ahab) occupied and oppressed Moab for forty years (*ANET*, p. 320).

Bibliography.–J. W. Jack, *Samaria in Ahab's Time* (1929); E. G. H. Kraeling, *Aram and Israel* (1918). For Ahab's palace and ornamentation, see J. W. Crowfoot, *PEQ* (1932), pp. 132ff.; (1933), pp. 7ff., 130ff.

S. K. MOSIMAN
M. S. SEALE

2. Son of Koliah, one of two false prophets (*see* ZEDEKIAH) among the Babylonian exiles. Jeremiah's condemnation of them included the prophecy that their fate would become a curse formula for the exiles (Jer. 29:20-23).

AHARAH ä'har-ə, ə-här'ə [Heb. *'aḥraḥ*–'brother of Raḥ' or 'a brother's follower,' though some regard it as a textual corruption for Ahiram; Gk. B *Iaphaēl,* A *Aara*]. A son of Benjamin (1 Ch. 8:1). *See* AHIRAM.

AHARHEL ə-här'hel [Heb. *'^{a}harḥēl*–'brother of Rachel'; Gk. *adelphoú Rēchab*]. A son of Harum of the tribe of Judah (1 Ch. 4:8).

AHASAI ä'hə-zī, ə-hā'zī (Neh. 11:13, AV). *See* AHZAI.

AHASBAI ə-has'bī [Heb. *'^{a}ḥasbay*–'blooming']. The father of Eliphelet, a Maacathite, a soldier in David's army (2 S. 23:34). He was either a native of Abel-beth-maacah (20:14) or, more probably, of Maacah in Syria (10:6). The list in 1 Ch. 11:35f. gives different names entirely, indicating textual corruption.

AHASUERUS ə-hazh-o͞o-er'əs [Heb. *'^{a}ḥašwērôš*; Gk. *Assouēros*].

1. A Persian king (*khshayarsha*) who married Esther (Est. 2:17). The LXX reads Artaxerxes throughout, and some have therefore identified him with Artaxerxes II (404-359 B.C.). More probably, however, he is Xerxes I of Persia (485-465 B.C.), a son of Darius the Great. This man is the Ahasuerus of Ezr. 4:6.

2. In Dnl. 9:1, the father of Darius the Mede.

3. [Gk. *Asyēros*] (Tob. 14:15); AV ASSUERUS. One who destroyed Nineveh with Nebuchadnezzar. Actually it was Cyaxares who helped Nebuchadnezzar overthrow Nineveh.

See also DARIUS **1.**

R. K. H.

AHAVA ə-hā'və [Heb. *'ah^{a}wā'*]. A river in Babylonia on the banks of which Ezra and his party encamped for three days in preparation for the journey to Jerusalem (Ezr. 8:15ff.). From here Ezra sent to Casiphia for temple servants, since no Levites were present in the assembled group. His appeal was successful. Then after Ezra had proclaimed a fast to seek of God "a straight way," the company "departed from the river Ahava," and journeyed in safety to Jerusalem.

This river or canal remains unidentified, though many conjectures have been made. Most probably it was one of the numerous canals that intersected Babylonia, flowing from the Euphrates apparently toward some town or district named Ahava (Ezr. 8:15). If so, identification is impossible.

S. F. HUNTER
R. E. HAYDEN

AHAZ ā'haz [Heb. *'āḥāz*–'he has grasped'; cf. the Assyrian records of Tiglath-pileser III, "Yauhazi of Judah," perhaps indicating that Ahaz is an abbreviated form of Jehoahaz]. The twelfth king of Judah, and son of Jotham. The biblical account of his reign is given in 2 K. 16; 2 Ch. 28; and Isa. 7.

Ahaz began his reign in 735 B.C. as co-regent with his father, who died in 732. With the support of the pro-

Assyrian party he very likely assumed active leadership of Judah immediately. International problems plagued Ahaz during most of his reign, as Assyria extended its control into Palestine. Religiously, Ahaz reversed the policy of Uzziah his grandfather. He erected molten images to Baal in the Hinnom Valley, burned his son in the fire, and generally conformed to heathen practices (2 Ch. 28:1-4). Although Isaiah was active throughout the time of Ahaz, this idolatrous tide was not reversed until Hezekiah's reign.

In 734 Tiglath-pileser III marched his armies down into the maritime plain. This may have been in response to an appeal by Ahaz for relief from the Philistines, who were raiding extensively in the outlying districts of Judah. After the Assyrians withdrew, Ahaz faced serious problems with Israel and Syria.

Pekah and Rezin, kings of Israel and Syria respectively, championed an anti-Assyrian policy with the purpose of terminating the extension of Assyrian control in Palestine. To make sure they would not be endangered by a neutral or potentially hostile nation behind them, they declared war on Ahaz, hoping to force Judah into their alliance. Their intention was to place the Aramean ben Tabeel (Isa. 7:6) on the Davidic throne instead of Ahaz.

When the news of the Syro-Ephraimitic declaration of war reached Jerusalem, the people were thrown into consternation (Isa. 7:1f.). At this crucial moment when Ahaz was on his way out of Jerusalem to inspect his defenses, the prophet Isaiah was sent to advise the king to put his trust in God. Ahaz, however, defied the prophet's advice and sent an enormous gift to Tiglath-pileser III, who responded in due time.

Meanwhile the Syro-Ephraimitic invaders besieged Jerusalem and took thousands of captives up to Samaria and Damascus (2 Ch. 28:5-15). The Judean captives taken to Samaria were released in accordance with the advice given by a prophet named Oded. Simultaneously Ahaz lost his control over the Edomites. The Syrians dislodged the Judean troops from Elath (Ezion-geber), so that Edomites were enabled to reoccupy this important seaport city.

The Assyrian pressure in response to the appeal for help by Ahaz brought temporary relief to Judah. Tiglath-pileser III marched his armies into Palestine, capturing numerous cities (2 K. 15:29). By 732 both Rezin and Pekah were killed; Damascus was occupied by the Assyrians and Samaria was ruled by Hoshea, who pledged tributary allegiance to the Assyrian king.

Isaiah had boldly assured Ahaz and the Judean citizens that the two kings from the north were but a temporary threat (Isa. 7:4-9). Like smoking firebrands they would last but a short time. Within a few years the predictions of Isaiah were fulfilled. Although the Assyrian advance provided temporary relief, it had foreboding implications. Isaiah explicitly warned that God would use the king of Assyria as a razor to shave Judah from head to toe (Isa. 7:20). Equally clear is the prophet's warning that God would cause Assyria to extend like a river into Palestine submerging Judah to its neck (Isa. 7:5-8). Significantly, however, the prophet did not predict the termination of Judah's national existence — a fate foretold regarding Ephraim and Syria — under the Assyrian advance southward in the Fertile Crescent. Under Hezekiah the Assyrian aggression became a realistic threat to Judah.

Significant indeed was the Damascus meeting of Ahaz and Tiglath-pileser III in 732 B.C. With the capitulation of Rezin, the kingdom of Syria ended, so that it was no longer a buffer state between Judah and Assyria. Ahaz met the Assyrian king as a servant, having sent him a heavy tribute of silver and gold which depleted both the royal and temple treasuries. Politically Ahaz became a vassal, not an ally, of Assyria (2 Ch. 28:16-21).

Inscribed seal (and a copy of its impression) "belonging to Ušna [Ašna?] minister [servant] of Ahaz" (American Schools of Oriental Research)

In their religious practice the citizens of Judah were made keenly aware of the visit of their king to Damascus. In accordance with specific instructions the priest Urijah constructed a model of an altar that Ahaz had seen in Damascus. This altar, erected in the temple court for the king, placed idol worship in juxtaposition with the altar where daily sacrifice was made in their worship of God (2 K. 16:10-16). Numerous other changes were made in Judah's religion because of the king of Assyria (vv. 17f.). At the same time Ahaz wanted to inquire personally at the brazen altar.

Other religious innovations charged to Ahaz are summarized in 2 Ch. 28:22-25. The doors of the temple porch were shut, the golden candlestick was not lit, the offering of incense was not made, and other solemnities were suspended. It is likely that Ahaz also erected the horses dedicated to the sun that are mentioned in 2 K. 23:11. Verse 12 of this chapter indicates that altars had been erected on the roof of the chambers of Ahaz that were destroyed in the reformation under Josiah. The leadership of Ahaz in religious matters consequently sanctioned idolatry and seemed to be diametrically opposed to the influence of Isaiah.

Little is known about the rest of the reign of Ahaz. In all likelihood he pacified the Assyrian kings with sufficient tribute so that Judah continued without serious international intervention during the period of the fall of Samaria in 722.

Ahaz died in 716 B.C., leaving the throne to Hezekiah. He was buried in Jerusalem with his fathers but not in the sepulchre of the kings of Judah (cf. 2 K. 16:20; 2 Ch. 28:27). Isaiah records a prophecy concerning Philistia in the year of Ahaz' death (Isa. 14:28-32). Ahaz is mentioned in the royal genealogies in 1 Ch. 3:13 and Mt. 1:9.

W. S. CALDECOTT
S. J. SCHULTZ

AHAZ, DIAL OF. *See* DIAL OF AHAZ.

AHAZIAH ā-hə-zī'ə [Heb. *'ᵃḥazyâ, 'ᵃḥazyāyû*–'Yahweh has grasped (sustained)'].

1. King of Israel (*ca.* 853-852 B.C.), and son of Ahab and Jezebel (1 K. 22:51–2 K. 1:18). Ahaziah succeeded his father as king in the seventeenth year of Jehoshaphat of Judah and reigned two years (for the chronological problem involved in a comparison of 1 K. 16:29; 22:41, 51; 2 K. 1:17, *see* CHRONOLOGY OF THE OT V.B). He was a Baal worshiper like his parents, and according to 2 K. 1:2ff. seems to have been particularly attracted to the Baal that was the deity of the Philistine city of Ekron.

The accession of Ahaziah encouraged Moab to rebel against Israel (cf. 2 K. 3:5); this revolt is the subject of the Hebraic stele of the Moabite King Mesha, known as the Moabite Stone. S. R. Driver, however (*Notes on the Hebrew Text of the Books of Samuel* [2nd ed. 1913], p. lxxxviii), thinks this revolt began in the reign of Ahab.

According to 2 Ch. 20:35-37, Ahaziah had an alliance with Jehoshaphat of Judah to revive the ancient maritime trade with Tarshish, but the fleet was broken up at Ezion-geber. 1 K. 22:48f. seems to imply that Ahaziah's attempt to form an alliance failed after Jehoshaphat had tried on his own to trade with Ophir. J. Skinner (*Century Bible*) thinks the Chronicles account probable, "since Jehoshaphat was no doubt still a vassal of Israel" (cf. H. L. Ellison, *NBC* on 1 K. 22:48f.).

As a result of his fall from an upper window, Ahaziah consulted Baal-zebub, the god of Ekron. His messengers were sent back by Elijah with the brusque reminder that Yahweh was the God of Israel. Three attempts to capture the prophet failed, and the message of judgment on Ahaziah's apostasy was speedily followed by his death.

2. King of Judah (842 B.C.), youngest son of Jehoram and Athaliah, and grandson of Ahab and Jezebel (2 K. 8:25-29; 9:16-29; 2 Ch. 22:1-9). His name is given as Jehoahaz in 2 Ch. 21:17; 25:23 (a transposition of the component parts of "Ahaziah") and as Azariah in 2 Ch. 22:6 (AV), an error corrected in fifteen Hebrew MSS and all the versions.

He came to the throne in the twelfth year of Jehoram of Israel, though 2 K. 9:29 states that it was Jehoram's eleventh year, a discrepancy variously explained as an editorial correction or as the result of the difference in the Hebrew and Greek methods of computation (cf. Thiele, *MNHK*, pp. 35, 68f.). The reason Ahaziah, the youngest son, succeeded to the throne was that his elder brothers had been slain by a band of invading Arabians (2 Ch. 22:1; cf. Josephus *Ant.* ix.5.3). In view of Athaliah's actions after his death, it may be significant that he was made king by "the inhabitants of Jerusalem." He was, however, under the domination of his mother (2 Ch. 22:3), even though it is recorded that he consecrated gifts to the temple of Yahweh (2 K. 12:18).

He joined his uncle, Jehoram of Israel, in an expedition against Hazael of Syria in which Ramoth-gilead was captured (2 K. 8:28f.; 9:14f.). Jehoram was wounded and returned to Jezreel, and later Ahaziah came to visit him there. He thus became involved in the coup d'etat in which Jehu slew Jehoram and Jezebel and other members of the royal family, and Ahaziah was himself killed. According to 2 K. 9:27f. he was mortally wounded as he fled in his chariot near Ibleam; he made his way to the fortress of Megiddo and died there. His body was conveyed to Jerusalem and there buried. Later his kinsmen were slain (2 K. 10:12-14). In 2 Ch. 22:7-9, his kinsmen are reported to have been killed first, and Ahaziah himself brought out of hiding in Samaria and executed. This may reflect a different tradition followed by the Chronicler, or it may be "a case of major textual disorder" (*NBC, in loc.*).

Bibliography.–J. A. Montgomery and H. S. Gehman, *ICC* on Kings (1951); E. L. Curtis and A. A. Madsen, *ICC* on Chronicles (1952).

J. G. G. NORMAN

AHBAN ä'ban [Heb. *'aḥbān*–'brother of an intelligent one' (?); Gk. *Achabar*]. The son of Abishur of the tribe of Judah (1 Ch. 2:29).

AHER ā'hər [Heb. *'aḥēr*–'another'; Gk. *Aer*]. A man of Benjamin (1 Ch. 7:12), his name here apparently a contracted form, perhaps the same as AHIRAM (Nu. 26:38) or Aharah (1 Ch. 8:1).

AHI ā'hī [Heb. *'ᵃḥî*–'my brother,' or perhaps a contraction from AHIJAH].

1. A member of the tribe of Gad (1 Ch. 5:15).

2. A member of the tribe of Asher (1 Ch. 7:34, AV, NEB).

AHIAH ə-hī'ə [Heb. *'ᵃḥîyâ*]; AV AHIJAH. A leader who set his seal to the covenant under Nehemiah (Neh. 10:26).

AHIAM ə-hī'əm [Heb. *'ᵃḥî'ām*–'mother's brother']. One of David's thirty heroes. He was the son of Sharar (2 S. 23:33), or according to 1 Ch. 11:35 of Sachar, the Hararite.

AHIAN ə-hi'ən [Heb. *'aḥyān*–'brotherly'(?)]. A son of Shemida of the tribe of Manasseh (1 Ch. 7:19).

AHIEZER a-hī-ē'zər [Heb. *'ᵃḥî'ezer*–'brother is help'].

1. A son of Ammishaddai, a Danite prince, who acted as representative of his tribe on several occasions (see Nu. 1:12; 2:25; 7:66, 71; 10:25).

2. One of the mighty men or warriors who joined David at Ziklag when David was a fugitive before Saul (1 Ch. 12:3).

AHIHUD ə-hī'hud [Heb. *'ᵃḥîhûḏ*–'brother is majesty'].

1. One of the chief men of the tribe of Asher. He was selected by Moses to help divide the land W of the Jordan (Nu. 34:27).

2. A son of Ehud of the tribe of Benjamin (1 Ch. 8:6f.). The text here is obscure and probably corrupt.

AHIJAH ə-hī'jə [Heb. *'ᵃḥîyâ* or *'ᵃḥîyāhû*–'brother of Yahweh' or 'Yahweh is my brother']; AV also AHIAH.

1. One of the sons of Jerahmeel the great-grandson of Judah (1 Ch. 2:25).

2. A descendant of Benjamin (1 Ch. 8:7).

3. AV Apoc. ACHIAS. The son of Ahitub, priest in the time of King Saul (1 S. 14:3, 18). Elsewhere he is called Ahimelech, priest of Nob and father of Abiathar (1 S. 21f.). In 2 Esd. 1:2 he is listed as an ancestor of Ezra, but the name is omitted in other genealogies.

4. One of David's mighty men, according to the list in 1 Ch. 11:36. The corresponding name in the list in 2 S. 23:34 is Eliam the son of Ahithophel the Gilonite.

5. A Levite of David's time who had charge of certain treasures connected with the house of God (1 Ch. 26:20).

6. Son of Shisha and brother of Elihoreph (1 K. 4:3).

7. A prophet from Shiloh who, in Solomon's lifetime, told Jeroboam that he would rule over the ten tribes (1 K. 11:29-39). For his subsequent apostasy Ahijah pronounced doom upon his house (1 K. 14). In 2 Ch. 9:29 the "prophecy of Ahijah" is listed as one historical source for the Solomonic period.

8. The father of Baasha king of Israel (1 K. 15:27, 33; 21:22; 2 K. 9:9).

9. (Neh. 10:26, AV). *See* AHIAH.

AHIKAM ə-hī'kəm [Heb. *'ᵃḥîqām*–'my brother has risen up']. A prominent man of the time of King Josiah and the following decades (2 K. 22:12, 14; 25:22; 2 Ch. 34:20; Jer. 26:24; 39:14; 40:5ff.; 43:6). He was the son of Shaphan, and a member of the deputation sent by Josiah to the prophetess Huldah (2 K. 22:12-14; 2 Ch. 34:20). Jer. 26:24 depicts him as Jeremiah's protector, while in 2 K. 25:22; Jer. 39:14 he was described as the father of Gedaliah, the governor appointed by Nebuchadrezzar.

AHIKAR ə-hī'kär [Gk. *Achiacharos, Acheicharos*]; AV ACHIACHARUS. Nephew of Tobit (son of Tobit's brother Anael) and grand vizier of the Assyrian court (Tob. 1:21f.). Because of his high position, Ahikar was able to intercede for Tobit and enable his return to Nineveh, where his property had been confiscated when he fled Assyrian vengeance upon his charitable acts on behalf of the exiled Jews. Ahikar later assumed care of the blinded Tobit (2:10) and joined in the wedding celebration of his nephew Tobias (11:18).

Cupbearer to the king and bearing responsibilities for the royal seal and all royal administrative accounts, Ahikar apparently was given his position by Sennacherib and reappointed by Esarhaddon (1:22, RSV mg., NEB; RSV "appointed second to himself"; cf. *APOT*, I, 205 n.).

Depicting him as a legendary figure, Ahikar's story is known in several versions including the writings of Democritus (preserved by Clement of Alexandria), Aesop, and the *Arabian Nights*. Discovery of fragments of the story among the fifth-century B.C. Aramaic papyri from Elephantine suggests a time of origin of at least 600 B.C., thus a possible influence for the allusions in Tobit.

The story appears in numerous variations, in which Ahikar is generally portrayed as prestigious and wealthy, a sage and politician. Although he had sixty wives, he was childless and was instructed to raise as his heir Nadan (RSV NADAB; AV Nasbas), his sister's son. When Ahikar threatened to supplant the unresponsive and belligerent youth with his brother Nebuzardan, Nadan betrayed him to the king with forged diplomatic correspondence proposing the betrayal of Assyrian forces to Egypt and Persia. Condemned to death for treason, Ahikar was hidden by his appointed executioner in gratitude for a previous favor, and a condemned criminal was killed in his place. Subsequently the Egyptian pharaoh posed for Sennacherib the option of paying or receiving tribute, depending on the Assyrian's ability to help devise a palace to be built midway between heaven and earth. The king bemoaned the loss of Ahikar, who might have accomplished such an impossible feat, whereupon the servant confessed his substitution and produced Ahikar. Ahikar then sought to fulfil the pharaoh's demands by sending aloft two boys, carried by eagles, who demanded building supplies for the project, which the Egyptians were unable to provide. After solving various other puzzles, Ahikar received the Egyptian tribute. Sennacherib then restored him to high position and permitted his severe punishment of Nadan.

Reference to the respective rewards of Ahikar and Nadan in Tob. 14:10 indicates the author's reliance on older material apparently well known to his readers. The occurrence of many similar proverbs in Tobit reinforces the probability of literary dependency on the Ahikar story.

See *APOT*, I, 191f.; II, 715-784. A. C. M.

AHIKAR, BOOK OF. A didactic folktale based on the story of AHIKAR, which is embellished by proverbs and parables representing Ahikar's instructions to his adopted son.

At the core of the book is the narrative of Ahikar, a sage of high rank in the Assyrian court who adopts as heir his nephew Nadan (RSV NADAB). The unappreciative youth falsely accuses his benefactor of treason, whereupon Ahikar escapes death only through the intervention of an executioner whom he himself had once spared. When the Egyptian pharaoh confronts Sennacherib with a conundrum bearing political consequences, the king laments the alleged demise of Ahikar, who is then brought forth from hiding. The sage masters the Egyptian demands, for which he is restored to favor, while the villainous nephew is punished.

Several versions of the story exist, including Syriac, Arabic, Slavonic, and Armenian accounts. The earliest extant is found in fragments of the fifth-century B.C. Aramaic papyri from Elephantine. Parallels are found in Democritus, Aesop, Strabo, Shahrastani, the Koran, and the *Arabian Nights*. The second-century B.C. apocryphal book of Tobit is quite familiar with the story and represents Ahikar as Tobit's nephew (Tob. 1:21). Other parallels occur in the OT wisdom literature, the Apocrypha, and the NT parables and epistles (see *APOT*, II, 718f.). Of particular interest are similarities between the Ahikar story and the book of Daniel, especially the difficulty of interpreting Nebuchadrezzar's dreams (Dnl. 2:2, 11, 27), the king's offer of reward for their explanation (5:7, 16), and the beastlike appearance of the afflicted monarch (4:33 [MT 36]). The death of Nadan resembles that of Judas (Mt. 27:5; Acts 1:18f.).

An Assyrian origin for the story is quite possible. The name of the servant who spares Ahikar, Nabû-šum-iškun, occurs in Akkadian historical documents (*ANET*, p. 272), and Ahikar and Nadan (cf. Nadin and other variants) resemble in form many Assyrian names and name components. Curiously, however, the book depicts Sennacherib as the son of Esarhaddon.

Bibliography.–*ANET*, pp. 427-430; *APOT*, II, 715-784; A. E. Cowley, *Aramaic Papyri of the 5th Cent. B.C.* (1923), pp. 204-248.

A. C. M.

AHILUD ə-hī'ləd [Heb. *'ᵃḥîlûḏ*–'child's brother'(?)]. The father of Jehoshaphat, who is mentioned as "recorder" in both the earlier and the later lists under David, and in the list under Solomon (2 S. 8:16 and 1 Ch. 18:15; 2 S. 20:24; 1 K. 4:3).

AHIMAAZ a-hi-mā'əz, ə-him'ə-az [Heb. *'ᵃḥîma'aṣ*].

1. Father of Ahinoam the wife of King Saul (1 S. 14:50).

2. The son of Zadok the high priest (1 Ch. 6:8f., 53). With his father he remained loyal to David in the rebellions both of Absalom and of Adonijah. With Jonathan the son of Abiathar he carried information to David when he fled from Absalom (2 S. 15:27, 36; 17:17, 20). At his own urgent request he carried tidings to David after the death of Absalom (18:19ff.). He told the king of the victory, and also, by his reluctance to speak, informed him of Absalom's death. There is no evidence that he succeeded his father Zadok as high priest.

3. In Naphtali, one of Solomon's twelve commissary officers (1 K. 4:15), who married Basemath the daughter of Solomon. It is not impossible that he was Ahimaaz the son of Zadok, though there is no proof to that effect.

W. J. BEECHER

AHIMAN ə-hī'mən [Heb. *'ᵃḥîman*].

1. One of the three "descendants of (the) Anak" (Nu. 13:22; Josh. 15:14; cf. Nu. 13:28; 2 S. 21:16, 18), or "sons of (the) Anak" (Josh. 15:14; Jgs. 1:20). The three names (Ahiman, Sheshai, Talmai) occur together also in Jgs. 1:10.

The word ANAK in the MT has the definite article except in Nu. 13:33 and Dt. 9:2. The Anakim were pre-Israelite settlers in Hebron. Their name may mean "tall people." Ahiman, whether an individual or a tribe, was defeated in Hebron (Josh. 15:14; Jgs. 1:10).

2. A Levite, one of the gatekeepers of late OT times (1 Ch. 9:17). He is associated with Akkub and Talmon and their brothers; cf. Neh. 11:19.

AHIMELECH ə-him'ə-lek [Heb. *'ᵃḥîmeleḵ*–'brother of a king' or 'my brother is king'].

1. The son of Ahitub of the house of Eli, and father of Abiathar (1 S. 21:2f., 8; 22:9-20; 30:7). Ahijah (1 S. 14:3, 18) may be the same person or Ahimelech's brother.

Ahimelech was high priest at Nob, the site of which is not known exactly though it was probably near Jerusalem (Isa. 10:29-32). It was here that the tabernacle had been transferred after the desolation of Shiloh. The priestly establishment at Nob existed on a fairly large scale, for eighty-five priests (LXX 305, Josephus 385) perished in the massacre (1 S. 22:18). The priests had families residing at Nob (v. 19). Among the votive offerings deposited at Nob was Goliath's sword, which was later taken back by David (21:9). The priests at Nob had authority to detain people, such as Doeg the Edomite, for religious purification or as punishment for some crime (21:7). It was customary to inquire of Yahweh there (22:10, 15), and the custom of the showbread or bread of the Presence was maintained (21:6). In the light of all this it is clear that Nob was an important religious center of the time.

David fled from Saul to Nob, and Ahimelech expressed surprise at his arrival and was in great fear. Anxious to preserve his own life and that of his men, David resorted to deception and pretended that he was on a royal commission from Saul: "The king hath commanded me a business" (21:2). Whether he believed him or not, Ahimelech cooperated with David by giving him the shewbread and Goliath's sword. This service was to have disastrous consequences, for Doeg, a royal servant, had witnessed the transaction and later told it to Saul, who interpreted it as treason on the part of Ahimelech. Despite Ahimelech's noble defense of David, he was ordered to be slain along with the rest of the priests. This command by Saul shows how completely deranged his mind was. The shocking nature of Saul's order is reflected in that even his own guard refused to lift a hand. He found a willing executioner in Doeg, however, perhaps because as an Edomite he did not share this reverence for the priesthood. Certainly the cruelty he showed is paralleled in others of his race. By killing the priests Saul cut all ties with the old amphictyonic order and drove its priesthood into the arms of his rival David. Abiathar, Ahimelech's son, was the only escapee (22:20). Ps. 52 was written in memory of this dastardly act.

2. A son of Abiathar and grandson of the above (1 Ch. 24:3, 6, 21). In a list of the heads of departments under David, this Ahimelech, the son of David's friend Abiathar, is mentioned as sharing with Zadok a high position in the priesthood. In this capacity he later shared with David and Zadok in the apportionment of the priests into twenty-four ancestral classes, sixteen of the house of Eleazar and eight of the house of Ithamar. No doubt his father Abiathar was too old for such administrative duty. It was quite common for a grandson to be named after his grandfather (cf. 1 Ch. 5:30-41).

In 2 S. 8:17 the phrase "Ahimelech the son of Abiathar" is most probably a copyist's inversion; this interpretation is supported by the Syriac and Arabic versions and by the history of the period. It must be remembered that this verse gives the list of David's *chief* officers. The parallel verse in 1 Ch. 18:16 is likewise an inversion, though here the name reads Abimelech, a copyist's error (corrected in the RSV and NEB).

3. A Hittite, a companion and friend of David when he was hiding from Saul in the wilderness (1 S. 26:6).

W. J. BEECHER
J. A. BALCHIN

AHIMOTH ə-hī'moth [Heb. *'ᵃḥîmôṯ*]. A descendant of Kohath the son of Levi (1 Ch. 6:25); ancestor of Elkanah the father of Samuel. The name Mahath holds a similar place in the list that follows (6:35).

AHINADAB ə-hin'ə-dab [Heb. *'ᵃḥînāḏāḇ*–'brother is noble']. The son of Iddo, and one of Solomon's twelve commissary officers (1 K. 4:14), whose district was Mahanaim.

AHINOAM ə-hi'nō-əm [Heb. *'ᵃḥînō'am*–'my brother is pleasantness'].

1. Daughter of Ahimaaz, and wife of King Saul (1 S. 14:50).

2. The woman from Jezreel whom David married after Saul gave Michal to another husband. She and Abigail, the widow of Nabal, seem to have been David's only wives prior to the beginning of his reign in Hebron. His marriage to Abigail is mentioned first, with some details, followed by the statement, easily to be understood in the pluperfect, that he had previously married Ahinoam (1 S. 25:39-44). Three times they are mentioned together, Ahinoam always first (1 S. 27:3; 30:5; 2 S. 2:2); Ahinoam is the mother of David's first son Amnon, and Abigail of his second (2 S. 3:2; 1 Ch. 3:1).

W. J. BEECHER

AHIO ə-hī'ō [Heb. *'aḥyô*–'fraternal'].

1. One of the sons of Beriah son of Elpaal, the son of Shaharaim and Hushim, reckoned among the families of Benjamin (1 Ch. 8:14). Beriah and Shema are described as ancestral heads "of the inhabitants of Aijalon, who put to flight the inhabitants of Gath."

2. A descendant of Jeiel ("the father of Gibeon") and his wife Maacah (1 Ch. 8:31; 9:37). King Saul apparently came from the same family (8:30, 33; 9:39).

3. One of the men who drove the new cart when David first attempted to bring the ark from the house of Abinadab to Jerusalem (2 S. 6:3f.; 1 Ch. 13:7). In Samuel, Uzza and Ahio are called sons of Abinadab.

AHIRA ə-hī'rə [Heb. *'ᵃḥîra'*]. A leader of Naphtali contemporary with Moses, who assisted in the census (Nu. 1:15).

AHIRAM ə-hī'rəm [Heb. *'ᵃḥîrām*–'exalted brother' or 'my brother is exalted']. A son of Benjamin, mentioned third of the five in Nu. 26:38f. In 1 Ch. 8:1 five sons are likewise mentioned, explicitly numbered; the third name, Aharah (*'aḥraḥ*), is conjectured to be either a corruption of Ahiram or a different name for the same person. In 1 Ch. 7:6ff. is a fuller list of Benjamite names, but it is fragmentary and not clear. In it occurs Aher (*'aḥēr*), which may be either Ahiram or Aharah with the end of the word lost. In Gen. 46:21 ten sons of Benjamin are mentioned, some being there counted as sons who, in the other lists, are spoken of as more remote descendants. In this list Ehi (*'ēḥī*) is perhaps Ahiram apocopated. *See* AHARAH; AHER.

AHIRAMITE ə-hī'rəm-īt [Heb. *'ᵃḥîrāmî*]. The family name of AHIRAM (Nu. 26:38).

AHISAMACH ə-his'ə-mak [Heb. *'ᵃḥîsāmāḵ*–'my brother supports']. A man of the tribe of Dan, father of Oholiab (Ex. 31:6; 35:34; 38:23).

AHISHAHAR ə-hish'ə-här [Heb. *'ᵃḥîšaḥar*–'brother of dawn']. One of the sons of Bilhan, the son of Jediael, the son of Benjamin (1 Ch. 7:10).

AHISHAR ə-hish'är [Heb. *'ᵃḥîšār*–'my brother has sung']. Mentioned in Solomon's list of heads of departments as "royal chamberlain" (1 K. 4:6).

AHITHOPHEL ə-hith'ə-fel [Heb. *'ᵃḥîṯōpel*–'brother of foolishness' (?)]. The real leader of the Absalom rebellion against David. He is described as "the king's counselor," in a context connected with events some of which are dated in the fortieth year of David (1 Ch. 27:33f.; cf. 26:31). His wisdom was such that his words were taken prophetically as a divine oracle (2 S. 16:23). A full account of his part in the rebellion is found in 2 S. 15:12ff. He joined Absalom's entourage after the coronation ceremony, and when Jerusalem was occupied he suggested that Absalom take token possession of the kingdom (2 S. 16:20-22). Following this he advised pursuit of David, but his plans were thwarted by Hushai who urged delay (17:5-14). Seeing that this scheme would implicate him, Ahithophel left Jerusalem and hanged himself (17:23). His son Eliam was loyal to David, being one of his thirty heroes (2 S. 23:34).

R. K. H.

AHITUB ə-hī'tub [Heb. *'ᵃḥîṭûḇ*–'brother of goodness.' i.e., 'good brother' or 'my brother is goodness'].

1. The brother of Ichabod and son of Phinehas the son of Eli (1 S. 14:3; 22:9, 11f., 20). According to 1 Ch. 24 he and his line were descended from Aaron through Ithamar. *See* AHIJAH **3.**

2. A Levite, the son of Amariah (1 Ch. 6:7f.), father of Meraioth and evidently grandfather of Zadok (2 S. 8:17; 1 Ch. 18:16; Ezr. 7:2; cf. 1 Ch. 9:11; Neh. 11:11).

3. [Gk. *Achitob*]; AV Apoc. ACHITOB. In the genealogies, in the seventh generation from Ahitub the descendant of Eleazar, appears another Ahitub, the son of another Amariah and the father (or grandfather) of another Zadok (1 Ch. 6:11 [MT 5:37]; 9:11; Neh. 11:11). The list in Ezr. 7 omits a block of names, and the Ahitub there named may be either **2** or **3**. He is mentioned in 1 Esd. 8:2 and 2 Esd. 1:1, and the name occurs in Jth. 8:1.

W. J. BEECHER

AHLAB ä'lab [Heb. *'aḥlāḇ*–'fat, fruitful'] A town of Asher from which the inhabitants were not driven out (Jgs. 1:31), formerly identified with Gush Halab (Gischala) in Galilee. In the related text, Josh. 19:29, the name Meheleb is found by some scholars (the MT as pointed reads "from Heleb"), and they suggest that Ahlab and Helbah in Jgs. 1:31 are misreadings from Meheleb (RSV Mahalab). On this basis Ahlab is identified with Khirbet el-Maḥâlib, about 5 mi. (8 km.) NNE of Tyre. Maḥalib was captured by Tiglath-pileser III in 734 B.C. and later by Sennacherib (cf. *Iraq*, 18 [1956], 129).

See *GTTOT*, §§ 332, 528.

AHLAI ä'lī [Heb. *'aḥlay*–'O would that!'].

1. A son of Sheshan (1 Ch. 2:31), or according to v. 34 a daughter of Sheshan.

2. The father of Zabad, a soldier in David's army (1 Ch. 11:41).

AHOAH ə-hō'ə [Heb. *'ᵃḥô(a)ḥ*–'brotherly'(?)]. A son of Bela of the tribe of Benjamin (1 Ch. 8:4). The apparent dittography in 1 Ch. 8:7 suggests that the name is an error for Ahijah.

AHOHI ə-hō'hī [Heb. *'ᵃḥôḥî*]. The father of Dodo and grandfather of Eleazar, who was the second of David's three heroes (2 S. 23:9).

AHOHITE ə-hō'hīt [Heb. *'ᵃḥôḥî*]. The patronymic form of AHOHI (2 S. 23:28; 1 Ch. 11:12, 29; 27:4).

AHOLAH ə-hō'lə. *See* OHOLAH.

AHOLIAB ə-hō'li-ab. *See* OHOLIAB.

AHOLIBAH ə-hō'li-bə. *See* OHOLIBAH.

AHRIMAN ä'ri-män. *See* RELIGIONS OF THE BIBLICAL WORLD: PERSIA.

AHUMAI ə-hoo'mə-ī, ə-hōō'mī [Heb. *'ᵃḥûmay*]. A descendant of Shobol of the tribe of Judah (1 Ch. 4:2).

AHURA-MAZDA ə-hōō'rä-mäz-də. *See* RELIGIONS OF THE BIBLICAL WORLD: PERSIA.

AHUZZAM ə-huz'əm [Heb. *'ᵃḥuzzām*–'possessor'] (1 Ch. 4:6); AV, NEB, AHUZAM. A son of Ashahur of the tribe of Judah; his mother's name was Naarah.

AHUZZATH ə-huz'əth [Heb. *'ᵃḥuzzaṯ*–'possession'] (Gen. 26:26). An adviser of Abimelech king of Gerar. He together with Phicol, commander of the army, accompanied their sovereign to Beer-sheba to make a covenant with Isaac.

AHZAI ä'zī [Heb. *'aḥzay*]; AV AHASAI. A priest who resided in Jerusalem (Neh.11:13).

AI ī, ā'ī.

1. [Heb. *hā'ay*–'the heap, ruin']; also **AIATH** ā'yath [Heb. *'ayyaṯ*] (Isa. 10:28); **AIJA** ā'jə [Heb. *'ayyā* or *'ayyā'*] (Neh. 11:31); AV also HAI (Gen. 12:8; 13:3). A town in central Palestine just E of Bethel and in Ephraimite territory originally (1 Ch. 7:28), but inhabited after the Exile by Benjaminites (Neh. 11:31). Abraham pitched his tent there when journeying to Egypt (Gen. 12:8) and again on his return (Gen. 13:3), during which time an altar was erected in the locality.

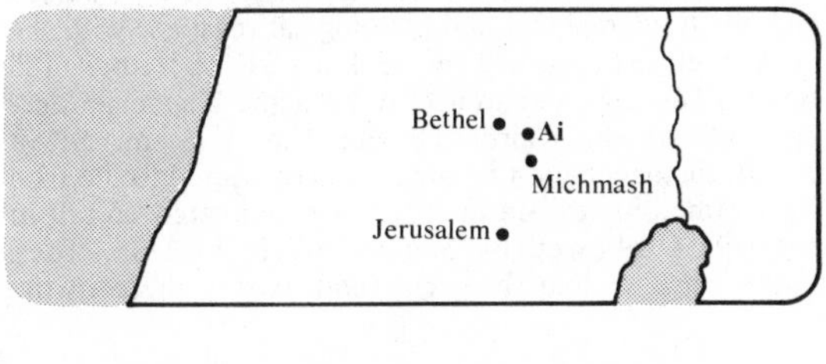

Aerial view of Ai (et-Tell) and Wâdī el-Jaya (center), which leads eastward to the Jordan valley just N of Jericho. The wadi is thought to be the ravine mentioned in the account of Joshua's capture of the city (Josh. 8:11). (J. A. Callaway)

Ai is prominent in the conquest narratives, where it is described as being adjacent to Beth-aven (Josh. 7:2). It was the next location to be reduced after Jericho, but despite its smallness its defenders routed an Israelite attack. This setback was attributed to the sin of Achan in appropriating material from the devoted spoil of Jericho, and after confession and expiation a second attack on Ai was successful. As the result of a stratagem the city was taken, the defensive area was demolished, and the site left a ruined heap. The king and his people were killed, and only the cattle were kept as spoil by the Israelites (Josh. 7:8). When the book of Joshua was being written the area was still in ruins (Josh. 8:28). The fall of Ai enabled the Israelites to penetrate deep into the interior of Canaan, where they quickly established themselves. Ai was rebuilt at a later period, being mentioned in Isa. 10:28 in connection with the approach of the Assyrian armies. Its location N of Michmash corresponds with the identification given above. This city was mentioned in postexilic times in Ezr. 2:28 and Neh. 7:32; 11:31, being associated in each case with nearby Bethel.

The site of the Late Bronze Age Ai seems best identified, for topographical and philological reasons, with the modern et-Tell, about 2 mi. (3 km.) SE of Bethel (Tell Beitîn). The town mentioned by Ezra and Nehemiah may be identified with Khirbet Haiyân, 1 mi. (1.6 km.) SE of et-Tell, the occupation of which was restricted to the Iron Age. Mme. Judith Marquet-Krause excavated et-Tell in 1933-1935, followed by Samuel Yeivin in 1936. They showed that a flourishing city had existed there in the 3rd millennium B.C., protected by an elaborate defense system of three walls. From the ruins of a temple were recovered numerous vessels of stone, alabaster, and ivory, the latter two varieties having doubtless been imported from Egypt.

The city arose *ca.* 3000 B.C., and seems to have been destroyed a millennium later, perhaps by Amorite invaders. In the Early Iron Age, after 1200 B.C., a new and smaller settlement arose which lasted for a century or so, and which made use of the earlier ruins. From the archeological evidence it would appear that the site was actually uninhabited at the time of the thirteenth-century B.C. Israelite conquest. Those who accept the identification of Ai with et-Tell have made various attempts to explain the discrepancy. For some the narrative is an example of the way all Israelite conquests over several centuries were referred to the time of Joshua, with Ai falling in the Early Iron Age. Others have regarded the Joshua narrative as an etiological legend, attempting to explain how the site received the name of "ruin" in antiquity. Still others have propounded the more probable suggestion that Ai was fortified hurriedly in the 13th cent. B.C. by the neighboring peoples as a temporary stronghold which it was hoped would stem the Israelite advance. Some have thought in consequence that the Joshua narrative referred to the destruction of nearby Bethel rather than Ai (*see* BETHEL). Since there is no clear distinction in the narratives between the soldiers of the two cities (Josh. 8:17), it may be that Ai was actually being used as a fortified outpost on the edge of Bethel. This procedure

Excavated area at et-Tell, including the Early Bronze Age temple and citadel (lower center) and the Iron Age village (upper center) (J. A. Callaway)

would be justified by the strategic role Ai had played prior to 2300 B.C. and would help to account for the mention of Ai in a narrative dealing with the conquest of Bethel.

The account of the battle for Ai describes, however, a firm defensive stand by the enemy at that location, which indicates an inhabited or at the very least an occupied site with its own ruler. If Ai was little more than a defensive strongpoint protecting the environs of Bethel, the ruler would be more of a military commander than a "king." That Ai was in fact a fortified outpost is implied by the narrative of its capture, which exhibits clear military purpose and tactical planning by Joshua and his forces. A careful examination of the topography of the area shows that the Israelites maneuvered their forces so as to take maximum advantage of the terrain in launching an ambush. The Israelite base camp was situated N of Bethel and Ai in "dead ground" beyond the valley, which contained seasonal wadis (Josh. 8:11, 13). The problem facing Joshua was how best to attack the ruin and its strong enemy force without exposing his flank and rear, and without losing the element of surprise. He solved the difficulty by appearing to repeat his earlier tactical mistake (Josh. 8:14f.), but in actuality moving secretly a large ambush of thirty thousand men into position W of the ruin some thirty-six hours before the main attack began. The smaller ambush of about five thousand men needed to be assigned to their positions only on the eve of battle (Josh. 8:12). When all preparations were complete, Joshua encamped in the valley N of Ai. When the reserve troops of Bethel hurriedly pursued the supposedly fleeing Israelites (Josh. 8:15ff.), the thirty-thousand men rose up and attacked the enemy in the rear while the smaller force sacked and burned Bethel (Josh. 8:19f.).

This account of events notes that "the city" and "the ruin" are apparently used interchangeably in the Hebrew text; and since the words differ only by one character (*h'yr,* "the city"; *h'y,* "the ruin"), there is an understandable element of confusion in their precise application to Bethel as the city and Ai as the ruin. In Josh. 8:12 "Beth-aven" should be read for "Bethel," following the consonantal form of the Eastern text and the Lagarde LXX edition (cf. Josh. 7:2).

A joint expedition to Ai was directed by J. A. Calloway between 1964 and 1972; supplementary expeditions followed which cast serious doubts on Albright's identification of Ai with et-Tell (cf. J. A. Callaway, in M. Avi-Yonah, ed., *Encyclopedia of Archaeological Excavations in the Holy Land,* I [1975], 36-52). No completely satisfactory solution to the problems presented by the excavation of Ai has yet been advanced, and it may be that the archeological evidence is inconclusive because of the erosion of Late Bronze Age strata at the site, as at Jericho. It is also possible that Ai has been incorrectly identified with et-Tell, and that Mme. Marquet-Krause did not actually excavate the Ai of Joshua's time. Further exploration of the area is clearly necessary before the archeological picture can be clarified fully.

2. [Heb. *'ay*]. An Ammonite city in Moab of uncertain location (Jer. 49:3). The text may be a corruption of Heb. *'ar* or *hā'îr,* "the city."

Bibliography.–W. F. Albright, *AASOR*, 4 (1924), 141-49; *BASOR*, 74 (Apr. 1939), 11-23.
R. K. HARRISON

AIAH ā'yə [Heb. *'ayyâ*–'falcon'].

1. AV also AJAH (Gen. 36:24). A Horite, son of Zibeon and brother of Anah, who was father of one of Esau's wives (Gen. 36:24; 1 Ch. 1:40).

2. Father of Rizpah, a concubine of Saul, about whom Ishbosheth falsely accused Abner (2 S. 3:7), and whose sons were hanged to appease the Gibeonites, whom Saul had wronged (2 S. 21:8-11).

AIATH (Isa. 10:28). *See* AI.

AIDE [Heb. *šālîš*] (2 K. 9:25); AV CAPTAIN; NEB LIEUTENANT. *See* BIDKAR.

AIJA (Neh. 11:31). *See* AI.

AIJALON ā'jə-lon [Heb. *'ayyālôn*–'deer-field']; AV also AJALON.

1. A town allotted to the tribe of Dan (Josh. 19:42) that was also designated a Levitical city (Josh. 21:24) and assigned to the Sons of Kohath (1 Ch. 6:69). It is mentioned in the Amarna Letters by the name Aialuna. It has been identified with the modern Yâlō, 14 mi. (23 km.) NW of Jerusalem. Excavations at Tell el-Qoqa' near the village have yielded traces of occupation as early as 2000 B.C.

The Danites failed to take it from the Amorites (Jgs. 1:35), although the men of Ephraim held it in vassalage. Here Saul and Jonathan won a great victory over the Philistines (1 S. 14:31). At one time it was held by the tribe of Benjamin (1 Ch. 8:13); Rehoboam fortified it against the kingdom of Israel (2 Ch. 11:10). In the days of King Ahaz it was captured by the Philistines (2 Ch. 28:18).

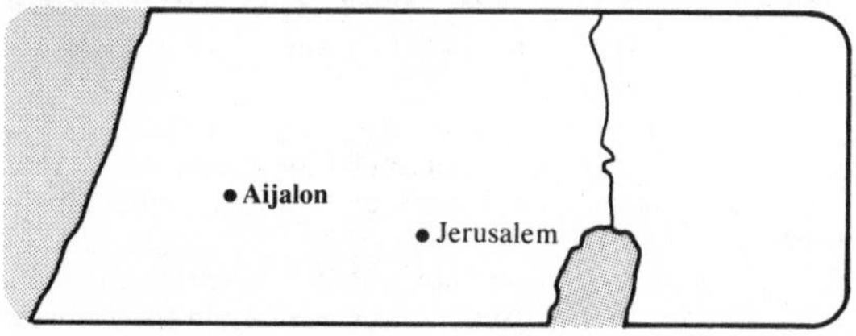

2. A valley named after the town, the natural approach to Jerusalem from the northwest, located at Wâdī Selmân. It is the battlefield where Joshua defeated the Amorite kings after commanding, "Sun, stand thou still at Gibeon, and thou Moon in the valley of Aijalon" (Josh. 10:12). Since the days of Joshua this valley has been the scene of many decisive battles. Here in 166 B.C. Judas Maccabeus defeated Gorgias (1 Macc. 3:40; 4:1-15). Vespasian assembled his Roman legions in this valley for their march against Jerusalem in A.D. 70 (Josephus *BJ* iv.8). The Moslems and later the Crusaders gathered here for their attacks on Jerusalem. In the First World War the British fought here, and in 1948 the Israeli army fought desperately in this valley attempting to secure communications with Jerusalem.

3. A town in the tribe of Zebulun where Elon the judge was buried (Jgs. 12:12). The site is uncertain.

E. MACK
J. F. PREWITT

AIJELETH SHAHAR ā'jə-leth shā'här (Ps. 22 title, AV); RSV "The Hind of the Dawn." *See* MUSIC III.B; PSALMS II.C; SONG.

AIL. The expression "What ails you?" in Jgs. 18:23f.; Ps. 114:5, renders the Heb. *mah-lᵉḵā*, literally "what to you?" Cf. 1 S. 11:5, *mah-lā'ām*, "What ails the people?"

AILMENT [Gk. *asthéneia*] (Gal. 4:13; 1 Tim. 5:23); AV INFIRMITY; NEB also ILLNESS. *See* DISEASE.

AIM [Heb. *dāraḵ*–'bend,' 'tread'?] (Ps. 64:3 [MT 4]); AV "bend their bows to shoot"; NEB "wing (like arrows)"; [polel of *kûn*–'fix,' 'make ready'] (Ps. 21:12 [MT 13]); AV "make ready (thine arrows upon thy strings)"; [Gk. *diṓkō*] (1 Cor. 14:1; 1 Tim. 6:11; 2 Tim. 2:22); AV FOLLOW AFTER, FOLLOW; NEB PUT FIRST, PURSUE; [*philotiméomai*] (2 Cor. 5:9); AV LABOUR; NEB AMBITION; [*pronoéō*] (2 Cor. 8:21); AV PROVIDE FOR; [*télos*] (1 Tim. 1:5); AV END; [*próthesis*] (2 Tim. 3:10); AV PURPOSE; NEB RESOLUTION; **(NOT) AIMLESSLY** [Gk. (*ouk*) *ádēlōs*] (1 Cor. 9:26); AV (NOT) UNCERTAINLY; NEB "with a clear goal."

This word is a translation of a number of words in the Pauline correspondence, all of which have to do with the Christian life. It is used to describe the strivings of Christians toward some end or goal. "The setting of a goal is a feature shared with OT and Rabbinic piety and Hellenistic moralism, but there is here a religious foundation and in consequence a greater intensity and depth" (*TDNT*, II, 230). In 1 Tim. 6:11 and 2 Tim. 2:22 the sequence "shun . . . aim at" is repeated, followed by a catalogue of virtues including righteousness, faith, and love. The greatest of the virtues, love (1 Cor. 13:13), is what is to be pursued and "prosecut[ed] to its goal" (*diṓkō*; Expos.G.T., II, on 1 Cor. 14:1), and it is also the true end or final goal of all the exhortations to Timothy.

It was Paul's ambition in life (*philotiméomai*)—whether at home in or away from the body—to please God (2 Cor. 5:9) by "taking thought for" or "having regard for" (*pronoéō*) what is honorable in God's sight and in man's (2 Cor. 8:21). This purpose (*próthesis*) and chief aim in life issue in Christian virtues that Timothy is exhorted to continue (2 Tim. 3:10, 14).

The strivings of the Christian life are directed toward this outcome in character so that Paul did not run "aimlessly," i.e., not as one who has no fixed goal (*ádēlōs*), but pressed on toward that goal for the "prize of the upward call of God in Christ Jesus" (Phil. 3:14).

Bibliography.–*Expos.G.T.*, II; *TDNT*, II, *s.v.* διώκω (Oepke); Bauer, pp. 16, 200, 819.
D. K. MCKIM

AIN ā'ən [Heb. *'ayin*–'eye' or 'spring (of water)'].

1. A town in the extreme northwest of Canaan. In Nu. 34:11 it appears W of Riblah (possibly modern Ribleh), and is evidently not far from the Sea of Chinnereth (Galilee). Its site is uncertain. The Vulgate reads *Rebla contra fontem Daphne*, "Riblah opposite the spring of Daphne," and rabbinical texts have Daphne for Ain, hence some locate Ain in the vicinity of Dan at modern Khirbet Dafneh.

2. A Levitical city given to the descendants of Aaron (Josh. 21:16). Some suggest the reading "Ashan" here after the parallel in 1 Ch. 6:59 (also Codex Vaticanus), but this is not certain. The passage in Joshua is the earlier of the two and has support in Codex Alexandrinus. That Ain is several times named in immediate connection with Rimmon has lent plausibility to the view that we have here a compound word that should be read En-rimmon (Heb. *'ên rimmôn*; cf. Josh. 15:32; 19:7; 1 Ch. 4:32). *See* EN-RIMMON; AYIN.
W. W. DAVIES

AIN FESHKHA. *See* DEAD SEA SCROLLS; QUMRAN IV.

AIR [Heb. *šāmayim, rû(a)ḥ* (Job 41:16; Jer. 14:6), *harîm* (Ps. 50:11); Aram. *šᵉmayyā'* (Dnl. 2:38; 4:12,21); Gk. *ouranós, aḗr*]; AV also HEAVEN, MOUNTAINS (Ps. 50:11), WIND (Jer. 14:6); NEB also HEAVEN, SKIES (Jer. 15:3), FLIES (Acts 10:12), FLY (Acts 11:6), HILLS (Ps. 50:11), WIND (Jer. 14:6); for the Heb. *'ôp haššāmayim* and the Gk. *peteiná toú ouranoú* the NEB has "birds", "birds on the wing" (Hos. 7:12), and "birds of prey" (Jer. 34:20).

In the OT, "air" most commonly signifies the region through which the birds fly. In Ps. 50:11 the RSV has emended *harîm* ("mountains") to read *šāmayim*, in accordance with the LXX, Syriac, and Targum texts. The Gk. *aḗr* is distinguished from the *aithḗr,* which is the rarified air of higher altitudes.

Aḗr is the term employed in the phrase rendered "speaking into the air" (1 Cor. 14:9), meaning "waste words," "talk to the wind," "talk in a vain and empty manner" (cf. Bauer, p. 19). The phrase "smiting the air" (also *aḗr*, 1 Cor. 9:26) is parallel to Vergil's *vires in ventum effudit* (*Aen.* v.446) and refers to a gladiator who misses a stroke.

The much disputed "prince of the power of the air" (*aḗr,* Eph. 2:2) probably refers to demonic activity in the region inhabited by man, i.e., the air or atmosphere in which man himself moves. In other words, Satan is active in the region where man is active. J. T. DENNISON, JR.

AIRUS ā-ī'rəs, âr'əs (1 Esd. 5:31, AV). *See* REAIAH.

AJAH ā'jə (Gen. 36:24, AV). *See* AIAH.

AJALON aj'ə-lon. *See* AIJALON.

AKAN ā'kən [Heb. *'ᵃqān*–'twisted']. A son of Ezer, a descendant of Esau of Seir (Gen. 36:27). He is called Jaakan in 1 Ch. 1:42.

AKELDAMA ə-kel'də-mə [Gk. *Akeldamach* (B), other MSS *Akeldama* (C, Koine), etc.]; AV ACELDAMA. A field said in Acts 1:19 to have been bought by Judas with the "thirty pieces of silver." In Mt. 27:6-10 it is narrated that the priests took the silver pieces which Judas had thrown down into the sanctuary and "bought with them the potter's field, to bury strangers in. Therefore that field has been called the Field of Blood to this day." Doubtless it was a supposed connection between this potter's field and the potter's house (Jer. 18:2) and the valley of the son of Hinnom (19:2) that influenced the selection of the present site, which, like the Aram. *hqldm'* (Dalman), is today known as *haqq ed-dumm,* "price of blood."

Tradition, which appears to go back to the 14th cent., points to a level platform on, and some distance up, the southern slope of the Wâdī er-Rabâbeh (Valley of Hinnom) just before it joins the Kidron Valley. Upon this spot there is a very remarkable ruin (78 by 57 ft., 24 by 17 m.) which for many centuries was used as a charnel house. The earth here was reputed to have the property of quickly consuming dead bodies. So great was its reputation that vast quantities of it are said to have been transported in A.D. 1215 to the Campo Santo at Pisa. When this building was standing entire, the bodies were lowered into it through five openings in the roof and then left to disintegrate, so that until recently there were bones to a depth of many feet all over the floor. These have now been removed. A little SE of this ruin is a Greek monastery erected in recent times over the remains of a large number of cave tombs; many of the bones from "Akeldama" are now buried here. E. W. G. MASTERMAN

AKKAD ak'ad; **AKKADIANS** ə-kā'dē-ənz. *See* AGADE.

AKKO ak'ō. *See* ACCO.

AKKUB ak'ub [Heb. *'aqqûḇ*–'pursuer'].

1. A son of Elioenai, a descendant of Zerubbabel (1 Ch. 3:24).

2. [Gk. *Akoub,* A *Dakoubi*]; AV Apoc. DACOBI; NEB Apoc. DACUBI. The head of a family of Levite porters in the second temple (1 Ch. 9:17; Ezr. 2:42; Neh. 7:45; 11:19; 12:25; 1 Esd. 5:28).

3. [Gk. *Akoud*]; AV Apoc. ACUA; NEB Apoc. ACUD. The head of a family of temple servants (*see* NETHINIM) who returned from exile under Zerubbabel (Ezr. 2:45; 1 Esd. 5:30).

4. [Gk. *Iakoubos*]; AV and NEB Apoc. JACUBUS. A Levite who helped in the exposition of the law (Neh. 8:7; 1 Esd. 9:48).

AKRABATTENE ak-rə-ba'tə-nē [Gk. *Akrabattēnē*] (1 Macc. 5:3); AV ARABATTINE; NEB ACRABATTENE. A place in Idumea where Judas Maccabeus defeated the Edomites, near the ascent of Akrabbim.

AKRABBIM, ASCENT OF ə-krab'im [Heb. *ma'ᵃleh 'aqrabbîm*–'scorpion pass'] (Nu. 34:4; Josh. 15:3; Jgs. 1:36); AV also MAALEH-ACRABBIM (Josh. 15:3), "the going up to Akrabbim" (Jgs. 1:36). A place on the southern border of Judah with Idumea (Edom), at modern Naqb eṣ-Ṣafā.

ALABASTER [Heb. *šēš*] (Cant. 5:15); AV, NEB, MARBLE; **ALABASTER JAR** (Mt. 26:7; Mk. 14:3); **FLASK** [Gk. *alábastron*] (Lk. 7:37); AV "alabaster box"; NEB "small bottle," "small flask." In modern mineralogy alabaster is crystalline gypsum or sulphate of lime. The Gk. word *alábastron* or *alábastos* meant a stone casket or vase, and *alabastítēs* was used for the stone of which the casket was made. This stone was usually crystalline stalagmitic rock or carbonate of lime, now often called oriental alabaster to distinguish it from gypsum. *See* Plate 2.

In the Gospel story a woman anointed Jesus with costly oil from an alabaster bottle. "She broke the jar" (Mk. 14:3) means that she broke the seal, not the bottle itself.

Alabaster vase with name of Artaxerxes I inscribed in Old Persian, Elamite, Babylonian, and Egyptian (University Museum, University of Pennsylvania)

ALAMETH (1 Ch. 7:8, AV). *See* ALEMETH **2.**

ALAMMELECH (Josh. 19:26, AV, NEB). *See* ALLAMMELECH.

ALAMOTH ə-la'mōth [Heb. *'ᵃlāmôṯ*]; NEB omits. A musical term of uncertain meaning. A group of musicians in David's court "were to play harps according to [*'al*] Alamoth" (1 Ch. 15:20). The term occurs also in the MT heading of Ps. 46 ("According to Alamoth").

Several possible interpretations have been suggested. Wellhausen read "with Elamite instruments" (cf. *BH* mg. *'al-'ēlamîṯ*). BDB and others translate as if from *'almâ*, "in the manner of young women," i.e., soprano (possibly falsetto boys). (BDB also reads this notation, by emendation, in the headings of Pss. 9 and 49.) *See* MUSIC III.B.

Most Gk. MSS transliterate in 1 Ch. 15:20; the reading *perí tṓn kryphíōn* in L assumes Heb. *(ta)'ᵃlumôṯ*, as does *hypér tṓn kryphíon* at Ps. 45:1, LXX (=MT 46:1). Even if this correctly reflected the original, its significance would be uncertain. J. W. D. H.

ALAR (1 Esd. 5:36, NEB). *See* IMMER **3.**

ALARM [Heb. *paḥaḏ* (Cant. 3:8), piel of *bāhal* (Dnl. 11:44); Aram. pael of *bᵉhal* (Dnl. 4:5 [MT 2], 19 [16]; 5:6, 10; 7:15, 28), hithpaal of *bᵉhal* (Dnl. 5:9); Gk. *phóbos* (2 Cor. 7:11), *throéō* (Mt. 24:6; Mk. 13:7), *thorybéō* (Acts 20:10), *émphobos gínomai* (Acts 24:25)]; AV FEAR, TROUBLE, TREMBLE; NEB also "demon" (Cant. 3:8), DISMAY, APPREHENSIVE, COMMOTION. A state of mind or disposition involving fear. "To be alarmed" is used in the sense of being distressed or being troubled with regard to such persons as Nebuchadnezzar (Dnl. 4:5, 19), Belshazzar (Dnl. 5:6, 9), Daniel (7:15, 28), and Felix (Acts 24:25). Jesus comforts His followers and tells them not to be alarmed during the time of great judgments (Mt. 24:6; Mk. 13:7). And finally, Paul encourages those concerned for Eutychus' health with the words, "Do not be alarmed, for his life is in him" (Acts 20:10). D. H. ENGELHARD

ALARM [Heb. *tᵉrû'â* (Nu. 10:5f.; 31:6; Ps. 31:22; Jer. 4:19; 20:16), *rû(a)'* (Nu. 10:1, 9; Hos. 5:8; Joel 2:1), *šāma'* (Ezk. 19:4)]; AV SHOUTING, BLOWING TRUMPETS; NEB SIGNAL, SHOUT, UPROAR. A warning signal. The alarm in Israel was most often sounded by means of a trumpet and was primarily used to alert the wilderness community that it was time to break camp and begin their journey. It was also used to summon the people to war (Nu. 31:6; Jer. 4:19; cf. 49:2, AV), and on at least two occasions it alerted the community to impending doom (Hos. 5:8; Joel 2:1). The regulations for the alarm are recorded in Nu. 10:5ff.

Ezk. 19:4 has been translated by the RSV as "the nations sounded an alarm against him." The RSV has followed the suggestion in the textual apparatus of *BH* in changing the MT qal form of *šāma'* to its hiphil vocalization. This suggestion lacks textual support from any ancient versions, and is therefore very dubious. The RSV is followed in this by the NEB with "the nations shouted at him," although the NEB has the AV reading in a footnote.

See also BLAST; BLOW **1;** SHOUT.

D. H. ENGELHARD

ALASA al'ə-sə (1 Macc. 9:5, NEB). *See* ELASA.

ALCIMUS al'si-mus [Heb. *'elyāqûm*–'God will rise'; Gk. *Alkimos*–'valiant']. A high priest for three years, 163-161 B.C., the record of whose career may be found in 1 Macc. 7:4-50; 9:1-57; 2 Macc. 14; see also Josephus *Ant.* xii. 9-11; xx.10 (sometimes "Iacimus").

Alcimus was a descendant of Aaron, but not in the high-priestly line (1 Macc. 7:14); and being ambitious for the office of high priest, he hastened to Antioch to secure the favor and help of the new king, Demetrius, who had just overthrown Antiochus Eupator. Alcimus was of the hellenizing party, and therefore bitterly opposed by the Maccabees. Demetrius sent a strong army under Bacchides to establish him in the high-priesthood at Jerusalem. The favor with which Alcimus was received by the Jews at Jerusalem on account of his Aaronic descent was soon turned to hate by his cruelties. When Bacchides and his army returned to Antioch, Simon Maccabeus attacked and overcame Alcimus, and drove him also to Syria. There he secured from Demetrius another army, led by Nicanor, who, failing to secure Simon by treachery, joined battle with him, but was defeated and killed. A third and greater army, under Bacchides again, was dispatched to save the falling fortunes of Alcimus. Now Simon was overwhelmed and slain, Alcimus established as high priest and a strong force left in Jerusalem to uphold him. But he did not long enjoy his triumph, as he died soon after from a paralytic stroke. E. MACK

ALDEBARAN. A red star in the eye of Taurus, the NEB interpretation of Heb. *'āš, 'ayiš* in Job 9:9; 38:32 (AV "Arcturus"; RSV "the Bear"). *See* ASTRONOMY II.C.

ALEMA al'ə-mə [Gk. *Alemois*]. A city in Hellenistic Gilead, mentioned once (1 Macc. 5:26), where Jews had been imprisoned by the gentile inhabitants. Judas Maccabeus, when he relieved other of the Gileadite cities, also probably aided Alema, though it is not mentioned. The site is unknown, but a suggested identification is the modern 'Alma, 8.5 mi. (13.5 km.) SW of Buṣr el-Ḥarîrī (Bosor).

J. W. WHEDBEE

ALEMETH al'ə-meth [Heb. *'ālemeṯ*–'concealment'].

1. A town of Benjamin near Anathoth (1 Ch. 6:60), identical with ALMON.

2. AV ALAMETH. A son of Becher and grandson of Benjamin (1 Ch. 7:8).

3. A descendant of Saul in the fifth generation after Jonathan, and son of Jehoaddah (1 Ch. 8:36) or Jarah (9:42).

ALEPH ä'ləf [א]. The first letter of the Hebrew alphabet, transliterated by an apostrophe ('), not to be confused with the smooth-breathing mark in Greek orthography. It became the symbol for the number one, and also that of the famous Greek biblical MS Codex Sinaiticus. *See* WRITING; NUMBER; TEXT AND MSS OF THE NT.

ALEPPO ə-le'pō. *See* BEROEA **2.**

ALEXANDER al-əg-zan'dər [Gk. *Alexandros*–'defender of man']. A name occurring in five passages in the NT (Mk. 15:21; Acts 4:6; 19:33; 1 Tim. 1:19f.; 2 Tim. 4:14). It is not certain whether the third, fourth, and fifth of these passages refer to the same man.

1. A son of the man who carried the cross of Christ, Simon of Cyrene (Mk. 15:21). Alexander therefore may have been a North African by birth. All three Synoptic Gospels record, with varying detail, that Simon happened to be passing at the time when Christ was being led out of the city to be crucified. Mark alone tells that Simon was the father of Alexander and Rufus. From this statement of the

Evangelist it is apparent that at the time the Second Gospel was written Alexander and Rufus were Christians, and were well known in the Christian community. Mark takes it for granted that the first readers of his Gospel will at once understand whom he means.

There is no other mention of this Alexander in the NT, but it is usually thought that his brother Rufus is the person mentioned by Paul in Rom. 16:13, "Greet Rufus, eminent in the Lord, also his mother and mine." *See* RUFUS.

2. A relative of Annas the Jewish high priest (Acts 4:6). He is mentioned by Luke as having been present as a member of the Sanhedrin, before which Peter and John were brought to be examined for what they had done in the cure of the lame man at the gate of the temple. Nothing more is known of this Alexander than is here given in Acts. It has been conjectured that he may have been the Alexander who was a brother of Philo, and who was also the alabarch or magistrate of the city of Alexandria. But this conjecture is unsupported by any evidence at all.

3. A Jew mentioned in Acts 19:33 in connection with the riot at Ephesus: "Some of the crowd prompted Alexander, whom the Jews had put forward. And Alexander motioned with his hand, wishing to make a defense to the people." Recognizing that he was a Jew, the crowd raised a commotion that prevented him from speaking.

The riot was entirely the responsibility of Demetrius the silversmith. In his anger against the Christians generally, but especially against Paul, because of his successful preaching of the gospel, he had called together a meeting of the craftsmen; the trade of the manufacture of idols was in jeopardy. From this meeting there arose the riot, in which the whole city was in commotion. The Jews were wholly innocent in the matter: they had done nothing to cause any disturbance. Instantly recognizing that the fury of the Ephesian people might expend itself in violence and bloodshed, and that in that fury they would be the sufferers, the Jews "put forward" Alexander, so that by his skill as a speaker he might clear them, either of having instigated the riot, or of being in complicity with Paul. Cf. Ramsay, *SPT*, p. 279.

4. One of two heretical teachers at Ephesus—the other being HYMENAEUS—against whom Paul warns Timothy in 1 Tim. 1:19f. The teaching of Hymenaeus and Alexander was to the effect that Christian morality was not required—antinomianism. They put away faith and a good conscience; they wilfully abandoned the great central facts regarding Christ, and so they made shipwreck of the faith.

In 2 Tim. 2:17 Hymenaeus is associated with Philetus, and further details are there given regarding their false teaching. Their heresy consisted in saying that the resurrection was past already, and they had been so far successful as to overthrow the faith of some. The doctrine of these three heretical teachers, Hymenaeus, Alexander, and Philetus, was accordingly one of the early forms of Gnosticism. It held that matter was originally and essentially evil; that for this reason the body was not an essential part of human nature; that the only resurrection was that of each man as he awoke from the death of sin to a righteous life; that thus in the case of everyone who had repented of sin, "the resurrection is past already"; and that the body did not participate in the blessedness of the future life, but salvation consisted in the soul's complete deliverance from all contact with a material world and a material body.

So pernicious were these teachings of incipient Gnosticism in the Christian Church that they quickly spread, eating "like gangrene" (2 Tim. 2:17). The denial of the future resurrection of the body involved also the denial of the bodily resurrection of Christ, and even the fact of the incarnation. In dealing with those who taught such deadly error, Paul resorted to the same extreme measures as he had employed in the case of the immoral person at Corinth; he delivered Hymenaeus and Alexander "to Satan that they may learn not to blaspheme" (1 Tim. 1:20; cf. 1 Cor. 5:5); i.e., he excluded them from the Church, in the hope that this strong treatment might drive them back to the truth.

5. Alexander the coppersmith, mentioned in 2 Tim. 4:14f.: "Alexander the coppersmith did me great harm; the Lord will requite him for his deeds. Beware of him yourself, for he strongly opposed our message." It is quite uncertain whether this Alexander should be identified with **4,** and even with **3.** All three of these Alexanders were resident in Ephesus; and the fourth and fifth of that name resided there at much the same time; the interval between Paul's references to these two was not more than a year or two, as not more than that time elapsed between his writing 1 and 2 Timothy. It is therefore quite possible that **4** and **5** are the same person.

In any case, it is said of this last Alexander that he had shown the evil which was in him by doing many evil deeds to the apostle, evidently on the occasion of a recent visit paid by Paul to Ephesus. These evil deeds had taken the form of personally opposing the apostle's preaching. As Timothy was now in Ephesus, in charge of the church there, he is strongly cautioned by the apostle to be on his guard against this opponent. J. RUTHERFURD

ALEXANDER BALAS bä'ləs [Gk. *Alexandros ho Balas legómenos*] A man who contended against Demetrius I of Syria for the throne and succeeded in obtaining it. He was a youth of mean origin, but was put forth by the enemies of Demetrius as being Alexander the son and heir of Antiochus Epiphanes. He received the support of the Roman senate and of Ptolemy VI of Egypt, and because of the tyranny of Demetrius he was favored by many of the Syrians. The country was thrown into civil war, and Demetrius was defeated by Alexander in 150 B.C. and was killed in battle. Demetrius II took up the cause of his father; and in 147 B.C. Alexander fled from his kingdom, and was soon after assassinated.

Our chief interest in Alexander is his connection with the Maccabees. Jonathan was the leader of the Maccabean forces, and both Alexander and Demetrius sought his aid. Demetrius granted Jonathan the right to raise and maintain an army. Alexander, not to be outdone, appointed Jonathan high priest, and as a token of his new office sent him a purple robe and a diadem (Josephus *Ant.* xiii.2.2). This was an important step in the rise of the Maccabean house, for it insured them the support of the Hasidim. In 153 B.C. Jonathan officiated as high priest at the altar (1 Macc. 10:1-14; *Ant.* xiii.2.1). This made him the legal head of Judea. In 1 Macc. 10:1 Alexander is called Alexander Epiphanes. A. W. FORTUNE

ALEXANDER THE GREAT [Gk. *Alexandros*].

I. Parentage and Early Life.–Alexander of Macedon, commonly called "the Great" (b. 356 B.C.), was the son of Philip king of Macedon, and of Olympias daughter of Neoptolemos, an Epeirote king. Although Alexander is not mentioned by name in the canonical Scriptures, in Daniel he seems to be designated by a transparent symbol (8:5, 21). In 1 Macc. 1:1 he is expressly named as the overthrower of the Persian empire and the founder of the Greek empire.

As with Frederick the Great, the career of Alexander would have been impossible had his father been other than he was. Philip had been for some years a hostage in Thebes. While there he had learned to appreciate the changes intro-

ALEXANDER THE GREAT

duced into military discipline and tactics by Epaminondas. Partly no doubt from the family claim to Heracleid descent, deepened by contact in earlier days with Athenians like Iphicrates and the personal influence of Epaminondas, Philip seems to have united to his admiration for Greek tactics a tincture of Hellenic culture and something like a reverence for Athens, the great center of this culture. In military matters his admiration led him to introduce the Theban discipline to the rough peasant levies of Macedon, and the Macedonian phalanx proved the most formidable military weapon that had yet been devised. The veneer of Greek culture he had taken on led him on the one hand—laying stress on his Hellenic descent—to claim admission to the comity of Hellas, and on the other to appoint Aristotle as a tutor to his son. By a combination of force and fraud, favored by circumstances, Philip had himself appointed generalissimo of the Hellenic states; further, he induced them to proclaim war against the "Great King." In all this he was preparing the way for his son, soon to be his successor.

II. Preparation for His Career.–He was also preparing his son for his career. Partly no doubt from being the pupil of Aristotle, Alexander was yet more imbued with Greek feelings and ideas than was his father. He was early introduced into the cares of government and the practice of war. While Philip was engaged in the siege of Byzantium, he sent his son to replace Antipater in the regency; during his occupancy of this post, Alexander, then only a youth of sixteen, had to undertake a campaign against the Illyrians, probably a punitive expedition. Two years later at the decisive battle of Chaeroneia (338 B.C.), which fixed the doom of the Greek autonomous city, Alexander commanded the feudal cavalry of Macedon, the "Companions." He not only saved his father's life, but by his timely and vehement charge contributed materially to the victory.

III. His Accession to the Hegemony of Greece.–In 336 B.C., when he had completed all his plans for the invasion of Persia and a portion of his troops had already crossed the Hellespont, Philip was assassinated. Having secured his succession, Alexander proceeded to Corinth, where he was confirmed in his father's position of leader of Hellas against Darius. But before he could cross into Asia he had to secure his northern frontier against possible raids of barbarian tribes. He invaded Thrace with his army and overthrew the Triballi, then crossed the Danube and inflicted a defeat on the Getae. During his absence in these slightly known regions, the rumor spread that he had been killed, and Thebes began a movement to throw off the Macedonian yoke. On his return to Greece, therefore, he wreaked terrible vengeance on Thebes, which was not only promoter of this revolt but also the most powerful of the Greek states.

IV. Campaign in Asia Minor.–Having thus secured his rear, Alexander collected his army at Pella to cross the Hellespont in order to punish Persia for indignities suffered at the hands of Xerxes, who having "become strong through his riches," stirred up "all against the kingdom of Greece" (Dnl. 11:2). When he came to the site of Troy, Alexander honored Achilles, whom he claimed as his ancestor, with games and sacrifices. This may have been an expression of his own romantic nature, but there was also wise policy in it; the Greeks were more reconciled to the loss of their freedom when it was yielded up to one who revived in his own person the heroes of the *Iliad.* From Troy he advanced southward and encountered the Persian forces at the Granicus, exhibiting the skill of a consummate general and the bravery of a Homeric hero. The Persian army was dispersed with great slaughter. Before proceeding farther into Persia, by rapid marches and vigorously pressed sieges he completed the conquest of Asia Minor. He showed his sensitivity to the legendry of the Asiatic peoples by cutting the knot tied about the yoke of the chariot of the Phrygian king Gordius—the knot on which, according to an oracle, depended the empire of Asia.

Alexander the Great on tetradrachma issued by Lysimachus of Thrace, one of Alexander's "Successors" (*ca.* 295 B.C.) (W. S. LaSor)

V. Battle of Issus and March through Syria to Egypt.–What had been accomplished symbolically now had to be effected by the sword. Having learned that Darius was coming to meet him with an army estimated at a half-million men, Alexander hastened to encounter him. Rapidity of motion (symbolized in Dnl. 8:5 by the "he-goat" that "came from the west . . . across the face of the whole earth, without touching the ground"), was Alexander's great strength. In 333 B.C. the two armies met in the relatively narrow plain of Issus. Here the Persians lost, to a great extent, the advantage of their numbers; they were defeated with tremendous slaughter, Darius himself being put to flight. Alexander pursued the defeated army only far enough to break it up utterly. He then began his march southward along the seacoast of Syria toward Egypt, a country that had always impressed the Greek imagination. Though most of the cities on his march opened their gates to the conqueror, Tyre and Gaza yielded only after a prolonged siege. Enraged at the delay occasioned by the resistance of Gaza, Alexander emulated his ancestor by dragging its gallant defender Batis alive behind his chariot as Achilles had dragged the dead Hector. (It should be noted that this episode does not appear in Arrian, usually regarded as the most authentic historian of Alexander.) Josephus relates that after he had taken Gaza, Alexander went up to Jerusalem and saw Jaddua the high priest, who showed him the prophecy of Daniel concerning him. The fact that none of the classic historians takes any notice of such a detour renders the narrative doubtful; still it is not improbable that during the siege of Gaza Alexander might have taken a small company into the hill country of Judea, both to secure the submission of Jerusalem, which occupied a position threatening to his communications, and to see something of that mysterious nation who worshiped one God and had no idols.

VI. Founding of Alexandria and Visit to the Shrine of Jupiter Ammon.–When Alexander entered Egypt in 333 B.C., the whole country submitted without a struggle. Influenced both by the fact that Pharos is mentioned in the *Odyssey,* and that he could best rule Egypt from the seacoast, he founded Alexandria on the strip of land opposite Pharos, which separated Lake Mareotis from the Mediterranean. The island Pharos formed a natural breakwater that made possible a spacious double harbor; the lake, communicating with the Nile, opened the way for inland navigation. The city thus founded became the capital of the Ptolemies, and the largest city of the Hellenistic world.

The most memorable event of Alexander's stay in Egypt was his expedition to the oracle of Jupiter Ammon (Amen-Ra), where he was declared the son of the god. To the Egyptians this meant no more than that he was regarded a lawful monarch, but he pretended to take this declaration as assigning to him a divine origin like so many Homeric heroes. Henceforward there appeared on coins Alexander's head adorned with the ram's horn of Amen-Ra. This impressed the Eastern imagination so deeply that Muhammad, a thousand years later, calls him in the Koran *Iskander ḏu al-qarnain,* "Alexander of the two horns." In the face of the universal attribution of the two ram's horns to Alexander, it seems impossible that the author of Daniel could represent Persia, the power he overthrew, as a two-horned ram (Dnl. 8:3, 20), unless he had written before the expedition into Egypt.

VII. Last Battle with Darius.–Having arranged the affairs of Egypt, Alexander set out for his last encounter with Darius. In vain had Darius sent to Alexander offering to share the empire with him; Alexander "was enraged against him" (Dnl. 8:7) and would have nothing but absolute submission. Darius had no choice but to prepare for the final conflict. He collected a yet greater host than that he had had at Issus, and assembled it on the plain of the Tigris. Alexander hastened to meet him. Although the plain around Gaugamela was advantageous to the Persian troops (which consisted largely of cavalry), giving them the opportunity to use their great numerical superiority to outflank the small Greek army, the result was the same as at Issus — overwhelming defeat and immense slaughter. The consequence of this victory was the submission of the greater portion of the Persian empire.

After making some arrangements for the government of the new provinces, Alexander set out in pursuit of Darius, who had fled in the care or custody of Bessus, satrap of Bactria. At last, to gain the favor of Alexander—or failing that, to maintain a more successful resistance—Bessus murdered Darius. Alexander hurried on to the conquest of Bactria and Sogdiana, in the course of his expedition capturing Bessus and putting him to death. In imitation of Bacchus, he then proceeded to invade India. He conquered all before him until he reached the Sutlej; at this point his Macedonian veterans refused to follow him further.

VIII. His Death.–Thus compelled to give up hopes of conquests in the Far East, he returned to Babylon, which he purposed to make the supreme capital of his empire, and set about to organize his dominions and fit Babylon for its new destiny. While engaged in this work he was seized with malaria, which, aggravated by his recklessness in eating and drinking, took his life in his thirty-third year (323 B.C.).

IX. His Influence.–Alexander is not to be estimated merely as a military conqueror. Had he been only this, he would have left no deeper impress on the world than Tamerlane or Attila. While he conquered Asia, he endeavored also to Hellenize her. He everywhere founded Greek cities that enjoyed a municipal autonomy. With these, Hellenic thought and the Hellenic language were spread all over southwestern Asia, so that philosophers from the banks of the Euphrates taught in the schools of Athens. It was through the conquests of Alexander that Greek became the language of literature and commerce from the shores of the Mediterranean to the banks of the Tigris. It is impossible to estimate the effect of this spread of Greek on the promulgation of the gospel.

See MAP XIII. J. E. H. THOMSON

ALEXANDRA al-eg-zan'drə. Jewish ruler 76-67 B.C. Salome Alexandra was the wife of the Jewish ruler Aristobulus I (104-103 B.C.), one of the three sons of John Hyrcanus who succeeded to power when his father died in 105 B.C. Aristobulus was the first of the Hasmoneans to claim the title of king, but reigned only one year, succumbing apparently to a painful disease. Alexandra then married Aristobulus' younger brother, Alexander Janneus, who reigned 104-76 B.C. He was a weak, dissolute individual who supported Hellenistic ideals enthusiastically, and it was this which provoked serious differences with the Pharisees, whom he subjugated cruelly toward the end of his reign. On his death Salome Alexandra succeeded to the throne. During her reign of nine years she reversed Janneus' policy towards the Pharisees to the point where they became the real rulers in Judea. A notable Pharisee, Simon ben Shetach, was Alexandra's brother. R. K. H.

ALEXANDRIA al-əg-zan'drē-ə [Gk. *Alexandreia*].

I. Foundation and Geographical Setting
II. History in Biblical and Apocryphal Sources
III. Description of Ancient Alexandria
IV. Cultural Contribution
V. Jews in Alexandria
 A. Their Condition
 B. Their Religious Life
 C. Their Literature
VI. Alexandria in the NT
VII. Early Christianity in Alexandria

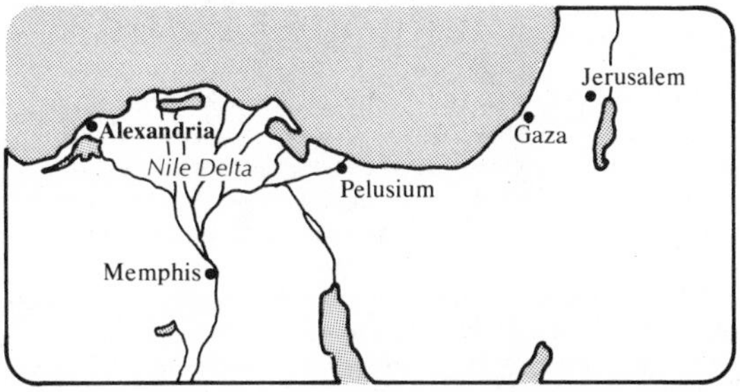

I. Foundation and Geographical Setting.–Alexandria in Egypt was founded by Alexander the Great in 331 B.C. after he had wrested Egypt from Persian control. Alexander's conquest of the Persian empire is symbolically described in Dnl. 8:5-7. A dream is said to have indicated to Alexander this site in the west corner of the Nile Delta, on a neck of land between Lake Mareotis and the Mediterranean Sea. Other factors that may have influenced his choice include: the island of Pharos, furnishing a natural breakwater at this point; the story of the Greek hero Menelaus' visit to Pharos after the Trojan War (Homer *Od.* iv.354ff.); the availability both of fresh water and of communication with the interior by water through Lake Mareotis the Canopic branch of the Nile 12 mi. (19 km.) to the east; the neighboring Greek commercial colony at Naucratis; and finally the existence at the site of Rakotis, an ancient Egyptian coast guard post and fishing town (Egyp. Raqety). Alexander entrusted the planning of the city to Deinocrates, the architect of the temple of Artemis at Ephesus, one of the seven wonders of the ancient world.

II. History in Biblical and Apocryphal Sources.–Ptolemy, a Macedonian general under Alexander, took Egypt in the partition of Alexander's empire after the latter's death (Dnl. 11:4). Ptolemy made Alexandria his capital, where he ruled as satrap (323-305 B.C.) and King Ptolemy I Soter (305-285 B.C.). This Ptolemy and his successors on the throne at Alexandria are referred to as "the kings of the south" in Dnl. 11:5-43—Ptolemy I Soter I in Dnl. 11:5; Ptolemy II Philadelphus (285-246 B.C.) and his daughter Berenice, who married the Seleucid Antiochus II Theos, in 11:6; Ptolemy III Euergetes I (246-221) in 11:7; Ptolemy IV Philopator (221-204) in 11:11; Ptolemy V Epiphanes (204-181) in 11:14; his wife Cleopatra, daughter of the Seleucid Antiochus III, in 11:7; and Ptolemy VI Philometor (181-146) in 11:25. These verses deal chiefly with the wars between the Ptolemies of Alexandria and the Seleucids of Antioch, who finally wrested Palestine from Ptolemaic control in 198 B.C. (Dnl. 11:16). Verse 14 may refer to the revolt of the Alexandrians against the oppressive regent Agathocles during the minority of Ptolemy V. It was doubtless to Alexandria that ships came with the Roman embassy to halt Antiochus Epiphanes' advance against Alexandria in 169 B.C. (11:30).

The Ptolemies of Alexandria are also mentioned in some books of the Apocrypha: Ptolemy IV Philopator in 3 Maccabees *passim*, though the attempt to kill Jewish leaders of Alexandria with elephants took place under Ptolemy Physkon according to Josephus (*CAp* ii.5); Ptolemy VI Philometor in 1 Macc. 1:18; 10:51-57; 11:3, 8, 13, 15-18; 2 Macc. 4:21 (his enthronement, which was probably celebrated in Alexandria as well as in Memphis); 9:29; 10:13; 4 Macc. 4:22; Ptolemy VII Euergetes II Physkon (169-164 B.C. with Ptolemy Philometor, sole ruler 145-116 B.C.) in 1 Macc. 15:16; prologue to Sirach; and Ptolemy VIII Soter II Lathyros (116-108, 88-80 B.C.) in Ad. Est. 11:1.

In collecting the biblical references to Alexandria one should note that the Vulgate mistakenly translates No (Thebes) by Alexandria in Jer. 46:25; Ezk. 30:14-16; Nah. 3:8.

The three centuries of Ptolemaic rule in Alexandria came to an end when Cleopatra VII took her own life rather than become a prisoner of Rome (30 B.C.). During the remainder of the biblical period Alexandria was part of the Roman empire and was governed by an imperial prefect (Strabo *Geog.* xvii.1.12).

III. Description of Ancient Alexandria.–The Pontian geographer Strabo spent five years in Alexandria using its great library in preparing his *Geography* (completed 7 B.C.), in bk. xvii of which he carefully describes the city. In common with the Jewish historian Josephus, who visited the city in the time of Vespasian and married an Alexandrian woman, Strabo notes the following districts: (1) the royal palaces covering one-quarter of the walled city on and near the promontory called Lochias (Arab. Râs al-Silsilah); (2) the Jewish quarter, corresponding to modern Shatby, E of Lochias; (3) Rakotis on the west, the original Egyptian town, around the modern Minā' al-Baṣal and Kom al-Shuqāfah; (4) the island of Pharos (modern al-Anfushy and Râs al-Tīn), united to the mainland by a mole, the Heptastadium (7 stadia = 1.3 km. = .8 mi.). Outside the city walls on the west was the Necropolis, a cemetery, modern al-Qabbāri. To the east was a residential suburb called Nicopolis, modern al-Raml.

The main street, Canopic Street, about 200 ft. (60 m.) wide, ran on the line of the present Shāri' al-Ḥurrīyah (formerly Rashīd) for about 30 stadia (5.5 km.) NE-SW, parallel to the sea. The width of the city was only 7–10 stadia (1.3–1.8 km., 0.8–1.2 mi.), confined to the strip of land between sea and lake. The other streets were laid out at right angles, like a chessboard.

A canal from the Nile brought fresh water, and underground channels distributed the water to different parts of the city. This canal was also used for travel or commerce to the town of Schedia (Kom al-Jīzah) on the Canopic branch of the Nile or to Canopus (Abū Qīr).

Several harbors made Alexandria the busiest port of the ancient world. E of the Heptastadium was the Great Harbor, with a special royal port on Lochias. The Great Harbor is now called al-Minā' al-Sharqīyah, "the Eastern Harbor," and is used only by fishing and pleasure craft. To the west was the harbor called Eunostos, now al-Minā' al-Gharbīyah, "the Western Harbor." This is the modern commercial harbor in which oceangoing vessels can dock. Off this harbor was a small inner harbor called Kibotos, connected by a canal with Lake Mareotis. To the harbor on this lake came the products of Egypt, Africa, and the East to be distributed to the Mediterranean world.

The chief buildings of the city as noted particularly by Strabo may be classified as follows: (1) *Commercial Buildings*. The Lighthouse, at the eastern point of the island of Pharos on the site of Fort Qā'it Bey, was about 400 ft. high; and its light, reflected by bronze mirrors, was visible 30 furlongs (3.8 mi., 6 km.) at sea. It was counted among the seven wonders of the ancient world. The Emporium was the business exchange. Great warehouses and docks lined the harbors. (2) *Political Buildings*. The extensive royal palaces faced the eastern part of the Great Harbor. The Soma (Body) or Sema (Tomb), including the mausolea of Alexandria and of the Ptolemies, has been traditionally located at the Mosque of Nabī Danyāl. There is no specific evidence for the suggestion that a marble-lined tomb discovered under the Latin Cemetery is that of Alexander. The Court of Justice was in the center of the city. (3) *Cultural Buildings*. Connected with the palace complex, the famous Museum and Library furnished scholars with books, laboratories, and living quarters. The Theater was perhaps where the Government Hospital now is. (4) The Paneum was a park of the god Pan on a hill, the modern Kom al-Dikkah, where a Roman theater was discovered in 1964. The Gymnasium, with porticoes over a stadium long, was near the Court of Justice. Outside the Canopic Gate to the east was the Hippodrome. (5) *Religious Buildings*. In the Serapeum the distinctive god of Alexandria, Serapis, was worshiped and the "daughter" library was housed near Pompey's (really Diocletian's) Pillar (Arab. 'Amūd al-Sawārī, "Column of the Pillars").

① Poseidium
② Obelisks (later Cleopatra's Needles)
③ Caesarium
④ Stadium
⑤ Library and Museum
⑥ Amphitheater
⑦ Sports Grounds
⑧ Serapeion

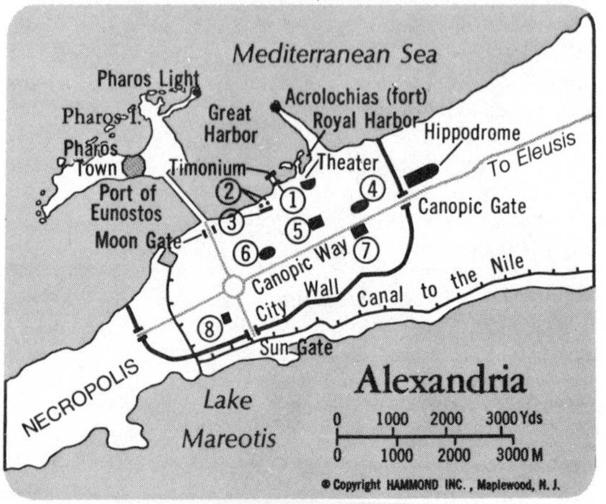

The Poseidon, the temple of the god of the sea, was naturally near the Great Harbor. The Caesareum was begun by Cleopatra, the last reigning Ptolemy, in honor of Antony, then devoted to the cult of Caesar Augustus, later converted into a Christian church of St. Michael, and finally destroyed by the Arabs. Philo describes this temple as including porticoes, libraries, rooms for functionaries, groves, gateways, and open courts, and encircled with statues of gold and silver (*De legatione ad Gaium* 22). In front of the Caesareum were erected two obelisks of Thutmose III, brought from Heliopolis in 13 B.C., and which have been taken, one to London in 1877 and the other to New York in 1879. The main Jewish Synagogue, in the form of a basilica, was called in Hebrew Diuploston, from Gk. *diplḗ stoá,* so named because it had a double gallery. In front were seventy-one golden, bejewelled chairs for the elders. This synagogue was so large that the ḥazzan, or sexton, had to stand on a platform in the middle to signal with a flag so that those in the back would know when to join in the amens (T.B. *Sukkah* 51b).

As late as the 7th cent. A.D., when Alexandria's glory had waned, the Arab conquerors were literally dazzled by its white marble buildings. The Arab general 'Amr reported that he had taken a city of four thousand villas with four thousand baths, four hundred places of entertainment for royalty, and ten thousand groceries (Ibn 'Abd al-Ḥakam, p. 82).

The population of ancient Alexandria included Macedonians, Greeks, Persians, Jews, and Egyptians. Diodorus Siculus (xvii.52) in 60 B.C. estimated the population at 300,000 citizens. Including slaves, the total was probably about 500,000.

IV. Cultural Contribution.–Alexandria was first of all a commercial city, "the greatest emporium of the inhabited world" (Strabo *Geog.* xvii.1.13). Its exports included wheat (Acts 27:38), papyrus, books, linen, tapestry, articles made of glass, of ivory, of tropical woods, of alabaster, of precious metals, and of bronze (like the great doors for the temple in Jerusalem, T.B. *Yoma* 38a), perfumes, cosmetics, domestic animals (Mish. *Bekhoroth* iv.4), and rare beasts and birds. Among the imports were wine and olive oil from Greece, metals from Cyprus, timber from Asia Minor, horses from Syria, precious stones, ivory, tropical woods, perfumes, and silk from Africa and the East. Thus Alexandria served as a commercial link between the East and Africa on the one hand and the Mediterranean countries on the other.

The art and architecture of the city were Hellenistic rather than specifically Alexandrian. The famous Lighthouse on Pharos may have influenced other lighthouses and also the form of some church towers and minarets of mosques. Some pieces of heroic statuary were produced in Alexandria; but more delicate art forms such as carved gems, vessels of glass and of precious metals, and many terra-cotta figurines (some pretty, some amusing, and some obscene), were more common. Sometimes Greek and Egyptian motifs were combined as in the reliefs of the Catacombs of Kom al-Shuqāfah (2nd cent. A.D.).

The scientists who studied in the Museum under royal patronage made significant contributions in various fields. Connected with the Museum were not only the Library but also an observatory, botanical and zoological gardens, and an anatomical laboratory. Eratosthenes, the librarian, calculated the circumference of the earth. Aristarchus proposed a heliocentric solar system. Claudius Ptolemy's geocentric system and world map were influential till Copernicus and Columbus. Theophrastus collected and described hundreds of plants. Euclid is the father of

Pompey's Pillar (actually dedicated to Diocletian *ca.* A.D. 297), located on the highest point in Alexandria (W. S. LaSor)

geometry. Archimedes of Syracuse studied in Alexandria and made advances in geometry (calculating the area of a circle), hydraulics, and mechanics, inventing a screw for raising water which is still used in Egypt. Hero invented a force-pump and described a primitive steam engine. In physiology Herophilus differentiated sensory and motor nerves, and Erasistratus came near to stating the circulation of the blood. In 239 B.C. the scientists of the Museum proposed a calendar with an extra day for leap year.

The scholars of the Museum copied and edited the Greek classics and scientific works. Zenodotus, the first librarian, divided the Iliad and the Odyssey into books and led the way in literary criticism by emending the text and marking doubtful verses. The Greek accents, still used in modern Greek, were introduced in Alexandria, and here the first Greek grammar was produced. In the reign of Ptolemy III the main library had 490,000 volumes, and the daughter library at the Serapeum had 42,800.

The original Greek literature produced in Alexandria was often contrived and sentimental. For example, Callimachus, librarian under Ptolemy III, wrote a poem about a lock of Queen Berenice's hair, which had disappeared from a temple and was then identified with a constellation of stars. Apollonius, another librarian, wrote a romance about the Argonauts. Theocritus was a master of the poetic dialogue called the idyll and of the pastoral poem.

The distinctive philosophies of Alexandria combined Eastern and Western elements. Philo tried to synthesize Moses and Plato. The semi-Christian Gnostics like Valentinus, and the pagan Neoplatonists like Plotinus, conceived of a God from whom proceeded successive emanations, until the evil material world was reached, from which the soul seeks to escape to return to God. These doctrines influenced Christian asceticism.

A similar fusion of East and West appears in the pagan religion of Alexandria. Serapis, the chief deity of Alexandria, was the Egyptian Osiris, god of the dead, identified with the bull-god Apis; but in Alexandria Serapis is depicted in a Greek form, something like Zeus with the addition of a basket on his head to signify abundance. The worship of Serapis and his consort Isis and their son Horus-Harpocrates spread into Europe, reaching even Pannonia (modern Hungary) and Britain. There were several temples in the city honoring members of the royal family, like the Arsinoeum in honor of Arsinoe, sister and wife of Ptolemy Philadelphus. The Greek god Hermes was identified in Alexandria with the Egyptian Hermanubis (Horus-Anubis), who guided the dead before Osiris. Hermes was also identified with the Egyptian Thoth, god of wisdom, and was given the title Trismegistus, about whom a body of syncretistic philosophical and religious literature, called the Corpus Hermeticum, developed. Magic was very popular in Alexandria, as evidenced by many magical inscriptions on papyri and potsherds.

V. Jews in Alexandria.–*A. Their Condition.* According to Josephus (*CAp* ii.4), Alexander himself granted the Jews a place and special rights in the city. Ptolemy I brought back Jewish captives to Egypt after his campaigns in Palestine; and some of these were freed under Ptolemy II, though pseudo-Aristeas' estimate (v. 12) of 100,000 such Jewish captives is probably exaggerated. At all events, by the 1st cent. B.C. many Jews were settled in Alexandria, E of the royal palaces in a district called Delta (Josephus *CAp* ii.4; *BJ* ii.18.8). Josephus says that fifty thousand rebellious Jews were killed in Alexandria in the reign of Nero, but this number seems excessive. 'Amr ibn 'Ās, the Arab general who took Alexandria in A.D. 642, estimated the Jews there at forty thousand (Ibn 'Abd al-Ḥakam, p. 82).

The Jewish community in Alexandria had some measure of autonomy, and special rights were guaranteed by Alexander, Ptolemy I, and Julius Caesar (Josephus *CAp* ii.4). According to Strabo *Geog.* xiv.7.2, they were ruled by an ethnarch, and then beginning with the time of Augustus by a gerusia or senate, presided over by archons (Philo *In Flaccum* 10). In Roman times a Jewish official, the alabarch, is mentioned, but his functions are not clear (Josephus *Ant.* xviii.6.3; 8.1; xx.7.3).

Some Alexandrian Jews were given responsible positions in the army and the civil government. Josephus (*CAp* ii.5) states that Ptolemy VI Philometor placed his army under Jewish generals, Onias and Dositheus. Cleopatra III also made two Jews, Chelkias and Ananias, generals of her army in her struggles with her son Ptolemy VIII Lathyrus (Josephus *Ant.* xiii.10.4; 13.1). In the reigns of Nero and Vespasian an apostate from Judaism, Tiberius Alexander, was governor of the city (Josephus *BJ* ii.15.1; 18:7; iv.10.6; v.1.6). In Roman times Jews were collectors of the taxes on the river traffic (*CAp* ii.5).

The Jews of Alexandria played an important role in the economy and especially the trade of the city. Philo speaks of the many articles in the shops of the Jews (*In Flaccum* 8). In the main synagogue, Dioploston, there were special sections for goldsmiths, silversmiths, blacksmiths, metalworkers, and weavers (T.B. *Sukkah* 51b). Jews largely controlled the wheat exports, which were important for feeding the people of Rome and Greece.

B. Their Religious Life. The corporate religious life of the Jews of Alexandria centered in their synagogues. In addition to the great Dioploston described above, there were other synagogues in every quarter of the city (Philo *De legatione ad Gaium* 20). To the regular Hebrew feasts the Jews of Alexandria added one in honor of the LXX translation of their holy books into Greek (Philo *Vita Mosis* ii.7), and another in memory of their deliverance from the elephants of Ptolemy VII Physkon (Josephus *CAp* ii.4).

Most of the Alexandrian Jews remained faithful to their traditions in spite of the surrounding pagan pressures. Philo, for example, went at least once to Jerusalem to offer prayers and sacrifice (*De providentia* ii.64). Alexandrian Jews showed their concern for the minutiae of the traditional law by submitting twelve questions to Rabbi Joshua ben Hananiah in Palestine (T.B. *Niddah* 69b-71a). The Ptolemies released Jews from religious observances honoring the royal family and Jewish soldiers from marching on the sabbath. According to 3 Macc. 7:10-15, three hundred apostates from Judaism were killed by faithful Jews in the time of Ptolemy IV Philopator. A few like Tiberius Alexander (see above) deserted Judaism to gain political positions, but his uncle Philo rebukes those who for the sake of temporal prosperity "transgress the laws in which they were born and bred" (*Vita Mosis* i.6).

The scorn of the Alexandrian Jews for the idolatry around them is evident in Wisd. 13:10–14:31 and in the taunts against Isis and Serapis in the Sibylline Oracles v.484, 487. They were so scandalized by the statues of the emperor Caligula that had been forced into their synagogues that they sent a delegation headed by Philo to Rome to protest to the emperor (Philo *De legatione ad Gaium, passim*).

C. Their Literature. The most important book produced by Alexandrian Jews was the LXX translation of the OT, perhaps the most influential translation in history. The story of the origin of the LXX as told by pseudo-Aristeas has been proved unhistorical at several points. This account, however, illustrates some features of Ptolemaic Alexandria: the royal palace where Ptolemy II Philadelphus is said to have banqueted the seventy-two elders from Palestine (v. 173), the library containing 200,000 volumes

(v. 10), the Heptastadium over which the visiting Jewish elders walked to the island of Pharos on which they carried out their translation (v. 301), the gathering of the Jewish community on Pharos to approve the translation (vv. 308-311), and the typical Alexandrian products sent by Ptolemy to Jerusalem as gifts: couches with silver legs, robes, purple cloth, a crown, linen, bowls, dishes, and two golden beakers (v. 320). Probably this translation was begun, but not completed, under Ptolemy II, and probably the work was done by Alexandrian Jews rather than by Palestinians. At all events, Tertullian in the 2nd cent. A.D. reports that the LXX translation with the Hebrew original was preserved in the daughter library at the Serapeum (*Apol.* 18).

This translation opened the OT not only to the Greek-speaking Jews of the Diaspora but also to the pagans. Thus it prepared the way for the Greek NT and is the source of most OT quotations and allusions in the NT. Furthermore, it was the basis for most early Christian translations of the OT into other languages, such as the Coptic, Ethiopic, Armenian, and Old Latin.

See also SEPTUAGINT.

The Jewish philosopher PHILO, in his attempt to harmonize Moses and Plato, is typical of the Alexandrian synthesis of East and West. Previously another Alexandrian Jew, Aristobulus, known only by quoted fragments, had tried to prove that Pythagoras and Plato borrowed much from Moses. Philo interprets Gen. 1:1 as the forming of an incorporeal pattern, like a Platonic "idea" (*De opificio mundi* 29). In connection with the six days of creation, his discussion of the qualities of the number "six" shows Pythagorean influence (*op. cit.,* 13). He gives the meaning of the four rivers of Paradise as prudence, self-mastery, courage, and justice, the cardinal Platonic virtues (*Legum allegoriae* i.63). This allegorical method of interpreting the Bible influenced the Alexandrian school of Christian exegesis. Some have pointed out parallels in method and wording between Philo and John (1:3), where the Logos, the Word, is the agent in creation; and between Philo (*Vita Mosis* ii.15f., 26) and Hebrews (chs. 8f.), where the earthly tabernacle is the copy of the heavenly.

Among the Apocrypha and Pseudepigrapha are some important Alexandrian Jewish writings and translations into Greek. Alexandrian books in the Apocrypha include: Wisdom of Solomon, 2 and 3 Maccabees, and the Greek translation of Sirach. Among the so-called Pseudepigrapha the following are of Alexandrian origin: Letter of Aristeas, Sibylline Oracles (in part), 4 Maccabees, 2 Enoch, and 3 Baruch. Thus Alexandria was the intellectual capital of Hellenistic Judaism.

VI. Alexandria in the NT.–Alexandria and Alexandrians are referred to particularly in the book of Acts. Some of the Jewish visitors to Jerusalem at the time of the Pentecostal outpouring of the Holy Spirit were from Egypt (Acts 2:10), probably mostly from Alexandria. The Hellenistic Jews at Jerusalem who opposed Stephen included some Alexandrians (6:9). It is in keeping with the tradition of pagan and Jewish learning at Alexandria that Apollos of that city was eloquent in Greek and also well versed in the Scriptures (18:24-28). Others from Alexandria were to follow Apollos in the scholarly presentation of the Christian faith. The Egyptian Jew who stirred up insurrection in Jerusalem (21:38) may have been from Alexandria.

It was an Alexandrian ship on which Paul as a prisoner sailed from Myra on his way to Rome (Acts 27:6) and in which he suffered shipwreck. This ship was carrying wheat (27:38), one of Alexandria's most important exports to Italy. The ship in which Paul proceeded from Malta was also from Alexandria (28:11). The Twins Castor and Pollux, represented on the figure-head of this ship, were the seamen's protectors, the "savior gods" to whom the lighthouse of Pharos was dedicated according to its inscription. The Mishnah also refers to Alexandrian ships (*Kelim* xv.1; *Oholoth* viii.2).

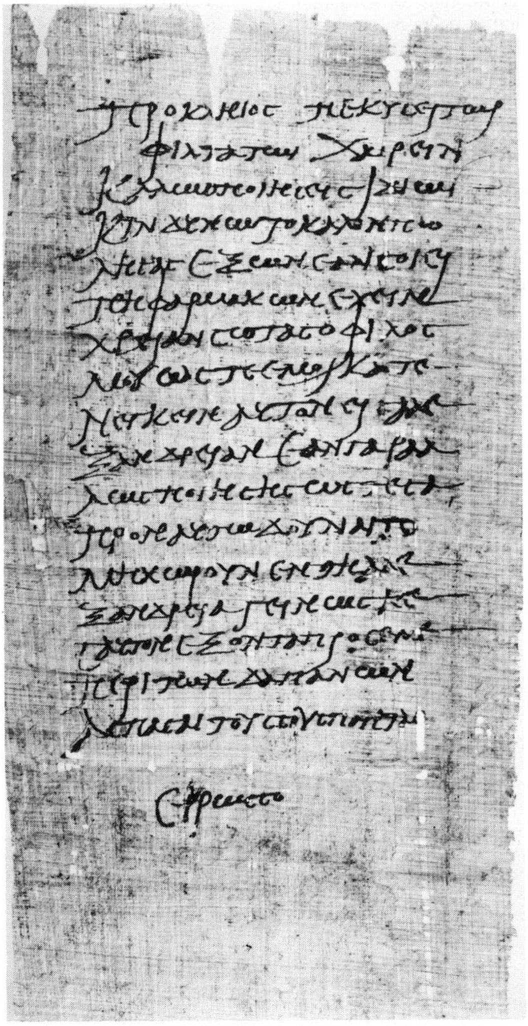

A typical letter written in Coptic on papyrus, in which a certain Procleius asks Pecusis to have his friend Sotas bring some drugs to Alexandria (1st cent. A.D.) (Trustees of the British Museum)

VII. Early Christianity in Alexandria.–The first to bring the gospel to Alexandria may have been some of the Alexandrian Jews who heard the message at Pentecost in Jerusalem (Acts 2:10). According to Eusebius (*HE* ii.16), John Mark, the writer of the Second Gospel, was the first preacher of the gospel in Alexandria. Unfortunately, earlier writers are silent about Mark's activity here. A supposed letter of Clement (announced in 1960) referring to Mark in Alexandria is suspect because of the modern date of the MS and because of Gnostic elements in the letter. In any case, the Coptic Orthodox patriarchs are counted in succession from Mark. According to tradition, after his martyrdom Mark was buried in the Jewish quarter, where the Church of St. Mark was built. In A.D. 828 Venetians took the reputed bones of Mark to Venice, where they were reburied in the Cathedral of St. Mark. The *libelli,* certificates of having performed pagan sacrifices and thus repudiations of Christianity, are evidences of the growth and of the persecution of the new faith. But in spite of the slaughter of thousands of martyrs, or perhaps partly because of these martyrdoms, Christianity triumphed. In A.D. 391 the Christians pulled down the statue of Serapis, and the Serapeum was converted into a church of St. John the Baptist.

For a time Alexandria was the intellectual center for the Christians, as it had been for the Hellenists and for the Hellenistic Jews. The Christian School in Alexandria, called the Didaskaleion (Eusebius *HE* v.10), produced some of the greatest scholars of the early Church, notably Clement and Origen. They had to face perversions of Christianity by Gnostics like Valentinus and also attacks on Christianity by Neoplatonic philosophers like Celsus. In the early 4th cent. A.D., both the heretical leader Arius and the champion of the true deity of Christ, Athanasius, were Alexandrians. From Alexandria missionaries took the gospel to Abyssinia.

Some of the activities now carried on by Bible societies were first performed in Alexandria. Attention has already been called to the LXX translation of the OT into Greek. Also some of the most important Greek MSS of the Bible were written in Alexandria, among them probably Codex Vaticanus (B) and Codex Sinaiticus (א), both of the 4th cent. A.D.

Bibliography.–H. I. Bell, *Cults and Creeds in Graeco-Roman Egypt* (1954); *Egypt, from Alexander the Great to the Arab Conquest* (1948); E. Bevan, *A History of Egypt: The Ptolemaic Dynasty* (1927); C. Bigg, *The Christian Platonists of Alexandria* (1913); E. Breccia, *Alexandria ad Aegyptum* (1922); A. J. Butler, *The Arab Conquest of Egypt* (1902); *CAH*, VII (1928); H. T. Davis, *Alexandria, the Golden City* (1957); P. G. Elgood, *The Ptolemies of Egypt* (1938); E. M. Forster, *Alexandria, a History and a Guide* (1922); Ibn 'Abd al-Ḥakam, *Futūḥ miṣr*, ed. C. C. Torrey (1922); J. Marlowe, *Golden Age of Alexandria* (1971); J. G. Milne, *A History of Egypt under Roman Rule* (1924); J. E. L. Oulton and H. Chadwick, *Alexandrian Christianity* (1954); E. A. Parsons, *The Alexandrian Library* (1952); Muḥammad 'Awad Husayn, ed., *Ta'rīkh al-iskandarīyah mundhu aqdam al-'uṣūr* (1963); Yāqūt, *Mu'jam al-buldān*, ed. F. Wüstenfeld, I (1866), *s.v. al-iskandarīyah*. J. ALEXANDER THOMPSON

ALEXANDRIANS [Gk. *Alexandreis*]. Jews of Alexandria who had, with the Libertines and Cyrenians, a synagogue in Jerusalem. They were among those who disputed with Stephen (Acts 6:9).

ALEXANDRINUS. *See* TEXT AND MSS OF THE NT I.A.2; SEPTUAGINT.

ALGUM al'gum [Heb. *'algûmmîm*] (2 Ch. 2:8; 9:10f.); **ALMUG** [Heb. *'almugîm*] (1 K. 10:11f.). The location of Ophir in these references is connected with the identification of these trees. Ophir was first mentioned during the early monarchy as the source of gold left by David for the temple (1 Ch. 29:4), and the location from which Solomon obtained further amounts (1 K. 9:28; 10:11). Despite the occurrence of the name on a potsherd from Tell Qasileh, its location is uncertain; and India, the Arabian peninsula, and East Africa have been suggested at various times as the area where Ophir was to be found. Almug (Ugar. *almg*) was imported by Hiram of Tyre; and if the usual identification with red sandalwood (*Pterocarpus santalinus* L.) is correct, it would locate Ophir in India or Ceylon, where the tree is indigenous. The white sandalwood (*Santalum album* L.), a small aromatic shrub native to the Orient, is less probable, since the wood is unsuitable for building purposes.

The passage in 2 Ch. 9:10f. reads "algum" for "almug" (LXX Gk. *peúkina*, "pine"), perhaps through transposition of two consonants, since the Ugaritic spelling supports that in Kings. But if algum refers to a different species, it may be the eastern savin (*Sabina excelsa*), a pyramidal tree growing in the Lebanon Range. Such an identification presents difficulties for any location of Ophir, and makes it impossible to describe the trees, if two species were meant to be understood, with any confidence.

R. K. H.

ALIAH ə-lī'ə [Heb. *'alyâ*] (1 Ch. 1:51); **ALVAH** [Heb. *'alwâ*] (Gen. 36:40). The second of eleven Edomite clan-chiefs dwelling in Edom.

ALIAN ə-lī'ən [Heb. *'alyān*] (1 Ch. 1:40); NEB ALVAN; **ALVAN** [*'alwān*] (Gen. 36:23). The first son of Shobal and the progenitor of a Horite group in Edom. Because of contextual differences Alian should not be identified with Aliah.

ALIEN. *See* STRANGER.

ALIENATE [Heb. *'āḇar, yāqa', pāraḏ*; Gk. *apallotrióō*]; AV also SEPARATE, DEPART; NEB variously. In the OT, it is used for the break between husband and wife caused by unfaithfulness to the marriage vow (Jer. 6:8); it is also applied to the diversion of property (Ezk. 48:14).

The NT speaks of the alienation of the soul from God (Eph. 2:12; 4:18; Col. 1:21, AV). The Gk. *allótrios,* which is the root of the verb, is the opposite of *ídios,* "one's own." The word implies a former state, whence the person or thing has departed, and that, generally, by deterioration. See *TDNT,* I, *s.v.* ἄλλος κτλ. (Büchsel).

ALIVE. *See* LIFE.

ALL; ALL IN ALL. The abundant use of "all" in Scripture can be variously treated. Where the meaning goes beyond the self-evident and the mundane, three categories predominate.

(1) Under *completeness* belong the affirmations about God that relate to His causation, control, and reconstitution of all things. This spectrum is grandly summarized in the Pauline doxology: "From him and through him and to him are all things" (Rom. 11:36). God's love and grace have all mankind as their object (Jn. 3:16; Tit. 2:11). His renewing work at the consummation will counteract all the disorder and devastation wrought by sin (Rev. 21:5). Completeness may also be involved at times when the frame of reference is less than universal (e.g., Acts 2:1). All believers are the recipients of all spiritual blessings which accrue to those who are in Christ (Eph. 1:3), even though these mercies are not always fully understood or appropriated.

(2) Some uses of the term are best described as connoting *comprehensiveness*. It is said of Moses that he was instructed in all the wisdom of the Egyptians (Acts 7:22). Broadly phrased axioms belong here also: "All who take the sword will perish by the sword" (Mt. 26:52).

(3) At times "all" is used for the sake of *emphasis.* Here should be put hyperbolic statements such as the note about Jerusalem and all Judea going out to John the Baptist (Mt. 3:5); also the assertion that the faith of the church at Rome had reached to all the world (Rom. 1:8) and the claim that the preaching of the gospel message had been similarly diffused (Col. 1:23).

Occasionally Scripture assigns limits to the meaning of "all," relieving uncertainty, as when the phrase "all that is in the world" (1 Jn. 2:16) is specifically confined to three items. Often the context gives help in setting the limits for the intended meaning, as when Peter in the house of Cornelius asserted concerning Jesus Christ that "he is Lord of all" (Acts 10:36). The reference is probably to Jew and Gentile. As another example, the "all things" of 1 Cor. 2:15 cannot properly be treated absolutely but should be restricted to spiritual truth.

Paul's statement that "one man's act of righteousness leads to acquittal and life for all men" (Rom. 5:18) raises a question. Does this statement teach universal salvation? The answer would seem to be that the provision is indeed adequate for all but is actually enjoyed only by those who put their trust in the Savior (cf. Rom. 3:22).

The somewhat baffling phrase "all in all" occurs twice in the RSV and four times in the AV. Each occurrence must be studied in the light of its setting. In 1 Cor. 12:6 (AV) God is pictured as working all (spiritual gifts) in all (believers). In 1 Cor. 15:28 (AV) the ultimate end of the whole creation-redemption process is stated in terms of unquestioned divine supremacy—God will be all (not pantheistically but sovereignly) in all (men and things). In Col. 3:11 Christ is all (as the Creator of the new man where human distinctions are transcended) and in all (as uniting and enriching His people in spite of their diversity). In Eph. 1:23 the interpretation of the phrase is more difficult because the translation of Gk. *plērouménou* is uncertain. *See* FULNESS for the various possibilities. E. F. H.

ALLAMMELECH ə-lam'ə-lek [Heb. *'alammeleḵ*–'king's oak']; AV, NEB, ALAMMELECH. A town in the tribe of Asher, the location of which is not known (Josh. 19:26).

ALLEGE. The AV rendering of Gk. *paratíthēmi* in Acts 17:3. RSV "prove" is a more accurate modern equivalent. The NEB has "apply" (scripture quotations). The word here indicates some form of setting forth Scripture by way of proof or demonstration. See Bauer, p. 628; MM, p. 490.

ALLEGIANCE. In 1 Ch. 12:29 the RSV uses the phrase "kept their allegiance" (cf. AV "kept the word"; NEB "remained loyal") to translate Heb. *šōmᵉrîm mišmereṯ*; both the participle and the noun are based on the verb *šāmar*, "watch, guard, keep," thus the phrase denotes constant attention and obedience to a person (cf. usage in Gen. 26:5; Lev. 8:35). In 1 Ch. 29:24 the RSV renders *nāṯan yāḏ taḥaṯ*, literally "place (or give) the hand under," with the phrase "pledge allegiance to" (cf. AV "submit to"; NEB "swear fealty to"). Both the RSV and NEB use "swear allegiance" in Isa. 19:18 to render the niphal of *šaḇa'*, the usual term for "swear" or "take an oath." N. J. O.

ALLEGORY [Heb. *māšal*] (Ezk. 17:2; 20:49; 24:3); AV PARABLE; NEB PARABLE, "song of derision"; [Gk. *allēgoréō*<*állo agoreúō*–'say something other (than what the words normally imply)'] (Gal. 4:24); **ALLEGORICALLY** [Gk. *pneumatikṓs*] (Rev. 11:8); AV SPIRITUALLY; NEB "in allegory." The word "allegory" etymologically can mean any verbal form of figurative expression. In actual usage in theology the term has a restricted sense, but it is used in three ways: rhetorically, hermeneutically, and homiletically.

I. Rhetorical.–The ordinary allegory of rhetoric is usually defined as an extended or continued metaphor, this extension expanding from two or more statements to a whole volume, like Bunyan's *Pilgrim's Progress*. Allegories of this character abound in the Scriptures both in the OT and NT. Instructive examples of this kind are found in Ps. 80:8-19; Eccl. 12:3-7; Jn. 10:1-16; Eph. 6:11-17. According to traditional interpretation both of the Jewish exegesis and of the Catholic and Protestant churches the entire Song of Solomon is such an allegory.

II. Hermeneutical.–In the history of biblical exegesis allegory represents a distinct type of interpretation, dating back to pre-Christian times, practiced particularly by the Jews of Alexandria, and adopted by the early church fathers and still practiced and defended by the Roman Catholic Church. This method insists that the literal sense, particularly of historical passages, does not exhaust the divinely purposed meaning of such passages, but that these latter also include a deeper and higher spiritual and mystical sense. The fourfold sense ascribed to the Scriptures finds its expression in the well-known saying: *Littera gesta docet; quid credas, allegorica; moralis, quid agas; quid speres, anagogica* ("The letter shows things done; what you are to believe, the allegoric; what you are to do, the moral; what you are to hope, the anagogic"), according to which the allegorical is the hidden dogmatic meaning to be found in every passage.

H. Cremer shows that this method of finding a hidden thought behind the simple statement of a passage, although practiced so extensively on the Jewish side by Aristobulus and especially Philo, is not of Jewish origin, but was taken, particularly by Philo, from the Alexandrian Greeks (who before this had interpreted Greek mythology as the expression of higher religious conceptions) and applied to a deeper explanation of OT historical data, together with its theophanies, anthropomorphisms, anthropopathies, and the like, which in their plain meaning were regarded as unworthy of a place in the divine revelation of the Scriptures (*Biblico-Theological Lexicon of NT Greek* [Eng. tr. 4th ed. 1895, repr. 1954], pp. 96f.). Such allegorizing became the common custom of the early Christian Church, although not practiced to the same extent in all sections, the Syrian Church exhibiting the greatest degree of sobriety in this respect. Only Jewish precedent was followed; the paraphrases of the Targums, the Midrash, and later most extremely of the Cabala, all showed this mark of "eisegesis" instead of exegesis.

This whole false hermeneutical principle and its application originated doubtless in an unhistorical conception of what the Scriptures are and how they originated. It is characteristic of the NT, and one of the evidences of its inspiration, that in the entire biblical literature of that age, both Jewish and Christian, it is the only book that does not practice allegorizing but abides by the principle of literal interpretation. Nor is Paul's exegesis in Gal. 4:21-31 an application of false allegorical methods. Here in v. 24 the Gk. *allēgoroúmena* need not be taken in the technical sense as expressive of a method of interpretation, but is merely a paraphrase of the preceding thought; or, if taken technically, the whole can be regarded as an *argumentum ad hominem*, a way of demonstration found also elsewhere in Paul's writings. The Protestant Church, beginning with Luther, has at all times rejected this allegorizing and adhered to the safe and sane principle, practiced by Christ and the entire NT, of *Sensum ne inferas, sed efferas* ("Do not carry a meaning into [the Scriptures] but draw it out of [the Scriptures]"). It is true that the older Protestant theology still adheres to a *sensus mysticus* in the Scriptures, but by this it means those passages in which the sense is conveyed not *per verba* (through words), but *per res verbis descriptas* ("through things described by means of words"), as, e.g., in the parable and the type.

III. Homiletical.–In homiletics allegorizing is applied to the method that draws spiritual truths from common historical statements, as, e.g., when the healing of a leper by Christ is made the basis of an exposition of the healing of the soul by the Savior. Naturally this is not interpretation in the exegetical sense. G. H. SCHODDE

IV. Biblical Occurrences of the Term.–On the meaning of

Heb. *māšal* in Ezekiel (and elsewhere), *see* PARABLE.

In Rev. 11:8, RSV, Gk. *pneumatikōs* is translated "allegorically" (NEB "in allegory"). Schweizer (*TDNT*, VI, *s.v.*) thinks "prophetic" is closer to the meaning. "A text relating to Sodom and Egypt is not applied to Jerusalem, nor is Jerusalem given an allegorically concealing name; Jerusalem is seen with prophetic eyes and identified with the biblical Sodom and Egypt." Cf. Bauer, p. 685.

See also INTERPRETATION.

ALLELUIA al-ə-lōō'yə. *See* HALLELUJAH.

ALLIANCE [Heb. *b^erîṯ*; cf. Akk. *birit*–'betweenness,' 'mutuality']. A covenant, treaty, or agreement, generally between tribes, states, or nations. There are two types of alliance: (1) parity, in which the two parties are more or less of equal status, and (2) suzerainty, in which a dominant party imposes a treaty on the weaker.

I. Nature of an Alliance.–Excavations in ancient sites throughout the Near East have yielded evidence of a wide variety of such agreements, ranging from simple agreements between individuals to interstate treaties. While alliances were necessary for trade and commerce, and could hardly be avoided if a powerful nation conquered Israel and imposed a suzerainty treaty, the voluntary formation of alliances with pagan nations, especially for protection, was discouraged, and even forbidden in certain areas of the legislation (Ex. 23:32; 34:12, 15; Lev. 18:3f.; 20:22ff.; Dt. 7:2; Jgs. 2:2f.). Such alliances both compromised the kingship of Yahweh and led to intermarriages. Isaiah, Hosea, Jeremiah, Ezekiel, and others warned Israel of the dangers of foreign alliances that placed the people too much in the hands of pagan kings (Isa. 7:3-9; 36:12-18; 37:5-7; Hos. 7:11; 8:9; Ezk. 23:5-7, 11-21).

If, on the other hand, an alliance had to be made for some reason, Israel was bound to be loyal, since her oath was taken in the name of Yahweh and the alliance was therefore His (Hos. 10:4; Ezk. 17:15-21). Presumably there was no objection to Israel's imposing a vassal treaty on a defeated enemy, for in that case Yahweh's sovereignty was not in danger.

II. Hebrew Alliances.–*A. Early Alliances.* The book of Genesis refers to a number of simple alliances between tribes or small groups. Abraham was linked in a confederacy of petty kings in the Dead Sea area (Gen. 14:13) and made an agreement with Abimelech of Gerar (21:22-34). Isaac also formed an agreement with Abimelech (26:26-34); both these agreements were concerned with land and water rights. Jacob and Laban made an agreement over Laban's daughters and over encroachment on one another's property (31:44-55). The nature of Israel's relationship with the Kenites, who were later linked closely with Israel, and from whom Moses took a wife (Jgs. 1:16; 4:11), is not clear, but there may have been some kind of alliance. Again, the attachment of Israel to the daughters of Moab in Shittim, and the consequent departure of some Israelites into false worship, may point to an alliance (Nu. 25:1-3; Hos. 9:10; Mic. 6:5).

B. Conquest and Judges Periods. A concrete example of an alliance is given in the case of the Gibeonites (Josh. 9). Other alliances may be inferred (11:10-16). The absence of fighting in the center of the land and Israel's later being in possession of the Shechem area suggest an alliance (cf. Jgs. 9:1-6).

C. David and Solomon. David became an ally of Achish of Gath (1 S. 27:2-12). Later he formed an alliance with Abner, the captain of the armies of Saul's son. This led to the consolidation of Judah and Israel into one kingdom (2 S. 3:12-21; 5:1:3). When David carried out his wars of expansion, he must have made several alliances, probably of the suzerainty type. King Toi of Hamath formed an alliance with David when they were both opposed to Hadadezer of Zobah (8:3-10). Possibly David had an alliance with Hiram of Tyre (1 K. 5:1).

Solomon maintained David's empire and kept the alliances his father had made. In addition he arranged trade treaties with Hiram of Tyre (1 K. 9:9-12) and probably with the pharaoh of Egypt (9:16).

D. Divided Kingdom. When war broke out between Asa of Judah and Baasha of Israel, Asa made an alliance with Ben-hadad of Damascus (1 K. 15:18-20). There had been a previous alliance between these two states, and later Omri and Ahab had an alliance with Ben-hadad (20:34). Assyrian records indicate that both Ahab and Ben-hadad were in a coalition of twelve kings which fought Assyria. On occasion Israel and Judah were in alliance, as when Jehoshaphat and Ahab joined in a war against Syria (22:2-4), or Jehoshaphat and Jehoram against Moab (2 K. 3:4-7).

Rezin of Damascus and Pekah were allied in a parity treaty and attacked Ahaz of Judah, whereupon Judah allied with Assyria (2 K. 16:6-9; Isa. 7). This latter alliance, certainly of the suzerainty type, led to the subjection of both Israel and Judah, and to the introduction of pagan cults into Judah (2 K. 16:10-18). Toward the close of Israel's life as a state, Hoshea made an alliance with Egypt that brought about the downfall of Israel (17:4).

E. Kingdom of Judah after 722 B.C. Hezekiah, when attacked by Sennacherib's armies, sought the help of Egypt (2 K. 19:8f.). The Assyrian king sought to force him into an alliance with Assyria but failed (18:29-32; 19:6f.). He may have had an alliance with Merodach-baladan (20:12-18). After the fall of Assyria in 612 B.C. Egypt came into Judah, deposed her king, and appointed Jehoiakim. When Egypt was expelled by Nebuchadnezzar, Jehoiakim remained, but his loyalty was suspect. He died, but his son was taken to Babylon as an exile, and Zedekiah his uncle was appointed king in his place. He too made an alliance with Egypt, and Nebuchadnezzar destroyed Jerusalem and Judah (2 K. 25).

F. Postexilic Alliances. The remnants of Israel and Judah were subservient to Babylon, Persia, and Greece. In the days of the Seleucid rulers they rebelled under the Maccabean leaders. Judas Maccabeus sought an alliance with the Romans (1 Macc. 8; Josephus *Ant.* xii.10.6), which was renewed by Jonathan (1 Macc. 12:1; *Ant.* xiii.5.8) and by Simon (1 Macc. 15:17; *Ant.* xiii.7.3). Treaties were concluded with the Spartans (1 Macc. 12:2; 14:20; *Ant.* xii.4.10; xiii.5.8). The Roman alliance was again renewed by Hyrcanus *ca.* 128 B.C. (*Ant.* xiii.9.2). This alliance proved to be fatal to the independence of the Jews (xiv.4.4; xiv.5).

For details of the normal content of an alliance and the rites and ceremonies associated with the establishment of an alliance *see* COVENANT.

Bibliography.–*ANET*, pp. 199ff., 531-541; V. Korošec, *Hethitische Staatsverträge* (1931); D. J. McCarthy, *Treaty and Covenant* (Analecta Biblica, 21; 1963); G. E. Mendenhall, *Law and Covenant in Israel and the Ancient Near East* (1955); D. J. Wiseman, *IRAQ*, 20/1 (1958). J. ARTHUR THOMPSON

ALLOM al'əm (1 Esd. 5:34, AV). *See* AMI.

ALLON al'ən [Heb. *'allôn*–'oak'].

1. A prominent descendant of the tribe of Simeon (1 Ch. 4:37).

2. According to Josh. 19:33, AV, a town of Naphtali. The better reading is *'ēlôn*, "oak" (in Za-anannim), as the RSV (NEB Elon-bezaanannim).

ALLON-BACUTH al'ən ba'kəth [Heb. *'allôn bāḵûṯ*–'oak of weeping']; AV ALLON-BACHUTH; NEB ALLON-BAKUTH. In Gen. 35:8, the burial place of Deborah, nurse of Rebekah, probably located between Bethel and Ramah (cf. Jgs. 4:5).

ALLOTMENT [Heb. *gôrāl, ḥēleq*]. A concept of land-tenure in which certain holdings in the total community property were distributed by lot. In Josh. 13–19 the tribes acquired territory by being alloted different sections of the land of Canaan. Because of this procedure the individual segment could be designated as a "lot" (cf. Jgs. 1:3) or a "portion" (*ḥēleq*). In Nu. 26:52-56 it was also called an "inheritance" (*naḥ*ᵃ*lâ*). The regulations for the jubilee year (v. 25) were intended to restore allotments to their original owners so as to preclude monopolies. Under the law the Levites received no specific allotment because the Lord was their portion (Nu. 18:20; Dt. 10:9; Josh. 13:14), receiving instead places of residence among the various tribes. In Isa. 34:17 Edomite territory was assigned by lot to the wild beasts as divine punishment for national wickedness.

Bibliography.–J. T. E. Renner, *A Study of the Word Goral in the OT* (1958), pp. 19ff.; *TDOT*, II, *s.v.* "gôrāl" (Dommershausen).

R. K. H.

ALLOW. In the AV the word has the sense "consent to" in Lk. 11:48 (Gk. *syneudokéō*), "accept" or "admit" in Acts 24:15 (*prosdéchomai*), "understand" in Rom. 7:15 (*ginṓskō*), and "approve" in Rom. 14:22; 1 Thess. 2:4 (*dokimázō*).

ALLOWANCE; FOOD ALLOWANCE [Heb. *ḥōq* (Gen. 47:22), *leḥem* (1 K. 11:18; Neh. 5:14, 18), *'ᵃruḥâ* (2 K. 25:30; Jer. 40:5; 52:34)]; AV also PORTION, VICTUALS, BREAD, DIET; NEB also MAINTENANCE. All the references are to food provided by a ruler to a subject, usually on a regular basis.

ALLOY [Heb. *bᵉḏîl*] (Isa. 1:25); AV TIN; NEB IMPURITIES. In this figure, the alloy is cheaper metal diluting the quality of precious metal, and hence to be purged away. *See* METALLURGY.

ALMIGHTY. A translation of Heb. *'ēl šadday* and Gk. *pantokrátōr*. *See* GOD, NAMES OF II.

ALMODAD al-mō'dad [Heb. *'almôḏāḏ*]. The first mentioned of the thirteen sons of Joktan (Gen. 10:26; 1 Ch. 1:20). The LXX reads *Elmōdad;* but if a South Arabian tribe is indicated, perhaps Al-Murad would be more accurate, involving only one consonantal change in the MT. R. K. H.

ALMON al'mən [Heb. *'almôn*]. A Levitical city in the tribe of Benjamin (Josh. 21:18), the same as Alemeth of 1 Ch. 6:60. It is probably to be identified with Khirbet 'Almît, NE of Anathoth.

ALMON-DIBLATHAIM al'mən dib-lə-thā'əm [Heb. *'almōn diḇlāṯayim*]. A station in the wilderness journeyings of the Israelites, located in Moab between Dibon-gad and the mountains of Abarim (Nu. 33:46f.). It was near the end of the forty years' wanderings. The site is not certain. It was probably the same place as BETH-DIBLATHAIM of Jer. 48:22, mentioned in the prophet's oracle against Moab.

ALMOND [Heb. *šāqēḏ* (Gen. 43:11; Nu. 17:8; etc.), *lûz* Gen. 30:37)]; AV also HAZEL (Gen. 30:37). Apparently originating in western India and Persia, the almond (*Amygdalus communis* L.) spread westward in early times and grew in Palestine during patriarchal times. That Jacob intended his sons to take almonds to Egypt as a delicacy (Gen. 43:11) may indicate that the tree was not established there during the patriarchal period.

Somewhat similar to a peach tree, the almond attains a height of about 25 ft. (7.5 m.), and in Palestine it blooms toward the end of January. Even in antiquity the almond was a welcome harbinger of spring. The blooms precede the leaves, and vary from pink to pure white. The fruit is an oval drupe with fibrous husk that splits as it ripens. The ancients extracted the oil and esteemed it for its fragrance.

In descriptions of the sacred candlesticks (Ex. 25:33ff.; 37:19f.) references to the blossoms should read "calyx" for "knop" (Heb. *kaptōr*; RSV "capital") and "petals" for "flower" (*peraḥ*). The almond rod (*lûz*, incorrectly "hazel" in the AV) is referred to in Gen. 30:37 and Nu. 17:2f., the latter rod apparently having come from Egypt during the Exodus. In connection with the story of Aaron's rod it should be noted that the almond is remarkable for the rapidity with which it can produce premature blossoms.

In Jer. 1:11f. there is a play on the word "almond" in which God informs the prophet, who has seen the almond tree (*šāqēḏ*), that He will watch over (*šōqēḏ*) His word to accomplish it. In Eccl. 12:5 the blossoming tree is likened to the white hair of old age. R. K. H.

ALMOST. In Acts 26:28 the Gk. *en olígō* does not mean "almost," although scholars have for centuries translated the clause "Almost thou persuadest me to become a Christian" (cf. AV). The RV does not make this error; but its explanation of the sentence is erroneous, for the Greek cannot mean "With but little persuasion thou wouldst fain make me a Christian." Paul's reply proves that *en olígō* must be taken with the last word *poiḗsai*, not with *peítheis*, since he takes up Agrippa's *en olígō*, couples it with *en megálō*, and continues with *genésthai*, which is the regular passive of *poiḗsai* (cf. Lysias xii.71 with 72). And the idea of "Christian" is also taken up and repeated in *hopoíos kaí egṓ eimi*.

An investigation of the usage of *en olígō* shows that it was never used in the sense of "almost" (cf. Bauer, p. 566; MM, p. 445). In the NT it means rather "a little," and is equivalent to *olígōs* in 2 Pet. 2:18. In classical writers the idea would have been expressed by *olígon*, or *kat' olígon*.

The King James translators disregarded the real significance of *poiḗsai*, or adopted the reading of the inferior MSS (*genésthai*), so as to make the rest of the sentence harmonize with their translation of the first two words; and the RV forces the last two words into an impossible service, since the object of *poiḗsai*, of which *christianón* is the factitive predicate, must be a third person, but certainly not Agrippa.

Some scholars are of the opinion that the thought is: "You are trying to persuade me so as to make me a Christian." (Cf. the NEB, "You think it will not take much to win me over and make a Christian of me.") But examples show that *peíthein* with the infinitive may have a different sense. The verb may mean "believe," or "earnestly desire," not "persuade." Cf. Herodotus v.93; Plato *Protagoras* 329d; Aeschylus, Sophocles, Euripides, etc. Agrippa is asking, "What do you want, Paul? What are you trying to do? Make me a Christian?" (The RSV reads, "In a short time you think to make me a Christian!") The implication in Paul's reply is that he is very desirous indeed of making him a Christian. And this interpretation harmonizes with the scene. The apostle's business at this juncture is not to convert heathen to Christianity; for he is in chains before Agrippa, Berenice, Festus, and prominent men of Caesarea, *metá pollḗs phantasías* (v. 23), to answer the charges brought against him by the Jews. But he holds forth at length and with such ardor that the Roman king says (though not necessarily in irony): "You seem to be anxious to make me a Christian in small measure." And Paul responds: "both small and great."

J. E. HARRY

For other possible interpretations see *TDNT*, VI, *s.v.* πείθω (Bultmann), where it is maintained that *peíthein* must mean "persuade" in this verse. Note especially the reference there to A. Nairne, *JTS*, 21 (1920), 171f., who would translate, "Soon thou persuadest me to play the Christian" (so also F. F. Bruce, comms. *in loc.*).

ALMS; ALMSGIVING [Gk. *eleēmosýnē*] (Mt. 6:2-4; Lk. 11:41; 12:33; Acts 3:2f., 10; 10:2, 4, 31; 24:17); NEB CHARITY, ACTS OF CHARITY, "beg" (Acts 3:2, 10), "give to help" (Acts 10:2), GOOD DEEDS, CHARITABLE GIFTS. The OT has no specific term for almsgiving, but several Hebrew terms and phrases are used to refer to this activity, e.g.: *ṣᵉdāqâ*–"righteous deeds" (Ps. 11:7; Dnl. 9:18), *pāṯaḥ 'eṯyāḏ*–"open (your) hand" (Dt. 15:8, 11), *ḥānan*–"be gracious" (Ps. 37:21, 26), *raḥᵃmîn*–"compassion" (Zec. 7:9), *nāṯan*–"give" (Dt. 15:10). The term *ṣᵉḏāqâ* referred to a broad spectrum of worthy deeds in accord with truth and justice. Specific acts of charity were often included. Later, the term came to be equated with gifts to the poor. The LXX uses both *dikaiosýnē* ("righteousness," "justice") and *eleēmosýnē* to translate both *ḥeseḏ* and *ṣᵉḏāqâ*. The Eng. "alms" comes from *eleēmosýnē*, as "charity" comes from Gk. *cháris* ("grace," "favor").

Almsgiving, approved in some form by most religions, ancient and modern, is a specific expression of a broad, general concern for the well-being of the poor. The sharing of one's possessions with those less fortunate arises basically from the desire to alleviate human suffering (Lev. 19:9f.; 23:22; Est. 9:22; Ruth 2:2-8; Amos 5:24; Isa. 10:1f.).

I. In the OT.–Several OT references express concern for the poor, especially those within the community. Lev. 19:9f. places a legal obligation on the rich to aid the poor in an agrarian economy. Minimal limits for this aid were set in the Mishnah (cf. *Peah* i.1f.). Ex. 23:11 and Dt. 14:28 speak of special concern which is to be demonstrated every three years and every seven years. Dt. 15 is particularly illustrative of the desired spirit of giving: the attitude toward fellow Hebrews in the year of release is to be one of generosity. The motive here is partly the expectation of God's blessing (v. 10), but basically it is a grateful response to God's prior merciful action to the owner, both as an individual (v. 14) and as a member of the redeemed community (v. 15). In every case the gifts are to be given freely and not grudgingly (cf. the "cheerful giver" of 2 Cor. 9:7; also Rom. 12:8 and Tob. 4:7).

II. In the NT.–For NT writers almsgiving is a fundamental expression of righteous life (Mt. 5:42; 19:21; Lk. 12:33; Acts 3:3; Rom. 12:6ff.; Jas. 2:15f.), especially toward other Christians (Gal. 6:10; 1 Jn. 2:10; 3:11); but the words of Jesus and His followers were directed primarily to the spirit and manner of the deed (Mt. 6:2-4; Mk. 12:41-44; Lk. 11:41; cf. Acts 20:35). Paul also gave directions as to how gifts should be made (Rom. 12:8; 2 Cor. 9:7); he brought his own alms (NEB "charitable gifts") to the saints in Jerusalem (Acts 24:17) and urged others to contribute also (1 Cor. 16:1-3; 2 Cor. 8:2; 9:1f.). Paul's reasons for the collection, however, included the theological concern for breaking down the wall of hostility between Gentile and Jew as well as the humanitarian concern for alleviating suffering.

III. Motivation.–The reason for charity to the poor and the sojourner was simply that this was an act pleasing to God (Ps. 11:7; Prov. 21:13; Ezk. 3:20; *Sukkah* 49b; Mt. 6:3; Acts 10:4). However, the idea of recompense, by which the almsgiver will receive benefits in this life, also appears in the OT and is stressed in later literature. Such good deeds deliver from death (Prov. 11:4; Tob. 4:10), bring happiness (Prov. 14:21), make one's children a blessing (Ps. 37:26), lengthen tranquility (Dnl. 4:27) and life (Tob. 12:8f.), rescue from all affliction (Sir. 29:12f.), and atone for sin (Sir. 3:30). (See also 2 Cor. 9:6.) Belief in a reward in some future life, "laying up treasures in heaven" (cf. Mt. 6:19; Lk. 12:33), was another frequently cited reason for almsgiving (e.g., Tob. 4:9; 1 Tim. 6:17ff.).

Early and late, however, there are evidences that all acts of charity were to be made not for the good they would bring the giver in the immediate or distant future, but in response to the mercy God had already bestowed upon the faithful community. Israel was frequently enjoined to remember her deliverance from bondage as the reason *sine qua non* for all genuine worship, and she was to be righteous because her God was righteous (Dt. 15:15; Ps. 11:7; Dnl. 9:18). When Jesus sent out the Twelve, His instructions included the rationale: "You received without pay, give without pay" (Mt. 10:8). The general theological basis for love and concern is further elucidated by Paul (see Romans, 1 Corinthians, Galatians), John (1 Jn. 3:17; 4:10, 19), and Peter (1 Pet. 4:10).

IV. Distribution.–As is frequently the case, some apparently abused this generous spirit so that all did not receive their equal share (e.g., Acts 6:1; 1 Cor. 11:17ff.). The church had to exercise care in distributing its limited funds. Those who falsely claimed to be widows (1 Tim. 5:6), the false prophets (Didache 12:2-5), and others who "received without need" (1:5) became a troublesome burden. One remedy given by the Didache was: "Let your alms sweat in your hand until you know to whom you are giving" (1:6).

Ignatius stressed the importance of the office of deacon: "For they are not the ministers of food and drink [only? never?], but servants of the Church of God; they must therefore guard against blame as against fire." Perhaps this was a subtle hint that they should be more liberal in their distribution, based on Sir. 3:30: "As water quenches a blazing fire, so almsgiving atones for sin." The overall economic situation in a given period always seems to be a factor in determining the attitude and form of almsgiving.

V. Status of Charity as a Virtue.–Essential to an adequate understanding of almsgiving in NT times and later is a recognition of the growing attitude that the world—and especially its riches — is evil, or at least a dangerous temptation (1 Jn. 2:15f.; 1 Tim. 6:8-10). The rich are under special obligation (1 Tim. 6:17-19), and, in fact, poverty *per se* is sometimes held as a virtue (Lk. 6:20; Jas. 2:5). At one stage there is a clear recognition of the mutuality of rich and poor; the former gives alms, the latter offers prayers, presumably for the giver. The Shepherd of Hermes elaborates this relationship in his parable of the elm and the vine and concludes: "Both . . . share in the righteous work" (Sim. 2:9).

Almsgiving and prayer were, along with fasting, the traditional expressions of piety in Judaism and early Christianity, and were frequently mentioned together and compared as to their value. The gnostic Gospel of Thomas rejects all three of the traditional virtues (Logion 14). 2 Clement placed the highest value on charity: "Fasting is better than prayer, but the giving of alms is better than both" (16:4). *See also* ABSTINENCE V. Refusal to give alms, on the other hand, was known to prompt the wrath of God, for as the author of Prov. 14:31 says:

He who oppresses a poor man insults his Maker,

but he who is kind to the needy honors him.

In the NT James puts it this way: "For judgment is without mercy to one who has shown no mercy; yet mercy triumphs over judgment" (2:13).

Some of the biblical characters who were noted for their generosity were Job (31:19ff.), Zacchaeus (Lk. 19:8), Tabitha (Acts 9:36), and Cornelius (Acts 10:2).

Bibliography.–R. de Vaux, *Ancient Israel: Its Life and Institutions* (Eng. tr. 1961), esp. pp. 72-76, 514f.; J. Lawson *Theological and Historical Intro. to the Apostolic Fathers* (1961); *TDNT*, II, *s.v.* ἔλεος (R. Bultmann), pp. 477-487.

J. T. CLEMONS

ALMUG al'mug. *See* ALGUM.

ALNATHAN al'na-thən, al-nā'thən (1 Esd. 8:44, AV). *See* ELNATHAN **2.**

ALOES al'ōz [Heb. *'ahālîm*; Gk. *alóē*]; AV, NEB, also LIGN ALOES (Nu. 24:6). An aromatic substance referred to in Nu. 24:6; Ps. 45:8; Prov. 7:17; Cant. 4:14; Jn. 19:39. Of these references, the Johannine one alone refers to the true aloes (*Aloë succotrina* Lam.).

Most OT references to aloes or lign-aloes (*lignum aloes*, "wood of aloes") are probably to the eaglewood (*Aquilaria agallocha* Roxb.), a lofty tree native to India and Malaya. When decaying the wood is fragrant, and in antiquity it was employed as a fumigant and perfume. The lign-aloes (RSV "aloes") of Nu. 24:6, which Balaam saw as a symbol of the exalted position of Israel, could not have been eaglewood, which is not native to Palestine. The reference is probably to some tree as the oak or terebinth; possibly Heb. *'ēlîm* ("terebinths") became corrupted in transmission to *'ahālîm*.

The thickened juice of aloes forms a pharmaceutical purgative and is used as an inducement to menstrual flow. This substance was familiar to the ancient Egyptians, who used it in the process of embalming.

R. K. H.

The true aloe (*Aloë succotrina* Lam.), which was mixed with myrrh for embalming (Religious News Service)

ALOTH ā'loth (1 K. 4:16, AV, NEB). *See* BEALOTH.

ALOUD. This English adverb has no direct equivalent in Hebrew or Greek, but occurs as a translation device in four different verb phrases.

(1) WEEPING ALOUD; also "mourning aloud," "weeping with a loud voice" [Heb. *bāḵâ* (e.g., Gen. 29:11; 1 S. 11:4; 2 S. 15:23; Ezr. 3:12), etc.; Gk. *penthéō* (e.g., Rev. 18:15), *klaíō* (e.g., Mt. 26:75; Rev. 5:4), etc.]; AV also WEEPING, WAILING; NEB also "moved to tears," "breaking into lamentation," WEEPING LOUDLY. "Aloud" in these and similar cases expresses the depth and intensity of the grief. *See* BURIAL II.C.

(2) SINGING ALOUD [Heb. *rānan* (e.g., Ps. 51:14; 59:16; Jer. 31:7, 12; Zeph. 3:14), hiphil of *šāma'* (e.g., Ps. 26:7)]; AV also "sing with gladness," SING, etc.; NEB also SING, SINGING OUT, "shouts of joy," etc. "Singing aloud" occurs in poetical and covenantal contexts, as a hopeful response or challenge resulting from gratifying deliverance. *See also* SINGERS; SHOUT.

(3) CRYING ALOUD; also "proclaiming aloud," "calling aloud," "shouting aloud," "shouting" [Heb. *qārā'* (e.g., Jgs. 9:7; 1 K. 18:27f.; Ps. 3:4; 27:7; Isa. 58:1; Jer. 4:5), *ṣā'aq* (e.g., Job 19:7; Ps. 77:1; Lam. 2:18), *rû(a)'* (e.g., Zeph. 3:14; Zec. 9:9), etc.; Gk. *krázō* (e.g., Mt. 9:27), *kraugázō* (e.g., Mt. 12:19), *boáō*, etc.]; AV also CRY; NEB also APPEAL, "cry at the top of one's voice," CALL LOUDLY, SHOUT ALOUD, PROCLAIM, etc. Heb. *qārā'* denotes shouting loudly in order to make oneself heard; Heb. *ṣā'aq*, Gk. *krázō* in the passages cited focus around the notion of bitter lament, distress; *rû(a)'* emphasizes the shout of exuberance and exultation. *See* SHOUT.

(4) READING ALOUD; also "read in the hearing of," "read before" [Heb. *qārā'* (e.g., Ex. 24:7; Dt. 31:11; 2 K. 22:10; 23:2; Jer. 36:13); Gk. *anaginṓskō* (Rev. 1:3)]; AV also "read in the audience," "read in the ears," etc.; NEB also "read publicly," "read out," etc. *See* READING.

Only in Rev. 1:3 is *anaginṓskō* translated "reading aloud" (AV and NEB use "read" here as in all other cases). However, the context indicates oral or public reading (contrasted with reading to oneself, or the figurative "reading" in 2 Cor. 3:2) in this and other NT passages (e.g., Lk. 4:16; Acts 8:30; 13:27; 15:21; 2 Cor. 3:15; Col. 4:16; 1 Thess. 5:27). The RSV legitimately adds "aloud" in Rev. 1:3, since it is suggested by the fact that an audience hears what is read. Indeed the pattern here of reader-congregation follows the typical Jewish liturgical format (cf. Lk. 4:16; Acts 15:21; 2 Cor. 3:15). Undoubtedly this lectionary precedent gave added significance to apostolic communications, which were publicly read in various congregations alongside the OT books (Col. 4:16; 1 Thess. 5:27; cf. 2 Clem. 19:1; Shep. Herm. Vis. 5:5; J. B. Lightfoot, comm. on Col. 4:16 [1900]). Within this developing tradition of publicly reading the NT John self-consciously places his "revelation of Jesus Christ," strengthening his assertion by promising blessings only to those who take it seriously, and by deliberately labeling it "prophecy."

C. G. CHRISTIANS

ALPHA AND OMEGA al'fə, ō-meg'ə [Gk. A and Ω–'A' and 'O']. The first and last letters of the Greek alphabet, hence symbolically "beginning and end." Cf. Theodoret *Historia ecclesiastica* iv.8: "We used alpha down to omega, i.e., *all*." A similar expression is found in Latin (Martial v.26). In the Jewish tradition, God blesses Israel from *aleph* to *taw* (Lev. 26:3-13), but curses from *waw* to *mem* (Lev. 26:14-43). So Abraham observed the whole law from *aleph* to *taw*. Consequently, "Alpha and Omega" may be a Greek rendering of the Hebrew phrase that expressed among later Jews the whole extent of a thing.

In Revelation the expression means "the Eternal One." It is used as a self-designation by the Father in 1:8 and 21:6, and by the Son in 22:13. In patristic and later literature the phrase is regularly applied to the Son.

Bibliography.–*TDNT*, I, *s.v.* AΩ (Kittel); comms. on Revelation.

J. E. HARRY

ALPHABET. *See* WRITING.

ALPHAEUS al-fē'əs [Gk. *Halphaios*].

1. The father of the second James in the list of the apostles (Mt. 10:3; Mk. 3:18; Lk. 6:15; Acts 1:13).

2. The father of Levi the publican (Mk. 2:14). Levi is designated as Matthew in Mt. 9:9. There is no other reference to this Alphaeus.

Some writers, notably Weiss, identify the father of Levi with the father of the second James; but that seems improbable. If Levi and James were brothers they would quite likely be associated as are James and John, Andrew and Peter. Chrysostom says James and Levi had both been tax-gatherers before they became followers of Jesus. This tradition would not lend much weight as proof that they were brothers, for it might have arisen through identifying the two names. Some MSS do read James instead of Levi in Mk. 2:14, but this is undoubtedly a corruption of the text. If it had been the original it would be difficult to explain the later substitution of an unknown Levi for James who is well known.

Many writers identify Alphaeus, the father of the second James, with Clopas of Jn. 19:25. This had early become a tradition, and Chrysostom believed they were the same person. Their identity rests on four suppositions, all of which are doubtful:

(1) That the Mary of Clopas was the same as the Mary who was the mother of the second James. There is a difference of opinion as to whether "Mary of Clopas" should be understood to be the wife of Clopas or the daughter of Clopas, but the former is more probable. We know from Mt. 27:56 and Mk. 15:40 that there was a James who was the son of Mary, and that this Mary belonged to that little group of women who were near Jesus at the time of the crucifixion. It is quite likely that this Mary is the one referred to in Jn. 19:25. That would make James, the son of Mary of Mt. 27:56, the son of Mary of Clopas. But Mary was such a common name in the NT that this supposition cannot be proven.

(2) That James the son of Mary was the same person as James the son of Alphaeus.

(3) That Alphaeus and Clopas are variations of a common original, and that the variation has arisen from different pronunciations of the first letter *ḥeth* (ḥ) of the Aramaic original.

(4) That Clopas had two names, as was common at that time.

It seems impossible to determine absolutely whether or not Alphaeus the father of the second James, and Clopas of Jn. 19:25, are the same person; but it is quite probable that they are, if for no other reason than the strength of the tradition.

See also CLOPAS.

A. W. FORTUNE

ALREADY. *See* NOW.

ALTANEUS al-tə-nē'əs (1 Esd. 9:33, AV); **ALTANAEUS** (NEB). *See* MATTENAI.

ALTAR [Heb. *mizbē(a)ḥ*–'place of slaughter or sacrifice,' from *zbḥ*–'slaughter,' 'sacrifice'; Gk. *bōmós*, from a root meaning 'to approach'; *thysiatḗrion*, from *thýō*–'to sacrifice'].

- I. Classification of Hebrew Altars
  - A. Forms
    - 1. Earth, Stone, and Rock Altars
    - 2. Bronze and Gilded Altars
  - B. Functions
    - 1. Lay Worship
    - 2. Temple Worship
- II. Archeological Evidence
- III. Altars in Israel's Worship
  - A. Pre-tabernacle Altars
  - B. Tabernacle Altars
  - C. Altars of Solomon's Temple
  - D. Ezekiel's Temple Altars
  - E. Altars of the Second Temple
  - F. Altars of Herod's Temple
  - G. Altars in the NT

I. Classification of Hebrew Altars.–*A. Forms. 1. Earth, Stone, and Rock Altars.* Biblical and archeological evidence combines to show that at least two, and possibly more, types of altars existed in the world of the Bible. The first was a simple altar consisting of earth or unhewn stones with no fixed shape. It might consist of a single rock (Jgs. 13:19; 1 S. 14:33-35), or several stones (Dt. 27:5f.; Josh. 8:31), or simply a heap of earth, perhaps in blocks of dried clay (Ex. 20:24).

2. Bronze and Gilded Altars. Other passages mention altars with horns, fixed measurements, a particular pattern, and bronze or gold overlay as the material. That these altars form a separate category is evident from the accounts in which the two types appear, for such items as horns and patterns would obviously be impossible in the simple construction required in most settings. The highest expression of such an altar in OT times came with the construction of the bronze altar of burnt offering in response to directions given Moses on the mountain (Ex. 27:1-8; 38:1-7). This tabernacle altar was to be of shittim or acacia wood covered with brass (bronze). It was to be five cubits long by five broad and three high. The four corners were to have horns of one piece with it, while a network of bronze was to reach halfway up the altar to a ledge. In some way it was to be hollow with planks, and it was to be equipped with rings and staves for facility of transport. Although the precise construction cannot be determined, the altar was rectangular, with a square surface at the top framed by horns at the four corners.

Such an altar may have functioned as a prototype for the altar built by David on the threshing floor of Araunah (2 S. 24:25) and again for Solomon in building the temple (1 K. 8:64). Although we have in 1 Kings no account of the construction, according to 2 Ch. 4:1 the altar was made of bronze and was twenty cubits by twenty by ten. That the material was bronze is confirmed by 1 K. 8:64 and 2 K. 16:10-15. Such an altar would have been considerably larger than the tabernacle altar, and in fact the Chronicler's dimensions are doubted by some in light of the apparently small size indicated by 1 K. 8:64.

That the former altar was movable is indicated also by the account of Ahaz's journey to Damascus and subsequent replacement of the Solomonic altar with another, more splendid version patterned after a Syrian model seen during the visit (2 K. 16:10-16). Solomon's altar was then set up to the north of the new altar, and may well have been restored to its former place in Hezekiah's reform. The new altar probably was to be approached by steps (Ahaz went up to it, v. 12), though it is possible that a ramp provided the access.

In contrast to the large, bronzed altar for whole offerings, the OT also speaks of a small (one cubit by one by two) horned altar for burning INCENSE (Ex. 30:1-10). This

Canaanite burnt-offering altar at Megiddo (*ca.* 2500-1800 B.C.), reconstructed. Access was by stairs (left), at the base of which was found a large deposit of bones of sacrificial animals. (A. C. Myers)

altar, too, was made of acacia wood, but its top and sides were overlaid with gold and it was surrounded by a crown or rim of gold. It is clear both in the Exodus account and in the subsequent record of Solomon's altar of incense (1 K. 6:20; 7:48; 1 Ch. 28:18) that gold was used as some kind of overlay, though cedar also is mentioned for the altar of Solomon's temple (1 K. 6:20). The use of gold overlay is made more likely by the size of this altar alone, together with the fact that the altar was placed inside a tent in contrast to the great bronzed altar which stood in the court. Some have therefore suggested that in the latter case the bronzed part of the altar may have been no more than a grating.

B. Functions. 1. Lay Worship. The earliest legislation as well as the earliest practice presupposes the use of altars in a worship attended by no special priesthood. In the Book of the Covenant (Ex. 20:24-26) the regulation is given in the 2nd person singular: "An altar of earth you shall make for me and sacrifice on it your burnt offerings and your peace offerings, your sheep and your oxen; in all the place where I cause my name to be remembered I will come to you and bless you. And if you make me an altar of stone, you shall not build it of hewn stones; for if you wield your tool upon it you profane it. And you shall not go up by steps to my altar, that your nakedness be not exposed on it." It applies in "all the place" (i.e., throughout the territory of Israel) rather than in "every place" (i.e., the special sites of theophanic appearances, or other sanctuaries). In the records of the patriarchal period there is abundant corroboration of the custom of throwing up what must have been rude earthen or rock altars for the purpose of offering in worship. Gen. 8:20; 12:7; 13:4 and probably 31:54, together with 1 S. 20:6, 29, describe this practice of family or lay worship, presumably in every case using an altar. Abraham's sacrifice of Isaac (Gen. 22) and also Jacob's covenant with Laban at the "heap of stones" (31:46) would both fit into such a category.

That these lay altars were something quite different from the elaborate structures described in the priestly ritual (Ex. 27:1-8 and 30:1-10) should be obvious to even the casual reader. It is for this reason that it seems best to find in the primitive regulations of the Book of the Covenant the kind of altar widely attested from ancient sources as a rough cairn, with the prohibition against tooled work and steps more in response to Canaanite cult worship than a rejection of what in other places is legitimate for the temple system.

2. Temple Worship. In the stipulations for priestly service explicit direction is given for at least two kinds of altar. Ex. 27:1-8 (cf. 38:1-7) orders the construction of a bronze-overlaid altar of burnt offering, to be attended by the caste of priests. In the service of this altar, which was set at the door of the tabernacle or the tent of meeting (Ex. 40:29; *see* TABERNACLE), no lay person was allowed, and the regulations of Ex. 20, alluded to above, would have been quite out of place.

A second type of altar provided for priestly service was found inside the sacred tent (Ex. 40:26) and was primarily for the burning of incense. Ex. 30:1-10 (see above) gives directions for its construction and use.

II. Archeological Evidence.–Evidence from archeological research has turned up a variety of Canaanite altars, with excellent examples available from Early Bronze times (*ca.* 3000 B.C.) to late in the Iron Age. In the OT specific instructions separate these Canaanite altars from the Hebrew ones, though whether the prohibition against using heathen altars relates to their form or to the innate impurity of such worship is not clear. Ex. 20:25f. prohibits both the use of hewn stone and any construction using steps, presumably both features of some Canaanite structures. Jgs. 6:25f. calls for the destruction of the altar of Baal, together with its accompanying "asherah" (a wooden symbol of a goddess), prior to the construction of Gideon's altar of Yahweh. Finally, the action of King Ahaz in importing a Syrian altar from Damascus (2 K. 16:10ff.) and the implicit condemnation of the act in the biblical source clearly show that the pattern of altars was not interchangeable.

From the ancient sites perhaps the best preserved examples of Canaanite altars come from Bronze Age Megiddo. A possible table or deposit-altar, dated to *ca.* 3000 B.C., is little more than a platform built into the rear wall of a temple. A more obvious altar is the large (*ca.* 26 ft. in diameter) stone, stepped structure still visible on the tell from the Middle Bronze Age city. Such a platform no doubt required officials to climb it for ceremonial purposes, perhaps exposing some part of the body considered immodest or improper in Israel (see the prohibition against steps, above). Other clearly pagan altars are either of the large, rubble type (burnt offering altars?) or the small table type (incense or possibly image-bearing altars) and appear in various levels at such ancient sites as Ai, Lachish, Alalakh, and Beth-shean. Also discovered are what have been called "altar blocks," large hewn-out stones (or sometimes natural rock platforms) that seem to have had basin systems for blood. Such artifacts have been found at Hazor and Hamath on the Orontes. It can readily be seen that none of these types of altars is easily identifiable with the altars described in the OT, though the prohibitions against certain forms seem directed more against the worship conducted at them than against simply the constructions themselves.

Of special interest to the Bible student are two "horned" altars, each with dimensions roughly equal to those prescribed in Ex. 27:1 (five cubits square by three cubits high), with horns on each corner (Ex. 27:2). Both the Arad and the Beer-sheba altars are of stone, though the former was unworked while the latter is not only made of smooth ashlar masonry (in defiance of biblical law, Dt. 27:5) but even contains an engraved decoration of a twisted snake. Both altars come from the Israelite monarchy. Y. Aharoni dates the Arad temple to the 10th cent. (Solomonic) and the Beer-sheba construction to the 8th century. He considers both these southern temples to be part of royal border sanctuaries and thus evidence for competing Israelite cultic structures prior to Hezekiah's and Josiah's reformations (Y. Aharoni, *BA*, 31 [1968], 19-21; 37 [1974], 2-5).

Finally, two small, four-sided terra-cotta structures have been found at Taanach, both of which relate to the Iron Age. The earlier, discovered in 1902 and designated by E. Sellin as an "incense-altar," is about 3 ft. (1 m.) high, hollow, with four sides like a truncated pyramid. In 1968 P. W. Lapp found buried in a cistern a tenth-century "cultic stand" (his terminology) which, when reconstructed, became a hollowed square 20 in. (50 cm.) high. It contains four registers of terra-cotta figures in relief with some resemblance to orthostats associated with Syrian temples. The form of both of these altars (if altars they may be called) is as contrary to the principles of the pentateuchal law as anything could be, and they stand as grim commentary on the religious practices to which the Israelites were exposed. (Cf. *BASOR*, 195 [Oct. 1969], 42-44.)

III. Altars in Israel's Worship.–*A. Pre-tabernacle Altars.* In the Bible, sacrifices are prior to altars, and altars prior to sacred buildings. The first reference to an altar is to the one built by Noah after the flood (Gen. 8:20). Abraham is the next builder of altars, the first three of which seem to have related to his circuit of wanderings within Canaan. His first altar, at Shechem, seems to have been the symbolic means of his formal possession of the land (Gen. 12:7), while the two subsequent structures, one between Bethel and Ai (12:8) and the other in the south at Hebron (13:18), marked the limits of his normal sojourning. At each place he sacrificed and called upon the name of Yahweh. His final altar was built on the top of a mountain in the land of Moriah (identified with Jerusalem in later Hebrew tradition) for the sacrifice of Isaac (22:19).

Four-horned limestone altar from Israelite Megiddo (*ca.* 1000-800 B.C.), possibly a house altar or incense altar (Oriental Institute, University of Chicago)

Each of these four spots was the scene of some special revelation of Yahweh; possibly to the third of them (Hebron) we may attribute the memorable vision and covenant of Gen. 15. To them Isaac added an altar at Beer-sheba (26:25), probably a re-creation, on the same site, of an altar built by Abraham, whose home for many years was at Beersheba. Jacob built no new altars, but repeatedly repaired those at Shechem and Bethel. There were thus four or five spots in Canaan (Shechem, Bethel, Hebron, Moriah, and Beer-sheba) associated both with the worship of Yahweh and with the names of the patriarchs. In later years these locations were to become important sanctuaries, not only for the worship of Yahweh but for the preservation and proclamation of family traditions.

With the growth of the family to a nation, provision is made for some regulation of altar-building immediately after the promulgation of the Decalogue (Ex. 20:24ff.). The instructions relate to "lay" rather than tabernacle altars (see above), as the pattern of patriarchal or clan worship had still not been supplemented by any developed national cult. In the same period, before the arrival at Sinai, during the war with Amalek, Moses built an emergency altar to which he gave the name Yahweh-Nissi (Ex. 17:15). This was probably only a memorial altar, a function attested again in the controversial structure built by the two and one-half tribes in Transjordan (Josh. 22:21-29).

These patriarchal or "lay" altars continued in use well into the period of the monarchy, withstanding both the centralizing tendency first apparent in David and Solomon's institution of worship at Jerusalem and later the iconoclastic reactions to potentially divisive or Baal-tainted shrines during the reigns of Hezekiah and Josiah. Joshua's altar on Mt. Ebal (Josh. 8:30-34) follows the Deuteronomic regulations for lay altar construction, and is used for sacrifices accompanying a ceremony of national covenant renewal. Gideon at Ophrah (Jgs. 6:24), the people of Israel at Bethel (21:4), Samuel at Ramah (1 S. 7:17), Saul at Michmash (14:35), and David at the threshing floor of Araunah (2 S. 24:25) all fit this pattern. Of the days between David and Hezekiah we know less, but it is apparent that such activity continued, and probably the reaction against Baalism, evidenced in Elijah's contest on Mt. Carmel (1 K. 19), led to the eventual disrepute into which these lay altars fell.

B. Tabernacle Altars. In the worship of Israel, as formalized in the Sinai covenant, two priestly altars become central to the ritual of the tabernacle in the wilderness. As we have seen, the directions for the construction of both the altar of burnt offering (*mizbaḥ hā'ôlâ*, or brazen altar *mizbaḥ hannᵉḥōšeṯ*) and the altar of INCENSE (*mizbaḥ haqqᵉṭōreṯ*, or golden altar *mizbaḥ hazzāhāḇ*) are given in great detail. Such exact direction seems to have related to the symbolic functioning of both structures with their central place in the sacrificial system of the nation.

The altar of burnt offering, much the larger of the two, was set up in front of the doorway of the tabernacle (Ex. 40:6) where it was used for the daily burnt and meal offerings (*see* SACRIFICES V). It was there that the priests made atonement for various sins of the people, according to the sacrificial system outlined in Lev. 1–7, and it stood as witness to the fact that any entry into the presence of God must be preceded by atonement for sin. The doorway to the tent of meeting was doubly important, as it was there that the worshiper met with the intermediary, the priest.

The second altar, the altar of incense, was also in the category of "most holy" things (Ex. 30:10). Speculation about whether it stood just inside the Holy of Holies (He. 9:4) or just before the veil (Ex. 40:26) separating the two inner rooms is useless. What is clear is that the altar was accessible to the priests who were commanded to burn daily upon it the sweet incense so that a cloud of smoke might rise to fill the inner chamber at the moment when the sacrificial blood was sprinkled. The symbolism of the incense is clearly that of offered prayer (cf. Rev. 8:3, where the golden altar stands before the throne of God and the priest is replaced by an angel).

C. Altars of Solomon's Temple. What happened to the tabernacle between the destruction of Shiloh (*ca.* 1050 B.C.) and the erection of Solomon's temple remains an enigma. Something of the wandering of the ark is known, but whether the altars and other tabernacle furniture were complete in such sanctuaries as Nob (1 S. 21:1-6) and Gibeon (2 Ch. 1:3) must remain unclear. The service of the Lord at the former site and the events of the removal to Jerusalem from the latter (cf. 1 K. 8:4 with 2 Ch. 1:3; 5:3) seem to indicate a continuous succession for the organized cult. According to 2 Ch. 1:5, the bronze altar made by Bezalel for Moses was at Gibeon, whereupon Solomon offered a thousand burnt offerings prior to its removal.

When Solomon built his new temple, he had new altars made in keeping with the fresh requirements. From the Chronicler's account (2 Ch. 4:1) we learn that one was a brazen altar, forming a square of 20 cubits (about 30 ft. or 9 m.) with a height of 10 cubits (about 15 ft. or 4.5 m.). This first and greatest altar, which with the molten sea dominated the middle of the court that was before the temple, remained the center of Israelite worship for two and one-half centuries, before Ahaz removed it to the northern side of his Damascene altar (2 K. 16:14), a travesty probably corrected by Hezekiah (2 Ch. 29:18). Its function was the same as the smaller structure in the tabernacle and, much older critical opinion notwithstanding, it was probably constructed on the model of the latter.

In like manner, the smaller tabernacle incense altar was superseded by Solomon's cedar structure, overlaid (like everything else in the inner rooms) with gold (1 K. 6:20, 22), and thereafter called the golden altar to distinguish it from the brazen courtyard altar. Of the size of this altar, which also functioned as its predecessor, we know nothing, but it was undoubtedly small and was part of the "vessels of the house of God" which Nebuchadrezzar took to Babylon (2 Ch. 36:18). Possibly as a consequence of this Ezekiel planned a wooden altar of incense with larger dimensions than before (Ezk. 41:22).

D. Ezekiel's Temple Altars. The purpose of Ezekiel's vision was to draw the attention of the exiles to their return and the restoration of God's direct dealings with them in a rebuilt Jerusalem, in order that "they may be ashamed of their iniquities" (Ezk. 43:10). The altar of burnt offering was a rather large and elaborate structure, measured out by the larger cubit (43:13) and consisting of four stages lying one above another. In the account of its construction and use emphasis seems to be on the real need in Israel for atonement, with the resulting impression being one of the holiness of God and the sinfulness of the people. The altar, promising as it did cleansing from the accumulated sins of exile, was clearly the focal point of the new temple and pointed graphically to the lack of such cleansing in the conditions of exile.

E. Altars of the Second Temple. The second temple likewise preserved the tradition of two altars. Ezr. 3:3 describes the laying of a foundation for the altar of burnt offerings, though of the altar itself no measurements are given. That there was also an altar of incense is clear because it was carried off by Antiochus Epiphanes (1 Macc. 1:21) and restored by Judas Maccabeus (1 Macc. 4:49), together with the altar of burnt offering.

F. Altars of Herod's Temple. The continued importance of both altars is reflected in their presence in the great sanctuary built by Herod. Although there is some difficulty in harmonizing the accounts of the Mishna and Josephus as to the size of the altar of burnt offering (*see* TEMPLE) the use of the altar is not in doubt. It was the one valid place of sacrifice and the place of which it was said, "Leave your gift there before the altar and go; first be reconciled to your brother, and then come and offer your gift" (Mt. 5:24). Also from the NT we know of an incident at the smaller altar. It was there that Zechariah had a vision of "an angel . . . standing on the right side of the altar of incense" (Lk. 1:11).

G. Altars in the NT. In addition to references to Herod's temple with its altars, the NT used the concept of the temple in a figurative sense, especially in Revelation. What is vitally significant is that in the future temple of God there is no need for an altar of burnt offering, since atonement is now complete and the re-establishment of a sacrifice would violate all the canons of NT thought. In Revelation, however, the altar of incense still stands immediately before God (8:3; 9:13) and indeed once speaks a word of confirmation to God's work of judgment (16:7). It is, like the golden altar of the ancient ritual, the place from which the sweet smell of spice arises to God, and 8:3 makes it plain that this pleasing odor is indeed the prayers of the saints. Thus the great truths continue: the atonement of the great altar of burnt offering is no more. It has been accomplished once and for all by the sacrifice of God's Son. But the role of the smaller, golden altar will continue into eternity.

See also HORNS OF THE ALTAR.

Bibliography.–*ARI*; K. Galling, *Der Altar in den Kulturen des Alten Orients* (1925); R. de Vaux, *Ancient Israel* (1961).

H. M. WIENER
W. S. CALDECOTT
C. E. ARMERDING

AL-TASCHITH al-tas'kith. The AV transliteration of Heb. *'al-tašḥēṯ* in the headings of Pss. 57–59, 75. The RSV translates "Do not destroy"; the NEB omits. The phrase occurs in Isa. 65:8, which may indicate that it is the name of a vintage song. *See* SONG; MUSIC III.B; PSALMS II.C.

ALTER [Heb. *šānâ*] (Ps. 89:34); NEB CHANGE; [*'āḇar*] (Est. 1:19); NEB REVOKE; [Aram. haphel of **šᵉnāy*] (Ezr. 6:11f.); NEB TAMPER WITH. The references in Ezra and Esther reflect the sacrosanct nature of official decrees in the ancient world, the penalty for tampering with which was generally death. The covenant stipulations were equally inviolable both for the old (Dt. 4:2; 12:32) and the new (Rev. 22:18f.) dispensations. The man of faith could undertake to live strictly by the covenantal promises (Ps. 89:34). R. K. H.

ALUSH ā'lush [Heb. *'ālûš*]. A desert camp of the Israelites between Dophkah and Rephidim (Nu. 33:13f.), possibly the modern Wâdī el-'Eshsh.

ALVAH al'və. *See* ALIAH.

ALVAN al'vən. *See* ALIAN.

ALWAY. An archaic and poetic form of "always" occurring frequently in the AV (e.g., Ps. 9:18; Mt. 28:20).

AMAD ā'mad [Heb. *'am'āḏ*]. A town allotted to the tribe of Asher in the division of Palestine (Josh. 19:26). Its place in the list of names suggests a location in the northwest, N of Mt. Carmel.

AMADATHUS a-mə-da'thəs (Ad. Est. 12:6, AV). *See* HAMMEDATHA.

AMAL ā'mäl [Heb. *'āmāl*]. A son of Helem of the tribe of Asher (1 Ch. 7:35).

AMALEK; AMALEKITES am'ə-lek, ə-mal'ə-kīts [Heb. *'ᵃmālēq, 'ᵃmālēqî*]. The son of Eliphaz and grandson of Esau (Gen. 36:12, 16), and as a collective noun, his descendants (Ex. 17:8; Nu. 24:20; Dt. 25:17; Jgs. 3:13; etc.). His mother was Timna, Eliphaz' concubine. He was one of "the chiefs of Eliphaz in the land of Edom" (Gen. 36:16).

Some writers distinguish the nomadic Amalekites normally found in the Negeb and Sinai area from the descendants of Esau, because Gen. 14:7, which antedates Esau, refers to the "country of the Amalekites." This may be merely an editorial note, although no doubt some of the descendants of Esau became incorporated into Amalekite groups, as they did into other tribes in Transjordan.

The origin of the Amalekites is obscure. They do not appear in the list of the nations in Gen. 10, although it is likely that they were of Semitic origin. Their first contact with Israel was at Rephidim in the wilderness of Sinai, where they made an unprovoked attack on the Israelites and were defeated after a desperate conflict (Ex. 17:8-13; Dt. 25:17f.). Because of this attack the Amalekites were placed under a permanent ban and were to be destroyed (Dt. 25:19; 1 S. 15:2f.; cf. Ps. 83:7). A year later, following the report of the spies, Israel ignored the advice of Moses and sought to enter southern Palestine. They were defeated by the Amalekites at Hormah (Nu. 14:43, 45). The spies had reported their presence in the south along with Hittites, Jebusites, and Amorites (Nu. 13:29).

From the days of the judges two encounters are recorded. The Amalekites assisted Eglon king of Moab in his attack on Israelite territory (Jgs. 3:13). Later they combined forces with the Midianites and the "people of the East" (*bᵉnê qeḏem*), and raided Israelite crops and flocks in the days of Gideon, who was able to drive them out (Jgs. 6:3-5, 33; 7:12).

During these years the Amalekites were to be found mainly in the Negeb region, although for a time they gained a foothold in Ephraim (Jgs. 12:15). The foreign prophet Balaam looked away to their lands from his vantage point in Moab and described them as the "first of the nations" (Nu. 24:20), which may mean in regard either to origin or to status. When Samuel commanded Saul to destroy them they were in the Negeb area, S of Telaim in Judah. Saul drove them toward Shur in the wilderness toward Egypt (1 S. 15:1-9). On that occasion Saul spared Agag their king, for which he was rebuked by Samuel, who slew Agag personally (1 S. 15:33).

David fought the Amalekites in the area of Ziklag, which Achish king of Gath had given to him (1 S. 27:6; 30:1-20). It was an Amalekite who brought to David the news of the deaths of Saul and Jonathan (in which he had a part), and who was put to death by David (2 S. 1:1-16).

After David's time the Amalekites seem to have declined. In Hezekiah's day the sons of Simeon attacked "the remnant of the Amalekites that had escaped," taking their stronghold in Mt. Seir (1 Ch. 4:43).

J. ARTHUR THOMPSON

AMAM ā'mam [Heb. *'ᵃmām*]. An unidentified town in southern Palestine, which was allotted to Judah in the division of the land. The name occurs only in Josh. 15:26. The LXX B reads *Sēn*, which Simons (*GTTOT* § 317) connects with Bîr el-Esani and Wâdī el-Esani, NW of el-Ḫalaṣah (which is about 12 mi. [19 km.] SW of Beer-sheba).

AMAN ā'man. AV Apoc. for NADAB (Tob. 14:10) and HAMAN (Ad. Est.).

AMANA ə-mā'nə, ə-mä'nə [Heb. *'ᵃmānâ*]. A mountain mentioned along with Lebanon, Senir, and Hermon in Cant. 4:8, and probably one of the mountains of the Anti-Lebanon, modern Jebel Zebedâni, near the source of the river Abana, or Amana.

AMARIAH am-ə-rī'ə [Heb. *'ᵃmaryâ, 'ᵃmaryāhû*].

1. A Levite in the line of Aaron-Eleazar; a son of Meraioth and grandfather of Zadok (1 Ch. 6:7, 52) who lived in David's time. Cf. Zadok (2 S. 15:27, etc.); also Josephus *Ant.* viii.1.3; x.8.6.

2. A Levite in the line of Kohath-Hebron referred to in 1 Ch. 23:19 and 24:23 at the time when David organized the Levites into divisions.

3. [Gk. *Amarias*, B *Amartheias*]; AV Apoc., NEB (1 Esd. 8:2), AMARIAS. A Levite in the line of Aaron-Eleazar; a son of Azariah who "executed the priest's office in the house that Solomon built" (1 Ch. 6:10f.). Cf. Ezr. 7:3, where in the abbreviated list this Amariah is mentioned as an ancestor of Ezra.

4. Chief priest and judge "in all matters of the Lord,"

appointed by Jehoshaphat (2 Ch. 19:11); possibly identical with **3.**

5. A descendant of Judah in the line of Perez and an ancestor of Ataiah who lived in Jerusalem after the Babylonian Exile (Neh. 11:4). Cf. Imri (1 Ch. 9:4) and **7** below, who seems to be of the same family.

6. A Levite and an assistant of Kore who was appointed by Hezekiah to distribute the "oblations of the Lord" to their brethren (2 Ch. 31:15).

7. A son of Bani who had married a foreign woman (Ezr. 10:42). See **5** above.

8. A priest who with Nehemiah sealed the covenant (Neh. 10:3); he had returned to Jerusalem with Zerubbabel (12:2) and was the father of Jehohanan (cf. Hanani, Ezr. 10:20), priest at the time of Joiakim (Neh. 12:13). Cf. Immer (Ezr. 2:37; 10:20; Neh. 7:40; 1 Esd. 5:24).

9. An ancestor of Zephaniah the prophet (Zeph. 1:1). A. L. BRESLICH

AMARIAS am-ə-rī'əs (1 Esd. 8:2, AV, NEB; 2 Esd. 1:2, AV). *See* AMARIAH **3.**

AMARNA TABLETS. An important cache of cuneiform documents discovered at TELL EL-AMARNA in Middle Egypt. The name derives from that of a local bedouin tribe, the Beni 'Amrân.

I. Discovery
II. Contents
III. Linguistic Value
IV. Historical Value
V. OT Relationships: The 'Apiru

I. Discovery.–As in the case of many other archeologically significant finds, the Amarna Tablets were discovered accidentally and by a nonspecialist. In 1887 an Egyptian peasant woman, while digging in the ruins of el-Amarna for a type of nitrous soil which is formed by the gradual decomposition of mud bricks and which can be used as a fertilizer, stumbled upon several hundred clay tablets covered with peculiar nail-like markings. Ignorant of their value, she sold them to a neighbor for two shillings. After changing hands several times the tablets eventually came to the attention of antiquities experts. Jules Oppert, the noted Franco-German Assyriologist, promptly pronounced them forgeries, while G. M. E. Grébaut, Director of the Service of Antiquities, ventured no opinion about their genuineness. It remained for the British Orientalist E. A. Wallis Budge to recognize their age as well as their authenticity.

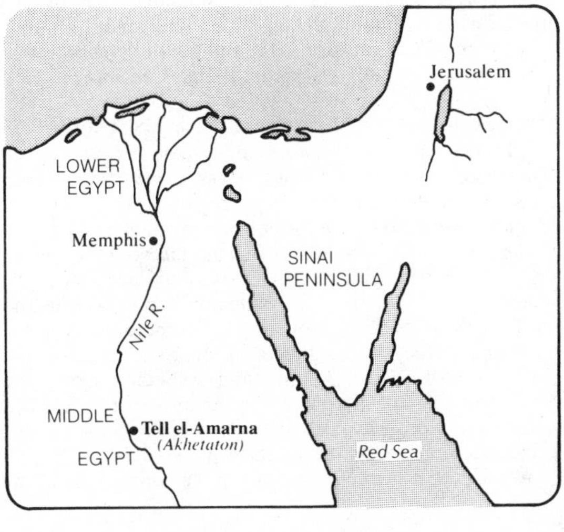

Unfortunately, many of the tablets in the original find had been damaged in various ways before the authorities became aware of their existence. It has been estimated that as many as two hundred of them were completely destroyed, whether deliberately or through rough handling, soon after their discovery. It may even be that the major portion of the archive has been irretrievably lost. Nevertheless, the surviving tablets are doubtless typical and enable us to formulate a fair evaluation of the original collection. At any rate, the 1887 find attracted the attention of archeologists to the site itself. The most important excavations at Tell el-Amarna were undertaken by W. M. Flinders Petrie in 1891, the Deutsche Orientgesellschaft from 1911 to 1914, and the Egypt Exploration Society in an almost uninterrupted series of campaigns from 1921 to 1937. In addition to the tablets found at Tell el-Amarna from the first horde in 1887 to the last group in the campaign of 1933/34, a letter of the same type and from the same period was unearthed by Frederick J. Bliss from the ruins of Tell el-Ḥesi (perhaps EGLON) in 1892. Other cuneiform documents have been found at Palestinian sites such as Gezer, Hazor, Jericho, Megiddo, Shechem, and Taanach, dating for the most part *ca.* 1450-1350 B.C.; but the Tell el-Ḥesi letter remains thus far the only "Amarna" tablet to be discovered in Palestine.

II. Contents.–Of the 379 published Amarna documents now extant, 358 items were already known by 1915 and were included by J. A. Knudtzon in his monumental edition of that year. He attempted to arrange the tablets in a N-S geographical order as well as chronologically within each group, and his system of numbering each individual tablet is still used. Samuel A. B. Mercer, *The Tell el-Amarna Tablets* (1939), added a few items that had been uncovered in the interim, but his publication unfortunately turned out to be little more than an English translation of Knudtzon's work and contained numerous errors not found in the original. As of this writing, therefore, the scholarly world still awaits a definitive, up-to-date edition of the cuneiform Amarna materials. More than half of the tablets are currently in the Berlin Museum. Budge acquired a total of eighty-two items from the original find for the British Museum, while a smaller group remained in the Egyptian Museum in Cairo. Other still smaller collections are in the possession of other museums and private individuals throughout the world.

Three hundred forty-nine of the Amarna Tablets are epistolary in nature and constitute part of the diplomatic correspondence of the Egyptian pharaohs Amenhotep III (*ca.* 1398-1361 B.C.) and IV (Akhenaten, *ca.* 1369-1353) with kings of other nations and with Egyptian officials and vassals in Palestine and Syria. The dates given for these two rulers are only approximate. They assume a coregency to which the Amarna Tablets and other evidence seem to point but concerning which there is still room for considerable debate. Since the thirty-second year of Amenhotep III is probably mentioned in a hieratic docket written in ink on one of the letters, and since Tutankhamen, Akhenaten's son-in-law, appears to be named in another, the Amarna Tablets cover a period of about thirty years encompassing roughly the second quarter of the 14th cent. B.C., the heart of the so-called Amarna age. Over forty of the letters consist of correspondence between the pharaonic court on the one hand and the kings of Alashia (biblical Elishah), Assyria, Babylonia, Hatti, and Mitanni on the other. That of the last two countries has enriched our understanding of the Hittite and Hurrian (biblical Horite) languages respectively. The other approximately three hundred letters were written by scribes who were nearly all Canaanites, who had learned cuneiform second- or third-hand, and who lived in Palestine, Phoenicia, and southern Syria. Of these three hundred about half were written either from or to Palestine or discuss affairs in Palestine, and thus are of supreme importance for OT studies.

The thirty nonepistolary Amarna Tablets include syllabaries, lexical lists, and practice-copies of sections of Akkadian mythological texts for the training of Egyptian apprentice scribes. The last, consisting of portions of *Adapa and the South Wind, Nergal and Ereshkigal,* and the *King of Battle* epic, contain frequent epigraphic indications of vowel length, colored dots serving as word dividers, and almost no logograms.

III. Linguistic Value.–Akkadian, firmly entrenched as the lingua franca of the Near East during the Amarna age, is the basic language of the Amarna Tablets. As might be expected, these documents have thus assisted scholars in solving certain grammatical and lexical problems inherent in the Akkadian of the period, even though Amarna Akkadian exhibits numerous linguistic archaisms. At the same time, however, the epistolary materials often reveal Amorite, Egyptian, Hittite, Hurrian, and (most importantly) Canaanite linguistic substrata, reflecting the mother tongues of the native scribes. All the Canaanite Amarna Letters display a mixture of Akkadian and Canaanite dialects, although a few are almost completely Canaanite with only the thinnest of Akkadian veneers. Amarna Canaanite and the Ugaritic documents from Râs Shamrah have helped immeasurably to establish the nature of proto-Hebrew and to trace its development into the classical language of the OT. Often the Canaanite *Vorlage* was all-pervasive, reaching not only into vocabulary, grammar, syntax, morphology, and phonology but also into phraseology and mode of expression, so that, e.g., when a scribe from Byblos wished to verbalize the concept of "from time immemorial" he did not write, in standard Akkadian parlance, *ištu labiriš* (or, as in later times, *ultu ulla*), but coined the phrase *ištu dārīti*, an Akkadian rendering of such Canaanite equivalents as Heb. *mēʿôlām*. Canaanite scribes also frequently glossed Akkadian words and phrases with their Canaanite counterparts. For example, the difficult Akk. *ḫuḫāru,* "trap, snare," which appears often in the Byblian letters, is usually explained immediately thereafter by Can. *kilūbu* (=Heb. *k^{e}lûḇ*), which has the same meaning. Needless to say, the scribes themselves did not always agree as to proper procedure in various matters. The Jerusalem Amarna correspondence, for example, exhibits scribal peculiarities demonstrating it to be the product of a scribal tradition different from that of the other Canaanite Amarna dialects.

IV. Historical Value.–The Amarna Tablets have helped to make the Amarna age one of the best-known periods in ancient history. It was supremely a time of international diplomacy, one of the first such times in the annals of mankind. Egypt had been in control of Syro-Palestine for almost two centuries but was now in decline there. Nevertheless, it was still in many respects the dominant power in the Near East. The Hittite kingdom of Asia Minor was at its height under the leadership of the great Šuppiluliuma I, and was threatening the very existence of Tušratta's Hurrian kingdom of Mitanni located in the bend of the upper Euphrates River. East of Mitanni was the rising power of Assyria under Erība-Adad I and Aššur-uballiṭ I, while the Kassite dynasty of Babylon under Kadašman-Enlil I and Burnaburiaš II exercised control over the lower Tigris-Euphrates basin. Diplomatic marriages, such as that of Tadu-ḫepa (a daughter of Tušratta) to Amenhotep III, attempted to upset the delicate balance of political power in the Near East during the Amarna age.

The chief Egyptian administrative centers in occupied Palestine were Gaza and Joppa, while strategic Egyptian outposts were located at Beth-shan and elsewhere. Although native Canaanite princely dynasties were in nominal control of the city-states into which Palestine was divided, Egyptian agents known as "commissioner" (Akk. *rābiṣu*, Can. *sōkinu* [=Heb. *sōḵēn*]) and "envoy" (Egyp. *wpwty*) closely supervised their activities. Such officials, often called simply *rabû,* "great one," by the Canaanite scribes, were usually native Egyptians, and bribery and other forms of corruption were common among them. On occasion a trustworthy Canaanite might be permitted to rise to a position of prominence in the Egyptian bureaucracy. One such bore the Amorite name Yanḫamu. His importance is attested by his appearing in the correspondence of various princes throughout Syria and Palestine and his being in charge of the food supplies stored in the territory of Yarimmuta, the location of which remains uncertain. The career of Yanḫamu is strongly reminiscent of that of the OT patriarch Joseph, with whom he has been implausibly identified by certain scholars. Many of the Amarna Letters reveal that the Egyptian overlords exacted tribute from their Palestinian subjects. They also demanded *corvée* contingents to be used in Egyptian construction and other projects that required large supplies of cheap labor.

Most of the Amarna Letters reveal an unsettled state of affairs in Syro-Palestine itself, which belies the superficial appearance of unity implied by the Egyptian presence in Hither Asia. The morale of the Canaanite princelings had greatly deteriorated during the period of Egyptian decline with the result that they were often at war with each other. In their correspondence they occasionally stooped to hurling mutual accusations of treason against the crown and disloyalty toward one another. Under such circumstances they were vulnerable to attack by dissident elements within their own domains as well as by enemies from without, and in their letters to the pharaohs we frequently read their desperate pleas for fresh supplies of Egyptian and Nubian archers to man their garrisons. Such requests were met uniformly with a stony silence by the Egyptian court. The dissolution of the Egyptian empire in Syro-Palestine, already under way during the rule of Amenhotep III, was greatly accelerated under Akhenaten, who was preoccupied with domestic affairs for most of his reign.

Although most of the Palestinian chieftains bore Northwest Semitic names, Indo-Aryan names are also well represented. At least one non-Semitic name common to both Amarna age onomastics and the OT is Ara/iwana, who was a prince in the region of Damascus and whose name must be compared with that of Araunah the Jebusite. The official title of such native princelings was "(free)man" (*amīlu*), while their official position in the scheme of things was that of "governor, mayor" (*ḫazānu*). Within Canaanite circles, however, the prince was referred to as "king," a usage reflected also in such OT passages as Josh. 11:1 and Jgs. 9:6.

It is clear from the Amarna Letters themselves that each Palestinian chieftain held sway over a city-state, which often controlled a rather large region surrounding it. Megiddo and Hazor were the two most strategic city-states in the north, Shechem dominated the hill country, Gezer and Jerusalem maintained extensive holdings in central Palestine, and Lachish was of major importance in the south. Correspondence from and concerning these cities, as well as other Syro-Palestinian sites such as Byblos, Beirut, Sidon, Tyre, Accho, and Ashkelon along the Mediterranean coast, constitutes the bulk of the Amarna archives and provides us with essential information about Canaanite civilization during the Amarna age.

Among the disruptive elements in the political life of the

Letter of Šipti-ba'al of Lachish (Am.Tab. 330) assuring the king that he and Yanḫamu remain loyal (Trustees of the British Museum)

Lab'ayu prince of Shechem protests that his hostile activity was only to repel aggression against his native town (Am.Tab. 252). (Trustees of the British Museum)

Second part of letter from Birdiya of Megiddo (Am.Tab. 245) accusing Zurata of Acco of treason against Lab'ayu (Trustees of the British Museum)

period was the notorious Lab'ayu ("lion man"), the prince of Shechem who seems to have controlled all the territory in the central ridge from N of Jerusalem to N of his own city. He and his sons, rebelling against their Egyptian overlords and in league with the 'Apiru (see below), terrorized the countryside and attempted to capture Megiddo. At the other end of the political spectrum is a man like the prince of Byblos, Rib-Addi, whose nearly seventy letters (the largest single group of Amarna documents) tell a tale of loyalty to the Egyptian court and cooperation with the Egyptian commissioners. The domain of Rib-Addi comprised the northern half of the modern Lebanese coastal plain, a strip of territory stretching northward from Byblos to Simyra. He was embroiled in a more or less continuous struggle with 'Abdi-Aširta and his sons, the princes of the region of Amurru, which extended to the east and north of Byblos. Although the feud was local in nature, Rib-Addi found himself in desperate straits as his enemies almost succeeded in driving him into the sea. His letters to the pharaohs, like those of his compatriots, request reinforcements and disclaim responsibility for military failure if Egypt refuses to supply them.

According to the Amarna Tablets, only rarely did the contingents of archers requested by the Canaanite princes exceed two hundred, and they were usually far smaller. On the basis of such evidence we may assume that the population of Palestine was small during the Amarna age. There were probably no more than 250,000 people there at the time, a figure comparable to the population total in Palestine under the Turks in A.D. 1800. The Cisjordanian inhabitants of the country were apparently concentrated in the coastal plains and adjacent hills, the plain of Jezreel, the towns of the central ridge, and the Jordan Valley. Nomadic tribes were the chief occupants of Transjordan except in the Jordan Valley and the northernmost areas. The population was ethnically mixed and socially stratified, a situation reflected, e.g., in the Byblian letters, in which *ḫupšu*, "tenant farmer," is apparently a loanword from Hurrian.

V. OT Relationships: The 'Apiru.–Attempts to find in the Amarna Tablets specific references to OT personalities or events have been uniformly unsuccessful. The idea that the names "Joshua" and "Benjamin" occur in them was thoroughly discredited long ago. The patriarchal period of Israel's history preceded the Amarna age; Jacob and his sons almost certainly migrated to Egypt in the early 17th cent. at the latest. The exodus period of Israel's history followed the Amarna age; Joshua and his armies almost certainly did not conquer the cities of Canaan until the late 13th cent. at the earliest. The Amarna age is thus to be sought somewhere in the "four hundred and thirty years" of Ex. 12:40, a period concerning which the OT is virtually silent. However, scholars have turned their attention increasingly in recent years to the possible relationship between the OT Hebrews and the Amarna 'Apiru.

Superficially, the terms *'apiru* and *'iḇrî* ("Hebrew") appear to differ in derivation and in morphology. It is now generally recognized, however, that the difficulties involved in equating them are not insuperable and that the possibility of an ultimate common origin cannot be excluded. SA.GAZ and its variants, the Sumerian logographic equivalents of Semitic *'apiru,* are found in cuneiform texts from *ca.* 2500 B.C. down to the 11th cent. B.C. In addition to its numerous Akkadian syllabic spellings, *'apiru* appears as *'pr* in Ugaritic and occurs also in Egyptian transcriptions. Among the Amarna Tablets, the Jerusalem letters write the term syllabically, whereas elsewhere SA.GAZ and its variants are uniformly used. SA.GAZ also stood for Akk. *ḫabbātu*, a word that seems to have meant originally "migratory worker" but that later came to signify "bandit, brigand." It may well be that this semantic evolution reflected historical development also, since from the most ancient times *'apiru* itself had similarly good and bad connotations. Politically, economically, and socially inferior malcontents, as were the 'Apiru, need little inducement to turn their backs on commendable endeavors, such as the seasonal harvesting of crops, in favor of less reputable activities, such as pilferage, plunder, or worse.

Request by Yapaḫu ruler of Gezer (Am.Tab 299) for assistance against the 'Apiru (Trustees of the British Museum)

During the Amarna age, *'apiru* was a pejorative term, denoting a population element composed of stateless and reputedly lawless individuals and groups of diverse ethnic origins and speaking a number of different languages. Although they were indigenous to Syro-Palestine, their social status was generally inferior. They therefore rebelled against native princes and Egyptian officials alike, raiding the towns and pillaging the countryside. It was for help against such forays that the Canaanite chieftains directed their frequent requests to the pharaohs. Similar bands of outlaws are not unknown in the OT; cf., e.g., Jgs. 9:3; 11:3; 1 S. 22:1f.

The Northwest Semitic word *'apiru* may have originally meant "dusty one, (donkey) caravaneer." Abraham himself may have been just such an 'apiru; it is instructive to note that he was the first individual in the OT to bear the title *'iḇrî* (Gen. 14:13). In Gen. 18:27 Abraham calls himself "dust [Heb. *'āpār*] and ashes" in terms reminiscent of those craven expressions of obedience and submission so common to the Amarna Tablets. Recent evidence has suggested that the Mari *Banū-yamīna,* with which may be compared Heb. *binyāmîn* (Benjamin), had affinities with the 'Apiru of the patriarchal period, and that the ancestral "Hebrews," understood in the broadest sense, founded the 1st Dynasty of Babylon.

Donkey caravaneers continued to ply their trade down to the Amarna age (cf. esp. letter no. 96) and beyond (cf. Jgs. 5). Eventually, however, the decline of their profession forced them into less nomadic occupations such as viticulture, a transition strikingly reflected in the description of Judah in Gen. 49:11:

Binding his donkey to the vine,
  His ass's colt to the tendril,
He washed his garment in wine,
  His robe in the blood of grapes.

Bibliography.–W. F. Albright, *CAH* (rev. ed. 1966), II, ch. 20; *Yahweh and the Gods of Canaan* (1968), pp. 73-91; P. Artzi, *Orientalia,* 36 (1967), 432; F. F. Bruce, *AOTS,* pp. 3-20; E. F. Campbell, Jr., *BA,* 23 (1960), 2-22; *Chronology of the Amarna Letters* (1964); M. Greenberg, *The Ḫab/piru* (*American Oriental Series*, 39, 1955); J. A. Knudtzon, *et al., Die El-Amarna-Tafeln* (2 vols., 1915); A. R. Millard, *PEQ*, 100 (1965), 140-43; C. F. Pfeiffer, *Tell el Amarna and the Bible* (1963); H. H. Rowley, *From Joseph to Joshua* (1950), pp. 37-56, 109-163; R. F. Youngblood, *BASOR,* 168 (Dec. 1962), 24-27.

R. F. YOUNGBLOOD

AMASA ə-mā'sə [Heb. *'ᵃmāśā'*].

1. According to 2 S. 17:25, the son of Abigail, the sister of Zeruiah and David, and Ithra, an Israelite; but another source, 1 Ch. 2:17, calls his father Jether the Ishmaelite. The RSV and NEB read "Ishmaelite" in both places. He was a nephew of David and a cousin of Absalom, who made him commander of the army of rebellion. When the uprising had been quelled, David, in order to conciliate Amasa, promised him the position held by Joab, who had fallen from favor (2 S. 19:13ff.). When a new revolt broke out under Sheba the son of Bichri (2 S. 20), Amasa was entrusted with the task of assembling the men of Judah. But Joab was eager for revenge upon the man who had obtained the office of command that he coveted. When Amasa met Joab at Gibeon, Joab murdered him while pretending to salute him (2 S. 20:8-10; 1 K. 2:5).

2. An Ephraimite, the son of Hadlai, who, obeying the words of the prophet Oded, refused to consider as captives the Judeans who had been taken from Ahaz king of Judah by the victorious Israelites under Pekah (2 Ch. 28:12).

H. J. WOLF

AMASAI ə-mā'sī [Heb. *'ᵃmāśay*].

1. A son of Elkanah, a Levite of the Kohathite family (1 Ch. 6:25, 35; 2 Ch. 29:12).

2. Chief of the captains who met David at Ziklag and tendered him their allegiance (1 Ch. 12:18). Some have identified him with Amasa and others with Abishai. The difficulty is that neither Amasa nor Abishai occupied the rank of the chief of thirty according to the lists in 2 S. 23 and 1 Ch. 11, the rank to which David is supposed to have appointed him.

3. One of the trumpet-blowing priests who greeted David when he brought back the ark of the covenant (1 Ch. 15:24).

AMASHSAI ə-mash'sī [Heb. *'ᵃmaššay,* probably a textual error for *'ᵃmāšay*]. A priestly name in the postexilic list of inhabitants of Jerusalem (Neh. 11:13). In 1 Ch. 9:12 the name is given as Maasai.

AMASIAH am-ə-sī'ə [Heb. *'ᵃmasyâ*–'Yahweh has borne'] (2 Ch. 17:16). One of the captains of Jehoshaphat.

AMATHEIS am-ə-thē'əs (1 Esd. 9:29, AV). *See* EMATHIS.

AMATHIS am'ə-this (1 Macc. 12:25, AV). *See* HAMATH.

AMAVITES (Nu. 22:5, NEB). *See* AMAW.

AMAW a'mô [Heb. *'ammô*; Gk. *laós autoú*] (Nu. 22:5); AV "his people"; NEB AMAVITES. The country from which Balak summoned Balaam, and which included Pethor, the seer's home city, located near the Euphrates. Amaw had as its capital the city of Emar, located about 50 mi. (80 km.) S of Carchemish. According to the Idrimi Inscription (*ca.* 1450 B.C.) the contemporary king of Alalakh also governed Amaw. R. K. H.

AMAZE; AMAZEMENT. Besides the ordinary usages, the words occur archaically in the AV for "distress" (Mk. 14:33, Gk. *ekthambéō*) and "terror" (*ptóēsis,* 1 Pet. 3:6).

The Gk. *ékstasis,* translated "amazement" in Mk. 5:42; Lk. 5:26; Acts 3:10, indicates that the people were "beside themselves" with astonishment, unable to comprehend fully what they witnessed (cf. Eng. "ecstasy")—in each case a miraculous healing, of a girl who had "died," of a paralytic, and of a lame man.

AMAZIAH am-ə-zī'ə [Heb. *'ᵃmaṣyâ*, *'ᵃmaṣyāhû*–'Yahweh is mighty'].

1. The son and successor of Jehoash, and the eighth king of Judah after the breach with Israel (2 K. 14:1-20; 2 Ch. 25). Amaziah had a peaceable accession at the age of twenty-five. Judah had suffered considerably at the hands of Syria during his father's reign, but Amaziah's reign marked the beginning of a new period of prosperity for the two Hebrew kingdoms. In Judah, however, this prosperity was not fully realized till the reign of his son Azariah (Uzziah), for Amaziah picked an ill-advised quarrel with Jehoash of Israel and suffered a severe defeat at his hands.

Amaziah's first action as king was to punish his father's assassins. Then he made preparations for war against Edom, which had for many years been subject to the kings of Judah, but had been independent since Jehoram's reign (2 Ch. 21:8-10). The control of Edom was not only important to the prestige of Judah, but was also essential to her commercial prosperity, since a hostile Edom could cut off Judah from her southern port Elath. The logical conclusion of Amaziah's victory over Edom was to retake and reopen Elath, which was in fact done by Azariah (2 K. 14:22).

Collecting a large army, Amaziah attacked and routed the Edomites in the Valley of Salt, causing great slaughter. Then the army moved on to Sela (Petra). This city lies in a hollow, shut in by mountains, and approached only by a narrow ravine, through which a stream of water flows. Amaziah took it by storm. Great execution was done, many of the captives being thrown from the rock, the face of which is now covered with rock-cut tombs of the Greco-Roman age.

Flushed with his success, Amaziah sent a foolish challenge to Jehoash of Israel. The account in 2 K. 14 gives no reason for his action, but 2 Ch. 25 gives rather more detail. At the beginning of his campaign against Edom he had engaged a large body of Israelite mercenaries, but had been dissuaded by a prophet from employing them. They were accordingly sent off home, but en route they vented their annoyance by plundering a number of the villages of Judah. Amaziah seized this as an excuse for challenging Jehoash. The latter was in no mood to fight, and his reply was the well-known parable of the thistle and the cedar. Amaziah failed to heed his good advice, and the battle of Beth-shemesh followed. Judah was utterly routed, and Amaziah himself taken prisoner. Jehoash contented himself with taking hostages, plundering the treasuries of the temple and palace, and breaking down 400 cubits (almost 600 ft., 180 m.) of the wall of Jerusalem at the northwest corner of the defense (2 K. 14:13f.; 2 Ch. 25:22-24). But he did not harm Amaziah, nor did he seek to incorporate Judah into his kingdom.

Amaziah had no one but himself to blame for this humiliation. His challenge to Jehoash had been presumptuous and unnecessary. Further, the Chronicler attributes his downfall to his religious apostasy in worshiping Edomite gods (2 Ch. 25:14-16); yet prior to the Edomite campaign his conduct had been exemplary (2 K. 14:3). So deep was his disgrace now and so profound the sense of national humiliation that a party in the state determined on Amaziah's removal, as soon as there was another to take his place. The age of majority among the Hebrew kings was sixteen; and when Amaziah's son was of this age, the conspiracy against his life grew so strong and open that he fled to Lachish. Here he was followed and killed; his body was insultingly carried to Jerusalem on horses, and not conveyed in a litter or coffin (2 K. 14:19f.; 2 Ch. 24:27f.). Uzziah succeeded him.

Amaziah is credited with a reign of twenty-nine years (2 K. 14:2; 2 Ch. 25:1), and 2 Ch. 25:25 states that he outlived Jehoash of Israel by fifteen years. It does not, however, seem possible on chronological grounds that he can have reigned for so long. Some scholars have suggested that twenty-nine is an error for nineteen or even nine; W. F. Albright ignores the figure of twenty-nine altogether, and gives Amaziah's dates as 800-783 B.C. It may be, however, that 2 K. 14:19 telescopes events; possibly Amaziah lived some twelve years at Lachish, while his son acted as king in Jerusalem. The statement of 2 K. 14:22 implies that Uzziah had some powers before his father's death at any rate. E. R. Thiele credits Amaziah with a twenty-nine-year reign, 796-767 B.C., but with Uzziah as coregent from 791 to 790 (*MNHK*, pp. 81-87).

Amaziah is mentioned in the royal genealogy of 1 Ch. 3:12, but not in that of Mt. 1, where there is a leap from Jehoram to Uzziah; and Ahaziah, Jehoash, and Amaziah are omitted.

2. A Simeonite (1 Ch. 4:34).

3. A Levite of the house of Merari (1 Ch. 6:30, 45).

4. A priest of Bethel (Am. 7:10ff.) who accused the prophet Amos of conspiracy against Jeroboam II of Israel. Amaziah advised Amos to return to his native Judah, to which the prophet replied: "I am no prophet, nor a prophet's son; but I am a herdsman, and a dresser of sycamore trees, and Yahweh took me from following the flock, and Yahweh said to me, 'Go, prophesy to my people Israel' " (7:14-17). W. S. CALDECOTT
D. F. PAYNE

AMBASSADOR [Heb. *ṣîr* (Isa. 18:2), *mal'āḵ*–'messenger' (Ezk. 17:15); Gk. *presbeúō*–'act as an ambassador,' lit. 'be older' (2 Cor. 5:20; Eph. 6:20), *presbýtēs* (see below, on Philem. 9)]; AV also "the aged" (Philem. 9); NEB also ENVOY, MESSENGER. An official representative of a king or government. On the OT references *see* ENVOY.

In the NT the term is used in a figurative sense. As the imprisoned representative of Christ at Rome Paul calls himself "an ambassador in chains" (Eph. 6:20); and in 2 Cor. 5:20 includes, with himself, all ministers of the gospel as "ambassadors for Christ," commissioned by Him as their sovereign Lord for the ministry of reconciling the world to God. The Bible contains no finer characterization of the exalted and spiritual nature of the minister's vocation as the representative of Jesus Christ, the King of kings and Savior of the world.

In Philem. 9 most MSS have Gk. *presbýtēs,* "old man." Both the RSV and NEB accept the conjectured emendation to *presbeutḗs,* "ambassador," which is possible in view of the dialectal interchange between *y* and *eu* in koine Greek (cf. 1 Macc. 14:22; 2 Macc. 11:34; 2 Ch. 32:31, LXX B, etc.). Others maintain that Paul's reference here to his old age is appropriate (*TDNT,* VI, *s.v.* [Bornkamm]). For references on both sides see Bauer, p. 707; and see MM, p. 535.

D. M. PRATT
J. W. D. H.

AMBASSAGE (Lk. 14:32, AV). *See* EMBASSY.

AMBER (Ezk. 1:4, 27; 8:2, AV). *See* ELECTRUM.

AMBITION [Gk. *philotiméomai*–'make it one's aim'] (Rom. 15:20); AV "strive"; **SELFISH AMBITION** [Gk. *eritheía*] (Jas. 3:14, 16); AV STRIFE. The Greek verb *philotiméomai* (lit. "be fond of honor") denotes a positive kind of ambition or aim to accomplish a particular goal. Thus it expresses Paul's pioneering ambition to carry the Good News to those places it had not previously reached (Rom. 15:20; cf. 2 Cor. 5:9 and 1 Thess. 4:11 for other uses of this term).

By way of contrast, the Gk. *eritheía* denotes a negative kind of ambition that is motivated by a selfish spirit bent on immediate personal gain at any cost. It is therefore quite appropriate that the RSV renders "selfish ambition" in the James passages (cf. NEB Rom. 2:8; Gal. 5:20; Jas. 3:14). The negative force of the term is further suggested by its presence in two separate lists of the "works of the flesh" (2 Cor. 12:20; Gal. 5:20). Both in these lists and in the James passages, *eritheía* stands alongside of "jealousy," which suggests a similarity of meaning.

The sin of selfish ambition runs contrary to the very heart of the Christian ethic, an ethic based on sacrificial love and humble service of the brethren, as so vividly portrayed in the life of Our Lord (e.g., Mk. 10:43-45). To promote one's own welfare at any cost is to become arrogant and divisive, and ultimately issues in every kind of evil practice (Jas. 3:16).

Bibliography.–W. Barclay, *NT Words* (1974), pp. 99f.; *TDNT,* II, *s.v.* ἐριθεία (Büchsel); C. L. Mitton, *Epistle of James* (1966), pp. 136f.

A. J. BIRKEY

AMBUSH [Heb. *'ārab̲*–'lie in wait,' *mā'ᵃrāb̲*]; AV also AMBUSHMENT; [Gk. *enédra, enedreúō*–'lie in wait']; AV "lie in wait"; NEB also "lie in wait." A military stratagem in which a body of men are placed in concealment to surprise an enemy unawares, or to attack a point when temporarily undefended. This stratagem was employed successfully by Joshua at Ai (Josh. 8). Jeremiah commanded the Medes to prepare ambushes (Jer. 51:12). Paul's enemies lay in ambush for him at Jerusalem (Acts 23:16, 21) and planned a further attempt at capture (25:3). The Hebrew verb is often used in the OT to describe the wiles of the wicked (Ps. 10:8; 59:3; Prov. 1:11; Jer. 9:8; etc.).

AMEN ā-men' (in ritual speech and in singing ämen', ä'men) [Heb. *'āmēn* < *'mn*–'be firm,' 'be reliable'; Gk. *amḗn*]. A particle expressing affirmation, equivalent to "so be it." It occurs twice as a noun in Isa. 65:16, "God of truth" (NEB "God of Amen"). Elsewhere in the OT it is used as a solemn formula by which an individual or the whole nation confirms a covenant or an oath (Nu. 5:22; Dt. 27:15ff.; Neh. 5:13; etc.). The prophet Jeremiah uses it to endorse the message of Hananiah (Jer. 28:6). It is also used as a liturgical formula by which the listeners join themselves to a doxology (esp. at the end of a Psalm) or to a prayer.

In the NT *amḗn* occurs frequently as a liturgical formula, usually at the end of a doxology (e.g., Rom. 1:25; 9:5; 11:36; 15:33; 16:27; Gal. 1:5; Eph. 3:21; Phil. 4:20; 1 Tim. 1:17; 16:16; 1 Tim. 4:18; He. 13:21; 1 Pet. 4:11; etc.). It is evident from 1 Cor. 14:16 that in the early Church the congregation was expected to respond with a spoken "Amen." This practice is reflected in the book of Revelation (5:13f.; 22:20).

In the Gospels a new and unique use of *amḗn* appears with the sayings of Jesus. Here the term means "surely" or "truly." All four Gospels record Jesus' use of the term as an introductory formula (*amḗn légō hymín,* "truly I say to you") emphasizing the authority of what He has to say, somewhat analogous to the messenger-formula of the OT prophets, "Thus says the Lord." (Cf. Mt. 5:18, 26; 6:2, 5, 16; etc.; Mk. 3:28; 8:12; etc.; Lk. 4:24; 12:37; etc.; Jn. 1:51; 3:3, 5, 11; etc. [always *amḗn amḗn* in John].)

See J. Jeremias, *NT Theology* (1971), pp. 35f.

J. MILLAR N. J. O.

AMETHYST. *See* STONES, PRECIOUS.

AMI ā'mī, ä'mē [Heb. *'āmî*; Gk. *Ēmi,* Apoc. *Amōn,* B *Allōn,* A *Adlōn*]; AV Apoc. ALLOM; NEB Apoc. ADLON. Ancestor of a family among "Solomon's servants" in the Return (Ezr. 2:57; 1 Esd. 5:34); the same as Amon in Neh. 7:59. *See* NETHINIM.

AMIABLE. Archaic in the AV for Heb. *yāḏîḏ*, "beloved," RSV "lovely," NEB "dear" (Ps. 84:1).

AMINADAB (AV NT). *See* AMMINADAB.

AMITTAI ə-mit'ī [Heb. *'ᵃmittay*–'faithful']. The father of the prophet Jonah. He was from Gath-hepher in Zebulun (2 K. 14:25; Jonah 1:1).

AMMAH am'ə [Heb. *'ammâ*]. A hill near Giah in the territory of Benjamin where the road from Gibeon begins its descent through the wilderness to the Jordan Valley (2 S. 2:24). Abner, pursued by the men of Joab, made a stand here and effected a truce (2:26-28; cf. Josephus *Ant.* vii.1.3).

W. S. L. S.

AMMI am'ī [Heb. *'ammî*–'my people'] (Hos. 2:1 [MT 3], AV). Hosea's symbolic name for Israel, indicating the state of restoration in contrast to sinful and rejected Israel represented by Hosea's son, who had been named LO-AMMI, "not my people" (1:9f.; cf. 2:21, 23, quoted in Rom. 9:25f.). *See* HOSEA.

AMMIDIANS ə-mid'ē-ənz [Gk. *Ammídioi*] (1 Esd. 5:20); AV AMMIDOI; NEB AMMIDAEANS. One of the families returning from exile under Zerubbabel in 537 B.C. This name is not found in the corresponding lists of the canonical books, Ezr. 2 and Neh. 7. Their identity is uncertain.

AMMIEL am'ē-əl [Heb. *'ammî'ēl*–'my kinsman is God'].

1. One of the twelve spies sent into Canaan by Moses; son of Gemalli, of the tribe of Dan (Nu. 13:12).

2. A Benjaminite, the father of Machir, a friend of David, living at Lo-debar in Gilead (2 S. 9:4f.; 17:27).

3. Father of Bathshua (or Bathsheba), one of David's wives, who was mother of Solomon (1 Ch. 3:5). In the parallel 2 S. 11:3, by transposition of the two parts of the name he is called Eliam, meaning "my God is a kinsman."

4. The sixth son of Obed-edom, a Levite, one of the doorkeepers of the tabernacle of God in David's lifetime (1 Ch. 26:5).

E. MACK

AMMIHUD ə-mī'hud [Heb. *'ammîhûḏ*–'my kinsman is glorious'; Gk. *Emioud, Semioud, Amioud*].

1. Father of Elishama, who in the wilderness was head of the tribe of Ephraim (Nu. 1:10; 2:18; 7:48, 53; 10:22; 1 Ch. 7:26).

2. Father of Shemuel, who was appointed by Moses from the tribe of Simeon to divide the land among the tribes after they should have entered Canaan (Nu. 34:20).

3. Father of Pedahel, who was appointed from the tribe of Naphtali for the same purpose as **2** (Nu. 34:28).

4. NEB AMMIHUR. Father of Talmai king of Geshur (2 S. 13:37). The NEB follows the MT (*'ammîḥûr*), while the AV and RSV read with the *qere*.

5. A descendant of Judah through the line of Perez (1 Ch. 9:4).

E. MACK

AMMIHUR ə-mī'hur (2 S. 13:37, NEB). *See* AMMIHUD **4.**

AMMINADAB ə-min'ə-dab [Heb. *'ammînāḏāḇ*–'my people (kinsman) is generous (noble)'].

1. One of David's ancestors (Ruth 4:19f.; 1 Ch. 2:10). He was the great-grandson of Perez son of Judah (Gen. 38:29; 46:12; cf. Mt. 1:4), and the great-grandfather of Boaz, who was the great-grandfather of David. Aaron's wife Elisheba was a daughter of Amminadab (Ex. 6:23), while one of the sons, Nahshon, occupied an important position in the Judah clan (Nu. 1:7; 2:3; 7:12; 10:14).

2. Son of Kohath (and therefore a grandson of Levi) and father of Korah (1 Ch. 6:22). However, in other genealogical passages (Ex. 6:18; Nu. 3:19; 1 Ch. 6:2) the sons of Kohath are Amram, Izhar, Hebron, and Uzziel; and in two places (Ex. 6:21; 1 Ch. 6:38) Izhar is mentioned as the father of Korah.

3. A priest who took part in the removal of the ark to Jerusalem (1 Ch. 15:10f.). He was the son of Uzziel, and therefore a nephew of Amminadab son of Kohath.

T. LEWIS

AMMI-NADIB ə-mi'nə-dib. The AV for Heb. *'ammînāḏîḇ* in Cant. 6:12: "my soul made me/Like the chariots of Ammi-nadib." Various other textual readings and translations have been proposed. The RSV has "my fancy set me in a chariot beside my prince"; the NEB "she made me feel more than a prince reigning over the myriads of his people"; JB "my desire had hurled me on the chariots of my people, as their prince"; RV "chariots of my princely people," The LXX renders *hármata Aminadab*.

AMMISHADDAI am-i-shad'ī [Heb. *'ammîšadday*–'Shaddai is my kinsman']. The father of Ahiezer, a Danite captain or "head of his fathers' house," during the wilderness journey (Nu. 1:12; 2:25; etc.).

AMMIZABAD ə-miz'ə-bad [Heb. *'ammîzāḇāḏ*–'my kinsman has made a present']. The son of Benaiah, one of David's captains for the third month (1 Ch. 27:6).

AMMON am'ən; **AMMONITES** am'ən-īts [Heb. *'ammôn, 'ammônîm*]. According to Hebrew tradition, the descendants of Ben-ammi, the son of Lot by his daughter (Gen. 19:30-38). As such they were regarded as related to Israel, a relationship reflected in the names *ben 'Ammi* ("son of my people") and *b^e^nê 'Ammôn* ("children of Ammon"). Hence the Israelites were commanded to treat them kindly (Dt. 2:19).

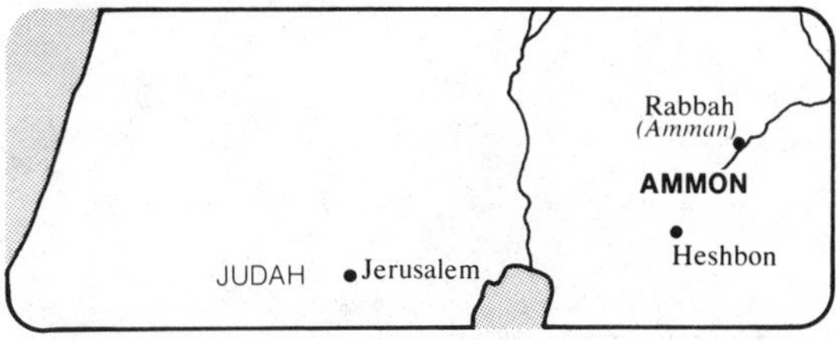

At an early date the Ammonites occupied the territory of the Zamzummim between the rivers Arnon and Jabbok (Dt. 2:20f., 37; 3:11). Later part of this territory was taken from them by the Amorites, and they were confined to an area E of the river Jabbok where it runs N-S (Nu. 21:24; Dt. 2:37; Josh. 12:2; 13:10, 25). Modern archeological discovery has shown that the Ammonites, like the Edomites, Moabites, and Amorites, surrounded their territories with small fortresses (Nu. 21:24).

At the time of the Exodus, Israel did not conquer Ammon (Dt. 2:19, 37; Jgs. 11:15). Later the Ammonites were condemned for joining the Moabites in hiring Balaam, and were forbidden to enter the congregation of Israel to the tenth generation (Dt. 23:3-6). Their chief town was Rabbah, or Rabbath-ammon, where in the days of the Exodus the ironstone sarcophagus ("bedstead of iron") of Og king of Bashan rested (Dt. 3:11). The town features much in later history.

In the days of the judges the Ammonites helped Eglon of Moab subdue Israelite territory (Jgs. 3:13). Again at the time of Jephthah they encroached on Israelite lands E of the Jordan (Jgs. 11) and were driven out. Their religion influenced some of the Israelites (Jgs. 10:6), and this caused the Ammonite oppression in Gilead and led to the campaign of Jephthah (Jgs. 11).

When Nahash king of Ammon besieged Jabesh-gilead just before Saul became king, Saul rallied the men of Israel and drove off the Ammonites, thus establishing his reputation as a military leader (1 S. 11:1-11; 12:12; 14:47). A few years later Nahash was a friend of David (2 S. 10:1f.), but his son Hanun rejected a kindly visit from David's ambassadors and insulted them. He hired Syrian mercenaries and went to war against Israel. David's generals Joab and Abishai defeated them (2 S. 10; 1 Ch. 14). A year later the Israelites captured the Ammonite capital of Rabbah (2 S. 12:26-31; 1 Ch. 20:1-3) and put the people to work in all their cities. Some Ammonites later befriended David when he fled from Absalom, among them being Shobi son of Nahash (2 S. 17:27-29), and Zelek, who was one of his thirty mighty men (2 S. 23:37; 1 Ch. 11:39).

Solomon included Ammonite women in his harem and worshiped Milcom (Molech) and Chemosh their gods (1 K. 11:1, 5, 7, 33). In the days of Jehoshaphat the Ammonites joined the Moabites and Edomites in a raid on Judah (2 Ch. 20:1-30).

The Assyrian records refer to a contingent of troops from

Theater at Roman Philadelphia (modern Amman), which as the ancient capital Rabbah was the only Transjordanian city clearly designated by the Bible as Ammonite (W. S. LaSor)

Ammon at the Battle of Qarqar in 853 B.C., when a coalition of twelve kings, including Ahab of Israel and Ben-hadad of Damascus, fought Shalmaneser III of Assyria. About 800 B.C. Zabad and Jehozabad, both sons of an Ammonitess, conspired to slay Joash king of Judah (2 Ch. 24:26). Later in the century both Uzziah and Jotham of Judah received tribute from the Ammonites (2 Ch. 26:8; 27:5).

In the days of the Assyrian ruler Tiglath-pileser III (744-727 B.C.) Sanipu king of Ammon paid tribute to the Assyrians along with others including Jehoahaz of Judah. Ammon was also listed among those who opposed Sennacherib (704-681 B.C.) in the days of King Hezekiah of Judah, but they submitted. Josiah of Judah defiled the high place that Solomon had erected (2 K. 23:13) and to that extent checked religious influence from Ammon.

In the days of Esarhaddon of Assyria (680-669 B.C.), Puduil king of Ammon is listed as one who paid tribute. Ammonites joined others in troubling Jehoiakim (2 K. 24:2); and after the fall of Jerusalem in 587 B.C., Baalis their king provoked further trouble (2 K. 25:25; Jer. 40:11-14).

The Ammonites were bitterly attacked by the prophets as inveterate enemies of Israel (Jer. 49:1-6; Ezk. 21:20; 25:1-7; Am. 1:13-15; Zeph. 2:8-11).

After the return from exile, Tobiah the Ammonite joined others in hindering the building of the walls of Jerusalem by Nehemiah (Neh. 2:10, 19; 4:3, 7). Intermarriage between the Jews and the Ammonites was censured by both Ezra and Nehemiah (Ezr. 9:1f.; Neh. 13:1, 23-31).

The Ammonites as a recognizable group persisted until the 2nd cent. B.C. Important graves, seals, and inscribed statues from Ammon of the 7th and 6th cents. B.C. suggest a vitality and political significance that outlasted Moab and Edom. The family of the Tobiads persisted from the 5th to the 2nd cent. B.C., as important archeological evidence from both Transjordan and Egypt demonstrates. Judas Maccabeus fought the Ammonites in his day (1 Macc. 5:6). The full story awaits further archeological discovery.

Bibliography.–G. L. Harding, *PEQ* (1958), pp. 10-12; J. B. Hennessey, *PEQ* (1966), pp. 155-162; S. H. Horn, *BASOR*, 193 (Feb. 1969), 2-19.

J. ARTHUR THOMPSON

AMMONITESS am-ən-ī'təs [Heb. *'ammōnîṯ*]. A woman of the Ammonites, Naamah the mother of Rehoboam (1 K. 14:21, 31; 2 Ch. 12:13; 24:26).

AMNON am'non [Heb. *'amnôn*–'faithful'].

1. The eldest son of David, by Ahinoam of Jezreel (2 S. 3:2). As the crown prince and heir presumptive to the throne, he was intensely hated by Absalom, who was, therefore, doubly eager to revenge the outrage committed by Amnon upon his sister Tamar (2 S. 3:2; 13:1ff.; 1 Ch. 3:1).

2. A name in the genealogy of Judah (1 Ch. 4:20).

AMOK ā'mok [Heb. *'āmôq*–'deep']. A chief priest who returned from exile to Jerusalem with Zerubbabel (Neh. 12:7). He was an ancestor of Eber, a priest in the days of Joiakim (12:20).

AMON ā'mən [Heb. *'āmôn*–'trustworthy'].

1. A governor of Samaria (1 K. 22:26) to whom the prophet Micaiah was committed by Ahab after the prophet had predicted Ahab's death in battle.

2. King of Judah (642-640 B.C.), the son and successor of

Manasseh (2 K. 21:19; 2 Ch. 33:21). Amon followed the idolatrous traditions of his father and was assassinated by his servants, who placed his eight-year-old son Josiah on the throne.

3. A descendant of the servants of Solomon who returned to Palestine in the postexilic period (Neh. 7:59), the same as Ami in Ezr. 2:57; 1 Esd. 5:34.

4. (Mt. 1:10, AV, NEB). *See* AMOS (NT).

AMON [Heb. *'āmôn*; Assyr. *āmūnû*; Egyp. *imn*] (Jer. 46:25); AV "the multitude." The Egyptian local deity of THEBES (No).

AMORITES am'ə-rīts [Heb. *'ĕmōrî* (always sing.); Sum. mar-tu; Akk. *amurru(m)*–'the West'; Egyp. *Amuru*/*Amarra* or *'imr*; Ugar. *'amr*; Gk. *'Amorraíos*].

I. In the OT.–The name Amorite is used in the OT to denote (1) the inhabitants of Palestine generally, (2) the population of the hills as opposed to the plain, and (3) a specific people under a king of their own. Thus (1) we hear of them on the west shore of the Dead Sea (Gen. 14:7), at Hebron (Gen. 14:13), and Shechem (Gen. 48:22), in Gilead and Bashan (Dt. 3:10), and under Hermon (Dt. 3:8; 4:48). They are named instead of the Canaanites as the inhabitants of Palestine whom the Israelites were required to exterminate (Gen. 15:16; Dt. 20:17; Jgs. 6:10; 1 S. 7:14; 1 K. 21:26; 2 K. 21:11); the older population of Judah is called Amorite in Josh. 10:5f., in conformity with which Ezk. 16:3 states that Jerusalem had an Amorite father; and the Gibeonites are said to have been "of the remnant of the Amorites" (2 S. 21:2). On the other hand (2) in Nu. 13:29 the Amorites are described as dwelling in the mountains like the Hittites and Jebusites of Jerusalem, while the Amalekites or bedouin lived in the south and the Canaanites on the seacoast and in the valley of the Jordan. Lastly (3) we hear of Sihon, "king of the Amorites," who had conquered the northern half of Moab (Nu. 21:21-31; Dt. 2:26-35). While nonbiblical evidence on the subject is lacking and biblical evidence faces notable difficulties, it appears certain that the scriptural use of the word depends on the general Syro-Palestinian pattern of the end of the 2nd millennium.

II. In Mesopotamia and the Ancient Near East.–*A. Varying Use of the Name.* Amorites appear first in Mesopotamia in a divinatory text of the time of Sargon I (*ca.* 2360-2305). There they are a nomadic people, possibly from the northwestern hill countries, but more likely (so Dossin) from the western deserts (kur-mar-tu=the desert countries). The name ("the Westerners") is therefore a purely geographical indication of their immediate origins, from the perspective of Mesopotamia, and conveys no information about their ethnic composition or their real name. The highly civilized Sumerians considered them as barbarians. The name is used also for the northwestern countries: Syria, Lebanon, and Palestine; the Mediterranean appears sometimes as the "Sea of Amurru."

B. Early Amorite Kingdoms and Nomads in Syria and Mesopotamia. Between the 23rd and 21st cents. B.C. the Amorites penetrated into Babylonia, where, after the fall of the 3rd Dynasty of Ur (*ca.* 1950), they settled down. Thereafter Northwest Semitic dynasties ruled over Larsa (*ca.* 1961-1699), Isin (*ca.* 1958-1733), Mari (until 1693), and Babylon (*ca.* 1830-1531, the 1st Dynasty of Babylon), further in Syria over Aleppo, Qaṭna, Alalakh, etc., showing a consistent ethnic and institutional pattern from Mesopotamia to Syria. Evidence comes also from the Egyptian Execration Texts (19th-18th cents.; see *ANET*, pp. 328ff.) and from a list showing the presence of Amorite slaves in Egypt (18th cent.). The end of Amorite rule came after the conquest and sack of Babylon *ca.* 1531 by the Hittites, when its remains were overrun by the Kassites, who were to hold the region for some four hundred years. The archives of Mari reveal another wave of Amorite nomads, plundering and trying whenever possible to settle down. Their linguistic pattern shows affinities with names and idioms of Biblical Hebrew, on which ground M. Noth has called them "Proto-Arameans." This has lately been challenged. The title "Northwest Semites" is more pertinent, therefore, although "Amorites" remains as a conventional name.

C. The God Amurru. The first Amorites had an eponymous god Martu, who was soon included into the Sumerian pantheon as son of Ninḫursanga and husband to Ašratum/Aširtum (=the Syrian Astarte). Martu is once identified with the storm-god (H)Adad.

D. The Amorite Kingdom During the Amarna Age. During the 14th cent. Amurru appears as the name for a Syrian kingdom, whose frontiers reach N to Arwad, S to Sidon,

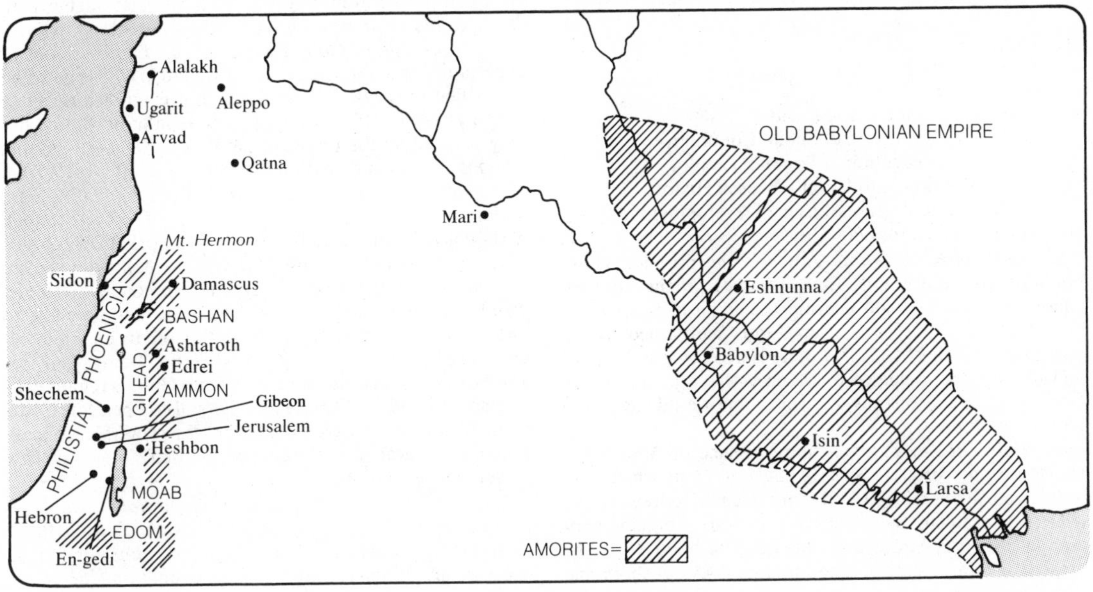

and E to Damascus. Any ethnic significance of the name seems here to have been lost and replaced by one merely political. The kingdom Amurru appears in Hittite and Ugaritic treaties, and through the latter one can reconstruct a genealogy of eight kings of Amurru (cf. M. Liverani, *Storia di Ugarit* [1962], ch. 2). The name appears also in Egyptian and Mesopotamian sources, respectively from Seti I and Tukulti-Ninurta I onward. In the Annals of Sennacherib (cf. *ANET*, p. 287 b), "kings of Amurru" are those of Phoenicia, Philistia, Ammon, Edom, and Moab, an evidence for a much broader use of the word.

E. Physical Characteristics of the Amorites. Because of the complicated history of the Amorites, great caution is needed when investigating their ethnic and racial background. The ancient statues of Amorite kings are often too damaged in relevant features (e.g., the nose) and too stylized to be of much use (cf. *ANEP*, nos. 429ff.), while Mari wall paintings tend not to classify the people there represented into racial types known to us. The Egyptian reliefs of Medinet Habu (12th cent.; cf. *ANEP*, nos. 7, 9, 346) refer to the inhabitants of the *kingdom* of Amurru, not to the original Amorites. From the language we can, however, safely consider the Amorites of Semitic stock, with probably a few Indo-Aryan elements.

Bibliography.–F. Böhl, *Kananäer und Hebräer* (1911); H. Bauer, *Die Ostkananäer* (1926); E. Dhorme, "Les Amorrhéens," *Recueil E. D.* (1956), pp. 81ff.; M. Noth, *ZAW*, 58 (1940/41), 182-89; *Der Ursprung des alten Israel im Lichte neuer Quellen* (1961); *Die Welt des AT* (4th ed. 1962); H. B. Huffmon, *Amorite Personal Names in the Mari Texts* (1965); G. Buccellati, *Amorites of the Ur-III Period* (1966); K. M. Kenyon, *Amorites and Canaanites* (1966); M. Liverani, *Oriens Antiquus*, 9 (1970), 5-27; C. H. J. de Geus, *Ugarit-Forschungen*, 3 (1971), 41-60; J. VanSeters, *VT*, 22 (1972), 64-81.

A. H. SAYCE
J. A. SOGGIN

AMOS ā'məs [Heb. *'āmôs*–'burdensome' or 'burden-bearer']. A prophet of the 8th cent. B.C., and the third book of the Minor Prophets.

- I. The Prophet
  - A. Name
  - B. Native Place
  - C. Personal History
  - D. Preparation
    1. Knowledge of God
    2. Acquaintance with History and Geography
  - E. Date
- II. The Book
  - A. Divisions
  - B. Theology
  - C. Historical and Critical Value
    1. As a Reflection of Social Conditions
    2. As a Reflection of Popular Theology
    3. As Witness to Israel's Sacred History
    4. As a Reflection of Legal Development in Israel
- III. Amos and the Prophetic Office

I. The Prophet.–*A. Name.* Amos is the prophet whose book stands third among the "Twelve" in the Hebrew canon. No other person bearing the same name is mentioned in the OT. There is an Amos mentioned in the genealogical series Lk. 3:25, but he is otherwise unknown, and although the spelling is the same as that for Amos in the Greek OT, we do not know how his name would have been written in Hebrew.

B. Native Place. TEKOA, the birthplace of Amos, was situated 6 mi. (10 km.) S of Bethlehem, from which it is visible, on a hill 2700 ft. (820 m.) high, overlooking the wilderness of Judah. The name has survived in contemporary Arabic society (Teqû'), and the neighborhood is at the present day the pasture-ground for large flocks of sheep and goats. From the high ground on which the modern village stands one looks down on the bare undulating hills of one of the bleakest districts of Palestine, "the waste howling wilderness," which must have suggested some of the startling imagery of the prophet's addresses. The place may have had—as is not seldom the case with towns or villages—a reputation for a special quality of its inhabitants; for it was from Tekoa that Joab fetched the "wise woman" who by a feigned story effected the reconciliation of David with his banished son Absalom (2 S. 14). There are traces in the book of Amos of a shrewdness and mother wit that are not so conspicuous in other prophetic books.

C. Personal History. The particulars of a personal kind noted in the book are few but suggestive. Amos was not a prophet or the son of a prophet (7:14), i.e., he did not belong to the professional class which frequented the so-called schools of the prophets. He was "among the shepherds (*nōqᵉḏîm*) of Tekoa" (1:1), the word here used being found only once again in biblical usage (2 K. 3:4), applied to Mesha king of Moab. An additional reference in the Ugaritic poem of Baal and Anath points to a cultic servant whose function included dictation of poetry in addition to whatever herding may have been required (*ANET*, p. 141b, colophon). In 7:14 the word rendered "herdsman" is different (*bôqēr*) and from its etymology denotes an owner of cattle, though some, from the LXX rendering, think that the word should be the same as in 1:1. He was also "a dresser of sycamore trees" (7:14). The word rendered "dresser" (AV "gatherer") occurs only here, and from the LXX (*knízon*) it is conjectured that there is reference to a squeezing or nipping of the sycamore-fig to make it more palatable or to accelerate its ripening.

D. Preparation. Nothing is said as to any special preparation of the prophet for his work: "The Lord took me from following the flock, and the Lord said to me, Go, prophesy to my people Israel" (7:15). In these words he put himself in line with all previous prophets who, in various modes of expression, claimed a direct revelation from God. There is, however, significance in the mention of the prophetic call in association with the statement about his occupation. There was apparently no period interposed between the one and the other, no cessation of husbandry to prepare for the work of prophesying. Amos was already prepared for that task, and when God's time came he took it up. Such preparation involved both his relationship with God and his awareness of the world in which he lived.

1. Knowledge of God. First of all, he had no doubt or uncertainty as to the character of the God in whose name he was called to speak. The God of Amos is one whose sway is boundless (9:2ff.), whose power is infinite (8:9f.), not only controlling the forces of nature (4; 5:8f.) but guiding the movements and destinies of nations (6:1ff., 14; 9:7ff.). Moreover, He is righteous in all His ways, dealing with nations on moral principles (1:3ff.; 2:1ff.), and, though particularly favorable to Israel, yet making that very choice of them as a people a ground for visiting them with sterner retribution for their sins (3:2). In common with all the prophets, Amos gave no explanation of how he came to know God and to form this conception of His character. It was simply assumed that God is such a Being; and this knowledge, as it could come only from God, is regarded as undisputed and undisputable. The call to speak in God's name may have come suddenly, but the prophet's conception of the character of the God who called him was no new or sudden revelation.

2. Acquaintance with History and Geography. Amos had a broad knowledge of the affairs of his own nation and those surrounding Israel. His opening words (chs. 1f.) demonstrate an ability to interact with events outside of the chosen nation, while various references (cf. below) show how well-informed the prophet was in the past and present of Israel's life. Such careful attention to national and international history has caused speculation to the effect that Amos was not the rustic he is often depicted to be. Further evidence in that direction comes from his acute awareness of the geography of his own country. Whether by personal travel as a wool-merchant or flock-master, or simply as one whose wanderlust led him to many places, the prophet seems to have visited various towns (e.g., Samaria, Bethel, Gilgal, Beer-sheba), particularly those which were religious and market centers.

Basic to all his knowledge is the influence of his own home, the scenery of the barren hills of the Judean wilderness, and the simple occupations of his daily life. The landscape surrounding Tekoa was such as to make a solemn impression on a reflective mind: the wide-spreading desert, the shimmering waters of the Dead Sea, the high wall of the distant hills of Moab. And as he tended his flock, or defended them from the ravages of wild beasts, this sublime setting nourished that exalted view of the divine Majesty which we find in his book, and furnished the imagery in which his thoughts are set (1:2; 3:4f.; 4:13; 5:8; 9:5f.). Rustic he may be; but his style is one of natural and impassioned eloquence, coming from a mind which saw God's working in all nature and His presence in every phenomenon.

E. Date. The date of the prophet Amos can be fixed approximately from the statement in 1:1 that his activity fell "in the days of Uzziah king of Judah and in the days of Jeroboam the son of Joash king of Israel, two years before the earthquake." Both these monarchs had long reigns, that of Uzziah (Azariah) extending from 767 to 740/39 B.C. and that of Jeroboam II from 782/1 to 753 B.C. Since Jotham probably acted as co-regent with Uzziah after 750 B.C., we may safely take the years of their concurrent reign and put the ministry of Amos between 760 and 750 B.C. The earthquake reference, though long preserved in Israel's memory (Zec. 14:5), is of no help to modern chronologists. The period thus fixed was one of peace and prosperity in both north and south. The troublesome Syrians had been reduced in 802 B.C. by the destruction of their capital Damascus at the hand of the Assyrian Adadnirari III, and for the next fifty years Israel was to grow at their expense. In Assyria itself a period of weakness followed Adadnirari's early successes and no serious threat to Palestine arose until after the accession of Tiglath-pileser III in 745. During the reign of Jeroboam II the northern kingdom reached its zenith of wealth and power with the attendant results of luxury and excess, a situation reflected constantly in the prophetic visions of Amos. Whether those prophecies were spread over a long period of time we cannot tell, though there is some indication that the brief biographical sketch (7:10ff.) is set chronologically within a series of consecutive proclamations.

II. The Book. The arrangement of the book is clear and simple, falling naturally into three parts, recognizable by certain recurring formulas and general literary features. The text has been, on the whole, faithfully preserved, and various attempts to find traces of later editorial hands rest mainly on grounds of content rather than style.

A. Divisions. (1) The first section embraces chs. 1 and 2. Here, after the title and designation of the prophet in 1:1, there is a solemn proclamation of divine authority for the prophet's words: "The Lord roars from Zion, and utters his voice from Jerusalem" (v. 2). This is notable in one who throughout the book recognizes God's power as worldwide and His operation as extending to all creation; and it should challenge, on the one hand, the assertion that the temple of Jerusalem was not more sacred than any of the numerous "high places" throughout the land, and, on the other hand, the superficial manner in which some writers speak of the Hebrew notion of a deity whose dwelling-place was restricted to one locality beyond which His influence was not felt. For this God, who has His dwelling-place in Zion, now through the mouth of the prophet denounces in succession the surrounding nations for breaches of a universal law binding on all humanity. It will be observed that the nations denounced are not named in geographical order, and the prophet exhibits remarkable rhetorical skill in the order of selection. The interest and sympathy of the hearers is secured by fixing the attention on the enormities of guilt in their neighbors, and curiosity is kept awake by the uncertainty as to where the next stroke of the prophetic whip will fall. Beginning with the more distant and alien peoples of Damascus, Gaza, and Tyre, he wheels round to the nearer and kindred peoples of Edom, Ammon, and Moab, till he rests for a moment on the brother tribe of Judah, and thus, having relentlessly drawn the net around Israel by the enumeration of seven peoples, he swoops down upon the northern kingdom to which his message is particularly addressed.

(2) The second section embraces chs. 3–6 and consists apparently of a series of discourses, three of which are introduced by the formula: "Hear this word" (3:1; 4:1; 5:1), and two others introduced by a comprehensive: "Woe to them . . ." (5:18; 6:1). Some would divide this section into a larger number of subsections (e.g., separating 4:1-3 from 4:4ff.); some, indeed, have described the whole book as a collection of ill-arranged fragments. Such views, however, popular with an earlier generation, are now treated with considerable reserve.

(3) The third section has some well-marked characteristics, although it is even less uniform than the preceding. The outstanding feature is the phrase, "Thus the Lord God showed me" (7:1, 4, 7; 8:1), varied at 9:1 by the words, "I saw the Lord standing beside the altar." We have thus a series of "visions" bearing upon, and interpreted as applying to, the condition of Israel. It is in the course of one of these, when the prophet comes to the words, "I will rise against the house of Jeroboam with the sword" (7:9), that the interposition of Amaziah the priest of Bethel is recorded, with the prophet's noble reply as to his divine call, and his rebuke and denunciation of the priest, ending with a prophetic announcement of the downfall and captivity of Israel (7:14-17).

B. Theology. Amos is sometimes considered to be the prophet of wrath in contrast to his contemporary Hosea, the prophet of God's love. Such a contrast is inconsistent with a balanced picture of both prophets as men whose theology was grounded in the covenant of love between God and Israel. Even if, as some critics (e.g., Eissfeldt) maintain, the closing passage of Amos (9:11-15) is a secondary addition, there is still no reason to believe that Amos—harsh though his words were—believed that the God of Israel would make a full end of His people in captivity. Judgment is pronounced on the false religion that claimed national security in the Lord but could ignore the ethical demands of the covenant. Woes are called down upon those who looked for the Day of the Lord as a day when Israel would triumph over all enemies. Such a Day, for disobedient Israel, was to be a day of darkness and not light (5:18), a day of national destruction rather than imperial expansion. Although Amos seems to have had no hope for the nation as a whole, he did enunciate the doctrine of the remnant (9:8), begun earlier under Elijah and developed fully by Isaiah. In view of these commitments to the mainstream of prophetic theological thought, it would seem strange if, as some scholars still maintain, Amos 5:21-23 were a rejection of cultic religion completely. One feels, rather, that Amos' God had rejected both cult and nation in their corrupt form, but any restoration of an Israelite remnant would certainly have included a reformed and revived ritual system.

C. Historical and Critical Value. The book of Amos is particularly valuable as a contemporaneous document from a period of great significance in the history of Israel. It not only gives graphic sketches and illuminating hints of the life and religious condition of the people, but furnishes a trustworthy standard for estimating the value of some other books whose dates are not so precisely determined, a definite starting-point for tracing the course of Israel's history.

1. As a Reflection of Social Conditions. The book is valuable as embodying a contemporary picture of society and the condition of religion. From the abuses which the prophet denounces and the lifelike sketches he draws of the scenes amid which he moved, taken along with what we know otherwise of the historical movements of the period, we are able to form a fairly adequate estimate of the condition of the age and the country. During the reign of Jeroboam II the kingdom of Israel rose to a degree of extent and influence unparalleled since the days of Solomon (2 K. 14:25), and we are not astonished to read in Amos the haughty words he puts into the mouth of the people of his time, who speak of Israel as the "first of the nations" (6:1). But success in war, if it encouraged this boastful spirit, brought also inevitable evils in its train. Victory meant plunder, an extension of territory and increase of wealth for the warrior-landowner class. The peasant, however, required to take up arms without promise of great spoil, was often taken away from the labors of the field, which at best were for a time neglected, and in the worst event were wasted and rendered unproductive. The wealth secured by men of strong hand led to the increase of luxury in its possessors, and became actually the means of still further adding to the burdens of the poor, who were dependent on the rich for the means of earning their livelihood and for basic justice in society. The opening denunciation of Israel for oppression of the poor (2:6f.) is reechoed and amplified in the succeeding chapters (3:9f.; 4:1; 5:11f.; 8:4-6). The luxury of the rich, who fattened on the misfortune of their poorer brethren, is castigated in biting irony in such passages as 6:3-6. Specially noticeable in this connection is the contemptuous reference to the luxurious women, the "cows of Bashan" (4:1), whose extravagances are maintained by the oppression of the poor. The situation, in short, was one that has found striking parallels in modern despotic countries in the East, where the people are divided into two classes, the powerful rich and the poor oppressed, men who have no helper, dependent on the rich and influential and tending to greater poverty under greedy patrons.

2. As a Reflection of Popular Theology. In a northern version of what was later denounced by Isaiah and Jeremiah, the people prided themselves on what they regarded as the worship of the national God, thinking that so long as they honored Him with costly offerings and a gorgeous ritual, they were pleasing Him and secure in His protection. Though lacking the strong prop of a Davidic monarchy and Jerusalem temple, crowds of worshipers resorted to Bethel, Dan, Gilgal, and even Beer-sheba with all the accompaniments of ceremony and ritual which the newly found wealth put in their power. The people seem to have settled down to a complacent optimism, nourished no doubt by a national prosperity; and though there had not been wanting reminders of the sovereignty of a righteous God, in convulsions of nature—drought, famine, pestilence, and earthquake (4:6-11)—these had been of no avail in awakening the sleeping conscience. They put the evil day far from them (6:3), for the Lord was their national God and "the Day of the Lord," the good time coming (5:18), when God would come to their help, was more in their minds than the imperative duty of returning to Him (4:6, 8, etc.).

3. As Witness to Israel's Sacred History. A past generation of scholars argued that the great historical sources of the Pentateuch which they designated J and E were composed at or shortly before the time of Amos and Hosea. References to events portrayed therein, as reflected in Amos, provided a reliable historical peg for affirming that the accounts in J and E were circulating by the 8th century. It was argued by not a few that the J and E documents were original compositions, bearing little resemblance to whatever history Israel may actually have experienced, and providing no faithful picture of what had really transpired. Contemporary scholarship offers no such facile solutions, and most would agree that the traditions contained in the Pentateuch, if not the actual writings themselves, were very old at the time Amos and his contemporaries appeared. It is not surprising, then, that within the compass of even a small book we should find references to outstanding events and stages of the past history presented as matters known to all his hearers. Such incidental notices as a reference to the house of Isaac (7:16), another to the house of Jacob (3:13), and another to the enmity between Jacob and Esau (1:11), certainly imply a familiarity with a connected patriarchal history such as found in Genesis. Again, references to the overthrow of Sodom and Gomorrah (4:11), to the "whole family" whom the Lord "brought up out of the land of Egypt" (3:1), to the divine leading of the people "forty years in the wilderness" (2:10), are not odds and ends of popular story but links in a chain of national history.

4. As a Reflection of Legal Development in Israel. The silence of Amos concerning the duties and perquisites of legitimate priests and Levites and the priority of the Jerusalem temple have led many to the conclusion that the prophet was unfamiliar with distinctly Levitical legislation. Adherents of the old JEDP documentary hypothesis have generally held that this material came either from D, written for Josiah's reformation in 622/621 B.C., or from P, a composition of the priests in the postexilic theocracy.

At the outset we must bear in mind the condition of the people whom Amos addressed, and the purpose and aim of his mission to the northern kingdom. As we are told in Kings (1 K. 12:25ff.), Jeroboam I deliberately sought to make a breach between the worship of Jerusalem and that of his own kingdom, while persuading his people that the worship of the Lord was being maintained. The schism occurred some 170 years before the time of Amos, and it is improbable that the worship and ritual of the northern kingdom tended in that interval to greater purity or greater conformity to what had been the authoritative practice of the undivided kingdom at the temple of Jerusalem. When, therefore, Amos, in face of the corrupt worship combined with elaborate ritual that prevailed around him, declared that God hated and despised their feasts and took no delight in their solemn assemblies (5:21), we are not justified in pressing his words into a sweeping condemnation of all ritual. On the contrary, when in the very same connection (5:22) he specified burnt offerings and meal offerings and peace offerings, and, in another passage (4:4, 5), daily sacrifices and tithes, sacrifices of thanksgiving, and freewill offerings, it is natural to infer that by these terms, which are familiar in the Pentateuch, he is referring to those statutory observances which were part of the national worship of united Israel, but had been overlaid with corruption and become destitute of spiritual value as practiced in the northern kingdom. Having condemned in such scornful and sweeping terms the worship that he saw going on around him, what was Amos to gain by entering into minute ritual prescriptions or defining the precise duties of priests and Levites? Having condemned the pilgrimages to the shrines of Bethel, Gilgal, Beer-sheba and Dan, what was he to gain by substituting for such meaningless activity an equally insincere attendance at a central sanctuary? Amos' problem was not one of form but one of content. No attempt is made even to reckon with questions of Jerusalem *v.* Bethel, Levite *v.* non-Levitical priest, because none of this could have been meaningful until the prior question of the heart and its attitude was settled. Thus the argument from silence cannot serve as proof of a late date for D or P material, inasmuch as the question simply was not one on which we might expect Amos to comment.

If we sense an ambiguity in Amos' handling of ritual law, there is no such response when we consider his ethical sources. His appeals are in striking agreement with the specifically ethical demands of the law books, and in phraseology they resemble them so much as to warrant the conclusion that the requirements of the law on these subjects were known and acknowledged. Thus his denunciations of those who oppress the poor (2:7; 4:1; 8:4) are quite in the spirit and style of Ex. 22:21f.; 23:9. His references to the perversion of justice and taking bribes (2:6; 5:7,10ff.; 6:12) are rhetorical enforcements of the prohibitions of the law in Ex. 23:6-8. When he reproves those that "lay themselves down beside every altar upon garments taken in pledge" (2:8) we hear an echo of the command: "If ever you take your neighbor's garment in pledge, you shall restore it to him before the sun goes down" (Ex. 22:26); and when he denounces those who make "the ephah small and the shekel great, and deal deceitfully with false balances" (8:5) his words are in close agreement with the law, "You shall do no wrong in judgment, in measures of length or weight or quantity. You shall have just balances, just weights, a just ephah, and a just hin" (Lev. 19:35f.).

In addition to an affirmation of those ethical parts of the law which lie at the foundation of all prophecy, Amos is remarkable in that his phraseology often agrees with Deuteronomy, the most ethical book of the Pentateuch. He does not, indeed, like his contemporary Hosea, dwell on the *love* of God as Deuteronomy does, but, in sterner mold, citing almost the very words of Deuteronomy, emphasizes the keeping of God's commandments, and denounces those who despise the law (cf. 2:4 with Dt. 17:19). Among verbal coincidences have been noticed the combinations "oppress" and "crush" (4:1; Dt. 28:33), "blasting" (RSV "blight") and "mildew" (4:9; Dt. 28:22), "gall" and "wormwood" (6:12; Dt. 29:18). In view of this it seems that the silence of Amos with reference to the centralization of worship, on which Deuteronomy is so explicit, is not to be seen as conclusive in judging the critical question of D.

III. Amos and the Prophetic Office.–With the possible exception of Joel, Amos is the earliest prophet whose oracles have been collected in written form. This fact, and the apparent dissociation from normative prophecy (7:14), has led some scholars to see in Amos a sharp break with earlier professional prophets and the institution of a new movement. However, Am. 7:14 is still the subject of lively academic discussion, with some translating the pertinent phrase "I *was* no prophet," indicating only a lack of early association with the office, while others opt for "I *am* no prophet," and argue about Amos' relationship with the guild prophets (some of whom may indeed have been ecstatics) and the normative tradition represented by Samuel and Elijah.

What is certainly clear, whatever the meaning of Am. 7:14, is that prophecy was no new thing in eighth-century Israel, and that Amos identified squarely with what he considered a known and accepted office within the nation. He begins by stating boldly, "Surely the Lord God does nothing without revealing his secret to his servants the prophets" (3:7). We need not search further for a definition of the prophet as understood by him and other OT writers: the prophet is one to whom God reveals His will, and who comes forward to declare that will and purpose to man. A great deal has been made of the words of Amaziah the priest of Bethel (7:12), as if they proved that the prophet in those times was regarded as a wandering rhetorician, earning his bread by reciting his speeches; and we must indeed admit that there were prophets whose motives and methodology were less than God-directed (Mic. 3:5, 11). Nevertheless, there were evidently true prophets, well known in the history of Israel, to whose tradition Amos appealed and with whose ministry he identified (2:11; 3:7f.). They were called by God to their office, and, far from echoing merely patriotic and nationalistic sentiments of the people, they were unpopular preachers of judgment whose message had, from the first, evoked a negative response (2:12).

Amos also gives a valid picture of prophetic religion. His God is a God of the universe, controlling the forces of nature (4:6ff.; 5:8f.), ruling the destinies of nations (6:2, 14; 9:2-6), searching the thoughts of the heart (4:13), inflexible in righteousness and dealing with nations and men on the basis of equal justice (1 and 2; 9:7), but most severe to the people who have received the highest privileges (3:2). This is the God whose laws Israel has broken (2:4; 3:10) and for whose just judgment she is warned to prepare (4:12). There is no rejection of cult except insofar as it has conflicted with God's true law. There is no exaltation of ethics apart from the ethic of Deuteronomy and the rest of the Pentateuch. There is no false assurance of God's choice of Israel apart from a reiteration of the covenant responsibilities inherent in that choice. In short, prophetic religion is the religion of normative spokesmen for God from Moses onward.

Bibliography.–Comms. by S. Amsler (1965); R. S. Cripps (2nd ed. 1955); S. R. Driver (*CBSC*, 1915); E. A. Edghill (1914); W. R. Harper (*ICC*, 1905); J. Marsh (*Torch*, 1965); J. L. Mays (1969); T. H. Robinson (1923); G. A. Smith (1940). H. W. Wolff (*Hermeneia*, 1977).

Comms. on Minor Prophets by J. A. Bewer (1949); B. Duhm (Eng. tr. 1912); A. van Hoonacker (*EtB*, 1908); R. F. Horton and S. R. Driver, eds. (1904-1906); K. F. Keil (1868); W. Nowack (*Handkommentar zum AT*, 1897, 1922); C. von Orelli (1893); G. L. Robinson (1926; 1964 simplified ed. by H. R. Boer); T. H. Robinson (*HAT*, 1954); E. Sellin (*KZAT*, 1929-1930); G. A. Smith (1928); A. Weiser (*ATD*, 5th ed. 1964); J. Wellhausen (1893). See also R. Calkins, *Modern Message of the Minor Prophets* (1947); H. L. Ellison, *Prophets of Israel* (1969).

Also on Amos: K. Cramer, *Amos* (1930); R. L. Honeycutt, *Amos and His Message* (1963); J. K. Howard, *Amos among the Prophets* (1968); A. S. Kapelrud, *Central Ideas in Amos* (2nd ed. 1961); V. Maag, *Text, Wortschatz und Begriffswelt des Buches Amos* (1951); A. Neher, *Amos* (1950); H. Reventlow, *Das Amt des Propheten bei Amos* (1962); J. M. Ward, *Amos and Isaiah* (1969); J. D. W. Watts, *Vision and Prophecy in Amos* (1958); A. Weiser, *Die Profetie des Amos* (1929); H. W. Wolff, *Amos geistige Heimat* (1964); *Die Stunde des Amos* (1969).

J. Morgenstern, *HUCA*, 11 (1936), 19-140; 12/13 (1937/38), 1-53; 15 (1940), 59-305; 32 (1961), 295-350; R. Gordis, *HTR*, 33 (1940), 239-251; J. P. Hyatt, *Interp.*, 3 (1949), 338-348; E. Würthwein, *ZAW*, 62 (1950), 10-52; W. S. McCullough, *JBL*, 72 (1953), 247-254; S. Terrien, *Israel's Prophetic Heritage* (1962), pp. 108-115; R. Smend, *EvTh*, 23 (1963), 404-423; W. Schmidt, *ZAW*, 77 (1965), 168-192; A. S. Kapelrud, "New Ideas in Amos," in *SVT*, 15 (1966), 193-206; M. Weiss, *JBL*, 86 (1967), 416-423; S. Gevirtz, *JBL*, 87 (1968), 267-276; G. W. Ramsey, *JBL*, 89 (1970), 187-191.

J. ROBERTSON C. ARMERDING

AMOS (NT) [Gk. *Amōs*]. An ancestor of Jesus in Luke's genealogy, the eighth before Joseph the husband of Mary (Lk. 3:25). The name occurs also, according to most Greek MSS, in Matthew's genealogy (Mt. 1:10), followed by the RSV. The AV and NEB read with a few MSS Amon, which is historically correct (cf. 1 Ch. 3:10ff.).

AMOZ ā'moz [Heb. *'āmôṣ*–'strong']. The father of Isaiah the prophet (2 K. 19:2, 20; 20:1; 2 Ch. 26:22; 32:20, 32; Isa. 1:1; 2:1; 13:1; 20:2; 37:2, 21; 38:1).

AMPHICTYONY [From Gk. *amphiktyonía*]. A confederation or league of political units focused on a central religious shrine. On the basis of twelve-member leagues known from ancient Greece, particularly the Pylean-Delphic league, and Etruria, Martin Noth and other biblical scholars have suggested such an organization for the pre-monarchic period in Israel. Biblical accounts, however, do not mention that specific type of arrangement. Rather, the loose tribal association probably resembled the situation at Mari. The Israelite tribes were linked by a covenant of allegiance to a common overlord, Yahweh, and the alliance was depicted in terms of kinship.

See ISRAEL, HISTORY OF THE PEOPLE OF V; JUDGES, PERIOD OF.

Bibliography.–A. Malamat, *JAOS*, 82 (1962), 143-150; G. E. Mendenhall, *Tenth Generation* (1973), pp. 1-31, 174-197; M. Noth, *Das System der zwölf Stämme Israels* (1930); *NHI*, pp. 85-109; H. M. Orlinsky, *Oriens Antiquus*, I (1962), 11-20. A. C. M.

AMPHIPOLIS am-fi'pə-lis [Gk. *Amphípolis*–'around the city']. An ancient city of Macedonia situated on a terraced hill on the east bank of the river Strymon, which curved about the north, west, and south sides of the city. The river drained Lake Cercinitus near the city and then flowed into the sea some 3 mi. (5 km.) downstream. The name of the city is derived either from its being nearly surrounded by a stream or from its being conspicuous on every side (Thucydides iv.102).

The Thracian tribe that founded it (Herodotus vii.114; cf.110) called it Nine Ways (Gk. *Ennéa hodoí*), a testimony to its general strategic and commercial importance. It guarded the main route from Thrace into Macedonia and later became an important station on the Via Egnatia, a main highway of the Roman empire. It lay in a fertile district, producing wine, oil, and figs. In addition, it was a depot for ship timber and for gold and silver produced in mines of the district, and also was a manufacturing center, especially of woolen stuffs.

After successfully resisting a number of attempts at colonization by Greek forces—in 497, 476, and 465 B.C.—it was colonized in 437 by Athenians and other Greeks under the leadership of Hagnon. However, the mixed population surrendered to the Spartan leader Brasidas in 424 and thereafter resisted Athenian reconquest. Philip of Macedon occupied the city in 357. When the Romans conquered and partitioned Macedonia after the battle of Pydna (168 B.C.) they made Amphipolis a free city and capital of the first district of Macedonia (Macedonia Prima).

On his second missionary journey, Paul, with Silas, passed through the city en route from Philippi, which lay some 30 mi. (50 km.) NE, to Thessalonica. Numerous inscriptions and coins have been found there, as well as traces of a Roman aqueduct and ancient fortifications.

Bibliography.–S. Casson, *Macedonia, Thrace and Illyria* (1926); Pauly-Wissowa, I/2, 1949-1952. R. P. MEYE

AMPLIAS am'plē-əs (Rom. 16:8, AV). *See* AMPLIATUS.

AMPLIATUS am-ple-ā'təs [Gk. *Ampliatos*, some MSS *Amplias* (D K L, etc.)]; AV AMPLIAS. A member of the Christian community at Rome, to whom Paul sent greetings (Rom. 16:8). He is designated "my beloved in the Lord." It is a common name and is found in inscriptions connected with the imperial household. The name is found twice in the cemetery of Domitilla, the earlier inscription being over a cell which belongs to the end of the 1st or the beginning of the 2nd century. The bearer of this name was probably a member of her household and conspicuous in the early Christian church in Rome.

AMRAM am'ram [Heb. *'amrām*–'people exalted'].

1. Father of Aaron, Moses, and Miriam (Ex. 6:20; Nu. 26:59; 1 Ch. 6:3; 23:13); and a son of Kohath the son of Levi (Ex. 6:18; Nu. 3:19; etc.). Perhaps he was not literally the son of Kohath, but rather his descendant, since there were ten generations from Joseph to Joshua (1 Ch. 7:20-27), while only four are actually mentioned from Levi to Moses for the corresponding period. Moreover, the Kohathites at the time of the Exodus numbered 8600 (Nu. 3:28), which would have been an impossibility if only two generations had lived. It seems best to regard Amram as a descendant of Kohath, and his wife Jochebed as a "daughter of Levi" in a general sense.

2. One of the Bani, who in the days of Ezra had taken a foreign wife (Ezr. 10:34; 1 Esd. 9:34).

3. (1 Ch. 1:41, AV, NEB). *See* HAMRAN.

AMRAMITES am'rəm-īts [Heb. *'amrāmî*]. The descendants of Amram, one of the Levitical families mentioned in Nu. 3:27 and 1 Ch. 26:23, who had the charge of the tabernacle proper.

AMRAPHEL am'rə-fel [Heb. *'amrāpel*]. The king of Shinar who fought against Sodom and the Cities of the Plain in alliance with Arioch king of Ellasar, Chedorlaomer king of Elam, and Tidal king of nations. His name is found only in Gen. 14:1, 9.

Certain difficulties are associated with the identification both of the individual and of his territory. The MT, the Sam. Pent. (Gen. 14:1), the LXX, and the Syriac all designated him clearly as "king of Shinar." However, the Sam. Pent. (v. 9), the Targums, and 1QapGen specifically recorded that he was king of Babel.

Shinar was the land in which the great Babylonian cities of Erech and Accad were situated (Gen. 10:10). It lay in a plain in which early migrants settled and founded the city and *ziggurat* of Babel (Gen. 11:2). The LXX interpreted "Shinar" (Heb. *šin'ār*) to mean "Babylonia" or "the land of Babylon," following the traditions of Gen. 10:10. On philological and other grounds it is improbable that Shinar can be equated with Sumer, or southern Babylonia. It is of some interest that although Syr. *Sen'ar* designates the country around Baghdad, no earlier name for Babylonia that might correspond to Shinar has yet come to light. Albright suggested that the land over which Amraphel ruled might have been the West Semitic Sangar in Syria, known to the Egyptians of the Amarna period by that name and appearing in the Amarna Letters as Akk. *Šankar*. However, a Syrian location for the kingdom seems unlikely, since the narrative of Gen. 14 appears to consider Mesopotamia as the home of Amraphel. Possibly the reference is to the district of Singar in Upper Mesopotamia, although this cannot be substantiated at present.

From the narrative of Gen. 14 it seems that Bera king of Sodom, Birsha king of Gomorrah, Shinab king of Admah, Shemeber king of Zeboiim, and the king of Bela (Zoar) had been tributaries of Chedorlaomer for twelve years, had rebelled in the thirteenth, and in the following year were attacked and defeated in the Vale of Siddim or Salt Sea by a punitive coalition led by Chedorlaomer. But before this onslaught the Mesopotamian allies had campaigned against the Rephaim in Ashtaroth-karnaim, the Zuzim in Ham, the Emim in Shaveh-kiriathaim, and the Horites living in the vicinity of Mt. Seir. Once these had been rendered powerless to assist the revolted vassals, the Mesopotamian coalition marched to Kadesh, attacked the Amalekites, and fought against the Amorites of Hazazon-tamar (possibly En-gedi).

The thoroughness with which the campaign was executed suggests that Amraphel and his allies were interested in the agricultural and mineral resources for which the locality was famous in antiquity. Despite the opposition they mounted, the rulers of the cities in the valley were forced to succumb to the Mesopotamian invaders in the Vale of Siddim. The kings of Sodom and Gomorrah were trapped with some of their allies among the numerous bitumen pits of the valley, while those who were able escaped to the hills. The equipment of the defenders was captured by the invading coalition, who, after pillaging Sodom and Gomorrah, marched in the direction of their native land.

Among those enslaved by the Mesopotamians was Lot the nephew of Abram. News of this event was carried by messenger to Abram, who was encamped at the terebinth plantation in Mamre, a place in the Hebron district westward from Machpelah (Gen. 23:17, 19). The patriarch immediately set out with a raiding party and followed the withdrawing invaders to Laish (Dan). He divided his forces, attacked the enemy by night, and sent them fleeing as far as Hobah, N of Damascus. As a result of this attack Abram was able to rescue Lot, with the women and other people, as well as recover the booty that the Elamite coalition had removed from Sodom, where Lot was living.

The discovery at Susa in 1901 of the celebrated Code of Hammurabi led many contemporary scholars to identify Amraphel with that renowned Akkadian monarch. However, there were some immediate philological problems that proved difficult to resolve. The *l* at the end of Amraphel was a particular matter of contention. Some scholars maintained that it was in fact the Akkadian determinative *ilu* ("god"). This view is improbable, since in cuneiform the determinative symbol invariably precedes the particular name. If the *l* is linked with the following word *meleḵ*, as others have argued, it destroys the sense of the phrase, which is clearly a standardized literary expression. Other inconclusive approaches include the suggestion that Heb. *'amrāpel* is a scribal error for 'MRPY (*'Ammurapi = Hammurapi*), or that it is a compressed transcription of the Akkadian title *Ammurapi-ili* ("Hammurabi is my god"). Such arguments tend to posit corruptions of the text for which there is no factual evidence, and at best are unconvincing philologically. There would therefore appear to be no sound reason for maintaining that Amraphel can be identified with Hammurabi, particularly as such a procedure is unsubstantiated by Mesopotamian archeology and history. If HAMMURABI were really Amraphel, it is difficult to see why he should be occupying a subordinate position to that of Chedorlaomer, unless Hammurabi happened to be a crown prince at the time. But here it has to be recognized that the Palestinian expedition itself has not been discovered to date among the recorded campaigns of Hammurabi. The identity of Amraphel king of Shinar must therefore remain uncertain for the moment.

See R. K. Harrison, *Intro. to the OT* (1969), pp. 159, 164.

T. G. PINCHES
R. K. H.

AMULET [Heb. *laḥaš*] (Isa. 3:20); AV EARRING; NEB CHARM. A small object worn on the body and generally hanging from the neck, supposed to afford protection against evil spirits. Amulets were common in all periods of Near Eastern antiquity, and many fine specimens have survived. Near Eastern amulets assumed many shapes, with animal and human figurines especially popular. The crescents (Heb. *śahᵃrōnîm,* Jgs. 8:21, 26) and female ornaments (Isa. 3:20) were fundamentally of this nature, as were possibly the earrings (*nezem*) of Ex. 32:2. Phylacteries (frontlets, *ṭôṭāpôṯ*; Gk. *phylaktḗria*) can also be regarded as amulets (Ex. 13:16; Dt. 6:8; 11:18; Mt. 23:5; cf. Prov. 6:21), while wisdom itself was described as a pendant (Heb. *'ᵃnāq,* Prov. 1:9), again reflecting the custom of amulet-wearing. This custom also seems indicated by Prov. 17:8, where the MT has "a stone bestowing favor." In the NT the personal articles of Acts 19:12 come into the category of amulets, though healing in the name of Jesus (Eph. 1:21; Phil. 2:9) precluded their use and relegated them to the area of magic and superstition (Acts 19:13-19). *See also* CHARM.

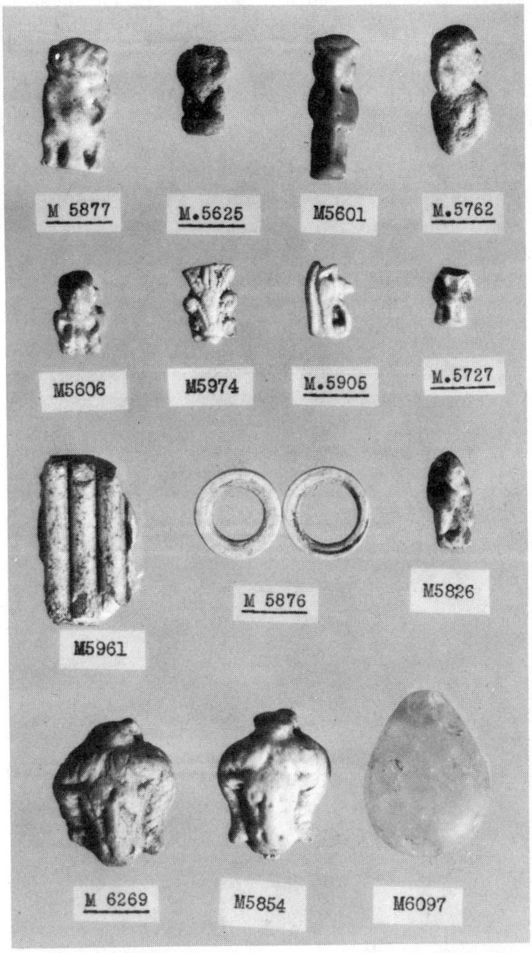

Amulets from Megiddo, largely of Egyptian style (Oriental Institute, University of Chicago)

See E. A. W. Budge, *Amulets and Superstitions* (1930).

R. K. H.

AMZI am'zī [Heb. *'amṣî*–'my strength'].

1. A Levite of the family of Merari (1 Ch. 6:46).

2. A priest of the family of Adaiah in the second temple, the son of a Zechariah (Neh. 11:12).

ANAB ā'nab [Heb. *'ᵃnaḇ*–'grape']. A place mentioned in the list of cities that fell to Judah (Josh. 15:50). In the list it follows Debir, from which it was a short distance to the southwest. It was a city of the Anakim, from whom Joshua took it (Josh. 11:21). In Egyptian texts of the 19th Dynasty it is called *Qrt 'nb,* indicating that the full name of the city was Kiriath-anab, "city of grapes." The site is identified as Khirbet 'Anâb, about 15 mi. (24 km.) SW of Hebron.

ANAEL an'ə-el [Gk. *Anaēl*]. A brother of Tobit, and father of Ahikar (Tob. 1:21).

ANAH ā'nə [Heb. *'ᵃnâ*]. A Horite clan name (Gen. 36).

1. In Gen. 36:2, 14, 18, the father (or mother) of Oholibamah, one of the wives of Esau. The LXX, Syriac, and Sam. Pent. read "son" of Zibeon in Gen. 36:2, 14, followed by the RSV and NEB; the AV has "daughter."

2. The fourth son of Seir, one of the Edomite chiefs (Gen. 36:20, 25, 29; 1 Ch. 1:38, 41).

3. A son of Zibeon (Gen. 36:24; 1 Ch. 1:40), who discovered thermal springs (AV, NEB, "mules") in the wilderness.

Aside from being members of Horite clans, the relationship among the above persons is obscure.

ANAHARATH ə-nā'hə-rath [Heb. *'ᵃnāḥᵃrāṯ*]. A place that fell to the tribe of Issachar in the division of the land (Josh. 19:19), the *'nḫrt* among the conquered cities listed by Thutmose III. It is identified as en-Na'ûrah, 6 mi. (10 km.) E of Afula in the Valley of Jezreel.

ANAIAH ə-nī'ə [Heb. *'ᵃnāyâ*–'Yahweh has answered'; Gk. *Ananias, Anaia*]; AV and NEB Apoc. ANANIAS. A Levite who assisted Ezra in reading the law to the people (Neh. 8:4; 1 Esd. 9:43). He was one of those who sealed the covenant (Neh. 10:22).

ANAK ā'nak [Heb. *(hā)'ᵃnāq*]; **ANAKIM** an'ə-kim [Heb. *'ᵃnāqîm;* Gk. *Enakim, Enakeim*]; AV ANAKIMS. Some of the pre-Israelite inhabitants of Canaan, descendants of Arba (Josh. 15:13; 21:11). Their name may mean "people of the necklace." They resided in the Hebron area, but may have occupied considerably more terrain originally (Josh. 11:21f.). Hebrew tradition uniformly regarded the Anakim as a formidable people (cf. Dt. 2:10, 21; 9:2), who in Nu. 13:33 are regarded as descendants of the Nephilim (Gen. 6:4). While Joshua dispossessed them from the hill-country, it was left to Caleb to drive them out of Hebron completely.

The eighteenth-century B.C. Egyptian Execration Texts seem to point to the presence in Palestine *ca.* 2000 B.C. of a tribe named Anak whose leaders bore Semitic names, but apart from this possible allusion there is no extrabiblical evidence for this ancient people. R. K. H.

ANAMIM an'ə-mim [Heb. *'ᵃnāmîm*]; NEB ANAMITES. Descendants of Mizraim (Gen. 10:13; 1 Ch. 1:11). *See* TABLE OF NATIONS.

ANAMMELECH ə-nam'ə-lek [Heb. *'ᵃnammeleḵ*–possibly 'Anu is king']. One of the gods of SEPHARVAIM, along with ADRAMMELECH, to whom the Sepharvites burned their children (2 K. 17:31). Formerly, Sepharvaim was identified with Sippar, and the two deities were thought to be Babylonian. However, Sepharvaim is grouped together with Arpad and Hamath (2 K. 17:24; 18:34), strongly suggesting that it was an Aramean (Syrian) city-state. The identification with Sibraim, on the border between Damascus and Hamath (Ezk. 47:16), has been suggested, but there are phonetic difficulties in such an identification. Moreover, there is no evidence of the immolation of children as part of the cultus of any Babylonian deity. On the other hand, sacrifice by fire was practiced in various portions of Syria and Palestine. We may tentatively conclude, therefore, that Anammelech and Adrammelech were Syrian, or possibly Canaanite, deities.

W. S. L. S.

ANAN ā'nən [Heb. *'ānān*–'cloud'].

1. One of those who, with Nehemiah, sealed the covenant (Neh. 10:26).

2. (1 Esd. 5:30, AV, NEB); RSV HANA. *See* HANAN **4.**

ANANI ə-nā'nī [Heb. *'ᵃnānî*–'(Yahweh) has revealed Himself'(?)]. A son of Elioenai of the house of David, who lived after the Captivity (1 Ch. 3:24).

ANANIAH an-ə-nī'ə [Heb. *'ᵃnanyâ*–'Yahweh has revealed Himself'(?)].

1. Grandfather of Azariah (Neh. 3:23).

2. A town of Benjamin mentioned along with Nob and Hazor (Neh. 11:32). It is perhaps to be identified with modern el-'Azarîyeh, the NT Bethany, nearly 2 mi. (3 km.) E of Jerusalem.

ANANIAS an-ə-nī'əs [Gk. *Hananias*<Heb. *ḥᵃnanyâ*–'Yahweh has been gracious']. A common Jewish name occurring several times in Acts, and in the Apocrypha. The OT form of the name is HANANIAH.

1. A member of the church at Jerusalem, the husband of Sapphira (Acts 5:1-10). He and his wife sold their property, and gave to the common fund of the church part of the purchase money, pretending it was the whole. When his hypocrisy was denounced by Peter, Ananias fell down dead; and three hours later his wife met the same doom.

The following points are of interest. (1) The narrative immediately follows the account of the intense brotherliness of the believers resulting in a common fund, to which Barnabas had made a generous contribution (Acts 4:32-37). The sincerity and spontaneity of the gifts of Barnabas and the others set forth in dark relief the calculated deceit of Ananias. The brighter the light, the darker the shadow. (2) The crime of Ananias consisted not in his retaining a part, but in his pretending to give the whole. He was under no compulsion to give all, for the communism of the early Church was not absolute, but purely voluntary (see esp. 5:4). Falsehood and hypocrisy ("lie to the Holy Spirit," v. 3), rather than greed, were the sins for which he was so severely punished. (3) The severity of the judgment can be justified by the consideration that the act was "the first open venture of deliberate wickedness" (Meyer) within the Church. The punishment was an "awe-inspiring act of Divine church-discipline." The narrative does not, however, imply that Peter consciously willed their death. His words were the occasion of it, but he was not the deliberate agent. Even the words in v. 9b are a prediction rather than a judicial sentence.

2. A disciple in Damascus, to whom the conversion of Saul of Tarsus was made known in a vision, and who was the instrument of his physical and spiritual restoration, and the means of introducing him to the other Christians in Damascus (Acts 9:10-19). Paul mentions him with great favor in his account of his conversion spoken at Jerusalem (Acts 22:12-16), where we are told that Ananias was held in high respect by all the Jews in Damascus, on account of his strict legal piety. No mention is made of him in Paul's address before Agrippa in Caesarea (Acts 26). In late tradition he is placed in the list of the seventy disciples of Jesus, and represented as bishop of Damascus, and as having died a martyr's death.

3. A high priest in Jerusalem, A.D. 47-59. From Josephus (*Ant.* xx.5.2; 6.2; 9.2; *BJ* ii.17.9) we glean the following facts: He was the son of Nedebaeus (or Nebedaeus) and was nominated to the high-priestly office of Herod of Chalcis. In A.D. 52 he was sent to Rome by Quadratus, legate of Syria, to answer a charge of oppression brought by the Samaritans, but the emperor Claudius acquitted him. On his return to Jerusalem he resumed the office of high priest. He was deposed shortly before Felix left the province, but continued to wield great influence, which he used in a lawless and violent way.

He was a typical Sadducee, wealthy, haughty, unscrupulous, filling his sacred office for purely selfish and political ends, antinationalist in his relation to the Jews, friendly to the Romans. He died an ignominious death, being assassinated by the popular zealots (*sicarii*) at the beginning of the last Jewish war.

In the NT he figures in two passages. (1) The first is Acts 23:1-5, where Paul defends himself before the Sanhedrin. The overbearing conduct of Ananias in commanding Paul to be struck on the mouth was characteristic of the man. Paul's ire was for the moment aroused, and he hurled back the scornful epithet of "whitewashed wall." On being called to account for "reviling God's high priest," he quickly recovered the control of his feelings, and said," "I did not know, brethren, that he was the high priest; for it is written, 'You shall not speak evil of a ruler of your people.'"

This remark has greatly puzzled the commentators. The high priest could have been easily identified by his position and official seat as president of the Sanhedrin. Some have wrongly supposed that Ananias had lost his office during his trial at Rome, but had afterward usurped it during a vacancy (John Lightfoot, Michaelis, etc.). Others take the words as ironical: "How could I know as high priest one who acts so unworthily of his sacred office?" (so Calvin). Others (e.g., Alford, Plumptre) take it that owing to defective eyesight Paul knew not from whom the insolent words had come. Perhaps the simplest explanation is that Paul meant, "I did not for the moment bear in mind that I was addressing the high priest" (so Bengel, Neander, etc.).

(2) In Acts 24:1 we find Ananias coming down to Caesarea in person, with a deputation from the Sanhedrin, to accuse Paul before Felix.

4. (1 Esd. 5:16, AV). *See* ANNIAS.

5. (1 Esd. 9:21, AV, NEB). *See* HANANI **3.**

6. (1 Esd. 9:29, AV, NEB). *See* HANANIAH **9.**

7. (1 Esd. 9:43, AV, NEB). *See* ANAIAH.

8. (1 Esd. 9:48, AV, NEB). *See* HANAN **5.**

9. Ananias the Great, son of Shemaiah the Great; a kinsman of Tobit. The angel Raphael, disguised as a man, pretended to be his son (Tob. 5:12f.).

10. NEB omits. An ancestor of Judith, and son of Gideon (Jth. 8:1).

11. (Song Three 66, AV). *See* HANANIAH **7.**

D. M. EDWARDS

ANANIEL ə-nan'ē-əl [Gk. *Ananiēl*–'God is gracious']; NEB HANANIEL. An ancestor of Tobit (Tob. 1:1).

ANATH ā'nath [Heb. *ʿanāṯ*; cf. Ugar. *ʿnt*]. The father of Shamgar (Jgs. 3:31; 5:6). Some scholars and the NEB emend "Shamgar ben Anath" to read "Shamgar of Beth-anath," designating either the Galilean city mentioned in Jgs. 1:33 or some other place where the Semitic goddess Anath had a sanctuary. Since, however, the goddess Anath (the sister and consort of Baal) appears in Ugaritic literature as the goddess of war as well as of love, the phrase "Shamgar ben Anath" could possibly mean "Shamgar the warrior."

D. MCINTOSH

ANATHEMA ə-nath'ə-mə [Gk. *anáthema*<LXX and Attic *anáthēma* < *anatíthēmi*]. This word occurs only once in the AV, in the phrase "Let him be anathema, Maranatha" (1 Cor. 16:22); elsewhere the AV renders *anáthema* by "accursed"; the RSV has "cursed" and "accursed"; the NEB "outcast" and "a curse on" (Rom. 9:3; 1 Cor. 12:3; Gal. 1:8); in Acts 23:14 the AV has "curse," the RSV and NEB "oath."

Both words—*anáthēma* and *anáthema*—were originally dialectical variations and had the same connotation, "offering to the gods." The non-Attic form *anáthema* was adopted in the LXX as a rendering of the Heb. *ḥērem* (*see* ACCURSED), and gradually came to have the significance of the Hebrew word—"anything devoted to destruction." Whereas in the Greek fathers *anáthema*—as *ḥērem* in rabbinic Hebrew—came to denote excommunication from society, in the NT the word has its full force.

In common speech it evidently became a strong expression of execration, and the term connoted more than physical destruction; it invariably implied moral worthlessness. In Rom. 9:3 Paul does not simply mean that, for the sake of his fellow countrymen, he is prepared to face death, but he is ready to endure the moral degradation of an outcast from the kingdom of Christ. In 1 Cor. 12:3 the expression "Jesus is anathema," with its suggestion of moral unfitness, reaches the lowest depths of depreciation, as the expression "Jesus is Lord" reaches the summit of appreciation.

The Gk. *anáthēma* occurs in Lk. 21:5 with the sense "votive offering" (NEB; RSV "offering"; AV "gift").

T. LEWIS

ANATHOTH an'ə-thoth [Heb. *ʿanāṯôṯ*]. A Levitical town in the tribal division of Benjamin (Josh. 21:18; cf. 1 Ch. 6:60), about 3 mi. (5 km.) NE of Jerusalem, best known as the home of the prophet Jeremiah. The modern village of ʿAnâtâ preserves the name, but the ancient city is represented by Râs el-Kharrûbeh, about a half-mile (1 km.) to the southwest. In an elevated position at the desert's edge, it was subject to drought and to the blasting east wind, elements that influenced the prophet's figures of speech (cf. Jer. 4:11; 17:8; 18:7; etc.).

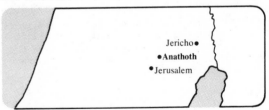

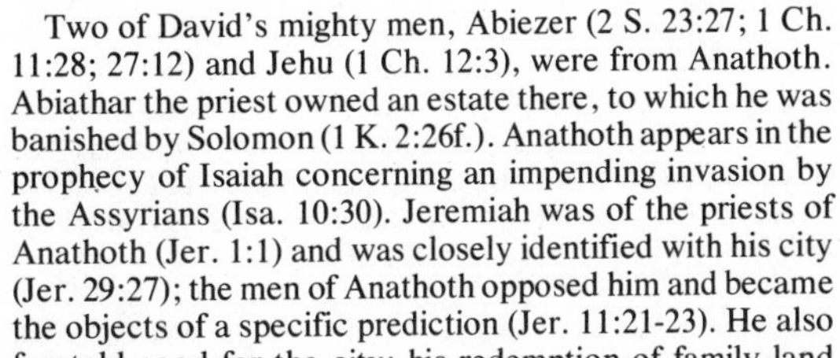

Two of David's mighty men, Abiezer (2 S. 23:27; 1 Ch. 11:28; 27:12) and Jehu (1 Ch. 12:3), were from Anathoth. Abiathar the priest owned an estate there, to which he was banished by Solomon (1 K. 2:26f.). Anathoth appears in the prophecy of Isaiah concerning an impending invasion by the Assyrians (Isa. 10:30). Jeremiah was of the priests of Anathoth (Jer. 1:1) and was closely identified with his city (Jer. 29:27); the men of Anathoth opposed him and became the objects of a specific prediction (Jer. 11:21-23). He also foretold good for the city; his redemption of family land there indicated God's assurance for its future (Jer. 32:6ff., esp. vv. 7-9).

Men of Anathoth are listed among the people who returned from the Exile (Ezr. 2:23; Neh. 7:27); these Benjaminites reoccupied the city (Neh. 11:32).

C. E. DEVRIES

ANCESTOR [Heb. *'āḇ*] (Josh. 19:47; Jgs. 18:29); AV FATHER; NEB also FOREFATHER; [Gk. *patḗr*] (He. 7:10); AV FATHER; **ANCESTRAL TRIBE** [Heb. *'āḇôṯ*] (Nu. 1:16, 47); AV TRIBE OF THEIR FATHERS; NEB FATHER'S TRIBE, FATHER'S FAMILY.

Cultural anthropology has provided us information and insight into the ancient (and sometimes primitive) conceptions of the relationship between the living and the dead. These conceptions of the relationship can range from abject fear to reverential awe. Many cultures have "deified" their human ancestors; and at least one known culture has the category of "ancestor" among the deities (the Hittite "former deities").

These insights are valuable for cultural studies in general, but have a limited value for understanding the ancestor in the OT. The ancestors receive frequent mention in the OT (Heb. *'āḇ* is usually rendered "father"), but there is never the hint that they are or should be the object of worship. The scriptural view of God and history precludes such notions about the ancestors. The OT's seeming preoccupation with the earlier generations has a historico-legal basis, viz., the covenantal relationship between Yahweh and His people. The corporate nature of the covenant community is expressed in terms of solidarity within a given generation as well as a oneness with previous generations. One's ancestors were not to be worshiped, but they were not to be forgotten either. It is Yahweh, the God of Abraham, Isaac, and Jacob, the God of one's ancestors/forefathers, with whom each contemporary generation must be personally and covenantally related.

See also CLAN; TOTEMISM.

D. H. ENGELHARD

ANCHOR [Gk. *ángkyra*] (Acts 27:29f., 40; He. 6:19). Every ship carried several anchors, which at successive periods have been made of stone, iron, lead, and perhaps other metals. Each had two flukes and was held by a cable or chain. Stern-anchoring, described in Acts 27:29, was very unusual, but a necessity in the circumstances. In Acts 27:13, "they weighed anchor" translates Gk. *árantes,* from *aírō,* "take up" (AV "loosing thence").

The figurative usage of the word occurs in He. 6:19, where the hope of the gospel is likened to "a sure and steadfast anchor of the soul."

T. NICOL

ANCIENT. This word renders several Hebrew terms: (1) *qeḏem,* denoting the remote past (Dt. 33:15; Isa. 19:11; etc.); (2) *'ôlām,* indicating lengthy duration (Prov. 22:28; Jer. 18:15; Ezk. 36:2; etc.); (3) *'attîq,* a rare word denoting spatial removal (Isa. 28:9) or an ancient tradition (1 Ch. 4:22).

See also ELDER IN THE OT.

ANCIENT OF DAYS [Heb. *'attîq yômîm*; Gk. *palaiós hēmerṓn*]; NEB ANCIENT IN YEARS. In Dnl. 7:7-22, the venerable judge who presided as the books were opened. Heb. *'attîq,* "of ancient tradition," means "aged," as with Ugar. *ab šnm* ("father of years"). The title alternated with "Most High" (7:18-27) and appears to depict God enthroned in judgment over the great world empires.

R. K. H.

AND IF. Archaic for "if" (Gk. *eán*) in the AV, e.g., Mt. 24:48; Jn. 6:62.

ANDREW an'drōō [Gk. *Andreas*–'manly,' or perhaps 'mighty one,' 'conqueror']. The first called of the twelve apostles.

I. In the NT.*–A. Early History and First Call.* Andrew belonged to Bethsaida of Galilee (cf. Jn. 1:44). He was the brother of Simon Peter and his father's name was John (cf. Jn. 1:42; 21:15-17). He occupies a more prominent place in the Gospel of John than in the Synoptics, and this is explicable at least in part in that Andrew was Greek both in language and sympathies (see below), and that his subsequent labors were intimately connected with the people for whom John was immediately writing.

There are three stages in the call of Andrew to apostleship. The first is described in Jn. 1:35-40. Andrew had spent his earlier years as a fisherman on the Sea of Galilee, but on learning of the fame of John the Baptist, he departed along with a band of his countrymen to Bethany (AV Bethabara) beyond Jordan, where John was baptizing (1:28). Possibly Jesus was of their number, or had preceded them in their pilgrimage. There Andrew learned for the first time of the greatness of the "Lamb of God" and "followed him" (v. 40). He was the means at this time of bringing his brother Simon Peter also to Christ (v. 41).

Andrew was probably a companion of Jesus on his return journey to Galilee, and was thus present at the wedding in Cana (Jn. 2:2), in Capernaum (v. 12), at the Passover in Jerusalem (v. 13), at the baptizing in Judea (3:22), where he himself may have taken part (cf. 4:2), and in Samaria (4:5).

B. Second Call and Final Ordination. On his return to Galilee, Andrew resumed for a time his old vocation as fisherman, till he received his second call. This happened after John the Baptist was cast into prison (cf. Mk. 1:14; Mt. 4:12) and is described in Mk. 1:16-18; Mt. 4:18f. The two accounts are practically identical, and tell how Andrew and his brother were now called on definitely to forsake their mundane occupations and become "fishers of men" (Mk. 1:17). The corresponding narrative of Luke varies in part; it does not mention Andrew by name, and gives the additional detail of the miraculous draught of fishes. By some it has been regarded as an amalgamation of Mark's account with Jn. 21:1-8.

After a period of companionship with Jesus, during which, in the house of Simon and Andrew, Simon's wife's mother was healed of a fever (Mk. 1:29-31; cf. Mt. 8:14f.; Lk. 4:38f.), the call of Andrew was finally consecrated by his election as one of the twelve apostles (Mt. 10:2; Mk. 3:18; Lk. 6:14; Acts 1:13).

C. Subsequent History. Further incidents recorded of Andrew are: At the feeding of the five thousand by the Sea of Galilee, the attention of Jesus was drawn to the lad with five barley loaves and two fishes (Jn. 6:8f.). At the feast of the Passover, the Greeks who wished to "see Jesus" inquired of Philip, who turned for advice to Andrew, and the two then told Jesus (Jn. 12:20-36). On the Mt. of Olives, Andrew along with Peter, James and John, questioned Jesus regarding the destruction of Jerusalem and the end of the world (Mk. 13:3-23; cf. also Mt. 24:3-28; Lk. 21:5-24).

II. In Apocryphal Literature.–The name of Andrew's mother was traditionally Joanna; and according to the "Genealogies of the Twelve Apostles" (E. A. Wallis Budge, *Contendings of the Apostles* [1901], II, 49) he belonged to the tribe of Reuben. A fragment of a Coptic gospel of the 4th or 5th cent. tells how not only Thomas (Jn. 20:27), but also Andrew was compelled, by touching the feet of the risen Savior, to believe in the bodily resurrection (H-S, I, 197). Various places were assigned as the scene of his subsequent missionary labors. The Syriac *Doctrine of the Apostles* (ed. W. Cureton, *Ancient Syrian Documents* [repr. 1967], p. 34) mentions Bithynia, Eusebius gives Scythia (*HE* iii.1.1), and others Greece. The Muratorian Fragment relates that John wrote his Gospel in consequence of a revelation given to Andrew, and this would point to Ephesus (cf. H-S, I, 43).

The *Contendings of the Twelve Apostles* contains several parts dealing with Andrew: (1) The "Preaching of Andrew and Philemon among the Kurds" (Budge, II, 163ff.) narrates the appearance of the risen Christ to His disciples, the sending of Andrew to Lydia, and his conversion of the people there. (2) The "Preaching of Matthias in the City of the Cannibals" (Budge, II, 267ff.) tells of how Matthias, on being imprisoned and blinded by the cannibals, was released by Andrew, who had been brought to his assistance in a ship by Christ; but the two were afterward again imprisoned. Matthias then caused the city to be inundated, the disciples were set free, and the people converted. (3) The "Acts of Andrew and Bartholomew" (Budge, II, 183ff.) gives an account of their mission among the Parthians. (4) According to the "Martyrdom of Andrew" (Budge, II, 215) he was stoned and crucified in Scythia.

In the surviving fragments of the "Acts of Andrew," a heretical work dating probably from the 2nd cent., and referred to by Eusebius (*HE* iii.2.5), the scene of Andrew's death was laid in Achaia. There he was imprisoned and crucified by order of the proconsul Eges (or Aegeates), whose wife had been estranged from him by the preaching of Andrew (cf. H-S, II, 416-423).

The relics of Andrew were discovered in Constantinople in the time of Justinian, and part of his cross is now in St. Peter's, Rome. St. Andrew is the patron saint of Scotland; his arm is said to have been transferred there by St. Regulus. The ascription to him of the decussate cross is of late origin.

See also Acts of Andrew under APOCRYPHAL ACTS.

III. Character.–There is something significant in Andrew's being the first called of the apostles. The choice was an important one, for the action of the others depended upon the lead given by Andrew. Christ perceived that the soul's unrest, the straining after higher things and a deeper knowledge of God, which had induced Andrew to make the pilgrimage to Bethany, gave promise of a rich spiritual growth, which no doubt influenced Him in His decision. His wisdom and insight were justified by the results. Along with a keenness of perception regarding spiritual truths was coupled in Andrew a strong sense of personal conviction, which enabled him not only to accept Jesus as the Messiah, but to win Peter also as a disciple of Christ.

The incident of the feeding of five thousand displayed Andrew in a fresh aspect: there the practical part which he played formed a striking contrast to the simplemindedness of Philip (Jn. 6:5ff.). Both these traits—his missionary spirit, and his decision of character which made others appeal to him when in difficulties—were evinced at the time when the Greeks sought to interview Jesus. Andrew was not one of the greatest of the apostles, yet he is typical of those men of broad sympathies and sound common sense without whom the success of any great movement cannot be assured.

See P. M. Peterson, *Andrew, Brother of Simon Peter* (1958).

C. M. KERR

ANDRONICUS an-dron'i-kəs [Gk. *Andronikos*].

1. A deputy of Antiochus Epiphanes who, while ruling at Antioch, excited the Jews by the murder of Onias, and upon their formal complaint was executed by his superior (2 Macc. 4:32-38).

2. Generally distinguished from **1,** another officer of the same name, also under Antiochus (2 Macc. 5:23).

3. A kinsman of Paul, residing at Rome (Rom. 16:7). He had been converted to Christianity before Paul, and like Paul had suffered imprisonment, although when and where can only be surmised. When he and Junias, another kinsman of Paul, are referred to as "of note among the apostles," this may be interpreted either as designating the high esteem in which they were held by the Twelve, or as reckoning them in the number of apostles. The latter is the sense, if "apostle" be understood here in the more general meaning, used in Acts 14:14 of Barnabas, in 2 Cor. 8:23 of Titus, in Phil. 2:25 of Epaphroditus, and in the Didache of "the traveling evangelists or missionaries who preached the gospel from place to place." On this assumption, Andronicus was one of the most prominent and successful of the traveling missionaries of the early Church.

H. E. JACOBS

ANEM ā'nəm [Heb. *'ānēm*–'two springs'; Gk. *Anam*]. A place mentioned with Ramoth among the cities of Issachar assigned to the Gershomite Levites (1 Ch. 6:73). In the parallel list (Josh. 21:29) are mentioned Jarmuth and En-gannim, corresponding to Ramoth and Anem; therefore Anem and En-gannim (Jenîn) may be identical. As the names denote (En-gannim="the spring of gardens"), it was well watered. *WHAB* suggests 'Olam, about 7 mi. (11 km.) E of Mt. Tabor, as its location.

ANER ā'nər [Heb. *'ānēr*; Sam. *'anrām*–'spout, waterfall'; Gk. *Aunan*]. One of the three "confederates" of Abraham in his pursuit after the four kings (Gen. 14:13, 24). Of the two other names, Mamre is the name of the sacred grove or tree and synonymous with Hebron, and Eshcol is the name of a valley (lit. "grape cluster"); thus Aner may perhaps be explained in a similar way. Dillmann suggested a range of mountains in that vicinity (comm. *in loc.*). S. COHON

ANER ā'nər [Heb. *'ānēr*]. A Levitical town in Manasseh W of the Jordan (1 Ch. 6:70 [MT 55]). Gesenius and others identified it with Taanach of Josh. 21:25, reading *ta'ᵃnaḵ* for *'ānēr*. There is, however, no agreement as to its location.

ANETHOTHITE an'ə-thoth-īt (2 S. 23:27, AV); **ANETOTHITE** an'ə-toth-īt (1 Ch. 27:12, AV). *See* ANATHOTH.

ANEW [Gk. *ánōthen*] (Jn. 3:3, 7); AV AGAIN; NEB OVER AGAIN; [Gk. *ana-* (in *anagennáō*–'cause to be born again')] (1 Pet. 1:3, 23); AV AGAIN; NEB also "new."

In Jn. 3:3, 7, the story of Jesus and Nicodemus, the important question is whether Gk. *ánōthen* here means "again" or "from above." While the English versions take it in the former sense, the other is possible, and not without support. Indeed, elsewhere in John *ánōthen* clearly means "from above" (3:31; 19:11, 23). Büchsel (*TDNT*, I, *s.v.*) argues strongly for this meaning, pointing out that John "always describes birth in terms of its origin, i.e., of God (1:13; 1 Jn. 2:29; 3:9; 4:7; 5:18), of the Spirit or flesh (3:6), of water and the Spirit (3:5)." In making his case he appeals also to a possible underlying Hebrew or Aramaic (on this see SB, II, 420f.), to ecclesiastical tradition, to a connection with Job 3:4, and to the psychology of the story.

In Bauer (p. 76) it is suggested that the usage is purposely ambiguous; Büchsel considers such an interpretation "both superfluous and unprovable," but Leon Morris (*NIC* [1971], *in loc.*) argues well for it, quoting Barclay's translation "reborn from above." (Morris also notes that in any case "anew" is preferable to "again.")

Those who argue for "anew" as the unambiguous meaning include Calvin and Westcott; but few modern commentators deny that the meaning "from above" is present at least in part. In all events, it is clearly a "new birth" that Jesus is talking about, whatever the connotations of *ánōthen*. That new birth is spoken of also by Peter (1 Pet. 1:3, 23), using a much less ambiguous word.

See also REGENERATION. J. W. D. H.

ANGEL [Heb. *mal'āḵ*; Gk. *ángelos*–'messenger'].

I. Definition and Terms
II. In the OT
  A. Nature, Appearances, and Functions
  B. Angelic Host
  C. Angel of the Theophany
III. In the NT
  A. Appearances
  B. Teaching of Jesus
  C. Other NT References
IV. Development of the Doctrine
V. Reality of Angels

I. Definition and Terms.–The word angel is applied in Scripture to an order of supernatural or heavenly beings whose function it is to act as God's messengers to men, and as agents who carry out His will. Both in Hebrew and Greek the word is also applied to human messengers (1 K. 19:2; Lk. 7:24); in Hebrew it is used in the singular to denote a divine messenger, and in the plural for human messengers, although there are exceptions to both usages. It is applied to the prophet Haggai (Hag. 1:13), to the priest (Mal. 2:7), and to the messenger who is to prepare the way of the Lord (Mal. 3:1).

Fresco of an angel in one of the Cappadocian "dark churches" at Göreme, Turkey. Pictured below are Christ with "Mary the Mother of God" (left) and the apostle John (right). (B. K. Condit)

Other Hebrew words and phrases applied to angels are *bᵉne ha'ᵉlōhîm* (Gen. 6:2, 4; Job 1:6; 2:1) and *bᵉne 'ēlîm* (Ps. 29:1; 89:6), i.e., sons of the *'ᵉlōhîm* or *'ēlîm*; this means, according to a common Hebrew usage, members of the class called *'ᵉlōhîm* or *'ēlîm,* the heavenly powers. It seems doubtful whether *'ᵉlōhîm,* standing by itself, is ever used to designate angels, although the LXX so translates it in a few passages. The most notable instance is Ps. 8:5, where the RSV reads, "Thou hast made him little less than God," while the AV has "the angels" for "God" (cf. He. 2:7, 9). Other terms are *qᵉḏōšîm,* "holy ones" (Ps. 89:5, 7), a name suggesting that they belong to God; and Aram. *'îr, 'îrîm,* "watcher," "watchers" (Dnl. 4:13, 17, 23). Still other expressions are used to designate angels collectively: *sôḏ,* "council" (Ps. 89:7), where the reference may be to an inner group of exalted angels; *'ēḏâ* and *qāhāl,* "congregation" (Ps. 82:1; 89:5); and finally *ṣāḇā', ṣᵉḇā'ôṯ,* "host," "hosts," as in the familiar phrase "the God of hosts."

In the NT the Gk. *ángelos,* when it refers to a divine messenger, is frequently accompanied by some phrase that makes this meaning clear, e.g., "the angels of heaven" (Mt. 24:36). Angels belong to the "heavenly host" (Lk. 2:13). In reference to their nature they are called "spirits" (He. 1:14).

Paul evidently referred to the ordered ranks of supramundane beings by a group of words that are found in various combinations, viz., *archaí,* "principalities," *exousíai,* "powers," *thrónoi,* "thrones," *kyriótētes,* "dominions," and *dynámeis,* also translated "powers." The first four are apparently used in a good sense in Col. 1:16, where it is said that all these beings were created through Christ and unto Him; in most of the other passages in which words from this group occur, they seem to represent *evil* powers. We are told that our wrestling is against them (Eph. 6:12), and that Christ triumphs over the principalities and powers (Col. 2:15; cf. Rom. 8:38; 1 Cor. 15:24). In two passages the word *archángelos,* "archangel" or chief angel, occurs: "the voice of the archangel" (1 Thess. 4:16), and "Michael the archangel" (Jude 9).

II. In the OT.–*A. Nature, Appearances, and Functions.* Everywhere in the OT the existence of angels is assumed. The creation of angels is referred to in Ps. 148:2, 5 (cf. Col. 1:16). They were present at the creation of the world, and were so filled with wonder and gladness that they "shouted for joy" (Job 38:7). Of their nature we are told nothing. In general they are simply regarded as embodiments of their mission. Though presumably the holiest of created beings, they are charged by God with folly (Job 4:18), and we are told that He "puts no trust in his holy ones" (Job 15:15). References to the fall of the angels are found only in the obscure and probably corrupt passage Gen. 6:1-4, and in the interdependent passages 2 Pet. 2:4 and Jude 6, which draw their inspiration from the pseudepigraphical 1 Enoch. Demons are mentioned (*see* DEMON); and although Satan appears among the sons of God (Job 1:6; 2:1), there is a growing tendency in later writers to attribute to him a malignity that is all his own (*see* SATAN).

As to their outward appearance, it is evident that they bore the human form, and could at times be mistaken for men (Ezk. 9:2; Gen. 18:2,16). There is no hint that they ever appeared in female form. The conception of angels as winged beings, so familiar in Christian art, finds no support in Scripture (except, perhaps, Dnl. 9:21; Rev. 14:6, where angels are represented as "flying"). The CHERUBIM and SERAPHIM are represented as winged (Ex. 25:20; Isa. 6:2); winged also are the symbolic living creatures of Ezk. 1:6 (cf. Rev. 4:8).

As stated above, angels are messengers and instruments of the divine will. As a rule they exercise no influence in the physical sphere. In several instances, however, they are represented as destroying angels: two angels are commissioned to destroy Sodom (Gen. 19:13); when David numbers the people, an angel destroys them by pestilence (2 S. 24:16); it is by an angel that the Assyrian army is destroyed (2 K. 19:35); and Ezekiel hears six angels receiving the command to destroy those who were sinful in Jerusalem (Ezk. 9:1, 5, 7). In this connection should be noted the expression "angels of evil," i.e., angels that bring evil upon men from God and execute His judgments (Ps. 78:49; cf. 1 S. 16:14).

Angels appear to Jacob in dreams (Gen. 28:12; 31:11). The angel who meets Balaam is visible first to the ass, and not to the rider (Nu. 22:22ff.). Angels interpret God's will, showing man what is right for him (Job 33:23). The idea of angels as caring for men also appears (Ps. 91:11f.), although the modern conception of the possession by each man of a special guardian angel is not found in the OT.

B. Angelic Host. The phrase "the host of heaven" is applied to the stars, which were sometimes worshiped by idolatrous Jews (Jer. 33:22; 2 K. 21:3; Zeph. 1:5); the name is applied to the company of angels because of their countless numbers (cf. Dnl. 7:10) and their glory. They are represented as standing on the right and left hand of the Lord (1 K. 22:19). Hence God, who is over them all, is continually called throughout the OT "the God of hosts," "the Lord of hosts," "the Lord God of hosts"; and once "the Prince of the host" (Dnl. 8:11).

One of the principal functions of the heavenly host is to be ever praising the name of the Lord (Ps. 103:21; 148:1f.). In this host there are certain figures that stand out prominently, and some of them are named. The angel who appears to Joshua calls himself "commander of the army of the Lord" (Josh. 5:14f.). The glorious angel who interprets to Daniel the vision that he saw in the third year of Cyrus (Dnl. 10:5), like the angel who interprets the vision in the first year of Belshazzar (Dnl. 7:16), is not named; but other visions of the same prophet were explained to him by the angel Gabriel, who is called "the man Gabriel," and is described as speaking with "a man's voice" (Dnl. 9:21; 8:15f.). In Daniel we find occasional reference made to "princes": "the prince of Persia," "the prince of Greece" (10:20). These are angels to whom is entrusted the charge of, and possibly the rule over, certain peoples. Most notable among them is Michael, described as "one of the chief princes," "the great prince who has charge of your people," and, more briefly, "your prince" (Dnl. 10:13; 12:1; 10:21); Michael is therefore regarded as the patron-angel of the Jews.

In the Apocrypha Raphael, Uriel, and Jeremiel are also named. Of Raphael it is said that he is "one of the seven holy angels who present the prayers of the saints" to God (Tob. 12:15; cf. Rev. 8:2, "the seven angels who stand before God"). It is possible that this group of seven is referred to in the above-quoted phrase, "one of the chief princes."

Some (notably Kosters) have maintained that the expressions "the sons of the *'ᵉlōhîm,*" God's "council," and "congregation" refer to the ancient gods of the heathen, now degraded and wholly subordinated to Yahweh. This rather daring speculation has little support in Scripture; but we find traces of a belief that the patron-angels of the nations have failed in establishing righteousness within their allotted sphere on earth, and that they will accordingly be punished by Yahweh their Sovereign (Isa. 24:21f.; Ps. 82; cf. Ps. 58:1f., RSV; cf. Jude 6).

C. Angel of the Theophany. This angel is spoken of as "the angel of the Lord," and "the angel of the presence [or face] of the Lord." The following passages contain references to this angel: Gen. 16:7ff.—the angel and Hagar; Gen. 18—Abraham intercedes with the angel for Sodom; Gen. 22:11ff.—the angel interposes to prevent the sacrifice of Isaac; Gen. 24:7,40—Abraham sends Eliezer and promises him the angel's protection; Gen. 31:11ff.—the angel who appears to Jacob says, "I am the God of Bethel"; Gen. 32:24ff.—Jacob wrestles with the angel and says, "I have seen God face to face"; Gen. 48:15f.—Jacob speaks of God and the angel as identical; Ex. 3 (cf. Acts 7:30ff.)—the angel appears to Moses in the burning bush; Ex. 13:21; 14:19 (cf. Nu. 20:16)—God or the angel leads Israel out of Egypt; Ex. 23:20ff.—the people are commanded to obey the angel; Ex. 32:34–33:17 (cf. Isa. 63:9)—Moses pleads for the presence of God with His people; Josh. 5:13–6:2—the angel appears to Joshua; Jgs. 2:1-5—the angel speaks to the people; Jgs. 6:11ff.—the angel appears to Gideon.

A study of these passages shows that while the angel and Yahweh are at times distinguished from each other, they are with equal frequency, and in the same passages, merged into each other. How is this to be explained? It is obvious that these apparitions cannot be the Almighty Himself, whom no man has seen, or can see. In seeking the explanation, special attention should be paid to two of the passages cited above. In Ex. 23:20ff. God promises to send an angel before His people to lead them to the Promised Land; they are commanded to obey him and not to provoke him, "for he will not pardon your transgression; for my name is in him." Thus the angel can forgive sin, which only God can do, because God's name, i.e., His character and thus His authority, are in the angel. Further, in the passage Ex. 32:34–33:17 Moses intercedes for the people after their first breach of the covenant; God responds by promising, "behold, my angel shall go before you"; and immediately after God says, "I will not go up among you." In answer to further pleading, God says, "My presence will go with you, and I will give you rest." Here a clear distinction is made between an ordinary angel and the angel who carries with him God's presence. The conclusion may be summed up in the words of A. B. Davidson in his *OT Theology* (1904): "In particular providences one may trace the presence of Jehovah in influence and operation; in ordinary angelic appearances one may discover Jehovah present on some side of His being, in some attribute of His character; in the angel of the Lord He is fully present as the covenant God of His people, to redeem them."

The question still remains, Who is the theophanic angel? To this many answers have been given, of which the following may be mentioned: (1) This angel is simply an angel with a special commission; (2) he may be a momentary descent of God into visibility; (3) he may be the Logos, a kind of temporary preincarnation of the second person of the trinity. Each has its difficulties, but the last is certainly the most tempting to the mind. Yet it must be remembered that at best these are only conjectures that touch on a great mystery. It is certain that from the beginning God used angels in human form, with human voices, in order to communicate with man; and the appearances of the angel of the Lord, with his special redemptive relation to God's people, show the working of that divine mode of self-revelation which culminated in the coming of the Savior, and are thus a foreshadowing of, and a preparation for, the full revelation of God in Jesus Christ. Further than this it is not safe to go.

***III. In the NT.–A.** Appearances.* Nothing that is related of angels in the NT is inconsistent with the teaching of the OT on the subject. Just as they are specially active in the beginning of OT history, when God's people is being born, so they appear frequently in connection with the birth of Jesus, and again when a new order begins with the Resurrection. An angel appears three times in dreams to Joseph (Mt. 1:20; 2:13,19). The angel Gabriel appears to Zechariah, and then to Mary in the annunciation (Lk.1). An angel announces to the shepherds the birth of Jesus, and is joined by a "multitude of the heavenly host," praising God in celestial song (Lk. 2:8ff.). When Jesus is tempted, and again during the agony at Gethsemane, angels appear to Him to strengthen His soul (Mt. 4:11; Lk. 22:43). The verse that tells how an angel came down to trouble the pool (Jn. 5:4) is now omitted from the text as not being genuine. An angel descends to roll away the stone from the tomb of

Jesus (Mt. 28:2); angels are seen there by certain women (Lk. 24:23) and (two) by Mary Magdalene (Jn. 20:12).

An angel releases the apostles from prison, directs Philip, appears to Peter in a dream, frees him from prison, smites Herod with sickness, appears to Paul in a dream (Acts 5:19; 8:26; 10:3; 12:7ff.; 12:23; 27:23). Once angels appear clothed in white; they are so dazzling in appearances as to terrify beholders; hence they begin their message with the words "Fear not" (Mt. 28:2-5).

B. Teaching of Jesus. It is quite certain that Our Lord accepted the main teachings of the OT about angels, as well as the later Jewish belief in good and bad angels. He speaks of the "angels in heaven" (Mt. 22:30), and of "the devil and his angels" (Mt. 25:41). According to Our Lord the angels of God are holy (Mk. 8:38); they have no sex or sensuous desires (Mt. 22:30); they have high intelligence, but they know not the time of the Parousia (Mt. 24:36); they carry (in a parable) the soul of Lazarus to Abraham's bosom (Lk. 16:22); they could have been summoned to the aid of Our Lord, had He so desired (Mt. 26:53); they will accompany Him at the Parousia (Mt. 25:31) and separate the righteous from the wicked (Mt. 13:41, 49).

They watch with sympathetic eyes the fortunes of men, rejoicing in the repentance of a sinner (Lk. 15:10; cf. 1 Pet. 1:12; Eph. 3:10; 1 Cor. 4:9); and they will hear the Son of man confessing or denying those who have confessed or denied Him before men (Lk. 12:8f.). The angels of the presence of God, who do not appear to correspond to our conception of guardian angels, are specially interested in God's little ones (Mt. 18:10). Finally, the existence of angels is implied in the Lord's Prayer in the petition, "Thy will be done, /On earth as it is in heaven" (Mt. 6:10).

C. Other NT References. Paul refers to the ranks of angels ("principalities, powers," etc.) only in order to emphasize the complete supremacy of Jesus Christ. He teaches that angels will be judged by the saints (1 Cor. 6:3). He attacks the incipient Gnosticism of Asia Minor by forbidding the worship of angels (Col. 2:18). He speaks of God's angels as "elect," because they are included in the counsels of divine love (1 Tim. 5:21). When Paul commands the women to keep their heads covered in church because of the angels (1 Cor. 11:10) he may mean that the angels, who watch all human affairs with deep interest, would be pained to see any infraction of the laws of modesty.

In He. 1:14 angels are described as ministering spirits engaged in the service of the saints. Peter also emphasizes the supremacy of Our Lord over all angelic beings (1 Pet. 3:22). The reference to angels in 2 Peter and Jude are colored by contact with pseudepigraphical literature.

In Revelation, where the references are obviously symbolic, there is very frequent mention of angels. The angels of the seven churches (1:20) are the guardian angels or the personifications of these churches. The worship of angels is also forbidden (22:8f.). Of special interest is the mention of elemental angels — "the angel of water" (16:5), and the angel "who has power over fire" (14:18; cf. 7:1; 19:17). Reference is also made to the "angel of the bottomless pit," who is called ABADDON or Apollyon, evidently an evil angel (9:11). In 12:7ff. we are told that there was war between Michael with his angels and the dragon with his angels.

IV. Development of the Doctrine.–In the childhood of the race it was easy to believe in God, and He was very near to the soul. In Paradise there is no thought of angels; it is God Himself who walks in the garden. A little later the thought of angels appears; but God has not gone away, and as "the angel of the Lord" He appears to his people and redeems them. In these early times the Jews believed that there were multitudes of angels, not yet divided in thought into good and bad; these had no names or personal characteristics, but were simply embodied messages.

Till the time of the Captivity the Jewish angelology shows little development. During the dark period they came into close contact with a polytheistic people, only to be more deeply confirmed in their monotheism thereby. They also became acquainted with the purer faith of the Persians, and in all probability viewed the tenets of Zoroastrianism with a more favorable eye, because of the great kindness of Cyrus to their nation. There are few direct traces of Zoroastrianism in the later angelology of the OT. It is not even certain that the number seven as applied to the highest group of angels is Persian in origin; the number seven was not wholly disregarded by the Jews. One result of the contact was that the idea of a hierarchy of the angels was more fully developed. The conception in Daniel of angels as "watchers," and the idea of patron-princes or angel-guardians of nations may be ascribed to Persian influence. It is probable that contact with the Persians helped the Jews to develop ideas already latent in their minds. According to Jewish tradition, the names of the angels came from Babylon. By this time the consciousness of sin had grown more intense in the Jewish mind, and God had receded to an immeasurable distance; the angels helped to fill the gap between God and man.

The more elaborate conceptions of Daniel and Zechariah are futher developed in the Apocrypha, especially in 2 Esdras, Tobit, and 2 Maccabees.

In the NT we find that there is little further development; and by the Spirit of God its writers were saved from the fanciful teachings of contemporary Rabbinism. We find that the Sadducees, as contrasted with the Pharisees, did not believe in angels or spirits (Acts 23:8). We may conclude that the Sadducees, with their materialistic standpoint and denial of the resurrection, regarded angels merely as symbolical expressions of God's actions. The book of Revelation naturally shows a close kinship to Ezekiel and Daniel.

Regarding the rabbinical developments of angelology, some beautiful, some extravagant, some grotesque, but all fanciful, it is not necessary here to speak. The Essenes held an esoteric doctrine of angels, in which most scholars find the germ of the gnostic aeons.

V. Reality of Angels.–A belief in angels, if not indispensable to the faith of a Christian, has its place there. In such a belief there is nothing unnatural or contrary to reason. Indeed, the warm welcome human nature has always given to this thought is an argument in its favor. Why should there not be such an order of beings, if God so willed it?

For the Christian the whole question turns on the weight to be attached to the words of Our Lord. All are agreed that He teaches the existence, reality, and activity of angelic beings. Was He in error because of His human limitations? That is a conclusion which it is very hard for the Christian to draw, and we may set it aside. Did He then adjust His teaching to popular belief, knowing that what He said was not true? This explanation would seem to impute deliberate untruth to Our Lord, and must equally be set aside. So we find ourselves restricted to the conclusion that we have the guarantee of Christ's word for the existence of angels; for most Christians that will settle the question.

The visible activity of angels has come to an end, because their mediating work is done; Christ has founded the kingdom of the Spirit, and God's Spirit speaks directly to the spirit of man. This new and living way has been opened up to us by Jesus Christ, upon whom faith can yet behold the angels of God ascending and descending. Still they watch the lot of man, and rejoice in his salvation; still they join in the praise and adoration of God, the Lord of hosts; still can they be regarded as "ministering spirits sent forth to serve for the sake of those who are to obtain salvation" (He. 1:14); still they shall accompany Christ at His coming.

Bibliography.–All OT and NT theologies contain discussions. The ablest supporter of the theory that the "sons of the Elohim" are degraded gods is Kosters, *Theologisch Tijdschrift*, 10 (1876). For Jewish beliefs see also *LTJM*, II, appendix xiii, and Bousset-Gressmann, 320-331. Among more recent articles cf. E. Bishop, *ATR*, 46 (1964), 142-154; G. Cooke, *ZAW*, 76 (1964), 22-47; M. Takahashi, *ZAW*, 78 (1966), 343-350; R. North, *CBQ*, 29 (1967), 419-449.

J. M. WILSON

ANGELS OF THE SEVEN CHURCHES. It is evident from the contexts of the various biblical passages in which the word "angel" appears that the word does not always represent the same idea. In such passages as Dnl. 12:1 and Acts 12:15 it would seem that the angel was generally regarded as a superhuman being whose duty it was to guard a nation or an individual, not unlike the *jenei* of the Arabs. However, in Mal. 2:7 and 3:1 the Heb. *mal'āḵ* is clearly used to represent men. In the NT also there are passages, such as Jas. 2:25, in which the Gk. *ángelos* is applied to men.

The seven angels of the seven churches (Rev. 1:20) received seven figurative letters, and therefore it would seem that the seven angels are also figurative. They may refer to the seven bishops who presided over the seven churches of Asia, or else the angels may be regarded as the personifications of the churches. E. J. BANKS

ANGER. The commonest Hebrew term is *'ap*, denoting either divine or human anger. The term means "nostril," which was thought of as the locale of anger. The related word *'ānap*, however, is used only of divine anger. The quickening of anger is described by the verb *ḥārâ*, "burn" (Nu. 22:27; Jonah 4:1), and the phrase *ḥarôn 'ap* is also restricted to God's anger (Ex. 32:12). Other common Hebrew synonyms include *za'am*, "indignation" (Jer. 15:17); *zā'ap*, "be enraged" (2 Ch. 26:19); *kā'as*, "be angry," "be irritated" (1 S. 1:6); and *'eḇrâ*, "boiling rage" (Est. 1:12).

In the LXX, Gk. *thymós*, *orgḗ*, or their derivatives were used indiscriminately to render the Hebrew terms, a pattern followed in the NT. In the RSV *thymós* is always rendered "wrath," whereas *orgḗ* can be either "anger" or "wrath." *See also* WRATH. R. K. H.

ANGLE (Isa. 19:8; Hab. 1:15). *See* FISHING; HOOK.

ANGLE, THE [Heb. *hammiqṣô(a)'*]; AV "the turning of the wall"; NEB ESCARPMENT. One segment of the Jerusalem ramparts, apparently located near the palace and fortified by Uzziah (2 Ch. 26:9). It was restored in the time of Nehemiah (Neh. 3:19f., 24f.).

ANGLO-SAXON VERSIONS. *See* ENGLISH VERSIONS.

ANGUISH [Heb. *ḥîl*, *ḥûl* (Dt. 2:25; Ps. 48:6; 55:4; Isa. 13:8; 23:5; Jer. 5:3; Joel 2:6; Zec. 9:5), *šāḇāṣ* (2 S. 1:9), *ṣar* (Job 7:11), *mᵉṣûqâ* (Job 15:24; Zeph. 1:15), *ḥēḇel* (Ps. 116:3), *māṣôq* (Ps. 119:143), *ṣûqâ* (Prov. 1:27; Isa. 8:22; 30:6), *mûṣāq* (Isa. 9:1 [MT 8:23]), *ḥalḥālâ* (Isa. 21:3; Ezk. 30:4; Nah. 2:10), *šēḇer* (Isa. 65:14), *mē'eh* (Jer. 4:19), *ṣārâ* (Jer. 4:31; 6:24; 49:24; 50:43), *'îr* (Jer. 15:8), *qᵉpāḏâ* (Ezk. 7:25); Aram. *'ᵃṣîḇ* (Dnl. 6:20); Gk. *odynáomai* (Lk. 16:24f.), *odýnē* (Rom. 9:2), *thlípsis* (Jn. 16:21), *synochḗ* (2 Cor. 2:4), *basanízō* (Rev. 12:2), *pónos* (Rev. 16:10)]; AV also PAIN, SORE PAINED (Ps. 55:4), SORROW, VEXATION, BOWELS (Jer. 4:19), etc.; NEB also TREMBLE, PAIN, "(refuse to) learn" (Jer. 5:3), TERROR, "throes of death" (2 S. 1:9), etc.

All of these terms denote extreme distress of mind or spirit. The Heb. *'îr* (Jer. 15:8) is rendered by the AV with its first meaning of "city," while the RSV and NEB render its second meaning with "anguish" and "terror" respectively. The term *mē'eh* (RSV "anguish," Jer. 4:9) refers to the internal organs which are viewed as the seat of the emotions, thus the source of anguish. The Hebrew verb *ḥîl* means "be in labor," or writhe with the sort of pain a woman experiences in childbirth.

In some instances anguish is associated with suffering caused by political involvements or anticipation of unhappy circumstances (Isa. 23:5; 30:6; Jer. 15:8; Zec. 9:5; Dt. 2:25); sometimes it is associated with the dreaded darkness, particularly that anticipated on the Day of the Lord (Prov. 1:27; Isa. 9:1; 8:22; Zeph. 1:5). The Greek verb *odynáomai* is associated particularly with the torment of flames in hell (Lk. 16:24f.). J. R. PRICE

ANIAM ə-nī'nim [Heb. *'ᵃnî'am*–'lament of the people']. A son of Shemidah of Manasseh (1 Ch. 7:19).

ANIM ā'nim [Heb. *'ānîm*–'springs']. One of the cities of the hill country of Judah mentioned immediately after Eshtemoh (Josh. 15:50). The Amarna Letters refer to the city as Ḫawini, while Eusebius (*Onom.* 26.9) calls it Anaia, "a very large village of Jews . . . , 9 [Roman] miles south of Hebron." It is probably Khirbet Ghuwein et-Taḥtā, 2.5 mi. (4 km.) S of es-Semû' (Eshtemoa), 13 mi. (21 km.) S of Hebron.

See *GP*, II, 244.

ANIMAL. *See* ZOOLOGY, and individual entries.

ANISE. *See* DILL.

ANKLET [Heb. *'eḵes*; Gk. *himatismós*] (Isa. 3:18); AV "tinkling ornaments about their feet." Part of the finery of the apostate women of Jerusalem in Isaiah's prophecy. Probably the "tinkling with their feet" in Isa. 3:16 refers to these anklets; part of the punishment threatened was the removal of these luxurious ornaments. Numerous bronze anklets measuring between 2½ and 4½ in. (6 and 11 cm.) in diameter have been recovered from graves at Lachish.

R. K. H.

ANNA an'ə [Gk. *Hanna* <Heb. *ḥannâ*–'grace' (cf. 1 S. 1:2)].

1. The wife of Tobit (Tob. 1:9, 20, etc.). The NEB follows Codex Sinaiticus in 1:9, which reads, "I took a wife from our kindred," omitting the name.

2. A "prophetess," daughter of Phanuel, of the tribe of Asher, and thus a Galilean, living in Jerusalem at the time of Jesus' birth (Lk. 2:36-38). "Of a great age," she must have been considerably over a hundred years, having been a widow eighty-four years after a short married life of seven. Exceptionally devout and gifted in spirit, she worshiped so constantly "with fasting and prayer night and day," that it is said she "did not depart from the temple." Some have mistakenly supposed that this signified permanent residence in the temple.

That her lineage is recorded indicates the distinction of her family. Tradition says that the tribe of Asher was noted for the beauty and talent of its women, who, for these gifts, were qualified for royal and high-priestly marriage. While the tribe of Asher was not among the tribes that returned from the Babylonian exile to Palestine, many of its chief families must have done so as in the case of the prophetess.

The period of war and national oppression through which Anna's early life was passed created in her, as in the aged SIMEON, an intense longing for the "redemption" promised through the Messiah. This hope of national deliverance sustained her through more than four decades of patient waiting. In the birth of Jesus her faith was abundantly rewarded, and she became a grateful and ceaseless witness, "to all who were looking for the redemption of Jerusalem," that the day of their spiritual deliverance had come.

3. In NT apocryphal writings, notably the Protevangelium of James, the mother of Mary and grandmother of Jesus. *See* APOCRYPHAL GOSPEL II.B.

D. M. PRATT

ANNAAS an'a-əs (1 Esd. 5:23, AV). *See* SENAAH.

ANNAN an'ən [Gk. *Annan,* A *Annas*] (1 Esd. 9:32); AV, NEB, ANNAS. The head of a family who returned from exile with Ezra, called Harim in Ezr. 10:31.

ANNAS an'əs [Gk. *Hannas,* Josephus *Ananos* or *Hananos*<Heb. *ḥānān*–'merciful, gracious' (cf. Neh. 8:7, etc.)].

1. A high priest of the Jews, the virtual head of the priestly party in Jerusalem in the time of Christ. He was a man of commanding influence.

The son of Seth (Josephus "Sethi"), he was elevated to the high-priesthood by Quirinius, governor of Syria, A.D. 7. At this period the office was filled and vacated at the caprice of the Roman procurators, and Annas was deposed by Valerius Gratus, A.D. 15. But though deprived of official status, he continued to wield great power as the dominant member of the hierarchy, using members of his family as his willing instruments.

That he was an adroit diplomat is seen in that five of his sons (Josephus *Ant.* xx.9.1) and his son-in-law Caiaphas (Jn. 18:13) held the high-priesthood in almost unbroken succession, though he did not survive to see the office filled by his fifth son Annas or Ananus II, who caused James the Lord's brother to be stoned to death (*ca.* A.D. 62). Another mark of his continued influence is that long after he had lost his office he was still called "high priest," and his name appears first wherever the names of the chief members of the sacerdotal faction are given. Cf. Acts 4:6, "with Annas the high priest and Caiaphas and John and Alexander, and all who were of the high-priestly family." Annas is almost certainly called high priest in Jn. 18:19, 22, though in vv. 13 and 24 Caiaphas is mentioned as the high priest. Note especially the remarkable phrase in Lk. 3:2, "in the high-priesthood of Annas and Caiaphas," as if they were joint holders of the office. The cases in which Josephus gives the title "high-priest" to persons who no longer held the office afford no real parallel to this. The explanation seems to be that owing to age, ability, and force of character Annas was the virtual, though Caiaphas the titular, high priest.

Annas belonged to the Sadducean aristocracy, and, like others of that class, he seems to have been arrogant, astute, ambitious, and enormously wealthy. He and his family were proverbial for their rapacity and greed. The chief source of their wealth seems to have been the sale of requisites for the temple sacrifices, such as sheep, doves, wine, and oil, which they carried on in the four famous "booths of the sons of Annas" on the Mt. of Olives, with a branch within the precincts of the temple itself. During the great feasts, they were able to extort high monopoly prices for their goods. Hence Our Lord's strong denunciation of those who made the house of prayer "a den of robbers" (Mk. 11:15-19), and the curse in the Talmud, "Woe to the family of Annas! woe to the serpent-like hisses" (*Pesahim* 57a).

As to the part he played in the trial and death of Our Lord, although he does not figure very prominently in the Gospel narratives, he seems to have been mainly responsible for the course of events. Renan's emphatic statement is substantially correct, "Annas was the principal actor in the terrible drama, and far more than Caiaphas, far more than Pilate, ought to bear the weight of the maledictions of mankind" (*Life of Jesus*). Caiaphas, indeed, as actual high priest, was the nominal head of the Sanhedrin which condemned Jesus; but the aged Annas was the ruling spirit. According to Jn. 18:12f., it was to him that the officers who arrested Jesus led Him first. "The reason given for that proceeding ["*for* he was father-in-law of Caiaphas"] lays open alike the character of the man and the character of the trial" (Westcott, *in loc.*). Annas (if he is the high priest of Jn. 18:19-23, as seems most likely) questioned Him concerning His disciples and teaching. This trial is not mentioned by the Synoptists, probably because it was merely informal and preliminary and of a private nature, meant to gather material for the subsequent trial. Failing to elicit anything to his purpose from Jesus, "Annas then sent him bound to Caiaphas the high priest" (Jn. 18:24; the AV "had sent" is incorrect and misleading) for formal trial before the Sanhedrin, "but as one already stamped with a sign of condemnation" (Westcott).

Doubtless Annas was present at the subsequent proceedings, but no further mention is made of him in the NT, except that he was present at the meeting of the Sanhedrin after Pentecost when Peter and John defended themselves for preaching the gospel of the resurrection (Acts 4:6).

2. (1 Esd. 9:32, AV, NEB). *See* ANNAN.

D. M. EDWARDS

ANNIAS a-nī'əs [Gk. B *Anneis,* A *Annias*] (1 Esd. 5:16); AV ANANIAS. A family in the list of the returning exiles, omitted in the parallel lists in Ezra and Nehemiah.

ANNIUTH a-nī'əth [Gk. B *Anniouth,* A *Annous*] (1 Esd. 9:48); AV ANUS; NEB ANNUS. One of the Levites who interpreted the law to the people, listed as Bani in the parallel Neh. 9:48.

ANNUL [Heb. *pārar, kāpar*; Gk. *athetéō, akyróō*]; AV DISANNUL, BREAK; NEB also FRUSTRATE, SET ASIDE, INVALIDATE.

God, as the Supreme Ruler, can annul His covenant for a cause (Isa. 28:18); man, through wilfulness and transgression, as party of the second part, may break the contract and thus release the Lord as party of the first part (Isa. 14:27), though there are some purposes and laws which the Almighty will carry out in spite of ungodly rage and ravings (Gal. 3:15); or an old law or covenant might be conceived as annulled, either by a new one (Gal. 3:17) or simply because it has become obsolete and ineffective (He. 7:18).

For the first idea the Bible employs Heb. *kāpar,* "cover," "expiate," "condone," "cancel," "annul," "put off" (Isa. 28:18); and Gk. *athetéō* (Gal. 3:15), "set aside," "disesteem," "neutralize," "violate," "frustrate." Heb. *pārar,* "break," "make void," is used for the second idea (Isa. 14:27; Zec. 11:10f., 14). One covenant annulling another by "conflict of laws" is expressed by Gk. *akyróō,* "invalidate," "annul," "make of no effect." Gk. *athetéō* is employed also to express annulling through age and disuse (He. 7:18; RSV "set aside").

In Job 40:8, the AV "wilt thou also disannul [*pārar*]

my judgment?" becomes in the RSV, "Will you even put me in the wrong?" and in the NEB, "Dare you deny that I am just . . . ?" F. E. HIRSCH

ANNUNCIATION. The term generally employed for the advance announcement of the conception and birth of Jesus, usually in reference to the angel Gabriel's visit to Mary (Lk. 1:26-38). Joseph also received word (Mt. 1:20f.). In both instances indication is given of the agency of the Holy Spirit in the conception of the child and of the name to be given to Him. His mission is stated to Joseph in terms of redemption from sin, to Mary in terms of His kingly role.

Similarly, the birth of John the Baptist was intimated by angelic announcement to Zechariah the father (Lk. 1:11-20). Included were the following items: the name to be given, his greatness in the eyes of the Lord, his ascetic manner of life, his equipment with the Holy Spirit and his mission "to make ready for the Lord a people prepared."

The pattern of annunciation occurs in the OT in connection with Samson (Jgs. 13:2-5), including his status as a Nazirite and his mission as the deliverer of Israel from the Philistines.

In all these cases the solicitude of God for His people is revealed along with His sovereignty in executing His purposes. E. F. H.

ANNUNUS an'nōō-nəs [Gk. *Announos*]; AV ANNUUS. One who returned with Ezra from Babylon to perform the functions of a priest in Jerusalem (1 Esd. 8:48); omitted in Ezr. 8:19.

ANNUS an'əs (1 Esd. 9:48, NEB). *See* ANNIUTH.

ANOINT; ANOINTING [Heb. *māšaḥ* (Ex. 28:41; 29:7, 36; 30:26, 30; 40:9ff.; 1 S. 9:16; 15:1; 16:3, 12; etc.), *dāšan* (Ps. 23:5), *sûḵ* (Dt. 28:40; Ruth 3:3; Dnl. 10:3; Mic. 6:15), *mišḥâ* (Ex. 25:6; 29:7, 21; 30:25; Lev. 8:2, 10, 12, 30; etc.); Gk. *aleíphō* (Mt. 6:17; Mk. 6:13; 16:1; Lk. 7:38, 46; Jn. 11:2; 12:3; Jas. 5:14), *enchríō* (Rev. 3:18), *chríō* (Lk. 4:18; Acts 4:27; 10:38; He. 1:9), *chrísma* (1 Jn. 2:20, 27)]; NEB also OINTMENT (Rev. 3:18), INITIATION (1 Jn. 2:20, 27).

Post-Reformation Protestantism is not very familiar with ritual anointing. The early and medieval Church, nonetheless, practiced anointing with some regularity for new believers as well as at the end of life in extreme unction. Anointing oil symbolized the presence of the Lord's Spirit to give wholeness to the total person (explicitly expressed in the fifth-century A.D. Gelasian sacramentary formula).

The ecclesiastical practice of anointing is firmly rooted in the biblical tradition. Several words are used in the OT to express the idea of anointing; however, the main one is *māšaḥ* (from which comes the word "Messiah"). While *māšaḥ* basically means "spread a liquid over something" (e.g., oil on wafers, Ex. 29:2; a house with paint, Jer. 22:14; a body with cosmetics, Am. 6:6), it is most frequently used in the sense of "anoint" or "consecrate to service" persons and objects.

The LXX uses *chríō* and *aleíphō* to translate *māšaḥ*, and these same Greek words, in addition to *enchríō*, are used in the NT for "anoint."

It has already been indicated that not only persons but also objects were anointed. Some suggest that shields were anointed and consecrated for battle (Isa. 21:5; cf. 2 S. 1:21), while others maintain that this was simply a process of preparing leather shields. The tabernacle (Ex. 40:9), the altar and its utensils (40:10; 30:28), the laver and its base (40:11; 30:28), were all anointed with oil and consecrated for the worship and service of Yahweh (Ex. 30:29f.).

Persons would also anoint themselves with oil for cosmetic reasons (Ruth 3:3; cf. Dt. 28:40). The soothing effect and the fragrant odors produced (Prov. 27:9; Eccl. 9:8) were so desirable that a lack of anointing oils in the land is a serious covenantal curse (Dt. 28:40; cf. Mic. 6:5).

Prophets (1 K. 19:16), priests (Ex. 28:41), and kings (1 S. 10:1; etc.) were anointed for office in Israel. It is only once explicitly mentioned that a prophet should be anointed (1 K. 19:16), but the patriarchs (esp. Abraham) are referred to as "my anointed ones" and "my prophets" (Ps. 105:15; 1 Ch. 16:22; cf. Gen. 20:7). Priests, beginning with Aaron (Ex. 29:7; Lev. 8:12) and including the high priests (Lev. 21:10), were also anointed and consecrated for service. They were set apart for a special office and to perform a special task in Israel. They were anointed as mediators between Yahweh and His people.

Royal anointings appear to have played a very prominent part in Israel's history. Both priests (1 K. 1:39; 2 K. 11:12) and prophets played a role in the anointing ritual. Several accounts are given of the actual anointing ceremonies: e.g., those of Saul (1 S. 10:1), David (1 S. 16:3), Solomon (1 K. 1:39), Jehu (2 K. 9:6), and Joash of Judah (2 K. 11:12). Israelite kings were not the only ones anointed, as we know from texts from several other ancient Near Eastern cities (Amarna Letters and Hittite sources). The Jotham fable also reflects the anointing of kings in pre-monarchic Israel (Jgs. 9:15).

Anointing was not treated as a light matter: as a matter of fact there was a law prescribing the making of special anointing oil by authorized personnel in a specified way (Ex. 30:22ff.). *See* OIL, ANOINTING. One who would dare to make the oil illegally and anoint an outsider "shall be cut off from his people" (v. 33). Such precaution was no doubt initiated because the anointing oil was a symbol of the Lord's appointment and consecration for office (1 S. 10:1, 9; Isa. 61:1; Zec. 4:11-14; Acts 10:38). Anointing, then, was viewed as God's act and as the outpouring of the Spirit to equip for service.

Whereas in the OT only special persons were anointed for office, in the NT all believers receive the anointing by the Holy One (1 Jn. 2:20). This anointing abides in the believer so that, as John says, "you have no need that any one should teach you" (1 Jn. 2:27); this latter statement is a clear reference to the presence of the new covenant era as promised in Jer. 31:34.

See also MESSIAH II.B. D. H. ENGELHARD

ANON. Archaic for "immediately" in the AV of Mt. 13:20 (Gk. *euthýs*) and Mk. 1:30 (*euthéōs*).

ANOS ā'nos (1 Esd. 9:34, AV, NEB). *See* VANIAH.

ANSWERABLE. Archaic in Ex. 38:18, AV, for Heb. *'ummâ*, with the sense "corresponding (to)."

ANT [Heb. *nᵉmālâ*<Arabic; Gk. *mýrmēx*]. The word occurs only twice in the Bible, in the familiar passages in Proverbs (6:6; 30:25), in both of which this insect is made an example of the wisdom of providing in the summer for the wants of the winter. Not all ants store up seeds for winter use; but among the ants of Palestine there are several species that do so, and their well-marked paths are often seen about Palestinian threshing-floors and in other places where seeds are to be obtained. The path sometimes extends for a great distance from the nest. A. E. DAY

ANTEDILUVIAN PATRIARCHS. The ancestors of the human race who lived prior to the flood and consisted of ten men, from Adam to Noah, plus Noah's three sons.

ANTEDILUVIAN PATRIARCHS

Most of their data is concentrated in the genealogies of Gen. 4:17–5:32.

I. Individuality.–On the existence of the antediluvians as individual persons locatable within history, J. D. Davis, among evangelicals, advocated the concept of family or group identification rather than individual. Calling attention to the appearance within the postdiluvian genealogies of tribal or place names (e.g., Elam and Aram as sons of Shem, Gen. 10:22), of plurals (e.g., Caphtorim and Philistines, v. 14), and of forms with definite articles (e.g., the Jebusites, v. 15), Davis interpreted 5:6-8 as follows: "In Seth, 105 years after it attained headship, the family of Enosh took its rise. Seth, after being at the head of affairs for 912 years, was succeeded by the family of Enosh" (*ISBE* [1929], I). His motive was commendable, to account for the patriarchal life-spans; but the antediluvians act as persons (cf. 4:17; 5:29), the genealogies of chs. 4 and 5 do not exhibit the features listed above for ch. 10, and even that postdiluvian table seems best understood from the viewpoint of a family's taking its name from an individual progenitor (cf. 10:15). Many scholars today lean toward dismissing the antediluvian patriarchs as nonhistorical borrowings from Mesopotamian folklore (cf. *IDB,* III, *s.v.* "Patriarchs"). Despite increasing recognition of the historicity of the later patriarchs, from Abraham onward (*see* PATRIARCHS), the presuppositions underlying the work of today's skeptical theologians do not permit them to hold to a literal understanding of the biblical account of individuals such as Adam or Noah.

II. Identity.–Scripture distinguishes two antediluvian genealogies (see chart). Interpreters who accept Wellhausen's framework, however, regularly assign Gen. 4 to two recensions of a J document, and ch. 5 to a P document (Wellhausen, pp. 8-14; Skinner, pp. 2, 14, 99). Since the names of both Adam and Enosh mean "man(kind)," all the lists are treated as corrupted forms of one original tradition beginning with "man's" son Cain (=Kenan) and ending with a family of four children (or three).

Actually, however, the only two patriarchs with identical names (Enoch and Lamech) exhibit sharply contrasted character (4:19, 23; 5:25, 28f.); some of the names that appear similar in English have distinct original meanings (e.g., Methushael, "man of God," but Methus(h)elah, "man of the javelin"), while others are radically different in the Hebrew (Irad, Heb. *'yrd,* and Jared, *yrd*); there is difference in order between Enoch and Mehujael ("smitten of God") or Mahalalel (in contrast, "praise of God"); and the Cainite Lamech's sons are pre-Noachian, as contrasted with Noah's sons (see Green, *Unity of Genesis,* pp. 43-49). The names of the twelve kings of Judah that were contemporary with the nineteen kings of northern Israel show almost as many resemblances to the latter as do those of the eight generations (including Adam) of the Cainites to the ten generations of the Sethites. Thus, the similarities in name could merely reflect contact between the two early branches of humanity (Leupold, *Exposition of Genesis* [1942], p. 217).

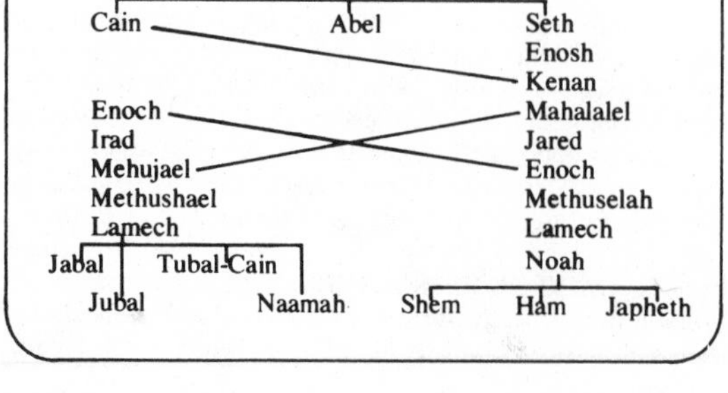

Confirmatory parallels to the Sethite patriarchs arise from the history of Berosus, a Babylonian priest of 300 B.C., who tells of ten kings who reigned thousands of years over Chaldea before the flood. The third king is Amelu, "man," cf. Enosh; the fourth is Ummanu, "artificer," matching the fourth patriarch Kenan, meaning "fabricator"; the seventh is Enmeduranki, reputed to be acquainted with the secrets of heaven and earth, while Enoch the seventh patriarch walked with God; and the tenth king, like the tenth patriarch, was the hero of the flood.

III. Longevity.–According to the biblical account, most of the antediluvian patriarchs lived over nine hundred years, a phenomenon which negative criticism explains as an attempt to idealize the remote past through the device of exaggeration. Yet even pagan Sumerian legend preserved the memory of extended life spans prior to the flood — although eight kings are reputed to have reigned a total of 241,200 years! (T. Jacobsen, *Sumerian King List* [1939]). The gradual reduction within Genesis of longevity, moreover, down to the almost normal 110 years of Joseph at the close of the book (50:26), casts doubt on theories either of special methods for counting time or of an unexplained shifting from legend to history. The decrease may have been due to a progressive manifestation of the effects of sin following Adam's fall from paradise (Prov. 10:27).

IV. Chronology.–The time covered by the antediluvian period depends upon ascertaining the figures employed in the original revelation of Genesis and then correctly interpreting them. While these figures appear in three differing pre-Christian texts (see chart), those of the LXX and Samaritan text represent systematic distortions of the

TEN PATRIARCHS FROM ADAM TO NOAH	HEBREW TEXT			SAMARITAN TEXT			SEPTUAGINT*		
	Age at Son's Birth	Remaining Years	Length of Life	Age at Son's Birth	Remaining Years	Length of Life	Age at Son's Birth	Remaining Years	Length of Life
Adam	130	800	930	130	800	930	230	700	930
Seth	105	807	912	105	807	912	205	707	912
Enosh	90	815	905	90	815	905	190	715	905
Kenan	70	840	910	70	840	910	170	740	910
Mahalalel ..	65	830	895	65	830	895	165	730	895
Jared	162	800	962	62	785	847	162	800	962
Enoch	65	300	365	65	300	365	165	200	365
Methuselah.	187	782	969	67	653	720	167†	802†	969
Lamech ...	182	595	777	53	600	653	188	565	753
Noah	500	....	....	500	....	....	500	....	....
To the Flood	100	....	....	100	....	....	100	....	....
Creation of man to the Flood	1656 years			1307 years			2242 years		

*Josephus (*Ant.* i.3.4) states only the age at son's birth and the total length of life; and in texts O and E (see Niese) agrees with the LXX as tabulated, except that the longevity of Jared is given as 969 (but texts S. P. and L as 962) and of Lamech as 707, and the age of Methuselah at his son's birth as 187 (texts S and P, 177).

†So Lucian; but A reads 187 and 782, and compare Josephus.

MT. That is, the LXX adds a hundred years wherever the Hebrew states that a patriarch begat his first son before the age of 150, while the Samaritan text reduces by a hundred the three who became parents after 150. Reductions are then introduced to insure death no later than the year the flood commenced. Yet if one accepts the validity of the MT figures, he must still establish the method of chronological interpretation. Three major examples may be mentioned.

(1) The name of Archbishop Ussher is associated with a minimal methodology, which counts for each antediluvian only the years prior to the birth of his first son. This theory of overlapping patriarchs, adopted by Ussher in A.D. 1650, produced the date of 4004 B.C. (more accurately, 4142, assuming Abraham's birth in 2133 B.C.; *see* CHRONOLOGY OF THE OT; cf. also *Zondervan's Pictorial Encyclopedia of the Bible*, I, *s.v.* [J. B. Payne]) for the creation of Adam.

(2) Interpreters such as Green (cf. Warfield, pp. 2-11; Kidner, pp. 82f.) have preferred to compare the two sets of ten antediluvian and postdiluvian patriarchs with the three sets, each of fourteen ancestors, in the genealogy of Christ (Mt. 1:1-17), and have concluded that just as the latter could omit three generations (v. 8, "Joram begat [an ancestor of] Uzziah"; cf. Ezr. 7:3's omission of six generations that are found in 1 Ch. 6:7-10), so also Genesis may have omitted a number of links. A theory of disconnected antediluvians could thus allow Adam to be dated, say, 100,000 B.C. While granting freedom for anthropological theories, it leaves the OT's lists of figures relatively pointless and must posit an unusually high proportion of omitted links.

(3) Another approach stresses W. F. Albright's observation that ancient Near Eastern peoples "dated long periods by lifetimes, not by generations" (*BASOR*, 163 [Oct. 1961], 50; cf. Kitchen, p. 54). Thus in Gen. 15, Israel's four hundred years in Egypt (v. 13), which actually covered some ten generations (1 Ch. 7:25-27), is said to entail four such lifetime generations (Gen. 15:16). Applied to Gen. 5, this counting by "successive" patriarchs would mean, e.g., that while Adam begat an ancestor of Seth when he was 130 (5:3), Seth (vv. 6-8) historically arose as Scripture's next prominent figure only after Adam's full life of 930 years (v. 4). Adam would then, theoretically, date from 13,652 B.C.; but since Seth was probably not born in the immediate year of Adam's death, man's creation may perhaps be dated 15,000 B.C., a millennium before the famous Lascaux cave paintings (*Journal of the American Scientific Affiliation*, 11:1 [1959], 8, though cf. 17:2 [1965], 43-47).

V. Characteristics.–Apart from Scripture's documentation for the initial careers of Adam and his sons, and for the terminal careers of Noah and his sons, the chief events chronicled under the antediluvian patriarchs can be summarized briefly. At the birth of Cain's son Enoch came the first settlement building (Gen. 4:17); and at the birth of Seth's son Enosh, the beginnings of public worship, "calling upon the name of Yahweh" (v. 26). Four generations later a parallel cleavage in interest appears as the Cainite sons of Lamech introduced cattle raising, the arts, and metallurgy (vv. 20-22), and their father—in a song perhaps to be associated with the metal sword — boasted of polygamy, violence, and vindictiveness (vv. 23f.); but the Sethite Enoch, walking in fellowship with Yahweh (5:22; cf. 6:9), was translated without experiencing death (5:24; cf. He. 11:5). Yet by the time of Noah even "the sons of God" (not angels, but presumably those Sethites who still worshiped Yahweh, Ex. 4:22; Dt. 14:1, 32; Isa. 1:2; 43:6; 45:11; Hos. 1:10; 11:1) had corrupted themselves by indiscriminate marriages (Gen. 6:2); and the NEPHILIM, those men of renown who witnessed the corruption (v. 4), became, as their name seems to suggest, "fallen ones" (Payne, pp. 205-207).

Bibliography.–J. D. Davis, *Genesis and Semitic Tradition* (1894); *Dictionary of the Bible* (1898), pp. 132-34; W. H. Green, *Bibliotheca Sacra*, 47 (1890), 285-303; *Unity of Genesis* (1895); T. Hartman, *JBL*, 91 (1972), 25-32; D. Kidner, *Genesis* (1967); K. A. Kitchen, *Ancient Orient and OT* (1966); J. B. Payne, *Theology of the Older Testament* (1962), pp. 204-208; J. Skinner, *ICC* on Genesis (1935); B. B. Warfield, *Princeton Theological Review*, 9 (1911), 1-25; J. Wellhausen, *Composition des Hexateuchs* (3rd ed. 1899).

J. B. PAYNE

ANTELOPE [Heb. *t*e*'ô*] (Dt. 14:5); AV WILD OX; NEB "long-horned antelope"; [*tô'*] (Isa. 51:20); AV WILD BULL. Several varieties of ruminant mammals similar to the Bovidae are designated by this term. The gazelle (*Gazella dorcas*) was widely distributed throughout Syria, Palestine, and Arabia, and this was probably the most familiar species of antelope in antiquity. In Dt. 14:5 the LXX renders *t*e*'ô* by Gk. *óryx*, perhaps indicating the *oryx beatrix*.

R. K. H.

ANTHEDON an-thē'dən. A city of Palestine, rebuilt along with Samaria, Ashdod, Gaza, and other cities, at Gabinius' command (Josephus *Ant.* xiv.5.3).

ANTHOTHIJAH an-tho-thī'jə [Heb. *'an*e*ṯōṯîyâ*]; AV ANTOTHIJAH; NEB ANTOTHIAH. A son of Shashak of Benjamin (1 Ch. 8:24).

ANTHROPOLOGY [<Gk. *ánthrōpos*–'man' + *lógos*–'study']. In general, the study of man. This definition obviously opens up a vast field that might be extended to cover all aspects of the being, life, character, history, and achievements of men, of groups of men, or of the human race as a whole. It is thus necessary to see first in what sense, with what delimitation, and with what claim one may speak of a biblical or theological anthropology. Otherwise the biblical data will be only too easily emptied of their distinctive content and incorporated into more general forms of anthropology.

I. Types of Anthropology
II. Nature of Biblical Anthropology
III. Content of Biblical Anthropology
  A. Terms
  B. Origin of Man
  C. Man's Relation to God
  D. Man's Relation to Men
  E. Constitution of Man
  F. Man and the Cosmos
  G. Fall of Man
  H. Salvation and Destiny of Man
IV. Biblical and Other Anthropologies
  A. Data from Other Sciences
  B. Basic Presupposition

I. Types of Anthropology.–There are, of course, many forms of study that might properly be regarded as branches of anthropology, e.g., primitive anthropology, psychology, physiology, sociology, even history. But if we adopt this mode of classification, it is obvious that what the Bible has to say could easily be subdivided under these various heads. It is better, then, to recognize at the outset two contrasting possibilities in anthropology: (1) that in which man is simply set in relation to himself and his world, and (2) that in which man is also and primarily set in relation to God. On the one side is scientific anthropology in the sense of an empirical study of man in his world; on the other is theological or biblical anthropology in the sense of a study of man in God's world.

This does not mean that the two possibilities are hostile or mutually exclusive. No irrevocable choice has to be made between them; indeed, a scientific anthropology can be theological, and a theological anthropology must be scientific. The difference between the two lies in the method, or, more precisely, in the terms of reference. A scientific anthropology recognizes that it can deal with man only in the given setting of the cosmos and that its knowledge must be gained from empirical investigation of man in this setting. It cannot legitimately go beyond man in his world, and any philosophical conclusions it may reach concerning the wider aspects of man's nature and destiny can only be speculative and in the last analysis improper. Its function is descriptive. Theological anthropology, however, has the primary task of studying man in the revealed setting of his dealings with God, and it realizes that in this task it can only give an exposition of what God Himself has made known. It cannot legitimately go beyond man in God's world, and attempts to draw wider deductions in the various scientific provinces cannot share the authority of the data that belong strictly to its own sphere.

The validity of both types of anthropology is not to be questioned. Many true aspects of man can be brought to light by scientific investigation, and there would be no sense in pretending that all there is to be known about man is disclosed in the Bible. But the scientific world needs to see the limitations of its own type of inquiry. A mere presentation of empirical data without any philosophical interpretation is not always an exciting or rewarding exercise. There is always a strong temptation to go further and fashion an understanding of man and the world. Strictly within the scientific method, however, this can only be an understanding of man and his world as a self-enclosed entity; and this involves a basic theological decision that the cosmos is a self-enclosed entity of this kind. To adopt this as a working methodological principle is one thing; to adopt it as a general principle for the understanding of things is quite another. It involves a very dubious process, a begging of the question that can turn a competent scientist into an incompetent theologian.

Truly to know man as he is, one must set him in his true and full context. The contention of theological anthropology, on the basis of the data of revelation, is that this true and full context involves a primary and ultimate relationship with God—a relationship that scientific anthropology cannot uncover except on its subjective side, which it necessarily has to leave out of account for its own more limited purpose, but which is not for that reason devoid of genuine objectivity or deprived of sovereign significance. As the theological anthropologist recognizes that his scientific counterpart may discover many things in his own sphere, so he claims validity for the many things that, taught by the divine self-revelation, he himself has to expound in the higher and ultimate sphere of the relation of man and his cosmos to God, i.e., of man in God's world.

II. Nature of Biblical Anthropology.–Theological or biblical anthropology is primarily concerned with man in relation to God, and with the origin, nature, life, and destiny of man against this background. Incidentally, this impinges at many points upon matter dealt with in scientific anthropology, e.g., matters of history, physiology, psychology, etc. But the orientation of biblical anthropology is different from the outset, for the factor that scientific anthropology must omit if it is to be true to itself is the basic and central theme in biblical anthropology. Furthermore, the approach is different, for, although both types of anthropology display the same rigorous objectivity, the objective data are very different. The data of scientific anthropology are men themselves, their bodies, minds, achievements, relics, and records. These things are of very little value in determining the objective relation of man to God, since they can approach this theme only from the side of man himself, i.e., the subjective side. Hence the most they can offer in themselves is information about what man has imagined this relation to be or made of it, which in itself is not theological anthropology, but only the anthropology of religion or philosophy.

To know man's relation to God, if there is such, it is necessary for God to be known as well as man and for man to be known with reference to God, not God with reference to man. For this purpose it is essential that there be objective data concerning God in His relation to man, and man as he is seen by God. In other words, God Himself must be the object of study, and man with this reference. But scientific anthropology methodologically excludes the existence of any such object of study. God Himself supplies the data with His self-revelation in word and act as recorded in the Bible, but scientific anthropology is bound by its own self-limitation to treat these data merely as the data of human religion. Theological anthropology, however, is prepared to take them seriously as data concerning God in relation to man, and man in relation to God. Its task is thus to study and expound the data of revelation, setting man and his origin, nature, and destiny in this final context. In so doing, it cannot become a branch of ordinary anthropology, which, rightly enough from its own standpoint, restricts itself to the data supplied by man and the cosmos. It deals with a broader picture. Yet it does so with its own objectivity, not speculatively, submitting itself rigorously to its own data. It is confident that in so doing it can finally give the picture of man the depth, perspective, and ultimate validity that scientific anthropology, as a restricted and provisional study, can never do.

III. Content of Biblical Anthropology.–*A. Terms.* Several words are used for man in the Bible.

The Heb. *'āḏām* (Gk. *ánthrōpos*; Vulg. *homo*) is either the name of the first man (cf. Lk. 3:38; Rom. 5:14; 1 Cor. 15:45); an appellative, "the man"; or a generic name of the race. Various derivations have been suggested for the word, e.g., Heb. *'^{a}ḏāmâ*, "of the earth"; Assyr. *admu*, "child"; Eth. *adma*, "pleasant"; but the origin is obscure.

The Heb. *ben-'āḏām*, "son of man," is used especially to denote man in his weakness and frailty before God (cf. Nu. 23:19; Job 25:6; Ezk. 2:3); *b^{e}nôṯ hā'āḏām*, "daughters of men," appears in Gen. 6:2.

The Heb. *'^{e}nôš* (Ps. 8:4; 10:18; 90:3; 103:15, often in Job) also denotes man in his weakness, frailty, and mortality (Gk. *brotós*), as compared with *'îš*, referring to man in his strength. It is used as a proper name in Gen. 4:26. Some have derived it from the root *'ānaš*, "to be or become frail" (cf. also Ps. 10:18).

The Heb. *'îš* (Gk. *anḗr*; Vulg. *vir*) is the male, as distinct from the female (cf. Gen. 7:2); the husband as distinct from the wife (Heb. *'iššâ*, Gen. 2:23f.); man in his dignity and excellence (Jer. 5:1); the man of standing (Prov. 8:4; cf. the contrast with *b^{e}nê 'āḏām*; also the Attic *andrés* and *ánthrōpoi*). Heb. *'îš* can also be used as the indefinite pronoun (e.g., Gk. *tis*, French *on*; cf. Ex. 21:14; 16:29).

The Heb. *geḇer*, *gibbôr*, is used for man in his strength (in contrast to women and children, Job 3:3); the male child (as distinct from the female, Gk. *ársēn*); the fighter (as distinct from noncombatants, Ex. 10:11); in the phrase "mighty man of valor" (Jgs. 6:12). It is also used for a strong beast (Prov. 30:30), or even God (Isa. 10:21) or the Messiah (Isa. 9:6). It may be combined with *'îš* to give intensity (1 S. 14:52).

The Gk. *ánthrōpos* is used in its main Greek sense for

man as a species (Mt. 12:12, etc.); sometimes there is an emphasis on his transitoriness and weakness (Jas. 5:17, etc.); other times a contrast between the outer and the inner man (2 Cor. 4:16); or between the natural and the psychic or pneumatic (1 Cor. 2:14); or between the old and the new (Rom. 6:6; Col. 3:4; Eph. 4:22).

The Gk. *anḗr* (Lat. *vir*) is used in the Bible in the various senses the Greek term may have, e.g., for man with some other designation (Acts 18:24); for the species (Lk. 5:8); for the male (Mt. 14:21); for man as opposed to woman (Gal. 3:28); for the husband (Mk. 10:2, 10); for the adult (1 Cor. 13:11); or for the honorable and mature man (Lk. 23:50; Acts 6:3, 5). In the plural *anḗr* can be used of the total population (Mt. 14:35).

B. Origin of Man. Like all else in the cosmos, man is revealed in the Bible to be the creature of God. While a scientific anthropology, restricted to cosmic data, is tempted to try to account for the existence of creatures in terms of continuity or self-origination, theological anthropology can tell us plainly that the beginning of man is to be found with God (Gen. 1:1ff.). Man is the consummation of God's creative work. He owes his origin to the divine counsel and fiat (Gen. 1:26f.). He is created (Heb. *bārā'*), and with his creation he is given dominion over other creatures (Gen. 1:28). He is presumably created with the endowment necessary for the fulfillment of this task. His position is one of honor and dignity (Ps. 8:4-6).

Man is part of creation, not merely in the sense that he derives his being from God, but also in the sense that he belongs to earth. He is fashioned (Heb. *yāṣar*) from the dust of the earth (Gen. 2:7). It is into this earthly vessel that God breathes the breath of life so that he becomes a living soul. His setting is on earth, not in heaven. His tasks relate to the soil, to plants and trees, to rivers. Even if the beasts cannot provide a suitable helpmeet for him, he is a companion to them. While he gives them their names, and is ordained to rule over them, and has a higher being and destiny, there is also a measure of kinship. Man's being divinely created does not mean at all that he is set in sharp antithesis to other creatures, or that physiological similarities (as well as differences) should occasion surprise or alarm. On the contrary, he shares his divine creation, and his creatureliness, with the whole world and all that is in it.

Nor is man created in human isolation. According to biblical anthropology sexual differentiation is part of creation. This again is something man shares at the physical level with other creatures. Yet for man sexual differentiation also means sexual interrelation (Gen. 2:20ff.). Man is from the very first a duality in unity, male and female. If the word "man" can be used for the first male, it cannot be used for the male in isolation. There is no such thing as man without the interrelation of male and female. Male or female in isolation is incomplete and doomed to extinction. The man needs a helpmeet. True man is achieved when the man cleaves to his wife and the two are one flesh.

From the very origin of man it may be seen at once that he stands in a threefold relation — to God, to his fellow man, and to the cosmos. Perhaps one might add that in terms of his human constitution man also stands in relation to himself. Biblical anthropology is a development of this fourfold relation of man as the creature of God.

C. Man's Relation to God. God is the author of man's life. He has provided him lavishly with all the means for living it. He has given man his task and man is responsible to Him. Man is not an automaton; within the possibilities and limitations of existence and under the ultimate divine sovereignty he is endowed by God with volition and has a measure of choice. God preserves and accompanies and overrules man. God is his ultimate end. He is the one from whom man comes and to whom he goes. Human life is inexplicable apart from God. It can be neither understood nor lived in terms of autonomy on the one side or a simply cosmic relation on the other. It is life from, with, by, and to God.

Since the relation between God and man is personal rather than mechanical, it has from the very first a covenantal aspect. There is election and promise on the one side, required response on the other. There is task on the one side, responsibility and obedience (or disobedience) on the other. Grace is balanced by gratitude, faithfulness by fidelity, the initiative of love by the response of love. Many of these themes are not developed in the creation narratives as such. But they are implicit from the outset and they occupy a predominant place in the further outworking of the relation of man to God. The cosmos is the theater for the great dialogue of drama between God and man. Because of the fall of man this takes the form of a drama of redemption, but even had there been no fall the great lines of interrelation could hardly have been different.

That the relationship between God and man has certain special characteristics is clearly intimated in the Bible. We have no information on the specific form of God's relation to birds or animals or plants. But in relation to man we do have the very definite statement that God created man in His image (Heb. *ṣelem*; Gk. *eikṓn*; Lat. *imago*) and after His likeness (Heb. *d*ᵉ*mûṯ*; Gk. *homoíōsis*; Lat. *similitudo*) (*see* Image of God). The exact meaning of this statement has been much debated. Even the detailed words "image" and "likeness" have called for minute investigation; and attempts have been made to differentiate between the two, e.g., physical image and ethical likeness, impressed image and acquired likeness, concrete image and abstract likeness, or original image and ideal likeness.

It has been asked what is the original of which man is the image or likeness. Tertullian sees a reference to the coming Christ. Others have argued that man is made after the image of the Logos. The Bible itself, with its plural ("our image"), seems at least to suggest that the reference is in some way to the whole trinity. The form of the biblical statement is also to be noted, for it does not say that man *is* the image of God but that he is made in the divine image.

The problem arises in what the likeness consists. Various qualities have been suggested, e.g., will, reason, love. Man's being spirit has also been named by some. Calvin thought in terms of the excellence or perfection of man rather than individual constituents; more recently Barth has argued strongly for the inner relationship of unity in plurality, though this also implies the personal qualities intrinsic in such a relationship.

There are, however, certain facts that are beyond dispute. Man is clearly represented as standing in a special relation to God. This relation is of such a kind that there may be personal dealings with God. Hence an element of relationship is implied in the *imago*, but it is a relationship that presupposes the likeness of man's created constitution to the Creator, especially on the psychical and spiritual side. From the NT we learn that the *imago* is of eternal significance, for in spite of the fall man is renewed in the divine image by conformity to Christ, and thus has a destiny of eternal sonship. Necessarily the *imago* also involved interrelationship between men, so that the principle of such interrelationship in the basic form of man's existence as male and female may not unjustly be regarded as at least one important aspect of the *imago*. That there is unlikeness as well as likeness is also plainly illustrated at this point.

D. Man's Relation to Man. Man's personal life involves

a horizontal relationship between men as well as a vertical one toward God. The basic form of this relationship is the man-woman — more specifically, the husband-wife — relation of marriage. Marriage is given with creation itself (Gen. 2:21ff.; Mt. 19:4ff.). While it is an end in itself, it is also the means to the further end of the family. Hence the husband-wife relation carries within it implicitly the parent-child relation (Ex. 20:12; Eph. 6:1ff.), and from the family circle there is a rapid extension to the varied individual and social relationships that constitute the common life of man.

Biblical anthropology makes it clear that by creation man is set in society. He cannot live by himself; but he is dependent on God and his fellow men, and he has obligations to them. Autonomous goals are a denial of humanity. If man is to love God, he must also love his neighbor as himself. However, in the Bible the internal relation of man to men, which is perceived in all anthropology, cannot stand alone. It cannot be the theme of an independent sociology, whether descriptive or prescriptive. Given in and with creation, this eternal relation always stands in the context of man's relation toward God. It is in a very real sense a reflection of the inner relation in the Godhead, and it stands under the direction of the reciprocal relation of God and man. The imperative nature of this relationship of man to man stands in the great imperative to love God, for the second commandment has no autonomous validity but is like the first. The indicative that underlies the imperative is not just that men are here and have to live together, like it or not. It is that God has put us here, in a relation analogous to that within Himself, and that He has made us in such a way that true humanity is possible only if there is love for God corresponding to God's love for man, and inner love of men corresponding to the inner love of the triune Godhead.

For the Christian, of course, the indicative is rather more than this. The gospel takes account of the fall, and the new indicative is that God has made us again in Jesus Christ. He has given us new life in the Son and with it new life in the family of God. He has fashioned us in the image of Christ. Having new fellowship with the Son, we have new fellowship one with the other. Yet the fact remains that, while this is a new creation, it is not unrelated to the first creation. Even in the world it is still true that by a common creation, in virtue of the common image and in terms of the common command, men belong inescapably to one another and can fulfil their destiny only in this relation. Fallen man rebels against this but cannot alter it. Redeemed man enters in a new and even more glorious way into the wonder of its fulfillment.

The implied solidarity of the race is a clear datum of biblical anthropology. It is seen already in the creation stories, for the whole race derives from the single couple. It finds expression in the OT and NT genealogies. Paul states it firmly in Acts 17:26. As the race derives from the one couple (Gen. 1:27), so the woman is from the man (1 Cor. 11:8), so that ultimately all men are in Adam (Rom. 5:12ff.), and Adam can be a term for man generally as well as for the first man. "Sons of Adam" is used for the human race (Dt. 32:8, AV).

The unity of the race has several important implications in theology and ethics. It means equality before God. It means corporate as well as individual responsibility. It makes nonsense of Cain's suggestion that he is not his brother's keeper. It underlies the various ramifications of the doctrine of original sin. It is also the basis of God's saving work in Jesus Christ. Because the race is a unity, the one can act for all. The first Adam can find his counterpart in the Lord from heaven (Rom. 5:14ff.; 1 Cor. 15:21f., 47-49). A new people can rise up in place of the old, those who belong to Christ and who thus belong no less indissolubly to one another. Whether by creation or by redemption, this unity of the race, this membership one of another in God, provides a solid basis for true ethical responsibility. It is because our fellow man is bone of our bone and flesh of our flesh that we ought to love him, that we are condemned because we do not, and that in the new body in Christ we finally can and shall.

E. Constitution of Man. Man is made of the dust of the earth, and God has breathed into him the breath of life so that he is a living soul. This means that at the least man is made up of body and soul. Some would add spirit, and argue that his being is tripartite (1 Thess. 5:23). This factor of spirit (or Spirit) has certainly to be taken into account, more particularly when the psyche is connected with mind. Yet there is a certain flexibility in the biblical usage that rules out making definition too precise. Man has a physical side and he has a spiritual side. Both are from God. Both belong together in a psychosomatic unity. Both are integral to human life. Man is not a soul imprisoned in a body. He is certainly not a pure soul in an evil body. Nor is he a body that has of itself, and as part of itself, produced the rudiments of mental, emotional, and spiritual life. Man is rather a body-soul, in which the soul is the vital principle, almost at times the individual essence, the ego. In a suggestive phrase of Barth (*CD*, III/2), man is the soul of his body, an embodied soul, a besouled body. If there is differentiation, there is also unity. But if there is unity, there is also order. The body is finally subordinate to the soul, not the soul to the body.

The implications of man's constitution as body and soul are significant. The body as such is not to be despised. It is the vehicle of life in the soul (Dt. 12:23). The word can sometimes be used to denote the whole man (Phil. 1:20). It is to be presented to Christ (Rom. 12:1; possibly the reference is again to the whole self). Even if it is secondary in importance (Mt. 6:25ff.; Phil. 3:21), its ills were healed by the Lord and His disciples (cf. Mt. 10:8). Paul emphasized both that the body is for the Lord (1 Cor. 6:13) and that it has its place in the resurrection (1 Cor. 15:23ff.). Christ Himself took a body (Jn. 1:14; He. 10), and the Church is the body of Christ (Rom. 12:5; 1 Cor. 10:16; Eph. 1:23).

In sum, the body is not to be cultivated for its own sake in abstraction from the psyche. True humanity consists in the harmony of body and soul under the direction of soul; this is supremely illustrated in the life of Jesus Himself. Yet the body has its place even in the new life. Hence Christians await not merely the immortality of the soul, but also the resurrection of the body. If there is change (cf. the spiritual body [Gk. *sṓma pneumatikón*] of 1 Cor. 15:44), there is also identity. A guarantee of this is that salvation itself was wrought in the body. If Jesus yielded up His spirit to God, He gave His body and blood a ransom for many. Similarly, the dedicated body is the instrument for the outworking of the purposes of God in and by the Christian (cf. Rom. 12:1). The body of the believer is the member of Christ and the temple of the Spirit (1 Cor. 6:15, 19).

In sum, man is the unity of soul and body both in the life of creation and in that of redemption. There is no dualism in the sense of separation, as though there could be full man either as body alone or as soul alone. Yet monistic explanation, whereby body is subsumed under soul or soul under body, is also excluded. Both body and soul are from God. Both are given for a purpose. Both are to work in integration, in ordered unity, as together they make up the one man. Both are assumed by Christ in His coming into the world for us. Both are redeemed so that they may be Christ's in the new life of the Christian. Both have an eternal destiny in the resurrection from the dead.

For a fuller discussion of "soul" and "spirit" *see* PSYCHOLOGY V.

F. Man and the Cosmos. A brief word may be said about the relation of man to the cosmos. Man is created with the cosmos and is part of it (Gen. 1). But he is no mere transient speck of cosmic dust; he also has a history with God. The cosmos is the setting of this history. It is also the sphere of the task God has given to man, for man is to have dominion over other creatures (Gen. 1:26). This means that the cosmos is the area of human possibilities (cf. Gen. 1:29ff.; 2:8ff.). Man's achievements are to be in relation to this world. A rich field of opportunity is thereby opened up. On the other hand, the cosmos also imposes on man his limitations. He is in space and time. He cannot break out of creation or arrest its ordered course. He is finite and he has to accept his finitude. If man is given a place of honor and dignity (Ps. 8), it is not a transcendent place. It is a place in the cosmos. Even in the world to come man will be set in a new heaven and a new earth. To this degree, and also in terms of the millennial kingdom (cf. Rom. 8:22), the cosmos is linked irrevocably to man and man to the cosmos in the outworking of the divine purpose. To put it as a simple truism, man as a creature is part of creation, and man as the new creature is part of the new creation. While it is true that man has a special position and specific gifts, it is also true that he cannot be abstracted from the world in which God has set him. Disorder in and revolt against this relation plays no little part in the fall and sin of man.

G. Fall of Man. Thus far man has been discussed primarily in terms of his creation and restoration. Man as he is, however, is neither man as he was to be nor man as he will be. Theological anthropology makes it plain that man as he is, as he now presents himself for scientific investigation, is fallen man. Gen. 1 and 2 are succeeded at once by Gen. 3, and if the doctrine of the fall is not greatly developed in the rest of Scripture, the biblical records from Gen. 4 make it quite evident that the sin of Adam is also the sin of the race. In fact, all the essential elements of fallen human nature may be seen already in the story of the original sin. In terms of specific offenses, the fall involves doubt, disobedience, covetousness, self-will, pride, and falsehood. In terms of relationship, it carries with it a fourfold breach. Communion with God is broken. Adam and Eve are brought into discord; Eve takes a false initiative; Adam throws the blame on Eve; and both have a new sense of shame. This sense of shame also involves an inner conflict in man, which finds further expression in his feeble attempt at self-exculpation. Finally, his harmony with the cosmos is broken; the garden is forfeited; and man goes forth to the place of thorns and thistles where he must eat his bread in the sweat of his brow. The implications of the fall provide the very stuff of human history, and nowhere is the nature of fallen man portrayed with greater candor and insight than in the historical records of Scripture.

Many problems arise in relation to the fall. Does it mean that the *imago* is impaired or obliterated? Is it total in the sense that everything man does is wholly evil? How is it transmitted from generation to generation? What is the relation of individual sins to corporate sin, or of individual responsibility to corporate guilt? To some of these questions it is not possible to give any full answer, since Scripture merely records the data without any full doctrinal exposition. But at least it may be said that even scientific observers of man, if they are candid, must admit the tragic inconsistency in man's heart between glory and shame, grandeur and squalor, greatness and pettiness. The ordinary data of history and sociology force anthropologists to consider some explanation, if only with a view to a remedy. This explanation may take various forms, some more optimistic, some more pessimistic. Without considering the data of revelation, the final result is a hopeless riddle that can certainly provide neither reason nor imperative for attempted human solutions.

The plight of man is not to be understood except in terms of the theological data. Man, created good, has fallen from his first estate. Man as he is now is a perversion of man as he was to be and as he will be. His relationships are soured and spoiled. The good that he desires issues only in evil. Over all his work, great and imposing though it be, lies the curse of his fall from God. Human nature has come to mean fallible, erring, sinful nature. Man's divinely given task is not properly discharged. His possibilities are possibilities of evil as well as good. His limitations are necessary restraints. His life has become an enigma to himself, and he has lost the very data by which he might understand it. The very fact that there can be a self-contained and secular anthropology is a final witness to the truth of theological anthropology. Only fallen man could even think of an anthropology without God. But fallen man has to think of this because he *is* man without God and without hope (Eph. 2:12). He cannot make his way back to God. If there is to be true fulfillment of the divine purpose, the initiative must again be from the side of God.

H. Salvation and Destiny of Man. At this point anthropology merges into soteriology and eschatology. The account of man is the account of his salvation and final destiny. It is hardly possible or necessary to go into this aspect of the matter in the present context, but a few points of importance should be noted.

(1) The anthropology of the Bible is not a study of man in the abstract, but of the specific man whom God created, who fell from God, and on whose behalf God pursues His revealing and reconciling purpose.

(2) The reconciling purpose involves a fulfillment of the original plan of God in creation, so that God is neither deflected from nor frustrated in His purpose in regard to man.

(3) The fulfillment of the purpose of God in man's restoration is accomplished in and by the God-man, Jesus Christ, and a wholly new turn is thereby given to anthropology; for (a) Jesus is Himself the divine Son; (b) He is as such the express image of God; (c) He is the one of and by and for whom all things are made; (d) God Himself becomes man in Him; (e) man, reconstituted in Christ, is thus advanced to a destiny and inheritance of sonship that transcends the original glory of creation. Incidentally, this raises the question to which Karl Barth has attempted an answer in his anthropology, namely, whether all anthropology does not necessarily have a christological orientation and basis in view of the incarnation.

(4) The supreme question for man becomes the question of the relation of God to man in Jesus Christ. This is the hinge of human meaning and destiny.

(5) The life of man in this world acquires significance and purpose, not just in relation to itself, but in relation to life in the world to come. As Christ is the decisive question put to man, so He is also the end and the goal. Life has relevance only in eschatological and theological terms. Apart from God's saving work in Christ, man is doomed to futility. He can never be true man. His frantic search for autonomous humanity can end only in the denial of humanity. As man has been irrevocably set in the context of this world, so life in this world has been irrevocably set in the context of life in the world to come. Anthropology can never be divorced from eschatology because it can never be divorced from Christology. If man tried to set up an independent anthropology, the fact that God has become man in Christ,

and invaded this sphere, has negated this attempt once and for all. The fulfillment of humanity does not lie in fallen Adam, but exclusively in the Second Adam, the Lord from heaven. It is the life of the new man in Him.

IV. Biblical and Other Anthropologies.–There are two main points at which biblical anthropology impinges on the various forms of secular anthropology.

A. Data from Other Sciences. It is inevitable that biblical anthropology should also include historical, physiological, psychological, and sociological data. Hence the question arises how far these coincide with the findings of scientific anthropology. It should be noted, of course, that in theological anthropology these data are in fact very selective. In many cases they are only incidental and secondary. They are not to be studied and classified merely or primarily along the lines adopted in scientific anthropology. Their presentation is mainly more general or popular, for the Bible is a book for everyman, not for this or that specialist alone. Scientific anthropology is not the purpose of the Bible. Nevertheless, there is a certain overlap, and possibility of cross-checking thus arises.

In general it may be affirmed with all confidence that the accounts given in the Bible conflict in no way with the data uncovered by scientific investigation. Physiologically and psychologically, the most that can be said is that biblical terminology is imprecise; but this is irrelevant in terms of the Bible's purpose. Historically and archeologically, too, the biblical stories stand up well at points of demonstrated overlapping.

It is, in fact, only in the sphere of the origins of the human race that a clash seems to arise between the stories in Gen. 1ff. and findings that seem to date back the history of the race thousands of years and to establish a possible line of derivation from closely related animals. In face of this problem various solutions have been proposed: (1) that the biblical records in Genesis are purely theological and not historical; (2) that the biblical records are an account of real events in the genre, not of exact history, but of poetic saga; (3) that the biblical records allow for long periods of development by natural processes; (4) that the early men of primitive archeology are not true men, and that God later either introduced a new race or brought about the decisive change that instituted true humanity. Other points that might be considered are that the data of primitive archeology are far less reliable than sometimes alleged, and that *creatio ex nihilo* cannot in any case be the object of scientific investigation, since the new creation will necessarily carry the implication of a prior history (e.g., the bread in the feeding of the five thousand, if it were subjected to scientific analysis). The problems are hardly severe enough to warrant an abandonment of the factual authenticity of the biblical account, and the final point is a pertinent reminder that for all the points of contact the approach, the purport, and the data of theological anthropology are by no means the same as those of scientific anthropology.

B. Basic Presuppositions. It is inevitable that biblical anthropology should impinge upon scientific anthropology in the area of basic presupposition. The scientist, justifiably for his own purpose, has to operate with a closed mind. He is giving an account of the creaturely within the creaturely context alone. This is legitimate so long as he recalls that his work is purely descriptive. But the human mind finds it very hard to stop at description. It wants to move on to interpretation. Here, however, the empiricist is in danger of arguing in a circle. Concentrating by choice on the creaturely data, he is in danger of explaining them solely in terms of themselves, and of then claiming that they prove the explanation. In other words, the methodology is made into an argument. The ignoring of the divine work of creation becomes an argument for its denial. The truth is, of course, that by entering the sphere of interpretation, scientific anthropology becomes philosophical anthropology. Indeed, it is this from the very outset if it treats its working principle as a basic principle. But the moment it becomes philosophical anthropology it comes into contact with theological anthropology. In this case it does so at some disadvantage, for theological anthropology is pursuing its proper task and doing so in a rigorously scientific manner, whereas in far too many cases scientific anthropology is here indulging merely in dilettante and obscurantist speculation.

In the sphere of interpretation, then, biblical anthropology need make no apology for its work. On the contrary, it may rightly call other anthropologies to account. On what grounds and with what basic knowledge does psychology adopt a materialistic view of man? or biology an explanation in terms of creative evolution? or physics and eternity of the cosmos? On what grounds and with what basic knowledge does anthropology exclude an interpretation in which man is related to the Creator as well as the creature? On what grounds and with what basic knowledge does science turn the modesty of its inquiry into the arrogance of denial of the Creator?

To be sure, man cannot see God. The eternal dimension of human life escapes ordinary observation. The claim of biblical anthropology, however, is that what man cannot perceive for himself, God has revealed to him. New data have been given. God Himself has revealed Himself as Creator. In so doing He has declared man's first, central, and final relation, the relation to Him. In so doing He has shown the nature of fallen man, but He has also exhibited true man in Jesus Christ and the restoration and eternal destiny of man in Him. These are the data on which alone a true and full anthropology can rest.

Bibliography.–*BDTh, s.v.* "Man"; *TDNT,* I, s.v. ἀνήρ (Oepke); ἄνθρωπος (Jeremias); Barth, *CD,* III/2; E. Brunner, *Man in Revolt* (Eng. tr. 1947); D. Cairns, *Image of God in Man* (1953); J. Jeremias, *Jesus als Weltvollender* (1930); J. G. Machen, *Christian View of Man* (1937); R. Niebuhr, *The Nature and Destiny of Man* (1953); H. W. Robinson, *Christian Doctrine of Man* (3rd ed. 1947); T. F. Torrance, *Calvin's Doctrine of Man* (1949).

G. W. BROMILEY

ANTHROPOMORPHISM [<Gk. *ánthrōpos*–'man' + *morphḗ*–'form']. The manifestation or depiction of God in human terms or as having the characteristics of man. Anthropomorphism is very common in the Bible.

I. Its Use in the Bible
II. The Dangers Involved
III. Its Necessity
IV. Its Justification
V. The Incarnation and Anthropomorphism

I. Its Use in the Bible.–*A. Data.* In Gen. 1 God is represented as speaking (v. 3), then as seeing (v. 4). He walks in the garden in the cool of the day (3:8). Elsewhere we read of the human form of God (Nu. 12:8), of the feet of God (Ex. 24:10), of the hand of God (Isa. 50:11), of the heart of God (Hos. 11:8). In addition to physical characteristics, emotional qualities appropriate to man are also ascribed to God. Thus He is jealous (Ex. 20:5), angry (Ps. 77:9), merciful (Jonah 4:2), mighty (Ps. 147:5), gracious and loving (Ps. 103:8). The Lord can resolve and He can also repent (1 S. 15:11). He is a shepherd (Ps. 23:1), a bridegroom (Isa. 62:5), and a warrior (Ex. 15:3).

While anthropomorphisms are in general less frequent in the NT, they do occur. There is a reference to the finger of God in Lk. 11:20. In Mt. 19:10 the angels behold the face of God. In Jn. 10:29 it is said that none can pluck the disciples out of the hand of God. In Jn. 1:18 the only begotten Son is in the bosom of the Father. The ascended Christ is seated at God's right hand (He. 1:3). In many verses (e.g., 2 Tim. 2:13; Eph. 2:8; 1 Tim. 1:16; Eph. 2:4; 1 Jn. 3:1) we read of the faithfulness, wisdom, longsuffering, mercy, and love of God. God can also act as man acts. He speaks (He. 1:1f.), sends (Jn. 17:18), chooses (Eph. 1:4), purposes (Eph. 3:11), is wrathful (Rom. 1:18), judges (Rom. 2:2f.), reconciles (2 Cor. 5:18f.), loves (Jn. 3:16). He is described in human categories as father (Mt. 6:9, etc.) or as king (Rev. 4:2).

B. Use. An interesting feature of the biblical use, especially in the OT, is that there is no very apparent development from anthropomorphism to more abstract terms. It is often said that cruder ideas of God give way to more lofty conceptions as one moves from the earliest documents to the later writings. But this is not very well substantiated by the facts. Thus if it were argued that Gen. 3 is of an earlier date than Gen. 1, the most that could be said is that there is a change in the nature of the anthropomorphism from walking to speaking and seeing. Perhaps there is a greater refinement in speaking and seeing than in walking, for the former denote more intellectual activity and the latter more physical. Or perhaps it could be argued that there is a greater awareness of the figurative nature of the usage in the so-called later writing. But the anthropomorphism itself remains. Moreover, some of those parts of Scripture that represent the sovereignty of God in the loftiest terms, e.g., the second part of Isaiah, are even more strongly anthropomorphic in expression than others that are supposed to belong to a more primitive stage.

The revolt against anthropomorphism in principle did not seem to affect the OT until the time of the LXX translation, in which pains are sometimes taken to avoid any anthropomorphic implication (e.g., Ex. 24:10). Even the more common introduction of angels in some of the later works is not without parallels in the earlier theophanies. Only with the increasing stress on the divine transcendence between the Testaments is there any real sense that anthropomorphism is in some way derogatory to God. If the NT displays a greater reserve in this respect than the OT, it has a special reason that will be seen later.

C. Meaning. The question arises whether the Bible really teaches that human attributes may be ascribed to God in the strict sense. Various answers may be given. In the first place, a distinction certainly has to be made between the various kinds of attributes. Thus ethical and spiritual qualities such as wisdom, power, mercy, righteousness, and love are obviously intended literally when posited of God, whereas a figurative meaning is in many cases no less apparent in the case of physical attributes or members. In the Psalms or Isaiah, for example, the anthropomorphisms have a vivid poetic quality when there is reference to the hand or face of God. God did not literally extend a giant arm from heaven when He protected Israel and overthrew Egypt at the Red Sea. The almost stereotyped metaphor is simply a graphic way of expressing the truth that God Himself did in fact intervene to save His people and to destroy the oppressor. The finger of God in the dominical saying in Luke is of the same genre.

Is this true of all physical anthropomorphism in the Bible? It could be argued, of course, that at an earlier stage God was thought to have a human form, that this underlies or finds expression in a story like Gen. 3, that it forms the basis of the later usage, and that many Israelites continued to believe it even when the great prophets had a clearer insight into the true nature of God. But, while it may be admitted that the individual beliefs of many Israelites, perhaps a majority at times, were crudely anthropomorphic, this does not mean that the usage in the text is necessarily of this kind. Indeed, one might suppose that the divine walking of Gen. 3 could be happily retained in the text because, in its charming poetic form, it represents so vividly the closeness of the relationship with God that was forfeited in the fall. If one considers the purpose of Bible study to be the reconstruction of the beliefs of the Israelites, then traces of inadequate conceptions, even illicit images, of God can easily be detected. If, on the other hand, one reads the Bible to hear the revelation of God, things take on a very different aspect.

That the Bible itself is very conscious of the limitation of anthropomorphism may be seen from the many verses that emphasize the transcendence of God in relation to man or to the cosmos at large. Thus Dt. 4:12 states categorically that when God met with Israel at Sinai they heard the voice of the words but saw no form. Again, when Moses sought the vision of God in Ex. 33, he asked only to be shown God's way of glory, and even the glory of God was seen only in passing: "You cannot see my face; for man shall not see me and live" (v. 20). Isaiah, in spite of all his anthropomorphisms, flings out the tremendous question: "To whom then will you liken God, or what likeness compare with him?" (40:18). God is the high and lofty one who inhabits eternity (Isa. 57:15). The same witness is carried through into the NT: "No one has ever seen God" (Jn. 1:18); "God is spirit" (Jn. 4:24). God alone has immortality "and dwells in unapproachable light, whom no man has ever seen or can see" (1 Tim. 6:16). Even the ways and thoughts of God are not as man's ways and thoughts (Isa. 55:8), and the natural man does not receive the things of the Spirit of God (1 Cor. 2:14).

II. The Dangers Involved.–The seriousness of the dangers of anthropomorphism may be seen from the crudities of myths in which gods share not only the attributes but also the vices and failings of men, albeit on a larger scale. What has happened is that God has been made in the image of man. He is simply an enlarged projection. The reverse side of the same error is divinization, for if the gods are no more than men writ large, there is no intrinsic reason why men, or at least some men, should not become or be gods.

Already in Greek philosophy Xenophanes recognized the danger of making God in the image of man, or indeed of any creature: "There is one God, greatest of all gods and men, who is like to mortal creatures neither in form nor in mind." But this opens the way only too easily to abstraction or to agnosticism. Either we cannot know or say anything concerning God, or we conceive of Him in abstract categories that deprive Him of any true and dynamic life. The Bible, on the other hand, uses anthropomorphic forms of speech, but it recognizes their limitation. Obvious crudities must be avoided. God cannot be shaped according to the physical, mental, ethical, or spiritual pattern of man. God has His own transcendent life and being that defy human depiction. He is not just an enlarged man. He certainly does not display human faults and failings. Nevertheless, He may still be presented in human categories and in terms of human attributes. With careful avoidance of extravagances, the Bible maintains a proper use, and it continues to do so even in the later books of the OT and on into the NT. Why is this so?

III. Its Necessity.–A first point is that anthropomorphism is subjectively necessary (*see* ACCOMMODATION III). If man is to hear or speak about God at all, it must be in intelligible terms. But man is limited by his own creatureliness. He can embrace the cosmos, but he cannot climb up to the sphere of God. He has no words or thoughts by which to describe transcendent deity. Even if he takes refuge in abstraction, his very abstractions have an ultimate creaturely basis. To say that God is the infinite is to define Him negatively in terms of the finite, and the finite involves spatial or temporal measurement. To take the way of negativity is here shown to be no true help, for this in turn involves definition in terms of the human or the creaturely, as though God were simply the opposite of the human.

The best that man can do, it might seem, is to take refuge in silence, to think and say nothing about God at all. But this is obviously impossible in face of the reality of God. The only other option is to be frank about anthropomorphism as the Bible is, to admit at once that some kind of anthropomorphism is needed, to avoid the supercilious contempt for the anthropomorphic that has come to characterize some theological and philosophical schools. There is a difference between cruder and more instructed anthropomorphism. Depiction of God as a cruel, carousing giant is not comparable with His depiction as the merciful Father. It is important that the right kind of anthropomorphism be found and that its limitation be recognized. But the fact remains that there is no escaping anthropomorphism as such. It is imposed by the ineluctable necessity of the very fact that seems to call it in question, namely, that man is man and not God. If on the one side this means that man cannot reduce God to human categories, it also means on the other that he has none but human categories in which to speak of God.

IV. Its Justification.–The limitations of man do not in themselves justify anthropomorphism. Perhaps man is unable to think or speak of God in any other way than that of anthropomorphism (unless, of course, he chooses to think and speak of Him in terms of other aspects of the organic or inorganic world). But one could deduce from this that he is in fact unable to think or to speak about God at all. God is so different from man that He transcends human comprehension altogether. To say that man is condemned to anthropomorphism is to say that he is condemned to ignorance or error. Even when it has been established that man has to learn and to speak about God in this way, it has still to be asked by what right and with what justification he may do so.

The answer to this question is twofold. First, the Bible itself does so, and the Bible is not just man's thinking and speaking about God. It is God's own address to man. Hence God Himself speaks concerning Himself in anthropomorphic terms, and this constitutes for man both a permission and a command to do the same. Anthropomorphism within the biblical limit is justifiable because it is God Himself who authorizes it. Second, God authorizes it, not under the pressure of an imposed necessity, nor by an act of irrational caprice, but because it corresponds to the facts of the situation. God has made man in His own image and after His own likeness. Between God and man, by God's own appointment and according to His own revelation, there is similarity as well as dissimilarity. If man, especially fallen man, is not to make God in his own image, he has to recognize that he himself, for all his present corruption, is made in the image of God.

This means that man's wisdom is in fact a copy of God's wisdom, man's love a copy of God's love, man's righteousness a copy of God's righteousness. Even the body of man, his capacity to act, to express himself, to fulfil his decisions and plans in the material cosmos, is in its own way a copy of God's superior power of action. Hence, so long as man remembers that he is the copy and God the original, not vice versa, there is every reason why anthropomorphism should contribute not to ignorance or error but to a true knowledge of God. Anthropomorphism is justified in relation to God because God Himself uses it, and God Himself uses it because its real basis is the divinely created theomorphism of man.

V. The Incarnation and Anthropomorphism.–This truth finds supreme illustration and support in the climax of God's revealing and reconciling action in the incarnation of the Word. The astonishing truth of the gospel is that God did in fact take human form even to the point of a human body. As mentioned earlier, the NT is comparatively reserved in its individual anthropomorphisms, but the special reason for this is that the basic NT witness and confession is to the supreme anthropomorphism of the God-man. In the NT God is not just depicted metaphorically in anthropomorphic terms. A reality of the most literal kind is now seen to underlie the metaphors. God has revealed Himself with all the attributes of humanity. "And the Word became flesh and dwelt among us" (Jn. 1:14). He "emptied himself, taking the form of a servant, being born in the likeness of men. And being found in human form he humbled himself" (Phil. 2:7f.). "Sacrifice and offerings thou hast not desired, but a body hast thou prepared for me . . . Lo, I have come . . ." (He. 10:5, 7). "That . . . which we have heard, which we have seen with our eyes, which we have looked upon and touched with our hands, concerning the word of life" (1 Jn. 1:1), "He who has seen me has seen the Father" (Jn. 14:9).

All this means that in Jesus Christ God has actually assumed human form in fulfillment of His revealing and reconciling purpose. Hence in relation to Jesus one can speak quite literally, not merely of the love, compassion, righteousness, or holy wrath of God, but of the hand or arm or eyes or feet of God. While God in His eternal deity is a Spirit, there is nothing incongruous or impossible in His assuming human form. Within the context of the divine self-revelation, anthropomorphism is fully vindicated, not as a general principle, but as a christological reality.

Several troublesome questions remain. Is there a sense in which humanity is intrinsic to God? Was the humanity of Christ the prototype of man as originally created? Will our knowledge of God always be in terms of the divine humanity of Christ? Would it have been this way even had there been no fall? Speculation on such matters can lead to some curious developments, e.g., the Scholastic problem whether there would have been an incarnation whatever happened, or the suggestion in Luther that somewhere a *Deus absconditus* still lurks behind the *Deus revelatus* in Christ, as though Christ were not the fulness of the Godhead bodily, as though some part of God were not revealed in Him. Behind this type of reasoning, and the implied wish that we may see God other than in Christ, there probably lies a recollection of the limitation of anthropomorphism, of the witness to divine transcendence.

Quite apart from all such questions, however, the incarnation does have at least three clear implications which may be accepted as criteria in this whole question of anthropomorphism. First, it leaves us in no doubt that there is nothing inconsistent in the bearing of human form by God. Second, it thereby establishes and reconstitutes the creation, not of God in man's image, but of man in God's. Man is truly theomorphic in Christ, and this theomorphism is the basis of legitimate anthropomorphism. Third, it makes it plain that anthropomorphism is not just a device; it is a divinely given task. Man has not just to learn about God in human terms. He has to find his true humanity in God and to work it out in terms of being made conformable to Christ as the image of the invisible God.

Set in the light of the incarnation, biblical anthropomorphism takes on a completely different aspect from the crass and dubious anthropomorphism that arouses justifiable objection. It starts not with man but with God. It has its basis in creation. It is sponsored by divine revelation. It teaches man his true relation to God. It gives him his real dignity and humanity. It poses his ethical task, and sets him the eschatological goal not of divinization but of assumption to eternal sonship in, with, and by the one Mediator between God and man, the man Christ Jesus.

See also IMAGE OF GOD; PERSON OF CHRIST.

Bibliography.–BDTh; Sch.-Herz.: *CD*, III/1f.; also OT theologies, esp. Eichrodt, II (Eng. tr. 1967). G. W. BROMILEY

ANTICHRIST [Gk. *antíchristos*]. The word "antichrist" occurs only in 1 Jn. 2:18, 22; 4:3; 2 Jn. 7, but the concept appears frequently in Scripture.

I. In the OT
II. In the NT
  A. The Gospels
  B. Pauline Epistles
  C. Johannine Epistles
  D. Revelation
III. In Apocalyptic Writings
IV. In Patristic Writings
V. Medieval Views
  A. Christian
  B. Jewish
VI. Post-Reformation Views

I. In the OT.–As in the OT the doctrine concerning Christ was only suggested, not developed, so is it with the doctrine of the antichrist. That the Messiah should be the divine Logos, the only adequate expression of God, was merely hinted at, not stated: so the antichrist was exhibited as the opponent of God rather than of His anointed. In the historical books of the OT "Belial" is used as of a personal opponent of the Lord; thus the shamefully wicked are called in the AV "sons of Belial" (Jgs. 19:22; 20:13), "daughter of Belial" (1 S. 1:16), etc. Modern versions translate the expression in an abstract sense, e.g., "base fellows," "scoundrels," "wicked woman." In Dnl. 7:7f. there is the description of a great heathen empire, represented by a beast with ten horns; its full antagonism to God is expressed in a little eleventh horn which had "a mouth speaking great things" and "made war with the saints" (vv. 8, 21). He was to be destroyed by the "Ancient of Days," and his kingdom was to be given to a "son of man" (vv. 9-14). Similar yet differing in many points is the description of Antiochus Epiphanes in 8:9-12, 23-25.

II. In the NT.–*A. The Gospels*. In the Gospels the activity of Satan is regarded as specially directed against Christ. In the Temptation (Mt. 4:1-10; Lk. 4:1-13) the devil claims the right to dispose of "all the kingdoms of the world," and has his claim admitted. The temptation is a struggle between the Christ and the antichrist. In the parable of the tares and the wheat, while He that sowed the good seed is the Son of man, he that sowed the tares is the devil, who is thus the antichrist (Mt. 13:37-39). Our Lord felt it the keenest of insults that His miracles should be attributed to satanic assistance (Mt. 12:24-32). In Jn. 14:30 there is reference to the "ruler of this world" who "has no power over" Christ.

B. Pauline Epistles. The Pauline Epistles present a more developed form of the doctrine. In the spiritual sphere Paul identifies the antichrist with Belial. "What accord has Christ with Belial?" (2 Cor. 6:15). 2 Thessalonians, written early, affords evidence of a considerably developed doctrine being commonly accepted among believers. The exposition of 2 Thess. 2:3-9, in which Paul exhibits his teaching on the "man of lawlessness," is very difficult, as may be seen from the number of conflicting attempts at its interpretation. (*See* LAWLESS, LAWLESSNESS.) Here we would indicate only what seems to be the most plausible view of the Pauline doctrine.

It had been revealed to the apostle by the Spirit that the Church was to be exposed to a more tremendous assault than any it had yet witnessed. Some twelve years before the Epistle was penned, the Roman world had seen in Caligula the portent of a mad emperor. Caligula had claimed to be worshiped as a god, and had a temple erected to him in Rome. He went further, and demanded that his own statue should be set up in the temple at Jerusalem to be worshiped. As similar causes might be expected to produce similar effects, Paul, interpreting what was "indicated by the Spirit of Christ within him," may have thought of a youth reared in the palace, who, raised to the awful, isolating dignity of emperor, might like Caligula be struck with madness and demand divine honors, and might be possessed with a thirst for blood as insatiable as his. The fury of such an enthroned maniac would, with too great probability, be directed against those who, like the Christians, would refuse as obstinately as the Jews to give him divine honor, but were not numerous enough to make Roman officials pause before proceeding to extremities. So long as Claudius lived, the manifestation of this "lawless one" was restrained; when, however, the aged emperor should pass away, or God's time should appoint, that "lawless one" would be revealed, whom the Lord would "slay with the breath of his mouth" (v. 8).

C. Johannine Epistles. Although many of the features of the "man of lawlessness" were exhibited by Nero, yet the messianic kingdom did not come, nor did Christ return to His people at Nero's death. Writing after Nero had fallen, the apostle John, who, as noted above, alone of the NT writers uses the term, presents us with another view of the antichrist (1 Jn. 2:18, 22; 4:3; 2 Jn. 7). From the first of these passages ("as you have heard that antichrist is coming"), it is evident that the coming of the antichrist was an event generally anticipated by the Christian community, but it is also clear that the apostle shared to but a limited extent in this popular expectation. He thought the attention of believers needed rather to be directed to the antichristian forces that were at work among and around them ("so now many antichrists have come"). From 1 Jn. 2:22; 4:3; 2 Jn. 7 we see that the apostle regards erroneous views of the person of Christ as the real antichrist. To him the Docetism (i.e., the doctrine that Christ's body was only a *seeming* one) which portended Gnosticism, and the elements of Ebionism (Christ was only a man), were more seriously to be dreaded than persecution.

D. Revelation. In the book of Revelation the doctrine of antichrist receives a further development. If the traditional date of the Apocalypse is to be accepted, it was written when the lull that followed the Neronian persecution had given place to persecution under Domitian—"the bald Nero." The apostle now feels the whole imperial system to be an incarnation of the spirit of Satan; indeed, from the identity of the symbols, seven heads and ten horns, applied both to the dragon (12:3) and to the beast (13:1), he appears to have regarded the *raison d'être* of the Roman empire to be found in its incarnation of Satan. The ten horns are borrowed from Dnl. 7, but the seven heads point, as seen from Rev. 17:9, to the "seven hills" on which Rome sat. As for the "image of the beast" (13:14f.), possibly this symbolizes the cult of Rome, the city being regarded as a goddess, and worshiped with temples and statues all over the empire. Inasmuch as the seer endows the beast that comes out of the earth with "two horns like a lamb" (13:11), the apostle must have had in his mind some system of teaching that resembled Christianity; its relationship to Satan is shown by its speaking "like a dragon" (v. 11).

The number 666 given to the beast (v. 18), though presumably understood readily by the writer's immediate public, has proved a riddle capable of too many solutions. The favorite explanation *nerôn qēsar* (Nero Caesar), which suits numerically (*see* NUMBER VI), becomes absurd when it implies the attribution of seven heads and ten horns. There is no necessity to make the calculation in Hebrew; the corresponding arithmogram in Sib.Or. 1:328-330, in which 888 stands for *Iesous,* is interpreted in Greek. On this hypothesis *Lateinos,* a suggestion preserved by Irenaeus (*Adv. haer.* v.30), would suit. If we follow the analogy of Daniel, which has influenced the Apocalyptist so much, the Johannine antichrist must be regarded not as a person but as a kingdom. In this case it must be the Roman empire that is meant.

III. In Apocalyptic Writings.–Although from their eschatological bias one would expect that the Jewish apocalyptic writings would be full of the subject, mention of the antichrist occurs in only a few of the apocalypses. The earliest certain notice is found in the Sibylline books (1:167). We are there told that "Beliar shall come and work wonders," and that "he shall spring from the Sebasteni (Augusti)," a statement that, taken with other indications, inclines one to the belief that the mad demands of Caligula were threatening the Jews when this was written. There are references to Beliar in the Testaments of the Twelve Patriarchs, which, if the date ascribed to them by Charles is correct, i.e., the reign of John Hyrcanus I, are earlier. The accuracy of this conclusion is doubtful, however. Further, Charles admits the presence of many interpolations, and even though one might assent to his opinions as to the nucleus of the work, yet these Beliar passages might be due to the interpolator. In only one passage is "Beliar" *antíchristos* as distinguished from *antítheos,* T. Dan 5:10f. (Charles' translation): "And there shall arise unto you from the tribe of [Judah and of] Levi the salvation of the Lord; And he shall make war against Beliar. And execute an everlasting vengeance on our enemies; And the captivity shall he take from Beliar . . . And turn disobedient hearts unto the Lord. . . ." Charles thinks he finds an echo of this last clause in Lk. 1:17; but may the case not be the converse?

The fullest exposition of the ideas associated with the antichrist in the early decades of Christian history is to be found in the Ascension of Isaiah. In this we are told that "Beliar" (Belial) would enter into "the matricide king" (Nero), who would work great wonders and do much evil. After the expiration of 1332 days during which he has persecuted the plant which the twelve apostles of the Beloved have planted, "the Lord will come with his angels and with armies of his holy ones from the seventh heaven, with the glory of the seventh heaven, and he will drag Beliar into Gehenna and also his armies" (4:3, 13, Charles' translation). If the date at which Beliar was supposed to enter into Nero was the night on which the great fire in Rome began, then the space of power given to him is too short by 89 days. From the burning of Rome till Nero's death was 1421 days. It is to be noted that there are no signs of the writer having been influenced by either Paul or the Apocalypse. As he expected the coming of the Lord to be the immediate cause of the death of Nero, we date the writing some months before that event. It seems thus to afford contemporary and independent evidence of the views entertained by the Christian community as to the antichrist.

IV. In Patristic Writings.–Of the patristic writers, Polycarp is the only one of the Apostolic Fathers who refers directly to the antichrist. He quotes John's words, "Whosoever doth not confess that Jesus Christ has come in the flesh is antichrist" (Polyc. Phil. 7:1), and regards Docetism as antichrist in the only practical sense. Barnabas, although not using the term, implies that the fourth empire of Daniel is antichrist; this he seems to identify with the Roman empire (4:5). Irenaeus is the first writer known to occupy himself with the number of the Beast. While looking with some favor on *Lateinos,* he himself prefers *Teitan* as the name intended (*Adv. haer.* v. 30). His view is interesting as showing the belief that the arithmogram was to be interpreted by the Greek values of the letters.

More particulars as to the views prevailing can be gleaned from Hippolytus, who has a special work on the subject, in which he exhibits the points of resemblance between Christ and the antichrist (*Demonstratio de Christo et antichristo* 4, 14f., 19, 25). In this work we find the assertion that the antichrist springs from the terms of Jacob's blessing to Dan. Among other references, the idea of Commodian (A.D. 250) that Nero *redivivus* (risen from the dead) was to be the antichrist has to be noticed. In the commentary on Revelation attributed to Victorinus of Petau there is, inserted by a later hand, an identification of Genseric with the "beast" of that book. It is evident that little light is to be gained on the subject from patristic sources.

V. Medieval Views.–*A. Christian.* The Christian was mainly occupied in finding methods of transforming the names of those whom monkish writers abhorred into a shape that would admit of their being reckoned 666. The favorite name for this species of torture was naturally *Maometis* (Muhammad). Gregory IX found no difficulty in accommodating the name of Frederick II so as to enable him to identify his great antagonist with "the beast coming up out of the sea." This identification the emperor retorted on the pope. Rabanus Maurus gives a full account of what the antichrist was to do, but without any attempt to label any contemporary with the title. He was to work miracles and to rebuild the temple at Jerusalem.

The view afterward so generally held by Protestants that the papacy was the antichrist had its representatives among the sects denounced by the hierarchy as heretical, as the *Kathari.* In various periods the rumor was spread that the antichrist had already been born. Sometimes his birthplace was said to be Babylon, sometimes this distinction was accorded to the mystical Babylon, Rome.

B. Jewish. The Jewish views had little effect on Christian speculation. With the Talmudists the antichrist was named Armilus, a variation of Romulus. Rome evidently is primarily intended, but the antichrist became endowed with personal attributes. He makes war on Messiah son of Joseph, and slays him, but is in turn destroyed by Messiah son of David.

VI. Post-Reformation Views.–In immediately post-Reformation times the divines of the Roman Church saw in Luther and the Reformed churches the antichrist and beast of Revelation. On the other hand the Protestants identified the papacy and the Roman Church with these, and with the Pauline man of sin. The latter view had a certain plausibility, not only from the many undeniably antichristian features in the developed Roman system, but from the relation in which the Roman Catholic Church stood to the city of Rome and to the imperial idea. That the beast that came out of the earth (Rev. 13:11) had the horns of a lamb points to some relation to the lamb that had been slain (5:6).

Futurist interpreters have sought the antichrist in historical persons, as Napoleon III. These persons, however, did not live to realize the expectations formed of them. The critical consensus is that Nero is intended by the beast of the Apocalypse, but this, on many grounds, as seen before, is not satisfactory. Some future development of evil may more exactly fulfil the conditions.

See W. Bousset, *The Antichrist Legend* (Eng. tr. 1896).

J. E. H. THOMSON

ANTILEBANON [Gk. *Antilibanon*] (Jth. 1:7); AV ANTILIBANUS. A mountain range E of the Lebanon and parallel to it, including Mt. Hermon as its southernmost extension, and terminating in the north at Emesa (Homs). *See* LEBANON I.

ANTILEGOMENA an-ti-lə-gom'ə-nə [Gk. *antilegómena* < *antilégō*–'speak against']. Eusebius' term (*HE* iii.25; cf. iii.3, 24) for seven disputed books of the NT: Hebrews, James, 2 Peter, 2 and 3 John, Jude, Revelation. *See* BIBLE III.D; CANON OF THE NT.

ANTILIBANUS (Jth. 1:7, AV). *See* ANTILEBANON.

ANTIMONY an'tə-mō-nē [Heb. *'aḇnê-pûḵ*] (1 Ch. 29:2); AV "glistering stones"; NEB "stones for mosaic work" (with following word *riqmâ*); cf. RV "stones for inlaid work"; [Heb. *pûḵ*] (Isa. 54:11); AV "fair colours"; NEB "the finest mortar." As an element, antimony is a metallic substance gleaming silver-white; as a compound, "stibnite," it is a gray mineral powder.

In two other passages Heb. *pûḵ* is used of black eyepaint (2 K. 9:30; Jer. 4:30). *See* PAINT. In 1 Ch. 29:2, however, *'aḇnê-pûḵ* is usually taken to mean stones set in mortar, and *pûḵ* may also refer to mortar in Isa. 54:11 (BDB, p. 806, "dark cement setting off precious stones"; KoB, p. 754, *Hartmörtel* for both passages). It is likely that 1 Ch. 29:2 describes something on the order of mosaic work, as the NEB suggests. Another possibility is that the stones had the "brilliant hue of antimony" (BDB).

J. W. D. H.

ANTINOMIANISM an-ti-nō'mē-ən-iz-əm [<Gk. *antí*–'against' + *nómos*–'law']. The view that Christians are exempt from the demands of the moral law by reason of their reliance upon divine grace alone for salvation. Although the expression is not found in Scripture, it is evident that Paul was libelously accused by his detractors of holding such a false doctrine. In Rom. 3:8 he denied heatedly the accusation that he had called right conduct irrelevant to Christian experience, and again made this repudiation in Rom. 6:1f., 15f.

The gospel brings freedom *from* sin but not freedom *to* sin. It is true that in the new dispensation of Christ the believer is no longer under obligation to the Mosaic law, in the sense that he is emancipated from its frustrating impositions upon an incapable human will. His obedience is not rendered directly to the commandment, but represents his response to the person of Christ. But this reorientation does not supply him with a license to transgress with impunity. "The freedom from the moral law which the believer enjoys," writes Robert Haldane, "is a freedom from an obligation to fulfil it in his own person for his justification—a freedom from its condemnation on account of imperfection of obedience. But this is quite consistent with the eternal obligation of the moral law as a rule of life to the Christian" (*Epistle to the Romans* [repr. 1966], p. 259).

The Epistle of James provides a further NT corrective to any such misconception of the Christian faith. James would appear to have been confronting a popular abuse, perhaps current in gentile Christian circles (as Sieffert conjectures), which laid such exaggerated emphasis upon faith in the scheme of salvation that a certain indifference to morality was inadvertently encouraged. James's stress on "the perfect law of liberty" (1:25) and "the royal law" of love (2:8), combined with his recognition that works must necessarily evidence the reality of faith, completes Paul's protest against the unwarranted preference of any antinomian charge against Christianity. Positive warnings about the insidious nature of the heresy are found in 2 Cor. 6:14-18; 12:21; Eph. 5:9; 2 Pet. 2:18f.; and 1 Jn. 3:7f.

The reference in 1 John reminds us that some of the Gnostic sects of the 1st and 2nd cents. were antinomian in their teaching. The Nicolaitans, mentioned in Rev. 2:6, 14f. as well as in the writings of the early fathers, advocated a return to sub-Christian morality. The Ophites inverted the accepted standards of moral judgment, and the Cainites exalted Cain and others who withstood the God of the OT. In the Valentinians we meet "the most frank and definite statement of antinomianism in its widest and most immoral form" (J. M. Sterrett, *ERE,* I, 582). The licentious practices of these Gnostics (standing in such marked contrast with the severe asceticism of other schools within the movement) arose from an unscriptural dualism that erroneously divorced matter from spirit. Since matter was thought to be irredeemably corrupt, the bodily passions could be indulged without inhibition, and in fact should be, so that the soul might shine in brighter splendor by comparison. The maxim of Gnostic antinomianism was: "Give to the flesh the things of the flesh and to the spirit the things of the spirit." The Circumcellions of the 4th cent. laid themselves open to the charge of antinomianism, and one of Augustine's treatises was entitled *Against the Enemies of the Law and Prophets.*

The actual term "antinomian" was first employed, so far as is known, by Martin Luther in his controversy with Johannes Agricola. The latter denied that the preaching of law should precede or accompany the preaching of the gospel in order to arouse a sense of sin. "The decalogue," he declared, "belongs to the courthouse, not the pulpit." His slogan was "To the gallows with Moses." In the later Majoristic dispute even more extreme forms of antinomianism were defended by Andreas Poach and Anton Otto on the ground that the Christian is "above all obedience" (see R. Seeberg, *History of Doctrines* [Eng. tr. 1952], II, 251, 365f.).

Luther opposed his former pupil Agricola in six disputations against the antinomians. The reformer maintained that, although the new obedience of the believer no longer requires the coercive stimulus of the Mosaic code, the law nevertheless serves as a mirror, a guide, and a restraint. A specific proscription of antinomianism was written into the Formula of Concord, where it was firmly asserted that the liberty of Christians with respect to the demands of the law must not be misconstrued in the sense "that it were optional with them to do or omit them or that they might or could act contrary to the Law of God and nonetheless could retain faith and God's favor and grace" (Art. IV). Bente shrewdly assessed the situation when he asserted that the intrusion of antinomianism was "a veiled effort to open once more the doors of the Lutheran Church to the Roman work-righteousness which Luther had expelled" (F. Bente, *Concordia Triglotta,* Historical Introductions, p. 161).

Antinomian echoes may be heard in succeeding centuries among the Anabaptists in Germany and Holland, the Illuminati in Spain, and the Camisards in France. During the Evangelical Awakening in Britain, John Wesley had occasion to warn his followers against "the bane of true religion" (*Letters,* ed. Telford, VII, 169) and John Fletcher issued his celebrated *Checks to Antinomianism.* While some of the conclusions drawn, e.g., by R. A. Knox in his study of Enthusiasm, are to be resisted, the caveat of Wesley ought to be observed: "I have found that even the precious doctrine of salvation by faith has need to be guarded with the utmost care, or those who hear it will slight both inward and outward holiness" (*Letters*, V, 83). A. S. WOOD

ANTIOCH (PISIDIAN). A city evangelized by Paul and Barnabas (Acts 13:14; 14:19, 21; 2 Tim. 3:11) during the first missionary journey, possibly visited again in the second and third missionary journeys (Acts 16:6; 18:23). The city is identified in the NT as Pisidian Antioch (*Antiocheia hē Pisidia*; var. *tēs Pisidias*). Strabo (*Geog.* xii.3.31; 6.4; 8.14) names it "Antioch toward Pisidia," a more precise description since the city lay in Phrygian territory near the Pisidian border (W. M. Calder, ed., *Monumenta Asiae Minoris Antiqua*, VII (1956), p. xi). Its Phrygian character is shown by Phrygian inscriptions found near Antioch. Later, *ca.* A.D. 297, it became the metropolis of the new Roman province of Pisidia. The city was located on the right bank of the Anthius River between Sultan Dağ to the NE and Eğridir Gölü on the S at an elevation of about 3600 ft. (1100 m.), NE of the modern village of Yalvaç in west central Turkey.

I. History.–The city was founded *ca.* 350 B.C. by either Seleucus Nicator or his son Antiochus I on territory devoted to the Phrygian god Mên. Settlers included Greeks, Jews, and Phrygians from nearby areas (*ca.* 200 B.C. two thousand Jewish families were brought to Phrygia from Babylonia [Josephus *Ant.* xii.3.4]). The early history of Antioch was a struggle between mountain tribes and coastal peoples until Augustus created *Provincia Galatia* upon the death of Amyntas in 25 B.C. (Dio Cassius *Hist.* liii.26.3). Antioch, as a Roman colony, was entitled *Colonia Caesareia Antiocheia.* Its location, on a major junction of the Via Sebaste built by Augustus in 6 B.C. to link his colonies, was both economically and militarily important. Situated on the east-west highway from Syria to Ephesus, it provided commercial attractions to merchants. Historical data and epigraphical evidence indicate that it was a prominent city at the time of Paul's visit(s). Levick (pp. 43-45) considers the colony to have been of moderate size, the city wall enclosing an area of about 115 acres (47 hectares) and the *territorium* of Antioch covering about 540 acres (219 hectares).

II. Jews in Antioch.–The existence of a synagogue in Antioch indicates a sizable Jewish population. Ramsay concluded that the Phrygian Jews were largely the nobles and the rich, who adapted their religion and culture to Roman and local customs, although retaining basically their Jewish feeling and religion (*Bearing*; *Cities*, 255-59). Paul's ministry in Antioch, given in detail in Acts, was his first full-scale encounter with Hellenized and Greek-speaking Diaspora Jews who were citizens of a Roman colony. It began in the synagogue where the audience was augmented by proselytes (Acts 13:43) and God-fearers (v. 16) who were directly addressed along with the Jews. Perhaps this Hellenized character of Diaspora Judaism in Asia Minor has not always been adequately appreciated in discussing the Galatian problem. The power and status of the Jewish community in Antioch forced the banishment of Paul and Barnabas from the city (Acts 13:50) and Antiochene Jews pursued them to Lystra (14:19).

III. Language and Culture.–Phrygian, Latin, and Greek inscriptions have been found in and around Antioch — Latin usually in official documents and Greek in the popular and private documents. Latin did not decline as rapidly in Antioch as in other colonies (Levick, pp. 130-144) because of the presence of Roman colonists and veterans located there to Romanize the subjugated peoples (indigenous Phrygians and Pisidians and Diaspora Jews). These Roman (and Greek) influences, along with the local worship of Mên and Judaism, shaped the culture

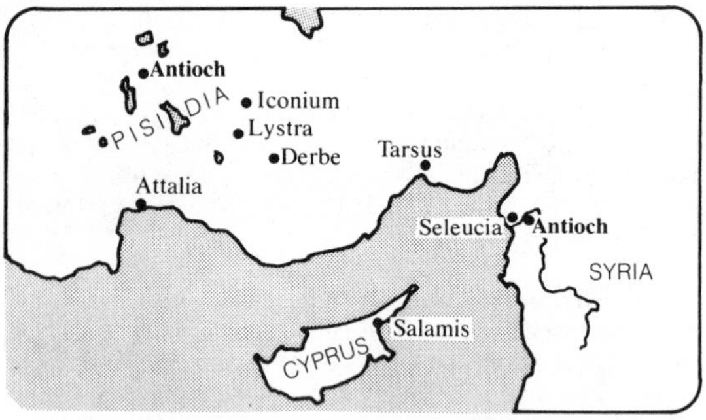

and religion, so that the city was both a model Roman colony and a striking mix of local and imported cultures (Levick, pp. 190-92). In this setting Paul confronted elements and issues that were formative factors in his succeeding ministry: the mission to acculturated Jews, to proselytized Gentiles (Gk. *éthnē*, Acts 13:48), and to the religious and secular pagans and Roman colonists. Paul's message had a mixed reception — enthusiastic interest, negative reaction, and political opposition. But in this first major confrontation with a heterogeneous culture being romanized, the gospel not only survived but triumphed, and Antioch became a paradigm for Paul's continuing ministry in Asia Minor, Greece, and Italy.

IV. Remains of the City.–The ruins of the city include remains of the Roman aqueduct which brought water from Sultan Dağ to the city, traces of the city wall on the NW, and on the W the ruins of the monumental Triple City Gate from early 3rd cent. A.D. Excavations by Ramsay and D. M. Robinson (*American Journal of Archaeology*, 28 [1924], 435-444) have uncovered remains of the first-century city: its squares, archways, reliefs, sculptures, and an elaborate temple dedicated to the god Mên. The architecture is a blend of Roman and Greek features. Inscriptions from the city and environs reflect its political, economic, and cultural prominence. A large Christian basilica with elaborate mosaics was built in the late 4th century.

Bibliography.–B. Levick, *Roman Colonies in Southern Asia Minor* (1967); W. M. Ramsay, *Bearing of Recent Discovery on the Trustworthiness of the NT* (2nd ed. 1915), pp. 353-369; *Cities of St. Paul* (1907, repr. 1970), pp. 245-314. B. VAN ELDEREN

ANTIOCH (SYRIAN), A city in ancient Syria (now Antakya, Turkey), founded by Seleucus I Nicator (300 B.C.) and named for his father Antiochus. It became the western capital of the Seleucid empire. The city enjoyed a beautiful site and an abundant supply of water from the springs of the suburb Daphne, 5 mi. (8 km.) S of the city, which was famous throughout antiquity as a pleasure resort. From early times, when the Seleucid kings rewarded their Jewish mercenaries with grants of land, Antioch had an important Jewish community.

When the deterioration of the Seleucid dynasty led to the Roman occupation of Syria (64 B.C.), Antioch became the capital of the new province of Syria and was beautified by Augustus and Tiberius, aided by Herod the Great. As a prosperous commercial center Antioch was a meeting point of the Greek and the oriental civilizations. When persecution broke out in Jerusalem following the death of Stephen, many of the followers of Jesus fled to Antioch. Some of these undertook the customary preaching to the Jews in the city. Others who were "Hellenist" (Greek-speaking) Jews, finding themselves in a Greek city, began to preach to the Greek-speaking Gentiles (Acts 11:19-21), some of whom had been attending the synagogue services, attracted by the Jewish ethical teaching; one of these may have been Nicolaus of Antioch,

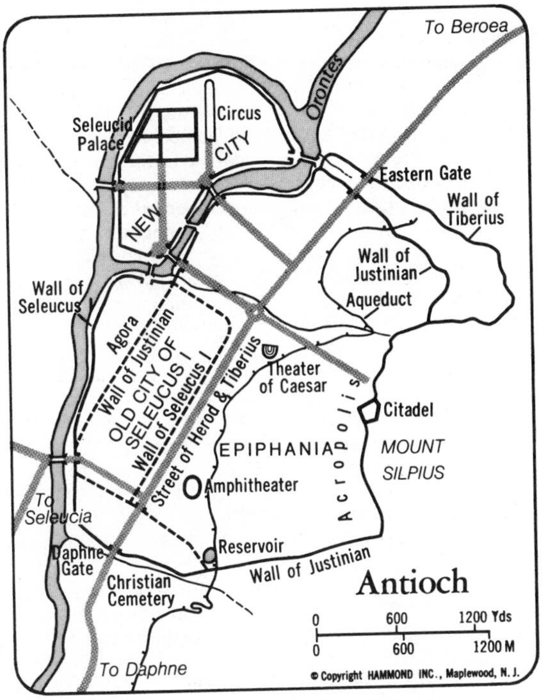

an early proselyte and one of the seven deacons in Jerusalem (Acts 6:5).

Following the success of the first preachers, Barnabas and Paul began to work in Antioch, and it was here that the name Christians was first used (Acts 11:22-26), the term apparently having been adopted by the Roman authorities as a means of describing the group. We hear of an *ekklēsía* including "prophets and teachers," named as Barnabas, Symeon Niger, Lucius of Cyrene, Manaen a "companion" of Herod the tetrarch, and Saul (Acts 13:1); but there is no indication of "elders" such as the leaders in Jerusalem. Jewish Christians and gentile Christians at first presumably met separately because of the Jewish law concerning association with Gentiles. About A.D. 46 the community was strong enough to send famine relief to Jerusalem by the hand of Barnabas and Paul (Acts 11:27-30). The question now arose of applying Jewish ritual law to the gentile converts. After a discussion in Jerusalem followed by a dispute in Antioch, Peter and Paul separated, the former to work among the Jews and the latter among the Gentiles, who were to be exempt from the law (Acts 15:1ff.; 2:1-21). Paul made Antioch the headquarters for his three missionary journeys in Asia Minor and Greece (Acts 13:1ff.; 15:40ff.; 18:23ff.). Local tradition made Peter the first "bishop" of the city, but the evidence for this is weak. Another tradition, equally dubious, made Luke the Evangelist a native of Antioch.

Led by Lucian of Antioch, early in the 4th cent., Antioch became an important center for biblical studies. The "Antiochene" text of the Greek NT was the forerunner of the "Constantinopolitan" text, and so of the Textus Receptus.

The celebrated Chalice of Antioch, reputed to have been found in or near the city about 1910, is now owned by the Metropolitan Museum of Art in New York. The original owners claimed that this was the cup used at the Last Supper, but scholarly opinion now dates it in the 4th century. Excavations were begun at Antioch in 1932 by a group of American sponsors and the Louvre, Paris, but were interrupted by war in 1939.

Bibliography.–G. Downey, *A History of Antioch in Syria from Seleucus to the Arab Conquest* (1961), with full bibliography; *Ancient Antioch* (1963); A. D. Nock, "*Isopolitea* and the Jews," in Z. Stewart, ed., *Essays on Religion in the Ancient World* (1972), II, 960-62. G. DOWNEY

ANTIOCHIANS an-tē-ok'e-ənz [Gk. *Antiocheís*]; NEB ANTIOCHENES; RSV "citizens of Antioch." An honorary title that Jason promised to confer on Hellenized Jews of Jerusalem in return for his appointment as high priest (2 Macc. 4:7-9).

Antiochus IV Epiphanes, who ruled Syria from 175-164 B.C., had determined to Hellenize the entire kingdom, but found the Jews stubbornly opposed to the policy. Jason, the brother of the high priest Onias III, bribed Antiochus, with money as well as promises of Hellenizing efforts, to get Antiochus to appoint him high priest. With the founding of a gymnasium (2 Macc. 4:12) and the increase of adopted foreign ways (4:13; cf. 1 Macc. 1:14f.), he succeeded not only in "an extreme of Hellenization" but even in turning the priests from their service at the altar to "unlawful proceedings in the wrestling arena," etc. (2 Macc. 4:14). When the quinquennial games were held at Tyre (174 B.C.), Jason sent "Antiochians" from Jerusalem with money for a sacrifice to Hercules (4:18f.). The money was used, however, toward the construction of triremes (4:20).

The suggestion has been made that the name of Jerusalem was actually changed to Antioch—which would certainly be in line with the policy of Antiochus throughout his kingdom—but there is no positive evidence to support this theory. E. Bickermann argues that the text simply means "to register the Antiochenes in Jerusalem"; in other words, as Bruce explains, the "'Antiochenes of Jerusalem' probably formed a distinct corporation in Jerusalem and enjoyed the privileges granted to a free Greek city."

Jason and the hellenization movement were opposed by devout Jews (1 Macc. 1:15) who banded together as Hasidim ("Pious"), the precursors of the Pharisees; but they could not halt the trend.

Bibliography.–*HNTT*, pp. 10-12; F. F. Bruce, *Israel and the Nations* (1963), pp. 134-37; Josephus *Ant.* xii.5; E. Bickermann, *Der Gott der Makkabäer* (1973), pp. 59-65. W. S. L. S.

ANTIOCHIS an-tī'ə-kis [Gk. *Antiochis*]. A concubine of Antiochus Epiphanes whom he presented with the two Cilician cities Tarsus and Mallus, which caused the cities to revolt (2 Macc. 4:30).

ANTIOCHUS an-tī'ə-kəs [Gk. *Antiochus*–'opposer,' 'withstander'].

1. The father of Numenius, who in company with Antipater, son of Jason, was sent by Jonathan on an embassy to the Romans and Spartans to renew "the friendship" and "former confederacy" made by Judas (1 Macc. 12:16; 14:22).

2. The favorite name of the Seleucid kings, whose history with reference to Jewish affairs is contained particularly in the books of Maccabees, and is predicted with remarkable minuteness in Dnl. 11. The name was first borne by one of the generals of Philip, whose son SELEUCUS, by the hold of the first Ptolemy, established himself as ruler of Babylon. In the Macedonian calendar the Seleucid era began with Dios 1 (Oct. 7), 321 B.C.; in the Babylonian it began with Nisanu 1 (Apr. 3), 311 B.C. Parker and Dubberstein cautioned: "The beginnings and ends of their reigns cannot always be determined with exactitude" (*Babylonian Chronology* [1956], p. 20). When Ptolemy, son of Lagus, became master of Southern Syria, the line dividing Seleucus and his successors from the Ptolemies (cf. "king of the north" and "king of the south" in Dnl. 11) was drawn somewhat to the north of Damascus, the capital of Coele-Syria.

The reigns are as follows:

1. Seleucus I Nicator, 312-281 B.C.
2. Antiochus I Soter, his son, 280-261 B.C.
3. Antiochus II Theos, his son, 261-246 B.C.
4. Seleucus II Callinicus, his son, 245-225 B.C.
5. Seleucus III Soter, 225-223 B.C.
6. Antiochus III the Great, his brother, 223-187 B.C.
7. Seleucus IV Philopator, his son, 187-175 B.C.
8. Antiochus IV Epiphanes, his brother, 175-164 B.C.
9. Antiochus V Eupator, his son, 164/163-162 B.C.
10. Demetrius I Soter, son of Seleucus IV Philopator, 161-150 B.C.
11. Alexander Balas, a usurper, who pretended to be son of Antiochus Ephiphanes, and was acknowledged by the Romans, 150-146 B.C.
12. Antiochus VI, Dionysus, son of the preceding (murdered by the usurper Tryphon, who contested the kingdom till 137 B.C.), 145-142/141 B.C.
13. Demetrius II, Nicator, son of Demetrius I, Soter, 145-139/138 B.C.
14. Antiochus VII, Sidetes, his brother, 139/138-129 B.C.

Bibliography.–For a summation of modern literature see V. Tcherikover, *Hellenistic Civilization and the Jews* (1961), p. 470. In addition, S. Tedesche and S. Zeitlin, *First Book of Maccabees* (1950), *passim*; M. Rostovtzeff, *Social & Economic History of the Hellenistic World* (3 vols., 2nd ed. 1953), *passim*; J. C. Dancy, *Comm. on I Maccabees* (1954), *passim*; R. A. Parker and W. H. Dubberstein, *Babylonian Chronology 626 B.C.-A.D. 75* (2nd ed. 1956), pp. 37-44; G. Downey, *History of Antioch in Syria* (1961), pp. 87-142; S. K. Eddy, *The King is Dead* (1961), *passim*; Y. H. Landau, *IEJ*, 11 (1961), 118-126; S. Zeitlin, *Rise and Fall of the Judaean State*, I (1962), *passim*; Y. H. Landau, *IEJ*, 16 (1966), 54-70. D. S. Russell, *The Jews from Alexander to Herod*, Vol. V of *New Clarendon Bible* (1967), *passim*; B. Reicke, *NT Era* (1968), pp. 48-73.

B. K. WALTKE

ANTIOCHUS I SOTER sō'târ [Gk. *Sōtēr*–'savior']. Born 324 B.C., son of Seleucus Nicator. He fell in love with his stepmother, Stratonike, and became very ill. His father, when he discovered the cause of his son's illness, gave her to him in 292 B.C., and yielded to him the sovereignty over all the countries beyond the Euphrates, as well as the title of king. When Seleucus returned to Macedonia in 281 B.C., he was murdered by Ptolemaeus Ceraunus. Antiochus thus became ruler of the whole Syrian kingdom. At this time the Hellenistic state was already organized, most of the new Hellenic cities founded, the economic organization functioning, and the social classes well established. But at the same time a new series of wars, which heavily involved Syria, Babylonia, and Cilicia, the "Syrian Wars," began between the Seleucids and the Ptolemies. The "First Syrian War," waged *ca.* 280-270 B.C., occasioned heavy fighting and considerable civil effort by both sides. Antiochus I lost important districts of Asia Minor and Syria to Ptolemy II Philadelphus (*see* PTOLEMY). Antiochus also waged war on Eumenes of Pergamum, but without success. For the victories of his elephant corps over the Gauls, who had settled Asia Minor, he received the surname of Soter. It was in a battle with these inveterate foes of his country that he met his death (261 B.C.).

J. E. HARRY
B. K. WALTKE

ANTIOCHUS II THEOS the-os' [Gk. *Theos*–'god,' so surnamed "by the Milesians because he overthrew their tyrant Timarchus" (Appian *Syr.* 65)]. Born 286 B.C., son and successor of Antiochus I, 261-246 B.C. In the "Second Syrian War" (260-253 B.C.) he regained from Ptolemy II Philadelphus of Egypt much of what Antiochus I had lost, but was obliged to buy peace in 253 B.C. by divorcing his wife Laodice and marrying Ptolemy's daughter Berenice (the incident in view in Dnl. 11:6) with the understanding that the kingdom should go to Berenice's son. After the death of Ptolemy, "the king of the south" (Dnl. 11:6), Antiochus recalled Laodice and named her eldest son (Seleucus Callinicus) as his successor to the throne. But Laodice (probably because she feared a second repudiation) had Berenice, her child, and Antiochus all murdered in 246 B.C. After the death of Antiochus, Ptolemy Euergetes the brother of Berenice ("out of a branch of her root," Dnl. 11:7) exacted vengeance for his sister's death by an invasion of Syria in which Laodice was killed, her son Seleucus Callinicus driven for a time from the throne, and the whole country plundered (Dnl. 11:7-9).

J. E. HARRY B. K. WALTKE

ANTIOCHUS III THE GREAT [Gk. *Megas*–'The Great']. Born 242 B.C., Seleucid king of Syria 223-187 B.C., second son of Seleucus II Callinicus (246-226 B.C.); brother and successor of Seleucus III Soter (226-223 B.C.).

After stabilizing the Seleucid Empire, Antiochus began the "Fourth Syrian War" by seeking to wrest southern Syria and Palestine from Ptolemy IV Philopator, who had previously neglected foreign affairs. His second campaign (219 B.C.) took him S of Mt. Carmel to the fortress of Dura. Misinformed about the Egyptian strength, he agreed to a four months' truce and led his army into winter quarters (Polybius v.60; Justinus xxx.1.2; cf. Dnl. 10:11). By spring 218 B.C. Antiochus had seen through the negotiations and began methodically to reduce Coele-Syria. In 217 B.C. he advanced beyond the frontier town of Raphia (Rafa, S of Gaza), where Ptolemy IV utterly defeated him. The Egyptian king reclaimed southern Syria, Palestine, and Phoenicia (Polybius v.79f., 82-86; Strabo *Geog.* xvi.2.31; cf. Dnl. 11:11).

Antiochus now undertook to bring under his sway again all the territory of the Near East. His expedition against Bactria and Parthia gained for him the surname "The Great." When Ptolemy IV died in 204 B.C. and was succeeded by his four-year-old child Ptolemy V Epiphanes, Antiochus saw his opportunity to retake the three countries. After concluding a pact with Philip the son of Demetrius, Antiochus attacked Coele-Syria in 202 B.C. Although details of the campaign(s) are obscure, it is clear that by 199 B.C. Antiochus considered the conquest of Coele-Syria, Phoenicia, and Palestine achieved, for he then invaded the undefended territory of Pergamos. But during his absence Ptolemy, aided by Scopas, formerly a *strategos* of the Aetolian League, invaded Coele-Syria and obtained possession of Jerusalem. Antiochus returned to confront this challenge and won a decisive victory at Panias (NT Caesarea Philippi) in 198 B.C. This battle denotes the final and definite replacement of Ptolemaic rule by the Seleucids in Palestine (Polybius xv.20; xvi.18f.; xviii.1; Appian *Syr.* 1; Livy xxxiii.19; Josephus *Ant.* xii.3.3; cf. Dnl. 11:13-16). The bulk of the Jewish population in Jerusalem opened its gates and assisted in the expulsion of its Egyptian garrison. Antiochus rewarded the Jews for their "splendid reception" by restoring those parts of Jerusalem destroyed by the war, freeing its citizens from taxes for three years, guaranteeing an inviolate and subsidized temple, and in general permitting "members of the nation to have a form of government in accordance with the laws of the country" (Josephus *Ant.* xii.3.4).

After completing a treaty with Ptolemy Epiphanes in which Antiochus betrothed his daughter Cleopatra to the young king (Polybius xxviii.20; Appian *Syr.* 5; cf. Dnl. 11:17), Antiochus turned to the West and encountered

Rome. He launched his forces upon Asia Minor in 197 B.C. and Greece in 194 B.C., but the Romans defeated him at Thermopylae (191 B.C.) and at Magnesia in Lydia (190 B.C.). According to the treaty signed at Apamea in 189 B.C., the Asiatic monarch was obliged to renounce everything on the Roman side of the Taurus and to pay enormous reparations over the course of twelve years (Appian *Syr.* 36-39; Polybius xx-xxi; Livy xxxvi-xxxvii; Josephus *Ant.* xii.10.6; 1 Macc. 1:11; 8:6-8; cf. Dnl. 11:18f.).

In 187 B.C. Antiochus marched against the Armenian revolt. In order to replenish his exhausted treasury, he attempted to plunder a temple; but both he and his soldiers were slain by the Elymaeans.

J. E. HARRY   B. K. WALTKE

ANTIOCHUS IV EPIPHANES ə-pi'fə-nēz [Gk. *Epiphanēs*–'illustrious'; nicknamed *Epimanēs*–'madman' (Polybius xxvi.10); on coins *Theos Epiphanēs*–'god manifest']. Younger son of Antiochus the Great (Appian *Syr.* 45; 1 Macc. 1:11), born 215 B.C., ruler 175-163 B.C. His career with respect to Palestine is recorded in 1 and 2 Maccabees, and remarkably predicted in Dnl. 11:21-35. Although some modern scholars speak sarcastically of the Jewish books that represent the events in Judea as of central importance, E. R. Bevan observed, "In regard to the influence destined to be exerted upon the subsequent history of mankind . . . the Jewish books were right. Of all that was happening in the kingdom of Antiochus, the events in Judea were by far the most important in consequence for the mind of man in ages to come" (*CAH,* VIII [1930], 514).

After the battle of Magnesia, Antiochus lived in Rome as a hostage in connection with the reparations Antiochus the Great had to pay. In 175 B.C. he was released by the intervention of his brother Seleucus IV Philopator, who substituted his own son Demetrius I as hostage. While Antiochus was at Athens, Seleucus IV was assassinated by his chief minister, Heliodorus. Antiochus IV, with the military sanction of the Pergamene monarch Eumenes II, expelled Heliodorus and usurped the throne to the exclusion of both Demetrius and the late king's younger son Antiochus, still a baby in Syria. The evidence, both from contrasting coins bearing either the image of the baby Antiochus or the image of the uncle Antiochus, and from cuneiform documents dating from 175 to 169 B.C. with the reading "Antiochus and Antiochus kings," indicates a struggle for power between the nephew and uncle. Commenting on Dnl. 11:21, E. R. Bevan concluded, "our scrappy data indicate that it required a good deal of dexterity and intrigue on the part of Antiochus for him to establish his position in Syria, but that he did get the better of the opposing elements" (*CAH,* VIII, 498).

His intervention in Jerusalem was brought about in part by the factions within the Jewish high-priestly state. The personal strife for power between Ḥonya III (Gk. Onias), his brother Yeshua (Jesus, called Jason by the Greeks), and a certain Menelaus of the tribe of Benjamin supported by the powerful house of Tobiah, was exacerbated by the fact that Jason and Menelaus wished to introduce Hellenistic culture while Onias stood by the traditional custom and law. By the promise both of a larger tribute and of habituating the Jews to Greek customs Jason induced Antiochus, an intense champion of Hellenization, to establish him as high priest in place of his brother (2 Macc. 4:7-20). Jerusalem under Jason was thus converted into a Greek city.

When Antiochus' sister Cleopatra I, the queen-regent of Egypt, died and the power was seized by two palace servants of the minor king Ptolemy Philometor, the war party at Alexandria, which wanted to recover Coele-Syria, gained the ascendancy. Antiochus moved south as far as Joppa with a force to encounter a possible invasion. The war did not come to pass, however, and after paying a visit to Jerusalem he returned to Antioch.

In 171 B.C. the blatant opportunist Menelaus, with the support of the Tobiads, purchased the venerable office of high priest from the "incarnate Zeus," who had to worry about military expenses. Menelaus came to Antioch in 170/169 B.C., during the absence of Antiochus in Cilicia, and persuaded a certain Andronicus to murder Onias, who had taken refuge in Antioch. At the same time Andronicus murdered the nephew king Antiochus. While Menelaus was at Antioch and desperate for money, his brother Lysimachus, whom he had left in command, robbed some of the temple's golden furniture. Although this provoked rioting in which Lysimachus was killed, Menelaus, through bribery, had the king reestablish him (2 Macc. 4:24-50).

From 170 to 168 B.C. Antiochus engaged in the "Sixth Syrian War," in the course of which he twice marched against Egypt. During the first attack, probably in 169 B.C., most of Egypt fell to him, including Memphis where he held the young Ptolemy captive. The people at Alexandria put the king's younger brother (Ptolemy Euergetes II) upon the throne. Toward the end of 169 B.C. Antiochus withdrew from Egypt, leaving Ptolemy Philometor king in Memphis and the younger Ptolemy king in Alexandria (cf. Dnl. 11:25-27).

While Antiochus was in Egypt a false rumor ran through Palestine that he was dead, and as a result Jason, who had fled to Transjordan, broke into Jerusalem and began killing the adherents of Menelaus (2 Macc. 4:39ff.). V. Tcherikover argues convincingly that the opponents of the king — the enemies of the Hellenizers — then defeated Jason and forced him back to the country of the Ammonites (*Hellenistic Civilization and the Jews* [1961], p. 187; 2 Macc. 5:7). On returning from Egypt, Antiochus, knowing that Jerusalem, a vital point in his frontier defenses, was in the hands of his opponents, stormed the city, killing thousands of Jews and selling thousands more into slavery. Moreover, he entered the holy of holies and carried off a quantity of gold and silver vessels from the temple (1 Macc. 1:20-42; 2 Macc. 5:1-23; Josephus *Ant.* xii.5.3; *CAp* ii.83; Dnl. 11:28). At some point before his next retributive raid the insurgents must have again taken the city.

In 168 B.C., in his second attack upon Egypt, Antiochus marched against Alexandria with even stronger forces, furious at a temporary collaboration of the two Ptolemies against him. After capturing Memphis he once again marched upon Alexandria. But then "ships of Kittim" arrived (Dnl. 11:30); at Eleusias, the eastern suburb of Alexandria, the Roman legate C. Popilius Laenas handed Antiochus an ultimatum from the senate, arrogantly drew a circle around Antiochus, and demanded his answer before he stepped outside the circle. Antiochus was forced to retreat to Syria within a specified time (Polybius xxix.2.1-4; 27.1-8; Livy xlv.12.1-6; Diodorus xxxi.2; Appian *Syr.* 66; Justinus xxxiv.3; Dnl. 11:28-30).

With the independence of Egypt and the threat of Rome from the south, the tyrannical king determined to secure his southern Palestinian border by organizing a solid Seleucid province. To Antiochus it evidently appeared that transforming the city into a settlement of gentile soldiers (1 Macc. 1:35f.; 3:45) was the only means of achieving political stability in Palestine, since that country's religion was out of place in a predominantly Hellenized empire and its conservative party opposed

Antiochus IV Epiphanes, on silver tetradrachma (168 B.C.) (W. S. LaSor)

him. In 167 B.C. he detached a body of troops to Jerusalem. They took the city by assault on the sabbath, slaughtered a large part of the inhabitants, and gave up the city to a general sack (1 Macc. 1:30ff.; 2 Macc. 5:24ff.; cf. Dnl. 11:31ff.). Then followed the decrees that have rendered his name infamous: the Jews were compelled under penalty of death "to depart from the laws of their fathers, and to cease living by the laws of God. Further, the sanctuary in Jerusalem was to be polluted and called 'Jupiter Olympius' " (2 Macc. 6:1f.), probably a Syrian deity in Hellenistic garb (E. Bickermann, *Der Gott der Makkabäer* [1937], pp. 111ff.). On Chislev 15 Antiochus instituted the pagan festival of "light," which celebrated the rebirth of the sun, and had a Greek altar erected upon the old altar in the temple court (Dnl. 11:31; cf. Josephus *Ant.* xii.5.4); the first victim was sacrificed to Jupiter Olympius on the twenty-fifth (Dec. 16, 167 B.C.) of the same month. Such an offering to Antiochus was to be made on the twenty-fifth of every month, since that date was celebrated as his birthday. All of this was a serious error on Antiochus' part. Instead of consolidating his empire around the Hellenic culture and religion, he sparked the Maccabean revolution (*see* MACCABEES).

Antiochus did not personally oversee the implementation of these policies but turned to campaigns in Parthia and Armenia (Josephus *Ant.* xii.7.2; Appian *Syr.* 45). Having heard of the riches of the temple of Nanaea in Elymais (1 Macc. 6:1ff.), hung with the gifts of Alexander, he resolved to plunder it. Although he did not fall like his father in the act of sacrilege, the event hastened his death. He retired to Babylon and then to Tabae (Isfahan) in Persia. Here, having first heard of the successes of the Maccabees in restoring the temple worship at Jerusalem, he died insane in 164 B.C. (1 Macc. 6:1-16; Appian *Syr.* 66; Polybius xxi.11; xxxi.9; Josephus *Ant.* xii.8.1ff.).

See also DESOLATING SACRILEGE. B. K. WALTKE

ANTIOCHUS V EUPATOR ū-pä'tōr [Gk. *Eupatōr*–'having a noble father']. Son (born 173 B.C.) and successor (163-162 B.C.) of Antiochus Epiphanes.

When he departed for the East Antiochus IV left his infant son Antiochus in Syria. A certain Lysias, who had the rank of Kinsman, was to act for the king in Syria during his absence. With his father's untimely death, Antiochus V succeeded to the throne in 164 B.C. while yet a child (of nine years according to Appian *Syr.* 66; or twelve years according to Porphyry in Eusebius *Chronicon*–Armenian i.348).

Antiochus Epiphanes had precipitated an internal division in his kingdom by his deathbed nomination of Philip as regent and guardian (1 Macc. 6:14ff., 55; 2 Macc. 9:29). With Philip still in Persia, Lysias held his position as regent, and together with Antiochus V directed a large army against Judea, complete with elephants, to relieve a hard-pressed garrison at Jerusalem in 162 B.C. They repulsed Judas Maccabeus at Beth-zecharia, and took Beth-zur after a vigorous resistance (1 Macc. 6:31-50). But when the Jewish force in the temple was on the point of yielding, Lysias persuaded the king to conclude a hasty peace in order that he might advance to meet Philip, who had returned from Persia and made himself master of Antioch (1 Macc. 6:51-63; Josephus *Ant.* xii.9.5ff.). Lysias defeated Philip, but in 162 B.C. Demetrius Soter son of Seleucus Philopator, now a young man of twenty-five, escaped from Rome with the aid of the historian Polybius and reached Syria by way of Lycia. The population of Syria quickly rallied to the legitimate heir of Seleucus IV, and the army abandoned the cause of Lysias and the young boy-king, putting them both to death (1 Macc. 7:14; 2 Macc. 14:1f.; Justinus xxxiv.3; Josephus *Ant.* xii.10.1; Polybius xxxi.11; Appian *Syr.* 46f., 67; Livy *Epit.* xlvi). B. K. WALTKE

ANTIOCHUS VI (surnamed *Epiphanes Dionysus*–'illustrious Bacchus' on coins; but *theós*–'god' by Josephus *Ant.* xiii.7.1). Son of Alexander (Balas) king of Syria, who claimed to be the son of Antiochus Epiphanes; ruled 145-142 B.C.

Though still a child, Antiochus VI was brought forward from Arabia by Diodotus (who assumed the name Tryphon [Strabo xvi.752]), who had been one of his father's chief ministers, as a claimant of the throne of Syria against Demetrius Nicator. Tryphon forced the Syrians to recognize his protege (1 Macc. 11:39, 54; Justinus xxxvi.1; Appian *Syr.* 68). The kingdom was thereby divided between Tryphon, who had mastery of the Orontes Valley with headquarters in Antioch, and Demetrius, who had mastery of most of the seaboard and of the provinces beyond the Euphrates with headquarters in Seleucia. By transferring his allegiance to Antiochus Dionysus, Jonathan Maccabeus was installed in the high priesthood, and his brother Simon was appointed commander of the royal troops in Palestine (1 Macc. 11:57ff.). Jonathan subjected the whole land from Damascus to Antioch (v. 62), defeated the troops of Demetrius (v. 63), and even sucfully repelled a fresh incursion of Demetrius into Palestine (12:24ff.).

As soon as the monarchy had been firmly established, Tryphon unmasked his long-cherished plan of seizing the royal power for himself (1 Macc. 12:39). First he had put to death Jonathan, whom he had seized at Ptolemais separated from his main body of troops. On his return to Syria he dethroned Antiochus and in 142 B.C. procured his assassination by surgeons in an operation (1 Macc. 13:31ff.; Josephus *Ant.* xiii.5.6; Appian *Syr.* 68; Livy *Epit.* lv).

B. K. WALTKE

ANTIOCHUS VII SIDETES si-dēt'ēz (so called because he was born in Sida in Pamphylia [Eusebius *Chronicon*–Armenian i.349]; called also *Eusebēs*–'pious' [Josephus *Ant.* xii.8.2]; on coins *Euergetēs*–'benefactor'). Born 159 B.C., second son of Demetrius I; ruled 139/138-129 B.C.

After his brother Demetrius II Nicator was captured by Mithridates king of Parthia in 139 B.C., temporarily leaving Tryphon sole king in Syria, Antiochus set foot quickly in Syria and took up the task of restoring Seleucid authority in the land. He married (as her third husband) Cleopatra Thea, his captive brother's wife (Justinus xxxvi.1), captured Tryphon and compelled him to commit suicide in 138 B.C. (Strabo *Geog.* xiv.886), and ruled for nine years as the last strong representative of the old royal house.

Before making his invasion Antiochus gained the allegiance of Simon by confirming to him concessions granted by his predecessors and adding the right to coin money (1 Macc. 15:1-9; Josephus *Ant.* xiii.7.1). But when he grew independent of Simon's help, Antiochus withdrew the concessions and demanded the surrender of the fortresses beyond the frontier of Judea, Joppa and Gezer, and of the Akra at Jerusalem, or an equivalent in money (1 Macc. 15:26-31; Josephus *Ant.* xiii.7.3). Simon refused the payment. Antiochus then sent a detachment under a certain Cendebaeus in 138 B.C., which was defeated by Simon's two sons, John Hyrcanus and Judas (1 Macc. 16:1-10). The land had rest for the next three years. Then in 135 B.C., while he was heavy with wine, Simon was assassinated at Jericho by a son-in-law, Ptolemy, who was in league with Antiochus VII (1 Macc. 16:11-20). John Hyrcanus forestalled Ptolemy's attempt to seize the chief power and had himself installed as high priest.

Antiochus, who had by this time returned from pursuing Tryphon, invaded Judea in person, reoccupied the frontier fortresses, and besieged Jerusalem for more than a year, after which it surrendered in 134 B.C. Although his councillors urged him to exterminate the turbulent people, he refused. Instead, through fear of the Romans, he did not reimpose the tribute and gave back the places the Jews had conquered beyond their frontiers. But he did insist that the Jews pay a tribute for these and a war indemnity of five hundred talents. The high priest also had to give hostages—including his own brother—and the fortifications of Jerusalem were demolished. Antiochus conciliated the Jews by marks of respect for their religion, but politically the Jews were subject to the house of Seleucus (Josephus *Ant.* xiii.8.3f.; cf. Eusebius *Chronicon*–Armenian i.349).

Having restored the kingdom in Syria, Antiochus set himself against the eastern provinces with some initial success against the Parthians in 130 B.C. But in 129 B.C. the Parthians set his brother Demetrius II free to create a diversion in Syria. In the same year Antiochus was entirely defeated by Phraortes II (Arsaces VII) king of Parthia, and fell in battle (Josephus *Ant.* xiii.8.4; Justinus xxxviii.10; Appian *Syr.* 68).

B. K. WALTKE

ANTIPAS an'tə-pəs [Gk. *Antipas,* abbr. of *Antipatros* (Antipater)].

1. A martyr of the church of Pergamum, described as "my witness, my faithful one" (Rev. 2:13).

2. *See* HEROD V.

ANTIPATER an-tip'ə-tər [Gk. *Antipatros*–'instead of (his) father']. The name of several men in the books of Maccabees and Josephus.

1. One of two envoys sent by the Jews in the time of the Maccabees to confirm the former amity with the Romans and Spartans (1 Macc. 12:16; 14:22).

2. The father of Herod the Great. According to Josephus (*Ant.* xiv.1.3) he was the son of a noble Idumean, to whom the government of that district had been given by Alexander Janneus and his queen Alexandra, at whose court he was raised. Antipater married an illustrious Arabian lady, Cypros, by whom he had four sons — Phasael, Herod, Joseph, and Pheroras — and a daughter, Salome.

He served as a counselor to Hyrcanus II against his brother Aristobulus II. When Pompey captured Jerusalem and took Aristobulus with his family to Rome in 63 B.C., Antipater continued to exercise his influence on the high priest and labored to ingratiate himself with the Romans. From the Roman occupation in 63 B.C. until 55 B.C., he was the unofficial ruler of the land. In 62 B.C. he assisted Scaurus, Pompey's legate to Syria, in his punitive campaign against the Nabateans. When Gabinius became proconsul of Syria, a rebellion broke out in Judea that had to be put down three times between 57 and 55 B.C. With the full support of Antipater, Gabinius and his daring cavalry commander Mark Antony succeeded in the suppressions. In 55 B.C., during the third campaign, Antipater, who had also recently helped Gabinius in connection with a change of regime in Egypt, was made Roman procurator (Gk. *epimelētēs*) in Jerusalem (Josephus *Ant.* xiv.1-7).

After Gaius Julius Caesar occupied Rome, he liberated a number of political prisoners, including Aristobulus II, whom he sent to Syria against Pompey. Pompey's supporters, however, soon eliminated Aristobulus and his elder son Alexander. In 48 B.C. Pompey was defeated at Pharsalus in Thessaly and slain by the ministers of Ptolemy when he sought refuge in Egypt. Caesar now rushed to Alexandria and occupied both the city and the land. This began the Alexandrian War in 48-47 B.C. When Caesar was in a desparate strait for reinforcements and supplies, and found himself in mortal danger, Antipater appeared as *deus ex machina* (Josephus *Ant.* xiv.8.1). With a combination of friendly influence on Syrian neighbors, speedy intervention of Jewish troops, and pressure on the Egyptian Jews, he made it possible for the popular Roman hero to continue his rise to dictatorship (Caesar, *Bellum alexandrinum* xxvi.1-3).

In grateful repayment for this assistance, Caesar granted a series of privileges to Antipater and the Jews. B. Reicke concluded: "These privileges remained extremely important even in the NT period, because Antony and Octavian, Caesar's successors, were prepared to continue his policies" (*NT Era* [1968], p. 88). Thus in 47 B.C. Hyrcanus II was confirmed in his high priesthood, and Antipater was granted Roman (city) citizenship as well as made procurator of the Roman Republic over the territory of the Jews. He in turn appointed his sons Phasael and Herod governors respectively of Jerusalem and Galilee. Moreover many courtesies were extended to the Jews: taxes were reduced, several towns in the Valley of Jezreel added to the land, exemption from the usual obligation of providing auxiliary troops, and freedom in their synagogues (Josephus *Ant.* xiv.9). B. Reicke observed: "One should not overlook the significance this freedom was later to have for the spread of the Gospel, which took place in and through the synagogues of the Diaspora, including their membership and adherents" (*op. cit.,* p. 89). In 46 B.C. Antipater dissuaded Herod from attacking Hyrcanus, and in 43 B.C. (after Caesar's death) he regulated the tax imposed by Cassius upon Judea for her support of the Roman troops. In 43 B.C. Malichus, whose life Antipater had twice saved, bribed Hyrcanus' cupbearer to poison him.

3. The eldest son of Herod by his first wife Doris. After his marriage to Mariamne the Hasmonean, Herod sent Doris and Antipater away. But when Herod, being suspicious of Mariamne's loyalty, ordered her execution in 29 B.C., tensions arose between him and her sons, Alexander and Aristobulus. In order to humble them Herod restored Antipater to court. Antipater now sought to annihilate Mariamne's sons by circulating calumnies against them. Even after Herod sent Antipater to Rome as the apparent crown prince in 12/11 B.C., he continued to send back false reports against his brothers. Inflamed by these reports Herod took the case before

Caesar, who, finding nothing of substance, effected a temporary reconciliation. But Herod continued in his suspicions and in the end Antipater and his allies gained their objective: Alexander and Aristobulus were executed on Herod's orders and Antipater became joint ruler with his father in 7 B.C. Testimony later came to light exposing both Antipater's seditious activity against his brothers and a plot to murder the aged Herod. Antipater was condemned to death and the sentence carried out five days before Herod's own death in March/April, 4 B.C.

See H. W. Hoehner, *Herod Antipas* (1972).

See also HEROD. B. K. WALTKE

ANTIPATRIS an-tip'ə-tris [Gk. *Antipatris*]. A town mentioned in Acts 23:31 as the end of the first stage of Paul's transfer, under a guard of 470 Roman soldiers, from Jerusalem to Caesarea. The site is located near Râs el-'Ain at the headwaters of the Yarkon, about 16 km. (10 mi.) north of Lydda (Lud), 65 km. (40 mi.) from Jerusalem and 40 km. (25 mi.) from Caesarea. Antipatris was built by Herod the Great in 9 B.C. and named in honor of his father Antipater, who had been procurator of Judea under Julius Caesar. The site was previously occupied by Kfar Saba (Josephus *Ant.* xvi.5.2 [143]; xiii.15.1 [390]; and *BJ* i.21.9 [417]). This is also the site of OT APHEK. In Roman times Antipatris served as a military relay station. It also was recognized as the border between Samaria and Judea.

The third season of excavations at Tell Aphek was conducted jointly in 1974 by Tel Aviv University Institute of Archeology, New Orleans Baptist Theological Seminary, Baylor University, the municipality of Petah Tikva, and the Department of Antiquities and Museums of the Ministry of Education and Culture, State of Israel. During this season a street of Antipatris bordered by a row of shops was uncovered; it had been destroyed during the conquest of Herodian Antipatris by Vespasian in A.D. 67. Occupation of Tell Aphek, one of the largest tells in the state of Israel, dates from the beginning of the Early Bronze Age, *ca.* 3000 B.C., and its importance as a crossroads is apparent in every period of its history. The ruins of the castle of Mirabel form a picturesque part of Râs el-'Ain. W. S. L. S.

ANTONIA an-tō'nē-ə. A fortress in Jerusalem N of the temple, rebuilt from the ancient Baris by Herod the Great *ca.* 24 B.C., and named after Antony, who had appointed Herod king of Judea. It was considerably larger than the Baris, and had four lofty corner towers.

ANTOTHIAH an-tō-thī'ə (1 Ch. 8:24, NEB); **ANTOTHIJAH** an-tō-thī'jə (AV). *See* ANTHOTHIJAH.

ANTOTHITE an'tə-thīt (1 Ch. 11:28; 12:3, AV). *See* ANATHOTH.

ANUB ā'nub [Heb. *'anûḇ*–'ripe']. A descendant of Judah and son of Koz (1 Ch. 4:8).

ANUS ā'nəs (1 Esd. 9:48, AV). *See* ANNIUTH.

ANVIL [Heb. *pa'am*]. The word is used once only to mean anvil (Isa. 41:7), and is perhaps descriptive of the "inverted foot" shape, since *pa'am* also means "foot" (Ps. 58:11; 85:14; etc.).

ANXIETY; (BE) ANXIOUS [Heb. *dā'ag* (1 S. 9:5; 10:2; Jer. 17:8), *d^e'āgâ* (Prov. 12:25), *'eṣeḇ*–'pain,' 'toil' (Ps. 127:2), *śî(a)ḥ* (1 S. 1:16), *ḥālâ* (Mic. 1:12); Aram. *k^erā'* (Dnl. 7:15)]; AV HEAVINESS, COMPLAINT, SORROWS, GRIEVED, etc.; NEB WORRY, CARE, GRIEF, TROUBLED, GREATLY ALARMED (Mic. 1:12), etc.; [Gk. *merimnáō* (Mt. 6:25ff.; 10:19; Lk. 10:41; 12:11ff.; 1 Cor. 7:32ff.; Phil. 2:20; 4:6), *mérimna* (2 Cor. 11:28; 1 Pet. 5:7), *promerimnáō* (Mk. 13:11), *amérimnos* (1 Cor. 7:32), *baréomai* (2 Cor. 5:4), *meteōrízomai* (Lk. 12:29), *odynáō* (Lk. 2:48), *álypos* (Phil. 2:28)]; AV TAKE THOUGHT, BE CAREFUL, GROAN (2 Cor. 5:4), "of doubtful mind" (Lk. 12:29), SORROWING (Lk. 2:48), etc.; NEB also LOOK AFTER (Mt. 6:34), CARE FOR (1 Cor. 7:32ff.), "take a genuine interest in" (Phil. 2:20), FRETTING (Lk. 10:41), SORROW (Phil. 2:28), etc.

In the OT the concerns and fears of everyday life are vividly portrayed in the vocabulary of "anxiety." For example, the Heb. *dā'ag* is used of a father's rightful concern over the delayed return of his son (1 S. 9:5; 10:7) and of the fear of famine in a year of drought (Jer. 17:8). Its derivative *d^e'āgâ* occurs in a familiar proverb: "Anxiety in a man's heart weighs him down, but a good word makes a man glad" (Prov. 12:25). Hannah's "great anxiety" (NEB "grief") over her childlessness is conveyed by the Heb. *śî(a)ḥ* (1 S. 1:16). The Aram. *k^erā'* describes Daniel's distress over his vision of the four beasts (Dnl. 7:15). A key OT passage is the reference to "eating the bread of anxious toil" (Heb. *'eṣeḇ* in Ps. 127:2; the preceding verse makes the point that any human effort that leaves God out is performed in vain. Only as man recognizes his own weakness and learns to trust in God's providence and care is he rescued from the treadmill of futile self-effort and spared "the bread of anxious toil" (see Weiser, pp. 764-66).

In the NT the subject of anxiety receives more extensive treatment, but moves in the same general direction that has been observed in the OT. Of the twenty-six occurrences of "anxiety" in the RSV NT, twenty-two are translations of *merimnáō* and its cognate forms. The essential meaning of this family of terms is given as "anxiety," "worry," or "care" (see Bauer, p. 506); however, apart from context, one cannot determine whether "anxiety" is used in a good sense or a bad sense. On the one hand, there are the recognized concerns of life that are both presupposed and expected. (The recurring "take no thought" of the AV is an unfortunate translation in its apparent denial of necessary foresight and planning.) For example, Paul is hard pressed to find anyone like Timothy who will be "genuinely anxious" for the welfare of the Philippians (2:20). He intends to send Epaphroditus to them momentarily in order that he may be "less anxious" (2:28; cf. NEB "to relieve my sorrow"). In another context, Paul alludes to "the daily pressure upon me of my anxiety for all the churches" (2 Cor. 11:28). These references illustrate some of the legitimate concerns of an apostle for his converts, and this is only one of many areas of human concern that are either implicitly or explicitly legitimized in Scripture.

On the other hand, there are those forbidden concerns that originate from a distorted perspective of life. The key NT teaching in this regard is found in the Sermon on the Mount (Mt. 6:25-34; Lk. 12:22-31). Here Jesus prohibits anxiety about even the most basic needs of life (i.e., food, drink, and clothing), not to mention the luxuries of life. Surely this does not mean that man is to fold his hands and to cease providing for himself and his household, for the Scriptures themselves teach otherwise (e.g., Prov. 6:6-11; 1 Tim. 5:8). A clue to the proper understanding of this and related passages is found in the word "first" in Mt. 6:33: "But seek first his kingdom and his righteousness, and all these things shall be yours as well." The emphasis in the Gk. *prṓton* ("first") as used here is not so much one of chronological priority as one of priority in degree or importance (see Bauer, p. 734). E. J. Goodspeed's translation of this verse is quite appropriate: "But you must make his kingdom and uprightness before him, *your greatest care* . . . " (italics added). Jesus warns elsewhere against the "cares of the world." the "delight in riches," and the "desire for other things" (Mk. 4:19). Whenever these concerns are given priority, the more important concerns of God's kingdom are crowded out and man's perspective on life becomes perilously distorted. The solution to anxiety lies in casting every concern upon God with thankful heart in the full realization of His care for His people (1 Pet. 5:7; Phil. 4:6).

Bibliography.–W. Barclay, *NT Words* (1974), pp. 198-203; *TDNT*, IV, *s.v.* μεριμνάω κτλ. (Bultmann); *RTWB*, *s.v.* "Care" (Cranfield); *IDB*, I, *s.v.* "Anxiety" (Davies); A. Weiser, *Psalms* (*OTL*, 1962), pp. 764-66. A. J. BIRKEY

APAME ə-pā'mə [Gk. *Apamē*]. A concubine of Darius and a daughter of Bartacus the Illustrious. Her behavior toward the king is referred to in a speech of Zerubbabel before the king to prove to him the great power of women (1 Esd. 4:29). *See* BARTACUS.

APART [Heb. *baḏ, bāḏal, qāḏaš, ḥûṣ, sāḇaḇ, 'āḇar, pālâ, nāṯan, rûm*; Gk. *chōrís, kat' idían, aphorízō, diaspáō* (Mk. 5:4)].

The Heb. *baḏ* contains the idea of separation and is frequently translated "alone," "by itself," or occasionally "apart." The verb *bāḏal* means "separate" or "set apart" for a special task or purpose. It may be used in reference to someone set apart for sacred purposes, e.g., the tribe of Levi to carry the ark (Dt. 10:8), Aaron to consecrate holy things (1 Ch. 23:13), sons of Asaph, etc., for temple service, and priests for priestly service (Ezr. 8:24). Or it may refer to something set apart for non-sacred use; e.g., cities set apart as cities of refuge (Dt. 4:41; 19:2, 7) or for the Ephraimites (Josh. 16:9), certain animals as unclean (Lev. 20:25), certain men to bury dead bodies (Ezk. 39:14).

The term *qāḏaš* is normally narrower in meaning and refers to that which is set apart exclusively for sacred use. This is the case with the portions set apart for the Levites and sons of Aaron (Neh. 12:47) and the sheep for sacrifice (here referring to the wicked, Jer. 12:3) and those who boast of their holiness (Isa. 65:5). However, in Josh. 20:7 *qāḏaš* seems to be used interchangeably with *bāḏal* for the cities of refuge which were set apart from other cities.

There are several other Hebrew words which the RSV rarely renders as "apart." In Eccl. 2:25 *ḥûṣ* is rendered "apart" instead of the more frequent "outside." Twice in 2 S. 14:24 Absalom "dwells apart" (*sāḇaḇ*) from David's quarters. Twice *'āḇar* is translated "set apart," once of the firstborn (Ex. 13:12) and once of temple officials who attend the Levites (1 Ch. 25:1). In Ex. 8:22 *pālâ* indicates that Goshen will be treated differently from the rest of Egypt. The same sense of *pālâ* seems to be in view in Ps. 4:3, which would then mean "the Lord works wonders for" (instead of "set apart") the one devoted to him. In Ezk. 45:6 *nāṯan* refers to an area given to each town. Four times in Ezekiel the verb *rûm* refers to the portion of land to be offered or set apart to God (45:1; 48:8f., 20). Finally, the Hebrew in Ps. 16:2 is difficult. However, the general sense of the RSV translation is probably correct if *'al* is translated "beyond" or "apart from."

In Gk. *chōrís* is used mostly as a preposition meaning "apart (from)" or "without." The latter translation is the consistent rendering of the AV where RSV has "apart." The verb *diaspáō* in Mk. 5:4 refers to the demoniac who wrenched apart (NEB snapped) his chains. The phrase *kat' idían*, translated "apart" in Mt. 14:13; 17:1; Mk. 9:2; Lk. 9:10, has the idea of "privately" or "alone." In each case the reference is to Jesus seeking privacy, alone or with His disciples, apart from the crowds. Finally, the verb *aphorízō* is used of the setting apart of Paul (Rom. 1:1; Gal. 1:15) and Barnabas and Saul (Acts 13:2) to preach the gospel.

Bibliography.–*TDOT*, I, *s.v.* "badhādh" (Zobel); II, *s.v.* "bdl" (Otzen). J. C. MOYER

APE [Heb. *qôp̱*]. Mentioned only in 1 K. 10:22 par. 2 Ch. 9:21, the ape was one of the imported luxury items in the Solomonic period. The Hebrew is the equivalent of Egyp. *gwf*, Akk. *uqūpu*, and Syr. *qûpa*. Probably the reference is not to apes as such, which are tailless, but to monkeys or baboons, the latter being well known in Egypt.

APELLES ə-pel'ēz [Gk. *Apelles*]. A Christian at Rome to whom Paul sent greetings (Rom. 16:10). He is described by Paul as "the approved in Christ," i.e., "that approved Christian" (Denney). In some way unknown to us Apelles had been tested and he had proved faithful (cf. Jas. 1:12; 2 Tim. 2:15). It is a common name.

APHAIREMA ə-fâr'ə-mə [Gk. *Aphairema, Apherema*]; AV, NEB, APHEREMA. One of three districts taken from Samaria and added to Judea by Demetrius Nicator (1 Macc. 11:34). Cf. Josephus *Ant.* xiii.4.9.

APHARSACHITES ə-fär'sə-kīts [Aram. *'ᵃparsᵉḵāyē'*]. The AV translation of a word in Ezr. 5:6; 6:6 formerly taken to be a tribe living in Samaria, but now generally recognized to be officials (cf. RSV "governors"; NEB "inspectors"). The word has been connected with Old Persian *frasaka* and is found in cuneiform texts as *iprasakku*, which agrees with the consonantal form (but not as vocalized) in Ezra. These officials complained to Darius about the rebuilding of the temple by the Jews who had returned from exile.

See also APHARSATHCHITES; APHARSITES; GOVERNOR.

APHARSATHCHITES ə-fär'sath-kīts, af-ar-sath'kīts [Aram. *'ᵃparsaṯᵉḵāyē'*]. The AV translation of a word in Ezr. 4:9 formerly identified with the APHARSACHITES and taken to be a tribe living in Samaria, transplanted from Persia by Asnapper (Ashurbanipal), but now generally recognized to be officials (cf. RSV "governors"; NEB "commissioners"). The word has been suggested as Old Persian *frēstak*, "messenger," but this does not quite fit he consonantal form of the word found in Ezra.

See also APHARSITES; GOVERNOR.

APHARSITES ə-fär'sīts [Aram. *'ᵃpārsayē'*]. The AV translation of a word in Ezr. 4:9 (cf. RSV "Persians"; NEB "chief officers") formerly identified as another tribe (along with the APHARSATHCHITES in the same verse) transplanted from the Trans-Euphrates province or from Persia by Asnapper (Ashurbanipal); see v. 10. Verse 9 is difficult, with three Masoretic emendations to complicate it further. The first four words after the athnaḥ (approximately equivalent to a colon) can be taken as gentilic forms (i.e., peoples) or as titles. The MT accents seem to oppose the RSV change from title to gentilic after the first three words: "the judges, the governors, the officials, the Persians." The following words all seem to be gentilics. To translate "Persians" is to ignore the *aleph* at the beginning of the word.

See also APHARSACHITES. W. S. L. S.

APHEK ā'fek [Heb. *'ᵃpēq*–'enclosure' or 'fortress'].

1. A city in the plain of Sharon NE of Joppa near Râs el-'Ain, the site of springs that form the main source of the Nahr el-'Aujā or Yarkon River. Joshua defeated the king of this city in his conquest W of the Jordan (Josh. 12:18; cf. v. 19, NEB). In the days of Samuel the Philistines set themselves at Aphek against the forces of Israel encamped at Ebenezer (1 S. 4:1). Later the Philistines again gathered their forces at Aphek preparing to engage the Israelites who were "pitched by a fountain which is in Jezreel" (1 S. 29:1). Aphek is mentioned in several Egyptian texts, including those of Thutmose III, Amenhotep II, Ramses II, and Ramses III, and also Josephus (*BJ* ii.19.1). About 35 B.C. Herod the Great built a fortress at Aphek and named it Antipatris in honor of his father.

Archeological investigations have revealed that the site has been almost continuously occupied since the Early Bronze Age (*ca.* 3000 B.C.). The discovery of cuneiform tablets indicates the importance of Aphek in the Late Bronze Age, at the end of which (*ca.* 1200 B.C., period of Israelite conquest) it was apparently destroyed by fire. Numerous artifacts from the time of the Israelite monarchy have been discovered also. *See also* ANTIPATRIS.

2. A city in the north listed as territory not conquered at the end of Joshua's life (Josh. 13:4). It is apparently N of Sidon and may be Afqā NE of Beirût.

3. Also **APHIK** [Heb. *'ᵃpîq*] (Jgs. 1:31). A town in the territory assigned to the tribe of Asher (Josh. 19:30). It has been identified with Tell Kurdâneh about 6 mi. (10 km.) NE of Haifa. The Asherites did not drive out the inhabitants and soon integrated with them (Jgs. 1:31).

4. A city on the plateau E of the Jordan where disaster befell Ben-hadad (1 K. 20:26, 30; also referred to in 2 K. 13:17). The modern Fîq on the brow of the hill beyond Qal'at el-Ḥuṣn E of the Sea of Galilee probably represents this ancient city.

J. F. PREWITT

APHEKAH ə-fē'kə [Heb. *'ᵃpēqâ*–'force' or 'strength']; NEB APHEK. A city in the hill country of Judah (Josh. 15:53), listed with places W of Hebron. A. Alt proposes Khirbet eḍ-Ḍarrameh (*PJ*, 28 [1932], 16f.), while Abel prefers Khirbet Kana'an (*GP*, II, 247; cf. *GAB*).

The NEB seems to identify it with APHEK **1.**

APHEREMA ə-fer'ə-mə (1 Macc. 11:34, AV, NEB). *See* APHAIREMA.

APHERRA ə-fer'ə [Gk. *Apherra*]. One of Solomon's servants whose descendants are mentioned collectively in the postexilic list at 1 Esd. 5:34, but not in Ezr. 2:57 or Neh. 7:59.

APHIAH ə-fī'ə [Heb. *'ᵃpîaḥ*]. A Benjaminite ancestor of King Saul (1 S. 9:1).

APHIK ā'fik. Variant of APHEK **3.**

APHRAH af'rə (Mic. 1:10, AV). *See* BETH-LE-APHRAH.

APHSES af'sēz (1 Ch. 24:15, AV, NEB). *See* HAPPIZZEZ.

APIS ā'pis. The sacred bull of Egypt, symbolizing Ptah, worshiped at Memphis as a fertility-god from at least the Old Kingdom period (*ca.* 2700-2200 B.C.). The name is read by the RSV and NEB at Jer. 46:15, "Why has Apis fled?" reading Heb. *maddûa' nās ḥap* instead of MT *maddûa' nisḥap,* which the AV renders, "why are thy valiant men swept away?"

See J. Černý, *Ancient Egyptian Religion* (1952), pp. 136-38.

R. K. H.

Bronze statuettes of Apis bull, from hoard of bronzes discovered at Ashkelon (4th cent. B.C.) (Israel Department of Antiquities and Museums)

APOCALYPSE. *See* Apocalyptic Literature; Revelation, Book of.

APOCALYPSE OF BARUCH. *See* Apocalyptic Literature III.H.

APOCALYPTIC LITERATURE. The word "apocalypse" appears as the first word in our NT apocalypse, the Revelation of John, meaning "disclosure" or "revelation." In this book it designates "what must soon take place": the consummation of God's redemptive purposes. The revelations were imparted to John in a series of ecstatic experiences (see "in the Spirit" at Rev. 1:10; 4:2; 17:3; 21:10) when Christ revealed to him the events that would attend the consummation of the age and the establishing of God's rule in the world. The term "apocalypse" has been borrowed from the Revelation and applied to a whole genre of Jewish literature produced between 200 B.C. and A.D. 100. The earliest apocalypse is the book of Daniel, and the subsequent apocalypses were written in imitation of it.

The word "apocalyptic" is used to designate two distinct things: the group of writings, and the kind of eschatology they contain. These two uses of "apocalyptic" need to be clearly distinguished.

I. Apocalyptic as Literature
  A. Revelatory Character
  B. Artificial Nature
  C. Pseudonymity
  D. Pseudo-Prophecy
  E. Symbolism
II. Apocalyptic as Eschatology
  A. Dualism
  B. History and Eschatology
  C. Pessimism
  D. Determinism
  E. Ethical Passivity
III. Apocalyptic Writings
  A. First (or Ethiopic) Enoch
  B. Book of Jubilees
  C. Testaments of the Twelve Patriarchs
  D. Psalms of Solomon
  E. Assumption of Moses
  F. Second (or Slavonic) Enoch
  G. Fourth Ezra
  H. Apocalypse of Baruch

I. Apocalyptic as Literature.–We do not know with certainty what circle in Judaism produced the apocalypses, nor how widely they were known and read in NT times. Albright held that Jewry swarmed with apocalyptists (*FSAC,* p. 374), while G. F. Moore thought they were only a small group of enthusiasts who were practically ignored by the masses of the people and their religious leaders (*Judaism in the First Centuries of the Christian Era,* I [1927], 127). Extensive new information about first-century Judaism has come to hand in the so-called Qumrân literature, and one fact at least is clear: the Qumrân community prized the apocalyptic writings. This is proved by the fact that fragments of several apocalyptic books, or of sources of some of these books, have been found in the Qumrân caves, including fragments of ten MSS of Jubilees, fragments of ten MSS of four of the five parts of Enoch, and fragments of the sources of the Testaments of Levi and Naphtali (see J. T. Milik, *Ten Years of Discovery in the Wilderness of Judaea* [1959], pp. 32-35). This fact has led some scholars to conclude that the Qumrân community, or rather the proto-Essenes of which it was one community, produced and preserved the apocalyptic literature, and that these writings should be interpreted in the life situation of the thought of this community (F. M. Cross, Jr., *Ancient Library of Qumran and Modern Biblical Studies* [1957], pp. 142ff.; H. H. Rowley, *Jewish Apocalyptic and the Dead Sea Scrolls* [1957]). However, H. Ringgren admits only the possibility of an Essenic source for the apocalyptic writings ("Jüdische Apokalyptik," *RGG,* I, 464); and while there are marked similarities between the eschatological ideas of the apocalypses and the other Qumrân literature, there are also striking differences (see Millar Burrows, *Dead Sea Scrolls* [1955], p. 261). Perhaps this problem could be solved if we had sufficient knowledge of the intertestamental period to reconstruct accurately the history of the Essene movement, but we must deal with the apocalypses as they stood and await further light upon their historical milieu.

"The Four Horsemen" — Death, Famine, Pestilence, and War — trampling men and women, with Dragon of Hell at lower left. Fourth print in Albrecht Dürer's fifteen-part woodcut series "The Apocalypse" (1498) (National Gallery of Art, Washington, Rosenwald Collection)

As a genre of literature, apocalyptic is notable for several features that set it apart from prophetic literature. In fact, a popular critical view is that prophetic eschatology and apocalyptic eschatology are two mutually exclusive kinds of eschatology in the OT and Judaism. According to this view, prophetic eschatology expected the kingdom of God to arise out of history and to be an earthly kingdom within history. However, when this historical hope was not realized, the Jews came to despair of history and to expect the kingdom of God to come from outside of history—i.e., directly from God—to involve a cosmic catastrophe, and to issue in a kingdom so different from earthly experience that it could only be described as a kingdom "beyond history" (see S. Mowinckel, *He That Cometh* [1956]; P. Volz, *Die Eschatologie der jüdischen Gemeinde* [1934], ch. 23). Prophetic eschatology looked for the coming of an earthly Davidic king (Messiah); apocalyptic eschatology looked for the coming of a heavenly Son of Man. However, the present author has argued that the expectation of a cata-

APOCALYPTIC LITERATURE

clysmic irruption into history is intrinsic to the prophetic hope of the OT. The kingdom of God will be established in this world, but with an entirely new quality of life (see G. E. Ladd, *Presence of the Future* [1974], pp. 55ff.). T. C. Vriezen describes the eschatology of Isaiah and his contemporaries as one that is "historical and at the same time supra-historical. It takes place within the framework of history but is caused by forces that transcend history, so that what is formed is a new order of things in which the glory and the Spirit of God (Isa. 11) reveals itself" ("Prophecy and Eschatology," in *Supplements to Vetus Testamentum,* I [1953], 222). Vriezen finds an even more distinct contrast between the old order and the new in Deutero-Isaiah. Certainly the eschatology of such scriptures as Isa. 24–27, Zephaniah, Joel, Zec. 9–14 expects to see the kingdom of God established only by a cosmic act of God. This is the most notable feature of apocalyptic eschatology, and it has its roots in the OT. *See* ESCHATOLOGY.

A. Revelatory Character. The apocalyptic literary genre has several outstanding characteristics. First, it is revelatory of the future. In this matter, apocalyptic differs from most of the writings of the prophets. The prophets claimed to receive revelations, as did the apocalyptists; but the central content of prophetic revelation was the will of God, and the chief means of revelation was the word of God. The prophets often foretold God's action in the future, but they did so that in the light of future judgment and salvation they might enforce the demands of the divine will in the present. Furthermore, while the prophets received revelations through dreams and visions (e.g., Isa. 6; Ezk. 1; Jer. 24), these were not central. "The word of the Lord," the dynamic message of the living God, was the center of their experience. Dreams and visions were never an end in themselves but were accompanied by an explanatory, accosting word.

With the apocalyptists, the center of interest has shifted. The living word of the Lord has given way altogether to revelations and visions. God no longer speaks by His Spirit to the prophet. The seer learns the solution to the problem of evil and the coming of God's kingdom through dreams, visions, or heavenly journeys. By means of these media the apocalyptist discovers the secrets of the hidden world, the reason for the suffering of the righteous on earth, and when and how the Kingdom will come.

We should note that some of the books usually called apocalyptic are not true apocalypses in that they are not revelations of this sort. The Testaments of the Twelve Patriarchs contain eschatology of an apocalyptic character, but the literary form is not that of an apocalypse. Each of the twelve patriarchs gives a brief resume of his life, makes a moral application, and usually utters a brief prediction of the future of his descendants. In form the book is imitative prophecy rather than apocalyptic. The Psalms of Solomon are not apocalyptic, i.e., revelatory, but are patterned after the OT Psalms. Since two of the Psalms anticipate the coming of Messiah and of the kingdom of God, they are usually included in the survey of Jewish apocalyptic literature. Those two books illustrate that apocalyptic literature and apocalyptic eschatology are not identical; the apocalyptic eschatology found expression in works that were not apocalyptic in literary form.

B. Artificial Nature. A second characteristic of apocalyptic literature is the imitative and artificial nature of its revelations. This stands in contrast to the visions of the canonical prophets, which involved genuine subjective experiences. In apocalyptic, visions and dreams have become a form of literature. While a few of the apocalyptists may have undergone some sort of subjective experience as a result of brooding over the problem of evil (see G. H. Box, *Ezra-Apocalypse* [1912], p. lxvii), Porter is correct in saying that "the visions described in the apocalypses are beyond doubt in the majority of cases not real visions at all but literary fictions" (F. C. Porter, *Messages of the Apocalyptical Writers* [1905], pp. 40f.).

C. Pseudonymity. A third characteristic of Jewish apocalyptic is pseudonymity. Usually, the apocalyptists employed the transparent fiction of using the name of an OT saint long dead as a means of validating their revelations. Many critics feel that the real authors did not intend to deceive their readers by this devout fiction; however, if the prevailing interpretation of the reason for pseudonymity is valid, the authors did expect their pious fraud to be taken seriously. After the days of Ezra and Nehemiah, Judaism felt that the age of the prophets was over, for no one stood up among the people to announce, "Thus saith the Lord." The Qumrân community believed that the Holy Spirit inspired their leaders, but the purpose of this inspiration was the correct interpretation of the Word of God, not the utterance of a fresh word from God. If the age of prophecy was over, how could the revelations of the apocalyptists gain a hearing? Since the apocalyptist could not speak as a prophet, "Thus saith the Lord," he borrowed an OT saint and attributed his visions to him, that the writing might receive the sanction of the prophetic name, whether Enoch, the Twelve Patriarchs, Moses, Ezra, or Baruch.

In this connection, we must observe that Daniel is not pseudonymous, for Daniel is not an OT saint whose name could be used to lend authority to a book. Apart from the stories in the book of Daniel, he is a nonentity. This fact lends some evidence to the view that, whatever the date of composition of Daniel, it embodies traditions of a historical person who lived in the time of Captivity.

Here too is one of the most notable differences between the Revelation and Jewish apocalyptic. The Revelation was written by a living author who was well known to those to whom he wrote.

D. Pseudo-Prophecy. Pseudonymity may be accompanied by pseudo-prophecy. The author not only borrowed an OT saint as the alleged author of his book; he often rewrote the history of Israel from the time of the alleged author to his own time, but cast it in the form of prophecy.

The prophets were men known to their audiences, who took their stand in their own historical situations and proclaimed their messages to their own generations against the background of the coming kingdom of God. Each prophetic writing reflects the events of the author's own time, which the critic must study to determine the date of the book. The prophets also predicted both historical and eschatological events that yet lay in the future. The apocalyptists often took their stand in the distant past and rewrote history as though it were prophecy, attributing the pseudo-prophecy to the pseudo-author. It is frequently possible to follow the course of the alleged prophecy down to the author's own time, when the historical predictions become vague and the Kingdom is expected to come.

It is significant that the Revelation does not use this technique, nor does Our Lord in his apocalyptic sayings. Both take their stand in their own day and predict both historical and eschatological events to come.

E. Symbolism. A final characteristic of the apocalyptic genre is the use of symbolism in declaring the will of God to the people and in predicting future events. This goes back to the prophets. To illustrate Israel's corruption, Jeremiah buried a linen cloth until it was spoiled (Jer. 13:1-11). Ezekiel's vision of the valley full of bones depicted the revival of Israel to national life (Ezk. 37). With Zechariah symbolic visions reach a new dimension. The first six chapters contain eight visions, each involving developed symbolism. The last vision is of four chariots with red, black, white, and dappled-gray horses that came from between the two mountains of bronze to patrol the four corners of the earth (Zech. 6:1-8). These chariots are symbolic of the accomplishment of God's will in all the earth. They are not designed to be identified with specific historical events or personages.

In the use of symbolism, Daniel goes beyond the other prophets and introduces a usage that is imitated by later apocalypses. He uses symbolism to represent events in history. The great image of gold, silver, brass, and iron represents four successive nations in history before the coming of God's kingdom (Dnl. 2), as do the four beasts of Dnl. 7. This device is greatly elaborated in subsequent apocalypses (see 1 En. 85–90), and the symbolism of the beast in Rev. 13 is clearly dependent on Daniel.

II. Apocalyptic as Eschatology.–We have examined the main features of the apocalyptic genre of literature. We must turn now to a consideration of the main features of the type of eschatology embodied in the apocalypses.

A. Dualism. The first and most important characteristic of apocalyptic eschatology is eschatological dualism. The apocalyptists see a sharp contrast between the character of this age and that of the age to come. The present is the age of sin and evil; the future will see the establishment of the kingdom of God, when God's people will be redeemed from all traces of sin and all the effects of evil will be removed from the earth. The transition from this age will not be achieved by historical processes, but only by an unmediated cosmic act of God.

This apocalyptic dualism is a development of the theology of the prophets, who were conscious of the contrast between God's ideal world and the actual world of nature and history. Although nature and history were under the divine sovereignty, both lay under the curse of sin and the burden of evil. God's kingdom would be established only by an inbreaking of God into history that would result in both a moral and a physical transformation of the present order.

This dualistic eschatology appears distinctly in one of the earliest prophets, Zephaniah. He begins his prophecy with an announcement of divine judgment in which God will "sweep away everything from the face of the earth" (Zeph. 1:2), including man and beast. "In the fire of his jealous wrath shall all the earth be consumed; for a full, yea, sudden end he will make of all the inhabitants of the earth" (v. 18). Yet beyond judgment Zephaniah sees a time of salvation when a remnant of Israel, redeemed, will be gathered in Zion, and even the Gentiles will be converted and worship God in the language of Zion (3:9-20).

Zephaniah does not emphasize the redemption of nature as do other prophets. Amos sees an earth that has become rich and abundant in harvest. So abundant will be the grain that the harvest will take all summer. The vines will yield so richly that the work of the treader of grapes in the wine press and that of the sower in the fields will overlap. The mountains and hills on whose slopes the vineyards lay will seem to stream with the flow of the wine (Am. 9:13). Isaiah paints the familiar picture of the wolf lying down with the lamb, the calf with the lion—of a nature so transformed that these fierce beasts become the pets of little children (Isa. 11:6-9). Second Isaiah describes the new age in terms of a new heaven and a new earth (65:17; 66:22), so different will the new order be from the old order. There is, in short, the *idea* of the contrast between this present world with its burden of evil and the new world transformed by a divine act of redemption.

This dualistic eschatology gradually developed the terminology of "this age" and "the age to come." This terminology begins to appear in I Enoch (16:1; 48:7; 71:15), but it makes its clear appearance first in 4 Ezra and in the NT. Fourth Ezra, written at the end of the 1st cent. A.D., says, "The Most High has made not one Age but two" (7:50, *APOT*); "This age the Most High has made for many, but the age to come for few" (8:1). If our Gospels accurately report Jesus' saying, he *may* have been among the first to use this idiom (Mk. 4:19; 10:30; Mt. 12:32; Lk. 16:8; 20:34). The expression also appears in the Pauline correspondence (Gal. 1:4; Eph. 1:21; 1 Cor. 2:6; 3:18). The theology of eschatological dualism is that the powers of evil are so dominant in this age that only a direct unmediated act of God can destroy them; and this redemptive act of God will deliver not only God's people but the very world of nature from the grip of evil. "The creation itself will be set free from its bondage to decay and obtain the glorious liberty of the children of God" (Rom. 8:21). This is a thoroughly apocalyptic saying.

B. History and Eschatology. A second characteristic of apocalyptic eschatology is its non-prophetic view of history. The prophets see a dynamic tension between the immediate historical future and the more distant eschatological future. For instance, Amos describes the day of the Lord as a day of darkness, when a historical judgment would overtake Israel (5:18-20). This means nothing less than captivity beyond Damascus (8:27). Yet beyond this historical judgment Amos sees a further visitation: the eschatological Day of the Lord. The future holds a day of universal judgment (7:4; 8:8f.; 9:5) and, beyond that, a day of salvation when the house of David will be revived, Israel restored, and the earth become a blessing (9:11-15). God will judge His people for their sins in a historical judgment, but He will finally redeem them in the kingdom of God.

The apocalyptists lost this tension between history and eschatology. The present and the future were seen as quite unrelated. The apocalyptists could not understand the prophetic interpretation of present historical experience as God's judgment upon His people for their apostasy, for Israel was no longer faithless. After the days of Ezra and Nehemiah, the Law assumed a role of new importance in the experience of Israel. Israel in OT times again and again neglected the Law and apostatized to foreign gods; but in NT times, under the influence of Pharisaic and scribal religion, many Jews were utterly devoted to obedience to the Law. In fact, religion had become a life of strict obedience to a mass of rules. Here then was Israel's problem: "Israel has received and kept God's law; why then are God's people suffering under the heel of godless pagans? This cannot be God's doing." The only answer given is that God's ways are inscrutable. There is no other answer. After the destruction of Jerusalem in A.D. 70, a very sensitive spirit, pondering this problem, wrote 4 Ezra 3:32-36: "Has another nation known Thee besides Israel? Or what tribes have so believed Thy covenants as these tribes of Jacob? Yet their reward has not appeared and their labor has borne no fruit, . . . when have the inhabitants of the earth not sinned in Thy sight? Or what nation has kept Thy commandments so well [as Israel]? Thou mayest indeed find individual men who have kept Thy commandments, but nations Thou wilt not find." The response to this problem is one of utter despair: "It would be better for us not to be here than to come here and live in ungodliness, and to suffer and not understand why" (4:12). The only solution offered is that God will yet act to rectify the evil of the present. The age will finally come to its end, and God will inaugurate the new age of righteousness. However, this final redemptive act has no bearing upon the present.

"Christ in Majesty," popular twelfth-century A.D. concept of Christ as judge, seated on rainbow with world at His feet and holding sealed book. Beasts at corners represent the four Evangelists (cf. Ezk. 1:5-19; Rev. 4:2–5:1). Enamel plaque from book cover, Limoges, France (Metropolitan Museum of Art, gift of J. Pierpont Morgan, 1917)

While the NT shares the eschatological dualism of Jewish apocalyptic, it does not share its despair over history. In fact, the NT revives the prophetic tension between history and eschatology. Jesus' view of the divine acts in the future includes both judgment in history and judgment at the end of history. He wept over Jerusalem because the Holy City had rejected the divinely appointed messenger: "Behold, your house is forsaken and desolate" (Mt. 23:38). He foretold the destruction of the holy temple; not one stone was to be left standing upon another (Mt. 24:2). He predicted the destruction of Chorazin and Bethsaida because of their unrepentant spirit (Mt. 11:20-22). God was again seen as active in history to challenge and to judge His people. Jesus also announced that Israel is to be dispossessed as the covenant people of God and that a new people will be raised up to take her place (Mt. 21:43).

At the same time, Jesus looked beyond this historical judgment to a final eschatological judgment. This is clear from the parables; in the day of judgment the wheat and the tares will be separated and the bad fish gathered out from among the good (Mt. 13).

This tension between history and eschatology (cf. G. E. Ladd. *Presence of the Future* [1974], pp. 64ff.) is seen most vividly in the Olivet discourse. According to Matthew, the disciples asked two questions: when will the temple be destroyed, and what will be the sign of the close of the age? In answer, Jesus seems to have conflated these two events, and to have viewed the eschatological future through the transparency of the nearer historical future. Mk. 13 and Mt. 24 emphasize the eschatological aspect — the appearance of the Antichrist and the last great tribulation (Mt. 24:15ff.). In the parallel passage, Luke writes of Jerusalem being surrounded by armies (Lk. 21:20). God, who will act at the end of history to establish His kingdom, is working in history in His kingly power. This tension between history and eschatology is one of the most distinctive marks of prophetic eschatology in contrast to Jewish apocalyptic. While Jesus shares the eschatological dualism of apocalyptic, with its expectation of a cosmic catastrophe, He stands squarely in the prophetic tradition in that He also sees the hand of God in historical events.

C. Pessimism. Jewish apocalyptic may also be described as pessimistic about history. Some scholars (e.g., H. H. Rowley, *Relevance of Apocalyptic* [1947], p. 36) object to the use of the term "pessimistic." As Rowley writes, it is erroneous to call the apocalyptists pessimists in their ultimate outlook, for they never lost their confidence that God would finally triumph. They possessed an ultimate optimism that was born of an unshakable faith. Indeed, the very purpose of their writings was to assure God's people that God had not really forsaken them, but that in His own good time He would arise to save Israel and punish the wicked.

But it is also true that the apocalyptists had not only lost the sense of the divine activity in history; they had become utterly pessimistic about the evil character of this age: the blessings of God's kingdom could not be experienced in the present, for God had abandoned this age to suffering and evil. Such a theology was forced upon devout Jews as the only possible explanation for their evil plight. The solution to the problem of evil was thrown altogether into the future; the present was seen as irremediably evil. The righteous could only submit patiently to suffering, sustained by the assurance that deliverance would surely come when the evil age was past and the new age of the Kingdom had arrived.

The most vivid illustration of this is found in the dream-visions of 1 Enoch (chs. 83–90). According to the second vision, God personally guided the experiences of Israel throughout its history until the Babylonian captivity. Then God withdrew his personal leadership, forsook the temple, and surrendered his people to wild beasts to be torn and devoured. God "remained unmoved, though He saw it, and rejoiced that they were devoured and swallowed and robbed, and left them to be devoured in the hand of all the beasts" (1 En. 89:58, *APOT*). Then God turned the fortunes of the nation over to seventy angel-shepherds, instructing them as to the number of Jews who might be slain. However, the shepherds were self-willed and faithless, ignoring the divine directive, and permitting fearful evils to befall God's people. When reports of the evil conduct of the shepherds were brought to God, He laid them aside and remained unmoved and aloof (1 En. 89:71, 75). A record was made of the angels' faithlessness that they might be punished on the day of judgment when Israel would be delivered. Between the years 586 and 165 B.C., God was conceived to be inactive in the fortunes of Israel. God's people found themselves at the mercy of faithless angels. No deliverance could be expected until the messianic era.

APOCALYPTIC LITERATURE

The apocalypse of Ezra reflects an equal pessimism. Ezra's problem is found in the fact that Israel has received and kept God's Law (4 Ezr. 6:55-59), while the Gentiles have rejected it (3:31-34; 7:20-24); yet God has spared the ungodly and preserved His enemies, but has destroyed His people (3:30). This insoluble problem casts Ezra into abject despair. He wishes he had never been born (4:12). Dumb beasts are better off than the righteous, for they cannot think about their fate (2:66). The only hope lies in the future. By divine decree, there are two ages: the present age is hopelessly evil, but the future age will witness the solution to the problem of evil (4:26-32; 7:50; 8:1-3). The righteous, therefore, must now patiently resign themselves to evil in the confidence of a solution in the age to come, and are not to be disturbed because the masses perish. God himself is not moved by the death of the wicked (7:60f., 131; 8:38, 55). This age is evil; hope belongs altogether to the age to come.

The NT shares the view of Jewish apocalyptic that this age is evil (Gal. 1:4). Satan is even called the god of this age (2 Cor. 4:4). But no NT writer shares the Jewish pessimism about this age. In fact, the heart of the gospel is found in the fact that in Jesus of Nazareth God has acted to bring to men the blessings of His kingly rule. The kingdom of God, which belongs to the age to come, has actually come to men in history (Mt. 12:28). While Satan is the god of this age, the mission of Jesus accomplishes a binding of Satan (Mt. 12:29). By His death, Jesus has "destroyed him who has the power of death, that is, the devil" (He. 2:14). Our NT apocalypse shares this redemptive view of history. John sees the scroll of human destiny resting in the hand of God, but the scroll is firmly sealed with seven seals so that no one can open the book and read its contents. When John weeps because the book can not be opened, he is told, "Weep not; lo, the Lion of the tribe of Judah, the Root of David, has conquered [lit., has won a victory], so that he can open the scroll and its seven seals" (Rev. 5:5). When John turns to see the Lion—the Davidic King—he sees instead a lamb, bearing the marks of slaughter. The Davidic King will be able to bring history to the kingdom of God only because He was first the suffering Lamb of God. He won a victory in history that will lead into the kingdom of God. This is the theme of the entire NT: the redemptive work of God in the historical Jesus of Nazareth, which will issue finally in Jesus' apocalyptic coming as the Son of Man to establish the glorious kingdom of God.

D. Determinism. Another characteristic of Jewish apocalyptic is determinism. The course of this age is predetermined and must run to its completion. The Kingdom does not come even though the righteous deserve it, because certain fixed periods must first unfold. Therefore, the Kingdom must await its appointed time. Little emphasis is placed on a sovereign God who is acting through these appointed times to carry out His purposes. Rather, God Himself is awaiting the passing of the times He has decreed. "For he has weighed the age in the balance, and measured the times by measure, and numbered the times by number; and he will not move nor arouse them until that measure is fulfilled" (4 Ez. 4:36f.). The entire course of human history is prerecorded in heavenly books (1 En. 81:1-3; 103:1f.).

Since the time of the end is fixed, the present age is often thought to be divided into certain determined periods. The dream-visions of Enoch divide time, from the captivity to the end, into seventy periods during which Israel is given into the care of seventy shepherds (1 En. 89:72; 90:1, 5). Only when the seventy periods have passed can the end come. The apocalypses usually assume that the fixed periods have nearly run out, and therefore that the end is about to come.

In contrast to this stand Jesus' words: "But of that day and hour no one knows, not even the angels of heaven, nor the Son, but the Father only" (Mt. 24:36); "Watch therefore, for you do not know on what day your Lord is coming" (v. 42); "The master of that servant will come on a day when he does not expect him and at an hour he does not know" (v. 50).

E. Ethical Passivity. A final characteristic may be called ethical passivity. The apocalyptists were not motivated by strong moral or evangelical urgency. The prophets continually appealed to Israel to repent and to turn from their sins to God. They prophesied that judgment would fall upon a sinful nation, but that the kingdom would one day come for a righteous remnant. The prophets were not interested in the future for its own sake, however, but only for its impact upon the present. They predicted future judgment and salvation in order that, in light of that future, they might confront Israel with the will of God.

As the apocalyptists perceived it, however, the problem in their day was not the need for national repentance. Rather, the problem arose out of their conviction that the Israel of their day was the righteous remnant—yet the Kingdom did not come. The apocalyptic and rabbinic definitions of righteousness were basically the same: obedience to the Law of Moses; and the circles in which the apocalyptists moved were faithful to the Law. The literature from the Qumrân caves, e.g., shows that the Qumranians were strict legalists. Therefore most of the apocalypses devote very little space to ethical exhortation. The two notable exceptions are the Testaments of the Twelve Patriarchs and the last part of Enoch (chs. 92–105). The Testaments have a strong ethical emphasis with a noteworthy stress on inward righteousness and the ethic of love; but this sets the book apart from the usual atmosphere of apocalyptic literature. The book is not in fact apocalyptic in form, but is imitative prophecy. The last section of Enoch defines righteousness in terms of obedience to the Law (99:2, 4) and has little apocalyptic material in the strict sense of the word. The scholars who insist upon a strong ethical emphasis in apocalyptic literature draw most of their illustrations from the two canonical apocalypses, Daniel and Revelation, and from the Testaments of the Twelve Patriarchs.

Ethical exhortation is lacking because there is a loss of a sense of sinfulness. The problem of the apocalyptists is found in the fact that the true Israel *does* keep the law and therefore *is* righteous—and yet is permitted to suffer. Fourth Ezra seems to be an exception to this statement, for the author at several points expresses a profound sense of sinfulness (4:12; 7:118). This, however, is counterbalanced by a sense of the righteousness of God's people, who have received the Law (3:32; 5:29; 8:29), have kept it (3:35; 7:25), and therefore have a treasury of works before God (6:5; 7:77; 8:33). Nevertheless, Jerusalem has been destroyed by the Romans and the temple leveled, and according to prophetic theology this must be a judgment for Israel's sins. But just there is the problem: as a matter of fact, Israel is not sinful! She has kept the Law. This problem created a tension in the author's mind that led to deep despair (7:118) and to a pitiful cry to God to deal with his people in terms of grace (8:6). Thus, Ezra's sense of sinfulness is more the result of theoretical theology than deep conviction. Throughout the book we meet the contrast between the righteous few who have kept the Law—the faithful of Israel—and the mass of men who perish, but about whose fate God is unconcerned (8:56; 7:61, 131; 8:38).

Both Jesus' teachings and the Revelation reflect prophetic rather than apocalyptic theology on this point. Jesus' forecast of the future has an ethical purpose.

"*Watch* [lit., be awake], therefore, for you do not know on what day your Lord is coming. But know this, that if the householder had known in what part of the night the thief was coming he would have watched and would not have let his house be broken into. Therefore you must always be ready" (Mt. 25:42-44).

The seven letters of Rev. 2–3 are replete with ethical warnings. Most of them contain a summons to repentance. The Revelation as a whole concludes with an evangelical summons for men to come and drink of the water of life (Rev. 22:17).

III. Apocalyptic Writings.–Included here are the several books that are usually grouped under the heading of apocalyptic writings, even though some of them are not, strictly speaking, apocalyptic in form.

A. First (or Ethiopic) Enoch. Three apocalyptic books bearing the name of Enoch have come down to us, known as Ethiopic Enoch (1 Enoch), Slavonic Enoch (2 Enoch), and Hebrew Enoch (3 Enoch). Since the last of these lies beyond the period of our interest, it will receive no attention.

First Enoch is obviously a composite work, consisting of at least five different parts. The third part (chs. 72–82) is an astronomical treatise containing no eschatology and may here be ignored. Since Aramaic fragments of ten different MSS, representing four parts of the book, have been found in the Qumrân caves, it is quite certain that the book in its several parts was originally written in Aramaic and then translated into Greek at an early date. Considerable fragments of the Greek version have been found; these have recently been re-edited by Matthew Black (*Apocalypsis Henochi Graece* [1970]). The Greek version was translated into Ethiopic. In 1773 a traveller, James Bruce, brought three MSS in Ethiopic from Abyssinia to Britain. We now possess twenty-nine MSS, but all of them more or less corrupt. We have no materials to trace the history of the five parts of Enoch as individual books or as a collection.

Few objective criteria exist by which to date the production of these books and their collection. Most scholars believe they were written between 165 and 64 B.C., but conclusions vary considerably.

The central motif of Enoch is easy to understand. According to Gen. 5:24, Enoch was caught up from the earth to be with God. The books of Enoch relate many of the heavenly secrets that Enoch allegedly saw on his journeys through the heavens. He learned not only secrets about the end of the age and the coming of the kingdom of God, but also secrets about many of the mysteries of life and the world.

The first book (chs. 1–36) opens with a brief introduction (chs. 1–5) that contains a short passage quoted in Jude 14f.: "And behold! He cometh with ten thousand of His holy ones to execute judgment upon all and to destroy all the ungodly, and to convict all flesh of all the works of their ungodliness which they have committed, and of all the hard things which ungodly sinners have spoken against Him" (1:9). In this part of Enoch there is no messianic personage; it is God who comes.

The main part of the first book is concerned with the problem of evil. Evil is traced to the fallen angels who lusted after the daughters of men. The fallen angels instructed men in many arts and crafts of civilization. Furthermore, all sin is ascribed to these fallen angels (10:8). They are allowed to plague mankind throughout human history, but Enoch foresees their final doom. This book pictures the coming of the kingdom of God, but in very crude terms, "Then shall all the righteous escape, and shall live till they beget thousands of children. And all the days of their youth and their old age shall they complete in peace" (10:17). There is no messiah of any kind.

In his travels, Enoch visits Sheol. The depiction of Sheol shows considerable development beyond the OT conception of a place where all the dead have a shadowy existence. In Enoch's description there are several compartments into which men are separated according to the good and evil of their lives. The righteous are gathered into a place that has a bright fountain of water (ch. 22). Although it is not explicitly stated, Enoch probably expected a resurrection before the day of judgment.

The second book, called the Parables or Similitudes (chs. 37–71), is of great interest for NT studies. It differs significantly from the first book in that it makes no reference to the fallen angels. Instead, the wicked are said to be subject to Satans (54:6) who, unlike the fallen angels, have access to heaven (40:7f.) to accuse men. The Similitudes is of particular interest because of its distinctive doctrine of the Son of Man and the kingdom of God. In Dnl. 7 "one like a son of man" comes to the throne of God to receive the kingdom of God. Scholars disagree as to whether this passage refers to a specific individual or merely to a symbol representing the saints of God (cf. the four beasts). In any case, in Enoch the Son of Man has become an individual who is also called the Elect One. He is a superhuman, heavenly, preexistent being to whom God has given all dominion, who comes to raise the dead and to sit in judgment over all men. Twice in Enoch this Son of Man is called the "messiah" (48:10; 52:4), but as the Psalms of Solomon shows, the messiah was thought to be an earthly, human, Davidic king, not a heavenly supernatural being. Therefore it is well to distinguish between the earthly Davidic messiah and the heavenly preexistent Son of Man.

In Enoch the righteous will be raised to a glorious Kingdom. They will be "clothed with garments of glory" (62:16). Both the earth and the heaven will be transformed (45:4) as the final dwelling place for the righteous. This reflects the theology of the new heaven and a new earth in Isaiah 65:17; 66:22.

A few scholars have maintained that the figure of the heavenly Son of Man in the similitudes can be used to explain our Lord's use of the term. Others have argued that the Son of Man passages in Enoch are the result of a Christian redaction of a Jewish book. The situation is further complicated by the fact that fragments of the other four books of Enoch have been found in Qumrân; and some scholars have used this fact to argue that the Similitudes is a Christian work. However, there is no distinctive Christian element in the book. The Son of Man theme can be accounted for as a midrash on the Son of Man in Dnl. 7. This book is of great value to Gospel study because it shows how some circles in Judaism interpreted Dnl. 7.

The fourth book (chs. 83–90) is the account of two visions seen by Enoch in his dreams. The second vision uses elaborate animal symbolism to trace the history of the world down to the establishment of the messianic Kingdom. We can trace this history down to Maccabean times. In the final period the Gentiles will launch an attack upon Israel; but they will not prevail, because a deliverer will arise, who is pictured as a mighty horn sprouting on one of the sheep (90:9ff.). The judgment will take place, the wicked will be destroyed, and the surviving Gentiles will be converted to serve Israel (90:30). A new Jerusalem replaces the old, the righteous dead arise, and the messiah will lead them (90:37). He is not called "messiah," but the idea is present.

The fifth book (chs. 92–105) contains an apocalypse of weeks, in which human history is divided into a period of ten weeks. The seventh week is marked by apostasy; the eighth week is a time of righteousness; the ninth week will see the destruction of the works of the godless; and the tenth week will witness the final judgment of the angels. This apocalypse is notable in that the kingdom of God is in a new heaven (91:16); there is no mention of a new earth.

B. Book of Jubilees. In form Jubilees is an apocalypse, for it allegedly records the revelation God made to Moses on Mt. Sinai. "The angel of the Presence" dictates the history of the world beginning at creation and ending with Moses on Mt. Sinai. The book is called Jubilees because of its way of calculating time. History is divided into a series of forty-nine Jubilees of forty-nine years each. It has also been called the "Little Genesis," not because of its size but because it tells the story found in Genesis in much greater detail.

Scholars are generally agreed that the book was written in the 2nd cent. B.C. Fragments of the book in Hebrew have been found in three of the Qumrân caves, representing ten different MSS. The Hebrew text as a whole has been lost, and so has most of a Greek translation. We possess four Ethiopic translations of the Greek, and a sizeable fragment in Latin.

The book, although technically an apocalypse, contains very little eschatology. Its main purpose is to prove that the cultic and religious practices accepted by the author actually go back to Moses. This reflects the Jewish tradition that both the written Law and the oral interpretation of the Law go back to Moses. The author rewrites the whole history of Genesis to prove that the patriarchs observed the customs of the author's own day. It is primarily a book glorifying the Law and Israel, and urging separation from Gentile practices. Thus, e.g., the angels were created circumcised (15:27).

What little eschatology the book contains is significant. A time of decadence and apostasy will set in; but this will be followed by a renewed study of the law and obedience to the commandments. This will result in the coming of the Kingdom, which is described in very earthly terms—men will live to be 1000 years old (23:27). There is no hint of a resurrection; instead, "their bones will rest in the earth, and their spirits will have much joy" (23:31)—a very unusual teaching in Judaism.

C. Testaments of the Twelve Patriarchs. This book (abbr. XII P.) belongs to the PSEUDEPIGRAPHA rather than to apocalyptic literature, for it consists of twelve pseudoprophecies allegedly uttered by each of the patriarchs before his death. Usually each of the twelve parts consists of a resume of the life of the given patriarch, emphasizing his particular merits or weaknesses; a moral application urging his sons to follow his example in the good things and warning them to avoid his sins; and a prediction of the future of the tribe. The book contains a strong eschatological element, and for this reason is usually included in the discussion of apocalyptic literature.

The text of XII P. is an unsolved problem. It exists in Greek translation and in Armenian and Slavonic translations of the Greek. Numerous fragments in Aramaic of Levi and Naphtali have been found in the Qumrân caves; but these look like fragments of sources used by the authors rather than fragments of the Semitic original. The problem of the text is further complicated by the fact that there are some obvious Christian passages in the Testaments, e.g., "In thee shall be fulfilled the prophecy of heaven, concerning the Lamb of God, and Savior of the world" (T. Benj. 3:8, *APOT*). The Armenian version lacks the Christian glosses that appear in the Greek. These facts have led to diverse conclusions. The most obvious conclusion is that XII P. is a Jewish book that has been interpolated by a Christian hand. Although some scholars have argued that XII P. *in toto* is a Christian production, the Christian passages are so obvious and interrupt the context so abruptly that this seems unlikely. One scholar has said, "Given such a history of the text it is apparently hopeless to try to unscramble the present omelet" (M. Smith, *IDB*, IV, 578).

The date of the book is difficult to determine. It has been dated as early as the 3rd to 2nd cent. B.C., but the prevailing date chosen by those who accept it as a Jewish work is the Maccabean period, probably in the reign of John Hyrcanus, between 140 and 110 B.C.

The book has strong moral and ethical emphasis. Dan warns against anger and sums up the law in these words: "Love the Lord throughout your life, and one another with a true heart" (T. Dan 5:3). Gad hates Joseph and warns against hatred. Joseph dwells at length on his refusal to yield to Potiphar's wife and urges mutual love that covers one another's faults.

Throughout the book, the moral law is stressed rather than the ceremonial. Sin results from the evil impulse in man, which is personified in Beliar, the prince of evil, and his seven false spirits—lust, greed, hostility, hypocrisy, arrogance, falsehood, and injustice (T. Reub. 3:3-6). The seven false spirits are therefore evil tendencies rather than demons. Repentance receives considerable attention. "For true, godlike repentance drives away the darkness, illuminates the eyes, gives knowledge to the soul, and leads the mind to salvation" (T. Gad 5:7). There is a passage in Joseph (1:5f.) that is strikingly similar to Mt. 25:35f.

Beliar plays an important role in the book and is frequently mentioned. He is the lord of darkness (T. Jos. 20:2); he can rule men (T. Dan 4:7). In the last days men will serve Beliar (T. Iss. 6:1). One is to arise (Messiah) who will make war on Beliar and deliver men from his captivity (T. Dan 5:10f.). He will bind Beliar (T. Levi 18:12) and cast him into the fire (T. Jud. 25:3). Beliar stands over against God; he is the embodiment of evil as God is of goodness. H. H. Rowley thinks that Beliar corresponds to Antichrist (*Relevance of Apocalyptic* [1963], p. 72); and although he is not a human figure, he is the personification of opposition to the will of God, and thus fills the role of Antichrist.

There are several striking similarites to the Qumrân literature, especially in the opposition of light to darkness (T. Levi 19:1; T. Jos. 20:2). The office of the priesthood is exalted over the office of the king. The descendants of Levi are urged to revere Levi and Judah — the priesthood and the Kingdom; but God "set the kingdom beneath the priesthood" (T. Jud. 21:3). Before the Qumrân materials had been published, G. R. Beasley-Murray defended the thesis that there were two messiahs in the Testaments (although they are not called "messiah"), with the kingly messiah subordinate to the priestly messiah (*JTS*, 48 [1947], 1-13); and this apparently is the messianic theology of Qumrân. "The Lord shall raise up from Levi as it were a High-Priest, and from Judah as it were a King" (T. Sim. 7:2; see also T. Iss. 6:7). Judah says, "To me the Lord gave the kingdom, and to him (Levi) the priesthood. He set the kingdom beneath the priesthood. To me He gave the things upon the earth, to him the things in the heavens. As the heaven is higher than the earth, so is the priesthood of God higher than the earthly kingdom, unless it falleth away through sin from the Lord and is dominated by the earthly king" (T. Jud. 21:2f.; cf. *APOT*).

It is clear that a messianic king is expected who will "make war against Beliar, and execute an everlasting vengeance on our enemies" (T. Dan 5:10). Israel is to be restored to her land (T. Iss. 6:4). There will be a resurrection of the patriarchs (T. Jud. 25:1), martyrs (v. 4) and all the saints (T. Levi 18:14). There will be a judgment of men, of angels and Beliar (T. Levi 3:2f.); the ungodly will be cast into eternal fire (T. Zeb. 10:3). God will visit

His people (T. Ash. 2:3), and "the saints shall rest in Eden, and in the New Jerusalem will the righteous rejoice . . . and no longer shall Jerusalem endure desolation, nor Israel be led captive, for the Lord shall be in the midst of it, and the Holy One of Israel shall reign over it" (T. Dan 5:12f.). The saints will enter into eternal life (T. Ash. 6:6).

D. Psalms of Solomon. These Psalms are not properly apocalyptic, but since they contain one of the most important eschatological passages in Jewish literature they are usually discussed in connection with this genre. Why the Psalms are ascribed to Solomon is a matter of conjecture.

The Psalms reflect a definite historical situation. Judea was plunged into war (1:2), invaded by a foreigner (17:8) who comes from the ends of the earth (8:16). The authorities opened the gates of Jerusalem to him (8:18f.), but he met stiff resistance within the walls (8:21). He broke down the walls with a battering ram (2:1) and trod Jerusalem under foot (2:20), desecrating the santuary (2:2). Multitudes were slain (8:23) and many taken away into captivity in the west (8:24; 17:13f.). However, the destroyer soon met his doom on the mountains of Egypt by the seashore. His body was thrown to the waves with none to bury him (2:30f.).

The situation depicted here corresponds to the historical situation in 63 B.C., when the Roman general Pompey came to Jerusalem. Aristobulus II and Hyrcanus II were contending for the position of leadership of the Jews. When Pompey arrived they sent ambassadors to him bearing gifts. Hyrcanus opened the city to Pompey, but Aristobulus fortified himself on Mt. Zion; and Pompey had to lay seige and break down with rams the walls protecting the temple area. He entered the holy of holies to see what was there, thus desecrating it. He carried Aristobulus and his children back to Rome as captives. Some years later (48 B.C.) Pompey was engaged in civil war with Caesar. Defeated at Pharsalus, he fled to Egypt, where he was murdered and decapitated. His body lay for some time unburied and was finally burned on a pile of spars. The allusions to these facts indicate that the book was written shortly after 48 B.C.

The tone of the Psalms is distinctly Pharisaic. Israel is divided into the righteous poor who fear the Lord, and the sinners or transgressors who are the priestly or Sadducean aristocracy. The pious, or Hasidim, are humble and poor (16:12-15), quiet souls who seek peace (12:6), enduring patiently the chastisement of the present distress (14:1; 16:11). They look forward to a reward after death (13:9-11; 14:3; 15:15; 16:1-3) and the coming of the messianic kingdom.

The author prays for the coming of the king, the Son of David, who is called "the anointed of the Lord" (17:36; 18:8), i.e., "the Lord's Christ." He will destroy his enemies with the word of his mouth (17:37f.), purify Jerusalem, gather the righteous in Israel together under his rule. Thus "the Lord Himself is our King for ever and ever" (17:51, *APOT*).

Here is a messianic concept very different from that found in the Similitudes of Enoch. The latter, following Dnl. 7, looks for the coming of a preexistent, supramundane, heavenly figure at whose coming the very earth will be transformed. The Psalms look for the coming of a Davidic kingly messiah, arising from among men, human but divinely empowered to destroy the enemies of Israel, purify Jerusalem, and gather God's people together in an earthly kingdom. These two concepts should be kept distinct in the study of the NT.

E. Assumption of Moses. This book is extant in a single sixth-century Latin MS discovered in 1861 in Milan. The Latin is obviously translated from the Greek, and the Greek from either Hebrew or Aramaic. It is allegedly a prophecy made by Moses to Joshua on the threshold of entering the Promised Land. Moses forecasts the future of Israel down to the coming of the Kingdom. It is largely didactic prophecy and does not use the elaborate animal symbolism of Daniel or the dream visions of Enoch. Events can be identified that belong to the Maccabean period. The insolent king (6:2) is probably Herod the Great, and the King of the West (6:8) Varus, governor of Syria, who quelled a rebellion in 4 B.C. This is followed by a time of trouble and then God's kingdom comes. The book therefore is easy to date; it must have been written shortly after the death of Herod the Great in 4 B.C.

It is quite certain that ch. 8 is out of place and belongs between chs. 5 and 6. Some scholars think ch. 9 also is out of place. It contains a reference to a mysterious figure Taxo (9:1), who had seven sons. Some think this is a reference to Eleazar of Maccabean times (2 Macc. 6:18-31); others think he is an unknown contemporary of the author. S. Mowinckel (*He That Cometh* [1956], p. 301) suggests that the word "Taxo" comes from the Gk. *táxōn,* "the orderer," the one who expounds the law and establishes right order. Mowinckel thinks Taxo is identical with the Teacher of Righteousness of the Qumrân community.

Scholars disagree as to the nature of the Kingdom in the book. One thing is clear: there is no messianic figure for "the Most High God, the Eternal and Only God shall arise and manifest Himself to punish the nations" (10:7). "Then shalt thou be happy, O Israel, and shalt mount on the neck and wings of the eagle . . . And God shall exalt thee, and bring thee to the heaven of the stars, the place of His habitation. And thou shalt look from on high and behold thy adversaries on the earth, and shalt know them and rejoice, and give thanks, and acknowledge thy Creator" (10:7-10). It is possible that instead of "earth" (Gk. *gḗ*) we should read "Gehenna," for *gḗ* can stand alone to represent Heb. *gê-hinnōm.* Some scholars think this is a nationalistic earthly eschatology, others a wholly supramundane eschatology.

F. Second (or Slavonic) Enoch. A second book bearing the name of Enoch has been preserved only in a Slavonic version. It is not at all clear that this book belongs to NT times, for some scholars have found strong reason for dating it much later (see K. Lake, *HTR* 16 [1923]). Rowley says, "it is improbable that the first-century date will maintain itself" (*Relevance of Apocalyptic* [1963], p. 110). The book describes the things seen in the seven heavens as Enoch ascended from earth to the dwelling place of God. In the first heaven he sees the angels who guard the ice and snow and dew; in the second he sees the fallen angels in torment waiting their final doom. In the third heaven he sees both the paradise of the righteous and the place of torment for the wicked. In the fourth heaven are the sun, moon, and stars and their attending angels. In the fifth he sees the watchers who revolted against God, and their chief, Satan. In the sixth he sees the angels who superintend the forces of nature. In the seventh heaven he comes to the throne of God himself, with the archangels and the heavenly glory.

The book contains several items of interest. Enoch is told about the souls who have been created from eternity (23:5). He is told about the course of creation, which will last seven thousand years—a thousand years for each day (33:1f.). The seventh thousand years will be a period of rest, corresponding to the sabbath. Here is the one place in Jewish literature where we find the idea of a millennium—a thousand-year interim kingdom. At the end of the thousand years time shall come to an end. There will be "no computations and no end; neither months, nor weeks, nor days, nor hours" (32:2). Here is a very un-Jewish idea, for our other literature considers "eternity" to be unending time in the age to come. There is no reference to a messiah and no description of a messianic kingdom.

G. Fourth Ezra. This book was originally written in either Hebrew or Aramaic, which was in turn translated into Greek. From it have descended versions in Latin, Syriac, Ethiopic, Arabic, Armenian, and Coptic. Of these, the Latin is the best. The Latin contains four additional chapters—two at the beginning and two at the end—that are obviously not a part of the apocalypse. The translation of the Latin, including the four additional chapters, is included in our English versions of the Apocrypha as 2 Esdras. The apocalypse alone is usually called 4 Ezra.

The book contains a series of seven visions allegedly given to Ezra in Babylon, but it was clearly written shortly after the fall of Jerusalem in A.D. 70. This is by far the most profound and moving apocalypse we possess. "Ezra" is deeply troubled that such a terrible fate could have befallen God's people, who have received and who keep God's Law. He descends to the depth of pessimism and despair, cries to God for help, and prays for a new heart (8:6, 31-33). He feels it would have been better if the human race had not been created and given the power of choice (7:116). "It would be better for us not to be here than to come here and live in ungodliness, and to suffer and not understand why" (4:12).

In answer to his despair, Ezra is told that God's ways are inscrutable (4:7-11), that human intelligence is finite and limited (4:12-21), that human history has been predetermined (4:33-43), and that God does love Israel (5:31-40). The most fundamental answer is that the evils of the present age will be righted in the future age (7:1-16). Suffering in this age is the way to future blessing. While God loves Israel, he does not love the mass of sinners (7:60f., 131). God is patient with men not because he loves men but because the times have been ordained (7:74).

The eschatology of the book is notable for its explicit dualism. "The Most High has made not one world but two" (7:50; cf. 6:7; 7:113; 8:1, 4-6). "This age is full of sadness and infirmities" (4:27); the present age has grown tired and lost the strength of youth (5:55); this age must pass away to make room for a new age (4:29).

In the first vision (3:1–5:19), Ezra is told that the end of the present age is not far off (4:44-50). The signs of the end will be widespread desolation, portents in the heavens, monstrous births, and universal wickedness (5:1-5). Ezra is also told that "one shall reign whom those who dwell on earth do not expect" (5:6)—probably the antichrist.

In the third vision (6:35–9:25) Ezra is told how the New Jerusalem will appear (7:26) and the messiah will be revealed together with those who have not tasted death. The messiah is called "my Son the Messiah." The messiah will remain for four hundred years "and those who remain shall rejoice" (7:28). Here again, as in 2 Enoch, is the idea of a temporal earthly kingdom before the age to come. After this "millennium" the messiah dies, and all men die with him. This is the one place in apocalyptic literature where we find the idea of a dying messiah. However, no reason or value is ascribed to his death. There follow seven days of silence on the earth, after which will come the resurrection of all men for the great judgment (7:31-35). Gehenna and Paradise will stand over against each other (7:36), and the judgment period will last a week of years (7:43).

Here the messiah is mortal and does not play a significant role in the Kingdom or in the Judgment. Resurrection is universal, and there is no enduring earthly kingdom, but a temporal earthly kingdom followed by the age to come.

In the fourth vision (9:26–10:59) Ezra beholds a sorrowful woman, who represents Jerusalem in all its misery and desolation. The sanctuary is laid waste and the altar broken down (10:21); the cultus and sacred songs are no more, and exile, bondage, and dishonor are the lot of the people (10:22). This passage, representing the desolation of Jerusalem, points to a date for the book shortly after A.D. 70. Suddenly the woman is transfigured so that she is no longer a woman but the New Jerusalem, surpassing in beauty. Thus the seer is assured of a blessed future for the Holy City.

The fifth vision (11:1-12:51) is the Eagle vision. The vision is of a twelve-winged eagle with three heads, which is interpreted as the fourth kingdom of Dnl. 7. The eagle thus represents Rome, whose emperors are indicated by the wings and heads. The three heads probably represent Vespasian, Titus, and Domitian, who reigned as emperors A.D. 70-96. Then appears a lion, who announces the destruction of the eagle. Thereupon the eagle is destroyed and burned. The lion is declared to be the messiah, who will execute judgment upon the oppressors, deliver the righteous with mercy, and make them joyful until the day of judgment. Little is said here of the reign of the messiah, and he functions only in the role of deliverer. He merely brings joy that shall last until the unspecified time of the Judgment.

The sixth vision (ch. 13) is of interest because of the appearance of the Son of Man figure. Ezra beholds a storm-tossed sea and emerging from it is the figure of a man, who comes with the clouds of heaven. A multitude of men gather to do battle with him. He makes for himself a mountain, later explained as Mt. Zion, and flies upon it. He consumes his foes with the breath of his mouth, then calls forth a peaceable multitude. In the interpretation the deliverer is called "my Son" (13:32). The fact that he flies with the clouds of heaven shows that he is not a human messiah of the seed of David, but the heavenly transcendental figure of Dnl. 7. However, his mission is to destroy his foes and deliver the saints. Little is said about the blessings he will bestow on the righteous in the Kingdom.

The seventh vision (ch. 14) assures Ezra that he is to be translated out of the world together with "my Son" (14:9), and together with those who are like him until the time of the end; and he is told that nine of the twelve parts into which the age is divided have already passed.

In conclusion, Ezra experiences a remarkable inspiration. He takes five men into the field, and after drinking from the cup of inspiration he dictates to the five scribes for forty days and nights without stopping. During these forty days, ninety-four books are written: the twenty-four of the Hebrew canon that are for all men to read, and seventy books that are to be given "to the wise among your people" (14:46). These were apparently apocalyptic books, and this incident suggests that the apocalypses were not widely read among the people at large but were the particular possession of small esoteric groups.

These seven visions contain very diverse eschatologies and messianic ideas, and have led to theories of various sources for the apocalypse. One thing is clear: there was no "orthodox" eschatology in Judaism.

Several items in this book are of great interest. In comparison to 1 Enoch, there is little angelology. This shows that an elaborate angelology and demonology is not essential to an apocalyptic view of history. Sin did not originate with fallen angels as in Enoch, but springs from an evil heart (3:20, 22). Sin is indeed attributed to Adam, but Adam sinned because he had an evil heart (3:21). The book has quite a bit to say about faith; but faith for Ezra is not personal commitment as in the NT, but is faith in the law

(5:20). The Gentiles are condemned because they have not had faith in the law (7:24). On the other hand, Ezra frequently speaks of treasures of works laid up before God (7:27; 8:33).

H. Apocalypse of Baruch. Also dating from the late 1st cent. A.D., the Apocalypse of Baruch is similar to 4 Ezra in its theology, but is far less profound and original. Most scholars think it was written in imitation of 4 Ezra. It has been preserved in a single Syriac version.

The book opens with Baruch, the scribe of Jeremiah, in Jerusalem. God announces to him the destruction of the Holy City. The next day the Chaldeans besiege the city; but before they take it, it is destroyed by four angels, who bury the sacred vessels of the temple. The Chaldeans then take possession of the city. Jeremiah goes into exile, but Baruch remains in Jerusalem lamenting its fate. He cannot understand why, if the world was made for God's people, such great evils should befall them. (As in 4 Ezra, the actual historical situation is the fall of Jerusalem in A.D. 70.) In answer, Baruch is told that men have sinned deliberately; therefore they deserve to suffer (15:6). A future world is destined for the righteous. Here again appears the eschatological dualism of the two ages (15:7; see also 44:13-15; 51:3; 83:8). If man is prospered in the end, then everything is in order (19:7); it is the end that should be considered (19:5). Meanwhile, Zion's fate will hasten the divine visitation and the coming of the end (20:1f.). There follows a series of revelations of the final woes, judgment, the messiah, and the messianic kingdom. These events are revealed not by the medium of visions or dreams, but in the form of a dialogue with God.

The revelations begin with a time of tribulation when men will abandon hope (25:4). The tribulation is divided into twelve disasters which will precede the messianic age. These woes will affect the whole earth (29:1), but those who are in the land will be protected (29:2). "The Messiah shall then begin to be revealed" (29:4), and the Kingdom—portrayed in crudely materialistic terms—will be established. Two great monsters, Leviathan and Behemoth, which have been kept in the sea since the fifth day of creation, will come up from the sea to serve as food for those who enter the Kingdom (29:4). "The earth also shall yield its fruit ten thousandfold, and on one vine there shall be a thousand branches, and each branch shall produce a thousand clusters, and each cluster shall produce a thousand grapes, and each grape shall produce a cor (120 gal.) of wine" (29:5). Manna will again descend from on high.

"And it shall come to pass after these things, when the time of the advent of the Messiah is fulfilled, that He shall return in glory" (30:1, *APOT*). This is a perplexing passage, for the messiah seems to be revealed before the beginning of the Kingdom. Many interpret this passage as saying that the messiah will return to heaven after his reign in the Kingdom. It is possible, however, that it refers to his coming to earth. He only *begins* to be revealed before the Kingdom; his advent occurs after the Kingdom. In any case, we have here a temporal earthly Kingdom, which is followed by the resurrection of "all who have fallen asleep in hope of Him" (30:2). The souls of the wicked, however, will waste away in torment (30:4f.). This is to be followed by the renewal of creation (32:6). In this passage the messiah seems to be only a conventional figure, without any significant function.

In the second section (chs. 36–40) Baruch is given a dream-vision of the coming of the Kingdom. In the vision, he sees a forest that represents the four kingdoms of Dnl. 7. In the forest is one great cedar. Then he sees a peaceable fountain that submerges the forest, rooting out the greater part of the trees so that none is left except the great cedar. Finally the fountain destroys also the cedar.

Baruch's interpretation of this vision takes the fountain to be "the principate of My Messiah" (39:7). The tall cedar is "the last leader of that time" (40:1), possibly the antichrist. The victory of the fountain over the cedar means that "My Messiah shall convict him of all his impieties . . . and afterwards he shall put him to death, and protect the rest of My people which shall be found in the place which I have chosen. And his principate shall stand for ever, until the world of corruption is at an end, and until the times aforesaid are fulfilled" (40:2f.). Here the Kingdom is an everlasting earthly kingdom, and the messiah a warlike deliverer who does not destroy by the word of his mouth but by the sword in his hand. The antichrist is apparently a human figure, the last Roman sovereign; and Messiah's Kingdom lasts forever. Nothing is said about the Age to Come.

A third section (chs. 49–52) is important for its teaching on the resurrection. Baruch asks in what shape men will come forth in the resurrection. He is told that men will first come to life again in the same form in which they died, in order that they may recognize one another. After this recognition, they will be changed. "Those who have now been justified by My law" (51:3) shall be "turned into the light of their beauty," that they may inherit the world that does not die. They shall be transformed into the splendor of angels because they have been "saved by their works" and the Law has been to them a hope. They shall dwell "in the heights of that world" and "be made like unto the angels, and be made equal to the stars, and they shall be changed into every form they desire" (51:10, *APOT*) in paradise.

A final apocalypse is found in chs. 53–74. In it Baruch sees another dream-vision in which the entire course of history is disclosed to him in the likeness of twelve white and black waters pouring upon the earth from a great cloud. The black waters represent evil periods in Israel's history, the last of which is the Roman period, and the bright waters represent good periods in history. Finally, he sees lightning on the summit of the cloud, which shines so brightly that it illuminates the whole earth, and heals the place of the last black waters and has dominion over all the earth. The lightning represents "My Messiah" who shall "summon all the nations, and some of them He shall spare, and some of them he shall slay . . . Every nation which knoweth not Israel and hath not trodden down the seed of Jacob shall indeed be spared" (72:2, 4, *APOT*). Those who have ruled over Israel shall be given to the sword. Here the messiah is a warlike being who slays Israel's enemies with his own hands. Thus the Kingdom is established.

It is clear that Baruch's concept of righteousness is legalistic. The righteous can die in peace because "they have with Thee a store of works preserved in treasuries" (14:12). Paradise will be opened to "those who have been saved by their works" (51:7). Baruch, like 4 Ezra, has no doctrine of fallen angels. However, his theology of sin is different. In 4 Ezra sin is due to an evil heart; but in Baruch every man is free. Adam was indeed the first to sin; but Adam's successors are responsible for their own sin. Man may choose torment or glories to come. "Adam is therefore not the cause, save only of his own soul, but each of us has been the Adam of his own soul" (54:19, *APOT*).

See also APOCRYPHAL APOCALYPSES; PSEUDEPIGRAPHA.

Bibliography.–*HJP*, II/3, § 32; G. H. Box, *The Ezra-Apocalypse* (1912); R. H. Charles, ed., *APOT* (Charles has also published commentaries on Jubilees, 1 Enoch, The Testaments of the Twelve Patriarchs, 2 Enoch, Apocalypse of Baruch; many of the texts have been printed in the series *Translations of Early Documents*); R. H. Charles, *Critical History of the Doctrine of a Future*

Life in Israel, in Judaism, and in Christianity (1913); F. C. Burkitt, *Jewish and Christian Apocalypses* (1914); C. C. Torrey, *Apocryphal Literature* (1945); H. H. Rowley, *Relevance of Apocalyptic* (rev. ed. 1946)–includes an extensive bibliography; *HNTT*; J. Klausner, *The Messianic Idea in Israel* (1955); D. S. Russell, *Method and Message of Jewish Apocalyptic* (*OTL*, 1964); J. M. Schmidt, *Die jüdische Apokalyptik* (1969); K. Koch, *Rediscovery of Apocalyptic* (1972); L. Morris, *Apocalyptic* (1972); W. Schmithals, *Apocalyptic Movement* (1972); P. D. Hanson, *Dawn of Apocalyptic* (1975).

G. E. LADD

APOCRYPHA.

I. Definition
II. Usage
  A. Original Meanings
    1. Classical
    2. Hellenistic
    3. In the NT
    4. Patristic
  B. "Esoteric"
  C. Early Christian Usage
  D. Eastern Church
    1. "Esoteric" Literature
    2. Noncanonical "Religious" Books
    3. "Spurious" Books
    4. "List of Sixty"
  E. Western Church
    1. The Decretum Gelasianum
    2. "Noncanonical" Books
  F. Reformers
  G. Hebrew Words for Apocrypha
  H. Summary
III. Contents of the Apocrypha
  A. List of Books
  B. Classification
IV. Original Languages
V. Dates

I. Definition.–The word "Apocrypha," as usually understood, denotes the collection of religious writings that the LXX and Vulgate (with trivial differences) contain that are not included in the Jewish and Protestant canon. This is not the original or the correct sense of the word, as will be shown, but the one it bears almost exclusively in modern speech.

It is customary to speak of the collection of writings now in view as the OT Apocrypha, because many of the books at least were written in Hebrew, the language of the OT, and because all of them are much more closely allied to the OT than to the NT. But there is a "New" as well as an "Old" Testament Apocrypha consisting of gospels, epistles, etc. Moreover the adjective "apocryphal" is also often applied in modern times to what are now generally called "pseudepigraphical" writings, so designated because ascribed in the titles to authors who did not and could not have written them (e.g., Enoch, Abraham, Moses). The persons thus connected with these books are among the most distinguished in the traditions and history of Israel, and there can be no doubt that the reason for using such names is to add weight and authority to these writings. *See* PSEUDEPIGRAPHA.

II. Usage.–When the word "apocryphal" was first used in ecclesiastical writings it bore a sense virtually identical with "esoteric," as we shall see, so that "apocryphal writings" were such as appealed to an inner circle and could not be understood by outsiders. The present connotation of the term did not become fixed until the Protestant Reformation had set in, limiting the biblical canon to its present dimensions among Protestant churches.

A. Original Meanings. 1. Classical. The Gk. adjective *apókryphos* denotes strictly "hidden," "concealed," of a material object (Euripides *Hercules furens* 1070). Then it came to signify what is obscure, recondite, hard to understand (Xenophon *Memorabilia* 3.5, 14). But in classical Greek it never has any other sense.

2. Hellenistic. In Hellenistic Greek as represented by the LXX and the NT there is no essential departure from classical usage. In the LXX (or rather Theodotion's version) of Dnl. 11:43 it stands for "hidden" as applied to gold and silver stores. But the word has also in the same text the meaning "what is hidden away from human knowledge and understanding." So Dnl. 2:20 (Th.), where the *apókrypha* or hidden things are the meanings of Nebuchadnezzar's dream revealed to Daniel though "hidden" from the wise men of Babylon. The word has the same sense in Sir. 14:21; 39:3,7; 42:19; 48:25; 43:32.

3. In the NT. In the NT the word occurs but thrice, viz., Mk. 4:22 par. Lk. 8:17; Col. 2:3. In the last passage Lightfoot thought we have in the word *apókryphoi* (treasures of Christ *hidden)* an allusion to the vaunted esoteric knowledge of the false teachers, as if Paul meant to say that in Christ alone we have true wisdom and knowledge and not in the secret books of these teachers. Assuming this, we have in this verse the first example of *apókryphos* in the sense "esoteric." But the evidence is against so early a use of the term in this — soon to be its prevailing — sense. Nor does exegesis demand such a meaning here, for no writings of any kind seem intended.

4. Patristic. In patristic writings of an early period the adjective *apókryphos* came to be applied to Jewish and Christian writings containing secret knowledge about the future, etc., intelligible only to the small number of disciples who read them and for whom they were believed to be specially provided. To this class of writings belong in particular those designated apocalyptic (*see* APOCALYPTIC LITERATURE), and it will be seen that *apókryphos* as thus employed has virtually the meaning of the Gk. *esōterikós*.

B. "Esoteric." From quite early times the philosophers of ancient Greece distinguished between the doctrines and rites which could be taught to *all* their pupils, and those which could profitably be communicated only to a select circle called the initiated. The two classes of doctrines and rites—they were mainly the latter—were designated respectively "exoteric" and "esoteric." Lucian (d. 312; see *Vitarum Auctio* 26), followed by many others, referred the distinction to Aristotle, but wrongly as modern scholars agree, for the *exōterikoí lógoi* of that philosopher denote popular treatises. The Pythagoreans recognized and observed these two kinds of doctrines and duties, and there is good reason for believing that they created a corresponding double literature, though unfortunately no explicit examples of such literature have come down to us. In the Greek mysteries (Orphic, Dionysiac, Eleusinian, etc.) two classes of hearers and readers are implied all through, though it is a pity that more of the literature bearing on the question has not been preserved. Among the Buddhists the *Samga* forms a close society open originally to monks or *bhikhus* admitted only after a most rigid examination; but in later years nuns *(bhikshunis)* also have been allowed admission, though in their case too after careful testing. The *Vinaya Pitaka* or "Basket of Discipline" contains the rules for entrance and the regulations to be observed after entrance. But this and kindred literature were and are still held to be caviar to outsiders.

It must be borne in mind that the word "apocrypha" is really a Greek adjective in the neuter plural, denoting strictly "things hidden." But almost certainly the noun *bíblia* is understood, so that the real implication of the word is "apocryphal books" or "writings." In this article apoc-

APOCRYPHA

rypha will be employed in the sense of this last, and apocryphal as the equivalent of the Gk. *apókryphos*.

C. Early Christian Usage. The word "apocrypha" was first used technically by early Christian writers for the Jewish and Christian writings usually classed under "apocalyptic" (*see* APOCALYPTIC LITERATURE). In this sense it takes the place of the classical Greek word *esōteriká* and bears the same general meaning, viz., writings intended for an inner circle and capable of being understood by no others. These writings give intimations regarding the future, the ultimate triumph of the kingdom of God, etc., beyond, it was thought, human discovery and also beyond the intelligence of the uninitiated. In this sense Gregory of Nyssa (d. 395; *In suam ordinationem* 2.44) and Epiphanius (d. 403; *Haer*. 51:3) speak of the Apocalypse of John as "apocryphal."

D. Eastern Church. Christianity itself has nothing corresponding to the idea of a doctrine for the initiated or a literature for a select few. The gospel was preached in its first days to the poor and ignorant, and the reading and studying of the sacred Scriptures have been urged by the churches (with some exceptions) upon the public at large.

1. "Esoteric" Literature. The rise of this conception in the Eastern Church is easily understood. When devotees of Greek philosophy accepted the Christian faith it was natural for them to look at the new religion through the medium of the old philosophy. Many of them read into the canonical writings mystic meanings, and embodied those meanings in special books, these last becoming esoteric literature in themselves; and as in the case of apocalyptic writings, this esoteric literature was more revered than the Bible itself. In a similar way there grew up among the Jews side by side with the written law an oral law containing the teaching of the rabbis and regarded as more sacred and authoritative than the writings they profess to expound. One may find some analogy in the fact that among many Christians the official literature of the denomination to which they belong has more commanding force than the Bible itself. This movement among Greek Christians was greatly aided by Gnostic sects and the esoteric literature to which they gave rise. These Gnostics had been themselves influenced deeply by Babylonian and Persian mysticism and the corresponding literature. Clement of Alexandria (d. 220) distinctly mentions esoteric books belonging to the Zoroastrian (Mazdean) religion.

Some Oriental and especially Greek Christians tended to give to philosophy the place which the NT and western Christianity assign the OT. The preparation for the religion of Jesus was said to be in philosophy as well as in the religion of the OT. It will be remembered that Marcion (d. end of 2nd cent. A.D.), Thomas Morgan, the Welsh eighteenth-century deist (d. 1743), and Friedrich Schleiermacher (d. 1834) taught this even more strongly.

Clement of Alexandria recognized 2 Esdras, the Assumption of Moses, etc., as fully canonical. In addition to this he upheld the authority and value of esoterical books, Jewish, Christian, and even heathen. But he is of most importance for our present purpose because he is probably the earliest Greek writer to use the word "apocrypha" as the equivalent of *esōteriká*, for he describes the esoteric books of Zoroastrianism as apocryphal.

But the idea of esoteric religious literature existed at an earlier time among the Jews, and was borrowed from them by Christians. It is clearly taught in 2 Esd. 14, where it is said that Ezra aided by five amanuenses produced under divine inspiration ninety-four sacred books, the writings of Moses and the prophets having been lost when Jerusalem and the temple were destroyed. Of this large number of sacred books twenty-four were to be published openly, for the unworthy as well as the worthy, these twenty-four books representing undoubtedly the books of the Hebrew OT. The remaining seventy were to be kept for the exclusive use of the "wise among the people," i.e., they were of an esoteric character. Perhaps if the Greek original of this book had been preserved the word "apocrypha" would have been found as an epithet attached to the seventy books. Our English versions are made from a Latin original (*see* ESDRAS, BOOKS OF). Modern scholars agree that in its present form this book arose in the reign of Domitian A.D. 81-96. Thus the conception of esoteric literature existed among the Jews in the 1st cent. A.D., and probably still earlier.

It is significant of the original character of the religion of Israel that no one has been able to point to a Hebrew word corresponding to "esoteric" (see below). When among the Jews there arose a literature of oral tradition it was natural to apply to this last the Greek notion of esoteric, especially as this class of literature was more highly esteemed in many Jewish circles than the OT Scriptures themselves.

2. Noncanonical "Religious" Books. The next step in the history of the word "apocrypha" is that by which it came to denote religious books inferior in authority and worth to the Scriptures of the OT and NT. This change of attitude toward noncanonical writings took place under the influence of two principles: (1) that no writer could be inspired who lived subsequent to the apostolic age; (2) that no writing could be recognized as canonical unless it was accepted as such by the churches in general (in Latin the principle was: *quod ubique, quod semper, quod ab omnibus)*. Now it was felt that many if not most of the religious writings which came in the end of the 2nd cent. to be called "apocryphal" in a disparaging sense had their origin among heretical sects like the Gnostics, and that they had never commanded the approval of the great bulk of the churches. Origen (d. 253) held that we ought to discriminate among books called "apocryphal," some such having to be firmly rejected as teaching what is contrary to the Scriptures. More and more from the end of the 2nd cent., the word "apocrypha" came to stand for what is spurious and untrustworthy, and especially for writings ascribed to authors who did not write them, the "pseudepigraphal" books.

Irenaeus (d. 202) in opposition to Clement of Alexandria denies that esoteric writings have any claims to credence or even respect. To him, as later to Jerome (d. 420), "canonical" and "apocryphal" were antithetic terms.

Tertullian (d. 230) took the same view: "apocryphal" to him denoted noncanonical. But both Irenaeus and Tertullian meant by "apocrypha" in particular the apocalyptic writings. During the Nicene period, and even earlier, sacred books were divided by Christian teachers into three classes: (1) books that could be read in church; (2) books that could be read privately, but not in public; (3) books that were not to be read at all. This classification is implied in the writings of Origen, Clement of Alexandria, Athanasius (d. 373), and in the Muratorian Canon (*ca.* A.D. 200).

3. "Spurious" Books. Athanasius, however, restricted the word "apocrypha" to the third class, thus making the corresponding adjective synonymous with "spurious." Nicephorus, patriarch of Constantinople (A.D. 806-815), in his chronography (belonging essentially to A.D. 500 according to Zahn) divides sacred books thus: (1) the canonical books of the OT and the NT; (2) the Antilegomena of both Testaments; (3) the Apocrypha of both Testaments.

The details of the Apocrypha of the OT are thus enumerated: (1) Enoch; (2) Twelve Patriarchs; (3) Prayer of

Joseph; (4) Testament of Moses; (5) Assumption of Moses; (6) Abram; (7) Eldad and Modad; (8) Elijah the Prophet; (9) Zephaniah the Prophet; (10) Zechariah, father of John; (11) Pseudepigrapha of Baruch, Habakkuk, Ezekiel, and Daniel.

The books of the NT Apocrypha are thus given: (1) Itinerary of Paul; (2) Itinerary of Peter; (3) Itinerary of John; (4) Itinerary of Thomas; (5) Gospel According to Thomas; (6) Teaching of the Apostles (the Didache); (7) and (8) Two Epistles of Clement; (9) Epistles of Ignatius, Polycarp, and Hermas.

The above lists are repeated in the "Synopsis of Athanasius." The authors of these so-called apocryphal books being unknown, it was sought to gain respect for these writers by tacking onto them well-known names, so that, particularly in the Western Church, "apocryphal" came to be almost synonymous with "pseudepigraphal."

Of the OT lists given above, nos. 1, 2, 4, 5 are extant wholly or in part. Nos. 3, 7, 8, 9 are lost though quoted as genuine by Origen and other Eastern Fathers. They are all of them apocalypses designated apocrypha in accordance with early usage.

4. "List of Sixty." In the anonymous "List of Sixty," from the 7th cent., we have represented probably the attitude of the Eastern Church. It divides sacred books into three classes: (1) Sixty canonical books, thirty-four of the OT and twenty-six of the NT (lacking Revelation). (2) Books excluded from the sixty, yet of superior authority to those mentioned as apocryphal in the next class. (3) Apocryphal books, the names of which are as follows: (*a*) Adam; (*b*) Enoch; (*c*) Lamech; (*d*) Twelve Patriarchs; (*e*) Prayer of Joseph; (*f*) Eldad and Modad; (*g*) Testament of Moses; (*h*) Assumption of Moses; (*i*) Psalms of Solomon; (*j*) Apocalypse of Elijah; (*k*) Ascension of Isaiah; (*l*) Apocalypse of Zephaniah (see no. 9 of the OT Apocrypha the Chronography of Nicephorus above); (*m*) Apocalypse of Zechariah; (*n*) Apocalyptic Ezra; (*o*) History of James; (*p*) Apocalypse of Peter; (*q*) Itinerary and Teaching of the Apostles; (*r*) Epistles of Barnabas; (*s*) Acts of Paul; (*t*) Apocalypse of Paul; (*u*) Didascalia of Clement; (*v*) Didascalia of Ignatius; (*w*) Didascalia of Polycarp; (*x*) Gospel According to Barnabas; (*y*) Gospel According to Matthew. (See H-S, I, 51f.)

The greater number of these books come under the designation "apocryphal" in the early sense of "apocalyptic," but by this time the word had taken on a lower meaning, viz., books not good for even private reading. Yet that these books are mentioned at all show that they were more highly esteemed than heathen and than even heretical Christian writings. The Eastern churches down to the present day reject the meaning of "apocrypha" current among Protestants (see definition above), and their Bible includes the OT Apocrypha, making no distinction between it and the rest of the Bible.

E. Western Church. 1. The Decretum Gelasianum. In the Western Church the words "apocrypha" and "apocryphal" had a somewhat different history. In general it may be said that the Western Church did not adopt the triple division of sacred books prevalent in the Eastern Church. Yet the Decretum Gelasianum (6th cent. in its present form) has a triple list which is almost certainly that of the Roman synod of 382 under Damasus bishop of Rome (366-384). It is as follows: (1) the canonical books of both Testaments; (2) writings of the fathers approved by the Church; (3) apocryphal books rejected by the Church. Then there is added a list of miscellaneous books condemned as heretical, including even the works of Clement of Alexandria, Tertullian, and Eusebius, these works being all branded as "apocryphal." On the other hand Gregory of Nyssa and Epiphanius, both writing in the 4th cent., use the word "apocrypha" in the old sense of apocalyptic, i.e., esoteric.

2. "Noncanonical" Books. Jerome (d. 420) in the *Prologus Galeatus* (so called because it was a defense and so resembled a helmeted warrior) or preface to his Latin version of the Bible uses the word "Apocrypha" in the sense of noncanonical books. His words are: *Quidquid extra hos* [i.e., the 22 canonical books] *inter Apocrypha ponendum*: "Anything outside of these must be placed within the Apocrypha" (when among the fathers and rabbis the OT is made to contain 22 [not 24] books, Ruth and Lamentations are joined respectively to Judges and Jeremiah). He was followed in this by Rufinus (d. *ca.* 410), in turns Jerome's friend and adversary, as he had been anticipated by Irenaeus. The Western Church as a whole departed from Jerome's theory by including the antilegomena of both Testaments among the canonical writings: but the general custom of western Christians about this time was to make apocryphal mean noncanonical. Yet Augustine (d. 430; *Civ. Dei* xv.23) explained "apocrypha" as denoting obscurity of origin or authorship, and this sense of the word became the prevailing one in the West.

F. Reformers. But it is to the Reformers that we are indebted for the habit of using Apocrypha for a collection of books appended to the OT and generally up to 1827 appended to every printed English Bible. Bodenstein of Carlstadt, usually called Carlstadt (d. 1541), an early Reformer, though Luther's bitter personal opponent, was the first modern scholar to define Apocrypha quite clearly as writings excluded from the canon, whether or not the true authors of the books are known, in this going back to Jerome's position. The adjective "apocryphal" came to have among Protestants more and more a disparaging sense.

Protestantism was in its very essence the religion of a book, and Protestants would be sure to see to it that the sacred volume on which they based their religion, including the reforms they introduced, contained no book but those which in their opinion had the strongest claims to be regarded as authoritative. In the Eastern and Western churches under the influence of the LXX and Vulgate the books of the Apocrypha formed an integral part of the canon and were scattered throughout the OT, generally placed near books with which they have affinity. Even Protestant Bibles up to 1827 included the Apocrypha, but as one collection of distinct writings at the end of the OT. It will be seen from what has been said that notwithstanding the favorable attitude toward it of the Eastern and Western churches, from the earliest times, our Apocrypha was regarded with more or less suspicion, and the suspicion would be strengthened by the general antagonism toward it. In the Middle Ages, under the influence of Reuchlin (d. 1532)—great scholar and Reformer—Hebrew came to be studied and the OT read in its original language. That the Apocrypha is absent from the Hebrew canon must have had some influence on the minds of the Reformers. Moreover in the Apocrypha there are parts inconsistent with Protestant principles, as for example the doctrines of prayers for the dead, the intercession of the saints, etc.

The Jews in the early Christian centuries had really two Bibles: (1) There was the Hebrew Bible which does not include the Apocrypha, and which circulated in Palestine and Babylon; (2) there was the Greek version (LXX) used by Greek-speaking Jews everywhere. However, instigated by the use made of it by Christians against themselves, the Jews condemned this version and made the Hebrew canon their Bible, thus rejecting the books of the Apocrypha from their list of canonical writings, and departing from the custom of Christian churches which continued with isolated remonstrances to make the Greek OT canon, with which the Vulgate agrees almost completely, their standard. It is known that the Reformers were careful students of the Bible, and that in OT matters they were the pupils of Jewish scholars—there were no other competent teachers of Hebrew. It might therefore have been expected that the OT canon of the Reformers would agree in extent with that of the Jews and not with that of the Greek and Latin Christians. Notwithstanding the doubt which H. E. Ryle (*Canon of the OT* [2nd ed. 1895], p. 156) casts on the matter, all the evidence goes to show that the LXX and therefore the other great Greek versions included the Apocrypha from the first onward.

But how comes it to be that the Greek OT is more extensive than the Hebrew OT? Up to the final destruction of Jerusalem in A.D. 71 the temple with its priesthood and ritual was the center of the religious thought and life of the nation. But with the destruction of the sanctuary and the disbanding of its officials it was needful to find some fresh binding and directing agency, and this was found in the collection of sacred writings known by us as the OT. By a national synod held at Jamnia, near Jaffa, in A.D. 90, the OT canon was practically though not finally closed, and from that date one may say that the limits of the OT were once and for all fixed, no writings being included except those written in Hebrew, the latest of these being as old as 100 B.C. The Jews of the Dispersion spoke and wrote Greek, and they continued to think and write long after their fellow countrymen of the homeland had ceased to produce any fresh original literature. What they did produce was explanatory of what had been written and practical.

The Greek Bible—the LXX—is that of the Jews in Egypt and of those found in other Greek-speaking countries. John Wyclif (d. 1384) put the Apocrypha together at the end of the OT and the same course was taken by Luther (1546) in his great German and by Miles Coverdale (d. 1568) in his English translation.

G. Hebrew Words for Apocrypha. Is it quite certain that there is no Hebrew word or expression corresponding exactly to the word "apocrypha" as first used by Christian writers, i.e., in the sense "esoteric"? One may answer this by a decisive negative as regards the OT and the Talmud. But in the Middle Ages *qabbālâ* (lit. "tradition") came to have a closely allied meaning (cf. our "cabalistic").

Is there in Hebrew a word or expression denoting "noncanonical," i.e., having the secondary sense acquired by "apocrypha"? This question does not allow of so decided an answer, and as a matter of fact has been answered in different ways.

Zahn, Schürer, Porter, and others maintained that "*Apocrypha (Biblia)*" is a translation of the Heb. *s^e^pārîm g^e^nûzîm,* lit. "books stored away." If this view is the correct one it follows that the distinction of canonical and noncanonical books originated among the Jews, and that the fathers in using the word "apocrypha" in this sense were simply copying the Jews, substituting Greek words for the Hebrew equivalent. But there are decisive reasons for rejecting this view.

(a) The verb *gānaz* of which the passive participle occurs in the above phrase means "store away," "remove from view" — of things in themselves sacred or precious. It never means exclude as from the canon.

(b) When employed in reference to sacred books it is only of those recognized as canonical. Thus after copies of the Pentateuch or of other parts of the Hebrew Bible had, by age and use, become unfit to be read in the home or in the synagogue they were "buried" in the ground as being too sacred to be burned or cut up; and the verb denoting the burying is *gānaz*. But those buried books are without exception canonical.

(c) The Hebrew phrase in question does not once occur in either the Babylonian or Jerusalem Talmud, but only in rabbinical writings of a much later date. The Gk. *apókrypha* cannot therefore be a rendering of the Hebrew expression. The Hebrew for books definitely excluded from the canon is *s^e^pārîm ḥîṣônîm,* "outside" or "extraneous books." The Mishnah or oral law with its additions came to be divided analogously into (1) the Mishnah proper; (2) the external (*ḥîṣônâ*) Mishnah.

H. Summary. (1) Among the Protestant churches the word "Apocrypha" is used for the books included in the LXX and Vulgate, but absent from the Hebrew Bible. This restricted sense of the word cannot be traced farther back than the beginning of the Reformation.

(2) In classical and Hellenistic Greek the adjective *apókryphos* denotes "hidden" (of visible objects), or obscure, hard to understand (of certain kinds of knowledge).

(3) In early patristic Greek this adjective came into use as a synonym of the classical Gk. *esōterikós*.

(4) In later patristic Greek (Irenaeus, etc.) and in Latin works beginning with Jerome, Gk. *apókryphos* meant noncanonical, implying inferiority in subject-matter to the books in the canon.

(5) By the Protestant Reformers the term "apocrypha" ("apocryphal books") came to stand for what is now called the "OT Apocrypha." But this usage is confined to Protestants, since in the Eastern Church and in the Roman branch of the Western Church the OT Apocrypha is as much an integral part of the canon as Genesis or Kings or Psalms or Isaiah.

(6) There are no equivalents in Hebrew for *apókryphos* in the sense of either "esoteric" or "noncanonical."

III. Contents of the Apocrypha.–*A. List of Books.* The books of the Apocrypha in the order in which they occur in the English versions are: (1) 1 Esdras; (2) 2 Esdras; (3) Tobit; (4) Judith; (5) Additions to the Book of Esther; (6) Wisdom of Solomon; (7) Ecclesiasticus (Sirach); (8) Baruch, with the Letter of Jeremiah; (9) Song of the Three Young Men; (10) Susanna; (11) Bel and the Dragon; (12) Prayer of Manasseh; (13) 1 Maccabees; (14) 2 Maccabees.

No. 5 in the above, "Additions to Esther," consists of 107 (out of 270) verses of the book of Esther that occur in the best MSS of the LXX and in the Vulgate but not in the Hebrew Bible. These six additions are in the LXX scattered throughout the book and are intelligible in the context thus given them, but not when brought together as they are in the collected Apocrypha of the AV, ERV, and RSV, and as they are to some extent in Jerome's Latin version and the Vulgate (the NEB Apocrypha translates the whole LXX version of Esther). Nos. 9-11 in the above enumeration are additions made in the LXX and Vulgate versions of Daniel to the book as found in the MT. It would be well to name them "Additions to Daniel." The bringing together of the writings of the Apocrypha into a separate collection was due in a large measure to Jerome, who separated many of the apocryphal additions from their original context because he suspected their genuineness. His version influenced the Vulgate, which follows Jerome's version closely.

Though it is generally true that the Apocrypha is the excess of the Greek (LXX) and Latin (Jerome, Vulgate) over the Hebrew (MT) Bibles, the statement needs qualification. 2 Esdras (4 Ezra) is absent from the LXX, from Jerome's version, and also from Luther's Bible, but it occurs in the Vulgate and in the English and other modern versions of the Apocrypha. On the other hand 3 and 4

APOCRYPHAL ACTS

Maccabees occur in the best MSS of the LXX, but the Vulgate, following Jerome's version, rejects both as do modern versions of the Apocrypha. Moreover, in the Vulgate proper the Prayer of Manasseh and 1 and 2 Esdras are appended to the NT as apocryphal.

B. Classification. 1. Historical. (a) 1 and 2 Esdras; (b) 1 and 2 Maccabees; (c) Additions to Daniel (nos. 9-11 in the above list); (d) Additions to Esther; (e) Letter of Jeremiah (usually appended to Baruch); (f) Prayer of Manasseh.

2. Legendary. (a) Baruch (sometimes classed with prophetic books, sometimes with apocalypses); (b) Tobit; (c) Judith.

3. Apocalyptic. 2 Esdras.

4. Didactic. (a) Wisdom of Solomon; (b) Sirach (Ecclesiasticus).

IV. Original Languages.–The bulk of the Apocrypha was written originally in Greek and existed at first in that language alone. The following books, however, were written in Hebrew: Tobit, Judith, Sirach, Baruch (part probably in Greek), and 1 Maccabees. In these cases some prefer regarding Aramaic as the original language in at least parts of the above books. For detailed information see articles on individual books.

V. Dates.–The dating of the books is discussed in the separate articles. But a general statement regarding the extreme limits between which all the books were completed may safely be made. The oldest apocryphal book is Sirach, which in its original Hebrew form belongs to the period 190-170 B.C. In its Greek form the best modern scholars agree in fixing it at 130-120 B.C. None of the books can well belong to a date later than A.D. 100, though some (e.g., 2 Esdras) may be as late as that. The whole of the Apocrypha may with more than average certainty be said to have been written some time between 200 B.C. and A.D. 100. It is inaccurate to assume that the Apocrypha was in all its parts of later date than the latest parts of the OT. Many think the canonical book of Daniel and many of the Psalms are of later date than Sirach and 1 Esdras, and there are reasons for giving the canonical Esther a later date than any of the books named and perhaps than Judith as well (*see,* however, DANIEL; ESTHER). But it is quite certain that by far the greater part of the Apocrypha is of later date than the OT; it is therefore of the utmost importance as reflecting the state of the Jews and the character of their intellectual and religious life at the various periods represented. And in later years much use has been made of it.

See also APOCRYPHAL ACTS; APOCRYPHAL APOCALYPSES; APOCRYPHAL GOSPELS; APOCRYPHAL EPISTLES.

Bibliography.–*ANT; APOT*; E. J. Goodspeed, *The Apocrypha: An American Translation* (1938); *HNTT*; H-S; B. M. Metzger, *Intro. to the Apocrypha* (1957); R. Meyer and A. Oepke in *TDNT*, III, 978-1000; W. O. E. Oesterley, *Books of the Apocrypha* (1916); C. C. Torrey, *Apocryphal Literature* (1945). T. W. DAVIES

APOCRYPHAL ACTS. A body of extracanonical writings of the 2nd and 3rd cents. A.D.

Originally the designation apocryphal meant "hidden" [<Gk. *apokrýptō*–'hide'], particularly in reference to the claims of some sects to preserve a tradition of secret doctrine of Christ or the apostles. The nature of these sects and the Church's insistence that the tradition of the apostles was openly preserved in the NT naturally added the connotation of spuriousness and even of heresy to the term, and "apocryphal" is used in this sense by Irenaeus and Tertullian. By the time of Jerome, however, "apocryphal" describes any writings ostensibly giving information about the Lord or the apostles but not recognized by the Church (whether doctrinally suspect or not). In this sense of "extracanonical" it is used here.

It is not known whether Luke or his transmitters named his second volume Acts of the Apostles, but the title, like much else in the book, was freely borrowed for a crop of second- and third-century writings. These writings were also influenced by another popular form of Christian writing also called *Acta*—the accounts of the trials and passions of the martyrs. Consideration must here be limited to some of the earlier and more influential apocryphal acts, but their manufacture went on for centuries, especially in the Eastern Church. Older legends were refurbished, new ones begun, and sometimes, one suspects, pagan stories adapted. Most apocryphal acts consequently present complex literary problems.

General Introduction
I. Characteristics
II. Origin
III. Sources
IV. Ecclesiastical Testimony
V. Value
The "Leucian" Acts
I. Acts of Paul
II. Acts of Peter
III. Acts of John
IV. Acts of Andrew
V. Acts of Thomas
Other Acts
I. Acts of Thaddaeus
II. Acts of Philip
III. Acts of Andrew and Matthias

GENERAL INTRODUCTION

I. Characteristics.–The apocryphal acts are surviving examples of early Christian popular literature. They reflect not only the doctrinal concerns of their authors, but also the tastes of their readers and the convictions and ideas of the past entertained by numerous humbler Christians both orthodox and heretical. Not all literate Christians spent their leisure hours studying Origen's *De principiis*.

A. Romance. These acts set out to tell a good story: to entertain as well as to edify. They succeed in various degrees, but most of all they reflect the reading public's craving for marvels, strange adventures, and the triumph of piety. Thomas' wonderful travels in India and Andrew's among the cannibals are related in detail; Peter's witness against Simon Magus is assisted by a dog with human speech. The ascetic fervor of the Acts of John is leavened with anecdotes like the curious story of the apostle and the bugs. The apostles, more than life-size, stride invincibly through the stories (none of the writers has Luke's observation or gift of characterization). Supernatural intervention by dream, vision, voice from heaven, and Christophany becomes commonplace. God fights for his martyrs: the wild beasts are tamed or killed, the fire goes out; and when the time for death finally comes, the martyr dies transfigured in unearthly glory. The apocryphal acts are in general unrealistic, fetid, and unutterably vulgar; and they witness, incidentally, to the probability that the real age of miracles lay already in the past.

B. Sexual Asceticism. Christians in the 2nd and 3rd cents. faced countless problems arising from the sexual promiscuity of the times. Pagan popular literature was blatantly erotic in interest and a strain of sexual asceticism ran through Christian popular literature. Continence ranked high, even supreme, among Christian virtues—thus the Acts of Paul (written by an orthodox presbyter) summarized Paul's preaching as "the word concerning abstinence and the Resurrection." Other acts, of more dubious doctrinal pedigree, are even more extreme in their insistence on celibacy; and many of their stories center upon disrupted brothels or withdrawal from conjugal relations

— often displayed as the direct result of apostolic preaching. The subject takes an unhealthy proportion of space, and its treatment at times (notably in the Acts of John) is indelicately explicit. Christian and pagan popular literature, in fact, arise from the same social background; and the writers of the acts are guided in varying degrees by horror of immorality, false ideals, and the horrible fascination of that which is loathed.

C. Heretical Teaching. Besides this ascetic stress, some of the earlier acts contain traces of dogmatic heresy; and it is possible that this type of literature arose first in unorthodox circles, other writers being influenced by the popular success of the (undoubtedly heretical) "Leucius" of the Acts of John. The latter work has a thoroughly docetic Christology, in which the human Jesus is little more than a specter; and it displays a naive modalism without clear distinction between the Father and the Son. According to this work, Christ left no footprints; and the apostle, trying to touch Him, put his arm through His apparent form. While apparently being crucified on Calvary, Jesus was in fact talking to John on the Mt. of Olives.

Less extreme are the docetic traces in the Acts of Peter, which probably reflect more of crude popular devotion than of self-conscious Gnostic rationalism. Moreover, this book is concerned to combat, under the symbol of Simon Magus, certain other forms of heresy. The Acts of Paul actually incorporates a pseudo-Corinthian correspondence that is specifically anti-Gnostic. Many of the acts, however, have images and aspirations drawn from the fringes of Gnosticism, like the mystic dance in the Acts of John, and the hymn of the pearl in the Acts of Thomas. References by some Christian fathers suggest that they knew versions more heretical than our present texts; and it is probable, and in the case of the Acts of Andrew virtually certain, that we possess in some instances disinfected copies, with the worst offenses removed, a process that strikingly testifies to the popularity of this type of literature.

D. Religious Feeling. Despite the unfavorable impression created by their vulgar, unpleasant, or unorthodox features, the apocryphal acts manifest unmistakably over large sections the rapture of a great spiritual enthusiasm. There are passages (supremely in the Acts of Thomas) of rare poetic beauty, full of religious warmth, mystic fervor, and moral earnestness. The rank superstition and the traces of unconquered heathenism should not blind us to the fact that we have in the apocryphal acts what is often a genuine, though greatly distorted, expression of Christian faith.

II. Origin.–*A. Reverence for the Apostles.* The apostles were recognized throughout the early Church as the normative interpreters of Jesus, commissioned by the risen Lord Himself and uniquely invested with His authority. As early as Ignatius the difference in kind between the apostolic and the fullest ecclesiastical authority is manifest (Ign. Trall. 3; Ign. Rom. 4). This recognition must be borne in mind when considering some types of apocryphal literature. The sanction of some apostle was often claimed for a form of doctrine or local custom.

Eventually it became clear that the traditions of apostles could not be pitted against each other, and that true apostolic tradition was substantially coterminous with the NT; but in days when the possibility of genuine tradition surviving orally was conceivable, these principles were not everywhere obvious. Among the motives that produced the apocryphal acts we may trace both the natural tendency of piety to glorify the apostles and the desire to appropriate apostolic authority.

B. Desire for Apostolic Authority. The Acts of John, for instance, undoubtedly seeks to justify outrageously sectarian views of Christ by using the name of the great apostle, ostensibly reported by a companion. The Acts of Thomas has affinities with other works to which Thomas' name is attached, and which represent him as the apostle most favored with stores of knowledge (*see* APOCRYPHAL GOSPELS V.J.1), perhaps partly because Thomas was traditionally associated with the areas in which they were produced. The author of the Acts of Paul, quite orthodox in his central theology, had a concern for sexual abstinence, which, while he doubtless believed it to be scriptural, he did not find clearly enough expressed in Scripture for his purpose. Accordingly, he attributes his concern to Paul himself, whom we find preaching a new form of the Beatitudes:

> "Blessed are the pure in heart, for they shall see God.
> "Blessed are they that keep the flesh chaste, for they shall become the temple of God.
> "Blessed are the continent, for unto them shall God speak. . . ."

C. Glorification of Martyrdom. The 2nd cent. saw the development, accentuated in later centuries, of a cult of the martyrs. This produced a body of literature of its own. We have moving early accounts of judicial processes leading to martyrdom that were treasured in the churches and elaborated by later generations. But those who revered the martyrs revered the apostles still more; and to such the silence of the canonical Acts on the last crises of the greatest apostles was inexplicable. Even the author of the Muratorian Canon felt he must explain this: "Luke has included for good Theophilus [only] the things done in his presence, as the omission of Peter's passion clearly shows, and the departure of Paul from Rome en route for Spain." Such pious, if misguided, sentiment filled in vivid pictures of the martyrdoms; and later generations concentrated their attention on these "contendings," or glorious sufferings, of the apostles.

D. Local Patriotism. But if the apostle is glorious, some of his glory is reflected on the area in which he worked. Early church controversies (above all the Quartodeciman) show how apostolic tradition was invoked to support local practice. Some features of some of the apocryphal acts may be due to such local patriotism: the Thecla stories in the Acts of Paul, for instance, associate the apostle with a heroine of local fame.

E. Dogma. The heretical tendency of many of the apocryphal acts has obscured that some of them are in fact antiheretical. The Acts of Paul, as we have seen, has a vigorous anti-Gnostic polemic; and the Acts of Peter, in spite of all its docetic touches, raises its banner against those who proclaim that Jesus was misunderstood by His disciples (cf. Acts of Peter 10, which is interesting to link with Tertullian *De praescr. haer.* 32). We may be satisfied that among the motives that produced this literature was the desire to set forth doctrine in an attractive form. Sometimes that doctrine was pernicious, sometimes eccentric, but occasionally it was catholic. Generally speaking it is the earlier acts that show the clearest dogmatic interest; later ones are usually simply mythopoeic.

III. Sources.–By far the most important source of the apocryphal acts is the imagination of their authors. At certain points, however, the influence of other forms of literature can be traced.

A. The Canonical Acts. The influence of the canonical Acts, both as an inspiration and as a model, is beyond doubt. Incidents and phraseology are borrowed from Acts, or remodeled, to lend verisimilitude to the narrative. In some cases the authors apparently propose a form of supplement to Acts. Thus the Roman section of the Acts of Peter opens with Paul's journey to Spain after the events of

Acts 28; and the Acts of Paul, though it is sometimes said to use the framework of Acts, probably intends to describe an assumed eastern ministry of Paul after the first imprisonment. Most of the personal names are fictitious, but of those taken from the NT not one occurs in Acts, and most come from the Pastorals. John, Andrew, Thomas, and the others play little or no part in the canonical Acts. Of twelve (or thirteen) apostles, the sacred writer had related the "acts" of only two. The impulse to supply parallels for the others proved irresistible.

B. Martyrologies. As we have seen, by second-century standards the canonical Acts were also deficient in having no accounts of the last crises of their heroes. People who treasured the stories of the trial and death of Polycarp and Justin would wish parallel accounts for the great apostles. It should be noted how large a proportion of many apocryphal acts is given to these stories, which in many cases (notably the Acts of Paul and the Acts of Peter) have circulated separately and have a literary history of their own. The inspiration for these stories comes from contemporary martyrologies, and sometimes local martyr stories (like the Thecla incidents?) have been incorporated.

C. Travel Romance. Among the contemporary forms of pagan literature that have influenced some of the apocryphal acts we may include that of the travel romance. The most famous example of this romantic literature is the *Life* of Apollonius of Tyana, the neo-Pythagorean preacher and great wonder-worker, who died about the end of the 1st cent. A.D. The marvelous deeds reported to have been wrought by him on his travels were freely transferred in a somewhat less striking form to other teachers. It is in the atmosphere of these romances that the apocryphal acts had their birth. In particular the Acts of Thomas recalls the history of Apollonius. For just as Thomas was a missionary in India, so "Apollonius as a disciple of Pythagoras had traveled, a peaceful Alexander, to the Indian wonderland and there preached his master's wisdom" (J. Geffcken, *Christliche Apokryphen* [1908], p. 36).

IV. Ecclesiastical Testimony.–From the nature of his reference to the canonical Acts it is probable that the writer of the Muratorian Canon (*ca.* A.D. 190) had the existence of other acts in mind. "The acts of all the apostles," he says, "are written in a single book. Luke relates them admirably to Theophilus, confining himself to such as fell under his own notice, as he plainly shows by the omission of all reference either to the martyrdom of Peter or to the journey of Paul from Rome to Spain." During the 3rd cent. there are slight allusions to certain of the apocryphal acts, but it is only in the 4th cent. that distinct references are frequent in writers both of the East and of the West. A few of the more important references follow (for a full account see A. Harnack, *Geschichte der altchristlichen Literatur* [2nd ed. 1958], I, 116ff.).

A. Eastern Testimony. Among Eastern writers Eusebius is the first to make any clear reference to apocryphal acts. He speaks of "Acts of Andrew, of John, and of the other apostles," which were of such a character that no ecclesiastical writer thought it proper to invoke their testimony. Their style and their teaching showed them to be so plainly of heretical origin that he would not put them even among spurious scriptures, but absolutely rejected them as absurd and impious (*HE* iii.25.6f.). Ephraem (d. 373) declares that these acts were written by the Bardesanites to propagate in the name of the apostles unbelief that the apostles had destroyed. Epiphanius (*ca.* 375) repeatedly refers to individual acts that were in use among heretical sects. Amphilochius of Iconium, a contemporary of Epiphanius, declares that certain writings emanating from heretical circles were "not acts of the apostles but accounts of demons." The Second Council of Nicea (A.D. 787), in the records of which those words of Amphilochius are preserved, dealt with apocryphal literature, and had under special consideration the Acts of John, to which the Iconoclasts appealed. In the synod's finding these acts were characterized as "this abominable book," and on it the judgment was passed: "Let no one read it; and not only so, but we judge it worthy of being committed to the flames."

B. Western Testimony. In the West from the 4th cent. onward, references are frequent. Philastrius of Brescia (*ca.* 387) testifies to the use of apocryphal acts among the Manichaeans, and declares that although they are not suitable for general reading they may be read with profit by mature Christians (*De haeresibus* 88). The reason for this favorable judgment is to be found in the pronounced ascetic tendency of the acts, which was in line with the moral ideal prevalent at that time in the West. Augustine refers repeatedly to apocryphal acts in use among the Manichaeans and characterizes them as the work of "cobblers of fables" (*sutoribus fabularum*). The Manichaeans accepted them as true and genuine; in reference to this claim Augustine says: "They would in the time of their authors have been counted worthy of being welcomed to the authority of the Holy Church, if saintly and learned men who were then alive and could examine such things had acknowledged them as speaking the truth" (*Contra Faustum Manichaeum* xxii.79). The Acts of John and the Acts of Thomas are mentioned by Augustine by name. He also refers to Leucius as the author of apocryphal acts. Turribius of Astorga (*ca.* 450) speaks of acts of Andrew, John, and Thomas and attributes them to the Manichaeans. Of the heretical teaching in the Acts of Thomas, Turribius singles out for special condemnation baptism by oil instead of by water. Leucius is mentioned as the author of the Acts of John. The acts of Andrew, Thomas, Peter, and Philip are condemned as apocryphal in the Gelasian Decree (A.D. 496; *see* APOCRYPHA II.E.1); and in the same condemnation are included "all books written by Leucius, a disciple of the devil."

C. Photius. The fullest and most important reference to the apocryphal acts is found in Photius, the patriarch of Constantinople in the second half of the 9th century. In his *Bibliotheca,* which contains an account of 280 different books that he had read during his absence on a mission to Baghdad, we learn that among these was a volume, "the so-called Wanderings of the Apostles, in which were included Acts of Peter, John, Andrew, Thomas, Paul. The author of these Acts, as the book itself makes plain, was Leucius Charinus." The language had none of the grace that characterized the evangelical and apostolic writings. The book teemed with follies and contradictions. Its teaching was heretical. In particular it taught that Christ had never really became man. Not Christ but another in His place had been crucified. After referring to the ascetic doctrine and the absurd miracles of the acts and to the part the Acts of John had played in the Iconoclastic controversy, Photius concludes: "In short this book contains ten thousand things which are childish, incredible, ill-conceived, false, foolish, inconsistent, impious and godless. If anyone were to call it the fountain and mother of all heresy, he would not be far from the truth."

D. Ecclesiastical Condemnation. There is thus a consensus of ecclesiastical testimony as to the general character of the apocryphal acts. They were writings used by a number of heretical sects but regarded by the Church as unreliable and harmful. It is probable that the corpus of the acts in five parts referred to by Photius was formed by the Manichaeans of North Africa, who attempted to have them accepted by the Church in place of the canonical Acts, which they had rejected. These acts in consequence were stamped by the church with a heretical character. The sharpest condemnation is that pronounced by Leo I (*ca.* 450), who declares that "they should not only be forbidden but should be utterly swept away and burned. For although there are certain things in them which seem to have the appearance of piety, yet they are never free of poison and secretly work through the allurements of fables so that they involve in the snares of every possible error those who are seduced by the narration of marvelous things."

The Acts of Paul, which shows no trace of dogmatic heresy, was included in the ecclesiastical censure inasmuch as it had received a place at the end of the corpus. Many teachers in the Church, however, made a distinction between the miraculous details and the heretical doctrines of the apocryphal acts. While they rejected the latter they retained the former. Witness the words of an orthodox reviser in regard to his heretical predecessor: *Quaedam de virtutibus quidem et miraculis quae per eos Dominus fecit, vera dixit; de doctrina vero multa mentitus est*—"he had told the truth about apostolic virtues and miracles, but had lied shamefully about their doctrine."

E. Influence. Ecclesiastical censure could not check the appeal of the stories, and for centuries Christians from Persia to Spain repeated and embroidered them. Apostolic legends appeared in poetry, martyrologies, and calendars; they were solemnly recounted in sermons on the saints' festal days. Their influence on Christian art has also lasted for centuries. Of the general effect of such literature as a staple diet, Harnack's words are still appropriate: "Whole generations of Christians, whole Christian nations, were intellectually blinded by the dazzling appearance of these tales. They lost the eye not only for the true light of history, but also for the light of truth itself" (tr. from I, 26).

*V. **Value***.–As historical records, the apocryphal acts have negligible worth. If some of the earlier ones do preserve valid traditions from the 1st cent., it is now impossible to sift them out. But as records of early Christianity they are of immense, and often underrated, value.

A. Records of Popular Christianity. Some insight into the masses of common people who were born amid degradation and superstition, and came, sometimes very imperfectly, under the influence of the gospel, is provided by the apocryphal acts. These people are not represented by the productions of most of the early church fathers. One can see the sort of stories that delighted them, and in the better works their aspirations, concerns, and problems. In some of the stories in the Acts of Peter, for example, one hears echoes of conflicts with the Jews, the problem of apostasy, the puzzle of unhealed illness, the controversies with pseudo-Christian sects who despised the apostles.

The apocryphal acts also recall that in many ill-instructed congregations there must have been a no-man's-land between orthodoxy and heresy. Their first readers were children of the soil in which Gnosticism flourished, and people who were not intentionally sectarian might hold gnosticizing views of the gospel. A contempt for matter is basic to Gnostic teaching, and when Gnosticism attached itself as a parasite to Christianity it had two effects that are marked even in the nonsectarian acts: docetic Christology and sexual asceticism.

B. Other Values. Some of the acts are, indeed, useful witnesses to Gnostic teaching and practice. They also preserve traces of liturgy and hymnody to which we would never have had access in orthodox sources. Nor should it be forgotten how the apocryphal acts show both the uniqueness of Luke's canonical work and its universal recognition and influence in the 2nd century.

The "Leucian" Acts

In the notice of Photius (*Bibliotheca* 114) the whole corpus made up of the acts of Peter, John, Andrew, Thomas, and Paul is ascribed to Leucius Charinus; but earlier writers speak of Leucius (a supposed disciple of John) as the ostensible author of the Acts of John; and his name has probably been transferred to the corpus as a whole.

Undoubtedly these acts have had a complicated editorial history. There seems to have been a bowdlerization to eliminate heretical elements. Many Gnostic features have been retained, however—some probably because the reviser did not understand their true meaning.

*I. **Acts of Paul***.–*A. Ecclesiastical Testimony*. Hippolytus (d. A.D. 235) in his commentary on Daniel argues from a lion's refusal to attack Paul in the arena to the credibility of a similar immunity for Daniel (3.29; the story about Paul occurs in the Hamburg Greek fragment of the Acts of Paul). Tertullian attests the popularity of the work while exposing its origin and date (*De baptismo* 17). Origen twice quotes the Acts of Paul with approval, though not as authoritative (*De prin.* i.2.3; *In Ioannem* xx.12). Both Eusebius (*HE* iii.25.4) and a stichometry attached to the (sixth-century?) Codex Claromontanus rank it with works that are catholic but subcanonical. Many writers reflect the popularity of the Thecla story; and another constituent element, "3 Corinthians," had an eventful history of its own.

B. Contents. From the notes given of extent in Codex Claromontanus and in the Stichometry of Nicephorus it seems that we possess rather over half of the ancient form of the book. Three of its constituents, the Acts of Paul and Thecla, the Corinthian correspondence, and the Martyrdom of Paul, are separately attested many times over and in several languages. In 1904 Carl Schmidt published a mutilated Coptic version that demonstrated that all three were part of the same work; in 1936 he published a Greek fragment that supplied some of the missing material. Further help may be expected from recently discovered Coptic material in the Bodmer papryi.

1. The Acts of Paul and Thecla. After some incidents preserved fragmentarily in Coptic, the first major surviving section is the Acts of Paul and Thecla. Thecla of Iconium, a betrothed maiden, is so fascinated by Paul's preaching on virginity that she repudiates her husband-to-be. Urged on by her mother and two scoundrels called Demas and Hermogenes, he brings Paul before the proconsul. Paul is imprisoned; Thecla visits him there and is condemned to be burned. The fire, however, is miraculously quenched, and Thecla seeks out Paul (who has been banished) and accompanies him to Antioch. There the official Alexander interferes with her; Thecla defends herself and is condemned to the beasts; but the beasts refuse to touch her, a lioness attacking instead those that come near. Thecla, after praying, throws herself into a tank of seals with the cry, "In the name of Jesus Christ I baptize myself on the last day." The seals perish in a flash of fire. From the first Thecla had engaged the sympathy of Queen Tryphena. When it was proposed to have Thecla torn asunder by maddened bulls Queen Tryphena fainted, and through fear of what might happen the authorities released Thecla and handed her over to Tryphena. Thecla once again sought Paul, and having found him was commissioned by him to preach the Word of God. This she did first at Iconium and then in Seleucia, where she died. Various later additions described Thecla's end, and in one of them it is narrated that she went underground from Seleucia to Rome that she might be near Paul. Finding that Paul was dead she remained in Rome until her death.

Although the Thecla story is a romance designed to

secure apostolic authority for the ideal of virginity, it is probable that it had at least a slight foundation in fact. The existence of an influential Thecla-cult at Seleucia favors the view that Thecla was a historical person. Traditions regarding her association with Paul, which clustered round the temple built in her honor in Seleucia, may have provided the materials for the romance. In the story there are clear historical reminiscences. The historicity of Tryphena is established by coins. She was the mother of King Polemon II of Pontus and a relative of the emperor Claudius. There are no grounds for doubting the information given us in the acts that she was living at Antioch at the time of Paul's first visit. The acts further reveal striking geographical accuracy in the mention of "the royal road" by which Paul is stated to have traveled from Lystra on his way to Iconium—a statement that is all the more remarkable because, while the road was in use in Paul's time for military reasons, it was given up as a regular route in the last quarter of the 1st century. In the acts Paul is described as "a man small in stature, baldheaded, bow-legged, of noble demeanor, with meeting eyebrows and a somewhat prominent nose, full of grace. He appeared sometimes like a man and at other times he had the face of an angel." This description may quite well rest on reliable tradition. On the ground of the historical features in the story, Ramsay (*CRE,* pp. 375ff.) argued for the existence of a shorter version going back to the 1st cent.; but this view has not been generally accepted.

The Acts of Paul and Thecla was very widely read and had a remarkable influence owing to the widespread reverence for Thecla, who had a high place among the saints as the first female martyr. References to the acts in the church fathers are comparatively few, but the romance had an extraordinary vogue among Christians both of the East and of the West. In particular, veneration for Thecla reached its highest point in Gaul; and in a poem entitled "The Banquet" (*Caena*) written by Cyprian, a poet of southern Gaul in the 5th cent., Thecla stands on the same level as the great characters of biblical history. The later Acts of Xanthippe and Polyxena is entirely derived from the Acts of Paul and Thecla.

2. 3 Corinthians. Another important fragment of the Acts of Paul is that containing the so-called Third Epistle to the Corinthians. Paul is represented as being in prison at Philippi (not at the time of Acts 16:23ff., but at some later time). His incarceration was due to his influence over Stratonice, the wife of Apollophanes. The Corinthians, who had been disturbed by two teachers of heresy, sent a letter to Paul describing their pernicious doctrines, which were to the effect that the prophets had no authority, that God was not almighty, that there was no resurrection of the body, that man had not been made by God, that Christ had not come in the flesh or been born of Mary, and that the world was not the work of God but of angels. Paul was very distressed on receipt of this epistle, and "under much affliction" wrote an answer in which the popular Gnostic views of the false teachers are vehemently opposed (*see* APOCRYPHAL EPISTLES I.A).

3. Martyrdom of Paul. The Coptic and Greek portions, and some citations, preserve in whole or part certain other incidents, notably Paul's healing a man with dropsy at Myra, which leads to an attempt on his life (his would-be murderer is struck blind), and a fight with wild beasts at Ephesus in which the lion proves friendly. Clement of Alexandria (*Misc.* vi.5.42f.) and the twelfth-century John of Salisbury (*Policraticus* iv.3) have accounts of Paul's missionary preaching that may be derived from the Acts of Paul.

There are several versions of the martyrdom of Paul, which takes place during the Neronian persecution. As the executioner beheads Paul, milk spurts upon his cloak. Paul appears in vision to Nero and his officers and prophesies judgment: the prefect and centurion in charge of Paul are converted, and Titus and Luke baptize them.

C. Authorship and Date. Tertullian (*De baptismo* 17), denying suggestions that Thecla's self-baptism was a sound precedent for female ministry, says that the author of the Acts of Paul was "a presbyter of Asia, who wrote the book with the intention of increasing the dignity of Paul by additions of his own." He adds that he was deposed from office, despite his confession that he had acted "out of love for Paul." The exact knowledge of the topography and local history of Asia Minor that the book demonstrates supports an Asian origin. F. C. Conybeare argued that the Armenian version preserved an earlier form of the Acts of Paul and Thecla than do the Greek and Latin, removing anachronisms and an apparent confusion of Pisidian with Syrian Antioch. Perhaps the author belonged to a town where Thecla was especially revered. The incident was a thing of the past when Tertullian wrote, and the acts probably belong to *ca.* A.D. 160-180, though C. Schmidt dated them rather later, holding them to be dependent on the Acts of Peter. Recently M. Testuz has argued that the Corinthian correspondence, with its different textual history, doctrinal interests, and purposes, is the work of an earlier author, which has been incorporated in the Acts of Paul; but this is not necessary. The same concern over Gnostic teaching on the Resurrection is visible in various parts of the acts.

II. Acts of Peter.–A. *Contents.* A large portion (to judge from the Stichometry of Nicephorus, nearly two-thirds) is preserved in a Latin translation found at Vercelli, and consequently known as the *Actus Vercellenses.* The latter part of this, describing the martyrdom, circulated separately in many languages, and two Greek MSS survive. There is a later recension entitled *Martyrium Beati Petri Apostoli a Lino conscriptum.* A number of fragments and stories about Peter probably belong to this work, notably one in Coptic published by Schmidt and headed "An Act of Peter." References in Philastrius of Brescia, Isidore of Pelusium, and Photius make it practically certain that the *Actus Vercellenses* belongs to the writing known in antiquity as the Acts of Peter and condemned in the rescript of Innocent I (A.D. 405) and in the Decretum Gelasianum.

1. The Coptic Fragment. This "Act of Peter" contains the story of the apostle's paralytic daughter. One Sunday, while Peter was healing (apparently in Jerusalem), a bystander asked why he did not heal his own daughter. To prove God's power, Peter did so, and then commanded her to return to her paralysis, explaining that he had had a vision on the day she was born that if she remained whole she would be a sore trial. There is a gap in the MS here, but from what follows one can gather that she was desired by Ptolemaeus, a rich man, and saved from ruin only by the affliction for which her father prayed. Ptolemaeus, grief-stricken, goes blind, repents, is healed, and bequeaths some land for the girl, which Peter sells and gives to the poor. Augustine (*Contra Adimantum* 17.5) and the Acts of Titus allude to a story that may come from the same context: Peter's prayers are sought for a gardener's daughter, who immediately falls dead. Her father begs for her restoration, and she recovers, only to be kidnapped shortly after. Both stories probably reflect concern with the problem of disease.

2. Actus Vercellenses. The first three chapters of the *Actus Vercellenses* are clearly a continuation of some other narrative. They could easily be added to the canonical Acts to tell of Paul's departure to Spain.

The longest section of the acts (chs. 4–32) gives an account of the conflict between Peter and Simon Magus at Rome. Paul had not been gone many days when Simon, who "claimed to be the great power of God," came to Rome and misled many of the Christians. Christ appeared in a vision to Peter at Jerusalem and bade him sail at once for Italy. Peter confirmed the congregation in Rome, declaring that he came to establish faith in Christ not by words alone but by miraculous deeds and powers (allusion to 1 Cor. 4:20; 1 Thess. 1:5). At the request of the brethren, Peter went to seek out Simon in the house of one named Marcellus, whom the magician had led astray; and when Simon refused to see him, Peter unloosed a dog and commanded it to go and deliver his challenge. The result of this marvel was the repentance of Marcellus. A section follows describing the mending of a broken statue by sprinkling the pieces with water in the name of Jesus. Meanwhile the dog had given Simon a lecture and had pronounced on him the doom of unquenchable fire. After reporting on its errand and speaking words of encouragement to Peter, the dog expired at the apostle's feet. A smoked fish is next made to swim. The faith of Marcellus was strengthened by the wonders Peter worked, and Simon was driven out of his house with every mark of contempt.

Simon, enraged at this treatment, came to challenge Peter. An infant of seven months speaking in a manly voice denounced Simon and made him speechless until the next sabbath day. Christ appeared in a vision during the night encouraging Peter, who when morning came narrated to the congregation his triumph over Simon, "the angel of Satan," in Judea. Shortly afterward, in the house of Marcellus, which had been "cleansed from every vestige of Simon," Peter unfolded the true understanding of the gospel.

The adequacy of Christ to meet every kind of need is shown in a characteristic passage that reveals docetic traits: "He will comfort you that you may love Him, this Great and Small One, this Beautiful and Ugly One, this Youth and Old Man, appearing in time yet utterly invisible in eternity, whom a human hand has not grasped, who yet is now grasped by His servants, whom flesh had not seen and now sees." Next, in a wonderful blaze of heavenly light, blind widows received their sight and declared the different forms in which Christ had appeared to them. A vision of Marcellus is described in which the Lord appearing in the likeness of Peter struck down with a sword "the whole power of Simon," which had come in the form of an ugly Ethiopian woman, clad in filthy rags.

Later, there was a conflict with Simon in the forum in the presence of the senators and prefects. First the combatants exchanged words; then the contest switched and the power of Peter was signally exhibited as greater than Simon's in raising the dead. Simon was now discredited in Rome, and in a last attempt to recover his influence he declared that he would ascend to God. Before the assembled crowd he flew up over the city, but in answer to Peter's prayer to Christ he fell down and broke his leg in three places. He was removed from Rome and, after having his leg amputated, died.

The *Actus Vercellenses* closes with an account of Peter's martyrdom (chs. 33–44). Peter had incurred the enmity of several influential citizens by persuading their wives to separate from them. The well-known *"Quo vadis?"* story follows: Peter, being warned of the danger he was in, fled from Rome; but meeting Christ and learning that He was going to the city to be crucified again, Peter returned and was condemned to death. At his own request he was crucified head downward, explaining the symbolism of this in obscure, and probably gnosticizing, words. He prays, and as the crowd says "Amen," he dies. Marcellus buries him in his own tomb, and Peter appears to him in a vision. Nero, who had intended to torture Peter, is angry at his summary execution, but is withheld by a vision from a general persecution (Vouaux considers this incident an addition).

B. Authorship, Date, General Features. Nothing can be said with certainty on the authorship of the Acts of Peter. James (*ANT,* p. 300) apparently retracted his earlier opinion (*Apocrypha Anecdota,* II, p. xxiv) that linguistic parallels indicated the same authorship as that of the Acts of John. The religious atmosphere is that of Asia Minor, though Schmidt has urged that Syria or Palestine is more likely. At any rate, the writer is not at home in Rome. Schmidt, who believed the work dependent on the Acts of Paul, thought the Acts of Peter might have been written *ca.* A.D. 180; it is not likely to be later than 200.

While obviously used, and possibly modified, by heretical sects, the Acts of Peter may well have originated within the catholic Church. Its gnosticizing ideas belong to its environment: great stress is laid on understanding the Lord. Scripture is supplemented by a secret tradition committed to the apostles. Peter communicates what he received in a "mystery," and on the cross reveals another. There are here and there traces of docetic language, but the writer seems to have believed in the reality of the Lord's sufferings and in their atoning efficacy. Water is used at the eucharist. A notable and welcome concern of the work is the stress on the mercy of God in Christ toward the backslider—probably one of the concerns of the writer in an age when some Christians were urging that postbaptismal sin was inexpiable. Altogether it is an eloquent mixture of theology, morality, and superstition.

***III. Acts of John.**–A. Contents.* According to the Stichometry of Nicephorus the complete Acts of John was a book about the length of Matthew's Gospel. We have perhaps two-thirds of the whole, in Greek. From late witnesses Bonnet deduces that the lost beginning contained John's summons from Ephesus to Rome, his trial, and his banishment to Patmos. When the first extant long Greek section begins, John is hastening to Ephesus. Lycomedes, the Ephesian praetor, beseeches him to heal his paralyzed wife Cleopatra. Lycomedes dies from grief, but John restores them both and agrees to stay with them. An incident follows that was to be discussed at large at the Second Council of Nicea. Lycomedes commissioned a friend to paint a picture of John, which he put in his bedroom with an altar and candlesticks. John, discovering this, accused Lycomedes of worshiping a heathen god, and only then found that the portrait was of himself. The picture, John says, is of a dead man; let Lycomedes paint his own soul, with such colors as faith in God, knowledge, godly fear, friendship, communion.

John next heals a group of aged women, and improves the occasion with an address to the Ephesians on the deadliness of fleshly passion. In answer to his prayer the temple of Artemis falls down, the priest killed in the collapse is revived and converted, and many are won to Christ. After further wonders (including the pleasant story of the bugs) comes the repulsive story of Drusiana, rescued by John from necrophilia (the theme also of a poem by the nun Hrotswitha [Roswitha] of Gandersheim in the 10th cent.). A lengthy discourse by John on the life, death, and ascension of Jesus is characterized by strong docetic traits, a long passage dealing with Christ's appearance in many forms and with the peculiar nature of His body. In this section occurs the strange hymn used by the Priscillianists, which purports to be the one Jesus sang after supper in the upper room (Mt. 26:30), the disciples dancing around Him in a ring and responding with an amen. Here too we find the mystic doctrine of the cross revealed to John by Christ.

Chapters 106–115 narrate the death of John. After addressing the brethren and dispensing the sacrament of the Lord's supper with bread alone, John ordered a grave to be dug; and when this was done he prayed, giving thanks that he had been delivered from "the filthy madness of the flesh" and asking a safe passage through the darkness and dangers of death. He lay down quietly in the grave and gave up the ghost.

B. Historical Value. The Acts of John, it need hardly be said, have not the slightest historical value. They are a tissue of legendary incidents that by their miraculous character served to insinuate into the popular mind the dogmatic conceptions and the ideal of life the author entertained. The acts are, however, in harmony with the well-founded tradition that Ephesus was the scene of John's later activity. Very remarkable is the account of the destruction of the Artemis temple by John—a clear proof that the acts were not written in Ephesus, for the Ephesian temple of Artemis was destroyed by the Goths in A.D. 262.

C. General Character. The Acts of John are the most clearly heretical of all the acts. The docetic traits have already been referred to. The unreality of Christ's bodily existence is shown by the changing forms in which He appeared (chs. 88–90), by His ability to do without food (ch. 93), and without sleep ("I never at any time saw His eyes closing but only open," ch. 89), by His leaving no footprint when He walked (ch. 93), by the varying character of His body when touched, now hard, now soft, now completely immaterial (ch. 89, 93). The crucifixion of Jesus, too, was entirely phantasmal (chs. 97, 99). the Ascension followed immediately on the apparent crucifixion; there was no place for the resurrection of someone who had never actually died.

Gnostic features are further discernible in the disparagement of the Jewish laws (ch. 94), in the emphasis on a secret tradition committed by Christ to the apostles (ch. 96), and in the contempt for those who were not enlightened ("Care not for the many, and them that are outside the mystery despise," ch. 100). The historical incidents of Christ's sufferings are sublimated into something altogether mystical (ch. 101); they are simply a symbol of human suffering, and the object of Christ's coming is represented as being to enable men to understand the true meaning of suffering and thus to be delivered from it (ch. 96). The real sufferings of Christ are those caused by His grief at the sins of His followers (chs. 106f.). He is also a partaker in the sufferings of His faithful people, and indeed is present with them to be their support in every trial (ch. 103). The Acts of John also reveal a strong ascetic tendency, although it is not so pronounced as that in the Acts of Andrew and of Thomas. Nowhere, however, is there a more horrifying glimpse into the depths of corrupt sexualism than in these acts. The writing and circulation of the story of Drusiana cast a lurid light on the gross sensual elements that survived in early Hellenic Christianity. Apart from this there are passages that reveal a warm and true religious feeling, and some of the prayers are marked by glow and fervor (cf. chs. 112ff.). The acts show that the author was a man of considerable literary ability.

D. Authorship, Date, Influence. The author represents Himself as a companion of the apostle. Testimony going back to the 4th cent. calls him Leucius; perhaps this name occurred in some part of the acts now lost. A passage in Clement of Alexandria's *Hypotyposeis* on 1 John (Lat. version in Stählin, *Clemens Alexandrinus,* III, 210; cf. Eng. tr. in *Ante-Nicene Fathers,* II [repr. 1971], 574) betrays knowledge (not necessarily firsthand) of these acts as a source of traditions about John. The book seems to belong to Asia Minor between A.D. 150 and 180.

The Acts of John was widely influential. It is probably the earliest of the apocryphal acts, and to some extent the model of the others. The reference in Clement of Alexandria suggests that the work was read in quite sophisticated, orthodox circles, as well as among ruder folk. Later opinion is represented by Augustine's severe animadversions on the hymn that he found being used by the Priscillianists, and by the severe judgment of the Second Council of Nicea. By this time, however, the stories had passed into orthodox tradition, and had been used by Prochorus (5th cent.), a supposed disciple of John, and Abdias, whose *Apostolic History* contains material from older acts not otherwise preserved. The Syriac Acts of John (in W. Wright) appear to be almost, if not entirely, independent of the "Leucian" acts.

IV. Acts of Andrew.–Eusebius (*HE* iii.25.6) is the earliest of many writers to mention this work, which he rejects as impious and absurd. Epiphanius (*Haer.* 47, 61, 68) refers to it as being in use among ascetic heretical sects. Some early writers attribute it to the author of the Acts of John, but in modern times the tendency has been to date it rather late in the 2nd cent.; but the use of the book by the author of the Acts of Paul means that it originated before the last decade of the 2nd century.

A. Contents. The general shape of the book is given in an abstract by Gregory of Tours. He says it was considered apocryphal because of its inordinate length, but either he or the version he used has eliminated repulsive elements referred to by other writers, and thoroughly worked over the stories. As with other acts, we have separate texts and different versions of the martyrdom. For the rest, only fragments remain, and it is not always certain that they are rightly attributed. The stories about Andrew and Matthias with the cannibals seem to belong to a different work.

An important fragment published by G. Quispel in 1956 describes how a soldier sent to arrest Andrew is convulsed by a demon, and, being healed, leaves the army. We hear also how his believing sister has resisted a magician's attacks on her virginity. There is a Gnostic flavor about the whole that is missing from Gregory's abstract. Euodias of Uzala (d. 424), attacking the Manichaeans' regard for the book, alludes to a story describing the deceits that enabled a certain Maximilla to resist the conjugal claims of her husband the proconsul.

The longest section of the acts deals with Andrew's imprisonment because he had induced Maximilla to separate from her husband "Aegeates" and to live a life of chastity. ("Aegeates," which occurs as the name of Maximilla's husband, denotes in reality "a native of Aegae," a town in the vicinity of Patrae, where Andrew was described as carrying on his work.) The section opens in the middle of an address spoken to the brethren by Andrew in prison, in which they were enjoined to glory in their fellowship with Christ and in their deliverance from the baser things of earth. Maximilla and her companions frequently visited the apostle in prison. Aegeates argued with her and warned that if she did not give up her life of chastity he would subject Andrew to torture. Andrew counseled her to resist the importunity of Aegeates, and delivered an address on the true nature of man, stating that torture had no terrors for him. If Maximilla should yield, the apostle would suffer on her account. Through her fellowship with his sufferings she would know her true nature and thus escape from affliction. Andrew next comforted Stratocles, the brother of Aegeates, who declared his need of Andrew, who had sown in him the "seed of the word of salvation." Andrew then announced his crucifixion on the following day. Maximilla again visited the apostle in prison, "the Lord going before her in the form of Andrew."

To a company of the brethren the apostle delivered an address, in which he discoursed on the deceitfulness of the devil, who first had dealt with men as a friend but now was manifest as an enemy.

When brought to the place of crucifixion Andrew addressed the cross, which he joyfully welcomed. After being bound to the cross he hung smiling at the failure of Aegeates' vengeance, for (as he explained) "a man who belongs to Jesus because he is known of Him is armed against every vengeance." For three days and nights Andrew addressed the people from the cross, and they, moved by his nobility and eloquence, went to Aegeates, demanding that he should be delivered from death. Aegeates, fearing the wrath of the people, went to take Andrew down from the cross, but the apostle refused deliverance and prayed to Christ to prevent his release. After this he gave up the ghost. He was buried by Maximilla, and Aegeates soon afterward cast himself down from a great height and died.

B. General Character. The ascetic ideal in its most pronounced form is exhibited in the Acts of Andrew. In view of this, and of Andrew's association elsewhere in ecclesiastical tradition with a strict asceticism, there is a curious irony in that in some parts of Germany Andrew is the patron saint of young girls seeking husbands. In the Harz and in Thüringen St. Andrew's Night (Nov. 30) is considered by unmarried women to be the most favorable time for having a vision of their future husbands. The Gnostic spirit is revealed in the feeling for the preeminent worth of the spiritual man (ch. 6). The true nature of man is pure; his weakness and sin are the work of the "evil enemy who is averse to peace." In seducing men he does not come out openly as an enemy but pretends friendship. When the light of the world appeared, the adversary of man was seen in his true colors. Deliverance from sin comes through enlightenment. The mystical view of sufferings (ch. 9) reminds us of the similar view in the Acts of John. The addresses of the apostle are characterized by religious earnestness and warmth (words flow from his lips "like a stream of fire," ch. 12), and by a profound sense of the divine pity for sinful and tempted men.

The only detail in the Acts of Andrew that has any claim to be considered historical is his activity at Patrae on the Corinthian Gulf.

*V. **Acts of Thomas**.*–These acts alone of the Leucian corpus are extant in their entirety, and appear in many MSS. They appear to have been composed in Syriac and later translated into Greek and worked over from a nonoriental standpoint.

A. Contents. The Stichometry of Nicephorus gives the work sixteen hundred stichoi (a fifth fewer than Mark's Gospel). Our present versions are much more extended.

At a meeting of the apostles in Jerusalem, Thomas is appointed to India. He is unwilling to go, but the Lord sells him as a slave to a messenger of the Indian king Gundaphorus. At the city of Andrapolis on the way, the nuptials of the king's daughter are in progress. The apostle sings a hymn in praise of the heavenly wedding; the king asks Thomas to pray for his daughter, and the Lord (appearing in the form of Thomas) wins the bridal couple to a life of sexual abstinence.

On arrival in India Thomas undertakes to build a palace for Gundaphorus, but gives the poor the money received for the work. The king imprisons him, until an appearance of his dead brother shows that Thomas has built a heavenly palace for him.

Farther east Thomas discovers a youth killed by a dragon in a quarrel over a woman. Thomas orders the dragon to suck the poison from the youth's body; the dragon dies; and the youth accepts sexual abstinence. A colt of the stock of Balaam's ass salutes Thomas as Christ's twin. Thomas delivers a woman from an unclean spirit; she is baptized, and the eucharist, celebrated with bread alone, and with a Gnostic prayer, follows. A youth partakes and becomes paralyzed. He confesses to the murder of a girl, whom Thomas raises, and who describes what she saw in hell.

Further anecdotes relate how Thomas is asked to exorcize the wife and daughter of a commander called Siphor. On the way the carriage animals are exhausted, but four wild asses allow themselves to be yoked. One of them assists Thomas at the exorcism, and afterward reminds him of his duty. Mygdonia, a relative by marriage of the king, Misdai, hears Thomas and repudiates marital relations; her husband secures Thomas' imprisonment as a magician. At their request, Thomas prays for his fellow prisoners, and recites the famous Gnostic Hymn of the Pearl. Thomas, miraculously released, meets Mygdonia and baptizes her; and another eucharist without wine is held. Siphor and his family are also baptized. Tertia the queen seeks to bring Mygdonia to reason, but is herself won to the new way. Misdai, enraged, has Thomas roughly brought to judgment. Vazan, the king's son, is converted. An attempt to torture Thomas with red-hot irons is foiled by a flood. The women and Vazan visit Thomas in prison; Thomas transfers to Vazan's house for the latter's baptism and the eucharist.

Thomas is later put to death by four spears. He appears to Siphor and Vazan (now a presbyter and a deacon). Mygdonia and Tertia are left in peace. Later Misdai seeks a bone from Thomas' tomb to cure a possessed son; but the body has already been transported to Mesopotamia (a significant bit of local patriotism on the part of the author). Dust from the tomb, however, is enough to effect the cure, and Misdai is converted.

B. Character and Tendency. The Acts of Thomas is a product of Syriac Christianity, in which, even in nonsectarian circles, asceticism and the requirement of celibacy are paramount. It is a work of intense earnestness, and in the speeches of Thomas positive Christian virtues are stressed. In particular, the duty and recompense of compassion are strongly exhibited in the story of the heavenly palace. A Gnostic origin seems certain, though orthodox revisers have been at work; they have left much in the hymns and dedication prayers, probably because they did not always understand their Gnostic significance. The Hymn of the Pearl, almost certainly older than the acts (some have ascribed it to the heresiarch Bardesanes), is usually interpreted as an allegory of the descent of the soul into the world of sense, its deliverance by the revelation of God, and its ascent to the heavenly house whence it came; though it may represent rather the descent of the Gnostic redeemer. Either way, it is a hymn of beauty and rich imagery. Christ frequently appeared in the likeness of Thomas, who is represented as His twin and designated "Judas Thomas"—a title that reappears in the Nag Hammadi Gospel of Thomas, with which there are other links (*see* APOCRYPHAL GOSPELS V.J.1; NAG HAMMADI LITERATURE).

The Acts of Thomas is not a historical source for the life of the apostle. That some of the situations described are true to life is beyond doubt. The story of Mygdonia and her husband is drawn with real insight, and must have represented the course of many marriages disrupted by such preaching as that attributed to Thomas. Furthermore, King Gundaphorus (Vindafra) is known from other sources as an Indo-Parthian ruler of the 1st cent., and other indications have been found of genuine knowledge of Indian topography. It is still possible that the tradition of Thomas' residence in India, maintained for centuries by the ancient

Indian Christian communities, has factual basis. It is difficult to date the Acts of Thomas: a reference in the Hymn of the Pearl implies that the Parthian kingdom, which fell in A.D. 227, still existed; but the hymn is probably older than the rest of the book.

OTHER ACTS

The five "Leucian" acts are by far the most important; but the early Christian centuries produced countless others. "Put very broadly the development is from rather dim historical reminiscences used as a framework for doctrinal teaching, to thaumaturgy plus doctrine, to pure thaumaturgy without any doctrine of significance" (*ANT*, p. 474). Syriac, Coptic, and Ethiopic sources are particularly fertile. Large numbers of texts have been published; many still lie unedited. Only a few of these minor acts will be mentioned here.

I. Acts of Thaddaeus.–Eusebius (*HE* i.13) tells the legend of the evangelization of Edessa. King Abgar Uchama (4 B.C.–A.D. 50) wrote to ask Jesus for healing and invited Him to stay in Edessa. Jesus wrote back declining, but promising to send a disciple. In due time Thaddaeus healed the king and converted the territory. Various elaborations of the story exist. The Greek form is the Acts of Thaddaeus; the Syriac form (where a verbal, not epistolary, reply comes from Jesus) is the Doctrine of Addai.

II. Acts of Philip.–This catholic novel (after the form of the Acts of Thomas) describes Philip's adventures in Greece, Parthia, and Carthage "which is in Azotus" (!). The martyrdom exists separately.

III. Acts of Andrew and Matthias.–This startling tale describes the adventures of these two apostles among the cannibals. Formerly, it was often thought to be part of the Acts of Andrew.

Bibliography.–*I. General:* The standard collection of Gk. and Lat. texts is R. A. Lipsius and M. Bonnet, *Acta Apostolorum Apocrypha* (1891-1903, repr. 1959); J. A. Fabricius, *Codex Apocryphus Novi Testamenti* (1719-1743), is still in use. Some Syr. texts with Eng. tr. are given in W. Wright, *Apocryphal Acts of the Apostles* (1871); Eth. in E. A. Wallis Budge, *Contendings of the Apostles* (1901); Arab. in A. S. Lewis, *Mythological Acts of the Apostles* (*Horae Semiticae*, 1904). (There is no necessary correspondence between some of the oriental acts and Gk. or Lat. acts with the same titles.)

The intros., trs., and comms. in H-S have largely replaced *ANT*. Many new texts have been published since the standard collections; J. Quasten, *Patrology*, I (1950), is helpful in tracing some of them.

II. Leucian Acts: A. Acts of Paul: Coptic with Ger. tr. in C. Schmidt, *Acta Pauli* (2nd ed. 1905). Nonoriental versions of Thecla and Martyrdom separately in Lipsius-Bonnet, I; for oriental versions see W. Wright, *Apocryphal Acts of the Apostles* (1871), which gives Eng. tr.; F. C. Conybeare, *The Armenian Apology and Acts of Apollonius* (Eng. tr., 2nd ed. 1896). More recently discovered Gk. fragments in W. Schubart and C. Schmidt, *Acta Pauli* (1936); H. A. Sanders, *HTR*, 31 (1938), 73ff.; G. D. Kilpatrick and C. H. Roberts, *JTS*, 47 (1946), 196ff.

Comms. in *ANT* and L. Vouaux, *Les Actes de Paul et ses lettres apocryphes* (1913) (both works appeared before publication of the Hamburg fragment). Also, M. R. James, *JTS*, 6 (1905), 244ff.; E. Peterson, *VC*, 3 (1949), 142ff.; R. Kasser, *Revue d'histoire et de philosophie religieuses*, 40 (1960), 45ff; H-S, II, 322-390. *See also* bibliography for Corinthian correspondence under APOCRYPHAL EPISTLES.

B. Acts of Peter: Gk. and Lat. texts of separate recensions in Lipsius-Bonnet, I; Coptic with Ger. tr. in C. Schmidt, *Die alten Petrusakten* (*TU*, 24, 1903); Eth. in S. C. Malan, *Conflicts of the Holy Apostles* (1871), Eng. tr. in *ANT*; H-S, II, 259-322; Fr. tr. and comm. in Vouaux, *Les Actes de Pierre* (1922). Also see G. Ficker, *Die Petrusakten* (1903); C. H. Turner, *JTS*, 32 (1931), 19ff. (important for Lat. readings); C. Schmidt, *Zeitschrift für Kirchengeschichte*, 47 (1926), 481ff.; *ZNW*, 29 (1930), 150f.

C. Acts of John: Gk. text in Lipsius-Bonnet, II; Lat. Abdias (*Historia Apostolica* v) in Fabricius, Eng. tr. in *ANT*; H-S, II, 188-259. See also T. Zahn, *Acta Johannis* (1880); M. R. James, *Apocrypha Anecdota*, II (1897); B. H. Streeter, *The Primitive Church* (1929).

Acts of Andrew: Long Gk. fragment and Gk. and Lat. recensions of the martyrdom in Lipsius-Bonnet, II; the best text of the abstract by Gregory of Tours, *Liber de miraculis Beati Andreae Apostoli*, is M. Bonnet, *Monumenta Germaniae Historiae* (1885); Eng. tr. in *ANT*; H-S, II, 390-425. Later discoveries by G. Quispel, *VC*, 10 (1956), 129ff.; and (perhaps) J. Barns, *JTS*, N.S. 11 (1960), 70ff; also J. Flamion, *Les Actes Apocryphes de l'Apôtre André* (1911). For the elaboration of the Andrew legend, F. Dvornik, *Idea of Apostolicity in Byzantium and the Legend of the Apostle Andrew* (1956); P. M. Peterson, *Andrew, Brother of Simon Peter* (1958).

E. Acts of Thomas: Gk. in Lipsius-Bonnet, II; Eng. tr. in *ANT*; H-S, II, 425-531; Syr. with Eng. tr. in Wright; A. S. Lewis, *Mythological Acts of the Apostles* (1904); F. C. Burkitt, *Studia Sinaitica*, 9 (1900). For a derivation with the same name, see M. R. James, *Apocrypha Anecdota*, II (includes Gk. text and S. C. Malan's Eng. tr. of its Ethiopian counterpart).

Comms. in F. C. Burkitt, *Early Christianity Outside the Roman Empire* (1899), pp. 63ff.; G. Bornkamm, *Mythos und Legende in den apokryphen Thomasakten* (1933). On the Hymn of the Pearl, see A. A. Bevan, *Hymn of the Soul* (*Texts and Studies*, 5 [1897]); A. F. J. Klijn, *VC*, 14 (1960), 154ff. On Thomas in India, see J. N. Farquhar, *BJRL*, 10 (1926), 80ff.; 11 (1927), 20ff.; A. Mingana, *BJRL*, 10 (1926), 435ff.

III. Other Acts: A. Acts of Thaddaeus: Gk. texts in Lipsius-Bonnet, I; Doctrine of Addai, ed. with Eng. tr. by G. Phillips (1876); L. J. Tixeront, *Les Origines de l'Église et la Légende d'Abgar* (1880); H. C. Youtie, *HTR*, 23 (1930), 299; 24 (1931), 61ff.; H-S, I, 437-444.

B. Acts of Philip: Gk. in Lipsius-Bonnet, II, partial Eng. tr. in *ANT*; Syr. fragment in W. Wright; see also J. Flamion in *Mélanges Ch. Moeller*, I (1914); E. Peterson, *ZNW*, 31 (1932), 97ff.; H-S, II, 577.

C. Acts of Andrew and Matthias: H-S, II, 576; texts, comm., and Ger. tr. in F. Blatt, *Acta Andreae et Matthiae apud anthropophages* (1930); see also under Acts of Andrew, above.

A. F. FINDLAY
A. F. WALLS

APOCRYPHAL APOCALYPSES.

I. Introduction
II. Apocryphal Apocalypses
  A. Ascension of Isaiah
  B. Apocalypse of Peter
  C. Coptic Apocalypse of Peter
  D. Apocalypse of Paul
  E. Christian Sibylline Books
  F. Apocalypse of John
III. Summary

I. Introduction.–The missionary outreach of the early church was undergirded by the written word. The literary form first employed was the letter, but primitive Christianity soon created new forms, like the gospel, and adopted from Palestinian Judaism older forms, like the apocalypse, to convey its message. The general recognition of the power of the written page as literary propaganda in support of the Christian movement stimulated the production of other documents which were similar in form, if not in content. Many of these asserted or implied a claim to apostolic origin. The distinction between authentic apostolic literature and other compositions, which resulted ultimately in the recognition of the authority of the documents comprising the NT, was made only after an extended process of use, examination and debate. Even then apocryphal accounts continued to appear and were widely circulated. They exerted a discernible impact upon the theology of the developing Church, and especially upon popular thinking, from the 2nd cent. to the medieval period. Study of the Apocrypha frequently puts the student in touch with grass-roots Christianity in the place and period in which a particular document first appeared.

There is evidence that APOCALYPTIC LITERATURE held a peculiar fascination among early Christians. The concept of revelation is integral to Christianity. Moreover, the Christian mission was supported by apocalyptic ideas and expectations. These factors created a climate of interest for this form of literature. The concept of an apocalypse, i.e. a writing disclosing the secrets previously hidden from men in the counsel of God, was familiar from the book of Daniel in the OT, and from the book of Revelation in the NT. The designation of this type of literature as "apocalypse" can be traced directly to Rev. 1:1, where the content of the book is characterized as "the revelation [Gr. *apokálypsis*] of Jesus Christ, which God gave to him to show his servants those things which must shortly take place." Here the word "apocalypse" is used for the first time to designate the disclosure of what must occur in the course of history under the sovereignty of God. The term was first used to designate a particular type of document when the title "Apocalypse of John" was attached to the Revelation. The authority and significance of the canonical Apocalypse explains why the word "apocalypse" subsequently became a literary title and the designation of related Christian compositions. Already in the 2nd cent. the Muratorian Canon (*ca.* 180) speaks of "the apocalypse of John, and of Peter" (lines 71f.).

In the canonical book of Revelation the writer clearly identifies himself by name and circumstances (1:9). All Christian apocryphal apocalypses, however, are pseudonymous — the apocalyptist does not write under his own name, but assumes the mask of one of the great personages from the past. The literary device of pseudonymity served two purposes: it permitted the writer to claim the authority of a prophet or an apostle; and it lent to his composition a fictitious aura of antiquity. The primary vehicle for conveying his message is an account of a revelation received through visionary ecstasy and mystical ascent into the presence of God and His angels. The apocalyptic seer claims to have been shown the regions of heaven and hell. What he has seen becomes the basis for exhortations to repentance, conversion, and correction. Having penetrated the veil of mystery surrounding the destiny of men, he can speak with conviction about the imminence of the consummation and the finality of the judgment of God.

In the patristic era Christians read and adopted for their own purposes several of the Jewish apocalypses that were produced during the INTERTESTAMENTAL PERIOD. Dogmatic additions to the text created the impression that respected seers from the past had prophesied the coming of "the lamb of God," who would be "put to death upon a tree," or the bestowal of the Holy Spirit upon the Gentiles (e.g. T. Benj. 3:8; 9:3-5; 10:7-9; 11:1-5). The extent and character of the Christian interpolations in one Jewish apocalypse can be gauged by comparing the Greek text of the Testaments of the Twelve Patriarchs, which contain insertions of a universal and patripassionist character, with the Armenian version, which appears to be relatively free from Christian alteration. Jewish apocalypses also provided models for the composition of distinctly Christian documents that were attributed to persons well known from the OT or to individuals from the apostolic age.

Numerous works of this type are known only by title; of others, only fragments or late versions survive. Nevertheless, the works which have been preserved provide a sufficient indication of the concerns of those Christians who were responsible for their production and circulation. The several apocryphal apocalypses which have survived are probably not the isolated statement of an individual; they represent the convictions of a larger group of Christians. They are therefore important sources for understanding the concerns and beliefs of broad segments of the Christian community in the post-apostolic period. As such, they modify and qualify the intellectual portrait of Christianity sketched by the Apologists and the church fathers. The range and variety of the apocryphal apocalypses that have survived the accidents of history can be gauged by the following examples.

II. Apocryphal Apocalypses.*–*A. Ascension of Isaiah. This apocryphon is composite in character. The first part (1–5) purports to narrate the circumstances under which Isaiah experienced martyrdom at the hands of Manasseh. Apart from an extraneous unit that is clearly a Christian insertion (3:13–5:1), the Martyrdom is a Jewish writing of uncertain date. The substance of the tradition that Isaiah was sawed in two (1:9; 5:1-14) was known in the 1st cent. A.D. (cf. Heb. 11:37), and it may be proper to assign the Jewish composition to the early years of the Christian era. To this account a Christian later added a description of the visionary ascent of Isaiah into the presence of God in the seventh heaven (6–11). The fusion of the two narratives shows little skill, for the martyrdom takes place under Manasseh, but the visionary experience of the prophet occurs while he is talking to Hezekiah (6:10-12). The person responsible for bringing the two accounts together failed to make the seam less obvious by identifying the visionary ascent of the seer with the vision in which Isaiah became so totally absorbed at the time of his ordeal that he became oblivious to the presence of his tormentors or the excruciating pain (5:7).

The composite character of the Ascension of Isaiah is confirmed by the textual history of the work. Various fragments of the document are available in Greek, Latin, Old Slavonic, and Coptic, but the entire work has been preserved only in an Ethiopic version. The Latin text, which has been known in published form since 1522, and the three Slavonic versions, contain only chs. 6–11, i.e., the visionary ascent of Isaiah into the presence of God. These versions carry the title "The Vision which Isaiah the son of Amoz saw," which is sufficient indication that the account of the seer's heavenly journey existed quite independent of the Martyrdom (1–5). The agreement of the Latin and Slavonic texts upon the omission of 11:2-22, the account of the vision of a small child granted to Joseph and Mary prior to Jesus' birth, indicates that this unit was not originally an integral part of the Ascension of Isaiah. It is now impossible to reconstruct the several stages of the growth of the document, although the seams are easily detected with the assistance of the manuscript tradition.

The Christian insertion in the Martyrdom of Isaiah (3:13–5:1) speaks of Beliar's wrath toward Isaiah because of a vision he received of Christ's incarnation, death, and resurrection, and of the experience of the Church following his ascension. The persecution of believers is the occasion for widespread apostasy encouraged by the reign of a godless world-ruler who claims to be God and opposes himself to the people of God (cf. 2 Thess. 2:3-12). The vision concludes with the coming of the Beloved One to vindicate the people of God and initiate the final judgment. This vision of the course of history, which is climaxed by the overthrow of Beliar (4:14), is introduced to explain why Beliar stirred the heart of Manasseh to consign Isaiah to be "sawn asunder with a tree saw" (5:1). It is the only genuinely "apocalyptic" element in the Martyrdom.

The Ascension of Isaiah (6–11) is also an account of what the prophet saw while in a visionary trance, but there is no indication that it is by the same hand responsible for 3:13–5:1. In contrast to the prophecies found in the canonical book of Isaiah, the writer states explicitly "the vision which he saw was not of this world, but from the world which is hidden from all flesh" (6:15). The unique character of the revelation is stressed by the repeated statement that the vision granted to the seer had never before been given to a man (8:11f.; 11:34). Isaiah is conducted by an angel from the seventh heaven on a journey that takes him through the firmament, which serves as the realm of the fallen angels (7:9-12; 10:29-31), to an experience of ascent through successive realms of the heavenly spheres. What he sees and hears in each of the heavens is a chorus of angels engaged in the praise of God. What he experiences is an increasing awareness of glory, so that the prophet himself becomes transformed as he ascends from one realm to the next (7:25). His destination is the seventh heaven where he beholds the ineffable glory of "the Lord of all those heavens" and is privileged to see the mystery of the Son of God laying aside His glory progressively as He descends through the seven heavens and the firmament in the course of the incarnation (8:9f; 10:7ff.). In the sixth heaven (8:16-22) and in the seventh (9:28-30, 33) Isaiah himself had joined in the chorus of praise-songs addressed to the Lord, but as the Son of God descends, unrecognized, through the realms of heaven to the earth he can only reflect in awe. The account follows Jesus' life from His birth to His ascension, in capsule fashion, until He ascends through each of the heavens and sits down on the right hand of the ineffable glory of the Father (11:2-33). The vision is brought to an end on the note of assurance that all of this will occur "in the last generation" (11:37f.).

This Apocryphon is interesting because it indicates two kinds of reflection that some Christians were bringing to biblical statements. One such statement is Jn. 12:41, "Isaiah . . . saw his glory and spoke of him." Throughout the account there is repeated emphasis upon the quality of glory associated with each of the realms of heaven, the glory of the Son eclipsing that of all the realms. Even the Son, who is designated "the Lord of all glory" (cf. 2 Cor. 2:8) engages in the worship of the Father, whom Isaiah describes as "the glorious One whose glory I could not see" (10:2). The striving after a conceptualization of the glory of the Lord appears to account for this dominant note in the Apocalypse. But a second kind of reflection is also evident here: What was involved in the incarnation of the Lord who possessed such glory?; How could Christ Jesus, who was in the form of God, lay aside His robes of glory and assume human form (cf. Phil. 2:6-8)? It is in response to such questions that the Ascension of Isaiah makes its boldest suggestion. The Son descended from the seventh heaven through each of the heavenly realms, and from the fifth heaven downward He was unrecognized because His appearance became like that of those who inhabited that realm. Isaiah had observed an increasing gradation of glory as he travelled from the first to the seventh heaven; the Son divested Himself by degrees of the glory He possessed with the Father (cf. Jn. 17:5, 24) as He made His way to the earth, until finally He bore the image and likeness of man (8:9f.). Behind the expression of the text can be detected an earnest searching after understanding by segments of the Church as men reflected upon the Incarnation in the light of such texts as Jn. 12:41 or 17:5, 24. This document may have originated in the 2nd or 3rd cent. A.D.

B. Apocalypse of Peter. In the 2nd cent. an apocalypse attributed to Peter circulated widely. Although its reception in the Church was not uniform, it was highly regarded by many orthodox Christians in the East and the West. Among the books received as authoritative by the Church of Rome, the Muratorian Canon lists "the apocalypse . . . of Peter," but with the qualification that "some of our people will not have it read in the church" (lines 72f.). Evidence that the greater part of the Western Church received this document as Scripture is provided by its inclusion in the Latin catalogue of biblical books in the Codex Claromontanus. Clement of Alexandria regarded it as Petrine, citing the work by title (*Eclogae ex scripturis propheticis,* 41, 48f.) and commenting upon it in his *Hypotyposeis* (Eusebius *HE* vi.14.1). Although the Stichometry of Nicephorus placed it among the disputed books, and Eusebius rejected it as spurious, claiming that no orthodox writer had made use of its testimony (*HE* iii.3.2 [he had forgotten, apparently, about Clement]), Methodius Olympius alluded to it as inspired Scripture (*Symposium* 2.6), and according to Sozomenus (*HE* vii.19) the book was read publicly on Good Friday in certain Palestinian communities as late as the 5th century. Yet in the modern period this work was known only through patristic reference and citation until the close of the 19th century.

The first large segment of the Apocalypse of Peter was recovered through a Greek fragment in 1887 and was published in 1892. It had been found in the grave of a Christian monk who was buried in the 8th or 9th cent. at Akhmim in Upper Egypt, together with a fragment of the Gospel of Peter and portions of the Book of Enoch in Greek. Although the new text was untitled, agreement with a quotation from the Petrine Apocalypse preserved by Clement of Alexandria (*Eclogae* 41.2) served to identify it. The Akhmim fragment begins abruptly with Jesus' words to His apostles, at the end of a discourse reminiscent of Mk. 13 (and parallels). In a first person account, Peter reports that Jesus led the disciples to the Mount of Olives. There, in response to a request to see the state of the blessed righteous who have died, two men appear to them clothed in resplendent light. At the request of Peter, the disciples are shown the regions of light where the righteous live with the angels. They are engaged in the joyous praise of God. Beyond this realm Peter can discern a dark place of torment, which is described in vivid detail. It is the final abode of unrighteous men, who are enumerated according to their chief offenses. Their punishment is administered by angels in dark robes. The narrative is broken off abruptly in a description of men and women "who have abandoned the way of God."

The complete text of the Apocalypse came to light in 1910 in an Ethiopic translation. It was recognized by M. R. James as an older work interpolated into a shapeless pseudo-Clementine collection of materials. Since the Ethiopic text contained all the previously known citations from the Apocalypse of Peter, including those which had not been verified by the Akhmim fragment, distributed over chapters 4, 5, 8, 10, 12, and 14, its identity was established beyond question. The Ethiopic text supplemented the Greek fragment by providing the extended discourse with which the Apocalypse begins and by carrying the narrative to a point of conclusion. The Lord promises Peter that He will return to resurrect the dead and to judge all men. The description of the torments suffered by the condemned closely parallels the Greek fragment but is more complete. The blessedness of the elect is only briefly described. The narrative concludes with the Transfiguration, which becomes the occasion for Jesus to ascend to heaven with Moses and Elijah in the company of other men.

Comparative study of the Greek and Ethiopic texts points up the problem of recovering the original form of the Apocalypse of Peter. (1) The Ethiopic account is almost three times as long as that of the Akhmim fragment. Yet it exceeds only slightly the figures which are given for the Apocalypse of Peter in the Stichometry of Nicephorus (300 lines) and in the Codex Claromontanus (270 lines). On this basis it can be assumed that the Ethiopic document approximates the original length of the Apocalypse of Peter. (2) The consideration of parallel passages reveals noticeable differences in content. The two accounts display extensive agreement in the description of hell, but striking differences exist in the treatment of paradise. The Ethiopic text simply alludes to the place of the elect in chs. 14 and 16. Its primary focus is upon the Transfiguration, where Moses and Elijah appear with Jesus, clothed in radiant light. In the Akhmim fragment there is no material parallel to ch. 14, but the Transfiguration account has become the basis for a genuine description of paradise. The two transfigured men who appear on the mountain are not identified as Moses and Elijah but as two of the "righteous brothers" whose form the disciples had requested to see. Their appearance is the introduction to the vision of the realm from which they come and the life of praise they share. This drastic alteration of the Transfiguration narrative in the Synoptic Gospels appears to be a secondary development and is unsupported by any of the older citations. (3) The sequence of the descriptions differs in the two principal witnesses. In the Akhmim fragment the description of paradise precedes the account of the condemned; in the Ethiopic text the order is reversed. The description of the condemnation awaiting the unrighteous follows rather naturally upon Christ's assurance that He will return as the Judge of all men. The sequence in the Ethiopic text should be followed, for it has the support of a secondary witness to the original order in Sibylline Oracles ii.238-338, a third-century document which used the Apocalypse of Peter.

In addition to the two primary witnesses to the text, there exist two small Greek fragments on papyrus: the Bodleian Fragment, a fifth-century scrap, contains verses 33f.; the Rainer Fragment, a larger piece from the 3rd or 4th cent., corresponds to ch. 14 of the Ethiopic translation.

The Apocalypse of Peter is an early and important exemplar of this literary genre. The citations preserved by the church fathers indicate it was in circulation prior to A.D. 180. The reference to a messianic deceiver who will persecute Christians and put them to death appears to be an allusion to the militant messianic claimant Simon bar Cochba, who led the Jewish revolt against Rome in A.D. 132. If this is so, the Apocalypse of Peter may have been written during the period of the revolt to encourage Christians to be faithful to Jesus, even in the face of death. The allusion to the prophetic word received on the mount of Transfiguration in 2 Pet. 1:16-19 appears to have prompted the writer to prepare the Apocalypse, with its twofold development of the coming in majesty of the Lord, and the experience of glory at the Transfiguration. The focus upon the situation in the afterlife, the different classes of sinners and their punishments, as well as the salvation experienced by the righteous, however, is distinctively his own. Before the end of the 2nd cent. his work was known in the West as well as in the East. The vision of the underworld and its torments put forth in the Apocalypse was picked up by later apocalyptists (Sibylline Oracles ii; Apocalypse of Thomas 55-57; Apocalypse of Paul) and so exerted an immense impact upon popular conceptions. As the first Christian book that attempted to represent through pictorial language what hell and heaven were like, the position of the Apocalypse of Peter in the history of ideas is secure.

C. Coptic Apocalypse of Peter (CG VII.3). Among the Coptic documents found at Nag Hammadi in Upper Egypt was one that excites particular interest, for it claims to be "The Apocalypse of Peter." The title occurs before the beginning of the text (70:13) and again at its conclusion (84:14). The document is clearly an apocalypse, but it bears no obvious relationship to the work discussed above. It is an account of a visionary revelation granted by the Savior to Peter during the night prior to the crucifixion (cf. 84:13, "When these things were said, Peter came to himself"). An oblique reference to Satan, who will accuse Peter "three times during this night" (72:4), situates the entire exchange on the evening of Jesus' betrayal and arrest. The central element in the Apocalypse is a long discourse in which Jesus provides assurance and consolation to His anxious follower and discloses what will take place in the period following His death. The setting for the vision is the temple, presumably in Jerusalem (perhaps under the influence of Mk. 14:49). Jesus identifies Himself as the Revealer, whose task was to reveal life to those chosen by the Father. His concern is that those who have been established in the truth should continue to "hear his word" and be able to distinguish truth from falsehood. What follows is a clear distinction between the group to which Peter gives leadership, "the remnant, whom I have called to understanding" (71:20), and another group, called "the men of the constitution of deceit" (74:10f.). This latter group "cleave to the name of a dead man, thinking they will become purified" (74:14f.). They experience deception and heresy (74:16-22), and from that perspective they attack the truth entrusted to Peter and his followers. The Apocalypse is thus a polemical document that reflects a struggle in the early Church over the fundamental issue of authority and truth. The community responsible for the Coptic Apocalypse of Peter grounds the authority of its tradition in the primacy of Peter, to whom Jesus entrusted a secret tradition that is clearly in conflict with the tradition observed by "the children of this age."

The revelation that Peter receives from the Savior centers in his destiny. He has been chosen by the Son of Man to "become perfect with me through your name" (71:16f.). The reference may be to martyrdom, if the word "perfect" carries the same nuance it does in He. 5:9, 14; 12:23; Eusebius *HE* v.2.3. In John 13:36; 21:18f. Peter is told in an elusive way that the form of his death will identify him as a follower of Jesus (cf. 71:25-32, where Peter is told he has been called to know the Son of Man through an act he is to perform, which has to do with "the distance which divides him, and the joints of his hands and feet, and the crowning by those of the center," an apparent reference to crucifixion). In his vision Peter sees the priests and the people running toward him, intent upon stoning Jesus and His disciple, and betrays deep anxiety in the face of death. But Jesus calms his fears by disclosing to him the character of the blindness in his adversaries (they are blind because they have no leader) and the vindication which will follow the apparent humiliation of the Savior. Like Jesus, he will be the object of rejection and humiliation, for this is the common lot of all who are worshippers of the Word (73:19-30).

Although Peter can expect humiliation, he is also assured that he has been chosen to be "a ruler over the remnant" of those whom the Savior has called to understanding (71:19-21). He is clothed with the robe of the primate, and at one point the eyes embroidered upon the garment play a special role in disclosing to Peter the Savior's nature (72:14-29). It is because He is the ruler of "the man of understanding" that the Revealer entrusts to Peter "a mystery" to be guarded from "the children of men." The mystery consists of the teaching of the two kinds of souls found in men, the mortal soul that exhausts itself upon the material creation (75:10-26), and the immortal soul that has its source in truth and continually strives for reunion with "the Living One" (75:26–76:18). Between men who possess these two different types of souls conflict is inevitable. Only those with an

APOCRYPHAL APOCALYPSES

immortal soul know the mysteries of the Revealer, while all others only pretend to know, but satisfy themselves with falsehood and deception. They not only oppose the truth, but "they make merchandise of my Word" (77:23–78:1). Actually they are followers of a dead man and are sons of darkness, not of light (78:15-30). The reference to the "dead man" appears to be to the crucified Jesus, for the larger context focuses upon an ecclesiastical struggle between the group for whom the Apocalypse was prepared and a hierarchically-constituted community led by bishops and deacons (79:23-31). The depreciation of the material world and the claim to exclusive knowledge of the mysteries of God as a result of esoteric teaching entrusted to Peter may serve to identify the first group as a gnostic sect, and the community which opposes them as the more numerous exponents of "orthodox" Christianity. When Peter expresses his concern that "there are multitudes who will certainly lead astray other multitudes of these who are living" who will be destroyed because they have believed those deceivers who have spoken "your name" (80:2-6), he is assured that the age of deception has an appointed limit. Then the age of immortal thought will be renewed and the members of the sect who have kept alive "the truth" will be vindicated. It is on the ground of this assurance that suffering and martyrdom can be embraced (80:25–81:4).

What follows is a vision of Jesus' arrest and crucifixion that makes clear the docetic orientation of the sect. A clear distinction is made between Jesus and the Savior: Jesus is arrested in the garden, but it is the Savior who restrains Peter from intervening; Jesus is "struck upon his feet and his hands" but the Savior is the "glad one above the tree who is laughing" in derision (81:5-13). "The Savior said to me: 'The one whom you see above the tree, who is glad and laughing, is the living Jesus. But his fleshly counterpart, into whose hands and feet they are driving the nails, is the substitute whom they put to shame. He it is who was in his likeness. Now look at him and me' " (81:15-25, cf. Acts of John 97-101). The assurance that the living Savior cannot be humiliated marks the transition to the high point of the Apocalypse. Peter sees the Holy Spirit ("one who will command us, who resembles him," 82:5f.) and the Laughing One surrounded by an ineffable light, receiving the unbroken praise of a multitude of invisible angels. The Savior is revealed as the one who bestows glory on men. He was *in* the one who was arrested, but the spiritual and the fleshly Jesus were separated. The men who put the fleshly Jesus on the cross simply demonstrated their blindness and lack of perception. It is the living Jesus who promises to be with Peter "so that none of your enemies will have power over you" (84:9f.).

On the surface, this document is a word of encouragement for Peter in the face of impending suffering and martyrdom. But behind the figure of Peter can be discerned an oppressed community of a distinctly docetic, if not gnostic, character, who receive the assurance that they possess the secret tradition entrusted to Peter that guarantees the presence of the Savior. In this apocalypse Peter is the recipient, transmitter, and guarantor of authentic gnosis. He functions as the base of authority for the teaching embraced by the sect. It is possible that Peter was chosen as the one to whom the revelation was purportedly entrusted because the opponents of this community appealed to Peter for their tradition. The function of the Revealer's visionary appearance to Peter is to ground his authority in an experience granted to him alone (cf. 2 Pet. 1:15-17). Although incidental references to Jesus' appearance to Peter after the Resurrection (Lk. 24:34; 1 Cor. 15:5) might have invited the kind of account found here, the clear situating of the visionary experience on the night of Peter's denials suggests that it was prompted by the promise of a future knowing given to Peter in the Upper Room (cf. Jn. 13:7, 36). There Jesus alluded both to Satan's desire for Peter, and to the special provision Jesus had made for him, in the light of his responsibility to strengthen his brothers (Lk. 22:31-33). Peter's experience of stupor and sleep in the Garden (Lk. 22:45) may have suggested an appropriate occasion for a visionary experience. This would explain the emphasis upon Peter's anxiety and the experience of Jesus with the arresting party. All of this, however, was only the vehicle for the word of consolation addressed to the members of the sect in their struggle with the "heresy" of orthodox Christianity. The Coptic Apocalypse of Peter may be dated tentatively in the late 2nd or early 3rd cent. A.D. It provides an important source for understanding the response of an unorthodox community to the heresiological struggles in which it found itself involved.

D. Apocalypse of Paul. The Apostle Paul's reluctantly-given report of his visionary ascent into paradise and the third heaven (2 Cor. 12:1-4) found in the late 4th cent. a literary sequel, the Apocalypse of Paul. It proved popular among monks and nuns of the period, but was rejected by churchmen who investigated its claims. Augustine (*ca.* A.D. 416) commented that some have concocted an Apocalypse of Paul "which is full of fables" regarding the unutterable words which Paul had heard, but the true Church does not receive it (*On John,* tractate 98.8). Sozomenus is even more explicit: "The book now circulated as the Apocalypse of Paul the Apostle, which none of the ancients ever saw, is commended by most monks; but some contend that this book was found in the reign of which we write (i.e. Theodosius). For they say that by a divine manifestation there was found at Tarsus in Cilicia, in Paul's home, a marble chest, and that in it was this book" (*HE* vii.19). That Sozomenus has in view the Apocryphon which has been preserved in a variety of versions and recensions is clear from the detail of the finding of the document, which corresponds to the opening paragraphs of the work. He adds that he investigated this claim, but learned from an aged presbyter at Tarsus that no such discovery had been made in the city and that he had not previously heard the story. The prefatory note to the Apocalypse (which begins at para. 3) states that it was discovered in Tarsus but was sent to Jerusalem. This is a virtual declaration that Jerusalem, or Palestine, is its place of origin. The Decretum Gelasianum (6th cent.) consigns the Apocalypse of Paul to the category of apocrypha which were not accepted by the Church. Nevertheless, later testimony confirms the continued knowledge of the work and an unchecked extension of its influence. It was actually quoted by Dante, who drew many of his conceptions from it (*Inferno* 2.28).

The manuscript tradition confirms the popularity of this work. The original Greek text has been preserved only in a fragmentary, abbreviated form, which may be no more than a summary of the document. The most complete and reliable witness to the extent and form of the text is the old Latin translation published by M. R. James on the basis of a MS at Paris. This text can be corrected by a whole series of Latin recensions, and by versions preserved in Syriac, Armenian, Coptic, and Slavonic texts. Of these, the most important witness to the text is the Coptic version, published by E. A. Wallis Budge in 1915, which begins with para. 15 of the Latin edition.

The revelation begins abruptly with the declaration: "The Word of God addressed me in these terms," followed by the exhortation to reprove men for their faults and to urge them to lead godly lives. The urgency for repentance is evident, for the creation continually reminds God of the transgression of men, and only divine forbearance delays the imposing of final punishment (para. 3-6). The complaints of the creation are verified by the reports about the deeds of men which the angels present to God each evening and morning (para. 7-10). Paul is then guided by angels through the regions where the righteous experience rest and the unrighteous receive the punishment their deeds have merited. He is shown that impiety covers the whole earth like a fiery cloud. Angels conduct the just and the unjust before God for judgment, and Paul participates in the judgment of two men, one of whom is righteous, the other unrighteous. Both holy and fallen angels are present at the judgment. When the fallen angels find nothing with which to accuse the righteous man, he is led to the place of rest by the holy angels; but the unrighteous man is accused by the guardian angel appointed to watch over him, and when he stands condemned before the tribunal of God the fallen angels are allowed to lead him to the inferno. The time of repentance is past, and the sinner is condemned to outer darkness because of his deeds (para. 11-18).

Paul is then shown the character of the two regions to which men are assigned following their death. The realm of the just resembles a city. Within the city of God the righteous of all ages are comforted, and Paul sees the patriarchs, the prophets whose word was scorned, the children of Bethlehem whom Herod slew, together with others, each occupying places which reflect the virtues that each one displayed in his life. In the center of the city the sweet singer of Israel, David, sings "alleluiah" before the heavenly altar, especially when the sacrifice of the body and blood of the Lord is repeated in the Mass upon earth (para. 19-30).

The region of darkness lies at the extreme west of the city, and there Paul sees those who have been justly condemned for their crimes. At this point the apocalyptist subjects the Church of his day to searching criticism, for in the lake of fire is a bishop who failed to fulfill his responsibilities to the poor. Beside him are a priest and a deacon who carelessly broke their fast before serving at the altar. Their faithlessness merits the punishment they now receive. In the abyss Paul is shown those who refused to receive the teaching of the Church. Included are those who failed to recognize Mary as the mother of God and who say that the Lord was not made incarnate through her, and those who deny that the bread of the eucharist or the wine of the chalice is really the body and blood of the Lord. Those who denied the factuality of the resurrection are also there, weeping and gnashing their teeth (para. 31-44).

It is especially in the depiction of the region of hell that this apocryphon provides an indication of popular thinking in the 4th cent., at a time when the theology of the Church had become encrusted with traditions alien to the Scriptures. Thus in para. 43 those who have been condemned to eternal torment beg Gabriel to intercede for them with Jesus that they may experience respite from their pain. As a result of his intercession, and for the sake of Paul, their punishment is relaxed "in the night and the day of the holy Sunday when Christ was raised from the dead." It is not clear from the text whether this provision was thought to apply to every Sunday or to Easter alone. But it is ironical that Augustine, who rejected the Apocalypse of Paul as a fraudulent document, should show the impact of its teaching upon his own thinking when he speaks of the relief experienced by those in hell on the day of the Lord (*Ench.* 112f.; cf. Prudentius *Cathemerinon* 5.125ff.). Another popular notion is reflected in Paul's admonition to praise God at sunset, for that hour marks the return of the guardian angels to adore God and to report on the actions of men. Such reflections of popular thinking permit a more accurate evaluation of the state of the Church in a period when Christianity was no longer being refined by the fires of persecution.

It is probable that the original Apocalypse of Paul ended with para. 44, but in all existing copies there is now found a second vision of paradise, in which he has an opportunity to speak with many of the great figures of the OT (45-51). The second tour of paradise entails obvious repetition and may tentatively be regarded as a secondary element. Greek, Latin, and Syriac texts speak of Paul's introduction to distinctly OT figures, but the Coptic version extends the account to include the priest Zacharias and his son John the Baptist. Once the convention had been established, it became possible to extend it to include persons from the NT as well.

In the 7th cent. (or later) a parallel work appeared, the Ethiopic Apocalypse of Mary the Virgin. This consists of an adapted translation of para. 13-44 of the Apocalypse of Paul, and tends to support the conclusion that the original Apocryphon concluded with para. 44. A closely related work, the Apocalypse of the Holy Mother of God concerning Those Who are Punished, is preserved in Greek, Armenian, Ethiopic, and Old Slavonic versions. It shows a dependency upon the Apocalypses of Peter and Paul, and may be assigned to the 9th century. In both of these later works Mary, the mother of Jesus, is accorded the experience previously claimed for Paul. She tours the regions of the condemned and assists in the judgment. As a result of her intercession for those who were not Christians and for Christians guilty of crimes which merited eternal punishment she obtains for them a suspension of torment during the days of Pentecost. The modern view of Mary's role as intercessor has its root in such popular conceptions as find expression in these apocrypha, which assign to Mary a function she nowhere has in Scripture.

Among the Coptic documents found at Nag Hammadi was a fragmentary work entitled the Apocalypse of Paul (CG V.2). Preliminary study has indicated that it is an independent work that was prompted by reflection of 2 Cor. 12:1-4. It situates Paul on the way to Jericho, and later "on the mountain of Jericho" (19:11ff.), reflecting the biblical convention of the mountain as the place of revelation. Paul's mystical ascent actually begins at the third heaven, from which he passes into the fourth heaven where a man is being examined at the judgment tribunal. When he is condemned by the mouth of three witnesses (cf. Deut. 19:15), his soul is cast into a body. In the fifth and sixth heavens Paul recognizes that he is being accompanied by his "fellow apostles." In the seventh heaven Paul has a long discussion with an old man who functions as a guardian to the upper regions. He will not permit Paul to ascend further until he presents an acceptable sign. His ascent continues to the tenth heaven, but no real description of the upper realms is presented. It is possible that the Coptic Apocalypse of Paul has some connection with a work mentioned by Epiphanius (*Haer.* 28.2) entitled the Ascension of Paul. Epiphanius traced its origin to the Cainite Gnostics, but gave no indication of its content.

E. Christian Sibylline Books. The earliest reference to the oracles of the Sibyl occurs in a quotation from Heraclitus preserved by Plutarch (*De Pythiae oraculis* 6 [397 A]): "The Sibyl, with frenzied mouth uttering things not to be laughed at, unadorned and rough, yet reaches to a thousand years with her voice by aid of the god." Plutarch described the oracles, which were the classical pagan counterpart to prophecy, as poems which spoke of "many revolutions and upheavals of Greek cities, many appearances of barbarous hordes and murders of rulers." They were uttered by a woman in a state of ecstasy under the prompting of some deity. The writers of the classical period knew of only one Sibyl, but later others were recognized. Their oracles were collected and commanded deep respect even in imperial times.

It was a specifically Jewish idea to attribute to the pagan Sibyl utterances that directed men to the one God. The Jewish Sibylline Oracles (Books iii-v, and fragments preserved in Theophilus *Ad Autolycum*) effectively brought together authentic ancient oracles and verses newly composed on the hexameter pattern of the Sibyl in the praise of monotheism and the Jewish people. These works furnished literary propaganda in support of the mission of Diaspora Judaism to the Gentiles at Alexandria and elsewhere in the second half of the 2nd cent. B.C. Christian apologists from Clement of Rome, who alludes to the Sibyl's prophecy that the world will perish by fire, to Lactantius, whose writings are a mine of Sibylline verses, generally accepted these compositions as genuine. Augustine even assigned the Sibyl a place among those who dwell in the City of God because of her service to the truth (*Civ. Dei* xviii.23).

In the second half of the 2nd cent. A.D., or early in the 3rd cent., Christians borrowed from Hellenistic Judaism the literary convention of Sibylline oracles. The success of the Jewish compositions indicated that the Sibyl could become an appropriate vehicle for the truth in the struggle to affirm Christian faith in a pagan world. The first step appears to have been the insertion of Christian verses into existing collections, and finally the creation of distinctly Christian oracle collections. Of the Oracles which have been preserved, it is commonly felt that books vi-viii are Christian, books xi-xiv are Jewish but have been subjected to Christian interpolation, and books i-ii, though of Jewish origin, have been completely revised by a Christian hand. Not all of these collections of verse are apocalyptic in nature. Book vi, for example, consists of only twenty-eight verses and is a hymn in honor of Christ, reviewing His earthly ministry from the moment of His baptism to His triumph upon the cross. But other segments of the Oracles clearly belong to the category of apocryphal apocalypses.

Particular importance attaches to book viii, a collection of 500 lines representing the work of two different writers. The first part (lines 1-216) contains nothing that is necessarily Christian. Its fierce invective against Rome was kindled by persecution. The punishment that will descend upon the imperial capital, where all vice increases, is detailed, together with the general judgment that will determine the destiny of all offenders against the law of God. The second part, however, is distinctly Christian, beginning with an acrostic on the words "Jesus Christ, Son of God, Savior, Cross" (lines 217-250). A translation of the passage in Latin verse, preserved by Augustine, is quite successful in maintaining the acrostic (*Civ. Dei* xviii.23). The acrostic rapidly sketches the events that herald the end of the world and provides a transition to a theological reflection upon the nature of the person of Christ (lines 251-323). The statement is interrupted by an exhortation to faithfulness (lines 324-358) and then is continued, developing the concepts of the unity of the Father and the Son, the function of the Word in creation and His incarnation in time (lines 369-470). The work is terminated with a final exhortation (lines 480-500). While the first part of book viii may date from the last quarter of the 2nd cent., critical opinion assigns the distinctly Christian portion of the work to the second half of the 3rd century. Its theological significance derives from the fact that distinctively Christian documents are rare in this period, and the light it sheds upon the history of doctrine is welcome.

Apocalyptic passages are scattered throughout the several collections, but they determine the character of books i and ii, which are sometimes joined together in the manuscript tradition. They form a unity in describing the general history of mankind by grouping events within a framework of ten generations. The tenth generation is concluded with the fall of Rome (ii.34ff.), which is itself the prelude to the great reversals that signal the consummation of history and the end of the world. The eschatological descriptions are familiar from other apocalypses, but have been disturbed by the insertion of the verses of pseudo-Phocylides (ii.56-148). The resurrected dead are made to pass through a river of fire which leaves unharmed the righteous but swallows up the sinners (ii.313ff.; cf. Isa. 43:2). The description of the destiny of those condemned to punishment and of the bliss of the righteous that brings the collection to a conclusion appears to be narrowly connected with the conceptions informing the Apocalypses of Peter and Paul. A prominent role in the final judgment is assigned to Jesus as Lord. In book i, lines 1-323 may be assigned to a Jewish hand (apart from the interpolation in lines 137-146), but lines 324-400, which speak of the appearance of Christ and of Israel's sin against him, resulting in the nation's fall, are Christian in origin. In book ii it is no longer possible to distinguish the Jewish element from the Christian, so thoroughly has it been revised by a Christian writer. The Christian redaction of this collection may be assigned tentatively to the middle of the 3rd century.

F. Apocalypse of John. A relatively late apocryphon, which was composed at the earliest in the 5th cent., is to be distinguished from the canonical book of Revelation, which is often designated the Apocalypse of John. It consists of a dialogue concerning the end of time that the apostle John is purported to have had with the exalted Lord after His ascension. By means of John's questions and the response of the Lord, many details of the coming age are disclosed. John is shown the character of the signs that herald the end and the last judgment that will ensue. The popular conception of the antichrist is expressed through grotesque imagery. The seer is assured by the two witnesses of Rev. 11, Enoch and Elijah, that the antichrist will be overcome. The fate of individuals in the resurrection is discussed in detail, as John sees the punishments of hell and the blessings of heaven. An insight into a current view of the resurrection is provided when John is told that the dead will be raised in the same form and the same age they had attained at the time of their death. After the judgment, those condemned will be consigned to the abyss with its darkness, but a distinction will be made between two classes of sinners. Gentiles who have maintained their pagan stance will be cast into the lake of fire; but the Jews, who were responsible for putting Jesus to death, will be cast into Tartarus. Christians who have sinned will be punished in accordance with the seriousness of their offense. Only baptized Christians who have died in a state of righteousness will be allowed to participate in the judgment. Their reward is to shine like the sun. Once the judgment has been accomplished there will remain no vestige of evil or vice or anything associated with Satan, but a renewed earth will provide the home of the one flock under the one Shepherd.

Most of these conceptions are familiar from the earlier apocalypses. Their appearance in a later document such as the Apocalypse of John simply attests a continuation of the Christian apocalyptic tradition from the early patristic era to the close of the medieval period, when they received classic formulation in the *Inferno* of Dante. The reason for assigning the Apocalypse of John to the 5th cent. is its apparent dependence upon Ephraem for its description of the antichrist. The oldest testimony to its existence, however, comes from the 9th century.

III. Summary.–These examples may be sufficient to indicate the kind of material to be found in documents that are apocryphal and apocalyptic in nature. There are other works of a later date that fall into this category, but they add nothing to the common stock of ideas from which they borrow. It is expected that new light will be shed on the subject from the publication and discussion of apocalypses of the Coptic library at Nag Hammadi. *See* NAG HAMMADI LITERATURE.

Common to the several documents discussed here is a desire to conceptualize what Scripture had left relatively veiled, i.e., the course of history toward the consummation and the nature of heaven and hell. The several apocalypses constitute primary evidence for a widespread wish on the part of the Old Catholic Church to know more than what Scripture had revealed. Apologetic motifs are skillfully woven into the fabric of apocalyptic fictions, and it is not difficult to demonstrate that these works made a profound impression upon popular thinking. One of their primary values is their witness to grass-roots Christianity in the postapostolic period, when increasingly the biblical core of the Church's thinking was overlaid with alien traditions, many of which had their origin in pagan conceptions. The neglect of the apocryphal apocalypses by the church historian and the student of the history of dogma can only result in a distorted picture of the developing church and the adjustments it made to the world of ideas in which it found itself.

Bibliography.–O. Bardenhewer, *Geschichte der altkirchlichen Literatur,* Vols. I-V (1913-1932); A. Böhlig and P. Labib, *Koptisch-gnostische Apokalypsen aus Codex V von Nag Hammadi* (1963); F. C. Burkitt, *Jewish and Christian Apocalypses* (1914); A. Harnack, *Geschichte der altchristlichen Literatur* (2nd ed. 1958); H-S, II, 579-803 (with extensive bibliography); M. R. James, *ANT*; *Apocrypha Anecdota,* I (Texts and Studies; 1893); M. Krause and V. Girgis, "Die Petrusapokalypse," in *Christentum am Roten Meer,* II (1973), 152-179; W. Michaelis, *Die apokryphen Schriften zum NT* (2nd ed. 1958); C. Tischendorf, *Apocalypses apocryphae* (1866); H. Weinel, "Die spätere christliche Apokalyptik," in *Eucharisterion. Studien zur Religion und Literatur des AT und NT* (Gunkel Festschrift, II; 1923), pp. 141-173; A. Werner, *TLZ,* 99 (1974), 575-584.

W. L. LANE

APOCRYPHAL EPISTLES. A body of early Christian writings, either letters purporting to be from Paul, or types of literature having the form of letters, or romantic forgeries resembling novels. Paul himself evidently knew of unauthorized letters sent in his name (cf. 2 Thess. 2:2; 3:17), but remarkably few indisputably apocryphal epistles are known. "The epistle was on the whole too serious an effort for the forger, more liable to detection, perhaps . . . and not so likely to gain the desired popularity as a narrative or an Apocalypse" (James, *ANT*, p. 476).

James's point is noteworthy in view of the facility with which pseudonymity has sometimes been attributed to the NT Epistles. In second-century orthodox circles some reticence is discernible in publishing letters (cf. the anonymous writer who is quoted in Eusebius *HE* v.16.3; Dionysius of Corinth, quoted in *HE* iv.23.12; W. C. van Unnik, *VC,* 3 [1949], 1ff.); and the "catholic epistle" was so sacrosanct a form that to write one was "aping the apostle" (Apollonius, quoted in *HE* v.18.5). This notion passed, but few of the later apocrypha bear even formal resemblance to the NT Epistles. The whole literature produced nothing really like 2 Peter.

I. Pseudo-Pauline Letters.*–A. "3 Corinthians."* The Acts of Paul (*see* APOCRYPHAL ACTS) contains an additional Corinthian correspondence set in a Philippian imprisonment. The Corinthians complain that Simon and Cleobius forbid their use of the OT, attribute creation to the angels, not God, and deny the Incarnation and Resurrection (these are standard Gnostic positions). Paul's reply, using 1 Cor. 15 and other Scripture in pastiche, stresses redemption through the Incarnation (there is no mention of the cross) as well as resurrection and judgment.

This correspondence was accepted by fourth-century Syriac authorities (Ephraem expounds 3 Corinthians in his comm. on the Pauline Epistles), and it appears regularly in Armenian, and very rarely in Latin Bibles long after. The Bodmer papyri have now provided a third-century Greek version, without the narrative setting. The correspondence is usually regarded as integral to the Acts of Paul, in which case its author was Tertullian's "presbyter of Asia," and its pseudonymity is a piece of historical imagination arising from his novelistic purpose. M. Testuz, however, argues that the letters were a separate late-second-century anti-Gnostic polemic, incorporated later by the Acts of Paul. This would be a very rare example of orthodox resort to pseudepigraphy to make an antiheretical point. If so, it was neither successful nor necessary. The work, though faithful enough to Pauline language, says nothing that the canonical Pauline Epistles do not say better.

B. Laodiceans. Col. 4:16 probably indicates that Paul sent a letter to Laodicea. Marcion apparently called Ephesians "Laodiceans," but the Muratorian Canon, which knows Ephesians, speaks of epistles to the Laodiceans and Alexandrians "forged in Paul's name for [possibly by mistranslation for "against"?] the heresy of Marcion." Jerome (*De viris illustribus* 5) and some Greek fathers speak slightingly of a forged Laodicean epistle, and the Second Council of Nicea (A.D. 787) rejects it. Many Latin MSS, however, beginning in the 6th cent. with Codex Fuldensis and continuing through the Middle Ages, contain an epistle to the Laodiceans: a feeble and formless collection of Pauline phrases, plagiarized mainly from Philippians, with no obvious motive other than filling out Col. 4:16. It bears marks of being translated from the Greek; the existence of an Arabic version also suggests this. It cannot be later than the 4th cent., but it is unlikely to be the second-century epistle attacked in the Muratorian Canon. It does not have a Marcionite, anti-Marcionite, or any other theological character at all.

C. Alexandrians. Only the Muratorian Canon names this epistle. Identifications with Hebrews, 3 Corinthians, or a homiletic section from a Bobbio missal headed "Colossians" (T. Zahn, *Geschichte des NT Kanons* [1892], II, 586ff.), involve extensive conjectures.

D. Paul and Seneca. Western Christians often esteemed Seneca. Tertullian calls him *saepe noster*. Jerome (*De viris illustribus* 12) classes him among his illustrious men on account of a correspondence "read by some" between him and Paul. No other authorities before the 9th cent. except Augustine (*Ep.* 153.14, perhaps following Jerome) and Pseudo-Linus, *Passio Pauli* (H-S, II, 134), show knowledge of it. It is doubtless identical with a set of fourteen Latin letters in several medieval MSS. These contain little but mutual compliments, some circumstantial historical detail, and reflections by Seneca (who sends Paul a book for improving his style) on the confluence of divine knowledge and uncultivated expression. They doubtless belong to the 4th cent., and reflect a recognition of Christian affinities in Seneca and sensitivity to criticisms that Christian writings were deficient in art. They are poor work by any standard, and went largely unnoticed.

II. Letters by Literary Convention.–Certain types of literature, neither epistles nor imitations of any of the NT categories, conventionally took some apparatus of the epistolary form. To some extent apocalypses followed this pattern (*see* APOCALYPTIC LITERATURE). Revelation itself contains a general epistolary address from John as well as the seven letters to the churches. The forms mentioned here bear some relation to apocalyptic.

A. Epistle of the Apostles. Preserved in Coptic and Ethiopic with one Latin scrap, this purports to be a letter to the churches of East, West, South, and North, from the Eleven (John is named first, then Thomas and Peter), describing the teaching of the Lord just before the Ascension. The core is an apocalypse; but there are reflections on evangelic matter, and a curious account of the Annunciation in which the Logos assumes the form of Gabriel. The work uses all four Gospels and independent tradition. The theology is essentially orthodox and anti-Gnostic, but with some eccentricities. It has usually been dated in the middle of the 2nd cent., and from Asia; but de Zwaan made a good case for an Edessene origin near the end of the 2nd cent., among Syrian Christians resentful of Roman pretensions.

B. The Didascalia. This was an influential Syrian work of the 3rd cent., claiming to represent the joint work of the apostles after the Jerusalem Council. It contains various materials on church order and discipline. Such epistolary indications as exist are consequent on the fiction (probably not intended seriously) of its historical setting.

C. Other Church Orders. Features noticeable in the Epistle of the Apostles and in the Didascalia were combined in a considerable pseudo-apostolic literature of church orders (such as the *Testamentum Domini* and the Apostolic Constitutions), which contain epistolary elements.

III. Romantic and Novelistic Forgeries.–Some famous examples of this genre must suffice. The independent Syrian buffer state of Carhoene was evangelized during the 2nd cent., and became the first state to acknowledge Christianity. Eusebius, in the early 4th cent. (*HE* i.13), transcribes a correspondence obtained from its capital Edessa. In this king Abgar Uchama (4 B.C.–A.D. 50; *see* ABGAR) invites Jesus to Edessa. Jesus replies by letter, commending Abgar's faith, declining the invitation, and promising to send one of His disciples when "all is fulfilled." This is the earliest known form of a legend originating in local patriotism and extant in many highly colored forms, notably the Greek Acts of Thaddaeus and the Syriac Doctrine of Addai (*see* APOCRYPHAL ACTS). In some versions a picture and an oral message replace the letter of the Lord.

The Clementine Homilies represent one form of a popular, if theologically dubious, Christian novel of the 2nd or 3rd century. They open with a letter in which Peter, whose sermons are allegedly abstracted by Clement, exhorts James the Just to secrecy on their contents. An equally worthless letter of Clement to James indicates what is to follow.

The Letter of Lentulus, supposedly by a Roman official in Palestine under Tiberius, has achieved celebrity as a contemporary description of Jesus' appearance; but it is a valueless medieval Latin creation. It "follows the traditional portraits closely, and was no doubt written in the presence of one" (*ANT*, p. 478).

The Sunday Letter. In a category apart stands a letter, found in many languages and versions (the oldest perhaps going back to the 6th cent.), supposedly from the Lord, said to have dropped out of heaven onto various altars, denouncing the profanation of Sunday.

Bibliography.–Eng. tr. of many texts can be found in H-S and also E. von Dobschütz, *Christusbilder* (*TU,* 18, 1899); *ANT.* Lat. texts of pseudo-Paulines, with Fr. tr. and comm. in R. Vouaux, *Les Actes de Paul et ses lettres apocryphes* (1913).

Gk. text of the Corinthian correspondence, with notice of later Lat. discoveries, can be found in M. Testuz, *Papyrus Bodmer X-XII* (1959); *see also* bibliography for Acts of Paul under APOCRYPHAL ACTS; M. Rist, *JR,* 22 (1942), 39ff.; M. Testuz in *Littérature et Théologie Pauliniennes* (1960), pp. 217ff. On Laodiceans, H-S, II, 128-132; J. B. Lightfoot, *Colossians* (3rd ed. 1879), pp. 272ff. On Alexandrians, H-S, II, 91. On Seneca, H-S, II, 133-141; C. W. Barlow, *Epistolae Senecae ad Paulum et Pauli ad Senecam* (1938); text reproduced in Migne-Hamman, *Patrologiae Cursus Completus Supp.,* I (1959), 674ff.; J. B. Lightfoot, *Philippians* (1879), pp. 220f.; J. N. Sevenster, *Paul and Seneca* (1961), pp. 11ff.

Eds. of Epistle of the Apostles by C. Schmidt, *Gespräche Jesu mit seinen Jüngern . . .* (*TU,* 43, 1919); H. Duensing, *Epistula Apostolorum* (*Kleine Texte,* 1925); Eng. tr. in *ANT*; H-S, I, 189-227; also J. de Zwaan in H. G. Wood, ed., *Amicitiae Corolla* (1933), pp. 344ff. Best ed. of Didascalia is R. H. Connolly, *Didascalia Apostolorum* (1929). On the relations of church orders see Connolly, *The So-Called Egyptian Church Order* (1916); on their pseudo-apostolicity, A. F. Walls, *Studia Patristica,* II (1957), 83ff.

On the Abgar legend, *see* bibliography under APOCRYPHAL ACTS. Text of Clementine Homilies by B. Rehm (1953); Eng. tr. in *Ante-Nicene Fathers* (repr. 1970), VIII; H-S, II, 532-570; see also O. Cullmann, *Le Problème Littéraire et Historique du Roman Pseudo-Clémentin* (1930). On the Sunday Letter, A. de Santos Otero, *Studio Patristica* (*TU,* 78, 1961), 290-96.

A. F. WALLS

APOCRYPHAL GOSPELS.

- I. Introduction
  - A. Description
  - B. Attestation and Extant Copies
  - C. Types
  - D. History of Research
- II. Gospels of Jesus' Infancy and Parents
  - A. Origins
  - B. Protevangelium of James
  - C. Infancy Gospel of Thomas
  - D. Pseudo-Matthew
  - E. Arabic and Armenian Infancy Gospels
  - F. Assumption of the Virgin Mary
  - G. History of Joseph the Carpenter
- III. Gospels of Jesus' Passion and Ressurection
  - A. Gospel of Peter
  - B. Gospel of Nicodemus (=Acts of Pilate)
- IV. Jewish-Christian Gospels
  - A. Gospels of the Nazarenes
  - B. Gospel of the Ebionites
  - C. Gospel of the Hebrews
- V. Heretical Gospels
  - A. Gospels of Heretical Teachers
  - B. Gospel of Eve
  - C. Gospel of Judas
  - D. Works Associated with Bartholomew
  - E. Gospel of the Egyptians
  - F. Gospel of Matthias
  - G. Pistis Sophia
  - H. Books of Jeu
  - I. Gospel of Mary (Magdalene)
  - J. Nag Hammadi Gospels
    1. Gospel of Thomas
    2. Gospel of Philip
    3. Gospel of Truth
    4. Gospel of the Egyptians
- VI. A Secret Gospel of Mark?
- VII. Evaluation

I. Introduction.–*A. Description.* The apocryphal gospels are a motley group of noncanonical writings about the purported deeds and revelations of Jesus Christ. Though the Greek word *apocrypha* originally meant "hidden," the church fathers used it to describe spurious gospels. Irenaeus refers to "an unspeakable number of apocryphal

APOCRYPHAL GOSPELS

and spurious writings, which they themselves [i.e., heretics] had forged, to bewilder the minds of the foolish" (*Adv. haer.* i.20.1). Though some are patterned after the canonical Gospels, many bear little resemblance to them.

B. Attestation and Extant Copies. As Origen noted, "The Church possesses four Gospels, heresy a great many" (First Homily on Luke, cited in H-S, I, 55). Of the approximately fifty apocryphal gospels, many are known by title only or by a few scattered quotations and allusions in the patristic writers. We know nothing more than the title of four of the nine apocryphal works titled "Gospels" in the sixth-century Decretum Gelasianum (*see* APOCRYPHA II.E.1). A number of works, especially of the popular infancy gospels, have been preserved in late MSS and versions. Egypt has preserved some early papyrus and parchment copies, most notably in the Gnostic library discovered at NAG HAMMADI.

C. Types. In addition to apologetic works such as the Gospel of Peter, most apocryphal gospels fall into two categories: (1) legendary, or (2) sectarian or heretical. The former category encompasses the infancy gospels, which are highly imaginative accounts of the Virgin Mary, the Nativity, and the childhood of Jesus. The latter category includes works which were written to set forth the peculiar views of Jewish-Christian sects, Encratites, and Gnostics. Eusebius (*HE* iii.25) describes such works as the Gospels of Peter, of Thomas, and of Matthias as follows: "Again, nothing could be farther from apostolic usage than the type of phraseology employed, while the ideas and implications of their contents are so irreconcilable with true orthodoxy that they stand revealed as the forgeries of heretics."

D. History of Research. Until the 19th cent. our only evidence for the apocryphal gospels apart from late MSS or versions consisted of patristic notices and extracts. Within the last century fragments and even entire copies of apocryphal gospels have been discovered in Egypt.

In 1886 five leaves of a parchment codex were discovered at Akhmim in the grave of a Christian monk of the 8th century. These contained a portion of the Gospel of Peter.

Between 1897 and 1907 second- to fourth-century papyri containing sayings of Jesus were discovered at Oxyrhynchus (*see* AGRAPHA IV.C). We now know that these are from a Greek version of the sectarian Gospel of Thomas.

In 1934 the British Museum acquired two damaged leaves and a fragment of a papyrus, Pap. Egerton 2, which combined elements from the four canonical Gospels. Published by Bell and Skeat in 1935, the papyrus dates to *ca.* 130 and is an important witness to the early circulation of the Gospels in Egypt.

The most important recent development has been the discovery in 1945 of the Nag Hammadi codices. These date to the 4th cent. and contain a number of apocryphal gospels in their entirety, including the Gospel of Truth, first translated in 1956, and the Gospel of Thomas, first translated in 1959.

In 1924 M. R. James published a handy collection of extracts and abstracts of the apocryphal gospels. This work has now been superseded by E. Hennecke and W. Schneemelcher's *NT Apocrypha,* I (Eng. tr. 1963).

II. Gospels of Jesus' Infancy and Parents.–A. Origins. The accounts of the birth of Jesus in Matthew and Luke, and the one account of Jesus as a child in Lk. 2:40-52, did not satisfy the curiosity of many Christians. Some, therefore, invented infancy gospels which attributed numerous miracles to the baby Jesus and the child Jesus. The Jesus who is thus portrayed appears as a grotesquely petulant and dangerously powerful youngster.

A desire to glorify Mary and to establish her perpetual virginity motivated some writers to describe the "brethren" of Jesus as the children of Joseph by a previous marriage.

The Protevangelium of James and the Infancy Gospel of Thomas, both from the 2nd cent., served as a basis for the later Pseudo-Matthew, the Arabic and the Armenian infancy gospels, and the Nativity of Mary. These expanded accounts were incorporated in the *Golden Legend,* which had an enormous influence upon medieval Europe.

B. Protevangelium of James. The History of James Concerning the Birth of Mary was given the title Protevangelium or "First Gospel" by the Frenchman Postel, who first published a Latin translation of it in 1552. The Gelasian Decree refers to it as The Gospel of James the Less, though the work itself implies that its author is James the Lord's brother.

There are possible allusions to elements contained in this work as early as Justin Martyr *Dial.* 78.5, and Clement *Misc.* vii.93.7. The earliest explicit reference is in Origen's commentary on Mt. 13:55, which cites The Book of James as the source for the tradition that Jesus' brethren were from Joseph's previous marriage.

The Protevangelium was composed in Greek in the mid 2nd cent., probably in Egypt by an author who was quite ignorant of Palestinian customs. The rather extensive work of 25 chapters or paragraphs is preserved in some 30 MSS which date from after the 10th century. Portions are represented in a fifth- or sixth-century papyrus published by Grenfell in 1896, and in Pap. Bodmer V of the 3rd cent., published by Testuz in 1958. Versions are extant in Syriac, Armenian, Ethiopic, Georgian and Slavonic, but surprisingly not in Latin.

The Protevangelium describes the parents of Mary as the aged Anna and the wealthy Joachim. In a narrative patterned after the story of Samuel, Mary is dedicated at the age of three as a kind of Jewish "vestal virgin." She is nurtured at the temple by angels until the age of twelve, when she is betrothed to Joseph, who is miraculously selected from a number of suitors.

Joseph is portrayed as a widower with sons, an attempt to explain away the reference to "first-born" in Lk. 2:7. Before the consummation of the marriage Joseph is horrified to discover that Mary is already six months pregnant. Both Mary and Joseph, however, demonstrate their innocence by drinking the waters of conviction (cf. Nu. 5:11-31).

The birth of Jesus takes place in a cave, a tradition mentioned by Justin Martyr also. Mary is assisted in her delivery by a Hebrew midwife, and her virginity notwithstanding the birth is attested by Salome.

The final chapters recount how Herod killed the Baptist's father, Zacharias, and how he sought the Baptist, who escaped by hiding with his mother in a hollow mountain.

C. Infancy Gospel of Thomas. The Gospel of Thomas that describes Jesus' childhood is quite distinct from the Gospel of Thomas discovered at Nag Hammadi (see V.J.1 below). The titles as given in the MSS are Infancy of the Lord Jesus and Account of the Infancy of the Lord by Thomas, the Philosopher of Israel.

Irenaeus alludes to the learning of the alphabet by Jesus, an incident related in this gospel. The Gospel of Thomas was therefore composed in the 2nd century. It is extant in two recensions: an older and longer form with nineteen chapters, and a shorter form with eleven chapters. Most Greek MSS are later than the 13th century. There are Syriac, Latin, Ethiopic, Georgian, and Slavonic versions.

The Infancy Gospel of Thomas purports to describe the miracles which Jesus, a veritable "enfant terrible," performed between the ages of five and twelve. When Jesus was five he made twelve sparrows from clay, and then caused them to fly. When the son of Annas the scribe scattered the water that Jesus had collected into a pool, Jesus cursed the child: "You insolent, godless dunderhead, . . . See, now you also shall wither like a tree." A lad who accidentally bumped into Jesus was smitten dead. Those who accused him were blinded. A teacher who attempted to teach the Alpha and the Beta was rebuked by the precocious Jesus. As an assistant in his father's carpenter shop, Jesus was able to stretch beams of wood to the proper size!

D. Pseudo-Matthew. A work known as Pseudo-Matthew is a Latin composition from the 6th-8th cent. preserved in numerous MSS dating from the 11th. cent. and later. Chs. 1–17 are based on the Protevangelium, and chs. 25–42 on the Infancy Gospel of Thomas. The intervening chapters recount miracles which took place during the Holy Family's flight to Egypt.

We are told that at the Nativity of the holy Infant was worshiped by the ox and the ass (cf. Isa. 1:3). Wild animals pay homage to the child en route to Egypt (cf. Isa. 11:6ff.). When Mary becomes hungry, the child commands the palm tree to bow down and proffer its dates. The thirty-day journey to Egypt was completed in one. In the capital of Egypt, Sotinen in the region of Hermopolis, 365 pagan idols fall down as Mary and the child enter the temple.

Based on Psuedo-Matthew is a Latin work, *Evangelium de nativitate Mariae,* The Gospel of the Nativity of Mary. It purports to be the work of Jerome, but was composed during the 6th to 8th centuries. It served as one of the principal sources of Marian legends.

Another Latin infancy gospel, preserved in the fourteenth-century Arundel MS, has the following testimony of the midwife who assisted at the Nativity: ". . . he had no weight like other children who are born. . . . I wondered greatly because he did not cry as new-born babes are accustomed to cry" (H-S, I, 414).

E. Arabic and Armenian Infancy Gospels. The Arabic Infancy Gospel, which is based upon the Protevangelium and the Infancy Gospel of Thomas, seems to have been composed originally in Syriac. The Arabic MS, first published in a Latin translation in 1697, is now lost. Its stories, which resemble those of the Arabian Nights, were known to Muhammad and appear in Islamic traditions.

This gospel recounts that on the trip to Egypt the Holy Family encountered two robbers, Titus and Dumachus. The young Jesus prophesies, "In thirty years, mother, the Jews will crucify me in Jerusalem, and those two robbers will be fastened to the cross with me, Titus on my right hand and Dumachus on my left" (H-S, I, 408).

The Armenian Infancy Gospel is a long text which also relies upon a Syriac work based on the Protevangelium and the Infancy Gospel of Thomas. Among the added features is a detailed description of the Magi: Melqon from Persia, Balthasar from India, and Gaspar from Arabia.

F. Assumption of the Virgin Mary. The Gelasian Decree condemns a work which is known in Latin as *Transitus Mariae* and in English as The Assumption of Mary. This was composed in Greek in Egypt *ca.* 400. It is preserved in eleventh- to fourteenth-century MSS and in Latin, Syriac, Coptic and Arabic versions, as well as in a discourse on St. John the Divine.

Two years after His ascension Jesus Himself appears to Mary to announce her impending demise. After her death miracles of healing take place through the agency of her corpse. Mary, restored to life in her body, is then transported to Paradise. This document played a role in the formulation of the dogma of the assumption of the Virgin promulgated by Pius XII in 1950.

G. The History of Joseph the Carpenter. The otherwise neglected Joseph is the subject of this work. Originally composed in Greek in Egypt *ca.* 400, it is preserved in Latin, Coptic, and Arabic versions. Like the infancy gospels in general, it assumes that Joseph was a widower before his marriage to Mary. The narrative relates that he was first married at 40, and was widowed when he was 89. Two years later he wed Mary. He died at the advanced age of 111.

III. Gospels of Jesus' Passion and Resurrection.–*A. Gospel of Peter.* Origen in his commentary on Mt. 10:17 claimed that a Gospel of Peter was used by those who held that Jesus' "brethren" were Joseph's sons by a previous marriage. Theodoret of Syria (5th cent.) also mentions a Gospel of Peter used by the Nazaraeans. Eusebius (*HE* vi.12) includes a very instructive account from the writings of Serapion, Bishop of Antioch (190), who discovered that the Christians at Rhossus in Syria were using a Gospel of Peter. After giving his preliminary approval to their reading it, he later examined the work more carefully and concluded "that while most of it accorded with the authentic teachings of the Savior, some passages were spurious additions."

One of the earliest noncanonical gospels, the Gospel of Peter was composed early in the 2nd cent., probably in Syria by Docetists who maintained that Christ only appeared to have a human body. In 1886 a Greek manuscript containing a portion of this gospel was discovered at Akhmim, Egypt.

The Gospel of Peter makes use of the four canonical Gospels. It shifts the blame for Christ's condemnation from Pilate entirely upon Herod and the Jews. When Jesus was crucified he "kept silence as one feeling no pain" in accordance with a docetic understanding of the crucifixion. On the cross he cried out, "My power, my power, thou hast forsaken me," and was then "taken up."

The miraculous element is also heightened. The guards actually witnessed the Resurrection taking place before their eyes: "they saw three men coming out from the sepulchre, and two of them sustaining the other, and a cross following them, and the heads of the two reaching as far as heaven, but that of him whom they led by the hand overpassing the heavens."

B. Gospel of Nicodemus (=Acts of Pilate). The Acts of Pilate became known after a Latin tradition (13th-14th cent.) as the Gospel of Nicodemus. A Christian named Ananias claims to have translated into Greek, in 425, the Hebrew account of Nicodemus, who is identified as the man whom Jesus healed of a thirty-eight-year-old paralysis.

Justin (*Apol.* i.35.9) mentions an Acts of Pilate, as does Tertullian (*Apol.* 21.24), but these references seem to be to the alleged official reports of Pilate. Epiphanius (*Haer.* 50.1.5) is the first to refer to a Christian Acts of Pilate.

Although some of the elements may go back to the 2nd cent., the work as it now stands does not date prior to the 4th-5th centuries. It is extant in Latin MSS, some of the 5th cent., and in Greek MSS, the oldest of which dates to the 12th century. It was also widespread in Coptic, Syriac, and Armenian versions.

It is possible that the work was written as a Christian answer to the anti-Christian Acts of Pilate introduced by the emperor Maximinus II into the schools in 311 (Eusebius *HE* ix.5). As in the Gospel of Peter, the blame for Jesus' condemnation is placed on the Jews rather than on Pilate, to avoid giving offense to the imperial authorities.

The gospel consists of two quite distinct parts. The first describes in chs. 1–11 the crucifixion and burial of Christ, and in chs. 12–16 the Sanhedrin's investigations which prove the Resurrection. The second part, which may have been added to the first because of the prominence of Joseph of Arimathea in both sections, describes in chs. 17–27 the Descent of Christ to the nether world (cf. 1 Pet. 3:19).

When Jesus first enters before Pilate, the Roman standards automatically bow down. The Jews charge Jesus: "Firstly, that you were born of fornication; secondly, that your birth meant the death of the children in Bethlehem; thirdly, that your father Joseph and your mother Mary fled into Egypt because they counted for nothing among the people." Twelve men step forward to affirm that Joseph and Mary were indeed married, and that Jesus' birth was therefore legitimate.

A number of other witnesses appear on behalf of Jesus, including Nicodemus and Bernice (Lat. Veronica), the woman who was healed of a hemorrhage. Despite Pilate's perception of Jesus' innocence, he is forced by the Jews to crucify Him. The robbers who are crucified with Jesus are identified as Dysmas and Gestas. The soldier who thrust a spear into Jesus is called Longinus.

After the Resurrection the Jews send three of their rabbis to investigate. These return and testify that they have seen the risen Christ teaching and then ascending into heaven.

The *Descensus* portion describes how Christ's arrival in the nether world strikes terror among Satan and his minions, a theme elaborated in the later Harrowing of Hell traditions. Christ raises the dead, including Adam and the penitent thief, Dysmas.

At a much later date were added appendices which related Pilate's end and which even described him as "blessed" because in his governorship "all was fulfilled." This tendency eventually led to the canonization of Pilate's wife, Procla, by the Greek Orthodox Church, and the celebration of St. Pilate's Day by the Ethiopian Orthodox Church.

IV. Jewish-Christian Gospels.–The question of the gospels used by early Jewish-Christian groups such as the Nazarenes and the Ebionites is very complex. The difficulty revolves around whether or not there were three separate gospels: (1) The Gospel of the Nazarenes (G. Naz.), (2) The Gospel of the Ebionites (G. Eb.), and (3) The Gospel of the Hebrews (G. Heb.), or whether G. Naz. = G. Heb. and G. Eb. = G. Heb. Quispel (*VC*, 11 [1957], 190f.) suggests that G. Naz. and G. Eb. are but recensions of an underlying G. Heb.

Eusebius (*HE* iv.22.8) reports that Hegesippus (A.D. 170) relied "occasionally on the Gospel of the Hebrews, on the Syriac Gospel, and particularly on works in Hebrew (i.e. Aramaic), showing that he was a believer of Hebrew stock." Clement of Alexandria cites a Gospel according to the Hebrews in his discussions on marriage (cf. *Misc.* ii.45.5).

Epiphanius speaks of a gospel used by the Ebionites, also called a Gospel of the Hebrews, which he considers a falsified and truncated Matthew (*Haer.* 30.3.7). He also says that the Nazoraeans (cf. Nazaraeans, Nazarenes), Jewish-Christians of Syria, have a Hebrew Gospel, which he thinks is the original Aramaic of Matthew (*Haer.* 29.9.4).

Jerome mentions a Hebrew Gospel used by the Ebionites, and a Hebrew Gospel used by the Nazaraeans, Jewish-Christians of Beroea near Aleppo, Syria. He says that he translated such a Gospel of the Hebrews into Latin, and reproduces many citations from it. A copy of the Gospel of the Hebrews was kept in the library at Caesarea.

Some scholars, such as P. Vielhauer (H-S, I, 117-165), believe that Jerome has falsified or at least confused his information. Vielhauer would distinguish three distinct Jewish-Christian gospels as follows:

A. Gospel of the Nazarenes. The Gospel of the Nazarenes was composed in Aramaic (or Syriac) early in the 2nd cent. in northern Syria, where it was used by the Nazarenes. Attested by Hegesippus (cited in Eusebius), Epiphanius and Jerome, it was apparently a targumic rendering of Matthew with various deletions and additions.

In the gospel the man with a withered hand, who was healed by Jesus (Mt. 12:10), says, "I was a stonemason, earning my living with my hands. I pray you, Jesus, restore my health to me, so that I may not be shamefully reduced to begging my food." When the disciples ask how often they should forgive, they are told that they should forgive seventy times seven (Mt. 18:15-22) "for in the prophets also . . . the sinful word was found." The story of the reluctant rich man (Mt. 19:16-22) was expanded to include two rich men, one of whom scratches his head in perplexity (*See* AGRAPHA IV.D.2-3). The parable of talents (Mt. 25:14-30) describes the three servants as follows: "One of them greatly multiplied his stock-in-trade, one hid his talent, and one consumed his master's property with harlots and flute-girls." At Jesus' death "the lintel of the temple, which was of immense size, was cracked in two" (cf. Mt. 27:51).

B. Gospel of the Ebionites. The Ebionites were heretical Jewish-Christians who lived in Transjordan. They rejected the OT sacrificial laws and were vegetarians. They denied the Virgin Birth and held that Christ's divinity depended on His union with the Holy Spirit at the time of His baptism.

That this gospel, written *ca.* 150, was composed in Greek is shown by the substitution of the Gk. *enkrís,* "cake" for *akrís,* "locust" in the Baptist's diet. It also omitted the narrative of the Nativity. As noted by Epiphanius, our chief witness for this work, the Gospel of the Ebionites was a "falsified and abridged" Matthew.

Christ is made to say, "I came to abolish sacrifices, and if you do not cease from sacrificing, the wrath of God will not cease from you" (cf. Mt. 5:17). His disapproval of the Passover is raised in the question, "Do I desire with desire at this Passover to eat flesh with you?" (cf. Mt. 26:17; Lk. 22:15).

C. Gospel of the Hebrews. According to Vielhauer this title should be reserved for a gospel composed in Greek in the first half of the 2nd cent. and in use in Egypt among Greek-speaking Jewish Christians. It is known chiefly from Clement, Origen, and Jerome. According to the Stichometry of Nicephorus it had but 300 lines less than Matthew.

The citation, "Even so did my mother, the Holy Spirit, take me by one of my hairs and carry me away on to the great mountain Tabor" (H-S, I, 164; cf. Mt. 4:1), would seem to betray a Semitic background as the Hebrew/Aramaic word for spirit is feminine. The saying, "He that marvels shall reign and he that has reigned shall rest" (H-S, I, 164), is paralleled in the Coptic Gospel of Thomas, logion 2, leading scholars to conclude that the latter has incorporated materials from the Gospel of the Hebrews.

The high regard for James, the Lord's brother, among Jewish-Christians is prominent in a passage in which the risen Lord appears to him, "For James had sworn that he would not eat bread from that hour in which he had drunk the cup of the Lord" (H-S, I, 165).

V. Heretical Gospels.–*A. Gospels of Heretical Teachers.* The church fathers attributed numerous gospels to heretical leaders, chiefly of Gnostic sects. The Gospel of Marcion was a redaction of Luke shorn of its first two chapters and adapted to Marcion's hostility to Judaism, to the OT, and to marriage.

The Gnostic Basilides "compiled twenty-four books on the gospel," which indicates that the gospel of Basilides was probably not his own composition but an altered gospel, perhaps of Luke. Clement, *Misc.* iv.81-83, cites from the 23rd book, called the Exegetica: "I will say that any man you may name is a man; the just one is God (Lk. 18:19)." A fourth-century work, *Acta Archelai* lxvii.5.7-11, preserves comments on the parable of the rich man and the beggar (Lk. 16:19-31), which according to a Gnostic point of view "shows us a nature without Root and without Place returning above to the things from which it had originated."

Other gospels, of which we know scarcely more than their names, are ascribed to Apelles, Bardesanes, Mani, etc.

B. Gospel of Eve. Epiphanius *Haer.* 26.3.1 quotes from a Gnostic work called The Gospel of Eve: "I stood upon a high mountain and saw a tall man, and another of short stature, and heard as it were a sound of thunder and went nearer in order to hear. Then he spoke to me and said: 'I am thou and thou art I, and where thou art there am I, and I am sown in all things; and whence thou wilt, thou gatherest me, but when thou gatherest me, then gatherest thou thyself.' " We know little else of this work, which seems to have been composed in the 2nd century.

C. Gospel of Judas. Irenaeus (*Adv. haer.* i.31.1) describes a Gospel of Judas (Iscariot), used by the perverse Cainites, Gnostics who esteemed the villains of Scriptures. This work, composed between 130 and 170, maintained that Judas, "alone knowing the truth as no others did," betrayed Jesus so that the mystery of redemption might be accomplished.

D. Works Associated with Bartholomew. Jerome in his commentary on Matthew mentions a Gospel of Bartholomew. Apart from its condemnation by the Decretum Gelasianum we know little about this work.

It may, however, be reflected in another work, The Questions of Bartholomew. Composed between the 3rd and 5th cent., this is preserved in Greek, Latin, and Slavonic recensions. Bartholomew (who is identified with Nathanael, cf. Jn. 1:50f.) asks a series of questions addressed to Jesus, to the Virgin Mary, and to Satan. When Bartholomew asks, "Tell me, Lord, who was he whom the angels carried in their arms, that exceedingly large man?," Christ answers that it was Adam, whom He raised from Hades. The answer to the question of how many souls leave the world every day is "thirty thousand," of which number only three are admitted into Paradise.

The text concludes with a comment on the issue of digamy or second marriage: "A single marriage belongs to chaste living. For truly I say to you: 'He who sins after the third marriage is unworthy of God.' " The fourth-century Apostolic Constitutions likewise maintained that to marry once is righteous, that second marriage is permissible for young widows, but that marriages beyond the third are "manifest fornication and unquestionable uncleanness."

The Book of the Apostle Bartholomew, composed in Egypt during the 5th or 6th centuries, is preserved in several Coptic MSS, the most important dating from the 12th century. It has Bartholomew relating to his son Thaddaeus the resurrection of Adam. "Doubting" Thomas is absent from the rendezvous with the risen Christ because of the death of his son Siophanes in a distant land. After raising his son from the dead and baptizing 12,000 natives, Thomas is transported back to the Mount of Olives on a cloud.

E. Gospel of the Egyptians. There are numerous patristic citations from the Gospel of the Egyptians, a work written in Greek in Egypt early in the 2nd century. It is quite distinct from a work with the same title found at Nag Hammadi (see V.J.4 below). It was a heretical gospel used by the Sabellians (Epiphanius *Haer.* 62.4), by the Naassene Gnostics (Hippolytus *Ref.* v.7.9), and by the Encratites or "Continent Ones," who discouraged marriage and procreation.

Clement of Alexandria cites the work a number of times in attempting to demonstrate the legitimacy of marriage: (1) In *Misc.* iii.6.45 (cf. iii.9.64) he accuses the Encratites of misquoting from the Gospel of the Egyptians when they refer to the Lord's answer to Salome's question, "How long shall death hold sway?" His answer, "As long as you women bear children," implied simply that birth was followed by death and was not a denigration of marriage. The same passage is cited by Clement in his excerpts from the Gnostic Theodotus (*Excerpta Theodoti* 67). (2) In *Misc.* iii.9.63 he notes that the Encratites quote the words of the Savior, "I came to destroy the works of the female," from this apocryphal gospel. (3) In *Misc.* iii.9.66 he accuses them of quoting very selectively Salome's reply, "I would have done better had I never given birth to a child," without also citing the Lord's reply, "Eat of every plant, but eat not of that which has bitterness in it." (4) In *Misc.* iii.13.92f. Clement says that Julius Cassianus, the originator of Docetism, cites the passage, "When Salome asked when she would know the answer to her questions, the Lord said, 'When you trample on the robe of shame, and when the two shall be one, and the male with the female, and there is neither male nor female.' "

As the latter saying is reproduced in logion 22 and logion 37 of the Coptic Gospel of Thomas, scholars have concluded that the latter is partly dependent upon the Gospel of the Egyptians.

F. Gospel of Matthias. The Gospel of Matthias (cf. Acts 1:26) is cited by Origen (*In Luc. Hom.* 1), and by Eusebius (*HE* iii.25.6). Hippolytus (*Ref.* vii.20.1) and Clement (*Misc.* vii.17.108) speak about secret traditions which the Basilidians had inherited from Matthias. Clement (*Misc.* iii.4.26) reports: "It is said that Matthias also taught that one should fight the flesh and abuse it, never allowing it to give way to licentious pleasure, so that the soul might grow by faith and knowledge."

Doresse (*Secret Books,* pp. 226, 336) has argued for the identification of the Gospel of Matthias with a work found at Nag Hammadi, The Book of Thomas the Contender (CG II.7), "which he wrote for the perfect ones," inasmuch as the work contains "secret sayings that the Savior told to Jude-Thomas, and that I myself have written, I, Matthew." Like the Gospel of Matthias it condemns sexuality: "woe to you who love intimacy with that which is feminine." But Puech (H-S, I, 313) objects that the transcriber is Matthew and not Matthias. The names are two different Greek transliterations that ultimately derive from the Hebrew or Aramaic *Mattathiah.*

G. Pistis Sophia. A Gnostic work known as the Pistis Sophia, "Faith Wisdom," has been preserved in the Coptic Codex Askewianus, a parchment from *ca.* 350-400 acquired by the British Museum in 1785. This was first translated in 1851 and retranslated in 1905 by C. Schmidt. The three sections of the Pistis Sophia were composed originally in Greek *ca.* A.D. 250-300; the fourth untitled section of the codex was composed *ca.* 200-250.

This treatise consists of a series of 46 questions posed to the Lord in the 12-year interval after the Resurrection; of these 39 are asked by Mary Magdalene. The answers are written down by Philip. The prominence of Mary exasperates Peter, who cries out, "My Lord, we shall not be able to endure this woman, for she takes our opportunity, and has not let any of us speak, but talks all the time herself" (Pistis

Sophia 146). Similar resentment against her is expressed in the Gospel of Mary (see V.I. below), and in the last logion of the Coptic Gospel of Thomas.

Jesus informs his disciples of his victory over the evil celestial powers, and of his encounter with Pistis Sophia, who sorrows because of her fall from the Pleroma. He tells his disciples that they must learn the mysteries of the Books of Jeu (see V.H. below). Jesus informs them about a baptism of the first oblation, a baptism of fire, and a baptism of the Holy Spirit.

H. Books of Jeu. The Coptic Codex Brucianus contains A Great Treatise according to the Mystery or The Books of Jeu. The papyrus codex, dated to the 4th to 6th centuries, was acquired by the Bodleian Library in 1769. It is a translation of a Greek work composed in the first half of the 3rd century. The work received a preliminary translation in 1891, and was retranslated by C. Schmidt in 1905.

Jesus reveals how the Father projected from his bosom Jeu, the true God, who dwells in the Treasury of Light. He warns his disciples not to reveal secrets to the licentious Gnostics. After reciting magical prayers, Jesus administers to his disciples baptisms of water, of fire, and of the Holy Spirit. As a preparation for the baptisms the disciples bring to Jesus various plants, the juniper, the terebinth, etc., probably for their magical properties. An untitled section of the codex gives a description of the various emanations from the supreme God.

I. Gospel of Mary (Magdalene). The Coptic papyrus Codex Berolinensis 8502, dated to the 5th cent., was acquired in 1896. It was lost during the Second World War, but W. Till was able to publish a translation in 1955 from C. Schmidt's notes. The codex contains an apocryphal Acts of Peter and three Gnostic works: (1) the Apocryphon of John, a work which is also contained in three NAG HAMMADI codices (CG II.1, CG III.1, CG IV.1); (2) the Sophia of Jesus, also contained in a Nag Hammadi codex (CG III.4); and (3) the Gospel of Mary.

The Gospel of Mary was composed in Greek in the 2nd century. A portion of it is also contained in a Greek papyrus, Pap. Rylands 463, dated to the 3rd century.

In this gospel the Savior tells the disciples, "Sin as such does not exist, but you make sin when you do what is of the nature of fornication, which is called 'sin.' " He reveals other mysteries only to Mary Magdalene, whom he loves above all women. She in turn describes to the disciples how the soul is questioned by such powers as Darkness and Ignorance during its ascent to heaven.

Peter is indignant at the favoritism shown to Mary, and bursts out, "Did he then speak secretly with a woman, in preference to us and not openly?" Whereupon Mary is aggrieved and protests, "My brother Peter, what do you think? Do you think that I thought this up myself in my heart or that I am lying concerning the Savior?" Levi comes to her defense and rebukes Peter, "But if the Savior made her worthy, who are you to reject her?"

J. Nag Hammadi Gospels. The discovery by accident in 1945 (or 1946) of twelve Coptic codices and a fragment of a thirteenth near Nag Hammadi in upper Egypt ranks as one of the most significant of all times. The codices date from the 4th cent. and were buried early in the 5th century. The texts are cited as follows: CG stands for Cairensis Gnosticus, the name of the collection; the Roman numeral corresponds to the number of the codex and the Arabic numeral to the tractate in a given codex. Among the fifty-three treatises are a number of gospels used by Gnostics.

1. Gospel of Thomas (CG II.2). Quite distinct from the Infancy Gospel of Thomas (see II.C. above) is the Coptic Gospel of Thomas. References in Origen *In Luc. Hom.* 1, in Eusebius *HE* iii.25.6, and in Ambrose *In Luc.* I.2 may be to this Gospel of Thomas. Hippolytus *Ref.* v.7.20 says that a Gospel of Thomas was used by the Naassenes, and cites a sentence from this work.

The Gospel of Thomas was originally composed in Greek, probably in Edessa in Syria *ca.* 140. It consists entirely of logia or sayings of Jesus, a number of which are also contained in Greek Oxyrhynchus Papyri, dated *ca.* 150. A number of the sayings are also paralleled in the Gospel of Hebrews (IV.C. above) and in the Gospel of the Egyptians (V.E. above) as well as in later Manichaean writings.

The 114 logia of the Gospel of Thomas represent the most extensive collection of noncanonical sayings of Jesus extant. Forty of these are entirely new. Some scholars, such as Koester (in *Trajectories Through Early Christianity* [1971], pp. 128-143) and Quispel (*NTS,* 12 [1966], 372), maintain that these sayings are based on an independent Aramaic tradition. A number of the logia may preserve genuine agrapha (*see* AGRAPHA IV.D).

The sayings are colored by Naassene Gnosticism according to Grant (*VC,* 13 [1959], 174-180), by Valentinian Gnosticism according to Gärtner and L. Cerfaux (*Muséon,* 70 [1957], 321), and by Encratism according to Quispel (in *Bible and Modern Scholarship,* ed. J. P. Hyatt [1965], pp. 252-58) and Grobel (*NTS,* 8 [1962], 367-373). In any case they stress perfection obtained through sexual abnegation and asceticism.

Among the three new parables are: (1) logion 21, a parable of children who take off their clothes in a field, i.e. Gnostics or Encratites who die and discard their bodies; (2) logion 97, the parable of a woman who was unaware that her jar was leaking grain, a warning against self-confidence; and (3) logion 98, the parable of the killing of a mighty man: "The Kingdom of the Father is like a man who wishes to kill a powerful man. He drew the sword in his house, he stuck it into the wall, in order to know whether his hand would carry through; then he slew the powerful (man)" (cf. Lk. 14:28-32).

The final logion reads: "Simon Peter said to them: 'Let Mary (Magdalene) go out from among us, because women are not worthy of the Life.' Jesus said: 'See, I shall lead her, so that I will make her male, that she too may become a living spirit, resembling you males. For every woman who makes herself male will enter the Kingdom of Heaven.' " This refers to the ultimate reunification of the sexes, as the Gnostics maintained that the separation of the sexes was responsible for the origin of evil.

2. Gospel of Philip (CG II.3). The Pistis Sophia declares that the three disciples who wrote down the Savior's revelations were Matthew, Thomas, and Philip. Apart from the title at the end and paragraph 91, Philip is not mentioned in this work. The title The Gospel of Philip may therefore have been secondary. Epiphanius (*Haer.* 26.13.2f.) refers to a Gospel of Philip used by Egyptian Gnostics, but the words which he cites are not found in this gospel.

The original Greek composition dates to the 2nd century. The Gospel of Philip is a Valentinian work with 127 paragraphs expounding Gnostic doctrines, often through parables. There is a particular stress on sacraments — baptism, chrism, "redemption," and a "bridal chamber" — which recalls the Valentinian Marcosians.

The Gospel of Philip, p. 104, lines 26-30 (para. 23), seems to be an attack on those who maintain a mere resurrection of the flesh: "Some are afraid lest they rise naked. Because of this they wish to rise in the flesh, and they do not know that those who bear the flesh [it is they who are] naked." The Gospel of Philip 121.1-5 (90) seems to defend the concept of a present spiritual resurrection (cf. 2 Tim. 2:18): "Those who say, 'They will die first and rise again,' are in error. If they do not first receive the resurrection while they live, when they die they will receive nothing.' "

A passage in 130.2-6 (122) speaks of the mystery of the undefiled marriage, a reference to the Valentinian concept of marriage as a positive symbol of the reunification of the sexes. Similar is the reference in 117.1-4 (73) to a "bridal chamber" which "is not for the beasts, nor is it for the slaves, nor for the women defiled; but it is for the free men and virgins."

3. Gospel of Truth (CG I.2). Irenaeus (*Adv. haer.* iii.11.9) writes, "But they who are from Valentinus . . . boast of having more gospels than there are. In fact they have gone to such lengths of audacity as to entitle what was not long ago composed by them [the] Gospel of Truth, though it in no way agrees with the Gospels of the Apostles." Since a further reference, *Adv. haer.* ii.24.6 (cf. i.16.2), and the Gospel of Truth 31.4-32.17 both refer to the counting of the ninety-nine sheep with the fingers of the two hands, we may identify the latter as the work written by Valentinus himself, perhaps *ca.* 140-145, before his break with the orthodox church. There are allusions in this work to eighteen books of the NT, including the four Gospels and the Apocalypse.

The Gospel of Truth is found in the codex bought for the Jung Institute in Zurich. It was the first of the Nag Hammadi works to be translated, appearing in 1956 as the *Evangelium Veritatis*. Several pages of this gospel were among the 38 pages of the codex which became detached and were sold to the Coptic Museum in Cairo. These were translated in 1961 as a supplement.

The maddeningly unsystematic essay is a meditation on the Gnostic understanding of the universe and salvation. Its opening words are: "The Gospel of Truth is a joy for them who have received the boon, through the Father of Truth, of knowing it by virtue of the Word who came from the Pleroma." Ignorance about the Father produces anguish and terror; man without gnosis is like one who is enmeshed in a fog.

It is *Planē* or Deceit who elaborated matter by a process of emanation, and who in anger nailed Jesus to a tree. Thereupon "having divested himself of these perishing rages, he (Jesus) clothed himself with the imperishability which none has power to take from him" (20.30-34).

4. Gospel of the Egyptians (CG III.2, IV.2). A Coptic work called The Sacred Book of the Invisible Great Spirit also has the title The Gospel of the Egyptians. It is quite distinct from another work with the latter title (see V.E. above). It contains a passage cited by Epiphanius *Haer.* 26.13 as coming from a Gospel of Philip.

This Sethian or Barbelo-Gnostic work is similar to the anonymous treatise in the Codex Brucianus. It describes how there emerge from the Ineffable Father the three powers of the Father, the Mother, and the Son, "issuing from the living Silence." There then proceeds emanation upon emanation so that five ogdoads (groups of eight beings) are formed. The mother of angels, a grotesque Plesithea, appears. Her four breasts produce the fruit of Gomorrha and Sodom.

A parody of the OT Yahweh, the demiurge Sacla, cries out: "I am a jealous god and there is no other beside me." Heaven responds with the declaration, "Man exists, and so does the Son of Man."

Three divine visitations, including a flood, are announced. Seth is given a holy, magical baptism which will enable his race to escape from the evil god. The final section contains a series of magical vowels similar to the formulae found in the Egypto-Hellenistic magical texts edited by Preisendanz.

VI. A Secret Gospel of Mark?–In 1973 Morton Smith published a MS which he had discovered in 1958 at the monastery of Mar Saba, SE of Jerusalem. The eighteenth-century MS, copied on two and a half blank pages of a book, contains part of a letter ascribed to Clement of Alexandria.

The letter maintains that the Carpocratian Gnostics derived their doctrines from a secret Gospel of Mark. It asserts that, after Peter's death at Rome, Mark came to Alexandria and composed a more spiritual gospel for those who were being perfected. Passages which are cited from this gospel include the description of the raising of a dead youth by Jesus. After his resurrection the youth came to Jesus with only a linen cloth over his nude body, "and he remained with him that night, for Jesus taught him the mystery of the kingdom of God."

Smith has drawn the most unwarranted conclusions from what is obviously but another apocryphal gospel. He not only asserts that this new gospel is earlier than canonical Mark but even argues that it reveals that the essence of Christianity was erotic magic.

VII. Evaluation. The apocryphal gospels, even the earliest and soberest among them, can hardly be compared with the canonical Gospels. They are all patently secondary and legendary or obviously slanted. Commenting on the infancy gospels, Morton Enslin concludes: "Their total effect is to send us back to the canonical gospels with fresh approval of their chaste restraint in failing to attempt to fill in the intriguing hidden years" (*IDB*, I, 167).

A. Roberts and J. Donaldson, the editors of the Ante-Nicene Library, observe that while the apocryphal gospels afford us "curious glimpses of the state of the Christian conscience, and of modes of thought in the first centuries of our era, the predominant impression which they leave on our minds is a profound sense of the immeasurable superiority, the unapproachable simplicity and majesty, of the Canonical Writings."

Though the authentic gold of possibly genuine AGRAPHA contained in the massive dross of the apocryphal gospels is minute, their influence on literature and art through the Middle Ages (especially the 13th-15th cent.) was enormous and even greater than that of the canonical Gospels themselves. The legendary account of Pilate in the Gospel of Nicodemus influenced the passion plays of the 15th century. The Marian legends of the infancy gospels, especially as incorporated by Jacobus de Voragine in *The Golden Legend* (A.D. 1298), became widely known. These stories inspired Giotto to paint "The Exclusion of Joachim from the Temple," Raphael to paint "The Betrothal of the Virgin," and Titian to paint "The Presentation of the Virgin in the Temple." They have contributed to the development of the Roman exaltation of Mary in no insignificant measure.

The Aquarian Gospel, produced by Levi Dowling (1844-1911) and derived in part from the Protevangelium, and numerous other examples described by Edgar Goodspeed demonstrate that the motivation which inspired the creation of the apocryphal gospels is still very much alive.

Bibliography.–*I. General:* C. Tischendorf, *Evangelia Apocrypha* (2nd ed. 1876, repr. 1966); *ANT*; H. I. Bell and T. C. Skeat, *Fragments of an Unknown Gospel* (1935); R. M. Grant and D. N. Freedman, *Secret Sayings of Jesus* (1960); H-S; J. Finegan, *Hidden Records of the Life of Jesus* (1969); F. F. Bruce, *Jesus and Christian Origins Outside the NT* (1974).

II. Heretical Gospels: C. A. Baynes, *A Coptic Gnostic Treatise Contained in the Codex Brucianus* (1933); W. C. Till, *Die gnostischen Schriften des koptischen Papyrus Berolinensis 8502* (1955); C. Schmidt and W. C. Till, *Koptisch-gnostische Schriften I* (3rd ed. 1959, repr. 1962); R. M. Grant, *Gnosticism* (1961).

III. Nag Hammadi Gospels: A. General: J. Doresse, *Secret Books of the Egyptian Gnostics* (Eng. tr. 1960); A. K. Helmbold, *Nag Hammadi Gnostic Texts and the Bible* (1967); D. M. Scholer,

Nag Hammadi Bibliography 1948-1969 (1971); "Bibliographia Gnostica Supplementum," *Nov.Test.*, 13 (1971), 332-336; 14 (1972), 312-331; 15 (1973), 327-345; W. Foerster, ed., *Gnosis II: Coptic and Mandaean Sources* (1974).

B. Gospel of Thomas: G. Quispel, *VC*, 11 (1957), 189-207; A. Guillaumont *et al.*, eds., *Gospel according to Thomas* (1959); G. W. MacRae, *CBQ*, 22 (1960), 56-71; R. McL. Wilson, *HTR*, 73 (1960), 231-250; B. Gärtner, *Theology of the Gospel according to Thomas* (1961); R. E. Brown, *NTS*, 9 (1963), 155-177; G. Quispel, *NTS*, 12 (1966), 371-382; W. H. C. Frend, *JTS*, 18 (1967), 13-26.

C. Gospel of Philip: E. Segelberg, *Numen*, 7 (1960), 189-200; R. M. Grant, *VC*, 15 (1961), 129-140; R. McL. Wilson, *Gospel of Philip* (1963).

D. Gospel of Truth: M. Malinine *et al.*, *Evangelium Veritatis* (1956); *Evangelium Veritatis Supplementum* (1961); E. Segelberg, *Orientalia Suecana*, 8 (1959), 1-42; K. Grobel, *Gospel of Truth* (1960).

E. Gospel of the Egyptians: J. Doresse, *Journal asiatique*, 254 (1966), 317-435; A. Böhlig, *Muséon*, 80 (1967), 5-26, 365-377; H.-M. Schenke, *NTS*, 16 (1970), 196-208; A. Böhlig and F. Wisse, *Gospel of the Egyptians* (1975).

IV. A Secret Gospel of Mark: M. Smith, *Clement of Alexandria and a Secret Gospel of Mark* (1973); *Secret Gospel* (1973); J. A. Fitzmyer, *America*, June 23, 1973, 570-72; Aug. 4, 1973, 64f.; H. Merkel, *ZTK*, 71 (1974), 123-144; E. Yamauchi, *Christian Scholar's Review*, 4 (1974), 238-251.

V. Modern Apocryphal Gospels: E. J. Goodspeed, *Modern Apocrypha* (1956).

E. M. YAMAUCHI

APOLLONIA ap-ə-lō'nē-ə [Gk. *Apollōnia*]. A town in Mygdonia, a district in Macedonia, to be distinguished from the many other cities bearing this name. It was situated a little S of Lake Bolbe, on the Via Egnatia, the great Roman road leading from the coast of the Adriatic to the river Hebrus (*Maritza*), one of the main military and commercial highways of the empire: it lay between Amphipolis and Thessalonica, a day's journey (Livy xlv.28) or about 30 Roman mi. (27.6 mi., 44.4 km.) from the former and 38 (35 mi., 56.2 km.) from the latter. The foundation of the town may perhaps be dated *ca.* 432 B.C.; in any case, coins are extant that attest its existence in the 4th cent. B.C. (B.V. Head, *Historia Numorum* [n.d.], p. 181). Paul and Silas passed through the town on their journey from Philippi to Thessalonica, but apparently did not stay there (Acts 17:1).

See Pauly-Wissowa II/1, 114.

M. N. TOD
R. P. MEYE

APOLLONIUS ap-ə-lō'nē-əs [Gk. *Apollōnios*]. A common name among the Syro-Macedonians.

1. Governor of Coelesyria under Seleucus Philopater (2 Macc. 3:5ff.). In v. 5 the AV and NEB, following the Greek text, read "son of Thras(a)eus," while the RSV has "of Tarsus." By his authority in that province he supported Simon the governor of the temple at Jerusalem against Onias the high priest. He was also chief minister of state to Seleucus. But on the accession of Antiochus Epiphanes, Apollonius, in some way incurring the disfavor of the new king, left Syria and retired to Miletus.

2. A son of **1** who, while his father resided at Miletus, was brought up at Rome along with Demetrius son of Seleucus Philopator, and at that time held as a hostage by the Romans. This Apollonius lived in great intimacy with Demetrius, who, on recovering the crown of Syria, made him governor of Coelesyria and Phoenicia, the same position his father held under Seleucus Philopator. He seems to have been continued in the same capacity by Alexander (1 Macc. 10:69), but he revolted from him to embrace the interest of Demetrius.

3. Son of Menestheus, and favorite and chief minister of Antiochus Epiphanes (2 Macc. 4:21). He went as ambassador from Antiochus, first to Rome (Livy xlii.6) and afterward to Ptolemy Philometor, king of Egypt.

This is generally held to be the same man who is said to have been over the tribute (1 Macc 1:29; 2 Macc. 5:24) and who, on the return of Antiochus from his last expedition into Egypt, was sent with a detachment of 22,000 men to destroy Jerusalem. He attacked the Jews on the sabbath and killed great numbers of them (2 Macc. 5:24-27).

4. Governor of Samaria in the time of Antiochus Epiphanes. He was slain in battle by Judas Maccabeus (1 Macc. 3:10f.; Josephus *Ant.* xii.7.10).

5. Son of Gennaeus (2 Macc. 12:2). As governor of a toparchy in Palestine under Antiochus Eupator he proved a bitter enemy of the Jews.

J. HUTCHISON

APOLLOPHANES ap-ə-lof'ə-nēz [Gk. *Apollophanēs*]. A Syrian killed by Judas Maccabeus (2 Macc. 10:37).

APOLLOS ə-pol'əs [Gk. *Apollōs*, abbr. of *Apollōnios* (Apollonius)]. A Jew of Alexandria (Acts 18:24) who reached Ephesus in the summer of A.D. 54, while Paul was on his third missionary journey, and there "spoke and taught accurately the things concerning Jesus" (18:25).

That he was eminently fitted for the task is indicated by his being a "learned man," "mighty in the scriptures," "fervent in spirit," "instructed in the way of the Lord" (vv. 24f.). His teaching was incomplete however, in that he knew "only the baptism of John" (v. 25); and this has given rise to some controversy. According to Blass, his information was derived from a written gospel which reached Alexandria, but it was more probably the fruits of what Apollos had heard, either directly or from others, of the preaching of John the Baptist at Bethany beyond Jordan (cf. Jn. 1:28).

Upon receiving further instruction from Priscilla and Aquila (Acts 18:26), Apollos extended his mission to Achaia, being encouraged thereto by the brethren of Ephesus (v. 27). In Achaia "he helped them much that had believed through grace; for he powerfully confuted the Jews, and that publicly, showing by the scriptures that Jesus was the Christ" (vv. 27f.). During Apollos' absence in Achaia, Paul had reached Ephesus and learned of what had been taught by Apollos there (19:1). As Paul was informed that the Ephesians still knew nothing of the baptism of the Spirit (vv. 2-4), it is probable that Apollos had not imparted to his hearers the further instruction he had received from Priscilla and Aquila, but had departed for Achaia shortly after receiving it. Paul remained upward of two years among the Ephesians (vv. 8,10), and in the spring of A.D. 57 he wrote the First Epistle to the Corinthians. By this time Apollos was once more in Ephesus (cf. 1 Cor. 16:12).

It is incredible that this Epistle of Paul could have been prompted by any feelings of jealousy or animosity on his part against Apollos. It was rather the outcome of discussion between the two regarding the critical situation then existing in Corinth. The mission of Apollos had met with a certain success, but the breeding of faction, which that very success, through the slight discrepancies in his teaching (cf. 1 Cor. 1:12; 3:4) with that of Paul or of Cephas, had engendered, was utterly alien to his intentions. The party spirit was as distasteful to Apollos as it was to Paul, and made him reluctant to return to the scene of his former labors even at the desire of Paul himself (16:12). The Epistle voiced the indignation of both. Paul welcomed the cooperation of Apollos (3:6: "I planted, Apollos watered"). It was not against his fellow evangelist that he fulminated, but against the petty spirit of those who loved faction more than truth, who saw not that both he and

Apollos came among them as "God's fellow workers" (3:9), the common servants of the one Lord and Savior Jesus Christ. This view is also borne out by the tenor of Clement's Epistle to the Corinthians; nor does it conflict with the passages 1 Cor. 12:1-7; 2 Cor. 3:1; 11:16, where Paul seems to allude to Apollos' eloquence, wisdom, and letter of commendation. Paul wrote thus not in order to disparage Apollos, but to affirm that, even without these incidental advantages, he would yield to none in the preaching of Christ crucified.

The last mention of Apollos is in Titus, where he is recommended along with Zenas to Titus (3:13). He was then on a journey through Crete (1:5), and was probably the bearer of the Epistle. The time of this is uncertain, as the writing of Titus, though generally admitted to have been after Paul's release from imprisonment at Rome, has been variously placed at A.D. 64-67. C. M. KERR

APOLLYON ə-pol'ē-ən [Gk. *Apollýōn* < *apollýō*–'destroy']. A name found only in Rev. 9:11, as a translation of the Hebrew name "Abaddon," designating an angel or prince of the lower world. In the OT ABADDON and the accompanying terms Death and Sheol are personified (as in Job 28:22) and represented as living beings who speak and act (cf. Rev. 6:8).

The starting point of the Apocalyptist's use of "Apollyon" is to be found in the fundamental meaning of "Abaddon" as moral destruction in the underworld, together with the occasional personification of kindred terms in the OT. The imagery was in general terms familiar, while the NT writer felt perfectly free to vary the usage to suit his own particular purposes.

(1) Since Apollyon is a personification he is not to be identified with Satan (cf. Rev. 9:1, where Satan seems to be clearly indicated) or with any other being to whom historical existence and definite characteristics are ascribed. He is the central figure in a mental picture of evil forces represented as originating in the world of lost spirits and allowed to operate destructively in human life. They are pictured as locusts, but on an enlarged scale and with the addition of many features inconsistent with the strict application of the figure (see vv. 7-10). The intention is, by the multiplication of images which the author does not appear to harmonize, to convey the impression of great power and far-reaching destructiveness.

(2) This interpretation finds additional support in the writer's significant departure from the familiar usage. In the OT the *place* of destruction is personified; in Rev. 9:11, personal forces *issue* from the Abyss, of which the presiding genius is Destruction in person. The seer's picture is equally independent of the tradition represented by the Talmud (*Shabbath* 55f.), where Abaddon is personified as jointly with Death president over six destroying angels. These modifications are evidently due to the exigencies of the pictorial form. It is clearly impossible to portray forces proceeding from the place of ruin as in charge of the place itself.

The importance of the conception of Apollyon to the completeness of the picture should not be overlooked. It is intended to represent these forces as having a certain principle of internal unity and as possessors of the power of effective leadership.

As to the specific significance of the vision of the locusts as a whole it is not easy to reach a conclusion. H. B. Swete suggests (comm. [1908] *in loc.*) that "the locusts of the abyss may be the memories of the past brought home at times of divine visitation; they hurt by recalling forgotten sins." It seems to us more probable that it represents an actual historical movement, past or to come, demoniacal in origin and character, human in the mode of its operation and the sphere of its influence, used by God for a scourge upon mankind and kept in restraint by His grace and power. L. M. SWEET

APOLOGETICS, BIBLICAL [<Gk. *apologētikós* < *apó*–'from' + *lógos*–'speech']. Passages in the Bible dealing with the knowledge of God or the veracity of the system of biblical faith, or discussing criteria for establishing the biblical faith.

I. Old Testament
   A. Foundations of OT Theism
   B. Yahweh as the Living God
II. New Testament
   A. Vocabulary of Apologetics
   B. Particularized Apologetics of the NT
      1. Christological
         a. Christianity *v.* Judaism
         b. Christianity *v.* Philosophy
      2. Revelational
         a. General Revelation and Sin
         b. Soteric Revelation

I. Old Testament.–*A. Foundations of OT Theism.* The OT contains a rich theistic interpretation of God and the world, constructed around the three fundamental concepts of election, revelation, and redemption.

It is the clear witness of the OT that Israel became God's people through an election of grace (cf. Dt. 1–10). Israel was not great nor holy, but small and stubborn (Dt. 9:6). Her history began concretely in the call of Abraham, which in turn was reaffirmed and enlarged in the revelation to Moses. Therefore, the root of OT theism is the gracious election of Israel (cf. H. H. Rowley, *Biblical Doctrine of Election* [1950]).

This election became manifest through divine revelation: "the God of glory appeared to our father Abraham" (Acts 7:2). The knowledge of God possessed by Abraham was founded in revelation, and this tiny stream of patriarchal revelation eventually became the great river of revelation of the major and minor prophets.

Election and revelation are incomplete without redemption. The fundamental redeeming act of God in the history of Israel was her deliverance from Egypt in a display of God's power and a manifestation of His glory.

The negative conclusions at this point are: (1) Israel did not first understand Yahweh as Creator and then as a consequence come to know Him as Elector, Revealer, and Redeemer; rather it was the other way around (cf. Vriezen, p. 187); (2) Israel's faith was not philosophically grounded in the sense of being a product of a rational interpretation of nature, religion, or experience.

B. Yahweh as the Living God. Israel's faith was held within a polytheistic group of cultures. Speculative atheism was hardly known in the ancient world; the atheism referred to in the OT (Jer. 5:2; Ps. 10:4; 14:1) is a so-called practical atheism. The OT emphasizes differentiation of the God of Israel from the pagan gods and religions of the surrounding cultures (cf. G. E. Wright, *The OT Against Its Environment* [1950]). The OT speaks much more of the living God than of the true God. A living God does something; He possesses power; He is spirit; He can answer by fire (1 K. 18:24). The pagan gods are essentially lifeless, breathless, and powerless.

(1) The God of Israel is a living God because He is the Lord of history. The living God can control the affairs of men and the destinies of nations. According to the taunt of Elijah (1 K. 18:27), the lifeless god is always meditating, or gone away, or on a journey, or asleep and in need of being awakened. But the living god can turn the heart of kings.

He can make Nebuchadnezzar live like a beast until he recognizes that the Lord of Israel rules the kingdoms of men (Dnl. 4:25).

Furthermore, the living Lord knows what will come to pass, whereas the idol is speechless about the future. Isaiah taunts the gods to declare the future so that "we may know that you are gods" (41:23). He calls upon them to act in history—to do good or do harm, so that "we may be dismayed or terrified" (v. 23). But the gods are lifeless, hence powerless; so Isaiah says, "Behold, you are nothing" (v. 24).

(2) The God of Israel is the living God because He can speak. The pagan gods are lifeless and therefore speechless. Habakkuk writes: "Woe to him who says to a wooden thing, Wake; to a dumb stone, Arise! Can this give revelation? Behold it is overlaid with gold and silver, and there is no breath in it" (2:19).

OT theism is therefore firmly grounded in revelation: in the remarkable revelatory person of the prophet, in the revelatory modalities of dreams, visions, and the divine speaking, and in the revelatory content (conceptions of God and of morality, and the schemata of blessing/judgment and prophecy/fulfillment).

(3) The God of Israel is the living God because He is Creator of all. According to the fullest revelation of the prophets He is the one and only God. There are no others. No representation may be made of Him and no idol may be worshiped, for in both instances His spirituality would be misrepresented. He is the Creator and must never be confused in any way with His creation.

In contrast the pagan idols are constructed by men from materials (cf. Ps. 96:5; Jer. 10:1-16). Such gods need nourishment from their worshipers; if they would change residence they must be picked up and carried. But the God of Israel is the sustainer of his worshipers.

God's action in history, God's revelation through his prophets, and God's creation and control of the universe are the criteria that show Him to be the living Lord, whereas the pagan gods and idols are speechless, powerless, and helpless. It is therefore the presupposition of the entire corpus of OT writings that the God of Israel is the true and living God, and that the faith He founded in Israel corresponds to the reality as it is in Yahweh.

***II. New Testament.**–A. Vocabulary of Apologetics.* Although the word apologetics [Gk. *apologētikós*] does not appear as such in the NT, the NT uses the vocabulary of apologetics, which is derived from Greek legal practice, in a popular and technical way. In Greek law an accusation (*katēgoría*) was lodged against a person, who then attempted to vindicate himself with a reply, an answer, a defense (*apología*, vb. *apologéomai*). If a person had no defense against the accusation, he was called *anapológētos*, "without excuse," a term Paul uses in Rom. 1:20; 2:1.

A classic example is the case of Socrates. The accusation (*katēgoría*) against him was that he was an atheist—in that he did not accept the gods of the state—and that he was a corrupter of the youth of Athens. To this charge Socrates made his famous defense (*apología*), preserved in Plato's dialogue *Apology*.

Paul's speeches before the various officials are called apologies (Acts 22:1; 24:10; 25:8; 26:1,24). Peter says that Christians ought always to be ready to give an *apología* for the hope that is within them (1 Pet. 3:15). Paul says that he is set for the *apología* of the gospel (Phil. 1:16). Jesus told his disciples not to frame their defense ahead of time whenever they might be brought into court for loyalty to Him, but that at that time they were to trust the Holy Spirit to make His defense through them (Lk. 12:11; 21:14).

The translators of the LXX made little use of this vocabulary. In the rare times they did, it was to translate the Heb. *rîḇ*, "to strive, contend, dispute, conduct a legal suit" (cf. B. Gemser, "The *rîb*- or Controversy-pattern in Hebrew Mentality," in M. Noth and D. Winton Thomas, eds., *Wisdom in Israel and the Ancient Near East* [*SVT*, 3, 1955], pp. 120-137).

B. Particularized Apologetics of the NT. The basic apologetic stance of the NT is the same as that of the OT. The writers of the NT believed that God did act in Israel's history, that the prophetic word is God's truth, that Yahweh is the Creator of the universe, and that idolatry is worthy of the severest judgments (cf. 1 Cor. 8:1-6; Eph. 2:1f.). However, upon this foundation the NT authors constructed a more particularized apologetic centering in the two foci of Jesus Christ and special revelation.

1. Christological. The Scriptures are nowhere concerned with the theistic proof or proofs for the existence of God, such as are found throughout the history of philosophy and theology: first, because the knowledge of God in Scripture is essentially revelational, thus displacing the function of such proofs; second, because the knowledge of God's being from the human side is everywhere intuitional (cf. Mt. 5:8 — hence the immense scriptural data on hearing and seeing, which are intuitional terms); and third, because such a simple or abstract statement as "God is" cannot begin to carry all the weight necessary for a meaningful theology and religion. Therefore the emphasis in this article, as in Calvin, is on the knowledge of God rather than on the existence of God.

The NT expresses often and forcefully that the knowledge of God is brought fully and authentically in Jesus Christ by virtue of His being God manifest in the flesh (cf. Jn. 1:1, 14, 18). Therefore the root of the NT apologetic is christological and incarnational.

a. Christianity v. *Judaism.* This controversy began with the debates between Jesus and the Jewish leaders. The issue behind the particular controversies was the authority of Jesus Christ; and behind that was the fundamental question whether or not Jesus Christ was the Messiah, the Son of man, with whose appearing came the fulfilment of the OT and the inbreaking of the kingdom of God. It was at root a christological controversy.

The apologetic method of Christ in these controversies was fivefold: (1) He appealed to the OT as being on His side rather than that of His opponents; (2) He argued from logic, e.g., when He demonstrated the logical absurdity in saying that He was in league with the devil in casting out demons (Mt. 12:22-25); (3) He argued from analogy in His parables and in various sayings; once, e.g., He argued that if it is right for a man to rescue a sheep on the sabbath, it ought to be more than right to heal a man on the sabbath (Mt. 12:9-12); (4) He appealed to the verifying function of signs (cf. Jn. 2:18-22; Lk. 7:18-23); (5) He placed great emphasis on the spiritual hearing of the Word of God as a self-authenticating experience (e.g., Jn. 5:24; 10:3; Mt. 11:15).

The debate with Judaism was carried on in Stephen's ministry (Acts 6f.), in some of Paul's letters (Romans, Galatians, 2 Corinthians, and Philippians), and in Hebrews, everywhere having this christological basis. The promises made to the fathers are fulfilled in Jesus Christ; the full knowledge of God shines in Jesus' face, not Moses' (2 Cor. 3f.); the shadows and types of the old covenant find their substance in Jesus Christ; the new covenant promised by Jeremiah was ratified in Jesus Christ; the sacrificial intentions of the Levitical system are fulfilled and ended in Christ crucified. Thus the great themes of the old covenant, the great institutions, and the representative persons find their consummation in Jesus

APOLOGETICS, BIBLICAL

Christ. The Jewish person with seeing eyes thus finds in Jesus Christ the complete vindication of the Christian religion, for in His person and work He sums up the entire reality of the old covenant (cf. 2 Cor. 3:7-18).

b. Christianity v. *Philosophy.* According to Paul, the norm for all knowledge of God is the knowledge of God in Jesus Christ (cf. 2 Cor. 10:5; Phil. 3:10; Col. 2:2f.). In Jesus Christ, the Lord of glory and the image of the invisible God, God has become fully known for the spiritual purposes of the human race; and, consequently, any proposed philosophical knowledge of God cannot be considered to compete with the knowledge of God in Jesus Christ. Thus on Mars' Hill Paul accuses the audience, which included Stoics and Epicureans, of ignorance; and he sets out the true knowledge of God as that known by creation (Acts 17:24) and Jesus Christ (17:31). In 1 Cor. 1:20-22 he claims that the wise men of Greece have produced theological foolishness, for in their proposed wisdom they failed to know God (note Paul does not speak of the existence of God, but of the knowledge of God). In 1 Cor. 2:1-6 Paul emphatically declares that Christian faith does not rest upon the methodology followed by the philosophers. Christianity does not rest upon "lofty words or wisdom," nor upon "plausible words of wisdom," nor upon the "wisdom of men."

In a passage replete with military metaphor (2 Cor. 10:4f.) Paul says that in the contest for theological truth the Christian is guided by the knowledge of God as it is in Jesus Christ. In contesting Gnosticism in the Colossian letter, Paul again makes the issue one of tempting human philosophy or beguiling human wisdom over against the full knowledge of God in Jesus Christ (2:4, 8). Christ is the only image of the invisible God. Only in Christ is the vast storehouse of the true knowledge of God (cf. Col. 1:15-20; 2:1-4; 2:8–3:5).

According to Paul the Resurrection put the status of the person of Christ beyond dispute. The early Church had composed a list of "official" appearances of the risen Lord (1 Cor. 15:3-11). Remarkably, this list did not include the appearances to the women, but did include the appearance to Paul. This also constituted the objective basis for Paul's apostleship (1 Cor. 9:1). The Resurrection marked out Jesus Christ as the powerful Son of God, thus setting the issue above equivocation (cf. G. Kock, *Die Auferstehung Jesu Christi* [1959]).

The christological knowledge of God is opposed to specific humanly constructed philosophies that compete against it, not to rationality as such. The elaborate emphasis of the NT on truth is not to be overlooked. It is referred to more than 170 times in the NT. Many traditional forms of logic were employed by Jesus and Paul. In the debates of Jesus with His contemporaries He made repeated appeals to the rational powers of His hearers ("What do you think?"— Mt. 17:25; 18:12; 22:17; Lk. 10:36). Paul carries on profound discourses in his Epistles, leading one to conclude that he expected his readers to use their minds to the fullest. Writing to the Corinthians he says: "I speak as to sensible men [Gk. *phrónimos,* "intelligent, wise"]; judge for yourselves what I say" (1 Cor. 10:15). For the balance between theology and philosophy, cf. *CD,* I/2, 607-609, 727-736.

2. *Revelational.* The NT teaches that our knowledge of God is revelational. The existence of God is neither rationally demonstrated nor presumed, but revealed.

a. General Revelation and Sin. The NT teaches that all men are under a general revelation of God. In Acts 10:35 Peter says that men in all nations may fear God and do right, which implies some witness of God's being and holiness. In Acts 14:17 Paul says that God's witness to the gentile world was His goodness in the fruitfulness of the earth; in Acts 17 he promulgates the theses that man is God's offspring, that He is near the seeking pagan, and that He is the Creator, who gives life to all things (vv. 24-28). In Rom. 1:19f. Paul argues that God reveals Himself through the things He has created; and in Rom. 1:32; 2:6-11, 14f., 26-29, he implies that Gentiles have some apprehension of God's moral order (cf. B. Gärtner, *The Areopagus Speech and Natural Revelation* [Eng. tr. 1955]).

Sinful man, according to the NT, perverts this general revelation. The argument of Paul in Rom. 1:19ff. is that the knowledge of God in general revelation is not honored by sinners but perverted. The Athenians are accused of ignorance of God (Acts 17:23). Idol worshipers are in ignorance of God as Creator and of Christ as co-Creator (1 Cor. 8:6f.). The pagan nations of the world have walked in their own erring ways (Acts 14:16). Man outside of Israel and the Church leads a Godless and Christless existence (cf. 1 Cor. 8:1-9; Gal. 4:1; Eph. 2:11f.; 1 Thess. 1:9). In that they pervert a valid general revelation, they are not innocent but without excuse (Gk. *anapológētos,* Rom. 1:20; 2:1).

Sinful men pervert general revelation and reject special revelation. The sinner is blind (2 Cor. 4:3f.); he possesses a fleshly mind hostile to the truth of God (Rom. 8:7); he considers the gospel foolishness (1 Cor. 1:18, 23); and he has no powers to apprehend a spiritual revelation (1 Cor. 2:14; cf. also R. Mehl, *La Condition du philosophe chrétien* [1947]).

b. Soteric Revelation. Man's recovery of a true knowledge of God is through soteric (i.e., healing, saving, and restoring) revelation. Man in sin does not have the will or the means to recover a true knowledge of God. The special revelation of God is "a secret wisdom of God" (1 Cor. 2:7). Its content could never be deduced from man's religious speculations (v. 9), and his natural mind is not at all favorably disposed toward such a revelation (v. 14).

This special revelation is communicated through the Holy Spirit. The Spirit knows the depths of God (1 Cor. 2:10) and the thoughts of God (v. 11). The depths and thoughts of God known by the Spirit may be communicated to Christians, who have received Him. This is what it means to have the mind of Christ (v. 16). This is the direct epistemological linkage in the communication of soteric revelation from God's mind to the human mind.

The content of soteric revelation is Jesus Christ and His cross. Paul speaks of the "word of the cross" (1 Cor. 1:18) when he opposes human wisdom. The "word of the cross" is the "testimony of God" (1 Cor. 2:1) and "spiritual truths" (v. 13) and "the mind of Christ" (v. 16). The intention of special revelation is to heal and restore; therefore, its content must be redemptive. In broad terms, special revelation is Christ crucified (Gal. 3:1). In this gospel there is the power of God unto salvation (Rom. 1:16). Special revelation cannot be discussed apart from its concrete expression in Jesus Christ as Redeemer, nor can apologetics be truly Christian if it does not draw into its discussion the apologetic significance of both special revelation and the word of the cross.

Special or soteric revelation became embodied in the NT. Just as the Church of the OT eventually cast her revelations into the documents of the ancient Scriptures, so the Church of the NT eventually cast her revelation in the form of Scripture. The word of the cross eventually became transcribed on papyrus just as the words of the divine Logos were eventually embodied in the records of the Evangelists. For all concrete theological and apologetical purposes, the NT is for the Church the special, soteric revelation of God.

Soteric revelation becomes actualized in sinners by the witness of the Holy Spirit. If human depravity causes the sinner to pervert general revelation and reject soteric revelation, something more powerful than his depravity must function if he is to be saved. At this point the general work of the Holy Spirit and His particular work of witnessing within the human heart come into consideration. In this witness, depravity is overcome, illumination takes place, and the believing sinner has a full assurance (Gk. *plērophoría*) of the truth of the gospel (cf. B. Ramm, *Witness of the Spirit* [1959]).

Bibliography.–In addition to the works cited in the text, for apologetics in the OT, see E. Jacob, *Theology of the OT* (Eng. tr. 1958); Y. Kaufmann, *Religion of Israel* (Eng. tr. 1960); *TDNT,* III, *s.v.* κτίζω (Foerster); IV, *s.v.* λέγω (Debrunner, *et al.*); G. A. F. Knight, *A Christian Theology of the OT* (1959); H. W. Robinson, *Inspiration and Revelation in the OT* (1946); E. C. Rust, *Nature and Man in Biblical Thought* (1953); T. C. Vriezen, *Outline of OT Theology* (Eng. tr. 1958).

For apologetics in the NT, see G. C. Berkouwer, *General Revelation* (Eng. tr. 1955); *Evangelisches Kirchenlexicon,* I, *s.v.* "Apologeten" (B. Lohse), "Apologetik" (K. Stürmer); A. D. Heffern, *Apology and Polemic in the NT* (1922); E. Kamlah, *et. al.,* "Apologetik," *RGG,* I, 477-496; J. Macgregor, *Studies in the History of Christian Apologetics; NT and Post-Apostolic* (1894); B. Ramm, *Pattern of Religious Authority* (1957); *Special Revelation and the Word of God* (1960); *The God Who Makes a Difference* (1973); E. F. Scott, *Apologetic of the NT* (1907).

B. RAMM

APOSTASY [Heb. *m^e^šûḇâ*] (Jer. 2:19; 5:6); AV BACKSLIDING; [Gk. *parapíptō*] (He. 6:6); AV, NEB, FALL AWAY. Defection from the faith. The English word occurs only in the passages above (thrice in the RSV, twice in the NEB); the Gk. *apostasía* occurs also in Acts 21:21 ("forsake") and 2 Thess. 2:3 ("rebellion"; AV "falling away"). But the concept of apostasy is found throughout Scripture.

"Forsaking the Lord" was the characteristic and oft-recurring sin of the chosen people, especially in their contact with idolatrous nations. It constituted their supreme national peril. The tendency appeared in their earliest history, as abundantly seen in the warnings and prohibitions of the laws of Moses (Ex. 20:3f., 23; Dt. 6:14; 11:16). The fearful consequences of religious and moral apostasy appear in the curses pronounced against this sin, on Mt. Ebal, by the representatives of six of the tribes of Israel, elected by Moses (Dt. 27:13-26; 28:15-68). So wayward was the heart of Israel even in the years immediately following the national emancipation, in the wilderness, that Joshua found it necessary to repledge the entire nation to a new fidelity to the Lord and to their original covenant before they were permitted to enter the Promised Land (Josh. 24:1-28). Infidelity to this covenant blighted the nation's prospects and growth during the time of the judges (Jgs. 2:11-15; 10:6, 10, 13; 1 S. 12:10). It was the cause of prolific and ever increasing evil, civic and moral, from Solomon's day to the Assyrian and Babylonian captivities. Many of the kings of the divided kingdom apostatized, leading the people, as in the case of Rehoboam, into the grossest forms of idolatry and immorality (1 K. 14:22-24; 2 Ch. 12:1). Conspicuous examples of such royal apostasy are Jeroboam (1 K. 12:28-32); Ahab (16:30-33); Ahaziah (22:51-53); Jehoram (2 Ch. 21:6, 10, 12-15); Ahaz (28:1-4); Manasseh (33:1-9); Amon (33:22). *See* IDOLATRY. Prophecy originated as a divine and imperative protest against this historic tendency to defection from the religion of the Lord.

Paul was falsely accused of teaching the Jews apostasy from Moses (Acts 21:21); he predicted the great apostasy from Christianity, foretold by Jesus (Mt. 24:10-12), which would precede "the Day of the Lord" (2 Thess. 2:2f.). Apostasy, not in name but in fact, meets scathing rebuke in the Epistle of Jude, e.g., the apostasy of angels (v. 6). It is foretold, with warnings, as sure to abound in the latter days (1 Tim. 4:1-3; 2 Thess. 2:3; 2 Pet. 3:17).

Causes of apostasy include persecution (Mt. 24:9f.); false teachers (24:11); temptation (Lk. 8:13); worldliness (2 Tim. 4:4); defective knowledge of Christ (1 Jn. 2:19); moral lapse (He. 6:4-6); forsaking worship and spiritual living (10:25-31); unbelief (3:12).

Some additional biblical examples: Saul (1 S. 15:11); Amaziah (2 Ch. 25:14, 27); many disciples (Jn. 6:66); Hymenaeus and Alexander (1 Tim. 1:19f.); Demas (2 Tim. 4:10). For further illustration see Dt. 13:13; Zeph. 1:4-6; Gal. 5:4; 2 Pet. 2:20f.

In classical Greek, apostasy signified revolt from a military commander. In the Roman Catholic Church, it denotes abandonment of religious orders; renunciation of ecclesiastical authority; defection from the faith. The persecutions of the early Christian centuries forced many to deny Christian discipleship and to signify their apostasy by offering incense to a heathen deity or blaspheming the name of Christ. The emperor Julian, who probably never vitally embraced the Christian faith, is known in history as "the Apostate," having renounced Christianity for paganism soon after his accession to the throne.

An apostate's defection from the faith may be *intellectual,* as in the case of Ernst Haeckel, who, because of his materialistic philosophy, publicly and formally renounced Christianity and the Church; or it may be *moral and spiritual,* as with Judas, who barely betrayed his Lord.

See *Jew.Enc., s.v.* D. M. PRATT

APOSTLE [Gk. *apóstolos* < *apostéllō*–'send' (with stress on the commission and authorization of the sender)]. A missionary, envoy, ambassador; in the NT, one of those who, having seen the risen Christ, is a witness of His resurrection, and, commissioned by Him, preaches the gospel to all the nations.

In classical usage the Greek verb *apostéllō* generally referred to the sending of a fleet or an embassy, but is also used by Epictetus to describe Zeus's sending a teacher of philosophy as his messenger. This would make the messenger a minister of the god, but scarcely, as with Paul, his bondservant. OT parallels to the office have been sought in God's sending Moses and Aaron to Pharaoh, Elijah to Ahab, and Isaiah to callous Israel, as well as in the religious consciousness of Jeremiah. Ahijah was an apostle with hard tidings for Jeroboam (1 K. 14:6).

Rabbinic Judaism used the Heb. *šālî(a)ḥ* or *šālû(a)ḥ* to describe an agent authorized by someone else to act for the sender in personal, legal, or financial matters. In such cases a man's ambassador was as himself (cf. 1 S. 25:40ff.; 2 S. 10:1ff.). If unable to complete his task, the embassy had no authority to commit the job to another. When Paul started to Damascus with letters of accreditation, he may have been a *šālî(a)ḥ* of the Sanhedrin, as were later emissaries of Judaism who opposed the Christian message (Justin *Dial.* 17, 108). The rabbinical concept, however, lacked the religious missionary obligation that is essential for the Christian apostle (Rom. 1:14-17; 15:16). The nearest to a Christian equivalent of the rabbinical concept seems to be the apostles sent by congregations to bring help to Paul (Phil. 2:25) or to the poor saints in Jerusalem (2 Cor. 8:23).

I. NT Usage
II. The Twelve
III. Paul
IV. Apostolic Authority

I. NT Usage.–There is some variety in the NT usage of the term "apostle." The supreme example of an apostle is Jesus Christ Himself. There is also a broad usage referring to many of His missionaries, but most frequently the word is applied to the Twelve and to Paul.

Jesus Christ is the Apostle and High Priest of our profession (He. 3:1), the Son through whom God has spoken His final word to men (He. 1:1), the High Priest who has made propitiation for the sins of His people once for all (He. 2:17; 9:26). Whoever receives Him, receives Him that sent Him (Mk. 9:37). As the Father sent Jesus, He has also sent His apostles to preach the gospel to all the world (Jn. 20:21; 1 Clem. 42), nor are the disciples to expect a better treatment than that accorded their Master (Mt. 10:24f.; Jn. 13:16).

The expression "all the apostles" in 1 Cor. 15:7 seems to include more than the twelve referred to in v. 5. Here, as in Gal. 1:15, James is designated as an apostle; and he worthily performed the duties of that office for a generation as a home missionary to Jerusalem, as the chief minister of the church there, and as a witness for Jesus to Jewry. Barnabas is designated an apostle in Acts 14 (cf. 11:22f.; 13:1-4), and Junias and Andronicus, kinsmen of Paul, in Rom. 16:7. In 1 Cor. 3:5, Apollos is called a minister (Gk. *diákonos*); hence he is hardly to be included as an apostle in 4:6, 9. Likewise Timothy is a brother, a minister, and a fellow laborer in 1 Thess. 3:2, and he is probably not designated an apostle in 2:6. The wider circle is intimated in 1 Cor. 9:5 and is presupposed in Didache 11:4-6. Paul's reference to false apostles in 2 Cor. 11:13 certainly goes beyond the Twelve and himself. In this broad usage, then, an apostle was a first-century evangelist who bore witness to the resurrection of Christ, an itinerant missionary sent by Him to make disciples of all nations.

In most of the approximately eighty cases in which the word "apostle" occurs in the NT, it refers to the Twelve or to Paul. Their unique place is based upon the resurrected Jesus' having appeared to them and having commissioned them to proclaim the gospel as the eschatological action of God in Christ. As witnesses of Jesus' resurrection (Mt. 28; Lk. 24; Acts 1:22; 10:41; 1 Cor. 9:1; 15:4) and sole witnesses of His ascension (Acts 1:9-13), they are the guarantors of His resurrection, even as the resurrection is the demonstration that He is the Messiah of prophecy and the Lord of glory (Acts 2:36; Rom. 1:4). Moreover, the risen Lord has particularly empowered them by the Holy Spirit for their whole ministry of witnessing, preaching, working miracles, establishing and guiding churches (Jn. 20:22; Acts 1:8; 2 Cor. 12:12; Rom. 15; 1 Cor. 2), and bearing hardships, shame, and suffering for Jesus' sake (Acts 5:40f.; 12:1-4; Phil. 3:8; 1 Cor. 9:1). In the case of the Twelve, an additional qualification for their special apostleship is having had fellowship with the Lord from the baptism of John until Jesus was received up from them (Acts 1:21f.); thus they had personal knowledge of the Incarnate Word.

The apostles are regarded as setting the norms of doctrine and fellowship (Acts 2:42), the marking posts (Gal. 2:9), the rule by which one must measure his preaching (Gal. 2:2), the foundation (Eph. 2:20; Rev. 21:14; 1 Cor. 3:11), so that there is no way to Christ that detours around them. Their importance is due to their function of presenting the authentic interpretation of their Lord. With the increasing Gnostic claims for oral tradition an added emphasis accrued to the writings authorized by the apostles. Their common testimony is based on OT prophecy and is preserved in the NT. Since they saw, heard, and handled the Word of life and gave eyewitness testimony to decisive events (1 Jn. 1:1-3), and since no foundation repeats itself, they are irreplaceable in any subsequent generation.

II. The Twelve.–In His itinerant ministry, Jesus called men to repent and receive the yoke of the kingdom (Mk. 1:14-20; Jn. 1:35-51). From those who heard He gathered disciples, and from among them He called twelve (Simon Peter, James and John sons of Zebedee, Andrew, Philip, Bartholomew, Matthew, Thomas, James son of Alphaeus, Thaddaeus, Simon the Cananaean or Zealot, Judas Iscariot) to be with Him (Mk. 3:15), that they might learn of Him such things as humility (Mt. 11:28-30; Lk. 18:9-14), prayer (Lk. 11:1-13), service to others (Mt. 20:20-28), the characteristics and responsibilities of the children of the kingdom (Mt. 5–7; 13), the person and mission of Himself (Mt. 16:13f; 20:28). Then, delegating some of His own authority to them, Jesus sent out the Twelve as apostles on limited assignments, to preach, to cast out demons, and to heal (Mk. 6:7; Lk. 9:1-6; Mt. 10:1). Their temporary mission accomplished, they returned to Jesus, reporting what they had done and taught (Mk. 6:30; Lk. 9:10). Seeing one casting out demons in the name of Jesus, without specific authorization by the Master, they had forbidden him (Mk. 9:38-41). Jesus assured them that even a cup of cold water given an apostle because he is Christ's is given to his sender (Mk. 9:41; Mt. 10:40). In these ways Jesus trained an inner circle of twelve to become the permanent apostles of the Lamb (Rev. 21:14), the "twelve tribes" of the New Israel (Mt. 19:28).

The Lord celebrated the Last Supper with the Twelve (Lk. 22:14f.) and used that occasion to teach them of the coming of the Holy Spirit (Jn. 14–17), who would interpret to them the meaning of His message, His acts, and His person. By the Spirit's abiding presence, their witnessing is not left to their unaided impressions and recollections, but is so directed by Him as to become the authentic interpretation of Christ. The arrest and the crucifixion scattered the Twelve, but their resurrected Lord appeared to Peter and to the Twelve (1 Cor. 15:5; Lk. 24:34f.). He breathed His Spirit upon them (Jn. 20:22f.; Acts 2), and thus empowered and commissioned them as permanent apostles sent by the risen Redeemer to carry His gospel to all nations (Mt. 28:19; Lk. 24:47; cf. Eph. 4:11; 1 Cor. 12:28).

The inner core of the Twelve consisted of Peter, James, and John (Mt. 17:1; 26:37). As Peter had been the spokesman of the Twelve in the great confession (Mt. 16:16), so with him begins the apostolic faith in Jesus' resurrection (1 Cor. 15:5; Lk. 24:34), as well as the apostolic interpretation of His death from such OT passages as Isa. 53 (Mk. 10:45; Acts 10:43; 1 Pet. 1:11, 19; 2:4; 3:18). In Jerusalem Peter led the disciples in appealing to the Lord to designate a successor to Judas as a witness to His resurrection (Acts 1:15-26). Peter with the Eleven proclaimed the risen Christ who sent the Spirit from God's right hand. Three thousand were baptized in the name of Jesus Christ and continued in the apostles' doctrine, fellowship, and prayers (Acts 2). In Christ's name Peter and John proclaimed healing to the lame man, and Peter used the occasion to preach again the resurrection of Jesus (Acts 3), as a result of which they were temporarily imprisoned. Speaking for the apostles, Peter condemned Ananias and Sapphira (Acts 5). With John he was sent to Samaria to seal with the Holy Spirit the newly baptized disciples (Acts 8:14). Thereafter Peter extended his missionary activities to Lydda, Joppa, and Caesarea, where he opened the doors of the Church to Cornelius, a Gentile who feared God (Acts 9:32–11:18). Later his missionary activities reached Antioch (Gal. 2) and Corinth (?) (1 Cor. 1:12; 9:5), and probably extended to a martyrdom in Rome.

The apostolic proclamation, that the God of Israel had raised from the dead and glorified as the Messiah the Jesus

Apostles gathered at the Last Supper. Fresco from the interior of a rock-carved church at Gőreme, Turkey (B. K. Condit)

whom Jerusalem had crucified, aroused animosity. The broadening of the Church, first by the preaching of the Seven and later by Peter's reception of Cornelius, accentuated the opposition, particularly toward the inner three. Herod killed James the brother of John with the sword, and put Peter in prison, expecting to treat him the same way in order to please the Jews. But the angel of the Lord delivered Peter from prison (Acts 12).

In Antioch, Paul pleaded with Peter to stand by his own true principles of receiving Gentiles and not to play the hypocrite in order to please the Judaizers (Gal. 2:11f.). Thus for the truth of the gospel even Peter, the Rock apostle, was corrected by an associate; and at the Council of Jerusalem Peter told how God had used him to proclaim the gospel and minister faith to the household of Cornelius. He begged the apostles and elders to lay no additional yoke upon these gentile believers (Acts 15:6-11). In Corinth some called themselves disciples of Cephas (1 Cor. 1:12; 3:22), but Peter seems to have been as careful as Paul to have his associates rather than himself baptize (Acts 10:48), lest men should say that the apostles baptized in their own names (1 Cor. 1:17). Thus Peter was the decisive figure among the Twelve.

III. Paul.–Unlike the Twelve, Paul had not accompanied Jesus during His preaching ministry. Nevertheless, he regarded himself and was accepted by the primitive Church as manifesting the signs of an apostle. While Acts gives Paul the title only in ch. 14, where some understand the reference to be to apostles of the church in Antioch, nevertheless the paramount place this book gives to Paul's ministry attests his full recognition. In its three accounts of the Lord's initial encounter with Paul as well as in the apostle's own writing (e.g., Gal. 1:16; 2 Cor. 4:6), his apostleship is presented as the direct action of the risen Lord Jesus. He is an apostle, not from men nor through a man, but through Jesus Christ and God the Father who raised Him from the dead (Gal. 1:1). This encounter is not a mere subjective vision, but an objective event, an act of God, a Christophany (1 Cor. 9:1; 15:8).

As Paul preached the gospel of Christ (Rom. 15:16-21), Gentiles were brought into the obedience of the faith, and churches were established throughout the Roman world. The fruits of his ministry, miraculous signs (1 Cor. 9:2; 2 Cor. 12:12; Gal. 2:8; cf. Jn. 14:12), his labors and sufferings for the name of Jesus Christ (Col. 1:14; 2 Cor. 1:5f.; 4:5f.; cf. Lk. 21:12), were truly apostolic.

In their ministry to the Jews and the God-fearers, the Twelve could presuppose OT theism, i.e., the living God, His righteousness, judgment to come, and the hope of Israel. Building on this, they sounded the call to repentance and offered men the Lord Jesus as the messianic Savior. In preaching to the Gentiles, Paul was given the additional task of first reasoning of the Most High God (Acts 16:17), the Maker and Governor of all things (Acts 17:24-28), and also of righteousness, self-control, and judgment to come (Acts 24:25; cf. Rom. 1:18–3:19). Then, having sought conviction under the law written in the hearts of men as well as on the tablets of Moses, he called sinners to Christ, the one Mediator between God and men (1 Tim. 2:5).

The most significant characteristic of Paul's apostleship is the graciousness of the Lord's action in converting His most formidable opponent into His most effective minister. The first word of the encounter recorded in Acts is "Saul, Saul, why do you persecute me?" In the Epistles, Paul never forgets that as a persecutor injurious to the Church, he is less than the least of all the saints and not worthy to be called an apostle (Eph. 3:8; 1 Cor. 15:9; 1 Tim. 1:12-16). In such a situation it was only grace on top of grace that made Paul an apostle. Here is grace most clear: Christ is for Paul even when Paul is most actively against Him. Thus is it most evident that the glory is not of men but of God. God is willing to work more abundantly in this very earthen vessel than in others (1 Cor. 15:10; 2 Cor. 4:7f.; Eph. 3:8f.; 1 Tim. 1:14, 16).

By his apostolic commission Paul was separated from all other interests to God's gospel concerning His Son (Rom. 1:1-3; 1 Cor. 1:1, 17; Gal. 1:15; 2:7; Acts 22:14-17). Other disciples had a long period of training for their apostleship, but by this great encounter Christ made Paul forever His bond slave, debtor, and apostle (Rom. 1:1, 15). In the case of Paul there was an immediate surrender, his consciousness was completely dominated by the will of God (1 Cor. 1:1; 2 Cor. 1:1; Eph. 1:1), which he beheld working from his birth to fit him for his particular place in God's plan (Gal. 1:15; Eph. 1:5; 3:2-9). Here is the recovery of that prophetic consciousness that gives the dominant place to the thought of God. In his letters to the church in Corinth Paul is constantly wringing all self-adulation out of his ministry that men may glory only in Christ, whom God has made unto us wisdom, righteousness, sanctification, and redemption.

Paul is careful not to base his apostleship on ecstatic gifts, lest by magnifying his own individuality he overshadow the grace of God (1 Cor. 12; 2 Cor. 12). It is by God's grace that he is an apostle, commissioned not to honor himself but to serve God in preaching the gospel of His Son (Rom. 1:9; 15:19; 1 Cor. 1:17). Even the signs of an apostle are given Paul only to further his ministry, to magnify God, not himself (1 Cor. 2:5).

IV. Apostolic Authority.–In the NT there is always a decisive distinction between the Lord Jesus and His apostles. While He has full authority in Himself, their power is only in His Name and in the Spirit given by Him (Acts 3:6, 12; 9:34; Jn. 15:5). Even so His majesty and might stand behind them. As His witnesses, ambassadors, and vicars (Mt. 10:40; Lk. 10:16), they hold the first and most significant place in the primitive Church (1 Cor. 12:28; Eph. 4:11). Accordingly, they exercise great authority in matters of discipline (Acts 5:1-11; 1 Cor. 5:1-7; 2 Cor. 2:1-10; Jn. 20:23; Mt. 16:19; 18:15-22) and other problems facing the churches (2 Cor. 13:2, 10; 1 Thess. 4:2; 2 Thess. 3:4, 6). Yet they treasure the precept, "you have one teacher, and you are all brethren" (Mt. 23:8; cf. 10:44). Paul sought to increase the joy of others, not to lord it over their faith (2 Cor. 1:24). He insisted that his own preaching as truly as Peter's conduct must be in accord with the gospel (Gal. 1:18; 2:14). Peter felt obligated to defend his in receiving Cornelius to the other apostles and the brethren (Acts 11:1-18).

The explanation of this paradox is to be found in the missionary situation in the primitive fellowship. In a sense the apostolate was prior to the Church as a sociological gathering. As the foundation pillars they spoke with authority, but it was an authority that sought to bring out and develop the local ministry. The earliest disciples put forward two, of whom the Lord chose Matthias to replace Judas (Acts 1:15, 23), and the enlarged body selected the Seven, whom the apostles ordained with the laying on of hands and prayer (Acts 6:1-6). The elders shared with the apostles in the decision at Jerusalem (Acts 15), and government appears as a gift distinct from apostleship in 1 Cor. 12:28f. Paul participated with the congregational presbytery in ordaining Timothy (1 Tim. 4:14; 2 Tim. 1:6). Nor did the apostles take the leading place in administering the sacraments, as the bishops did in the 2nd cent. (1 Cor. 1:14; Acts 10:48). Through the local ministers the apostles made provision for the Church's worship, government, and discipline to be carried on in their absence and after their decease. The writings of the Apostolic Fathers show the advance of this process.

Later in the 2nd cent. a more strenuous effort was made to ward off the dangers of speculation, schism, and apostasy brought about by persecution. Added stress was placed upon the Apostolic Rule of Faith, the Apostolic Canon of Scripture, and the Apostolic Office, that is, the bishops in churches that had been founded by apostles. These tests were expected to keep church proclamation in conformity with the word and witness of the dominically chosen and commissioned body of apostles.

In the final analysis the apostles were officers not of the Church but of the risen Lord, who proclaimed Himself through their preaching of Him and so built His Church through their labors. In their activities, the ministry of the Church was so related to the ministry of Christ that it was Christ Himself who was nourishing, sustaining, and directing His Church. And the Church is authentically apostolic only when her thought and action are governed and guided by her Lord, that is, when He rules and teaches His Church through His Spirit and Word by the ministry of men. Through their faithful exposition of the apostolic gospel the risen Lord is still heard proclaiming Himself as the Savior of sinners.

Bibliography.–*TDNT,* I, *s.v.* ἀποστέλλω (Rengstorf); *Encyclopaedia of Christianity* (1962); *NBD*; *BDTh*; *RGG*; *DTC,* I; J. L. McKenzie, ed., *Dictionary of the Bible* (1965). For further reference, see E. Schweizer, *Church Order in the NT* (Eng. tr. 1961); C. F. D. Moule, *Birth of the NT* (1962); T. F. Torrance, *Royal Priesthood* (1955); A. Schlatter, *Church in the NT Period* (Eng. tr. 1955); E. D. Burton, *Galatians* (*ICC,* 1920), appendix I; F. V. Filson, *Three Crucial Decades. Studies in the Book of Acts* (1962); O. Cullman, *Peter* (Eng. tr. 1953); T. W. Manson, *The Church's Ministry* (1948); H. E. Kirk, ed., *Apostolic Ministry* (1948); H. Diem, *Dogmatics* (Eng. tr. 1959); H. D. Betz, *Der Apostel Paulus* (1972).

W. C. ROBINSON

APOSTLES' CREED. *See* CREEDS AND CONFESSIONS IV.A.

APOSTOLIC AGE. The period from Pentecost to the death of John, the last of the twelve apostles (*ca.* 100), when the Church was under the guidance of Paul (till his death) and the apostles, especially Peter and John.

I. The Mission.–When the disciples realized that they had seen the risen Christ for the last time and that it had now become their duty to spread His message, they gathered themselves together and restored the number of "witnesses" to the appointed Twelve. Immediately afterward the outpouring of the Holy Spirit gave them the signal to begin work. At first this work was rigidly centered in Jerusalem, and the first journeyings were the result of forcible dispersion and not of planned effort (Acts 11:19).

APOSTOLIC AGE

(Left) Thomas, Philip, Andrew, and Peter. Jamb figures on south porch of cathedral of Notre Dame, Chartres. (Right) Paul, John, James the Great, and James the Less. Figures right of central door, south porch (A.D. 1194-1260)

But pilgrims to the feasts had carried away the gospel with them, and in this way Christianity had been spread at least as far as Damascus (9:2, 19). The dispersion itself widened the circle to Cyprus and to Antioch and marked the beginning of the gentile work (11:19f.).

The extreme prominence of Paul's ministry in the NT should not obscure the success of the other missionaries. When the apostles began their journeys we do not know, but at the time of Gal. 1:19 only Peter represented the Twelve in Jerusalem. Paul mentions their extended work in 1 Cor. 9:5f., and it seems certain that Peter was in Rome shortly before his death. The troubles caused Paul by the Judaizers at least give evidence of the missionary zeal of the latter. Barnabas and Mark worked after their separation from Paul (Acts 15:39), and gentile Christianity existed in Rome long before Paul's arrival there (Rom. 1:13). By the year 100 it appears that Christianity extended around the Mediterranean from Alexandria to Rome (and doubtless farther, although data are scanty), while Asia Minor was especially pervaded by it.

Many factors cooperated to help the work. Peace was universal and communication was easy. Greek was spoken everywhere. The protection given Judaism sheltered from civil interference. The presence of Judaism insured hospitality and hearers for at least the first efforts to convert. The Jews' proselytizing zeal (Mt. 23:15) had prepared Gentiles to receive Christianity. And not the least element was the break-up of the old religions and the general looking to the East for religious satisfaction.

Paul's procedure is probably typical. Avoiding the smaller places, he devoted himself to the cities as the strategic points and traveled in a direct route, without side-journeys. In this way a "line of fire" (Harnack) was traced, and the flame could be trusted to spread of its own accord to each side of the road. So as fruits of Paul's work at Ephesus there appear churches at Colossae and Laodicea some 120 mi. (200 km.) away (Col. 2:1; 4:16). The churches founded needed revisiting and confirming; but when the apostle felt that they could shift for themselves, he felt also that his work in the East was over (Rom. 15:23).

II. Jerusalem Church.–The members of the earliest Jerusalem church thought of themselves simply as Jews who had a true understanding of the Messiah and so constituting a new "way" or "party" (hardly "sect") in Judaism (Acts 22:4, esp.). At first they were allowed to grow unmolested, and their right to exist was apparently unquestioned, for the Sadducean actions of Acts 4:1; 5:17 were in the nature of police precautions. And it is significant that the first attack was made on a foreigner, Stephen. He seems to have angered the crowds by preaching the impending destruction of the temple, although he was martyred for ascribing (practically) divine honors to Jesus (7:56). Yet the apostles were not driven from the city (8:1) and the church was able to continue its development.

In 41, the Roman representatives gave way to the pharisaically inclined Agrippa I, and (for reasons that are not clear) persecution broke out in which James was martyred and Peter delivered only by a miracle (Acts 12). With the resumption of Roman rule in 44 the persecution ceased. Some peaceable mode of living was devised, as appears from the absence of further allusions to troubles (cf Acts

21:17-26) and from the accounts of Josephus and Hegesippus of the esteem in which James the Lord's brother was held. His martyrdom (in 62?) was due to the tension that preceded the final revolt against Rome, in which the Christians of Jerusalem took no part. Instead, they retired across the Jordan to Pella (Rev. 12:13-17), where they formed a close, intensely Jewish body under the rule of the descendants of Christ's brethren according to the flesh. Some mission work was done farther to the east, but in the 2nd cent. they either were absorbed in normal Christianity or became one of the factors that produced Ebionism.

III. Judaists.–Many members of this body (and, doubtless, other Jewish Christians outside it) showed various degrees of inability to understand the gentile work. The acceptance of an uncircumcised Christian as "saved" offered fairly slight difficulty (Gal. 2:3; Acts 15). But to eat with him was another thing and one that was an offense to many who accepted his salvation (Gal. 2:12f.). The rigorous conclusion that the Law bound *no* Christian was still another thing and one that even James could not accept (Acts 21:21). At the time of Gal. 2:9, the "pillars" were as yet not thinking of doing gentile work. Paul's controversies are familiar, and probably the last friction did not end until the fall of Jerusalem. But the difficulties grew gradually less, and 1 Peter is evidence that Peter himself finally accepted the full status of Gentiles.

IV. Relations with Rome.–From the Roman power Christianity was safe at first, as the distinctions from Judaism were thought too slight to notice (Acts 18:14-16; 25:19). (Troubles such as those of Acts 17:9 were due to disturbance of the peace.) So the government was thought of as a protector (2 Thess. 2:7) and spoken of in the highest terms (Rom. 13:1; 1 Pet. 2:13f.). But, while absolute isolation was not observed (1 Cor. 10:27), yet the Christians tended more and more to draw themselves into bodies with little contact with the world around them (1 Pet. 4:3-5), so provoking suspicion and hostility from their neighbors. Hence they were a convenient scapegoat for Nero after the burning of Rome. It is uncertain how far his persecution spread or how far persecutions occurred from his time until the end of the reign of Domitian (*see* PETER, FIRST EPISTLE OF II), but in Revelation Rome has become the symbol for all that is hostile to Christ.

V. "Hellenism."–Influence of the "pagan" religions on Christianity is not very perceptible in the 1st century. But syncretism was the fashion of the day and many converts must have attempted to combine the new religion with views that they held already (or that they learned still later). Apparently little attention was paid to this attempt if it was restricted to entirely minor details (1 Cor. 15:29?), but in Col. 2:8-23 a vital matter is touched. The danger appears more acute in the Pastorals (1 Tim. 1:4; 4:3; Tit. 3:9), and according to Rev. 2 great harm was being done. Also, Jude, 2 Peter, and 1 John contain direct polemics against the systems so arising, the beginnings of what in the 2nd cent. appeared as Gnosticism.

For further details *see* esp. MINISTRY; CANON OF THE NT; and (for life in the apostolic age) SPIRITUAL GIFTS.

Bibliography.–L. W. Barnard, *Studies in the Apostolic Fathers and their Background* (1966); C. K. Barrett, *NT Background: Selected Documents* (1956); F. C. Burkitt, *Church and Gnosis* (1932); *CAH,* XII (1939); T. R. Glover, *Conflict of Religions in the Early Roman Empire* (10th ed. 1923); C. G. A. von Harnack, *Expansion of Christianity in the First Three Centuries,* I, II (Eng. tr. 1904, 1905); H. Lietzmann, *History of the Early Church* (Eng. tr., 2nd ed. 1949-1950); E. Lohse, *NT Environment* (Eng. tr. 1976); A. C. McGiffert, *History of Christianity in the Apostolic Age* (1897); G. F. Moore, *Judaism in the First Centuries of the Christian Era* (1927); K. von Weizsäcker, *Apostolic Age of the Christian Church,* I, II (Eng. tr., 3rd ed. 1907, 1912).

B. S. EASTON

APOSTOLIC CONSTITUTIONS AND CANONS. A pseudepigraphical work usually dated in the 4th cent. A.D. and thought to be Syrian in origin. It consists of a collection of independent treatises on doctrine, worship, and discipline collected into eight books, with eighty-five appended canons, and seems to be designed predominantly as a manual for the clergy. The ostensible author is Clement of Rome, who, it is claimed, edited apostolic materials, although as early as the Trullan Council of 692 it was recognized that neither the apostolic origin nor Clement's editorship was authentic.

The general dating of the Constitutions has not given rise to serious controversy. Many of the underlying materials obviously come from the third century or even (in a few instances) earlier, but since the rulings of the Council of Antioch in 341 are incorporated the compilation can hardly precede this date. On the other hand there is no reference to the Nestorian or Monophysite debates, so that a date past *ca.* 420 is excluded. References by Eusebius, Epiphanius, and Athanasius might be to constituent materials and not necessarily to the full collection.

The books of the Constitutions come from various sources. Bks. 1–6 rest on a third-century collection known as the Didascalia, which is fully extant only in Syriac. One part of bk. 7 incorporates the moral teaching of the Didache, while the rest is from an unknown source. Bk. 8 brings together various materials. It seems to use at the outset the treatise of Hippolytus on spiritual gifts. Other sections show evident kinship to the Egyptian Church Order, and the familiar Clementine Liturgy is included also. The work of redaction is usually traced to a single, if unknown, hand, since the style in the editorial sections is obviously uniform. A semi-Arian trend has been seen in the work by some, but others suspect Apollinarianism. More plausibly the editor has been identified as pseudo-Ignatius, the writer responsible for the longer recension of the epistles of Ignatius of Antioch.

The contents of the first set of books—those based on the Didascalia—give evidence of careful grouping. Bk. 1 is devoted to the duties of ordinary Christians and prescribes a strict although not wholly ascetic manner of life. Soberness in adornment and caution in respect of the public baths might be mentioned as examples. In contrast, bk. 2 deals with the qualifications and duties of the clergy. An interesting account of penitential practice is added, and many ceremonial details are given. Widows and their office receive attention in bk. 3, as do also deacons and baptism, while charity comes under discussion in bk. 4. In bk. 5 duties toward the persecuted are set out, and martyrdom comes under discussion, along with idolatry as the main threat to Christians and the chief object of the martyrs' protest. Finally, bk. 6 offers a survey of the history and teachings of the different movements of schism and heresy in the early Church.

The part of bk. 7 that derives from the Didache provides moral instruction according to the familiar schema of the Two Ways. The second part consists of liturgical directions, an interesting point here being that some of the prayers suggest Jewish origins. Bk. 8, apart from the opening section on charismata, deals predominantly with matters of order and worship. Finally, the appended canons turn again to the important subject of the selection, ordination, and duties of the clergy. Also given is a list of canonical writings which omits Revelation but recognizes 3 Maccabees, 1 and 2 Clement, and the Constitutions themselves. Fifty of these canons came into the West and found a home in the Isidorian Decretals and Gratian's codification. The full eighty-five were adopted by John of Constantinople in the East and came to be invested with considerable authority.

APOSTOLIC COUNCIL

Certain features of the Constitutions and Canons call for special notice. Occasional extravagant mystical interpretations of Scripture characterize and mar the work. If a certain friendliness toward Jews may be discerned, opposition to Jewish Christians is severe, possibly because of local rivalries. Sharp separation from the pagan world is demanded, including the laying aside of all pagan literature. A full round of observances is also required of all Christians, including brief services twice a day, the keeping of both the sabbath and the Lord's Day, and various fasts and festivals. Exaggerated respect must be paid to the clergy and especially the bishop. The bishop should not even be approached except through deacons or servants, just as God should not be approached except through Christ. Deaconesses are to be esteemed as the Holy Spirit and presbyters as the apostles, while teachers deserve more respect that princes or magistrates. The clericalism of a later period found welcome ammunition in this set of documents.

The intricate problems associated with the sources of the Constitutions have given rise to an extensive literature. This is, however, a specialized field which, in view of the inauthenticity of the work, has little bearing on the church's life, teaching, or discipline today. The main interest in the Constitutions for the average Christian lies in the picture that they give of practical, liturgical, and clerical life in the early centuries, the measures in which this conforms to authentically apostolic precept and precedent, its influence in succeeding centuries, and the positive and negative lessons that might still be learned from it.

Bibliography.–J. Quasten, *Patrology* (1953), II, 119f., 147-152, 180-190 offers a fairly up-to-date survey of the literature, which it is unnecessary to list in the present context.

G. W. BROMILEY

APOSTOLIC COUNCIL. A meeting between delegates from the church at Antioch (Paul, Barnabas, and others) and those from the mother church at Jerusalem, convened to settle a dispute raised by some Jewish-Christians from Jerusalem who had come to Antioch teaching that gentile converts could not be saved apart from the Mosaic rite of circumcision. The Council probably took place between Paul's first and second missionary journeys and is recorded in Acts 15:1-35. Schlatter (p. 125) suggests that the term "Apostolic Council" is not entirely appropriate, since the apostles were not the only active participants. It is also called the Jerusalem Council.

I. Critical Problems
II. Occasion
III. The Council
IV. Apostolic Decree
V. Outcome

I. Critical Problems.–Whether we may supplement the Acts 15 account with information from Paul's report in Gal. 2:1-10 (his encounter with "those who were of repute") depends upon our decision regarding the relationship between Paul's visits to Jerusalem as recorded in Galatians and those recorded in Acts. If these are two accounts of the same incident we will have to conclude that Paul played a much more active role than is suggested by the passing references to him in Acts (15:4, 12), and also that the decisions of the Council were considerably broader in scope than a mere rejection of the Jewish-Christian proposal for gentile circumcision.

Briefly stated the problem is this. In his letter to the Galatians Paul indicates with great care that subsequent to his conversion he had been in Jerusalem on but two occasions. The first (Gal. 1:18-24) was a fortnight spent with Peter during which he saw none of the other apostles except James. The second (Gal. 2:1-10) was "after fourteen years," at which time he gave an account of his gospel. The leaders of the Jerusalem church, recognizing that the gospel to the uncircumcised had been entrusted to him, extended to him the right hand of fellowship. Nothing was added to his gospel. In fact, even an apparent attempt to have Titus circumcised failed.

In what has traditionally been taken as the same span of time, Acts lists not two but three visits to Jerusalem. The first follows Paul's escape from Damascus (Acts 9:26-30). This is quite widely identified with the first visit of Gal. 1:18-24. The second visit in Acts is the so-called famine visit (Acts 11:30; 12:25) and the third is the Jerusalem Council. The essential problem is which, if either, of these two latter visits in Acts coincides with Gal. 2:1-10. The problem is made acute by the absolute necessity to Paul's argument that all his contacts with Jerusalem be mentioned. The very point he wants to establish is that his apostolic commission is independent of the authorities in Jerusalem. Deliberately to omit a significant contact would be to falsify the record and discredit himself as a true apostle. Innocently to overlook the visit would undermine his argument and afford his opponents a splendid opportunity for rebuttal.

The view that Gal. 2:1-10 is Paul's account of the Jerusalem Council (described by Luke in Acts 15) is most often associated with the name of J. B. Lightfoot (*St. Paul's Epistle to the Galatians* [1900], pp. 123-28). He argues the striking coincidence of circumstances between the accounts (in matters of geography, time, persons, subject of dispute, character of conference, and result) and concludes that it is unlikely that two conferences so similar could have occurred within such a few years (p. 124). He supports his position negatively by pointing out difficulties with alternative solutions.

A great number of scholars from Irenaeus in the 2nd cent. (cited by Lightfoot, p. 123 n. 1) to Burton (Galatians [*ICC*, 1920], pp. 115ff.), Ridderbos (comm. on Galatians [*NIC*, 1953], pp. 78-80), and Filson (*IDB*, I, 701f.) in the 20th have been in essential agreement with Lightfoot. Writing at the turn of the century W. M. Ramsay was forced to admit that "scholars who agree in regard to scarcely any other point of early Christian history are at one in this" (*SPT*, p. 154). Filson holds that although the accounts of Acts 15 and Gal. 2 differ "in important respects" there is nevertheless broad agreement between the accounts. Of the various solutions proposed "none is so convincing as the view that Gal. 2:1-10; Acts 15:1-29 describe the same conference" (p. 711; cf. also O. Moe, *The Apostle Paul: His Life and His Work* [Eng. tr. 1950], pp. 221ff.; D. J. Selby, *Toward the Understanding of St. Paul* [1962], pp. 196-204).

The other classic solution is connected with the name of William Ramsay. He accepted as historical the three visits recorded by Luke and held that the private consultation of Gal. 2:1-10 took place during the second (or famine) visit, (pp. 54ff., 152ff.). This view has gained a great number of adherents (cf. the bibliographic note in Bruce, *Book of the Acts*, pp. 300f. n. 10) and is apparently the revival of Calvin's position in his commentary on Galatians published in 1548. It is the prevailing view among British scholars.

There are three basic arguments against the equation of Gal. 2 with Acts 15 that make many scholars look with favor on an alternate solution. First, attention is drawn to the discrepancies between the accounts. Lightfoot is certainly right when he argues the similarity of geography and persons (in the matter of time he is begging the question) but wrong when he holds that the subject of dispute, the character of the conference, and the result are the same.

The subject of the Galatians meeting was not circumcision but the sufficiency of Paul's gospel and the appropriateness of his ministry to the Gentiles. The question of circumcision arose at the instigation of some false brethren, and receives the mention it does because it serves to establish the point Paul is making in his letter, namely, the independence of his gospel. In the case of Acts 15 the Council is convened to deal with the subject of gentile acceptance into the Church. Here circumcision is the occasion of the meeting. It is interesting to note, however, that after the preliminary hearing (Gal. 2:5) it is not mentioned again in the entire conference.

Neither is the character of the conference the same in the two accounts. Lightfoot's description of the Council as a "prolonged and hard-fought contest" (p. 124) captures the feeling of the Galatians account but not that of Acts. The strong dissension and debate took place in Antioch, not Jerusalem. While the opposition gave clear statement to their opinion (Gal. 2:5), the Council itself is represented by Luke as conciliatory and moving rather easily toward a practically unanimous verdict (cf. esp. vv. 12, 22).

The results of the two meetings are not the same. In Galatians a division between spheres of missionary activity is recognized and accepted. Not yielding to circumcision is a parenthetical event within the conference, not the outcome of it. In Acts the result is a decision against the imposition of either circumcision or Mosaic law upon gentile converts. Along with it goes a request that for the sake of fellowship the Gentiles abstain from certain practices abhorrent to the Jews.

Certain other discrepancies may be mentioned. Paul portrays his opponents as "false brethren" who slipped in secretly to enslave the gentile converts (Gal. 2:3f.). Luke calls them "believers" (Acts 15:5) and gives no indication of any lack of integrity. Galatians suggests that for a time the Jerusalem leaders were willing to compromise with the antagonists (Burton says that the pillar apostles for a time "urged that Paul should waive his scruples and consent to the circumcision of Titus" but later "yielded and gave assent to Paul's view" [p. 77]), but Luke presents Peter and James in unwavering support of the Pauline position. In Galatians Paul is portrayed as pressing home his case, unwilling to allow even Titus to be circumcised, and securing the confidence of the Jerusalem leaders. In Acts Paul is hardly more than an interested onlooker who gives an account of what God has done through him among the Gentiles but leaves the deliberations in the hands of the Jerusalem authorities. In Galatians Paul is fiercely independent and depreciates the rank (if not the person) of those "reputed to be something" (Gal. 2:6, 9). In Acts he is a part of the team. (It is common for writers who distinguish between Gal. 2 and Acts 15 to point out still other discrepancies, but many of these are of dubious validity. For example: the motives for going ["by revelation"; "appointed to go"] are not mutually exclusive; the decree concerning table fellowship does not mean that something was added to Paul's gospel; and the problem of private or public council is extremely unconvincing.)

Two approaches have been taken to alleviate the problem. One is to hold that most of the account in Galatians describes the private consultation and that Acts records the public meeting (Ridderbos follows this approach). But the overall tone of the two meetings is too divergent to explain Galatians as a caucus before the Acts convention. Is it psychologically reasonable that the rugged champion of gentile freedom (Galatians) would act as nothing more than a witness (Acts) when the crucial question came out into the open for final disposition?

The other approach is to stress the difference between external and internal history (cf. R. B. Rackham, comm. on Acts [*WC*, 1902], p. 240). Paul is seen as revealing his own personal involvement to a specific group for a specific reason (Galatians). Luke writes as an objective historian to the entire Church and reports the major result. That the perspectives of Paul and Luke would differ is undeniable, but that this difference in perspective is adequate to explain the marked dissimilarities is highly questionable.

A second basic problem with the Gal. 2–Acts 15 equation is created by Paul's omissions. What possible explanation could there be for his failure to include the famine visit in his Gal. 2 listing of his contacts with the Jerusalem leaders? Would not this omission—deliberate or accidental—undermine the very point he was trying to establish?

The weight of this argument depends upon one's interpretation of why Paul in Galatians lists his visits to Jerusalem. Some hold that the visits are mentioned in Galatians not to show that it would have been geographically impossible for him to have received his gospel, but to illustrate that when he did have contact with the apostles his purpose was not to secure authorization for his gospel. However, the text seems to emphasize the significance of the actual contacts (e.g., Gal. 1:16, "I did not confer with flesh and blood"; Gal. 2:19, "I saw none of the other apostles"; Gal. 2:22, "I was still not known by sight to the churches of Christ in Judea"). The idea that Paul could defend the omission before the Council by retorting, "Don't you recall that this visit was made during a time of persecution when all Christians of rank had fled from Jerusalem?" and thus score a debating point, is overly subtle and in conflict with the pattern found in Acts 8:1.

Short of the critical reconstruction that maintains that both Paul and Barnabas were appointed to go on the famine visit but for some unexplained reason only Barnabas went, there is no reasonable explanation for Paul's neglect. (Renan's suggestion is that Luke was simply mistaken about the identity of Barnabas' colleague and Paul never did go. Cf. B. H. Streeter, *The Four Gospels* [rev. ed., repr. 1964], pp. 556f. n. 1; also E. J. Goodspeed, *Paul* [1948], p. 35)

Another serious omission by Paul is his lack of reference to the restrictive clauses of the decree. In Galatians he reports "mission accomplished" and adds that the only obligation was that "they would have us remember the poor" (Gal. 2:10). In view of the specific instructions to gentile Christians, would not Paul be guilty of playing fast and loose with the decision by presenting it in such a general way? It is no answer to say that Galatia was far removed from Palestine and the problem was less acute. The matter of Jewish-Gentile fellowship was as broad as the early Church itself. It reached even to Corinth (1 Cor. 8–10) and Rome (Rom. 14).

It is also difficult to understand why Paul did not report to the Galatians the major decision of the Council, namely, that the Gentiles need not be circumcised or take upon themselves the yoke of Mosaic legislation. While the reference to Titus' not being compelled to be circumcised would be important as a specific example, the final decision of the authorities at Jerusalem would have settled the matter for good.

The third problem is to account for the actions of Peter and Barnabas at Antioch on the assumption that they *follow* the Council (Gal. 2:11-21). In Acts, Peter gives the keynote address and, arguing from the Cornelius episode, becomes an outstanding advocate of gentile freedom. In Antioch he quickly abandons his convictions upon the arrival of a Jewish delegation and withdraws from table fellowship with the gentile believers. In Acts 15:2 Barnabas strenuously resists the men from Judea but immediately following the Council, which gave official support to his position, weakly acquiesces to their demands. Ramsay writes with eloquent disapproval, "We are asked to accept as a credible narrative this recital of meaningless tergiversation" (p. 164).

All three of these problems disappear when the Galatians account is identified with Acts 11 rather than Acts 15. The discrepancies no longer exist, there are no omissions, and the behavior of Peter and Barnabas offers no problem. (Some evade this last problem by explaining that Paul has arranged the material in Gal. 2 in a logical rather than chronological order; cf. Zahn and Turner).

An Acts 11 equation is also favored by Paul's remark that he "went up by revelation" (Gal. 2:2). The answer that Paul is supplying the inner motive while Luke is recording the external details is a bit beside the point, because in both cases the men are delegated by the Antiochene church. "By revelation" refers not to a divine impulse but to the prophecy of Agabus, who foretold the great famine (Acts 11:28). It was in response to this revelation of God that the men of Antioch determined to send relief to the brethren in Judea.

That the circumcision party was already questioning the inclusion of Gentiles even before the founding of the church at Antioch is seen in Acts 11:2f., where Peter is forced to defend his actions at Caesarea.

Ramsay's view gains credence when compared with the numerous alternatives that have been suggested. The most important of these is the Wellhausen-Schwartz hypothesis (*BC,* V, 195-212) that the visits of Acts 11 and 15 are really one. When Luke came across two variant traditions he failed to recognize that they referred to the same event and kept them separate in his reconstruction. (This view is widely accepted in Europe: Goguel, Jeremias, Bultmann. It is also the later view of Lake and others. Cf. the bibliographic note in Bruce, *Book of the Acts,* p. 300.)

Characteristic of this approach is a lack of confidence in Luke's record. A mild position is that of Foakes-Jackson, who says that although "it is not possible to deny the accuracy of the impression he [Luke] has conveyed" it is "unquestionable that St. Paul's statements in Galatians are to be preferred to those of Luke" (comm. on Acts [*MNTC,* 1931], pp. 137, 132). Others, however, are more radical. Sahlin rejects the historicity of Acts completely (*Der Messias und das Gottesvolk* [1945]). Haenchen's view is that the Apostolic Council "is an imaginary construction answering to no historical reality" (*The Acts of the Apostles* [Eng. tr. 1971], p. 463). Dibelius' view (*Studies in the Acts of the Apostles* [Eng. tr. 1956], pp. 93-101) is that Luke's treatment is literary-theological and can make no claim to historical worth. Luke has taken the account of Cornelius (originally a "simple conversion story") and written it into the story of the Council to propagate his thesis that the conversion of the Gentiles was dependent upon the will of God rather than a decision by Peter or Paul.

Against those who hold a low view of Luke as a historian (to say nothing of the implications concerning his intelligence) Filson replies, "If Acts is so confused on this crucial point, we can hardly hope to reconstruct a convincing history of the apostolic age" (p. 711).

Other alternatives involve the rearrangement of material or the creation of new visits. Lampe favors the view that Luke has fused together two different stories (one about circumcision and the other a dispute about food laws) and arranged his materials in a historically mistaken order (*Peake's Comm. on the Bible* [rev. ed. 1962], pp. 907f.). J. Knox (pp. 47f.) notes that Acts has two more visits than Paul. He finds two sets of doublets (Acts 11:27-30 = Acts 20:3–21:17 = Rom. 15:25; and Acts 15 = Acts 18:21–19:1 = Gal. 2:1ff.) and holds that the Council of Acts 15 took place after the second missionary journey. The Acts 11 account was created to find a place for the famine visit, which was actually Paul's last visit to Jerusalem (Acts 20:3–21:17). T. W. Manson (*BJRL,* 24 [1940], 58-80) devises the theory that the Gal. 2 account is a visit not recorded in Acts but taking place on the eve of the first missionary journey (*ca.* A.D. 47/48). (Cf. Lightfoot, p. 123 nn. 2, 3, for other views from earlier writers; also C. S. C. Williams, comm. on Acts [*HNTC,* 1957], pp. 28-39, for more recent "imaginative reconstructions.")

Several arguments have been raised against the equation of Gal. 2 and Acts 11:

(1) If the question of circumcision was settled in Acts 11 why was it brought up again in Acts 15?

The "question of circumcision" was not the same on the two occasions. In Acts 11 it arose in connection with the independence of Paul's gospel. In Acts 15 it is only a symbol of the real problem—that of gentile acceptance into the Church.

(2) The famine visit of Acts 11 is historically suspect because Josephus dates it after the death of Herod Agrippa and Luke places it before.

The answer to this objection is that the events of Acts 12 took place between the time of Agabus' prophecy and the departure of Paul and Barnabas for Jerusalem. It would require some little time to collect the material for famine relief. Acts 11:30 is an example of the normal procedure of ancient historians to carry an account to a suitable stopping place before turning to another source (cf. W. L. Knox, comm. on Acts [1948], pp. 36f.).

(3) The visit recorded in Acts 11 is too early to be equated with Gal. 2, which is specifically dated either fourteen or seventeen years after Paul's conversion.

But if the famine is dated A.D. 46, then Paul's conversion would be 32/33, a perfectly acceptable date although a bit earlier than most commentators have it. The lack of Damascus coins indicating Roman occupation between 34-62 and the mention of King Aretas of Nabataea in 2 Cor. 11:32 allow a conversion date as early as A.D. 31.

(4) It would be anachronous to assume that the "developed outlook" of Paul in Gal. 2 could be true at an early date when he was still subordinate to Barnabas.

This objection misunderstands the relationship between Paul and Barnabas (placing unwarranted significance on the order of names) and overlooks the vigorous activity of Paul in Damascus *immediately* after his conversion (Acts 9:20-22), to say nothing of the eleven intervening years.

(5) Why should two accounts of the "famine visit" be so different?

Notice, however, that we have but one account (Gal. 2); in Acts there is no more than a reference. Paul relates certain developments of the visits for personal reasons and Luke refers to the incident as one step in the shift of primitive Christianity from Jerusalem to the gentile world.

(6) Filson holds that "the council of Acts 15 implies that no previous conference on Gentile Christianity had been held" (p. 711).

A careful reading of the text fails to reveal any such implication. Besides, the former meeting (Gal. 2; Acts 11) was not a conference on gentile Christianity but a meeting in which Paul's authority as an apostle was fully recognized and a division of the missionary task was effected.

We conclude that since the Gal. 2–Acts 11 equation provides "a perfectly clear historical development" (W. L. Knox, p. 49) there is no need to assume the essential untrustworthiness of Luke, develop an ingenious system of doubtlets, or manufacture new visits in Acts. Thus in our treatment of the Jerusalem Council we take as our source of information Acts 15 without modification.

II. Occasion.–Paul and Barnabas returned from their

first missionary journey into Asia Minor and reported to the church at Antioch all that God had done with them (Acts 14:27). Here they remained with the disciples for a considerable period of time (Gk. *ouk olígos* is a characteristic Lukan understatement). During this period "certain men" came from Judea and began to teach (*edídaskon* is probably to be taken as an inceptive impf.) the brethren at Antioch that circumcision was necessary for salvation. The exact identity of these men is not known but they were probably believing Pharisees who had recently joined the Christian movement. They are the *tinas apó Iakōbou* of Gal. 2:12.

The rapid expansion of the Christian Church into gentile territory posed a crucial problem for the Jerusalem church. Although they had accepted in principle the inclusion of Gentiles (had not Peter's vision indicated God's approval?) they were not prepared for the full implication of their concession. Now they realized that Christianity would be a break with the Mosaic religion and constitute a denial that they were the chosen people of God. From a practical standpoint there would soon be more Gentiles than Jews in the Church, and this could have serious effects upon the level of Christian morality. Since Christ had specifically denied the abolition of the law (Mt. 5:17f.) the Jew would also feel that he had tradition squarely on his side.

But while the Jew viewed Christianity as the consummation of his faith, thus stressing its continuity with the past, the Gentile adopted the forward look and conceived of his newfound faith as dissociated from Judaism. For the Gentile the idea of circumcision was both unneccessary and unwise: unnecessary because salvation is by faith, and unwise because it would seriously hinder the propagation of the faith among those who looked with great disfavor upon any form of bodily mutilation (cf. A. D. Nock, *St. Paul* [1938], p. 104). The seriousness of the situation is aptly stated by W. F. Burnside: "Judaism . . . was the birthplace of Christianity and it threatened to be its grave" (comm. on Acts [*CGT*, 1916], p. 171).

The answer of the more legalistic element of the Jewish wing was that all Gentiles should undergo circumcision and thus come under the legal prescriptions of the Mosaic law. Since Antioch was a thriving center of gentile Christianity it was soon investigated by proponents of this point of view. Not only did they stir up controversy about the way of salvation but they completely upset the existing practice of table fellowship. Gal. 2:11ff. is an illustration of the persuasiveness of their approach. Peter had learned at Joppa and Caesarea that no man was to be considered unclean and excluded from the fellowship (Acts 10:28). Acting in good faith he came to Antioch and joined in the table fellowship. But upon the arrival of the Pharisaic group he lost his nerve and separated himself from the Gentiles. The Jewish Christians at Antioch followed his example and even Barnabas, who recently had returned with Paul from a tour of evangelizing in gentile territory, contravened his convictions. Paul, realizing the implications of the withdrawal (that it would ultimately destroy the basic principle of salvation by grace), opposed Peter openly and pointed out the inconsistency of his action.

Considerable dissension and debate followed. It soon became apparent that the question was too important to be decided apart from consultation with the Jerusalem leaders. That the Antiochene church was willing to consult the mother church indicates that they were not at all persuaded that the emissaries represented the majority opinion of the Jewish church. Thus Paul and Barnabas, along with some others, were appointed to take the issue to Jerusalem. (The subject of Gk. *étaksan,* Acts 15:2, is disputed. While the Western text rewrites the verse to indicate that "those who had come from Jerusalem" charged them to go, it is more probable that the verb is an impersonal plural and best translated by the passive.) Although it must have been a temptation to Paul to repudiate his opposition and "establish Gentile Christianity in a sphere free from the power, influence, and bigotry of Pharisaism" (E. M. Blaiklock, comm. on Acts [Tyndale, 1959], p. 113), his sense of propriety and his willingness to negotiate for the freedom of the gospel determined his course of action. En route to Jerusalem they passed through Phoenicia and Samaria reporting the conversion of Gentiles and bringing great joy to the hearts of the brethren (15:3).

III. The Council.–Arriving in Jerusalem the delegation was warmly received by the apostles and elders. They recounted what God had accomplished through them. Losing no time a group of believing Pharisees seized the opportunity to raise the problem of circumcision and law. Some commentators hold that the legalists had already given some ground in that Acts 15:5 says nothing specific about the relationship of legal obligations to salvation. It is possible that they made a strategic retreat to ground more theologically firm and were content to press their point of view in regard only to social intercourse.

Those who equate Gal. 2 with Acts 15 usually insert the "private conference" at Acts 15:6. But the reference to "all the assembly" (v. 12) and "the whole church" (v. 22) indicate that what followed was a general meeting of the entire congregation. After much debate (*zḗtēsis* ranges in meaning from "investigation" to "controversy") Peter took the floor and presented the crucial argument. He reminded the Council that the issue in question had already been settled in principle. At the house of Cornelius God Himself bore witness to the believing Gentiles by giving them the Holy Spirit. In cleansing their hearts by faith He had erased the line of distinction between Jew and Gentile. How then could the Jews make trial of God by challenging His acceptance of Gentiles and attempting to impose additional requirements? Peter boldly likens circumcision and the law to a yoke that neither their fathers nor they had been able to bear (v. 10). Since they had failed to fulfil the law they must realize that their own salvation, as well as that of the Gentiles, must come as the free gift of God.

It has been argued that a man so devoted to the law as Peter (cf. Acts 10:14) could never have spoken of it as a yoke. Was not the attitude of the pious toward the law one of intense pride and joy (cf. Ps. 119)? Perhaps Luke inadvertently gave Peter's speech a "Pauline accent." And what of such Pauline traces as the antithesis of faith to law (Acts 15:9) and salvation by grace (v. 11)?

All such reconstructions reflect the Tübingen assumption of a Petrine-Pauline schism in primitive Christianity. Although laid to rest by the end of the 19th cent., this point of view continues to haunt twentieth-century scholarship. Actually, Peter's speech is true to what we know of him elsewhere. He states his opinion with an enthusiasm that is almost guilty of bending the evidence. (On the Jewish attitude toward the law during this era cf. Bruce, *Acts of the Apostles,* p. 294.)

Following Peter's speech Barnabas and Paul gave witness to the signs and wonders God had done through them among the Gentiles. This served to answer any objection that the Cornelius episode was an isolated example and not intended as normative. Since Luke is primarily interested in the testimony of Peter and James (the readers of Acts had already learned in narrative form the substance of Paul and Barnabas' remarks in chs. 13f.), he passes by this stage of the Council with no more than a brief reference.

The time for decision had arrived. Peter had established the basic principle by reference to God's acceptance of Cornelius. Barnabas and Paul had given ample illustration of what God was in fact doing among the Gentiles. As leader of the Jerusalem church and moderator of the Council, James, the brother of Jesus, summarized the salient points of the discussion, related it to prophetic declaration, and offered a final decision. In that James was by no means a Paulinist by background or temperament (he was the one who later requested Paul to demonstrate his fidelity to his Jewish heritage by undergoing ceremonial purification, Acts 21:18ff.), what he would say would be widely acceptable among the stricter group.

The crucial point in the entire argument was Peter's experience at Caesarea. It is to this that James redirected the thinking of the Council. God had indicated his own will in visiting the Gentiles and taking out of them a people for His name (Acts 15:14). Luke's use of Gk. *episképtomai* ("visit") had a note of divine intention (cf. such verses as Lk. 1:68 and 7:16). The remarkable thing about James's statement is not discernible in English translation. The juxtaposition in Greek is significant: *ex ethnō̃n laón* ("out of Gentiles a people"). Gk. *laós* was a word used regularly for the Jews. But the new *laós,* the Christian community, was to come from the *éthnē,* Gentiles, as well. The implication of the Caesarean incident was that the Church was to be constituted of Gentiles as well as Jews.

The clinching argument was that this "new departure" was in perfect harmony (Gk. *symphōnéō*; cf. symphony) with prophetic promise. James quotes from the LXX text of Am. 9:11f. and applies it to the immediate situation. It should be noted that the LXX text has several significant deviations from the MT. In the MT the passage means that Israel will be restored and rule the nations inhabiting the territory of David's kingdom. The LXX reads "man" (from Heb. *'āḏām*) for "Edom," making it subject rather than object, and has "they will seek" for "they will inherit." This has a meaning decidely different from the MT. James quotes the LXX, and relates the first part of the prophecy (rebuilding of David's dwelling) to the resurrection of Christ and the founding of His Church on Jewish soil, and the second part (Acts 15:17) to the inclusion of believing Gentiles (the *kai,* "and," in this verse is epexegetic and places the two clauses in apposition). The presence of gentile believers, such as Cornelius and those reached by Paul and Barnabas, is not a novel departure but the fulfillment of prophecy.

The conclusion follows naturally. If God has allowed the Gentiles entrance and included them as part of His people, who are we to trouble them with legal requirements that are strictly Jewish? The conclusion is not handed down *ex cathedra* but comes as a respected opinion of the leader (Gk. *egṓ krínō* may be translated, "I, for my part, judge . . ."; cf. Bruce, *Acts of the Apostles,* p. 299). It is high time to stop troubling (note the present tense, *parenochleín*) the gentile converts. Thus the Judaizers' complaint is overruled and the threat of a divided Church is averted. There is but one way of salvation and one qualification for entrance into the Christian fellowship.

IV. Apostolic Decree.–Once it had been determined that gentile converts had no obligation to Jewish ceremonial law, the problem of table fellowship would become that much more acute. How could the Jew, with his conscience sensitive to traditional religious taboos, enter wholeheartedly into fellowship with converts out of paganism who were not only uninformed about Jewish phobias but would be unable to appreciate the "weaker conscience" of the Jew? As a partial answer to this inevitable problem James suggests that the Gentiles abstain from certain practices especially offensive to the Jew. These prohibitions (known now as the Apostolic Decree) are recorded three times in Acts: as suggested by James (Acts 15:20), as stated in the letter (15:29), and as referred to at a later date (21:25).

Whether the Decree, which prohibits pollutions of idols, fornication, things strangled, and blood, is to be taken as moral or ceremonial depends upon one's evaluation of the critical variations between the Alexandrian and Western texts. The Alexandrian text has the fourfold prohibition and understands it as a food regulation against meat offered to idols or from which the blood has not properly been drained, and a request that Gentiles conform to the high code of conduct between sexes as maintained in the Jewish community. The Western text omits Gk. *pniktoú* ("what is strangled") and understands the Decree as a threefold moral prohibition against idolatry, unchastity, and murder. It also adds a negative version of the Golden Rule (in 15:20 and 15:29, but not in 21:25).

In favor of the Western text it has been argued: (1) The addition of *pniktoú* by a scribe who misunderstood "blood" in a ceremonial sense, and wanted to clarify the prohibition, is more acceptable than the omission of *pniktoú* if it were original. (2) An admonition to gentile converts to avoid their former heathen worship in its three most characteristic features — idolatry, temple prostitution, blood baths of the mystery cults (cf. the suggestion in *IB,* IX, 204) — would be appropriate to the context. (3) It explains why Paul makes no later reference to the Decree when dealing with the problem of meat offered to idols at Corinth (1 Cor. 8–10). (4) The uncial support of the Alexandrian text is from the 4th cent., while the Western reading is confirmed by Irenaeus in the 2nd and Tertullian in the 3rd.

In favor of the Alexandrian text: (1) The weight of MS evidence (the trustworthiness of the textual family still takes precedence over date). (2) The Gk. *alisgēmátōn* ("pollutions") is a hapax legomenon; and the entire phrase, as defined by 15:29 (*eidōlothýtōn,* "things offered to idols"), is distinctly ceremonial rather than moral. (3) "To abstain [*apéchesthai,*" hold oneself away"] from blood" is a curious way of saying "Thou shalt not kill." (4) Instructions to gentile converts regarding Jewish scruples would be expected in this context. Filson writes, "Respect for Jewish aversion to meat containing blood and taken from strangled animals is as intelligible as not serving pork at a modern conference of Jews and Christians" (*IDB,* I, 711). (5) Although the inclusion of fornication in a series of regulations about food may seem strange, the purpose of the Decree was not to be a model of homogeneity, but a reminder of those things especially offensive to Jewish sensitivities. Bruce mentions an interesting emendation, Gk. *porkeías* ("swine flesh") for *porneías* ("fornication"), but notes that *porkeía* is not found in Greek and *porkos* only as a transliteration of the Latin *porcus* (*Acts of the Apostles,* p. 300). (6) It would be far more natural for a specific regulation about foods to be broadened at a later time into a general statement of morality than for the reverse to take place. With the passing of time and the shift to a predominantly gentile Church we would even expect some scribe to rescue the relevancy of the regulation by transforming it into a moral code.

One interesting explanation for the critical variants is that the Alexandrian text was original but consisted of only two prohibitions: one against meat offered to idols and another against meat from which the blood had not properly been drained. The textual group represented by $\mathfrak{p}^{45}$ (Chester Beatty) and Ethiopic, which have no reference to fornication, understood it as a food law and added "what is strangled" as explanation. The Western group took it as moral and added a third major sin, fornication.

Since the evidence favors the fourfold Alexandrian text, we interpret the Decree as relating to those gentile practices that were abhorrent to the Jew and would seriously impair the table fellowship in the local congregation. Since blood was considered a delicacy in pagan society but prohibited to the Jews (Lev. 17:10ff.) on the basis that the "life of the flesh is in the blood," imagine the horror of Jewish Christians at a fellowship meal where recent gentile converts were relishing meat with the blood in it!

Some have traced the background of the Decree to the so-called Noachic precepts. It was believed by later rabbis that prohibitions against blasphemy, idolatry, murder, incest, robbery, resistance to magistrates, and the eating of blood, were enjoined upon the sons of Noah as representatives of the whole human race. This stems from Gen. 9, where murder and the eating of meat containing blood are forbidden. These Noachic prohibitions are taken as an elementary code of universal obligation in existence before the perfect law of God given through Moses. Hence James could make valid appeal to them in his attempt to regulate gentile conduct. The planting of such a subtle scheme in the mind of James, however, seems to be an unnecessary tour de force. All he was doing was giving practical advice on how gentile converts could avoid offending the weaker conscience of their Jewish friends.

Some have doubted the genuineness of the Decree, holding that it originated at a later date (e.g., H. Lietzmann, *Beginnings of the Christian Church* [Eng. tr. 1937], p. 109). It is said that James's reference to the Decree in Acts 21:25 indicates that Paul had never heard of it. A careful reading of the text, however, indicates that such an inference is unwarranted.

It is also argued that Paul would have referred to the Decree in his extended discussion with the Corinthians about meat offered to idols (1 Cor. 8–10). But in 1 Corinthians Paul is arguing for a principle and could achieve little by bringing up as evidence a decision given in a totally different situation. At Antioch the problem was one of instruction so as to avoid offense; at Corinth of wilful disregard of the weaker brother. Reference to a Council decision before the disorderly element at Corinth would have been utterly futile. Even if such an appeal to an external authority would have carried the day in Corinth it would have laid Paul wide open to the criticism of those who refused to recognize him as an apostle in the full sense.

The relationship of James's concluding statement (v. 21) to the preceding Decree is obscure. Among the more plausible explanations are: (1) This proposal will not undermine Israel's impact upon the gentile world because there is ample opportunity for them to learn the law of Moses. (2) These precautions are necessary because Jewish worshipers reside in every gentile community and the majority must make concession to the scruples of the minority. (3) The gentile God-fearers are so accustomed to hear the law of Moses that they will readily see the wisdom in avoiding offense. (4) Moses would not lose out by not gaining a people who were never his.

V. Outcome.–James's proposal won acceptance among the leaders of the Jerusalem church (Gk. *édoxe,* "it pleased," is used regularly for taking a decision in assembly). Judas (presumably a brother of Joseph, mentioned in Acts 1:23) and Silas (Silvanus of 2 Cor. 1:19) were chosen by the leaders to accompany Paul and Barnabas to Antioch. They were to confirm by word of mouth the written report (Acts 15:27).

The letter is sent by the apostles and elders of Jerusalem. They are further designated "brethren," although some join Gk. *adelphoí* to *presbýteroi* and read "elder brethren." It is addressed to the gentile brethren in Antioch, Syria, and Cilicia. In view of those who had reportedly gone out from the Jerusalem church to trouble with words and subvert the faith of the converts, it seemed appropriate not only to write the decision of the Council but to send along official spokesmen. When the entourage reached Antioch the letter was read and the church received the exhortation with great rejoicing. After a period Judas returned to Jerusalem but Silas remained in Antioch.

The significance of the Jerusalem Council is that in the first great threat to the unity of the early Church, intelligent arbitration prevented a drastic division along ethnic and religious lines. "Ultimately, the [Judaizing] movement developed into Ebionism, which in time became a great force in world-history in Islam, with its passionate protest against the Son of God" (Schlatter, p. 128). But within the Christian Church a major step forward was taken. The Jewish wing, with its ceremonial practices, agreed that God was accepting Gentiles on the basis of faith alone, and the gentile wing willingly altered their cultural pattern so as not to be offensive to their Jewish brethren and thus undermine the possibility of genuine harmony within the Church.

Bibliography.–F. F. Bruce, *Acts of the Apostles* (Gk. text; 2nd ed. 1952); *Book of the Acts* (*NIC,* 1954); M. Dibelius, *Studies in the Acts of the Apostles* (Eng. tr. 1956), pp. 93-101; E. Haenchen, *Acts of the Apostles* (Eng. tr. 1971); J. Knox, *Chapters in a Life of Paul* (1950), pp. 61-73; K. Lake, *BC,* V, 195-212; M. Simon, *BJRL,* 52 (1970), 437ff.; *SPT,* pp. 152-177; A. Schlatter, *The Church in the NT Period* (1926; Eng. tr. 1955), pp. 125-138.

R. H. MOUNCE

APOSTOLIC FATHERS. Any attempt to classify the Christian literature of the second and early third centuries under distinct headings is bound to be somewhat arbitrary. The original editors of *ISBE* included in "Subapostolic Literature" the writings more commonly known as the "Apostolic Fathers" (except for the Martyrdom of Polycarp) plus the fragments of Papias, and two of the early apologists, Aristides and Justin Martyr. These were the documents believed to have been written before A.D. 156, the date of the death of Polycarp who was, according to Irenaeus, a disciple of the apostle John and therefore presumably the last surviving disciple of an apostle. Excluded from the list (even if they fell within the stipulated dates) were writings falsely attributed to apostles (i.e., the NT Apocrypha) and writings which by later standards were judged to be "heretical" (e.g., the fragments of the Gnostics Basilides and Valentinus).

Such a method of classification exhibits many arbitrary features and creates a number of problems. For example, there is now wide agreement that the so-called Epistle to Diognetus belongs not to this early period but to the end of the 2nd and the beginning of the 3rd century. Moreover, the thirteen papyrus codices discovered in 1945 near NAG HAMMADI on the banks of the Nile in Upper Egypt, have enriched and virtually revolutionized our picture of this "subapostolic age." Although they may generally be described as Gnostic, some of them, such as the Valentinian Gospel of Truth and Epistle to Rheginos, stand almost as close to "orthodoxy" (depending on how that term is defined) as parts of the Apostolic Fathers and the Apologists. The "subapostolic age" was in any case a period in which the bounds of orthodoxy and heresy had not yet been firmly established. All sides on virtually every question seem to have claimed support for their views in some kind of apostolic tradition. It is historically misleading to abstract one group of early second-century writings, no matter how diverse a group it may be, from the rest and distinguish it with the title of "subapostolic literature." Only on the basis of tradition, remembering the subsequent influence which the "Apostolic Fathers" have had on the Christian Church, can such a procedure be justified. These documents have functioned as a kind of secondary "canon" for centuries, and as such

"Lives of the Fathers" (*Vitae Patrum*), fourteenth-century A.D. manuscript from Naples (Trustees of the Pierpont Morgan Library)

are entitled to separate treatment. The only misconception to be avoided is that they offer anything like a complete picture of the era immediately following the death of the last apostles.

With these considerations in mind, this article will confine itself to the works included in the series *The Apostolic Fathers: A New Translation and Commentary,* ed. Robert M. Grant (1964).

I. First Clement
II. Second Clement
III. Barnabas
IV. Didache
V. Ignatius
VI. Polycarp
VII. Martyrdom of Polycarp
VIII. Papias
IX. Shepherd of Hermas

I. First Clement.–This epistle is the earliest and best known of the so-called "Apostolic Fathers." It is extant in two Greek MSS: the fifth-century biblical Codex Alexandrinus, where it stands at the end of the NT, and the Constantinople MS written in 1056 and rediscovered by Philotheos Bryennios in 1873, containing both 1 and 2 Clement, as well as Barnabas, Didache, and a long recension of the letters of Ignatius. In addition there are Latin, Syriac, and Coptic versions of 1 Clement, as well as extensive quotations by Clement of Alexandria.

The salutation of this letter designates it as an epistle from the church at Rome to the church at Corinth. No author is mentioned by name, but tradition uniformly identifies the author as Clement. As early as A.D. 170 Dionysius bishop of Corinth wrote to Soter bishop of Rome in answer to a letter received from Rome by the Corinthian church: "Today we observed the holy day of the Lord, and read out your letter, which we shall continue to read from time to time for our admonition, as we do with that which was formerly sent to us through Clement" (Eusebius *HE* iv.23.11). Clement of Alexandria quotes this letter frequently, referring to it both as "the letter of the Romans to the Corinthians" (*Misc.* v.80.1) and as the letter of "Clement" (i.38.5), or even "the apostle Clement" (iv.105.1).

This Clement of Rome is probably to be identified with the Clement whom Eusebius mentions as the third bishop of Rome after Peter (*HE* iii.4.9; iii.15.1f.). Eusebius' assumption that the Roman church at this early period was ruled by a single bishop is in all likelihood an anachronism, even though it was believed already by Irenaeus near the end of the 2nd cent. (*Adv. haer.* iii.3). Much earlier, when Ignatius wrote his letter to the Roman church, the monarchical bishop is conspicuously absent, while 1 Clement itself speaks consistently in terms of a body of presbyters rather than a single ruling bishop. Clement was therefore most likely one of the chief presbyters in the Roman church near the end of the 1st cent. and wrote his epistle on behalf of the congregation (cf. Eusebius *HE* iii.38.1). In the Shepherd of Hermas (Vis. 2:4:3) a Clement is mentioned whose duty it was, presumably in the church of Rome, to send messages to other cities, and it is possible that the same individual is in view.

Two other identifications are more speculative: the ancient one of Origen and Eusebius that this Clement is also Paul's co-worker mentioned in Phil. 4:3, and the modern one that he is the same as, or belonged to the household of, the consul Titus Flavius Clemens who was put to death about A.D. 95 for disloyalty to the gods and pro-Jewish tendencies (Dio Cassius *Hist.* lxvii.14). These are no more than guesses. Essentially 1 Clement is not the product of an identifiable "great personality," but a letter from one important church to another in response to a particular crisis.

The situation in the Corinthian church is sketched in the first three chapters. Chs. 4-36 consist of a general discourse on the Christian virtues (with the Corinthian problem in view). Chs. 37-61 bring the argument to bear on the immediate crisis. Chs. 62-65 function as a summary and final exhortation from the Roman church.

The author begins by apologizing for the congregation's delay in addressing itself to the predicament of its sister church. He refers vaguely to "misfortunes and calamities" in Rome which have hindered this ministry of exhortation (1:1). We have no way of knowing what these troubles were, but possibly the reference is to provocations against Christians late in the reign of the Emperor Domitian (A.D. 81-96). The threat in Corinth, however, was from within, an "abominable and unholy schism" (1:1) in which there had been a rebellion against those in authority in the church (3:1-4). The description becomes more explicit later on when the author states that "in spite of their good service you have removed some from the ministry which they fulfilled blamelessly" (44:6). He contrasts the present sedition with an idealized past when Corinthians were obedient to their leaders and wholly at peace among themselves (1:2–2:8). The reader of the NT will think that the divisions Paul faced at Corinth have been overlooked, but Clement later qualifies this simplistic picture by admitting that when "the blessed Paul the Apostle" wrote his epistle, "even then you had made yourselves partisans" (47:3). But in those days they had at least aligned themselves with apostles (cf. 1 Cor. 1:12), "men of high reputation," while now they had overturned all authority, so that "on account of one or two persons the old and well-established church of the Corinthians is in revolt against the presbyters'' (47:6).

The central section of 1 Clement (4:1–36:6) draws on many sources for examples to combat the rebellion. Jealousy and envy have brought about all kinds of evil in the past, not only in the OT (4:1-13) but in ''our own generation'' in the trials which confronted Peter and Paul and the other martyrs (5:1–6:4). But God has always given repentance to those who will turn to Him, and according to the ''venerable rule of our tradition'' (7:2) has made this repentance available to all through Jesus Christ (7:1–8:5). Thus Clement anticipates the outright appeal for repentance which he will make in ch. 57. He similarly extols the virtues of obedience, faithfulness, and hospitality as exemplified in such OT figures as Abraham, Lot, and Rahab (9:1–12:8). These were evidently the qualities he felt to be conspicuously lacking in the rebels at Corinth. The frequent mention of hospitality in particular suggests that antagonism had been directed not only toward the Corinthian presbyters, but perhaps toward emissaries from other churches as well, possibly to messengers from Rome (cf. 63:3; 65:1). What is needed above all else is humility, and Clement speaks of many who exemplified this virtue (13:1–19:1), preeminently Christ Himself (16:1-17) and David (18:1-16).

The keynote of the next subsection is peace and harmony, which Clement illustrates from the natural creation (19:2–20:12). He reinforces his appeal to the Corinthians by pointing to the reality of divine judgment and the hope of resurrection (21:1–28:4). Creation and redemption are inextricably bound together as the basis on which he presses home his argument. To support the idea of a future resurrection he can appeal without much distinction to Scripture, to the raising of Jesus Christ, to the regularity of nature, and even to the strange legend of the phoenix bird who renews himself every fifty years (25:1-5), a legend which is paralleled in several of the pagan ''natural histories.'' Clement brings to a close his general discourse on the Christian life with an emphasis on holiness as the way to the blessedness that comes from God (29:1–36:6). Here his argument is heavily laced with Scripture citations, not only from the OT but from the NT as well (esp. in ch. 36, the Epistle to the Hebrews). The words of 36:6, ''Who then are the enemies?'' anticipate the last main section of 1 Clement, which turns once more to the Corinthian situation.

Clement adopts military imagery as the framework for his solution to the problem afflicting the church. He reiterates the divinely established order which must govern all things (37:1–43:6) and simultaneously pleads with and warns those who he feels have violated this order (44:1–48:6). After a short excursus on love (49:1–50:7) he renews his appeal for repentance (51:1–59:2), closing with a long liturgical prayer for harmony (59:3–61:3) and a summary of his argument (62:1–65:2). The epistle is carried from Rome to Corinth by ''faithful and prudent men, who have lived among us without blame from youth to old age, and they shall be witnesses between you and us'' (63:3). These three messengers are named in 65:1 with the request that they be allowed quickly to return to Rome, hopefully with news of reconciliation.

1 Clement has considerable historical importance as a witness to the authority exercised by the church of Rome over a sister church near the end of the 1st century. Such authority is not surprising in view of the city of Rome's relation to Corinth as a Roman colony, and in any case it should not be forgotten that two decades later Ignatius bishop of Antioch does not hesitate to instruct the churches of Asia Minor. There is therefore no reason to assume that the authority reflected in 1 Clement belonged to the Roman church in any exclusive way.

II. Second Clement.–The designation of Clement's epistle as ''first'' is really a misnomer, for there is no authentic ''second'' letter from him to any church. The document known in tradition as 2 Clement is not an epistle but an anonymous sermon of uncertain date. Doubt was expressed about its authenticity as early as Eusebius (*HE* iii.38.4). It generally circulated with 1 Clement in the later Church, and is extant in the same two Greek manuscripts and Syriac version as the other writing, though it is not found in the Latin or Coptic versions. Codex Alexandrinus breaks off after ch. 12 so that the complete Greek text was unknown until the Bryennios discovery of the Constantinople manuscript in 1873. This find made it clear that the document was indeed a sermon, for a specific occasion of public worship is presupposed. The hearers are exhorted to ''pay attention'' both ''now'' and ''when we have gone home,'' and to ''try to come here more frequently'' (17:3; cf. 19:1).

The traditional association with 1 Clement suggests that it was written in Rome, though its non-epistolary character weakens Harnack's theory that it is the lost letter of Bishop Soter to the Corinthian church. Certain similarities with the Shepherd of Hermas (e.g., 2 Clem. 8:6) tend to confirm Roman origin. The use of material otherwise more familiar to us in Gnostic writings suggests that 2 Clement comes from a time and place in which orthodox and Gnostic alike drew on a common stock of traditions. In 12:2-6 the author takes a saying now known to us from the Nag Hammadi Gospel of Thomas Logion 22 and (with no trace of polemic) attaches to it a wholly orthodox interpretation (much as the Gnostics took apostolic traditions and without hesitation interpreted them in Gnostic fashion). R. M. Grant feels that such a practice points to the time around A.D. 140 when such Gnostic teachers as Marcion and Valentinus were active in Rome without being immediately rejected as heretics. This is possible, though there is every likelihood that this kind of fluidity between ''orthodox'' and ''Gnostic'' traditions existed in many times and places in the 2nd century.

This ancient Christian sermon begins with a reflection on the salvation which God has granted to the gentile hearers (1:1–4:5). They must not take lightly either the salvation itself or Jesus Christ through whom it has come. He must be acknowledged as Lord, along with God the Father, not only with words but with deeds as well. The preacher appeals to Isa. 54:1 and to certain sayings of Jesus (cf. Mk. 2:17; Lk. 19:10) to make his point that those who were lost are now saved (2:1-7). It is perhaps significant for an understanding of authority in the second-century Church that the author appeals to Scripture and tradition, and to the OT and ''the Gospel'' (8:5; cf. 2:4) in much the same way. He confronts his hearers with the choice between this world and the world to come (5:1–7:6) and calls them to repentance (8:1–20:5). This repentance is defined as ''self-control'' (15:1) or ''keeping the flesh pure'' (8:6). This demand is grounded in the complicated argument that Christ (and with Him the Church) was originally ''spirit'' but became ''flesh,'' and that in the resurrection the flesh will rise again as it ''receives the Spirit'' (9:1-5; 14:1-5). More broadly and simply, the demand is grounded in the fear of judgment and hope of the kingdom of God (10:1–12:6; 16:1-3; 17:4-7). Again and again the preacher renews his call to repentance (8:1f.; 13:1; 16:1; 17:1; 19:1), urging that if they repent, his hearers will save both themselves and him their counsellor (15:1; cf. 19:1). Like the ancient prophets, he sees his own fate intertwined with those to whom he ministers.

III. Barnabas.–Once again the title (the Epistle of Barnabas) is a misnomer. Though Clement of Alexandria (e.g., *Misc.* ii.31.2) and Origen (*Contra Celsum* i.63) attributed it to Barnabas the companion of Paul, it is an anonymous work, and Eusebius classed it among the "spurious" (*HE* iii.25.4) or at least "disputed" (vi.13.6; 14.1) books circulating in the ancient Church. Yet its inclusion in the fourth-century Greek manuscript of the Bible, Codex Sinaiticus, testifies to the great esteem and near-canonical status it enjoyed in some sectors of the Church. In addition it is contained in the Constantinople manuscript (see above under First Clement), and in a family of nine Greek manuscripts in which Barn. 5:7ff. is abruptly joined to Polycarp's Epistle to the Philippians (after 9:2) without a break of any kind. There is also a Latin version, in somewhat abridged form, of the first seventeen chapters of Barnabas, as well as a few Syriac fragments and a number of quotations by Clement of Alexandria.

The date of this work cannot be established with any certainty. A statement in 16:4 indicates that the Jerusalem temple is in ruins, thus supporting a date between A.D. 70 and 135, but attempts to be more specific are only conjectures. The reference in 4:4 to the ten kingdoms of Dnl. 7:24 is simply traditional apocalyptic language and should probably not to be made the basis for any conclusions about the epistle's date.

Though it cannot be proved that Barnabas the companion of Paul did *not* write this book, neither the range of possible dates nor the nature of the document itself makes the tradition that he did very plausible. The author is apparently writing to Gentiles who have been saved out of darkness and idolatry (14:5-8; 16:7), and he claims to write as one of their own (1:8; 4:6). The most obvious affinities of Barnabas are with Alexandrian Christianity, as evidenced on the one side by similarities in its OT exegesis with Philo, and on the other by the acquaintance with Barnabas shown by Clement and Origen. Barnabas is more likely the work of a gentile Christian of Alexandria in the early 2nd cent. than of the Jewish Christian from Cyprus mentioned in the book of Acts.

The introduction (1:1–2:3) is rather general and gives only a slight indication of what is to follow. The author presents himself as one whose task it is to impart perfect knowledge to his readers (1:5), not as a teacher (which he apparently is), but as a father to the children he loves. This knowledge has to do with the past, the present, and the future (1:7; cf. 5:3). The knowledge about the future turns out to be conventional eschatological teaching (e.g., ch. 4); the knowledge of past and present, which comprises most of the epistle, turns out to be a series of allegorical interpretations of the OT.

In the ancient prophetic tradition, the author makes it clear that God does not desire ceremonial fasts and sacrifices, but justice and mercy (2:4–3:6). The readers are called on to be ready for the eschatological crisis and not to be lured into the false security that deceived the Jews under the old covenant (4:1-14). He underscores the greatness of the Christian calling by a discussion of the work of Christ, who suffered to prepare a new people and to bring to completion the sins of the old Israel. He illustrates many aspects of Jesus' career by quotations and allegorical interpretations of OT passages (5:1–8:7). Especially elaborate is his exegesis of Gen. 1:26, 28 and Ex. 33:1, 3 (6:8-19), of the ritual of the Day of Atonement (7:3-11) and of the red heifer ritual of Nu. 19:1-10 (8:1-7). Then he offers "spiritual" interpretations of such Jewish institutions as circumcision and the various Mosaic food laws (9:1–10:12). His procedure is to reinterpret ceremonial rules as moral and ethical exhortations. Even though he employs these interpretative principles in the framework of a polemic against the Judaism of his day, the author of Barnabas had ample precedent for his sometimes fanciful exegesis within Judaism itself (notably Philo and the Letter of Aristeas).

Turning his attention to what is distinctly Christian, "Barnabas" finds many subtle intimations in the OT of the water of baptism, the wood and the shape of the cross, and even the name and person of Jesus Himself (11:1–12:11). Here Barnabas exhibits several of the same interpretative traditions which show up in more detail in the writings of Justin Martyr.

The heart of the Epistle of Barnabas is the contrast between the old covenant and the new, with the assertion that God's true covenant belongs not to the Jews but to the Christians (13:1–14:9). Correspondingly the ancient sabbath has given way to the Christian "eighth day," or Sunday, in which Jesus rose from the dead (15:1-9), just as the physical temple in Jerusalem has been replaced by the spiritual temple, the Christian community where God has made his dwelling (16:1-10). Chapter 17 reads like a conclusion; though there is more he could write about present and future (cf. 1:7; 5:3), it is "hidden in parables" and he judges that what he has said is sufficient (17:2).

There is thus a definite break at the end of ch. 17 and in fact the Latin version ends at this point. But the Greek manuscripts make a new beginning with the words, "But let us move on to other knowledge and teaching" (18:1). This begins the famous "Two Ways" section of Barnabas (18:1–21:9), which is paralleled in Did. 1:1–6:2. The way of light (ch. 19) is under the rule of God through his angels, while the way of darkness (ch. 20) belongs to the angels of Satan (18:1f.). This "Two Ways" teaching is by no means profound or "hidden in parables," but sounds more like elementary instruction for new converts (which is exactly how it functions in the Didache). Older commentators argued for literary dependence of Barnabas on the Didache or of the Didache on Barnabas, but the more recent tendency has been to favor the dependence of both on a common primitive source. There are, for example, close parallels between the "Two Ways" tradition and the Qumrân Manual of Discipline (1QS 3:18ff.). It is surprising to find in such an anti-Jewish document as Barnabas a section like this in which there is little or nothing that is distinctively Christian, but in which all that is said can function appropriately in either a Christian or a Jewish setting. The most plausible explanation is that Barnabas comes from a gentile Christian community in which the basic instruction given to new converts from idolatry and paganism necessarily focused as much on general moral principles and things which Christianity inherited from Judaism as it did on the distinctively new Christian message of the cross. New converts needed to be taught to love each other and give alms, and to shun idolatry, murder, lies, and witchcraft. Nothing could be assumed. There is some evidence that "Barnabas" is at times alluding to this moral catechism even in the earlier parts of his epistle (e.g., 1:4; 2:9; 4:1, 10; 5:4), and chs. 18–21 give the impression that the author (or someone else) has simply appended the full text of his source for the sake of completeness. Certainly the Latin tradition witnesses to the fact that Barnabas circulated without this material as well as with it. But in any case the author or final editor has attached a summary which draws together chs. 1–17 and 18–20 and serves as the conclusion to both (ch. 21). The very first verse of this concluding statement makes it clear that "Barnabas" has made use of the primitive "Two Ways" material in written form (21:1). Like the NT writers, the author knows that his readers are never too mature to be reminded of what they have been taught at conversion.

*IV. **Didache***.–The longer title of this work, "The Teaching of the Lord, through the Twelve Apostles, to the Gentitles," gives a clue to its nature. It seems to be a work conceived against the background of Mt. 28:18-20, purporting to give the content of that which the twelve apostles taught to the "Gentiles" or "nations" of the things which Jesus the Lord had commanded. It therefore stands in a tradition somewhat different from the one which sees Paul as the apostle to the Gentiles par excellence and the Twelve as missionaries to the Jews (cf., e.g., Gal. 2:9); instead the Twelve, representing the whole Church, are sent to the whole world, and indeed especially to the Gentiles. Shorter variations of this title (e.g., Teaching [or Teachings] of the Apostles) are cited by several patristic writers (e.g., Eusebius *HE* iii.25.4; Athanasius *Festal Letter* 39; the ninth-century Stichometry of Nicephorus), but there is no way to be sure that they are identical to the work now known by this name.

This work really came to light for the first time in the Constantinople MS discovered by Bryennios. As a result of the publication of the full text of the Didache in 1883, the "canon" of the Apostolic Fathers was enlarged by one. It then became possible to go back and see that the Didache in Greek was actually to be found (in a somewhat revised form) in book vii of the fourth-century Egyptian Apostolic Constitutions. In addition there are fragments in Greek (Oxyrhynchus Papyrus 1782), Coptic, and Ethiopic, and a complete Georgian version. For the "Two Ways" section there is (besides the witness of Barn. 18–20) a Latin version (the *Doctrina*) the fourth-century Apostolic Church Order, and three other manuals of the 4th cent. or later. There is no way of being sure that the Constantinople MS represents the "original" Didache nor even what the term "original" exactly means in such a context. We are not dealing here simply with textual variants as we do when studying the NT, but with a developing tradition, and our various witnesses to the Didache merely afford us glimpses of this tradition at various stages. Total agreement is seldom possible as to which forms are primitive and which are later adaptations. Therefore it is difficult to speak about dates, but the compilation of purportedly apostolic material under the name of the apostles as a group indicates that the apostles are already figures of the past. This together with the apparent use of Matthew's Gospel tends to suggest a date of composition in the 2nd cent., though many specific elements (e.g., the prayers, the "Two Ways," and the eschatological teaching) may well go back to the apostolic age and even perhaps to the early days of the Jerusalem church.

The "Two Ways" section of the Didache comes at the beginning (1:1–6:2) rather than at the end as in Barnabas. The "way of life" is found in 1:2–4:14 and the "way of death" in 5:1f., with a brief summary in 6:1-3. The parallels with Barnabas are rather close, though by no means verbal. Didache contains an interpolation in its "Two Ways" material, consisting of words of Jesus based on Matthew and Luke and/or an unknown collection of traditional sayings (1:3b–2:1). This section is missing from the "Two Ways" both in Barnabas and in the *Doctrina*. It has been inserted here as the "teaching" or explanation of the negative form of the Golden Rule found in 1:2. Thus 2:2-7 (which does belong to the "Two Ways") becomes the *second* such explanation (2:1), this time using a traditional list of prohibitions based on the Ten Commandments.

Didache 3:1-6 is another interpolation into the "Two Ways," this time designed to warn against certain attitudes and practices which lead to the more serious sins enumerated in ch. 2. In good rabbinic fashion the author or compiler is "building a fence around the law" (cf. Mish. *Pirke Aboth* i.1) by avoiding even that which might lead to sin. Unlike the NT, however, the Didachist seems to locate the real sin in the act rather than in the heart. The attitudes are dangerous because of what they engender, not because they indicate a sinful nature already at work. In his appended conclusion to the "Two Ways" (6:1-3) the editor adds a pragmatic touch to bring the commands within reach of everyone: if the readers can bear the whole "yoke of the law" they will be perfect, but if not, they must simply do the best they can (6:2).

In 7:1-4 the theme is baptism, with a clear indication that the "Two Ways" material has functioned in the Didache as instruction designed for baptismal candidates. After reviewing "all these things" the community is to "baptize in the name of the Father and of the Son and of the Holy Spirit" (7:1). This closely parallels Mt. 28:19f., where "teaching the Gentiles" to obey Jesus' commands is linked to baptism involving the same trinitarian formula. Ch. 8 deals with fasting and prayer, centering on a version of the Lord's Prayer quite similar to that found in Matthew. Here for the first time a doxology is attached to the prayer; this doxology is repeated twice in chs. 9f., and along with a shorter formula ("To thee be glory forever") is used to punctuate the eucharistic meal prayers found in those chapters. These prayers, before (9:1-5) and after (10:1-7) the meal, are traditional and very ancient, exhibiting a number of parallels with Jewish table prayers, and embodying traces of a primitive Palestinian Christology which described Jesus as God's servant or as the "holy Vine of David."

The rest of the Didache addresses itself to other concerns of the ancient Church in no particularly logical sequence: the testing of traveling teachers and prophets to tell the true from the false (11:1–12:5); the responsibility of the congregation to those who are found to be worthy (13:1-7); the Sunday gatherings for worship (14:1-3, possibly eucharistic again as in chs. 9f.); the qualifications for resident leaders (bishops and deacons) with an appeal to have respect for them and to be at peace with one another (15:1-4); and finally a chapter of eschatological instruction, including a call to readiness and a small apocalypse (not unlike Mt. 24) which sets forth the events leading up to the end of the age and the return of Christ (16:1-8).

Thus the Didache as we know it is a compendium of practical teaching on various subjects which must have come up in the course of the Church's fulfillment of its commission to teach the Gentiles. The Jewish or Jewish Christian origin of much of the material makes the Didache (along with Matthew) an important witness to the fact that segments of Jewish Christianity besides the Apostle Paul took seriously their calling to be a light and a blessing to the nations. Syria is a plausible locale for such a community of Jewish Christians. Though recensions of the Didache, or parts of it, can be traced to Egypt, Ethiopia, Rome, etc., many scholars have suggested Syria or Palestine as the setting of the form of the tradition found in the Bryennios MS. The parallels with Matthew and the references to bread or wheat gathered from the "mountains" (9:4) point in this direction, but no one really knows.

*V. **Ignatius***.–The letters of Ignatius, bishop of Antioch at the beginning of the 2nd cent., are known to us in three recensions.

(1) The short recension, accepted today as the authentic collection of Ignatius' writings, consists of the seven letters mentioned by Eusebius in *HE* iii.36.5-11: four from

Smyrna, to the churches of Ephesus, Magnesia, Tralles, and Rome; and three from Troas (after leaving Smyrna), to the churches of Philadelphia and Smyrna, and to Smyrna's bishop, Polycarp. They were said to have been written while Ignatius was en route from Syria to Rome to suffer martyrdom (*HE* iii.36.3f.; cf. Ign. Rom. 5:1).

(2) The long recension consists of thirteen letters in all, in the following order: two from Antioch — one from a certain Mary of Cassobola (a neighboring town) to Ignatius, and Ignatius' letter to her in reply; the four from Smyrna and three from Troas found in the short recension; three from Philippi, to Tarsus, Antioch, and Hero (Ignatius' successor as bishop of Antioch); and one from Italy to Philippi. In addition there are some extensive interpolations in the seven letters from Smyrna and Troas mentioned by Eusebius. In the early Middle Ages this collection was enlarged still further by two letters to the apostle John, one to Mary the mother of Jesus, and one from Mary to Ignatius in return! Even though these latter were soon rejected as forgeries, the works of Ignatius continued to be known in the Church only in the long recension until the middle of the 17th century.

(3) The Syriac abridgement, discovered by W. Cureton in 1845, is a Syriac version consisting of only three epistles (to the Ephesians, to the Romans, and to Polycarp), similar in form to the short recension.

The dominance of the long recension began to be broken in 1644 when Archbishop James Ussher published an edition of Ignatius based on two medieval Latin MSS which, while containing all the letters of the long recension, provided an uninterpolated text of the seven core epistles known to Eusebius. Soon afterward a Greek MS was found which confirmed the existence of the short recension. It contained the epistles of the short recension in the same uninterpolated form, except for Romans; a martyrological text discovered a few decades later supplied this lack with a similarly short text of Romans. Since then, as the result of careful investigations of Theodor Zahn, J. B. Lightfoot, and others, scholarship came to a point of virtual consensus in favor of the short recension. Though some for a time defended the originality of the Syriac abridgment, the consensus still stands. In addition to the Greek and Latin witnesses and the Syriac abridgment mentioned above, there are fragments in Greek, Syriac, and Coptic, and an Armenian version.

In his letter to Polycarp, Ignatius states that he was unable to write to all the churches because he was taken on short notice from Troas to Neapolis on the Macedonian coast. He asks Polycarp to write to the churches that lay ahead on his itinerary, so that they might have news of Ignatius and send messengers or letters to him (Ign. Polyc. 8:1). The first of these churches would be the one at Philippi, and we have Polycarp's letter to this church, in which he states clearly that he is sending them "the letters of Ignatius, which were sent to us by him, and others which we had by us" (Polyc. Phil. 13:2). Presumably these would include Ignatius' letters to Smyrna and to Polycarp as well as copies of the four letters written from Smyrna (i.e., all the letters except that to the Philadelphians, a copy of which *may* have been sent to Polycarp as well). Thus Polycarp was the earliest collector of the Ignatian corpus and the person chiefly responsible for its preservation.

Without discussing each of Ignatius' letters in detail, it can be said that they share a common structure which enables the reader to know more or less what to expect: first there is an elaborate salutation with praise for the church and its bishop; then often an appeal to live in harmony with the bishop; then usually some attention to the particular heresy threatening the church; and finally some reference to Ignatius' own situation and that of the church in Syria.

The theology and Christology of Ignatius arises out of a life situation in which three factors were at work: (1) his sense of impending martyrdom, (2) his awareness of the threat of heresy and schism, and (3) his concern for unity in the churches under the authority of the bishop.

(1) The factor of martyrdom looms largest in his letter to the Romans, where his aim is to make sure that the church at Rome does nothing to prevent his execution by the Roman authorities. For him to die as a martyr is to "attain to God" (Ign. Rom. 1:2; 2:1; 9:2) or to Christ (5:3), to "become a disciple" (4:2; 5:1, 3) or a true Christian (3:2), to be reborn (6:1) and thus fully to "become a man" (6:2). His death is a sacrifice (2:2; 4:2), sometimes specifically a eucharistic sacrifice. For Ignatius, violent death means participation in the sacrifice of the flesh and blood of Jesus Christ. To be martyred is to receive the sacrament of the eucharist in the ultimate sense (7:3). He longs to be devoured by wild beasts and ground as wheat so as to become the "pure bread of Christ" (4:1). If the beasts are reluctant, he will entice and compel them to destroy him (5:2). Such language has led to a widespread characterization of Ignatius as morbid and fanatical in his longing for self-annihilation, but two qualifying factors must be kept in mind: first, his language is only an extension and a heightening of similar phrases used by the apostle Paul (e.g., Phil. 1:23; 2:17; 3:10; Col. 1:24;ff.); second, he saw his death as virtually inevitable and so addressed his concern to the one church which, for its own sake, most needed to see Ignatius' death as a victory and to interpret it in this way to other Christians and to the world.

Ignatius draws freely on Pauline language, and a case can be made that he, like Paul, sees himself as a decisive figure in the redemptive historical plan of God for the world. Though (like Paul) he is the "least" and like an "untimely birth" (Ign. Rom. 9:2; cf. 1 Cor. 15:8f.), his great journey from East to West is as crucial to him as Paul's collection journey to Jerusalem (and from there to Rome and possibly Spain) was to the apostle (cf. Paul in Rom. 15:16-33; also 1 Clem. 5:5-7). Mal. 1:11 seems to stand behind Ignatius' thinking here as a kind of hidden Scripture citation: observance of the eucharist in the gentile churches "from furthest east to furthest west" is the proof that now God's name is "great among the nations" (cf. Did. 14:3; Justin Martyr *Dial.* 41.2; 117:1). To Ignatius this eucharistic sacrifice finds supreme expression in the sacrifice of his own life (Ign. Rom. 2:2; 7:3).

(2) The threat of false teaching comes to the surface especially in his letters to the Magnesians, Trallians, Smyrneans, and Philadelphians. Heresy is compared to a deadly poison (Ign. Trall. 6). It seems to have confronted Ignatius in two forms: a re-Judaizing of the Christian message not unlike the threat which Paul faced, and a docetic denial of the reality of Jesus' human nature. With regard to the first, Ignatius follows Paul in warning that "if we are still living according to Judaism, we acknowledge that we have not received grace" (Ign. Magn. 8:1; cf. Ign. Philad. 6:1). He argues that even the ancient prophets were disciples of Jesus Christ in the Spirit (Ign. Magn. 9:2; cf. 8:2), and that we who stand in their tradition must therefore observe not the sabbath but the Lord's Day, on which Christ rose from the dead (9:1). Though Ignatius retains and respects the OT, his supreme authority is Jesus Christ whom he knows first of all not through ancient Jewish prophecies but through the proclaimed message of the gospel (Ign. Philad. 8:2; 9:2). Having placed his faith firmly in Christ on this basis, Ignatius then goes back

and "after the fact" sees the prophets and the OT scriptures as witnesses to him. His answer to the Judaizers is to test the Jewish Scriptures by means of the new Christian tradition, not the tradition by the Scriptures. It is no accident that he seems much more influenced by Paul and John and certain freely quoted sayings of Jesus than by the OT. We have no way of knowing who these Judaizers were, but one statement (Ign. Philad. 6:1) suggests that they may have been gentile converts to Judaism and Jewish Christianity who developed an extreme zeal for the law. We are reminded of the references in the book of Revelation (2:9; 3:9) in letters to Smyrna and Philadelphia (!) to "those who claim to be Jews, but are not."

With regard to Docetism, the second heresy which he faced, Ignatius even provides us with the derivation of the term. He speaks of those who say that the suffering of Jesus was unreal, a semblance (Gk. *tó dokeín*), and condemns them by claiming that it is they who are unreal, for they shall become like phantoms, without bodies (Ign. Trall. 10:1; cf. Smyrn. 2:1). He affirms that Christ *really* suffered and *really* rose from the dead (Ign. Smyrn. 2:1). Because they deny this, the heretics abstain from the eucharist, which witnesses to the reality of Jesus' flesh (7:1). Once again Ignatius' appeal is to the validity and necessity of this sacrament, the "medicine of immortality" and antidote to all such poisonous teachings (Ign. Eph. 20:2); more immediately, he argues from his own experience of imminent death. If Christ's sufferings are unreal, then why is Ignatius a prisoner, longing for the sword and the beasts of the arena? (Ign. Smyrn. 4:2; Trall. 10:1). His campaign against heresy is thus not waged in a vacuum but always and inevitably within the context of his life (and death) situation.

(3) The third concern of Ignatius has to do with church order and submission to the bishop's authority. His theology may be described as *sacramental* in both a narrower and a broader sense. In the narrow sense it is clear that he puts great emphasis on the sacrament of the Lord's Supper. But in the broad sense his thought is sacramental in its insistence that spiritual realities must find their embodiment in that which is visible and physical. Just as Jesus was no phantom but actually "became flesh" (cf. Jn. 1:14), so the Spirit must "become flesh" in different ways in order to have any validity or authority. Flesh is not a worldly or evil principle opposed to the Spirit, as it is sometimes in Paul, but rather as in John the natural and appropriate sphere in which the Spirit must express Himself. This is clear in Ignatius' theology of the eucharist, which builds upon Jn. 6:52-58 with its demand to eat the flesh and drink the blood of the crucified and risen Lord (see Ign. Eph. 20:2; Smyrn. 7:1). But where John limited his insistence on "flesh" to the sacrament and to the historical reality of Jesus Christ, Ignatius extends it also to the matter of church organization. In fact there can be no valid eucharist unless the bishop (or someone he appoints) is present to celebrate it (Ign. Smyrn. 8:1f.; cf. Magn. 4:1). John's sacramentalism is combined with virtual silence about particular offices or ministries, but to Ignatius spiritual realities must find their embodiment in the structure of the institutional Church. Ignatius is the first real advocate of episcopacy in the ancient Church — probably not episcopacy in the modern sense of one bishop supervising a group of churches each with its individual pastor, but in an incipient form involving "one man rule" in each local congregation. This is of course a form of "episcopacy" which is found today in the vast majority of Christian denominations, even those which follow a "congregational" type of church government, but it is not characteristic of the NT period.

Ignatius undergirds his high view of episcopal authority with theological arguments and elaborate imagery. At Ephesus the presbytery "is attuned to the bishop like the strings of a harp" so that "by your concord and harmonious love, Jesus Christ is sung" (Ign. Eph. 4:1). Unity is essential to the Church, and for Ignatius this means unity with the bishop, even as the Church is united with Jesus Christ and Jesus with the Father (5:1). The bishop is sent from the Lord and is therefore to be regarded as if he were the Lord himself (6:1; cf. Mt. 10:40). Sometimes the bishop represents Jesus Christ (e.g., Ign. Trall. 2:1); at other times the bishop represents the Father, while the deacons represent Christ the servant, and the presbytery the apostles (Ign. Trall. 3:1; cf. Magn. 6:1). While on the one hand he is the divine representative, on the other he is the embodiment of the whole congregation, especially as it ministers to the needs of Ignatius himself, the prisoner (e.g., Ign. Eph. 1:3, Trall. 1:1). The churches must recognize and submit to his authority and do nothing apart from him, just as Jesus did nothing apart from the Father (Ign. Magn. 7:1; Trall. 2:2). Even though his function is not primarily that of prophecy or teaching, his authority is beyond question (Ign. Eph. 6:1; 15:1), for he is the administrative leader of the church. There can be only one bishop even as there is only one eucharist (Ign. Philad. 4:1). Nevertheless, Ignatius knows that the bishop is not absolutely essential for a church. His own church at Antioch is of course without its bishop for a time. God is its shepherd in place of Ignatius, and Jesus Christ alone is its bishop (Ign. Rom. 9:1). For this reason, however, the other churches are to support Antioch with their prayers. The one church in which nothing is said of a bishop is the church of Rome, and it is possible that the supreme authority there still lies with the presbytery, as it did a short time earlier according to the witness of 1 Clement.

There is every indication that these major theological concerns of Ignatius are all tied together in his mind. His martyrdom is a kind of ultimate expression or illustration of the reality of the eucharist; the eucharist depends for its validity on the authority of the bishop; the sacrament and the episcopal office together bring about and guarantee the unity of the Church so as to furnish the antidote to the deadly poison of false teaching. This means that Ignatius is also a pivotal figure in preserving and drawing together several strands from the NT: Paul's intense consciousness of mission, John's emphasis on the reality of the "flesh" both in the Incarnation and the sacraments, the developing institutionalism which can be seen in Matthew and in the Pastoral Epistles, and the concern over heresy which appears conspicuously in the Pastoral and the Catholic Epistles (e.g., 2 Peter, Jude, 1-3 John). Perhaps more than any other theologian, Ignatius bridges the apostolic and the subapostolic periods.

An especially valuable feature of Ignatius' corpus, from the standpoint of the history of Christian thought, is his preservation of earlier creedal formulations, some of which must reach well back into the NT era. Even more conspicuous here than the customary emphasis on the cross and the resurrection is the particular attention given to the birth of Jesus, somewhat in the manner of the Pauline formula in Rom. 1:3. Jesus is born of Mary from the family of David (see Ign. Eph. 18:2; Trall. 9:1; Smyrn. 1:1; cf. Ign. Eph. 7:2; Magn. 11:1). The virgin birth takes its place in the core of the Christian message, not primarily as a proof of Jesus' deity, but as a witness to his humanity and his messianic descent from David (cf. Mt. 1f.). A different expression of this theology of birth comes in the great hymn in Ign. Eph. 19 to the new revelation in Jesus Christ by which God broke the ancient powers of

APOSTOLIC FATHERS

magic and wickedness. Mary's virginity and childbearing introduce nothing less than the manifestation of God to man "for the newness of eternal life" (19:3).

VI. Polycarp.–The letter of Polycarp bishop of Smyrna to the church at Philippi appears to be a kind of "covering letter" for the Ignatian corpus which Polycarp sends on to the Philippians (Polyc. Phil. 13:2; and see above). It exists in nine Greek MSS, all apparently based on a single archetype. These MSS break off after ch. 9 (see above on Barnabas), though there exists a Latin version which is complete. Thus most of chs. 10–14 are known to us only in Latin. Ch. 13, however (all but the last sentence), can be found (along with ch. 9) quoted in Greek in Eusebius *HE* iii.36.13-15.

As a man — though not as a theologian — Polycarp stands even more than Ignatius as a link between the apostolic and the subapostolic ages (*HE* iii.36.1, 10). Irenaeus, who claims to remember him, identifies him as a disciple of the apostle John, and an opponent of Gnosticism (*Adv. haer*. iii.3.4; cf. his letter to Florinus in Eusebius *HE* v. 20.4-8). Polycarp's traditional connection with John on the one hand and Irenaeus on the other makes Irenaeus' testimony to the apostolic authorship of the Fourth Gospel a particularly weighty piece of evidence. Polycarp seems to have been involved not only in the Church's conflict with Gnosticism, but also (somewhat more amicably) in the early disputes over the date of Easter (Irenaeus, in Eusebius *HE* v.24.14-18).

Irenaeus speaks of several letters of Polycarp to various churches, but only the letter to the Philippians is now extant. It may be dated as roughly contemporary with the letters of Ignatius (i.e., within the reign of Trajan, and probably around A.D. 110). P. N. Harrison argued that the Philippian epistle is really two epistles copied on the same scroll: the first, consisting of chs. 13f., was the original covering letter for the Ignatian epistles, while the second was written perhaps twenty years later, when the name of "blessed Ignatius" the martyr had become a memory (see 9:1f.). This is possible, but MS evidence for it is lacking. Moreover, (a) it is not altogether certain that Ignatius is assumed to be dead in 9:1; (b) sufficient time may have elapsed between Ignatius' letter to Polycarp and Polycarp's letter to the Philippians for Polycarp to assume that Ignatius was by this time a martyr; (c) it is not entirely clear whether the end of 13:2 refers to an inquiry about Ignatius' current situation or about the circumstances of his death.

Whether regarded as one letter or two, the Epistle to the Philippians is a rather conventional document, especially in contrast with the writings of the creative and almost flamboyant Ignatius. To a considerable extent it is a patchwork of allusions to NT books (e.g., 1 Peter, 1 Timothy, and most of the rest of the Pauline letters) and to 1 Clement. Polycarp commends the Philippians for their faith and endurance, and summons them to continue in the service of God (chs. 1f.). He speaks to them of righteousness at their invitation, though he declines to compare himself with "the blessed and glorious Paul" who had taught the word of truth and written letters to them. In the Pauline tradition, Polycarp sees righteousness as coming through faith, hope, and love (ch. 3). He sets forth the duties of groups in the church, husbands, wives, widows, deacons, younger men, and presbyters (chs. 4–6; no bishop is mentioned). He then warns against heresy in terms reminiscent of John: "Everyone who does not confess that Jesus Christ has come in the flesh is an anti-Christ" (7:1; cf. 1 Jn. 4:2f.; 2 Jn. 7). In the face of denials of resurrection and judgment, the Church must return to the tradition it received in the beginning (7:2), and imitate the endurance of Christ and the martyrs (chs. 8f.). Christian believers are to love each other and give alms (ch. 10), avoiding the greed that has led some astray (e.g., a certain presbyter named Valens, 11:1–12:1). Polycarp closes the epistle with a benediction, an appeal to pray for fellow Christians and for rulers, some final remarks about Ignatius and his letters, and a word of recommendation for the messenger who will bring the epistles to Philippi (12:2–14:1).

If any one theme can be singled out, it is expressed by the phrase "concerning righteousness" in 3:1 (cf. 3:3; 4:1; 8:1; 9:1f.). Though Polycarp connects this theme with Paul, he develops it not in the Pauline sense but in terms of rather conventional exhortations to virtue and faithfulness. He is more concerned to preserve and hand down traditions of generally-accepted Christian truth than to shape or adapt them to particular needs or situations, much less to move out in any new directions. Polycarp's epistle is of more interest for its sources than for itself.

VII. Martyrdom of Polycarp.–This most ancient of Christian martyr accounts takes the form of a letter from the church of Smyrna to the church of Philomelium in Phrygia, and beyond that church "to all the parishes of the holy universal church in every place" (Mart. Polyc., inscr.; cf. 20:1 and 1 Cor. 1:1). It gives every evidence of being what it claims to be, an eyewitness report (15:1), apparently written within a year of the event it describes (18:3).

The Martyrdom of Polycarp is known in six Greek MSS, in extensive quotations by Eusebius (*HE* iv.15) and a Latin version (Armenian, Syriac, and Coptic versions are simply based on Eusebius). The most reliable Greek witness is generally considered to be the so-called Moscow MS. Several appendices volunteer information about the Martyrdom's transmission: a certain Gaius claims to have copied it from papers belonging to Irenaeus (a disciple of Polycarp), and at a later time a certain Pionius claims to have transcribed it from a copy whose location was revealed to him by "the blessed Polycarp" himself in a vision (22:2f.). Another conclusion, found only in the Moscow MS, seems to attribute the actual writing of the Martyrdom to Irenaeus and goes to great lengths to emphasize the close connection of Irenaeus with Polycarp. (At the exact moment when Polycarp died in Smyrna, Irenaeus heard a voice in Rome saying, "Polycarp has been martyred"!) Such traditions seem to be shaped by a desire to reinforce the links between the orthodox fathers and the apostles. Though the reference to Gaius may well be authentic, much of the rest is open to serious question. Still another appendix (21:1) offers an exact date for the martyrdom (Feb. 23, 155, or Feb. 22, 156, according to different methods of reckoning), which disagrees with the date of 166/167 fixed by Eusebius in his *Chronicon*. The ruling officials mentioned in 21:1 and 12:2 suggest in any case a date before 160. But in general the epistle itself carries more marks of its own authenticity than do the appendices which were written to validate it.

The writer introduces his narrative as a "martyrdom in accord with the Gospel" (1:1), and prefaces the actual story of Polycarp with a few briefer accounts of those who had just previously suffered for Christ (2:1–4:2). He makes the point that to give oneself up voluntarily or to seek martyrdom is not in accordance with the teaching of the gospel (4:2). Polycarp's martyrdom was thus "in accord with the Gospel" by virtue of the fact that "he waited to be betrayed, as also the Lord had done" (1:2). Such martyrdom is also "in accord with the will of God" (2:1). This theme of not forcing God's hand or the hand of the oppressors is part of a larger complex, in which parallels between Polycarp's death and the death of Christ are noted and stressed. After withdrawing from the city, Polycarp is hunted by a police captain named Herod and betrayed by young slaves who belong to his own house (6:2). He is arrested late in the evening in an "upper room" by police armed as if advancing against a robber (7:1; cf. Mt. 26:55). He refuses to flee, but like Jesus in Gethsemane says "the will of God be done." After a long prayer (7:3) he is taken back to the city riding on an ass on a "great Sabbath day" (8:1). Because of his great age, he is urged to say "Caesar is Lord," offer the right sacrifices, and so spare himself; but he refuses and is taken to the arena (8:2f.). Here he is questioned and commanded to denounce Christ and the Christians by shouting "Away with the atheists" (i.e., those who deny the Roman gods). Instead he motions to the pagan crowds looking on and says of *them,* "Away with the atheists" (9:2). He then confesses that he is a Christian and has been for 86 years (thus dating his birth at A.D. 70 or earlier), and refuses to renounce his faith, even under the severest threats (9:3–11:2). The martyrdom itself is described in some detail (12:1–16:2), focusing on such features as the particular role of the Smyrnean Jews — even in violation of the sabbath (12:2; 13:1; 17:2; 18:1; cf. Rev. 2:9), the last prayer of Polycarp (14:1-3), and the miracles attending the death itself (15:2; 16:1). He is burned alive, in fulfillment of his own vision (cf. 5:2).

It is clear from this account that although there is an interest in showing similarities between the martyr's death and that of his Lord, this interest has not been pushed so far as to violate the probabilities of what actually happened. Several features (e.g., Polycarp's great age, the death by burning, the "great Sabbath day"), do not fit this pattern and are not forced. Though he is like a ram to be sacrificed he is not nailed but bound in the fire (14:1). Moreover the element of the miraculous, though present, is somewhat more restrained than in later martyr accounts.

After his death Polycarp's body is destroyed and his bones are taken by the Christians to an appropriate place (17:1–18:2) where they intend to celebrate "the birthday of his martyrdom" (18:3). Here we have the beginning of the later custom of treasuring the relics of the saints, but also the concept that martyrdom is not an end, but a birth into another life. It is fully in accord with Ignatius' notion that he will truly become a disciple only when he gives up his life.

The concluding chapters summarize Polycarp's career (19:1f.), and identify a certain Marcion (not the heretic) as the one who drafted the letter on behalf of the church of Smyrna (20:1f.). Though we know nothing else of this person, he probably deserves to be called the author of this church epistle just as much as Clement deserves to be called the author of the famous letter from the Romans to the Corinthians (see above).

In the appendices (21:1–22:3) a noteworthy feature is the exact time reference in 21:1, where the names of the asiarch and the proconsul are given, but instead of naming the emperor the text concludes "Jesus Christ was reigning for ever, to whom be glory, honor, majesty, and an eternal throne. . . ." Whatever its claim to authenticity, this citation has caught the point of Polycarp's confession (see 8:2; 9:2f.). Not Caesar but Christ is Lord.

VIII. Papias.–Papias, like Polycarp, was traditionally believed to have been a disciple of the apostle John (Irenaeus *Adv. haer.* v.33.4). He was bishop of Hierapolis in Phrygia during the first half of the 2nd cent. A.D. (Eusebius *HE* iii.36.2), whose writings are known to us only in fragments quoted by later fathers. At first (in his *Chronicon*) Eusebius accepted the claim that Papias was a hearer and eyewitness of the apostles, but later disputed it on the basis of an interpretation of one of Papias' own statements (*HE* iii.39.2). He attributes to Papias a work consisting of five treatises and entitled "Interpretation of the Sayings of the Lord," in which Papias claims to draw much of his information from "the presbyters" or their followers concerning what the Lord's disciples had said or were saying (iii.39.1-4). Eusebius argues that this puts intermediaries between Papias and the apostles. But the case is not conclusive, for a few lines later Eusebius himself speaks of "the apostles" and "their followers" (iii.39.7), apparently as a clarification of Papias' reference to the presbyters and their followers. It is hard to avoid the conclusion that for Eusebius no less than for Papias, "presbyters" and "apostles" can be used interchangeably. This raises a serious question about Eusebius' effort in the context to draw a sharp distinction between the two, especially between John the apostle (whom Papias mentions with other members of the Twelve), and John the presbyter (named with a certain Aristion as Papias' contemporary). Many theories have been built on Eusebius' exegesis here, but it should not be too quickly assumed that two Johns are mentioned, especially since: (a) both times the name occurs, it refers to a "disciple of the Lord," and (b) both times it is found in close association with "presbyter." It is clear that Eusebius is not self-consistent at this point, and the traditional view that Papias speaks of the aged apostle John first as a man of the past and then as a contemporary should not be summarily ruled out. All this has considerable bearing on the traditions about the Fourth Gospel, but does not enable us to fix the role of Papias with any exactness. Whether mediated by "presbyters" or simply by "followers," Papias' knowledge does seem to be at least once removed from the apostles themselves. In this respect Eusebius is right.

Another tradition preserved by Papias describes the Gospels of Mark and Matthew. According to Eusebius, Papias attributes to "the Presbyter" a statement that Mark presented his Gospel without making an ordered arrangement of what Jesus had said and done. He simply followed the oral teaching of Peter, becoming in effect Peter's recorder (*HE* iii.39.15). Matthew on the other hand did what Mark did not do: he made an ordered arrangement of the gospel in the Hebrew language (or a Hebraic style). Thus each of them presented the gospel according to the possibilities open to him (iii.39.16). We have no statement of Papias preserved about Luke and John, but the Gospels are presumably the "interpretations" or "presentations" which he proposes to supplement with the oral traditions of the presbyters (iii.39.3). Though he does not disdain the written Gospels, he attributes equal or greater authority to "the living and abiding voice" of the apostles or of those who (like Mark) were their followers (iii.39.4).

Other statements attributed to Papias reflect this interest in oral traditions. He cites, for example, otherwise unknown sayings of Jesus about a coming thousand-year reign on earth (iii.39.11f.; cf. Rev. 20:1-6), and about unbelievably plentiful harvests of grapes and wheat on the earth in those days (Irenaeus *Adv. haer.* v.33.3f., a tradition supposedly from Jesus by way of John and the "presbyters"). He also preserves stories of apostolic miracles involving in one case the daughters of Philip (cf. Acts 21:8), and in another the Justus Barsabbas of Acts 1:23f. (Eusebius *HE* iii.39.8-10). He refers to an account of a woman accused of many sins in the Lord's presence (*HE* iii.39.17; cf. Jn. 7:53–8:11), and is said to have been responsible for a particularly gruesome report of the death of Judas Iscariot now found in commentary fragments of a fourth-century writer named Apollinaris of Laodicea. A number of other statements are assigned to Papias by late historians and epitomists, including references to a martyrdom of the apostle John, and even a legend that Papias wrote the Gospel of John at the apostle's dictation! In such accounts the uncertainty about Papias himself is compounded by the tendentious and confusing growth of legends about him and about the apostles he is supposed to have known.

Largely because of his extravagant depictions of millennial plenty, Eusebius described Papias as a "man of very little intelligence" (*HE* iii.39.13). Though this verdict is perhaps unfair on such limited data, Papias seems to have been a person who was fascinated by eschatological hopes, especially when they involved extravagant and bizarre projections of certain features of the present life into the future.

IX. Shepherd of Hermas.–The longest of the writings of the Apostolic Fathers is also one of the most remarkable. The Shepherd of Hermas is part novel and part apocalypse, with the literary features of both of these genres directed toward an overall purpose of edification and moral exhortation. It is divided into three sections, commonly known as the Visions, the Mandates, and the Similitudes.

The work is found in three Greek MSS: the fourth-century biblical Codex Sinaiticus, containing only Vis. 1:1:1 through Mand. 4:3:6; Codex Athous, from the 15th cent., ending at Sim. 9:30:2; and Papyrus 129, containing Sim. 2:8 through Sim. 9:5:1. In addition there are a number of Greek fragments, two complete Latin versions (the Vulgate and the Palatine version), an Ethiopic version, and a few fragments in Coptic and Middle Persian. This means in Sim. 9:30:3 through 10:4:5 we are mainly dependent on the Latin for our text.

The first four visions form a literary unit. The fifth and last of the visions is really the introduction to the twelve Mandates and ten Similitudes which are to follow, and in a very real sense belongs with them in the structuring of the book. This is acknowledged even in the MS tradition. Codex Sinaiticus entitles the fifth Vision the fifth "Revelation"; before the fifth Vision the Palatine version says, "Here begin the Twelve Mandates of the Shepherd," and (most significantly) the Vulgate says, "The fifth Vision is the beginning of the Shepherd." There is indeed a sense in which the Shepherd of Hermas proper begins with the fifth Vision. The Coptic Sahidic version and apparently Papyrus 129 originally began at this point, and some of the patristic citations provide further evidence that at times the book circulated in this shorter form. The most obvious difference between the two major divisions is that in the first four Visions the Church in the form of a woman is the revealer of what is seen, while in the fifth Vision to the end the mysterious figure known as the "Shepherd" assumes this role.

The Visions are unusual among apocalyptic writings in that the author writes in his own name instead of assuming the guise of some great man of the past. He begins in an autobiographical vein, introducing himself as a former slave in Rome who entertains desire in his heart for a woman named Rhoda, who had once been his owner. She reproves him in an initial vision by a river for his evil desire, and warns him to repent (Vis. 1:1:1-9). In subsequent visions an aged woman (representing the Church) appears to him assuring him that his sin is thus far potential rather than actual, but that he must take steps to convert and discipline his family (1:2:1–1:4:3). More important he is to bring a message to the Church that a limiting day has been fixed: Christians who have sinned and repent before that day will be forgiven, but those who have not repented by that time will not be forgiven (second Vision). He is shown a tower being built, which like the aged lady represents the Church. The different kinds of stones put into the tower represent various types of Christian believers who comprise the Church which, though old as creation, is nevertheless still in process of being completed. Around the tower are seven maidens representing the virtues which must belong to those who find a place in the tower (third Vision). Finally he sees a vision of a great dragon or Leviathan, representing the great persecution to come and is shown how to escape it through faithfulness (fourth Vision).

In the fifth Vision Hermas meets the shepherd to whom he has been "handed over" (5:1:3f.), and who dictates to him the Mandates and the Similitudes (Vis. 5:1:5f.). In spite of the familiarity of the biblical image of the Good Shepherd (e.g., Jn. 10), this shepherd is not Christ. Elsewhere the Son of God is identified with the "glorious man" who appears in a later sequence as the lord of the tower (Sim. 9:12:8), and even he is not so much Christ himself as the Spirit of God manifest in human flesh, whether of Jesus or of Christians (see Sim. 5:6:5f.; cf. 9:1:1). As for the shepherd, he is identified as the "angel of repentance" (e.g., Vis. 5:7; Mand. 12:4:7). He is a christological figure in that he carries out certain functions normally assigned to Christ. But in himself he is simply an angel sent to watch over and instruct Hermas.

The Mandates are a series of moral injunctions (not unlike the Didache) perhaps intended in part for new converts. They urge such things as belief in God, simplicity and generosity, truth, purity, faith, and cheerfulness, and warn against bitterness, double-mindedness, grief, and evil desire. They grapple with the specifics of such problems as divorce and second marriage and the testing of false prophets. They bear the marks of very early traditional material and, like the "Two Ways" in Barnabas, recognize two angels at work in man, one of righteousness and one of wickedness. Their aim is to help believers to know the difference and to choose always what is good.

The Similitudes, or Parables, are told to Hermas by the shepherd to illustrate the things he has learned from the Visions and the Mandates. Among these are the parables of the two cities (on the heavenly citizenship of the Christian), the elm and the vine (on mutual responsibilities of rich and poor), the trees in winter and summer (on the differences between the righteous and the sinners, which become apparent only in the "summer" of the world to come), the vineyard (on the Christian's stewardship of the Spirit that God has given him), and the willow tree (on different types and classes of believers, distinguished by the use they have made of their gifts and by the quality of their repentance).

The ninth Similitude, the so-called parable of the tower, is by far the longest, and in fact encompasses more than a fourth of the whole Shepherd of Hermas. Essentially it is a long elaboration and reinterpretation of the third Vision, the vision of the Church as a tower. It is set apart from the first eight Similitudes by a time lapse of a few days (Sim. 8:11:5) and seems to presuppose that Hermas has already written down the rest of the Similitudes and Mandates (9:1:1). This distinction of the ninth Similitude from the rest is anticipated as early as Vis. 5:5, in which the shepherd tells Hermas, "First of all write my commandments and the parables; but *the rest* you shall write as I shall show you." Some have argued from this that the ninth Similitude is a later addition, but if so the final editor has prepared for it carefully and woven it skillfully into the literary structure of the whole work. Possibly the first four Visions represent a substratum (either of traditions or of personal visionary experiences) which the author has drawn up and made the basis of a moral appeal to the Church. Thus the ninth Similitude in particular would be a special adaptation of the third Vision to the needs of a somewhat later time. Certainly the ninth Similitude speaks more overtly to a real ecclesiastical situation. The Church is no longer an idealized eschatological community as in the third Vision but a real institution existing in history. Instead of being kept out of the tower altogether (Vis. 3:2:7-9; 3:7:5) the unsuitable stones are already there and need to be removed (Sim. 9:4:7; 9:6:5), like the bad fish in Jesus' parable of the net (Mt. 13:44-50).

Such signs of development in the tradition suggest that the dating of the Shepherd of Hermas is no simple matter, and the external evidence and internal evidence confirm this. The threat of persecution in the fourth Vision and the apparent absence of a monarchical bishop suggest the last decade of the 1st cent. or slightly later. The locale is clearly Rome (Vis. 1:1:1), and the mention of Clement in Vis. 2:4:3 may indeed refer to the Roman presbyter who wrote 1 Clement. There is even a remarkable confirmation of the "limiting day" for the forgiveness of sins committed after baptism (Vis. 2:2:4f.) in a tradition recorded by Hippolytus of Rome that a Jewish Christian (Ebionite) prophet named Elkesai announced just such a day in the third year of Trajan (i.e., about A.D. 100; *Ref.* ix.13). A multitude of distinctly Jewish features in the thought and terminology of the Shepherd of Hermas suggest that this document's tradition arises not in the church of Rome as such but probably in a distinctly Jewish Christian subculture within, or on the property of, the church from which Clement wrote and to which Ignatius addressed his letter.

Over against the evidence for an early date is the witness of the Muratorian Canon (from Rome shortly before 200) that "Hermas composed the Shepherd quite recently in our times in the city of Rome, while his brother Pius held the office of bishop." This would yield a date close to 150. Though certainty is impossible, perhaps a series of visions originating in a small Jewish Christian community in Rome were later made available and began to circulate in the mainstream of the Roman church, and in the process were greatly enlarged (by either the original author or someone else) and adapted to the needs and ecclesiastical situation of a larger Christian community made up of Jews and Gentiles.

In any case there is no doubt that the Shepherd of Hermas became popular in the later Church; it was an exciting story with allegorical features (like *Pilgrim's Progress* in another era), and it spoke pointedly to the ever-recurring problem of sin and repentance in the life of the baptized Christian. Origen considered it inspired and identified its author with the Hermas of Rom. 16:14 (*Comm. on Romans, in loc.*). Though Eusebius rejected it, he admitted that it was widely quoted and read publicly in the churches, being considered especially valuable "for those who need elementary instruction" (*HE* iii.3.6). Irenaeus' quotation of the elementary instruction in the first Mandate as "Scripture" (*Adv. haer.* iv.20) seems to support this, though it is not impossible that Irenaeus is drawing on an earlier catechism to which Hermas itself is also indebted. The value of the Shepherd of Hermas today does not lie in its theology; its author can hardly be called one of the "Fathers" (apostolic or otherwise!). Rather, like the somewhat later NT apocrypha, it is worthwhile because of the vivid glimpse it affords of the "grass roots" piety and the practical concerns of the churches around Rome in the 2nd century.

Thus the so-called "Apostolic Fathers," though brought together in later tradition arbitrarily and seemingly almost by chance, offer to the student of the Bible by their very diversity at least a cross section of the Christian literature produced in the first few decades after the NT period. If he is perceptive they will teach him that diversity is no scandal for the Church, but is always the inevitable and healthy result when revealed truth confronts a variety of life situations.

Bibliography.–J. B. Lightfoot, *Apostolic Fathers,* I (1890), II (1889); K. Lake, ed. and tr., *Apostolic Fathers* (*LCL,* 1930); R. M. Grant, *Apostolic Fathers: A New Translation and Commentary* (1964); D. R. Bueno, ed., *Padres Apostolicos. Edicion Bilingue Completa* (1965); E. J. Goodspeed, *History of Early Christian Literature* (rev. ed. 1966); M. Dibelius, *Der Hirt des Hermas* (*HNT* 20, 1923).

J. R. MICHAELS

APOTHECARY. *See* PERFUME.

APPAIM ap'ə-im [Heb. *'appayim*–'nostrils']. A son of Nadab of the house of Jerahmeel, of Judah (1 Ch. 2:30f.).

APPAREL. *See* GARMENTS.

APPARENTLY. Archaic in Nu. 12:8, AV, for Heb. *mar'eh,* "clearly," "openly."

APPARITION [Gk. *epipháneia*] (2 Macc. 5:4; also 3:24, AV, NEB). Besides the two incidents in 2 Macc. 3:24 and 5:14, the Apocrypha mentions apparitions in Wisd. 17:3, 15 ("monstrous specters"); 18:17; etc. The ERV uses "apparition" to translate Gk. *phántasma* in Mt. 14:26 par. Mk. 6:49; the AV has "spirit," the other English versions "ghost."

APPEAL. In the sense of a request for review of a lower-court decision by a higher court, we find no such instance either in the OT or the NT. In the institution of judges by Moses (Ex. 18:26), the statement "hard cases they brought to Moses, but any small matter they decided themselves," indicates simply a distribution of cases between two courts, but gives no evidence that appeal could be made to Moses of a decision made by lower court. In Dt. 17:8-13 directions are given that a lower court, under certain conditions, shall ask a higher for instructions as to procedure, and shall strictly follow the order prescribed; nevertheless, the decision itself belongs to the lower court. When its sentence was once given, there was no appeal.

In the NT, the provision of the Roman law for an appeal from a lower to a higher court is clearly recognized, although the case of Paul in Acts 25 does not strictly fall within its scope. The Roman law originally gave a citizen the right of appeal to the tribune of the people; but with the establishment of the empire, the emperor himself assumed this function of the tribune, and became the court of last resort. The case of Paul, however, had not been tried before Festus, nor any verdict rendered, when (Acts 25:10f.) he uttered the proper legal formula: "I appeal to Caesar" (Gk. *Kaisara epikaloúmai*). That Roman citizens could insist upon such procedure, as a right, is not perfectly certain (*HJP,* II/2, 279). Paul evidently acted upon the suggestion of the governor himself (v. 9), who seems to have been desirous of avoiding the responsibility of a case involving questions most remote from his ordinary attention.

At first sight, Paul's decision to appeal seems premature. He throws away his chance of acquittal by Festus, and acts upon the assumption that he has been already condemned. Acts 26:32 shows that the possibility of his acquittal had amounted almost to a certainty. His course is explicable only by regarding his appeal the master stroke of a great leader, who was ready to take risks. In the proposition of Festus, he grasps at what had been an object of hope long deferred. For many years he had been desiring and praying to get to Rome (Acts 19:21; Rom. 1:11, 15; 15:23f.). The Lord had just assured him (Acts 23:11) that as he had testified at Jerusalem, "so you must bear witness also at Rome." With this promise and direction in view, he hastens toward the world's capital and the center of the world's influence, in the seemingly precipitate words, "I appeal," which a lower order of prudence would have deferred until he had first been condemned.

Bibliography.–E. Haenchen, *Acts of the Apostles* (Eng. tr. 1970), pp. 667f.; H. J. Cadbury, *BC,* V, 297-338.

H. E. JACOBS

APPEAR. The usual Hebrew word is *rā'â,* used mainly of God's self-revelations in person and in dreams and visions: "The Lord appeared to Abram" (Gen. 12:7); to Moses (Ex. 3:2); to Solomon (1 K. 3:5).

In the NT, Gk. *ṓphthēn,* passive of *hōráō,* "see," is used especially of angelic revelations and visions: as on the Mount of Transfiguration (Mt. 17:3); an angel (Lk. 1:11); the risen Lord (24:34; cf. *optánomai* in Acts 1:3); cloven tongues at Pentecost (Acts 2:3); vision to Paul (Acts 16:9); a great wonder in heaven (Rev. 12:1).

Other NT words are: *phaínomai,* "shine," with the thought of a resplendent, luminous revelation, as of the Bethlehem star (Mt. 2:7); and *phaneróō,* "make manifest," used of the postresurrection appearances and second coming of Christ, and of the disclosures of the great judgment day. See Col. 3:4; 2 Cor. 5:10; 1 Jn. 2:28; etc.

D. M. PRATT

APPEARANCE. In the OT, Heb. *mar'eh* occurs especially in Ezekiel and Daniel in describing supernatural visions (e.g., Ezk. 1:5, 16, 26-28; 8:2; 10:9f; 40:3; Dnl. 1:13; 10:6, 18; also Joel 2:4).

The main NT word is Gk. *prósōpon,* as in Lk. 9:29 of Jesus on the mount of the Transfiguration, and in Mt. 16:3 par. Lk. 12:56, the "appearance of (earth and) sky." Other words are Gk. *eidéa* (Mt. 28:3) and *ópsis* (Jn. 7:24, "Do not judge by appearances"); also *lógos* (Col. 2:23), *homoíōma* (Rev. 9:7).

APPEARING [Gk. *epipháneia*–'manifestation']. A term referring to the parousia of Christ (2 Thess. 2:8 [AV "brightness"]; 1 Tim. 6:14; 2 Tim. 1:10; 4:1,8; Tit. 2:13); for 1 Pet. 1:7, AV, the word is *apokálypsis* (RSV "revelation").

APPENDAGE OF THE LIVER [Heb. *yōṯereṯ 'al-hakkāḇēḏ*] (Ex. 29:13, 22; Lev. 3:4, 10, 15; 4:9; etc.); AV "caul above the liver"; NEB "long lobe of the liver." The large lobe or flap of the liver, which is usually mentioned together with the kidneys and the fat as the special portions set aside for the burnt offering. H. L. E. LUERING

APPERTAIN. Archaic in Jer. 10:7, AV, for Heb. *yā'â,* "be fitting"; cf. RSV, "this is thy due"; NEB, "is thy fitting tribute."

APPETITE [Heb. *nep̱eš, ḥayyâ* (Job 38:39); Gk. *koilía* (Rom. 16:18)]; AV also SOUL, GREEDY, "herself" (Isa. 5:14), BELLY, etc.; NEB also DESIRE, GREEDY, HUNGER, RELISH, THROAT, etc.

Appetite is most often a translation of *nep̱eš*. Cognate with the Akkadian term for "neck" or "throat," the Heb. *nep̱eš* sometimes retains that meaning, but by extension came to signify the most vital function of the throat: breathing. It was natural, then, for *nep̱eš* to become equated with the living and active expression of life, or life itself. As a description of human vitality, it came to embrace all the basic human urges and emotions. The *nep̱eš* can thirst (Prov. 25:25), hate (2 S. 5:8), rejoice (Ps. 35:9), etc. Hence, a full life includes a joyous satisfying of the appetites for food and drink (Dt. 14:26). The appetite is a constant constituent of man's life (Prov. 16:26; Eccl. 6:7), and while the wicked are ceaselessly driven by it (Isa. 56:11), the righteous are satisfied (Prov. 13:25). Therefore, self-control over one's appetite is a recommended virtue (Prov. 23:2; cf. vv. 20f.).

Paul's reference to those who "do not serve our Lord Christ, but their own appetites" (Rom. 16:18) is probably a sardonic jab at Judaizers who sought to graft Jewish food laws to the gospel.

Bibliography.–W. Eichrodt, *Theology of the OT* (Eng. tr. 1967), II, 134-142; *TDNT,* III, *s.v.* κοιλία (Behm). K. H. MAAHS

APPHIA af'ē-ə, ap'fē-ə [Gk. *Apphia*] (Philem. 2). A Christian of Colossae, probably the wife of Philemon; certainly a member of his household, greeted as "sister." In the Greek Church Nov. 22 is sacred to her memory. It has been supposed, since this Epistle concerns one household exclusively, that Apphia was Philemon's wife and the mother or sister of Archippus. Tradition says she was stoned to death with Philemon, Onesimus, and Archippus in the reign of Nero.

APPHUS af'əs, ap'fəs [Gk. *Apphous*–'cunning']. A name borne by Jonathan, the fifth son of Mattathias (1 Macc. 2:5). All the brothers, according to this passage, had double names; John is said to have been called Gaddis; Simon, Thassi; Judas, Maccabeus; Eleazer, Avaran; Jonathan, Apphus (1 Macc. 2:2-5).

APPIUS ap'ē-əs, **FORUM OF** [Gk. *Appiou Phóron*; Lat. *Appii Forum*] (Acts 28:15); AV, NEB, APII FORUM. A station at the forty-third milestone on the Appian Road (39.5 mi. [63.5 km.] from Rome, a single day's journey for energetic travelers).

Its existence probably dates from the time of Appius Claudius Caecus (Suetonius *Tiberius* 2; cf. T. Mommsen, *Römische Forschungen,* I [2nd ed. 1864], 308), who laid out the famous highway from Rome to Capua in 312 B.C. In the 1st cent. it had the rank of a municipality (Pliny *Nat. hist.* iii.64). Its importance as a highway station is due chiefly to the canal which ran by the side of the road from there to within a short distance of Tarracina (at the sixty-second milestone), affording an alternative means of conveyance (Strabo *Geog.* v.3.6). It was customary to cover this section of the journey, passing through the Pontine marshes, by night in canal boats drawn by mules. Horace (*Satires* i.5) offers a lively picture of the discomforts of the trip, mentioning the importunate innkeepers and intolerable drinking water at Appii Forum, the gnats and frogs which were enemies to repose, and the exasperating procrastination of the muleteer.

The Christian brethren in Rome went out along the Appian Road to welcome the apostle Paul upon hearing of his arrival at Puteoli. One party awaited him at Three Taverns while another proceeded as far as the Forum of Appius (Acts 28:15). G. H. ALLEN

APPLE; APPLE-TREE [Heb. *tappû(a)ḥ*; Gk. *mḗlon*]; NEB also APRICOT(-TREE). The identity of the biblical apple is one of the most puzzling questions of biblical botany. The common apple *(Malus pumila* Mill.) is of recent introduction to Palestine, and in its wild form would not match the elegant OT descriptions of it.

Some botanists have favored identifying the apple of the OT with the citron (*C. medica* L.); but the tree affords little shade, and the fruit, though pleasantly scented, is bitter. The citron is a native of India, and it probably was unknown in ancient Palestine. The "apple" of Cant. 2:3, 5; 7:8; 8:5 has been identified as the quince (*Cydonia oblonga* Mill.), a native of Asia Minor bearing a yellowish fragrant fruit that is exceedingly acrid to taste.

The OT descriptions of "apple" and "apple tree" seem to indicate the apricot (*Prunus armeniaca* L.), a native of China that was introduced into Mesopotamia and Palestine prior to the patriarchal period. The apricot is now widespread there, and in a favorable environment grows to 30 ft. (9 m.) in height. The spreading branches make it a desirable shade tree, and it yields abundant harvests. The apricot may very well have been the "forbidden fruit" of Eden. R. K. H.

APPLE OF THE EYE. An old English expression denoting the pupil of the eye, used metaphorically of something extremely precious and jealously protected. In Dt. 32:10; Prov. 7:2 the Heb. *'îšôn* ("little man") evidently refers to the beholder's reflection in the eye of another, while in Ps. 17:8 the apple is the "daughter of the eye" (*bat-'āyin*; cf. Lam. 2:18, MT). The word *bāḇâ*, "gate," "opening" (Zec. 2:8), is also rendered "apple" in the RSV and NEB. R. K. H.

APPLES OF SODOM. A name often associated with the Vine of Sodom (*see* SODOM, VINE OF), but designating more likely the Jericho potato or Palestine nightshade (*Solanum sanctum* L.). It is probably referred to by Josephus (*BJ* iv.8.4), who describes fruits of Sodom that "dissolve into smoke and ashes" when picked, supposedly giving evidence of the city's destruction by fire. The shrub has coarse, low brier-like branches, and bears a yellow fruit which when ripe contains a dusty pulp. It is reportedly abundant in the Dead Sea region. R. K. H.

APPLY [Heb. *nāṯan* (Eccl. 1:13, 17; 8:9, 16), *bô'* (Prov. 23:12), *māraḥ* (Isa. 38:21), *m^eyuššār* (1 K. 6:35), *šîṯ* (Prov. (22:17); Gk. *proïstēmi* (Tit. 3:8, 14), *metaschēmatízō* (1 Cor. 4:6)]; AV also GIVE, FIT, MAINTAIN, "in a figure transferred" (1 Cor. 4:6); NEB also ENGAGE IN, OPEN (Prov. 22:17), BRING.

"Apply" occurs most frequently in the sense of devoting one's attention or efforts toward a specific end or activity. Four times (Eccl. 1:13, 17; 8:9, 16) the Preacher says he applied his heart (RSV "mind") to the search for wisdom, but he found nothing of enduring significance in this futile venture. However, the writer of Proverbs looks more positively upon the pursuit of applying the heart (RSV "mind") to knowledge (22:17) and instruction (23:12). Paul exhorts the people to apply themselves to the doing of good deeds, or to engage in honorable occupations (Tit. 3:8, 14).

Elsewhere "apply" is used of laying some material over something else, such as gold over carved work (1 K. 6:35) or a cake of figs over a boil (Isa. 38:21).

"Apply" occurs once in a third sense, viz., for utilizing something (e.g., a teaching) with reference to a particular person, situation, etc. In 1 Cor. 4:6 Paul uses *metaschēmatízō* (lit. "transform") to inform his readers that he is bringing his teaching to bear upon his relationship with Apollos. Apollos and Paul are thus used as examples for the early Church. Because there was no contention between the apostle and Apollos, it follows that the Church has no ground to form opposing parties.

B. L. BANDSTRA

APPOINT [Heb. *pāqaḏ* (Gen. 41:34; Lev. 26:16; Nu. 1:50; 3:10; 27:16; Jer. 15:3; 49:19; 50:44; 51:27; Ps. 109:6; Est. 2:3), *śîm* (Ex. 21:13; Nu. 4:19; Dt. 1:13; 1 S. 8:5, 11f.; 2 S. 7:10; 1 Ch. 17:9; Hos. 1:11), *nāṯan* (Ex. 30:16; Dt. 16:18; Josh. 20:2; Ezk. 44:14), *'āmaḏ* (1 Ch. 15:16; Neh. 7:3), *ṣiwwâ* (2 S. 6:21), *šîṯ* (Job 14:13), *lāqaḥ* (Ps. 75:2), *yāsaḏ* (Ps. 104:8); Aram. *m^enâ* (Ezr. 7:25), *n^eṯan* (Dnl. 2:16); Gk. *diatíthēmi* (Lk. 22:29), *kathístēmi* (Acts 6:3; Tit. 1:5), *procheirízomai* (Acts 26:16)]; AV also SET, MAKE, ORDAIN, RECEIVE, FIND, GIVE; NEB also COMMIT, ORDAIN, BRING, PUT (UP), "round up" (Jer. 49:19; 50:44), "set to a task" (Nu. 4:19), "set in authority" (Dt. 1:13), ASSIGN, CHOOSE, APPLY, INSTALL, GIVE, VEST, INSTITUTE.

Of the thirty-two times that "appoint" occurs in the OT, roughly a third of the instances translate the word *pāqaḏ*, which can mean either "visit" or "establish or set in authority." It is the latter usage which is relevant here. *Śîm* (with variant *śûm*) means "put" or "place (a time, place, event)"; thus its meaning becomes extended to mean "establish, set up." *Nāṯan* is the normal Hebrew word for "give," but it is one of the most flexible words in the language, having meanings that range from "permit" to "pay." In some cases *nāṯan* is almost synonymous to *śîm* and is often found parallel to it (esp. in the P source of the Pentateuch and Ezekiel). *'Āmaḏ* in the qal means "stand," or "take a stand" (1 S. 26:13), but when put into the hiphil it means "cause to stand, establish, appoint" (1 Ch. 15:16).

The most common meaning for *ṣiwwâ* (in the piel) is "command," but it also may mean "lay a charge upon" (2 S. 6:21). *Šîṯ* is very similar to *śîm*. It may mean "lay" or "put," but it may also take on the meaning "fix" or "make (someone) into something" (1 K. 11:34, where the RSV translates it "I will make him ruler," or Isa. 5:6, "I will make it a waste"). In Job 14:13 the RSV translates *šîṯ* as "appoint" in the clause, "that thou wouldst appoint me a set time, and remember me." In Ps. 75:2 the RSV translates the word *lāqaḥ* (lit. "take") as "appoint," whereas the NEB gives a more usual translation, "seize," in the clause, "I seize the appointed time." *Yāsaḏ* has as its basic meaning "establish, found, set." In Ps. 104:8 the word is translated by the RSV "appoint." Earlier in the same Psalm (v. 5), *yāsaḏ* is translated as "set" in "Thou didst set the earth on its foundations."

Two Aramaic words are translated as "appoint" by the RSV. *M^enâ*, which in the peal means "number" (cf. Heb. *mānâ*), in the pael means "assign." So, in Ezr. 7:25 (Artaxerxes' letter to Ezra) we find ". . . appoint magistrates and judges." *N^eṯan* (cf. Heb. *nāṯan*) is not the common Aramaic word for "give." The more common word by far is *y^ehaḇ* (Dnl. 2:48; 5:17; etc.). *N^eṯan* is used (in Dnl. 2:16) in a way comparable to that in which *nāṯan* is used in Josh. 20:2 (see above), and is probably a Hebraism.

NT usage is confined to four passages. *Diatíthēmi* means literally "put through (by means of)," or "put throughout." It is the common term used to translate "decree." It also has a very common meaning, "dispose of something by means of a will," although this meaning is not found in the NT. The noun *diathḗkē* (usually translated as "covenant," but with the original meaning "last will and testament") comes from this verb. This understanding of *diatíthēmi* can give us an important clue to understanding Jesus' statement about the kingdom which he is "appointing" to his followers. If the idea of covenant (with all its OT heritage behind it) and the idea of a will are kept in mind, the matter of an inheritance is the natural outcome. When it is remembered that the one who "appointed" the kingdom to Jesus is the God Almighty, then it is easy to see that the inheritance which Jesus is "willing" to his followers is also eternal.

Kathístēmi is usually translated "bring, ordain, make (someone) to become something." The literal meaning is probably "set down." In the LXX of Nu. 3:10 *kathístēmi* translates the Heb. *pāqaḏ*. In Mt. 24:45 and Lk. 12:42 *kathístēmi* is translated as "set over" by the RSV. Tit. 1:5 uses the word in connection with ordaining elders.

Procheirízomai is a middle deponent from *procheirízō*, literally "hand forth." In Acts 26:16 Paul uses this term in recounting his experience with the risen Christ. God has "handed Paul forth" into His service. The idiom is very forceful, and gives one the mental picture of God picking Paul up and pushing him in the direction He intends.

T. R. ASHLEY

APPOINTED FEAST [Heb. *mô'ēḏ* (Lev. 23:2, 4, 37, 44; Nu. 10:10; 15:3; 29:39; etc.), *ḥag* (Ezk. 45:17), *'ᵃṣārâ* (Isa. 1:14)]; AV FEAST, SOLEMN DAY, SOLEMN FEAST, SET FEAST, ASSEMBLY; NEB APPOINTED SEASON, APPOINTED FESTIVAL, "sacred season appointed by the Lord" (Ezr. 3:5), SACRED FEAST, PLACE OF ASSEMBLY, etc.

When *mô'ēḏ* means "appointed feast" it is usually in the plural (but cf. Lam. 2:6.; Hos. 12:9). When it is in the singular, a more normal rendering is "set time, season." Although *ḥag* is translated "appointed feast" in Ezk. 45:17, its more usual meaning is "pilgrim feast" (the verbal form, *ḥāgag*, means to "make a pilgrimage"). The term *'ᵃṣārâ* has the more usual meaning of "assembly," coming from a verb meaning to "hold in."

The festal times, exclusive of the sabbath, were kept three times a year. This threefold pattern of "appointed feasts" may reflect the agricultural environment of Canaan; they correspond to the times connected with planting, harvest, etc. The feast of the Passover is kept, along with the Feast of Unleavened Bread, for seven days, starting "in the first month, on the fourteenth day of the month" (Lev. 23:5). This means that the dates are Nisan 14-21. Framing the feast time are two convocations, one on the first day and one on the last. The ordinances for the keeping of the Passover and Feast of Unleavened Bread are found in Ex. 12:1–13:16; 23:15; 34:18ff.; Lev. 23:5-14; Nu. 28:16-25; Dt. 16:1-8.

The Feast of Weeks was a one-day celebration, and although no precise date is given for it, the regulation states that it be fifty full days after the bringing of the barley offering at the Feast of Unleavened Bread (cf. Lev. 23:15f.). This would put the Feast of Weeks in the early part of the third month. The basic texts ordaining this "appointed feast" are Lev. 23:15-21; Ex. 23:16; 34:22; Nu. 28:26-31; Dt. 16:9-12.

The Feast of Booths is ordained, among other places, in Lev. 23:33: "On the fifteenth day of this seventh month and for seven days is the feast of booths." This feast corresponds in time of year to the autumn ingathering of the crops. Earlier in the month (on the first day) the ram's horn is sounded, and on the tenth of the month the solemn fast (Heb. *ṣôm*) of *Yôm Kippur* ("day of atonement") occurs. For further details on the Feast of Booths see Ex. 23:16; 34:22; Lev. 23:33-36, 39-43; Nu. 29:12-32; Dt. 16:13-16.

There are several feasts celebrated in later Judaism which are not set out in the Torah. Two of these are *Ḥᵃnukkâ* ("dedication"), also known as the Festival of Lights, and *Pûrîm*. *Ḥᵃnukkâ* celebrates the cleansing of the temple of Judas Maccabeus in December, 164 B.C. (1 Macc. 4:52-59). It is observed starting on the twenty-fifth day of the ninth month. *Pûrîm* is a joyful celebration on the fourteenth day of the twelfth month, commemorating the Jews' deliverance from Haman by Mordecai and Esther (Est. 9:23ff.).

See also FEASTS.

Bibliography.–Hans-Joachim Kraus, *Worship in Israel* (Eng. tr. 1965); M. Noth, *Leviticus* (Eng. tr. 1965). T. R. ASHLEY

APPORTION [Heb. *ḥālaq*] (Josh. 18:2, 10); AV RECEIVE, DIVIDE; NEB TAKE POSSESSION, DISTRIBUTE; [*nāṯan*] (2 Ch. 31:14); AV DISTRIBUTE; [*mānâ*] (Job 7:3); AV APPOINT; NEB LOT; [*nāpal*] (Ps. 78:55); AV DIVIDE; NEB ALLOT; [*nāḥal*] (Isa. 49:8); AV "cause to inherit"; NEB "sharing out afresh"; [Gk. *diairéō*] (1 Cor. 12:11); AV DIVIDING; NEB DISTRIBUTING; [*merízō*] (2 Cor. 10:13; He. 7:2); AV DISTRIBUTE, GIVE; NEB LAY DOWN, GIVE.

There is little apparent uniformity in translation; the context and the translator are the major determinants. The Heb. *ḥālaq* is a basic term meaning "divide" with a noun form that means "portion" or "territory." Even more common and general is *nāṯan*, meaning essentially "give." "Count" or "number" is the root idea of *mānâ*. *Nāpal* is the common verb for "fall." More to the point is *nāḥal*, which means "get or take as a possession" (Gesenius). The Gk. *diairéō* is found only twice in the NT; it means "divide into parts" or "distribute." More common is *merízō*, also meaning "divide," "distribute," or "separate into parts." A significant cognate is *méros*, which has two basic uses in the NT: it is seen as a "part" of something or it conveys the idea of "share," whether relating to a person, group, thing, or event (Schneider).

An important concept in 1 Cor. 12:11 is that the Holy Spirit is one, and that He is the author of the various gifts given to men at His discretion. Since men are not complete in themselves, they must be joined into Christ with others of like faith. Thus the Spirit ministers to the various parts of the body with a diversity of gifts intended to make the body complete in Christ, individual members becoming vital channels of God's grace to the whole body. Paul recognizes that such interdependence presupposes limitations. No member can get along without the others, because his gifts and role are restricted by God's design. Paul acknowledges that he and Timothy operate within distinct limits (2 Cor. 10:13f.). God had apportioned to them a ministry of being the first to come to the Corinthians with the gospel. Paul wanted them to remember that he led them to Christ, but also that his rights were not unlimited; he wanted to operate only within divine appointment.

See *TDNT*, IV, *s.v.* μέρος (J. Schneider).

G. H. HOVEE

APPREHEND. In Phil. 3:12f., AV, an archaic rendering of Gk. *katalambánō*; the RSV renders "make (one's) own," the NEB "take (get) hold of"; cf. Eph. 3:18, "comprehend." The same word in Jn. 1:5 is translated "overcome" in the RSV.

APPROACH [Heb. *qāraḇ*; Ugar. *qrb*]. The Hebrew verb is commonly used in the normal sense of "draw near," the causative form being particularly prominent in the prescriptions for sacrificial offerings. It was also used to mean sexual intercourse in Gen. 20:4; Lev. 18:6, 14, 19; 20:16; Dt. 22:14; Isa. 8:3; Ezk. 18:6. R. K. H.

APPROVE. Biblical and archaic usages of the word often intend a stronger meaning than the ordinary "have a favorable opinion of," especially in the NT. As a translation of Gk. *dokimázo, dókimos* ("approved"), it implies a testing or proving. The RSV often uses a stronger or more specific word, such as 1 Cor. 16:3, "accredit"; 11:19, "genuine"; 2 Cor. 13:7, "to have met the test." Similarly, *apodeíknymi* in Acts 2:22, RSV, is "attested"; and *synistáō* is rendered "commend" in 2 Cor. 6:4 and "prove" in 7:11.

The Gk. *dókimos* is frequently used extrabiblically for the testing of ores. That which does not stand the test is *adókimos;* that which passes the test is *dókimos.* "Greet Apelles, who is approved in Christ" (Rom. 16:10). "Present yourself to God as one approved" (2 Tim. 2:15). See also Rom. 14:22 and 1 Thess. 2:4 (AV "allow"); Rom. 2:18; 14:18; Phil. 1:10.

Other words translated "approve" or "approved" in the RSV are Heb. *rā'â* (Lam. 3:36), *bārar,* "purify" (1 Ch. 7:40), *'ûḏ* (Job 29:11), *rāṣâ* (Eccl. 9:7); Gk. *syneudokéō* (Acts 22:20; Rom. 1:32), and *cháris* (1 Pet. 2:19). "Approval" translates Gk. *épainos* (Rom. 13:3), *martyréō* (He. 11:2, 4), and *cháris* (1 Pet. 2:20).

APRON [Heb. *ḥ^agôrâ*] (Gen. 3:7); NEB LOINCLOTH; [Gk. *simikínthion*] (Acts 19:12); NEB SCARF.

In Gen. 3:7, Heb. *ḥ^agôrâ* is used for mankind's first garment — the fig leaves sewed together by Adam and Eve. The word comes from *ḥāgar,* "gird," and elsewhere means "girdle" (2 S. 18:11; 1 K. 2:5; Isa. 3:24). It undoubtedly covered only the loins.

The Gk. *simikínthion* in Acts 19:12 is a dialectic form of *sēmikínthion,* from Lat. *semicinctium,* normally a workman's apron, or "half-girdle" (i.e., covering only the front). Some other possibilities have been suggested, however, for this passage. MM (p. 575) cites Nestle, *Expos.T.,* 13 (1901), 282, who thinks the reference is to an undergarment which had been in contact with Paul's skin. Others suppose it may have been a scarf or band, which is easily removable.

See also GARMENTS V. J. W. D. H.

APT. In 1 Tim. 3:2; 2 Tim. 2:24 the RSV has "an apt teacher" for Gk. *didaktikós* (AV "apt to teach"; NEB "a good teacher"); in both passages it is a qualification for leadership in the church. The word is very rare, found elsewhere only in Philo and Philodemus, although it may be a late form of the classical Greek *didaskalikós* (cf. MM, p. 158), "fit for teaching."

AQUEDUCT. *See* CISTERN.

AQUILA ak'wi-lə [Gk. *Akylas*–'eagle']. A Jew at Corinth, a refugee along with his wife Priscilla (diminutive form of Prisca) from Rome, who became a friend of Paul (Acts 18).

Aquila was a native of Pontus, doubtless one of the colony of Jews mentioned in Acts 2:9; 1 Pet. 1:1. They were victims of the cruel and unjust edict of Claudius which expelled all Jews from Rome *ca.* A.D. 49. The decree, it is said by Suetonius, was issued on account of tumults raised by the Jews, and he especially mentions one Chrestus (Suetonius *Claudius* 25). Since the word Christus could easily be confounded by him to refer to some individual whose name was Chrestus and who was an agitator, resulting in these disorders, it has been concluded that the fanatical Jews were then persecuting their Christian brethren and disturbances resulted. The cause of the trouble did not concern Claudius, and so without making inquiry, he expelled all Jews.

The conjecture that Aquila was a freedman and that his master had been Aquila Pontius, the Roman senator, and that from him he received his name, is without foundation. He doubtless had a Hebrew name, but it is not known. It was a common custom for Jews outside of Palestine to take Roman names.

Driven from Rome, Aquila sought refuge in Corinth, where Paul on his second missionary journey met him because they had the same trade: that of making tents of Cilician cloth (Acts 18:3). The account does not justify the conclusion that he and his wife were already Christians when Paul met them. Had that been the case Luke would almost certainly have said so, especially if it was true that Paul sought them out on that account. Judging from their well-known activity in Christian work they would have gathered a little band of inquirers or possibly converts, even though they had been there for but a short time. It is more in harmony with the account to conclude that Paul met them as fellow tradespeople, and that he took the opportunity of preaching Christ to them as they toiled. There can be no doubt that Paul would use these days to lead them into the kingdom and instruct them in it, so that afterward they would be capable of being teachers themselves (Acts 18:26).

Not only did they become Christians, but they also became fast and devoted friends of Paul, and he fully reciprocated their affection for him (Rom. 16:3f.). They accompanied him when he left Corinth to go to Ephesus and remained there while he went on his journey into Syria. When he wrote the first letter to the church at Corinth they were still at Ephesus, and their house there was used as a Christian assembly place (1 Cor. 16:19).

The decree of Claudius excluded the Jews from Rome only temporarily, and so afterward Paul is found there; his need of friends and their affection for him doubtless led Aquila and Priscilla also to go to that city (Rom. 16:3). At the time of the writing of Paul's second letter to Timothy they have again removed to Ephesus, possibly sent there by Paul to further the work in that city (2 Tim. 4:19). While nothing more is known of them they doubtless remained the devoted friends of Paul to the end.

That Priscilla's name is mentioned several times before that of her husband has called forth a number of conjectures. The best explanation seems to be that she was the more active Christian. J. W. KAPP

AQUILA. A proselyte to Judaism in the time of Hadrian, and like the Aquila of the NT a native of Pontus, who translated the Hebrew OT into very literal Greek. *See* SEPTUAGINT.

AR är; **AR OF MOAB** mō'ab [Heb. *'ār, 'ār mô'āḇ*; Gk. *Ēr, Aroēr, Sēeir*]. A Moabite site located on the southern bank of the Arnon River (Nu. 21:28). At the time of the Israelite Exodus it lay on the northern border of Moab (Nu. 21:15; Dt. 2:18). There is some question as to whether Ar refers to a city or a region. It may be the place called the city of Moab (Nu. 22:36; cf. NEB). It is probably also intended by "the city that is in the middle of the valley" (Dt. 2:36; Josh. 13:9, 16; 2 S. 24:5). In Dt. 2:9, however, Ar may be a synonym of Moab. Dt. 2:29 speaks of Moabites living in Ar and Edomites in Seir. The term, therefore, may refer to both a city and a region. Ar has been identified with Areopolis and Rabbath Moab; but this is unlikely, since the location of this latter site is 14 mi. (22.5 km.) S of the Arnon.

See *GP,* II, 248. J. W. WHEDBEE

ARA ā'rə [Heb. *'^arā*]. A son of Jether of the tribe of Asher (1 Ch. 7:38).

ARAB âr'ab [Heb. *'ᵃrāḇ*–'ambush']. A city in the hill country of Judah (Josh. 15:52), probably er-Râbiyeh, 7½ mi. (12 km.) SW of Hebron. The gentilic form *'arbî*, "Arbite," occurs in 2 S. 23:35.

ARAB; ARABIANS. *See* ARABIA.

ARABAH ar'ə-bə [Heb. *hā'ᵃrāḇâ*]; AV usually PLAIN. The term frequently used in the OT of one of the principal geographical areas of Palestine, as contrasted with the coast lands, the Shephelah, the Negeb, and the mountainous regions. Variously translated as "plain," "plains," "desert," "valley," or "wilderness," its root meaning is uncertain, but it most probably indicated an arid region.

I. Usage
II. Natural Dimensions
III. Minerals
IV. Routes
V. History

I. Usage.–The term was applied specifically in part or wholly to the depression of the Jordan Valley, extending from Mt. Hermon, a 9100-ft. (2775-m.) elevation in the Anti-Lebanon Range, due S beyond the Sea of Chinnereth (Galilee), and including both sides of the river Jordan, the Dead Sea, and the region slightly to the southwest as far as the head of the Gulf of Aqabah.

In the AV the term was transliterated once only (Josh. 18:18), in describing the border of Benjamin, being rendered "plain" elsewhere, and once "champaign" (Dt. 11:30). But in the RSV and NEB it is normally transliterated "Arabah." The rendering "plain" is misleading, since the Arabah constitutes a depression between areas of considerably higher ground, and is actually below sea level for much of its length. The designation "Arabah" almost always occurs with the article, and it is used topographically in the OT to designate any specific area of the rift-valley. Because it was sometimes applied to the arid and sterile land lying S of the Dead Sea (Dt. 2:8), the word was employed by Judean writers in the sense of "desert" or "steppe" (Ps. 68:4 [MT 5]; Isa. 33:19; Jer. 17:6). In Josh. 11:16; 12:8 it is used to describe one of the great natural divisions of the country W of the Jordan, while in Dt. 4:49 it refers to an area E of the river.

Its location is connected variously with the Sea of Chinnereth (Dt. 3:7; Josh. 11:2; 13:3) and with the area far S of the depression, around Elath and the Red Sea (Dt. 1:1; 2:8). In 2 S. 4:7 the word describes the entire length of the Jordan Valley below the Sea of Chinnereth, while in Josh. 3:16; 12:3; Dt. 4:49; 2 K. 14:25 the expression "Sea of Arabah" is applied to the Dead Sea. In many places the designation "Sea of the Arabah" is qualified by the addition of "the Salt Sea." The plural (*'ᵃrāḇôṯ*) generally indicates specific waste sections within the depression, such as the "plains of Moab" (Nu. 22:1; Dt. 34:1), which are clearly distinguished from the pastoral and cultivated lands of the plateaus above the rift-valley. Similarly, the "plains of Jericho" (Josh. 4:13; 5:10) designate an infertile tract of territory in the Arabah near Jericho. The "plains of the wilderness" (2 S. 15:28; 17:16, AV) no doubt allude to that section of the Arabah that merges into the wilderness of Judah, although the RSV emends the Hebrew to read "fords of the wilderness," making the reference doubtful.

Although largely ignored by earlier commentators, the topographical usage of the designation "Arabah" carried a precise connotation for many OT writers. For Jeroboam II the "Sea of the Arabah" marked one of the limits of his kingdom (2 K. 14:25), the reference being to the entire eastern boundary of Israel as far S as the southerly reaches of Moab. The expression *naḥal hā'ᵃrāḇâ* (Am. 6:14), rendered "river of the wilderness" by the AV, "Brook of the Arabah" by the RSV, and "gorge of the Arabah" by the NEB, is paralleled exactly by the Arabic expression Wâdī el-'Arabah, which describes the region between the southern end of the Dead Sea and the Gulf of Aqabah. Almost certainly Amos had this territory in mind, the southerly limit of the nation, which included Judah, being marked by the beginning of the wadi. The "Brook of the Willows" (*naḥal hā'ᵃrāḇîm*) of Isa. 15:7 was probably some specific stream flowing into the Dead Sea, such as the Wâdī Qelt or the "brook Zered" (Wâdī el-Ḥesā).

II. Natural Dimensions.–The Arabah consists of three distinct areas, comprising the Jordan Valley, the Dead Sea region, and the territory from the southern end of the Dead Sea to the Gulf of Aqabah. Starting S of the Sea of Chinnereth, the Jordan Valley or Ghôr runs for about 65 mi. (105 km.) before entering the Dead Sea. It slopes southward from 696 ft. (212 m.) below sea level at the Sea of Chinnereth to 1286 ft. (392 m.) below sea level at the Dead Sea. For the first 25 mi. (40 km.) the valley is about 12 mi. (20 km.) wide and is fed by a number of streams including the Yarmuk, 'Arab, Taiyibeh, Ziqlâb, and Yâbis. The Yarmuk enters the Jordan from the east about 5 mi. (8 km.) S of the Sea of Chinnereth, doubles the volume of water flowing in the river, and makes for a progressive deepening of the Jordan bed. In this region the land has always been comparatively fertile and well watered, and lines of communication were established early by means of numerous fords.

Opposite Samaria, where the rift is crossed by the line of the Judean-Gilead dome, the river narrows for a distance of 5 mi. (8 km.) and the land grows progressively infertile. The last 30 mi. (48 km.) of the valley are augmented by the waters of the Wâdī Fâr'ah from the west, and those of the Jabbok River and the Shu'aib from the east. South of Gilead the trough becomes much drier—little more than 5 cm. of mean annual rainfall can be measured at the head of the Dead Sea. The valley exhibits three physical zones, consisting of the broad terrace of the Pliocene trough, the Ghor proper; the dissected soft marl and clay slopes of the Qattara badlands; and the lower Quaternary terrace and flood plain of the river, known as the Zor. The Zor is characterized by an impenetrable jungle of tamarisks and other shrubs, whose vivid green vegetation is in sharp contrast to the Qattara wastes. The Qattara and the Zor have combined to constitute a formidable natural barrier to human communication in this area.

The Dead Sea region is about 50 mi. (80 km.) long and nearly 11 mi. (18 km.) wide, of which the sea itself occupies the major part. The rift-valley reaches its lowest point at the Dead Sea basin, whose surface is 1286 ft. (392 m.) below sea level and whose deepest point is some 1300 ft. (395 m.) lower still. On the western side the narrow Judean shore is bounded by numerous terraces, but apart from a few springs the district is arid and barren. So rapid is the rate of evaporation that the combined inflow of the Jordan and the four main streams of Zerqa, Ma'în, Arnon, and Kerak from the east barely manage to keep the sea level constant. Luxurious vegetation abounds at the mouths of the inflowing streams, or where fresh-water springs occur. The rugged terrain of Moab stands E of the Dead Sea, comprising a plateau of some 3000 ft. (915 m.) in height, deeply dissected by gorges.

The modern Wâdī el-'Arabah stretches for about 100 mi. (160 km.) slightly W of S from the Dead Sea to the Gulf of Aqabah. Immediately S of the Dead Sea is the

Sebkha, a mud-flat area watered by the Wâdī el-Jeib and its tributaries. Here the Arabah is 1275 ft. (388 m.) below sea level, but farther to the south in the area W of Sela, an ancient Edomite stronghold, it rises to 300 ft. (90 m.) above sea level, the highest point being reached near Jebel er-Rishe. Here the valley widens out to as much as 25 mi. (40 km.) in places, but narrows again as it slopes downward to the Gulf of Aqabah, terminating at Elath (Ezion-geber). The entire region is barren save for occasional oases, and even the careful irrigation procedures of Nabatean times produced indifferent results.

III. Minerals.–Mineral deposits are not especially prominent in the Jordan Valley, being sparse in the agricultural area S of Chinnereth. But E of the valley, in Gilead, there were considerable iron deposits; and the mine at Magharat Warda, between the Jabbok and the Wâdī Râjeb, was undoubtedly worked in antiquity. From ore mined in this area may have come the bed of Og king of Bashan (Dt. 3:11), although more probably the Heb. *'ereś* meant "throne" rather than "bed," reflecting Hittite traditions. The copper-mining industry was also developed in the Jordan Valley between Succoth (Tell Deir 'allā) near the Jabbok, and Zarethan (perhaps Tell es-Sa'īdîyeh), 12 mi. (19 km.) NE of Adamah.

The entire region between Succoth and Zarethan furnished suitable clay for the molds in which the copper was cast. In the Dead Sea region are heavy chemical deposits of sodium, potash, magnesium, calcium chlorides, and bromide, and in solution these constitute about one quarter of the liquid in the Dead Sea, giving it a peculiar buoyancy. In Nabatean times there was a limited trade in the bitumen that collected on the surface.

The southern extent of the Arabah contained the only mines for iron and copper found in Canaan. The presence of iron slag at certain mining and smelting camps along the Arabah indicates commercial production of this metal in the Iron Age, although the exact site of the mines is uncertain. A large deposit of iron ore exists in the Wâdī es-Sabrah, about 5 mi. (8 km.) SE of Petra; but this was probably worked only by the Nabateans in the 2nd cent. B.C. Copper ore, principally malachite, is found on both sides of the Wâdī el-'Arabah, with heavy deposits in certain tributary wadis from the east, some sandstone veins containing up to 40 percent of metal. They are associated with the geology of the Sinai Peninsula, where the metal was mined at Serābîṭ el-Khâdim (perhaps Dophkah) and elsewhere from predynastic times. The earliest mining in the Arabah was undertaken at Punon (modern Feinân), from 2200 B.C., principally at a site now named Umm el-'Amad, some 2 mi. (3 km.) to the southeast. In the Iron I-II Age (1200-550 B.C.) the Arabah copper deposits were developed extensively, first probably by the Kenites ("coppersmiths"), who had their center at Sela (Nu. 24:21), the later Edomite city of Petra. Probably the chief cause of hostility between Judah and Edom was the desire to control the mineral resources of the Arabah. To the north the most important mining area was at Khirbet en-Nahas, nearly 17 mi. (27 km.) S of the Dead Sea, while in the south the heavy ore deposits at Mene'iyyeh, some 22 mi. (35 km.) from the head of the Gulf of Aqabah, made it an important location for mining and smelting. Clearly this area of the Promised Land was one "whose stones are iron, and out of whose hills you can dig copper" (Dt. 8:9).

IV. Routes.–Only one major road in antiquity, the "King's Highway" (Nu. 20:17), followed the direction of the Arabah as a whole. It ran from the Gulf of Aqabah to Syria, skirting the Dead Sea and the Jordan Valley on the east and passing through Edom, Moab, Ammon, Gilead, and Bashan. Early Bronze Age settlements along its extent show that it was in use from the 23rd cent. B.C. Further datable ruins between the 13th and 6th cents. B.C. indicate that the road was controlled by Edomites and Ammonites when Moses and the Hebrews desired to use it (Nu. 20:17). A number of smaller transverse routes joined the King's Highway, notably the most southerly one, where Arabian and oriental commerce came through Sela to Beer-sheba and Gaza. An important link with the Jordan Valley was provided by the road between Jericho, Bethel, and Joppa, while further north lay the route connecting Gilead, Adam, Shechem, and Joppa (Josh. 3:16). Yet another important transverse road lay between Gilead, Megiddo, and Esdraelon.

V. History.–The lower Arabah witnessed the semi-sedentary activities of the early patriarchs, who had migrated from Ḥarrân along the western extremity of the Fertile Crescent. Scarcity of pasture land (Gen. 13:5) caused Abraham to move to the Hebron uplands, whereas Lot chose the area around Sodom. The latter was very fertile prior to the catastrophe that overtook the "cities of the plain," for fresh mountain streams from Moab made the location most productive. Its agricultural and mineral wealth apparently attracted invaders from the east under Chedorlaomer, who were initially successful in securing tribute from the region before being pursued up the King's Highway by Abraham (Gen. 14:14).

The southern Arabah was crossed by the wandering Israelites on their journey from Egypt to Canaan. Dt. 2:8 shows that they traveled down the Arabah from a point near Kadesh-barnea to Ezion-geber, after which they turned northward through the Wâdī Yitm to skirt the borders of Edom and Moab. Subsequently the Moabite part of the Arabah was conquered by the Amorite King Sihon (Nu. 21:26). When Sihon was killed by the Israelites at Jahaz, his territory was occupied by the victorious invaders. It was the site alike of the apostasy at Abel-Shittim (Nu. 25:1) and the final acts of Moses (Dt. 1:1). From there Joshua crossed into the Jericho Arabah, establishing Gilgal and gaining access to Canaan with the fall of Jericho.

The northern Arabah is mentioned occasionally in subsequent historical narratives. Abner fled through it after being vanquished at Gibeon (2 S. 2:29), and the murderers of Ish-bosheth crossed its terrain to bring his head to David at Hebron (2 S. 4:7). At the time of the captivity of Judah, Zedekiah was fleeing there for refuge from Jerusalem when he was taken prisoner by the Babylonians (Jer. 39:4). The southern Arabah was prominent in the time of Solomon, furnishing much of his mineral wealth. Glueck discovered what he first identified as the remains of the Solomonic copper refinery at Ezion-geber (Tell el-Kheleifeh), constructed in the 10th cent. B.C. by Phoenician workmen. Subsequently he regarded the site as some kind of storehouse, of approximately the same period. At Timna in 1941 Glueck observed a large slag heap that indicated mining activities. Thirty years later B. Rothenberg uncovered a complex of copper mines and shafts that antedate any others in the Near East of comparable size and sophistication by at least a millennium. Mining operations at Timna were such as to suggest that they could have been conducted throughout the year. At Khirbet en-Nahas and Ezion-geber enclosures were unearthed that seem to have comprised some sort of compound for accomodating the laborers, who would doubtless have been slaves. Khirbet en-Nahas ("copper ruin") may perhaps be identified with Ir-nahash, the "copper city" of 1 Ch. 4:12. Ezion-geber was also an important base for the trading activities of Solomon, whose merchantmen sailed to southwest Arabia and elsewhere carrying smelted copper. Solomonic control of the sea trade and overland caravan routes in the south posed a serious economic threat to the Sabeans of southwest Arabia. The visit of their queen to Jerusalem (1 K. 10:1ff.) was most likely prompted by commercial considerations.

Edom attempted to reoccupy portions of the southern Arabah whenever Judah was weak (2 Ch. 20:1) and suffered periodic reprisals (2 K. 14:7). Later prophets spoke of the restoration of the productivity of this barren territory (Ezk. 47:1; Zec. 14:8). After the 3rd cent. B.C. it was occupied by the Nabateans.

See MAP II.

Bibliography.–*SSW*; J. S. Golub, *Geography of Palestine* (1939); N. Glueck, *The River Jordan* (1946); *Rivers in the Desert* (1959); M. du Buit, *Géographie de la Terre Sainte* (1958); B. Rothenberg, *God's Wilderness* (1961); Baly, *GB*; *Geographical Companion to the Bible* (1963). R. K. HARRISON

ARABATTINE ar-ə-bə-tī'nē (1 Macc. 5:3, AV). *See* AKRABATTENE.

ARABIA ə-rā'bē-ə [Heb. *'ᵃraḇ*; NT Gk. *Arabia*]. The large peninsula lying between Asia and Egypt, generally considered a part of southwest Asia but actually as much a part of Africa. It has often been termed "the home of the Semites."

- I. Arabia In the Bible
  - A. Names
  - B. In the OT
  - C. In the Apocrypha
  - D. In the NT
- II. Size and Location
- III. Physical Description
  - A. Interior
  - B. Coastal Regions
  - C. Mountains
  - D. Rivers
  - E. Climate
  - F. Flora and Fauna
- IV. Peoples and Languages
- V. Literature
- VI. Arts and Crafts
- VII. Cities
- VIII. Caravan Routes
- IX. Discoveries
- X. History

I. Arabia in the Bible.–*A. Names*. The Heb. root *'rb* has a basic meaning of "to be arid," and *'ᵃraḇ* means "steppe, desert-plateau." Accordingly, *'ᵃraḇ* is "the steppe-dweller," and the name can be used as a collective of the people, "the Arab," or by extension to the area in which the people dwell. The gentilic form *'arḇî* means "the Arabian." Another word, usually taken to be from a distinctly different root, is *'ēreḇ*, "mixed company," which is used of the people who joined the Israelites at the time of the Exodus (Ex. 12:38). It is at once obvious that there is no clear-cut term for "Arabia" in the OT. Moreover, no occurrence of Gk. *Arabia* is found in the LXX. (The word does, however, occur in the NT, Gal. 1:17; 4:25.) The terms *bᵉnê qeḏem*, "sons of (the) East" (Gen. 29:1, etc.), and *'ereṣ qeḏem*, "land of (the) East" (Gen. 25:6), are found, and numerous names of tribes and peoples of Arabia are scattered throughout the OT.

B. In the OT. In the Table of Nations (Gen. 10) a number of Arabian tribes are mentioned: among the descendants of Joktan (of the line of Shem), Hazermaveth, Sheba, Havilah, and others (10:26-29); and among the descendants of Cush (of the line of Ham), Seba, Havilah, and others (10:7). If Cush is to be taken to mean Ethiopia, then the relationship of the south Arabian peoples and the Ethiopic peoples (or some of them), which is clearly indicated linguistically, may lie behind the dual reference in the Semite and Hamite genealogies. We also find northern Arabian tribes mentioned among the descendants of Abraham by Keturah (Gen. 25:1-4) and by Hagar (25:12-15), and among the descendants of Esau (Gen. 36). At the time of Solomon, contacts with the Arabian peninsula are indicated, both in the visit of the Queen of Sheba (1 K. 9:26ff., etc.) and in the tribute from the "kings of (the) Arab" (2 Ch. 9:14).

Jehoshaphat king of Judah received tribute from the "Arabian" (2 Ch. 17:11). The wives, sons, and possessions of his son Jehoram were carried off by "the Arabs who are near the Ethiopians" (2 Ch. 21:16f.), which may mean tribes of south Arabia. Isaiah proclaims an oracle concerning "the Arab" (RSV "Arabia"), mentioning the caravans of Dedanites and the inhabitants of the land of Tema (Isa. 21:13f.), which would seem to refer to the nearer or northwestern portion of Arabia. The mention of "Kedar" (21:16f.) indicates the same. Jeremiah includes the "kings of (the) Arab" (RSV "Arabia") in his "cup of wrath" prophecy (Jer. 25:24), along with Dedan, Tema, and possibly other Arabic tribes (e.g., Uz and Buz). In the prophecy against Tyre Ezekiel mentions many of the nations and peoples who were engaged in commerce with Tyre, including "(the) Arab" (RSV "Arabia"), Dedan, the princes of Kedar, Sheba, and Raaman (Ezk. 27:20-22). The context indicates that he is referring to areas S of Damascus in northwest Arabia. In Ezk. 30:5, reference is made to "all the Arab" (RSV "all Arabia"), which in context seems to refer to south Arabia as well as the nearer parts of the peninsula. Joel 3:8 refers to the Sabeans, "a nation far off," referring no doubt to south Arabia. Geshem "the Arab" (Neh. 2:19; 6:1) is clearly from the nearby region of Arabia.

The book of Job is generally considered to be set in Arabia, i.e., in nearer Arabia. The land of Uz (Job 1:1) cannot be positively located; it has been tentatively placed between Edom and Arabia, or in the Ḥaurân S of Damascus, or near Palmyra NE of Damascus. Eliphaz is called a Temanite (Job 2:11), and Teman was in Edom (Am. 1:11f.). Job's home was located where the Sabeans (Job 1:15) and the Babylonians (or Chaldeans, 1:17) alike could raid them. Once again it is clear that we are dealing with the portion of Arabia that borders on Transjordan. The OT, then, is principally concerned with nearer Arabia, and references to south Arabia are very few.

Traditionally the Queen of Sheba is considered to have come from south Arabia. However, this question needs careful study (*see* QUEEN OF SHEBA).The names Sheba and Seba both occur in the OT; and Seba is clearly to be located in south Arabia, probably to be identified with the Sabeans. The location of Sheba is less certain; some authorities argue for its location in north Arabia, while others are convinced that it is in the south. If we can form a conclusion from phonemic data (which are not always reliable in the case of proper names), the South Arabic word for the kingdom of the Sabeans is to be related to the Hebrew word for Sheba, not Seba. (For discussion of the phonemic problem, cf. W. S. LaSor, *JQR*, 48 [1957/58], 161-173.)

C. In the Apocrypha. The word Arabia is used of the Nabatean kingdom (in north Arabia) in 1 Macc. 11:16. In Jth. 2:25 the term, according to the context, refers to the region around Damascus. The "dragons from Arabia" of 2 Esd. 15:29 cannot be geographically located.

D. In the NT. Jesus refers to "the Queen of the South," referring to the visit of the Queen of Sheba (Mt.

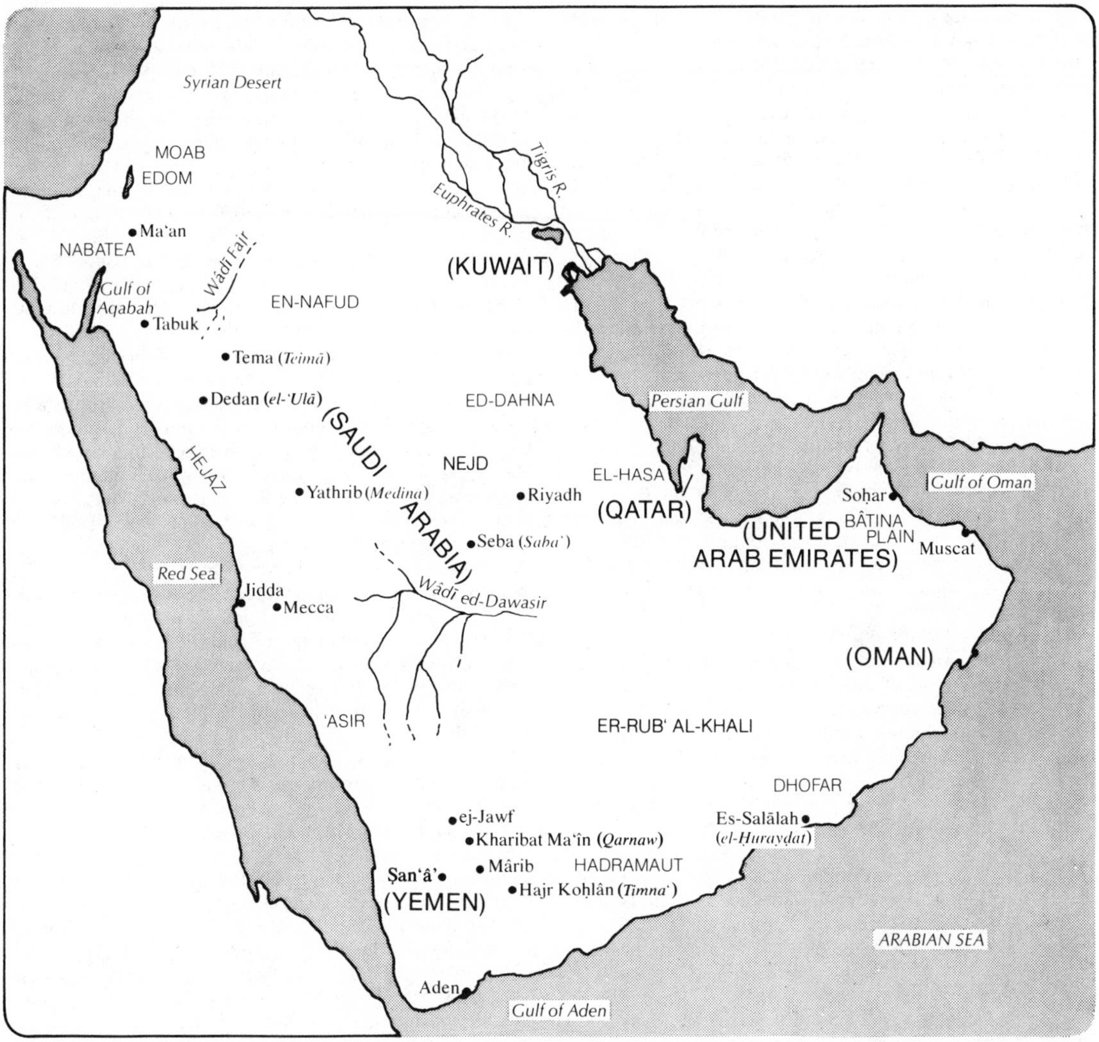

12:42; Lk. 11:31), which some would equate with Yemen, since *yemen* means "south" as well as "right hand" in Hebrew. Paul speaks of going to "Arabia" after his Damascus experience (Gal. 1:17), which has been taken to refer to (1) the region E of Damascus, or (2) that S of Damascus, or (3) Mt. Sinai. He includes Sinai in Arabia in Gal. 4:25, following the classical view of *Arabia Petrea*; but this is hardly sufficient evidence to decide the location of his postconversion visit. King Aretas, elsewhere identified as an Arabian (cf. Josephus *Ant.* xiv.1.4), is mentioned in 2 Cor. 11:32, and we are reasonably certain that he is to be identified with Aretas IV, king of the Nabateans, whose kingdom extended E and S of Damascus, with its capital at Petra.

II. Size and Location.–Arabia is the largest peninsula in the world, occupying more than 1,000,000 sq. mi. (2,600,000 sq. km.), almost one-quarter the size of all Europe, and one-third the size of continental USA. The peninsula is almost a right triangle in shape, with the altitude lying along a line running NW-SE, about 1400 mi. (2250 km.) in length, the base on a line running NE-SW, approximately 1100 mi. (1770 km.) in width, and the hypotenuse roughly forming the northeast side of the triangle. The peninsula is bounded on the southwest by the Red Sea, on the southeast by the Gulf of Aden and the Arabian Sea, on the northeast by the Gulf of Oman and the Persian Gulf, and on the north by the modern borders of Iraq and Jordan. Where the Arabian Desert ends and the Syrian Desert begins is not easily determined. If we were to take the Arabic name as a guide ("the island of the Arabs"), we should consider the Euphrates River and the Mediterranean Sea as the northern and western limits of Arabia.

III. Physical Description.–The entire peninsula can be thought of as a plateau raised along the southwest (the Red Sea) side, with the highest point at the south (about 10,700 ft., 3250 m.), and sloping gradually toward the northeast. The northeast side (along the Persian Gulf) is but little above sea level. At the eastern corner the mountain peaks of Oman form an exception to the general description. In general the peninsula is a desert surrounded by the more or less fertile coastal regions; however, this simple description needs to be developed to suit the complexities of Arabia.

Classical geographers speak of three main divisions: *Arabia Petrea* (Arabia of Petra), including Petra and the Arabah, Edom, Moab, and Transjordan; *Arabia deserta* (Desert Arabia), the northern and central portion including the Syrian Desert and the Nejd; and *Arabia felix* (Fortunate Arabia), the southern portion. This is not completely satisfactory for modern study. We shall consider first the interior, and then the coastal regions.

A. Interior. A rocky spur, running approximately N-S, and the high land on its west side (called the Nejd), divide the interior of Arabia into desert areas, the smaller toward the north called en-Nafud, and the larger toward the south called er-Rub' el-Khali ("the empty quarter"). The Nafud, which is about 400 mi. (650 km.) E-W, and about half as wide, is almost waterless, but during the rainy season it produces good pasture. It is crossed by many large sand dunes. The Rub' el-Khali, which is well named, is almost devoid of plant and animal life. It is roughly triangular in shape, about 800 mi. (1300 km.) NE-SW and nearly 400 mi. (650 km.) wide at the northeast end. Toward the east there are huge sand dunes, some more than 500 ft. (150 m.) high. The southwest portion of the Rub' el-Khali lies at an altitude of about 2000 ft. (600 m.), and the east portion about 600 ft. (180 m.). A desert strip connecting the Nafud with the Rub' el-Khali, lying between the Nejd and the coastal region (the Hasa) along the Persian Gulf, is known as the Dahna, about 400 mi. (650 km.) N-S and averaging about 30 mi. (50 km.) in width. This is described as consisting of seven longitudinal bands of sand separated by sandy valleys about a mile across. In the northern Dahna, peaks of pure red sand rise to heights of 200 to 300 ft. (60 to 90 m.). The southern Dahna yields rich pasture in the winter and spring.

Lying within this desert encirclement is the Nejd, which is the principal part of interior Arabia, and according to some theories the source of the Arab peoples. It is a region of numerous oases, traversed by three wadi systems that flow W-E in addition to mountain chains and a strip of desert.

At one time there were volcanoes along the western part of the interior, and large lava fields separate the Nejd from the coastal regions of the Hejaz and the Tehâma. In Arabic such an area is designated as *harrä*, and on the map we may note Harrat el-'Uwairidh (W of the Nafud), Harrat Khaibir (N of Medina), Harrat el-Kishib (NE of Mecca), and Harrat Nawasif (E of Mecca). Another lava field, Hadhaudha Mukhaidhir, lies E of Wâdī Sirḥân, near the present Jordan border, in the north.

B. Coastal Regions. We shall describe the coastal regions beginning in the west (at the north end of the Red Sea) and continuing counterclockwise. The most important region, from the religious point of view, is the Hejaz, which stretches from S of the Gulf of Aqabah to about the vicinity of Jidda (some 500 mi. [800 km.]), and extends inland from 100 to 200 mi. (160 to 320 km.). This region includes the sacred cities of Mecca and Medina. Southeast of the Hejaz is the Tehâma, a narrow fringe of well-watered land between the Red Sea and the high mountains that form the southwest side of the peninsula. The mountainous region lying between Tehâma and the Nejd is 'Asîr, separated from the Tehâma by the range known as Jebel Hijaz. The southern corner is Yemen, a region of many mountains and valleys, and of great fertility. In this region were some of the earliest civilizations of Arabia.

The southern coast on the Gulf of Aden is known as Hadramaut (probably the OT Hazarmaveth), while the eastern coast on the Arabian Sea and the Gulf of Oman is Oman, marked by a mountain mass, cut by rugged valleys, and of unusual fertility. The coastal region along the Persian Gulf is known as Hasa; here are Trucial Oman, Qatar, and the offshore island of Bahrain.

If we are to follow the natural boundaries we must include the fertile strip along the Euphrates (modern Iraq), the Syrian Desert, the Transjordanian plateau, and the eastern shore of the Gulf of Aqabah, to conclude the circuit of Arabia.

C. Mountains. Mountain peaks in the Hejaz reach heights of 6000 to 8461 ft. (1800 to 2580 m.). In the Tehâma, just S of Mecca, one peak rises to 9400 ft. (2865 m.) while in Yemen several peaks are above 10,000 ft. (3050 m.) and one near Ṣan'â' rises to an elevation of 12,336 ft. (3760 m.). In Oman there is one peak (Jebel esh-Sham) reaching 11,000 ft. (3350 m.). In the central area (the Nejd) there are scattered peaks rising to elevations from 3500 to 4500 ft. (1070 to 1370 m.), and one range (Jebel et-Tuwaiq) running S from Riyadh with one peak of 2766 ft. (843 m.). A mountainous region SW of Riyadh in the Nejd is known as Jebel el-'Alaiya (3547 ft. [1081 m.]). A range of mountains (the Jebel Hijaz), as we have noted, separates 'Asîr from the Tehâma.

D. Rivers. There are no true rivers in the Arabian peninsula. There are, however, numerous seasonal river beds (wadis), some of which are murderous torrents after a sudden rain. Three main wadi systems run W-E across the Nejd. In the northern part, Wâdī er-Rima rises in the Harrat Khaibar and ultimately loses itself in the sand. Wâdī es-Surra rises in the western Nejd, cuts its way through the Jebel et-Tuwaiq, and under several different names can be traced until it reaches the Persian Gulf near Qatar. Wâdī ed-Dawasir, formed by several wadis rising in 'Asîr and Yemen, cuts through the lower end of Jebel et-Tuwaiq, and loses itself in the sand of er-Rub' el-Khali. Because of its significance as a trade route, we should mention the Wâdī Fajr, in the extreme northwest, which opens into the Wâdī Sirḥân, E of Amman in Transjordan. We shall not mention here the names of the numerous wadis that cut the ranges bordering the Hejaz, the Tehâma, Yemen, Hadramaut, or Oman. In spite of these, some of which reach the sea, there are no good harbors in the Arabian peninsula with the exception of Aden at the extreme south, and Muscat in Oman.

E. Climate. The weather is hot and humid in the coastal regions, and since these are the areas best known to travelers, inaccurate generalizations have been drawn. Actually, the interior is often quite pleasant. Maximum summer temperature in the Nejd is about 112°F (44°C), and a low of 18°F (-8°C) has been recorded in the northern Nejd, where frost is not uncommon in winter. The high plateau and mountains of western Arabia as well as the mountainous region of Oman are pleasant at all times. Snow falls on the higher parts of Yemen in December; but the temperature at the Red Sea, perhaps 100 mi. (160 km.) distant, remains around 80°F (27°C). Snow falls also in the Oman massif, and in the high regions in the extreme northwest.

Along the precipitous southwest edge of the plateau, in 'Asîr, Yemen, and part of Hadramaut, the annual rainfall may exceed 20 in. (50 cm.), extending inland 50 mi. (80 km.) or more; and settled habitation is possible. This was the *Arabia felix* of the ancients. Likewise there is sufficient rainfall in Oman to support a settled population. For the rest of the peninsula the rainfall is minimal, although it is sufficient to cause the desert to blossom in the spring; only nomadic life is possible, supported by wells and oases. In the region around the cities of Mecca and Medina, rainfall, although scant, is often in the form of thundershowers that result in flooding and erosion.

The northern part is in the area of the etesian winds, which blow prevailingly from the west. This is the area of two seasons, rainy and dry, the rainy season coming in the winter. Yemen, on the other hand, is in the monsoon area, getting heavy rain in the late summer months. For the rest of the peninsula, winds are generally either from the north or from the south, the south wind bringing heat in summer and rain in winter. The Nafud and the Empty Quarter are sand deserts, the latter being the largest in the world.

ARABIA

F. Flora and Fauna. It is unnecessary to name in detail all of the flora of Arabia, for it is typical of any region of desert and steppe. Of biblical relevance we mention first frankincense, which is often named in connection with various peoples of Arabia (e.g., Havilah, Gen. 2:12; Sheba, 1 K. 10:2; Ishmaelites, Gen. 37:25). The date palm is also of importance, but specific reference to it as being on Arabian soil is limited to Sinai (Ex. 15:27; Nu. 33:9). In Job typical desert flora is mentioned, such as the mallow, bushes, broom (30:4-7). Almug wood (1 K. 10:11f.) and ebony (Ezk. 27:15) were not indigenous to Arabia, hence must have been imported, probably from eastern Africa to Sheba, as part of the extensive commerce of south Arabia.

Likewise it is unnecessary to list all of the animals and birds to be found in Arabia. The most important of all animals to the Arab is the camel, and biblical references to the camel are numerous: in connection with the Ishmaelites, Midianites, and Amalekites (Gen. 37:25ff.; Jgs. 6:3-5), with Kedar (Jer. 49:29), with the Queen of Sheba (1 K. 10:2), etc. Next in importance for the Arab were his sheep and particularly goats (cf. Ezk. 27:21). Before the domestication of the camel the Arab was doubtless among the ass-nomads, and mention of asses is found among the booty taken from the Midianites (Nu. 31:1-47, esp. vv. 34, 39). Cattle belong to pasture land, not to steppe; and the cattle mentioned in this account properly belong to the fertile area in northwest Arabia — which must be taken into consideration when we try to locate the land of Midian. The horse, mentioned in Job 39:19ff., was a later import of the Arabians, now considered one of their prize animals. A long list of wild animals and birds could be added, particularly from Job 38f.; but this article is not the place for such a treatise. The reference to "peacocks" or "baboons," however the word is to be translated, and to apes (1 K. 10:22), is to be taken as part of the commerce of south Arabia and not necessarily to indigenous fauna. We might mention the oysters of the Persian Gulf, from which were gotten the exquisite pearls of the ancient Middle East; but there is no specific reference to them in the OT (Heb. *gāḇîš* in Job 28:18 is properly translated "crystal").

IV. Peoples and Languages.–It is reasonably certain that there were two racial stocks in Arabia, which can possibly be identified with the sedentary population of the south and the nomads of the north. The nomads of the Nejd seem to belong to the same stock as those of the south, judging from the linguistic evidence. The northern nomads spoke a language akin to Aramaic or Canaanite, or more likely the common ancestor of these languages. The other peoples spoke a language more closely related to Arabic, probably the ancestor of South Arabic and North (or Classical) Arabic. It has been customary to refer to periodic irruptions of the desert Arabs into the "sown," or the Fertile Crescent. Some of these periodic migrations can be traced with great probability: one just before the patriarchal period, and another around the time of the Israelite conquest of Canaan. These "invasions" seem to have been by groups of north Arabian peoples, from what meager linguistic evidence has come down to us. The later invasion, at the time of the Muhammedan conquest, was accomplished by south Arabians. We may note in passing, with cautious restraint, that the genealogical tables in Gen. 10 likewise indicate both Hamitic (Gen. 10:7) and Semitic (Gen. 10:23) origins for the peoples of Arabia.

The languages of Arabia likewise confirm this duality of origin, with West Semitic (Proto-Canaanite[?]-Aramaic) and South Semitic (Proto-North-South-Arabic), but in addition indicate a clear development of two branches of South Semitic, namely Old South Arabic and North Arabic. In south Arabia we know principally the languages of the early kingdoms: Sabean, Minaean, Qatabanian, Hadramauti, and Awsani. These exist almost exclusively in inscriptional materials, several thousands of inscriptions having been recovered over the past century and a quarter. The script, which is very neat and regular and which is clearly related to Ethiopic, seems to be independent of Canaanite or Phoenician alphabetic writing, and is the only system of Semitic writing known to us that preserves all twenty-nine of the parent phonemes. Unfortunately, the material is limited to votive inscriptions, dedications, and the like, with a very small vocabulary, a limited set of formulaic expressions, and very little to help us reconstruct the history or the life of the people. These dialects, generally classified as Old South Arabic, or Epigraphic South Arabic, are closely related to Classical Arabic, but there are a number of significant differences. The serious Semitist therefore must give careful attention to Old South Arabic evidence — a fact that has not always been apparent.

The inscriptions from the northern region are in related dialects known as Liḥyanite, Thamudic, and Safaitic. These dialects are generally classified as North Arabic, and are closer to Classical (Koranic) Arabic than is Old South Arabic. Classical Arabic developed from the dialect of Mecca through the tremendous influence of the Koran, and represents a later stage of development (approximately a thousand years later than the early OSA inscriptions).

It seems likely that both South Arabic and North Arabic are to be traced to a common origin, with North Arabic developing from colonial extensions of the south Arabian kingdoms. On the other hand, the nomadic peoples of north Arabia, as far as we have been able to study them linguistically — and it must be admitted that we are seriously handicapped, since they have left little if any material that we can use for the study of their language — are perhaps to be classified as non-Arabic. The Nabateans and Palmyrenes, of the southern and northern portions of the extreme northwest of the Arabian peninsula respectively, were Aramaic-speaking peoples, although admittedly they may have adopted Aramaic as a trade-language.

V. Literature.–Within the period of our present discussion there are few literary remains. It is obvious, however, that the peoples of the desert must have had a rich literary heritage, for much of it is reflected in the literature of later periods. Arabic poetry, for example, is known to us only from the centuries immediately preceding the rise of Islam (7th cent. A.D.). But it is already well developed in form and style, which to most scholars suggests a long period of preparation. This, of course, is not an infallible principle, for frequently we find the sudden appearance of some literary or art form of excellence due to the advent of a genius. In the case of Arabic literature, one of the chief figures is the prophet Muhammad. But the imagery of the language, the richness of the vocabulary, and many other features, all seem to point to a long period of development. We could wish that we had other types than inscriptional material in Old South Arabic!

VI. Arts and Crafts.–Moscati says, "Art does not flourish in the desert" (p. 207). This statement is open to question. It is probably true that the life of the nomad does not offer the time or the opportunity for the cultivation of artistic skills and crafts that a settled civilization does. On the other hand, there is opportunity for the development of the imagination, and creative work comes from the imagination. The discoveries in south Arabia by the expedition of the American Foundation for the Study of Man have brought to light a number of interesting items, including fine bronze statues, stone statues and reliefs, and articles of jewelry. The craftsmanship is often rough and primitive. South Arabian architecture was largely dependent on the granite found in the area, and buildings were made of great stone blocks, often with drafted margins and pecked faces, laid up without mortar and therefore depending on careful fitting and finishing. Pillars were fitted into sockets, and there was extensive use of pilasters and columns. G. W. van Beek has traced the style to Assyria about the middle of the 7th cent. B.C. (in *Archaeological Discoveries in South Arabia* [1958], Appendix v, pp. 287-295). Temples were elliptical or rectangular in plan. Castles, walls, and towers have also been discovered. Of particular note are the numerous structures for water storage, particularly dams and dikes, which were essential to the large and flourishing civilization in south Arabia for centuries. One of these, the great dam at Mârib, at first built of packed earth, was later constructed of limestone finely cut and well engineered. The collapse of this dam after A.D. 542 is credited by Arab historians with the collapse of the entire south Arabian civilization. It is more reasonable to suppose that the mastery of navigation by the Romans, using the monsoon winds to reach India and thus by-passing Arabia, and the constant warfare of the south Arabian tribes, were the most significant reasons.

VII. Cities.–Due to the physical nature of Arabia, which is for the large part desert and steppe, there are few important cities. In the extreme north in the Syrian desert NE of Damascus was Palmyra (TADMOR), one-time kingdom of Queen Zenobia, an oasis city-state on an important caravan road. Tadmor is attributed to Solomon in 2 Ch. 8:4, but possibly this is a textual error (cf. 1 K. 9:18). The Palmyrene inscriptions came from this location. On the western edge of the Syrian desert is DAMASCUS, called in Arabic esh-Shâm ("the North"), also an oasis city-state at the junction of important caravan routes, and most significant of the Aramean city-kingdoms. In the mountains SE of the Dead Sea is Petra (Sela, 2 K. 14:7), one-time capital of the Nabatean kingdom. Possibly there is a connection between Nabateans and the Nebaioth of Gen. 25:13, etc. As we have seen, Palmyrene and Nabatean are Aramaic dialects, hence we assume that these cities were properly Aramean rather than Arabian.

Southwest of the Nafud is the important oasis of Teimā (Tema, Gen. 25:15; Job 6:19), and about 100 mi. (160 km.) SSW is el-ʻUlā, often identified with biblical Dedan (Isa. 21:13; Jer. 25:23, etc.). In the Hejaz, nearly 100 mi. (160 km.) inland from the Red Sea, is the important city of Yathrib, better known as Medina, lying in a fertile plain; it was to this city that Muhammad made his epochal hegira in A.D. 622, from which the Muhammadan calendar takes its starting point. About 200 mi. (320 km.) further S is Mecca, birthplace of the Prophet and the holiest city of Islam. Jidda, the port and airport for Mecca, lies on the Red Sea, about 45 mi. (75 km.) W of Mecca. These cities are north Arabian, possibly originating as we have suggested as colonial outposts of south Arabian kingdoms.

In the extreme south, in the region known as Yemen ("South," possibly in contrast to esh-Sham, "the North," or Damascus), were several cities in biblical times, but it would appear that none of them is named in the Bible. We might mention, for the record, Qarnaw the capital of Maʻîn, Mârib the capital of Saba', Timnaʻ the capital of Qatabân, and Shabwa the capital of Hadramaut. Today, the only significant cities in the area are Aden on the coast of the Gulf of Aden, and Ṣanʻâ' the capital of Yemen, about 170 mi. (275 km.) NNW of Aden and inland about 100 mi. (160 km.) from the Red Sea. In east Arabia, Muscat the capital of Oman is a city of significance, partly because of its natural harbor. Finally, Riyadh the capital of Saudi Arabia is in the heart of the Nejd and close to the center of the Arabian peninsula.

Cameo carved facade of the Nabatean Treasury at Petra, seen from the "Siq," a mile-long narrow gorge with walls 200 ft. (73 m.) high, the only entrance to the site (Jordan Information Bureau, Washington)

VIII. Caravan Routes.–There are many indications of the importance of caravan trade in Arabia in antiquity, and it would seem that a number of items were imported from eastern Africa and probably India to south Arabia, thence to Gaza and Egypt, to Damascus and regions N and W from there, and to Mesopotamia. One route led from Yemen by Mârib, Qarnaw, and the wadis and oases of Tehâma to the vicinity of Mecca. From Mecca one route led across the peninsula, through the Nejd, to the Persian Gulf in the vicinity of Bahrein (ancient Dilbat?) and along the coast to what is now Iraq. Another route led by an interior valley to Yathrib (Medina), where again the route divided, the one way crossing the southern edge of the Nafud going on to Babylon, and the other proceeding northwestward, via el-ʻUlā (probably Dedan), to Madâ'în Ṣâliḥ, Tebuk, Maʻan, to Gaza, Egypt, etc. Since Maʻan is the present-day entrance to Petra, which was once the capital of the Nabatean kingdom, we can readily understand why the Nabateans rose to power by control of this caravan road. From Madâ'în Ṣâliḥ another route branched northward by Wâdī Sirḥân into Transjordan and on to Damascus. This, too, came under the control of the Nabateans toward the beginning of the Christian era. The important King's Highway skirted the edge of the desert from the Gulf of Aqabah (Ezion-geber) to Damascus, and from Damascus several routes branched east, north, and west.

Starting again at Yemen, we can trace a spice route northeastward via Shabwa in Hadramaut to Dhofar, where the "frankincense mountains" were located (about halfway between Aden and Muscat), thence to Oman. Another route ran from Mârib and Qarnaw almost due N across the peninsula through the Nejd, to the Persian Gulf

Arabs mounted on camels battle Assyrian forces. Relief from Ashurbanipal's palace, Nineveh (Trustees of the British Museum)

near Bahrain. A further route connected with this route somewhere in the general vicinity of modern Riyadh and led to Oman.

IX. Discoveries.–Exploration in Arabia has been carried out since the 18th cent., but archeological work has been undertaken only within the past few decades and that has been largely confined to north Arabia. *See* ARCHEOLOGY OF ARABIA.

X. History.–The history of ancient Arabia is not yet clear. It would seem that there were two different peoples in north Arabia and in south Arabia by the end of the Paleolithic era. It has generally been proposed that the Semitic peoples of south Arabia came there from the north in the 2nd millennium B.C. Basing our hypothesis upon the evidence of language and phonetic shifts, we have suggested that these Semites may rather have come from the Nile Valley, through Abyssinia, and across the Bâb el-Mandeb into Yemen — but this is far from proven. At any rate, toward the end of the 2nd millennium there were several peoples who were later to become the Sabeans, the Minaeans, the Qatabanians, the Hadramauti, and the Awsani. Perhaps as early as 1200 B.C. these peoples had developed a remarkable civilization, with public buildings, political organization, agricultural and commercial achievements, and other indications of wealth and cultural achievement.

The kingdom of Saba' is the first to come to light historically, with inscriptions probably from the 8th cent. B.C. indicating a well-organized city-state under a *mkrb* (*mukarrib*), who was evidently a high priest. Later (in the 5th cent.) the term *mlk* (*malk*?), "king," replaced the term *mkrb*, marking a "transition to a lay form of government based on the oligarchy of a small number of military and landed families" (Moscati, p. 185). The kingdom of Maʿîn (the Minaeans) began to challenge Sabean supremacy by the end of the 5th cent., and in the following century the kingdom of Qatabân was a third important power. The kingdom of Hadramaut (often incorrectly spelled Hadhramaut, but the letter is ḍ, not ḏ) also came into the political picture, and the fortunes favored first one and then the other. Finally, the region came under the dominion of the Ḥimyarites. Moscati dates the Minaean period from *ca.* 400 B.C. to the end of the 1st cent. B.C., the Qatabân *ca.* 400 to 50 B.C., and the Hadramaut *ca.* 450 B.C. to the 2nd cent. A.D. The Ḥimyarites he identifies as a Sabean tribe that rose to power in the 2nd cent. B.C. and welded south Arabia into a single state until the Ethiopian Christians occupied Yemen in A.D. 525. By the time the great dam at Mârib collapsed, perhaps *ca.* 575 A.D., the death knell had sounded for the south Arabian civilization.

Saba' is mentioned in a number of Assyrian inscriptions. Tiglath-pileser III (744-727 B.C.) mentions two queens of Arabia by name, Zabiba and Samsi (*ARAB*, I, §§ 778, 817; *ANET*, p. 283), Sargon II (721-705 B.C.) also mentions Samsi the queen of Arabia as well as It'amra the Sabean (*ARAB*, II, § 18; *ANET*, p. 286; N. Abbot, *AJSL*, 58 [1941], 1-22). It is not always clear that south Arabia is in view in the Assyrian inscriptions, and in some cases it would seem that there were colonial centers in the north, indicating the extent of south Arabian control of the trade routes.

The history of north Arabia is not known to us until a somewhat later date. From remote antiquity there were nomads in the area, but our first knowledge of "Arabs" is found in an inscription of Shalmaneser III (858-824 B.C.) in which he mentions "Gindibu' the Arabian" (*ARAB*, II, § 611; *ANET*, p. 279). Thereafter the Arabians, who are camel-riding raiders, are found often in Assyrian inscriptions, and are portrayed in Ashurbanipal's bas-reliefs at Nineveh. The Nabateans had developed control of the trade routes and probably become a political entity by the 4th cent. B.C., but the earliest known ruler is Aretas I (*ca.* 170 B.C.; cf. 2 Macc. 5:8). Nabatean villages and towns and the cultivation of the desert can be traced to the same time and a bit earlier. The capital was at Petra, and the kingdom extended N to Damascus. The Nabatean period ended with the Roman occupation in A.D. 106. The oasis-state of Palmyra (Tadmor) became important in the 1st cent. B.C., and rose to power until it was conquered by the emperor Aurelian in A.D. 272. It was located in the Syrian desert, NE of Damascus, and its best-known ruler was Queen Zenobia. Both the Nabatean and the Palmyrene kingdoms were Aramaic-speaking. Further S, in the region about Dedan (modern el-'Ulā), which had been a Minaean colony, the kingdom of the Liḥyanites developed and reached its zenith at the beginning of the Christian era. The rise of Mecca and the Islamic state is beyond the scope of this present article.

Bibliography.–S. Moscati, *Ancient Semitic Civilizations* (1957), pp. 181-207, and Bibliography, p. 243; R. L. Bowen and F. P. Albright, eds., *Archaeological Discoveries in South Arabia* (1958); W. Phillips, *Qataban and Sheba* (1955); also in paperback, *Sheba's Buried City* (1958); H. von Wissman and Maria Höfner, *Beiträge zur historischen Geographie des vorislamischen Südarabiens. Mainz Akademie der Wissenschaften und der Litteratur. Abhandlungen der geistes- und sozialwissenschaftlichen Klasse* (1952, 1954), pp. 364-370; W. F. Albright, *BASOR*, 119 (Oct. 1950), 5-15; 129 (Feb. 1953), 20-24; G. W. van Beek, *BASOR*, 143 (Oct. 1956), 6-9; A. Grohmann, *Südarabien als Wirtschaftsgebiet II. Schriften der Philosophischen Fakultät der Deutschen Universität in Prag*, XIII (1933), 101-131 (on the land and sea trade routes); G. Ryckmans, *Les religions arabes préislamiques* (2nd ed. 1951); W. Caskel, *Das altarabische Königreich Lihjan* (1950); J. Starcky, *Palmyre* (1952); R. Blachère, *Histoire de la littérature arabe des origines à la fin du XVe siècle de J.-C.* (1952); C. Doughty, *Travels in Arabia Deserta* (2 vols., 1884); J. Starcky, *BA*, 18 (1955), 4; M. Höfner, *Altsüdarabische Grammatik* (1943); *National Geographic* map "Southwest Asia," 1:1,750,000 (1952).

W. S. LASOR

ARABIC GOSPEL OF THE INFANCY. *See* APOCRYPHAL GOSPELS II.E.

ARABIC LANGUAGE. For the student of the Bible the Arabic language is of interest, first, as one of the members of the Semitic group of languages, to which belong the Hebrew and Aramaic tongues of the Bible; second, as one of the languages into which the Bible and other church literature were early translated and in which a Christian literature was produced; and third, as the vernacular of Muhammad and his followers, the classical tongue of Islam.

I. Philological Characterization.–Scholars are generally agreed in grouping the Arabic and Ethiopic together as a South Semitic branch of the Semitic stock. For the geographical and ethnological background of the Arabic language, *see* ARABIA III, IV. A general characteristic of this tongue of the desert is its remarkable retention, into a late historical period, of grammatical features obliterated or in process of obliteration in other Semitic tongues at their earliest emergence in literature, so that in the period since the golden age of its literature, Arabic has been undergoing changes in some respects analogous to those which its sister dialects underwent in their preliterary or earliest literary stage. Thus, e.g., the case-endings of nouns, lost in Aramaic and Canaanitish (including Hebrew), all but lost in the Abyssinian dialects, beginning to be disregarded in even the early (popular) Babylonian, lost also in the dialects of Modern Arabic, are in full vitality throughout the classical period of Arabic literature.

The Arabic language itself, ancient and modern, divides into a vast number of dialects, many of which have attained the distinction of producing a literature greater or less. But the dialect of the tribe of Koreish, to which Muhammad belonged, is the one that, by the circumstances of the Koran's composition and diffusion, has become the norm of pure Arabic. Old Arabic poems, some of them produced in "the Ignorance," that is, before the days of Muhammad, are in substantially the same dialect as that of the Koran, for it appears that bedouin tribes ranging within the limits of the Arabian desert spoke an Arabic little differentiated by tribal or geographical peculiarities. On the other hand the inhabitants of the coast of the Indian Ocean from Yemen to Oman, and of the island of Socotra off that coast, spoke an Arabic differing widely from that of the northern tribes. The various dialects of this "South Arabic," known partly through their daughter dialects of today (Mehri, Socotri, etc.), partly from the numerous and important inscriptions ("Minaean" and "Sabean") found in Yemen by modern travelers, notably Halévy and Glaser, show a closer affinity than do the "North Arabic" with the Abyssinian dialects (Ge'ez, i.e., "Ethiopic," Tigre, Tigriña, Amharic, etc.), as might indeed be expected from the admitted south Arabian origin of the Habesh tribes or Abyssinians.

For the interpretation of the OT the Arabic language has been of service in a variety of ways. In the department of lexicography it has thrown light not only on many a word used but once in the Bible or too seldom for usage alone to determine its meaning, but also on words which had seemed clear enough in their biblical setting, but which have received illustration or correction from their usage in the immense bulk and range of Arabic literature with its enormous vocabulary. For the modern scientific study of Hebrew grammar, with its genetic method, Arabic has been of the greatest value, through the comparison of its cognate forms, where in the main the Arabic has the simpler, fuller, and more regular morphology, and through the comparison of similar constructions, for which the highly developed Arabic syntax furnishes useful rubrics. In addition to this the Arabic language plays a prominent part, perhaps the foremost part, in the determination of those laws of the mutation of sounds which once governed the development and now reveal the mutual relationships of the various Semitic languages.

The script which we know as Arabic script, with its numerous varieties, developed out of the vulgar Aramaic alphabet in north Arabia; diacritical points were added to many of those letters, either to distinguish Arabic sounds for which no letter existed, or to differentiate letters the forms of which had become so similar as to create confusion. In Yemen another script arose early, that of the inscriptions above mentioned, admirably clear and adapted to express probably all the chief varieties of consonantal sounds in actual use, though entirely without vowels.

II. Christian Arabic Literature.–For Arabic versions of the Bible, *see* VERSIONS. Outside of the Scriptures themselves there was felt by Christian communities living in the Arabic-speaking world (primarily, though not exclusively, in Egypt and Syria) the need of a Christian literature suited to the tastes of the time and region. Apocryphal and legendary material makes up a large part, therefore, of the list of Christian Arabic literature. *See* APOCRYPHAL GOSPELS. But this material was not original. With the small degree of intellectual activity in those circles it is not surprising that most of such material, and indeed of the entire literary output, consists of translations from Syriac, Greek, or Coptic, and that original productions are few.

Of these last the most noteworthy are the following: theological and apologetic tracts by Theodore bishop of Haran, the same who held the famous disputation with Muhammadan scholars at the court of Caliph al-Mamun early in the 9th cent.; apologetic and polemic writings of Yahya ibn-Adi of Tekrit, and of his pupil abu-Ali Isa ibn-Ishaq, both in the 10th cent.; the Arabic works of Bar-Hebraeus, better known for his numerous Syriac compositions, but productive also of both historical and theological works in Arabic (13th cent.); in Egypt, but belonging to the same Jacobite or Monophysite communion as the above, the polemic and homiletic productions of Bishop Severus of Eshmunain (10th cent.), and, a generation earlier than Servus and belonging to the opposing or Melkite Egyptian Church, the chronicle of Eutychius patriarch of Alexandria, continued a century later by Yahya ibn-Said of Antioch; large compilations of church history, church law, and theological miscellany by the Coptic Christians al-Makin, abu-Ishaq ibn-al-Assal, Abu'l Barakat, and others, the leaders in a general revival of Egyptian Christianity in the 13th cent.; on the soil of Nestorianism, finally, the ecclesiastical, dogmatic, and exegetical writings of Abulfaraj Abdallah ibn-at-Tayyib (11th cent.), the apologetic compositions of his contemporary, Elias ben Shinaya the historian, and the Nestorian church chronicle begun in the 12th cent. by Mari ibn-Suleiman and continued two centuries later by Amr ibn-Mattai and Saliba bar Johannan. After this date there is no original literature produced by Arabic-speaking Christians until the modern intellectual revival brought about by contact with European Christianity.

III. Literary Vehicle of Islam.–What Aramaic, Greek, and Latin have been successively in the history of Christianity, all this and more Arabic has been in the history of Islam. The language of its founder and his "helpers," the language of the Koran "sent down" from God to Muhammad by the angel Gabriel, the language therefore in which it has always been preserved by the faithful, untranslated, wherever it has spread in the wide world of Islam, Arabic is identified with Islam in its origin, its history, its literature, and its propaganda. All the points of contact between the religion of the Bible and the religion of the Koran, literary, historical, apologetic, and missionary, are alike in this, that they demand of the intelligent student of Christianity a sympathetic acquaintance with the genius and the masterpieces of the great Arabic tongue.

J. O. BOYD

ARABIC VERSIONS. *See* VERSIONS.

ARAD âr'ad [Heb. *ʿᵃrāḏ*]. One of the descendants of Elpaal son of Shaharaim, mentioned among the descendants of Benjamin (1 Ch. 8:15).

ARAD. An important biblical town in the eastern Negeb that dominated the frontier region and the outset of the highway to Edom and to the harbor of Elath.

I. Biblical Data.–In the desert traditions Arad figured as the main obstacle on the direct way of the Israelites to the land of Canaan. "The Canaanite, the king of Arad, who dwelt in the Negeb," withstood the assault of the tribes on their approach from Kadesh-barnea by way of Atharim (Nu. 21:1; 33:40), defeating them at neighboring Hormah

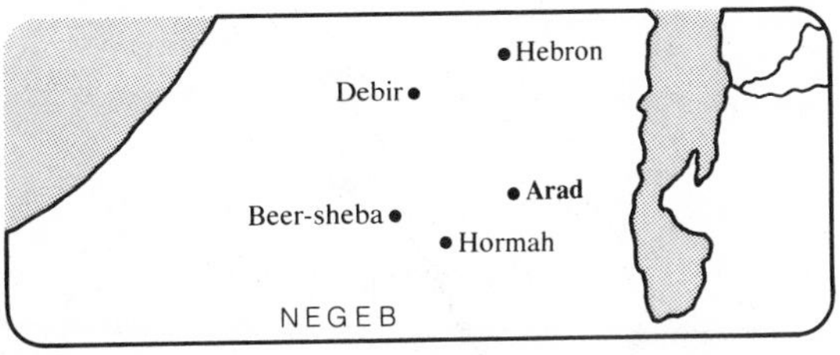

(Nu. 14:44f.; Dt. 1:44). That the latter detail may be a popular explanation of the origin of the name (from the root *ḥrm,* "ban, devote to destruction") is indicated by the divergent tradition of the defeat at Hormah of the king of Arad due to a second Israelite assault (Nu. 21:2f.). Both neighboring cities were enumerated in the list of the defeated Canaanite kings (Josh. 12:14). According to Jgs. 1:16 "the descendants of [LXX "Hobab"] the Kenite, Moses' father-in-law, went up with the people of Judah from the city of palms into the wilderness of Judah, which lies in the Negeb near [lit. "of"] Arad; and they went and settled with the people" (LXX "the Amalekite"; cf. 1 S. 15:6). This information has taken on a very special meaning with the discovery of an Israelite sanctuary in the excavations (see below).

In the list of cities conquered by Pharaoh Sheshonq (Shishak) after the death of Solomon (*ca.* 920 B.C.) the following names are mentioned among other places in the Negeb: *ḥqrm. ʿrd. rbt. nbt. yrḥm.* (nos. 107-112), i.e., "the fortresses Arad the Great and Arad of the House of *Yrḥm*" (=Jerahmeel? cf. 1 S. 27:1; 30:29). The last biblical reference to Arad lists the city in the Negeb district of Judah (Josh. 15:21, corrupted to Heb. *ʿeḏer*, LXX B Gk. *Ara*; Lucianic MSS *Arad*). Eusebius (*Onom.* 14.2) still knew a village called Arad 20 Roman mi. from Hebron and 4 mi. from Malaatha (Moleatha), distances that fit modern Tell ʿArâd, situated about 20 mi. (32 km.) ENE from Beer-sheḇa.

II. Archeology.–In excavations carried out by an Israeli expedition during 1962-1967 two different settlements were discovered at Tell Arad:

(1) A large fortified city of the Early Bronze Age II (*ca.* 2900-2700 B.C.) preceded by an open settlement of the Late Chalcolithic period. It was surrounded by a stone wall about 8 ft. (2.4 m.) thick supported by projecting semicircular towers. The city was divided into quarters, and the houses were built according to a fixed architectural concept of a distinct "broad house" (with an entrance at one of the longer sides). A unique find is a clay model of one of these houses. Other remarkable finds are vessels imported from Egypt and an abundance of painted and well-burnished local pottery known hitherto mainly from Egyptian 1st Dynasty tombs (Abydos ware). They give evidence of the intense trade with Egypt in this early age and are of much importance for its chronology. The early city was completely destroyed and deserted before the end of the Early Bronze Age II, i.e., not later than 2700 B.C.

(2) The site lay deserted for over fifteen hundred years, and a new settlement was founded on its southeast ridge only during the 12th–11th cent. B.C. It was a small, open village built around the hill, and in its center was a paved *témenos* with a crescent-shaped *bāmâ* and a square altar. This evidently was a Kenite high place, where the venerated priestly family related to Moses served (Jgs. 1:16). On its place a temple was erected during the 10th cent., which now became part of a strongly fortified royal citadel, founded possibly by Solomon. During the period of the monarchy it was six times destroyed and burned

Excavations at Tell Arad, which determined two distinct sites (Consulate General of Israel in New York)

(the first time evidently by Shishak), but always was quickly rebuilt, and served until the end of the first temple as the royal military and administrative center of the border area. Later, fortresses stood on the site, in the Persian, Hellenistic, and Roman periods up to the Early Arab period.

III. Ostraca.–Much information about the royal Judean administration is obtained from the Hebrew inscriptions found at the place. The excavations have resulted in almost two hundred inscribed potsherds (ostraca), nearly half Aramaic from *ca.* 400 B.C., and the rest Hebrew from the period of the monarchy. This is the largest and most varied find of early inscriptions in any Palestinian excavation. The Aramaic ostraca are mainly dockets of the Persian garrison, containing lists of names and troops (*dgl*) and quantities of various commodities like wine, oil, flour, and silver. The Hebrew ostraca derive from different Iron Age strata (which increases their paleographic importance); most are letters and dockets from the royal archives of the various citadels. Some contain lists of private names, occasionally with the addition of numerals and an indication of the produce, such as wheat (*ḥṭm*).

Several ostraca were found in rooms bounding the temple and apparently connected with it. Some of these contain only the name of a single person, two of them names of well-known biblical priestly families: Meremoth and Pashhur. They served probably as lots for the priestly terms, similar to the custom in the Jerusalem temple. On a fragment of a large bowl, names of families and numerals were written in various directions, among them the "sons of Korach" (*bny qrḥ*). This may be a list of donations for the temple. Most illuminating are a group of letters from the archive of Eliashib son of Eshyahu, who was a high official, possibly the commander of the last citadel (*ca.* 600 B.C.). Their main contents are orders to provide certain peoples with rations of wine and bread, among them Kittim (*ktym*), probably mercenaries of Aegean stock in the service of Judah. In one is a reference to Beer-sheba and in another to the "house of Yahweh" (*byt yhwh*), probably the Jerusalem temple. This is the first and only instance of a direct reference to the temple in Hebrew epigraphy.

A letter from the same period contains a strict order to dispatch reinforcements of men from Arad and Kinah (Josh. 15:22) to Ramath-negeb (Josh. 19:8; 1 S. 30:27) against a threatening Edomite attack. This is probably the assault hinted at in the Bible in the days of Jehoiakim, preceding Nebuchadrezzar's first campaign (1 K. 24:2; Jer. 35:11, reading Edom instead of Aram).

IV. The Temple.–The most surprising discovery at Arad is the temple occupying the northwest corner of the citadel. It is the only Israelite temple discovered by archeology. Its direction, general plan, and contents stand in basic agreement with the Solomonic temple and especially with the tabernacle. It consists of one main room, the (Heb.) *hêḵāl*, and to the west of it a raised cella, the holy of holies or *d*^{e}*ḇîr*. Flanking the entrance of the latter were two incense altars, and inside were a small *bāmâ* and a *maṣṣēḇâ*. East of the building was a relatively large courtyard, divided into a large outer and smaller inner part (the *'ûlām*). Flanking the entrance to the *hêḵāl* were two stone slabs, probably bases of pillars, evidently similar to the biblical Jachin and Boaz (cf. 2 Ch. 3:17!). In the outer court was the altar for burnt offerings. It was built of earth and unhewn stones (cf. Ex. 20:25, etc.) and its measurements were a square of 5 cubits, 3 cubits high, like the altar in the tabernacle (Ex. 27:1; cf. 2 Ch. 6:13!).

The history of the temple seems to correspond to the development of worship in Israel. It was built on a sanctified place in the days of the united monarchy; its altar went out of use at the end of the 8th cent. and the temple was finally destroyed with the erection of the last Israelite citadel in the second half of the 7th century. The two phases of its abolition belong evidently to the days of Hezekiah and Josiah, the two reformers who concentrated the worship in Jerusalem. Its foundation at Arad may be explained as a royal border sanctuary like Dan and Bethel in Israel and probably Beer-sheba in Judah (cf. Am. 5:5; 7:13; 8:14).

V. Identification.–The results of the excavations contradict the accepted identification of the Canaanite city with Tell 'Arâd, which lacks remains of the Middle and Late Bronze Ages. On the other hand its identification with the Israelite city has been further confirmed by the appearance of the name Arad in two Hebrew ostraca. Two possible solutions have been suggested: (1) In the Canaanite period no city of Arad existed, but this was the name of the whole region, the Negeb of Arad. (2) Canaanite Arad was located at Tell el-Milḥ, 8 mi. (13 km.) SW of Tell 'Arâd, where strong Hyksos fortifications have been discovered. This suggestion is strengthened by the double appearance of the name in the Shishak list. We may assume that "Arad of the House of *Yrḥm*" is the early city, which was settled by Jerahmeelite families; "Great Arad" is then the strong citadel on the outstanding hill dominating the Negeb of Arad, which was founded by Solomon on the site of the venerated Kenite high place.

Bibliography.–*GP*, pp. 248f.; N. Glueck, *Rivers in the Desert* (1959), pp. 50-53, 114f.; Y. Aharoni and Ruth Amiran, *IEJ*, 14 (1964), 131-147; *Archaeology*, 17 (1964), 43-53; B. Mazar, *JNES*, 24 (1965), 297-303; V. Fritz, *ZDPV*, 82 (1966), 331-342; Y. Aharoni, *BASOR*, 184 (Dec. 1966), 14-16; *Fourth World Congress of Jewish Studies, Papers*, I (1967), 11-13; *BA*, 31 (1968), 1-32; Y. Aharoni, *Arad Inscriptions* (1975).

Y. AHARONI

ARADUS ar'ə-dəs [Gk. *Arados*]. The Greek name for a Phoenician island-fortress (Ruad) and its homonymous city (1 Macc. 15:23). Named Arvad in the OT, it is located off the Syrian coast above Tripoli, opposite Tartus (Antarados). *See* ARVAD. A. H. LEWIS

ARAH âr'ə [Heb. *'āraḥ*–'traveler'(?)].

1. The son of Ulla, an Asherite (1 Ch. 7:39).

2. [Gk. *Ares, Aree*]; AV and NEB Apoc. ARES. The head of a family that returned from the Exile with Zerubbabel (Ezr. 2:5; Neh. 7:10; 1 Esd. 5:10). He is usually identified with Arah of Neh. 6:18, whose granddaughter became the wife of Tobiah, the Ammonite who tried to thwart Nehemiah in rebuilding Jerusalem.

ARAM âr'əm [Heb. *'ᵃrām*; Gk. *Aram*].

1. A son of Shem (Gen. 10:22f.; 1 Ch. 1:17). *See* SYRIAN III.

2. A grandson of Nahor (Gen. 22:21).

3. A descendant of Asher (1 Ch. 7:34).

4. (AV, Mt. 1:3f; Lk. 3:33). *See* ARNI; RAM.

ARAM OF DAMASCUS [Heb. *'ᵃrām dammeśeq*] (2 S. 8:6); AV SYRIA OF DAMASCUS; NEB "these Aramaeans"; also **ARAM** [*'ᵃrām*] (2 S. 15:8; 1 Ch. 2:23; Hos. 12:12; Zec. 9:1); AV also "man" (Zec. 9:1, for MT *'āḏām*). A Syro-Aramean city-state that rose to prominence during the reign of David. It was still important enough in Isaiah's time to be called the "head of Syria" (Isa. 7:8). Its site was in the immediate vicinity of DAMASCUS. *See* SYRIAN. A. H. LEWIS

ARAMAEAN âr-ə-mē'ən. *See* SYRIAN.

ARAMAIC ar-ə-mā'ik [Heb. *'ᵃramîṯ*]; AV SYRIAN, SYRIAC. A language or group of languages of the Semitic family, closely related to Hebrew. Biblical Aramaic, formerly called Chaldee, is the name given to the Aramaic occasionally found in the OT, viz.: (1) two words in Gen. 31:47 used by Laban, whereas Jacob expressed the same idea in Hebrew; (2) one verse in Jer. 10:11 representing the testimony that the house of Israel was to make to the nations; (3) two portions in Ezra (4:8–6:18; 7:12-26), being principally correspondence between the enemies of the Jews and the Persian King Darius, and a letter from Artaxerxes to Ezra; (4) the central portion of Daniel (2:4b–7:28). The language is called "Aramaic" (improperly translated "Syriac" in the AV) in Ezr. 4:7 and Dnl. 2:4.

Aramaic words or forms called "Aramaisms" are often pointed out in other parts of the OT; and a number of Aramaic words, expressions, or names (such as *marana tha* [1 Cor. 16:22], *ephphatha* [Mk. 7:34], *talitha cumi* [Mk. 5:41], Tabitha [Acts 9:36, 40], Cephas [Jn. 1:42; 1 Cor. 1:12; etc.]), are recorded in the NT.

I. History of the Language
II. Description
  A. Phonetics
  B. Morphology
    1. Nouns
    2. Verbs
  C. Syntax
III. Date of Biblical Aramaic
IV. Aramaic and the NT

I. History of the Language.–Aramaic takes its name from the Arameans, or the people of Aram. These strange people, whose origins are unknown, probably occupied the stage of history for a longer period of time than any others, yet never developed an empire or even a strong kingdom. They furnished a language that became the medium of international communication in the days of the Assyrian, Babylonian, and Persian empires, and faded only gradually in the Hellenistic period; yet they gave the world no great literature (others who used their language did) nor indeed any other form of art. They borrowed an alphabet and gave it, in its many forms, to most of the literate world (including even the names for the Greek letters, in most cases); yet the alphabet was so poorly suited to their speech that scholars become confused by the orthography when discussing the phonetics and phonemics of Aramaic. And if any other paradox needs to be mentioned, the Arameans were often the enemies of the people of the OT — even though the Israelite was constantly reminded that "a wandering Aramean" was his father (Dt. 26:5).

Aram is a place name in Old Akkadian writings, from the middle of the 3rd millennium B.C., referring to the region of the Tigris N of Elam and E of Assyria. Some scholars think the name is non-Semitic. Tiglath-pileser I (*ca.* 1100 B.C.) gave the name Aramean to the Semitic nomads in that area who were troubling his borders. Aram is also a personal name, found in the 3rd dynasty of Ur (*ca.* 2000 B.C.) and at Mari (*ca.* 1800 B.C.). In the Table of

Nations, Aram is named as one of the sons of Shem along with Elam and Asshur (Gen. 10:22). At least two of the "sons" of Shem listed are not "Semitic," linguistically speaking, viz., Elam and Arpachshad.

The *Aḫlamê*, long identified with the Arameans, are mentioned in cuneiform texts from Mesopotamia from about the 26th cent. B.C. on; they were principally troublesome marauders, nomads who moved with the flocks according to the season, knowing no boundaries, and constantly raiding the borderlands of civilized peoples. Along with them we should probably group similar nomads, such as the Suti, the Kaldi, and the Arami. They seem to have come from the Arabian Desert, and they spread into Mesopotamia, Egypt, and the western and northern edge of the Syrian Desert, better known as the Fertile Crescent. They doubtless spoke a common language or closely related dialects of a language, to which we might give the name Proto-Aramaic, although we have no literary remains to support this theory. There is, however, much evidence in written records of their existence (cf. Dupont-Sommer, *Les Araméens*). Their principal location was in upper Mesopotamia, within the great bend of the Euphrates known as Aram-Naharaim, "Aram of the Two Rivers" (the Euphrates and the Habor), or Paddan-aram (Gen. 28:6). According to Israelite tradition, this was where Abram and his father and brother located after leaving Ur (Gen. 11:31); to this region Abraham sent his servant to get a wife for Isaac (Gen. 24:10), and Isaac in turn sent Jacob to get a wife (Gen. 28:2); and here the sons of Jacob, the heads of the twelve tribes, were born, excepting Benjamin (Gen. 29:31–30:24). It was following the departure of Jacob and his sons, when Laban pursued and overtook him, that the cairn of stones was named "Jegar-shadutha" in Aramaic and "Galeed" in Canaanite (or Hebrew) (Gen. 31:47). We are led to the conclusion that Aramaic (in an early form) was spoken in Paddan-aram.

In the 12th cent. B.C., groups of nomads are found along the Tigris and Euphrates from the Persian Gulf to Aram-Naharaim, and along the Levantine coast as far as north Arabia. In the 11th cent. we find the beginnings of the Aramean states, actually small kingdoms consisting of a city or town and its surroundings, with such names as Aram-Zobah, Aram-Maacah, Aram-Dammesek, Aram-Rehob, as well as names not compounded with Aram, such as Geshur, Hamath, and Bit-Adini (Beth Eden). By the 10th, or at the latest the 9th cent., Aramaic inscriptions begin to appear, and the study of Aramaic is put on a basis no longer highly speculative.

Aramaic, however, was already a lingua franca of the merchants who traveled the highways from town to town. This hypothesis alone can explain the next development, when Aramaic became the official language of trade and diplomacy. Aramaic "dockets" began to be attached to Assyrian and Babylonian tablets. The records were kept in the languages of the kingdoms, but brief descriptions were attached in Aramaic — obviously because more persons could understand it. (For these texts, see L. Delaporte, *Épigraphes Araméens* [1912].) In some Assyrian tablets "Aramaic scribes" (*dupšarrê armaya*) are mentioned — certainly meaning that they could write Aramaic as well as (or instead of) Assyrian. Aramaic inscriptions appear on weights, seals, and vessels. The statue of Bar Rekub, found at Zenjirli (in the Kara Su Valley, now in Turkey), includes a scribe who has pen and ink: Akkadian tablets were pressed with a stylus, but Aramaic was usually written with ink. Similarly, a relief from Nimrûd shows two scribes recording the booty taken by Tiglath-pileser III (*ca.* 740 B.C.); one scribe has a stylus in the right hand and a tablet in the left, the other has a pen and a scroll of leather or papyrus.

Evidence of the use of Aramaic is found in the story of the siege of Jerusalem by Sennacherib, where Hezekiah's representatives plead with the Assyrian official to speak in Aramaic so the common people will not understand the plight (2 K. 18:26). Aramaic inscriptions are found in Egypt from the time of Esarhaddon of Assyria (681-669 B.C.). But it was in the time of the Persian empire that Aramaic flourished as the official language. Correspondence between the priests of a Jewish colony in Upper Egypt and the Persian governor in Jerusalem were written

Folded and sealed contracts from Elephantine. The legends written on the outside in Official Aramaic identify the contents. (Brooklyn Museum)

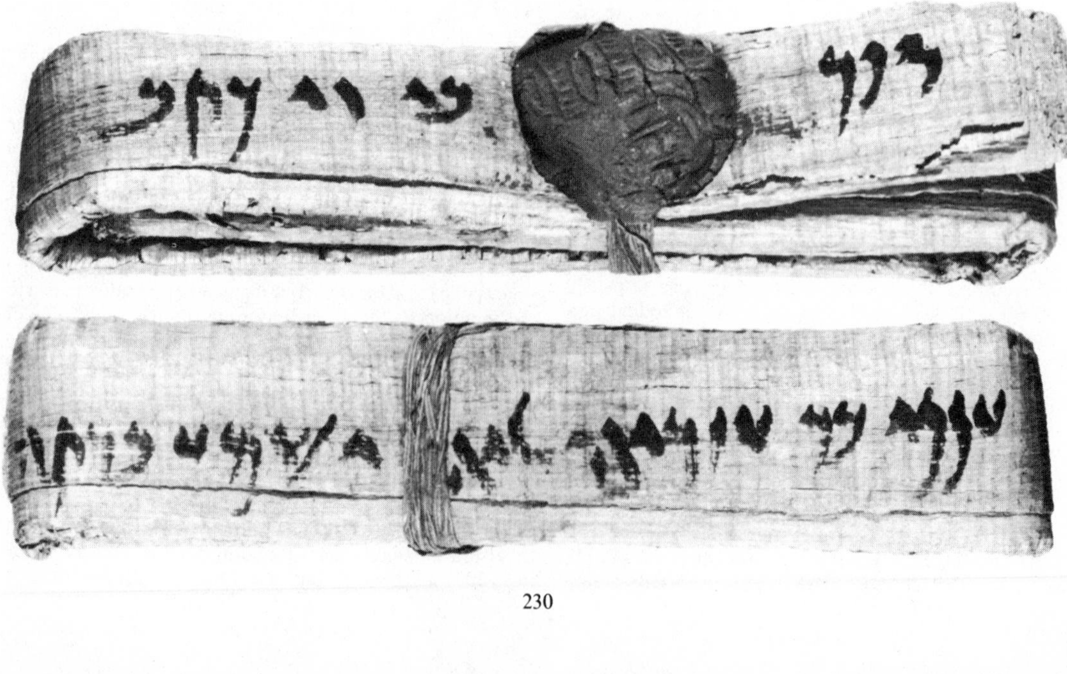

in Aramaic (the Aramaic papyri from Elephantine, 5th cent. B.C.). An Aramaic copy of the famous Behistun inscription of Darius I was found in Egypt (Cowley, pp. 251-54). Even a Persian satrap sent his orders to an Egyptian boat builder in Aramaic (Cowley, no. 26)! Aramaic inscriptions of various types, including some on metal objects and coins, have been found in many parts of the Middle East, from Greece to Pakistan, and from the Ural Mountains to Arabia. The biblical use of Aramaic for official correspondence, as found in Ezra, and for description of events in the palace concerning a Hebrew youth, as found in Daniel, is fully in accord with the custom of the times.

With the spread of Hellenism, including the deliberate attempt to extend the usage of the Greek language, Aramaic all but vanished. In three areas, however, it survived: in Arabia, among the Nabateans and the Palmyrenes, down into the Christian era; in Palestine, among Jews and later among the Melkite Christians, until the conquest by Islam; and in Mesopotamia, among Jews, Christians, and Mandeans, in some cases right to the present day. Jewish literature in Aramaic includes the Targums (translations of the OT into Aramaic), the Palestinian Talmud and Midrash, and the Gemara of the Babylonian Talmud — though these are not all in the same dialect. Christian literature includes the Old Syriac and Peshitta versions of the Bible, or portions of the Bible, and a wide variety of religious and historical literature. The term "Syriac" is usually applied to the dialect of Aramaic used by Christians in the East; and it spread eastward as far as India and even to China, and westward to Asia Minor, Egypt, and Arabia. Christian communities in Syria, Iraq, and Iran still speak subdialects of Syriac. The Mandeans of Iraq have a considerable religious literature in a dialect supposedly preserved from impurities that Jewish and Christian backgrounds have imposed on their respective bodies of literature. Lady Drower has recently published extensively on the Mandeans. Some liturgical use of Aramaic is found in the Jewish prayer book and also in Syriac Christian groups.

II. Description.–Within the limits of this article we can give only the most salient features of the language. For further information, any of the recognized grammars may be consulted, particularly the standard work by Bauer and Leander. But until one has worked extensively in Aramaic dialects of several different periods, he should hesitate to speak categorically on these subjects.

A. Phonetics. In the parent language (generally called "Proto-Semitic"), there were at least twenty-nine consonantal phonemes and three vocalic phonemes. The vowels were further distinguished by long and short forms. (A *phoneme* is a discretely meaningful basic unit of sound in a given language or dialect.) Through the centuries, various phonetic shifts have occurred, contributing to the development of dialects and languages within the family derived from the parent. Where written remains have accurately reflected the phonetic patterns we can trace some of these shifts — but we must always use caution when following out this line of research, for the written form of the language does not always accurately represent the phonetic form.

In Aramaic, the twenty-nine parent consonantal phonemes seem to have been reduced to twenty-two or twenty-three, while the vowels, particularly the short vowels, developed additional gradations. To demonstrate these changes we may use Arabic, Aramaic, and Hebrew for comparison, although this is not in any way to be considered a complete picture.

Proto-Semitic	*Arab.*	*Aram.*	*Heb.*
d as in day	d	d	d
ḏ like th in then	ḏ	d	z
z as in zoo	z	z	z
t as in stop	t	t	t
ṯ like th in thin	ṯ	t	š like sh in ship (?)
ŝ perhaps s in see	s	t	š like sh in ship
s perhaps Ichlaut	s	s	s s (?); used by Greeks for ks
ś perhaps sh in ship	š	s/ś	ś s (?); used by Greeks for s
ḍ emphatic ɹd (?)	ḍ	q/ʿ	ṣ s as in sought
ṯ̣ emphatic th (?)	ẓ	ṭ	ṣ s as in sought
ṭ emphatic t (?)	ṭ	ṭ	ṭ t as in taught
ṣ emphatic s (?)	ṣ	ṣ	ṣ s as in sought
â a in far	â	â (â')	ô o as in notable

It will be seen that the fricatives (such as *th* in *then* and *th* in *thin)* tended to drop out of both Aramaic and Hebrew; but whereas in Hebrew they became sibilants (*z* and *s*), in Aramaic they became stops (*d* and *t*). The shift of the long *â* to *ô* is a feature of the Canaanite dialects and is not found in Aramaic (nor, for that matter, in Ugaritic). However, in eastern Syriac dialects (and probably in the Hebrew of the Masoretes, who used the same sign for the *qāmāṣ* as for the *qāmāṣ-ḥaṭûp̱*), both long *â* and short *a* (under certain conditions) shifted to *ô*/*ŏ*. In certain Aramaic dialects, we should add, fricatives shifted to sibilants rather than to stops.

Both Aramaic and Hebrew developed vocalic gradations, so that in addition to the basic *a, i,* and *u,* we find *e* and *o* (in long and short quantitative forms). But whereas Hebrew tended to avoid short *i* (developing to *e* or *ē*), Aramaic often keeps the i-vowel. On the other hand, just prior to Masoretic times Hebrew attenuated short *a* in unaccented, closed syllables to short *i,* but Aramaic (except Biblical Aramaic) and Syriac kept the short *a* in such a position.

B. Morphology. Like all Semitic languages, Aramaic is chiefly triconsonantal in word-formation; in other words, a "root" consists of three consonants that carry a root meaning, while the various developments, whether as nouns or verbs, give precision to the general root meaning by vocalic alteration and/or the addition of prefixes, infixes, and suffixes.

1. Nouns. Instead of a prefixed definite article, as is found in Hebrew and Arabic, Aramaic uses the emphatic state (or determinate state), which in the singular may generally be described as a long *-ā* (*-ā',* sometimes *-â*) affixed to the noun or adjective, with vocalic alteration of the basic word depending upon the effect of the shift of accent occasioned by the addition of the afformative. Thus, *mélek̲* means "king," and *malkâ'* "the king." Nouns built on the CvCC pattern (C=root consonant, v=vowel), whether *qatl, qitl,* or *qutl* formations, undergo anaptyxis (vowel insertion), in Hebrew retaining the accent on the basic vowel, but in Aramaic tending to shift the accent to the anaptyctic (inserted) vowel thus forming a new pattern. This can be seen in the following illustrations: Arab. *'alf,* Heb. *'élep,* Aram. *'ᵃláp,* "thousand"; Arab. *milḥ,* Heb. *mélaḥ,* Aram. *mᵉláḥ,* "salt"; Akk. *šuršu,* Heb. *šôreš,* Aram. *šᵉráš,* "root." In Biblical Aramaic, however, this is not consistent, and many "segholates" are found with the same development as in Hebrew (cf. *mélek̲,* mentioned above). It is possible that this resulted from Hebrew influence in the Hebrew Bible.

One other feature of noun morphology worthy of mention is the use of *-în* for the masculine plural absolute ending (contrast Heb. *-îm*).

2. Verbs. As in Hebrew, the verb develops "stems" from the basic root, indicating repetition, causation, etc.

The common stems are the G (Ground-stem, Heb. *qal*, Aram. *pᵉal*), the D (Double-stem, Heb. *piel*, Aram. *pael*), and the H (Causative, Heb. *hiphil*, Aram. *haphel*). These are usually described, with great oversimplification, as the "simple," "intensive," and "causative" stems, respectively. The passive voice in a number of Semitic languages is formed by internal vocalic change, generally a u-type vowel after the first radical of the root or after the prefixed causative morpheme (thus, Heb. *pual, hophal*). However, in some of the Semitic languages, including Aramaic, a prefixed middle or reflexive morpheme, *hiṯ-* or *'iṯ-*, came into general use for the passive, more or less replacing the passive formed by vocalic change (or "internal passive"). Thus in Aramaic we find *'ethpᵉel* used for the passive of the G-stem, *'ethpael* for the passive of the D, and *'ettaphal* for the passive of the H (or A) causative stem. Once again, however, Biblical Aramaic has not completely moved in the direction of other Aramaic dialects, and we find internal passives (the *pᵉil* for G-passive, the *pual* for D-passive, often; and the *huphal* for H-passive always). The N-stem (Heb. *niphal*, used as passive of G-stem) is not found in Biblical Aramaic. Instead of the H-stem (*haphel*), the A-stem (*'aphel*) is sometimes found in Biblical Aramaic; and instead of the *hiṯ*-morpheme the *'eṯ*-morpheme is occasionally found. The Š-causative stem also occurs (active *shaphel*, passive *hishtaphal*).

In verbal inflection to show person, number, and aspect ("tense"), we may note the following characteristics of Biblical Aramaic. In the perfect, 3 f.s. *-aṯ* (Heb. *-ā*), 2 m.s. *-t* (Heb. *-tā*), 1 s. *-ēṯ* (Heb. *-tî*), 2 m.pl. *--tûn* (Heb. *-tem*), 2 f.pl. *-tēn* (Heb. *-ten*); in the imperfect, 2 f.s. *t---în* (Heb. *t---î*), 3 m.pl. *y---ûn* (Heb. *y---û*), 3 f.pl. *y---ân* (Heb. *t---nā*), 2 m.pl. *t---ûn* (Heb. *t---û*), 2. f.pl. *t---ân* (Heb. *t---nā*). In the verb *hᵉwâ*, "he was," the imperfect 3 m.s., 3 m.pl., and 3 f.pl. forms have the preformative *l-* instead of the regular *y-* (*lehᵉwē*, "he will be"). The G-stem infinitive in Aramaic has preformative *m-* (*miḵtaḇ*; cf. Heb. *kāṯôḇ*, "to write"); and the G-passive participle has *î* as the second vowel (Aram. *kᵉṯîḇ*; cf. Heb. *kāṯûḇ*), a formation often found in Biblical Hebrew but not recognized as a passive formation (cf. *nāḇî'*, "one called, prophet," and *nāśî'*, "one lifted up, prince").

C. Syntax. Syntax is always a very complicated subject, and there is risk in picking out a few characteristics in any language, since personal style is often involved. We suggest the following noteworthy points in Biblical Aramaic. (1) The verb "to be" is used as an auxiliary verb to form compound tenses: the perfect with the participle to indicate continuous action in past time (*hᵃwā' 'āḇēḏ*, "he was doing," Dnl. 6:11), and the imperfect with the participle to indicate continuous action in future time (*miṯ'ārᵉḇîn lehᵉwôn*, "they will be mixing," Dnl. 2:43). In fact, the participle comes to be used in Aramaic as a present tense, and stands alone as the verb in a clause, sometimes as a historical present (cf. *'ānēh wᵉ'āmar*, "he answered and said," lit. "answering and saying," Dnl. 2:5).

(2) The direct object of the verb is often indicated by the prefixed preposition *lᵉ-* (*dānîyē'l bāriḵ le'ᵉlāh šᵉmayyā'*, "Daniel blessed the God of Heaven," Dnl. 2:19).

(3) The genitive relationship can be indicated, as in Hebrew, by the use of the construct state (two words joined into a single phrase with but one major accent). In Aramaic, however, there are two other means commonly used to express the genitive, the ruling element in the emphatic state followed by the particle *dî*, and the ruling element with an anticipatory suffix followed by *dî*. The following examples illustrate all three methods: *millaṯ malkā', millᵉṯā dî malkā', millᵉṯēh dî malkā'*, "the word of the king."

III. Date of Biblical Aramaic.–The discussion of the date of Biblical Aramaic involves other issues over which there is deep disagreement among scholars. Thus, Montgomery assigns chs. 1–6 of Daniel to the 3rd cent. and chs. 7–12 to 168-165 B.C. (*ICC*, p. 96), though he agrees with Wilson in taking issue with Driver over the late character of the Aramaic of Daniel (p. 20 n. 5). On the other hand, E. J. Young writes, "Even if it could be conclusively demonstrated that the Aramaic of our Bibles was from the 3rd cent. B. C., this would not preclude authorship by Daniel in the 6th century B. C." (*Prophecy of Daniel* [1949], p. 23).

Leaving aside the matter of interpretation as well as authorship, we believe we are able to place the Aramaic of the Bible in the 5th or 4th cent. B.C. In the first place, there is little objective reason to attempt to remove either the Hebrew or the Aramaic of Ezra from the time of Ezra. The critical view does not attempt to date the Chronicler later than "between 350 and 250" (R. H. Pfeiffer in *IDB*, II, 219), and it is generally admitted that the Chronicler is the author of Ezra-Nehemiah. It is admitted by nearly all scholars that there is little if any difference between the Aramaic of Ezra and the Aramaic of Daniel (e.g., C. C. Torrey, *Ezra Studies* [1910], p. 162, says, "there is not a single particular, major or minor, in which one of them can be said with confidence to belong to a more advanced stage of development than its fellow"). Therefore, there is little if any linguistic reason to date the Aramaic later than the 4th century. If we press for the unity of authorship of Daniel and of Ezra, we can argue that the language of the Hebrew portions of these books is certainly not as late as that of Ecclesiastes. Rather, it is quite like that of Esther, which again puts it not later than the 4th century.

In the second place, the Aramaic of Daniel is not greatly different from that of the Elephantine papyri. The whole matter of dialectal differences enters into this discussion, and it is admittedly complex. Rowley, who is committed to a second-century date for Daniel, concludes that Biblical Aramaic is later than the papyri, "but as to how much later, we have scant means of judging" (p. 154). The Aramaic papyri from Elephantine can be absolutely dated, since they contain date formulas in the 5th century. It seems clear that the Aramaic of Daniel is much more closely related to that of the papyri than either to that of the Zenjirli inscriptions of the 8th cent. B.C. on the one hand, or to that of the Nabatean inscriptions of the 1st cent. B.C. on the other. We therefore would hesitate to argue that the Aramaic of the Bible is much earlier (or much later) than the Aramaic of the papyri.

When we take these two lines of evidence as our guides there seems to be little doubt that the Aramaic of the OT must be placed in the 5th or 4th cents., with a possible deviation of a half-century on either side, in other words, between 550 and 250 B.C., probably around 400 or the time of Ezra.

What bearing does this have on the authorship of Daniel? E. J. Young, who insists on the Danielic authorship of the entire work, claims that this is no problem (see quotation above). We are forced to recognize later editorial work, particularly in spelling and linguistic matters, for several portions of the Scripture, otherwise we cannot explain the great uniformity of Biblical Hebrew over a period of nearly a millennium (let us say, from Moses to Haggai). We should not be embarrassed, then, to admit editorial alterations to Daniel if it becomes necessary.

What bearing does this have on the critical position? The burden would seem to be on the critics to explain the nature of the Aramaic of the OT, including the great similarity of the Aramaic of Daniel to that of Ezra, the difference between the Aramaic of Daniel and that of 1QapGen, and similar matters, which they have generally ignored while insisting on a second-century date for Daniel. The critic must certainly be willing to subject his own theories to rigid critical methodology!

*IV. **Aramaic and the NT**.*–It is commonly accepted that Jesus spoke Aramaic. As a matter of fact, one writer has made quite a reputation by his translation of the Bible from the "original Aramaic," which, he assures us in many popular presentations, is "the language Jesus spoke." Paul on occasion spoke "in the Hebrew dialect" (Acts 21:40; 22:2; 26:14), which according to most commentaries and lexicons is to be translated as "the Aramaic vernacular of Palestine." This view is so common that we need waste no space on presenting it; it is the contrary view that needs to be defended.

With the discovery of the Dead Sea Scrolls in 1947ff. it became obvious that Hebrew was indeed not a "dead" language in Palestine in the 1st cent. A.D. In fact, it was used by the Qumrân sectarians not only for the commentaries and religious writings (e.g., 1QpHab, 1QM, 1QH), but even for 1QS; hence it was understood by the rank-and-file. Slowly this has opened up anew the question of the language of Jesus and Paul, in fact, the language of Palestine in the 1st century.

In a compelling article on "Hebrew in the Days of the Second Temple" (*JBL*, 79 [1960], 32-47), J. M. Grintz has offered several lines of evidence to show that Hebrew, rather than Aramaic, lay behind the Gospel of Matthew. A number of expressions in the Gospel can only be explained on the basis of Hebrew, where the Aramaic would not lend the same interpretation, such as the use of "Israel" (Aram. regularly uses "Jews"), "gentiles" (Aram. has no word like *gôyîm*), "Canaanite" (Aram. has no such word), "flesh-and-blood" for "human being" (Aram. uses "son of man"), "Queen of the south" for "Sheba" (in Heb. but not in Aram. *yémen* means "south"; cf. Yemen), etc. After a study of the references in Josephus, Grintz states: ". . . [Josephus] means precisely what he says: Hebrew and not Syrian [=Aramaic]" (p. 44). He finally concludes that "in the last days of the Second Temple, Hebrew was a living language. And it continued to be so seventy years later, though the destruction of Jerusalem wreaked terrible havoc among the speakers of Hebrew. The final blow to Hebrew as a spoken language was a direct outcome of the disastrous wars of 132-35 C.E." (p. 47).

This does not mean that Aramaic was not used in Palestine. There is positive evidence in the NT in the form of Aramaic words. But perhaps we should look upon these as the uncommon, unusual words. Possibly the exact words of Jesus were remembered at certain times just because He uttered Aramaic on those occasions. Possibly "in the Hebrew dialect" is noted with reference to Paul on occasion because he more often spoke in Aramaic or even in Greek. The entire subject needs very careful restudy, and theories of Aramaic backgrounds to the Gospels, etc., must not be allowed to distort this study.

Bibliography.–R. D. Wilson, *Aramaic of Daniel* (1912); *Studies in the Book of Daniel* (1917); J. A. Montgomery, *Book of Daniel* (*ICC*, 1927), pp. 15-20; H. H. Rowley, *Aramaic of the OT* (1929); F. R. Blake, *A Resurvey of Hebrew Tenses* (1951), Appendix, pp. 81-96; A. Dupont-Sommer, *Les Araméens* (1949); E. G. H. Kraeling, *Aram and Israel or the Arameans in Syria and Mesopotamia* (1918); R. A. Bowman, *JNES*, 7 (1948), 65-90; F. Rosenthal, *Grammar of Biblical Aramaic* (1961); H. Bauer and P. Leander, *Grammatik des Biblisch-Aramäischen* (1927); W. B. Stevenson, *Grammar of Palestinian Jewish Aramaic* (1924); K. Marti, *Kurzgefasste Grammatik der biblisch-aramäischen Sprache* (3rd ed. 1925).

G. A. Cooke, *A Text-book of North-Semitic Inscriptions* (1903); A. E. Cowley, *Aramaic Papyri of the 5th Cent. B.C.* (1923); M. Lidzbarski, *Handbuch der nordsemitischen Epigraphik* (2 vols., 1898); *Altaramäische Urkunden aus Assur* (1921); E. G. Kraeling, *Brooklyn Museum Aramaic Papyri* (1953); A. Dupont-Sommer, *Les Inscriptions araméennes de Sfiré* (1958); J. Cantineau, *Grammaire du Palmyrénien épigraphique* (1935); F. Rosenthal, *Die Sprache der palmyrenischen Inschriften* (1936); J. Cantineau, *Le Nabatéen* (2 vols., 1930-1932); G. Dalman, *Aramäische Dialektproben* (2nd ed. 1927); H. Odeberg, *The Aramaic Portions of Bereshit Rabba, with Grammar of Galilean Aramaic* (2 vols., 1939); J. A. Montgomery, *Aramaic Incantation Texts from Nippur* (1913); T. Nöldeke, *Mandäische Grammatik* (1875); *Compendious Syriac Grammar* (1904); C. Brockelmann, *Syrische Grammatik* (7th ed. 1955).

W. S. LASOR

ARAMAIC VERSIONS. *See* TARGUM; VERSIONS.

ARAM-DAMMESEK âr′əm-dam′əs-ek. *See* ARAM OF DAMASCUS.

ARAMEAN âr-ə-mē′ən. *See* SYRIAN.

ARAMITESS âr-əm-īt′əs, âr′əm-īt-əs [Heb. *ʾᵃrammîyâ*]. An Aramean woman. This designation is applied to the concubine mother of Machir, the father of Gilead (1 Ch. 7:14); the inhabitants of Gilead were thus in part Arameans (Syrians) by descent.

ARAM-MAACAH âr′əm-mā′ə-kə. *See* MAACAH; SYRIAN.

ARAM-NAHARAIM âr′əm-nā-hə-rā′əm. *See* SYRIAN II.

ARAM-ZOBAH âr′əm-zō′bə. *See* ZOBAH; SYRIAN.

ARAN âr′an [Heb. *ʾᵃrān*–'wild goat']. A son of Dishan the Horite (Gen. 36:28; 1 Ch. 1:42). Many more of the sons of Seir bear animal names, as do the clans of the Edomites connected with them.

ARARAH ar′ə-rə (Josh. 15:22, NEB). *See* ADADAH.

ARARAT ar′ə-rat [Heb. *ʾᵃrāṭ*]; AV also ARMENIA (2 K. 19:37 par. Isa. 37:38); AV Apoc. ARARATH (Tob. 1:21). A country in the region of Lake Van in Armenia, where today the borders of Russia, Iran, and Turkey converge. It was inhabited by the people known to us from Assyrian inscriptions as URARTU.

*I. **Biblical Ararat**.*–The name, mentioned four times in the OT, has achieved fame because of its connection with Noah's ark. At the end of the Flood, the ark is said to have come to rest "upon the mountains of Ararat" (Gen. 8:4), i.e., in the mountainous region of Armenia. The use of the plural indicates that the author does not have in mind the high mountain peak known traditionally as Mt. Ararat, but rather the general region of what was later called Armenia. Adrammelech and Sharezer, the sons of Sennacherib, are said to have fled to that land for asylum following their assassination of their father (2 K. 19:37 par. Isa. 37:38). Jeremiah (51:27) associates Ararat with the nations of Minni and Ashkenaz in the call to rise up against the tyranny of Babylonia. The AV reads "Armenia" in 2 Kings and Isaiah, which is a fairly accurate representation of the region designated.

*II. **History**.*–The country of the Urartu is first mentioned in an inscription of Shalmaneser I (1274-1245 B.C.) when it was still a tiny kingdom. Its rise to importance came during the decline of Assyrian power during the following centuries. In the 9th cent. Urartu is mentioned in the inscriptions of Ashurnasirpal II (884-859 B.C.) and Shalmaneser III (859-824 B.C.) as an important power.

Ashurnasirpal lists Urartu as one of the boundaries of his conquests; his successor reports several campaigns against the Urartian king Sarduri I, who founded a new dynasty *ca.* 830 B.C. During this time the Urartian kings built strong cities, which were partly carved out of the rocks and were served by elaborate aqueducts and irrigation systems. The capture of some of these mountain fortress-cities by Shalmaneser III is depicted on the bronze gates from Balawat. Throughout the 7th and 6th cents. the kingdom of Urartu was continually attacked and invaded by the surrounding nations until it ceased to exist as an independent unit. The region subsequently became a part of Armenia.

III. Archeology.–Fairly extensive excavation has been done in the region of Lake Van in recent years by British, Turkish, and Russian archeologists. The most detailed information has come from the Russian excavations at Kamir Blur. Approximately two hundred inscriptions written in the Urartian language, which adopted and modified the cuneiform script, have been discovered. In these inscriptions the land is referred to as *Biai-nae,* from which the modern name Van is derived; and its inhabitants are "children of [the god] Haldi." Many objects of bronze and other metals have been found, demonstrating that Urartu was the center of an important metal industry. Urartian bronzes have been discovered elsewhere in Asia Minor, Greece, and even Italy. Excavations are being carried on at present by various Turkish universities in cooperation with the Department of Antiquities, as well as by the British Institute of Archeology at Ankara.

Bibliography.–A. Goetze, *Kleinasien,* II, pt. 2 of *Kulturgeschichte des alten Orients* (2nd ed. 1957), pp. 187-200, 215f.; S. Lloyd, *Early Anatolia* (1956), pp. 27-29, 183-190; B. B. Piotrovsky, *Urartu: The Kingdom of Van and Its Art* (Eng. tr. 1967).

W. W. GASQUE

ARARATH ar'ə-rath (Tob. 1:21, AV). *See* ARARAT.

ARATUS ar'ə-təs [Gk. *Aretos*]. A Stoic poet of Soli in Cilicia who died about 240 B.C. He wrote and taught under the patronage of Antigonus Gonatas, king of Macedonia, and Antiochus I of Syria. His most famous work — the only one extant in a complete form — is *Phaenomena,* a didactic poem about astronomy. This work was quite popular in the 1st cent., so it is not surprising that Paul quotes from it in his speech on the Areopagus (Acts 17:28). The passage Paul quotes, "For we are indeed his offspring," is from an introductory dedication to Zeus.

Aratus was born in Cilicia, and was thus a fellow countryman of Paul. Yet it could also be said that he belonged to Athens ("even some of your poets have said"), for he studied there during a formative period of his life.

See G. R. Mair, ed. and tr., *Aratus* (with *Callimachus* in *LCL,* 1921). G. A. VAN ALSTINE

ARAUNAH ə-rô'nə [Heb. *'ᵃrawnâ* (2 S. 24:16, 20ff.), *'ᵃranyâ* (v. 18)]; **ORNAN** ôr'nən [*'ornān*] (1 Ch. 21:15ff.; 2 Ch. 3:1). A Jebusite from whom David at the request of the prophet Gad bought a threshing floor located upon Mt. Moriah, as a site for an altar of the Lord at the time of the great plague (2 S. 24:15ff.; 1 Ch. 21:15ff.), and upon which Solomon later erected the temple (2 Ch. 3:1).

ARBA är'bə [Heb. *'arba'*–'four'] (Josh. 14:15; 15:13; 21:11). An important inhabitant of Kiriath-arba (Hebron) in the time of Joshua, and the ancestor of the gigantic Anakim. While the MT regarded Arba as a personal name, the LXX suggests that it was a shortened form of Kiriath-arba, making that city, rather than Arba himself, the source of the Anakim. This interpretation is questionable, since it was common in antiquity for cities to be named after their founders. R. K. H.

ARBATHITE är'bə-thīt [Heb. *hā'arḇāṯî*]. A resident of Beth-araba, notably Abi-albon (2 S. 23:31), also named Abiel (1 Ch. 11:32), one of David's heroes.

ARBATTA är-bat'ə [Gk. *en Arbattois*] (1 Macc. 5:23); AV ARBATTIS. Apparently a district in the neighborhood of Galilee, from which the Jews who were in danger of attack by the heathen were carried by Simon Maccabeus to Jerusalem (1 Macc. 5:21ff.). It cannot be identified with certainty. Ewald (*History of Israel* [Eng. tr. 1883], V, 314) favored el-Baṭeiḥa, the plain through which the Jordan flows into the Lake of Galilee. *EB* suggests "the Arabah, or Araboth of Jordan"; and *GAB* suggest a possible connection with ARUBBOTH. Possibly, however, we should look for it in the toparchy of Akrabattis, SE of Shechem (Josephus *BJ* iii.3.4f.). W. EWING

ARBELA är-bē'lə [Gk. *Arbēla*]. The name of several sites in biblical times.

1. Erbil (Arbil), in Mesopotamia, near Gaugamela, E of Nineveh, near the site of Alexander's decisive victory over Darius in 331 B.C.

2. Khirbet Irbid, in Galilee on the southern bank of Wâdī el-Haman (Arbel Valley), 2½ mi. (4 km.) W of the Sea of Galilee, the probable site mentioned in 1 Macc. 9:2, and by Josephus (*Ant.* xii.11.1), as an encampment of the Syrian army under Bacchides in his line of invasion against Judas Maccabeus in 161 B.C., although the site in Gilead and sites in Samaria and by Aijalon have been suggested (see *EB*; *HDB*). If this be so the "Messaloth in/near Arbela" (1 Macc. 9:2) besieged by Bacchides may refer to the fortified, terraced caves of Jewish refugees, robbers, and insurgents mentioned elsewhere by Josephus (*BJ* ii.20.6, etc.).

Josephus gives a vivid account of the stout resistance put up by the Jews when the caves of Arbela were later stormed by Herod in the winter of 39 B.C. (*Ant.* xiv.15.4f.; *BJ* i.16.204). Afterward Josephus himself fortified the caves for the great war (*Vita* 37) and held an important conference with the Jews of Galilee in Arbela (*Vita* 60). Noted for its wheat and durable thick linen (Midr. *Gen. Rabbah* xix.38b; *Eccl. Rabbah* i.18.75b), the "plain of Arbela" was used in Jewish literature as a site for messianic redemption of the Jews from foreign domination (T.P. *Berakoth* 2e, 5a; *Maḥzor Romania* 143b).

The present unexcavated ruins of Khirbet Irbid, including a synagogue of the 3rd cent. A.D., reflect its importance for several centuries. The site may have been visited by Jesus during His Galilean ministry on His way from Nazareth to Capernaum (Mt. 4:13; Mk. 1:16f.; Jn. 2:11f.).

3. A suggested emendation for RIBLAH in Nu. 34:11, which would then be identified with modern Hermel at the source of the Orontes (see *GAB,* pp. 160f.).

4. *See* BETH-ARBEL.

Bibliography.–*SSW,* pp. 116-120; *GP,* II, 249; *GTTOT,* pp. 406, 411.

ARBITE är'bīt [Heb. *hā'arbî*]. A resident of Arabia temporarily in southern Judah (cf. Josh. 15:52). The epithet described either the person or the home of Paarai (2 S. 23:35), who was known in 1 Ch. 11:37 as Naarai son of Ezbai.

ARBONAI är-bō'nī (Jth. 2:24, AV). *See* ABRON.

ARCH (Ezk. 40:16ff., AV). *See* VESTIBULE.

ARCHANGEL [Gk. *archángelos*] (1 Thess. 4:16; Jude 9). *See* MICHAEL **11.**

ARCHELAUS är-kə-lā'əs [Gk. *Archelaos*] (Mt. 2:22). The son of Herod the Great by his wife Malthace. He succeeded on his father's death to the government of Judea, Samaria, and Idumea, but was deposed by the Romans for misgovernment in A.D. 6. *See* HEROD IV.

ARCHEOLOGY. The scientific study of the material remains of past human life and activities.

I. Definition
II. Materials
III. Geological and Cultural Levels
IV. The Task
V. Methods
VI. Dating the Finds
VII. Archeology and the Bible
VIII. Evidential Value of Archeology

I. Definition.–The word archeology (British archaeology), which is derived from Gk. *archaio-* + *logos*, "orderly arrangement of ancient [things]," can be defined broadly to include all study of antiquity, and this use of the word indeed is found in works of the 19th century. Accordingly, subjects included are often more properly covered under physical anthropology or human paleontology. In the narrower sense, which is the scope of this article, archeology deals with the material remains of human life in antiquity. Thus the Zinjanthropus skull, for example, would be more properly studied under anthropology, while the stone artifacts found in the vicinity of the skull would be treated under archeology. The distinction, obviously, is a tenuous one, and overlapping can hardly be avoided. Some scholars limit the study of archeology to the study of artifactual remains, i.e., those which have been made by man, while others include also the nonartifactual materials, or those things that were used, but not made or fashioned, by man. Since "nonartifactual materials" is a rather unwieldy term, I suggest "usuquid" as a term to indicate anything used, but not made or fashioned, by man.

Biblical archeology is a specialized branch of archeology that is devoted to the gathering and classification of archeological data that come from or relate to the areas included in the biblical world and the times pertinent to the biblical story. There is no special technique in biblical archeology; indeed, some scholars would deny that there is such a discipline as "biblical archeology," any more than there are such disciplines as "biblical geology" or "biblical mathematics." The difference, however, lies not in methods or results but in the definition of purpose. Just as there are valid studies of "biblical metrology" (i.e., those weights and measures that are specifically mentioned in the Bible) and "biblical Hebrew" (the specific kinds of Hebrew that are used in the Bible), so there is a valid limitation of archeology to shed light on the social and political structures, the religious concepts and practices, and other human activities and relationships that are found in the Bible or pertain to peoples mentioned in the Bible.

But just as it is difficult if not impossible to decide where to draw the line between archeology and physical anthropology, so it is to establish the limits of biblical archeology. In Egypt, for example, the first biblical situation is in the time of Abraham (Gen. 12:10), and we are given details of Egyptian life only in the time of Joseph (Gen. 37:38). But it is unrealistic to start our study of the material remains of man in Egypt at one of these points, for the cultural level of Egypt in Joseph's day had its own antecedents, and Egyptian archeology, as it contributes to our understanding of the closing portion of Genesis and the opening chapters of Exodus, must include some of those earlier elements. We want to know, for example, what evidence there is of merchant caravans traveling through Canaan to Egypt, or what the social structure of Egypt was and the status of slaves within it. We want to know something about the "divining cup" (Gen. 44:5, 15), and many other details, to help us understand the biblical account. As the biblical scholar searches for such details, he finds himself going further and further back in the findings reported by Egyptian archeologists. Where does he stop? Usually this is determined by the time and patience he has, rather than by some definition of the limits of the subject. Biblical archeology, then, is the study of any of the material remains of man's activity that may properly be used to shed further light on the biblical story.

II. Materials.–According to our definition, anything made by man (artifact) or used by him (usuquid) is properly a subject for study by the archeologist. Artifacts include tools, household utensils, furnishings, ornaments, buildings, weapons, fortifications, coins, sculpture, paintings, mosaics, and all other things made or fashioned by man. Usuquids include such things as bones, shells, teeth, etc., of animals that served for food or other domestic purposes, traces of plants that were collected or cultivated for food, weaving, basket-making, or other purposes (but not the finished item, which is an artifact), mineral items such as semiprecious stones (unfashioned) used for decorative or other purposes (for example, to be inlaid in mosaics or worn as ornaments), charcoal from the hearth, and any other materials occurring in nature that were adapted for use by man. A special category, which some scholars (e.g., Braidwood) would not consider under archeology, includes any kind of written material, whether carved in stone, impressed in clay, stamped in metal, written with ink on papyrus or parchment, or produced in any other way. The list is long, and grows longer as our knowledge of the past and our areas of interest expand, and the study of many items requires high levels of specialization. Accordingly, modern archeological excavations generally are done by groups or teams of scholars that include experts in many fields.

Several subdivisions of the materials have been suggested; quite frequently these follow the peculiar interests of the person making the division. For example, we might separate the materials that remain above ground (such as the pyramids, the Parthenon, or the Colosseum) from those which have been excavated from the earth (such as Sargon's palace at Khorsabad, or Pompeii). Or we might distinguish between the prehistoric and the historical remains — which would require definition of our terms. Or we might simply separate artifactual from nonartifactual materials. Any method has advantages and disadvantages; perhaps the greatest disadvantage is the artificial fragmentation of a very complex subject and the resulting tendency to ignore what lies outside one's own special interests. The biblical archeologist, for example, could never dismiss the documentary remains as lying outside his field, for without the religious, legal, historical, and other writings that have been recovered in Mesopotamia, or Egypt, or Râs Shamrah, or Boghazköy — to mention just these few places — the interpretation of the other data and the interpretation of the Bible itself would be filled with all sorts of fantasy. In a very definite way, the documentary materials of archeology provide the necessary controls for interpreting much of the other data.

One has only to recall the strange interpretations that were placed on Egyptian archeological materials prior to the decipherment of Egyptian inscriptions!

III. Geological and Cultural Levels.–A person coming to the study of archeology for the first time finds himself encountering a large number of unfamiliar terms, or familiar terms used in unfamiliar ways. Geologists refer to the last million years of earth's history as the Pleistocene (or Glacial) Epoch, which extended from about 1,000,000 B.P. (= Before the Present) to about 11,000 B.P., and the Holocene (or Recent) Epoch, since about 11,000 B.P. (= 9000 B.C.). During the Pleistocene there were alternating periods of advance and retreat of the great ice sheets that covered the northern latitudes. The periods of extensive glaciation are generally called by the names that originated in the Alps: Günz, Mindel, Riss, and Würm glacial periods. With the last ice age (the Würm), the Pleistocene ended and the Holocene began.

Anthropologists distinguish the cultural levels of man with terms such as Paleolithic (Old Stone) Age, Mesolithic (Middle Stone) Age, and Neolithic (New Stone) Age. The principal characteristic distinguishing the New Stone Age from the Old Stone Age is the fact that during the Old Stone Age man was a food-gatherer, a hunter and fisher, whereas in the New Stone Age man became a food-producer, having cultivated cereals and domesticated cattle. The Paleolithic Age lies within the Pleistocene Epoch, and the Neolithic Age began in Europe-Asia-Africa approximately with the Holocene Epoch, in other words, *ca.* 9000 B.C. (some scholars would reduce this to *ca.* 8000 B.C.).

It appears obvious, from passages such as Genesis 2:19; 4:2, 20-22, etc., that the life-situation (or *Sitz im Leben*) of the earliest portions of the biblical story is the New Stone Age. This would seem to provide a reasonable beginning-point for biblical archeology. While it may be interesting to study the bifacial-tool traditions of Abbevillian and Acheulean, and the flake-tool traditions of Clactonian and Levalloisian cultural levels of the second and third interglacial periods, it is open to serious question whether these areas of study make any significant contribution to understanding the Bible. At best we might conclude that the Old Stone Age was one of the final steps of God's creative activity before He created Adam in His own image.

Biblical archeology, then, lies within the Holocene Epoch of geological study. It may expect to find its most meaningful contributions for biblical study in the anthropological cultural levels of the New Stone Age and later. For the biblical world, these may be conveniently listed as follows:

Aceramic (Prepottery) Neolithic Age	*ca.* 9000-6000 B.C.
Neolithic-with-Pottery Age	*ca.* 6000-5000 B.C.
Chalcolithic Age (introduction of copper tools)	*ca.* 5000-3200 B.C.
Early Bronze Age (copper tools predominate)	*ca.* 3200-2000 B.C.
Middle Bronze Age	*ca.* 2000-1600 B.C.
Late Bronze Age	*ca.* 1600-1200 B.C.
Iron Age (introduction of iron tools)	*ca.* 1200- 300 B.C.
Hellenistic Period	*ca.* 300- 63 B.C.
Roman Period	63 B.C.-A.D. 323

Further subdivision of the Early Bronze (E.B. I, II, III, IV), the Middle Bronze (M.B. I, IIa, IIb, IIc), Late Bronze (L.B. I, II, III), and Iron (Iron I or Early Iron [E.I.], Iron II [M.I.], Iron III [L.I. or Persian]) are commonly found. Within the past twenty-five years there have been some alterations of terminology by certain scholars, such as the use of "Urban" instead of "Bronze," and some slight shifting of the dates given (E.U. 3300-1850, M.U. 1850-1550, L.U. 1550-1200). For the Greek mainland, archeologists use the terms Early Helladic, Middle Helladic, and Late Helladic, and for Crete they use the terms Early Minoan, Middle Minoan, and Late Minoan. Within reasonable limits we may make the following equations: E.B. = E.H. = E.M., M.B. = M.H. = M.M., and L.B. = L.H. = L.M.

Obviously, the end of Aceramic Neolithic did not occur simultaneously throughout the world of the Bible. The discovery of how to make plastic clay, fashion it, fire it, and so fabricate pottery was localized to one, or more likely to several places, from which the craft spread into other areas. Likewise the discovery of metallurgical crafts spread, probably more slowly because of the relatively limited sources of copper ore and the higher levels of skill needed in making copper tools as compared to making pottery. As recently as the time of World War II aboriginal tribes were living in the Paleolithic cultural level in Australia, and in the 1970's a Paleolithic group was discovered in a remote section of Mindanao in the Philippines. But when all factors are taken into consideration and the problems of terminology are understood, the terms and dates given above are a satisfactory working basis for all of the areas included in biblical archeology.

IV. The Task.–The work of the archeologist may be divided into three main areas: recovery of the data, reporting the discovery, and interpreting the significance of the finds. In the early days of archeology only the recovery (or discovery) seemed to be important. That was the day of antiquities-collecting, and many museums and private collections were the recipients of rare treasures. In some cases, unfortunately, exhibits are marked "provenance unknown." Human curiosity and pride were served, but knowledge was not advanced by such collections. With the rise of scientific methodology in archeology, the exact reporting of all details of the discovery became of primary importance. We are no longer interested in the mere collecting of treasures; we now want to know as much as possible of the life and thought of the people who produced the items, lived in the place where the "treasures" were discovered, and were part of a larger community with complex sociological, political, and religious relationships with still other communities. In the past century and the first half of this century, there was a great effort to explore as many sites as possible; often an archeologist began work at a new site before he had published the detailed reports for the excavation just completed. Today, the writing of the report is considered to be as important as the discovery, for the discovery has little value if other scholars do not have access to the details.

Interpretation is a necessary part of the task — and here the work may be done by "armchair" archeologists. Indeed, Professor G. Ernest Wright has defined biblical archeology as "a special 'armchair' variety of general archaeology" (*WBA*, p. 17). The best interpretation of the finds at one site will be made against the background of discoveries at other sites. The archeological term used here is *typology,* which is the classification of the various types of objects that have been found in an excavation, and the study of their relationship to earlier and later finds of the same types at that location as well as to the same or similar types that have been discovered at other locations.

The archeologist who spends twenty-five years exclusively at one location may become somewhat myopic, particularly if he fails to keep up with the discoveries in other areas. In fact, this specialization had progressed to such extent that until about 1950 very little effort was made to integrate the archeology of Egypt, to take just one example, with that of other parts of the Near East. In December, 1952, the American Anthropological

Association and the Archaeological Institute of America held a symposium on "The Integration of Relative Chronologies in Old World Archaeology." The publication of their discussions in *Relative Chronologies in Old World Archaeology,* edited by R. W. Ehrich (1954), was a major step in the integration of archeological knowledge, principally but not exclusively for the Near East. Such integration is necessary if sound interpretation is to be formulated. The "armchair archeologist," therefore, is not working from ignorance; rather, he should be fully cognizant of all the significant discoveries in all of the periods and locations that comprise his area of study.

*V. **Methods.***–The most obvious — and in some ways the simplest — method is *surface exploration.* Travelers to the Arabian peninsula in the 19th cent. brought back our first, and for a long time our only, knowledge of southern Arabia, including many inscriptions that had been laboriously copied. Napoleon's scholars, who accompanied him on his expedition to Egypt in 1798, brought back a vast storehouse of knowledge and this greatly accelerated Egyptological studies. One of the most significant finds of this expedition was the Rosetta Stone, which gave Champollion the bilingual inscription needed for the decipherment of Egyptian hieroglyphic inscriptions. The Behistun inscription, from which Rawlinson was able to decipher Babylonian cuneiform writing, was likewise a surface discovery, in this instance in Persia (modern Iran).

Usually, however, we think of *excavation* when we speak of archeology. But before we attempt to discuss archeological excavation, it will be helpful to know something about archeological sites. The Arabic word *tell,* commonly meaning "hill," has been taken over by archeologists to designate a hill that has been formed by successive occupations of the location. There are thousands of tells of this nature in the Near East.

In its earliest stage, the tell was sometimes a natural rise of ground, but more often a level surface. Among the reasons the first community located there would be its location on a trade route, or, more important, a supply of water to meet the needs of the community. The houses were built close together, a wall was built for protection, and the people used the surrounding fields for farming and grazing. During the lifetime of that first community, which may have been fifty or one hundred years, garbage and trash accumulated in the lanes, dust blown by the wind settled against the walls of the houses and the city wall, and gradually the level of the town was raised, sometimes making it necessary to raise the earth floors in the houses in order to keep water from flowing in during the rainy season. At last the community came to an end, whether by pestilence, earthquake, or warfare. At a later period, perhaps a dozen or a score of years after the first community ceased to exist, a new community located there, for the water supply was still ample. Some of the old walls may have been reused; others were levelled, resulting in raising the base of the new city. Years later, the second community, too, met its fate. Over a span of perhaps as much as four thousand years, the same story was repeated many times, and from these superimposed layers of human occupation the tell was formed. The hill had grown possibly 10 or 20 m. (33 or 66 ft.) in height, and was composed of perhaps 15 to 30 levels of occupation. Finally, when great empires gobbled up the small city-states, military governors were appointed, and aqueducts were built to bring in water, such walled cities were no longer necessary, and many tells were no longer occupied. A few cities, however, can still be seen "sitting on their tells" (cf. Josh. 11:13).

The archeologist locates a tell which, from various kinds of evidence, such as references in ancient documents, types of pottery scattered around the sloping sides, the imposing size of the tell, and other facts known to the archeologist, seems to be a likely location for an ancient city, e.g., Gath or Lachish. Then he prepares to excavate the site.

Ash layer indicating violent destruction of community at Qumrân (W. S. LaSor)

Three types of excavation have been used: trenching, stepping (or step-trenching), and area excavation. A modified kind of trenching, seldom used, was tunneling. Today, as a general rule, only area excavation or stratigraphy is used.

Trenching, as the name suggests, consists of digging a trench across a portion of a tell, going as deep as possible, noting the levels that appear, and collecting the materials that are found at each level. Tunneling consisted of digging down to the desired level, possibly a wall, and then tunneling along that structure. In several instances in the past century, tunneling was used to excavate parts of Jerusalem, with results that were little short of disastrous from a modern archeologist's point of view. Trenching has several disadvantages, principally that of the limited amount of area that will be excavated in each stratum. Since all levels were not formed in exactly the same way, it is entirely possible to miss a complete stratum in trenching. It is even more likely that the most significant parts of any level (such as the palace, the library, etc.) will not be discovered. Trenching was relatively inexpensive and quick. It served the purpose for collecting "treasures." It is still valuable for exploration, as for example when the archeologist wants to determine the limits of the palace.

Stepping consists of digging a series of steps or a step-trench at the edge of the tell, possibly 5 or 10 m. (16½ or 33 ft.) in width, each step reaching the next successive stratum of the mound. Since the sides of a tell slope, generally at the natural angle of repose of the earth that forms the tell, the steps will roughly follow the contour of the slope. But once again, this method is highly subject to chance, and therefore to misleading or erroneous interpretation. For example, the lowest level (the first occupation level) was quite likely much smaller than the area covered by the sloping sides, for they have been spreading out through the centuries, as successive communities have thrown earth, rubbish, rocks, and many other items outside the walls, and the rains have washed this debris down the slope. Furthermore, the very fact that debris from various occupation levels has been washed down and mixed with materials from other levels increases the possibility of later intrusions in the finds of lower levels. Stepping is used occasionally (as at Tell Arad) to locate the outer walls of the successive levels

 ARCHEOLOGY

Step-trench at Tell Judeidah in Syria, showing occupation levels and corresponding artifacts (Oriental Institute, University of Chicago)

Canaanite temple at Mekal, oldest of a succession of five temples in the south flank of Tell el-Ḥuṣn (Beth-shean). Level IX (14th cent. B.C.) (University Museum, University of Pennsylvania)

Surveyor checking grid at Tell Beth-Yerah (W. S. LaSor)

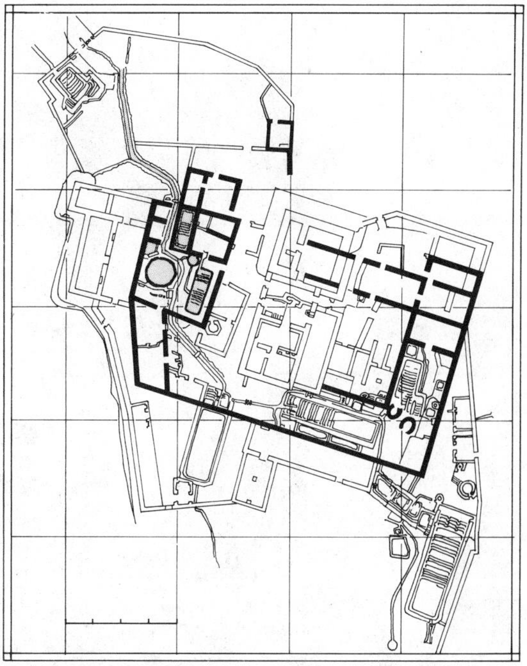

Plan of Khirbet Qumrân excavations. Solid lines indicate Level Ia (prior to 135 B.C.) (after a plan from R. de Vaux, *L'Archéologie et les manuscrits de la Mer Morte*)

of occupation, and it does make a graphic display of the successive strata (as at Tell ej-Judeideh).

Area stratigraphy, the favored method at present, is carried out in somewhat the following manner. First a surveyor establishes a grid for the surface of the mound, setting pegs or concrete blocks on the surface to mark the grid. The recorder will use this grid as a reference for all the data of the excavation. A zero-datum or bench mark is established and the vertical location (or elevation) of each stratum will be measured with surveying equipment from that mark. Thus the exact vertical and horizontal location of every significant find can be determined. The archeologist and his team of experts meanwhile have decided where to begin digging, and he will mark out a square or oblong area that includes a number of the 5-meter (16½-foot) squares of the grid. His excavation will be strictly confined to this area and he will leave balks standing along the grid-lines as long as possible. Thus the visitor who sees the excavation after it is well under way notes that it is crisscrossed by straight walls of untouched earth at 5- or 10-meter intervals. He may even see cards tacked into one of these walls marking the levels that have been uncovered.

Why does the archeologist not take off the entire top of the mound down to the first level of occupation below the surface, and get a complete picture of that level? For one thing, it is too expensive and time-consuming. For another, the uppermost level is generally of lesser interest; the deeper levels are most significant, for they go back to periods where our interests are centered. (At one site, however, a portion of the top level seemed to be Chalcolithic!) But most important, all archeology is destructive. The archeologist, in order to discover what lies below the level he has uncovered, must destroy that stratum. Once excavated, it cannot be put together again. It is essential that the archeologist keep in mind the limitations of his knowledge, no matter how great his knowledge may be. Fifty years, or possibly even ten years later, as a result of other discoveries in other places, entirely new light will be shed on the materials to be found at this site. It will be necessary to excavate again, and to revise the former interpretations in the light of the new knowledge. Therefore the archeologist must leave part of the tell untouched for the next round of studies.

So the archeologist digs away the earth — or more precisely, the actual digging is done by those members of his expedition who handle the rough excavation (with picks and shovels). Then, as signs appear that they are nearing the floor of that occupation level, those with special training do the more careful work with hand picks and trowels, and finally with penknives, icepicks, teaspoons, and soft brushes. With experience the archeologist learns to recognize (by feel and by coloration) different types of soil such as surface humus, subsoil, rubble that has been used to level off an area, the tamped earth floor of the occupation level, the sub-floor, etc. Since significant artifacts and usuquids will be found on or in the floor level, the excavator must approach the floor level with extreme care. The first excavated stratum may be labeled "Level I." The level is carefully cleared, every artifact and usuquid is carefully marked, recorded, and, if significant, photographed where found (*in situ*). The entire level is photographed and sketched to scale. When this is done, so that the entire level can be reconstructed in the minds of other scholars, the archeologist prepares to go down to the next stratum (Level II). This continues until the season is over, and may be resumed in subsequent seasons. An archeological "season" is determined by the weather (avoiding excessively hot or cold periods, rainy seasons, etc.), religious holidays, the amount of money available, and other factors. It may be several weeks or months in length. If the archeologist has sufficient means, he may continue the excavation until he reaches the bottom level. If the tell is quite large (most tells are less than a city-block [approximately 4 hectares or 10 acres] in size), and if the resources are sufficient, the archeologist and his staff may excavate two or three areas in different parts of the

Danish archeologists at Bahrain (Dilmun) sorting pottery fragments (Religious News Service)

tell. This increases the chance of hitting the important parts of each level, and diminishes the possibility of missing a stratum entirely.

The record of the digging is now an inverted history of the mound, i.e., Level I is the latest, and Level IX (or whatever the lowest stratum happens to be) is the earliest. In the final form of the report, the order may be reversed, and the chronological sequence followed.

Each day, usually in the late afternoon and evening, the finds of the day are carefully sorted and indexed. Pottery fragments are washed. Preliminary interpretation comes out in the discussion held by the staff, and questions are raised that will sharpen the observations of the following day. One who has never seen a "dig" may have little idea of how meaningless a stone, or a jar, or a hearth may be when first uncovered. The entire picture takes shape slowly, and usually it requires the trained observation of the veteran to put it all together. Maps, sketches, drawings, and prints of the photographs shot during the day have to be made. Artist, architect, surveyor, photographer, the chief archeologist and members of his staff are busy until bedtime — and the next day probably begins with a truck ride to the tell at 5 A.M.! Archeology to the uninitiated is glamorous; to the person at the dig, it is dust and dirt and flies and heat and backbreaking work — and significant discoveries are relatively rare.

Modern techniques have added many variations to the archeological method. For example, at Tell Arad electrodes were inserted in the surface of the mound at regular intervals, and the current was measured across them in order to identify the probable locations of walls under the surface. With the help of the electrodes, stepping was highly successful at Arad. At Gordion, an oil rig was used to make a test boring in a tumulus, and the tomb covered by the mound was quickly located. In Italy, small holes have been drilled and tubes with lights, mirror, and lenses have been inserted so that the contents of tombs could be photographed without any excavation. In England, aerial photography and infrared film have been combined to locate ancient roads, walls, and other features. The great pyramid of Gizeh was explored by X-ray in an effort to locate a second burial chamber (the tests proved negative).

Of particular significance are tombs and other types of burial. Because of religious beliefs and other customs, personal items were often buried with the dead, and in the case of royal burials sometimes personal servants, oxen or horses, and large quantities of valuable goods were included. Because of the great value of some of the items, there has been much plundering of tombs, but those that remained undisturbed, such as the tomb of Tutankhamen ("King Tut") or of Queen Shub-ad at Ur, have provided us with finds of unusual significance. Often the best of the art and craft of the period will be found in a royal tomb, and comparison of these items with those found in tombs of commoners provides interesting sidelights on social structures. Pottery and other fragile items, which are almost always broken in excavated sites, may be unbroken or only slightly damaged in tombs. In some cases, inscriptions provide important information. In a few cases, as for example in an Egyptian royal tomb, small figurines and models (miniature housing complexes complete with furnishings, boats with oarsmen and sails, etc.) may furnish evidence for many of the details of daily life, such as grinding flour, slaughtering cattle, cooking, making beer, and other activities. As a result, the daily life of that period can be reconstructed. Skeletons give us evidence of the size of the people and in some cases the hair and clothing are sufficiently well preserved to furnish details of dress and appearance. Mummified remains from Egypt even let us see the person much as he looked (e.g. Seti I and Ramses II).

Cave archeology has not been described, since it lies

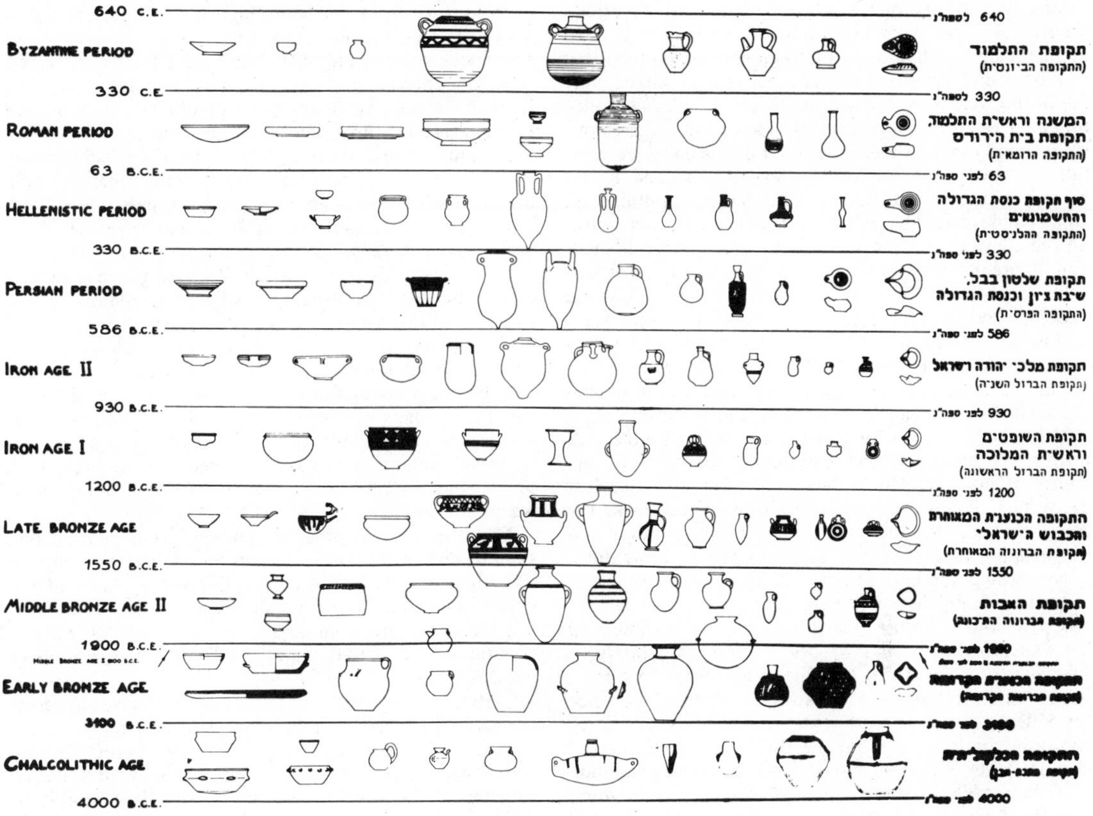

Sequence of pottery types from the Chalcolithic to the Byzantine periods (Israel Department of Antiquities and Museums)

principally outside the period of biblical archeology. Those who are interested in Palestinian Paleolithic and Mesolithic eras will of course fault us for this omission — but there must be limits to this article.

VI. Dating the Finds.–Chronology is a subject of great importance, and because of the complexity of the methods, can be presented here only in general outline.

Relative chronology is to be carefully distinguished from *absolute* chronology. Most archeological data provide us at best with relative chronology: Level II was later than Level III and earlier than Level I. Accordingly, the types of materials found in those levels can be arranged typologically and sequentially. The pottery, for example, can be put in relative chronology. If similar types are found at other tells, the pottery of Level II of Tell "A" may be compared with the pottery of Level IV of Tell "B" and the chronology of those strata can probably be related. If this process is continued for enough types, for many tells, and for a representative sequence of strata at each tell, it is possible to build up a relative chronology for all those tells, and even for the general area in which those particular tells are located. In the work to which we have already referred, *Relative Chronologies in Old World Archaeology*, and in its sequel, *Chronologies in Old World Archaeology* (1965, also edited by Robert W. Ehrich), this method has been carried out for Palestine, Egypt, Syria, Mesopotamia, Iran, the Aegean, and for other areas that lie beyond that in which biblical archeology is principally interested.

The term *absolute chronology* is used with reference to a year-by-year chronology for a given area and period of time, and it is also used to mean a calendar date. On the basis of king lists, which give the names of successive kings and the number of years each king reigned, *limmu*-lists, which name the officials for whom the successive years in a sequence were named, and similar data, we may be able to construct an absolute chronology for a certain period. For example, the names and lengths of reign of the kings of Israel and Judah, which are given in the books of Kings, supply the data for an absolute chronology of the period (with a few problem points). Scholars have reconstructed similar absolute chronologies for lengthy periods of Mesopotamian and Egyptian history. In a more popular sense, absolute chronology means calendar dates, whether converted to our Julian calendar or based on some other system of calendration such as the Seleucid era. If a calendar date can be attached to one item in an absolute chronology, such as the solar eclipse at Assur in the *limmu* of Buru-Sagale (established by astronomers at June 15, 763 B.C.), this provides calendar dates for the other parts of the absolute chronology.

One of the most important items in establishing a chronological sequence is pottery. Contrary to popular belief, a scholar cannot pick up a piece of broken pottery and place an exact date on it. If it lies within the area of his expertise, he can put a probable date on it. But how does he do this?

There are several features that make pottery the ideal material for relative chronology. For one thing, pottery style changed rather frequently. Second, pottery is relatively inexpensive, and therefore quite plentiful, in all communities of the Near East. (This is not true everywhere, and archeologists who specialize in American archeology have been known to become quite excited upon seeing the hundreds of fragments of pottery that can be found lying on the ground around almost any tell in the Near East.) Third, pottery is fragile, and once broken it is practically useless. Gold, silver, precious stones, and other valuables, even if damaged, were carefully treasured, but broken pottery was kicked into a corner or thrown outside. Fourth, sherds of pottery are almost indestructible. After a certain point, depending on the curvature of the vessel, one can step on a sherd and it breaks no further. Moreover, it does not dissolve in water and it is not consumed by fire. (My son and I picked up four pieces of a bowl that were lying on the surface of the mound at Rayy, near Tehran — and they proved to be about 5,000 years old!) As a result of all these factors, pottery is the most plentiful and the most reliable means of building a relative chronology.

The expert — e.g., in Palestinian Early Bronze Age pottery — has seen and handled thousands of fragments of pottery. He knows the color, the glaze or decoration (if any), the general shape of the neck, the base, the handle, the spout, and other details, and by breaking pieces he has come to recognize texture. Through long and careful study he has put the typology of pottery found in Early Bronze Age strata of tells in Palestine into a chronological sequence. By combining his expertise with that of other scholars who have specialized in Nabatean, Israelite, Chalcolithic, or other pottery, it is possible to construct a pottery sequence for Palestine that extends from Ceramic Neolithic to Byzantine or Islamic. Combine this with similar studies in other parts of the Near East, and the result is a study like that in *Chronologies of Old World Archaeology,* mentioned above. Examination of either of the volumes mentioned will show at once the large part that pottery plays in chronological study.

Absolute chronology requires other data besides pottery. Coins found in the ruins at Qumrân, for example, could be dated by the names of kings issuing the coins, and these dates could, with reasonable certainty, be applied to the strata in which the coins were found. This in turn dates the pottery found in those strata. Egyptian scarabs found in Palestinian sites were likewise used to synchronize the levels in which they were found with the pharaohs whose seals they included. The pottery fragments which we found at Rayy could be dated because that type of pottery was produced only at that place *ca.* 3200 B.C. — the date being established by other means.

Thus we see that synchronisms are of very great importance in establishing chronology for the entire Near East. A scarab in a certain level of a Palestinian tell synchronizes that level with a certain Egyptian pharaoh, e.g., Ramses II. A letter is found that is part of the correspondence between Ramses II of Egypt and Hattushilish III of the Hittite Empire, thus synchronizing the Hittite ruler not only with Ramses II but also with the stratum of a Palestinian mound. A wine jar or oil jar found in a lower level of the Palestinian mound may synchronize that level with a certain period in Crete, and a cylinder seal in another tell may synchronize that stratum with a certain ruler in Babylon. A building inscription of a Babylonian king may record a victory of that king over the king of another land. What we have is a number of portions of chronological ladders which can be tied to each other by synchronistic data.

Building the chronology of the ancient Near East, therefore, consists in building chronological ladders for each locality from the many bits of data that are available (relative chronology), and from whatever fixed sequences such as king lists, etc., have been discovered (absolute chronology), and joining as many rungs of these ladders as possible with those of other areas by data that provide synchronisms. If we add firm calendar dating at various points (such as solar eclipses, synchronisms with the Sothic cycle in Egypt, or with other systems of calendration that are reasonably reliable [e.g., the Seleucid era]), we can apply calendar dates to much of the structure we have built.

Obviously, this is a long and detailed process, which only in the past two decades has been worked out to any satisfactory extent. If we had enough ladders of chronology to cover the entire history of each area, and enough correlations to tie all the chronological ladders together, and enough absolute chronology to fit dates to significant rungs of these ladders, we could account for every year. At present, we fall short of this desideratum by small amounts back to *ca.* 1200 B.C., by perhaps ± 75 years back to 2000 B.C., and by inceasing amounts as we go further back in time.

There are several other methods of establishing dates, such as carbon-14 dating, dendrochronology (analysis of the annular rings in trees), varve analysis (study of the deposit-lines left by the receding water at the end of the last ice age), potassium-argon dating, etc. With the exception of carbon-14 dating, these lie outside the limits of our discussion.

Carbon-14 has been used in thousands of cases to determine the dates of materials found in archeological excavations, with varying results. A certain amount of radioactive carbon, or the isotope of carbon with fourteen neutrons in the atom instead of the customary twelve, is produced in the upper atmosphere, and this ultimately finds its way into the soil about us. This is taken up by organic matter such as plants, trees, and animals. Since it is constantly replaced, as long as the life process continues, the proportion of radioactive carbon remains constant, but when the life process ends, i.e. when the tree is cut down or the animal dies, the radioactive isotope deteriorates at a fixed rate, defined as the "half-life." In other words, after approximately 5500 years (which is the half-life of carbon-14), only half the amount of the radioactive carbon will be present. The scientist, with very delicate instruments, can measure the amount of radioactive carbon that remains, and from this he can determine when the life process ended. Because of the geometric nature of the half-life (one-half remains after 5500 years, one-quarter after 11,000 years, one-eighth after 16,000 years, one-sixteenth after 22,000 years, etc.) the test is valid only for the past 25,000 or 50,000 years. Obviously it applies only to organic material. The most useful materials for dating by this process are wood, charcoal, shell, antler, burned bone, dung, and peat. For various reasons, unburned animal and human bone do not provide satisfactory results, and most other organic material decays rather quickly. In order to make the test, a measurable amount of material must be burned, so the archeologist is reluctant to apply the test to finds that should be preserved.

The results of carbon-14 dating have been irregular. In some locations, all the tests have yielded results remarkably close to the dates that could be determined by other means, thus yielding a "control" for the process. In other cases, however, the results of carbon-14 dating have varied widely, both with duplicate tests of the same material and with control dates. It therefore follows that some scholars remain highly skeptical of dates established by carbon-14. While such skepticism seems unwarranted, in the face of thousands of highly satisfactory results, we still must remember that this science is young (about twenty-five years old), that scientists are constantly refining the process and rechecking their results, and that the dates obtained are at best approximations with a margin of error of approximately 5 percent. The *limmu*-lists of the 8th cent. B.C. will therefore give far greater accuracy than carbon-14 tests from the same period (at 750 B.C., ± 5 percent amounts to about 137 years on either side, or between 887 and 613 B.C.!).

VII. Archeology and the Bible.–For a century and a quarter biblical studies have been influenced to some extent by the results of archeological discovery. It is not our purpose to give a detailed study of the finds; the more significant discoveries will be discussed either in the individual articles on areas of archeology that follow, or in articles particularly concerned with some of the most significant finds. A general summary statement can be made: archeology has added a tremendous amount to our knowledge and understanding of the Bible.

The Babylonian creation and flood stories, the discoveries of early villages in northern Iraq, and other materials have given us a background for our studies of the early chapters of Genesis. From Nuzi and Mari we have material that throws light on several points in the patriarchal narratives. The Joseph-cycle of Genesis is illuminated by materials from Egypt. From Egyptian, Ugaritic, and Mesopotamian sources we are able to draw a rather full picture of the land of Canaan both at the time of the patriarchs and later in the period of Israelite occupation. Babylonian, Assyrian, and Hittite legal codes provide a very full background for the study of Mosaic legislation, while the materials from Râs Shamrah supply details for the study of Wilderness cultic provisions. The Egyptian tales of Sinuhe and Wen-amon and the Amarna Letters add further details concerning the land of Canaan and its customs, and Greek legends probably supply still more.

Probably our greatest help, both in quantity and relevance, comes from the royal annals of Assyria, Babylonian chronicles, and similar material contemporary with the kings of Israel and Judah. A few details are added by the Mesha Inscription (MOABITE STONE) and by Phoenician and Old Aramaic inscriptions. The great stumbling block to the Israelites was Baal worship, introduced on a grand scale by Jezebel the Phoenician princess. From the Ugaritic materials we have a firsthand presentation of the religion of Baal and other deities in the Canaanite pantheon, and the teachings of the prophets have taken on new dimensions of reality. Egyptian and Mesopotamian wisdom literature helps us understand the nature of this literary genre and brings biblical wisdom writings into clearer focus.

For the Exile and the postexilic period we have documents of Babylonian kings, the Cyrus inscription, correspondence in Aramaic from Elephantine, and additional details from Persian and Greek sources that have once and for all destroyed the theory that there was no Exile, while helping us understand both the return to the land and the reestablishment of the Jerusalem cultus on the one hand, and the establishment of Diaspora Judaism on the other.

The DEAD SEA SCROLLS have filled in many details of the rise of sectarian Judaism, and help us see how Christianity as a Jewish sect could be so quickly established. Sir William Ramsay's extensive and intensive explorations in Asia Minor put Pauline studies on a more solid basis. Many incidental archeological discoveries have added significant details about the Roman empire, its administration (including the offices and many of the officials named in the NT), its changing attitudes toward the Jews and later the Christians, and other matters that come into the NT account.

For those who wish to study certain of these matters in detail, there are many reliable books (see the bibliography, below). The value of various discoveries for biblical study is often a matter of personal axiology: for the person who wants "archeological proof" of the Bible, the inscription mentioning the proconsulship of Gallio in Corinth is far more significant than the Admonitions of Ipuwer or the Wisdom of Amenemope, and reports of the discovery of "Noah's Ark" on Mount Ararat are of greater import than the Dead Sea Scrolls. Some want proof to bolster faith, others want knowledge to make faith more certain, and still others want knowledge to replace faith. Archeology serves each in his own way.

VIII. The Evidential Value of Archeology.–The materials and techniques of biblical archeology must be precisely the same as those of all archeology. Only the purpose is different, for the biblical archeologist is interested in applying the results to the study of the Bible. But what, precisely, is meant by this? In the 19th and early 20th cents., the expression "archeology proves the Bible" was often used. It is the opinion of many scholars today, including many who are personally committed to faith in the Bible as the word of God, that the evidential value of archeology is not properly understood if it is taken to mean that archeology proves the Bible. Just what, then, does archeology prove? The Bible tells us, among other things, that the Israelites under Joshua went in and took possession of the land of Canaan. Archeological evidence indicates that certain Canaanite cities, including some of those specifically mentioned in the book of Joshua, were destroyed in the 13th cent. B.C. — which corresponds with the time of the Israelite invasion, according to one system of biblical chronology — and that the Canaanite culture was for a time replaced by a different (and inferior) culture. The Bible tells us that the reason the Israelites were able to capture Canaanite territory was that Yahweh their God fought their battles. Archeology has nothing to say on this point. Archeology, then, "proves" that some people — probably Israelites, for they are found in the land at a subsequent time — conquered the land of Canaan. Archeology does not and cannot prove that Yahweh fought the battles and gave the Israelites the land. This was a matter of Israelite faith, and it remains a point of faith for all who accept the Bible by faith.

Similar points could be set forth for other parts of the Bible for which archeology has provided material for study. An inscription proves that Gallio was proconsul of Achaia in A.D. 51-52. This and other archeological data help us establish a reasonable chronology for Paul's ministry. But the most significant fact in the life of Paul, namely, that when he was a persecutor of the Church he was confronted by the risen Jesus, is not capable of archeological proof. No item of faith is dependent on proof. Once we insist on proof we no longer have faith.

Nevertheless, there is evidential value in the study of biblical archeology. It is a unique doctrine of the religion of the Bible, both in the OT and in the NT, and therefore believed by Jews as well as Christians, that the God of the Bible, the Yahweh of the Israelites and the Father of Jesus Christ, revealed Himself to His people in historical situations in time and space. He called Abram (later Abraham) out of Ur to go to the land of Canaan. He brought Israel into Egypt; and after the time He had ordained, He led Israel out of Egypt and subsequently into the land of Canaan. He used the Assyrians as the rod in His hand to punish the Israelites. He took Judah into exile in Babylonia, and later returned them to the land by the agency of His anointed Cyrus (Isa. 45:1). He sent His son, Jesus, to the little country of Palestine, more specifically to Nazareth in Galilee in the days of Herod the Great. Jesus was crucified in Jerusalem after suffering under the Roman procurator Pontius Pilate. The tomb in which Jesus was buried and from which He rose belonged to Joseph of Arimathea. From beginning to end, the Bible is filled with the names of peoples and places, of kings and commoners. No other religion has its faith so thoroughly intermingled with historical and geographical details. It therefore becomes necessary to include the study of peoples and places with our study of the Bible. Archeology brings to life these peoples and places.

There were nineteenth-century scholars who were convinced that Abraham, Isaac, Jacob, and perhaps even Moses were simply imaginary creations of later Israelite authors. But archeology has put these persons in a real world. As a result, a scholar such as J. Bright, after devoting thirty-six pages to the subject, can write, "the Bible's picture of the patriarchs is deeply rooted in history" (*BHI*, p. 102).

Faith that requires proof is no faith, but faith that says, "Help my unbelief!" is quite common among human beings. Archeology supplies means for understanding many of the biblical situations, it adds the dimension of reality to pictures that otherwise would be strange and somewhat unreal, and therefore it provides an element of credibility. While the person of faith does not ask for proof, he does want to feel that his faith is reasonable and not mere fantasy. Archeology, by supplying him with material remains from biblical times and places, and by interpreting these data, provides a context of reality for the biblical story and reasonability for biblical faith.

Bibliography.–*Method:* K. M. Kenyon, *Beginning in Archaeology* (1952); L. Woolley, *Digging Up the Past* (1930); O. G. S. Crawford, *Archaeology in the Field* (1953); R. F. Heizer and S. F. Cook, eds., *Application of Quantitative Methods in Archaeology* (1960); W. F. Badè, *Manual of Excavation in the Near East* (1934).

Source Materials: ANET; *ANEP*; J. B. Pritchard, ed., *Ancient Near East: Supplementary Texts and Pictures* (1969); *ARE*; *ARAB*; *DOTT*; F. Michaeli, *Textes de la Bible et de l'ancien Orient* (1961).

General: W. F. Albright, *AP*; *FSAC*; *ARI*; *IB*, I (1951), 233-271; *OTMS*, pp. 27-47; K. M. Kenyon, *Archaeology in the Holy Land* (1960); G. L. Harding, *Antiquities of Jordan* (1959); A. Jirku, *Die Welt der Bibel; Fünf Jahrtausende in Palästina-Syrien* (1957); C. C. McCown, *The Ladder of Progress in Palestine* (1943); *WBA*; R. J. Braidwood, *The Near East and the Foundations for Civilization* (1952); V. G. Childe, *What Happened in History?* (1942); *New Light on the Most Ancient East* (1957); H. Frankfort, *et al.*, *Intellectual Adventure of Ancient Man* (1946; paperback title *Beyond Philosophy*, 1961); E. Anati, *Palestine Before the Hebrews* (1963); S. Piggott, ed., *Dawn of Civilization* (1961); E. A. Speiser, *Beginnings of Civilization in the Orient* (*JAOS* Supplement 4, 1939); L. Woolley, *History Unearthed* (1958); *BANE*.

Area Studies: S. Lloyd, *Foundations in the Dust* (1947); S. N. Kramer, *From the Tablets of Sumer* (1956); M. E. L. Mallowan, *Twenty-five Years of Mesopotamian Discovery* (1956); J. Laessøe, *People of Ancient Assyria* (1963); A. Pallis, *Antiquity of Iraq* (1957); A. L. Perkins, *Comparative Archeology of Early Mesopotamia* (1949); A. Parrot, *Archéologie mésopotamienne* (2 vols., 1953); L. Woolley, *Ur: The First Phases* (1946); *The Sumerians* (1928); E. Drioton and J. Vandier, *Peuples de l'Orient méditerranéen*, II, *L'Égypte* (3rd ed. 1952); R. Engelbach, *Introduction to Egyptian Archaeology* (1946); G. Jéquier, *Manuel d'archéologie égyptienne* (1924); J. Vandier, *Manuel d'archéologie égyptienne* (2 vols., 1952); H. T. Bossert, *Altsyrien* (1951); S. Lloyd, *Early Anatolia* (1956); R. Ghirshman, *Iran* (1954); L. Vanden Berghe, *Archéologie de l'Irān ancien* (1959); V. G. Childe, *Dawn of European Civilization* (6th ed. 1957); R. W. Hutchinson, *Prehistoric Crete* (1962); G. L. Huxley, *Aegeans and Hittites* (1960); S. Marinatos and M. Hirmer, *Crete and Mycenae* (1960); F. Matz, *Kreta, Mykene, Troja* (1956); P. MacKendrick, *Greek Stones Speak* (1962); J. Vercoutter, *Essai sur les relations entre Égyptiens et Préhellènes* (1954); B. Rothenberg, *Discoveries in Sinai* (1961); S. Piggott, *Prehistoric India* (1950); R. L. Bowen and F. P. Albright, *Archaeological Discoveries in South Arabia* (1958); C. B. M. McBurney, *Stone Age of North Africa* (1960); see also the bibliographies of the articles on archeology of specific areas.

Art: S. Lloyd, *Art of the Ancient Near East* (1961); H. Schäfer und W. Andrae, *Kunst des Alten Orients* (1925); E. D. Ross, *Art of Egypt through the Ages* (1931); M. M. Rutten, *Arts et styles du Moyen Orient ancien* (1950); W. S. Smith, *Art and Architecture of Ancient Egypt* (1958); H. Frankfort, *Art and Architecture of the Ancient Orient* (1954); A. U. Pope and P. Ackerman, eds., *Survey of Persian Art from Prehistoric Times to the Present*, (7 vols., 1938); E. Akurgal, *Art of the Hittites* (1962); E. Bell, *Early Architecture in Western Asia, Chaldean, Hittite, Assyrian, Persian* (1924); C. L. Woolley, *Development of Sumerian Art* (1935); F. Matz, *Crete and Early Greece, the Prelude to Greek Art* (1962); C. Zervos, *L'art de la Crète néolithique et minoenne* (1956).

Daily Life: National Geographic Society, *Everyday Life in Ancient Times: Highlights of the Beginnings of Western Civilization in Mesopotamia, Egypt, Greece, and Rome* (1958); A. Erman, *Ägypten und ägyptisches Leben im Altertum* (2nd ed. 1923; Eng. tr. from 1st ed., *Life in Ancient Egypt*, 1894); W. Corswant, *Dictionary of Life in Bible Times* (1960); R. de Vaux, *Ancient Israel: Its Life and Institutions* (1961); A. E. Baily, *Daily Life in Bible Times* (1943); G. Bibby, *Four Thousand Years Ago: A Panorama of Life in the Second Millennium B.C.* (1962); A. C. Bouquet, *Everyday Life in New Testament Times* (1954); J. Carcopino, *Daily Life in Ancient Rome* (1940); G. Haddad, *Aspects of Social Life in Antioch in the Hellenistic-Roman Period* (1949); M. and C. B. Quennell, *Everyday Life in Prehistoric Times* (1959; 2-vol. ed. 1955).

Chronology: R. W. Ehrich, ed., *Chronologies in Old World Archaeology* (1965); P. van der Meer, *Ancient Chronology of Western Asia and Egypt* (2nd ed. 1955); R. A. Parker and W. H. Dubberstein, *Babylonian Chronology 626 B.C. — A.D. 75* (1956); *IDB*, III, *s.v.* "Pottery" (J. L. Kelso); *MNHK*.

Interpretation: LAP; J. A. Thompson, *Bible and Archaeology* (1972); C. H. Gordon, *World of the Old Testament* (1958); *BASOR*, 66 (Feb. 1937), 25-27; *BA*, 3 (1940), 1-9; *JBR*, 21 (1953), 238-243; J. Gray, *Archaeology and the Old Testament World* (1962); *OTMS*; M. Noth, *Welt des Alten Testaments* (1964; Eng. tr. *Old Testament World*, 1966); W. F. Albright, *History, Archaeology, and Christian Humanism* (1964); E. M. Yamauchi, *Stones and the Scriptures* (1972). W. S. LASOR

ARCHEOLOGY OF ARABIA. Archeology in Arabia is still at a very early stage, although the archeological information to be found in the reports of many travelers and especially the results of the few limited excavations portend a wealth of data still hidden under the sand.

I. Northwest.–Tema and Dedan are mentioned in Genesis, TEMA as son of Ishmael (25:15) and DEDAN as descendant of Ham (10:6f.). In antiquity these two cities (modern Teimā and el-'Ulā) were important commercial centers at crossings of incense trade routes. Teimā, renowned for its springs, is mentioned by Tiglath-pileser III (745 B.C.), and became the residence of Nabonidus. Circular tumuli with steps leading to rectangular tombs and Thamudic graffiti were found in the vicinity, as well as a stele. The text of the stele is Aramaic (6th cent. B.C.), the god and his priest (the author) are Assyrian, and the name of the author's father Egyptian. Dedan was populated by Dedanites and Liḥyanites when (6th cent. B.C.) Minaeans from south Arabia founded there an important trading center, which included a temple dedicated to their lunar god Wadd.

 ARCHEOLOGY OF ARABIA

Dedan became a Minaean colony (3rd cent. B.C.), which was conquered by Nabateans shortly before the Christian era. The cultural characteristics of all the populations are found in many different inscriptions and beautiful monuments in el-'Ulā and vicinity, especially the necropolis on the flank of the mountain Khureybeh and the ruins of tombs and of a sanctuary at el-Ḥajrâ (modern Medâ'în Ṣâliḥ).

***II. Southwest.*–*A. Ma'în*.** This is the only ancient south Arabian kingdom still awaiting excavators. The relatively small country ej-Jawf (about 75 mi. [120 km.] NE of Ṣan'â') contains ruins of several Minaean cities. Kharibat Ma'în (ancient Qarnâwû, capital of the Minaean kingdom) is a huge field of ruins of a walled city with two rectangular temples. The smaller one is inside the wall, and the larger one, Risâf(um) (modern el-'Urayš), dedicated to the stellar god 'Aṯtar, is outside the wall. It is preceded by a monumental vestibule. The crenelated wall of Barâqiš (ancient Yaṯil, SW of the preceding city) is well preserved; the two remaining temples have been located inside the wall. Other important ruins are located at el-Bayḏâ' (ancient Našq), es-Sawdâ' (ancient Našân), Kharibat Sa'ûd (ancient Kutal) and Kamina (ancient Kamnahû).

B. Saba'. The first excavations in south Arabia were conducted by C. Rathjens and H. von Wissman in 1928, in a small rectangular temple at el-Ḥuqqat (about 14 mi. [22 km.] NNW of Ṣan'â') dedicated to the solar goddess Ḏât-Ba'dân, which had been in use for several centuries before the Christian era. The 1951-1952 American excavations in the peristyle of Maḥram Bilqîs (the elliptic 'Awwâm temple built in the 8th cent. B.C., SE of Mârib) cleared the entrance court almost completely. Among the numerous discoveries, those worthy of special mention are Ma'adkarib's bronze statue with Syro-Hittite features (7th cent. B.C.) and the complex of remains in and facing the southern entrance of the elliptic wall (inside the peristyle). The latter was used for an ablution ritual, by immersion and aspersion, in which the faithful engaged before entering the temple. Further, more than three hundred new texts, unearthed in the peristyle, contain priceless data for Sabaean studies. The famous dam of Mârib and the ruins of el-'Amâyid (the ancient temple Bara'ân) are located NW and SE of Mârib, respectively. Other major ruins are found in Ṣirwâḥ (with its monumental temple) and Ṣan'â' (with its fortress Gumdân and the church built by the Ethiopian viceroy 'Abraha).

C. Qatabân. The American excavations worked in 1950/51 at Hajr Koḥlân (ancient Timna', capital of the Qatabanian kingdom), its necropolis called Ḥeid bin 'Aqîl, and Hajr bin Ḥumeid and vicinity. Of particular importance are the following discoveries. One of the wooden beams from stratified Hajr bin Ḥumeid is dated from *ca.* 852 B.C. (± 160 years) by radiocarbon analysis, thus providing a basis for dating the jar with a monogram found below the beams. The first typological sequence of pottery from the same site will help in dating the different strata of the site itself and of other Qatabanian sites. The remains in Wâdī Beiḥân of an irrigation system, whose origin in the middle of the 2nd millennium B.C. is proved by the rate of silt accumulation found below the first occupation of Hajr bin Ḥumeid, indicate that the sedentary occupation in Wâdī Beiḥân goes back at least to 1500 B.C. The two bronze lionesses with infant riders testify to a strong Hellenistic influence in the 1st cent. B.C., and the stele from Hajr bin Ḥumeid is an adaptation from Syrian art. A drain facing the entrance of the temple Riṣâfum dedicated to the lunar god 'Anbay, at Ḥeid bin 'Aqîl, is similar to that of the peristyle of Maḥram Bilqîs near Mârib. Finally, most of the tombs of the cemetery at Ḥeid bin 'Aqîl are dug in the rock and divided by stone slabs in the manner of the boxes of a wine cellar. Other important ruins are located at 'Imm'adîyah (E of Mukerâs) and Hajr Ḥenû ez-Zurîr (in Wâdī Ḥarîb).

***III. Central South.*–**In 1937-1938, G. Caton Thompson excavated a small, rectangular temple dedicated to the lunar god Sîn (ENE of el-Ḥuraydat in Wâdī 'Amid), a "farm house," and two tombs. Benches, bones, ashes, crudely-made statues in the apsidal shrines at el-Ḥuraydat, as well as in the small temple excavated by F. P. Albright at Khôr Rôrî (ancient Sumhuram), are best interpreted as evidence for practice of a ritual repast, associated with some ancestor or other deceased person represented by a statue. Connected with the frankincense trade are the seasonal collecting station, excavated by R. L. Cleveland at Ḥânûn (about 25 mi. [40 km.] N of eṣ-Ṣalâlah), the fortress at Anḏûr (about 43 mi. [69 km.] NNE of Khôr

Old South Arabic inscription from Mârib. Dedication of building named Yafud by three brothers in reign of Karib'il Watar Yuhamin king of Saba' (1st cent. B.C.) (W. S. LaSor)

Rôrî), and especially the clay stamp discovered by J. L. Kelso at Beitîn (biblical Bethel) in 1957 and its identical counterpart found at el-Mashad (Wâdī Du'ân, Hadramaut) almost sixty years before. These two stamps testify to incense trade between the two cities in the 9th cent. B.C.

IV. Southeast.–Soundings made by R. L. Cleveland at Soḥar (about 65 mi. [105 km.] NE of Muscat) and in several other places in the Bâṭina Plain present late remains of about the 6th or 7th centuries.

V. Eastern Center.–R. LeBaron Bowen, Jr. made excavations in the necropolis at Jâwân, and a Danish expedition in 1957 discovered remains of Sumerians in the island of el-Baḥrayn (Bahrain).

See ARABIA Map.

Bibliography.–*Encyclopedia of World Art,* I (1959), *s.v.* "Arabia," "Arabian Pre-Islamic Art" (A. Grohmann); *BANE*, pp. 229-248.

A. JAMME (1965)

ARCHEOLOGY OF ASIA MINOR. The area generally included in the designation ASIA MINOR is what today comprises the greater part of Turkey, especially the large peninsula lying between the Black Sea and the Mediterranean Sea. Frequently, when the earlier periods are considered, the name Anatolia is used for this area. The beginning and development of archeological research in this area were slow since the areas to the west (classical archeology in Greece), to the south (biblical archeology in Syria and Palestine), and to the southeast (Mesopotamian archeology) commanded greater interest and attention. Presently, however, Anatolian archeology has developed and expanded to such a degree that scholars working in the eastern Mediterranean area must reckon with the significant contributions from Asia Minor. These contributions date from prehistoric to Islamic times and deeply influence the discussions relating to all the archeological periods.

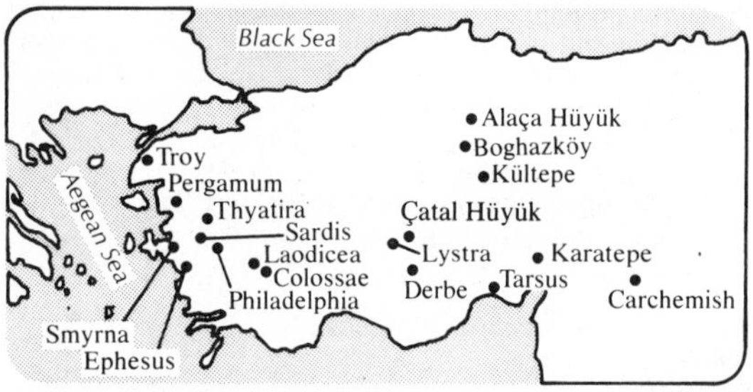

Asia Minor illustrates *inter alia* the glamorous excitement of archeology (Schliemann's discovery of Troy), the frustration and persistence of the archeologist (Wood's discovery of the temple of ARTEMIS at Ephesus), the unparalleled contributions of archeology (the discovery of the remains of the Hittite empire), and the growing frontiers of archeology (the identification of numerous prehistoric sites).

As was true of other areas in the Middle East, modern knowledge of ancient Asia Minor first came from accounts by nineteenth-century travelers. In the last three decades of that century some excavations of sites were undertaken (e.g., cities of Iona, MYSIA, and CARIA), although these were often more quarrying and treasure hunting than scientific and systematic excavating. Perhaps the best-known of the responsible excavations was H. Schliemann's work at Troy, which, although conducted somewhat haphazardly and with inaccurate conclusions, did arouse unending interest in archeology. Regrettably, before World War I the antiquities of Turkey were frequently plundered by foreign expeditions and some of the most prized monuments were transferred to European museums. On the other hand, between the two world wars Continental, British, and American scholars and institutions contributed significantly to the development and expansion of the archeology of Asia Minor. Many foreign academic and archeological institutions now sponsor excavations.

Concomitant with and encouraged by these foreign expeditions has been the development of Turkish interest in the heritage of the land. Following the political reforms of Kemal Atatürk, faculties and departments of ancient history and archeology were established in the universities, and scientific institutes were founded. Public interest was stimulated through local museums and the expansion of museums in major cities by the addition of excellent new facilities. The enlarged Department of Antiquities properly and scientifically controls and supervises archeological work. These developments have given rise to a generation of competent Turkish scholars and archeologists, whose contributions, with those of foreign expeditions, have made Turkey one of the most productive areas in archeological research.

The first major contribution of Anatolian archeology to biblical studies was the identification of the Hittite empire, previously know only from the biblical documents. Sayce's initial identification (1876) of pictographs in several remote places in Asia Minor with the HITTITES of the OT spurred a more extensive search for, and collection of, Hittite antiquities. Between 1907 and 1911 Winckler found cuneiform tablets at Boghazköy. B. Hrozný deciphered them in 1915, identifying the Hittite language as Indo-European. Several Hittite sites were excavated, the principal ones being CARCHEMISH, Alaça Hüyük, Boghazköy, Kültepe, Karatepe, and Alişar. "Hittite archeology" and "Hittitology" became significant disciplines in the scholarly world. A bilingual inscription found at Karatepe in 1945 provided H. T. Bossert the key to the deciphering of the Hittite hieroglyphs. This new body of literature and the related archeological data have added major new dimensions to historical, economic, and political studies of the 2nd millennium B.C. In addition, the legal codes of the Hittites have illumined the parallels in the OT.

Asia Minor was the scene of extensive apostolic mission activity, especially by Paul, who devoted most of his work to this area and was himself a native of Tarsus (*see* ASIA MINOR V.A). Scholars have identified all the sites in Asia Minor mentioned in the NT. A pioneer in the archeology of Asia Minor of the Roman period was W. M. Ramsay (1851-1939), a classicist at the University of Aberdeen. Through his extensive travels in Turkey, begun in 1880, he was able to identify numerous sites with certainty and to define the major roads and trade routes of ancient Anatolia. In NT studies his identification of biblical sites and corroboration of related details have greatly supported the accuracy and reliability of the Lucan writings. His scholarship and contributions have been very significant in the development of the archeology of Asia Minor as it relates to the NT period (cf. W. W. Gasque, *Sir William Ramsay: Archaeologist and NT Scholar* [1966]).

Some of the NT sites have been or are being extensively excavated, e.g., EPHESUS, SARDIS, and HIERAPOLIS. Others farther inland still await the archeologist's spade, e.g., COLOSSAE, LYSTRA, and DERBE. The epigraphical evidence dating to the early Christian centuries is very extensive (cf. *Monumenta Asiae Minoris Antiqua* [8 vols., 1925-1962]). Continuing investigations of these documents and remains with artifacts of the sites are delineating more precisely the religious character of the 1st cent. A.D.: a syncretism of Greco-Roman religions and local deities and practices.

ARCHEOLOGY OF ASIA MINOR

Hittite Sphinx Gate at Alaca Hüyük (Euyuk), suggesting Egyptian influence (B. K. Condit)

Postern tunnel with corbeled arch at Boghazköy (Hittite Hattusas) (B. K. Condit)

Excavated site at Çatal Hüyük providing evidence of early urbanization (B. K. Condit)

ARCHEOLOGY OF EGYPT

It was into this environment that Paul brought Christianity.

The seven cities of Rev. 2 and 3 (EPHESUS, SMYRNA, PERGAMUM, THYATIRA, SARDIS, PHILADELPHIA, LAODICEA) have been identified and some of their individual features can be correlated with allusions in the scriptural accounts (*see also* ASIA MINOR V.D). New light on the provincial boundaries of the Roman empire and the administration of these as shown by epigraphical and literary sources will soon lay to rest the problem of North Galatia or South Galatia in favor of the latter (*see also* GALATIA; GALATIANS, EPISTLE TO THE III). Similarly, as collections of Greek inscriptions of Asia Minor become more available, there will be new insights into the vocabulary and syntax of the Northeast Mediterranean Greek of the NT.

Evidence of early Christianity can be found throughout Asia Minor. Although no systematic study of this vast and scattered body of evidence has been undertaken, preliminary surveys and a few major excavations (e.g., Alahan, Ephesus) indicate that much information about history, art, architecture, worship, and life in the early Christian and Byzantine periods must still be uncovered by the archeologist.

Anatolian archeology in recent years has acquired an exciting new dimension: the study of prehistoric and Bronze Age man. Some of the best preserved and earliest forms of civilization have been found in south central Turkey. The Neolithic site at Çatal Hüyük (near Konya) provides evidence of early urbanization, of developed art forms in frescoes and statues over 8500 years old, and of humanity's religious and economic quests. Other sites in the same area have produced similar evidence. Surveys by I. Todd and others have identified numerous prehistoric and Bronze Age sites (cf. U. B. Alkim, *Anatolia I* [1968]; J. Mellaart, *Çatal Hüyük. A Neolithic Town in Anatolia* [1967]).

Bibliography.–*American Journal of Archaeology*; *Anatolian Studies*; *Anatolica*; T. Dowley, ed., *Eerdmans' Handbook to the History of Christianity* (1977), pp. 53-83; J. A. Thompson, *Bible and Archaeology* (rev. ed. 1972), pp. 375-424.

B. VAN ELDEREN

ARCHEOLOGY OF EGYPT.

I. Limits of This Article.–A complete study of archeological discoveries in Egypt would exceed the space available and go far beyond the purpose of a Bible encyclopedia. Archeological discoveries from Egypt are very abundant, because the area has an extremely long history of continuous habitation by productive civilizations and because the climate of Egypt favors the preservation of nearly all kinds of artifacts and usuquids (non-artifactual materials). But only an extremely small proportion of Egyptian material is directly relevant to biblical studies.

That there is relevance, however, is unquestionable. The biblical account includes a brief visit to Egypt by Abraham and Sarah (Gen. 12:10-20), a long period when the sons of Jacob and their descendants dwelt in Egypt (Gen. 39:1–Ex. 14:31), several references to Egyptian pharaohs during the periods of the Israelite monarchy and the divided kingdom, the mention of a colony of Jews in Egypt in the days of Jeremiah (Jer. 43–44), and the visit of Jesus' family to Egypt in the days of Herod the Great (Mt. 2:13-21).

Moreover, evidence of many significant contacts between Egypt and Palestine is found in extrabiblical sources. From the earliest period of which we have record Egypt maintained trade with Byblos, principally to obtain timber for building purposes. "Asiatics" (*'Aamu*)—certainly including Palestinians—visited Egypt for commerce and, in times of famine, for food. In the middle of the 2nd millennium B.C. Asiatic invaders took control of Lower Egypt (and, according to the words attributed to Manetho by Josephus, even Upper Egypt; cf. *CAp* 1.14 [§ 77]). Thutmose I marched to Nahrin, the region beyond the Euphrates known in the Hebrew Bible as Aram-naharaim. Thutmose III likewise marched to the Euphrates and undertook to expand the borders of Egypt. Between the twenty-third and thirty-ninth years of his reign he conducted fourteen campaigns into Palestine and Syria and erected forts at several places, including Beth-shean. In the following century Egypt seemed to be concerned principally with other matters, and the kings of small city-states in Palestine were pleading with the ruler of Egypt to send help against the SA.GAZ or Ḫabiru (*see* AMARNA TABLETS V). The Egyptian Aramaic papyri reveal the existence of a Jewish colony at Elephantine (near Aswan), in addition to that at Tahpanhes (Jer. 2:16; Ezk. 30:18; Jth. 1:9), and the production of the LXX at Alexandria in the 3rd and 2nd cents. B.C. testifies to a large and important Jewish colony there.

But how much of Egyptian history and archeology is necessary for biblical study? The answer is complicated by several factors. First and perhaps most important is the problem of dating the entrance of the sons of Jacob into Israel and the Exodus of the Israelites from Egypt (*See* EXODUS). Working from figures in Josephus and from certain biblical data, we might put the entrance of Joseph as early as the 20th century, and if we follow Montet's thesis that the pharaoh of the Exodus was Siptah or even Seti II, we could date the Exodus around the end of the 13th century. To examine the various theories carefully the biblical scholar is obliged to consider details in Egyptian history and geography within that span of seven hundred years. The whole picture is further complicated by the conservatism of Egypt. Many customs, for example, that might be found in the New Kingdom (18th to 20th Dynasties) had their origin in the Old Kingdom (4th to 6th Dynasties), the Archaic Period (1st to 3rd Dynasties), or even in the Predynastic Period (*ca.* 4000-3200 B.C.). Quite often a study of the earlier periods is necessary for a clear understanding of a later incident.

Obviously, then, it is necessary to make a selection from the vast amount of material to be handled, and any

ARCHEOLOGY OF EGYPT

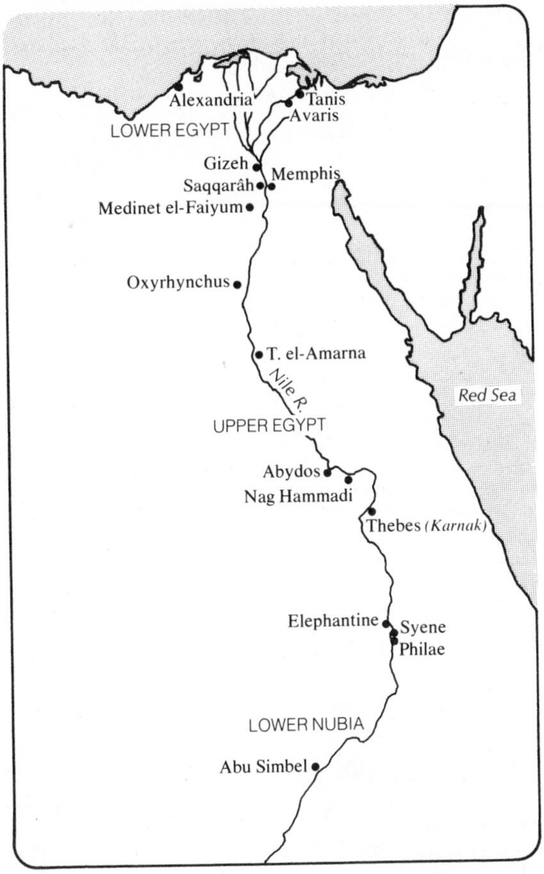

Rosetta Stone, fragment of a stele commemorating the coronation of Ptolemy V Epiphanes as king of all Egypt (186 B.C.). The Greek inscription (bottom) was a major key to decipherment of the hieroglyphic and demotic Egyptian (above). (Trustees of the British Museum)

such choice will be largely subjective. This article selects aspects of Egyptian archeology that seem to have greater significance for biblical studies, and refers to other works for further study.

II. History of Egyptian Archeology.–*A. General Survey.* In general, the history of Egyptian archeology has two main periods, before and after Napoleon's campaign into Egypt, A.D. 1798-1799. Pre-Napoleonic archeology consists of references to monuments, inscriptions, and the like, e.g., the report of Thutmose IV (1413-1405 B.C.) that he cleared the sand away from the Sphinx, or reports of Greek and Latin visitors or of medieval pilgrims to several of the great monuments. These give us valuable information about the condition of the monuments, and in some cases, the location of monuments no longer extant. Important as such data are, they cannot be considered scientific archeology.

Napoleon, in a campaign that was planned to go to India but turned back after a year in Egypt, took with him a staff of 175 scientists, including orientalists, geographers, cartographers, and many other specialists, as well as a large library and a shipload of scientific instruments. These scientists explored Egypt from the Mediterranean coast to the Sudan. Among many other kinds of data, they brought back casts of statues, copies of inscriptions, and many valuable records of monuments that they uncovered. Among their discoveries was a slab of black basalt inscribed in what appeared to be three languages, now known from the place of discovery as the Rosetta Stone, which was very important for the deciphering of the Egyptian language (see II.B). The publication of ten volumes of texts and fourteen volumes of plates describing the discoveries of Napoleon's expedition, plus the deciphering of Egyptian hieroglyphs by J. F. Champollion and others, greatly increased the desire to know more about Egyptian antiquities.

Also important were discoverers and explorers, such as G. B. Belzoni, who explored the Nile Valley to Abu Simbel, and who found the tomb of Seti I, among other achievements. Twenty important items in the British Museum were acquired through Belzoni's expeditions. He was a collector, however, rather than an archeologist. About the same time (first quarter of the 19th cent.), H. Salt, British Consul-General in Egypt, and W. J. Bankes explored the length of Egypt. Salt removed a colossal head of Ramses II from Thebes, and correctly diagnosed the direction that hieroglyphs should be read. Bankes discovered a list of kings at Abydos, which was useful to T. Young and Champollion in their deciphering of Egyptian inscriptions. R. Howard-Vyse, whose work in Egypt had the advantage of beginning after Champollion and who had completed his work of deciphering the inscriptions, worked at Gîzeh. He rejected the fantastic notions about the pyramids and concluded that they were tombs of pharaohs. He discovered the entrance of the tombs of Mycerinus, discovered chambers in the pyramid of Cheops that had not previously been found, and uncovered some of the polished limestone casing that had once covered the entire pyramid of Chephren. There were several others, but all of them were more interested in collecting than in studying and interpreting. Some of their efforts were destructive, but like the work of H. Schliemann at Troy and elsewhere, the formed a necessary step to true investigation.

R. Lepsius led a Prussian expedition to Egypt in 1842, to catalogue and to classify, and to make the first steps toward a chronological framework for the materials. Over the next few years the expedition conducted a careful survey of Gîzeh, the Faiyûm, Tell el-Amarna, Thebes, Philae, Abu Simbel, and other sites, and produced *Monuments of Egypt and Ethiopia* (12 vols., 1849-1859). Lepsius' chronological work appeared in *Egyptian Chronology* (1849) and *Book of Egyptian Kings* (1850). Besides his cataloging and classifying, he sent 15,000 objects to Berlin for the museum that was yet to be built. He rationalized, as others have done, that if he had not taken the treasures to Europe they would have been stolen or destroyed by vandals — and to some extent he was right.

With the appointment of A. Mariette as Director of the Service of Antiquities in 1858, Egyptian archeology was placed under supervision. For the next ninety-four years this position was held by French scholars. Only experience can lead to sound principles, and Mariette had a few things to learn. He established the rule that all antiquities found in Egypt were to stay in Egypt — basically a sound principle, but one not easy to enforce — and he refused to allow anyone else to conduct an archeological excavation. His own efforts at thirty-seven locations, by lack of supervision and unsatisfactory cataloguing, proved that it takes more than one man to excavate Egypt. Still, his work was tremendous by any standard, and by no means the least of his achievements was the founding of the museum at Bulaq, later moved to Gîzeh, and now located in Cairo.

W. M. Flinders Petrie (1853-1942), the first, if not the only, person who could appropriately write a book entitled *Seventy Years in Archaeology,* is credited with opening the age of scientific archeology in Egypt, and to a degree in other parts of the Near East. His book *Inductive Metrology* (1877) and his use of "Sequence Dating" provided the basis for relative chronology. Simply stated, Sequence Dating (abbr. S.D.) is the arrangement of different styles (principally of pottery) in accordance with the sequence of their appearance in successive levels of an excavation, and, by comparing these styles with those found at other sites, the construction of a sequence for a larger area. This method is accepted today as a matter of course, but it was indeed revolutionary when Petrie introduced it. With no way to establish dates based on our calendar or on any other continuous calendration, Petrie took what appeared to him to be the earliest style in wavy-handle pots, and arranged a sequence. Starting with S.D. 30 (to allow for later discoveries that would prove to be earlier), Petrie developed a sequence to S.D. 77, which corresponded with the beginning of the 1st Dynasty. His foresight was rewarded when Badarian remains were dated S.D. 21-29. S.D. 30-39 are now identified as Amratian, and S.D. 40-62 as Gerzean. The dates that Petrie hazarded (Faiyûm 9000, Badarian 7400-7100, Menes 4236 B.C.) now seem fantastic.

Only a few of the great scholars who have contributed to Egyptian archeology since the days of Petrie can be listed here. J. H. Breasted edited the five-volume collection *Ancient Records of Egypt* (1906-1907). A. Erman and H. Grapow edited the seven-volume *Wörterbuch der ägyptischen Sprache* (1926-1963), and Erman and his pupils, notably K. Sethe, laid the foundations of scientific grammar. A. H. Gardiner made the results available to the English-speaking world in his *Egyptian Grammar* (1st ed. 1927; 3rd ed. 1957). Erman also produced the very valuable *Ägypten und ägyptisches Leben im Altertum* (rev. ed. by H. Ranke, 1923; Eng. tr. of 1st German ed. 1894). American, British, French, German, and Egyptian archeologists, as well as those of several other nations, have provided us with important excavations, writings, interpretations, and other works.

B. Deciphering the Language. The Rosetta Stone, which fell into British hands when they took possession of Egypt in 1802, was actually written in two languages: Egyptian in two forms (hieroglyphic and demotic) and Greek. It was correctly assumed that the Egyptian inscriptions were substantially the same as the Greek, and scholars went to work at deciphering the Egyptian. S. de Sacy identified several names. J. D. Åkerblad identified all the names and added a few other words, but he was working on the mistaken hypothesis that demotic was an alphabetic system of writing. T. Young, a physicist, physician of Cambridge, and an Egyptologist by hobby, made considerable advance on the others. But it is to the French scholar J. F. Champollion that credit is usually given for deciphering the work. A genius who could read Arabic, Syriac, and Coptic at the age of thirteen, and who was made a member of the faculty of the Lycée in Grenoble at seventeen, Champollion determined to solve the riddle of Egyptian hieroglyphs. He applied himself to intensive study of Coptic — a later form of Egyptian written in an alphabet largely borrowed from Greek — and in 1808 started work on the Rosetta Stone. It took him fourteen years, and in 1822 he published the results of his study. He had succeeded partly as a result of comparing the inscription on the Philae Obelisk, which mentioned the names of Ptolemy and Cleopatra (as did the Rosetta Stone), but mostly because he correctly concluded that hieroglyphic writing is a mixture of alphabetic, phonetic, and ideographic symbols. Although Champollion had never visited Egypt up to that time, he was made director of the Egyptian collection in the Louvre and professor of Egyptology at the Collège de France. Before his death at the age of 42 he was privileged to make an expedition to Egypt (1828-1829). His works, *Grammaire Égyptienne* and *Dictionnaire Égyptienne,* published after his death in 1832, served as a foundation for other scholars. The standard work in English today is Gardiner's *Egyptian Grammar* (3rd ed. 1957).

Prior to the decipherment of Egyptian, fantastic explanations of hieroglyphic writings had been made. Even the name "hieroglyph" is a fantasy, for it is composed of the Greek elements *hierós* "sacred," and *glýphein* "carve in stone," suggesting that these inscriptions were some religious or cultic secret. Champollion's work, at first opposed by other scholars, ultimately led to a scientifically acceptable knowledge of Egyptian and placed Egyptological studies on a firm basis.

C. Establishing Chronology. Egyptian history, even today, is almost always related to the system of dynasties established by the priest-historian Manetho. He compiled a list of the kings of Egypt for a history of Egypt which he wrote for Ptolemy I Soter (304-285 B.C.). Manetho had worked from earlier lists similar to those found in the Turin Papyrus and the Palermo Stone. These are fragmentary, and can be augmented by the list of Thutmose III, the list of Seti I, and the Saqqârah list. (See IV.I below.) On the basis of synchronisms it is possible to put approximate dates on some of the kings named, and from data in the king lists, other dates can be calculated; but because of gaps in the lists, coregencies, and other factors, the results are far from satisfactory.

For many years Egyptian scholars worked more or less in isolation, and Egyptian chronology was considerably out of phase with other chronologies of the ancient Near East. The union of Upper and Lower Egypt and the beginning of the 1st Dynasty was formerly dated *ca.*

4200 or *ca.* 4400 B.C. Today scholars generally agree that it should be dated *ca.* 3200 B.C. The later date, established by synchronistic evidence, was confirmed by radiocarbon dating of wood from a roof beam of a first-dynasty tomb at Saqqârah. Tests gave the following dates: 4803 B.P. (before the present) ± 260 (= 3112-2592 B.C.); 4961 B.P. ± 240 (=3250-2770 B.C.). For a discussion of radiocarbon dates, see the general article ARCHEOLOGY VI.

Early in history the Egyptians had developed a calendar of 365 days, consisting of 12 months of 30 days each, plus 5 epagomenal days added at the end of the year. A theory that this was intended to be an agricultural calendar is suggested by the division of the year into three seasons of four months each, called "inundation," "winter," and "summer"; but this theory is not convincing because the Egyptians made no effort to keep the calendar in phase with the seasons until the time of Ptolemy III Euergetes (247-221 B.C.). Because of the importance of the annual inundation of the Nile for agriculture, the Egyptians had also noted from early times that the beginning of the rising of the Nile occurred about the same time as the heliacal rising of the star Sirius (called by the Egyptians Sopde, in Greek Sothis; *see* ASTRONOMY I.A). Accordingly, the festival of "the going up of Sothis" was observed either on the day of the first observation of Sothis or shortly thereafter. Later the divergences between the "going up of Sothis" and the New Year's Day of the civil calendar were noted. Unfortunately, only a very few of these synchronisms have been preserved. The heliacal rising of Sothis occurred on the 16th day of the 8th month of the 7th year of Sesostris III (12th Dynasty). The Roman scholar Censorinus reported that the calendar New Year coincided with the Sothic festival in A.D. 139. Since the divergence is ¼ day per year, other Sothic cycles would have begun at intervals of 1460 (365 times 4) years, i.e., in 1321 B.C. and 2781 B.C. From this a date of 1877 B.C. for the 7th year of Sesostris III can be calculated. (The rising was 226 days out of phase — 30 days for each of the 7 months plus 16 days of the 8th month — and each full day out of phase represents 4 years, so this was 904 years after the beginning of a cycle. Subtracting this from 1321 yields 417 B.C., obviously too late for the 12th Dynasty; so it must be 904 years after 2781 B.C.) Another synchronism is recorded for the 9th day of the 11th month of the 9th year of Amenhotep I (= 1536 B.C.), and for the 28th day of the 11th month of an unspecified year of Thutmose III (= 1469 B.C.). These figures are reasonably satisfactory, but several facts must be borne in mind. First, it is uncertain where the observations of Sothis were made; observations made at Thebes would be slightly different from observations made at Memphis. Second, it is uncertain whether the festival of the "going up of Sothis" occurred on the day of the observation of the heliacal rising or a day or two later. Third, the atmospheric conditions could obscure the faintly visible star, making the observation a day or two late. Furthermore, each day's difference amounts to four years in the calculations. The 7th year of Sesostris III, according to Gardiner (*Egypt of the Pharaohs,* p. 66), is probably 1872, five years later than the figure obtained from the Sothic synchronism, while the 9th year of Amenhotep I is probably 1543, or seven years earlier than the Sothic calculation.

In general, Egyptian chronology is established principally from relative chronology developed from the various king lists, aided by synchronisms. Most significant for our purposes are the synchronisms found in the Amarna correspondence and the treaty between Ramses II and the Hittite king Ḫattusilis III in the 5th month of the 21st year of Ramses' reign. From these data we know that: Ramses II fought with the Hittite king Muršilis II, and made the treaty with his son Ḫattusilis III; the treaty is mentioned in a letter from Ḫattusilis to the Kassite king Kadašman-ḫarbe II; Amenhotep III died very shortly before Kadašman-ḫarbe II; both Amenhotep III and Amenhotep IV (Akhenaten) were contemporaries with Aššur-uballiṭ of Assyria. (The complete data available to us from the king lists are found in Gardiner, *Egypt of the Pharaohs* [1962], pp. 429-453.)

III. Outline of Egyptian History.–For a more complete study see the article on EGYPT. This brief survey is included here so that the pertinent details of Egyptian archeology to be recorded may be quickly placed into historical perspective.

Since the days of Manetho, Egyptian history has been divided into thirty-one dynasties. (A dynasty is generally understood to be a continued reign by members of the same family.) Manetho's 1st Dynasty begins with the union of Upper and Lower Egypt, but obviously this was preceded by a period when Upper and Lower Egypt were not united. Thus, we must preface the dynastic history with a predynastic or prehistoric period — which is what Flinders Petrie accomplished with his Sequence Dating. Also, Manetho's arrangement ends with the conquest of Egypt by Alexander the Great; but for purposes of biblical study the history is extended to Roman times.

A. Predynastic Period (*ca.* 5000-3200 B.C.). In the Lower Pleistocene period the waters of the Mediterranean, which had spread far into the Nile Valley, receded and the water level in the Nile Valley dropped. Periodic pauses in this process left their marks in successively lower gravel terraces along the sides of the valley, beginning at 295 to 148 ft. (90 to 45 m.) above the present level of the Nile River. The first evidence of human presence is found in the 98-foot (30-meter) terrace, and since the remains are Paleolithic they lie beyond our present interest. The Neolithic "revolution" seems to have reached the Nile Valley around 5000 B.C., and Neolithic communities have been discovered at Merimda (Beni Salameh), about 30 mi. (48 km.) NW of Cairo on the edge of the desert, and at Der Tasa and Badari, between Asyut and Akhmim in Upper Egypt. Typical finds are called "Tasian" and "Badarian." At Nagada (Naqada) N of Luxor on the west bank, two types were identified, now called "Amratian" and "Gerzean." That humanity had passed into the Chalcolithic Age is inferred from the presence of copper artifacts among the finds.

A number of small areas, probably controlled by individual clans, were governed by petty rulers. The historian Herodotus called the areas "nomes" and the rulers "nomarchs." At some time prior to the 1st Dynasty the twenty-two nomes of southern Egypt federated to form Upper Egypt, and the twenty nomes of the northern Egypt united to form Lower Egypt. Writing does not yet appear in this period, and our reconstructions are made from low-relief carvings on flat palettes of stone. The introduction of Babylonian influence, according to H. Frankfort and other scholars, is found just before the 1st Dynasty, and a synchronism with the Jemdet-Nasr period of Babylonia is established.

B. Archaic Period (*ca.* 3200-2700 B.C.). Upper and Lower Egypt were united, probably by Narmer (= Menes), although Egyptologists are still debating this problem. Memphis was built and became the capital. Writing was introduced, perhaps from Mesopotamian influence, but it quickly went in an independent direction. Architecture and art were revolutionized.

C. Old Kingdom (*ca.* 2700-*ca.* 2400 B.C.). The 3rd Dynasty, located at Memphis, began the building of

ARCHEOLOGY OF EGYPT

Narmer, wearing white crown of Upper Egypt, subduing prisoner. Slate palette from Hierakonpolis, 1st Dynasty (*ca.* 3000 B.C.) (Egyptian Museum, Cairo)

pyramids, notably the Step Pyramid of Djoser (Zoser), the first large stone building, probably the work of Djoser's architect Imhotep. The 4th Dynasty (*ca.* 2620) included Cheops (Khufu) and Chephren (Khafre), who built the greatest of the pyramids. Art and architecture were formalized; literature developed; campaigns were conducted against Nubia and Libya; trade with Byblos (by sea) was conducted, and some have suggested that Byblos was actually an Egyptian colony. In the minds of some, this was the apogee of Egyptian history.

D. First Intermediate Period (*ca.* 2400-2150 B.C.). The period between the 6th Dynasty and the 11th (or 12th) was a time of decline. The Memphite rule was replaced by rulers in various parts of Egypt, suggesting to some scholars a separation of Upper and Lower Egypts, and Thebes in Upper Egypt rose to prominence.

E. Middle Kingdom (*ca.* 2134 or 1991-1786 B.C.). Scholars divide on the question of where to put the 11th Dynasty. Gardiner, for example, puts it at the close of the 1st Intermediate Period, and W. Stevenson Smith takes it as the beginning of the Middle Kingdom. The 11th Dynasty was located at Thebes in Upper Egypt. Mentuhotep I is credited with reuniting Egypt. The 12th Dynasty was inaugurated by Amenemhet I (1991 B.C.). Thebes continued to be honored, but the second king of the dynasty, Sesostris I, saw the need of establishing a capital midway between Memphis and Thebes. Asiatics came into the Delta. Turquoise mines were worked in the peninsula of Sinai. "Upper Retjenu" extended to Byblos, and relations

Facade of temple dedicated to cult of Ramses II at Abu Simbel. The facade was raised to a cliff site 200 ft. (73 m.) above its original setting to escape flooding upon completion of the Aswan High Dam. (B. K. Condit)

ARCHEOLOGY OF EGYPT

between Egypt and Retjenu were amicable, at least at the beginning. Sesostris III (1878-1843 B.C.), however, traveled to Sekmem, generally identified as Shechem, to overthrow the Asiatics (*'Aamu*), and Egyptian remains have been found at Qatna (N of Homs), Ugarit, and as far as Atçana, not far from the mouth of the Orontes. Certain kinds of art, notably jewelry and cloisonné, reached its highest level, while great literary remains have come down from the Middle Kingdom, including the Story of Sinuhe and the Prophecy of Neferti. Many scholars consider the Middle Kingdom the golden age of Egyptian literature. The visit of Abraham to Egypt is generally placed in this period.

F. Second Intermediate Period (*ca.* 1786-1573 B.C.). A combination of internecine strife and foreign restlessness brought about the end of the glorious Middle Kingdom. The 15th Dynasty, according to Africanus' report of Manetho, consisted of six "Shepherd Kings," generally known as the Hyksos. The 16th and 17th Dynasties also were led by "Shepherd Kings." The combined reigns of the 217 kings of these three dynasties according to Manetho would be 1590 years. But the date of the end of the 12th Dynasty involves the Sothic date (1877; see II.C above); and the founding of the Hyksos capital of Avaris according to the Stele of the Four Hundred was 400 years before a celebration that Seti I offered to the god Seth Nubti, dated *ca.* 1330 B.C., hence 1730 B.C. Therefore, this period must be compressed to about 200 years. The descent of Joseph followed by that of his father and brothers is generally placed in this period.

G. New Kingdom (Empire) (1570-1085 B.C.). Ahmose (1573-1550), the first king of the 18th Dynasty, is credited with driving the foreign rulers from Egyptian soil. Although Josephus connected the Hebrew Exodus from Egypt with this event, this is highly unlikely (*see* EXODUS). Under Amenhotep I, Thutmose I, and Thutmose III, Egypt pushed its frontiers to the Euphrates (into Nahrin of the kingdom of the Mitanni). There were numerous campaigns into Asia and Egyptian remains can be found at many places. The Egyptian capital, however, was at Thebes — an important point to bear in mind when considering the date of the Exodus. Amenhotep IV revolted against the Amon priesthood, changed his name to Akhenaten and located his capital at Akhetaton, known today as Tell el-Amarna. The art of the Amarna age represents a revolution in several areas of Egyptian art. The Amarna Letters tell of great disturbances in Retjenu (Palestine), in which the SA.GAZ or Ḫabiru were prominent; the Egyptian kings seem to have lost interest in their satellite kings in Palestine. One of Akhenaten's successors was Tutankhamen, "King Tut," whose tomb yielded such a fabulously rich collection. The 19th Dynasty was inaugurated by Ramses I (1314-1309), who was succeeded by Seti I (1309-1291). The greatest king, however, was Ramses II (1290-1224), who left colossal monuments over all of Egypt from Abu Simbel on the border of Nubia to Tanis in the Delta. The building of Pithom and Raamses by the Hebrew slaves (Ex. 1:11) is connected by some scholars with the building operations of Ramses II. Of great significance for the date of the Exodus is the fact that Ramses II had a second capital at Avaris. The other kings of the 18th and 19th Dynasties, except for Akhenaten, had their capital at Thebes, 500 mi. (800 km.) to the south. Ramses extended the borders of Egypt southward into Nubia, and claimed victory over the Hittites at Qadesh on the Orontes; but subsequent history indicates that the battle of Qadesh was the end of Ramses' operations in Asia. Merneptah, successor of Ramses II, has left the first known reference to Israel in his stele. The 20th Dynasty (1197-1085 B.C.) is known as the Ramesside Dynasty, for after the first king, Sethnakht,

Mummy and lower part of painted wooden coffin of An-tjau, son of Ankh-Hor and the lady Tjes-Net-peret (*ca.* 7th-6th cent. B.C.) (Royal Ontario Museum, Toronto)

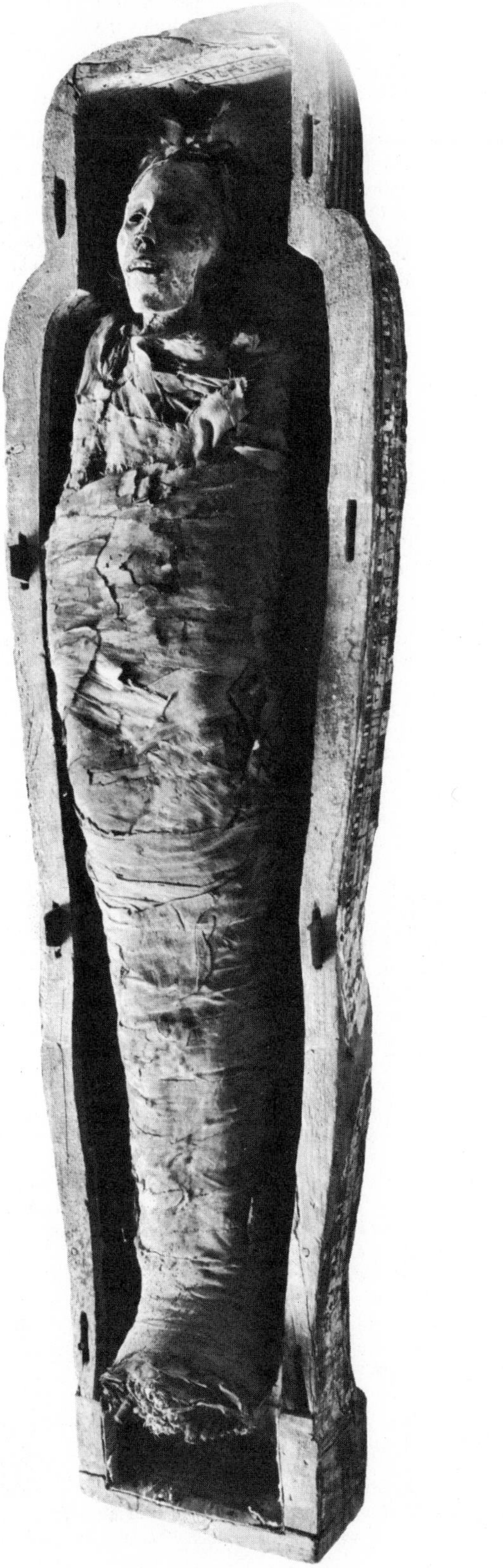

ARCHEOLOGY OF EGYPT

all the kings were named Ramses (III to XI). The great days of Egypt were over.

H. Late Dynastic Period (1085-332 B.C.). The closing period of Egypt's dynastic history is of relative insignificance, from artistic or political viewpoints, but it is in this period that the names of Egyptian pharaohs first come into the biblical account. Sheshonq I (950-930) is generally identified as the pharaoh who gave Gezer as a dowry to Solomon (1 K. 9:16; cf. 11:40). The mummy of Sheshonq was found at Tanis. There is considerable confusion about the chronology of the 22nd to 25th Dynasties, and considerable overlapping must be allowed. Pharaohs of the 25th (Cushite or Ethiopian) Dynasty are mentioned in the biblical account, including So (2 K. 17:4; the identification is very problematic) and Tirhakah (2 K. 19:9; Isa. 37:9). Esarhaddon captured Memphis in 671 and Ashurbanipal sacked Thebes in 663. Neco II of the 26th Dynasty is mentioned in 2 K. 23:29-35 and 2 Ch. 35:20-24; 36:4. Hophra (Jer. 44:30) is identified with Apries (588-568) of the same dynasty. The 27th Dynasty was Persian (Cambyses to Darius II). From the Aramaic papyri discovered in Egypt we know that there was a Jewish colony at Elephantine. With the conquest of Egypt by Alexander the Great, the dynastic history came to an end (332 B.C.).

I. Ptolemaic Period (332-30 B.C.). After the division of Alexander's empire, the Ptolemies (I to XIII) ruled Egypt, followed by Cleopatra VII (44-30 B.C.). The Romans occupied Egypt in 30 B.C.

IV. Archeological Discoveries of Significance for Biblical Studies.–*A. Pyramids*. On the surface, there is no reason to connect the great pyramids (built *ca.* 2600 B.C.) with biblical studies. However, in the 19th cent. fantastic theories were published, and received widespread acceptance, suggesting that the Great Pyramid of Gîzeh (i.e., that of Cheops or Khufu) is the monument mentioned in Isa. 19:19, and that all of its dimensions have significance. Even the date of the Second Coming of Christ was supposedly foretold by these measurements. More recently a Swiss author has suggested that the great pyramids were built by "gods" who visited this planet from outer space. The biblical scholar would do well to study the works by I. E. S. Edwards, *The Pyramids of Egypt* (rev. ed. 1960) and A. Fakhry, *The Pyramids* (1961), and become acquainted with the factual material. The pyramids are truly tremendous monuments of Egyptian architectural and engineering genius. They are tombs of the pharaohs. They are neither charts to foretell the future, nor monuments of the so-called gods from another solar system.

B. Tombs. Except for those who built pyramids, the pharaohs were commonly buried in tombs, many of them in the Valley of the Kings near Luxor. The best known of these is the spectacular tomb of Tutankhamen, discovered by H. Carter in 1922. The evidence of great wealth found in these tombs is impressive, but of little value for biblical studies. More important are the wall decorations, which show many of the details of everyday life in ancient Egypt.

C. Mummies. The Egyptian custom of mummification, preserving the body of the dead king, queen, or person of noble birth, is mentioned in connection with the deaths of Jacob and Joseph (Gen. 50:2f., 26). Because the bodies were so well preserved we have visual access to the mummified persons of kings Seti I, Ramses II, Sheshonq, and others. Thus their historic reality helps make biblical interpretation more vivid.

D. Inscriptions. The exceedingly great number of inscriptions (cf. J. H. Breasted, *Ancient Records of Egypt* [5 vols., 1906-1907]) on walls, stelae, statues, etc., makes it impossible for the biblical scholar to have more than a passing acquaintance with some of them. We have already mentioned several king lists, important for chronology, and the Merneptah stele with the first mention of Israel (*yśrr*; Egyptian has no sign for *l*, so *n* and *r* are often used to represent *l*, and scholarly consensus holds that Israel is intended). A number of inscriptions by "King" Hatshepsut, the woman who ruled Egypt (1490-1468), may be worth studying, particularly because she is sometimes put forth as the "Pharaoh's daughter" who adopted the baby Moses (Ex. 2:3-10), or because the miraculous birth of Hatshepsut is proferred to counteract the effect of biblical miracle stories. *The Seven Lean Years* is an account of seven years of famine which were to be followed by years of plenty according to the promise of the god Khnum. The setting is in the reign of Djoser of the 3rd Dynasty (*ca.* 2700 B.C.), but the inscription is from the Ptolemaic period, around the end of the 2nd cent. B.C. (cf. J. Vandier, *La famine dans l'Égypte ancienne* [1936], pp. 132-39; *ANET*, pp. 31f.). The *Hymn to Aton* is often compared to Ps. 104 (cf. J. H. Breasted, *Dawn of Conscience* [1933], pp. 366-370). It sets forth the "monotheism" of Amenhotep IV (Akhenaten), and deserves careful study in view of extreme claims that have been made both with reference to monotheism and concerning the relationship of this "hymn" to Ps. 104 (cf. N. de G. Davies, *Rock Tombs of El Amarna*, VI [1908], plate XXVII; *ANET*, pp. 369-371). Many other inscriptions of significance for OT studies are readily available in works such as *ANET*, *DOTT*, and Breasted, *Ancient Records of Egypt*.

E. Excavations at Tanis. Because of the Egyptian religious beliefs, buildings for this life (built mostly on the east bank of the Nile) were made of rather temporary materials, while those for the *ka* (the protective genius, the vital force, the true self) and the purified body were made of permanent materials. As a result, little is known of the common buildings. At Tanis, however, we see the remains of buildings or storerooms built of mud brick, some of the bricks bearing the stamp-seal of Ramses II (cf. Ex. 1:14; 5:7f.). The biblical account of the plagues suggests that the Israelites and Moses were located reasonably near the dwelling of Pharaoh (cf. Ex. 7:15). According to one tradition, which claims support from the fact that the nearby river is called Baḥr Yûsûf, "river/sea of Joseph," the Hebrew slaves were in the Faiyûm. But the story of the actual flight of the Hebrews from Egypt (Ex. 13:17-20) seems to require a location in the eastern Delta, and the subsequent events suggest that Pharaoh's forces were stationed nearby (Ex. 14:5-10). The location of Tanis, on the very edge of the fertile region of the eastern Delta, fits these requirements. The pharaohs of the 18th Dynasty (except for the brief Amarna period) had their capital at Thebes. Ramses II and succeeding kings of the 19th and 20th Dynasties had an alternate capital at Avaris. It is remarkable that the name Ramses (Ramesses or Ra'messe) comes into Egyptian history for the first time in the 19th Dynasty, while the name Raamses (Ra'amses) is used in the Exodus account in Ex. 1:11. A few scholars, however, locate Ramses' capital at Qantir, 11 mi. (18 km.) S of Tanis.

F. Hatshepsut. Since Queen Hatshepsut (1490-1468 B.C.), has sometimes been identified as the "Pharaoh's daughter" who took the baby Moses and raised him as her son, some attention may be given to certain details known of her reign. There is some confusion, but it appears that Hatshepsut was the daughter of Thutmose I and the wife of Thutmose II; hence, she had a strong claim to the throne. There was another claimant, a son of Thutmose II by a concubine who reigned as Thutmose III (1490-1436), but who was apparently kept under ward by Hatshepsut for more than twenty years, during which time she reigned as "king," wearing men's clothing and sometimes also the symbolic false beard. Her funerary temple at Deir el-Baḥri is one of the noblest architectural remains in all Egypt. Among other archeological remains is an inscription on the north wall of a portico between the Fourth and Fifth Pylons at Karnak, telling of the queen's miraculous conception and birth. Guides at Karnak have been known to point to this inscription and tell how it records the miraculous finding of her "son," suggesting the Moses story. But there are serious objections to identifying Hatshepsut as Moses' adoptive mother. For one thing, the 18th Dynasty was located at Thebes and had no known building complexes in the eastern Delta. Then there is the matter of chronology: if the Exodus occurred in 1446 B.C. when Moses was 80 years of age (he died forty years later at 120), then he was born in 1526 and became a fugitive *ca.* 1486 — at which time Hatshepsut would have been the reigning "king." It is unlikely that we can apply Ex. 2:15 to Hatshepsut, and it is even less likely that the daughter of Thutmose I would have been bathing in the Nile in the eastern Delta or that the baby Moses would have been placed in a basket among the reeds at Thebes.

G. Papyrus Discoveries. A great many documents written on papyrus have been discovered in Egypt. Some of these are noteworthy for biblical studies. The *Story of Sinuhe* dates from the 20th cent. B.C., and MSS are found from *ca.* 1800 to *ca.* 1000 B.C. It tells of the exile of an Egyptian official, and describes life of that period in Canaan (for the text, see A. M. Blackman, *Middle-Egyptian Stories* [1932], pp. 1-41; *ANET*, pp. 18-22). The *Tale of Two Brothers* is sometimes suggested as the original of the story of Joseph and Potiphar's wife, but without good reasons (cf. A. H. Gardiner, *Late-Egyptian Stories* [1932], pp. 9-29; *ANET*, pp. 23-25). The *Travels of Wen-Amon* tells of a journey by an official of the temple of Amon to Byblos to procure lumber (cedars of Lebanon?), in the 12th or 11th cent. B.C., and furnishes many details of geography and customs in Canaan (cf. Gardiner, *Late-Egyptian Stories*, pp. 61-76; *ANET*, pp. 25-29). The *Wisdom of Ptahhotep* is a compilation of wisdom sayings supposedly from Ptahhotep, the vizier of King Djedkare Isesi (5th Dynasty, *ca.* 2450 B.C.). (Cf. G. Möller, *Hieratische Lesestücke* [2nd ed. 1927], I, 2f.; E. Dévaud, *Les Maximes de Ptah-hotep* [1916]; *ANET,* pp. 412-14.) The early date of this type of literature is particularly significant in view of many claims that wisdom literature came very late to Israel. The *Instruction of Ani* is also a type of the wisdom genre, instructions from a "father" to his "son," dating from the Empire (*ca.* 12th cent. B.C.), although the principal MS is a papyrus of the 21st or 22nd Dynasty (11th-8th cent. B.C.). (Cf. E. Suys, *La sagesse d'Ani* [1935]; *ANET*, pp. 420f.). The *Wisdom of Amenemope* is remarkably like Prov. 22:17–24:22, and the claim has often been made that it is the source of these biblical proverbs (cf. A. Erman, "Eine ägyptische Quelle der 'Sprüche Salomos,' " *Sitzungsberichte der preussischen Akademie der Wissenschaften* [May 1924], pp. 86-93; H. Gressmann, *ZAW*, 42 [1924], 273-296; standard text: H. O. Lange, *Das Weisheitsbuch des Amenemope* [1925]; *ANET*, pp. 421-25). The *Admonitions of Ipuwer* is sometimes described as "prophetic," in the sense that Ipuwer stood before a pharaoh (possibly one of the last rulers of the 16th Dynasty) and placed the blame for deteriorating conditions on the past and present administrations (cf. A. H. Gardiner, *Admonitions of an Egyptian Sage* [1909]; *ANET*, pp. 441-44).

The Aramaic papyri from Elephantine contain various types of documents from the 5th cent. B.C., most of them precisely dated in the Persian period (cf. A. E. Cowley, *Aramaic Papyri of the Fifth Century B.C.* [1923]). For studies of the text of the NT the papyri found at Oxyrhynchus have been very important (cf. G. Maldfeld and B. M. Metzger, *JBL*, 68 [1949], 359-370). The Coptic Gnostic documents discovered at Nag Hammadi in the 1940's were published in the 1970's. They lie just beyond the biblical period, but will be of considerable value in the study of the development of Gnostic and early Christian thought. *See also* PAPYRUS.

H. Amarna Letters. A flood of light was thrown on several problems by the accidental discovery and subsequent publication of the tablets from Tell el-Amarna. They have been helpful for such matters as the synchronizing of Egyptian history with that of the Hittites, Assyrians, and other nations; details of Palestinian political and social conditions in the 15th and 14th cent. B.C.; linguistic fine points (with the aid of Canaanite "glosses" in the Akkadian documents, as well as for dialect studies in Akkadian); treaties both in Hittite and Akkadian; and internal problems in the Egyptian political structure. (*See also* AMARNA TABLETS.)

I. Manetho's List and other King Lists. Egyptian history has long been reconstructed on the basis of a chronicle of Egyptian kings made by Manetho, priest of Heliopolis early in the 3rd cent. B.C. The original work is not extant, but there are edited extracts in the writings of Josephus, and an abridgement, somewhat garbled, in the works of Sextus Julius Africanus (early 3rd cent. A.D.) and Eusebius (early 4th cent. A.D.), edited by Syncellus *ca.* A.D. 800. This work is now supplemented by other discoveries. The Turin Papyrus, a hieratic papyrus from the early 13th cent. B.C., agrees closely with Manetho's list for the first six dynasties, but after the 12th Dynasty it adds many names, some of which are "of so fantastic an appearance that they are unlikely to have belonged to any real kings" (Gardiner). The Table of Abydos is a list of kings inscribed on the walls of the temple at Abydos, in which Seti I (1309-1291) and his son Ramses are making offerings to seventy-six of their ancestors. The Table of Saqqârah originally had the cartouches of fifty-seven kings honored by Ramses II, but, because of damage to the wall, only about fifty can now be read. In the great temple of Karnak, the Table of Karnak contained sixty-one names, of which forty-eight were legible when the table was discovered in 1825. The names of the kings in this list are not given in order, hence certain names that were omitted in the other lists cannot be inserted with any assurance.

Bibliography.–W. M. F. Petrie, *Seventy Years in Archaeology* (1931); S. R. K. Glanville, *Growth and Nature of Egyptology* (1947); E. Drioton and J. Vandier, *L'Égypte* (*Les Peuples de l'Orient mediterranéen*, II; 3rd ed. 1952); J. A. Thompson, *Bible and Archaeology* (rev. ed. 1972), pp. 37-75; W. S. Smith, *Art and Architecture of Ancient Egypt* (1958); I. E. S. Edwards, *The Pyramids of Egypt* (rev. ed. 1960); J. Vandier, *Manuel d'archéologie égyptienne* (2 vols., 1952-1955); H. E. Winlock, *Models of Daily Life in Ancient Egypt* (1955); *CAH* (3rd ed.; I.1.2, II.1.2).

W. S. LASOR

ARCHEOLOGY OF GREECE AND ROME. Before the 19th cent. neither Greece nor Italy was in a position to preserve or to investigate adequately her past. Greece did not win formal independence from the Ottoman empire until 1832, and Italy did not become a fully united power with Rome as capital until 1870. Before these pivotal dates ancient structures often were valued only as quarries for building material, and clandestine hunts for museum pieces frequently passed for archeological investigations. When an opportunity to begin archeological projects did exist, neither government found itself with sufficient funds or qualified personnel. So, at least in the early days, these

ARCHEOLOGY OF GREECE AND ROME

governments turned to foreign help. Now, however, highly qualified archeologists of both countries are in the field. Nationals now conduct most archeological work in Italy, but in Greece important projects remain in the hands of foreign teams.

I. Greece
  A. History of Greek Archeology
  B. Sites of Biblical Significance
    1. Amphipolis
    2. Athens
    3. Corinth
    4. Cenchreae
    5. Philippi
    6. Delphi
    7. Eleusis
II. Roman Italy
  A. Rome
    1. Palatine
    2. Forum
    3. Nero's Golden House
    4. Mausoleum of Augustus
    5. Tomb of Peter
  B. Pompeii
  C. Ostia

***I. Greece.**–A. History of Greek Archeology.* Soon after Greek independence, interest was kindled in antiquities of that country. The Greek Archaeological Society was founded in 1836, the French in 1846, the German in 1874, the American in 1882, the British in 1886, the Austrian in 1898, the Italian in 1909, and the Swedish after World War II.

Even before these schools went into action, some individual efforts were begun. But Greek archeology did not develop effectively until the last decades of the 19th cent. and did not come to full flower until the 20th century. To a real extent the story of Greek archeology began not in Greece but in Asia Minor; the two areas are linked in what is called Aegean archeology. H. Schliemann's successes at Troy, beginning in 1870, led him to work at Mycenae on mainland Greece. There in 1876 he announced that he had found the remains of Agamemnon. Actually he had uncovered Grave Circle A, with its magnificent collection of Mycenaean gold objects. He also worked at the nearby Mycenaean center of Tiryns.

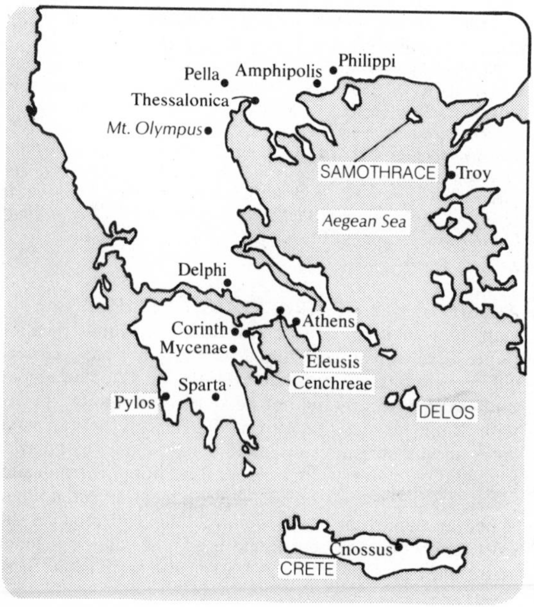

Meanwhile, three other important excavations were launched in the Greek world. In 1872 on the Aegean island of Delos the French school began a dig that has continued intermittently until the present. At Olympia, beginning in 1874, the Germans launched a project that brought the ancient center back to life. Simultaneously the Austrians were digging on the island of Samothrace. The Germans and Austrians introduced a discipline and scientific spirit to Greek archeology that was to affect not only that field but others of the Mediterranean and Near East as well.

In the 1880's and 1890's extended excavations were launched in several parts of Greece. Greek archeologists D. Filios and A. Skias excavated the site of the Eleusinian Mysteries (1882-1910). Greek archeologists dug the whole Athenian acropolis area down to bedrock (1884-1891); C. Tsountas initiated a major dig for the Greek Archaeological Society at Mycenae (1884-1903). The Society also excavated the temple of Zeus in Athens (1886-1901). Three extensive campaigns began in the 1890's. In 1890 the Greek Archaeological Society began a dig at the Roman market in Athens that continued intermittently until 1931, the French School uncovered much of the site of Delphi (1892-1903), and in 1896 the American School of Classical Studies began the massive task of uncovering ancient Corinth, where they have continued to work.

During the 20th cent. Greek archeology has continued to improve. Archeological technique has been extensively refined. Minoan culture has been discovered and the knowledge of it amplified with continuing exploration. Numerous excavations have increased the knowledge of previously known Mycenaean culture. Work at Corinth has gone forward steadily, and the Athenian Agora has been almost completely uncovered. Sparta has been extensively studied, as has Philippi. Interesting work has been done at Pella, birthplace of Alexander the Great.

Lion Gate, entrance to citadel of Mycenae. The stress-relieving triangle above the lintel is the oldest monumental sculpture in Europe. Late Helladic IIIb (*ca.* 1250 B.C.) (B. K. Condit)

ARCHEOLOGY OF GREECE AND ROME

It is not germane to biblical study to note numerous other digs relating to classical or early Hellenic periods.

Comments on Minoan and Mycenaean cultures of the Aegean area do deserve mention, however, because artifacts produced by these two cultures are found in excavations throughout the eastern Mediterranean world, and have significance for biblical studies. Moreover, if one is to accept the commonly held view that Crete is Caphtor (home of the Philistines) and that the Philistines are somehow connected with Mycenaean developments, it is necessary to give attention to early Aegean archeology.

Foremost in Minoan studies was A. Evans, who worked at Knossos in northern Crete from 1900 until his death in 1941, and uncovered the site that first revealed Minoan culture. J. Evans (1958-1961) and S. Hood 1960-1961) led subsequent British excavations at Knossos. L. Pernier began an extended Italian School dig at the Cretan palace of Phaistos in the south of Crete beginning in 1900. Late in the 1950's and the 1960's the Italians returned to Phaistos under the leadership of D. Levi. Several other Minoan sites have been investigated.

Meanwhile, considerable work has been done on Mycenaean sites. At Mycenae itself Greek expeditions conducted excavations before World War I and A. J. B. Wace worked there between the wars and from 1950 to 1955; since 1963 excavation there has been entrusted to G. Mylonas. Nearby Tiryns drew the attention of W. Dorpfeld before World War I and K. Müller after the war. In 1939 C. Blegen found at Pylos what he identified as the palace of Nestor; he returned in 1952 for extended excavations at the site. Discoveries at numerous sites of tablets written in an early Greek script known as Linear B provided M. Ventris with materials on which he based a successful decipherment in 1952.

In addition to the extensive attention to Minoan and Mycenaean sites in this century, and the continuing projects already noted at places like Corinth, Athens, and Delos, numerous other significant excavations have been carried on in Greece. For example, the British School excavated at Sparta (1906-1910, 1924-1929), the French School at Philippi (1914-1938), Greek archeologists at Eleusis (1919-1932), the American School of Classical Studies on the north slope of the Athenian Acropolis (1931-1939), the American School in the Athenian Agora (1931-1940, since 1946), the Germans at Olympia since World War II, the American School at the Isthmus of Corinth (since 1952), and the Greek Archaeological Service at Pella (since 1957).

B. Sites of Biblical Significance. Nine Greek cities are mentioned in the NT in connection with the ministry of Paul and his companions. Four have undergone no organized excavation (Apollonia, Beroea, Neapolis, and Thessalonica) and hence receive no comment here. The other five (Amphipolis, Athens, Corinth, Cenchreae, and Philippi) are noted briefly; more extensive comments appear in the separate articles in this encyclopedia. In addition, since excavations at Eleusis and Delphi have significance for the religious development of Greece, they require attention here.

1. Amphipolis. Paul's first stop on the road from Philippi to Thessalonica was AMPHIPOLIS, about 30 mi. (50 km.) SW of Philippi. The Greek Archaeological Service excavated S of the acropolis of Amphipolis in 1920, uncovering the foundations of an early Christian basilica and the "Lion of Amphipolis," a stone sculpture (4th cent. B.C.) commemorating a victory. The lion has been properly mounted once more along the highway. The excavators also worked in the necropolis, about one mi. NW of the ancient town. There has not been a detailed archeological survey of the site, however.

2. Athens. ATHENS was still the great cultural center of Greece in NT times, though political prominence had passed to such cities as Corinth and Thessalonica. Much of the archeological effort in Athens has significance for

Classical Doric limestone temple "of Poseidon" (actually dedicated to Hera) at the Greek colony Posidonia (Paestum) in Italy (5th cent. B.C.) (B. K. Condit)

ARCHEOLOGY OF GREECE AND ROME

NT study. The hub of Athenian life was the *agora* (marketplace), and there Paul reasoned daily with prospective converts (Acts 17:17). The American School of Classical Studies worked in the agora from 1931 to 1940 and from 1946 to 1960, and is now engaged in a campaign to complete excavation of the north end. The task has been prodigious, involving the removal of over 250,000 tons of earth and the discovery of about 68,000 objects in addition to 94,000 coins. The archeologists rebuilt the magnificent Stoa of Attalos (385 by 64 ft. [117 by 19.5 m.]) as the Agora Museum.

A few hundred feet E of the Greek agora lay the Roman market (forum), which housed wine and oil shops and which was dominated by the tower of the winds (a hydraulic clock). The Greek Archaeological Society undertook excavation of this area in 1890 and carried on intermittently until 1931.

From 1884 to 1891 Greek archeologists examined the entire Acropolis area down to bedrock. The Greek Archaeological Society also excavated the remains of the Odeion of Pericles in the 1920's. Several German scholars studied the theater of Dionysus. The American School of Classical Studies excavated the north slope of the Acropolis from 1931 to 1939 under the direction of O. Broneer. The great temple of Zeus, unfinished when Paul visited Athens, was excavated by the Greek Archaeological Society between 1886 and 1901, and by the German School in 1922-1923.

3. Corinth. Because the apostle Paul spent eighteen months ministering at CORINTH (second only to Ephesus, where he stayed more than two years), the site holds special interest for biblical studies. The American School of Classical Studies began to excavate there in 1896 and has continued, except during war years.

The city and its acropolis were enclosed by a wall over 6 mi. (10 km.) long. Inside the city the agora (700 by 300 ft. [215 by 90 m.]), the Odeion (music hall), the theater, and the Asklepion (health center) have been excavated.

About 6 mi. (10 km.) E of Corinth at the Isthmus of Corinth was a sanctuary of Poseidon where games were held in honor of that god every two years. The American School of Classical Studies has been making annual digs there since 1952. They have excavated the temple of Poseidon, the 650-foot (200-meter) stadium, the theater, and an impressive propylaeum to the sanctuary with adjacent structures. Roman baths also have come to light there.

4. Cenchreae. CENCHREAE (Acts 18:18), the eastern port of Corinth, lay on the Saronic Gulf and so handled the city's Aegean and Asian trade. In 1963 and 1964 R. L. Scranton led a joint University of Chicago and Indiana University expedition there and worked on some remains at the water's edge, which were once thought to be a church but seem instead to have been a center of Isis worship later used as a warehouse.

5. Philippi. PHILIPPI stood inland, some 10 mi. (16 km.) NW of Neapolis (its port). The French School at Athens worked at the site from 1914 to 1936, and the Greek Archaeological Service has been active there since World War II. While important beginnings have been made, much remains to be excavated at Philippi. As usual, attention has focused on a limited number of major structures in the middle of the town (such as the agora). The agora, center of Greek life, where the mob scene took place and accusations were leveled against Paul and Silas (Acts 16:19f.), is a large rectangular area 300 ft. (90 m.) long and 150 ft. (45 m.) wide.

The success of the gospel at Philippi is evident from the imposing ruins of great churches. At the south side of the agora stand the remains of a sixth-century church known as Basilica B. North of the agora lie the ruins of a large fifth-century church known as Basilica A. East of the agora in an area of more recent excavation may be seen the remains of another fifth-century church flanked by a third-century bath. Over 1000 ft. (300 m.) above the town towers the acropolis of Philippi. On its eastern slope are the well-preserved remains of a Greek theater built in the 4th cent. B.C., and nearby was a temple to Egyptian gods constructed early in the 1st cent. A.D.

6. Delphi. The oracle at Delphi, about 100 mi. (160 km.) NW of Athens, was significant in the ancient world from the 2nd millennium B.C. to the end of the 4th cent. A.D. There the Pythian Games took place, in honor of Apollo. The first private excavations at Delphi were made by a British officer, W. M. Leake, in 1806. He was followed by five others in a private capacity and by brief expeditions of the French School of Archaeology in Athens. The French School carried on the definitive campaign there from 1892 to 1903 and again in 1920.

The total results of all efforts have been impressive. There is the great hillside enclosure of Apollo, with its sacred way angling up to the temple itself past treasuries of various city-states designed to house votive offerings. Adjacent to the temple is a well-preserved theater and a magnificent stadium, both seated in stone. At a lower level may be seen a gymnasium with two racecourses and baths.

7. Eleusis. The site of Eleusis, 14 mi. (23 km.) W of Athens, is particularly interesting because here it is possible to see the center of operations of a mystery religion. After brief earlier excavations, Filios and Skias made real progress in uncovering the sacred complex (1882-1910). K. Kuruniotis took over leadership of the dig from 1919 to 1932. The sanctuary on the east slope of the acropolis was surrounded by a wall with a massive entrance propylaeum. Inside the gateway the marble sacred way ascended the hill past sanctuaries of Pluto (god of the underworld) and Demeter (goddess of the mysteries) to the large initiation room (56 by 59 yds., 51 by 54 m.). *See* RELIGIONS OF THE BIBLICAL WORLD: GRECO-ROMAN.

II. Roman Italy.–Although Italy is important for biblical studies, few of its cities are mentioned in Scripture. Only PUTEOLI, FORUM OF APPIUS, THREE TAVERNS, and ROME appear as stops on Paul's Italian itinerary; and of these sites archeological work of note has been done only in Rome. Therefore, limitations of space and orientation of interest seem to dictate omission here of a survey of the history of Italian archeology with its heavy emphasis on Etruscan and Roman themes that have no real bearing on Scripture. Attention is focused instead on the city of Rome and only on those structures that Paul may have known or that may have been significant when he was there, with supplementary comments on Pompeii and Ostia as cities where one may learn something of life during NT times.

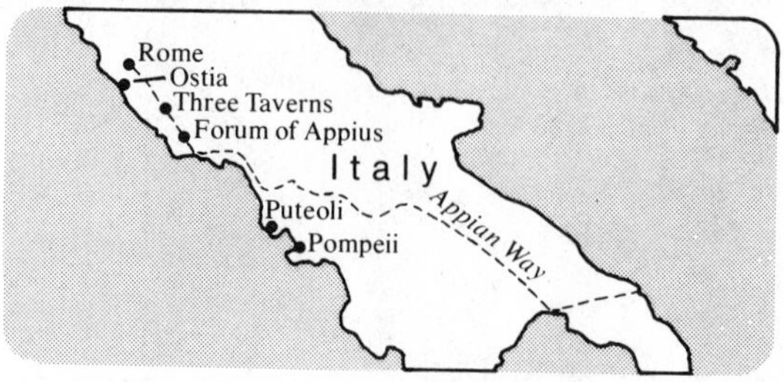

A. Rome. As Paul walked up the Appian Way and entered the city of Rome, he undoubtedly passed the Palatine Hill with its palaces of the Caesars. He may

ARCHEOLOGY OF GREECE AND ROME

have been arraigned before Nero in the Forum, possibly in the Basilica Julia; and he may have been imprisoned in the Mamertine Prison, near the west end of the Forum. Nero's Golden House was largely completed by the time of Paul's martyrdom; and the Mausoleum of Augustus was an important monument of the city at that time. Moreover, there is the persistent tradition that Peter was buried in the Vaticanus section of Rome during Nero's persecution; and the Roman Church claims that his tomb is under the high altar of St. Peter's Cathedral.

1. Palatine. Systematic excavations on the Palatine began about 1724 under the auspices of Francis I of Parma, who concentrated on the area of the official palace of Domitian (who sent the apostle John to Patmos). About a half century later the French abbot Rancoureuil worked on Domitian's residential palace. After sporadic excavations during the first half of the 19th cent., in 1860 Napoleon III launched a campaign under the direction of P. Rosa, who explored the palace of Tiberius Caesar beneath the Farnese gardens. After the Italian State took over Rome in 1870, Rosa continued to dig on the Palatine and excavated, among other things, the stadium of Domitian. Italian excavators have been busy on the Palatine during most of this century, but especially noteworthy has been the work of A. Bartoli, who worked there during most of the period between World Wars I and II and uncovered and studied the whole residential palace of Domitian.

2. Forum. Archeological investigation in the Forum took its first feeble steps in 1788 when the Swedish ambassador in Rome excavated there briefly. C. Fea became Commissioner for Roman Antiquities in 1803, and conducted work there for over thirty years. The government of the Roman Republic prepared an extensive plan of excavation which the papacy continued. After the new government of Italy obtained Rome for its capital in 1870, a new phase in excavation of the Forum began. P. Rosa supervised the work until 1885. G. Boni directed the excavations from 1898 to 1925 and began the practice of excavating down to bedrock. He was followed by A. Bartoli. Work has continued at the Forum since World War II.

As the hub of Roman life, the Forum became altogether too small with the growth of the empire. Adjacent to it Julius Caesar added his own forum, as did Augustus and Nerva and Trajan. C. Ricci won permission from Mussolini in 1924 to excavate these forums and uncovered them all by 1932.

3. Nero's Golden House. When Nero's palace went up in flames during the fire of Rome in A.D. 64, he determined to build a massive new palace complex across the whole center of Rome, with a total area of 125 acres (50 hectares), including the palace, parks, groves, and a lake. Archeologists have been working on the site since 1906, when the German F. Weege squeezed his way through a hole in the wall of the baths of Trajan and began to explore Nero's palace on the Oppian Hill. Thus far eighty-eight rooms have been cleared.

4. Mausoleum of Augustus. Begun in 28 B.C. in northwestern Rome, this imperial tomb was to resemble an Etruscan burial mound. It had a core of concrete covered with soil and planted with cypress trees, and was surmounted with a statue of Augustus. By the time Paul came to Rome, Augustus, Caligula, and Claudius had been buried there, and Vespasian and Nerva would follow. Italian excavators stripped the soil from the concrete core in 1935 and thoroughly investigated the structure.

5. Tomb of St. Peter. Excavations were conducted under St. Peter's Basilica from 1940 to 1949 and again in 1953. What was found has led to considerable debate, with the Roman Church taking the stand that the bones of Peter were found, though others are not so certain of this identification. G. F. Snyder has written an excellent survey of the situation in *BA*, 32 (1969), 2-24.

Appian Way, oldest Roman road (built in 312 B.C.), from Rome to Campania and southern Italy. Monuments and inscriptions flank the first few miles outside Rome. (B. K. Condit)

Ruins of the Roman Forum with a portion of the preserved temple of Saturn in the foreground (B. K. Condit)

Interior of Colosseum, the Amphitheater of Flavius (begun in A.D. 75). Below the arena floor are remains of chambers for human and animal participants. (A. C. Myers)

B. Pompeii. Because life in this city was frozen in action, the study of Pompeii offers a glimpse of what life was like in a typical Roman city of the NT period. Food was deserted as it was cooking on the stove, dishes were left in the pantry, and furniture was left in place throughout the house when Mt. Vesuvius erupted in A.D. 79, destroying the city and burying it to a depth of 19 to 23 ft. (6 to 7 m.) with volcanic ash. Probably about two thousand perished of its population of twenty thousand.

Excavations began at Pompeii in 1748 on a more or less exploratory basis. Between 1806 and 1832 most of the public buildings of the forum and several important private structures were excavated. Systematic, house-by-house excavation began in 1860 under the direction of G. Fiorelli and has continued sporadically to the present. Now some three-fifths of this city of 161 acres (65 hectares) has been uncovered.

C. Ostia. Ostia, the great port of Rome, did not die all at once like Pompeii but gradually declined until its end *ca.* A.D. 500. Therefore it does not offer the same insights on first-century life that Pompeii does; but many of its structures originated in the 1st cent., and a study of the place is useful for biblical backgrounds.

Of some 160 acres (65 hectares) of Ostia, about half have now been excavated. During the last years of the 19th cent. Pius VII and Pius IX began excavations at Ostia. The first systematic excavations began only in 1909 and have been continued by the Italian Government with few interruptions. Especially fruitful campaigns were led by G. Calza (1938-1942) and P. Romanelli (1950-1953). Today if one walks down the streets of Pompeii and Ostia it is possible to imagine life there as it must have been during NT times.

Bibliography.–G. Calza and G. Becatti, *Ostia* (1965); O. Cullmann, *Peter* (Eng. tr. 1962); M. Grant, *Cities of Vesuvius* (1971); M. Guardicci, *Tomb of St. Peter* (1960); E. Kirschbaum, *Tombs of St. Peter and St. Paul* (1959); P. MacKendrick, *The Greek Stones Speak* (1962); *The Mute Stones Speak* (1960); P. Romanelli, *The Palatine* (1956); *Roman Forum* (1959); E. Yamauchi, *Greece and Babylon* (1967).

H. F. VOS

ARCHEOLOGY OF IRAN. Archeological work in Iran goes back to the early part of the 19th century. In 1835 H. C. Rawlinson discovered the large inscription of Darius I on the side of the cliff at Behistun. This inscription, written in three languages (Old Persian, Akkadian, and Elamite), gave scholars the key to unlock the mysteries of Akkadian cuneiform script (*see* ARCHEOLOGY OF MESOPOTAMIA II).

In 1851 another Englishman, W. K. Loftus, did some digging at Susa and salvaged a large number of figurines. More scientific field research was undertaken by the French expedition to Susa in 1884, led by M. Dieulafoy, which excavated the acropolis and unearthed the Archer Frieze. Under the direction of J. de Morgan the famous diorite stele of the Code of Hammurabi was discovered at Susa in 1901-1902. R. de Mocquenem was director from 1912 to 1939. R. Ghirshman became supervisor in 1946, and the work has continued since that time. Excavations have disclosed that SUSA was occupied for over five thousand years, from 4000 B.C. to A.D. 1200. During the Persian period Susa shared with Ctesiphon, Ecbatana, and Persepolis the honor of being a royal capital.

Susa and Ecbatana have special interest for biblical studies. At Susa Nehemiah served as cupbearer to Artaxerxes I (Neh. 1:1, 12; 2:1), and Esther lived with her cousin Mordecai and was chosen queen by Ahasuerus (Xerxes I) (Est. 2:5-8). At ECBATANA Darius I found a scroll which

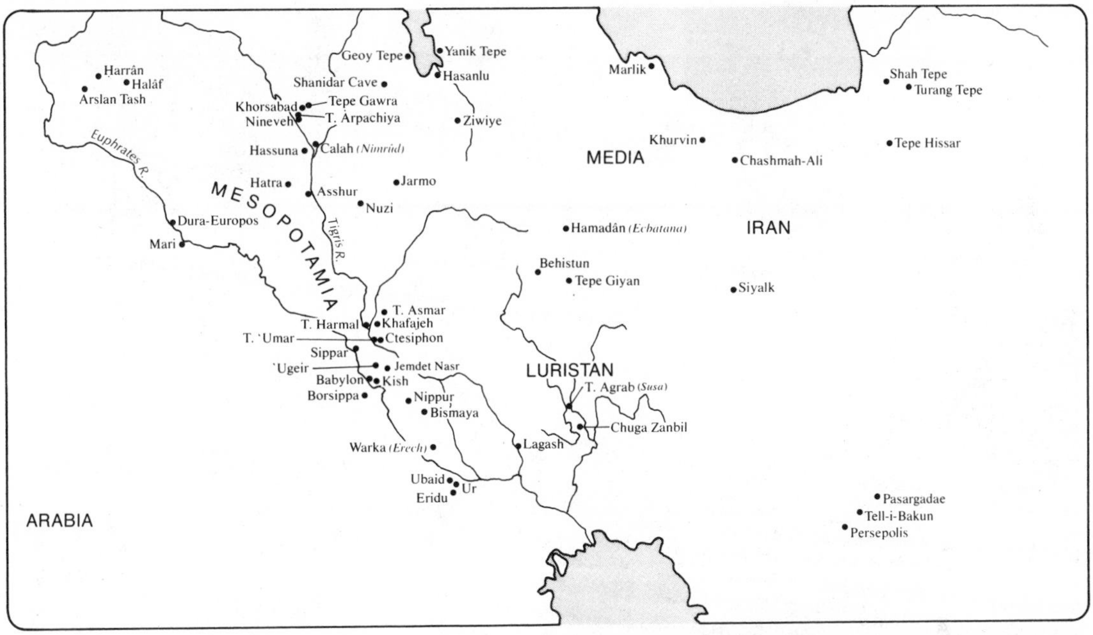

contained the decree of Cyrus authorizing the return of the Jews to Jerusalem and the rebuilding of the temple (Ezra 6:2). Ecbatana is mentioned several times in the apocryphal literature. Arphaxad is portrayed as king over the Medes in Ecbatana (Jth. 1:1-14). According to 2 Macc. 9:3 Antiochus Epiphanes stopped at Ecbatana on his retreat from Persepolis. At Ecbatana Tobias met and married Sarah, Raguel's daughter (Tob. 7–8).

Completely scientific expeditions in Iran date from 1931 and are attributed mainly to R. Ghirshman and G. Contenau, who worked at Tepe Giyan. This site, together with excavations at Tepe Siyalk in 1933, made possible the establishment of a relative chronology for the prehistoric levels in western Iran. In the 1930's excavations were carried out at Tureng Tepe, Tepe Hissar Damghan, Shah Tepe, Jamshidi, Chashmah-Ali, Surkh Dum, Chuga Zambil, and Persepolis. World War II interrupted the work. Several expeditions have been undertaken since 1946, investigating such major sites as Susa, Hasanlu (where a gold bowl and a silver and electrum cup have been recovered), Ziwiyeh (which yielded a group of gold and ivory objects in a bronze sarcophagus), the necropolis of Khurwin, Tell-i-Bakun, Tureng Tepe, Marlik at Rudbar, and British expeditions at Geoy Tepe, Yanik Tepe, Yarim Tepe, and Pasargadae.

The only written records from before the Achaemenid period found in Iran are proto-Elamite tablets discovered at Susa and Siyalk. Most of our knowledge of Iran during the 3rd and 2nd millennia B.C. has to do with the Elamites, but much of the available information about their political and military history comes from foreign sources: the cuneiform material from Mesopotamia. The archeologist is dependent on pottery and other human remains to reconstruct the history of pre-Achaemenid Iran. The beautiful painted pottery, architecture, and art give evidence of a highly developed culture.

Thousands of bronze objects have come from Luristan, where a peasant's discovery of a tomb while plowing a field in 1928 set off a rash of unsupervised excavations, mainly by peasants. These bronze pieces include weapons (daggers, swords, arrowheads, lances, and axes), personal ornaments (bracelets, earrings, necklaces, pins, and buckles), and equipment for horses (harnesses, bits, and rein-stalls).

Rock-cut tombs of Darius I and Artaxerxes I at Naqsh-i-Rustam (Oriental Institute, University of Chicago)

This material has been dated to anywhere between 2000 and 600 B.C. Additional information from supervised digs is necessary to clear up the vexing problem of date.

Architecture in ancient Iran reached its zenith during the Achaemenid period. A good example is PERSEPOLIS, at a site probably chosen by Cyrus, but built by Darius I,

ARCHEOLOGY OF IRAN

Eastern stairway of Apadana (audience hall) at Persepolis, with relief showing Susian and Persian guards (*ca.* 485 B.C.) (Oriental Institute, University of Chicago) *See also* Plate 1.

Persepolis, an Achaemenean capital, with Apadana of Darius I (left) and palace (center) and harem (reconstructed, right) of Xerxes I (University Museum, University of Pennsylvania)

Plate 1. Apadana (audience hall) at Persepolis, begun by Darius I. Seventy-two columns once supported the roof of the chamber, which covered nearly thirty thousand sq. ft. (2800 sq. m.). (Oriental Institute, University of Chicago)

Plate 2. Alabaster-and-gold votive figurine from Nippur (*ca.* 2800 B.C.). Sumerian worshipers left such figures at temples to pray to the gods in their absence. (Oriental Institute, University of Chicago)

Plate 3. Bronze model of the ritual of the dawn (*ṣît šamši*), including representations of stepped temples, altars of sacrifice, and libation bowls. One figure extends his hands while the other holds purification water for the ablution. (Susa, 12th cent. B.C.) (Louvre; photo Éditions "TEL," Paris)

Plate 4. Winged bull, relief from Susa (5th-4th cents. B.C.). The ancient Mesopotamian art of enameled brick was revived by the Achaemenean kings in decorating their luxurious palaces. (Louvre)

Plate 5. Gold plate deposited by Darius I in the foundation box of the Persepolis apadana. It records in Old Persian, Elamite, and Old Babylonian the boundaries of the Persian empire — "from the Saka beyond Sogdiana to Ethiopia, from India to Sardis." (W. S. LaSor)

Plate 6. Ishtar Gate and Procession Way at Babylon, *ca.* 605-562 B.C. (painting by M. Bardin, based on reconstruction by E. Unger) (Oriental Institute, University of Chicago)

Plate 7. Ceiling of the Great Hypostyle Hall in the temple of Amon-Re at Karnak, with inscriptions bearing royal titulary. Numerous additions to the twelfth-dynasty (*ca.* 2000 B.C.) shrine of a then obscure local deity make the temple a showcase for nearly twenty centuries of architecture. (A. C. Myers)

Plate 8. Mock tomb of a lower middle class Egyptian family of the 18th Dynasty (*ca.* 1350 B.C.) from the cemetery at Deir el-Medina, western Thebes. Included are coffins of a man, woman, and infant child, canopic equipment, and funerary offerings. (Royal Ontario Museum, Toronto)

Plate 9. Samples of pigment used by ancient Egyptians to impart color. Blue (top and center): frit made by heating copper compound with powdered quartz, limestone, and natron; black: charcoal; green: artificial frit from malachite; red (bottom): red ochre; white: carbonate of lime. The medium for these pigments was water with size, gum, or eggwhite. (Royal Ontario Museum, Toronto)

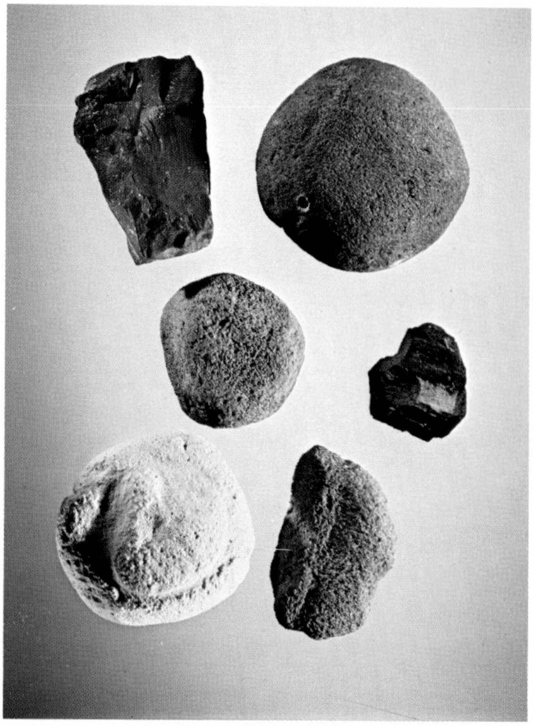

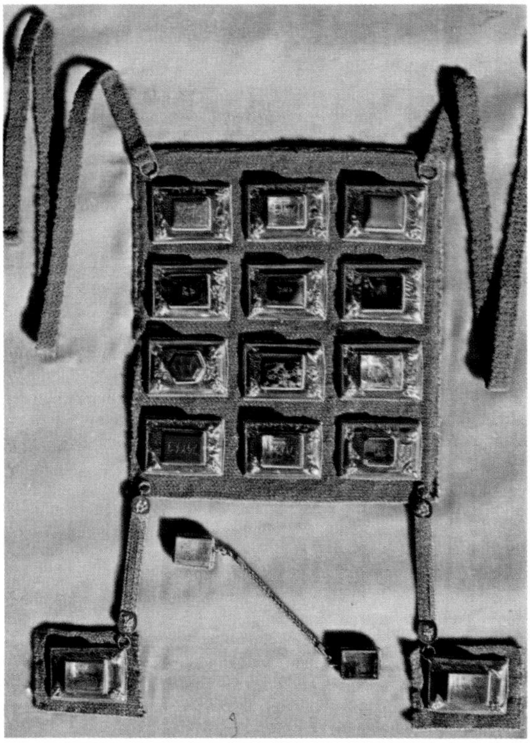

Plate 10. Replica of Aaron's breastplate in gold and precious stones representing the twelve tribes (cf. Ex. 28, 39) (American Baptist Assembly, Green Lake, Wisconsin)

Plate 12. Jordan Valley, north-south rift from the Beqaʿ (top) to the Wâdī el-ʾArabah (bottom). Multi-spectral image, composite of three photos from satellite Landsat-1, 1973. (NASA)

Plate 11. Gold glass bowl of a style found in the eastern Mediterranean region in the late 3rd-2nd cents. B.C. (Corning Museum of Glass)

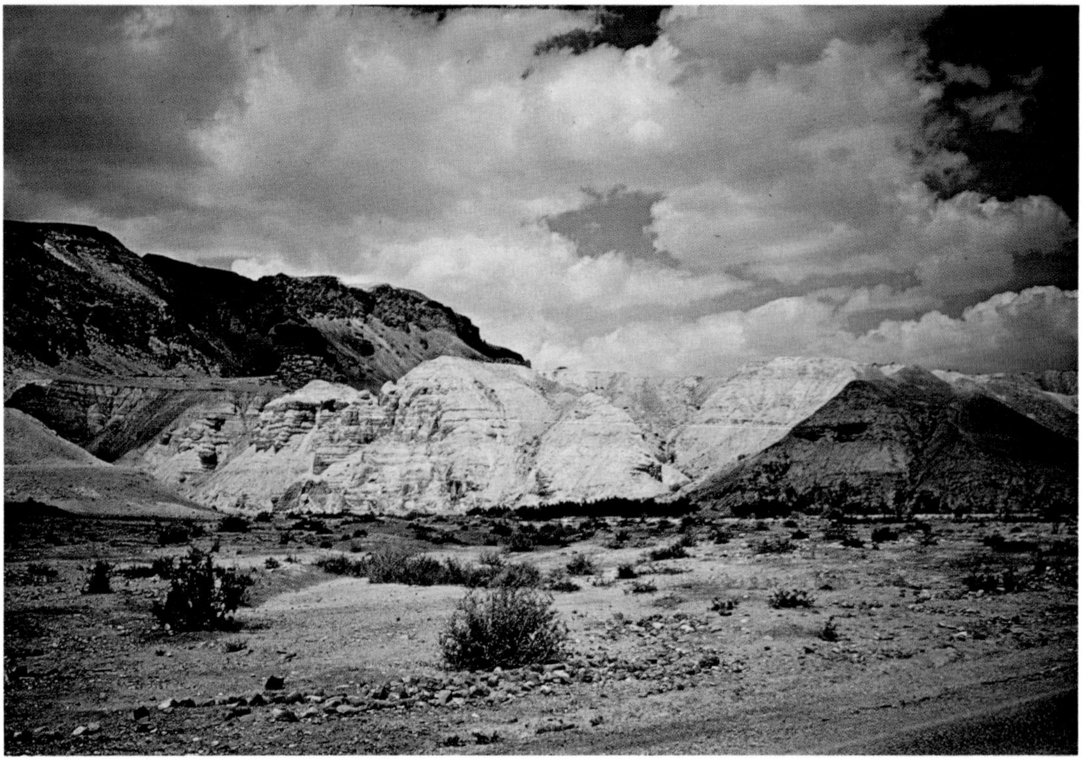

Plate 13. Wâdī Qumrân from the southeast. Towering above are the plateau of Khirbet Qumrân and the cliffs with the caves where the scrolls were discovered. (J. C. Trever)

Plate 14. Fragment of the Fouad papyri, oldest Greek text of Deuteronomy (2nd cent. B.C.), using Hebrew letters for the name Yahweh (Courtesy Société Egyptienne de Papyrologie. From *The Interpreter's Bible*, vol. 12; copyright 1957, Abingdon Press; used by permission)

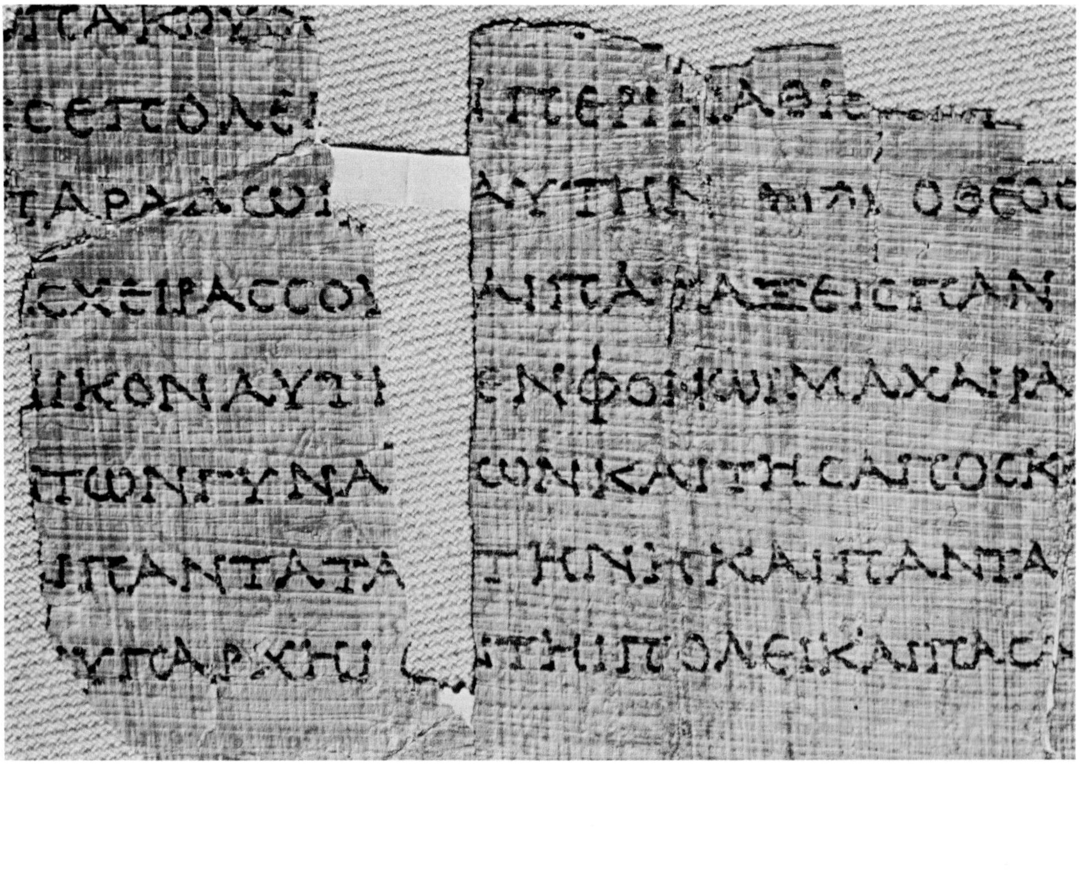

Plate 15. Qumrân caves 4 and 5, which contained more than forty thousand fragments of biblical, pseudepigraphal, and sectarian documents (W. S. LaSor)

Plate 16. Col. 10 of the Habbakuk commentary (1QpHab), which quotes and interprets Hab. 2:13f. Archaic script in lines 7 and 14 distinguishes Yahweh (*YHWH*) as a sacred name. (J. C. Trever, copyright 1964)

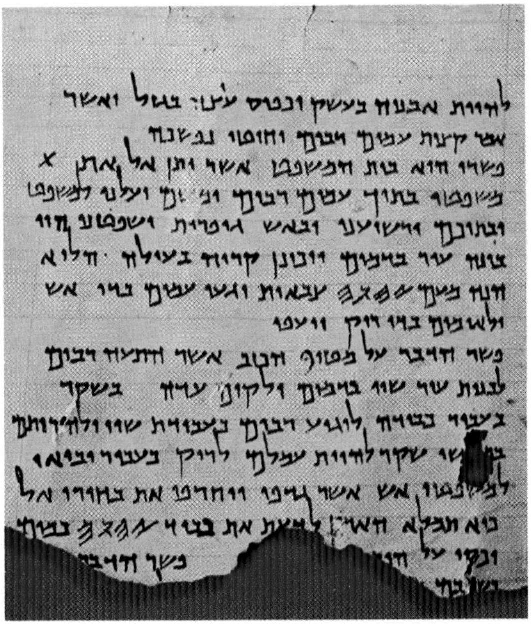

Plate 17. Fragments of the Dead Sea Scrolls (nonbiblical Hebrew text), jar, and linens used to wrap scrolls (Oriental Institute, University of Chicago)

Plate 18. Remains of defenses and public buildings overlooking the harbor at Assos on the Gulf of Adramyttium. Paul walked the 20 mi. (32 km.) from Troas, while his companions sailed round Cape Lectum (Acts 20:13f.). (D. H. Condit)

Plate 19. Shepherds' field at Bethlehem, with Tell Herodium in distance (A. C. Myers)

Plate 20. Kenyon Excavations in Canaanite Jericho (Tell es-Sultan) down to the Neolithic level, looking west to the Mount of Temptation (J. C. Trever)

Plate 21. Fresco of the crucifixion, from a rock-hewn church at Göreme (Ürgüp) in Cappadocia (W. S. LaSor)

Xerxes I, and Artaxerxes I. An outstanding feature of this architecture is the vast pillared (or hypostyle) hall. This type of structure was not new to Iran, but the use of new materials — the long cedar beams from Lebanon — allowed a reduction in the number of pillars needed to support the ceiling. The Apadana is supported by only thirty-six pillars set thirty feet apart. Another hall at Pesepolis, known as the hall of "hundred pillars," was even larger than the Apadana.

See also PERSIA; RELIGIONS OF THE BIBLICAL WORLD: PERSIA.

Bibliography.–Journals: *Iranica Antiqua* (since 1962); *Iran* (since 1963). *Books:* J.-L. Huot, *Persia,* I (*Archaeologia Mundi,* 1965); A. Godard, *Art of Iran* (1965); E. Porada, *Art of Ancient Iran* (1965); W. Culican, *Medes and Persians* (1965); D. N. Wilber, *Persepolis* (1969); R. Collins, *Medes and Persians* (1974).

R. E. HAYDEN

ARCHEOLOGY OF MESOPOTAMIA. The archeology of Mesopotamia holds special interest for Bible students because so much of the OT narrative is linked with this area. In this general vicinity the Garden of Eden was located and civilization began. Later Noah's ark came to rest on the mountains of Ararat at the northern fringe of Mesopotamia; and after the flood descendants of Noah founded such cities as Babylon, Calah, Erech, and Nineveh (Gen. 10:10f.). Abraham was born in Ur, one of the greatest cities of the region. Subsequently he moved to Haran in northern Mesopotamia. At Haran some of Abraham's relatives remained; there Abraham sought a wife for his son Isaac (Gen. 24), and there Jacob married Leah and Rachel and lived for twenty years. In the 8th cent. B.C., Assyria subjugated the kingdom of Israel and carried thousands of Hebrews into captivity in Mesopotamia. Early in the 6th cent. Babylon destroyed the kingdom of Judah and deported additional thousands of Hebrews to Mesopotamia, where they remained until the Persians subjugated the area and permitted those who wished to return home.

The archeology of Mesopotamia commands interest among students of general culture, too. Civilization began in Mesopotamia. Social organization, the origin of writing, formulation of law codes, effective use of the wheel, discovery of the principle of the arch as a weight-carrying device, and much more apparently must be attributed to early Mesopotamians. Therefore, these peoples deserve much archeological attention to see what yet can be learned about the origins of civilization.

The term "Mesopotamia" has been subject to a diversity of usage over the millennia. Today it generally applies to the entire area between the Tigris and Euphrates rivers from the mountains of Armenia to the Persian Gulf, and even includes some land to the east and west of those great rivers. Roughly, the dimensions of the area may be put at 600 mi. (1000 km.) northwest to southeast and 300 mi. (500 km.) from east to west. It is included within the modern state of Iraq, but is not exactly coextensive with it. It is difficult to determine exactly the boundaries of Mesopotamia with Persia on the east, Turkey (Anatolia) on the north, Syria on the northwest, and Arabia on the west. Therefore some rather arbitrary decisions have been made concerning which excavations to include in this article.

I. History of Mesopotamian Archeology
   A. Early Explorers
   B. Nineteenth-Century Beginnings
   C. Scientific Advances
   D. Between the Wars
   E. Postwar Developments
II. Decipherment of Cuneiform
III. Biblical Sites Individually Considered
   A. Asshur
   B. Babylon
   C. Calah
   D. Erech
   E. Haran
   F. Nineveh
   G. Ur

I. History of Mesopotamian Archeology.–*A. Early Explorers.* The first significant western explorer of Mesopotamia was the learned Jewish merchant Benjamin Bar Jona of Tudela (in the kingdom of Aragon in Spain). Although primarily interested in Jewish communities of the East as he traveled in 1160, he made significant notes on Nineveh and Babylon and what he considered to be the Tower of Babel at Birs Nimrûd, ancient Borsippa. After they were translated from Spanish into English and French, his writings made an increasing impact on European scholars.

Many followed in Benjamin's train. One of the most important was an Italian nobleman, Pietro della Valle, who visited Babylon in 1616 and Ur in 1625. Apparently he was the first to send copies of cuneiform inscriptions back to Europe and the first to engage in limited rummaging among the ruins of Babylon with the aid of a pick. The Danish scholar Carsten Niebuhr published an account of his travels in 1788, and receives credit for having more positively identified the sites of Nineveh and Babylon than previous visitors. The Abbé de Beauchamp, papal vicar-general at Baghdad, made extended visits to the ruins of Babylon and engaged in minor excavations (the first known, 1781-1786), collecting inscribed bricks and other small antiquities which he brought back to France. His detailed and accurate accounts of Babylon helped to spur interest in Mesopotamian antiquities, especially in British East India Company circles in London. The company authorized their agents in Baghdad to do archeological prospecting. Of special importance in this connection was C. J. Rich, resident of the company in Baghdad from 1808 until his death from cholera in 1821. A gifted linguist, Rich was fluent in Turkish, Arabic, and several other languages. His informative memoirs on Babylon, Nineveh, and other Mesopotamian sites, and the collection of antiquities he accumulated for the British Museum, did much to kindle a desire for actual excavation in the area.

B. Nineteenth-Century Beginnings. But the French, not the English, were destined to begin large-scale and more or less systematic excavation in Mesopotamia. In 1842 the French government established a vice-consulate at Mosul, on the west bank of the Tigris opposite the ruins of ancient Nineveh, and named P. E. Botta vice-consul. His responsibilities were to be in part archeological. In December he began to dig at Nineveh, but after three fruitless months decided to abandon the effort in favor of Khorsabad, 14 mi. (23 km.) to the northeast. The site proved to be the magnificent capital of Sargon II (722-705 B.C.) with its 25-acre (10-hectare) palace complex. After two successful years, Botta sent his extensive finds to the Louvre in Paris. V. Place, Botta's successor at Mosul, continued excavations at Khorsabad (1851-1855) with a French government grant, inspired by Botta's accomplishments. Although many of Place's finest discoveries sank to the bottom of the Tigris en route to Paris, some reached their destination; and Place and his architects were able to complete a systematic study of the palace and reconstruct its ground plan. Discoveries at Khorsabad were important in confirming the existence of Sargon II (disputed by biblical critics) and in throwing light on the reign of this king who claimed to be conqueror of the kingdom of Israel.

The second pioneer archeologist of Mesopotamia was A. H. Layard, an Englishman of Huguenot descent who had made Botta's acquaintance in Mosul and had been inspired by his successes at Khorsabad. Layard began his work at Nimrûd (biblical Calah). At first supported only by a few friends, he gained a sponsorship by the British Museum after his discovery of a royal palace at Calah. Layard's efforts were crowned with much good fortune. In 1846 he found the famous Black Obelisk of Shalmaneser III (859-824 B.C.); and by the time he returned to England in 1847 he had partially explored palaces of Ashurnasirpal I, Shalmaneser III, Adadnirari III, and Esarhaddon at Calah (which had served as one of Assyria's great capitals). In addition, in a brief campaign of only one month at Nineveh he had found and partially excavated Sennacherib's palace. Commissioned a second time by the British Museum to direct their work in Mesopotamia, Layard alternated his supervision between digs at Calah and Nineveh (1849-1851). During those years he concentrated on Sennacherib's palace, with its almost two miles of halls and galleries faced with bas reliefs, and the ziggurat of Calah. His most significant find was part of the great Assyrian library.

With Layard's return to England, H. C. Rawlinson, decipherer of cuneiform, was dispatched to take charge of all excavations of the British Museum in Assyria, Babylonia, and Persia (1851-1855). H. Rassam, a native of Mosul who had worked under Layard, was retained as excavator of Nineveh (1852-1854). He located Ashurbanipal's palace and the major part of his library. Including as it did a wide variety of Assyrian and Babylonian literature, this constitutes one of the most important archeological discoveries ever made.

During this period some successful attempts were made in Babylonia. W. K. Loftus worked briefly at biblical Erech (modern Warka, ancient Uruk) about 40 mi. (65 km.) NW of Ur (1850). Initial successful reports from his dig led the French to lay plans in 1851 to work at Hilla (Babylon) and Birs Nimrûd (Borsippa) under the leadership of J. Oppert. Returns there were minimal because the team had to spend most of their time and effort clearing debris from the site.

J. E. Taylor, British vice-consul at Basra, worked under Rawlinson's supervision at el-Muqaiyar (Ur) in 1854, examining the ziggurat, the famous temple of the moon-god Sin, and finding some valuable inscriptions. In the same year Rawlinson himself examined the great ziggurat at Birs Nimrûd and found some important inscriptions dating to the reign of Nebuchadrezzar (605-562 B.C.). After this, interest in excavation seems to have declined for several decades. Scholarly efforts in part turned to decipherment and interpretation of the scores of thousands of tablets and inscriptions already in hand.

Interest in Mesopotamian antiquities was suddenly rekindled in December, 1872, when G. Smith reported on the discovery of a Babylonian flood story from the library of Ashurbanipal. In response to demands for reopening the Nineveh excavations in order to find the missing portion of the account, the *Daily Telegraph* agreed to finance the expedition in return for exclusive reporting rights. Smith arrived at Nineveh the following May, and had unbelievable success in finding the flood fragment after only about one week of excavation. But Mesopotamian archeology during the last quarter of the 19th cent. proved not to be quite the same hunt for museum pieces that earlier campaigns had been.

Now French and Americans chose to settle down to extended excavation of a single site, and the focus of attention shifted southward to Babylonia, with the realization that there was a culture in ancient Mesopotamia older than that of the Assyrians. (Later it became known that the Sumerians were responsible for the earliest cultural developments in Mesopotamia, during the 5th to the 3rd millennia B.C.) E. de Sarzec, French vice-consul at Basra, began to work at the Sumerian site at Telloh, 50 mi. (80 km.) N of Ur, in 1877, and continued intermittently until his death in 1901. Other French archeologists continued the work for nine more seasons. It is one of the most important sites of Mesopotamia, yielding a large quantity of sculptures, inscriptions, and tablets (30,000 business documents were found in one room alone), which have added much to our knowledge of early Babylonia.

A. H. Layard copying reliefs from the Hall of Archives in Sennacherib's palace at Kuyunjik. From Layard, *Discoveries in the Ruins of Nineveh and Babylon* (1853) (Oriental Institute, University of Chicago)

Another major Sumerian site was Nippur, the religious center of Sumerian times, about 100 mi. (160 km.) S of Baghdad and unconvincingly identified with the biblical Calneh (Am. 6:2). There a University of Pennsylvania team conducted four campaigns (1888/89; 1889/90; 1893-1896; 1898-1900), under the general direction of J. P. Peters, with J. H. Haynes as field director and leader of the fourth expedition. The first expedition surveyed the ruins, began systematic excavation of the temple of Bel, and unearthed over two thousand cuneiform documents. The second expedition recovered, among other things, about eight thousand tablets. The third concentrated on the temple mound and netted about 21,000 largely fragmentary tablets. The fourth definitely located the famous temple library of Nippur, from which thousands of tablets had been already obtained, and excavated about 23,000 tablets and fragments, mostly of a literary character and including parts of a Sumerian flood and creation account.

C. Scientific Advances. About the turn of the century Near Eastern archeology in general and Mesopotamian archeology in particular entered a new phase. No longer was its primary objective the accumulation of museum pieces but rather rediscovery of the past by means of systematic uncovering of the remains of civilizations buried in layers in the tells or mounds of the region. This shift occurred for five reasons. First, the excavators themselves became increasingly concerned about the destruction wrought when museum pieces were removed from meaningful contexts in the ruins, making future interpretation difficult or impossible. Second, the Turkish government became increasingly interested in the preservation of antiquities and the recovery of a knowledge of the past. Third, archeology itself was maturing; better ways of understanding the past began to present themselves. Fourth, enough museum pieces had been collected in centers like Paris, London, Philadelphia, and elsewhere to stir an interest in the founding of archeological societies and the subsidizing of digs by wealthy donors. Thus it was now possible to finance prolonged expeditions dedicated to a more scholarly interpretation of the ruins.

Fifth, the Germans entered the field with their more strict, meticulous scholarship; architects turned archeologists were more concerned with the layout of cities, functions of buildings, diagrams of structures and sites than some of the earlier excavators. They turned away from tunneling into mounds and sinking shafts down through them to the practice of removing a part or entire layer of a mound at a time to reveal the stratigraphic sequence. The Germans especially focused attention on Babylon, Asshur, and Erech, with minor activity elsewhere.

The newly-formed German oriental society (Deutsche Orientgesellschaft), under the patronage of Emperor Wilhelm II, decided to make its first major task the excavation of Babylon, and appointed R. Koldewey to leadership of the operation. Digging continued through all seasons of the year from the spring of 1899 to the spring of 1917, a feat in itself remarkable considering the high summer temperatures in the area. Since the ground water had risen considerably during the millennia, the Babylon of Hammurabi's day was under water and could not be excavated. Therefore Koldewey was forced to concentrate on the level of Nebuchadrezzar's day.

With the aid of competent architects Koldewey successfully recreated the main features of Nebuchadrezzar's city — its walls, palaces, temples, and parts of the residential areas. Although he found a few inscriptions, Koldewey was not destined to unearth at Babylon the vast treasure troves of antiquities located elsewhere. This was partly because the Babylonian plain had no stone; so the statuary and bas reliefs appearing in Assyrian palaces and temples were not to be found in the south. The Babylonians built largely in sun-dried brick, which in time became solid masses of clay almost indistinguishable from the surrounding soil. It is important, therefore, that the early excavators did not extensively dig away the mounds of Babylonia, for they had not yet developed techniques equal to the task of excavating cities of mud. In his brief attack on the site Layard had been unable to detect the difference between the mud of walls and mud of debris and quickly reached the conclusion that "nothing" could "be hoped for from the site of Babylon." Happily Koldewey proved him wrong.

Under Koldewey's general direction, J. Jordan dug at Erech (Warka) in 1912-1913, uncovering much of the great temple of Ishtar, part of the city wall, many houses, and tablets. A pupil of Koldewey, W. Andrae, directed an excavation at Qal'ât Sherqâṭ (ancient Asshur [Gen. 10:10f.] from which Assyria was named). Andrae's excavation technique was of especially high quality, considering the relative infancy of Assyriology. His work enabled him to reconstruct the history of the site from *ca.* 3000 B.C. to the 3rd cent. A.D. He found inscriptions from every period of Assyrian history and uncovered palaces and temples. At Halâf, in the upper reaches of the Habor River, M. von Oppenheim excavated during 1911-1913, finding a whole new culture dating to *ca.* 4500 B.C. Especially noteworthy among his finds was a magnificent collection of pottery decorated in two or three colors, with figures of human beings or animals.

Although the Germans dominated the archeological scene in Mesopotamia during the years prior to World War I, others worked in the area. For instance, Henri de Genoillac led a French dig at Kish near Babylon in 1914, discovering the temple of the god of Kish. E. J. Banks in 1903 led a University of Chicago expedition to Bismaya (ancient Adab) near Nippur.

D. Between the Wars. A wholly new political situation existed in Iraq between World Wars I and II. With the dissolution of the Ottoman Empire at the end of World War I, the League of Nations assigned Britain a mandate over Iraq. The British established a department of antiquities in 1924. Two years later the Iraqi Museum was established at Baghdad. In 1932 Iraq became an independent, sovereign nation and gradually developed its own qualified staff of archeologists.

During the years between the wars archeological research gathered momentum and there was unbroken advance in excavation technique. The use of pottery as a means of dating was increasingly refined. Moreover, the basic chronological framework of the area was established. With the aid of the accumulation of evidence from the excavations, it was largely regularized by the Eighteenth Congress of Orientalists in 1931, which agreed that prehistoric periods were to be named after sites where a culture was first found. Thus, Ubaid (Obeid), Uruk (Warka), and Jemdet Nasr periods (in that order) were prehistoric and the Early Dynastic was the first historic period. Halâf and Pre-Halâf (Hassuna) periods were later introduced before Ubaid. An approximate chronology has now been adopted for these periods: Hassuna (5000-4500 B.C.); Halâf (4500-4000 B.C.); Ubaid (4000-3500 B.C.); Uruk (3500-3200 B.C.); Jemdet Nasr (3200-2800 B.C.); Early Dynastic (2800-2350 B.C.). (For a generally accepted chronology of the more recent periods of Mesopotamian history, see *LAP*, pp. 36-73; 196-246.)

Even before the British signed the 1918 armistice British Museum archeologist R. C. Thompson was in the field, working at Ur and Eridu. Within a few months his brief campaign led to another, under H. R. Hall. Hall found Ubaid 4 mi. (6.5 km.) W of Ur and excavated a temple platform there. The work of Thompson and Hall was taken over by C. L. Woolley, who led an expedition sponsored jointly by the British Museum and the University of Pennsylvania Museum. During the years 1922-1934 he concentrated on Ur but spent several seasons at Ubaid, where distinctive finds established a whole new culture period of Mesopotamian prehistory. At Ur itself Woolley's greatest successes illuminated two periods in the city's history: Ur I and Ur III. Dating to the Ur I period (*ca.* 2500 B.C.) were the magnificent royal tombs with treasures that caused a sensation in the popular mind somewhat comparable to the discovery of King Tutankhamen's tomb in Egypt. As a result, the Sumerian culture that they represented was soon known all over the world. Woolley was able to document the Ur III period (*ca.* 2000 B.C., approximately the time of Abraham) in an entirely different way: with walls, temples, houses, streets, the ziggurat, and scores of thousands of cuneiform tablets.

At the same time other significant excavations were in progress. S. Langdon directed a joint Oxford–Field Museum (Chicago) dig at Kish, 8 mi. (13 km.) E of Babylon (1923-1933), and Jemdet Nasr, 18 mi. (29 km.) NE of Kish (1926-1928). At the former site a palace, a temple, and important tablets came to light; at the latter, important documents and distinctive cultural elements that bore witness to a whole new culture period in Mesopotamian history. Americans cooperated also in an excavation at Nuzi, SE of Nineveh. E. Chiera led the first seasons of excavation, which continued from 1925 to 1931. The American Schools of Oriental Research and the Iraqi government backed the project, and other American institutions joined later. Nuzi was significant for the light it shed on Hurrian civilization and for the clay tablets from private homes with striking parallels to biblical passages (e.g., sale of birthright and oral blessing).

Americans were busy elsewhere in Mesopotamia. E. A. Speiser of the University of Pennsylvania led an extended dig at Tepe Gawra, 4 mi. (6.5 km.) NE of Khorsabad (1927-1938). The venture, a cooperative effort of the University of Pennsylvania, the American Schools of Oriental Research, and Dropsie College, was important both for the history of archeological technique (as it systematically uncovered the mound layer by layer) and the history of Mesopotamian culture (as it confirmed the development of Halafian culture and helped to round out understanding of the 5th millennium B.C.). L. Waterman of the University of Michigan worked at Tell 'Umar (1927-1932), a site which proved to be the Babylonian Opis (Hellenistic Seleucia). The Oriental Institute of the University of Chicago entered the field in 1928 and conducted a very successful campaign at Khorsabad until 1936, under the leadership of E. Chiera and H. Frankfort. Although they excavated parts of the complex not previously dug and added considerably to knowledge of the site, one of the most important discoveries was the Khorsabad king list, which helped to establish the chronology of ancient Mesopotamia. At the same time the Oriental Institute was digging at Tell Asmar, Khafaje, and Tell Agrab in the Diyala region east of Baghdad.

At Erech Germans dug for eleven seasons (1928-1939) under the leadership of J. Jordan, A. Nöldeke, and E. Heinrich, concentrating on some of the important temples of the site. Also, in 1929 von Oppenheim returned to Halâf, from which he recovered numerous large stone monuments and much pottery.

The British returned to Nineveh in 1927 and continued to work there until 1932. R. Campbell Thompson cut a 70-ft. shaft to virgin soil, locating in stratified sequence all the periods of Mesopotamian history from Assyrian back through pre-Halâfian, thus confirming the commonly accepted arrangement of periods of Mesopotamian culture. In 1933 M. E. L. Mallowan and his wife Agatha Christie excavated for the British Museum at Arpachiyah just N of Nineveh. The not-unreasonable 1933 antiquities law of Iraq (to the effect that unique finds could no longer leave the country and that only half of the rest might be exported) led Mallowan and others to set up operations elsewhere. Several went to Syria.

One Syrian site that belongs to Mesopotamian studies was Tell Hariri (ancient Mari), a French dig in the middle Euphrates region. A. Parrot of the Louvre led excavations there in 1933-1939. Most dramatic of the finds were the royal palace, covering more than 8 acres (3.2 hectares), and its archive of over 20,000 tablets. These tablets are important for the establishment of the chronology of the 2nd millennium B.C., and contain names appearing in Gen. 11:16, 23f., 27 (e.g., Peleg, Serug, Nahor).

E. Postwar Developments. With the outbreak of World War II all excavation did not cease as it did during World War I. Iraqi archeologists worked at 'Uqair (1940-1941), Hassuna (1943-1944), Tell Harmel (1943-1945) and Eridu 1946-1949). Of special interest were the results at Hassuna, where materials similar to those in the lowest levels at Nineveh came to light. So the tendency today is to call the earliest period of Mesopotamian culture "Hassuna" and to label the five periods of Mesopotamian prehistory at Hassuna, Halâf, Ubaid (Obeid), Uruk (Warka), and Jemdet Nasr. In the 1960's Iraqi expeditions worked at Ḥaṭra, the strange capital of a pre-Islamic Arab kingdom dating *ca.* 140 B.C.–A.D. 226, and at Tell es-Sawwan, which had village life going back to *ca.* 5500 B.C.

Other important developments in Mesopotamian archeology since World War II were a new museum, a new technique, and participation by two more nations. The Iraqi Museum's new building in Baghdad (1966) at last brought together in one place many of the magnificent treasures of the region. The new technique was carbon-14 dating (not restricted to Mesopotamia, of course), a scientific means of determining the validity of earlier conclusions about chronology and of establishing new ones (*see* ARCHEOLOGY VI). New participants in Mesopotamian archeology were the Danes and Japanese. P. V. Glob of Aarhus worked on the island of Bahrain at the head of the Persian Gulf during the 1950's and concluded that it was the land of Dilmun, home of Utnapishtim, the Babylonian Noah. In the 1960's Glob excavated on the Kuwaiti island of Failaka with considerable success. In 1956 the Dane H. Ingold visited the sixteen tells of the Little Zab valley in northeast Iraq, which was to be flooded on completion of the Dokan reservoir, and found interesting clay tablets. N. Egami of the University of Tokyo in 1956 began a dig at Telul ath-Thalathat, 37 mi. (60 km.) W of Mosul and found, among other things, a temple thought to be one of the oldest and best preserved in Mesopotamia.

Much of the postwar archeological development in Iraq was a continuation of previous activity. German excavators, this time under the leadership of H. Lenzen, resumed work at Uruk in 1954. A. Parrot dug at Mari again in 1951-1956. After a seventy-year lapse the British returned to Nimrûd. M. E. L. Mallowan led the campaign on behalf of the British School of Archaeology in Iraq (1949-1961). Special finds included the Banquet Stele of Ashurnasirpal, which celebrated the king's completion of his palace; a fine collection of ivories; the great fort of Shalmaneser III; and his throne base. Americans, this time the Oriental Institute of the University of Chicago and the University of Pennsylvania, resumed excavations at Nippur in 1948 on a plan to work there every second year. D. E. McCown and R. C. Haines led the campaigns through the 1950's and 1960's, with concentration on the great temple of Inanna but with attention to other structures of the main tell and the surrounding area.

A new feature of excavation in postwar years has been attention to the earliest life in the area. R. J. Braidwood of the Oriental Institute, beginning in 1948, spent three seasons at Jarmo, 30 mi. (50 km.) E of the modern oil town of Kirkûk in northeastern Iraq, where he found a village site dated by carbon-14 to *ca.* 6750 B.C. R. S. Solecki of the Smithsonian Institution excavated in the Shanidar Cave in the Zagros Mountains in northeastern Iraq (1951, 1953, and 1956/57) and found three Neanderthal adults and an infant dated about 50,000 years before the present.

After almost two hundred years of digging in the soil of Mesopotamia it is now possible to write the history of the region, at least in outline, from *ca.* 7000 B.C. to the present. But only a beginning has been made. The Iraqi Department of Antiquities has records of over 6500 tells in the country; well over 6000 of them have not yet been excavated at all.

II. Decipherment of Cuneiform.–The herculean efforts of Mesopotamian excavators would be of little value in reconstructing the past if we could not read the hundreds of thousands of texts they uncovered. Ultimately what made decipherment possible was that the Persians did not have their own system of writing when they conquered the Babylonians. Therefore they adopted the Babylonian script for the writing of Persian, and, because their empire was so ethnically diverse, they then wrote many of their public documents and inscriptions in three languages: Persian, Elamite, and Assyro-Babylonian (now called Akkadian).

Pietro della Valle was the first to bring back to Europe some of the Persian inscriptions from Persepolis. T. Hyde of Oxford coined the term cuneiform ("wedge-shaped") to apply to this writing (1700). C. Niebuhr made additional copies of Persepolis inscriptions (1765). This provided only a little raw material — no clues to decipherment.

Several individuals had a part in translating cuneiform. S. de Sacy, a French scholar, deciphered (1789-1791) some late Persian inscriptions (Sassanid, A.D. 226-640, written when cuneiform had given way to the Phoenician alphabet). In those materials he continually found a formula, "X, the great king, king of kings, son of Y, etc." In 1802 G. Grotefend, a German scholar, read a paper before the learned society of Göttingen in which he claimed to have worked out the value of thirteen cuneiform signs and to have identified the names of Darius and Xerxes and the words "king" and "son." He had used Niebuhr's texts, which had appeared over the heads of kings, and had guessed that de Sacy's formula was represented in them. But he could go no further. Finally in 1836 Bonn professor C. Lassen and French scholar E. Burnouf completed the translation of Grotefend's two texts.

Paralleling the work of Grotefend was that of H. C. Rawlinson, an officer of the British army in India who was later stationed in Persia (1833). He was very much intrigued by the trilingual inscriptions on the cliffs of Behistun 65 mi. (105 km.) W of Hamadan, not far from his camp. In 1835 he began copying these texts, which had been carved in the side of the cliff by Darius the Great (522-486 B.C.) 400-500 ft. (120-150 m.) above the plain. He guessed that Class I, the simplest of the inscriptions, was Old Persian and that the decipherment of Class I would be the clue to decipherment of Classes II and III. He realized that in order to identify all the signs in Class I he would have to work through a large number of proper names. He had already learned late Persian in India and so had the benefit of that background. Rawlinson guessed that words occurring many times would be common nouns like "king." Using a combination of shrewd guesses, clues from late Persian (such as the formula noted above) and other helps, he made amazing progress. By 1839 he had worked out the whole alphabet and translated 200 lines and was able to read a survey paper before the Royal Asiatic Society of London. He realized that many imperfections still existed. Finally, however, he was able to publish a full interpretation of the Persian column in 1846. Then Rawlinson began work on Class II, which he assumed to be Babylonian. This was much more difficult. Persian was alphabetic and Indo-European; Babylonian was syllabic ideographic and Semitic. Nevertheless, Rawlinson was able to publish 112 lines in 1851. He was not able to decipher the Elamite (Class III), however.

Cuneiform is not a language but a script in which many languages of Western Asia have been written. The decipherment of one language will often lead to the decipherment of another. For instance, the translation of Akkadian led to translation of Sumerian, the oldest written language of Mesopotamia. The Sumerians were writing in cuneiform before 3000 B.C. and apparently invented it. When Semites came in contact with the Sumerians they evidently borrowed their script, as the Persians were to do later. To promote understanding by ancient scribes, "syllabaries" were drawn up listing Sumerian signs and their Semitic (Akkadian) equivalents; some have been found in the excavations. Thus, the decipherment of Akkadian led, in the 20th cent., to the ability to read Sumerian, Elamite, and several other very difficult Near Eastern languages written in cuneiform. *See also* CUNEIFORM.

III. Biblical Sites Individually Considered.–Information about biblical sites that is found throughout the chronological presentation of Mesopotamian archeology is here summarized.

A. Asshur. This was the ancient city that gave Assyria its name. Its site is modern Qal'ât Sherqâṭ, about 60 mi. (100 km.) S of Nineveh on the west bank of the Tigris. Layard, Rassam, and Place dug briefly there. The major campaign was led by W. Andrae and the German oriental society (1903-1914). Andrae was able to work out the general history of the site from 3000 B.C. to A.D. 300 and to study its palaces and temples.

Asshur began to assume significance in the 19th cent. B.C., after the end of the Ur III period. At that time the city was well fortified, had a fine temple to its god, and enjoyed the success of a well-established merchant colony in central Asia Minor. After a period of decline late in the century, there was a political revival during the 18th cent., until Hammurabi absorbed Assyria into his empire (*ca.* 1700). After Hammurabi's dynasty ended in 1550 Assyria was relatively free to expand once more. Although Asshur was the capital during much of the following millennium, Nineveh became an alternate royal residence in the 12th cent. and the main capital during the height of empire in the 7th century.

Among important texts excavated at Asshur were a fragmentary Assyrian law code dating to *ca.* 1100 (more severe than Hammurabi's) and part of a creation account dating to *ca.* 1000 B.C.

B. Babylon. The Abbé de Beauchamp cut the first archeological trenches in the ruins in the 1780's. Rich visited Babylon in 1811 and 1818, measured the various mounds that encased the ruins, and made the first accurate plan of the site. In 1828 R. Mignan cut a shaft into the site and removed a number of clay tablets. In 1850 A. H. Layard dug into three mounds but soon concluded that the place was not worth his time. His assistant Rassam came back in 1879 for a quick dig, at which time he unearthed a large collection of business documents and the famous Cyrus Cylinder (giving Cyrus' account of his conquest of Babylon). Meanwhile, in 1852 the French had begun an expedition under the direction of J. Oppert and others. They extracted numerous small objects from the mounds and began to ship them back to France in 1855. Unfortunately, all was lost when their rafts overturned in the Euphrates. Finally a more scientific team led by R. Koldewey systematically worked at the site (1899-1917).

J. H. Breasted, founder of the Oriental Institute, examining excavations along the Procession Way at Babylon (Oriental Institute, University of Chicago)

Black Obelisk of Shalmaneser III (841 B.C.) from Nimrûd. The second panel from the top depicts "Jehu son of Omri" kneeling as Israelite porters present tribute. (Oriental Institute, University of Chicago)

For a description of the large and complex site with information gained from the archeological work there *see* BABYLON.

C. Calah. Biblical CALAH (Gen. 10:11) is the mound known today as Nimrûd, about 20 mi. (32 km.) S of Nineveh. A. H. Layard excavated there from 1845 to 1848 and M. E. L. Mallowan led a dig there for the British School of Archaeology in Iraq from 1949 to 1961. Though Calah has a history extending from prehistoric to Hellenistic times, it enjoyed real prosperity only when Assyrian kings chose to bestow their blessings on the site. Around 1250 B.C. Shalmaneser I rebuilt Calah and brought a period of prosperity. Ashurnasirpal II, *ca.* 879, made the town his capital and built a magnificent palace covering 6 acres (2.4 hectares), of which Mallowan completed excavation and a plan. This is now the best preserved of Assyrian royal dwellings. In 1951 Mallowan found the king's banquet stele, which describes a great feast for about 70,000 to celebrate completion of the palace. This would have included more than the entire population of the city, estimated at about 60,000. Mallowan also found a number of fine pieces of ivory inlay in the palace. Ashurnasirpal's son Shalmaneser III (859-824) also built himself a palace at Calah and set up his Black Obelisk (a kind of victory monument, found by Layard in 1846; *see* JEHU) in the public square. Mallowan discovered and largely excavated Shalmeneser's great 18-acre (7.3-hectare) fort, which lay just inside the 5-mi. (8-km.) circuit of the city wall at its southeast edge. This is the most extensive military installation yet discovered in ancient Assyria. Sargon II (722-705) made his capital at Asshur, Calah, and Nineveh before building Khorsabad. In fact, it was from Calah that he launched attacks on the Israelites and to Calah that he brought the booty after the fall of Samaria.

D. Erech. Biblical ERECH (modern Warka, ancient Uruk) lies 40 mi. (65 km.) NW of Ur. In 1850 Loftus investigated the site, as did Rawlinson on occasion during the years he supervised British Museum work in Mesopotamia (1851-1855). Jordan, for the German oriental society, conducted the first scientific excavation there in 1912-1913, discovering the great temple of the goddess Ishtar and part of the city wall. German teams led by Jordan and others worked again at Erech from 1928 to 1939, and after World War II returned to the site in 1954.

To date no city can be described at Erech, but the earliest ziggurat, the earliest cylinder seals, and the earliest known writing (*ca.* 3300 B.C.) appeared at this site. This early writing, apparently in Sumerian, was found on a number of clay tablets in a pictographic script in the Red Temple (one of three located there). Most of the finds at Erech date to the period 3500-3200 B.C.

Several mounds (the highest about 100 ft. [30 m.]) encase the ruins of ancient Uruk. Four of these cover the remains of temples, the largest of which was dedicated to Inanna, Lady of the Heavens. Another mound contains the palace of a Babylonian king. Though all these structures have been partially excavated, work has centered on the great Inanna temple. Occupation of the site apparently goes back to the 5th or 4th millennium B.C. Numerous houses of the 1st millennium B.C. (Assyrian and Persian) have been uncovered. The whole area of the city, surrounded by a wall, is 5½ sq. mi. (14 sq. km.).

E. Haran. HARAN stands 10 mi. (16 km.) N of the Syrian border inside the Republic of Turkey, at a point almost equidistant from the Tigris and Euphrates rivers. Since medieval and modern towns have occupied most of the ancient site, large-scale excavations have been impossible. An Anglo-Turkish expedition began work in the region in 1951, concentrating on the nearby mound of Sultan Tepe, which may have been a part of ancient Haran. In Sultan Tepe excavators found an Assyrian sanctuary with dependent buildings. The prize discovery was a rich collection of literary and religious texts belonging to Qurdi Nergal, priest of the moon-god, and dating from 648 to 612 B.C. This library, written in Sumerian and Assyrian, included literary texts (poems of Gilgamesh, creation, etc.), prayers and rituals, medical texts, and astronomical materials.

In 1956 D. S. Rice found in the mosque of Haran three reused stelae of Nabonidus' day, probably originally erected in the temple of the moon-god Sin. The three slabs bear a continuous text and include an autobiographical account by Nabonidus' mother telling why her son usurped the throne, Nabonidus' mission of restoring the temple at Haran, and other interesting details of the king's life.

F. Nineveh. The ruins of NINEVEH cover an area of 1800 acres (730 hectares) surrounded by remains of a brick wall almost 8 mi. (13 km.) long and still standing to a height of over 10 ft. (3 m.). Within this area are two large mounds, Kuyunjik and Nebi Yûnus, and a number of smaller ones. Kuyunjik is unoccupied and the site of most of the archeological work at Nineveh. Nebi Yûnus is occupied by a village, so little excavating can be done there.

The first to excavate briefly at Nineveh was P. E. Botta (1842), followed by A. H. Layard in 1845. Most of the work there has been done by British expeditions: H. Rassam (1852-1854); G. Smith (1872-1873, 1876); Rassam (1878-1882); E. A. W. Budge (1888-1891); L. W. King and R. Campbell Thompson (1903-1905); Thompson (1927-1932); Iraqi Department of Antiquities (1954). Thompson was especially responsible for bringing a degree of order out of the chaos created by previous campaigns at the site. He cut down to virgin soil and established the history of the site from 612 B.C. (when the Babylonians destroyed the city) back to almost 5000 B.C.

Nineveh was periodically the capital of Assyria, along with Nimrûd and Asshur; but from Sennacherib's reign on (705-682) it was permanently the capital. To Sennacherib goes credit for the city wall, an aqueduct that brought water from about 30 mi. (50 km.), and a great palace. His palace, at the southern edge of Kuyunjik, had more than seventy rooms decorated with sculptured stone slabs for a total of almost two miles of reliefs. In the middle of Kuyunjik stood Sennacherib's temple to Nabû (god of writing), where he deposited his royal library (found by Layard). At the northern edge of the mound was the palace of Ashurbanipal (Osnappar of Ezr. 4:10), where Rassam found the rest of the royal library (perhaps totaling more than 100,000 texts, including Babylonian accounts of creation and the flood). Palaces of Shalmaneser I, Tiglath-pileser I, Adadnirari II, Ashurnasirpal, and Tukulti-Ninurta II also came to light at Kuyunjik, and a palace of Esarhaddon on Nebi Yûnus. The site of Nineveh is so huge that work there has hardly begun.

G. Ur. The home of Abraham was first excavated briefly by J. E. Taylor for the British Museum in 1854. He found inscriptions at the ziggurat which demonstrated

Relief from palace of Ashurbanipal (668-633 B.C.) at Kuyunjik. The king pours a libation over four dead lions before an offering table and incense stand. (Trustees of the British Museum)

ARCHEOLOGY OF PALESTINE AND SYRIA

that Tell el-Muqaiyar was truly Ur. In 1918 R. Campbell Thompson worked there briefly, followed a few months later by H. R. Hall, who concentrated on the ziggurat area but also uncovered tombs and houses. The main campaign, however, was a cooperative effort of the British Museum and the Museum of the University of Pennsylvania under the direction of C. L. Woolley (1922-1934).

Most interesting for biblical studies, as possibly the time when Abraham lived there, is the Ur III period (2070-1960 B.C.), which saw the city at its height. Woolley estimated the population of the city and its environs at about 250,000. The wall around the city proper was some 2½ mi. (4 km.) in circumference and 77 ft. (23 m.) thick. In the northwestern part of the city was the sacred enclosure of the moon-god Nanna, within which stood the great brick ziggurat measuring 200 ft. (60 m.) in length, 150 ft. (45 m.) in width, and 70 ft. (21 m.) in height. The city had two harbors and numerous business houses with sales representatives scattered far and wide. Houses of the middle class normally had ten to twenty rooms in two stories arranged around a central court. Education was quite highly developed. In mathematics one not only knew multiplication and division but also could extract square roots and do exercises in practical geometry. Scores of thousands of clay tablets have come to light, a large percentage of which are bills of lading, invoices, records of court cases, tax records, and the like, demonstrating the prosperity and social and economic advancement of the community.

Later, during the 17th cent., the city was badly damaged by Hammurabi's son when Ur rebelled against her overlords, but it was restored to greatness by Nebuchadrezzar and Cyrus. For a general description of the city's history and significance *see* UR.

Bibliography.–E. Bacon, *Archaeology: Discoveries in the 1960's* (1971); G. Barton, *Archaeology and the Bible* (7th ed. 1937); M. A. Beek, *Atlas of Mesopotamia* (1962); G. E. Daniel, *A Hundred Years of Archaeology* (1950); J. Finegan, *LAP*; H. V. Hilprecht, ed., *Explorations in Bible Lands During the Nineteenth Century* (1903); G. A. Larue, *Babylon and the Bible* (1969); S. Lloyd, *Foundations in the Dust* (1947); M. E. L. Mallowan, *Nimrud and Its Remains* (2 vols., 1966); A. Parrot, *Nineveh and the OT* (1955); C. F. Pfeiffer, ed., *The Biblical World* (1966); G. Roux, *Ancient Iraq* (1964).

H. F. VOS

ARCHEOLOGY OF PALESTINE AND SYRIA. The ancient areas of Palestine, Phoenicia, and Syria are now incorporated into four modern nations: Israel, Jordan, Lebanon, and Syria. The modern nation Israel was formed in 1948. The wars of 1967 and 1970 resulted in Israeli occupation of the Sinai and Gaza Strip territories of Egypt, the Golan Heights of Syria, and the West Bank of Jordan. The last is a large area of Cisjordan that includes Samaria, the Old City of Jerusalem, and many other important biblical sites. The Hashemite Kingdom of Jordan includes the transjordanian areas of ancient Gilead, Ammon, Moab, and Edom.

Modern Lebanon, a small country about 135 mi. (215 km.) long and no broader than 50 mi. (80 km.), includes the ancient Phoenician coast, the Lebanon Mountains, and the fertile Beqa' Valley.

The Syrian Arab Republic extends 350 mi. (560 km.) inland to include the northwestern area of ancient Mesopotamia — the region of the upper Euphrates River and its major tributary, the Khābûr (Habor) River. Although the mouth of the Orontes lies in the district of Alexandretta ceded to Turkey in 1939, this important area of ancient Syria will be included in the following discussion.

I. History of Archeological Investigation
   A. Syria
   B. Phoenicia
   C. Palestine
   D. Transjordan
II. Significant Archeological Discoveries
   A. Surveys
   B. Mesolithic and Neolithic Ages
   C. Chalcolithic Age
   D. Early Bronze Age
   E. Middle Bronze Age
   F. Late Bronze Age
   G. Early Iron Age
   H. United Monarchy
   I. Divided Monarchy
   J. Babylonian Conquest
   K. Persian and Hellenistic Periods
   L. Herodian Period
   M. NT Period
   N. Dead Sea Scrolls and the Bar Cochba Finds
   O. Late Roman and Byzantine Periods

I. History of Archeological Investigation.–*A. Syria.* Major excavations in Syria began in the early 20th century. From 1911 to the outbreak of World War I, R. C. Thompson, T. E. Lawrence (of Arabia), D. G. Hogarth, and C. L. Woolley worked at Carchemish on the Euphrates River near the Syrian-Turkish border, uncovering a large number of Syro-Hittite reliefs. Carchemish was the site of the battle in 605 B.C. between Nebuchadrezzar and Neco (2 Ch. 35:20; Jer. 46:2). The excavators found evidence of this battle, including the shield of a Greek mercenary soldier in the hire of Neco.

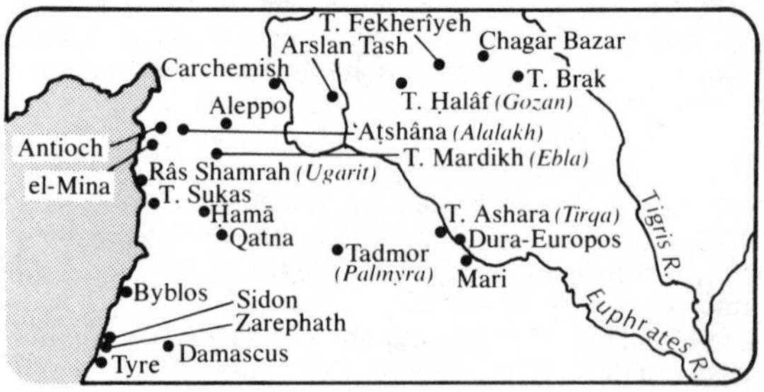

On the Habor (Khābûr) River near the Turkish border is Tell Halâf, ancient GOZAN. Max von Oppenheim excavated the site in 1911-1913 and 1927-1929. An inscribed altar from Halâf yields our oldest Aramaic text, dated to 925 B.C. Under the Assyrians Gozan was a provincial capital. Israelites were sent there by Tiglath-pileser III in 734-732 B.C. (1 Ch. 5:26) and by Shalmaneser V and Sargon II in 722 (2 K. 17:6; 18:11).

DURA-EUROPAS is a huge settlement of 160 acres (65 hectares), 25 mi. (40 km.) up the Euphrates from the Iraqi border. Eminent Belgian, French, and American scholars worked at the site in 1922-1923 and from 1928 to 1937. Among their significant discoveries were a Mithraeum (2nd cent. A.D.), a synagogue (3rd cent. A.D.), and a church (3rd cent. A.D.) which is the earliest yet found. All these buildings were decorated with frescoes.

Tell 'Asharah is situated 15 mi. (25 km.) below the confluence of the Habor and the Euphrates. It was identified by E. Herzfeld as ancient Terqa, the capital of the kingdom of Ḫana in the Old Babylonian period. In 1923 F. Thureau-Dangin conducted a short season there. At that time the mound measured 2600 by 2000 ft. (800 by 600 m.), but erosion by the Euphrates has reduced this to only 1870 by 1670 ft. (570 by 510 m.). In 1974 T. H. Carter began new excavations at the site; these were continued by G. Buccellati.

From 1924 to 1929 R. du Mesnil du Buisson excavated ancient Qatna, the capital of an important kingdom that

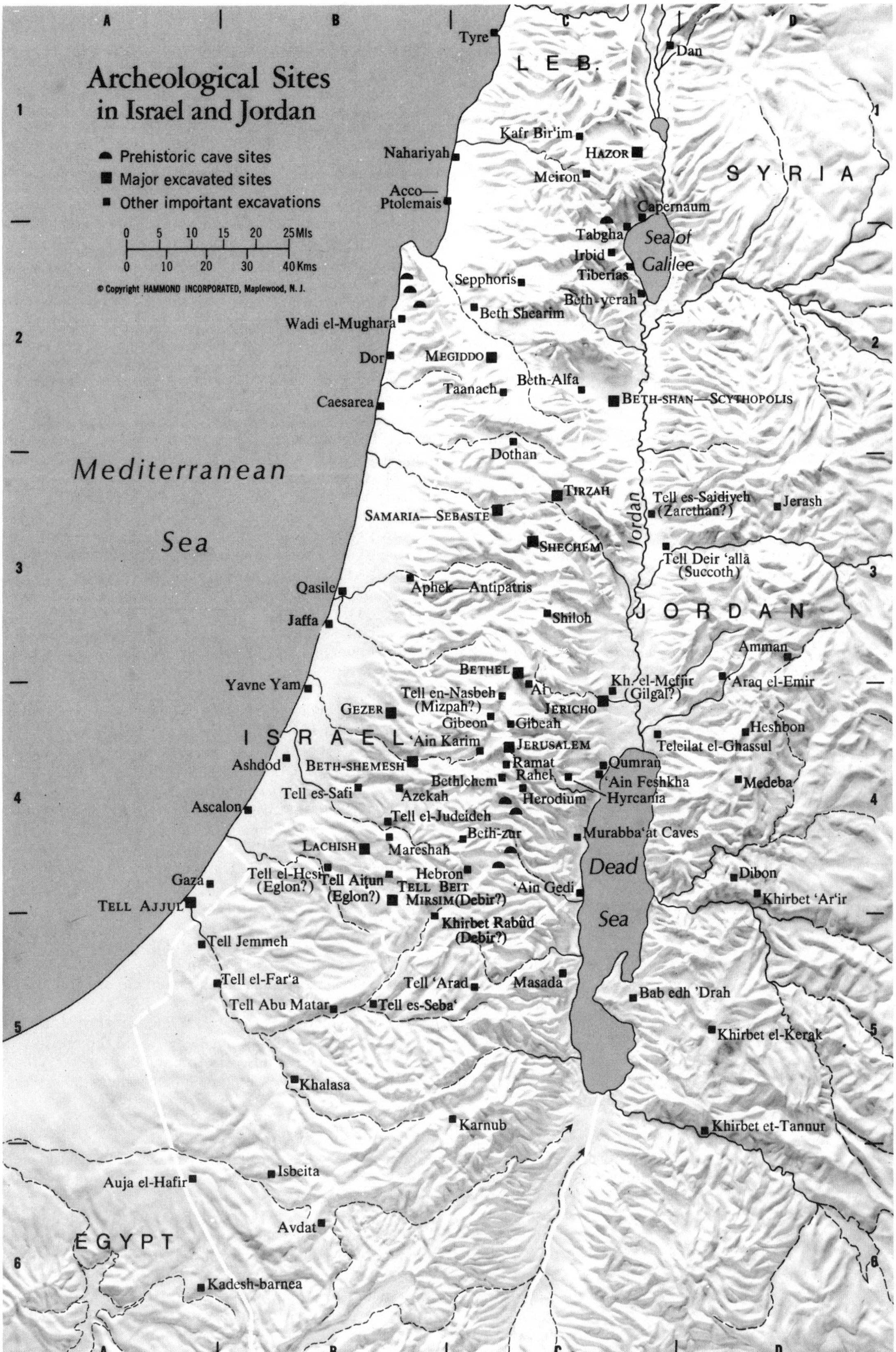
Archeological Sites
in Israel and Jordan
Prehistoric cave sites
Major excavated sites
Other important excavations
0 5 10 15 20 25 Mls
0 10 20 30 40 Kms
© Copyright HAMMOND INCORPORATED, Maplewood, N. J.
Mediterranean
Sea
LEB.
SYRIA
JORDAN
ISRAEL
EGYPT
Sea of Galilee
Dead Sea
Jordan
Tyre
Dan
Kafr Bir'im
Hazor
Nahariyah
Meiron
Acco—Ptolemais
Capernaum
Tabgha
Irbid
Tiberias
Sepphoris
Beth-yerah
Beth Shearim
Wadi el-Mughara
Dor
Megiddo
Beth-Alfa
Taanach
Caesarea
Beth-shan—Scythopolis
Dothan
Tirzah
Tell es-Saidiyeh (Zarethan?)
Jerash
Samaria—Sebaste
Shechem
Tell Deir 'allā (Succoth)
Qasile
Aphek—Antipatris
Shiloh
Jaffa
Amman
Bethel
Ai
Kh. el-Mefjir (Gilgal?)
'Araq el-Emir
Yavne Yam
Tell en-Nasbeh (Mizpah?)
Gezer
Jericho
Gibeon
Gibeah
Heshbon
'Ain Karim
Jerusalem
Teleilat el-Ghassul
Ashdod
Beth-shemesh
Ramat Rahel
Qumran
'Ain Feshkha
Bethlehem
Medeba
Tell es-Safi
Azekah
Herodium
Hyrcania
Ascalon
Tell el-Judeideh
Beth-zur
Murabba'at Caves
Lachish
Mareshah
Gaza
Tell el-Hesi (Eglon?)
Tell Aitun (Eglon?)
Hebron
Tell Beit Mirsim (Debir?)
'Ain Gedi
Dibon
Khirbet 'Ar'ir
Tell Ajjul
Khirbet Rabûd (Debir?)
Tell Jemmeh
Tell el-Far'a
Tell 'Arad
Masada
Bab edh 'Drah
Tell Abu Matar
Tell es-Seba'
Khirbet el-Kerak
Khalasa
Karnub
Khirbet et-Tannur
Isbeita
Auja el-Hafir
Avdat
Kadesh-barnea
A
B
C
D
1
2
3
4
5
6

ARCHEOLOGY OF PALESTINE AND SYRIA

flourished during the Old Babylonian period. The site, about 3300 ft. (1000 m.) square, was protected by steep "Hyksos" ramparts, some 50 ft. (15 m.) high.

F. Thureau-Dangin excavated Arslan Tash, ancient Hadâtu, from 1927 to 1929. He found an important collection of ivories in a magnificent provincial palace of Tiglath-pileser III.

On the coast E of the tip of Cyprus is one of the most important sites in the Near East, Râs Shamrah, ancient UGARIT. The initial discovery was made accidentally in 1928 by a farmer whose plow struck a tomb. This led to the excavation of the tell of Ugarit less than a mile away. Begun in 1929 by C. Schaeffer, excavations continued until 1939. They were resumed in 1948.

Ugarit flourished between 2100 and 1200 B.C. The excavators have uncovered a palace, and temples of Dagon and Baal. Most important are the archives, with numerous clay tablets in Akkadian and the previously unknown Ugaritic. The latter was deciphered concurrently in 1930 by H. Bauer of Germany and by E. Dhorme and C. Virolleaud of France. As recently as 1960 excavators came upon a new archive, which produced thirty boxes of texts. The Ugaritic texts are of paramount importance to OT studies because the religion of Baal, Anath, and other Ugaritic gods is similar to that of the Canaanites of Palestine. The literary style and vocabulary of texts such as the epics of Aqhat and of Keret are very similar to the poetic portions of the OT.

Ancient HAMATH on the Orontes was investigated by the Danes under H. Ingholt between 1931 and 1938. Hamath was an independent kingdom conquered by Jeroboam II (2 K. 14:28).

Tell Ta'yinat near Antioch was excavated by C. W. McEwan from 1932 to 1938. He found a Syro-Hittite temple of the 9th cent. B.C. with a ground plan similar to that of Solomon's temple.

Ancient ANTIOCH (SYRIAN) was the third largest city in the Roman empire. Joint American-French excavations were conducted between 1932 and 1939 under G. Elderkin, C. Morey, and R. Stillwell. Hundreds of fine mosaics were recovered from twenty churches of the 4th century. Unfortunately, little of the earlier levels was recovered, as these are now under the water table of the Orontes. Only one inscription and a marble fragment bear witness to the Jews of ancient Antioch, who comprised one-seventh of the population. At the famous suburb of DAPHNE, 5 mi. (8 km.) S of Antioch, excavators found the Roman theater built by Vespasian on the site of the Jewish synagogue.

On the Euphrates just across from the Iraqi border is one of the most important sites in the Near East, ancient MARI, a major city that flourished until it was destroyed by Hammurabi in the 18th cent. B.C. Bedouin accidentally discovered the site in 1933. The French under A. Parrot have excavated Mari in more than twenty seasons (1933-1939, 1951-1956, and since 1960). They cleared a royal palace of the 2nd millennium B.C., covering 15 acres (6 hectares) and including 270 rooms, some with striking frescoes. Of the greatest significance are more than twenty thousand cuneiform tablets, which provide us with (among other things) names similar to those found in Abraham's genealogy. Recently published texts from Mari provide the first substantial parallels to biblical prophecy.

Tell Chagar Bazar, on a branch of the Habor about 20 mi. (30 km.) S of the Turkish border, was excavated under M. E. L. Mallowan (1935-1937). Its identification is uncertain. It is significant that an Old Babylonian text from the site mentions horses, for this area became part of the state of Mitanni, which flourished because of its charioteers. Just S of Tell Chagar Bazar, Tell Brâk also was excavated by Mallowan between 1937 and 1939. In the temple terrace (2900 B.C.) were thousands of black and white alabaster "eye idols," figurines of gods consisting of pairs of eyes. An unexpected discovery was a palace belonging to Naram-Sin of Akkad (2250 B.C.).

From 1937 to 1939 and from 1946 to 1949 C. L. Woolley labored at the large mound of ancient Alalakh on the Orontes in Turkish territory, and also at the port of el-Mina (Gk. Poseideion), located at the mouth of the Orontes. A total of 466 Akkadian texts from Alalakh sheds important light on the background of the biblical patriarchs. El-Mina was the major Greek outpost for trade with Syria and Mesopotamia from the 8th to the 4th cents. B.C.

Biblical TADMOR (2 Ch. 8:4), the famous oasis city of Palmyra during Roman times, attained its apogee under Queen Zenobia, who dared to challenge the Roman emperor Aurelian (A.D. 271). The extensive ruins, including over one hundred columns still in place, were seen by the Jewish traveler Benjamin of Tudela in A.D. 1172, and were then rediscovered by English merchants at the end of the 17th century. Between the World Wars French scholars such as R. Dussaud, C. Virolleaud, A. Gabriel, and M. Dunand worked at Palmyra. In 1939 H. Seyrig investigated the agora. Just before World War II Chinese silks of the 1st-2nd cents. A.D. were discovered. From 1954 to 1961 Swiss excavators under P. Collart worked in the Baalshamin temple area. Since 1959 Polish scholars under K. Michalowski have been excavating the camp of Diocletian. From 1963 to 1966 Syrians under A. Bounni uncovered the temple of Nebo.

The capital of Syria, DAMASCUS, was also the capital of the Arameans (2 S. 8:5f.) until its conquest by Tiglath-pileser III in 732 B.C. The outline of "the street called Straight" (Acts 9:11) is still preserved by the modern Sharia' et-Tawwil, which ends at the Eastern Gate (Bâb esh-Sharqi). In 1947 the Syrians discovered a Roman arch about 13 ft. (4 m.) below the present street level. The eastern triple gate (now largely restored) at the end of the street also dates from the Roman period.

In 1955-1956 the West Germans under A. Moortgat worked at the great mound of Tell Fekherîyeh, E of Tell Halâf on the Habor River. They uncovered a Hurrian settlement of the mid-2nd millennium B.C., which may have been ancient Waššukanni, the capital of the kingdom of Mitanni.

The Danes under P. Riis excavated the site of Tell Sukas on the coast from 1958 to 1963. Sukas is probably the Šuksi mentioned in Ugaritic texts. Gifted with two harbors, Sukas served as an important Greek trading outpost from 850 to 550 B.C.

Ancient ARPAD has been excavated by British archeologists since 1960. They have uncovered the remains of the Aramean city whose destruction by the Assyrians left such a deep impression on biblical writers (2 K. 18:34, par. Isa. 36:19; Jer. 49:23).

Between 1968 and 1974 the Syrians built a major dam on the Euphrates at Tabqa, about 90 mi. (145 km.) E of Aleppo. The new lake created by the dam, 50 mi. (80 km.) long and 5 mi. (8 km.) wide, has covered many tells, including those of the southern part of the kingdom of Carchemish and the eastern part of the kingdom of Yamḫad (Aleppo). Emergency salvage excavations were conducted by many nations at Tell Frey, 12 mi. (20 km.) upstream from the dam. A palace of the 17th-16th cents. B.C., with a number of cuneiform texts, was cleared. Another site, Tell Selenkahiyah, which flourished from 2400 to 2200 B.C., also was subject to salvage excavations.

ARCHEOLOGY OF PALESTINE AND SYRIA

Third-millennium temple at Byblos. During the Amorite period (2nd millennium B.C.) the site was occupied by the "obelisk temple" of Resheph (reconstructed at left). (W. S. LaSor)

The Italians under P. Matthiae have been working since 1964 at TELL MARDIKH, 43 mi. (70 km.) SW of Aleppo. This large tell of 140 acres (56 hectares) has turned out to be one of the most spectacular sites ever excavated, for it was ancient EBLA, one of the main kingdoms of the area. Over twenty thousand cuneiform tablets in Sumerian and in a new dialect, Paleo-Canaanite, have come from its archives, dated to 2400-2250 B.C. Of great significance is the appearance of a king named Ebrum (cf. Eber in Gen. 10:21). Also, cities of Palestine such as Salem, Hazor, Lachish, Megiddo, Gaza, Joppa, etc., are mentioned.

B. Phoenicia. The earliest explorations in Phoenicia were conducted by the French scholar E. Renan, who came to the Levant in 1860 with troops sent by Napoleon III.

The most famous site in Lebanon is the spectacular Roman temple complex of BAALBEK (Gk. Heliopolis) in the Beqa' Valley. Some scholars have sought to associate Aven (Am. 1:5) with the area. Baalbek was first brought to Europe's attention by P. Belon in 1555, and was then accurately described by Wood and Dawkins in 1751. After the visit in 1898 of Emperor Wilhelm II, the German scholars O. Puchstein and B. Schulz worked at the site. Since World War II excavations and reconstruction have been directed by M. Chehab and H. Kalayan. Soundings have revealed Persian and Hellenistic remains.

The French have excavated the port of Byblos under M. Dunand and P. Montet (1921-1924, 1933-1938, 1960-1962, and since 1968). The Egyptians traded with Byblos for the famous cedars of Lebanon from the 3rd millennium B.C., and many Egyptian objects have been recovered from the site. In 1923 the sarcophagus of Ahiram was discovered. Inscribed in archaic Phoenician, it is one of the oldest extant alphabetic inscriptions (early 10th cent. B.C.).

Ancient SIDON was a great Phoenician city (Gen. 10:19; 1 K. 5:6 [MT 20]; 16:31). In 1855 the black basalt sarcophagus of Eshmun'azar, with an important Phoenician inscription, was discovered at Sidon. Thirty-two years later the sarcophagus of his son Tabnit, "priest of Astarte," was found. At the end of the 19th cent. the Turkish archeologist O. Hamdi discovered four carved sarcophagi, which are the finest Hellenistic sculptures on display in the Istanbul Museum. Outstanding is the "Alexander Sarcophagus," which depicts a battle between Alexander and the Persians.

Bronze figure of Syrian god discovered near Tyre (Trustees of the British Museum)

The temple of Eshmun at Bostan esh-Sheh, 3 mi. (5 km.) N of Sidon, was partly excavated by Macridi-Bey and Van Landau in the early 20th century. Work was resumed in 1963 by M. Dunand, who discovered eleven statues of squatting children dedicated to Eshmun. Four of these have Phoenician inscriptions, one with a text naming a series of three kings and a prince from the 5th-4th cents. B.C.

The Phoenician city of TYRE was renowned for its maritime trade (Ezk. 26:4-14). It was actually an island that was transformed into a peninsula by Alexander the Great's causeway. Aerial and underwater surveys of the harbor installations were conducted in 1934-1936 by A. Poidebard. Since 1947 systematic excavations under M. Chehab have uncovered 40 acres (16 hectares) in the Roman Byzantine necropolis on the mainland and in the area of the southern harbor on the peninsula. On the mainland at Tyre hundreds of carved sarcophagi (2nd-7th cents. A.D.) have been uncovered on both sides of a columned roadway with a monumental gateway. Most impressive is a well-preserved hippodrome (4th cent. A.D.) which seated 100,000 spectators. In the area of the peninsula the excavators have uncovered marble and mosaic pavements of the 4th cent. A.D. and a square arena for two thousand spectators. Unfortunately, pre-Roman levels have proved elusive.

German scholars under R. Hachmann conducted excavations from 1963 to 1970 at the site of Kamed el-Loz,

ARCHEOLOGY OF PALESTINE AND SYRIA

ancient Kumidi, in the Beqa' Valley. Important finds include a fortress and temple with early (13th cent. B.C.) alphabetic ostraca. Also discovered were four cuneiform tablets, similar to the Amarna Letters, which refer to the deportation of some Ḫabiru to Nubia.

Midway between Sidon and Tyre lies the site of ZAREPHATH (1 K. 17:8-24; Lk. 4:26). J. B. Pritchard conducted systematic excavations from 1969 to 1974, uncovering for the first time stratified Iron Age (9th-6th cents. B.C.) remains of the Phoenicians. The site yielded painted clay masks, a small shrine, and an ivory plaque with an inscription to Tanit-Ashtart (RSV "Ashtaroth," Jgs. 10:6; 1 K. 11:5). This is the first inscriptional reference in the East to Tanit, who was the goddess worshiped at Carthage.

C. Palestine. In 1838 an American seminary professor E. Robinson, with his former student E. Smith, made a pioneer survey of sites and established many important identifications. From 1872 to 1878 the British Palestine Exploration Fund sponsored a topographical survey of Cisjordan, conducted by C. R. Conder and H. H. Kitchener. In 1884 and the following years G. Schumacher explored northern Transjordan.

The first excavation was undertaken in Jerusalem in 1863 by F. de Saulcy at the so-called "Tombs of the Kings" N of the present walled city. He believed that he had found the mausoleum of the kings of Judah. One tomb, which has a rolling stone, is actually that of Helena,Queen of Adiabene, who was converted to Judaism in A.D. 48.

The first important excavator in Palestine was the British Egyptologist Flinders Petrie, who dug in 1890 at Tell el-Ḥesī (mistakenly identified with Lachish, but now believed to be Eglon). He was able to synchronize Palestinian pottery with that found in Egypt. Petrie later dug SE of Tell el-Ḥesī at Tell Jemmeh in 1926-1927, at Tell el-Fâr'ah (S) in 1928-1930, and at Tell el-'Ajjûl in 1930-1934. His identifications of these sites are not maintained today.

R. A. S. Macalister of Ireland excavated the site of GEZER (Tell Jezer) from 1902 to 1909. An important find was the Gezer Calendar (10th cent. B.C.), the oldest Hebrew text yet discovered. (See also below.)

At TAANACH (Tell Ta'annak) E. Sellin initiated Austrian involvement with campaigns from 1902 to 1904. The cache of twelve cuneiform texts that he discovered is the largest corpus of Akkadian texts found in Palestine. (See also below.)

From 1908 to 1910 G. Reisner, who had worked in Egypt, excavated SAMARIA (Sebasṭiyeh), introducing more exact techniques into Palestinian archeology.

Excavations were conducted by D. MacKenzie in 1911-1912 at BETH-SHEMESH (Tell er-Rumeileh). His earlier work in the Aegean enabled him to identify Philistine sherds.

Because of faulty techniques and inadequate records, most of the results of excavations before World War I are difficult to use. The liberation of Palestine from the Turks by General Allenby opened a period of many fruitful excavations.

W. F. Albright, who was to become a leading biblical archeologist, began his career by digging at Tell el-Fûl in 1922-1923. Early Iron Age materials that he discovered strongly support its identification with GIBEAH, Saul's capital.

The Germans, who began excavations at SHECHEM (Tell Balâṭah) in 1913-1914, returned to the site from 1926 to 1934. Unfortunately, digging proceeded without adequate supervision, evidence of pottery was neglected until 1934, and Sellin's files were destroyed by the American bombing of Berlin in 1943. (See also below.)

Tell el-Ḥuṣn (ancient Beth-shean), from Roman theater. The site has been occupied almost continuously since Chalcolithic times. (W. S. LaSor)

Excavations at BETH-SHEAN (Tell el-Ḥuṣn) were conducted from 1921 to 1933 by C. S. Fisher, A. Rowe, and G. M. Fitzgerald. Nearly all the top five levels were removed and a sounding to virgin soil went through 70 ft. (21 m.) of debris. Four Canaanite temples (1400-1000 B.C.) with evidence of a serpent cult were uncovered. Prized discoveries were inscribed stelae of Seti I and Ramses II. That the Egyptians used Philistine mercenaries at this key outpost is evidenced by numerous anthropoid coffins with Philistine features.

The most ambitious excavation undertaken in Palestine was that of the Oriental Institute of Chicago at MEGIDDO (Tell el-Mutesellim). The work, directed in turn by C. S. Fisher, P. L. O. Guy, and G. Loud, continued from 1925 to 1939. The five top strata, dating from 350 to 1000 B.C., were completely removed, but in only one area was bedrock reached. The most noteworthy of the discoveries are the so-called stables of Solomon, which were later proved to be from the period of Ahab (9th cent. B.C.). (J. Pritchard has argued that these structures are storehouses, but Y. Yadin would still maintain that they are stables.) Also remarkable are a shaft and tunnel cut to give access to water 118 ft. (36 m.) below the surface.

On the boundary between Judah and Israel W. F. Badè excavated the site of Tell en-Naṣbeh from 1926 to 1935. The tell is identified with Mizpah (1 K. 15:21f.). Badè cleared a large city gate (9th cent. B.C.) equipped with benches, and found a seal of Jaazaniah (2 K. 25:23) dated to 600 B.C. *See* MIZPAH **3.**

Shiloh (Seilûn) was excavated by the Danes under H. Kjaer from 1926 to 1932. The results indicate that the site was destroyed *ca.* 1100 B.C. *See* SHILOH **2.**

W. F. Albright and M. G. Kyle excavated Tell Beit Mirsim from 1926 to 1932. They found a seal of Eliakim, steward of Jehoiachin (2 K. 24:6). Albright's publication of the stratification and pottery provided the definitive framework for subsequent work in Palestine. He persisted in his identification of the site with biblical DEBIR (originally called Kiriath-sepher); but see II.F below.

Improved methods of analysis developed by M. Wheeler were introduced by the British excavations of J. W. Crowfoot and K. Kenyon at Samaria from 1931 to 1935. From the NT period is preserved a large basilica and the broad staircase of Herod's temple to Augustus. (See also II.I below.)

R. W. Hamilton excavated Tell Abū Hawâm on the Bay of Haifa in 1932-1933. He found imported Mycenaean pottery and Greek ware of the 10th-9th cents. B.C. The latter are among the earliest Greek wares exported to the Near East after the inception of the Dark Age in 1200 B.C.

Work on the great mound of LACHISH (Tell ed-Duweir) begun by J. Starkey in 1932 was cut short by his murder by bandits in 1938. Sennacherib captured Lachish in 701 B.C. (2 K. 18:13f.), a feat proudly recorded on reliefs in his palace. The remains of fifteen hundred victims desecrated by a layer of pig bones, and an Assyrian helmet, arms, and arrows are grim remnants of the siege. In 1966 Y. Aharoni excavated the "solar shrine."

BETHEL (Beitîn) was excavated in 1934 by W. F. Albright and J. L. Kelso and by the latter in 1954, 1957, and 1960. They found a Canaanite temple and well-built houses. Bethel was burned in the late 13th cent. B.C. and covered with ash nearly 2 m. (6.5 ft.) thick in places (Jgs. 1:22-26). The Canaanite structures were followed by poorly-built Israelite houses.

In JERUSALEM C. N. Johns conducted excavations in the citadel area between 1934 and 1940. He found eighth- to seventh-century B.C. pottery, and walls from the Maccabean period. Excavations in the 1930's by L. H. Vincent under the building of the Sisters of Zion near the Ecce Homo Arch uncovered what he interpreted as remains of the Herodian fortress Antonia. P. Benoit, however, has argued that the striated flagstones are not part of the Lithostroton where Jesus was tried (Jn. 19:13) but the eastern forum of Hadrian's Aelia Capitolina. (See also II.L below.)

With the outbreak of World War II, followed by fighting between Jews and Arabs, excavations in Palestine ceased almost completely during the 1940's. One exception was the excavation at Tell el-Fâr'ah (N) begun in 1946 by R. de Vaux and continued until 1960. This was the site of TIRZAH, the capital of some of the Israelite kings before Omri founded Samaria. In 1947 a Canaanite temple was discovered at Nahariyah. Excavations there by I. Ben-Dor in 1947, by M. Dothan in 1954-1955 and by D. Barag in 1968 recovered Canaanite figurines and a mold for casting them.

The year 1948 marked the establishment of the state of Israel. In Jordan (including the West Bank) foreign archeologists continued to dominate the work of excavation, but in the new Jewish state Israeli archeologists themselves took the lead.

In 1950-1951 J. L. Kelso and J. B. Pritchard, working at the site of NT JERICHO, uncovered Herodian buildings, including a sunken garden and a reflecting pool. From 1952 to 1958 K. Kenyon reexcavated the site of OT Jericho (Tell es-Sulṭân), which had been worked earlier by E. Sellin and C. Watzinger in 1907-1909, and by John Garstang in 1930-1936. The latter believed that he had found the walls that had fallen flat in Joshua's siege, an event that he dated to *ca.* 1400 B.C. Kenyon demonstrated that Garstang's walls belonged instead to a far earlier period. Her expedition found very little from Joshua's day, for most of the material from this period seems to have been eroded away. Her greatest achievement was the demonstration that Jericho is the oldest Neolithic city in the world, dated to 7000 B.C.

From 1953 to 1964 J. P. Free excavated the site of DOTHAN (Tell Dôthā). At this site rectangular cisterns 10 ft. (3 m.) deep may illustrate the type of pit into which Joseph was placed by his brothers (Gen. 37:24).

Y. Aharoni, an Israeli archeologist, excavated Ramat Raḥel, just S of Jerusalem, from 1959 to 1962. He believed that he had discovered the palace built by Jehoiakim and denounced by Jeremiah (Jer. 22:13-19).

Israeli archeologist Y. Yadin excavated the massive site of HAZOR (Tell el-Qedaḥ) between 1955 and 1958. Among the significant discoveries were numerous Canaanite shrines, and a clay liver model (for extispicy; *see* BABYLONIA IX.D) inscribed in cuneiform. (See also II.I below.)

Jaffa (Yâfā) was excavated by Y. Kaplan from 1955 to 1961. An important find was part of the city gate, inscribed with the name of Ramses II (13th cent. B.C.). *See* JOPPA.

J. B. Pritchard worked at the site of GIBEON (el-Jîb) from 1956 to 1962. Among his finds were inscriptions with the name Gibeon. The most spectacular discovery was an elaborate water system involving an enormous "pool" with a spiral stairway (cf. 2 S. 2:13).

A major salvage expedition was directed from 1957 to 1966 at SHECHEM by G. E. Wright. Shechem served as the training ground for a new generation of American archeologists. A large fortress-temple from the Hyksos period was uncovered. A Canaanite shrine at nearby Tananir, built *ca.* 1400 B.C., may have served as the central shrine for a league of seminomadic tribes.

'Avdat, about 30 mi. (50 km.) S of Beersheba, was excavated between 1958 and 1960 by M. Avi-Yonah and A. Negev. There are remains from its Nabatean, Roman, and Byzantine eras. Among the discoveries from the last phase are well-preserved churches and a monastery.

From 1959 to 1961 an Italian expedition led by Antonio Frova excavated Qeiṣâriyeh, the Herodian port of CAESAREA. The archeologists cleared the theater that was the scene of Herod Agrippa's fatal stroke (Acts 12:23) and found an inscription naming Pilate. In 1962 M. Avi-Yonah cleared the remains of a fourth-century A.D. synagogue and found fragments of an inscription mentioning Nazareth—the only occurrence of its name on an inscription.

K. Kenyon directed a major expedition designed to investigate the area of OPHEL, OT Jerusalem, from 1961 to 1968. Her work was begun when the area was in Jordanian hands and was completed after the capture of the Old City by the Israelis. (See also II.I, K below.)

Excavations from 1962 to 1972 were conducted by by M. Dothan, D. N. Freedman, and J. L. Swauger at the major Philistine settlement of ASHDOD (Esdûd). Mycenaean goddess figurines and Cypro-Minoan texts were among the finds. (See also II.I below.)

Between 1962 and 1967 Y. Aharoni worked at Tell 'Arâd in the Negev. The identification of the site was confirmed by a bowl with the name ARAD incised upon it. Arad was rich in inscribed ostraca from the 9th-4th cents. B.C. The greatest surprise was an Israelite sanctuary from the Solomonic period.

From 1962 to 1967 an Italian expedition under V. Corbo worked at Herodium (Jebel Fureidîs), where Herod the Great was buried. Many of the structures were uncovered, including a double concentric wall, towers, and a Roman bath. (See also II.L. below)

Y. Yadin excavated es-Sebbeh, the spectacular Herodian stronghold of MASADA, from 1963 to 1965. He found valuable remains of the last stand of the Jewish zealots in A.D. 73 against the Romans. (See II.L below.)

Between 1963 and 1968 P. W. Lapp reexcavated Taanach. Numerous objects used in Canaanite religion were found, including a terra-cotta mold for the mass production of nude fertility-goddess figurines.

A major excavation was conducted at Gezer (see also above) under the directorship of G. E. Wright, W. G. Dever, and others from 1964 to 1974. They cleared the famous row of Canaanite pillars (apparently legal symbols of a treaty) that Macalister had discovered and dated them to *ca.* 1600 B.C.

In 1966 an expedition led by A. Biran began excavations

ARCHEOLOGY OF PALESTINE AND SYRIA

at the northern city of DAN. The finds include a monumental Israelite city gate and a high place.

B. Mazar conducted extensive excavations between 1968 and 1977 in the area S of the temple platform in JERUSALEM. He recovered materials from the Herodian period and evidence of the Roman attack in A.D. 70 that destroyed the temple. (See also II.I, L below.)

In 1969 Y. Aharoni began excavations at BEER-SHEBA (Tell es-Seba'). He found extensive structures from the period of the Israelite monarchy. The displacement of a horned altar may have been a result of Josiah's reforms.

D. Transjordan. 'Arâq el-Emîr, about 11 mi. (18 km.) W of Amman, was discovered in 1817. The site was the home of the influential Tobiad family (cf. Neh. 2:19). H. C. Butler made a study of the palace in 1904-1905; further excavations were undertaken by P. W. Lapp in 1961. (See II.K below.)

Jerash (Roman GERASA) was excavated by the British from 1928 to 1929 and by Americans between 1930-1931 and 1933-1934. They traced the two-mile circuit wall and found 150 inscriptions. Among the well-preserved structures are Hadrian's triumphal arch, the famed elliptical forum, a colonnaded street 2000 ft. (600 m.) long, and thirteen churches.

Khirbet et-Tannur, about 14 mi. (23 km.) E of the southern tip of the Dead Sea, was excavated by N. Glueck in 1937-1938. Its Nabatean temple yielded architectural fragments and sculptured reliefs of such deities as Atargatis and Zeus-Hadad.

Between 1938 and 1940 Glueck worked at the small mound of Tell el-Kheleifeh on the Gulf of Aqabah. Glueck, who discovered evidence of copper smelting, identified the site with EZION-GEBER, Solomon's seaport (1 K. 9:26). A building with holes in its walls was originally interpreted by Glueck as a smelter, but B. Rothenberg has demonstrated that the building was simply a storehouse or granary. (*See also* ELATH.)

In 1950 and 1956 F. V. Winnett, W. L. Reed and G. W. Van Beek worked at Dhībân (DIBON, or Dibon-Gad). They found fragments of a Moabite stele, the first Moabite ostracon, and the first Moabite structure ever recovered.

Excavations were conducted at PETRA, the famous Nabatean capital, from 1958 to 1964 by P. J. Parr and P. Hammond. The Roman theater was cleared.

Between 1964 and 1967 J. B. Pritchard worked at the large mound of Tell es-Sa'īdîyeh. The excavator identified the tell with biblical ZARETHAN, a bronze-working center in the days of Solomon (1 K. 7:45f.).

Excavations were conducted in 1960-1962 and 1964 at Tell Deir 'allā, just N of the Jabbok and E of the Jordan, by the Dutch scholar H. J. Franken. The site was identified as Succoth by Glueck, but Franken rejects this identification. Among the rich finds of this cult center are tablets in a unique script similar to the Aegean linear scripts and a wall inscribed in Aramaic mentioning the words of Balaam (Nu. 23). (*See* SUCCOTH **1**.)

In 1967 R. H. Smith was able to work briefly at PELLA before fighting broke out between Israel and Jordan. He reached only Byzantine levels but found a sarcophagus which may be descended from the first-century ossuary style.

HESHBON (Tell Ḥesbân) was excavated between 1968 and 1976 by S. H. Horn, R. S. Boraas, and L. Geraty. As no Late Bronze remains have been found, Sihon's capital city (Nu. 21:21-30) must have been located elsewhere. A large plastered cistern from the 9th cent. B.C. has been found (cf. Cant. 7:4). Among the extensive remains from the Roman period are two tombs with rolling stones and a lead flogging head used for scourging.

C. M. Bennett conducted a decade-long examination of Edomite sites. In 1960, 1962, and 1965 she worked at Umm el-Bayyârah, which rises almost 1000 ft. (300 m.) above Petra. Her finds include a royal seal with the name "Qos Gabr," an Edomite king mentioned in the Assyrian annals of the 7th cent. B.C. In 1968-1969 she excavated Tawīlân, E of Petra. The site proved to be a large Edomite settlement that flourished from the 8th to the 6th cents. B.C. In 1971 she worked at Buṣeirah, which is possibly biblical BOZRAH (Am. 1:12; Isa. 34:6), one of the great Edomite cities.

A major development in Jordanian archeology has been the training of Jordanian students by American archeologists at the University of Jordan in Amman, established in 1963.

II. Significant Archeological Discoveries.–*A. Surveys.* From extensive surface surveys in Transjordan between 1932 and 1947 N. Glueck concluded that there was a major break in intensive sedentary occupation between 1900 and 1300 B.C., a conclusion that would support the late date of the Exodus and the Conquest in the 13th century. The German scholar S. Mittmann surveyed the area between the Jabbok and the Yarmuk Rivers from 1963 to 1966, mapping about 350 sites. A survey was also conducted by the Heshbon excavations within a 6-mi. (10-km.) radius of the site. Both of these surveys support in general Glueck's basic thesis. The Spanish scholar E. Olávarri, who excavated Aroer between 1964 and 1966, found an occupational gap between 2050 B.C. and the end of the Late Bronze period (1550-1200 B.C.).

On the other hand, Middle Bronze materials have come to light at Mt. Nebo, Nā'ûr, and Amman, and L.B. materials at Medeba and Amman. In 1955 a bulldozer on a runway at the Amman airport uncovered a L.B. shrine. Salvage operations by G. L. Harding and later work in 1966 by J. B. Hennessy showed that the temple contained a large quantity of imported Mycenaean ware. It has been suggested that this was a tribal-league shrine for seminomadic peoples.

Between 1952 and 1964 Glueck surveyed the southern area of the Negeb in Israel and discovered over 1500 sites. In 1963 Lapp estimated that out of 5000 sites in Palestine there had been scientific excavations at about 150, including twenty-six major excavations. Since 1967 Israeli surveys have uncovered thousands of new sites. Of 2500 sites plotted in the Golan Heights and in Judah in 1967-1968, 1000 were hitherto unknown. Thus, in spite of the great increase in excavations, only a very small percentage of the known sites has been excavated.

B. Mesolithic and Neolithic Ages (*ca.* 10,000-4300 B.C.). Important finds from the Mesolithic Natufian culture (10,000-7000 B.C.) were discovered in the caves at the base of Mt. Carmel by D. Garrod between 1929 and 1934.

In addition to the major Neolithic (*ca.* 7000-4300 B.C.) materials from Jericho, other remains from this period have been found at Abū Ghôsh by J. Perrot and at Beidha (near Petra) by D. Kirkbride.

C. Chalcolithic Age (4300-3200 B.C.). Between 1929 and 1938 A. Mallon and R. Koeppel excavated Teleilât el-Ghassûl NE of the Dead Sea. They discovered houses with multicolored frescoes of animals. Excavations in the area of Tel Azor, just SE of Tel Aviv, have yielded ossuary tombs in the shape of dwellings. At Tell Abū Maṭar and other sites in the Beersheba Valley excavations by J. Perrot and others have uncovered Chalcolithic settlements. At En-gedi ('Ain Jidi) B. Mazar in 1949 and 1961-1962 uncovered a Chalcolithic temenos. In 1960 the Israelis recovered over four hundred cultic objects from a cave in Naḥal Mishmar near En-gedi.

D. Early Bronze Age (3200-*ca.* 2000 B.C.). On the

ARCHEOLOGY OF PALESTINE AND SYRIA

southwest shore of the Sea of Galilee is the 50-acre (20-hectare) site of Khirbet Kerak, identified as Beth-Yerah. This was excavated between 1944 and 1964 by B. Mazar and others. The red and black burnished pottery, named Khirbet Kerak ware (2550-2275 B.C.), may have had its origins in Anatolia.

Excavations by J. Marquet-Krause from 1933 to 1935 and by J. Callaway between 1964 and 1972 have revealed a 28-acre (11-hectare) E.B. city at et-Tell (identified by Albright with biblical AI). Work at the E.B. lower city of ARAD by R. Amiran from 1962 to 1966 and since 1971 has uncovered a towered wall and evidence of contacts with Egypt. S. Yeivin conducted excavations at Tell Sheikh Aḥmed el-ʿAreini (near modern Tel Gat) from 1956 to 1961. He found a sherd with the name of Narmer, the earliest of the Egyptian pharaohs (3100 B.C.).

On the peninsula el-Lisan of the Dead Sea are the walled city and cemetery of Bâb edh-Dhrâʿ, discovered in 1924 by A. Mallon. Excavations by Lapp in 1965 and 1967 at the 10-acre (4-hectare) E.B. town revealed that the cemetery with its shaft tombs and charnel houses contained an estimated 500,000 individual burials. Surveys in the area by W. Rast and T. Schaub in 1973 indicated that there are four other impressive E.B. settlements in the area, which was noted in the OT for its five CITIES OF THE VALLEY (Gen. 14:2).

E. Middle Bronze Age (*ca.* 2000-1550 B.C.). Archeologists disagree about the parameters and the designation of the earliest phase of the Middle Bronze Age in Palestine. While Albright favored 2000-1800 as the M.B. I period, K. Kenyon preferred to speak of an Intermediate E.B.-M.B. Age with the M.B. I Age proper beginning *ca.* 1900, and W. Dever preferred to begin the M.B. I period *ca.* 2100.

This era witnessed major destructions caused by the incursions of nomads, whose presence is indicated by large cemeteries. Lapp believed that the newcomers included non-Semitic elements from beyond the Caucasus, whereas Dever and Kenyon identified the invaders as Amorites from Syria.

In the 1960's Dever and Lapp investigated M.B. I settlements and burials at Jebel Qaʿaqir (8 mi. [13 km.] W of Hebron) and at Dhahr Mirzbaneh (7 mi. [11 km.] NE of Bethel). In 1970 Yeivin investigated forty-four tombs at ʿAin Samiya (9 mi. [14 km.] NE of Ramallah) and found a silver cup with Mesopotamian mythological motifs. It appears that the nomadic M.B. I tribes also set up some of the dolmens in the Golan area. Hut foundations were found in the rocky Har Yeruḥam by M. Kochavi.

Albright, who dated Abraham *ca.* 1800 B.C., associated the patriarchal movements with caravan sites that flourished in the M.B. I period in Transjordan and in the Negeb. By using a magnetometer P. C. Hammond discovered some M.B. remains at Jebel er-Rumeide, a terraced hill W of Hebron. In 1971 he cleared a thick wall from the late 18th century. On the other hand, excavations at Tell es-Sebaʿ (Beer-sheba) have failed to produce any M.B. materials.

Excavations at Aphek (Râs el-ʿAin), begun in 1972 by M. Kochavi, have revealed a major M.B. IIA (1900-1750 B.C.) palace with large courtyards. In 1974-1975 several cuneiform lexical fragments were discovered, including a trilingual text in Sumerian, Akkadian, and Canaanite. (*See* APHEK 1; ANTIPATRIS.)

Middle Bronze and Late Middle Bronze (*ca.* 2000-1500 B.C.) pottery from Megiddo, a period of prosperity but little peace, indicated by numerous strata and phases of strata (Oriental Institute, University of Chicago)

ARCHEOLOGY OF PALESTINE AND SYRIA

The M.B. IIB-C (1750-1550 B.C.) period is the age of the Hyksos domination of Egypt, when Jacob and his descendants emigrated to Egypt. Excavations at Dan, Beer-sheba, Tell Malḥata, etc., have uncovered "Hyksos" sloped ramparts. A large fortress temple of this period was found in Shechem.

Religious structures of the Canaanites during the M.B. II period include the spectacular row of pillars at Gezer (see above I.C). At Bethel, Kelso found traces of blood — which he interpreted as evidence of Canaanite sacrifices — under a gate destroyed in the 16th century. C. Epstein discovered a *bāmâ*, or open-air precinct (*see* BAMAH), marked off by cyclopean stones at Turbo Mecha just S of Beth-shemesh.

F. Late Bronze Age (1550-1200 B.C.). The L.B. I (1550-1400) was a period dominated by the expansionistic activities of the 18th Dynasty of Egypt. Vivid evidence of the devastation by Thutmose III's campaign in 1468 B.C. has been found at GEZER.

The L.B. II period covers the 14th and 13th centuries. In the 14th cent. Palestine was threatened by the Ḫabiru during the Amarna age of Akhenaten. The Mycenaean pottery imported from the Aegean in the L.B. II can be used for dating strata.

Egyptian interest in controlling the Via Maris from Egypt along the Philistine coast has been illuminated by finds from Deir el-Balah, SW of Gaza. In 1972 T. Dothan found about forty anthropoid clay coffins in a cemetery used by an Egyptian garrison from the 14th to the 11th. centuries. These served as the prototypes for the later Philistine coffins.

Important evidence of the Egyptians in the Negeb was discovered by B. Rothenberg in 1969 at Timna. An Egyptian temple, with inscriptions from Seti I (1318-1304) to Ramses V (1160-1156), was uncovered at the base of the so-called Solomon's pillars. In opposition to Glueck's attribution of copper mining in the ARABAH to Solomon, Rothenberg suggests that these operations were conducted at an earlier date by the Egyptians.

There are only minimal L.B. remains from Jericho and Gibeon and none from Ai, cities associated with Joshua's campaigns. Scholars who believe that Joshua's campaign can be dated to the 13th cent. cite a number of Canaanite cities that were attacked at this time. The burning of Hazor (Josh. 11:1-11) is assigned by Yadin to *ca.* 1230 B.C. on the basis of Mycenaean pottery. The thirteenth-century devastation of Bethel is also attributed to the Israelites by Kelso.

Albright identified Tell Beit Mirsim, which was destroyed in the 13th cent., with Debir (see I.C above). Khirbet Rabûd, 9 mi. (14 km.) S of Hebron, excavated by M. Kochavi in 1968-1969 has now been proposed as a better candidate for DEBIR.

The biblical account which indicates that Shechem passed peacefully into Israelite hands is confirmed by its transition from L.B. to Iron I without a major destruction.

G. Early Iron Age (12th-11th cents. B.C.). The E.I. IA-B period was the time of the settlement of the Philistines along the coast and their conflict with the Israelites during the days of the judges and of Saul.

The excavations at Taanach confirm the biblical record that the city was captured not by Joshua but later (*ca.* 1125) under Deborah (Jgs. 5:19). The destruction of Dan in the 12th cent. is believed by A. Biran to be the result of the invasion of the tribe of Dan (Josh. 19:47; Jgs. 18:29). The devastation of Shechem in the 12th cent. is attributed to Abimelech (Jgs. 9). (*See also* SHECHEM II.)

In the late 13th and early 12th centuries the sea-peoples from the Aegean invaded the Levant and Egypt during the reigns of Merneptah and Ramses III. The newcomers may have been responsible for the shrine with a lion's skull discovered in the thirteenth-century level at Jaffa.

The most famous of the sea-peoples were the Philistines. Impressive Philistine objects, which betray their Aegean origins (Am. 9:7), have been recovered from Ashdod. A unique Philistine temple with two column bases, reminiscent of the temple destroyed by Samson (Jgs. 16:29), was uncovered by A. Mazar in 1971-1972 at Tell el-Qasîleh. The penetration of the Philistines into the interior has been illustrated by extensive remains at Gezer and by Philistine objects found as far north as Dan.

H. United Monarchy (10th cent. B.C.). The mastery of iron smelting, which gave the Philistines an upper hand until the reign of Saul, is vividly illustrated by the discovery of an iron plow in Saul's palace at Gibeah, reexcavated by Lapp in 1964.

David's capture of Jerusalem from the Jebusites has been illuminated by the excavations of K. Kenyon, who found a massive corner of the wall of the Jebusite city on the slope above the spring Gihon.

Unfortunately, almost all of Solomon's extensive building projects in Jerusalem have been obliterated. One possibly Solomonic structure is a fragmentary casemate wall. Kenyon believes that the enigmatic MILLO, "filling," which was repaired by David (2 S. 5:9) and by Solomon (1 K. 9:15), referred to the massive platforms on the eastern edge of Ophel, which were in constant need of repair.

Striking evidence to illustrate the biblical statement that Solomon built "Hazor, Megiddo, and Gezer" (1 K. 9:15) has come from the discovery of nearly identical gates at these sites. Yadin, recalling that the earlier excavation at Megiddo had uncovered a gate with three chambers on each side, anticipated the discovery of a similar gate at Hazor. His reexamination of Macalister's report on GEZER (see also above) led to the discovery of an identical gate there. The gateway at Gezer was destroyed late in the 10th cent., probably by Pharaoh Shishak (Sheshonq), who invaded Palestine five years after Solomon's death (1 K. 14:25). Shishak's raid at Megiddo was confirmed by a fragment (published in 1929) of his monumental stele.

I. The Divided Kingdom (9th-7th cents. B.C.). Upon Solomon's death his kingdom split into the southern kingdom of Judah, headed by his son Rehoboam, and the northern kingdom of Israel, led by the rebel Jeroboam I. The northern kingdom, which was more open to the influence of its pagan neighbors in Phoenicia and Syria, had a history characterized by spiritual apostasy and political instability. The northern kingdom was also the first to succumb to the expansion of the powerful Assyrian empire in the 8th century.

Phoenician materials from the 8th-6th cents. have been recovered from Achzib on the coast, where I. Ben-Dor cleared seventy tombs in 1941-1942 and 1944. Additional tombs were excavated between 1958 and 1970 by M. Prausnitz. (*See* ACHZIB **2.**)

Omri, the sixth king of Israel, transferred his capital from Tirzah to Samaria (1 K. 16:23f.). This transfer is confirmed by the discovery of unfinished buildings from Omri's time at Tell el Fâr'ah (N), identified with Tirzah (see I.C above). Omri's son Ahab married the notorious Phoenician princess Jezebel; this explains the presence of fine Phoenician masonry at Samaria. Ivory fragments found there illustrate the reference to Ahab's "ivory palace" (1 K. 22:39). Ahab's reign has also been credited with a number of constructions at Hazor, including the large pillared hall and the impressive water system, which descended 130 ft. (40 m.) to a spring. The so-called

ARCHEOLOGY OF PALESTINE AND SYRIA

stables of Solomon at Megiddo have been redated to Ahab's reign.

In the 8th cent. Judah was threatened and Israel was destroyed by the Assyrian expansion to the west. HAZOR was destroyed by Tiglath-pileser III in 732, during the reign of Pekah (2 K. 15:29); in the burned debris of the acropolis was found an ostracon with Pekah's name. At the site of ACCO (Tel 'Akko) M. Dothan, who began excavations in 1973, has found further evidence of the Assyrian attack. Lapp discovered a small fortress, destroyed probably by Tiglath-pileser III, at Tell er-Rumeith in Gilead.

After completing the siege of Samaria in 722, Sargon II sent further armies against the rebel Yamani ("Greek") of ASHDOD in 721. J. Kaplan, who excavated the seaport of Ashdod-Yam from 1965 to 1968, believed that he had found the wall built by Yamani. M. Dothan discovered at Ashdod a fragment of an Assyrian stele which confirms the reference (Isa. 20:1) to the campaign of Sargon's field marshal at Ashdod.

The presence of the paganism denounced by the prophets of Judah has been vividly illustrated by K. Kenyon's work at Jerusalem. Along the east slopes of OPHEL she discovered a ritual complex, including two stone pillars and a cultic cave dated *ca.* 800 B.C. (2 K. 12:3; 14:4). She also found a cave deposit dated *ca.* 700 with thirteen hundred pottery vessels and numerous human and animal figurines.

B. Mazar has found eighth- to seventh-century tombs near the southwest corner of the temple platform; he suggested that these may represent a royal cemetery. In the Jewish quarter of the walled city of Jerusalem, which N. Avigad has excavated since 1969, a city wall (cf. Neh. 3:8) 23 ft. (7 m.) broad was found. This wall, which enclosed the *mišneh,* "second quarter" (2 K. 22:14), was probably built by Hezekiah as a defense against Sennacherib's attack in 701. An inscription discovered at the Pool of Siloam in 1880 describes Hezekiah's construction of the Siloam tunnel.

In Transjordan, also, key discoveries have been made for this era. In 1879 H. Clermont-Ganneau was able to secure for the Louvre the important Mesha Stele (MOABITE STONE) from DIBON, the capital of Moab. It gives the Moabite king's version of his conflict with the Israelites in the 9th cent. (2 K. 3:4-27).

In 1961 a stone slab with eight lines in Ammonite was discovered on the citadel mound at Amman. This rare inscription, which includes a reference to the god Milcom (1 K. 11:5), is dated by F. Cross to the 9th cent. and

Objects identified as manger and hitching post from level IV at Megiddo. Once identified as "Solomon's stables," the building complexes have been dated to Ahab's time, and their function is open to question. (B. Van Elderen)

by S. Horn to the 8th century. In 1972 excavations under H. Thompson at Tell Siran on the campus of the University of Jordan in Amman uncovered a unique bronze bottle with eight lines of Ammonite. The text contains an inscription of the king of Ammon in the 7th cent. B.C.

J. Babylonian Conquest (6th cent. B.C.). In 1960 J. Naveh excavated the fortress of Meṣad Ḥashavyahu on the coast between Jaffa and Ashdod. The large quantity of Greek pottery indicates that this was held by Greek mercenaries in the service of Pharaoh Neco. Neco was defeated in 605 B.C. at Carchemish by Nebuchadrezzar, who also employed Greek mercenaries. From Arad have come ostraca from a fort destroyed by Nebuchadrezzar. They include instructions for the distribution of supplies to the KITTIM, who according to Aharoni were Greek mercenaries fighting for Judah. The abundant evidence of Greeks in the Near East at this early date indicates that the presence of Greek words in the Aramaic of Daniel is not an anachronism.

In 1942 an Aramaic papyrus was found at Saqqârah in Egypt. It is a letter, dated 604 B.C., from a King Adon to Pharoah Neco. Adon, who was probably the king of ASHKELON, asks for aid against the invading forces of Nebuchadrezzar (2 K. 24f.).

Epitaph of Sheban-yahu (Shebna), a royal steward of the early 7th cent. B.C. (cf. Isa. 22:15f.), written in archaic Hebrew (Phoenician) script (outlined in white for clarity). From rock-cut tomb at Siloam. (Trustees of the British Museum)

 ARCHEOLOGY OF PALESTINE AND SYRIA

Round tower from the Hellenistic second defense system, which replaced the Israelite inner wall around the summit at Samaria (B. Van Elderen)

Ostraca from Lachish reveal the tense situation before Nebuchadrezzar's attack. In 1975 N. Avigad discovered arrowheads and charred wood near a defensive tower in Jerusalem dating to the Babylonian king's assault in 586 B.C.

A vivid memorial of one man's faith in the face of the Babylonian invasion has been found at Khirbet Beit Lei, 5 mi. (8 km.) E of Lachish. F. Cross has translated the inscription, first published by J. Naveh in 1963, as follows: "I am Yahweh thy God; I will accept the cities of Judah and will redeem Jerusalem," and has suggested that this may have been incised by a refugee who thus expressed his trust in God's faithfulness in spite of the desolation of the Holy City (Lam. 3:22-24).

In addition to the well-known sites that were devastated by the Babylonians, the Israeli surveys of Judah in 1967-1968 uncovered many previously unknown settlements that are small and nameless. S. Weinberg has suggested that we may obtain a truer picture of Palestine in this period by the excavation of these sites, which have sixth- to fifth-century sherds.

K. Persian and Hellenistic Periods (5th-2nd cents. B.C.). From the second temple of Zerubbabel the only visible remains may be a straight joint about 100 ft. (30 m.) N of the southeast corner of the temple platform, noted by K. Kenyon in 1966. Kenyon's excavations revealed that in Nehemiah's day the perimeter wall was reduced to about 8500 ft. (2600 m.), which explains how the walls could be repaired within fifty-two days (Neh. 6:15).

On the cliff face at 'Arâq el-Emîr in Jordan is an inscription with the name Tobiah (Neh. 2:19). This is dated to the 6th or 5th cent. B.C. by B. Mazar but to the 3rd cent. B.C. by Albright.

In the Persian period the Sidonians established a colony at DOR on the coast. Dor was closely allied with Athens in the 5th cent., as indicated by its inclusion in the Athenian tribute lists and as confirmed by the presence of Attic pottery.

At Wâdī ed-Dâliyeh NW of Jericho, bedouin discovered a cave in 1962 and removed rare fourth-century papyri which contain the name of a Sanballat, perhaps the grandson of the governor of Samaria in Nehemiah's day (Neh. 2:10). Lapp, who explored the cave in 1963-1964, discovered grim remains of about two hundred men, women, and children from Samaria who had tried unsuccessfully to flee from the troops of Alexander the Great in 331 B.C.

BETH-ZUR (Khirbet eṭ-Ṭubeiqah) was excavated in 1931 by W. F. Albright and O. R. Sellers, and in 1957 by Sellers. The excavators recovered a dozen bathtubs from the Maccabean era, Beth-zur's period of greatest prosperity.

At ACCO (Roman Ptolemais) in the Bay of Haifa, while clearing the crusader castle between 1955 and 1964, S. Applebaum discovered a Hellenistic temple with an inscription of Antiochus V.

Between 1968 and 1973 S. Weinberg excavated Tel Anafa, an important Hellenistic site N of the Sea of Galilee. The settlement, founded before 200 B.C. and destroyed *ca.* 80 B.C., has yielded an unparalleled amount of molded glass and striking architectural ornaments.

L. The Herodian Period (1st cent. B.C.). Herod the Great built at numerous sites during his reign (37-4 B.C.). In JERUSALEM, B. Mazar has cleared the area S of the great temple platform (see I.C above). He has uncovered magnificent ashlars of the platform, some 30 ft. (9 m.) long (cf. Mk. 13:1), a street, and a staircase 215 ft. (64 m.) wide which leads up to the Huldah Gates. A Herodian aqueduct has been traced underground for over 600 ft. (180 m.). Among the most significant objects uncovered are a fragment of a sundial, a limestone object inscribed *qrbn* ("offering"; cf. Mk. 7:11), and the inscription

ARCHEOLOGY OF PALESTINE AND SYRIA

Excavations along the southwest corner of the retaining wall surrounding the temple mount in Jerusalem. An inscription found in this area confirmed that a tower stood here, from which a priest sounded the beginning of the sabbath. (Consulate General of Israel in New York)

"for the place of the blowing [of the trumpet]" on the cornerstone of the parapet of the royal stoa. Fragments with gold leaf enable one to visualize the grandeur of the temple. Evidence of the destruction of the temple in A.D. 70 includes 6 ft. (2 m.) of debris and ash, and an inscription of Vespasian and Titus discovered in 1970.

In the Jewish quarter W of the temple platform N. Avigad uncovered in 1969 a Herodian building with frescoes and a depiction of a menorah. Another house contained mortars, weights, and a mold for coins. The excavators cleared a sewage canal, which may have served as a temporary refuge for Jews fleeing from the Romans in A.D. 70.

In the citadel area of Jerusalem Israeli archeologists in 1970-1971 found Herodian remains believed to be extensions of structures found by Tushingham in 1967 in the Armenian gardens to the south. They interpret these structures as part of a huge platform, perhaps 1000 to 1150 ft. (300 to 350 m.) long, which would have served as the foundation for Herod's palace. Some scholars believe that the praetorium of Pilate, where Jesus was tried, was at Herod's palace rather than at the fortress Antonia, which overlooked the temple area.

Yadin uncovered spectacular remains at Herod's fortress of Masada (see I.C above), including Herod's palaces and the first synagogue from the 1st cent. A.D. Over four thousand coins, numerous cosmetic objects, and a few MSS were found. Yadin discovered about thirty skeletons of the 960 men, women, and children who perished. Among the remains of the Roman assault still visible are the siege ramp, the circumvallation wall, and several camps.

The Herodian fortress of Machaerus in Jordan, where John the Baptist was imprisoned, was excavated by J. Vardaman in 1968. He found aqueducts, bath installations, and evidences of the Roman siege of A.D. 72.

At NT Jericho, E. Netzer in 1972-1974 uncovered on the north bank of the Wâdī Qelt a palace complex with a swimming pool. This may have been the pool where the young high priest Aristobulos III was drowned at Herod's orders.

At Herodium, work since 1969 by G. Foerster and E. Netzer has uncovered a large reservoir, 150 by 230 ft. (45 by 70 m.), at the base of the hill.

M. NT Period (1st cent. A.D.). Locating Jesus' exorcism of the so-called Gadarene demoniac has been a problem because of the textual variants in the name of the site (Mt. 8:28; Mk. 5:1; Lk. 8:26; some MSS read "Gerasene" and others "Gergesene"). Origen's comment that there was a village called Gergesa on the eastern shore of the Sea of Galilee was confirmed in the course of road-building operations in 1970. D. Urman has excavated a first-century A.D. fishing village, called Kursi in Jewish sources, and a fifth-century A.D. church that commemorated the site of the miracle.

Excavations begun by G. Foerster in 1973 at TIBERIAS (cf. Jn. 6:23) have uncovered a gate complex dated to the reign of Herod Antipas, who founded the city and named it in honor of the emperor Tiberius. South of Tiberias by the warm springs at Hamath-Tiberias, work by M. Dothan in 1961 cleared a building that may have been used as a synagogue as early as the 1st cent. A.D.

The synagogue at CAPERNAUM (Tell Ḥûm), which may rest upon the site of the synagogue attended by Jesus, has been dated to the 2nd cent. A.D. But V. Corbo and S. Loffreda, who reexcavated Capernaum in 1968, now date the building to the 4th cent. on the basis of coins. Digging under an octagonal structure about 30 ft. (9 m.) from the Capernaum synagogue, the excavators uncovered the remains of a household church. They have suggested, on the basis of graffiti at the site and references by pilgrims (4th-6th cents. A.D.), that it was built upon the home of Peter.

In 1968 the first physical evidence of crucifixion as a form of punishment was recovered from an ossuary at Giv'at ha-Mivtar in northeastern Jerusalem. The ossuary, which dates to between A.D. 6 and 66, contained heel bones still transfixed by an iron nail. A crease in the radial bone indicates that the victim had been pinioned in his forearms, rather than in the palms as in the traditional picture of Christ's crucifixion (Gk. *cheír* in Jn. 20:27 can mean "arm"). The victim's calf bones had been shattered (cf. Jn. 19:32). (*See also* CROSS; CRUCIFY VI.)

Excavations in and around the Church of the Holy Sepulchre have helped to demonstrate that it lay outside the wall in Jesus' day. There is therefore no reason to doubt its authenticity as the site of Calvary and the empty tomb. Shafts dug in the church show that the area was used as a quarry and was therefore extramural, a conclusion also supported by Kenyon's excavation in the adjoining Muristan area.

In the area N of the present walled city of Jerusalem, L. Mayer and E. Sukenik discovered in 1925-1927 and 1940 what they believed were sections of the "third wall" of Herod Agrippa I. Subsequent discoveries, including the clearing of a tower facing north in 1972 by S. Ben-Aryeh and E. Netzer, have extended the line of the wall to 3950 ft. (1200 m.) and have confirmed the identification. This means that by the time of Agrippa I (A.D. 40-44) Jerusalem had expanded to 450 acres (180 hectares), and housed 120,000-150,000 people.

N. Dead Sea Scrolls and the Bar Cochba Finds (2nd

cent. B.C.-2nd cent. A.D.). An outstanding development for biblical studies was the discovery between 1947 and 1956 of the DEAD SEA SCROLLS in the caves of QUMRÂN. The MSS include copies of the OT a thousand years older than the Hebrew texts previously available, and sectarian compositions of a community that many scholars identify with the Essenes.

From 1951 to 1956 R. de Vaux and G. L. Harding excavated the khirbeh, or ruins, of the monastery at Qumrân, which flourished from *ca.* 130 B.C. to A.D. 68. In 1958 the community's farm buildings at 'Ain Feshkha were excavated. De Vaux also investigated forty-three of the more than eleven hundred tombs in the cemeteries. In 1966-1967 S. Steckoll uncovered ten skeletons from the main cemetery.

P. Bar-Adon discovered the site of 'Ain Ghuweir, 9 mi. (15 km.) S of Qumrân, in 1969. He uncovered a banquet hall, the burials of twelve men, seven women, and a child, and a jar inscribed with the same script as that used in the Dead Sea Scrolls.

In 1952 Harding and de Vaux investigated caves at Wâdī Murabba'ât, 11 mi. (18 km.) S of Qumrân, where the bedouin had discovered letters and contracts from the Bar Cochba revolt in A.D. 132-135. In 1960 and 1961 at Naḥal Ḥeber, just N of Masada, the Israelis found additional materials from this period, including letters and documents in Aramaic, Hebrew, Nabatean, and Greek.

O. Late Roman and Byzantine Periods (2nd-6th cents. A.D.). BETH-SHEARIM (Sheikh Abreiq) was famous as a rabbinic center from the 2nd to the 4th cents. A.D. Excavations by B. Mazar and N. Avigad between 1936 and 1958 have uncovered numerous sarcophagi, some with mythological motifs. Inscriptions bear witness that notable Jewish dead were brought there from Syria, Phoenicia, Mesopotamia, and Arabia.

Khirbet Shema' was the burial place of Rabbi Shimon bar Yokhai, revered as the author of the Zohar. Between 1970 and 1975 E. Meyers excavated the site, which flourished from A.D. 135 to 360. Its noted synagogue is dated to A.D. 300. Other synagogues of the 4th-5th cents. A.D. have been cleared at Ḥammath-Gader, at Chorazin (Mt. 11:21), and at Beth-Alfa. The last building has a mosaic with the signs of the zodiac encircling the figure of Helios-Apollo.

The tradition of Jesus' birth in a cave in BETHLEHEM (Beit Laḥm) was known to Justin Martyr in the 2nd cent. A.D. In 325 Helena, the mother of Constantine, had a church built over the traditional site. Investigations by W. Harvey in 1934 proved that the present Church of the Nativity dates only to Justinian (6th cent. A.D.). He uncovered remains of the Constantinian structure at a depth of 4 ft. (1.3 m.) below the present floor. At Beit Sahur to the E of Bethlehem, in the Greek Orthodox site of the shepherds' field, V. Tzaferis discovered in 1972 a well-preserved fourth-century chapel. This is the earliest Christian monument in the Holy Land in such an excellent state of preservation.

In 1973 R. Bull discovered a fourth-century A.D. Mithraeum at Caesarea, the first found in Palestine. Soundings were also made in the third-century A.D. hippodrome.

MEDEBA (Mâdebā) in Jordan is noted for an important mosaic map of Palestine, dating from the 6th cent. A.D., on the floor of a Greek Orthodox church. Other Byzantine mosaics may still be seen in private houses.

Bibliography.–*AOTS*; *AP*; Archaeological Institute of America, *Archaeological Discoveries in the Holy Land* (1967); M. Avi-Yonah, *et al.*, eds., *Encyclopedia of Archaeological Excavations in the Holy Land* (4 vols., 1975-1978); J. Finegan, *Archaeology of the NT* (1969); D. N. Freedman and J. C. Greenfield, eds., *New Directions in Biblical Archaeology* (1969); N. Glueck, *Other Side of the Jordan* (rev. ed. 1970); *Rivers in the Desert* (rev. ed. 1968); D. Harden, *The Phoenicians* (1963); G. L. Harding, *Antiquities of Jordan* (rev. ed. 1967); K. M. Kenyon, *Archaeology in the Holy Land* (1960); *Jerusalem: Excavating 3000 Years of History* (1967); *Royal Cities of the OT* (1971); P. J. King, *BASOR*, 217 (Feb. 1975), 55-65; H. Klengel, *Art of Ancient Syria* (1972); P. Lapp, *Tale of the Tell* (1975); *LBHG*; B. Mazar, *Mountain of the Lord* (1975); C. C. McCown, *Ladder of Progress in Palestine* (1943); S. M. Paul and W. G. Dever, *Biblical Archaeology* (1974); M. Pearlman and Y. Yannai, *Historical Sites in Israel* (1965); C. F. Pfeiffer, ed., *The Biblical World* (1966); C. F. Pfeiffer and H. F. Vos, *Wycliffe Historical Geography of Bible Lands* (1967); J. B. Pritchard, *Archaeology and the OT* (1958); J. A. Sanders, ed., *Near Eastern Archaeology in the Twentieth Century* (1970); E. B. Smick, *Archaeology of the Jordan Valley* (1973); J. A. Thompson, *Bible and Archaeology* (rev. ed. 1972); E. K. Vogel, *HUCA*, 42 (1971), 1-96; *WBA*; G. E. Wright, *Eretz-Israel*, 9 (1969), 120-133; E. M. Yamauchi, *Journal of the American Academy of Religion*, 42 (1974); 710-726; *The Stones and the Scriptures* (1972); S. Yeivin, *A Decade of Archaeology in Israel 1948-1958* (1960).

Preliminary reports of current excavations appear in the following periodicals: *AASOR*; *ADAJ*; *BA*; *BASOR*; *Berytus*; *IEJ*; *Levant*; *PEQ*; *Quarterly of Department of Antiquities in Palestine*; *RB*; *Syria*; *ZDPV*.

E. M. YAMAUCHI

ARCHEOLOGY OF THE INDUS VALLEY. The Indus Valley forms the eastern limit of the region that we may designate "the biblical world," viz., the region between the great deserts of Africa and Arabia and the mountains that extend almost unbrokenly from the Pyrenees to the Himalayas. It was at the Indus that Alexander the Great was forced by his soldiers to turn back. Millennia earlier trade between the Indus and Mesopotamia (and probably even Egypt) left its traces. We therefore include a brief summary of the archeology of the region.

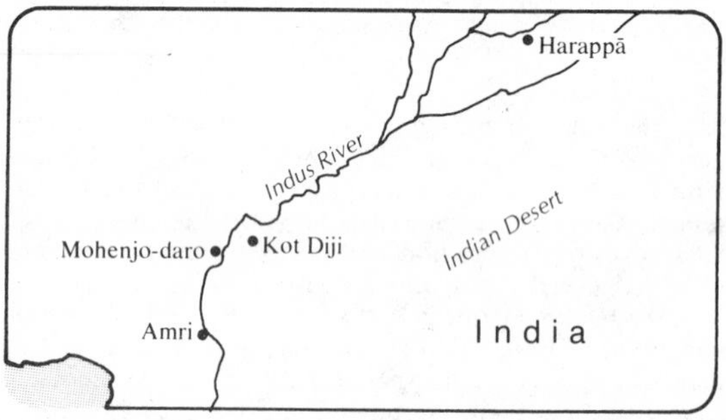

Archeological findings since 1920 have revealed the existence of an advanced, distinct, and independent civilization in the great river system of what now is Pakistan. The Indus civilization flourished from 2500 to 1500 B.C., and ranks as one of the first three literate civilizations of the world, following closely upon those of Mesopotamia and Egypt. Nearly one hundred sites have been discovered in an area over 1000 mi. (1600 km.) in length, making the Indus larger in area than any other known preclassical civilization.

I. Sites.–Knowledge of the Indus civilization comes primarily from excavations at two principal sites: Mohenjo-daro and Harappā. These "twin capitals," 400 mi. (650 km.) apart but joined by a continuous river, were constructed of baked bricks; and some authorities believe this innovation stems from here rather than Mesopotamia. Both cities consisted of carefully engineered civic layouts, containing elaborate drainage systems, well-ventilated granaries, large public baths, and a high citadel-mound from which governmental authority was enforced, as evidenced by the numerous weights, measures, and seals that have been discovered.

Stamp seal with image of "unicorn," from Mohenjo-daro (*ca.* 15th cent. B.C.). The inscription is as yet undeciphered. (W. S. LaSor)

II. Economy.–Although the Indus civilization derived its wealth from both agriculture and trade, its basic economy was agricultural. A variety of crops existed, but the most interesting finds of all are traces of cotton cloth which have survived at Mohenjo-daro. This is by far its earliest known occurrence.

III. Arts and Crafts.–In general the artistry of the Indus civilization is not comparable with that of contemporary work found in Mesopotamia and Egypt. The best products uncovered are the stone sculptures. Some animal and human figures are reminiscent of Mesopotamian religious mythology and suggest a possible link between East and West in this area. Several bronze figurines have been unearthed, but the vast number of terra-cotta figurines are especially characteristic. They exist at all known periods and are quite like those of Mesopotamia, consisting of animal and human forms and various toy miniature vessels.

Indus pottery is a mass of inchoate material and more exploration is needed in this area. As a whole it is without analogy, and thus helps to isolate this civilization as independent of other cultures.

Beads are abundant, varied in form and material and important historically. Their similarity with Mesopotamian beads of the Sargonid period indicates their derivation from a common source, and possible use in export trade from the Indus.

Seals constitute the outstanding contribution of the Indus civilization to ancient craftsmanship. Over twelve hundred have been found at Mohenjo-daro alone. The most typical animal is an oxlike beast with a single horn and therefore nicknamed "unicorn." Aristotle ascribed the unicorn to India and called it the Indian ass. The animal seals always include a standard that possibly represented an offering of food or incense. Series of composite animal monsters suggest their religious character. One seal suggests a scene of human sacrifice and several contain obvious images of deities. The Babylonian Tree of Life may even have had its counterpart in Mohenjo-daro and Harappā, where seals often display the sacred tree.

IV. Dating.–The Indus civilization is dated primarily on the basis of its commercial and trade contacts with Mesopotamia. Indus seals have been found in Ur, Kish, Susa, Lagash, Umma, and Tell Asmar, in layers allowing a maximum period from 2500 to 1500 B.C. It is safe to assume a trade link between Ur and the Indus valley during the time of Abraham.

V. Conclusion.–Skeletal remains at Mohenjo-daro suggest a sudden and tragic end to the city, probably caused by invading hordes of Indo-Aryans. Thus many gaps are left in our knowledge of this civilization. The undeciphered pictographic script of the seals and tablets still constitutes one of the major mysteries. It bears no apparent relationship to any script of that period.

Finally, recent excavations at Kot Diji and Amri indicate the existence of an Indus civilization earlier than and alien to that of Mohenjo-daro and Harappā. These discoveries are still under study and only preliminary reports on them have been published, but they may be expected to throw light on the beginnings of Harappā and Mohenjo-daro and their connection with this earlier culture. S. C. PITTMAN

ARCHER; ARCHERY [Heb. *ba'al ḥiṣṣîm* (Gen. 49:23), qal part. of *dāraḵ qešeṯ* (Jer. 51:3), qal part. of *yārâ* (2 Ch. 35:23), hiphil part. of *yarâ* (*qešeṯ*) (1 S. 31:3; 2 S. 11:24; 1 Ch. 10:3), qal part. of *rāmâ qešeṯ* (Jer. 4:29), *qešeṯ* (Isa. 21:17), *raḇ* (Job 16:13; Jer. 50:29; Prov.

Archers stringing and testing composite bows. Relief from Ashurbanipal's palace (Trustees of the British Museum)

26:10)]; AV also SHOOTERS, BOWMEN, etc.; NEB also BOWS, ARROWS, etc. While the MT of Prov. 26:10 is admittedly difficult, it seems best to follow the RSV, which translates *raḇ* as "archer," rather than following the AV, which reads it as "great (God)." In Jgs. 5:11 the RSV has altered the AV translation of Heb. *m^ehaṣṣîm* from "archer" to "musician," and is followed in this change by the NEB.

Prior to the widespread use of guns (15th cent. A.D.), the bow and arrow were the principal weapons of war. The Greeks and Romans were not known particularly for their skill in archery, but are known to have employed Asiatic mercenaries for this important kind of warfare. The armies of Assyria, Babylonia, Egypt, Hatti, Israel, Philistia, and Ugarit were served well by their archers, as is attested both by written documents and by pictorial representations. Both the infantries and the cavalries of these ancient Near Eastern nations were well staffed by trained and experienced archers.

Curiously enough the OT gives very little information with regard to the status, training, or even employment of archers in Israel. Except for Jonathan in 1 S. 20, most of the archers mentioned are of foreign armies: Philistines who killed Saul (1 S. 31:3; 1 Ch. 10:3); archers of the city Rabbah who killed Uriah the Hittite with one of their arrows (2 S. 11:24); a Syrian archer who hit Ahab (1 K. 22:34); and the Egyptian archer who killed Josiah (2 Ch. 35:23). Only by way of inclusion in a genealogical account are we apprised of the existence of archers (RSV "bowmen") in Israel (1 Ch. 8:40). We have some indirect hints about the archer's importance in the nation: David's lament over Saul (2 S. 1:17ff.) was apparently used to teach the men of Judah the bow (RSV mg. of 1:18). The RSV has chosen to emend this passage on basis of a Greek text; the *lectio difficilior* would suggest the MT reading. Furthermore, the virility and manliness of the archer is evident in the imagery of the psalmist, wherein the archer's equipment becomes the symbol of great fertility (Ps. 127:3-5).

Both Isaiah and Jeremiah picture the weakness of a nation in terms of a lack of, or inability on the part of, its archers (Jer. 51:3; Isa. 21:17). A would-be conqueror is required to "summon archers" (Jer. 50:29) in order to gain a victory. Jacob's final words to his sons use the imagery of archers to depict those who would harass Joseph (Gen. 49:23).

See also WEAPONS OF WAR.

See Y. Yadin, *The Art of Warfare in Biblical Lands* (1963).

D. H. ENGELHARD

ARCHEVITES är'kə-vīts [Heb. *K 'arkāwê, Q 'ark^ewāyē'*] (Ezr. 4:9, AV). One of the tribes transplanted by Ashurbanipal (Asnapper, Osnapper) to swell the mixed multitudes in the cities of Samaria. The word is taken as a gentilic and generally identified with ERECH.

ARCHI är'kī (Josh. 16:2, AV). *See* ARCHITE.

ARCHIPPUS är-kip'əs [Gk. *Archippos*] (Col. 4:17; Philem. 2). Probably a member of Philemon's family circle who held some official position in the church. He is addressed by Paul as "our fellow soldier" (Philem. 2). The tradition that he was one of the seventy disciples, became bishop of Laodicea, and later became a martyr, seems to have little historical foundation. *See also* APPHIA.

ARCHITE är'kīt [Heb. *hā'arkî*]; AV pl. ARCHI (Josh. 16:2). A member of a Benjaminite clan, notably David's friend HUSHAI (2 S. 15:32; 16:16; 17:5, 14; 1 Ch. 27:33). The clan is also mentioned in connection with the marking of the southern boundary of Joseph (Josh. 16:2). The Heb. *g^eḇûl hā'arkî '^aṭārôṯ* offers difficulties, and it has been suggested that the order of the last two words be changed to read "the border of Ataroth-of-the-Archites." *See* ATAROTH **2.**

H. J. WOLF

ARCHITECTURE. Near Eastern archeology has uncovered many palaces, temples, private houses, walls, city gates, and fortifications. Egypt, Mesopotamia, Persia, Greece, and Rome had well-developed architectural traditions. So dependent upon these arts and skills was Israel that it is debatable whether one can properly think of a distinctive Israelite architecture (S. Moscati, *Face of the Ancient Orient* [Eng. tr. 1960], p. 264).

"What the Hebrews were forbidden to make with their hands they made with words." This oft repeated aphorism is applicable, as in other areas of culture, to architecture in the Bible. The words "architecture" and "architect" do not occur in the OT or in the NT. The literature shows little concern with the aesthetics of building in general, no awareness of styles that are so characteristic of architecture in other cultures, and no detailed consideration of construction techniques.

The land offered the builder materials that were useful for such basic structures as houses, walls, and gates. On the other hand, it would appear that none of the available raw materials (mainly stone or wood) by its inherent beauty or excellence challenged the artist to creative experimentation, again in contrast to the experience of neighboring peoples. The people of the Bible did engage in building from the time of entry into Canaan, but the archeologically known remains support the literature in the conclusion that the performance was unpretentious and unprofessional, the main wall form being of home-dressed stones laid in mortar by common laborers. When the Hebrew author sought to describe a different form of building from that to which he was accustomed, he wrote of the substitution of "brick for stone and slime for mortar" (Tower of Babel, Gen. 11:3). The regular result was walls of rubble stone, sometimes reinforced by long stones and, if desired, sealed outside and in with mud mortar. Incidentally, it would be difficult for any save perhaps a professional thief (Mt. 6:20) visually to distinguish a house wall built of stone covered with mud from a house wall built of mud bricks or adobe. Indicative of Israel's pre-Davidic building is "Gibeah of Saul" (1 S. 15:34, i.e., Tell el-Fûl) with its massive stone walls and towers, a castle rather than a royal palace. W. F. Albright remarks, "Saul was only a rustic chieftain, as far as architecture and the amenities of life were concerned" (*FSAC*, p. 292).

The technique of using waterproof lime plaster, Albright holds, was developed in Palestine at precisely the time Israel was populating the previously unusable hill country (*AP*, p. 113). There may be a relation between this observation and the fact that aqueducts and water systems demonstrate most clearly the engineering skills of biblical builders. Hezekiah's tunnel at Jerusalem and the pool at Gibeah would be illustrations. Neither is ornamented or decorated as one might expect of architecture but each demonstrates, as a piece of engineering, forethought and precise planning.

Until the Persian period, when the vault and arch were introduced to Palestine, roofing was done simply with timber or stone beams laid from wall to wall or supported by interior columns, usually wooden. As Nelson Glueck discovered at Ezion-geber, the rough boards supported brush into which clay had been impacted by rolling, the whole being covered over with a layer of stone chips. The roofs of Jerusalem, being covered with white limestone

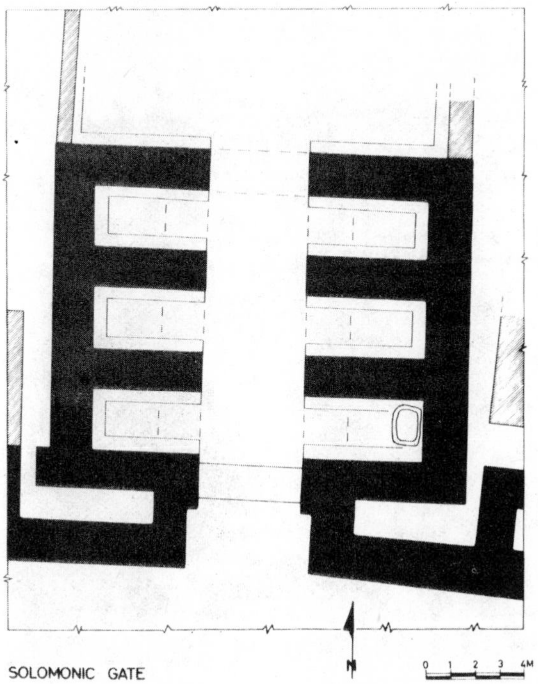

Plan of earliest phase of Solomonic gate at Gezer. An elaborate system of stone benches around the three sides of each room suited the gate's function as a civic, judicial, and mercantile center. (American Schools of Oriental Research)

Reconstruction of Solomon's temple by C. F. Stevens from specifications by W. F. Albright and G. E. Wright (*Biblical Archeologist*)

chippings, must have reflected sun by day and moon by night, thus adding attractiveness to the city.

Recent excavation has shown that in the Iron Age (as at Lachish, Gezer, Mizpah, Megiddo, Hazor) Palestinian builders gave thought and effort to making efficient and defensible city gates. Here human requirements for the military guards and "judiciary" at the city gate, as well as a certain feeling for symmetry and proportion, are in evidence. In the city gates is to be found the earliest finely dressed and deliberately laid masonry in styles borrowed from the Phoenicians. Is it simply coincidence that during the same period there came into being the Bible's most famous buildings, those of the Jerusalem "suburb" Solomon developed around the site of the tabernacle?

1 Kings 5–8 tells of the building of Solomon's temple, his palace, and the other state buildings erected simultaneously in the same location, with much the same materials and by the same Phoenician craftsmen. From the accounts as we have them no assuredly accurate reconstruction is possible. They are not primarily concerned with architectural terms of detail. Yet by coupling the texts as understood by competent linguists with what is known by archeological investigation, it is possible to indicate the main arrangements and proportions of at least the temple. Neither text nor archeological discoveries give the same opportunity for a reconstruction of the other buildings — palace, Hall of Cedars, etc.

What is demonstrated by such a work as the Howland-Garber model reconstruction of Solomon's temple (1950) is that the sanctuary, as described in the Bible and illustrated by archeological findings relevant to the early Iron Age, architecturally belongs to its age. The "style" or fashion of building temples in the Middle East was followed. The raised basement, the two columns, the "liwan" porch, the two rooms of the house arranged lengthwise, and the appended storage chambers are all features that can be observed in recently excavated temples at Shechem, Hazor, and Arad. Some innovations, as the lavish use of bronze, reflecting Solomon's vast

Herodian temple at Caesarea, dedicated to Caesar Augustus. Located near the harbor, the temple contained colossal statues of Augustus and Roma. (B. Van Elderen)

economic interests in this and other metals, may have been included. But by and large, for the "house of Yahweh" the Phoenician builders who worked under Solomon's sponsorship employed that sort of architecture with which they were familiar, including the form of cherub, the proto-Ionic capitals for the holy-place pilasters, the Egyptian streamlined cornice, the bulls, the repeated symbolism of the pomegranates, the lotus plant, and blossom. It was by contributions to the temple's significance, and these of a nonmaterial sort, that the Hebrews over a period of nearly four centuries made the temple a national symbol of their own particular religious faith and devotion.

Other Hebrew kings who were noteworthy for their building accomplishments include Asa (1 K. 15:23), Baasha (15:17), Omri (16:24), Ahab (16:23; cf. the excavations at Samaria), Hezekiah (2 K. 12:11; cf. the Siloam tunnel and inscription), and Jehoiakim (Jer. 22:14; 36:22). After the return from Exile the Jewish community's poverty made possible only the most modest repair of the walls and construction of a temple (Ezr. 3:8; 5:8; Neh. 2:8).

Near the end of the divided kingdom, Persian influences appear. Architecturally interesting in this connection is the governor's residence at Lachish, a building distinguished for its long chamber with an impressive vaulted roof whose stones were laid in diagonal lines. Thus inner supports were eliminated and a roof of unusual appearance in Palestine was produced.

Second only to Solomon as a builder mentioned in the Bible was Herod, who as an Idumaean had had a detailed introduction to Greco-Roman decorative arts. The Maccabees before him had responded in one degree or another to the Greco-Roman influences as mediated to them through Syria. Excavations tend to reveal a greater influence than the literature suggests. "Huge Roman-type buildings appeared in Palestine, undoubtedly employing the newly invented Roman concrete" (*WBA*, p. 243). Herod's building activities according to Josephus (*Ant.* xv.7ff.) included rebuilding Samaria/Sebaste, the new city of Antipatris, a palace and a tower near Jericho, a Pythian temple on the island of Rhodes, aid to Caesar Augustus in building Nicopolis near Actium in western Greece, and providing the broad, paved and colonnaded main street of Antioch in Syria. Certainly one of Herod's chief accomplishments as a builder, even beyond the spectacular, remote fortress-palaces of Alexandrium, Herodium, and Masada, was the creation of Caesarea Maritima, a place named in honor of Caesar Augustus and so closely resembling the ideal of a Greco-Roman city that the Procurators made it their provincial political capital. What Herod contributed to the Jerusalem temple during the long years (Jn. 2:20; Josephus *BJ* v.5) of his efforts is not known in detail. It may be surmised that the architecture generally followed Greco-Roman models as suggested by the rock-cut tombs of the Jerusalem area and perhaps, as Muehsam's study suggests, by ancient Jewish coins. The provisions and appearance of the Herodian constructions may be projected by impressions drawn from the earlier mausoleum at 'Arâq el-Emir as well as from the later synagogues of Capernaum and Dura-Europus.

In architecture as otherwise, the literature and the remains indicate that Palestine was no backwoods, isolated province but rather a forum for worldwide exchange of knowledge and techniques as well as of ideas.

Bibliography.–A. Badawy, *Ancient Egyptian Architectural Design* (1965); D. Baramki, *Phoenicia and the Phoenicians* (1961); H. K. Beebe, *BA*, 21 (1968), 38-58; W. Culican, *First Merchant Venturers*, (1967); R. de Vaux, *Ancient Israel: Its Life and Institutions* (1961); P. L. Garber, *BA*, 14 (1951), 2-24; K. M. Kenyon, *Archaeology in the Holy Land* (1960); C. H. Kraeling, "The Synagogue," Final Report VII, pt. 1, *The Excavations at Dura Europos* (1956); A. Muehsam, *Coin and Temple* (1966); M. Noth, *The OT World* (1966); E. L. Sukenik, *Ancient Synagogues in Palestine and Greece* (1934).

P. L. GARBER

The Areopagus, meeting place of the council before whom Paul preached at Athens (W. S. LaSor)

ARCHIVES, ROYAL. [Aram. *bêṯ ginzayyā' dî-malkā'*] (Ezr. 5:17); AV "king's treasure house"; **HOUSE OF THE ARCHIVES** [Aram. *bêṯ siprayyā'*] (6:1); AV "house of the rolls." A section of the royal treasury in which official memoranda, public records, and historical documents were housed. Subsequently the Aram. *geniza* was used to describe a repository for used scrolls.

R. K. H.

ARCTURUS ärk-to͞o'rəs (AV Job 9:9; 38:32). *See* ASTRONOMY II.C.

ARD ärd [Heb. *'ard*–'humpbacked'] (Gen. 46:21; Nu. 26:40). A descendant of Benjamin. Nu. 26:38-40 mentions five sons of Benjamin, together with Ard and Naaman, the sons of Bela, Benjamin's oldest son, counting all seven as ancestors of Benjaminite families. In 1 Ch. 8:1-3 Addar and Naaman are mentioned, with others, as sons of Bela, Addar and Ard being apparently the same name with the consonants transposed. In Gen. 46:21 ten sons of Benjamin are counted, including at least the three grandsons, Ard and Naaman and Gera.

ARDAT är'dat [Lat. *Ardat*; Syr. and Eth. *Arphad*]; AV ARDATH. A certain field where Ezra communed with God (2 Esd. 9:26).

ARDITES är'dīts [Heb. *hā'ardî*] (Nu. 26:40). Family name of ARD.

ARDON är'don [Heb. *'ardôn*]. One of the three sons of Caleb and Azubah, of the tribe of Judah (1 Ch. 2:18).

ARELI ə-rē'lī [Heb. *'ar'ēlî*]. A son of Gad son of Jacob (Gen. 46:16; Nu. 26:17).

ARELITES ə-rē'līts [Heb. *'ar'ēlî*] (Nu. 26:17). Family name of ARELI.

AREOPAGITE ar-ē-op'a-jīt [Gk. *ho Areopagitēs*]. *See* DIONYSIUS.

AREOPAGUS ar-ē-op'ə-gəs [Gk. *Areios Pagos*] (Acts 17:19, 22); AV MARS' HILL (v. 22); NEB "Court of Areopagus." A hill NW of the Acropolis in ATHENS.

There are two traditions as to how the hill got its name. According to one, it was named for Ares the god of War, who was put on trial there for the slaying of Halirrhotios the son of Poseidon; hence the AV designation in Acts 17:22 (Ares has been identified with the Roman god Mars). The other tradition understands the name Areopagus to mean the "hill of the Arai." The Arai ("curses"), more popularly known as the Furies, were goddesses whose task was avenging murder. If this tradition is true the name was very fitting, for the Areopagus was the place where cases of homicide were tried. Moreover, at the foot of this hill there is a cave wherein the shrine of these goddesses was located. The goddesses are also known by the names Semnai and Erinyes. Pausanias of Sparta tells of a tradition that the first trial on the Areopagus was that of Orestes, whom the goddesses cursed and pursued relentlessly for the murder of his own mother, Clytemnestra.

A staircase hewn out of the rock leads to the summit of this hill (which is about 370 ft. [113 m.] high), where traces of benches are visible forming three sides of a square, also cut out of the stone. At one time, two white stones were also there, upon which the defendant and his accuser stood. They were named "The Stone of Shamelessness" and "The Stone of Pride," respectively.

The name of the hill was given later to the council whose meetings were held upon it. The council of the Areopagus retained this name even when its meetings were transferred from the hill to the Royal Stoa, which should, perhaps, be identified with the stoa of Zeus Eleutheros in the agora. It is suggested that the council met at times on the Acropolis as well. The council of the

Areopagus was similar to a council of elders, and was subject to the king of Athens. It was very influential in the formation of the aristocracy. Aristotle (*Pol.* viii.2) describes the scope of its power as including the appointment to all offices, the work of administration, and the right to punish all cases. Through the reforms of Solon (594 B.C.) the authority of the Areopagus was greatly limited, though the council did maintain jurisdiction in cases of conspiracy against the state. During the time of Pericles its functions were mainly those of a criminal court. Further transfers of its functions to the Boule, the Ecclesia, and the Popular Court of Law detracted from the prestige of the court, though it retained jurisdiction in cases of homicide. Under Demosthenes it recaptured some of its power and was able to annul the election of certain officers. In times of Roman domination the council of the Areopagus concerned itself with cases of forgery, maintaining correct standards of measure, supervision of buildings, and matters of religion and education. The Areopagus was the court where Socrates met his accusers.

The apostle Paul was brought to the Areopagus by certain Epicureans and Stoics who wished to hear more of his teaching about Jesus and the Resurrection. Since the name Areopagus may be applied to the hill or to the council, there is an ambiguity which has given rise to debate as to whether Paul spoke publicly on the hill or was examined for his religious teaching before the council. Ramsay (*SPT*) rejected the view that they took Paul to the summit of the Areopagus in an effort to find a more suitable place for him to address the crowd. He considers that pride would have prevented the Athenians from asking Paul, a despised person, to address them in such an honored locality. Furthermore, he asserts that the language of the text will not allow it, for one cannot stand "in the midst of the hill." It is likely that Paul was examined by the council on account of the religious tenets he was proclaiming. The control the council exercised over public instruction is illustrated by Plutarch's statement with respect to Cratippus the peripatetic, that Cicero "got the court of Areopagus, by public decree, to request his stay at Athens, for the instruction of their youth, and the honor of their city" (Plutarch *Cicero* 24.5). Although it is recognized that the council met in various places, its common practice to convene on the hill from which it took its name makes plausible the position of Wright and certain others who consider that Paul stood before the council on the hill of the Areopagus.

Bibliography.–*SPT*; *WBA*; F. F. Bruce, *Book of the Acts* (*NIC*, 1954); W. A. McDonald, *BA*, 4 (1941), 1-10; O. Broneer, *BA*, 21 (1958), 2-28.

D. H. MADVIG

ARES âr'ēz (1 Esd. 5:10, AV, NEB). *See* ARAH.

ARETAS ar'ə-təs [Gk. *Haretas*–'virtuous, pleasing' < *ḥâriṭat,* found on Nabatean inscriptions]. A common name among Arabian rulers, mentioned in the Apocrypha, in the NT, and in Josephus.

1. An Arabian king who accused (Gk. and NEB "imprisoned") Jason, causing him to become a fugitive (2 Macc. 5:8). He was a contemporary of Antiochus Epiphanes (*ca.* 170 B.C.).

2. An Arabian prince surnamed Obodas, who defeated Antiochus Dionysius and reigned over Coele-Syria and Damascus (Josephus *Ant.* xiii.15.2; 16.2; xvi.9.4). He participated with Hyrcanus in the war for the Jewish throne against his brother Aristobulus; but the allies were completely defeated at Papyron by Aristobulus and Scaurus, the Roman general. Scaurus carried the war into Arabia and forced Aretas to make an ignominious peace, at the price of 300 talents of silver. Of that event a memorial denarius still exists; one side shows a Roman chariot in full charge while the other has a camel by the side of which a kneeling Arab holds out a branch of frankincense.

3. Aretas IV, the successor of Obodas, apparently surnamed Aeneas; the Arabian king who figures in the NT (2 Cor. 11:32; cf. Acts 9:24). He was the father-in-law of Herod Antipas, who divorced his wife to marry Herodias, the wife of his brother Philip (Mt. 14:3; Mk. 6:17; Lk. 3:19).

Josephus (*Ant.* xviii.5.1, 3) provides a circumstantial narration of the events leading up to and following the conduct of Antipas. Coupled with a boundary dispute, it occasioned a bitter war between the two princes, in which Antipas was completely overwhelmed, and thereupon invoked the aid of the Romans. Tiberias ordered Vitellius, proconsul of Syria, to make war on Aretas and to deliver him dead or alive into the hands of the emperor. On the way, at Jerusalem, Vitellius received intelligence of the death of Tiberius, Mar. 16, A.D. 37, and stopped all warlike proceedings.

According to 2 Cor. 11:32, Damascus, which had formerly belonged to the Arabian princes, was again in the hands of Aretas when Paul escaped from it, not immediately after his conversion, but on a subsequent visit, after his Arabian exile (Gal. 1:16f.). It is inconceivable that Aretas should have taken Damascus by force in the face of the almost omnipotent power of Rome. Moreover, the picture that Josephus draws of the Herodian events points to a passive rather than an active attitude on the part of Aretas. The probability is that the new emperor Caligula, wishing to settle the affairs of Syria, freely gave Damascus to Aretas, inasmuch as it had formerly belonged to his territory.

As Tiberius died in A.D. 37, and as the Arabian affair was completely settled in 39, it is evident that the date of Paul's conversion must lie somewhere between 34 and 36. This date is further fixed by a Damascus coin, with the image of King Aretas and the date 101. If that date points to the Pompeian era, it equals A.D. 37, making the date of Paul's conversion A.D. 34 (T. E. Mionnet, *Description des médailles antiques greques et romaines,* V [1811], 284f.).

H. E. DOSKER

ARGOB är'gob [Heb. *'argōḇ*–'mound']. A district in northern Transjordan, apparently identified as the kingdom of Og in Bashan (Dt. 3:4). The name occurs four times in the OT, once with the definite article, "the Argob," and always preceded by Heb. *ḥeḇel,* "the measured region of [the] Argob."

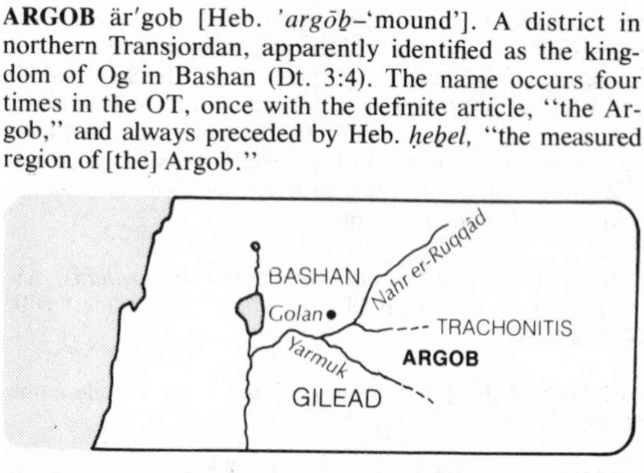

When the Israelites were advancing from the wilderness to the crossing of the Jordan, they "turned and went up on the way to Bashan" (Dt. 3:1), where they were confronted by Og king of Bashan. When Og was defeated the land was allotted, and Jair the Manassite "took all the region of Argob, that is, Bashan, as far as the border of the Geshurites and the Maacathites, and called the villages after his own name, Havvoth-jair, as it is to this day'' (3:14). In spite of the obvious clarity of the description, we are faced with difficulties that make positive identification all but impossible.

Judging from the words ''as it is to this day,'' Dt. 3:14 is a gloss. Furthermore, the reference to HAVVOTH-JAIR is problematical. Havvoth-jair, ''the tent-villages of Jair,'' were in Gilead, and are clearly distinguished from the cities of Bashan in 1 K. 4:13. It would of course be possible to assume that there were other Havvoth-jair in Bashan, but this needs further confirmation. The territory of the Geshurites and the Maacathites can be located with little hesitation on the eastern edge of the Jordan rift, stretching from Mt. Hermon on the north to the Yarmuk River on the south, and extending east to the plateau of Bashan, the boundary of which may have been the tributary of the Yarmuk that divides the region of Golan (Jaulan); the Maacathites occupied the northern part and the Geshurites the southern part. Hence we would assume that the district of Argob lay E of the Nahr er-Ruqqâd.

But there are other factors that must be taken into consideration. The Targum translates Argob by *ṭarkônâ,* reflected in the Gk. *Trachōn* from which is derived ''Trachonitis,'' which is the modern el-Lejâ, a volcanic region about 30 mi. (50 km.) E of the Sea of Galilee. This region is clearly defined by natural characteristics resulting from the hardening of the lava flow. Moreover, the ruins of many cities have been discovered, leading earlier writers to find the sixty great cities of 1 K. 4:13 and Dt. 3:4. But if the meaning of Argob is indeed ''clod'' or ''region of clods,'' i.e., arable land, this name does not fit the region of el-Lejâ. Turning again to the reference to ''sixty great cities with walls and bronze bars'' (1 K. 4:13) we find that Josephus locates these in Gaulanitis or Golan (*Ant.* viii.2.3), which lies W of the eastern border of the Geshurites and Maacathites as defined in Dt. 3:14. Further, ruins of ''cities'' or villages can be found in almost any district in northern Transjordan.

It is possible to read 1 K. 4:13 so as to make the district of Argob a portion of Bashan (this is not so easy to do in the other references): ''to him the district of Argob, which is in the Bashan. . . .'' Possibly the solution to the problem is to be found in this direction, although we must not shut our eyes to the difficulties it raises with the other texts. The district of Argob is certainly in Bashan; it may be a synonym for Bashan, or it may be a part of Bashan. If the latter is to be accepted, we might suggest that portion of Bashan lying E of Nahr er-Ruqqâd and extending to Wâdī el-Ehreir or even to the edge of el-Lejâ.

See also BASHAN; TRACHONITIS.

Bibliography.–*GTTOT*, §§ 21, 302, 307; B. Mazar, *JBL*, 80 (1961), 16-28.

W. S. LASOR

ARGOB AND ARIEH är′gob, âr′ē-ə [Heb. *'argōḇ*–'mound,' *hā'aryēh*]. Names occurring in 2 K. 15:25, AV, following the MT, but removed to the margin by the RSV and NEB. The RSV mg. suggests they may belong with v. 29. They could also be conspirators with Pekah or officers of Pekahiah who were slain with him.

See J. A. Montgomery, *ICC* (1951 ed.), *in loc.*

ARGUE; ARGUMENT [Heb. *yāḵaḥ* (Job 13:3; 15:3; 19:5; 40:2), *riḇ* (Prov. 25:9), *šāpaṭ* (Prov. 29:9; Isa. 43:26), *tôḵaḥaṯ* (Job 23:4); Gk. *dialégomai*, *dialogízomai*, *dialogismós* (Lk. 9:46), *logismós* (2 Cor. 10:5), *logízomai* (Mk. 11:31), *syzētéo* (Mk. 8:11; 9;14)]; AV also CONTEND, DEBATE, DISPUTE, IMAGINATIONS, PLEAD, QUESTION, REASON, REPROVE; NEB also BANDY, DISCOURSE, DISPUTE, ''go to law,'' ''engage in discussion,'' ''hold discussions,'' SOPHISTRIES, etc.

The RSV uses ''argue'' to translate various Hebrew and Greek words whose contexts suggest spirited controversy (Mk. 9:14). Most instances indicate an attempt to prove oneself right (Isa. 43:26), the very meaning of the causative form of *yāḵaḥ*. *Dialégomai,* frequently used of Paul's ''arguing'' in the Diaspora synagogues (Acts 17:2, 17; 18:4, 19; 19:8f.), does not refer to public debates but to religious discourses (Bauer, p. 184; cf. Acts 24:25, NEB). The LXX used *dialégomai* as the primary translation for the intensive form of *dāḇar,* with the predominant meaning ''say'' or ''speak.'' A material parallel to Paul's practice may be found in Jesus' Sabbath teaching (Mk. 1:21 par.; see *TDNT*, II, 94f.). Similarly, *dialogízomai* probably indicates group reflection or discussion rather than argumentation (Mt. 21:25; Mk. 11:31). *See also* DISCUSSION.

''Argument'' is used in two senses. It may mean a dispute involving two or more people: ''And an argument arose among them'' (Lk. 9:46; cf. Prov. 29:9), or a reason advanced as proof of a position: ''I would . . . fill my mouth with arguments'' (Job 23:4; cf. 19:5). The latter sense is probably in view when Paul speaks of destroying ''arguments and every proud obstacle to the knowledge of God'' (2 Cor. 10:5); they are the ''sophistries'' (NEB) of a reason which is earth-bound and devoid of spiritual enlightenment.

See also DISPUTE.

Bibliography.–Bauer, pp. 184f.; *TDNT,* II, *s.v.* διαλέγομαι (Schrenk); *TDNT,* IV, *s.v.* λογίζομαι (Heidland).

K. H. MAAHS.

ARIARATHES ar-ē-ə-rā′thēz [Gk. *Ariarathēs*] (1 Macc. 15:22). King of Cappadocia, 163-130 B.C. Educated in Rome, he imbibed Roman ideas and became a faithful ally of the Romans, in conformity with whose wishes he declined a proposal of marriage with the sister of Demetrius Soter. Demetrius declared war, drove Ariarathes from his kingdom, and set up Holophernes in his stead. He fled to Rome about 158, and through the good offices of the Romans succeeded in obtaining for himself a participation in the government of Cappadocia. Later he again became sole king.

In 139 B.C., as a result of an embassy sent by Simon Maccabeus, the Romans wrote letters to Ariarathes (1 Macc. 15:22) and other eastern kings in behalf of the Jews. See Diodorus xxxi.19, 28, 32; Polybius iii.5; xxxii. 20-30; xxxiii.12.

J. E. HARRY

ARIDAI âr′ə-dī [Heb. *'ᵃrîḏay*]. A son of Haman (Est. 9:9). The name may be related to Pers. *Hari-dayas,* ''delight of Hari.''

ARIDATHA âr-ə-dā′thə [Heb. *'ᵃriḏāṯā'*]. A son of Haman (Est. 9:8). Perhaps the name is related to Pers. *Hari-dâta,* ''given by Hari.''

ARIEH. *See* ARGOB AND ARIEH.

ARIEL âr′ē-əl [Heb. *'ᵃrî'el*–'lion of God'].

1. A member of the delegation sent by Ezra to secure ministers for the temple (Ezr. 8:16). In par. 1 Esd. 8:43 he appears as ''Iduel'' (NEB ''Iduelus'').

2. A cryptic name for Jerusalem (Isa. 29:1f., 7) as the principal stronghold of divine worship.

3. TWO ARIELS [Heb. *šnê 'ᵃri'ēl*] (2 S. 23:20; 1 Ch. 11:22); AV ''two lionlike men''; NEB ''two champions.'' Moabites who were slain by David's warrior Benaiah. The LXX has *dýo hyioí ariel.* The meaning of the term is not clear.

4. In Ezk. 43:15f., a name for the altar of burnt offering ("altar hearth"; AV "altar"), a structure which may have resembled that mentioned in line 12 of the Mesha Inscription. *See* MOABITE STONE.

ARIMATH(A)EA ar-ə-mə-thē'ə [Heb. *Arimathaia*]. "A city of the Jews," the home of Joseph, in whose sepulchre the body of Jesus was laid. The place is mentioned once in each Gospel (Mt. 27:57; Mk. 15:43; Lk. 23:50; Jn. 19:38). In the Davidic account, the home of Samuel is called Ramah (1 S. 19:19) and Ramathaim (1 S. 1:1), always with the definite article. Often the word is formed with *he*-directive ("toward Rama"), hence Heb. *hārāmāṯâ*, which becomes in the LXX Gk. *Armathaim*. This agrees with the early identification of Arimathea and Ramathaim-zophim (cf. Eusebius *Onom.* 144.28). Eusebius further identified Arimathea with Remphis, elsewhere called Remtis, probably the modern village of Rentîs, 9 mi. (14.5 km.) NE of Lydda (Lod). Arimathea is mentioned in 1 Macc. 11:34, and, as Ramatha, in Josephus *Ant.* xiii.4.9.

See *GTTOT*, § 646; *GP*, II, 428f.

S. F. HUNTER
W. S. L. S.

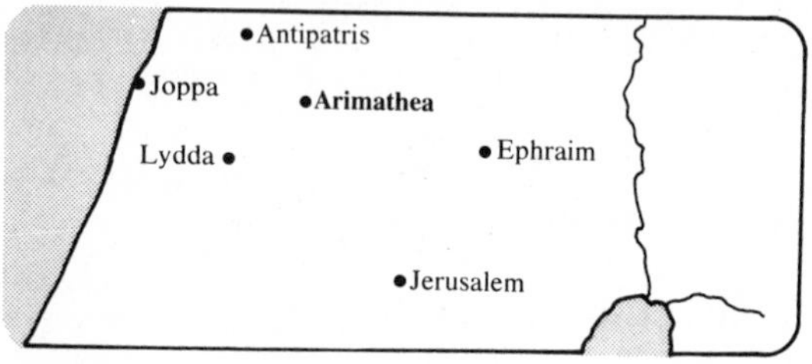

ARIOCH ar'ē-ok [Heb., Aram., *'aryôḵ*].

1. The vassal king of Ellasar who was an ally of Chedorlaomer of Elam and Amraphel king of Shinar, and undertook with them a punitive expedition against five south Palestinian kings, routing them in the Valley of Siddim (Gen. 14:1, 9).

The identification of the name is uncertain, despite the attempts of earlier Assyriologists to connect Arioch with Eri-Aku (Warad-Sin) king of Larsa, and to regard Ellasar as the Hebrew form of al-Larsa. The name Arioch is evidently of Hurrian origin, and was found in the Mari correspondence as the name (Arriwuk) of the fifth son of Zimri-Lim, king of Mari *ca.* 1750 B.C. In the form *Ar-ri-uk-ki* this Hurrian cognomen also occurred in the Nuzi documents from the 15th cent. B.C. Thus the name, with slight variants, seems to have been in use somewhat frequently in the 2nd millennium B.C., and this fact alone should preclude a definite identification of any particular individual with Arioch.

The district over which Arioch ruled is also uncertain in locale and extent. While the Hebrew text spoke of it as "Ellasar," 1QapGen favored *kptwk,* possibly a corruption of *kptwr* (Caphtor). Recent scholars have suggested Ilanzura, a city located between Carchemish and Harran, as comprising Ellasar.

2. Captain of the bodyguard of Nebuchadnezzar (Dnl. 2:14f., 24f.), who introduced Daniel to the king.

R. K. HARRISON

ARISAI âr'ə-sī [Heb. *'ᵃrîsay*]. One of Haman's sons, slain by the Jews (Est. 9:9).

ARISTARCHUS ar-is-tär'kəs [Gk. *Aristarchos*–'best ruler']. One of those faithful companions of the apostle Paul who shared with him his labors and sufferings. He is first mentioned along with Gaius as having been seized by the excited Ephesians during the riot stirred up by the silversmiths (Acts 19:29). They are designated "men of Macedonia, Paul's companions in travel." We learn later that he was a native of Thessalonica (20:4; 27:2). They were probably seized to extract from them information about their leader Paul, but when they could tell nothing, and since they were Greeks, nothing further was done to them.

We do not know when Aristarchus attached himself to Paul, but he seems to have remained in Paul's company ever after the Ephesian uproar. He was one of those who accompanied Paul from Greece via Macedonia (20:4). Having preceded Paul to Troas, where they waited for him, they traveled with him to Palestine. He is next mentioned as accompanying Paul to Rome (27:2). There he attended Paul and shared his imprisonment.

He is mentioned in two of the letters of the Roman captivity, viz., Colossians (4:10) and Philemon (v. 24), in both of which he sends greetings. In the former Paul calls him "my fellow prisoner." According to tradition he was martyred during the persecution by Nero.

S. F. HUNTER

ARISTEAS ar-is-tē'əs. *See* PSEUDEPIGRAPHA II.

ARISTOBULUS ar-is-tob'ū-ləs [Gk. *Aristoboulous*–'best counselor'].

1. Son of the Maccabean John Hyrcanus. He assumed the power and also the title of king after his father's death (105 B.C.). He associated with himself, as co-regent, his brother Antigonus (Josephus *Ant.* xiii.11), though by the will of his father the government was entrusted to his mother. He cast three older brothers and his mother into prison, where they died of starvation. He murdered Antigonus, and died conscience-stricken himself in 104 B.C. *See* MACCABEES.

2. Nephew of **1.** He dethroned his mother Alexandra (69 B.C.), and forced his brother HYRCANUS to renounce the crown and mitre in his favor. In 64 B.C. Pompey came to Palestine and supported the cause of Hyrcanus. Aristobulus was defeated and taken prisoner, and Hyrcanus was appointed ethnarch in 63 B.C. Aristobulus and his two daughters were taken to Rome, where he graced the triumph of Pompey. Aristobulus escaped later (56 B.C.) and appeared in Palestine again as a claimant to the throne. Many followers flocked to his standard, but he was finally defeated, severely wounded, taken prisoner a second time, and with his son Antigonus taken again to Rome. Julius Caesar not only restored him to freedom (49 B.C.), but also gave him two legions to recover Judea and to work in his interest against Pompey. But Quintus Metellus Scipio, who had just received Syria as a province, had Aristobulus poisoned as he was on his way to Palestine.

3. Grandson of **2**, and the last of the Maccabean family. *See* HASMONEANS.

4. The Jewish teacher of Ptolemy VII (2 Macc. 1:10).

5. An inhabitant of Rome, certain of whose household are saluted by Paul (Rom. 16:10). He was probably a grandson of Herod and brother of Herod Agrippa, a man of great wealth, and intimate with the emperor Claudius.

M. O. EVANS

ARITHMETIC. *See* NUMBER III.

ARIUS âr'ē-əs [Gk. *Areios*]; AV AREUS. A king of Sparta, Arius I (309-265 B.C.), who wrote a letter to Onias the high priest (1 Macc. 12:7, 20-23). There were two Spartan kings named Arius, and three high priests named Onias.

ARK OF BULRUSHES. *See* BASKET.

ARK OF NOAH [Heb. *tēḇâ*; Gk. *kibōtós*] (Gen. 6:14ff.; Mt. 24:38; Lk. 17:27; He. 11:7; 1 Pet. 3:20). A vessel built by Noah at the command of God to preserve from the Flood a remnant of the human race and of the animals associated with man.

The Hebrew word for the ark is related to the Egyptian *ḏb't* "chest," "box," "coffin," and is used only to designate Noah's vessel and the reed vessel in which the infant Moses was saved (Ex. 2:3, 5). The Greek term means "box," "chest," "coffin." Accordingly, Heidel (p. 235) proposes that the ark "was a flat-bottomed, rectangular construction, square on both ends and straight up on the sides. Such a craft is represented on bronze coins from the Phrygian city Apameia."

The ark was made of GOPHER WOOD, coated inside and out with pitch, or bitumen, to make it watertight, and contained numerous unspecified cells or compartments (Gen. 6:14). The obscure Hebrew text of Gen. 6:16 is normally taken to mean that the ark had three stories, with a door in its side and probably an opening for light below the roof.

Reckoning the cubit at 17.5 inches, the ark was about 437.5 feet long, 72.92 feet wide and 43.75 feet high (Gen. 6:15), giving it, according to Whitcomb and Morris, a total deck area of 95,700 sq. ft. and a total volume of 1,396,000 cubic feet. This size should be contrasted with the much smaller size of ancient vessels, which seldom exceeded 150 to 200 ft. at the most, and with Utnapishtim's unfloatable cubical vessel described in the Gilgamesh Epic.

The ark carried Noah, his wife, his three sons and their wives, every kind of animal dependent upon the earth for food, and the required amount of food. More precisely, there were seven of every clean animal — i.e., three pairs and probably one supernumerary for sacrifice after the termination of the Flood — and one pair of every unclean animal (Gen. 7:2f.). The instruction concerning the animals has raised both literary and logistical problems. The supposed clash between Gen. 6:19f. (cf. 7:8f.) and 7:2f. over "two by two" or "seven pairs" is imaginary; for the first set of passages, probably using "pairs" as a collective, is a general statement, while 7:2f. is specific. Logistical problems pertain (1) to the gathering of the animals, (2) to the capacity of the ark, and (3) to the caring for the animals. Concerning these objections Whitcomb and Morris plausibly suggest: (1) that the climate, and the geography and topography of the earth differed before the Flood, making it probable that representatives of each created kind of animal lived in that part of the earth when Noah was building the ark; (2) that according to the best estimates of modern taxonomy only 35,000 individual vertebrate animals need to have been on the ark, a number easily accommodated according to the stated dimensions; and (3) that the animals probably hibernated.

Persistent rumors of the discovery of the ark on the slopes of Mt. Ararat have never been confirmed.

Peter uses the salvation of the few persons in the ark as a type of the believers' salvation in Christ (1 Pet. 3:20). Warning of the Flood was given 120 years beforehand (Gen. 6:3; 1 Pet. 3:20; 2 Pet. 2:5), during which time Noah, while preparing the ark, became a preacher of righteousness.

See also FLOOD (GENESIS).

Bibliography.–A. Heidel, *Gilgamesh Epic and OT Parallels* (1946); J. C. Whitcomb and H. M. Morris, *Genesis Flood: The Biblical Record and its Scientific Implications* (1946); J. W. Montgomery, *The Quest for Noah's Ark* (1972).

B. K. WALTKE

ARK OF THE COVENANT [Heb. *'ărôn habbᵉrîṯ*]. A portable chest of acacia wood containing various articles and serving as the meeting place of Yahweh with Israel.

- I. Biblical Data
  - A. Pentateuch
  - B. Historical Books
  - C. Prophetic and Poetic Books
  - D. New Testament
- II. Form of the Ark
- III. Contents
- IV. Names
- V. Origin
- VI. Significance

I. Biblical Data.*–A. Pentateuch.* Ex. 25:10-22 records the command to Moses to build an ark of acacia wood. Within this ark were to be placed the "testimony" (Heb. *'eḏûṯ*), an apparent reference in this context to the tables of the law that God was about to give to Moses. Upon the top of the ark, probably not as a lid but above the lid, the mercy seat (Heb. *kappōreṯ*; Gk. *hilastḗrion*, He. 9:5) was to be placed. This was a golden plate upon which two cherubim, with raised wings and facing each other, covered the ark. From the place between the two cherubim God promised to speak to Moses, and the whole structure was to be placed in the innermost room (holy of holies) of the tabernacle (Ex. 26:33).

In Deuteronomy the ark's origin is the subject of a much abbreviated narrative, the command to build and its execution forming part of the account of Moses' creation of the second two tablets of the law (Dt. 10:1-5). Commentators have often pointed out that the parallel account in Exodus would be found in Ex. 33:1-6, and many have argued that following v. 6 there must originally have been a statement concerning the erection of the sacred ark. Adherents to the documentary theory hold that this material, which consists of E-document narrative interposed within the dominant P source for the legal prescriptions, was originally separate from the entire section on the tabernacle and its furnishings, and should therefore contain some record of the making of the ark. If the material is parallel to that in Dt. 10, however, it is not clear that the making of the ark should in fact be introduced in Ex. 33 rather than in Ex. 34, following the commandment to make two additional tablets of stone. What has given rise to the suggestion is not some kind of exact parallel with the Deuteronomic material, but rather the enigmatic nature of the reference to God's withdrawal in Ex. 33:1-6 and the subsequent apparent reversal of this action in vv. 7ff. If the ark is the symbol of God's presence in Israel, it should logically figure in the narrative at some point; thus the attempt to match this narrative with that of Dt. 10.

A final reference of note is found in Nu. 10:33-36, in which appears the so-called Song of the Ark. This passage, considered to be very early by most critics, establishes the ark's position as accompanying Israel in its wilderness journeying. The "Song," which will be considered again below, seems to identify Yahweh and the ark in the closest possible fashion.

B. Historical Books. According to the narrative in Josh. 3 the ark cooperated at the crossing of the Jordan in such a way that the waters of the river ceased to flow as soon as the feet of the priests who were carrying the ark entered the water, and that they stood still above that point until these priests left the bed of the river. In the account of the solemn march around Jericho, which according to ch. 6

caused the walls of the city to fall, the carrying of the ark around the city is regarded as an essential feature in vv. 4, 7, 11. In ch. 7 it is narrated that Joshua, after the defeat of the army before Ai, lamented and prayed before the ark. In 8:30-34 the ark is mentioned as forming the central focus for the assemblage of Israel on Ebal and Gerizim, an action reminiscent of the later assembly in Shechem (ch. 24) which contains, however, no record of the ark.

Just where the ark was during the period of the judges is still a matter of some uncertainty. According to Josh. 18:1 the center of the amphictyony had moved to Shiloh during the time of Joshua, though the tent of meeting, not the ark, is mentioned in this connection. A brief reference in Jgs. 2:1 to a movement of "the angel of the Lord" from Gilgal to Bochim (LXX adds "unto Bethel") has given rise to the idea that at least one tradition saw the ark in Bethel during the entire period. This, so the argument goes, is confirmed by the ark's appearance in Bethel at the close of the period of the judges (Jgs. 20:18, 26-28), and the lack of mention of Shiloh in Jgs. 20. Such arguments are not entirely convincing when it is noted that Judges does, like Joshua, place the religious center of the amphictyony in Shiloh (18:31). Furthermore, the cult center is called the house of God (*bêṯ ha'elōhîm*) in that passage, and it is quite possible that the reference to Bethel (Heb. *bêṯ-'ēl,* "house of God") in ch. 20 is also a reference to the ark or tent of meeting in Shiloh. Conversely, the ark could well have been resident in Shiloh but simply moved to Bethel for convenience at the battle, although 20:27 seems to indicate a period of general residence for the ark in that place. In view of the otherwise unbroken testimony to the ark's presence in Shiloh (excepting only the LXX of Jgs. 2:1) it seems best to explain the Bethel reference by some means such as that suggested above.

At the time of Eli the ark stood in the sanctuary at Shiloh (1 S. 3:3). It was taken from this place after Israel had been defeated by the Philistines at Ebenezer, in order to assure the help of Yahweh to the people, but instead of this the ark fell into the hands of the Philistines (ch. 4). The various misfortunes that then afflicted the Philistines induced them to regard the possession of the ark as a calamity (ch. 5), and they sent it back to Israel (ch. 6). It was taken first to Beth-shemesh in the border-country between Philistia and Judah and soon after to Kiriath-jearim about 7½ mi. (12 km.) NW of Jerusalem. There the ark remained for years (unless 1 S. 14:18 be an exception, but cf. the LXX where "ephod" is read in place of "ark") in the house of a man named Abinadab, whose son was its guardian (7:1), until David had it removed to Mt. Zion after he had established his camp and court there. He placed it in a tent (*see* TABERNACLE) prepared for it (2 S. 6; 1 Ch. 16:1).

In David's time the ark was taken again into battle (2 S. 11:11). When David fled from Absalom the priests wanted to accompany him with the ark, but he sent it back (2 S. 15:24f.). David had also intended to build a temple in which the ark was to be located, since before this it had always found its resting-place in a tent. But God forbade this through Nathan, because He was willing to build a house for David, but unwilling that David should build one for Him (2 S. 7). Solomon then built the temple and placed the ark of the covenant in the holy of holies, where it was located under the wings of two mighty cherubim images (1 K. 8; 2 Ch. 5).

C. Prophetic and Poetic Books. Jer. 3:16 states that in the future new Jerusalem nobody will concern himself about the ark, nor make an attempt to rebuild it — presumably in view of the ark's loss or destruction in the collapse of the city in 586 B.C. Only one reference in the Psalms explicitly mentions the ark (Ps. 132), but recent study of this psalm in connection with 2 S. 6 has convinced commentators that there is a whole genre of praise literature properly associated with the ark narratives in Samuel. Even considering the excesses to which this kind of scholarship has tended in modern times, it is certainly reasonable to see in various references within the Psalms (e.g., 78:61; 26:8) allusions to the ark. One need not reorient Israel around an illusionary New Year's Festival to appreciate the enthronement nature of certain psalms and the reenactment of the ascent of the ark in connection with the liturgical celebration of the new king, or the ultimate position of Yahweh as the truly enthroned monarch of Israel. To say that the king and the ark were probably in close contact does not, however, justify claims that the ark was considered a repository for Yahweh or that the king represented Yahweh in a cultic reenactment. The Lord was from the beginning in heaven, although His presence was somehow implied in the possession of the little rectangular chest that figured so prominently in Israel's history and, undoubtedly, its worship as well.

D. New Testament. In the NT the ark of the covenant is mentioned only in He. 9:4, in the description of the Jewish tabernacle, though a heavenly counterpart does appear in Rev. 11:19.

II. Form of the Ark.–The ark was a chest made of acacia wood, 2½ cubits long. 1½ cubits wide, and 1½ cubits high. That there are two widely varying traditions, whereby the ark is represented in the so-called P document as an elaborate golden shrine, and in the earlier narratives as a simple wooden chest, is not clear from the Scriptures themselves. The statement of Dt. 10:3 and the full account of instructions in Ex. 25 are in agreement so far as they go. Exodus, in addition to mentioning an acacia-wood chest, goes on to prescribe an overlay of gold within and without, and a molding of gold running all around. At the feet of the ark were to be four rings of gold for use with the gold-covered carrying staves. These staves are also mentioned in 1 K. 8:7f.; 2 Ch. 5:8f., while reference is often made to those who carried the ark (2 S. 6:13; 15:24). Such carefully crafted wooden chests with gold overlay are known from the time of Tutankhamen and earlier (*ANEP,* nos. 318, 548) and need cause no incredulity when set in the context of Israelite handiwork following the exodus from Egypt.

On top of the ark was the gold *kappōreṯ* or "mercy-seat," flanked by two gold cherubim (*see* CHERUBIM) with outstretched wings. In the later temple of Solomon the ark was placed between two much more massive cherub figures (1 K. 6:19, 23ff.; 8:6), a fact which does not prove that there were no cherubim on the ark itself, or even that those cherubim, which according to Ex. 25:19 were found on the ark, were nothing else than those of Solomon's days transferred in imagination to an earlier period. Excavations from Syria-Palestine have uncovered a variety of symbolic winged creatures from the late 2nd and early 1st millennium B.C. (*ANEP,* nos. 644-659).

III. Contents.–Unbroken tradition in the pentateuchal narratives (including both the so-called P and D sources) affirms that from the beginning the ark served as a container for the tables of the law (Ex. 25:16; 40:20; Dt. 10:5; 1 K. 8:9). Arguments of older critics who felt that the receptacle concept of the ark was incompatible with the idea of the ark as a dwelling place or throne for Yahweh have now been set aside by evidence from the ancient Near East (cf. deVaux, p. 301) showing that the covenant or treaty was often placed beneath the feet of a god who served as witness to it. In similar form, the Ten Words form the basis for the covenant of which the ark was the

Relief of Torah shrine (ark of the law) from second-century A.D. Jewish catacomb at Beth Shearim (Consulate General of Israel in New York)

symbol. Note that the common Deuteronomic term "ark of the covenant" is replaced in Exodus by the term "ark of the testimony," similarly a reference to the tables of the law as covenant witnesses.

Additional objects within the ark were but two. According to Ex. 16:33f. a pot of manna was to be placed "before the Lord" or "before the testimony" as a witness throughout the generations. Nu. 17 furnishes evidence that Aaron's rod was similarly placed "before the testimony," this time as a sign for would-be rebels in Israel; and He. 9:4 confirms the tradition that the testimony spoken of in both passages was, or became, the law tablets within the ark of the covenant.

IV. Names.–Over twenty different designations appear with reference to the ark, and discerning any invariable pattern in usage is difficult. Certainly the long narratives of Exodus in which directions are given for the tabernacle favor the designation "ark of the testimony" or simply "the ark." The so-called Deuteronomic term "ark of the covenant of the Lord" is uniformly used in Deuteronomy, but also appears in the very old "Song of the Ark" passage of Nu. 10:33-35 (JE). Joshua seems to use "ark of the covenant of the Lord" and "ark of the Lord" indiscriminately, as do the Samuel-Kings narratives, which add frequently the term "ark of God." Some indication of the complexity of the problem is found in an examination of Josh. 4, where the ark is mentioned seven times. It is called the "ark of the Lord" (vv. 5, 11), the "ark of the covenant of the Lord" (vv. 7, 18), the "ark of the covenant" (v. 9), the "ark" (v. 10), and the "ark of the testimony" (v. 16). The last designation is especially significant, as it appears nowhere else outside of the pentateuchal narratives claimed for the P document, and is considered a clear mark of P.

V. Origin.–Nineteenth-century scholarship produced various suggestions concerning the ark's origin, including the view that it was a shrine taken over by Israel from the Canaanites after the entry into Palestine. Another theory saw in the ark an ancient palladium of the tribe of Ephraim which was only at a later period recognized by all Israel. Contemporary scholarship recognizes that the Mosaic connection with the ark, deeply embedded in each of the traditions (cf. Ex. 25; Nu. 10:33-36; Dt. 10), must reflect the situation in the desert, confirming the Bible's own testimony that the ark accompanied the children of Israel from Sinai onward.

VI. Significance.–The ark has been variously interpreted as (1) the extension or embodiment of the presence of Yahweh; (2) a war palladium of Israel's amphictyony; (3) a container for the tables of the law; and (4) a portable throne for the invisible presence of Yahweh. We have already shown that the container idea is both original and compatible with other concepts put forth. Proposal (2) is favored in light of texts such as 1 S. 4 and 2 S. 11:11 which show that the ark was taken into battle in order to enlist the divine help. Note also the word of Moses which he spoke when the ark was taken up to be carried: "Arise, O Lord, and let thy enemies be scattered" (Nu. 10:35). However, nothing of what we know or presuppose concerning the form and contents of the ark points to an original military purpose, and in other statements concerning the ark a much more general significance is assigned to it. The importance of the ark for Israel in connection with her wars is only the outcome of the significance as the symbol of the presence of Yahweh, a God whose presence was necessary if His people were to be victorious in their struggle.

Proposals (1) and (4) may be taken together, as both refer to the deeply rooted idea that the ark somehow meant Yahweh was present. The throne concept has arisen from the epithet of Yahweh of Hosts who is "enthroned upon the cherubim" (1 S. 4:4; 2 S. 6:2; 2 K. 19:15; etc.). In postexilic times it was promised that Jerusalem itself would be the throne of Yahweh, a fact that would render the ark superfluous (Jer. 3:16f.); and in the prophecy of Ezekiel it is specifically said that the temple is both throne and footstool for the Lord (Ezk. 43:7). Much was made of this material, and parallels have been drawn from various areas of the ancient Near East in which empty thrones were a part of the sacred furnishings of a temple. However, inasmuch as the ark in the OT is always described as an ark (Lat. *arca,* "chest") and never as a throne or seat, it seems best to take these references to a throne in a somewhat figurative sense. What is clear is that the ark was designed to be a symbol of the presence of God in the midst of His people. When the people were to leave the mountain where God had caused them to realize His presence (Ex. 30:6), the ark was made to serve as a comfortable assurance that He would indeed accompany them on the journey. In Ex. 25:21f., God promised to meet with Moses and to speak with him from above the *kappōreṯ,* between the two cherubim upon the ark. When Israel in the time of Eli was overpowered by the Philistines, the Israelites sent for the ark in order that Yahweh should come into the camp of Israel, and this was also believed to be the case by the Philistines (1 S. 4:3ff.). After the ark had come to Beth-shemesh and a pestilence had broken out there, the people did not want to keep the ark, because no one could live in the presence of Yahweh, this holy God (1 S. 6:20). Jeremiah says (3:16f.) that an ark of the covenant would not be made again after the restoration, because the city itself, as God's throne, would guarantee the presence of God at least as much as the ark formerly did.

In all the discussion it is foolish to press the aspect of physical presence to great lengths. That Yahweh was present with His people is clear from the texts. But that Yahweh was confined to the ark runs counter both to Hebrew notions about the nonspatial nature of God, and to the explicit statements of Scripture which, dating from the same times, mention God dwelling in many places both within and outside of Canaan. The statement of Moses, "Arise, O Lord, and let thy enemies be scattered" (Nu. 10:35), is not the command addressed to those who carry the ark to lift it up and thereby elevate Yahweh for the journey, but is a demand made upon Yahweh, in accordance with His promise, to go ahead of Israel as the ark does. According to 1 S. 4:3 the Israelites did not say, "We want to go and get the Lord," but "We want to go and get the ark of the Lord, that he may come among us." They accordingly wanted only to induce Him to come by getting the ark. This, too, the priests and the soothsayers of the Philistines say: "Do not send away the ark of the God of Israel empty [i.e., without a gift]" (1 S. 6:3), but they do not speak as though they really thought Yahweh was Himself confined therein. That Samuel, who slept near the ark, when he was addressed by the Lord did not at all originally think that the Lord was addressing him, proves that at that time the view did not prevail that He was in the ark or had His seat upon it. Ancient Israel was therefore evidently of the conviction that the ark was closely connected with Yahweh, and that something of His power was inherent in the ark; consequently the feeling prevailed that when near the ark they were in a special way in the presence of the Lord. But this is something different from the opinion that the ark was, in the very literal sense, a seat or dwelling place of Yahweh. Ancient man was not conscious to the extent we are of the difference between the symbolic presence and the literal reality, but that this difference was felt is not a matter of doubt.

That the ark was built to embody the presence of God among His people seems equally clear from each one of the supposed documents of the documentary theory, though the tables of the law, rather than Yahweh Himself, constituted the contents of the ark. What would have been better adapted to make the presence of God felt as a reality than the stone tables with the Ten Words, through which the Lord had made known to His people His ethical character? For the words on these tables were a kind of spiritual portrait of the God of Israel, who could not be pictured in a bodily form, but whose living, holy presence was a vital element in His people's daily life.

Bibliography.–M. Dibelius, *Die Lade Jahves* (1906); H. Gressmann, *Die Lade Jahves* (1920); D. W. Gooding, *Account of the Tabernacle* (1959); R. de Vaux, *Ancient Israel* (Eng. tr. 1961), pp. 297-302; W. Eichrodt, *Theology of the OT*, I (Eng. tr. 1961), 107-119; P. D. Miller and J. J. M. Roberts, *Hand of the Lord: A Reassessment of the "Ark Narrative" of 1 Samuel* (1977); G. von Rad, *OT Theology*, I (Eng. tr. 1962), 234-241; R. Smend, *Yahweh War and Tribal Confederation* (Eng. tr. 1970).

H. G. May, *AJSL*, 52 (1935/36), 215-234; O. Eissfeldt, *ZAW*, 58 (1940/41), 190-215; J. Morgenstern, *HUCA*, 17 (1942/43), 153-266; *HUCA*, 18 (1943/44), 1-52; A. Bentzen, *JBL*, 67 (1948), 37-53; J. R. Porter, *JTS*, N.S. 5 (1954), 161-173; M. Haran, *Eretz-Israel*, 5 (1958), 83-89; *IEJ*, 9 (1959), 30-38; E. Nielsen, "Some Reflections on the History of the Ark," in *SVT*, 7 (1960), 61-74; G. von Rad, *Problems of the Hexateuch and Other Essays* (Eng. tr. 1966), article from *Neue Kirchliche Zeitschrift*, 42 (1931), 476-498; J. Blenkinsopp, *JBL*, 88 (1969), 143-156.

W. LOTZ
M. G. KYLE
C. E. ARMERDING

ARK OF THE TESTIMONY. *See* ARK OF THE COVENANT.

ARKITE ärk'īt [Heb. *'arqî*]. An inhabitant of Arqat (Irqata), a town on the Phoenician border about 11 mi. (17.5 km.) N of Tripoli, Lebanon. The Arkites are mentioned in Gen. 10:17 and 1 Ch. 1:15 as descendants of Canaan. Arqat is mentioned in the Amarna Letters: ^{al}*ir-qat*^{ki} (62.13), $^{m\bar{a}t}$*ir-qa-ta* (140.10), etc. It was conquered by Thutmose in his sixteenth or seventeenth campaign and was conquered again by Tiglath-pileser III. In Roman times it was known as Caesarea Libani, and it was the birthplace of Alexander Severus. The site is marked today as Tell 'Arqah. W. S. L. S.

ARM [Heb. *z^{e}rô(a)'* (Ex. 6:6; 15:16; etc.), *'ezrô(a)'* (Job 31:22; Jer. 32:21), *yāḏ*–'hand' (1 K. 10:19; 2 K. 5:18; 2 Ch. 9:18; Ezk. 17:9); Aram. *d^{e}rā'* (Dnl. 2:32); Gk. *brachíōn* (Lk. 1:51; Jn. 12:38; Acts 13:17)]; AV also HELP (Ps. 83:8), POWER (Ezk. 17:9), STAYS (1 K. 10:19; 2 Ch. 9:18); NEB also POWER, "lending aid" (Ps. 83:8), HANDS (Ezk. 17:9), STRENGTH (2 Ch. 32:8), SUPPORT (Jer. 17:5), INFLUENCE (Dnl. 11:6), etc.

The usual term *z^{e}rô(a)'*, is used surprisingly infrequently in its literal meaning (2 S. 1:10; Isa. 44:12). As the natural instrument of human volition, the arm became a metaphorical symbol of effective power. It is in this sense that the word is most often used. A king's arms represented his ability to muster and project an effective military force (cf. *z^{e}rô(a)'*, RSV "forces," "armies," in Dnl. 11:15, 22, 31). Hence, to break the arms of an enemy nation is to break its power (Jer. 48:25; Ezk. 30:21f.).

In the vast majority of usages, this word denotes the awesome might of Yahweh. The "descending blow of his arm" is as swift and overwhelming as a bolt of lightning (Isa. 30:30). Defeating the chaos monster, Rahab (Ps. 89:10; Isa. 51:9), it had both brought the universe into existence (Jer. 27:5; 32:17) and created the nation of Israel. The latter theme is by far the most typical motif associated with the arm of God. With "an outstretched arm" He had delivered His people from bondage (Ex. 6:6; Dt. 4:34; Ps. 44:3). Because of that mighty display of power, Israel knew that her national life rested upon "the everlasting arms" of her God (Dt. 33:27). This experience of deliverance also provided the basis for Israel's eschatological hope (Isa. 40:10f.; 51:5, 9; Ezk. 20:33ff.).

The NT saw the arm of God at work in the birth (Lk. 1:51) and ministry (Jn. 12:38) of Jesus. In Him the promises of old were being fulfilled.

See *TDNT*, I, *s.v.* βραχίων (Schlier). K. H. MAAHS

ARMAGEDDON är-mə-ged'ən [Gk. *Harmagedon*]. A name found only in Rev. 16:16. It is described as the rallying place of the kings of the whole world who, led by the unclean spirits issuing from the mouth of the dragon, the beast, and the false prophet, assemble here for "the war of the great day of God, the Almighty."

Although the author designates the name as Hebrew, it appears nowhere else in that language and its derivation is uncertain. The generally accepted view is that the word *har* means mountain (or mountains) and that *magedon* refers to Megiddo, the biblical city near which many notable battles were fought. Here the armies of Israel defeated Sisera and his host (Jgs. 5:19), and later it was the scene of the fatal struggle between Josiah and Pharaoh Neco (2 K. 23:29f.; 2 Ch. 35:22). There was, therefore, a peculiar appropriateness in the choice of this as the arena of the last mighty struggle between the powers of good and evil. This is apocalyptic language, and it is possible that Armageddon is used not as a name for a particular locality but as a symbolic term for the final decisive conflict.

Because the phrase "mountains of Megiddo" does not

occur elsewhere, some scholars have conjectured interpretations such as "city of Megiddo," "land of Megiddo," or "mount of assembly"; but none has met with general acceptance. "Mountains" seems to be the best translation for *har*. Megiddo itself was a hill town, and the district was in part mountainous (cf. Mt. Tabor, Jgs. 4:6, 12; "the heights of the field," 5:18). Also, as Charles has pointed out (*ICC*), the final conflict is pictured by the prophet Ezekiel — in a passage that influenced Rev. 20:8-11 — as taking place on "the mountains of Israel" (38:8, 21; 39:2, 4, 17). W. W. BUEHLER

ARMENIA. *See* ARARAT.

ARMENIAN VERSIONS. *See* VERSIONS.

ARMHOLE. *See* ARMPIT.

ARMLET [Heb. *'eṣ'āḏâ, ṣe'āḏâ* (Isa. 3:20)]; AV CHAIN (Nu. 31:50), BRACELET (2 S. 1:10), ORNAMENT OF THE LEGS (Isa. 3:20); [*kûmāz*] (Ex. 35:22); AV TABLET; NEB PENDANT. A band or ring worn on the upper arm, and different from a bracelet, which was worn around the wrist. The Midianites (Nu. 31:50) wore these luxury items (cf. Isa. 3:20), which were also favored by the Israelite nobility (cf. 2 S. 1:10).

See also BEADS. R. K. H.

ARMONI är-mō'nī [Heb. *'armōnî*]. One of the two sons of Saul by Rizpah, the daughter of Aiah (2 S. 21:8). David delivered them over to the blood vengeance of the Gibeonites.

ARMOR; ARMS. *See* WEAPONS OF WAR.

ARMOR-BEARER [Heb. *nōśē' kelî*; Gk. *ho aírōn tá skeúē*]. One who carried the large shield and perhaps other weapons for a king (1 S. 31:4), commander-in-chief (2 S. 23:37), captain (1 S. 14:7), or champion (17:7). All warriors of distinction had such attendants.

Rather than perish by the hand of a woman, Abimelech called upon his armor-bearer to give him the finishing stroke (Jgs. 9:54); and when King Saul's armor-bearer refused to do this for him that he might not become the prisoner of the Philistines, he took a sword himself and fell upon it (1 S. 31:4). David had been Saul's armor-bearer for a time. Jonathan's armor-bearer was a man of resource and courage (1 S. 14:7).

The shield-bearer was a figure well known in the chariots of Egypt, Assyria, and the Hittites, his business being to protect his fighting companion during the engagement. T. NICOL

ARMORY [Heb. *bêṯ kelî*] (2 K. 20:13; Isa. 39:2); AV HOUSE OF ARMOR; [*nešeq*] (Neh. 3:19); NEB emends with LXX AB; [*'ôṣār*] (Jer. 50:25); NEB ARSENAL. A storehouse for weapons, such as that of Hezekiah (2 K. 20:13 par.). In Jer. 50:27 the use is figurative, of the Lord's "weapons of wrath," unleashed in judgment. The same word designates the temple treasury in 1 K. 7:51; Neh. 10:38. In Neh. 3:19 the text is uncertain. *See also* ARSENAL.

ARMPIT [Heb. *'aṣṣî*]; AV ARMHOLES. In Jer. 38:12 the word is used of the shoulder-joints. Ropes were put under the prophet's arms, protected with rags, and he was pulled from the cistern. The same word in Ezk. 13:18 refers to the joints of the hands.

ARMY [Heb. *ḥayil, ṣāḇā', maḥaneh, geḏûḏ, ma'arāḵâ* (1 S. 17, etc.), also *ḥêl, ḥêl ṣāḇā'* (2 Ch. 26:13), *'am, zerō'ôṯ* (Dnl. 11:22); Gk. *stráteuma* (Rev. 19:14, 19), *stratópedon* (Lk. 21:20), *parembolḗ* (He. 11:34)]; AV also HOST, PEOPLE (*'am*), SOLDIERS (1 Ch. 7:4), POWER (*ḥayil*, Est. 1:3), ARMS (Dnl. 11:22), "to war" (Dt. 24:5), "to battle" (1 S. 28:1); NEB also COMPANY, TROOPS, INFANTRY, FORCES, FIGHTING MEN (1 Ch. 7:4), HOST (Joel 2:5), "forces of opposition" (Dnl. 11:22); in Cant. 6:4, 10, AV, RSV, "an army with banners" translates Heb. *niḏgālôṯ*, lit. "raising banners," NEB "the starry heavens."

While the Israelites were not distinctively warlike, their geographical position in Canaan necessitated some means of self-defense. During patriarchal times the able-bodied men were mustered when the enemy threatened. In Gen. 14 Abram prosecuted a typical bedouin night-attack with 318 followers, the usual size of raiding parties described in the Amarna tablets. Although army commanders were mentioned in the Wilderness narratives (cf. Nu. 31:14), men were mustered at the summons of a leader such as Joshua (Ex. 17:9ff.) or Gideon (Jgs. 6:34). The *geḏûḏîm* of the judges period were individual marauding companies which sometimes served the national cause with fidelity and usefulness (Jgs. 11:3). The first standing army was formed in the time of Saul, consisting mostly of his personal retinue (cf. 1 S. 13:2); and under David the numbers increased considerably by the addition of mercenaries (2 S. 15:18). Even in spite of this they were outnumbered by the Philistines (cf. 1 S. 13:5).

Under Joab the Israelite army became an efficient fighting force, adept at siege warfare (cf. 2 S. 20:15). Solomon introduced the iron-fitted chariot as a military weapon (1 K. 10:26-29), following Egyptian tradition; but chariots were distrusted by the prophets generally (cf. Isa. 2:7; Hos. 1:7; etc.) if only because enemy chariots invariably outnumbered those of Israel (cf. 2 K. 18:23). Also introduced under Solomon were cavalry units, in disregard of the Torah (Dt. 17:16; cf. 20:1).

Under Mosaic law all males became liable for military service (Nu. 1:3; 26:2; 2 Ch. 25:5), but Levites (Nu. 2:33), those with newly acquired property, the recently married, and the timid were exempt from battle (Dt. 20:1-9). These exemptions were still being maintained in the Maccabean period (1 Macc. 3:56). Very little is known about preexilic army organization, despite the mention of officers and corps of troops. The term *'elep* ("thousand") is not necessarily a strictly literal number, and could perhaps be as low as 200. Prior to the monarchy, soldiers provided both their own food and weapons (1 S. 17:17f.), but on foreign soil they were allowed to pillage. Occasionally they were maintained by regular pay (1 K. 4:27). After the exile there was no Israelite army until the Maccabean period, when guerilla bands rose to the defense of the nation. Under the Hasmoneans a standing army was formed, and augmented by mercenary soldiers (Josephus *BJ* i.2.5) at considerable expense (cf. 1 Macc. 14:32). Though Jewish soldiers are mentioned in Mk. 6:27; Lk. 3:14; 23:11, it is the Roman army that is prominent in the NT (Acts 10:1; 27:1; Phil. 1:13; etc.).

See also ARMY, ROMAN; WEAPONS OF WAR.

R. K. HARRISON

ARMY, ROMAN. The treatment will be confined to (I) a brief description of the organization of the army and (II) a consideration of the allusions in the NT to the Roman military establishment.

I. Organization.–Originally there were no standing forces, but citizens of the wealthier classes performed

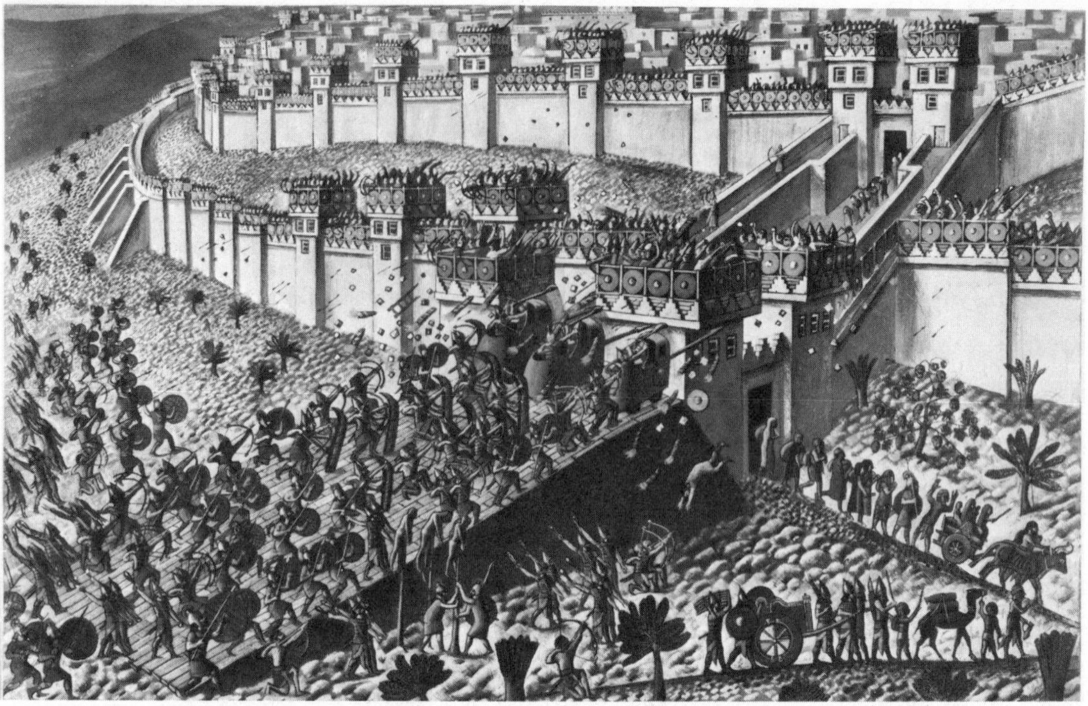

Assault and surrender of Lachish *ca.* 700 B.C., reconstructed from Assyrian reliefs. Bowmen man both walls, as soldiers hurl stones and firebrands on the attackers. (Trustees of the British Museum, A. Sorrell, 1957)

military service when summoned by the magistrates, providing their own equipment. The gradual development of a military profession and standing army culminated in the admission of the poorest classes to the ranks by Marius (107 B.C.). Henceforth the Roman army was made up of men who were essentially mercenaries, with periods of service ranging from sixteen to twenty-six years. In the civil wars of the late Republic their loyalty toward their commanders was often greater than toward the state.

The forces that composed the Roman army under the empire may be divided into the following five groups: (1) the imperial guard and garrison of the capital, (2) the legions, (3) the *auxilia,* (4) the *numeri,* (5) the fleet.

A. The Imperial Guard. The imperial guard consisted of the *cohortes praetoriae,* which together with the *cohortes urbanae* and *vigiles* made up the garrison of Rome. In the military system established by Augustus there were nine cohorts of the praetorian guard, three of the urban troops, and seven of the vigiles. Each cohort numbered a thousand men, and was commanded by a tribune of equestrian rank. The praetorian prefects (*praefecti praetorii*), of whom there were usually two, were commanders of the entire garrison of the capital, and stood at the highest point of distinction and authority in the equestrian career.

B. The Legions. There were twenty-five legions in A.D. 23 (Tacitus *Ann.* iv-v), which had been increased to thirty at the time of the reign of Marcus Aurelius, A.D. 161-180 (*CIL,* VI, 3492 a-b) and to thirty-three under Septimius Severus (Dio Cassius iv.23f.). Each legion was made up, ordinarily, of six thousand men, who were divided into ten cohorts, each cohort containing three maniples, and each maniple in turn two centuries.

The *legatus Augusti pro praetore,* or governor of each imperial province, was chief commander of all the troops within the province. An officer of senatorial rank known as *legatus Augusti legionis* was entrusted with the command of each legion, together with the bodies of *auxilia* that were associated with it. Besides, there were six *tribuni militum,* officers of equestrian rank (usually sons of senators who had not yet held the quaestorship), in each legion. The centurions commanding the centuries belonged to the plebeian class, but were the mainstay of the whole system both in discipline and in the actual fighting. Under them served the *principales* of lower noncommissioned rank.

C. The "Auxilia." The *auxilia* were organized as infantry in *cohortes,* as cavalry in *alae,* or as mixed bodies, *cohortes equitatae.* Some of these divisions contained approximately a thousand men (*cohortes* or *alae miliariae*), but most divisions only about five hundred (*cohortes* or *alae quingenariae*). They were commanded by *tribuni* and *praefecti* of equestrian rank. The importance of the *auxilia* consisted originally in the diversity of their equipment and manner of fighting, since each group adhered to the customs of the nation in whose midst it had been recruited. But with the gradual romanization of the empire they were assimilated more and more to the character of the legionaries.

D. The "Numeri." The *numeri* developed out of the auxiliary forces, additional infantry and cavalry who retained their local character (cf., e.g., Tacitus *Hist.* i.6; *Agricola* 18; Pliny *Ep.* x.29). Their commanders were also of equestrian rank.

E. The Fleet. The Roman fleet, which had first achieved strength in the Punic Wars, was not organized as a state force until after the death of Julius Caesar. It consisted chiefly of triremes and quinqueremes, and was commanded by high-ranking equestrian officers (*praefecti classis*). The principal naval stations were at Misenum (near Naples) and Ravenna.

F. Defensive Arrangements. Augustus established the

northern boundary of the empire at the Rhine and at the Danube, throughout the greater part of its course, and bequeathed to his successors the advice that they should not extend their sovereignty beyond the limits he had set (Tacitus *Ann.* i.11; *Agricola* 13). Although this policy was departed from in many instances, such as the annexation of Thrace, Cappadocia, Mauretania, Britain, and Dacia, not to mention the more ephemeral acquisitions by Trajan, yet the military system of the empire was arranged primarily with the view of providing for the defense of the provinces and not for carrying on aggressive warfare on a large scale. Thus Palestine generally was dependent on the four legions stationed in Syria, Rome's most important frontier to the east. Nearly all the forces, with the exception of the imperial guard, were distributed among the provinces on the border of the empire; and the essential feature of the disposition of the troops in these provinces was the permanent fortress in which each unit was stationed. The combination of large camps for the legions with a series of smaller forts for the *alae,* cohorts, and *numeri* was the characteristic arrangement on all the frontiers. The immediate protection of the frontier was regularly entrusted to the auxiliary troops, while the legions were usually stationed some distance to the rear of the actual boundary. This system of "defense in depth," based on the *limites* (fortified posts) and their linking roads, proved generally satisfactory in view of the conditions that prevailed, and secured for the millions of subjects of the Roman empire the longest period of undisturbed tranquility known to European history.

G. Recruiting System. In accordance with the arrangements of Augustus, the *cohortes praetoriae* and *cohortes urbanae* were recruited from Latium, Etruria, Umbria, and the older Roman colonies (Tacitus *Ann.* iv-v), the legions from the remaining portions of Italy, and the *auxilia* from the subject communities of the empire.

But in course of time the natives of Italy disappeared, first from the legions and later from the garrison of the capital. Antoninus Pius established the rule that each body of troops should draw its recruits from the district where it was stationed. Henceforth the previous possession of Roman citizenship was no longer required for enlistment in the legions. The legionary was granted the privilege of citizenship upon entering the service, the auxiliary soldier upon being discharged (O. Seeck, *Geschichte des Untergangs der antiken Welt* [1897-1920], I, 250).

II. Allusions in the NT to the Roman Military Establishment.–Such references relate chiefly to the bodies of troops that were stationed in Judea. Agrippa I left a military establishment of one *ala* and five cohorts at his death in A.D. 44 (Josephus *Ant.* xix.9.2; *BJ* iii.4.2), which he had doubtless received from the earlier Roman administration. These divisions were composed of local recruits, chiefly Samaritans (O. Hirschfeld, *Die Kaiserlichen Verwaltungsbeamten bis auf Diocletian* [1876; 3rd ed. 1963], p. 395; T. Mommsen, *Hermes,* 19 [1884], 217 n. 1). The *Ala I gemina Sebastenorum* was stationed at Caesarea (Josephus *Ant.* xx.6; *BJ,* ii.12.5; *CIL,* VIII, 9359).

A. Augustan Band. Julius, the centurion to whom Paul and other prisoners were delivered to be escorted to Rome (Acts 27:1), belonged to one of the five cohorts stationed at or near Caesarea. This *speíra Sebastḗ,* "Augustus' Band" or "Cohort," was probably identical with the *Cohors I Augusta* (Dessau, no. 2683) based in Syria, and is to be distinguished from the *Cohors Augusta Sebastenorum* consisting of men from the town of Sebaste (Josephus *BJ* ii.3.4).

B. Italian Band. There was another cohort in Caesarea, the "Italian band" (*Cohors Italica,* Vulg.), of which Cornelius was centurion (Acts 10:1: Gk. *ek speíres tḗs kalouménēs Italikḗs*). The *cohortes Italicae* were made up of Roman citizens (Marquardt, II, 467). Our earliest evidence of such a cohort is from Syria in A.D. 69 (Dessau, no. 9168), but a similar unit was evidently at Caesarea at this time (cf. F. F. Bruce, *Acts of the Apostles* [2nd ed. 1952], *in loc.*).

C. Praetorian Guard. One of the five cohorts was stationed in Jerusalem (Mt. 27:27; Mk. 15:16), the "chief captain" of which was Claudius Lysias. His title, *chiliárchos* in the Greek (Acts 21:31; 23:10, 15, 17, 19, 22, 26; 24:7, AV), meaning "leader of a thousand men" (Vulg. *tribunus*), indicates that this body of soldiers was a *cohors miliaria.* Claudius Lysias sent Paul to Felix at Caesarea under escort of two hundred soldiers, seventy horsemen, and two hundred spearmen (Acts 23:23). The spearmen (Gk. *dexioláboi,* a very rare word; cf. Bauer, p. 173) are thought to have been a party of provincial militia. Several centurions of the cohort at Jerusalem appear during the riot and subsequent rescue and arrest of Paul (Acts 21:32; 22:25f.; 23:17, 23). A centurion, doubtless of the same cohort, was in charge of the crucifixion of Jesus (Mt. 27:54; Mk. 15:39, 44f.; Lk. 23:47). It was customary for centurions to be entrusted with the execution of capital penalties (Tacitus *Ann.* i.6; xvi.9, 15; *Hist.* ii.85).

The AV contains the passage in Acts 28:16, "The centurion delivered the prisoners to the captain of the guard" (Gk. *stratopedárchēs*), which rests on doubtful MS authority (cf. RSV, NEB). This officer was perhaps the prefect of the praetorian guard (Lat. *praefectus praetorii*), who at this time was Sextus Afranius Burrus (Tacitus *Ann.* xii.42, 69; xiii.2ff.; xiv.7ff.). But this Greek title is nowhere used for the praetorian prefect, and Mommsen's view is more likely, that the *stratopedárchēs* was the centurion in command of the *frumentarii* at Rome (*princeps castrorum peregrinorum*). These troops served as military couriers between Rome and the provinces, as political spies, and as imperial police; the reading in question thus no doubt preserves an authentic tradition.

Bibliography.–Comprehensive discussions of the Roman military system will be found in K. J. Marquardt, *Römische Staatsverwaltung* (1884), II, 319-612; Pauly-Wissowa, III/2, 1962-65; VI/2, 1589-1679; XII, 1186-1837; H. M. D. Parker, *The Roman Legions* (rev. ed. 1958); Y. Yadin, *The Art of Warfare in Biblical Lands* (1963); G. Webster, *Roman Imperial Army* (1969); G. R. Watson, *Roman Soldier* (1969).

G. H. ALLEN
B. F. HARRIS

ARNA är'nə [Lat. *Arna*]. One of the ancestors of Ezra given in 2 Esd. 1:2, evidently identical with Zerahiah of Ezr. 7:4 and Zaraias of 1 Esd. 8:2, AV (NEB Zaraeus).

ARNAN är'nən [Heb. *'arnān*; Gk. *Orna*]. A descendant of David (1 Ch. 3:21).

ARNI är'nī [Gk. *Arni*] (Lk. 3:33); AV ARAM. An ancestor of Jesus Christ. But in the AV, following TR, and in the genealogical list of Mt. 1:3f., the name is Aram (Gk. *Aram*); in the latter passage, however, the RSV and NEB have "Ram," like the OT name (Heb. *rām*) for the great-grandson of Judah and ancestor of David (Ruth 4:19; 1 Ch. 2:9f.).

See also ADMIN.

ARNON är'non [Heb. *'arnōn*; Gk. *Arnōn*]. A river flowing into the Dead Sea on the east. Apart from 2 K. 10:33; Isa. 16:2; Jer. 48:20, this river is mentioned only in Numbers through Judges, and always as marking the boundary be-

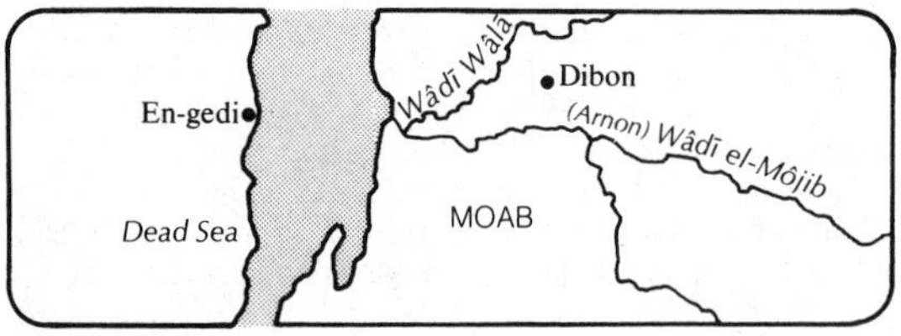

tween Moab to the south, and first the Amorites, then Israel, to the north.

The high plateau of Moab is drained by two streams, the Seil Hedān or Wâdī Wâlā to the north and Seil el-Môjib to the south, and by their tributaries — the valleys (AV "brooks") of Arnon (Nu. 21:14) — which for most of their course flow through gorges about 2 mi. (3 km.) wide at the top and about 120 ft. (37 m.) wide at the bottom; at points the depth is nearly 2300 ft. (700 m.). About 13 mi. (21 km.) E of the Dead Sea they unite to form the Arnon (Wâdī Môjib), which continues through the gorge to discharge its water into the sea just about halfway down its length. The depth of its gorge is one of the reasons "the King's Highway" (Nu. 20:17; 21:22) ran so far E of the Jordan Valley.

In spite of the apparent suitability of the Arnon as a natural frontier, it is clear that the essential continuity of the land on either side was more potent than the influence of the gorge. Not only had Sihon been able to carve out a kingdom N of it at the expense of Moab (Nu. 21:26), but the Ammonites also claimed the territory as traditionally theirs (Jgs. 11:13). When Israel was weak, Moab was able to recapture much of the area, as Mesha claims in his inscription; many of the Moabite towns listed in Isa. 15 traditionally belonged to Israel. H. L. ELLISON

AROD âr'od [Heb. *'ᵃrôḏ*]. The sixth son of Gad (Nu. 26:17).

ARODI âr'ə-dī [Heb. *'ᵃrôḏî*] (Gen. 46:16). The descendants of AROD.

ARODITES âr'ədīts [Heb. *hā'ᵃrôḏî*] (Nu. 26:17). The family name of AROD.

AROER ə-rō'ər [Heb. *'ᵃrô'ēr*].

1. An Amorite city situated on the northern rim of a canyon overlooking the Arnon River (Dt. 2:36; 3:12; 4:48), the southern boundary of the Amorite kingdom of Sihon (Josh. 12:2). Following the Israelite conquest it was assigned to the tribe of Reuben (Josh. 13:15f.). The men of Gad, co-sharers with Reuben in the land of the Amorites, later fortified Aroer (Nu. 32:34). The census taken by David started in Aroer (2 S. 24:5). In the 9th cent. B.C., Hazael the Syrian occupied Aroer (2 K. 10:33); and according to the Moabite Stone, Mesha king of Moab fortified it against Israelite attack. The last reference to Aroer in the OT ascribes it to the Moabites (Jer. 48:19). The modern city is 'Arâ'ir.

2. A town in Gilead, "east of Rabbah" (Josh. 13:25), forming part of Israel's boundary with Ammon. Although the exact location of this site remains unknown, it has been suggested that it might be found S of Rabbah ('Ammân) in the vicinity of es-Sweiwina.

3. A town about 12 mi. (19 km.) SE of Beer-sheba. David shared with the elders of this town the spoils taken in a military engagement with the Amalekites (1 S. 30:28). The location today is 'Ar'arah. F. E. YOUNG

AROERITE ə-rō'ər-īt [Heb. *hā'ᵃrō'ērî*]. A native of Aroer, notably Hotham, father of two of David's heroes (1 Ch. 11:44).

AROM âr'əm [Gk. *Arom*]. Ancester of a family that returned to Jerusalem with Zerubbabel (1 Esd. 5:16); omitted in Nehemiah. Hashum is found in place of Arom in Ezr. 2:19.

AROMA (2 Cor. 2:15, RSV). *See* SAVOR.

AROMATIC CANE (Ex. 30:23). *See* CALAMUS.

AROUSE. The most significant use of the term is in Isa. 45:13, where it renders the hiphil of Heb. *'ûr*. "Arouse," "stir up," "awaken," and "incite" are all better translations here than the AV "raise up" (cf. NEB "rouse"). In 41:2, 25 the RSV renders "stir up" for the same Hebrew verb form; a further similarity is the use of Heb. *ṣeḏeq* in both 41:2 (RSV "victory") and 45:13 (RSV "righteousness"). All three passages point to the sovereignty of Yahweh over history as displayed in His use of Cyrus, who came from both the east (41:2) and the north (v. 25), to accomplish His will, i.e., "righteousness," "justice," "deliverance" (*ṣeḏeq*). N. J. O.

ARPACHSHAD är-pak'shad [Heb. *'arpaḵšaḏ*; Gk. *Arphaxad*]; **ARPHAXAD** är-fak'sad (NT, Apoc., and AV, NEB).

1. Third son of Shem, grandfather of Eber (Gen. 10:22-24) and ancestor of the Hebrews (cf. Gen. 11:10-13; 1 Ch. 1:17f., 24), The common identification is with the *Arrapḫu* of cuneiform inscriptions, perhaps to be identified with Kirkuk. Following Jth. 1:1 an Iranian etymology has been proposed, but this appears doubtful.

See also TABLE OF NATIONS.

2. A king of the Medes who ruled in Ecbatana (Jth. 1:1). He was defeated and killed by Nebuchadrezzar.

R. K. H.

ARPAD är'pad [Heb. *'arpāḏ*–'support']; AV ARPHAD. A city-state in Syria 25 mi. (40 km.) NNW of Aleppo, modern Tell Erfâd. In biblical references Arpad is always mentioned with Hamath, and they serve as examples of places destroyed by the Assyrians in the third year of Tiglath-pileser III. Rabshakeh mentions the place as one of the cities he conquered (2 K. 18:34; 19:13; Isa. 36:19; 37:13). Isaiah also mentions Arpad in the boast that he puts in the mouth of the Assyrian king (Isa. 10:9). Jeremiah includes the place in an oracle concerning Damascus (Jer. 49:23). A treaty between Matti'el king of Arpad and Barga'yah king of Katka is included in the Aramaic inscriptions from Sfire. The site has been excavated by Hrozný in 1924 and by the British since 1960.

Bibliography.–*ARAB*, I, §§ 769, 821; II, §§ 5, 55, 134, 589, 590, 1196; A. Dupont-Sommer, *Les Inscriptions Araméenes de Sfiré* (1958); B. Mazar, *BA*, 25 (1962), 118. W. S. L. S.

ARPHAXAD. *See* ARPACHSHAD.

ARRANGEMENT. In Ex. 40:4, 23, Heb. *'ereḵ* refers to the setting out of the bread of the Presence in layers on the table in the tabernacle. In Ezk. 42:11, "arrangements" is the RSV rendering of Heb. *mišpaṭîm*, "rules," AV "fashions," NEB "general character." In 43:11 "arrangement" translates *tᵉḵûnâ*, AV "fashion," NEB 'fittings." Both these passages are descriptions of the second temple.

ARRAY. (1) [Heb. *lāḇēš*, *lāḇaš*–'put on, clothe'; Gk. *periballō*–'put on, clothe,' *endýo*–'dress, clothe' (Rev. 19:4), *hetoimázō*–'prepare' (Rev. 9:7)]; AV also PUT ON, CLOTHE, PREPARE (Rev. 9:7); NEB DRESS, "in shining armour," CLOTHE, ATTIRE, EQUIP, etc. When it translates these terms "array" denotes putting on fine clothing (cf. Gen. 41:42; 2 Ch. 5:12; Est. 6:9:11; Mt. 6:29 par.; Lk. 23:11; Rev. 19:14; etc.) or clothing suitable for battle (Rev. 9:7).

(2) [Heb. *h^{a}ḏārâ*–'adornment, attire']. In 1 Ch. 16:29; 2 Ch. 20:21; Ps. 29:2, 96:9 the expression *hadraṯ-qōḏeš* (RSV "holy array"; AV "beauty of holiness"; NEB "splendor of holiness"; NEB mg. "holy vestments") refers to garments worn in worship.

(3) [Heb. *'āraḵ*–'arrange, put in order,' *'āmaḏ*–'take a stand,' 'set' (Jgs. 6:31; Ps. 55:18), hiphil of *kûn*–'prepare' (Nah. 2:3 [MT 4]); Gk. *parístēmi* (Acts 4:26)]; AV also PREPARATION, STAND (UP), "that could keep rank" (1 Ch. 12:38 [MT 39]); NEB also REFORMED, "TAKE UP POSITION," MARSHAL, etc. These terms are used in reference to the deployment of military forces prior to battle. The most common OT term is *'āraḵ*, from a root designating "orderly arrangement." In the quotation of Ps. 2:2 in Acts 4:26, Gk. *parístēmi* appropriately translates the hithpael of Heb. *yāṣaḇ*, "take one's stand." N. J. O.

ARREST AND TRIAL OF JESUS. *See* JESUS CHRIST, ARREST AND TRIAL OF.

ARROGANCE; ARROGANT; ARROGANTLY [Heb. *gē'eh* (Ps. 140:5), *ga'^{a}wâ* (Ps. 10:2; 36:11; Isa. 9:9; 13:11), *gā'ôn* (Prov. 8:13; Isa. 16:6; Jer. 48:29), *gē'ûṯ* (Ps. 17:10), hithpael of *gāḇar* (Job 36:9), *gāḇō(a)h* (Prov. 16:5), *gōḏel* (Isa. 10:12), *hālal* (Ps. 73:3), *zēḏ* (Mal. 3:15; 4:1 [MT 3:19]), *zîḏ* (Ex. 18:11), *yāhîr* (Hab. 2:5), *'^{e}ḇrâ* (Prov. 21:24), *'āṯāq* (1 S. 2:3; Ps. 94:4), *rāḥāḇ* (Ps. 101:5), *ša'^{a}nān* (2 K. 19:28; Isa. 37:29); Gk. *alazoneía* (Jas. 4:16), *alazṓn* (2 Tim. 3:2), *authádēs* (Tit. 1:7), *physióō* (1 Cor. 4:18f.; 5:2; 13:5)]; AV also ARROGANCY, BOASTINGS, FOOLISH, HARD, HAUGHTINESS, PRIDE, "proud in heart," PUFFED UP, SELFWILLED, STOUT HEART, TUMULT, etc.; NEB also BLUSTER, BOASTFUL, "the boasts of sinners," BRAG, CONCEIT, "filled with self-importance," HAUGHTY, OVERBEARING, POMPOUS, etc.

There are many Hebrew and Greek words that express the multifaceted problem of arrogance. This is probably because it is the radical expression of the cardinal biblical evil — pride. "A distinctive feature of biblical religion," writes Richardson, "is its teaching about pride and its converse, humility; this is unparalleled in other religious and ethical systems. According to the Bible . . . pride is the very root and essence of sin" (*RTWB*, p. 176). Given this biblical perspective, it is only natural that arrogance, whether viewed as a self-existent entity (n., Prov. 8:13), a mode of being (adj., Ps. 101:5), or a mode of action (adv., Ex. 18:11; cf. Ps. 94:4-7), is taken with utmost seriousness. Arrogance and its various modes of expression assume a pretentious and unwarrantable claim to human superiority and control over life which is horrendous, especially when contrasted with the biblical view of the Creator who alone is Lord of history.

When Isaiah speaks of the arrogance of the king of Assyria, he uses Hebrew parallelism, whereby a line of thought is reiterated and clarified by a subsequent one, to indicate that his arrogant pretensions to control history are nothing less than a mad raging against God Himself (2 K. 19:28; par. Isa. 37:29). Such arrogant madness pointedly shows a lack of real knowledge (1 S. 2:3ff.) or a proper understanding of man's true position in the world (cf. Ps. 73:3ff. with vv. 16ff.).

From the Judeo-Christian perspective arrogance and its concomitant boasting is simply an aberrant perception of reality that does not acknowledge or understand the larger picture (Jas. 4:13-15); therefore "all such boasting is evil" (v. 16). It insists that it is capable of controlling reality without recourse to God. This is why Paul insists that a bishop, as leader of a Christian congregation, "must not be arrogant" (Tit. 1:7; the LXX uses the same word in Prov. 21:24), but on the contrary must be "hospitable, a lover of goodness, master of himself, upright, holy, and self-controlled; he must hold firm to the sure word . . ." (Tit. 1:8f.).

Just as James sees that arrogant boasting (Gk. *alazoneía*) indicates a distorted view of the world, so John understands that those who are spellbound by the "glamour of its life" (NEB's translation of *alazoneía* in 1 Jn. 2:16) are entranced by a false reality, i.e., a world already in process of passing away (v. 17).

Bibliography.–*TDNT*, I, *s.v.* ἀλαζών, ἀλαζονεία (Delling); I, *s.v.* αὐθάδης (Bauernfeind); *THAT*, I, *s.v.* גָּאָה (H.-P. Stählin); *TDOT*, II, *s.v.* "gā'āh" (Kellermann). K. H. MAAHS

ARROW [Heb. *ḥēṣ, ḥēṣî, ḥāṣaṣ, rešpeh* (Ps. 76:3), *ben qešeṯ*–'son of the bow' (Job 41:28), *ben ('ašpâ)*–'son of (the quiver)' (Lam. 3:13)]. *See* ARCHER; WEAPONS OF WAR.

ARROWS, DIVINATION BY. *See* DIVINATION.

ARSACES är-sā'sēz, är'sə-sēz [Gk. *Arsakēs*]; NEB ARSAKES. The common name assumed by all the Parthian kings. The name is mentioned in 1 Macc. 14:1-3 in connection with the history of Demetrius, one of the Greek (Seleucid) kings of Syria, and successor of Antiochus Epiphanes the oppressor of the Jews who caused the Maccabean uprising against the Syrian domination. This particular Arsaces was the sixth of the line of independent Parthian rulers that had been founded in 250 B.C. by Arsaces I, who revolted from Antiochus Theos, killed the Syrian satraps, and with his successor Tiridates I firmly established the independence of the Parthian kingdom. About 243 B.C. Tiridates added Hyrcania to his dominions; but it was not until the reign of Arsaces VI, whose preregnal name was Mithridates, that Parthia, through the conquest of Bactria, Media, Persia, Armenia, Elymais, and Babylonia, threatened the very existence of the kingdom of the Seleucids and became a dangerous competitor of Rome itself. It was this king who *ca.* 141 B.C. was attacked by Demetrius Nicator, king of Syria.

Arsaces VI is mentioned also in 1 Macc. 15:22 as one of the kings whom the Romans forbade to make war on their Jewish allies. R. D. WILSON

ARSARETH är'sə-reth (2 Esd. 13:45, AV). *See* ARZARETH.

ARSENAL [Heb. *talpîyôṯ*] (Cant. 4:4); AV ARMOURY; NEB "(with) winding courses." The meaning of the Hebrew word is uncertain. BDB (p. 1069) says it may be poetical for "weapons," while KoB (p. 1030) suggests "courses of stones."

ARSIPHURITH är-sə-fo͞o'rəth (1 Esd. 5:16, NEB). *See* JORAH.

ART. A skill or ability; more specifically, the application of a skill to produce a pleasing effect.

I. Definition
II. Classification
III. Matter, Form, and Content
IV. Art and Science
V. History of Art
VI. Art and the Bible
VII. Art and Eschatology

I. Definition.–Any attempt to define "art" runs into subjective problems. A person who has acquired a skill is an *artisan* or an *artist*. The product of that skill is an *artifact* or *art*. But when is it *art*? We speak of "the art of cooking," but is it the same application of skill as "the art of painting," or, for that matter, "the art of gardening"? The bricklayer who lays up a solid wall with no variation in pattern is an artisan, but is he an artist if the wall contains an intricate and pleasing design or pattern? The application of some skill in all cases is doubtless present. As for the pleasing effect, to whom must it be pleasing? In art appreciation, as in eating, there is no argument concerning taste.

One definition that seeks to be objective distinguishes between the utilitarian and the nonutilitarian. Art is nonutilitarian. But what of architecture, to cite just one example? Some might say that a cathedral is nonutilitarian, but would they say that of a beautiful home or hotel? It seems that the difference is not as clearly objective as we first thought, particularly when we take into consideration that the psychological effects of a "beautiful" office are demonstrably productive of "useful" work.

Another definition distinguishes between the "fine arts" and the "liberal arts." The fine arts (from the French *beaux arts*) are those that are related to the beautiful, whereas the liberal arts are such things as grammar, logic, and rhetoric. Most music, we would probably agree, would be in the category of fine arts, whereas mathematics as a kind of logic belongs to liberal arts. But what of music that is composed by a computer using mathematical formulae? Is it art? If so, who is the artist? When we turn to rhetoric we find that many modern grammars include a section on "style." But style is more a matter of what is pleasing than what is useful, and certainly great oratory and literature belong with the fine arts.

In this article it becomes necessary to make a subjective decision. The term "art" will deal with the "fine arts" as commonly defined, viz., architecture, painting, sculpture, the dance, music, and literature. These subjects can be dealt with only generally and briefly, since separate articles deal with each one in more depth, and the entire article is rather severely restricted to those elements that may be of significance to Bible students.

II. Classification.–The arts can be classified as *spatial* and *temporal*. Architecture, sculpture, and painting are spatial arts. Music and literature are temporal arts. The dance extends over both categories. Spatial art must be seen as a whole before the parts become meaningful; temporal art, on the other hand, must be seen or heard in the parts before the whole can be comprehended. Greater use of the memory is therefore required in the temporal arts, and the artist must make use of repetition and interpretation to convey his message.

The arts can also be classified as *aural* and *visual*. Music and, in spoken form, literature are aural arts. Music must be heard to be comprehended. The dance often involves hearing as well as seeing, as when some rhythmic noise (tapping or clapping) is produced as part of the dance. The other senses are usually not involved in art appreciation.

III. Matter, Form, and Content.–In each of the arts we speak of matter, form, and content. Certain *materials* are available to the artist to which he can apply his skill. Phidias, we know, could not have created the classical beauty of Athens if the marble resources of Mt. Pentelicus had not recently been made available. There was no great architecture or sculpture in early Babylonia, probably not because there were no artists who could develop the required skills, but because there was no stone in Babylonia. The composer must work with the musical instruments that are available, the painter with both the materials on which to paint and those with which to paint. Of course, new materials may become available, and the artist may even be responsible in part for their creation, such as painting with resins, or building with reinforced concrete or with glass.

Form is the use that the artist makes of his material. *Content* pertains to what is expressed when he has finished his artistic creation. The artist's skill is demonstrated by his selection and arrangement of materials to create effect.

It is apparent that the artist's purpose must be compatible with matter and form. If an artist, for example, wished to move men's emotions in some area of civil rights, he could hardly do so by electing to use architecture as his art. Nor would a composer be likely to describe the flight of a bumblebee by writing a duet for tuba and tympani.

Each art, therefore, has limitations imposed upon its content. Music is often called "the universal language," but while it is almost universal in conveying emotional concepts, it is limited in the intellectual message it can convey. Sculpture and painting, on the other hand, are probably more limited than music in expressing emotion. Literature is by far the most communicative of the arts — unless, of course, we include theater or drama, which is a combination of literature with one or more of the other arts.

IV. Art and Science.–According to one view, art and science are both concerned with the pursuit of truth. The scientist breaks things down (analysis); the artist puts things together (synthesis). The scientist tends to become a specialist, the artist a universalist. The scientist strives to isolate the smallest of the component parts; the artist puts the parts together to create a world. The scientist formulates a theory that is temporary, that must be changed when further observations are made. The artist creates something that is permanent; once finished it

Backrest of Tutankhamen's throne (1352 B.C.) depicting king and queen in a family scene typical of Amarna Age Egypt. Wood overlaid with sheet gold, silver, blue faience, calcite, and glass, from Tutankhamen's tomb at Thebes (Egyptian Museum, Cairo)

stands (or at least, it could conceivably stand, barring some destruction) forever.

But is this view entirely correct? The characteristic of art is *creativity*. Let the scientist become creative and to that degree he is no longer a scientist. His sole responsibility is to observe and report the world as it is. When he alters any portion of it to what he would like it to be, he falsifies and is no longer a pure scientist. But the artist, in contrast, makes his world as he thinks it is or as he wants it to be. The artist may want to paint a landscape, but in his creative imagination, there should be a boy in a red sweater with a fishing-rod on a bicycle riding along that road in the foreground, and a few cumulus clouds in the sky, with perhaps a glow of early-morning sun. And so he paints it. He has not falsified; he has created.

Statue of he-goat with forelegs in a tree, probably an incense or offering-bowl holder. Discovered in the "Great Death Pit" at Ur (*ca.* 2500 B.C.), it is made of silver, gold, lapis lazuli, and white shell on a wooden core. (Trustees of the British Museum)

Some would rule out the photographer just at this point. The photographer simply records the world as it is, even to the wart on the nose. The artist removes the wart. But again we see how tenuous is the dividing line, for what is the difference between painting out the wart or turning the subject's head so the wart does not show in the photograph? The scientist must be creative if he is to develop theories that lead into new fields of observation. The photographer is a scientist when he records a portion of the world exactly as it is; but when he selects that portion with an eye to composition, distribution, balance, or radiation, and when he uses light and shadow to bring out the message he wishes to convey, is he scientist or artist?

Perhaps we should say that art and science are both concerned with the *communication* of truth: the scientist with truth as he has found it, and the artist with truth as he imagines it. But again we discover that there are complicating factors that make a simple statement less than satisfactory. The scientist not only conveys truth as he has found it, but also suggests truth as he creates it on the basis of observation, viz., his scientific theory. And the artist likewise sometimes creates a world in his imagination that is so far removed from the world of reality that it becomes fantastic or even schizophrenic.

Even with the problems of imprecision, we can say that communication of feeling is the essence of art. By a combination of sounds, or colors, or lines, or masses, or motions, or words, the artist conveys to me a bit of the world as he thinks it ought to be, or shocks me into seeing it as it appears to him. The ability to produce a pleasing effect is of less importance than the ability to produce the desired emotional effect. If this is so, then the measure of an artist is his ability to communicate through the art he has chosen, and the artist who is able to maintain that communication to generations of men in many nations, in all races and social strata, is therefore a greater artist than one who speaks only to a small segment, perhaps the *avant garde*, of a single time and place.

V. History of Art.–If it is difficult to define art, it is equally difficult to determine its appearance in history. If art is simply the application of a skill to produce a pleasing effect, then we must admit that the first man who fashioned a stone axe that gave him pleasure when he looked at it was an artist. If art is merely communication, then the first man who scratched a picture on the wall of a cave to say that he had gone hunting was an artist. And what shall we say of the man who painted a corpse with red ochre, or covered the mud floor with lime, or added a pattern when building a wall?

It is generally conceded that art, in the sense of the acquisition and use of an emotive skill, could not develop until man had available the time needed. As long as he was a "food gatherer," i.e., in the Stone Age when men were hunters and fishers, there was little time to develop artistic abilities. It was only with the "Neolithic revolution," when man became a "food producer," when he built a village with some of his fellow men and they produced the food there by the cultivation of cereals and the domestication of animals, that he at last had time for the arts.

In the undated past, some Cain built the first city (Gen. 4:17). Whether it was in Jordan, Iran, or Anatolia, we must leave to the archeologists to decide. By 7000 B.C. agriculture was well established in these areas. (Cain's brother, we remember, was a "tiller of the ground," Gen. 4:2.) The development of the arts quickly followed. Some Jubal invented the lyre and the flute (Gen. 4:21), and composers were developing their skill with music. Lyres and flutes can be seen among the archeological discoveries from early Mesopotamia and Egypt. Pottery, a kind of "sculpture," was invented, and soon it was decorated with lines scratched in the clay before baking, and then the painter began to paint figures on the pottery. Wall paintings seem to have been produced earlier in Egypt than in Mesopotamia, and the dance, as well as the accompanying musical instruments, are shown in some of the paintings. Sculpture, in low relief (as at el-'Obeid) and in the round (as at Tell Asmar), made its appearance in Mesopotamia and soon after in Egypt. Writing was invented, perhaps simultaneously and independently, in Egypt and Mesopotamia, and while no literary compositions from the earliest period have been found, it is obvious, from the well-established literary forms, that a preliterary literature (epic tales, annals, ritual, etc.) was already in existence in spoken form. Temples had been built (as at Eridu and Tepe Gawra), showing clear evidence of architectural design. The same was true of pyramids (as at Sakkara).

We can therefore conclude that by the end of the fourth millennium (3000 B.C.) or soon thereafter, all six of the arts were known, some of them before 4000 B.C.

VI. Art and the Bible.–God the Creator is the great Artist. He set the dome of the heavens and fashioned the universe. He created the music of the stars and set the heavenly bodies whirling in a great cosmic dance. He paints the sky of man's earth with clouds and sunsets, and the ground with flowers and streams. He fashioned man out of dust of the earth. He tells the greatest love story of time and eternity, and unfolds it in a drama unlike any that man has ever created. He uses every art and every medium.

He created man in His own image, and man, too, is a creator and an artist. The art of storytelling was developed quite early, when the serpent attempted to achieve an effect by the tale he communicated to Eve, who in turn used the art to achieve her purpose with Adam, who likewise attempted to use the art to achieve his purpose with God (Gen. 3:1-12). The Bible presupposes the existence of preliterary forms of literature by including genealogies, poetry, historical narrative, and other literary genres, from the period before the Flood — literary forms that could only have been preserved by oral transmission until they were written down at a much later time. We shall return to this after we have discussed the appearance and development of other arts in the biblical account.

There can be no doubt that all of the arts were well developed by the time of the appearance of the Israelite nation. Some Bible students appear to resent any suggestion that the "chosen people" were inferior in any way to their idolatrous neighbors. This attitude is unrealistic, and refuses to accept not only the facts recovered by the archeologist's spade but even the clear declarations of the Bible itself. Israel was not chosen because of superior value, whether in number, or intellectual ability, or even moral excellence. The choice of Israel was a sovereign act of God (Dt. 8:11-18; 9:4-6; etc.). The simple fact is that the Israelites developed a severely limited number of artistic skills.

Part of this poverty in artistic ability was doubtless due to the lack of materials and time to develop skills. Where would desert bedouin find the materials or the time to become sculptors? Or the slaves in Egypt the time to become painters? Or farmers and shepherds in the land of Canaan the time to become architects?

Part of the failure to develop certain artistic abilities was no doubt due to the teachings of the religion of Yahweh the God of Israel. Take architecture as an example. In the biblical account, the first builders attempted to build a tower reaching to heaven. God was displeased. He is the God who comes to earth in order to bring men to Himself. He will not tolerate a religion that expresses the humanistic concept that man can by his own efforts get to heaven. So the Israelites did not become builders.

They built the tabernacle in the wilderness, of course, and, to judge by the detailed description, it was a work of art. But while it required certain skills, it was not the type of building that required or developed architects. When Solomon, centuries later, wished to build a house for the Lord, it was necessary for him to import Tyrian (Phoenician) architects to supply the artistic skill. The Israelites were useful only for hauling the cedar logs from Lebanon or for cutting the soft limestone from the strata that underlay Jerusalem. The casting of bronze, the ornamentation, the true "art work" had to be done by the artists furnished by King Hiram of Tyre (1 K. 5–7).

Sculpture and painting, likewise, were not developed arts among the Israelites. No favorable mention of these arts is found in the Bible except for the gem-cutting and wood-carving that was part of the building of the tabernacle (Ex. 35:33; 36:38). Archeologists have commented on the lack of sculpture (whether large figures or small figurines) in Israelite sites. Since the materials were available, and since the non-Israelite peoples in the same region did develop the art of sculpture and some kinds of painting, we must conclude that there was a religious taboo among the Israelites. In Ex. 32:2ff., soon after their departure from Egypt, the Israelites made a "molten calf," i.e., they cast a figure in the round. It would have been necessary for them to carve such a figure from wood or fashion it in clay, in order to make the mold for the casting. We conclude that the innate artistic ability was present, and needed only the development of the skills.

But this was at once forestalled by the divine commandment, "You shall not make for yourself any graven image, or any likeness of anything that is in heaven above, or that is in the earth beneath, or that is in the water under the earth; you shall not bow down to them or serve them . . ." (Ex. 20:4f.). It can be demonstrated exegetically that the purpose of this commandment was not to prohibit painting and sculpture but rather to prohibit the worship of images. Whenever we find any prophetic word on the subject, it is not directed against the art, but against the idolatry (Isa. 30:22; Hos. 13:2; etc.). It can be argued, of course, that the image leads to the sin of idolatry — but a similar argument can be made concerning many amoral things, such as money, intellectual ability, physical strength, sex, etc. The ambivalent nature of certain things does not make them sinful; rather it imposes upon man an obligation to use them sinlessly. Still, the fact remains that the people of the OT showed no inclination to develop sculpture and painting within their religious system. Under the impact of Hellenism, toward the end of the pre-Christian era, we find for the first time any measurable artistic effort in these categories. NT references are almost nonexistent. We might note, in passing, that when Paul saw the magnificent beauty of Athens, he was apparently unimpressed, concerned only with the rampant idolatry. However, he was not above using one of their altars as the opening illustration by which he could go on to preach Jesus and the resurrection (Acts 17:22-29).

But if architecture, sculpture, and painting were undeveloped artistic skills among the people of the Bible, the same cannot be said for the remaining arts. Music and to a lesser extent dancing were part of their life and their worship. It would take an extended study of the subject (*see* MUSIC) to cover all the ways that music was used, the various instruments that are named, and the development

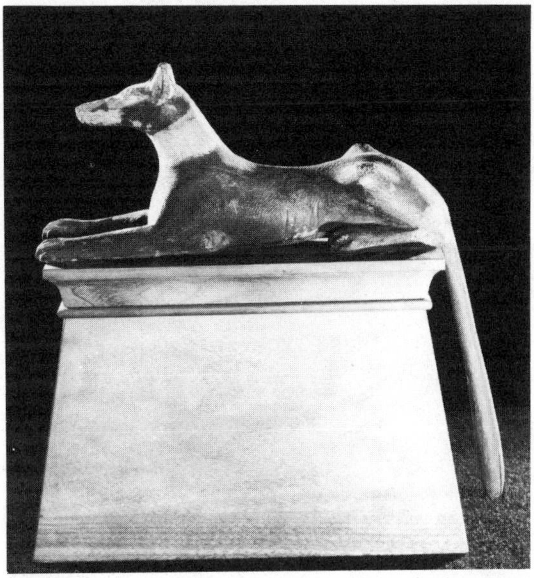

Wooden figure of the Egyptian god Anubis in animal form. Painted black, the collar and probably the ears were originally metal foil (*ca.* 7th-6th cents. B.C.) (Royal Ontario Museum, Toronto)

Head of a female clay figurine from the Israelite period (*ca.* 12th-11th cents. B.C.) at Dan (Tell el-Qâḍī) (Israel Department of Antiquities and Museums)

South porch of the Erechtheion, an Ionic temple of Athena on the Acropolis at Athens. The six caryatids (sculptured female figures taking the place of columns) portray maidens in the service of the goddess (*ca.* 420 B.C.). (W. S. LaSor)

Relief showing wheeled structure, possibly representing the ark of the covenant, from the Capernaum synagogue (early 4th cent. A.D.). The synagogue's unorthodox ornamentation includes animal, mythological, and geometric figures, perhaps magical symbols. (Israel Department of Antiquities and Museums)

of the musical part of worship in the temple. We have recovered no musical scores and virtually no musical instruments in Israelite archeology. But we do have a fairly large and varied vocabulary of musical instruments in the OT, in most cases as incidental parts of the story, and therefore not merely the effort of some writer to mention instruments that he had only heard about. In addition, we have, in the Psalms and elsewhere in the OT and NT, various types of songs, indicative of a rather well-developed hymnody. The literary part of hymnody properly belongs to the study of literature. We mention it here because some kind of musical arrangement or accompaniment is associated with it, whether by the mention of instruments or by the reference to choirs. Music, as an integral part of worship, was taken over by early Christians, partly because it was their heritage as Jews and partly, no doubt, because of the example of their Master, who, with His apostles, closed the Last Supper with the singing of a hymn (Mt. 26:30).

Wall painting on a Roman tomb at Ashkelon (3rd cent. A.D.), showing nymphs against a background of Nilotic reeds and lotus blossoms. Hellenistic and Roman influence dominated this center of literature and scholarship until the 4th century. (W. S. LaSor)

To judge from references scattered through the Bible, dancing was also an artistic form of expression, in both the secular and the religious life of the people. Dancing was part of the scene that Moses beheld, along with the golden calf, when he returned to the camp (Ex. 32:19). We assume that it was part of the people's religious expression along with the singing and the idolatrous image. When the Israelites were delivered from the Egyptian armies by the miracle at the Red Sea, Miriam and "all the women" joined in praising the Lord, with timbrels and dancing (15:20). Likewise, "when David returned from slaying the Philistine," the women came out to meet King Saul singing and dancing "with timbrels, with songs of joy, and with instruments of music" (1 S. 18:6). This dancing is usually described as having religious significance, but the biblical account says nothing about any religious motive; it appears to be hero-worship directed toward David, and Saul apparently understood it as such (vv. 8f.). It is true, however, that when David "danced before the Lord with all his might" (2 S. 6:14) and was rebuked by his wife Michal for such a vulgar display, he replied, "It was before the Lord, . . . and I will make merry before the Lord" (6:21). In the NT there is likewise little if any religious significance in the dance, whether it was the dance of Salome the daughter of Herodias (cf. Josephus *Ant.* xviii.5.4) at Herod's birthday party (Mt. 14:6; Mk. 6:22), or the dance that was given when the Prodigal Son returned home (Lk. 15:25). Since no representations of the dance have been recorded, such as those in Egyptian wall paintings, we can only conjecture about the form of Israelite dancing.

By far the most thoroughly developed art in Israel was literature. Thanks to the extensive archeological discoveries of the past 150 years, we have a vast knowledge of the literature of the peoples of the ancient Near East. We have quantities of religious literature, hymns, epics, and other genres, from the Sumerians, the Babylonians, the Egyptians, the people of Ugarit, the Greeks, and others. It is in no way derogatory to these other peoples to say that we have far more religious literature from the Israelites than from any other single people. There seems to be no doubt that the people of the OT originated some forms earlier than any other people, and that they developed other forms to a greater extent, even if they were not the originators. This is often referred to as "the Semitic genius for religion," but this is a misnomer, for the Babylonians and the Canaanites (Ugaritians) were also Semites. The phenomenon is uniquely Israelite.

Just as the very limited extent to which Israel developed the spatial arts can be traced at least in part to a religious taboo, so the extensive development of literature can be linked with their religious heritage. Their God, far beyond the gods of the nations, was a God who communicated. To speak of Him merely as "the God who acts" is to miss the genius of the OT faith. He did act (and still does), and the religious significance of history was therefore developed in Israel to an extent not matched anywhere else in religious literature. But this is only part of the story. God not only acted; in addition, to His servants the prophets (using the term broadly to include Abraham, Moses, and others, as well as those more commonly called "prophets") He revealed the significance of what He was going to do or had done.

This revelation became the basis for the Scriptures. The people told and retold the stories of how their God had revealed Himself. They used many types of literature: historical recitation, poetry, legal proscriptions, lists of names, and others — but always with religious significance. The people of Yahweh developed the art of literature because their God encouraged them to tell the stories

Detail of mosaic pavement from church at Khirbet el-Mekhaiyeṭ (7th cent. A.D.). One of the largest mosaics known, it is almost intact, showing vines, harvest scenes, fishing, and landscapes with bulls and sheep. (Jordan Information Bureau, Washington)

to their children and their children's children, and because He provided the example. Literature is the most perfect form of art for the communication of ideas that are designed to reach the mind, the heart, and the will. God not only communicated to His people, He wanted them to be faithful in communicating His message to all men.

VII. Art and Eschatology.–Little has been written about the place of art in the age to come, but there are some significant points revealed in Scripture.

One of the most striking, perhaps, is the revelation that in the New Jerusalem that is to be let down from heaven, there is no temple (Rev. 21:22). Little is said concerning the architecture of the Holy City, but we are told instead of its river and its trees and their health-giving nature (Rev. 22:1f.). It would seem that problems of ecology, the curse brought about by the building of cities, will be no problem in the Heavenly City.

Nor is anything said about statues and paintings in the New Jerusalem. The walls, the gates, even the very streets of the city are adorned, but their adornment come from nature, from the precious and semiprecious (Rev. 21:17-21); and since it is a city not made with hands, we assume that these are not the artistic creations of men. Paintings, as we know them, in a land of endless day (therefore no sunsets) and a glassy sea (hence no clouds, no waves, no storms), would lack excitement and would fail to convey an emotional message. Besides, if these forms of art are an attempt on the part of the artist to create a world according to his own ideal, why are they needed in an ideal world? How can an artist improve on perfection? How can we move men when nothing is lacking? The glory of the Holy City is the Lamb. What painting or what sculpture can fully convey that message?

The spatial arts, it would seem, are lacking in the world to come. But how could it be otherwise? Spatial arts must

Silver "Chalice of Antioch" (4th-5th cents. A.D.), once thought to be that used at the Last Supper. The metal work includes two representations of Christ, eight apostles, and two evangelists, all subordinate to highly stylized vines. (Metropolitan Museum of Art, Cloisters Collection)

have boundaries. The viewer must be able to see the whole in order to comprehend its message — and how can we see the whole of eternity or infinity?

But there will be music there, and it will be a new song (Rev. 5:9). Music, the art that best conveys emotion even though it falls short in communicating factual expression, is well suited to the age of perfection. The communication of truth is necessary in this age because we know in part, but it becomes unnecessary when knowledge is perfect. On the other hand, the expression of feelings is a basic part of perfected man, even as it is a basic part of the God in whose image man was created. As a temporal art, music does not have to be presented in the whole in order to be understood. It can continue to unfold and to express new feelings through all eternity. The word has become flesh and dwells with man. Literature has been transformed into life. The books have been closed. But the song continues into endless ages.

See Plates 4, 7, 21.

Bibliography.–T. M. Greene, *The Arts and The Art of Criticism* (1940); *Enc.Brit.* (1970), II; H. Frankfort, *Art and Architecture of the Ancient Orient* (1954); S. Lloyd, *Art of the Ancient Near East* (1961); *ANET*; *ANEP*; H. Schäfer and W. Andrae, *Kunst des Alten Orients* (1925); H. Frankfort, *et al.*, *Intellectual Adventure of Ancient Man: An Essay on Speculative Thought in the Ancient Near East* (1946); H. A. Groenewegen-Frankfort, *Arrest and Movement: An Essay on Space and Time in the Representational Art of the Ancient Near East* (1951).

S. Cole, *Neolithic Revolution* (3rd ed. 1963); A. Reifenberg, *Ancient Hebrew Arts* (1950); Albright, *AP;* E. Anati, *Palestine Before the Hebrews* (1963); H. Th. Bossert, *Altsyrien: Kunst und Handwerk in Cypern, Syrien, Palästina, Transjordanien und Arabien* (1951); S. Moscati, *World of the Phoenicians* (Eng. tr. 1968), chs. 5, 11.

H. Frankfort, *Sculpture of the Third Millennium from Tell Asmar and Khafajah* (1939); S. N. Kramer, *The Sumerians* (1963); H. R. Hall, *Babylonian and Assyrian Sculpture in the British Museum* (1928); H. Th. Bossert, *Altanatolien: Kunst und Handwerk in Kleinasien* (1942); Maurice Vierya, *Hittite Art, 2300-750 B.C.* (1955); A. U. Pope, *A Survey of Persian Art from Prehistoric Times to the Present* (4 vols., 1938).

W. S. Smith, *Art and Architecture of Ancient Egypt* (1958); I. Woldering, *Art of Egypt* (1963); C. Desroches-Noblecourt, *Le style égyptien* (1946); C. Aldred, *Old Kingdom Art in Ancient Egypt* (1949); *Middle Kingdom Art in Ancient Egypt* (1950); *New Kingdom Art in Ancient Egypt* (1951); J. Vandier and M. Naguib, *Egypt: Paintings from Tombs and Temples* (1956); H. Kees, *Ägypten: Kulturgeschichte des Alten Orients,* I (1933); A. Erman, *Literature of the Ancient Egyptians* (Eng. tr. 1927).

R. W. Hutchinson, *Prehistoric Crete* (1962); S. Marinatos and M. Hirmer, *Crete and Mycenae* (1960); G. E. Mylonas, *Ancient Mycenae* (1957); L. R. Palmer, *Mycenaeans and Minoans* (2nd ed. 1965); C. Zervos, *L'Art de la Crète Néolithique et Minoenne* (1956).

Paul MacKendrick, *Greek Stones Speak* (1962); T. B. L. Webster, *Art of Greece: The Age of Hellenism* (1967); *Hellenistic Poetry and Art* (1964); P. Demargne, *Aegean Art* (1964); A. W. Lawrence, *Greek Architecture* (1957); M. Bieber, *Sculpture of the Hellenistic Age* (1961); G. Lippold, *Die griechische Plastik* (1970); A. Lesky, *History of Greek Literature* (1966).

Chapters on Art and Architecture and splendid photographic plates in the following volumes in the series *Ancient Peoples and Places*: J. Gray, *Canaanites* (1964); W. Cullican, *Medes and the Persians* (1965); M. Wheeler, *Early India and Pakistan* (1959); C. Aldred, *Egyptians* (1961); W. Taylor, *Mycenaeans* (1964); D. Harden, *Phoenicians* (1962); J. M. Cook, *Greeks in Ionia and the East* (1962); A. G. Woodhead, *Greeks in the West* (1962); R. M. Cook, *Greeks Until Alexander* (1962); R. Bloch, *Origins of Rome* (1960); D. Diringer, *Writing* (1962). W. S. LASOR

ARTAXERXES är-tə-zûrk'sēz [Heb. and Aram. *'artaḥšastā'*, with vowel variants; Gk. *Artaxerxēs*].

1. Artaxerxes I Longimanus (464-424 B.C.), son of Xerxes I, who subdued revolts in Egypt between 460 and 545 B.C. He permitted Ezra to visit Jerusalem as Commissioner for Jewish Affairs (Ezr. 7:7-26; Neh. 2:1; etc.) in 458 B.C. He also authorized the mission of Nehemiah twelve years later (Neh. 1:2, etc.).

2. The LXX reads Artaxerxes for Ahasuerus throughout Esther; and some scholars have thought that Artaxerxes II Mnemon (404-359 B.C.) was being envisaged, son of Darius I and grandson of Artaxerxes I, who defeated his brother Cyrus at the battle of Cunaxa in 401 B.C. More probably, however, the reference is to Xerxes I (486-485 B.C.). R. K. H.

ARTEMAS är'tə-məs [Gk. *Artemas*] (Tit. 3:12). An associate of Paul, whom he planned to send ("or Tychicus") to Crete to replace Titus, so that Titus could join Paul at Nicopolis. Tradition names him as bishop of Lystra, and as one of the seventy disciples.

The name is probably Greek, perhaps a masculine form of Artemis, or, as has been suggested, a short form of Artemidorus, a common name in Asia Minor. (These contracted forms were by no means rare in the Greek world. The Athenian orator Lysias was doubtless named after his grandfather Lysanias, and at first may even have been called Lysanias himself.)

ARTEMIS är'tə-məs [Gk. *Artemis* (Acts 19:35), Latinized as DIANA (AV)]. The Greek goddess of wild animals, wild nature, chastity, and childbirth, and the Ephesian goddess of fertility, superficially with little but the name in common.

The Greek goddess Artemis, identified by the Romans as Diana, was the virgin huntress in the *Hippolytus* of Euripides, but behind that figure apparently was the goddess of wild nature, who was to be found in mountains and forests accompanied by nymphs. Worship of Artemis may be traced to Crete and the Greek mainland. The Cretan Mother Goddess had three roles: goddess of vegetation, mistress of animals, and goddess of the household. Each of these roles is perhaps reflected in the names by which she was known: Demeter, Artemis, and Athene. The problems of etymology of the names, relationships to other deities in other places, and the like, lie beyond our purpose here. It has been suggested that the name Artemis, which has defied all attempts to find an Indo-European or Greek etymology, may be Minoan. However, there are non-Minoan elements in the worship of Artemis as it developed, such as phallic dances and symbols, the concept that she was the sister of Apollo (who was not introduced to Greece until after the early Hellenic settlement), and her healing properties as reflected in the *Iliad* (v.311-13), with reference to Aeneas. Since the Mycenean princes encountered nature rarely except during the hunt, Artemis in Homer is essentially the archer and huntress (*Il.* vi.428; xvi.183; xx.39, 71; xxiv.606). From her relationship with Apollo developed a further relationship, that she was the daughter of Zeus and Leto. On a limestone tablet from Mycenae, she appears as the shield goddess (if correctly identified, as seems likely), hence the protectress of the citadel. In this capacity she can be compared with Athene. The comparison is further strengthened by the fact that Athene was associated with snake, bird, shield, and tree in the Erechtheon on the Acropolis of Athens, and in the epics of Homer she acts as protectress of her favorite heroes. These various strands yield a rather complex picture of Artemis, one who protected the chastity of her nymphs and was accordingly the goddess of maidens of marriageable age. As the goddess of animals, she on occasion required human sacrifices, yet she was at other times worshipped as the goddess who helped women in childbirth and gave gentle death to women. She was also a moon-goddess. The refining of her complex nature into the virgin huntress can be traced to the influence of poets such as Homer and Euripides.

Artemis of Ephesus is often described as having little in common with the Greek goddess Artemis (and the Roman Diana), but study of the early portrayal of Artemis shows how the Ephesian, Greek, and Roman goddess could have been derived from a common prototype. Artemis of Ephesus, perhaps best known from the "many-breasted" statues that have been discovered at Ephesus, is principally the Earth Mother (Demeter; Gk. *Dēmēter*), the Anatolian *Magna Mater* (Great Mother), or Cybele the goddess of fertility or fructification. It is possible to trace this concept in the religious ideas and practices of Asia Minor, Syria, Phoenicia, and other areas to the east of Ephesus. Thus, Artemis of Ephesus has sometimes been related to Atargatis, Astarte, Ishtar, and other deities of the ancient Near East. Some of the efforts along this line are rather convincing, while others seem to verge on the fantastic. It is particularly difficult to separate the complex and often confused notions of the common people from the systematized pantheons of the cultic leaders — and at times it seems that even their systems have been superimposed on them by modern scholars. A wiser course, it would seem, is to set down the known characteristics of each god and goddess in each of the religious systems, compare and contrast their similarities and differences, and draw whatever conclusions seem to be well supported by the data.

Statue of Artemis Polymastros ("many-breasted") from Ephesus. Goddess of fertility and childbirth, she is represented as a form of the Great Mother. (W. S. LaSor)

Artemis of Ephesus was born, according to tradition, in the woods near Ephesus, or rather, near the mouth of the Caÿster River, long before the city of Ephesus was founded by Greek colonists (*ca.* 1100 B.C.). She was a goddess of fecundity or fertility in man, beast, and nature. She was worshipped in crude shrines, and her worship spread into many cities of Asia Minor, Syria, the Greek mainland, and ultimately to Rome and southern Gaul. At some point she was adopted by the Greek colonists at Ephesus, and a large temple was built for her — indeed, it was one of the seven wonders of the ancient world (*see* EPHESUS). It was not her home, however, simply the principal shrine. Pilgrims came in great numbers to worship Artemis at her shrine. The guide will point out the road leading from the ancient harbor to the great theater, and he may even delight the visitor by describing how the pilgrims came along this way singing, "Great is Artemis of Ephesus!" He may forget to mention that this Arkadiane way was named for the emperor who rebuilt it (Arcadius, A.D. 395-408). A large statue of Artemis Polimastros ("many-breasted") was discovered in 1956 and is in the museum at Ephesus today; but this is not the object that was venerated in the temple (Acts 19:35, "the sacred stone that fell from the sky"), which is generally believed to have been a meteorite. The "silver shrines of Artemis" (Acts 19:24) are believed to have been replicas of the earlier shrine that was replaced by the Artemissium (the great temple), which the pilgrims carried back home with them, possibly to serve as local or house-shrines.

The temple of Artemis, according to Pliny, was completed in 120 years and was destroyed and rebuilt seven times; it was to be rebuilt the eighth time in the 2nd cent. B.C. Many historians question or reject Pliny's statements. Contributions came from all Asia Minor. The completed temple was 425 ft. by 225 ft. (130 m. by 69 m.) and had 127 columns each 60 ft. (18 m.) in height and each representing a king. Thirty-six of the columns were decorated with high reliefs, and at least one was the work of Scopas, a renowned sculptor. (Cf. Pliny *Nat. hist.* xxxvi.21 [95-97].) According to tradition, the great temple was destroyed by fire on the night of the birth of Alexander the Great (356 B.C.); the arsonist was a deranged man named Erostratos who committed the act to achieve immortality in history. When Alexander reached Ephesus on his famous march (334 B.C.), he offered to rebuild the temple on the condition that it bear his name, but the people of Ephesus declined his offer, saying that it would not be appropriate for one god to build a temple to another.

The temple was attended by a very large hierarchy of religious persons, of which the chief were the Megabizes (cf. Pliny *Nat. hist.* xxxv.40 [132]), eunuchs, and young virgins. There were male and female priests, receptionists, supervisors, drummers, bearers of the scepter, cleaners and chambermaids, acrobats, and flute players. One month every year was entirely devoted to impressive ceremonies in honor of Artemis. No work was done during this month, and there were athletic games at the Stadium, plays at the Theater, and concerts at the Odeon. The people made offerings at the sacred grove that was Artemis' birthplace, gave great banquets, sang to the accompaniment of the flutes, and had a time of carnival. There was also a bank at the temple, and the chief Megabize was the treasurer of the goddess. According to one tradition (Plutarch *Moralia* 828c-d) the temple was a sanctuary for debtors.

Bibliography.–M. P. Nilsson, *Geschichte der griechischen Religion*, I (2nd ed. 1955); L. R. Palmer, *Mycenaeans and Minoans* (2nd ed. 1965), pp. 138ff.; W. Taylour, *Mycenaeans* (1964), pp. 63ff.; T. B. L. Webster, *From Mycenae to Homer* (1958), pp. 46 *et passim*; *Enc.Brit.*, II (1970), 507f.; Pliny *Nat. hist.* xxxv.40; xxxvi.21.

W. S. LASOR

ARTIFICER (Gen. 4:22; 1 Ch. 29:5; 2 Ch. 34:11; Isa. 3:3, AV). *See* INSTRUMENT; CARPENTER; MAGIC.

ARTILLERY (1 S. 20:40; 1 Macc. 6:51, AV). *See* WEAPONS OF WAR.

ARTISAN; ARTS. *See* CRAFTS.

ARUBBOTH ə-rub'oth [Heb. *'ᵃrubbôt*]; AV, NEB, ARUBOTH ə-ro͞o'both. One of the twelve districts from which food supplies for Solomon's household were obtained (1 K. 4:10). With Arubboth are mentioned "Socoh, and all the land of Hepher"; and since Socoh lay in the Shephelah (Josh. 15:35), Arubboth probably lay in the southern part of the Shephelah. However, 'Arrâbeh near Dothan has been suggested as a possible identification.

J. F. PREWITT

ARUMAH ə-ro͞o'mə [Heb. *'ᵃrûmâ*–'lofty']. The town in which Abimelech the son of Jerubbaal (Gideon) dwelt when driven from Shechem (Jgs. 9:41). The ruins el-'Ormeh, 5 mi. (8 km.) SE of Shechem and 3½ mi. (5.5 km.) E of Huwwara, may be the site, though its position is not known with certainty. In Jgs. 9:31 the RSV follows the emendation of Heb. *bᵉṯormâ* (AV "privily") to *ba'ᵃrûmâ* ("at Arumah"). The NEB reads "he resorted to a ruse."

ARVAD är'vad [Heb. *'arwaḏ*; Gk. *Arados*] (Ezk. 27:8, 11); **ARVADITE** [Heb. *hā'arwāḏî*] (Gen. 10:18; 1 Ch. 1:16). One of the four major cities of Phoenicia.

Arvad, modern Erwâd, is located on an island 2½ mi. (4 km.) from the coast and about 30 mi. (50 km.) N of Tripoli. This island has a low, flat, rocky surface approximately 800 yds. (730 m.) in length and 500 yds. (460 m.) in width, and has neither water nor natural soil. Consequently, the city was dependent upon the mainland for its supplies and water. Rainwater was stored on the island in tanks and reservoirs. There is a fresh-water spring, it is said, issuing from the ocean floor midway between Arvad and the mainland. In times of emergency water was ingeniously piped from this spring to boats moored at the surface.

Houses several stories high were built close together in the western and southern sectors of the island. Remnants of an ancient wall may be found on three sides of Arvad. In some places the massive stones are still standing, five to six courses high. Since the island lacked a natural harbor, one was constructed on the east toward the mainland by means of three piers 70 to 100 yds. (64 to 90 m.) long, made of immense sandstone blocks. This artificial harbor, protected from winds on the fourth side by the mainland, made possible Arvad's famous and powerful navy. In Ezk. 27:8, 11 it is stated that the men of the city were employed by Tyre as sailors and soldiers.

The inhabitants of Arvad (Arvadites) are correctly identified in Gen. 10:18 as Canaanites.

One of the earliest references to Arvad is its capture, mentioned in the Annals of Thutmose III (*ca.* 1475 B.C.). The decline of Egyptian power after Ramses II afforded the opportunity for Arvad to assume leadership over a hegemony in northern Phoenicia similar to that of Sidon in the south. The extent of Arvad's influence on the mainland is indicated by Strabo, who lists six cities over which Arvad exercised control. The Amarna Tablets record that Arvad supported the Amorites in their attacks upon Egyptian possessions in Syria (Am.Tab. 101, 149). Arvad was first made tributary to Assyria by Tiglath-pileser I. Mattan Baal king of Arvad is listed among the enemies defeated by Shalmaneser III at the battle of Qarqar (853 B.C.). About fourteen years later Shalmaneser forced the city to surrender and to pay tribute.

The hexagonal prism of Sennacherib (ii.52) lists Abdilihit of Arvad as one of three Phoenician kings from whom he received tribute in 701 B.C. In the Annals of Ashurbanipal (ii. 63-67) it is stated that Yakinlu king of Arvad, in submitting to Assyria, sent his own daughter to Nineveh with a large tribute in the form of a dowry (*ca.* 664 B.C.). During the years of Persian domination, Arvad, Tyre, and Sidon were permitted to form a federation with a common council in Tripoli. As one of the first cities of Phoenicia to surrender to Alexander the Great, Arvad lent its formidable fleet to the conqueror for his attack upon Tyre. Arvad is also mentioned in a list of cities in 1 Macc. 15:23, in the Greek form ARADUS.

Bibliography.–D. Harden, *The Phoenicians* (1962); P. K. Hitti, *Lebanon in History* (1957).

D. H. MADVIG

ARZA är'zə [Heb. *'arṣā*]. A steward of King Elah, in whose house at Tirzah Zimri murdered the king at a drinking debauch (1 K. 16:9).

ARZARETH är'zə-reth [cf. Heb. *'ereṣ 'aḥereṯ*–'another land' (Dt. 29:28 [MT 27])]; AV ARSARETH. A land to which the ten tribes were deported (2 Esd. 13:45), described as lying "a journey of a year and a half" beyond the river, i.e., the Euphrates. According to Josephus, people were still believed to be there in countless numbers (*Ant.* xi.5.2), and in the last days they will return from that place.

W. S. L. S.

ASA ā'sə [Heb. *'āsā*–'healer,' or perhaps a contraction of *'ᵃsāyâ*–'Yahweh has healed'; Gk. *Asa* (Mt. 1:7f.)].

1. A king of Judah, the third one after the separation of Judah and Israel. Asa was the son (or less probably the younger brother) of Abijah, the son and successor of Rehoboam. Absalom's granddaughter Maacah is called his mother (1 K. 15:10); she indeed acted as queen mother, but more probably was Asa's grandmother. She was at any rate the mother of Abijah (1 K. 15:2). The first ten years of his reign were prosperous and peaceful (2 Ch. 14:1). He introduced many reforms, such as putting away the sodomites or male cult prostitutes, removing idols from holy places, and breaking down altars, pillars, and Asherim. He even deposed the queen mother because of her idolatrous practices and the image she had made for Asherah (1 K. 15:12ff.; 2 Ch. 14:3). Despite the continued existence of the high places, Asa was held blameless (2 Ch. 15:17).

The first military event of Asa's reign was the repulse of an attack by Zerah "the Ethiopian" (2 Ch. 14:8-15), although the numbers of the troops recorded on both sides seem impossibly high (580,000 in Asa's army; 1,000,000 of the enemy). It is uncertain who this foe was; some have suggested that he was Osorkon I king of Egypt, but it is more probable that he was the military commander at the frontier garrison of Gerar (cf. v. 14). The epithet "Cushite" may mean that he was an Ethiopian or an Arabian. At any rate, Asa routed him completely at Mareshah in the lowlands of Judah (14:6ff.). Directed and encouraged by Azariah the prophet, he carried on an important revival. Having restored the great altar of burnt offering in the temple, he assembled the people for a renewal of their covenant with Yahweh. On this occasion seven hundred oxen and seven thousand sheep were offered in sacrifice.

The hostility between Israel and Judah, which had continued unbroken since the disruption of the monarchy, showed itself again in one incident. The king of Israel, Baasha, encroached and finally fortified Ramah as a frontier fortress. Asa, fainthearted, instead of putting his entire trust in Yahweh, made an alliance with Ben-hadad of Damascus. The Syrian king, in consideration of a large sum of money and much treasure from the temple at Jerusalem, consented to attack the northern portion of Baasha's territory. It was at this favorable moment that Asa captured Ramah; and with the vast building material collected there by Baasha, he built Geba of Benjamin and Mizpah (1 K. 15:16-22). This lack of faith in Yahweh was severely criticized by Hanani the prophet. Asa, instead of listening patiently to this prophet, was greatly offended and enraged, and Hanani was put in prison (2 Ch. 16:1-10). Three years later, Asa was attacked by gout or some disease of the feet (cf. DISEASE III.J). Here again he was accused of lack of faith, for "he did not seek the LORD, but sought help from physicians" (2 Ch. 16:12). Having ruled forty-one years, he died and was buried with great pomp in a tomb erected by himself in the city of David, Jerusalem. On the whole his reign was very successful, but it must be sadly recorded that as the years rolled on he became less and less faithful to Yahweh and His Law.

Asa reigned *ca.* 913-873 B.C. It is uncertain when exactly Baasha sought to fortify Ramah, in view of the discrepancy between 1 K. 16:8 and 2 Ch. 16:1. Probably the simplest explanation is that the numeral of the latter verse has suffered in transmission; perhaps "sixteenth" was the original reading.

2. A son of Elkanah, a Levite, who dwelt in one of the villages of the Netophathites (1 Ch. 9:16).

W. W. DAVIES
D. F. PAYNE

ASADIAS as-ə-dī'əs (Bar. 1:1, AV). *See* HASADIAH.

ASAEAS ə-sī'əs (1 Esd. 9:32, NEB). *See* ASAIAS.

ASAEL as'ə-el (Tob. 1:1, AV). *See* ASIEL **3.**

ASAHEL as'ə-hel [Heb. *'ᵃśâ'ēl*–'God is doer' or 'God has made'].

1. The brother of Joab and Abishai and son of Zeruiah, one of David's sisters (1 Ch. 2:15f.; 2 S. 2:18; etc.). With his two brothers Asahel was an early adherent of David and later became one of the famous "thirty" (2 S. 23:24; 1 Ch. 11:26).

Asahel was renowned for his swift running, which was the cause of his downfall. After the battle of Gibeon (which in fact was more of a border skirmish than a battle), in which Abner lost 360 men to Joab's twenty (2 S. 2:30f.), Asahel pursued Abner. Being "swift of foot as a wild gazelle" he overtook him. Abner, confident that he could slay the smaller man, magnanimously tried to persuade him to go after the spoil of a younger man, but without success, whereupon Abner killed him with a backward thrust of his spear. His death had important repercussions, including the delay of David's accession to the throne. Abner later transferred his loyalties; but this made no difference to Joab, who later slew him, both out of revenge for Asahel and out of jealousy (2 S. 3:26f.). Asahel was buried in his father's tomb at Bethlehem.

Asahel is also mentioned as the fourth of David's month-by-month captains (1 Ch. 27:7); and although he died rather earlier than this, it may show that the division was of long standing, though in a less developed form. On the other hand, it may be that he is mentioned only *honoris causa*. The honor of being head over such a division may in some cases have been posthumous, the deceased man being represented by someone else, perhaps his own son. This would explain the addition of the words "and his son Zebadiah after him."

2. A Levite of the commission of captains and Levites and priests that Jehoshaphat, in his third year, sent among the cities of Judah with the book of the law to spread information among the people (2 Ch. 17:7-9).

3. One of the keepers of the storechambers in the temple in the time of Hezekiah (2 Ch. 31:13).

4. The "father" or ancestor of Jonathan, who was one of the two elders who opposed Ezra in his reforming policy of putting away the foreign wives of the Jews after the return from exile (Ezr. 10:15). The phrase translated in the AV of this verse "were employed" has a variety of translations, but the most likely one is that given by the RSV — "opposed."

W. J. BEECHER
J. A. BALCHIN

ASAHIAH as-ə-hī'ə (2 K. 22:12, 14, AV). *See* ASAIAH **1.**

ASAIAH ə-sā'yə [Heb. *'ᵃsāyâ*].

1. AV also ASAHIAH (2 K. 22:12, 14). A member of the delegation sent by Josiah to Huldah concerning the law scroll found in the temple (2 K. 22:12-14; 2 Ch. 34:20).

2. A Simeonite leader who dispossessed the Meunim (1 Ch. 4:36).

3. A Levite of the family of Merari who assisted in bringing the ark to Jerusalem (1 Ch. 6:30; 15:6, 11).

4. A Shilonite resident in Jerusalem (1 Ch. 9:5), called Maaseiah in Neh. 11:5.

ASAIAS ə-sī'əs [Gk. *Asaias*]; AV ASEAS; NEB ASAEAS. A son of Annan who put away his foreign wife (1 Esd. 9:32). *See* ISSHIJAH.

ASAL ā'səl (Zec. 14:5, NEB). *See* AZAL.

ASAMIAS a-sə-mī'əs (1 Esd. 8:54, NEB). *See* HASHABIAH **8.**

ASANA as'ə-nə (1 Esd. 5:31, AV, NEB). *See* ASNAH.

ASAPH ā'saf [Heb. *'āsāp*; Gk. *Asaph*].

1. Ancestor of Hezekiah's recorder Joah (2 K. 18:18, 37).

2. One of David's three chief musicians, along with Heman and Jeduthun (Ethan), and the reputed author of Pss. 50 and 73-82; the son of Berechiah (1 Ch. 6:39). After the ark was taken to Jerusalem (15:16-19), he conducted with cymbals the music performed in the tent of the ark (16:5, 7, 37). Heman and Jeduthun did the same at Gibeon (vv. 41f.). Four of Asaph's sons (fellow guild members?) were among those appointed to conduct under him sections of the great chorus (25:1ff.), and all took part at the dedication of the temple (2 Ch. 5:12). The "sons of Asaph" formed a musical guild and were prominent in temple worship, especially as singers (cf. 1 Ch. 25:1ff.; 1 Esd. 1:15).

Asaph is said to have "prophesied under the direction of the king," through his music (1 Ch. 25:2); and Jeduthun and Heman are called "royal seers" (v. 5; 2 Ch. 35:15); cf. 1 S. 10:5.

3. NEB EBIASAPH (cf. 1 Ch. 9:19). A name in the list of divisions of gatekeepers in the second temple (1 Ch. 26:1).

4. Keeper of the royal forest under Artaxerxes I (Neh. 2:8).

ASAPPHIOTH ə-sa'fē-ōth (1 Esd. 5:33, NEB). *See* SOPHERETH.

ASARA as'ə-rə (1 Esd. 5:31, NEB). *See* HASRAH.

ASARAMEL ə-sar'ə-mel [Gk. *Asaramel, Saramel*]; AV SARAMEL. A name of uncertain nature in 1 Macc. 14:28, occurring in an inscription. The Vulg., AV, RSV, and NEB take it as a place name. If it was originally Heb. *w^{e}śar 'am'ēl* ("a prince of the people of God"), it might be a title of Simon the high priest.

ASAREL as'ə-rel [Heb. *'^{a}śar'ēl*]; AV, NEB, ASAREEL. A descendant of Judah and son of Jehallelel (1 Ch. 4:16).

ASARELAH as-ə-rē'lə (1 Ch. 25:2, AV, NEB). *See* ASHARELAH.

ASBASARETH as-bas'ə-reth (1 Esd. 5:69, NEB). *See* ESARHADDON.

ASCALON as'kə-lon [Gk. *Askalōn*] (Jth. 2:28; 1 Macc. 10:86; 11:60; 12:33); RSV also ASKALON (1 Maccabees). *See* ASHKELON.

ASCENSION. The departure of Christ from earth to the presence of the Father. Although the Ascension as an event is more often assumed than described in the NT, the Ascension of Jesus Christ is an important article of the Christian faith, declaring the victory of Jesus and pointing to his present lordship over the events of human history.

- I. Biblical Accounts
  - A. Matthew, Mark, and John
  - B. Luke and Acts
- II. Proclamation
- III. Significance
  - A. As the Conclusion of Jesus' Earthly Activity
  - B. As Exaltation of Jesus
  - C. For Christian Life
  - D. For the Future

I. Biblical Accounts.–*A. Matthew, Mark, and John.* Since the Ascension is the event that concludes the historical appearances of Jesus, one would assume that all the Gospels would end with an account of it. However, only Luke includes an Ascension scene. In the other Gospels the final scenes of Jesus' earthly life are Resurrection appearances.

The longer ending of Mark (16:9-21), which was recognized by the Church for many centuries as part of the canonical text, does contain an explicit reference to the Ascension: "So then the Lord Jesus, after he had spoken to them, was taken up [Gk. *anelḗmphthē*] into heaven, and sat down at the right hand of God" (16:19). However, in terms of the present understanding of the text of Mark, the original Gospel ended with the announcement that Jesus would appear to His disciples in Galilee. The story of that appearance in Galilee is the final scene in the Gospel of Matthew. This story contains the theme of the Ascension, viz., "all authority in heaven and on earth has been given to me" (Mt. 28:18), but no direct account of the Ascension. In addition, both Matthew and Mark contain Jesus' apocalyptic sayings about the Son of man coming on the clouds of heaven (Mt. 16:27; 24:30; 26:64; Mk. 8:38; 13:26), sayings that imply Jesus' Ascension but do not declare it.

The Gospel of John contains three specific references to the Ascension (Gk. *anabaínein*) but only by way of anticipation. The first is the difficult saying in Jn. 3:13, "No one has ascended into heaven but he who descended from heaven, the Son of man." In Jn. 6:62 Jesus asks His disciples, "What if you were to see the Son of man ascending where he was before?" And in Jn. 20:17 Jesus says to Mary Magdalene, "Do not hold me, for I have not yet ascended to the Father; but go to my brethren and say to them, I am ascending to my Father and your Father, to my God and your God." This saying of Jesus has been interpreted by W. Michaelis as implying that all subsequent Resurrection appearance are post-Ascension events, i.e., they are all manifestations of Jesus from heaven, and the Ascension story in Acts is then simply the last of these appearances. However, most have not been convinced by this interpretation.

The Gospel of John also contains implicit references to the Ascension both in those sayings in which Jesus speaks about going away or departing to His Father (Gk. *poreúesthai*: Jn. 14:2, 12, 28; 16:7, 28; *hypágein*: 7:33; 8:14, 21; 13:33; 14:4; 16:5, 10, 17), and in the significant theme of the glorification (Gk. *doxázein*) of Jesus. Although Jesus' glorification begins with the cross, it cannot be said to be completed until Jesus' return to His Father (Jn. 7:39; 12:16, 23; 13:31, 32; 17:5). Thus, in the Gospel of John the Ascension is presented within the pattern of descent/ascent, i.e., the origin and destiny of Jesus transcend the limits normally applied to human origin and destiny. Jesus comes from God and returns to God, and His person and ministry cannot be understood apart from either His origin or His return to the Father (Jn. 8:14) where He was before (Jn. 17:5). Yet this Gospel contains no specific account of the Ascension.

B. Luke and Acts. For a descriptive account of the Ascension we are dependent solely upon the writings of Luke. Midway in the Gospel of Luke the Ascension is already anticipated: "When the days drew near for him to be received up [Gk. noun *análēmpsis*]" (Lk. 9:51). The story of the Ascension in Luke has been transmitted in two textual versions. The longer one reads, "While he blessed them, he parted [Gk. *diéstē*] from them and was carried up [Gk. *anephéreto*] into heaven," whereas the shorter version omits "and was carried up into heaven."

The majority of textual critics have traditionally defended the shorter text as the more authentic. However, many have argued that the shorter version arose either by an accidental scribal oversight, or by a deliberate attempt to harmonize this account with Acts 1 resulting from the fact that Lk. 24 mentions no forty-day interval and seems to describe the Ascension as occurring on Easter Sunday. Since the discovery of a more ancient manuscript (p^{75}) and the consequent discrediting of the theory on which the arguments for the shorter text were based (Western non-interpolation), the longer text is increasingly favored as the more authentic. However, whether one selects the shorter or the longer text, it is clear from Acts 1:2 that Luke intended to narrate in his Gospel the work of Jesus "until the day when he was taken up [Gk. *anelḗmphthē*]." Thus Luke himself informs his readers that his first book ends with the Ascension of Jesus.

Since Luke wrote both versions of the Ascension story, it would seem best to account for the differences between the Gospel and Acts in terms of Luke's intention. Calvin, for example, handled the differences very simply by affirming that Luke abbreviated the account in the Gospel because he intended to write a longer narrative. Today scholars attempt to be more specific concerning Luke's intention.

Luke's Gospel ends as it begins, on a note of joy. At the Incarnation the angels announced the "good news of great joy" (Lk. 2:10). At the Ascension the departing Lord bestows a priestly blessing, and the disciples respond with worship, praise, and joy. The joy promised by the angels has now been realized in the community of the disciples of Jesus. Thus the Ascension story forms a fitting conclusion to the Gospel of Luke.

Although the only day mentioned in Lk. 24 is Easter Sunday, there is no explicit reference to the day in the latter part of the chapter. Consequently, since at other places also the Gospels do not present a rigid chronological ordering of events, there is no reason to assume that Luke intends to date the Ascension on Easter Sunday and thereby create a conflict with the time of the event in Acts 1.

The Ascension story of Acts 1 is told with greater detail, but remains a sober account told with great reserve. It does not directly describe Jesus' entrance into heaven, but is rather a farewell scene described from the perspective of the spectators. Jesus is removed from their presence and a cloud takes Him out of their sight. Whether this was a natural cloud hiding a mystery or the cloud of the divine presence is a matter of some debate. In either case the story neither assumes nor depends upon a particular cosmological theory regarding the location of heaven. To approach the story from such a perspective is to miss the point. The Ascension story is a farewell scene in which Jesus visually demonstrates that until His return He will no longer be visibly present with them. The Ascension is a visible sign revealing a new relationship of Jesus to His disciples.

Both Lk. 24 and Acts 1 contain Jesus' words concerning the world mission of His disciples; yet there is a distinctive difference in emphasis. The Ascension story in Lk. 24 focuses on the disciples in an attitude of worship and joy. Acts 1, however, begins with a stress on the necessity of the mission to the nations. The fulness of the promised eschatological joy has not yet come. That fulness of joy is reserved for the future because Jesus will return in the same way that He departed into heaven. Thus the Ascension story of Acts 1 is focused on the Parousia of Jesus. Until Jesus' return the mission to the world must be carried out. Ascension, mission, and Parousia are essentially related. The first vision of the ascended Lord presented in Acts is one in which Jesus appears "standing at the right hand of God" (Acts 7:56). The Ascension into heaven is the beginning of Jesus' session at the right hand of God. Paul's visions of the ascended Lord imply the same heavenly reign of Jesus (Acts 9:3-5; 22:6-8; 26:13-15). Hence the mission of the Church to the nations can be carried out — until the Lord returns — with the assurance that all authority belongs to the ascended Lord.

II. Proclamation.–In the NT Epistles, the Ascension of Jesus is more assumed than described. Nowhere do we find a further description of the Ascension. Neither the apostles nor the early Church dwell upon the Ascension as a visible event. Instead, the early Christian confession and proclamation declare the basis for, and the significance of, the Ascension: Jesus has been raised from the dead and exalted to power. "God has made him both Lord and Christ" (Acts 2:36).

Frequently, the confession of the Resurrection includes the Ascension. In 1 Thess. 1:10 the Church is described as waiting "for his Son from heaven, whom he raised from the dead, Jesus who delivers us from the wrath to come." Here the Resurrection is proclaimed as the reason Jesus

"The Ascension," part of a triptych by A. Mantegna (1431-1506) in the Uffizi Gallery, Florence (Religious News Service)

can and will return from heaven, and it forms the basis for the authority Jesus will exercise in the final judgment. The Ascension is not mentioned, but the Resurrection includes the exaltation of Jesus.

Similarly, in Rom. 1:4 Paul proclaims that Jesus was "designated Son of God in power, according to the Spirit of holiness, by his resurrection from the dead." The proclamation of the Resurrection includes the significance of the Ascension, viz., Jesus is exalted to power. The confession proceeds in Rom. 8:34 from Jesus' death and resurrection to his session and intercession: "Is it Christ Jesus who died, yes, who was raised from the dead, who is at the right hand of God, who indeed intercedes for us?" The Resurrection is the basis for Jesus' role as heavenly intercessor. (Cf. also Eph. 1:20.) Phil. 2:8f. announces the death on the cross as the reason that God "has highly exalted him and given him the name which is above every name." Both Resurrection and Ascension are assumed under exaltation.

Among the Epistles, 1 Pet. 3:22 contains the most specific reference to the Ascension. Between the confession of the resurrection of Jesus and His session at the right hand of God, the phrase is inserted, "who has gone into heaven." The perspective of Hebrews is primarily from the vantage point of Jesus' activity in heaven (He. 6:19f.; 7:26; 9:11f., 24). Yet the phrase "who has passed through the heavens" (He. 4:14) may include a reference to the Ascension itself though it clearly goes beyond that event. Similarly, the phrase "taken up in glory," from the early hymn quoted in 1 Tim. 3:16, announces both the Ascension and the exaltation that follows.

Thus the NT Epistles are not concerned primarily with the story of the Ascension itself as a separate event in the life of Jesus. Instead, the Epistles focus on the exaltation of Jesus, which begins with the Resurrection, continues in His session at the right hand of God, and will culminate in His return from heaven.

III. Significance.–*A. As the Conclusion of Jesus' Earthly Activity.* The Ascension, not the Resurrection, brings Jesus' earthly ministry to its conclusion. Although the Resurrection altered the manner of Jesus' association with His disciples, the forty days until the Ascension continue to be an essential part of Jesus' earthly ministry, during which He proclaims the kingdom of God (Acts 1:3). According to Luke, Jesus' earthly ministry extends "from the baptism of John until the day when he was taken up" (Acts 1:22). This period between baptism and ascension is the decisive period of Jesus' action and teaching (Acts 1:1f.), the time in which the Law and the Prophets are fulfilled (Lk. 4:21). Consequently, association with Jesus during this period of revelation and fulfillment is the essential qualification for admission to the office of apostle (Acts 1:22). Thus the Ascension brings to an end the time of Jesus and begins the time of the Church. The Ascension is the event that, on the one hand, distinguishes the time of Jesus' earthly ministry from the time of the Church, while, on the other hand, it forms the point of continuity between what Jesus "began to do and teach" (Acts 1:1) and what Jesus continues to do and teach through His apostles and the Church.

B. As Exaltation of Jesus. The Ascension reveals Jesus' exaltation to the right hand of God (Acts 2:33). Jesus is exalted because He is the righteous one (Jn. 16:10), and He is entitled to be restored to the glory that He had with the Father before the world was made (Jn. 17:5). Hence the appearances of Jesus after the Ascension are quite different from Resurrection appearances. They are visionary in character and reveal Jesus in His glory. The post-Ascension appearances are clearly manifestations from heaven and not on earth (Acts 7:56; 9:3f.; 18:9; 22:6f.; 22:17f.; 26:13f.; Rev. 1).

The Ascension declares Christ's enthronement as cosmic ruler. Using the language of Psalms 68 and 110, the apostle Paul announces Christ's victory over all the principalities and powers that had been vying for world dominion. Christ is enthroned at their expense (Eph. 1:20-23; 4:8-10). The enthronement is for the sake of the Church of which Christ is the head (Eph. 1:22), and it is the source of abundant blessing because the enthroned king gives gifts to men (Eph. 4:8ff.). These gifts enable the Church to attain to "the measure of the stature of the fulness of Christ" (Eph. 4:13).

This enthronement motif is found also in Hebrews. Here again the language of the Psalms is employed to describe the event. In addition to Ps. 110, Pss. 2 and 8 are employed. Jesus has been declared to be the Son of God (He. 1:5; 5:5), "has sat down at the right hand of the Majesty on high" (He. 1:3; 8:1; 10:12; 12:2), and all things have been put "in subjection under his feet" (He. 2:8). The Ascension is Christ's accession to power.

The primary message of Hebrews, however, concerns the significance of Jesus' exaltation for atonement. Jesus Christ is the "great high priest who has passed through the heavens" (He. 4:14) and has entered the Holy Place with His own blood to secure an eternal redemption (He. 9:12). Both as high priest and sacrifice, Jesus has appeared "in the presence of God on our behalf" (He. 9:24). He is the "forerunner on our behalf" (He. 6:20) so that we also may now enter the holy place (He. 10:19f.). Thus the Ascension of Jesus secures our salvation. The exalted high priest now lives "to save those who draw near to God through him, since he always lives to make intercession for them" (He. 7:25f.; 4:15f.; 2:18).

C. For the Christian Life. The Ascension of Jesus is not the means by which Jesus escapes from the world. On the contrary, it is an expression of the redemption of the world, for in the Ascension Jesus takes into heaven the humanity that He assumed in the Incarnation. Thereby mankind is restored into fellowship with God, and the creation is on the way to its final liberation (Rom. 8:21).

The Ascension is not only an event in the life of Jesus, but it is an event in the life of believers as well. Because of the corporate relationship to Christ, what has happened to Him happens also to those who are His. This involves not only death and resurrection (Rom. 6:4), but also sitting with Him in the heavenly places (Eph. 2:6) at the right hand of God (Col. 3:1-4). Thus the Ascension contains not only a hope concerning the future, but it also gives transcendent meaning to Christian suffering and joy in the present. The Ascension relates earthly existence to heaven and present existence to the future.

The Holy Spirit is the agent through whom Christian life is related both to heaven and to the future. The Ascension was the essential prerequisite for the outpouring of the Holy Spirit (Jn. 7:39; 16:7; Acts 1). Thus the Ascension inaugurates the coming into being of the new people of God, because the gift of the Spirit fulfills the promises made through the OT prophets. The Holy Spirit creates a people fit for service and mission, and for fellowship with God Himself.

D. For the Future. The Ascension proclaims victory both for Christ and for Christians. However, this victory has not yet been made fully visible. Although the Spirit is the gift of the end time (Joel 3), Christians receive only the "firstfruits of the Spirit" (Rom. 8:23). The redemption accomplished in Christ must still work its way through the history of the nations, and heaven must receive Jesus "until the time for establishing all that God spoke by the mouth of his holy prophets from of old" (Acts 3:20f.).

The Ascension reveals the victory of Jesus only to the eyes of faith, but hides it from the world. Therefore, the Ascension anticipates the return of Christ. In fact, it is a picture of the Parousia: "This Jesus, who was taken up from you into heaven, will come in the same way as you saw him go into heaven" (Acts 1:11). Until then the Christian life is a life of hope, lived with the assurance that the ascended Lord is with His people always, even to the close of the age (Mt. 28:20).

See also EXALTATION OF CHRIST.

Bibliography.–H. B. Swete, *Ascended Christ* (1911); W. Michaelis, *Erscheinungen des Auferstandenen* (1944); C. F. D. Moule, "The Ascension — Acts 1:9," *Expos.T*, 68 (1957), 205-09; J. G. Davies, *He Ascended Into Heaven* (1958); P. A. Van Stempvoort, *NTS*, 5 (1958), 30-42; P. Brunner, *Dialog*, 1 (1962), 38f.; B. Metzger, *Historical and Literary Studies* (1968), pp. 77-87;

E. Haenchen, *The Acts of the Apostles* (Eng. tr. 1971), pp. 135-152; G. Lohfink, *Die Himmelfahrt Jesu* (1971); M. Barth, *Ephesians* (*AB*, 1974); *TDNT*, I, *s.v.* ἀναβαίνω (Schneider); IV, *s.v.* ἀναλαμβάνω (Delling); νεφέλη (Oepke); VI, *s.v.* πορεύομαι (Hauck, Schulz). D. E. HOLWERDA

ASCENSION OF ISAIAH. *See* APOCRYPHAL APOCALYPSES II.A.

ASCENT [Heb. *maʿaleh*; Gk. *anábasis*]. (1) In Ezk. 40:31, 34, 37; Neh. 12:37, a flight of steps, or stairway. (2) A topographical designation of a climbing road or pass, such as that up the Mt. of Olives (2 S. 15:30), the road leading to the Jerusalem armory (Neh. 3:19), or to the royal tombs (2 Ch. 32:33). The mountain passes thus described were: the ascent of Beth-horon (Josh. 10:10f.); the ascent of Gur (2 K. 9:27); the Scorpion pass (Akrabbim) (Nu. 34:4; Josh. 15:3; Jgs. 1:36); the ascent of Ziz (2 Ch. 20:16); the ascent of Adummim (Josh. 15:7; 18:17); the ascent of Luhith (Isa. 15:5; Jer. 48:5); and the ascent of Heres (Jgs. 8:13). R. K. H.

ASCENTS, SONG OF [Heb. *šîr hammaʿalôṯ*]; AV SONG OF DEGREES; NEB omits. The title prefixed to Pss. 120-134. The meaning is still doubtful, but there are four main views as to its significance: (1) The Jewish interpretation. According to the Mishnah (*Middoth* ii.5; cf. *Sukkah* 51b), there was in the temple a semicircular flight of stairs with fifteen steps which led from the court of the men of Israel down to the court of the women. Upon these stairs the Levites played on musical instruments on the evening of the first day of Tabernacles. Later Jewish writers say that the fifteen psalms derived their title from the fifteen steps. (2) Gesenius, Delitzsch, and others affirm that these psalms derive their name from the step-like progressive rhythm of their thoughts. They are called Songs of Ascents because they move forward climactically by means of the resumption of the immediately preceding word. But this characteristic is not found in several of the group. (3) Theodoret and other early church fathers explain these fifteen hymns as traveling songs of the returning exiles. In Ezr. 7:9 the return from exile is called "the going up (*hammaʿalâ*) from Babylon." Several of the group suit this situation quite well, but others presuppose the temple and its stated services. (4) The most probable view is that the hymns were sung by pilgrim bands on their way to the three great festivals of the Jewish year. The journey to Jerusalem was called a "going up," whether the worshipper came from north or south, east or west. All of the songs are suitable for use on such occasions. Hence the title Pilgrim Psalms is preferred by many scholars. J. R. SAMPEY

ASCETICISM [Gk. *askēsis*–'exercise, training']. The term is not found in the canonical biblical text (the verb *askéō* occurs in Acts 24:16), but this does not of itself determine whether asceticism is scriptural or not. Among the Greeks considerable development is observable in the use of the word — from physical ability (athletic prowess) to mental discipline, especially in philosophy, then on to the achievement of virtue, and finally to the pursuit of piety. Similar language is used at times in the NT, as in Paul's portrayal of stern self-discipline couched in the language of the athlete (1 Cor. 9:24-27) and in the admonition to Timothy, "Train yourself in godliness" (1 Tim. 4:7), where the verb is *gymnázō*.

Asceticism is not easily defined because of its diverse manifestations, but in general it involves self-deprivation and is usually pursued out of a desire to glorify God by avoiding what is harmful and by limiting oneself to what is necessary to maintain life. It is unfortunately susceptible to the danger that the pursuit may become subtly diverted to a desire to outstrip one's fellows and to be credited with a holiness of life unattained by ordinary mortals. These spiritually elite, in turn, may seek to dominate other lives. "There is no pride like that which bases on ascetic austerity the claim to direct with authority the life and conduct of others" (James Denney).

Historically, asceticism has often been fostered by a dualistic outlook that pronounces the body (in contrast to the soul) as basically evil and its desires as requiring suppression if one would qualify for the ideal life (E. Rhode, *Psyche* [Eng.tr. 1925], pp. 302, 343). This was congenial to the Greek point of view but not to the Hebrew. Almost nothing in the OT fits the category of the ascetic. The Day of Atonement called for "afflicting" oneself (Lev. 23:27), which was understood as a requirement to fast. The Rechabites drank no wine and dwelt in tents, adopting a nomadic type of life as a protest against the settled life that Israel had maintained since the conquest of Canaan. Although the Nazirite vow called for abstention from wine and strong drink, it was usually only for a limited period. At a later time the Qumrân group adopted a somewhat rigorous type of communal living, but they did not glorify this as central to the genius of their movement. The typical Hebrew outlook was to regard food and drink, marriage, and material goods as gifts of God to be gratefully enjoyed but not abused.

Whereas John the Baptist was called to an ascetic type of life (Lk. 1:15, 80; Mk. 1:6; Mt. 11:18), he did not impose this standard on his disciples. Jesus fasted in connection with the temptation, but this was not a continuing feature of his life-style (Mt. 11:19), differentiating him from the Pharisees (Lk. 18:12). On the other hand, he left home and kindred as well as his means of livelihood. Those who would follow him were made to understand that a similar pattern applied to them. But there is no suggestion that in these various forms of self-deprivation lay the key to holiness. "Rigorism has nothing to do with one's own private spiritual holiness; it is not that leaving home and property is in itself a holier thing than retaining both. Rather is it that the man who in principle has given up everything can in practice be called upon to give up anything, when the needs of the kingdom, or of mission, dictate" (J. A. Ziesler, p. 54).

This observation explains the attitude and practice of the apostle Paul (1 Cor. 9:24-27). As far as one can tell, his choice of the single life was dictated by the determination that in his particular calling he was able to serve the will of God more efficiently in this way. An ascetic tendency that was disturbing the Colossian church received his strong rebuke to the effect that the measures advocated were "of no value in checking the indulgence of the flesh" (Col. 2:23). There is a similar rebuke for those who forbid marriage and enjoin abstinence from certain foods (1 Tim. 4:3).

In the postapostolic period the inclination of some sections of the Church toward asceticism grew, probably influenced by Greek thought and the desire not to be outdone by movements that were not Christian. Renunciation of marriage is prominent in the apocryphal Acts. Willingness to endure social disfavor and persecution for advocating this shows how deep-seated and earnest was the conviction that this form of asceticism represented the Christian ideal. It was not a case of denying that marriage had its place for the rank and file (the human family must not die out), but rather that marriage involved fleshly desire which the truly devoted should be willing to suppress.

Eventually the monastic movement combined celibacy with withdrawal from society. Rigid adherence to ascetic theory changes the biblical aphorism, "in the world but not of it," to "in the world but not part of it." There is a not inconsiderable difference.

See also ABSTINENCE; CELIBACY; FAST.

Bibliography.–F. Pfister, in *Festgabe für Adolf Deissmann* (1927), pp. 76-81; *ODCC, s.v.*; *TDNT*, I, *s.v.* ἀσκέω (Windisch); J. A. Ziesler, *Christian Asceticism* (1973).

E. F. HARRISON

ASCHENAZ ash'ə-naz (Jer. 51:27, AV). *See* ASHKENAZ.

ASEAS ə-sē'əs (1 Esd. 9:32, AV). *See* ASAIAS.

ASEBEBIA a-seb-ə-bī'ə (1 Esd. 8:47, AV); **ASEBEBIAS** (NEB). *See* SHEREBIAH.

ASEBIA as-ə-bī'ə (1 Esd. 8:48, AV); ASEBIAS (NEB). *See* HASHABIAH **7**.

ASENATH as'ə-nath [Heb. *'āsᵉnaṯ*]. The wife of Joseph, daughter of Potiphera, and mother of Manasseh and Ephraim (Gen. 41:45, 50; 46:20). She was evidently an Egyptian woman. The Masoretic pointing *'āsᵉnaṯ* appears in the LXX as *aseneth*. The name is typically Egyptian, the first two consonants corresponding to "she belongs to . . ." and the final element determining the possessor, in this case perhaps the deity Neit. Such names were common in the Middle Kingdom and Hyksos periods (*ca.* 2000-1500 B.C.). *See also* PSEUDEPIGRAPHA V.E.

R. K. H.

ASER ā'sər (Lk. 2:36 and Rev. 7:6, AV). *See* ASHER **1**.

ASERER as'ə-rər (1 Esd. 5:32, AV). *See* SISERA **2**.

ASH. *See* CEDAR.

ASHAMED. *See* SHAME.

ASHAN ā'shan [Heb. *'āšan*]. A city originally cited in the inheritance list of the tribe of Judah (Josh. 15:42). It was granted to Simeon (19:7; 1 Ch. 4:32) when Judah's territory was adjudged too large (Josh. 19:9), and finally given to the sons of Aaron as one of the priests' cities, listed in 1 Ch. 6:59 (MT 44). In Josh. 21:16 Heb. *'ayin* is a corruption of *'āšān*. Borashan (Heb. *bôr- 'āšān*, "well of Ashan") in 1 S. 30:30 (the AV has Chorashan, an error resulting from a misprint in an early Heb. ed.) is the same as Ashan. The site is to be identified with Khirbet 'Asan, about 5 mi. (8 km.) WNW of Beer-sheba.

R. E. W. BASON

ASHARELAH ash-ə-rē'lə [Heb. *'ᵃśar'ēlâ*]; AV, NEB, ASARELAH. One of the Asaphites appointed by David to the temple service (1 Ch. 25:2). In v. 14 he is called Jesharelah, whence the RSV spelling here; but cf. Asarel in 4:16.

ASHBEA ash'bē-ə, ash-bē'a (1 Ch. 4:21, AV, NEB). *See* BETH-ASHBEA.

ASHBEL ash'bel [Heb. *'ašbēl*]. The second son of Benjamin (Gen. 46:21; Nu. 26:38; 1 Ch. 8:1). In 1 Ch. 7:6 "Jediael" ("known to God") is substituted for the heathen-sounding "Ashbel" (Ishbaal, "man of Baal"). The Chronicler, in this case, conforms literally to the principle laid down in Hos. 2:17; the title "Baal" ("lord") was applied in early days (e.g., in the days of Saul) to the national God of Israel, but in later days the prophets objected to it because it was freely applied to heathen gods (*see* ISH-BOSHETH). In 1 Ch. 8:1, however, the three names Bela, Ashbel, Aharah (=Ahiram), are taken from Nu. 26:38 without change.

H. J. WOLF

ASHBELITES ash'bə-līts [Heb. *hā'ašbēlî*] (Nu. 26:38). The family name of Ashbel.

ASHDOD ash'dod [Heb. *'ašdôḏ*–'stronghold, fortress'; Gk. *Asdōd, Asedōth, Azōtos*, etc.]; Apoc. and NT **AZOTUS** a-zō'təs [Gk. *Azōtos*]. One of the five chief cities of the Philistines, about 18 mi. (29 km.) NE of Gaza. Its strength may be seen in that Psamtik I of Egypt besieged it for many years (Herodotus says 29). Some of the Anakim were found there in the days of Joshua (Josh. 11:22), and the inhabitants were too strong for the Israelites at that time. It was among the towns assigned to Judah, but was not occupied by them (13:3; 15:46f.). It was still independent in the days of Samuel, when, after the defeat of the Israelites, the ark was taken to the house of Dagon in Ashod (1 S. 5:1f.). We have no report that it was occupied by David, although he defeated the Philistines many times; and we have no definite knowledge that it was ever subdued by Judah before the time of Uzziah (2 Ch. 26:6).

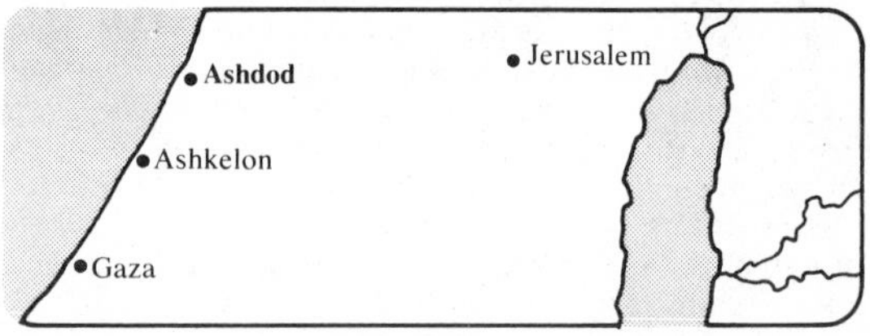

Ashdod, like the other Philistine towns, came under the authority of the Assyrian monarchs and is mentioned in their extant records. It revolted against Sargon in 711 B.C. and deposed the Assyrian governor Ikhmiti, who had been appointed by Sargon in 720. Sargon at once dispatched a force to subdue the rebels, and the city was severely punished. This is referred to by Isaiah (20:1). Amos had prophesied such a calamity some years before (1:8), and Jeremiah refers to "the remnant of Ashdod" as though it had continued weak until his day (25:20). Zephaniah (2:4) refers to the desolation of Ashdod, and Zechariah (9:6) to its degraded condition. It continued to be inhabited, however, for Jews intermarried with women of Ashdod after the return from Babylon (Neh. 13:23f.).

In the Maccabean period Judas and Jonathan both took it and purified it of idolatry (1 Macc. 5:68; 10:84). In these passages it is called Azotus, as it is also in the NT (Acts 8:40). In the 4th cent. A.D. it became the seat of a bishopric. It had been restored in the time of Herod by the Roman general Gabinius, and was presented to Salome the sister of Herod by the emperor Augustus.

H. PORTER

Recent excavations at the site of ancient Ashdod have greatly expanded our knowledge of that prominent city on the coastal plain of southwest Palestine. By combining pertinent data from literary sources (including chiefly the Bible, classical writers, and ancient historical inscriptions and business documents) with the results of several seasons of archeological work, we can now trace the major cultural phases of Ashdod's history, link the city effectively with political and social movements of ancient times, and fill out the general picture with numerous de-

Clay figurine of lyre player from Ashdod (Iron II), indicating that the early Philistine tradition of men playing the lyre continued into the 8th cent. B.C. (Israel Department of Antiquities and Museums)

"The Ashdoda," an early Philistine figurine of a seated goddess with the lower part of her body in the form of a throne. Although painted black and red in Philistine style, the basic concept is Mycenaean. (Israel Department of Antiquities and Museums)

tails. Five major seasons of excavations were carried out at Ashdod between 1962 and 1969 under the field direction of Moshe Dothan, representing the Israel Department of Antiquities and Museums, with additional smaller operations to deal with special problems.

Early and Middle Bronze Age. There is little substantive evidence for an Early Bronze Age occupation of the site. Some stray Chalcolithic and E.B. sherds were found during the survey of the tell and in stratum 20. They represent a settlement of insignificant proportions. The first fortified city originated in the M.B. II period, about the 17th cent. B.C. In this respect Ashdod is like a number of other prominent cities in Palestine, including Shechem, Tell Beit Mirsim, Gezer, Tell el-ʿAjjûl, and Tell Jemmeh. Its cultural history in this period was roughly parallel to that of Ashkelon, Ashdod's neighbor to the south.

Late Bronze Age. In the Late Bronze Age Ashdod was a prominent commercial center. The archeological evidence is supported by epigraphic data. The city is mentioned in a number of Ugaritic business documents, including a list of Ashdodite merchants with both Hurrian and Semitic personal names who apparently were resident in the north Syrian metropolis. Several levels of Canaanite occupation can be identified during the 15th and following centuries. The last of these cities came to a violent end in the latter part of the 13th cent. B.C. Recent evidence from the excavations has shown that after this destruction there was a brief occupation characterized by distinctive pieces of Mycenaean ware, reflecting the presence of the sea-peoples. It is reasonable to suppose that they were responsible for the attack on the city. The first Philistine settlement of the 12th cent. is a separate phase following the occupation by the sea-peoples.

The Philistine City. The first Philistine city was modelled on the earlier Canaanite city, and like its predecessor apparently did not extend beyond the upper mound (about 17 acres [7 hectares] in extent). The Iron I strata yielded large quantities of distinctive Philistine pottery. Massive public buildings dominated by a fortress-like structure have been uncovered, reflecting the preeminence of Ashdod in the Philistine pentapolis (cf. 1 S. 5). A figurine of a female deity forming a throne (the "Ashdoda") from the early Philistine period sheds light on the probable Aegean origin of the Philistines. Seal impressions with an undeciphered Cypro-Minoan script were also found in the Philistine strata.

Iron II Period. During the Iron II period the city expanded significantly in size and wealth. The slopes and plains around the mound were occupied and a second outer wall was built to encompass the lower city. This period of Ashdod's growth and prosperity, during which the transition from an Aegean to a Semitic culture was completed, matches the general decline in the fortunes of its neighbors, Judah and Israel, following the death of Solomon and the division of the kingdom. There were four major destructions of Ashdod during the Iron II period — all of them marked by thick ash layers in the area of the lower city. They should be attributed to Uzziah of Judah (stratum 4); Sargon II of Assyria (stratum 3b); Psamtik of Egypt (stratum 3a); and Nebuchadrezzar of Babylonia (stratum 2). The capture of Ashdod by Sargon II in 712/11 B.C. is described at length in the annals of that monarch, and is mentioned in Isa. 20:1. Fragments of a monumental cuneiform inscription found at Ashdod in 1963 reflect the same event.

Of unusual significance for interpreting the religious practices of the inhabitants are the many cultic objects found in the vicinity of a small temple in the lower city. There are several kinds of ceramic figurines including a unique group of strange-looking male (human) heads, some of which were originally attached to small offering tables or couches, as well as the familiar Astarte plaques found all over Palestine. Fragments of *kernoi*, or hollow-ringed vessels to which animal heads were attached, have turned up in large numbers, indicating that these served an important function in worship. It is of interest that the nearest affinities of the reclining figures and *kernoi* are with the centers of Indo-European culture in the eastern Mediterranean and Asia Minor, i.e., the areas in which the Philistines were resident or through which they passed. Inscribed materials of this period, including a potsherd with the word *pḥr* (perhaps "potter") and a weight with the word *nṣp*, indicate that Philistia was in close contact with Judah.

Persian Period. Not much is known of Ashdod during the Persian period, though its existence and importance as a provincial capital are attested in the extant sources. Excavations have revealed a substantial public building of the Persian period and an ostracon bearing an Aramaic inscription datable to the 5th cent. B.C. The latter contains the name Zebadiah, which also occurs in biblical writings of the same period, i.e., the Chronicler's work. A remarkable gold earring in the form of an ibex head also comes from the Persian era.

Greco-Roman Times. The archeological evidence, including major structural remains and a rich assortment of artifacts, supports the impression of a large and flourishing community in Greco-Roman times. The historical sources, including especially the Apocrypha, the NT, and Josephus, provide important information about the vicissitudes of Ashdod during these troubled times. Its changing fortunes are dramatically attested by successive occupation and destruction levels. A coin of Antiochus VIII discovered in Area A provides a *post quem* date for the conquest of Ashdod by John Hyrcanus. This date, 114 B.C., contributes to the discussion of this problem, and means that earlier proposals must be reduced by several years. In later Roman times the inland city *Azotus mesogeius* was surpassed by its seaport *Azotus paralius*; the former gradually declined in size and importance until the major part of the ancient site of the city was abandoned in early Arabic times. The village of Isdud on the adjoining hill continued to preserve the name and mark the site until it too was abandoned a few years ago.

Bibliography.–M. Dothan and D. N. Freedman, *Ashdod I. The First Season of Excavations, 1962* (1967); M. Dothan, *Ashdod II-III. The Second and Third Seasons of Excavations* (1971); "Ashdod of the Philistines" in *New Directions in Biblical Archeology* (1971), pp. 17-27; *IEJ*, 23 (1973), 2-17. D. N. FREEDMAN

ASHDODITES ash'dod-īts [Heb. *'ašdôḏî*]. (Neh. 4:7); also AV ASHDOTHITES (Josh. 13:3). Inhabitants of ASHDOD.

ASHDOTH-PISGAH ash'doth piz'ga [Heb. *'ašdôṯ happisgâ*– 'slopes of Pisgah']. The AV for RSV "slopes of Pisgah"; NEB "watershed of Pisgah" (Dt. 3:17; Josh. 12:3; 13:20), though in Josh. 10:40; 12:8 the AV translates "springs." The reference is to the spurs and ravines of Pisgah. The Heb. *'ašēḏâ* means "a pouring out," and *'ašēḏôṯ* are the slopes of a mountain from which springs gush forth.

See also PISGAH. J. W. WHEDBEE

ASHER ash'ər [Heb. *'āšēr*–probably derived from the West Semitic goddess Asherah; Gk. *Asēr*]; AV NT ASER.

1. The second son of Zilpah, Leah's maid, and the eighth son of Jacob born at Paddan-aram (Gen. 30:12f.); and the tribe named for him.

According to the genealogical list in Numbers, the tribe of Asher consisted of six families, viz., three sons, one daughter, and two grandsons (Nu. 26:44). A similar list is found in 1 Ch. 7:30; in this list four sons and one daughter are mentioned (i.e., one son has been added and to one of the grandsons, Heber, more descendants are attributed). In the list in 1 Chronicles there are at least six names that can be identified with geographical place names. Strangely, some of them are situated not within the historical territory of Asher (see below) but within that of Rachel's descendants: Ephraim, Manasseh, and Benjamin.

When settling in Canaan the tribe of Asher took possession of the western slopes of Galilee, part of the plain of Esdraelon (Josh. 17:2), and the main part of the plain of Acre (Josh. 19:22-31). The boundaries of Asher as given in the last-mentioned passage are not sufficiently clear, and the possibility exists that two separate lists, one describing the boundaries and one naming the cities within the territory, were combined. In addition, a third list giving the names of the Canaanite settlements that the Israelites were unable to subdue can also be traced (Jgs. 1:31). Not all place names mentioned in Joshua have yet been identified, nor is there agreement regarding those which have been.

The name Shihor-libnath (Josh. 19:26) has given rise to discussions in connection with the southern border of Asher. Alt held that it was the Nahr ez-Zerga S of Mt. Carmel, (so *GAB*) and was convinced that this was the southern boundary of Asher; but its identification with the lower or southern part of the Kishon, suggested by Mazar, is more likely and fits better the description in the Bible. Asher's southern border then continues to the west along the northern slopes of Mt. Carmel. Mazar also identified other cities in this list: the city of Achsaph with Tell el-Harbaj, Mishal with Tell en-Naḥl, and Aphek with Tell Kurdâneh, all of them in the plain of Acre.

The eastern and northern borders are more difficult to trace but it is possible that its eastern end was the Valley of Netophah (identified with the Valley of Iphtah-el), which was the western boundary of Zebulun. From there it ran to the area of Cabul, situated on the western slopes of lower Galilee, and then N to the city-state of Sidon (Josh. 19:28), a name that is thought to be a later addition to the biblical account, since Sidon was not the actual border but a desirable one. In any case, the names of settlements in this area have not been identified. The western boundaries of Asher reached the sea near Tyre and again from S of Achzib to the northern slopes of Mt. Carmel. The stretch of the coast between the two points last mentioned was in the hands of the Phoenicians.

To summarize, the territory of Asher consisted of the hinterland of the city-states of Tyre and Sidon, the whole plain of Acre from the neighborhood of the Ladder of Tyre to Mt. Carmel, and the western slopes of upper and lower Galilee.

The settlement of Asher in its territory is reflected in the Bible and in additional historical documents. In the Amarna Letters (14th cent. B.C.) Abi-milki king of Tyre complains that the king of Sidon had attacked Tyre with the help of the SA.GAZ (sometimes identified with the Hebrew tribes) and had conquered part of its territory. Farther east the same complaints were voiced by the king of Megiddo. This would mean that at the beginning of the 14th cent. a wave of Hebrew tribes came from the east and after having crossed the Valley of Esdraelon continued to the plain of Acre. The larger cities withstood the attacks, whereas the smaller settlements were conquered. Possibly among the SA.GAZ were the tribes of Asher and Issachar, who later settled in this area. When at the end of the 18th Dynasty Egypt's hold on Palestine weakened, the kings of the large Canaanite cities Hazor and Acre conquered both plains and pushed the newcomers back into the hill region. Issachar was subdued (Gen. 49:15), and Asher was confined to Galilee on one side and the hills of Ephraim on the other. At this time the tribe of Asher began to intermarry with Ephraim, Manasseh, and Benjamin.

The tribe of Asher appears in the lists of the pharaohs of the 19th Dynasty recording their reconquest of Palestine: Seti I mentions the tribe once, Ramses II twice. Asher is also mentioned in Papyrus Anastasi I, which was written at the same time. Another mention of the name of Asher is quoted by Gauthier from an unpublished papyrus.

When the tribes of Rachel conquered the hills of Ephraim at the end of the 14th cent., some Asherite families were swallowed up by the newcomers, whereas the rest were pushed north toward western Galilee and the plain of Acre. A similar fate befell the Asherite families in the Valley of Esdraelon, who were replaced by families from the tribe of Zebulun (Gen. 49:13; Dt. 33:19), so that the territory of Asher was confined to western Galilee and the plain of Acre.

Besides the tribes of Reuben and Simeon, who were destroyed in fighting their neighbors, Asher was the only tribe that did not have a judge of its own. In the Song of Deborah, Asher is reproached for lack of patriotism while Zebulun and Naphtali engage in the struggle against Sisera. The Asherites did, however, assist Gideon against the Midianites (Jgs. 6:35; 7:23).

During the reign of David the territories of Asher were administered by the central government, as is shown by the administrative division that found its expression in the list of cities granted to the Levites; four of these cities had previously belonged to Asher (Josh. 19:30f.). Among the administrative districts of Solomon, Asher was the ninth (1 K. 4:16). Solomon gave part of the territory of Asher, the Cabul territory, to the king of Tyre (1 K. 9:11-13); as compensation he gave Asher an area in Galilee (1 K. 4:16).

After the fall of the northern kingdom Asher was included in the Assyrian province of Megiddo, but the king of Judah tried to seize its territory (2 Ch. 30:10-12). This, however, happened only during the reign of Josiah (2 Ch. 34:6).

The Hasmoneans were unable to conquer Asher, i.e., the city of Acre and the coast stretching north. According to the rabbinical Halakah this coast did not belong to Israel. According to the NT, Anna the prophetess came from the tribe of Asher (Lk. 2:36).

See Map VI.

Bibliography.–Y. Aharoni, *Settlement of the Israelite Tribes in Upper Galilee* (1957), p. 76; *ARI*, pp. 59-61, 121, 132; A. Alt, *PJ*, 20 (1924), 35ff.; 21 (1925), 100-116; *KS*, I, 89-126; *ZAW*, 65 (1927), 59-81; C. F. Burney, *Israel's Settlement in Canaan* (1921), *s.v.* "Asher"; K. Elliger, *ZDPV*, 53 (1930), 265-301; J. Lewy, *HUCA*, 18 (1944), 461f.; E. Meyer, *Die Israeliten und ihre Nachbarstämme* (1906), pp. 540ff.

W. M. Mueller, *Asien und Europa nach altägyptischen Denkmälern* (1893), pp. 236-39; M. Noth, *IP*, p. 131; *Das System der zwölf Stämme Israels* (1930); *ZDPV*, 58 (1935), 215-230; H. Ranke, *Die ägyptischen Personennamen* (1935), p. 46; A. A. Saarisalo, *JPOS*, 8/9 (1928/1929); C. Steuernagel, *Die Einwanderung der israelitischen Stämme in Kanaan* (1901), pp. 30ff.; R. de Vaux, *RB*, 53 (1946), 263, 272. A. A. SAARISALO

2. A town on the southern border of Manasseh (Josh. 17:7). The site is unknown.

3. NEB HAZOR. A place mentioned in Tob. 1:2, identified with HAZOR in Naphtali.

ASHERAH ə-shē'rə [Heb. *'ªšērâ*]; pl. **ASHERIM,** also **ASHERAHS** (2 Ch. 19:3; 33:3), **ASHEROTH** (Jgs. 3:7); AV GROVE (following LXX and Vulgate); NEB SACRED POLE. The name of a goddess whose worship was widely spread throughout Syria and Canaan; and the objects of worship erected to her.

Her "image" is mentioned in the OT (1 K. 15:13; 2 K. 21:7; 2 Ch. 15:16) as well as her prophets (1 K. 18:19) and the vessels used in her service (2 K. 23:4). In Assyria the name appears under the two forms Asratu and Asirtu; it was to Asratu that a monument found near Diarbekir was dedicated on behalf of Hammurabi, "king of the Amorites"; the Amorite king in the Amarna Tablets bears the name Ebed-Asrati or Ebed-Asirti.

Like so much else in Canaanite religion, the name and worship of Asherah were borrowed from Assyria. She was the wife of the war god Asir, whose name was identified with that of the city of Ashhur, and thus became the national god of Assyria. Since Asirtu was merely the feminine form of Asir, "superintendent" or "leader," it is probable that it was originally an epithet of Ishtar (Ashtoreth) of Nineveh. In the West, however, Asherah and Ashtoreth came to be distinguished from one another, Asherah being exclusively the goddess of fertility, whereas Ashtoreth passed into a moon-goddess.

The Assyr. *asirtu,* which appears also under the forms *asrātu, esrēti* (pl.), and *asru,* had the further meaning of "sanctuary". Originally the wife of Asir, and *asirtu,* "sanctuary," seem to have had no connection with one another, but the identity in the pronunciation of the two words caused them to be identified in meaning. As the tree trunk or cone of stone that symbolized Asherah was regarded as a (Heb.) *bêṯ-'ēl,* "house of a deity," wherein the goddess was immanent, the word Asirtu, Asherah, came to denote the symbol of the goddess. The trunk of the tree was often provided with branches, and assumed the form of the tree of life. It was as a trunk, however, that it was forbidden to be erected by the side of the "altar of the Lord" (Dt. 16:21; Jgs. 6:25, 28, 30; 2 K. 23:6). Accordingly, Asa "cut down" the symbol made for Asherah by his mother (1 K. 15:13). Asherim or symbols of the goddess were put on the high places under the shade of a green tree (Jer. 17:2; 2 K. 17:10). Manasseh introduced one into the temple at Jerusalem (2 K. 21:3, 7).

In the Râs Shamrah texts Asherah is the consort of El, the supreme god. She is mentioned as "creatress of the gods" and as "Lady Asherah of the sea," titles that are given to the most important goddess of the pantheon. In the Ugaritic Keret text Asherah is said to have a shrine in Tyre, which would indicate her supremacy there also. She is the adversary of Baal. When Baal, the fertility god of the Canaanites, is defeated by Mot, god of death and aridity, and sent to the nether regions, Asherah is quick to appoint her son Aṯtar to the throne as substitute king in place of Baal.

As the role of Baal grows in importance and overshadows that of El, Asherah's interest seems to shift more toward Baal. When a house is to be built for Baal, he and Anat, his sister-consort, bribe Asherah with gold and silver in order to persuade her to intervene for them before El, a mission she gladly undertakes. Again, in a myth stemming from the Late Bronze Age (W. F. Albright, *Yahweh and the Gods of Canaan* [1968], p. 107), Asherah attempts to seduce Baal. Asherah's interest in Baal stimulates considerable competition between her and Anat.

Asherah, the goddess of fertility, represented the Babylonian Ishtar in her love-goddess aspect. In one of the cuneiform tablets found at Taanach by Sellin, written by one Canaanite sheikh to another shortly before the Israelite invasion of Palestine, reference is made to "the finger of Asherah" from which oracles were derived. The "finger" seems to signify the symbol of the goddess; at any rate it revealed the future by means of a "sign and oracle." The practice is probably alluded to in Hos.. 4:12. The existence of numerous symbols, in each of which the goddess was believed to be immanent, led to the creation of numerous forms of the goddess herself, which, after the analogy of the Ashtaroth (Jgs. 2:13), were described collectively as the Asherim. K. G. JUNG

ASHERITES ash'ər-īts [Heb. *hā'āšērî*] (Jgs. 1:32). The descendants of Asher, Jacob's eighth son. *See also* ASHURITES.

ASHEROTH ə-shē'rōth [Heb. *'ᵃšērôṯ*] (Jgs. 3:7). *See* ASHERAH.

ASHES [Heb. *'ēper, dešen,* vb. *dāšēn* ("take away ashes," Ex. 27:3; Nu. 4:13), *'āpār, pî(a)ḥ* (Ex. 9:8, 10); Gk. *spodós,* vb. *tephróō* ("turn to ashes," 2 Pet. 2:6)]. Ashes are mentioned frequently in connection with sacrifice (Nu. 19:9-17), mourning, and fasting (Isa. 58:5; Jonah 3:6). Among the ancient Orientals, to sit in or be covered with ashes was a sign of grief, mourning, humiliation, or penitence. Grief for the dead was expressed by placing ashes on the head (2 S. 13:19), as was national humiliation (Neh. 9:1; Jonah 3:5f.; cf. 1 Macc. 3:47). Like other afflicted persons, Job sat in ashes (Job 2:8; cf. 42:6), as wilful Israel was advised to do (Jer. 6:26). The distraught mariners of Tyre were depicted as placing ashes on their heads to indicate their distress (Ezk. 27:30f.). NT mourning and purification rites employed ashes (Mt. 11:21; Lk. 10:13; He. 9:13). The word "ashes" also designated worthlessness or insignificance (Gen. 18:27; Job 30:19).

On 1 K. 20:38, 41 *see* BANDAGE. R. K. H.

ASHHUR ash'ər [Heb. *'ašḥûr*]; AV ASHUR. The father (or founder) of Tekoa (1 Ch. 2:24; 4:5). The LXX and Vulg. (cf. RSV, NEB) understood him to be the son of Caleb and Ephrathah (the Ephrath of 2:19). In 2:19 Hur would probably be an abbreviation of Ashhur.

ASHIMA ə-shī'mə [Heb. *'ᵃšîmā'*]; RSV and NEB also **ASHIMAH** (Am. 8:14). A deity worshiped by the residents of Hamath who were resettled in Samaria by the Assyrians after the fall of Israel (2 K. 17:30). It has been suggested that "Ashimah of Samaria" (RSV; NEB "Ashimah, goddess of Samaria") should be read for "sin of Samaria" (AV) in Am. 8:14. While this would require only a change of vocalization (*'ašma* to *'ᵃšîmâ*), it is unnecessary since the guilt of Samaria, like the guilt of Judah, was its idolatry (2 Ch. 24:18).

Neither the identification of Ashima with the Elephantine colony of Ashema-bethel, nor the suggestion that Ashima is a deliberate corruption of Asherah the Canaanite mother-goddess, is without difficulty. The extent of our present knowledge does not permit a positive identification of this deity.

***Bibliography*.**–S. Amsler, "Amos," in R. Martin-Achard, ed., *Commentaire de l'AT,* XIa (1965), 237; R. de Vaux, *The Bible and the Ancient Near East* (Eng. tr. 1971), pp. 97-110.

D. McINTOSH

ASHKELON ash'kə-lon [Heb. *'ašqᵉlôn*]; AV also ASKELON; Apoc. ASCALON; RSV Apoc. also **ASKALON.** A maritime town 12 mi. (19 km.) N of Gaza and 10 mi. (16 km.) S of Ashdod. The name in NT times was Ascalon; the modern name is Ashqelon. It was one of the five chief cities of the Philistines.

Excavations of the site show that it was occupied by the Middle Bronze period or earlier. It is first mentioned in the Execration Texts of Egypt (1850 B.C.) and in the Amarna Tablets (1400 B.C.). In response to a revolt in 1280 B.C., Ramses II sacked the city and inscribed a record of the battle on the wall of the great temple at Karnak in Upper Egypt.

Israel failed to take Ashkelon during the conquest by Joshua (Josh. 13:3). In the period of the judges it was temporarily occupied by the tribe of Judah (Jgs. 1:18), but it had reverted to the Philistines before the days of Samson (Jgs. 14:19). Ashkelon contributed one of the golden tumors (AV "emerods") sent to Israel when the Philistines returned the ark, which had been taken in battle (1 S. 6:17). David couples Ashkelon with Gath in his lament over Saul and Jonathan (2 S. 1:20). It is joined with Gaza, Ashdod, and Ekron in the denunciations of Amos (Am. 1:7f.), and is referred to in a similar way by Jeremiah (Jer. 25:20; 47:5-7). Zephaniah (2:4-7) speaks of the impending desolation of Ashkelon and then prophesies that "the seacoast shall become the possession of the remnant of the house of Judah, on which they shall pasture, and in the houses of Ashkelon they shall lie down at evening. For the Lord their God will be mindful of them and restore their fortunes." (The new city established in 1953 is dedicated to Zephaniah the prophet.) Zechariah also speaks out against Ashkelon (Zec. 9:5).

Tiglath-pileser III named Ashkelon among his tributaries; and its disloyal king Mitinti is said to have become insane when he heard of the fall of Damascus in 732 B.C. Ashkelon revolted again in the reign of Sennacherib and was punished. It remained tributary to Assyria until the decay of that power.

After the conquest by Alexander the Great, Ashkelon embraced Hellenism and became a wealthy Greek city and a center of literature and scholarship. In Maccabean times it was captured by Jonathan (1 Macc. 10:86; 11:60). In 104 B.C. it was declared a "free city." Tradition says that Herod the Great was born there (Eusebius *HE* i.6.2; Justin Martyr *Dial.* 52.3). Herod lavished baths, costly fountains, colonnaded courts, and other splendid buildings upon the city (Josephus *BJ* i.21.11). After Herod's death, the royal palace of Ashkelon was bestowed upon his sister Salome (*BJ* ii.6.3).

By the 4th cent. A.D. the city had become a Christian community and the seat of a bishopric. In the 7th cent. the conquering Moslems claimed it. During the Crusades, a series of memorable sieges involving Saladin and Richard Coeur de Lion took place at Ashkelon. The famous walls built by Richard are still visible in places. It was an important fortress because of its vicinity to the trade route between Syria and Egypt. But from the end of the Crusader period until modern times, the site was uninhabited ruins.

The first excavations were carried out in 1815 by Lady Hester Stanhope, an English noblewoman, who was in search of gold and silver reputedly buried at Ashkelon. During 1920-1922 John Garstang, working for the Pales-

Remains of a wall constructed at Ashkelon by Richard I Coeur-de-Lion in 1191 A.D. Under terms of a truce the walls were again demolished the following year and the city abandoned. (W. S. LaSor)

tine Exploration Fund, carried out a serious archeological excavation, which brought to light extensive finds from the Hellenistic and Roman periods and allowed the history of the city to be traced as far back as the Middle Bronze Age. The state of Israel has converted the site into a park and an open-air museum. J. F. PREWITT

ASHKENAZ ash'kə-naz [Heb. *'aškᵉnaz*]; AV also ASHCHENAZ. A son of Gomer son of Japheth (Gen. 10:3; 1 Ch. 1:6), and eponymous ancestor of a nomadic kingdom also known as SCYTHIANS. *See also* TABLE OF NATIONS.

ASHNAH ash'nə [Heb. *'ašnâ*]. Two sites in the inheritance list of the tribe of Judah.

1. A site in the lowlands of Judah, probably near Eshtaol and Zorah (Josh. 15:33). The small ruin 'Aslîn between those two places may retain an echo of the old name.

2. A site farther S, possibly to be identified with Idhna, near Mareshah (Josh. 15:43). R. E. W. BASON

ASHPENAZ ash'pə-naz [Heb. *'ašpᵉnaz*]. A highly placed court official under Nebuchadrezzar, mentioned only in Dnl. 1:3. His task was to recruit intelligent Jewish captives for the royal service.

ASHRIEL ash'rē-el (1 Ch. 7:14, AV). *See* ASRIEL.

ASHTAROTH ash'tə-roth [Heb. *'aštārôṯ*]; AV ASTAROTH as'tə-roth. The plural form of ASHTORETH, the Canaanite goddess of fertility, used as the name of a place in Bashan in Transjordan, possibly ASHTEROTH-KARNAIM (Gen. 14:5), although these are best considered as two neighboring cities (*LBHG,* p. 50), and certainly Be-eshterah (NEB Be-ashtaroth) in Josh. 21:27 (cf. 1 Ch. 6:71); also, images to ASHTORETH (Jgs. 2:13; 10:6; 1 S. 7:3f.; 12:10).

Ashteroth-karnaim, possibly referring to the region around these cities, was the scene of the defeat of the Rephaim by Chedorlaomer (Gen. 14:5). Ashtaroth was the capital city of Og king of Bashan (Dt. 1:4, etc.). Located in the territory of Manasseh E of the Jordan, it was one of the Levitical cities (Josh. 21:27; 1 Ch. 6:71). Carnion or Carnaim of 1 and 2 Maccabees may be identified either with Ashteroth-karnaim or with Karnaim as a separate city.

Ashtaroth was located on the important King's Highway, thus comes into history at various points. The name is read by some scholars on figurines of princes among the Execration Texts from the 19th cent. B.C. (*LBHG,* p. 133). It is twenty-eighth in the roster of cities of Thutmose III, being spelled *'-s-t-r-t* and *'-ś-t-r-t*. In the Amarna Letters the name occurs as *ᵃˡaš-tar-te* (197:10) and *ᵃˡaš-tar-ti* (256:21); the latter reference occurs in the only Amarna text containing the name Jashuia, sometimes identified as the biblical Joshua — though this is impossible in the total context of the letter. In 732 Tiglath-pileser III exiled the people of Ashtaroth. A bas-relief discovered at Nimrod, which portrays a walled city with the name *as-tar-tu* (*ANEP,* no. 336), may refer to the same event.

In Eusebius (*Onom.*) two forts bearing the name Ashteroth-karnaim are mentioned, 9 mi. (14.5 km.) apart, as well as a Carnaim Ashtaroth; but the identifications seem to be badly confused, and the account must be rejected. Ashtaroth is probably to be identified with Tell 'Ashtarah, about 3 mi. (5 km.) S of Sheikh Sa'd (supposedly the site of Karnaim), about 20 mi. (32 km.) E of the sea of Galilee, and about 12 mi. (19 km.) NW of Der'ā (Edrei). Traces can be seen of an ancient wall, and evidence of occupation during all the Bronze Age and Iron I.

See *GP,* II, 255. W. S. L. S.

ASHTERATHITE ash'tə-ra-thīt [Heb. *hā'ašṭᵉrāṯî*]. A native of Astaroth, viz., Uzzia, one of David's heroes (1 Ch. 11:44).

ASHTEROTH-KARNAIM ash'tə-roth kär-nā'əm [Heb. *'ašṭᵉrôṯ qarnayim*–'Ashteroth of two horns']. A city of the Rephidim "subdued" by Chedorlaomer (Gen. 14:5). Modern scholars understand the name to mean either "Ashtaroth near Karnaim" or a location near ASHTAROTH with the name Ashteroth-karnaim. In either event, it is identified with Ashtaroth in Gilead.

The name Karnaim occurs in Am. 6:13, possibly a pun on the name of the town, and in 1 Macc. 5:26 and 2 Macc. 12:21, 26, as Carnaim or Carnion. The latter passages refer to a postexilic city of Jews and Greeks which was captured and destroyed by Judas Maccabeus.

W. S. L. S.

ASHTORETH ash'tə-reth [Heb. *'aštōreṯ,* pl. *'aštārôṯ*; Gk. *Astartē*]. A goddess of Canaan and Phoenicia whose name and cult were derived from Babylonia, where Ishtar represented the evening and morning stars and was accordingly androgynous in origin. Under Semitic influence, however, she became solely female, although retaining a trace of her original character by standing on equal footing with the male divinities. From Babylonia the worship of the goddess was carried to the Semites of the West, and in most instances the feminine suffix was attached to her name; where this was not the case the deity was regarded as a male. On the Moabite Stone, for example, 'Ashtar is identified with Chemosh, and in the inscriptions of southern Arabia 'Athtar is a god. On the other hand, in the name Atargatis (2 Macc. 12:26), 'Atar, without the feminine suffix, is identified with the goddess 'Athah or 'Athi (Gk. *Gatis).* The cult of the Greek Aphrodite in Cyprus was borrowed from that of Ashtoreth; that the Greek name also is a modification of Ashtoreth is doubtful. It is maintained, however, that the vowels of Heb. *'aštōreṯ* were borrowed from *bōšeṯ* ("shame") in order to indicate the abhorrence the Hebrew scribes felt toward paganism and idolatry.

In Babylonia and Assyria Ishtar was the goddess of love and war. An old Babylonian legend relates how the descent of Ishtar into Hades in search of her dead husband Tammuz was followed by the cessation of marriage and birth in both earth and heaven; and the temples of the goddess at Nineveh and Arbela, around which the two cities afterward grew, were dedicated to her as the goddess of war. As such she appeared to one of Ashurbanipal's seers and encouraged the Assyrian king to march against Elam. The other goddesses of Babylonia, who were little more than reflections of a god, tended to merge into Ishtar, who thus became a type of the female divinity, a personification of the productive principle in nature, and more especially the mother and creatress of mankind.

In Babylonia Ishtar was identified with Venus. Like Venus, Ishtar was the goddess of erotic love and fertility. Her chief seat of worship was Uruk (Erech), where prostitution was practiced in her name and she was served with immoral rites by bands of men and women. In Assyria, where the warlike side of the goddess was predominant, no such rites seem to have been practiced, and instead prophetesses to whom she delivered oracles were attached to her temples.

From various Egyptian sources it appears that Astarte or Ashtoreth was highly regarded in the Late Bronze Age. As goddess of war she is seen unclothed, weapons in hand, on a galloping stallion, charging into war. Other figures depicting the nude goddess have been unearthed in Syria and Palestine. In 1935 excavations were begun in ancient Mizpah, or Tell en-Naṣbeh, that unearthed a temple dedicated to Ashtoreth.

Strangely, Ashtoreth is seldom mentioned in the Râs Shamrah texts, which fact has led several scholars to assume that Ashtoreth and Asherah were two names for the same goddess. The evidence to warrant such a conclusion, however, is at most meagre. In the Râs Shamrah texts Ashtoreth is mentioned in connection with Baal in his conflict with the sea, but from the fragmentary text it is not possible to determine the exact role of the goddess.

It is quite possible that Ashtoreth, in distinction to the male god 'Ashtar, dropped her warlike attributes in Canaanite mythology and became, on the one hand, the colorless consort of Baal, and on the other hand, an astral deity. In the Râs Shamrah texts the most prominent goddess is not Ashtoreth, but Anat, the sister-consort of Baal. Ashtoreth plays a very inconspicuous role in the Baal passages. That Ashtoreth the goddess of the Sidonians belonged to the astral cult is supported by the fact that she is mentioned in connection with Chemosh the god of Moab and Milcom the god of the Ammonites, both of whom were probably astral deities. Solomon, having forsaken Yahweh, worshiped Ashtoreth, Chemosh, and Milcom (1 K. 11:5, 33; cf. 2 K. 23:13).

Hence there were as many "Ashtoreths" or Ashtaroth as Baals. They represented the various forms under which the goddess was worshiped in different localities (Jgs. 10:6; 1 S. 7:4; 12:10; etc.). Sometimes she was addressed as Naamah, "the delightful one," Gk. *Astro-noē,* the mother of Eshmun and the Cabeiri. The Philistines seem to have adopted her under her warlike form (1 S. 31:10, AV, NEB, LXX). Generally, however, she was worshiped locally as the consort of Baal, depicted in the nude with horns on her head, and was thus a member of the fertility cult. At Ashkelon, where Herodotus (i. 105) places her most ancient temple, she was worshiped under the name *Atargatis,* as a woman with the tail of a fish, and fish were accordingly sacred to her. The immoral rites with which the worship of Ishtar in Babylonia was accompanied were transferred to Canaan (Dt. 23:18) and formed part of the idolatrous practices that the Israelites were called upon to extirpate.

A. H. SAYCE
K. G. JUNG

Ashtoreth wearing diaphanous robe and composite crown with sheep horns. The stele is from the temple of Amenhotep III at Beth-shan, where her cult was prominent in the 15th-13th cents. (cf. 1 S. 31:10). (University Museum, University of Pennsylvania)

Ashurbanipal hunting lions. Carved on flat slabs of alabaster, this and other reliefs lined the walls of the king's palace at Nineveh. (Trustees of the British Museum)

ASHUR ash'ər. *See* ASSYRIA.

ASHURBANIPAL ash-ər-ban'i-pal [Assyr. *aššur-bāni-apli*–'Ashur (is) creating an heir']. The last great king of Assyria, 668-626 (?) B.C., son of ESARHADDON.

Before Esarhaddon set out on his last campaign against Egypt, he named Ashurbanipal as crown prince of Assyria, and Šamaš-šum-ukīn, another son, as crown prince of Babylonia (*ARAB*, II, § 766). Esarhaddon died on the way to Egypt, and Ashurbanipal claimed the supreme title, permitting his brother to be called only viceroy of Babylon. Ashurbanipal began his reign by continuing the policies of his father, waging war against Egypt. In 663 he even succeeded in advancing as far south as Thebes (Karnak), which he destroyed (*ARAB*, II, §§ 771, 778). It is probably this destruction of Thebes to which Nah. 3:8 refers, for No-Amon, "the city of Amon," is generally identified as Thebes.

The western frontier of Assyria at that time was Lydia in Asia Minor, whose king Gyges was under pressure from the Cimmerians, and sought Ashurbanipal's aid (*ARAB*, II, §§ 784, 849). The northern frontier, which was some distance south of Lakes Van and Urmia, was inhabited by the kingdom of Urartu, the Manneans, and other smaller groups of people. They were an almost constant source of trouble (cf. *ARAB*, II, § 786, etc.). In the east, the Elamites were continually in revolt until Ashurbanipal finally ravaged the land and destroyed the capital Susa (*ARAB*, II, §§ 805-832). In the south, Šamaš-šum-ukīn apparently brooded over the situation whereby his brother had taken over the entire empire of their father. In 652, Šamaš-šum-ukīn rebelled (*ARAB*, II, § 789). Possibly he thought the other nations on Assyria's borders would join the revolt, as they were to do forty years later when Babylon overthrew Assyria. But the time was not yet ripe; Babylonia was surrounded by well-disciplined Assyrian garrisons, and the Elamites were too weak to be effectual. Ashurbanipal crushed the revolt, after a two-year siege of Babylon (650-648), and went on to punish Elam and the Arab tribes who had attempted to support Babylonia (*ARAB*, II, § 817ff.). The annals of Ashurbanipal leave much to be desired from the point of view of chronology, possibly because they were written down quite a few years later, and we are unable to put all of the details of Ashurbanipal's many campaigns in order with certainty.

"The great and noble Osnapper" of Ezr. 4:10 (AV Asnapper) is generally identified as Ashurbanipal, although it is uncertain whether the biblical name is derived from the Assyrian form known to us. The description of Osnapper's deportation and resettlement of the peoples he conquered is in accord with what we know of Ashurbanipal's policies — and with the Assyrian kings in general from Tiglath-pileser III on. According to 2 Ch. 33:11, "commanders of the army of the king of Assyria" took Manasseh king of Judah (co-regent from 696, reigned 687-642) "with hooks and bound with fetters of bronze" to Babylon. This probably took place under Esarhaddon (*ANET*, p. 291). Manasseh was released, however, and permitted to return to Jerusalem and to resume his reign. In the course of his first campaign against Egypt, Ashurbanipal lists twenty-two kings from whom he received tribute, including Manasseh of Judah (*ARAB*, II, § 876; *ANET*, p. 294); hence we assume that Manasseh regained his throne by becoming a tributary of Assyria. It is interesting to note in this connection that Ashurbanipal records that he carried the leaders of the Egyptian insurrection to Nineveh in chains (*ARAB*, II, §§ 771-74). Among these was Neco (AV Necho), who had entered into coalition with Tirhakah. Later, Neco was released and permitted to take up his rule at Sais (*ANET*, p. 295). This is similar to the biblical account of Manasseh's capture and subsequent restoration.

We have no records from Ashurbanipal after the year 639, even though he reigned until at least 633, possibly to 626. Internal affairs were apparently chaotic, and it is obvious that the Assyrian empire fell apart during the reign of Sin-šar-iškun (?-612). There is much evidence that Ashurbanipal devoted himself to the arts, particularly to architecture, sculpture, and the formation of his library; this shift from militarism to the more peaceful arts took place in the second half of his reign. Psamtik the son of Neco (who had remained faithful to Assyria after his restoration) declared Egypt's independence, and Assyria did not contest it. The tribes on the west and north became increasingly inclined to revolt, and quickly joined Babylon in 612. It is not unlikely that Sin-šar-iškun's failure to hold the empire together was directly related to Ashurbanipal's de-emphasizing the military might of the nation.

Ashurbanipal built a palace in Nineveh that was embellished by rich ornamentation and many fine sculptures, some of which are displayed at the British Museum. In other cities he restored, enlarged, or refurbished many temples and shrines (cf. *ARAB*, II, §§ 951-1000, etc.). The sculptures from this period represent the zenith of that form of Assyrian art. But above all, Ashurbanipal's great interest in literature, the training of scribes to read the ancient Sumerian literary remains, which resulted in bilingual and trilingual word-lists and sign-lists (which, in turn, have made possible the great achievements in modern study of Assyrian and Sumerian), not to speak of the preservation of great quantities of the ancient literature of Sumer and Akkad, is, beyond cavil, Ashurbanipal's greatest monument. To say that Ashurbanipal, who boasted of his ability to read and write (*ARAB*, II, §§ 767, 843), "is perhaps to be considered the greatest known patron of literature in the pre-Christian centuries" (A. T. Clay, *ISBE,* 1st ed.), is to qualify the statement unnecessarily.

See also ASSYRIA III. E. 9.

Bibliography.–*ARAB*, II, §§ 762-1129; *ANET,* pp. 294-301; A. C. Piepkorn, *Historical Prism Inscriptions of Ashurbanipal* (1933).

W. S. LASOR

ASHURITES ash'ər-īts [Heb. *hā-'ᵃšûrî*]; NEB ASHERITES. According to the MT of 2 S. 2:9, a tribe located between Gilead and Jezreel, which was included in the short-lived kingdom of Saul's son Ishbosheth. There is some question as to the accuracy of the text here, with the Targum reading "Asherites" and the Vulg. and Syr. preferring "Geshurites." The latter, however, seems precluded because Geshur was independent at this time (2 S. 3:3; 13:37).

ASHVATH ash'vath [Heb. *'ašwāṯ*]. A man of Asher, of the house of Japhlet (1 Ch. 7:33).

ASIA [Gk. *Asia*]. A Roman province including in the first three centuries A.D. nearly the whole of the western part of Asia Minor and some of the coastal islands such as Samos and Patmos. Most of the area comprising the provinces of Mysia, Lydia, Caria, and Phrygia had been bequeathed to the Romans by King Attalus III in 133 B.C. It was governed by a proconsul who had his headquarters at Ephesus, but the title "First of Asia" (Gk. *prṓtē tḗs Asias*) was also claimed by Pergamum and Smyrna.

In the 1st cent. B.C. there was a large Jewish population whose relations with the Greek provincials were bad. Dolabella, governor of Asia in 43 B.C., and others took steps to prevent the Greek city oligarchies from discriminating against the Jews in their midst (see Josephus *Ant.* xiv.10). Paul intended to preach in the cities of Asia on his second missionary journey but was prevented (Acts 16:6); on his third he took up residence in Ephesus,

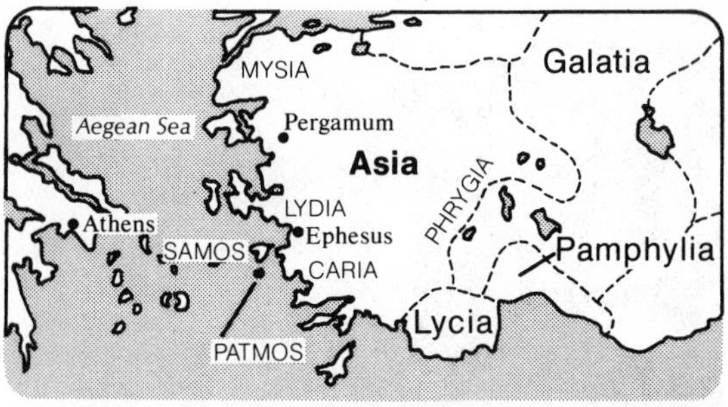

where he stayed over two years, so that "the entire population of Asia heard the word of the Lord, both Jews and Greeks" (Acts 19:10).

By the end of the 1st cent. A.D., Christianity was strongly represented in the provincial cities, and had aroused the enmity of the Jewish and Greek population, as revealed in the book of Revelation. The "seven churches" that are in Asia (Rev. 1:11) contained relatively large Christian communities and may have been missionary centers (W. M. Ramsay's theory: *LSC*).

In the early 2nd cent., anti-Christian outbreaks by the population were checked by Hadrian's rescript to the proconsul Minucius Fundanus in 124/25, ordering that procedure against Christians must be kept within the framework of the law and protecting Christians against vexatious attacks by informers. Justin Martyr was converted and held his celebrated debate with the Jew Trypho at Ephesus *ca.* 137. Later under Antoninus Pius and especially Marcus Aurelius there were severe local persecutions directed against the Christians, the most prominent victim being Polycarp at Smyrna (in either 156 or 166/67) (Eusebius *HE* iv.15). In the Decian persecution (250/51) the Christians in the cities of Asia were again affected (martyrdom of Pionius).

In the reign of Diocletian (284-305) the province of Asia was greatly reduced in size, and Ephesus lost some of its preeminence among the Christian churches in Asia Minor, though it continued to assert a right to patriarchal status, based on a claim to apostolic foundation through the apostle John. In the 5th cent., partly out of resentment at the predominance of Constantinople, Ephesus and the province of Asia generally tended toward support of Cyrilline theology and Monophysitism. Ephesus was the scene of Nestorius' condemnation in 431 and of Dioscorus' short-lived triumph at the "Robber Council" in 449. In 475 at Ephesus yet another Monophysite Council was held which conferred on the city the patriarchal status it had never renounced. It failed to gain acceptance for this and remained simply a see of metropolitan rank. Considerable areas of paganism remained in the province until the long and successful mission of John of Amida, acting on the orders of the emperor Justinian. John was elected Monophysite bishop of Ephesus in 558 and is known to history as John of Ephesus.

Bibliography.–V. Chapot, *La province romaine proconsulaire d' Asie* (1904); *CERP*; LSC; RRAM; references in W. H. C. Frend, *Martyrdom and Persecution in the Early Church* (1965).

W. H. C. FREND

ASIA MINOR.

I. The Country
  A. Name
  B. General Description
  C. Routes
II. History
  A. Early Times

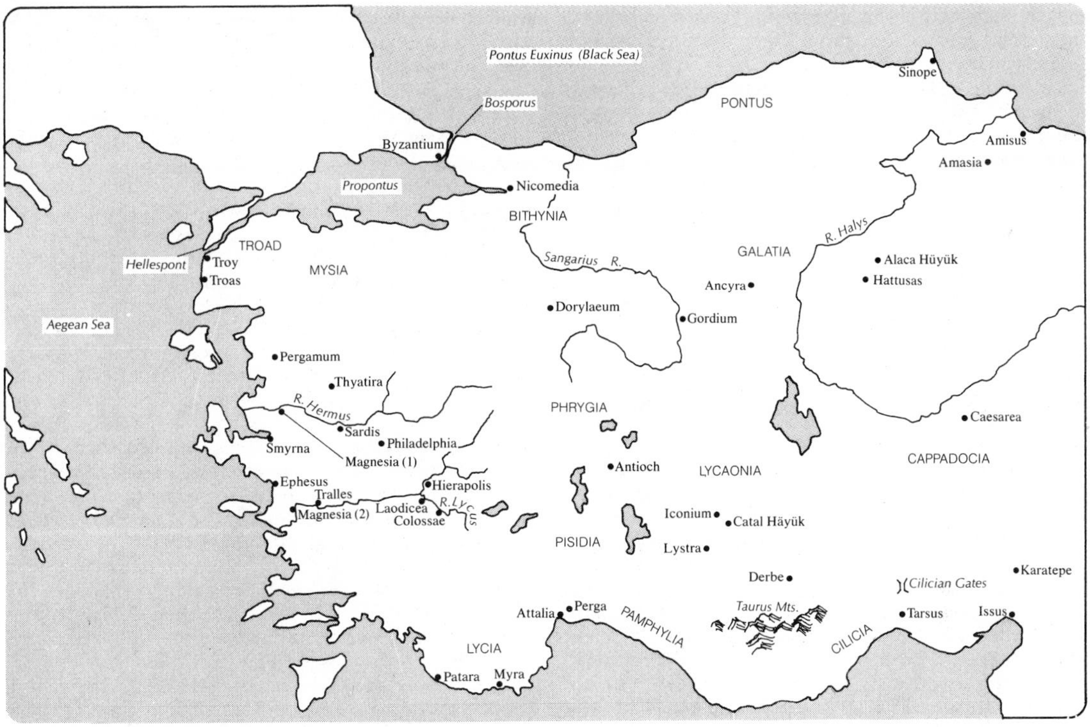

- B. Phrygians, Lydians, Persians, and Greeks
- C. From Alexander to the Romans

III. Asia Minor in the OT

IV. Asia Minor in NT Times
- A. General
- B. Life and Religion

V. Asia Minor in the NT
- A. Paul
- B. Peter and the General Epistles
- C. The Johannine Literature
- D. The Revelation
- E. After the NT

***I. The Country.**–A. Name.* The term "Asia Minor" does not occur in the Bible, nor is it known from Bible times. As a Latin phrase in its modern sense it is first extant in Orosius (5th cent. A.D.), though a Greek counterpart goes back to Ptolemy in the 2nd century. The land to which this name has been applied, however, plays an important part in some periods of Bible history, and a central part in the history of the earliest Christian mission. The term is now commonly used of the peninsula that forms the western half of modern Asiatic Turkey, approximately W of a line from Amisus (modern Samsun) on the Black Sea southward to the Gulf of Issus at the northeast corner of the Mediterranean. This includes all the country W of about longitude 36°E; it excludes such places in eastern Turkey as Mt. Ararat and northern Mesopotamia.

The only early name for this peninsula was the ambiguous "Asia" (later also Gk. *Anatolē*, the "east land," whence the Byzantine and modern "Anatolia"). The term "Asia" in different times and contexts could variously denote the continent, the whole peninsula, or a much smaller area on its western seaboard. The qualification "Asia Minor" distinguished the peninsula from the continent, but this name must be very carefully distinguished in turn from the "Asia" of the NT, which is normally to be equated with the Roman administrative province often known as "proconsular Asia" in the West.

B. General Description. The country forms an elevated land-bridge between central Asia and southeastern Europe, shaped and structured rather like a human hand stretching west. The central plateau, like the hollow of the palm, is bordered by a rim of coastal mountains along the Black Sea (Pontus Euxinus) to the north and another along the Mediterranean to the south. Eastward, too, the ranges converge into the highland block of Armenia. West of the central plateau longitudinal mountain ridges extend W like fingers, divided by fertile E-W river valleys and terminating in a raggedly indented western coastline. At the northwest corner the peninsula is separated from Europe by the Bosporus, the Sea of Marmora (Propontis), and the Dardanelles (Hellespont).

The high central tableland lies at an altitude of 3000 to 4000 ft. (900 to 1200 m.), stretching across large parts of Galatia, Lycaonia, and Cappadocia. There is much internal drainage into seasonal swamps and ultimately into the great central depression of the salty Lake Tatta (Tuz Gölü). The more important rivers cut their way outward through gaps in the mountain rim. They flow mostly to the north and west: the plateau is tilted down to these sides, and the mountains there are not so high as the Taurus on the south and southeast. The Taurus closely follows the contour of the south coast for most of its length, receding only where the fertile coastal plains of Cilicia and Pamphylia interpose. It reaches an average height of 7000 to 10,000 ft. (2100 to 3000 m.), but rises to 12,000 ft. (3600 m.) in the hinterland of Cilicia. There are no sizable plains below the mountains of Pontus in the north, and Sinope offers the only sheltered anchorage of that inhospitable coast. Only on the west is the ascent from the littoral to the plateau more gradual. Here the river valleys of the Caicus, Hermus, Cayster, and Maeander with their tributaries provide easy access through the Phrygian mountains to the western edge of the plateau. These western coastlands resemble Greece and its islands. In fact the chain of islands across the Aegean Sea encouraged very early navigation between East and West. Greece and Asia Minor had close relations from the earliest times.

Other major geographical features of the country are less immediately important for the understanding of its history. Its highest mountain is actually Mt. Argaeus (Erciyas Dağ), rising almost in isolation to 12,548 ft. (3823 m.) near Caesarea in Cappadocia (Kayseri). The longest river is the Halys (Kızıl Irmak), which describes a huge bend before escaping NE from the plateau through narrow gorges to the Black Sea. Its valley offers no important routes. There are also notable lakes, both of fresh and salt water, especially to the southwest, near the northern edge of the Pisidian Taurus. These include the Limnae (Eğridir Gölü) and Lake Caralis (Beyşehir Gölü).

This brief description will give some idea of the diversity of the land, which has remarkably varied climate and scenery. It also highlights the fact that Asia Minor has rarely functioned as a political or cultural unit. The western coast belongs to the Aegean world and enjoys a typically Mediterranean climate. The plateau is largely dry and empty, with extremes of temperature, locally diversified with ranges of bare hills. Ancient irrigation doubtless improved this land, but it remained largely a rural and static area, relatively slow to accept western influences. The northern and southern coasts had largely independent histories, both being almost isolated by their mountainous hinterlands. Communication was by sea. The grain and metals of the southeastern shores of the Black Sea attracted Greek commerce and colonization despite the perils of the Straits and the treacherous storms of this exposed coast. In the warm Mediterranean South, Pamphylia and Cilicia prospered, but the latter had closer contact with the Semitic lands to the southeast. While eastern Pontus had a mild and very wet climate with prolific harvests, the highlands of the interior suffered long winters of extreme severity.

C. Routes. The predominantly E-W grain of the country has determined the course of its principal roads and profoundly influenced the whole pattern of its history. The easiest route from the Euphrates went by Caesarea and Laodicea Combusta (Lâdik) to Apamea (Dinar), and then down the gentle gradient of the Lycus (Çoruk Su) to the more famous Laodicea (Col. 4:13f.; Rev. 3:14-22). Thence the broad valley of the Maeander (Büyük Menderes) led to the western ports of Miletus and Ephesus. An important branch of the road ran from the Lycus-Maeander confluence to the old western metropolis of Sardis, and thence down the Hermus (Gediz Nehri) to Smyrna. A further branch led to Pergamum at the time when that city achieved its political ascendancy.

Though this route and its ramifications marked the natural path of trade, political considerations dictated the use of a more northerly route over rougher gradients in early times to link the Hittite capital of Ḫattusas (Boğazköy) with Sardis and the Aegean ports. This was the course of the later Persian "Royal Road," which thus reflected the political realities of a much earlier time.

The few passes through the Taurus were of special importance. The famous road through the Cilician Gates linked Tarsus and Syria with the interior of Asia Minor and joined the great trade route westward. A corresponding outlet to the Black Sea ran through Amasia (Amasya) to Amisus.

The Roman peace led to a great development of the road system. An important branch of the central route ran through Iconium and Pisidian Antioch to Apamea, but was vulnerable to attack by the Pisidian brigands. Augustus based on Antioch a chain of new military "colonies," including Lystra, linked by a military road (6 B.C.). Many of these routes mentioned were used by the earliest Christian mission. Later the roads NW from Ancyra (Ankara) and Dorylaeum (Eskişehir) became more important when the political focus moved to Byzantium.

The Roman peace also opened the seas. The pirates were cleared from the rugged western section of Cilicia. The ports of Asia Minor began to play an important part in the new systems of integrated communication which focused on Rome. Navigation was always essentially seasonal, and depended on the regularity of the north and northwest winds of the Eastern Mediterranean summer. The Aegean crossing, the coasting traffic, and the region of the Straits all assumed a new importance. The artificial harbor at Troas gave needed shelter near the mouth of the Hellespont, and the crossing to Neapolis (Kavalla) in Macedonia linked with the Egnatian Way, the principal route from Rome to the East. And in Paul's time Claudius (A.D. 41-54) organized the Alexandrian grain fleet to supply Rome. Its ships beat against the wind from Egypt to gain the shelter of Patara or Myra on the southern coast of Asia Minor (cf. Acts 27:5f.). These aspects of travel illustrate further the setting of the NT journeys.

II. History.–*A. Early Times.* Asia Minor has always been a bridge between peoples, a land subject to new invaders and influences, which have repeatedly left a lasting mark. It has rarely been the seat of a homogeneous political unit.

Its history begins with one of the oldest town sites in the world, recently excavated at Çatal Hüyük near Konya. The excavation revealed remarkable Neolithic wall paintings of the 7th millennium B.C. In the 3rd millennium notable Bronze Age cultures appeared at Troy in the west and at Alaca Hüyük, over 100 mi. (160 km.) ENE of Ankara, where the people properly called Ḫatti flourished *ca.* 2500-2000. The Hittites who succeeded them at nearby Ḫattusas were evidently a mixed nation who appropriated the older name but incorporated an Indo-European immigrant element. Their empire reached its height *ca.* 1600-1200 B.C. Winckler's discovery of the royal archives at Ḫattusas in 1906 opened a new chapter of history. The Hittites emerged as one of the great empires of the day, with a complex history of foreign relations with Egypt and the Mesopotamian kingdoms. The great Assyrian trading colony at Kültepe (Kanesh) near Kayseri had flourished even earlier (*ca.* 1900 B.C.). Its cuneiform tablets are the earliest samples of writing yet known from Anatolia.

The latest phase of Hittite civilization shifts its focus to the southeast and to Syria, where it continued into the 1st millennium. This phase preserved the language known as "hieroglyphic Hittite," distinct from but resembling the Indo-European "cuneiform Hittite" (properly Nesian), which had been the principal language of the older empire. An important bilingual inscription of the 8th cent., in hieroglyphic and Phoenician, has been found at Karatepe in eastern Cilicia. The study of the several early Anatolian languages now known from the Hittite sites is a valuable and expanding source of knowledge of the ancient Near East. *See* HITTITES.

B. Phrygians, Lydians, Persians, and Greeks. The end of the 2nd millennium was a time of confusion and migration. Troy was destroyed. Phrygian and Bithynian immigrants arrived from southeastern Europe. Greek colonial

"King's Gate" at Boghazköy (ancient Hattusas). The figure at left represents a god, not a king as once thought. (B. K. Condit)

settlement began on the west coast at places like Miletus and Ephesus, and subsequently spread from them to the Straits and the Black Sea.

The kingdom of Phrygia was finally established in the 8th cent. in an extensive area around the west side of the central plateau, and the name and language long persisted there. The political ascendancy of Phrygia, centered on its capital at Gordium, was relatively short-lived, but it made a deep impression on the early Greeks, and its king Midas loomed large in Greek tradition.

About 700 Lydia, centered upon Sardis in the west, replaced Phrygia as the leading power. Gyges, the traditional founder of its dynasty, became a proverb for aggression and has been considered the prototype of Ezekiel's Gog (Ezk. 38–39; cf. Rev. 20:8). The last and most famous of the Lydian kings was Croesus (*ca.* 560-546), whose name is still proverbial for wealth. He conquered the Greek cities of the west coast, but then treated them generously, inaugurating a new temple of Artemis at Ephesus. (Smyrna had earlier been destroyed by his father Alyattes.) Yet the formidable citadel of Sardis itself fell unexpectedly to Cyrus of Persia in 546. It became a classic example of pride before a fall: Croesus had neglected to watch (Herodotus i.84; cf. Rev. 3:3). *See* SARDIS.

The fall of Sardis brought Persia to the Aegean. The city now became the western metropolis of the new empire, and evidently an early and principal seat of the Jewish Dispersion; it was probably the "Sepharad" of Obad. 20. The land was now assigned to satraps (provincial governors) or to native princes or Greek dynasts who recognized the suzerainty of Persia. The repulse of the Persian attack on Greece under Xerxes in 480/479 gave freedom to the Greek cities of Asia Minor during the time of Athenian greatness, but Sparta yielded them back to Persia in 386.

C. From Alexander to the Romans. Alexander the Great crossed the Hellespont in 334, winning all Asia Minor from the weakened control of Persia after decisive battles at the Granicus in the far northwest in 334 and at Issus in 333. He briefly united the whole country under Greek rule and began the eastward spread of Greek language and civilization. But his premature death in 323 brought new power struggles between his generals, the Successors (Diadochi). Most of Asia Minor fell initially to Antigonus, but he was defeated and killed by his rivals at Ipsus in Phrygia in 301. The country then became divided between Lysimachus of Thrace and Seleucus, who held the remnants of Alexander's conquests in the East. Lysimachus was active in the West, resiting Ephesus and refounding Smyrna, and fortifying Antigonus' seaport foundation of Alexandria (Troas). In 281 Seleucus defeated and killed Lysimachus at Corupedium in Lydia, but his successors, the Seleucid kings of Syria, lost something of the ascendancy he had won in Asia Minor. New dynasties arose, first in Bithynia in the northwest, then

Port of Antalya (biblical Attalia), from which Paul and Barnabas set sail for Antioch. The walled city was founded in the 2nd cent. B.C. by Attalos II king of Pergamum, whose heirs bequeathed it to the Romans. (B. K. Condit)

at Pergamum, where Philetaerus, the custodian of Lysimachus' war treasure, had rebelled in 282 and placed himself under Seleucid protection.

In 278 Nicomedes I of Bithynia brought a Celtic army across the Bosporus as allies, but they escaped his control and terrorized large tracts of Asia Minor for many years until finally restricted to a territory on the northeast side of Phrygia, around Ancyra and the bend of the Halys. This land of the Gaulish Celts was named "Galatia" (the Greek for "Gaul"). Gaulish speech persisted there in the time of Jerome (4th cent. A.D.).

The initially insignificant principality of Pergamum came to play a focal part. Attalus I (241-197) defeated the Gauls and assumed the titles King and Soter ("savior"), giving his name to the Attalid dynasty. He and his successors Eumenes II (197-159) and Attalus II Philadelphus (159-138) raised Pergamum almost to a great power, but at the cost of bringing Rome to Asia and finally becoming subservient to her. Only Rome could curb the ambition of the Seleucid Antiochus III the Great (223-187). When his power was broken at Magnesia (Manisa) in 190, the Romans gave the government of a vast tract of country to their ally Eumenes. In 133 Attalus III, the last king of Pergamum, bequeathed his kingdom to Rome. The Romans organized their wealthy province of Asia from its territory.

The policies and achievements of the Seleucids and Attalids had a great bearing on the political, religious, and social conditions of the land in NT times. Both dynasties were great founders of cities. The Seleucids peopled the area with cities called Antioch, Seleucia, Laodicea, or Apamea from their recurring dynastic names. They gave special privileges to the Jews, both in the cities that they founded and in existing towns like Tarsus and Ephesus, to which they granted new constitutions. Antiochus III, according to Josephus (*Ant.* xii.3.4), settled two thousand Jewish families from Mesopotamia in Lydia and Phrygia.

Thyatira and Philadelphia were Attalid frontier cities at successive stages of the expansion of Pergamum. The Attalids developed centrally the resources of their kingdom: they had the timber and metals of the Troad and the command of the Hellespont. They also made state religion an instrument of policy, exploiting more deliberately than some of the other Hellenistic monarchs the oriental tendency to ascribe divinity to rulers. They made of Pergamum a brilliant focus of religious architecture, culture, and art. Later a strategic road extension SE from Laodicea on the Lycus gave them a south coast port at Attalia in Pamphylia (modern Antalya).

After 133 the rich new province of Asia was ruthlessly plundered by Roman officials. About 102 the province of Cilicia was organized in southern Asia Minor to safeguard the way to the East, though its sphere at first did not even include the land of Cilicia proper. Mithridates VI the Great of Pontus (115-63) emerged as Rome's most formidable and persistent antagonist: in 88 he briefly overran most of Asia Minor, and was welcomed widely as a liberator. Nicomedes IV of Bithynia bequeathed his kingdom to Rome in 74, and it became another province. Pompey finally overthrew Mithridates and established Rome's position in the East. He added much of Pontus to the province of Bithynia.

Augustus brought the benefits of peace to Asia Minor and won spontaneous acclaim there. He continued the policy of exercising influence through native dynasties until the time was ripe for direct Roman rule of a territory. When the client-king Amyntas of Galatia was killed fighting the Homonades, a tribe on his southern border, in 25 B.C., Augustus made a province of his kingdom, an area which then extended far S of the Celtic homeland. Cappadocia was annexed in A.D. 17. There were many subsequent major or minor alterations of the provincial boundaries. The most important was by Vespasian, who after A.D. 72 combined Galatia with Cappadocia into a strategic military command.

III. Asia Minor in the OT.–Though this land lay within the perspective of the early biblical nations it played only a peripheral part in the OT. There are scattered references to places and peoples which may with more or less confidence be identified here.

The most important and obvious link is with the Hittites, a people first known from the OT. But the OT refers explicitly only to the Hittites of Syria and Palestine, who persisted later than the Hittites of the empire in Anatolia. Yet indications of their wider importance are not lacking. The "sons of Heth" appear in Gen. 10:15. Their early greatness emerges in Josh. 1:4. "Tidal king of Goiim" ("nations," Gen. 14:1) seems to bear a Hittite name, Tudhalias. *See* HITTITES.

The repeatedly associated Meshech and Tubal (Gen. 10:2; etc.) evidently denote nations of Asia Minor, and are referred to the Moschi and Tibareni of Herodotus. Javan suggests the Ionians (Greeks) of the distant coastlands (Gen. 10:2, 4; Isa. 66:19), Lud perhaps the Lydians. Tarshish is much disputed; it is possible that in at least some places it denotes Tarsus. These are all thought to have been ancient indigenous names. We have already noted possible later references in Gog and Sepharad.

The migrations of the disturbed period at the end of the 2nd millennium have probably left their indirect mark on the ethnography of the OT. The "sea-peoples," who included the Philistines, evidently came from or through the Aegean or Anatolian coastlands.

IV. Asia Minor in NT Times.–*A. General.* The country was now a political and ethnic complex with little intrinsic unity. There were old indigenous nations, whose lands were designated by traditional names still in current use: Lydia, Mysia, Phrygia, Pisidia, Lycaonia, etc. There were also Roman political divisions, which sometimes cut very arbitrarily across the natural ethnic boundaries. Some terms, notably "Galatia," present special difficulty, often because they had two or more senses.

The predominant language at this time was Greek, and almost all the literate remains are in Greek or Latin. The western and coastal areas were thoroughly hellenized, but Greek had not ousted native languages from the remoter parts. Lycaonian was still the popular speech of Lystra (Acts 14:11), and Phrygian and Celtic were spoken even later. In this hinterland Hellenism was only superficial.

Roman rule continued to favor Jewish settlement, despite anti-Semitic outbreaks at Ephesus and elsewhere. The presence of flourishing synagogue communities in many cities attracted Gentiles who sought a purer monotheism, and opened the way for the Christian mission. A very rich and important synagogue of the 3rd cent. A.D. has been excavated in Sardis.

B. Life and Religion. Greek city life in Asia Minor was superimposed on a very different Anatolian substratum. The ancient village system had been theocratic and matriarchal, centered on the temple, where the god, through his priests, exercised a close supervision over his people. The ancient gods and goddesses in whom the power and fertility of nature were embodied and localized became fused with Olympian Greek deities, but their alien character persisted. The goddess of Ephesus or of Sardis was represented by a grotesque image very different from the virgin huntress Artemis (Diana) by whose name she was called.

The unit of Greek life was the city. Thousands of surviving inscriptions and the coins of scores of cities testify to the activities of civic life. The city was an intricately organized entity in which citizenship, business, social life, and religion were interwoven. The trade guilds, for instance, often sponsored religious festivals or public benefactions, whose pagan basis posed problems for the Christian whose livelihood might depend on membership.

The vaunted privileges of the cities depended on the goodwill of Rome (cf. Acts 19:40). There was spontaneous gratitude for the peace and the facility of travel and trade that the Augustan empire had brought. Emperor worship was the natural result, at first sanctioned only reluctantly. Temples of Rome and Augustus were first established at Pergamum and at Nicomedia in Bithynia (29 B.C.). Only later, particularly under Domitian (A.D. 81-96), did the enforcement of this cult become a matter of Roman policy.

V. Asia Minor in the NT.–*A. Paul.* Paul was born in Tarsus, a great cosmopolitan university and commercial city, the capital of Cilicia. Though his education may have owed more to Jerusalem than to Tarsus, he returned there some time after his conversion (Acts 9:30), and his subsequent travels were largely directed to the evangelization of Asia Minor. The country thus became a principal center of the earliest Christianity, especially when it was displaced from Jerusalem and not yet established in Rome. A high proportion of the NT Epistles was written to or from localities in this land.

Paul's first journey took him and Barnabas over the dangerous Pisidian Taurus mountains from Perga in Pamphylia to Pisidian Antioch (Yalvaç), and thence through Iconium (Konya) to Lystra and Derbe, in Lycaonia. Lystra is beside Hatunsaray; the location of Derbe was identified in 1956 at Kerti Hüyük, N of Karaman. This visit marks Paul's first coming to provincial Galatia (cf. Gal. 4:13). He usually found an opening through the synagogue, but at his unintended visit to Lystra he encountered the native religious system.

The second journey went overland, doubtless by the Cilician Gates, to revisit the same district. The route entailed crossing a section of the land still held by the client-king Antiochus IV of Commagene. The subsequent itinerary has been the subject of controversy. "The Phrygian and Galatian country" (Acts 16:6), if so rendered, probably refers to the Phrygian district which overlapped the provincial boundary of Galatia and included Iconium and Pisidian Antioch. This concurs with the belief that Paul's dealings with "Galatia" were wholly with the southern part of the extended province. This view permits an early dating of the Epistle (*ca.* 48/49) and a natural integration of the biographical evidence of Gal. 1–2 with the sequence of Acts: it immediately preceded the Council in Jerusalem. *See* GALATIA.

"Asia" in Acts 16:6 was also in current usage the Roman province (*contra* E. Haenchen, *Acts of the Apostles* [Eng. tr. 1970]). Paul must have seen it as a strategic target, one of the most prosperous and sophisticated parts of the Roman world, a focus of Greek culture, whose greatest cities had hundreds of thousands of people. Mysia and Troas lay within Asia; the ban on preaching there did not preclude crossing the territory. From perhaps Dorylaeum, near the border of forbidden Bithynia, he travelled W to Troas. This was a strategic point (cf. 2 Cor. 2:12; etc.), for it was from here that Paul started for Europe, though this is not stressed in Acts. On his return to Jerusalem, he stopped only briefly at Ephesus (Acts 18:19-21).

Paul subsequently resided more than two years in Ephesus (*ca.* 52-55), and all Asia heard the word of the Lord (Acts 19:10). He reached the city "through the upper country" (19:1), possibly by a direct hill-road that bypassed the great crossroads of Laodicea. This accords with the probable implication of Col. 2:1 that he had not at that date visited the Lycus cities. The Ephesian residence and its aftermath were the occasion of the Corinthian correspondence, and ended after a time of special danger (cf. 1 Cor. 15:32; 2 Cor. 1:8, 10) in a journey N to Troas *en route* again for Macedonia (2 Cor. 2:12f.; cf. Acts 20:1). *See* EPHESUS. Paul returned by a coasting ship in haste to be at Jerusalem for Pentecost. He gave Troas the longest time possible, but then went past Ephesus, perhaps because of prospective delays in negotiating the silting port, and called the Ephesian elders to Miletus.

Paul's last recorded visit to Asia Minor was on his voyage as a prisoner to Rome. The ship clung to the shores of Cilicia and Pamphylia, where a westward coastal current offsets the northwest winds. At Myra in Lycia the party transferred to a ship of the Alexandrian grain fleet (Acts 27:5).

The Epistles provide evidence for Paul's later dealings with the churches of this land. Philem. 22 shows that Paul had some hope of visiting Colossae after release from imprisonment. In my opinion, Paul wrote Philemon from Rome. On the hypothesis that he was in fact released after two years, the references to Ephesus and to Troas and Miletus in the Pastorals suggest that he had then revisited them all.

The geographical perspective helps in resolving the vexed questions surrounding the relation of Acts with the Epistles and the reliability of Acts itself. The classic case is the question of the usage of the term "Galatian": the "South Galatian" view adopted here interlocks fruitfully with Acts. Ephesians, Colossians, and Philemon are ostensibly linked. Ephesians may have been an encyclical to the churches of Asia, delivered first in Ephesus and ending its course as the "letter from Laodicea" that Paul commended to nearby Colossae (Col. 4:16). Laodicea was then the principal city of the district and overshadowed its close neighbors Hierapolis and Colossae (cf. Col. 4:13). All three were important in the early Church, but Colossae (near Honaz), now deserted and unexcavated, was the destination of two Epistles (Colossians and Philemon). According to 1 Tim. 1:3 Paul left Timothy, himself probably a native of Lystra (Acts 16:1), at Ephesus, and at least the first letter was ostensibly sent there to him. Some or all of the Captivity Epistles have often been ascribed to a hypothetical imprisonment in Ephesus, but this is questionable.

B. Peter and the General Epistles. 1 Peter is addressed to the "Dispersion" in Pontus, Galatia, Cappadocia, Asia, and Bithynia (1 Pet. 1:1). These names are all to

Roman bridge at Assos, a Greek city of the Troad and the only good harbor on the north shore of the Adramyttian Gulf. There Paul rejoined his companions to return via Macedonia to Jerusalem. (B. K. Condit)

be taken in their provincial sense. Bithynia, though forbidden to Paul, must have received the gospel early. The Roman governor Pliny found Christianity in great strength in Pontus (rather than Bithynia proper) *ca.* A.D. 110 (Pliny *Ep.* x.96). F. J. A. Hort argued long ago that the list in 1 Peter represents the sequence of Silvanus' projected route. The present writer has suggested that this probably involved using the important road from Amisus on the Pontic coast through Amasia in Pontus Galaticus, in the eastern part of what was then the province of Galatia. This suits the provincial terminology used before Vespasian's reorganization. It also suggests that the Celtic territory of North Galatia was not in view here any more than elsewhere in the NT, for the continuation of Silvanus' route to Asia presumably crossed the Pauline districts of the south.

On any view of 2 Peter it seems that 2 Pet. 3:1 is intended to refer to 1 Peter and to imply a destination among the same recipients in Asia Minor. This cannot, however, be used to shed light on the destination of Jude.

C. The Johannine Literature. This literature poses complex problems, but strong traditions link both the Fourth Gospel and the Epistles with Ephesus. Irenaeus is explicit in locating the Gospel there (*Adv. haer.* iii.1.2). The First Epistle combats a form of Docetism which is often referred to John's traditional opponent Cerinthus at Ephesus. It is hazardous to argue an Asian setting from such other supposed parallels as Nicolaitanism or the teaching opposed by Paul at Colossae.

D. The Revelation. The book is addressed to "the seven churches of Asia" (Rev. 1:11; 2–3). These were certainly not the only churches of the province. Geographical considerations confirm Ramsay's suggestion that these seven were chosen as the best postal stages for the whole Church in Asia, placed in sequence along the messenger's route. On landing from Patmos at Ephesus he went N to Smyrna (İzmir) and Pergamum (Bergama), and then turned SE along the great road through Thyatira (Akhisar) and Sardis (Sart, near Salihli) to Philadelphia (Alaşehir) and Laodicea (near Denizli). It is possible that this route had already long been in use for the distribution of Christian letters. The same concern with communication is relevant to 1 Pet. 1:1 and perhaps to Ephesians, if that was in fact an encyclical.

The words of Christ in the seven letters are full of OT language applied to the particular needs of the named churches. They show an intimate knowledge of the cities of Asia and are rich in local allusion, reflecting what was probably a situation of impending persecution under Domitian. The Sardis letter, for instance, recalls the proverbial unpreparedness of Croesus (Rev. 3:2f.), and the Laodicean letter alludes to the tepid and emetic water of the city's aqueduct, in contrast to the scenic hot cascades of Hierapolis (Pamukkale) and the cold water of Colossae (Rev. 3:15f.). More important are the allusions that may shed light on the larger historical situation of the Church in Asia: pressures from the new enforcement of the emperor cult and from both Jewish and antinomian opponents. The Revelation is a classic document of an obscure phase of church history, and the study of contemporary Asia is a focal point of approach to it.

E. After the NT. It is beyond the scope of this article to relate in detail the later history of the Church in Asia Minor. Yet this land was so important that extrabiblical personalities and writings obtrude here on biblical debates. Ignatius of Antioch (*ca.* 115) was escorted through Asia Minor for martyrdom in Rome, and wrote epistles from Smyrna to the churches in Ephesus, Magnesia, and Tralles, and later from Troas to Smyrna and Philadelphia. These letters have an obvious bearing on three of the churches of the Revelation. W. Bauer has built a precarious argument from silence here into his view of orthodoxy and heresy in the early Church. Polycarp, to whom Ignatius addressed another letter, spans the history of the church in Smyrna from the days of John to his martyrdom there in extreme old age about A.D. 155. Philip (probably the apostle) is said to have died at Hierapolis, where also lived Papias, who transmitted through Eusebius traditions about the apostolic writings.

Bibliography.–*General and Historical:* W. J. Hamilton, *Researches in Asia Minor, Pontus and Armenia* (2 vols., 1842); W. M. Ramsay's works, especially *The Historical Geography of Asia Minor* (1890); *CBP*; *Asianic Elements in Greek Civilization* (1927); *The Social Basis of Roman Power in Asia Minor* (2nd ed. 1967); E. R. Bevan, *The House of Seleucus* (1902); V. Chapot, *La province romaine proconsulaire d' Asie* (1904); E. V. Hansen, *The Attalids of Pergamon* (1947); D. Magie, *RRAM*; O. R. Gurney, *The Hittites* (1952); S. Lloyd, *Early Anatolia* (1956); W. M. Calder and G. E. Bean, *A Classical Map of Asia Minor* (1957); L. Robert, *Villes d' Asie Mineure* (2nd ed. 1962); G. E. Bean, *Aegean Turkey: An Archaeological Guide* (1966); B. Levick, *Roman Colonies in Southern Asia Minor* (1967); D. J. Georgacas, *The Names for the Asia Minor Peninsula* (1971); E. Akurgal, *Ancient Civilizations and Ruins of Turkey* (3rd ed. 1973); J. M. Cook, *The Troad* (1973).

Biblical: Here many classic old works have not been superseded: J. B. Lightfoot, *St. Paul's Epistles to the Colossians and to Philemon* (1875), Intro.; Ramsay, *CRE*; *SPT*; *Historical Comm. on St. Paul's Epistle to the Galatians* (1899); *Letters to the Seven Churches of Asia* (1904); *Cities of St. Paul* (1907); F. J. A. Hort, *First Epistle of St. Peter I.1–II.17* (1898), pp. 157-185; for more recent work on specific matters see C. J. Hemer, "Unto the Angels of the Churches," *Buried History,* 11 (1975), four articles; "Alexandria Troas," *Tyndale Bulletin,* 26 (1975), 79-112; and "The Address of 1 Peter," *Expos.T.,* 89 (1977/78).

Epigraphy: There are large collections of inscriptions in the Corpora, and in *Inscriptiones Graecae ad Res Romanas Pertinentes,* ed. R. Cagnat *et al.* (4 vols., 1911-1927); in *Monumenta Asiae Minoris Antiqua,* ed. W. M. Calder *et al.* (8 vols., 1928-1962); and in *Tituli Asiae Minoris,* ed. E. Kalinka *et al.* (1901ff.). See also the journal *Anatolian Studies.* Other material is extraordinarily scattered in many publications. C. J. HEMER

ASIARCH ā'zhi-ärk [Gk. *Asiarchēs*] (Acts 19:31); AV "chief of Asia"; NEB "dignitaries of the province." The title given to certain men of high honorary rank in the Roman province of Asia. What their exact functions were is not altogether clear. They derived their appellation from the name of the province over which they presided (cf. Bithyniarch, Cariarch, Syriarch). Brandis has shown that they were not "high priests of Asia," as some have thought, but delegates of individual cities to the provincial council (*Commune Asiae*) which regulated the worship of Rome and of the emperor. They were probably assembled at Ephesus, among other places, to preside over the public games and the religious rites at the festival, in honor of the gods and the emperor, when they sent word to Paul and gave him a bit of friendly advice, not to present himself at the theater (Acts 19:31).

The title could be held along with any civil office and with the high-priesthood of a particular city. An Asiarch served for one year, but reelection was possible (the tenure of office, according to Ramsay, was four years). The municipalities must have shown the Asiarchs high honor, as we find the names of many perpetuated on coins and inscriptions. The office could be held only by men of wealth, as the expenses of the provincial games were for the greater part defrayed by the Asiarchs.

Bibliography.–Pauly-Wissowa, II/1, 471-483; II/2, 1564-1578; Eusebius *HE* iv.15; Strabo *Geog.* xiv.1.42 [649]; *CBP,* I, 55-58; II, ch. 11; L. R. Taylor, "The Asiarchs," in *BC,* V, 256-262; *RRAM,* pp. 449f., 1298-1301, 1526. M. O. EVANS

ASIBIAS as-ə-bī'əs [Gk. *Asibias*]. One who put away his foreign wife (1 Esd. 9:26). Cf. MALCHIJAH **3** (Ezr. 10:25).

ASIEL as'ē-əl [Gk. *Asiēl*].

1. Grandfather of Jehu, one of the Simeonite "princes" mentioned in 1 Ch. 4:35 as sharing Judah's inheritance (see Josh. 19:9).

2. A scribe engaged by Ezra to write down Scripture (2 Esd. 14:24).

3. AV ASAEL. An ancestor of Tobit (Tob. 1:1). Cf. Jahzeel (Gen. 46:24).

ASIPHA ə-si'fə (Esd. 5:29, AV, NEB). *See* HASUPHA.

ASK [esp. Heb. *šā'al*; Gk. *aitéo, erōtáō, eperōtáō, pynthánomai*].

A distinction can probably be made between Heb. *šā'al*/Gk. *(ep)erōtáō*, which imply the request of an equal, and *aitéō*, the word commonly used with reference to prayer, where the petition is by an inferior asking from a superior (Mt. 6:8; 7:7f.; Mk. 10:35; Jn. 14:13; etc.). It is not, however, asking in the sense of begging, but rather as a child making request of its father. The petitioner asks both because of his need and out of the assurance that he is welcome. He is assured before he asks that the petition will be granted, if he asks in accordance with God's will (1 Jn. 3:22; 5:15). *See also* PRAYER.

The normal sense of *pynthánomai* is "request information or explanation" (e.g., Lk. 15:26; Acts 4:7; 10:18, 29; 23:19).

In Dnl. 2:10, AV "ask at" is archaic for "ask of."

J. W. KAPP

ASKALON as'kə-lon [Gk. *Askalōn*] (1 Macc. 10:86; 11:60; 12:33); AV, NEB, ASCALON. *See* ASHKELON.

ASKELON as'kə-lon (AV, Jgs. 1:18; 1 S. 6:17; 2 S. 1:20). *See* ASHKELON.

ASLEEP. *See* SLEEP.

ASMODEUS az-mō-dē'əs [Heb. *'ašmeḏay*; Gk. *Asmodaios*]; NEB ASMODAEUS. An evil spirit figuring in the apocryphal book of Tobit. The name is probably derived from Heb. *šāmaḏ,* "destroy"; and it may be related as well to the Persian *Aesma Daeva,* or spirit of lust, of Zoroastrianism. In Jewish tradition Asmodeus was thought equivalent to Abbadon (Job 31:12) and Apollyon (Rev. 9:11). In Tobit the spirit was enamoured of Sarah to the point of killing her seven successive husbands on their wedding nights. Asmodeus was ultimately dispelled by a magical potion (Tob. 6:15; 8:3). R. K. H.

ASMONEANS. *See* HASMONEANS.

ASNAH as'nə [Heb. *'asnâ*–'thornbush'; Gk. *Asana*]; AV and NEB Apoc. ASANA. One of the Nethinim, who returned with Zerubbabel from exile (Ezr. 2:50; 1 Esd. 5:31).

ASNAPPER as-nap'ər (Ezr. 4:10, AV, NEB). *See* OSNAPPAR; ASHURBANIPAL.

ASOM ā'səm (1 Esd. 9:33, AV, NEB). *See* HASHUM.

ASP [Heb. *peṯen* (Dt. 32:33; Job 20:14, 16; Isa. 11:8); Ugar. *bṯn*; Akk. *bašmu*; Gk. *aspís* (Rom. 3:13)]. Any species of poisonous snake would suit the above references, though *peṯen* is rendered "adder" in Ps. 58:4; 91:13 by the AV and RSV. The biblical usage is uniformly metaphorical.

See also ADDER; SERPENT; VIPER.

ASPALATHUS as-pal'ə-thəs (Sir. 24:15, AV). *See* CAMEL'S THORN.

ASPATHA as-pā'thə [Heb. *'aspāṯâ*]. One of the ten sons of Haman killed by the avenging Jews (Est. 9:7).

ASPHALT. *See* BITUMEN.

ASPHAR as'fär [Gk. *Asphar*]. A pool in the wilderness of Tekoa, near which Jonathan and Simon Maccabeus camped when fleeing from Bacchides (1 Macc. 9:33; Josephus *Ant.* xiii.1.2). J. Simons (*GTTOT,* § 1152) says that the identification with ez-Za'ferân is doubtful, since that name occurs at several places.

ASPHARASUS as-fär'ə-səs (1 Esd. 5:8, AV, NEB). *See* MISPAR.

ASRIEL as'rē-əl [Heb. *'aśrî'ēl*]; AV also ASHRIEL (1 Ch. 7:14; NEB omits). A man of the tribe of Manasseh (Nu. 26:31; Josh. 17:2). According to 1 Ch. 7:14 he was born to Manasseh by an Aramean concubine.

ASRIELITES as'rē-ə-līts [Heb. *hā'aśri'ēlî*]. The family name of Asriel (Nu. 26:31).

ASS [Heb. *ḥ^a^môr, 'aṯôn, 'ayir*; Akk. *atânu*; Gk. *ónos, hypozýgion* (Mt. 21:5; 2 Pet. 2:16)]; AV also ASS COLT (*'ayir,* Jgs. 10:4; 12:14), YOUNG ASS (*'ayir,* Isa. 30:6, 24); NEB also DONKEY, BEAST OF BURDEN (Mt. 21:5), BEAST (2 Pet. 2:16); **HE-ASS** [Heb. *ḥ^a^môr* (Gen. 12:16), *'ayir* (32:15)]; AV also FOAL (Gen. 32:15); **SHE-ASS** [*'āṯôn*]; **SWIFT ASS** [*'ārôḏ*] (Job 39:5b); AV, NEB, WILD ASS; **WILD ASS** [*pere', 'ārôḏ* (Jer. 48:6, emended from MT *'^a^rô'ēr,* with LXX A *ónos ágrios*; but cf. 17:6); Aram. *'^a^rāḏ* (Dnl. 5:21)]; AV also "heath" (Jer. 48:6); NEB also "sand-grouse" (Jer. 48:6); **YOUNG ASS** [Gk. *onárion*] (Jn. 12:14); NEB DONKEY. The ass had been domesticated in Mesopotamia by the 3rd millennium B.C., being used as a beast of burden from the patriarchal period in Israel (Gen. 42:26; Isa. 16:20; 25:18; etc.). It was

Asses at the harvest. Painted wall sculpture in limestone, probably from the tomb of Metjetjy at Saqqârah (late 5th-early 6th Dynasty Egypt, *ca.* 2400 B.C.) (Royal Ontario Museum, Toronto)

renowned for its strength (cf. Gen. 49:14), and was the animal normally ridden by nonmilitary personnel (cf. Nu. 22:21; Jgs. 10:4; 1 S. 25:20; etc.). The Messiah's use of the ass (Zec. 9:9; Mt. 21:1-7; Jn. 12:14) thus depicts Him as the Prince of Peace.

The Torah prohibited the use of an ass and an ox yoked together for plowing (Dt. 22:10). While ass meat was eaten in emergencies (cf. 2 K. 6:25), the dietary laws regarded it as unclean (Lev. 11:1-8; Dt. 14:3-8). As one of the most common domestic animals the ass was virtually indispensable to sedentary life, and was thus one indication of wealth (cf. Gen. 12:16; Job 1:3; Ezr. 2:66f.; etc.). The animal symbolized wildness (Gen. 16:12; Hos. 8:9), strength (Gen. 49:14), contempt (Ezk. 23:20), and the dishonoring of a corpse (Jer. 22:19).

Like the ox, the ass participated in sabbath rest (Dt. 5:14); it also received proper care on that day (cf. Lk. 13:15; 14:5). The ass was once employed miraculously to give fresh direction to Balaam's prophetic abilities (Nu. 22–24). R. K. H.

ASSAILANTS. In Ps. 18:39; 92:11; Lam. 3:62; etc., derivatives of Heb. *qûm,* "arise," are used to describe those who rose in opposition to the aspirations or the behavior of the godly. They sometimes employed physical force (cf. Ps. 18:39), but their downfall was always confidently expected by the righteous (cf. 92:11; 109:28). The AV translates "those that rise up against (me)"; the NEB has "foes," "adversaries," "opponents," "enemies."

ASSALIMOTH ə-sal'i-mōth (1 Esd. 8:36, AV, NEB). *See* SHELOMITH.

ASSANIAS a-sə-nī'əs (1 Esd. 8:54, AV). *See* HASHABIAH **8.**

ASSASSINS [Gk. *sikárioi*] (Acts 21:38); AV MURDERERS; NEB TERRORISTS. The Sicarii, an outlaw band described by Josephus, and mentioned in Acts because Lysias mistook Paul for their Egyptian leader.

Josephus (*BJ* ii.13.3; cf. ii.17) relates that "there sprang up in Jerusalem a class of robbers called Sicarii, who slew men in the daytime, and in the midst of the city. This they did chiefly when they mingled with the populace at the festivals, and, hiding short daggers in their garments, stabbed with them those that were their enemies. The first to be assassinated by them was Jonathan the high priest, and after him many were slain daily" (see also *Ant.* xx.8.6; xx.9). The name is derived from Lat. *sica,* "a dagger." The Sicarii were implacable in their hatred to Rome and to those Jews who were suspected of leaning toward Rome. They took a leading part in the Jewish rebellion and in the disturbance previous to it, and also in the faction quarrels during the war. After the war they continued their nefarious practices in Egypt and Cyrene, to which they had fled. S. F. HUNTER

ASSAY. Archaic in the AV for "attempt," "venture." In the RSV and NEB of Jer. 6:27 it renders Heb. *bāḥan,* "test," "prove" (AV "try"), with reference to the role of Jeremiah as "assayer and tester" (*bāḥôn, mibṣār*; AV "a tower and a fortress") of Israel.

ASSEMBLIES, MASTERS OF (Eccl. 12:11, AV). *See* COLLECTED SAYINGS.

ASSEMBLY [Heb. *qāhāl,* also *qᵉhillâ, miqrā', mô'ēḏ, 'ēḏâ, môšāḇ*; Gk. *ekklēsía, plḗthos, synagōgḗ* (Jas. 2:2, and LXX)]; AV also CONGREGATION, CONVOCATION, MULTITUDE; NEB also COMMUNITY, COMPANY, "place of worship" (Jas. 2:2). The Heb. *qāhāl* and Gk. *ekklēsía,* both with the root idea "call," mean in strictest usage a meeting called together by a crier, and can refer to any gathering of people called for any purpose (Nu. 10:7; 2 Ch. 30:13; Neh. 7:66; Acts 19:32, 39, 41). But in the OT especially (where the LXX often uses *ekklēsía* to render *qāhāl*), the "assembly" is most often the people of God gathered for worship and sacrifice. (On *ekklēsía, see also* CHURCH.)

The root of Heb. *miqrā'* also means "call," and the usual rendering is "convocation" (e.g., Ex. 12:16, AV; Lev. 23:2ff.; but "assembly" in Isa. 1:13; 4:5). It usually occurs with *qōḏeš* ("holy assembly," Ex. 12:16; cf. Lev. 23; Nu. 28f.; NEB "sacred assembly") and indicates a day set aside for religious observance, when no work may be done. *See* CONVOCATION. The RSV "assembly" in Mic. 6:9 (AV "he who hath appointed") is based on a textual emendation, following the Greek.

In the NT, Gk. *plḗthos,* normally "multitude," refers also to the Council of Jerusalem (Acts 15:12) and once to the Sanhedrin (23:7). The Gk. *synagōgḗ,* which often translates Heb. *qāhāl* in the LXX, is used in Jas. 2:2 for the regular assembly places of Jewish Christians. On He. 12:22f. *panḗgyris, see* FESTAL GATHERING.

See also COMPANY; CONGREGATION. J. W. D. H.

ASSEMBLY, MOUNT OF [Heb. *har-mô'ēḏ*] (Isa. 14:13); AV MOUNT OF THE CONGREGATION; NEB "mountain where the gods meet." What is evidently meant is the fancied Olympus of the gods on some lofty northern height. The king vaunted that he would make his abode with the gods in heaven; now he is cast down to the depths of Sheol. J. ORR

ASSENT. Archaic in the AV, meaning "voice" (Heb. *peh,* 2 Ch. 18:12) and "join in the attack" (Gk. *synepitíthemai,* Acts 24:9).

ASSESSMENT [Heb. *'ēreḵ* < *'āraḵ*–'arrange,' 'estimate']; AV "that every man is set at" (2 K. 12:4), TAXATION (23:25). *See* VALUATION.

ASSHUR ash'ər [Heb. *'aššûr*]. The name for the people or nation of ASSYRIA, or the city that was sometimes the capital. It is also the name of the national god (spelled Ashur in this encyclopedia), forms of which appear in the names of rulers, e.g., ESARHADDON and ASHURBANIPAL (possibly the Osnappar of Ezr. 4:10). On the city, *see* ARCHEOLOGY OF MESOPOTAMIA III.A.

ASSHURIM ə-shōō'rim [Heb. *'ăššûrîm*]. An obscure Arabian tribe descended from Abraham and Keturah through Dedan (Gen. 25:3).

ASSIDEANS as-ə-dē'ənz (1 Macc. 2:42, etc., AV). *See* HASIDEANS.

ASSIGN [Heb. *nāṯan, pāqaḏ,* also *'āmar* (1 K. 11:18), *mānâ* (Dnl. 1:5), *sāpar* (2 Ch. 2:2), *'āśâ* (2 Ch. 2:18), *śîm* (Prov. 8:29); Gk. *dídōmi* (1 Cor. 3:5), *merízō* (Rom. 12:3; 1 Cor. 7:17)]; AV also GIVE, APPOINT, RECKON, PUT TO (2 Ch. 2:14), SET TO BE (2 Ch. 2:18), DEAL (Rom. 12:3), DISTRIBUTE (1 Cor. 7:17); NEB also GIVE, ALLOT, STATION, ENGAGE (2 Ch. 2:2), SUBMIT TO (2 Ch. 2:14), PRESCRIBE (Prov. 8:29), DEAL (Rom. 12:3), GRANT (1 Cor. 7:17), ARRANGE (Nu. 8:26).

The verb "assign" is frequently used of the delegation of certain duties, tasks, or obligations. Often the notion of authority is present, as when Joab assigned Uriah a place in battle where he surely would be killed (2 S. 11:16), or when Solomon assigned men their tasks in the building of the temple (2 Ch. 2:2, 14, 18). In Prov. 8:29 God, with Wisdom, creates the boundaries of the seas beyond which they cannot pass.

Likewise in Rom. 12:3 it is God who does the assigning. He measures out to each person his portion of faith. In 1 Cor. 3:5 and 7:17 it is God who gives to each man his particular calling and position in life. It is interesting to note the individualistic reference in each of these three NT uses of "assign." In each case it is to the individual (Gk. *hekástō*) that the faith and vocation is assigned, and it is always assigned by God Himself.

B. L. BANDSTRA

ASSIR as'ər [Heb. *'assîr*–'captive'].

1. A Levite of the family of Korah (Ex. 6:24; 1 Ch. 6:22).

2. A son of Ebiasaph and grandson of Assir. Samuel was descended from him (1 Ch. 6:23, 37).

3. According to 1 Ch. 3:17, AV, a son of Jeconiah. The RSV, however, takes the word not as a name but as a common noun, "captive," as also the NEB, "prisoner."

ASSOCIATES [Aram. *kᵉnaṯ*; Akk. *kinātu*]; AV COMPANIONS; NEB COLLEAGUES. An Aramaic term occurring in Ezr. 4:7–6:13 to describe a "colleague" in some particular enterprise.

ASSOS as'os [Gk. *Assos*]. An ancient city of Mysia in the Roman province of Asia at which Paul and Luke rested while on their way from Troas to Mitylene (Acts 20:13).

Assos, or Assus, as it is also spelled, stood on a volcanic hill some 700 ft. (215 m.) in altitude. Since it was located on on the Gulf of Adramyttium and faced south toward Lesbos, it is not at all surprising that it was founded by Aeolians of Lesbos (Mitylene), *ca.* 900 B.C.

This virtually impregnable site rose in steep cliffs sheer from the sea. Its sides were covered with both natural and artificial terraces.

Assos was successively a part of the Lydian kingdom, the Persian empire, Alexander's empire, the kingdom of Pergamum, and the Roman empire. Aristotle taught there for three years (348-345 B.C.), and Cleanthes the Stoic philosopher was born there.

An American Archaeological Institute team explored and excavated at Assos 1881-83. Upon the terraces of the hill they found such public buildings as the gymnasium, treasury, baths, marketplace, and theater. The marketplace (agora) was nearly rectangular in shape, and along its north and south sides were long stoas of typically Pergamene form. Around the base of the hill stood a Hellenistic wall about 2 mi. (3 km.) in length and 30 ft. (9 m.) high. A second wall at the site dated to the Byzantine period. On the summit of the acropolis stood a Doric temple which the excavators assigned to the 5th cent. B.C. but which many others date a century earlier. The harbor from which Paul sailed to Mitylene has since silted up and is covered with gardens. Modern inhabitants of the town (called Behramköy, a Turkish corruption of the Byzantine name) have constructed an artificial harbor at its side. *See* Plate 18. H. F. VOS

ASSUAGE. In Job 16:5f., the rendering of Heb. *ḥāšak* (AV "asswage"), and in Nah. 3:19 of *kēhâ* (AV "healing"). The AV uses it at Gen. 8:1 for *šākak*, of the subsiding flood waters.

ASSUMPTION OF MOSES. *See* APOCALYPTIC LITERATURE III.E.

ASSUR as'ər (1 Esd. 5:31, AV). *See* ASUR.

ASSURANCE [Heb. *'āman* (Dt. 28:66); Gk. *pístis, plērophoría, hypóstasis* (He. 11:1)]; AV, NEB, also SUBSTANCE (He. 11:1); NEB also SECURITY; **ASSURED** [Heb. *'emet* (Jer. 14:13); Gk. *plērophoría* (Col. 2:2), *plēróō* (4:12)]; AV also COMPLETE (Col. 4:12); NEB LASTING, CONVICTION. These words are exceptionally rich in spiritual meaning, signifying the joyous unwavering confidence of an intelligent faith, the security of a fearless trust. They have to do with the heart of vital religion.

In the OT Heb. *'āman* means "support," hence "confide in, trust." Jesus repeatedly used this word "amen" to express the trustworthiness and abiding certainty of His sayings. Heb. *'emet* is the most important OT word for "truth." In Jer. 14:13 it occurs with *šālôm*, "assured peace," NEB "lasting prosperity" — but this is the lie of false prophets.

The NT terms are Gk. *pístis*, "faith," *plēróō*, "fill," *plērophoría*, "bearing fullness," and *hypóstasis*, "firm conviction" or else "essential reality." This last word is difficult, because of the possible philosophical connotations. Perhaps the best suggestion is the RV mg., "the giving substance to." Faith makes the things hoped for *real* to the soul. Cf. He. 1:3.

The confidence of faith is based not on "works of righteousness which we have done" (cf. Tit. 3:4f., AV) but on the high-priesthood and atoning sacrifice of Christ (He. 10:21f.; cf. v. 19, "boldness to enter . . . by the blood of Jesus," AV). Assurance is the soul's apprehension of its complete emancipation from the power of evil and from consequent judgment, through the atoning grace of Christ. It is the exact opposite of self-confidence, being a joyous appropriation and experience of the fulness of Christ — a glad sense of security, freedom, and eternal life in Him.

This doctrine is of immeasurable importance to the life of the Church and of the individual believer, as a life of spiritual doubt and uncertainty contradicts the ideal of liberty in Christ Jesus which is the natural and necessary fruit of "the washing of regeneration and renewing of the Holy Spirit . . . shed on us abundantly, through Jesus Christ our Savior." Paul unhesitatingly said, "I know" (2 Tim. 1:12) — a word which, oft-repeated in 1 John, furnishes the groundwork of glad assurance that runs through the entire Epistle. For the classic passage on "full assurance" see Col. 2:1-10. D. M. PRATT

ASSURBANIPAL as-ur-bä'ni-pal. *See* ASHURBANIPAL.

ASSYRIA ə-sir'ē-ə. The upper Tigris region, which took its name from its capital city Asshur (Heb. *'aššûr*, Gen. 10:11). From the first millennium B.C. until its subjugation by Babylonia, its inhabitants (Assyrians) were the major opponents of the kingdoms of Israel and Judah.

I. Geography
II. People
III. History
  A. Sources
  B. Early History
  C. Old Assyrian Period
  D. Middle Assyrian Period
  E. Neo-Assyrian Period
    1. Ashurnasirpal II
    2. Shalmaneser III
    3. Adadnirari III
    4. Tiglath-pileser III
    5. Shalmaneser V
    6. Sargon II
    7. Sennacherib
    8. Esarhaddon
    9. Ashurbanipal
  F. The Fall of Nineveh
IV. Exploration and Excavation
V. Texts
  A. Libraries
  B. Rituals
  C. Letters
  D. Laws
VI. Institutions
  A. King
  B. Government
  C. Military
VII. Economy
VIII. Architecture and Art
IX. Technology

I. Geography.–The fertile heartland of Assyria lay between the Syrian desert, Anatolia, and the Kurdish hills, and was separated from its southern neighbor BABYLONIA by the Hamrin hills. It was well watered by the swift-flowing river Tigris (Heb. *ḥiddeqel*, Gen. 2:14), which flowed E of the first capital Asshur and past the other capitals of NINEVEH and CALAH (Gen. 10:11f.), which is situated near its confluence with the upper Zab.

II. People.–Assyria's mixed population was predominantly Semitic. They had many of the strong characteristics of the hill people who surrounded them. Their language, a dialect related to Babylonian, was written in the cuneiform script following the first use of that script at Uruk (modern Warka; *see* ERECH) by the Babylonians, who thereafter influenced them culturally.

III. History.–*A. Sources.* In addition to archeological evidence, the history can be reconstructed from king lists, royal annals, building inscriptions, and many references in correspondence and other texts. The Assyrians dated by eponym of an official (*limmu*), using his name to mark a year, and by regnal years.

B. Early History. The land seems to have been inhabited from early prehistoric times. Middle Paleolithic finds from Barda-Balka (about 120,000 years ago), the Mousterian culture in the Shanidar Cave, and evidence of the early Neolithic and Chalcolithic from the Barodost caves overlooking the upper Zab continue the history. The Neolithic revolution *ca.* 7000 B.C. can be seen in the agricultural village life of ancient Jarmo. The subsequent prehistoric periods Hassuna-Samarra, Halâf (first known from Assyria), the later Ubaid, Uruk, and Proto-literate (or Early Dynastic but not Jemdet Nasr) similar to those known from the south have been traced at Nineveh, Arpachiyah, Tepe Gawra and the Jebel Sinjar and Kirkûk areas.

The king-list tradition is of early nomads under Ušpia who founded a settlement at Asshur *ca.* 2800 B.C. in the Early Dynastic period. Sargon of Agade (Akkad) (*ca.* 2350 B.C.) built at Nineveh, and his son Maništusu at Asshur. A successor Naram-Sin continued to control the region for the Babylonians. Gen. 10:11f. records the foundation of Asshur, Nineveh, and Calah (modern Nimrûd) by immigrants from Babylonia (*see* NIMROD; attested by archeological discoveries at Nimrûd). Amar-Sin of Ur and his dynasty mastered Assyria until their own city fell and Assyria won its independence during the Puzur-Ashur dynasty.

C. Old Assyrian Period. By 1900 B.C. the individual cities had established caravan links with Cappadocia (Kanish), trading copper for tin. They were also closely associated with the tribes of the west desert. Following a brief domination by Eshnunna (Diyala region), a strong family under its energetic head Šamši-Adad I (*ca.* 1814-1782) controlled even distant Mari through his son Yasmaḫ-Adad. On the latter's death Zimri-Lim of Mari reasserted his authority with the help of the peoples of Yamḫad (Aleppo), Eshnunna, and Babylon. Hammurabi of Babylon warred with Assyria until Mari was taken.

Ashurnasirpal II and protective genius, a human figure with eagle head and wings. The spirit, representing the king's vitality and potency, holds a bucket and cone, symbols associated with the Tree of Life. Gypsum relief from Nimrûd (Trustees of the British Museum)

Assyria broke up into small city-states under the Hurrians (*see* HORITES), though its agricultural prosperity continued, as attested by the documents from NUZI (Yorgan Tepe, near Kirkûk).

D. Middle Assyrian Period (1300-900 B.C.). Aššur-uballiṭ (1365-1330) reunited Assyria under a strong central control. He corresponded with Amenhotep IV of Egypt, much to the objection of Burnaburiaš II of Babylon, who reckoned him a vassal (so Am.Tab.). With the recession of Mitannian power, trade routes to the west were reopened and Arik-dēn-īli (1319-1308) and Adadnirari I (1307-1275) regained land westward to Carchemish which had been lost since the days of Šamši-Adad. Further rapid expansions followed, and Assyria became one of the most powerful states in the ancient Near East.

Shalmaneser I (1274-1245) had to battle to keep his northern and eastern frontiers against recurrent Hurrian attacks. These he thwarted by conquering Ḫanigalbat. A new capital was established at Calah (Nimrûd). His son Tukulti-Ninurta I (1244-1208) was primarily engaged against Babylon, which he overcame; so it was left to Tiglath-pileser I (1115-1077) to settle the dynastic disputes that had meanwhile weakened Assyria. He struck first against the Muški (*see* MESHECH) and Subarian tribes. With these nearer frontiers secure, he was the first Assyrian king to march to the Mediterranean. He received tribute from Byblos (Gebal), Sidon, and Arvad and imposed taxes on the king of Ḫatti (north Syria). He reached Tadmor (Palmyra) in his many campaigns against the emergent Aramean (Aḫlamu) tribes. These Assyrian preoccupations left David and Solomon free to extend their own territory into south Syria. The intruders from the Syrian desert impoverished Assyria under the aged Ashurnasirpal I, the uncle of Tiglath-pileser.

E. Neo-Assyrian Period (900-612 B.C.). *1. Ashurnasirpal II* (885-860 B.C.) followed his father, Tukulti-Ninurta II, in taking strong military action that led to the reestablishment of the empire. His first move was to attack the Arameans in the upper and middle Euphrates Valley. In seven years he stopped their incursions by imposing tribute and taxes on the rulers of Laqe and Ḫindanu, while further north he struck at the people of Na'iri who had been attacking the Assyrian garrison town of Damdusa from their strong base at Kinabu. The whole region of the Kashiari hills (Tušḫan) was incorporated as an Assyrian province. Tribute was taken from Amme-Ba'al, who was, however, soon assassinated by local rebels; so the Assyrian army was dispatched to take revenge (879). Assyrian arms were carried as far as the land of Kummuḫ in the upper Tigris, where tribute was taken from the Muški.

In the east Zamua (modern Sulaimania) was taken over, and the rebels holding the Babite Pass, a key eastern trade route, were ousted. His ability to control the hill peoples enabled Ashurnasirpal to march beyond the rivers Habor (Ḫābûr) and Balîkh to the Euphrates, invade Bīt-Adini (the Beth-Eden of Am. 1:5; 2 K. 19:12; Isa. 37:12; Ezk. 27:23), and take tribute from the defeated ruler Aḫuni. This prepared the way for a major expedition to Syria in 877 to receive tribute from Tyre, Sidon, and Byblos and then march home via the Amanus Mountains, leaving reinforcements with his garrisons on the middle Euphrates and at Tušḫan (upper Tigris).

Much of the booty from these campaigns, as well as prisoner labor force, was devoted to the rebuilding of the capital at Calah about 875 B.C. Here a temple to Ninurta, a royal palace decorated with sculptured reliefs, irrigation works, and botanical and zoological gardens, was constructed. The new population (50,000) and 19,574 guests were entertained for ten days (cf. 1 K. 8:65f.). A statue of this king stands in the British Museum.

2. Shalmaneser III continued his father's policy during a long and active reign (859-824 B.C.). Thirty-one years were spent in campaigning to extend Assyrian rule to Cilicia, Palestine, and the Persian Gulf. His first three campaigns were directed to the capture of Carchemish (857) and the incorporation of Bīt-Adini, whose capital Til-Barsip (Tell el-Aḥmar) was captured in 856 and renamed Kār-Šulmanašaridu ("Shalmaneserburg"). The alarmed Syrian states were ready to oppose his return in force in 853. Irḫuleni of Hamath and Adad-'idri (Hadadezer, possibly the Ben–hadad II of 1 K. 20) massed a coalition of "twelve kings of the sea-coast" with 62,900 infantry, 1,900 cavalry, 3,900 chariots, and 1,000 Arabian fighting camels at Karkara (Qarqar). "Ahab the Israelite" (Akk. *A-ḫa-ab-bu* ^{māt}*Sir-'i-la-a-a*) supplied 10,000 men and 2,000 chariots according to the first reference to Israel in Assyrian annals (See *ANET,* pp. 278f.). The clash was so fierce that the Assyrians did not return for three years (1 K. 16:29; 20:20; 22:1). Neither Hamath nor Damascus was taken, and it was a few years before the Assyrian attacks were resumed; and even then Hadadezer held firm.

When Hadadezer was assassinated (842), Shalmaneser took the opportunity to march against his successor Hazael, "the son of a nobody" (i.e., a usurper), whose army was routed at Mt. Senir (Hermon). While claiming the defeat of Hazael, the Assyrians failed to capture either him or Damascus, where he had taken refuge. They ravaged the surrounding countryside, plundered the rich Hauran plain, and marched to the Mediterranean coast at Carmel (*Ba'li-ra'si*), where tribute was received from Tyre, Sidon, and "Jehu son of Omri" (*Yaua mār Ḫumri*); the event is not recorded in the OT but was perhaps induced by Israel's need of support against Hazael's raids into their territory (2 K. 10:32). If this was Jehu's plan, it was unsuccessful. The submission of the Israelite is depicted on the Black Obelisk (British Museum). JEHU, or his ambassador, is portrayed kneeling before Shalmaneser while porters bring "silver, gold, golden bowls, vases, cups, buckets" and other objects as tribute. After a further attempt to take Damascus in 838 Shalmaneser undertook no further campaign in the west, a sure witness to the growing power of the Syrian city-states.

To the north Shalmaneser had to continue pressure on the Urarṭian kingdom of Van. He had reached Tarsus in Cilicia in 858 and captured the silver and salt mines of Tabal (Tubal). In the east he held Zamua. In Babylonia his contemporary Nabû-apla-iddina (885-852) had repaired the damage caused by Aramean invaders, but dissension following his death led one Marduk-zākir-šumi to call for Assyrian aid. Shalmaneser defeated the rebels, entered Babylon, and made a parity treaty with Marduk-zākir-šumi (shown on the Nimrûd throne bas-relief by their shaking hands), who was now confirmed on the throne.

Shalmaneser moved against the Chaldeans (Kaldu) and took tribute from two of their tribal chiefs (Mušallim-Marduk and Adini), but this was merely a police operation combined with a show of force as far as the Persian Gulf. The end of his reign was saddened by domestic revolution. One son, Aššur-danin-apli, stirred up Asshur, Nineveh, Arbela (Erbil), and Arrapḫa (Kirkûk) so that the aged king was confined to Calah, where he had built a palace and arsenal. For four years another son Šamši-Adad V fought the rebels and then succeeded his father (824/3-811 B.C.).

3. Adadnirari III (810-783 B.C.) took five years to quell the widespread revolt led by nobles, high officials, and some provincial governors who, like Dayan-Aššur, the army commander of Shalmaneser, had accumulated much local power. He had to reassert Assyrian authority also over tribes to the north and east who had meanwhile withheld their taxes. This was the beginning of the internal resistance to the central authority of the king which was to recur and ultimately lead to Assyrian weakness in the following century.

When Šamši-Adad died, his queen Sammu-ramat (in part the legendary Semiramis) took over command as co-regent for five years during the minority of her son Adadnirari. In 806 B.C. the young king undertook an expedition to north Syria, reaching the Mediterranean (Arpad), and another the following year, when he took Hazazu and broke up the powerful coalition developing between Damascus and states as far afield as Malatya. In 804 he struck further southwest to Tyre and Sidon. Joash of Israel, anxious to annul the burdensome treaty imposed on him by Hazael, seems to have taken this opportunity, as had Jehu before him, to obtain Assyrian help. The evidence for this is a royal stele (from Tell ar Rimah, Iraq) in which Adadnirari lists tribute from "Joash of Samaria" (*Yu'asu* ^{māt}*Samerinā*) before that of Tyre and Sidon. When the Assyrian entered Damascus and took spoil from Ben-hadad it is likely that Israel was allowed to strengthen trade relations with that city and recover some lost territory (2 K. 13:25).

Adadnirari received the submission of all the Chaldean chiefs; but his early death led to disturbed conditions, since his eldest son Shalmaneser IV (782-772) seems to have had limited authority, his general Šamši-ilu claiming credit for successes against the Urarṭians. A second son (Aššur-dân III, 771-754) campaigned unsuccessfully in Syria, the event being marked by the ominous sign of a solar eclipse on June 15, 763 B.C. (which serves as a check on Assyrian chronology). At home there was a plague and revolt in the cities of Asshur, Gozan, and Arrapḫa. The third son, Aššur-nirari V (753-746), was probably killed in a palace revolution, and years of ineffectual rule ended when his younger brother Tiglath-pileser mounted the throne.

4. Tiglath-pileser III (745-727 B.C.) took immediate and vigorous action to strengthen the central royal authority by subdividing provinces, thereby giving them the same direct allegiance as the home districts had to the king in person. By reestablishing control over outlying regions he aimed at bringing conquered territories into a close-knit empire. He first marched to the Karûn River, reminding Nabû-naṣir (Nabonassar) of Babylon and the Chaldean chiefs of his superior military power. Sacrifices were offered in their principal shrines. However, the growing might of a new Syro-Urarṭian coalition under Mati'-ilu of Arpad demanded his attention. Sardur III of Urarṭu was defeated at Samosata (Samsat) on the Euphrates, and Arpad was besieged for three years until it was finally incorporated as an Assyrian provincial capital in 741. Tiglath-pileser next campaigned against a south Syrian group whose revolt had been instigated by Azriyau of Yaudi, more likely to be identified with Azariah of Judah than with a king of the same name ruling at Ya'diya (Sam'al, modern Zenjirli). If so, it shows that Judah was strong before Azariah's death (2 K. 15:7). Judeans are named among prisoners settled at Ullabu (near Bitlis). This victory opened the way for Assyrian arms to reach Phoenicia and for north Syria to be counted as the Assyrian province of Unqi and Ḫatarikka (738). During the siege of Arpad, Raṣunu (or Raḫianni, biblical Rezin) of Damascus and Meniḫimme (Menahem) of Samaria brought tribute. The 1,000 Israelite talents were calculated on the number of males of military age at the current Assyrian value of a slave (50 shekels.) This action was sufficient for Tiglath-pileser to confirm Menahem in power (2 K. 15:19f.).

The Assyrian was now free to turn to the east, where a series of expeditions led to the subjugation of the Zamua (Zagros) region as a new province. Some detachments sent against the Medes penetrated as far as the desert of Teheran. An unsuccessful siege of Tušpa, Sardur's capital on Lake Van, implies further intrigues in the north.

In 734 Tiglath-pileser intervened again in Palestine, where Hiram of Tyre was allied with Rezin of Damascus. Tyre, Sidon, and neighboring Maḫalib (Ahlab of Jgs. 1:31) were laid under tribute. The latter, with Kashpuna, was included in a new province of Ṣimirra, and the whole area W of Damascus (Bīt-Ḫazael) to Samaria (Bīt-Humria) including Gilead was overrun. Ḫanunu (Ḫanno) of Gaza fled to Egypt as the Assyrian advanced to Naḫal-muṣur ("Wadi of Egypt"; RSV "Brook of Egypt") and set up a golden image of the king there and in Gaza itself. Idi-bi'li was made local governor to watch the Egyptian frontier. When the king of Ashkelon was killed, his successor with Sanipu of Amman, Quaš(Chemosh)-Malaku of Edom, Salamanu of Moab, and Jehoahaz of Judah (*Yauḫazi* ^{māt}*Yaudaya*) sent tribute. It may have been on this basis that Ahaz appealed for Assyrian aid against Rezin and Pekah of Israel. Despite his acceptance of vassal status (2 K. 16:7), Ahaz received little help and Judah was invaded, Jerusalem itself being besieged (2 K. 16:5f.; 2 Ch. 28:17). Two years later Tiglath-pileser captured Damascus (732), annexed part of Israel (2 K. 15:29), and, according to his annals, set up Hoshea (*Ausi'*) as king there after the removal of Pekah (*Paqaḫa*) by assassination (2 K. 15:30).

Meanwhile in Babylonia disturbances followed the death of Nabû-naṣir (Nabonassar) in 734. An Aramean chief claimed the throne, and the Assyrian tried hard to persuade the Babylonians to rise against him, with promises of tax exemption. When this failed, Tiglath-pileser himself marched to defeat the usurper and lay the tribal lands waste. He took over personal rule in Babylon in 729, participating in the New Year Festival under his native name of Pul(u) (so 2 K. 15:19; 1 Ch. 5:26).

5. Shalmaneser V (727-722). The reign of Tiglath-pileser's son is obscure, since no annals survive. His actions have to be reconstructed from a broken Assyrian eponym list and references in the Babylonian Chronicle. The former states that he besieged Samaria for three years (see also 2 K. 18:9) in reprisal for Hoshea's failure to pay tribute (also 2 K. 17:3-6). The Babylonian Chronicle tells how Shalmaneser "broke [the resistance of] the city of Šamara'in [Samaria]." 2 K. 17:6 does not name the king of Assyria to whom Samaria fell; and though this might be Shalmaneser, it could equally well apply to his successor Sargon, who claimed to be the conqueror of Samaria in his accession year. He may have taken over the army on the premature death of his father, or there may have been joint participation in the siege (so the plural "they took it," 2 K. 18:10). The matter must remain in debate, since Sargon makes no claim to be the conqueror of Samaria in his earlier annals from Asshur, Nineveh, and Calah. It is certain that when the citizens of Samaria refused to pay their tribute, encouraged by Yau-bi'di (Ilu-bi'di) of Hamath, Sargon marched against the city in 722/1 B.C. and claimed 27,270 (or 27,290) prisoners.

6. Sargon II (722-705 B.C.). Sargon had to counter the increasing interference of Egypt in Palestinian affairs and of Elam in Babylonia. Both were the result of Assyrian expansion that had cut them off from trade with their neighbors. Whenever there were dissidents among these peoples they could now turn to these outside powers for help. But first Sargon had to settle disturbances among his own citizens, who had reacted against his father's heavy demands for men and taxes for military service.

In Babylonia Marduk-apla-iddina (*see* MERODACH-BALADAN) took the opportunity of these changes in Assyria to mount the throne in Babylon with the help of Humbanigaš I of Elam. In 720 Sargon's forces clashed with the rebels at Dēr and claimed a victory, though the Babylonian Chronicle marks it as an Elamite and Chaldean success. Marduk-apla-iddina certainly remained in control of the main Babylonian cities for the next ten years.

About this time Yau-bi'di (Ilu-bi'di) of Hamath, the sole remaining independent Syrian prince, attempted to meet the Assyrian in another battle at Qarqar. Despite Egyptian help sponsored by the exile Ḫanunu of Gaza, he was unsuccessful and Hamath was reduced to provincial status. Isaiah saw the lesson to be drawn from this (Isa. 10:5f.). Gaza, aided by an Egyptian, So (perhaps Sib'e, a general, 2 K. 17:4), was involved in this rising. In a battle near Raphia (Rapihu) on the Egyptian border they were defeated, Ḫanunu was captured with 9,053 prisoners, and the Egyptian fled. Eight years later the Egyptian pharaoh (*pi'ru*) — probably Bocchoris — stirred up Ashdod. Once again the Assyrian won and "the rulers of Palestine, Judah, Edom, and Moab brought tribute and gifts for the god Ashur." Though Judah (*Yaudi*) is named, this does not necessarily imply that Sargon entered their territory. Isaiah again interpreted the defeat of Ashdod by the Assyrian (Isa. 20:1-6). Even the Egyptian king (*Šilḫanni*) — either Osorkon III or IV — sent tribute. It was certainly vain for Judah to look to Egypt for help, for that king simply handed over Yamani of Ashdod, who had fled to him for refuge to the Assyrians.

It was probably the Elamites who stirred up the Zagros hill-peoples. In 713 Sargon raided the region of Hamadân and Kermanshah and took booty from the Medes. Further north a revival of Urarṭian intrigue was reported to Sargon by his ever watchful local officials. Ursâ (Rusas I) continually harassed the Assyrian garrisons until in 714 Sargon directed his eighth campaign as a major offensive to capture Muṣaṣir (where Ursâ committed suicide) and defeat the Manneans (the Minni of Jer. 51:27). The expedition is reported in detail both in the Annals and in a letter to the god, which was perhaps read at a victory parade at Asshur. In 717-712 Sargon kept the pressure on Carchemish (now another Assyrian province), Cilicia, and all the neo-Hittite states in the Taurus (Melid, Kummuh, and Tabal) which had been influenced by Ursâ and Mida (Midas) of Phrygia but now turned to him for help against the westward thrust of the Cimmerians (Assyr. *Gimirraya*; Gomer of Ezk. 38:6).

It was now time for Sargon to try to bring Babylonia under his sway. He marched down the eastern bank of the Tigris, forcing the Chaldean tribes to retreat southward. In their wake the cities, tired of ten years of rule under tribesmen, opened their gates and welcomed the deliverers. Sargon, as "vice-regent of Babylon," celebrated the New Year Festival, showing that this act of itself was no mark of kingship. Marduk-apla-iddina's land of Bīt-Yakin was overrun after two years of hard struggle, but on Sargon's withdrawal he was left in charge. Upēri of Dilmun (modern Bahrain) sent Sargon gifts.

Sargon himself lived at Calah until *ca.* 706, when he moved to a new capital Dūr-Šarrukin (Khorsabad) 15 mi. (25 km.) NE of Nineveh, on which he had spent eleven years labor. He did not enjoy it long, for in the next year he was killed at war in Tabal (*see also* SARGON).

7. Sennacherib (705-681 B.C.). While crown-prince, Sennacherib had served his father as a military advisor on the northern frontier. This knowledge served him well, for he was to enjoy calm there and to the east. This enabled him to concentrate on other fields, except for brief displays of strength in Zagros, Cilicia, and Tabal. His work on the restoration of Nineveh was soon interrupted by the need to go to Babylonia, where Marduk-apla-iddina, faithful to Sargon since 710, now made another bid for the kingship. He had the support of the Arameans, Elamites, and Arabs, and had made overtures for support to Hezekiah (Isa. 39; 2 K. 20:12-19). Marduk-apla-iddina, following the disappearance of a little-known Marduk-zākir-šumi II, held the throne with the title "King of Babylon" until defeated with his allies by Sennacherib near Kish in 703 B.C. (J. A. Brinkman, in *Studies Presented to A. L. Oppenheim* [1964], p. 24). Sennacherib plundered Babylon, deported 208,000 prisoners to Nineveh, and set up a young friend Bēl-ibni as ruler. He had to move into the southern marshes to follow up Marduk-apla-iddina, who had reappeared in Bīt-Yakin. The latter was this time driven to flee to Elam. An expedition was mounted with ships built at Nineveh, carried overland from Opis on the Tigris, and manned by Phoenicians. It embarked with troops at Bab-Salimeti; but it was too late, for by then the wily old Chaldean had died in exile (694). The Elamites invaded Babylonia, captured Sippar, and removed the pro-Assyrian Aššur-nadin-šumi from the throne in Babylon. For seven years the struggle continued until the Babylonians, again with Elamite auxiliaries, met the Assyrian army at Ḫalule. Though the Arameans and their allies were defeated, Assyrian casualties were heavy. Angered, Sennacherib laid siege to the Chaldeans within the sacred city of Babylon for nine months before he sacked it. The statue of the god Marduk was carried off to Assyria. Sennacherib took the ancient title "King of Sumer and Akkad" and resistance ceased.

In Palestine also rebellion had broken out. Sennacherib marched in 701 to the Phoenician coast and reimposed control and taxation on Little Sidon, Ṣariptu (Zarephath), Maḫalib (Mahalab, Ahlab), Ušu, and Akku (Acco). Luli of Sidon fled and was replaced by Tuba'lu (Ethba'al, 1 K. 16:31). Tyre was bypassed but the rulers of Arvad, Byblos, Beth-Ammon, Moab, and Edom submitted. Since Ashkelon and the neighboring towns of Beth-Dagon and Joppa resisted, they were sacked. The Assyrian claimed the defeat of the Egyptian army at Eltekeh and the slaughter of the elders of Ekron. At this time they ravaged Judah, taking forty-six towns and villages with 200,150 captives and thus isolating Hezekiah in Jerusalem. The Judean capital may well have been left under blockade while the Assyrians protected their flank against a possible Egyptian capture of Lachish. From there Sennacherib sent to Hezekiah demanding the release of Padi, the pro-Assyrian ruler of Ekron. Hezekiah appears to have paid some tribute (2 K. 18:13-16; Isa. 36:1; 2 Ch. 32:9; Assyrian Taylor prism dated 691 B.C.). Padi was freed and Hezekiah "besieged in his capital city of Jerusalem like a bird in a cage" (Sennacherib prism), though the Assyrians soon raised the siege (cf. 2 K. 19:32-34). The reason given for this is "the angel of the Lord" (v. 35) or, by Herodotus (ii.141), a plague of mice devouring the Assyrian bow-strings and shield-straps, interpreted usually as descriptive of a plague. The Assyrian annals are noticeably silent as to the cause for their withdrawal, which might also have been precipitated by the troubles in Babylonia.

The reference to the approach of Egyptian forces under

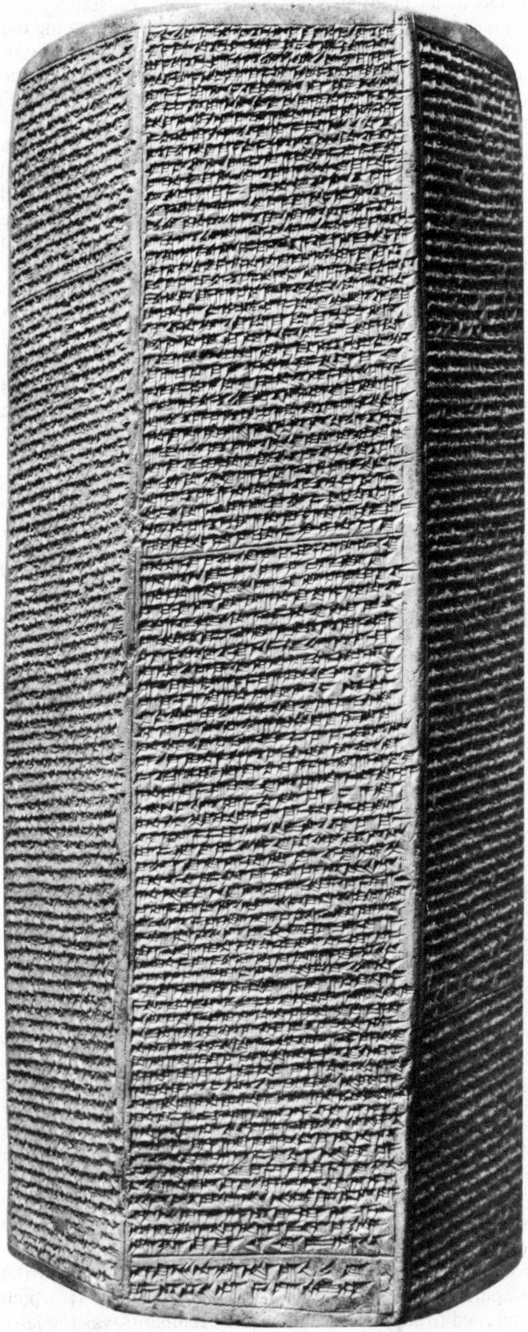

Six-sided clay prism containing the final edition of Sennacherib's annals. Included is an account of the Assyrian siege of Jerusalem and "forty-six of [Hezekiah's] strong cities, walled forts, and countless small villages." (Oriental Institute, University of Chicago)

"Tirhakah [Akk. *Tarqû*] King of Ethiopia" (2 K. 19:9; Isa. 37:9) is considered by many scholars to be an anachronism, since his regnal dates were taken to be *ca.* 690-664 B.C. They thus postulate a second Assyrian campaign in Palestine *ca.* 688 B.C. This is not attested by any extant source and it is preferable to envisage a single campaign in 701. Some Egyptologists assume an earlier co-regency for Tirhakah since there is no certain evidence for his precise regnal years in Cush. The two-campaign theory is sometimes supported by the presumption that Sennacherib's death followed immediately, or soon, after his return from Palestine (2 K. 19:36; Isa. 27:37). The time between the events recorded in 2 K. 19:36 and v. 37 is of unspecified duration.

Sennacherib's death was interpreted by the Babylonians as divine punishment for his action against their capital. The Babylonian Chronicle states that he was murdered by a son, 2 K. 19:36f. by two sons in the temple of Nisroch (Ninurta'). He died on 20th Tebītu (January, 681 B.C.) and was succeeded by his youngest son Esarhaddon.

8. Esarhaddon (681-669 B.C.). Sennacherib's death plunged Assyria into a dynastic crisis. Esarhaddon had earlier taken refuge in Cilicia or Tabal to escape his brothers while they fought for the throne. His supporters called for his return to Nineveh, where he was crowned in 681. He immediately restored Babylon, which his gods had earlier decreed should lie in ruins for 70 years. This involved a reversal of destiny (whereby the Babylonian numeral for 60 + 10 became 10 + 1 years). The work, which was not completed till 669, won over the Babylonians. They repulsed an Elamite attack in 675 and helped Assyria against the son of Marduk-apla-iddina, who attempted to recapture Ur, and against the Bīt-Dakkuri tribe, which siezed land near Babylon. Their chief was replaced by a pro-Assyrian.

The major pressures against Assyria proper came from the nomadic Scythians (Assyr. *Iškuzai*), who drove through Tabal and Cilicia towards Šupria. At first Esarhaddon warred successfully against Teušpa and his hordes, diverting them against the Phrygians. An Assyrian princess may have been given in marriage to the Scythian Bartatua, but by the end of the reign Assyria had lost Ḫilakku (Cilicia) and Tabal and had made little headway in the east, where the Manneans were largely independent despite many punitive raids. Some Medean chiefs were made vassals and the central Zagros and Gambulū tribes quieted to form a buffer between Assyria and Elam, where on the death of Ḫumba-Ḫaldaš II a pro-Assyrian, Urtaki, ascended the throne (675).

Phoenicia was quelled by strong reprisal action against rebels in Sidon. The king Abdi-Milkuti was executed (677), the city sacked, and its land given to Tyre. The border garrison near Egypt at Arzani had been reinforced in 679, and three years later Esarhaddon quelled the Arabs in a series of raids.

In public ceremonies in May, 672, Esarhaddon, mindful of the trouble at his own accession, appointed Aššur-bāni-apli (Ashurbanipal) as crown-prince of Assyria and Šamaš-šum-ukīn, his twin or a brother of equal status by a different mother, as crown-prince of Babylonia. The vassal-rulers present were given an oral and written confirmatory treaty listing the conditions they had to fulfil to maintain this arrangement, on pain of curse for default. As well as the eastern vassals, rulers of Syria and the west whom Esarhaddon names in his annals must have been present. These included Manasseh (*Menasī*) of Judah (cf. 2 Ch. 38:11), Ba'lu of Tyre, Quaš-gabri of Edom, Musuri of Moab, Ṣilli-Bēl of Gaza, Metinti of Ashkelon, Ikausu of Ekron, Pudu-il of Beth-Ammon, Aḫimilki of Ashdod, and the rulers of Cyprus and the Greek islands. A list of payments from Palestine about this time tells of gold sent from Beth-Ammon and Moab, silver from Edom, and "ten minas of silver from the people of Judah."

The way was thus open by the spring of 671 for Esarhaddon's ambitious project: the subjugation of Egypt. Avoiding rebellious Tyre, which was contained by a siege force, the Assyrian army marched via Raphia (S of Gaza) across the Sinai desert to Memphis. Despite the defense by Tarqū (Taharqa), Memphis fell and the Ethiopians were deported, leaving local native princes (among them Neco of Sais) to be appointed as governors, officers, harbor overseers, and other officials under the surveillance of Assyrians.

Tribute and taxes were imposed and some statuary and other Egyptian treasures removed before the army withdrew to Nineveh. Soon Taharqa reappeared, stirred the native princes to declare their independence of Assyria, and retook Memphis. Esarhaddon was on his way to remedy this when he died at Ḫarran in December, 669 B.C., and was succeeded by his sons as planned.

9. Ashurbanipal (669-*ca.* 627 B.C.) had already held responsibility at court and in state building projects as well as in the appointment of governors and prefects. His assumption of the royal powers was vigorous and complete. Before he could take over the punitive expedition against the Egyptian rebels he settled the Tyrian confrontation with a treaty whereby the king became his vassal again, led an expedition into the eastern hills, and installed his brother on the Babylonian throne. In 667 B.C., backed by contingents from the twenty-two vassals in Syria, Phoenicia, Palestine, and Cyprus, the Assyrian marched into Egypt and defeated Taharqa, who again withdrew from Memphis. Egypt was again in Assyrian hands. The twenty native kings, governors, and regents who had left their office under Taharqa's threats were now reinstated. Those who connived with Taharqa in his exile were removed to Nineveh. Yet Ashurbanipal followed his father's policy, choosing among others Neco I of Sais as an important local ruler. Taharqa's successor and son-in-law Ta-net-Amon (Tandamane) made a further bid to retake the Delta in 664. Memphis was retaken by the Assyrians and Thebes was sacked (Nah. 3:8). Psamtik I was appointed to succeed Neco who died in 663. A few years later, with the backing of Greek mercenaries and troops from Lydia, he forced the Assyrian garrisons to withdraw to Ashdod.

These upheavals in Egypt encouraged Ba'lu of Tyre and Yakinlu of Arvad to make bids for independence, but these failed after sieges (665). A campaign against the Manneans and an alliance with Madyes the Scythian helped to relieve the pressure of the Cimmerians on the Assyrian border tribes. Nonetheless, when Gyges of Lydia asked for assistance against these Cimmerians he was refused because of his support for Egypt.

In the south Ashurbanipal fought against Urtaki of Elam, who had invaded Babylonia. Assyria had long had some direct control in that area (e.g., Nippur) and had worked in harmony with Urtaki's brother for sixteen years before the Elamites fomented trouble. Tept-Humban, the Elamite usurper of Urtaki, was killed, and Ashurbanipal supported the claims of Humbanigaš II and Tammaritu, sons of Urtaki who had earlier taken refuge in Nineveh. They were given separate regions to govern within the reconquered Elamite borderlands. Ashurbanipal may have directed this action in part to assist his own brother in Babylon. The citizens of Babylonia sent a deputation professing loyalty, while the Gambulū tribe E of the Tigris was punished for its part in the Elamite troubles.

Šamaš-šum-ukīn seems to have succumbed to the local spirit of nationalism and independence, perhaps interpreting Ashurbanipal's action as weakness. He seems to have plotted with Elam, Egypt, Phoenicia, and Judah, as well as with the local Arab and Chaldaean tribes to move against Assyria. Ashurbanipal appealed for loyalty and only when this was refused began war with Babylonia, a war that was to continue for three years. Elam, divided in its internal politics, was of no assistance, and famine led the Arabs within Babylon to desert. Seeing the hopelessness of further resistance, Šamaš-šum-ukīn committed suicide in the conflagration which swept his palace (648). A Chaldean, Kandalanu, was appointed as vice-regent of Babylon.

Ashurbanipal followed up the fall of Babylon with action against the Arabs, especially the Qedar (Kedar) and Nabatean tribes. The booty taken was so plentiful that the current market price for a camel fell to one silver shekel in Nineveh. War against Elam dragged on until Susa was sacked in 639 B.C., the year in which Ashurbanipal celebrated a triumph in Nineveh. The last years of his life are obscure, due to a lack of direct historical sources after 639 B.C. He may have associated his sons Aššur-etil-ilāni and Sin-šar-iškun as governors and later as co-regents. Under these rulers Assyria lost territory. According to Herodotus, Phraortes the Mede made an attack on the Assyrians. Certainly by 626 B.C. the Chaldean Nabû-apla-usur (Nabopolassar) had won independence for Babylon and was recognised as king there; by 617 the Assyrian garrison had withdrawn. Assyrian affairs in the south seem to have been the responsibility of Sin-šar-iškun, who commanded the army against Babylon. Aššur-etil-ilāni (627-623 B.C.) may have been coregent in Assyria proper, succeeded briefly by Sin-šum-lišir before the last king of Assyria ruling at Nineveh, Sin-šar-iškun, held sole sway (627-612).

F. The Fall of Nineveh. In 616 Assyria began to lose further territory to Nabopolassar, who defeated them at Qablinu and took over the middle Euphrates and raided the Balîkh. A Babylonian raid against Madanu (near Kirkûk) was repulsed. In 615 Asshur was raided and the Medes overran the Arrapḫa province; in the following year they moved against Tarbiṣu in alliance with the Babylonians and against Nineveh. The siege may have been raised by some sort of Scythian intervention. Nabopolassar suppressed a rebellion in the middle Euphrates by the Suḫu tribe but withdrew from 'Anah when the Assyrian army approached. In 614 Asshur fell, and by 612 the Medes and Babylonians marched up the Tigris to Nineveh. They laid siege to the city for the months Simānu-Abu (*ca.* June-Aug., 612), making only slight progress. The final breach seems to have been the result of flooding (Nah. 1:8; Xenophon *Anabasis* iii.4.7-12; Diodorus ii.27.1). Sin-šar-iškun (classical Sardanapalus) threw himself into the flames. Some escaping Assyrians were followed as far as Nisibin by the Babylonians, while Cyaxares (son of Phraortes) and the Medes withdrew with their loot.

The Assyrian supporters under Aššur-uballiṭ II raised the banners of an independent Assyria at Ḫarran. In 609 B.C. the Babylonians and the Umman-manda peoples forced him and his Egyptian allies to withdraw W of the Euphrates. The Egyptian army under Neco II which marched to support these Assyrian remnants was too late. Josiah's fatal intervention at Megiddo marked his own siding with the enemies of Assyria (2 K. 23:29f.). Assyria as a political unit now ceased to exist. From this point on it formed part of the Persian, Seleucid, and Parthian empires. But the name (Pers. *Athura*) continued as a designation of Assyria's former homelands (Ezk. 16:28; 23:5-23).

IV. Exploration and Excavation.–Early travelers reported the site of biblical Nineveh opposite Mosul. C. J. Rich was the first to examine its ruins (Kuyunjik and Nebi Yûnus) in 1820. The Frenchman P. E. Botta excavated there briefly (1842) before working at Dūr-Šarrukin (Khorsabad) 15 mi. (25 km.) NE, thinking the latter to be Nineveh. A. H. Layard worked at both Nineveh and Nimrûd (Calah) 22 mi. (35 km.) S in 1845-1851. His work was continued by H. Rassam (1851-1854), W. K. Loftus 1854/55), British Museum expeditions (1927-1931), and recently the Iraqi Department of Antiquities (1957, 1967-). The British School of Archaeology continued work at Nimrûd (1949-1963), finding a remarkable series of ivories and tablets in the palaces and arsenal. Further work has been done there by the Iraqis and Poles (1967-). Prehistoric sites cleared include Arpachiyah, Hassuna, and Thalthat. The Deutsche Orientgesellschaft excavated Asshur (Qal'ât Sherqâṭ) in 1903-1904. Other sites dug include Imgur-Bēl (Balawat, 1956-1957); Shibaniba (Tell Billa, 1846, 1930-1931), Karanā (Tell ar Rimah, 1964-1971), and Tell Taya (1968-). (*See also* ARCHEOLOGY OF MESOPOTAMIA.)

V. Texts.–A. *Libraries.* Babylonian literature was much used and influential in Assyria. Because of the importance of tradition, kings used to accumulate collections of texts in their palace libraries for use by specialists. In this way Tiglath-pileser I and his successors at Asshur and Sargon II and his family at Calah amassed libraries, part of which were transferred to Nineveh by Ashurbanipal. The latter also sent scribes to Babylon to copy texts not already in his hands. Of the approximately eighteen thousand tablets and fragments (perhaps representing more than five thousand individual works), the majority are reference works used by scribes in divination and related "sciences." Catalogues (especially of myths, epics, tables, and incantations) were kept, and some texts have labels or the royal library colophon added or bear library notes in Aramaic. The whole range of classical Babylonian literature is represented, as well as some texts only known from Assyrian copies ("The Poor Man of Nippur") or versions. The extant texts probably represent only a part of the original collection of tablets, papyri, writing-boards, and other documents.

B. Rituals. Some cultic rituals known only from Assyrian relate to operations requiring the royal person and his purification in a ritual bath (*bīt rimki*) and cleansing (*bīt mesēri*) or sprinkling with water (*sala' me*). The appropriate actions, prayers, and incantations to be recited in each room of the palace are given. The rites for the manufacture, consecration, and induction of divine statues, whose mouths were "opened" to give them existence, are followed by rules for their feeding (*tākultu*) and service. Details of the cult at Asshur imply that the main New Year Festival (*akītu*) differed in time and style from that at Babylon.

C. Letters. Apart from the libraries' literary texts, a large number of letters have survived both from the early Assyrian period of Šamši-Adad I and from the last ruling Sargonid dynasty. Some are royal correspondence or palace edicts, but most are administrative documents which give valuable insights into personal histories. More than three hundred reports from the astrologers advise the king of the implications of astronomical or other omens thought to affect affairs of state. Among these are warnings (e.g., of a solar eclipse) that the royal person was endangered. In this event a substitute king (*šar pūḫi*) was appointed for a hundred days while the king remained in his palace. It is assumed, but by no means certain, that the substitute was then killed.

D. Laws. Surviving fragments of middle Assyrian laws from the 14th-13th cents. are drafted in a form similar to those from Babylon itself (*see* BABYLONIA VII). This may indicate an independent collection of local cases rather than any mere supplementation of general precedents compiled by earlier kings (*see* HAMMURABI). Most legal clauses relate to the rights and duties of women, marriage (including a type of *erēbu*-marriage by which the wife visits her husband's family), levirate marriage (less restricted than the Hebrew), veiling, and widows. Some fragments deal with theft, assault, murder, sexual offenses, slander, trial by ordeal, and witchcraft; others with pledges for debt, the control of corporal and other punishments, and the classification and inheritance of land. A few of the latter correspond directly to certain royal decrees and grants, the legal procedure by which they were effected.

Assyria maintained interstate relations with her neighbors by means of treaties or covenants made with equals (parity) or subordinates (vassal). Part of a parity agreement between Šamši-Adad V (824-815) and Marduk-zākir-šumi I of Babylon survives (cf. that made by his predecessor Shalmaneser; see III.E.2 above). Vassal treaties between Aššur-nirari VI (753-746) and a ruler in north Syria (Mati'-ilu) and between Esarhaddon and Ba'lu king of Tyre can be compared with additional stipulations imposed by Esarhaddon on his existing vassals when he made his son Ashurbanipal crown prince in 672. Manasseh of Judah would have been among those present to reaffirm their trust in Assyria and her gods, declare their loyalty, and promise support under oath and supernatural sanction (including the threat of invasion). Many curses are recorded in these texts, inviting self-judgment in case of rejection of Assyrian physical and spiritual overlordship.

VI. Institutions.–A. *King.* The Assyrian king, like his Babylonian counterpart, acted as representative of man to the gods and was also responsible to the god, as his steward, for the welfare of the land and people. Accordingly he made reports to the national god of the way he had exercised wisdom, ruled, and extended the god's fame (e.g., Sargon II's report to Aššur on his eighth campaign). This was one basis of Assyrian historiography; these reports were often incorporated in inscriptions. In the cult of Aššur the king played a leading role, though probably different from that of the Babylonian king, especially in the New Year Festival. Though not high priest, he was a prime participant in rituals that may have included the royal hunt.

B. Government. The king was served by his palace household under a vizier, majordomo, and chief secretary, supported by specialists in foreign affairs (and languages) and many nobles and courtiers. The army commander (*turtānu*, the Tartan of 2 K. 18:18; Isa. 20:1), chief butler (*see* RABSHAKEH), and other high officials were responsible to the king. Like the city and district governors, among whom they were included, they were required to make an oath of loyalty and report any subversive activities directly to the king. He was usually careful not to alienate these dignitaries upon whom his throne depended. There are relatively few instances of rebellion against the highly developed Assyrian administration.

The royal harem was controlled by the queen ("she of the palace") who, like the queen-mother Sammu-ramat (Semiramis) and Adad-guppi', mother of Nabonidus, was sometimes influential in state affairs. It was governed by strict protocol and guarded by eunuchs.

Assyria annexed territories adjacent to her homeland when this was necessary for defense, security, or safeguarding trade routes. The gradual assimilation of these areas under provincial governors was the basis of the Assyrian empire. Such governors gave their names to the years by turn as eponyms (*limmi*). To prevent power from falling into the hands of any of the twenty-eight provinces formed by Ashurnasirpal II, Tiglath-pileser III subdivided them into smaller areas. Each governor had to collect local taxes and to store supplies for military operations. Syria was so subdivided in 738-734 B.C., and this prepared the way for expansion toward Israel and Egypt.

Beginning with Shalmaneser I (1264-1245 B.C.), Assyrian rulers often deported conquered peoples and resettled their lands with their own or other conquered peoples, a tactic apparently adopted from the 3rd Dynasty of Ur. Such "colonization" was employed most extensively by Tiglath-pileser III, who carried away portions of the Israelite population of Galilee and the Transjordan *ca.* 733 B.C. After the fall of Samaria, Sargon II claims to have deported the inhabitants, and it was he who repopulated the area with the captives of other campaigns.

C. Military. Some kings prided themselves in leading their armies personally, while others left the hard campaigning to their field marshals (*turtānu*). By the time of Sargon II the earlier system of call-up for military or corvée service was replaced by a royal bodyguard and standing army divided into named units. These army groups (twenty thousand) were composed of armies (ten thousand) arranged in units of a hundred, fifty, and ten, with the bulk supplied by the district governors. Chariots, cavalry, pioneers, and sappers were supporting arms (*see* WAR). The Assyrian development of mobile warfare, siege, and psychological warfare (Isa. 36) accounts for their success. It was regularly backed up by a display of arms and organization which helped to maintain control of even the most distant province or source of supplies.

VII. Economy.–The economy was basically agricultural, supplemented by imports of raw materials (iron, copper, silver) along routes dominated by military forces. Local taxes on grain, straw, and herds were imposed, as were other dues; exemption was given rarely by charter. By Neo-Assyrian times such exemptions, as for the city of Asshur, were highly prized. Taxes were supplemented by various dues and tribute (*biltu u mandattu*) imposed on the conquered territories. After an initial heavy exaction (as in 2 K. 18:14-16), annual dues were set which were usually payable in local produce or currency. Other payments included war indemnity (as tax instead of slave service; e.g., 2 K. 15:20) and gifts on appearing before a suzerain. Such income played a large part in the economy of the first millennium B.C.

Slaves played only a small part in the economy, being mainly in private hands and able to work for their release. Prisoners of war were employed on large-scale public works such as the construction of Calah (about fifty thousand were employed there in 879-865 B.C.). With the declining power of the central authority after 632 B.C., and rebellions in the outer empire which could not be controlled, most external sources of income dried up and the Assyrian economy failed quickly.

VIII. Architecture and Art.–Most attention was paid to the embellishment of the capital cities of Asshur, Nineveh, and Calah, where successive kings repaired and rebuilt the citadels in which were located the royal palaces, administrative buildings, public squares, and principal temples. The massive defense walls of the citadel were extended to include the town proper and an "arsenal," or military barrack and store area (*ekal māšarti*). Some new foundations were attempted at Kār-Tukulti-Ninurta and Dūr-Šarrukin (Khorsabad, by Sargon II), but these did not outlive their founders. The basic forms were similar to the Babylonian, but the proximity of abundant stone and wood led to increasing use of these materials, and some innovations. The royal palaces, some temples, and

The God Aššur with outstretched wings and drawn bow, encircled by an aura of flames, amidst rain clouds. Fragment of brick with colored glaze, from Asshur (reign of Tikulti-Ninurta II, 890-884 B.C.) (Trustees of the British Museum)

facades were lined with stone orthostats or panels, which formed an integral part of the architectural design and construction. These stone slabs were carved in bas-relief depicting war and victory, the royal hunt, religious acts by priests or demons, or symbolic "sacred trees" or griffins. The style changed from the early open drawings to crowded attempts at perspective and detail (e.g., Sennacherib at Lachish). The doorways were built around large protective colossi or figures either in the round or in semi-relief. Sculptured stelae, obelisks, and columns were set up in public places and temples, where also stood statues of gods and kings made of decorated metal, stone, or wood.

Though the temples were made of mud brick, they were often elaborately furnished. At Asshur the ziggurat (temple tower) was a twin construction; here and elsewhere access was directly from the court, from a roof, or by ramps. Some early temples (Rimah) had facades of mud brick shaped like palm trunks or other patterns. Roofs, domes, or vaulting made of large tree trunks were often gilded or painted. Some buildings were of the open portico style (*bīt ḫilāni*) adopted from Syria. Glazed panels or orthostats are also found, some of which were used as decorated walls or friezes above the stone sculptures, or as roof tiles.

In the applied arts the best furniture was of elaborate ivory or wood with gold overlaid, or of wood with bronze fittings. Thrones, couches, stools, screens, and smaller objects have been found in abundance. Doors were overlaid similarly or with sculptured bronze (Balawat). As depicted in the reliefs and paintings, doorsills were sometimes carved with intricate patterns similar to those used on carpets and embroidered garments.

As in Babylonia, stone or frit cylinder seals were carved with scenes in a local style reminiscent of the larger art forms. Sometimes they used the flowing style of outline figures made with a few carving strokes or the marks of a drill.

IX. Technology.–Assyria paralleled Babylonia in its development and applications of the wheel, glass-making, dyeing, refining, and other tools and crafts. Mathematics, medicine, tanning, and chemical technology played a large part in daily life. Military necessity led to experimentation in the development of weaponry, chariotry, siege engines, road-building, and other arts. Royal botanical and zoological gardens constructed at the capital cities housed

Colossal winged bull, a protective genius that guarded the doorway of Ashurnasirpal's palace at Nimrûd. Five legs are shown so the figure might be viewed from the front and side. (Trustees of the British Museum)

plants and animals collected during campaigns. These gardens and the cities they served were watered by elaborate irrigation systems. Sennacherib constructed barrage and dam control of the rivers (Bavian, Jerwan, and Ageila) and an underground system (*qana'at*), as well as water-hoists (*šaduf*), for these purposes. He introduced cotton plants ("wool-bearing trees") and new techniques of casting bronze. Earlier irrigation systems had brought water to Calah from the river Zab by tunnel and open canal (Negub).

See Map X.

Bibliography.–E. Forrer, *Die Provinzeinteilung des Assyrischen Reiches* (1921); B. Meissner, *Babylonien und Assyrien* (1925); R. C. Thompson, *Dictionary of Assyrian Chemistry and Geology* (1936); *Dictionary of Assyrian Botany* (1949); H. Frankfort, *Art and Architecture of the Ancient Orient* (1954); D. J. Wiseman, *Vassal-Treaties of Esarhaddon* (1959); H. W. F. Saggs, *The Greatness that was Babylon* (1962); P. Garelli, *Les Assyriens en Cappadoce* (1963); A. L. Oppenheim, *Ancient Mesopotamia* (1964); G. Cardascia, *Les lois assyriennes* (1969); G. Van Driel, *The Cult of Assur* (1969); S. Parpola, *Letters from Assyrian Scholars* (1970); E. Ebeling, *et al.*, eds., *Reallexikon der Assyriologie*, I-IV (1932-1975); D. J. Wiseman, ed., *Peoples of OT Times* (1973); *CAH*; *ANET*.

D. J. WISEMAN

ASSYRIA AND BABYLONIA, RELIGION OF. *See* RELIGIONS OF THE BIBLICAL WORLD: ASSYRIA AND BABYLONIA.

ASSYRIANS ə-sir'ē-ənz [Heb. *'aššûr*]. The people of Assyria. In Hebrew the name of the people is the same as that of the country. *See* ASSYRIA.

ASTAA as-tā'ə (1 Esd. 5:13, NEB). *See* AZGAD.

ASTAROTH as'tə-roth. *See* ASHTAROTH.

ASTARTE as-tär'tē; **ASTORETH**. *See* ASHTORETH.

ASTATH as'tath (1 Esd. 8:38, AV, NEB). *See* AZGAD.

ASTONISHMENT [Heb. *šammâ*] (2 Ch. 29:8); NEB HORROR; [Gk. *ékstasis*] (Mk. 16:8); AV AMAZED; NEB "beside themselves with terror"; **ASTONISHING THINGS** [Heb. niphal pl. part. *pālā'*] (Dnl. 11:36); AV MARVELLOUS THINGS; NEB MONSTROUS BLASPHEMIES; **ASTONISHED** [Heb. *šāmēm*] (Lev. 26:32); NEB APPALLED; [Aram. *tᵉwah*] (Dnl. 3:24); AV ASTONIED; NEB AMAZED; [Gk. *ekpléssomai*] (Mt. 7:28; 13:54; Mk. 6:2; 10:26; Lk. 2:48; 9:43; Acts 13:12; etc.); AV also AMAZED; NEB also "struck with awe," ASTOUNDED, "in amazement," etc.; [*thámbos*] (Lk. 5:9); NEB AMAZED; [*thaumázō*] (Lk. 11:38; Gal. 1:6); AV MARVEL; NEB also "notice with surprise"; **ASTOUNDED** [Heb. *tāmah*] (Job 26:11; Ps. 48:5; Jer. 4:9; Hab. 1:5); AV also MARVEL(LOUSLY); NEB also AGHAST, DUMBFOUNDED, "struck with amazement"; [Gk. *exístamai*] (Mk. 6:51); AV AMAZED; NEB DUMBFOUNDED; [*ékthambos*] (Acts 3:11); AV GREATLY WONDERING.

Of the three Hebrew roots in question here, *tāmah* is the nearest equivalent to our Eng. "astonish, astound" (its Aramaic cognate, *tᵉwah,* connotes more precisely "startle, alarm"); *šāmēm* has about it the aura of "horror, desolation," while *pālā'* means basically "be extraordinary, miraculous." Of the Greek words noted, the *exístamai*/*ékstasis* complex is perhaps the most intriguing, having as its basic meaning "change of place, displacement," from which derives the idea of "being driven out of one's senses, being beside oneself" (cf. "ecstasy"), and finally "astonishment" of the sort that "boggles the mind."

Where the concept of "astonishment" is found in the OT, the nuance of "dread" is usually not far away; and when God is its object, one finds himself in the presence of the *mysterium tremendum* as it is called by Rudolf Otto in *The Idea of the Holy* (2nd ed. 1958). While the same emphasis is continued in the NT, a more positive element becomes prominent as well; one is not so much "struck by awe" as he is, in the words of C. S. Lewis, "surprised by joy." For the believer in Christ, the ultimate astonishment of all will be experienced when he casts his crown before Him and finds himself "lost in wonder, love and praise" (Charles Wesley).

R. F. YOUNGBLOOD

ASTROLOGY [< Gk. *ástron*–'star' + *lógos*–'meaning']. The study of the professed effect of heavenly bodies on human personality and affairs.

I. Introduction
II. Origins
III. Development
IV. In the OT
V. In the NT

A. In General
B. The Star in the East

I. Introduction.–Both astronomy and astrology are concerned with the heavenly bodies. Astronomy classifies the laws (Gk. *nómos)* of their movement and nature, while astrology looks for intelligible meaning in their relationship to people and things on earth.

Of the many methods of attempting to discover the future by technical methods, astrology has been the most persistent among civilized peoples, although it is matched by the consultation of clairvoyants and mediums who claim to be able to foresee the future. *See* DIVINATION; MAGIC.

Modern astrology is based on exact mathematics. If a person supplied the precise data of the time and place of his birth to any number of trained astrologers, each would produce a basically identical horoscope, showing the position of the sun, moon, and planets in relation to the birth of the person in question. The astrologer does not observe the heavens himself, but uses detailed technical tables, which he adjusts according to the latitude and longitude of the place of birth. Indeed, actual observation would be misleading, since the signs of the zodiac (which is divided into twelve equal segments for the placing of the sun, moon, and planets) have gradually changed their position down through the ages.

Although each astrologer would produce the same basic horoscope, the interpretations might differ. The astrologer holds that the position of the planets in the zodiac, and their angles to each other, both at the moment of birth and from day to day, indicate the helpful or hampering influences in the individual's life. Here there is obviously room for a variety of interpretations. Astrologers are divided over whether the planets actually exert an influence or whether they are merely indicators of how a person of a particular temperament is likely to fare.

II. Origins.–It is difficult to draw a line between primitive observation of the heavens and early theories of a connection between the heavenly bodies and earthly events. A people soon learns to associate the apparent movement of the sun, the phases of the moon, and the position of certain stars, with a simple calendar system for the agricultural year. Thus, not long after 3000 B.C. the Egyptians noted the rising at dawn of the bright star Sothis, or Sirius, and regarded this as the beginning of their year.

Unexpected events, such as eclipses, comets, and meteors, would be dreaded as portents, and some contemporary event could easily be connected with their appearance. The other exceptions to the ordinary movement of the stars are the planets, which change their relative positions in the sky, and must have caused much speculation among the early observers. We have Babylonian records of the rising and setting of the bright planet Venus from the 17th cent. B.C. Names were naturally given to individual stars and groups of stars, and particular attention was paid to those that were associated with the changing position of the sun during the year; these make up the zodiac.

III. Development.–At some time before the 7th cent. B.C. the wise men in Mesopotamia thought they had found correspondence between things in heaven and things on earth. Astrological documents are found in the time of Ashurbanipal king of Assyria (668-633 B.C.). Thus a priest writes to him: "The planet Venus is approaching the constellation Virgo. The appearance of the planet Mercury is near. Great wrath will come" (MacNeice, p. 110). Egyptian astrology does not appear until after this date.

Astrological predictions at this time were concerned with the destiny of the nation, or of the king as head of the nation. The heavens, as well as sacrificial omens, pointed to lucky and unlucky times for undertaking projects. After the fall of Babylon the art of astrology was spread by traveling Chaldeans, and *ca.* 280 B.C. Berossus, a Babylonian priest, is said to have set up a school for astrologers on the island of Cos. Greeks and Romans adopted astrology almost as a substitute religion, and from this time onward astrologers offered horoscopes for individuals. Cicero attacked it in *De divinatione* (*ca.* 43 B.C.), but he was fighting a losing battle. It became rife in Egypt, and in the 2nd cent. A.D. Ptolemy of Alexandria wrote the fullest book yet produced on the subject.

The early Church opposed astrology, although occasional writings, such as the *Clementine Recognitions* (early 3rd cent..), supported it. Augustine, who had formerly believed in it, attacked it repeatedly in *The City of God.* In the 2nd cent. B.C. the Jewish work known as the Sibylline Oracles (3:227) praised the Jewish nation because it did not "study the predictions of Chaldaean astrology"; yet after the time of Christ and in the Middle Ages many Jews became powerful exponents of astrology, coupling it with a belief in angels and demons as lords of the planets who regulated the destinies of mankind.

IV. In the OT.–One must distinguish between references to stars and constellations (*see* ASTRONOMY) and references to astrology. Thus, it is possible to see a link between the blessings of Jacob's sons in Gen. 49 and certain stars and constellations; but this would have been for purposes of memory, since there is no hint here of the influence of the stars.

The following references should be noted:

In Gen. 1:14 the purpose of the heavenly bodies as *signs* is indicated by the context as referring to the calendar of the year. Comparisons are naturally made between this verse and the lines in the Babylonian Creation Epic

Jewish zodiac, intended as a liturgical calendar, with the twelve zodiacal signs indicating months. At the center are the sun-god and chariot against a starry sky (representing day and night); the corner figures are the four seasons. Floor mosaic from Beth-alpha synagogue (6th cent. A.D.) (Consulate General of Israel in New York)

(*Enuma Elish*). There are variant translations of words and phrases in Marduk's creation of the stars and planets, and it cannot be proved that the lines are astrological rather than astronomical, in the sense that Marduk appoints the stars to be a reliable guide for the farmer and calendar-fixer. E. A. Speiser in *ANET* translates: "He constructed stations for the great gods, fixing their astral likenesses as constellations. He determined the year by designating the zones: He set up three constellations for each of the twelve months. After defining the days of the year by means of (heavenly) figures, He founded the station of Nebiru (probably Jupiter) to determine their (heavenly) bands, that none might transgress or fall short." The date of extant copies of this epic is after 1000 B.C., but scholars date the original early in the 2nd millennium; however, astrological references, if the above lines are astrological, could conceivably have been worked in later.

In Dt. 4:19 Israel is forbidden to worship the heavenly bodies, which God created for the benefit of all nations; but such worship is not at this stage astrology. Astrologers are not specifically included among the diviners and the like who are denounced in the law (e.g., Dt. 18:9-14).

The stars in their courses are said by Deborah (Jgs. 5:20) to have fought against Sisera. In the context the reference is to the flooded river, and the stars are in their springtime position associated with the melting of the snows or with sudden heavy storms; thus poetically they are responsible for incapacitating the Canaanite chariots.

Amos (5:26) refers to the northern kingdom's worship of Sakkuth and Kaiwan, which are generally regarded as Assyrian names for the planet Saturn. Similarly, Jeremiah has several references to the worship of the QUEEN OF HEAVEN, who is Ishtar, the planet Venus (e.g., 7:18; 44:17-19), and to the worship of the heavenly bodies (8:2; 19:13). By this time also, as we have seen, astrologers in Mesopotamia found portents in the sky; and Jer. 10:2 tells the Jews not to be dismayed, as the nations are, at the signs of the heavens.

Jeremiah 31:35, like Isa. 40:26, speaks of God as the Creator and Ruler of the sun, moon, and stars, thus indicating that the people of God must neither worship nor fear them.

Isaiah 47:13 is the first passage to refer specifically to astrologers as those who divide out the heavens into what later became known as *houses,* who observe the movements of the stars, and who at each new moon make predictions for the fortunes of Babylon. Isaiah declares that they have no power even to save themselves.

The book of Daniel contains several likely references to astrologers along with enchanters and magicians (e.g., 2:27; 4:7; 5:7, 11). The RSV is probably correct in translating Aram. *gāzᵉrîn* (lit. "dividers, determiners") as "astrologers." In these passages and elsewhere in Daniel the technical use of the name "Chaldeans" occurs. From the 10th cent. B.C. the area around Babylon appears in inscriptions as the land of Kaldu, though the Hebrew equivalent of Chaldeans is always *kaśdîm,* with the Aram. *kaśdāy'ē*. After the collapse of the Babylonian empire the term gradually came to mean wise men of Babylonian descent who practiced astrology. In Daniel's day it would still have had the racial sense, and would have included all Babylonians, as indeed it does in Dnl. 1:4; 5:30; 9:1. Thus some scholars regard the technical use in Daniel as a mark of the late date of the book. However, Daniel himself may originally have written *galdu,* which on Babylonian inscriptions appears to mean "astrologers." A later copyist, not knowing the word *galdu,* associated it with *kaldu,* and rendered it by the word for Chaldean, which in his day had come to mean "astrologer." The alteration may have occurred when 2:4b–7:28 was translated into Aramaic (*see* DANIEL, BOOK OF), since the technical occurrences are in the Aramaic section (apart from 2:2, 4, which would then naturally have been changed to match the Aramaic).

It might be argued that Daniel's appointment as head of the wise men (2:48; 5:11) suggests compromise with astrology, but this would not be a fair interpretation in the light of the failure of astrology and other forms of magical wisdom to interpret the king's dream in Dnl. 2. Daniel declares publicly that God alone is the source of true revelation and interpretation (2:27f.; 5:14-16).

The term "host(s) of heaven" is used both of the heavenly bodies (e.g., Dt. 4:19; Isa. 40:26; Jer. 8:2) and of the angels (1 K. 22:19; Ps. 103:21). The angels are given the title "morning stars" in Job 38:7, as the parallelism shows; and the king of Babylon is compared in Isa. 14:12 to a "Day Star, son of Dawn," who fell from heaven; this Star is commonly identified with Satan, the fallen angel. The probability is that, just as "heaven" is used both of the natural sky and of the sphere where God rules absolutely, so the term "hosts of heaven" is used both of the multitude of stars in the natural sky and of the multitude of bright angels round the throne of God. But Jewish astrologers took the further step, which the Bible does not take, and identified individual stars and planets with individual angels, fallen or unfallen, or with their spheres of influence.

Wisdom 13:1-4 makes reference to foolish men who regard fire, wind, air, the circle of the stars, the violent water, or the lights of heaven, as the gods that govern the world. The whole passage resembles the argument of Rom. 1:19-23.

V. In the NT.–*A. In General.* Possible general references to astrology in the NT are capable of several interpretations, but none is favorable to it.

The books of magic that Christian converts burned at Ephesus may have included astrological writings (Acts 19:19).

Gal. 4:3 and Col. 2:20 speak of Christian deliverance from *tá stoicheía toú kósmou,* variously translated as "the rudiments of the world," or "the elemental spirits of the universe." These could be the influences of the planets with their governing principalities and powers (Col. 2:15). *See* ELEMENT. One may accept the fact of fallen angelic principalities and powers, as in Eph. 6:12, without linking them with the planets or stars.

Some commentators regard the words "height" (Gk. *báthos*) and "depth" (*hypsṓma*) in Rom. 8:39 as astrological. They are more likely to be astronomical, denoting the expanse of the sky above and the sphere below the horizon from which the heavenly bodies rise. If Paul had intended "height" to denote the sign in which a planet is said to be exalted, which is the astrological use of the Greek word, he would almost certainly have matched it with the usual astrological opposite, Gk. *tapeínōma* (lit. "abasement"), although admittedly there is a single use quoted of *báthos* in this sense in a second-century astronomical writer (Vettius Valens 241.26).

B. The Star in the East. Matthew relates that after the birth of Jesus wise men came from the East to find Him, since they had seen His star (2:1f.). The Greek term for the men is *mágoi,* or "Magi," from which our word "magic" comes. The verb and noun are used of magicians in Acts 8:9; 13:6, 8. Herodotus says that the Magi were priests of the race of the Medes. It is likely that they were astrologers. It may seem strange that these Medians should have known of the Jewish Messiah, but the Jews had spread through the former Persian empire and many would have spoken of the promise found throughout the OT. Daniel the Jew had also gained a reputation as a wise man under the Babylonian and Persian empires. Thus wise men of the East would have been aware of the belief that a great Ruler was to be born among the Jews.

As to the nature of the star, some have supposed that a special constellation was regarded as the sign of Judah, and that some phenomenon appeared there. All the Magi say is that they had seen the Messiah's star "in the East." If this is the correct translation, it means that while they were still east of Palestine they had seen the star. But many translate, "We have seen his star in its rising." This would mean that they noticed this star as it rose one night and were attracted by it, either because of its position in a certain constellation or because of its own appearance.

It may have been a comet. Halley's comet appeared in 11 B.C., which is rather too early; and there are records of another comet *ca.* 4 B.C. This need not be too late if, as is commonly believed nowadays, Jesus was born *ca.* 6 B.C., since Jesus may have been up to two years old when the Magi came (Mt. 2:16), and the Magi could have observed the comet at its earliest appearance. Or there may have been yet another comet of which we have no record.

The star may have been a nova, which is an explosive flare-up of a star, lasting for several weeks or months before dying away.

It has also been suggested that the Magi observed a conjunction of Jupiter, Mars, and Saturn in Pisces, which has been calculated as taking place in 7 B.C. and recurring in 6 B.C. The difficulty here is that the Magi refer to a single star, although one of these planets by itself could have been associated with Judah or the Messiah, so that the Magi were impressed by its proximity to the other two.

No difficulty need be felt about the statement that the star went before the Magi and came to rest over the house where Jesus was (Mt. 2:9). As they traveled from Jerusalem to Bethlehem the star was ahead of them to the south. As they came near to Bethlehem the star was low enough in the sky to appear to touch down over the roof of the house they were seeking. Wordsworth uses similar language in one of his Lucy poems, when he rides toward Lucy's house and watches the moon descending toward it and finally dropping behind its roof.

Although the Magi were astrologers, the story does not encourage astrology in general, any more than the appearances of Moses at the Transfiguration supports the practice of spiritualism. There will be signs in the heavens before the Second Coming (Lk. 21:25); the sun was darkened before Christ died on the cross; and Josephus says that a comet was seen for a whole year before the destruction of Jerusalem (*BJ* vi.5.3). Thus we need not be surprised if some phenomenon such as a comet appeared at the time of Christ's birth. (*See also* CHRONOLOGY OF THE NT I.A.3.)

Bibliography.–*Catholic Encyclopedia* (15 vols., 1907-1914); *Colliers Encyclopedia*; *Jew.Enc.*; L. MacNeice, *Astrology* (1964); R. Campbell Thompson, *Reports of the Magicians and Astrologers of Nineveh and Babylon* (1897). J. S. WRIGHT

ASTRONOMY. The science dealing with the celestial bodies and their motions, origins, evolution, and composition. In a biblical encyclopedia the discussion of astronomy is properly limited to the material mentioned in the Bible and such additional data as may be useful in understanding or interpreting biblical statements.

I. Historical Background
   A. Development of Astronomy
   B. Astronomy in the Ancient Near East
II. Astronomical Elements in the Bible
   A. Biblical Attitude toward Astronomy
   B. Sun, Moon, and Planets
   C. Stars and Constellations
   D. Astronomical Miracles in the Bible

I. Historical Background.–*A. Development of Astronomy.* Astronomy, the oldest of all the sciences, has existed since the beginning of recorded civilization. Its development can be divided into three major periods: (1) the astronomy of the ancients, until the time of Ptolemy of Alexandria, 2nd cent. A.D.; (2) medieval astronomy; (3) modern astronomy, from the time of Copernicus (1473-1543). In this article we are concerned only with the first period.

Western astronomy began with the peoples of the Fertile Crescent, particularly with the peoples in Babylonia. These early astronomers were acute observers and were aware of many celestial phenomena. Their interest in the heavenly bodies arose alongside the concept that the sun, moon, and stars were deities, and they developed the belief that the movements of the astral bodies could reveal the intentions of the deities. At an unknown date the ancients learned that the heavenly bodies were useful as guides to travelers, first in crossing deserts with few landmarks, and later in navigating the seas.

The ancients also came to use celestial bodies, especially the sun and moon, for calendration. The phases of the moon led to the development of the "month," while the cycle of seasons led to the concept of the "year." The period between new moons is 29½ days; hence the months were alternately 29 and 30 days in early Babylonian calendration. Twelve lunar months add up to only 354 days, which was a "lunar year." This was satisfactory for nomads, who had no reason to prepare the ground for planting, but it was not sufficiently accurate for agricultural purposes. Hence, intercalation was necessary. Seven times in nineteen years an extra month was added to bring the lunar year into phase with the seasons. In ancient Babylonia this was done by royal or priestly decrees every second or third year as necessary. The ancient Egyptian calendar consisted of 12 months of 30 days, plus 5 extra year-end days. It therefore fell one-fourth day short of a true solar year; hence, like the lunar calendar it moved out of phase with the seasons, but at a much slower pace.

As the earth rotates upon its axis, it also revolves about the sun. A "day," by definition, is the period between the moment when the sun is directly overhead and the next moment when that occurs. (In practice, we may mark the day from sunset to sunset or from midnight to midnight, but the period is the same.) But, because of its revolution about the sun, the earth actually rotates on its axis one extra time each year. In other words, it rotates about 361° in 24 hours. The position of the stars, however, is independent of the relationship between our planet and our sun. The period of time between the moment when a certain star — let us say Sirius — is overhead and the next moment it is directly overhead, is 3 minutes and 56.55 seconds less than our twenty-four-hour day. The stars that are overhead at midnight on the spring equinox will have advanced 90° by the summer solstice, and will be setting at midnight.

Early in the history of astronomy, men observed that the stars remained in relatively fixed positions and that the sun, moon, and planets moved with respect to the stars. They called the path that these "moving stars" took the "ecliptic" or "zodiac," and they were aware that the sun followed this path as the year progressed. Precession of the vernal equinox was also observed by the ancients.

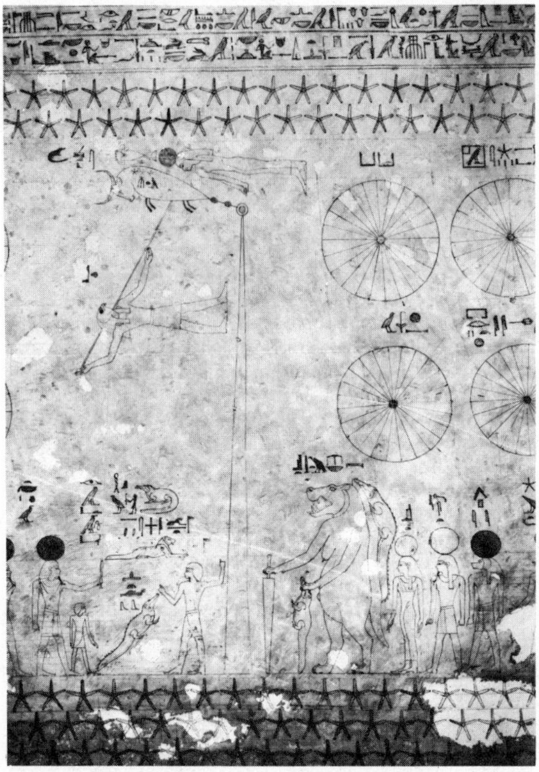

Mural from tomb of Hatshepsut's vizier Senmut (18th Dynasty, *ca.* 1500 B.C.) at Deir el-Bahri, with lists of decans (circles, divided into twenty-four hours) and a procession of the celestial bodies of the northern sky. Artistic principles rather than astronomical accuracy determined the arrangement. (Metropolitan Museum of Art)

Early astronomical records have proved helpful in establishing the chronologies of ancient civilizations. Babylonian records of solar eclipses are important in establishing fixed points in Babylonian chronology. Similarly, Egyptian records that reconcile the Sothic cycle with the civil (or solar) year are significant in establishing Egyptian chronology. If the star Sothis (Sirius) is just rising as the sun rises, it will be invisible, since it is beyond the sun. But since it rises approximately 4 minutes earlier each day, after about 11 days it will be just faintly visible about 42 minutes before sunrise. This is the "heliacal rising." The ancient Egyptian astronomers marked "the going up of Sothis," for it foretold the flooding of the Nile, and the farmers knew when to prepare the fields for the inundation. Because the Egyptian civil calendar lost one-fourth day each year, there were 1460 years between the times when the civil year coincided with the going up of Sothis. This period came to be known as a "Sothic cycle." Egyptian kings sometimes marked the number of days and months that the civil calendar deviated from the Sothic calendar, which gives us a basis for Egyptian chronology. The Sothic cycle, however, because of irregularities in the earth's movements, is not so mathematically precise that we can make exact synchronizations. Moreover, the observation of the heliacal rising may be obscured by haze — and a difference of a day in observation amounts to a difference of four years in chronology.

Because all observations were earth-centered, ancient descriptions of astronomical phenomena naturally assumed a geocentric universe. Certain Greek scientists, prior to the time when inductive observation was subjugated to the systems of the philosophers, seem to have come to the conclusion that the earth moved about the sun (e.g., Aristarchus of Samos, 3rd cent. B.C.). Strabo records that scholars had observed that, on the summer solstice, a man's shadow was exactly under him at noon in Syene (Aswan, Egypt), which is located on the Tropic of Cancer. Eratosthenes (*ca.* 276-*ca.* 194 B.C.) had even calculated the circumference of the earth to be 252,000 stadia (Strabo *Geog.* ii.5.7), which, according to one estimate of the stadium, comes within 50 mi. (80 km.) of the present estimate of the earth's size. In the 2nd cent. A.D. Ptolemy, using ancient observations, devised a mathematical explanation of celestial movements, published in his *Almagest*. In his system the earth was the center of the universe, and the sun, moon, stars, and planets revolved around it. Because this theory predicted the motions of the sun, moon, and planets with reasonable accuracy, it was used throughout the Middle Ages.

Few advances were made during the medieval period of astronomy. Medieval science was unlike modern science, and was heavily influenced by religious and philosophical considerations. Ptolemy's theory was studied and revised, and by the late Middle Ages was discovered to be woefully inadequate in predicting the actual positions of the celestial bodies.

The modern period of astronomy began in 1543 with the theory of Copernicus, who suggested that many of the inadequacies of Ptolemy's theory would be solved by placing the sun, rather than the earth, at the center of the universe. This theory, which at first came under much attack, was supported by the careful naked-eye observations of Tycho Brahe and the telescopic observations of Galileo. In 1609 and 1619, using the observations of Tycho Brahe, Johannes Kepler published his three laws of planetary motions. After this, the heliocentric system, although still the object of official disapproval, was gradually accepted as scientifically sound. In the late 17th cent. Isaac Newton refined and generalized Kepler's laws and produced his famous laws of motion. These laws still provide the basis of modern celestial mechanics. In the 20th cent. the theory of relativity and new, specialized branches of astronomy have affected the character of astronomy. Now it is often concerned with the origin, evolution, and composition of celestial bodies as well as their motions.

B. Astronomy in the Ancient Near East. The period in the history of astronomy most relevant to study of the Bible is the period from *ca.* 2000 B.C. to A.D. 150. In the ancient Near East, where western astronomy began, the two major centers of civilization were Egypt and Mesopotamia. Hebrew astronomy was almost certainly influenced by the astronomical observations of these areas.

Egyptian astronomy was crude; this was partially because of the deficient nature of Egyptian arithmetic. The Egyptians did, however, make some notable contributions to astronomy. The first of these was their calendar. It is often thought that their calendar was agricultural, rather than astronomical, in origin. But since the Egyptians never attempted to bring their 365-day calendar into phase with the solar year, it is now considered unlikely that the origin was agricultural.

The Egyptians also devised the idea of dividing the day and night into 24 hours (the Sumerians had used a system of "double-hours"), with 12 hours of daylight varying in length according to the season of the year. In Hellenistic times, hours of equal length, divided into 60 minutes, were introduced. The Egyptians also developed a "star-clock" in which the rising of a certain star marked the last hour of the night. There were thirty-six of these stars or "decans," and every 10 days a different decan marked the last hour of the night. Astrological texts, the idea of the zodiac, and numerical predictions of astronomical phenomena appeared only under Ptolemy. Until the Hellenistic period, the achievements of Egyptian astronomy were few and had little influence on the rest of the ancient world.

Mesopotamian astronomy, on the other hand, was the most sophisticated of the ancient astronomies and greatly influenced surrounding civilizations. It has been commonly believed that Babylonian astronomy was guided by mysticism and magic, and not by scientific considerations. The worship of the sun, moon, stars, Venus, and Saturn was part of the religion of Babylon, and provided much motivation for the study of astronomy; but this astrological religion should not be allowed to obscure the achievements of Babylonian astronomy.

Astronomical references first occur during the Kassite period (*ca.* 1650-1175 B.C.), and tablets recording observations of Venus have been important in determining the chronology of the period of Hammurabi. Tablets have been found that indicate that by 700 B.C. the Babylonians had acquired a fair amount of astronomical knowledge. These texts are descriptive, and deal with observations of celestial phenomena and with solar and lunar eclipses. About this time omens and reports to the Assyrian court were also important. Some time after 500 B.C. mathematical astronomy arose, and by 400 B.C. the Babylonians had made considerable advances, including the following developments: a zodiac as a reference for solar and planetary motion, a fixed luni-solar calendar, basic period relationships for the moon and planets, a knowledge of the variation in the length of day and night, and a numerical method that could be used in astronomical calculations.

Mesopotamian astronomy reached its greatest maturity during the Seleucid period. Texts from this period fall into two categories, the procedure texts and the ephemerides. The ephemerides were tables of celestial phenomena; the procedure texts told how to compute the ephemerides. These texts show that the Babylonians had developed a highly complex lunar theory and were able to predict lunar eclipses. They did not, however, have the data needed to predict solar eclipses. Greek astronomy before A.D. 150 was heavily influenced by the Babylonians. The Greeks used the empirical data of the ephemerides to develop many of their astronomical theories, and combined Babylonian arithmetical methods with their own geometrical methods to produce the beginnings of a highly mathematical astronomy.

In all probability the ancient Hebrews gained most of their astronomical knowledge from the Babylonians. They may have adopted the idea of the Egyptian star-clock. But in general, Egyptian astronomy had little to offer a nomadic, largely nonagricultural people like the early Israelites. The Hebrews could have gained little astronomical knowledge from the Greeks, because even during intertestamental and NT times Greek astronomy was only in its fledgling stage. Also, since Israel was culturally and politically involved with other Mesopotamian nations and had a lunar calendar similar to that of the Babylonians, it is not unreasonable to suppose that she obtained most of her astronomical knowledge from Babylonia. One major question is: To what extent did Israel absorb the astrological and religious interpretations along with the scientific data? Obviously, worship of the celestial bodies was unthinkable to the devout Hebrew and was not officially welcome in Israel. In the OT, however, there are indications that such idolatry was practiced in Israel (Am. 5:26f.), and that the Israelites learned astrological practices as well as astronomical science from the Babylonians.

II. Astronomical Elements in the Bible.–A. *Biblical Attitude toward Astronomy.* There is no scientific astronomy, in the modern sense, in the Bible. The ancient Hebrews were, however, familiar with the motions of the heavenly bodies. Observing the positions of the sun, moon, and stars was a practical necessity to ancient man, who depended on celestial data in order to determine the time of day and the time of year. In this sense the people of the Bible were much closer to the heavens and knew them much more intimately than most moderns. This familiarity with the heavens is evidenced by the abundance of astronomical similes and metaphors in Hebrew literature. Astronomy had a great effect on the philosophical attitudes of the peoples in the ancient Near East, and the Hebrews were no exception.

Our source book for the study of Hebrew astronomy is the Bible, and none of the books of the OT or NT gives any record of systematic astronomy. Astronomical data are incidental and few in number. This is to be expected, for the Bible's main purpose is to reveal God to man, and astronomical phenomena are recorded only when they assist in that revelation. The God of the Bible is the God who created the heavens "for signs and for seasons and for days and years, and . . . [to] be lights in the firmament of the heavens to give light upon the earth" (Gen. 1:14f.). All heavenly bodies have their origin with God, and God created them for specific purposes. To the biblical writers these celestial objects are also a sign of God's otherness in relation to men. They are the created works of God and are insignificant in comparison with Him. They remind the psalmist of God's majesty and His grace in caring for men: "When I look at thy heavens, the work of thy fingers, the moon and the stars which thou hast established; what is man that thou art mindful of him, and the son of man that thou dost care for him?" (Ps. 8:3f.). Astronomical references occur most frequently in passages dealing with the beginning and end of the world and with the intervention of God in history, for events in heaven foreshadow the mighty working of God. Above all else, the heavens bear witness to God. The beginning of Ps. 19 is an apt summary of the biblical view of celestial bodies: "The heavens are telling the glory of God; and the firmament proclaims his handiwork. Day to day pours forth speech, and night to night declares knowledge. There is no speech, nor are there words; their voice is not heard; yet their voice goes out through all the earth and their words to the end of the world."

The theological attitude of the Hebrews toward the heavens differed in one very significant respect from the attitude of other peoples in the ancient Near East — they did not sanction worship of the heavenly bodies as deities nor the practice of astrology. The celestial bodies were the creations of God and certainly not deities in their own right. God had ordained that men should use the heavenly bodies to determine calendars and festivals, and as guides for nighttime travel; but they were not to be used as guides for predicting terrestrial happenings. A certain disdain toward those who practice astrology, instead of worshiping the true God, is shown throughout the Bible: "Learn not the way of the nations, nor be dismayed at the signs of the heavens because the nations are dismayed at them. . . . Thus shall you say to them: 'The gods who did not make the heavens and the earth shall perish from the earth and from under the heavens' " (Jer. 10:2, 11).

B. Sun, Moon, and Planets: In the Bible, references to the sun and the moon are both astronomical and symbolic. As stated in Gen. 1, the sun and moon were placed in the heavens not only "for days and for years" but also "for signs." References to the signs of the sun and moon occur most frequently in passages dealing with the end of the world or great, catastrophic events. All four Gospels assert that the sun was darkened when Jesus Christ was crucified. The sun and moon will also be darkened at the time of the End, although at God's triumph they will shine again even more brightly (Isa. 13:10; 30:26). The most terrible and impressive signs of the sun and the moon are solar and lunar eclipses. These phenomena are briefly but unmistakably described in several passages, e.g., Joel 2:31. To God's people eclipses were signs of the power and authority of God, who forbade them to be alarmed at portents that distressed the heathen.

The word used most frequently in the OT for "sun" is Heb. *šemeš*, a word common to all Semitic languages. Less common OT terms for the sun are: *'ôr*, meaning "light" (Job 31:26); *ḥammâ*, meaning "heat" and usually used with *l^eḇānâ* for the moon (Isa. 24:23); *ḥeres,* meaning "blister" (Jgs. 8:13). The NT word is Gk. *hḗlios*. The sun is often used in Hebrew poetry as a symbol of permanence: "May his name endure for ever, his fame continue as long as the sun" (Ps. 72:17). In Ecclesiastes the expression "under the sun" denotes man's earthly existence. In Gen. 1 the sun is referred to as "the greater light." The metaphor "wings of the morning" (Ps. 139:9) probably refers to the long streamers seen when the sun rises behind the bank of clouds. In prophecy the messenger of the Lord is called "the sun of righteousness" (Mal. 4:2). The NT writers take over this sun imagery and refer to Jesus Christ as "the light of men" (Jn. 1:4).

The most common Hebrew word for "moon" is *yārē(a)ḥ*, a word common to all Semitic languages. Other terms used for the moon include *l^eḇānâ*, meaning "white" and usually used in conjunction with *ḥamma* for the sun (Isa. 24:23); *ḥōḏeš,* meaning "new moon" or "month" (Gen. 7:11); *kissē',* meaning "full moon" (Job 26:9); and *yeraḥ,* which is usually translated "month" (Dt. 33:14). In the NT, Gk. *selḗnē* is used. It is interesting that there is no direct mention of the phases of the moon in the Bible. The Israelites could hardly have failed to notice this phenomenon, and that it is not directly mentioned strongly suggests that the Hebrews were aware of more astronomical phenomena than are actually recorded in the Bible. The Hebrews used a lunar calendar based on the actual observation of the young crescent moon. To ancient peoples moonlight was very important for travel and nighttime activity, and the return of the moonlit portion of the month was a cause for rejoicing. The moon was also used to determine religious festivals. The moon, like the sun, was used in Hebrew poetry as a symbol of permanence: "as long as the moon [endures], throughout all generations" (Ps. 72:5). In Gen. 1 it is called "the lesser light."

The planets seem to have played a very small role in Hebrew astronomy, for there are only two possible references to planets in the Bible. The first is found in Am. 5:26. Here the Hebrew name *kîyûn* probably refers to Saturn, one of the major planets in the Babylonian astrology-religion. The Gk. *rhaiphán* in Acts 7:43 may be another name for the planet Saturn. *See also* KAIWAN.

C. Stars and Constellations. In the OT the stars are usually called Heb. *kôḵāḇîm*. As with the sun and the moon, the stars were created by God for giving light and measuring time. The other expression used for the stars, *ṣeḇā' haššāmayim*, means "host of heaven" (Gen. 2:1). This term usually means stars in general, but may also refer to the stars and planets worshiped by the Babylonians and by some Hebrews at the time of the last kings of Israel. The Hebrews were especially aware of three characteristics of the stars: their number, their distance or height, and their brightness. The great number of the stars made them a symbol of God's prodigality and of any limitless number: "Look toward heaven, and number the stars, if you are able to number them. . . . So shall your descendants be" (Gen. 15:5). The distance of the stars was seen as a symbolic measure of God's mercy and faithfulness: "Can you find out the limit of the Almighty? It is higher than heaven" (Job 11:7f.). Their brightness and infinitude often led the Hebrews to consider them as a type of the other celestial host, the holy angels: "The seven stars are the angels of the seven churches" (Rev. 1:20). The word star is also used to imply dignity: "And those who are wise shall shine like the brightness of the firmament; and those who turn many to righteousness like the stars for ever and ever" (Dnl. 12:3). The expression "day star" or "light-bringer" is used in a metaphoric reference to Christ as the one who causes God's truth to illumine men's hearts (2 Pet. 1:19).

One of the first astronomical accomplishments of any people is the grouping of stars into constellations. There are three present-day constellations that are readily grouped and were known to nearly all ancient peoples: Ursa Major, Orion, and the Pleiades. The Hebrews certainly knew these and other constellations; but whether they are mentioned in the Bible is a matter of debate. Names that seem to refer to stars or constellations appear in the Bible. These names are so ancient that even the translators of the LXX had difficulty, and there is little agreement about which constellations some of these designate. Job 9:9 mentions Heb. *'āš* (=*'ayiš* in 38:32), *k^esîl* (cf. *k^esîlîm*, Isa. 13:10), *kîmâ,* and *haḏrê ṯēmān*. Other terms are *m^ezārîm* (Job 37:9) and *mazzārôṯ* (38:32) or *mazzālôṯ* (2 K. 23:5). The AV translation "Arcturus" for *'āš*/*'ayiš* is almost certainly incorrect, for the word is generally considered a reference to Ursa Major and Ursa Minor (cf. RSV "the Bear"). Cases have also been made for its identification with Capella, the Hyades (cf. NEB), and the Pleiades. Most scholars think that *m^ezārîm* (RSV "scattering winds") also refers to Ursa Major and Ursa Minor. *K^esîl* means "foolish," probably a name for Orion, which could have been seen as the figure of a foolish man. The plural *k^esîlîm* is a way of referring to all the constellations of the heavens. *Kîmâ* is almost certainly to be identified with the Pleiades. *Haḏrê ṯēmān,* translated "chambers of the south," could refer to the very bright section of the sky from Argus to Centauri that would have been visible on the southern horizon in Israel. It could also refer to the zodiac, or perhaps only the southern portion of the zodiac. The term *mazzārôṯ* (untranslated in Job 38:32, RSV) or *mazzālôṯ* (RSV "constellations") is the most difficult to identify. It is similar to the Babylonian word for "planet" and the word for "section," and is most often considered to be a term for the zodiac. It has also been regarded as the word for the morning and evening appearances of Venus, the five larger planets, or the stars that kept the hours of the night.

Other stellar phenomena besides constellations are mentioned in the Bible. The Hebrews, like the Egyptians, might have marked the passing of the year by noting which stars were the last to rise before the sun. They were aware that the stars had paths, or "courses," as they moved through the night sky (Jgs. 5:20) and thus could be used to measure time. These timekeeping stars are probably what are indicated by "morning stars" (Job 38:7). There is some debate as to whether comets or meteorites are mentioned in the Bible. Astronomical phenomena are often used in descriptions of the End (cf. Mk. 13:25). It seems that the star Wormwood (Rev. 8:11) is a meteorite, and that a meteor shower is one of the apocalyptic phenomena (6:13). The Greek expression *astéres planḗtai* ("wandering stars") in Jude 13 appears to be a reference not to the planets but to comets, as a metaphor for apostate teachers.

D. Astronomical Miracles in the Bible. In the Bible at least three astronomical miracles are recorded: Joshua ordering the sun to "be still" (Josh. 12:14), the shadow going back on the DIAL OF AHAZ (2 K. 20:8-11), and the star of Bethlehem (Mt. 2:1-11). There are three common ways of attempting to understand miracles in the biblical narratives. The first is to try to find a natural explanation for an apparently supernatural phenomenon. Another way of interpreting the record is to understand it as poetical hyperbole. The third way is to regard the biblical narrative as an essentially accurate account of a truly supernatural event. The Bible itself suggests that these miracles are the mighty work of God and not astronomical flukes. The God of the Bible is the creator of all celestial objects and they bear witness to Him. He can certainly intervene and change their natural course.

Many explanations have been offered for the narrative of Joshua. Some have suggested that refraction was responsible for an optical illusion. Others have thought that the verb translated "stand still" should really be translated "be silent," and that Joshua was commanding a cloud to cover the sun and shield his army from the heat. E. W. Maunder suggests that saying the sun "did not hasten to go down" is a way of saying that the Hebrew army did more than was usually possible in one afternoon. Whatever the explanation, it is certain that God intervened in some way and saved the Israelite nation. (*See* BETH-HORON, THE BATTLE OF.)

The narrative of the dial of Ahaz contains few details, so it has been difficult for anyone to form a convincing explanation. It is probably wisest to say that one cannot know what really happened, but that it is clear that the Lord did act and did save Hezekiah's life.

One of the questions most commonly asked of astronomers and planetariums is: "What was the star of Bethlehem?" Various explanations have been offered. It could have been a comet, a new star, a variable star, Venus, a supernova, or a conjunction of Mars, Jupiter, and Saturn. All of these explanations fail in important ways. Another explanation is that it might have been a ball of fire especially created by God, similar to the pillar of fire that guided the Hebrews in the Sinai wilderness. One must realize that the narrative does not give a detailed description because the star itself was not important. It was mentioned only because it was a guide to the Christ child and a sign of His birth.

See also ASTROLOGY; CALENDAR.

Bibliography.–A. Duveen and L. Motz, *Essentials of Astronomy* (1966); E. W. Maunder, *Astronomy of the Bible* (1908); O. Neugebauer, *Exact Sciences in Antiquity* (1957); G. V. Schiaparelli, *Astronomy in the OT* (1905); G. de Vaucouleur, *Discovery of the Universe* (1957); R. de Vaux, *Ancient Israel* (1961), pp. 178-194.

J. M. EVERTS

ASTYAGES as-tī'ə-jēz [Gk. *Astyagēs*] (Bel 1). The last king of Media (585-550 B.C.), the son of Cyaxares I and predecessor of Cyrus. His name is also spelled Istuvigu. His wife was the daughter of Alyattes king of Lydia.

The daughter of Astyages (Mandane) married a Persian, Cambyses; and a son was born to them who later became Cyrus the Great. Astyages had given orders to expose the baby, but a shepherd reared it to adolescence (Herodotus i.108-116). Cyrus II later revolted against his grandfather Astyages, who was defeated when his own vassals deserted him. Cyrus, the founder of the Persian empire, treated the dethroned monarch kindly.

See also CYRUS.

ASUPPIM ə-sup'im (1 Ch. 26:15, 17, AV). *See* STOREHOUSE.

ASUR as'ər [Gk. *Asour*] (1 Esd. 5:31); AV ASSUR. A family of NETHINIM, perhaps the same as Harhur of Ezr. 2:51.

ASYLUM. *See* ALTAR; REFUGE, CITIES OF.

ASYNCRITUS ə-sin'kri-təs [Gk. *Asynkritos*–'incomparable']. An unknown Christian at Rome to whom Paul sent an affectionate salutation (Rom. 16:14).

ATAD ā'tad [Heb. *'āṭāḏ*–'thorn'] (Gen. 50:10f.). *See* ABEL-MIZRAIM.

ATAR ā'tär (1 Esd. 5:28, NEB). *See* ATER.

ATARAH at'ə-rə, ə-tā'rə [Heb. *'ᵃṭārâ*–'crown']. One of Jerahmeel's wives and mother of Onam (1 Ch. 2:26).

ATARGATIS ə-tär'gə-tis [Gk. *Atargatis* (2 Macc. 12:26), transliterating Heb. *'tr'th*; the shortened form *tr'th* yields Gk. *Derketō*, "Derceto"]. The great goddess of the Arameans, consort of Hadad, called the "Syrian goddess" by the Greeks and Romans. Knowledge of her cult is obtained in part from Lucian *De dea Syria* (On the Syrian Goddess) and Apuleius *Metamorphoses* 8f. Her name is compounded from *'atar* (the Aramaic reflex; Bab. Ishtar, Sabean and Ugar. *'ṯtr*, Heb. Ashtoreth, Gk. Astarte) and *'attah* (possibly Ate, a Greek goddess, or Attis, a Phrygian god, but this is quite uncertain; the Greek form with *gamma* suggests an original *ǵáyin* [cf. Gaza, Gomorrah, etc.]).

The principal cult center of Atargatis was at Hierapolis (Bambyce, modern Membidj) in Syria, NE of Aleppo. As a fertility-goddess, however, she was named Baalat (Lady, mistress) of numerous cities, just as we find city names compounded with "Baal." Her temple at Karnaim (Carnaim) in Gilead is mentioned in 2 Macc. 12:26, where Judas Maccabeus slaughtered those who had fled there for refuge.

Atargatis had attributes that can be compared with those of the Phoenician Astarte, to which have been added elements of the Babylonian Ishtar and the Anatolian mother-goddess Cybele. She is commonly portrayed wearing the mural crown, holding a sheaf of grain, and sitting on a throne supported by lions. Nero was said to be a devotee of her cult, and Roman soldiers carried the Syrian Goddess as far as northern Britain.

Bibliography.–J. A. Garstang and H. A. Strong, *Syrian Goddess* (1913); E. O. James, *Ancient Gods* (1960), pp. 86, 297, 307, 348.

W. S. L. S.

ATAROTH at'ə-roth [Heb. *'ᵃṭārôṯ*–'crowns, wreaths'].

1. A town E of the Jordan, in Reubenite territory, fortified and occupied by Gadites (Nu. 32:3, 34). Represented by modern Khirbet 'Aṭṭārûs, it stands 4 mi. (6.5 km.) W of Jebel 'Aṭṭārûs in fertile grazing country. It was later taken by the Moabites (*see* MOABITE STONE IV).

2. A place on the border between Ephraim and Benjamin, toward the west (Josh. 16:2); probably the same as Ataroth-addar of 16:5 and 18:13. Smith (*HGHL*) identified this place with the present Atara on the high road from Jerusalem to Bethel, 3.5 mi. (5.5 km.) S of Bethel and 6 mi. (10 km.) E of upper Beth-horon.

3. A place in northeast Ephraim (Josh. 16:7), not far from Jericho; possibly modern Tell Sheikh edh-Dhiab.

4. 1 Ch. 2:54 (RSV ATROTH-BETH-JOAB) may read, "the crowns [chiefs] of the house of Joab," referring to Bethlehem and Netophathi. The NEB reads as two names, Ataroth and Beth-joab; the AV has Ataroth and "the house of Joab." If this "Ataroth" is a place, its location is unknown. D. B. PECOTA

ATAROTH-ADDAR at'ə-roth ad'är [Heb. *'ăṭrôṯ 'addār*–'crowns of Addar'] (Josh. 16:5; 18:13). *See* ATAROTH **2.**

ATEPHA ə-tē'fə (1 Esd. 5:32, NEB). *See* HATIPHA.

ATER ā'tər [Heb. *'āṭēr*–'crippled'; Gk. *Atēr, Atar*]; AV Apoc. ATEREZIAS (1 Esd. 5:15), JATAL (5:28); NEB also ATAR (5:28). The ancestor of a family that returned to Palestine under Zerubbabel (Ezr. 2:16; Neh. 7:21; 1 Esd. 5:28). Some family members were gatekeepers (Ezr. 4:42; Neh. 7:45; 1 Esd. 5:28). Ater was one who sealed the covenant of Nehemiah (Neh. 10:17).

ATEREZIAS a-tər-ə-zī'əs (1 Esd. 5:15, AV, combining Gk. *Atēr* with the following *Ezekiou*). *See* ATER; HEZEKIAH **4.**

ATETA ə-tē'tə (1 Esd. 5:28, NEB). *See* HATITA.

ATHACH ā'thak [Heb. *'ᵃṯāḵ*–'lodging place']; NEB ATHAK. A village in Judah to which David sent some of the booty that had been taken from Ziklag (1 S. 30:30), possibly that which had been taken by the Amalekites from Philistine and southern Judah communities (1 S. 30:14, 16).

Many scholars are convinced, on the basis of Josh. 15:42; 19:7, that the text should read "Ether." The LXX of 1 S. 30:30 is indefinite, with readings of *Noo, Athach, Athag, Nageb,* etc., for "Athach." Likewise the text of Josh. 15:42 has *Ithak* in the B-text and *Ather* in A, where the MT has Heb. *'eṯer*. On the other hand, a comparison of the place names in Josh. 15:42; 19:7; 1 Ch. 4:32 with those listed in 1 S. 30:27-31 really gives no firm basis for considering the lists as parallel. The B reading of Josh. 15:42 is not convincing, for in Josh. 19:7 (A and B) the place is called *Ether*. The identification therefore remains uncertain.

See *GTTOT*, § 321. W. S. L. S.

ATHAIAH ə-thā'yə [Heb. *'ᵃṯāyâ*–'Yahweh is helper'] (Neh. 11:4). A descendant of Judah and the son of Uzziah. After the return from Babylon, he dwelt in Jerusalem. He is perhaps the same as Uthai in the parallel list at 1 Ch. 9:4.

ATHALIAH ath-ə-lī'ə [Heb. *'ᵃṯalyā, 'ᵃṯalyāhû*–'Yahweh is exalted'; Gk. *Gotholia*].

1. The daughter of King Ahab (2 K. 8:26; 11:1ff.; 2 Ch. 22:2ff.). Her mother is nowhere named; the only wife of Ahab mentioned in Scripture is the notorious Jezebel, but clearly he had other wives (cf. 2 K. 10:1). It is difficult on chronological grounds to make Athaliah Jezebel's daughter, but Jezebel certainly exercised a strong influence over Athaliah, as the sequel shows.

During the childhood of Athaliah, the political relations of the kingdoms of Judah and Israel had, after many years of strife, become friendly; and she was married to Jehoram, eldest son of King Jehoshaphat of Judah (2 K. 8:18). The marriage was one of political expediency, and is a blot on the memory of Jehoshaphat.

When Jehoram was thirty-two years of age he succeeded to the throne, and Athaliah became queen of Judah. Like Jezebel, she exhibited a fanatical devotion to the cultus of the Tyrian Baal Melqart. Elijah's blow against the worship of Baal in Samaria shortly before her accession to power did nothing to mitigate her zeal; it probably intensified it. The first recorded act of Jehoram's reign is the murder of his six younger brothers. Some princes of the realm, who were known to favor the ancient faith of the nation, were also destroyed (2 Ch. 21:4). There can be little doubt that these deeds of blood were supported, and perhaps instigated, by Athaliah, who was a much stronger character than her husband.

After eight years of royal life, Athaliah became a widow, and her son Ahaziah, then twenty-two years old (2 K. 8:26; not 42 as in 2 Ch. 22:2), ascended his father's throne. As queen mother Athaliah was now supreme in the councils of the nation, as well as in the royal palace. Within a single year the young king fell (*see* JEHU), and the only persons who stood between Athaliah and the throne were her grandchildren. Ambition, fired by fanaticism, saw its opportunity; and the massacre of the royal seed was planned and carried out. One of them, however, the baby Jehoash, escaped by the intervention of his aunt Jehosheba (1 K. 11:2; 2 Ch. 22:11).

With the palace cleared of its royal occupants, Athaliah had herself proclaimed sovereign. No other woman, before or since, sat upon the throne of David; and it is a proof of her energy and ability that, in spite of her sex, she was able to keep the throne for six years.

From 2 Ch. 24:7, where she is called "that wicked woman," we gather that a portion of the temple of Yahweh was pulled down and the material used in the structure of a temple to Baal.

The high priest at this time was Jehoiada, who had married Jehosheba the daughter of Jehoram (2 Ch. 22:11). He proved staunchly, if secretly, true to the religion of Yahweh. For six years he and his wife concealed in their apartments, near the temple, the young child of Ahaziah. In the seventh year a counterrevolution was planned. The details are given with unusual fulness in Kings and Chronicles, the writings of which supplement one another, even if it is difficult to reconcile all the details of the two accounts. At the time of her deposition, Athaliah was resident in the royal palace. When roused to a sense of danger by the acclamations that greeted the coronation ceremony, she made an attempt to stay the revolt by rushing alone into the temple court; her guards, according to Josephus, had been prevented from following her (*Ant.* ix.7.3). With a quick glance she saw the lad standing on a raised platform before the temple, holding the Book of the Law in his hand and wearing the crown. Rending her robe and shouting "Treason! Treason!" she fled. Some were for cutting her down as she did so, but this was objected to as defiling the temple with human blood. She was therefore taken out, and killed at the palace entrance. It is clear from the two accounts (2 K. 11:4-20; 2 Ch. 23) that the counterrevolution was instigated by the priesthood, naturally enough in view of Athaliah's predilection for Baal worship, and also that it had full popular support. The only allies Athaliah had were her personal troops, and presumably it was only their influence that kept her in power so long. Jehoiada's first action was of necessity to win over their allegiance to Jehoash.

The Tyrian Baal cult perished from Judah with the death of Athaliah (2 K. 11:3; 2 Ch. 22:12). Her first year synchronizes with the first of Jehu of Israel, and may be dated 842 or 841 B.C.

2. A leading Benjaminite, resident in Jerusalem (1 Ch. 8:26-28).

3. Also **GOTHOLIAH** goth-ə-lī'ə [Gk. *Gotholios*] (1 Esd. 8:33); AV, NEB, GOTHOLIAS. The father of Jeshaiah, who returned with Ezra (8:7). W. S. CALDECOTT D. F. PAYNE

ATHANASIAN CREED. *See* CREEDS AND CONFESSIONS IV.C.

ATHARIAS ath-ə-rī'əs (1 Esd. 5:40, AV). *See* ATTHARIAS.

ATHARIM ath'ə-rim [Heb. *'ᵃṯārîm*]. AV SPIES. The route being followed by Moses and the Israelites when they were attacked by the king of Arad (Nu. 21:1). The location remains unidentified.

ATHBASH ath'bash. An artificially contrived term designating a Semitic cipher. In this word (for Heb. *'tbš*) the first alphabetic consonant is followed by the last, and the second by the next to the last. To form a cipher, the consonants from the beginning of the alphabet are substituted for those at the end of the alphabet in corresponding order, and vice versa. Thus the letters *lbqmy* of Jer. 51:1 become *kśdym* (*kaśdîm*), i.e., the Chaldeans. The clue for this was provided by the LXX of 28:1, which reads *Chaldaious*. In 51:41, *ššk* (AV Sheshach) is athbash for *bbl*, i.e., Babylon (cf. LXX 28:41). Why the cipher was used when elsewhere the nations are condemned so explicitly is unknown. R. K. H.

ATHEISM [< Gk. *átheos*–'without God' (Eph. 2:12)]. Ordinarily this word is interpreted to mean a denial of the existence of God, a disbelief in God, the opposite of theism. But it seems better that we should consider it under four heads, in order to obtain a clear idea of the different meanings in which it has been used.

(1) *Classical* atheism does not mean a denial of the existence of a divine being, but the denial of the existence or reality of the god of a particular nation. Thus the early Christians were repeatedly charged with atheism, because of their disbelief in the gods of heathenism. Socrates' teaching cast a shadow on the reality of the existence of the gods, and this charge was brought against him by his contemporaries. Cicero also uses the word in this sense in his charge against Diagoras of Athens. Indeed, such use of it is common in all classical literature.

(2) *Philosophic* atheism does not necessarily imply lack of any belief in a divine being; but it is in contrast to the theism that affirms that God is a person, a self-conscious being, not merely a first cause or force. To deny this fundamental affirmation of theism is to make the teaching atheistic, a denial of that which is essential to theism (He. 11:3).

(3) *Dogmatic* atheism is the absolute denial of the existence of God. It has often been held that this kind of atheism is, in fact, impossible. It is true, however, that in all ages there have been persons who declared themselves absolute atheists. Especially is this true of the 18th cent., a period of widespread skepticism when many, particularly in France, professed themselves atheists. In many cases, however, it resulted from a careless use of the word, loose definition, and sometimes from the spirit of boastfulness.

(4) *Practical* atheism is to live as though there were no God. It takes the form of complete indifference to the claims of the divine being, or of outspoken and defiant wickedness (Ps. 14:1). That this form of atheism is widely prevalent is well known. It is accompanied in many cases with some form of unbelief or prejudice or false opinion of the Church or Christianity. Dogmatic atheism is no longer a menace or even a hindrance to the progress of Christianity, but practical atheism is widespread in its influence and a dangerous element in our modern life (cf. Isa. 31:1; Jer. 2:13, 17f.; 18:13-15).

Whatever the form, whether it be that of religious agnosticism, denying that we can know that God exists; or critical atheism, denying that the evidence to prove His existence is sufficient; or dogmatic, or practical atheism, it is always a system of negation and as such tears down and destroys. It destroys the faith upon which all human relations are built. If there is no God there is no right nor wrong, and human action is neither good nor bad, but convenient or inconvenient. It leaves human society without a basis for order and human government without foundation (Rom. 1:18-32). All is hopeless, all is wretchedness, all is tending to the grave and the grave ends all.

Arguments against atheism may be summarized as follows: (1) It is contrary to reason. History has shown again and again how impossible it is to bring the mind to rest in this doctrine. Although Buddhism is atheistic in its teaching, idolatry is widespread in the lands where it prevails. While the Positive Philosophy of Auguste Comte was based on a denial of the existence of God, his attempt to found the new religion of humanity with rites and ceremonies of worship reveals how the longing for worship cannot be suppressed. It is a revelation of the fact so often seen in the history of human thought, that the mind cannot rest in the tenets of atheism.

(2) It is contrary to human experience. All history testifies that there are deep religious instincts within the human breast. To regard these as deceptive and unreasonable would itself be utterly unreasonable and unscientific. But the fact of such spiritual longing implies also that there is a Being who is responsive to and can satisfy the cry of the heart (He. 11:6).

(3) It fails to account for the evidence of design in the universe.

(4) It fails to account for the existence of man and the world in general. Here is the universe: how did it come to be? Here is man: how is he to be accounted for? To these and like questions, atheism and atheistic philosophy have no adequate answer. J. W. KAPP

ATHENIANS ə-thē'nē-ənz [Gk. *Athēnaioi*]. People of Athens. Luke remarks on their curiosity and their delight in novelty (Acts 17:21). *See* ATHENS.

ATHENOBIUS ath-ə-nō'bē-əs [Gk. *Athēnobios*]. An envoy of Antiochus VII (Sidetes), who was sent to Jerusalem by the king to protest against the occupation of Joppa and Gazara, and the citadel Jerusalem. A demand was made on Simon Maccabeus to give up all the places he had taken or pay 1000 talents in silver. Simon declined to pay more than 100 talents, and Athenobius returned to Antiochus from his fruitless mission (1 Macc. 15:28-36).

ATHENS ath'enz [Gk. *Athēnai*]. The most important city of Attica in antiquity, the capital of the same district in NT times, and the capital of the Republic of Greece in the modern era. The name has been derived, so it would seem, from that of the patron goddess Athena.

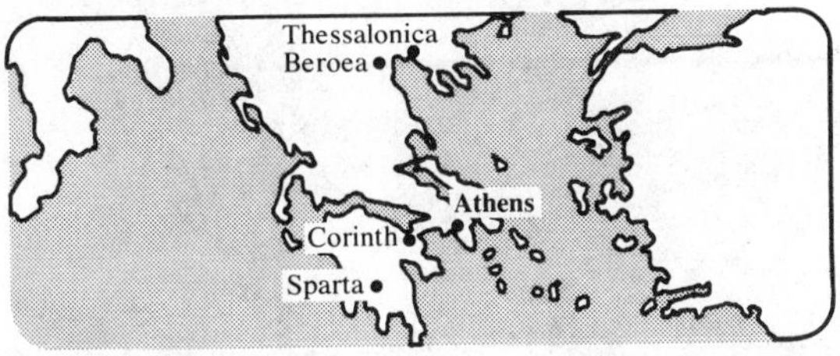

The city of Athens is important to biblical studies as the scene of Paul's famous Areopagus address (Acts 17:15-34). Having been driven from Beroea by the antagonism of the Jews, Paul waited in Athens for the arrival of his companions, who had remained in Beroea for a short time. It is not known whether Athens was included in Paul's program of evangelization or whether the opportunity and stimulus for his preaching in that city were provided by the circumstances he encountered.

The account in Acts does not make clear whether Paul approached Athens by land or by sea. If he came by sea he would have landed at Piraeus, which was the seaport of Athens and the base for her navy. Located 5 mi. (8 km.) from Athens, Piraeus was joined to the city by a corridor about 250 ft. (75 m.) wide protected by walls about 50 ft. (15 m.) high. Most likely Paul would have traveled outside these walls in a northeasterly direction, on the road leading to Athens. On this road Pausanias claims to have observed "altars to gods called unknown." The existence of inscriptions worded in the singular in accordance with the statement of Paul (Acts 17:23) has been questioned. McDonald, however, asserts knowledge of two late literary passages that refer to *an* unknown god (*BA*, 4 [1941], 1). Coming by this way, Paul would have entered the city from the west through the "dipylon" (double gate), from which a road continuing to the southeast led directly to the agora.

The agora in an ancient city was the focal point of political, commercial, and social life. Here, as well as in the synagogue, Paul engaged in discussion with the people, conspicuous among whom were the Stoics and Epicureans. The agora was a large open space enclosed by civic and religious buildings. Modern excavators have discovered the foundations of buildings that correspond substantially with the description of the agora given by the historian Pausanias. Among these were the Odeion, or music hall, the stoa of Attalos on the east, and two long parallel stoas on the south. A stoa was a long narrow pavilion with a colonnade on one side and a wall on the other. The stoas were the scene of public lectures and discussions. The circular Tholos on the west was the meeting place of the executive sections of the Athenian Council of five hundred. Also on the west were: the Bouleuterion, where the Council met; the Metroön, the sanctuary of the Mother of the Gods; the temple of Apollo Patroös; and the stoa of Zeus Eleutherios. The temple of Ares was toward the center of the open area of the agora.

The AREOPAGUS was directly S of the agora, and the Acropolis was to the southeast. The Acropolis, a commanding hill 512 ft. (156 m.) high was customarily approached from the west, through an ornamental gateway known as the Propylaea. Here on the south stood the small temple of Wingless Victory. The top of the hill was dominated by the Parthenon, which contained a gold and ivory statue of Athena made by Phidias, Pericles' sculptor. The Erechtheion stood on the north. This was a temple erected in honor of Erechtheus, the semidivine hero who is reputed to have been the first king of Athens, though we cannot be sure that he was more than a legendary character. The Prytaneion, or town hall, where the sacred fire of the city was always kept aflame, was on the north slope of the Acropolis, E of the Agora. North of the Prytaneion the Roman Forum was built through the generosity of the Caesars, Julius and Augustus. When Paul visited Athens, the temple of Olympian Zeus stood unfinished, SE of the Acropolis. When it was completed, this structure, known as the Olympeion, was the largest temple in all Greece. The Odeion, or music hall of Pericles, and the theater of Dionysos stood S and SW of the Acropolis, respectively. The temple of Hephaistos was located W of the agora on a small hill known as the Kolonos Agoraios. In the past this temple has been identified wrongly, at times, as the temple of Theseus. That it is indeed the Hephaisteion, the temple of the god of fire and metallurgy, has been confirmed by the discovery of numerous metalworking shops on the slopes of the hill on which it stands. The Acropolis, which is ideally situated for defense and water supply, bears evidence of having been inhabited from earliest times.

Athens was made the capital of the twelve communities

Ionic colonnade of the Roman agora. Planned by Julius Caesar in 44 B.C., the "new agora" was probably primarily an olive oil market. (W. S. LaSor)

Ruins of the Hellenistic agora at Athens. The stoa of Attalos II (top, reconstucted) contained a row of twenty-one single-roomed shops on each of its two stories, each with a double colonnade. (W. S. LaSor)

The Acropolis at Athens, with the Odeion (concert hall) of Herod Atticas, a wealthy Athenian, at its base. Constructed mostly during the "Golden Age of Pericles" (5th cent. B.C.), the site is an outstanding example of architectural planning of buildings in groups. (Ewing Galloway)

of Attica through the skillful leadership of Theseus. After more than four hundred years in which Athens was ruled by archons, Solon (*ca.* 594 B.C.), himself an archon, with the approval of the aristocracy changed the whole organization of the state, encouraging agriculture and commerce. The period 560-510 B.C. was one of despotism, and one of prosperity as well. Cleisthenes founded the democracy in the years following 509 B.C. He succeeded in removing class distinctions, forming a constitution, and establishing the Popular Assembly (Gk. *ekklēsía*), the Council (*boulḗ*), and the Popular Court of Law (*hēliaía*). Although Athens defeated the Persians at Marathon in 490 B.C., the city was threatened by Persian invasion again in 480. At this time, under the leadership of Themistocles, the fleet was enlarged and victory was gained. The golden years of Athens were those between 443 and 429 B.C. when with the leadership of Pericles the democracy was developed fully. More spectacular than the political progress, however, were the cultural attainments — the erection of temples and public buildings, the creation of works of art, and the development of drama, ethics, rhetoric, logic, and history.

Athens responded willingly to Philip of Macedon when he called for her aid. Later on, however, her refusal to give continued assistance led to the city's subjugation by him. After the death of Alexander the Great, the city of Athens once again regained a position of independence, international prestige, and cultural prominence, which she then held until overshadowed by the city of Alexandria. War with Rome reduced the populace to poverty and submission, but freedom and pardon were later granted to Athens because of her illustrious past. Accordingly, although the time of her greatest glory was gone forever, Athens could still boast of her right to be called a great center of philosophy, architecture, and art when the apostle Paul made his celebrated visit.

Bibliography.–O. Broneer, *BA,* 21 (1958), 2-28; I. T. Hill, *Ancient City of Athens* (1953); W. A. McDonald, *BA,* 4 (1941), 1-10; A. N. Oikonomides, *The Two Agoras in Ancient Athens* (1964); *WBA*.

D. H. MADVIG

ATHLAI ath'lī [Heb. *'aṯlay*–'afflicted'(?)]. A Jew, the son of Bebai, who was influenced by Ezra to put away his wife (Ezr. 10:28).

ATHLETE [Gk. *agōnizómenos* (1 Cor. 9:25), *athléō* (2 Tim. 2:5)]. *See* GAMES.

ATIPHA at'ē-fə (1 Esd. 5:32, AV). *See* HATIPHA.

ATONE; ATONEMENT [Heb. *kāpar*–'cover,' *kippurîm*–'coverings']; AV also RECONCILE (Lev. 6:30; 16:20; Ezk. 45:20), RECONCILIATION (Lev. 8:15; Ezk. 45:15, 17; Dnl. 9:24), PURGE (Prov. 16:6; Ezk. 43:20, 26), PUT OFF (Isa. 47:11); NEB EXPIATE, EXPIATION (but "Day of Atonement" in Lev. 23:27; 25:9), also SECURE PARDON (Ex. 32:30), RANSOM (Nu. 31:50), "wipe out" (Prov. 16:6), "master" (Isa. 47:11). To atone is to bring together in mutual agreement, with the added idea, in theology, of reconciliation through the vicarious suffering of one on behalf of another. *See also* RECONCILIATION; RANSOM.

The English word "atonement" traces its origin to the 16th century. The *New Oxford Dictionary* indicates that in the first instance it appeared as two separate words "at onement" (cf. Acts 7:26, AV; Gk. *eis eirḗnēn*), but it soon became a quasi-technical theological term. Sir Thomas More employed it in 1513, and in 1526 William Tyndale used it to translate Gk. *katallagḗ* in 2 Cor. 5:18. In the Bible the idea of atonement occurs much more widely than the actual use of either *kāpar* or *katallagḗ* would seem to indicate.

I. Atonement in the Bible
II. Interpreting the Atonement
III. History of the Doctrine
  A. Fathers

B. Schoolmen
C. Reformers
D. Liberal Thinkers
E. Conservative Theologians

I. Atonement in the Bible.–The doctrine of the atonement holds a central place in biblical doctrine. Both the OT and NT continually deal with the subject, for the concept of "the covenants" or "testaments" is fundamentally bound up with the idea of atonement for sin (Lk. 22:19f.; He. 9). Moreover, the origin of atonement is always referred back in the Bible to the eternal plan, purpose, and grace of God (2 Tim. 1:9f.; Eph. 1:4; Jn. 17:6ff.). Thus it appears as a basic and altogether indispensable theme of Christianity.

As a presupposition to the doctrine of atonement, however, one must consider the doctrine of the fall of man. Gen. 1f. teaches that God created all things perfect and according to His own sovereign plan and purpose. At the summit of this creation He placed man, who possessed a free will. At the same time God subjected man to a test, so that he could attain to a knowledge of good and evil by facing temptation, which he might overcome or to which he might succumb, by the use of his will. Man failed this test, falling into sin by his denial of the sovereignty of God and his assertion of independence from the Creator (Gen. 3:4ff.). This disobedience immediately brought man under the condemnation of God, who punished him with both physical and spiritual death. This punishment applied not merely to the original offenders, but, by virtue of the solidarity of the human race, to all those physically descending from Adam (Rom. 5:12ff.).

No sooner had God revealed to man this judgment than He also set before him the promise of redemption. Gen. 3:15 contains the promise (often known as the protevangel) in which God says that the "seed of the woman" will crush the head of the tempter. Here one finds a revelation of ultimate salvation. In the meantime, however, ritual sacrifice came into the picture, for Cain and Abel offered sacrifices to God, apparently for the expiation of sin (Gen. 4:3-7). Cain offered of the fruit of the ground, while Abel offered animal sacrifice. Whether the differences in the sacrifices had any importance is not explained, but in He. 11:4 the writer states that the reason Abel's offering achieved acceptance while Cain's did not was that Abel offered his sacrifice in faith. Thus from the beginning of redemption-history, sacrifices offered in faith assumed a central place in the matter of atonement.

During the patriarchal period sacrifice held a similar position in the lives of God's people. One of the first actions taken by Noah after he came out of the ark was to build an altar and offer sacrifices to God, who because of the sacrifice promised never again to destroy man from the earth (Gen. 8:20ff.). Abraham and his descendants likewise sacrificed to God, apparently looking forward to the time when one would come who would make full atonement for their sins (Gen. 13:18; 26:25; 33:20; 35:6; cf. Jn. 8:56ff.; Rom. 4:3ff.). How clearly the patriarchs understood the meaning of their sacrifices one cannot say, but that they had a concept of vicarious atonement seems quite clear (cf. Job 1:5).

The Exodus of Israel from Egypt brings forth a much clearer revelation of atonement. Israel had no doubt identified herself with her masters to such an extent that she had lost much of her knowledge of the divine revelation to the patriarchs. When God in accordance with His covenant called His people forth from Egypt, He did so by vicarious sacrifice, which stood for atonement. For Egypt's rebellion against His commands the eldest sons died; only those protected by the blood of the Passover lamb escaped (Ex. 12:27; cf. Jn. 2:29). Thus at the heart of the Passover stands the idea of atonement through believing sacrifice. Release from Egypt was its fruit.

The Mosaic law contains even fuller reference to the concept of atonement by sacrifice. Lev. 1–7 shows clearly what emphasis the ritual of the tabernacle laid upon this theme. The covenant between God and Israel as represented by the services of the sanctuary had its roots firmly embedded in this teaching, the ultimate manifestation coming upon the Day of Atonement (*see* ATONEMENT, DAY OF). At that time the priest both offered a sacrifice and sent forth the scapegoat as atonements for the people (Lev. 16:1-34; 23:27-32; cf. He. 9:7-12). In all the teaching involved in the Mosaic law, God made it very clear that atonement, the covering of sin, could result only from some innocent individual's taking upon himself the penalty due, although not the guilt of, the sinner. Such atonement now lost the purely individual or family character it had had during patriarchal times, and, mediated by the Aaronic priesthood, took on a national character by virtue of the covenant relation between God and Israel.

Following the conquest of Palestine, Israel's adherence to the Mosaic law and to the requirements of the covenant rose and fell frequently. Under the judges the people set up high places for sacrifice in various parts of the country; but under the unifying influence of the monarchy, particularly during the reigns of David and Solomon, the sacrifices became, as they had been intended to be, the prerogative of the priesthood serving the tabernacle and later the temple in Jerusalem. God required that one could find atonement for sin only through the sacrifice offered by the appointed priest, or, in certain extraordinary cases, a prophet (1 S. 13:8; 1 K. 18:21ff.). Furthermore, the sacrifices had to originate in the sinner's repentance and faith. Thus, while Israelites might perform the ceremonies, unless these two subjective elements indwelt the sinners, no covering of sin availed (Isa. 1:10ff.; Jer. 7:21). After the division of the kingdom and the steady spiritual decline first of Israel and then of Judah, the prophets continually stressed the need for atoning sacrifice whereby repentant believers might find redemption and reconciliation. At the same time they suggested more and more that this would ultimately find fulfillment in one who was to come (Isa. 53; 63:9; Jer. 23:6; 33:15f.).

The captivity of Israel and Judah in Assyria and Babylonia did much to turn Israel's mind toward the importance of sacrifice, while at the same time it had certain unfortunate results. Although the believing remnant continued to trust in God's ordained means of atonement even though sacrifice at Jerusalem had ceased, many of the people prided themselves increasingly on their covenant relationships and on fulfillment of the law as their means of forgiveness (2 Ch. 36:14ff.). Yet the postcaptivity prophets continually taught that forgiveness and acceptance by God could come to man only through atoning sacrifice accepted by faith. Based upon all the earlier teaching, the prophets pointed forward to the coming of one whom Zechariah called "the branch" (6:12), and Malachi "the messenger" (3:1) and "the sun of righteousness" (4:2), who would redeem and save His people.

By the close of OT times, therefore, the Jews had a well-developed concept of atonement. In the minds of most of them, no doubt, it had a largely mechanical character, repentance and faith being for the most forgotten while they laid great stress upon ceremonial and legal exactitude. Nevertheless, for the believing remnant their hope had its focus on Him who would come with healing in His wings to atone for sin. To announce this promised One, John the Baptist came preaching repentance. The OT economy had fulfilled its function of preparing the way for the Redeemer (Gal. 3:19ff.).

The Synoptic Gospels, Matthew, Mark, and Luke, set forth very clearly that the Lord Jesus Christ was the fulfillment of the OT types and prophecies concerning a Redeemer and that He fulfilled His office by substitutionary atonement. In both accounts of the Annunciation, it is stressed that the promised child would save His people from their sins (Mt. 1:21; Lk. 1:31ff.). During the early part of His ministry as reported by the Synoptics, Christ seems to have laid great emphasis upon a demand for repentance and for righteousness that exceeded that of the Pharisees. Nevertheless, underlying all the accounts one finds a constant reference to His saving power, which Matthew links directly to Isa. 53 and the concept of substitution (Mt. 8:17). From the time of Peter's confession of His deity, Christ continually reiterated that He had come to die for men, although the disciples did not understand His statements (Mt. 16:20ff.; Lk. 9:18ff.). Not until the eve of the crucifixion did it become clear that He must die, shedding His blood and giving His body for the remission of sins (Mt. 26:26ff.; Mk. 14:22ff.; Lk. 22:19ff.). Even after His resurrection the Synoptists show that the disciples did not yet fully understand His work (Lk. 24:13ff.).

With the coming of the Holy Spirit on Pentecost, the apostles gained a clearer understanding of the atoning character of Christ's work on Calvary. Through the leading, revelation, and inspiration of the Holy Spirit, Peter, Paul, and others set forth in their preaching and their letters with increasing clarity what Christ had achieved by His death and resurrection. Romans, Galatians, and Colossians expound His atoning work most clearly, but none more than Hebrews or the writings of Peter. To the NT Church, Christ had fulfilled all the prophecies and types of the OT by making final and full atonement for sin.

One must see the writings of John in the light of this NT development, for in his work one obtains some of the clearest statements of the doctrine of atonement. In his accounts of Christ's various sermons (Jn. 3, 6, 8, 10) he brings out points that the other Evangelists do not stress. Here, as in his Epistles, the concept of vicarious atonement accepted in repentance and faith becomes crystal clear (1 Jn. 2:2; 3:5; Rev. 5:9). Thus by the close of the canon of the NT a doctrine of atonement had come to full expression, although even to this day the Church has not brought forth a complete systematic statement of the doctrine (see III below).

II. Interpreting the Atonement.–The Scriptures lay down certain basic statements and principles that seem to point quite clearly to the proper interpretation of the atonement.

(1) The need for atonement. The Bible plainly sets forth the doctrine that man as a sinner is guilty of breaking the law of God, of contravening His righteousness. God has, therefore, judicially delivered man over to his own will so that corruption has entered in, whereby he has lost all desire to serve God (Rom. 1:17ff.; 5:12ff.). This means that man has no ability to save himself, for he does not realize his need nor has he the righteousness to provide atonement for his sin.

(2) God's love. Although God has given man over to his own sinful waywardness, He has not ceased to love man. Man has not ceased by his sin to be God's creature and a man. Therefore, despite his sinfulness God desires fellowship with him, and this can be restored only by divine forgiveness (Jn. 3:16; Acts 4:4).

(3) God's justice. God is love; He is also righteousness and truth. Consequently in His righteousness and truth He cannot accept sinful man as though he were perfect. Man's rebellion and sin merit, even demand, just punishment, for he has denied God, worshiping the creature rather than the Creator (Rom. 1:17ff.). The divinely ordained penalty for sin, which is in reality the denial of God, is God's denial of man, bringing death (Jer. 31:30; Rom. 6:23). Thus, in the face of God's justice man must pay the penalty before God will accept and forgive him.

(4) God's eternal covenant. To fulfil both God's love and His justice, only God could take the initiative. This He did in eternity by His covenant of grace. Within the triune Godhead a covenant was established whereby the second person of the trinity, the Son, took upon Himself the representation of God's elect, for whom He would obtain salvation; and to Him it was covenanted that in His mediatorial work as God incarnate He would receive the fulness of the Holy Spirit that He might accomplish the work of atonement (Jn. 6:37f.; 17:6; Gal. 3:17; Eph. 1:44ff.; He. 2:11ff.).

(5) Accomplishment of atonement. As the God-man, the Lord Jesus Christ became man and obeyed the law of God perfectly on man's behalf, fulfilling all righteousness. Then He suffered and died on Calvary's cross, bearing the penalty of man's rebellion. He could not take unto Himself man's guilt since He had not sinned, but He could and did assume the penalty of sin: eternal death. Thus He made atonement for sin, voluntarily submitting Himself to the law in both its positive and negative aspects, manifesting both active and passive obedience, that man might be saved from the just wrath of God (Isa. 53; Jn. 10:11ff.; Rom. 3:24ff.; Gal. 3:13; 4:5; He. 8).

(6) The scope of atonement. The question then arises as to the identity of those for whom Christ made atonement. Did He atone for all sin? That He *could,* no Christian would deny. Some declare that He did atone for all, so that eventually He will save all men. Others hold that He atoned "hypothetically" for all, but in actuality only for those who believe on Him. Others teach that He atoned sufficiently for all but effectively only for His elect people. This is usually known as the doctrine of the "limited" or "definite" atonement. What it affirms is that although God loves the world and would that all men should repent, He has sovereignly willed that Christ should make atonement only for those chosen in Him before the foundation of the world (Eph. 1:4; Jn. 6:39; 10:15; 17:6, 9, 12, 19f.). Thus Christ effectively atoned for the sins of His people and for them alone.

(7) The application of the atonement. Sinful man participates in the benefits of Christ's atoning work only by faith. Such faith, however, comes not out of man's own will or heart but by the work of God, for faith is the gift of God's Spirit as a result of the Covenant of Grace. By the Spirit Christ applies the atonement to those for whom He has made atonement. The application is as wide as its scope (Jn. 6:57; 14:16ff.; Rom. 8:15, 28ff.; 1 Cor. 1:26ff.; Eph. 2:5ff.; Col. 2:13ff.).

(8) The atonement and the world. In the mystery of God's action He offers the atonement to the world sincerely and freely. But in so offering it He also judges the world, for it refuses the benefits of the atoning death of Christ, counting it an unholy thing and preferring to assert either its own independence and self-righteousness or its indifference. Yet the world cannot escape the effects of the atonement, for God by His common grace restrains sin and the chaos it would bring, for the sake of the elect, that they may be brought to faith in the atoning work of Christ.

(9) The consummation of the atonement. The atonement will reach its consummation when Christ as the glorified redeemer returns to take His people unto Himself. Then shall His work have full manifestation in that all those for whom He made atonement will be revealed in eternal glory (Mt. 24:34ff.; Rom. 8:19ff.; 1 Thess. 4:13ff.).

Thus in summary one may say that the doctrine of the atonement as revealed in the Scriptures is centered on the work of Christ and forms the core of the Christian faith, the heart of the Christian interpretation of history.

Bibliography.–E. Brunner, *The Mediator* (Eng. tr. 1934); *Divine Imperative* (Eng. tr. 1937); R. W. Dale, *Theory of the Atonement* (1895); J. Denney, *Death of Christ* (1902); *Christian Doctrine of Reconciliation* (1917); P. T. Forsyth, *Work of Christ* (1910); L. W. Grensted, *Short History of the Atonement* (1920); A. A. Hodge, *The Atonement* (1867); J. N. D. Kelley, *Early Christian Doctrines* (1958); J. Murray, *Redemption — Accomplished and Applied* (1955), pt. 1; H. Rashdall, *Idea of the Atonement in Christian Theology* (1919); B. B. Warfield, *Biblical Doctrines* (1929), chs. 9-11.

W. S. REID

III. History of the Doctrine.–Since the atonement is a work of inexhaustible significance, and the NT presentation is itself so rich and varied, one need not be surprised that from early times different understandings have competed with or complemented one another. Thus already in the Apostolic Fathers and Apologists, though one finds no specific or comprehensive statements, several aspects of God's reconciling work receive mention and emphasis.

A. Fathers. In Ignatius, for example, the death of Christ is part of the reality of His incarnation (Smyrn. 2). The same point is made by Justin in *Dial.* 99. Justin also sees in the atonement a supreme fulfillment of prophecy, so that there is a divine ineluctability about it (ch. 89). If atonement is linked to the Incarnation on the one side, it is also a step to the Resurrection on the other (Barn. 5:6f.). Christ's work expresses the divine sympathy with us (Justin *Apol.* ii.12f.). It serves as an example of obedience (Ign. Rom. 2:2). It is also a moving demonstration of love (1 Clem. 7:4). If all Christ's life is the ground of reconciliation, forgiveness is specifically through faith and hope in the blood of Christ (12:7). As regards response, love and works also play some part (e.g., *Dial.* 45, 123). But this is possible only because the devil has been defeated by God in Christ (ch. 30). If in these works there is little thought of Christ's death as a penalty or sacrifice, the Epistle to Diognetus finely expresses the element of substitution ("O sweet exchange"). In this connection it quotes the ransom saying from the Gospels and also 1 Pet. 3:18 (cf. Diogn. 9).

The same variety remains as one passes into the fuller patristic era. Yet now two new tendencies emerge. The first is that one of the forms of presentation — the redemption-liberation understanding — begins to attain a dominant position. The other is that there is a certain bifurcation between the more objective western school and the more subjective or Alexandrian theology, although this is a point to be made with considerable caution.

Here as always, Irenaeus of South Gaul is an important figure. On the basis of parallels between the fall and the work of salvation, i.e., the tree, the new Adam, and the new Eve (*Adv. haer.* v.19.1), he sees in the atonement a recapitulation or restoration (iii.19.6). Man, who fell in Adam, is now represented by the new Adam, Christ. As man was slain by the first man, so sin is now slain by the second or new man. The victory had to be won by man to be just, but to be secure it had to be won by God; this is why the second man had to be the incarnate Son of God (*loc. cit.*). The representing of man by Christ involved an exchange: "He was made what we are that we might become what he is" (bk. v pref.). It also involved substitution, his flesh instead of ours. Yet the victory is viewed primarily as an act of liberation. A ransom was paid. In slaying Christ, however, the devil exacted more than his due and thus lost all claim to us (v.1.1; cf. iii.32.2). Appropriation is by faith, though this faith is accompanied by love (ii.44.1).

Tertullian, too, speaks of a rescue from the devil's sway (*De carne Christi* 17). But he also has the idea of substitutionary merit, satisfaction, or compensation for the debt of fallen man (*Adv. Marc.* iv.21). The Incarnation as a whole saves (ii.27), but especially the death, which is a reversal of the fall (v. 14) and the fulfillment of prophecy (*Adv. Judaeos* 10). Entrance into the atonement is by faith and baptism (*De anima* 41), or by martyrdom (*Scorpiace* 6).

On the Alexandrian side Clement points out that the life of Christ equals the world in value (*Quis dives salvetur?* 37). Its main force, however, seems to be as an example. When there is reference to the slaying of the serpent, this is highly figurative (*Protrepticus* 11.111). Salvation is through the incarnate Logos who brings knowledge of God (*Paed.* i.3.7). Sin is ignorance, Christ is the teacher, knowledge brings repentance (i.6.32), and baptism signifies illumination (i.6.28). The concept of punishment occurs, but it is presented as educative rather than penal (i.8.70). To be noted is Clement's variation on the principle of Irenaeus: "The Word of God became man that you also may learn from a man how a man becomes God" (*Protrepticus* 1.8).

Origen, Clement's successor in the cathechetical school at Alexandria, helped to introduce an influential idea into the ransom concept, namely, that of defeating the devil by a stratagem, i.e., the humanity of Christ, in order to secure our liberation from the devil's sway (*Comm. in Mt.* 16.8). In most of his references to the atonement Origen repeats early patristic phrases or ideas, including propitiation (*Comm. in Rom.* 3.8) and punishment (*Comm. in Joannem* 28.19). Christ's death also has value as an example (*Contra Celsum* iii.2.8), and it is as exemplary rather than imputed that the righteousness of Christ saves. The subjective trend in Origen is very clear in his interpretation of the saying of Paul: "So you also must consider yourselves dead to sin," for he takes this to mean that we are to be dead, not in fact, but in thought (*Comm. in Rom.* 5.10). The power of Christ's death to evoke a response of love also occurs (4.10). In addition to the death of Christ and faith, works are necessary to salvation (4.11). Freedom of the will and a speculative transmigration and universalism complete the picture.

The Nicene age produced important thinking on the atonement in both East and West. In the East Athanasius saw how essential was Christ's deity as well as his humanity for full and true atonement. If a man must die for sin, since man is the sinner, only God can so do with saving validity and power (*De incarnatione Verbi* 6). Hence, the Son of God became man for us men and our salvation. Naturally the Incarnation alone did not save; the incarnate Son of God, very God and very man, died on our behalf. His death was a ransom for us. By His life, death, and resurrection He overcame both sin and death. Bearing our corruption even to Golgotha, He also clothed us in His own incorruptibility by His resurrection (9.1). His death was representative; all died in Him. Its aim was to exalt us to divine sonship with Himself; He became man that we might be made gods (54.3). Yet this was a renewal rather than a completely new work; by it the purpose of God in creation, temporarily arrested by sin, came to fulfillment (6.4). Reconciliation in Christ was also accompanied by revelation as its complement, or as another aspect of God's saving work. Through Christ, very God and very man, ignorant man was again enlightened to know God.

Among other Eastern fathers, Eusebius of Caesarea stressed the vicarious aspect. Christ bore the punishment, retribution, or curse in our stead (*Demonstratio evangelica* 10.1). Eusebius also depicted Christ's work as a conquest of demons and as a sacrifice (*Praep. ev.*). This work avails for us by identification. A new note is sounded when the ransom theory comes in for criticism by pseudo-Origen, who asks: "Who is the seller [of Christ]? . . . the devil then holds the blood of Christ as the price of man, What immense and blasphemous folly!" But even so eminent a theologian as Gregory of Nyssa could restate the view with an even more dramatic feature. For him the deity of Christ is the fish-hook that catches the devil when he greedily gulps down "the bait of flesh" (*Oratio catechetica magna* 22, 23). Gregory suggests that since the devil is himself a deceiver, he is justly repaid in his own coin. The ransom itself is an exchange, and it is possible only by God's identification with us in Christ (ch. 26). The Resurrection, as in Athanasius, secures our incorruptibility (ch. 25). Appropriation is sacramental (chs. 33, 37), though conversion is seen to be essential (ch. 40). Gregory of Nazianzus attempts a new version of the ransom understanding in which the ransom is paid to the Father rather than the devil, but he does not seem to see how this can be carried through with consistency (*Oratio* 45.22). He can still speak of a trick played on the devil through Christ's divine humanity (39.13). When discussing Christ's being made a curse for us, he argues that this is not to be taken literally; Christ was not in fact made a curse but was called a curse. Basil of Caesarea repeats the same thought in *Epistula* 261.2, though he can describe Christ quite definitely as an equivalent for us all (*In Ps.* 68.6). Cyril of Jerusalem again alludes to the trick on the devil, but a more interesting concept is that the righteousness of Christ is more than adequate to counterbalance the sin of man: "We did not sin so much as he who laid down his life for us did righteously" (*Catechesis* 13.33).

Chrysostom in a much fuller analysis presents the same idea: "Christ hath paid down more than we owe" (*Homiliae in Rom.* 10.3). He emphasizes the universal character of Christ's death; it is equal "to the death of us all" (*Hom. in Hebr.* 17.2). He tries to find illustrations for the transfer of liability, e.g., a king giving his son for a bandit (*Hom. in 2 Cor.* 11.4). The injustice of Christ's death counterbalances the justice of our own condemnation, so that freedom is secured for the guilty (*Hom. in Ioann.* 62.2f.). Cyril of Alexandria strongly holds that in Christ's flesh an equivalent is paid "for the flesh of us all" (*De recta fide* 21). He describes this payment as a punishment (*De incarnatione* 27). In answer to the possible objection that only the man Jesus died, he replies that by virtue of the *enhypostasis* the one person of Jesus Christ died, so that His death has the scope and efficacy of that of the eternal Son (ch. 16). It is interesting that Cyril's great rival, Nestorius of Constantinople, also spoke of Christ paying our penalty "by substitution for our death." In the final stages of Greek patristic theology John of Damascus referred to a sacrifice for us all (*Expos. Orth.* iv.4f.). While rejecting any payment to the devil, John was still attracted to the metaphor of the deity as a hook on which to catch the devil (iii.27). The relationship to Christ by which the benefits of his reconciling work are secured is primarily sacramental (iv.9,13), though faith, primarily perhaps as orthodox belief, is also required. John's final picture is of all-conquering life in Christ. "Destruction is driven away at the onset of life, and life comes to all, while destruction comes to the destroyer" (iii.27).

In the West, Augustine, as always, exerted a powerful influence, but some development had taken place already in earlier fathers. Cyprian construed Christ's work mainly as a sacrifice which is a fount of sacramental efficacy (*Epistula* 76.2). He also introduced the thought of placation through good works and the merits of martyrs, though this was secondary to the basic work and merit of Christ (cf. *De lapsis, passim*). In Hilary the penal aspect received attention (*in Ps.* 53.12). Arnobius, like many others, quoted Isa. 53, but with an emphasis on the exemplary side (*Inst. Divin.* 4.24f.). Ambrose stood by the ransom idea and offered an elaborate comparison in which sin is a burdened estate on which Christ wipes out the arrears of interest and becomes the new and good creditor (*in Ps.* 36.46). A dangerous idea in the light of future Mariology was the inclusion of Mary's virginity as part of the stratagem by which the devil was defeated. Ambrosiaster also espoused the ransom view, the main point being that the unjust treatment of Christ is to be set over against our just bondage, so that the devil forfeits all claim and has to let us go (*in Col.* 2.15).

Turning to Augustine, we find that he shares the common understanding. Christ's death is a payment that frees us from just enslavement in Satan (*De trin.* xiii.12ff.). In this whole dealing with the devil, Christ's humanity plays the same part as the bait in a mousetrap (*Sermo* 263.1). Yet Augustine digs deeper than this. He sees not merely the payment of a debt whereby the release of justly held debtors is secured, but also the vicarious suffering of a penalty. Emphasis is laid by Augustine on (a) the innocence of Christ (*De trin.* xiii.14) and (b) the efficacy of the work as a work done by God as well as man (ch. 16). While he does not claim that this is the only possible way of atonement, which would seem to imply limitation for God, he likes to point out the congruity of what was in fact done: the priest is the victim; the flesh which sinned also saves; the pure-born body has power to purify (iv.14). With his strong doctrine of predestination Augustine ascribes a crucial role to grace in the application of the work done by Christ. Faith is needed (primarily as belief), but grace works through the sacraments divinely appointed to this end. It should also be noted that since justification tends to be predominantly a making righteous, faith naturally includes good works, especially asceticism.

After Augustine we find little new. Leo combines restoration by Christ's incarnation with the concept of his righteousness counterbalancing our sin (*Sermo* 22.4). Gregory the Great uses the category of penalty: Christ suffers without guilt the penalty of our sins (*Moral.* xiii.30, 34). He displays a tendency to set the Father's justice in some kind of antithesis to the Son's pity (ix.38.61). John Scotus Erigena follows Leo in linking salvation by incarnation to the traditional ransom idea. He seems to suggest that a general resurrection implies universal salvation (*De div. nat.* v.29).

B. Schoolmen. The preparatory scholastic age saw two great but conflicting reinterpretations of the atonement. The first was that of Anselm, who, following his principle of faith seeking understanding, tried to work out a rationale of the biblical teaching in his great work *Cur deus homo?* In so doing Anselm tactfully but firmly resisted the ideas (a) that the devil has rights and (b) that payment is thus in any sense made to him. In place of the devil he sets the divine justice. This demands that sinners be punished by death, so that, if they are to be saved as God's love requires, there must be an equivalent satisfaction which, as death, meets the just demand (i.13). Since sin is an affront to the divine honor, the satisfaction must also make good the affront (i.11). Since sin, as sin against the infinite God, is infinite, the satisfaction must be infinite too (i.21). Man offered the affront and therefore it is incumbent that man also offer the satisfaction, but in fact only God can do this. This leads to the answer to the question in the title. Why the God-man? Because only He who is both God and man can on man's behalf make the satisfaction that will both meet the justice of God and also fulfil the merciful love of God. In detail Anselm works this out clearly and coherently. A virgin birth breaks sin's entail, a life of obedience means that the death is that of the innocent (ii.6-10), and the infinite merit acquired thereby offsets and indeed exceeds the infinite debt (ii.11,14). The reward for this merit is not needed by Christ, who as God already has all things; and so He passes it on to sinners as forgiveness and renewal with a surplus of merit still to spare (ii.19f.). By means of this, and by His example, Christ continues His mediatorial work in the postbaptismal life.

Abelard, too, rejected the ransom view, but apart from some conventional references to satisfaction, he followed a very different line. The main point for him was the teaching of Christ and the response it evoked. Christ became man in order that He might enlighten the world by His wisdom and excite it to love for Himself (*Ep. ad Rom., Opera* [ed. Cousin], II, 207). His death was both a lesson and also an example. Its intended effect was the kindling of a responsive gratitude and love which "should not be afraid to endure anything for his sake" (pp. 766f.). When the sinner was stimulated to amendment of life in this way, God could remit eternal punishment in virtue of the conversion rather than any objective or external equivalent (p. 628). The work of Christ was thus a demonstration of divine love which removed the obstacle between God and man, not by a work for man, but by the effect in him.

In Scholasticism proper neither Anselm nor Abelard found any direct following. The tendency of the movement was toward comprehensive rather than exclusive presentation. Appeal might be made to a thinker like the English theologian Robert Pullan, who rejected the ransom view and in good Abelardian fashion stressed the noetic aspect that Christ "by the greatness of the price" made known to us "the greatness of his love and of our sin" (*Sent.* viii.4.13). But a more representative treatment is that of Lombard, who combines several aspects. Thus a ransom is paid and the devil is caught as in a mousetrap (*Sermo* i.30.2). Yet Christ's death is also seen from the standpoint of satisfaction or merit (*Sent.* iii.18.2). It exerts a moral influence too, for by it we "are moved and kindled to love God who did such great things for us" (19.1).

Thomas Aquinas is even more comprehensive, for when he comes to speak of Christ's reconciling work he lists seven important aspects. (1) Christ's merit outweighs our demerit (*Summa Theol.* iii.48.1). (2) It applies to us by means of union with the head (art. 2). (3) It is a ransom, though the idea of tricking the devil is omitted (art. 4). (4) It moves us to responsive love (49.1). (5) It is a placating sacrifice (art. 4). (6) It represents a vicarious satisfaction or punishment (50.1). (7) It brings remission by way of efficiency, i.e., as the source of grace, prevenient, cooperating, congruous, and condign (art. 6). As in Augustine, this grace is mediated through the sacraments.

Among the later schoolmen the main interest is the new twist that was given to the doctrine by the emphasis on the divine freedom or transcendence. Thus Scotus did not see that Christ's death was a punishment or that God's justice necessarily demanded it. He could regard it as in fact a (nonsubstitutionary) satisfaction, but only because God in love freely willed to accept it as such (a doctrine known as acceptilation). Nor did it have to be infinite in scope but merely sufficient to merit initial grace for man, for which implicit faith was enough on man's part. Occam, too, laid the main stress on the divine good-pleasure. Christ's work did not have to be an exact equivalent. So long as God willed to view it thus, no more was needed. Similarly, God needed only to will that faith, works, and the sacraments be the means by which sinners enter into the accepted merits of Christ. This no doubt spares theologians the difficult task of showing how or why the death of Christ serves as an atonement for sin, but it seems to introduce an element of arbitrariness and even irrationality into God. If God's will is abstractly exalted in this way, He might just as well have called sinners righteous quite apart from Christ. While the fact of atonement through Christ is accepted, its inner logic is ignored and even, in principle, denied.

C. Reformers. Although at some points the Reformers are heirs of the later Nominalism represented by Occam, it would obviously be a mistake to try to understand their theology exclusively from this standpoint. Thus one might argue that if justification means declaring righteous, then in fact believers are justified only because God freely wills and declares them to be so. But this would miss the all-important point that justification by faith is possible only because it is justification in Christ. Behind the declaring just, there lies the atoning work of Christ in virtue of which the declaration is made. Nor is the work of Christ merely accepted by God as a reconciling equivalent even though it is not so in fact. We may be justified by faith through or in Christ because Christ did in fact do a full work of reconciliation in our stead and on our behalf.

Luther, indeed, can even go back to the ransom theory, though perhaps with a greater emphasis on the victorious liberation than on the payment. For him satisfaction is also an important concept (*WA*, x1/1, 503f.). But what really counts in Luther is the vicarious action of Christ, and he makes this point with a vigor that many find distasteful. Christ assumed our sins (pp. 433ff.). He made them His own so that the Father could say to Him: "Thou art that Peter the denier, that Paul the violent persecutor and blasphemer, that David the adulterer, . . . the person of all men who committed the sins of all men" (p. 437, 23). Christ was ready to be the chief murderer, adulterer, thief, blasphemer (p. 433, 26). He was ordained to "eternal punishment on our behalf . . . as if he were a man to be eternally condemned to hell" (*Romans* [ed. Ficker], II, 218). Luther can even speak of the Father being placated by the Son, although it is everywhere evident that it was the Father who in love sent the Son to bear our sins. To Luther the vicarious fulfillment of the law was important as well as the vicarious death. "The law has been fulfilled, that is, by Christ, so that it is not necessary for us to fulfil it" (*WA*, x1/1, 105). Naturally, Luther has justification in view here, for in Christian life believers are, of course, "to be conformed to him who fulfils it." The victorious Christ and the vicarious Christ correspond to the kingly and the priestly offices of Christ in His atoning work.

Calvin developed the doctrine of the atonement much more systematically than Luther did, but the basic elements are much the same. For Calvin the necessity of the atonement is grounded in the divine decree of predestination (*Inst.* ii.12.1). This in turn finds its root or cause in the triune love of God expressed in grace to the elect. Ultimately, then, the atonement is the work of the whole trinity, and this must be remembered when there appears to be an antithesis between the love of Christ and the wrath of God (the Father). Christ executed the work by His substitutionary ministry in which He experienced "all the signs of an angry and punishing God" (*Inst.* [1553] 7.29). He paid the penalty of our sin (*Inst.* ii.16.2). He came as the mediator "to satisfy God by the effusion of his blood" (iv.14.21). The focus is on Christ's death, but Calvin has a much broader view than is sometimes allowed. The self-offering or death of Christ is part of His ministry as priest. This ministry includes the total obedience by which He abolished the disobedience of man and also, of course, the heavenly intercession. Furthermore, the office of Christ is threefold. While He is priest to offer satisfaction for us, He is also prophet to declare the truth of God and king to establish and govern the kingdom of grace.

This threefold work of mediation is developed with great thoroughness by the theologians of the 17th century. (For details of the seventeenth-century theologians, see H. Heppe, *Reformed Dogmatics* [1950].) Here again the heart of it is that "by his blood Christ hath intervened," so that "from a condemning judge God has become a judge who pardons" (Heidegger *Corp. Theol.* XIX, 22). This is done by merit and efficacy (cf. Polanus *Synth. Theol. Christ.* VI, 27). Yet more than the death is involved, for "he opposed a triple cure to sweep away this triple misery," i.e., a prophetic work for ignorance, a priestly for alienation, and a kingly for impotence (Heidegger XIX, 26).

The prophetic work comprises "the external promulgation of divine truth" and "the internal illumination of hearts by the Holy Spirit" (Polanus VI, 29). It is both legal and evangelical, being done by Christ yet to be incarnate as well as by Christ incarnate (*loc. cit.*). It includes not only teaching but also signs, miracles, and even prayer (Alstedtius *Theol. Scol.* 574). It can be indirect (through the disciples) as well as direct (Leiden *Syn.* XXVI, 41).

The priestly work received greater elaboration. It is "a propitiatory offering along with intercession" (Olevianus *De subst. foed.* I, 3). The offering or satisfaction, in the form of obedience, is both active and passive. The active obedience is that of the life of Christ, especially as a federal obedience for us (Wollebius *Christ. Theol. Compend.* 81). The passive obedience comprises the whole passion before death, in death, and after death, in which Christ bore the weight of sin and wrath (Keckermann *Syst. Sacros Theol.* 346). Christ suffered thus after the human nature, so that the man died, but "divine weight is added" (Wendel in *Collat. doctrin.* 211). The active and passive obedience must "not be torn apart"; "from the joining of the two full satisfaction arises" (Burmann *Synop. Theol.* IV, 19, 3). This satisfaction is vicarious (Leiden *Syn.* XXIV, 4), necessary (Cocceius *Summa Theol.* LXI, 5-10), and full (not just by acceptilation [Turrettini *Compend. Theol.* XIV, 10, 14]). In spite of some of the expressions used it involves no change in God: "Not that he transformed God . . . from one who hated us to one who loved us" (Maresius *Colleg. Theol.* X, 41). It is universal in sufficiency but limited to the elect in efficacy: "For all sufficiently . . . efficaciously only for the elect" (Olevianus, 67f.). Intercession is also part of the priestly work. This is twofold, the intercession in the days of humility and the intercession in glory (a Diest *Theol. Bibl.* 207). It consists "rather in things than in words" (Turrettini XIV, 15, 13). This ministry is restricted to the elect (Heidegger XIX, 95).

The kingly work is specifically related to the exaltation of Christ which follows the central priestly work of his exinanition (self-humiliation). In its special sense (donative, economic, and dispensative) "the kingly office is to govern and preserve the church" (Wollebius, 79). It covers (a) vocation (both general and effectual) and (b) government. It is exercised by Christ as both God and man and is for ever (Heidegger XIX, 103, 112). It is now indirect (through rulers, pastors, etc.), but in heaven it will be direct (Leiden, *Syn.* XXVI, 52). It will not finally merge into the essential government of Christ as the eternal Logos but will change in form (Riissen), so that Wollebius can say: "The economic kingship he will exercise for ever" (VIII, 80).

D. Liberal Thinkers. As compared with the teaching of the Reformation churches, and indeed with the Roman Catholic restatement of Anselm or Thomas Aquinas, the humanist or liberal doctrines of the atonement purchase simplicity at the cost of fulness and profundity. Already at the end of the 16th cent. and the beginning of the 17th, various schools were foreshadowing things to come with their reductions. Grotius, for instance, abandoned true satisfaction for a new and juridical form of Scotus' "acceptilation." Since law and punishment are enactments, Grotius argued, God is not tied to them (*Defensio fidei* [1614], III, 60, 110). Salvation is by relaxation of the law, not satisfaction (311). This is not abrogation, for the interests of moral government must not be harmed (V). Instead, God accepts Christ's death as a nominal equivalent, a quid pro quo (VI). This is pure mercy, but God gives and accepts a ransom in which the deliverer bears something similar to the penalty, and the evil consequences of relaxation are thus averted (VI, VIII, IX). Although Grotius denies that this is formally acceptilation, and there are obvious differences, it amounts in fact to very much the same thing.

Some Arminians viewed the atonement along similar lines. They espoused substitution, but a substitute for the penalty rather than penal substitution. The term "offering" was thus preferred to "satisfaction." The offering might be called satisfaction in the sense of being pleasing, or satisfactory, to God's benevolence. Even the offering, however, was more a precondition of forgiveness than its basis, since, it was argued, God's justice could have required nothing more had this offering been the basis of forgiveness. As it is, however, forgiveness comes through faith and obedience; but it would not do so if Christ had not made His self-offering. In other words, once the condition of this offering has been met, God may now require faith and obedience, and those who believe and obey are forgiven.

Socinianism went even further, opening the door to the fully developed subjective understanding that has dominated liberal Protestantism. Like Grotius, Socinus argued that justice is not essential. It depends, as mercy also does, on God's will (*Praelectiones theologicae* [1609], XVI). A doctrine of satisfaction makes the mistake of upholding justice at the expense of mercy (XVIII). In any case, substitution is impossible for Socinus, since punishment is personal. At the most, only a substitute for the penalty might be offered (XVIII). It is to be argued against penal satisfaction (a) that Christ's death was not eternal (*loc. cit.*), (b) that Christ's obedience cannot be vicarious, since he also owed obedience (*loc. cit.*), (c) that imputation by faith is self-contradictory (*De Christo Servatore* [1594], IV, 3), and (d) that satisfaction destroys sanctification (*loc. cit.*). Atonement is secured instead by penitence and a will to obey. The role of Christ's death is that of an example of obedience.

The subjective view naturally found support and expression in the various anthropocentric theologies of the age that followed. Thus the German Neology taught that the force of Christ's death is to be found in its example and inspiration. Kant in his clumsy jargon specifically attacked and rejected an objective atonement; according to his moral subjectivism man must first earn forgiveness by doing his duty, and then God will grant it to him (*Religion Within the Limits of Reason Alone* [1793]). Schleiermacher was more profound. Christianity is the basic and true religion because it perceives the antithesis between

God and man, and synthesis or reconciliation is achieved in Christ the God-man. As always in Schleiermacher, however, the doctrine is finally no more than a description of the inner state (*Speeches* V). F. D. Maurice, who in any case objected to eternal punishment, could find little place for an objective work for us. Ritschl, with his value judgments, presented what is in many ways a new version of acceptilation. The historical death of Jesus has the value of an act of reconciliation. In this case, however, the value is for us rather than for God, so that the essence and effect are inward. The new historicism thus turns out to be an old subjectivism. Bushnell emerged as another prominent proponent for understanding the atonement in terms of moral influence. Rashdall in the 20th cent., in his learned but biased Bampton Lectures entitled *The Idea of the Atonement in Christian Theology* (1920), castigated the immoralities and irrationalities of all objective understandings and came out strongly for atonement by the combined example and effect of the obedience of Jesus, which carried Him to the cross. Ironically the ink was hardly dry on Rashdall's rational subjectivism before a far-from-rational existentialism was beginning to find the atonement in the transition from death to life, or darkness to light, of which Christ's historical death and (less than historical) resurrection are little more than symbols or ciphers, even if it is the preaching of these that produces the result (Bultmann). Perhaps the logical end of subjectivism is the complete absorption of God in Death-of-God theology, in which God achieves total immanence by the crucifixion, and there is thus a universal or even cosmic atonement by identification of God and man or God and creation. But this is after all only a variation of the triadic theme of Schleiermacher and his contemporaries Schelling and Hegel.

E. Conservative Theologians. A survey of the liberal and predominantly subjective presentations might suggest that the older emphases have been completely ousted. In reality, however, this is not the case. Throughout the last two centuries the objective view has found vigorous champions both in traditional forms and also in attempted reformulations. Furthermore, the basic NT evidence has received a new and better attention than in a sketch like Rashdall's. Both studies of individual words, as in *TDNT,* and also more general accounts, such as Leon Morris' *Apostolic Preaching of the Cross* (3rd ed. 1965), have confirmed that an objective and even a substitutionary doctrine is not a later invention of theology, nor even a Pauline peculiarity, but an inherent part of the total event, record, and interpretation of Christ's saving work.

Among proponents of a penal understanding one might refer first to J. K. Mozley, who concludes his competent and comprehensive survey by stating: "I do not therefore think that we need shrink from the fact that Christ bore penal suffering for us and in our stead" (*Doctrine of Atonement* [1915, 1947], p. 216). Denney, too, has an able and forthright presentation of the objective work for us: "I do not know of any word which conveys the truth of this [Paul's teaching] if 'vicarious' or 'substitutionary' does not" (*Death of Christ,* p. 126). In his well-known work, *Theory of the Atonement,* Dale contends that Christ's death is "the objective ground on which the sins of men are remitted" as "an act of submission to the righteous authority of the Law by which the human race was condemned." This act atones in virtue of Him who did it, our relation to Him, His making our sufferings His own, and its imposing of a similar obligation of submission on all who believe in Him. Being performed in our stead, it is really ours. Furthermore, Christ's death is also the objective ground of remission, because it makes possible the restoration of the original relation to God that sin had dissolved and the loss of which was the supreme penalty of transgression. Again, it is the objective ground in that "it involved the actual destruction of sin." Finally, it is the objective ground because God's righteousness was revealed in such sort that God "endured the penalty instead of inflicting it" (pp. 430ff.). Along rather different lines R. L. Ottley, while defending the thought of Christ as substitute, emphasizes the enclosing or including of all men in Him by reason of the Incarnation (*Doctrine of the Incarnation,* II [1896], 315). W. Temple, in his essay in *Foundations* (1912), pp. 252-58, follows a similar line of thought. Christ is not just one man but man generically, so that what He does, all do in Him. Even the ancient redemption or liberation view has been revived in *Christus Victor* (1935), a fine book by G. Aulen, who points out that for all the curious distortions it suffered, this understanding expresses the sound and biblical concept of the active and triumphant Christ.

Already in Aulen's book we are perhaps more in the realm of restatement rather than reiteration of the traditional objective teaching. In this area the 20th cent. has perhaps been a more fruitful period than its predecessor. At the beginning, R. C. Moberly in his *Atonement and Personality* (1901) made an important if not entirely successful attempt to present Christ's work more in terms of vicarious penitence than vicarious punishment. This preserves the equation of Christ and mankind, and undoubtedly has the twofold merit (1) of doing greater justice to the life as well as the death of Christ, and (2) of making a firmer link with the repentance required and evoked in us. More traditionally but with great freshness and force, P. T. Forsyth (e.g., *Cruciality of the Cross* [1909, 1965]) contends that the work of Christ, if not precisely penal, is a substitutionary cost-bearing. His thought would seem to be that sin, like crime, involves cost. Hence, even though forgiveness is freely bestowed in love, the cost has to be paid by the one who forgives. God carries the cost for us in the expiatory work of Christ. At many points this obviously merges into a penal understanding. The cost of sin, which is death, has the characteristics, not of a blow to God, but of a penalty or consequence for sinners themselves. Yet God Himself absorbs it.

A new and powerful voice rang out across the theological world with the publication of Emil Brunner's *The Mediator.* Here Brunner sees and discusses two great lines of understanding in Scripture, the legal one with Christ's death as penalty and the cultic one with Christ as sacrifice. Brunner himself develops the doctrine along both lines. If he maintains a certain caution — these are interpretations rather than the fact itself — he stands firmly by the objective reality of the fact. Christ did something for us in accomplishment of our reconciliation with God. This is presented in legal and cultic analogues in Scripture, and it is along such lines that we can best understand it.

An even more comprehensive and searching restatement, with a bolder emphasis on vicariousness, is to be found in Barth's volume on reconciliation in *CD* (IV/1-3). Barth combines many themes here: the execution of election; the fulfillment of the covenant; the Incarnation and Christ's role as very God, very man, and God-man; justification, sanctification, and vocation; the gathering, upbuilding, and sending of the Church; the faith, love, and hope of the individual Christ. His basic scheme is the traditional Reformed one of the triple office of Christ, but he rearranges the order. Christ does His priestly work as the Son of God, the Lord who has become a servant; He does His kingly work as the Son of man, the servant who is exalted to be Lord; and He does His prophetic work as the victorious God-man, the true witness and guarantor. All these are essential parts or aspects of the one work of reconciliation. So far as the death of Christ is concerned, Barth allows with Brunner that one might follow a cultic or indeed a military or financial model, but even though this is Christ's priestly work, Barth himself prefers the judicial model. Christ is the judge, judged in our place and establishing judgment and justice. Quite naturally, this presentation is strongly penal, but the real heart of it — and this would apply in the other categories too — is the representative, vicarious, and substitutionary work of Christ as very God made man, living the obedient life we ought to live and also dying the penal death we ought to die in order that these may be ours in Him. The same vicariousness applies to the kingly work of Christ as Son of man, both in the life of royal obedience that He lived in order that our life may be sanctified in Him, and also in His raising up to eternal life which may equally be ours in Him. Objectively, Barth's stress on Christ for us leads him to stress also the universal reality of the atonement, although he leaves as an open question, subject to the sovereignty of the Spirit, whether or not all men enjoy its benefits.

On balance one may say that while the temper of much Protestant theology has been that of anthropocentric subjectivity, the objective presentation has not only held its own but has in fact displayed far greater force, freshness, and versatility. Apart from the existentialist variations, more recent subjective statements have been little more than stale and platitudinous repetitions that answer to the biblical data only by discarding the biblical norm. The main reaction either to solid biblical expositions or to vast and penetrating reinterpretations, such as that of Barth, is to ignore them. Of course, an objective understanding does not itself see a rival but rather a friend and complement in the subjective understanding. The work for us can and must and does push on to the work in us. Only when the work in us tries to stand on its own feet, to renounce the prior and underlying work for us, does the dispute arise, whose only consequence is a necessary qualifying of the work in us. Yet even though this seems plain enough, it is unlikely that the plea for an independent work in us will be abandoned unless theologians recover from the "pre-Copernican" illusion that God revolves around man instead of man around God. An anthropocentric theology has no proper place for God, and therefore for the work of God for us. A theocentric theology assures to man, and therefore to the work of God in man, a true and proper place.

Bibliography.–G. Aulen, *Christus Victor* (1935); K. Barth, *CD*, IV/1-3; E. Brunner, *The Mediator* (Eng. tr. 1934); H. Heppe, *Reformed Dogmatics* (1950) — esp. for many works from 17th cent.; J. N. D. Kelly, *Early Christian Doctrines* (1958); *LCC*, V-XI; H. Rashdall, *Idea of Atonement in Christian Theology* (1920); P. Schaff, *Creeds of Christendom* (1938). For details consult also works mentioned in the article. G. W. BROMILEY

ATONEMENT, DAY OF [Heb. *yôm hakkippurîm*–lit. 'day of the covering over,' i.e., 'day of appeasement']. The fourth of the five annual feasts of preexilic Israel.

The name *yôm hakkippurîm* (more familiarly Yom Kippur) is derived from the Heb. noun *kôper*, "ransom" or "hush money" (Ex. 30:12; 1 S. 12:3; KoB, p. 453; R. Laird Harris, *Bulletin of the Evangelical Theological Society*, 4 [Apr. 1961], 3). KoB comment that "the aim of [*kipper*] . . . always is to avert evil, especially punishment" (p. 452). Yom Kippur was the day above all others on which Israel, as a nation, sought the propitiation of the God against whom they had sinned, together with the consequent blessing of His forgiveness and of reconciliation to Him.

The Day of Atonement fell on the tenth day of the seventh month (Tishri = Sept./Oct.), nine days after the Feast of Trumpets and five days before the coming of Tabernacles, or Ingathering. This last feast had been revealed to Israel at the time of its arrival at Sinai (Ex. 23:16; cf. 19:1), late in the spring of 1446 B.C. according to one system of biblical chronology. Soon thereafter, according to Ex. 30:10 (directions for the construction of the altar of incense), Aaron was instructed to make an atonement once a year on the horns of the altar with the blood of "the sin-offering of atonement." But not until the following year, after the completion of the tabernacle (Ex. 40:17; Nu. 10:11), was full divine revelation granted to Moses concerning the Day of Atonement (Lev. 16).

- I. Its Institution
  - A. Position in Leviticus
  - B. Legal Enactment, Lev. 16
  - C. Unity of the Chapter
- II. Significance
  - A. Contemporary Symbolism
  - B. Typology
- III. History
  - A. Relative Silence of the OT History
  - B. Historicity
  - C. Further Development

I. Institution.–*A. Position in Leviticus.* Chapter 16 occupies a well-established place in Leviticus. This "book of life" has as its purpose the presentation of God's "judgments: which if a man do, he shall live in them" (18:5). Thus, even as the salvation of men involves both God's acts of redemption and man's own response of appropriation through sincere commitment to Him, so Leviticus contains two parts: On the way of access to God (chs. 1–16) and on the way of living for God (chs. 17–27, holiness according to ceremonial, moral, and devotional standards). The former, which describes the propitiation of God's wrath through sacrifice (chs. 1–7), intercession by a priestly ministry (chs. 8–10), and the purification of God's people (chs. 11–15), is climaxed by a visible enactment of reconciliation: the Day of Atonement service (ch. 16). Lev. 16:1 refers back to the events of ch. 10. (This, however, does not mean that ch. 16 has been displaced by an interpolation, chs. 11–15. It implies merely that both sections, chs. 11–15 and ch. 16, were revealed shortly after ch. 10. Even critical scholars recognize that the position occupied by chs. 11–15 "is a thoroughly appropriate one" [S. R. Driver, *Intro. to the Literature of the OT* (9th ed. 1913), p. 46].) A clear transition, moreover, to the thoughts of Lev. 16 appears in 15:31 with its mention of the uncleanness of the Israelites, which contaminates the dwelling place of Yahweh that is in their midst (cf. 16:16-20).

B. Legal Enactment, Lev. 16. Lev. 16:1-28 contains instructions given by Yahweh to Moses for his brother Aaron (vv. 1f.). (1) Verses 1-10 contain presuppositions, preparations, and summary statements of the ceremonies on the Day of Atonement. According to vv. 1f. Aaron is not allowed to enter the holy place at any time whatever, lest he die as did his sons with their unholy fire offering (cf. Lev. 10:1ff.); vv. 3-5 tell what is necessary for the ceremony: for Aaron four things — a young bullock as a sin offering (cf. vv. 6, 11, 14f., 27), a ram for burnt offering (cf. v. 24), sacred garments (cf. vv. 23, 32), a bath; for the congregation — two goats, one for a sin offering and the other for a scapegoat (cf. vv. 7-10, 15-22, 25, 27f., 32f.) and a ram as a burnt offering (cf. v. 24). The passages in parentheses show how closely the succeeding parts of this account are connected with this introductory part.

In other parts of Leviticus also it is often found that the materials used for the sacrifices are mentioned first, before anything is said in detail of what is to be done with this material. Cf. 8:1f. with vv. 6-26 and 9:24 with vv. 7-18. In v. 6 Aaron's sin-offering bullock is to be used as an atonement for himself; vv. 7-10 refer to the two goats: they are to be placed at the door of the tent of meeting (v. 7); lots are to be cast upon them for Yahweh and Azazel (v. 8); the first is to be prepared as a sin offering (v. 9); the second, while not an offering, is yet to be used for atonement by being sent into the desert (v. 10).

(2) Verses 11-24 describe the ceremony itself and give fuller directions as to how the different sacrificial materials mentioned under (1) are to be used by Aaron. Verses 11-14 speak of the atonement for Aaron and his house — v. 11 of his sin-offering bullock to be killed; v. 12 of burning coals from the altar and incense to be placed behind the veil; v. 13 of the cloud of incense to be made in the holy of holies over the mercy seat so that Aaron is protected from the danger of death; v. 14 of Aaron's second passing within the veil, with some of the bullock's blood to be sprinkled on and in front of the mercy-seat. Verses 15-19 prescribe the ceremony with the first, the sin-offering goat, for the congregation — vv. 15, 16a, Aaron enters a third time within the veil, and the ceremony described in v. 14 is directed also to be carried out with the goat, as an atonement for the inner sanctuary, cleansing it from blemishes; v. 16b, the same thing is directed to be done in regard to the holy place; v. 17, no one is permitted to be present even in the holy place when these ceremonies transpire; vv. 18f., the altar too is directed to be cleansed by an atonement with some of the blood of both sin-offering animals. Verses 20-22 prescribe the ceremony with the second, the scapegoat, for the congregation — v. 20 directs it to be brought in; v. 21, the transfer of guilt takes place as Aaron confesses all Israel's sins over its head; v. 22, the goat is sent away, an "escape goat," carrying the nations's guilt into the uninhabited desert. Verses 23f. mark the concluding act as Aaron takes off his linen garments, bathes in the holy place, resumes his usual priestly garments, and presents the burnt-offering rams for himself and his people.

(3) Verses 25-28 are explanatory, with four additional directions — v. 25, the fat of the sin offering is directed to be consumed on the altar; v. 26, he who has taken away the second goat must wash his clothes and bathe himself, and only then is he permitted to enter the camp; v. 27, the flesh and stomach contents of the sin-offering animals are to be burned outside the camp; v. 28; the one who burns them must wash, as in v. 26.

(4) Verses 29-34. Over against sections (1)-(3) (vv. 1-28), a fourth (vv. 29-34), phrased in the 2nd person plural, is addressed to the congregation. In vv. 29-31, the demand is made that Israel "afflict their souls," a general expression for self-humiliation (cf. Dt. 8:2f., 16; Nu. 30:13), signifying sincere repentance. It might include such elements as bowed heads, prayer, fasting, or the use of sackcloth and ashes (Ps. 35:13; Isa. 58:3-6); cf. Ezr. 8:21, "a fast, that we might humble ourselves" (RV). The OT, however, never specifically legislates a regular fast (*see* FAST, FASTING). The congregation was also to observe "a sabbath of solemn rest," by abstaining from all work on the tenth day of the seventh month. In vv. 32-34, a number of directions are given, summarizing the previous statements; and in v. 34 the service is declared to be an everlasting statute, an annual Day of Atonement for all sins.

C. Unity of the Chapter. An attempt is made by almost all modern critics to destroy the above-demonstrated unity of Lev. 16. The general critical approach is to distinguish three rituals: a purification ceremony, making possible the high priest's entry into the most holy place (vv. 1-6, 34b; R. H. Pfeiffer includes vv. 1-4; 6 [11], 12-13, 23-24a, 34b, under "P^s" [Priestly Code, secondary], p. 251); a scapegoat ritual of magic, dating back to immemorial antiquity and tolerated in more enlightened times only as "a concession to popular demands" (vv. 7-10; cf. *IB,* II, 77f.); and an annual atonement service (vv. 29-34a, a secondary version, according to Pfeiffer, of Lev. 23:26-32, "P" [p. 266]). These would then have been combined in postexilic days and elaborated according to vv. 11-28 (cf. W. Eichrodt, *Theology of the OT* [Eng. tr. 1961], I, 130). As S. R. Driver long ago cautioned, however, "it may be doubted whether the successive stages in the amalgamation and development . . . can be distinguished by means of a literary analysis" (*HDB,* I, 201). The phrase "not at all times" in Lev. 16:2 suggests a specific occasion of the high priest's entry, viz., the Day of Atonement (vv. 29f.); and the atonement-making of v. 30 (cf. 23:28) presupposes certain already articulated regulations, viz., the ceremonies of vv. 3-28. Scripture itself pronounces the whole chapter to be one unified message of Yahweh.

***II. Significance.**–A. Contemporary Symbolism.* In accordance with its name, Yom Kippur was designed to effect atonement. The blood of sacrifices, suffering death in the place of sinful men, symbolized the propitiation of God's wrath first of all against Aaron and his priestly family (Lev. 16:6, 11); for even the high priest stood before God as a death-guilty sinner (v. 13). On this day, with the exception of the miter, he does not wear the insignia of his high-priestly office but dons white garments, which in their simplicity represent the earnestness of the situation. The repetition of the bath, both in his case and in that of the other persons engaged in the ceremony (vv. 4, 24, 26, 28), was necessary, because the mere washing of the hands and feet (Ex. 30:19f.) would not suffice on this occasion (cf. Nu. 19:7ff., 19, 21). Correspondingly, the flesh of the sin-offering animals was not permitted to be eaten but had to be burned (v. 27) because it was sacrificed also for Aaron's sin (compare Lev. 16:27 with 6:23; 4:11f., 21; Ex. 29:14; Lev. 8:17; 9:11; 10:19). Atonement is further wrought for the sanctuary, which has been defiled by the contamination of Israel (Ex. 30:10; Lev. 16:16-20, 33; cf. also Ezk. 45:18-20). In particular, the holy of holies is mentioned (Lev. 16:33), then the holy place (vv. 16b, 20, 33), and then the altar (vv. 18, 20, 33). With the way thus prepared, a climactic atonement takes place for all the transgressions of the congregation since the last Day of Atonement (cf. vv. 21f., 30, 34). Particularly significant is the departure of the sin-laden scapegoat (vv. 8, 10, 20-22; cf. Lev. 14:7, 53; Zec. 5:5-11; and numerous parallels in other religions), not as a sin offering (for God's people are not to sacrifice to demons, Dt. 32:17), but symbolizing the sending back to its satanic source the guilt of Israel (*see* AZAZEL). Thus Delitzsch correctly called the Day of Atonement "the Good Friday of the Old Testament." Furthermore, even as salvation requires both God's redemptive activity and man's response of faith, so also the ritual of atonement remained ineffective unless accompanied by sincere repentance (cf. Nu. 15:30). As the Talmud later cautioned, there could be no forgiveness for a man who sinned, counting on Yom Kippur for atonement (*Yoma* viii-ix). In comparison, however, with the consciousness of sin that had been aroused, how great must God's grace have appeared when once in each year a general remission of sins was vouchsafed!

B. Typology. But just as with the tabernacle and the sacrificial system, so too the Day of Atonement contained only the shadow of future good things, but not these things themselves (He. 10:1). Its intrinsic limitations are manifest, both in the repetitiveness of its numerous atoning acts and by its recurrence year after year (He. 7:27). Yom Kippur was an acted prophecy or type of Christ, who has entered into the holy place not made with hands, viz., into heaven itself, and has now appeared before God, by once for all giving Himself as a sacrifice for the removal of sin (9:23ff.). Like the first goat, burned outside the camp, He died outside the walls of Jerusalem for us (13:12); and like the second, the scapegoat, He suffered substitutionary condemnation, sending sin back to its demonic author and abrogating Satan's claims over the fulness of Israel (2:14f.; 1 Jn. 3:8). By this act, the purpose of OT sacrificial worship in its highest development (viz., the Day of Atonement) has been fulfilled. Accordingly our hope too, like an anchor (He. 6:19), penetrates to the inner part of the veil in the higher sense of the term, i.e., to heaven.

***III. History.**–A. Relative Silence of the OT History.* Shortly after its primary revelation in Lev. 16, Moses again mentions the Day of Atonement in 23:26-32, in the list of Israel's annual festivals. It is ordered that for this day there shall be a holy convocation at the sanctuary, a humbling of the heart, and sabbath rest from labor, under threat of divine destruction (cf. Nu. 29:7). Then according to Lev. 25:9 the Year of Jubilee begins with the Day of Atonement. Lev. 16 closes, however, with the statement that Aaron (cf. v. 2) did as Yahweh commanded Moses. The first full observance of Yom Kippur must therefore have taken place in the fall of that year, possibly 1445 B.C. Nu. 18:7 subsequently states that Aaron and his sons, in contrast to the ordinary Levites, are to perform the duties of the priesthood "within the veil," by which reference is again made to the ceremony of the Day of Atonement. Thirty-eight years later Nu. 29:7-11 once more validates the observance when it speaks of offerings on this day additional to those which are brought for the purposes of atonement for sin. But the OT makes no further explicit mention of the Day of Atonement. Jeremiah's "fast day" (36:6) was a special observance in the ninth month (v. 9). Similarly Ezekiel, in his vision of the new temple (chs. 40–46), gives a series of enactments for the festivals that includes an atonement service in the first month (45:18-25). But while vv. 18-20 appear to present an analogy to Lev. 16, they cannot be put on the same level as the Mosaic enactments. They are to be regarded as an ideal scheme, the realization of which was conditioned on a degree of popular obedience that failed to materialize among those Jews who returned from Babylon (cf. 43:10f.). Neh. 9:1 records a gathering in Jerusalem in the seventh month of 444 B.C. for the purpose of confession, with fasting and sackcloth. This appears to represent Ezra's reestablishment on the Day of Atonement. The time of its observance, however, was postponed two weeks that year, until the twenty-fourth day of the month, presumably to allow for the Feast of Tabernacles from the fifteenth to the twenty-second, which seems to have suffered similar postexilic neglect, and had even been completely forgotten until that very time (cf. 8:14).

B. Historicity. Many critical OT scholars have assumed that the elaborate rituals of the Day of Atonement could have arisen only at a late postexilic date in the history of Israel (*see* LEVITICUS). They have relegated all the above-listed references to the so-called Priestly Code, claiming that the day originated in the days of atonement mentioned in Ezk. 45:18-20, in the four national fast days of Zec. 7:5 and 8:19, and in the day of penance of 444 B.C., just mentioned, on the twenty-fourth day of the seventh month. It is thought that in this way Lev. 16:29ff. came into being, and that at a later time the complicated blood ritual was added (see I.C above). But it is to be observed that in still later times there is found no more frequent mention of the Day of Atonement than in the earlier. Sir. 50:5ff. refers to the high priest Simon on Yom Kippur, although no further mention is made at this place of the ceremony as such. Except for a similar allusion in 3 Macc. 1:11, there is then a further silence on the subject down to Philo (*De specialibus legibus* ii.193-223 [ch. 32]), Josephus (*Ant.* xiv.4.3), and the NT (Acts 27:9; He. 6:19; 9:7, 13ff; 10:1ff.), which shows how carefully we must handle the argument from silence if we do not want to arrive at uncomfortable results.

Actually, the Day of Atonement is stated to have been instituted in the times of Moses (Lev. 16:1); the ceremony takes place in the Mosaic tabernacle; the people are presupposed to be in the camp (vv. 26ff.); Aaron is still the high priest; and even the most extreme critics admit that the references to the ark must be "in some sense preexilic" (*IB*, II, 81). Indeed, it is impossible to separate Lev. 16 from the other priestly ordinances, because the name of the lid of the ark of the covenant (Heb. *kappōreṯ*, Ex. 25:17ff.; 26:34) stands in the clearest relation to the ceremony that takes place on the Day of Atonement. If the ark was no longer in existence after the Exile, and if, as according to Jer. 3:16, the Israelites no longer expected its restoration, then it would have been impossible to connect the most important ceremony of the Yom Kippur ritual with the ark and to base the atonement on this. Finally, the Passover festival is mentioned in prophetic literature, in addition to the mere reference in Isa. 30:29, only in Ezk. 45:21; the ark of the covenant only in Jer. 3:16; the Feast of Tabernacles only in Hos. 12:9; Ezk. 45:25; Zec. 14:16-19; and the Feast of Weeks is mentioned incidentally only in 2 Ch. 8:13, and possibly in 1 K. 9:25, and is not found at all in Ezekiel (cf. 45:18ff.).

C. Further Development. The Day of Atonement came more and more into the foreground in later times and was called "the great fast" (cf. Acts 27:9), "the great day," or merely "the day." Its ritual was further enlarged and the special parts mentioned in the law were fully explained, fixed, and specialized (cf. esp. Mish. *Yoma*). Modern Jews, no matter how indifferent they may otherwise be to old customs and festivals, generally observe "Yom Kippur." Since the destruction of the Jerusalem temple in A.D. 70 the blood offerings have necessarily ceased. Judaism, paradoxically, explains its loss of objective atonement as a punishment for its sins. Indeed, no man may come unto the Father but by Jesus, the Lamb slain to take away the sin of the world (Jn. 1:29; 14:6).

Bibliography.–H. Cohen, *Judaism*, 17 (1968), 352-57; 18 (1969), 86-90, 216-222; W. Eichrodt, *Theology of the OT* (Eng. tr. 1961), I, 130f., 163-65; J. G. Frazer, *The Scapegoat* (*The Golden Bough* [3rd ed. 1913], IX); S. Landersdorfer, *Studien zum biblischen Versöhnungstag* (1924); M. Löhr, *Das Ritual von Lev. 16* (1925); N. Micklem, *IB*, II, 77-85; W. G. Moorehead, *Studies in the Mosaic Institutions* (*ca.* 1895), ch. 5; G. Oehler, *Theology of the OT* (Eng. tr. 1883), pp. 309-319; J. B. Payne, *Theology of the Older Testament* (1962), ch. 28-C; *ILC*, I-II, 454-460; III-IV, 447, 453f., 464; *PIOT*, pp. 251, 255, 261f., 266; R. Rendtorff, *Die Gesetze in der Priesterschrift* (1954), pp. 59ff.; N. H. Snaith, *Leviticus and Numbers* (1967), pp. 109-118; G. von Rad, *Die Priesterschrift im Hexateuch* (1934), pp. 85ff.

W. MÖLLER
J. B. PAYNE

ATROTH-BETH-JOAB at'roth-beth-jō'ab [Heb. *'aṭrôṯ bêṯ yô'āḇ*–'crowns of the house of Joab'] (1 Ch. 2:54);

AV "Ataroth, the house of Joab"; NEB "Ataroth, Beth-joab." *See* ATAROTH **4.**

ATROTH-SHOPHAN at'roth-shō'fan [Heb. *'aṭrôṯ šôpān*; Gk. *gēn sōpár*]. A town built or fortified by the tribe of Gad in Transjordan (Nu. 32:35). The AV reads "Atroth, Shophan" as two places, but this is contrary to the LXX reading. Likewise, attempts to identify the site with Khirbet 'Aṭṭārûs or Rujm 'Atarus fail to account for the LXX reading of the second element (Shophan/Sophar) as the place name. W. S. L. S.

ATTAI at'ī [Heb. *'attay*–'timely'(?)].

1. A son of Jarha the Egyptian, by a daughter of Sheshan (1 Ch. 2:35f.).

2. A Gadite soldier who joined David's army at Ziklag (1 Ch. 12:11).

3. A son of Rehoboam and grandson of Solomon (2 Ch. 11:20).

ATTAIN. Archaic, difficult, or otherwise important occurrences include the following: In 2 S. 23:19, 23 (par. 1 Ch. 11:21, 25) the meaning of Heb. *bô'* is clearest in the NEB, "he did not *rival* the three." In Prov. 1:5, *qānâ* ("buy") is best translated as in the RSV and NEB, "acquire."

In the NT, Gk. *katantáō* is used both of a ship "reaching" a harbor (Acts 27:12) and of "attaining" the resurrection (Phil. 3:11; NEB "arrive at"). In Phil. 3:12 the word is *lambánō* (RSV "obtained"; NEB "achieved"; cf. Rom. 9:30, *katalambánō*), and in 3:16 *phthánō* is used: "let us hold true to what we have attained." The idea of "attaining to the resurrection" is found in the words of Jesus in Lk. 20:35, where the Greek word is *tynchánō* (AV "obtain"; cf. 2 Tim. 2:10; He. 11:35).

In Rom. 9:31 the AV has "attained to the law of righteousness" (*phthánō*), which the RSV interprets as "succeed in fulfilling." "Attained" in 1 Tim. 4:6, AV (*parakolouthéō*), is better rendered "followed," as in the other versions. J. W. D. H.

ATTALIA at-ə-lī'ə [Gk. *Attalia*]. A harbor city on the southwest coast of Asia Minor in the region of Pamphylia; modern Adalia.

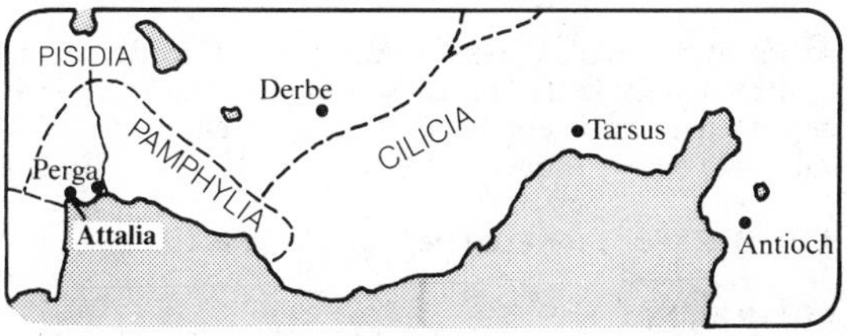

Attalia stood on a flat terrace of limestone about 120 ft. (37 m.) above the Catarrhactes River, which flowed directly into the sea. The river has now all but disappeared, its waters having been diverted for irrigation purposes. The port served the rich district of southwest Phrygia, and an important trade route passed through it en route to the Lycus and Meander valleys, and so to Ephesus and Smyrna. It was in turn the preferred route to Syria and Egypt. It was accordingly overrun by the successive Persian, Macedonian, Seleucid, Attalid, and Roman invaders. Paul and Silas passed through it as they returned to Antioch from their first missionary journey (Acts 14:25). Although it originally served as the port for Perga, some 8 mi. (13 km.) inland, by early Christian times it had become the area metropolis.

The town holds considerable archeological interest. There are extensive remains of the ancient wall, which, with its towers, protected the outer harbor. The entrance to the harbor was closed by means of a chain; the inner harbor was just a recess in the cliff. The city itself was surrounded by two walls, with a moat protecting the outer wall. The inscribed and arched triple gateway of Hadrian and the ancient aqueduct are the chief monuments to antiquity.

See K. Lanckoronski, *Städte Pamphyliens und Pisidiens* (1890). E. J. BANKS R. P. MEYE

ATTALUS at'ə-ləs [Gk. *Attalos*]. King of Pergamum, mentioned in 1 Macc. 15:22 among the kings to whom was sent an edict from Rome forbidding the persecution of the Jews (Josephus *Ant.* xiv.8.5).

ATTEND; ATTENDANCE. In 1 Tim. 4:13, AV, "give attendance to" (Gk. *proséchō*) means "devote your attention to" (NEB); cf. Acts 16:14; He. 7:13. The AV "attend upon the Lord" in 1 Cor. 7:35 follows the TR *euprósedros*, "constant"; the correct reading is *euparedros*, with the same meaning: "devoted" to the Lord.

ATTENDANT. The term occurs in Jgs. 3:19 for Heb. *hā'ōmᵉḏîm* (AV "[all] that stood by him"); in Dnl. 11:6 for *mᵉḇî'ay*, "followers (AV "they that brought her"; NEB "escort"); in Mt. 22:13 for Gk. *diákonoi*, "servants" (so AV); and in Lk. 4:20 for *hypērétēs*, "synagogue official" (AV "minister").

ATTENT; ATTENTIVE. In 2 Ch. 6:40; 7:15 the AV uses "attent" archaicly for "attentive" (Heb. *qaššuḇ*), "Very attentive" in Lk. 19:48, AV, translates Gk. *ekkrémamai*, "hang upon": "the people hung upon his words" (RSV, NEB).

ATTHARATES ə-thär'ə-tēz [Gk. *Attaratēs*] (1 Esd. 9:49); NEB "the governor." A Greek rendering of the Persian title Tirshatha, "governor," which in Neh. 8:9 is applied to Nehemiah, probably by a later editor (Heb. *hatiršāṯā'*).

ATTHARIAS a-thə-rī'əs [Gk. *Attharias*] (1 Esd. 5:40); AV ATHARIAS; NEB "the governor." An official under Nehemiah who had supervision of the priests during the return from exile; or a title of Nehemiah himself. Cf. Ezr. 2:63, RSV and NEB "the governor"; AV "the Tirshatha." *See* ATTHARATES.

ATTIRE. *See* GARMENTS.

ATTITUDES. *See* POSTURES.

ATTUS at'əs (1 Esd. 8:29, NEB). *See* HATTUSH **1.**

AUDIENCE. In the OT the AV has "audience" for Heb. *'ōzen*, "ear," where the RSV and NEB usually have "hearing" (e.g., Gen. 23:10; Ex. 24:7; 1 Ch. 28:8; Neh. 13:1).

In the NT the expression "give audience" (Acts 13:16; 15:12; 22:22) translates Gk. *akoúō*, "hear," and means "listen," "pay attention." Cf. Lk. 7:1; 20:45, where the usage is similar to that of the OT.

The only RSV occurrence is Acts 25:23, where Gk. *akroatḗrion*, AV "place of hearing," is rendered "audience hall" (NEB "audience-chamber"). The word is an equivalent of Lat. and Eng. "auditorium," and refers here to a room, probably in Agrippa's praetorium, used for hearing criminal cases.

AUGIA ô'gē-ə (1 Esd. 5:38, AV, NEB). *See* AGIA.

AUGUR; AUGURY [Heb. *nāḥaš*–'look for an omen']; AV ENCHANTER, ENCHANTMENT(S); NEB DIVINER, DIVINATION. *See* DIVINATION.

AUGUSTAN COHORT [Gk. *speíra Sebastḗ*] (Acts 27:1); AV AUGUSTUS' BAND. *See* ARMY, ROMAN.

AUGUSTUS ô-gus'təs [Gk. *(Kaisar) Augoustos*].

1. The first Roman emperor, noteworthy in Bible history as the emperor in whose reign the Incarnation took place (Lk. 2:1). His original name was Gaius Octavius, and he was born in 63 B.C., the year of Cicero's consulship. He was the grandnephew of Julius Caesar, his mother Atia having been the daughter of Julia, Caesar's younger sister. He was only nineteen when Caesar was murdered in the Senate house (44 B.C.); but with a true instinct of statesmanship he steered his course through the intrigues and dangers of the closing years of the republic, and after the battle of Actium was left without a rival.

Some difficulty was experienced in finding a name that would define exactly the position of the new ruler of the state. He himself declined the names of *rex* and *dictator,* and in 27 B.C. he was by the decree of the senate styled Augustus. The Greeks rendered the word by *Sebastós,* "reverend" (cf. Acts 25:21, 25; 27:1). The name was connected by the Romans with Lat. *augur* — "one consecrated by religion" — and also with the verb *augere*. In this way it came to form one of the German imperial titles "Mehrer des Reichs" (extender of the empire). The length of the reign of Augustus, extending as it did over forty-four years from the Battle of Actium (31 B.C.) to his death (A.D. 14), doubtless contributed much to the settlement and consolidation of the new regime after the troublous times of the civil wars.

It is chiefly through the connection of Judea and Palestine with the Roman empire that Augustus comes in contact with early Christianity, or rather with the political and religious life of the Jewish people at the time of the birth of Christ: "In those days a decree went out from Caesar Augustus that all the world should be enrolled" (Lk. 2:1). During the reign of Herod the Great the government of Palestine was conducted practically without interference from Rome except, of course, as regarded the exaction of the tribute; but on the death of that astute and capable ruler (4 B.C.) none of his three sons among whom his kingdom was divided showed the capacity of their father.

In A.D. 6 the intervention of Augustus was invited by the Jews themselves to provide a remedy for the incapacity of their ruler Archelaus, who was deposed by the emperor from the rule of Judea; at the same time, while Caesarea was still the center of the Roman administration, a small Roman garrison was stationed permanently in Jerusalem. The city, however, was left to the control of the Jewish Sanhedrin with complete judicial and executive authority, except that the death sentence required confirmation by the Roman procurator.

There is no reason to believe that Augustus entertained any specially favorable appreciation of Judaism, but from policy he showed himself favorable to the Jews in Palestine and did everything to keep them from feeling the pressure of the Roman yoke. To the Jews of the eastern Diaspora he allowed great privileges. It has even been held that his aim was to render them pro-Roman as a counterpoise in some degree to the pronounced Hellenism of the East; but in the West autonomous bodies of Jews were never allowed (see T. Mommsen, *Provinces of the Roman Empire* [Eng. tr. 1886, repr. 1909], ch. 11).

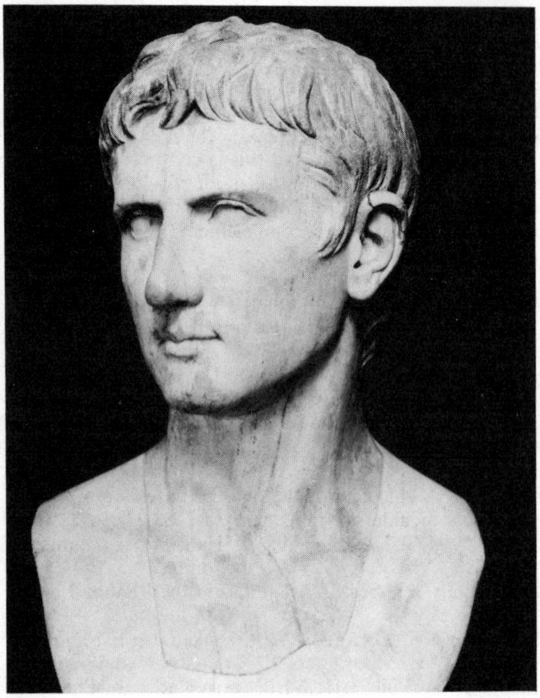

Augustus Caesar, Emperor of Rome (29 B.C.–A.D. 14), shown in the prime of life. Bust of fine Greek marble (Trustees of the British Museum)

2. For Augustus in Acts 25:21, 25, AV, *see* EMPEROR.

J. HUTCHISON

AUL. *See* AWL.

AUNT [Heb. *dôḏâ*] (Lev. 18:14; cf. 20:20; Ex. 6:20). *See* RELATIONSHIPS, FAMILY.

AURANITIS ô-rən-ī'təs. *See* HAURAN.

AURANUS ô-rān'əs [Gk. *Auranos*]. The leader of an insurrection in Jerusalem caused by Lysimachus. He is described as "a man advanced in years and no less advanced in folly" (2 Macc. 4:40).

AUTHOR. *See* PIONEER (He. 12:2); SOURCE (5:9).

AUTHORITY.

- I. The Term
  - A. Greek Equivalent
  - B. Meanings
- II. Biblical Material
  - A. OT
  - B. LXX
  - C. NT
- III. Historical Survey
  - A. Early Church
  - B. Medieval West
  - C. Reformation
  - D. Liberal Protestantism
  - E. New Alternatives
- IV. Civil Authority
  - A. In the NT

B. In the Middle Ages
C. Reformation Views
V. Conclusion
A. God and the Word
B. God and the Church
C. God and Civil Authority

I. The Term.–A. Greek Equivalent. In biblical and Christian usage authority is predominantly the equivalent of the Greek *exousía,* which derives from *éxestin.* "Power" in one of its senses can also be a rendering of the same Greek noun, although it more commonly represents the distinct, if materially related, *dýnamis.* Other words that underlie the Eng. "authority" are *epitagḗ,* "command" (Tit. 2:15), *hyperochḗ* (1 Tim. 2:2), *dynástēs* (Acts 8:27), and *authentéō* (1 Tim. 2:12).

B. Meanings. Primarily the verb *éxestin* has two interconnected senses: (1) "be free, unimpeded," and (2) "have the right or permission," which may include moral as well as legal right. What is suggested is a possibility of doing (or not doing) something because (1) there are no impediments and (2) there is, positively, the necessary permission or authorization.

The noun expresses the same concepts as the verb. Hence the first meaning is of *exousía* is that of power to do something because nothing stands in the way. The difference from *dýnamis* is that this is power based on extrinsic considerations, whereas *dýnamis* is intrinsic ability. Nevertheless, the two terms obviously overlap in the power or capability itself.

The second meaning is naturally that of authorization. In this case the power has been conferred by a superior power, court, or norm, whether this be political (the king or ruler), judicial (the law), or something more general (e.g., custom). Authorized power, which may be conferred corporately as well as individually, constitutes a right. Within the political and social structure, for instance, this may be the right of officials, parents, property-owners, or rulers, while in the cultural sphere it may be the right to act without question as custom allows.

Yet the right expressed by *exousía* is not abstract. It carries with it real power, even though this be extrinsically rather than intrinsically derived. The third nuance, then, brings once again a very close kinship to *dýnamis.* In practice the real power based on authorization, or lack of obstacles, cannot easily be differentiated from the power that is innate. Negatively, potential obstacles might vary, but positively, the ability amounts to the same thing. Sometimes, of course, the source of power matters a great deal, as in a question whether the power of a ruler is innate or derived. In many practical instances, however, the source is of no account whatever. For this reason "power" can often be a better rendering of *exousía* than "authority" or "right," even though the latter might still be implied.

By a strange if not illogical development, *exousía* can come to stand in antithesis to law rather than dependence on it. This gives us the fourth sense, "freedom." At this point a tension between the first and second senses is resolved in favor of the first. What can authorize (e.g., custom), can also restrain or impede. Ability in the sense of freedom from external obstacle can thus mean freedom from external power, even though in another setting it might mean authorization by it.

A final important usage, however, rests on the second sense. This is the employment of *exousía* for "office," "office-bearer," "ruler," or, in the plural, "authorities." The main concept here is that of wielding a power conferred. The authorities are the offices—or, more properly, the officers—to whom power has been officially entrusted. It is perhaps worth noting that the term does not seem to be used for government as such.

***II. Biblical Material.**–A. OT.* Two Hebrew words are translated "authority" in the OT but the examples are extraordinarily sparse and contribute little to the development of the concept. The first word, *rᵉḇôṯ,* occurs in Prov. 29:2. The usual rendering is to the effect that the people rejoice when the righteous are "in authority" (part. of *rāḇâ,* "be great," "increase"). The second term, *tōqep,* is found in Est. 9:29. Here "full written authority" is given by Esther and Mordecai in confirmation of the second letter about Purim. A parallel statement in v. 32 says that the command of Queen Esther fixed these practices of Purim.

B. LXX. In the sphere of biblical and Judaic literature we find the normal uses of *exousía.* However, the LXX also made a distinctive application of the term, which from the standpoint of biblical and theological development was of almost incalculable significance. It found in *exousía* the most suitable term to express the sovereignty of God (His complete freedom from all restraints) as distinct from His might or power. The Greek word thus acquired a new sense in which it came to stand not for authorization but for the absolute divine freedom that is also the source of all authorization. Even the regular meanings, then, were brought in the last analysis into a new theological relation.

In this regard the Greek word came to borrow in part from the Hebrew, which also seems to have shaped the LXX use of *exousía* for "sphere of power." Furthermore, *exousía* became virtually coextensive with the rabbinic *rᵉšûṯ,* which may well have made some contribution to the distinctive nuances of NT usage.

C. NT. 1. God. The most significant NT usage is the application of *exousía* to God as in the LXX. God has authority both in the sense that He has absolute possibility or freedom of action, being under neither necessity nor restraint, and also in the sense that He is the only ultimate source of all other authorization and power (cf. Lk. 12:5; Acts 1:5; Jude 25). So complete is the authority of God that it may be compared with the power of the potter over the clay (Rom. 9:21). In relation to the universe the authority of God is indeed that of creator as well as ruler. It is worked out in both nature and history. Thus God controls the natural and historical forces that fulfil His purposes (Rev. 6:8; 9:3, 10, 19).

2. Powers and Rulers. Thus far the NT does not differ substantially from the LXX in its use of *exousía,* or from rabbinic theology in its use of *rᵉšûṯ.* The same might be said when the term is specifically applied to subordinate powers or authorities as in 1 Cor. 15:24; 1 Pet. 3:22; Eph. 1:21, or to the civil authority exercised by kings, magistrates, priests, or stewards, as in Lk. 7:8; Mk. 13:34; Acts 9:14; Rom. 13:1-3; Tit. 3:1. Indeed, the same is still true when *exousía* is rather oddly used of Satan. In this connection "sphere of power" obviously comes into the picture, and yet also the sense of "authorization" or at least "permission," since neither the demonic not the political world has the same kind of authority as God but can function only within or under the divine sovereignty. If in relation to evil or evil forces this creates a problem, it is plain that dualism would create a more serious problem. Hence the Bible makes it clear beyond question that all subsidiary forces, including Satan and his world, can have power only inasmuch as this is conferred by God. Even if antichrist seems to derive his authority from Satan (Rev. 13:2), the final authority of God is always presupposed (cf. Lk. 22:53).

3. Christ. If there is little new in all this, the situation changes radically when we come to the authority of Christ. To be sure, the power that Christ exercises within His earthly commission, e.g., that of forgiving sins (Mk. 2:10), or exorcism (3:15), or teaching (Mt. 7:29), or judgment (Jn. 5:27), is a power granted by the Father. The great truth brought to light in the NT, however, is that Christ is more than a man who is commissioned by God. He is Himself God. This means that His authority, as divine authority, is also self-grounded.

The power He enjoys is thus the power of His own sovereignty in concert with that of the Father (Jn. 10:18; Rev. 12:10ff.). It is an absolute power free from all limitations (Mt. 28:18). It is also a power that underlies all other authority, as in the charges of Christ to His disciples (Mk. 6:7ff.) and to the apostles (Jn. 20:22f.). The particular sphere of this power is the world of men (Jn. 17:2), and it includes the right of final judgment (5:27). Recurrent references to the giving of this authority by the Father make it plain that no rivalry with God's power is intended. Absolute authority pertains to Christ, and indeed to the Holy Spirit too, because this authority is seen in fact to be one and the same as the authority of the Father; i.e., it is the authority of the triune God.

4. The Apostles. Christ, however, is not alone. He is accompanied by the apostles whom He Himself chose, associated with Himself, and sent out with His own authorization. It is natural, then, that there should be an authority of the apostolate. This is supported by the practice of the apostles. It is also formulated expressly, not only in the charge of Mk. 6:7, but also in the saying of Paul in 2 Cor. 10:8; cf. also Mt. 10:1; Mk. 3:15; 2 Thess. 3:9. (*See also* BIND; KEY.)

This is not, of course, an absolute or inherent authority. It is an authority of commissioning by the Lord. Hence the elements of derivativeness and responsibility are prominent. The apostle is put in charge by His Lord, and it is essential that he make a proper use of his authority (cf. Mk. 13:34). Nevertheless, the authority also carries with it certain rights, e.g., that of support by the churches (1 Cor. 9:4ff.). More broadly, the teaching and guiding authority of the apostle is a mediation of the authority of Christ. His ministry is backed by Christ Himself. This is what makes it possible. This is also what gives it incontestable validity in the Church.

5. The Church. If Christ is accompanied by the apostles, He is also accompanied by believers in general. It is not surprising, then, that the NT can also speak of the *exousía* of the Church and of individual Christians. What is surprising, however, is what is said about that authority. For (1) Christians have the authority to become the children of God (Jn. 1:12). The two primary senses of the word may both be seen here. On the one hand they are given a new possibility that they could not have in themselves. On the other hand, they are granted a right or title. Inasmuch as they receive the one Son of God, they themselves have a legitimate sonship conferred upon them.

Then (2) Christians are also granted freedom in the sense of the right to do certain things (1 Cor. 6:12). Now it is true that in the passages in 1 Corinthians Paul is more concerned about a right or wrong use of this "authority." We are to do what is appropriate and what is of service to edification. Nevertheless, even when faced by possible misuse, the apostle does not deny the authority as such. All things are indeed lawful even if all are not expedient and all do not edify. For this is a freedom, an authorization, a permission which Christ Himself has conferred and which is received in faith: the freedom of the children of God. The true answer to misuse is not surrender but true and proper use. Although enigmatic, *exousía* in 1 Cor. 7:37 might well be grouped in the same category.

III. Historical Survey.–*A. Early Church. 1. Basis.* The chief lesson of the NT — viz., that authority finally rests in God and that this authority is embodied in Jesus Christ — was well learned in the early Church. The Church grounded itself upon the fact that God in Jesus Christ stands behind both the faith that is believed and also the faith that believes it. God in Jesus Christ is the authority that establishes the Christian life with its new possibilities; and God in Jesus Christ is also Lord of the Church, exercising this lordship by the Holy Spirit, so that all decisions and actions, whether doctrinal or practical, must derive from Him and take their validity from Him. Whatever difficulties or ambiguities there might have been both in the first centuries and later, the authority of God was accepted and advocated as the fundamental principle.

A further lesson was also learned: that this authority is exercised through the apostles and the community. Even though serious divergence later arose, this common presupposition was always held. As God the Father sent Christ, so Christ commissioned, equipped, and sent the apostles. He gave them divine authority to preach the gospel, to instruct in Christian knowledge, and to exercise control over the churches. Apostolic right and privilege, of course, were not inherent power. The apostles had authority because they were authorized by God Himself. Put another way, Christ exercised His own rule and authority through them.

2. Scripture and Church. Nevertheless, the death of the apostles posed a new question, one that received different answers, or at least an ambivalent answer, in the age of the fathers. The question was an obvious one: What is the locus of apostolic authority after the passing of the apostles themselves? How does God — Father, Son, and Spirit — exercise His own absolute authority in the postapostolic Church? On whom or what does authorization come in succession to the apostles?

A single and straightforward answer to this question was difficult. For one thing, there seemed at the very outset to be two alternatives: (1) the apostolic writings, added to the existing and accepted canon of OT Scripture, and (2) the ongoing authority of the Church, including the special authority vested in those who are set up apostolically as its pastors and teachers. Even if Scripture is adopted as the supreme and normative source, however, there are in the NT itself different forms and areas and levels of authority, and many issues — especially those of minor importance — will still have to be decided according to other criteria. On the other hand, if a greater function is ascribed to the Church a variety of further alternatives opens up when the center of ecclesiastical authority is sought. Is it to be found in the community as such, in its bishops or ministers, in synods (local, provincial, or ecumenical), in creeds, in traditions, in the fathers, in a combination of these, or in one or the other according to the subject at issue?

As regards the fundamental choice between Scripture and the Church, it might seem that Scripture is a new factor that does not arise at all in what the NT itself has to say about *exousía*. In fact, however, the NT does recognize Scripture as the voice of God. As the OT writers introduced their messages with the daring "Thus saith the Lord," so our Lord Himself and the NT authors quote OT statements as authoritative: "As Scripture says. . . ." It is natural and inevitable, then, that the immediate postapostolic Christians should inherit the same approach to the OT; and it is no less natural and inevitable that they should extend this approach to the works of the divinely commissioned and authorized apostles (works that later became the NT Canon), finally introducing their copious quotations (as in 2 Clem. 2:4) with the time-honored formulas. In other words, all the holy writings came to be seen and accepted as an established form in which the authority of God, mediated through the biblical authors, should be permanently exercised in the Church.

In fact, the fathers are virtually unanimous in ascribing a normative role to Scripture as a primary source of revelation. In addition to the continuous appeal to Scripture in patristic writings, the care for a proper recognition of the NT canon, and the labor expended on exposition of the biblical books, one might quote the rejection of purely oral tradition in Irenaeus *Adv. haer.* iii.2.1. Athanasius also makes a distinction between the "holy and inspired writings," which are self-sufficient, and other works that are a commentary on them (*Contra Gentes* 1). Origen states firmly: "We must needs call the holy scripture to witness; for our judgments and expositions without these witnesses are worthy no credit" (*In Jer. Hom.* 1). Basil asks that convincing and convicting words and deeds "be confirmed by the testimony of God's scriptures" (*Moralia* xxvi.1). Augustine, referring to Cyprian's works, says that he "weighs them by the canonical writings" (*Contra Cresconium grammaticum Donatistam* ii.32). John of Damascus, pointing to his basic authority, says: "All that was ever delivered by the law, the prophets, the apostles, and the evangelists, we receive, acknowledge, and give reverence unto them, searching nothing besides them" (*De Fide Orthodoxa* 1).

On the other hand, the fathers had a strong sense that authority resided also in the ongoing apostolic tradition as represented especially in the orderly ministry and the rule of faith. Irenaeus and Tertullian both found the appeal to this authority especially valuable in refutation of Gnosticism, for it provided (a) an answer to Gnostics who would not accept Scripture but spoke of a secret tradition, (b) a historico-geographical basis for the authenticity of orthodox teaching, and (c) a useful hermeneutical principle in meeting Gnostic interpretations of Scripture. Tertullian can even complain that Scripture without tradition is ambiguous (*De praescr. haer.* 19), although both he and Irenaeus seem to view Scripture and tradition, or the rule of faith, as substantially one and the same thing, or at least as two different and complementary forms of the same thing.

The situation had changed, however, by the 4th century. If Basil of Caesarea demanded Scriptural confirmation, he also argued that the tradition preserved in Scripture is incomplete (*De Spiritu sancto* 27 [66]; cf. Epiphanius *Haer.* 61.6). Jerome too, although he can speak strongly of the need for the authority and testimony of Scripture (*Comm. on Haggai* i), can refer at the same time to many things that are accepted on the basis of tradition alone (*Dialogus contra Luciferianos* 8). Chrysostom even appeals to the Scriptures themselves (2 Thess. 2:15) in support of the view that the apostles transmitted many things not put in writing (*Hom. 4 in 2 Thess.*). Along different lines, Vincent of Lérins (d. before 450) finally subjects Scripture to the Church with his principle that, while Scripture is intrinsically adequate, a regulative interpretation is needed, this being supplied not by tradition alone but by the threefold criterion of what is held "everywhere, always, by all." As Barth observes (*CD*, I/2, pp. 550f.), the addition "by all" means in effect the enforcement of an official understanding, and this is the more dangerous in that Vincent's opposition to change does not rule out a progress controlled by the teaching office in its consensus. The significant point in all this is that not only has tradition emerged as supplementary to Scripture, but Scripture itself has been deprived of any effective authority through its hermeneutical subjection to the Church — or rather, in practice, to the Church's hierarchy.

B. Medieval West. 1. Developments. The pattern set by Vincent of Lérins tended to dominate the understanding of authority throughout the Middle Ages. In the West it resulted in a tilting of the scales in favor of the authority of the Church. This may be seen at four points. First, a more-or-less general acceptance of the fourfold scheme of exegesis helped to shackle the Bible by making its exposition extremely complicated. Second, dogmatic definitions such as that of transubstantiation promoted development under alien norms beyond the limits of legitimate interpretation. Third, canon law codified ecclesiastical authority in an effective, practical form that enhanced the power of the hierarchy. Finally, the papacy, while challenged from time to time as in the Conciliar Movement of the 14th cent., focused ultimate authority on the bishop of Rome both as heir to the supreme apostolic authority of Peter and also, on this basis, as vicar of Christ Himself, enjoying and exercising the plenitude of power that properly belongs to the Lord. Naturally, these developments met with opposition. The Eastern Churches provided some counterbalance with their stress on the authority of the ecumenical synods. The limits of allegorical exegesis were frequently recognized. On political as well as ecclesiastical and doctrinal grounds, challenges were issued again and again against the papal claims. The unfortunate thing, however, is that for many years these forces were not sufficient to put up effective resistance against the Church's exploitation of its own authority in all branches of ecclesiastical life in the West.

2. Problems. Thus, the development of doctrine ineluctably led to changes, and even innovations, which Vincent of Lérins had neither anticipated nor desired. Medieval practice, while authorized and commanded by canon law, seemed in the event to produce a monstrous caricature of NT Christianity. The Church's authoritative exposition of Scripture turned out to be far from infallible when brought under the scrutiny of Renaissance scholarship, which also served to spotlight the vast difference between medieval practice and thinking on the one side, and that of the apostolic Church on the other.

C. Reformation. 1. Scripture Principle. Once the issues began to come out into the open with Luther's theses of 1517 and the ensuing controversy, it quickly became apparent that the protest involved a drastic rethinking of the way in which Christ's authority is exercised, and particularly of the relationship between Scripture and Church in the mediation of apostolic authority to and through the postapostolic community. The reformers cannot deny, of course, that the Church and its various expressions (e.g., ministry, confessions, synods, and fathers) do have a lawful measure of authority. Their contention is, however, that it is in and through the prophetic and apostolic writings of Holy Scripture that God exercises supreme and ultimate authority in the Church, whether in doctrine or practice. Other authorities are subsidiary and derivative.

2. Confessions. The Reformation confessions make this point and bring out its ramifications with a happy blend of force, comprehensiveness, and conciseness. Thus the French Confession (1559) states that "the Word contained in these books receives its authority from God alone" and that "all things should be examined, regulated, and reformed according to these books." The Belgic Confession (1561) approves the Scriptures "because the Holy Ghost witnesseth in our hearts that they are from God"; with them nothing can be compared, and "whatsoever doth not agree with this infallible rule" is to be rejected. The Westminster Confession (1647) concludes its more extended discussion with the notable statement (I,10) that the supreme judge in controversies and in the examinations of Church Decisions "can be no other but the Holy Ghost speaking in the scripture." This accords with the earlier teaching of Heinrich Bullinger in the Second Helvetic Confession (1566) that in matters of faith "we cannot admit any other judge than God himself, pronouncing by the holy scripture what is true. . . ." The Epitome of the Lutheran Formula of Concord (1576) advances a similar understanding: "We believe, confess, and teach that the only rule and norm according to which all dogmas and all doctors ought to be esteemed and judged is no other whatever than the prophetic and apostolic writings of both the Old and the New Testament. . . . Holy scripture alone is acknowledged as the judge, norm, and rule according to which, as by the (only) touchstone, all doctrines are to be examined and judged." As Quenstedt puts it, holy scripture is judge as the voice of the supreme and infallible Judge, the Holy Spirit.

As noted, a proper place can be found for secondary authorities. Both the Scots Confession (1560) and the Anglican Articles (1571) may be quoted in favor of the common view that the Church has authority to institute and reform traditions, "so that nothing be ordained against God's word." The Second Helvetic Confession, too, concedes that in the interpretation of Scripture the fathers and councils should be taken into account, so long as the duty of modest dissent is recognized when they set down things not in agreement with the Scriptures.

To summarize, three points are made here. First, absolute authority lies with God himself, exercised through Christ and the Holy Spirit. Second, the voice of God is heard primarily in Holy Scripture, not merely because this is historically the first and authentic deposit of the prophetic and apostolic record, but because God Himself has raised it up to fulfil this purpose. Third, subsidiary authorities have a valid function, but discharge it properly only in submission to the divine authority expressed primarily in and through Scripture.

3. Roman Reply. Unfortunately, Roman Catholicism did not accept — nor even perhaps understand — this position. It naturally did not dispute the supreme authority of Christ. It also gave to Scripture an eminent place. Yet even in the Reformation age it defended its doctrines and practices by invoking the complementary authorities of fathers and tradition. Thus, in the Leipzig Disputation (1519) Eck hurled not only texts but also the interpretations of the fathers against Luther and accused him of arrogance when, faced by the latter, "he contradicted them all without a blush, and said that he would stand alone against a thousand." As regards tradition, Trent took the decisive step in Session IV (1546) when it made the pronouncement: "This synod receives and venerates, with equal pious affection, all the books both of the New and the Old Testaments, since one God is the author of both, together with the said traditions, as well those pertaining to faith as those pertaining to morals. . . ." According to this dogma, traditions found in apostolic sees such as Rome can also claim to be of apostolic or even dominical origin, even though not preserved in the apostolic writings; and they may thus be accorded a status equal to that of written Scriptures.

4. Papal Infallibility. In the post-Reformation era, however, the Roman understanding of authority has taken a different turn. Greater stress has been laid on the authority of the Church rather than tradition. Already in Reformation days it was argued that Christians accept Scripture basically because it has been authored and authorized by the Church. For a time, indeed, the curious and self-destructive thesis was advanced in some circles, that by reason of its obvious fallibility Scripture would not be credited without the Church's backing. Later, attention shifted back again to the interpretative role of the Church, or of the Church's teaching office, and finally of the pope. The argument here is simple. Scripture is indeed the ultimate norm. Nevertheless the Church, enlightened by the Holy Spirit, has the task of correctly expounding and applying Scripture. In this task it is guided and governed by its head. Its ultimate Head, of course, is Christ Himself, but in terms of Christ's earthly representation the head is Peter's successor, the bishop of Rome. The infallibility decree of 1870 brings this understanding to its logical conclusion and climax: "The Roman Pontiff, when he speaks *ex cathedra* [i.e., when in fulfilling the office of Pastor and Teacher of all Christians on his supreme apostolical authority, he defines a doctrine concerning faith or morals to be held by the Universal Church], through the divine assistance promised him in blessed Peter, is endowed with that infallibility, with which the divine Redeemer has willed that His Church — in defining doctrine concerning faith or morals — should be equipped: And therefore, such definitions of the Roman Pontiff of themselves — and not by virtue of the consent of the Church — are irreformable." What is biblical is held to be authoritative. In the last resort, however, the Pope expounds and declares what is biblical. Effective authority thus comes to be vested not in Scripture but in its hermeneutical master, whose decisions are final and irrevocable.

D. Liberal Protestantism. 1. Reason. The modern age has brought different but no less radical challenges through the Liberal Protestantism that began to flourish in the latter part of the 17th century. In an early form this involved the exaltation of human reason to a highly authoritative role in doctrinal and moral teaching. On this view "reason is not less from God than revelation; 't is the candle, the guide, the judge he has lodged within every man that cometh into the world" (Toland, *Christianity not Mysterious* [1696]). To the dictates of reason, then, revelation itself must submit (M. Tindal, *Christianity as Old as the Creation* [1730]). God Himself maintains ultimate authority. Here, however, He exercises it in a completely different way, choosing reason rather than Church or Scripture as His primary instrument. A problem, of course, is that reason can just as easily exalt itself against God so that He Himself comes under its dictates. This is precisely what happened in many circles in the rational subjectivism of the 18th cent., which made man himself the ultimate arbiter of all truth.

2. Religious A Priori. As it turned out, the older rationalism proved much less than adequate when it came under the scrutiny of Hume's scepticism and the withering epistemological analysis of Kant. Other expressions of human domination thus arose to replace it in the form of the so-called religious *a priori* in man. Kant's moral imperative, Schleiermacher's sense of absolute dependence, and the consciousness of Hegel's religious philosophy all play this role. Common to all these self-contradictory reconstructions is the refusal to let God Himself be the true authority even in the things of God and the committal of this authority to man himself, whether corporately or in the highly individualistic form in which each man fashions and chooses his own God — or even proclaims the total absence of God in the form of the secularization or humanization of the gospel.

E. New Alternatives. 1. Catholic Consensus. Between the extremes of Roman ecclesiasticism and Liberal subjectivism some fresh alternatives to the Reformation view have been attempted. Building on one aspect of the Reformation appeal, some movements have proposed the authority of an early Catholic consensus somewhat along the lines of Eastern Orthodoxy. Anglican groups have been leaders in this field. With their fears of the evils of private judgment, the Mercersburg theologians, especially Nevin, worked along not dissimilar lines although with a stronger emphasis on the authority of Holy Scripture. The difficulty, of course, is that consensus among the fathers is hard to come by, and even if it is attained there is no reason to suppose that the early Church was any less fallible than the medieval or modern Church. On many occasions, even in early days, the minority has been right and the majority tragically wrong. Such attempts to achieve consensus might even result in the absurdity that the expert in church history becomes the new pope.

2. Experience. Pietism, on the other hand, has tended at some points to seek authority in evangelical experience. This canon might be applied apologetically: Christianity is true because I have found it so in my own life. It might also be applied in relation to aspects of Christian practice: this form of worship is the right one because it is the most meaningful to me. The ministry can be conducted along the same line: we ought to follow this or that course of action because it works out best in the actual experience of the individual or Church. Even biblical interpretation can be subjected to the same canon: the right meaning of a verse or passage is that from which I derive doctrinal, devotional, or practical benefit. Fortunately, experience has seldom if ever been set up as a final or sole authority, for it obviously gives rise to rampant individualism and anthropocentricity with its assertion that God exercises His authority specifically through me and Scripture is an infallible rule of faith and practice according to my particular interpretation. At the same time the chaos of conflicting experiences produces an inevitable crisis of authority when God is apparently saying different things to different individuals, and thousands of popes are claiming infallible discharge of the teaching office.

3. Roman Catholic Trends. Roman Catholicism, under the pressure of its new stress on biblical study, has been forced to do some rethinking on the matter of authority. The interrelation of oral and written tradition has come under new discussion, especially in relation to early patristic thinking. Sharp differences have arisen on the sources of revelation, and the view has even been advanced (e.g., by Hans Küng) that Scripture has always been the primary source according to true Catholic theology. The infallibility of the pope has also been called in question, either in itself, or in its exercise apart from the official participation of other bishops, priests, or even the Church as a whole. If few positive results have thus far been achieved in this process, the rigidity of the Tridentine statement and the Infallibility Definition has been broken and important modifications are by no means out of the question.

4. Barth's Discussion. Possibly the most constructive of recent dogmatic contributions to the theme of authority is to be found in the section that Karl Barth devotes to it in *CD,* I/2. This section falls within the chapter on Holy Scripture as the second of the three forms of the Word of God (the Word revealed, written, and preached). Authority is thus considered specifically in relation to the Word — first as the authority *of* the Word and secondly as authority *under* the Word. (The parallel section on the freedom of the Word and freedom under the Word offers some important complementary insights.)

As regards the authority of the Word, Barth first deals with the question whether Scripture can claim precedence of authority simply by virtue of its historical position as the apostolic deposit. He concludes that at best this argument can yield only an indirect, formal, and relative authority, which can make Scripture only the first among equal competitors. Final authority resides with the revelation event itself, the first form of the Word of God. Nevertheless, this revelation stands in a unique relation to the prophets and apostles and therefore to their writings too, since both the men and their works were raised up by God specifically to be witness to revelation, and hence to be God's written Word. In virtue of this unparalleled relationship between event and witness, Scripture has then a direct, material, and absolute authority that marks it off from all its competitors. Even preaching, as the third form of God's Word, cannot be its rival in this regard, since the preached Word is known only from the written Word. Thus the written Word has a normative function in relation to the preached Word.

As regards authority *under* the Word, Barth's main point is that subsidiary authorities cannot be in competition with the authority of the written Word but are in fact established by it. This applies primarily and prototypically to the Church, which undeniably has authority but which derives this authority wholly from the Word, i.e., by authorization. This authority then comes to focus in the Church's confession, which is not a rival authority, nor a hermeneutical norm, nor indeed a sum of biblical teaching, but the Church's hearing of the Word. Finally, it takes historical form in the canon, in fathers old and new, and in the historical confessions. All these are relative, indirect, and formal authorities. All stand under, and must be tested by, the supreme authority of the Word. All are thus reformable in principle, as the written Word, in virtue of its unique relation to revelation, is not.

***IV. Civil Authority.**–A. In the NT.* Concentration on the problems of ecclesiastical authority should not cause us to overlook the fact that civil authority has also constituted a difficulty throughout Christian history. The NT, e.g., in Rom. 13, gave recognition to the divinely given authority of civil office-bearers. However, it was not long before conflicts arose between the authority of church and state — especially with the rise of professedly Christian rulers from the time of Constantine, and consequent approximations to the OT model — and a demarcation of authority was demanded.

B. In the Middle Ages. In the Middle Ages the divine authorization of rulers found expression in the idea of the Holy Roman Empire and in the impressive coronation rituals. At the same time, however, the popes resisted the attempt of temporal rulers to interfere in ecclesiastical matters, since such interferences usually made the Church subservient to political and material interests. This was the reason for the drastic medieval principle of a separation of church and state, which went to the length of excluding the clergy from secular justice and taxation as well as ensuring that churches and monasteries would not come under military attack. Rulers, of course, opposed this obvious threat to their own supremacy, finding in the pretensions of the clergy an infringement on their rightful temporal and spiritual authority and responsibility; and they constantly played a part in church matters wherever these had obvious civil implications.

The more powerful popes tried to solve the problem by arguing that while the powers are separate, the ecclesiastical power is superior. Gregory VII (1073-1085) was already claiming the right, as the vicar of Christ, to depose or set up rulers. Innocent III (1198-1216), who imposed this right more successfully, compared church and state to the two lights of Gen. 1, the church being the greater light, the sun, and the state the lesser light, the moon, which draws its radiance from the sun. Boniface VIII (1294-1303) put the matter even more forcefully in his bull Unam Sanctam (1302), when he stated that the two swords — the temporal and the spiritual — are both in the hands of Peter, the one to be used *by* the church and the other *for* it. He failed dismally, however, in his attempt to bring England and France under this rule.

C. Reformation Views. A sharp reversal of this position came with the Reformation period when the reformers, often finding civil rulers more ready to instigate reforms than the clergy, recalled the godly princes of the OT and saw it as within the authority of Christian magistrates, and indeed as their duty, to take action for the spiritual welfare of their subjects. Thus Luther leaned on the electors of Saxony; Zwingli brought about reformation through the city council of Zurich; and Henry VIII set a pattern in England that led ultimately to the authorization of the prayer book and articles by crown and parliament as well as by convocation.

Nevertheless, the reformers were not unaware of the dangers of this course. Rulers might be ill-disposed to the gospel, or to some aspects of it, as Calvin found in his dealings both with the Geneva councils and also with the French crown. They might also use reformation to their own selfish ends, as Cranmer and Ridley learned to their own cost when Northumberland would not permit the proper redeployment of ecclesiastical endowments. Furthermore, even in their exercise of civil authority they might indulge in wicked or despotic actions. An attempt was thus made to set the limits of temporal power by subjecting it plainly to God, from whom it derives, and to the Word of God, which is its norm. Heinrich Bullinger of Zurich states the position forcefully and clearly in *Decades* ii. He argues that distinctions should be made between "the office, which is the good ordination of God, and the evil person." Tyranny should not be tolerated on the ground that "it is of God." As every magistrate "is ordained of God, and is God's minister, so he must be ruled by God, and be obedient to God's holy word and commandment."

In the last resort this means that an evil power may be resisted or, finally, overthrown, so long as this is done responsibly. Unlike the Lutherans and Anglicans, the Reformed were thus prepared for the extreme action of civil revolt as this found historical expression in the overthrow of Mary Guise in Scotland, the war of independence in Holland, and the unfortunate civil wars in France. It was emphasized, however, that resistance to the powers is justified only when the gospel is threatened or excessive tyranny is enforced. Patient submission to authority, or at the most passive resistance in religious matters, was seen to be the biblical rule.

The Reformed understanding as Bullinger succinctly states it tries to avoid the clash of eccleciastical and civil power by relativizing both in the same way. As the church derives its authority from God, so does the state. Neither has inherent power. Neither, indeed, has power that can ever become independent of the God who gives it. The freedom of God is not restricted by the authorization that He grants. The human institution thus authorized is no autonomous competitor. If it draws its right and power from God, it does so only in subjection to the rule which God still exercizes by His Word.

The so-called radical reformers, of course, approached the matter very differently. Certain violent leaders attempted a fusion of religious and civil authority in Münster, the "new Jerusalem," the kingdom of the saints; but when this proved to be illusory, the dominant motif became the strict separation advocated and practiced by the Swiss and South German Anabaptists. On this view the secular authorities are ordained by God, but their function of restraint and force is incompatible with true Christianity. They are to be honored and obeyed in virtue of their divine ordination, but Christians can have no part in their work and must not become entangled in the evils of temporal office. If a conflict arises between civil authority and true Christianity, no resistance is to be offered; but the authority of God must also take precedence, so that patient endurance of persecution is the only legitimate course. In no circumstances are the children of the light to make use of the weapons of the present world, since their victory will come in and through affliction and by the weapons of spiritual warfare. With the emergence of the modern secularist state and pluralist society the thinking of the radical reformers has taken on new relevance today, although whether or not there should be abstraction from all temporal exercise of power is a question to which very different answers will obviously be given.

V. Conclusion.–*A. God and the Word.* It might be accepted as a basic principle that God exercises authority through the Word. In the ultimate sense, since Christ is the Word, the Word is God Himself. God exercises His own authority. Nevertheless, the Word takes form not only in the Incarnation but also in the words spoken and written by the prophets and apostles, i.e., in the Scriptures of the OT and NT. These words or Scriptures, having divine authorization, carry the authority of God Himself. Similarly, being God's Word, they have the freedom of God, not innately or inherently, but in virtue of their divine authorship or authorization.

B. God and the Church. God also exercises His authority through the Church and its confessions, rulings, and teachings. Here again one might say that since the Church is Christ's body, Christ Himself is the Church. In the Church, therefore, Christ exercises His own authority. At the same time, in terms of its human members and structures, the Church does not have the same immediate authorization as the apostles and prophets. It has indirect authorization by the Word of God that gives it birth and that comes through the prophetic and apostolic words. Hence the freedom it enjoys is, as Barth observes, freedom under the Word, not freedom from or over the Word. The Church achieves its true authority not when it makes a direct claim to declare the voice of God, but when it seeks to speak God's Word in accordance with the Word already spoken and written, so that the authority with which it is invested is authentically that of the Word.

C. God and Civil Authority. In another sense and sphere, civil authorities are also means by which God exercises His authority. Outside the sphere of revelation rulers have only an indistinct and perverted apprehension of this truth. They thus tend to think in terms of absolute or inherent power or to confuse divine authorization with a transferred right to do all things at will. This can raise acute problems for the Church and can produce the clash of authority that brings tension, persecution, or compromise. Even where rulers are Christians and know clearly the source of their authority, they may still fail to see that this authority can be properly exercised only according to the Word of God and within the sovereign authority that God always reserves to Himself. This is equally true no matter what the human form of authority might be.

God grants authorization, but in so doing He does not reduce or transfer His own divine authority. Neither church nor state, then, has any mandate for tyranny.

Neither church nor state can issue any edict it pleases and demand absolute submission on the basis of divine authorization. Indeed, even Holy Scripture, for all the uniqueness of its origin and role, is not to be treated as though it had autonomous authority apart from God Himself, who is its ontic, noetic, and dynamic basis. God indeed rules through Scripture. The ultimate stress, however, lies not on Scripture but on the God who rules. "To the only God our Savior, through Jesus Christ our Lord, be glory, majesty, dominion, and authority, before all time and now and for ever. Amen" (Jude 25).

Bibliography.–*TDNT*, II, *s.v.* ἔξεστιν, ἐξουσία (Foerster); H. J. D. Denzinger, *Sources of Catholic Dogma* (Eng. tr. 1957); J. H. Bullinger, *Decades*, ed. T. Harding (1849-1852; repr. 1968); Calvin *Inst.* iv.8-11, 20; W. Whitaker, *Disputation on Holy Scripture* (1588); P. Schaff, *Creeds of Christendom* (3 vols., 1877); H. Bettenson, *Documents of the Christian Church* (2nd ed. 1967); J. Martineau, *Seat of Authority in Religion* (1890); P. W. Forrest, *Authority of Christ* (1914); R. W. Harding, *Authority of Jesus* (1922); R. H. Strachan, *Authority of Christian Experience* (1931); H. Cunliffe-Jones, *Authority of the Biblical Revelation* (1948); R. H. Thouless, *Authority and Freedom* (1954); *CD*, I/2 §§ 20f.; J. K. S. Reid, *Authority of Scripture* (1957); D. M. Lloyd-Jones, *Authority* (1958); R. C. Johnson, *Authority in Protestant Theology* (1959); R. R. Williams, *Authority and the Church* (1965); D. G. Miller, *Authority of the Bible* (1972).

G. W. BROMILEY

AUTHORIZED VERSION (AV). The King James translation of the Bible. *See* ENGLISH VERSIONS.

AUTUMN [Heb. *ḥōrep̄, yôreh* (Jer. 5:24); Gk. *phthinopōrinós* (Jude 12)]; AV "of my youth" (Job 29:4), "cold" (Prov. 20:4), "former" (Jer. 5:24), "whose fruit withereth" (Jude 12); NEB also "of my prime" (Job 29:4), "in season" (Jude 12). The period ushering in the winter, which was the season of rain (Lev. 26:4; Dt. 11:14; etc.) and stormy weather (Job 37:9; Isa. 25:4; etc.). By this time the summer fruits and olives had been harvested (Sept. to Nov.).

AVA a'və (2 K. 17:24, AV). *See* AVVA.

AVARAN av'ə-ran [Gk. *Hauran*]; (1 Macc. 2:5); AV SAVARAN. A surname of Eleazar, fourth son of Mattathias, who died at Beth-zechariah (1 Macc. 6:32-46).

AVEN ā'vən [Heb. *'āwen*–'iniquity,' 'idol'].

1. A shortened form of BETH-AVEN in Hos. 10:8, used contemptuously for Bethel.

2. The Valley of Aven (Am. 1:5), mentioned in context with Damascus and located perhaps somewhere between the Lebanon and Anti-Lebanon ranges.

3. A deliberate pun or a misvocalization for ON in Ezk. 30:17, MT, followed by the AV. The RSV and NEB have "On"; cf. the LXX Gk. *hēlíou póleōs* (Heliopolis being the Greek name for the Egyptian city On).

R. F. YOUNGBLOOD

AVENGE [Heb. *nāqam, nāqam nᵉqāmâ* (Nu. 31:2), *nāṯan nᵉqāmâ, yāšā'* (1 S. 25:33), *dāraš, rîḇ* (1 S. 25:39), *śîm* (1 K. 2:5); Gk. *ekdikéō, poiéō ekdíkēsin* (Acts 7:24)]; AV also REQUIRE (1 Ch. 24:22), "cleanse" (Joel 3:21; RSV emends *nāqâ* to *nāqam*), TAKE VENGEANCE (Jgs. 11:36), "plead the cause" (1 S. 25:39), RETURN (2 S. 16:8), MAKE INQUISITION (Ps. 9:12), SHED (BLOOD) (1 K. 2:5), etc.; NEB also (TAKE or EXACT) VENGEANCE, "exact the penalty" (2 Ch. 24:22), (SEEK) REVENGE, PUNISH (1 S. 25:39), "giving way [to anger]" (1 S. 25:33), "breaking [the peace]" (1 K. 2:5), SPILL (BLOOD) (Joel 3:21), etc.

I. Terms.–The Hebrew words most frequently translated by "avenge" are the verb *nāqam* and the noun *nᵉqāmâ* (often the object of *nāṯan*, "take vengeance," or *nāqam*, "avenge"). In 2 Ch. 24:22 and Ps. 9:12 the RSV renders *dāraš* as "avenge." Here *dāraš* has the sense of "require [vengeance]." 1 K. 2:5 has *śîm*, lit. "place, put," here "put blood," i.e., "avenge." 1 S. 25:33 has *yāšā'* in the hiphil, lit. "help, save," here "save myself by my hand," i.e., "avenge myself." The term in 1 S. 25:39 is *rîḇ*, usually "contend," here "contend" in the sense of righting a wrong, i.e., "avenge." The NT and LXX have either the verb *ekdikéō*, "avenge," "punish," or the noun *ekdíkēsis* "revenge," "punishment," "retribution." Both the notion of "avenging" and "punishing" (in a forensic sense) are found.

II. In the Ancient Near East.–To avenge a wrong seems to have been a legal custom in the ancient Near East. In tribal society, the "avenger of blood" (Heb. *gô'ēl haddām*, Nu. 35:9-34; cf. Gen. 9:5f.; *see* AVENGER) was the kinsman obligated to exact retribution for the death of a family member.

III. In the OT.–The OT mentions several provocations of human "vengeance." Samson avenges murder (Jgs. 15:7), Saul seeks vengeance on his military foes (1 S. 14:24; 18:25), as does Israel on the Midianites (Nu. 31:2). Samson avenges himself on the Philistines for the loss of his eye (Jgs. 16:28). In Est. 8:13 the Jews avenge themselves on those who planned to murder them. Joab avenges the death of his brother in battle (1 K. 2:5; here it is not in his avenging that Joab is blameworthy, but in his doing it in a period of truce).

Other passages mention acts that need not or should not be avenged — at least not by killing, or not by men. Had David avenged an insult (1 S. 25:33), this would have caused "blood-guilt," probably because the provocation was not sufficient to warrant killing. However, the tradition maintains that Yahweh avenged this insult (v. 39). A vengeance "overkill" is also found in the Song of Lamech, Gen. 4:23, in which Lamech says that he slew a man who struck him. That this response is out of proportion to the provocation is clear in v. 24, "If Cain is avenged seven-fold, truly Lamech seventy-sevenfold." (On Lamech's boasting song, see C. Westermann, *Genesis* [*BKAT*, I/6, 1970], pp. 453f.)

God acts to avenge in several situations. He may avenge individuals (Jgs. 11:36; 1 S. 24:12; 25:39; 2 S. 4:8; 16:8), or Israel — on her enemies or His (Joel 3:21; Nah. 1:2; Isa. 1:24; Jer 46:10 [Day of Yahweh]). He avenges the "blood of his prophets" (2 K. 9:7), or the "blood of his servants" (Dt. 32:43; Ps. 9:12). In Ps. 79:10, the tradition that Yahweh avenges is presupposed by the petitioner, who invokes Yahweh's vengeance. In addition, Yahweh avenges Himself *upon* Israel (Jer. 5:9, 29; 9:9). The use of the term in the OT suggests that the shedding of blood or the plotting thereof was the only legitimate provocation for "avenging."

IV. In the Apocrypha.–"Avenge/take vengeance" in the Apocrypha follows OT usage. Gentiles seek to revenge themselves against Israel (1 Macc. 3:15; Jth 1:12; 2:1; cf. 1 Macc. 6:22, where "ungodly" Israelites ask the Seleucid king to "avenge our brethren"). The Maccabean revolution was seen as Israel's avenging itself against the gentile enemies (1 Macc. 2:67, death-bed speech of Mattathias); cf. also 13:6 (Simon), and Jonathan and Simon's avenging "the blood of their brother" (1 Macc. 9:42). The prayer of the priests that God avenge Himself on Nicanor, who threatened to destroy the temple (1 Macc. 7:38), is reminiscent of Ps. 79:10. The promise of God in 2 Esd. 15:9, that He will avenge the "souls of the righteous," expresses an idea similar to those in Dt. 32:43; 2 K. 9:7;

Ps. 9:12. Sir. 30:6 cites as a boon of having children, that after one's death his son remains as an avenger against his enemies.

V. At Qumrân.–At Qumrân the concept of vengeance is similar to that in the NT: avenging is God's prerogative. In the Damascus Document this is treated twice. First, in a commentary on Lev. 19:18 ("You shall not take vengeance [Heb. *lô tiqôm*] on the children, nor bear any rancor against them"): "If any member of the covenant accuses his companion without first rebuking him before witnesses; if he denounces him in the heat of his anger or reports him to his elders to make him look contemptible, he is one that takes vengeance and bears rancor" (CD 9:2-5; Vermes, p. 110). Here Heb. *nāqam* has a new meaning. Not only is avenging in the usual OT meaning forbidden; here several ways of rebuking one's companions are equated with "avenging." (Note also the parallel term "bear rancor" [Heb. *nāṭar*], also in Lev. 19:18.)

A second occurrence of this concept is in the description of the "Princes of Judah," who "have not turned from the way of traitors but have wallowed in the ways of whoredom and wicked wealth. They have taken revenge or borne malice, every man against his brother, and every man has hated his fellow, and every man has sinned against his near kin, and has approached for unchastity, and has acted arrogantly for the sake of riches and gain" (CD 8:4-5; Vermes, p. 105). Note also that when the Kittim "took vengeance" on the "Priest who rebelled" (1QpHab 9:2), this was his punishment (Vermes, p. 240).

The Qumrân texts speak of God's being avenged in the final war. In the War Scroll, note the "names" on the trumpets: "Formations of the Divisions of God for the Vengeance of His Wrath on the Sons of Darkness," and "Reminder of Vengeance in God's Appointed Time" (1QM 3:6f.; Vermes, p. 127); note also the inscription on a battle standard: "Vengeance of God" (1QM 4:12; Vermes, p. 129). That the final war was regarded in terms of divine vengeance is shown by the hymn at the end of the Manual of Discipline: "I will not grapple with the men of perdition until the Day of Revenge [Heb. *ywm nqm*]" (1QS 10:19; Vermes, p. 91). Also in 1QS, the Levites are to curse the "men of the lot of Belial": "May he deliver you up for torture at the hands of the vengeful Avengers [Heb. *nwqmy nqm*]. . . . May He raise his angry face toward you for vengeance [Heb. *nqmtkh*]" (1QS 2:6, 9; Vermes, p. 73). Here the "vengeful Avengers" may be angels. Thus, the Qumrân texts use "avenge" in the OT sense, but maintain that avenging is God's.

VI. In the NT.–Although Stephen recounts Moses' avenging an oppressed Israelite by striking an Egyptian (Acts 7:24), the notion that avenging belongs to God is found in the NT also in Paul's quotation of OT tradition (Rom. 12:19). The context of the OT passage (Dt. 32:35) indicates that God stands ready to vindicate His people when their enemies mistreat them. Vengeance, like judgment (Mt. 7:1), should be left in His hands. In Rev. 6:10, martyrs cry out to God that He avenge their blood, and in 19:2 we find a reference to God's avenging the blood of "his servants" (on the "great harlot"), in terms reminiscent of Dt. 32:43; Ps. 9:12; 79:10; 2 Esd. 15:9.

See also AVENGER; VENGEANCE.

Bibliography.–*TDNT*, II, *s.v.* ἐκδικέω (Shrenk); G. Vermes, *Dead Sea Scrolls in English* (repr. 1970). F. B. KNUTSON

AVENGER. The RSV translation of the Hebrew participial forms of *gā'al* and *nāqam*, and the Greek substantive *ékdikos*.

Gō'ēl is rendered by "avenger" only in the expression *gō'ēl haddām*, "the avenger of blood." In Nu. 35:12 "blood" is omitted in the MT but found in the LXX and other versions.

The *gō'ēl* was the protector or defender of his family's interests. As the nearest male relative he was responsible for protecting the property (Lev. 25:25-34), liberty (vv. 35-54), and posterity (Ruth 4:5, 10; Dt. 25:5-10) of his next of kin, in addition to protecting their lives through the avenging of blood (Nu. 35:9-28; Dt. 19:4-10; Josh. 20:1-9; 2 S. 4:7, 11).

The legislation giving the *gō'ēl* both the right and responsibility to avenge his kinsman's blood distinguished two types of criminal bloodshed, "murder" and "manslaughter," both expressed by the same Hebrew word *rāṣaḥ*, found in the sixth commandment (cf. Ex. 20:13). Whereas in the case of "murder" the *gō'ēl* killed the offender (Nu. 35:19, 21; Dt. 19:12), in the case of "manslaughter" he could do so only if the offender left the assigned city of refuge prior to the death of the high priest (Nu. 35:12, 24f., 27; Dt. 19:6; Josh. 20:3, 5, 9). The human avenger of blood is used as a figure of Yahweh's role as *gō'ēl* for His people in passages such as Isa. 49:26.

The custom of avenging blood has not been limited to the ancient Hebrews. In ancient times it was practiced by, among other nations, the Greeks; and in present times has been attested among the Arabians, Persians, and other Oriental peoples.

In contrast to *gā'al, nāqam* is the Hebrew equivalent of the Eng. "avenge" in the sense of "exact satisfaction for a wrong by punishing the wrongdoer." It occurs twice in the Psalms (Ps. 8:2 [MT 3]) and 44:16 [MT 17]) in connection with Israel's enemies as a hithpael (intensive, reflexive) participle meaning "they that avenge themselves." Perhaps the poet is implying a contrast to Israel, who has Yahweh as his avenger. In Ps. 99:8 the *qal* participial form is used to denote Yahweh's vengeance against the misdeeds of His servants.

The Gk. *ékdikos,* describing the Lord (1 Thess. 4:6), means "one who satisfies justice," i.e., by punishing the evildoer (cf. Rom. 13:4).

See also AVENGE; VENGEANCE. B. K. WALTKE

AVIM; AVIMS; AVITES. *See* AVVIM.

AVITH ā'vith [Heb. *'ᵃwîṯ*; Gk. *Getthaim*–'two presses' (?)]. The royal city of Hadad, son of Bedad king of Edom (Gen. 36:35; 1 Ch. 1:46), identified by Abel (*GP,* II, 257) with Khirbet el-Jiththeh between Ma'ân and el-Basṭa. The Arabic and Greek words are obviously similar, but no phonetic relationship with the Hebrew is possible.

W. S. L. S.

AVOID. Archaic in 1 S. 18:11, AV, for "escape."

AVVA a'və [Heb. *'awwā*] (2 K. 17:24); AV AVA. A province whose people Shalmaneser king of Assyria relocated to cities of Samaria, replacing the Israelites whom he took into exile. *See* IVVAH.

AVVIM av'im; **AVVITES** av'īts [Heb. *'awwîm*]; AV AVIM; AVIMS; AVITES. The name of a people and a place.

1. The Avvites were early inhabitants of Canaan in the region later known as the Philistine plain, "as far as Gaza." They were destroyed by the invading Caphtorim (*see* CAPHTOR) (Dt. 2:23; cf. Josh. 13:3; 2 K. 17:31).

2. Avvim was one of the cities of the tribe of Benjamin (Josh. 18:23), probably near Bethel. However, since the form is gentilic and occurs with the definite article, it is tempting to read "Bethel and (the village of) the Avvim" — although one hesitates to suggest that they were the people of Ai. W. S. L. S.

AWAKE. Usually the translation of Heb. *'ûr, qîṣ,* or *yāqaṣ*, or Gk. *grēgoréō*. Other terms are Heb. *šāqaḏ* ("be awake, watchful," Ps. 102:7; 127:1) and *qāḏam* ("be early," Ps. 119:148), and Gk. *diagrēgoréō* ("keep awake," Lk. 9:32), *exypnízō* ("arouse," Jn. 11:11), and *egeírō* ("rise, get up!" Eph. 5:14). Heb. *qîṣ* is used only in the hiphil in the sense of awaking someone else. *'Ûr* occurs in both the qal and the hiphil, meaning either to arouse oneself or to stir up or incite someone else. Gk. *grēgoréō* generally means to be alert or vigilant.

In addition to the ordinary usage for awaking from sleep, "awake" is used in several figurative senses: (1) waking from moral, spiritual, or emotional sleep (Jgs. 5:12; Cant. 2:7; Isa. 52:1); (2) waking from death, either physical or spiritual (Isa. 26:19; Dnl. 12:2; Eph. 5:14); (3) waking from drunkenness (Joel 1:5); (4) in apostrophe to address musical instruments (Ps. 57:8; 108:2), the north wind (Cant. 4:16), a sword (Zec. 13:7); (5) in addressing God, as a plea that He respond to prayer (Ps. 7:6; 35:23; 44:23; Isa. 51:9). N. J. O.

AWAY WITH. Archaic in Isa. 1:13, AV, for "endure, bear with" (Heb. *yāḵōl*).

AWE; AWESOME; AWFUL [Heb. *gûr* (1 S. 18:15; Ps. 22:23; 33:8), *ḥāṯaṯ* (Mal. 2:5), *yārē'* (Gen. 28:17; Dt. 28:58; Josh. 4:14; 1 K. 3:28; 1 Ch. 16:25), *'āraṣ* (Isa. 29:23), *pāḥaḏ* (Ps. 119:161); Gk. *déos* (He. 12:28), *phobéō* (Mt. 17:6; 27:54; Mk. 4:41), *phóbos* (Lk. 5:26; Rom. 11:20)]; AV also AFRAID, DREADFUL, FEAR, FEARED, FEARFUL, GODLY FEAR; NEB also AFRAID, AWESTRUCK, "be on your guard," DREADED, FEARED, FEARSOME, TERROR, THRILLS. A heightened emotional state characterized by a commingling of fear, astonishment, and terror with wonder, veneration, and reverence.

When evoked by men, awe is directed toward the unique and charismatic qualities of the human personality. Thus, Israel held Joshua in highest esteem: "they stood in awe of him, as they had stood in awe of Moses" (Josh. 4:14). The nation similarly "stood in awe of the king [Solomon], because they perceived that the wisdom of God was in him" (1 K. 3:28). Awe can also denote simple fear or dread, such as Saul had of David (cf. 1 S. 18:12, 15). One can also be in awe of a place in which some dramatic and inspirational event has happened; hence, Jacob says of Bethel, "How awesome is this place!" (Gen. 28:17).

But awe is most typically directed to the Deity or His actions. When so directed, awe is that state of mind which contemplates "the 'wholly other' . . . that which is quite beyond the sphere of the usual, the intelligible, and the familiar, which therefore falls outside the limits of the 'canny', and is contrasted with it, filling the mind with blank wonder and astonishment" (Otto, p. 26). Yahweh "is to be held in awe above all gods. For all the gods of the peoples are idols; but the Lord made the heavens" (1 Ch. 16:25f.). Because He is the Creator of nature and history, writes the psalmist, "let all the inhabitants of the world stand in awe of him!" (Ps. 33:8). His name is awful (Dt. 28:58; Mal. 2:5) and His words also are held in awe (Ps. 119:161). Therefore, reverential awe is one of the constituents of acceptable worship (Ps. 22:23 [MT 24]; He. 12:28). Paul speaks of godly awe as the opposite of human pride (Rom. 11:20); it is the realization that one's life and destiny are in the hands of the "wholly other."

The Gospels observe that the disciples and others were frequently astonished at events surrounding the life of Jesus. When Jesus healed and forgave the paralytic, a whole crowd was "filled with awe, saying, 'We have seen strange things today' " (Lk. 5:26). When He spoke a calming word to nature, the disciples "were filled with awe" (Mk. 4:41). Again, the disciples "fell on their faces, and were filled with awe" at the transfiguration (Mt. 17:6). And finally, even a Roman centurion and his soldiers were struck with awe during the last hours of Jesus' life and concluded, "Truly this was the Son of God" (Mt. 27:54).

See also FEAR; REVERENCE.

Bibliography.–R. Otto, *Idea of the Holy* (Eng. tr. 1950); *THAT*, I, *s.v.* יָרֵא (Stähli). K. H. MAAHS

AWL [Heb. *marṣē(a)'*]; AV AUL. A pointed tool that was used for boring through a slave's ear (Ex. 21:6; Dt. 15:17).

AWNING [Heb. *m^{e}ḵasseh*] (Ezk. 27:7); AV "that which covered thee"; NEB AWNINGS. A poetic reference to the deck-coverings of Phoenician ships. If the MT is repointed *miḵseh* (Ugar. *mks*) it could refer to a skin roof of the same kind that covered the ark (cf. Gen. 8:13) or the tent of meeting (Ex. 26:14). R. K. H.

AXE. Several types of axes are mentioned in Scripture:

(1) The Heb. *garzen* unquestionably was one of the larger chopping instruments, as the uses to which it was put would imply (Dt. 19:5; 20:19; 1 K. 6:7; Isa. 10:15). It was used by stonemasons, and appears in the Siloam Inscription as a tool for excavating.

Bronze ceremonial axehead from the upper altar room at Beth-shan (13th cent. B.C.). The form is an open hand with outstretched fingers. (Israel Department of Antiquities and Museums)

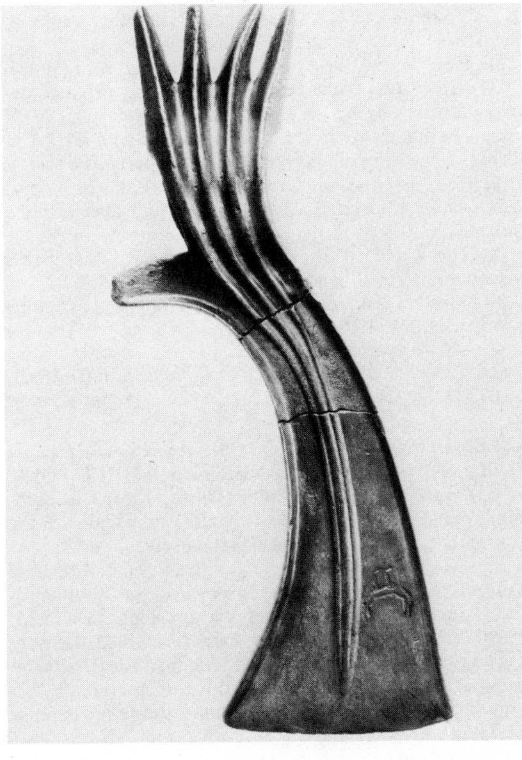

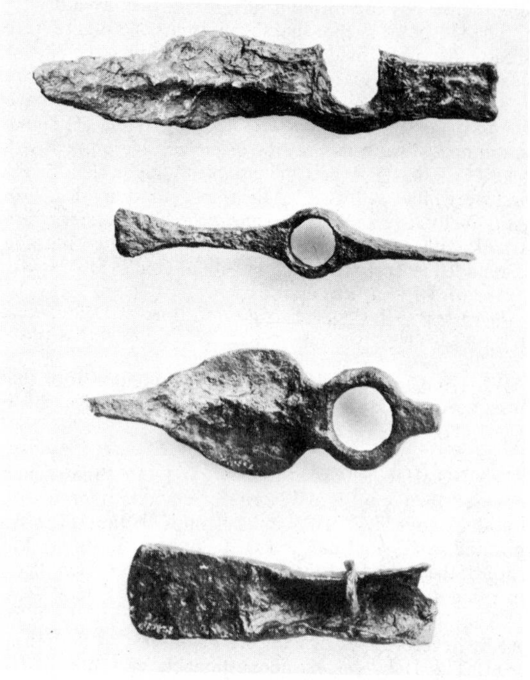

Top to bottom: (1) pick-axe from Ramah; (2) small axe-adze; (3) pick-axe, probably from Ramah; (4) adze from Bittîr. All are iron, from the Hellenistic or Roman periods. (Royal Ontario Museum, Toronto)

(2) The *ma'aṣār* (Jer. 10:3) was a hand tool, probably an adze (cf. Isa. 44:12, MT).

(3) Heb. *qardōm* is used in Jgs. 9:48; 1 S. 13:20f.; Ps. 74:5; Jer. 46:22. This was evidently another name for an adze.

(4) Heb. *barzel,* lit. "iron" (Dt. 19:5; 2 K. 6:5; Isa. 10:34), indicates a characteristic Iron Age product developed originally by the Hittites.

(5) The *magzērâ* of 2 S. 12:31 and *megērâ* of 1 Ch. 20:13 is some form of cutting instrument, perhaps a saw.

(6) Heb. *ḥereḇ* is rendered "axe" in Ezk. 26:9 only. It is usually translated "sword"; it could also mean a pickaxe.

(7) The *kaššîl* of Ps. 74:6 (RSV, NEB, "hatchet") is probably a small hand-axe.

(8) In the NT, Gk. *axínē* designates a tool used in cutting down trees (Mt. 3:10; Lk. 3:9).

See also WEAPONS OF WAR.

See Y. Yadin, *Art of Warfare in Biblical Lands* (1963), I, 11f., 59, 77, 126-184. R. K. H.

AXLE [Heb. *seren*] (1 K. 7:30); AV PLATE; [*yāḏ*] (7:32f.); AV AXLETREE; NEB also WHEEL-FORK (v. 32). Part of the ornamental bronze wagons in Solomon's temple, In v. 32 *yāḏ* ("hand") may indicate the axle-mounts rather than the axles themselves.

AYIN ä'yēn, ä'yin [ע, Heb. *'ayin*–'eye' or 'fountain']. The sixteenth letter of the Hebrew alphabet, so named, probably, because the original form resembled the eye. It is commonly pronounced by producing a rough guttural sound at the back of the throat and is transliterated by '.

In some cases the LXX substituted the letter *gamma* (*g*). The numerical value is 70.

See WRITING.

AYYAH a'yə [Heb. *'ayyâ,* Bomberg ed. and Targ. *'azzâ*; Gk. *Gaia, Gaza*] (1 Ch. 7:28); AV, NEB, GAZA. An Ephraimite possession, but not the Philistine city of Gaza. Some site close to Ai has been proposed (cf. Ezr. 2:28; Neh. 11:31), but this is uncertain. R. K. H.

AZAEL ā'zə-el [Gk. *Azaēl, Aziēlos*]; AV AZAELUS. An Israelite who divorced his foreign wife (1 Esd. 9:34). The name is omitted in Ezr. 10:41.

AZAELUS a-zə-ē'ləs (1 Esd. 9:34, AV). *See* AZAEL.

AZAL ā'zəl [Heb. *'āṣāl*; Gk. *Iasol, Asaēl,* etc.] (Zec. 14:5, AV); RSV "the side of it"; [Heb. *'eṣlô*]; NEB ASAL. Perhaps a place near Jerusalem. The Gk. *Iasol* has been compared with Wâdī Yasûl, a tributary of the Kidron. The RSV emendation is supported by Symmachus. W. S. L. S.

AZALIAH az-ə-lī'ə [Heb. *'aṣalyāhû*–'Yahweh has set aside']. A son of Meshullam and father of Shaphan the scribe, famous in connection with the discovery of the law in the reign of King Josiah (2 K. 22:3).

AZANIAH az-ə-nī'ə [Heb. *'azanyâ*–'Yahweh has heard']. A son of Jeshua, a Levite who signed the covenant of Nehemiah (Neh. 10:9).

AZAPHION ə-zā'fē-ən (1 Esd. 5:33, AV). *See* SOPHERETH.

AZARA az'ə-rə (1 Esd. 5:31, AV). *See* HASRAH.

AZARAEL a-zä'rə-el; **AZAREEL** a-zä'rə-el. *See* AZAREL.

AZAREL az'ə-rel [Heb. *'azar'ēl*–'God has helped']; AV AZAREEL, also AZARAEL (**6**); NEB also AZAREEL (**1-4**); [Gk. Apoc. *Ezril*]; AV ESRIL; NEB EZRIL.

1. A Korahite who entered the army of David at Ziklag (1 Ch. 12:6).

2. A musician in the temple appointed by lot; son of Heman (1 Ch. 25:18; cf. Uzziel, v. 4).

3. A captain of the tribe of Dan in the service of David (1 Ch. 27:22).

4. One of those who divorced foreign wives; a son of Bani (Ezr. 10:41; 1 Esd. 9:34).

5. The father of Amashsai, a priest who dwelt in Jerusalem after the Exile (Neh. 11:13).

6. A priest's son who played the trumpet in the procession when the wall was dedicated (Neh. 12:36). A. L. BRESLICH

AZARIAH az-ə-rī'ə [Heb. *'azaryâ, 'azaryāhû*–'Yahweh has helped'; Gk. Apoc. *Azarias, Ezerias* (1 Esd. 8:1)].

1. King of Judah. *See* UZZIAH.

2. A Judahite of the house of Ethan the Wise (1 Ch. 2:8).

3. The son of Jehu, descended from an Egyptian through the daughter of Sheshan (1 Ch. 2:38f.).

4. A son of Ahimaaz and grandson of Zadok (1 Ch. 6:9).

5. A son of Zadok the high priest and an official of Solomon (1 K. 4:2).

6. A high priest and son of Johanan (1 Ch. 6:10f.).

7. A Levite, ancestor of Samuel and of Heman the singer (1 Ch. 6:36).

8. A son of Nathan and captain of Solomon's tax collectors (1 K. 4:5).

9. A prophet in the reign of King Asa; his father's name was Oded (2 Ch. 15:1-8).

10, 11. Two sons of Jehoshaphat king of Judah (2 Ch. 21:2).

12. (2 Ch. 22:6, AV). *See* AHAZIAH **2.**

13. A son of Jeroham, who helped to overthrow Athaliah and place Joash on the throne (2 Ch. 23:1).

14. A son of Johanan and a leading man of Ephraim, mentioned in connection with the emancipated captives taken by Pekah (2 Ch. 28:12).

15. A Levite of the family of Merari, who took part in cleansing the temple in the days of Hezekiah (2 Ch. 29:12).

16. A high priest who rebuked King Uzziah for arrogating to himself priestly functions (2 Ch. 26:16-20).

17. The father of Seraiah and son of Hilkiah and grandfather of Ezra (1 Ch. 6:13f.; 9:11; Ezr. 7:1; 2 Esd. 1:1).

18. A son of Hoshaiah, and a bitter enemy of Jeremiah (Jer. 43:2ff.).

19. AV Apoc. AZARIAS. One of the royal captives taken to Babylon, whose name was changed to Abednego (Dnl. 1:7; Song Three 2, 66).

20. The son of Maaseiah, who helped repair the walls of Jerusalem (Neh. 3:23f.).

21. AV and NEB Apoc. AZARIAS. A Levite who assisted Ezra in expounding the law (Neh. 8:7; 1 Esd. 9:48).

22. A priest who sealed the covenant (Neh. 10:2).

23. A prince of Judah mentioned in connection with the dedication of the walls of Jerusalem (Neh. 12:32f.).

24. AV Apoc. EZERIAS, AZIEI; NEB Apoc. EZERIAS, AZIAH. An ancestor of Ezra (Ezr. 7:3; 1 Esd. 8:1; 2 Esd. 1:2).

25. AV, NEB, AZARIAS. One who divorced his foreign wife (1 Esd. 9:21); cf. UZZIAH (Ezr. 10:21).

26. AV, NEB, AZARIAS. One who stood at the right side of Ezra when the law was read to the people (1 Esd. 9:43); omitted in Ezr. 8:4.

27. AV, NEB, AZARIAS. A general in the service of Judas Maccabeus (1 Macc. 5:18, 56, 60).

AZARIAS az-ə-rī'əs [Gk. *Azarias*]. A name assumed by the angel RAPHAEL (Tob. 5:12; 6:6, 13; etc.). *See also* AZARIAH **19, 21, 25, 26, 27.**

AZARU az'ə-ro͞o [Gk. *Azarou, Azourou*]; AV AZURAN; NEB AZURUS. A family that returned with Zerubbabel to Jerusalem (1 Esd. 5:15); cf. Azzur (Neh. 10:17).

AZAZ ā'zaz [Heb. *'āzāz*–'powerful']. A descendant of Reuben (1 Ch. 5:8).

AZAZEL ə-zā'zel [Heb. *'ᵃzā'zēl*] (Lev. 16:8, 10, 26); AV SCAPEGOAT; NEB PRECIPICE. The goat banished into the wilderness during the Day of Atonement ceremonies. It had received the "lot for Azazel," and therefore was not to be sacrificed to God but made symbolic of atonement for Israel through its release in the desert. The term Azazel has been interpreted as follows:

(1) By the LXX of Lev. 16:8, 10 as "escape goat" (*trágos apopompaíos*) and of v. 26 as *trágos diestálmenos eis áphesin,* where the idea of remission is evident. (Cf. AV.)

(2) By rabbinic authorities as the place where the goat was sent. This is likely only if the Israelite camp remained in one place for most of the wilderness wanderings. (Cf. NEB.)

(3) As the name of a demon living in the desert (cf. Ps. 106:37; Dt. 32:17; Isa. 13:21; Mt. 12:43ff.; etc.), perhaps the Azael (Azazel) of 1 En. 6:7; 8:1; 9:6; 10:4; etc. However, the very concept of setting up a deity of this kind in contrast to God is entirely foreign to OT thought. Furthermore, no ancient Near Eastern culture offered scapegoats to demons in this way.

The goat appears to symbolize the transfer of guilt from the nation, and its complete removal from their midst, never to return.

See also ATONEMENT, DAY OF II. R. K. H.

AZAZIAH az-ə-zī'ə [Heb. *'ᵃzazyāhû*–'Yahweh is strong (strengthens)'].

1. A Levite musician who participated in the services held on the return of the ark to Jerusalem (1 Ch. 15:21). His name is omitted from the list in v. 18.

2. Father of Hoshea, who was the leader of Ephraim at the time David numbered the people (1 Ch. 27:20).

3. A Levite who had charge of the offerings brought to the temple in the days of Hezekiah (2 Ch. 31:13).

AZBAZARETH az-baz'ə-reth (1 Esd. 5:69, AV). *See* ESARHADDON.

AZBUK az'buk [Heb. *'azbûq*]. The father of a certain Nehemiah — not the great governor of the same name, though a contemporary (Neh. 3:16).

AZEKAH ə-zē'kə [Heb. *'ᵃzēqâ*–'hoed, bared ground']. An isolated fortress city situated in the Shephelah of Judah (Josh. 15:35), 9 mi. (15 km.) N of Eleutheropolis (Beit Jibrîn) and 15 mi. (24 km.) NW of Hebron, controlling the entrance into the valley. The plateau on the summit is about 350 by 150 yds. (320 by 135 m.). A well-fortified enclosed citadel sat atop the highest point. Today the site is called Tell ez-Zakarîyah, and evidences of ruined towers and an ancient wall atop the mound may still be seen.

After coming to the aid of besieged Gibeon, Joshua and his men chased the remnant of the Canaanite coalition, led by Adonizedek of Jerusalem, to Azekah and beyond to Makkedah (Josh. 10:10f.). A sudden downpour of rain and hailstones aided Joshua's men in achieving the victory.

In 1 S. 17:1ff. it is stated that Goliath and the Philistine army were encamped between Azekah and Socoh in Ephes-dammim. Saul and the Israelite hosts were encamped on the opposite hillside. David's conquest of the Philistine giant opened the way for an eventual Israelite victory.

Following the revolt of the northern kingdom, Rehoboam (*ca.* 922-915 B.C.) strengthened many Judean cities, including the fortifications of Azekah (2 Ch. 11:9). This involved fortifying the enclosed citadel on the highest point of the hill on which Azekah was built. He also stationed a garrison there and supplied it with food, oil, wine, and weapons.

Azekah was one of the last Judean cities to capitulate to the forces of Nebuchadrezzar (*ca.* 588 B.C., Jer. 34:7). On one of the clay documents found by excavators in the debris of a Lachish building, Hoshaiah, the commanding officer of the army N of Lachish, tells his commanding officer Yoash, whose headquarters were in Lachish, that he can no longer see the smoke (fire) signals from Azekah, implying that the city had already fallen to the enemy from Babylon.

After the Exile, Jews who returned from Babylon reoccupied Azekah (Neh. 11:30). F. E. YOUNG

AZEL ā'zəl [Heb. *'āṣēl*–'noble']. A descendant of King Saul, through Jonathan (1 Ch. 8:37f.; 9:43f.).

AZEM ā'zəm (AV Josh. 15:29; 19:3). *See* EZEM.

AZEPHURITH az-ə-fo͞o'rəth (1 Esd. 5:16, AV). *See* JORAH.

AZETAS ə-zē'təs [Gk. *Azētas*]. The head of a family accompanying Zerubbabel out of captivity (1 Esd. 5:15); omitted in Ezr. 2:16; Neh. 7:21.

AZGAD az'gad [Heb. *'azgāḏ*–'strong is Gad'; Gk. *Asgad, Argai, Astad, Astaa*]; AV Apoc. SADAS; ASTATH; NEB Apoc. ASTAA; ASTATH. A family that returned from exile with Zerubbabel (Ezr. 2:12; Neh. 7:17; 1 Esd. 5:13; 8:38), and some with Ezra (Ezr. 8:12).

AZIAH ə-zī'ə (2 Esd. 1:2, NEB); **AZIEI** ə-zī'yī (AV). *See* AZARIAH **24.**

AZIEL ā'zē-əl [Heb. *'ᵃzî'ēl*]. A Levite who played the harp when the ark came back to Jerusalem (1 Ch. 15:20), the same as Jaaziel of v. 18.

AZIZA ə-zī'zə [Heb. *'ᵃzîzā'*–'the powerful']. One who divorced his foreign wife (Ezr. 10:27). Cf. Zerdaiah in 1 Esd. 9:28.

AZMAVETH az-mā'vəth [Heb. *'azmāweṯ*]; NEB AZMOTH.

1. One of David's thirty mighty men (2 S. 23:31; 1 Ch. 11:33).

2. A descendant of Jonathan the son of Saul (1 Ch. 8:36; 9:42).

3. Father of two warriors who joined David at Ziklag (1 Ch. 12:3).

4. A man put in charge of David's treasuries (1 Ch. 27:25).

AZMAVETH az-mā'vəth [Heb. *'azmāweṯ*–possibly 'Mot is strong'; Gk. *Asmōth, Azmōth*]; NEB BETH-AZMOTH. A place settled by forty-two "sons of Azmaveth" who returned from the Babylonian Captivity with Zerubbabel (Ezr. 2:24). In Neh. 7:28 it is called Beth-azmaveth, "the place of Azmaveth," indicating that Azmaveth is a personal or family name. Singers from this village took part in the dedication of the wall of Jerusalem (Neh. 12:29). It has been identified with Ḥizmeh, about 1.5 mi. (2.5 km.) N of *'Anâtâ* (Anathoth). W. S. L. S.

AZMON az'mon [Heb. *'aṣmôn*–'strong'; Gk. *Asemōna*]. A site named to define the southwest border both of the land given to Israel (Nu. 34:4f.) and of the tribal inheritance of Judah (Josh. 15:4). It was near the Brook of Egypt (Wâdī el-'Arîsh); a location near 'Ain el-Qeṣeimeh, about 10 mi. (16 km.) NW of 'Ain Qedeis (Kadesh-barnea), has been suggested. W. S. L. S.

AZMOTH az'mōth (NEB 2 S. 23:31; 1 Ch. 8:36; etc.). *See* AZMAVETH **1-4.**

AZNOTH-TABOR az'noth-tā'bər [Heb. *'aznôṯ tāḇôr*–'ears (?) of Tabor']. A site in the southwest (?) of the portion given to the tribe of Naphtali (Josh. 19:34), obviously related somehow to Mt. Tabor. In order to count a total of "nineteen cities" (v. 38), we are forced to understand some of these names as other than towns, and Aznoth-tabor is probably some other kind of landmark.

See *GTTOT*, §§ 334f. W. S. L. S.

AZOR ā'zôr [Gk. *Azōr*]. An ancestor of Jesus Christ (Mt. 1:13f.).

AZOTUS ə-zō'təs [Gk. *Azōtos*] (1 Macc. 4:15; 5:68; 9:15; 10:77f., 83f.; 11:4; etc.; Acts 8:40). The Greek name of ASHDOD, although S. E. Johnson suggests in the *Oxford Annotated Apocrypha* (1965) that Mt. Azotus in 1 Macc. 9:15 may be el-'Asur, 6 mi. (10 km.) NE of el-Bîreh, since Ashdod is too far removed from the scene of battle.

AZRIEL az'rē-əl [Heb. *'azrî'ēl*–'God is my help'].

1. One of the leading men of the half-tribe of Manasseh, E of the Jordan, who with others of his tribe was carried captive by the king of Assyria (1 Ch. 5:24ff.).

2. The father of Jerimoth of the tribe of Naphtali in the reign of King David (1 Ch. 27:19).

3. The father of Seraiah, one of the officers sent by Jehoiakim to arrest Jeremiah and Baruch (Jer. 36:26).

AZRIKAM az-rī'kəm [Heb. *'azrîqām*–'my help has arisen'].

1. A descendant of King David through Zerubbabel (1 Ch. 3:23).

2. A prince of Judah in the time of Ahaz. He was slain by Zichri, an Ephraimite soldier (2 Ch. 28:7).

3. One of Azel's sons, a Benjaminite, descended from King Saul (1 Ch. 8:38; 9:44).

4. A Levite of the house of Merari and a resident of Jerusalem (1 Ch. 9:14; Neh. 11:15).

AZUBAH ə-zo͞o'bə [Heb. *'azûḇâ*–'desolation'].

1. A wife of Caleb, by whom she had three sons (1 Ch. 2:18f.).

2. The daughter of Shilhi and mother of King Jehoshaphat (1 K. 22:42; 2 Ch. 20:31).

AZUR ā'zər (AV Jer. 28:1; Ezk. 11:1). *See* AZZUR **1, 3.**

AZURAN az'ə-ran, (1 Esd. 5:15, AV); **AZURUS** az'ə-rəs (NEB). *See* AZARU.

AZZAH az'ə (AV Dt. 2:23; 1 K. 4:24; Jer. 25:20). *See* GAZA.

AZZAN az'ən [Heb. *'azzan*–'strong']. Father of Paltiel of the tribe of Issachar (Nu. 34:26).

AZZUR az'ər [Heb. *'azzûr*–'helpful']; AV also AZUR **(1, 3).**

1. The father of Hananiah, a false prophet of Gibeon in the days of Zedekiah (Jer. 28:1ff.).

2. One of those who, with Nehemiah, sealed the covenant on the return from Babylon (Neh. 10:17).

3. The father of Jaazaniah (Ezk. 11:1).

BAAL bā'əl [Heb. *ba'al* < Bab. *Belu.* or *Bel*–'lord'; Gk. *Baal*]. The supreme fertility-god of the Canaanites.

I. Name
II. Character
III. Worship
IV. Various Forms of Baal

I. Name.–In the Râs Shamrah texts, the first of which were discovered in 1929, the designation "Baal" is found about 240 times either alone or in a compound. The combination *aliyn b'l,* referring to the same god, is specified about seventy times and mainly in those passages where sacrifices are offered to Baal. The name is most widely employed alone as a title; as such it occurs about 150 times. About twenty times Baal is called Hadad or is used in a compound form of Hadad, the Semitic storm-god of the ancient Near East who was perhaps universally known in the ancient world. Though Hadad (Addu of the Amarna Letters) and Baal were two separate gods, the Râs Shamrah tablets indicate no differentiation. The two names are employed as though they belonged to the same god, giving a strong indication that the characteristics of Baal were similar to those of Hadad. Hadad's mission, as well as his symbol (the bull, a symbol of fertility), was assumed by the Canaanite Baal. Baal is further mentioned as *bn dgn,* i.e., "son of Dagan," the fertility-god who was also worshiped by the Philistines (Jgs. 16:23; 1 S. 5:2). His close relationship to Hadad and Dagan leaves no doubt that Baal was considered the fertility-god of the Ugaritic religion.

"Baal of the lightning," stele from Râs Shamrah. The small human figure may be a deity or a person in the god's care. (Louvre)

The Râs Shamrah tablets give no indication that Baal was in any sense a local god. As the word in Hebrew also means "possessor," however, it is quite possible that when used in a religious sense the name signified the god of a particular area of land or soil. Thus the forms under which Baal was worshiped were necessarily as numerous as the communities that worshiped him. Each locality had its own Baal or divine lord who frequently took his name from the city or place to which he belonged. Hence there were Baal-meon ("Baal of Meon," Nu. 32:38), Baal-hermon ("Baal of Hermon," Jgs. 3:3), Baal-hazor ("Baal of Hazor," 2 S. 13:23), Baal-peor ("Baal of Peor," Nu. 25:3). At other times the title was affixed to the names of an individual god; thus there were Bel-Marduk ("the lord Marduk") at Babylon, Baal-Melqart at Tyre, and Baal-gad (Josh. 11:17) in the north of Palestine. Occasionally the second element was a noun, as in Baal-berith ("lord of the covenant," (Jgs. 9:4), Baal-zebub ("lord of flies," 2 K. 1:2), and Baal-hamon ("lord of abundance or wealth," Cant. 8:11). All these various forms of the fertility-god were collectively known as the Baalim (b^{e}'*ālîm*, Heb. pl. of Baal).

II. Character.–The Râs Shamrah tablets, as well as the statuettes and stelae found there, have produced an abundance of information relating to the character of Baal. His character as the storm-god is expressed on a sculptured stele. In his left hand he is seen grasping a thunderbolt, the extension of which converts into a spearhead, and in his right hand he is swinging a club overhead. He dons a helmet adorned with the horns of a bull, which emphasizes his role as the supreme fertility-god of the Ugaritic religion.

The Râs Shamrah texts praise Baal as the god who has power over rain, wind, clouds, and therefore over fertility. His control over nature, however, fluctuates in accord with his victories or defeats in his encounters with Mot, god of death, sterility, and aridity. In emphasizing the cycle of the seasons the Râs Shamrah texts tell of Baal's repeated defeats by Mot, who brings forth scorched and barren fields. During these periods of aridity Baal's power is eclipsed, but only temporarily. Baal will be victorious again; he will defeat Mot and return to grant rich, fertile fields to his people.

After one such struggle in which Baal is defeated, he is commanded by Mot to descend to the underworld. Before he does, however, he copulates with his sister-consort, the goddess Anat, to produce an heir in order to guarantee the continued fertility of the land. Here Baal appears as a bull and Anat as a heifer. The goddess Anat laments over the death of Baal and searches for him. She finds him and returns him to the heights of Sapan, buries him there, and sacrifices seventy wild oxen, seventy bulls, seventy sheep, seventy deer, seventy wild goats, and seventy asses. Anat pleads with Mot to raise Baal from death, but he refuses. During this time, of course, the rains cease falling, the sun scorches the earth, the vegetation is burned, the fields are unproductive, and the drought continues.

Finally the time arrives for Anat to bring vengeance against the evil Mot. She attacks him, cleaves him with a sword, burns him with fire, grinds him with millstones, and sows him in the fields, so that the birds will eat his remains. The aftermath of Anat's victory over Mot is the reappearance of Baal. But, even as the Babylonian Marduk had to defeat Tiâmat before regaining his supremacy over the gods, so Baal must recapture his rightful throne on Sapan, the mountain of the gods. Consequently, Baal drives Aṯtar, the son of Asherah, from the throne and in a short but fierce battle again defeats Mot. Now the fields can once again be fertile and productive.

III. Worship.–The Canaanite religion had a strong influence on the Hebrews. During the time of Balaam and Balak, Baal was worshiped in Moab (Nu. 22:41). Saul, Jonathan, and David had sons who were named Esh-baal (1 Ch. 8:33), Merib-baal (8:34), and Beeliada (14:7). During Ahab's reign, however, the name became associated with the worship and rites of the Tyrian deity introduced into Samaria by Jezebel, and its idolatrous associations accordingly caused it to fall into disrepute. Hosea (2:16) declares that henceforth the God of Israel should no longer be called BAALI, "my Baal," and that the "names of the Baals . . . shall be mentioned by name no more" (2:17).

Temples of Baal at Samaria and Jerusalem are mentioned in 1 K. 16:21 and 2 K. 11:18. They had been erected at the time when the Ahab dynasty endeavored to fuse the Yahweh worshipers and the Baal worshipers into a single people under the same national Tyrian god. Altars on which incense was burned to Baal were erected in the streets of Jerusalem (Jer. 11:13), apparently on the flat roofs of the houses (32:29). The temple of Baal contained an image of the god in the shape of a pillar (2 K. 10:26f.). In the reign of Ahab, Baal was served by 450 priests (1 K. 18:19), as well as by prophets (2 K. 10:19). Baal worshipers wore special vestments when the ritual was performed (2 K. 10:22). The ordinary offering made to the god consisted of incense (Jer. 7:9). On extraordinary occasions the sacrifice was a human being (Jer. 19:5). At times the priests worked themselves into a state of ecstasy and slashed themselves with knives as they danced (1 K. 18:26, 28).

Being fully aware of the religious danger of the Baal cult to Israel, the prophet Elijah challenged Ahab, his pagan wife Jezebel, the prophets of Baal, and Baal himself (1 K. 18:20-29). The blood purge against the Baal worshipers continued under the leadership of Jehu and finally concluded after King Jehoram was killed. Jezebel was thrown out of a window to be trampled by the soldiers' horses, and the remaining Baal worshipers were slaughtered in the temple (2 K. 9f.). The cult was revived in Judah by Athaliah, Jezebel's daughter (2 Ch. 17:3; 21:6; 22:2). After Athaliah was killed the temple of Baal was razed and the chief priest, Mattan, was slain before the altar (2 K. 11:18). Ahaz made molten images for the Baalim (2 Ch. 28:2); and despite Hezekiah's reformation his son Manasseh erected altars to Baal (2 K. 21:3). During Josiah's reform Hilkiah the chief priest was commanded to remove the vessels of Baal from the temple and destroy them, as well as to depose all the idolatrous priests. Obviously, Baalism was and continued to be a pronounced threat to the Hebrews throughout their history, perhaps more in Israel than in Judah.

IV. Various Forms of Baal.–*Baal-berith* (Heb. *ba'al b^erîṯ*; Gk. *Baalberith*), "covenant Baal," was worshiped at Shechem after the death of Gideon (Jgs. 8:33; 9:4). In Jgs. 9:46 "El" is substituted for "Baal," and the temple is referred to as that of El-berith, "covenant god." Whether the covenant referred to was one made between Baal and his worshipers or between the Hebrews and the Canaanites is a matter of speculation. *See* BAAL-BERITH.

Baal-gad (Heb. *ba'al gāḏ*; Gk. *Balagada*), "Baal of good fortune," was probably the god of a town called after his name. The place may have been located in the valley of Lebanon below Mt. Hermon (Josh. 11:17) on the northern border of the land captured by Joshua (12:7; 13:5). The god is termed simply "Gad" in Isa. 65:11, where it has been translated "Fortune" and "Destiny" by the RSV and "god of Fate" and "Fortune" by the NEB. The exact location of the town is unknown, but it may be the modern Hasbeiyah. *See* BAAL-GAD.

Baal-hamon (Heb. *ba'al hāmôn*; Gk. *Beelamōn*), "lord of abundance or wealth," is mentioned only as a place where Solomon had an extremely fertile vineyard (Cant. 8:11). The site of this place is unknown.

Baal-hermon (Heb. *ba'al ḥermôn*; Gk. *Balaermōn*), "Baal of Hermon," was perhaps a place on the northern border of Israel near or on Mt. Hermon. Apparently it was not involved in war during the conquest of Israel (Jgs. 3:3; 1 Ch. 5:23). The exact site is unknown, but some scholars believe it to be another name for Baal-gad. *See* BAAL-HERMON.

Baal-peor (Heb. *ba'al p^e'ôr*; Gk. *Beelphegor*), "Baal of Peor," was the god of the Moabite mountains who took his name from Peor. When the Israelites dwelt in Shittim they "played the harlot with the daughters of Moab," i.e., took part in the rituals of the pagan cult and linked themselves to Baal-peor. Because of this defection 24,000 Israelites were struck and slain by a plague (Nu. 25:1-9; Dt. 4:3; Ps. 106:28; Hos. 9:10).

Baal-zebub (Heb. *ba'al z^e'ḇûḇ*; Gk. *Baalmyia Theos*) is generally interpreted to mean "Baal the fly god." BAAL-ZEBUB was the Philistine god at Ekron. King Ahaziah, having fallen through the lattice of his upper chamber and desiring to know whether or not he would die from his fall, sent messengers to Baal-zebub. By this act he kindled the wrath of God, and as a result he had to die (2 K. 1:1-17). Some have held that Baal-zebub was the god who could drive pesky flies away; others hold that he was able to give oracles by the buzzing of a fly.

Bibliography.–W. F. Albright, *History, Archaeology and Christian Humanism* (1964); *Yahweh and the Gods of Canaan* (1968); G. R. Driver, *Canaanite Myths and Legends* (1956); C. H. Gordon,

Ugarit and Minoan Crete (1966); *Ugaritic Literature* (1949); J. Gray, *The Canaanites* (1965); A. Jirku, *Kanaanäische Mythen und Epen aus Ras Schamra-Ugarit* (1962); A. S. Kapelrud, *Baal in the Ras Shamra Texts* (1952); *Ras Shamra Discoveries and the OT*, tr. G. W. Anderson (1963). K. G. JUNG

BAAL bā'əl [Heb. *ba'al*–'lord, master, possessor'].

1. A descendant of Reuben, Jacob's firstborn son, and the father of Beerah, prince of the Reubenites (1 Ch. 5:5).

2. The fourth of ten sons of Jeiel, father and founder of Gibeon. His mother was Maacah, his brother Kish the father of Saul (1 Ch. 8:29f.; 9:35f., 39; cf. 1 S. 14:50f.).

3. In composition, often the name of a man and not of the heathen god, e.g., Baal-hanan, a king of Edom (Gen. 36:38; 1 Ch. 1:49); also a royal prefect of the same name (1 Ch. 27:28).

4. A city of the tribe of Simeon (1 Ch. 4:33). *See* BAALATH-BEER. D. M. PRATT

BAALAH bā'ə-lə [Heb. *ba'ᵃlâ*–'mistress'].

1. The same as KIRIATH-JEARIM (Josh. 15:9f.; 1 Ch. 13:6).

2. Also (probably) **BALAH** [Heb. *bālâ*] (Josh. 19:3); **BILHAH** [Heb. *bilhâ*] (1 Ch. 4:29). A city in the Negeb of Judah (Josh. 15:29). The site is unknown.

3. Mt. Baalah (Josh. 15:11), a narrow ridge between Ekron and Jabneel marking part of the territory allotted to the tribe of Judah. D. D. GERARD

BAALATH bā'ə-lath [Heb. *ba'ᵃlāṯ*; Gk. *Baalath, Baalōn*]. A town on the border of Dan (Josh. 19:44) associated with Eltekeh and Gibbethon. It was a store-city of Solomon mentioned with Beth-horon (1 K. 9:18; 2 Ch. 8:6), and is possibly to be identified with "Baalah which is Kirjath-jearim" (Josh. 15:9). According to Josephus (*Ant.* viii.6.1) it was near Gezer. J. F. PREWITT

BAALATH-BEER bā'ə-lath-bē'ər [Heb. *ba'ᵃlaṯ bᵉ'ēr*–'lady of the well'] (Josh. 19:8); **BAAL** bā'əl [Heb. *ba'al*–'lord'] (1 Ch. 4:33). A village included in the inheritance of Simeon. It is also designated as "Ramah [high place] of the South [or Negeb]" while in 1 S. 30:27 it is described as "Ramoth [high places] of the Negeb." It must have been a prominent hill in the far south of the Negeb and near a well. The site is unknown.

See also RAMAH **5.** D. D. GERARD

BAALATH - JUDAH (2 S. 6:2, NEB). *See* KIRIATH-JEARIM.

BAALBEK bal'bek [<*Ba'al*–'lord' + *Biq'â* (valley)]. A site with impressive ruins, located in the Beqa', a large fertile area between the Lebanon and Anti-Lebanon ranges, the watershed between the Orontes flowing north and the Litani flowing south. Baalbek is at an elevation of 3800 ft. (1155m.), the highest point of the plain.

The Beqa' was one of the large grain-producing areas for ancient Rome. The Baalbek region of the plain was especially noted for its grapes and wines. It is not surprising, then, that the "little temple" of the Baalbek acropolis was a temple to Bacchus. It remains one of the best-preserved of ancient buildings.

The ancient Semitic peoples of Syria worshiped as chief deity Hadad, who was lord of the sky. In the Greek period this god was identified with Helios, the sun-god, and hence the Greek name for Baalbek became Heliopolis, "city of the sun." The Romans built the magnificent temple to Jupiter at Baalbek, six of whose original

Ruins of the temple of Jupiter at Baalbek. Completed *ca.* A.D. 60, the temple was dedicated to three gods: the Syrian storm-god Hadad, equated with Jupiter; the nature-goddess Atargatis (Venus); and a youthful vegetation-god (Hermes or Mercury). (B. K. Condit)

fifty-four Corinthian columns still tower in lonely majesty over the ruins.

There have been various attempts to identify Baalbek with biblical places, e.g., Baal-gad (Josh. 11:17), or Baalath, one of the frontier cities of Solomon's time, or Baal-hamon, referred to in Cant. 8:11. None of these identifications is certain.

The early history of Baalbek is obscure. The first certain reference comes from the Roman days when Augustus made Baalbek a Roman colony under the name of *Colonia Julia Augusta Felix Heliopolitana*. There is no certainty as to who was responsible for building the Baalbek acropolis. Some authorities believe the temple to Jupiter was Nero's work; others (and more generally), that Antoninus Pius (A.D. 138-161) was responsible. Caracalla (211–217) did much building and restoration at Baalbek.

The practice of polytheism was stopped by Constantine early in the 4th cent., following his conversion. The temple to Venus in Baalbek (located outside the acropolis proper) was specifically ordered to be destroyed. One Christian tradition says that Constantine made Baalbek the site of an episcopal see. Another tradition, however, dates the first bishopric of Baalbek from near the beginning of the 2nd century. When Theodosius (379-395) became emperor, he ordered the great altar in the Baalbek acropolis torn down and had a church built in the great court in its place. The church was destroyed by the French in modern times to make possible the excavation of the court.

The Arabs came to Baalbek in A.D. 635 and transformed the acropolis into a fortified citadel. They also replaced the Greek name HELIOPOLIS by the ancient name Baalbek. The subsequent history of Baalbek is an unhappy record of conflict, sieges, and massacres. It was not until *ca.* 1850 that any lasting peace and stability existed there. After a long period of wars and several serious earthquakes, the marvel is that the ruins are as well preserved as they are.

There are some interesting traditions regarding Baalbek. One is that Cain founded the city as a place of refuge. Another insists that Nimrod built high towers there to fight the gods. Still another says that Seth lived near Baalbek, and that Noah's son Shem was buried only 20 mi. (32 km.) S of Baalbek.

Bibliography.–M. I. Aluf, *History of Baalbek* (21st ed. 1953); G. Haddad, *Baalbak* (1st ed. 1953); D. M. Robinson and G. Hoyningen-Huene, *Baalbek, Palmyra* (1946); J. Huxley, *From an Antique Land* (1966); Report of the UNESCO Mission of 1953, *Lebanon.*

R. A. GWINN

BAAL-BERITH bāl-bə-rith' [Heb. *ba'al bᵉrîṯ*–'lord of covenant']. A deity also known as EL-BERITH (Jgs. 9:46) and worshiped by the Israelites at Shechem (9:4) after Gideon's death (8:33). Albright (*ARI,* p. 113) suggests that this deity belongs to "the sons of Hamor" (Josh. 24:32), since the slaying of an ass (Heb. *ḥᵃmôr)* was an essential part of their treaties. However, the scant evidence does not permit a precise identification of this god.

D. McINTOSH

BAALE-JUDAH bāl'ə-jōō'də; **BAALE OF JUDAH** (2 S. 6:2). *See* KIRIATH-JEARIM.

BAAL-GAD bāl-gad' [Heb. *ba'al gāḏ*; Gk. *Balagada, Balgad*]. A place in the valley of Lebanon, under Mt. Hermon, the northern limit of Joshua's conquest of Canaan (Josh. 11:17). This passage definitely locates it in the valley between the Lebanons, W or NW of Hermon. It must not be confused with Baal-hermon. Conder thought it might be represented by 'Ain Jedeideh; *GAB* suggests Hasbeiyah.

BAAL-HAMON bāl-hā'mən. *See* BAAL IV.

BAAL-HANAN bāl-hā'nən [Heb. *ba'al ḥānān*–'the Lord is gracious'].

1. A king of Edom (Gen. 36:38f.; 1 Ch. 1:49f.).
2. A gardener in the service of David (1 Ch. 27:28).

BAAL-HAZOR bāl-hā'zôr [Heb. *ba'al ḥāṣôr*; Gk. *Bailasor, Bellasōr*]. A place on the property of Absalom where his sheepshearers were gathered, near Ephraim (2 S. 13:23). The sheepshearing was evidently the occasion of a festival, which was attended by Absalom's brothers. Here he accomplished the death of Amnon in revenge for the outrage upon his sister.

The place may be identified with Jebel 'Asûr, a mountain that rises 3386 ft. (1032 m.) above the sea, 4.5 mi. (7 km.) NE of Bethel. The oft-mentioned Tell 'Aṣûr is nonexistent (*GTTOT,* § 775).

BAAL-HERMON bāl-hûr'mən [Heb. *ba'al ḥermôn*]. A place named in the description of the half-tribe of Manasseh (1 Ch. 5:23), E of the upper Jordan Valley and near Mt. Hermon. In Jgs. 3:3 "Mount Baal-hermon" is named as one of the limits of the Hivites. However, in Josh. 13:5, which seems to be a parallel passage, "Baal-gad" is named. Simons (*GTTOT*, § 112) suggests that the texts may originally have read "Baal-Gad near Mount Hermon."

BAALI bā'ə-lī [Heb. *ba'ᵃlî*–'my master']. A generic title of deity in the ancient Near East. In Hos. 2:16f. God rejects this in favor of Ishi ("my husband"), in order to repudiate the ethos of Canaanite religion and reassert the obligations of the Sinai covenant.

BAALIM bā'ə-lim [Heb. *habbᵉ'ālîm*]. The collective designation for the various forms of the god BAAL. (Cf. Asherim, Ashtaroth.) The RSV has "Baals" (e.g., Jgs. 2:11, 13; 3:7; 1 S. 7:4; 2 Ch. 28:2; 33:3; Jer. 2:23; 9:14; Hos. 2:13, 17; 11:2).

BAALIS bā'ə-lis [Heb. *ba'lîs*; Gk. *Belisa, Baalis,* Josephus *Baalimos*]. King of the Ammonites, and instigator of the murder of Gedaliah (Jer. 40:14; cf. Josephus *Ant.* x.9.3).

BAAL-MEON bāl-mē'on [Heb. *ba'al mᵉ'ôn*]. A town built by the sons of Reuben (Nu. 32:38), probably identical with Beon of v. 3. As BETH-BAAL-MEON it was assigned to the tribe of Reuben (Josh. 13:17).

Mesha reports that he fortified it (cf. Moabite Stone); hence *ca.* 830 B.C. it was in Moabite hands. Ostracon 27 from Samaria tells of "Baala the Baal-meonite," indicating Israelite possession *ca.* 772 B.C., if this is the same city. Later it returned to Moabite rule (Jer. 48:23 [BETH-MEON]; Ezk. 25:9). It has been identified with Ma'în, ruins about 4 mi. (6.5 km.) SW of Medeba. The ruins now visible, however, are not older than Roman times.

W. EWING J. W. WHEDBEE

BAAL-PEOR bāl-pē'ôr. *See* BAAL IV.

BAAL-PERAZIM bāl-pə-rā'zim [Heb. *ba'al-pᵉrāṣîm*–'lord of breakings through'; Gk. *Baal pharasein*]. The place in or near the valley of Rephaim where David obtained a signal victory over the Philistines soon after he was anointed king (2 S. 5:20; 1 Ch. 14:11). The Mt. Perazim mentioned in Isa. 28:21 appears to be a reference to the same spot.

The identification is uncertain and two locations have been suggested: (1) If the valley of Rephaim is the Baqa', the open valley running SW between Jerusalem and Mar Elias, then Baal-perazim may possibly be the mountains to the east near what is called the "Hill of Evil Counsel," or Mar Elias itself. (2) It has further been suggested that the parallelism with the valley of Gibeon in Isa. 28:21 may indicate that the site is N of Jerusalem, possibly Sheikh Bedr about 3 mi. (5 km.) NW of Jerusalem, above Nephtoah.

R. E. W. BASON

BAALSAMUS bāl'sə-məs [Gk. *Baalsamos*]; AV BALASAMUS. One who stood at the right side of Ezra when the law was read to the people (1 Esd. 9:43). Cf. Maaseiah (Neh. 8:7).

BAAL-SHALISHAH bāl-shal'i-shə [Heb. *ba'al šālišâ*]; AV, NEB, BAAL-SHALISHA. A place near Gilgal. The report in 2 K. 4:42 that the bread of the first fruits was brought to Elisha by a man from this locality, and the statement in the Talmudic text (*Sanhedrin* 12a) that fruits ripened more quickly here than elsewhere, may indicate that this site was in a most productive and fertile area of Palestine. Eusebius calls the place "Baithsarith" (Jerome: "Bethsalisa") and locates it 15 mi. (24 km.) N of Diospolis (Lydda). Khirbet Sirīsiā fits this description almost exactly. Gilgal lies in the plain about 4.5 mi. (7 km.) NW. Some scholars have also suggested Kefr Thilth, 3.5 mi. (5.5 km.) farther N, as a possible location, inasmuch as the Arab. *ṯilṯ* corresponds exactly to the Heb. *šālišâ.*

W. EWING
K. G. JUNG

BAAL-TAMAR bāl-tā'mər [Heb. *ba'al tāmār*–'lord of the palm tree']. A site between Bethel and Gibeah where the Israelites drew up for the final attack on the city of Gibeah when the tribe of Benjamin was destroyed (Jgs. 20:33); possibly a seat of heathen worship (cf. 18:31). The place was known to Eusebius (*Onom.*), but all trace of the name is now lost. A connection has been suggested with the palm tree of Deborah (Jgs. 4:5). It may have been a well-known landmark rather than a city.

R. E. W. BASON

BAAL-ZEBUB bāl-zē'bub [Heb. *ba'al zeḇûḇ*–'lord of flies'; Gk. *Baal-myian*]. A god worshiped in the Philistine city of Ekron and consulted by Ahaziah king of Israel regarding his recovery from a sickness (2 K. 1:2f., 6, 16).

Since the Heb. *zeḇûḇ* means "fly" (as LXX Gk. *myían*; cf. Josephus *Ant.* ix.2.1), some scholars regard this as an oriental "Baal of flies" similar to the Greek Zeus Apomyios ("fly-averting Zeus") or the Roman god Myagros. It is unlikely, however, that a god representing the flies that swarm around a sacrifice should be sought after for an oracle regarding the fate of a man injured in a fall. It is more probable that *b'l zbl*, which can mean "lord of the (heavenly) dwelling" in Ugaritic, was changed to *b'l zbb* to make the divine name an opprobrius epithet. The reading Beelzebul in Mt. 10:25 would then reflect the right form of the name, a wordplay on "master of the house" (Gk. *oikodespótēs*). Another suggestion that must be considered is that Baal-zebub is the right spelling of a Philistine word representing a god who gave oracles by the flight of a fly. An accurate identification is not yet possible.

See also BEELZEBUL. D. McINTOSH

BAAL-ZEPHON bāl-zē'fon [Heb. *ba'al ṣepôn*–'lord of the north']. A place along the route of the Exodus used to locate Pi-hahiroth (which was "in front of Baal-zephon," Ex. 14:2, 9, or "east of Baal-zephon," Nu. 33:7; the encampment is further described as "between Migdol and the sea"). The location of Baal-zephon has become central to the discussion of the route of the EXODUS.

Since the publication by O. Eissfeldt of his *Baal Zaphon, Zeus Kasios und der Durchzug der Israeliten durchs Meer* (1932), many scholars have adopted the view that the Israelites proceeded directly from Egypt toward Canaan by the shortest route, viz., along the Mediterranean. The account of the journey in the wilderness and to Sinai is, for any who hold this view, an intrusion into the original story for obvious theological purposes.

Baal-zephon, it is now clear, was a god associated with the sea and maritime commerce, and his name associates him with the north. In the Râs Shamrah texts *ṣpn* is generally identified with Mt. Casius, N of Ugarit alongside the mouth of the Orontes. It seems logical to assume that a site to the north in Egypt would be chosen for worship of the same deity, and this is supported by a Phoenician papyrus that associates Baal-zephon with the Egyptian port of Tahpanhes (Tell Defneh). On the other hand, it is also clear that Zeus Casios, whom Eissfeldt identifies as Baal-zephon, was worshiped at several places in Egypt, not all of them on the northern boundary, including Tahpanhes and Memphis.

If we accept the biblical record of the stages of the Exodus journey as authentic, we note that the Israelites started out to worship Yahweh at the mountain of Moses' revelation experience, that they proceeded to Etham on the edge of the desert (Ex. 13:20; Nu. 33:6), then turned back (Ex. 14:2; Nu. 33:7) to Pi-hahiroth E of Baal-zephon, where Pharaoh's hosts overtook them (Ex. 14:9). The miraculous deliverance through the parted waters of the "Sea of Reeds," or "Red Sea," occurred there. In Hebrew "Sea of Reeds" can refer both to the Red Sea and to the Gulf of Aqabah; the Greek term is even more vague, referring to the Red Sea, the Arabian Sea, and the Persian Gulf. But in any event, neither term is applied to the Mediterranean Sea or any of its arms. It seems, then, that if we are to handle the biblical text — not to mention the long and unbroken tradition that stems from it — as definitive, we must locate Baal-zephon somewhere between the eastern Delta and the Wilderness of Sinai, possibly in the region of the Bitter Lakes, somewhat to the north of the route from which the Israelites had to turn back.

Bibliography.–W. F. Albright, *BASOR,* 109 (Apr. 1948), 14ff.; *Festschrift Alfred Bertholet* (1950), pp. 1-14; H. Cazelles, *RB,* 62 (1955), 321ff., for the northern route; and for a full discussion, with representative bibliography, *GTTOT,* §§ 417-425.

W. S. L. S.

BAANA bā'ə-nə [Heb. *ba'anā*–'son of oppression'].

1, 2. AV, NEB, also BAANAH (v. 16). Two of Solomon's district governors (1 K. 4:12, 16).

3. Father of Zadok the builder (Neh. 3:4).

4. (1 Esd. 5:8, AV, NEB). *See* BAANAH **3.**

BAANAH bā'ə-nə [Heb. *ba'anâ*–'son of oppression'; Gk. *Baana*].

1. Captain in the army of Ish-bosheth (2 S. 4:2ff.).

2. Father of Heleb (2 S. 23:29; 1 Ch. 11:30).

3. AV and NEB Apoc. BAANA. A leader of the return from exile with Zerubbabel, who sealed the covenant of Nehemiah (Ezr. 2:2; Neh. 7:7; 10:27; 1 Esd. 5:8).

BAANI bā'ə-ni (1 Esd. 9:34, NEB). *See* BANI **5.**

BAANIAS bā-ə-nī'əs (1 Esd. 9:26, AV). *See* BENAIAH **9.**

BAARA bā'ə-rə [Heb. *ba'arā'*]. A wife of the Benjaminite Shaharaim (1 Ch. 8:8).

BAASEIAH bā-ə-sē'yə [Heb. *ba'aśēyâ,* perhaps for *ma'eśēyâ*; Gk. B *Maasai*]. An ancestor of Asaph the musician (1 Ch. 6:40).

BAASHA bā'ə-shə [Heb. *ba'šā'*]. King of Israel *ca.* 900-877 B.C.; the son of Ahijah, and of common birth (1 K. 16:2). Baasha usurped the throne of Nadab the son of Jeroboam, killed Nadab, and exterminated the house of Jeroboam. He carried on a long warfare with Asa king of Judah (cf. Jer. 41:9); he began to build Ramah, but was prevented from completing this work by Ben-hadad king of Syria. He was told by the prophet Jehu that because of his sinful reign the fate of his house would be like that of Jeroboam. Baasha reigned twenty-four years. His son Elah who succeeded him, and all the members of his family, were murdered by the usurper Zimri (1 K. 15:16ff.; 16:1ff.; 2 Ch. 16:1ff.). The fate of his house is referred to in 1 K. 21:22; 2 K. 9:9.

A. L. BRESLICH

BABBLER [Gk. *spermológos* < *spérma*–'seed' + *légo*–'gather'] (Acts 17:18); NEB CHARLATAN. The Greek word is used of birds, such as the crow, that live by picking up small seeds, and of men, for "hangers on" and "parasites" who obtained their living by picking up odds and ends off merchants' carts in harbors and markets. It carries the "suggestion of picking up refuse and scraps, and in literature of plagiarism without the capacity to use correctly" (Ramsay, *SPT,* p. 242; cf. 243). The Athenian philosophers in calling Paul a *spermológos,* or "ignorant plagiarist," meant that he retailed odds and ends of knowledge which he had picked up from others, without possessing any system of thought or skill of language, i.e., without culture. In fact it was a fairly correct description of the Athenian philosophers themselves in Paul's day.

On Eccl. 10:11, AV *see* CHARM; CHARMER. T. REES

BABE. *See* CHILD.

BABEL. *See* BABYLON.

BABEL bā'bəl, **TOWER OF.** The popular designation of the tower (Heb. *migdōl*) described in Gen. 11, which people migrating from the East built in the midst of their city in the plain of Shinar.

I. The Narrative
II. Type of Story
III. Origin of Languages
IV. The Name Babel
V. Historical Details
VI. Brevity of the Story
VII. Setting
VIII. Theological Implications
IX. Composition of the Story
X. Archeological Evidences
  A. The Ziggurat
  B. Location of the Tower of Babel
  C. A Babylonian Description
XI. Destruction of the Tower

I. The Narrative.–Early in the history of mankind, as repopulation was taking place after the ravages of the Flood, a number of people settled in the "land of Shinar." Here they decided to build a city and erect a tower, "its top in the heavens." Their stated purpose was to make a name for themselves, and for this reason the project displeased Yahweh, who put an end to it by scattering the builders far and wide, with consequent diversity of languages; and in the confusion, the project remained incomplete. The narrative finally reveals the name of the city concerned: it is Babel (or Babylon), and the writer links the name with the Heb. *bālal,* "He confused" (v. 9).

II. Type of Story.–It is easy enough to dismiss the whole story as legendary, and deny any historicity in it. But this is an unscholarly procedure; the first step logically must be to endeavor to find out what the narrative means to say. Is its primary purpose to explain the diversity of languages in the world, to explain how Babylon got its name, or to account for the ruined ziggurats that were so plentiful in Mesopotamia? If any of these is the sole answer, then the story may be described as etiological, but completely unhistorical. A further possibility is that the story is basically historical, though interpreted etiologically by the compiler of the stories of Genesis. See VII below.

III. Origin of Languages.–It is difficult to concede at once that the wide diversity of tongues could have originated in such a way. Certainly, at the present stage of philological inquiry, it seems hardly likely that the many languages of the world have a common origin, however remote. Even in the case of Middle Eastern tongues that do perhaps share a common origin, such as the Semitic and Hamitic language groups, it may be argued that this origin must be placed in the very earliest, prehistoric times, long before civilization reached the stage of culture and achievement basic to Gen. 11. On the other hand, the incident described is in terms of a catastrophic happening rather than the prolonged development that linguistic research presupposes.

IV. The Name Babel.–The name Babel has no connection with the Heb. *bālal,* "He confused." Its meaning is in fact patent in its Assyrian form, *Bāb-ilī,* "gate of god." The final syllable, *'ēl* in Hebrew, is common to all Semitic languages, and means "god"; while *bâb* is well-known in Assyrian, Arabic, Aramaic, and late Hebrew. It seems probable, then, that the narrator of Gen. 11:9 is indulging in a play on words, a verbal irony, or else relating a folk etymology, rather than attempting a serious etymology of the name. He must surely have known that such a word could not possibly derive from a root *b-l-l.*

V. Historical Details.–The two preceding paragraphs might seem to indicate that the story is purely etiological and totally unhistorical. Yet a number of details of the story bear the stamp of historicity. The name Shinar, for instance, was evidently well known for Babylonia in early times; cf. Gen. 10:10. It is possibly cognate with Sumer. The mention of a tower in Babylonia is certainly an authentic touch; the ziggurats of Babylonia known to archeologists are many (see X below). Above all, the reference to brick and bitumen is strikingly accurate, for Babylonia did not possess the stone that was so commonplace a building material in Palestine. Baked mud bricks and bitumen were widely used in the vast Tigris-Euphrates plain.

VI. Brevity of the Story.–It is difficult to deny the historical accuracy of some details of the story, then. But it is not easy to get a clear picture of any historical event from Gen. 11:1-9, since the narrative is so brief and condensed. There are a number of omissions that cause problems. Was the purpose of the tower religious or secular? (Note that the narrative does not state that the builders were trying to reach heaven thereby; the Hebrew idiom signifies merely that the tower was to be very high.) What exactly was the builders' sin? How did Yahweh scatter them? How did He confuse their language? Without the answers to these questions, we can only guess what historical event, if any, was in the mind of the author.

VII. Setting.–The story, like the others of Gen. 1–11, is in a Mesopotamian setting. This is too easily obscured by such phrases as "the whole earth" (11:1); the Hebrew word is *hā'āreṣ,* which may mean "the land" or "the world"; and it need not be doubted that the author of this story was concerned with just his own immediate surroundings, southern Mesopotamia. This is the stage, then, and the date is probably the 3rd millennium B.C. The situation is that there is at first one language, and a political unity; the story ends with some political upheaval. If we wish to link this with known historical developments, it seems possible that it refers to one of the periodic shifts of population in the Middle East; and a distinct possibility is the influx of Semites, the Akkadians, into the territory of the Sumerian city-states during the first half of the 3rd millennium B.C. This certainly brought with it a linguistic confusion that lasted some hundreds of years, till eventually the Akkadian tongue displaced the Sumerian.

VIII. Theological Implications.–The writer viewed the builders of Babel as guilty of some sin (probably that of pride, the besetting sin of Babylon at a later date), and to him the linguistic and political confusion that ensued was Yahweh's punishment upon them. A lofty monotheism is here displayed; it is not the local deities but Yahweh who controls the vicissitudes of Mesopotamian history. It has also been remarked that the writer exhibits a profound insight when he observes the divisions caused by diversity of language.

IX. Composition of the Story.–According to source-critical theories of the composition of the Pentateuch, this story belongs to the original document (or stratum) known for convenience as J (*see* CRITICISM II; PENTATEUCH). The chief indications of this are the use of the name Yahweh for God, and the anthropomorphic style. A number of scholars have contended that the narrative is a conflation of two accounts (J^1 and J^2?); it is suggested that in one account a city was built, in the other a tower. Another supporting argument is that the "Let us go down" of v. 7 is inconsistent with the previous remark, "And Yahweh came down," of v. 5. When it is understood, however, that such anthropomorphisms are not in any case to be taken literally, the inconsistency is purely verbal, and needs no explaining away. The mere reference to a city and a tower together is not in itself a very secure basis for a theory of conflated accounts, and the present trend of opinion (e.g., Parrot) appears to uphold the unity of the narrative.

Bibliography.–S. R. Driver in *HDB*; comms. on Genesis, esp. those of J. Skinner (*ICC*, 1935); Ryle (*CBSC*, 1914); and G. von Rad (Eng. tr., *OTL*, 1961); A. Parrot, *Tower of Babel* (Eng. tr. 1955).

D. F. PAYNE

X. Archeological Evidences.–*A. The Ziggurat.* Babylonian temple towers differed significantly from the Canaanite *migdōl* or watchtower. The watchtower was simply a high structure, probably without any special shape or form, as this depended upon the will of the architect and the nature of the ground upon which it was erected. The tower of Babel or Babylon, however, was a structure peculiar to Babylonia and Assyria. According to all accounts, and judging from the extant ruins of the various buildings in those countries, Babylonian towers were always rectangular, built in stages, and provided with an inclined ascent continued along each side to the top. Since religious ceremonies were performed thereon, they were generally surmounted by a chapel in which sacred objects or images were kept.

These structures had, with the Babylonians, a special name: *ziqqurratu,* apparently meaning "peak," or the highest point of a mountain. This word was applied to the mountain height upon which Utnapishtim, the Babylonian Noah, offered sacrifices on coming forth from the ark (or ship) when the waters of the great Flood had sufficiently subsided. It has also been thought that these towers were used as observatories when the Babylonians studied the starry heavens. This is probable; but these structures were of no great height, and in the clear atmosphere of the Babylonian plains perhaps there was no real necessity to go above the surface of the earth to make their observations.

B. Location of the Tower of Babel. There has been much difference of opinion about the location of the tower of Babel. Most writers upon the subject, following the tradition handed down by the Jews and Arabs, have identified it with the great temple of Nabû (Nebo) in the city of Borsippa, now called the Birs Nimrûd (explained as a corruption of Birj Nimrûd, "tower of Nimrod"). This building, however, notwithstanding its importance, was to all appearance never regarded by the Babylonians as the tower of Babel, for the very good reason that it was not situated in Babylon but in Borsippa, which, though called in later times "the second Babylon," was naturally not the original city of that name. The structure regarded by the Babylonians as the great tower of their ancient city was *É-temen-an-ki,* "the temple of the foundation of heaven and earth," called by Nabopolassar and Nebuchadrezzar *ziqqurrat Bābilī*, "the tower of Babylon" — the world-renowned temple tower dedicated to Marduk, Babylon's chief deity, and his consort Ṣarpānītum.

This structure was situated in the southern portion of the city, not far from the right bank of the Euphrates, and according to Weissbach is now represented by a depression within which is the original rectangular core of unbaked brick. From its shape the Arabs have named this site *Ṣaḥn,* "the dish." Within the memory of men not so very old, these remains of the great temple of Babylon towered, even in the ruined state, high above the surrounding plain. The burnt bricks of the ancient Babylonians, however, who "had brick for stone, and bitumen for mortar" (Gen. 11:3), are still good and have a commercial value; so they were all cleared out, along with whatever precious material in the way of antiquities they may have contained, to repair, it is said, the banks of the Hindīyah Canal. Certain records in the shape of conical "cylinders," however, came into the market and were acquired by the museums of Europe and America. As these refer to the restoration of the building by Nabopolassar, and the part taken by his sons Nebuchadrezzar and Nabû-šumu-līšir in the ceremonies attending the rebuilding, it is very probable that they formed part of the spoils acquired.

C. A Babylonian Description. É-temen-an-ki is generally believed to have consisted of six square stages built upon a platform, topped with a small sanctuary. Primary sources for reconstruction of the tower include a ground plan uncovered in R. Koldewey's 1913 excavations, a third-century B.C. copy of an earlier Akkadian text, and the description of Herodotus, who visited the city *ca.* 460 B.C.

The pilastered walls of the É-temen-an-ki complex enclosed a large open square, 460 by 408 by 456 by 412 yds. (420 by 373 by 417 by 377 m.). Surrounding the square were several small buildings variously interpreted as storehouses or shrines of miscellaneous deities.

The main feature of the complex, the ziggurat, is described by the Esagil Tablet, which indicates dimensions in terms of the *suklum*-cubit, as used by the Assyrian kings Sennacherib and Esarhaddon: "60.60.60 [is] the length, 60.60.60 the breadth. . . . To produce the reckoning of it, 3x3." The height of the *kigal* (tower) of É-temen-an-ki was equal to the length and to the breadth. A second, more cryptic description gives the dimensions in the larger "step-cubit." Detailed measurements of the tower are indicated in the tablet as follows: 1st story–length 90 m., breadth 90 m., height 33 m.; 2nd story–78 by 78 by 18 m.; 3rd story–60 by 60 by 6 m.; 4th story–51 by 51 by 6 m.; 5th story–42 by 42 by 6 m.; (6th story–33 by 33 by 6 m.); 7th story–24 by 24 by 15 m. Details of the 6th story, omitted by scribal error, are conjectural.

It cannot be said that it was by any means a beautiful structure, but there was probably some symbolism in its measurements. Although various artistic representations have been proposed, in appearance it probably resembled (except the decoration) the temple tower of Calah as restored in the frontispiece to Layard's *Monuments of Nineveh* (1st series), in which a step-pyramid with a similarly high basement-stage is shown.

With this detailed description the account in Herodotus (i.181ff.) agrees. He states that it was a temple square in form, two furlongs (1213 ft., 370 m.) each way, in the midst of which was built a solid tower a furlong square (nearly 607 ft., 185 m.). This, however, must have been the platform, which, with the six stages and the chapel on the top, would make up the total of eight stages of which Herodotus speaks. Parrot, E. Unger, and others so interpret the Esagil Tablet. The ascent by which the top was reached he describes as running "outside round about all the towers" — wording which suggests, though not necessarily, that it was spiral — i.e., one had to walk round the structure seven times to reach the top.

Model of the ziggurat at Babylon, based on E. Unger's interpretation of the Esagil Tablet (Oriental Institute, University of Chicago)

Representations on Babylonian boundary-stones suggest that this view would be correct, though a symmetrical arrangement of inclined paths might have been constructed which would have greatly improved the design. At the middle of the ascent, Herodotus says, there was a stopping-place with seats to rest upon, which rather favors this idea. At the top of the last tower there was a large cell, and in the cell a large couch was laid, well covered, and by it a golden table. There was no image there, nor did any human being spend the night there, except only a woman of the natives of the place chosen by the god, "as say the Chaldeans who are the priests of this god." These men told Herodotus that the god often came to the cell and rested upon the couch; "but," he adds, "I do not believe them." After mentioning parallels to this at Egyptian Thebes and Patara in Lycia, he goes on to speak of another cell below, wherein was a great image of Zeus (Bel/Marduk) sitting, with a footstool and a large table, all of gold, and weighing no less than 800 talents. Outside of this cell was an altar to the god, made of gold; and also another altar, whereon full grown animals were sacrificed, the golden altar being for sucklings only. The Chaldeans also told him that there was, in the precincts of the building, a statue 12 cubits (5.5 m.) high, and of solid gold. Darius I Hystaspes desired to take possession of this valuable object, but did not venture. His son Xerxes, however, was not so considerate of the feelings of the people and the priesthood, for he also killed the priest when the latter forbade him to meddle with it.

Koldewey's excavations reveal the remarkable accuracy of the Esagil Tablet as well as Herodotus' account. Located in a large rectangular enclosure with external dimensions 500 by 450 yds. (460 by 410 m.) the square foundation of the tower measures approximately 298 ft. (91 m.) on each face. The tower was formed with a core of sun-dried bricks ensheathed with an exterior shell (49 ft. [15 m.] thick) of baked bricks. Three staircases, two against the south face and the third centrally located, at right angles to the façade, provided access to the upper stories from ground level. Extrapolation from archeological data supports the height suggested by the literary evidence, 295 to 300 ft. (90 to 92 m.).

*XI. **Destruction of the Tower**.*–There is a Jewish tradition that the tower was split through to its foundation by fire that fell from heaven — suggested probably by the condition of the tower at "second Babylon," i.e., the Birs Nimrûd. Another tradition, recorded by Eusebius (*Praep. ev.* ix; *Chronicon* 13; *Chronicon*-Syncellus 44) says it was blown down by the winds: "but when it approached the heavens, the winds assisted the gods, and overturned the work upon its contrivers; and the gods introduced a diversity of tongues among men, who, until that time, had all spoken the same language."

That the building of the city would have been stopped when the confusion of tongues took place is natural — the departure of the greater part of the inhabitants made this inevitable. When the population increased again, the building of the city continued, with the result that Babylon ultimately became the greatest city of the then known world. The tower, notwithstanding the traditions concerning its destruction, remained; and when, as happened from time to time, its condition became ruinous, some energetic Babylonian king would restore it. Nabopolassar (625-605) and Nebuchadrezzar II (604-562) refurbished the tower, covering the upper temple with blue enameled bricks. Alexander and Philip of Macedon began clearing away the rubbish to rebuild the great temple of Zeus Belos (Bel/Marduk) connected with it, and there is hardly any doubt that the tower would have been restored likewise; but the untimely death of the former, and the deficient mental caliber of the latter for the ruling of a great empire, put an end to the work. The tower therefore remained unrepaired — "The tower was exceedingly tall. The third part of it sank down into the ground, a second third was burned down, and the remaining third was standing until the time of the destruction of Babylon" (Rabbi Yehanan, *Sanhedrin* 109a).

Bibliography.–A. Parrot, *Tower of Babel* (Eng. tr. 1955); E. Unger, *Babylon, die heilige Stadt* (1931), pp. 191-200.

T. G. PINCHES

BABI bā'bī (1 Esd. 8:37, AV, NEB). *See* BEBAI.

BABYLON ba'bə-lon; **BABEL** bā'bəl (Gen. 10:10; 11:9) [Heb. *bāḇel*–'gate of god'; Akk. *bāb-ili, bāb-ilāni*–'gate of god(s)'; Gk. *Babylōn*; Pers. *Babirush*]. The capital city of Babylonia.

I. Location
II. Name
III. Early History
    A. Foundation
    B. Old Babylonian Period
    C. Middle Babylonian Period
    D. Neo-Assyrian Supremacy
    E. Chaldean Rulers
IV. Description
    A. Walls
    B. Gates
    C. Streets
    D. Citadel
    E. Palaces
    F. City Quarters
    G. Temple Tower (Ziggurat)
    H. Esagila
    I. Other Temples
    J. Private Houses
    K. Documents
V. Later History
    A. Fall of Babylon, 539 B.C.
    B. Achaemenid City
    C. Hellenistic Period
    D. Seleucid-Parthians

E. Later City
VI. Exploration and Excavation

I. Location.–Babylon lay on the bank of the Euphrates in the land of Shinar (Gen. 10:10), in the northern area of Babylonia (now southern Iraq) called Accad (as opposed to the southern area called Sumer). Its ruins, covering 2100 acres (890 hectares), lie about 50 mi. (80 km.) S of Baghdad and 5 mi. (8 km.) N of Hillah. The ancient site is now marked by the mounds of Bâbil to the north, Qaṣr ("the Citadel") in the center, and Merkes, 'Amran Ibn 'Alī Ṣaḥn, and Homera to the south. The high water and long flooding of the whole area render the earlier and lower ruins inaccessible.

II. Name.–The oldest attested extrabiblical name is the Sumerian ká-dingir-ki (usually written ká-dingir-ra, "gate of god"). This may have been a translation of the more commonly used later Babylonian *Bāb-ilī*, of which an etymology based on Heb. *bālal*, "confused," is given in Gen. 11:9. Throughout the OT and NT, Babylon stands theologically for the community that is anti-God. Rarely from 2100 B.C. and frequently in the 7th cent. Babylon is called TIN.TIR.KI, "wood (trees) of life," and from the latter period also E.KI, "canal zone(?)." Other names applied to at least part of the city were ŠU.AN.NA, "hand of heaven" or "high-walled(?)," and the Heb. *šēšak* (Jer. 25:26; 51:41), which is usually interpreted as a coded form (ATHBASH) by which *š* = *b*, etc. The proposed equation with ŠEŠ.KU in a late king list has been questioned, since this could be read equally well as (É).URU.KU.

III. Early History.–*A. Foundation.* Genesis ascribes the foundation of the city to Nimrod prior to his building of Erech (ancient Uruk, modern Warka) and Accad (Agade), which can be dated to the 4th and 3rd millennia B.C. respectively. The earliest written reference extant is by Šar-kali-šarri of Agade *ca.* 2250 B.C., who claimed to have (re)built the temple of Anunītum and carried out other restorations, thus indicating an earlier foundation. A later omen text states that Sargon (Šarrukīn I) of Agade (*ca.* 2300) had plundered the city.

B. Old Babylonian Period. Šulgi of Ur captured Babylon and placed there his governor (*ensi*), Itur-ilu, a practice followed by his successors in the Ur III Dynasty (*ca.* 2150-2050 B.C.). Thereafter invading Semites, the Amorites of the 1st Dynasty of Babylon, took over the city. Their first ruler Sumu-abum restored the city wall. Though few remains of this time survive the inundation of the river, Hammurabi in the Prologue to his laws (*ca.* 1750) recalls how he had maintained Esagila (the temple of Marduk), which by the time of his reign was the center of a powerful regime with wide influence. Samsu-iluna enlarged the city, but already in his reign the Kassites were pressing in from the northeast hills. It actually fell in 1595 to Hittite raiders under Mursilis I, who removed the statue of Marduk and his consort Ṣarpānītum to Ḫana. (Possession of a city's gods [their statues] symbolized control.) The city changed hands frequently under the Kassites (Meli-Šipak [Meli-Šiḫu] and Marduk-apla-iddina I) amid the rivalry of the local tribes. Agum-kakrime recovered the captive statues, but that of Marduk was again removed at the sack of the city by Tukulti-Ninurta I of Assyria (1250) and by the Elamite Kudur-Naḫḫunte II (1176).

C. Middle Babylonian Period. The recovery of Marduk's statue was the crowning achievement of Nebuchadrezzar I (1124-1103), marking an end to foreign domination of the city. He restored it to Esagila amid much public rejoicing and refurbished the cult places. Although Babylon retained its independence despite the pressure of the western tribes, this required help from the Assyrians, one of whom, Adad-apal-iddina, was given the throne (1067-1046). By the following century, however, the tribesmen held the suburbs and even prevented the celebration of the New Year Festival by Nabû-mukīn-apli of the 8th Babylonian Dynasty.

D. Neo-Assyrian Supremacy. Shalmaneser III of Assyria was called to intervene in the strife that broke out on the death of Nabû-apla-iddina in 852 B.C. He defeated the rebels, entered Babylon, treated the inhabitants with respect, and offered sacrifices in Marduk's temple. This action inaugurated a new period of Assyrian intervention in the southern capital, with the result, according to Herodotus, that Sammu-ramat (Semiramis), mother of Adadnirari III, carried out restoration work there.

The citizens' independent spirit was never long suppressed; and Arameans from the southern tribes seized the city, made Erība-Marduk their leader, and refused to pay allegiance to the northern kingdom. To remedy this Tiglath-pileser III began a series of campaigns to recover control. First he won over the tribe of Puqūdu (Pekod of Jer. 50:21; Ezk. 23:23), who lived to the northeast, leaving Nabonassar (*Nabû-nāṣir*) as governor of Babylon to pursue a pro-Assyrian policy until his death in 734 B.C., whereupon Ukīn-zēr of the Amukkani tribe seized the city.

The Assyrians then tried to gain the support of the other tribal chiefs, including Marduk-apla-iddina (MERODACH-BALADAN of the OT) of Bīt-Yakin, who, however, took over the city on the death of Tiglath-pileser's successor Shalmaneser V in 721. He proclaimed the city's independence and maintained it for ten years. Either toward the end of this period or more probably in 703 B.C., when he again held Babylon, Merodach-baladan sought Hezekiah's help against the Assyrians (2 K. 20:12-17). Sargon II recaptured the city in 710 and celebrated the New Year festival by taking the hands of Marduk/Bēl and the title "viceroy of Marduk."

To revenge Merodach-baladan's later seizure of the capital, Sennacherib marched south to remove the traitor Bēl-ibni and set his own son Aššur-nadin-šumi on the throne. The latter was soon ousted, however, by local revolutionaries, who in turn were defeated by Sennacherib in 689 when he besieged the city for nine months, sacked Babylon, and removed the statue of Marduk and some of the sacred soil to Nineveh. Though this act brought peace, it broke any trust the citizens ever had in the Assyrians, despite Esarhaddon's efforts to restore the decrepit town. Esarhaddon claimed to have revoked his father's decree imposing "seventy years of desolation upon the city" by reversing the Babylonian numerals for 70 to make them 11. Many refugees returned, and the city again became a prosperous center under his son Šamaš-šum-ukīn (669-648). He was isolated, however, by the surrounding tribes, who eventually won him over to their cause. His twin brother Ashurbanipal of Assyria laid siege to the city, which fell after four years of great hardship. Šamaš-šum-ukīn died in the fire that destroyed his palace and the citadel.

E. Chaldean Rulers. Reconstruction work began under the Chaldean Nabopolassar (*Nabû-apla-uṣur,* 626-605 B.C.), who was elected king following a popular revolt after the death of the Assyrian nominee Kandalanu. His energetic son Nebuchadrezzar (II) with his queen Nitocris restored not only the political prestige of Babylonia, which for a time dominated the whole of the former Assyrian empire, but also the capital city, to which he brought the spoils of war including the treasures of Jerusalem and Judah (2 K. 25:13-17). Texts dated to this reign list Jehoiachin king of Judah (*Ya'ukin māt Yaḫudu*), his five sons, and Judean craftsmen among recipients of corn and oil from the king's stores. It is to the city of this period, one of the glories of the ancient world, that the extant texts and archeological remains bear witness. Nabonidus (555-539 B.C.) continued to care for the temples of the city, though he spent ten years in Arabia, leaving control of local affairs in the hands of his son and co-regent Belshazzar, who died when the city fell to the Persians in 539 (Dnl. 5:30).

IV. Description.–*A. Walls.* Babylon lay in a plain, encircled by double walls. The inner rampart (*dūru*), called "Imgur-Enlil," was constructed of mud brick 6.50 m. (21 ft.) thick. It had large towers at intervals of 18 m. (60 ft.) jutting out about 3.5 and .75 m. (11.5 and 2.5 ft.) and rising to 10-18 m. (30-60 ft.). It has been estimated that there were at least a hundred of these. The line may well have followed that laid down by Sumu-abum of the 1st Dynasty. Over 7 m. (23 ft.) away lay the lower and double outer wall (*šalḫu*) called Nimit-Enlil, 3.7 m. (12 ft.) thick, giving a total defense depth of 17.4 m. (57 ft.). Twenty m. (65 ft.) outside these walls lay a moat, widest to the east and linked with the Euphrates to the north and south of the city, thus assuring both river passage and water supply and a flood defense in time of war. The quay wall nearest the city was of burnt brick set in bitumen, and this too had observation towers. The outermost wall of the moat was of beaten earth. The inner area, including Babylon W of the river, which remains unexcavated, measured 8.35 sq. km. (3.2 sq. mi.) and the eastern city alone encompassed an area of about 2.25 sq. km. (.87 sq. mi.). Nebuchadrezzar and, according to Herodotus, his queen Nitocris made significant additions to the defenses begun by his father. These now incorporated his "Summer Palace" (Bâbīl) 2 km. (1.2 mi.) to the north. He also added an enlarged northern citadel and enclosed a large area of the plain with yet a third wall, forming an "armed camp" in which the surrounding population could take refuge in time of war. This ran 250 m. (820 ft.) S of the inner walls and projected about 1.5 km. (1 mi.) beyond the earlier wall systems.

Herodotus, who describes the city and walls some seventy years after the damage done by Xerxes in 478 B.C. (i.178-187), appears to exaggerate the size. He says that the height of the walls, beyond the moat, was 200 cubits (about 90 m. or 300 ft.) by 50 royal cubits thick (= 87 ft., 26.5 m.). The width was sufficient for a chariot and four horses to pass along them. Moreover, the estimate of the total length of the walls as 480 stades (about 95 km. or 60 mi.) is difficult to reconcile with the archeological evidence, though the figures are close to those given by Ctesias (300 furlongs = 68 km. or 42 mi., with the walls 300 ft. [90 m.] high and 60, 40, and 20 furlongs in length respectively). Herodotus viewed the city as a rectangle. Unfortunately no excavations to confirm this have yet been possible West of the river.

B. Gates. Babylonian inscriptions give the names of the eight major entrances to the city itself, but of these only four have been excavated. The southwest gate of Uraš was probably typical in general plan. The approach was by a dam across the moat through a wide gateway in the outer wall with recessed tower chambers and thence by a deep gateway in the inner wall. The other gate in the south wall was named after Enlil, since it faced southeasterly toward his sanctuary at Nippur. In the east wall were the gate called "Marduk is merciful to his friend" and, S of this, the Zababa gate facing Kish. In the north wall the Ishtar gate was specially decorated and renovated

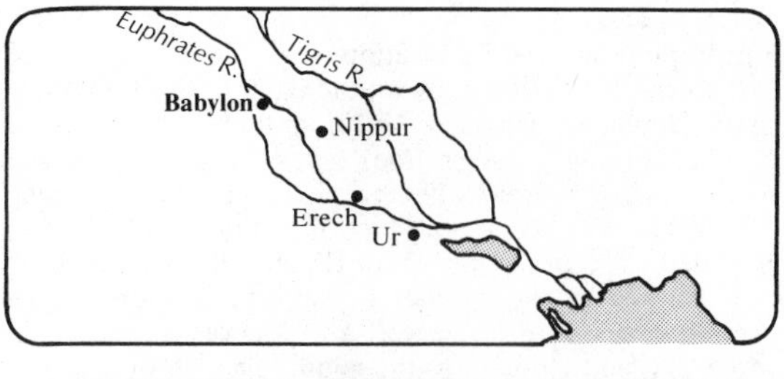

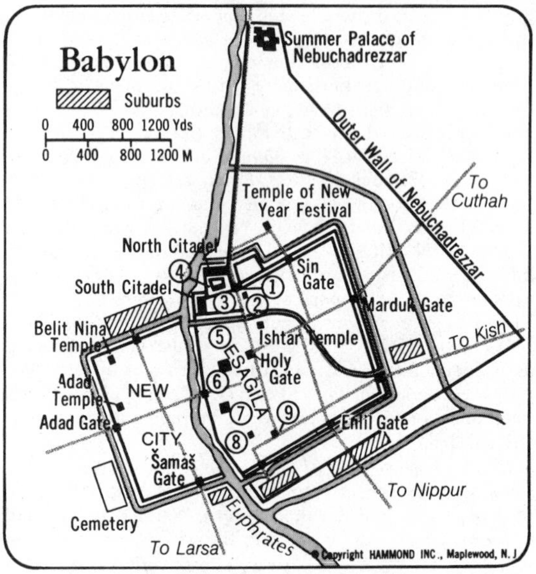

1	Ishtar Gate	6	Temple Tower (Tower of Babel?)
2	Ninmaḫ Temple	7	Marduk Temple
3	Hanging Gardens	8	Gula Temple
4	Museum	9	Ninurta Temple
5	Inner Town		

by Nebuchadrezzar at the time of his enlargement of the citadel.

The Sin gate in the north wall and the Šamaš and Adad gates in the west are known only from references in the texts. These gates may well be identified with the five named by Herodotus as Semiramis (Ishtar), Nineveh (Sin to the north?), Chaldean (Enlil? to the south), Kissian (Zababa), and Zeus Belos (Marduk). He further mentions one hundred gates of bronze in the outer walls, which may be "the well-built wide gates with doors of bronze-covered cedar" made by Nebuchadrezzar. Excavations show that the Ishtar gate consisted of a double tower 12 m. (40 ft.) high, decorated with blue and black glazed bricks with alternate rows in yellow relief of 575 *mušruššu* (a symbol of Marduk, a combination of a serpent with lion's and eagle's legs) and the bulls of (H)adad.

C. Streets. The layout of the principal streets was determined by the line of the river and of the main gates and was virtually unchanged from Old Babylonian times. The main thoroughfare, called Ai-ibūr-šābū ("the enemy shall not prevail"), was the sacred procession way running from the Ishtar gate SSE, parallel with the Euphrates. Completed by Nebuchadrezzar, it ran for more than 900 m. to the temple Esagila before joining the main east-west road between that temple and the sacred area of Etemenanki and then turning to the Nabonidus wall on the river. There the crossing was made by a stone bridge, 6 m. wide, supported by eight piers, each 9 by 21 m. (29 by 69 ft.), the six amid stream being of burnt bricks

Western towers of the Ishtar gate, with reliefs of animals. Constructed by Nebuchadrezzar II (605-562 B.C.), the gate led to the sacred processional street. (Oriental Institute, University of Chicago) *See* Plate 6.

that still show traces of wearing by the current. The bridge was 123 m. (403 ft.) long, shortened to 115 m. (377 ft.) when Nabonidus built his quay. Herodotus ascribed the bridge to Nitocris (i.186; cf. Diodorus ii.8) and speaks of it as an "open bridge," perhaps with a removable center section to enable the two parts of the city to be defended independently.

The Procession Way was 11-20 m. (36-66 ft.) broad and paved with colored stone from Lebanon, red breccia, and limestone. Some paving stones were inscribed "I Nebuchadrezzar, king of Babylon, paved this road with mountainstone for the procession of Marduk, my lord. May Marduk my Lord grant me eternal life." The parapet of the raised road was decorated with 120 lions in relief.

The other main roads intersected the city at right angles and bore names associated with the gates from which they led: "Adad has guarded the life of the people"; "Enlil establisher of kingship"; "Marduk is shepherd of his land"; "Ishtar is the guardian of the folk"; "Šamaš has made firm the foundation of my people"; "Sin is stablisher of the crown of his kingdom"; "Uraš is judge of his people"; and "Zababa destroys his foes." There were also other procession streets named after deities — Marduk ("Marduk hears him who seeks him") and Sibitti — and also after earlier kings (Damiqilišu).

D. Citadel. The northern wall was extended in the center by Nebuchadrezzar to form an additional defense for the palaces to the south and to provide more accommodation. This complex appears to have been used by his successors as a storehouse (some think as a "museum"), for here were found objects from earlier reigns including inscriptions of the Assyrian kings Adadnirari III and Ashurbanipal from Nineveh, a Hittite basalt sculpture of a lion trampling a man ("the lion of Babylon"), and a stele showing the Hittite storm-god Tešub from seventh-century (B.C.) Sam'al.

E. Palaces. In the southern citadel, bounded by the Imgur-Enlil wall (N), the river (W), the Procession Way (E), and the Libilḫegalla canal (which was cleared by Nebuchadrezzar and linked the Euphrates and the Banitu canal E of the city with the canal network in the New City, thus providing the city with a system of internal waterways), was a massive complex of buildings covering more than 360 by 180 m. (400 by 200 yds.). Here lay the vast palace built by Nabopolassar and extended by his successors. The entrance from the Procession Way led to a courtyard (66.5 by 42.5 m., 218 by 140 ft.), flanked by quarters for the royal bodyguard, which in Nebuchadrezzar's time largely consisted of foreign mercenaries. A double gateway led into the second court, off which lay reception rooms and living quarters. A wider doorway gave access to a third court (66 by 55 m., 218 by 180 ft.); to its south lay the Throne Room, the external wall of which was decorated in blue glazed bricks bearing white and yellow palmettes, pillars with a dado of rosettes and lions. This large hall (52 by 17 m., 170 by 57 ft., partially restored in 1968) could have been that used for state occasions, such as Belshazzar's feast for a thousand persons (Dnl. 5). Two further wings of the palace overlooking the river to the west may have been the quarters of the king, his queen, and their personal attendants. It is more likely that this was the building used by Belshazzar for his feast rather than the "Palace of the Crown Prince" (*ekal mār šarri*) said to have been used later by Xerxes.

In the northwest angle of this complex, adjacent to the

Ishtar gate, lay another large building (42 by 30 m., 140 by 98 ft.) consisting of fourteen narrow rooms leading off a long central walk. Since it was at some time walled off from the new palace, it has been thought to have been the substructure of that wonder of the ancient world, the Hanging Gardens of Babylon. According to Ctesias in Diodorus (ii.10) and Strabo (xvi.1.5), this was a series of garden-laid terraces supported by arches designed by Nebuchadrezzar (so Berossus in Josephus *Ant.* x.11.1 [226]) for his queen, to remind his new bride, Amyitis daughter of Astyages the Mede, of her mountain-fringed homeland. This description might, however, equally apply to the ziggurat (see G below).

The presence of administrative texts within these subterranean rooms more likely indicates that these were palace stores. Included among the tablets found here and dated to the tenth to thirty-fifth years of Nebuchadrezzar (i.e., 595-570 B.C.) were lists of recipients of rations of corn and oil distributed to foreigners, men from Judah, Ashkelon, Gebal, Egypt, Cilicia, Greece (Yamanu), and Persia. Among the men of Judah were Jehoiachin and his sons and craftsmen, some with such OT names as Gaddiel, Shelemiah, and Samakiah (E. F. Weidner, *Mélanges offerts à M. Dussaud,* II [1939], 924ff.). Nebuchadrezzar also built himself a "Summer Palace" outside the main citadel but within the defense walls. This was set 9 m. (30 ft.) high (it was 100 m. [328 ft.] long) to catch the cooler northeast winds.

F. City Quarters. Tablets name the various parts of the city, which included the citadel itself (*ālu libbi āli,* "city within a city") with at least nine temples. It was described as near ká-dingir-ra, which name also applied to the whole city. The citadel included the royal palace as far as Esagila. Here were to be found the temples of Ishtar and Ninmaḫ. Other quarters were named Kaṣiri, Kullab, and Kumari. The "New City" (*ālu eššu*) lay on the west bank of the Euphrates and was part of the Chaldean extension. Large areas within the city walls were given up to parks and squares.

G. Temple Tower (Ziggurat). The ziggurat of Babylon, *É-temen-an-ki* ("building [of] the foundation of heaven and earth"), lay in the center of the city, S of the citadel, now marked by the ruin-area Ṣaḥn ("the Pan"), a deep depression near the mausoleum of 'Amrān Ibn 'Alī founded A.D. 680. It lay in a square double-casemate walled enclosure, forming a rectangular courtyard measuring about 420 by 375 m. (460 by 410 yds.). Entry was by two doors in the north and ten elaborate gateways. The enclosure was frequently repaired, and bricks marking this activity in the reign of Esarhaddon and Ashurbanipal of Assyria and of Nebuchadrezzar have survived. The area was subdivided into a long narrow western court, a northern court in which towered the ziggurat with its adjacent monumental buildings, wall shelters for the pilgrims, housing for the priests, and storerooms. The main approach from the Procession Way led between two long storerooms. One late Babylonian text, the Esagila tablet AO 6555, gives the dimensions of the courts and the names of the gates: "grand"; "the rising sun"; "the great gate"; "gate of the guardian colossi"; "canal-gate"; and "gate of the tower-view."

Opposite the main gate lay the stepped tower on a platform with shrines grouped around. The stages are given as 91 m. sq. by 34 m. high (300 ft. sq. by 110 ft. high) for the lowest, the next 80 m. sq. by 18 m. high (260 ft. sq. by 60 ft. high), the next three diminishing stages each 6 m. (20 ft.) high and 61, 52, and 43 m. (200, 170, and 140 ft.) square. Originally each stage, as at Ur, may have been of different color. The sanctuary of Marduk (Bēl) on top,

Ruins of Nebuchadrezzar's "Summer Palace," just inside the outer fortification line on the bank of the Euphrates (W. S. LaSor)

15 m. (50 ft.) high, gave a total height of 85 m. (280 ft.). However, nothing remains of the tower except the lower stairs, the whole having been plundered for its bricks by local villagers. There is no reason to doubt the identification of this site with the Tower of Babel (Gen. 11:1-11), the building of which had been terminated. The inscriptions refer only to rebuilding and repair work by the later kings of Babylon. The common identification of the Tower of Babel with the remains of the ziggurat at Borsippa, 7 mi. (11 km.) SSW, is open to question on a number of grounds, not the least that that edifice was in a separate city. The extant vitrified ruins there are of a temple tower also rebuilt by Nebuchadrezzar II.

Herodotus (i.181-183) described Etemenanki, which he called the "sanctuary" of Zeus Belos. It was, he wrote, 2 stadia (400 m. or 1300 ft.) sq. and was entered through a bronze gate. The temple tower stood in the center of the sanctuary, its sides 1 stadium (200 m., 650 ft.) long, with eight towers, one on top of the other. It also had slopes or steps rising on each level. (*See* BABEL, TOWER OF.) In the large topmost temple was a couch covered in beautiful rugs with a golden table. There was no image of the deity, and the Chaldean priests informed Herodotus that one unmarried native woman spent the night there to be visited by the deity. Though Herodotus did not believe the story, it conforms to the known Babylonian view of the sacred marriage.

H. Esagila. The principal temple of Babylon, Esagila ("house of the uplifted head"), was dedicated to the patron deity of the city Marduk. It lay S of Etemenanki, which must have overshadowed it. The excavations by Koldewey in the 'Amrān Ibn 'Alī mound disclosed sufficient evidence to recover the ground plan of two building complexes. The main shrine to the west (10 by 79 m., 33 by 260 ft.) was entered by four doors, one on each side. At a lower level than the principal shrine, that of Marduk, were chapels and niches for lesser deities around the central courtyard. Nabopolassar claimed to have redecorated the Marduk shrine with gypsum and silver alloy, which Nebuchadrezzar replaced with fine gold. The walls were studded with precious stones set in gold plate, and stone and lapis lazuli pillars supported cedar roof beams. The texts describe the god's gilded bedchamber adjacent to the throne room.

Herodotus (i.183) described two statues of the god, one seated. The larger was said to be 12 ells (6 m., 20 ft.) high, but Herodotus did not see it, being told that it had been carried off by Xerxes. This was the usual practice of those kings who wished to curb the independent citizens of Babylon. The opposite action, that of "taking the hand of Bēl (Marduk)" to lead the statue out of the *akitu* (New Year) house and into Esagila, ensured their authority and usually acceptance by the people. Herodotus was told that 800 talents (16.8 metric tons) of gold were used for these statues and for the table, throne, and footstool. A thousand talents of incense were burned annually at the festivals while innumerable sacrificial animals were brought in to the two golden altars, one used for large, the other for small victims.

Esagila was first mentioned by Šulgi of Ur, who restored it *ca.* 2100 B.C. Sabium, Hammurabi, Samsu-iluna, Ammi-ditana, Ammi-ṣaduqa and Samsu-ditana all refer to their devotion to the temple during the 1st Dynasty of Babylon (1894-1595), a care that was to be continued by every king and conqueror of Babylon except Sennacherib. Some refer to their dedications to Marduk and Ṣarpānītum or to Nabû and Tašmetum in their twin shrine at Ezida ("house of knowledge"). One of the best-known of these votive gifts was the diorite stele engraved with the laws of Hammurabi and set up in Esagila as a record of the manner in which that king had exercised justice. The standard brick inscription of Nebuchadrezzar describes him as "provider for Esagila and Ezida." At a lower level in Esagila were located the shrines of Ea to the north, Anu to the south, and elsewhere Nusku and Sin. To the east of Esagila lay a further complex of buildings (89 by 116 m., 292 by 380 ft.) the precise purpose of which is not known.

I. Other Temples. In addition to Ezida, Babylonian texts refer to at least fifty other temples by name, Nebuchadrezzar himself claiming to have built fifteen of them within the city. Excavations have uncovered the temple of Ishtar of Agade (Emašdari) in the area of private houses (Merkes), E of the Procession Way. This faced toward the southwest and was rectangular in form (37 by 31 m., 111 by 102 ft.) with two entrances, S and E, leading into an inner court. The plan was similar to others of the period (e.g., Ezida of Borsippa) with six antechambers alongside the antechapel and shrine, which led directly off the court. This temple was kept in order by Nebuchadrezzar and Nabonidus and lasted into the Persian era.

Koldewey also cleared two temples E of 'Amrān Ibn 'Alī in the Išin-Aswad mound. One cannot be identified as yet due to the absence of inscriptions, hence its designation "Z" temple. This was in continual use over at least seventeen hundred years. To the east lay the shrine of Ninurta (Epatitilla, "temple of the staff of life") built by Nabopolassar, according to its foundation cylinder. This was restored by Nebuchadrezzar. Here the plan (190 by 133 m., 623 by 436 ft.) differs, the main entry being to the east, with subsidiary doors to the north and south. Off the courtyard to the west lay three interconnected equal shrines, each with a dais perhaps dedicated to Ninurta and his wife Gula and son Nusku.

Near the Ishtar gate stood the well-preserved temple of Ninmaḫ, goddess of the underworld, constructed by Ashurbanipal *ca.* 646 B.C. Outside this massive building, called Emaḫ, stood an altar. Passing this to the main door on the north side, worshipers would then traverse the courtyard, passing a well, to enter the shrine in the antechapel. Here they would kneel before the statue of the goddess splendidly clothed and standing on its dais. The architect, Labāši, had designed the surrounding storerooms with a view to security, since many valuable votive offerings must have been hoarded there together with the many fertility figurines found in them. The outer wall was defended by towers, since the shrine may have lain outside the main city defenses. This building has now been fully restored by the Iraqi Department of Antiquities. The cuneiform texts imply that there were many shrines in the city, "180 open-air shrines for Ishtar" and "300 daises for the Igigi gods and 1200 daises of the Anunnaki gods." There were also more than two hundred pedestals for other deities mentioned. The open-air shrines were probably similar to those for the intercessory Lama goddess found at crossroads at Ur.

J. Private Houses. A series of mounds to the north of Išin Aswad at Babylon are called locally Merkes, "trade center." Since the levels containing houses were easier to excavate, being on raised ground, it was possible for Koldewey to trace occupation here almost continuously from the Old Babylonian period to the Parthian period. Here too the streets ran almost straight and crossed at right angles. The houses consisted of a series of rooms around a central courtyard. They were made of mud brick roofed with mats set over wooden beams, and many showed signs of the fire that had raged in the destruction of the city at the hands of the Hittites, Sennacherib, or Xerxes. Several of the buildings had foundation walls 1.8 m. (6 ft.) thick; and, like "the Great House" in Merkes, this may indicate that they supported more than one story. Nevertheless, Herodotus' observation that "the city was filled with houses of three or four stories" cannot now be checked. Some houses may have been built on higher ground than others. Moreover, his expression *órophos* could be rendered "roofs" rather than "story."

K. Documents. Apart from the architectural remains, the decorations of the Ishtar gate, and small objects, the most significant finds from ancient Babylon are more than thirty thousand inscribed tablets. Since apart from the Merkes the Old Babylonian levels have not been explored, mainly because of the high water table of the region, most of these are dated to the Chaldean dynasty or later. They provide an intimate knowledge of personal dealings by merchants until the Seleucid era. Many were obtained by locals in their illicit diggings and cannot now be associated with their original context. These tablets are mainly contracts and administrative documents. There are, however, a number of literary and religious texts originating in the temples in the post-Achaemenid period up to A.D. 100. A few of these traditional "school-texts" are in Greek on clay tablets. These continued to be copied long after Aramaic had become the official language written on more perishable materials, and they include astronomical observations, diaries, almanacs, and omens.

V. Later History.*–*A. Fall of Babylon, 539 B.C. In 544 Nabonidus returned from Teimā to Babylon, with which he had been in contact throughout his ten-year exile. He does not, however, appear to have taken over control of the city itself again from Belshazzar when, according to the Babylonian Chronicle for his seventeenth year, the gods of the chief cities of Babylonia, except Borsippa, Kutha, and Sippar, were brought into the capital for safe-keeping. During Cyrus' attack on Opis the citizens of Babylon apparently revolted but were suppressed by Nabonidus with some bloodshed. He himself fled when Sippar fell on the 15th of Tešrītu, and the next day Ugbaru, the governor of Gutium, and the Persian army entered the city without a battle. This appears to have been effected by the strategem of diverting the river Euphrates, thus drying up the moat defenses and enabling the enemy to enter the city by marching up the dried-up river bed. This may also imply some collaboration with sympathizers inside the walls. That night Belshazzar was killed (Dnl. 5:30). For the remainder of the month Persian troops occupied Esagila, though without bearing arms or interrupting the religious ceremonies.

On the 3rd of Araḫ-samnu (Oct. 29, 539 B.C.), sixteen days after the capitulation, Cyrus himself entered the city amid much public acclaim, ending the Chaldean dynasty as predicted by the Hebrew prophets (Isa. 13:21; Jer. 50f.). Cyrus treated the city with great respect, returning to their own shrines the statues of the deities brought in from other cities. The Jews were sent home with compensatory assistance. He appointed new governors, so ensuring peace and stable conditions essential to the proper maintenance of the religious centers.

B. Achaemenid City. In Nisānu 538, Cambyses II son of Cyrus II "took the hands of Bēl," but left the city under the control of a governor, who kept the peace until Cambyses' death in 522 B.C. There followed the first of the recurrent revolts. Nidintu-Bēl seized power, taking the emotive throne-name Nebuchadrezzar III (Oct.–Dec. 522). Darius, the legitimate king (520-485), put down a further rebellion in the following year but spared the city, building there an arsenal, a Persian-style columned hall (*appa danna*), as an addition to the palace he used during his stay in the city.

Xerxes, possibly the Ahasuerus of Ezr. 4:6, maintained Babylon's importance as an administrative center and provincial capital, but the town declined after an uprising that he successfully suppressed. Another rebellion in his fourth year (482) led him to destroy the ziggurat and to remove the statue of Marduk. The walls remained standing in good enough repair for Herodotus, who probably visited the city *ca.* 460 B.C., to describe them in detail (i.178-188), vindicated to a large measure by subsequent researches. There is no evidence that the decree of Xerxes imposing the worship of Ahuramazda was ever taken seriously.

Economic texts from the Egibi family and the Murašu archives from Nippur (460-400 B.C.) show continued activity despite increasing inflation which more than doubled the rent on a small house, from 15 shekels per annum under Cyrus II to almost 40 shekels in the reign of Artaxerxes I (Longimanus, 465-424), when Ezra and Nehemiah left Babylon to return to Jerusalem (Ezr. 7:1; Neh. 2:1). Artaxerxes II (404-359), according to Berossus, was the first Persian ruler to introduce the statue of Aphrodite or Anahita into the city. Artaxerxes III (Ochus, 358-338) could be the builder or restorer of the *appa danna* found by Koldewey.

C. Hellenistic Period. After his victory at Gaugamela near Arbela (Erbil), Oct. 1, 331 B.C., Alexander marched to Babylon, where the Macedonian was triumphantly acclaimed, the Persian garrison offering no opposition. He offered sacrifices to Marduk, ordered the rebuilding of temples that Xerxes allegedly had destroyed, and then a month later moved on to Susa. He later returned to further his elaborate plans for the sacred city, on which he paid out 600,000 days' wages for clearing the rubble from the precincts of Esagila (Strabo xvi.1). This debris was dumped on that part of the ruins now called Ḥomera. The Jews who had fought in his army refused to take any part in the restoration of the temple of Bēl (Josephus *CAp* i.192). Alexander also planned a new port, but this too was thwarted by his death, June 13, 323. The Greek theater inside the east wall (Ḥomera), cleared by Koldewey and Lenzen, may have been built at this time, though it was unquestionably restored in the time of Antiochus IV.

D. Seleucid-Parthians. A king list from Babylon written soon after 175 B.C. names the successors of Alexander who ruled the city — Philip Arrhidaeus, Antigonus, Alexander IV, and Seleucus I (323-250). Before Seleucus died Babylon's economic but not its religious importance had declined sharply, a process hastened by the foundation of a new capital at Seleucia (Tell 'Umar) on the Tigris by his successor Antiochus I, in 274 B.C.

E. Later City. Babylon's attraction as a "holy city" continued. The satrap Hyspaosines of Characene suppressed a revolt led by a certain Hymerus in 127 B.C. when the priests of Esagila were active. Hymerus issued coins as "king of Babylon" in 124/23, but by the following year Mithradates II had regained control. An independent ruler Gotarzes I was recognized as ruler in 91-80, and the city lay in Parthian hands (Mithradates III, 58-55) until taken over by a rebel Orodes. It remained a center of Hellenism, despite the opposition of a significant traditional Babylonian priestly party and of a minority of Jews, from among whom may have come Hillel. Babylon supported the Jews in Palestine who opposed Herod (Josephus *Ant.* xv.2.1-3). The close association between these Jews in Babylon, who enjoyed self-government there in the 1st cent., and their fellows in Jerusalem is suggested in Acts 2:9-11. Dated cuneiform texts up to A.D. 110 show that the site was still occupied. While Babylon may have been the site of an early Christian church (1 Pet. 5:13), there is no evidence (*see* BABYLON IN THE NT). When Trajan entered the city in 115 he sacrificed to Alexander's *manes* but made no reference to the continued existence of other religious practices or buildings. According to Septimius Severus the site was deserted by A.D. 200.

VI. Exploration and Excavation.–Since the ancient city of Babylon long lay deserted and unidentified, many early travelers, including Schiltberger (*ca.* 1400), di Conti (1428-1453), Rauwolf (1574), and John Eldred (1583), thought it lay elsewhere, probably at the upstanding remains of 'Aqar Qūf, W of Baghdad, which resembled the Tower of Babel. Benjamin of Tudela (12th cent.), however, considered that the ruins of Birs Nimrûd covered ancient Babylon.

Pietro della Valle, visiting Bâbil in 1616, correctly equated it with Babylon, as did Emmanuel Ballyet in 1755 and Carsten Niebuhr some ten years later. Surface exploration was undertaken by C. J. Rich (1811/12, 1821) and J. S. Buckingham and Mellino (1827). Ker Porter mapped the ruins (1818), as did Coste and Flandin (1841), while soundings were made by R. Mignan (1828) and more seriously by A. H. Layard (1850).

The first systematic excavations were directed by a French consul, Fresnel, with Oppert and Thomas in 1852. Their finds were regrettably lost when a boat containing them foundered at Qurna. Work was continued by E. Sachau in 1897/98, but it was left to the Deutsche Orientgesellschaft under Robert Koldewey to plan and carry out scientific excavations throughout the years 1899-1917. Work began with the Procession Way, the temple of Ninmaḫ, and the palaces (1900), the Ninurta temple (1901), the Ishtar gate (1902), the Persian buildings (1906/07), Merkes (1908), and the rest of the Qaṣr (1911/12).

From 1955 to 1968 the Iraqi Department of Antiquities carried out further clearances, especially of the Ishtar gateway, which was partially restored together with the Procession Way and the palaces. The Ninmaḫ temple was reconstructed, and a museum and rest house built on the site, which is also partially covered by the village of Jumjummah. The German Archaeological Institute has continued its interest in the site by excavating the quay wall and the Greek theater.

See also ARCHEOLOGY OF MESOPOTAMIA.

Bibliography.–R. Koldewey, *Excavations at Babylon* (1914); E. Unger, *Babylon, die heilige Stadt* (1931); "Babylon" in *Reallexikon der Assyriologie,* II (1932); O. E. Ravn, *Herodotus' De-*

scription of Babylon (1932); W. Andrae, *Babylon, die versunkene Weltstadt und ihr Ausgräber Robert Koldewey* (1952); F. Wetzel, *Das Babylon der Spätzeit* (1957); A. Parrot, *Babylon and the OT* (1958); H. J. Klengel, in *Forschungen und Berichte*, 5 (1962); J. Neusner, *History of the Jews in Babylonia: The Parthian Period* (1965); H. W. F. Saggs, in *AOTS*, pp. 39-56.

D. J. WISEMAN

BABYLON IN THE NT. Babylon (Gk. *Babylōn*) is used in the NT both literally and symbolically. In Mt. 1:11f., 17; Acts 7:43 the old Mesopotamian city is plainly meant. These all refer to the Captivity in Babylon.

All the references to Babylon in Revelation are evidently symbolic: cf. 14:8; 16:19; 17:5; 18:2, 10, 21. In 17:5 Babylon is designated as *mystḗrion*. This undoubtedly indicates that the name is to be understood figuratively. A few interpreters believe that Jerusalem is the city here designated as Babylon, but most scholars hold that Rome is meant. This interpretation goes back at least to the time of Tertullian (*Adv. Marc*. iii.13). It was adopted by Jerome and Augustine and has been commonly accepted by the Church. There are some strong reasons for accepting it.

(1) The characteristics ascribed to this Babylon apply to Rome rather than to any other city of that age: (a) as ruling over the kings of the earth (17:18); (b) as sitting on seven mountains (17:9); (c) as the center of the world's merchandise (18:2f.; 19:2); (d) as the persecutor of the saints (17:6).

(2) Rome is designated as Babylon in the Sibylline Oracles (5:143), and this is perhaps an early Jewish portion of the book. The comparison of Rome to Babylon is common in Jewish apocalyptic literature (see 2 Esdras and 2 Baruch).

(3) Rome was regarded by both Jews and Christians as being antagonistic to the kingdom of God, and its downfall was confidently expected. This conception is in accord with the predicted downfall of Babylon (Rev. 14:8; 18:2, 10-21). As Babylon had been the oppressor of Israel, it was natural that this new power, which was oppressing the people of God, should be designated as Babylon.

In 1 Pet. 5:13 Babylon is designated as the place from which 1 Peter was written. Down to the time of the Reformation this was generally understood to mean Rome, and two cursives added *en Roma*. Since the Reformation, many scholars have followed Erasmus and Calvin and have urged that the Mesopotamian Babylon is meant. Three theories may be noted:

(1) That the Egyptian Babylon, or Old Cairo, is meant. Strabo (xvii.1.30), who wrote as late as A.D. 18, says the Egyptian Babylon was a strong fortress, founded by certain refugees from the Mesopotamian Babylon. But during the 1st cent. this was little more than a military station, and it is quite improbable that Peter would have gone there. There is no tradition that connects Peter in any way with Egypt.

(2) That the statement is to be taken literally and Babylon in Mesopotamia is meant. Many good scholars hold to this view, among them Weiss and Thayer; but there is no evidence that Peter was ever in Babylon, or that there was even a church there during the 1st century. Mark and Silvanus are associated with Peter in the letter and there is no tradition that connects either of them with Babylon. According to Josephus (*Ant*. xviii.9.5-9), the Jews at this time had largely been driven out of Babylon and were confined to neighboring towns, and it seems improbable that Peter would have made that his missionary field.

(3) That Rome is here again the city designated as Babylon. The Apocalypse would indicate that the churches would understand the symbolic reference, and it seems to have been so understood until the time of the Reformation. The denial of this position was in line with the Reformers' effort to refute Peter's supposed connection with the Roman church. Ancient tradition, however, makes it quite probable that Peter did make a visit to Rome (see J. B. Lightfoot, ed., *Apostolic Fathers*, I, *Clement*, Part 2 [1890], 493-97).

Internal evidence helps to substantiate the theory that Rome was the place from which the letter was written. Mark sends greetings (1 Pet. 5:13), and we know he had been summoned to Rome by the apostle Paul (2 Tim. 4:11). The whole passage, "She who is at Babylon, who is likewise chosen, sends you greetings," seems to be figurative, and that being true, it is natural that Babylon should have been used instead of Rome. The character of the letter as a whole would point to Rome as the place of writing. Ramsay thinks this book is impregnated with Roman thought beyond any other book in the Bible (see *CRE*, p. 286).

A. W. FORTUNE

BABYLONIA bab-ə-lō'nē-ə. Southern Mesopotamia (modern south Iraq) was the site of the first civilization (Gen. 10:10), first called SUMER and Akkad and later Chaldea. Abraham migrated from here to Palestine (Gen. 11:31). The Babylonian army overran Judah and took the Jews into exile there. Throughout the OT Babylonia and its inhabitants, "Babylonians" (Heb. *bᵉnê baḇēl*–'sons of Babylon') were a symbol of opposition to God's people (*see also* BABYLON).

I. Geography
II. Peoples
III. Languages
IV. History
  A. Prehistory
  B. Sumerians
  C. Akkad
  D. Ur III Dynasty
  E. Isin and Larsa
  F. Amorite Dynasty
  G. Kassites
  H. Middle Babylonian Period
  I. Assyrian Supremacy
  J. Chaldeans
  K. Achaemenids
  L. Hellenistic Rulers
V. Discovery
  A. Exploration
  B. Excavation
  C. Decipherment
VI. Writing
  A. Script
  B. Methods and Materials
  C. Scribes and Education
  D. Nonliterary Texts
VII. Law
VIII. Historiography
IX. Literature
  A. Epics
  B. God lists
  C. Wisdom Literature
  D. Omens
  E. Prophecies
  F. Rituals
  G. Prayers and Hymns
X. Science and Technology
  A. Astronomy
  B. Medicine
  C. Technology
  D. Music
XI. Institutions
  A. Social System
  B. The King

C. Cities
XII. Arts
XIII. Legacy

I. Geography.–Babylonia designates the plain of Iraq S of the Hamrīn hills, themselves the border with her northern neighbor Assyria. It is bounded on the east by the Persian (Elamite) hills, to the west by the Syrian desert, and to the south by the Persian Gulf. The whole is divided and watered by the slow-flowing river Euphrates and swift Tigris (Gen. 2:14), which flowed southward through steppe and marshes to the Persian Gulf (Kaldu or Chaldea). The southern area has been subject to a geosyncline in which the land levels have risen where silting has occurred, but the coastline may not have changed. To the west lies the desert stretching from Syria to Arabia.

The main rivers, fed from the northern hills and from tributaries (e.g., Diyala), formed the source from which a network of canals made the region very fertile when supplemented with winter rain. The wheat, date groves, and grazing-land supported a large population. The principal cities lay on or near the river Euphrates. In the north (called Akkad) were Babylon the capital, Agade (Gen. 10:10), Sippar, Borsippa, Kutha, and Kish, and in the south (Sumer) were Nippur, Uruk (Erech, Gen. 10:10), Umma, Lagash, and Ur. Although the designation "Sumer and Akkad" was retained as the official title of the country, from *ca.* 1800 B.C. it was called after its capital Babylon (hence Gk. *Babylonia*). When Babylon fell to the southern tribesmen in 626 B.C. it was externally known as "the land of the Chaldeans" (Jer. 24:5; Ezk. 12:13).

II. Peoples.–Though it cannot be certain, the earliest inhabitants appear to have been Semites, according to the evidence of early place names and some texts from *ca.* 2800 B.C. (Abu Ṣalabīḫ). Till the mid-2nd millennium the non-Semitic Sumerians appear to have lived amid a predominantly Semitic population. Babylonia was in contact with Assyrians, Amorites, Chaldeans, and Arabs and Elamites on its borders and, by trade, with Syria and Egypt. Hittites invaded *ca.* 1645 B.C., and Kassites and Gutians from the eastern hills took over control for a time. The Judeans were exiled there for at least seventy years from 604 B.C. (Jer. 25:11).

III. Languages.–The earliest identifiable language used in Babylonia is the non-Semitic agglutinative Sumerian employing the cuneiform script (*see* WRITING). It cannot yet be identified with any known language group, though it bears several characteristics which later appear in different branches of languages.

Several local Semitic dialects appear from *ca.* 2800 B.C., the most influential being the Amorite Old Babylonian, which became the diplomatic lingua franca of the whole ancient Near East (see 2 K. 18:16). With the rise of the Chaldeans *ca.* 626 B.C. Aramaic was clearly influencing the local Neo-Babylonian dialect. Aramaic itself became the dominant Semitic dialect in use alongside the local "Late Babylonian" in Achaemenid times as the diplomatic language of the period. Babylonian dialects continued in use, with the cuneiform script for religious purposes at Babylon, until the 1st cent. A.D.

IV. History.–*A. Prehistory.* The earliest human traces in Mesopotamia in the northern hills (Sulaimania) include Middle Paleolithic implements usually dated about 120,000 years ago. Mousterian skeletons from the Shanidar Caves are said to be about 45,000 years old. The Neolithic revolution (*ca.* 7000 B.C.) resulted in the settlement of villages with a pre-ceramic culture on irrigated sites. Farming settlements were devoted to cereal crops, husbandry, and early iron and bronzeworking. Some have identified this with the environment portrayed in Gen. 3–5. Phases of culture named after sites where distinctive finds were made include Eridu (possibly Irad, Gen. 4:18) with its early series of temples, Hajji Muhammad, Ubaid, Uruk, and Jemdet Nasr ("Protoliterate"). The "birth of civilization" in this region, which antedates that of Egypt, was marked by the use of writing (Uruk IV, Kish), irrigation, and urbanization. The Sumerian civilization now blossomed around the temple-cities with a social system that was to remain unchanged for many centuries.

B. Sumerians. The origin of these early settlers is much questioned, the prevailing view being that they entered from the east and south. Their tradition was that "kingship was lowered from heaven" first to Eridu. Their king lists name five pre-Flood cities where eight (or ten) kings reigned a total of 241,200 years. "Then the Flood swept over" (*see* DELUGE OF NOAH). Kingship was resumed at Kish but soon wrested from there by Uruk (biblical Erech, modern Warka), where a powerful dynasty (Enmerkar, Lugalbanda, Dumuzi [Tammuz], and Gilgamesh) held sway. Although a cycle or series of epics has clustered round these figures, especially that of Gilgamesh, the hero of the Babylonian flood story (see IX.A below), there is accumulating evidence of their historical basis. Gilgamesh mastered Agga of Kish in this spectacular period of which the splendor can be seen in the royal cemetery at Ur. This dynasty traded with Syria, Persia, and perhaps as far as the Indus Valley.

With the breakup of the Uruk dynasty, Sumer fragmented into thirteen city-states each under a chief (en-si) governing on behalf of the city-god. In the 1st Dynasty of Kish, Enmebaragesi had built the temple of the supreme god Enlil at Nippur, which thereafter became a special sacred capital city. When the power of Kish was curtailed by Gilgamesh, Ur took up the leading role under Mesanne-pada. In its turn it was overriden by Ur-Nanshe of Lagash. His grandson Eannatum (*ca.* 2550 B.C.) freed Sumer of Elamite raiders, won over Ur and Kish, and warred with his neighbor Umma. His nephew Entemena continued this hostility but made a pact with Uruk and Ur. Lagash revived for a while under the reformer Urukagina, but was destroyed by Lugalzaggesi, who captured Uruk and Nippur and claimed dominion from the Persian Gulf to the Mediterranean. His claim may be true, as it was for succeeding Semitic rulers of Babylonia. *See also* SUMER.

C. Akkad. Sargon (Šarrukīn I), a vizier of Kish, founded a strong dynasty at a new city, Agade, which gave its name to the line of successors (Akkadians), 2370-2190 B.C., and to the northern part of Babylonia (Akkad). He gained control of Uruk, dismantled the walls of that and other cities, and took over Lugalzaggesi's wide realm. Trade with Mediterranean and Anatolian peoples flourished. He maintained suzerainty over Assyria and for this reason some identify him with Nimrod of Gen. 10:9-12. His grandson Naram-Sin held the empire together, maintaining garrisons in the north (Nineveh, Brâk). The Gutian invasion from the eastern hills is described as the action of the goddess Inanna abandoning her cursed city of Agade. These newcomers (2230-2120 B.C.) assimilated the Semitic customs and language. Then Lagash, which had suffered little, flourished under Gudea, who controlled Nippur and Uruk, until by 2100 B.C. most of the former city-states reasserted their independence.

D. Ur III Dynasty. This new regime at Ur (2113-2006 B.C.) witnessed a renaissance of Sumerian civilization well attested by numerous documents. The founder, Ur-Nammu, rebuilt his capital and restored the temples at

"War panel" of an Early Dynastic III (25th cent. B.C.) standard from Ur, showing a victorious king, soldiers, and prisoners. Mosaic of shell, lapis lazuli, and red limestone set in bitumen on wood (Trustees of the British Museum)

his vassal-cities Eridu, Lagash, Isin, Nippur, and Uruk. More than 1100 brickmakers worked for a year to build the temple-tower and sacred precinct of Ur. He maintained close links with outlying governors (e.g., in Babylon and Assyria) through a messenger service and traded between the Persian Gulf and India.

Ur-Nammu was followed by a series of vigorous rulers (Šulgi, Amar-Sin [Amar-Su'en], Šu-Sin) each of whom had once been a local governor. Despite defensive measures and punitive raids it proved impossible to withstand the armed incursions of the Semites from the western desert. The Amorite tribesmen isolated the city from its empire; and amid the collapse of central authority, raiders from Elam captured the last king Ibbi-Sin, sacked Ur, and brought the Sumerians to an end as a political force. It may be that the migration of Terah and Abraham (Gen. 11:31) took place about this time (*see* ABRAHAM).

E. Isin and Larsa. The West Semites who now took over the main cities brought a new conception of kingship, in which the palace controlled the land, and state institutions existed alongside the temple economy and private enterprise that had characterized their Sumerian predecessors. Some of the latter still controlled some centers. For example, Išbi-Irra, governor of Isin, won back Ur, Nippur, and Dēr and restored the trade that had dwindled during the unrest. Išme-Dagan, however, faced increasing incursions from the western tribes as well as from Assyria (under Ilušuma), which claimed to have "freed" the southern cities. Lipit-Ishtar of Isin faced opposition from Larsa, whose ruler Gungunum had captured Ur and absorbed Nippur and Uruk into his kingdom. Lipit-Ishtar's successor was a West Semite, Sumu-ilum, who inaugurated the well-known Amorite 1st Dynasty of Babylon whose growing power led to an inevitable clash with Larsa, which controlled the south despite raiders from the eastern hills. Isin was won back by an Elamite sheikh Kudur-Mabuk (*see* CHEDORLAOMER), who placed his son Warad-Sin on the throne. A revolution led by his brother Rîm-Sin of Larsa brought yet another change. This powerful personality was to rule all central and southern Babylonia for thirty-six years.

F. Amorite Dynasty. At Babylon, Hammurabi (1792-1750 B.C.) consolidated his position and, as can be judged from the Mari Letters, dominated a coalition of ten kings, the same number as followed Rīm-Sin of Larsa, Ibal-pī-'el his contemporary at Eshnunna, and the kings of Qatanum, but fewer than those owing allegiance to Yarīm-Lim of Yamḫad (Aleppo). At this time Mari on the Euphrates was ruled by Yasmaḫ-Adad, son of Šamši-Adad I of Assyria. In his seventh year Hammurabi captured Uruk and Isin and destroyed Malgium. While the uneasy truce with Assyria and Eshnunna lasted, Hammurabi devoted himself to local affairs. He strengthened the palace's hold over land, which he distributed on "feudal" terms to ex-soldiers and other palace dependents. In his twenty-ninth year a dramatic victory over the rulers E of the Tigris opened the way for a major assault on his old rival Rīm-Sin of Larsa. When this was accomplished, together with victories over Eshnunna and Mari, Babylon controlled a wide area of diverse cities and peoples. The internal stability throughout the reign owed much to Hammurabi as judge (see VII below) and his piety toward the gods of the major cult centers. (*See also* HAMMURABI).

Hammurabi's successors had to face a revolt by the Sea-Land tribes of the southern marshes. In 1595 the Hittite Mursilis I swept from Aleppo to Babylon. His withdrawal left a weakened regime to face inroads from the Kassites, mountain folk from the northeast.

G. Kassites. The newcomers under Agum-kakrime gradually infiltrated Babylonia and, once in command of Babylon itself, united the whole country against pressure from the Mitanni rulers of Assyria. Their liberal attitude toward Babylonian religion, learning, trade, and institutions, which continued unchanged, was a major unifying factor. It enabled them also to quiet the rebellious south, though here military force was required. Agum-kakrime's successor Kara-indaš was allied by marriage with Amenhotep (Amenophis) III of Egypt, and these relations were maintained by his successors. Kurigalzu II (*ca.* 1345-1324) restored Ur and founded a new capital at Dūr-Kurigalzu ('Aqar Qūf). The Kassites were much interested in Babylonian religion, rebuilding the shrines, and recopying religious texts. Secular administrative control, to judge from the names of officials, remained in the hands of native Babylonians. Grants of royal land recorded as

Cuneiform tablet (*ca.* 600 B.C.) containing a map of the world showing the surrounding oceans (ring) and designating Babylon as the center. The map illustrates the campaigns of Sargon of Agade (*ca.* 2300 B.C.), who invaded Asia Minor. (Trustees of the British Museum)

charters (sometimes with tax exemption) are found on boundary stones (*kudurru*) of the period. This decentralization undoubtedly decreased the power of the central authority to withstand the incursions of the Aramean tribesmen from the western desert. This allowed Assyrian action against Babylonia, and enabled Elam to rule Babylon itself for a while (*ca.* 1151 B.C.).

H. Middle Babylonian Period. Nebuchadrezzar I (*ca.* 1124-1103) accumulated support from the Babylonian tribes and landowners on the eastern frontier sufficient to mount a highly successful campaign against Elam. He plundered Susa and restored the exiled god Marduk to his place in Babylon amid public rejoicing, an act long to be remembered in Babylonian literature. However, this was not enough to unite local factions for long in the face of constant attacks from nomads, floods, and famine. For more than a century Babylonia was dominated by the southern tribes of the 2nd (or Paše) Dynasty of Isin (called the Sea-Land Dynasty, 1026-987) and the House of Bazi (987-977) until finally control returned to the 8th Dynasty at Babylon itself.

I. Assyrian Supremacy. Freed from Mitanni domination, the Assyrians under Ashurnasirpal (883-859) controlled northern Babylonia and held the southern tribes (Kaldu) in check. His son Shalmaneser III (858-824) consolidated this hold after a show of force against the Kaldu (Chaldean) chiefs, who were now made tribute-paying vassals. Šamši-Adad V had to fight Marduk-balāssu-iqbi of Babylon, who had allied himself with Elam, and entered Babylon in 811 B.C. This led to a series of raids directed to control the southern tribes.

Ashurbanipal king of Assyria carrying a basket for the rebuilding of the temple Esagila at Babylon (Trustees of the British Museum)

Tiglath-pileser III of Assyria, "king of Sumer and Akkad," took the title of "king of Babylon" in 729 B.C., having claimed the throne in 745 under his native name Pul(u) (2 K. 15:19; 1 Ch. 5:26). He had earlier recovered ground lost to the Aramean tribe of Puqudu (Pekod, Jer. 50:2) and reinstated a native Nabû-nāṣir (Nabonassar) as king in Babylon. When he died in 734, Ukīn-zēr, a sheikh of the Amukkani tribe, seized the throne. The situation was restored only by Tiglath-pileser's acceptance of support from the Chaldean Marduk-apla-iddina (*see* MERODACH-BALADAN) while his army besieged the other tribes.

Tiglath-pileser's son Sargon II called himself "vice-regent of Babylon" when he was welcomed into the city, and Marduk-apla-iddina submitted to him, being allowed to retain his chieftainship of the Bīt-Yakin tribe. Sargon's own account of the desolation of Babylon in 709 B.C. has much in common with Isa. 13:1-22. When Marduk-apla-iddina later seized Babylon with Elamite assistance, Sennacherib marched to defeat the coalition in 703 B.C. and sack the city. While Marduk-apla-iddina was left to retreat to the southern marshes. Bēl-ibni was set up as a puppet ruler dependent on Assyria. This did not last, for Marduk-apla-iddina sought outside help for his renewed resistance, including overtures to Judah (2 K. 20:12-19; Isa. 39; *see* HEZEKIAH). Once more the Assyrian army raided the tribal lands and Marduk-apla-iddina fled into exile. In 692 a further Assyrian campaign led to the defeat of Aramean rebels and their Elamite supporters at Ḫalule. Babylon was sacked after a siege of nine months. These events form the background of Isaiah's prophecies against Babylon (chs. 14; 39; 43:14).

Esarhaddon's conciliatory policy toward Babylon enabled peace and trade to be restored so that an Elamite raid there in 675 B.C. elicited no welcome from the

Winged deity (right), armed with swords and lightning, driving out lion-headed monster. Reconstruction of limestone relief from temple at Nineveh, reign of Ashurnasirpal II (883-859 B.C.) (From A. H. Layard, *Monuments of Nineveh*, 1849) (Trustees of the British Museum)

independent tribes. Esarhaddon appointed one of his sons Šamaš-šum-ukīn, of equal status (perhaps a twin) to Ashurbanipal, as crown prince of Babylon in 672 B.C. He took over in 668 but his jurisdiction was limited, as some major cities (Nippur) and several Assyrian garrisons and officials owed allegiance directly to Ashurbanipal in Nineveh. It seems that by 652 B.C. pressure from the tribes and Elam, combined perhaps with a misplaced belief in Ashurbanipal's weakness and conciliatory advances, led to open rebellion. But the Arabian and other tribes gradually forsook Babylon under famine and siege. When the Elamites also were defeated, Šamaš-šum-ukīn committed suicide in his burning palace, and Babylon fell into Assyrian hands (648 B.C.). Despite further raids against the Arab tribes (642-638) the southern tribesmen never lost their spirit of independence.

J. Chaldeans. The gap in the Assyrian annals after 639 makes it difficult to trace the decline of that power under aging Ashurbanipal. The Babylonian tribes were not slow to strive for total independence. The Babylonian Chronicles tell of their attack on the Assyrian garrisons of Sin-šar-iškun in northern Babylonia in 627 B.C. When the Assyrian army marched to relieve Nippur they were forced to retreat. The Babylonian commander Nabû-apla-uṣur (Nabopolassar) successfully defended Babylon and six weeks later was acclaimed king (Nov. 22, 626) in place of the Assyrian successor of Šamaš-šum-ukīn, Kandalanu, who had died a year earlier. The Assyrians repeated the attempt to reinforce the Nippur garrison but were unsuccessful. In 616/615 they were defeated by the crown prince of Babylon, Nebuchadrezzar, in the middle Euphrates and driven back to the heart of Assyria proper. This prepared the way for the Babylonian attack on Asshur (614) and, with the Medes, the final sack of Nineveh in August 612 (Nah. 1:8; *see* NINEVEH). The same Chronicles report further expeditions, which culminated in the defeat of the Assyrians and Egyptians at Ḫarran (609) and of the Egyptians at Carchemish in 605 B.C. Then Nebuchadrezzar "conquered the whole of Syro-Palestine" (so also 2 K. 24:7; Josephus *Ant.* x.6.86). The crown prince, who was at Ribleh (Riblah, Jer. 39:5) when he heard of Nabopolassar's death, rode home to succeed to the throne (Sept. 6, 605) and then returned for another campaign in Palestine.

In the following year "all the kings of Syro-Palestine," including Jehoiakim of Judah (2 K. 24:1), became his vassals. However, when in 601 Nebuchadrezzar II was defeated by Neco II of Egypt in a fierce battle, Jehoiakim switched his allegiance. Two years later the Babylonians raided the Arab tribes (Jer. 49:28-33) and so prepared the way for retaliation on Judah. In Nebuchadrezzar's seventh year "he besieged the city of Judah, capturing it on the second day of the month Adaru [= Mar. 16, 597 B.C.]. He took the king [JEHOIACHIN] and put a king of his own choice [Mattaniah/Zedekiah] on the throne. Having taken much spoil from the city, he sent it back to Babylon" (Babylonian Chronicle BM 21946; cf. 2 K. 24:10-17; 2 Ch. 36:5-10; Jer. 37:1). Jehoiachin's captivity is confirmed by texts from Babylon. A revolt by Zedekiah led to another attack on Judah in the course of which Jerusalem was sacked (587 B.C.; 2 K. 24:25–25:26). The Babylonians later besieged Tyre and invaded Egypt (568/567 B.C.; Jer. 46).

Nebuchadrezzar rightly boasted of his architectural achievements at Babylon and of his control of an empire almost equivalent to that of the Assyrians at the height of their power. He was succeeded by a son Amēl-Marduk (2 K. 25:27-30; *see* EVIL-MERODACH), who enhanced the status of the Judean princes at his court, and then by a fellow army officer Neriglissar or Nergal-šar-uṣur (560-558) and Labāši-Marduk (557 B.C.). These for a time acted as intermediaries between the mounting rival powers of Media and Lydia on their borders. Nabonidus (Labynetus of Herodotus) acted similarly until for the years 553-543 he moved to Tema (Teimā) in northwest Arabia and set up a kingdom in exile there. Then with the support of the king of Egypt and the king of the Medes (probably Cyrus, who may be identified with "Darius the Mede" of Dnl. 6:28) he returned to Babylon. Soon the Persians attacked Opis and then Babylon when his coregent and son Bēl-šar-uṣur (Belshazzar) was killed (Dnl. 5:30). Cyrus entered Babylon on Oct. 29, 539 B.C., but spared Nabonidus (who may have died in exile in Carmania). Independent Babylonia now ceased to exist.

See also CHALDEA V; Map XI.

K. Achaemenids. Under Cyrus II conditions changed little. He entrusted local government in Babylonia to Gubaru (Gobryas), a former general and perhaps a district governor (*see* DARIUS 1). His own son Cambyses II (Akk. *Kambuziya*) acted as viceroy from 538 until his father's death in 530 B.C. On Cambyses' death (522) local unrest followed his brother Bardiya's usurpation. The Babylonians supported Nidintu-Bēl, who took the title of Nebuchadrezzar III (Oct.-Dec., 522). Next year another rebel (Arakha as Nebuchadrezzar IV) aroused the masses but was put to death. Darius (II) was then acknowledged ruler (520-485 B.C.). Babylonian administration was now reshaped under satraps and local governors, royal inspectors and tax inspectors, who did away with much corruption under rigid control but heavy taxation. In the fourth year of Xerxes (485-465, = Ahasuerus of Ezr. 4:6) the Babylonians made a last attempt to win independence but were crushed by Megabyzus, Xerxes' brother-in-law. Little attention was paid to ruined Babylon while Xerxes was at war with Greece. Herodotus may have visited Babylon about this time (*see* BABYLON). The larger centers, Babylon, Borsippa, Kish, Nippur, Uruk, and Ur continued as independent trading centers under Artaxerxes II and III (404-338).

L. Hellenistic Rulers. The subsequent history of Babylonia centers on the capital itself, due to the lack of sources from other cities. Alexander III (330-323 B.C.) captured the city and planned to rebuild it, but little was done under his generals Philip Arrhidaeus (323-316) and Alexander IV (316-312). The Seleucids moved the capital to their new city of Seleucia. While Ur died slowly, Uruk flourished. There, as through the Parthian and later Seleucid control, the major cult centers maintained the ancient traditions. Texts continued to be copied in Babylon into the 1st cent. A.D. (cf. 1 Pet. 5:13). Parthian occupation has been traced at Babylon, Kish, Nippur, Uruk, and Lagash, though the temples were now rededicated to other deities. There is evidence of the spread of Christianity in Mesopotamia under the Sassanids (A.D. 227-636).

***V. Discovery.**–A. Exploration.* Early travelers, including Herodotus in the middle 5th cent. B.C., recorded their description of Babylon or of a land mentioned in the OT. Few accounts survive, and some authors, as Marco Polo (1271-1295) and "John Mandeville" (1322-1356), failed even to note the ruins of the ancient kingdom. Once interest had been focused on the supposed ruins of Babylon and the Tower of Babel, reports became more frequent. The capital was variously reported as at 'Aqar Qūf by Nicolo di Conti (1428-1453), at Birs Nimrûd by Benjamin of Tudela (1160-1173) and Carsten Niebuhr (1765), or, correctly, near Hillah by Pietro della Valle in 1616. Closer observation followed, by de Beauchamps (1784) and by C. J. Rich (1811, 1817), through whom the first antiquities found their way to Europe (the Louvre and British Museum). There followed activity by local diplomats and the first excavations. W. K. Loftus explored many a tell at Nuffar (Nippur), Senkereh (Larsa), Warka (ancient Uruk, biblical Erech), and el-Muqaiyar (Ur). In this he followed up Henry Layard's initial work at Babylon, Borsippa, and Nippur. The first scientific expeditions were conducted by the French at Babylon (1850) and Telloh (Girsu, 1877-1909); by the British at Babylon (1879/80), Dilbat (1880), and Sippar (Abū Ḥabbah, 1881/82); the Americans at Nippur (1889-1900), and the Germans at Adab (1903).

B. Excavation. Excavations in south Iraq in the modern sense of scientific archeology may be said to date from the systematic work of the Deutsche Orientgesellschaft at Babylon under R. Koldewey (1899-1917). The joint British Museum–University Museum, Philadelphia work at Ur under Sir Leonard Woolley (1922-1934) is justly famous for its discoveries, including the Royal Graves. The French worked at "Lagash" and Larsa (1929-1934, 1967ff.) while the Americans concentrated on surface surveys and digs in the Diyala region and in 1948 resumed work at Nippur. In the same year the Iraqi Department of Antiquities excavated 'Uqair, Eridu, and Dūr-Kurigalzu. Several expeditions are currently at work at Al Hiba (Lagash), Dēr, Abu Salabīkh, Seleucia, and Babylon.

C. Decipherment. Curiosity over the cuneiform inscriptions brought to Europe from Babylon, Ur, and Persepolis by Pietro della Valle, Niebuhr, Rich, and other travelers soon aroused scholarly curiosity. Work concentrated on the bi- and trilingual inscriptions from Persia, especially from Behistun where identical texts were extant in Old Persian, Elamite, and Babylonian. Since the Old Persian system used the fewest signs it was deciphered by Grotefend, Rask, Bernouf, Rawlinson, and Oppert by 1847 on the basis of groups of signs used for royal names and titulary. Then the Babylonian column gradually yielded its secrets to the patient work of Grotefend (1814), Hincks (1847), Rawlinson (1850), and Oppert (1857). In 1857 a trial translation of an inscribed prism of Tiglath-pileser I was arranged by the Royal Asiatic Society. The similarity of results among these scholars proved their ability to read the script. The Elamite cuneiform yielded to F. H. Weisbach in 1892.

A non-Semitic language represented by an increasing number of cuneiform texts from Babylonia was identified as Sumerian by Oppert (1869). Detailed linguistic analysis had, however, to await the work of A. Poebel, C. J. Gadd, T. Jacobson, S. N. Kramer (literary texts), and A. Falkenstein (Gudea inscriptions) in the years 1925-1960. Both Sumerian and Akkadian (Assyrian and Babylonian) are now represented by a large literature (in volume some ten times that of the OT). The study of these languages has a prominent place in comparative Semitic studies and helps to elucidate Biblical Hebrew at many points.

***VI. Writing.**–A. Script.* The cuneiform script, originally pictographic, was first employed for memoranda and administrative purposes. By 2500 B.C. its extensive use alongside oral tradition is attested by numerous documents of many different types and purposes (see IX below). Signs were used as ideograms and logograms, and the occurrence of polysyllables and of signs used as markers or determinatives (e.g., for gods, professions, cities, lands) indicates a large development and a skilled use before 3000 B.C. The script was adapted for writing many languages (Hittite, Hurrian, Elamite, Amorite, and Old Persian), and its use together with the scribal schools on which it was based proved an important focus for the spread of Babylonian literature and ideas. There is no proven relationship of the earliest script with later Proto-Elamite, Egyptian hieroglyphs, or with the origin of the alphabet; but an original development from one Babylonian center is not impossible (*see* WRITING).

B. Methods and Materials. One reason for the survival, and consequent unearthing during excavation, of at least a quarter-million inscribed documents from Babylonia is its unique use of the sun-dried or kiln-baked clay tablet (*ṭuppu*). These were in vogue continuously from *ca.*

3000 (mainly pictographs) to the 6th cent. B.C. Thereafter such tablets continued to be used for some types of legal contracts and religious texts until Seleucid times. They were still used by at least one major temple for copies of "canonical" texts until *ca.* A.D. 100. From the 8th cent. B.C. there was increasing use of wooden writing-boards (*lē'u*; cf. Heb. *lû(a)ḥ,* "tablet" of stone, wood, or metal) filled wtih wax, and of scrolls (*magallatu*; cf. Heb. *m^e^gillâ*) of leather or papyrus (*niāru*) for the Aramaic script with brush or pen. Parchment (*mašak šipirtum*) is first mentioned in the Achaemenid period.

C. Scribes and Education. From the late Uruk periods scribes were apprenticed as pupils ("sons") to temple or secular schools (é-dub-ba, "tablet-house"). All education was bilingual, in Sumerian and Akkadian, the student progressing through the signs (about 500) and syllabary to copying lists of ideographs, words, and then all types of texts (see IX below). A scribe might specialize in accountancy, medicine, or state, religious, or general secretarial work. As an expert (*ummānu*) he had a highly prized profession, often hereditary. He could rise to high administrative positions such as Chancellor or Secretary of State (Ezra held such a position for Jewish affairs).

From Old Babylonian times many scribes, the poor aristocracy, were trained in local schools and would serve the public, waiting outside public buildings for customers. Literacy was low; only a few kings, Šulgi of Ur, Lipit-Ishtar of Isin, and Darius of Persia claimed, like Ashurbanipal of Nineveh, to be able to read, write, and know the scribal arts.

D. Nonliterary Texts. Babylonia developed a bureaucratic administration centered on the temple and palace. Many tablets written by the scribes were individual accounts (daily, monthly, or annual) of rations, offerings, taxes, and even land disbursed or received. Letters giving effect to local decisions are particularly numerous in the Old Babylonian period (Babylon, Lagash, and Mari). Many refer to interstate diplomacy between kings, e.g., Hammurabi of Babylon and Zimri-Lim of Mari, or between Kassite kings and the Egyptian pharaohs. The majority of the texts written were personal contracts of purchase, sale, loan, hire, rent, gift, inheritance, marriage, or other legally binding event. Evidence before a judge was also recorded (cf. Nu. 27:1-11; 1 K. 3:16-28) as were oaths taken before a god (in a temple) or king.

See also III above.

VII. Law.–The Babylonian held a strong concept of authority and law. Law (*kittum*) is truth; law and justice or order (*kittum u mēšarum*) was received from the supreme god. It was the responsibility of the king to exercise it so as "to destroy the evil and the wicked that the strong might not oppress the weak"; equally he had "to protect the fatherless and the widow." Because the human ruler was answerable to powers outside himself his subjects were protected from autocracy. This made for order and stability, with all men as equals before the law and the god who gave it. The king, as chief judge, decided hard cases, some referred to him by local and lesser magistrates. All decisions were recorded in writing to be valid, the summary form used as protasis, "If a man / It was decided that a man had . . .," the apodosis recording the royal decision spoken "He shall die/pay a fine," etc. They then omit the detail needed for a modern legal analysis, though full accounts of evidence do exist (see VI.D above). The major Babylonian rulers made selections of decisions taken partly as precedent but mainly to report to this god the discharge of responsibility and god-given wisdom (cf. 1 K. 3:28). These summary collections of laws are not a code (many categories, e.g., murder, sale, are omitted). One large group of laws was collected by Hammurabi of Babylon and recorded on a stone stele set up in the temple of Marduk in Babylon. The 282 cases are only roughly grouped and cover property, marriage and divorce, false witness, corruption, theft, looting, tenants of the crown, commercial law, inheritance, priestesses, adoption, assault, agricultural work, rates of hire, slaves, courts and punishment. Several cases were copied as precedents while a number are similar to those recorded by earlier kings, Lipit-Ishtar of Isin (*ca.* 1836) and the ruler of Eshnunna. Even earlier collections of laws came from the Sumerian Ur-Nammu of Ur. This literary form remained unchanged throughout Babylonian history. There is no evidence that the few similarities between Babylonian and Hebrew laws are more than the result of common practice.

Royal edicts or decrees enforcing law and justice include some issued by Urukagina of Lagash (*ca.* 2300) and Ammi-ṣaduqa of Babylon (1645 B.C.). These call for remittance of debt, taxes, and of some forms of slavery. Similar *mēšarum*-edicts were issued in the first full and sole regnal year of Babylonian kings in addition to special occasions. By this means (and the tariffs associated with the collections of law) the economic and social life of the community was regulated according to a constant norm of "law" (i.e., a religious basis). Similar ideal practice could account for the so-called reforms of Hezekiah (2 K. 18:6) and Josiah, whose actions the historian judges by the law of Moses. The phrase "he did the right (Heb. *hayyāšār*) in the eyes of the Lord" may imply the issue of similar decrees and the acknowledgement of the law also by Asa (1 K. 15:11; 2 Ch. 14:2), Jehoshaphat (1 K. 22:43), and Azariah (2 K. 15:3).

International treaties or covenants are known from Sumer, terminating war or settling boundaries (e.g., the Stele of Vultures between Lagash and Umma). That similar legal documents, based on historical data, were drawn up by the Later Babylonians may be surmised both from the pictorial representation of a parity pact between Shalmaneser III of Assyria and the Babylonian Marduk-zākir-šumi (*ca.* 846 B.C.), and the partial text of a later agreement between the latter and Šamši-Adad V of Assyria.

Royal land grants were recorded, as most permanent royal legal and religious enactments, on stone (cf. Ex. 24:12). Boundary markers or stones (Bab. *kudurru*) were set up as public witness to a deed and placed in the temple, showing the title and extent of ownership. These large oval or cylindrical stones were sometimes ornamented with protective divine symbols and curses on any who should remove them (cf. Dt. 19:14; 27:17; Job 24:2).

VIII. Historiography.–Sumerian historical writing was allied to other genres (e.g., epic; see IX.A below); but separate detailed accounts, such as the border dispute between Lagash and Umma, show that earlier events had been recorded and transmitted both orally and in writing in sufficient detail for later evaluation. Lists of rulers and cities headed the king lists, and genealogies and historical incidents, which can be checked from several sources, are included in omen texts. These attest the careful recording of past events that have some parallel with Gen. 5, 11 (cf. 1 Ch. 1–9). One list gives the full ancestry of the Hammurabi dynasty and includes names otherwise known only as persons, tribes, or toponyms (cf. Gen. 11:10-28). King lists naming rulers before and after the Flood are the framework on which the chronology has been reconstructed. All kings were included in the native Babylonian King List (A), and local year-formulas, citing an outstanding event for each regnal year, were used for dating purposes until the Middle Babylonian period. Thereafter regnal years numbered from each accession were used. Beginning with Seleucus I (312/311 B.C.) an era dating was introduced. Events were usually recorded in expanded form in annals, reports to gods, and dedicatory inscriptions. A reliable source, unique to Babylonia, is the Babylonian Chronicle, which relates specific events in each year. The major Chronicles extant are:

1. Sargon of Agade–Kaštiliašu (*ca.* 2350-1600 B.C.).
2. The Babylonian Chronicle: Nabonassar–Šamaš-šum-ukīn (747-648).
3. Esarhaddon Chronicle (680-667).
4. Chronicle of the Years 680-626.
5. Nabopolassar–Nebuchadrezzar II (626-595). (Missing: Nebuchadrezzar II year 11–Neriglissar year 2.)
6. Neriglissar 3 (556).
7. Nabonidus (555-539).
8. Various Seleucid Chronicles and King Lists (306-175).

In these such events as the fall of Nineveh (612), the siege of Ḫarran by Neco II with Assyrian help (609), the Babylonian defeat of the Egyptians at Carchemish and the overrunning of Syria and Palestine (605), the Egyptian defeat of the Babylonians (601), the capture of Jerusalem by Nebuchadrezzar II (Mar. 16, 597 B.C.), and the fall of Babylon to Cyrus (Oct. 29, 539 B.C.) are independently attested from extrabiblical sources.

From astronomical diaries kept at Babylon (as yet unpublished) it is possible to reconstruct precise datings for political, economic, and other historical events in the Seleucid period. (For Seleucid period chronicles see A. K. Grayson, *Assyrian and Babylonian Chronicles* [1975].)

***IX. Literature.**–A. Epics.* Sumerian literature is rich in epical material mostly preserved in Old Babylonian (18th cent.) copies. An early Semitic epic of *Atra-ḫasis* ("the very devout one") includes an account of creation, the earliest rulers, and the Flood in a single work (as does Gen. 1–11). It names the five principal cult-centers that were the seats of the antedeluvian kings. The existence and roles of the gods are assumed; the lesser gods toil in support of the great gods. Following strike action by the former, the great gods plan to create man to relieve these gods of labor. "Let one god be slaughtered so that all the gods may be cleansed in one dipping. From his flesh and blood let the birth-goddess (Nintu) mix clay so that god and man be thoroughly mixed in the clay. . . . Let there be a spirit in the god's flesh" (lines 208-215). The increase in population and man's rebellion (cf. Gen. 6:1-8) are met by divinely sent plagues, which are averted only when man withholds his service of the gods. Man's evil conduct, ending in violence, is the reason the gods eventually send the Flood. There is a period of "grace" before the judgment (cf. Gen. 6:3). The story of the Flood then given is similar to that known from Tablet XI of the later (11th cent. B.C.) epic of Gilgamesh, but shows that the Sumerian Flood story is itself a translation from an earlier Semitic version.

The Gilgamesh Epic (composed *ca.* 2000 B.C. and recorded on eleven tablets to which a twelfth, describing the afterlife, was added later) is but one of a cycle of earlier epics surrounding this king of Uruk. Basically the story is of the king's rebellion against the idea of death following the loss of his friend Enkidu. In his quest for immortality Gilgamesh punts across the waters of death to meet Utnapishtim, who recounts his own preservation, due to the revelation of the god's plan by Ea, and his survival of the Flood in a large reed boat accompanied by his family, animals, and birds. Gilgamesh himself, however, fails to pass three tests necessary to become immortal. He is unable to stay awake for six days and nights, he does not drink from the "fountain of youthful life," though he bathes in it, and he loses the "plant of life" to a snake and must return to his earthly city. Any similarities between this Babylonian story and the Genesis narrative are best explained as derived from an earlier source. Copies of this epic were known in Palestine at Megiddo (14th cent.), southern Syria (Ugarit, 13th cent.) — here the hero introduces the Flood story himself in first-person narrative style — and at the Hittite capital of Boghazköy.

The most copied and recited Babylonian account of creation was *Enuma Elish* ("When on high . . ."), known, as all literary texts, from its opening words. This was composed in the mid to late 2nd millennium B.C. It was originally written on six tablets, to which a seventh was added later to list the fifty titles of the god Marduk, in whose praise the whole was written in hymnal poetic style. The development of the early pantheon is traced from the primeval sweetwater Apsû and the saltwater Tiâmat to Enki and Ea. There was a clash between the younger noisy gods and the aged Tiâmat, who threatened their destruction. The gods found a champion in Marduk son of Ea, who offered to fight Tiâmat's forces in return for elevation to supreme authority among the gods. He battles with his magic weapons, takes the Tablet of Fate/Destiny from the rebel leader Kingu, and cleaves Tiâmat in two to make the heaven and earth. Next Marduk sets in order the planets and stars and then kills Kingu, whose blood mixed with clay becomes the substance of man. The gods are given their stations and tasks and in return build Babylon and Marduk's temple Esagila there. In the final joyful assembly they recite Marduk's fifty names, which bring together all the epithets of the major gods. The epic is thus a cosmology rather than a creation story. Parallels with Genesis are not generally supported. Lambert has shown that the "deep" (*t^ehôm*, Gen. 1:2) does not presuppose mythological content. The only major similarities between the Hebrew and Babylonian are the existence of water at the initial creation and divine rest at the end. The purposes of the accounts are differently construed.

Other Sumerian epics or myths relate the existence of paradise (Dilmun), the golden age when men and beast did not contend and all men praised the gods in unison. The creation of a woman (nin) is linked with sickness, and other epics mention early medicine, agriculture, horticulture, world peace and harmony.

The epic of the *Anzū* bird (Zū), found in copies from Assyria, Egypt (Amarna), and Elam (Susa), is of Sumerian origin. It relates the recapture of the "tablet of fate," which was thought to control the correct functioning of every element of the universe. The *Descent of Ishtar* (or the Sumerian goddess Inanna) through the seven gates of the underworld in search of her dead husband Dumuzi (Tammuz) is unfinished. It seems that Tammuz was allowed out for six months of the year; the older view that this was a seasonal ritual is now much questioned. The emphasis is on the weeping for his death (as Ezk. 8:14). *Nergal and Ereškigal* tells how Nergal became king of the underworld and *Adapa* how a mortal of divine origin at Eridu broke the south wind which had overturned his boat. Called to answer for this, on the advice of Ea his father he refused the food and drink offered by Anu and thus lost the chance for immortality. This etiological story explains the powers of exorcism granted him and his followers as compensation. The Babylonian Adapa/Oannes was believed to have received the revelation of first things from the gods and so reappears, like Ea, as the original author of a number of works.

Etana, also originally a Sumerian story about this pre-flood king of Kish, describes his desire for a son. The sun god Šamaš introduces him to an eagle on whose back he flies heavenward in an attempt to gain the "plant of birth."

B. God lists. The Babylonian scribes compiled lists of divine names and epithets as part of their school exercises. Since the ranking of the gods (e.g., Marduk) is not the same in all and some are arranged theologically, they show something of the development of religion and the attempt in Middle Babylonian times at a move toward monotheism. The genealogical position of gods and their epithets, which sometimes came to be thought of as separate deities, can also be traced. The elevation of Marduk (Merodach, Jer. 50:2) as chief god of Babylon was complete by the late 1st millennium B.C.

See also RELIGIONS OF THE BIBLICAL WORLD: ASSYRIA AND BABYLONIA II.

C. Wisdom Literature. Babylonian writings concerned with moral and social attitudes, life and nature, and man's evaluation of it based on direct observation, reveal a concern for ethical values and an aesthetic appreciation from the earliest period.

A religious poem *Ludlul Bēl Nēmeqi* ("I will praise the Lord of Wisdom"), which has sometimes been called the Babylonian Job, describes the dilemma of the personal sufferer, as do variants of the same poem (in Akkadian from Ugarit) and the earlier Sumerian "A man and his god." The man is stripped of possessions and smitten with diseases, and no priestly help avails. The action of the gods is inscrutable and he is resigned to his fate. Withal he seems to have preserved faith in his ultimate recovery and vindication following various dream experiences.

The Babylonian *Theodicy* is a dialogue, written in stanzas as an acrostic poem (cf. Ps. 119). The man's misfortunes are contrasted with the prosperity of the ungodly; human effort is worthless, and social justice is lacking. His pious opponent praises the gods who allocate man's fate and recommends acceptance of the good and evil they send equally. Pessimistic literature is represented by a *Dialogue of Man and His God* (*ANET,* pp. 589-591; cf. Ecclesiastes). Precepts include those counseling a king how to behave, with special reference to the Babylonian cult-centers. They promise due rewards or punishment. For the individual many precepts (like Egyp. *sb'ʒyt,* "instruction," and many verses in Proverbs) are based on long experience. They are collections or books of proverbs in Sumerian and Babylonian, some bilingual, and often with no specific arrangement. Some are similar to Proverbs but this indicates only their wide usage in the ancient Near East. Some proverbs are cited in later Aramaic by AHIKAR (whose name appears in cuneiform texts also). Proverbs are found in letters and other literature (as Gen. 10:9; 1 S. 10:12; 1 K. 20:11; Jer. 22:28). Advice and practical instruction are given in a number of texts. One from Ugarit addresses Šube'awelum on leaving home, with special reference to street women, parents, the choice of a wife, buying an ox, fools and wise men. The conclusion is that all is misery and vanity (as in Eccl. 1:17; 12:8). *Counsels of Wisdom* cover different topics in each section: the avoidance of bad companions, altercations, improper speech, pacification of enemies, the undesirability of marrying a slave girl or prostitute, the temptation of being a vizier, deception by friends.

There are satirical dialogues and disputations arguing intrinsic worth, e.g., Winter and Summer; the Pickaxe and the Plough; Tamarisk and Date Palm; Truth and Falsehood; Fox, Dog, Wolf, and Lion; Ox and Horse (cf. 1 Esd. 3:1–4:63). Pre-Aesopic animal fables are grouped according to the principal animal actor. For OT fables see Jgs. 9:7-15; 2 K. 14:19; Isa. 10:15; 29:16; Ezk. 17:3-10; 19:1-14. Folk tales so far recovered are few and didactic in purpose. Humor is apparent in the tale of *The Poor Man of Nippur* who takes revenge for mistreatment by officialdom. The story survives in Babylonian texts from Sultantepe, Nineveh, and in later Arabic sources. Parables are rare in Babylonian literature, as in the OT (cf. 2 S. 12:1-4; Isa. 28:4). So also are allegories (cf. Isa. 5:1-7). Riddles are found copied out in Sumerian school texts together with their solution (cf. Jgs. 14:14; 1 K. 10:1). Love poems or songs relate to the sacred marriage of the king (acting as Tammuz?) and the representative of the goddess of love (contrast Song of Solomon) or to participants in the New Year Festival. Lamentations bewailing the destruction of cities, as Nippur, Lagash, and Ur (cf. Lamentations on the destruction of Jerusalem and Vergil *Aen.* ii.157 on Troy), were probably composed prior to their reconstruction, as a liturgical apology to the deity for the razing of buildings. In a Sumerian text, Lugaldingirra bemoans in hyperbolic terms the death of his father and wife.

D. Omens. The Babylonians believed that what the gods planned in heaven was knowable by direct observation on earth. This led to serious and systematic observation and recording of all events (hence historiography; see VIII above) and especially of unusual actions or aspects of men, animals, plants, and objects. These were recorded in a specific form of protasis (*šumma,* "If/It happened that. . . .") and apodosis (the concomitant result) or prognostication. These were built up into "scientific" texts by diviners (*bārû, mašmāšu*). It is noteworthy that this type of literature, though common in Babylonia, is absent from the OT, which is nevertheless cognizant of these pagan practices.

Astrology, the commonest of omens, led to the Babylonians being renowned as astrologers (*see* ASTROLOGY; CHALDEA VI). Astrological omens were recorded on a series of seventy-seven tablets entitled *Enūma-Anu-Enlil.* Twenty-three tablets cover observations of the moon; others list omens derived from the sun, weather (predominantly clouds, wind, waves, and earthquakes), planets, and fixed stars. Their rising and setting, relation to other planets, eclipses, halos, color, intensity, and duration are all noted. Horoscopes are first found in the 4th cent. B.C., and predict the future of a child according to the astronomical setting of its birth.

Extispicy is the examination of the liver, lungs, gallbladder, kidneys, or intestines of slaughtered animals, usually sheep, to see the god's "writing" there in response to the diviner's prayer. This was usually performed for the king in matters of war or state. The interpreter had available clay models of the organs (examples were found at Hazor and Mari in the west) as well as tablets that gave in standardized form the phenomena to be observed and the predictions, largely relating to historical events and the fate of earlier rulers. These gave the priest a direct affirmative or negative answer to questions posed by him to the gods.

Medical omens are found in an omen series entitled "If the exorcist goes into the house of a patient," which runs to forty tablets beginning in the Old Babylonian period. The main purpose (tablets 3-34) is the diagnosis and prognosis of disease based on external observation, beginning at the hand and working down to the feet. The prognosis (a percursor of Hippocrates' formulas) states whether the patient will live or die, or the length of illness. Other tablets (35-36) relate to pregnancy and to the birth of children (39-40). A further series of omens (*šumma izbu*) is derived from monstrous or multiple births of infants or animals. Physionomical omens were derived from bodily characteristics, eccentricities, the color of hair or skin, location of moles, and mannerisms in speech or gait.

In another type of text, dream omens are usually linked with events. A Dream Book brought together omens derived from activities taking place in dreams. Thus eating (including cannibalism) and traveling to heaven, the underworld, or to a named country or city were made the basis of prognostications. The role of dreams here differs from their usual role in the OT (but cf. Gen. 41:15-32). The largest collection of omens, the series *šumma ālu ina mēlê šakin* ("If a city is set on a hill"), runs to 110 tablets. It appears to have originated in the Middle Babylonian period. These omens refer to incidents in cities, houses, the behavior of or encounter with animals and reptiles of all kinds, fire, agriculture, and human relations. Since the apodosis often refers to national events, these collections made at Uruk in Babylonia (as at Nineveh, Asshur, and Calah in Assyria) may have been compiled for state purposes. Other omens were compiled to interpret the patterns formed by oil on water or the flight of birds.

See also RELIGIONS OF THE BIBLICAL WORLD: ASSYRIA AND BABYLONIA VI.

E. Prophecies. The so-called Akkadian prophecies describe the reigns of unnamed kings or princes, and are cast in the form of predictions describing each rule as "good" or "bad" in a form similar to that commonly found in the apodoses of omens. One appears to predict a reign of twenty-seven years followed by one of seven years, and others associated with historical events of the period Meli-šipak to Enlil-nadin-aḫḫe can be shown to have been written *post eventum*. A few set out as forecasts of unnamed kings who will ascend the throne, and in this are parallel to Dnl. 8:23-25; 11:3-45. (See A. K. Grayson, *Babylonian Historical-Literary Texts* [1975], pp. 24-37, for a dynastic prophecy describing the fall of Assyria, the rise and fall of Babylonia and of Persia, and the rise of the Hellenistic monarchies.) These prophecies are not related to the West Semitic practices at Mari by "ecstatic" priests and priestesses (*muḫḫ[tu]*). The latter were of lower status than the *âpilu* ("answerer"), whose name implies that he was the agent through whom revelations were given after questioning the deity through divination (see D above), the paramount means of knowing the divine will. The prophecies were primarily about the temple and its interests, and the person of the king and his military success.

F. Rituals. Royal rituals are known mostly from Assyrian or Mari sources describing the part the king played in the cult. In Babylon the primary occasion was the New Year Festival (*akītu*). The development of this festival from a seasonal rite to the most important cultic and social event of the Mesopotamian calendar in the cities of Babylon, Uruk, Dilbat, Sippar, Kish, and Ur cannot yet be traced. There were many local variations. At Babylon the god Marduk was led by the king in procession from his temple Esagila (*see* BABYLON IV.H) with other gods who came into the city, as Nabû from Borsippa. (The king had earlier come before the god and had been deprived of his insignia and been granted it back. The Epic of Creation had been recited, as commonly in the ritual.) The procession went out by chariot and barge to the *akītu*-house on the ninth day of the first month. Then the gods in parliament (*Ubšukinna*) decided the fates for the following year, and the "sacred marriage" was sometimes performed. On the eleventh of the month the procession returned amid public rejoicing. The king's legitimate position was not affected by any failure to celebrate the festival. In later Babylonian times the *akītu* was performed on more than one occasion in the year. Descriptions of the New Year Festival, offerings, and ritual (*dullu*) have survived from Uruk in Seleucid times. The ritual feeding (*tākultu*) of deities was associated with the New Year Festival. The daily care of the gods, the sanctuary, and its offerings was the special responsibility of classes of priests.

The individual sufferer had recourse to an incantation-priest who might consult the *Šurpu* ("burning") texts to ascertain the cause. These enumerate all types of sins and petition Marduk, the supreme god of exorcist power, the fire, or other substances that might eradicate the failure. The *Maqlû* series describes the binding, burning, or cursing of figurines representing the man whose illness was due to evil magic. The accompanying prayers invoked or praised the deity who was thought to have been involved.

See also RELIGIONS OF THE BIBLICAL WORLD: ASSYRIA AND BABYLONIA IV.

G. Prayers and Hymns. The "lifting up of hands" prayers (*šu-íl-lá*) were an established part of the ritual from Old Babylonian times. After the invocation and praise to a named god, the worshiper's complaint and request were followed by the words expressing thanks for the blessings to be received. There were lamentations (*šigû*), benedictions (*ikribū*), and prayers for special occasions. In some cases "letter-prayers" of similar form were written and placed before the god's statue. These bore epistolary greeting formulas. Most were petitions for relief from sickness or for long life. This type of text (*Gottesbrief*) is a more extensively used literary form than has hitherto been recognized. There are also examples of letters from a god to a king in response to requests.

Hymns to deities or planets stem from the earliest period. Some are straightforward praise and worship, others are for processional or liturgical use. A few (e.g., hymns to Šamaš) are preceptive hymns replete with ethical injunctions. More than a hundred royal hymns in Sumerian laud the rulers of the dynasties of Ur, Isin, Larsa, and Babylon (i.e., *ca*. 2100-1700 B.C.). The first may be Gudea of Lagash's hymn to Bau (Baba) *ca*. 2150, and the last comes from the Sea Land Dynasty *ca*. 1500 B.C. W. Hallo has argued that these emphasize the theoretical concept of Mesopotamian unity by recognizing a single dynast as the earthly holder of a divinely granted primacy over his fellow rulers. Hymns appear to have been composed freely using existing topoi (cf. "Prayer to the Gods of the Night"). They were also composed for the king's coronation, marriage (cf. Ps. 45), victory, death, and other momentous occasions.

X. Science and Technology.–Babylonian "science" was thought to be by revelation or divine instruction to those initiated into a craft. The secret was transmitted orally or in "obscure" writing. The basic data (the lists), however, were available to all skilled scribes.

A. Astronomy. Texts from the 20th to the 1st cent. B.C. constitute the most significant body of scientific texts from a pre-Hellenistic civilization. Positional notations, decimal and sexagesimal systems, and later a zero mark made possible advanced calculations using basically algebraic methods. For practical purposes multiplication, division, and square and cube root tables were available. Exercises also were of an essentially practical nature (estimating for building or financing, etc.). Geometrical problems show a pre-Pythagorean knowledge of theorem

($\pi = 3\frac{1}{8}$; cf. 1 K. 7:23, $\pi = 3$). By the 7th cent. Babylonian astronomy with its arithmetical methods was concerned with the accurate observation of the appearance and disappearance of the sun, moon, and planets in order to fix the calender. The zodiac was described and various planetary and stellar movements plotted in sufficient detail to lead to predictions. Rules for computing their positions ("procedure texts") and the results were listed ("ephemerides"). The goal of all their lunar theory was to determine the precise length of the month. They aimed to find the place of any heavenly body at a given time and thus predict the new moon, its last visibility, and eclipses. These lists are precursors of modern astronomical and nautical almanacs.

B. Medicine. In addition to the omen-type texts already described (see IX. D above), which gave the diagnosis and prognosis of disease, the Babylonians listed in a pharmaceutical series (uru-anna = *maštakal*) all plants, drugs, and their substitutes. Prescriptions based on these are preserved. Though often combined with magical or psychological medicine using ritual folklore (*ašipūtu*), the purely therapeutic texts outline the symptoms and diagnosis, and give advice to the physician (*asû*) on treatment. Court physicians, as at Babylon, Mari, and Nineveh, were highly skilled and foreigners were accepted. Fevers, women's diseases, and the treatment of wounds were the subject of special study. Epilepsy, jaundice, malaria, rheumatism, and skin diseases ("leprosy") were identified. The pressure points were noted and, in addition to common remedies, some surgery (*šipir bēl imti*) was carried out, e.g., opening a cranial abscess, trepanning, treatment of caruncle of eye (Hammurabi Laws, §§ 215, 218), clearing cutaneous infection, treatment of fractures (and possibly amputation), and what some think was an early attempt at a Caesarean section.

C. Technology. The listing of animals, plants, minerals, etc., led to what may justly be called the first short step toward empirical science. Mineralogy and metallurgy from the 3rd millennium had always some practical end. Thus silver and gold were separated from impurities and assayed *ca.* 2000 B.C., metals were refined by cupellation, and silver and lead smelted by air reduction. Glass, glaze-making, dying, and textile embroidery may have come from the West, for Babylonia was always open to the influence of new ideas through booty taken in war or by trade. Certainly writing (the cuneiform script), the wheel, water clock, seeder plough, and seal-stone cutting seem to have been local and influential inventions which, like the "sciences" of astronomy and medicine, were passed on through Anatolia to ancient Greece.

D. Music. Musical life and practice is known largely from the instruments discovered. Fifty-three different instruments are listed: percussion (drums, cymbals, gongs, and clackers), wind (wood and reed pipes, flutes), and string (harp, lyre, lute). All the instruments of Nebuchadrezzar's orchestra (Dnl. 3:5, 7, 10, 15) are attested in sixth-century texts or archeological finds. The names of nine strings and of the intervals and tunings are listed. Thus the lyres from Ur, strung like the modern Ethiopian *bagana,* were tuned to a scale equivalent to C major or to a seven-tone species similar to, but far antedating, the heptatonic scale known from Greek sources. Musicians and singers of various vocal ranges performed solo or in unison. Šulgi king of Ur claimed to be adept at all musical arts, performing and also tuning and restringing instruments. Tunes (or instruments) to accompany certain hymns, laments, or songs are noted in some texts (cf. the headings of some Psalms). No written musical notation has been identified with certainty.

XI. Institutions.–A. *Social System.* The Babylonian concept of law required that all men be considered equal, but at all times there were distinct groups (prisoners of wars, debtors, etc.) who were enslaved. Outside the palace and temple these were not numerous and played a minor part in the economy until the late 1st millennium. A small group won special rights (tax and other exemptions) which enabled them to attain privilege and power. Contrary to many interpretations, the laws (e.g., Hammurabi) rarely refer to a "freeman" (*awēlum* also stands for "man"), though they legislated for dependents of the palace (*muškēnum*) and slaves (*wardum*) in Old Babylonian times. These classes are rarely noted outside these texts. Slaves had privileges, could marry a freeman or woman, hold property or office, and earn redemption. All men could be called up for military or corvée duties (though substitutes could be provided). The corvée was mainly for the constant renewal required of irrigation ditches due to salination, and for harvest or special works. Army service soon called for mercenaries in view of the constant campaigning in Chaldean times.

The main distinction was between nomads (or seminomad tribesmen) and the urban population. The interaction and absorption of nomads led to many political changes. The major cities (Babylon and Nippur) had a unique status and were usually free of royal taxation.

The economy was primarily agricultural. Since this was dependent on security and irrigation, control of land centered in the cities and manorial estates. Villages were comparatively few. The seminomads were dependent on their wool-bearing sheep and goats or, in the marshes, on fishing. The temple and palace held large estates, which enabled them to support flocks, fishing, industry (mainly weaving; cf. Josh. 7:21), shipping, and trade. Guilds of craftsmen attached to temples flourished from Neo-Babylonian times.

Trade was by traveling agents, financed by traders (*tamkaru*) and protected by interstate agreement. Thus Babylonia was linked with Egypt, the Mediterranean, Persia, Arabia, and possibly India. Finance houses (and tax-farmers) sprang up under the Achaemenids and their successors.

B. The King. The king (LU.GAL/*šarru*) was originally the chief temple official (en-si) or city governor holding supreme power over a tribe or district. Less is known of his functions in Babylonia than in Assyria, but in Babylonia he held a lesser place in the cult and never acted as chief priest. With the advent of the Amorites there was a new concept of kingship and an increasing distinction between palace and temple. The king was surrounded by court administrators headed by a vizier (*sukallu*) after the Middle Babylonian period. His palace acted as state treasury, receiving tribute, taxes, and dues, and redistributing them in kind through the stores and workshops to the army, civil service, and retainers, many of whom were also tied to the palace by services (*ilku*) due on their crown holdings. There is no certainty that kings of the Ur III or Amorite periods were considered divine, though they shared in the splendor of deity with robes and horned headdresses while acting on behalf of the state god. They were not worshiped, though their names were sometimes prefixed with the determinative used for divine names. It is probable that this, like some of the hymns addressed to them, was part of the ancestral cult after death.

C. Cities. Cities played an important part from their early development in Babylonia. It seems that the early city assembly (*puḫrum*) exercised certain primitive democratic rights. The "city fathers" were consulted on questions of war and peace (as 1 K. 20:7f.; 2 Ch. 25:17).

Gilgamesh of Uruk, facing an ultimatum from Agga of Kish, appealed first to the elders and then to the "young warriors," as did Rehoboam (1 K. 12:8). This shows a certain lack of freedom in the independent exercise of the ruler's prerogative of decision, at least in matters requiring national support expressed in the vox populi. The Babylonian kings paid particular attention to the maintenance of the fabric, funds, and offerings of the main sanctuaries and thus usually avoided friction between the palace and temple.

These temples acted in much the same way as the palace, being the economic center of large estates that supplied their needs. The *šangû*-priest headed the administration. In Neo-Babylonian times royal appointees (*šatammu*) sat with the committees of priests and citizens who managed temple affairs. Part of the temple upkeep was derived from temple taxes, collection boxes (*quppu*), and votive gifts.

XII. Arts.–The most distinctive characteristic of Babylonian architecture was the temple-tower (*ziqqurratu*). Originally this was a small temple on a raised platform (as at 'Uqair); it was then placed at a higher level above the surrounding town (the Diyala city oval temples). Later the temple tower became a series of recessed stepped platforms one above the other rising to three (Ur-Nammu ziggurat at Ur) or to seven stages surmounted by a small chapel (Babylon). Ascent was by direct staircase, or spiral stairs or slopes. These temple-towers sometimes stood within their own walled enclosures adjacent to the temple proper. *See* BABEL, TOWER OF X.

In Babylonia the principal building material was sun-dried or kiln-baked clay brick, sometimes with the royal builder's name stamped upon it. Bitumen and mud mortar were available locally. Despite the limitations of the material, domes, barrel-vaults, or facades decorated with columns, plastered in color or ornamented with mosaics of colored clay cones (Early Dynastic Uruk), are found. Some Kassite reliefs were made by the insertion of premolded bricks. In Nebuchadrezzar's restoration of Babylon much use was made of bricks with colored glaze surfaces.

The temple, like the palace, had storerooms built around complexes of courtyards. The main sanctuary was approached across one of these paved courts in which were wells or basins for lustrations. The crowned and bedecked statue of the god stood within the small dark *naós*. The commonest plan required the worshiper to enter and then turn to face the deity from the antecella. Wayside shrines and domestic chapels have been excavated.

Stone was used for boundary stones (*kudurru*) engraved with symbols, for life-size or smaller statues (e.g., the Warka head, Gudea statues), the stelae of laws (Hammurabi), and commemorative reliefs (Ur-Nammu). All of these were stationed in temples. The commonest use of small stones, apart from jewelry, was for the characteristic cylinder or stamp seal, which was also used as a personal amulet. The iconography is important for the study of religion. The size, stone, and style of workmanship varied according to the provenance, period, and purpose of each seal. Stones such as haematite in Old Babylonia and chalcedony in Neo-Babylonia, scenes of a worshiper introduced to a deity, and conical stamp seals in Neo-Babylonia, are particularly characteristic of the Babylonian seal-cutter's craft.

XIII. Legacy.–Babylonia early influenced Egypt, giving that country the cylinder seal and its system of cuneiform script, which also influenced the writing of the Elamites, Syrians, and Hittites. (*See* WRITING.) Babylonian literary forms and educational practices may have influenced the OT scribes, though the contents, historiography, prophecy, and laws of the OT are unique. Babylonia's sciences and military might played their part in the spread of her ideas, which were incorporated into succeeding civilizations.

Bibliography.–*CAH*; *ANET*; A. Heidel, *The Gilgamesh Epic and OT Parallels* (1949); *Babylonian Genesis* (1951); J. Bottéro, *La Religion babylonienne* (1952); Wiseman, *CCK*; S. N. Kramer, *From the Tablets of Sumer* (1956); W. G. Lambert, *Babylonian Wisdom Literature* (1960); H. W. F. Saggs, *The Greatness that was Babylon* (1962); A. L. Oppenheim, *Ancient Mesopotamia* (1964); S. N. Kramer, *The Sumerians* (1964); J. Brinkman, *A Political History of Post-Kassite Babylonia, 1158-722 B.C.* (1968); W. G. Lambert and A. R. Millard, *Atra-Ḫasīs: The Babylonian Story of the Flood* (1969). D. J. WISEMAN

BABYLONIA AND ASSYRIA, RELIGION OF. *See* RELIGIONS OF THE BIBLICAL WORLD: ASSYRIA AND BABYLONIA.

BABYLONIAN CAPTIVITY. *See* CAPTIVITY.

BABYLONIANS [Heb. *bᵉnê-ḇāḇel*]. The inhabitants of BABYLONIA. They were among the colonists planted in Samaria by the Assyrians (Ezr. 4:9). The "picture of Babylonians" (Ezk. 23:15) refers to the bas-reliefs that decorated the walls of Babylonian palaces. The reports of them heard in Jerusalem or copies of them seen there awakened the nation's desire for these unknown lovers, of which Judah had ample occasion to repent (vv. 17, 23; cf. 2 K. 24).

BACA, VALE OF bā'kə [Heb. *bāḵā*] (Ps. 84:6); NEB "thirsty valley." A valley so named because it contained trees that exuded resin or gum, perhaps several species of balsam. The valley of Rephaim has been suggested, but the identification is uncertain (cf. 2 S. 5:23f.; 1 Ch. 14:14f.).

BACCHIDES bak'ə-dēz [Gk. *Bakchidēs*]. Ruler over Mesopotamia and a faithful friend of both Antiochus Epiphanes and Demetrius Soter. He established at the request of the latter the rulership over Judea for Alcimus, who, desiring to become high priest, had made false accusations against Judas Maccabeus (1 Macc. 7:8ff.; Josephus *Ant.* xii.10.2). Bacchides was sent the second time to Judea after the Syrian general Nicanor was killed near Adasa and Judas Maccabeus had gained control of the government (1 Macc. 9:1ff.). After an unsuccessful battle near Bethbasi he was forced to make peace with Jonathan, the brother of Judas (9:58ff.; *Ant.* xiii.1). In 1 Macc. 10:12 and 2 Macc. 8:30 reference is made to the strongholds Bacchides built during his second campaign against Jerusalem (1 Macc. 9:50). A. L. BRESLICH

BACCHURUS ba-kū'rəs (1 Esd. 9:24, AV, NEB). *See* ZACCUR **6.**

BACCHUS bak'əs [Gk. *Dionysos,* later *Bakchos*]. The Greek and Roman god of wine, whose rites in the pre-Christian era were synonymous with drunkenness and immorality. His worship was probably introduced into Egypt under Ptolemy Philopator (227-204 B.C.). Antiochus IV Epiphanes, endeavoring to hellenize the Judean Jews, compelled them to participate in the Dionysian rites (2 Macc. 6:7). Some years later Nicanor, when he was fighting Judas Maccabeus, threatened to destroy the Jerusalem temple and build a shrine to Bacchus on the site (2 Macc. 14:33).

See also DIONYSUS. R. K. H.

BACENOR bə-sē'nôr [Gk. *Bakēnōr*]. An officer in the army of Judas Maccabeus engaged in war against Gorgias, governor of Idumea (2 Macc. 12:35, AV, RSV; cf. NEB "Tubian"). See Josephus *Ant.* xii.8.6.

BACHRITES bak'rīts. The AV for "Becherites," the descendants of BECHER (Nu. 26:35).

BACK. The "back" (Heb. *'ᵃḥôr*; AV "back parts") of Yahweh is referred to in Ex. 33:23 as an anthropomorphic image signifying the reflection of the divine glory, in contrast to the "face" of Yahweh (vv. 20, 23). The expression "cast . . . behind the back (*gaw*)," as used in 1 K. 14:9; Ezk. 23:35 of the Lord as object, in Neh. 9:26 of His law, and in Isa. 38:17 (*gēw*) of the sins of Hezekiah, means "forget utterly," "reject," or "neglect."

BACKBITE. To slander the absent, like a dog biting behind the back, where one cannot see; to go about as a talebearer. The only RSV occurrence is Prov. 25:23, which speaks of "a backbiting tongue," lit. "a tongue of secrecy" (Heb. *seṯer*).
See also SLANDER.

BACKSIDE. In the AV archaic for BACK (Ex. 3:1; 26:12).

BACKSLIDING. *See* APOSTASY.

BADGER. *See* ROCK BADGER.

BAEAN bē'ən, **SONS OF** [Gk. *hyioí Baian*]; AV BEAN; NEB BAEANITES. An unknown tribe hostile to the Jews (1 Macc. 5:4). Their hatred of the Jews' religion and attempts to disrupt the rebuilding of their sanctuary duplicated the conspiracy of Sanballat and his confederates against the restoration of Jerusalem and the temple in the days of Nehemiah (cf. Neh. 4:7f.). They were utterly exterminated by Judas Maccabeus, who burned alive, in towers, many of the imprisoned people. Cf. Beon in Nu. 32:3.

BAETERUS bē'tər-əs (1 Esd. 5:17, NEB). *See* BAITERUS.

BAG [Heb. *kᵉlî, kîs, ḥāriṭ, ṣᵉrôr*, vb. *ṣûr*; Gk. *pḗra*]; AV also SACK, VESSEL, SCRIP (NT); NEB also BAGGAGE (Gen. 43:11), BUNCH (Cant. 1:13), PURSE (Hag.1:6), PACK (NT). Bags of various kinds are mentioned in the Bible, but the type of bag intended is often unclear in English translations.

Cotton bag from Faiyum, Egypt. Formed from two pieces of netted material, with a woolen drawstring (Oriental Institute, University of Chicago)

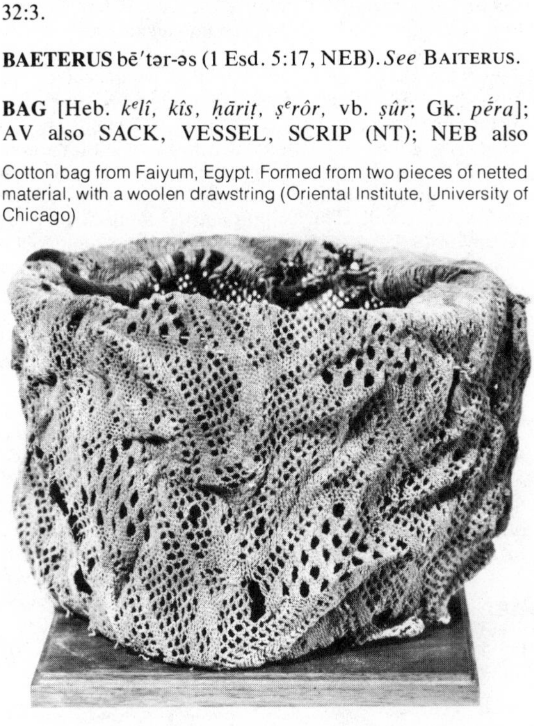

The "shepherd's bag" (Heb. *kᵉlî*) of 1 S. 17:40 is given the specific designation *yalqûṭ*, which the AV renders "scrip," the RSV "wallet," and the NEB "pouch." This "bag" of the shepherd or "haversack" of the traveler was of a size sufficient for one or more days' provisions. It was made of the skin of animals, ordinarily undressed, like most of the other "bags" of ancient times, and was carried slung across the shoulder. This is the "scrip for the journey" (Gk. *pḗra*) mentioned in Mt. 10:10 par., AV ("scrip" is now obsolete; cf. RSV "bag," NEB "pack").

The small bag (Heb. *kîs*) used by merchants for carrying their weights is mentioned in Dt. 25:13; Prov. 16:11; Mic. 6:11. The same word designates a money purse in Prov. 1:14; Isa. 46:6.

The *ṣᵉrôr* was often a cloth tied up in a bundle, or a sack tied with a string, and was used for carrying jewels and money (Prov. 7:20; Hag. 1:6). A figurative usage occurs in Job 14:17, "my transgression would be sealed up in a bag"; this may refer to the practice of putting a seal upon the knot of the bag. The verb *ṣûr*, "tie up in a bag," occurs in 2 K. 12:10 (MT 11). The NEB reads this verse differently: they "melted down the silver . . . and weighed it."

The Heb. *ḥāriṭ* (Arab. *ḥariṭat*) is used, on the one hand, for a "bag" large enough to hold a talent of silver (see 2 K. 5:23, "bound two talents of silver in two bags"), and, on the other, for a lady's dainty satchel, such as is found in Isa. 3:22 (RSV "handbag"; wrongly rendered "crisping pins" in AV). This is the most adequate Hebrew word for a large bag.
See also MONEY BOX; PURSE. J. W. D. H.

BAGGAGE [Heb. *kᵉlî*] (1 S. 10:22; 17:22; etc.; Isa. 10:28; Jer. 46:19; Ezk. 12:3-12); AV CARRIAGE, STUFF, "furnish" (Jer. 46:19); NEB also THINGS, STORES, BAGGAGE-TRAIN, BELONGINGS; [Gk. *aposkeuḗ*] (Jth. 7:2; 1 Macc. 9:35, 39; 2 Macc. 12:21); NEB BAGGAGE TRAIN. The words denote various kinds of portable equipment for travel or for battle, or supplies (Lat. *impedimenta*) for an army.

The Heb. *kᵉlî* is a very general word meaning "article," "implement," "vessel," etc. Its various contexts indicate its use for "luggage" (1 S. 17:22), "stores" (1 S. 30:24, where David decrees that those who stay behind to guard the supplies shall share equally in the spoils of victory with those who fight), and "belongings" packed for exile (Ezk. 12). The "keeper of the baggage" with whom David left his things is called a "quartermaster" in the NEB (1 S. 17:22).

In the Apocrypha, Gk. *aposkeuḗ* again means the supplies of an army. The verb *aposkeuázomai* occurs in Acts 21:15, where the NEB has "packed our baggage," the RSV "made ready." J. W. D. H.

BAGO bā'gō (1 Esd. 8:40, AV, NEB). *See* BIGVAI **1**.

BAGOAS bə-gō'əs [Gk. *Bagṓas*]. A personal aide to Holofernes (Jth. 12:11f.; 13:1, 3; 14:14).

BAGOI bā'goi (1 Esd. 5:14, AV, NEB). *See* BIGVAI **1**.

BAGPIPE [Aram. *sûmpōnyâ, sûppōnyâ*] (Dnl. 3:5, 10, 15); AV DULCIMER; NEB MUSIC. The Aramaic is probably a loanword from the Greek (*symphōnía*), and is usually thought to indicate a bagpipe or similar musical instrument (cf. BDB, p. 1104; KoB, p. 1103). A contemporary Greek usage is in Polybius xxvi.31, where the *symphōnía* is said to have been played, along with the horn, at the feasts of Antiochus Epiphanes (cf. E. J. Young, comm. [1949] *in loc.*).

The ancient bagpipe was made of goatskin and had two pipes; it is uncertain, however, whether it existed at the time the story of Daniel takes place. J. W. D. H.

BAHARUM bə-här'əm [Heb. *habbaḥ^a rûmî*] (1 Ch. 11:33); AV BAHARUMITE; NEB "from Bahurim." A gentilic form, probably of BAHURIM, referring to Azmaveth, one of David's mighty men.

BAHURIM bə-hū'rim [Heb. *baḥûrîm*–'young men']; prob. also BAHARUM (1 Ch. 11:33); AV BAHARUMITE, also BARHUMITE (2 S. 23:31). A site E of Jerusalem in the territory of Benjamin, on the old Jerusalem-to-Jericho highway, upon which David fled during the uprising of his son Absalom (2 S. 16:5). The Talmud locates it E of Mt. Scopus near Anathoth at modern Râs eṭ-Ṭmîm. At a nearby brook, Wâdī Farah, Abner parted Paltiel from his wife Michal as she was being returned to David (2 S. 3:16). It was the home of Shimei, a man from the house of Saul who cursed as he stoned the fleeing David (2 S. 16:5; 19:16; 1 K. 2:8). In Bahurim, Jonathan and Ahimaaz, sons of the priests Abiathar and Zadok and spies for David, were hidden in a well by a loyal woman (2 S. 17:18-20).

Comparing the variant gentilic forms in 2 S. 23:31 and in 1 Ch. 11:33 it has been conjectured that Azmaveth, one of David's mighty men, was a native son of the village Bahurim. F. E. YOUNG

BAITERUS bā'tə-rəs [Gk. *Baitērous*]; AV METEKUS; NEB BAETERUS. A family that returned from exile with Zerubbabel (1 Esd. 5:17; omitted in Ezr. 2 and Neh. 7).

BAITHER bā'thər [Gk. *Baithēr*]. A town of Judah listed only in Josh. 15:59, NEB, following the LXX (v. 59a).

BAJITH bā'jith [Heb. *bayiṯ*–'house'] (Isa. 15:2, AV). If a proper noun (probably correct), a Moabite town mentioned with Dibon; if a common noun, which requires some textual change (the MT is supported by 1QIsa[a]), either "house of" or (as RSV) "daughter of" (Dibon). That the definite article is used supports this rendering. Cf. the construct form "Beth-" frequently used in compounds. The NEB has "the people of Dibon go up."

D. B. PECOTA

BAKBAKKAR bak-bak'ər [Heb. *baqbaqqar*] (1 Ch. 9:15). A Levite of the sons of Asaph, living in Jerusalem; perhaps the same as Bakbukiah of Neh. 11:17.

BAKBUK bak'bo͞ok [Heb. *baqbûq*; Gk. *Bakbouk, Akoub, Akouph, Akoum*]; AV Apoc. ACUB; NEB Apoc. ACUM. A family that returned from exile with Zerubbabel (Ezr. 2:51; Neh. 7:53; 1 Esd. 5:31).

BAKBUKIAH bak-bə-kī'ə [Heb. *baqbuqyâ*].

1. A Levite who lived in Jerusalem after the return from exile (Neh. 11:17); perhaps the same as Bakbakkar of 1 Ch. 9:15.

2. A Levite who returned from exile with Zerubbabel (Neh. 12:9).

3. A Levite and guard of the temple storehouse (Neh. 12:25).

BAKEMEATS. Archaic in Gen. 40:17, AV, for "every kind of food which the baker prepares" (NEB); Heb. *ma'^a kāl ma'^a śēh 'ōpeh*.

BAKER [Heb. *'ōpeh*]. The term was derived from a verb meaning "bake bread," but from an early period included miscellaneous cooking also (Gen. 40:1–41:13; 1 S. 8:13; Hos. 7:4). Bread was usually baked in an oven or on the surfaces of heated stones. Confections were baked in pans or on griddles (Lev. 2:4ff.). The titles in Gen. 40:1, etc., belonged to high Egyptian court officials; and the duties of the holders may well have undergone significant modification from the time the offices were first devised. Hosea is supposed to have been a baker, but there is no evidence to support this contention. R. K. H.

BAKERS' STREET [Heb. *ḥûṣ hā'ôpîm*] (Jer. 37:21); NEB STREET OF THE BAKERS. An area in Jerusalem where the bakers had their ovens and shops. Unlike modern Western cities, where this would be considered wasteful competition, the cities of the ancient Middle East (and even the modern Middle East) had areas where various crafts and guilds were concentrated. Jeremiah received a daily ration of a loaf of bread from the bakers' street by order of King Zedekiah (Jer. 37:21). W. S. L. S.

BAKING. *See* BREAD I, IV.

BAKING PAN. *See* BREAD IV; PAN.

BALAAM bā'ləm [Heb. *bil'ām*–etymology disputed, perhaps 'devourer'; Gk. *Balaam*]. A man of Pethor, a city in Mesopotamia lying S of Carchemish; the son of Beor. The narrative describing this enigmatic individual is contained in Nu. 22:2–24:25. Subsequent allusions to him are found in Nu. 31:8, 16; Dt. 23:4f.; Josh. 13:22; 24:9f.; Neh. 13:2; Mic. 6:5; 2 Pet. 2:15f.; Jude 11; Rev. 2:14.

I. The Narrative.–Balak king of Moab, alarmed at the encampment of the Israelites in the Jordan Valley adjacent to his own territory after their overwhelming victories over the Amorites, entered into an alliance with the Midianites and sought the aid of Balaam, a renowned diviner by whose agency he hoped that Israel might be brought under a curse. Balaam's hesitancy in responding to this invitation, which carried with it a handsome reward, is ascribed to his deference to the will of Yahweh (Nu. 22:8, 13). At the same time he appears from the first to be rather less than wholehearted in his acquiescence to Yahweh's will. This impression is confirmed by his reception of Balak's second and more imposing deputation. God permitted Balaam this time to accompany the messengers but admonished him of his complete subservience to the divine will (Nu. 22:20f.). His encounter with the angel of Yahweh and the rebuke administered to him miraculously by his ass serve to show that this permission was granted to Balaam as a judgment upon him for his cupidity (cf. 2 Pet. 2:15f.).

Having reached Moab, Balak led Balaam up to the heights above the Dead Sea whence he might gain a view of Israel encamped below. But neither elaborate sacrificial ritual, nor changing position from one peak to another, availed to produce the desired curse upon Israel. Instead, Balaam was gripped by the Spirit of God (Nu. 24:2) and was powerless to do other than pronounce blessing upon blessing. In all he uttered four memorable oracles (Heb. *māšāl* is used in each case and signifies here a "prophetic figurative discourse" [BDB]). In the final oracle he adumbrates, among other things,

Israel's conquests under the monarchy and in particular the subjugation of Moab (Nu. 24:17).

This concluded, Balak and Balaam part company and the latter is described as returning "to his place" (Nu. 24:25). It is widely held that this implies that Balaam returned to his home in Mesopotamia. Yet Nu. 25 is represented as the sequel to the narrative concerning Balaam. The idolatry of the Israelites in participating in the immoral rites associated with the worship of Baal-peor is attributed to "the counsel of Balaam" (Nu. 31:16) and it is twice affirmed that Balaam was put to death by the Israelites (Nu. 31:8; Josh. 13:22). For this reason some dispute the location of Pethor in Mesopotamia and claim the support of the Samaritan Pentateuch and LXX that it was located in Ammonite territory (cf. Marsh, *IB*, II, *in loc.*).

II. Alleged Inconsistencies.–That Balaam's character poses problems can scarcely be denied. A non-Israelite, he yet acknowledged the supremacy of Yahweh and evinced a desire to please Him (Nu. 22:34; 24:1). At the same time he was famed for his skill as a diviner (Heb. *qôsēm*) and for his ability to use enchantments (Heb. *n^eḥāšîm* — the noun occurs only twice in the OT, in Nu. 23:23; 24:1; the cognate verb *nāḥaš* occurs frequently); both terms are used subsequently in the OT in connection with the false prophets of Israel (cf. Dt. 18:10; Ezk. 13:6; Mic. 3:7, 11; etc.). His prophecies were clearly given to him by Yahweh (Nu. 23:5, 16) and were uttered under the constraint and inspiration of the divine Spirit (Nu. 24:2).

At first sight what is most perplexing of all is that, although God had given Balaam permission to go with Balaak's second deputation, "God's anger was kindled because he went" (Nu. 22:22). A closer examination of the narrative suggests that this apparent inconsistency arises from Balaam's character. The categorical prohibition of Nu. 22:12 was modified as a judicial penalty for Balaam's venality.

Many scholars accept the inconsistencies as real and not merely apparent. Some allege that the unfavorable references to Balaam are later additions attempting to discredit a heathen prophet who appears to act as a true spokesman of Yahweh. Various attempts have been made to analyze the narrative into its original sources, but no suggested analysis has met with universal approval. Source critics concur in regarding the narrative about the ass and the angel of Yahweh (Nu. 22:22-35a) as from a source different from that of the rest of the story, viz., J. The oracles, which are in poetic form, are now held to be earlier than the prose narrative, having been committed to writing, it is conjectured, perhaps as early as the 10th cent. (Albright). The sequel recording Balaam's death and charging him with responsibility for Israel's sin in the worship of Baal-peor (Nu. 31:1-54) is unanimously ascribed to P.

III. The Oracles.–The oracles of Balaam (Nu. 23:7-10, 18-24; 24:3-9, 15-24) are significant alike for their content and for the accompanying account of the experience of the prophet himself. The first two oracles are directly attributed to the activity of Yahweh, who "put a word in [Balaam's] mouth" (23:3, 16). Yet it would appear from 24:1 that on both occasions he had recourse to divination. It is noteworthy that the two final oracles are introduced with precisely the same words (24:3, 15) and imply a measure of progress in Balaam's spiritual experience. He speaks of himself as "the man whose eye is opened" (cf. BDB, p. 1060 [*šāṯam*]), as if he has come to see the worthlessness of heathen divination and has come to recognize that he must henceforth forego all effort to turn Yahweh from His purpose to bless Israel. The manner of his inspiration also undergoes a change. The apparently somewhat mechanical communication of Yahweh's word in the delivery of the first two oracles is replaced by the direct operation of the Spirit of God upon him (Nu. 24:2b).

In the first two oracles Balaam declares his impotence to curse Israel when Yahweh is manifestly intent on blessing them. He acknowledges their uniqueness as a people. Unlike the other nations Israel had no use for divination and augury (Nu. 23:23, RV). God Himself was among them and by His counsel they were guided. Having enlarged upon Israel's prosperity and invincibility as the outcome of their deliverance from Egypt, Balaam proceeds in the third oracle to affirm positively, "Blessed be everyone who blesses you, and cursed be everyone who curses you" (24:9). The last of the oracles is the most striking of them all. General predictions of Israel's future prosperity give way to specific details. The "star out of Jacob" and the "scepter" (v. 17) undoubtedly point beyond the military conquests of David (though this is widely disputed; cf. *NBC*), and must ultimately be given messianic import (cf. Gen. 49:10, and KD). The *terminus ad quem* of the prophecy is not agreed. The reference to ships from KITTIM (v. 24) is of particular interest in view of the allusion in Dnl. 11:30 and subsequent references in the literature of the Qumrân sect.

IV. Balaam's Character.–Though an element of mystery surrounds Balaam in the OT narratives, the Scriptures leave us in no doubt as to what conclusions to draw with regard to his character. He is represented as the archetype of the false teachers of the Christian Church who pervert the truth of the gospel in the interests of personal gain (2 Pet. 2:15) and under the guise of Christian liberty advocate compromise with the world (Rev. 2:14).

Bibliography.–Comms. on Numbers in *ICC*, *CBSC*, *IB*; S. Mowinckel, *ZAW*, 48 (1930), 233-271; O. Eissfeldt, *ZAW*, 57 (1939), 212-241; W. F. Albright, *JBL*, 63 (1944), 207-233.

J. C. J. WAITE

BALAC bā'lak (Rev. 2:14, AV). *See* BALAK.

BALADAN bal'ə-dən [Heb. *bal^adān*]. In 2 K. 20:12; Isa. 39:1, the father of MERODACH-BALADAN king of Babylon (721-710; 704 B.C.), whose native name was Marduk-apla-iddina II.

BALAH bā'lə [Heb. *bālâ*; Gk. *Bōla*]. An unidentified town in southwest Palestine in the territory of Simeon (Josh. 19:3). It is called Bilhah in 1 Ch. 4:29 and may be identified with BAALAH in Judah (Josh. 15:29).

BALAK bā'lak [Heb. *bālāq*–'devastator'; Gk. *Balak* (Rev. 2:14)]; AV NT BALAC. King of Moab, mentioned in connection with the story of BALAAM (Nu. 22:24; cf. Josh. 24:9; Jgs. 11:25; Mic. 6:5; Rev. 2:14). He hired Balaam to pronounce a curse on the Israelites.

BALAMON bal'ə-mən [Gk. *Balamōn*]; AV BALAMO. In the field between Balamon and Dothaim, Manasses the husband of Judith was buried (Jth. 8:3). Cf. Baal-hamon (Cant. 8:11).

BALANCE [Heb. *mō'znayim*, the usual word, a dual form referring to the two scale pans; *qāneh* (Isa. 46:6), lit. "reed" or "staff" and thus the beam of a balance; *peles* (Prov. 16:11; Isa. 40:12), a balance as being level; Gk.

zygós, basically "yoke," used of the beam of a balance in Rev. 6:5].

The form of the balance has hardly altered since OT times. Egyptian and Assyrian sculptures and paintings show portable balances with the crossbeam suspended from a cord or hook at the center, held in the hand, with a pan hanging from each end (*ANEP*, nos. 117, 133). For weighing large quantities or heavy objects the beam was balanced on a fixed stand (*ANEP*, nos. 360, 639). In the Roman period the steelyard came into general use. Instead of an equiarmed beam with two pans, the beam was suspended from a point nearer to the one end from which hung the pan. On the other part weights were hung at graduated spaces from the fulcrum.

Before the introduction of coinage (i.e., pieces of precious metal of guaranteed standard weight), exchange often involved weighing the money (Gen. 23:16; Jer. 32:10). A properly constructed balance would give accurate results, but the owner could easily cheat by shortening one arm slightly so that the object placed in the pan on that side appeared to be lighter than it actually was. Such underhand practice is repeatedly condemned in Scripture ("A false balance is an abomination to the Lord, but a just weight is his delight" [Prov. 11:1; cf. 20:23; 16:11; Hos. 12:7; Am. 8:5; Mic. 6:11]) and in other ancient writings (cf. e.g., *ANET*, p. 388b). By law Israelites were required to be fair in this as in all their business (Lev. 19:36).

See also WEIGHTS AND MEASURES. A. R. MILLARD

BALASAMUS bə-las′ə-məs (1 Esd. 9:43, AV). *See* BAALSAMUS.

BALBAIM bal-bā′əm [Gk. *Belbaim*] (Jth. 7:3); AV BELMAIM; NEB BELBAIM. A place near Dothan, perhaps the same as BELMAIN.

BALD LOCUST. *See* LOCUST.

BALDNESS; MAKE BALD; BALD HEAD; etc. [Heb. *qorḥâ* (Isa. 3:24; Ezk. 7:18; etc.), *qāraḥ* (Jer. 16:6; Ezk. 27:31; etc.), *qērē(a)ḥ* (Lev. 13:40; 2 K. 2:23), *qāraḥaṯ* (Lev. 13:42f.), *gabbaḥaṯ* (Lev. 13:42f.), *gibbē(a)ḥ* (Lev. 13:41)]; NEB also SHAVE, SHORN, "hair is torn," etc.; **TONSURE** [*qorḥâ*] (Lev. 21:5); AV BALDNESS; NEB BALD PATCHES. The reference in the Bible to baldness is not to the natural loss of hair, but to baldness produced by shaving the head. This was practiced as a mark of mourning for the dead (Lev. 21:5; Isa. 15:2; 22:12), or as the result of any disaster (Am. 8:10; Mic. 1:16). The custom arose from the hair's being regarded as a special ornament. Such shaving of the head was the custom of the people of the land, and the Israelites were strictly forbidden to practice it (Lev. 21:5; Dt. 14:1). To call one a "bald head" was an epithet of contempt, and was sometimes applied to persons who were not naturally bald. It was the epithet applied by certain infidel young men to Elisha (2 K. 2:23f.). In a figurative sense it is used to express the barrenness of the country (Jer. 47:5).

See also HAIR. J. W. KAPP

BALL [Heb. *dûr*]. A rare word occurring only in Isa. 22:18 and referring to a round object. Cf. the translation "circle" for the same Hebrew term in 29:3. *See also* GAMES.

BALLAD SINGERS [Heb. *hammôšᵉlîm*] (Nu. 21:27); AV "they that speak in proverbs"; NEB BARDS. Professional compounders of proverbial sayings, whose compositions resembled folk songs.

Egyptian goldsmiths determining weights with a balance. Wall painting from the tomb of Amenemhet at Beni Hasan (12th Dynasty, 1971-1928 B.C.) (Egypt Exploration Society)

BALM [Heb. *ṣᵉrî, ṣᵒrî*; Gk. *rētínē*]; NEB also BALSAM (Gen. 43:11; Ezk. 27:17). An aromatic resin mentioned six times in the Bible and claiming widespread therapeutic usage in the ancient Near East. Its true identity is nonetheless difficult to establish. It was brought by Ishmaelites journeying from Gilead to Egypt (Gen. 37:25). In Gen. 43:11 it was included in the gifts sent by Jacob to Joseph, while Ezk. 27:17 mentioned it as one of the Judean exports to Tyre. Classical writers referred to balm by a variety of names, and appear to have alluded mainly to *Balsamodendron opobalsamum* L. or BALM OF GILEAD. This is not a Palestinian shrub, however, being native to Arabia. Strabo and Pliny recorded that it grew at Jericho, but it does not exist there today.

In Jeremiah (8:22; 46:11; 51:8) its medicinal properties as an unguent and sedative are referred to figuratively, and probably here as in Gen. 37:25 the Jericho balsam, *Balanites aegyptiaca* (L.) Delile, was envisaged. This small shrub still grows in North Africa, and yields a sticky exudate of reputed medicinal value. Since healing qualities are not mentioned, the allusion in Gen. 43:11 may be to the mastic tree, *Pistacia lentiscus* L., from which a yellow aromatic resin was derived by incising the branches. Balm has dropped out of modern pharmacopoeias. R. K. H.

BALM OF GILEAD. In antiquity this substance was reputed for its medicinal qualities, but it presents problems of identification. It has been held to be the aromatic resin exuded by the shrub *Balsamodendron opobalsamum* L., otherwise known as *B. gileadense* or *Commiphora opobalsamum* (L.) Engl. Perhaps no single shrub was envisaged, however, since the substance received its name because it was exported from Gilead to Egypt and Phoenicia (Gen. 37:25; Ezk. 27:17). R. K. H.

BALNUUS bal-nū′əs (1 Esd. 9:31, AV, NEB). *See* BELNUUS.

BALSAM. *See* SPICE; BALM; INCENSE.

BALSAM TREES [Heb. *bāḵā'*; Gk. *klauthmṓn*] (2 S. 5:23f.; 1 Ch. 14:14f.); AV MULBERRY TREES; NEB ASPENS. In these passages, as probably in Lev. 23:40; 26:36; Ps. 137:2; Isa. 7:2 (*see* WILLOW), the references appear to be to a species of aspen, perhaps the Euphrates aspen (*Populus euphratica* Oliv.), which is distributed throughout Palestine. Mulberry leaves are softly textured, and do not rustle in the breeze.

BALTHASAR bal-tha′zər.

1. (Bar. 1:11, AV). *See* BELSHAZZAR.

2. The supposed name of one of the three Magi who according to legend visited Jesus at Bethlehem: Melchior from Nubia, Balthasar from Godolia, and Caspar from Tharsis.

BAMAH bä′mə, bā′mə [Heb. *bāmâ*–'high place']; NEB "hill-shrine." The word appears in Ezk. 20:29, where reference is made to former "high-place worship," the prophet speaking with contempt of such manner of worship. It is possible that reference is made to a prominent high place like the one at Gibeon (cf. 1 K. 3:4; 1 Ch. 16:39; 21:29; 2 Ch. 1:3) for which the name "Bamah" was retained after the reform mentioned by the prophet.

BAMOTH bā′moth; **BAMOTH-BAAL** bā′moth-bāl [Heb. *bāmôṯ-ba'al*–'high places of Baal'] A station in the journeyings of Israel N of the Arnon (Nu. 21:19f.). It is probably the same place as the Bamoth-baal of Nu. 22:41, RSV, to which Balak king of Moab conducted Balaam to view and to curse Israel (here the AV has "high places of Baal," NEB "Heights of Baal"). Bamoth-baal is named in Josh. 13:17 as one of the cities given to Reuben. Mesha on the Moabite Stone speaks of having "rebuilt" Beth-bamoth. Its precise location is unknown, though it certainly is on a height on the western edge of the Transjordan plateau in the area of Mt. Nebo. J. W. WHEDBEE

BAN ban (1 Esd. 5:37, AV, NEB). *See* TOBIAH **2.**

BAN [Heb. *bāḏal*] (Ezr. 10:8); AV SEPARATE; NEB EXCLUDE. *See* EXCOMMUNICATION; DEVOTE.

BANAEAS bə-nē′əs (1 Esd. 9:35, NEB); **BANAIAS** bə-nā′əs (AV). *See* BENAIAH **12.**

BAND [Heb. *gāḏaḏ* (Ps. 94:21), *gᵉḏûḏ* (1 S. 30:8, 15, 23; 2 S. 4:2; 1 K. 11:24; 2 K. 13:20f.; etc.), *gûr* (Ps. 56:6; 59:3), *ḥeḇel* (1 S. 10:5, 10), *ḥeḇer* (Hos. 6:9), *ḥayil* (Ezr. 8:22), *ḥayyâ* (2 S. 23:13), *ḥēšeḇ* (Ex. 28:8, 27f.; 39:5, 20f.; Lev. 8:7), *ḥāṯal* (Ezk. 16:4), *ḥᵃṯullâ* (Job 38:9), *'ᵃguddâ* (2 S. 2:25), *keseṯ* (Ezk. 13:18, 20), *mᵉlō'* (Isa. 31:4), *sāḇîḇ* (1 K. 7:35), *sûr* (Hos. 4:18, Heb. uncertain), *'ᵃḇōṯ* (Hos. 11:4), *'ēḏâ* (Ps. 86:14), *pᵉlēṭâ* (2 K. 19:31; Isa. 37:32); Aram. *'ᵉsûr* (Dnl. 4:15, 23 [MT 12, 20]); Gk. *speíra* (Jn. 18:3, 12)]; AV also ASSEMBLIES, COMPANY, COMPASS, GATHER(ED), GIRDLE, MULTITUDE, PILLOWS, SWADDLINGBAND, TROOP, etc.; NEB also BLANKET, BONDS, COMPANY, DETACHMENT, ESCORT, FREEBOOTERS, MAGIC BANDS, MOB, MUSTER, RAIDERS, RAIDING PARTIES, REMNANT, RING, SWADDLING CLOTHES, etc.

The English word comprehends two general definitions; each has many specific usages: (1) a uniting force or implement that binds together, restrains, or encircles; a bond; (2) a group of men united by common purposes. Both meanings are represented in the OT and NT by the several Hebrew, Aramaic, and Greek words noted.

(1) Many types of restrictive bonds are mentioned in the OT: (a) A "skilfully woven band (*ḥēšeḇ*) . . . of gold, blue and purple and scarlet stuff, and fine twined linen" bound the ephod to its wearer (Ex. 28:8). (b) The circular borders at the top of the temple's laver stands that Solomon had constructed (1 K. 7:35) were apparently ornamental as well as practical (vv. 36f.). (c) Figuratively, the dark clouds that envelop the sea are spoken of as its "swaddling band" (Job 38:9). (d) "Magic bands" that were placed on the wrists are mentioned in Ezk. 13:18, 20. These were used in magical practices that involved "the hunt for souls" and "delusive visions" (v. 23); their precise nature is unknown. (e) There are also the "bands of love" with which Yahweh had led Israel, only to see her rebel (Hos. 11:4). (f) The deranged Nebuchadnezzar was to be tethered by "a band of iron and bronze" in the dream Daniel interpreted (Dnl. 4:15, 23).

(2) A group of men: (a) Saul was to join himself to "a band of prophets" (1 S. 10:5, 10). Israel's earliest prophets seem to have grouped together into schools, i.e., itinerant bands of men dedicated to a rather ecstatic prophetic way of life. See J. Lindblom, *Prophecy in Ancient Israel* (1962), pp. 48, 65ff.; *see also* PROPHECY. (b) Isa. 31:4 speaks of "a band of shepherds." (c) Often hostile bands of foreign raiders are referred to (1 S. 30:8, 23; 1 K. 11:24; 2 K. 13:21; 24:2; 1 Ch. 12:21; 2 Ch. 22:1), but Israel too had bands of commando forces (2 S. 4:2). (d) Escort troops can be called "a band of soldiers" (Ezr. 8:22). (e) "Band" is also used as a synonym for the remnant that God would cause to survive the Exile (2 K. 19:31 par. Isa. 37:32). (f) The evil "band themselves together" against God's people (Ps. 56:6 [MT 7]; 59:3 [MT 4]; 94:21). (g) John speaks of "a band of soldiers" that Judas led to arrest Jesus (Jn. 18:3). In light of the "captain" (v. 12, lit. "tribune") who was in charge of this band, John is probably speaking of a Roman cohort, the Roman army unit consisting of six hundred men, although it may stand for a smaller unit, the maniple, with two hundred soldiers. See C. K. Barrett, Comm. on John (1958), p. 433.

See also ARMY, ROMAN. K. H. MAAHS

BANDAGE [Heb. *'ᵃpēr*] (1 K. 20:38, 41); AV "ashes"; [*ḥittûl*] (Ezk. 30:21); AV ROLLER; [Gk. *keiría*] (Jn. 11:44); AV GRAVE-CLOTHES; NEB LINEN BANDS. Heb. *'ᵃpēr* represents a cloth wrapped around the prophet's head to disguise himself as he tricked Ahab into condemning himself (1 K. 20:38, 41); the AV reads it as *'ēper,* "ashes." Another type (*ḥittûl*) was used as a sling for a broken arm (Ezk. 30:21). The NT term refers to the material used to wrap a body for burial, as in Lazarus' case (Jn. 11:44). These passages are the only occurrences of these Hebrew and Greek terms in Scripture. R. J. HUGHES, III

BANDITS [Heb. *gᵉḏûḏ*] (Hos. 7:1); AV "troops of robbers"; NEB ROBBERS. A group of men intent on plunder. Cf. 1 S. 30:8, 15; 2 S. 3:22; etc.

BANDS, BEAUTY AND (Zec. 11:7, 10, AV). *See* GRACE AND UNION.

BANI bā′nī [Heb. *bānî*].

1. A Gadite, one of David's mighty men (2 S. 23:36).

2. A Levite whose son was appointed for service in the tabernacle at David's time (1 Ch. 6:46).

3. A Judahite whose son lived in Jerusalem after the Captivity (1 Ch. 9:4).

4. A family that returned with Zerubbabel (Ezr. 2:10), and who had taken foreign wives (10:29); the same as Binnui of Neh. 7:15.

5. [Gk. *Bani,* Apoc. *Baani*]; AV Apoc. MAANI; NEB Apoc. BAANI. A family some of whom had taken foreign wives (Ezr. 10:34; 1 Esd. 9:34).

6. (Ezr. 10:38, AV). The AV follows the MT in reading "Bani, and Binnui." The RSV and NEB, following the LXX, read simply "Binnui." *See* BINNUI **3.**

7. Father of Rehum, a Levite and builder (Neh. 3:17).

8. One who instructed the people at Ezra's time (Neh. 8:7).

9-11. Three Levites mentioned in connection with the temple worship at Ezra's time (Neh. 9:4f.).

12. A Levite who sealed the covenant with Nehemiah (Neh. 10:13).

13. A leader of the people who also signed the covenant (Neh. 10:14).

14. Father of Uzzi, overseer of the Levites at Jerusalem (Neh. 11:22).

15. [Gk. *Bani*]; AV BANID. A family that returned from exile with Ezra (1 Esd. 8:36). The name is omitted from Ezr. 8:10, perhaps due to a mistaken reading of *bᵉnê,* "sons of," for *bānî.*

BANID bā'nid (1 Esd. 8:36, AV). *See* BANI **15.**

BANISHMENT. *See* EXCOMMUNICATION.

BANK [Heb. *śāpâ, gāḏâ, giḏyâ*; Gk. *krēmnós, trápeza, chárax*]; AV also BRINK, BEFORE (THE RIVER), SIDE, PLACE, COAST, STEEP PLACE, TRENCH (Lk. 19:43); NEB also RIVER-BANK, BESIDE, GORGE (Dt. 2:37), BY, EDGE, SIEGE-WORKS (Lk. 19:43).

All the OT occurrences refer to the bank(s) of a river: Heb. *śāpâ* means "lip"; *gāḏâ* and *giḏya* (Josh. 3:15; 4:18; 1 Ch. 12:15; Isa. 8:7) mean "cutting" (descriptive of the action of a river upon its banks); and the RSV uses "bank" in translating prepositional expressions such as "at hand" (*'al-yāḏ,* Jgs. 11:26; Dnl. 10:4; cf. *kol-yaḏ,* Dt. 2:37), "before" (*lipnê,* Dnl. 8:3, 6), and "between" (*bên,* Dnl. 8:16). In the NT, the uses of Gk. *krēmnós* (Mt. 8:32 par.) refer to the bank of the Sea of Galilee; *trápeza* in Lk. 19:23 is a table, one at which a money-changer sits (*see* BANK; BANKING); and *chárax* in Lk. 19:43 is a palisade for military purposes, hence the NEB "siege-works." F. B. KNUTSON

BANK; BANKING. Banking is the business of receiving, disbursing, exchanging, safeguarding, and lending money. Institutional banking in the modern sense did not begin until the founding of the Banco di Rialto in Venice, Italy, in 1587, and similar institutions in Amsterdam in 1609 and Hamburg in 1619. Banking functions can, however, be traced from early times through the development of media of exchange, the coining of money for the purpose of exchange, the storing of treasure for safekeeping, and the appearance of the money changer.

I. Safekeeping.–Perhaps the earliest banking was that of deposit for safekeeping. As early as 2000 B.C. Babylonians placed their treasure for safekeeping with trusted men, to whom they paid as much as one-sixtieth of the treasure for that service. The statutes of Hammurabi addressed that practice by providing that "if a man gives to another silver, gold, or anything else to safeguard, whatsoever he gives he shall show to witnesses, and he shall arrange the contracts before he makes the deposits." Egypt and Greece also had treasure houses. The Greeks used their temples for this purpose. Religious principles made the temple relatively inviolate in turbulent times, for a thief would not dare arouse the anger of the gods by taking what the gods protected. At first "presents" were made to the priests for their safekeeping service. Later, business charges were instituted. Eventually money changers had strongboxes in which they kept their money, and people began to leave their own coins with the money changers for safekeeping in the strongboxes. The revision of the Justinian code of laws in Rome, in A.D. 534, showed that there were many regulations of "banking" of this kind at that time.

In Palestine, as in Greece, temples were used for storing treasures in the absence of banks. During the contest between the Egyptians and Syrians for Palestine in the early 2nd cent. B.C. the pro-Syrian faction of the Jews alerted Seleucus that much money belonging to his opponents was stored in the temple. Seleucus' attempts at that time to seize the money and other treasures, however, were unsuccessful.

II. Media of Exchange and Currency.–The earliest trade was in direct barter of goods. Nomadic Aryans used cattle as one of the earliest media of exchange. When a cow or ox was the standard medium of exchange, the crude cattle pens in which those forerunners of modern currency were confined became, in effect, the first banks. Indeed, the English word "pecuniary" is derived from the Latin word *pecus,* meaning "cattle." Homer relates that when the direct transfer of cattle became inconvenient among the Greeks or Trojans, a weight of uncoined gold, equal in value to an ox, was fixed and called a "talent." Later, ox talents were coined with the head of an ox impressed on one side, and came to be called "oxen." The first general coining of gold and silver was probably accomplished by the Lydians in the early 7th cent. B.C. (Herodotus i.94).

Until the Exile the Jews had little need either for money as a medium of exchange or for other banking functions. Palestine's economy was essentially agricultural, and the Hebrews were probably the least commercial people of civilized antiquity, though they were surrounded by other Semitic groups who had developed business as a fine art. The laws of the Israelites were unfavorable to the financing of trade or the development of banking. Lending of money at interest, except to foreigners, was illegal (Ex. 22:25; Lev. 25:37; Dt. 23:19f.; *see* USURY). Until the 2nd cent. B.C., Jews weighed out silver and gold as payment, or used the currency of other nations. They probably first used coined money during the Exile, and must have used their conquerors' coins except during their brief periods of independence. Simon the Maccabee is said to have been the first to issue the shekel as a coin. In addition to facilitating increased commercial trade, coined money became a convenient way of paying taxes and tribute.

III. Money Changing.–As the variety of coins multiplied, money changing became increasingly important in order both to exchange the currencies of different countries and to "give change" in smaller coins for the larger currency of the same country. Money changing is the banking function most prominently involved in biblical passages. For a fee, money changers would provide the desired currency at their table (Gk. *trápeza*) or bench ("bank"), from which they derived the name *trapezítēs* ("banker" or "money changer," Mt. 25:27).

The annual temple tax of one-half shekel, and additional freewill offerings were put into chests placed in the temple court of the women (Mk. 12:41). This money was required to be in native coin, necessitating the exchange of foreign coins brought by Jews from the foreign lands in which they lived. Exchange of currency to provide correct denominations for the purchase of animals to be sacrificed, or for other purposes, may also have been necessary. The money changers who provided this service had stalls in the city, and as the feast approached they were admitted to the temple area and placed their tables in the Court of the Gentiles. The commission paid for a half-shekel was, according to the Talmud, a *kóllybos,* equal to twelve grains of silver. From this the money changer was sometimes called a *kollybistḗs* (Mt. 21:12).

On two occasions Jesus expressed His disapproval of their activities in the temple by overturning the tables of the money changers and driving out those who sold animals for sacrifice. The first is recorded in Jn. 2:14-16, where the emphasis is on the mere presence of commercial activity: "You shall not make my Father's house a house of trade." The second occasion is recorded in Mt. 21:12f. and Mk. 11:15-17. In this case the complaint is dishonesty: "It is written, 'My house shall be called a house of prayer'; but you make it a den of robbers" (Mt. 21:13).

IV. Moneylending.–Money changers were often also

moneylenders. The Phoenicians and Greeks, as well as the Romans, had a range of banking fuctions that included receiving money on deposit, paying interest, and lending it out at a higher rate. The row along the north side of the Roman Forum, on the street of Janus, housed the banking establishments with their facilities not only for money changing, but also for deposit of monies. They paid interest on time deposits, made loans, purchased mortgages, and issued bills of exchange and letters of credit. Despite OT prohibitions on the lending of money at interest except to foreigners, Jesus' parable of the talents (Mt. 25:14-30) and the parable of the pounds (Lk. 19:11-27) indicate that it was the practice to leave money with the money changers and receive interest from it; and the fearful servant was chastised because he did not at least put the money into the "bank" (Lk. 19:23; "bankers," Mt. 25:27) to draw interest. "Bank" and "banker" in these passages refer to the *trapezítēs* rather than to the *kollybistḗs,* suggesting a greater tolerance for the activities of the moneylender in the city than of the money changer in the temple.

See also LEND; MONEY; USURY.

Bibliography.–N. F. Hoggson, *Banking Through the Ages* (1926); S. Grayzel, *History of the Jews* (1968); *World Book Encyclopedia* (1966), II, *s.v.* "Banks and Banking" (E. W. Reed).

M. W. CALL

BANNAEAS bə-nē′əs (1 Esd. 9:26, NEB). *See* BENAIAH **9.**

BANNAIA bə-nā′ə (1 Esd. 9:33, AV). *See* ZABAD **5.**

BANNAS ban′əs [Gk. *Bannos*]; AV BANUAS; NEB BANNUS. A family that returned from the Captivity with Zerubbabel (1 Esd. 5:26). Bannas and Sudias are replaced by Hodaviah in the list of Ezra (Nehemiah "Hodevah").

BANNER [Heb. *degel* (Cant. 2:4), *dāgal* (Ps. 20:5 [MT 6]; Cant. 6:4, 10), *nēs* (Ex. 17:15; Ps. 60:4 [MT 6]; Jer. 50:2)]; AV also "nissi" (Ex. 17:15), STANDARD; NEB also "nissi," "starry heavens" (Cant. 6:4; cf. KoB, p. 203; *CHAL,* p. 68), etc. The RSV's rendering of the obscure Ex. 17:16 is based simply on conjecture.

A banner was usually a flag, streamer, or wrought emblem affixed to the end of a standard. It was common in the ancient world for banners to be used for military, national, or religious purposes in much the way they are today. The purpose of the banner was to indicate the rallying point for any group holding a common cause (Jer. 50:2).

Perhaps the oldest use of this word in the OT took place at Rephidim where Israel battled the Amalekites, and Moses himself, with arms outstretched, became a living banner symbolizing God's presence. At the close of this successful engagement, Moses built an altar and called its name "The Lord is my banner" (Ex. 17:15). While in the wilderness, and no doubt afterward, each Israelite clan had its own individual banner (lit. "standard, ensign"; cf. Nu. 1:52; 2:2f.). The principal OT usage is military, in which the banner is seen as the rallying point of Yahweh's faithful and their armies (Ps. 60:4; cf. vv. 5, 10-12). The awesome grandeur of a marching army is reinforced by the fearsome parade of its proud banners (Cant. 6:4, 10), but in Israel, when the king was victorious, it was due to the intervention of Yahweh; hence, banners were to be set up in His name (Ps. 20:5).

It is not known what Israelite banners looked like, but banners were widely used by other nations in antiquity and commonly took the form of symbolic animals. It is conceivable that some of these clan symbols, animal and otherwise, are reflected in Gen. 49.

There is an intriguing correspondence between the cruciform stance taken by Moses with Aaron and Hur on either side at Rephidim (Ex. 17:12) and John's depiction of Jesus' crucifixion: ". . . and with him two others, one on either side, and Jesus between them" (Jn. 19:18). "The meaning of the Evangelist would seem to be: Just

Commemorative stone palette of Narmer (1st Dynasty, *ca.* 3000 B.C.) from Hierakonopolis. Preceded by men bearing banners, the king marches to view the bound and decapitated bodies of his northern enemies. (Egyptian Museum, Cairo)

as Moses with arms outstretched before Israel was a standard or banner proclaiming Yahweh's victory, so also was Christ raised up on the cross the proclamation of God's victory over sin" (Plastaras, p. 299).

See J. Plastaras, *God of Exodus* (1966), pp. 297-99.

K. H. MAAHS

BANNUS ban'əs.

1. (1 Esd. 5:26, NEB). *See* BANNAS.

2. (1 Esd. 9:34, AV, NEB). *See* BINNUI **3.**

BANQUET [Heb. *mišteh*; Gk. *deípnon*]; AV also FEAST SUPPER; NEB also DINNER PARTY, DINNER-TIME. The Hebrew word is derived from the verb "to drink," and conveys the fact that wine was consumed at banquets. The RSV has translated *mišteh* as "banquet" only in Esther, translating it elsewhere as "feast." In Esther the term refers to a festive meal, held either by the king or queen. Gk. *deípnon* can mean either supper, the main meal of the day, or a formal supper, feast, or banquet (Mt. 23:6; Mk. 12:39; Lk. 20:46; Rev. 19:9, 17). The RSV translates *deípnon* as "banquet" only in Mk. 6:21, referring to a birthday banquet of Herod, and in Lk. 14:12ff., the "parable of the banquet."

A *mišteh* is always a "secular feast," held on a variety of occasions: the weaning of a son (Gen. 21:8), a wedding (Gen. 29:22; Jgs. 14:10), the birthday of a king (Gen. 40:20), in response to a royal vision (1 K. 3:15), upon the arrival of guests (Gen. 19:3; 2 S. 3:20). A sign of wealth was the ability to "feast" often (1 S. 25:36; Job 1:4f.). The association of "feasting" with drinking is assumed in the oracle of Jer. 51:39.

The "banquets" in Esther (1:3, 5, 9) are similar to others in the OT. Much is made of the drinking: "and drinking was according to the law, no one was compelled; for the king had given orders to all the officials of his place to do as every man desired" (Est. 1:8). One of the banquets is most extravagant: it is said to last 180 days! Another is seven days long (cf. the wedding feast in Jgs. 14:12).

See also DINNER.

Votive plaque with relief of ritual banquet, from the temple of Inanna at Nippur (Early Dynastic IIIa, *ca.* 2550 B.C.). Wine is consumed (top), while attendants bring bulls (center). (Oriental Institute, University of Chicago)

Bibliography.–H. Bardtke, *Das Buch Esther* (*KZAT*, 2nd ed. 1963), pp. 276f.; A. C. Bouquet, *Everyday Life in NT Times* (1954), pp. 66-79.

F. B. KNUTSON

BANQUET HALL; BANQUET HOUSE [Heb. *bêṯ hayyāyin* (Cant. 2:4); Aram. *bêṯ mišteyā'* (Dnl. 5:10)]; NEB also WINE-GARDEN (Cant. 2:4). Ancient Near Eastern banquets were characterized by rich foods and abundant supplies of wine. Many occasions prompted banquets (cf. Gen. 19:3; 21:8; Jgs. 9:27; 2 Ch. 7:8; etc.), and in large houses or palaces they were usually held in a dining room. The Hebrew and Aramaic terms imply that the banquet hall was synonymous with a place where wine was drunk.

R. K. H.

BANUAS ban'ū-əs (1 Esd. 5:26, AV). A misprint for BANNAS.

BAPTISM.

NT REFERENCES

This first article is designed simply to present the references to baptism in the NT. No attempt will be made to interpret the data; for in this area, in view of the different possibilities of understanding, neutral interpretation is especially difficult. For some of the ways in which baptism is understood and practiced in various churches, readers may consult the specialized articles that follow.

I. The Words
II. Synoptic References
III. Johannine References
IV. References in Acts
V. Pauline References
VI. References in Hebrews
VII. References in the General Epistles
VIII. References in the Revelation

I. The Words.–The words used in relation to baptism should be briefly noted.

The basic verb is Gk. *báptō*, meaning "dip in or under," also "dye." In the NT this word occurs only rarely and always with its literal sense, as in Lk. 16:24. It never has the sense "baptize."

The form *baptízō* is the term which in different constructions is employed in the NT for "baptize." This verb can have varied but related senses as "immerse, sink, drown, go under, sink into, and bathe." The range of meaning adds to its suitability for an act which itself has different connotations and can be given, in the context of the gospel, such a richly diversified significance.

The noun for baptism is *báptisma*, which occurs only in the NT, only in the singular, and only for baptism. The term seems to denote not only the external act but also the inner meaning and force. Thus the baptism denoted may be that of the Spirit as well as water, and even the baptism of the cross.

An associated term is *baptismós*. This is found elsewhere, occurs in the plural as well as the singular, and seems to refer simply to the act of washing. In two instances at least it carries a plain reference to Jewish ablutions. The use in He. 6:2 is contested.

Another word used by the NT is *baptistḗs*. This is a descriptive nickname for John. Mark sometimes has instead *ho baptízōn*, "the baptizer," but the nickname has stuck, as in the Eng. "John the Baptist."

II. Synoptic References.–*A. John's Baptism.* In the Synoptics the first references to baptism occur in relation to John, who is called the baptizer or baptist in Mk. 1:4; Mt. 3:1. In Mk. 1:5; Lk. 3:3 John is said to preach a baptism of repentance for the remission of sins. Mt. 3:2 puts it differently: John proclaims, "Repent, for the king-

"The Baptism of Christ" by Andrea Pisano, panel from bronze door of the baptistery, Florence (1330-1336)

dom of heaven is at hand." All the Synoptists speak of great crowds coming (from Jerusalem, Judea, and the Jordan area) to be baptized by John in the Jordan. Mk. 1:5; Mt. 3:6 state specifically that those baptized by John confessed their sins. Lk. 3:10ff. gives concrete examples of acts of repentance that John demanded. All three Gospels (Mk. 1:7f.; Mt. 3:11; Lk. 3:15ff.) record that John spoke of one mightier than he who was coming and who would not just baptize with water as he did, but baptize with the Spirit (and with fire, Matthew and Luke).

B. Baptism of Jesus. All the Synoptists (and also John) have accounts of the baptism of Jesus by John. Mt. 3:14 adds that John was reluctant to baptize Jesus but consented when Jesus said it was fitting for them to fulfil all righteousness. Lk. 3:21 notes that Jesus prayed when He came up from the water. All the Synoptists (Mk. 1:11f.; Mt. 3:16f.; Lk. 3:21f.) tell us that three things took place after the baptism: the opening of heaven, the descent of the Spirit like a dove, and the voice from heaven calling Jesus the beloved Son in whom God is well pleased. In all three accounts it is also stated that immediately after the baptism the Spirit drove (Mk. 1:12) or led (Mt. 4:1; Lk. 4:1) Jesus into the desert, where He was tempted by Satan (Mk. 1:13) or the devil (Mt. 4:1; Lk. 4:3).

C. Baptism and the Cup. Although baptism seems so important at the beginning of the Synoptic records, it is little mentioned after the ministry of Jesus commences. We are not told in these Gospels that Jesus or His disciples baptized. Indeed, there are few references of any kind to it. Nevertheless, baptism has not lost its significance, as may be seen from the incident reported in Mk. 10:35ff.; Mt. 20:20ff. Jesus here has just been talking about His coming passion; and when the sons of Zebedee (and their mother) ask for places of special honor in His kingdom (or glory), He asks them whether they too can drink His cup (Mt.), or be baptized with His baptism and drink His cup (Mk.). In another context in Lk. 12:50 Jesus says that He has a baptism to be baptized with, and how He is constrained until it is accomplished. In the light of the cup saying, and the further references to the cup at the last Supper and in Gethsemane, it seems evident that by this baptism He means His vicarious death and passion.

D. Authority of John's Baptism. During the last week, when He taught in the temple, Jesus had to answer many questions put to Him by various adversaries. The most direct challenge came from the chief priests (and scribes) and elders (Mk. 11:27-33; Mt. 21:23-27; Lk. 20:1-8) when they asked Him by what authority He did what He was doing, and who gave Him that authority. In reply Jesus put the counter-question: Did John's baptism have a divine or a human origin? When they answered that they did not know, Jesus refused to answer their initial question. By raising the question of John's baptism Jesus obviously put them in a dilemma, but He also related John's baptism very plainly to Himself and thus accepted its validity. This is confirmed by the forthright endorsement of John in the address that follows in Mt. 21:28ff. and also by similar endorsements in Mk. 9:13; Mt. 11:11ff.; 17:12f.; Lk. 7:24ff.

E. Baptism and the Great Commission. Matthew and Luke tell us after the resurrection Jesus gave the disciples a worldwide commission of preaching and teaching. Lk. 24:44 sees in this a prophetic fulfillment: "It is written that . . . repentance and forgiveness of sins should be preached in His [Christ's] name to all nations." No reference is made here to baptism, but repentance and remission remind us of what is said about John's baptism at the outset. Mt. 28:16ff. records a direct commissioning by Jesus. In it He claims full authority and sends out the disciples to make disciples, baptizing and teaching. In a phrase that has aroused much debate, but whose textual credentials are sound enough, this baptizing is to be "in the name of the Father and of the Son and of the Holy Spirit" (Mt. 28:19). It may be noted that grammatically the commission is the single one of making disciples; baptizing and teaching are included within this in dependent clauses. The Markan ending, generally accepted as inauthentic, has no command to baptize, but after the preaching commission states that whoever "believes and is baptized will be saved," while those who do not believe will be condemned (Mk. 14:16). The reference to baptism in the triune name is peculiar to Matthew.

III. Johannine References.*–*A. John's Baptizing. Like the Synoptics, John's Gospel opens with the story of the Baptist (Jn. 1:19ff.). The initial concern here is to show that John did not claim to be the Messiah but had come to prepare His way. That he administered baptism comes out incidentally in the question of why he was doing this if he was not the Christ. His reply is that he baptizes with water but that among them is one who comes after him, the thong of whose sandal he is not worthy to untie. (No reference is made as yet to Jesus' baptizing with the Spirit.) It is noted that John baptized at a place called Bethany beyond the Jordan (1:21).

B. John and Jesus. John records the baptism of Jesus by John the Baptist, but with some special touches of his own. Jesus is hailed by John as the Lamb of God (1:29). The purpose of John's baptism is to reveal Him to Israel (v. 31). The Baptist himself sees the Spirit descend like a dove and rest on Jesus (v. 32), and he says that he had been told that he to whom this happens will be "he who baptizes with the Holy Spirit" (v. 33). Witness to the divine Sonship — given in the Synoptics by the voice from heaven — is now borne by John on the ground of what he has seen (v. 34).

C. Baptizing of the Disciples. John's Gospel gives some further information about baptism that none of the Synoptists records. The Baptist's ministry did not stop with the baptism of Jesus. He continued to baptize at Aenon near Salim, where "there was much water" (3:23). Meanwhile Jesus also was baptizing in Judea (v. 22), although it is explained later that the disciples, not Jesus, did the actual baptizing (4:2). While some people still came to John, more were now going to Jesus (3:26; 4:1). The Baptist, however, refused to be put out by this (3:27ff.), since he was the bridegroom's friend, not the bridegroom himself. The attention of the Pharisees naturally shifted to Jesus (4:1), and this is perhaps why He moved to Galilee, passing on the way through Sychar, where He appropriately described Himself at the well-side as the giver of eternal water (4:14).

D. Baptism and New Birth. In addition to what he says about the practice of baptism, John speaks also about its significance. The setting is the interview with Nicodemus. In response to Nicodemus' introductory flattery, Jesus abruptly poses the requirement of a new birth, or a birth from above, if one is to see God's kingdom (3:3). When Nicodemus does not understand this, Jesus then says that being born anew is being born of water and the Holy Spirit (v. 5). Commentators expound this saying in different ways. Some find in water, i.e., baptism, an indispensable instrument or agency of regeneration. Others spiritualize water in such a way that it is virtually the same as Spirit and no reference to water baptism is seen at all. In the general context of chs. 1–4 it seems probable that there is at least an allusion to the baptism of water and the baptism of the Spirit (possibly as remission and regeneration). At the same time the rite of water baptism is not expressly mentioned, nor is it said to be an essential vehicle of the new birth. In reflecting on 3:5, comparison should perhaps be made with 7:37ff. Here there is obviously no reference to baptism, since Jesus is summoning the thirsty to come to Him and drink. Yet water and the Spirit are again associated, v. 39. The drinking of water is important as well as washing by water in the teaching of the Johannine Jesus, especially in relation to its life-giving significance.

E. The Footwashing. Washing, of course, recurs in the footwashing of ch. 13. Primarily Jesus washes the disciples' feet as an example of humility (vv. 12ff.). In the exchange with Peter, however, there is at least a hint of spiritual as well as physical washing. When Peter, after initial resistance, asks for his head and hands to be washed too, Jesus makes the enigmatic reply that he who has bathed does not need to wash except for his feet, "and you [plural] are clean, but not all of you" (v. 10). The reference is to Judas, and it can hardly mean that the others have had a bath and he has not.

F. The Cross. In John's Gospel Jesus does not call His cross a baptism, but the Evangelist may be alluding to this when he notes that water as well as blood flowed from the pierced side of Jesus (19:34).

G. The Commission. No equivalent of the Great Commission occurs in John, nor is there an express command to baptize. Yet the incident in 20:22 may perhaps point to Jesus as the One who baptizes with the Spirit and who thus gives the apostles authority for their mission: "Receive the Holy Spirit. If you forgive the sins of any. . . ."

IV. References in Acts.*–*A. Pentecost. Acts opens with the promise of baptism with the Holy Spirit (1:5) and the summoning of the disciples to a worldwide ministry. The outpouring of the Spirit follows on the day of Pentecost (2:1ff.) and is described as a filling with the Holy Spirit (2:4). Yet this does not abrogate water baptism, for when the people, cut to the heart, ask what to do, Peter tells them to repent and be baptized for the forgiveness of sins (2:37f.). "Those who received his word were baptized, and there were added that day about three thousand souls" (v. 41).

B. Samaria. Philip's mission to Samaria brought many people to faith in Christ and these "were baptized, both men and women" (8:12). As Philip had preached "the good news about the kingdom of God and the name of Jesus Christ," this baptism was given "in the name of the Lord Jesus" (8:16). The Holy Spirit, however, did not fall on the new believers when Philip baptized them, but only when Peter and John came and laid their hands on them (v. 17). Whether this descent of the Spirit is baptism with the Spirit, and whether the laying on of the apostles' hands, with their prayer, is necessary for it, the passage does not explicitly say.

C. The Eunuch. Continuing his ministry on the Gaza road, Philip preached Christ to the Ethiopian eunuch on the basis of Isa. 53. In his teaching Philip must have spoken about baptism, for when they came to water the eunuch asked what prevented him from being baptized (8:36). In the next verse, which is textually insecure, Philip asks for a confession of faith and the eunuch expresses belief in Jesus Christ as the Son of God. Both of them went down into the water and Philip baptized the eunuch (v. 38). No reference is made to a descent of the Spirit.

D. Paul. After Paul was granted his vision of the risen Lord and then brought blind into Damascus, Ananias, acting by divine command, went to him and laid hands on him, telling him that he, Ananias, had been sent in order that Paul might regain his sight and be filled with the Holy Spirit (9:3ff., 10ff., 17). Paul's sight returned, and he rose up and was baptized (v. 18). In Paul's later account Ananias told him: "Rise and be baptized, and wash away your sins, calling on his name" (22:16).

E. Cornelius. The baptism of Cornelius follows a common pattern, but as the first recorded gentile baptism it also has some distinctive features. Peter was given a special vision to remove his prejudice against preaching to Gentiles (10:9ff.). Then, while he was still preaching, "the Holy Spirit fell on all who heard the word" (v. 44) so that they spoke with tongues and praised God (v. 46). In the astonishment that this caused (v. 45), Peter asked who could "forbid water for baptizing these people who have received the Holy Spirit just as we have" (v. 47). Not Cornelius alone but also his relatives and close friends were then baptized at Peter's command (v. 48). In his report of the incident in Jerusalem, Peter said that when the Holy Spirit fell on them he "remembered the word of the Lord, 'John baptized with water, but you shall be baptized with the Holy Spirit' " (11:16; cf. 1:5).

F. Philippi. During the Galatian ministry of Paul and Barnabas no direct reference is made to the baptism of converts. In the ministry at Philippi, however, two baptisms are noted, that of Lydia (16:15) and that of the jailer (16:33). The baptisms are interesting because in each case the household or family also is baptized. In the case of the jailer Paul and Silas told him that if he believed in the Lord Jesus he would be saved, he and his household. The word of the Lord was then spoken to him and to all who were in his house (16:31f.). Their baptism then followed (v. 33). Of Lydia we simply read that after "the Lord opened her heart to give heed to what was said by Paul . . . she was baptized, with her household" (16:14f.).

G. Ephesus. After a long stay in Corinth, where many believed and were baptized, including Crispus and his household (18:8), Paul called briefly at Ephesus (18:19), went back to Antioch, revisited Galatia and Phrygia, and then returned to Ephesus (19:1). There he found disciples who not only had not received but had not even heard of the Holy Spirit (19:2). When Paul asked them about their baptism, they said that they had been baptized into John's baptism (v. 3). Paul then explained that John had baptized "with the baptism of repentance" but had also told the people "to believe in the one who was to come after him, that is, Jesus" (v. 4). When they heard this the twelve disciples of Ephesus were "baptized in the name of the Lord Jesus" (v. 5). Paul then laid hands on them, the Holy Spirit came on them, and like the disciples at Pentecost and Cornelius and his company, "they spoke with tongues and prophesied" (v. 6).

V. Pauline References.*–A. Romans.* Paul does not speak much about baptism in his Epistles. This general rule applies to Romans, where there is indeed only one reference in 6:3f. Nevertheless, the passage is an important one, for in it the apostle interrelates the death and resurrection of Christ and the dying and rising of His people in and with Him. The issue is whether, with the superabounding of grace, we might continue in sin. For Paul this idea is ludicrous. How can those who have died to sin still live in it? (v. 2). All who are baptized into Christ are baptized into His death (v. 3). They are buried with Him by baptism into death so that as He rose again they can now "walk in newness of life" (v. 4). Union with Christ in death means union with Him in resurrection. The old self being crucified, freedom from sin is secured by death. We are dead to sin and alive to God in Jesus Christ (vv. 5ff.).

B. Corinthians. 1 Corinthians contains rather more references to baptism, although, in contrast, 2 Corinthians has none at all. In 1 Cor. 1 Paul responds to party groupings in Corinth by asking whether he was crucified for them or they were baptized in his name. In view of the rise of parties appealing to himself or Peter or Apollos, he is glad that he personally baptized so few, only Crispus and Gaius (v. 14), the household of Stephanas, and perhaps one or two others (v. 16). The task that Christ had given him was not to baptize but to preach the gospel (v. 17).

There is a possible allusion to baptism in 6:11. Here Paul is saying that the wicked will not inherit the kingdom of God (v. 9). He then names sinners of various kinds, such as idolaters, adulterers, and thieves (v. 10). Some Corinthian believers were formerly among these flagrant offenders, but they have been washed, sanctified, and justified "in the name of our Lord Jesus Christ and in the Spirit of our God" (6:11). While there is no literal reference to baptism here, being "washed" may well carry a reference to the meaning of baptism, especially in the context of the ministry, not only of Christ, but also of the Spirit.

Baptism is mentioned expressly in the admonition in ch. 10. Paul introduces here a comparison to OT Israel. Israel had its own baptism in the great act of deliverance out of Egypt. Israel was baptized into Moses in the cloud and the sea (10:2f.). It also received spiritual food and drink (vv. 3f.). Yet through its wicked acts it still came under God's displeasure (vv. 5ff.). Christians should learn from this, especially by avoiding idolatry (vv. 11ff., 14ff.).

Another important reference comes in the chapter on gifts. No one can say that Jesus is Lord except by the Spirit (12:3). This Spirit gives different gifts, but the difference does not mean disunity. As with the body and its members, so it is with Christ and His people (12:12). "By one Spirit we were all baptized into one body . . . and all were made to drink of one Spirit" (v. 13). It should be noted that baptism and Spirit are closely associated here, that baptism is into Christ's body, and that drinking as well as washing is in view (cf. Jn. 4; 1 Cor. 10:1ff.).

An enigmatic baptismal saying occurs in the discussion of the Resurrection in 1 Cor. 15. As a subsidiary point, Paul shows in 15:29 that baptism on behalf of the dead makes no sense if there is no resurrection. Expositions of this verse, which has, of course, the form of a question, differ widely. Some think there must have been a regular custom of baptizing the dead vicariously; others suggest an irregular practice of which Paul does not necessarily approve; while others find only a general relation between baptism, death, and resurrection. Since no agreed interpretation can be offered, Paul's actual words might be cited: "Otherwise, what do people mean by being baptized on behalf of the dead? If the dead are not raised at all, why are people baptized on their behalf?"

C. Galatians. Paul mentions baptism in Galatians only at 3:27, but here, as in Romans, the context is important. The line of thought is that in Christ, the one seed of Abraham, all are sons of God through faith, whether or not they fulfil the law (3:27). Baptism is, for all who receive it, a putting on of Christ (3:27). In Christ all divisions are broken down: "There is neither Jew nor Greek. . . . All are one in Christ Jesus" (3:28; cf. 1 Cor. 12:13f.). "Those who are Christ's are, in him, Abraham's seed and heirs according to the promise" (3:29).

D. Ephesians. Unity is again connected with baptism in Eph. 4. The author is here summoning his readers to lowliness, forbearance, and unity in the Spirit. Unity should be maintained because there is one body and one Spirit. Similarly believers are called to one hope, and there is "one Lord, one faith, one baptism, one God and Father of us all" (4:5f.). The one baptism here would seem to mean not that we are baptized only once, but that the baptism received in the name of Christ, or of Father, Son, and Spirit, is one and the same for all Christians. As in 1 Cor. 12 diversity of gifts accompanies the unity of the body, the Spirit, and baptism.

An allusion to baptism is sometimes seen in Eph. 5:26. In his admonition to husbands and wives the apostle asks from the former the same love as Christ showed for the Church when He gave Himself for it so as to sanctify it, having cleansed it by the washing of water with the word. Particularly to be noted here is the connection of the washing of water and the word.

Some commentators think that sealing with the Spirit in 1:13 carries an allusion to baptism, while others question or deny it. If baptism is the seal, a relation of baptism and the Spirit takes place as in ch. 4, though the nature of the relation, apart from the thought of marking, is not clearly specified.

E. Colossians. In answer to false teaching at Colossae, Paul has an interesting passage on circumcision and baptism. Believers do not need the OT sign but they have been circumcized with a circumcision without hands. They have put off the body of the flesh with the circumcision of Christ (2:11). Through faith, and by the work of God who raised Him from the dead, they have been buried (and raised again) with Christ in baptism (2:12). Inner circumcision (the putting off of the body of the flesh) and baptism (burial with Christ) are thus brought into a close relation which is developed by the apostle in v. 13, where the uncircumcision of the flesh is equated with deadness in trespasses, but is remedied by renewal and forgiveness, not by physical circumcision.

F. Titus. The Pastoral Epistles do not use the term baptism but a reference to it is usually seen in Tit. 3:5. The readers have just been reminded that Christians were once foolish, disobedient, and wicked (v. 3). They did not save themselves but were dependent on the goodness and kindness of the Savior God. When He appeared, He saved us, not by our works, but by His mercy. This He did through the washing of regeneration and renewal in the Holy Spirit (v. 5). The washing (water) and Spirit in this verse remind us of Jn. 3:5 and of the basic NT concept of baptism by water and the Spirit.

VI. References in Hebrews.–It is apparent from the context that the washings of He. 9:10 do not imply baptism but relate to provisions of the OT law. Whether or not the washings of He. 6:2 bear a similar reference to ablutions is debatable. As noted under I, we have here a plural of *baptismós*, which suggests washings in a more general sense. Yet the other "elementary doctrines" listed in the verse — repentance, faith, laying on of hands, resurrection, and judgment — point more naturally to baptism. It has sometimes been suggested that the plural is used because instruction is given about different baptisms, viz., John's, water baptism, and baptism by the Spirit. If baptism is in view, the point is that we cannot keep on laying, destroying, and relaying the foundation. Baptism is not to be accepted, renounced, then accepted again. We must move on from the basis to the building.

He. 10:22 carries a fairly obvious allusion to baptism which links the outer and the inner action. The passage is speaking of the access to God which Jesus has opened by His blood. We are thus to draw near in faith, our hearts sprinkled clean from a bad conscience, our bodies washed with pure water. The physical washing has a spiritual counterpart. The language reflects the background of the ceremonial law.

VII. References in the General Epistles.–*A. 1 Peter.* A similar thought to that of He. 10:22 occurs in 1 Pet. 3:21.

Staircase leading to a cistern at Qumrân. Purification by means of a ritual bath was an important part of the life of the covenantal community. (W. S. LaSor)

Baptism is here compared to the ark in which Noah and his family were saved by water when the rest were destroyed by it. In baptism we again have saving water. The washing, however, is not a removing of bodily dirt. It is the answer of a good conscience, or the appeal for it, through the resurrection of Jesus Christ. An inner cleansing is again linked to the outer act.

B. 1 John. A possible allusion to baptism is made in 1 Jn. 5:6ff. Here Jesus is said to have come by water and blood. The Spirit is then adduced as the witness. The Spirit, the water, and the blood are three witnesses whose testimony agrees. One is reminded here of the twofold baptism of water and the Spirit and also of the baptism of Jesus which is His death and passion (cf. also the water and blood of Jn. 19:34). In his characteristic way the author does not make an express reference to baptism. Intentional ambivalence, however, leaves the door open for a wealth of associations and cross-connections.

VIII. References in the Revelation.–Something of the same result is achieved by the vivid imagery of Revelation. Here again baptism is not mentioned, but an interrelating of water and blood occurs in 7:13: "They have washed their robes and made them white in the blood of the Lamb." The rope dipped in blood and the linen white and pure are again set in juxtaposition in 19:13f. Water and blood can also be seen together, of course, in the death and judgment of 16:3f. At the same time a significant feature of the eternal city is the life-giving water that flows from the throne of God and of the Lamb (22:1ff.). As in John, the thought is extended to include not only washing in water (22:14) but also the drinking of it (v. 17). Baptism as a rite is no longer the point here. The water of baptism is associated with the ministry of the Lamb and the Spirit (cf. v. 17), and its eternal significance is poetically developed and presented.

G. W. BROMILEY

BAPTIST VIEW

- I. Meaning of Baptism
  - A. Terminology
  - B. Proselyte Baptism
  - C. Greek Usage
  - D. NT Usage
  - E. The Didache
  - F. Baptismal Regeneration
- II. Subjects of Baptism
- III. Present Obligation

I. Meaning of Baptism.–*A. Terminology.* The verb used in the NT is Gk. *baptízō*. The nouns *báptisma* and *baptismós* occur, though the latter is not used in the NT of the ordinance of baptism except by implication, as in He. 6:2 ("instruction about ablutions"), where the reference is to the distinction between the Christian ordinance and the Jewish ceremonial ablutions. Some MSS have it also in Col. 2:12 (cf. He. 9:10, "various ablutions") for a reference solely to the Jewish purifications (cf. the dispute about purifying in Jn. 3:25). The verb *baptízō* appears in this sense in Lk. 11:38, where the Pharisee marveled that Jesus "did not first wash before dinner."

The Mosaic regulations required the bath of the whole body (Lev. 15:16) for certain uncleannesses. Tertullian (*De baptismo* 15) says that the Jew required almost daily washing. Herodotus (ii.47) says that if an Egyptian should "in passing accidentally touch a pig, he instantly hurries to the river and plunges in [*báptō*] with all his clothes on." See also the Jewish scrupulosity illustrated in Sir. 34:25 and Jth. 12:7, where *baptízō* occurs. The same thing appears in the correct text in Mk. 7:4, "And when they come from the market place, they do not eat unless they bathe themselves." Here *baptízō* is the true text. The use of *rhantízō* ("sprinkle") is due to the difficulty felt by copyists not familiar with Jewish customs. Note also the omission of "couches" in the same verse. The couches were "pallets" and could easily be dipped into water. It is noteworthy that here *rhantízō* is used in contrast with *baptízō,* showing that *baptízō* did not mean "sprinkle."

The term *baptismós* occurs in Josephus (*Ant.* xviii.5.2) in connection with John's baptism (cf. also Irenaeus *Adv. haer.* ii.22 on Christ's baptism). In general, however, *báptisma* is the noun found for the ordinance. The verb *baptízō* is in reality a frequentative or intensive of *báptō* ("dip"). Examples occur where that idea is still appropriate, as in 2 K. 5:14 (LXX), where Naaman is said to have "dipped himself seven times in the Jordan" (*ebaptísato*). The notion of repetition may occur also in Josephus (*Ant.* xv.3.3) in connection with the death of Aristobulus, brother of Mariamne, for Herod's friends "dipped him as he was swimming, and plunged him under water, in the dark of the evening." But in general the term *baptízō,* as is common with such forms in the late Greek, is simply equivalent to *báptō* (cf. Lk. 16:24) and means "dip," "immerse," just as *rhantízō,* like *rhaínō,* means simply "sprinkle."

If *baptízō* never occurred in connection with a disputed ordinance, there would be no controversy on the meaning of the word. There are, indeed, figurative or metaphorical uses of the word, but the figurative use is that of immersion, like our "immersed in cares," "plunged in grief," etc. It remains to consider whether the use of the word for a ceremony or ordinance has changed its significance in the NT as compared with ancient Greek.

It may be remarked that no Baptist has written a lexicon of the Greek language, and yet the standard lexicons, like that of Liddell and Scott (LSJ), uniformly give the meaning of *baptízō* as "dip," "immerse." They do not give "pour" or "sprinkle," nor has anyone ever adduced an instance where this verb means "pour" or "sprinkle." The presumption is therefore in favor of "dip" in the NT.

B. Proselyte Baptism. Before we turn directly to the discussion of the ceremonial usage, a word is called for in regard to Jewish proselyte baptism. It is still a matter of dispute whether this initiatory rite was in existence at the time of John the Baptist or not. Schürer argues ably, if not conclusively, for the idea that this proselyte baptism was in use long before the first mention of it in the 2nd cent. (*HJP,* II/2, 319ff.; also Edersheim, *LTJM,* appendix 12). It matters nothing at all to the Baptist contention what is true in this regard. It would not be strange if a bath was required for a Gentile who became a Jew, when the Jews themselves required such frequent ceremonial ablutions. But what was the Jewish initiatory rite called proselyte baptism? Lightfoot (*Horae Hebraicae et Talmudicae,* Mt. 3:7) gives the law for the baptism of proselytes: "As soon as he grows whole of the wound of circumcision, they bring him to Baptism, and being placed in the water they again instruct him in some weightier and in some lighter commands of the Law. Which being heard, he plunges himself and comes up, and, behold, he is an Israelite in all things." To this quotation Marcus Dods (Presbyterian) in *DCG* adds: "To use Pauline language, his old man is dead and buried in the water, and he rises from this cleansing grave a new man. The full significance of the rite would have been lost had immersion not been practised." Lightfoot says further: "Every person baptized must dip his whole body, now stripped and made naked, at one dipping. And wheresoever in the Law washing of the body or garments is mentioned, it means nothing else than the washing of the whole body." Edersheim (*loc. cit.*) says: "Women were attended by those of their own sex, the rabbis standing at the door outside." Jewish proselyte baptism, an initiatory ceremonial rite, harmonizes exactly with the current meaning of *baptízō* already seen. There was no peculiar "sacred" sense that changed "dip" to "sprinkle."

C. Greek Usage. The Greek language has had a continuous history, and *baptízō* is used today in Greece for baptism. As is well known, not only in Greece, but wherever the Greek Church prevails, immersion is the unbroken and universal practice. The Greeks may surely be credited with knowledge of the meaning of their own language. The substitution of pouring or sprinkling for immersion, as the Christian ordinance of baptism, was late and gradual and finally triumphed in the West because of the decree of the Council of Trent. But the Baptist position is that this substitution was unwarranted and subverts the real significance of the ordinance. The Greek Church does practice trine immersion, one immersion for each person of the trinity, an old practice (cf. *ter mergitamur,* Tertullian *De baptismo* 6), but not the scriptural usage. A word will be needed later concerning the method by which pouring crept in beside immersion in the 2nd and later centuries. Before we turn directly to the NT use of *baptízō* it is well to quote from the *Greek Lexicon of the Roman and Byzantine Periods* by E. A. Sophocles, himself a native Greek. He says (p. 297): "There is no evidence that Luke and Paul and the other writers of the NT put upon this verb meanings not recognized by the Greeks." We expect therefore to find in the NT "dip," as the meaning of this word in the ceremonial sense of an initiatory Christian rite. Thayer's *Lexicon* likewise defines the word in this ceremonial Christian use to mean "an immersion in water, performed as a sign of the removal of sin."

Baptists could very well afford to rest the matter right here. There is no need to call for the testimony of a single Baptist scholar on this subject. The word of scholarship has rendered its decision with impartiality and force on the side of the Baptists in this matter. Alfred Plummer (Church of England) in his comm. on Matthew (2nd ed. 1910), p. 28, says that the office of John the Baptist was "to bind them to a new life, symbolized by immersion in water." Swete (Church of England) in his comm. on Mark (3rd ed. 1909) speaks of "the added thought of the immersion, which gives vividness of the scene" (on 1:9). The early Greek ecclesiastical writers show that immersion was employed; cf. Barn. 11:11, "We go down into the water full of sins and filth, and we come up bearing fruit in the heart." For numerous ecclesiastical examples see Sophocles' *Lexicon*.

D. NT Usage. But the NT itself makes the whole matter perfectly plain. The uniform meaning of "dip" for *baptízō* and the use of the river Jordan as the place for baptizing by John the Baptist makes inevitable the notion of immersion, unless there is some direct contradictory testimony. It is a matter that should be lifted above verbal quibbling or any effort to disprove the obvious facts. The simple narrative in Mt. 3:6 is that "they were baptized by him in the river Jordan." In Mk. 1:9f. the baptism is sharpened a bit in the use of *eis* and *ek*. Jesus "was baptized by John in [*eis*] the Jordan. And when he came up out of [*ek*] the water, immediately he saw." So in Acts 8:38 we read: "They both went down into [*eis*] the water, Philip and the eunuch, and he baptized him. And when they came up out of [*ek*] the water, the Spirit . . . caught up Philip."

If one could still be in doubt about the matter, Paul adds further evidence by the symbolism used in Rom. 6:4, "We were buried therefore with him by baptism into death, so that as Christ was raised from the dead by the glory of the Father, we too might walk in newness of life." The submergence and emergence of immersion thus, according to Paul, symbolize the death and burial to sin on the one hand and the resurrection to the new life in Christ on the other. Sanday and Headlam (Church of England) put it thus in their comm. on Romans (*ICC*, 14th ed. 1913), *in loc.*: "It expresses symbolically a series of acts corresponding to the redeeming acts of Christ. Immersion=Death. Submersion=Burial (the ratification of death). Emergence=Resurrection." In Col. 2:12 Paul again says: you were buried with him in baptism, in which you were also raised with him through faith in the working of God, who raised him from the dead." The same image is here presented. J. B. Lightfoot (Church of England) in his comm. on Colossians (1900), *in loc.*, says: "Baptism is the grave of the old man, and the birth of the new. As he sinks beneath the baptismal waters, the believer buries there all his corrupt affections and past sins; as he emerges thence, he rises regenerate, quickened to new hopes and new life."

There is nothing in the NT to offset this obvious and inevitable interpretation. The objections that are occasionally raised vanish on examination. The use of "with" after "baptize" in the AV is appealed to as disproving immersion. But the Committee of the American Standard Revision, which had no Baptist member at the final revision, substituted "in" for "with." Thus, "I indeed baptize you in water unto repentance" (Mt. 3:11; cf. also Mk. 1:8). The use of both "with" and "in" in Lk. 3:16 is a needless stickling for the use of the Gk. *en* with the locative case. In Mk. 1:8 *en* is absent in the best MSS, and yet the American Revisers correctly render "in." In Acts 1:5 they seek to draw the distinction between the mere locative and *en* and the locative. As a matter of fact the locative case alone is amply sufficient in Greek for the notion of "in." Cf. Jn. 21:8, "in the boat." The presence or absence of *en* with *baptízō* is wholly immaterial. In either case "dip" is the meaning of the verb.

The objection that three thousand people could not have been immersed in Jerusalem on the day of Pentecost is superficial. Jerusalem was sufficiently supplied with pools. There were 120 disciples on hand, most of whom were probably men (cf. the seventy sent out before by Jesus). It is not at all necessary to suppose that the twelve (Matthias was now one of them) apostles did all the baptizing. But even so, that would be only 250 apiece.

It is sometimes objected that Paul could not have immersed the jailer in the prison (Acts 16:25-34); but Luke does not say they stayed in the prison; indeed he implies just the opposite: "And he took [took *along*, Gk. *pará*] them the same hour of the night, and washed their wounds, and he was baptized at once." He took Paul and Silas with him and found a place for the baptism, probably somewhere on the prison grounds.

E. The Didache. Appeal has been made to the Didache, which may belong to the first half of the 2nd century. Here for the first time pouring is distinctly admitted as an ordinance in place of immersion. Because of this remarkable passage it is argued by some that, though immersion was the normal and regular baptism, yet alongside of it pouring was allowed, and that in reality it was a matter of indifference even in the 1st cent. whether pouring or immersion was used. But that is not the true interpretation of the facts in the case. The passage deserves to be quoted in full and is here given in the translation of Philip Schaff (Presbyterian) in his edition of the Didache (pp. 184ff.): "Now concerning baptism, baptize thus: Having first taught all these things, baptize ye into [*eis*] the name of the Father, and of the Son, and of the Holy Ghost, in living water. And if thou hast not living water, baptize into other water; and if thou canst not in cold, then in warm [water]. But if thou has neither, pour water thrice upon the head in [*eis*] the name of the Father, and of the Son, and of the Holy Ghost." There is thus no doubt that early in the 2nd cent. some Christians felt baptism was so important that, when the real baptism (immersion) could not be performed because of lack of water, pouring might be used in its place. This is all that can be deduced from this passage. It is to be noted that for pouring another word (*ekchéō*) is used, clearly showing that *baptízō* does not mean "pour." The very exception filed proves the Baptist contention concerning *baptízō*.

There is no thought of denying that pouring early in the 2nd cent. came to be used in place of immersion in certain extreme cases. The question remains as to why this use of pouring in extreme cases grew. The answer is that it was due to a mistaken and exaggerated estimate put upon the value of baptism as essential to salvation. Those who died without baptism were felt by some to be lost. Thus arose "clinic" baptisms.

F. Baptismal Regeneration. Out of this perversion of the symbolism of baptism grew both pouring as an ordinance and infant baptism. If baptism is necessary to salvation or the means of regeneration, then the sick, the dying, infants, must be baptized, or at any rate something must be done for them if the real baptism (immersion) cannot be performed because of extreme illness or want of water (cf. Justin *Apol.* i.61). The Baptist contention is to protest against this perversion of the significance of baptism as the ruin of the symbol. Baptism, as taught in the NT, is the picture of death and burial to sin and resurrection to new life, a picture of what has already taken place in the heart, not the means by which spiritual change is wrought. It is a privilege and duty, not a necessity. It is a picture that is lost when something else is substituted in its place. *See* BAPTISMAL REGENERATION.

II. Subjects of Baptism.–It is significant that even the Didache with its exaggerated notion of the importance of baptism does not allow baptism of infants. It says: "Having first taught all these things." Instruction precedes baptism. That is a distinct denial of infant baptism. The uniform practice in the NT is that baptism follows confession. The people "confessing their sins" were baptized by John (Mt. 3:6). It is frankly admitted by paedobaptist scholars that the NT gives no warrant for infant baptism. Thus Jacobus (Congregationalist) in the *Standard Bible Dictionary* says: "We have no record in the NT of the baptism of infants." Scott (Presbyterian) in *HDB* (1 vol. ed.) says: "The NT contains no explicit reference to the baptism of infants or young children." Plummer (Church of England), *HDB,* says: "The *recipients* of Christian baptism were required to repent and believe." Marcus Dods (Presbyterian), *DCG,* calls baptism "a rite wherein by immersion in water the participant symbolizes and signalizes his transition from an impure to a pure life, his death to a past he abandons, and his new birth to a future he desires." It would be hard to state the Baptist interpretation in better terms.

Thus no room is found in the NT for infant baptism, which would symbolize what the infant did not experience or would be understood to cause the regeneration in the child, a form of sacramentalism repugnant to the NT teaching as understood by Baptists. The dominant Baptist note is the soul's personal relation to God apart from ordinance, church, or priest. The infant who dies unbaptized is saved without baptism. The baptized individual, whether child (for children are often baptized by Baptists, children who show signs of conversion) or adult, is converted before his baptism. The baptism is the symbol of the change already wrought. So clear is this to the Baptist that he bears continual protest against that perversion of this beautiful ordinance by those who treat it as a means of salvation or who make it meaningless by performing it before conversion. Baptism is a preacher of the spiritual life. The Baptist contention is for a regenerated church membership, placing the kingdom before the local church. Membership in the kingdom precedes membership in the church.

The passages quoted from the NT in support of the notion of infant baptism are wholly irrelevant, Acts 2:39, where there is no such idea as baptism of infants, and 1 Cor. 7:14, where the point is that the marriage relation is sanctified and the children are legitimate, though husband or wife be heathen. It is begging the question to assume the presence of infants in the various household baptisms in Acts. In the case of the family of Cornelius they all spoke with tongues and magnified God (Acts 10:46). The jailer's household "rejoiced greatly" (Acts 16:34). We do not even know that Lydia was married. Her household may have been merely her employees in her business. Thus the NT presents no exceptions.

III. Present Obligation.–The Baptists make one more point concerning baptism. It is that, since Jesus himself submitted to it and enjoined it upon His disciples, the ordinance is of perpetual obligation. The arguments for the late ecclesiastical origin of Mt. 28:19 are not convincing. If it seem strange that Jesus should mention the three persons of the trinity in connection with the command to baptize, one should remember that the Father and the Spirit were both manifested to Him at His baptism. It was not a mere ceremonial ablution like the Jewish rites. It was the public and formal avowal of fealty to God, and the names of the trinity properly occur. The new heart is wrought by the Holy Spirit. Reconciliation with the Father is wrought on the basis of the work of the Son, who has manifested the Father's love in His life and death for sin. The fact that in Acts in the examples of baptism only the name of Jesus occurs does not show that this was the exact formula used. It may be a mere historical summary of the essential fact. The name of Jesus stood for the other two persons of the trinity. On the other hand the command of Jesus may not have been regarded as a formula for baptism; while in no sense sacramental or redemptive, it is yet obligatory and of perpetual significance. It is not to be dropped as one of the Jewish excrescences on Christianity. The form itself is necessary to the significance of the rite.

Hence Baptists hold that immersion alone is to be practiced, since immersion alone was commanded by Jesus and practiced in NT times. Immersion alone sets forth the death to sin, burial in the grave, and the resurrection to new life in Christ. Baptism as taught in the NT is "a mold of doctrine," a preacher of the heart of the gospel. Baptists deny the right of disciples of Jesus to break that mold. The point of a symbol is the form in which it is cast. To change the form radically is to destroy the symbolism. Baptists insist on the maintenance of primitive NT baptism because it alone is baptism, it alone proclaims the death and resurrection of Jesus, the spiritual death and resurrection of the believer, the ultimate resurrection of the believer from the grave. The disciple is not above his Lord, and has no right to destroy this rich and powerful picture for the sake of personal convenience, nor because he is willing to do something else which Jesus did not enjoin and which has no association with Him. The long years of perversion do not justify this wrong to the memory of Jesus, but all the more call upon modern disciples to follow the example of Jesus who himself fulfilled righteousness by going into the waters of the Jordan and receiving immersion at the hands of John the Baptist.

A. T. ROBERTSON

Bibliography.–*Reference:* Bauer, pp. 131f.; *TDNT,* I, *s.v.* βάπτω κτλ. (Oepke); A. Gill, *Bibliography of Baptist Writings on Baptism, 1902-1968* (1969); E. C. Starr, *Baptist Bibliography* (1947ff.); *Southern Baptist Encyclopedia.*

Ancient: Didache; Tertullian *De baptismo*; Cyril of Jerusalem *Catecheses.*

Early Anabaptist: G. Blaurock, *Reminiscences*; C. Grebel, *On Baptism*; M. Hofmann, *Ordinance of God*; B. Hübmaier, *Works.*

Modern: K. Aland, *Did the Early Church Baptize Infants?* (1963); K. Barth, *Teaching of the Church Regarding Baptism* (1948); G. R. Beasley-Murray, *Baptism in the NT* (1962); A. Carson, *Baptism in its Mode and Subjects* (1844); E. T. Hiscox, *New Directory for Baptist Churches* (1970); W. H. Pardee, *Baptism* (n.d.); H. W. Robinson, *Baptist Principles* (4th ed. 1966); J. Schneider, *Baptism and Church in the NT* (1957); J. Warns, *Baptism* (1957); R. E. O. White, *Biblical Doctrine of Initiation* (1960).

Baptist journals: Baptist History and Heritage; *Baptist Quarterly*; *Foundations*; *Review and Expositor.* A. G. CRAWFORD

REFORMED VIEW

I. Scriptural Names for the Rite
II. Pre-Christian Baptism
  A. Baptism of Proselytes
  B. Baptism of John
  C. Baptism in the Pagan Mysteries
III. Christian Baptism
  A. Administration of the Rite
  B. Mode
    1. Immersion
    2. Affusion
    3. Aspersion
  C. Who May Perform Baptism
  D. Who May Receive Baptism
    1. Baptism of Infants
    2. Baptism for the Dead
IV. Formula of Baptism
V. Doctrine of Baptism

Baptism has been from the earliest times the initiatory rite signifying the recognition of entrance into or of presence within the Christian Church. We find the earliest mention of the ceremony in Galatians (3:27), written about twenty years after the death of Jesus. There and in 1 Corinthians (1:13; 12:13) Paul takes for granted that everyone who becomes a Christian (himself included) must be baptized. The rite seems also to have existed among the discipleship of Jesus before His death. We are told (Jn. 4:1f.) that, although Jesus Himself did not baptize, His disciples did, and that their baptisms were more numerous than those of John.

I. Scriptural Names for the Rite.–The words commonly used in the NT to denote the rite are the verb *baptízō*, and the nouns *báptisma* and *baptismós*; but none is employed in this sense alone. The verb is used to denote the ceremonial purification of the Jews before eating, by pouring water on the hands (Lk. 11:38; Mk. 7:4); to signify the sufferings of Christ (Mk. 10:38f.; Lk. 12:50); and to indicate the sacrament of baptism. It is the intensive form of *báptein,* "to dip," and takes a wider meaning. The passages Lk. 11:38 and Mk.7:4 show conclusively that the word does not invariably signify to immerse the whole body. Some have held that *baptismós* invariably means ceremonial purification, and that *báptisma* is reserved for the Christian rite; but the distinction can hardly be maintained. The former certainly means ceremonial purification in Mk. 7:4, and in 7:8 (AV); but it probably means the rite of baptism in He. 6:2. Exegetes find other terms applied to Christian baptism. It is called 'water' in Acts 10:47 ("Can anyone forbid water for baptizing these people?"); the laver of the water in Eph. 5:26 (RV mg.) (where baptism is compared to the bridal bath taken by the bride before she was handed over to the bridegroom); and perhaps the laver of regeneration in Tit. 3:5 (RV mg.) (cf. 1 Cor. 6:11), and enlightenment in He. 6:4; 10:32.

II. Pre-Christian Baptism.–*A. Baptism of Proselytes.* Converts in the early centuries, whether Jews or Gentiles, could not have found this initiatory rite, in which they expressed their newborn faith, utterly unfamiliar. Water is the element naturally used for cleansing the body and its symbolical use entered into almost every cult, and into none more completely than the Jewish, whose ceremonial washings were proverbial. Besides those, the Jew had what would seem to the convert a counterpart of the Christian rite in the baptism of proselytes, by which Gentiles entered the circle of Judaism. For the Jews required three things of strangers who declared themselves to be converts to the law of Moses: circumcision (men only), baptism, and to offer sacrifice. It is somewhat singular that no baptism of proselytes is forthcoming until about the beginning of the 3rd cent.; and yet no competent scholar doubts its existence. Schürer (*HJP*) has contempt for those who insist on the argument from silence. The presence of this rite enables us both to see how Jews accepted readily the baptism of John and to understand the point of objectors who questioned his right to insist that all the Jews had to be purified before they could be ready for the messianic kingdom, although he was neither the Messiah nor a special prophet (Jn. 1:19-23).

B. Baptism of John. The baptism of John stood midway between the Jewish baptism of proselytes and Christian baptism. It differed from the former because it was more than a symbol of ceremonial purification; it was a baptism of repentance, a confession of sin and of the need of *moral* cleansing, and was a symbol of forgiveness and of moral purity. All men, Jews who were ceremonially pure and Gentiles who were not, had to submit to this baptism of repentance and pardon. It differed from the latter because it only symbolized preparation to receive the salvation, the kingdom of God which John heralded, and did not imply entrance into that kingdom itself. Those who had received it, as well as those who had not, had to enter the Christian community by the door of Christian baptism (Acts 19:3-6). The Jewish custom of baptizing, whether displayed in their frequent ceremonial washings, in the baptism of proselytes, or in the baptism of John, made Christian baptism a familiar and even expected rite to Jewish converts in the 1st century.

C. Baptism in the Pagan Mysteries. Baptism, as an initiatory rite, was no less familiar to gentile converts who had no acquaintance with the Jewish religion. The ceremonial washings of the priests of pagan religions have been often adduced as something that might familiarize gentile converts with the rite that introduced them into the Christian community, but they were not initiations. A more exact parallel is easily found. It is often forgotten that in the earlier centuries when Christianity was slowly making its way in the pagan world, pagan piety had deserted the official religions and taken refuge within the mysteries, and that these mystery religions represented the popular pagan religions of the times. They were all private cults into which men and women were received one by one, by rites of initiation that each had to pass through personally. When admitted the converts became members of coteries, large or small, of like-minded persons, who had become initiated because their souls craved something they believed they would receive in and through the rites of the cult. These initiations were secret, jealously guarded from the knowledge of all outsiders; still enough is known about them for us to be sure that among them baptism took an important place (Apuleius *Metamorphoses* xi). The rite of baptism was therefore as familiar to pagan as to Jewish converts, and it was no unexpected requirement for the convert to know that baptism was the doorway into the Church of Christ. These heathen baptisms, like the baptism of proselytes, were for the most part simply ceremonial purifications; for while it is true that both in the cult of the mysteries and beyond it a mode of purifying after great crimes was baptizing in flowing water (Euripides *Iphigenia in Tauri* 167) or in the sea, yet it would appear that only ceremonial purification was thought of. Nor were ceremonial rites involving the use of water confined to the paganism of the early centuries. Such a ceremony denoted the reception of the newly born child into pagan Scandinavian households. The father decided whether the infant was to be reared or exposed to perish.

If he resolved to preserve the babe, water was poured over it and a name was given to it.

III. Christian Baptism.–*A. Administration of the Rite.* In the administration of the rite of Christian baptism three things have to be looked at: the act of baptizing; those who are entitled to perform it; and the recipients or those entitled to receive it. A complete act of baptizing involves three things: the material of the sacrament; the method of its use; and the form of the sacrament, the baptismal formula or form of words accompanying the use of the water. The material of the sacrament is water, and for this reason baptism is called the water sacrament. The oldest Christian ecclesiastical manual of discipline that has descended to us, the Didache, says that the water to be preferred is "living," i.e., running water, water in a stream or river, or fresh flowing from a fountain. "And if thou hast not living water, baptize in other water; and if thou canst not in cold, then in warm" (ch. 7). In those directions the prescriptions of the ceremonial for the Jewish baptism of proselytes are closely followed. The earlier canons of the Church permit any kind of water, fresh or salt, provided only it be true and natural water (*aqua vera et naturalis*).

B. Mode. The use of the water is called ablution. According to the rules of by far the largest portion of the Christian Church the water may be used in any one of three ways: *immersion,* where the recipient enters bodily into the water, and where, during the action, the head is plunged either once or three times beneath the surface; *affusion,* where water is poured upon the head of the recipient who stands either in water or on dry ground; and *aspersion,* where water is sprinkled on the head or on the face.

1. Immersion. It has frequently been argued that the word *baptízein* invariably means "to dip" or "immerse," and that therefore Christian baptism must have been performed originally by immersion only, and that the two other forms, affusion and aspersion, are invalid — that there can be no real baptism unless the method of immersion be used. But the word that invariably means "to dip" is not *baptízein* but *báptein*; *baptízein* has a wider signification; and its use to denote the Jewish ceremonial of pouring water on the hands (Lk. 11:38; Mk. 7:4), as has already been said, shows that it is impossible to conclude from the word itself that immersion is the only valid method of performing the rite. It may be admitted at once that immersion, where the whole body including the head is plunged into a pool of pure water, gives a more vivid picture of the cleansing of the soul from sin; and that complete surrounding with water suits better the metaphors of burial in Rom. 6:4 and Col. 2:12, and of being surrounded by cloud in 1 Cor. 10:2.

2. Affusion. On the other hand affusion is certainly a more vivid picture of the bestowal of the Holy Spirit, which is equally symbolized in baptism. No definite information is given of the mode in which baptism was administered in apostolic times. Such phrases as "And when he came up out of the water," "went down into the water" (Mk. 1:10; Acts 8:38), are as applicable to affusion as to immersion. The earliest account of the mode of baptizing occurs in the Didache (ch. 7), where it is said: "Now concerning baptism, baptize thus: Having first taught all these things, baptize ye into the name of the Father, and of the Son, and of the Holy Ghost, in living water. And if thou hast not living water, baptize into other water; and if thou canst not in cold, then in warm. But if thou has neither, pour water thrice upon the head in the name of the Father, and of the Son, and of the Holy Ghost." This seems to say that to baptize by immersion was the practice recommended for general use, but that the mode of affusion was also valid and enjoined on occasions.

What is here prescribed in the Didache seems to have been the practice usually followed in the early centuries of the Christian Church. Immersion was in common use; but affusion was also widely practiced, and both were esteemed usual and valid forms of baptizing. When immersion was used the head of the recipient was plunged thrice beneath the surface at the mention of each name of the trinity; when the mode was by affusion the same reference to the trinity was kept by pouring water thrice upon the head. The two usages that were recognized and prescribed by the beginning of the 2nd cent. may have been in use throughout the apostolic period, although definite information is lacking.

When we remember the various pools in Jerusalem, and their use for ceremonial washings, it is not impossible to suppose that the three thousand who were baptized on the day of Pentecost may have been immersed; but when the furnishing and conditions of Palestinian houses and of oriental jails are taken into account, it is difficult to conceive that at the baptisms of Cornelius and of the jailer the ceremony was performed otherwise than by affusion.

It is a somewhat curious fact that if the evidence from written texts, whether ancient canons or writings of the earlier fathers, be studied by themselves, the natural conclusion would seem to be that immersion was the almost universal form of administering the rite; but if the witness of the earliest pictorial representations be collected, then we must infer that affusion was the usual method and that immersion was exceptional; for the pictorial representations, almost without exception, display baptism performed by affusion, i.e., the recipient is seen standing in water while the minister pours water on the head. It may therefore be inferred that evidence for the almost universal practice of immersion, drawn from the fact that baptisms took place in river pools (it is more than probable that where we find the names of local saints given to pools in rivers, those places were their favorite places of administering the rite), or from the large size of almost all early medieval baptisteries, is by no means so conclusive as many have supposed, such places being equally applicable to affusion.

It is also interesting to remember that when most of the Anabaptists of the 16th cent. insisted on baptism upon confession of faith, immersion was not the method practiced by them. During the great baptismal scene in the marketplace of the city of Münster the ordinance was performed by the ministers pouring three cans of water on the heads of the recipients. They baptized by affusion and not by immersion. This was also the practice among the Mennonites or earliest Baptists. This double mode of administering the sacrament — by immersion or by affusion — prevailed in the churches of the first twelve centuries, and it was not until the 13th that the practice of aspersion or sprinkling was almost universally employed.

3. Aspersion. The third method of administering baptism, by aspersion or sprinkling, has a different history from the other two. It was in the early centuries exclusively reserved for sick and infirm persons too weak to be submitted to immersion or affusion. There is evidence to show that those who received the rite in this form were somewhat despised; for the nicknames *clinici* and *grabatorii* were (unworthily, Cyprian declares) bestowed on them by neighbors. The question was even raised in the middle of the 3rd cent. whether baptism by aspersion was a valid baptism, and Cyprian was asked for his opinion on the matter. His answer is contained in his 75th epistle (69 in Hartel's ed.). There he contends that the ordinance administered this way is perfectly valid, and quotes in support of his opinion various OT texts that assert the purifying effects of water sprinkled (Ezk. 36:25f.; Nu. 8:5-7; 19:8f., 12f.). It is not the amount of the water or the method of its application that can cleanse from sin: "Whence it appears that the sprinkling also of water prevails equally with the washing of salvation . . . and that where the faith of the giver and receiver is sound, all things hold and may be consummated and perfected by the majesty of God and by the truth of faith." His opinion prevailed. Aspersion was recognized as a valid, though exceptional, form of baptism. But it was long in commending itself to ministers and people, and did not attain to almost general use until the 13th century.

The idea that baptism is valid only when practiced in the one method of immersion can scarcely be looked on as anything else than a ritualistic idea.

C. Who May Perform Baptism. The Scripture nowhere describes or limits the qualifications of those who are entitled to perform the rite of baptism. We find apostles, wandering preachers (Acts 8:38), a private member of a small and persecuted community (Acts 9:18) performing the rite. In the subapostolic Church we find the same liberty of practice. Clement of Alexandria tells us that the services of Christian women were necessary for the work of Christian missions, for they alone could have access to the *gynaeceum* and carry the message of the gospel there (*Misc.* iii.6). Such women missionaries did not hesitate to baptize. Whatever credit may be given to the Acts of Paul and Thecla, it is at least historical that Thecla did exist, that she was converted by Paul, that she worked as a missionary, and that she baptized her converts.

Speaking generally, as participation in a sacrament has always been looked upon as the recognition of one's presence within the Christian Church, it is an act of the Church and not of the individual believer; therefore no one is entitled to perform the act who is not in some way a representative of the Christian community — the representative character ought to be maintained somehow. As soon as the community had taken regular and organized form the act of baptism was suitably performed by those who, as office-bearers, naturally represented the community. It was recognized that the pastor or bishop (for these terms were synonymous until the 4th cent. at least) ought to preside at the administration of the sacrament; but in the early Church the power of delegation was recognized and practiced, and elders and deacons presided at this and even at the eucharist. What has been called lay baptism is not forbidden in the NT and has the sanction of the early Church. When superstitious views of baptism entered largely into the Church and it was held that no unbaptized child could be saved, the practice arose of encouraging the baptism of all weakling infants by nurses. The Reformed Church protested against this and was at pains to repudiate the superstitious thought of any mechanical efficacy in the rite by deprecating its exercise by any save approved and ordained ministers of the Church. Still, while they condemned lay baptism as irregular, it may be questioned whether they would assert any administration of the rite to be invalid, provided only it had been performed with devout faith on the part of giver and receiver.

D. Who May Receive Baptism. The recipients of Christian baptism are all those who make a presumably sincere profession of repentance of sin and of faith in the Lord Jesus Christ, the Savior, together with the children of such believing parents. The requirements are set forth in the accounts given us of the performance of the rite in the NT, in which we see how the apostles obeyed the commands of their Master. Jesus had ordered them to "make disciples of all nations, baptizing them in the name of the Father and of the Son and of the Holy Spirit" (Mt. 28:19) — to "preach the gospel to the whole creation. He who believes and is baptized will be saved; but he who does not believe will be condemned" (Mk. 16:15f.). The apostle Peter said to the inquirers on the day of Pentecost, "Repent, and be baptized every one of you in the name of Jesus Christ for the forgiveness of your sins; and you shall receive the gift of the Holy Spirit" (Acts 2:38); and three thousand were added to the Church through the initiatory rite of baptism. The Samaritans, who believed on Jesus through the preaching of Philip, were admitted to the Christian community through baptism; though in this case one of the baptized, Simon Magus, after his reception, was found to be still in "the bond of iniquity" (Acts 8:12, 23).

The jailer *with all his family,* Lydia *with her household,* were baptized at Philippi by Paul on his and her profession of faith in Jesus. There is no evidence in any of the accounts we have of apostolic baptisms that any prolonged course of instruction was thought to be necessary; nothing of classes for catechumens such as we find in the early Church by the close of the 2nd cent., or in modern missionary enterprise. We find no mention of baptismal creeds, declarative or interrogative, in the NT accounts of baptisms. The profession of faith in the Lord Jesus, the Savior, made by the head of the family appears, so far as the NT records afford us information, to have been sufficient to secure the baptism of the "household" — a word which in those days included both servants and children.

1. Baptism of Infants. This brings us to the much debated question whether infants are to be recognized as lawful recipients of Christian baptism. The NT Scriptures do not in so many words either forbid or command the baptism of children. The question is in this respect equivalent to the change of the holy day from the seventh to the first day of the week. No positive command authorizes the universal usage with regard to the Christian sabbath day; that the change is authorized must be settled by a weighing of evidence. So it is with the case of infant baptism. It is neither commanded nor forbidden in so many words; and the question cannot be decided on such a basis. The strongest argument against the baptizing of infants lies in the thought that the conditions of the rite are repentance and faith; that these must be exercised by individuals, each one for himself and for herself; and that infants are incapable either of repentance or of faith of this kind. The argument seems weak in its second statement; it is more dogmatic than historical, and will be referred to later when the doctrine lying at the basis of the rite is examined.

On the other hand a great deal of evidence supports the view that the baptism of infants, if not commanded, was at least permitted and practiced within the apostolic Church. Paul connects baptism with circumcision and implies that under the gospel the former takes the place of the latter (Col. 2:12); and as children were circumcised on the eighth day after birth, the inference follows naturally that children were also to be baptized. In the OT, promises to parents included their children. In his sermon on Pentecost Peter declares to his hearers that the gospel promise is "to you and to your children" and connects this with the invitation to baptism (Acts 2:38f.). It is also noteworthy that children shared in the Jewish baptism of proselytes. Then we find in the NT narratives of baptisms that "households" were baptized — of Lydia (Acts 16:15), of the jailer at Philippi (16:32), of Stephanas (1 Cor. 1:16). It is never said that the children of the household were exempted from the sacred rite. One has only to remember the position of the head of the household in that ancient world, to recollect how the household was thought to be embodied in its head, to see how the repentance and faith of the head of the household was looked upon as including that of all the members, not merely children but servants, to feel that had the children been excluded from sharing in the rite the exclusion would have seemed such an unusual thing that it would have at least been mentioned and explained. Our Lord expressly made very young children the types of those who entered into His kingdom (Mk. 10:14-16); and Paul so unites parents with children in the faith of Christ that he does not hesitate to call the children of the believing husband or wife "holy," and to imply that the children had passed from a state of "uncleanness" to a state of "holiness" through the faith of a parent. All these things seem to indicate that the rite that was the door of entrance into the visible community of the followers of Jesus was shared in by the children of believing parents.

Moreover, evidence for the baptism of children goes back to the earliest times of the subapostolic Church. Irenaeus was the disciple of Polycarp, who had been the disciple of John, and it is difficult to draw any other conclusion from his statements than that he believed that the baptism of infants had been an established practice in the Church long before his days (*Adv. haer.* ii.22; cf. 39). The witness of Tertullian is specially interesting; for he himself plainly thinks that adult baptism is to be preferred to the baptism of infants. He makes it plain that the custom of baptizing infants existed in his days, and we may be sure from the character and the learning of the man that had he been able to affirm that infant baptism had been a recent innovation and had not been a long-established usage descending from apostolic times, he would certainly have had no hesitation in using what would have seemed to him a very convincing way of dealing with his opponents. Tertullian's testimony comes from the end of the 2nd cent. or the beginning of the 3rd. Origen, the most learned Christian writer during the first three centuries and who comes a little later than Tertullian, in his 14th Homily on Luke bears witness to the usualness of the baptism of infants when he argues that original sin belongs to children because the Church baptizes them.

At the same time it is plain from a variety of evidence too long to cite that the baptism of infants was not a universal practice in the early Church. The Church of the early centuries was a mission Church. It drew large numbers of its members from heathendom. In every mission Church the baptism of adults will naturally take the foremost place and be most in evidence. But it is clear that many Christians were of the opinion of Tertullian and believed that baptism ought not to be administered to children but should be confined to adults. Nor was this a theory only; it was a continuous practice handed down from one generation to another in some Christian families. In the 4th cent. few Christian leaders took a more important place than Basil the Great and his brother Gregory of Nyssa. They belonged to a family who had been Christians for some generations; yet neither of the brothers was baptized until after his personal conversion, which does not appear to have come until they had attained the years of manhood.

The whole evidence seems to show that in the early Church, down to the end of the 4th cent. at least, infant and adult baptism were open questions and that the two practices existed side by side without disturbing the unity of the churches. In the later Pelagian controversy it became evident that the theory and practice of infant baptism had been able to assert itself and that the ordinance was always administered to children of members of the Church.

2. *Baptism for the Dead.* Paul refers to a custom of "baptizing on behalf of the dead" (1 Cor. 15:29). What this "vicarious baptism" or "baptism for the dead" was it is impossible to say, even whether it was practiced within the primitive Christian Church. The passage is a very difficult one and has called forth a very large number of explanations, which are mere guesses. Paul neither commends it nor disapproves of it; he simply mentions its existence and uses the fact as an argument for the resurrection. *See* BAPTISM FOR THE DEAD.

IV. Formula of Baptism.–The formula of Christian baptism, in the mode that prevailed, is given in Mt. 28:19: "I baptize you in the name of the Father, of the Son, and of the Holy Ghost." But it is curious that the words are not given in any description of Christian baptism until the time of Justin Martyr, and there they are not repeated exactly but in a slightly extended and explanatory form. He says that Christians "receive the washing with water in the name of God, the Ruler and Father of the universe, and of our Savior, Jesus Christ, and of the Holy Spirit" (*Apol.* i.61). In every account of the performance of the rite in apostolic times a much shorter formula is in use. The three thousand believers were baptized on the day of Pentecost "in the name of Jesus" (Acts 2:38); and the same formula was used at the baptism of Cornelius and those who were with him (10:48). Indeed it would appear to have been the usual one, from Paul's question to the Corinthians: "Were you baptized into the name of Paul?" (1 Cor. 1:13). The Samaritans were baptized "in the name of the Lord Jesus" (Acts 8:16); and the same formula (a common one in acts of devotion) was used in the case of the disciples at Ephesus. In some instances it is recorded that before baptism the converts were asked to make some confession of their faith, which took the form of declaring that Jesus was the Lord or that Jesus Christ was the Son of God. It may be inferred from a phrase in 1 Pet. 3:21 that a formal interrogation was made, and that the answer was an acknowledgement that Jesus Christ was Lord.

Scholars have exercised a great deal of ingenuity in trying to explain how, with what appear to be the very words of Jesus given in the Gospel of Matthew, another and much shorter formula seems to have been used throughout the apostolic Church. Some have imagined that the shorter formula was that used in baptizing disciples during the lifetime of Our Lord (Jn. 4:1f.), and that the apostles having become accustomed to it continued to use it during their lives. Others declare that the phrases "in the name of Jesus Christ" or "of the Lord Jesus" are not meant to give the formula of baptism, but simply to denote that the rite was Christian. Others think that the full formula was always used and that the narratives in Acts and in the Pauline Epistles are merely brief summaries of what took place — an idea rather difficult to believe in the absence of any single reference to the longer formula. Others, again, insist that baptism in the name of one of the persons of the trinity implies baptism in the name of the Three; while others declare that Matthew does not give the very words of Jesus but puts in His mouth what was the common formula used at the date and in the district where the First Gospel was written.

Whatever explanation be given it is plain that the longer formula became universal or almost universal in the subapostolic Church. Justin Martyr has already been quoted. Tertullian, nearly half a century later, declares expressly that the "law of baptism has been imposed and the formula prescribed" in Mt. 28:19 (*De baptismo* 13); and he adds in his *Adv. Prax.* (26): "And it is not once only, but thrice, that we are immersed into the Three Persons, at each several mention of Their names." The evidence to show that the formula given by Matthew became the established usage is overwhelming; but it is more than likely that the use of the shorter formula did not altogether die out, or, if it did, that it was revived. The historian Socrates informs us that some of the more extreme Arians "corrupted" baptism by using only the name of Christ in the formula; while injunctions to use the longer formula and punishments, including deposition, threatened to those who presumed to employ the shorter, which meet us in collections of ecclesiastical canons (*Apostolic Canons* 43, 50), prove that the practice of using the shorter formula existed in the 5th and 6th cents., at all events in the East.

V. Doctrine of Baptism.–The sacraments, and baptism as one of them, are always described to be (1) signs representing as in a picture or figure spiritual benefits (1 Pet. 3:21), and also (2) as seals or personal tokens and attestations confirmatory of solemn promises of spiritual benefits. Hence the sacrament is said to have two parts: "the one an outward and sensible sign, used according to Christ's appointment; the other an inward and spiritual grace thereby signified." It is held, moreover, that when the rite of baptism has been duly and devoutly performed with faith on the part of both giver and receiver, the spiritual benefits do follow the performance of the rite. The question therefore arises: What are the spiritual and evangelical blessings portrayed and solemnly promised in baptism?

In the NT we find that baptism is intimately connected with the following: with forgiveness of sins, as in Acts 22:16 ("Rise and be baptized, and wash away your sins"), and in He. 10:22; with regeneration or the new birth, as in Tit. 3:6 and Jn. 3:5 (this idea also entered into the baptism of proselytes and even into the thought of baptism in the mystery religions; neophytes were taught that in the water they died to their old life and began a new one [Apuleius *Metamorphoses* xi]); with ingrafting into Christ, with union with Him, as in Gal. 3:27 — and union in definite ways, in His death, His burial, and His resurrection, as in Rom. 6:3-6; with entering into a new relationship with God, that of sonship, as in Gal. 3:26f.; with the bestowal of the Holy Spirit, as in 1 Cor. 12:13; with belonging to the Church, as in Acts 2:41; with the gift of salvation, as in Mk. (?) 16:16; Jn. 3:5.

From these and similar passages theologians conclude that baptism is a sign and seal of our ingrafting into Christ and of our union with Him, of forgiveness of sins, regeneration, adoption, and life eternal; that the water in baptism represents and signifies both the blood of Christ, which takes away all our sins, and also the sanctifying influence of the Holy Spirit against the dominion of sin and the corruption of our human nature; and that baptizing with water signifies the cleansing from sin by the blood and for the merit of Christ, together with the mortification of sin and rising from sin to newness of life by virtue of the death and resurrection of Christ. Or to put it more simply: Baptism teaches that all who are out of Christ are unclean by reason of sin and need to be cleansed. It signifies that just as washing with water cleanses the body so God in Christ cleanses the soul from sin by the Holy Spirit, and that we are to see in this cleansing not merely pardon but also an actual freeing of the soul from the pollution and power of sin and therefore the beginnings of a new life. The sacrament also shows us that the cleansing is reached only through connection with the death of Christ, and further that through the new life begun in us we become in a special way united to Christ and enter into a new and filial relationship with God.

Probably all Christians, Reformed or not, will agree in the above statement of the doctrinal meaning in the rite of baptism; and also that when the sacrament is *rightly used* the inward and spiritual grace promised is present along with the outward and visible signs. But Roman Catholics and Protestants differ about what is meant by the *right use* of the sacrament. They separate on the question of its efficacy. Roman Catholics understand by the *right use* simply the correct performance of the rite and the placing no obstacle in the way of the flow of efficacy. Protestants insist that there can be no *right use* of the sacrament unless the recipient exercises faith, that without faith the sacrament is not efficacious and the inward and spiritual blessings do not accompany the external and visible signs. Whatever minor differences divide Protestant evangelical churches on this sacrament they are all agreed upon this, that where there is no faith there can be no regeneration. Here emerges doctrinally the difference between those who give and those who refuse to give the sacrament to infants.

The latter, taking their stand on the fundamental doctrine of all evangelical Christians that faith is necessary to make any sacrament efficacious, and assuming that the effect of an ordinance is always tied to the precise time of its administration, insist that infants cannot form such a conscious, intelligent, and individually independent act of faith as they believe all Protestants insist on scriptural grounds to be necessary in the *right use* of a sacrament. Therefore they refuse to baptize infants and young children.

The great majority of evangelical Protestants practice infant baptism and do not think, due explanations being given, that it in any way conflicts with the idea that faith is necessary to the efficacy of the sacrament. The Baptist position appears to them to conflict with much of the teaching of the NT. It implies that all who are brought up in the faith of Christ and within the Christian family still lack, when they come to years of discretion, that great change of heart and life which is symbolized in baptism, and can receive it only by a conscious, intelligent, and thoroughly independent act of faith. This seems in accordance neither with Scripture nor with human nature. We are told that a child may be full of the Holy Spirit from his mother's womb (Lk. 1:15); that little children *are* in the kingdom of Christ (Mt. 19:14); that children of believing parents are holy (1 Cor. 7:14). Does it mean nothing that in the NT as in the OT the promise is "to you and your children"? Besides, the argument of those who oppose the baptism of infants, if logically carried out, leads to consequences few of them would accept. Faith is as essential to salvation, in all evangelical theology, as it is for the *right use* of the sacrament; and every one of the arguments brought against the baptism of infants is equally applicable to the denial of their salvation.

Nor can the Baptist position be said to be true to the facts of ordinary human nature. Faith, in its evangelical sense of *fiducia* or trust, is not such an abrupt thing as they make it. Their demand for such a conscious, intelligent, strictly individualist act of faith sets aside some of the deepest facts of human nature. No one, young or old, is entirely self-dependent; nor are our thoughts and trust always or even frequently entirely independent and free from the unconscious influences of others. We are interwoven together in society; and what is true generally reveals itself still more strongly in the intimate relations of the family. Is it possible in all cases to trace the creative effects of the subtle imperceptible influences that surround children, or to say when the slowly dawning intelligence is first able to apprehend enough to trust in half-conscious ways? It is a shallow view of human nature that sets all such considerations aside and insists on regarding nothing but isolated acts of knowledge or of faith.

With all this in mind, the great majority of evangelical churches admit and enjoin the baptism of infants. They believe that the children of believing parents are "born *within* the church and have interest in the covenant of grace and a right to its seal." They explain that the efficacy of a sacrament is not rigidly tied to the exact time of administration, and can be appropriated whenever faith is kindled and is able to rest on the external sign, and that the spiritual blessings signified in the rite can be appropriated again and again with each fresh kindling of faith. They declare that no one can tell how soon the dawning of intelligence may awaken to the act of appropriation. Therefore these churches instruct their ministers in dispensing the sacrament to lay vows on parents that they will train up the infants baptized "in knowledge and fear of the Lord," and will teach them the great blessings promised to them in and through the sacrament and teach them to appropriate these blessings for themselves. They further enjoin their ministers to admonish all who may witness a baptismal service to look back on their own baptism in order that their faith may be stirred afresh to appropriate for themselves the blessings that accompany the proper use of the rite.

Bibliography.–*HERE*; *TDNT,* I, *s.v.* βάπτω κτλ. (Oepke); Calvin *Inst.* iv.14-16; Zwingli, *Of Baptism* (*LCC,* XXIV); W. Wall, *History of Infant Baptism* (1705); J. B. Mozley, *Review of the Baptismal Controversy* (2nd ed. 1895); W. R. Flemington, *NT Doctrine of Baptism* (1949); O. Cullmann, *Baptism in the NT* (Eng. tr. 1950); P. C. Marcel, *Biblical Doctrine of Infant Baptism* (1953).

T. M. LINDSAY

LUTHERAN VIEW

I. The Term
II. The Ordinance
  A. Teaching of Scripture
  B. Biblical History of the Ordinance
  C. Types of Baptism
III. Difficulties
  A. Are Mt. 28:18-20 and Mk. 16:15f. Genuine?
  B. Was the Trinitarian Formula Used in NT Times?
  C. Was Christian Baptism Really a New Ordinance?
  D. Should Infants Be Baptized?
  E. Why Did Paul Not Baptize?
  F. What Is the Baptism for the Dead?

I. The Term.–The word "baptism" is the Anglicized form of the Gk. *báptisma,* or *baptismós*. These Greek words are verbal nouns derived from *baptízō,* the intensive form of the verb *báptō*. "*Baptismós* denotes the act as a fact, *báptisma* the result of the act" (Cremer, p. 130). This distinction differs from, but is not necessarily contrary to, that of Plummer, who infers from Mk. 7:4 and He. 9:10 that *baptismós* usually means lustrations or ceremonial washings, and from Rom. 6:4; Eph. 4:5; 1 Pet. 3:21 that *báptisma* denotes baptism proper.

The Greek words from which our English "baptism" has been formed are used by Greek writers, in classical antiquity, in the LXX, and in the NT, with a great latitude of meaning. It is not possible to exhaust their meaning by any single English term. The action the Greek words express may be performed by plunging, drenching, staining, dipping, sprinkling. The nouns *báptisma* and *baptismós* do not occur in the LXX; the verb *baptízō* occurs in only four places, two of them in a figurative sense (2 K. 5:14; Jth. 12:7; Isa. 21:4; Sir. 34:25). Wherever these words occur in the NT, the context or, in the case of quotations, a comparison with the OT will in many instances suggest which of these renderings should be adopted (cf. Mk. 7:4; He. 9:10 with Nu. 19:18f.; 8:7; Ex. 24:4-6; and Acts 2:16 and 41 with Joel 2:28). But there are passages in which the particular form of the act of baptizing remains in doubt. "The assertion that the command to baptize is a command to immerse . . . [is] utterly unauthorized" (C. Hodge, *Systematic Theology* [1876], III, 527).

In the majority of biblical instances the verbs and nouns denoting baptism are used in a literal sense and signify the application of water to an object or a person for a certain purpose. The ceremonial washings of the Jews, the baptism of proselytes to the Jewish faith, common in the days of Christ, the baptism of John and of the disciples of Christ prior to the day of Pentecost, and the Christian sacrament of baptism, are literal baptisms (*baptismus fluminis,* "baptism of the river," i.e., water). But Scripture speaks also of figurative baptisms, without water (Mk. 10:38 and Lk. 12:50 refer to the sufferings that overwhelmed Christ and His followers, especially the martyrs [*baptismus sanguinis,* "baptism of blood]; Mt. 3:11; Mk. 1:8; Lk. 3:16; Acts 1:5; 11:16 refer to the outpouring of the miraculous gifts of the Holy Spirit, which was a characteristic phenomenon of primitive Christianity [*baptismus flaminis,* "baptism of wind, breeze," i.e., "spirit"]). Some even take Mt. 21:25; Mk. 11:30; Acts 18:25; 1 Cor. 10:2 in a synecdochical sense, for doctrine of faith, baptism being a prominent feature of that doctrine (*baptismus luminis,* "baptism of light").

Scripture occasionally alludes to Christian baptism without employing the regular term. Thus in Tit. 3:5 and Eph. 5:26 we have the term *loutrón*, "washing," instead of *báptisma.* From this term the Latin Church derived its *lavacrum* (Eng. "laver") as a designation of baptism. In He. 10:22 the verbs *rhantízō* and *loúō*, "sprinkle" and "wash"; in Eph. 5:26 the verb *katharízō,* "cleanse"; and in 1 Cor. 6:11 the verb *apoloúō,* "wash," are evidently synonyms of *baptízō*.

II. The Ordinance.–*A. Teaching of Scripture*. Christian baptism as now practiced is a sacred ordinance of evangelical grace, solemnly appointed by the risen Christ prior to His entering into the state of glory by His ascension, and designed to be a means, until His second coming, for admitting people to discipleship with Him. Mt. 28:18-20 and its parallel Mk. 16:15f. are the principal texts of Scripture on which the Church in all ages has based every essential point of its teaching regarding this ordinance. The host of other baptismal texts of Scripture expand and illustrate the contents of these two texts. We have in these texts:

(1) *An authoritative* (Mt. 28:19) *command,* issued in plain terms: "Make disciples . . . baptizing." This command declares (*a*) *speciem actus*, i.e., it indicates with sufficient clearness, by the use of the term "baptize," the external element to be employed, viz., water, and the form of the action to be performed by means of water,

viz., any dipping, or pouring, or sprinkling, since the word "baptize" signifies any of these modes. On the strength of this command Luther held: "Baptism is not simple water only, but it is the water comprehended in God's command"; and the Westminster Shorter Catechism (Q. 94) calls baptism "a washing with water." Water is distinctly mentioned as the baptismal element in Acts 8:38; 10:47; Eph. 5:26; He. 10:22. "There is no mention of any other element" (Plummer). The phraseology of Eph. 5:26, "the washing of water with the word," shows that not the external element alone, nor the physical action of applying the water, constitutes baptism; but "the word" must be added to the element and the action, in order that there may be a baptism. "Remove the word and what is water but water? The word is added to the element and it becomes a sacrament" (Augustine). "Without the Word of God the water is simple water, and no baptism" (Luther). The command prescribes (b) *exercitium actus,* i.e., it enjoins a continued exercise of this function of the messengers of Christ for all time.

(2) *A clear declaration of the object in view.* The participle "baptizing" qualifies the imperative "make disciples" and expresses the means by which that end is to be attained. The participle "baptizing," again, is qualified by "teaching" (v. 20). The second participle is not connected by "and" with the first, hence is subordinate to the first. Discipleship is to be obtained by baptizing-teaching. There is no rigid law regarding the order and sequence of these actions laid down in these words; they merely state that Christ desires His disciples to be both baptized and fully informed as to His teaching.

(3) *A definite promise:* salvation (Mk. 16:16), i.e., complete and final deliverance from all evil, the securing of "the faith" (1 Pet. 1:9). This is a comprehensive statement, as in 1 Pet. 3:21, of the blessing of baptism. Scripture also states, in detail, particular baptismal blessings: (a) *Regeneration* (Tit. 3:5; Jn. 3:3, 5). Despite Calvin and others, the overwhelming consensus of interpreters still agrees with the ancient Church and with Luther in explaining both these texts of baptism. (See d below.) (b) *Remission of sins,* or justification (Acts 2:38; 22:16; 1 Cor. 6:11; Eph. 5:26; He. 10:22). This blessing, no doubt, is also intended in 1 Pet. 3:21, where *eperṓtēma* has been rendered "answer" by the AV (RV "interrogation"; RSV "appeal"). The word denotes a legal claim, which a person has a right to set up (see Rom. 8:1). (c) *The establishment of a spiritual union with Christ,* and a new relationship with God (Gal. 3:26f.; Rom. 6:3f.; Col. 2:12). In this connection the prepositions with which *baptízein* occurs in the NT may be noted. The phrase *baptízein eis,* "to baptize into," always denotes the relation into which the party baptized is placed. The only exception is Mk. 1:9. The phrase *baptízein en* or *epí,* "to baptize in" (Acts 10:48; 2:38), denotes the basis on which the new relation is made to rest (Crem., p. 128). (d) *The sanctifying gifts of the Holy Spirit* (1 Cor. 12:13; Tit. 3:5). All these blessings Scripture declares to be effects of baptism. "Baptism is called 'washing of regeneration,' not merely because it symbolizes it, or pledges a man to it, but also, and chiefly, because it effects it (Holtzmann, Huther, Pfleiderer, Weiss). . . . Regeneration or being begotten by God does not mean merely a new *capacity* for change in the direction of goodness, but an actual change. The legal washings were actual external purifications. Baptism is actual internal purification" (Plummer). To these modern authorities Luther can be added. He says: "Baptism worketh forgiveness of sin, delivers from death and the devil, and gives eternal salvation to all who believe, as the words and promises of God declare" (Smaller Catechism). In Tit. 3:5, AV, the force of the preposition *diá,* "by," deserves to be noted: it declares baptism to be the regenerating, renewing, justifying, glorifying medium to the heirs of eternal life. The baptismal promise is supported, not only in a general way, by the veracity and sincerity of the Speaker, who is the divine Truth incarnate, but also in a special way, by the Author's appeal to His sovereign majesty (Mt. 28:18), and by the significant assurance of His personal ("I" =*egṓ* is emphatic) presence with the disciples in their aforementioned activity (Mt. 28:20; cf. Mk. 16:20). *See also* BAPTISMAL REGENERATION.

(4) *A plain indication of the scope:* "all nations," "the whole creation" (*pásę tę́ ktísei* to be understood as in Col. 1:23, "all people"). Baptism is of universal application; it is a cosmopolitan ordinance before which differences such as of nationality, race, age, sex, social or civil status, are leveled (cf. Col. 3:11 with 1 Cor. 12:13). Accordingly, Christ orders baptism to be practiced "always, to the close of the age," i.e., until the second advent of the Lord. For throughout this period Christ promises His cooperative presence with the efforts of His disciples to make disciples.

(5) *A prescribed formula for administering the ordinance:* "in the name of the Father and of the Son and of the Holy Spirit." Belief in the trinity is fundamental to Christianity; accordingly the sacred rite by which people are initiated into the Christian religion justly emphasizes this belief. The three persons are mentioned as distinct from one another, but the baptismal command is issued upon their joint and coequal authority ("in the name," not "names"), thus indicating the unity in trinity.

B. Biblical History of the Ordinance. After the Lord had entered into His glory, we find that in the era of the apostles and in the primitive Christian Church baptism is the established and universally acknowledged rite by which persons are admitted to communion with the Church (Acts 2:38, 41; 8:12f., 36, 38; 9:18; 10:47f.; 16:15, 33; 18:8; 22:16; Rom. 6:3; 1 Cor. 12:13; Gal. 3:27). Even in cases where an outpouring of the special gifts of the Holy Spirit had already taken place, baptism is still administered (Acts 10:44ff.; 11:15f.). Therefore, baptism came to occupy the same place in the new covenant as circumcision had in the old covenant (Col. 2:11f.; cf. Gal. 5:2ff.). The one baptism in Christ was recognized from the beginning as one of the bases for the unity of the Christian community (1 Cor. 12:13; Gal. 3:27f.; Eph. 4:5).

C. Types of Baptism. In 1 Cor. 10:1f. the apostle states that the Israelites were all "baptized into Moses in the cloud and in the sea." F. W. Farrar attempts the following solution of this type: "The passing under the cloud (Exod. xiv.19) and through the sea, constituting as it did their deliverance from bondage into freedom, their death to Egypt, and their birth to a new covenant, was a general type or dim shadow of Christian baptism (compare our collect, 'figuring thereby Thy holy baptism'). But the typology is quite incidental; it is the moral lesson which is paramount. . . . By this 'baptism' they accepted Moses as their Heaven-sent guide and teacher" (p. 322). In 1 Pet. 3:21 the apostle calls baptism the *antítypon* of the Deluge. Delitzsch (on He. 9:24) suggests that *týpos* and *antítypon* in Greek represent the original figure and a copy made therefrom, or a prophetic foretype and its later accomplishment. The point of comparison is the saving power of water in either instance. Water saved Noah and his family by floating the ark which sheltered them, and by removing from them the disobedient generation that had sorely tried their faith, as it had tried God's patience. In like manner the water of baptism bears up the ark of the Christian church and saves its believing members by separating them from their filthy sins.

***III. Difficulties.**–A. Are Mt. 28:18-20 and Mk. 16:15f. Genuine?* Feine (p. 396f.) and F. Kattenbusch (Sch.-Herz., I, 435-440) argue that the trinitarian formula in Mt. 28:19 is spurious, and that the text in Mark belongs to a section that was added to this Gospel at a later time. Thus far research has produced no good reason for rejecting the genuineness of the formula in Matthew. As to the concluding section in Mark (16:9-20), the so-called Longer Ending, its omission from such important MSS as ℵ and B has long cast doubt on its originality; yet no doctrinal scruple can arise on account of this section; for it contains nothing that is contrary to the doctrine of Scripture in other places on the same subject.

B. Was the Trinitarian Formula Used in NT Times? No record of such use can be discovered in the Acts or the Epistles of the apostles. The baptisms recorded in the NT after Pentecost are administered "in the name of Jesus Christ" (Acts 2:38), "in the name of the Lord Jesus" (8:16), "into Christ" (Rom. 6:3; Gal. 3:27). This difficulty was considered by the fathers. Ambrose says: "What had not been mentioned in words is expressed in belief" (*De Spiritu Sancto* i.3.43). On close inspection the difficulty is found to rest on the assumption that the above passages are records of baptismal formulas used on those occasions. The fact is that these records contain no baptismal formula at all, but "merely state that such persons were baptized as acknowledged Jesus to be the Lord and the Christ" (Plummer). The same can be said of any person baptized in our day with the trinitarian formula. That this formula was the established usage in the Christian Church is proven by records of baptisms in Justin (*Apol.* i.61) and Tertullian (*Adv. Prax.* 26).

C. Was Christian Baptism Really a New Ordinance? Baptism was practiced among the Jews prior to the solemn inauguration of this ordinance by the risen Christ. The ceremonial washings of the Jews are classed with the transient forms of the Levitical worship (He. 9:9f.), which had not been intended to endure except "until the time of reformation." They were removed when Christian baptism was erected into an abiding ordinance of the Church (Col. 2:11-13). It would be erroneous to say that those ancient washings developed into Christian baptism; a shadow does not develop into a substance. Nor do we find the origin of Christian baptism in the baptism of proselytes, which seems to have been a Jewish custom in the days of Christ. Though the rite of baptism was not unknown to the Jews, still the baptism of John startled them (Jn. 1:25). Such passages as Isa. 4:4 (1:16); Ezk. 36:25; 37:23; Zec. 13:1 had, no doubt, led them to expect a rite of purification in the days of the Messiah, which would supersede their Levitical purification. The delegation they sent to John was to determine the messianic character of John and his preaching and baptizing.

John's baptism has been a fruitful theme of debate. The question does not affect the personal faith of any Christian at the present time; for there is no person living who has received John's baptism. The entire subject and certain features of it, as the incident recorded in Acts 19:1-7, will continue to be debated. However, attention to a few essential facts will make clear the scriptural estimate of the baptism of John. John had received a divine commission to preach and baptize (Lk. 3:2; Jn. 1:33; Mt. 21:25). He baptized with water (Jn. 3:23). His baptism was honored by a wonderful manifestation of the holy trinity (Mt. 3:16f.) and by the Redeemer in His capacity as the representative of sinful mankind, the sin-bearing Lamb of God, accepting baptism at John's hand (Mt. 3:13-17; Jn. 1:29-34). It was of the necessity of receiving John's baptism that Christ spoke to Nicodemus (Jn. 3:3ff.). The Pharisees invited their eternal ruin by refusing John's baptism (Lk. 7:30); for John's baptism was to shield them from the wrath to come (Mt. 3:7); it was for the remission of sin (Mk. 1:4); it was a washing of regeneration (Jn. 3:5). When Jesus began His public ministry, He took up the preaching and baptism of John, and His disciples practiced it with such success that John rejoiced (Jn. 3:22, 25-36; 4:1f.). All this evidence fairly compels the belief that there was no essential difference between the baptism of John and the baptism instituted by Christ; that what the risen Christ did in Mt. 28:18-20 was merely to elevate a rite that had previously been adopted by an order "from above" to a permanent institution of His Church, and to proclaim its universal application. The contrast that John himself declares between his baptism and that of Christ is not a contrast between two baptisms with water. The baptism of Christ, which John foretells, is a baptism with the Holy Spirit and with fire, the pentecostal baptism. But for the general purpose of begetting men unto a new life, sanctifying and saving them, the Spirit was also bestowed through John's baptism (Jn. 3:5).

D. Should Infants Be Baptized? The command in Mt. 28:19; Mk. 16:16 is all-embracing; so is the statement concerning the necessity of baptism in Jn. 3:5. After reading these statements, one feels inclined to ask, not "Should infants be baptized?" but "Why should they *not* be baptized?" The *onus probandi* rests on those who reject infant baptism. The desire to have their infants baptized must have been manifested on the day when the first three thousand were baptized at Jerusalem, assuming that they were all adults. The old covenant had provided for their children; was the new to be inferior to the old in this respect? (See Plummer.) The baptism of entire households is presumptive evidence that children and infants were baptized in apostolic times (Acts 16:15, 33; 18:8; 1 Cor. 1:16). The arguments against infant baptism imply defective views on the subject of original sin and the efficacy of baptism. Infant faith — for faith is as necessary to the infant as to the adult — may baffle our attempts at explanation and definition; but God who established His covenant even with beasts (Gen. 9:16f.) extends His promises also to children (Acts 2:39); Christ who blessed also little children (Mk. 10:13-16) and spoke of them as believers (Mt. 18:6), certainly does not consider the regeneration of a child or infant a greater task than that of an adult (cf. Mt. 18:3f.).

E. Why Did Paul Not Baptize? Paul did baptize Crispus, Gaius, and Stephanas with his household. These baptisms he performed at Corinth alone; we have no record of his baptisms at other places. What Paul declares in 1 Cor. 1:14-17 is that by his baptizing he could not have become the cause of the divisions in the Corinthian congregation, because he had baptized only a few persons at Corinth and, moreover, had not baptized in his own name, hence had attached no one to his person. The statement, "Christ did not send me to baptize," is made after the Semitic idiom, and means: "not so much to baptize as to preach" (Farrar). If his words are taken in any other sense, it is impossible to protect Paul against the charge that he did something he was not authorized to do when he baptized Crispus, etc.

F. What is the Baptism for the Dead? 1 Cor. 15:29 is sometimes taken to mean that the early Christians practiced baptism by proxy. After they had been converted to Christianity, it is held, they desired to convey the benefits of their faith to their departed friends who had died in paganism, by having themselves baptized in their behalf, perhaps on their graves. We have no evidence from history that such a practice prevailed in the early Christian churches. Nor does the text suggest it. The Gk. *hýper* expresses also the motive that may prompt a person to a certain action. In this case the motive was suggested by the dead, viz., by the dead insofar as they shall rise. The context shows this to be the meaning: If a person has sought baptism anticipating that the dead are to rise to be judged, his baptism is valueless if the dead do not rise. *See* BAPTISM FOR THE DEAD.

Bibliography.–H. Cremer, *Biblico-Theological Lexicon of NT Greek* (4th ed. 1895, repr. 1954) *s.v.* βαπτίζω, βαπτισμός; F. W. Farrar, Comm. on 1 Cor. (*Pulpit Comm.*, repr. 1962); *HDB*, I, *s.v.* (Plummer); M. Luther; "The Holy and Blessed Sacrament of Baptism," *Luther's Works*, ed. J. Pelikan and H. T. Lehman, XXXV (1960), 25-43; *Three Treatises*, ed. C. M. Jacobs, A. T. W. Steinhäuser and W. A. Lambert (1960), pp. 178-198; P. Melanchthon, *Loci communes theologici* (*LCC*, XIX), esp. pp. 136-140; J. Herzog and A. Hauck, eds., *Realencyklopädie für protestantische Theologie und Kirche* (3rd ed. 1896ff.), XIX, *s.v.* "Taufe" (P. Feine); P. Schaff, *Creeds of Christendom*, III (4th ed. 1919).

W. H. T. DAU

BAPTISM FOR THE DEAD [Gk. *baptízomai hypér tṓn nekrṓn*]. As a subsidiary argument to combat the Corinthian denial of resurrection, Paul suggests that this denial deprives of all point the practice of baptism for the dead (1 Cor. 15:29). To what does he here refer, and what is the true force or drift of his argument?

A first and obvious suggestion is that there was in Corinth an actual practice "of survivors allowing themselves to be baptized on behalf of (believing?) friends who had died without baptism" (Alf., *in loc.*). This certainly seems to be the plain meaning of the phrase, but there are some good reasons for rejecting this interpretation. (1) Apart from a possible reference in Tertullian (*De res.* 48c), there is evidence of such a practice only among heretical groups like the Cerinthians and the Marcionites. (2) The practice as such seems inconsistent with Paul's general teaching. (3) If the practice existed without his approval, he would hardly be likely to appeal to it as the ground of so important a doctrine.

Many alternatives have been suggested, though most of them are strained and artificial. The following may be mentioned as perhaps the most helpful. First, baptisms often took place through the influence of dead friends, or through the actual witness of Christian death; but this would be nonsensical if there were no resurrection of the dead. Second, baptism is with a view to the dead, i.e., to their resurrection; but again this is pointless if there is no hope of resurrection.

The main difficulty with this kind of interpretation is that it does not give a strict rendering of what Paul actually says. On the other hand, it may be that Paul is here inserting a hurried parenthetical question which, like the similar question in 15:30, is a little obscure in its phrasing, because it has its main force by allusion rather than by full and clear statement. There can certainly be no doubt as to the underlying interconnection of baptism, death, and resurrection. Thus the question must mean: What is the value of a baptism unto death, or of the death signified in baptism, if there is no resurrection?

G. W. BROMILEY

BAPTISM OF FIRE [Gk. (*baptísei*) *en* (*pneúmati hagíǭ kaí*) *pyrí*]. This expression is found in Mt. 3:11 and Lk. 3:16. Two explanations are advanced. The first is that these are two different baptisms, the one of life (the spirit) and the other of judgment (fire). Arguments for this view are (1) that Luke immediately refers in v. 17 to the judicial work of Christ in terms of fire; (2) that baptism carries with it the thought of death and judgment as well as life and salvation; and (3) that Christ in relation to His atoning work links fire and baptism in the important sayings in Lk. 12:49f.

The second explanation is that the Holy Spirit and fire are here equated. In development of this interpretation it is argued (1) that the copulative demands equation; (2) that the Spirit is linked with tongues like as of fire in Acts 2:3; and (3) that fire may equally well symbolize the purifying, energizing, and even enlightening work of the Spirit.

Probably we should be wiser to think in terms of an interconnection of these various motifs instead of a stark alternative, since the work of the Spirit is also connected with judgment (Jn. 16:8), and the evangelical word and sacraments can be the savor of death to unbelievers as well as of life to believers (2 Cor. 2:15f.). In any case we are not to think of a literal baptism of fire as reported of the Origenists and others.

See also BAPTISM; FIRE. G. W. BROMILEY

BAPTISM OF THE HOLY SPIRIT.

I. Biblical Material.–The expression "baptism of the Holy Spirit" is based on a number of predictions found in our four Gospels and the record of their fulfillment in the book of Acts. The passages in the Gospels are as follows: Mt. 3:11: "I baptize you with water for repentance, but he who is coming after me is mightier than I, whose sandals I am not worthy to carry; he will baptize you with the Holy Spirit and with fire." The last clause is Gk. *autos hymās baptísei en pneúmati hagíǭ kaí pyrí*. In Mk. 1:8 and Lk. 3:16 we have the declaration in a slightly modified form; and in Jn. 1:33 John the Baptist declares that the descent of the Spirit upon Jesus at His baptism marked out Jesus as "he who baptizes with the Holy Spirit." Again in Jn. 7:37f. we read: "Now on the last day of the feast, the great day, Jesus stood up and proclaimed, 'If anyone thirst, let him come to me and drink. He who believes in me, as the scripture has said, "Out of his heart shall flow rivers of living water." ' " Then the Evangelist adds in v. 39: "Now this he said about the Spirit, which those who believed in him were to receive; for as yet the Spirit had not been given, because Jesus was not yet glorified." These are the specific references in the four Gospels to the baptisms of the Holy Spirit. In Acts we find direct reference by Luke to the promised baptism in the Holy Spirit. In 1:5 Jesus, just before His ascension, contrasts John's baptism in water with the baptism in the Holy Spirit that the disciples are to receive "before many days," and in v. 8 power in witnessing for Jesus is predicted as the result of the baptism in the Holy Spirit. On the evening of the resurrection day Jesus appeared to the disciples and "he breathed on them, and said to them, 'Receive the Holy Spirit' " (Jn. 20:22). This was probably not a wholly symbolic act but an actual communication to the disciples, in some measure, of the gift of the Spirit, preliminary to the later complete bestowal.

We observe next the fulfillment of these predictions as recorded in Acts. The gift of the Holy Spirit on the day of Pentecost and the miraculous manifestations that followed are clearly the chief historical fulfillment of the prediction of the baptism of the Holy Spirit. Among the manifestations of the coming of the Spirit at Pentecost were first those that were physical, such as "a sound . . .

like the rush of a mighty wind, and it filled all the house where they were sitting" (Acts 2:2), and the appearance of "tongues as of fire, distributed and resting on each one of them" (v. 3). Second, there were spiritual results: "And they were all filled with the Holy Spirit and began to speak in other tongues, as the Spirit gave them utterance" (v. 4). In vv. 16-21 Peter declares that this bestowal of the Holy Spirit is in fulfillment of the prediction made by the prophet Joel, and he cites the words in 2:28-32 of Joel's prophecy.

There is one other important passage in Acts in which reference is made to the baptism of the Holy Spirit. While Peter was speaking to Cornelius (Acts 10:44) the Holy Spirit fell on all that heard the word, and the Jews who were with Peter "were amazed, because the gift of the Holy Spirit had been poured out even on the Gentiles." When giving the brethren at Jerusalem an account of his visit to Cornelius, Peter declares that this event he had witnessed was a baptism of the Holy Spirit (Acts 11:16): "And I remembered the word of the Lord, how he said, 'John indeed baptized with water, but you shall be baptized with the Holy Spirit.' "

II. Significance.–*A. From the Point of View of OT Teaching as to the Gift of the Spirit.* The prophecy of Joel quoted by Peter indicates something extraordinary in the gift of the Spirit at Pentecost. The Spirit now comes in new forms of manifestation and with new power. The various classes mentioned as receiving the Spirit indicate the wide diffusion of the new power. In the OT the Spirit was usually bestowed upon individuals; here the gift is to the group of disciples, the Church. Here the gift is permanently bestowed, while in the OT it was usually transient and for a special purpose. Here again the Spirit comes in fulness as contrasted with the partial bestowal in OT times.

B. From the Point of View of the Ascended Christ. In Lk. 24:49 Jesus commands the disciples to tarry in the city "until you are clothed with power from on high," and in Jn. 15:26 He speaks of the Counselor "whom I shall send to you from the Father, . . . he will bear witness to me." In Jn. 16:13 Jesus declares that the Spirit when He comes will guide the disciples into all truth, and He will show them things to come. In this verse the Spirit is called the Spirit of truth. It was fitting that the Spirit who was to interpret truth and guide into all truth should come in fulness after, rather than before, the completion of the life-task of the Messiah. The historical manifestation of divine truth as thus completed made necessary the gift of the Spirit in fulness. Christ Himself was the giver of the Spirit. The Spirit now takes the place of the ascended Christ, or rather takes the things of Christ and shows them to the disciples. The baptism of the Spirit at Pentecost thus inaugurates, on the basis of the completed work of Christ, the worldwide mission of the Church in fulfillment of the Great Commission and with the promised presence and empowering of Mt. 28:19f.

C. From the Point of View of the Disciples. It can hardly be said with truth that Pentecost was the birthday of the Church. Jesus had spoken of His Church during His earthly ministry. The spiritual relation to Christ that constitutes the basis of the Church existed prior to the baptism of the Holy Spirit. But the baptism established the Church in several ways. It did so in unity, the external bond being strengthened by an inner spiritual bond of common quickening and endowment. Second, the Church now became conscious of a spiritual mission, and the material expectations the disciples had had right up to the Ascension in Acts 1 now disappeared. Third, the Church was now endued with power for its work. Among the gifts bestowed were the gift of prophecy in the large sense of speaking for God, and the gift of tongues, which enabled disciples to speak in foreign tongues. The account in Acts 2 admits of no other construction. There was also bestowed power in witnessing for Christ. This was indeed one of the most prominent blessings named in connection with the promise of the baptism of the Spirit. The power of working miracles was also bestowed (Acts 3:4ff.; 5:12ff.). Later in the Epistles of Paul much emphasis is given to the Spirit as the sanctifying agent in the hearts of believers. In Acts the word of the Spirit is chiefly messianic, i.e., the Spirit's activity is all seen in relation to the extension of the messianic kingdom. The occasion for the outpouring of the Spirit is Pentecost, when men from all nations were assembled in Jerusalem. The symbolic representation of tongues of fire is suggestive of preaching, and the glossolalia — or speaking with tongues — that followed, so that men of various nations heard the gospel in their own languages, indicates that the baptism of the Spirit had a very special relation to the task of worldwide evangelization for the bringing in of the kingdom of God.

III. Finality of the Baptism of the Holy Spirit.–The question is often raised whether or not the baptism of the Holy Spirit occurred once for all or has been repeated in subsequent baptisms. The evidence seems to point to the former view to the extent at least of being limited to outpourings that took place in connection with events recorded in the early chapters of Acts. The following considerations favor this view:

(1) In Acts 1 Jesus predicts, according to Luke's account, that the baptism of the Holy Spirit would take place "before many days" (Acts 1:5). This would seem to point to a definite and specific event rather than to a continuous process.

(2) Peter's citation in Acts 2:17-21 of Joel's prophecy shows that in Peter's mind the event his hearers were witnessing was the definite fulfillment of the words of Joel.

(3) The one other event that is described in the NT as the baptism of the Holy Spirit may be regarded as the completion of the pentecostal baptism. The passage is that contained in Acts 10:1–11:18, in which the record is given of the following events: (a) a miraculous vision is given to Peter on the housetop (10:11-16), indicating that the things about to occur are of unique importance; (b) speaking in tongues occurs (10:45f.); (c) Peter declares to the brethren at Jerusalem that the Holy Spirit fell on the Gentiles, in this instance Cornelius and his household, "as on us at the beginning" (11:15); (d) Peter also declares that this was a fulfillment of the promise of the baptism of the Holy Spirit (11:16f.); (e) the Jewish Christians who hear Peter's account acknowledge this as proof that God has also extended the privileges of the gospel to the Gentiles (11:18). The baptism of the Holy Spirit bestowed upon Cornelius and his household is thus directly linked with the first outpouring at Pentecost, and as the event signaling the formal opening of the door of the gospel to Gentiles, it is in complete harmony with the missionary significance of the first great pentecostal outpouring. It marks a turning point or crisis in the messianic kingdom, for it completes the pentecostal gift by showing that Gentiles as well as Jews are to be embraced in all the privileges of the new dispensation.

(4) Nowhere in the Epistles do we find a repetition of the special baptism of the Spirit. This would be remarkable if it was understood by the writers of the Epistles that this baptism was frequently to be repeated. There is no evidence outside the book of Acts that the baptism of the Spirit ever occurred in later NT times. In 1 Cor. 12:13 Paul says, "For by one Spirit we were all baptized into one body . . . and all were made to

drink of one Spirit." But here the reference is not to the baptism of the Spirit, but rather to a baptism into the Church, which is the body of Christ. We conclude, therefore, that according to the NT teaching the pentecostal baptism, taken in conjunction with the baptism of the Spirit in the case of Cornelius, completes the baptism of the Holy Spirit as a special event. The baptism of the Spirit as thus bestowed was, however, the definite gift of the Spirit in His fulness for every form of spiritual blessing through the divinely ordained ministry of word and sacrament. All subsequent NT writings assume this presence of the Spirit and His availability for all believers. The various commands and exhortations of the Epistles are based on the assumption that the baptism of the Spirit has already taken place, and that, according to the prediction of Jesus to the disciples, the Spirit is to be with them forever (Jn. 14:16). We should not therefore confuse other forms of expression found in the NT with the baptism of the Holy Spirit. When Christians are enjoined to "walk by the Spirit" (Gal. 5:16) and "be filled with the Spirit" (Eph. 5:18), or when the Spirit is described as an anointing (Gk. *chrísma*) as in 1 Jn. 2:20-27, and as the "guarantee of our inheritance" (*arrabṓn*) as in Eph. 1:14, and when various other similar expressions are employed in the Epistles of the NT, we are not to understand them as references to the baptism of the Holy Spirit. These expressions indicate aspects of the Spirit's work in believers or of the believer's appropriation of the gifts and blessings of the Spirit, rather than the historical baptism of the Spirit.

Three final points require brief attention, viz., the relation of the baptism of the Spirit to baptism in water, to baptism with fire, and to the laying on of hands.

(1) The baptism of the Spirit was not meant to supersede water baptism. This is clear from the whole history of Acts, where water baptism is uniformly administered to converts after the pentecostal baptism of the Spirit, as well as from numerous references in the Epistles (cf. Rom. 6:3; 1 Cor. 1:14-17; 10:2; 12:13; Gal. 3:27; etc.). On the contrary, the baptism of the Spirit brings out the true significance of the rite, inward baptism being the regeneration that the work of the Spirit accomplishes on the basis of the death and resurrection of Christ and through the ministry of the gospel.

(2) The relation of the baptism of the Spirit to that of fire is discussed in BAPTISM OF FIRE. If the two are complementary, we are to refer the latter to judgment; if they are parallel, we are to think in terms of the phenomenon of Acts 2:3 and of the convicting as well as the converting ministry of the outpoured Spirit.

(3) In Acts 8:17 and 19:6 an endowment with the Spirit is connected with the laying on of hands. Three problems arise: (a) whether this is a genuine repetition of the baptism of the Spirit; (b) what is its relation to baptism; (c) whether the practice mentioned is to be continued in the Church. As regards the first, we are to note that this is an individual reception of spiritual gifts rather than the specific and nonrecurrent descent of the Spirit at Pentecost. As regards the second, the new birth of the Spirit is linked with baptism and may be presumed of all believers, but obviously does not preclude special spiritual endowments. As regards the third, we have no command to follow the example of the apostles, nor is there evidence of any definite conveyance of spiritual blessing, e.g., in confirmation or ordination. Continuation of the practice also involves the danger of minimizing the regenerative work of the Spirit at the expense of subsequent endowment. On the other hand, there is no reason why the scriptural practice of laying on of hands with prayer should not be continued as such, i.e., so long as there is no thought of a necessary bestowal of spiritual gifts by this means. *See also* HANDS, LAYING ON OF.

E. Y. MULLINS
G. W. BROMILEY

BAPTISMAL REGENERATION. This conjunction of the sign of baptism and its meaning is not wholly unscriptural or objectionable so long as it is correctly understood. Thus Jn. 3:5 speaks of being "born of water," and Tit. 3:5 refers to the "washing of regeneration," so that water and the new birth are brought into close interrelationship. This connection may be validly defended either in terms of the sign alone or in terms of the thing signified alone. On the one side, all those who have external baptism may be said to have the sign of regeneration and thus to be regenerate in sign, i.e., baptismally. On the other side, all those who are regenerate by faith in Christ have the thing signified in baptism and may thus be described as truly baptized, i.e., to regeneration. Indeed, there is no particular danger in seeing a connection between the sign on the one hand and the thing signified on the other so long as this is not conceived in causal or instrumental terms. Thus the sign of baptism undoubtedly points us to regeneration as its meaning, and regeneration gives meaning to the baptismal sign. Or, to state it another way, Christian regeneration is that which is signified in baptism, and baptism is that which signifies regeneration.

The introduction of causal notions, however, brings about an inevitable distortion of the phrase, since it overthrows the two basic principles of sacramental theology: (1) that there is a distinction between sign and thing signified, and (2) that these coincide not in terms of cause and effect but only by the sovereign activity of the Holy Spirit. Hence we cannot speak legitimately of baptismal regeneration in the sense of the effective conferring of regeneration by means of or through the instrumentality of the external rite. Where baptismal regeneration is taught in this sense, it results in a depreciation of the word, in a mistaken sense of assurance, in a false problem or dilemma of the postbaptismal life, and in a restriction of the sovereignty of the Spirit.

The Roman Catholic Church accepts baptismal regeneration in the instrumental sense. It can claim certain passages in the fathers that obviously equate baptism and regeneration, though not necessarily in causal terms. Following Augustine, it can also argue from the divine sovereignty itself, counting upon God to work through the means of grace that He Himself has appointed. It thus administers baptism with the belief that the graces of cleansing, regeneration, and habitual righteousness are infallibly conveyed, that they will be enjoyed except where an obstacle of unbelief or insincerity is posed, and that in any case an indelible "character" is impressed on all the baptized.

A similar view is held by some High Church Anglicans, though without the accompanying insistence on the absolute necessity of the sacrament in all normal cases, and frequently with a distinction between baptismal regeneration and the full renovation envisaged in Scripture. On this view, baptism is a normal channel for the mediation of grace. Administered to infants, it brings forgiveness of sins and at least the germ of new life. This does not give absolute assurance, nor does it preclude the need for subsequent conversion in many recipients. Always there is need of the fostering of the new life not merely by Christian instruction but also by such additional special means of grace as confirmation and holy communion. It need hardly be said that this is not the teaching of the Anglican Reformers or of the Formularies in their original Reformation setting.

Lutheranism, too, has a doctrine of baptismal regeneration in a modified sacramentalist sense. Here regeneration is given its fuller meaning and implies true spiritual quickening and the kindling of saving faith, with which is naturally connected the justification of the sinner. This regeneration is called baptismal regeneration insofar as this occurs in the event and as an application of Christian baptism, which is plainly linked with it in the texts quoted earlier. Lutheranism emphasizes that the external sacrament does not confer regeneration *ex opere operato*. The Spirit alone does this through the Word of God as His giving hand. Lutheranism also emphasizes that there is no operation without faith. Faith is awakened in the sacrament as man's receiving hand. This is a mystery in infants; but so, too, is the miracle by which the adult is brought from spiritual darkness to light. In adults, faith is more directly kindled by the Word, but even here it is relevant to speak of baptismal regeneration, because the sacrament is a seal of righteousness and a summons to daily renewal.

In these views there are real elements of truth that we should not ignore because of the doubtful nature of the whole understanding. Particularly important is the stress on the sovereignty of God and the miraculous rather than the rationalistic nature of faith. On the other hand, we have to note such serious consequences as the gravitation to more mechanical or formal understanding, the equation of sign and thing signified in more causal terms, the creation of a false antithesis between the status and the reality of the lives of some of the baptized, and the fostering of resistance to evangelism within the Church on the ground of its supposed superfluous character.

We may conclude that if the term baptismal regeneration is to be used at all it should be with reference to the sign alone, to the thing signified alone, or preferably to the work of Christ, in which the sign and the thing signified are truly one and the same. G. W. BROMILEY

BAR bär (prefix). Aramaic for the Heb. *bēn*, "son." Cf. Aramaic sections of Ezra and Daniel. In the OT the word is found three times in Prov. 31:2 and once in Ps. 2:12 (Jerome translates "pure"). In the NT "Bar" is frequently employed as prefix to names of persons. Cf. Barabbas; Bar-Jesus; Bar-Jonah; Barnabas; Barsabbas; Bartholomew; Bartimaeus. *See* BEN-.

BAR. (1) [Heb. *b^e^rî(a)ḥ*]. (a) A part of the framework of the tabernacle, made of acacia wood and plated with gold (Ex. 26:26-29; 35:11; 36:31-34; 39:33; Nu. 3:36; 4:31).

(b) A bolt, part of the securing mechanism of a gate (Dt. 3:5; Jgs. 16:3; 1 S. 23:7; 1 K. 4:13; 2 Ch. 8:5; 14:7; Neh. 3:3, 6, 13-15; Job 38:10 ["bars and doors" of the sea]; Ps. 107:16; 147:13; Prov. 18:19 ["the bars of a castle"]; Isa. 45:2; Jer. 51:30; Lam. 2:9; Nah. 3:13; Jonah 2:6 [the bars of the earth]). The lack of bars is a sign that a city is at peace (Jer. 49:31; Ezk. 38:11). The NEB also has "barred gates," "doors," "gates," "gate-bars."

(c) Two passages do not fit with the above definitions easily: Am. 1:5 and Isa. 43:14. The latter is a difficult verse in which the RSV interprets *bārîḥîm* as a form of *b^e^rî(a)ḥ*; thus it refers to the bars of Babylon that had been broken down. The AV and NEB take it to be from *bārāḥ* (to "flee"), thus "their nobles" or "great men," those most likely to flee. The NEB follows the AV, "as they flee." The RSV and AV both speak of the destruction of "the bar of Damascus" (Am. 1:5), meaning the bolt of a gate. The NEB has "great men."

(2) [Heb. *môṭâ*]. A pole, part of a yoke, symbol of oppression (Lev. 26:13; Jer. 28:13; Ezk. 34:27). The AV has "bonds," "bands," "yokes."

(3) [Heb. *lāšôn*]. A large piece of gold, weighing fifty shekels (Josh. 7:21, 24; AV "wedge").

(4) [Heb. *baḏ*]. A bolt, of Sheol (Job 17:16; NEB follows the LXX, "with me"); of gates (Hos. 11:6; AV "branches"; NEB emends).

(5) [Heb. *m^e^ṭîl*]. Something wrought by striking, "a wrought-metal rod," figuratively of the limbs of Behemoth, the hippopotamus (Job 40:18).

(6) [Heb. *min'āl*]. A bolt (Dt. 33:25; NEB "bolts"; AV "shoes" from *na'al*, "sandal, shoe").

J. R. PRICE

BARABBAS bä-rab'əs [Gk. *Barabbas* < Aram. *bar'abbā'*–'son of the father' or (Harclean Syr.) *bar-rabban*–'son of the teacher']. Origen knew and did not absolutely reject a reading of Mt. 27:16f. giving the name "Jesus Barabbas," but although it also occurs here in a few other witnesses, it is probably due to a scribe's error in transcription. If the name was simply Barabbas or Barrabban, it may still have meant that the man was a rabbi's son, or it may have been a purely conventional proper name]. The criminal chosen by the Jerusalem mob, at the instigation of the priests, in preference to Jesus, for Pilate to release on the feast of Passover (Mk. 15:15; Mt. 27:20f.; Lk. 23:18; Jn. 18:40). Matthew calls him "a notorious prisoner" (27:16). Mark says that he was "among the rebels in prison, who had committed murder in the insurrection" (15:7). Luke states that he was cast into prison "for an insurrection started in the city, and for murder" (23:19; cf. Acts 3:14). John calls him a "robber" or "brigand" (18:40). Nothing further is known of him, nor of the insurrection in which he took part.

Luke's statement that he was a murderer is probably a deduction from Mark's more circumstantial statement, that he was only one of a gang who in an uprising had committed murder. Whether robbery was the motive of his crime, as John suggests, or whether he was "a man who had raised a revolt against the Roman power" (Gould) cannot be decided. But it seems equally improbable that the priests (the pro-Roman party) would urge the release of a political prisoner and that Pilate would grant it, especially when the priests were urging, and Pilate could not resist, the execution of Jesus on a political charge (Lk. 23:2). The insurrection may have been a notorious case of brigandage. To say that the Jews would not have been interested in the release of such a prisoner is to forget the history of mobs. No extrabiblical sources refer to the custom of releasing a prisoner on the Passover.

For a view of the incident as semilegendary growth, see *EB*, I, *s.v.* (Schmiedel). See also comms. *in loc.* (esp. *ICC* — Allen on Matthew and Gould on Mark), and *HDB*, *s.v.* (Plummer).

See also JESUS CHRIST, ARREST AND TRIAL OF.

T. REES

BARACHEL bar'ə-kel [Heb. *bāraḵ'ēl*–'God blesses']. A Buzite of the family of Ram, and father of Elihu, who was the last one to reason with Job (Job 32:2, 6). *See* BUZ; RAM.

BARACHIAH bar-ə-kī'ə [Gk. *Barachias*] (Mt. 23:35); AV BARACHIAS. Father of the Zechariah who was murdered between the sanctuary and the altar. It is possible that the reference is to Zechariah the son of Jehoiada (2 Ch. 24:20ff.), and that Matthew gives the name incorrectly. Lk. 11:51 omits the name of the father.

BARACHIAS bar-ə-kī'əs (Mt. 23:35, AV). *See* BARACHIAH.

BARAK bâr'ək [Heb. *bārāq*]. The son of Abinoam of Kedesh, a refuge city in Naphtali. He was summoned by the prophetess Deborah to lead his countrymen to war against Jabin king of the Canaanites, whose army was under the leadership of SISERA. The story of the battle is recorded in both prose (Jgs. 4) and poetry (the celebrated Song of Deborah, ch. 5).

According to both accounts, Israel was suffering under the oppression of the Canaanites (Jgs. 4:2f.), and the land was in a state of near anarchy: the caravan roads were in danger and traffic almost ceased; the cultivated lands were plundered; the fighting men in Israel were disarmed, and neither a shield nor a spear could be found among forty thousand in Israel (5:6-8). According to the prose narrative, Barak was summoned in the name of Yahweh by the prophetess Deborah, who was judging Israel at that time, to gather an army of ten thousand on Mt. Tabor and meet Jabin's army near the brook Kishon (4:6f.). Barak refused to go unless Deborah would accompany him. Deborah consented to go with him, but apprised him that the glory of bringing down Sisera would go not to him but to a woman (vv. 8f.).

With an army of ten thousand men — according to Jgs. 4:10 they were all drawn from Zebulun and Naphtali, but the account in ch. 5 adds Benjamin, Machir (Manasseh), and Issachar to the list of faithful tribes (vv. 13-18)— Barak, accompanied by Deborah, went up to Mt. Tabor, about 12 mi. (19 km.) NE of Megiddo. This location was favorable to the poorly armed Israelites, for the wooded slopes protected them against the iron chariots of the Canaanites. Sisera, informed that the Israelites were positioning themselves on Mt. Tabor, mustered his troops and approached from Harosheth-ha-goiim to the brook Kishon in the Valley of Jezreel. With Deborah's assurance that Yahweh would bring them victory, Barak and his army rushed down upon the Canaanites, completely routing them. The victory, however, is attributed to Yahweh, for He fought against the Canaanites with a storm that caused the brook Kishon to become a raging torrent overflowing its banks. Thus the plain became a morass in which Sisera's troops found it impossible to maneuver. Barak pursued the Canaanite army all the way to Harosheth-ha-goiim, "and all the army of Sisera fell by the edge of the sword; not a man was left" (4:16). Sisera, however, fled on foot; and Deborah's prophecy was fulfilled when Barak found him murdered by JAEL in her tent (4:22; 5:24-27).

Barak is mentioned in Samuel's farewell address as one of the judges who delivered the Israelites from the hand of their enemies (1 S. 12:11; RSV and NEB correctly follow the LXX and Syriac in rendering "Barak" rather than "Bedan" [MT; cf. AV]). His name also appears in He. 11:32 on the list of ancient heroes of the faith.

See also DEBORAH **2**; DEBORAH, SONG OF.

S. COHON
N. J. O.

BARBARIAN [Gk. *bárbaros*] (Rom. 1:14; Col. 3:11); NEB also NON-GREEK. Elsewhere the RSV renders "natives" (Acts 28:2, 4), "foreigner" (1 Cor. 14:11); the NEB also renders "(rough) islanders" and paraphrases in 1 Cor. 14:11 "words will be gibberish." The Greek word was probably formed by imitation of the unintelligible sounds of foreign speech, and hence in the mouth of a Greek it meant anything that was not Greek in language, nationality, or customs. With the spread of Greek language and culture, it came to be used generally for all that was non-Greek. Philo and Josephus sometimes called their own Jewish nation "barbarians," as Roman writers did their country up to the Augustan age, when the Romans adopted Greek culture and reckoned themselves with the Greeks as the only cultured people in the world. Therefore "Greek and barbarian" meant the whole human race (Rom. 1:14).

In Col. 3:11 "barbarian, Scythian" is not a classification or antithesis but a "climax" (Abbott, comm. on Colossians [*ICC,* 1905], *in loc.*) — "barbarians, even Scythians, the lowest type of barbarians." In Christ all racial distinctions, even the most pronounced, disappear.

In 1 Cor. 14:11 Paul uses the term in its more primitive sense of one speaking a foreign and therefore unintelligible language: "But if I do not know the meaning of the language, I shall be a foreigner [*bárbaros*] to the speaker and the speaker a foreigner [*bárbaros*] to me." Speaking in tongues would not be a means of communication unless someone had the gift of interpretation.

In Acts 28:2, 4 the writer, perhaps from the Greco-Roman standpoint, calls the inhabitants of Melita *bárbaroi,* as being descendants of the old Phoenician settlers, or possibly in the more general sense of "strangers." For the later sense of "brutal," "cruel," "savage," see 2 Macc. 2:21; 4:25; 15:2. T. REES

BARBER [Heb. *gallāḇ*]. One who shaves the head or beard, or styles and trims the hair. The term occurs once only, in Ezk. 5:1. Shaving is referred to in Gen. 41:14, where the bearded Semites are contrasted to the clean-shaven Egyptians. Beard-trimming is mentioned in 2 S. 19:24 (Heb. *śāpām*, "beard," "moustache"), while neglect of the beard is associated with madness in 1 S. 21:14. In Lev. 21:5 the priests are forbidden to shave their heads or the corners of their beards, these perhaps being pagan practices. The prohibition is extended to the Zadokite priesthood in Ezk. 44:15, 20.

See also BEARD. R. K. H.

BARCHUE bär'kū (1 Esd. 5:32, NEB). *See* BARKOS.

BAREFOOT [Heb. *yāḥēp*] (2 S. 15:30; Isa. 20:2-4). In biblical times it was customary for people to walk barefoot indoors and to put on sandals to go out (cf. Ex. 12:11). The dusty roads made it necessary, for the sake of comfort, to take them off and wash the feet when coming into the house (Gen. 18:4; 19:2; 24:32; 43:24; Jgs. 19:21; 1 S. 25:41; Lk. 7:38, 44; Jn. 13:5ff.; 1 Tim. 5:10).

To walk outside with bare feet, however, had special significance. It was a sign of mourning (2 S. 15:30; Ezk. 24:17, 23) and of poverty (Lk. 15:22). It also implied captivity or slavery (Isa. 20:2; Mic. 1:8, LXX; cf. Job 12:17, 19 [esp. v. 19 in Moff.]). Any form of nakedness was shameful; even, according to J. Pedersen, "if one pulls off the sandal of a man, one puts him to shame" (*ILC*, I, 242). This seems to be implied by Dt. 25:9f., where the loosing of the shoe is linked with the idea of renunciation or transference of rights (cf. Ruth 4:7f.; T. Zeb. 3:4ff.).

The origins of such customs are obscure. They seem to have been general among Semitic peoples and have been regarded as remnants of animism, or perhaps of ancestor worship; but no certainty is possible. Mt. 10:10 has been interpreted by some, e.g., Francis of Assisi, as a command to go barefoot.

The removal of shoes also had a ritual significance. To be barefoot was a sign of reverence, and so Moses and Joshua were commanded to remove their sandals when on "holy ground" (Ex. 3:5; Josh. 5:15), in the presence of a theophany, which made the surrounding place holy or taboo. Sandals that have been in contact with common ground must not be brought into contact with sacred ground lest they bring in any contagion from the secular world, and, similarly, lest they carry away the sacredness of the holy place, which would prevent the ordinary usage of the sandals again. Also, since bare feet were a sign of mourning, they may have been thought appropriate as denoting a humble approach to the deity. Again, to remove sandals in the presence of God may indicate the renunciation of all rights before Him. Thus Martin Buber, writing on Ex. 3:5 and comparing Ruth 4:7, says: "The reason may possibly be because, being holy ground, it should not be trodden by any occupying or possessing shoe" (*Moses* [1946], p. 42). Originally, religious rites must have been performed without shoes; and this practice continued after shoes had become general, so that priests officiated in the temple with bare feet.

See *ERE, s.v.* "Shoes and Sandals."

J. G. G. NORMAN

BARGAIN [Heb. *kārâ*] (Job 6:27; 41:6); AV "dig a pit," "make a banquet"; NEB "hurl," HAGGLE; [*kāraṯ* (Isa. 57:8), *kāraṯ bᵉrîṯ* (Hos. 12:1)]; AV "make a covenant"; NEB also "make a treaty" (Hos. 12:1). The AV reflects an accepted meaning of the verb *kārâ* in Job 6:27; however, the RSV rendering is preferred (cf. KD, *in loc.*). The NEB reflects the emendation of the LXX (Gk. *enállomai*). The RSV and NEB take Job 41:6 (MT 40:30), which uses *kārâ 'al-* in exactly the same way as 6:27, to mean the capture and sale of Leviathan by barter to the merchants, rather than the butchering of him to make a banquet. The RSV and NEB emend Isa. 57:8 to read *kārâ* instead of *kāraṯ*, a term frequently used by the MT in the phrase *kāraṯ bᵉrîṯ* for making a covenant or treaty such as the alliance formed between Israel and Assyria in Hos. 12:1 (MT 2).

BARHUMITE bär′hū-mīt (2 S. 23:31, AV). *See* BAHURIM.

BARIAH bə-rī′ə [Heb. *bārî(a)ḥ*-'fugitive']. A descendant of David in the line of Solomon (1 Ch. 3:22).

BAR-JESUS bär-jē′zəs [Gk. *Bariēsous*]. "A certain magician (Gk. *mágos*), a Jewish false prophet" whom Paul and Silas found at Paphos in Cyprus in the company of Sergius Paulus, the Roman proconsul (Acts 13:6ff.). The proconsul was "a man of intelligence," of an inquiring mind, interested in the thought and magic of his times. This characteristic explains the presence of a *mágos* among his staff and his desire to hear Barnabas and Saul. Bar-Jesus was the magician's Jewish name. "Elymas" is said to be the interpretation of his name (v. 8). It is the Greek transliteration of an Aramaic or Arabic word equivalent to *mágos*. From Arab. *'alama*, "to know" is derived *'alīm*, "wise man" or "learned man." In Koran Sura 106, Moses is called *sāḥir 'alīm*, "wise magician." Elymas therefore means "sorcerer" (cf. Simon "Magus").

The East was flooding the Roman empire with its new and wonderful religious systems, which, culminating in Neo-Platonism, were the great rivals of Christianity both in their cruder and in their more strictly religious forms. Superstition was very widespread, and wonder-workers of all kinds, whether impostors or honest exponents of some new faith, found their task easy through the credulity of the public. Babylonia was the home of magic, for charms are found on the oldest tablets. "Magos" was originally applied to the priests of the Persians who overran Babylonia, but the title degenerated when it was assumed by baser persons for baser arts. Juvenal (vi.562, etc.), Horace (*Satires* i.2.1), and other Latin authors mention Chaldean astrologers and imposters, possibly Babylonian Jews. Many of the Magians, however, were the scientists of their day, the heirs of the science of Babylon and the lore of Persia, and not merely pretenders or conjurers (*see* MAGIC). It may have been as the representative of some oriental system, a compound of "science" and religion, that Bar-Jesus was attached to the company of Sergius Paulus.

Both Sergius and Elymas had heard about the teaching of the apostles, and this aroused the curiosity of Sergius and the fear of Elymas. When the apostles came, obedient to the command of the proconsul, their teaching apparently produced on him a considerable impression. Fearing that his position of influence and gain would be taken by the new teachers, Elymas "withstood them, seeking to turn away the proconsul from the faith" (v. 8). Paul, inspired by the Holy Spirit, struck him blind with his word, thus revealing to the proconsul that behind him was divine power. Sergius Paulus believed, "for he was astonished at the teaching of the Lord" (v. 12).

S. F. HUNTER

BAR-JONAH bär-jō′nə [Gk. *Bar-iōnas*]. Simon Peter's patronymic (Mt. 16:17). *Bar* is Aramaic for "son" (cf. Bar-timaeus, Bartholomew, etc.), and corresponds to Heb. *bēn*. This would indicate that Peter's father's name was Jonah. But in Jn. 1:42; 21:15-17, according to the best reading, his name is given as John (so RSV, instead of AV Jona, Jonas). There are two hypotheses to account for the difference: (1) *Iōnas* (Jonah) in Mt. 16:17 may be simply a contraction of *Iōanēs* (John); (2) Peter's father may have been known by two names, Jonah and John.

D. M. EDWARDS

BARKOS bär′kos [Heb. *barqôs*; Gk. B *Barchous*, A *Barchoue* (Apoc.)]; AV Apoc. CHARKUS (from Aldine ed. *Charkous*); NEB Apoc. BARCHUE. A family of temple servants who returned with Zerubbabel to Jerusalem (Ezr. 2:53; Neh. 7:55; 1 Esd. 5:32).

BARLEY [Heb. *śᵉʿōrâ*]. Several kinds of cultivated barley grow in Palestine, the most common being *Hordeum distichon* L., *H. vulgare* L., and *H. hexastichon* L. In ancient times barley was a characteristic Palestinian product (Dt. 8:8), and the failure of the crop was a national disaster (Joel 1:11). Barley bread was the common food of the poor (Ruth 2:17; 2 K. 4:42; Jn. 6:9, 13), and in Jgs. 7:13f. the barley loaf may have depicted the peasant origin of Gideon and his army. The grain was fed to horses, asses, and cattle. Ezekiel was requested to eat barley cakes under distasteful conditions (Ezk. 4:9, 12) as a sign to the people. He also accused the false prophetesses of profaning God for "handfuls of barley" (13:19). The five thousand were fed barley bread at the hands of Christ (Jn. 6:9ff.).

Barley is sown in the autumn following the "early rains" and ripens about a month earlier than wheat. In Palestine the harvest takes place in March or April, depending on the location. The barley harvest was a well-marked season of the year (*see* AGRICULTURE III.A; HARVEST), and the barleycorn was a familiar measure of length (*see* WEIGHTS AND MEASURES).

E. W. G. MASTERMAN
R. K. H.

BARN [Heb. *m^e^gûrâ*] (Hag. 2:19); [*'āsām*] (Dt. 28:8; Prov. 3:10); AV also STOREHOUSES; NEB GRANARIES; [Gk. *apothḗkē*] (Mt. 6:26; 13:30; Lk. 12:18, 24); NEB also STOREHOUSES. A place for storing grain; thus, better rendered "granary" (cf. Syr. *âsan*; Ugar. *'sm*).

Archeological excavations have revealed three devices for storing grain: jars, pits, and silos. Work at the Middle Bronze level of Jericho has unearthed jars containing charred grain (Kenyon, p. 187). A large pit (25 ft. [7.5 m.] in diameter and 19 ft. [6 m.] deep) has been uncovered at Beth-shemesh. The city of Gezer possessed public as well as private granaries. Macalister suggests that the silos found in Gezer were probably beehive-shaped with vents at the top. Storage of wheat, barley, and oats in pits and jars was also common at Gezer. The reference to "stores of wheat, barley, oil and honey hidden in the fields" (Jer. 41:8) probably refers to underground granaries.

The *apothḗkē* is, literally, a place where anything is stored; figuratively it represents heaven (Mt. 13:30). Our English word "apothecary" is a well-known derivative.

Bibliography.–*WBA*; E. Grant and G. E. Wright, *Ain Shems Excavations* (1939), pp. 40f.; K. Kenyon, *Archaeology in the Holy Land* (1965), p. 187; R. A. S. Macalister, *Excavation of Gezer, 1902-1905 and 1907-1909* (1912), I, 199-204; II, 22.

J. T. DENNISON, JR.

BARNABAS bär'nə-bəs [Gk. *Barnabas*–'son of exhortation' or possibly 'son of Nebo']. An associate of Paul, originally called Joses or Joseph (Acts 4:36). He was called Barnabas as a testimony to his eloquence. Its literal meaning is "son of prophecy" (Aram. *bar*, "son"; *n^e^ḇû'â*, "prophecy"; cf. Heb. *nāḇî'*; Aram *n^e^ḇî'*). This is interpreted in Acts 4:36 as "Son of encouragement" (RSV) or "son of consolation" (AV), expressing two sides of Gk. *paráklēsis* that are not exclusive. The office of a prophet being more than to foretell, all these interpretations are admissible in estimating Barnabas as a preacher. The interpretation "son of Nebo" is Deissmann's suggestion (G. A. Deissmann, *Bible Studies* [2nd. ed., Eng. tr. 1909], pp. 187ff.), taking "Barnabas" as the Jewish Greek form of the Semitic *Barnebon*. He is followed by Dalman and G. B. Gray.

Barnabas was a Levite from the island of Cyprus and a cousin, not "uncle" (AV), of the Evangelist Mark, the word *anépsios* (Col. 4:10) being used as in Nu. 36:11, LXX, "father's brothers' sons." When we first learn of him, he had moved to Jerusalem and acquired property there. He sold "a field," and contributed its price to the support of the poorer members of the church (Acts 4:36f.). In Acts 11:24 he is described as "a good man, full of the Holy Spirit [cf. Isa. 11:2; 1 Cor. 12:8, 11] and of faith," traits that gave him influence and leadership. Possibly on the ground of former acquaintanceship, interceding as Paul's sponsor and surety, he removed the distrust of the disciples at Jerusalem and secured the admission of the former persecutor to their fellowship.

When the preaching of some of his countrymen resulted in a movement toward Christianity among the Greeks at Antioch, Barnabas was sent from Jerusalem to give this movement encouragement and direction; and after a personal visit to Antioch, recognizing its importance and needs, he sought out Paul at Tarsus and brought him back as his associate. At the close of a year's successful work, Barnabas and Paul were sent to Jerusalem with contributions from the infant church for the famine sufferers in the older congregation (Acts 11:30). Ordained as missionaries on their return (13:3), and accompanied by John Mark, they proceeded upon what is ordinarily known as the "first missionary journey" of Paul (13:4f.). Its history belongs primarily to Paul's life (*see* PAUL THE APOSTLE VII.D). Barnabas as well as Paul is designated "an apostle" (14:14). Up until Acts 13:43, the precedence is always ascribed to Barnabas; from that point, except in 14:14 and 15:12, 25, we read "Paul and Barnabas" instead of "Barnabas and Saul." Paul became the chief spokesman. The people at Lystra named Paul, because of his fervid oratory, Hermes, while the quiet dignity and reserved strength of Barnabas gave him the title of Zeus (Acts 14:12). Barnabas escaped the violence Paul suffered at Lystra (14:19).

Upon their return from this first missionary tour they were sent, with other representatives of the church at Antioch, to confer with the apostles and elders of the church at Jerusalem concerning the obligation of circumcision and the ceremonial law in general under the new covenant; this conference was known as the Council of Jerusalem. A separation from Paul seems to begin with a temporary yielding of Barnabas in favor of the inconsistent course of Peter (Gal. 2:13). This was followed by a more serious rupture concerning Mark. On the second journey, Paul proceeded alone, while Barnabas and Mark went to Cyprus. Luther and Calvin regarded 2 Cor. 8:18f. as meaning Barnabas ("the brother whose praise is spread through all the churches"), and indicating, therefore, subsequent joint work. The incidental allusions in 1 Cor. 9:6 and Gal. 2:13 ("even Barnabas") show at any rate Paul's continued appreciation of his former associate. Like Paul, he accepted no support from those to whom he ministered.

Tertullian, followed in modern times by Grau, Zahn, and a few others, regarded him as the author of Hebrews. The document published among patristic writings as the Epistle of Barnabas, and found in full in Codex Sinaiticus, is universally assigned today to a later period. "The writer nowhere claims to be the apostle Barnabas; possibly its author was some unknown namesake of 'the son of consolation' " (J. B. Lightfoot, *Apostolic Fathers* [1912], pp. 239f.).

H. E. JACOBS

BARNABAS, EPISTLE OF. *See* APOSTOLIC FATHERS III.

BARODIS bə-rō'dis [Gk. *Barōdeís*] (1 Esd. 5:34). A family of the "sons of the servants of Solomon" who returned with Zerubbabel to Jerusalem. The name is omitted in Ezr. 2 and Neh. 7.

BARRACKS [Gk. *parembolḗ*] (Acts 21:34–23:32); AV CASTLE. *See* FORTIFICATION.

BARREL. *See* JAR.

BARREN; BARRENNESS. [Heb. *'āqār, galmûḏ* (1 S. 2:5; Job 3:7; Isa. 49:21), *'ōṣer* (Prov. 30:16); Gk. *steíros, nekrós* (Jas. 2:20), *nékrōsis* (Rom. 4:19)]; AV also SOLITARY, DESOLATE, DEAD, DEADNESS; NEB also CHILDLESS, DEADNESS. The term is generally applied to women who bear no children: Sarah (Gen. 11:30); Rebekah (25:21); Rachel (29:31); Manoah's wife (Jgs. 13:2f.); Hannah (1 S. 2:5); Elizabeth (Lk. 1:7, 36 [*steíros*]).

In Israel and among oriental peoples generally, barrenness was a woman's and her family's greatest misfortune. The highest sanctions of religion and patriotism blessed the fruitful woman, because children were necessary for the perpetuation of the tribe and its religion. It is significant that the mothers of the Hebrew race, Sarah, Rebekah, and Rachel, were by nature sterile; God's special intervention shows His particular favor to Israel. Fruitfulness was God's special blessing to His people (Ex. 23:26; Dt. 7:14; Ps. 113:9). A complete family is an emblem of beauty (Cant. 4:2; 6:6).

Metaphorically, Israel in her days of adversity, when her children were exiled, was barren, but in her restoration she will rejoice in many children (Isa. 54:1; Gal. 4:27). Jesus portrays the utter despair and terror of the destruction of Jerusalem when He speaks of a day when the barren will be called blessed (Lk. 23:29).

See also CHILD. T. REES

BARRIER [Heb. *g*^{e}*ḇûl*–'border'] (Ezk. 40:12); AV SPACE; NEB KERB. Perhaps the raised pavement of the side chambers in the gateways of Ezekiel's temple, which would be narrower in the first pair of side chambers to allow the gates to swing back. Another view is that the barrier is a boundary fence designed to enable a sentry to observe the people in the gateway without being disturbed by the traffic. (Cf. also Jer. 5:22, Heb. *ḥôq,* "prescribed limit.")

See *TDOT,* II, *s.v.* "g^{e}bhûl" (Ottosson). G. WYPER

BARSABBAS. *See* JOSEPH BARSABBAS; JUDAS BARSABBAS.

BARTACUS bär'tə-kəs [Gk. *Bartakos,* Josephus *Rhabezakēs*; Vulg. *Bezazes*]. The father of APAME (1 Esd. 4:29). He is called "the illustrious," probably because of rank and merits. The family seems to be of Persian origin, since the name Bartacus (Syr. *'rṭq)* in the form of Artachaeas is mentioned by Herodotus (vii.22.117) as a person of rank in the Persian army of Xerxes, and since the name of his daughter, Apame, is identical with that of a Persian princess who married Seleucus I Nicator and became the mother of Antiochus I. Apamea, a city in Asia Minor founded by Seleucus I, is named in honor of his wife Apame.

BARTER [Heb. *'āraḇ*–'exchange merchandise'] (Ezk. 27:9); AV "occupy (merchandise)"; NEB "market (wares)"; [*ma'*^{a}*rāḇ*–'articles for exchange'] (Ezk. 27:19); AV "were in thy market"; NEB "were among your imports." The exchange of merchandise without the use of money. The term occurs in the oracles against the Phoenician city of Tyre, which was renowned in the ancient world for its trade.

BARTHOLOMEW bär-thol'ə-mū [Gk. *Bartholomaios* – 'son of Tolmai or Talmai']. One of the twelve apostles (Mt. 10:3; Mk. 3:18; Lk. 6:14; Acts 1:13). There is no further reference to him in the NT. According to the "Genealogies of the Twelve Apostles" (E. A. Wallis Budge, *Contendings of the Apostles* [1901], II, 50), "Bartholomew was of the house of Naphtali. Now his name was formerly John, but Our Lord changed it because of John the son of Zebedee, His beloved." A Gospel of Bartholomew is mentioned by Jerome (*Comm. ad Matt.,* preface), and Gelasius gives the tradition that Bartholomew brought the Hebrew Gospel of Matthew to India. In the "Preaching of St. Bartholomew in the Oasis" (cf. Budge, II, 90), he is referred to as preaching probably in the oasis of Al Bahnâsâ; and according to the "Preaching of St. Andrew and St. Bartholomew" he labored among the Parthians (Budge, II, 183). The "Martyrdom of St. Bartholomew" states that he was placed in a sack and cast into the sea.

From the 9th cent. onward, Bartholomew has generally been identified with NATHANAEL; but this view has not been conclusively established. C. M. KERR

BARTHOLOMEW, GOSPEL OF. *See* APOCRYPHAL GOSPELS V.D.

BARTIMAEUS bär-tə-mē'əs [Gk. *Bartimaios,* hybrid < Aram. *bar*–'son' + Gk. *timaios*–'honorable,' or < Aram. *bar-timai*–'son of Timai' (=Timotheus?)]. In Mk. 10:46-52, the name of a blind beggar, whose sight Jesus restored as He went out from Jericho on His last journey to Jerusalem. An almost identical account is given by Luke (18:35-43), except that the incident occurred "as he drew near to Jericho," and the name of the blind man is not given. Again, according to Mt. 20:29-34, "as they went out of Jericho" (like Mark) *two* blind men (unlike Mark and Luke) received their sight.

It is not absolutely impossible that two or even three events are recorded, but so close is the similarity of the three accounts that it is highly improbable. Regarding them as referring to the same event, it is easy to understand how the discrepancies arose in the passage of the story from mouth to mouth. The main incident is clear enough, and on purely historical grounds the miracle cannot be denied. The discrepancies themselves are evidence of the wide currency of the story before the Gospels assumed their present form. Only a most mechanical theory of inspiration would demand their harmonization.

T. REES

BARUCH bä-rōōk', bâr'ək [Heb. *bārûḵ*–'blessed'; Gk. *Barouch*].

1. Son of Neriah and brother of Seraiah, King Zedekiah's quartermaster (Jer. 51:59). He was the devoted friend (32:12), the amanuensis (36:4ff., 32), and faithful attendant (36:10ff.; Josephus *Ant.* x.6.2) of the prophet Jeremiah. He seems to have been of noble family (see *Ant.* x.9.1; cf. Jer. 51:59; Bar. 1:1). He was also according to Josephus a man of unusual achievements (*Ant.* x.9.1). He might have risen to a high position and seemed conscious of this, but under Jeremiah's influence (Jer. 45:5) he repressed his ambition and was content to throw in his lot with the great prophet.

Jeremiah dictated his prophecies to Baruch, who read them to the people (ch. 36). The king (Jehoiakim) was greatly angered at these prophecies and had Baruch arrested and the roll burned. Baruch, however, rewrote the prophet's oracles. In the final siege of Jerusalem Baruch stood by his master, witnessing the purchase by the latter of his ancestral estate in Anathoth (ch. 32). According to Josephus (*Ant.* x.9.1) he continued to reside with Jeremiah at Mizpah after the fall of Jerusalem. Subsequent to the murder of Gedaliah, he was accused of having unduly influenced Jeremiah when the latter urged the people to remain in Judah — which shows how great an influence Baruch was believed to have had over his master (Jer. 43:3). He was carried with Jeremiah to Egypt (43:6; *Ant.* x.9.6), and thereafter our knowledge of him is merely legendary. According to a tradition preserved by Jerome (on Isa. 30:6f.) he died in Egypt soon after reaching that country. Two other traditions say that he went, or was carried by Nebuchadnezzar, to Babylon after the latter conquered Egypt.

The high character of Baruch and the important part he played in the life and work of Jeremiah induced later generations to enhance his reputation still further, and a large number of spurious writings passed under his name, among them the following: The Apocalypse of Baruch, the Book of Baruch, the Rest of the Words of Baruch, the gnostic Book of Baruch, the Latin Book of Baruch (composed originally in Latin), a Greek Apocalypse of Baruch belonging to the 2nd cent. A.D., another Book of Baruch belonging to the 4th or 5th century.

2. A son of Zabbai who aided Nehemiah in rebuilding the walls of Jerusalem (Neh. 3:20).

3. One of the priests who signed the covenant with Nehemiah (10:6).

4. The son of Colhozeh, a descendant of Perez the son of Judah (Neh. 11:5). T. W. DAVIES

BARUCH, APOCALYPSE OF. *See* APOCALYPTIC LITERATURE.

BARUCH, BOOK OF. A book of the OT Apocrypha.

I. The Text
II. Contents
III. Author
IV. Date
V. Original Language
VI. Selected Exegetical Notes
VII. Conclusion

I. The Text.–Whatever the original language of Baruch may have been, the most authoritative extant textual evidence is in Greek — all other versions are translations therefrom. Swete (*OTG,* III, 351-59) prints Codex Vaticanus (B) in full, with variants from Codex Alexandrinus (A), Codex Marchalianus (Q), and Codex rescriptus Cryptoferratensis (Γ). This critical apparatus, though not exhaustive, is sufficient for most purposes. For details of other Greek MSS, and of secondary versions in Syriac, Latin, Arabic, Ethiopic, Coptic, Armenian, indeed for anything else connected with the book, the most exhaustive of all published studies is that of J. J. Kneucker, *Das Buch Baruch* (1879). See in this connection pp. 91-97, 135-189; E. H. Gifford in Wace, II, 215f.; O. C. Whitehouse in *APOT,* I, 577-580; E. C. Bissell, *Apocrypha of the OT* (Lange, XV [1886]), pp. 410ff. The text of the more important of the Syriac versions will be found in Paul de Lagarde, *Libri Veteris Testamenti Apocryphi Syriace* (1861), pp. 93-100. The reconstructed Hebrew text of Kneucker (pp. 351-361), though purely conjectural in authority, is always of immense interest and exegetical suggestiveness.

II. Contents.–*APOT* (I, 570) divides Baruch into three parts, A, B, and C, which form a convenient basis of reference.

A. Chs. 1:1–3:8: Historical introduction, followed by penitential prayers, entirely in prose. The ostensible scene is the Babylonian Captivity, and the implied historical reference is 597 or 586 B.C. The choice between these dates, and the numerous errors and anachronisms, need concern only those anxious to uphold the authorship of the real Baruch; for others, they are mere pseudepigraphic embroidery or literary carelessness.

B. Chs. 3:9–4:4: Wisdom section, in poetry, with canonical and apocryphal counterparts.

C. Chs. 4:5–5:9: Further poetry, not of the wisdom type, with alternating strains of lamentation and comfort.

See also JEREMIAH, EPISTLE OF, sometimes incorrectly appended as a sixth chapter.

Baruch is minutely summarized in *HNTT,* pp. 409-411; and it is translated in full in *APOT*; Wace; Lange; etc.

III. Author.–The traditional or professed author of the book was of course Baruch, friend and amanuensis of Jeremiah. He certainly traveled to Egypt with the prophet, but his residence in Babylon possessed only a legendary attestation, invented perhaps to support the theory of his authorship, which in turn would lend considerable prestige to the book. The claim of the opening verses, unethical by modern literary standards, was a tolerated device of ancient authorship. The three parts A, B, and C probably originated from at least three different unknown authors, and may have been fused by one of them, or by yet another hand. See the elaborate study of Kneucker, pp. 1-76; this dry-looking volume contains some novel and interesting theories, though these have not been universally accepted. Kneucker feels (p. 61) that Baruch was compiled by a Jew reared in Palestine, but now in exile; that ancient Babylon is merely a type of contemporary Rome, and 588 B.C. is really A.D. 70 (p. 62). As rabbis Gamaliel II, Eleazar, Joshua, and Akiba were exiled the short distance from Jerusalem to Jabneh, and thereby just as effectively barred from the Holy City, Kneucker toys with the idea that A might have originated from one of their number (pp. 63, 67). These hypotheses all accord with his theory of a very late date (see further below).

IV. Date.–Only a few Roman Catholics pursue the lonely battle for a dating in the time of the real Baruch. Whitehouse (*APOT,* I, 569) urges that every part of the book was composed after A.D. 70, that the tragedy of 597 or 586 B.C. is merely a cryptogram for the final destruction of the Herodian temple, that Nebuchadnezzar and Belshazzar really mean Vespasian and Titus. He would further associate the pacifist attitude toward Rome with the celebrated Rabban Johanan ben Zakkai, who flourished before and after the destruction of the Herodian temple. (See *Jew.Enc.* for an excellent biography.) Kneucker dates entirely in the period A.D. 81-117. If the Catholic dating be rejected, need the pendulum be swung quite so radically? Pfeiffer (*HNTT,* pp. 413-423) cogently argues that A, B, and C may all be dated a hundred or more years before Christ; Wace, Toy in *Jew.Enc.,* Marshall in *HDB,* and many others share his doubts concerning so late a dating. The crucial factor is whether certain allusions, particularly in C, do or do not have a demonstrably Christian or post-temple reference, when ambiguity and possible interpolation are allowed for. Witton Davies (*ISBE* [1929]) urges the later dating for 1:1-14 and 4:5–5:9, but feels that some of the material in between may be earlier. There are some arguments and authorities at least for tracing the book back, in whole or in part, to the commonly accepted apocryphal period, and not divorcing it quite so radically from its sister writings.

V. Original Language.–It may be taken as reasonably well established that the Greek of A is translated from Hebrew; the original language of B and C, however, is more controversial. Several scholars claim a Hebrew inception for the entire book, and Kneucker's rendering into Hebrew is a very practical argument for his opinion. Others are convinced that B and C were composed in Greek. Primary Jewish Greek writing and Jewish translation Greek are never easy to differentiate, as other apocryphal sources have made clear. Marshall (*HDB*) argues with equivalent renderings of great learning that B was originally composed in Aramaic. This strengthens the Semitic claim, though certain scholars do not admit that he has demonstrated Aramaic as such. The book is unquestionably Hebraic in its thought molds, whatever answer may be given to the controversial issues.

VI. Selected Exegetical Notes.–*1:11f.* Despite prophetic precedent, prayer for a heathen overlord, Babylonian or Roman, would violently offend nationalistic Judaism. The close of v. 11 is a hyperbolic prayer, flattering but formalized, that the lives of the monarchs may last as long as the heavens. It echoes Dt. 11:21, where the reference is national, not personal. Cf. Dnl. 2:4 and Neh. 2:3. Oriental crowds shout the same thing to their rulers on the streets today, and the Western mind should not take the words too literally.

2:3. Anthropophagy, foretold as the punishment of sin

in Lev. 26:29; Dt. 28:53; Jer. 19:9, became a hideous reality in 2 K. 6:28f.; Lam. 4:10.

2:17. The sentiment, which sounds rather harshly in Christian ears, is really quite scriptural; see Ps. 6:5; 30:9; 88:10-12; 115:17; Isa. 38:18; Eccl. 9:5. Cf. also Sir. 17:27f. The Baruch passage has been interpreted as a throwback to an early Jewish Sheol theology, in which the concept of personal immortality was somewhat rudimentary (cf. Toy in *Jew.Enc.*). This is also used as an argument for an earlier dating. The hypothesis that mortal death is followed by oblivion lasting till the final resurrection could also be read into the passage. See further Wace, pp. 262f.; Kneucker, pp. 239f. When Scripture repeatedly states that the dead cannot praise God, this means that the physical tools of praise, organs of speech and song, perish with the material body, and also that a corpse cannot help the living. There is no denial of immortal soul or spirit, or of a final resurrection, or of the praise of God in higher realms than ours. See Matthew Henry on the scriptural passages.

2:18. Kneucker turns the tortured Greek of the verse opening into smooth Hebrew, drawing his vocabulary only partially from Dt. 28:65. His Hebrew means: "For the troubled heart and the foot which walks bent and stumbling. . . ." In the Greek, *psychḗ* could mean either life principle or immortal soul, and may have stood in antithesis to some part of the body mistranslated from Hebrew by the impossible *epí tó mégethos*. The writer's exact meaning is now a matter of conjecture.

2:19. A most interesting denial of the prevailing Jewish doctrine of merits.

2:29. For "multitude," the original probably used the biblical (Heb.) *hāmôn* (so Kneucker). The beautiful onomatopoetic *bómbēsis* of the LXX, "buzzing of bees," hence by metonymy "swarm" or "multitude," is not a mistranslation, as Kneucker maintains (p. 254), though it may be a happy coinage. The cognate Hebrew and Greek verbs are found in Jer. 31:35; 48:36, but the Greek noun is known only in this passage.

3:4. Much has been made of the supposedly praying dead. Cf. prayer for the dead in 2 Macc. 12:43ff., a passage important to Roman Catholics, and contrast Bar. 2:17. The word for dead, Heb. *mēṯê* (pl. construct), may also be read *m^{e}ṯê* (pl. construct), from *maṯ*, "man"; and the original text, written in Hebrew, may have postulated no other prayer than that of the men of Israel. The meaning of the whole verse outshines its textual confusions and changes of pronoun. It may reasonably be inferred that the plagues of the last clause represent sufferings recognized as deserved through personal sin, and do not violate the theological principle of Ezk. 18 or Jer. 31:29f.

3:24. For an exhaustive study of the phrase *ho oíkos toú theoú,* see *TDNT,* V, *s.v.* οἶκος (Michel). In the OT the term commonly means sanctuary (Michel), also holy place created by theophany, as in Gen. 28:17, 19. But why should the sanctuary contain (v. 26) the giants of Gen. 6:4? The meaning here must be wider, perhaps (with Philonic precedent) signifying the entire created universe. Or (Wace, p. 274), v. 24 may split into two halves the phrase under discussion meaning the heavens, God's residence, as in 2:16, and *tópos tḗs ktḗseōs autoú,* the earth beneath, which He has made.

3:32. An apparent doctrine of "earth abides," linking with Eccl. 1:4; Ps. 104:5; 119:90, and contrasting sharply with the more orthodox teaching of Ps. 102:26 (MT 27), which is so strongly confirmed by modern scientific opinion. The contradiction is resolved if Baruch and canonical parallels be understood comparatively—earth's duration is eternal, not absolutely, but in contrast to the transient life of man. In the Bible and elsewhere, many so-called contradictions are merely fruits of shifting emphasis, and of the inherent imperfection of all human language.

3:38. This verse has been variously interpreted as a genuine Jewish prophecy of Jesus Christ; as a spurious Christian interpolation; and as an authentic Jewish utterance, referring not to the Incarnation but to wisdom.

4:3. Many have taken the "strange nation" to mean the Christians (cf. esp. Kneucker, pp. 73ff., 315f.). This certainly suits theories of late dating; but Toy has pointed out (*Jew.Enc.,* II, 557 col. 1) that it is just as logical to regard this as Jewish propaganda against Hellenism, and to date it two centuries earlier.

4:5. "Be of good cheer" — cf. vv. 21, 27, 30 below. The LXX has *tharseíte* as in Mt. 24:27, etc. Kneucker renders *'al-tîr'û* "fear not," with tenfold MT and LXX precedent (see HR, p. 626 col. 3). See further *TDNT*, III, *s.v.* θαρρέω (Grundmann). Syriac uses in the first passage the word of the Peshitta in Isa. 40:1, meaning "to comfort" or "console."

4:6ff. Idolatry, captivity to correct this favorite sin, final restoration — these elements constitute a familiar prophetic picture.

4:28. Pfeiffer, arguing for a Hebrew original, remarks (*HNTT*, p. 423): "The presence of phrases like 'seek him ten times more,' which are not easily reproduced in Hebrew, merely prove that the Greek translation is occasionally rather free." LSJ records only one other, Philonic, occurrence of the Greek verb *dekaplasiázō,* "multiply by ten"; it may be that the writer's thought was not easily reproduced in Greek either! Kneucker translates by the piel of the Hebrew verb *'āśar*, "tithe," meaning here "multiply by ten." This he characterizes in his exegetical note (p. 336) as a "neuhebräische Bedeutung," a late-Hebrew meaning. But "neuhebräisch" roughly means "postbiblical," and includes the rabbinic language. There is no trace of this usage in rabbinic literature — it is entirely modern. See Yehudi-Gûr's contemporary *Hebrew Dictionary* (1946), or the smaller *Compendious Hebrew Dictionary* of Grossman, Sachs, Segal (1946). Kneucker's translation, delightfully neat as it is, constitutes a philological anachronism. A very rare Greek verb, and a Hebrew usage impossible at its implied date, cannot be claimed as a valid argument either way for the identity of the original language.

4:35. It is not necessary to examine all Kneucker's arguments for late dating. Here he invokes the fire as that of the eruption of Vesuvius in A.D. 79 (pp. 51ff.). It could also (Wace) refer immediately to Babylon, and backward to Sodom and Gomorrah, and be inspired by Isa. 13:19-21. The allusions are all too vague to constitute absolute proof in either direction.

It has been impossible in this brief compass to make any study of the numerous OT quotations in Baruch.

VII. Conclusion.–If there were an edition of the Greek text of Baruch that, like certain convenient Greek Testaments, printed the OT quotations in black type, their proportional bulk would be seen to be approximately in ratio to those of the Epistle to the Hebrews. If this quoted material were entirely removed from both writings, the residue of Baruch would be of much lesser significance than that of the Epistle, for Baruch's original contribution to theology and thought (making the fullest allowance for its most valuable part, the praise of wisdom in 3:9-38) is infinitely less. There is no doubt that the book was overestimated in early Christian patristic circles, owing to the mistaken idea that it emanated from one very close to the person of Jeremiah. Protestant thought assigns, without antagonism, a lesser valuation.

Bibliography.–JB, pp. 1128, 1353-1361; J. A. Soggin, *Intro. to the OT* (Eng. tr. 1974), pp. 458-461. R. A. STEWART

BARZILLAI bär-zil'ī [Heb. *bārzillay*; Gk. Berzelli]; AV Apoc. BERZELUS.

1. A Gileadite of Rogelim who brought provision to David and his army at Mahanaim in their flight from Absalom (2 S. 17:27-29). When David was returning to Jerusalem after Absalom's defeat, Barzillai conducted him over Jordan; but being an old man of eighty years, he declined David's invitation to come to live in the capital and sent instead his son Chimham (2 S. 19:31-39). David before his death charged Solomon to "deal loyally with the sons of Barzillai" (1 K. 2:7).

2. The father of a family of priests who in Ezra's time, after the return of the exiles, could not trace their genealogy, "so they were excluded from the priesthood as unclean." This Barzillai had taken "a wife of the daughters of Barzillai the Gileadite," and had adopted his wife's family name (Ezr. 2:61f.=Neh. 7:63f.). His original name is given as Jaddus (AV Addus) in 1 Esd. 5:38.

3. Barzillai the Meholathite, whose son Adriel was married to Saul's daughter, either Michal (2 S. 21:8) or Merab (1 S. 18:19). T. REES

BASALOTH bas'ə-loth (1 Esd. 5:31, AV). *See* BAZLUTH.

BASCAMA bas'kə-mə (1 Macc. 13:23, AV, NEB). *See* BASKAMA.

BASE. (1) [Heb. *'eḏen*]. A pedestal that gives support and upholds.

(a) AV FOUNDATIONS; NEB SUPPORTING PILLARS. The bases of the earth (Job 38:6).

(b) AV, NEB, SOCKET. Golden pedestals for alabaster columns (Cant. 5:15).

(c) AV, NEB, SOCKET. The bases that support the tenons of the planks and pillars of the tabernacle (Ex. 26:19ff.; 27:10ff.; 35:11, 17; 36:24ff.; 38:10ff.; 39:33, 40; 40:18; Nu. 3:36f.; 4:31f.). Ex. 38:12 is the only place the RSV translates *'eḏen* as "socket."

(2) [Heb. *y^esôḏ*]; AV BOTTOM. Foundation or bottom of the altar, where the blood of the sacrifices was poured (Ex. 29:12; Lev. 4:7, 18ff.; 5:9; 8:15; 9:9).

(3) [Heb. *yārēḵ*]; AV SHAFT; NEB STEM. Originally "thigh" or loins," now base (loins) of a candlestick (Ex. 25:31; 37:17; Nu. 8:4).

(4) [Heb. *kēn*]; AV FOOT; NEB STAND. Pedestal or support, the base of the laver of the tabernacle (Ex. 30:18, 28; 31:9; 35:16; 38:8; 39:9; 40:11: Lev. 8:11).

(5) [Heb. *'oreḵ*]; AV LENGTH. The Hebrew term means "length" (Ezk. 41:22). The RSV and NEB readings follow the LXX *basis*.

(6) [Heb. *ḥêq*]; AV BOTTOM. Primary meaning is "bosom," used of the hollow base of the altar (Ezk. 43:13f., 17).

(7) [Heb. *m^eḵonâ*]; NEB PLACE. The final resting place prepared for the ephah (Zec. 5:11).

(8) In 1 Cor. 1:28, AV "base" is an obsolete term for "low," as it is rendered in the RSV. J. R. PRICE

BASEMATH bas'ə-math [Heb. *bāś^{e}maṯ*–'balsam,' 'fragrance'].

1. AV BASHEMATH. A wife of Esau. Gen. 26:34 has her as "the daughter of Elon the Hittite." Gen. 36:2-4, however, lists Basemath as the daughter of Ishmael and sister of Nebaioth who bore Esau a son Reuel, and lists Adah as the daughter of Elon the Hittite. It is probable that Esau had only one wife Basemath, the daughter of Ishmael, and that the Gen. 26:34 (cf. 36:2) designation actually belonged only to Adah. It is also likely that Basemath is identical with Mahaleth (cf. 28:9), a daughter of Ishmael whom Esau married because his father was displeased with his Canaanite wives.

2. AV BASMATH. The daughter of Solomon and wife of Ahimaaz (1 K. 4:15). N. J. O.

BASHAN bā'shən [Heb. *habbāšān*–'fruitful,' possibly 'wheatland']. A fertile plateau E of the Sea of Galilee and N of Gilead, the borders of which are not precisely defined. When the Israelites were moving toward Canaan from the wilderness, Bashan was under King Og, who had his capital at Ashtaroth (Nu. 21:33; Dt. 29:7). Og was defeated at Edrei (Dt. 3:1-3), and the territory was given to the half-tribe of Manasseh (Dt. 3:13) except for the Levitical cities of Golan and Beeshterah (Josh. 21:27). The region was taken by Hazael the Aramean king in the days of Jehu (2 K. 10:33) and reconquered by Jeroboam II (2 K. 14:25). Tiglath-pileser III conquered a large portion of north Transjordan and Galilee in the days of Pekah (2 K. 15:29), including Bashan, which thereafter was outside the limits of the land of Israel. In the time of the Persian empire it was approximately equivalent to the district of Qarnaim, and in the Greek period it was known as Batanea, which has been taken to be a derivative of Arabic Bathaniyah, which in turn is cognate with Hebrew Bashan (*GP*, II, 9).

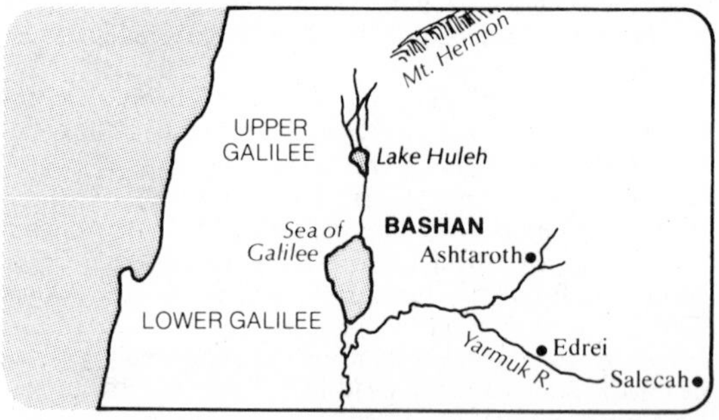

Most of Bashan is tableland, described by Baly as "wide open plains between 1600 and 2300 feet in height, and magnificently fertile" (*GB*, p. 220). It is generally considered to be the southern portion of Ḥaurân, which extends from Mt. Hermon to the Yarmuk River; but the borders of Bashan are not exact, and in some references the northern limit extends to Mt. Hermon (cf. Josh. 12:5; 13:1; 1 Ch. 5:23). Its western border is generally taken to be the edge of the plateau overlooking the Sea of Galilee (cf. Dt. 4:47; 33:22; Josh. 12:5; 13:11), and its eastern extent would seem to include the wooded slopes of Jebel Druze (Jebel Ḥaurân; cf. Ps. 68:16, "the many-peaked mountain of Bashan"). The relationship between Argob and Bashan remains a problem, hence we cannot be sure how many of the sixty cities of Argob actually were in the Bashan (cf. 1 K. 4:13); at any rate, Bashan included Ashtaroth, Qarnaim, Kenath, Edrei, and Salecah, the latter two possibly indicating the western and eastern limits of Bashan (Dt. 3:10). Mt. Zalmon (AV Salmon), on which snow fell (Ps. 68:14), is mentioned immediately before the mighty, many-peaked mountain of Bashan (68:15), hence is generally identified with Jebel Ḥaurân.

Because of the lower altitude of the hills in lower Galilee, rainfall in Bashan is above the normal for a region so far east, which, added to the volcanic nature of the soil, has produced rich land. The primary crop is wheat, and Bashan has long been one of the regions to serve as a "breadbasket." In NT times, when Bashan included Gaulanitis and Batanea, it was one of the important granaries of the Roman empire, and its wheat was transported across Galilee to be loaded on Roman grain ships at Ptolemais (Acre). Likewise the region provided good pasture land, and the "bulls of Bashan" (Ps. 22:12), the "cows of Bashan" (Am. 4:1), and the "fatlings of Bashan," including rams, lambs, goats, and bulls (Ezk. 39:18), appear to be proverbial figures of speech in Scripture. Lions are also mentioned (Dt. 33:22).

The trees of Bashan are often mentioned, particularly the oaks (Isa. 2:13; Zec. 11:2), which were used by Tyrian Phoenicians to make oars (Ezk. 27:5f.). Baly points out that since Bashan has been farmland for so many centuries, the ground must have been cleared comparatively early; hence we are probably to apply the references to trees to the eastern part, on the slopes of Jebel Ḥaurân, to which we might possibly add the southern region across the Yarmuk in north Gilead.

See also ARGOB; HAURAN.

Bibliography.–*GB*, pp. 219-226; *GP*, I, 274f., II, 8-11; *GTTOT*, §§ 33, 1685; Josephus *Ant.* xv.10.1; xviii.4.6. W. S. L. S.

BASHAN-HAVVOTH-JAIR bā'shən-hav'oth-jā'ər. *See* HAVVOTH-JAIR.

BASHEMATH bash'ə-math. *See* BASEMATH **1.**

BASIN [Heb. *mizrāq, sap̱, 'aggān,* '^{a}*garṭāl*; Gk. *niptḗr, kratḗr, trýblion, phiála, psyktḗr, lébēs*, etc.]; AV also BASON, BOWL, CHARGER (Ezr. 1:9); NEB also TOSSING-BOWL, BLANKET (2 S. 17:8).

The Heb. *mizrāq* (< *zāraq,* "toss, sprinkle") is a bowl used especially in connection with the sacrificial blood, thrown against the sides of the altar (Ex. 24:6; 29:16; etc.) or sprinkled on the participants in the ceremony (Ex. 24:8). Since it has to contain the blood of a slaughtered bull, ram, or lamb (2 Ch. 29:22), it must have been rather large and deep. Bronze basins are mentioned in connection with the tabernacle (Ex. 27:3; 38:3) and the temple (1 K. 7:45; cf. Jer. 52:18); silver ones in the description of the dedication of the altar of the tabernacle (Nu. 7:13-85, 14 times; in these exceptional cases they were filled with wheat groats mixed with oil, which was used as a cereal offering); silver or gold ones are mentioned in connection with the temple (2 K. 12:13; 25:15; cf. Jer. 52:19); for golden basins see 1 K. 7:50; 1 Ch. 28:17; 2 Ch. 4:8, 22, in descriptions of the temple.

Some of these bowls, captured by the Babylonians in 586, were sent back to Jerusalem to be used after the reinstatement of sacrificial worship there (Neh. 7:70). The weight of one silver *mizrāq* according to Nu. 7:13-85 was 70 shekels, i.e., about 28 oz. (794 grams). Inasmuch as they were used in the sacrificial cult, a special sanctity was ascribed to these vessels (Zec. 14:20). The blood of the sacrifice filled them to the rim (Zec. 9:15). Am. 6:6 mentions the use of such sprinkling bowls for drinking wine; this is both a profanation (cf. Dnl. 5:2) and an indication of greed. Many scholars, however, read here, following the LXX, "refined wines."

Evidently 1 K. 7:50 distinguishes between the *mizrāq* and the *sap̱*, both made of gold and both used in the temple. 2 K. 12:13 mentions *sippôṯ* of silver; cf. Jer. 52:19. The *sap̱* could be used for drinking (Zec. 12:2; cf. Ps. 75:8 [MT 9]; Isa. 51:17-22; Jer. 25:15-29, where *kôs*, a drinking cup, is used in the same way). Whereas the *kôs* had a large foot, the *sap̱* seems to have been a fairly flat bowl without foot. In Ex. 12:22 it is supposed that there was at least one *sap̱* in every household. In such cases it was of course one of earthenware. The *sappôṯ* of 2 S. 17:28 were probably not bowls but rather woolen blankets; cf. Bab. *šipātu,* "skin, wool," and Perles, *AfO*, 4 (1927), 220.

The *'aggān* is mentioned in Ex. 24:6 in connection with the blood of the covenant ceremony. According to Honeyman these basins were large, deep bowls, with two handles (cf. Cant. 7:2 [MT 3]; Isa. 22:24).

In Ezr. 1:9, '^{a}*garṭāl* is of uncertain meaning and origin. It may have been a basket (cf. BDB, KoB; the LXX, however, has *psyktḗres,* "wine-coolers." The RSV and NEB render "basins," while the AV has "chargers" (large flat platters).

In the NT, "basin" occurs only in Jn. 13:5 (Gk. *niptḗr* < *níptō,* "wash off"). Hands and feet were washed by pouring water on them, not by putting them into a basin of water. In order to purify, water should run. This is the general oriental conception to this day. The method of washing by using water in a basin is considered "washing in one's own uncleanness." Washing by pouring water is to be supposed in texts such as Gen. 18:4; 19:2; Lev. 15:11; 1 S. 25:41, and is explicit in 2 K. 3:11. So the *niptḗr* of Jn. 13:5 is not a basin to wash the feet in, but rather a jug of water to pour over the feet. Perhaps a basin was also used, to catch the water as it dripped from the feet, as is done nowadays in oriental countries. But the elaborate brass ewer with long spout, and basin with double bottom as described by E. W. Lane (*Manners and Customs of the Modern Egyptians* [2nd ed. 1908], ch. 5), have never been found in biblical excavations, and should be considered as rather modern. In biblical times people did not mind if the floor of the house got wet; note the Greek custom of pledging some of the wine to the gods by pouring it on the floor. It seems probable, therefore, that the *niptḗr* was a jug or ewer to be filled with water from larger pots standing ready near the wall of the room (Jn. 2:6). The large footbaths of Israelite times (K. Galling, *Biblisches Reallexicon* [1937], pp. 79-81) had handles so that they could be carried by two men, and therefore have nothing to do with the *niptḗr*, which was handled by the Master alone.

See also LAVER.

Bibliography.–A. M. Honeyman, *PEQ* (1939), pp. 76-90; *JTS*, 37 (1936), 56ff.; J. Kelso, "The Ceramic Vocabulary of the OT," *BASOR* Supplementary Studies 5-6 (1948). A. VAN SELMS.

BASKAMA bas'kə-mə [Gk. *Baskama*] (1 Macc. 13:23); AV, NEB, BASCAMA; Josephus (*Ant.* xiii.6.6) "Baska." A town in Gilead where the Syrian Trypho killed Jonathan Maccabeus son of Absalom. It is perhaps to be identified with el-Jummeimeh, NE of the Sea of Galilee.

D. B. PECOTA

BASKET [Heb. *dûḏ, ṭene', sal, k*^{e}*lûḇ, tēḇâ*; Gk. *kóphinos, spyrís, sargánē*]; AV also ARK (Ex. 2:3, 5), "pots" (Ps. 81:6).

I. OT Terms.–There is little in the Hebrew terms, or in the narratives where they occur, to indicate the exact differences in size and shape among the various baskets. The Mishnah refers to baskets of willow and of palm branches, of rushes and of leaves, some having lids, some with handles (Mish. *Kelim* xvi, xvii).

The Heb. *dûḏ* includes various kinds of baskets (note the variety of words used to translate it in the LXX). It is used as a symbol of slavery in Egypt (Ps. 81:6), referring probably to the large baskets in which clay was carried to the brick kilns. It was used, too, in fruit-gathering

Egyptian baskets illustrating coiled work (left) and plaited (or woven) construction (right) (Oriental Institute, University of Chicago)

Plaited basket (left) dating to the Egyptian New Kingdom (1580-1085 B.C.); open work basket (right) from the Roman period (30 B.C.-A.D. 324) (Oriental Institute, University of Chicago)

(Jer. 24:1f.), though this is distinguished from Amos' basket of summer fruit (*kᵉlûḇ*, Am. 8:1), and was counted a suitable receptacle in which to carry the heads of Ahab's slaughtered sons (2 K. 10:7). It stands, too, for a cooking pot (1 S. 2:14; Job 41:20), perhaps indicating that a pot-shaped basket was known by this name.

The *ṭene'*, a large, deep basket for carrying and storing crops (Dt. 26:2, 4), was a common household article along with the kneading trough (28:5, 17). The modern counterpart of it is possibly the *habya*, a basket of clay and straw used by peasants. Shaped like a jar, it is used for storing grain, which is poured in at the top, and removed as needed from an opening at the bottom.

The *sal* was the flat, lidless basket in which the court baker of Egypt carried his wares on his head (Gen. 40:16). As a basket for carrying foodstuffs (Jgs. 6:19), it was used in the offering of unleavened bread (Ex. 29:3; Lev. 8:2; Nu. 6:15). Some see a connection with Heb. *salsillâ* in Jer. 6:9, interpreting this as a grape-gatherer's basket (AV). More probably it refers to the shoots of the vine (BDB, RSV, NEB).

The *kᵉlûḇ*, found in Am. 8:1 for a fruitbasket, is used in Jer. 5:27 for a birdcage (cf. Am.Tab. *kilubi*, "bird net").

The basket of bulrushes in which the infant Moses was placed by his mother is called *tēḇâ*, the same word used of Noah's ark. Cf. Egyp. *tebt*; LXX *thíbis*. It was made of bulrushes (Heb. *gōme'*, "papyrus"), a species of reed used by the Egyptians for many different vessels, even small ships. It was made fit to float by plastering with a mixture of bitumen (*ḥēmār*) and Nile mud (*zepet*), then placed among the reeds in the shallow water at the edge of the Nile. A similar story is told of Sargon of Agade. *See* MOSES.

II. NT Terms.–The Gospel writers describe the baskets used in feeding the five thousand as Gk. *kóphinoi* (Mt. 14:20 par.), in contrast to the *spyrídes* (WH *sphyrídes*) of the miracle of the four thousand (Mt. 15:37; Mk. 8:8). That they are specifically contrasted (Mt. 16:9f.; Mk. 8:19f.) indicates that they are clearly distinguished from each other, though the distinction is probably one of material rather than size. The *kóphinos* was probably a basket of wickerwork, such as were carried by Jews as food containers, slung on the back by means of a cord handle (cf. *kûptā'* in the Mishnah). Evidence of its variation in size is found in certain military accounts (MM).

The *spyrís*, on the other hand, was a large hamper, possibly of rope, of sufficient size and strength for Paul to be lowered in it from the wall of Damascus (Acts 9:25). The apostle himself describes this basket as *sargánē* (2 Cor. 11:33), a plaited basket, sometimes more specifically a fish basket. G. I. EMMERSON

BASMATH bas'math. *See* BASEMATH **2.**

BASON. *See* BASIN.

BASSA bas'ə (1 Esd. 5:16, AV, NEB). *See* BEZAI **2.**

BASTAI bas'tī (1 Esd. 5:31, AV). *See* BESAI.

BASTARD [Heb. *mamzēr*] (Dt. 23:2); NEB "descendant of an irregular union"; **ILLEGITIMATE CHILDREN** [Gk. *nóthoi*] (He. 12:8); AV, NEB, BASTARDS. In Dt. 23:2 probably the offspring of an incestuous union or of a marriage within the prohibited degrees of affinity (Lev. 18:6-20; 20:10-21). He and his descendants to the tenth generation are excluded from the assembly of the Lord. In He. 12:8 "illegitimate children" means sons born "out of wedlock," and therefore not admitted to the privileges of paternal care and responsibility as legitimate sons.

See also MONGREL PEOPLE. T. REES

BASTHAE bas'thī (1 Esd. 5:31, NEB). *See* BESAI.

BAT [Heb. *'ᵃṭallēp̱*] (Lev. 11:19; Dt. 14:18; Isa. 2:20). Bats are the most widely distributed of mammals. Because it has not always been realized that they are mammals, it is not surprising that they should be mentioned at the end of the list of unclean birds in Lev. 11:19 and Dt. 14:18. It may, however, be significant that they are at the end of the list and not in the middle of it. The reference in Isa. 2:20, "cast . . . idols . . . to the moles and to the bats" refers to these animals as inhabitants of dark and deserted places. A. E. DAY

BATANEA bat-ə-nē'ə. The name used in Greek times for ancient BASHAN and for one of its four divisions. (Cf. Josephus *Vita* 11; *Ant.* xv.10.1; xvii.2.1, "toparchy of Batanea.") It was part of the kingdom of Herod the Great. D. B. PECOTA

BATH [Heb. *baṯ*]; NEB also GALLON (Isa. 5:10; Ezk. 45:10). A liquid measure equal to about 5½ U.S. gals. (21 liters). It seems to have been regarded as a standard for liquid measures (Ezk. 45:10) as in the case of the molten sea and the lavers in Solomon's temple (1 K. 7:26, 38), and for measuring oil and wine (2 Ch. 2:10; Ezr. 7:22; Isa. 5:10; Ezk. 45:14). The bath contained one tenth of a homer (Ezk. 45:11, 14).

See WEIGHTS AND MEASURES.

BATH KOL bath kōl [Heb. *baṯ qôl*–'daughter of the voice,' i.e., 'sound']. A rabbinic term signifying the divine voice, audible to man and unaccompanied by a visible divine manifestation. Thus conceived, *baṯ qôl* is to be distinguished from God's speaking to Moses and the prophets; for at Sinai the voice of God was part of a larger theophany, while for the prophets it was the resultant inward demonstration of the divine will, by whatever means effected, given to them to declare (*see* VOICE). It is further to be distinguished from all natural sounds and voices, even where these were interpreted as conveying divine instruction.

The concept appears for the first time in Dnl. 4:31 (MT 28), where, however, Aram. *qal,* "voice," stands without *bᵉraṯ,* "daughter": "A voice fell from heaven." Josephus (*Ant.* xiii.10.3) relates that John Hyrcanus (135-104 B.C.) heard a voice while offering a burnt sacrifice in the temple, which Josephus expressly interprets as the voice of God (cf. T.B. *Sotah* 33a and T.P. *Sotah* 24b where it is called *baṯ qôl*). In the NT, mention of "a voice from heaven" occurs in the following passages: Mt. 3:17; Mk. 1:11; Lk. 3:22 (at the baptism of Jesus); Mt. 17:5; Mk. 9:7; Lk. 9:35 (at His transfiguration); Jn. 12:28 (shortly before His passion); Acts 9:4; 22:7; 26:14 (conversion of Paul), and 10:13, 15 (instruction of Peter concerning clean and unclean).

In the period of the Tannaim (*ca.* 100 B.C.–A.D. 200) the term *baṯ qôl* was in very frequent use and was understood to signify not the direct voice of God, which was held to be supersensible, but the echo of the voice (*baṯ* being somewhat arbitrarily taken to express the distinction). The rabbis held that *baṯ qôl* had been an occasional means of divine communication throughout the whole history of Israel and that since the cessation of the prophetic gift it was the sole means of divine revelation. It is noteworthy that the rabbinical conception of *baṯ qôl* sprang up in the period of the decline of OT prophecy and flourished in the period of extreme traditionalism. Where the gift of prophecy was clearly lacking — perhaps even because of this lack — there grew up an inordinate desire for special divine manifestations. Often a voice from heaven was looked for to clear up matters of doubt and even to decide between conflicting interpretations of the law. So strong had this tendency become that Rabbi Joshua (*ca.* A.D. 100) felt it necessary to oppose it and to insist upon the supremacy and the sufficiency of the written law.

Bibliography.–F. Weber, *System der altsynagogalen palästinischen Theologie* (2nd ed. 1897), pp. 194ff.; J. Hamburger, *Real-Encyklopädie des Judentums,* II (1896); W. Bacher, *Agada der Tannaiten and Agada der palästinischen Amoräer* (see Index); *Jew.Enc.* II, 588ff.; Society of Biblical Archeology, *Transactions,* IX (1893), 18; *RGG* (1st ed. 1909), I, *s.v.* (P. Fiebig); *TDNT,* IX, 288-290 (O. Betz).

J. R. VAN PELT

BATHE [Heb. *rāḥaṣ*; Gk. *loúō* (Jn. 13:10)]; AV also WASH, DIP (Ps. 68:23); NEB also WASH, SPLASHED (Cant. 5:12), DABBLE (Ps. 68:23). The verb "bathe" appears thirty-four times in the RSV. Most of these instances occur in the ceremonial regulations of Lev. 15–17 and Nu. 19, where the Hebrew verb *rāḥaṣ,* "rinse," refers to Israel's washings in connection with sexual uncleanness (cf. Dt. 23:11), the Day of Atonement rites, food pollution, and defilement from death; cf. similar instances in Lev. 14:8f., on leprosy, and 22:6, on contact with unclean things. The process of bathing, however, occupies a greater place in Scripture than does the actual word "bathe."

Bathing is to be defined as washing one's body, as opposed to a mere washing of hands (also signified by Heb. *rāḥaṣ,* Job 9:30), face (Gen. 43:31; Mt. 6:17), or feet (particularly necessary because of the dusty, limestone soil of Palestine, and the open footgear of the Orient on stockingless feet) (Gen. 19:2; 2 S. 11:8; Cant. 5:3). Such partial bathing might carry a ritualistic meaning (Ex. 30:19; Mt. 15:2; cf. Lk. 11:38) or a symbolical one (Dt. 21:6; Ps. 26:6; cf. Mt. 27:24 on Pilate's vain handwashing), and was a particular sign of a host's hospitality (Gen. 18:4; Jgs. 19:21; Lk. 7:44; Jn. 13:5; 1 Tim. 5:10); but *see* WASH and FOOT WASHING. As used for full, bodily bathing the verb *rāḥaṣ* does not, moreover, distinguish between immersion in water (2 K. 5:13; cf. v. 14, Heb. *ṭāḇal,* "dip, plunge into") and the application of water through pouring or scrubbing (Ezk. 16:9; in parallelism with *šāṭap,* "wash away," here, of blood). A combination practice is suggested by the 800 B.C. pottery figurine from ez-Zîb, which depicts a woman bathing in a shallow tub. Streams and ponds, when available, were the usual resorts for bathing (Ex. 2:5; 2 K. 5:10); but the water supply of large cities, stored up in pools or large cisterns, was available to some degree for bathing (2 S. 11:2). Cleansing agents employed (cf. Jer. 2:22) consisted either of vegetable alkali, extracted from soap plants (KoB, p. 152; Heb. *bōrîṯ,* "soap"), or of mineral alkali (Heb. *neṯer,* "natron"; AV "nitre"; RSV "lye"). *See* SOAP.

The OT describes bathing for newborn children (Ezk. 16:4), but bathing was avoided at times of mourning (2 S. 12:10). Eight specific instances appear in which *rāḥaṣ* identifies full bodily bathing: the pharaoh's daughter washing in the Nile (Ex. 2:5), the ritualistic washing by Moses of Aaron and his sons at their priestly ordination (Lev. 8:6), Ruth's washing and anointing before meeting Boaz (Ruth 3:3), Bathsheba's washing herself at her house in Jerusalem (2 S. 11:2), David's bathing after the death of their child (12:20), the harlots at the pool of Samaria (1 K. 22:38), Naaman in the Jordan (2 K. 5:10-13), and the allegorical Oholah and Oholibah when preparing to receive guests (Ezk. 23:40). Additional figurative references occur in OT prophecy (Isa. 1:16; 4:4; Ezk. 16:9; not to be confused with the "washing" of Jer. 2:22, in which the verb is the piel of *kāḇas,* "launder" by pounding) and in poetry (Prov. 30:12); and OT law prescribes numerous ritualistic washings, as noted above (*see* ABLUTION; CLEAN AND UNCLEAN; etc.). Albright comments on the built-in basins for washing found in the guest house of preexilic Tell Beit Mirsim (*AP*, pp. 139f.). Thus, while it is true that certain Hebrews, particularly among the masses, may have had neither the privacy nor the inclination for bathing, still, the total OT picture suggests standards of cleanliness well above the average for the ancient world. The priests of Egypt took four baths daily (Herodotus ii.37; cf. the bathing of the Egyptian official Sinuhe, as recorded in *ANET,* p. 22a); but when one considers that in Palestine six months of the year are rainless, and how scarce water is at any season, the Mosaic law's rigid requirement of bathing for so many purposes is remarkable indeed.

Public baths are first constructed during the Greco-Roman period, when they are found to be regularly included in the *gymnasia,* or "places of exercise" (1 Macc. 1:14). A series of bath chambers was discovered by Macalister at Gezer in connection with a building supposed to be the palace of Simon Maccabeus. The Apocrypha speaks of Judith bathing in a fountain (Jth. 12:7), and of Susanna, in a garden, attended by maids (Sus. 15). Under Herod (37-4 B.C.) Greek ideas of bathing increasingly prevailed. The hot springs at Tiberias in Galilee and at Callirrhoë by the Dead Sea were sought out as health resorts (Josephus *Ant.* xvii.6.5; xviii.2.3), and elaborate public baths were eventually constructed in various cities (cf. xix.7.5). Herod's temple included a bathing room for priests (Mish. *Yoma* iii.2), and the name of the rabbi Gamaliel is associated with the public bath of Aphrodite in Acre.

In NT times, at the Essene community of Qumrân by the Dead Sea, most of the pools that have been excavated appear to have served simply as reservoirs, though some of the smaller were probably employed for daily priestly lustrations (cf. Josephus *BJ* ii.8.5) and for baths before the communion meal (F. M. Cross, *Ancient Library of Qumran and Modern Biblical Studies* [rev. ed. 1961], pp. 67f., 85, 234). Discovered remains of actual baths confirm the inscription found in the first-century Jerusalem synagogue of Theodotos near the Pool of Siloam, which mentions its "bathing establishment for those from abroad." Simons is willing to equate this structure with the synagogue of the Freedmen mentioned in Acts 6:9. The NT speaks of bathing in the Pool of Bethesda, for a cure (Jn. 5:7); and Christ illustrates the relationship of basic salvation to the need for daily cleansing by saying, "He who has bathed [Gk. *loúō*] does not need to wash [*níptō*] except for his feet" (Jn. 13:10); cf. 1 Cor. 6:11, "You were washed [*apoloúō*] . . . sanctified in the name of the Lord Jesus Christ. . . ."

Bibliography.–F. J. Bliss, *PEQ*, 27 (Oct. 1895), esp. 306-08; R. A. Stewart Macalaster, *PEQ*, 39 (Oct. 1907), esp. 258-262; J. Simons, *Jerusalem in the OT* (1952), pp. 75f.; R. de Vaux, *RB*, 63 (1956), esp. 539f. J. B. PAYNE

BATH-RABBIM bath-rab'im, **GATE OF** [Heb. *ša'ar baṯ-rabbîm*; Gk. *en pýlais thygatrós pollṓn*–'in the gates of the daughter of the many'] (Cant. 7:4); NEB "gate of the crowded city." A gate in Heshbon, near which were the pools to which the Shulammite's eyes are likened. *See* HESHBON.

BATHSHEBA bath-shē'bə [Heb. *baṯ-šeḇa'*]. The daughter of Eliam (2 S. 11:3) or Ammiel (both names have the same meaning), also called BATHSHUA (1 Ch. 3:5). She was the beautiful wife of Uriah the Hittite, who because of her beauty was forced by King David to commit adultery (2 S. 11:2ff.). When David learned that she had become pregnant, he sent an order that Uriah be treacherously killed (vv. 6ff.). After Uriah's death David made Bathsheba his wife, and she lived with him in the palace (v. 27). After their first child died (12:14ff.) she bore him four sons (2 S. 5:14; 1 Ch. 3:5).

With the help of the prophet Nathan she rendered futile the usurpation of Adonijah and secured the throne for her son Solomon (1 K. 1:11ff.). According to Jewish tradition, Prov. 31 was written by Solomon in memory of his mother. In the genealogy of Jesus (Mt. 1:6) Bathsheba is mentioned as the former wife of Uriah and the mother of Solomon by David.

See also DAVID II.F. A. L. BRESLICH

BATH-SHUA bath-shōō'ə [Heb. *baṯ-šûa'*–'daughter of opulence' or 'daughter of Shua'].

1. An alternative form of BATHSHEBA (1 Ch. 3:5).

2. A Canaanite woman who married Judah, bearing him Er, Onan, and Shelah (Gen. 38:2, 12; 1 Ch. 2:3). Her designation "daughter of Shua" is not a proper name.

BATHZACHARIAS bath-zak-ə-rī'əs (1 Macc. 6:32ff., AV). *See* BETH-ZECHARIAH.

BATTALION [Gk. *speíra*] (Mt. 27:27; Mk. 15:16); AV BAND; NEB COMPANY. The reference is to a *cohors miliaria*, which was stationed in Jerusalem under Claudius Lysias. *See* ARMY, ROMAN II.C.

Pottery figure of woman bathing in an oval tub, from the Phoenician cemetery at ez-Zib (8th-7th cents. B.C.) (Israel Department of Antiquities and Museums)

BATTERING RAM [Heb. *karîm* (Ezk. 4:2; 21:22), *m^{e}ḥî gōḇel* (26:9)]; AV also ENGINE OF WAR (26:9). *See* SIEGE.

BATTLE (GO OUT TO BATTLE; TAKE IN BATTLE; etc.) [Heb. *milḥāmâ, yāṣā' lammilḥâ, lāqaḥ ḇammilḥāmâ, 'ārak milḥāmâ*, etc.]; AV also FIGHT, WAR; NEB also FIGHT, ATTACK, WAR, FIELD, "take up position"; [*ṣāḇā'*] (Nu. 31:27f.); NEB CAMPAIGN, COMBATANTS; [*ma'^{a}rāḵâ*] ("field of battle," 1 S. 4:2; "battle line," 4:12); AV ARMY; NEB FIELD, BATTLEFIELD [*q^{e}rāḇ*]; NEB also MARCH (2 S. 17:11), BESET (Ps. 55:18 [MT 19]); [*maḥ^{a}nâ*] (1 K. 22:34; 2 Ch. 18:33); AV HOST; NEB LINE; [niphal of *lāḥam*] ("join battle," 2 Ch. 35:22); AV FIGHT; NEB FIGHTING; [*yāṣā'*] ("go forth to battle," 2 S. 11:1; 1 Ch. 20:1); NEB "take the field"; [*ḥ^{a}mušîm*] ("equipped for battle," Ex. 13:18); AV "harnassed"; [*kîḏôr*] (Job 15:24); [*nešeq*] (Ps. 140:7); [*sō'ēn b^{e}ra'aš*] ("battle tumult," Isa. 9:5 [MT 4]); AV "confused noise"; [*hêḏāḏ*] ("battle shout," Isa. 16:9); AV "shouting"; NEB "shouts"; [hithpael pl. of *rā'â pānîm*] ("faced one another in battle," 2 K. 14:11; 2 Ch. 25:21); AV "looked one another in the face"; NEB "met one another"; [hiphil of *rû(a)'*] ("sound the call to battle," 2 Ch. 13:12); AV "cry alarm"; NEB "signal the battle-cry"; [*ḥ^{a}ṣōṣ^{e}rôṯ hatt^{e}ru'â*] ("battle trumpets," 2 Ch. 13:12); AV "sounding trumpets"; NEB "trumpets"; [Gk. *pólemos*] (1 Cor. 14:8; Rev. 9:7, 9; 16:14; 20:8). *See* WAR.

BATTLE AXE (Jer. 51:20, AV). *See* WEAPONS OF WAR.

BATTLE BOW [Heb. *qešeṯ milḥāmâ*]; NEB WARRIOR'S BOW. Mentioned in the messianic prophecy of Zec. 9:10, describing the peace that the coming Prince will bring. This compound Asiatic bow required strong arms for proper use, but in battle was an extremely formidable weapon. *See also* WEAPONS OF WAR.

R. K. H.

BATTLEMENT. *See* FORTIFICATION; PARAPET (Dt. 22:8, AV); BRANCH (Jer. 5:10, AV).

BAVAI bav'ī. *See* BAVVAI.

BAVVAI bav'ī [Heb. *bawway*]; AV BAVAI; NEB BINNUI. The son of Henadad "ruler of half the district of

Keilah" (Neh. 3:18). He was from one of the levitical families that repaired the wall of Jerusalem after the return from Babylon (3:17f.). He may have been identical to or the brother of BINNUI (**5**) (Neh. 3:24).

BAY (Zec. 6:3, 7, AV). *See* COLOR V.D.

BAY [Heb. *lāšôn*–'tongue'] (Josh. 15:2, 5; 18:19); NEB INLET; [Gk. *kólpos*–'bosom, cavity, sinus, gulf, bay'] (Acts 27:39); AV CREEK. An inlet of the sea. The place referred to in Acts 27:39 has been identified as St. Paul's Bay, about 8 mi. (13 km.) NW of Valetta, on the island of MALTA. James Smith, *Voyage and Shipwreck of St. Paul* (4th ed. 1880), pp. 141ff., used the translation "creek" as the basis of his study, and suggested one of the two creeks on the west side of the bay. This interpretation, however, disregards the evidence that the Gk. *kólpos* (cognate with Eng. "gulf"), when used of the sea, means bay or gulf. W. S. L. S.

BAY TREE. The term occurs only in the AV for Heb. *'ezrāḥ* (Ps. 37:35), which means "native" or "indigenous." The RSV follows the LXX, reading "a cedar of Lebanon," while the NEB renders "a spreading tree in its native soil." R. K. H.

BAZAAR [Heb. *ḥûṣ*–'street of sale'] (1 K. 20:34); AV STREET; NEB TRADING QUARTER. A street given over to a market place. Ben-hadad of Syria conceded the right of the victorious Ahab to establish bazaars in Damascus.

BAZLITH baz'lith [Heb. *baṣlîṯ*] (Neh. 7:54); **BAZLUTH** [*baṣlûṯ*] (Ezr. 2:52); [Gk. *basalōṯ*] (1 Esd. 5:31); AV BASALOTH; NEB BAALOTH. The head of a family of temple-servitors who returned with Zerubbabel to Jerualem.

BDELLIUM del'ē-əm [Heb. *b^e^dōlaḥ*; Akk. *budulḫu*–'Indian myrrh']; NEB also "gum resin" (Nu. 11:7). A word that occurs twice in the Pentateuch: (1) in Gen. 2:12, in conjunction with gold and onyx, as a product of the land of HAVILAH, and (2) in Nu. 11:7, where the manna is likened to this substance in appearance. Cognate terms favor an identification with a resinous gum, which in droplet form might resemble stones or a pearl, depending on the color of the exudation.

BEACH [Gk. *aigalós*] (Mt. 13:2; Jn. 21:4; Acts 21:5; 27:39f.); AV, NEB also SHORE. The Gospel references are to the shore of the Sea of Galilee; those in Acts are to the Mediterranean.

BEACON. *See* STANDARD.

BEADS [Heb. *kûmāz*–some kind of golden ornament] (Nu. 31:50); AV TABLETS; NEB PENDANTS. Articles of gold jewelry, possibly pectorals, necklaces, or breastplates. *See also* ARMLET.

BEALIAH bē-ə-lī'ə [Heb. *b^e^'alyâ*]. A former friend of Saul who joined David at Ziklag (1 Ch. 12:5).

BEALOTH bē'ə-loth [Heb. *b^e^'ālôṯ*].

1. An unidentified city of Judah in the Negeb (Josh. 15:24), perhaps BAALATH-BEER.

2. AV, NEB, ALOTH. One of the places in Solomon's eleventh administrative district (1 K. 4:16), possibly the same as **1.**

BEAM. (1) [Heb. *mānôr*]. A part of a loom, used in comparison to indicate the great size of the spears carried by the enemy soldiers who were defeated by the heroes of Israel (1 S. 17:7; 2 S. 21:19; 1 Ch. 11:23; 20:5).

(2) Translation of a variety of building terms, all referring to constructional beams used in buildings for roofings, upper floors. *See also* ARCHITECTURE.

(a) [Aram. *'ā'*]; AV TIMBER. A punishment for anyone who altered the king's edict was that "a beam shall be pulled out of his house" (Ezr. 6:11; AV "timber").

(b) [Heb. *gēḇ*]. Part of the ceiling (1 K. 6:9).

(c) [Heb. *kāpîs*]. Used in Hab. 2:11 in the protest of inanimate things against sin.

(d) [Heb. *k^e^ruṯôṯ*]; NEB LENGTHS. Lit. "lengths"; cedar used in building courts and the House of the Forest of Lebanon, laid upon courses of stone or pillars (1 K. 6:36; 7:2, 12).

(e) [Heb. *qôrâ*]; NEB also RAFTERS. Literally "a thing meeting another" (2 Ch. 3:7; Cant. 1:17).

(f) [Heb. *qōrâ*]; AV also FLOOR. Timber purchased for buildings (2 Ch. 34:11; Neh. 2:8).

(g) [Heb. *qārâ*]; NEB also TIE-BEAM. Part of a gate (Neh. 3:3, 6); also used of the work of God (Ps. 104:3).

(h) [Gk. *toíchos*]. The AV, RSV, and NEB follow the LXX in 1 K. 6:6. J. R. PRICE

BEANS [Heb. *pôl*; Gk. *kýamos*]. A valuable article of ancient diet cultivated throughout the entire Near East. The beans of 2 S. 17:27f.; Ezk. 4:9 are undoubtedly the broad beans (*Faba vulgaris* Moench). The sowing took place in the autumn, and the crop was harvested just after the barley and wheat. The beans were threshed and winnowed like the other cereals, and while sometimes eaten raw, they were often cooked with oil and meat. R. K. H.

BEAR [Heb. *dōḇ, dôḇ*; cf. Arab. *dubb*; Gk. *árktos*]. Mentioned in 1 S. 17:34-37, where David tells Saul how as a shepherd boy he had overcome a lion and a bear. In 2 K. 2:24 it is related that two she-bears came out of the wood and tore forty-two of the children who had been mocking Elisha. All the other references to bears are figurative; cf. 2 S. 17:8; Prov. 17:12; 28:15; Isa. 11:7; 59:11; Lam. 3:10; Dnl. 7:5; Hos. 13:8; Am. 5:19; Rev. 13:2.

The Syrian bear, sometimes named as a distinct species, *Ursus Syriacus,* is better to be regarded as merely a local

Dancing bear, with donkey playing a lyre and jackal shaking a sistrum. Plaque of shell inlay set in bitumen, from the sound-box of a lyre discovered at Ur (Early Dynastic III, 25th cent. B.C.) (University Museum, University of Pennsylvania)

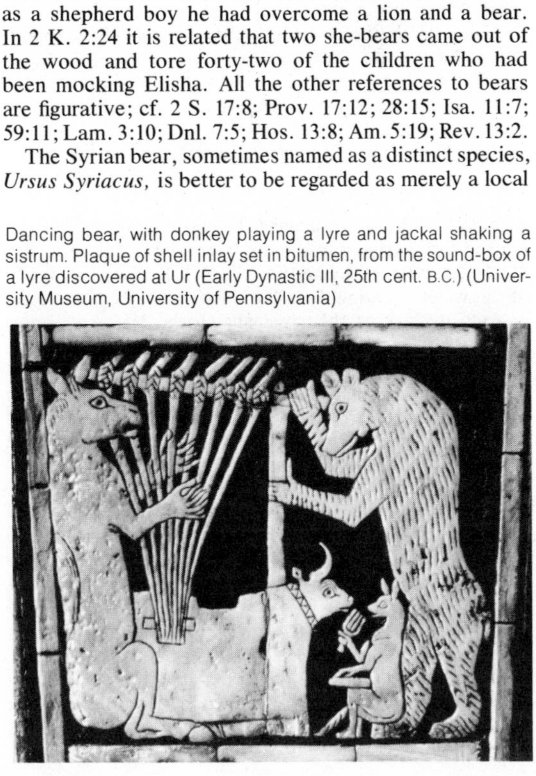

variety of the European and Asiatic brown bear, *Ursus arctos*. The figurative references to the bear take account of its ferocious nature, especially in the case of the bear robbed of her whelps (2 S. 17:8; Prov. 17:12; Hos. 13:8). Her transformation in the messianic age is envisaged in Isa. 11:7. A. E. DAY

BEAR, THE [Heb. *'aš, 'ayiš*]; AV ARCTURUS; NEB ALDEBARAN. A great northern constellation referred to in Job 9:9; 38:32. *See* ASTRONOMY II.C.

BEAR; BORN [Heb. *yālaḏ*]; AV also BEGET, BRING FORTH, COME OF, etc.; NEB also GIVE BIRTH, etc.; [Gk. *gennáō, tíktō, gínomai*]; AV also BEGOTTEN, MADE, SPRANG, BRING FORTH; NEB also GIVE BIRTH, SPRANG, etc.; [*teknagonéō*] ("bear a child," 1 Tim. 5:14); **UNTIMELY BORN** [Gk. *éktrōma*] (1 Cor. 15:8); AV BORN OUT OF DUE TIME; NEB ABNORMAL BIRTH; **BORN IN THE LIKENESS OF MEN** [Gk. *schḗmati heuretheís hōs ánthrōpos*] (Phil. 2:7); AV MADE IN THE LIKENESS OF MEN; NEB BEARING THE HUMAN LIKENESS. *See also* BIRTH.

In the OT the term used often is *yālaḏ*. The RSV also renders "born" certain Hebrew expressions that are translated more literally in the AV. In Gen. 25:23, e.g., the RSV translates *šnê lᵉ'ummîm mimmē'ayiḵ yippārēḏû* as "two peoples, born of you, shall be divided," while the AV gives a literal translation: "two manner of people shall be separated from thy bowels." Similarly, in 1 K. 8:19 and 2 Ch. 6:9 the RSV renders *hayyôṣē' mēḥᵃlāṣeyḵā* as "who shall be born to you," while the AV gives "that shall come forth out of thy loins." Again, the RSV renders "before you were born" for *ûḇᵉṭerem tēṣē' mēreḥem* (Jer. 1:5), while the AV gives "before thou camest forth out of the womb."

The NT term used most frequently for "bear, born" is Gk. *gennáō* — sometimes in the literal sense alluding to motherhood, but also in a figurative sense referring to the beginning of the spiritual life (e.g., Jn. 1:13; 3:3-8). In Gal. 1:15 the RSV renders "he who had set me apart before I was born" for *ho aphorísas me ek koilías mētrós*, which the AV translates literally as "who separated me from my mother's womb" (cf. NEB "who had set me apart from birth").

For a discussion of Jn. 3:7; 1 Pet. 1:3, 23, *see* ANEW.

N. J. O.

BEAR; BORNE. The usual OT word is Heb. *nāśā'*. It is used for bearing punishment (Gen. 4:13), iniquity (Ex. 28:38; Isa. 53:12), shame (Ezk. 32:24), honor (Zec. 6:13); of the waters bearing the ark of Noah (Gen. 7:17), priests bearing the ark of the covenant (Josh. 3:8), an armorbearer (1 S. 14:1), a tree bearing fruit (Joel 2:22). Other words include *kûl* (Am. 7:10), *sāḇal* (Gen. 49:15; Isa. 53:11; Lam. 5:7), *'āśâ* (2 K. 19:30; Ezk. 17:23). In Lam. 3:28 *nāṭal* is better rendered as in the RSV, "laid it on him." The RSV is to be preferred also at Ps. 75:3 ("keep steady," *tāḵan*) and Zeph. 1:11 ("weigh out," *nāṭîl*).

In the NT the most frequent words are Gk. *bastázō* (bear a cross, Lk. 14:27; Jn. 19:17; one another's burdens, Gal. 6:2; cf. also 6:5, 17; Mt. 8:17; Acts 15:10; Rev. 2:2), *phérō* (bear fruit, Jn. 15:2), *anaphérō* (bear sins, He. 9:28; 1 Pet. 2:24), *ekphérō* (He. 6:8), *phoróō* (Rom. 13:4; 1 Cor. 15:49), *aírō* (Mt. 4:6 par.), *anéchomai* (bear with, 2 Cor. 11:1). Gk. *stégō* means "endure" in 1 Thess. 3:5, and in 1 Cor. 13:7 may have the connotation "endure in silence." In Acts 27:15 *antophthalméō*, AV "bear up," means the ship could not head into the wind. J. W. D. H.

BEARD [Heb. *zāqān*]. The Hebrews generally wore full rounded beards, as contrasted with the desert nomads who frequently clipped or cut their beards (cf. Jer. 9:26; 25:23; 49:32; etc.). The Egyptians were clean shaven, although high officials wore artificial beards. In Babylonia and Assyria the aristocrats and rulers usually wore beards. The customary Hebrew word for beard (*zāqān*) was the term for "elder" or "old man." The term *śāpām* (2 S. 19:24) probably referred to the moustache.

The Torah forbad trimming the edges of the beard (Lev. 19:27), though Ezekiel was told to shave off his beard as a token of coming destruction (Ezk. 5:1). Among the Semites grief was indicated by cutting off the hair and beard, while anger could be shown by plucking out hair from one's head and beard. Mutilating the beard of another person, however, was considered an insult (cf. 2 S. 10:4; Isa. 50:6). The anointing of Aaron's beard (cf. Ps. 133:2) was probably part of the tabernacle ritual. R. K. H.

BEARERS (of a bier, Lk. 7:14) [Gk. *hoi bastázontes*]. *See* BIER; BURIAL II.D.

BEAST [Heb. *bᵉhēmâ*, *ḥayyâ nepeš* (Lev. 24:18), *bᵉ'îr* (Gen. 45:17; Ex. 22:5), *nᵉḇēlâ* (Lev. 7:24), *ḥay* (Gen. 8:1), *bᵉnê šāḥaṣ* ("proud beasts," Job 28:8), part. of *mûṯ* ("dead beast," Ex. 21:34f.), *gᵉnēḇâ* ("stolen beast," Ex. 22:4), *mᵉrî'* ("fed beast," Isa. 1:11), *ṭeḇaḥ* (Prov. 9:2); Aram. *ḥêwâ* (Dnl. 2:38; 4:12, 14ff.; 7:3; etc.); Gk. *thēríon* (Tit. 1:12; He. 12:20; Jas. 3:7; Rev. 6:8; etc.), *ktḗnos* (Lk. 10:34)]; AV also LIVING THING (Gen. 8:1), CATTLE (Dt. 28:4), LION'S WHELPS (Job 28:8), "multitude of the wicked" (Ps. 74:19), etc.; NEB also CATTLE, (WILD) ANIMAL, etc. In Ezk. 17:23 the RSV includes the phrase "all kinds of beasts," based on the LXX; the MT lacks the phrase, and is followed in this by the AV and NEB.

The word "beast" has been largely replaced in English by the word "animal." Nonetheless, the RSV and NEB have usually followed the tradition of the AV in translating the terms at the head of this entry as "beast" (although the NEB sometimes uses "[wild] animal" for *ḥayyâ*). Some of these terms probably refer to a particular species and/or genus, but it is most difficult to distinguish their original designations today. It is probably correct, however, to say that all the "beasts" designated by these terms belong to the general category of mammals.

"Beast" often refers to any animal at all in distinction from man (Eccl. 3:18-21), reptiles (Gen. 1:24), and (sometimes) cattle (Gen. 1:30). Two common uses of beasts were for food and for sacrifices. Beasts were divided into categories of CLEAN AND UNCLEAN (Lev. 11:1-8); only the clean ones could be eaten by the Israelites. Certain kinds of animals could be used for sacrifices, and these were sometimes fattened for the special occasions (Isa. 1:11; Am. 5:22; cf. Acts 7:42; He. 13:11).

In addition to the categories of clean and unclean, beasts were divided into those of wild and domesticated. "Wild beasts" (AV "beasts of the field") lived outside the civil community. These animals were predacious (cf. Gen. 37:20; Dt. 28:26). To the extent that this predatory nature was also characteristic of some people, the terms "wild beast" and "evil beast" became descriptive of Israel's enemies (Ps. 74:19; Jer. 12:9; cf. also 1 Cor. 15:32, where enemies of Paul are termed "wild beasts"). *See* WILD BEAST.

The term "beast" is also used for domesticated animals (though not necessarily "pets" as we think of the term). They received their food from their owners and did not have to plunder for it. Laws were formed to provide compensation for any violent act done against such animals (Ex. 22:10), and other laws proscribed any sexual activity between man and beast (Ex. 22:19; Lev. 18:23; Dt. 27:21). This anti-bestiality proscription may well have been formulated to distinguish the Israelites from the Canaanites, who are thought by some to have practiced a ritualistic copulation with beasts. (*See* CRIME.) Tamed animals were used for riding (Neh. 2:12, 14; Lk. 10:34) and probably also for pack purposes (Gen. 45:17; 2 K. 3:9). Furthermore, domesticated animals were subject to the laws of the sabbath (Dt. 5:14, Heb. *b^ehēmâ*; RSV "cattle") and of firstlings (Nu. 3:13; 8:17).

Whereas wild beasts will be the instruments of God's judgments (Ezk. 5:17), domestic animals will be the objects of God's wrath along with their owners (Jer. 7:20; 50:3; Ezk. 36:11). Nonetheless, when the Lord promises renewal to His people, both man and beast are included in the restoration (Jer. 31:27; Ezk. 36:11). *See also* CATTLE.

"The Beast" is used symbolically in the apocalyptic literature to represent the enemies of God and His people (Dnl. 7; Rev. 13:17). The OT already knew a metaphorical use of "beast" for enemies (Ps. 74:19; Jer. 12:9), and the apocalyptic usage may well be building on that.

Daniel in his vision saw "four great beasts" coming out of the sea, each with slightly different characteristics. "These four great beasts are four great kings who shall arise out of the earth" (Dnl. 7:17). Each shall make an onslaught against God's kingdom, but "the saints of the Most High shall receive the kingdom, and possess the kingdom for ever" (v. 18).

John in Revelation writes of "a beast rising out of the sea" (13:1) in an obvious allusion to the Daniel passage. John's "beast," however, is a composite figure that combines many of Daniel's characteristics into one. This seven-headed beast receives his authority from the dragon (Rev. 12:3; 13:4) and symbolizes the last enemy of God and His people (cf. Ps. 74:13f.). Yet another "beast" arises, but this one from the earth (Rev. 13:11ff.). This "lesser" beast seeks devotees for the "greater" beasts, and is referred to as the "false prophet" (16:13; 19:20; 20:10). The beast and this false prophet harass the Church but finally receive their decisive judgment (19:20) at Christ's appearing (cf. 2 Thess. 2:6ff.).

D. H. ENGELHARD

BEATEN GOLD. *See* GOLD.

BEATEN OIL. *See* OIL.

BEATING. *See* PUNISHMENTS.

BEATITUDES. Statements of blessedness, particularly those at the beginning of Jesus' great discourse commonly called the Sermon on the Mount (Mt. 5) or Sermon on the Plain (Lk. 6).

I. The Name.–The word "beatitude" is not used in the English Bible. It derives from the Lat. *beatitudo,* used by the Vulgate in Rom. 4:6, 9, where, with reference to Ps. 32:1f., David is said to pronounce a "beatitude" upon a certain type of man. "Beatitude" originally meant simply "blessedness," "happiness," "felicity." In church usage the term came to refer to biblical declarations of blessedness (makarisms), particularly the Psalms (32:1f.; 41:1; 65:4; etc.), but especially Jesus' pronouncements of blessing (Mt. 11:6; 13:16; 16:17; 24:46; Lk. 7:23; 10:23; 11:27f.; 12:37f., 43; Jn. 13:17; 20:29). Finally the plural form became the common designation for the series of blessings beginning both accounts of Jesus' great sermon. These beatitudes regularly consist of two clauses, the first pronouncing blessedness upon a certain type of person, the second giving the reason or ground for such blessedness: "Blessed . . ., for. . . ."

II. The Differing Forms.–Comparison of the two collections of beatitudes (Mt. 5:3-12; Lk. 6:20-23 [24-26]) immediately reveals their resemblances and differences. The ordinary reader, most familiar with Matthew's version, will notice first the differences, and will be apt to account for the discrepancy of the two reports as Augustine did, by assigning them to distinct occasions in the Lord's ministry. However, careful comparative study of the two passages raises serious questions regarding such a view. Some have proposed a varying oral tradition to account for the differences, but most scholars conclude that these are two versions of material drawn by the Evangelists from an underlying source consisting of sayings of Jesus (*see* SYNOPTIC GOSPELS). Numerous scholarly studies and proposals concern the extent of each Evangelist's freedom in using the hypothetical source and the possibility that the source itself had a prior redactional history. But the hosts of hypotheses have not yielded much scholarly consensus on the origin of the two collections or their present differences.

The form of the two collections differs markedly. Luke has a very balanced and orderly form: four blessings followed by four woes — the woes being exact counterparts to the respective blessings (blessed are you poor, woe to you that are rich; blessed are you that are hungry now, woe to you that are full now; etc.). Both the blessings and the woes are addressed directly to the audience in the 2nd person. Matthew on the other hand, has a series of eight blessings in the more general 3rd person, followed by a ninth blessing in the direct 2nd person form. As to content, Luke's first is the same as Matthew's first; Luke's second equals Matthew's third; Luke's fourth matches Matthew's ninth. Luke's third has no counterpart in Matthew; and Matthew's second, fourth, fifth, sixth, seventh, and eighth have no counterparts in Luke.

Although Greek literature has a few formulations that suggest beatitude collections, more likely antecedents to Matthew's and Luke's forms are found in the OT and other Jewish literature. Schweizer (p. 122) sees Luke's form as part of a continuation and gradual expansion of the prophetic-apocalyptic tradition of pronouncing series of woes on the hearers. Dodd has found precedents for both versions in the OT and Jewish literature. For Luke's antithetical scheme he cites Eccl. 10:16f. and rabbinic uses in T.B. *Berakoth* 61b and *Yoma* 87a. Dodd concludes, "The Lucan beatitudes and woes, forming a unitary whole, are composed on a well-established literary pattern" (p. 4). Dodd has more difficulty in finding parallels for Matthew's form, but he notes that some of the Psalms have at least a series of two beatitudes, e.g., Ps. 32:1f.; 84:4f., 12; sometimes the whole Psalm is simply an expansion of an initial beatitude, e.g., Ps. 112. But the closest literary analogy to Matthew's form he finds in Sir. 25:7-11, where, although the actual beatitude formula occurs only twice, in effect there is a series of ten beatitude statements. Dodd finds that "Matthew and the son of Sirach are composing within the same literary *genre*" (p. 7). He advises caution in drawing conclusions from the two literary forms of the Beatitudes: "Perhaps we can with confidence say little more than that when the tradition emerges into our ken, the Beatitudes had already taken two diverse forms represented by Matthew and Luke respectively. In that sense both are 'primitive'. But whether these traditional forms reflect distinct modes of presentation by the Lord himself on different occasions, or whether they developed in the course of giving shape to the Church's recollections of his teaching, is a question more difficult to answer" (pp. 9f.).

III. The Differing Emphases.–The beatitudes in the two collections as well as the single pronouncements of beatitudes found throughout the NT are expressions of the distinctive religious joy that comes to one sharing in the salvation of the kingdom of God. The beatitudes often resemble sacred paradoxes. For those who are citizens of God's kingdom, human estimations and values are radically reversed: the hungry, the meek, the weeping, the persecuted are pronounced blessed. In striking ways the beatitudes present the consolation and the challenge of the kingdom that Christ was bringing.

A. Luke. The beatitude collections in Matthew and Luke betray different emphases. Luke's emphasis is on the great reversal in personal and social relationships that the arrival of the kingdom will bring. The contrast between the present situation and that to come is expressed by the future tense of the verbs and is heightened by the fourfold occurrence of "now" in vv. 21 and 25. It is further heightened by the woes upon the counterparts of the blessed and the portrayal of the great reversal to come upon them in the eschaton. The poor, the hungry, the weeping, and the hated are pronounced blessed, but the rich, the full, the jovial, and the well-accepted are candidates for woe. Luke's words suggest social categories; no qualifying terms suggest religious commitment or a spiritualizing of the stance.

In Luke the sermon containing this beatitude collection is delivered on the plain where Jesus meets the crowds, after having returned from the hills where he chose his twelve disciples (6:17). Hence, Luke gives the sermon a general thrust, and it seems to speak of the broadest categories — the poor, the rich. His version is thus open to misunderstanding as presenting an "opiate of the people" type of religion: the poor and weeping will get their reward in the next life. The fact that Jesus "lifted up his eyes on his disciples" (v. 20a) immediately before speaking the beatitudes and woes in Luke's account does not limit Jesus' words to being specific instruction for the disciples alone. Their whole content is the broad address to the crowds on the plain.

Dupont proposes that the theological milieu for the Lucan beatitudes is not so much the Galilean plain, the mixed crowd, and the imminence of the messianic kingdom. Rather, Luke sees the social condition of the primitive Church in Acts, the poor saints of Jerusalem and the outcasts of this world. Here the poor, the hungry, the afflicted, and the dishonored have a theological interpretation; they are blessed because they cannot and do not live for this world but remain faithful to the Lord as they await their pleasures in the next life. As Dupont points out, this combination of social justice and Christian asceticism, together with an expectation of greater reward in the next life than in the present messianic kingdom, is typical of Luke's Gospel (cf. the rich man and Lazarus, 16:19-31; the dishonest steward, 16:1-15; the Baptist's advice to the crowd, 3:10-14; and Mary's song, 1:46-55). Luke's beatitudes offer eschatological consolation to suffering Christians.

B. Matthew. If Luke's beatitudes present eschatological consolation, Matthew's beatitudes present eschatological challenge. There is an ethical emphasis in Matthew, with no suggestion of a reversal in conditions or roles. The merciful, the pure of heart, and the peacemakers are pronounced blessed with no implications of their having afflictions from which one might anticipate alleviation. Rather, their behavior is clearly indicative of conduct that meets with God's approval and characteristic of eschatological blessedness in the kingdom of heaven. While the persecuted in Luke's setting could look forward to release from an unfavorable situation (Lk. 6:23), in Matthew's setting the persecution is "for righteousness' sake" (5:10), stressing the ethical quality of the martyr's sufferings. The next beatitude, in the 2nd person address of its Lucan counterpart, does not direct the attention of the persecuted to "that day" as in Luke; rather, they are to "rejoice and be glad" (by implication "now") as they find themselves in the situation of the prophets before them (Mt. 5:12). The "mourners" who shall be "comforted" (5:4) are reminiscent of the many during prophetic times who mourned over the sins of the covenant people and whom the prophets promised comfort (cf. Isa. 57:18; 61:2f.; Joel 2:12-14). Mourning thus suggests the present life of penitence for personal and national sin.

Nowhere is the ethical emphasis of Matthew's collection seen more clearly than in his beatitudes about the poor and the hungry. The poor in Matthew are "the poor in spirit," the pious and humble poor of a host of OT passages. By the times of later Isaiah, Jeremiah, and the postexilic Psalms, the term "poor" could be the practical equivalent of "the truly devout Israelite." Their poverty in spirit contrasts not with material riches or intellectual wealth, but with those who are rich in religious knowledge and achievement (*TDNT,* VI, 401 [E. Schweizer]). Matthew's poor are those whose sole help is God and who stand poverty-stricken in their own achievements. They are the humble and lowly as opposed to the Pharisees with their self-esteem and religious accomplishments. As for the hungry, in Matthew they hunger and thirst for righteousness. Hunger and thirst are spiritualized, indicating a driving desire for righteousness. Whether this righteousness is that which is the gift of salvation from God, or the righteousness that is the human activity of actualizing God's ways in our lives, is a question for continued scholarly debate (cf. Strecker, p. 265, and n. 1). Either way, the beatitude has an ethical thrust, for the righteousness that is a gift yields the activity of actualizing that salvation which has been given.

Matthew's beatitudes suggest more clearly than Luke's the inaugurated presence of God's kingdom in Jesus' present ministry. Luke stresses the future consummation of the kingdom that will come with the great reversal. Matthew's collection begins and ends (except for the added 2nd person beatitude) with the promises "for theirs is the kingdom of heaven" (vv. 3, 10). Clearly this is programmatic for the construction of the Matthean series. Matthew's beatitudes proclaim eschatological fact and eschatological promise. They present the challenge to actuate here and now what is ours as citizens of God's kingdom through Christ. However the differing forms of the two collections in Matthew and Luke are to be accounted for, there are clearly two distinct emphases. The two collections reflect the two poles of the "already but not yet" nature of God's kingdom through Christ.

Bibliography.–J. W. Bowman, *Review and Expositor,* 54 (1975), 377-392; G. Braumann, *Nov.Test.,* 4 (1960), 253-260; C. H. Dodd, *More NT Studies* (1968), pp. 1-10; J. Dupont, *Les Béatitudes* (2nd ed. 1969); E. Schweizer, *NTS,* 19 (1973), 121-26; G. Strecker, *NTS,* 17 (1971), 255-275; *TDNT,* IV, *s.v.* μακάριος κτλ. (Hauck, Bertram).

W. P. DEBOER

BEAUTIFUL GATE. *See* GATE, BEAUTIFUL.

BEAUTY [Heb. *yāp̱eh, y^epî, tip̱'ārâ, nō'am, hāḏār, ḥeseḏ* (Isa. 40:6), *mar'eh* (Isa. 53:2), *hôḏ* (Hos. 14:6), etc.]; AV also GOODLINESS (*ḥeseḏ*), GLORY (Isa. 62:3), etc.; NEB also GRANDEUR, DIGNITY, SPLENDOUR, "perfume" (Isa. 3:24), etc.; [Gk. *timḗ*] (Rom.

9:21); AV HONOUR; NEB "to be treasured"; [*euprépeia*] (Jas. 1:11); AV "grace of fashion"; NEB "what was lovely to look at." These biblical terms and their cognates describe aesthetic impressions without formulating theoretical propositions about beauty.

The Hebrews appreciated the aesthetic values of nature in Palestine (cf. Ps. 16:6; Jer. 3:19), but also saw beauty in Zion (Ps. 50:2; Lam. 2:15) and even in such places as Egypt (Ezk. 31:1ff.) and Tyre (Ezk. 27:1ff.). The handsome qualities of men such as David (1 S. 16:12), Absalom (2 S. 14:25), Daniel (Dnl. 1:4, 15) and others were paralleled by the feminine beauty of Sarai (Gen. 12:11, 14), Rebekah (Gen. 24:16; 26:7), Abigail (1 S. 25:3), and numerous others. The bride of Cant. 4:1-6 was the epitome of womanly beauty. Various parts of the body were credited with beauty, such as the lips (Cant. 4:3), the hair (4:1), and the neck (cf. Hos. 10:11), while elegant clothing of various kinds also had aesthetic appeal (cf. Gen. 41:42; 45:22; Ex. 26:36; 28:2, 40; Mt. 17:2; Rev. 3:4f.; etc.).

While the Hebrews did not build magnificent, structures on the scale of other nations, the expressed their aesthetic values in a variety of arts and crafts, and were outstanding musicians in the ancient Near East. Their speech, and especially their poetry, manifested a beauty and delicacy of linguistic expression that has seldom been exceeded. Beauty is accepted in Scripture as a concomitant of divine creativity, and thus it is hardly surprising that it plays so important a part in the eschatological passages of Revelation.

The biblical terms for the adjective "beautiful" include Heb. *yāpeh* (AV usually "fair"; NEB also "comely," "fine," etc.), *ṭôḇ mar'â* (AV "fair"), *ḥemdâ* (AV "pleasant"), *tip'ārâ* (NEB also "loveliest," "glorious," etc.), *ṣ^eḇî* (AV also "fair"); Gk. *hōraíos* (NEB also "well," "welcome"), *kalós* (AV "good"; NEB "fine"), *asteíos* (AV "fair," "proper"; NEB "pleasing," "fine"). The terms for the verb "beautify" include Heb. *yāpâ* (AV "make yourself fair"), *pā'ar* (NEB "add glory," "bring glory"). R. K. H.

BEAUTY AND BANDS (Zec. 11:7, 10, AV). *See* GRACE AND UNION.

BEBAI bē'bī [Heb. *bēḇay*; Gk. *Bēbai*].

1. AV also BABI; NEB also BABI, BEBAE. The head of a family that returned with Ezra to Jerusalem (Ezr. 8:11; 1 Esd. 8:37). One of his descendants was Zechariah, the son of Bebai (Ezr. 8:11; 1 Esd. 8:37). Of his descendants, 623 returned with Zerubbabel to Jerusalem (Ezr. 2:11; 1 Esd. 5:13; Neh. 7:16 gives the number 628); some of these had married foreign wives (Ezr. 10:28; 1 Esd. 9:29).

2. A chief of the people who sealed the covenant with Nehemiah (Neh. 10:15).

BEBAI [Gk. *Bēbai*]. An unknown town in Israel (Jth. 15:4). Omitted in B and the Vulgate.

BECAUSE. Archaic for "in order that" (Gk. *hína*) in Mt. 20:31, AV.

BECHER bē'kər [Heb. *beḵer*]; **BECHERITES**; AV, NEB, BACHRITE(S).

1. Second son of Benjamin (Gen. 46:21; 1 Ch. 7:6, 8).

2. Son of Ephraim, whose family is called the Becherites (Nu. 26:35); both names are omitted in the LXX. Cf. BERED in 1 Ch. 7:20.

BECHORATH (1 S. 9:1, AV, NEB). *See* BECORATH.

BECK. Archaic for "nod" (Gk. *neúma*) in 2 Macc. 8:18, AV.

BECKON [Gk. *neúō* (Jn. 13:24), *kataneúō* (Lk. 5:7)]; NEB SIGNAL, NOD. A nod would be appropriate in the context of Jn. 13:24, but in Lk. 5:7 a more visible signal such as a motion with the arm is no doubt intended. MM can cite no clear examples of *kataneúō*. The AV has "beckon" for *dianeúō* in Lk. 1:22, where the RSV has "made signs" (so NEB), more clearly describing the situation with the mute Zechariah.

See also GESTURE.

BECOME; BECOMING; BECOMINGLY. The notion of the fitting, the suitable, the proper, is not unknown to the Bible. The Heb. *nā'weh,* "fitting" or "beautiful," occurs in Prov. 17:7, "Fine speech is not becoming to a fool"; the same word occurs in 19:10, "It is not fitting for a fool to live in luxury," and 26:1, "honor is not fitting for a fool." The NEB has "out of place" in the first two instances and "unseasonable" in 26:1. Cf. Ps. 33:1. Ps. 93:5, AV, reads "Holiness becometh thine house"; the RSV reads "befits" (*nā'â*).

In the NT occurs Gk. *prépei,* "it is proper, fitting" (Mt. 3:15; Eph. 5:3; 1 Tim. 2:10; Tit. 2:1; He. 2:10; 7:26), translated "become" in the AV, as is *axíōs,* "worthily," in Rom. 16:2; Phil. 1:27. *See* FIT. The word "becomingly" is used in Rom. 13:13, RSV (AV "honestly"; NEB "with decency") to translate *euschēmónōs* (cf. 1 Thess. 4:12; RSV and NEB "command respect"). The Greek word means literally "in good form." Paul was concerned that outward appearance accurately reflect the Christian's renewed inner disposition; that the conduct of the Christian reflect Christian faith. J. W. D. H.

BECORATH bə-kôr'ath [Heb. *b^eḵôraṯ*]; AV, NEB, BECHORATH. An ancestor of Saul of the tribe of Benjamin (1 S. 9:1).

BECTILETH bek'tə-leth [Gk. *Baikteilaith*]. A plain, described as three days' march from Nineveh, "near the mountain which is to the north of Upper Cilicia" (Jth. 2:21). But upper Cilicia is N of the Taurus Mountains, 300 mi. (480 km.) from Nineveh, and far out of the way for Holofernes, according to the route described in the following verses. Hence scholars believe either that the text has been distorted or that the author is using symbolic language. (In Aramaic, Bectileth could mean "place of slaughter.") Some scholars identify Bectileth with the Beqa', the mountain with the Anti-Lebanon, and the possible location in the region between Beirût and Damascus.

Bibliography.–GTTOT, § 1601; F. Stummer, *Geographie des Buches Judith* (1947), p. 27. W. S. L. S.

BED [Heb. *yāṣa'*–'spread out' (e.g., Isa. 14:11), *yaṣû(a)'*–'that which is spread out' (e.g., Ps. 132:3), *miṭṭâ*–'place of reclining' (e.g., 2 K. 4:10), *miškāḇ*–'place of lying' (e.g., 2 S. 4:11), *'āpîq*–'channel, stream' (Joel 3:18), *'^arûgâ*–'garden terrace' (e.g., Ezk. 17:7, 10), *'ereś*–'couch, divan' (e.g., Job 7:13), *naḥal*–'stream' ("torrent bed," Job 22:24); cf. Arab. *'rš*–'booth,' 'shed,' or 'throne'; Gk. *klínē* (e.g., Mt. 9:2) and its diminutives *klinárion* (Acts 5:15) and *klinídion* (Lk. 5:19, 24), *koíte* (e.g., Lk. 11:7), *strōnnýō*–'spread out,' 'make one's bed' ("make your bed," Acts 9:34)]; AV also BROOKS (Job 22:24), "lie down" (Job 27:19), "spread under" (Isa. 14:11), FURROWS (Ezk. 17:7, 10), etc.; NEB also "lie down" (Job 27:19), PALLET, etc.; **BEDSTEAD** [Heb. *'ereś*] (Dt. 3:11); NEB SARCOPHAGUS; **BEDCHAMBER** [Heb. *ḥ^adar*

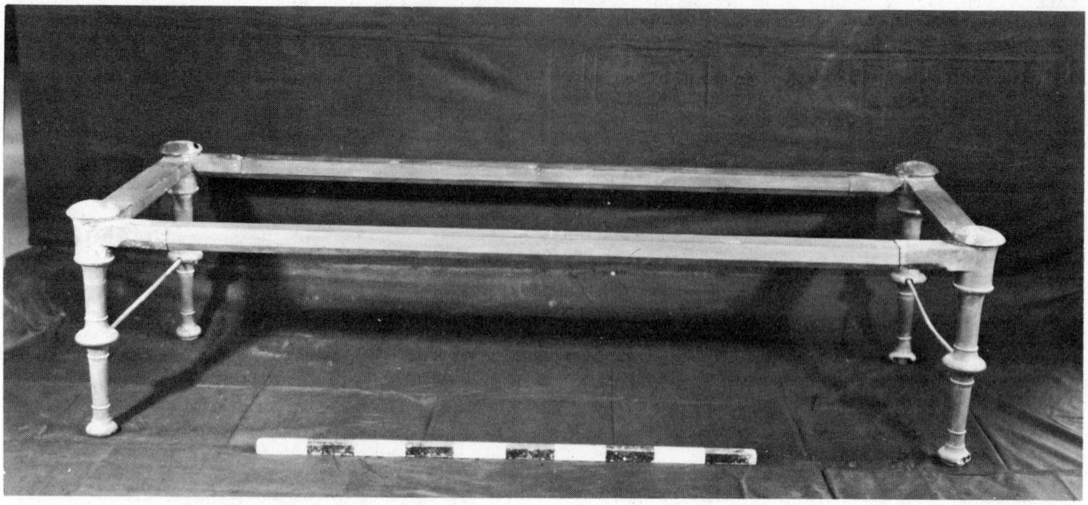

Bed with bronze fittings for the legs and iron tie-rods to hold them together (reconstructed, from Tell el-Fâr'ah, *ca.* 550-330 B.C.) (Israel Department of Antiquities and Museums)

miškāḇ (e.g., Ex. 8:3 [MT 7:28]), *ḥ^{a}ḏar miṭṭâ* (e.g., 2 K. 11:2)]; NEB also BEDROOM, "room where he was asleep"; **COUCH** [Heb. *yāṣû(a)'* (e.g., Gen. 49:4), *miškāb* (e.g., 2 S. 11:2), *miṭṭâ* (e.g., Est. 7:8), *'ereś* (e.g., Ps. 6:6), *mēsaḇ* (Cant. 1:12)]; AV often BED, also TABLE (Cant. 1:12); NEB also BLANKET (2 S. 11:13), "incest" (1 Ch. 5:1), etc.; **PALLET** [Gk. *krábattos*– 'mattress, pallet'] (e.g., Mk. 2:4); AV BED; NEB STRETCHER, BED.

I. Types of Beds and Couches.–The Hebrew and Greek words for "bed" and "couch" seem to overlap in usage with little detail given as to shape and structure. At times, no doubt, the bed was the ground or a mat laid out on the ground, with the person's garment as a covering (Ex. 22:27). But often the bed was laid somewhere in the house, sometimes in the bedchamber of the master of the house (2 K. 6:12). At other times it might be in a guest room in an upper story, i.e., a small roof chamber (2 K. 4:12; 1 K. 17:19).

Beds were sometimes quite short (Isa. 28:20), but at other times they seem to have been large and off the ground (2 K. 1:4, 6, 16) — at least high enough for a lamp to be placed under them (Mk. 4:21; Lk. 8:16). The bed could be simple, a mere portable mattress belonging to a poor man (Mk. 2:4); or it could be quite elaborate, with a frame covered with silver or gold (e.g., the couches used in the palace at Shushan, Est. 1:6); cf. the "stately" (RSV) couch mentioned by Ezekiel (23:41). Some couches, as noted in Am. 6:4 and in Hezekiah's tribute list given to Sennacherib (*ANET,* p. 288), were inlaid with panels of ivory. Holofernes had a canopied bed (Jth. 10:21). Josephus reports (*Ant.* xii.2.15) that Ptolemy Philadelphus of Egypt gave Eleazer the high priest of Jerusalem ten couches (*klínai*) with silver feet, along with accompanying furnishings.

Some beds or couches were undoubtedly portable and made with a wooden frame, e.g., the bed carried in to King Saul (1 S. 19:13, 15; cf. 2 S. 17:28); cf. also the mattress bed on which the paralytic man was carried to Jesus (Mt. 9:2; Lk. 5:18). Beds belonging to the wealthy or royalty were perfumed with myrrh, aloes, and cinnamon (Prov. 7:17), and might be covered with linen sheets or spreads from Egypt (v. 16). The Scriptures do not mention the wooden headrests connected with Egyptian beds; there is, however, the mention of a pillow of goat's hair (1 S. 19:13), or even of stone (Gen. 28:11).

II. Uses of Beds or Couches.–The most common use of the bed was for sleeping at night (cf. Job 7:13; Ps. 132:3; Lk. 11:5-8). The place of sleeping, especially in the case of royalty or the wealthy, could be in a room set aside as a bedchamber (cf. Ex. 8:3; 2 S. 4:5, 7; 2 K. 6:12). On occasion the bed was also used for taking a siesta at noon (2 S. 4:5, 7). Often the bed is referred to as the place of rest and recuperation for the sick (Gen. 48:2; Ps. 41:4; Acts 9:33); and sometimes a person sat on the bed while regaining his strength (1 S. 28:23). Being at times transportable, the pallet was used as a stretcher to carry those who were ill (Mk. 2:4, 9, 11f.; Lk. 5:18; Jn. 5:8-11). Misuses of the bed are also mentioned: the sluggard is warned against spending too much time in bed (Prov. 26:14); King Ahab used the bed as a place to do his sulking (1 K. 21:4).

Another common use of the couch was for reclining beside a table, either while beautifying oneself with cosmetics (Ezk. 23:40f.), or while taking meals; examples of this latter use are the couch of gold and silver in the Shushan (Susa) palace (Est. 1:6), the equally luxurious couches of ivory mentioned in Am. 6:4, and the ancient dining couch of Mk. 7:4, mentioned in some early Greek MSS.

There is considerable reference in Scripture to the bed used as a place of lovemaking (cf. Nu. 31:17, 35; Jgs. 21:11f.). This could be the legitimate and God-honoring use of the marriage bed (Cant. 3:1; He. 13:4). However, the bed is also described as being defiled through incest (Gen. 49:4; 1 Ch. 5:1) or other sexually immoral acts (Ezk. 23:17; He. 13:4b), e.g., homosexuality (Lev. 18:22; 20:13; Rom. 1:26f.). The Greek word *koítē,* which can have the general meaning of bed (Lk. 11:7), is sometimes used euphemistically for sexual intercourse (cf. LXX Lev. 15:21-26) or sexual excesses (Rom. 13:13, RSV "debauchery"), and in one instance refers to seminal emission in the conception of a child (Rom. 9:10).

One particularly specialized use of the bed is as a funeral bier. The Heb. *miṭṭâ* (2 S. 3:31) and *miškāḇ* (2 Ch. 16:14) and the Gk. *klínē* (LXX 2 K. 3:31; 2 Ch. 16:14; Josh. 7:40) are sometimes used in this sense in the OT; although *klínē* does not occur with this meaning in the NT, it is used thus by Josephus for Herod's golden bier studded with precious stones (*Ant.* xvii.8.3). Related to this usage is the figure of the grave as the bed for the individual (Job 17:13; cf. Ps. 139:8) or nation (Ezk. 32:24f.) at death.

The expression, a "short bed" (Isa. 28:20), seems to be a figure for difficult circumstances.

Beds are sometimes mentioned as places where acts of devotion (Gen. 47:31; 1 K. 1:47) and meditation (Ps. 63:6) are performed. Grief on account of sin against the Lord or the oppression of the enemy is also expressed in bed (Ps. 6:6).

It is not certain whether Og's "bedstead of iron" mentioned in Dt. 3:11 is anything other than a bed for sleeping; a sarcophagus has been suggested (cf. NEB).

See A. Edersheim, *Sketches of Jewish Social Life* (repr. 1957), pp. 86-102. W. H. MARE

BEDAD bē'dad [Heb. *b^{e}ḏaḏ*]. Father of Hadad king of Edom (Gen. 36:35; 1 Ch. 1:46).

BEDAN bē'dan [Heb. *b^{e}ḏan*].

1. (1 S. 12:11, AV). One of the leaders in Israel who with Jerubbaal, Jephthah, and Samuel is mentioned in the MT as a deliverer of the nation. The text is questioned because the LXX, Syriac, and Arabic read "BARAK" instead, and this is followed by the RSV and NEB.

2. A son of Ulam of the house of Manasseh (1 Ch. 7:17).

BEDCHAMBER. *See* BED.

BEDEIAH be-dē'yə [Heb. *bēḏ^{e}yâ*–'servant of Yahweh']. A son of Bani who married a foreign wife (Ezr. 10:35).

BEE [Heb. *d^{e}ḇôrâ*; cf. Arab. *dibr*–'a swarm of bees']. Honey is mentioned many times in the Bible, especially in the OT, but the word "bee" occurs only four times, and only one of the four times in connection with honey, in the story of Samson (Jgs. 14:8). Both wild and domesticated bees are found today in Palestine; though it is not clear that bees were kept in Bible times, it would seem very probable. The frequently recurring phrase, "a land flowing with milk and honey," certainly suggests that honey as well as milk was a domestic product.

In Jgs. 14:8 it is related that Samson found a swarm of bees and honey in the carcass of the lion he had killed on his previous visit. We are not told how much time had intervened, but it does not take long in the dry climate of Palestine for scavenging beasts and insects to strip the flesh from the bones and make the skeleton a possible home for a swarm of bees.

The other three passages refer to the offensive power of bees. In Dt. 1:44 Moses says, "The Amorites . . . chased you as bees do"; in Ps. 118:12 the psalmist says, "They surrounded me like bees"; in Isa. 7:18, the bee is the type of the chastisement that the Lord will bring from the land of Assyria. A. E. DAY

BEEF. *See* CATTLE.

BEELIADA bē-ə-lī'ə-də [Heb. *b^e'elyāḏā'*]. The name of a son of David born in Jerusalem (1 Ch. 14:7), but changed to ELIADA in order to remove the element of "Baal" from the name (2 S. 5:16; 1 Ch. 3:8).

BEELSARUS bē-el'sə-rəs (1 Esd. 5:8, AV, NEB). *See* BILSHAN.

BEELTETHMUS bē-əl-teth'məs (1 Esd. 2:16, 25, AV, NEB). *See* BELTETHMUS.

BEELZEBUB bē-el'zə-bub. *See* BEELZEBUL.

BEELZEBUL bē-el'zə-bul [Gk. *Beelzeboul* var. *Beezeboul*–'master of the (heavenly) dwelling'; Latin and Syriac versions have *Beelzebub*–'master of the flies'] (Mk. 3:22 par. Mt. 12:24 and Lk. 11:15; Mt. 12:27 par. Lk. 11:18f.; Mt. 10:25); AV, NEB, BEELZEBUB (following Vulg.). A relatively obscure name for Satan (Mk. 3:26 par. Mt. 12:26 and Lk. 11:18), or the prince of demons (Mt. 9:34), or an unclean spirit (Mk. 3:30), claimed by Jesus' enemies to be the supernatural agency through which Jesus performed miraculous deeds.

Etymologically, Beelzebul appears to be a compound word made up of the Aram. *b^e'ēl* ("master, lord") and the Heb. *z^{e}ḇul* ("height, abode, dwelling"), the only Hebrew word found on the lips of Jesus in the NT. The compound name may therefore be translated "master of the (heavenly) dwelling," and appears to have been a pejorative nickname for Jesus coined by his enemies (Mt. 10:25). This interpretation is made plausible in view of the play on words found in the saying of Jesus: "If they have called the master of the house (Gk. *oikodespotēn*, possibly translating Heb. *ba'al habbayiṯ* or Aram. *b^e'ēl d^{e}ḇayṯā'*) Beelzebul (i.e., "master of the [heavenly] dwelling"), how much more will they malign those of his household." In origin, Beelzebul may have been the name of the Canaanite god of Ekron, later altered to the opprobrious form BAALZEBUB found in 2 K. 1:2f., 6, 16; nevertheless it remains a mystery why Jerome and the unknown translators of the Syriac NT rendered the transliterated Greek name "Beelzebul" with the form "Beelzebub." A less likely etymology of Beelzebul is reflected in the translation "lord of dung," based on the valid contention that *zbl* in postbiblical Hebrew, as in Syriac and Arabic, can be translated "dung, manure."

Jesus and many of His Greco-Roman contemporaries believed that miraculous feats were accomplished through the possession of a spirit (Smith, pp. 220ff.). Jesus regarded His own miracles as empowered by the "finger of God" or the Holy Spirit (Lk. 11:20; Mt. 12:28; cf. Mk. 3:28-30 par. Mt. 12:31f. and Lk. 12:10), while His Jewish opponents were apparently convinced that His miracles were in fact feats of magic performed through the agency of Satan or the prince of demons, i.e., Beelzebul (Mk. 3:23, 26; Mt. 12:26; Mk. 3:22 par. Mt. 12:24 and Lk. 11:15), or simply an unclean spirit or demon (Mk. 3:29; Jn. 7:20; 8:48-52; 10:20), or possibly through the spirit of John the Baptist (Mk. 6:14-16 par. Mt. 14:1f. and Lk. 9:7-9; cf. Kraeling). In the NT era it was believed that a man might be possessed and victimized by a demon, or might have a demon under his control. The accusation that Jesus "has Beelzebul" (Mk. 3:22) or that He performs miracles "by Beelzebul" (Mt. 9:34; 12:24, 27; Lk. 11:15, 18f.) clearly presupposes the second type of possession (for a similar charge against John the Baptist, cf. Mt. 11:18; Lk. 7:33). In fact, the expression "by Beelzebul" is probably a shortened form of an original "by/in *the name of* Beelzebul" (Samain, p. 466); according to Origen, "those who invoke Beelzebul are magicians" (*In Numeros homilia* 13:5). Apart from the Beelzebul passages listed above, an analogous charge that Jesus has a demon, repeated three times in the Gospel of John (7:20; 8:48-52; 10:20), also appears to be an accusation that Jesus practiced magic, as is the charge that Jesus is an impostor in Mt. 27:63 (Samain, pp. 456-464, 473-484). The depreciating charge that Jesus was a magician has been preserved in both pagan and Jewish traditions and sources (Origen *Contra Celsum* i.6, 38, 49, 53, 68; Justin *Apol.* i.30; *Dial.* 69.7; T.B. *Sanhedrin* 43a; Koran 5:113; cf. Klausner, pp. 18-47; Hull, pp. 1-4).

Bibliography.–W. E. M. Aitken, *JBL*, 31 (1912), 34-53; J. M. Hull, *Hellenistic Magic and the Synoptic Tradition* (1974); J. Klausner, *Jesus of Nazareth* (1925); C. H. Kraeling, *JBL*, 59 (1940), 147-157; S. V. McCasland, *By the Finger of God* (1951);

P. Samain, *Ephemerides theologicae Lovanienses,* 15 (1938), 449-490; M. Smith, *Clement of Alexandria and a Secret Gospel of Mark* (1973). D. E. AUNE

BEER bē'ər [Heb. *b^e'ēr*; Gk. *phréar*–'well'; Lat. *puteus*]. The word for "well," used as a place name, usually in compounds. Two locations are called Beer.

1. A station on the march of the Israelites N of the Arnon (Nu. 21:16), the well that the Lord had promised. It is perhaps to be identified with Wâdī eth-Themed, where an adequate water supply can be easily attained by digging, and the BEER-ELIM of Isa. 15:8.

2. The town to which Jotham fled from his brother Abimelech after declaring his parable from Mt. Gerizim (Jgs. 9:21), identified as BEEROTH or as el-Bîreh (7 mi. [11 km.] N of Beth-shan).

BEERA bē'ə-rə [Heb. *b^e'ērā'*–'well']. A descendant of Asher (1 Ch. 7:37).

BEERAH bē'ə-rə [Heb. *b^e'ērâ*–'well']. A chieftain of the house of Reuben whom Tiglath-pileser carried away captive (1 Ch. 5:6). Cf. 2 K. 15:29; 16:7ff.

BEER-ELIM bēr-ē'lim [Heb. *b^e'ēr 'ēlîm*; Gk. *phéar toú Aileim*–'well of Elim' or 'terebinths' or 'chiefs']. A city mentioned in the oracle concerning Moab (Isa. 15:8). Some scholars identify it with BEER **1.** W. S. L. S.

BEERI bē'ə-rī [Heb. *b^e'erî*].

1. Father of Judith, one of Esau's wives (Gen. 26:34).

2. The father of the prophet Hosea (Hos. 1:1).

BEER-LAHAI-ROI bēr-lə-hī'roi [Heb. *b^e'ēr laḥay rō'î*–'well of the Living One that sees me,' possibly a folk etymology of a more ancient name, 'well of a jawbone of a *rō'î*']. The name given to "a spring of water in the wilderness" and "the spring on the way to Shur" (Gen. 16:7-14), which was the scene of Hagar's theophany, and by which Isaac dwelt for some time (Gen. 16:7f.; 24:62; 25:11). The site is in the Negeb between Kadesh and Bered (16:14). According to Arab tradition, it may possibly be identified with modern 'Ain Muweileh about 7 mi. (11 km.) W of Kadesh-barnea and about 47 mi. (75 km.) SW of Beer-sheba. D. D. GERARD

BEEROTH bē'ə-roth [Heb. *b^e'ērōṯ*; Gk. *Bērōt, Bērōth*]; AV and NEB Apoc. BEROTH (1 Esd. 5:19). A Canaanite city, one of four Hivite strongholds that followed the Gideonites in making a covenant with Israel (Josh. 9:17). Beeroth was assigned to Benjamin (2 S. 4:2f.), though located on the border between Benjamin and Ephraim.

The reference to a flight of Beerothites S to Gittaim may have resulted from Philistine pressure after the events at Mt. Gilboa. Naharai of Beeroth was the armor-bearer of Joab (2 S. 23:37; 2 Ch. 11:39). In 2 S. 4, two Beerothite brothers, Rechab and Baanah, were officers in Ishbosheth's forces and assassinated him in the seventh year of his reign. The site remains unidentified; el-Bîreh, Nebu Samwil, and Tell en-Naṣbeh have been suggested. R. K. H.

BEEROTH BENE-JAAKAN ben'ə-jā'ə-kən [Heb. *b^e'ērōṯ b^enê-ya'^aqān*–'the wells of the children of Jaakan'] (Dt. 10:6). A desert camp of the Israelites mentioned before Moserah. In Nu. 33:31f. the name is given simply "Bene-jaakan," and the location after Moseroth. *See* WANDERINGS OF ISRAEL.

BEEROTHITE bē'ə-roth-īt [Heb. *b^e'ērōṯî*] (2 S. 4:3, 5, 9; 23:37, AV). An inhabitant of BEEROTH.

BEER-SHEBA bēr-shē'bə [Heb. *b^e'ēr šeḇa'*; Gk. *Bērsabee*; Eusebius (*Onom.* 166.20f.) equates Gk. *phrear horkismou*–'well of swearing']. A site of major importance in the northern Negeb desert.

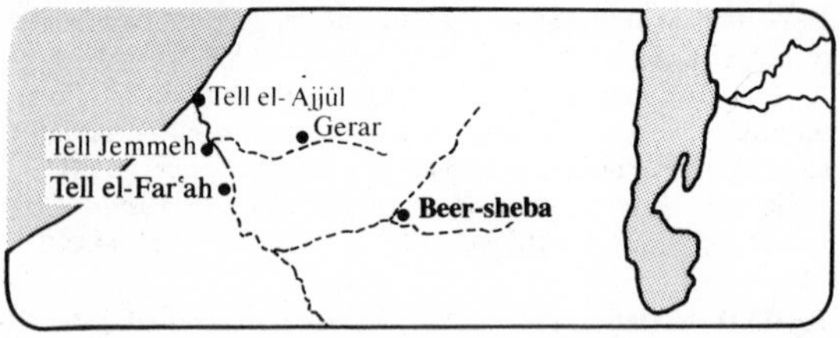

I. Significance of the Name.–The name of this venerable town means literally "the well of seven." The Semitic words for "oath" and "swear an oath" are derived from the consonantal root of the number seven, and this etymological relationship is stressed in the biblical explanations of the name Beer-sheba. The name was first given because there Abraham and Abimelech king of Gerar swore an oath of mutual allegiance (Gen. 21:31), and the ritual of swearing involved seven ewe lambs that Abraham gave to Abimelech (Gen. 21:28-30). The covenant agreement was aimed at resolving disputes between the two parties concerning the possession of certain wells. A similar dispute is recorded concerning Abimelech and Isaac. When agreement was finally reached and the oath duly taken, Isaac received a report from his servants that a new well had successfully been dug. In honor of this occasion, Isaac named the new well *šiḇ'â*, the numeral seven (masc.). "Therefore the name of the city is Beer-sheba to this day" (Gen. 26:33).

II. Geographical Situation.–The site of biblical Beer-sheba has been identified with Tell es-Seba', also known as Tell el-'Imshash, "mound of the wells," located at the juncture of the Wâdī Seba' with the Wâdī Khelil. The resultant stream bed continues WSW in a winding course for about 10 mi. (16 km.) before swinging northward in a wide arc past Tell el-Far'ah (Sharuhen) and Tell Jemmeh (probably Yurzah, known from Egyptian inscriptions), whence it continues NW, reaching the sea near Tell el-'Ajjûl (known from Byzantine sources as Beth-eglaim). The western segment of this stream bed was probably the biblical Besor; various wells, especially in the region of Tell es-Seba', serve to illustrate the appropriateness of the biblical passages cited above.

Beer-sheba is located in a topographical basin, the outline of which resembles an hourglass. As it extends eastward from the coastal plain, it narrows toward Beer-sheba; from there to the crest overlooking the Dead Sea it widens once again. Thus it serves to separate the populated region on the north, where the traditional topographical division into longitudinal belts prevails, and the desert highlands on the south, where the principal ridges swing round toward the southwest. Because of this position between the Judean mountains to the north and the Negeb highlands to the south, the Beer-sheba basin is an area of deposition rather than of erosion. This accounts for its rich alluvial soil, and especially its extensive regions of loess (a very fine blown sand). The basin itself marks the southern end of the region of permanent settlement; the 300 mm. (about 12 in.) per annum rainfall line, the border of aridity, passes through it. Below this line regular agriculture could not be maintained without an artificial water supply. Therefore, the southern boundary of settlement varied from N to S in accordance with prevailing weather conditions. This territory, of which Beer-sheba was the topographical pivot, embraced the biblical Negeb.

III. Chalcolithic Culture.–Extensive Chalcolithic settlement in the immediate vicinity of Beer-sheba is evidenced by numerous small mounds on both sides of the Wâdī es-Seba'. Each of these hillocks contained the remains of a small community of underground dwellings dug in the loess. The Chalcolithic culture of Beer-sheba evidently originated in the northern Negeb; its latest stage is closely related to that of Tuleilat Ghassul. But Chalcolithic culture in this region has no connection with any of the events or peoples referred to in the Bible even though Chalcolithic sherds have also been found at Tell es-Seba'.

IV. Patriarchal Associations.–More than a millennium separated the biblical patriarchs from the Chalcolithic occupants of Beer-sheba. The Genesis accounts make no mention of a king or even of a city at Beer-sheba. The absence of Middle and Late Bronze Age sherds from Tell es-Seba' and the immediate vicinity supports the assumption that the patriarchs encountered no sedentary population there. Accordingly, the area of Hagar's wanderings is called "the wilderness of Beer-sheba" (Gen. 21:14). The closest cultural and commercial center was evidently Gerar, whose rulers enjoyed hegemony over the Beer-sheba district. While Abraham was located on the vital artery connecting Shur (the famous Egyptian defense line on the east) and Kadesh(-barnea), he enjoyed the status of a sojourner at Gerar (Gen. 20:1). At the same time, he enjoyed water rights in the Beer-sheba area by virtue of an agreement with Abimelech, the ruler of Gerar (21:22-32). The earliest biblical reference to the sanctity of Beer-sheba is associated with this event. Soon after his covenant with Abimelech, Abraham planted a tamarisk tree at Beer-sheba; the religious nature of this act is stressed by the added statement that there he called on the name of Yahweh the everlasting God (21:33). He evidently continued to reside in that region for some time (cf. 22:19).

A similar situation prevailed during the sojourn of Isaac in the territory of Gerar. Although Isaac dwelt for a time in Gerar itself (Gen. 26:1-16), the envy of his agricultural success and renewed disputes over water rights forced him to move, first to the "valley of Gerar" (v. 17) and finally to Beer-sheba (v. 23). Here he was able to reach an agreement with Abimelech like that formerly extended to his father (vv. 23-33). Isaac must have remained in the Beer-sheba region for a long time; the disputes between his grown sons Jacob and Esau seem to have taken place there (28:10). But upon his return to Canaan, Jacob found his father at Hebron (35:27); Jacob evidently made this latter place his own headquarters until his descent to Egypt (cf. 46:1-7).

V. Southern Extremity of Israelite Territory.–From early in the period of settlement by the Israelite tribes Beer-sheba was reckoned as the southernmost extremity of the territory, as expressed in the familiar phrase "from Dan to Beer-sheba" (Jgs. 20:1; 1 S. 3:20). The same definition was applied to the territory encompassed by Saul's kingdom (2 S. 3:10) and maintained its validity during the reign of David (1 S. 24:2, 15; 1 Ch. 21:2). Under Solomon it served to distinguish Israel proper from the wider sphere of his dominions (1 K. 4:24f.). Even after the fall of the northern kingdom of Israel, when Hezekiah king of Judah sought to expand his own influence over the entire Israelite sphere, he had a proclamation made "from Beer-sheba to Dan" (2 Ch. 30:5). Meanwhile, Beer-sheba had represented the southern limit of the Judean kingdom, for example, under Jehoshaphat, who had exercised leadership "from Beer-sheba to Mount Ephraim" (2 Ch. 19:4). Although King Josiah had extended his own authority, at least in some measure, even as far as Galilee (2 Ch. 34:6), the immediate bounds of his own Judean kingdom extended "from Geba to Beer-sheba" (2 K. 23:8).

During the postexilic period Beer-sheba continued to mark the southern extent of Judean settlement (Neh. 11:30).

VI. Capital of the Negeb.–Beer-sheba was assigned to the tribe of Simeon (Josh. 19:2; 1 Ch. 4:28); but since that tribe had become so closely affiliated with Judah (Jgs. 1:3), the towns of Simeon also appear in the allotments made to Judah. Beer-sheba and the others are listed therefore among the towns in the "Negeb district" of Judah (Josh. 15:28; cf. vv. 21, 32). Beer-sheba's importance as an administrative center in the premonarchial period is underlined by Samuel's having stationed his sons there to act as judges (1 S. 8:2).

The role of Beer-sheba as capital of the Negeb, the southernmost district in David's kingdom (2 S. 24:2; 1 Ch. 21:2), is clearly seen in the record of Joab's census. The officials sent out to take this census went "to the Negeb of Judah at Beer-sheba" (2 S. 24:7). The same administrative arrangement seems to have prevailed under Solomon (1 K. 4:24). When the prophet Elijah wished to escape from the territory under Ahab and Jezebel's jurisdiction, he fled south; his first stop was evidently at "Beer-sheba, which belongs to Judah" (1 K. 19:3). Perhaps it was necessary to explain which Beer-sheba was intended so as to distinguish this town in the Judean Negeb from another Beer-sheba in Galilee (Josephus *BJ* iii.3.1).

A wife of Ahaziah king of Judah, named Zibia, came from Beer-sheba. It was her son, Joash/Jehoash, who was rescued from Athaliah's cruel slaughter of the royal sons (cf. 2 K. 11:2), and who was later enthroned by a palace coup (2 K. 12:2; 2 Ch. 24:1). Under King Jehoshaphat, Beer-sheba was apparently still the administrative center of southern Judah as indicated by 2 Ch. 19:4. Two allusions to Beer-sheba by the prophet Amos indicate that a shrine was located there (Am. 5:5; 8:14). Although Beer-sheba continued to be singled out as the southern extremity of Judean territory during the reign of Hezekiah (2 Ch. 30:5) and of Josiah (2 K. 23:8), it has been suggested that the capital of the Negeb of Judah was moved late in the Iron Age to the powerful fortress at Khirbet Gharrah, about 8 mi. (13 km.) E of Beer-sheba.

VII. Postexilic Period.–The presence of a Judean population at Beer-sheba and other neighboring towns is indicated by the book of Nehemiah (11:27), and the general sphere of Judean occupation is said to extend from "Beer-sheba to the Valley of Hinnom" (v. 30). The presence of Judeans in Beer-sheba and the Judean Negeb, even though the region was practically cut off from Jerusalem by the newly arrived Edomites who had settled in the southern Judean hill country (the Idumeans of NT times), suggests that perhaps the residents of these towns (and of the others in Neh. 11:25-35) may have escaped the Babylonian Exile.

VIII. Later History.–In spite of the presence of Jewish settlements, it is quite possible that Beer-sheba had become absorbed into Idumea during the intertestamental period. Under the Romans Beer-sheba was a major military center on the defense line that spanned southern Palestine from Raphia to the Dead Sea (Eusebius *Onom.* 50.1).

IX. Archeological Excavations.–Besides the excavation of the prehistoric Chalcolithic settlements along the stream bed there have been several trial digs in the modern town of Beer-sheba when new buildings were being constructed. An extensive Iron Age settlement was found to exist on the western bank of the Wâdī es-Seba'. Beginning in 1969, Tell es-Seba' (Modern Hebrew Tel Beer Sheva) became the subject of an intensive research project by the Institute of Archaeology, Tel Aviv University, under the direction of Y. Aharoni.

The earliest occupation (stratum VIII) is dated by painted Philistine ware to the late 12th century. Strata VII and VI represent further occupation levels of the Early Iron Age. There premonarchial remains have appeared mainly in the area beneath the later city gates. During the united monarchy (stratum V) a huge, artificial platform was created by laying down large quantities of gravel and dirt mixed with ash. A massive solid wall with salients and recesses surrounded the city. Stratum V was destroyed by fire; the city was rebuilt in the early 9th cent. B.C. and the solid wall and its gate were reused. Stratum IV was also destroyed by fire.

In the late 9th or early 8th cent. B.C. (stratum III) the city was reconstructed once again along lines similar to those of the preceding strata. However, a casemate wall was built over the remains of the former solid wall and a new gate, somewhat smaller than the older one, was constructed. The stratum III city seems to have suffered considerable damage but does not show signs of having been burned. The buildings were, for the most part, repaired and some of the floor levels were raised for the final Israelite city (stratum II). This latter occupation level was destroyed by a terrific conflagration (similar to strata V and IV), and afterwards there are only traces of a poor attempt by squatters to live for a short time among the ruins of the city (stratum I).

During the course of excavation, almost the entire plan of this Judean fortified center has been uncovered. In the stratum II gate house one sees rooms with plastered walls and benches round about. Through the streets ran a unique drainage system to carry the overflow water from the sudden winter rainstorms to safe storage areas outside the city gate. Inside the gate was a plaza (Heb. *r^eḥôḇ ša'ar hā'îr,* 2 Ch. 32:6) from which streets led in several directions through the town. One street followed a circular course parallel to the city wall; the zone between the street and the wall was taken up with small dwelling units. The inner quarters were bisected by lateral streets and contained larger buildings of a more impressive nature. A plastered pool, probably for ceremonial purposes, was found near the center of the town. A row of three storehouses at one side of the gate plaza resembled in many details the so-called stables at Megiddo, including small holes in the corners of some of the pillars; there is no doubt today that at Megiddo and elsewhere, the buildings of this type were for storage and not for keeping horses.

At the northeast corner of the mound a large flight of stairs was uncovered which seems to lead down into a water shaft. There is an obvious depression in the mound at this point which probably denotes the presence of an installation similar to those discovered at Megiddo and Hazor.

Small cult objects such as figurines, miniature incense altars, a broken kernos, etc., have come to light in various parts of the city. Of special interest is a krater bearing the Hebrew inscription *qdš,* which must represent the word *qōḏeš,* "holy." Epigraphic finds have generally been limited to incised personal names on vessels or fragments of ink inscriptions. One complete text, from a storehouse, bears the hieratic numerals for "fifteen" and records commodities (wine?) "from Tolad" and "from Beth-amam." Both (El)tolad (Josh. 15:30; 19:4; cf. 1 Ch. 4:29) and Amam (Josh. 15:26) were towns in the Negeb (15:21).

The most astonishing discovery from the Israelite period thus far has been the ashlar stones of a dismantled altar. The stones were found built into a storehouse wall; horns were preserved on three of them and a fourth showed signs of having its horn broken off. Though other stones are still missing, the provisional reconstruction of the altar is quite impressive. No cultic building has, as yet, been discovered, but the only large structure oriented directly E and W (a "four-unit" dwelling plus a deep cellar) was shown to date from stratum II; its predecessor(s) had been completely removed down to bedrock and this dwelling unit built in its place. Perhaps the dismantling of the altar accompanied the obliteration of its associated temple.

The date of the great devastation by fire that marked the end of Beer-sheba as an Israelite city is linked to the destruction of Lachish stratum III and Arad stratum VIII, since the pottery styles are identical in the three sites. Historically, the only reasonable date for the fall of Lachish III is 701 B.C. in the campaign by Sennacherib.

During the Persian period practically no structures were erected on the site, but the tell was used as a campground and for the storage of grain in pits. About fifty Aramaic ostraca record quantities of cereals in relation to personal names (Jewish, Edomite, and Arabian); sometimes the texts are dated.

The Hellenistic Period (strata H III and H II) saw the construction of a small fort with a temple nearby. Excavations uncovered many votive cult objects, including a Mesopotamian cylinder seal and Egyptian figurines, along with Hellenistic coins and lamps. The temple plan resembles closely the Israelite temple at Arad and the temple (also Hellenistic in date) at Lachish. The central axis was turned north of east, to line up with the summer solstice. Steps found earlier were seen to lead into the holy place; the holy of holies, if it existed, was not preserved. Two occupation phases were evident. The construction of the first cannot be earlier than *ca.* 125 B.C., as evidenced by three coins of Demetrius II; the second phase lasted until *ca.* 95-90 B.C., since Nabatean coins of Aretas II were present. Many cult objects, apparently discarded during the rebuilding of the second phase, were found buried in pits beneath the courtyard floor.

In the early Roman period (parallel to the Herodian dynasty in Judea; stratum H I) a massive structure stood on the western quarter of the tell. It included a deep plastered pool or cistern, water conduit(s), and a typical hot room for a Roman-style bathhouse.

On top of the tell and over the ruins of the Herodian-period building was erected a small fort. A coin from the age of Trajan found in the wall of this fort shows that it was built no earlier than the first quarter of the 2nd cent. A.D.

The adjacent ridge and plateau, both lower than Tell es-Seba', saw settlement at least in the late Israelite, Hellenistic, and Roman periods. It is worthy of note that late seventh-century B.C. pottery (like that of Arad VI and Lachish II) is entirely lacking on the high mound but present on the plateau below as well as in the settlement beneath modern Beer-sheba. The ostracon from Arad stratum VI concerning a shipment of supplies to Beer-sheba and the reference to Josiah's rule "from Geba to Beer-sheba" (2 K. 23:8) evidently refer to one of these unwalled towns, since the fortified city was in ruins.

Bibliography.–Y. Aharoni, "The Negeb," in D. Winton Thomas, ed., *Archaeology and OT Study* (1967), pp. 384-403; *IEJ,* 8 (1958), 26-38; 19 (1969), 245-47; 20 (1970), 227-29; 21 (1971), 230-32; (1972), 169f.; *BA,* 35 (1972), 111-127; "Excavations at Tel Beer-sheba — A Preliminary Report on the First Season (1969)," in Y. Aharoni, ed., *Excavations and Studies* (1973), pp. 13-20; ed., *Beer-sheba I: Excavations at Tel Beer-Sheba 1969-1971 Seasons* (1973); W. F. Albright, *JPOS,* 4 (1924), 131-161; Israel Department of Antiquities, *IEJ*, 2 (1952), 253; 3 (1953), 262f.; 4 (1954), 125f.; 5 (1955), 125f., 174f.; 6 (1956), 126f.; 8 (1958), 131-33; 9 (1959), 29, 141f., 267; 10 (1960), 120f.; 13 (1963), 145f., 260f.; J. S. Holladay, *JBL*, 96 (1977), 281-84; N. Liphschitz and Y. Waisel, *IEJ*, 23 (1973), 30-36; J. Perrot, *IEJ*, 5 (1955), 17-40, 73-84, 167-189.

A. F. RAINEY

BE-ESHTERAH bē-esh'tə-rə [Heb. *b^e'ešt^erâ*] (Josh. 21:27); NEB BE-ASHTAROTH. *See* ASHTAROTH.

BEETLE. *See* CRICKET.

BEEVES. *See* CATTLE.

BEG; BEGGAR; BEGGING. There are no OT terms for professional begging; the nearest are the expressions (Heb.) *baqēš leḥem*–"ask for bread" (Ps. 37:25) or *y^enû'ûn le'^ekōl*–"let them wander to eat" (Ps. 59:15 [MT 16]); the NT expressions formed with Gk. *aitéō* have the root idea of "asking," while *ptōchós* (Lk. 16:20, 22) suggests the cringing of a beggar.

I. OT Times.–While there are no provisions in the Mosaic law for beggars, the practice was not unknown to the ancient Jews. It developed with the growth of the larger cities and probably arose with the intermingling of other peoples. It is associated in the OT with the wicked, for the children of the righteous never have to ask for bread: "I have been young, and now am old; yet have I not seen the righteous forsaken or his children begging bread" (Ps. 37:25).

II. Jewish Literature.–The first denunciation of beggary and alms-taking in Jewish literature is found in Sir. 40:28-30, where the Hebrew for begging is the same as in the OT. The Jewish community was forbidden to support beggars from the general charity fund (*Baba Bathra* 9a; Jacob ben Asher, *Yoreh De'ah* 250.3). However, it was also forbidden to drive a beggar away without alms (Maimonides, *ha-Yad ha-Hazakah* vii.7).

III. Gospel Age.–Evidence of its prevalence in the gospel age is abundant. Beggars were to be found wherever crowds assembled or passed by, as at the entrance to Jericho or the gates of the temple (Mt. 20:30; Acts 3:2). This prevalence of begging was due largely to the want of any adequate system of ministering relief, to the lack of any true medical science and the resulting ignorance of remedies for common diseases like ophthalmia, and to the impoverishment of the land under the excessive taxation of the Roman government. M. A. MACLEOD

BEGGARLY [Gk. *ptōchós*] (Gal. 4:9). The Greek word has the thought of "crouch" or "cringe," such as is common with professional beggars. It is normally translated "poor," as in Mt. 5:3; both there and in Gal. 4:9 it means complete spiritual destitution. As used in Galatians it expresses the contrast between the Galatian Christians' present condition and the former state toward which Paul says they are again tending. He has in mind both the Jewish and heathen systems of religion with all their outward show. He therefore emphasizes the immeasurable superiority of the riches and liberty in Christ.

Paul expresses this same thought in reference to the law in Rom. 8:3; cf. He. 7:18. In view of the wretchedness of the condition indicated by "beggarly," he states his astonishment that they should so little appreciate the liberty and riches they now enjoy as even to think of going back to the former condition. J. W. KAPP

BEGIN [chiefly Heb. *ḥālal*; Gk. *árchomai*]. Those who interpret it in many passages pleonastically mean that in such passages as "began to teach" or "began to speak," nothing more is intended than to express vividly and graphically the thought of the dependent infinitive. Mt. 4:17; Lk. 3:23; Acts 1:1 are so understood. For contrary opinion see Thayer's *Lexicon* and Winer's *Grammar of NT Greek*. H. E. JACOBS

BEGINNING [Heb. *rē'šîṯ*; Gk. *archḗ*]. A word generally used with reference to time, but also having meaning in the categories of eternity and quality. The temporal use is found in Ex. 12:2; etc., and is probably found also in Gen. 1:1, where the construct state probably indicates a translation such as "When in the beginning God created the heavens and the earth. . . ." Certainly the sentence structure as well as the context of Gen. 1:1 requires that the word "beginning" be understood as the first stage of a historical process or sequence. This is the customary use of the word. Jn. 1:1, on the other hand, refers to the existence of the Word prior to creation or to any historical sequence, hence "in the beginning" is here equivalent to "before time," therefore "in eternity." The *en archḗ* of Jn. 1:1 is accordingly not to be equated with the *b^erē'šîṯ* of Gen. 1:1, but is anterior to the beginning of creation, as Jn. 1:3 clearly indicates. (This is not to deny, however, that the author of the Fourth Gospel may have drawn his terminology from the LXX of Gen. 1:1.) Christ is without beginning or end (He. 7:3).

The use of "beginning" to denote quality or excellence is found in Prov. 1:2, where "the fear of the Lord" is described as "the beginning," or the best or most significant element, of "wisdom."

See *TDNT*, I, *s.v.* ἀρχή (Delling). W. S. L. S.

BEGOTTEN [Heb. *yālaḏ* (Lev. 18:11; Job 38:28; Ps. 2:7; etc.); Gk. *gennáō* (Acts 13:33; He. 1:5; 5:5)]; NEB also SIRED, "become your father," etc. In the RSV the term occurs mainly of God's act in making Christ His Son: "You are my son; today I have begotten you" (Ps. 2:7), quoted in Acts (13:33) in reference to His resurrection (cf. Rom. 1:4). The same passage is cited in He. 1:5 as proving Christ's filial dignity, transcending the angels in that "the name he has obtained is more excellent than theirs," i.e., the name of son; and again (5:5) of God's conferring upon Christ the glory of the priestly office.

Commentators differ as to whether the act of begetting the Son in these two passages is (1) the eternal generation, or (2) the incarnation in time, or (3) the resurrection and ascension. The immediate context of He. 1:5 (see 1:3) seems to favor the last view (Westcott). The first view would not be foreign to the author's thought; with 5:5 cf. 6:20, "a high priest forever." The author of Hebrews thinks of the eternal and essential sonship of Christ as realized in history in His ascension to the "right hand of the Majesty" (1:3). And what is emphatic is the fact and status of sonship, rather than the time of begetting.

On the AV translation "only begotten Son," *see* ONLY BEGOTTEN. T. REES

BEGUILE; BEGUILING [Heb. *nāšā* (Gen. 3:13), *nāḵal* (Nu. 25:18); Gk. *paralogízomai* (Col. 2:4), *planáō* (Rev. 2:30)]; AV also SEDUCE (Rev. 2:20); NEB TRICK, "be the undoing of," SPECIOUS, LURE. The references in Genesis and in the NT have to do with attempts to corrupt by argument or teaching. In Nu. 25 the Midianites entice Israel to the service of idols and to intermarriage. "Beguile" appears in the AV also in Gen. 29:25; Josh. 9:22; 2 Cor. 11:3 (RSV "deceive"); and 2 Pet. 2:14 (RSV "entice"), where the words are Heb. *rāmâ*; Gk. *exapatáō*, *deleázō*.

BEHAVIOR. David "changed his behavior" when he feigned madness before Achish. The Hebrew word is *ṭa'am,* "taste," hence "intellectual taste," i.e., judgment. He acted as though he had lost his judgment, or sense.

"Behaved worse" in Jgs. 2:19 translates *šāḥaṯ*; the AV has "corrupted themselves more," the NEB "(relapsed into) deeper corruption," both of which render the word more specifically. In Job 36:9, "behaving arrogantly" better translates Heb. *gāḇer* than AV "exceeded" (cf. NEB "tyranny"). Other OT words are *dāḇār* (Est. 1:18; AV "deed"; NEB "conduct") and *dereḵ* (Ezk. 16:27; AV "way"; NEB "ways").

The Gk. *anastrépho* occurs in the NT in 2 Cor. 1:12 (AV "have conversation"; NEB "dealings") and 1 Tim. 3:15 (NEB "conduct oneself"); the noun *anastrophḗ* is used in 1 Pet. 3:1f., 16 (AV "conversation"; NEB v. 16 "conduct"). "Behave" also translates *peripatéo* (1 Cor. 3:3; AV "walk"; the NEB renders this passage "you are living on the purely human level of your lower nature") and *aschēmonéō* (7:36). "Behavior" translates *katástēma* in Tit. 2:3 (NEB "bearing") and a form of *gínomai* in 1 Thess. 2:10. J. W. D. H.

BEHEADING. *See* PUNISHMENTS.

BEHEMOTH be-hē'məth [Heb. *b^ehēmôṯ*] (Job 40:15). Apparently the intensive plural of *b^ehēmâ,* "beast," used of domesticated or wild animals. The same form, *b^ehēmôṯ,* occurs in other passages, e.g., Dt. 28:26; 32:24; Isa. 18:6; Hab. 2:17, where it is not rendered "behemoth" but "beasts." The reference in Job is to some marsh-dwelling mammoth such as the *Hippopotamus amphibius,* which inhabits the Nile and other African rivers. In the Apocrypha the name denotes the male counterpart of the Leviathan (2 Esd. 6:49, 52), while in the Targum on Ps. 50:10 it alludes to the "ox of the open field." R. K. H.

BEHISTUN bā-his-tōōn'. Village and precipitous rock (modern Bisitun in Iran) near Hamadan, on the road from Ecbatana to Babylon. In the face of the cliff, 500 ft. (150 m.) above the plain, Darius the Great (522-486 B.C.) carved a relief and trilingual inscription depicting his succession upon defeating the usurper Gaumata. The Old Persian and Babylonian portions of the text were copied by H. C. Rawlinson from 1835-1847 and recopied in 1948 by G. G. Cameron, who used latex "squeezes" (rubber molds) to recover the Elamite columns as well. Decipherment of the Behistun inscription proved the key to these languages and their cuneiform scripts.

See ARCHEOLOGY OF MESOPOTAMIA II; CUNEIFORM; DARIUS.

BEHOLDING. A significant occurrence is in 2 Cor. 3:18, where the Greek is *katoptrizómenoi,* "beholding the glory of the Lord." The AV renders "beholding as in a glass," thus giving something of the etymological sense of the word; a *kátoptron* was a mirror of polished metal. The NEB has "we all reflect as in a mirror the splendour of the Lord"; cf. also the ERV, ARV mg., and RSV mg., which all give "reflecting." For references on both sides, see Bauer, pp. 425f.; see also MM, p. 738; *TDNT,* II, *s.v.* ἔσοπτρον κτλ. (Kittel).

We cannot clearly and fully behold the spiritual grandeur that shines forth in Christ Jesus, but in the gospel God accommodates and adjusts the vision as we are able to bear it, and the glory beheld becomes glory imparted to (and reflected by) the beholder. M. O. EVANS

BEING [Heb. *baṭṭuḥôṯ*] ("in the inward being," Ps. 51:6 [MT 8]); AV "in the inward parts"; NEB "in darkness"; [*b^e'ôḏî*] ("while I have being," Ps. 104:33; 146:2); NEB "all my life"; [*nepeš*] (Gen. 2:7); NEB CREATURE; [Gk. *eimí*] ("have being," Acts 17:28); NEB EXIST; [*psychḗ*] (1 Cor. 15:45); AV SOUL. The NEB rendering of Ps. 51:6 reflects the LXX (*ádēlos*–'unseen') and the Vulgate (*incerta*–'uncertain').

The Hebrews thought of man as an animated body rather than an incarnated SOUL. In the creation story two distinct kinds of being are described: the infinite being of God, whose very nature is to exist; and the finite being of man, who is unique among living creatures. The vital relationship between the finite and the Infinite is suggested by God's animating man by His own breath, and by the psalmist's responding to God by that inner animation or spirit. G. WYPER

BEIRUT bā-rōōt'. *See* BERYTUS.

BEKA bē'kə [Heb. *beqa'*–'half']. Half a shekel, the amount contributed by each male of the Israelites for the use of the sanctuary (Ex. 38:26). Its value varied according to the standard used. *See* WEIGHTS AND MEASURES.

BEL bel [Heb. *bēl*]. Name of a Babylonian god, the counterpart of the Canaanite BAAL, identified in the OT and Apocrypha with Marduk or MERODACH, the tutelary deity of Babylon (cf. Isa. 46:1; Jer. 50:2; 51:44; Bar. 6 [Letter of Jeremiah]:41). See the discussion of Marduk in RELIGIONS OF THE BIBLICAL WORLD: ASSYRIA AND BABYLONIA.

BEL AND THE DRAGON; NEB DANIEL, BEL, AND THE SNAKE. A book of the OT Apocrypha, an addition to the book of Daniel along with SONG OF THE THREE YOUNG MEN and SUSANNA.

I. The Daniel Apocrypha: Texts and Versions.–*A. Greek.* The Hebrew Bible contains no trace of the Danielic Apocrypha. The earliest attestation is the LXX, where Daniel and its additions happen to be preserved only in a single ninth-century MS, Codex Chisianus. The additions are printed on the left-hand pages of *OTG,* III, 576-593. Theodotion's second-century Greek version (Th.) ousted the LXX of Daniel in Christian circles. (See *IOTG,* pp. 42-49, 165ff., 260ff.; for complete text, see the right-hand pages opposite Codex Chisianus, *OTG, loc. cit.*)

B. Latin. The Old Latin is available in fragmentary form, the Vulgate complete.

C. Syriac. The very literal Syriac rendering of Paul of Tella is contained in the sixth column of Origen's *Hexapla.* Its main textual significance, collated with Codex Chisianus and distilled into Greek, may be gleaned from Swete's critical notes to the LXX. The Syriac Peshitta text is splendidly printed in P. de Lagarde, *Libri Veteris Testamenti Apocryphi Syriace* (1861).

D. Other Languages. There are further versions in Sahidic, Bohairic, and Ethiopic. (See W.O.E. Oesterley, *Intro. to the Books of the Apocrypha* [1935]; *HNTT*; C. C. Torrey, *Apocryphal Literature: A Brief Intro.* (1945); *Jew.Enc.*; *HDB*; R. H. Charles, *Comm. on Daniel* [1929], Intro., pp. l-lviii; J. A. Montgomery, *ICC* on Daniel [1927], pp. 24-57; etc.)

E. Hebrew and Aramaic. The existence of Hebrew and Aramaic versions is unquestioned, their date controversial. Josippon (the Little Josephus) recounted the tales in Hebrew *ca.* A.D. 940, but this proves nothing before his date. M. Gaster claimed that the "Aramaic original"

is embedded in the medieval Chronicles of Jerahmeel; T. Witton Davies and others regard this as merely a late rendering into Aramaic of Th. The lateness of Josippon and Jerahmeel does not exclude a lost Semitic original. (See *APOT*, I, 655ff.; *HDB*, I, 267f.; *Jew.Enc.*, II, 651 col. 1; Wace, II, 344ff.; with further references in literature cited.)

II. The Stories of Bel and the Dragon.–The story of Daniel and Bel is recounted in vv. 1-22, that of Daniel and the dragon or serpent in vv. 23-42, with numerous discrepancies between the LXX and Th. In the LXX Daniel strews the ashes unbeknown to the king, making the plot coherent, while in Th. he strews them in his presence, utterly spoiling the story. (For a full translation of both Greek versions, see *APOT,* I, 658-664; for detailed separate summaries, *HNTT,* pp. 436f.; also Wace; and others *in loc.*)

Bel or Baʿal signifies here the Babylonian deity Marduk, worshiped as a temple idol, and reputed to consume daily quantities of food and drink faithfully offered. The pure monotheist Daniel refuses to worship Bel, incurring royal censure. He undertakes, on pain of death if he fails, to demonstrate Bel's inability to eat or drink a particle. The offerings are duly laid, the temple sealed, the priests confident. The next day everything has disappeared as usual, and Daniel impudently laughs. Unbeknown to priests or king, he has had fine ash sprinkled over the temple floor, which in the darkness of the night has become mysteriously covered with naked footprints. The secret trapdoor in the floor leading to the homes of the fraudulent servitors of Bel is unmasked, Daniel is justified, the priests are visited with condign punishment. Ludwig Couard (*Die Apokryphen und Pseudepigraphen* [1907], p. 5) describes Bel and Susanna as *pikante Kriminalnovellen.*

The recalcitrant Daniel refuses equally to worship the dragon (or serpent) revered by the Babylonians, impiously declaring that he will kill it. This he does by throwing into its mouth a cake composed of pitch, fat, and hair, which causes the corporeal explosion of the deity. The king is deeply impressed, but the angry mob clamors for Daniel's blood. For his theocide, he is cast into a den of hungry lions, where he remains unscathed for seven days, the distant prophet Habakkuk being miraculously brought to minister to him. Daniel emerges to enjoy royal and public favor, while his enemies discover that it is their turn to be cast to the lions.

III. Selected Exegetical Notes.–*v. 1.* In the LXX and Syrohexapla the composition of the work is referred to Habakkuk, Grecized for euphony *Ambakoum*. His authorship is not endorsed in Th. and Pesh., where a note of regal chronology is substituted.

v. 2. The LXX designates Daniel "priest," probably for apologetic motives. Th. enhances rather the lay prestige of the hero, while Pesh. carries this to still greater lengths. The Hebraism *kaí ḗn* (*wayᵉhî*) may be noted — see vv. 11-22 below. The Aram. *wahᵃwâ* without *waw* conversive might produce the same Greek.

v. 5. In Th. Daniel refuses his worship to *eídōla cheiropoiḗta,* "idols made with hands," which Pesh. renders "the work of the hands of the sons of men." Hatch and Redpath (HR, p. 1467 col. 1) record sixteen occurrences of the Greek adjective, ten without Hebrew equivalents, six translating Heb. *ʾᵉlîl* "worthless." All passages refer to idolatry. Classical usage is less restricted — *cheiropoiḗtos* means "man-made, artificial," the antonym of *autophyḗs,* "self-growing, natural." In the NT five passages describe the man-made temple or sanctuary, one in its actuality (Mk. 14:58), two in general concept (Acts 7:48; 17:24), two in special concept (He. 9:11, 24). In Hebrews the term is used of phenomenal, material, earthly sanctuaries, which are antitypes of the real, eternal ektypes in God's realm — an instance of idealist philosophy with a deeply spiritual insight. In Eph. 2:11 the reference is to the physical performance of the rite of circumcision.

v. 9. Th. and Pesh. speak of Daniel "blaspheming" Bel, which is the reverse of the customary usage of the term. For this important word, see *TDNT,* I, *s.v.* βλασφημέω (Beyer).

vv. 11-22. T. W. Davies (*APOT, in loc.*) makes strong points for a Hebrew rather than an Aramaic original:

(1) In v. 14 the LXX *sphragisámenos tón naón ekéleuse sphragísai* makes an intolerable tautological reading. The substitution of *kleísas* for the first word has the authority of Th., enhanced, as Davies brilliantly points out, by the ready confusability of Heb. *stm*, "to shut," with *ḥtm*, "to seal," in the postulated Hebrew original.

(2) The numerous verses beginning *kaí egéneto,* where Classical Greek would use an aorist participle followed by an indicative, suggest the familiar Heb. *wayᵉhî* — although Aramaic cannot be ruled out. See on v. 2 above.

(3) In v. 18a, where the LXX is classical and neat, Davies points out in Th. the same Hebraism conjoined with another: *kaí egéneto háma tṓ anoíxai tás thýras.* The Hebraist quickly perceives that *háma* represents the familiar Heb. *wayᵉhî* followed by an infinitive, corresponding to an English adverbial clause of time (cf. W. Gesenius, E. Kautzsch, and A. E. Cowley, *Hebrew Grammar* [1910], § 111 g). This clause can easily be translated into Hebrew as *wayᵉhî biptō(a)ḥ ʾeṯ-haddᵉlāṯîm.* Similar OT constructions are innumerable: cf. Gen. 19:29; 1 Ch. 15:26. While the LXX ends the verse in good Classical Greek, Th. ends it with a double negative — most un-Greek, but translatable, as Davies demonstrates, into excellent Hebrew.

v. 23. Is the *drákōn* of Babylonian worship a mythical dragon or an ordinary serpent? The Heb. *tannîḵ* is as ambiguous as the Greek. Pesh. favors "dragon," using a different word for "serpent" in Gen. 3:1 and Am. 9:3. However, the evidence on this important point remains ambiguous.

v. 25. Included in Th., lacking in the LXX; cf. v. 5. The "living God" is an important biblical concept, often found in polemic against idols.

v. 27. With the remains of the monster strewn over the ground, Daniel remarks (LXX) with delicious irony: *ou taúta sébesthe, basileú* — "You don't mean to tell me you worship these smithereens, O king?"

v. 32. Part of the planned punishment is that Daniel is to be unburied, a thought horrible to a Greek, worse to a Jew. See *Oxford Classical Dictionary* (1949), *s.v.* "Dead, Disposal of"; *HDB, s.v.* "Burial."

vv. 33-39. The Habakkuk incident may be a late interpolation.

v. 36. Gk. *epilambánesthai* may mean "to succor"; cf. He. 2:16; Sir. 4:11. Here it means "take hold of." The verb requires a genitive. In the LXX it is furnished with several genitives, awkwardly separated, but the sense is clear.

v. 41. The king's praise of God is significant, perhaps indeed the point of the story. In Th., in the 2nd person, it becomes almost the language of prayer.

IV. Original Language.–Six reasonable hypotheses may be considered: (1) That both versions were originally written in Greek. (2) That both versions are in a contemporary "Yiddish," a mixture of Greek and Hebrew elements. (3) That both versions are translated from the same Semitic document. (4) That the two versions are translated from two different Semitic documents. (5) That both versions rest on an oral, folkloristic Semitic source, maintaining substantial agreement, but liable to variation in detail. (6) That the original language was not Aramaic, but Hebrew.

The argument for (1) would be that a writer of Semitic background composed in Greek. The limits of reasonable expectation for such coloring seem here to have been exceeded. (2) was proposed and abandoned by Wellhausen (cf. *APOT,* I, 656). The Greek is just a little too good. The numerous variants rule (3) out of court. (4) and (5) are both possible, and (5) commends itself as more probable. Davies makes a good case for Hebrew (6), though it is only fair to set against this J. T. Marshall's arguments for Aramaic in *HDB,* which are based on Gaster's work. On balance, however, Davies seems worthy of the vote.

V. Author, Place, and Date.–On the identity of the author, it is idle even to speculate. The story professes a Babylonian setting, which may be fact or fiction. Editorial opinions on the dating are somewhat variant, but most of them fall within the 2nd cent. B.C.

VI. Evaluation.–The double version of Bel and the Dragon, with its many variants, can distract the reader and spoil the fun, unless he peruses one at a time. The two stories probably came together without any original connection, simply because both exalt the shrewdness of Daniel in the same sphere. The first story is logical, satisfying, free from the supernatural; the second somehow falls rather flat. The narrative may, of course, be entirely satirical in intent. The prophet Habakkuk seems to be dragged in in more senses than one, and he may be omitted without disruption. Both stories are intended to ridicule the excesses of heathen idolatry; the first does so with greater skill and success.

Without making any fresh contribution, this writing reiterates the unity and omnipotence of God, showing the impact of the Jewish faith on a heathen king.

R. A. STEWART

BELA bē'lə [Heb. *bela'*–'destruction']; AV also BELAH (Gen. 46:21).

1. Son of Beor and the first king of Edom previous to the kingdom of Israel. He reigned in the city of Dinhabah (Gen. 36:32f.; 1 Ch. 1:43f.). The LXX (A) calls him Balak; the Targum has Balaam.

2. The firstborn son of Benjamin (Gen. 46:21; 1 Ch. 7:6f.; 1 Ch. 8:1). He was the head of the family of the Belaites (Nu. 26:38), the father of Addar (called Ard, Nu. 26:40), Gera, Abihud, Abishua, Naaman, Ahoah, Gera, Shephuphan (cf. Shephupham, Nu. 26:39), Huram (1 Ch. 8:3-5).

3. A son of Azaz, of the tribe of Reuben, who had great power and wealth. His possessions reached from Nebo to the Euphrates (1 Ch. 5:8ff.).

A. L. BRESLICH

BELA. *See* ZOAR.

BELAITES bē'lə-īts [Heb. *bal'î*–'belonging to Bela']. The descendants of Bela (Nu. 26:38). *See* BELA **2.**

BELBAIM bel-bā'əm (Jth. 7:3, NEB). *See* BALBAIM.

BELEMUS bel'ə-məs (1 Esd. 2:16, AV, NEB). *See* BISHLAM.

BELIAL bē'lē-əl [Gk. *Beliar* and variants]. The name appears in the MT (as *b^elîya'al*) in Jgs. 20:13; 1 S. 10:27; 30:22; 1 K. 21:13; etc., generally rendered as a proper name by the AV, but by the RSV as "base fellows" and by the NEB as "scoundrels." In Jewish apocalyptic writing (Book of Jubilees, Ascension of Isaiah, Sibylline Oracles) the name was used to describe Satan or the antichrist. Paul used the word in this sense in 2 Cor. 6:15: "What accord has Christ with Belial?" The "man of lawlessness" in 2 Thess. 2:3 is probably an equivalent of the "man of Belial." *See* ANTICHRIST; MAN OF LAWLESSNESS.

See P. von der Osten Sacken, *Gott und Belial* (1969), esp. pp. 73-78.

R. K. H.

BELIE (Jer. 5:12, AV). Archaic for "speak falsely." The NEB has "denied."

BELIEF. *See* FAITH.

BELIEVERS [Gk. *(hoi) pisteúontes* (e.g., Acts 5:14; 1 Cor. 14:22; 1 Thess. 1:7), *hoi pistoí* (Acts 10:45; 2 Cor. 6:15 [sing.]; 1 Tim. 4:12; 6:2; Tit. 1:6)]. This and equivalent phrases occur frequently as a regular description of those who professed their faith in Christ, and attached themselves to the Christian Church. The one essential condition of admission into the Christian community was that one should believe in Jesus Christ (Acts 16:31). The actual experiences of the persons thus denoted varied with all the possible degrees and modifications of faith. Believers are nowhere in the NT distinguished as a subordinate class from the "Christians who know," as in the gnostic antithesis of *pistikoí* and *gnōstikoí*, "believers" and "knowers."

T. REES

BELL [Heb. *m^eṣillôṯ, pa'^{a}môn*]. In Zec. 14:20 the former term meant "that which tinkles," and was an ornament attached to the harness of horses. The latter term occurs only in Ex. 28:33f.; 39:25f., describing a golden object fastened to the high priest's robes, alternating with golden pomegranates. It served as a signal or warning of the high priest's movements (cf. Ex. 28:35).

BELLOWS [Heb. *mappu(a)ḥ*]. The word occurs only once in the AV and RSV, in Jer. 6:29 where the prophet is predicting the coming of the destroyer (v. 26), "a great nation" from "the north country" (v. 22), upon Israel

Traveling metalworker, from a wall painting in the tomb of Khnumhotep III at Beni Hasan (1892 B.C.). The donkey carries a bellows, a spear, and a throwing-stick. (Oriental Institute, University of Chicago)

because "all of them act corruptly" (v. 28). The imagery is drawn from the refiner's art, and the "bellows" are the instrument that blows air on the fire, thus making the refiner's fires burn fiercely. *See* METALLURGY.

BELLY [Heb. *gāḥôn*] (Gen. 3:14; Lev. 11:42); [*mē'eh*] (Dnl. 2:32; Jonah 1:17; 2:1); [*beṭen*]; NEB also "gorged," "go hungry," etc.; [*k^erēś*] (Jer. 51:34); NEB MAW; [*ḥōmeš*] (2 S. 2:23; 3:27); AV "under the fifth rib"; [Gk. *koilía*]; NEB also APPETITE. The term for belly used most often in the OT is *beṭen*. Heb. *gāḥôn* is used only with reference to reptiles; *mē'eh* for intestines or abdomen; *ḥōmeš*, "belly," is identical in form to the Hebrew term for "fifth." In the NT, *koilía*, a general term for the abdomen (Mt. 12:40), was sometimes regarded as the seat of appetite and carnal affection (Phil. 3:19).

BELMAIM bel-mā'əm (Jth. 7:3, AV). *See* BALBAIM.

BELMAIN bel-mā'ən [Gk. *Belmain*] (Jth. 4:4); AV BELMEN. A place to which warning was sent to prepare for the invasion of Holofernes. It may be the modern Tell Bel'ameh (Ibleam) S of Jenîn, and is perhaps the same as Balbaim (7:3) and possibly Balamon (8:3).

BELMEN bel'mən (Jth. 4:4, AV). *See* BELMAIN.

BELNUUS bel'nōō-əs [Gk. *Balnouos*, B *Balnous*, Lucian *Banoui*] (1 Esd. 9:31); AV, NEB, BALNUUS. One who put away his foreign wife. Cf. Binnui in Ezr. 10:30.

BELOVED [chiefly Heb. *dôḏ* (Cant. 1:13; etc.); Gk. *agapētós*]. A term of affectionate endearment common to both Testaments. In the OT it occurs about thirty-two times in the Song of Solomon, translating Heb. *dôḏ*. Other words include *'āhēḇ* (2 S. 1:23; Hos. 3:1), *yāḏîḏ* (Dt. 33:12; Ps. 60:5; etc.), *maḥmāḏ* (Hos. 9:16), *y^eḏiḏûṯ* (Jer. 12:7), and *ḥ^amûḏôṯ* (Dnl. 9:23; 10:11, 19). The words seem to have interchangeable significance, so usage is more important than etymology in determining shades of meaning.

In the NT "beloved" (Gk. *agapētós*) is used exclusively of divine and Christian love, an affection begotten in the community of the new spiritual life in Christ, e.g., "beloved in the Lord" (Rom. 16:8). The beauty, unity, endearment of this love is historically unique, being peculiarly Christian. "Brethren" in Christ are "beloved" (1 Thess. 1:4; 1 Cor. 15:58; Jas. 1:16; 2:5). Many individuals are specified by name: Timothy (2 Tim. 1:2); Philemon (Philem. 1); Epaenetus, Amplias, Urbane, Stachys, Persis (Rom. 16:5, 8f., 12), *et al.*

The aged John is the conspicuous NT illustration of the depth and tenderness of Christian love. In his Epistles alone he addresses his disciples twelve times as "beloved." Paul terms "God's elect" "holy and beloved" (Col. 3:12).

The term has still greater significance as an epithet of Christ, whom Paul, grateful for His "freely bestowed" grace, terms "the Beloved." This is the word used repeatedly to express God the Father's infinite affection for Jesus His "beloved Son" (Mt. 3:17; 12:18; 17:5; Mk. 1:11; 9:7; Lk. 3:22; 20:13).

Through the apostles the word has become familiar in pastoral and sermonic address. Few NT words better illustrate the power and impress of the Christian spirit on succeeding centuries than this.

See also LOVE; BROTHERLY LOVE. D. M. PRATT

BELSHAZZAR bel-shaz'ər [Aram. *bēlša'ṣṣar* or *bēl'šaṣṣar*; Bab. *bēl-šar-uṣur*–'may Bel protect the king']; AV also BALTHASAR (Bar. 1:11). The son of the last of the Neo-Babylonian kings (NABONIDUS, 556-539 B.C.) and co-regent with him (probably 553-539 B.C.).

Belshazzar appears in Dnl. 5, 7, and 8 as the last of the Neo-Babylonian kings, in succession to NEBUCHADREZZAR (Nebuchadnezzar). Ancient historians, however, knew the last of those rulers as Nabonnēdus (Berossus, quoted by Josephus (*CAp* 1.20 [149]), Naboandēlus (Josephus *Ant.* x.11.2 [232]), Labynētus (Herodotus i.77, 188), or Nabannidochus (Abydenus, quoted by Eusebius *Praep. ev.* ix.41), all variants of the name Nabonidus. The contemporary cuneiform inscriptions also make clear that Nabonidus (Bab. *Nabû-na'id*, "Nabû is awe-inspiring") was the last titular king of the neo-Babylonian empire (cf., e.g., the "Nabonidus Chronicle," *ANET*, pp. 305-307). Yet the book of Daniel does not mention Nabonidus and suggests that the empire fell with the death of Belshazzar (5:30).

However, the biblical account is not incorrect. The cuneiform literature shows that: (1) Nabonidus' son was named Bēl-šar-uṣur, i.e., Belshazzar (cf., e.g., S. Langdon, *Die neubabylonischen Königsinschriften* [1912], Nabonid. No. 5).

(2) In the third year of his reign (553 B.C.) Nabonidus "entrusted the 'Camp' to his oldest son Belshazzar, the first-born. . . . He let everything go, entrusted the kingship to him, and himself, he started out for a long journey" ("Verse Account of Nabonidus," *ANET*, pp. 312-15). So although Belshazzar is never called "king" in the cuneiform sources, and was unable to replace Nabonidus in the New Year Festival ritual, he clearly exercised many of the functions of kingship. He was still theoretically subordinate to Nabonidus, a situation reflected correctly in Dnl. 5:16, where he offers Daniel a position as "third ruler in the kingdom," or perhaps as "member of a triumvirate."

(3) Nabonidus seems to have remained absent from Babylon for nearly ten years. We know from the "Nabonidus Chronicle" (*ANET*, pp. 305-07) that the New Year Festival was cancelled in the seventh to the eleventh years of his reign because he did not return to Babylon from his new capital at Teima in northern Arabia. The wording of two legal documents, from his twelfth and thirteenth years, in which oaths are sworn not only by his name but also by that of Belshazzar (cf. T. G. Pinches, *PSBA*, 38 [1916], pp. 27-29), suggests that Nabonidus was no more than a nominal ruler, in Babylon at least. He did return to Babylon in 539 B.C., a few months before the city fell to the Persians, but whether he relieved Belshazzar of his responsibility we do not know.

There are two points at which the biblical narrative of Belshazzar appears impressionistic rather than formally precise. (1) Belshazzar's father is said in Dnl. 5:2, 11, 18, 22 to have been Nebuchadnezzar. In fact, Nebuchadrezzar's son and successor was Amēl-Marduk (EVIL-MERODACH; cf. 2 K. 25:27), while Belshazzar was the son of Nabonidus, an Aramean usurper from Ḫarran who brought Nebuchadrezzar's dynasty to an end. Yet "father" may simply have been a rather loose term for "predecessor." Some have argued that Nabonidus married Nebuchadrezzar's daughter Nitocris (R. P. Dougherty, pp. 42ff., following Herodotus i.188), thus making Nebuchadrezzar Belshazzar's grandfather, which is clearly sometimes meant by "father" (e.g., Gen. 28:13). This view is uncertain, however.

(2) Years are numbered in Dnl. 7:1; 8:1 by the reign of

Belshazzar, whereas contemporary Neo-Babylonian documents invariably number years by the reign of Nabonidus. It is not surprising, however, that the biblical narrator, having no occasion to mention Nabonidus, should number years by the reign of the co-regent who did figure in his story.

Two further elements in the Belshazzar narrative cannot be certainly confirmed from the cuneiform evidence. One of these is the report of his death on the night Babylon fell to the Persians. The Persian account is that Cyrus' army under Ugbaru (Gobryas) entered Babylon without a battle, and a fortnight later Cyrus' arrival was greeted with much enthusiasm ("Nabonidus Chronicle," *ANET*, pp. 305-07; Cyrus Cylinder, *ANET*, pp. 315f.). A mutilated passage of the "Nabonidus Chronicle" has, however, been understood by some scholars as recording that on Araḫ-samnu 11, one month after Gobryas' entry into Babylon, he slew Belshazzar (cf. H. H. Rowley, *Darius the Mede* [1935], p. 20). If this uncertain reading is correct, it would confirm the biblical report of Belshazzar's death, while implying that the narrator has compressed the events of one month into a single night. If it is incorrect, Belshazzar may well, of course, have been slain on the night of Gobryas' entry, whether by a Persian or by one of his own subjects.

The other element is the report that Babylon was taken by the Persians while the Babylonians were feasting. Although there is no contemporary evidence of these circumstances, Herodotus (i.191) and Xenophon (*Cyropaedia* vii.5.15-25) recount the same story. Nevertheless, the testimony of the extrabiblical sources is that Babylon was taken by Cyrus, not "Darius the Mede," as Dnl. 5:31 has it. On the identification of this figure, *see* DARIUS.

Bibliography.–J. N. Strassmeier, *Babylonische Texte. Inschriften von Nabonidus* (1887-1897); R. P. Dougherty, *Nabonidus and Belshazzar: A study of the closing events of the Neo-Babylonian empire* (Yale Oriental Series; Researches, 15; 1929); B. Alfrink, *Biblica*, 9 (1928), 187-205; W. Dommershausen, *Nabonid im Buche Daniel* (1964).

D. J. A. CLINES

BELT. *See* GARMENTS.

BELTESHAZZAR bel-tə-shaz'ər [Heb. *bēlṭᵉšaʾṣṣar*; Akk. *balaṭsu-uṣur*–'protect his life']. The Babylonian name given to Daniel (Dnl. 1:7; 2:26; 4:8; 5:12). In 4:8 King Nebuchadnezzar interprets the first syllable of the name as coming from the Babylonian god BEL. This is a folk etymology, unless the name is contracted from Akk. *Bel-balaṭsu-uṣur*. This name should not be confused with BELSHAZZAR.

BELTETHMUS bel-teth'məs [Gk. *Baaltam*]; AV, NEB, BEELTETHMUS. The title of a Persian officer in Palestine in the time of Artaxerxes (1 Esd. 2:16; cf. Ezr. 4:8).

BEN ben [Heb. *bēn*–'son']. A name found in the MT of 1 Ch. 15:18 and retained in the AV, but omitted in the RSV and NEB.

BEN- ben (prefix) [Heb. sing. *bēn*–'son of'; pl. *bᵉnê*– 'sons of'; cf. Aram. *bar* and related forms in most Semitic languages]. The term occurs in the construct to express a consanguine or affinel relationship or a particular condition. The Hebrew form is preserved in a number of personal or place names (Ben-Geber, Ben-Hadad, Bene-Berak), but for the most part the idiom is translated variously in the English versions. It can designate: (1) a direct male descendant (*see* SON); the plural may indicate children of both sexes (Gen. 3:16); in combination with other kinship terminology *bēn-* may designate a variety of relationships (*bᵉnê ʾāḇîḵā*, "your brothers," lit. "your father's sons," Gen. 49:8; *see* RELATIONSHIPS, FAMILY); (2) a member of a tribe or people, in construct with the name of the father or another ancestor ("sons [= children] of Esau," Dt. 2:4; "sons of Israel," Gen. 42:5); (3) a representative of a geographic or national entity, perhaps indicating place of birth ("son of Jabesh," 2 K. 15:10ff.; cf. Benjamin, lit. "son of the right hand" = "southerner"); (4) a member of a social or professional class (*bᵉnê hāʿām*, "the common people," 2 K. 23:6; *bᵉnê haggôlâ*, "[returned] exiles," lit. "sons of the exile," Ezr. 4:1 [cf. Aram. Dnl. 2:25]; *ben-hāraqqāḥîm*, "perfumer," Neh. 3:8).

It can also designate characteristics or conditions: (5) a person distinguished by a certain trait (*ben-ḥayil*, "valiant man," lit. "son of strength," 1 S. 14:52; *bᵉnê-merî*, "rebels," lit. "sons of rebellion," Nu. 17:10 [MT 25]); (6) a person's fate (*bᵉnê hattaʿᵃruḇôṯ*, "hostages," lit. "sons of pledges," 2 K. 14:14; *bᵉnê-māweṯ*, lit. "sons of death" [RSV "you deserve to die"], 1 S. 26:16); (7) a person's age (*ben-šᵉmōnaṯ yāmîm*, "eight days old," lit. "son of eight days," Gen. 17:12); (8) a member of a herd (*ben-bāqār*, "a cow," Gen. 18:7) or species (*bᵉnê-ṣōʾn*, "sheep," Ps. 114:4); (9) In this respect it also has various figurative uses (*ben-šāmen*, "very fertile," lit. "son of oil," Isa. 5:1; *bᵉnê-rešep*, "flames," lit. "sons of fire," Job 5:6 [MT 7]; NEB "birds").

See also BAR-.

Bibliography.–G. B. Gray, *Studies in Hebrew Proper Names* (1896), pp. 64-75; *IP*; *TDOT*, II, *s.v.* "ben" (J. Bergman-H. Ringgren, H. Haag).

A. C. M.

BEN-ABINADAB ben-ə-bin'ə-dab [Heb. *ben-ʾᵃḇînāḏāḇ*–'son of Abinadab']; AV SON OF ABINADAB. One of the twelve officers of Solomon who provided for the king and his household, each for a month in the year (1 K. 4:11). His district was the region of Naphath-dor. On the AV rendering, "the son of Abinadab," *see* BEN-. His wife was Taphath the daughter of Solomon.

BENAIAH bə-nā'ə, bə-nī'ə [Heb. *bᵉnāyâ*, *bᵉnāyāhû*–'Yahweh has built'].

1. The son of Jehoiada of Kabzeel (cf. Josh. 15:21), a man of "mighty deeds" and more honorable than any of the mighty men of David except the three chiefs. David therefore made him his chief counselor (2 S. 23:23; cf. 1 Ch. 27:34) and set him over the Cherethites (cf. Carites, 2 K. 11:4ff. and mg.) and Pelethites, and he was made the third captain of the host and chief over the division of the third month (2 S. 8:18; 11:22ff.; 20:23; 23:20ff.; 1 Ch. 18:17; 27:5f.). Being a true friend of David he did not take part in the usurpation of Adonijah (1 K. 1:8, 10, 26); therefore along with others he was chosen by the king to proclaim Solomon king over Israel (vv. 32ff.), and was later chosen by Solomon to execute Adonijah (2:25), Joab (vv. 29ff.), and Shimei (v. 46). In recognition of his services Solomon appointed him over the host in Joab's place (2:35; 4:4).

2. A Pirathonite, one of David's thirty mighty men (2 S. 23:30; 1 Ch. 11:31). He was captain over the division of the eleventh month numbering 24,000 (1 Ch. 27:14).

3. A prince of the house of Simeon (1 Ch. 4:36).

4. A Levite of the second order appointed as singer (1 Ch. 15:18) "to play harps according to Alamoth" (15:20; 16:5).

5. A priest appointed to "blow the trumpets before the ark of God" (1 Ch. 15:24; 16:6).

6. The father of Jehoiada (1 Ch. 27:34), but see **1** above.

7. An ancestor of Jahaziel of the house of Asaph (2 Ch. 20:14).

8. An overseer in the service of Hezekiah (2 Ch. 31:13).

9. [Gk. *Banaia* (Ezr. 10:25), Apoc. *Bannaias* (1 Esd. 9:26)]; AV Apoc. BAANIAS; NEB Apoc. BANNAEAS; **10, 11.** [Gk. *Banaia*] (Ezr. 10:30, 35); **12.** [Gk. *Banaia* (Ezr. 10:43), Apoc. *Banaias* (1 Esd. 9:35)]; AV Apoc. BANAIAS; NEB Apoc. BANAEAS. Four men of Israel who had taken foreign wives while in exile.

13. The father of Pelatiah who was seen by Ezekiel in his vision (Ezk. 11:1, 13). A. L. BRESLICH

BEN-AMMI ben-am'ī [Heb. *ben 'ammî*–'son of my kinsman' (Gen. 19:38)]. The progenitor of the Ammonites, a son of Lot's younger daughter, born after the destruction of Sodom. It was thought originally that the name Ben-ammi was derived from the deity Emu, an alternative name for Nergal. However, excavations at Ugarit (Râs Shamrah) have revealed that in the 15th cent. B.C. Ben-ammi was a genuine name in north Syrian onomastics. Lists of names from Alalakh also include what appears to be the form Ben-Ammi as a personal designation. During the Amarna age, therefore, it would seem to have been in fairly frequent use in Syro-Palestine. The fact that the name appears in the Râs Shamrah texts as the designation of both an individual and a clan supports the tradition that Ben-ammi was at once the name of the Ammonite clan and its progenitor.

See AMMON. R. K. H.

BENCH. *See* DECK; SEAT.

BEN-DEKER ben-dē'ker [Heb. *ben-deqer*–'son of Deker']; AV "son of Dekar"; NEB BEN-DEKAR. One of the twelve officers who provided food for King Solomon and his household (1 K. 4:9).

BENE-BERAK ben-ə-ber'ak [Heb. *b^e^nê b^e^raq*–'sons of lightning']. A town in the territory of Dan (Josh. 19:45). It was one of the cities besieged by Sennacherib and named on a hexagonal prism inscribed with the record of his conquest (*GAB*, p. 89). It has been identified with Ibn-ibrâq, now el-Kheiriyeh, about 4 mi. (6 km.) E of Jaffa. A few miles to the north a modern Israeli community was established in 1924 by orthodox Jews from Poland and named Bene Beraq. It has become a sizeable city. J. F. PREWITT

BENEDICTION. A declaration of, or supplication for, divine blessing. Pronouncing the benediction was a regular part of the temple service in Israelite times. It was assigned to the Aaronites, who preserved the benediction of Nu. 6:24-26 (cf. Lev. 9:22; Dt. 10:8; 2 Ch. 30:27). All Aaronites of proper age were entitled to perform this service except those who by previous conduct or on account of physical defect were disqualified. One who had killed another (intentionally or otherwise), violated the marriage vows, given himself excessively to wine drinking or other excesses, or been guilty of unrighteous conduct, was not only prohibited from pronouncing the blessing but was also required to withdraw before this part of the service was performed. If one was blind even of one eye, had a defect in his hands or speech, or was a hunchback, he was also excluded. Before the priest could engage in this service he was required to wash his hands. Then, with uplifted hands, while the people stood, he uttered the words of blessing. The main idea was that the name of Yahweh was thus put on the people. Later it came to be regarded as having some special blessing in and of itself, a development against which the more spiritual priests protested.

It was common to pronounce the benediction not only in the public worship but also in noncultic settings (Gen. 9:26f.; 27:27-30). This practice prevailed among the heathen as well as in Israel. We may readily see, therefore, that from the very beginning of the Christian Church the use of the benediction was common. In the course of time an extensive literature developed on this subject, and it may be said that there are now three distinct ideas in the Church as to the benediction. (1) One section of the Church holds that the blessings pronounced are actually conferred in the utterance of the words, because of the sacerdotal powers conferred upon the minister or priest when he was set aside for the sacred office. (2) Others hold that the benediction is merely a prayer that God may bestow certain blessings on the people. (3) Still others teach that it is the declaration of the special relation in which those stand who have entered into covenant fellowship with Christ, and that the blessings now declared are theirs by right of that relation and are conferred upon them by the Holy Spirit.

The Greek and Roman Catholic Churches take the first position, and therefore we find among them much detail as to the manner in which it should be pronounced. In the Greek Church the priest raises his hand with the thumb touching the third finger to signify the procession of the Holy Spirit from the Father alone, or according to others to form the sacred name IHS. In the Roman Church the thumb and first and second fingers are open in order to symbolize the trinity.

The apostolic benedictions in the Epistles present considerable variety. A striking feature in a number of cases is the omission of the Holy Spirit. The best explanation seems to be that the Father and the Son effect the redemption of the world, and the Holy Spirit applies this blessing. Thus, "grace, mercy, and peace" are sent from the Father and the Son, through the Holy Spirit, to be the possession of all who have come into the kingdom. Since the involvement of the third person of the trinity is in the application of the blessing, He is not mentioned. The fact that in other cases Father, Son, and Holy Spirit are mentioned indicates that the writers were aware of the work of the Holy Spirit. Familiar NT benedictions occur in Rom. 15:13; 2 Cor. 13:14; He. 13:20f.

See BLESSING; SALUTATION. J. W. KAPP

BENEFACTORS [Gk. *euergétai*] (Lk. 22:25). Probably an allusion to the practice among kings of assuming or accepting the surname "Euergetes," e.g., Ptolemy III (247-242 B.C.) and VII (147-117 B.C.) of Egypt. Jesus draws the contrast between worldly kingdoms, in which the title "benefactor" is given those who rule with all the splendor of earthly display and luxury, and His kingdom, in which it belongs only to those whose work is that of humble, obscure, and often menial service.

BENEFIT. In the OT Heb. *g^e^mûl* is thus rendered in 2 Ch. 32:25 (NEB "good") and Ps. 103:2. The usual meaning of the Hebrew term is "deed," but here the connotation of "good deed" is present. The cognate *tagmûl* in Ps. 116:12 is rendered "bounty" in the RSV (NEB "gifts").

The noun "benefit" occurs in the RSV NT in 1 Cor. 4:6 (Gk. *di' hymás*; AV "for your sakes"; NEB "on your account"); 7:35 (*symphérō*; AV "profit"; NEB "good"); Philem. 20 (*onínēmi*; AV "joy"; NEB paraphrases, "be generous with me"); "material benefits" occurs in 1 Cor. 9:11 (Gk. *tá sarkiká*; AV "carnal things"; NEB "material harvest"). The verb occurs for *ōpheléō* (AV "profit"; NEB "do good") in 1 Cor. 14:6; He. 4:2; 13:9; and for *euergesía* in 1 Tim. 6:2.

In the AV the word appears also for Gk. *cháris* in 2 Cor. 1:15, "a second benefit," where the RSV has "double pleasure," the NEB "the benefit of a double visit." The RSV is based on the variant *chará* found in a few MSS (including B). The AV also has "benefit" for *agathós* in Philem. 14 (RSV "goodness"; NEB "kindness").

J. W. D. H.

BENE-JAAKAN ben-ə-jā'ə-kən [Heb. *b*^{e}*nê ya'*^{a}*qān*] (Nu. 33:31f.). A desert camp of the Israelites. The name is given as BEEROTH BENE-JAAKAN in Dt. 10:6.

BENEVOLENCE. The TR has Gk. *eúnoia* in 1 Cor. 7:3, followed by the AV; the better reading, however, is simply *opheilḗ*, hence RSV "conjugal rights," NEB "her due." This reference to the marriage relation is explained in v. 4. Cf. Ex. 21:10.

BEN-GEBER ben-gē'bər [Heb. *ben-geḇer*–'son of Geber']; AV "son of Geber." One of the twelve commissariat officers in the service of Solomon (1 K. 4:13). He has been identified with GEBER son of Uri (v. 19).

See W. F. Albright, *JPOS*, 5 (1925), 17ff.

BEN-HADAD ben-hā'dad [Heb. *ben-hadad*; Gk. *hyiós Hader*]. The name of either two or three rulers of the Aramean kingdom of Damascus. Ben-hadad seems to have become a general designation for the kings of Syria (Am. 1:4; Jer. 49:27).

1. Ben-hadad I was called "son of Tabrimmon, son of Hezion, king of Aram" (1 K. 15:18), though his throne-name was probably Hadadezer (Akk. Adad-'idri). He is first mentioned as king of Damascus in connection with the attack of Baasha of Israel (909/08–886/85 B.C.) on Asa of Judah in the thirty-sixth year of the divided monarchy. In 879 Asa bribed Ben-hadad to break his treaty with Baasha, and when Ben-hadad invaded northern Israel Baasha was obliged to withdraw his forces in order to protect his own capital (1 K. 15:16ff.). Subsequently Omri of Israel (885/84–874/73) was compelled to admit the merchants of Damascus to the bazaars of Samaria (1 K. 20:34). Perhaps about 860, shortly after the accession of Pygmalion to the Tyrian throne, Ben-hadad I seems to have entered into some sort of alliance with him, and this doubtless provided the occasion for the erection of his votive stele to his "lord," the Tyrian Melqart. This stele was discovered in 1940 at a north Syrian site, and the text was translated the following year by W. F. Albright. While the stele confirmed the Syrian list contained in 1 K. 15:18, it failed to identify Rezon, who seized Damascus in the Solomonic period and established the Aramean dynasty. From his connections with Asa it would appear that Ben-hadad was ruling by *ca.* 895, and perhaps as early as 900.

2. If three Ben-hadads are to be distinguished, the second Damascene ruler of this name probably commenced his reign about 860 B.C., and as such would be the opponent of Ahab (874/73–853). According to 1 K. 20, Ben-hadad besieged Samaria and demanded the capitulation of the northern kingdom. His purpose seems to have been that of compelling Ahab of Israel to join the Syrians in resisting the military encroachments of Assyria, which had become a threat to the security of Palestine ever since 857, when Shalmaneser III of Assyria (859-824) had begun to launch annual campaigns against Syria. In one foray against Israel Ben-hadad was driven off (1 K. 20:21); and in a second attack near Aphek he suffered heavy losses, although Ahab spared his life (vv. 26-30) in return for commercial concessions in the

Monolith inscription of Shalmaneser III from Kurkh, Turkey (*ca.* 850 B.C.), in which the Assyrian claims victory over a Syrian coalition headed by Ben-hadad I in the battle of Qarqar. In reality, the coalition triumphed decisively. (Trustees of the British Museum)

bazaars of Damascus (v. 34) similar to those allowed the Syrian merchants in Samaria in the time of Omri. Ben-hadad was also required to return the border cities the Damascene regime had captured from Omri, after which a treaty was made (856) that resulted in three years of peace between Israel and Damascus (1 K. 22:1).

In 853 Ben-hadad joined with Ahab against a threatened attack from Shalmaneser III, and a full-scale battle was

Stele of Ben-hadad, dedicated to the Tyrian god Melqart. The inscription apparently commemorates a treaty with Tyre, perhaps made shortly after the accession of Pumiyaton (Pygmalion) in Tyre (*ca.* 860 B.C.). (James B. Pritchard)

fought at Qarqar on the Orontes in which huge numbers of Israelite and Syrian infantry and chariots inflicted a decisive defeat on the Assyrians. However, Shalmaneser claimed a great victory, and in his Monolith Inscription he stated among other things that Ahab the Israelite and Ben-hadad (Adad-'idri) led the opposing forces. When animosity between Israel and Syria flared up again shortly afterward, Ahab allied himself with Jehoshaphat of Judah in an attempt to capture Ramoth-gilead from Ben-hadad (1 K. 22:29); but the Syrians won the battle and Ahab was killed.

Ben-hadad II may be the "king of Aram" mentioned in the Elisha narratives who sent his officer Naaman for healing (2 K. 5:1-19) and later on sought aid for himself when ill. His servant Hazael, who bore the message to Elisha, was informed by the prophet that he would succeed to the Damascene throne; and on his return *ca.* 843 Hazael murdered Ben-hadad and usurped the rule (2 K. 8:14f.). The annals of Shalmaneser III recorded the incident by saying: "Adad-'idri forsook the land; Hazael, the son of a nobody, seized the throne."

3. The third Ben-hadad, following the above pattern, was the son of Hazael and reigned from *ca.* 796 to 770 B.C. He continued his father's oppression of Israel into the reign of Jehoash (798–782/81), who in fulfillment of the prophecy of the dying Elisha was able to repel Ben-hadad III (2 K. 13:14-19, 25). The latter was mentioned on the contemporary stele of Zakir king of Lu'ash and Hamath, which commemorated a victory of Zakir over the Syrian ruler *ca.* 775. The reference to an unnamed nation that delivered Israel from Syrian interference at this time may be to the Assyrian intervention under Adadnirari III (805-782), though this is uncertain.

Before the discovery of the Melqart stele it was usual to distinguish three Damascene rulers named Ben-hadad, as suggested above. Since that time many scholars have dropped the distinction between a Ben-hadad I of the time of king Asa of Judah and Baasha of Israel, and a Ben-hadad II who was contemporary with Ahab. On such a basis the son of Hazael, enumerated above as Ben-hadad III, would then be known as Ben-hadad II. However, there are certain problems that arise if only two Ben-hadads are postulated. If the one mentioned in connection with the reigns of Ahab and Joram is also the Ben-hadad associated with Asa of Judah, namely Ben-hadad I son of Tabrimmon, it would imply that he occupied the throne of Damascus for a period of about fifty-seven years (*ca.* 900-843 B.C.), which while not entirely without parallel would certainly be unusual. Albright thought in terms of a single Ben-hadad for this period, but seems to have based his estimate on a date of *ca.* 850 for the Melqart stele, arrived at on epigraphic grounds. It is equally possible from the style of the script, however, to date the stele as early as *ca.* 870, which would place it firmly within the time of Ben-hadad I and eliminate the need for telescoping two Ben-hadads into one. Furthermore, from 1 K. 20:34 it would appear that Omri had been defeated at an earlier time by Ben-hadad I, the father of Ben-hadad II who was the speaker and a contemporary of Ahab of Israel. Since the Melqart stele is partly mutilated and the patronymic has been lost, its evidence is less than decisive in identifying Ben-hadad I and Ben-hadad II.

Bibliography.–R. de Vaux, *RB*, 43 (1934), 512-18; A. Jepsen, *AfO*, 14 (1941-1944), 153-55; W. F. Albright, *BASOR*, 89 (Feb. 1942), 23-29; M. F. Unger, *Israel and the Arameans of Damascus* (1957).

R. K. HARRISON

BEN-HAIL ben-hā'il [Heb. *ben-ḥayil*–'son of strength']. One of the princes who was sent by Jehoshapat "to teach in the cities of Judah" (2 Ch. 17:7).

BEN-HANAN ben-hā'nan [Heb. *ben-ḥānān*–'son of grace']. A son of Shimon of the house of Judah (1 Ch. 4:20).

BEN-HESED ben-hē'sed [Heb. *ben-ḥesed*–'son of Hesed']; AV "son of Hesed." Commissariat officer over the third district in the service of Solomon (1 K. 4:10).

BEN-HINNOM ben-hin'em, **VALLEY OF** (NEB, and in Jer. 19:2, 6 in some editions of RSV). *See* HINNOM, VALLEY OF.

BEN-HUR ben-hûr' [Heb. *ben-ḥûr*–'son of Hur']; AV "son of Hur." Commissariat officer over the first district in the service of Solomon (1 K. 4:8).

BENINU bə-nī'no͞o [Heb. *b^e^nînû*–'our son']. A Levite who along with Nehemiah sealed the covenant under Ezra the scribe (Neh. 10:13).

BENJAMIN ben'jə-min [Heb. *binyāmîn*–'son of the right hand'].

1. The youngest of Jacob's sons, the only one to be born in Palestine; and the tribe named for him. According to tradition, his mother Rachel died in giving him birth (Gen. 35:16-20), and the name Ben-oni, "son of my sorrow" (Gen. 35:18), was given by the dying Rachel; Jacob, however, named him Benjamin.

Benjamin, Ephraim, and Manasseh formed a special group among the tribes, all of them being sons of Rachel. Some scholars believe that as "sons of Rachel" these tribes were goatherds at the time of their wanderings, since the name Rachel in Hebrew means "young goat," and that the other tribes were cattlebreeders inasmuch as they were related to Leah ("cow" in Akkadian; "wild cow" in Arabic). The tribes descendant from Rachel finally settled in Canaan in an uninterrupted stretch of country. As the territory of Benjamin lay S of that of Manasseh and Ephraim, i.e., to the right of them, some scholars have believed that their name was given them after their settlement. The tradition of Benjamin having been born in Palestine may mean, according to some scholars, that this tribe had already settled there before the coming to Canaan of Jacob and his sons.

At the time of the Exodus the number of men of war in the tribe is given as 35,400; at the time of the second census as 45,600 (Nu. 1:37; 26:41); their place was with the standard of the camp of Ephraim, W of the tabernacle; their leader was Abidan son of Gideoni (Nu. 2:22). Benjamin was represented among the spies by Palti son of Raphu (Nu. 13:9). At the time of the division of the land the leader of Benjamin was Elidad son of Chislon (34:21).

The tribe of Benjamin settled between Ephraim to the north and Judah to the south. To the west their neighbor was the tribe of Dan (Josh. 18:11).

The northern border started from the Jordan over against Jericho, then continued to the west toward Beth-aven, the northern part of the Wilderness of Judah. From there it turned NW to Bethel, then to Ataroth-addar and W to the neighborhood of Beth-horon. The western border crossed the town of Kiriath-jearim and then turned east. The southern border crossed the waters of Nephtoah and then ran S of Jerusalem through Beth-hoglah and joined the river Jordan again near its mouth (Jgs. 18:11-20).

The eastern parts of the territory of Benjamin were seized by force at the beginning of the Israelite conquest of Canaan. But most of their territory was acquired through the treaty between the Israelites and the four Hivvite cities (Josh. 9:7). This situation is reflected in the list of Benjaminite cities (18:21-28), which is divided into two groups of a dozen cities each. The first group, the conquered area, consists of the cities of the southern Jordan Valley E of the watershed; the second group of cities, which came to them through the treaty, lay W of the watershed.

The first of the judges that emerged in Israel after the conquest was Ehud of the tribe of Benjamin, who fought the Moabites. If we trace in the genealogical lists the names that reflect place names, it appears that during this period Benjamin expanded northward and southward, and later also to the west when the tribe of Dan left its previous territory. The Benjaminites were men of war and famous slingers (Gen. 49:27; Jgs. 3:15; 1 Ch. 8:40; 12:2). The story told in Jgs. 19–21 presents many difficulties that cannot be discussed here. The atrocity committed by the Benjaminites and the terrible punishment they suffered for it illustrate certain features of life in those lawless times when there was no king in Israel. The refusal of the men of JABESH-GILEAD (of the tribe of Manasseh) to take part in the battle of requital against Benjamin provides the background for the special relationship between the Benjaminites and the inhabitants of that city. It explains why Saul and the Benjaminites came to their aid when Jabesh-Gilead was attacked by the Ammonites (1 S. 11:1-3).

Benjamin was also the first tribe to oppose the Philistines. From among the Benjaminites arose the first king, Saul. After his death David a Judahite, became king. David did not easily win the loyalty of the Benjaminites; and one of them, Shimei son of Gera, a descendant of Saul, took part in Absalom's rebellion (2 S. 16:5). Sheba son of Bichri led the revolt against David after the quelling of Absalom's rebellion (2 S. 21:1f.). Owing to David's peaceful policy, however, the Benjaminites finally joined him and remained loyal to his son Solomon even after the division of the kingdom. From that time the history of the tribe is the history of the kingdom of Judah.

Other Benjaminites of distinction were the prophet Jeremiah (1:1), Esther and Mordecai (Est. 2:5), and the Apostle Paul (Rom. 11:1; Phil. 3:5).

See Map VI.

Bibliography.–W. F. Albright, *AASOR*, 4 (1922/23), *passim*; *BASOR*, 56 (Dec. 1934), 9ff.; 57 (Feb. 1935), 13; F. T. Cooke, *AASOR*, 5 (1923/24), 105ff.; A. Alt, *Die Landnahme der Israeliten in Palaestina* (1925); *PJ*, 31 (1934), 94ff.; A. Fernandez, *Studios ecclesiasticos*, 13 (1934), 6ff.; M. Noth, *ZDPV*, 58 (1935), 189-196; G. Dossin, *Mélanges Dussaud*, 2 (1939), 981-996; A. Malamat, *JNES*, 9 (1950), 226f.

2. A great-grandson of Benjamin, son of Jacob (1 Ch. 7:10).

3. One of those who had married a foreign wife (Ezr. 10:32, and probably also Neh. 3:23; 12:34).

W. EWING
A. A. SAARISALO

BENJAMIN, GATE OF. *See* JERUSALEM.

BENJAMINITE ben'jə-min-īt [Heb. *ben-y^e^mînî, ben-ḥaymînî*]; AV, NEB, BENJAMITE. One belonging to the tribe of BENJAMIN, such as Ehud (Jgs. 3:15), Saul (1 S. 9:1f.), Sheba (2 S. 20:1), Shimei (1 K. 2:8), etc.

BENO bē'nō [Heb. *b^e^nô*–'his son']. The son of Jaaziah of the house of Levi (1 Ch. 24:26f.).

BEN-ONI ben-ō'nī [Heb. *ben-'ônî*; Gk. *huiós odýnēs mou*–'son of my sorrow']. The name given by the dying Rachel to her newborn son; changed by his father Jacob to BENJAMIN (Gen. 35:18).

BENT OVER [Gk. *synkýptō*–'be bent over'] (Lk. 13:11); AV BOWED TOGETHER; NEB BENT DOUBLE. The woman who had the spirit of infirmity and was unable to straighten herself (Lk. 13:11-17) was afflicted with senile kyphosis, a chronic bone disease often found among aged men and, more frequently, women whose lives have been spent in agricultural labor. In these people the vertebrae become altered in shape so that it is impossible to straighten the back. Some rabbinical authorities believed all deformities to be due to Satan, and to this Jesus seems to have alluded in His rebuke to those who objected to His healing on the sabbath. This condition has been observed in some Egyptian skeletons, and a skeleton with a similar curvature was found buried under the threshold of a house at Gezer, where she had evidently been offered as a foundation sacrifice.

See also DISEASE IV.F. A. MACALISTER

BEN-ZOHETH ben-zō'heth [Heb. *ben-zôḥēṯ*–'son of Zoheth']. A son of Ishi of the house of Judah (1 Ch. 4:20).

BEON bē'on [Heb. *be'ōn*] (Nu. 32:3). *See* BAAL-MEON.

BEOR bē'ôr [Heb. *be'ôr*].

1. Father of Bela, the first king of Edom (Gen. 36:32; 1 Ch. 1:43).

2. [Gk. *Beōr*]. The father of the seer Balaam (Nu. 22:5; 24:3, 15; 31:8; Dt. 23:4; Josh. 13:22; 24:9 [omitted in the LXX]; Mic. 6:5; 2 Pet. 2:15; AV "Bosor" based on a different textual reading).

BERA bē'rə [Heb. *bera'*]. King of Sodom (Gen. 14:2) who in the battle of Siddim was subdued by Chedorlaomer.

BERACAH ber'ə-kə [Heb. *berāḵâ*–'blessing']; AV, NEB, BERACHAH. A Benjaminite who joined David at Ziklag (1 Ch. 12:3).

BERACAH, VALLEY OF [Heb. *'ēmeq berāḵâ*–'valley of blessing'; Gk. *koilás eulogías*] (2 Ch. 20:26); AV BERACHAH; NEB BERAKAH. A place where Jehoshaphat and his people met to bless the Lord for their victory over Moab and Ammon. The Wâdī el-Arrûb, on the main road from Hebron to Jerusalem and not far from Tekoa, suits the narrative well. E. W. G. MASTERMAN

BERAIAH bə-rī'ə [Heb. *berā'yâ*–'Yahweh has created']. A son of Shimei of the house of Benjamin (1 Ch. 8:21).

BEREA bə-rē'ə [Gk. *Berea*; Lat. *berethin*].

1. A place mentioned in 1 Macc. 9:4, whose location has not been identified with certainty. Two possibilities have been suggested: el-Bîreh, a city in Benjamin about 8 mi. (13 km.) N of Jerusalem; and Bir ez-Zait, a village about 13 mi. (21 km.) N of Jerusalem.

See F.-M. Abel, *RB*, 33 (1924), 381-83; 55 (1948), 187; J. C. Dancy, Comm. on 1 Maccabees (1954), p. 131.

2. (AV, Acts 17:10, 13; 20:4). *See* BEROEA.

D. H. MADVIG

BEREAVE [Heb. *šāḵal, šāḵōl*] (Dt. 32:35; Ezk. 36:12-14; Hos. 9:12); AV also DESTROY (Dt. 32:35); NEB "make orphans" (Dt. 32:35), "rob of children" (Ezk. 36:12-14), "make childless" (Hos. 9:12). In these passages, *šāḵōl* is in the piel (*šikkēl*). In the qal, *šāḵōl* is a stative verb meaning "be without children." The piel makes this verb active, "deprive of children."

In Ezk. 36:14 the form is *tekaššelî* in the *K*, but in the *Q* this is corrected to *tešakkelî*. The *K* reading would be a piel form of the verb *kāšal*, meaning "stumble" (cf. v. 15).

In Dt. 32:25 the word is found in connection with the judgment of God upon the people of Israel due to their violation of the first commandment. The whole of the pericope 32:1-43 is the so-called Song of Moses, which plays upon the themes of God's activity in history and the apostacy of the people.

In Ezk. 36 the passage is giving a picture of the new Israel. The whole of the unit 36:1-15 is directed to the mountains of Israel. Vv. 13f. probably refer to the child sacrifice that was a feature of Canaanite religion.

Hosea 9:12 is part of a judgment oracle against the people of Israel. A clue to the reason for the judgment is found in v. 10. The people were found by Yahweh and nurtured as a farmer nurtures his crops, but they chose to dedicate themselves to Baal instead of Yahweh. Therefore there shall be no hope for productivity in the land, and even those children who are born will be slain.

Bibliography.–W. Eichrodt, *Ezekiel* (*OTL*, Eng. tr. 1970); J. L. Mays, *Hosea* (*OTL*, 1969); G. von Rad, *Deuteronomy* (*OTL*, Eng. tr. 1966). T. R. ASHLEY

BERECHIAH ber-ə-kī'ə [Heb. *bereḵyâ, bereḵyāhû*–'Yahweh blesses'].

1. A descendant of David (1 Ch. 3:20).

2. The father of Asaph the singer (1 Ch. 6:39; AV "Berachiah"; 15:17).

3. A former inhabitant of Jerusalem, a Levite (1 Ch. 9:16).

4. A doorkeeper for the ark at David's time (1 Ch. 15:23).

5. One of the chiefs of the men of Ephraim (2 Ch. 28:12).

6. The father of Meshullam the builder (Neh. 3:4, 30; 6:18).

7. The father of the prophet Zechariah (Zec. 1:1, 7; cf. Mt. 23:35). *See also* BARACHIAH. A. L. BRESLICH

BERED bē'red [Heb. *bereḏ*–'hail']. The son of Shuthelah of the house of Ephraim (1 Ch. 7:20). *See* BECHER.

BERED [Heb. *bereḏ*; Gk. *Barad*]. A place in the Negeb mentioned in the story of Hagar (Gen. 16:14). The well Beer-lahai-roi was "between Kadesh and Bered." The Onkelos Targum renders it *Ḥagrā'*, the usual equivalent of Shur; the Jerusalem Targum renders it *Ḥalûṣâ*, also the equivalent of Shur (Ex. 15:22). *Ḥalûṣâ* is the Elusu mentioned by Ptolemy and from the 4th to 7th cents. by various ecclesiastical writers. It was an important town on the road from Palestine to Kadesh and Mt. Sinai, and can be identified with reasonable certainty with Khirbet Ḥalaṣeh, modern Ḥalutsah, about 15 mi. (24 km.) SW of Beer-sheba. The large ruins are of a city with a population of about twenty thousand, from the Byzantine period. The identification Bered = Shur = Ḥalutsah, however, is not positively established.

Bibliography.–*GP*, I, 458; II, 264; *GTTOT*, §§ 367f.

E. W. G. MASTERMAN
W. S. L. S.

BERI bē'rī [Heb. *bērî*]. A descendant of Asher (1 Ch. 7:36).

BERIAH bə-rī'ə [Heb. *berî'â*–'excellent'].

1. Son of Asher and father of Heber and Malchiel (Gen. 46:17; 1 Ch. 7:30f.); the head of the family of the Beriites (Nu. 26:44ff.).

2. Son of Ephraim, called Beriah by his father because "evil had befallen his house" (1 Ch. 7:23).

3. A descendant of Benjamin (1 Ch. 8:13, 16).

4. A Levite in the line of Gershon (1 Ch. 23:10f.).

BERIITES bə-rī'īts [Heb. *habberî'î*] (Nu. 26:44). The family name of BERIAH **1.**

BERITES bē'rīts (2 S. 20:14, AV). *See* BICHRITES.

BERITH bə-rith' (Jgs. 9:46, AV). *See* EL-BERITH.

BERNICE bər-nēs' [Gk. *Bernikē*–'victorious'] (Acts 25:13, 23; 26:30). The eldest daughter of Herod Agrippa I and sister of Herod Agrippa II. She was born *ca.* A.D. 28. Her life's story is told by Josephus (cf. also Juvenal *Satires* vi.156).

Her first marriage was to Marcus the son of Alexander Lysimachus the "alabarch" of Alexandria. After Marcus' death she married her uncle, King Agrippa's brother Herod, for whom Agrippa was able to procure the kingdom of Chalcis from Claudius (*Ant.* xix.5.1). This marriage produced two sons, Bernicianus and Hyrcanus (xx.5.2). After Herod's death in 48 she became involved in an incestuous relationship with her brother Agrippa II, with whom she listened to the defense of Paul at Caesarea before Festus. In an attempt to silence the rumors about her relationship with Agrippa, she persuaded Polemo king of Sicily to undergo circumcision and marry her; but soon after they were married she left him and returned to her brother (xx.7.3).

Josephus writes that she was in Jerusalem to perform a vow at the time when Procurator Florus slaughtered many of the Jews (A.D. 66). She pleaded with him to stop the massacre; but he refused to listen to her, and she herself was almost killed by his soldiers (*BJ* ii.15.1). During the war that ensued, her palace — as well as that of Agrippa — was set on fire by the Jews (ii.17.6).

In later years she and Agrippa took an oath of loyalty to the emperor Vespasian. It appears that *ca.* 75 they moved to Rome, where she became the mistress of Vespasian's son Titus.

See also HEROD. N. J. O.

BERODACH-BALADAN ber'ə-dak bal'ə-dən. (2 K. 20:12, AV). *See* MERODACH-BALADAN.

BEROEA bə-rē'ə [Gk. *Beroia, Berroia*]; AV BEREA.

1. A city of southwestern Macedonia in the district of Emathia; modern Verria. Lying 40 mi. (65 km.) W of Thessalonica and 25 mi. (40 km.) from the Gulf of Thermai, Beroea was situated on a tributary on the Haliacmon at the foot of Mt. Bermius. It was called "a town off the beaten track" by Cicero (*In Pisonem* 36) probably because it was not on one of the main Roman roads. The existence of the city by the end of the 4th cent. B.C. is verified by an ancient inscription (U. Koehler, ed., *Inscriptiones Graecae*, II/5 [1895], no. 296i). Moreover, it is mentioned twice by Polybius (xxvii.8; xxviii.8). After the battle of Pydna in 168 B.C., Beroea was the first city to surrender to Rome, and fell into the third of the four regions into which Macedonia was divided (Livy xliv.45; xlv.29).

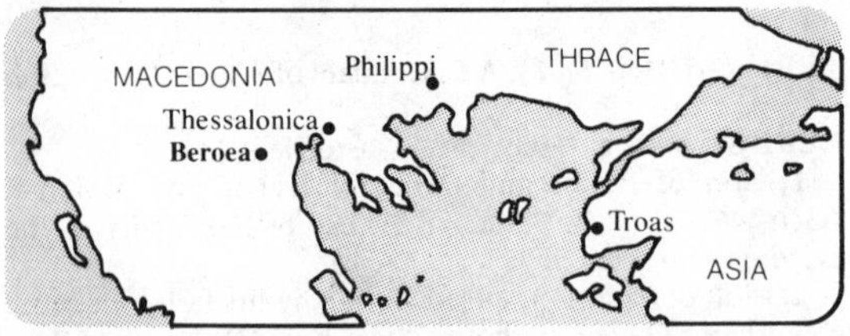

When they were driven out of Thessalonica, Paul and Silas came to Beroea, where they preached in the synagogue of the Jews. Many of their hearers came to believe, having first carefully examined the message in the light of the Scriptures (Acts 17:10f.). The work of Paul and Silas in Beroea terminated when a group of hostile Jews from Thessalonica created a disturbance in the city and thereby forced them to leave (vv. 12-15). Perhaps Sopater of Beroea, who accompanied Paul to Asia on his last journey, was one of his converts on this visit (20:4).

As one of the most populous cities of Macedonia, Beroea was made a bishopric under the metropolitan of Thessalonica and was itself made a metropolis by Andronicus II (1283-1328). According to tradition, Onesimus was the first bishop of the church. After playing a prominent role in the struggles between the Greeks and the Bulgarians and Serbs, Beroea was conquered by the Turks in 1373/74. A large number of inscriptions are the only known remains of the ancient city.

2. The city of Aleppo in northern Syria between the Orontes and the Euphrates rivers. It was renamed Beroea, after the Macedonian city, by Seleucus Nicator (312-280 B.C.). It is mentioned in 2 Macc. 13:3ff. as the site of the execution of Menelaus, the former high priest, by order of Antiochus Eupator, for inciting war with the Maccabees. The manner of the execution was one peculiar to the region, whereby the victim was thrown into a tower filled with ashes. The Semitic name of the city, Halab, from which "Aleppo" is derived, was revived by the Moslems in the Middle Ages when it was a city of some importance, being located on a vital trade route from Europe to Persia and Asia. Its importance declined, however, after the discovery of the route around the Cape. The Mosque Zakariyah in Aleppo is reported to contain the tomb of Zechariah, father of John the Baptist. For many years the city was the repository of the famous Aleppo Codex of the OT. D. H. MADVIG

BEROTH bē'roth (1 Esd. 5:19, AV, NEB). *See* BEEROTH.

BEROTHIAH bē-rō'thə [Heb. *bērôṯâ*] (Ezk. 47:16); NEB BERUTHA; **BEROTHAI** bē-ro'thī [Heb. *bērôṯay*] (2 S. 8:8). A town on the northern boundary between Zedad and Sibraim (Sepharvaim), just S of the kingdom of Hamath (Ezk. 47:16). 2 S. 8:8 identifies Berothai as one of the cities belonging to King Hadadezer from which David captured much bronze. The parallel passage, 1 Ch. 18:8, substitutes the name Cun. Etymological similarities have convinced some that it was identical with ancient Beirût (*Beruti* in Am. Tab.), but its position in the Ezekiel passage makes this unlikely. A more plausible site would be at Bereitan (Brital) 8 mi. (13 km.) S of Baalbek in the western foothills of Anti-Lebanon (*GTTOT*, p. 333).

A. H. LEWIS

BEROTHITE bē'roth-īt (1 Ch. 11:39, AV). *See* BEEROTHITE.

BERYL. *See* STONES, PRECIOUS.

BERYTUS bə-rit'əs. The ancient name of the city of Beirut, Lebanon. There seems to be no reference to the city in the Bible. Some have thought that Berothai (2 S. 8:8) and BEROTHAH (Ezk. 47:16) were references to Beirut, but the other names associated with these places make such an identification improbable. The name seems to have come from the Phoenician word for "wells."

R. A. GWINN

BESAI bē'sī [Heb. *bēsay*; Gk. *Basi, Bēsi*, Apoc. *Basthai*]; AV Apoc. BASTAI; NEB Apoc. BASTHAE. One whose descendants returned with Zerubbabel to Jerusalem (Ezr. 2:49; Neh. 7:52; 1 Esd. 5:31).

BESIDE. Often archaic in the AV for "besides"; e.g., Ex. 12:37; Nu. 5:20; Josh. 22:19, 29; Isa. 44:6; 45:5; Hos. 13:4; Mt. 14:21; 25:20; 2 Cor. 11:28.

BESIEGE. *See* SIEGE.

BESODEIAH bes-ə-dē'yə [Heb. *b^esoḏyâ*–'in the confidence or counsel of Yahweh' (cf. Jer. 23:18, 22)]. Father of Meshullam the builder (Neh. 3:6).

BESOR bē'sôr, **BROOK** [Heb. *naḥal b^eśôr*; Gk. *Bechōr, Beana*]; NEB "ravine of Besor." A torrent bed (*naḥal*) or wadi where David left two hundred of his men while the rest of his troops continued in pursuit of the Amalekites (1 S. 30:9f., 21). The incident is recalled by Josephus (*Ant.* vi.14.6). Some have identified it with Wâdī es-Sheriah, others with Wâdī Ghazzeh. Modern Israeli maps identify Wâdī Ghazzeh as Habesor or "the Besor." It enters the Mediterranean Sea S of Gaza.

J. F. PREWITT

BEST SEAT [Gk. *prōtokathedría*]; AV CHIEF SEATS, UPPERMOST SEAT, HIGHEST SEAT; NEB CHIEF SEAT, SEAT OF HONOUR. Jesus reproached the scribes and Pharisees for having the best seats in the synagogues (Mt. 23:6; Mk. 12:39; Lk. 11:43; 20:46). These were special chairs set in front of the ark and facing the congregation, reserved for those held in highest honor in the congregation, the teachers of the law. They may have been similar to the seventy-one special chairs in the great synagogue of Alexandria, which were occupied by the members of the great council in that city.

See also MOSES' SEAT; SYNAGOGUE. J. M. WILSON

BESTEAD. Archaic term for "beset" in Isa. 8:21, AV.

BESTIALITY. *See* CRIME.

BESTOW. Some occurrences in the AV are archaic for "lay up," "stow away," "store," as 2 K. 5:24 (Heb. *pāqaḏ*); Lk. 12:17f. (Gk. *synágō*). In 1 K. 10:26 (Heb. *nāḥâ*) and 2 Ch. 9:25 (*nû(a)ḥ*) it is replaced in the RSV by "station." Elsewhere "bestow" or "bestow on (upon)" means "give" or "provide."

BETAH bē'tə [Heb. *beṭaḥ*; Gk. *Masbak*, Lucian *matebak*; Syr. *Ṭeḇaḥ*] (2 S. 8:8). *See* TIBHATH.

BETANE bet'ə-nē [Gk. Baitanē] (AV Jth. 1:9). A place named among those to which the messengers of Nebuchadrezzar were sent. From the order in which they are named we should look for it S of Jerusalem. It may be identical with Beit 'Ainûn (Beth-anoth) about 3 mi. (5 km.) N of Hebron; or the RSV may be correct in identifying it with BETHANY (el-'Azarîyeh) 2 mi. (3 km.) SE of Jerusalem.

BETEN bē'tən [Heb. *beṭen*; Gk. *Batne*]. A city listed to designate the territory assigned to Asher when the land of Canaan was divided among the tribes of Israel following the conquest under Joshua (Josh. 19:25). It is probably modern Abtun, 2.5 mi. (4 km.) ENE of Mt. Carmel on the eastern edge of the Kishon River Valley.

R. J. HUGHES, III

BETH bāth [ב]. The second letter of the Hebrew alphabet. With the daghesh it is transliterated here as *b*, and without as *ḇ*. It came also to be used for the number two, and with the dieresis for two thousand. *See* WRITING.

BETH beth (in proper names) [Heb. *bêṯ*; Gk. *bēth, baith,* or *beth*]. The Heb. *bêṯ* means "house," "tent," "place." It occurs in many compound proper names and in expressions such as *bêṯ 'ᵃnāṯ* or *'ᵃnōṯ*–'house of replies' (Josh. 19:38; Jgs. 1:33); *bêṯ'ēl*–'house of God' (Gen. 12:8; 13:3); etc. We also find the word in hybrid formations, e.g., *Bēthphagē*–'fig house' (Mt. 12:1).

F. E. HIRSCH

BETHABARA beth-ab'ə-rə [Gk. *Bēthabara*]. The AV and RV mg. for Bethany in Jn. 1:28. The best MSS (p^{66} ℵ* A B C* W N Θ) have Bethany, obviously the original reading. In his Greek comm. on the Fourth Gospel Origen says: "We were persuaded it must not be read Bethany, but Bethabara." The only Bethany he knew was "the home town of Lazarus and Martha and Mary," near Jerusalem. This apparently explains the presence of Bethabara in the TR. A redactor of Codex Sinaiticus substituted Betharaba for Bethany, perhaps to identify it with a city of Judah and Benjamin (Josh. 15:6, 61; 18:22). Bethabara has also been identified with Beth-nimrah (Josh. 13:27); but this is 5 mi. (8 km.) E of the Jordan, about opposite Jericho. It is more probable that John would be baptizing at the Jordan.

Condor (*HDB*, I, 276) writes: "The name survives at the ford called *Abarah,* north-east of Bethshean, and this is the only place where this name occurs in Palestine." He favors this site, as being only a day's walk from Cana. But A. S. Geden observes: "The inference . . . which has been drawn from Jn. 2:1, that Bethabara or Bethany lay not more than a day's journey from Cana of Galilee, is precarious" (*DCG,* I, 193).

After a lengthy discussion, Gustaf Dalman fixes on the Wâdī el-Kharrâr, E of the Jordan near Jericho, as the best site (*SSW,* p. 89).

Perhaps the best suggestion is that of Pierson Parker. Pointing out that Gk. *péran* can mean "opposite" as well as "beyond," he paraphrases Jn. 1:28 thus: "These things took place in Bethany, which is across from the point of the Jordan where John had been baptizing" (*JBL,* 74 [1955], 258). That is, the reference here is to the well-known BETHANY, near Jerusalem.

See also BETH-BARAH. R. EARLE

BETH-ANATH beth-ā'nath [Heb. *bêṯ 'ᵃnaṯ*–'house of Anath,' a Canaanite goddess; Gk. *Baithanath*]. A fortified city (listed by several Egyptian rulers during the New Kingdom period) in the territory assigned to Naphtali when Canaan was divided among the tribes of Israel following the conquest under Joshua (Josh. 19:38). Instead of driving out the inhabitants, the Israelites used them as forced labor (Jgs. 1:33). If represented by modern el-Ba'neh, the city is located 10 mi. (16 km.) E of Acco (Ptolemais). R. J. HUGHES, III

BETH-ANOTH beth-ā'noth [Heb. *bêṯ 'ᵃnôṯ*; Gk. *Baithanam*–'house of Anoth' (to associate this name with the goddess Anath is not justified by the consonantal text)]. One of the cities in the hill country allotted to Judah (Josh. 15:59), often identified as Beit 'Ainûn, 2 mi. (3 km.) SE of Ḥalhûl and 3 mi. (5 km.) NE of Hebron. On the basis of the similarity of the names, this was sometimes identified as the Aenon of Jn. 3:23 — which is quite impossible. W. S. L. S

BETHANY beth'ə-nē [Gk. *Bēthania*].

1. A village 15 stadia (less than 2 mi., 3 km.) from Jerusalem (Jn. 11:18), on the southeast slopes of the Mt. of Olives, on the Jericho road (Mk. 11:1; Lk. 19:29). Here lived Simon the leper (Mk. 14:3), and Mary, Martha, and Lazarus (Jn. 11:18f.). Apparently Jesus usually spent the night there when He went to Jerusalem (Mt. 21:17; Mk. 11:11). On at least one occasion He was entertained in the home of Martha and Mary (Lk. 10:38-42). At Bethany He raised Lazarus from the dead (Jn. 11). In the home of Simon the leper He was anointed by Mary (Mt. 26:6-13;

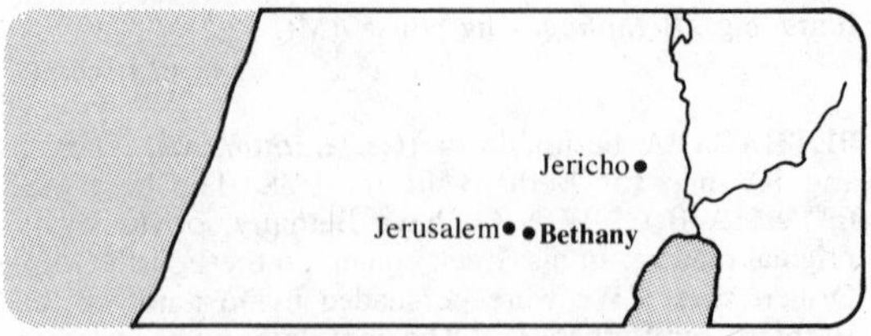

Mk. 14:3-9; Jn. 12:1-9). That Martha served the meal on this occasion (Jn. 12:2) suggests that this may also have been the home of Martha and Mary, though their relation to Simon is not stated.

The Ascension is commonly placed at Bethany, because of the statement in Lk. 24:50f., "Then he led them out as far as Bethany, and lifting up his hands, he blessed them. While he blessed them, he parted from them." The account of the Ascension in Acts 1:6-12 seems to suggest that it took place on the Mt. of Olives, which could include Bethany. But the phrase in Lk. 24:50 may be translated "over against Bethany" (RV). So the traditional site of the Ascension on top of the Mt. of Olives could be correct.

Today Bethany is called el-'Azarîyeh, a corrupted form of "Lazarus." Tourists are shown the tomb of Lazarus, as well as the house of Mary and Martha; but both sites are uncertain.

See also BETANE (Jth. 1:9).

2. "Bethany beyond the Jordan" (Jn. 1:28). For the probable location of this *see* BETHABARA. As indicated there, it may well be that this should be identified with the Bethany near Jerusalem. R. EARLE

BETH-APHRAH beth-af'rə (Mic. 1:10, NEB). *See* BETH-LE-APHRAH.

BETH-ARABAH beth-är'ə-bə [Heb. *bêṯ hā'ᵃrāḇâ*–'house (place) of the Arabah']. One of the six cities of Judah "in the wilderness" (Josh. 15:61). Also included in this group is En-gedi, a well-known location midway along the western shore of the Dead Sea, which suggests that the site is to be located in the barren land W of the Dead Sea. Since it is named both as a city of Judah and as a city of Benjamin (Josh. 15:6; 18:18), it must have stood on the border between the two tribes, somewhere near the north end of the Dead Sea. It is possibly to be identified with 'Ain el-Gharabah, on the north of Wâdî Qelt, SE of Jericho. J. F. PREWITT

BETH-ARAM beth-ā'rəm (Josh. 13:27, AV). *See* BETH-HARAM.

BETH-ARBEL beth-är'bəl [Heb. *bêṯ 'arbē'l*]. A place mentioned by Hosea — "as Shalman destroyed Beth-arbel" (Hos. 10:14) — identified in Eusebius *Onom.* 14.18 as Arbela in the region of Pella in Transjordan, and now generally as Irbid (Irbil), 20 mi. (32 km.) NW of 'Ammân. It is useless to speculate upon the historical situation that lay behind Hosea's prophecy. W. S. L. S.

BETHASHBEA beth-ash'bē-ə [Heb. *bêṯ 'ašbē(a)'*]; AV, NEB, "house of Ashbea." Evidently, the location of a guild of linen-workers (1 Ch. 4:21). Nothing further is mentioned of them or their town.

BETHASMOTH beth-az'moth [Gk. *Baithasmōth*]; AV BETHSAMOS. A place mentioned in the census of the men who returned from the Babylonian Captivity (1 Esd. 5:18), spelled "Beth-azmaveth" in Neh. 7:28. *See* AZMAVETH. W. S. L. S.

BETH-AVEN beth-ā'vən [Heb. *bêṯ 'āwen*–'house (place) of nothing'; Gk. *Baithōn, Baithaun*]. A place near Ai (Josh. 7:2), on the northern boundary of Benjamin (Josh. 18:12). According to 1 S. 13:5, Michmash was E of Beth-aven; but this cannot be if the latter was near Ai. The Greek texts indicate a basic problem throughout: in Josh. 7:2 there is no mention of Beth-aven; in 18:12, B reads *Baithōn* and A reads *Baithaun*; in 1 S. 13:5 some texts read *Baithōn*, others read *Baithōrōn*; and in 14:23 we find *Baithōn, Bamōth, Bēthaun,* or *Baithōrōn*.

Hosea (4:15; 10:5) uses the term Beth-aven as a symbol of reproach for Bethel, and Amos (5:5) makes a pun on the name, "Bethel shall come to nought" (Heb. *'āwen*). Even the word *'āwen* may be a pun, for with slightly different vocalization it becomes *'Ôn,* which was Heliopolis, the city of the Egyptian priestly caste, from which elements were imported for the idolatrous religion at Bethel. It seems likely, then, that Beth-aven is a surrogate for Bethel.

See *GP,* II, 268. W. S. L. S.

BETH-AZMAVETH beth-az-mā'vəth [Heb. *bêṯ 'azmāweṯ*]; NEB BETH-AZMOTH. A place named in the census of men who returned from the Exile (Neh. 7:28), identified with AZMAVETH on the basis of Ezr. 2:24.

BETH-AZMOTH beth-az'moth (NEB Ezr. 2:24; Neh. 7:28; 12:29). *See* AZMAVETH; BETH-AZMAVETH (Neh. 7:28).

BETH-BAAL-MEON beth-bāl-mē'on [Heb. *bêṯ ba'al mᵉ'ôn*–'Baal's dwelling place'] (Josh. 13:17). *See* BAAL-MEON.

BETH-BARAH beth-bâr'ə [Heb. *bêṯ bārâ*]. A place in the vicinity of the Jordan Valley, probably located between the Jordan and the modern Wâdī Fâr'ah. At this point the enemy could easily be taken. Gideon sent messengers to the Ephraimites directing them to seize these rivers "as far as Beth-Barah" in order to trap the fleeing Midianites (Jgs. 7:24). If, as some conjecture, it is the same as Bethabara (*bêṯ 'ᵃḇārâ*), guttural having been lost in copying (*HDB*), it may indeed have been a ford or crossing near the confluence of the two rivers. The exact location is unknown.

See BETHABARA. K. G. JUNG

BETHBASI beth-bā'sī [Gk. *Baithbasi,* perhaps < Heb. *bêṯ-bᵉṣî*–'place of marshes'] (1 Macc. 9:62, 64). A place in the Wilderness of Judah refortified by Jonathan and Simon Maccabeus. It was subsequently attacked by Bacchides, but he was driven off. Today it is identified with Khirbet Beit Baṣṣi, SE of Bethlehem and about 3 mi. (5 km.) NE of Tekoa.

BETH-BIREI beth-bir'ā (1 Ch. 4:31, AV, NEB). *See* BETH-BIRI.

BETH-BIRI beth-bir'ī [Heb. *bêṯ-bir'î*; Gk. *oíkos Braoumseōreim*]; AV, NEB, BETHBIREI. A site belonging to Simeon in the Negeb (1 Ch. 4:31). The consonants suggest a meaning "house (or place) of my Creator," but the vowel pointing does not, and the Greek seems to support a different reading. In Josh. 19:6 the same site, apparently, is called Beth-lebaoth ("abode of lionesses"). The name may survive in Jebel el-Biri, about 6 mi. (10 km.) SW of Ḥalutsah (el-Ḥalaṣeh) or about 20 mi. (32 km.) SW of Beer-sheba; but the site has not been identified.

BETH-CAR beth-kär' [Heb. *bêṯ-kār*–'house (place) of a lamb'; Gk. *Baithchor, Belchor*]. A place mentioned only in 1 S. 7:11, "And the men of Israel went out of Mizpeh and pursued the Philistines, and smote them, as far as below Beth-car." Ain Kârim has been suggested. If Mizpah is Nebī Samwîl or nearby Tell en-Naṣbeh, then this identification is possible, as the pursuit would be along the deep Wâdī beit Hannîneh — a natural line of retreat for the Philistines to take. But the route of pursuit is uncertain and the site of Beth-car unknown.

See also BETH-HACCHEREM. J. F. PREWITT

BETH-DAGON beth-dā'gən [Heb. *bêṯ-dāgôn*–'house of (the god) Dagon']. The name of at least five localities in Palestine. The frequency of the name points to the popularity of the cult of Dagon among the Canaanites.

1. A town belonging to Ṣidqa of Ashkelon, conquered by Sennacherib in 701 (Taylor Prism ii.65), on the Madeba Map "(bēto)degana." The name has been preserved in Beth Dejān, 6 mi. (10 km.) SE of Jaffa, identical with Caferdago (Eusebius *Onom.* 50.16).

2. Present-day Beth Dejān 7 mi. (11 km.) E of Nablus, with the ruins of a Samaritan synagogue.

3. A town in upper Galilee, mentioned in Tosephta, present-day Beth Jenn, 7 mi. (11 km.) W of Safed.

4. A town of Judah (Josh. 15:41), mentioned also in a list of Ramses III, where it is preceded by *rbnt*=Libnah (cf. Josh. 15:42). Probably it is to be looked for in the region of Lachish; some identify it with **1.**

5. A town near the boundary between Asher and Zebulun (Josh. 19:27), unidentified, probably about 3 mi. (5 km.) W of Galilean Bethlehem (Khirbet Buṣin?).

Bibliography.–M. Avi-Yonah, *The Holy Land from the Persian to the Arab Conquests* (1966), p. 158, Register; E. Honigmann, *Reallexikon der Assyriologie* (1929), *s.v.* "Ašqalûna"; J. Simons, *Handbook for the study of Egyptian Topographical Lists* (1937), p. 168; M. Noth, *Das Buch Josua* (2nd ed. 1953), *in loc.*

A. VAN SELMS

BETH-DIBLATHAIM beth-dib-lə-thā'im [Heb. *bêṯ diḇlāṯayim*–'house of Diblathaim']. A town in Moab mentioned with Dibon and Nebo (Jer. 48:22). It is probably identical with ALMON-DIBLATHAIM (Nu. 33:46f.), a stopping place during the Exodus. Mesha claims to have fortified it along with Medeba and Baal-meon (*see* MOABITE STONE). It may be Khirbet Deleilât esh-Sherqîyeh. D. B. PECOTA

BETH-EDEN beth-ē'dən [Heb. *bêṯ 'eḏen*–(as pointed) 'house (place) of delight']; AV HOUSE OF EDEN. A place named in the prophecy of Amos against Damascus (Am. 1:5). In view of the parallelism of Amos' words, it seems most likely that "Valley of Aven" should be read as *Biq'aṯ 'Ôn* (Valley of Heliopolis=Baalbek), the prophecy accordingly referring to the Aramean city-states of Damascus and Bit-adini. The LXX, in fact, lends support to this translation by reading "from the men of Haran" — for Haran was in Bit-adini. "The people of Eden" (AV "children of Eden") in 2 K. 19:12=Isa. 37:12, and "Eden" in Ezk. 27:23, likewise probably refer to (Bit-) Adini.

Bibliography.–A. Dupont-Sommer, *Les Araméens* (1949), pp. 22-24, 35; *GTTOT*, §§ 1494f.; S. Moscati, *Ancient Semitic Civilizations* (1957), pp. 169f. W. S. L. S.

BETH-EGLAIM beth-eg'lā-əm [Gk. *Bēthaglaim*]. The name, which does not occur in the Bible, is applied by some archeologists to the site of modern Tell el-'Ajjûl, 4 mi. (6.5 km.) SW of GAZA. Fruitful excavations have led to the discovery of fortifications and other structures, pottery, and other artifacts of the Hyksos and post-Hyksos periods of Egyptian history. With the onset of the Iron Age and the arrival of the Philistines, Egyptian influence and the importance of Beth-eglaim decreased. Cf. Eusebius *Onom.*, *s.v.* "Bethaglaim."

Bibliography.–W. F. Albright, *AJSL*, 55 (1938), 337-359; C. Eppstein, *PEQ*, 93 (1961), 137-142; *AOTS*, pp. 405-411.

G. WYPER

BETH-EKED beth-ē'kəd [Heb. *bêṯ-'ēqeḏ*; Gk. *Baithakad*, B *Baithakath*] (2 K. 10:12, 14); AV "shearing house"; NEB "shelter" (v. 12), Beth-eker (mg.), "(the pit) that was there" (v. 14). A place where Jehu met and killed forty-two men in the course of his extinction of the house of Ahab. Eusebius (*Onom.*, *s.v.*) calls it Bethacath and locates it 15 mi. (24 km.) from Legio in the plain. This points to identification with Beit Kâd, about 3 mi. (5 km.) E of Jenîn.

BETHEL beth'əl [Heb. *bêṯ-'ēl*–'house of God'; Gk. *Baithēl, oíkos theoú*].

1. A city located W of Ai on the main N-S watershed route near where the boundaries of Benjamin and Ephraim met. It was situated about 12 mi. (19 km.) N of Jerusalem, and was identified with the modern Tell Beitîn by Edward Robinson in the 19th century. This mound has been excavated at various times between 1934 and 1957 under Albright and Kelso. In antiquity the site was noted for the numerous springs present on the mountain ridge, and these have remained perennial features of the terrain.

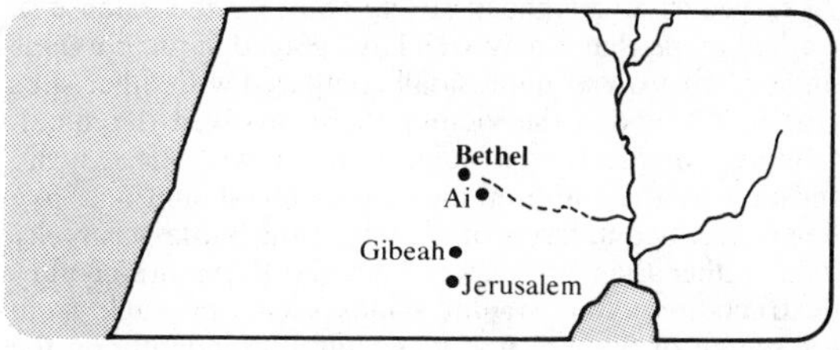

Although excavations have uncovered traces of earlier occupation, the city proper seems to have been founded somewhat prior to the Middle Bronze Age, perhaps *ca.* 2000 B.C. In the early Hyksos period, *ca.* 1750 B.C., a city wall on the north side constructed of well-fitted stones to a depth of about 11 ft. (3.3 m.) was reinforced with a wide clay revetment, and about a century later a number of defensive buildings were constructed inside the wall and close to the city gate. Another wall uncovered at the west of the tell was also early, but its gate had been replaced by a defensive tower with a Hyksos type of revetment.

The city was well established by the time it was mentioned in the patriarchal narratives in the Middle Bronze Age (*ca.* 1950-1550 B.C.). Abraham halted near Bethel on his way S from Shechem, and offered sacrifice to God. After visiting Egypt he returned there (Gen. 13:3). Bethel, originally known as Luz (Gen. 28:19), became particularly significant to the Hebrews in the time of Jacob, who received a divine revelation there from the "God of Bethel" (Gen. 31:13). Thereupon Jacob named the place "house of God," and set up a pillar as a memorial. (*See also* EL-BETHEL). On his return from Haran Jacob was summoned to Bethel, where he built an altar and set up another pillar, again giving the name "Bethel" to the site. Most probably the location (cf. Gen. 28:11) was the one where Abraham had offered sacrifice in an earlier generation. The site may be that of Burj Beitan, SE of Tell Beitîn (cf. Josh. 18:13, RSV). At about this time Jacob ordered his household to put away their Mesopotamian idols, and shortly afterward his name was changed to Israel. The renewal of the Abrahamic covenant with Jacob at Bethel (Gen. 35:10ff.) related the city intimately to the origins of Israelite faith. At Bethel, Deborah the nurse of Rebekah was buried (Gen. 35:6f.), and it was probably on the uplands E of the city that Abraham and Lot stood to look across the highlands to the rich terrain of the Jordan Valley.

At the beginning of the Late Bronze Age (*ca.* 1550 B.C.) a strong city wall was erected around Bethel, and this was accompanied by the construction of sturdy houses. Excavations at this level show that the period was one of considerable prosperity, with luxury goods being imported from Egypt to that part of the country. In the period of Joshua it was a royal city of the Canaanites (Josh. 12:16), and appears to have been captured by Joshua (8:7), though the destruction of Bethel was not mentioned specifically in the narrative. However, thirteenth-century B.C. levels at Bethel revealed that the city had been sacked and burned at that time, as indicated by the vast quantities of charred debris, burned brick, and ashes at the lower Bronze Age levels. On the basis of such evidence this destruction has been assigned to the Israelite invasion in the latter part of the 13th cent. B.C. (Josh. 12:16; Jgs. 1:22ff.).

The Israelite campaign against Ai and Bethel contains certain problematical features. Et-Tell, commonly identified with Ai, gives no indication of thirteenth-century destruction, yet Bethel, which was thoroughly obliterated, was unmentioned in this connection. The two sites were very close together, and it seems highly probable that Ai served as an advanced strong point for the defense of Bethel, a role that it may well have played in the previous millennium. Ai was quite small compared with other sites (Josh. 7:3); and if the victory there involved the simultaneous conquest of a neighboring town, there is no reason why the entire military operation should not have been described in terms of Ai, where the battle was really won, rather than of Bethel. That the thirteenth-century destruction was at Israelite hands seems probable from the nature of the city that was built subsequently on the site, where the crude constructional techniques contrast strongly with the elegance of earlier dwellings.

The Israelite conquest of Bethel marked the transition from the late Bronze Age to the Iron Age. The city was given to the tribes of the house of Joseph who had captured it, particularly to Benjamin (Josh. 18:22). The road from Jericho to Bethel formed the boundary between Ephraim and Benjamin (Josh. 18:13), and when the latter was virtually wiped out (Jgs. 20:1-48) the city seems to have passed into Ephraimite control (cf. 1 Ch. 7:28). The ark of the covenant was brought to Bethel from Gilgal (Jgs. 2:1, LXX), and during this period Bethel became an important center of worship (Jgs. 20:18). It was still a sanctuary in the days of Samuel, and he visited the city annually on circuit to judge the Israelites (1 S. 7:16; 10:3). Deborah the prophetess lived in the vicinity of Bethel (Jgs. 4:5). Toward the end of the judges period the ark was moved to Shiloh, probably to avoid capture by the Philistines. If one of the levels of destruction in the Iron Age occurred while the ark was still at Bethel, it would probably represent a Philistine attack earlier than the campaign against Shiloh (1 S. 4–6) in which the ark was captured and taken to Philistine territory. In the time of Saul, Bethel lost its prominence to nearby Gibeah, which was established in Benjaminite territory as the capital of the new ruler. Although the Philistines fought a battle near Bethel (1 S. 12–14), there is no archeological evidence that the city was actually conquered at that time. Under David its influence waned still further with the establishing of Jerusalem as the capital of the monarchy, though excavations have shown that Bethel was a prosperous farming center at that time.

With the disruption of the kingdom came Bethel's greatest period of splendor and prominence. To counteract the influence of Jerusalem as the national religious center, Jeroboam I erected an independent shrine in Bethel, instituted a new priesthood, adopted a different religious calendar, and set up the golden calves as new cultic images. The north sanctuary at Dan never equaled in splendor that of Bethel, which became the royal sanctuary and the focus of religious life in the northern kingdom (1 K. 12:29ff.; Am. 7:13). To Bethel came the man of God from Judah who pronounced doom against Jeroboam (1 K. 13). The Judean King Abijah (913-910 B.C.) captured it (2 Ch. 13:19), and his son Asa (910-869 B.C.) probably subjugated it also (cf. 2 Ch. 14:8).

A prophetic guild appears to have existed in Bethel and had some contact with Elisha (2 K. 2:3); but according to Amos and Hosea, Canaanite religion with its terrible moral, social, and religious degradations was dominant at Bethel. Because it was synonymous with the very worst elements of paganism and idolatry, these two prophets launched the most scathing denunciations against it. Amos condemned the rites of the royal sanctuary (Am. 4:4; 5:5f.; 7:13), while Hosea (10:15) prophesied the destruction of the king of Israel. Even Jeremiah commented in retrospect upon the futility of the cultic rites at Bethel (Jer. 48:13). With Hosea the name Beth-aven became a condemnatory surrogate for Bethel (Hos. 4:15; 5:8; 10:8), the place of supreme idolatry. The prophets pointed out that unless Israel repented and turned afresh in faith to God, such a gross violation of covenant love could only end in destruction. The latter came about when the Assyrians under Sargon II (722-705 B.C.) overthrew the northern kingdom and carried the tribes captive to Assyria. While Bethel shared in this general fate there is no specific mention in the OT or the cuneiform texts that it was destroyed, nor do excavations at the site give indication of damage or fire at Assyrian levels.

The territory around Bethel was repopulated by Assyrian colonists, who intermarried with the local population; and when a plague of mountain lions threatened community life the superstitious colonists sent to Assyria for a deported priest to instruct them in the law of Yahweh, god of the land (2 K. 17:28). This priest settled at Bethel, and was instrumental in building up the religious tradition that was later described as Samaritan. Worship continued in the area until King Josiah took advantage of a decline in Assyrian power to invade the northern territories and destroy the existing pagan sanctuaries. The shrine at Bethel was demolished and its priests were dispersed (2 K. 23:15ff.), but Bethel itself was spared. Perhaps the sanctuary lay outside the city proper, near the site of the patriarchal altars, since archeologists to date have been unable to locate any traces of it in the city mound. Nebuchadrezzar spared Bethel from destruction, probably because of its past association with Assyrian colonists; but during the 6th cent. B.C. the city was destroyed by fire, at the hands of either Nabonidus of Babylon or the Persian armies.

After the Exile the men of Bethel were among those who returned from Babylonia under Zerubbabel (Ezr. 2:28; Neh. 7:32), at which time the site was apparently reoccupied by Benjaminite families (Neh. 11:31). Bethel never again became a separate sanctuary, and worship from that time on was centered upon Jerusalem (Zec. 7:2). The city was one of the fortifications established by Bacchides in the time of the Maccabees, *ca.* 160 B.C. (1 Macc. 9:50; Josephus *Ant.* xiii.1.3), and was again mentioned as a town that, along with Ephraim, was captured in A.D. 69 by Vespasian as he approached Jerusalem (Josephus *BJ* iv.9.9).

The NT makes no reference to Bethel, although at that time the city was at its greatest size since OT days. It reached its highest level of population in the Byzantine period, and archeological excavations have so far been unable to explain why Bethel suddenly ceased to exist at the time of the transition from the Byzantine to the Arabic period. The site lay in ruins thereafter until the 19th cent., when it was reoccupied by Arabs from nearby Burka.

2. A city in Judah (1 S. 30:27) called in Josh. 19:4 "Bethul," and in 1 Ch. 4:30 "Bethuel." The site has not been identified to date.

Bibliography.–W. F. Albright, *BASOR*, 55 (Oct. 1934), 24f.; 56 (Dec. 1934), 1-15; J. L. Kelso, *BASOR*, 137 (Feb. 1955), 5-9; 151 (Oct. 1958), 3-8; Kelso, *et al., Excavation of Bethel (1934-1960)* (1968).

W. EWING
R. K. HARRISON

BETHEL (deity). A West Semitic god, originating perhaps among the Phoenicians or Arameans, current from the time of Esarhaddon of Assyria (7th cent. B.C.) until Darius II of Babylon (5th cent. B.C.). The name is also seen as part of some Jewish personal names from Elephantine, and in the documents from Râs Shamrah. Some scholars find a reference to this deity in Gen. 31:13; Jer. 48:13; Am. 5:5.

Bibliography.–J. P. Hyatt, *JAOS*, 59 (1939), 81-98; *ARI*, pp. 168-175.

G. WYPER

BETHEL, HILL COUNTRY OF [Heb. *har bêṯ-'ēl*] (1 S. 13:2); AV MOUNT BETHEL. The Heb. *har* can designate either "mountain" or "hill." The term here refers to no specific mountain, but a hilly area. Thus the RSV and NEB translation is preferable to the AV. In Josh. 16:1 the RSV and NEB read "hill country to Bethel," while the AV again has "mount Bethel," for Heb. *har bêṯ-'ēl*. *See also* HILL.

BETHEL, MOUNT (AV Josh. 16:1; 1 S. 13:2). *See* BETHEL, HILL COUNTRY OF.

BETHELITE beth'əl-īt [Heb. *bêṯ hā'ᵉlî*] (1 K. 16:34, AV). A man of Bethel. *See* HIEL.

BETH-EMEK beth-ē'mək [Heb. *bêṯ hā'ēmeq*–'house (place) of the valley']. A town in the territory of Asher (Josh. 19:27). The location is uncertain, but it may possibly be identified with modern Tell Mīmâs, about 6.5 mi. (10.5 km.) NE of Acre (Acco).

W. W. BUEHLER

BETHER bē'thər [Heb. *beṯer*; Gk. A *Baither*, B *Thethēr*] (Josh. 15:59). A village 5 mi. (8 km.) SW of Jerusalem in the allotment of Judah. Reference to "the mountains of Bether" in the AV of Cant. 2:17 is a dubious translation (but *see* MALOBATHRON); the RSV conjectures "rugged mountains," the NEB, "the hills where cinnamon grows." In 1 Ch. 6:59 (LXX 44), LXX A reads Gk. *Baiththēr* (instead of Beth-shemesh). This spelling is found also in Eusebius *HE* iv.6, and in the Talmud (*bttr*), and would explain the modern Arabic spelling Bittîr. It would also militate against the suggested etymology *Beṯer* < *Beṯ har*, "house of the mountain."

On the nearby height Khirbet ej-Jehûdiyeh, Bar Cochba had his capital and was besieged by the Romans in A.D. 135. A Latin inscription marks the location.

Bibliography.–*GP*, II, 271; W. D. Carroll, *AASOR*, 5 (1924/25), 77-103.

W. S. L. S.

BETHESDA bə-thez'də [Gk. *Bēthesda*, prob. < Aram. *bêṯḥisdā'*–'house of mercy'; Gk. variants *Bēth-zatha* and *Bēthsaida* have strong MS support]; RSV BETH-ZATHA. A pool in Jerusalem, mentioned in the NT only in Jn. 5:2 in the account of Jesus' healing by a word a man who had been sick for thirty-eight years and who was lying in a pillared porch of the pool. According to a less well-attested text (the koine recension; vv. 3b, 4) he was hoping to be the first to be carried into the pool after the waters had acquired momentary healing powers by being disturbed by an angel (cf. v. 7).

The story locates the incident near the Sheepgate of Jerusalem, which, since it was constructed by the priests (Neh. 3:1), must have been one of the entrances to the temple area. It is regularly placed on the north facing the suburb called Bezetha.

Early tradition speaks of twin pools having five porticoes and known as the Sheep Pool or Bethesda. Pilgrim reports locate the site more exactly by noting the erection of a church in the first half of the 5th cent. in memory of the healing of the "lame" man N of the temple not far from the city gate leading to the Kidron.

Archeological discoveries and excavations support the tradition that the Pool of Bethesda is to be found at the foot of Mt. Bezetha largely within the property of St. Anne's Church, which belongs to the White Fathers.

In the process of restoring the Church of St. Anne in 1866 a marble foot from the 2nd cent. A.D. was found bearing the Greek inscription "devoted by Pompeia Lucilia." This suggests that physical healing was associated by the Romans with this location. The two cisterns, of which the eastern is approached by a medieval staircase and is frequently shown as the Pool of Bethesda, are but a small part of the north pool and are later constructions, though the eastern cistern may date from the Roman period and have been used for storing drinking water.

Ruins of Byzantine and Crusader churches built over the Pool of Bethesda (B. Van Elderen)

In 1914 S of the two cisterns a second pool was discovered separated from the north pool by an east-west dike over 20 ft. (6 m.) in breadth. This wall is doubtless the site of the fifth pillared hall mentioned by Cyril of Jerusalem and Theodore of Mopsuestia. In 1938 van der Pliet suggested that the pools formed an unsymmetrical trapezoid. Vincent demonstrated that the columns were over 22 ft. (6.7 m.) high and the hall about 27.5 ft. (8.4 m.) high and of the Roman period. Recent extension of the excavations to the east uncovered a vaulted subterranean gallery covered with paintings no longer identifiable, which Rousée suggests may have been a sanctuary of Roman times.

The history of the site may be tentatively reconstructed as follows. Presumably during the time of Herod two large reservoirs were built in the valley coming down from the north. The location of the pools may have been determined by the presence of a seasonal intermittent spring as well as by the possibility of collecting the rainwater of the valley. Locally the site may have been known as the Sheep Pool because it was near the Sheep Gate; it could have been used for watering the flocks.

Vincent supposes that in connection with his building the temple, Herod the Great, because of the healing powers of the waters, constructed the splendid five-porticoed building. Presumably Sheep Pool would be too common a name for such a beautiful pool, and so Bethesda, suggesting the site where God's mercy was shown in healing, became the proper name. Since the pool was located in a district known in the time of Josephus as Bezetha, it may on occasion have been referred to as the Be(th)zatha pool.

In the 5th cent., in order to supplant the pagan sanctuary and to commemorate the healing of Jn. 5:2, a Byzantine church was built partly on the pools and partly on solid ground to the east.

On the ruins of the old Bethesda church the Crusaders built a chapel probably between 1177 and 1187 and constructed a stairway to the Roman cistern at the southeast corner of the north pool.

On the basis of excavations of a cave E of the two pools since 1956, Père Benoit has proposed an alternative view: that with Herod the Great's construction of the Pool of Israel closer to the temple those pools went out of use, and that the miracle should now be associated with the reddish-hued waters of that cave.

Bibliography.–*SSW*, pp. 335-342; J. Jeremias, *Die Wiederentdeckung von Bethesda* (1949); J. Rousée, *RB*, 69 (1962), 80-109; P. Benoit, in J. Aviram, ed., *Jerusalem through the Ages (Yerushalayim ledoroteha)* (1968), pp. 48*-57*; A. Duprez, *Jésus et les Dieux Guérrisseurs; à propos de Jean V* (1970).

D. J. WIEAND

BETH-EZEL beth-ē'zəl [Heb. *bêṯ hā'ēṣel*–lit. 'adjoining house'; Gk. *oíkos echómenos autḗs*]. A town in southern Judea mentioned in connection with other cities of the Shephelah and Philistine plain (Mic. 1:11). At one time it was thought to be the same as Azel of Zec. 14:5; but it has now been identified with Deir el-'Aṣal about 10 mi. (16 km.) SW of Hebron. J. F. PREWITT

BETH-GADER beth-gā'dər [Heb. *bêṯ-gāḏēr*–'house of the stone wall'(?)]. One of the descendants of Judah (1 Ch. 2:51), possibly the same as Geder (Josh. 12:13). Note that most of the names in this section of Chronicles are identical with place names: Salma was the "father" of Bethlehem, Hareph the "father" of Beth-gader, Shobal the "father" of Kiriath-jearim, etc. W. S. L. S.

BETH-GAMUL beth-gā'məl [Heb. *bêṯ gāmûl*–'house of reward'; Gk. *oíkos Gaimōl,* ℵ *Gamōla*]. An unwalled city in the plain country of Moab, denounced by Jeremiah (48:23). Since it does not appear in the earlier lists of Numbers and Joshua, it may be a city of late date or a city S of the Arnon, possibly Khirbet Jemeil. A Nabatean inscription dating perhaps from the 2nd cent. A.D. was discovered here. D. B. PECOTA

BETH-GILGAL beth-gil'gal [Heb. *bêṯ haggilgāl*]. A city likely settled by part of the temple singers of postexilic Israel (Neh. 12:29). Some suggest that it is the Gilgal of Benjamin's possession situated E of Jericho (Josh. 4:19, etc.), while others suggest the Gilgal of Judah's territory (Josh. 15:7). The latter passage is not clear, because the parallel passage in Josh. 18:17 calls the place Geliloth. The exact site is still unknown.

D. McINTOSH

BETH-HACCHEREM beth-ha-ke'rəm [Heb. *Bêṯ-hakkerem*–'house (place) of the vineyard'; Gk. *Bēthachcharma*]; AV BETH-HACCEREM; NEB BETH-HAKKEREM. A district in Judea ruled by Malchiah as governor in the days of Nehemiah (Neh. 3:14). Jeremiah seems to indicate that it was a vantage point from which signal fires could be seen throughout the surrounding territory (Jer. 6:1). On the top of Jebel Ali above the village of 'Ain Kârim are some remarkable cairns, which would appear to have been used as beacons.

Beth-haccherem is mentioned in 3QInv (3Q*15*) and 1QapGen. Both relate it with the Valley of the King in which stands the tomb of Absalom (2 S. 18:18). From its association with Tekoa (Jer. 6:1), and from the statement by Jerome that it was a village that he could see from Bethlehem, the Frank Mountain (Herodium) has been suggested. This identification is unlikely. Pfeiffer suggests that the ancient sources all support a location in the vicinity of modern Ramat Raḥel about midway between Jerusalem and Bethlehem. Modern Israel has assigned the name to a new community about 1.5 mi. (2.4 km.) SW of Jerusalem near Mt. Herzl on the road leading to the valley and village of 'Ain Kârim.

Bibliography.–Y. Aharoni, *IEJ*, 6 (1956), 102-111, 137-157.

J. F. PREWITT

BETH-HAGGAN beth-hag'ən [Heb. *bêṯ-haggān*–'house (place) of the garden']. A place toward which Ahaziah fled from Jehu (2 K. 9:27). The AV translates "garden house," but modern scholars incline to the identification with EN-GANNIM **(2)** (Josh. 19:21), called in NT times Ginaea, modern Jenîn, about 11 mi. (18 km.) SE of Megiddo. W. S. L. S.

BETH-HANAN beth-hā'nən (1 K. 4:9, NEB). *See* ELONBETH-HANAN.

BETH-HARAM beth-hā'rəm [Heb. *bêṯ hārām*] (Josh. 13:27); AV, wrongly, BETH-ARAM; **BETH-HARAN** beth-hā'rən [Heb. *bêṯ hārān*] (Nu. 32:36). An Amorite city taken and fortified by the Gadites. Beth-haran was probably the original form of the name.

It was in good pasture but in the valley, and therefore lacked the security of hill fastnesses. It corresponds to Betharamphtha of Josephus (*Ant.* xviii.2.1), which according to Eusebius was the name used by the Syrians. Here was a palace of Herod (*Ant.* xvii.10.6, here called Amathus; *BJ* ii.4.2). Eusebius (*Onom.*) says it was called Livias. Josephus says it was fortified by Herod Antipas, who called it Julias for the wife of Augustus (*Ant.* xviii.2.1; *BJ* ii.9.1). It is identified with modern Tell Iktanû 8 mi. (13 km.) NE of the mouth of the Jordan. D. B. PECOTA

BETH-HOGLAH beth-hog'lə [Heb. *bêṯ ḥoglâ*–'house (place) of partridge'; Gk. *Baithaglaam*] (Josh. 15:6; 18:19, 21). A city of Benjamin along its southern border and along the northern border of the tribe of Judah. The name is preserved in 'Ain Hajlah ("partridge spring") between Jericho and the Jordan.

G. F. WRIGHT

BETH-HORON beth-hôr'ən [Heb. *bêṯ-ḥôrôn*–prob. 'place of the hollow' (other Hebrew forms occur); Gk. *Bethōrōn*]. The name of two towns, Beth-horon the Upper (Josh. 16:5) and Beth-horon the Nether or Lower (Josh. 16:3), located a few miles apart in the pass that ascends from the plain of Aijalon (Yâlō) to the western plateau near Gibeon (el-Jîb). The lower city was at an elevation of about 1210 ft. (369 m.) above sea level. The upper city was about 2022 ft. (616 m.) above sea level. Although the pass was rugged and steep it was the great highway from the plain into the plateau that was the heart of Judea. The importance of this pass as the main approach to the interior of the country explains the frequent enlargement and fortification of these two towns through many centuries.

When Joshua overcame the Amorites, "Israel . . . slew them with a great slaughter at Gibeon, and chased them by the way of the ascent of Beth-horon . . ." (Josh. 10:10). When the land was apportioned to the Israelites the two Beth-horons were assigned to Ephraim and stood on the border between Ephraim and Benjamin (Josh. 16:5; 18:13f.). One of the cities was assigned to the Levite family of Kohath (21:22). Both cities were enlarged and fortified by Sheerah the daughter of Beriah (1 Ch. 7:24). When the Philistines were opposing King Saul at Michmash they sent a company of their men "toward Beth-horon" (1 S. 13:17f.). Solomon further expanded and fortified both Upper and Lower Beth-horon "with walls, gates, and bars" (1 K. 9:17; 2 Ch. 8:5).

From Egyptian sources it appears that Beth-horon was one of the places conquered by Shishak of Egypt from Rehoboam. Centuries later Bacchides repaired Beth-horon, "with high walls and gates and bars. And he placed garrisons in them to harass Israel" (1 Macc. 9:50f.). At another time the Jews fortified it against Holofernes (Jth. 4:4f.). Along this route came Canaanites, Israelites, Philistines, Egyptians, Syrians, Romans, Saracens, and Crusaders. Since the days of Joshua it has frequently been the scene of a rout. Here the Syrian general Seron was defeated by Judas Maccabeus (1 Macc. 3:13-24); and six years later Nicanor, retreating from Jerusalem, was defeated and slain (1 Macc. 7:39; Josephus *Ant.* xii.10.5). Along this pass in A.D. 66 the Roman general Cestius Gallus was driven in headlong flight before the Jews.

Today two villages occupy the sites, Beit 'Ur el-Fōqā (i.e., "the upper") and Beit 'Ur et-Taḥtā ("the lower").

Bibliography.–HGHL, pp. 248-250, 287-292; *GP,* II, 274f.

E. W. G. MASTERMAN
J. F. PREWITT

BETH-HORON, THE BATTLE OF.

I. The Political Situation.
II. Joshua's Strategy
III. Joshua's Command
IV. Astronomical Relations
V. The "Silence" of the Sun
VI. "The Lord Fought for Israel"
VII. The Afternoon's March
VIII. The Chronicle and the Poem
IX. Date of the Events
X. The Records Contemporaneous with the Events

I. The Political Situation.–The battle that gave to the Israelites under Joshua the command of southern Palestine has always excited interest because of the astronomical marvel recorded to have taken place at that time (Josh. 10:6-14). In invading Palestine the Israelites were not attacking a single coherent state, but a country occupied by different peoples and divided, like Greece at a later period, into a number of communities, each consisting of little more than a single city and the cultivated country around it. Thus Joshua destroyed the two cities of Jericho and Ai without any interference from the other Amorites. The destruction of Jericho gave him full possession of the fertile valley of the Jordan; the taking of

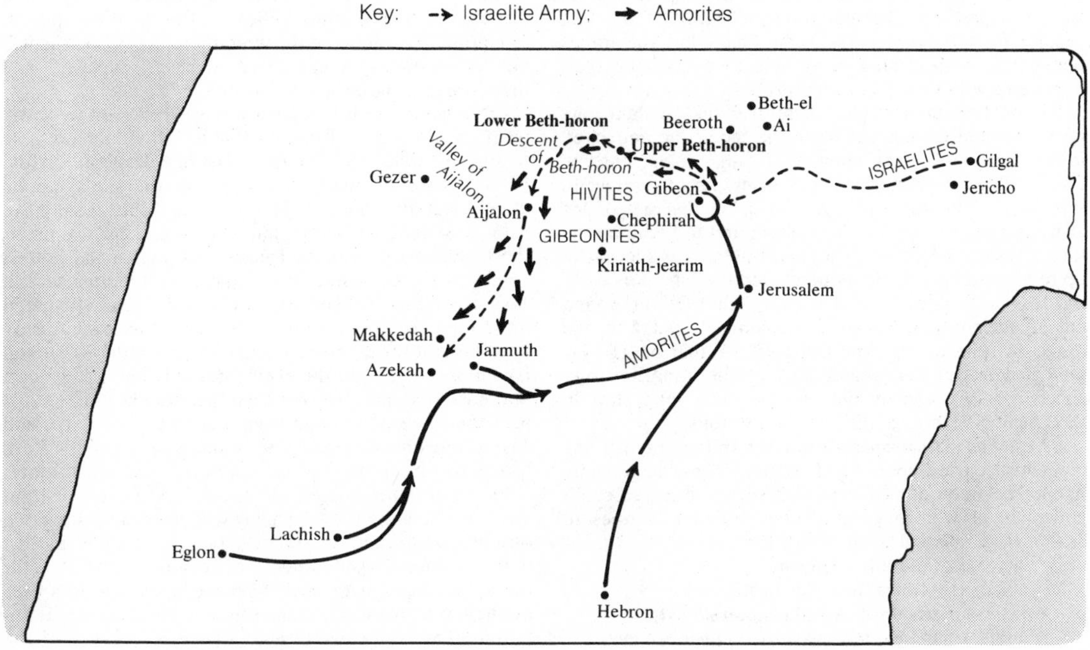

Ai opened his way up to the ridge that forms the backbone of the country, and he was able to lead the people unopposed to the mountains of Ebal and Gerizim for the solemn reading of the law. But when the Israelites returned from this ceremony a significant division showed itself among their enemies. Close to Ai, Joshua's most recent conquest, was Beeroth, a small town inhabited by Hivites; and no doubt because in the natural order of events Beeroth might be next attacked, the Hivites determined to make terms with Israel. An embassy was therefore sent from Gibeon, their chief city, and Joshua and the Israelites, believing that it came from a distant land not under the ban, entered into the proposed alliance.

The effect on the political situation was immediate. The Hivites formed a considerable state, relatively speaking; their cities were well placed on the southern highland, and Gibeon their capital was one of the most important fortresses of that district, and only 6 mi. (9 km.) distant from Jerusalem, the chief Amorite stronghold. The Amorites recognized at once that, in view of this important defection, it was imperative for them to crush the Gibeonites before the Israelites could unite with them, and this they endeavored to do. The Gibeonites, seeing themselves attacked, sent an urgent message to Joshua, and he at the head of his picked men made a night march up from Gilgal and fell upon the Amorites at Gibeon the next day and put them to flight.

II. Joshua's Strategy.–We are not told by which route he marched, but it is significant that the Amorites fled by the way of Beth-horon; that is to say, not toward their own cities, but away from them. A glance at the map shows that this means that Joshua had succeeded in cutting their line of retreat to Jerusalem. He had probably therefore advanced upon Gibeon from the south, instead of by the obvious route past Ai which he had destroyed and Beeroth with which he was in alliance. But coming up from Gilgal by the ravines in the neighborhood of Jerusalem he was exposed to a great danger, for the Amorites might have caught him before he had gained a footing on the plateau, and have taken him at a complete disadvantage. It was thus that the eleven tribes suffered such terrible loss at the hands of the Benjaminites in this very region during the first intertribal war; and probably the military significance of the first repulse from Ai was of the same character, the forces holding the high ground being able to overwhelm their opponents without any fear of reprisals.

It would seem possible, therefore, that Joshua may have repeated on a larger scale the tactics he employed in his successful attack upon Ai. He may have sent one force to draw the Amorites away from Gibeon, and when this was safely done, he may have led the rest of his army to seize the road to Jerusalem, and to break up the forces besieging Gibeon. If so, his strategy was successful up to a certain point. He evidently led the Israelites without loss up to Gibeon, crushed the Amorites there, and cut off their retreat toward Jerusalem. He failed in one thing. In spite of the prodigious efforts that he and his men had made, the greater part of the Amorite army succeeded in escaping him and gained a long start in their flight NW through the two Beth-horons.

III. Joshua's Command.–It was at this point that the incident occurred upon which attention has been chiefly fixed. The Book of Jashar (which seems to have been a collection of war songs and other ballads) ascribes to Joshua the command (Josh. 10:12f.):

"Sun, stand thou still at Gibeon,
and thou Moon in the valley of Ai'jalon."
And the sun stood still, and the moon stayed,
until the nation took vengeance on their enemies.

And the prose narrative continues, "The sun stayed in the midst of heaven, and did not hasten to go down for about a whole day."

IV. Astronomical Relations.–In these two, the ballad and the prose chronicle, we have several distinct astronomical relations indicated. The sun to Joshua was associated with Gibeon, and the sun can naturally be associated with a locality in either of two positions: it may be overhead to the observer, in which case he would consider it as being above the place where he himself was standing; or on the other hand, he might see the locality on the skyline and the sun rising or setting just behind it. In the present instance there is no ambiguity, for the chronicle distinctly states that the sun was in "the midst of heaven"; literally, in the halving of the heaven, that is to say overhead. This is very important because it assures us that Joshua must have been at Gibeon when he spoke, and that it must have been noonday of summer when the sun in southern Palestine is only about 8° or 12° from the exact zenith. Next, the moon appeared to be associated with the valley of Aijalon; i.e., it must have been low down on the horizon in that direction, and since Aijalon is NW of Gibeon it must have been about to set, which would imply that it was about half full, in its "third quarter," the sun being, as we have seen, on the meridian. Third, "the sun did not hasten to go down," that is to say, it had already attained the meridian, its culmination; and henceforward its motion was downward. The statement that it was noonday is here implicitly repeated, but a further detail is added. The going down of the sun appeared to be slow. This is the work of the afternoon, that is of half the day, but on this occasion the half-day appeared equal in length to an ordinary whole day. There is therefore no question at all of the sun becoming stationary in the sky: the statement does not admit of that, but only of its slower progress.

V. The "Silence" of the Sun.–The idea that the sun was fixed in the sky, in other words, that the earth ceased for a time to rotate on its axis, has arisen from the unfortunate rendering of the Hebrew verb *dûm*, "be silent," by "stand thou still." It is our own word "dumb," both being onomatopoeic words from the sound made when a man firmly closes his lips upon his speech. The primary meaning of the word therefore is "be silent," but its secondary meaning is "desist," "cease," and therefore in some cases "stand still."

From what was it that Joshua wished the sun to cease: from its moving or from its shining? It is not possible to suppose that, engaged as he was in a desperate battle, he was even so much as thinking of the sun's motion at all. But its shining, its scorching heat, must have been most seriously felt by him. At noon, in high summer, the highland of southern Palestine is one of the hottest countries of the world. It is impossible to suppose that Joshua wished the sun to be fixed overhead, where it must have been distressing his men who had already been on foot for seventeen hours. A very arduous pursuit lay before them, and the enemy not only had a long start but must have been fresher than the Israelites. The sun's heat therefore must have been a serious hindrance, and Joshua must have desired it to be tempered. And the Lord listened to his voice and gave him this and much more.

VI. "The Lord Fought for Israel."–A great hailstorm swept up from the west, bringing with it a sudden lowering of temperature, and no doubt hiding the sun and putting it to "silence." And "the Lord fought for Israel," for the storm burst with such violence upon the Amorites as they fled down the steep descent between the Beth-horons that "there were more who died because of the hailstones than the men of Israel killed with the sword" (v. 11). This was the culminating incident of the day, the one that so greatly impressed the sacred historian. "There has been no day like it before or since, when the Lord hearkened to the voice of a man" (v. 14). It was not the hailstorm in itself nor the veiling of the sun that made the day so remarkable. It was that Joshua had spoken, not in prayer or supplication, but in command, as if all Nature were at his disposal; and the Lord had hearkened and had, as it were, obeyed a human voice: an anticipation of the time when a greater Joshua would command even the winds and the sea, and they would obey Him (Mt. 8:23-27).

VII. The Afternoon's March.–The explanation of the statement that the sun "did not hasten to go down for about a whole day" is found in v. 10, in which it is stated that the Lord discomfited the Amorites before Israel, "who slew them with a greater slaughter at Gibeon, and chased them by the way of the ascent of Beth-horon, and smote them as far as Azekah and Makkedah." The Israelites had of course no time-keepers, no clocks or watches, and the only mode of measuring time available to them was the number of miles they marched. Now from Gibeon to Makkedah by the route indicated is some 30 mi. (48 km.), a full day's march for an army. It is possible that, at the end of the campaign, the Israelites on their return found the march from Makkedah to Gibeon heavy work for an entire day. Measured by the only means available to them, that afternoon seemed to be double the ordinary length. The sun had not hastened "to go down for about a whole day."

VIII. The Chronicle and the Poem.–Joshua's reference to the moon in connection with the valley of Aijalon appears at first sight irrelevant, and has frequently been assumed to be merely inserted to complete the parallelism of the poem. But when examined astronomically it becomes clear that it cannot have been inserted haphazardly. Joshua must have mentioned the moon because he actually saw it at the moment of speaking. Given that the sun was "in the midst of heaven," above Gibeon, there was only a very restricted arc of the horizon in which the moon could appear as associated with some terrestrial object; and from Gibeon, the valley of Aijalon does lie within that narrow arc. It follows therefore that unless the position assigned to the moon had been obtained from actual observation at the moment, it would in all probability have been an impossible position. The next point is especially interesting. The ballad does not expressly state whether the sun was upon Gibeon in the sense of being upon it low down on the distant horizon, or upon it, in the sense of being overhead both to Joshua and to that city. It becomes clear that the latter is the only possible solution. The moon was above the valley of Aijalon. The sun and moon cannot both have been setting — though this is the idea that has been generally held, on the supposition that the day was far spent and that Joshua desired it to be prolonged — for then sun and moon would have been close together and the moon would be invisible. The sun cannot have been setting and the moon rising; for Aijalon is W of Gibeon. Nor can the sun have been rising and the moon setting, since this would imply that the time of year was either about Oct. 30 of our present calendar, or about Feb. 12. The month of February was already past, since the Israelites had kept the Feast of the Passover. October cannot have come; for since Beeroth, Gibeon, and Jerusalem were so close together it is certain that the events between the return of the Israelites to Gilgal and the battle of Beth-horon cannot have been spread over several months, but must have occupied only a few days. The poem therefore contains implicitly the same fact that is explicitly stated in the prose narrative — that the sun was overhead — but the one statement cannot, in those days, have been inferred from the other.

IX. Date of the Events.–A third point of interest is that the position of the moon gives an indication of the time of the year. The valley of Aijalon is 17° N of W from Gibeon, of which the latitude is 31° 51′ north. With these details, and assuming the time to be nearly noon, the date must have been about the twenty-first day of the fourth month of the Jewish calendar, corresponding to July 22 of our present calendar, with an uncertainty of one or two days on either side. The sun's declination would then be about 21° N, so that at noon it was within 11° of the zenith. It had risen almost exactly at 5:00 A.M. and would set almost exactly at 7:00 P.M. The moon was now about third quarter, and in north latitude about 5°. It had risen about 11:00 the previous night, and was now at an altitude of under 7°, and within about half an hour of setting. The conditions are not sufficient to fix the year, since from the nature of the luni-solar cycle there will always be one or two years in each cycle of nineteen that will satisfy the conditions of the case, and the date of the Hebrew invasion of Palestine is not known with sufficient certainty to limit the inquiry to any particular cycle.

X. The Records Contemporaneous with the Events.–It will be seen, however, that the astronomical conditions introduced by the mention of the moon are much more stringent than might have been expected. They supply therefore proof of a high order that the astronomical details, both of the poem and prose chronicle, were derived from actual observation at the time and have been preserved to us unaltered. Each, therefore, supplies a strictly contemporaneous and independent record.

This great occurrence appears to be referred to in one other passage of Scripture — the Prayer of Habakkuk. Here again the rendering of the English versions is unfortunate, and the passage should stand:

The sun and moon ceased [to shine] in their habitation;
At the light of Thine arrows they vanished,
And at the shining of Thy glittering spear.
Thou didst march through the land in indignation,
Thou didst thresh the nations in anger (Hab. 3:11f.).

E. W. MAUNDER

BETH-JESHIMOTH beth-jesh′ə-moth [Heb. *bêṯ hayyᵉšîmōṯ*; Gk. B *Haisimōth,* A *Asimōth,* and other variants]. One of the final stopping places of the Exodus, mentioned as the point in the south from which the camp of Israel in the plains of Moab stretched N to Abel-shittim (Nu. 33:49). It was assigned to Reuben (Josh. 13:20), but later is mentioned as one of the important cities of Moab (Ezk. 25:9). It is most likely the modern Tell el-ʻAzeimeh near the northeast shore of the Dead Sea. Close by is a Roman settlement whose Greek name was Besimoth, the modern Khirbet es-Sweimeh. D. B. PECOTA

BETH-LE-APHRAH beth-lə-af′rə [Heb. *bêṯ lᵉʻaprâ*–ʻhouse of dust'; Gk. *ex oíkou katá gélōta*]; AV "house of Aphrah"; NEB BETH-APHRAH. A settlement in the Philistine plain mentioned only in Mic. 1:10. As in the other couplets in this passage (vv. 10-16), Micah puns on the name: "In Beth-le-aphrah / roll yourselves in the dust (*ʻāp̄ār*)." The word for "roll yourselves" (*hiṯpallāšiṯî*) may also be a pun on "Philistines" (*pᵉlištîm*). Cf. G. A. Smith, *Book of the Twelve Prophets* (rev. ed. 1928), *in loc.*; *IB*, VI, *in loc.*

BETH-LEBAOTH beth-lə-bā′oth [Heb. *bêṯ lᵉḇā'ôṯ*–ʻhouse

Manger Square and Church of the Nativity at Bethlehem. Marking the site of Constantine's basilica, the present church was built by Justinian I (A.D. 527-565). (W. S. LaSor)

of lionesses']. A town in the territory of Simeon (Josh. 19:6). In 1 Ch. 4:31 the name is given as BETH-BIRI.

BETHLEHEM beth'lə-hem [Heb. *bêṯ leḥem*–'house of bread' or possibly 'house of Lakhmu,' an Assyrian deity; Gk. A, NT, *Bēthleem,* B *Baithleem*; Josephus *Bēthleemōn, Bēthleemēs,* etc.].

1. Bethlehem-judah, or EPHRATH or Ephrathah, a town located on the edge of the desert of Judah, 5 mi. (8 km.) S of Jerusalem, 2500 ft. (760 m.) above sea level, situated on a rocky spur of the mountains of Judah just off the main road to Hebron and Egypt. It has a typical Mediterranean climate, which is made milder through its altitude and the nearness of the sea. The average temperature in summer is 73°F (23°C), in winter 57°F (14°C). The average annual rainfall has been 18.5 in. (47 cm.). Bethlehem is surrounded by fertile fields, fig and olive orchards, and vineyards.

I. OT History.–In 1 Ch. 2:51 Salma the son of Caleb is described as the "father of Bethlehem." In Gen. 35:19; 48:7 it is recorded that Rachel was buried in Bethlehem (*see* RACHAEL'S TOMB). The Levites mentioned in Jgs. 17 and 19 were Bethlehemites. Bethlehem is the stage for the love idyll of Ruth and Boaz (Ruth 4:11). Rehoboam, son and successor of King Solomon, fortified Bethlehem to guard the approach to Jerusalem (2 Ch. 11:5f.). After the return of the Jews from exile (*ca.* 538 B.C.). Bethlehem was sparsely populated (Ezr. 2:21; Neh. 7:26).

David himself is declared "the son of that Ephrathite of Bethlehem-judah, whose name was Jesse" (1 S. 17:12). Samuel was sent to Bethlehem to anoint David as successor to unworthy Saul (16:1f., 12). At Bethlehem David went about feeding his father's sheep (17:5). In the days of David the town was occupied by a garrison of the Philistines (2 S. 23:14; 1 Ch. 11:16). David's men broke through the host of Philistines to draw water out of the well of Bethlehem and brought it to David (2 S. 23:16). According to tradition, the well is a short distance NE of Bethlehem. David's nephews, the sons of Zeruiah (1 Ch. 2:15f.), came from Bethlehem; Asahel, one of the nephews, was buried "in the sepulchre of his father, which was Bethlehem" (2 S. 2:32).

Though Bethlehem became an insignificant town after the time of David, Mic. 5:2 indicates its future fame. Matthew and the Fourth Gospel acknowledge this to be a prophecy of the birth of the Messiah (Mt. 2:5f.; Jn. 7:42).

II. Christian Era.–In the NT Bethlehem is mentioned as the birthplace of the Messiah (Mt. 2:1, 5; Lk. 2:4, 15) and the locale of Herod's "massacre of the innocents" (Mt. 2:8, 16). The cave-stable is mentioned by Justin Martyr (*Dial.* 78.5f.), Origen (*Contra Celsum* i.51), and Jerome (*Ep.* 108.10). After the Romans conquered Bethlehem anew (A.D. 135) the site of the Nativity was desecrated, probably under Hadrian (117-138; cf. Jerome *Ep.* 58.3). Jerome lived for thirty-three years in Bethlehem (A.D. 387-420). Here he helped found and direct pilgrim hospices, convents for women, and a monastery. During this time, by the request of Pope Damasus, Jerome began his revision of the Latin NT and his comparison of the Greek version of the OT with the original Hebrew, which ultimately led to the composition of the Vulgate. The cell where Jerome made his famous translation is still maintained as a chapel in the Church of the Nativity.

The desert E of Bethlehem is still inhabited by Moslem bedouin who use this fertile land for grazing goats and sheep. A field located a short distance SE of Bethlehem

Grotto of the Nativity, with the crypt of the manger. The belief that Jesus was born in a cave dates at least to the time of Justin Martyr (middle 2nd cent. A.D.). (W. S. LaSor)

is designated as the place where the angels appeared to the shepherds to bring them the good tidings of the birth of the Savior (Lk. 2:8). *See* Plate 19.

Bethlehem has had an interesting history. The Persians spared it in A.D. 614, the Arabs in 636. The inhabitants invited the Crusaders to occupy the city in 1099. In the 12th cent. a Latin bishopric was erected in Bethlehem; in the 14th cent. an episcopal see was constituted there by the Greek Church; the same was done by the Armenian Church in the 17th century. The wall and the towers, symbolizing Bethlehem on the Madeba Map, were demolished and the moat was filled in 1489. Ibrahim Pasha, Egyptian general and son of Muhammed Ali, as punishment for a Moslem insurrection laid waste the Moslem section of the town in 1834.

III. Church of the Nativity.–Constantine erected the large basilica (*ca.* 325) over the hillside grotto that is identified by tradition and believed by most authorities to be the site of the birth of Jesus. Originally it was known as *S. Marie a Praesepio* (Church of St. Mary). The Church of the Nativity was never destroyed; it remains the oldest of the famous churches of the world.

Even though it was damaged by the Samaritans in A.D. 525, it was repaired and enlarged under the rule of the emperor Justinian. When the Persians invaded the Holy Land in 614 they left the church untouched, because they recognized the garb worn by the Magi pictured in the mosaic as their national attire. The three large gates of the basilica were changed into a small entrance in order to prevent riders from entering on their horses. Entering this 4-ft. (1.2-m.) high "Door of Humility," one proceeds through a vestibule to the main sanctuary.

The grotto of the Nativity is under the chancel. It occupies the center of the transept and is approached by steps leading down from each side of the choir. In a crypt at the front of the grotto is the manger where Jesus was born. A silver star on the marble floor at the east end of the crypt is inscribed with the words, *Hic de Virgine Maria Jesus Christus natus est* ("Here of the Virgin Mary Jesus Christ was born"). Of the fifteen lamps that burn day and night around this star, six belong to the Greek, five to the Armenian, and four to the Latin churches.

IV. Modern Bethlehem.–Bethlehem has become a city of international and ecumenical character. It became a part of Jordan in 1949, and residence for Jews was prohibited; in June, 1967, it was occupied by Israel. Its modern name is Beit Laḥm, "house of meat." The majority of its people belong to one of the various Christian confessions. Though the Bethlehemites prefer occidental clothing the national garb may still be seen, worn mostly by women.

Tourists and pilgrims are an important source of its income. Religious souvenirs are manufactured in private homes with primitive tools. Other small factories produce furniture, plastic, macaroni, and weaving equipment. Bethlehem also produces one of the finest wines in the Palestine area.

V. Archeology.–Bethlehem is among the ancient cities and villages that have been only slightly disturbed by excavations. Nevertheless, bones and teeth of monstrous rhinoceroses, hippopotamuses, elephants, and cave oxen have been discovered in the hills of Bethlehem, as well as tools used by pre-Chellean man over 100,000 years ago.

2. Bethlehem of Zebulun (Josh. 19:15f.), now the small village of Beit Laḥm located 7 mi. (11 km.) NW of Nazareth on the edge of the Oak Forest. A few antiquities have been found there showing that in earlier days it was a place of some importance. There are traces of the influence of Hellenism as well as the ruins of a synagogue.

Bibliography.–W. Harvey, *et al., Church of the Nativity at Bethlehem* (1910); *GP,* II, 276f.; C. Kopp, *Holy Places of the Gospels* (1963), pp. 1-47; *LBHG.* E. W. G. MASTERMAN K. G. JUNG

BETHLEHEM, STAR OF. *See* STAR OF THE MAGI.

BETHLEHEMITE beth'lə-hem-īt [Heb. *bêṯ hallaḥmî*]. An inhabitant of BETHLEHEM, a town in Judah, 5 mi. (8 km.) S of Jerusalem. Jesse is so named in 1 S. 16:18; 17:58, and Elhanan in 2 S. 21:19. The sons of Bethlehem are referred to in Ezr. 2:21; Neh. 7:26; 1 Esd. 5:17.

BETH-LOMON beth-lō'mən [Gk. *Baithlōmōn,* B *Rhagethlōmōn*]. A town in Judah whose inhabitants returned from Babylon with Zerubbabel (1 Esd. 5:17, Gk., AV, NEB), identified as Bethlehem in the RSV (cf. Ezr. 2:21).

BETH-MAACAH beth-mā'ə-kə. *See* ABEL-BETH-MAACAH.

BETH-MARCABOTH beth-mär'kə-both [Heb. *bêṯ hammarkāḇōṯ*–'the house (place) of chariots'; Gk. *Baithmachereb*]. A place mentioned along with Hazar-susah, "the station of horses," as cities in the Negeb near Ziklag (Josh. 19:5; 1 Ch. 4:31). It is tempting to connect these stations with "the cities for his chariots, and the cities for his horsemen" which Solomon built (1 K. 9:19; cf. 10:26). The site of Beth-marcaboth has not been identified, although in a partly parallel list in Josh. 15:31 its place is taken by Madmannah, which is also in the Negeb and may be identical (*GAB*). E. W. G. MASTERMAN

BETH-MEON beth-mē'on [Heb. *bêṯ meʿôn*–'dwelling place']. A city of Moab (Jer. 48:23), identical with BAAL-MEON.

BETH-MILLO beth-mil'ō [Heb. *bêṯ millô'*; Gk. *oíkos Maallōn*] (Jgs. 9:6, 20); AV "house of Millo." A quarter in Shechem associated with the armed forces of that city, perhaps to be understood as a civil defense center or barracks. It is not certain whether "the house of Millo" is identical with the TOWER OF SHECHEM (J. Simons, *Jerusalem* [1952]), nor how both are related to the shrine of BAAL-BERITH. The three seem to be connected with the city's considerable defense installations (see G. E. Wright, *Shechem* [1965]).

BETH-NIMRAH beth-nim'rə [Heb. *bêṯ nimrâ*] (Nu. 32:36; Josh. 13:27); **NIMRAH** nim'rə [Heb. *nimrâ*] (Nu. 32:3). A city in the plains of Moab built and fortified by the Gadites.

It is located on the north side of Wâdī Shu'eib at Tell Bleibil, about 1 mi. (1.6 km.) N of the Byzantine site of Tell Nimrîn. Because of the vegetation lining the banks of the streams on the east of the Jordan, the Gadites requested this city among others for grazing their cattle (Nu. 32:3, 36). In Isa. 15:6 the prophet, in an oracle against Moab, declared a blight on this land.

D. McINTOSH

BETHOMESTHAIM be-thō-məs-thā'əm (Jth. 4:6; 15:4, NEB). *See* BETOMESTHAIM.

BETH-PALET beth-pā'lət (Josh. 15:27, AV). *See* BETH-PELET.

BETH-PAZZEZ beth-paz'əz [Heb. *bêṯ paṣṣēṣ*–'house of dispersion'; Gk. *Bērsaphēs, Baithphrasēe*]. A town in the territory of Issachar, named with En-gannim and En-haddah (Josh. 19:21). The site has not yet been discovered, but is frequently identified with modern Kerm el-Ḥadîtheh. W. W. BUEHLER

BETH-PELET beth-pē'lət [Heb. *bêṯ-peleṭ*–'house of escape']; AV BETH-PALET (Josh. 15:27), BETH-PHELET (Neh. 11:26). An unidentified city in the extreme south (Negeb) of Judah, "toward the boundary of Edom." Some of the Judahites returned there after the Exile (Neh. 11:26).

BETH-PEOR beth-pē'ôr [Heb. *bêṯ peʿôr*–'house of the opening'; Gk. *oíkos Phogōr, Baithphogōr*]. A place in Moab, possibly N of Mt. Nebo, used to identify the valley where Moses recalled to Israel the covenant of Sinai (Dt. 3:29; 4:46) and where Moses was buried (Dt. 34:6). It was in the portion of land allotted to the tribe of Reuben by Moses (Josh. 13:20), near the mountain where Balaam had seven altars built and where Israel later "began to play the harlot with the daughters of Moab" and "yoked himself to Baal of Peor" (Nu. 25:1, 3, 5, 18; cf. Dt. 4:3; 31:16; Josh. 22:17; Ps. 106:28; Hos. 9:10).

According to Eusebius *Onom.* 48.3, Beth-peor was 6 mi. (10 km.) from Livias on the road to Ḥesbân (Heshbon). on a mountain of the same name, 7 mi. (11 km.) from Heshbon. The Taanaïtes said that the cult of Baal-phegor was still practiced in their time, and a Roman fort at that place overlooked the Jordan Valley. Khirbet esh-Sheikh Jâyel best fits this description, but identification with Beth-peor is not certain.

See *GP,* II, 278.

BETHPHAGE beth'fə-jē, beth'fāj [Gk. *Bēthphagē*–'house of figs']. A village near the Mt. of Olives and the Jericho road, mentioned three times in the NT. In Mk. 11:1 and Lk. 19:29 it is associated with Bethany, in connection with the Triumphal Entry. Only Bethphage is named in the parallel passage in Matthew (21:1).

Although not mentioned in the OT, the name occurs in the Talmud, where it is spoken of as being near Jerusalem. G. Dalman (*SSW,* pp. 252f.) says: "It must have been a district situated outside Jerusalem (in any case a suburb, but not a separate unit), beginning at the border of the sanctuary, i.e. before the eastern wall of Jerusalem." This would mean the western slope of the Mt. of Olives. Because Bethphage is mentioned before Bethany, many scholars locate it E of Bethany, on the lower slopes of the Mt. of Olives. The site is nonetheless uncertain. R. EARLE

BETH-PHELET beth-fē'lət (Neh. 11:26, AV). *See* BETH-PELET.

BETH-RAPHA beth-rā'fə [Heb. *bêṯ rāp̄ā'*–'house of Rapha,' a healing deity(?)]. A place mentioned in 1 Ch. 4:12, possibly to be located, according to Aharoni's reconstruction of the list, in the region between Bethlehem and Hebron. W. S. L. S.

BETH-REHOB beth-rē'hob [Heb. *bêṯ-reḥôḇ*–'place of street (or "market")'(?); Gk. *ho oíkos Rhaab*]. A principality of Aram along the southern border of Hamath; the northernmost point of the spies' journey (Nu. 13:21). The valley around Beth-rehob included the city of Dan, formerly Laish, according to Jgs. 18:28. Simons, however (*GTTOT,* p. 7), translates so that Dan was *near* [b^e; cf. 1 S. 29:1] the valley of Beth-rehob, rather than *in* it, thereby allowing for a location farther N and W, along the Syrian Beqa'. W. M. Thomson suggested present-day Bâniyâs in the general area of Dan (*Land and The Book,* II [1882], 547). According to 2 S. 10:6 Beth-rehob supplied mercenaries to fight David, along with the neighboring city-states of Zobah, Tob, and Maacah. A. H. LEWIS

BETHSAIDA beth-sā'ə-də [Gk. *Bethsaida*–'house of fishing' or 'fisherman's house']. A town on the north shore of the Sea of Galilee. Many scholars believe there were two towns of the same name, one to the east and the other to the west of the Jordan. The precise locations are disputed.

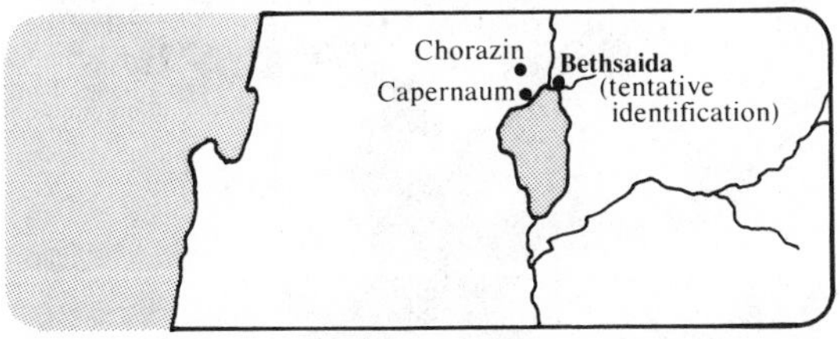

I. In the NT.–Bethsaida was the home of at least three of Jesus' disciples. In Jn. 12:21 Philip is identified as being from "Bethsaida in Galilee," and in Jn. 1:44 Bethsaida is described as "the city of Andrew and Peter." Some think James and John also came from the same city. There are reasons to believe that Bethsaida was a city of some importance. With Chorazin and Capernaum, it is one of the cities (Gk. *póleis,* although it is twice designated a *kṓmē,* "village," in Mk. 8:26) where Jesus did most of His mighty works (Mt. 11:20-24; Lk. 10:13-15). Further, if there were but one Bethsaida it would undoubtedly be the one lying E of the Jordan which Philip the tetrarch rebuilt in honor of Julia, the daughter of Caesar Augustus, and made into his capital (Josephus *Ant.* xviii.2.2). It was at Bethsaida that Jesus healed a blind man by spitting on his eyes and laying His hands on him (Mk. 8:22-26). Context would seem to locate this E of the Jordan (the "other side" from the district of Dalmanutha, Mk. 8:10, 13; on the way to the villages of Caesarea Philippi, Mk. 8:27), although the injunction not to enter the village (v. 26) is more in keeping with Jesus' practice in Jewish, rather than gentile, regions (cf. Mk. 5:43 with 5:19).

II. One Bethsaida or Two?–The evidence for a Bethsaida E of the Jordan is strong. Josephus, who identified Bethsaida as the site Philip developed into the city of Julias, located it as lying near the Jordan in "Lower Gaulanitis" (cf. *BJ* ii.9.1; 8.2; iii.10.7; with *Vita* 72). Both Pliny and Jerome agree with this location.

The problem arises with the Gospel materials. After the feeding of the five thousand in a place Luke connects with "a city called Bethsaida" (Lk. 9:10), Jesus sends His disciples by boat to "the other side, to Bethsaida" (Mk. 6:45). Jesus walks on the water to the disciples, who are rowing against a strong wind; and "when they had crossed over, they came to land at Gennesaret" (Mk. 6:53). John's account indicates that the disciples started across the sea to Capernaum. The following day the crowds, who had been miraculously fed on five barley loaves and two fish, follow by boat and find Jesus "on the other side of the sea," at Capernaum (Jn. 6:16-25). A normal reading of these verses assumes a Bethsaida W of the Jordan as well as another to the east.

The position is strengthened by several supporting considerations: (1) Philip, Peter, and Andrew are from "Bethsaida in *Galilee*" (Jn. 1:44 with 12:21); (2) in Acts 1:11 the disciples are called "men of Galilee," which would be incorrect if at least three were from Gaulanitis; (3) the close connection with Chorazin and Capernaum as the center of Jesus' mighty works does not favor a gentile city E of the Jordan (Mt. 11:20-24). In fact, Bethsaida is contrasted with the gentile cities of Tyre and Sidon. Further, we have recorded only three brief visits of Jesus to the foreign peoples E of the Sea of Galilee.

Those who argue against a second Bethsaida W of the Jordan point out how unlikely it would be that two towns of the same name should exist so close to each other. It is also stressed that Mark's "to the other side, to Bethsaida" (6:45) need not indicate a journey directly across the lake to the far side. John indicates the destination as Capernaum (Jn. 6:17), which lay a relatively short distance away; and Josephus uses a similar expression for a boat trip from Tiberias to Taricheae (3.7 mi. [6 km.]), both on the west shore of the lake. That three disciples came from "Bethsaida in Galilee" is answered by the claim that at one time the province of Galilee ran right around the lake (G. A. Smith) or that Galilee may here indicate a general geographical area rather than a province.

III. Location.–The exact location of Bethsaida Julias is still uncertain, although most scholars identify it with et-Tell, 2 mi. (3 km.) N of the Sea of Galilee just E of the Jordan, along with Khirbet el-Araj, the nearby fishing settlement on the shore of the lake. Traces of an aqueduct and a Roman road indicate a connection between the original fishing village and the larger city established by Philip on higher ground to the north. The transfer of the name "house of fishing" to the larger settlement is understandable. Et-Tell is located near an open plain (about 2 mi. [3 km.] down the east side of the lake) with rich soil and thick grass. This corresponds to the "green grass" of Mk. 6:39 and the "much grass" of Jn. 6:10 where Jesus fed the five thousand.

'Ain et-Tabigha, about 3 mi. (5 km.) SW of the mouth of the Jordan, is usually mentioned as the location of the "second Bethsaida" W of the Jordan.

A solution to the Bethsaida problem suggested by W. M. Thomson (*Land and the Book,* II [1882], 422) locates the city at el-Mas'adiyeh on the eastern bank of the river near the lake, and posits a Galilean suburb on the west bank. This double city would answer the problem raised by the data in the Gospels, but the boggy ground and the lack of any fording place or indication of connection by bridge argues against the site.

R. H. MOUNCE

BETHSAMOS beth-sā'məs (1 Esd. 5:18, AV). *See* BETH-ASMOTH.

BETH-SHEAN beth-shē'ən; **BETH-SHAN** beth'shan, beth-shan' [Heb. *bêṯ-šeʾān, bêṯ-šān*; Gk. usually *Baithsan, Bethsan,* with minor variants]; (1 and 2 Samuel); AV Apoc. BETHSAN; **SCYTHOPOLIS** sith-op'ə-lis [Gk. *Skythōn Pólis*] (Apoc.). A city located at the juncture of the Jezreel and Jordan valleys. Through here passed the main arteries of the ancient world, and Beth-shean saw almost continuous occupation from Chalcolithic times to the present. The numerous springs and wells, especially the Jālûd (now Nahal Harod) and its tributaries, have combined with the intense summer heat and rich soil to produce a subtropical paradise ideal for human habitation. During OT and prehistoric times the main settlement was on the site of Tell el-Ḥuṣn, an impressive mound just S of Nahal Harod, and some 650 ft. (200 m.) N of modern Beit Shan (formerly Beisan). The name can be interpreted "house of rest" but was more than likely called "the temple of Shan," the latter being a deity some have identified with the Sumerian serpent-god Šaḫan.

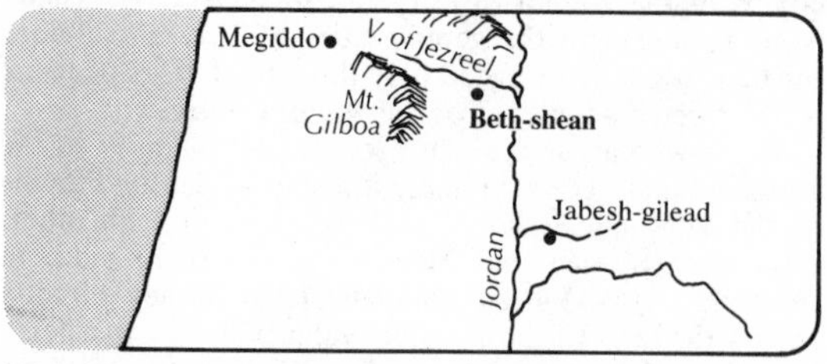

I. Late Bronze Age.–Beth-shean is mentioned among the "conquered" cities of Pharaoh Thutmose III, the name being spelled *btšîr*. Scarabs from these rulers were found in the temples of levels IX-VII. During the Amarna period (level IX) a garrison of troops from Gath-Carmel was posted at Beth-shean (*Bītsāni*). The king of Jerusalem felt that this was not in the best interest of Egypt (Am.Tab. 298:18-20).

By the time Seti I had risen to the throne of Egypt (1303 B.C.), Beth-shean was clearly in Egyptian hands. To this period (Late Bronze II) Mazar dates the temples of level IX. This was one of the richest strata to be uncovered in the excavation; it abounded in artifacts of Egyptian type. A stele found in the southern-most of these two temples was dedicated to "Mikkal, Lord of Beth-shean." A stone slab from the same place bore two carved scenes representing a lion and a dog (?) fighting.

Among the stelae of Seti I found at Beth-shean, two give glimpses of military action taken by this pharaoh to secure and maintain his control of this vital strategic region. The first indicates that Beth-shean served as the main Egyptian base in the area. The king of Rehob was evidently the principal vassal ruler in the valley, and an attack on him by his neighboring rivals could be accomplished only by neutralizing the garrison at Beth-shean. The troops from Gath-Carmel had probably been stationed there in the service of the pharaoh. Thus, the practice of manning this fortress by mercenary troops was well established before the Philistines appeared on the scene (cf. below). The other stele, on which the date is not preserved, records that the *'apiru* of *Yarmuth* with the *Tayaru* have attacked the *'Amu* (Asiatics) of *Rhm*. This Yarmuth is doubtless that belonging to Issachar (Josh. 19:21; cf. also 21:29; 1 Ch. 5:58). It is interesting to note that such disorders continued to take place among the tribes of Galilee at this time.

Level VIII also produced Egyptian-type artifacts. Level VII, which Mazar thinks lasted until *ca.* 1175, contained the commander's palace and another temple. In level VI another temple of similar plan was discovered and also a palace containing a stele of Ramses II and a statue of Ramses III. Beth-shean and its villages were in the territory of Issachar (Josh. 17:16) but were actually assigned to Manasseh (Josh. 17:11; 1 Ch. 7:29). However, not even this stronger tribe was able to conquer Beth-shean because the inhabitants were armed with "chariots of iron" (Josh. 17:12-16; Jgs. 1:27f.).

II. Iron Age.–The extent of Egyptian control during the early days of Israelite settlement (*ca.* 1200-1050) is difficult to determine. Level V at Beth-shean apparently represents this period, to which can be related the anthropoid coffins — pottery caskets bearing representations of faces, some of which have typically "Philistine" headdress. Except for two bowls, no Philistine ware was discovered at Beth-shean. However, there were some very interesting incense stands in the shape of houses, with human, animal, and reptile figures on them.

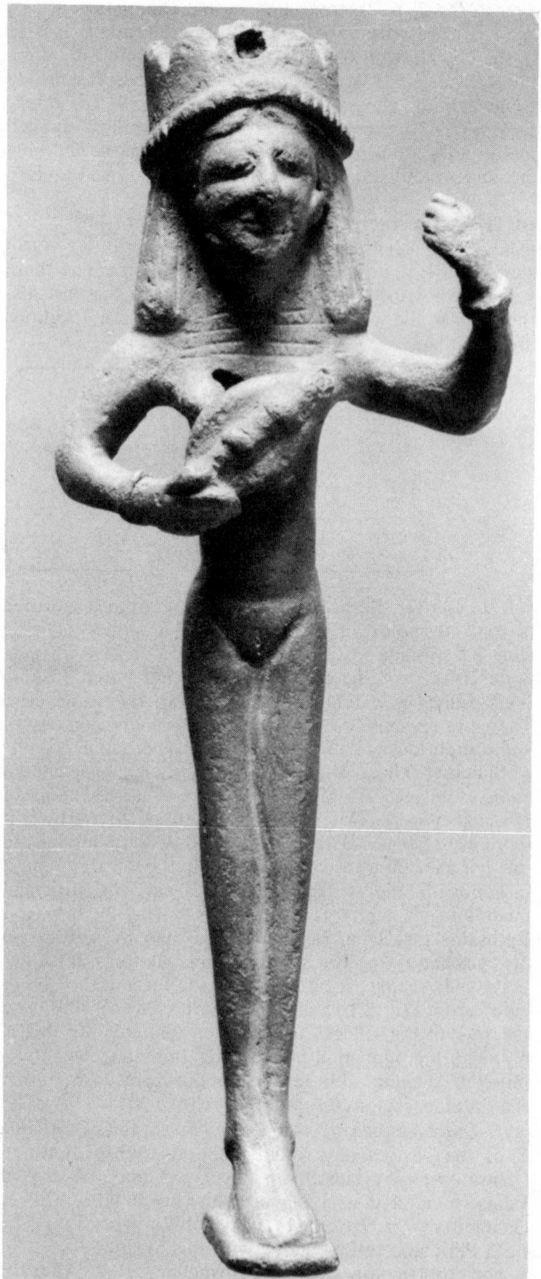
Bronze statuette of a girl playing the lute, discovered at Beth-shan (Israel Department of Antiquities and Museums)

By the end of Saul's reign, Israel was trying desperately to break the Philistine stranglehold on the Valley of Jezreel. This was Saul's intention when he mustered his troops for his last fateful battle (1 S. 28:4). The Israelites gathered at Gilboa, the high ground above Beth-shean, and the Philistines assembled at Shunem nearby. Like so

Tell el-Ḥuṣn, site of biblical Beth-shean. It was occupied intermittently for more than five thousand years. (Religious New Service)

many passages from this period, the account of this battle (ch. 31) reads like a page out of Homer's *Iliad*. The heroes, Saul and Jonathan, were carried as trophies to the Philistine garrison at Beth-shean, and while the heads were sent to the main center of Philistia as an announcement of victory (31:9), the decapitated bodies were hung on the wall of Beth-shean. The men of Jabesh in Gilead (Tell el-Maqlub), whom Saul had once saved from disaster (ch. 11), came by night and rescued the bodies from their ignominious display and gave them a hero's burial (31:11-13). Scholars have often suggested that this passage is spurious because it does not conform to the usual burial customs of ancient Israel. However, the burial rites described here are those carried out in honor of heroes, e.g., Achilles' friend Patroclos (*Iliad* xxiii), among the Homeric Greeks. It is no wonder that Aegean customs should be found at this time in which the Philistines (comprising several Aegean peoples) held sway at all the main centers of international commerce (cf. also 2 S. 21:12-14).

In honor of the two fallen heroes, David wrote his great lament (2 S. 1:17-27), "to teach the men of Judah the bow." Soldiers in training were to sing the chant about two mighty warriors who had fallen in battle. The hills of Gilboa were given the curse befitting the site of such tragic deaths: "no dew and no rain upon you!" The same curse is found in an Ugaritic legend about the death of a young warrior (*Aqhat* i.40-46).

The gateway of level V, which continued in use during much later periods, was doubtless that used by the garrison placed there later by Solomon (1 K. 4:12). Beth-shean was subject once more to destruction during the campaign of Pharaoh Shishak (*ca.* 920 B.C.). The period of Israelite occupation is represented by level IV, but the buildings were in such a ruined state due to the Assyrian and/or Babylonian onslaughts that the history of the period cannot be discerned in detail. Level IV seems to have lasted from *ca.* 815 to 700 B.C.

III. Hellenistic Period.–Level III of the tell and the large city area enclosed by the circumference wall represent this period. A temple to Dionysos existed on top of the mound. In fact the city was sometimes called Nysa-Scythopolis, or Nysa, in honor of Dionysus' nurse and the town of his birth. The name Scythopolis probably dates back not to the Scythian invasion of the Near East (Herodotus i.103-05) but rather to the founding of a Ptolemaic city (perhaps in 254 B.C.) to be inhabited by hellenized descendants of Scythian mercenaries who had served in the Ptolemaic army.

In 107 the city was occupied by the Jewish high priest John Hyrcanus, and it remained under Maccabean (Hasmonean) rule until 63 B.C. when Palestine became a Roman province. Under the Romans the city was one of the chief cities of the Decapolis (Josephus *BJ* ii.9.7), a league of ten cities with Greek culture and constitution (cf. Mt. 4:25; Mk. 5:20; 7:31). During the 1st cent. A.D. the population was therefore predominantly gentile (2 Macc. 12:30; *BJ* ii.18.1, 3f.; *Vita* 6), though a Jewish enclave remained. During the war against Rome (A.D. 68-70) the Jewish force raided Scythopolis several times, and the populace retaliated by attacking the Jewish residents there. The theater, now being restored, a hippodrome, an aqueduct and other public buildings, plus the great city wall and the ancient bridge, date back to this period. At the end of the 4th cent. the country under-

Connecting rooms with rich mosaic floors, the living quarters of a sixth-century A.D. monastery at Beth-shan (Consulate General of Israel in New York)

went an administrative reorganization, and Scythopolis became the capital of *Palestina Secunda,* a province that included the plain of Esdraelon, Galilee, and part of northern Transjordan.

IV. Byzantine Age.–This period is represented by level II, during which time Scythopolis was the see of a bishop. Among several churches erected here, the round church (no longer visible) found on top of the mound is worthy of note as being the same plan as the original Church of the Holy Sepulchre. Across the valley, N of the tell, a sixth-century monastery was excavated which contained lovely mosaic floors.

After the Arab conquest in A.D. 640 the old name Beisan came back into use. The town was utterly destroyed by the Crusaders and never regained its former prosperity. A mosque (the Mosque of the Forty Warriors) is located just outside of the town. The present structure is recent, but an inscription on the wall near the *minbar* or pulpit gives the year 1403 as the date of completion of the original mosque. The only traces of the Crusader period consist of a small castle called "the Old Serail," on a site now occupied by the girls' school. The original structure was destroyed by Saladin A.D. 1183.

Bibliography.–W. F. Albright, *AASOR*, 17 (1938), 76-79; *BASOR*, 125 (Feb. 1952), 24-32; M. Avi-Yonah, *IEJ*, 2 (1962), 123-134; G. M. Fitzgerald in *AOTS*, pp. 185-196; F. James, *Iron Age at Beth Shan* (1966); E. Oren, *Northern Cemetery at Beth Shan* (1973); H. O. Thompson, *BA*, 30 (1967), 110-135.

A. F. RAINEY

BETH-SHEMESH beth-shem'ish [Heb. *bêṯ šemeš*–'house of (the solar deity) Shemesh,' rather than 'house of the sun,' which would require *haš-šemeš*]. The name of four places mentioned in the OT, principally Beth-shemesh in Judah.

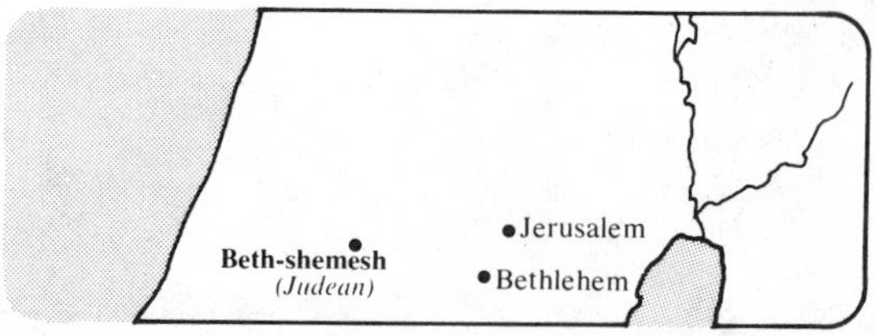

1. Judean Beth-shemesh was located on the northern border of the tribal allotment of Judah, named between Mt. Jearim (Chesalon) and Timnah in Josh. 15:10. If Beth-shemesh is to be equated with Ir-shemesh, it was originally allocated to Dan (Josh. 19:41), but was later considered to belong to Judah (2 K. 14:11), It is presently identified with Tell er-Rumeileh. (Earlier identification was with 'Ain Shems, which lies somewhat to the east, and preserves the ancient name.) The site is 18 mi. (29 km.) W of Jerusalem, 2 mi. (3 km.) SW of Eshta'ol, in the Valley of Sorek (Wâdī es-Sarâr) in the Shephelah (2 Ch. 28:18). Tell er-Rumeileh was excavated by the British in 1911/12, and by Haverford College in 1928-1932. It was settled before 2000 B.C., toward the end of the Early Bronze Age, and was occupied until the 6th cent. B.C., reaching its high point in the period of Egypt's 19th Dynasty.

It seems likely that the Israelites occupied the city after the tribe of Dan relocated to the north, and it was designated as one of the cities of the Levites (Josh. 21:16; 1 Ch. 6:59). After the capture of the ark by the Philistines and the subsequent events, the ark was returned to Israel by the expedient of placing it in a cart drawn by two fresh (milch) cows, and letting the cows take the cart where they would — which was to Beth-shemesh (1 K. 6:1-14). At that time the city was beyond the border of Philistine territory (6:12), although the quantity of Philistine pottery recovered from the site indicates that it had been strongly influenced by, and possibly even under control of, the Philistines at the close of the Late Bronze Age.

In the reign of Solomon Beth-shemesh was in the second administrative (or commissary) district (1 K. 4:11). In the fifth year of Rehoboam (*ca.* 927 B.C.) Shishak (Sheshonq) the king of Egypt invaded Judah and plundered Jerusalem. This was probably the time of the destruction of Beth-shemesh of which the archeological exploration gave evidence, although the Bible is silent on this point (cf. 1 K. 14:25-28). When Amaziah was king of Judah (796-767 B.C.) he challenged Jehoash king of Israel (798-782 B.C.), and the two met in battle at Beth-shemesh (2 K. 14:8-11). Judah was defeated and Amaziah was captured, following which Jerusalem was plundered (14:12-14). The date had to be between 796 and 782 B.C., probably toward the end of the reign of Jehoash, as this would best account for Amaziah's loss of popular support and ultimately his assassination.

During the reign of Ahaz king of Judah (735-716 B.C.) the Philistines captured Beth-shemesh (2 Ch. 28:18), along with other cities. The Edomites also were taking advantage of the situation, and were raiding cities of Judah. Ahaz therefore sent to Tiglath-pileser III king of Assyria for help (28:16). Tiglath-pileser marched against the west in 734, plundering Phoenician cities and laying Ashkelon and Gaza under tribute, but it would seem that the capture of Beth-shemesh was somewhat later, and Tiglath-pileser was of no help, even though Ahaz had already become his vassal (cf. 28:19-21). Beth-shemesh thereafter is unmentioned in the biblical narratives, and we know nothing more of it except that it was destroyed by Nebuchad-

Remains of a casemate wall at Beth-shemesh. After its destruction (probably by Shishak, late 10th cent. B.C.), the city never regained the strength it enjoyed under Solomon. (W. S. LaSor)

nezzar in the campaign of 588-587. The recovery of a jar handle bearing the name Yaukin (Jehoiachin) suggests that Beth-shemesh had once again come under the government of Judah, possibly at the time of Josiah's expansion.

Bibliography.–D. Mackenzie, *PEF*, 1 (1911), 41-94; 2 (1912/13), 1-100; E. Grant and G. E. Wright, *Ain Shems Excavations* (5 vols., 1931-1935); E. Grant and G. A. Barton, *BASOR*, 52 (Dec. 1933), 3-6; G. E. Wright and F. M. Cross, *JBL*, 75 (1956), 215-17.

2. A city of Beth-shemesh is mentioned in the territory allocated to the tribe of Issachar, located on the border and named between Shahazumah and the Jordan (Josh. 19:22). It has been identified with three sites: 'Ain esh-Shamsiyeh, about 7 mi. (11 km.) S of Beth-shan (Beisan); Khirbet Shemsin, 2 mi. (3 km.) NW of el-'Abeidiyeh; and el-'Abeidiyeh, a ford over the Jordan about 2 mi. (3 km.) S of the Sea of Galilee and E of Khirbet Shamsawi (which may preserve the ancient name). The last is the preferred identification at the present time.

See A. Saarisalo, *The Boundary Between Issachar and Naphtali* (1927), pp. 71-73, 119-120.

3. The Beth-shemesh allotted to Naphtali (Josh. 19:38) has not been identified. It would seem to lie N (and W?) of the Sea of Galilee. If the Beth-shemesh of Jgs. 1:33 is the same (note that Beth-anath is mentioned next to Beth-shemesh in both passages), it was occupied by the Canaanites, who became subject to Naphtali for forced labor. Some scholars identify this Beth-shemesh with **2**, although the geographical details in the texts seem to support separate identities.

4. Jeremiah mentions a Beth-shemesh (translated "Heliopolis" in RSV) in the land of Egypt (Jer. 43:13). Since the Gk. *hēlioúpolis* means "city of (the) sun," this is a logical identification. *See* ON.

W. S. LASOR

BETH-SHEMITE beth-she'mīt [Heb. *beṯ-šimšî*] (1 S. 6:14, 18). An inhabitant of Beth-shemesh in Judah. *See* BETH-SHEMESH **1.**

BETH-SHITTAH beth-shit'ə [Heb. *bêṯ haššiṭṭâ*–'house (place) of the acacia']. A place on the route followed by the Midianites in their flight before Gideon (Jgs. 7:22). Its association with Zererah seems to indicate a location in the Jordan Valley, S of Beth-shan, rather than the frequent identification with modern Shutta.

W. W. BUEHLER

BETHSURA beth-so͞o'rə (AV and NEB Apoc.). *See* BETH-ZUR.

BETH-TAPPUAH beth-tap'ū-ə [Heb. *beṯ-tappû(a)ḥ* – 'place of fruit trees']. A town in the hill country of Judah (Josh. 15:53). Tappuah was a "son of Hebron" (1 Ch. 2:43). The site is identified with the village of Taffûḥ 3.5 mi. (5.5 km.) WNW of Hebron. It stands on the edge of a high ridge surrounded by very fruitful gardens; an ancient highway runs through the village, and there are many old cisterns and caves nearby. Beth-tappuah is to be distinguished from Tappuah.

BETH-TOGARMAH beth-tō-gär'mə [Heb. *bêṯ tôgarmâ*]; AV HOUSE OF TOGARMAH; NEB also TOGARMAH (Ezk. 27:14). A place name in Ezk. 27:14; 38:6, probably the same as TOGARMAH.

BETHUEL bə-tho͞o'əl [Heb. *bᵉṯû'ēl*–'dweller in God']. A son of Nahor and Milcah; Abraham's nephew, and father of Laban and Rebekah (Gen. 22:22f.; 24:15, 24, 47, 50; 25:20; 28:2, 5). In 25:20 and 28:5 he is surnamed "the Aramean." The only place in the narrative where he has any significance is in connection with Rebekah's betrothal to Isaac; and even here, his son Laban stands out more prominently than he — a fact explainable on the ground of the brother's right to take a special interest in the welfare of the sister (cf. Gen. 34:5, 11, 25; 2 S. 13:20, 22). Josephus (*Ant.* i.16.2) says Bethuel was dead at this time.

F. E. HIRSCH

BETHUEL [Heb. *bᵉṯû'ēl*; cf. Can. personal name *Batti-ilu* (Am.Tab. 161:20)]. A town of Simeon near Hormah and Ziklag (1 Ch. 4:30). It is called Bethul in Josh. 19:4, but in what appears to be a parallel list the name Chesil occurs (Josh. 15:30). The name Bethel in 1 S. 30:27 is possibly a corruption (by mispointing) of Bethuel (so NEB).

W. S. L. S.

BETHUL beth'əl [Heb. *bᵉṯûl*] (Josh. 19:4). *See* BETHUEL.

BETHULIA bə-thōō'lē-ə [Gk. *Baithouloua*]. A town named only in Judith (4:6; 6:10ff.; 7:1ff.; 8:3; 10:6; 12:7; 15:3, 6; 16:21ff.). The references indicate that it stood above a valley on a hilltop, at the foot of which was a spring. The city was opposite Esdraelon toward the plain of Dothan, perhaps in the vicinity of modern Jenîn. It was a strategic site, guarding the passes by which an army might march to the south. It is often suggested that the name is a pseudonym for an important city, and Shechem has found considerable acceptance as a possibility.

See C. C. Torrey, *Apocryphal Literature* (1945), pp. 91-93.

W. W. BUEHLER

BETHZACHARIA beth-zak-ə-rī'ə; **BETH-ZACHARIAS** beth-zak-ə-rī'əs. *See* BETH-ZECHARIAH.

BETH-ZAITH beth-zā'ith [Gk. *Bēthzaith,* A *Bēzeth*]; AV BEZETH. The place to which Bacchides withdrew and where he slew several Jews (1 Macc. 7:19). It is identified with Khirbet Beit Zeita, about 3 mi. (5 km.) N of Bethzur (Bethsura), where a cave-cistern is pointed out as the "great pit" into which the bodies of the murdered Jews were thrown.

R. E. W. BASON

BETH-ZATHA beth-zā'thə [Gk. *Bethzatha*] (Jn. 5:2); AV, NEB, BETHESDA. The RSV reading is supported by Codex Sinaiticus and a few other MSS, and is accepted by many scholars today. *See* BETHESDA.

BETH-ZECHARIAH beth-zek-ə-rī'ə [Gk. *Baithzacharia*]; NEB BETHZACHARIA; AV BATH-ZACHARIAS. The place where Judas Maccabeus lost a battle to Antiochus Eupator, and his brother valiantly attacked and killed one of the elephants only to have it fall upon him and crush him (1 Macc. 6:32ff.). According to Josephus (*Ant.* xii.9.4), the place was located about 70 stadia (about 8 mi., 13 km.) from Bethsura, but the modern identification with Khirbet Beit Skâriā, 10 mi. (16 km.) SW of Jerusalem, puts it only about 6 mi. (10 km.) NE of Beth-zur.

W. S. L. S.

BETH-ZUR beth-zûr' [Heb. *bêṯ-ṣûr*–'house of rock']; AV and NEB Apoc. BETHSURA. A town in Judah (Josh. 15:58), the name of which survives in Burj eṣ-Ṣur, 4.5 mi. (7 km.) N of Hebron. The ancient town, however, has been found in Khirbet eṭ-Ṭubeiqah, 500 yds. [460 m.] to the northwest, where excavations were begun by W. F. Albright and O. R. Sellers in 1931 and resumed by Sellers in 1957. Traces from Early Bronze are scarce. Fortifications from the Middle Bronze period have been ascribed by the excavators to the Hyksos; after the defeat of the Hyksos in southern Palestine by the Egyptians the wall was destroyed.

Joshua 15:58 mentions Beth-zur as a town of Judah; 1 Ch. 2:45 reckons it part of the region of Caleb. Of the fortifications by Rehoboam (2 Ch. 11:7) no definite remains have yet been found. Beth-zur became very important as a fortress on the way from Hebron to Jerusalem in the Persian period, to which Albright now ascribes the "first citadel" with its water reservoir. It was the capital of one of the districts of the province Judah (Neh. 3:16).

Judas Maccabeus fortified it again (1 Macc. 4:61; 6:7, 26) as a boundary fortress against Idumea. In 163 B.C. he left the town, and it soon capitulated to the Syrians (1 Macc. 6:31f., 49). The Syrian general Bacchides fortified it again in 161 (9:52), building what is called by the excavators the "third fortress." According to 10:14 it was still a place of refuge for the Hellenistic Jews in 154 B.C.; but in 144 B.C. it was conquered by Simon the Maccabee, who placed there a Jewish garrison (11:65f.; cf. 14:7).

Numerous coins and amphora handles, the latter from Rhodes, attest the commercial importance of the town during the last centuries B.C. It declined and was abandoned during the first centuries A.D.

Bibliography.–O. R. Sellers, *Citadel of Beth-Zur* (1933); *AP,* pp. 150-152; *BASOR,* 150 (Apr. 1958), 8ff.

A. VAN SELMS

BETOLION bə-tō'lē-ən [Gk. A *Betoliō,* B *Bētoliō*]; AV BETOLIUS; NEB BETOLIO. A town whose inhabitants returned from Babylon with Zerubbabel (1 Esd. 5:21), identified as Bethel in Ezr. 2:28.

BETOMESTHAIM be-tō-məs-thā'əm [Gk. *Betomesthaim*] (Jth. 4:6); AV BETOMESTHAM; **BETOMASTHAIM** [Gk. *Baitomasthaim*] (Jth. 15:4); AV BETOMASTHEM; NEB (both references) BETHOMESTHAIM. A place that "faces Esdraelon opposite the plain near Dothan" (Jth. 4:6). The name may have been Beth Mastema, "place of Mastema (or 'Satan')," a name of derision; but the suggestion that this was intended for Samaria hardly fits the references that have been preserved in Judith.

W. S. L. S.

BETONIM bet'ə-nim, be-tōn'im [Heb. *bᵉṭōnîm*; Gk. *Botanei*]. A town in the territory of Gad (Josh. 13:26), identified by Eusebius (*Onom.* 48.11; 49.10) as Botnia or Bothnim, identified with Khirbet Baṭneh or Baṭana, about 4 mi. (6 km.) SW of es-Salṭ, and not to be confused with Baṭnah of the Talmud, which is toward Aleppo.

BETRAY; BETRAYER; DELIVER (UP) [Heb. *rāmâ* (1 Ch. 12:17), *mirmâ* (Prov. 14:25), *gālâ* (Isa. 16:3), *māḵar* (Neh. 3:4); Gk. *paradídōmi, prodótēs* (Acts 7:52), *poiéō dēlon*–'make clear' (Mt. 26:73)]; AV also BEWRAY (Isa. 16:3; Mt. 26:73), DECEITFUL (Prov. 14:25), SELL (Nah. 3:4); NEB also FALSE (Prov. 14:5), BEGUILE (Neh. 3:4), GIVE AWAY (Mt. 26:73), etc.

Nearly all the NT references are to the betrayal of Jesus by JUDAS ISCARIOT, where the word is uniformly *paradídōmi,* "give over." Judas' act was more than that of giving a person up to the authorities; he did it under circumstances of treachery, which modified its character: (1) he took advantage of his intimate relation with Jesus Christ as a disciple to put Him in the hands of His enemies; (2) he did it stealthily by night; and (3) by a kiss, an act that professed affection and friendliness; (4) he did it for money; and (5) he knew that Jesus Christ was innocent of any crime (Mt. 27:4).

Stephen charged the Jews with being betrayers of the Righteous One (Acts 7:52), i.e., as having made Judas' act their own; cf. the same word (*prodótēs*) in Lk. 6:16,

"Judas Iscariot, who became a traitor"; and also in 2 Tim. 3:4, "traitors." T. REES

BETROTH; BETROTHED [Heb. *'āraś, ḥārap̱* (Lev. 19:20); Gk. *mnēsteúō, harmózomai* (2 Cor. 11:2), *parthénos* (1 Cor. 7:36-38)]; AV also ESPOUSED (2 S. 3:14; Mt. 1:18; Lk. 1:27; 2:5; 2 Cor. 11:2), VIRGIN (1 Cor. 7); NEB also ASSIGNED, PLEDGED (in marriage), "partner in celibacy" (1 Cor. 7). On betrothal as a social custom *see* MARRIAGE III.

Hosea, in his great parable of the prodigal wife (2:19f.), surpassed only by a greater Teacher's parable of the Prodigal Son, uses betrothal as the symbol of the Lord's pledge of His love and favor to penitent Israel.

The passage 1 Cor. 7:36-38 has been interpreted in a number of ways, and presents crucial translation difficulties. The AV "virgin" for *parthénos* does not give a good sense here; the RV interprets it as "virgin daughter," thus making the advice apply to fathers. The RSV, however, renders *parthénos* as "betrothed," understanding Paul's advice as applying to a suitor. The NEB ("partners in celibacy") reflects the interpretation given by, among others, Delling in *TDNT,* V, *s.v.* παρθένος: "The reference is to women in the community who have agreed to set up house with a man in order that they may achieve the ideal of Christian asceticism in economic independence." See also comms. *in loc.*; Bauer, p. 150.

J. W. D. H.

BETWEEN THE TESTAMENTS. *See* INTERTESTAMENTAL PERIOD.

BEULAH bū'lə [Heb. *bᵉ'ûlâ*–'married'] (Isa. 62:4, AV, NEB). A name symbolically applied to Israel: "Thy land [shall be called] Beulah . . . thy land shall be married . . . so shall thy sons marry thee" (Isa. 62:4f.). In this figure, frequently used since Hosea, the prophet wishes to express the future prosperity of Israel. The land once desolate shall again be populated. The RSV has "Your land [shall be called] Married . . . and your land shall be married."

BEVELED WORK [Heb. *ma'ᵃśēh môrāḏ*–'work of descent'] (1 K. 7:29); AV THIN WORK; NEB "hammered work of spiral design." Scrollwork on the bronze stands of the laver in Solomon's temple.

BEWAIL [Heb. *bāḵâ*–'weep'; Gk. *kóptō*]. The Greek word (in the middle voice) has the thought of striking on the breast and of loud lamentation, so common among oriental people in time of great sorrow. It is used to express the most intense grief, a sorrow that compels outward demonstration (Lk. 8:52; 23:27). A poignant example of this grief is that of the daughter of Jephthah (Jgs. 11:37; Lev. 10:6).

See BURIAL II.C, D; IV.D-F; GRIEF.

BEWITCH [Gk. *baskaínō*] (Gal. 3:1). The meaning here is "captivate by falsehood." Paul castigates the Galatians in strong terms for being so dazzled by the message of the Judaizers as to have strayed from the gospel of faith in the crucified Christ. The Greek word is colored by a background in magical evil incantations and spell-casting (see esp. *TDNT,* I, *s.v.* βασκαίνω [Delling]).

In the AV "bewitched" appears also for *exístēmi* in Acts 8:9, 11 (RSV "amazed"; NEB "swept off their feet," "carried away"), referring to the people's reaction to Simon the magician.

See also ENCHANTER; EVIL EYE; MAGIC.

J. W. D. H.

BEWRAY. An archaic word in the AV meaning "reveal" or "disclose" (Heb. *nāgaḏ,* Prov. 29:24), "betray" (*gālâ,* Isa. 16:3; Gk. *poiéō dḗlon,* Mt. 26:73; cf. also Sir. 27:21; 2 Macc. 4:1). It occurs also for Heb *qārā',* "call," in Prov. 27:16, AV; "the ointment of his right hand which bewrayeth itself," i.e., a contentious woman is said to be like oil held in the hand — she cannot be restrained. Cf. the RSV, "to restrain her is to restrain the wind or to grasp oil in his right hand"; and the NEB, "As well try to pick up oil in one's fingers!"

BEYOND. In the RSV the Heb. *bᵉ'ēḇer* with *hayyardēn,* "the Jordan," is generally rendered "beyond the Jordan." The AV sometimes translates "beyond (the Jordan)" (Gen. 50:10f.; Dt. 3:20, 25; etc.), but in other contexts "on this side" (Dt. 1:1, 5; Josh. 1:14f.; 9:1; etc.), "on the other side" (Dt. 11:30; Josh. 12:1; etc.), "on the side . . . westward" (Josh. 5:1). The NEB also varies according to the context: "beside" (Gen. 50:10f.), "in Transjordan" (Dt. 1:1, 5), "on the other side" (Dt. 3:20; 11:30), "east of" (Josh. 1:14f.; 9:10), "west of" (5:1), "district of" (1 S. 31:7).

The RSV also gives "beyond" for Heb. *mē'ēḇer* where it occurs in connection with the Jordan. The AV renders these passages "on this side" (Nu. 34:15; 35:14) or "on the other side" (Josh. 13:32; Jgs. 7:25); the NEB "beyond" (Nu. 34:15), "east of" (Nu. 35:14; Josh. 13:32), "across" (Jgs. 7:25).

Similarly, the RSV consistently has "Beyond the River" for Heb. *'ēḇer hannāhār* or Aram. *'ᵃḇar nahᵃrâ,* which occur frequently in Ezra and Nehemiah. The AV gives "beyond" or "on this side of" the river, the NEB always "Beyond-Euphrates."

In the NT the Gk. *péran,* when used in connection with the Jordan, is generally rendered "beyond" by the RSV and AV. The NEB, however, gives a variety of readings: "Transjordan" (Mt. 4:25; Mk. 3:8), "across" (Mt. 19:1), "beyond" (Jn. 1:28), "the other side of" (3:26).

It is clear that in the RSV "beyond" may indicate either the eastern or the western side of the river and that it may refer to the side on which the writer stands (Josh. 5:1; 9:1; etc.); e.g., in Dt. 1:1, 5; 4:41, etc. the reference is to the country E of the Jordan, while in 3:20, 25; 11:30, the country W of the Jordan is indicated. N. J. O.

BEZAE bē'zī, **CODEX (D).** *See* TEXT AND MSS OF THE NT I.A.2.

BEZAI bē'zī [Heb. *bēṣay*].

1. A chief who with Nehemiah sealed the covenant (Neh. 10:18).

2. [Gk. Apoc. *Bassai*]; AV and NEB Apoc. BASSAI. One whose descendants returned with Zerubbabel to Jerusalem (Ezr. 2:17; Neh. 7:23; 1 Esd. 5:16).

BEZALEEL bez'ə-lē-əl. *See* BEZALEL.

BEZALEL bez'ə-lel [Heb. *bᵉṣal'ēl*–'in the shadow (protection) of 'El (God)'; Gk. *Beseleēl*]; AV BEZALEEL.

1. A master workman under Moses; son of Uri the son of Hur, of the tribe of Judah. Yahweh gave him special wisdom and skill for this task of supervising — with the assistance of Oholiab of the tribe of Dan — the making of the tabernacle and its furniture (Ex. 31:2; 35:30; 36:1f.; 37:1; 38:22; 1 Ch. 2:20; 2 Ch. 1:5).

2. An Israelite of the time of Ezra who divorced his foreign wife (Ezr. 10:30). F. K. FARR

BEZEK bē'zek [Heb. *bezeq*].

1. A town in the territory allotted to Judah. Jgs. 1:4f.

records its conquest by Judah and Simeon, who captured and mutilated its ruler, Adoni-bezek (vv. 6f.). It is somewhat doubtfully identified with Khirbet Bezqa, about 3 mi. (5 km.) NE of Gezer.

2. [Gk. B *Abiezek*]. The place where Saul marshaled his army before marching to the relief of Jabesh-gilead (1 S. 11:8). Eusebius (*Onom.*) speaks of two villages of this name 17 Roman mi. (25 km.) from Shechem, on the way to Scythopolis. No doubt Khirbet Ibzîq is intended. The army probably assembled here or on the neighboring height, Râs Ibzîq, a mountain 2404 ft. (732 m.) above sea level.

W. EWING

BEZER [Heb. *beṣer*–'strong'; Gk. A *Basar,* B *Sobal*]. A son of Zophah of the tribe of Asher (1 Ch. 7:37).

BEZER bē'zər [Heb. *beṣer*–'strong']. A city of refuge set apart by Moses for the Reubenites and located in the "plain country" (or tableland, Heb. *mîšôr*), E of the Jordan, later assigned to this tribe by Joshua (Dt. 4:43; Josh. 20:8). The NEB always lists it as "Bezer-in-the-wilderness." The same city was assigned by lot as place of residence to the Merarites of the tribe of Levi (Josh. 21:36; 1 Ch. 6:63, 78). According to the Moabite Stone it was fortified by Mesha. It has been identified provisionally with Umm el-'Amad, 8 mi. (13 km.) NE of Medeba.

W. S. L. S.

BEZETH bē'zeth (1 Macc. 7:19, AV). *See* BETH-ZAITH.

BEZETHA bə-zē'thə. An addition to JERUSALEM N of the temple, outside the second but included within the third wall. Josephus describes it in *BJ* v.4.2, where he calls it also the "New City." It may be the same as BETH-ZAITH.

BIATAS bī'ə-təs (1 Esd. 9:48, AV). *See* PELAIAH **2.**

BIBLE [Gk. *biblía*–'books'].

The word "Bible" designates the collection of the Scriptures of the OT and NT recognized and in use in the Christian churches. Different religions (such as the Zoroastrian, Hindu, Buddhist, Moslem) have their collections of sacred writings, sometimes spoken of as their "Bibles." The Jews acknowledge only the Scriptures of the (Protestant) OT. Christians add the writings contained in the NT. The present article deals with the origin, character, contents, and purpose of the Christian Scriptures, regarded as the depository and authoritative record of God's revelations of Himself and of His will to the fathers by the prophets, and through His Son to the Church of a later age (He. 1:1f.). Reference is made throughout to the articles in which the several topics are more fully treated.

- I. Names
  - A. Bible
  - B. Other Designations
  - C. OT and NT
- II. Languages
- III. Compass and Divisions
  - A. Jewish Bible
    - 1. Josephus
    - 2. Other Lists and Divisions
    - 3. NT References
  - B. The LXX
    - 1. Origin
    - 2. Apocrypha
    - 3. Ecclesiastical Use
  - C. Vulgate (OT)
  - D. The NT
    - 1. Acknowledged Books
    - 2. Disputed Books
- IV. Literary Origin and Growth — Canonicity
  - A. The OT
    - 1. OT Indications
      - a. Patriarchal Age
      - b. Mosaic Age
      - c. Judges
      - d. Monarchy
      - e. Wisdom Literature
      - f. Prophecy
      - g. Josiah's Reformation
      - h. Exilic and Postexilic
      - i. Daniel
      - j. Preexilic Bible
    - 2. Critical Views
      - a. Pentateuch
      - b. Histories
      - c. Psalms and Prophets
    - 3. Formation of Canon
      - a. Critical Theory
      - b. More Positive View
      - c. Close of Canon
  - B. The NT
    - 1. Historical Books
      - a. Synoptics
      - b. Fourth Gospel
      - c. Act
    - 2. Epistles
      - a. Pauline
      - b. Epistle to Hebrews
      - c. Catholic Epistles
    - 3. Book of Revelation
    - 4. Canonicity
- V. Unity and Spiritual Purpose — Inspiration
  - A. Scripture a Unity
  - B. Purpose of Grace
  - C. Inspiration
    - 1. Biblical Claim
    - 2. Marks of Inspiration
  - D. Historical Influence
- VI. Chapters and Verses

I. Names. *–A. Bible.* The word "Bible" is the equivalent of the Gk. *biblía* (diminutive < *bíblos,* the inner bark of the papyrus), meaning originally "books." The expression "the books" (*tá biblía*) occurs in Dn. 9:2 (LXX) for prophetic writings. In the prologue to Sirach ("the rest of the books") it designates generally the OT Scriptures; similarly in 1 Macc. 12:9 ("the holy books"). The usage passed into the Christian church for the OT (2 Clem. 14:2), and eventually (*ca.* 5th cent.) was extended to the whole Scriptures. Jerome's name for the Bible (4th cent.) was "the divine library" (*Bibliotheca Divina*). Afterward came an important change from plural to singular meaning. "In process of time this name, with many others of Greek origin, passed into the vocabulary of the western church; and in the thirteenth century, by a happy solecism, the neuter plural came to be regarded as a feminine singular, and 'The Books' became by common consent 'The Book' (*biblía,* sing.), in which form the word was passed into the languages of modern Europe" (Westcott, *Bible in the Church,* p. 5). Its earliest occurrences in English are in *Piers Plowman,* Chaucer, and Wyclif.

B. Other Designations. There is naturally no name in the NT for the complete body of Scripture, the only Scriptures then known being those of the OT. In 2 Pet. 3:16, however, Paul's Epistles seem brought under this category. The common designations for the OT books by Our Lord and His apostles were "the scriptures" (writings, Gk. *hai graphaí*) (Mt. 21:42; Mk. 14:49; Lk. 24:32; Jn. 5:39; Acts 18:24; Rom. 15:4; etc.), "the holy scriptures" (Rom. 1:2); once "the sacred writings" (2 Tim. 3:15). The Jewish technical division (see below) into the Law, the Prophets, and the Hagiographa (holy writings) is recognized in the expression "in the law of Moses, and the prophets, and the psalms" (Lk. 24:44). More briefly the whole is summed up under "the law and the prophets" (Mt. 5:17; 11:13; Acts 13:15). Occasionally even the term "law" is extended to include the other divisions (Jn. 10:34; 12:34; 15:25; 1 Cor. 14:21). Paul uses the phrase "the oracles of God" as a name for the OT Scriptures (Rom. 3:2; cf. Acts 7:38; He. 5:12; 1 Pet. 4:11).

C. OT and NT. Special interest attaches to the names "Old" and "New Testament," now and since the close of the 2nd cent. in common use to distinguish the Jewish and the Christian Scriptures. "Testament" (lit. "a will") is used in the NT (AV) to represent the Gk. *diathḗkē*, in classical usage also "a will," but in the LXX and NT employed to translate the Heb. *b^e rîṯ*, "a covenant." In the RV, accordingly, "testament" is, with two exceptions (He. 9:16f., RSV "will"), changed to "covenant" (Mt. 26:28; 2 Cor. 3:6; Gal. 3:15; He. 7:22; 9:15; etc.). Applied to the Scriptures, therefore, "Old" and "New Testament" mean, strictly, "old" and "new covenant," though the older usage is now too firmly fixed to be altered. The name is a continuation of the OT designation for the law, "the book of the covenant" (2 K. 23:2). In this sense Paul applies it (2 Cor. 3:14) to the OT law: "the reading of the old testament" (RV, RSV, "covenant"). When after the middle of the 2nd cent. a definite collection began to be made of the Christian writings, these were named "the New Testament," and were placed as of equal authority alongside the "Old." The name *Novum Testamentum* (also *Instrumentum*) occurs first in Tertullian (A.D. 190-220), and soon came into general use. The idea of a Christian Bible may be then said to be complete.

II. Languages.–The OT, it is well known, is written mostly in Hebrew; the NT is written in Greek. The parts of the OT not in Hebrew, viz., Ezr. 4:8–6:18; 7:12-26; Jer. 10:11; Dnl. 2:4–7:28, are in Aramaic (formerly called Chaldean), a related dialect which after the Exile gradually displaced Hebrew as the spoken language of the Jews (*see* ARAMAIC; HEBREW LANGUAGE). The ancient Hebrew text was "unpointed," i.e., without the vowelmarks that came into use as a result of the labors of the Masoretic scholars (after 6th cent. A.D.).

The Greek of the NT, on which so much light was thrown by the labors of Deissmann and others from the Egyptian papyri, showing it to be a form of the "common" or *koinē* (Hellenistic) speech of the time (*see* GREEK LANGUAGE), still remains — from its penetration by Hebrew ideas, the influence of the LXX, peculiarities of training and culture in the writers, and above all the vitalizing and transforming power of Christian conceptions in vocabulary and expression — a study by itself. "We impart this," the apostle says, "in words not taught by human wisdom but taught by the Spirit" (1 Cor. 2:13). This is not always remembered in the search for parallels in the papyri. (For translations into other languages, *see* VERSIONS.)

III. Compass and Divisions.–The story of the origin, collection, and final stamping with canonical authority of the books that compose our present Bible involves many points still keenly in dispute. Before touching on these debatable matters, certain more external facts fall to be noticed relating to the general structure and compass of the Bible, and the main divisions of its contents.

A. Jewish Bible. 1. Josephus. A first step is to ascertain the character and contents of the Jewish Bible — the Bible in use by Christ and His apostles. Apart from references in the NT itself, an important aid is here afforded by a passage in Josephus (*CAp* i.8), which may be taken to represent the current belief of the Jews in the 1st cent. A.D. After speaking of the prophets as writing their histories "through the inspiration of God," Josephus says: "For we have not myriads of discordant and conflicting books, but twenty-two only, comprising the record of all time, and justly accredited as Divine. Of these, five are books of Moses, which embrace the laws and the traditions of mankind until his own death, a period of almost three thousand years. From the death of Moses till the reign of Artaxerxes, the successor of Xerxes, king of Persia, the prophets who followed Moses narrated the events of their time in thirteen books. The remaining four books consist of hymns to God, and maxims of conduct for men. From Artaxerxes to our own age, the history has been written in detail, but it is not esteemed worthy of the same credit, on account of the exact succession of the prophets having been no longer maintained." He goes on to declare that in this long interval "no one has dared either to add anything to [the writings], or to take anything from them, or to alter anything," and speaks of them as "the decrees [*dógmata*] of God," for which the Jews would willingly die. Philo (20 B.C.–*ca.* A.D. 50) uses similar strong language about the law of Moses (in Eusebius *Praep. ev.* viii.6).

In this enumeration of Josephus, it will be seen that the Jewish sacred books — thirty-nine in our Bible — are reckoned as twenty-two (after the number of letters in the Hebrew alphabet), viz., five of the law, thirteen of the Prophets, and four remaining books. These last are Psalms, Proverbs, Song of Solomon, and Ecclesiastes. The middle class includes all the historical and prophetical books, likewise Job, and the reduction in the number from thirty to thirteen is explained by Judges-Ruth, 1 and 2 Samuel, 1 and 2 Kings, 1 and 2 Chronicles, Ezra-Nehemiah, Jeremiah-Lamentations, and the twelve minor prophets, each being counted as one book. In his twenty-two books, therefore, Josephus includes all those in the present Hebrew canon, and none besides — not the books known as the APOCRYPHA, though he was acquainted with and used some of these.

2. Other Lists and Divisions. The statement of Josephus as to the twenty-two books acknowledged by the Jews is confirmed, with some variation of enumeration, by the lists preserved by Eusebius (*HE* vi.26) from Melito of Sardis (*ca.* A.D. 172) and Origen (A.D. 186-254), and by Jerome (*Preface to OT, ca.* 400) — all following Jewish authorities. Jerome knew also of a rabbinical division into twenty-four books. The celebrated passage from the Talmud (*Baba Bathra* 14b; *see* CANON OF THE OT; cf. Westcott, p. 35; Driver, *Literature of the OT* [1913], p. vi) counts also twenty-four. This number is obtained by separating Ruth from Judges and Lamentations from Jeremiah. The threefold division of the books, into Law, Prophets, and Writings (Hagiographa), is old. It is already implied in the prologue to Sirach (*ca.* 130 B.C.), "the law, the prophets, and the rest of the books"; is glanced at in a work ascribed to Philo (*De vita contemplativa* 25); and is indicated, as seen above, in Lk. 24:44. It really reflects stages in the formation of the Hebrew canon (see below). The rabbinical division, however, differed materially from that of Josephus in reckoning only eight books of the prophets, and relegating 1 and 2 Chronicles, Ezra-Nehemiah, Esther, Job, and Daniel to the Hagiographa, thus enlarging that group to nine (Westcott, p. 28; W. Smith, *Dictionary of the Bible* [1860-1864], I, *s.v.* "Canon"). When Ruth and Lamentations were separated, they were added to the list, raising the number to eleven. Some, however, take this to be the original arrangement. In printed Hebrew Bibles the books in all the divisions are separate. The Jewish schools further divided the "Prophets" into "the former prophets" (the historical books — Joshua, Judges, Samuel, and Kings) and "the latter prophets" (Isaiah, Jeremiah, Ezekiel, and the twelve minor prophets as one book).

3. NT references. It may be concluded that the above lists, excluding the Apocrypha, represent the Hebrew Bible as it existed in the time of Our Lord (the opinion, held by some, that the Sadducees received only the five books of the Law rests on no sufficient evidence). This result is borne out by the evidence of quotations in Josephus and Philo (cf. Westcott). Still more is it confirmed by an examination of OT quotations and references in the NT. It was seen above that the main divisions of the OT are recognized in the NT, and that, under the name "Scriptures," a divine authority is ascribed to them. It is therefore highly significant that, although the writers of the NT were familiar with the LXX, which contained the Apocrypha (see below), no quotation from any book of the Apocrypha occurs in their pages. One or two allusions, at most, suggest acquaintance with the book of Wisdom (e.g., Wisd. 5:18-21 par. Eph. 6:13-17). On the other hand, "every book in the Hebrew Bible is distinctly quoted in the NT with the exception of Joshua, Judges, Chronicles, Song of Solomon, Ecclesiastes, Ezra, Nehemiah, Esther, Obadiah, Zephaniah, and Nahum" (Westcott). Enumerations differ, but about 178 direct quotations may be reckoned in the Gospels, Acts, and Epistles; if references are included, the number is raised to about 700 (*see* QUOTATIONS IN THE NT). In four or five places (Lk. 11:49-51; Jas. 4:5; 1 Cor. 2:9; Eph. 5:14; Jn. 7:38) apparent references occur to sources other than the OT; it is doubtful whether most of them are really so (cf. Westcott, pp. 46-48; Eph. 5:14 may be from a Christian hymn). An undeniable influence of apocalyptic literature is seen in Jude, where vv. 14f. are a direct quotation from 1 Enoch. It does not follow that Jude regarded this book as a proper part of Scripture. (*See* JUDE, EPISTLE OF V.)

B. The LXX. Hitherto we have been dealing with the Hebrew OT; marked changes are apparent when we turn to the Septuagint, or Greek version current in the Greek-speaking world at the commencement of the Christian era. The importance of this version lies in its having been practically the OT of the early Church. It was used by the apostles and their converts, and is freely quoted in the NT, sometimes even when its renderings vary considerably from the Hebrew as we have it in the MT. Its influence was necessarily, therefore, very great.

1. Origin. The special problems connected with the origin, text, and literary relations of the LXX are dealt with elsewhere (*see* SEPTUAGINT). The version took its rise, under one of the early Ptolemies, because of the needs of the Jews in Egypt, before the middle of the 2nd cent. B.C.; it was gradually executed, and completed hardly later than *ca.* 100 B.C.; thereafter it spread into all parts of the diaspora. Its renderings reveal frequent divergence in MSS from the present MT, but show also that the translators permitted themselves considerable liberties in enlarging, abbreviating, transposing, and otherwise modifying the texts they had, and in the insertion of materials borrowed from other sources.

2. Apocrypha. The most noteworthy differences are in the departure from Jewish tradition in the arrangement of the textbooks (this varies greatly; cf. Swete, *IOTG,* II, ch. 1), and in the inclusion in the list of the other books, unknown to the Hebrew canon, now grouped as the APOCRYPHA. These form an extensive addition. They include the whole of the existing Apocrypha with the exception of 2 Esdras and the Prayer of Manasseh. All are of late date, and are in Greek, though Sirach had a Hebrew original which has been partly recovered. They are not collected, but are interspersed among the OT books in what are taken to be their appropriate places. The Greek fragments of Esther, e.g., are incorporated in that book; Susanna, and Bel and the Dragon, form part of Daniel; Baruch is joined with Jeremiah; etc. The most important books are Wisdom, Sirach, and 1 Maccabees (*ca.* 100 B.C.). That Sirach, originally in Hebrew (*ca.* 200 B.C.) and of high repute, was not included in the Hebrew canon, has a weighty bearing on the period of the closing of that canon.

3. Ecclesiastical Use. It is, as already remarked, singular that, notwithstanding this extensive enlargement of the canon by the LXX, the books just named obtained no scriptural recognition from the writers of the NT. The more scholarly of the fathers (Melito, Origen, Athanasius, Cyril, Jerome, etc.) likewise adhere to the Hebrew list, and most draw a sharp distinction between the canonical books and the Greek additions, the reading of which is, however, admitted for edification (cf. Westcott, pp. 135f., 168, 180, 182f.). Where slight divergences occur (e.g., Esther is omitted by Melito, and placed by Athanasius among the Apocrypha; Origen and Athanasius add Baruch to Jeremiah), these are readily explained by doubts as to canonicity or by imperfect knowledge. On the other hand, familiarity with the LXX in writers ignorant of Hebrew could not but tend to break down the limits of the Jewish canon, and to lend a scriptural sanction to the additions to that canon. This was aided in the West by the fact that the Old Latin versions (2nd cent.), based on the LXX, included these additions (the Syriac Peshitta followed the Hebrew). In many quarters, therefore, the distinction is found broken down, and ecclesiastical writers (Clement, Barnabas, Irenaeus, Tertullian, Clement of Alexandria, Basil, etc.) quote freely from books like Wisdom, Sirach, Baruch, Tobit, 2 Esdras, as from parts of the OT.

C. Vulgate (OT). An important landmark is reached in the Vulgate or Latin version of Jerome (*see* VERSIONS). Jerome, on grounds explained in his Preface, recognized only the Hebrew Scriptures as canonical; under pressure he executed later a hasty translation of Tobit and Judith. Feeling ran strong, however, in favor of the other books, and ere long these were added to Jerome's version from the Old Latin. It is this enlarged Vulgate which received official recognition, under anathema, at the Council of Trent (1546), and, with revision, from Clement VIII (1592), though leading Roman Catholic scholars (Ximenes, Erasmus, Cajetan) had previously made plain the true state of the facts. The Greek Church vacillated in its decisions, sometimes approving the limited, sometimes the extended, canon (cf. Westcott, pp. 217-229). The churches of the Reformation (Lutheran, Swiss), as was to be expected, went back to the Hebrew canon, giving only a qualified sanction to the reading and ecclesiastical use of the Apocrypha. The early English versions (Tyndale, Coverdale, etc.) include, but separate, the apocryphal books (*see* ENGLISH VERSIONS). The Anglican Articles express the general estimate of these books: "And the other books (as Jerome saith) the Church doth read for example of life and instruction of manners; yet doth it not apply them to establish any doctrine" (Art. VIII). Modern Protestant Bibles often exclude the Apocrypha altogether.

D. The NT. It has been seen that a Christian NT did not, in the strict sense, arise till after the middle of the 2nd century. Gospels and Epistles had long existed, collections had begun to be made, and the Gospels, at least, were read weekly in the assemblies of the Christians (Justin *Apol.* i.67), before the attempt was made to bring together, and take formal account of, all the books which enjoyed apostolic authority (*see* CANON OF THE NT). The needs of the Church, however, and especially controversy with gnostic opponents, made it necessary that this work should be done; collections also had to be formed for purposes of translations into other tongues. Genuine gospels had to be distinguished from spurious; apostolic writings from those of later date, or falsely bearing apostolic names. When this task was undertaken, a distinction soon revealed itself between two classes of books, setting aside those recognized on all hands as spurious: (1) books universally acknowledged — those named afterward by Eusebius the *homologoúmena*; and (2) books only partially acknowledged, or on which some doubt rested — the Eusebian *antilegómena* (*HE* iii.25). It is on this distinction that differences as to the precise extent of the NT turned.

1. Acknowledged Books. The "acknowledged" books present little difficulty. They are enumerated by Eusebius, whose statements are confirmed by early lists (e.g., that of Muratori, *ca.* A.D. 170), quotations, versions, and patristic use. At the head stand the four Gospels and the Acts, then come the thirteen Epistles of Paul, then 1 Peter and 1 John. These, Westcott says, toward the close of the 2nd cent. "were universally received in every church, without doubt or limitation, as part of the written rule of Christian faith, equal in authority with the Old Scriptures, and ratified (as it seemed) by a tradition reaching back to the date of their composition" (p. 133). With them may almost be placed Revelation (as by Eusebius) and Hebrews, the doubts regarding the latter relating more to Pauline authority than to genuineness (e.g., Origen).

2. Disputed Books. The "disputed" books were the Epistles of James, Jude, 2 and 3 John, and 2 Peter. These, however, do not all stand in the same rank as regards authentication. A chief difficulty is the silence of the western fathers regarding James, 2 Peter, and 3 John. On the other hand, James is known to Origen and is included in the Peshitta; the Muratorian Fragment attests Jude and 2 John as "held in the Catholic Church" (Jude also in Tertullian, Clement of Alexandria, Origen); none of the books is treated as spurious. The weakest in attestation is 2 Peter, which is not distinctly traceable before the 3rd cent. (*see* CANON OF THE NT). It is to be added that, in a few instances, as in the case of the OT Apocrypha, early fathers cite as Scripture books not generally accepted as canonical (e.g., Barnabas, Hermas, Apocalypse of Peter).

The complete acceptance of all the books in our present NT canon may be dated from the councils of Laodicea (*ca.* A.D. 363) and of Carthage (397), confirming the lists of Cyril of Jerusalem, Jerome, and Augustine.

IV. Literary Origin and Growth — Canonicity.–Thus far the books of the OT and NT have been taken simply as given, and no attempt has been made to inquire how or when they were written or compiled, or how they came to acquire the dignity and authority implied in their reception into a sacred canon. The field here entered is one bristling with controversy, and it is necessary to choose one's steps with caution to find a safe way through it. Details in the survey are left, as before, to the special articles.

A. The OT. The OT, it is obvious and on all sides admitted, has a long literary history prior to its final settlement in a canon. As to the course of that history traditional and modern critical views differ widely. It may possibly turn out that the truth lies somewhere midway between them.

1. OT Indications. If the indications furnished by the OT itself be accepted, the results are something like the following:

a. Patriarchal Age. No mention is made of writing in the patriarchal age, though it is now known that a high literary culture then prevailed in Babylonia, Egypt, and Palestine, and it is not improbable, indeed seems likely, that records in some form came down from that age, and are, in parts, incorporated in the early history of the Bible. One theory has it that Gen. 1:1–37:2 consists of eleven tablets placed end-to-end, recording the history, in Mesopotamian fashion, of the period from Adam's time.

b. Mosaic Age. In Mosaic times writing was in use, and Moses himself was trained in the learning of the Egyptians (Ex. 2:10; Acts 7:22). In no place is the composition of the whole Pentateuch (as traditionally believed) ascribed to Moses, but no inconsiderable amount of written matter is directly attributed to him, creating the presumption that there was more, even when the fact is not stated. Moses wrote "all the words of the Lord" in the "book of the covenant" (Ex. 21–23; 24:4, 7). He wrote "the words of this law" of Deuteronomy at Moab, "in a book, to the very end" (Dt. 31:9, 24, 26). This was given to the priests to be put by the side of the ark for preservation (vv. 25f.). Other notices occur of the writing of Moses (Ex. 17:14; Nu. 33:2; Dt. 31:19, 22; cf. Nu. 11:26). the Song of Miriam, and the snatches of song in Nu. 21, the first (perhaps all) quoted from the "Book of the Wars of the Lord" (Nu. 21:14ff.), plainly belong to Mosaic times. In this connection it should be noticed that the discourses and law of Deuteronomy imply the history and legislation of the critical JE histories (see below). The priestly laws (Leviticus, Numbers) bear so entirely the stamp of the wilderness that they can hardly have originated anywhere else, and were probably then, or soon after, written down. Joshua, too, is presumed to be familiar with writing (Josh. 8:30-35; cf. Dt. 27:8), and is stated to have written his farewell address "in the book of the law of God" (Josh. 24:26; cf. 1:7f.). These statements already imply the beginning of a sacred literature.

c. Judges. The Song of Deborah (Jgs. 5) is an indubitably authentic monument of the age of the judges; and the older parts of Judges, at least, must have been nearly contemporary with the events they record. A knowledge of writing among the common people seems implied in Jgs. 8:14. Samuel, like Joshua, wrote "in a book" (1 S. 10:25), and laid it up, evidently among other writings, "before the Lord."

d. Monarchy. The age of David and Solomon was one of high development in poetical and historical composition: witness the elegies of David (2 S. 1:17-27; 3:33f.), and the finely finished narrative of David's reign (2 S. 9–20), the so-called Jerusalem Source, admitted to date "from a period very little later than that of the events related" (Driver, *Literature of the OT,* p. 183). There were court scribes and chroniclers.

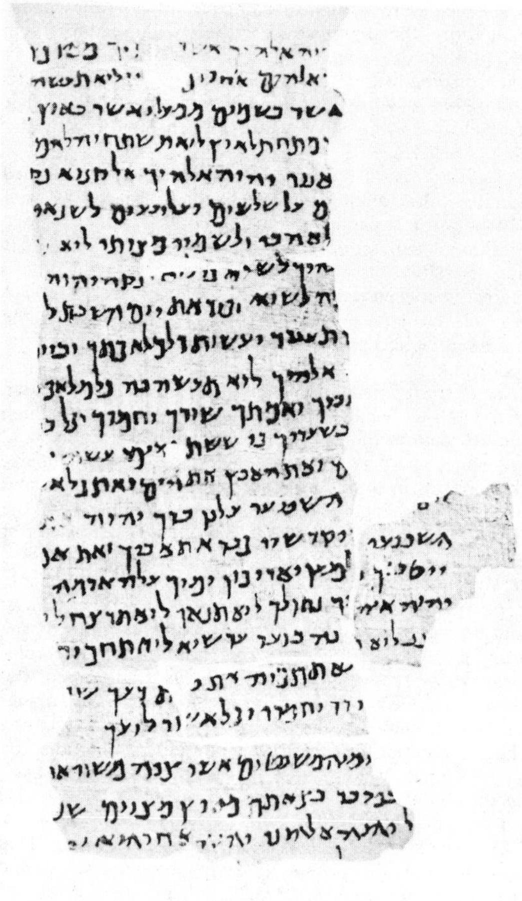

Nash Papyrus, containing the Ten Commandments and the Shema (Dt. 6:4) (1st or 2nd cent. B.C.) (*Biblical Archeologist*)

David, as befits his piety and poetical and musical gifts, is credited with laying the foundations of a sacred psalmody (2 S. 23:1ff.; *see* PSALMS), and a whole collection of Psalms (1–72, with exclusion of the distinct collection, 42–50), once forming a separate book (cf. Ps. 72:20), are, with others, ascribed to him by their titles (Pss. 1, 2, 10 are untitled). It is hardly credible that a tradition like this can be wholly wrong, and a Davidic basis of the Psalter may safely be assumed. Numerous Psalms, by their mention of the "king" (as Pss. 2, 18, 20, 21, 28, 33, 45, 61, 63, 72, 101, 110), are naturally referred to the period of the monarchy (some, as Ps. 18, certainly Davidic). Other groups of Psalms are referred to the temple guilds (Sons of Korah, Asaph).

During the monarchy, the prophets would seem to have acted as the "sacred historiographers" of the nation. From their memoirs of the successive reigns, as the later books testify (1 Ch. 29:29; 2 Ch. 9:29; 12:15; etc.), are compiled most of the narratives in our canonical writings (hence the name "former prophets"). The latest date in 2 Kings is 562 B.C., and the body of the book is probably earlier.

e. Wisdom Literature. Solomon is renowned as founder of the wisdom literature and the author of Proverbs (1 K. 4:32; Prov. 1:1; 10:1; Eccl. 12:9; Ecclesiastes itself appears to be late), and of the Song of Solomon (Cant. 1:1). The "men of Hezekiah" are said to have copied out a collection of his proverbs (Prov. 25:1; *see* PROVERBS). Here also may be placed the book of Job. Hezekiah's reign appears to have been one of literary activity: to it, probably, are to be referred certain of the Psalms (e.g., 46, 48).

f. Prophecy. With the rise of written prophecy a new form of literature enters, called forth by, and vividly mirroring, the religious and political conditions of the closing periods of the monarchy in Israel and Judah (*see* PROPHECY). On the older view, Obadiah and Joel stood at the head of the series in the pre-Assyrian period (9th cent.), and this seems the preferable view still. On the newer view, these prophets are late, and written prophecy begins in the Assyrian period with Amos (Jeroboam II, *ca.* 750 B.C.) and Hosea (*ca.* 745-735). When the latter prophet wrote, Samaria was tottering to its fall (721 B.C.). A little later, in Judah, come Isaiah (*ca.* 740-690) and Micah (*ca.* 720-708). Isaiah, in the reigns of Uzziah, Jotham, Ahaz, and Hezekiah, is the greatest of the prophets in the Assyrian age, and his ministry reaches its climax in the deliverance of Jerusalem from Sennacherib (2 K. 18f.; Isa. 36f.). It is a question whether some oracles of an Isaian school are not mingled with the prophet's own writings, and most scholars now regard the second part of the book (chs. 40–66) as exilic or (in part) postexilic in date. The standpoint of much in these chapters is certainly in the Exile; whether the composition of the whole can be placed there is extremely doubtful (*see* ISAIAH). Nahum, who prophesies against Nineveh, belongs to the very close of this period (*ca.* 660).

The prophets Zephaniah (under Josiah, *ca.* 630 B.C.) and Habakkuk (*ca.* 606) may be regarded as forming the transition to the next — the Chaldean — period. The Chaldeans (unnamed in Zephaniah) are advancing but are not yet come (Hab. 1:6). The great prophetic figure here, however, is Jeremiah, whose sorrowful ministry, beginning in the thirteenth year of Josiah (626 B.C.), extended through the succeeding reigns till after the fall of Jerusalem (586 B.C.). The prophet elected to remain with the remnant in the land, and shortly after, troubles having arisen, was forcibly carried into Egypt (Jer. 43). Here also he prophesied (chs. 43f.). From the reign of Jehoiakim, Jeremiah consistently declared the success of the Chaldean arms, and foretold the seventy years' captivity (25:12-14). Baruch acted as his secretary in writing out and editing his prophecies (chs. 36, 45).

g. Josiah's Reformation. A highly important event in this period was Josiah's reformation in his eighteenth year (621 B.C.), and the discovery, during repairs of the temple, of "the book of the law," called also "the book of the covenant" and "the law of Moses" (2 K. 22:8; 23:2, 24f.). The finding of this book, identified by most authorities with the book of Deuteronomy, produced an extraordinary sensation. On no side was there the least question that it was a genuine ancient work. Jeremiah, strangely, makes no allusion to this discovery, but his prophecies are deeply saturated with the ideas and style of Deuteronomy.

h. Exilic and Postexilic. The bulk of Isa. 40–66 belongs, at least in spirit, to the Exile, but the one prophet of the Exile known to us by name is the priestly Ezekiel. Carried captive under Jehoiaçhin (597 B.C.), Ezekiel labored among his fellow exiles for at least twenty-two years (Ezk. 1:2; 29:17). A man of the strongest moral courage, his symbolic visions on the banks of the Chebar alternated with the most direct expostulation, exhortation, warning, and promise. In the description of an ideal temple and its worship with which his book closes (chs. 40–48), critics think they discern the suggestion of the Levitical code.

i. Daniel. After Ezekiel the voice of prophecy is silent till it revives in Daniel, in Babylon, under Nebuchadnezzar and his successors. Deported in 605 B.C., Daniel rose to power, and "continued until the first year of King Cyrus" (539 B.C.; Dnl. 1:21). Criticism will have it that his prophecies are a product of the Maccabean age, but there are powerful considerations on the other side (*see* DANIEL, BOOK OF). Jonah may have been written about this time, though the prophet's mission itself was pre-Assyrian (9th cent.). The rebuilding of the temple after the return, under Zerubbabel, furnished the occasion for the prophecies of Haggai and Zechariah (520 B.C.). Scholars are disposed to regard only Zec. 1–8 as belonging to this period — the remainder being placed earlier or later. Malachi, nearly a century after (*ca.* 430), brings up the rear of prophecy, rebuking unfaithfulness, and predicting the advent of the "messenger of the covenant" (Mal. 3:1f.). To this period or later belong, besides postexilic Psalms (e.g., Pss. 124, 126), the books of Ezra, Nehemiah, Chronicles, Esther, and apparently Ecclesiastes.

j. Preexilic Bible. If in this rapid sketch the facts are correctly represented, it will be apparent that, in opposition to prevalent views, a large body of sacred literature (laws, histories, Psalms, wisdom-books, prophecies) existed and was recognized long before the Exile. God's ancient people had "Scriptures" — had a Bible — if not yet in collected form. This is strikingly borne out by the numerous OT passages referring to what appears to be a code of sacred writings in the hands of the pious in Israel. Such are the references to, and praises of, the "law" and "word" of God in many of the Psalms (e.g., 1, 19, 119, 12:6; 17:4; 18:21f.), with the references to God's known "words," "ways," "commandments," "statutes," in other books of the OT (Job 8:8; Hos. 8:12; Dnl. 9:2). In brief, Scriptures, which must have contained records of God's dealings with His people, a knowledge of which is constantly presupposed, "laws" of God for the regulation of the heart and conduct, "statutes," "ordinances," "words" of God, are a postulate of a great part of the OT.

2. Critical Views. The account of the origin and growth of the OT above presented is in marked contrast with that given in the textbooks of the more critical schools. The main features of these critical views are sketched in the article CRITICISM; here a brief indication will suffice. Generally, the books of the OT are brought down to late dates, and regarded as highly composite; the earlier books, because of their distance from the events recorded, are largely deprived of historical worth. Neither histories nor laws in the Pentateuch belong to the Mosaic age: Joshua is a "romance"; Judges may embody ancient fragments, but in bulk is unhistorical. The earliest fragments of Israelite literature are lyric pieces like those preserved in Gen. 4:23f; 9:25-27; Nu 21; the Song of Deborah (Jgs. 5) is probably genuine. Historical writing begins about the age of David or soon thereafter. The folklore of the Hebrews and traditions of the Mosaic age began to be reduced to writing about the 9th cent. B.C.

a. Pentateuch. Our present Pentateuch (enlarged to a "Hexateuch," including Joshua) consists of four main strands (themselves composite), the oldest of which (called J, from its use of the name Jehovah) goes back to *ca.* 850 B.C. This was Judean. A parallel history book (called E, from its use of the name 'Elohim, God) was produced in the northern kingdom about a century later (*ca.* 750). Later still these two were united (JE). These histories, "prophetic" in spirit, were originally attributed to individual authors, distinguished by minute criteria of style; later they were regarded as the work of "schools." Hitherto the only laws known were those of the (post-Mosaic) book of the covenant (Ex. 20–23). Later, in Josiah's reign, the desire for centralization of worship led to the composition of the book of Deuteronomy. This, secreted in the temple, was found by Hilkiah (2 K. 22), and brought about the reformation of Josiah formerly mentioned. Deuteronomy (D), thus produced, is the third strand in the pentateuchal compilation. After the destruction of the city and temple, under the impulse of Ezekiel a new period of law-construction began, now priestly in spirit. Old laws and usages were codified; new laws were invented; the history of institutions was recast; finally, the extensive complex of Levitical legislation was brought into being, clothed with a wilderness dress, and ascribed to Moses. This elaborate Priestly Code (P or PC), with its accompanying history, was brought from Babylon by Ezra, and, united with the already existing JE and D, was given forth by him to the restored community at Jerusalem (444 B.C.; Neh. 8) as "the law of Moses." Their acceptance of it was the inauguration of "Judaism."

b. Histories. In its theory of the Pentateuch reconstructive criticism lays down the determinative positions for its criticism of all the remaining books of the OT. The historical books show but a continuation of the processes of literary construction exemplified in the books ascribed to Moses. The Deuteronomic element, e.g., in Joshua, Judges, Samuel, and Kings, proves them, in these parts, to be later than Josiah, and historically untrustworthy. The Levitical element in Chronicles demonstrates its pictures of David and his successors to be distorted and false. The same rule applies to the prophets. Joel, e.g., must be postexilic, because it presupposes the priestly law. The patriarchal and Mosaic histories being subverted, it is not permitted to assume any high religious ideas in early Israel. David, therefore, could not have written the Psalms. Most, if not practically all, of these are postexilic.

c. Psalms and Prophets. Monotheism came in — at least first obtained recognition — through Amos and Hosea. The prophets could not have the foresight and far-reaching hopes seen in their writings: these passages, therefore, must be removed. Generally the tendency is to put dates as low as possible, and very many books, regarded before as preexilic, are carried down in whole or part to exilic, postexilic, and even late Greek times (P, Psalter, Job, Proverbs, Song of Solomon, Ecclesiastes, 2 Isaiah, Joel, Lamentations). Daniel is Maccabean and unhistorical (*ca.* 168-167 B.C.).

It is not proposed here to discuss this theory, which is not accepted in the present article, and is considered elsewhere (*see* CRITICISM; PENTATEUCH). The few points calling for remark relate to canonical acceptance.

3. Formation of the Canon. The general lines of the completed Jewish canon have already been sketched, and some light has now been thrown on the process by which the several books obtained a sacred authority. As to the actual stages in the formation of the canon opinions again diverge widely (*see* CANON OF THE OT).

a. Critical Theory. On the theory outlined above, no collections of sacred books were made prior to the return from Babylon. The only books that had authority before the Exile were, perhaps, the old book of the covenant, and, from Josiah's time, Deuteronomy. Both, after the return, were embodied with the JE histories and P in Ezra's completed book of the Law (with Joshua?), in which, accordingly, the foundation of a canon was laid. The fivefold division of the Law was later. Subsequently, answering to the second division of the Jewish canon, a collection was made of the prophetic writings. As this includes books which, on the critical view, go down to Greek times (Jonah; Zec. 9–14), its completion cannot be earlier than well down in the 3rd cent. B.C. Latest of all came the collection of the "Hagiographa" — a division of the canon, on this theory, kept open to receive additions certainly till the 2nd cent., some think after. Into it were received such late writings as Ecclesiastes, Maccabean Psalms, Daniel. Even then one or two books (Ecclesiastes, Esther) remained subjects of dispute.

b. More Positive View. It will appear from the foregoing that this theory is not here accepted without considerable modification. If the question be asked, What constituted a right to a place in the canon? the answer can hardly be other than that suggested by Josephus in the passage formerly quoted — a real or supposed inspiration in the author of the book. Books were received if men had the prophetic spirit (in higher or lower degree: that, e.g., of wisdom); they ceased to be received when the succession of prophets was thought to fail (after Malachi). In any case the writings of truly inspired men (Moses, the prophets, psalmists) were accepted as of authority. This article, however, has already sought to show that many of these books already existed from Moses down, long before the Exile (the law, collections of Psalms, of proverbs, written prophecies: to what end did the prophets write, if they did not mean their prophecies to be circulated and preserved?); and such writings, to the godly who knew and used them, had the full value of Scripture. A canon began with the first laying up of the "book of the law" before the Lord (Dt. 31:25f.; Josh. 24:26). The age of Ezra and Nehemiah, therefore, is not that of the beginning, but, as Jewish tradition rightly held (Josephus; 2 Macc. 2:13; Talmud), rather that of the completion, systematic delimitation, acknowledgment, and formal close of the canon. The divisions of "Law, Prophets, and holy Writings" would thus have their place from the beginning, and be nearly contemporaneous. The Samaritans accepted only the five books of the Law, with apparently Joshua (*see* PENTATEUCH, SAMARITAN).

c. Close of the Canon. There is no need for dogmatism as to an absolute date for the close of the canon. If inspired voices continued to be heard, their utterances were entitled to recognition. Books duly authenticated *might* be added, but the non-inclusion of a book such as Sirach (in Hebrew *ca.* 200 B.C.) shows that the limits of the canon were jealously guarded, and the onus of proof rests on those who affirm that there were such books. Calvin, e.g., held that there were Maccabean Psalms. Many modern scholars do the same, but it is doubtful if they are right. Ecclesiastes is thought on linguistic grounds to be late, but it and other books need not be so late as critics make them. Daniel is confidently declared to be Maccabean, but there are weighty reasons for maintaining a Persian date (*see* DANIEL VI). As formerly noticed, the threefold division into "the law, the prophets, and the rest [*tá loipá,* a definite number] of the books" is already attested in the prologue to Sirach.

B. The NT. Critical controversy, long occupied with the OT, has again keenly attached itself to the NT, with similar disturbing results (*see* CRITICISM II.E). More extreme opinions may be here neglected, and account be taken only of those that can claim reasonable support. The NT writings are conveniently grouped into the historical books (Gospels and Acts); Epistles (Pauline and other); and a prophetic book (Revelation). In order of writing, the Epistles, generally, are earlier than the Gospels, but in order of subject, the Gospels naturally claim attention first.

1. Historical Books. The main facts about the origin of the Gospels can perhaps be distinguished from the complicated literary theories which scholars are still discussing (*see* GOSPELS, SYNOPTIC). The first three Gospels, known as the Synoptics, evidently embody a common tradition and draw from common sources. The Fourth Gospel — that of John — presents problems by itself.

a. The Synoptics. The Synoptic Gospels (Matthew, Mark, Luke) fall in date well within the apostolic age, and are, in the 2nd cent., uniformly connected with the authors whose names they bear. Mark is spoken of as "the interpreter of Peter" (Papias, in *HE* iii.39); Luke is the well-known companion of Paul. A difficulty arises about Matthew, whose Gospel is stated (by Papias and others) to have been written in Aramaic, while the Gospel bearing his name is in Greek. The Greek Gospel seems at least to have been sufficiently identified with the apostle to admit of the early Church always treating it as his.

[The oral tradition theory of Gospel origins capitalizes on the fact that these documents were written not at the close of Jesus' earthly life but after an interval of several decades. Meanwhile, the apostles taught the Church what Jesus had said and done, and by repetition the instruction gradually assumed a fixed form. This approach helps to account for the agreements in the Synoptics but runs into trouble where the writers give differing reports of the same incident or the same address by our Lord.

Literary criticism, as the term suggests, uses a different approach. It postulates two written sources lying behind Matthew and Luke: Mark, the earliest Gospel, basically a record of the preaching of Peter; and a collection of the sayings and discourses of Jesus labelled by modern students Q (the initial letter of the German word for source). It is recognized, however, that both Matthew and Luke contain some unique material, leading some scholars to prefer a four-document hypothesis. The Q factor has proved the most elusive because of differences in the text of Matthew and Luke where this source is apparently used. Some have theorized that Q should be considered an oral rather than a written source.

Another approach reverses the position of Mark by placing his Gospel last in relation to Matthew and Luke (W. R. Farmer, *The Synoptic Problem* [1964]). On this assumption the difficulty is to account for the emergence of Mark's Gospel, since so much of it was already found in the other two Synoptics.

For further developments in the treatment of the Synoptics such as form criticism and redaction criticism, *see* GOSPELS, SYNOPTIC; CRITICISM. E. F. H.]

b. Fourth Gospel. The Fourth Gospel (John), the genuineness of which is assumed (*see* JOHN, THE GOSPEL ACCORDING TO), differs entirely in character and style. It is less a narrative than a didactic work, written to convince its readers that Jesus is "the Son of God" (Jn. 20:31). The Gospel may be presumed to have been composed at Ephesus, in the last years of the apostle's residence there. With this its character corresponds. The other Gospels had long been known; John does not therefore traverse the ground already covered by them. He confines himself chiefly to matters drawn from his personal recollections: the Judean ministry, the visits of Christ to Jerusalem, His last private discourses to His disciples. John had so often retold, and so long brooded over, the thoughts and words of Jesus, that they had become, in a manner, part of his own thought, and in reproducing them he necessarily did so with a subjective tinge, and in a partially paraphrastic and interpretative manner. Yet it is truly the words, thoughts, and deeds of his beloved Lord that he narrates. His Gospel is the

Miniature of Mark and opening verses of his Gospel, from a manuscript of the four Gospels (MS 30) dated May 31, 1430 (University of Michigan Library)

needful complement to the others — the "spiritual" Gospel.

c. Acts. This book narrates the origin and early fortunes of the Church, its special motif (cf. 1:8) being the extension of the gospel to the Gentiles through the labors of Paul. Its author is Luke, Paul's companion, whose Gospel it continues (1:1). Certain sections—the so-called we-sections (16:10-17; 20:5-15; 21:1-18; 27:1–28:16)—are transcribed directly from Luke's journal of Paul's travels. The book closes abruptly with Paul's two-year imprisonment at Rome (28:30f.; A.D. 60-61), and not a hint is given of the issue of the imprisonment — trial, liberation, or death. Does this mean that a 3rd "treatise" was contemplated? Or that the book was written while the imprisonment still continued? (thus Harnack). If the latter, the Third Gospel must be very early.

2. Epistles. a. Pauline. Doubt never rested in the early Church on the thirteen epistles of Paul. Following upon the rejection by the Tübingen school of all the Epistles but four (Romans, 1 and 2 Corinthians, Galatians), the tide of opinion has again turned strongly in favor of their genuineness. An exception is the Pastoral Epistles (1 and 2 Timothy, Titus), still questioned by some (*see* PASTORAL EPISTLES). The Epistles, called forth by actual needs of the churches, are a living outpouring of the thoughts and feelings of the mind and heart of the apostle in relation to his converts. Most are letters to churches he himself had founded (1 and 2 Corinthians, Galatians, Ephesians[?], Philippians, 1 and 2 Thessalonians): two are to churches he had not himself visited, but with which he stood in affectionate relations (Romans, Colossians); one is purely personal (Philemon); three are addressed to individuals, but with official responsibilities (1 and 2 Timothy, Titus). The larger number were written during his missionary labors and reflect his personal situation, anxieties, and companionships at the places of their composition; four are Epistles of the first Roman imprisonment (Ephesians, Philippians, Colossians, Philemon); 2 Timothy is a voice from the dungeon, in his second imprisonment, shortly before his martyrdom. Doctrine, counsel, rebuke, admonition, tender solicitude, ethical instruction, prayer, thanksgiving, blend in living fusion in their contents. So marvelous a collection of letters, on such magnificent themes, was never before given to the world.

The earliest Epistles, in point of date, are generally held to be those to the Thessalonians, written from Corinth (A.D. 52, 53). The church, newly founded, had passed through much affliction (1 Thess. 1:6; 2:14; 3:3f.; etc.), and Paul writes to comfort and exhort it. His words about the Second Coming (4:13ff.) led to mistaken expectations and some disorders. These his second Epistle was written to correct (2 Thess. 2:1-3; 3:6; etc.).

Corinth itself received the next Epistles — the first called forth by reports received at Ephesus of grave divisions and irregularities (1 Cor. 1:11; 3:3; 11:18ff; etc.), joined with pride of knowledge, doctrinal heresy (15:12ff.), and at least one case of gross immorality (ch. 5) in the church; the second, written at Philippi, expressing joy at the repentance of the offender, and removing the severe sentence that had been passed upon him (2 Cor. 2:1-10; cf. 1 Cor. 5:3f.), likewise vindicating Paul's own apostleship (chs. 10–13). The date of both is A.D. 57. 1 Corinthians contains the beautiful hymn on love (ch. 13) and the noble chapter on resurrection (ch. 15).

In the following year (58) Paul penned from Corinth the Epistle to the Romans — the greatest of his doctrinal Epistles. In it he develops his great theme of the impossibility of justification before God through works of law (chs. 1–3), and of the divine provision for human salvation in a "righteousness of God" in Christ Jesus, received through faith. He exhibits first the objective side of this redemption in the deliverance from condemnation effected through Christ's reconciling death (chs. 3–5); then the subjective side, in the new life imparted by the Spirit, giving deliverance from the power of sin (chs. 6–8). A discussion follows of the divine sovereignty in God's dealings with Israel, and of the end of these dealings (chs. 9–11); and the Epistle concludes with practical exhortations, counsels to forbearance, and greetings (chs. 12–16).

Closely connected with the Epistle to the Romans is that to the Galatians, in which the same truths are handled, but now with a polemical intent in expostulation and reproach. The Galatian churches had apostatized from the gospel of faith to Jewish legalism; and the apostle, sorely grieved, writes this powerful letter to rebuke their faithlessness, and recall them to their allegiance to the truth. It is reasonable to suppose that the two Epistles are nearly related in place and time. The question is complicated, however, by the dispute which has arisen as to whether the churches intended are those of northern Galatia (the older view; cf. Conybeare and Howson, Lightfoot, Kümmel) or those of southern Galatia (Wm. Ramsay, Ridderbos), i.e., the churches of Derbe, Lystra, Iconium, and Antioch, in Paul's time embraced in the Roman province of Galatia (*see* GALATIA IV; GALATIANS, EPISTLE TO THE). If the latter view is adopted, date and place are uncertain; if the former, the Epistle may have been written from Ephesus (*ca.* A.D. 57).

The four Epistles of the imprisonment all fall within the years A.D. 60-61. That to the Philippians, warmly praising the church, and exhorting to unity, possibly the latest of the group, was sent by the hand of Epaphroditus, who had come to Rome with a present from the Philippian church, and had there been overtaken by a serious illness (Phil. 2:25-30; 4:15-18). The remaining three Epistles (Ephesians, Colossians, and Philemon) were written at one time, and were carried to their destinations by Epaphras. Ephesians and Colossians are twin Epistles, similar in thought and style, extolling the preeminence of Christ; but it is doubtful whether the former was not really a "circular" Epistle, or even, perhaps, the lost epistle to the Laodiceans (Col. 4:16; *see* LAODICEANS, EPISTLE TO THE). The Colossian Epistle has in view an early form of gnostic heresy (cf. Lightfoot, comm. on Galatians). Philemon is a personal letter to a friend of the apostle at Colossae, whose runaway slave Onesimus, now a Christian, is being sent back to him with warm commendations.

Latest from Paul's pen are the PASTORAL EPISTLES (1 and 2 Timothy, Titus), implying his liberation from his first imprisonment and a new period of missionary labor in Ephesus, Macedonia, and Crete. Timothy was left at Ephesus (1 Tim. 1:3), Titus at Crete (Tit. 1:5), for the regulation and superintendence of the churches. The Epistles, the altered style of which shows the deep impress of advancing years and changed conditions, contain admonitions to pastoral duty, with warnings as to perils that had arisen or would arise. 1 Timothy and Titus were written while the apostle was still at liberty (A.D. 63); 2 Timothy is from his Roman prison, when his case had been partly heard and the end was impending (2 Tim. 4:6, 16f.).

b. Epistle to the Hebrews. Though ascribed to Paul in the title of the AV, it is not really his. It is an early writing (probably before the destruction of Jerusalem, A.D. 70) of some friend of the apostle (in Italy, cf. 13:23f.), designed, by a reasoned exhibition of the superiority of Jesus to Moses and the Levitical priesthood, and of the fulfillment of OT types and institutions in His person and sacrifice, to remove the difficulties of Jewish Christians who clung with natural affection to their temple and divinely appointed ritual. It was included by Eusebius, with others in the East (not, however, by Origen), among the Epistles of Paul; in the West the Pauline authorship was not admitted. Many, nevertheless, with Origen, upheld a connection with Paul ("the thoughts are Paul's"). Ideas and style suggest an Alexandrian training: hence Luther's conjecture of Apollos as the writer. There can be no certainty on the subject. The value of the Epistle is unimpaired, whoever was the author.

c. Catholic Epistles. Of the seven so-called Catholic Epistles, James and Jude are by "brethren" of the Lord (James, "the Lord's brother," was head of the church at Jerusalem, Acts 15:13; 21:18; Gal. 1:19; etc.); Peter and John, to whom the others were ascribed, were apostles. James and 1 Peter are addressed to the Jews of the Dispersion (1 Pet. 1:1; Jas. 1:1). The doubts respecting certain of these writings have already been mentioned. The early date and acceptance of James is attested by numerous allusions (Clement of Rome, Barnabas, Hermas, Didache). Many regard it as the earliest of the Epistles — before Paul's. Its tone is throughout practical. The seeming conflict with Paul on faith and works, which led Luther to speak slightingly of it, is only verbal. Paul, too, held that a dead faith avails nothing (1 Cor. 13:2; Gal. 5:6). 1 John, like 1 Peter, was undisputed (if the Fourth Gospel is genuine, 1 John is), and, on internal grounds, the shorter Epistles (2 and 3 John) need not be doubted (*see* JOHN, EPISTLES OF). Jude, rugged in style, with allusions to Jewish apocalypses (vv. 9, 14), is well attested, and 2 Peter seems to be founded on it. But 2 Peter must rely for acceptance on its own claim (2 Pet. 1:1, 18), and on internal evidence of sincerity. It is to be observed that, though late in being noticed, it never appears to have been treated as spurious. The style certainly differs from 1 Peter; this may be due to the use of an amanuensis. If accepted, it must be placed late in Peter's life (before A.D. 65). 1 Peter and Jude, in that case, must be earlier (*see* CATHOLIC EPISTLES).

3. Book of Revelation. The one prophetic book of the NT — the apocalyptic counterpart of Daniel in the OT — is Revelation. The external evidence for the Johannine authorship is strong (*see* APOCALYPSE). Tradition and internal evidence ascribe it to the reign of Domitian (*ca.* A.D. 95). Its contents were given in vision on the isle of Patmos (Rev. 1:9). The theory connecting it with the reign of Nero through the supposed fitness of this name to express the mystic number 666 is entirely precarious (cf. G. Salmon, *Historical Intro. to the Study of the Books of the NT* [2nd ed. 1886], pp. 245-254). The main intent is to exhibit in symbolic form the approaching conflicts of Christ and His Church with anti-

Christian powers — with secular world-power (Beast), with intellectual anti-Christianism (False Prophet), with ecclesiastical anti-Christianism (Woman) — these conflicts issuing in victory and a period of triumph, preluding, after a sharp, final struggle, the last scenes (resurrection, judgment), and the eternal state. When the visions are taken, not as poetic imaginings, but as true apocalyptic unveilings, the change in style from the Gospel, which may be regarded as already written, can readily be understood. These mighty revelations in Patmos brought about, as by volcanic force, a tremendous upheaval in the seer's soul, breaking through all previous strata of thought and feeling, and throwing everything into a new perspective. On the resultant high keynote: "Amen. Come, Lord Jesus" (Rev. 22:20), the NT closes.

4. Canonicity. The principal steps by which the books now enumerated were gradually formed into a NT "canon" have been indicated in previous sections. The test of canonicity here, as in the OT, is the presence of inspiration. Some would prefer the word "apostolic," which comes to the same thing. All the writings above reckoned were held to be the works of apostles or of apostolic men, and on this ground were admitted into the list of books having authority in the Church. Barnabas (*ca.* A.D. 100-120) already quotes Mt. 20:16 with the formula "it is written." Paul quotes as "scripture" (1 Tim. 5:18) a passage found only in Luke (10:7). Paul's Epistles are classed with "other scriptures" in 2 Pet. 3:16. Post-apostolic Fathers draw a clear distinction between their own writings and those of apostles like Paul and Peter (Polycarp, Ignatius, Barnabas). The fathers of the close of the 2nd cent. treat the NT writings as in the fullest degree inspired (cf. B. F. Westcott, *Intro. to the Study of the Gospels* [8th ed. 1895], appendix B). An important impulse to the formation of a definite canon came from the Gnostic Marcion (*ca.* 140), who made a canon for himself in two parts, "Gospel" and "Apostolicon," consisting of one Gospel (a mutilated Luke) and ten Epistles of Paul (excluding Pastorals). A challenge of this kind had to be taken up, and lists of NT writings began to be made (Melito, Muratorian Fragment, etc.), with the results previously described. By the commencement of the 4th cent. unanimity had practically been attained as regards even the ANTILEGOMENA. At the Council of Nicea (325), "the Holy Scriptures of the Old and New Testaments were silently admitted on all sides to have a final authority" (Westcott, *Bible in the Church,* p. 155). *See* CANON OF THE NT.

V. Unity and Spiritual Purpose—Inspiration.–*A. Scripture a Unity.* Holy Scripture is not simply a collection of religious books: still less does it consist of mere fragments of Jewish and Christian literature. It belongs to the conception of Scripture that, though originating "in many and various ways" (He. 1:1), it should yet, in its completeness, constitute a unity, evincing, in the spirit and purpose that bind its parts together, the divine source from which its revelation comes. The Bible is the record of God's revelations of Himself to men in successive ages and dispensations (Eph. 1:8-10; 3:5-9; Col. 1:25f.), till the revelation culminates in the advent and work of the Son, and the mission of the Spirit. It is this aspect of the Bible that constitutes its grand distinction from all collections of sacred writings — the so-called "Bibles" of heathen religions — in the world. These, as the slightest inspection of them shows, have no unity. They are accumulations of heterogeneous materials, presenting in their collocation no order, progress, or plan. The reason is that they embody no historical revelation working out a purpose in consecutive stages from germinal beginnings to perfect close. The Bible, by contrast, is a single book because it embodies such a revelation and exhibits such a purpose. The unity of the book, made up of so many parts, is the attestation of the reality of the revelation it contains.

B. Purpose of Grace. This feature of spiritual purpose in the Bible is one of the most obvious things about it. It gives to the Bible what is sometimes termed its "organic unity." The Bible has a beginning, middle, and end. The opening chapters of Genesis have their counterpart in the "new heaven and new earth" and Paradise restored of the closing chapters of Revelation (21f.). Man's sin is made the starting point for disclosures of God's grace. The patriarchal history, with its covenants and promises, is continued in the story of the Exodus and the events that follow, in fulfillment of these promises. Deuteronomy recapitulates the lawgiving at Sinai. Joshua sees the people put in possession of the Promised Land. Backsliding, rebellion, failure, do not defeat God's purpose, but are overruled to carry it on to a surer completion. The monarchy is made the occasion of new promises to the house of David (2 S. 7). The prophets root themselves in the past, but, at the very hour when the nation seems sinking in ruin, hold out bright hopes of a greater future in the extension of God's kingdom to the Gentiles, under Messiah's rule. A critical writer, E. F. Kautzsch, has justly said: "The abiding value of the OT lies above all in this, that it guarantees to us with absolute certainty the fact and the process of a divine plan and way of salvation, which found its conclusion and fulfilment in the new covenant, in the person and work of Jesus Christ" (*Bleibende Bedeutung des AT* [1902], pp. 22, 24, 28f., 30f.).

How truly all that was imperfect, transitional, temporary in the OT was brought to realization and completion in the redemption and spiritual kingdom of Christ need not here be dwelt upon. Christ is the prophet, priest, and king of the new covenant. His perfect sacrifice, "once for all," supersedes and abolishes the typical sacrifices of the old economy (He. 9f.). His gift of the Spirit realizes what the prophets had foretold of God's law being written in men's hearts (Jer. 31:31-34; 32:39f.; Ezk. 11:19f.; etc.). His kingdom is established on fixed foundations, and can have no end (Phil. 2:9-11; He. 12:28; Rev. 5:13; etc.). In tracing the lines of this redeeming purpose of God, brought to light in Christ, we gain the key that unlocks the inmost meaning of the whole Bible. It is the revelation of a "gospel."

C. Inspiration. "Inspiration" is a word round which many debates have gathered. If, however, what has been said is true of the Bible as the record of a progressive revelation, of its contents as the discovery of the will of God for man's salvation, of the prophetic and apostolic standing of its writers, of the unity of spirit and purpose that pervades it, it will be difficult to deny that a quite peculiar presence, operation, and guidance of the Spirit of God are manifest in its production. The belief in inspiration, it has been seen, is implied in the formation of these books into a sacred canon. The full discussion of the subject belongs to a special article (*see* INSPIRATION).

1. Biblical Claim. Here it need only be said that the claim for inspiration in the Bible is one made in fullest measure by the Bible itself. It is not denied by any that Jesus and His apostles regarded the OT Scriptures as in the fullest sense inspired. The appeal of Jesus was always to the Scriptures, and the word of Scripture was final with Him. "Have you not read?" (Mt. 19:4). "You are wrong, because you know neither the scriptures nor the power of God" (Mt. 22:29). This is because God speaks in them (Mt. 19:4f.). Prophecies and Psalms were fulfilled in Him (Lk. 18:31; 22:37; 24:27, 44). Paul esteemed the Scriptures "the oracles of God" (Rom. 3:2). They are "inspired by God" (2 Tim. 3:16). That NT prophets and apostles were not placed on any lower level than those of the OT is manifest from Paul's explicit words regarding himself and his fellow apostles. Paul never faltered in his claim to be "an apostle of Christ Jesus by the will of God" (Eph. 1:1, etc.) — "set apart for the gospel of God" (Rom. 1:1) — who had received his message, not from man, but by "revelation" from heaven (Gal. 1:11f.). The "mystery of Christ" had "now been revealed to his holy apostles and prophets by the Spirit," in consequence of which the Church is declared to be "built upon the foundation of the apostles and prophets, Christ Jesus himself being the corner-stone" (Eph. 2:20; 3:5).

2. Marks of Inspiration. It might be shown that these claims made by NT writers for the OT and for themselves are borne out by what the OT itself teaches of prophetic inspiration, of wisdom as the gift of God's spirit, and of the light, holiness, saving virtue, and sanctifying power continually ascribed to God's "law," "words," "statutes," "commandments," "judgments" (see above). This is the ultimate test of "inspiration" — that to which Paul likewise appeals — its power to "instruct you for salvation through faith in Christ Jesus" (2 Tim. 3:15) — its profitableness "for teaching, for reproof, for correction, and for training in righteousness" (v. 16) — all to the end "that the man of God may be complete, equipped for every good work" (v. 17). Nothing is here determined as to "inerrancy" in minor historical, geographical, chronological details, in which some would wrongly put the essence of inspiration; but it seems implied that at least there is no error which can interfere with or nullify the utility of Scripture for the ends specified. Who that brings Scripture to its own tests of inspiration will deny that, judged as a whole, it fulfils them?

D. Historical Influence. The claim of the Bible to a divine origin is justified by its historical influence. Regarded even as literature, the Bible has an unexampled place in history. Ten or fifteen MSS are thought a goodly number for an ancient classic; the MSS of whole or parts of the NT are reckoned by thousands, the oldest fragment going back to *ca.* A.D. 150 and several papyri dating from *ca.* 200. Another test is translation. The books of the NT had hardly begun to be put together before we find translations being made of them into Latin, Syriac, Egyptian, later into Gothic and other tongues (*see* VERSIONS). In the Middle Ages, before the invention of printing, translations were made into the vernacular of most of the countries of Europe. Today there is not a language in the civilized world into which this word of God has not been rendered. Thanks to the labors of Bible Societies, the circulation of the Bible in the different countries of the world in recent years outstrips all previous records. No book has ever been so minutely studied, has had so many books written on it, has founded so vast a literature of hymns, liturgies, devotional writings, sermons, has been so keenly assailed, has evoked such splendid defenses, as the Bible. Its spiritual influence cannot be estimated. To tell all the Bible has been and done for the world would be to rewrite in large part the history of modern civilization. Without it, in pagan lands, the arm and tongue of the missionary would be paralyzed. With it, even in the absence of the missionary, wondrous results are often effected. In national life the Bible is the source of the highest social and national aspirations. T. H. Huxley, though an agnostic, argued for the reading of the Bible in the schools on this very ground. "By the study of what other book," he asked, "could children be so much humanized, and made to feel that each figure in that vast historical procession fills, like themselves, but a momentary space in the interval between two eternities, and earns the blessings or the curses of all times, according to its effort to do good and to hate evil, even as they are also earning their payment for their work?" (*Critiques and Addresses* [1873], p. 61).

VI. Chapters and Verses–Already in pre-talmudic times, for purposes of reading in the synagogues, the Jews had larger divisions of the Law into sections called *pārāšôṯ*, and of the Prophets into similar sections called *hapṭārôṯ*. They had also smaller divisions into *p^{e}sûqîm*, corresponding nearly with our verses. The division into chapters is much later (13th cent.). It is ascribed to Cardinal Hugo de St. Caro (d. 1248); by others to Stephen Langton, archbishop of Canterbury (d. 1227). It was adopted into the Vulgate, and from this was transferred by R. Nathan (*ca.* 1440) to the Hebrew Bible (Bleek, Keil). Verses are marked in the Vulgate as early as 1558 and first appear in the NT in Robert Stephens' edition of the Greek Testament in 1551. Henry Stephens, Robert's son, reports that they were devised by his father during a journey on horseback from Paris to Lyons. J. ORR

Bibliography.–An extremely short selection from an enormous literature. Many of these works contain large sections of additional bibliographical material.

B. F. Westcott, *The Bible in the Church* (1875); W. Dittmar, *Vetus Testamentum in Novo* (1903); H. B. Swete, ed., *Cambridge Biblical Essays* (1909); A. S. Peake, *The Bible, Its Origin, Its Significance, and Its Abiding Worth* (1913); B. B. Warfield, *Inspiration and Authority of the Bible* (1927); C. H. Irwin, *The Bible, the Scholar and the Spade* (1932); H. E. Fosdick, *Guide to the Understanding of the Bible* (1938); J. Finegan, *Light From the Ancient Past* (1946); C. H. Dodd, *The Bible Today* (1946); N. B. Stonehouse, *et al., The Infallible Word* (1946); H. R. Willoughby, ed., *Study of the Bible Today and Tomorrow* (1947); L. Berkhof, *Principles of Biblical Interpretation* (1950); B. W. Anderson, *Rediscovering the Bible* (1951); D. Johnson, *The Christian and His Bible* (1953); J. N. Geldenhuys, *Supreme Authority* (1953); B. Ramm, *Protestant Biblical Interpretation* (1953); R. Preus, *Inspiration of Scripture* (1955); J. K. S. Reid, *Authority of Scripture* (n.d.); *Bible Today* (1955); E. J. Young, *Thy Word is Truth* (1957); G. E. Wright, *Biblical Archaeology* (1957); R. L. Harris, *Inspiration and Canonicity of the Bible* (1957); C. F. Henry, ed., *Revelation and the Bible* (1958); F. G. Kenyon, *Our Bible and the Ancient Manuscripts* (5th ed. 1958); K. J. Foreman, *et al., Introduction to the Bible* (1959); J. A. Thompson, *Bible and Archaeology* (1962); F. F. Bruce, *The Books and the Parchments* (1963); S. L. Greenslade, *Cambridge History of the Bible: The West from the Reformation to the Present Day* (1963); H. von Campenhausen, *Formation of the Christian Bible* (1972); J. Stott, *Understanding the Bible* (1972); J. B. Job, ed., *Studying God's Word* (1972); J. Barr, *Bible in the Modern World* (1973); S. Blanch, *For All Mankind* (1976).

OT Introductions by: G. L. Archer (1973), A. Bentzen (5th ed. 1959), J. A. Bewer (3rd ed. 1962), S. R. Driver (9th ed. 1913; repr. 1961), O. Eissfeldt (1965), N. K. Gottwald (1959), W. H. Green (1899), R. K. Harrison (1969), J. E. McFadyen (1932), W. O. E. Oesterley and T. H. Robinson (3rd ed. 1958), R. H. Pfeiffer (repr. 1957), A. Weiser (1961), E. J. Young (1949); NT Introductions by: B. W. Bacon (1900), A. E. Barnett (2nd ed. 1946), F. B. Clogg (3rd ed. 1948), W. D. Davies (1966), F. V. Filson (1950), E. J. Goodspeed (1937), R. M. Grant (1963), D. Guthrie (1970), E. F. Harrison (2nd ed. 1971), M. Jones (1914), A. H. McNeile (2nd ed. 1953), J. Moffatt (3rd ed. 1918), A. Wickenhauser (1958), T. Zahn (1909); and works listed in COMMENTARIES. R. K. H.

BIBLE DICTIONARIES AND ENCYCLOPEDIAS. Reference works giving information about biblical terms, names, doctrines, history, and culture.

The first such work was probably that of Eusebius of

Caesarea, a four-volume encyclopedia of which only one part is extant, *Onomasticon,* produced *ca.* A.D. 326. This dictionary lists and often describes approximately 600 names of towns, rivers, etc., of the OT and Gospels. Jerome, intimately acquainted with Palestine, translated this work into Latin, correcting some errors and adding much important material. Although within forty years, 1862-1904, German scholars produced three different editions of Eusebius' original Greek text together with Jerome's Latin version, no English translation has yet appeared. Around the end of the 4th cent., Augustine expressed in his "Rules for the Interpretation of Scripture" what must have been shared by many serious students of the Scriptures, a longing for a worthy biblical encyclopedia:

"What then some men have done in regard to all words and names found in Scripture in the Hebrew and Syriac and Egyptian and other tongues, taking up and interpreting separately such as were left in Scripture without interpretation; and what Eusebius has done in regard to the history of the past, with a view to the questions arising in Scripture that require a knowledge of history for their solution; — what, I say, these men have done in regard to matters of this kind, making it unnecessary for the Christian to spend his strength on many subjects for the sake of a few items of knowledge, the same I think might be done in regard to other matters, if any competent man were willing in a spirit of benevolence to undertake the labor for the advantage of his brother. In this way he might arrange in their several classes and give an account of the unknown places and animals and plants and trees and stones and metals and other species of thing that are mentioned in Scripture, taking up these only and committing his account to writing. . . . It might happen that some or all of these things have been done already (as I have found that many things I had no notion of have been worked out and committed to writing by good and learned Christians) but are either lost amid the crowds of the careless, or are kept out of sight by the envious" (*De doctrina christiana* ii.39).

Of the many responses to this longing that have been published in English, this article has a fairly complete listing up to 1900; works of a trivial nature published since 1900 are not included. Only brief mention will be made of lexicons, indexes, and handbooks to the Bible, and theological and denominational encyclopedias. For other biblical reference works see the articles on COMMENTARIES and CONCORDANCES.

Hebrew lexicons include that of F. Brown, S. R. Driver and C. A. Briggs, based on H. F. W. Gesenius' works (1833 and 1834), and the *Lexicon in Veteris Testamenti Libros* by L. Koehler and W. Baumgartner, with supplement (2nd ed. 1958). For NT Greek there are the indispensable volumes of H. Cremer (1872; Eng. tr. 1878), J. H. Thayer (1887), and W. Bauer (translated by W. F. Arndt and F. W. Gingrich, 1957).

Some valuable volumes that might be called indexes to the Bible include those of M. Pilkington (1749), R. Hitchcock (1869), N. West (1868), and A. J. Nave (1896).

Much material similar to that found in Bible dictionaries is often included in what may be called handbooks for Bible study, e.g., the excellent one by J. Angus, *Bible Handbook* (1865); the *Illustrated Bible Treasury* by W. Wright (new ed. 1897); *The Cambridge Companion to Bible Studies*; and the *Oxford Helps to the Study of the Bible*. Such works have frequently been revised and reprinted.

Some rich material relating to biblical subjects is included in theological encyclopedias, such as that by C. Buck (1802), followed by the huge volume by J. M. Brown (1836). Other important volumes include: J. H. Blunt, *Dictionary of Doctrinal and Historical Theology* (1872); L. Abbott (1871); S. Mathews (1921); *Baker's Dictionary of Theology* (1960); *Concise Dictionary of Religious Knowledge*, ed. S. M. Jackson (3rd ed. 1898); the *New Schaff-Herzog Encyclopedia of Religious Knowledge* (2nd ed. 1949-1952, based on an 1882-1884 work); and an earlier work (1891), which has been reprinted in twelve volumes, by J. McClintock and J. Strong, *Cyclopedia of Biblical, Theological and Ecclesiastical Literature*. Here also belong the standard Jewish and Roman Catholic encyclopedias, as well as the remarkable *Presbyterian Encyclopedia* (1884) and the *Baptist Encyclopedia* (1889).

W. Patten published the first English work that might be regarded as a Bible dictionary. A two-hundred-page volume issued in London in 1575, it was called *The Calendars of Scripture, whearin the Hebru, Chaldean, Arabian, Phenician, Syrian, Persian, Greek, and Latin names of Contreys, Men, Weemen, Idols, Cities, Hils, Rivers, and of Other Places in the Holy Byble Mentioned by Order of Letters, is set and Turned into Our English Toung*.

The first real Bible dictionary in English was that of T. Wilson, minister of St. George's, Canterbury (d. 1621). First appearing in 1612, his *Complete Christian Dictionary* enjoyed numerous editions; the 5th appeared in 1667, somewhat enlarged. The 3rd edition (1622), consisting of 948 unnumbered pages, includes a unique dictionary for the book of Revelation with 131 pages and a forty-nine-page dictionary of the Song of Solomon. The articles concern phrases as well as individual words.

During the following century no important English works of this nature appeared. To be comprehensive, however, the following volumes are noted.

The schoolmaster T. Hayne (1582-1645) published *The General View of the Holy Scriptures; or, the Times, Places, and Persons of the Holy Scriptures* (rev. ed. 1640). In 1642 a primarily theological work by R. Bernard (1568-1641) appeared, *The Bibles Abstract and Epitome, the Capitale Heads, Examples, Sentences and Precepts of all the Principal Matters in Theologie, Collected Together for the Most part Alphabetically . . . taken Out of the Best Moderne Divines*.

F. Roberts, who wrote several apologetic works, published in 1648 *Clavis Bibliorum: The Key of the Bible,* which had at least four editions by 1675. A volume more lexicon than dictionary appeared in 1660, comprehensively entitled *Scripture-Names Expounded, in this right profitable fruitfall, large, and ample, Alphabeticall Table: Containing the Interpretation of about foure thousand Proper Names (but halfe a dayes Reading in Newcastle, July 16, 1649) in the Hebrew, Caldean, Greeke, and Latine Tongues, dispersed throughout the whole Bible. Collected by R. F. H. Now again re-Printed by S. D. for the benefit of all that would soon Reade and understand the Scriptures of Truth, in their Originall Tongues, especially Hebrew; these Names containe all, or the most of the Primitives in Hebrew, which being all known, with their Significations, make a firmer impression of them in the Memory, than anyway else I know, all Names being reduced to their Primitives, which in a Moneth one unlettered in the Hebrew may doe, by a few directions, with much ease, profit and delight*.

More in the nature of a true dictionary was F. Shaw's *A Summary of the Bible; or the Principal Heads of Natural and Revealed Religion; alphabetically disposed in the Words of Scripture only* (1730).

A truly great Bible dictionary appeared in 1732, a translation of a work originally published in French in 1722, by A. Calmet (1672-1757). The momentous *Historical, Critical, Geographical, Chronological and Etymological Dictionary of the Holy Bible* appeared in three volumes (six parts), and contained almost 2,500,000 words. One of the most intriguing yet almost entirely ignored works in biblical interpretation is the last section, the second part of Vol. III. The first three hundred pages comprise an annotated "Bibliotheca Sacra, or a Catalog of the Best Books that can be Read in Order to Acquire a Good Understanding of the Scriptures." Most sections on the books of the Bible and biblical subjects have been recategorized in terms of Catholic and Protestant authors. Many books mentioned in this comprehensive bibliography are not likely to be found in any modern libraries of Europe or America. More than two thousand names are included in the alphabetical table of authors. Also included are a dissertation on Israelite military tactics by a noted French military expert, a survey of Hebrew coins, a chronological table of biblical history, and a remarkable "Preface to the Translation of the Hebrew, Chaldee, Syriac, and Greek Names in the Bible." Publication of this work continued for more than a century until 1847. An abridged one-volume edition edited by T. A. Buckley appeared as late as 1856, 135 years after the first French edition. Two supplementary volumes entitled *Fragments,* edited by C. Taylor, provide a good view of the interpretation of many biblical passages at the beginning of the 19th century.

In 1749 M. Pilkington (1705-1765), Prebendary of Lichfield, published in Nottingham *A Rational Concordance of an Index to the Bible.* Ten years later a three-volume work was published in London with no indication of authorship. It was entitled *A Dictionary of the Holy Bible . . . Serving in a Great Measure as a Concordance to the Bible.* Its nearly 1300 pages contain about 1,700,000 words. The work acknowledges the influence of Calmet's dictionary. Included are extensive quotations from Newton, Josephus, S. Bochart, H. Prideaux, and others. As in many contemporary dictionaries, various subjects receive disproportionate treatment. For example, more attention is devoted to "Ahab" than to either "Adam" or "Angel."

Perhaps the most frequently reprinted Bible dictionary of the latter half of the 18th cent. was edited by J. Brown of Haddington (1722-1787). It was called *A Dictionary of the Holy Bible Containing Definitions of All Religious and Ecclesiastical Terms . . . and a Biographical Sketch of Writers in Theological Science.* First published in 1768, the 6th edition (1816) claimed in the title *The Whole Comprising Whatever Important is Known Concerning the Antiquities of the Hebrew Nation and the Church of God.* The 6th edition was enlarged by Brown's three sons and contained the author's biography. The two volumes number 1270 pages, about 860,000 words. Editions appear as late as W. Brown's 1866 revision. Among several interesting articles, that on the Hebrews traces their history to modern times and includes the following speculation: "About A.D. 1866 or 2016, we suppose the offspring of Judah, together with the remains of the ten tribes, will by the power of God and to the great joy and advantage of the Gentiles, be converted to the Christian faith. It seems they will resist the opposers of Antichrist at Armageddon and greatly rejoice in his ruin. The Turks and their allies will try to dispossess them but shall perish in their attempt. Thence forward the twelve Hebrew tribes shall in the greatest harmony, peace, piety and order reside in their country til the end of the millennium." A new edition was issued in a single volume of 746 pages in 1823 under the editorship of T. Smith. The preface notes that at least five "spurious editions of Brown's dictionary had already appeared."

In 1770 T. Tooley published a volume entitled *Nomenclator Biblicus; or, An Index of Proper Names Occurring in the Old and New Testament; intended as a Supplement to the known defect of Concordances in that Necessary Article.*

There appeared in 1774 the most extensive Bible dictionary by an English scholar before that of Kitto. Its author, J. Fleetwood, who wrote one of the most widely used works on Christ to be published in the 18th or early 19th cent., is otherwise unknown, and many have thought the name to be a pseudonym. The complete title of Fleetwood's dictionary is: *The Christian's Dictionary; or, Sure Guide to Divine Knowledge. Containing a Full and Familiar Explanation of all the Words made use of in the Holy Scriptures, and Body of Divinity, as set forth in the Writings of the Most Eminent and Pious Divines; whether Ancient or modern . . . to which is added a Brief Explication of all the Proper Names found in Scripture, including the senses wherein they were used by the Jews; etc.* A quarto work (10½ x 8¼ in.) of more than five hundred pages, the text contains approximately 200,000 words. The author describes his book as follows: "To make Christians acquainted with every term made use of in the sacred scriptures, and in the writings of the most eminent divines, both ancient and modern, this work was undertaken on a plan never yet offered to the public. The author . . . has spent a great part of his time, during a course of nearly fifty years, in learning to acquire a perfect knowledge of these things. Few treatises on divinity, whether theological, polemical, critical or practical have escaped his notice. . . . The rise and progress of every heresy in the Christian church has been taken notice of." His interpretations were often novel. Of course, he interpreted the antichrist as the pope and the beast out of the earth as Rome. The "Dictionary of Scriptural Proper Names" treats nearly 1500 items, several with considerable detail.

A Dictionary of the Bible Historical and Geographical, Theological, Moral and Ritual, Philosophical and Philological (1779), by A. Macbean, was the most important Bible dictionary edited by a British writer in the latter part of the 18th century. The first American edition (1798) was developed from the enlarged second London edition.

An important Bible dictionary with no identification of its editor was published in 1792, entitled *The Dictionary of the Bible.* This was the first Bible dictionary to appear in America, published in Worcester, Mass. by I. Thomas in 1798.

A number of less important Bible dictionaries appeared toward the end of the 18th cent.: *A Comprehensive Dictionary of the Holy Bible: Containing a Biographical History, etc.* (1776), 504 pages; A. Fortescu, *A Dictionary of the Holy Bible* (1777, reprinted in 1792 and 1798); W. Button, *A Comprehensive Dictionary of the Holy Bible* (1796), based upon J. Brown's earlier work. Worthy of note is P. Oliver's *Scripture Lexicon, or a Dictionary of above Four Thousand Proper Names Mentioned in the Bible, with their Derivation, Description, Accentuations* (1787). New editions of this work of less than three hundred pages appeared in 1810 and 1818, both at Oxford, where it was used as a text. Oliver (1713-1791), a 1730 American graduate of Harvard, was judge of the Superior Court and Chief Justice before moving to England in 1776.

Bible dictionaries of the early 19th cent. reflected the influence of Calmet and Brown, as J. Wood (1751-1840) acknowledged in *A New Dictionary of the Holy Bible Extracted from Brown, Calmet, etc., collated with other works of Like Kind with Numerous Additions from Various Authors and a Considerable Quantity of Original Matter* (2 vols., 1804). A 12th edition was issued in 1863.

J. Morrison (1762-1809) is generally accepted as author of *Bibliotheca Sacra or Dictionary of the Holy Scriptures* (2 vols., 1806), an anonymous work that acknowledges its extensive borrowing from earlier writers.

In 1807 A. Arrowsmith published the first work of its kind, *A Geographical Dictionary of the Holy Scriptures*, with various editions appearing for the next fifty years. He also edited *A Bible Atlas*, and published more than 130 maps. In 1808 J. Creighton's *Dictionary of Scripture Proper Names* appeared, followed in 1810 by M. Martindale's two-volume *Dictionary of the Holy Bible*.

W. Jones (1762-1846), a Baptist minister at Finsbury, edited the famous two-volume *Biblical Cyclopaedia; or Dictionary of the Holy Scriptures* (1816). This unnumbered work, with 648 pages in the first volume and 564 in the second, includes beautiful steel engravings, excellent maps (for the period), and interesting bibliographies.

T. Hawker's *A Concordance and Dictionary to the Holy Scriptures* appeared in 1812, a work of some 880 pages, with later editions. In 1815 J. K. Whish published in Bristol *The Cottager's Dictionary of the Bible*, a small volume of 130 pages with definitions limited to one or two lines in length. Its purpose was "to facilitate the understanding of the Scriptures among the poor." Minor dictionaries published at this time include J. Robinson's *A Theological, Biblical and Ecclesiastical Dictionary, etc.* 1815-1816; rev. 1835). A small volume published in 1818, *The Youth's Spelling, Pronouncing, and Explanatory Theological Dictionary of the NT*, contained an introduction by E. Dowson.

The first Bible dictionary by a recognized biblical geographer, E. Robinson's (1794-1863) *A Dictionary of the Holy Bible*, appeared in 1822 with numerous revisions as late as 1879. It was followed in 1826 by G. Wall's *Domestic Dictionary of the Bible* and H. J. G. Dwight's *A Dictionary of the Proper Names in the NT with Other Helps* (2nd ed. 1828). In the same decade H. Malcolm (1799-1899) published *The Dictionary of the Bible*, of which more than 130,000 copies were sold within its first twenty years. The author of *Index to Religious Literature*, Malcolm also published *A New Bible Dictionary* (1852); *A Dictionary of the Most Important Names found in the Holy Scriptures* (1831); and *The Proper Names of the OT arranged Alphabetically* (1859). Princeton Seminary professor A. Alexander (1772-1851) prepared the 546-page *Pocket Dictionary of the Bible* (1829; rev. ed. 1831) for the American Sunday School Union.

R. Watson (1781-1833), author of the famous *Theological Institutes*, produced a work with the comprehensive title *A Biblical and Theological Dictionary: Explanatory of the History, Manners, and Customs of the Jews and Neighboring Nations. With an Account of the Most Remarkable Places and Persons Mentioned in Sacred Scripture; An Exposition of the Principal Doctrines of Christianity and Notices of Jewish and Christian Sects and Heresies* (1831, 1068 pages). This popular volume had at least ten editions within twenty years.

Also in 1831 there appeared an anonymous work, *A Dictionary of Important Names, Objects, and Terms Found in the Holy Scriptures intended principally for Youth*. A small work by J. H. Cotton, *A Short Explanation of Obsolete Words in Our Version of the Bible* (1832), should also be noted. Other contemporary works were *A Pocket Biblical Dictionary* by D. Davidson (new ed. 1837); J. Covel's *Bible Dictionary* (1838); and a sixty-page volume by T. Rowland, *An Exposition of the Names of Persons and Places Recorded in the Holy Scriptures*.

S. Green's *A Biblical and Theological Dictionary* first appeared in 1840 and was published for more than twenty-five years. The 1868 edition was reputedly the 28th. In 1841 W. Goodhugh (1799-1842) published the two-volume *Bible Cyclopedia, or Illustrations of the Civil and Natural History of the Sacred Writings by Reference to the Manners, Customs, Rites, Traditions, Antiquities, and Literature of Eastern Nations*. A universalist, S. B. Emmons, published his *Bible Dictionary* in 1841. In 1842 the American Sunday School Union published the widely circulated *Union Bible Dictionary*.

Also among the profusion of dictionaries released in the mid-19th cent. were the *Concordance and Dictionary of the Holy Scriptures* by R. Hawker (1753-1827) and J. Covel, Jr., *A Concise Dictionary of the Holy Bible Designed for the Use of Sunday School Teachers and Families*, both published in 1844. A 4th edition of S. Dunn, *A Dictionary of the Gospels with Maps*, etc. appeared in 1846. Also in 1846 J. R. Beard published his *Household Biblical Encyclopedia*, followed by *The People's Dictionary of the Bible* (1847 and 1861). A three-volume work, *The Bible Cyclopedia Containing the Biography, Geography and Natural History of the Holy Scriptures*, edited by J. P. Lawson, was issued in 1847. The first volume, devoted to biography, included "A List of Persons Mentioned in the Scriptures of Whom Little is Known," with about 2200 names. In 1869 Lawson joined J. M. Wilson to publish a two-volume work, *A Cyclopedia of Biblical Geography, Biography, Natural History, and General Knowledge*. Its bibliography was the most comprehensive of its time. Lawson and Wilson also produced the two-volume *Imperial Cyclopedia of Biblical Knowledge* in 1873.

The most important contribution of the period was the publication of the epochal *Cyclopedia of Biblical Literature* (1846) by J. Kitto (1804-1854). Acknowledging the increased information about ancient history and Palestinian geography, Kitto engaged the help of forty noted Bible scholars, such as G. Bush, J. Eadie, J. P. Smith, and the Germans E. W. Hengstenberg and F. A. G. Tholuck. Included were the first authoritative articles on geographical matters, as well as accounts of such topics as biblical criticism and Gnosticism. The 3rd edition of 1869, edited in three volumes by W. L. Alexander, incorporated the assistance of such additional scholars as F. W. Farrar, A. Geikie, R. S. Poole, H. Wace, and J. S. Candlish. Included was the first extensive article on biblical concordances and "Notices of the Life and Works of Biblical Scholars."

The most important single-volume Bible dictionary of its time was *The Biblical Cyclopedia* by J. Eadie (1810-1876), a work of nearly 700,000 words, which first appeared in 1849 and was revised and reprinted as late as 1901.

In 1850 there appeared Bible dictionaries by I. Cobbin (1771-1851), W. M. Engles (1797-1867), and an American Presbyterian author, as well as J. Jameson's *Glossary to the Obsolete and Unusual Words and Phrases of the Holy Scriptures in the Authorized English Version*.

The Bible Dictionary for the Use of Bible Classes, Schools, and Families was published in 1851. The 3rd edition of *Biblical and Theological Dictionary* by J. Farrar (1802-1884) appeared in 1852. J. Booker published a small work in 1853, *Obsolete Words and Phrases in the Bible*, etc., followed a year later by *The Pictorial Dictionary of the Bible* and J. Gardner's *Christian Cyclopedia or a Repertory of Biblical and Theological Literature*. Edited in 1855 by F. A. Packard, *The Union Bible Dictionary for the Use of Schools, Bible Classes and Families* was a new edition of the 1844 American Sunday School Union publication mentioned above. In 1858 Davies published his *Biblical Dictionary*. In 1859 the American Tract Society published *A Dictionary of the Holy Bible* by W. W. Rand (1816-1909), based upon E. Robinson's work and revised in 1886. Also in 1859 appeared a three-volume, condensed version of J. A. Bastow's 1848 *A Biblical Dictionary*, etc.

The 1st edition of what was to become the most important Bible dictionary of that generation appeared in 1860, the *Dictionary of the Bible* by W. Smith (1813-1893), which continued in publication for nearly fifty years. The most popular of its many editions was the American revision edited by H. B. Hackett, assisted by E. Abbot, a four-volume work totaling 3667 pages. The large editorial staff of the original edition was augmented by an additional twenty-seven American scholars.

Among the minor biblical dictionaries of this decade are *Cassell's Bible Dictionary* (1863, with frequent revisions); J. Ayre's *Treasury of Bible Knowledge, Being a Dictionary of Books, Persons, Places . . . in the Holy Scriptures* (1866); J. Eastwood and W. A. Wright, *Bible Word Book: A Glossary of Old English Bible Words* (1866); and S. W. Barnum, *A Comprehensive Dictionary of the Bible* (1867), a work of 1,500,000 words by sixty-nine contributors. An exceptional contribution of this decade was the *Imperial Bible Dictionary* edited by P. Fairbairn (1805-1874). The new edition of 1885 was extended to six volumes.

Dictionaries appearing in the early 1870's included: W. Henderson (1810-1872), *Dictionary and Concordance of the Names and Persons and Places in the Scriptures*, etc. (1869); S. O. Beeton, *Bible Dictionary* (1870); W. Gurney, *A Handy Dictionary of the Bible* (1870); W. Nicholson, *The Bible Explained; A Dictionary of the Names, Countries, etc. as Contained in the Old and New Testaments* (1870); J. A. Wylie (1808-1890), *The Household Bible Dictionary* (1870, 2 vols.); C. Boutell (1812-1877), *A Bible Dictionary etc. for Students of the Holy Scriptures* (1871; later editions in 1876 and 1879); and the unsigned *Dictionary of the Bible* (1872). The most beautiful Bible dictionary ever published in the United States was by W. Blackwood, *Potter's Complete Bible Encyclopedia*, etc. (1873), two quarto volumes of two thousand pages with three thousand illustrations. The work encompassed almost every conceivable biblical, theological, and ecclesiastical subject, as well as Christian biography. Perhaps because its cost was high for that period, this encyclopedia never received wide recognition.

An anonymous work appeared in 1877, *A New and Complete Pronouncing Bible Dictionary*. *The Handbook of Bible Words*, with an introduction by J. J. S. Perowne, appeared in 1878. In 1880 the Presbyterian Board of Education of Philadelphia published *The Westminster Bible Dictionary*, later the title of a more famous work by J. Davis. *Student's Illustrated Bible Dictionary* appeared in 1881, a small work also entitled *The Household Bible Dictionary*. The Southern Methodist Publication Society published J. C. Granberry's *Bible Dictionary* (1883). In the same year R. Young issued his *Dictionary and Concordance of Bible Words and Synonyms of the NT*. The revised edition of the earlier work by Eastwood and Wright appeared in 1884, edited by Wright himself (1831-1914). Carrying the title *The Bible Word Book, A Glossary of Archaic Words and Phrases in the Authorized Version of the Bible and the Book of Common Prayer*, this volume of nearly seven hundred pages became a standard work of reference.

The anonymous *New Biblical Dictionary for Students and Teachers*, a work of 1200 pages, appeared in 1859. In 1890 J. P. Boyd (1836-1910) published his *Self-Pronouncing Bible Dictionary*, often included in Holman's *Pronouncing Teacher's Bible*. F. Bourazan published in 1890 his *Sacred Dictionary and Explanation of Scripture Names and Terms*, etc. In 1891 appeared T. R. Safe's *Scriptural Dictionary of Personal Names Found in the OT*, etc. Also that year A. R. Fausset (1821-1910) published *The Englishman's Critical and Expository Bible Encyclopedia*. Republished as late as 1949, the work contained approximately 950,000 words. A prolific author on prophecy, Fausset co-authored the famous Jamieson, Fausset, and Brown Commentary, first published in six volumes (1864-1870) and reissued in many editions, complete or abridged.

Other Bible dictionaries published in the final decade of the 19th cent. include: J. Macpherson, *The Universal Bible Dictionary* (1892); A. Westcott and J. Watt, *The Concise Bible Dictionary* (1893), based on the *Cambridge Companion to the Bible*; N. G. Easton, *Illustrated Bible Dictionary and Treasury of Biblical History, Doctrine, and Literature* (1893); E. W. Rice, *The People's Dictionary of the Bible*, published by the American Sunday School Union (1893; rev. ed. 1904); and R. Hunter, *Concise Bible Dictionary* (1894). A new edition of this dictionary and index of the Bible was issued with the editorial help of A. J. P. McClure, under the title *The International Teacher's Handy Bible Encyclopedia and Concordance* (1944). The earlier edition formed a part of the "Bible Readers' Guide," which appeared in several editions of the Bible.

This was followed by C. J. Ball, *The Bible Student's Encyclopedia* (1897) and *A New and Concise Bible Dictionary* (1897-1900), edited by G. Morrish, approximately 600,000 words, originally issued in thirty-seven monthly parts, 1897-1900.

J. D. Davis (1854-1926) offered a significant contribution with his *Dictionary of the Bible* (1898). The 4th edition of 1924 was reprinted in 1954. Revised and rewritten by H. S. Gehman, the work was republished as *The Westminster Dictionary of the Bible* (1944), with more than 658 pages. Davis' work has proved one of the most helpful conservative Bible dictionaries in English. Gehman's revision was less conservative concerning the Scriptures. A completely revised edition was issued in 1970 (see below).

In 1899 the famous *Encyclopedia Biblica*, edited by T. K. Cheyne and J. S. Black, was published, embracing 5444 columns of text. Despite a vast amount of scholarly work by some of the writers, the book was drastically marred by its radical views. The *Expository Times* called it "not a dictionary of the Bible" but "a dictionary of the historical criticism of the Bible." B. B. Warfield, in a long review, said the entire work appears as "the determined and tireless opponent of the supernatural." Also in 1899, W. Baches edited the *Keswick Bible Dictionary*.

C. R. Barnes published his *Bible Encyclopedia* in 1900 as two volumes; in 1910 as three volumes; and in 1913 as a single volume with a short archeological supplement by M. G. Kyle, entitled *People's Bible Encyclopedia*. Reissued in 1928, it was one of the most comprehensive works of this kind in that decade. E. F. Cavalier's *Preacher's Dictionary* (1901; 2nd ed. 1904) was a unique volume. Cavalier, then Rector of Wramplingham, Norfolk, arranged his material under eighty major headings, which, with their subdivisions, embraced 558 subjects. After defining each subject, he summarizes the biblical teaching on that topic, quotes in full most of the verses, and offers the thoughts of ancient and modern writers. This work was followed by W. W. Davies (1848-1922), *The Universal Bible Encyclopedia* (1903), two volumes.

S. Fallows (1835-1922) was editor of the *Popular and Critical Encyclopedia and Scriptural Dictionary* (1901, 1904), three volumes totalling more than 1900 pages, including six hundred maps and engravings. There were 126 contributors, with C. A. Zenos and H. L. Willett as coeditors. This work was the basis for the *International Standard Bible Encyclopedia*.

In 1905 began the publication of the most important dictionary since that of W. Smith in 1860, *A Dictionary of the Bible*, edited by J. Hastings (1852-1922). This came out in five volumes, containing approximately 5,400,000 words. The fifth volume featured a series of important special articles as well as two hundred pages of index. W. Ramsay wrote two of the special articles, one on the religions of Greece and Asia Minor (forty-seven pages), the other on the numbers, hours, and years, and roads and travel in the NT (twenty-eight pages). These, along with a forty-five page article on the Sermon on the Mount by C. W. Votaw, were exceptional. A one-volume *Dictionary of the Bible*, also edited by Hastings, appeared in 1909. Not a condensation of the earlier work, it contained new articles. Hastings added in 1908 his *Dictionary of Christ and the Gospels*; the two-volume *Dictionary of the Apostolic Church* in 1916-1918; and the twelve-volume *Encyclopedia of Religion and Ethics* from 1908 to 1926.

F. Vigouroux's five-volume Roman Catholic *Dictionnaire de la Bible* was issued from 1905-1912, with supplements beginning in 1928.

A volume that had extensive circulation was *The Handy Bible Encyclopedia*, edited by J. L. Hurlbut (1834-1930), published in 1908. Also issued in 1908, *Murray's Bible Dictionary*, edited in 1957 by M. F. Unger (3rd rev. ed.) was a thousand-page work with ninety-four contributors. In 1909 Funk & Wagnalls published their *Standard Bible Dictionary*, edited by E. E. Nourse and A. C. Zenos. This was followed by a 2nd edition in 1925. A further revision was published in 1936, entitled *A New Standard Bible Dictionary*. *The Temple Dictionary of the Bible*, published in 1910, was edited by W. Ewing and J. E. H. Thomson, long-time missionaries in Palestine. *The Universal Bible Dictionary*, edited in 1957 by M. F. Unger (3rd rev. ed. 1960), was based upon C. R. Barnes' *Bible Encyclopedia*, assistance of Canon L. Williams.

The indispensable and consistently conservative *International Standard Bible Encyclopedia*, edited by J. Orr, first appeared in 1915. The five volumes, with hundreds of illustrations and exhaustive indexes, feature the efforts of more than two hundred contributors representing the best biblical scholarship of the English-speaking world. Many articles in this work, which totals more than four million words, and of which the present work is an extensive revision, remain the most comprehensive on many subjects. The most significant dictionary during the next thirty years was the revision of the 1909 *Standard Bible Dictionary*. Republished as *A New Standard Bible Dictionary* (1936), the work was edited by W. M. Jacobus, who was assisted by fifty-five contributors, and included nearly one million words. *The Theological Word Book of the Bible*, edited by A. Richardson (1950), is worthy of mention. The work includes articles on selective topics, with extensive bibliographies.

Harper's Bible Dictionary was published in 1952, edited by M. S. and J. L. Miller, who had published in 1944 their *Encyclopedia of Bible Life*. Heavy emphasis was placed here on sociology and natural history, and the sections on archeology included up-to-date work on pottery. The dictionary featured five hundred illustrations and the Westminster maps. The British edition bears the title *Black's Bible Dictionary*.

Stressing current evangelical scholarship, *Unger's Bible Dictionary*, edited in 1957 by M. F. Unger (3rd rev. ed. 1960), was based upon C. R. Barnes' *Bible Encyclopedia*, which first appeared in 1900. As Unger's preface says, it was "revised and rewritten in the light of the latest historical, archaeological, and linguistic discoveries in Bible lands." Although most of the five hundred photographs and drawings are new, as much as three-fourths of the material in this volume is taken directly from Barnes' earlier work without accounting for a half century of scholarship. However, Unger's articles on archeology, including the Dead Sea Scrolls, Abraham, etc., are excellent.

A very interesting work, which originally appeared in French in 1954, was published in 1958 as *A Companion to the Bible*, edited by J. J. Von Allmen, with the assistance of several French and Swiss Protestant scholars. H. H. Rowley has called it "a dictionary of the major theological terms and ideas found in the Bible."

Seventh Day Adventist's Bible Commentary, a large volume published in 1960, was edited by S. H. Horn, biblical archeologist.

Of two notable Bible dictionaries published in 1962, *New Bible Dictionary*, edited by J. D. Douglas (1390 pages), is probably the most important one-volume Bible dictionary yet published in the 20th century. Consulting editors included F. F. Bruce and D. J. Wiseman, and the 135 contributors are from many lands. Especially valuable are Wiseman's articles entitled "Writing," "Assyria and Babylonia," and, most of all, "Archeology," which features "A List of the Principal Excavated Sites in Palestine."

The four-volume *Interpreter's Dictionary of the Bible* also appeared in 1962, a typographically beautiful work with an extensively illustrated text exceeding four million words. Edited by G. A. Buttrick, the work includes the contributions of 253 Christian and Jewish scholars. On such topics as inspiration, predictive prophecy, historicity, and authenticity, the book is theologically inclined to a moderately liberal view. But conservative interpretations also occur, e.g., Bishop J. A. T. Robinson's long article on the Resurrection, which devotes three columns to the defense of the view that the tomb of Joseph of Arimathea was empty on Easter morning. The articles are often extensive, and many include practical bibliographies. A Supplementary Volume, published in 1976, contains many new articles as well as additions to the original articles.

In 1963 four quite dissimilar volumes of an encyclopedic nature were published. L. F. Hartman edited the large *Encyclopedic Dictionary of the Bible*, a translation of A. van den Born's *Bijbels Woordenboek*, a Roman Catholic work exceeding 2600 pages. The *Zondervan Pictorial Bible Dictionary* also appeared that year, edited by American NT scholar M. C. Tenney, a volume intended for those not interested in more exhaustive articles of the *New Bible Dictionary*. Of similar purpose is MacMillan's 1965 *Pictorial Biblical Encyclopedia, A Visual Guide to the Old and New Testaments*, edited by G. Cornfield. J. L. McKenzie's *Dictionary of the Bible* was also published in 1963.

More than half a century after its original publication, a thoroughly revised edition of the one-volume Hastings *Dictionary of the Bible* was issued, edited by F. C. Grant and H. H. Rowley. This edition is based on the RSV and contains many new entries. In 1968 Rowley contributed two specialized works, his *Dictionary of Bible Themes* and *Dictionary of Bible Personal Names,* concise tools that make biblical texts easily accessible.

In 1970, more than seventy years after its first edition (1898), a *New Westminster Dictionary of the Bible* appeared, edited by H. S. Gehman, who had prepared the 1944 edition. Improved and increased by three hundred pages over earlier editions, this edition has approximately three hundred new entries and 450 illustrations and reflects the influence of recent archeological discoveries.

A lavishly illustrated non-technical work is *Eerdmans' Handbook to the Bible,* edited by A. and P. Alexander and released in 1973. This popularly oriented reference volume is arranged in four sections, encompassing general biblical information, OT and NT topics including articles on "Critical Methods and Findings," and key scriptural themes and doctrines. Also in 1973, a revised edition of X. Leon-Dufour's *Dictionary of Biblical Theology* appeared, a translation by E. M. Stewart of the French work first published in 1962.

The five-volume *Zondervan Pictorial Encyclopedia of the Bible,* edited by M. C. Tenney, was published in 1975, the first completely new evangelical biblical encyclopedia in nearly forty years. Also published in 1975, the two-volume *Wycliffe Bible Encyclopedia* is a companion project to the *Wycliffe Bible Commentary* and the *Wycliffe Geography of Bible Lands* and includes articles on the proper names and places mentioned in the Bible. More than two hundred scholars, primarily Americans, have contributed to the work, edited by C. F. Pfeiffer, H. F. Vos, and J. Rea.

One of the most significant theological projects of the century, the *Theological Dictionary of the New Testament* (1964-1976) is G. W. Bromiley's English translation of the monumental *Theologisches Wörterbuch zum Neuen Testament* initiated in 1928 by G. Kittel (1888-1948) and completed by G. Friedrich. The ten-volume series, which includes an index volume, examines the detailed linguistic character as well as the related theological meanings of significant terms, with extensive articles on the most important terms. Its counterpart is the *Theological Dictionary of the Old Testament,* English translation of the *Theologisches Wörterbuch zum Alten Testament,* edited by G. J. Botterweck and H. Ringgren. Volume one of the projected twelve-volume series appeared in 1974.

Bibliography.–For further discussion see T. H. Horne, *Manual of Biblical Bibliography* (1839), pp. 369-372; MSt, II, 787-89; *Jew.Enc.,* IV, 577-79; E. C. Richardson, in *ISBE* (1939), II, 843ff. (encyclopedias other than biblical are also extensively noted here); C. T. Fritsch, *Interp.,* 1 (1947), 363-371; W. M. Smith, *Fuller Library Bulletin* (Sept. 1954) (includes theological and ecclesiastical dictionaries not discussed in this article).

W. M. SMITH

BIBLICAL CRITICISM. *See* CRITICISM.

BIBLICAL DISCREPANCIES. *See* DISCREPANCIES, BIBLICAL.

BIBLICAL THEOLOGY, HISTORY OF.

I. Middle Ages
II. Reformation
III. Orthodox Scholasticism
IV. Rationalist Reaction
V. Rise of the Philosophy of Religion
VI. Conservative Reaction
VII. Liberal Historicism in NT Theology
VIII. Victory of Religion over Theology
IX. Contemporary Return to Biblical Theology

I. Middle Ages.–Biblical theology as such is a modern discipline. During the Middle Ages biblical study was almost completely subordinated to ecclesiastical dogma. The theology of the Bible was used to reinforce the dogmatic teachings of the Church, which were founded upon both the Bible and church tradition. Not the Bible alone, historically understood, but the Bible as interpreted by tradition was the source of dogmatic theology.

II. Reformation.–The Reformers reacted against the unbiblical character of dogmatic theology and insisted that theology must be founded upon the Bible alone. Dogmatics should be the systematic formulation of the teachings of the Bible. This new emphasis led to a study of the original languages of Scripture and to a recognition of the role of history in biblical theology. The Reformers also insisted that the Bible should be interpreted historically and not allegorically; and this led to the beginnings of a truly biblical theology. However, the Reformers' sense of history was undeveloped, and they did not pursue biblical theology as a distinctive discipline.

III. Orthodox Scholasticism.–The gain in the historical study of the Bible made by the Reformers was partly lost in the post-Reformation period, and the Bible was once again used uncritically and unhistorically to support orthodox doctrine. The Bible was viewed not only as a book free from error and contradiction but also without development or progress. The entire Bible was looked upon as possessing one level of theological value. History was completely lost in dogma, and philology became a branch of dogmatics.

IV. Rationalist Reaction.–Biblical theology as a distinct discipline is a product of the impact of the Enlightenment (*Aufklärung*) upon biblical studies. A new approach to the study of the Bible emerged in the 18th cent. which gradually freed itself altogether from ecclesiastical and theological control and interpreted the Bible with what it claimed to be "complete objectivity," regarding it solely as a product of history. From this perspective, the Bible was viewed as a compilation of ancient religious writings preserving the history of an ancient Semitic people, and was studied with the same presuppositions with which one studies other Semitic religions. This conclusion was clearly articulated by J. P. Gabler, who in an inaugural address in 1787 distinguished sharply between biblical theology and dogmatic theology. Biblical theology must be strictly historical and independent of dogmatic theology, tracing the rise of religious ideas in Israel and setting forth what the biblical writers thought about religious matters. Dogmatic theology, on the other hand, makes use of biblical theology, extracting from it what has universal relevance and making use of philosophical concepts. Dogmatic theology is that which a particular theologian decides about divine matters, considered philosophically and rationally in accordance with the outlook and demands of his own age; but biblical theology is concerned solely with what men believed long ago.

Gabler was essentially a rationalist, and his approach to biblical theology prevailed for some fifty years. Works on the theology of the Bible were written by Kaiser (1813), De Wette (1813), Baumgarten-Crusius (1828), and von Cölln (1836). Some scholars of this period were extremely rationalistic, finding in the Bible religious ideas that were in accord with the universal laws of reason. Others tried to reconcile Christian theology with the thought forms of the modern period. While this rationalistic perspective as such is long since passé, it is obvious that this historical approach to the study of the Bible is still the fundamental assumption of modern scholarship; and even Evangelical scholars employ the historical method, although with limitations.

V. Rise of the Philosophy of Religion.–Rationalism was superseded under the influence of the idealist philosophy of Hegel (d. 1813), who saw the Absolute Idea or Absolute Spirit eternally manifesting itself in the universe and in human affairs. Hegel taught that the movement of human thought followed the dialectic pattern from a position (thesis) to an opposite position (antithesis), from which interaction emerged a new insight or aspect of reality (synthesis). Hegel saw in the history of religion the evolution of spirit in its dialectical apprehension of the divine, from nature religions, through religions of spiritual individuality, to the Absolute Religion, which is Christianity.

Under the influence of Hegel, Vatke wrote a biblical theology in 1835 in which the emerging critical views about the OT were combined with Hegel's evolutionary philosophy. His interpretation of the history of Israel's religion was much in advance of his day and was passed over for some thirty years until it was taken up and popularized by Wellhausen.

Under the influence of Hegel, F. C. Baur abandoned the rationalistic effort to find timeless truth in the NT, and instead found in the historical movements in the early Church the unfolding of wisdom and spirit. The teachings of Jesus formed the point of departure. Jesus' teachings were not yet theology but the expression of his religious consciousness. Theological reflection began over the question of the law. Paul, the first theologian, took the position that the Christian was freed from the law (thesis). Jewish Christianity, represented particularly by James and Peter, took the opposite position, that the law was permanently valid and must remain an essential element in the Christian Church (antithesis). Baur interpreted the history of apostolic Christianity in terms of this conflict between Pauline and Judaistic Christianity. Out of the conflict emerged in the 2nd cent. the Old Catholic Church, which effected a successful harmonization between these two positions (synthesis).

Baur was less concerned with the truth of the Scriptures than with the effort to trace historical development. He has made a lasting contribution, for the principle that biblical theology is rooted in history is sound, even though Baur's application of this principle is not. Baur's interpretation gave rise to the so-called Tübingen school, which had great influence in German NT studies.

VI. Conservative Reaction.–These new approaches to the study of the Bible naturally met with a strong resistance in orthodox circles, not only from those who denied the validity of a historical approach but also from those who tried to combine the historical approach with a belief in revelation. Influential was E. W. Hengstenberg's *Christology of the OT* (Eng. tr. 1829-1835) and *History of the Kingdom of God under the OT* (Eng. tr. 1869-1871). Hengstenberg saw little progress in revelation, made little distinction between the two Testaments, and interpreted the prophets spiritually with little reference to history. A more historical approach was structured by J. C. K. Hofmann in a series of writings beginning in 1841 (*Verheissung und Erfüllung*), in which he attempted to vindicate the authority and inspiration of the Bible by historical means, developing his *Heilsgeschichte* theology. Hofmann found in the Bible record of the process of holy or saving-history, which aims at the redemption of all mankind. This process will not be completed until the eschatological consummation. He tried to assign every book of the Bible to its place in this scheme of the history of redemption. This so-called Erlangen school (including also J. A. Bengel, J. T. Beck), did not regard the Bible primarily as a collection of proof texts or a repository of doctrine but as the witness to what God had done in saving-history. They held that the propositional statements in Scripture were not meant to be an end in themselves nor an object of faith, but were designed to bear witness to the redemptive acts of God.

The most important product of the conservative reaction for this discipline was G. F. Oehler's *Theologie des AT* (*Prolegomena* 1845, *Theologie* 1873; Eng. tr. 1883). Conservative in his critical views and holding to the revealed character of OT religion, Oehler also recognized that OT theology is a historical discipline which must describe the OT faith as a phenomenon in history. He criticized the older view, which limited theological exposition to the didactic contents of the Bible, insisting that the discipline must "exhibit properly the internal connection of the doctrine of Revelation with the revealing history" (p. 6). Thus he found the OT to be mediated through a series of divine acts and commands, and also through the institutions of a divine state. A condensation of Oehler's large work was made by R. F. Weidner (1896). Other conservative OT scholars were Baumgarten, C. A. Auberlen, and the commentator Franz Delitzsch.

The Erlangen school had great influence in conservative circles upon such scholars as Tholuck, T. Zahn, P. Feine, and is represented in the theologies of F. Büchsel (1937), A. Schlatter (1909), and Ethelbert Stauffer (1941; Eng. tr. 1955). Stauffer rejects the "systems of doctrine" approach and does not try to trace the development of the Christian understanding of the person and work of Jesus. Rather, he presents a "Christocentric theology of History in the NT," i.e., the theology of the plan of salvation enacted in NT history. The book does not distinguish between canonical and noncanonical writings and ignores the variety of the several interpretations of the meaning of Christ in the NT.

A new form of the *Heilsgeschichte* theology has emerged in recent years, for there is a widespread recognition that revelation has occurred in redemptive history and that *Heilsgeschichte* is the best key to understand the unity of the Bible. This will be developed later.

VII. Liberal Historicism in NT Theology.–Bultmann has pointed out that the logical consequence of Baur's method would have been a complete relativism (*NT Theology*, II [1955], 245), for the liberal mind could not conceive of absolute truth in the relativities of history. Under the influence of Ritschlian theology, the essence of Christianity was interpreted as a pure spiritual-ethical religion which was proclaimed by and embodied in the life and mission of Jesus. The kingdom of God is the highest good, the ethical ideal. The heart of religion is personal fellowship with God as Father.

This theological interpretation was reinforced by the solution of the Synoptic problem, with its discovery of the priority of Mark and the hypothetical document Q. Scholars of this "old liberalism" believed that in these most primitive documents historical science had at last discovered the true Jesus, freed from all theological interpretation. Biblical theologians of this school began with this "historical" picture of the ethical religion of Jesus and then traced the diverse systems of doctrine (*Lehrbegriffe*) that emerged as the result of later reflection and speculation. The great classic of this school is H. J. Holtzmann's *Lehrbuch der NT Theologie* (1896/97). Paul Wernle's *The Beginnings of Our Religion* (Eng. tr. 1903/04) is another example. Adolf von Harnack's *What Is Christianity?* (Eng. tr. 1901) is a classic statement of this liberal view.

This "old liberal" approach influenced even conserva-

BIBLICAL THEOLOGY, HISTORY OF

tive writers. Both B. Weiss (*Theology of the NT* [1868; Eng. tr. 1903]) and W. Beyschlag (1891; Eng. tr. 1895) interpreted Jesus primarily in spiritual terms, placing great emphasis upon the centrality of the Fatherhood of God. These men were conservative in that they recognized the reality of revelation and the validity of the canon; but their picture of Jesus shared the features of liberalism. They also employed the "systems of doctrine" method, Weiss going so far as to discover four different periods of theological development in Paul, which he treated separately. This approach is found in English in the writings of Orello Cone, *The Gospel and Its Earliest Interpreters* (1893), G. B. Stevens, *Theology of the NT* (1899), E. P. Gould, *Biblical Theology of the NT* (1900), and A. C. Zenos, *Plastic Age of the Gospel* (1927). The same method is used by even more conservative writers in Germany, such as T. Zahn, *Grundriss der NT Theologie* (1932), and P. Feine, *Theologie des NT* (1910).

VIII. Victory of Religion over Theology.–Along with liberalism developed the *religionsgeschichtliche Schule*. In 1883 appeared Julius Wellhausen's *Prolegomena zur Geschichte Israels,* which has been often called the most important work in OT criticism in the 19th century. Taking over Vatke's historico-philosophical interpretation, Wellhausen gave classic expression to the view that the story of Israel's religion was not to be interpreted in terms of divine revelation but in terms of evolutionary principles; the religious development of the OT period embodies particular examples of general religious laws manifesting themselves in history. Wellhausen popularized both the idea of evolutionary development of OT religion and the documentary hypothesis, illustrating how criticism and theology interact upon each other. In Wellhausen's reconstruction the religion of Israel began with Moses, not the patriarchs; the fundamental law of the Jewish community belongs to the postexilic community, not to Mosaic times; eschatology is a late postexilic development in the evolution of Hebrew religion; and the ethical monotheism of the prophets was the basic force that molded Israel's religion into a significant faith.

Wellhausen's work marks the beginning of the period that saw the apparent death of OT theology and the victory of the discipline called the "history of the religion of Israel." Even the name "theology of the OT" was seldom used; and when books were written with this title, as for instance by B. Stade (1905) and Kayser (1886), the contents were not theology but a history of Hebrew religion. Treatises on Hebrew religion were written by Smend (1893), K. Marti (Eng. tr. 1907), E. Kautzsch (*HDB,* V, 612-734), A. Loisy (Eng. tr. 1910), K. Budde (1910), E. Koenig (1915), R. Kittel (Eng. tr. 1921), G. Hoelscher (1922), and M. Loehr (Eng. tr. 1936). In English the approach is found in the misnamed work of A. Duff, *OT Theology* (1891), and it appears clearly in W. O. E. Oesterley and T. H. Robinson, *Hebrew Religion: Its Origin and Development* (1930), A. C. Knudson, *Religious Teaching of the OT* (1918), G. A. Barton, *Religion of Israel* (1919), and in the widely used book of H. E. Fosdick, *Guide to the Understanding of the Bible* (1938; see Eichrodt's criticism in *JBL,* 65 [1946], 205-217). Although this approach has now given way before the revival in interest in the theology of the Bible, it persists in such works as I. G. Matthews, *Religious Pilgrimage of Israel* (1947), S. V. McCasland, *Religion of the Bible* (1960), and R. H. Pfeiffer, *Religion in the OT* (1961).

The interpretation of the OT as the story of the evolution of one Semitic religion naturally led to a comparison between Hebrew religion and other Semitic religions, and to the search for common patterns, particularly of ritual practice. W. R. Smith in *Religion of the Semites* (1889) emphasized the common elements shared by the Hebrews with the neighboring religions. The interpretation of biblical religion in terms of its religious environment is called the *religionsgeschichtliche Methode*.

This approach still persists in contemporary scholarship, particularly in what is called the "myth and ritual school," which believes that a common culture pattern, at least in the sphere of religious belief and practice, had been diffused throughout the ancient Orient and is reflected in the OT. See S. H. Hooke, *Myth and Ritual* (1933); *The Labyrinth* (1935); E. O. James, *Myth and Ritual in the Ancient Near East* (1958). S. Mowinckel (*Psalmenstudien* [1922-24]; *He That Cometh* [Eng. tr. 1956]) traced the origin of eschatology to a New Year Festival in which the return of the rainy season with its resultant renewal of fertility was celebrated as an annual accession of the divine King to His throne when He resumed His divine reign. The existence of such an enthronement festival is not explicit in the OT but is assumed from the analogy of the Babylonian New Year ritual and from alleged traces of a supposed cult-myth in the Psalms. See also A. R. Johnson, *Sacral Kingship in Ancient Israel* (1955).

During the early part of this period, efforts were still made to interpret the religion of the OT from a theological point of view. A. Dillmann (1895) rejected the Wellhausen hypothesis and argued that a comparative study of Semitic religions would demonstrate the uniqueness of OT religion. Other works accepted the Wellhausen hypothesis, but tried to give a systematic view of Israel's religious outlook. C. Piepenbring (1886) found elements of permanent value in the historical development. H. Schultz adopted the Wellhausen hypothesis in the 2nd edition of his OT theology (1878), and tried to solve the problem of history and theology by giving first a historical account of the development of Israel's religion and then a topical treatment in which the several theological concepts were traced through the various periods. However, he felt that the diversity of religious ideas was so great that there were virtually different theologies in the different periods. In England, A. B. Davidson's *Theology of the OT* (1904) reflects the same uneasy truce between history and theology. Although he states that the proper subject of OT theology is the history of the religion of Israel (p. 11), he attempts to create a theology out of the religious beliefs and ideas in the OT, and in effect he has produced a theology of the OT. H. W. Robinson wrote a small book on *The Religious Ideas of the OT* (1913) in which he presented a few simple yet profound ideas which he found behind the variety of OT religion, and which he set forth with some indication of their theological value.

The works of Schultz and Davidson were the last efforts for a generation to attempt to set forth the theological significance of OT religion. The history-of-religion approach had triumphed. A philosophy of evolutionary naturalism was substituted for that of revealed religion. Many studies in the history of Israel's religion appeared, but even conservative writers did not attempt to write theologies of the OT.

This "comparative religions" approach also dominated NT study. Liberalism found the distinctive element of biblical theology in the simple ethical teaching of Jesus. While its representatives paid some attention to the influence of the religious environment of early Christianity (Holtzmann's *Theologie* devoted 120 pages to a sketch of Jewish and Hellenistic backgrounds), the essence of Christianity was treated as something unique, though Holtzmann recognized Hellenistic influences on Paul.

Otto Pfleiderer presaged a new approach. The 1st edition of *Das Urchristentum* (1887) took the same position as Harnack and Holtzmann; but in the 2nd edition (1902; Eng. tr. 1906, *Primitive Christianity*) he interpreted many elements in NT theology in terms of their religious environment. The program for this new approach was presented by W. Wrede in 1897 in a little book entitled *Über Aufgabe und Methode der sogenannten NT Theologie*. He attacked the prevailing method of interpreting NT theology as a series of doctrinal systems, for the Christian faith is religion, not theology or a system of ideas. NT theology has the task not of formulating timeless truths, whether these be mediated by a supernatural revelation or discovered by rational thought, but of formulating expressions of the living religious experiences of early Christianity, understood in light of the religious environment. Therefore the theology of the NT must be displaced by the history of religion in primitive Christianity. (See also A. Deissmann in *ZTK*, 3 [1893], 126-139.)

This new approach had two distinct centers of interest: the interpretation of NT ideas in terms of expressions of religious experience, and the explanation of the rise of these religious experiences and ideas in terms of the religious environment. One of the first to attempt the former task was H. Weinel in his *Biblische Theologie des NT* (1913). Weinel was not primarily interested in the value or truth of Christianity but only in its nature in comparison with other religions. He set forth types of religions against which Christianity is to be understood as an ethical religion of redemption. Books in English that reflect this influence are S. J. Case, *Evolution of Early Christianity* (1914), E. W. Parsons, *Religion of the NT* (1939), and E. F. Scott, *Varieties of NT Religion* (1943).

The basic assumption of this approach led to very different treatments of Jesus and Paul. In 1892, J. Weiss published a booklet of sixty-seven pages on *Die Predigt Jesu vom Reiche Gottes* in which he interpreted Jesus' message of the kingdom in terms of the milieu of Jewish apocalyptic. This approach was made famous by Albert Schweitzer's *Von Reimarus zu Wrede* (1906; Eng. tr. *QHJ*), which gives a history of the interpretation of Jesus and then in a hundred pages interprets Jesus in terms of "Consistent Eschatology," i.e., as a Jewish apocalyptist who belongs to first-century Judaism and has little relevance for the modern man. This preacher of eschatology was diametrically opposed to the ethical teacher of the pure religion of the Fatherhood of God as sketched by Harnack and Holtzmann, and it became clear that the "old liberal" Jesus was a distinct modernization. Eschatology, instead of being the husk (Harnack), was shown by Schweitzer to be the very kernel of Jesus' message.

If Jesus was interpreted in terms of the milieu of Jewish apocalyptic, Paul was interpreted in terms of Hellenistic Judaism or the Hellenistic cults and mystery religions. Some scholars, like Bousset, still interpreted Jesus along the lines of liberalism but applied the *religionsgeschichtliche Methode* to Paul. Brückner argued that Paul found a ready-made doctrine of a heavenly man in Judaism, which he applied to Jesus. Gunkel held that there had sprung up in the Orient a syncretistic religion, gnostic in character, with faith in the resurrection as its central doctrine. This pre-Christian Gnosticism had penetrated Judaism, and through this medium influenced Christianity, even before Paul. W. Bousset put this view on a firmer basis by arguing that Gnosticism was not a heretical new formation in Christianity, as Harnack had supposed, but was a pre-Christian pagan phenomenon, oriental rather than Greek, and religious and mystical rather than philosophical. In his *Kyrios Christos* (1913) Bousset traced the history of belief in Jesus in the early Church, and sharply distinguished between the religious consciousness of Jesus, the faith of primitive Christianity, which held Jesus to be the transcendental Son of man of Jewish apocalyptic, and the view of the Hellenistic Church and of Paul, who held Jesus to be a divinity, like the Greek cult lords.

The most important NT theology embodying this approach is Rudolf Bultmann's. Bultmann differed from Bousset in that he interpreted Jesus in terms of Jewish apocalyptic; but he followed Bousset in his understanding of the Hellenistic Church and Paul. However, Bultmann added a new feature in his existential understanding of these NT "myths," which will be discussed below.

IX. Contemporary Return to Biblical Theology.–During the 1920's a new viewpoint began to make itself felt which resulted in a revival of biblical theology. Factors contributing to this revival included a loss of faith in evolutionary naturalism, a reaction against the purely historical method, which claimed complete objectivity and believed in the adequacy of bare facts to disclose the truth of history, and the recovery of the concept of revelation. This led to the conviction that the OT contained both history and a word concerning the ultimate meaning of history. Thus the study of biblical theology turned its attention to discovering what is of permanent value in OT religion.

The first theological work on the OT in this period was by E. König (1922). König, however, wrote as an old man who had defended the conservative view of Israel's history against Wellhausenism, and who opposed the evolutionary method. The new emphasis is seen in essays by R. Kittel, C. Steuernagel, O. Eissfeldt, and W. Eichrodt published in *ZAW*. Rudolf Kittel (1921) admitted the shortcomings of the purely critical approach and urged scholarship to recapture the study of the OT as a theological discipline. Steuernagel (1925) recognized that the other theological disciplines needed a systematic presentation of OT theology which the history-of-religion method could not provide. Eissfeldt (1926) urged that there were two different methods of studying the OT, standing side by side: the historical method, which deals empirically with the history of Hebrew religion, evaluating the objective data by reason and critical methodology; and the theological method, which recognizes by faith the timeless truths embodied in the OT.

Eichrodt (1933) rejected Eissfeldt's view of two different disciplines and held that a fruitful combination of the two methods is possible. The task of theology is to penetrate to the essence of the OT religion and throw light on the inner structure of its theological system. When Eichrodt later published his OT theology (1933-1938) he took the idea of the covenant from the OT itself as a center in terms of which all the theology of the OT was to be understood, and produced a systematic synthesis of the essential doctrines of the religion of Israel.

In the years that followed, a succession of OT theologies was produced in Europe. E. Sellin (1933) viewed the entire Bible as an essential unity and presented the major ideas of the OT in systematic form; but he selected only those basic doctrines such as God, man, and salvation which are common to the various parts of the OT and which give to its theology a consistent unity. The revived theological approach to the OT is more vividly seen in W. Vischer's *Witness of the OT to Christ* (1934; Eng. tr. 1949). Vischer to a large degree disregarded the distinction between the Testaments and used allegorical exegesis to discover in the OT what Christ is.

Although L. Koehler's OT theology (1936) was more historical in approach, it attempted a synthesis of the thoughts and concepts of the OT that are or can be important. E. Jacob (1955) defended the view that the OT is one book, presenting one religion whose strands come together in Christ. He held that both the "religion of Israel" and the "theology of the OT" are historical disciplines, the former showing the variety of the history and its evolution, the latter displaying its unity. OT theology is the systematic account of the specific religious ideas which can be found throughout the OT and which form its profound unity. O. Procksch (1949) was influenced by von Hofmann and viewed OT theology from the perspective of saving-history.

T. C. Vriezen published an *Outline of OT Theology* in Dutch in 1949 which has been translated both into German and English (Eng. tr. 1958). OT theology has as its object not the religion of Israel but the OT; and the OT is not to be studied in isolated detachment but in its relationship to the NT. He therefore selected the central themes and materials that are important for Christian faith. A later German work, that of G. von Rad (1957, 1961), is a sort of *Heilsgeschichte*; yet it is not a theological interpretation of the modern historian's reconstruction of the events of Israel's history, but the theology of traditions that Israel held about its own history. He has therefore been criticized by critical scholars for placing a gulf between history and theology.

The new theological approach to the OT made a strong impact on Great Britain but by the mid-1970's had produced few full-scale OT theologies there. H. W. Robinson reflected the new trend in the second volume of essays by the Society for OT Study (*Record and Revelation*, ed. H. W. Robinson [1938]) in which he emphasized a *heilsgeschichtlich* (saving-history) approach to revelation. Revelation is not the communication of abstract truth but the gradual disclosure, through the concrete experiences of life, of a pattern of divine purpose steadily unfolding itself in history, and pointing to the climax in the NT without which it is incomplete. Later Robinson expanded this thesis in *Inspiration and Revelation in the OT* (1946), which was designed to be a prolegomena to an OT theology that he did not live to write.

N. H. Snaith vigorously criticized the comparative-religions approach because it ignored any distinctive elements in the Bible. He found theology in the distinctive beliefs in the OT which set it apart from other religions and which are further developed in the NT. H. H. Rowley wrote many volumes dealing with the thought of the OT, and in *The Faith of Israel* (1956) he, like Snaith, argued that OT theology is to be found in the distinctive elements in the religion of Israel. He recognized evolution and borrowing from other religions but was unable to account for the essence of Israel's religion in these terms. He saw within OT history and religion a self-revelation of God which results in something timeless and of enduring validity; this constitutes OT theology. The most thoroughgoing theological treatment was that of G. A. F. Knight, *A Christian Theology of the OT* (1959), which studies the OT not in terms of Israel's religion or historical development but in terms of the OT message to the 20th cent. in light of the Christian revelation as a whole. N. W. Porteous in the third volume of essays by the Society for OT study (*OTMS*) differentiated between OT religion and theology, finding theology in a critical evaluation of the knowledge of God resulting from the human reaction to the Word spoken in the events of OT history. This thesis is unfolded in his essay in the revised edition of Peake's *Comm. on the Bible* (1962).

The new theological concern also strongly influenced American scholarship. In 1940, W. F. Albright (*FSAC*) rejected positivistic historicism in favor of an "organismic" philosophy of history, defending the basic soundness of the main outlines of the OT tradition and tracing essential monotheism to Moses. This thesis was reinforced in *ARI* (1942). Millar Burrows in *An Outline of Biblical Theology* (1946) pointed out the loss of a note of authority in biblical preaching as a result of modern critical study of the Bible. Burrows then sketched the development of the several theological concepts throughout the entire Bible. He distinguished between history and theology by holding that theology asks for God's judgment on the religion of Israel and of primitive Christianity and seeks its modern significance. O. J. Baab in his OT theology (1949) admitted the sterility and failure of the pure objective-historical study of Israel's religion. He argued that we must interpret the biblical religion and history from the viewpoint of the faith by which the men of the Bible lived. R. C. Dentan in his *Preface to OT Theology* (1950) defined biblical theology as "that Christian theological discipline which treats the religious ideas of the OT systematically, i.e., not from the point of view of historical development, but from that of the structural unity of OT religion" (p. 48).

G. E. Wright showed that the OT teaching cannot be explained as a natural evolution resulting from environmental influences (*The OT Against Its Environment* [1950]). OT theology is neither a history of biblical ideas nor a systematic cross section of these ideas treated under the rubrics of dogmatic theology. It is rather a confessional recital of the redemptive acts of God in history together with their theological meaning (*God Who Acts* [1952]). This exposition Wright undertook in his essay on "The Faith of Israel" in the first volume of *IB* (1952).

Among modern Roman Catholic works is the *Theologie des AT* by Paul Heinisch (1940; Eng. tr. 1955). Heinisch does not make it his main purpose, as had earlier Roman Catholic writers, to use biblical theology as a tool for defending the doctrines of the Church. He interprets the OT in its historical setting. OT theology is the systematic presentation of what the OT leaders, who were raised up and inspired by God, required as to faith and morals; while the religion of Israel shows how the people responded to the directives of their religious teachers and how the environment and cultural progress affected the development of spiritual ideas.

In spite of this renaissance in biblical theology, conservative writers have had little to contribute to the dialogue, at least on the level of critical studies. R. B. Girdlestone's *OT Theology and Modern Ideas* (1909) is not a theology of the OT but a series of essays on various theological themes. In 1948, G. Vos' *Biblical Theology* was published posthumously. The work breaks off abruptly in the midst of a discussion of the revelation in Jesus' ministry, and it is more an extended essay on revelation in the OT than a biblical theology. A contemporary writer in the same conservative tradition, E. J. Young, wrote an introductory study under the title *The Study of OT Theology Today* (1958). See also his remarks in *EQ*, 31 (1959), 52f., 136-142. Young assumed such a very conservative stance that he denied that the modern movement was really a resurgence of true biblical theology, for any theology that does not accept the complete trustworthiness of Scripture "is not taught by God, does not teach God and does not lead to God" (*EQ*, 31 [1959], 53). Young's position has been criticized by other conservative scholars for "passing judgment by implication on all works on modern OT theology" (E. L. Ellison, *EQ*, 31 [1959], 52). J. B. Payne has produced a comprehensive *Theology of the Older Testament* (1962). Payne, like Eichrodt, takes the concept of the covenant as the integrating center for OT theology; but instead of finding the meaning of the covenant in the OT concept of *b^erîṯ*, he turns to the Greek meaning of *diathēkē* as it is used in He. 9:16ff., and structures the entire pattern of OT theology around this Greek concept.

The new approach to theology changed the complexion of NT studies. The historical assurance of liberalism was challenged by Martin Kähler in a book that has proved to be crucial for the modern debate. Kähler structured the problem in terms of *Der sogenannte historische Jesus und der geschichtliche biblische Christus* (1898). The *historische* Jesus, i.e., the Jesus reconstructed by the liberal critical method, never really existed in history but only in the critical imagination of scholarship. The only Jesus who possesses reality is the Christ pictured in the Bible, whose character is such that he cannot be reconstructed by the methods of scientific historiography. The Gospels are not historical (*historische*) documents in the scientific sense of the term, but witnesses to the Christ. They are kerygma, not "history"; and it is impossible to get behind the kerygma. Indeed, the "historical Jesus" serves only to obscure from us the living biblical Christ. The real *geschichtliche* Christ is the Christ who is attested in the Gospels and who is preached by the Church.

Another signpost pointing in the same direction was the book by W. Wrede, *Das Messiasgeheimnis in den Evangelien* (1901). Wrede shattered the liberal portrait of the historical Jesus by showing that the Jesus of Mark was not the inspired prophet but a messianic (divine) being. Wrede differed from Kähler in that he did not accept the Markan portrait of Jesus as true but attempted to explain historically how the nonmessianic, historical Jesus became the messianic Christ of the Gospels.

In the years that followed, gospel criticism turned to the study of the oral stage of the gospel tradition (*Formgeschichte*) to try to discover the laws controlling the tradition which could explain the transformation of the "historical" Jesus into the kerygmatic Christ. One outstanding aspect of this study was the admission that form criticism could not find in any stratum of the gospel tradition a purely historical Jesus. The resultant "kerygmatic" approach has issued in two very different interpretations of the NT.

On the one hand, E. H. Hoskyns and Noel Davey in *The Riddle of the NT* (1931) show that all the evidence of the NT converges on a single point: that in Jesus, God revealed Himself for man's salvation. The critical method has revealed most clearly the living unity of the NT documents. The historian is compelled to state that both the unity and uniqueness of this claim are historical facts. This claim, while occurring in history, transcends history, for it demands of the historian what he as a historian may not give: a theological judgment of ultimate significance.

This "kerygmatic" interpretation of NT theology received its greatest impetus through the writings of C. H. Dodd. In his inaugural lecture at Cambridge University, Dodd called for a new emphasis on the unity of NT thought in place of the analytic approach, which had prevailed throughout the preceding century. In the same year (1936) he implemented his own suggestion in *Apostolic Preaching and Its Developments*. Dodd finds the unity of the NT message in the kerygma, the heart of which is the proclamation that the new age has come in the person and mission of Jesus. Here for the first time, a single biblical concept was used to relate the NT materials to a unified development. Dodd has enlarged upon this thesis in *The Parables of the Kingdom* (1935) and *The Interpretation of the Fourth Gospel* (1935), interpreting both the message of Jesus and that of the Gospel of John in terms of the inbreaking of the age to come. While this approach is sound in principle, Dodd's work has the defect of understanding the age to come in terms of Platonic thought rather than biblical eschatology. The age to come is the "wholly other," the eternal breaking into the temporal, instead of the future age breaking into the present age.

This kerygmatic theology has produced an extensive literature. The outstanding American protagonist has been F. V. Filson. His *One Lord, One Faith* (1943) defends the unity of the NT message, and his *Jesus Christ the Risen Lord* (1956) argues that NT theology must understand NT history from the theological point of view, i.e., from the standpoint of the living God who acts in history, the most notable event being the resurrection of Christ. Filson interprets the entire NT theology in light of the Resurrection.

A. M. Hunter expounded *The Unity of the NT* (1944, American title *The Message of the NT*) in terms of One Lord, One Church, One Salvation. More recently, in a slim volume *Introducing NT Theology* (1957), he has expounded the "fact of Christ,"; he includes in this term "the totality of what Jesus Christ's coming involved, his person, work and words, of course, but also the Resurrection, the advent of the Spirit and the creation of the new Israel. . . " (p. 9).

Oscar Cullmann also follows the *Heilsgeschichte* interpretation, and provides an excellent corrective for Dodd's Platonic approach. In *Christ and Time* (1946; Eng. tr. 1950, 1964) he argues that the NT finds its unity in a common conception of time and history rather than in ideas of essence, nature, eternal or existential truth. Theology is the meaning of the historical in time. In Cullmann's work, *Heilsgeschichte* theology has emerged in a new form; and the principle of *Heilsgeschichte* as the unifying center of NT theology has been widely recognized. We can accept the basic validity of Cullmann's approach without agreeing with him that the NT shows no interest in questions of nature and being but only in "functional Christology."

(For the influence of this *Heilsgeschichte* theology, see A. N. Wilder in H. R. Willoughboy, ed., *Study of the Bible Today and Tomorrow* [1947], pp. 419-436; F. V. Filson, *JBR*, 19 [1951], 191-96; C. T. Craig, *JBR*, 19 [1951], 182-86; W. D. Davies, *JBR*, 20 [1952], 231-38 [Davies does not use the term, but he recognizes that in Bultmann's theology — of which Cullmann's is the antithesis — the "nature of Christianity as a historical religion . . . is at stake"]; C. Gamble, Jr., *Interp.*, 7 [1953], 466-480; J. W. Bowman, *Prophetic Realism and the Gospel: A Preface to Biblical Theology* [1955]; K. Stendahl, *IDB*, I, 423-25. F. C. Grant also recognized the validity of the concept in *An Intro. to NT Thought* [1958], p. 41.)

Alan Richardson in his *Intro. to the Theology of the NT* (1958) assumed the kerygmatic approach by accepting the hypothesis that the "brilliant re-interpretation of the OT scheme of salvation which is found in the NT" goes back to Jesus Himself and is not the product of the believing community. In an essay on "Historical Theology and

Biblical Theology," Richardson argued that biblical theology cannot use a purely objective, scientific, neutral approach, but must interpret the biblical history from the standpoint of a biblical faith (*Canadian Journal of Theology*, 1 [1955], 157-167).

The exponents of this "kerygmatic" approach assume that the Christ proclaimed in the kerygma is continuous with the historical Jesus. The "kerygmatic" factor is the interpretative element that necessarily accompanies the event. A radically different use of the kerygmatic approach, on the other hand, is found in the writings of Bultmann, who found no continuity between the historical Jesus and the Christ of the kerygma. The historical Jesus, for Bultmann, has been quite obscured behind the layers of believing tradition, which reinterpreted the significance of Jesus in mythological terms. Historically, Jesus was only a Jewish apocalyptist who proclaimed the imminent apocalyptic end of the world and warned people to prepare for the catastrophe of judgment. He conceived of Himself neither as Messiah nor as Son of man. He did, however, possess an overwhelming sense of the reality of God, and He realized that He was the bearer of the Word of God for the last hour, which placed men under the demand for decision. His death was an incomparable tragedy, though this was redeemed from meaninglessness by the emergence of belief in His resurrection. The early Church reinterpreted Jesus, first in terms of the Jewish apocalyptic Son of man, and then in terms of a conflation of the apocalyptic Son of man, the Gnostic heavenly man, and the dying and rising cult deity of the mystery religions. The kerygma, i.e., the early Church's proclamation of Christ, is a historical fact in the life of early Christianity; and therefore there is continuity between the historical Jesus and the kerygma. If there had been no Jesus there would have been no kerygma. The Christ who is proclaimed in the kerygma, however, is a mythological construction and had no existence in history, for mythology by definition is nonhistorical. Therefore, there can be no continuity between the historical Jesus and the Christ of the kerygma.

Bultmann's interpretation of NT theology was controlled by his view of God and theology. God is the wholly Other who by definition cannot break into history or act objectively in history. The place where God acts is in human existence. Theology consists not of eternal truths or revealed doctrines, but of theological thoughts explicated from believing authenticity. Theology is faith interpreting itself, i.e., it is the theological formulation of the meaning of authentic existence. Therefore, the order is: the kerygma, authentic existence, theological interpretation of authenticity (*Theology of the NT*, II, 237ff.).

Thus for Bultmann, NT theology was not the explication of what God has done in past history; it was the explication of what God does in man through the kerygma. The kerygma was a present fact, not an element of ancient history. Authentic existence must be faith in God and in God alone; it cannot rest upon objective events in past history. If it did, faith would be faith in history or in the historian, not faith in God. Therefore, the believer need not know much about the historical Jesus, only that this man lived and died and was the beginning point of the kerygma. Indeed, Jesus and His message were for Bultmann no part of NT theology, but only one of its presuppositions.

Bultmann's radical position stirred up a storm of discussion (see *Der historische Jesus und der kerygmatische Christus*, ed. H. Ristow [1960]), and even many of his followers have been disturbed by the extremeness of his position, which divorced the historical Jesus from the Christ of faith and removed Him from the orbit of NT theology. They have therefore initiated a "new quest for the historical Jesus" who will stand in a real measure of continuity with the Christ of the kerygma. The most notable products of this "post-Bultmannian" school to date have been Günther Bornkamm's *Jesus of Nazareth* (Eng. tr. 1960), James Robinson's *New Quest of the Historical Jesus* (1959), and Hans Conzelmann's *Outline of the Theology of the NT* (Eng. tr. 1969).

Two other notable works have appeared. In 1969, W. G. Kümmel published *Die Theologie des NT* (Eng. tr. 1973), a study of the theology only of the "major witnesses: Jesus — Paul — John," with a small section on the faith of the primitive community. For Kümmel, the message of the historical Jesus is essential for Christian faith. Kümmel is concerned primarily with the unity and diversity of the major witnesses. While fully recognizing their diversity, he finds a central unity in that all the major witnesses give common testimony to the fact that, in Jesus, God has initiated His eschatological salvation, and in the Christ event God encounters men. Thus we encounter in the canonical Scriptures the uniform witness to God's revelation in Jesus Christ.

In 1971 Joachim Jeremias published Volume I of his *NT Theologie* (Eng. tr. 1971). Jeremias' position is almost exactly opposite to that of Bultmann so far as the historical Jesus is concerned. By the use of *Formgeschichte*, Jeremias has attempted to recover the main outlines of the teaching of the historical Jesus. Furthermore, in his view it is in the *ipsissima vox* of Jesus that men stand face to face with God. The Epistles are not revelation but are the response of men to the revelation confronting them in the historical Jesus. (See Jeremias' important statement in *The Problem of the Historical Jesus* [Eng. tr. 1964].)

A position somewhat analogous to that of Bultmann was espoused by the American scholar John Knox in his *Criticism and Faith* (1952) and his books on Christology. Knox was concerned to make faith independent of historical criticism, and he did this by interpreting the "Christ event" as the historical Jesus plus the responses made to Him and the meanings found in Him by the Church. In his view, it is therefore not important what the historical Jesus said or thought, for what the Church thought about Him is included in the "Christ event" as the object of faith; and this area of meaning is independent of the findings of historical criticism. The "event" of Jesus Christ was the totality of fact and meaning — of fact responded to, remembered, and interpreted by the believing community.

One of the few NT theologies written in America is by F. C. Grant, entitled *Intro. to NT Thought* (1950). Grant's purpose was not primarily historical or descriptive; rather he tried to set forth the central concepts in the NT, such as God, man, Christ, salvation, and the Church. Although Grant found many different theologies, i.e., interpretations of the "divine event," he also recognized an underlying unity in the NT view of God, revelation, salvation, and the finality of Christ. Grant felt that we could not recover the historical facts about Jesus. He admitted that for the NT the risen Christ is identical with Jesus.

As in OT theology, Evangelical writers have made limited contributions to NT Theology. Vos's *Biblical Theology* (1948) breaks off abruptly in the middle of Jesus' ministry. His *Self-Disclosure of Jesus* (1926), although long out of date, has some excellent chapters on the christological problem in the Synoptic Gospels. Frank Stagg's *NT Theology* (1962) is a topical study designed more for pastors than for scholars. The present author has published his own *Theology of the NT* (1974), designed to be a seminary textbook, which views the NT as the trustworthy record by various witnesses, and the normative interpretation, of the redeeming revelatory event in Jesus Christ.

Bibliography.–*See* BIBLICAL THEOLOGY, NATURE OF.

G. E. LADD

BIBLICAL THEOLOGY, NATURE OF.

I. Introduction
II. Theology
III. Biblical
IV. Historical
V. Revelation
VI. Hermeneutics
VII. Unity and Diversity
VIII. Methodology
IX. Goal

I. Introduction.–Biblical theology is first of all a descriptive discipline. Its purpose is to set forth in its own historical and religious categories the teaching of the several parts of the Bible about God, man, redemption, ethics, and eternal destiny. This principle was long ago set forth by Gabler, and was more recently insisted on by Stendahl (*IDB,* I, 418f.). It is finally the task of systematic or dogmatic theology to decide what is normative for Christian theology.

Recognition of the descriptive character of biblical theology would appear to be a great achievement, in that it set men free from dogmatic presuppositions so that they could interpret the Bible in an objective fashion. However, such "objectivity" has proved to be an illusion, for it has led some to interpret the Bible from the perspective of modern, rationalistic, naturalistic categories instead of in the Bible's own thought forms. The most vivid illustration of this is the "search for the historical Jesus." "The historical Jesus" is a technical term designating a Jesus capable of being explained in naturalistic, rationalistic categories. Modern criticism recognizes that the Gospels represent Jesus as a divine man, having an innate consciousness of an intimate personal relationship with His Father. Rationalism, however, has no room for divine men. The historian qua historian has no category of divine transcendence. Therefore, modern scholars have tried to reconstruct a Jesus who would be completely compatible with the categories of critical historiography — i.e., a Jesus who is only human. In other words, the modern "historical-critical method" is not neutral and "objective"; it is utterly prejudiced against anything supernatural.

The entire NT regards Jesus as a supernatural being, and biblical theology must set the teachings of the Bible *in its own thought categories and forms.* The idea of a divine man may be unpalatable to the modern critic; but if he is true to the task, he will not try to dilute the biblical teaching to suit modern presuppositions.

The main theme of the Bible is the self-revelation of God. The Bible may be viewed exclusively as a record of historical people and events; however, the Bible itself is not interested in history for its own sake but only as it is the vehicle for the divine self-revelation. History is recorded, but the chief concern of the Bible is the God who acts in history.

The biblical theologian must ask: Is this claim true? Did God actually reveal Himself to men? The answer to this question transcends the tools of the historian qua historian. It can be answered only on the basis of faith. Only if the critic believes that there is a personal sovereign God who is Lord of both nature and history can he accept the Bible's witness. Furthermore, whether he accepts it or not will be a major determining factor in the way he writes biblical theology. This is why the present author has rejected the rationalistic "historical-critical method" and opted for the "historical-theological method" (see *NT and Criticism* [1967], pp. 14, 40), which approaches the task of biblical theology with the presupposition that such a God does exist.

In other words, if God does exist and has really revealed Himself in a series of historical events, only the critic who starts with this presupposition will be able to write biblical theology as it really is.

For the critic who takes this stance, biblical theology is both a descriptive and a normative discipline. What the theologian finds in Scripture of the self-revelation of God, he believes to be true. This is the stance from which the present article is written.

II. Theology.–Biblical theology has to do with *theology,* i.e., with the knowledge of the person and the creative and redeeming acts of God, of man seen in light of the knowledge of God, and of human destiny or salvation. Biblical theology therefore is to be distinguished from the religion of Israel and early Christianity. Much confusion has been caused by the frequent use of the term "biblical theology" by modern scholars synonymously with the history of the religion of Israel and of the early Church. The religion of Israel and of the early Church, however, included many elements of which the Bible disapproves. Israel frequently lapsed into the worship of pagan deities, for which the prophets rebuked a backsliding people. The early Church included Judaizers and Gnosticizers, who are reproved by the apostles. Historically speaking, the theology of the Bible represents only one strand, or rather several selected strands from a very complex religious situation; but theologically speaking it embodies the normative interpretation of God's redemptive acts.

At this point, however, another historical fact must be recognized. It is an altogether too simple and unhistorical solution to suggest that biblical theology stands at every point in contrast with its religious environment. Here is an involved historical and theological problem that Evangelical scholars need to take far more seriously. The extreme *religionsgeschichtliche* school in both the OT and NT regards biblical religion as a syncretistic product of the religious environment. An outstanding illustration is Bultmann, who believed that, historically, NT Christology reflects the interpretation of Jesus of Nazareth in terms of a synthesis of the Jewish apocalyptic Son of man, the mystery religions' dying and rising nature deity, and the Gnostic heavenly Lord who descends and ascends. The extreme conservative view, under the influence of supernaturalism, is that biblical theology is strictly unique at every point.

Little reflection is required to demonstrate that God's self-revelation in history has often caught up elements from the religous milieu and incorporated them in *Heilsgeschichte*, so that they become instruments of revelation. For instance, one of the most common names for God in the OT, 'El ('Elohim), is shared with Israel by its Semitic neighbors as the name of the chief God in the pagan pantheon. Again, the rite of sacrifice, providing the background for the meaning of the death of Christ, is not distinctive to OT religion but is common to most religions. The rite of circumcision, which in the OT is the sign of God's covenant with Israel, was practiced by most Semitic people. The sudden unexplained appearance of elders in the NT (Acts 11:30) appears to be nothing but the adaptation of the Jewish synagogue structure; and the pattern of early Christian worship was undoubtedly taken from the Jewish synagogue.

This points to the conclusion that the revelatory element in *Heilsgeschichte* is accompanied by ordinary historical development and interaction with the religious milieu. There is no evidence that the primitive "Christian communism" pictured in Acts 2 and 4 was occasioned by revelation or is a part of revelation; it was a historical manifestation of Christian love. Evangelical scholarship needs to devote far more attention than it has previously to the problem of the relation of history to revelation. The revelatory character of biblical theology is truly unique; but objective scholarship must freely recognize the degree to which revelation has made use of secular historical factors.

If biblical theology is the normative interpretation of God's redemptive acts, the question must be raised: What is theology? If theology is the permanent and normative element in biblical religion, tested by human reason and religious experience, or if theology is man's theological reflections based on authentic self-understanding (Bultmann), or if theology is the explication, the scientific self-consciousness of faith (Ott), we will have a very different understanding of biblical theology from that of those who regard theology as the theological truth in the inspired Word of God. One of the central doctrines of the Bible is revelation; and biblical theology must rest upon a biblical view of revelation. Traditionally, orthodox theology has tended to regard the Bible as the main vehicle of revelation. Since the entire Bible is equally inspired, it must be of equal theological worth; and theology has the sole task of synthesizing the many statements in the Bible into a coherent whole. However, the Bible is not *primarily* a book of theology but of history — the history of Israel, of Jesus, of the early Church. This leads to the insight that the divine revelation has occurred in historical events, the most important being the total event of Jesus of Nazareth. *Heilsgeschichte* designates the theology that sees the self-revelation of God in a select stream of historical events.

The events themselves, however, are not self-explanatory; there was always a divinely initiated prophetic or apostolic word of interpretation. That Jesus died is an objective fact that even the Pharisees could affirm. That Jesus died *for our sins* is no less an "objective" fact; but it is a theological event occurring within the historical fact which could be understood only from the prophetic word of interpretation. Revelation, therefore, occurred in the complex of event–Word. The normative, interpretative words giving the meaning of the redemptive events were sometimes immediately deposited in written form (the NT Epistles); but sometimes they were first given orally, preserved as an oral tradition, and finally committed to writing (the Gospels). Most of the references in the NT to the "Word of God" designate the spoken word, the gospel, the kerygma, not the written word of the Bible. An Evangelical theology believes that the Holy Spirit superintended the entire process. The Bible is, therefore, both the record of God's revealing redemptive acts and the final, normative, authoritative deposit of the divinely given word of interpretation. Thus revelation includes both the self-disclosure of God to men, and the disclosure of the theological meaning of God's revealing acts.

III. Biblical.–Our discipline has to do not only with theology, but with biblical theology in the stricter sense. This term can, of course, designate any theology that is consistent with biblical truth. Such diverse theologies as Calvinism and Dispensationalism consider themselves thoroughly "biblical." Our discipline, however, designates the theology of the Bible viewed in its own biblical and historical perspective.

Theologies that do not regard the Bible itself as the Word of God and the authoritative interpretation of God's redemptive acting, tend to distinguish sharply between biblical and dogmatic theology. The former is viewed in strictly historical terms as the theology or theologies found in the Bible, and is often indistinguishable from the history of religion. Biblical theology may also be regarded as a cross section of the theological ideas in the Bible which may or may not have normative value. Dogmatic theology is the theology that the modern theologian regards as normative. Such theologies often find their normative element in some modern philosophy such as rationalism, Hegelianism, Ritschlianism, or existentialism. The theological statements of the Bible are used to give greater or lesser support for what each theologian feels to be theologically true.

An Evangelical theology recognizes biblical and dogmatic (or systematic) theology to be equally normative. There are, however, distinct differences between the two disciplines. Biblical theology recognizes progressive revelation in the course of redemptive history and therefore traces the stages of revelation in the Bible to its fulfilment and consummation in Christ. In the course of this historical development, biblical theology must distinguish between that which is contingent and temporary and that which is permanent even though expressed in contingent forms. Systematic theology, on the other hand, is a systematic arrangement of the end product of the history of revelation. Biblical theology is primarily historical; systematic theology is primarily synthetic. Biblical theology, as we have seen, may be defined as the theology of the Bible viewed in its own biblical and historical setting.

A second difference between the two disciplines results from the systematizing principle of dogmatic theology. In pursuing this end, it must ask questions biblical theology does not ask. These questions admittedly come often from a Greek way of thinking. Some scholars insist that a theology that is biblical in any sense ought to be biblical in its form, and that a theology structured in terms of Greek categories must ipso facto be unbiblical. This does not follow. The very word "theology" is a Greek, not a biblical word. Since the theological materials in the Bible are not arranged systematically, any topical arrangement is in a sense artificial, for the Bible is a book of history and not a theology of the covenant. Biblical theology will endeavor so far as possible to retain the biblical order and its structure, while systematic theology may neglect the biblical form in favor of a synthetic or logical arrangement.

To illustrate: there cannot be said to be a "doctrine" of the trinity in the Bible. The very word "trinity" belongs to systematic theology. However, raw materials of a trinitarian theology are to be found in the Bible, for the Bible clearly teaches that the Father is God, that the Son is God, and that the Holy Spirit is God. Thus the Bible demands a trinitarian theology; but the Bible does not itself reflect on the problem of how there can be three persons in a single Godhead. The task of biblical theology is to discover what the various stages of redemptive history teach about God and Christ and the Holy Spirit and to go as far as the Bible itself goes. Systematic theology then takes the end product of biblical theology and asks additional theological and philosophical questions, going farther than the Bible goes in the formulation and expression of theology, yet remaining true to the biblical data.

A third difference is that systematic theology will often organize its materials around some single principle or scheme that may reflect the problems facing men at the time. Many diverse systems of theology appeal to the Bible, e.g., Calvinistic theology, Arminian theology, dispensational theology, and even dialectical and existential theology. Thus systematic theology deals with many questions that do not come within the purview of the biblical theologian, who is concerned with the theology of the Bible seen in its own biblical and historical setting.

*IV. **Historical.***–That revelation has occurred in historical events and that biblical theology must therefore be primarily historical in character and arrangement require further exposition; for the historical nature of revelation is the modern "scandal" of the gospel. Since G. E. Lessing, the modern mind has found it difficult to accept the view that eternal absolute truth can be embodied in the particular, contingent events of history. History by definition involves relativity, particularity, caprice, arbitrariness, whereas revelation must convey the universal, the absolute, the ultimate. History has been called "an abyss in which Christianity has been swallowed up quite against its will."

Further, God and history belong to two different categories. History is concerned with the observable, the natural, the human, while God belongs to the invisible, the supernatural, the spiritual. The historian, as a historian, feels that he can make no statement about God. He can observe what people have thought about God, but he does not feel he can observe God or the acts of God, because God stands above and outside human history and belongs to the realm of faith and spiritual experience.

It is for this reason that scholars like Bultmann have taken offense. It is to them incredible that God could act in history in the terms in which the Bible represents it. To Bultmann, "mythology" included not only ideas of angels, demons, heaven, hell, miracles, etc., but also every attempt to objectify God and His acts, to find the acts of God within the phenomena of world history. Bultmann thought that "we must speak of God as acting only in the sense that He acts with me here and now." For Bultmann, by definition, there could be no *Heilsgeschichte* in the sense in which we have described it; and he tried to reinterpret the meaning of God's redemptive activity in terms of personal human existence. He did this, however, only at the sacrifice of the gospel itself, which proclaims a redemptive history of which Christ is the end term. The fundamental issue at stake is not the nature of history but the nature of God: whether God is indeed Lord of history or stands quite apart from history.

A second difficulty must be faced. Not only is the Bible conscious that God has been redemptively active in one stream of history in a way in which He is not active in general history; it also is conscious that, at given points, God has acted in history in ways that transcend ordinary historical experience.

This can best be appreciated by a brief consideration of the nature of "history." The layman thinks of history as the totality of past events; but a moment's reflection will show that we have no access whatever to vast areas of past human experience. There can be no history unless there are documents — records of past events. Ancient records, however, do not themselves constitute "history." The writings of Herodotus are a sort of history, but they are replete with fancy, imagination, and errors. "History" therefore must be understood as the modern historian's reconstruction of the events of the past by the critical use of ancient documents. In such a reconstruction there must be accepted critical procedures, "ground rules." When one reads in Greek literature of the activities of the gods among men, he understands this not as history but as mythology.

Many historians feel that this same critical definition of history must be applied to the study of biblical history. This, however, runs head-on into a difficult problem. Frequently the Bible represents God as acting through "ordinary" historical events. The events that brought Israel into captivity in Babylon and later effected their restoration to Palestine were "natural" historical events. God used the Chaldeans to bring defeat to the chosen people and banishment from the land; but it was nonetheless a divine judgment. He also used Cyrus, "his anointed" (Isa. 45:1), as an agent to accomplish the divine purpose of restoring His people to the land. In such events, God was active in history, carrying forward His redemptive purposes through the nation Israel. This one stream of history carries a meaning that sets it apart from all others in the river of history. Within the historical events, the eye of faith can see the working of God.

Frequently, however, God is represented as acting in unusual ways. Sometimes the revelatory event assumes a character that the modern secular historian calls unhistorical. The God who reveals Himself in redemptive history is both Lord of creation and Lord of history, and He is therefore able not only to shape the course of ordinary historical events but to act directly in ways that transcend usual historical experience.

The most vivid illustration of this is the resurrection of Christ. From the point of view of scientific historical criticism, the Resurrection cannot be "historical," for it is an event uncaused by any other historical event, and it is without analogy. Indeed God, and God alone, is the cause of the Resurrection. It is therefore causally unrelated to other historical events. Furthermore, nothing like it ever occurred elsewhere. The resurrection of Christ is not the restoration of a dead man to earthly, mortal life but the emergence of a new order of life — resurrection life. If the biblical record is correct, there can be neither "historical" explanation nor analogy of Christ's resurrection. In fact, its very offense to scientific historical criticism is a kind of negative support for its supernatural character.

The underlying question is a theological one. Is such an alleged supernatural event consistent with the character and objectives of the God who has revealed Himself in holy history? Is history as such the measure of all things, or is the living God indeed the Lord of history? The biblical answer to this question is not in doubt. The Lord of history is transcendent over history yet not aloof from history. He is therefore able to bring to pass in time and space events that are genuine events yet that are "suprahistorical" in their character. This merely means that such revelatory events are not produced by history but that the Lord of history, who stands above history, acts within history for the redemption of historical creatures. The redemption of history must come from outside of history — from God Himself. This does not mean the abandonment of the historical method in studying the Bible. It does mean that at certain points the character of God's acts is such that it transcends the historical method, and that the historian qua historian can say nothing about them.

*V. **Revelation.***–That revelation has occurred in history leads to the important fact that revelation is progressive. We have said that *theology* must be concerned with that which is normative and permanently true; but this statement does not imply a static view of revelation. Not all truth was given at one time; and the truth was often conveyed in vehicles that were temporary and transitory. Animal sacrifice and circumcision embodied a permanent theological truth but were not themselves permanent. God in the OT shows Himself to be a God of wrath in ways that violate our modern sense of humanity. That

God is a God of wrath is a permanent theological truth emphasized in the NT; but the historical forms in which this truth is conveyed to Israel are temporary.

Because revelation is progressive, the OT cannot be finally understood by itself but must be interpreted in light of the completed revelation in Christ and the NT. The OT is itself conscious of being incomplete and of looking forward to something beyond itself to provide its fulfillment. While God rules over Israel as His people, the OT constantly looks forward to a day when the kingdom of God will be brought to consummation and God's rule over His people will be realized in its perfection. The institution of the written law is recognized as inadequate, for the prophets looked forward to a day when the law shall be written on the hearts of men (Jer. 31:33). The OT cult is not an end in itself, for the prophets anticipated a day when a true cleansing of the heart will be provided (Zec. 13:1; Ezk. 36:35). Even the OT covenant is not the final form of God's relationship with His people; a new covenant will be required which will accomplish what the old covenant could not do (Jer. 31:31). All these elements in which the theology of the OT looks beyond itself are fulfilled in the NT.

While there is progression in revelation, which comes to fulfillment in Christ, the OT must nevertheless be interpreted in its own historical setting. The meaning of the OT covenant must be interpreted in terms of OT history, not in terms of the Greek idea of a last will and testament, which is made use of by the book of Hebrews (G. B. Payne).

Progressive revelation explains the abolition of the OT cult in the NT, the discontinuance of circumcision, the substitution of the Church for a nation as the people of God, the transition from law to grace. Each stage of biblical theology must first be interpreted in terms of its own historical setting and then the difference discovered between the permanent and the contingent elements in every stage of revelation. This is even true of the NT and the revelation in Christ, for the NT repeatedly teaches that the revelation accomplished in the historical Jesus is yet to assume a different form at the eschatological consummation. Then, that which was accomplished as a mystery in Christ will be publicly displayed to all the world. "Christ" is the fulfillment of revelation, but the term "Christ" includes His parousia and the establishment of the kingdom in glory, as well as His life, death, and resurrection. Revelation still awaits its final consummation.

It simply is not true that the acceptance of the Bible's claim to inspiration means that everything in the Bible must be viewed on the same level of truth (H. Gunkel, *RGG* [2nd ed.], I, col. 1090). Inspiration means that the Scriptures are a faithful record of redemptive history and an authoritative interpretation of the revelatory meaning of this history. It does not mean that all Scripture is of the same theological value. It leaves room for progressive revelation and historical interpretation.

VI. Hermeneutics.–We have taken the stance that biblical theology is primarily a descriptive historical discipline, but that for the evangelical Christian, who believes that the Bible is the Word of God written, the findings of biblical theology are also of a normative character. This obviously does not mean a one-to-one equivalence. The writings of the NT are historically and culturally conditioned and therefore must be *interpreted.* No one in our western culture is troubled by the problem of meats offered to idols. Most modern Christians do not apply *literally* what Peter says about female dress (1 Pet. 3:3f.). Paul's instruction about the role of women is culturally conditioned. In fact, if Paul is taken literally, the evangelical Christian can have little interest in questions of social ethics. Paul explicitly commands his reader to "remain in the state in which he was called" (1 Cor. 7:20), even in slavery. Paul seems to regard all social institutions — whether of slavery or the family — as belonging to "the form of this world [which] is passing away" (1 Cor. 7:31). In such instances, the law of love must take precedence over the letter of Scripture. Scripture must be seen as a whole, not as a collection of legalistic proof texts.

Obviously this raises difficult questions, for equally devout and learned men will come to different conclusions as to the *meaning* of Scripture for us. Therefore it must be remembered that while the inspired Scripture is the only infallible rule of faith and practice, interpretation is a human discipline, which must be carried out in humility and in love.

VII. Unity and Diversity.–The study of biblical theology must bring out both the diversity and unity in the various portions of the Bible. Authors of several recent works in the field, e.g., F. C. Grant, E. Stauffer, A. Richardson, use the thematic or topical approach, which obscures the rich diversity of the NT. In this respect the historical approach, which studies NT theology in the Synoptics, John, Primitive Church, Paul, etc., is to be preferred.

An older approach to biblical theology was content to study the many diverse theologies in the Bible, but the modern approach seeks for some center of unity. The unity may be found in the stream of redemptive history. The Bible reveals one and the same God acting in the course of redemptive history to fulfil His purpose of salvation. "That which brings together indivisibly the two realms of the Old and New Testament — different in externals though they may be — is the irruption of the Kingship of God into this world and its establishment here" (Eichrodt). This is another way of describing the redemptive activity of God in history, which has as its goal the final establishment of the kingdom of God. There is therefore a common purpose running throughout the diversity of the Bible. There are vast differences between a small nomadic patriarchal family, a nation with a king, temple, and priestly cult, and the loose fellowship of believers, largely gentile, who welcomed Paul in Rome. Underlying all the diversity is a single redemptive purpose which unfolds itself throughout the history of Israel and of the Church.

VIII. Methodology.–This leads to the question of the method of structuring biblical theology. Should the approach be historical or topical? The older approach used a severe historical method because it found contradictory theologies, which of necessity must be analyzed separately. The modern method tends to use the topical approach, and to study the theology of both Testaments in a topical manner to bring out the basic unity.

Either method is valid; but when the topical approach is used, the historical development involved in the progressive revelation of the several theological concepts must be included. Because the historical period covered by the OT writings is so long and the historical problems are so difficult, it may be convenient to employ the topical method in studying the OT to seek out the underlying concepts of God, man, and salvation. The NT writings, however, have a much more explicit theological content than the OT, and the diversity is more patent. Therefore, lest the variety of interpretation of the meaning of Christ and His work be obscured, it may be preferable to structure NT theology historically along the traditional divisions of Synoptic, Johannine, Primitive Christian, Pauline, etc. In either method, biblical theology must preserve the diversity while showing how the diverse theologies illustrate the central theme of the divine redemptive purpose.

IX. Goal.–If biblical theology is the study of the meaning of God's redeeming acts in *Heilsgeschichte,* and if the purpose of God's redeeming acts is to disclose Himself to men and thus to bring men to Himself, it follows that biblical theology is far more than an intellectual discipline; it has a spiritual goal, namely, personal knowledge of God. When biblical theology becomes only an intellectual discipline, it is not really theology but the study of the history of religion. In other words, biblical theology cannot be the subject of purely objective neutral study. The historian can observe what the ancients, both in the OT and the NT, thought about God and God's redeeming works; but when the historian takes his task seriously, he "must state that the New Testament demands what he, as an historian, may not give, a judgment of the highest possible urgency for all men and women" (E. C. Hoskyns and F. N. Davey, *The Riddle of the NT* [1931], p. 263) — a decision for or against God in His self-revelation. This means that faith cannot be compartmentalized and made aloof from historical study; it means also that historical study must be carried on from the perspective of faith. The historian qua historian cannot talk about God; but the biblical student must be both historian and theologian, who recognizes God's redemptive acts in history, who hears the call of God in the interpretative Word of God, and who responds to God's self-revelation in faith. Biblical theology therefore has as its goal the description and the interpretation of God's redeeming acts in history, whereby God desires to bring men into fellowship with Himself. "Objectivity" means neutrality, noncommitment; biblical theology demands commitment, faith, or it is not true to its essential character. "In fact, New Testament scholarship fails in its task when the scholar precisely in his capacity as scholar thinks he has to exclude this claim" (W. G. Kümmel, *The NT: The History of the Investigation of its Problems* [Eng. tr. 1972], p. 405).

Bibliography.–L. Koehler, *TR,* N.F. 7 (1935), 255-318; 8 (1936), 55-69, 247-284; A. Richardson, *Theology,* 39 (1939), 166-176; C. T. Craig, *JBL,* 62 (1943), 281-294; J. D. Smart, *JR,* 23 (1943), 1-11, 125-136; P. S. Minear, *Theology Today,* 1 (1944), 47-58; W. A. Irwin, *JR,* 25 (1945), 235-246; M. Burrows, *JBR,* 14 (1946), 13ff.; F. V. Filson, *JBR,* 14 (1946), 22-28; *Interp.,* 2 (1948), 24-38; C. R. North, *Interp.,* 2 (1948), 3-16; *SJT,* 2 (1949), 113-126; O. Eissfeldt, *ZAW,* 62 (1949/50), 312ff.; W. Eichrodt, *Theology Today,* 7 (1950), 15ff.; R. L. Hicks, *ATR,* 32 (1950), 137-153; E. R. Lacheman, *JBR,* 19 (1951), 71-75; W. A. Irwin, *JBR,* 19 (1951), 183-190; P. E. Davies, *Interp.,* 5 (1951), 175-185; F. Baumgärtel, *TLZ,* 76 (1951), 257-272; C. Gamble, *Interp.,* 5 (1951), 462-67; F. V. Filson, *JBR,* 19 (1951), 191-96; A. J. B. Higgins, *SJT,* 6 (1953), 275-286; B. Reicke, *Theologische Zeitschrift,* 9 (1953), 401-415; C. Gamble, *Interp.,* 7 (1953), 466-480; N. Dahl, *TR,* N.F. 22 (1954), 21-49; A. M. Hunter, *Expos.T.,* 66 (1954/55), 269-272; G. Ebeling, *JTS,* N.S. 6 (1955), 210-225; A. Richardson, *Canadian Journal of Theology,* 1 (1955), 157-167; C. Gamble, *Interp.,* 9 (1955), 91-99; J. Hempel, *TLZ,* 81 (1956), 259-280; M. Albertz, *TLZ,* 81 (1956), 341-44; J. R. Branton, *Religion in Life,* 26 (1956/57), 5-18; J. D. Smart, *Religion in Life,* 26 (1956/57), 22-39; E. L. Allen, *JBR,* 25 (1957), 13-18; O. A. Piper, *JBR,* 25 (1957), 106-111; J. Muilenburg, *Union Seminary Quarterly Review,* 12 (1957), 29-37; H. G. Wood, *NTS,* 4 (1958), 169-182; H. Wildberger, *EvTh,* 19 (1959), 70-90; M. Martin-Achard, *Revue de théologie et de philosophie,* 3 (1959), 217-226; P. Wernberg-Möller, *HibJ,* 59 (1960), 21-29; H. Braun, *ZTK,* 2 (1961), 3-18; P. S. Watson, *Expos.T.,* 73 (1961/62), 195-200; D. H. Wallace, *Theologische Zeitschrift,* 19 (1963), 88-105; A. Richardson, *Expos.T.,* 75 (1963/64), 109-113; J. Blenkinsopp, *CBQ,* 26 (1964), 70-85; V. P. Furnish, *Perkins School of Theology Journal,* 19 (1965/66), 5/11; R. M. Grant, *JBL,* 87 (1968), 42-50; J. C. Beker *Theology Today,* 25 (1968), 185-194; G. E. Ladd, *Interp.,* 25 (1971), 41-62; E. Käsemann, *NTS,* 19 (1973), 235-245.

N. W. Porteous, *OTMS,* pp. 311-345; J. Hempel, *RGG,* I, 1256-59; *IDB,* I, *s.v.* "Biblical Theology, Contemporary" (K. Stendahl); "Biblical Theology, History of" (O. Betz); R. Schnackenburg, *NT Theology Today* (1963); A. A. Anderson, "OT Theology and its Methods," in F. F. Bruce, ed., *Promise and Fulfillment* (1963), pp. 7-19; H. Schlier, *Besinnung auf das NT* (1964), pp. 7-34; A. M. Hunter, "Modern Trends in NT Theology," in H. Anderson and W. Barclay, eds., *NT in History and Contemporary Perspective* (1965), pp. 133-148; R. Davidson, "Theology of the OT," in R. Davidson and A. R. C. Leaney, eds., *Biblical Criticism* (1970), pp. 138-165; B. S. Childs, *Biblical Theology in Crisis* (1970); G. Hasel, *OT Theology: Basic Issues in the Current Debate* (1972); W. Harrington, *Path of Biblical Theology* (1973); R. Morgan, *Nature of NT Theology* (1973); G. E. Ladd, *Theology of the NT* (1974).

G. E. LADD

BICHRI bik'rī [Heb. *biḵrî*]. Father of Sheba who rebelled against David. Bichri is of the house of Benjamin; the word probably means a "descendant of Becher" (2 S. 20:1ff.). Cf. BECHER **1.**

BICHRITES bik'rīts (2 S. 20:14); AV BERITES; NEB "clan of Bichri." The family or descendants of BICHRI. The RSV and NEB follow Klostermann's suggested emendation of the doubtful MT *bērîm* to *biḵrîm.* The Vulgate presupposes *baḥurîm,* "choice young men."

BID. The word occurs often in the AV, and rather less often in the RSV, for "command," "order," "tell," "invite." The NEB uses instead such words as "tell," "command," "urge." In Zeph. 1:7 the AV has "bid" for Heb. *qāḏaš,* for which the RSV more properly has "consecrate" (NEB "hallow").

BIDE. A variant of "abide," rendering Gk. *periménō,* in Wisd. 8:12, AV (RSV "they will wait for me"). In Acts 1:4 the same word is translated "wait for" in both the AV and RSV.

BIDKAR bid'kär [Heb. *biḏqar*–'son of Deker'(?)]. An aide in the service of Jehu, probably an adjutant or the carrier of Jehu's shield (2 K. 9:25).

BIER [Heb. *miṭṭâ*–'place of reclining,' 'bed'] (2 S. 3:31); [*miškāḇ*–'place of lying,' 'bed'] (2 Ch. 16:14); AV BED; [Gk. *sorós*] (Lk. 7:14); **COFFIN** [Heb. *'ᵃrôn*–'ark,' 'chest' (once meaning the Egyptian type of sarcophagus or mummy case)] (Gen. 50:26).

The Hebrew terms *miṭṭâ, miškāḇ,* and *'ᵃrôn* indicate "bier" or "coffin" only in contexts involving burials. In classical contexts (according to LSJ, p. 1621), the Gk. *sorós* was the vessel used for holding human remains — either a cinerary urn, a coffin (sometimes of stone), or a simple bier (Lk. 7:14).

That the bier was portable is seen from David's following Abner's bier (2 S. 3:31) and from the fact that the young man's bier touched by Jesus was being carried out of the city of Nain for burial (Lk. 7:12-14). These portable biers may have been like the wooden slabs used in Moslem funerals today. King Asa's funeral bier (2 Ch. 16:14, Heb. *miškāḇ*; LXX *klínē*), which was filled with various kinds of spices and placed in the tomb he had carved out in the city of David, must have been more impressive in construction.

In times subsequent to the NT the Gk. *sorós* could indicate a symbolic bier or coffin carved on an altar erected at a family vault, with a warning against intruders (*CBP,* II, 717, no. 651 [mid-3rd cent. A.D.]). It could also be used in this general period to indicate a sacrophagus (W. M. Calder, *Expos.* 7th series, 6 [1908], 387, inscr. 4th cent. A.D.).

See also BURIAL.

Bibliography.–R. de Vaux, *Ancient Israel,* I (1961), 56-61; A. Edersheim, *Sketches of Jewish Social Life* (1957), pp. 161-181.

W. H. MARE

BIGTHA big'thə [Heb. *bigᵉṯā'*; Gk. *Barazi,* B *Bōrazē,* A *Oarebōa*]. One of the seven eunuchs or chamberlains having charge of the harem of King Xerxes (Ahasuerus) and commanded to bring Vashti to the king's banquet (Est. 1:10).

BIGTHAN big'thən; **BIGTHANA** big-tha'nə [Heb. *bigᵉṯān, bigᵉṯānā'*]. One of the two chamberlains or eunuchs of Xerxes (Ahasuerus) who conspired against the king's life and were hanged after the conspiracy was detected by Mordecai (Est. 2:21; 6:2). Possibly these men had been partially superseded by the degradation of Vashti and were thus prompted to take revenge on Xerxes. Some have identified him with the BIGTHA of Est. 1:10.

BIGVAI big'vī [Heb. *bigway*; Gk. *Enēnios, Bagoi, Bago* (1 Esd. 5:8, 14; 8:40)].

1. AV Apoc., NEB Apoc., ENENIUS, BAGOI, BAGO. The head of one of the families who returned from Babylon with Zerubbabel (Ezr. 2:2; Neh. 7:7; cf. 1 Esd. 5:8; *see also* NAHAMANI). The household was a large one (2,056 according to Ezr. 2:14; 2,067 according to Neh. 7:19; 2,066 according to 1 Esd. 5:14), besides the seventy-two males who returned later under Ezra (Ezra 8:14; cf. 1 Esd. 8:40).

2. One of those who sealed the covenant with Nehemiah (Neh. 10:16).

BIKATH-AVEN bik-əth-ā'vən (Am. 1:5, AV mg.). *See* AVEN; BETH-EDEN.

BILDAD bil'dad [Heb. *bildaḏ*]. The second of Job's friends, who came to "bemoan and comfort" him (Job 2:11). That we can give no certain meaning to his name — "Bel has loved" is most improbable — and that we do not know where Shuah his home was, beyond the reasonable certainty that it was somewhere in Transjordan, is reasonable evidence that neither he nor his friends are to be understood in any typical sense.

Though he was evidently a rich chief, Bildad is presented like his friends primarily as one of the wise, and hence no details of his family are given, in contrast to Elihu. We gain the impression that he was somewhat younger than Eliphaz, and he was clearly above all a traditionalist (8:8-10). Hence he had far less sympathy with Job, for he considered the traditional teaching that suffering is the immediate outcome of sin to be an adequate explanation of what had come upon him.

He speaks three times (chs. 8, 18, 25). Already in his first speech he clearly hinted at the cause of Job's troubles (8:11-13), and he did not hesitate to refer to the fate of Job's children (8:4; 18:5f., 19). In his second speech he clearly used Job's own experience in his picture of the fate of the wicked. His third speech is very brief and is an appeal to the omnipotence of God and the depravity of man. Its brevity may be a sign that he no longer considered Job worth arguing with, or it may be due to textual corruption (*see* ZOPHAR). Bildad is so bound by tradition that he is hardly concerned with Job as a man; note the almost perfunctory promise of restoration in 8:20-22 in contrast to that by Eliphaz (5:17-26; 22:21-30).

H. L. ELLISON

BILEAM bil'ē-əm [Heb. *bil'ām*; Gk. *Iblaam*]. A town in the territory of Manasseh assigned to the Kohathite Levites (1 Ch. 6:70), probably the same as Ibleam (Josh. 17:11; etc.), and identical with the modern Tell Bel'ameh, half a mile S of Jenîn.

BILGAH bil'gə [Heb. *bilgâ*–'cheerfulness,' 'brightness']. A priest or priestly family (1 Ch. 24:14); the fifteenth of twenty-four divisions of priests who officiated in the temple. A chief of the priests by this name is listed among those who returned from exile with Zerubbabel (Neh. 12:5, 18); he is probably the same as Bilgai (Neh. 10:8).

W. S. L. S.

BILGAI bil'gī [Heb. *bilgay*] (Neh. 10:8). *See* BILGAH.

BILHAH bil'hə [Heb. *bilhâ*]. A slave girl whom Laban gave to Rachel (Gen. 29:29), and whom the latter gave to Jacob as a concubine (30:3f.). Bilhah was the mother of Dan and Naphtali (30:4, 7; 35:25; 46:25; 1 Ch. 7:13). Reuben committed incest with her (Gen. 35:22).

BILHAH bil'hə [Heb. *bilhâ*; Gk. A *Balaa,* B *Abella*]. A city in Simeon (1 Ch. 4:29), probably identical with BAALAH (2) (Josh. 15:29), Balah (19:3), and perhaps Baalath (19:44). The site is unknown.

BILHAN bil'han [Heb. *bilhān*].

1. A Horite chief, son of Ezer (Gen. 36:27; 1 Ch. 1:42).

2. A descendant of Benjamin, son of Jediael, father of seven sons who were heads of houses in their tribes (1 Ch. 7:10).

BILL [Heb. *sēper*] (Dt. 24:1, 3; Isa. 50:1); NEB NOTE, DEED; [Gk. *grámmata* (pl. of *grámma*–'letter, document')] (Lk. 16:6f.); NEB ACCOUNT.

The Heb. *seper kᵉrîṯûṯ* is used four times in the OT to indicate a "bill of divorce" (cf. Jer. 3:8, "decree of divorce"). In this usage the meaning is merely "certificate." *See* DIVORCE.

The two NT uses of the word refer to a notation of a commercial transaction, a certificate of indebtedness (Lk. 16:6f.). Elsewhere in the NT *grámma* is translated "letter," "scripture," "writing," "learning." It is used in Koine Greek to refer to letters of the alphabet and then to any letter or written document. MM give examples of usage in contemporary papyri in the sense of "bond" or "contract" (p. 131). Josephus used the word of a promissory note for money loaned to Herod Agrippa as his written bond and security (*Ant.* xviii.6.5 [156]).

The content of the contract of Lk. 16:6f. has been discussed but can hardly be determined because of lack of evidence. It could have been a note with a promise to repay the debt in kind at some future date, in accordance with the examples above. The other suggestion is that the contract was a rental contract specifying so much produce to be paid per year.

It is also questioned whether the debtor was to write a new bond or to alter the existing one. We may suppose he did the latter, which was easier and had less chance of being discovered. (*See also* BOND.) R. L. HARRIS

BILL OF DIVORCE. *See* DIVORCE.

BILLOWS [Heb. *gallîm*–'waves']. Figuratively, waves of trouble: "All thy waves and thy billows have gone over me" (Ps. 42:7; cf. Jonah 2:3).

BILSHAN bil'shan [Heb. *bilšān*; Gk. Apoc. *Beelsarus*

(1 Esd. 5:8)]; AV and NEB Apoc. BEELSARUS. An Israelite who returned with Zerubbabel (Ezr. 2:2; Neh. 7:7). The rabbis understood Bilshan as a surname of the preceding Mordecai, though this interpretation is questionable.

BIMHAL bim'hal [Heb. *bimhāl*]. A descendant of Asher (1 Ch. 7:33).

BIND. An important figurative usage occurs in Mt. 16:19; 18:18: "Whatever you bind (Gk. *déō*) on earth shall be bound in heaven," spoken by Jesus to His disciples. Necessarily certain powers for administration must be conferred on the company of men to carry out the purpose of Christ. That this power was not conferred on Peter alone is evident from Mt. 18:18, where clearly it is given to all the apostles. The use of the word in the NT is to declare a thing to be binding or obligatory (Jn. 20:23). In this sense this authority is used by some denominations in the service in preparation for the Lord's Supper, in which after the confession of sin by the people the minister says, "I declare to you who have sincerely repented of your sins and believe on the Lord Jesus Christ the entire forgiveness of your sins." This statement is followed by the further declaration that if any have not so repented God will not forgive them, but will retain them and call them to account. The claim of the Roman Catholic Church that these statements of Our Lord confer on the priests and bishops, or primarily on the pope, special power to retain or forgive sins, is without historical or scriptural validity. *See* FORGIVENESS; KEY; PETER.

J. W. KAPP

BINDERS (2 Ch. 34:11); **CLAMPS** (1 Ch. 22:3) [Heb. *m^e ḥabb^e rôt*]; AV COUPLINGS, JOININGS; NEB also RAFTERS (2 Ch. 34:11). Both references are to the temple. The "clamps" used in building it were of iron, whereas the "binders" employed in its rebuilding were timber, probably connecting beams running perpendicular to the main beams.

BINEA bin'ē-ə [Heb. *bin'â*]. A name in the genealogy of Benjamin (1 Ch. 8:37; 9:43).

BINNUI bin'ōō-ī [Heb. *binnûy*–'a building up'].

1. A Levite whose son Noadiah was among those in charge of weighing the gold and silver vessels brought up from Babylon by Ezra (Ezr. 8:33).

2. One of the sons of Pahath-moab who had taken foreign wives (Ezr. 10:30).

3. [Gk. Apoc. *Bannous*]; AV Apoc., NEB Apoc., BANNUS. One whose sons had taken foreign wives (Ezr. 10:38). He is probably identical with the Binnui son of Bani listed in 1 Esd. 9:34 as being among those who took foreign wives.

4. One whose descendants (a family of 648) returned with Zerubbabel (Neh. 7:15; cf. Ezr. 2:10, "Bani").

5. A Levite, of the family of Henadad, who repaired part of the wall of Jerusalem (Neh. 3:24) and sealed the covenant with Nehemiah (10:9). He is probably identical with "Bavvai the son of Henadad" mentioned in 3:18. "Bavvai" is either a corruption of "Binnui," or is the name of the Levitical house of which Bavvai was the chief representative.

6. A Levite who returned with Zerubbabel (Neh. 12:8).

7. (Neh. 3:18, NEB). *See* BAVVAI.

BIRDS.

I. Origin
II. Identification
III. In Legal Literature
IV. In Narrative Literature
V. In Prophetic and Poetic Literature
VI. In Apocalyptic Literature and Visions
VII. In the Teaching of Jesus

I. Origin.–It is agreed that birds appeared on this planet before man and in connection with the fish, whether one argues the case for the theory of evolution, which places the origin of birds at *ca.* 125,000,000 years ago, or for the doctrine of a creation in seven literal days. Just as the Bible associates the fashioning of the luminaries on the fourth day with the making of light on the first day, and the creation of land creatures, beasts, and man on the sixth day with the making of land and vegetation on the third day, so also it parallels the bringing forth of the fish and fowl on the fifth day with the separation of the water from the atmosphere on the second day. The fossils *Archeopteryx* and *Archaeornis* are often regarded as connecting links in the evolution of the reptile to the bird. However, they must be classified as birds because they had feathers, wings for flying, feet for perching, and were warm-blooded. Their lizardlike tails, teeth, and claws on wings may be features only of extinct species of birds.

Because birds were created by God (Gen. 1:20f.) and continue to owe their fecundity to His blessings (v. 22), they are both owned and known by Him (Ps. 50:10f.; Mt. 10:29), and they are called upon to praise Him along with all His creation (Ps. 148:1-14).

Because God's spokesman in Genesis refused to reduce Yahweh to a nature deity, but rather insisted that He was the Creator of the cosmos, the Israelites avoided the folly of the priests of the surrounding nature religions, who reduced man to the point of worshiping birds (Ex. 20:3f.; Rom. 1:23). Moreover, by separating the Creator from His creation, the Hebrews described birds not as gods empowered to act in unpredictable, magical ways, but as creatures of an orderly, predictable universe. The modern ornithologists R. C. Murphy and D. Amadon have said: "To judge from the Old Testament, the inheritors of the Land of Canaan were extraordinarily good naturalists" (cited by Parmelee, p. 20). Concerning the description of the behavior of an ostrich in Job 39:13-18 they note: "Few readers of the Bible realize how exact is this passage" (*ibid.*, p. 204).

II. Identification.–Created in the image of the eternal Ruler, man is given the mandate by Him to "have dominion" over the creation, including the birds (Gen. 1:26-28). To achieve this aim, God brought the creatures to man, and by labeling them, presumably according to their unique qualities, man began the process of reducing the world to a conceptual order (G. von Rad, *OT Theology*, I [Eng. tr. 1962], 158). Unfortunately this catalogue by the first naturalist, whose powers of observation were not jaded by the Fall, could not be recorded. But modern ornithologists of Palestinian birds resumed the task, beginning with Frederick Hasselquist in 1750. His list of fifteen birds was considerably expanded by Henry B. Tristram in his classic work, *Flora and Fauna of Palestine* (1884), to include 348 species. F. S. Bodenheimer (1953) listed 413 species and subspecies (cf. Ps. 104:24).

But the exegete's task of relating the birds mentioned in the Bible to these known species is complicated by two facts. First, the biblical writers speak of only some fifty birds, and therefore must have classified more than one species in some instances under one label. Second, the names mentioned once or twice with little clue as to their identity will always remain a difficulty. For G. R.

Driver's identification of the birds listed in Lev. 11:13-19, *see* Abomination, Birds of.

III. In Legal Literature.–The divine law specified that those too poor to offer animals from the herd or flock be allowed instead to offer turtledoves (Heb. *tōr*) or young pigeons (Heb. *yônâ,* covering all species of the large family designated *Columbidae*) as a burnt offering (Lev. 1:14; 14:22) — either as a sin offering or in connection with the reparation offering (Lev. 5:7), in the ritual cleansing of the leper (Lev. 14:22, 30), and for other purifications (Lev. 12:6, 8; 15:14, 29; Nu. 6:10). The turtledove and young pigeons are cousins, but their habits are different. The turtledove is a wild bird, never domesticated like the pigeon, for it has strong migratory habits (cf. Cant. 2:12). Only from April to October can turtledoves be obtained, for they spend the winter in Africa. Therefore the pigeon had to be authorized for winter sacrifices. The adjective "young" has significance. The common rock doves are extremely wary, fly fast, and cannot easily be trapped. But at any time of the year a search among the rocks discovers nests of these abundant birds with helpless young. In the rituals for cleansing a leper or a house, two birds (*ṣippor*, meaning any little bird) were used (Lev. 14:4-7, 49-53). In each case one was killed and the other let go. Perhaps this is a picture of the one "who was put to death for our trespasses and raised for our justification" (Rom. 4:25).

The law also distinguished the cultically acceptable birds from those cultically unacceptable (Lev. 11:13-19, 46; 20:25; Dt. 14:11-18). Israel was enjoined to eat clean birds (Dt. 14:11), i.e., those that fed on grain; but they were forbidden to eat Birds of Prey that fed on carrion or blood, because both were cultically unclean (Lev. 17:10-14; *see* Abomination, Birds of).

Finally, the law forbade robbing a nest and taking the mother bird as well (Dt. 22:6-7). This commandment, like the fifth of the Decalogue (Ex. 20:12), also has the promise "that it may go well with you, and that you may live long." This law was not only humane but also prudent, for it helped to conserve Israel's natural heritage.

IV. In Narrative Literature.–The accuracy with which birds are described in the historical literature is striking. The book of Genesis says that Noah used first the raven and then the dove to determine whether the water had subsided (Gen. 8:6-13). Whereas the raven continued flying to and fro from the ark until the water subsided, the dove returned quickly to the ark the first time she was let go, returned with a newly plucked olive leaf in her beak the second time, and did not return the third time. A. Heidel noted the superiority of the biblical account to the parallel account in the Babylonian Gilgamesh Epic where Utnapishtim, called "the exceedingly wise," first sent a dove, then a swallow, and finally a raven (A. Heidel, *Gilgamesh Epic and OT Parallels* [1963], pp. 252f.). Noah, whose wisdom is nowhere mentioned, showed much more knowledge about birds. Parmelee wrote: "In selecting the raven as his first scout Noah made an excellent choice, for [the raven] is a powerful and unusually astute bird. . . . With a wing spread of four feet and great strength and endurance, ravens survive where smaller, weaker birds perish. . . . they can fly without rest for long periods of time, covering immense distances. . . . Because they have heavy beaks and can eat almost anything including carrion, Noah's raven would have found enough to eat in the floating wreckage of a flooded world" (Parmelee, pp. 54f.). The dove, believed to be the ancestor of the message-carrying homer pigeon, was an excellent second selection. "When it flies it attains remarkable speed in its first moments and can cover long distances very rapidly. It nests in cliffs and on ledges, preferring pleasant valleys to barren wastes or wind-swept mountains" (Parmelee, p. 55).

In the episode where Yahweh confirmed His promise to give Abram the land of Israel, the relatively defenseless turtledove and fledgling lay exposed under the birds of prey that characteristically swooped down upon them (Gen. 15:9-12). The attack probably continued until nightfall, for the sudden dive of one is a signal to the others, who in turn transmit the signal until hungry birds from miles around gather at the feast. Their arrival, however, would have ceased at sunset, for recent experiments have shown that carrion-feeding birds locate their food by sight rather than smell (Parmelee, p. 63.). Throughout the attack Abram "blew" them away. Perhaps this incident is a cameo of Israel's future history in which foreign powers attempt to frustrate God's promise to give Israel the land, but by His vigilant care Israel possesses it.

The description of the very edible quail (undoubtedly the common quail, *Coturnix communis* or *C. dactylisonans*) that provided meat for the Israelites in the wilderness also corresponds accurately to modern observation in its details — the great multitude of the birds, their use of wind in their migration (during March and April, and August and September), the lowness of their flight, the ease with which they are netted when weary. "Pliny told the story of a boat crossing the Mediterranean on which so many quails alighted that it sank" (Parmelee, p. 76).

Both references to birds in the description of Solomon's glory are of uncertain derivation and meaning. The "fatted fowl" (Heb. *barburîm ʾᵃḇûsîm*, 1 K. 4:23 [MT 5:3]) may be derived from a root meaning "be white." L. Köhler proposed that it is cognate with Arab. *abu ḅurbur* ("the cuckoo"), presumably referring to a tidbit like the Roman dish of larks' tongues. J. Gray suggested "geese." G. R. Driver offered the best suggestion in deriving it from Arab. *birbir,* "chicken." This prolific bird, valuable for its eggs, originated as a wild, red, jungle fowl in India, Burma, and Malaya and is believed to have become domesticated before 2700 B.C. It was carried from its original home to all parts of the world and has become the world's most valuable bird (Parmelee, p. 122). The peacocks (Heb. *tukkiyîm*) mentioned in 1 K. 10:22 may be baboons, according to W. F. Albright (J. B. Gray, *I & II Kings* [OTL, 1970], pp. 142f., 262-68).

Rizpah had to protect the carcasses of her sons from the birds of prey only by day, for, as stated, birds of prey depend on sight. At night she had to protect them from the beasts of the field (2 S. 21:10).

The ravens in the Elijah pericope (1 K. 17:3-6) are also depicted according to the facts of their natural history. "It has been noted that ravens and other members of the crow family often store surplus food in rocky crevices or beneath a covering of leaves," and this habit may explain their action when commanded by Yahweh to feed Elijah (Parmelee, p. 149).

In accordance with the law (Lev. 12:6, 8; 15:14) Mary and Joseph, after the birth of Jesus, offered for Mary's purification two turtledoves or two young pigeons (Lk. 2:24). This information indicates that Mary and Joseph had to avail themselves of the provision for those too poor to offer a lamb with a bird.

It is also noteworthy that when Jesus cleansed the temple, the unscrupulous dealers and money changers — who were issued licenses by the Sadducees — were involved in the sale of pigeons, the sacrifice of the poor (Mt. 21:12; Mk. 11:15; cf. Lk. 19:45f. and Jn. 2:14-16).

The Holy Spirit descended on Jesus at His baptism

"in bodily form like a dove" (Lk. 3:22) to symbolize His character. The dove, as indicated above, is wise and strong (cf. Isa. 11:2) but at the same time guileless (Gk. *akéraios,* lit. "unmixed," Mt. 10:16).

The cock, which since the days of Solomon had become common in Palestine, appears in the account of Peter's denial of Christ (Mk. 14:30, 66-72). True to its character, this bird welcomed the light of day on the morning mankind revealed the depth of its own darkness.

V. In Prophetic and Poetic Literature.–The preachers and poets in the Bible made frequent use of the habits and habitat of birds to illustrate their message.

One of the most frequently mentioned birds is the griffon-vulture or golden eagel (Heb. *nešer*). The superb protection and care of Yahweh for His people is likened to that of a *nešer* (Ex. 19:4-6; Dt. 32:11-13). The nests of these birds are built in inaccessible places with great skill. The parent bird guards the nest with great ferocity, incubates the eggs by shielding them from too much sun and from cold winds, and feeds the nestlings until they are large enough to fly. Then the parent stirs up the nest and lures the fledglings out of it for their first flight. Sometimes the adult birds hover over them and flutter encouragingly around them. Although there is no reliable report of any bird actually flying with a smaller bird on its back, the fledglings sometimes appear to be carried, so that the poet speaks of the *nešer* bearing the young on its wings. The Hebrew poets also saw in the wings of these majestic birds a symbol of God's redeeming activity and of His care and protection of His people (Parmelee, pp. 99f.; cf. Ps. 17:8; 91:4; cf. Isa. 31:5). (The wings of God probably refer to the protective wings of the cherubim [Ps. 36:7; 57:1; 61:4; 63:7; Ruth 2:12].) *See also* EAGLE.

In likening the speed of Saul and Jonathan to the *nešer* David may have had in mind the golden eagle, which, pressing its wings against its sides, dives from great heights upon its victim, "usually taking it by surprise and striking it dead in an instant with its powerful, sharp talons" (Parmelee, p. 118; cf. 2 S. 1:23). "Jeremiah warned of a foe that would approach with an eagle's speed" (Parmelee, p. 157; cf. Jer. 4:13; cf. Hab. 1:8), and Job lamented that his days go by like an eagle swooping on its prey (Job 9:25f.).

The flight of other birds is also used in comparisons (cf., e.g., Jer. 48:9; Ezk. 13:20; Hos. 9:11). Birds' nests are used to illustrate security (Ps. 104:16f.; Prov. 27:8; Isa. 16:2; Jer. 49:16). "Birds were quick to notice that nests built within the sacred area of the Temple . . . were inviolate. Here both man and bird found peace and security in God's house" (Parmelee, p. 161; cf. Ps. 84:3f.). The proverb that compares the one who "gets riches but not by right" to "the partridge that gathers a brood which she did not hatch" (Jer. 17:11) refers to an erroneous popular belief widespread among the Israelites, without saying anything about its accuracy. The migratory habit of birds illustrates the return of Israel from the Diaspora (Hos. 11:11) and contrasts sharply with the ignorance of Israel (Jer. 8:7). Birds of prey feeding on carrion illustrate the fate of Israel (Dt. 28:26), of the northern kings (1 K. 14:7-11; 16:4; 21:22-24), of the house of the Lord (Hos. 8:1), of Egypt (Ezk. 29:5; 32:4), of Babylon at the hands of Cyrus (Isa. 46:11), of Gog (Ezk. 39:4), and of God's enemies at the end of time (Ezk. 39:17-20).

Birds, as part of the ecology, also illustrate the physical conditions of Israel. Songbirds suggest a well-cared-for land (mentioned only in Ps. 104:1-12; Cant. 2:11f.), but the absence of such birds indicates desolation (Jer. 4:25; 9:10; 12:4; Zeph. 1:3) and birds of prey indicate a state of chaos (Isa. 34:11, 13-15; Ps. 102:6f.). Likewise, the sounds of a dove or a raven suggest a melancholy or ominous situation (Isa. 59:11; Ezk. 7:16; Zeph. 2:14). Conditions during the times of the writing prophets can be inferred by their failure to refer to songbirds.

Job, an astute naturalist, saw the wisdom of the Creator in the ways of birds (12:7; 39:26-30). Job's poor opinion of the ostrich and the raven as parents was based on appearance rather than reality (39:14f.; 38:41).

The use of about a dozen different words for "net," "snares," "gins," and "traps" shows the popularity of this figure for destruction (cf. Hos. 9:8; Jer. 5:26-28). "Egyptian wall paintings illustrate the method of suddenly lowering a net over ducks resting on the water. Flocks of quails were often captured in nets thrown over the bushes in which they had taken refuge. When the birds flew up they became entangled in the meshes of the net" (Parmelee, p. 193). Birds were also hunted with bows and arrows (Ps. 11:1f.). When out in the wilderness David likened Saul's pursuit of him to the hunt for a partridge (1 S. 26:20), he probably had in mind Hey's sand partridge whose range is almost confined to this area. Deliverance is portrayed as an escape from the fowler either by flight (Ps. 55:6), breaking his snare (Ps. 124:7; cf. Ps. 91:4), or by being let loose (Prov. 6:5).

VI. In Apocalyptic Literature and Visions.–Birds appear in visions as symbols. The majestic, high flying eagle symbolizes heavenly beings (Ezk. 1:5-11; 10:14; Rev. 4:7). The wings of the eagle and stork symbolize great speed and/or strength (Dnl. 7:4; Zec. 5:9; Rev. 12:13f.). "Actually, even larger birds are able to lift only a little weight in addition to their own. It is believed that if the strongest eagles can lift as much as ten pounds, they cannot carry it far" (Parmelee, p. 156).

Birds in a tree symbolize the subject people in the kingdom and empire (Ezk. 31:6; Dnl. 4:11f.). God's command to Peter to eat unclean birds in the vision in the house of the tanner (an unclean trade) at Joppa, the Jewish port, teaches him that he should no longer consider unclean the Gentiles he is about to meet at Caesarea, the Roman port (Acts 10).

VII. In the Teaching of Jesus.–Like the prophets and poets of the OT, Jesus used the birds to illustrate His teachings. He described the care He desired to provide by comparing it to the protection given by the wings of a hen over her brood (Mt. 23:37). He illustrated a disciple's life without earthly comfort by contrasting it with that of the bird who has a nest (Mt. 8:20). W. M. Thomson noted that the bushes in the area around Capernaum where He taught this lesson "are stuffed full of bird's nests" (*Land and the Book*, II [1882], 410). Jesus also likened the destruction of the last day to the gathering of vultures (Mt. 24:28), and illustrated the day of judgment by a fowler's net (Lk. 21:35).

He deduced God's care for man and the value He placed upon him from His care for the birds (Mt. 6:25f.) and from the value He placed on the common sparrow (Lk. 12:6f.). His teaching contrasts markedly with Cicero's statement: "the gods care for the great, but they neglect the lowly" (cited by Parmelee, p. 245).

Bibliography.–G. R. Driver, *PEQ*, 87 (1955), 5-20; 90 (1958), 56ff.; A. Parmelee, *All the Birds of the Bible* (1969); *NBD, s.v.* (G. S. Candale).

B. K. WALTKE

BIRDS OF ABOMINATION. *See* ABOMINATION, BIRDS OF.

BIRDS OF PREY [Heb. *'ayiṭ*] (Gen. 15:11; Job 28:7; Isa. 18:6; 46:11; Jer. 12:9; Ezk. 39:4); AV FOWL, RAVENOUS

BIRD; [*'ayiṭ ṣāḇû(a)'*] ("speckled bird of prey," Jer. 12:9); AV SPECKLED BIRD; NEB "hyena's lair." In its translation of *ha'ayiṭ ṣāḇû(a)'* the NEB follows the LXX, which gives *spḗlaion hyaínēs*. The meaning of the phrase is disputed. KoB (p. 699) deletes *ha'ayiṭ* and renders *ṣāḇû(a)'* as "hyena." The NEB retains *ha'ayiṭ* but translates it as "lair," linking it with the Arab. *ghāṭa* ("enter to hide oneself") and *ghaiṭ* ("garden, lowland"). Elsewhere, however, the NEB (along with the RSV) translates *'ayiṭ* as "bird of prey." The RSV would judge the root of *ṣāḇû(a)'* to be *ṣāḇa'* ("dip, dye"; cf. Jgs. 5:30) and accordingly understands the passage in Jer. 12:9 to describe an attack upon an unfamiliar bird by those whose territory it had invaded.

Birds of prey were undoubtedly the first birds noticed by the compilers of biblical records. They were camp followers, which also swarmed over villages and perched on the walls of cities. They were offensive in manner and odor, and of a boldness unknown to us in birds. When they flocked in untold numbers there was small defense against them, and the largest and strongest not only carried away meat prepared for food and sacrifice but also preyed upon the much-prized house pigeons, the newly born of the smaller animals, and even at times attacked young children. Cf. Gen. 15:11, "And when birds of prey came down upon the carcasses, Abram drove them away." Because they were attracted from above the clouds by anything suitable for food, people recognized that these birds had unusual vision. When Job wanted to tell how perfectly the path to the gold mine was concealed, he wrote, "That path no bird of prey knows" (Job 28:7). The inference is that if the path were so perfectly concealed that it escaped the piercing eyes of these birds, it was not probable that man would find it.

These birds were so strong, fierce, and impudent that everyone feared them, and when the prophets gave warning that the people would be left for birds of prey to ravage, they fully understood what was meant, and they were afraid (Isa. 18:6). In His complaint against His heritage, Yahweh questions, "Is my heritage to me like a speckled bird of prey? Are the birds of prey against her round about?" (Jer. 12:9). And when he prophesied the destruction of Jerusalem, Jeremiah painted a dreadful picture, but one no doubt often seen in that land of pillage and warfare: "I will give their dead bodies for food to the birds of the air and to the beasts of the earth" (19:7).

See also ABOMINATION, BIRDS OF; BIRDS; EAGLE.

G. STRATTON-PORTER
G. WYPER

BIRDS, UNCLEAN. Whereas the birds proscribed for Israel's diet in Lev. 11:13-19 are "to be had in abomination" (Heb. *šāqaṣ*), meaning that they were cultically unacceptable, in the synoptic passage in Dt. 14:12-18 they are called by inference "unclean" (*ṭāmē'*, cf. vv. 10f.) and "abominable" (*tô'ēḇâ*, cf. v. 3), here meaning "loathsome to one's sensibilities." The latter term in Deuteronomy suggests that the flesh of these birds is distasteful, while the statement in Leviticus indicates that they were ritually unclean either because they eat blood or have contact with carcasses.

These lists, however, differ in two particulars. Whereas Lev. 11:14 reads *haddā'â*, "the kite," and omits *haddayyâ* after *hā'ayyâ*, "the falcon," Dt. 14:13 reads *hārā'â*, "the buzzard," and includes *haddayyâ*, "the kite," after *hā'ayyâ*. The text is probably corrupt and cannot be restored with certainty.

See ABOMINATION; ABOMINATION, BIRDS OF; BIRDS OF PREY.

B. K. WALTKE

BIRSHA bûr'shə [Heb. *birša'*]. The king of Gomorrah, who was defeated along with the rulers of Sodom, Admah, Zeboiim, and Bela, after an abortive rebellion against Mesopotamian suzerainty (Gen. 14:1-12). The defeat was inflicted near Sodom and Gomorrah by an Elamite coalition led by Chedorlaomer.

R. K. H.

BIRTH [Heb. *môleḏeṯ*] (Gen. 11:28; 24:7; 31:13; Jer. 46:16; Ezk. 16:3f.); AV NATIVITY, KINDRED; [*tôleḏôṯ*] (Gen. 25:13; Ex. 28:10); AV also GENERATIONS; NEB also SENIORITY; [*min-beṭen*] (Jgs. 13:5, 7; Ps. 22:10; 58:3; 71:6; Isa. 46:3; 48:8); AV WOMB, BELLY; [*yālaḏ*] (Gen. 5:7ff.; 11:11ff.; 1 S. 4:19 [emended]; 1 K. 3:17f.; Job 38:29; Eccl. 7:1; Isa. 23:4; 66:7; Jer. 2:27; Hos. 9:1); AV BEGET, BE DELIVERED, BRING FORTH, GENDER; NEB also "her time," BE MOTHER; [*min-reḥem*] (Job 3:11); AV WOMB; [*šāḇar*] (2 K. 19:3; Isa. 37:3; 66:9); NEB also "point of birth"; [*ḥûl*] (Dt. 32:18); AV FORM; [*zerā'*] (Dnl. 9:1); AV SEED; [*yôm*] (Job 3:1); AV DAY; [Gk. *génesis*] (Mt. 1:18; Lk. 1:14); [*gennáō*] (Mt. 19:12; Lk. 1:57); AV BROUGHT FORTH, WERE BORN; NEB WERE BORN; [*genetḗ*] (Jn. 9:1); [*tíktō*] (Lk. 2:7); AV BROUGHT FORTH; [*ōdínō*] (Rev. 12:2); NEB LABOR; [*apokyéō*] (Jas. 1:15); AV BRING FORTH; [*génos*] (Mk. 7:26); AV NATION; NEB NATIONALITY; [*eugenḗs*] (1 Cor. 1:26); AV NOBLE; [*phýsis*] (Gal. 2:15); AV NATURE; [*ek koilías*] (Acts 3:2; 14:8); AV "from the womb"; **UNTIMELY BIRTH** [Heb. *nepel*] (Job 3:16; Ps. 58:8; Eccl. 6:3); NEB ABORTIVE BIRTH, STILLBORN CHILD; [*neṣer*] (Isa. 14:19); AV "branch"; NEB "carrion." *See also* BEAR, BORN.

"Birth" is used with several meanings in the OT and NT. It is frequently found in its literal sense, referring to the birth of a child, a happy occasion in the life of any ancient Semitic family. It is found in expressions such as "land of his birth," i.e., native land; "from his birth/the womb," i.e., from the beginning of one's life, and "day of his birth." (*See* BIRTHDAY.) In poetic texts, the substantive forms of "birth" are often parallel to "womb," and in its verbal forms it is parallel to "deliver," "bring forth," and "travail."

The command to procreate is found in the creation story (Gen. 1:28), and giving birth was a primary role of the Israelite wife, as seen in passages such as Gen. 24:60: "And they blessed Rebekah, and said to her, 'Our sister, be the mother of thousands of ten thousands. . . .' " For a woman to be barren was considered a curse (1 S. 1:3ff.).

The mother was probably usually assisted by a midwife (Ex. 1:15; Gen. 35:17; 38:28), and giving birth was regarded as a painful experience (Gen. 3:16). The mother delivered squatting, or sitting on two "birthstones" (Ex. 1:16; *see* BIRTHSTOOL), and the newborn was perhaps placed on the knees of the father (Gen. 50:23) or mother Job 3:12). This may reflect an adoption rite, however, in the case of Gen. 30:13; 48:13 (de Vaux). The cord would be cut, the baby washed with water, rubbed with salt, and wrapped in cloths (Ezk. 16:4). Often the child was named at birth. According to Lev. 12:1-8, the mother was cultically "unclean" for forty to eighty days following the birth.

Since the birth of a child, especially a male, was so eagerly welcomed, a stillbirth or the birth of a deformed child (Heb. *nepel*, "untimely birth," means "a fallen thing") was a tragic occurrence. To "curse the day of one's birth" is an idiom reflecting extreme displeasure with one's life, i.e., in effect, wishing one had never been born (Job 3:11, 16).

The importance of birth, its defining the relationship between child and mother, and the tragedy of stillbirth form the background for the figurative use of the term in the OT. When the psalmist says of Yahweh, "upon thee was I cast from my birth" (Ps. 22:10; 71:6), he refers to God's care of him throughout his entire life. The wicked, on the other hand, "go astray from the womb, they err from their birth" (Ps. 58:3; cf. Ezk. 16:3f.). In Dt. 32:18 it is Yahweh who is credited with giving birth to Israel, hence when the Israelites say to the tree "You are my father," and to the stone "you gave me birth" (Jer. 2:27), their crime is apostasy. When Hosea pronounces judgment upon Israel, he uses language that describes starkly the fate of the nation: "No birth, no pregnancy, no conception" (Hos. 9:11). In Isa. 66:7-9, Zion is in labor and will "deliver." Here the birth will be that of the restored community of Israel. Yahweh has brought things to the point of birth, and He will complete the course of events, according to the prophet. Finally, God's role as creator is presupposed by Job 38:29: "Who has given birth to the hoarfrost?"

The NT has both literal and figurative uses of the term. It is used literally in referring to the birth of Jesus (Mt. 1:18; Lk. 2:7) and that of John the Baptist (Lk. 1:14 — as a cause for rejoicing). In Acts 3:2; 14:8, the phrase "from birth" (to describe a lifelong lameness) is parallel to the OT usage of Heb. *min-beṭen,* literally "from the womb."

Figurative usage is found in Jas. 1:15, where "desire" (Gk. *epithymía*) "gives birth" (*tíktō*) to sin, which in turn "brings forth" (*apokyéō*) death; and in Rev. 12:2, where the woman suffers the "birth pangs" of the Messiah (see S. Mowinckel, *He That Cometh* [1954], p. 272). *See also* Birth Pangs.

Bibliography.–A. C. Bouquet, *Everyday Life in NT Times* (1954), pp. 146f.; E. W. Heaton, *Everyday Life in OT Times* (1956), pp. 77f.; R. Patai, *Family, Love and the Bible* (1960), pp. 166-170; R. de Vaux, *Ancient Israel,* I (1961), 41-43; H. W. Wolff, *Anthropologie des AT* (1973), pp. 259-261.

F. B. KNUTSON

BIRTH, NEW. *See* Regeneration.

BIRTH, VIRGIN. *See* Virgin Birth.

BIRTHDAY [Heb. *yôm hulleḏeṯ*; Gk. *genésia*]. The term occurs in Gen. 40:20 ("birthday" of Pharaoh) and in Mt. 14:6; Mk. 6:21 ("birthday" of Herod Antipas). There is evidence for birthday celebrations in Greece and Persia. Herodotus refers to the birthday celebrations of individuals, a special meal (*Persian Wars* i.133); and of the king, an annual royal banquet with the dispensing of gifts to his subjects (ix.110). The pre-Hellenistic Greeks celebrated the birthdays of gods and prominent men. Gk. *genéthlia* designated these celebrations, while *genésia* meant a celebration commemorative of the birthday of a deceased important individual. In 2 Macc. 6:7 we find reference to a monthly *genéthlia* of Antiochus IV, during which the Jews were forced to "partake of the sacrifices." Josephus (*BJ* vii.3.1) refers to Titus' celebration of his brother's and father's birthdays (*genéthlia*) by slaughtering Jewish captives. By the time of the NT, *genésia* could be used to designate the birthday celebration of a living prominent person, hence Mt. 14:6; Mk. 6:21. When Herod celebrated his birthday he was acting in accord with a Hellenistic custom; there is no evidence for the celebration of birthdays in Israel in pre-Hellenistic times.

Likewise, other than Gen. 40:20, there is no evidence for a birthday celebration of a pharaoh in pre-Hellenistic times. Procksch suggests that the annual celebration of the pharaoh's enthronement in which he was "born as a god" might lie behind the tradition of Gen. 40:20. In the Ptolemaic period the pharaoh's birthday was celebrated, an amnesty being granted to prisoners. Josephus refers to a celebration (Gk. *genésia*) at the birth of a son to Ptolemy (*Ant.* xii.4.7-9).

Bibliography.–W. Schmidt, *Geburtstag im Altertum* (1908); *ERE, s.v.* (W. Kroll); O. Procksch, *Die Genesis* (3rd ed. 1924), p. 397; G. R. Driver, *Book of Genesis* (2nd ed. 1904), p. 338.

F. B. KNUTSON

BIRTH-PANGS [Gk. *ōdín*] (Mk. 13:8 par. Mt. 24:8); AV SORROWS; earlier RSV SUFFERINGS. Literally the physical pain accompanying childbirth. Strict literal usage of Gk. *ōdín* and its cognates *ōdínō* and *synodínō* is not found in the NT; rather the terms have symbolic meanings or appear in figurative expressions, e.g., the pains of the symbolic apocalyptic woman in Rev. 12:2, and Paul's application of Isaiah's metaphor of the barren woman who bore children without labor pains (Isa. 54:1) to the Gentiles who have become true Israelites (Gal. 4:27). Elsewhere, *ōdín* (and cognates) is to be understood figuratively of pain or anguish that is related to some anticipated or hoped-for event. The pain of childbirth was apparently among the more dreaded experiences in the ancient world; hence, to the claim that women's life is free from danger, Euripides has Medea respond that she would rather go to war three times than bear a child once (*Medea* 248-251). Elsewhere the point seems implicit that the "birth-pangs" are worth enduring because of the result: so (figuratively) Socrates serves as midwife for a student who agonizes (*ōdínō*) his way from ignorance to knowledge (Plato *Theaetetus* 148e, 151a, 210b). A similar notion is found in Gal. 4:19, but here Paul himself undergoes the agony (*ōdínō*) on behalf of the Galatian Christians in whom he wishes to see "Christ formed."

In several passages the birth-pangs result in the new situation brought about by Christ's return, and the pangs themselves correspond to the sufferings or tribulation expected to precede that event (Mk. 13:8 par.). The whole creation is already involved in this agony (*synōdínō*, Rom. 8:22). And for those who find "peace and safety" in the empire, the return of Christ will mean sudden judgment, as labor pains come suddenly to an expectant mother (1 Thess. 5:3). These eschatological birth-pangs are determined by the resurrection of Christ, whose death as inevitably led to resurrection as birth-pangs signal that a child is on the way (Acts 2:24; cf. *TDNT*, IX, *s.v.* ὠδίνω [Bertram]; cf. 4 Ezra 4:42 for a similar emphasis on the immediateness of birth after the beginning of labor, in an eschatological context).

See also Child-Bearing; Labor; Travail.

J. J. HERZOG

BIRTHRIGHT [Heb. *bᵉḵōrâ*; Gk. *prōtotókia*]. The right belonging naturally to the firstborn son, whether the offspring of a legal wife or a concubine. Such a person ultimately became the head of the family, the line being continued through him. As firstborn he inherited a double portion of the paternal estate.

Discoveries at Mari, Nuzi, and Alalakh, however, show that the father could disregard the law of primogeniture and divert the birthright to a younger son, as in the case of Reuben (Gen. 48:22; 49:3f.), of Shimri (1 Ch. 26:10), and of Joseph's children as they were blessed by Jacob (Gen. 48:13-20). They also indicate that the firstborn son by a concubine could be displaced if the father subsequently had a son by his legal wife (cf. Gen. 21:10). In the Deuteronomic version of the law, a provision is made prohibiting the father from making the younger son the possessor of the birthright just because his mother was especially beloved (Dt. 21:15ff.). At Mari and Nuzi, possession of the *t^e^rāpîm* or household images generally attested to ownership of the birthright, while texts from these localities show that, as with Jacob and Esau, the birthright could be traded for certain considerations among members of the same family.

On succeeding to the family property, the firstborn was responsible for maintaining the younger sons, the widow or widows, and any unmarried daughters, as well as exercising authority over the household as a whole. As the firstborn of God, Israel was accorded the protection of a loving and provident heavenly Father (Ex. 4:22f.; Jer. 31:9).

In the NT *prōtotókia* occurs once only (He. 12:16) in reference to Esau, while in Acts 22:28 Paul treated the privilege of Roman citizenship as a birthright.

See also INHERIT. J. M. WILSON R. K. H.

BIRTHSTOOL. Found only in Ex. 1:16, in connection with Hebrew women in Egypt when they were oppressed by Pharaoh. The Heb. *'oḇnāyim*, here rendered "birthstool," is used also in Jer. 18:3, where it is rendered "potter's wheel." The word is used in both places in the dual form, which points, no doubt, to the fact that the potter's wheel was composed of two discs, and suggests that the birth stool was similarly double.

BIRZAITH bûr-zā'əth [Heb. *birzāwiṯ*; Gk. *Berzaith, Bēzaith,* etc.] (1 Ch. 7:31); AV, NEB, BIRZAVITH. A great-grandson of Asher and son of Malchiel; or possibly a town founded by the latter, as the name would seem to suggest. The RSV spelling follows *Q,* LXX A, Vulgate, Symmachus, etc.

Modern Bîr-Zeit is located 13 mi. (21 km.) N of Jerusalem. W. W. BUEHLER

BISHLAM bish'ləm [Heb. *bišlām*–'peaceful'(?); Gk. *en eirḗnē*–'in peace,' Apoc. *Bēlemus*]; AV and NEB Apoc. BELEMUS. One of three foreign colonists who wrote a letter of complaint against the Jews to Artaxerxes (Ezr. 4:7; cf. 1 Esd. 2:16). The LXX renders Bishlam *en eirḗnē,* "in peace," as though it were an Aramaic phrase rather than a proper name.

BISHOP [Gk. *epískopos*; Lat. *episcopus*].

GENERAL

I. Use in the LXX and Classical Greek.–The LXX gives *epískopos* the generic meaning of "superintendency, oversight, searching" (Nu. 4:16; 31:14) in matters pertaining to the Church, the state, and the army (Jgs. 9:28; 2 K. 12:11; 2 Ch. 34:12, 17; 1 Macc. 1:54; Wisd. 1:6). Nor is it unknown to Classical Greek. Thus Homer in the *Iliad* applied it to the gods (xxii.255), as did Plutarch (*Camillus* 5). In Athens the governors of conquered states were given this title.

II. NT Use.–The word is once applied to Christ Himself, "the Shepherd and Bishop [RSV Guardian] of your souls" (1 Pet. 2:25, AV). It abounds in Pauline literature and is used as an alternative for *presbýteros*, "elder" (Tit. 1:5, 7; 1 Tim. 3:1; 4:14; 5:17, 19). The earliest ecclesiastical offices instituted in the Church were those of elders and deacons, or rather the reverse, inasmuch as the latter office grew almost immediately out of the needs of the Christian community at Jerusalem (Acts 6:1-6). The presbyterial constitution of Jerusalem must have been very old (11:30) and was distinct from the apostolate (15:2, 4, 6, 22f.; 16:4). As early as A.D. 50 Paul appointed "elders" in every church, with prayer and fasting (14:23), referring to the Asiatic churches before established. But in writing to the Philippians (1:1) he speaks of "bishops" and "deacons." In the gentile Christian churches this title evidently had been adopted; and it is only in the Pastoral Epistles that we find the name "presbyters" applied. The name "presbyter" or "elder," familiar to the Jews, signifies their age and place in the church, while the other term "bishop" refers rather to their office; both evidently refer to the same persons. Their office is defined as "ruling" (Rom. 12:8), "overseeing" (Acts 20:17, 28; 1 Pet. 5:2), caring for the flock of God (Acts 20:28). But the Gk. *archeín,* "to rule," in the hierarchical sense, is never used. Each church had a college of presbyter-bishops (Acts 20:17, 28; Phil. 1:1; 1 Tim. 4:14). During Paul's lifetime the Church was evidently still unaware of the distinction between presbyters and bishops.

Of a formal ordination, in the later hierarchical sense, there is no trace as yet. The word "ordained" used in the AV (Acts 1:22) is an unwarrantable interpolation, rightly emended in later versions. Neither the word *cheirotonḗsantes* (Acts 14:23, RSV "appointed") nor *katastḗsēs* (Tit. 1:5, RSV "appoint") is capable of this translation. In rendering these words invariably by "ordain," the AV shows a *vitium originis.* No one doubts that the idea of ordination is extremely old in the history of the Church, but the laying on of hands mentioned in the NT (Acts 13:3; 1 Tim. 4:14; 2 Tim. 1:6; cf. Acts 14:26; 15:40) points to the communication of a spiritual gift or to its invocation, rather than to the imparting of an official status.

III. Later Development of the Idea.–According to Rome, as finally expressed by the Council of Trent, and to the episcopal idea in general, the hierarchical organization, which originated in the 3rd cent., existed from the beginning in the NT Church. But besides the NT as above quoted, the early testimony of the Church maintains the identity of "presbyters" and "bishops." Thus: 1 Clem. 42:4f.; 44:1, 5; 57:1; Did. 15; perhaps Apos. Const. ii.33f., in the use of the plural form; Irenaeus (*Adv. haer.* iii.2f.); Ambrosiaster (on 1 Tim. 3:10; Eph. 4:11); Chrysostom (*Hom. 11 in 1 Tim.*), in an unequivocal statement, the "presbyters of old were called bishops . . . and the bishops presbyters"; just as unequivocally Jerome (comm. on Tit. 1:7), "the same is the presbyter, who is also the bishop." Augustine and other fathers of the 4th and 5th cents. held this view, and even Peter Lombard, who preceded Aquinas as the great teacher of the Church of the Middle Ages. Hatch and Harnack, in the face of all this testimony, maintain a distinction between the presbyters, as having charge of the law and discipline of the church, and the bishops, as being charged with the pastoral care of the church, preaching, and worship. This theory is built upon the argument of prevailing social conditions and institutions, as adopted and imitated by the Church, rather than on sound textual proof. The distinction between presbyters and bishops can be maintained only by a forced exegesis of the Scriptures. The later and rapid growth of the hierarchical idea arose from the accession of the Ebionite Christian view of the Church as a necessary continuation of the OT dispensation, a view that has so largely influenced the history of the inner development of the Church in the first six centuries of her existence. H. E. DOSKER

ANGLICAN VIEW

I. Episcopacy Defined.–Episcopacy is the government of the church having bishops as the chief ministers. According to the Eastern Orthodox, Roman Catholic, and Anglican churches, bishops can be consecrated only by existing bishops; presbyters and deacons are not to be ordained without bishops; bishops have the oversight of all spiritual functions; and a historical line of episcopal succession is traced back to apostolic or subapostolic times. Two points, however, should be remembered. First, episcopacy as such does not necessarily imply the monarchical form that has become customary from at least the end of the 2nd century. Second, a distinction is to be made between the dogmatic Episcopalianism which insists that there can be no valid ministry apart from (monarchical) bishops and the practical episcopacy which sees here only a matter of the most suitable order and administration.

II. Offices in the Early Church.–In the NT the office of bishop is not clearly defined. Indeed, there seem to have been many degrees or functions of ministry, which merge into one another. Some of these contribute more to a ministry of evangelism than to the settled pastoral ministry. We have perhaps to learn from the NT that function is more important than office and that the ministry has been perpetually hampered by the tendency to give to the pastoral ministry a primacy it ought not to have.

The *apostles* were undoubtedly first in the NT. In them rested a final and divinely conferred authority. On the other hand, while the apostles consisted of more than the Twelve, the apostolate could hardly be perpetuated in the full NT sense. In close proximity to the apostles we read of the *prophets* (Acts 11:27). Many important prophets seem to have resided at Antioch (Acts 13:1), and it is worth noting that Saul and Barnabas were set aside for their missionary work by the prophets and teachers. Judas and Silas are called prophets in Acts (15:32), and in the Pauline lists (1 Cor. 12:28 and Eph. 4:11f.) the prophets come second to the apostles. Prophecy is closely linked with the laying on of hands in 1 Timothy (1:18; 4:14). In Revelation the prophet is associated with saints and apostles (cf. 18:20). The exact function of the prophet is hard to determine. It can include foretelling, but is probably a more general ministry of exhortation and instruction. Prophetesses are also mentioned (cf. Miriam and others in the OT).

Elders or *presbyters* quickly appear as the men commissioned to supervise the early Christian congregations. They were probably modeled on the synagogue of Judaism, and seem to have discharged their responsibilities corporately rather than individually (cf. Acts 15:4, 6, 22; 16:4; 20:17; Jas. 5:14). There is no evidence for their popular appointment, though they may have been approved by the churches and then ordained or commissioned by the apostles, their delegates, or existing elders.

Teachers are most likely the equivalents of the "doctors" or catechists among whom the Lord was found as a boy in the temple. As distinct from *evangelists* with their office of proclamation, their task was to instruct in the faith. Paul calls himself a teacher in the Pastorals, just as Peter styles himself an elder in 1 Peter. This indicates not merely fluidity in usage but a conception in terms of function rather than office.

Whether the *bishops* referred to in the NT constitute a separate group or again denote a function that might be exercised by others is much debated. Some contend that according to Paul's address in Acts 20 all the Ephesian elders are obviously bishops, or exercise an episcopal function (v. 17). Others argue that, while all bishops are elders, not all elders are necessarily bishops. This seems, however, to be an artificial refinement. The word *epískopos,* as already noted, simply means "overseer" and might well be used of anyone who fulfils a task of oversight. Thus "bishopric" is used of the apostolic office in Acts 1:20; and in Acts 20:28 there is more general reference to the Ephesian ministry, which on any reading must include more than one "bishop." The Pastorals speak more fully of bishops, though there are hints (e.g., in Tit. 1:5) that these include the elders. The Pastorals show plainly that the two functions of episcopate and diaconate have established themselves as the main essentials of the settled pastoral ministry.

The seven men appointed to supervise the daily administration in Acts are usually regarded as the first *deacons.* Certainly, the later deacons came to fulfil this particular form of ministry, although after the pattern of the seven they were not excluded from more spiritual administration. By the time of the Pastorals we can see a more definite emergence of deacons (and possibly in some sense deaconesses), though again we do well to think primarily in terms of function rather than office.

III. Episcopacy in the NT.–The term *epískopos* appears so rarely that we may enumerate the occurrences. In Acts 20:17, 28 the elders of Ephesus are addressed as bishops. In Phil. 1:1 Paul and Timothy salute the bishops and deacons. In 1 Tim. 3:1f. and Tit. 1:7 there are references to the appointment and qualifications of bishops. In 1 Pet. 2:25 Christ Himself is called the "bishop of your souls."

From the NT we may rightly deduce that, under Christ the head, there is a ministry or function of pastoral oversight for the nurture of the churches. No clear information is given, however, on the many questions raised in subsequent discussion, e.g., whether there is a distinct order of bishops, whether this inherits the authority of the apostolate, what is its relation to the eldership, how many bishops there ought to be in one place, how they should be appointed and ordained, etc. The probability seems to be that as yet there is only the function of oversight, which might be exercised by apostles, prophets, elders, etc. On the other hand, there is a distinct NT tendency (1) for one man to emerge as at least the supreme overseer, possibly on the model of the ruler of the synagogue (cf. James, Timothy, Titus), and (2) for the various functions of prophecy, teaching, and even perhaps evangelism to be assimilated to that of oversight in more settled congregational conditions.

A dogmatic Episcopalianism would go much further, arguing that the apostles deliberately instituted the order of bishops (presiding elders or apostolic delegates) in order to perpetuate the permanent elements in their own ministry and especially to exercise supreme control over all branches of Christian preaching, teaching, sacramental administration, and congregational discipline. In fact, however, this is as difficult to establish from the NT as any other doctrinaire system. It thus seems best to keep to the incontestable fact that there is a function of episcopacy which may be exercised by many leaders, which is in a true sense the responsibility of every minister but which is important enough to require the appointment of specially qualified bishops and which seems to find its focus increasingly in a single figure in the church.

IV. Apostolic Fathers.–The data in the immediate post-apostolic age are as uncertain and almost as contradictory as in the NT. Thus in the Didache we still have reference to itinerant apostles and prophets, though apparently this ministry was falling into disrepute through self-seeking impostors, and worthy prophets might be invited to settle. There is also evidence of a more local ministry of bishops and deacons, which tends to be less glamorous but is still to be honored and gives signs of outlasting the itinerant form.

In 1 Clement we hear again of bishops and deacons, as also of elders. Some scholars argue that Clement refers to bishops and elders interchangeably, while others think that there is a selection of bishops from among the elders. There is, of course, the famous passage in 1 Clem. 44 that has been taken as the basis for an apostolic succession. But here again there is much doubt as to the true meaning. Does Clement really mean that the apostles arranged for successors to the bishops already appointed by them? Either way, his concern is not with the transference of grace and prerogatives, but with orderly continuation in ministry.

Ignatius of Antioch poses a more difficult problem, for in six of his epistles he presents us rather suddenly, as it were, with a developed threefold structure of one bishop supported by elders and deacons, rather after the manner of the high priest, priests, and Levites of the OT. It should be noted that the bishop does not stand alone. It should also be noted that some Presbyterians see here no more than an example of the pastor, ruling elders, and deacons of their own order. On the other hand, there now seems to be (1) a clear differentiation of terms and (2) the emergence of a single bishop as head of the church and true focus of its unity.

Rather strangely, the picture presented by Ignatius is not uniformly supported by other writings of the 2nd century. Justin refers only to the president and deacons. Even Polycarp, to whom Ignatius wrote, mentions only two orders of ministers, and the same is true of Hermas. Nevertheless, there can be little doubt that Ignatius depicts what was already emerging as a normal development of the NT pattern, any remaining confusion of terminology being probably because of the influence of NT usage and because the bishop was a presiding elder rather than a completely isolated and exalted successor of the apostles.

V. Later Development.–From the end of the 2nd cent. the common episcopal pattern established itself more or less universally, although there seems to have been an interesting form of presbyterianism in Alexandria which may have influenced the curious relationship of the monasteries to the bishops in the great age of Celtic evangelism. Even with the more uniform development, however, the interrelationship of bishops, elders, and deacons was still a subject of inquiry and debate. It could be generally admitted that deacons ought not to exercise spiritual functions except by special delegation from the bishop. But what about presbyters? Were they simply delegates of the bishops, in whom alone true ministry was thus invested? Or were they ministers in their own right, although under episcopal supervision for the sake of good order? Serious attempts were made to enforce the former view, e.g., at the Council of Vern in A.D. 755. The great Jerome, however, perhaps disappointed at his failure to attain to the Roman bishopric, emerged as a strong champion of the parity of essential ministry, and this was the view that finally seemed to prevail in medieval theology, in spite of the feudal exaltation of bishops and probably with the connivance of the papacy in its desire to depreciate all rival bishops. Thus presbyters and bishops together came to constitute the supreme and final order of ministry, and presbyters retained their historic right to participate in the ordination of new presbyters.

VI. The Reformation.–A great outcry arose against bishops from many Reformers. This was directed primarily against prelacy rather than episcopacy as such, i.e., against the worldliness and tyranny of bishops and their hostility to attempts at dogmatic and practical reform according to the Scriptures. Among the original leaders there was little opposition in principle to the episcopalian type of order. Calvin, for example, believed that he had reconstructed the ministry in Geneva on the NT pattern, but he would also allow that the original episcopal order was a tolerable and effective form of NT ministry. It was in an attempt to restore the episcopate to its original purity as a pastoral and preaching office that the Anglican leaders, many of whom were themselves bishops, retained episcopacy, for what they took to be good biblical, historical, and practical reasons, not claiming it as the exclusive NT form of government, nor investing it with doctrinal significance, but seeing in it a potentially effective form of church order which embodied the essential features of NT ministry and for which there were good historical precedents.

In its classical form as represented by Cranmer, Jewel, Whitgift, Hooker, and even many of the Carolines, Anglicanism does not deny a parity of essential ministry. It makes no claim that bishops have inherited apostolic authority or prerogatives. It does not dismiss nonepiscopal ministries as invalid. It makes no attempt to enforce Episcopalianism on all other churches as the only acceptable NT form. It stresses above all the pastoral and spiritual nature of the office and the basic humility and simplicity essential in the one who occupies it. If it retains episcopacy, this is because it finds in the structure a historically grounded and satisfactory mode of discharging the genuine NT function, not of autocratic rule, but of pastoral care and spiritual leadership. It thus exercises its right as a Church to take order according to the Scriptures and its own estimate of the needs of the situation.

Since the time of the Reformation there have been Anglican movements, especially Anglo-Catholicism, which have tried to go beyond this classical understanding to a dogmatic Episcopalianism that depreciates the presbyterate and invalidates nonepiscopal ministries and ministrations. Thus far, however, such movements have never been able to establish themselves in the Anglican world as more than private or partisan schools of thought, often influential, but not in any genuine way representative of the teaching of the church. The views enshrined in the formularies are still those of the classical Anglicanism of the Reformers, which accepts episcopacy as a matter of good order, which is prepared to see a historical succession of ministry from early days, but which denies apostolic succession in any dogmatic sense, and divests the external mode or structure of doctrinal significance.

G. W. BROMILEY

REFORMED VIEW

The Reformed churches stress that the word "bishop" in the NT is interchangeable with "presbyter." Both words seem to denote the same office.

Calvin believed that in NT times the distinct office of a bishop, as it was later established within the Catholic Church, had not emerged (cf., e.g., his comm. on 1 Tim. 3:1). He believed, however, that the form and order of the Church's life was not so fixed as to leave no room for good developments, and he seems to have had little objection to the emergence of such a bishop within the Church: "All those to whom the office of teaching was enjoined they called "presbyters." In each city these chose one of their number to whom they specially gave the title "bishop" in order that dissensions might not arise (as commonly happens) from equality of rank. Still, the bishop was not so much higher in honor and dignity as to have lordship over his colleagues. But the same functions that the consul has in the senate — to report on business, to request opinions, to preside over others in counseling, admonishing, and exhorting, to govern the whole action by his authority, and to carry out what was decreed by common decision — the bishop carried out in the assembly of presbyters" (*Inst.* iv.4.2). Accordingly Calvin wrote to the king of Poland recommending the setting up of an episcopal form of church government there.

Calvin did stress, however, that episcopacy was the custom of the Church rather than the Lord's actual arrangement, and in his letter to the king of Poland he can be interpreted as expressing a hope that episcopacy there would be only temporary. He often expresses disapproval of power resting in the hands of one man (cf., e.g., *Inst.* iv.11.4). He admits that the episcopal bishops have a "godly and excellent office, if only they would fulfil it" (*Inst.* iv.5.11). But he points out that in the course of church history the bishops have tended to forsake their true pastoral office, have neglected their duty to preach the Word, and have instead immersed themselves in administration and have loved power.

Calvin himself, however, seems to have fulfilled the role of a bishop in Geneva, and his teaching and activity seem to leave room for the emergence in the Reformed churches of a bishop who holds and exercises his distinctive episcopate only along with and in the midst of his fellow bishops in presbytery (cf. T. F. Torrance, *Conflict and Agreement in the Church* [1959], I, 97). Such a bishop would refrain from any show of dignity, would be a preacher and local pastor rather than an administrator. He would have no independent right to create presbyters (*Inst.* iv.5.4), and the people should have some say in his election. He might be permanent moderator of a presbytery (cf. Calvin's comm. on Tit. 1:7).

The Reformed churches did not follow up these hints in Calvin's practice and teaching. Beza ignored Calvin's suggestion that he should succeed him as the permanent moderator of the Consistory in Geneva, and the office was rotated. In Scotland, a tentative effort by Knox to have "superintendents" in synodical areas was not followed up, and "bishop" later on became an ugly word. More recently in Scotland the church has rejected the idea of a Reformed "bishop in presbytery." In France, the name "superintendent" occurs in the Gallican Confession (arts. 2, 30), but this was later defined as not implying any ministerial superiority of one pastor over another (cf. J. L. Ainslie, *Doctrine of Ministerial Order in the Reformed Church* [1940], pp. 90ff.). R. S. WALLACE

CONGREGATIONAL VIEW

I. The NT Church a Spiritual Democracy.–As a spiritual and social democracy, Congregationalism finds no warrant or precedent in the NT for the episcopal conception of the words "bishop," "presbyter," and "elder." It interprets *epískopos* literally as "overseer" — not an ecclesiastical dignitary but a spiritual minister. It finds the Roman Catholic view of Peter's primacy, founded alone on Mt. 16:18, contradicted by the entire trend of Christ's teaching, as, e.g., when referring to the Gentiles exercising *lordship* and *authority* Christ says, "It shall not be so among you" (Mt. 20:26ff.). He set the precedent of official greatness when He said, "the Son of man came not to be served but to serve," and that "whoever would be first among you must be your slave." Paul's testimony confirms this in suggesting no primacy among the apostles and prophets, but making "Christ . . . himself . . . the cornerstone" (Eph. 2:20). The organization and history of the early Christian Church establish this view of its simplicity and democracy. In Acts 1:20 the RSV corrects the rendering "bishoprick" (given by the King James translators, who were officers in the Episcopal Church) to "office," thus relieving the verse of possible ecclesiastical pretensions.

The Church formed on the day of Pentecost was the spontaneous coming together of the original 120 disciples and the 3000 Christian converts, for fellowship, worship, and work, under the inspiration and guidance of the Holy Spirit. Its only creed was belief in the risen Christ and the renewing power of the Holy Spirit; its only condition of membership was repentance and baptism.

II. Election of Officers by Popular Vote.–The apostles naturally took leadership but, abrogating all authority, committed to the Church as a whole the choice of its officers and the conduct of its temporal and spiritual affairs. Judas' place in the apostolate was not filled by succession or episcopal appointment (Acts 1:23-26). The seven deacons were elected by popular vote (Acts 6:1-6). One of the Seven — Philip — preached and, without protest, administered the rite of baptism (Acts 8:12f.).

The churches in the apostolic era were independent and self-governing, and the absence of anything like a centralized ecclesiastical authority is seen in that the Council of Jerusalem, called to consider whether the church at Antioch should receive the uncircumcised into membership, was a delegated body, composed in part of lay members, and having only *advisory* power (Acts 15:1-29).

III. The Epistles Not Official Documents.–The apostolic letters, forming so large a part of the NT, are not official documents but letters of loving pastoral instruction and counsel. The terms bishops, elders, pastors, and teachers are used synonymously and interchangeably, thus limiting the officers of the early Church to two orders: pastors and deacons. *See also* CHURCH GOVERNMENT.

IV. Restoration of Primitive Ideals.–Under the spiritual tyrannies of the Church of England, during the reigns of Henry VIII, Edward VI, "bloody" Mary, and Queen Elizabeth, the Dissenting bodies, chiefly the Congregationalists, returned to the simplicity and spiritual freedom of the primitive Church. The issue was forced by two arbitrary acts of Parliament under Elizabeth: the Act of Supremacy and the Act of Uniformity. Emancipation from the intellectual and religious tyranny of these acts was won at the cost of many martyrdoms. These struggles and persecutions wrought into the successors of Robert Browne, the father of modern Congregationalism, a deep-seated and permanent resentment against all forms of autocratic power in church and state. They challenged, at the cost of life, the divine right both of kings and of bishops. They believed that in Christ Jesus all believers are literally and inalienably made "kings and priests unto God" (Rev. 1:6, AV), actual spiritual sovereigns, independent of all human dictation and control in matters of belief and worship. The Pilgrims expatriated themselves to secure this spiritual liberty; and to their inherent antagonism to inherited and self-perpetuated power, whether civil or ecclesiastical, must be credited the religious freedom and civil democracy of America.

D. M. PRATT

BISHOPRICK. The AV translation of Gk. *episkopḗ* in Acts 1:20 (quoting Ps. 109:8). The RSV has "office," the NEB "charge." *See* BISHOP CONGREGATIONAL VIEW.

BISHOPS' BIBLE. *See* ENGLISH VERSIONS IV.

BIT [Heb. *meṯeg*–'bit,' 'bridle'; Gk. *chalinós* (Jas. 3:3)]; AV also BRIDLE; NEB also HOOK, BRIDLE; **BRIDLE** [Heb. *resen* (Ps. 32:9; Isa. 30:28), *maḥsôm*–'muzzle' (Ps. 39:1); Gk. *chalinós* (Rev. 14:20), *chalinagōgéō* (Jas. 1:26; 3:2)]; NEB also BIT, MUZZLE, etc. The two words occur in conjunction (*meṯeg wāresen*) in Ps. 32:9: "Be not like a horse or a mule . . . which must be curbed with bit and bridle. . . ." The bit is the metal bar which is fastened to the muzzle end of the horse's bridle or halter, and which by being inserted between the teeth when the horse is bridled, is used to control the animal. Some early types of bits in the Near East had spiked wheels

Bronze horse bit with circular cheek-pieces bearing sharp spikes (Tell el-'Ajjûl, *ca.* 1800 B.C.) (Israel Department of Antiquities and Museums)

Horse with bridle and jointed bit led by attendants, apparently Medes. The alabaster relief from Sargon II's palace at Khorsabad depicts an expedition to Media (*ca.* 721-705 B.C.) (Louvre)

on each end which rested against the horses' lips, while others were simply jointed.

The natural functions of the bit and bridle were applied metaphorically in both Testaments to refer to different forms of control; e.g., James says, "If any one thinks he is religious, and does not bridle his tongue . . . this man's religion is vain" (1:26), and "if any one makes no mistakes in what he says he is a perfect man, able to bridle the whole body also" (3:2; cf. 2 K. 19:28; Isa. 37:29).

R. K. H.

BITHIAH bi-thī'ə [Heb. *biṯyâ*–'daughter (worshiper) of Yahweh']. An Egyptian woman married to Mered, a descendant of Judah (1 Ch. 4:17). The RSV and NEB "daughter of Pharaoh" need only reflect a MT euphemism for "Egyptian lady," without necessarily implying that Mered had married a person of royal descent. The name Bithiah seems to designate one who had become converted to the worship of Yahweh.

BITHRON bith'ron [Heb. *habbiṯrôn*; Gk. *hólēn tḗn parateínousan*–lit. 'the entire extending (region)']. In the AV, a gorge or grove by which Abner approached Mahanaim. The LXX indicates that the Hebrew word was not considered as a proper name. Since the phrase "all that night" occurs in the first half of 2 S. 2:29, the RSV takes the word to mean "the whole forenoon," NEB "all the morning."

See W. R. Arnold, *AJSL*, 37 (1911/12), 278-283.

W. S. L. S.

BITHYNIA bi-thin'ē-ə [Gk. *Bithynia*]. The coastal province in northwestern Asia Minor on the Propontis and Black Sea. It adjoined Paphlogonia on the east and Mysia on the west and southwest. It was a mountainous area watered

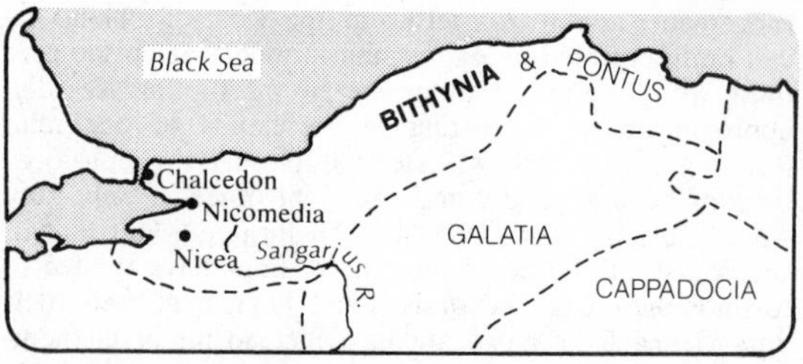

by the river Sangarius (modern Salcaria) with a fertile plain sloping toward the Black Sea coast.

The earliest recorded immigrants were Thracians. Herodotus (i.24) mentions the existence of Thyni and Bithyni, of whom the latter became the more important. They were incorporated by Croesus with the Lydian monarchy, and when this fell they also came under Persian control in 546 B.C. After the conquest of Persia by Alexander the Great, Bithynia became independent and the dynasty founded by Nicomedes I in 278 B.C. governed for more than two hundred years. In 74 B.C. Nicomedes III, unable to maintain himself against Mithradates of Pontus, bequeathed his kingdom to the Roman republic.

As a Roman province Bithynia was often united with Pontus, and this was the situation when Pliny the Younger was appointed *legatus pro praetore* by Trajan A.D. 111-113. As in other maritime provinces in Asia Minor, the social and cultural life of Bithynia depended upon the Greek cities, among the most important of which were Nicea, Nicomedia, Prusa, Chalcedon, and Heraclea. These and other smaller cities administered the whole area as their separate civic territories. It was to investigate the serious financial and administrative difficulties into which these had fallen that Pliny had been given special powers by Trajan.

When Pliny reached Amisus in the east of the province (autumn, 112) he encountered Christians. These were denounced to him as undesirables; the success of their mission was causing a serious decline in the trade of sacrificial animals. When Christianity reached Bithynia is not precisely known. "The Spirit" suffered Paul and Silas not to enter the province (Acts 16:7), but Bithynia was among the provinces addressed in 1 Pet. 1:1, and some of those who were brought before Pliny claimed to have lapsed from Christianity as much as twenty years before. Pliny's correspondence with Trajan concerning the Christians (*Ep.* x.96f.) is a landmark in the relations between the Church and the Roman empire. Christianity was not a legally sanctioned religion (*religio licita*) and Christians, if denounced as such, were liable for punishment; but Trajan states, "they are not to be sought out" (*conquirendi non sunt*) and they could only be charged in proper form by a private prosecutor (an *accusator* or *delator*). Anonymous accusations were to be disregarded. Christians, therefore, though members of an illegal organization, were not to be treated as common criminals liable to be "sought out"; and if they recanted they were to be freed. This remained the policy of successive emperors down to Constantine.

At the end of the 3rd cent. Diocletian fixed his capital at Nicomedia, and Hierocles the governor of Bithynia played a prominent part in the Great Persecution (303-312). Constantine chose Nicea as the site of the First Ecumenical Council in 325, and the province's proximity to Constantinople ensured its continued prominence in ecclesiastical affairs. In 451 the emperor Marcian convened the Fourth Ecumenical Council, devoted to Christology, at Chalcedon, immediately across the Bosporus from the capital.

Bithynia remained part of the Byzantine empire for a

thousand years, being finally overrun in the 1320's, when the Turkish sultan Orchan selected Brousa (Prusa) as his capital.

Bibliography.–No monograph has yet been devoted to the history of the province. Much material has been collected by Magie, *RRAM*. See also *CERP*, ch. 6; and A. N. Sherwin White, *The Letters of Pliny. A Historical and Social Commentary* (1966).

G. E. WHITE W. H. C. FREND

BITTER; BITTERNESS [Heb. *mar, mārar, mōrâ, m*^e^*rî, m*^e^*rōrâ, m*^e^*rōrîm, tamrûrîm, memer, mamm*^e^*rōrîm, m*^e^*rîrûṯ, mārûḏ*, also *la'*^a^*nâ*–'wormwood' ("bitter fruit," Dt. 29:18), *rō'š*–'gall' (Lam. 3:5), *nihyâ* (Mic. 2:4); Gk. *pikraínō, pikrós, pikría*]; AV also GRIEF, GRIEVE, MISERY, VEX, PROVOKE, GALL, WORMWOOD, HEAVY (Prov. 31:6), DOLEFUL (Mic. 2:4); NEB also CONTENTION, WORMWOOD, "great," RESENTFUL, CRUEL, EMBITTER(ED), "mighty," MISERY, "rebellion" (Jer. 4:18), "behind" (Lam. 3:5), GALL, "exaltation" (Ezk. 3:14), "thrice told" (Mic. 2:4), SAVAGE, SPITE, POISON, SOUR, etc.; **BITTERLY** [Heb. *'mar, mārar* (also "weep bitterly"), *beḵeh, b*^e^*ḵî gāḏôl, bāḵâ* with inf. abs., *dāma'* with inf. abs., "curse bitterly," *'ārar* with inf. abs.; Gk. *pikrṓs*]; AV also SORE; NEB also LOUD, etc.

The words denoting bitterness are used principally in the following ways: (1) the physical sense of taste; (2) a figurative meaning in the objective sense of cruel, biting words; intense misery resulting from forsaking God, from a life of sin and impurity; the misery of servitude; the misfortunes of bereavement; (3) more subjectively, bitter and bitterness describe emotions of sympathy; the sorrow of childlessness and of penitence, of disappointment; the feeling of misery and wretchedness, giving rise to the expression "bitter tears"; (4) the ethical sense, characterizing untruth and immorality as the bitter thing in opposition to the sweetness of truth and the gospel; (5) Nu. 5:18 speaks of "the water of bitterness that brings the curse." Here it is employed as a technical term, in connection with the trial by ordeal of a woman accused of adultery. The NEB has "the water of contention which brings out the truth." *See* ADULTERY II.

F. E. HIRSCH

BITTER HERBS [Heb. *m*^e^*rōrîm*; Gk. *pikrídes*]. The references to bitter herbs in the first Passover (Ex. 12:8; Nu. 9:11) were probably to a salad as an accompaniment to the roasted lamb, and would include lettuce, endive, chicory, and dandelion. The use of the term in Lam. 3:15 to parallel "wormwood" has led some to suggest the inclusion of the colocynth (*Citrullus colocynthis* [L.] Schrad.) or the squirting cucumber (*Ecbalium elaterium*). However, these two plants were renowned for their noxious effects, and would not knowingly be eaten as food.

R. K. H.

BITTER WATER. *See* MARAH.

BITTER-APPLES (2 K. 4:39, NEB). *See* GOURD **3**.

BITTERN. *See* HEDGEHOG.

BITTERNESS. *See* BITTER.

BITTERNESS, WATER OF. *See* ADULTERY II; BITTER.

BITUMEN [Heb. *ḥēmār*]; AV SLIME (Gen. 11:3; 14:10; Ex. 2:3); NEB also CLAY (Ex. 2:3). Heb. *ḥēmār* (LXX *ásphaltos*) stands for the more viscous natural hydrocarbons, also called asphalts. One such bitumenous material is found in solid black lumps in the cretaceous limestone on the west bank of the Dead Sea. Other, sometimes less viscous, examples can be seen at various points along the Euphrates and in the Levant.

In Gen. 11:3 the baked bricks of the "tower of Babel" are to be set in bitumen. The verse contains a pun, since the Hebrew word for mortar (*ḥômer*) has the same consonants as the word for bitumen. Herodotus (i.179) refers to the same practice in building the walls of the city of Babylon. The outer courses of the ziggurat at Ur also were set in this way.

Gen. 14:10 refers to bitumen pits, into which some of the kings of Sodom and Gomorrah are said to have fallen, in the Valley of Siddim. The location of the Valley of Siddim is usually thought to be the southern part of the Dead Sea, which Josephus calls Lake Asphaltites (*Ant.* i.9).

The caulking of the ark prepared for the infant Moses (Ex. 2:3) with bitumen was a common practice in the ancient Near East. The Legend of Sargon I, which is an older story based on the same epic paradigm, tells of his being cast upon a river in a basket of rushes sealed with bitumen. In the same manner the ark of Noah and the ark of Atra-ḫasis are caulked with bitumen.

See also PITCH.

D. E. SMITH

BIZIOTHIAH biz'ē-ō-thī'ə [Heb. *bizyôṯyâ*; Gk. *hai kṓmai autṓn*–lit. 'their villages']; AV BIZJOTHJAH; NEB "its villages." Following the MT, a town in the Negeb near Beer-sheba (Josh. 15:28). The LXX reading, followed by the NEB, is based on a very slight change in the MT, to *b*^e^*nôṯeyhā*, "her daughters," i.e., the villages surrounding Beer-sheba. This reading is almost certainly correct (cf. Neh. 11:27).

W. S. L. S.

BIZTHA biz'thə [Gk. *Mazan*; also *Bazan* and *Bazea*]. One of the seven eunuchs or chamberlains of King Ahasuerus (Xerxes). It is possible that the name is derived from the Pers. *besteh*, "bound," hence, "eunuch" (Est. 1:10).

BLACK. *See* COLORS.

BLACK OBELISK. *See* ASSYRIA III.E.2; JEHU.

BLACKNESS [Heb. *kimrîrîm*–'deep gloom'] (Job 3:5); [*qaḏrûṯ*] (Isa. 50:3); NEB MOURNING; [*šaḥar*] (Joel 2:2); AV MORNING. "Blackness" occurs three times only in the RSV: in Job 3:5, where Job curses the day of his birth; in Isa. 50:3, in which a darkened sky symbolizes apostate Israel's sin; and in Joel 2:2, relating to the coming day of divine judgment. Blackness is also implied in He. 12:18 and Jude 13, also relating to judgment against sin.

BLAINS. *See* SORE; BOIL.

BLASPHEME; BLASPHEMY [Heb. *nāqaḇ, n*^e'^*āṣâ, qālal, gāḏap*; Gk. *blasphēméō, blasphēmía, blásphēmos*]; AV also PROVOCATION (Neh. 9:18, 26), "make vile" (1 S. 3:13); NEB also "utter (the Name) (in blasphemy)," INSULT (vb.), SLANDER (noun, vb.), DISHONOUR (vb.), ABUSE (noun), "renounce one's faith," "pour contempt on." In classical usage the Gk. *blasphēmía* meant primarily "defamation" or "evil-speaking" in general; also "a word of evil omen." In the NT it often has the later sense of impious and irreverent speech against God. The RSV frequently has "revile" for AV "blaspheme," and also uses "curse," "defame," "despise," "discredit," "scorn," "slander," "abusive."

(1) In the OT the penalty for blasphemy against God is death by stoning (Lev. 24:16; cf. Jn. 10:33; Acts 6f. [Stephen]). According to 1 S. 3:13, Eli's sons blasphemed God (RSV and NEB, following LXX; the AV has "made

themselves vile," following MT). In Neh. 9:18, 26, Ezra refers to the "great blasphemies" of the Israelites of old. And Ezk. 20:27ff. speaks of the blasphemy of ancient Israel in sacrificing on the high places.

(2) In the NT, Jesus is accused by the Jews of blasphemy (Mt. 9:3; Lk. 5:21; Jn. 10:33), as is Stephen (Acts 6:11). But the Jews who boast of the law and yet fail to keep its basic precepts are themselves accused of blasphemy (Rom. 2:24). Paul confesses that before his conversion he tried to force Christians to blaspheme Christ (Acts 26:11), and himself blasphemed (1 Tim. 1:13). Others accused of blasphemy in the NT are Hymenaeus and Alexander (1 Tim. 1:20), and the rich who oppress the poor (Jas. 2:7). The blasphemy referred to in Acts 19:37 is not against God but against Diana (Artemis), goddess of the Ephesians. The beast of Rev. 13 bore blasphemous names and uttered blasphemies (cf. 17:3).

(3) Blasphemy against the Holy Spirit: ". . . every sin and blasphemy will be forgiven men, but the blasphemy against the Spirit will not be forgiven. And whoever says a word against the Son of man will be forgiven; but whoever speaks against the Holy Spirit will not be forgiven, either in this age or in the age to come" (Mt. 12:31f. par. Mk. 3:28f.; Lk. 12:10). As in the OT "to sin with a high hand" and to blaspheme the name of God incurred the death penalty, so the blasphemy against the Holy Spirit remains the one unpardonable sin. These passages at least imply beyond cavil the personality of the Holy Spirit, for sin and blasphemy can be committed only against persons. In Matthew and Mark a particular case of this blasphemy is the allegation of the Pharisees that Jesus Christ casts out devils by Beelzebub. The general idea is that to attribute to an evil source acts that are clearly those of the Holy Spirit, to call good evil, is blasphemy against the Spirit, and sin that will not be pardoned. "A distinction is made between Christ's other acts and those which manifestly reveal the Holy Spirit in Him, and between slander directed against Him personally as He appears in His ordinary acts, and that which is aimed at those acts in which the Spirit is manifest" (Gould, comm. on Mark [*ICC*, 1896], *in loc.*). Luke does not refer to any particular instance, and seems to connect it with the denial of Christ, although he too gives the saying that "every one who speaks a word against the Son of man will be forgiven." *See* HOLY SPIRIT II.B.

T. REES

BLAST [Heb. *nᵉšāmâ, rû(a)ḥ, māšaḵ* (Ex. 19:13; Josh. 6:5), *qôl-šôpār* (Ex. 19:16), *šôpār* (Zec. 1:16), *tᵉrû'â* (Lev. 23:24)]; AV also SOUNDETH, "voice of the trumpet," etc.; NEB also SOUNDS, ACCLAIMS.

The Hebrew words *nᵉšāmâ*, "breath" (2 S. 22:16; Job 4:9; Ps. 18:15), and *rû(a)ḥ*, "wind," "spirit," "breath" (Ex. 15:8; Isa. 25:4; 27:8), mean in these contexts the hot wind generated by God's anger that wreaks destruction. In Isa. 25:4 *rû(a)ḥ* is used also to depict man's anger. The two words occur together in Ps. 18:15, "at the blast [*nᵉšāmâ*] of the breath [*rû(a)ḥ*] of thy nostrils," and in parallel statements in Job 4:9. This depiction of God's anger and its destructive force is associated principally with the motif of Yahweh as the Divine Warrior (Ex. 15:1-21; Jgs. 5:4-23). As Divine Warrior, Yahweh comes to destroy His enemies who are also Israel's enemies, and thus to save His people. The battle is invariably portrayed in heightened — and often cosmic — imagery (Ps. 18:15; Ex. 15:8). Isa. 27:8 looks back to the time when Yahweh in His anger turned upon His people, who had been faithless and forsaken Him.

The Hebrew words *māšaḵ*, to "give a sound" with the ram's horn (*qeren-hayyôḇēl*) and *qôl-šôpār*, "voice of trumpet," describe the loud sounds that announced the call to assemble either for worship (Lev. 25:9) or for war (Jgs. 6:34). (*See also* BLOW 1.) Where the RSV translates "blast" the text announces that the people should be ready to go to Mt. Sinai (Ex. 19:13), or it signals the appearance of God (Ex. 19:16; cf. 20:18f.). The Heb. *tᵉrû'â* used in Lev. 23:24, translated "proclaimed with the blast of trumpets" by the RSV (NEB "acclaim"), usually means the shouting that accompanied the sound of trumpets. It is the SHOUT that is raised on the "day of trumpet blast [*yôm-šôpār*] and battle cry [*tᵉrû'â*]" (Zeph. 1:16; cf. Josh. 6:5), and often heralds the coming of God to fight for His people (1 S. 4:5ff.). It is also the jubilant shout that acclaims the presence of God in the temple (Ps. 47:5).

D. P. NILES

BLASTING [Heb. *šiddāpôn*–'scorching'] (Dt. 28:22); NEB BLACK BLIGHT. Dt. 28:22-24 describes the fiery east winds which still blow irregularly across Palestine for days at a time, drying up vegetation, ruining the crops, and damaging property. As reported by travelers the heat is fiery; it dries up the vegetation and blasts the grain; the sky is hazy and there is a glare as if the sun were reflected from a huge brass tray. Woodwork cracks and warps; the covers of books curl up. Instead of rain, the wind brings dust and sand which penetrate into the innermost corners of the dwellings. This dust fills the eyes and inflames them. The skin becomes hot and dry. To one first experiencing this storm it seems as though some volcano must be belching forth heat and ashes. No other condition of the weather can cause such depression. Such a pestilence, prolonged beyond endurance, was to be the fate of the disobedient.

Elsewhere in the RSV (1 K. 8:37 par. 2 Ch. 6:28; Am. 4:9; Hag. 2:17) *šiddāpôn* is translated as "blight."

J. A. PATCH

BLASTUS blas'təs [Gk. *Blastos*–'shoot'] (Acts 12:20). The chamberlain of Herod Agrippa I, whose services as an intermediary with the king were gained by the people of Tyre and Sidon. These cities were dependent on Palestine for corn and other provisions, and when Herod, on the occasion of some commercial dispute, forbade the export of footstuffs to Tyre and Sidon, they were at his mercy and were compelled to ask for peace. "Having persuaded Blastus, the king's chamberlain," probably by means of a bribe, the Phoenician embassy was given an opportunity to bring their case before Herod (Acts 12:20ff.).

S. F. HUNTER

BLAZE. The rendering of Gk. *diaphēmízein* in Mk. 1:45, AV. The RSV has "spread (the news)," NEB "spread it far and wide."

BLEACH (Mk. 9:3, RSV); **BLEACHER** (NEB). *See* FULLER.

BLEMISH [Heb. *mûm, K mu'wm* (Dnl. 1:4)]; also SPOT; NEB also DEFECT, FLAW, FAULT; [*šāḥaṯ*] (Mal. 1:14); AV CORRUPT (THING); NEB DAMAGED (VICTIM); [Gk. *mṓmos*] (2 Pet. 2:13); NEB BLOT; [*spilás*] (Jude 12); AV SPOT; NEB BLOT; **WITHOUT BLEMISH** [Heb. *tāmîm*]; AV also WITHOUT SPOT; NEB also WITHOUT DEFECT, PERFECT; [Gk. *ámōmos*] (Eph. 5:27; Phil. 2:15; He. 9:14; 1 Pet. 1:19; Jude 24); AV WITHOUT REBUKE, WITHOUT SPOT, FAULTLESS; NEB FAULTLESS, UNBLEMISHED, ABOVE REPROACH; [*amṓmētos*] (2 Pet. 3:14); AV BLAMELESS; NEB ABOVE REPROACH.

The adjective *tāmîm*, translated "without blemish," really represents a positive condition. The Hebrew root *tmm* has the idea of completeness or wholeness. Thus *tāmîm* can be translated "whole," as in Josh. 10:13. But when it is used to describe the type of animal to be used in sacrifice, the RSV translates "without blemish" to signify no physical imperfections.

Another Hebrew word, *mûm*, represents the negative condition, which can be translated "blemish" or "defect," usually referring to physical imperfections. Both words are used in Lev. 22:21 (*mûm* with a negative) to indicate animals that are acceptable for sacrifice. According to Lev. 22:22-25 animals that are blind, disabled, mutilated, or have a discharge, scab, or eruption are considered blemished, as are deformed animals and those whose testicles have been damaged. Finally, animals coming from a foreigner are also considered blemished.

This last item may indicate that the real concern in each of these prohibited cases is ritual impurity. Among the Hittites the king was a special object of purity, and he had an entourage of palace officials employed to protect his purity. In a text describing the duties of these officials (*ANET*, p. 207), the leatherworkers were specifically forbidden to use any hides except those from the royal kitchen, because only those were controlled to make certain they were pure. The king could send other hides abroad where the laws of purity might not be so stringent. Similarly, if Israel were the recipient of any foreign animals, she could not know for sure whether the animals were ritually pure by her own standards. Consequently, "blemishes" may have been associated with ritual impurity, and offering a ritually impure animal to God would be an affront to Him. The postexilic community of Malachi's day was guilty of just such a practice (Mal. 1:13f.).

Similar physical imperfections or defects also excluded a man from priestly service (Lev. 21:17f., 21, 23; on v. 20 *see* DEFECT). A man with blemishes would profane the sanctuaries of the Lord (Lev. 21:23). Here again the physical imperfections seem to be best explained as associated with ritual impurity.

In 2 S. 14:25 Absalom is pictured as the perfect physical specimen without blemishes. The same is true of the three young men in Dnl. 1:4. In Dt. 32:5 the context seems to require that *mûm* be taken in a figurative sense of "moral blemish." Still, the interpretation is difficult. Probably it means that Israel's iniquity has made them God's children no more.

In the NT, Christ is the antitype of the perfect sacrifice (He. 9:14; 1 Pet. 1:19). The Gk. *ámōmos* used here is used in the LXX to translate *tāmîm*. Here and elsewhere in the NT the meaning goes beyond the cultic and ritual sphere to the moral and religious. This is clear also in Eph. 5:27 — Christ's sacrifice was intended to sanctify the Church and remove all blemishes. The children of God are to be without blemish (Phil. 2:15; 2 Pet. 3:14). By contrast, false teachers are blemishes (*mṓmos*) among God's people (2 Pet. 2:13). The Gk. *amṓmētos* refers to the lack of moral blemishes which should characterize believers in the divine judgment (2 Pet. 3:14).

The use of *spilás* in Jude 12 causes difficulty. This context and a similar context in 2 Pet. 2:13 (*spílos*, "blot") seem to require something like "blemishes," though the translation "reef" is possible.

See also SPOT.

See *TDNT*, IV, *s.v.* μῶμος, ἄμωμος, ἀμώμητος (F. Hauck).

J. C. MOYER

BLESS [Heb. *bārak̲*–'bend the knee'(?); Aram. *b^e^rak̲*; Gk. *eulogéō*–'speak well of']; NEB also GIVE, GRANT, BRING, INVOKE, SAY, or SHARE A BLESSING, WORSHIP, PRAISE, GREET, CONGRATULATE, etc.; **BLESSED** [Heb. *'ašrê, bārûk̲*; Aram. *b^e^rik̲* (Dnl. 3:28), *m^e^bārak̲* (Dnl. 2:20); Gk. *eulogētós, makários, makarízō*– 'call blessed' (Lk. 1:48), *eneulogéō* (Acts 3:25; Gal. 3:8)]; NEB also HAPPY, etc.; **BLESSING** [Heb. *b^e^rāk̲â*; Gk. *eulogía*]; AV also MERCIES, GIFT, GRACE, BLESSEDNESS, etc.; NEB also FAVOR, PRAISE, HAPPINESS, etc. Several meanings occur, including "worship or praise," "bestow favor and goodness (sufficient to warrant adoration)," and "invoke such benefits upon others." (Cf. Akk. *karābu*, which encompasses these meanings.) Substantively, blessing is praise or favor, the act of bestowing such, or statement accompanying or recommending worship or beneficence.

When a human blesses God, the literal sense "bend the knee (in homage or adoration)" is expressed, indicating gratitude. Expressions of praise are especially frequent in the poetry and include appeals for worship by the speaker (Ps. 103:1f.; 104:1, 35) and others (Jgs. 5:2; AV "offered themselves"; Ps. 66:8; 67:5; 68:26 [MT 27]), as well as pledges of praise (Ps. 26:12; 63:4 [MT 5]; 115:18). These acts are often accompanied by relative clauses indicating the basis for the adulation (Gen. 24:48). Such statements often occur in liturgical settings (Dt. 11:29; NEB "pronounce the blessing"; 2 Ch. 20:26; Sir. 50:20). In wisdom literature, the author praises the source of his inspiration (Sir. 39:35; 50:22; 51:12). Isaiah reproves those who worship idols (66:3; RSV "bless a monster").

Statements of adoration or praise frequently follow a standard pattern or formula of blessing, as "blessed is" or "blessed be [someone]," usually expressed by passive participles, Heb. *bārûk̲* and Gk. *eulogēménos* (Ruth 4:14; 1 S. 25:32; 1 Ch. 29:10; Neh. 9:5; Mt. 25:34). When applied to God, they have the jussive sense "let us praise" or "let be praised" (Gen. 14:20; Ps. 28:6). NT utterances apply similarly to Jesus ("he who comes in the name of the Lord," Mt. 2:19; 23:39; Mk. 11:9; Lk. 19:38; Jn. 12:13), Mary (Lk. 1:42), and the kingdom of God (Mk. 11:10). God is often so cited in statements using Gk. *eulogētós* (Lk. 1:68; 2 Cor. 1:3; Eph. 1:3; 1 Pet. 1:3).

More frequently, to bless means to grant prosperity or well-being ("fortunate power," KoB, p. 153), and God is generally the subject, bestowing physical and spiritual grace upon man in the form of long life, affluence, and power (Gen. 39:5; Ps. 3:8 [MT 9]; 24:5; 129:8). He blesses mankind in creation (Gen. 5:2) and throughout history (26:3; Ex. 18:10). Such acts often provide fertility for man (Gen. 1:28; 17:16, 20; 22:17; 48:4), animals (1:22), and various forms of produce (Ex. 23:25; Dt. 7:13; Ps. 65:10 [MT 11]; 132:15). God blesses man for keeping His laws, implying sanction (Dt. 7:12-14; cf. Ex. 23:25).

People often bless each other, as when a father transfers goods and authority to his children prior to his death (Gen. 27; 31:55 [MT 32:1]; 48:9, 15, 20; 49:28; Dt. 33:1ff.; He. 11:20). This is accompanied by an invocation of God's favor upon one's descendants (Gen. 49:25f.; Dt. 33). Division of one's power and property among several children may have been possible, as suggested by Esau's request (Gen. 27:38). A family blesses members embarking on a journey (Gen. 24:60). Charismatic leaders bless the people (Lev. 9:23), as priests bless individuals (1 S. 2:20) and the entire congregation (Nu. 6:23-27; 2 Ch. 30:27). Balaam, the non-Israelite seer, blesses Israel (Nu. 23:11, 20) by announcing good fortune.

When people bless one another, they commend the recipient to God through laudatory petitions (Ruth 2:20; 1 S. 23:21; 2 S. 2:5; cf. Gen. 49:26; Ps. 72:15). Such petitions may include the formula "blessed be [someone]" or such variants as "may you be blessed" (Ruth 3:10) and "let . . . be blessed" (Prov. 5:18). God is recognized as the source of such benefits (cf. 1 S. 2:20), indicated by Heb. *bāraḵ b^e^šēm,* "bless by (or in) God's name" (Dt. 10:8; 21:5; 1 Ch. 23:13; Sir. 45:15; cf. Nu. 6:27). Such intercessory activity may include praying for another person (Mt. 5:44, RSV; cf. He. 11:20). Jesus instructs His followers to "bless those that curse you" (Lk. 6:28; Rom. 12:14; 1 Cor. 4:12). Invocation of God's blessing upon others may have been standardized in expressions of greeting or congratulation (1 S. 13:10; 2 S. 8:10 par. 1 Ch. 18:10; 2 K. 4:29; 10:15); the content of such statements may be indicated by Ruth 2:4; Ps. 129:8.

The sense "praise, do homage" may be indicated when men bless those of higher status (Gen. 47:7, 10; cf. Ex. 12:32). This is apparent when it is reported that Joab "fell on his face, did obeisance, and blessed the king" (2 S. 14:22). A debtor may bless a creditor (Dt. 24:15) and a subject bless his king (1 K. 8:66), perhaps seeking a blessing in return. The king's servants bless David (1 K. 1:47), asking God to make Solomon greater than David.

Men also bless themselves. In such instances, they may either "count themselves happy" (Ps. 49:18 [MT 19], AV "blessed his soul"), priding themselves on having been favored (cf. Dt. 29:19; NEB "inwardly flatter"), or invoke God's blessing upon themselves (Gen. 12:3, NEB "pray to be blessed").

Both God and men occasionally bless nonhuman objects. God blesses the sabbath (Gen. 2:3; Ex. 20:11) and Samuel blesses the sacrifice (1 S. 9:13), but they may thereby indirectly bless those who observe these occasions. God blesses work performed by men (Dt. 28:8, 12; Job 1:10; cf. Dt. 28:4f.) and "the latter days of (Job's) life" (Job 42:12). He also favors the abode of the righteous (Prov. 3:33) and the habitation of righteousness, the land of Judah (Jer. 31:23). Objects of blessing may include qualities, such as discretion (1 S. 25:33). Jesus blesses fish (Mk. 8:7) and, in the sense of giving thanks, bread (Mk. 6:41). Cf. also BLESSING, CUP OF (1 Cor. 10:16).

The state of being blessed, designated by a passive verb, may indicate receipt of both favor (Gen. 27:33; 2 S. 7:39) and adoration (Job. 1:21; Ps. 113:2). Gk. *eneulogēthḗsontai* is used to indicate the universal application of Abraham's blessing (Acts 3:25; Gal. 3:8; cf. LXX Gen. 12:3; 18:18). Heb. *'ašrê* and Gk. *makários* occur primarily with the sense "happy, fortunate," illustrating the joy of life unmarred by care, labor, or death. Generally found in blessing formulas, these expressions indicate the subject's having fulfilled certain obligations or stipulations. In the OT these include coming to Zion (Ps. 65:4 [MT 5]; 84:4 [MT 5]), being blameless in behavior (Ps. 119:1f.), seeking God's wisdom (Prov. 8:13, 33f.), and executing God's judgment against His enemies (Ps. 137:8). By extension of this principle, children of "a righteous man who walks in integrity" are blessed (Prov. 20:17). In the NT the blessed exhibit the traits of the faithful (Mt. 5:11; Lk. 11:28; Rev. 16:15), particularly suffering (Jas. 1:12; Lk. 6:20-22). The condition may be shared by parts of the body (Mt. 13:16; Lk. 10:23; 11:27). Generally applied to God with the sense "praised" or "praiseworthy" (Tim. 1:11; 6:15), Gk. *makários* occurs in the same sense with reference to actions (Acts 20:35) and qualities (Tit. 2:13). The rewards that accompany such favor are often reserved for the future (Ps. 128:2-4). *See also* BEATITUDES.

A related concept is a person's being named or called blessed (Heb. *'āšār*; Gk. *makarízō*). A woman's children call her blessed (Prov. 31:28) and the nations call God blessed (Ps. 72:17; Mal. 3:12); all generations will call Mary blessed (Lk. 1:48). Such acts may illustrate the close relationship between word and fact in the ancient Near East whereby making a statement establishes the fact (*see* CURSE). They may also indicate use of the blessing formula. A person can "be a blessing" if his acts warrant his being named in such a formula (Gen. 12:2; Ps. 37:26; Prov. 10:7; Isa. 19:24; Zec. 8:13; cf. Ps. 21:6 [MT 7]).

"Blessed" occurs substantively as a substitute for God's name, as in the use of "Lord," to prevent defilement of the name Yahweh. In Mk. 14:61, Jesus is called "son of the Blessed." The substantive also designates one who adheres to God's commandments and has received His favor, as "the blessed of the Lord" (Gen. 24:31; 26:29; Isa. 65:16) or "the blessed of my father" (Mt. 25:34).

"Blessing" may designate the actual words spoken ("blessed be [someone]" or similar phrases), the gift that is given, or the act by which it is bestowed. Dt. 33:1 indicates that the following statement contains Moses' very words and also outlines the nature of the blessing. Both the words uttered and the power or gifts evoked by their pronouncement are implied in the fathers' blessings (Gen. 48:15f.; 49) and elsewhere (Dt. 28:2; Prov. 10:6; 11:11, 26; 24:25; cf. Nu. 6:23-27), as when a person blesses "with a blessing" (Gen. 27:41; 49:28). The act of blessing and the powers that emanate from it are indicated in Prov. 10:22 and when God commands a blessing (Lev. 25:21; Dt. 28:8; Ps. 133:3). God's power and its effect may be identical (Ezk. 34:26; Sir. 40:27). Apparently in some instances a token gift or present accompanied the pronouncement of a blessing (AV Gen. 33:11; Josh. 15:19; Jgs. 1:15; RSV "gift, present"; cf. 2 K. 5:15). The words alone are designated in Prov. 10:7 (cf. Ps. 37:26; Mal. 2:2).

Blessing is common in Israelite liturgy, generally paired with the pronouncement of curses (Dt. 11:29; Josh. 8:34; cf. Dt. 27:12f.). God's favor is a positive sanction of one who follows His commandments as stipulated in the laws of the pertinent covenant. Man may choose to follow the law or not and thereby determine his reward (Dt. 11:26; 30:1, 19). Similar sanctions are found in ancient Near Eastern treaties. Occasionally Heb. *bāraḵ* is used euphemistically for *'ārar* and *qālal,* "curse" (1 K. 21:10, 23; Job 1:5, 11; 2:5, 9; Ps. 10:3; RSV "curses the Lord"; AV "blesses the covetous"; NEB "gives wickedness his blessing"). A negative form of the blessing formula occurs in Jer. 17:7, "let it not be blessed."

Although the blessing granted by Isaac to Jacob is irrevocable (Gen. 27:33-35), a curse may be transformed into a blessing (Dt. 23:5 [MT 6]; Jgs. 17:2; Neh. 13:2). Blessings may be cursed (Mal. 2:2).

"Blessedness" (Gk. *makarismós*) is rendered only by the AV in Rom. 4:6, 9 (RSV "pronounce a blessing," "the blessing pronounced"; NEB "happiness") and Gal. 4:13 (RSV "satisfaction"; NEB "how happy you thought you were").

"Most blessed" (AV Ps. 37:26; Prov. 10:6) translates Heb. *liḇrāḵâ,* lit. "for a blessing."

Bibliography.–*Bless: CAD,* VIII, *s.v.* "karābu"; F. C. Fensham, *ZAW,* 74 (1962), 1-9; *ILC,* I-II, 182-212; A. Murtonen, *VT,* 9 (1959), 157-177; *TDNT,* II, *s.v.* εὐλογέω (Beyer); *TDOT,* II, *s.v.* "brk" (Scharbert); G. Weimeier, *Der Segen im AT* (1970).

Blessed: W. Janzen, *HTR,* 58 (1965), 215-226; *TDNT,* IV, *s.v.* μακάριος (Bertram, Hauck); *TDOT,* I, *s.v.* "ashrê" (Cazelles); W. S. Towner, *CBQ,* 30 (1968), 386-399.

Blessing: F. M. Cross and D. N. Freedman, *JBL,* 67 (1948), 191-210; T. H. Gaster, *JBL,* 66 (1947), 53-62; E. M. Good, *JBL,* 82 (1963), 427-432; L. J. Liebrich, *JBL,* 74 (1955), 33-36; D. J. McCarthy, *Analecta Biblica,* 21 (1963); G. E. Mendenhall, *BA,* 17 (1954), 50-76; H. Mowvley, *Bible Translator,* 16 (1965), 74-80; C. Westermann, *Der Segen in der Bibel und im Handeln der Kirche* (1968).

A. C. MYERS

BLESSING, CUP OF [Gk. *tó potḗrion tḗs eulogías*–'the consecrated cup'] (1 Cor. 10:16). A technical term from the Jewish meals transferred to the Lord's supper, and signifying the cup of wine upon which a blessing was pronounced. The succeeding words, "which we bless," are equivalent to "for which we give thanks," for it was consecrated by thanksgiving and prayer. It is possible that the term here has a further significance, as a cup that brings blessing. *See also* CUP.

BLIGHT. *See* BLASTING.

BLINDING. *See* EYE.

BLINDNESS [Heb. *'iwwēr, 'iwwārôn, 'āwar, 'awwereṯ, 'ālam*; Gk. *typhlós, typhlóō*]. Blindness, defects of sight, and diseases of the eye are frequently mentioned in the Bible and were common maladies in the ancient world. In the Papyrus Ebers (1500 B.C.) several diseases of the eye are enumerated and nearly one hundred prescriptions are given for their treatment. That some diseases occurred in children and caused destruction and atrophy of the eyeball is attested by numerous mummy heads in which there is marked diminution in size of one orbit.

The most common eye disease in Palestine and Egypt was probably a purulent ophthalmia, a highly infectious inflammation of the conjunctivae, a malady that affected people of all ages, but especially children. It was propagated largely by flies that settled upon a diseased person's discharging eyes and transmitted the infection to others, especially sleeping infants. (In Egypt there is still a superstition that it is unlucky to drive away the flies.) Even when internal injury to the eye was avoided, the margins of the lids would exhibit chronic inflammation, and the cornea might become opaque. In cases of granular conjunctivitis, a viral keratoconjunctivitis (*trachoma* or Egyptian ophthalmia), the inflammation would be accompanied by hypertrophy of the conjunctivae and the growth of small granules of adenoid (lymphoid) tissue. When pustular conjunctivitis occurred, the conjunctivae would manifest small red nodules of lymph-type cells which would ulcerate at their extremity. Minor forms of the disease destroy the eyelashes and produce the unsightly "tender eyes" (not necessarily intended in Gen. 29:17, however, where Heb. *raḵ* may mean simply "weak" or "dull-eyed"). These conditions and others, which doubtless included glaucoma, leucoma (albugo), retinitis, cataract, cortical blindness, membranous conjunctivitis, and inflammation of the iris, must have been prevalent in biblical times. While no firm OT evidence can be adduced, it is highly probable that pannus, iridocyclitis, and other ophthalmic conditions were an accepted part of life in ancient Israel.

Blindness from birth is the result of a form of *ophthalmic neonatorum.* This is commonly due to an infectious gonococcal discharge with which the child comes into contact while in the birth canal; subsequently the infection results in an acute suppurating conjunctivitis which produces blindness. Sometimes ophthalmia accompanies malarial fever (Lev. 26:16, "sudden terror, consumption, and fever that waste the eyes"). The situation was worsened by environmental factors such as blowing dust and sand and the intense glare of the sun, which could be ruinous for eyes after some years.

Blindness incapacitated a man from serving in the priesthood (Lev. 21:16ff.), and blindness in an animal rendered it unfit to be offered as a sacrifice to the Lord (Lev. 22:22; Dt. 15:21; Mal. 1:8). Because poverty and hardship characterized their plight, care for the blind was enjoined in the law (Lev. 19:14; cf. Rom. 2:19), and mistreatment of them caused one to be accursed (Dt. 27:18).

The widespread incidence of blindness in NT times is indicated by the importance which the restoration of sight had in Christ's ministry of healing (cf. Mt. 9:27; 11:5 [par. Lk. 7:22]; Mt. 12:22; 15:30f.; 20:30-34 [par. Mk. 10:46-52; Lk. 18:35-43]; 21:14; Mk. 8:22-25; etc. In the 1st cent. A.D. blindness was generally regarded, in accordance with the OT tradition (cf. Ex. 4:11; Dt. 28:28; 2 K. 6:18; Ezk. 6:9), as a divine punishment for sin without any reflection on its possible incidence from purely physical and external causes. Jesus did not subscribe to the punitive view of blindness, however (Jn. 9:2f.), but instead used the condition from time to time as a means of manifesting divine love to an underprivileged segment of the community. The methods which He used in healing the blind differed somewhat from those applied to people suffering from other ailments, yet at the same time they were meant to elicit faith and trust in God's healing power. Consequently they were always symbolic rather than remedial in nature. Christ made a paste of saliva and dust for the congenitally blind man in Jerusalem (Jn. 9:6f.), and having anointed his eyes He commanded him to wash off the material. The response of obedience and faith resulted in restoration of the man's sight. A blind man at Beth-saida (Mk. 8:23) also was anointed with saliva as a means of eliciting his trust and arousing his expectation of divine healing. The restoration of this man's sight by stages enabled him to make a proper accommodation to the bright sunlight and to the flood of new sensory stimuli without experiencing concomitant psychic traumata. What appears to have been a case of ophthalmia is seen in the blind beggar Bartimaeus (Mk. 10:46-52), who in being healed demonstrated his faith in Christ's restorative powers. Two blind beggars near Jericho (Mt. 20:29-34) prayed for mercy as well as for the gift of sight and were similarly healed. Just as the miracles of Jesus, among which the curing of blindness held a prominent place, were regarded as manifestations of the kingdom of God (cf. Mt. 12:28), so OT prophecy saw the imparting of sight to the blind as one of the events which would occur in the day of the Lord, when His kingdom is established in Israel.

The foregoing cases appear to have represented organic diseases of the eyes, as distinct from certain other NT instances of blindness that are clearly psychogenic in nature. The most celebrated of these was the temporary amaurosis which Paul experienced at the time of his conversion (Acts 9:3-9). His recognition of the wrong that he had been doing to God's work came with blinding suddenness, and the intense emotional conflict which resulted from his inability to see his immediate future clearly expressed itself somatically in a temporary form of blindness that was independent of any lesion in the eye or the optic nerve. Once Paul's turbulent emotions had been calmed and his mind reoriented through spiritual assurances and the imposition of hands, his sight was restored. The "scales" (Acts 9:18), a rare word (Gk. *lepídes*) occurring nowhere else in the NT, were doubtless the initial imperfect visual impressions which he received as the physiological portion of the retina began to interpret stimuli once again. The affliction left behind a weakness of the eyes, evidence of which is attested by some in Paul's inability to recognize the high priest (Acts 23:5) and his employing an amanuensis to transcribe his Epistles (Rom. 16:22), as well as his writing in characters of a large size (Gal. 6:11). Another case of temporary amaurosis occurred in the case of Elymas, the sorcerer of Paphos (Acts 13:10), who was rebuked by Paul for his perfidy and wrongdoing. The degree of emotional tension and guilt involved in being exposed and denounced in the presence of the proconsul was so severe that he lost his sight for a time. The ability of his retinal cells to respond to sensory impressions was impaired dramatically, the process of degeneration being likened to a "mist and darkness." There are numerous clinical cases on record of people who have become blind temporarily for purely psychogenic reasons because under stress they have been unable to cope with a situation. Thus Elymas' sight would return only when the emotional tensions and conflicts had been resolved, thereby reversing the earlier somatic expression.

Though blindness was not necessarily a concomitant of senility, Isaac (Gen. 27:1), Eli (1 S. 3:2; 4:15), and Ahijah the prophet (1 K. 14:4) lost their sight in old age. Leah seems to have suffered from blepharitis or mucopurulent conjunctivitis (Gen. 29:17).

The most accurate description of a specific eye disease occurs in the Apocrypha. Tobit was evidently afflicted with a dense white opacity of the cornea (*leucoma*), caused usually by ophthalmia. According to the narrative, fish gall was applied to the cornea, presumably as an attempt at pigmentation, and this therapy resulted in healing (Tob. 11:4ff.).

Figuratively, blindness is used to represent spiritual imperceptiveness, inability to discern and heed the will of God (cf. Isa. 42:16ff.; 2 Cor. 4:4; 2 Pet. 1:9), and inability to perceive moral distinctions (Mt. 15:14; 23:16ff.). In Ex. 23:8; Dt. 16:19; 1 S. 12:3, blindness is used of the biased judgment that results from accepting bribes and subverts the cause of justice. Blindness is also used to refer to the spiritual imperception that makes one unable to understand the voice of prophecy (Isa. 29:9; cf. Jn. 12:40).

See also DISEASE III.G; IV.C.

A. MACALISTER R. K. HARRISON

BLINDNESS, JUDICIAL. *See* JURISPRUDENCE, ABUSE OF.

BLOOD [Heb. *dām,* prob. < *'āḏam*–'be red'; Gk. *haíma*]. Blood in the OT is the life principle, both animal (Lev. 17:11) and vegetable (Dt. 32:14, the "blood" of the grape). Its atoning power in the OT sacrifices foreshadows the ultimate atonement by the blood of Christ. The word has a figurative sense in both the OT and NT for bloodshed or murder (Gen. 37:26; Hos. 4:2; Rev. 16:6).

I. Primitive Ideas.–Although the real function of the blood in the human system was not fully known until the fact of its circulation was established by William Harvey in 1615, nevertheless from the earliest times a singular mystery has been attached to it by all peoples. Blood rites, blood ceremonies, and blood feuds are common among primitive tribes. It came to be recognized as the life principle long before its function was scientifically proved. Naturally a feeling of fear, awe, and reverence would be attached to the shedding of blood. With many uncivilized peoples scarification of the body until blood flows is practiced. Blood brotherhood or blood friendship is established by African tribes by the mutual shedding of blood and either drinking it or rubbing it on one another's bodies. Thus and by the intertransfusion of blood by other means it was thought that a community of life and interest could be established.

II. Hebrew and OT Customs.–Notwithstanding the ignorance and superstition surrounding this suggestively beautiful idea, it grew to have more than a merely human significance and application. For this crude practice of intertransference of human blood there came to be symbolic substitution of animal blood in sprinkling or anointing. The first reference in the OT to blood (Gen. 4:10) is figurative, but highly illustrative of the reverential fear manifested upon the shedding of blood, and the first teaching regarding it.

The rite of circumcision is an OT form of blood ceremony. Apart from the probable sanitary importance of the act is the deeper meaning in the establishment of a bond of friendship between the one upon whom the act is performed and the Lord Himself. In order that Abraham might become "the friend of God" he was commanded that he should be circumcised as a token of the covenant between him and God (Gen. 17:10f.; *see* CIRCUMCISION).

It is significant that eating blood was prohibited in earliest Bible times (Gen. 9:4). The custom probably prevailed among heathen nations as a religious rite (cf. Ps. 16:4). This and its unhygienic influence together doubtless led to its becoming taboo. The same prohibition was made under the Mosaic code (Lev. 7:26; *see* SACRIFICE).

Blood was commanded to be used also for purification or for ceremonial cleansing (Lev. 14:5-7, 51f.; Nu. 19:4), provided, however, that it be taken from a clean animal (*see* PURIFICATION).

In all probability there is no trace of the superstitious use of blood in the OT, except perhaps in 1 K. 22:38; but everywhere it is vested with cleansing, expiatory, and reverently symbolic qualities.

III. NT Teachings.–As in the transition from ancient to Hebrew practice, so from the OT to the NT we see an exaltation of the conception of blood and blood ceremonies. In Abraham's covenant his own blood had to be shed. Later an expiatory animal was to shed blood (Lev. 5:6; *see* ATONEMENT), but there must always be a shedding of blood. "Without the shedding of blood there is no forgiveness of sins" (He. 9:22). The exaltation of this idea finds its highest development then in the vicarious shedding of blood by Christ Himself (1 Jn. 1:7). As in the OT "blood" was used also to signify the juice of grapes; the most natural substitute for drinking blood would be the use of wine. Jesus takes advantage of this, and introduces the beautiful and significant custom (Mt. 26:28) of drinking wine and eating bread as symbolic of the primitive intertransfusion of blood and flesh in a pledge of eternal friendship (cf. Ex. 24:6f.; Jn. 6:53-56). This is the climactic observance of blood rites recorded in the Bible.

Bibliography.–*TDNT,* I, *s.v.* αἷμα (Behm); *TDOT*, III, *s.v.* "dām" (Bergman, Kedar-Kopfstein); L. Morris, *JTS*, N.S. 3 (1952), 216-227; 6 (1955), 77-82.

W. G. CLIPPINGER

BLOOD AND WATER [Gk. *haíma kaí hýdōr*]. An unusual phenomenon is related in Jn. 19:34 in connection with the death of Jesus. When the soldiers came to Jesus to perform the final step in His execution, viz., the breaking of His legs, they saw that He was already dead and omitted the act. "But one of the soldiers pierced his side with a spear, and at once there came out blood and water." Two things seem to be startling to the writer: the flow of blood and water, and the fact that it took place immediately, indicating that the fluids had accumulated prior to the piercing with the spear. In v. 35 he emphasizes that he was an eyewitness and not mistaken or lying about the remarkable event.

The fact that "dead bodies don't bleed" has often been thought to make this passage problematical, but physicians seem agreed that a flow of accumulated blood — as the "at once" seems to indicate — from a wound inflicted shortly after death is not impossible. The real difficulty is to understand how and why the water (sometimes thought to have been serum) and blood were so clearly separated and distinguishable.

One way of solving the problem has been to view the phenomenon as a miracle and to seek a mystical interpretation. Origen recognized that the blood is clotted in dead bodies and that water does not flow from them, and therefore he interpreted the blood and water as a miracle (*Contra Celsum* ii.36). Others have followed this line of reasoning and insisted that, since Jesus' body did not see corruption (Acts 2:31), it therefore did not undergo the changes that follow an ordinary human death.

The romantic notion that Jesus died literally of a broken heart — first advanced by Stroud in 1847 — has fallen from favor. Spontaneous rupture of the heart is not unknown, but it does not occur under the pressure of mental or emotional stress. It is the result of preexisting heart disease, for which, in the case of Jesus, we have no indication.

Pierre Barbet (*A Doctor at Calvary* [1953]) and others have argued that the blood came from within the heart and the water from the pericardial sac. A. F. Sava (*CBQ*, 19 [1957], 343-46) has taken issue with this on technical grounds and suggests that the blood and water were accumulated in the pleural cavity between the rib cage and the lung. He shows that severe nonpenetrating chest injuries are capable of producing such an accumulation, and suggests that a scourging such as Jesus received several hours before His death was sufficient to account for the accumulation that flowed forth when the chest wall was pierced. Also, there was enough time between the scourging and the piercing to allow the red blood cells to separate from the lighter clear serum.

John considered the event to be of considerable importance, but he does not state explicitly its theological significance. Perhaps he was concerned to refute early Docetic heresies by stressing the real death and true humanity of Jesus, as he does in his first Epistle. This was the view of Irenaeus (*Adv. haer.* iii.22.21).

Various interpretations have been given to the symbolism in this passage (for an excellent overview of these interpretations, along with a good bibliography, see R. E. Brown, *Gospel According to John, XIII-XXI* [*AB*, 1970], pp. 945-956). Brown recommends that the symbol of blood and water be interpreted in the light of their use elsewhere in the Johannine works. The shedding of blood would then be a sign that Jesus was actually dead — and therefore glorified — and the flow of water a sign of the Spirit; thus Jesus' prophecy concerning the Spirit in Jn. 7:38f. was proleptically fulfilled. "The soldier's lance thrust was meant to demonstrate that Jesus was truly dead; but this affirmation of death is paradoxically the beginning of life, for from the dead man there flows living water that will be a source of life for all who believe in him in imitation of the Beloved Disciple" (p. 950).

W. W. BUEHLER

BLOOD, AVENGER OF. *See* AVENGER.

BLOOD, FIELD OF. *See* AKELDAMA.

BLOOD, FLOW OF. *See* HEMORRHAGE.

BLOODGUILTINESS. The Heb *dām* is rendered "bloodguilt" six times in the RSV, the AV giving "blood" and the NEB "murder," "bloodshed," etc. "Bloodguiltiness" (*dām*) is found only in Ps. 51:14 in the AV and RSV, the NEB rendering it "bloodshed." Ezk. 18:13 seems to indicate that these terms do not necessarily signify bloodshed, but any grievous sin which, if it remains, will block God's favor to His land and people (cf. Dt. 21:8; Isa. 1:15).

BLOODTHIRSTY [Heb. *'anšê-dāmîm*–'men of blood'] (Ps. 5:6; 26:9; 59:2; Prov. 29:10); AV also BLOODY; NEB "men of blood," "men who have tasted blood," etc. *See* BLOODY.

BLOODY [Heb. *dām*]; NEB MURDEROUS, BLOODSTAINED, etc. Where the Hebrew employs the noun in construct form, "of blood," the RSV sometimes renders with the adjective "bloody," as with *'îr haddāmîm,* rendered "bloody city" (Ezk. 24:6). In 1 K. 2:32 the requiting of Joab's murderous deeds is at issue, while in Ezk. 7:23; 22:2; 24:6-9 the allusion is to the capital crimes committed by the wicked rulers of Jerusalem, and hence to the city itself. Nineveh is described in the same manner in Nah. 3:1.

A similar construction occurs in Ex. 4:25f., where the AV renders as "bloody husband" the Heb. *ḥ*ª*ṭan-dāmîm,* which the RSV translates "bridegroom of blood." The reference here is to the circumcision of the son of Moses, when his wife Zipporah threw the prepuce into his lap (AV, RSV, "feet"; NEB "touched him"). R. K. H.

BLOODY FLUX. *See* DYSENTERY.

BLOODY SWEAT. In Lk. 22:44 Our Lord's agony at Gethsemane is described with the words: "His sweat became like great drops of blood [Gk. *hōseí thrómboi haímatos*] falling down upon the ground." Most writers take this to mean that the perspiration dropped in the same manner as clots of blood drop from a wound, regarding the Gk. *hōseí* as expressing merely a comparison as in Mt. 28:3, where *leukón hōs chiṓn* means "white as snow." Cases of actual exudation of blood are described in several of the medieval accounts of stigmatization, and have even been reported in modern times (see *Enc.Brit.*, XXI, *s.v.* "stigmatization" for examples). As the agony of Our Lord was unexampled in human experience, it is conceivable that it may have been attended with physical conditions of a unique nature.

Important MSS, including p^{75} B A, omit Lk. 22:43f.

A. MACALISTER

BLOOM; BLOSSOM. *See* FLOWER.

BLOW [Heb. *makkâ* (Jer. 14:17; 30:14), *maḥaṣ* (Isa. 30:26)]; AV also WOUND, STROKE; NEB also STRIKE, etc.; [*naḥaṯ*] ("descending blow [of his arm]," Isa. 30:30); AV "lighting down"; NEB "sweeping down"; [*māḥaq* (Jgs. 5:26), *nāḵâ* (Nu. 35:21), *šānâ* (2 S. 20:10)]; AV SMITE, STRIKE; NEB STRIKE, etc. These nouns and verbs refer to a blow with the hand or weapon.

BLOW. 1. [Heb. *tāqa', ḥ*ª*ṣōṣēr* (1 Ch. 15:24)]; NEB also SOUND, etc.; [*t*ᵉ*rû'â*] ("blow the trumpets," Nu. 29:1); NEB ACCLAMATION; [Gk. *salpízō*] (Rev. 8:6, 13); AV SOUND. These terms are used with reference to sounding trumpets (*ḥ*ª*ṣōṣēr* and *salpízō* are used only in this connection) or alarms. Where the AV and RSV translate the Heb. *t*ᵉ*qa'tem t*ᵉ*rû'â* as "blow an alarm" (Nu. 10:5f.), the NEB gives "signal for a shout." The term *t*ᵉ*rû'â* can refer to a signal or to shouting—either for joy or in alarm (cf. Nu. 29:1). The alarm of Nu. 10:5f. was probably some sort of military call (cf. Am. 1:14) which could be distinguished from the blowing of trumpets that summoned the congregation (Nu. 10:7). *See also* BLAST; SHOUT.

2. [Heb. *pu(a)ḥ*]; NEB also "breathe out"; [*ḥārar*]; AV "are burned"; [*napaḥ*]. These terms are used with reference to fire and the wrath of God. The verb *ḥārar* is used by Jeremiah in a figurative description of God's judgment against Israel: "The bellows blow fiercely, the lead is consumed by the fire" (6:29). The verb *pu(a)ḥ* sometimes means "blast," as in Ezk. 21:31, "I will blow upon you with the fire of my wrath" (cf. 22:20f., where *napaḥ* is used as a synonym for *pu(a)ḥ*; but it can also be used of a breeze, as in Cant. 4:16: "Blow upon my garden, let its fragrance be wafted abroad."

3. [Heb. *'āḇar*] ("blow over," Gen. 8:1); AV, NEB, "pass over"; [*nāšap̱*] (Ex. 15:10); [*nāšaḇ*] (Ps. 147:18); [*nāsa'*] (Ps. 78:26); NEB "let loose"; [Gk. *pnéō*] (Rev. 7:1). These terms are used of the blowing of the wind, as is *pu(a)ḥ* in passages such as Cant. 4:16 (**2**).

BLUE. *See* COLORS.

BLUSH [Heb. *kālam*–'feel humiliated'] (Ezr. 9:6; Isa. 1:29; Jer. 6:15; 8:12). In contrast to Ezra, the people of God mentioned by Isaiah and Jeremiah were not ashamed of their iniquities as they ought to have been. Thus the Lord determined to teach them the shame of their acts by humiliating them in the eyes of their neighbors by means of a foreign conqueror.

BOANERGES bō-ə-nûr'jēz [Gk. *Boanērges* < Aram. < Heb. *b^enê regeš*–'sons of thunder']. The surname bestowed by Jesus upon James and John, the sons of Zebedee, when they were ordained to the apostleship (Mk. 3:17). *See* JAMES **1.** It has also been regarded as an equivalent of the "Heavenly Twins," the Sons of Zeus or Thunder. According to this interpretation, the name Boanerges would represent the Dioscuri in some form or other of their varied presentation in the cults of the Mediterranean (cf. J. R. Harris, *Expos.*, 7th series, 3 [1907], 146-152). C. M. KERR

BOAR [Heb. *ḥ^azîr*]. In lamenting the troubled state of the Jewish nation the psalmist (80:13) says: "The boar from the forest ravages it, and all that move in the field feed on it," with evident reference to Israel's enemies, the Assyrians, etc. The wild boar is abundant in certain parts of Palestine and Syria, especially in the thickets that border the lakes and rivers, e.g., the Sea of Galilee, the Jordan, and the deltas of streams flowing into the Dead Sea. *See* SWINE. A. E. DAY

BOARD. *See* PLANK.

BOAST; BOASTFUL; BOASTFULNESS; etc. [Heb. *hālal, gāḏal* (*peh*, Ob. 12), also *'āmar, kāḇaḏ, zāḵar*, etc.; Gk. *kaucháomai, kaúchēsis, kaúchēma, katakaucháomai, alazṓn*, also *tolmáō, perpereúomai* (1 Cor. 13:4), *megalauchéō, hypéronkos*]; AV also GLORY, REJOICE, MAGNIFY ONESELF, VAUNT ONESELF, BE BOLD, SPEAK PROUDLY, TRUST, REMEMBER, FOOLS, FOOLISH, SWELLING WORDS, "fruit of the stout heart" (Isa. 10:12), etc.; NEB also GLORY, EXULT, FLATTER ONESELF, PRIDE, ARROGANCE, BRAG, ENCROACH (Zeph. 2:8, 10), MAKE ONESELF SUPERIOR, SELF-SATISFACTION, TAKE CREDIT, VAUNTED, etc. Boasting has both a good and a bad sense in the Bible. The Heb. *hālal* means primarily "praise," and is used in that sense in Ps. 44:8, etc.; but in Ps. 5:5; 75:4 it has a negative connotation (AV "foolish," "fools"). In the NT the positive sense of Gk. *kaucháomai* is found, e.g., in 2 Cor. 1:12; 2 Thess. 1:4; and the negative sense in 1 Cor. 3:21; Jas. 4:16. Biblical teachings against undue boasting — that based on arrogance, false pride, or self-righteousness — include Ps. 5:15; Prov. 27:1; Rom. 2:17, 23; 1 Cor. 1:26-31; 4:6ff.; 2 Cor. 10:17f.; Eph. 2:9; Jas. 3:14; 4:16. Cf. Paul's "foolish boasting" in 2 Cor. 11:16ff.

BOAT. *See* SHIPS.

BOAZ bō'az [Heb. *bō'az* (Ruth 2–4; 1 Ch. 2:11f.); Gk. *Boes, Boos* (Mt. 1:5; Lk. 3:32)].

1. A resident of Bethlehem and kinsman of Elimelech, Naomi's husband. In Ruth 2:1 he is described as a *gibbōr ḥayil*, or aristocrat (cf. 1 S. 9:1). He owned fields outside the town, in which Ruth was allowed to glean. After she had revealed herself to him without compromising his integrity, he redeemed the family property and married Ruth. 1 Ch. 2:11f. makes him a descendant of Hezron, and thus perhaps a chief of the Hezronite clan in Bethlehem. A son, Obed, was subsequently born to Ruth and Boaz, and he was the ancestor of David.

2. The name of one of the two bronze pillars erected in front of Solomon's temple, the other being Jachin (1 K. 7:21; 2 Ch. 3:17). *See* JACHIN AND BOAZ. D. F. ROBERTS

BOCCAS (1 Esd. 8:2, AV). *See* BUKKI **2.**

BOCHERU bō'kə-rōō [Heb. *bōḵ^erû*]. A son of Azrikam, Saul's descendant (1 Ch. 8:38; 9:34). See *IP*, p. 239.

BOCHIM bō'kim [Heb. *habbōḵîm*–'the weepers']; NEB BOKIM. A place on the mountain W of Gilgal said to have been so named because Israel wept there at the remonstrance of the angel (Jgs. 2:1, 5). No name resembling this has been discovered. Many, following the LXX, identify it with Bethel.

BODY. The concomitant relation of form to being is fundamental to the biblical concept of the body. Man is viewed as a psychophysical unity in which, contrary to Greek philosophy and to some modern psychology, the body is not separated from the spiritual aspect of man.

- I. OT
- II. NT
- III. Related Concepts
  - A. Spiritual Body of 1 Cor. 15
  - B. Body of Christ
    1. The Physical Body of Jesus Christ
    2. Eucharistic Use
    3. Community of Believers

I. OT.–Properly speaking, the OT has no formal term for the body, although several words are so translated. Heb. *g^ewiyyâ* sometimes means living body (Ezk. 1:11, 23; Dnl. 10:6; cf. Aram. *g^ešēm*, Dnl. 3:27f.; etc.), though more normally *dead* body, i.e., a corpse (cf. *nepeš*, Lev. 21:11; Nu. 6:6; etc.; *n^eḇēlâ*, Dt. 21:23).

Occurring 266 times in the Hebrew OT, *bāśār* basically denotes bodily flesh, composed of *'āpār* (dust) and *n^ešāmâ* (breath), the material element of man (Gen. 2:21-24; Ezk. 37:6; cf. *še'ēr*, Prov. 5:11), but *bāśār* also is used for animal flesh (Gen. 6:17; 7:15, 21). Other terms occasionally translated "body" in the RSV basically designate specific parts, including *beṭen* ("belly" or "womb," Dt. 28:4, 11, 18, 53; etc.), *gûpâ* ("back," 1 Ch. 10:12), and *'eṣem* ("bone," Lam. 4:7).

Yet, man's *bāśār* is conjoined with his *rû(a)ḥ* (spirit) and *nepeš* (soul) in ways that refer to the whole man, not only as fleshly, but as rational, soulish (cf. Ps. 63:1 [MT 2]; 84:2). Body and soul are used almost interchangeably, soul to indicate man as a living being, and body (flesh) to denote him as a corporeally visible creature (Ps. 16:9; Isa. 10:18). This unity of body and soul have led some writers to conclude that the OT lacks a view of the physical body as a discrete entity, that "man is an animated body rather than an incarnated soul" (H. W. Robinson, *The People and the Book* [1925], p. 362; also, *The Religious Ideas of the OT* [1949], p. 90). More properly, however, the OT sees body and soul as coordinates interpenetrating each other in function to form a single whole.

II. NT.–The NT uses two distinct words for body: *sárx* and *sṓma*. The LXX writers uniformly used *sárx* (flesh) to translate *bāśār*, so its use in the NT builds upon the meaning of *bāśār* in the OT. Consequently, its basic NT meaning is bodily substance (Mt. 24:22; Jn. 3:6). Paul uses the word ninety-one times, and, while he accepts the basic connotation, he adds immeasurably to its meaning. For Paul, *sárx* has two principal meanings.

First, *sárx* designates the external, physical aspect of man's bodily existence (1 Cor. 15:50; Gal. 4:13). As *sárx*, man is mortal and subject to death (2 Cor. 4:11). Second, *sárx* represents flesh as a part of the natural human order in contrast to the divine order. As body, *sárx* is worldly, human nature under control of fleshly powers, obedient to the lust of the flesh rather than the power of the Spirit (Rom. 8:5-8). To be "in the flesh" is to be subject to the powers that control the flesh (cf. Gal. 4:3; Col. 2:8, 20). Hence, *sárx* is the aspect of man that is a part of the world-order that stands in opposition to God (Rom. 8:7f.).

Sṓma both identifies and expands the concept of the body as designated by *sárx*. As does *sárx, sṓma* also refers to the external physical aspect of man's bodily existence (Mt. 27:59; Jn. 19:31; 1 Cor. 9:27; Gal. 6:17) and that of an animal (Lk. 17:37). It is virtually equivalent to *sárx* in that it connotes the whole man in human weakness (Mk. 5:29) and is subject to the reign and judgment of sin (Rom. 7:22-25). Like *sárx*, the *sṓma* is mortal (Rom. 6:12; 8:11), and has its lusts (Rom. 6:12). But the use of *sṓma* uniquely expresses some essential differences.

To understand these differences, attention must be given to the distinctively Pauline use of *sṓma*. As J. A. T. Robinson states, ". . . the concept of the body forms the keystone of Paul's theology. . . . For no other New Testament writer has the word any doctrinal significance" (*The Body,* p. 9). It would be significant if a source of this aspect of Paul's theology could be identified. Several suggestions have been made: a carry-over from the rabbinic Adam-speculation (W. D. Davies, *Paul and Rabbinic Judaism* [2nd ed. 1955]), and the Stoic doctrine of the organic unity of the universe (S. Hanson, *Unity of the Church in the NT* [1946]). More probably, however, the concept arose out of Paul's own creative thinking, as F. W. Dillistone (*Structure of Divine Society* [1951]), among others, suggests.

The unique aspect of Paul's *sṓma* concept is his use of it to indicate that man has both physical and spiritual existence, and that his spiritual existence is an integral part of his total being. As J. A. T. Robinson states, "*Sṓma* . . . does not mean simply something external to a man himself, something he *has*. It is something he *is*" (*The Body,* p. 28). A. M. Hunter similarly describes Paul's use of body as "the organic principle of identity which persists through the years and all changes of substance" (*Interpreting Paul's Gospel* [1960], p. 54).

Paul uses this concept in at least five ways. First, *sṓma,* in a way impossible for *sárx,* expresses the identity of the whole person as an entity before God. It identifies bodily form with the inner person and as such is tantamount to being personality or the essential self (Rom. 12:1; 1 Cor. 9:27; 13:3; Phil. 1:20). *Sṓma* is an essential aspect of human personality, not just accidental as bodily form. *Sṓma,* as body, is therefore essential to the understanding of the self.

Second, as the body/self, *sṓma* is the locus of the spiritual in man. As *sárx* is the seat of man's bodily (fleshly) enmity toward God, so *sṓma* is the seat of man's spirituality. Since *sṓma* denotes both the body and the whole person, all spiritual relations must be in and through his somatic existence (Rom. 6:12). The body is the coordinate of the spirit in that it provides the spirit its agency of expression. Man is fully himself in the unity of body and spirit as both function within the integral whole. Neither takes precedence over the other, while each gains in relation to the other.

Third, as body *sṓma* means the whole man as destined for membership in God's kingdom. As *sárx* man is destined for death and destruction, but as *sṓma,* man as he is meant to be, he is in confrontation with God. As *sṓma* man serves God as a total being, not as divided into body and soul.

Fourth, the *sṓma* provides the vehicle for the resurrection. Since the body is not just an accidental part of the human personality to be detached at death, the whole person, not just a disembodied soul, is to be resurrected. At death the individual will not escape from his body, but will find it changed and glorified. Therefore, the *sṓma* must first die, for the resurrection is "of the dead" (cf. 1 Cor. 15:21). That the body is to be transformed is evidence that its fleshly form is not essential (Phil. 3:20f.). Yet Rom. 8:11 indicates that God will raise up "mortal" bodies and 1 Cor. 6:14 confirms this (cf. Rom. 6:12). Moreover, Rom. 8:23 asserts that the resurrection will be "of our bodies," not from our bodies.

Therefore, fifth, since the resurrection is associated with judgment, the body, in its earthly existence, is viewed as the site of spiritual testing, in terms of which the judgment will take place (2 Cor. 5:1-10). Consequently, the spiritual life, with the body/self as its locale, is regarded as a firstfruit of participation in Christ's own resurrection (Phil. 3:20f.).

Thus, it is clear that the body is used to represent the whole man, and militates against any idea of the biblical view of man as existing apart from bodily manifestation, unless it be during the intermediate state.

III. Related Concepts.–*A. Spiritual Body of 1 Cor. 15.* The interrelation of body and the totality of man's being is illustrated by the contrast between the physical and the spiritual body in 1 Cor. 15:44, 46: "It is sown a physical body; it is raised a spiritual body. If there is a physical body, there is also a spiritual body. . . . But it is not the spiritual which is first but the physical, and then the spiritual."

In response to a question about the nature or quality of the body to be raised in the resurrection (1 Cor. 15:35), Paul relates the body to be raised to that which is buried in death. His implicit answer is that the dead have a body that is altered in the resurrection. The body that is sown is the body that is raised. It is sown in one quality and raised in another, but it remains the same body. The physical body can be sown because it is subject to death. The body that is raised is spiritual, that is, renewed and governed by the Spirit.

The contrast between physical and spiritual has to do not with the substance of which the bodies are made but with the relation of the bodies. The spiritual body is related to the physical as Adam is a "living soul" and Christ is a "quickening spirit." This means that as a living soul Adam had a body. Body and soul are interwined as one entity. The existence of a physical body presupposes the existence of a spiritual body, just as the spiritual body does not come into being unless there is a physical body. The spiritual body follows the physical, and is not only the evidence of the resurrection, but shares the fruits of Christ's work (cf. 2 Cor. 3:18; 4:16f.; Phil. 3:21).

The spiritual body can be understood only against the background of Paul's understanding of the physical body. Paul does not claim, as was the Hebraic belief, that the physical body as such is to be raised. Paul's use of the word *sárx* (seventy times, thirty-six of which refer to man simply as a physical entity, and thirty-four to his sinfulness, under the domination of the "flesh") suggests his attitude toward the physical body. It is perishable, mortal, and weak (1 Cor. 15:44; cf. Rom. 8:21; 1 Cor. 15:50; 2 Cor. 4:16). Since "flesh and blood" cannot inherit the kingdom, it is not flesh that is to be raised but a body.

Furthermore, man's present weak and sinful body does not constitute the totality of his being, which is rather the "inner nature [which] is being renewed every day" (2 Cor. 4:16). Intrinsic to this is Paul's understanding of man's *psychḗ* and *pneúma*. *Psychḗ*, used only thirteen times by Paul, and always in relation to the present life (with 1 Thess. 5:23 a possible exception), is inextricably related to man's fleshly existence as the focus of his personality. *Pneúma*, used 110 times, clearly refers to the spirit of man, which is capable of relating to God, but which is also in danger of falling under control of the flesh.

In this age man is under both flesh and spirit. The struggle within man is not between body and spirit, but between flesh and spirit. Flesh may overcome the body (Rom. 8:10) but "he who raised Christ Jesus from the dead will give life to your mortal bodies also through his Spirit" (Rom. 8:11). The body is essential to the spirit. Consequently, Paul may boldly assert that what is "sown in dishonor [will be] raised in glory" (1 Cor. 15:43).

Paul makes no attempt, however, to explain the substance of the spiritual body. He is content to assert that in the resurrection that which is essential to man's being, i.e., his somatic existence, is raised, yet changed into its primary essence, i.e., spiritual. This seems to be the intention of the antithetical terms of 1 Cor. 15:42-44: imperishable/perishable, glory/weakness, physical body/spiritual body. The two primary emphases of these antitheses are individual and body. Body is indissolubly a part of the total being. Consequently, Paul sees the resurrection as a continuance of that total being, bodily in form, freed from the rule of the flesh, with spirit in triumph. This is accomplished through the transforming work of redemptive grace in this age, and completed in the resurrected spiritual body.

The spiritual body of 1 Cor. 15:44 is the proof of the spiritual life begun in Christ. In Rom. 6:5 Paul states, "For if we have been incorporated with him in a death like his, we shall certainly be incorporated with him in a resurrection like his." This incorporation speaks of identity. As Christ died "in the likeness of sinful flesh" (Rom. 8:3) yet not being sinful, so mankind, being sinful, died also to sin, hence must share the same resurrected life as Christ. This likeness is not just a symbolic conformity, but a redemptive-historical likeness by virtue of its oneness with Christ. The old man has been crucified, judged, with Him, so that the sinful body might be rendered powerless (6:6). The resurrection of Christ's own body assures the believer that, as this identifies with Christ's redemptive work, man's physical body (his soma-self) will share in His resurrection as a spiritual body.

B. The Body of Christ. This phrase has three uses in the NT.

1. The Physical Body of Jesus Christ. That the NT writers accepted the true humanity of Jesus is clearly indicated by Rom. 7:4, in which salvation is said to have come in dying to the law "through the body of Christ" (cf. He. 10:10). This is confirmed in references to His physical body at the time of His death (Mt. 27:58f.; Lk. 24:3, 23; Jn. 19:38, 40; 20:12). Col. 1:22 refers to "his body of flesh" (cf. Eph. 2:13-15). Though not using the exact phrase, Phil. 3:21 and 1 Cor. 15:12-28 affirm Christ's resurrection as bodily (cf. 35-58). This assurance of His bodily resurrection is the hope of believers in that it is presented as a prototype of their own resurrection.

2. Eucharistic Use. At the institution of the memorial meal Jesus broke the bread, saying, "This is my body" (Mt. 26:26; Mk. 14:22; Lk. 22:19; 1 Cor. 11:24; cf. 10:16). There is a double reference here: (1) *sṓma*, as "my body," referring to the totality of the person of Jesus, hence He says, "This is my total self, which I give to you"; and (2) the element of sacrifice, which is indicated both by the setting of the supper, at the Passover feast, and the reference to "broken" (cf. 1 Cor. 10:16; 11:24 mg.). Jesus joined the element of sacrifice, which was essential to the Passover celebration, with His earlier statements about Himself as the Bread of Life: "I say to you, it was not Moses who gave you the bread from heaven; my Father gives you the true bread from heaven. For the bread of God is that which comes down from heaven, and gives life to the world. . . . I am the bread of life" (Jn. 6:32f., 35). This act of sacrifice is confirmed by the interpretation given by later writers (e.g., He. 10:5, 10) as being efficacious for mankind.

3. Community of believers. The term "body" is applied to the Church as the body "in Christ" (Rom. 12:5), "of Christ" (1 Cor. 12:27), or simply as "his body" (Eph. 1:23).

Since this is a term unique to Paul, it is important to understand its development. The basic idea is the collective solidarity of Christ and believers. Assuming that 1 Corinthians is its earliest use, a progression can be at least tentatively suggested.

In 1 Cor. 6:15-17, Paul introduces the concept of body as participation: "Do you not know that your bodies are members of Christ?" Borrowing from the OT image of marriage as constituting "one flesh" (Gen. 2:24), he uses the sexual union (even with a prostitute) to conclude that "he who is united to the Lord becomes one spirit with him" (v. 17).

The first use of the phrase "body of Christ" (1 Cor. 10:16f.) furthers the idea of both collective solidarity and participation. Breaking of bread, symbolic of new-covenant concepts, is participating *in* the body of Christ. Just so, unworthy participation (without discernment) profanes the "body and blood of the Lord" (1 Cor. 11:27). This is followed by the enumeration of gifts emanating from the Spirit (ch. 12) and their direct application to "the body" (12:12-26) with its unity and diversity. Paul immediately proceeds to his next use of the term by concluding, "now *you* [emphatic *hymeís*] are the body of Christ and individually members of it." (While it may be argued that this refers primarily to the church at Corinth, this does not preclude its universal application.) This same sense of interrelatedness within the church is repeated in Rom. 12:3-8 where the term becomes "one body in Christ" (v. 5).

It may well be that since Paul in several places resorts to an analogical use of the marriage relation to illustrate his body-of-Christ concept (1 Cor. 6:15-17; Eph. 5:21-33) he has in mind the concept of Israel as the bride of God (Jer. 2:2), and through new-covenant theology develops the "body of Christ" as its parallel for the new Israel, the Church. Whether or not this concept developed in this way, the use of the term clearly emphasizes both corporate solidarity and participation.

The conceptual use of the body in relation to the Church is developed in three ways. First, the Church is the body of Christ as a community of fellowship "in Christ." The Church is understood in its pneumatic (spiritual) mode of existence as communion with the risen Christ. It is the body of Christ as the fellowship in which He dwells by His Spirit and which by His Spirit He sustains. The Church is not constituted merely by the assembly of believers, but is the community created by the incorporation of believers into Christ. 1 Cor. 12:13 makes it plain that Christians are baptized "into one body," which exists in Christ's redemptive work not merely as the totality of believers, but as the community created by the risen Christ Himself (v. 27).

This community exists as more than mere human fellowship. Paul uses the metaphor of the body to portray the correlation between the Church as a concrete entity on earth and the eschatological dimension of His redemptive person and work. The crucified body of Christ, risen now and actual within history, is at work in and through the Church. The community created by the presence of this earthly aspect of the risen Lord is the "body" into which believers are incorporated.

Second, as the body of Christ, the Church is a corporate unity in the relationship of believers to each other. Great stress is laid upon this unity in Paul's metaphor of the Church in Romans and 1 and 2 Corinthians. Its unity refers to both mutuality of identity and mutuality of service. Both Rom. 12:5 and 1 Cor. 12:12f. assert this mutuality: as Christians are one body in Christ, so they are individually members one of another. As members of the one body they stand in mutual relation with each other in the service of the kingdom of God.

Precisely in this unity lies the great truth about the nature of the Church as the body of Christ. The pronouncements of these passages confirm that underlying the unity into which the many are incorporated is an objective, historical entity into which they are individually baptized. The fundamental idea here is that the body of Christ exists in its concrete "objectivity" as the presence of Christ in the world into which believers are incorporated and by which they, through their corporate existence in Christ, exist in unity with each other. While the term may be metaphorical in use, it connotes a realistic understanding of the corporate unity among believers.

Third. as the body of Christ, the Church is the eschatological entity of which He is the Head. This imagery of Christ's headship is developed in both Colossians and Ephesians and adds a dimension to Paul's understanding of the Church not seen in Romans or Corinthians. The Church is still the body (Eph. 1:23; 4:12); believers are members of the body (Eph. 5:30), which is maintained through the work of the Spirit (Eph. 4:3; Col. 3:15); and unified in Christ (Eph. 2:14ff.). But a new concept is introduced: Christ as the Head of the body. As Head, He has been given the Church as His body (Eph. 1:22ff.). As Head, He has all spiritual gifts at his disposal (4:8ff.). The Church, as body, has fellowship with Him as its Head (Eph. 5:23; Col. 1:18; 2:19; cf. v. 10). The Church is to understand itself as His body and grow into fulness of its position in Him (Eph. 4:12f.).

The full meaning of headship is developed in Eph. 1:22f. and illustrated analogically in 5:21-33. After delineating the exalted position of the risen Lord "far above all rule and authority and power and dominion . . . not only in this age but also in that which is to come," Christ is declared to be "head over all things for the church, which is his body, the fulness of him who fills all in all" (1:21-23). Moreover, that headship is illustrated by the analogy of the marriage relationship — the husband is the head of the wife as Christ is the head of the Church. The emphasis here is the unity of the one flesh of husband and wife. Just so, the unity of Christ as Head with the Church as body is the identification of the Church with Christ's mission in the world.

Paul treats this identification in two ways. In Ephesians the purpose of Christ's redemptive work is the creation of "one new man" (2:15) and the joining of two into "one flesh" (5:31), of which Paul says, "This is a great mystery, and I take it to mean Christ and the church" (v. 32). Moreover, in Colossians Christ is said to have "fulness of life in him, who is the head of all rule and authority" (2:10). This "head" undoubtedly refers to the same headship of the body, the Church, mentioned in 1:18.

Consequently, three concepts emerge in Paul's extended treatment of the Church: the Head as the source and sustenance of the body; His rule over "all rule and authority and power and dominion"; and consequently, this rule in and through His presence in the world as His body, the Church. The Church may be said, then, to be the self-manifestation of Christ in the world, the body through which the Spirit extends the presence of Christ.

This concept is strengthened by a consideration of the meaning of "fulness" (*plḗrōma*) in Eph. 1:23, "the fulness of him who fills all in all." While subject to much debate, the passage seems to teach that it is Christ who "fills all in all" and that He does this through "His body." This establishes a dynamic unilateral relation between Christ as Head and the Church as body. This relation establishes Christ as the power who works in the world to subdue all things and also the cosmic role ascribed to the Church. The Church is to do the work of Christ, to stand against the attacks of the evil powers (Eph. 4:15f.). This it can do only as Christ fills it with His presence and power by the Spirit to do His redemptive work.

As surely as Christ is seen working cosmically in the world, so He works through His body, the Church. He who gave His body for the world now through His body still works redemptively in the world. As Christ's kingdom in the world in the present age must be viewed proleptically as eschatological, so must His "agency" of penetration of the evil age, His body the Church, be viewed as an eschatological entity.

Care must be taken, however, not to confer on the Church an inborn authority or nature that it does not have. The Church is always the body *of* Christ, always conjoined with Christ as *His* body. Its dynamic character as the activity of Christ is always functional, and always as the present ministry of Christ.

Bibliography.–R. Bultmann, *Theology of the NT* (2 vols.; Eng. tr. 1951, 1955), esp. I, §§ 17, 22; R. H. Gundry, *Soma in Biblical Theology* (1976); W. G. Kümmel, *Man in the NT* (Eng. tr. 1963); H. W. Robinson, *The Religious Ideas of the OT* (rev. ed. 1956); J. A. T. Robinson, *The Body: A Study in Pauline Theology* (*SBT*, 5, 1952); *TDNT*, VII, *s.v.* σάρξ κτλ. (Schweizer, Baumgärtel); *TDOT*, II, *s.v.* "bāśār" (Bratsiotis), "gᵉviyyāh" (Fabry).

C. B. BASS

BODY OF DEATH (Rom. 7:24). At the end of his description of man's predicament in relation to sin and the law, Paul writes, "Wretched man that I am! Who will deliver me from this body of death?" (Gk. *tís me rhýsetai* *ek toú sṓmatos toú thanátou toútou*). The expression "body of death" seems to be equivalent to "body of sin" in 6:6. "Body" here is used as Paul elsewhere uses the term "flesh," as the locus of the effect of sin, made known through the law.

The Greek syntax allows "this" to refer either to "body" or to "death," resulting in differing translations. The AV has "the body of this death," the NEB "this body doomed to death," mg. "the body doomed to this death." In spite of disagreement about the placement of "this," it is generally agreed that the expression as a whole denotes humanity as subject to sin, and therefore to death, until redeemed by Christ. E. W. S.

BODY OF HEAVEN. The AV translates the Hebrew expression *'eṣem haššāmayim* as "the body of heaven" (Ex. 24:10). The RSV gives a more correct rendering, "the very heaven," taking *'eṣem* in its idiomatic use as an intensive, which is derived from its literal meaning, "bone," as "strength," "substance," and then as "self" (cf. Job 21:23). The reference is to the substance of the blue, unclouded sky, hence the clear sky itself.

BODY, SPIRITUAL. *See* BODY III.A.

BODYGUARD [Heb. *mišma'aṯ*] (1 S. 22:14; 2 S. 23:23; 1 Ch. 11:25); AV BIDDING (1 S. 22:14), GUARD; NEB STAFF, HOUSEHOLD; [*šōmēr lᵉrō'šî*] (1 S. 28:2); AV "keeper of mine head"; [*ṭabbāḥîm*] (2 K. 25:8; Jer. 52:12); AV GUARD; [Gk. *hoi sōmatophýlakes*] (1 Esd. 3:4); AV GUARD. It appears that soldiers were favored with the position of bodyguard on account of feats of bravery; e.g., David defeats Goliath for Saul (1 S. 17) and the inhabitants of Shur for Achish, King of Gath (1 S. 27:8-12), and Benaiah kills a lion in the snow and an Egyptian (2 S. 23:20f.). The noun *mišma'aṯ* is derived from the root *šāma'*, "hear," and indicates one in a position of obedience. The LXX translates *šōmēr lᵉrō'šî* by the word *archisōmatophýlaka*—the same word used as the title for the chief of the royal bodyguard of the Ptolemies. The term *sōmatophýlax* (<Gk. *sṓma*–"body" + *phýlax*–"watcher, guard") is applied to three young men who guarded the life of the Persian king Darius (1 Esd. 3:4). One of these highly trusted officers was the Jew ZERUBBABEL. (Cf. Josephus *Ant.* xi.3.2.)

See also GUARD. J. T. DENNISON, JR.

BOHAN bō'han [Heb. *bōhan*–'thumb,' 'stumpy']. A son of Reuben according to Josh. 15:6; 18:17. No mention is made in the genealogies of Reuben. "The stone of Bohan" (*'eḇen bōhan*) was a boundary mark on the northeast frontier of Judah, separating it from Benjamin. A site SE of Jericho has been suggested, but is at best uncertain.

BOIL [Heb. *šᵉḥîn*; Gk. *hélkē*; Ugar. *šḥn*–'burn'; Akk. *šaḫānu*–'grow hot'; Egyp. *sḥn*]. *Furunculus,* an inflamed swelling of tissue surrounding a skin follicle, often followed by discharge of pus and necrosis of the core. The Hebrew term appears to have described a variety of swellings, not all of which were staphylococcal.

The boils of the sixth Egyptian plague (Ex. 9:9-11) were associated with blains (Heb. *'ᵃḇa'bu'â,* an inflammation of the skin), and followed an infectious disease that ravaged Egyptian herds and flocks. The symbolic sprinkling of ashes in the air (Ex. 9:10) demonstrated the helplessness of the Egyptian air-deity (Show) in the face of coming events. The modern concept of the atmospheric dissemination of germs and viruses was probably not envisaged. Some have regarded the affliction as elephantiasis, since Pliny (*Nat. hist.* xxvi.5) recorded that the disease was peculiar to Egypt. A less probable suggestion is that of confluent smallpox.

Some writers have seen it in terms of infection by the microscopic *streptococcus pyogenes,* which results in the common furuncle. These conjectures fail to notice that the affliction was visited upon animals as well as human beings. Therefore the most probable diagnosis is not a staphylococcal infection so much as cutaneous anthrax, characterized by small red papules surrounded by white vesicles.

Hezekiah's boil (2 K. 20:7; Isa. 38:21) was more localized, and was probably a furuncle or a carbuncle. The latter is a more extensive inflammation of the skin, usually attended by a lowering of bodily resistance, and it can prove fatal. Ugaritic tablets have shown that the fig poultice prescribed by Isaiah was both popular and effective for such conditions in contemporary therapeutics.

The malady from which Job suffered is difficult to pinpoint. His symptoms included irritating sores which were apparently invaded by larvae (7:5), and a general debility of the nervous system (3:26). The "oriental" or "Baghdad" boil, known in Algeria as "Biskra button," has been the diagnosis of some authorities. The affection, epidemic in parts of North Africa, Asia Minor, and India, consists of a localized infectious papule which enlarges and subsequently breaks down into an ulcer. The sores are irritating, and in multiple proportions on the upper extremities can be very disfiguring. Some form of variola (smallpox) has also been suggested, although the infectious nature of this disease does not accord very well with the conditions described in the book of Job. The boils may have been the result of infection by the pathogenic *Treponema pertenue,* producing framboesia (yaws). This tropical disease is marked by fever, rheumatic pains, and rounded or flattened eruptions of the skin crowned by a cheeselike crust.

Wyclif used the term "boil" (*bylis*) for the sores of Lazarus (Lk. 16:20), although these were more probably old varicose ulcers, such as are found on the legs of the old and poor alike throughout the world.

See also DISEASE III.I, J. A. MACALISTER
R. K. H.

BOLD; BOLDNESS [Heb. *bāṭaḥ, 'āz*; Gk. *parrhēsía, parrhēsiázomai, tharrhéō, tolmáō, tolmētḗs, tolmēróteron, apotolmáō*]; AV also FIERCE, HARDEN, "plainness of speech," PRESUMPTUOUS; NEB also "in repose" (Prov. 28:1), HARSH, OUTSPOKEN, DARING, BRAVE, BRAVERY, CONFIDENCE, COURAGE, RECKLESS. Many of the references are to boldness of speech; indeed the root of Gk. *parrhēsía* and *tharrhéō* implies a flow of words. Such boldness was one of the results of discipleship (Acts 4:13, 29, 31; Eph. 3:12). It was a necessary qualification for the work assigned them. They not only were subject to violent persecutions, but also were the constant subject of ridicule and contempt. In He. 10:19; 1 Jn. 2:28; 4:17, where the RSV has "confidence," *parrhēsía* has the sense of freeness resulting from trust. In Philem. 8, the reference is to the authority Paul claims in this case.

See also CONFIDENCE; COURAGE. J. W. KAPP

BOLLED [Heb. *giḇ'ōl*–'the calyx of flowers'] (Ex. 9:31, AV). The meaning is "in bloom," and it is so rendered in the RV. The RSV and NEB have "in bud."

BOLT [Heb. *man'ûl*]; AV LOCK; [vb. *nā'al*–'tie']. The ancient Hebrews had fastenings of wood or iron for the doors of houses (2 S. 13:17f.; Cant. 5:5), city gates

Libyan, Syrian, and Nubian prisoners with their arms lashed behind them. Gold-covered interior of a state chariot from the tomb of Tutankhamen (1361-1352 B.C.) at Thebes (H. Burton, Metropolitan Museum of Art)

(Neh. 3:3, 6, 13-15), prison doors, etc. (cf. Isa. 45:2), which were in the form of bolts. These were sometimes pushed back from within; but there were others which, by means of a key, could be unfastened and pushed back from without (Jgs. 3:23ff.). These were almost the only form of locks known. *See* BAR; LOCK. M. O. EVANS

BOND [Heb. *'ēsûr, mosēr, māsoreṯ* (all cognates of *'āsar*–'tie, bind'), *'aṣûr, harsubbâ* (Isa. 58:6); Gk. *desmós, sýndesmos, cheirógraphon* (Col. 2:14)]; AV also BAND; NEB also FETTERS, COLLAR, CORDS, TRACES. Used literally and figuratively for a condition of servitude or obligation as well as the instruments of restraint and contract.

In the OT, subjugation is literal in the phrase "bond (Heb. *'aṣûr*; AV "shut up"; NEB "not [under the protection of the family]") or free" (Dt. 32:36; 1 K. 14:10; 21:21; 2 K. 9:8; 14:26; cf. KoB, p. 729). Devices for restraining or confining the body, such as chains or shackles, are used to bind men (Jgs. 15:14; 2 K. 23:33; Ps. 107:14; Jer. 27:2) and animals (Job 39:5).

Figurative uses include bonds of oppression or imprisonment (Ps. 116:16; Isa. 52:2; Jer. 30:8; Nah. 1:13; cf. Ps. 69:33 [MT 34]), affliction (Isa. 28:22), royal authority (Ps. 2:3), and loyalty (Jer. 5:5). Job 12:18 seems to be a reference to symbols of royal office.

In Ezk. 20:37, the "bond of the covenant" (Heb. *māsoreṯ*; NEB "muster") is a contractual agreement. The AV infers a similar undertaking of moral obligation from Heb. *'issār* (Nu. 30:3ff. [MT 4ff.]; RSV "pledge"; NEB "binding obligation").

In the NT, Gk. *desmós* and *sýndesmos* mean, literally, the condition of imprisonment (Philem. 13; cf. Acts 22:5), prisoner's shackles (Lk. 8:29), or the sinews that knit together the body (Col. 2:19).

Figuratively, these terms indicate any hindrance that restricts use of the body or its members, such as infirmity (Lk. 13:16); or a uniting force, such as love (Col. 3:14; cf. 1 Clem. 49:2), peace (Eph. 4:3), or sin (Acts 8:23).

In the imagery of Col. 2:14, *cheirógraphon* (lit. "handwritten [document]") refers to a certificate of indebtedness (cf. Lk. 16:6f.), usually written by the debtor (cf. MM, p. 687; Bauer, p. 889).

See also BAND; BILL; CHAIN; FETTER; IMPRISONMENT; PLEDGE. A. C. M.

BONDAGE [Heb. *'ᵃḇōḏâ, 'ᵃḇāḏîm, 'aḇdûṯ* (Ezr. 9:8f.; Neh. 9:17), hiphil of *'aḇaḏ* (Ex. 6:5); Gk. *douleía* (Rom. 8:21; He. 2:15), *douleúō* (Jn. 8:33; Gal. 4:8), *katadoulóō* (Gal. 2:4)]; AV also BONDMEN, SERVANTS, SERVICE; NEB also SLAVERY, ENSLAVED, SHACKLES; SLAVES, SERVITUDE. This has in Scripture both a literal and a metaphorical sense. The literal bondage of the Hebrews, in Egypt, Babylonia, and Persia, was not so much personal as national. As a rule individuals were not subject to individuals, but the whole Hebrew people were subject to the Egyptian, Babylonian, and Persian states. They were forced to labor on public works, and otherwise, and were denied their own freedom when the exigencies of the state seemed to demand it.

It is used in the metaphorical sense only in the NT. Gk. *douleía* is the power of physical corruption as against the freedom of life (Rom. 8:21), the power of fear as over against the confidence of Christian faith (He. 2:15; cf. Rom. 8:15), and especially the bondage of the letter, of the elements, of a ceremonial and institutional salvation that must be scrupulously and painfully observed, as contrasted with the freedom of the children of God, emancipated by faith in Jesus Christ. This metaphorical usage is particularly characteristic of the apostle Paul, who was an advocate for Christian freedom (Gal. 2:4; cf. 4:3-11, 21-31; 5:1).

See SERVANT, SERVITUDE; SLAVE, SLAVERY.

W. J. MCGLOTHLIN

BONDMAID [Heb. *'āmâ*]. This term occurs only once in the RSV in the phrase "son of your bondmaid" (Ex. 23:12), which the AV renders as "son of thy handmaid" and the NEB as "your home-born slave." Whether the allusion is to a native Hebrew woman or a foreigner is unknown. Elsewhere the RSV renders *'āmâ* by "female slave," "maid," "maidservant." *See* SLAVE.

BONDMAN [Heb. *'eḇeḏ*]; AV also SERVANT; NEB SLAVE. This term occurs in the RSV only once in the singular (Dt. 15:17) and once more in the plural (Ezr. 9:9); elsewhere the RSV usually renders "servant." While the reference is to the Israelites, voluntary servitude was a common feature of ancient Near Eastern life. *See* SERVANT; SLAVE.

BONDSERVANT. *See* SERVANT; SLAVE.

BONE; BONES [Heb. *'eṣem,* pl. *'ōṣem, 'āṣam*–'break bones' (Jer. 50:17), *gerem* (Job 40:18; Prov. 17:22; 25:15); Aram. *g^e ram* (Dnl. 6:24); Gk. *ostéon*]; AV also LIFE (Job 7:15); NEB also BODY, LIMBS, MARROW, STRENGTH, etc. Very often we find these words used in metaphorical phrases, in which a disease or a discomfort of the body denotes certain emotions or mental attitudes. Thus the expression "rottenness of the bones" (Prov. 12:4; 14:30) signifies the feelings of a man whose wife causes him shame and confusion, or is equivalent to "envy," "jealousy." The translation of the LXX in these passages by *skṓlēx,* "worm," and *sḗs,* "maggot," "moth," is incorrect. The same phrase is used in Hab. 3:16 for utter dejectedness in the anticipation of approaching evil. Similarly the "shaking of the bones" (Job 4:14) is expressive of fear, and denotes dejection and sadness in Jer. 23:9. The "burning of the bones" is found as a symptom of Job's disease (Job 30:30), and stands for grief, depression of spirits in Ps. 102:3 and Lam. 1:13, and also for the feeling of Jeremiah when he attempted to hold back the Divine message (Jer. 20:9). "Dryness of bones" (Prov. 17:22) is the opposite of "good health."

Other similar expressions of mental distress are the "racking of the bones" (Job 30:17), the bones are "troubled" (Ps. 6:2), "out of joint" (Ps. 22:14), "waste away" (Ps. 31:10), are "broken" (Ps. 51:8; Lam. 3:4), "having no health" (Ps. 38:3). "Bone of my bones" (Gen. 2:23) can mean having the same nature, and being the nearest relation (2 S. 5:1). In Eph. 5:30 the RSV omits "of his flesh, and of his bones" as an interpolation from Gen. 2:23. The figures in Mic. 3:2f. are expressive of the most cruel oppression and murder. H. L. E. LUERING

BONNETS. *See* CAPS.

BOOK. The AV in Job 31:35, for RSV and NEB "indictment," translating Heb. *sēper.*

BOOK. *See* WRITING.

BOOK OF ABRAHAM. *See* PSEUDEPIGRAPHA V.

BOOK OF JUBILEES. *See* APOCALYPTIC LITERATURE III.B.

BOOK OF LIFE. The ancient practice of keeping various kinds of records has an analogy in the concept of heavenly record books. Although the only OT use of the complete expression "book of the living" (Heb. *sēper ḥayyîm*) is in Ps. 69:28, God's "book" in Ex. 32:32f. is part of the same concept. To be blotted out of this book means an (untimely) end of life. The use of the concept in Ps. 139:16 includes an expression of predestination, and in Isa. 4:3 it refers to those who will live in an ideal future state. The related idea of a record of deeds, found in Ps. 56:8 and perhaps 40:7, is associated with the "book of the living" in 69:28. There is more of a future reference in the similar BOOK OF REMEMBRANCE in Mal. 3:16. A further development is the conception of a book or books upon which the final judgment is to be based, in the apocalyptic writings (Dnl. 7:10; 12:1; Jub. 30:20, 22; 36:10; 39:6; 1 En. 47:3; 108:3; cf. also the BOOK OF TRUTH, apparently God's plan for history, Dnl. 10:21).

All NT uses of "book of life" (Gk. *hē bíblos* [*tó biblíon*] *tḗs zōḗs*), except for the mention of it in Phil. 4:3, are found in Revelation, where it refers to the en-enrollment for eternal life (21:27), sometimes with the implication of predestination (13:8; 17:8), once with an assurance against erasure (3:5, as in Joseph and Asenath 15:4). It is related to, but not the same as, the books of records on which judgment is based (20:12, 15). The expression is also used in Shep. Herm. Vis. 1:3:2; Sim. 2:9; and the concept is referred to in Lk. 10:20; He. 12:23; 1 Clem. 45:8; Shep. Herm. Mand. 8:6; Sim. 9:24:4.

Bibliography.–*APOT,* II, 216; Bousset-Gressmann, *Die Religion des Judentums* (*HNT,* 21, 1966), p. 258; L. Koep, *Das himmlische Buch in Antike und Christentum* (1952).

E. W. S.

BOOK OF MEMORABLE DEEDS (Est. 6:1). *See* MEMORABLE DEEDS, BOOK OF.

BOOK OF REMEMBRANCE [Heb. *sēper zikkārôn*–'book of record']. It occurs only once in the RSV (Mal. 3:16), referring to a list of the righteous. *See also* BOOK OF TRUTH.

BOOK OF TRUTH [Heb. *k^e ṯāḇ '^e meṯ*] (Dnl. 10:21; cf. 12:1, 4); AV SCRIPTURE OF TRUTH. This source, taken by the NEB to be an accredited book (Dnl. 10:21), seems to be closely related to, if not actually identical with, the book first alluded to by Moses (Ex. 32:32f.). The concept was that of a record made by God of the destinies of all human beings (cf. Ps. 40:7; 69:28; 87:6; 139:16). The ostensible purpose of the book was to serve as evidence of the quality of individual life lived against the background of revealed truth. In Mal. 3:16 a similar BOOK OF REMEMBRANCE contained the names of those who feared the Lord and lived by His power. The references in Dnl. 10:21; 12:1, 4 are also to the book of destiny in which God inscribed the future of men. The most developed form of such a record is seen in the NT BOOK OF LIFE. R. K. H.

BOOKS OF ADAM. *See* ADAM, BOOKS OF; PSEUDEPIGRAPHA V.H.

BOOT [Heb. *s^e 'ôn*]; AV BATTLE. The word *s^e 'ôn,* found only in Isa. 9:5 [MT 4], is probably from the Assyr. *šênu,* meaning "shoe," "sandal." Assyrian reliefs from the Sennacherib period depicted soldiers wearing leather boots laced up to the knee, in contrast to the Israelite sandal. *See also* GARMENTS VII. R. K. H.

BOOTH [Heb. *sukkâ, sōḵ* (Lam. 2:6); Gk. *skēnḗ*]; AV also TABERNACLE, PAVILION, COTTAGE, TENT; NEB SHELTER, TABERNACLE, HOUSE, ARBOUR, "under canvas" (2 S. 11:11), "their quarters" (1 K. 20:12, 16). The term *sukkâ* refers to a hut made of wattled twigs or branches. In countries where trees are abundant such wattled structures are common as temporary buildings as they can be constructed in a very short time. Cattle were probably housed in them (Gen. 33:17). Such hurriedly made huts were used by soldiers (2 S. 11:11; 1 K. 20:12) and by harvesters — hence the name feast of "booths" or "tabernacles" (*see* BOOTHS, FEAST OF). Job (27:18) uses booth (parallel to "spider's web" or "moth's house") as a symbol of impermanence. Similar huts were erected in vineyards, etc., to protect them from robbers and beasts of prey. The isolated condition of Jerusalem in the time of the prophet Isaiah is compared to a "booth in a vineyard" (Isa. 1:8). T. LEWIS

BOOTHS, FEAST OF. This festival, known variously as the Feast of Booths, (Lev. 23:34; Dt. 16:13), Tabernacles (2 Ch. 8:13; Jn. 7:2), or Ingathering (Ex. 34:22), was one of the three major feasts in which all Hebrew males were required to participate each year. It began on the fifteenth day of the seventh month (Tishri), i.e., mid-October, five days after the Day of Atonement (Tishri 10). It continued for one week, and was associated with the end of the year (Ex. 34:22) when agricultural work concluded. It was a "pilgrim" festival, the intent of which was to emphasize the nomadic character of the wilderness period (Lev. 23:43).

On the first day the congregation ceased from all normal activities and presented burnt offerings to the Lord, a procedure that was repeated on the eighth day, after the festival proper had terminated. Lev. 23:39-43 describes the ritual procedures that the Israelites were commanded to observe, and that gave the occasion its particular designation. The booths, which were simple shelters made of interlaced branches, were the people's living quarters during the festival. In each seventh year occurred a special ceremony, a public recitation of the covenant provisions agreed to on Mt. Sinai by the Israelites in time of Moses. This served the extremely important function of keeping at the forefront of the people's minds the obligations assumed on that occasion, as well as reminding them of the blessings that would follow as long as the provisions of the covenant were honored.

The feast was celebrated against a background of rejoicing for divine blessings, represented by the bounty of the year's harvest. This was reflected in its occasional designation as the "Feast of Ingathering" (Ex. 23:16; 34:22). The feast seems to have lapsed during the monarchy, so that the observance which occurred in Jerusalem during the time of Ezra was of particular significance. On that occasion a celebration of a character unknown since the time of Joshua took place (Neh. 8:13-18). The popularity of the feast was maintained throughout the postexilic period, and it became the occasion on which Jews from the eastern Diaspora visited Jerusalem for worship and celebration. In at least one instance Christ Himself was in the city when the festival was being observed (Jn. 7:2). By NT times it had become a custom on that feast for a procession to visit the Pool of Siloam and return with water, which was then poured out as a libation of thanksgiving to God. It may well have been as a result of witnessing this ceremony that Jesus was prompted to make His observations about living water and eternal life (Jn. 7:37-39).

See also FEASTS. R. K. HARRISON

BOOTY [Heb. *bāz* or *baz, malgô(a)ḥ, pereq* (Nah. 3:1), *m^{e}śissâ* (Hab. 2:7)]; AV also SPOIL, PREY, ROBBERY (*pereq*); NEB also PLUNDER, "all that has been captured," PREY (*pereq*), VICTIM (*m^{e}śissâ*); [*bāzaz, šālāl*]; AV "take spoil," "take for prey," etc.; NEB "carry off," PLUNDER, "kept for themselves," etc. Booty refers to anything that might be of personal service to the captor, including persons. *See also* SPOIL.

BOOZ (Mt. 1:5; Lk. 3:32, AV). *See* BOAZ.

BORASHAN bôr-ash'ən [Heb. *bôr-'āšān*]. A correction of the MT in the RSV and NEB in 1 S. 30:30 for AV "Chor-ashan." Probably the same as ASHAN (Josh. 15:42; 1 Ch. 4:32; 6:59).

BORDER [Heb. *qāṣeh*] (Ex. 16:35; 19:12; Josh. 4:19; Ezk. 48:1); AV also COAST; NEB also EDGE, DISTRICT, "extreme (north)"; [*qāṣû*] (Isa. 26:15); AV ENDS; NEB FRONTIERS; [*pē'â*] (Lev. 19:9; 23:22); AV CORNERS; NEB EDGES; [*śāpâ*] (Jgs. 7:22); NEB RIDGE; [*g^{e}ḇûl*] (Ex. 34:24; Nu. 20:23; 21:15; Dt. 3:14; 19:8; Josh. 13:23; 18:16, 19; Jgs. 1:36; 1 S. 6:12; 13:18; 27:1; 1 K. 4:21; etc.; NEB also FRONTIER, BOUNDARY, EDGE, TERRITORY, SIDE, PLOUGHLANDS, REALM (Ps. 147:14; Mal. 1:5), DISTRICTS, ANYWHERE (1 S. 27:1); [*gāḇal*] (Zec. 9:2); NEB FRONTIER; [*yāḏ*] (1 Ch. 7:29); NEB POSSESSION; [*yāṣā'*] (Josh. 17:18); AV "outgoings of it"; NEB "furthest limits"; [*y^{e}rēḵâ*] (Gen. 49:13); NEB FRONTIER; [*'al-hammiḏbār*] (Gen. 14:6); AV "by the wilderness"; NEB "edge of the wilderness"; [*'aḏ-l^{e}ḇô'* (2 Ch. 26:8); AV "entering of (Egypt)." These are geogaphical terms indicating outer territorial limits, that which separates one geographical region from another.

The borders of the Promised Land were described as being: "the Great Sea" (Mediterranean) on the west (cf. Nu. 34:6; Ezk. 47:20); a line from Aphek through the "entrance to Hamath" (=Lebo-Hamath; cf. Aharoni, pp. 65f.) to Zedad on the north (cf. Nu. 34:7-9; Ezk. 47:15-17; 48:1); the Jordan River and the Dead Sea ("east sea") on the east (cf. Nu. 34:10-12; Ezk. 47:18); a line from the southern tip of the Dead Sea through Tamar along the edge of the Wilderness of Zin to the Brook of Egypt on the south (cf. Nu. 34:3-6; Ezk. 47:19; 48:28; and Josh. 15:1-4, which describes the southern border of the tribe of Judah). Borders of the twelve tribes are found in Josh. 13–19.

Heb. *pē'â* (Ugar. *p't*; Akk. *pātu*) refers to the edge of a grain field intended for the relief of the poor and the sojourner (cf. Dt. 24:19-22; Ruth 2:15f.). *Śāpâ* (lit. "lip") can refer to (1) the edge of a valley (cf. Dt. 2:36; 4:48; Josh. 12:2; 13:9, 16), or (2) the lip of a wadi or stream (Ezk. 47:6f.). But in Jgs. 7:22, where it occurs in combination with a place name (Abel-meholah=Tell Abu Ṣûṣ [?]), it appears to be equivalent to another combination, *q^{e}ṣēh* plus a place name (cf. Josh. 18:15; 1 S. 14:2), which in turn refers to the borders of a city's territory (see *GTTOT*, p. 293).

G^{e}ḇûl (Ugar. *gbl*), in combination with the preposition *'al* (Nu. 20:23), is equivalent to *'el-g^{e}ḇûl* ("bordering on"); thus, Mt. Hor borders the west side of Edom (cf. *bîqṣēh,* Nu. 33:37). Dahood suggests reading "mountain" instead of "border" at 1 S. 13:18. Meek suggests "bottomland" at Dt. 3:17; Josh. 13:23, 27, since *g^{e}ḇûl* in these cases indicates the area bordering the Jordan River. The LXX reads "border of the Edomites" in Jgs. 1:36 (cf. Josh. 15:1ff.).

The "enlarging of the borders" of Israel was part of the patriarchal promise (Gen. 15:18; cf. Ex. 34:24; Dt. 12:20; 19:8) fulfilled in the reign of David and Solomon (1 K. 4:21). Under Jeroboam II (793-753 B.C.) the border of Israel once again reached Lebo-Hamath (2 K. 14:25). Concomitantly, Uzziah (791-739 B.C.) extended the border of Judah once again to Egypt (2 Ch. 26:8). A period of

Boundary stone (*kudurru*) of Nebuchadrezzar I, from Nippur (12th cent. B.C.). Such stones publicized royal grants, and the emblems of deities and inscribed curses and blessings discouraged their removal. (University Museum, University of Pennsylvania)

internal chaos in the Assyrian empire permitted this expansion; even Ammon gave tribute to Judah. On previous occasions, Ammon had manifested a penchant for "enlarging her borders" (cf. Jgs. 10:7f.; 11:4f.; 1 S. 11:1-11; 14:47f.); the opportunism mentioned by Am. 1:13-15 probably occurred during Hazael's campaign against Israel (*ca.* 825-815 B.C.) in the days of Jehu (841-814 B.C.); cf. 2 K. 10:32.

El-paran (Gen. 14:6) is apparently an old name for Elath, on the edge of the desert of Paran.

The border of Zebulun (Gen. 49:13; cf. Dt. 33:19; Josh. 19:10-16) did not actually reach the Mediterranean, though commerce may have flowed through the territory from coastal ports (cf. Isa. 9:1). The prepositions (*l*^{e}*ḥôp . . .'al*) may mean "toward"; thus, "toward the seashore" and "his border toward Sidon" (Gen. 49:13).

Bibliography.–*GTTOT*; *LBHG*; M. Dahood, *Bibl.*, 45 (1964), 396; T. J. Meek, *JQR*, 50 (1959), 45-54. J. T. DENNISON, JR.

BORE [Heb. *rāṣa'*–'pierce']. According to the Book of the Covenant (Ex. 20:20–23:33) a slave whom his master had purchased was to be released after six years. Should he choose to remain in his master's service a religious ceremony was necessary to ratify his decision (Ex. 21:6). Ancient Near Eastern slaves, including some HABIRU, were usually marked or branded in some way for purposes of identification. In Dt. 15:17 the ceremony followed voluntary and permanent identification of the slave with a particular household.

BORITH bôr'ith [Lat. *Borith*]. Mentioned in the genealogical table which traces the descent of Esdras (Ezra) from Aaron (2 Esd. 1:2). His name appears as BUKKI in 1 Esd. 8:2 (AV "Boccas"; NEB "Bocca"); 1 Ch. 6:5, 51; Ezr. 7:4.

BORN. *See* BEAR.

BORN AGAIN. *See* ANEW; REGENERATION.

BORNE. *See* BEAR.

BORROW. *See* LEND; LOAN.

BOSCATH bos'kath (2 K. 22:1, AV). *See* BOZKATH.

BOSOM [Heb. *ḥêq*]; AV also ARMS (Isa. 49:22); NEB also "the fold of your cloak," LAP (Ruth 4:16), ARMS, HEART, etc.; [*ḥōḇ*] (Job 31:33); NEB "to myself"; [*ḥēṣen*] (Ps. 129:7); NEB "armful"; [*daḏ*] (Ezk. 23:3, 8, 21); AV BREASTS, TEATS; [*šālôm*] (Ps. 41:9); AV FAMILIAR; [Gk. *kólpos*] (Lk. 16:22f.; Jn. 1:18); NEB "close beside," etc. The Heb. *ḥêq* often denotes the lap, or the part of the body where one clasps those one loves (e.g., Nu. 11:12; Ruth 4:16; 1 K. 1:2; 3:20; 17:19; Isa. 40:11); sometimes a fold in the garment above the belt, which could be used for hiding things (e.g., Ex. 4:6f.; Ps. 74:11; Prov. 17:23). The term *ḥōḇ* refers to a pocket in the bedouin's garment, *daḏ* to a woman's breasts.

Used in a figurative sense, the term "bosom" refers to closest intimacy (e.g., Dt. 13:6; Jn. 1:18) or tender care (Isa. 40:11).

See also ABRAHAM'S BOSOM. N. J. O.

BOSOM, ABRAHAM'S. *See* ABRAHAM'S BOSOM.

BOSOR bō'sôr [Gk. *Bosor*].

1. NEB BEZER. A city taken by Judas Maccabeus "in the land of Gilead" (1 Macc. 5:26, 36), identified with Buṣr el-Ḥarîri, on the southern edge of el-Lejā.

See *WHAB*, plate VIII; *GTTOT*, map V.

2. (2 Pet. 2:15, AV). *See* BEOR **2.**

BOSORA bos'ər-ə (1 Macc. 5:26, 28, AV). *See* BOZRAH **3.**

BOSS [Heb. *gaḇ*]. The word is used only once, in Job 15:26, in reference to the protuberant knob of a shield.

BOSTRA. *See* BOZRAH **3.**

BOTANY. *See* FLORA.

BOTCH (Dt. 28:27, 35, AV). Archaic term for BOIL.

BOTTLE [Heb. *nō'ḏ*] (Ps. 33:7; 56:8); AV also HEAP; NEB GOATSKIN, FLASK. The RSV and NEB readings at Ps. 33:7 are based on the reading *nōḏ* for MT *nēḏ* (cf. Gk. *askós*, "wineskin," and other ancient versions). Except for Ps. 56:8, the RSV elsewhere translates *nō'ḏ* as "skin" or "wineskin," though the AV has "bottle" (e.g., Josh. 9:4, 13; Jgs. 4:19; Ps. 119:83). "Bottle" is used in the

AV also for Heb. *'ôb, baqbûq, ḥēmâ* (Hos. 7:5; RSV "heat"), *ḥēmeṯ, nēḇel*; Gk. *askós*. *See* FLASK; JAR; WINESKIN. Ancient bottles were almost invariably made of animal skins, tanned or untanned (kid, goat, cow, camel, buffalo), since they were more easily carried about than earthenware vessels. J. W. D. H.

BOTTOM. The AV translates as "bottom" the Heb. *m^eṣullâ* in Zec. 1:8: "the myrtle trees that were in the bottom." The term denotes "depths" or "shadowy place." Thus, it probably refers to a valley of some sort, and the RSV's "glen" or the NEB's "hollow" would be a preferable translation.

The AV also translates as "bottom" the Heb. *qeṣeḇ* in Jonah 2:6 (MT 7); "I went down to the bottoms of the mountains." The Hebrew term connotes a "cutting off" or "extremity." The RSV renders the phrase "roots of the mountains" and the NEB "troughs of the mountains."

N. J. O.

BOTTOMLESS PIT. *See* ABYSS.

BOUGAEAN bo͞o-gē'ən [Gk. *Bougaíos*] (Ad. Est. 12:6); AV AGAGITE; NEB BUGAEAN. The LXX used this designation for Haman in Est. 3:1; 9:10, where the MT has Heb. *'^agāgî* ("Agagite"). Elsewhere the LXX omits, or has "Macedonian" (9:24).

BOUGH. *See* BRANCH.

BOUGHT (1 S. 25:29, AV mg.); also BOW. *See* HOLLOW.

BOUND. *See* BIND.

BOUNDARY. *See* TERRITORY.

BOUNDS [*g^eḇûl, g^eḇûlâ, ḥōq, q^eṣāṯ, ḥēl*]; AV also BORDER, WALL (*ḥēl*), DECREE, etc.; NEB also BARRIER, FRONTIERS, BOUNDARIES, BORDER, ORDINANCE, etc.; [*gāḇal* ("set bounds," Ex. 19:12), *'āḇar* ("know no bounds," Jer. 5:28), *pāras* ("break all bounds," Hos. 4:2)]; AV also "overpass" (*'āḇar*), "break out" (*pāraṣ*); NEB "put barriers," etc. Whereas *gāḇal* means "enclose" and *g^eḇûl* denotes a boundary, *ḥōq* has reference to a law, order, or regulation.

BOUNTIFUL EYE [Heb. *ṭôḇ-'ayin*] (Prov. 22:9); NEB KINDLY. The expression here refers to generosity; cf. the LXX rendering, Gk. *ho eleṓn ptōchón*, "he who shows a beggar mercy (or pity)."

BOUNTIFULLY [Heb. *gāmal*; Gk. *eulogía*] (Ps. 13:6; 116:7; 119:17; 142:7; 2 Cor. 9:6); NEB OT variously (see below). The Heb. *gāmal* is translated "deal bountifully" by the AV and RSV in the four passages in the Psalms. In other passages it is translated "reward," "recompense," "do (good or evil to)," etc.; it has the generalized meaning "deal" with someone, often "pay" or "pay back"; and the precise meaning must be gathered from the context.

The NEB renders the passages as follows: Ps. 13:6, "has granted all my desire"; 116:7, "has showered gifts upon you"; 119:17, "Grant this to me"; 142:7, "thou givest me my due reward."

For *eulogía* in 2 Cor. 9:6, cf. Bauer, p. 323.

J. W. D. H.

BOUNTIFULNESS (2 Cor. 9:11, AV). *See* GENEROSITY.

BOUNTY. In Gen. 49:26 the RSV has "bounties," the NEB "bounty," for Heb. *ta'^awâ*, which the AV renders "utmost bound." Philologically either meaning is possible, though most commentators today take it in the sense "desirable things" (cf. Gen. 3:6; Prov. 10:24; etc.; and see KoB, p. 1016; BDB, pp. 16, 1063).

Other words translated "bounty" in the RSV are Heb. *yāḏ*, "hand" (1 K. 10:13; Est. 1:7, AV "state," cf. NEB "as befitted a king"), *ṭôḇ* (Ps. 65:11; AV "goodness," NEB "good gifts"), *tagmûl* (Ps. 116:12; AV "benefits," NEB "gifts").

In addition, the AV and NEB have "bounty" for Gk. *eulogía* in 2 Cor. 9:5, where the RSV has "gift," referring to the offering of the Christians of Judea.

J. W. D. H.

BOW [Heb. *qešeṯ*; Gk. *tóxon*]. *See* ARCHER.

BOW; BOWING. *See* ADORATION II; POSTURES.

BOW IN THE CLOUD. *See* RAINBOW.

BOWED TOGETHER (Lk. 13:11, AV). *See* BENT OVER.

BOWELS [Heb. *mē'îm*; Gk. *splánchna*]; NEB also BODY, ENTRAILS. In the RSV the term literally means "intestines," but in the AV it refers more generally to various other organs, such as the heart or the womb. Used psychosomatically the term "bowels" symbolized powerful emotional forces, as in the AV Col. 3:12 "bowels of mercy" (RSV "compassion") or the AV Cant. 5:4 (RSV "heart"). In the RSV "bowels" occurs only once in the NT, in reference to the death of Judas (Acts 1:18).

BOWL [Heb. *sēpel*] (Jgs. 5:25; 6:38); AV also "lordly dish"; [*ṣ^elōḥîṯ*] (2 K. 2:20); AV NEW CRUSE; [*gullâ*] (Eccl. 12:6; Zec. 4:2f.; 1 K. 7:41f.; 2 Ch. 4:12f.); AV also POMMELS; NEB also "bowl-shaped capitals"; [*'aggān*] (Cant. 7:2); AV, NEB, ROUND GOBLET; [*kôs*] (Isa. 51:17, 22); AV CUP; [*mizrāq*] (Zec. 9:15; 14:20; 2 K. 25:15; Am. 6:6); NEB also TOSSING-BOWLS, BOWLFUL; [*miš'ereṯ*] (Ex. 8:3; 12:34); AV "kneading troughs"; [*m^enaqqîṯ*] (Ex. 25:29; 37:16; Nu. 4:7; Jer. 52:19); AV also CUPS; NEB also FLAGONS; [*sap*] (2 K. 12:13; Jer. 52:19); AV BASONS; NEB TOSSING-BOWLS, CUPS; [*k^epôr*]; AV GOLDEN BASONS (1 Ch. 28:17), SILVER (BASONS) (1 Ch. 28:17; Ezr. 1:10), BASONS (Ezr. 1:10; 8:27); NEB also GOLDEN DISHES (1 Ch. 28:17), SILVER DISHES (28:17); [Gk. *skeúos*] (Jn. 19:29); AV VESSEL; NEB JAR; [*phiálē*] (Rev. 5:8; 15:7; 16:1ff.; 17:1; 21:9); AV VIAL.

The RSV uses "bowl" for various types of containers made from wood, metal, or ceramics. J. L. Kelso has identified the various Hebrew terms in his monograph, *The Ceramic Vocabulary of the OT, BASOR* (1948), Supplementary Studies, nos. 5f.

The *sēpel* of Jgs. 5:25 (actually *sēpel 'addîrîm*) and 6:38 may be a species of large banquet bowl, although the cognate *spl* (Ugaritic; cf. Akk. *saplu*) of the Râs Shamrah tablets indicates a vase (cf. *Syria*, 28 [1951], 30f. l.17). The "lordly dish" of 5:25 may not be a bowl at all; Kaplan (*PEQ*, 97 [1965], 144-152), following Tur-Sinai, believes *'addîrîm* may also mean *rō'îm* (herdsmen). Thus, "lordly dish" becomes "herdsmen's container" and actually signifies a skin-bottle used for storing milk.

The *ṣ^elōḥîṯ* is a small bowl for salt; Kelso argues that it is not a flask because salt (a deliquescent) would cake in such a container.

The *gullôṯ* (Akk. *gullatu* or *gullu*; Sum. *gal*; Ugar. *gl*) of Solomon's temple were bowl-like or bowl-shaped capitals on the pillars Jachin and Boaz. A similar construc-

A bowl decorated in "chocolate-on-white" style from the Late Bronze I Canaanite temple (Stratum III) at Tell Kittan in the Jordan Valley (Israel Department of Antiquities and Museums)

tion is found in an incense stand from Megiddo (Early Iron Age) where the bowl forms the cresset (*BASOR*, 88 [Dec. 1942], 23ff.; cf. 85 [Feb. 1942], 25). The bowls on the lampstands (Zec. 4:2f.) contained oil for light. In Eccl. 12:6, the *gullâ* may be a lamp-like structure (silver chain and golden bowl signifying a hanging lamp) or a cup (cf. *VT*, 19 [1969], 158-160).

The *'aggān* (Assyr. *agan(n)u)* was probably a large bowl used for mixing water with wine. Other drinking vessels are *kôs* and *sap* (wine cup?).

The "tossing-bowl" (*mizrāq*) was used to splash the blood of the sacrifices against the altar (cf. Ex. 27:3; 29:16). It was also used for meal or cereal offerings (Nu. 7:13ff.). Other containers used for sacrifices were the *m^{e}naqqîṯ* (for drink offerings) and the *k^{e}pôr*.

Flour for bread was mixed in the *miš'ereṯ*. The Gk. *skeúos* at the foot of the cross was a drinking vessel. The *phiálē* was a common household bowl.

See also Plate 11. J. T. DENNISON, JR.

BOWMAN [Heb. *dōrḵê qešeṯ*–'bending the bow'] (1 Ch. 8:40); AV, NEB, ARCHERS; [*nōšqê qešeṯ*–'armed with bows'] (12:2); AV "armed with bows"; NEB "(they) carried bows." *See* ARCHER.

BOWSHOT [Heb. *m^{e}ṭaḥ^{a}wê qešeṯ*–'as far as an archer shoots']. Found only in Gen. 21:16 in the account of Hagar and her child: "Then she went, and sat down over against him a good way off, about the distance of a bowshot." This was a typical oriental way of indicating distance.

BOWSTRINGS, FRESH [Heb. *y^{e}ṯārîm laḥîm*] (Jgs. 16:7-9); AV GREEN WITHS. The Heb. *yeṯer,* used elsewhere for bowstring (e.g., Ps. 11:2) and perhaps tent cord (Job 4:21), used here with *laḥ* ("moist") apparently refers to the sinews of slaughtered cattle, which would contract in drying.

BOX. *See* ALABASTER JAR; FLASK.

BOX [Gk. *pykteúō*] (1 Cor. 9:26). *See* GAMES I.B.

BOX-TREE; BOXWOOD. *See* PINE TREE. For AV "box trees" in 2 Esd. 14:24, *see* WRITING TABLETS.

BOY [Heb. *yeleḏ*–'child,' *na'ar*–'lad,' 'youth'; Gk. *ho país*]; AV also CHILD, YOUNG (2 Ch. 34:3); NEB also YOUNG (1 S. 2:26), CHILD. The term "boy" refers to a child of any age (see, e.g., Joel 3:3; Mt. 17:18; Lk. 2:43; 9:42). In the East the word applies also to an adult who is a servant.

The boy occupied a place of special importance in the family life of all ancient peoples. As is true among all oriental peoples, the father had absolute control in the Jewish household, yet the boy received a consideration and advantages not accorded to the daughter. His religious life began at the fourth year. He was expected to learn the Scriptures at five, the Mishnah at ten, and to fulfil the whole law at thirteen. At twelve years he was expected to learn a trade, and attained to something of independence at that age, though he did not come into full rights as a citizen until he was twenty. Among many nations there was special rejoicing at the birth of the boy, and sometimes a feast. *See* CHILD; FAMILY; SON.

J. W. KAPP

BOZEZ bō'zez [Heb. *bôṣēṣ*; Gk. *Bazes*]. The northern of two cliffs that stand on each side of the gorge of Michmash (1 S. 14:4), on the Wâdī eṣ-Ṣuweinît. The name of the other cliff was Seneh. W. S. L. S.

BOZKATH boz'kath [Heb. *boṣqaṯ*–'stony'; according to the LXX the *qop* is not certain and either a *daleṯ* or a *reš* was read, hence Gk. *Basēdōth, Basourōth*]; AV also BOSCATH (2 K. 22:1). A village in the Shephelah between Lachish and Eglon (Josh. 15:39), the birthplace of Adaiah the mother of King Josiah (2 K. 22:1). Abel (*GP*) suggests the site Dawā'imeh. W. S. L. S.

BOZRAH boz'rə [Heb. *boṣrâ*–'sheepfold'; Gk. *Bosorra, Bosor*].

1. An oasis city of great antiquity, the capital and northern metropolis of Edom, through which ran the principal highways (Gen. 36:33; 1 Ch. 1:44; Isa. 34:6; 63:1; Jer. 49:13; Am. 1:12; [Mic. 2:12?]). It was noted for its weaving industry and its export of dyed garments. It may be modern Buṣeirah, 30 mi. (48 km.) SE of the Dead Sea.

2. A city in Moab mentioned in Jer. 48:24. It is probably identical with Bezer (*GAB*) the Levitical city of refuge, 15 mi. (24 km.) E of the point where the Jordan enters the Dead Sea. It cannot be identified with any certainty.

D. B. PECOTA

3. [Gk. *Bosorra*]; AV BOSORA. A city in Gilead captured by Judas Maccabeus (1 Macc. 5:26, 28). Probably identical with modern Buṣra-Eski Shâm, the Buṣruna of the Amarna Letters, and Roman Bostra, it was an important caravan center 67 mi. (108 km.) S of Damascus and 22 mi. (35 km.) E of Der'a (Edrei) on the southeast border of the Hauran at the foot of Jebel ed-Druz.

A Nabatean city in Herodian times, Bostra fell to the Romans in A.D. 105 and became capital of the province of Arabia. Alexander Severus declared it a colony, and Philip the Arab (Roman emperor, A.D. 244-249), a native of Bostra, made it a metropolis. Origen presided there at a council disciplining Beryllius the Monarchian. It became a bishop's see in the 4th century.

Muhammud visited Bostra and probably gained there much of his knowledge about Christianity. Bostra fell to the Arabs in 636. In the 12th cent. Crusaders captured and then lost it. An earthquake contributed to its decline. Extensive ruins include a fortress of Crusader times built around an ancient theater, temples, churches, and aqueducts. The Roman Catholic archdiocese is still called Bosra and Hauran.

See A. Alt, *ZDPV*, 68 (1951), 235-245. F. WEDDLE

BRACELET [Heb. *ṣāmîḏ*] (Gen. 24:22, 30, 47; Nu. 31:50; Ezk. 16:11; 23:42); [*šērôṯ*] (Isa. 3:19); NEB BANGLES. The "bracelets" referred to in these OT passages were decorative articles, usually gold, of female dress. Heb. *ṣāmîḏ* signifies jewelry worn on the lower arm or wrist; in Gen. 24 it is part of the bridal offering presented to Rebekah. *Šērôṯ* is similar to the Akkadian cognate *šemêru, šewêru*, which also means "bracelet"; whether it signifies jewelry for the arm or the neck (cf. Isa. 3:16) is not clear. J. T. DENNISON, JR.

Bracelet of gold and lapis lazuli made by Pharaoh Shishak (*ca.* 940 B.C.) for his son Nemareth. It portrays the infant god Harpocrates emerging from a lotus. (Trustees of the British Museum)

BRAIDED; BRAIDING [Gk. *plégma*] (1 Tim. 2:9); AV BROIDED; NEB "elaborate hair-styles"; [*emplokḗ*] (1 Pet. 3:3); AV PLAITING. These references to hairstyles of Christian women are in two passages where the apostles emphasize the superiority of good works and spiritual grace over outward adornment.

BRAMBLE. *See* THORN; FLORA.

BRANCH; BOUGH [Heb. *'ānāp* (Ezk. 17:8; Dnl. 4; Mal. 4:1; etc.), vb. *'ānēp* (Ezk. 19:10), *z^{e}môrâ* (Nu. 13:23; Ezk. 8:17; etc.), *pō'râ* (Ezk. 31), *pu'râ* (Isa. 10:33), *daliyyâ* (Jer. 11:16; Ezk. 17:6; etc.), *ṣemaḥ* (Isa. 4:2; Jer. 23:5; Zec. 3:8; etc.), *kippâ* (Job 15:32; Isa. 9:14; etc.), *kap* (Lev. 23:40), *qāṣîr* (Job 18:16, etc.), *nēṣer* (Isa. 11:1; Dnl. 11:7), *baḏ* (Ezk. 17:6; 19:14), *śārîgîm* (Gen. 40:10, 12; Joel 1:7), *ś^{e}rûqqîm* (Isa. 16:8), *s^{e}'appâ* (Ezk. 31:6, 8), *sar'appa* (Ezk. 31:5), *sa'îp* (Isa. 27:10), *n^{e}ṭîšôṯ* (Isa. 18:5; Jer. 5:10), *qāneh* (Ex. 25:31ff.; 37:17ff.), *amîr* (Isa. 17:6), *baṯ, bēn* (Gen. 49:22), *y^{e}'ôr* (Isa. 19:6), *yôneqeṯ* (Ps. 80:11), *salsillâ* (Jer. 6:9), *sansinnîm* (Cant. 7:8), *'aḇōṯ* (Ps. 118:27), *'āleh* (Neh. 8:15), *'^{o}pā'îm* (Ps. 104:12), vb. *pā'ar* (Dt. 24:20), *p^{e}rî* (Ezk. 17:9), *śôḇeḵ* (2 S. 18:9), *šibbōleṯ* (Zec. 4:12); Gk. *kládos* (Mt. 13:32; Mk. 4:32; Lk. 13:9; Rom. 11:16ff.; etc.), *klḗma* (Jn. 15:2, 4-6), *baíon* (Jn. 12:13), *stibás* (Mk. 11:8), *phoínix* (Rev. 7:9)]; AV also "principal plants" (Isa. 16:8), "battlements" (Jer. 5:10), "plants" (Jer. 48:32), "brooks" (Isa. 19:6), "baskets" (Jer. 6:9), "cords" (Ps. 118:27), "fruit" (Ezk. 17:9), "palms" (Rev. 7:9); NEB also "new growth" (Job 14:9), "red grapes" (Isa. 16:8), "streams" (Isa. 19:6), "fronds" (Cant. 7:8), "pilgrims" (Ps. 118:27), "fruit" (Ezk. 17:9), "palms" (Rev. 7:9). Most of the references are to literal branches of various kinds, but many figurative uses are included: e.g., Heb. *qāneh* in Ex. 25 and 37 refers to the "branches" of the golden candlesticks; *y^{e}'ôr* in Isa. 19:6 is a river branch; *ṣemaḥ* is the "branch" of messianic prophecy.

Vine branches are designated by Heb. *z^{e}môrâ* (Nu. 13:23; Ezk. 8:17; 15:2; Nah. 2:2). The references in Ezk. 8:17; Isa. 17:10 are apparently to some idolatrous practice. Other words for vine branches include Heb. *śārîgîm, n^{e}ṭîšôṯ*, and Gk. *klḗma,* a vine cutting ready for grafting. In Jer. 5:10, Heb. *n^{e}ṭîšôṯ* is translated "battlements" in the AV, perhaps owing to the obscurity of the form *šārôṯe(y)hâ* which precedes. Emended to *šurôṯe(y)hâ,* it becomes a form of either *šûrâ* ("vine-rows," RSV) or *šûr* ("wall") (see BDB, p. 1004). The AV, choosing the latter, which gives the figure of a city rather than a vineyard, perhaps conjectures "battlements" for *n^{e}ṭîšôṯ* in terms of the context (although it renders "branches" and "plants" in the other two uses of this term, Isa. 18:5 and Jer. 48:32).

The Heb. *kap* and *kippâ* indicate palm branches, as do Gk. *baíon* and *phoínix*.

Plant sprouts or shoots are intended by Heb. *yôneqeṯ* (Job 14:7, and figuratively in Ps. 80:11; Ezk. 17:22, AV; Job 8:16; etc.), *ṣemaḥ, nēṣer* (Dnl. 11:7; Isa. 11:1; 14:19; 60:21); Gk. *kládos*. Twigs are perhaps meant by Heb. *zāmîr, sā'îp, šibbōleṯ, n^{e}ṭîšôṯ, '^{o}pā'îm*; Gk. *stibás*.

Most of the other references are to ordinary branches, of the olive (e.g., Jer. 11:16) and other trees.

R. K. H. J. W. D. H.

BRAND [Heb. *'ûḏ*]; AV also FIREBRAND; [*zîqôṯ*]; AV SPARKS; NEB FIRE-BRANDS. The term *'ûḏ* is used in Am. 4:11 and Zec. 3:2 to signify a stick or small log on fire. Heb. *zîqôṯ* in Isa. 50:11 refers to flaming arrows. *See also* TORCH.

BRASEN. *See* BRASS.

BRASEN SEA [Heb. *yām hann^{a}ḥōšeṯ*]. *See* SEA, MOLTEN.

BRASEN SERPENT. *See* NEHUSHTAN.

BRASS; BRASEN [Heb. *n^{e}ḥōšeṯ*]. The term *n^{e}ḥōšeṯ* is translated "brass" by the RSV only where it describes tensile strength or symbolizes spiritual obduracy (Lev. 26:19; Dt. 28:23; Isa. 48:4); elsewhere, where the AV renders "brass" the RSV generally renders "bronze." *See* BRONZE.

BRAWLER [Heb. *hāmâ*]; AV RAGING; NEB "makes an uproar." The term is used once in the RSV: "Wine is a mocker, strong drink a brawler" (Prov. 20:1). The Hebrew verb literally means to make a noise or uproar.

BRAY [Heb. *nāhaq*]; NEB also HOWL (Job 30:7). The strident cry of a donkey is referred to in Job 6:5, and the term is used figuratively in 30:7 of those who mocked the afflicted patriarch.

BRAZEN. In Ezk. 16:30 the RSV renders as "brazen" (AV, NEB, "imperious") the Heb. *šalleṭeṯ* in the phrase, "the deeds of a brazen harlot."

BRAZIER [Heb. *'āḥ*] (Jer. 36:22f.); AV HEARTH. A fire-pot or firepan, probably portable, used for heating a room in cold weather.

BREACH [Heb. *pāraṣ* (Mic. 2:13), *pereṣ* (Gen. 38:29; Jgs. 21:15; 1 K. 11:27; Neh. 6:1; Job 16:14; 30:14; Ps. 106:23; Isa. 58:12; Ezk. 22:30), *peša'* ("breach of trust," Ex. 22:9), *bāqa'* (2 K. 25:4; Jer. 39:2; 52:7)]; AV also BREAKER (Mic. 2:13), GAP (Ezk. 22:30), TRESPASS (Ex. 22:9), "breaking in" (Job. 30:14), "be broken up" (2 K. 25:4; Jer. 39:2; 52:7); NEB also LAW-BREAKING (Ex. 22:9), LEADER (Mic. 2:13), GAP (Jgs. 21:15), "broken wall" (Isa. 58:12), "be thrown open" (2 K. 25:4; Jer. 39:2; 52:7), etc.

The verbal form of the root *prṣ* (*pāraṣ*), meaning to "break through," is only once rendered "breach" by the RSV. The noun form, *pereṣ,* literally means a "bursting through" or a "gap." Apart from *peša',* "breach of trust," and *ma'al* (*see* BREACH OF FAITH), *pereṣ* is the only noun translated as "breach" by the RSV.

Gen. 38:29 has an etiology of the name Perez (i.e., *Pereṣ,* one of the sons of Judah and Tamar). Because he had pushed his way out of the womb ahead of his brother, he was called Perez ("a bursting through").

Pereṣ can also refer to a literal gap or hole in a wall structure (1 K. 11:27; Neh. 6:1; Job 30:14). "Repairing the breach" in Isa. 58:12 probably means both a literal repairing of broken walls and a figurative repairing of the broken relationship between Yahweh and His people.

In Ezk. 22:30 the phrase "stand in the breach" indicates that Yahweh looked for one worthy man to stand in the righteousness-gap between a sinful people and Himself. If this righteous one could have been found, the disaster of the Exile could have been avoided. Related to this passage in thought is Ps. 106:23: Moses is that one who stands "in the breach," or righteousness-gap, between God and people.

The noun *pereṣ* can also be used as a figurative description of the "breaking forth" of God's wrath upon man (Job 16:14; Jgs. 21:15).

The verb *bāqa',* used in the niphal and the hophal with the meaning "be burst in upon," describes the condition of Jerusalem at the time of her fall (Jer. 52:7 uses 2 K. 25:4; cf. Jer. 39:2). T. R. ASHLEY

BREACH OF COVENANT. *See* CRIME.

BREACH OF FAITH [Heb. *ma'al, mā'al*] (Lev. 5:15; 6:2; Josh. 22:22); AV TRESPASS (Lev. 5:15; 6:2), TRANSGRESSION (Josh. 22:22); NEB OFFENCE (Lev. 5:15), GRIEVOUS FAULT (6:2), TREACHERY (Josh. 22:22).

The noun *ma'al* means "an unfaithful or treacherous act." It is found twice (Lev. 5:15; 6:2) in a cognate accusative relationship with the verb of the same root (*mā'al,* "act treacherously"). The act of treachery could be either planned or unplanned. An example of the latter is found in Lev. 5:15, where it is made clear that if anything is found wrong with the holy things of Yahweh (those things connected with the worship and sacrifice), and the act was an *unknowing* one, then it was pardonable by the payment of a fine plus restitution for the offence. If the deceit was planned, death was the judgment for the offender.

The deceit did not have to be against holy things, however, to be classified as a *ma'al.* Acting treacherously with regard to a fellow Israelite's property is also classified here (Lev. 6:2). This offence is obviously planned; but even so, it is remediable by the payment of a fine plus restitution (6:5b-6).

An important clue for our understanding of *ma'al* is gained in Josh. 22:22. Here "a treacherous act" (*ma'al*) is contrasted with open rebellion (*mereḏ*). It would seem that *ma'al* is something plotted in the secret recesses of the heart as opposed to open rebellion against authority.

See M. Noth, *Leviticus* (Eng. tr. 1965).

T. R. ASHLEY

BREACH OF RITUAL. *See* CRIME.

BREACH OF TRUST. *See* TRUST, BREACH OF.

BREAD [Heb. *leḥem*; Gk. *ártos*].

I. Antiquity of Bread-Making
II. Prominence in Diet
III. Ingredients
IV. Bread-Making
V. Eating Bread

I. Antiquity of Bread-Making.–The art of bread-making is very ancient. Neolithic communities, as for example in Jericho, were acquainted with agriculture. It is possible that the products of grain in the beginning were used for making porridge; but the art of baking must date from prehistoric times, for bread is mentioned in the oldest literatures of mankind. The first mention of bread in the Bible is in Gen. 3:19. The Heb. *leḥem* is generally connected with an Arabic and Syriac root meaning "make solid"; the word indicates "solid food" in general. Among the nomadic population of the desert the most common form of solid food is meat, so the cognate word in Arabic (*laḥm*) means "meat"; but among a sedentary population bread becomes the staple diet, and therefore is called *leḥem.* We find the same word in Ugaritic, many Aramaic dialects, and Phoenician, but not in Akkadian (though cf. the verb *laḥāmu,* "to eat" and "to drink").

II. Prominence in Diet.–Among the peasants in Palestine and elsewhere, bread is primary, other articles of solid food merely accessory. Many days will pass in the life of a peasant without any taste of meat, which is considered a festival dish among the sedentary population. "Bread" therefore often stands for solid food in general, not only because this is the original meaning of the word but also because bread is food par excellence. When people went out on a journey they took bread along with them (Josh. 9:5, 12). Nowadays the laborer in the Near East often wraps other kinds of food such as olives, cheese, or eggs in thin loaves of bread, or even inserts them within the crust of his bread; and it is quite possible that the same was done in biblical times; about this, however, we have no available information.

III. Ingredients.–From earliest times, several kinds of grains were well known in Palestine. Wheat, however, is most common today and there is no reason to suppose that it was otherwise in biblical times. When bread is mentioned without any further qualification, we may safely suppose that it was made of wheat. Palestine has excellent wheat varieties with great nutritive value.

Bread of other grains was not much appreciated, though the poor sometimes had to resort to it; and because barley was harvested a few weeks earlier in the year than wheat, there may have been a time of year when only barley flour was available. In the sanctuary it is only in connection with the offering of jealousy that barley is mentioned (Nu. 5:15). Barley bread is a symbol of the Israelite army in Jgs. 7:13, because the logic of the dream asks for a thick and heavy cake (see below); in 2 K. 4:42 and Jn. 6:9, 13 barley bread is mentioned in connection with the early season. The witches of Ezk. 13:19 sell their offices even for "handfuls of barley." Nevertheless barley is recognized as human food, but it takes the second place after wheat (2 S. 17:28; 2 Ch. 2:15 [MT 14]) and has only half its price (2 K. 7:18).

In Ezk. 4:9 millet is mentioned; this word occurs as a name for a kind of grain in Babylonian literature. It is doubtful whether it occurred in Palestine. The same text mentions also spelt (AV "fitches"), a cereal like wheat, which according to Ex. 9:32 (AV "rie") ripened at about the same time, and which was cultivated in Palestine (Isa. 28:25).

Apart from different kinds of grains, Ezk. 4:9 mentions also beans and lentils as ingredients for bread. This must be considered an exceptional case, as the symbolic action ordered in this verse is meant as a prefiguration of the hardships to be suffered during the siege of Jerusalem.

Clay figure of a woman kneading dough in a trough. From the Phoenician cemetery at ez-Zib (9th-early 6th cents. B.C.) (Israel Department of Antiquities and Museums)

Flour will become so scarce that people will not only put together the last remnants of different grains, but also mix it with crushed beans and lentils. There is no reason to suppose that these things happened in normal times.

Three different kinds of flour may be distinguished: (1) The flour or meal of ordinary use (1 S. 28:24; 2 S. 17:28; 1 K. 17:12, 14, 16; etc.) was made by rubbing grains between two stones and sifting the product in such a way that all larger pieces were removed. (2) Groats (AV often "fine flour"), as distinguished from common flour (cf. 1 K. 4:22 [MT 5:2]), were used for sacrificial purposes (Lev. 2:1, 4, 7; 5:11; 6:20 [MT 13]; etc.). In order to make groats one had to sift two times: once for removing the large pieces, and once in order to separate the groats from meal in powder form. Kings and honored guests were offered groats (Gen. 18:6); it was considered a luxury (Ezk. 16:13, 19). (3) Groats from fresh ears are mentioned in Lev. 2:14, 16 only. Though this kind of groats is used for making porridge nowadays, the mention of oil and of the burning in fire show that a kind of bread or cake could be made of it.

*IV. **Bread-Making.***–After the flour had been provided it was mixed with cold or warm water and kneaded to dough; the use of this as an offering is prescribed in Nu. 15:20f.; Ezk. 44:30; Neh. 10:37 (MT 38). The "kneading bowl" (Ex. 8:3 [MT 7:28]; Dt. 28:5, 17) must have been a small, light wooden box, for it could be bound up in clothes and carried on the shoulders (Ex. 12:34). For common use a piece of leavened dough of the preceding day's baking, preserved for the purpose, was mixed with the dough; the whole was then set aside and left standing until it was thoroughly leavened (*see* LEAVEN). For sacrificial use unleavened bread was the rule, and cakes of unleavened bread (Heb. *maṣṣôṯ*) were the only form of bread allowed for any Israelite during the Passover season. Leavened bread as an offering to the sanctuary is mentioned, however, in Lev. 7:13; 23:17, 20; Am. 4:5.

Every dough was mixed with salt; sometimes olive oil was added to the unbaked dough (Lev. 2:4f.; 7:12), but in other cases it was added only after the baking process.

Disk-shaped platter used to form or bake cakes of bread, from a fifteenth-century B.C. shrine at Lachish. The holes on the underside (right) are not bored through the pottery tray. (Israel Department of Antiquities and Museums)

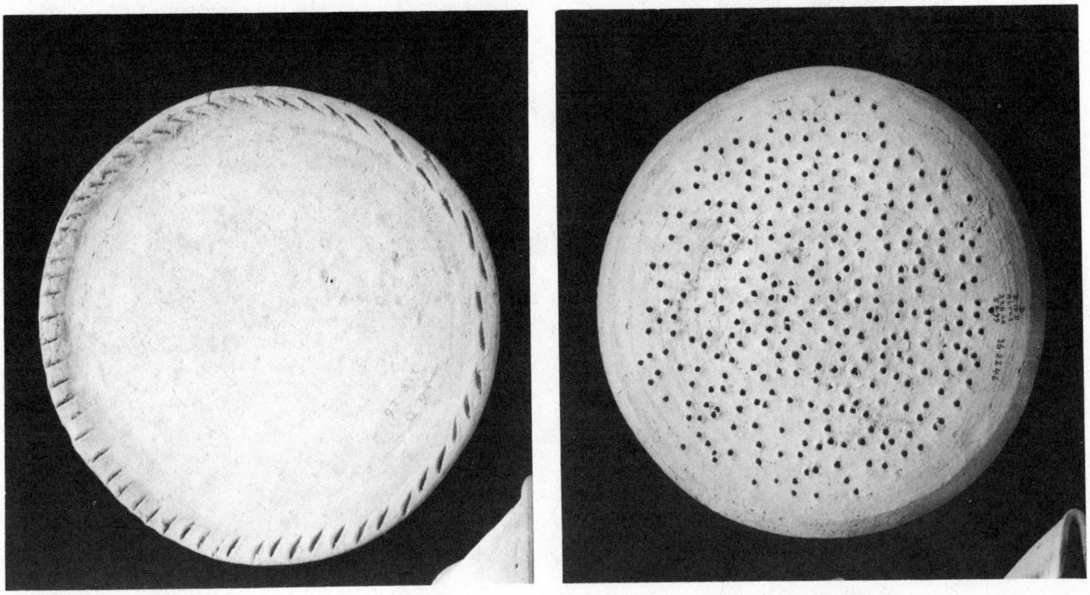

After the leavening process was finished, the dough was made into cakes. Thick and thin forms are distinguished, the choice being determined both by the material (it is not possible to bake "wafers" from barley flour) and by the method of baking: "ash-bread" (see below) cannot be as thin as oven-bread. Moreover, several varieties are possible, e.g., "ring-bread," often seen nowadays in the Near East, and perhaps intended by the frequent word *ḥallâ* (Lev. 2:4, etc.; see KoB); bread in the form of a heart (Heb. *lᵉḇîḇôṯ*, 2 S. 13:6, 8, 10), and others. The most common shape, however, is that of a disk (*kikkār*, Ex. 29:23) 7 in. (18 cm.) or more in diameter and half an inch thick. Thin disk-shaped bread is called *rāqîq* (Ex. 29:23, etc.). Unleavened bread is often very thin (cf. Ex. 29:2; Lev. 2:4; etc.).

Three methods of baking are indicated. The first could be called the direct way: a fire is built on some stones, and when these are well heated the cinders are raked off; the cakes are laid on the stones and ashes are heaped upon them. After some time the cakes are turned. Such a cake is called an *'ugâ*. This is the sort of bread baked by Sarah (Gen. 18:6) and by the Israelites after they left Egypt (Ex. 12:39). Elijah found such ash-bread ready when he awoke from his sleep (1 K. 19:6). Though this is certainly the most primitive way of baking bread, we find it also in NT times (Jn. 21:9) and even today among bedouin and travelers. The turning of the bread is mentioned in Hos. 7:8.

The second method is baking on a plate or in a pan. The baking plate (*maḥᵃḇaṯ*) is sometimes made of iron (Ezk. 4:3) but may be of earthenwork like those found in Gezer. It is a flat bowl, put with the convex side up over a fire; and the cakes are thrown on the outside. This instrument, mentioned in Lev. 2:5; 6:21 (MT 14); 7:9; 1 Ch. 23:29, is probably the same as that of 1 Ch. 9:31, though some scholars understand the word used there (Heb. *ḥᵃḇittîm*) as an indication of the product, namely, flat cakes baked on the baking plate (so RSV, NEB). Those cakes are hard and thin. Softer and thicker are those made with the help of the frying pan or *marḥešeṯ* (Lev. 2:7; 7:9), a deeper bowl which may have a lid. A variant of this is *maśrēṯ*, probably also a bowl or frying pan with a lid, but with a hole in the lid. It is mentioned in 2 S. 13:9 only. The frying pan in its two variants supposes the use of oil.

The third method is baking bread in an oven (*tannûr*), a cylinder of earthenwork, which might be dug into the soil but might also stand on the ground. A small hut of stones and clay is built around it. The oven is heated by grass (Mt. 6:30), stubble (Mal. 4:1 [MT 3:19]), thorns, and other dry twigs (Nah. 1:10), or dung (cf. Ezk. 4:15, where, however, the first method is probably meant). Cow dung is very frequently used as a fuel today. The *tannûr* has two openings: one at the bottom, from the side, through which the ashes may be removed, and one at the top, through which after the flames have died down the dough-cakes are stuck on the hot inside walls. The cakes are not turned. When ready they are taken out by hand. Such bread-cakes are rather thin and soft. It is impossible to break them, but they are torn by hand. The rule is that one person, sometimes assisted by a servant, makes use of one *tannûr*. It is a sign of dire need when there is so little dough that ten wives make use of one oven (Lev. 26:26). In such a case food is rationed by weight; in ordinary times an adult needs (according to Mish. *Kelim* as understood by Dalman)

Model of a house containing a brewery (top) and bakery, from the tomb of Meketre (11th Dynasty Egypt, 2135-2000 B.C.) at Thebes. Thirteen men and women (not all visible) crush and grind grain, mix dough, form cakes, and tend the ovens. (Metropolitan Museum of Art, 1919-1920 excavations)

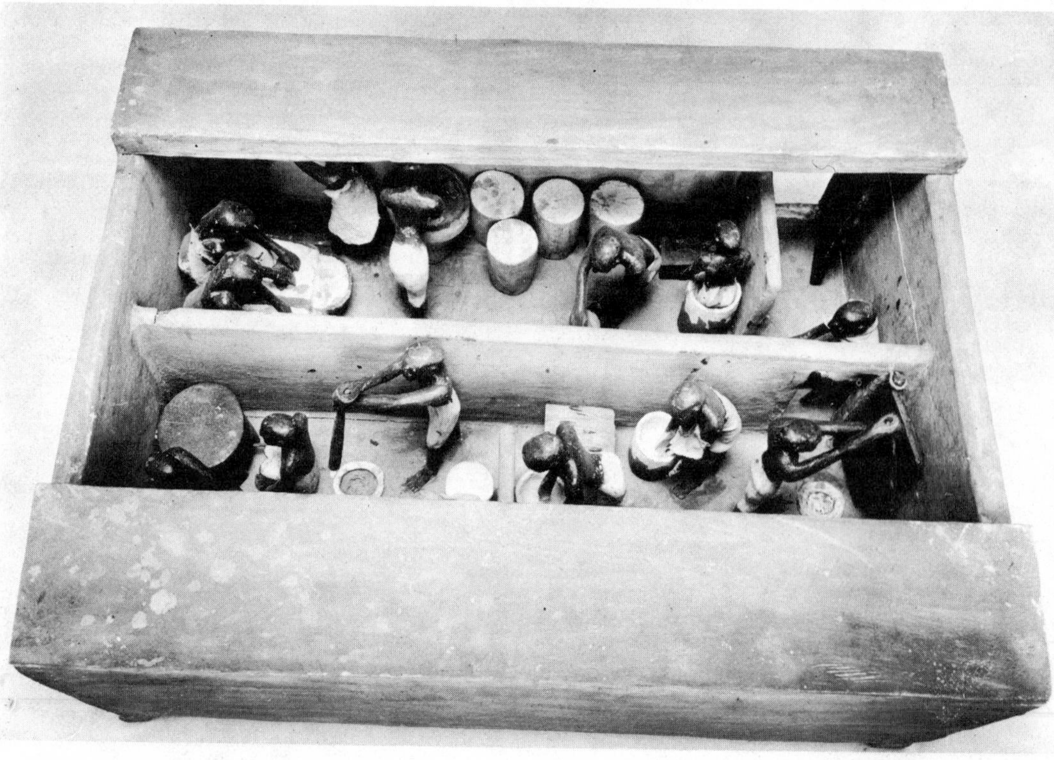

one-third of a *kab̲*, i.e., slightly over one pint, of flour a day. The three measures of flour mentioned in Gen. 18:6 and Mt. 13:33 are sufficient for fifty-four persons a day, or, if they take one meal only, for 162 persons. One needs a rather large *tannûr* to prepare such a quantity of bread; but as we have seen, Sarah as the wife of a tent-dweller probably baked in ashes.

Special kinds of bread were, in the first place, the unleavened bread of the Passover season, the *maṣṣôṯ* (see above). Ex. 16:31 mentions the *ṣappîḥiṯ*, according to the etymology of the word a flat cake, which was served with honey. We may suppose that the varieties of special bread and cake mentioned in the Talmud were also known in biblical times, but as a luxury only. The addition of oil or honey or several kinds of spices to the dough or to the baked cake allows an unending list of variations. The "bread of affliction" mentioned in 1 K. 22:27 and 2 Ch. 18:26 is not a special kind of bread but rather a small quantity (cf. the "water of affliction" mentioned alongside it, and Isa. 30:20). In the same way "bread of mourners" (Hos. 9:4; cf. Ezk. 24:17, 22) is not a special kind of bread but ordinary bread used in extraordinary circumstances. In mourning Daniel ate no "pleasant bread" (Dnl. 10:3), i.e., no bread that in any way was made more tasty, but simple bread without any addition of oil, honey, or spices.

Every oriental household used to make its own bread, and bread-making for the most part was in the hands of the women. Handmaids were often employed to grind the grains (Ex. 11:5; Job 31:10); Sarah kneaded and baked (Gen. 18:6), and so did the woman of Endor (1 S. 28:24). Jeremiah considers it the rule that children gather wood, fathers kindle fire, and women knead the dough to make cakes (Jer. 7:18). Even today this is the rule not only among nomadic people but also among sedentary peasants.

In a very large household, such as the king's, it might happen that some persons had baking as their sole task. 1 S. 8:13 assumes that even in such a case the baker will be a female; but at the court of the Egyptian king we find a male "chief of the bakers" (Gen. 40:2, etc.), and the form of the Hebrew word for "bakers" indicates that his helpers were male. Also the baker of Hos. 7:4, 6 is a man. Jer. 37:21 shows that in the metropolis Jerusalem there was a "bakers' street." Most commentators consider this an indication that there were private professional bakers in Jerusalem, brought together on one street as members of one guild, as were the goldsmiths and the traders in later times (Neh. 3:31f.). But Zedekiah's ordering a disk of bread to be delivered daily to Jeremiah, who was a prisoner in the king's palace, suggests direct authority of the king over these bakers. So they are to be considered workers in the royal household, which consumed large quantities of flour (1 K. 4:22), enough for the daily meals of 1620 persons. For such a multitude a fair number of bakers was needed, and it is evident that they needed a street, if not for their dwelling then certainly for the location of their ovens, each in its own shelter.

V. Eating Bread.–The thin, brittle forms of bread, especially the *maṣṣôṯ*, were broken; the softer and thicker varieties were torn apart. Sometimes oil was poured on the bread; we have no information of the use of butter in connection with bread. Bread was usually carried in a basket (Gen. 40:16f.; Ex. 29:3; Mt. 14:20; 15:37; etc.); when traveling one carried bread in a sack (1 S. 9:7, etc.). When bread was eaten by a group, the head of the household or the master of the community broke it or tore it and gave a portion to everybody present. If meat, fish, or other food was offered together with the bread, it was often handed out from the common cooking pot with the help of a piece of bread. The bread was folded into a kind of spoon and used to dip in the common dish without touching the broth or whatever with the fingers. So Mt. 26:23 is to be understood (cf. Jn. 13:26). After the meal the pieces that had not been consumed were gathered carefully into the basket again (Mt. 14:20, etc.). These remains are to be distinguished from the crumbs that fall on the ground and are left to be devoured by animals, and from the crumbs *(niqqûdîm,* Josh. 9:5, 12) to which bread is reduced when it is kept too long. The same word also denotes a special kind of cake, probably of very small size (1 K. 14:3; AV "cracknels").

Bread is considered a gift from God, by whose blessing the grain grows. Its sanctity therefore should always be respected. No oriental will tread on a piece of bread. When he sees it lying on the street, he will pick it up and give it to a dog or put it somewhere where a bird may get it. The general sanctity of bread makes it one of the most common forms of offering. Every burnt offering and many other kinds of sacrifices are accompanied by a *minḥâ,* the principal element of which is some form of bread (cf. Lev. 2). There were also offerings of bread independently from animal sacrifice: the oblation of two leavened disks of bread at Pentecost (Lev. 23:17), and the "shewbread" (AV) or "bread of the Presence" (RSV), twelve cakes according to tradition arranged in two rows, each of them consisting of six large rectangular cakes, with "horns" at their corners. After the replacement of this bread the old cakes were to be eaten by priests only; but note 1 S. 21:3-6 and Mt. 12:3f.

Bread became a symbol of different things, first of all one of hospitality. The stranger is to be offered bread and water (Neh. 13:1f.), and one should not send people away without having given them bread (Mt. 14:15-21, etc.). The disciples of Jesus could reckon on such hospitality and therefore were not to bring along their own bread (Mt. 10:10). The host will break off a piece of the cake he has in hand and give it to his guest; in such a way they partake of the same bread, and this becomes a symbol of community and mutual responsibility. By eating bread one becomes bound to his host. Prophets who ate from Jezebel's table were bound to speak their mistress' word (1 K. 18:19); the man of God sent to protest against Jeroboam's illegal worship was not allowed to eat bread in Jeroboam's realm (1 K. 13:9).

Both symbolic meanings of bread-eating have been taken over in Christian worship. The idea of hospitality developed into the ancient Christian custom of connecting the *agápē* (Jude 12; cf. 1 Cor. 11:21) with the Lord's Supper. Community by partaking of the same bread is expressed by Paul in 1 Cor. 10:17. But the first idea in the Lord's Supper is still another symbolism: the conception of the bread of life, the spiritual food given to mankind when Christ surrendered Himself unto death in order that His followers might find life eternal. This symbolism, expressed in the words of Christ at the institution of holy communion (Mt. 26:26), has been expanded largely in Jn. 6:32-58, words spoken when "the Passover . . . was at hand" (Jn. 6:4), and when Christ had shown Himself the divine host by the multiplying of bread. So the symbolism of bread in Israel's religion and the symbolism of bread in the common life of the eastern countries were joined to the central theme of the Lord's Supper: the sacrifice of Christ as the life-bread for His people.

Bibliography.–G. Dalman, *Arbeit und Sitte in Palästina,* IV: *Brot, Öl und Wein* (1935), pp. 1-152; M. Währen, *Brot und*

Gebäck im Leben und Glauben des Orients (1964); *TDNT*, I, *s.v.* ἄρτος (Behm). A. VAN SELMS

BREAK. The most common word is Heb. *šāḇar,* which is nearly always used literally, for breaking objects, e.g., a door (Gen. 19:9), bones (Ex. 12:46; Job 29:17), images and altars (Dt. 7:5; 2 K. 11:18; 2 Ch. 23:17; Jer. 43:13), weapons (Ps. 76:3; Hos. 1:5), yokes (Jer. 28; Neh. 1:13), bread (Lev. 26:26; Ezk. 5:16; 14:13). Occasionally it is used more abstractly, e.g., Lev. 26:19, "I will break the pride of your power," and Ps. 69:20, "Insults have broken my heart." The word most often used for breaking covenants is Heb. *pārar* (e.g., Gen. 17:14; Lev. 26:15, 44; Dt. 31:16, 20; Isa. 24:5; Ezk. 16:59).

In the AV "break up" is used for "break in(to)," in Ex. 22:2 (Heb. *maḥtereṯ*); 2 Ch. 24:7 (*pāraṣ*); Mt. 24:43 (Gk. *diorýssō*). Other AV usages of "break" that are replaced by more accurate expressions in the RSV or NEB include: Job 13:25, RSV "frighten," NEB "chase" (Heb. *'āras*); 38:10, RSV "prescribed," NEB "established" (*šāḇar*); 39:15, RSV and NEB "trample" (*dûš*); Ps. 119:20, RSV "is consumed," NEB "pines" (*gāras*); 141:5, RSV and NEB "anoint" (*nô*); Lam. 3:16, RSV "made my teeth grind" (*gāras*).

Important NT words include Gk. *kláō* (of breaking bread, e.g., Mt. 14:19 par.; Acts 20:7; 1 Cor. 10:16), *diarrhḗgnymi* (Lk. 5:6; 8:29), *katágnymi* (Mt. 12:20; Jn. 19:31-33), *syntríbō* (Mk. 5:4; 14:3 [*see* ALABASTER]).

See also BREACH. J. W. D. H.

BREAKFAST [Gk. *aristáō*–'eat breakfast'] (Jn. 21:12, 15); AV DINE. The regular morning meal, although in later times the term was applied to the main meal. Lk. 14:12 distinguishes between this meal and dinner, the evening meal.

While there is discussion as to whether the noun *áriston* always means breakfast or may mean the noon meal (*see* MEALS), there can be little doubt the instance mentioned in Jn. 21 is an early morning meal (cf. v. 4). If the word does relate to breakfast alone, the meal Jesus ate with the Pharisee (Lk. 11:37) should also be interpreted as a breakfast. It may have been a customary meal that took place immediately after the morning prayer in the synagogue. Some have argued that the parable of the wedding feast (Mt. 22:4ff.) is more meaningful if this is interpreted as breakfast, as this would have called those invited from their daily work and would have meant loss to them.

The meal Jesus cooked on the shore of the Sea of Galilee is described as fish roasting on a charcoal fire. While we do have record of more humble meals (Ruth 2:14), the Jew normally preferred to have meat or fish with his meal. The fish would be roasted either directly on the coals or on flat rocks that had first been heated by a charcoal fire.

D. W. WEAD

BREAST [Heb. *ḥāzeh* (Ex. 29:26f.; Lev. 7:30f., 34; 8:29; 9:20f.; 10:14f.; Nu. 6:20; 18:18), *lēḇāḇ* (Nah. 2:7), *mē'îm* (Ps. 22:14), *s^egôr* (Hos. 13:8), *šaḏ* (Gen. 49:25; Job 3:12; etc.), *šōḏ* (Job 24:9; Isa. 60:16; 66:11); Aram. *ḥ^aḏî* (Dnl. 2:32); Gk. *kólpos* (Jn. 13:23), *mastós* (Lk. 11:27; 23:29; Rev. 1:13), *stḗthos* (Lk. 18:13; 23:48; Jn. 13:25; 21:20; Rev. 15:6)]; AV also BOSOM, BOWELS, "the caul of their heart," PAPS, TEATS, etc.; NEB also BOSOM, RIBS, TEAT, etc. In Ps. 131:2 the RSV supplies "breast" where the Hebrew simply has *'ēm,* "mother."

Either of the two milk-producing glands located on the upper torso of the female, the frontal area of the chest or thorax of both male and female, and the seat or location of the emotions and affections, i.e., the consciousness: all are designated in the Bible at different times by the one word "breast."

Ḥāzeh occurs only in priestly material, where it refers solely to the breast meat of animals to be used in sacrifices. These sacrifices were always of the wave offering type and were connected with priestly ordination services (Ex. 29:26f.; Lev. 8:29), peace offerings (Lev. 7:29f.; 9:18, 20f.), and the concluding rites of a Nazirite vow (Nu. 6:20). This portion of the sacrifice was to be consumed exclusively by the priests (Ex. 29:26; Lev. 7:31).

The breasts are frequently associated with the blessing of God on life and motherhood (Gen. 49:25; Ps. 22:9; 131:2; Lk. 11:27). In keeping with this line of thought, they are also considered a feature of feminine charm (Cant. 4:5-7; 7:7f.; 8:10; Ezk. 16:7). Conversely, however, dry or unfulfilled breasts are sometimes marks of sin and judgment (Hos. 9:14; Lk. 23:29); and by extension, "to beat one's breast," the seat of the emotions, is to express pain, grief, and anguish (Isa. 32:12; Nah. 2:7; Lk. 18:13; 23:48; cf. Ps. 22:14).

In the Gospel of John, the disciple "whom Jesus loved" is distinguished by having lain close to Jesus' breast at the Last Supper (13:23, 25; 21:20). This was the place of honor, at the right hand of the host. Furthermore, this designation is meant to indicate the identity of the Gospel's author (21:24).

The term is also used figuratively. Israel is described allegorically as a beautiful, fully developed maiden whose "breasts were formed" when Yahweh betrothed Himself to her (Ezk. 16:7). But she had already practiced harlotry — i.e., idolatry — in Egypt and continued to do so later with the Assyrians and Babylonians, who also fondled her breasts (Ezk. 23:3-21). For this unfaithfulness, Judah is to be judged so horribly that she will be moved to tear off her breasts (23:24, NEB). But there is also a future hope for Jerusalem; she will be nourished again and draw strength from the nations by sucking at the "breast of kings" (Isa. 60:16). Then her own breasts will supply the milk of consolation to all who are needy; and then all may "drink deeply with delight from the abundance of her glory" (Isa. 66:11).

See *TDNT*, III. *s.v.* κόλπος (Meyer). K. H. MAAHS

BREASTPIECE OF THE HIGH PRIEST [Heb. *ḥōšen*]; AV BREASTPLATE. Apparently a pouch or bag referred to in the Torah (Ex. 25:7; 28; 29:5; 35:9, 27; 39; Lev. 8:8). Of obscure nature, it seems to have been a multicolored embroidered fabric square (Ex. 28:15f.), and was attached to the ephod by four golden rings. In or on it were twelve semi-precious stones symbolizing the Israelite tribes, as well as the Urim and Thummim, the latter used in the casting of lots. The pouch or bag was worn by the high priest as the representative of the Israelites when he entered the holy place, thereby bringing the nation vicariously into the divine presence (cf. Ex. 28:29).

R. K. H.

BREASTPLATE. *See* WEAPONS OF WAR.

BREATH [Heb. *n^ešāmâ, rû(a)ḥ, heḇel, nepeš* (Job 41:21), *'ap* (Cant. 7:8), *yāpaḥ* (Jer. 4:31); Gk. *pnoḗ, pneúma*]; AV also VANITY, WIND, SPIRIT, LIFE, INSPIRATION (Job 32:8), NOSE (Cant. 7:8), "bewaileth herself" (Jer. 4:31); NEB also BREATH OF WIND, VAPOUR, SPIRITS, COMMAND, PUFF OF WIND, PUFF OF AIR, WIND, etc.; **BREATH OF LIFE** [Heb. *nepeš ḥayyâ* (Gen. 1:30), *nišmaṯ ḥayyîm* (2:7), *rû(a)ḥ ḥayyîm* (6:17; 7:15), *nišmaṯ-rû(a)ḥ ḥayyîm* (7:22), *n^ešāmôṯ* (Isa. 57:16)]; AV also LIFE (Gen. 2:7), SOULS (Isa. 57:16); NEB also SPIRIT OF LIFE (Gen. 6:17), LIFE (7:22), "living (creatures)" (Isa. 57:16). The words *nešāmâ* and *rû(a)ḥ* both mean basically "wind," though the former suggests a gentler blowing, the latter often a blast (cf. 2 S. 22:16; Ps. 18:15; Isa. 11:4). As *rû(a)ḥ* is related most often to the will or emotions, it is translated more than 230 times as SPIRIT. The "breath of life" is in the second Creation story the vital principle, imparted to man by God when He "breathed into his nostrils" (Gen. 2:7); in the other references, however, it is no doubt merely an expression for "living," like the phrase "all that breathed" (*kol-hanneš̌āmâ,* Josh. 10:40) or "any that breathed," etc. (11:11, 14; Dt. 20:16; 1 K. 15:29; Ps. 150:6).

J. W. D. H.

BREATHE. The enemies of the psalmist "breathe out violence" (Ps. 27:12, Heb. *yāp̄aḥ,* "breathe hard," "snort"); and Saul of Tarsus was prior to his conversion "breathing threats and murder against the disciples of the Lord" (Acts 9:1, Gk. *empnéō*).

In Lam. 3:56 the AV has "hide not thine ear at my breathing [Heb. *rewāḥâ*], at my cry." The RSV reads, "Do not close thine ear to my cry for help!" with the marginal note "Heb. uncertain"; the NEB has: "Do not turn a deaf ear when I cry, 'Come to my relief.' " The AV "breathing" (cf. *rû[a]ḥ*) is least likely; see Ex. 8:15, where the same word is translated "respite." Many commentators emend the text (see BDB, p. 926; *IB, in loc.*; *BH*; LXX). The Hebrew word order casts some doubt on the RSV and NEB readings.

J. W. D. H.

BREECHES [Heb. *mik̲nāsayim*; Gk. *periskelḗ*]; NEB DRAWERS. Priestly garments covering the thighs for reasons of propriety and modesty, and worn by Aaron on the Day of Atonement and by the priests on ceremonial occasions (Ex. 28:42; 39:28; Lev. 6:10; 16:4; Ezk. 44:18; cf. Ex. 20:26). They "reached to the knees" (J. H. Hertz on Ex. 28:42). Josephus described them as worn in his time; they are "in the nature of breeches" with the upper half cut off, ending at the thighs and there tied fast (*Ant.* iii.7.1).

It is sometimes thought that one of the three articles of dress mentioned in Dnl. 3:21 may have been a trouser-like garment. The RV translates Aram. *sarbāl* as "hosen," and the NEB has "trousers"; but J. A. Montgomery (*ICC* on Daniel) thinks it more likely that this means "mantles" (as does the RSV; cf. AV "coats") and that the second article, *paṭṭîš,* refers to trousers. (See also S. A. Cook, *Journal of Philology,* 26 [1899], 306-313.)

J. G. G. NORMAN

BREED; BRED [Heb. qal and piel of *yāḥam*] (Gen. 30:38f., 41); AV CONCEIVE; NEB "be on heat," "feel a longing"; [*šāraṣ*] (Gen. 8:17); NEB SWARM; [*rûm*] (Ex. 16:20); NEB "become full of"; [hiphil of *rāb̲a'*] (Lev. 19:19); AV GENDER; NEB MATE TOGETHER; [piel of *'ab̲ar*] (Job 21:10); AV GENDER; NEB MOUNT; [Gk. *gennáō*] (2 Tim. 2:23); AV ENGENDER; **BREEDER** [Heb. *nōqēd̲*] (2 K. 3:4); AV SHEEPMASTER. In Dt. 28:54, 56; Jer. 6:2 the RSV supplies "bred," rendering Heb. *'ānōg* "delicately bred" (AV "delicate"; NEB "delicate," "lovely"). The thrust of these passages is that these people are so pampered that even at a time of trouble they can think only of themselves. The RSV also supplies "bred" in Est. 8:10, rendering "bred from the royal stud" for *benê hārammāk̲îm,* which the NEB translates "from the royal stables."

Used in the piel form *yāḥam* means "conceive," while in the qal it means "be in heat." Gen. 30:37-43 describes the trickery to which Jacob resorted in order to get the better of Laban. Ancient belief in magic held that the visual characteristics of certain objects placed in the sight of the mother at the time of intercourse would be reflected in the offspring. The NEB with its alternate use of "be on heat" and "feel a longing for" seems to suggest a possible original pun on the Heb. *yāḥam*. The hiphil form of *rāb̲a'* literally means "cause to lie down." The Israelites were not allowed to mate together two different kinds of animals (Lev. 19:19). Heb. *rûm*, literally meaning "rise up," is used in Ex. 16:20 to describe the manna that had become full of worms.

The term is used only once in the NT, in 2 Tim. 2:23. Gk. *gennáō*, which literally means to "beget" or "bear," is here used figuratively with the sense of "produce" or "bring forth."

D. P. NILES

BRETHREN. *See* BROTHER; BROTHERS OF THE LORD.

BRIBE; BRIBERY [Heb. *šōḥad̲, kōp̄er, mattānâ, beṣa'* (Ex. 18:21), *šillûm* (Mic. 7:3)]; AV also GIFT, REWARD, COVETOUSNESS (Ex. 18:21); NEB also REWARD, RANSOM, etc.; [*šādḥad*] (Job 6:22; Ezk. 16:33); AV HIREST, "give a reward"; NEB also "open your purses." The Hebrew law condemns everything that would tend to impair the impartial administration of justice, particularly the giving and receiving of gifts or bribes in order to pervert judgment (Ex. 23:8). There are frequent allusions to the prevailing corruption of judges and rulers (Job 15:34). In clearing himself of any suspicion, Samuel denied that he had ever been involved in bribery (1 S. 12:3). *See* JURISPRUDENCE, ABUSE OF; JUSTICE.

L. KAISER

R. K. H.

BRICK [Heb. *leb̲ēnâ*]. ***I. Mesopotamia.***–The Tower of Babel episode (Gen. 11:1-9) is set in stoneless southern Mesopotamia, where bricks have always been the primary building material. Baked bricks (11:3) were used for foundations, drains, pavements, etc. Walls were generally of sun-dried brick, which, although less permanent than the baked brick, had the advantage of making buildings cooler in summer and warmer in winter.

II. Egypt.–Prisoners were used for government building projects. The tomb painting of Rekhmire shows Egyptian taskmasters carrying sticks and supervising the making of bricks for workshops at Karnak. Water is brought from a pool; mud is mixed with a hoe and then carried to a spot convenient for the brickmaker. This mud is pressed into a wooden mold which the brickmaker holds to the ground. The mold is then lifted off, leaving a newly shaped brick to dry in the sun. Rows and rows of bricks are molded and, when dry, stacked preparatory to use. This procedure is still followed in the Near East.

The tomb painting is of special interest since it is nearly contemporary to the events in Ex. 5. The Israelites were, like prisoners, made to build the store-cities of Pithom and Ramses. They found it necessary to add straw and stubble to their bricks. Straw acts as a binder when the mud is poor in clay. Conversely, straw is added when the mud is too rich in clay, to prevent the bricks from warping and cracking while drying.

Although no straw is shown in the Rekhmire tomb painting, preserved Egyptian brick structures attest to its use. The importance of straw is also evident in the statement of an Egyptian official that, in his outpost, "there are neither men to make bricks nor straw in the neighborhood."

Brickmaking for the workshops of Amon at Karnak, wall-painting from the tomb of Rekhmire, vizier of Upper Egypt (*ca.* 1470-1445 B.C.). Syrians and Nubians mix water and mud, then mold and dry bricks. (Metropolitan Museum of Art, Egyptian Expedition)

Throughout Egyptian history sun-dried brick was the chief building material. Stone was reserved for temples and other monumental constructions. Baked bricks were not generally employed until Roman times.

III. Palestine.–As in Egypt, the baked brick was not common until Roman times. Houses were usually built of sun-dried bricks set on stone foundations. Although stone was recognized as a superior building material (Isa. 9:10), the superstructures of city walls and their gateways were generally of brick. Towers and glacis were designed to compensate for any lack of strength.

See also CLAY.

Bibliography.–A. Lucas, *Ancient Egyptian Materials and Industries* (4th ed. 1962); R. A. Caminos, *Late-Egyptian Miscellanies* (n.d.).

A. J. HOERTH

BRICK MOLD. *See* BRICKKILN.

BRICKKILN [Heb. *malbēn*]. Since Palestinian bricks were normally sun-dried in the OT period, the Hebrew word in 2 S. 12:31 is better translated "brick-mold" (Amer. Tr.) than "brickkiln" (AV, RV, RSV, NEB; cf. Nah. 3:14, where RSV has "brick mold," NEB "brickwork"). Making bricks was considered the task of prisoners. The ancestors of the new taskmasters had themselves been put to similar toil. The sense of the word is problematic in Jer. 43:9. "Pavement" (RSV, NEB) and "brickwork" (RV) have been suggested.

See also BRICK.

A. J. HOERTH

BRIDE [Heb. *kallâ*; Gk. *nýmphē*]. *See* MARRIAGE.

BRIDE CHAMBER, CHILDREN OF THE. In Mt. 9:15 par., the AV rendering of Gk. *huioí toú nymphṓnos*. A *nymphṓn* is a room where a wedding takes place, and the "sons" of the *nymphṓn* are the "wedding guests" (so RSV), or more correctly the "bridegroom's friends" (so NEB; Bauer, p. 547), who took part in the Eastern wedding ceremony. *See* CHAMBER; MARRIAGE.

BRIDE OF CHRIST [Gk. *nýmphē*–'bride'] (Jn. 3:29; Rev. 21:2, 9; 22:17); [*gynḗ*–'wife'] (Rev. 19:7; 21:9); [*parthénos*–'virgin'] (2 Cor. 11:2); [*kyría*–'lady'] (2 Jn. 1, 5). An image for the Church which emphasizes the ideas of purity, subjection, faithfulness, and intimate communion with Christ her bridegroom-husband; one constituent feature of a larger complex of nuptial imagery symbolizing the relationship between Christ and the Church (*see* MARRIAGE). While the OT is the primary source of this imagery, its application to the relationship between Christ and His Church in the NT was facilitated by (1) the messianic interpretation of some features of OT nuptial imagery in Judaism, (2) the tendency in Judaism to depict the messianic age as a wedding feast, (3) early Christianity's functional substitution of Jesus for Yahweh, and (4) the Greco-Roman penchant for personifying corporate bodies with feminine imagery.

The OT occasionally used the image of a bride (Heb. *kallâ, k^elûlâ*), together with other aspects of nuptial imagery, to depict Israel's relationship to Yahweh (2 S. 17:3 [var. adopted by RSV, NEB]; Isa. 49:18; 61:10; 62:5; Jer. 2:2, 32). Other OT references of particular interest, in view of later Jewish and early Christian allegorical interpretation, are found in Cant. 4:8-12; 5:1. This bridal imagery primarily emphasizes devotion (Jer. 2:2) and the joy of the bride (Isa. 61:10; 62:5); the voice of the bridegroom and the bride were proverbial for mirth and gladness (cf. Jer. 7:34; 16:9; 25:10; 33:11). In view of Israel's recrudescent tendency to seek illegitimate foreign alliances and to participate in the fertility rites of Canaanite religion, an even more frequent — though pejorative — image is that of the harlot or adulteress (Hos. 2:2–3:5; 4:14f.; Jer. 3:1; Ezk. 16:6-63; 23:1-49). These prophets use this negative image to condemn Israel's behavior as a heinous violation of the covenant relationship between Yahweh and Israel.

In interpreting the giving of the covenant at Sinai, later Judaism used the imagery of a marriage between Yahweh and Israel, with the Torah as the marriage contract, and Moses as the best man (*TDNT*, I, 654). Beginning with the 1st cent. A.D., the rabbis had interpreted the nuptial imagery of Canticles in terms of the love of God (=bridegroom) for Israel (=bride); cf. SB, I, 516f., 844, 898, 969f.; III, 501, 822. While it is technically correct to claim that the allegory of the bridegroom (=Yahweh) was never applied to the Messiah by Judaism (*TDNT*, IV, 1102), the messianic interpretation of the Royal Wedding Song preserved in Ps. 45 (which contains a wealth of nuptial imagery) saw the Messiah in the figure of the king-bridegroom (SB, III, 679f., quoting the Targum on Ps. 45). The Israelite king is rather astonishingly addressed as "God" in Ps. 45:6, and the NT applies the statements made in Ps. 45 to Christ in He. 1:8f. (cf. Justin, *Dial.* 56, 63, 86). Since Judaism also compared the Day of the

Messiah to a wedding feast (SB, I, 517f.), these factors undoubtedly facilitated the application of the bride-bridegroom imagery to Christ and the Church.

In the NT, Jesus used the parables of the wedding feast (Mt. 22:2-14; cf. Lk. 12:35-38), and the wise and foolish virgins (Mt. 25:1-13) to depict the coming kingdom of God; in neither parable does He refer to Himself as the bridegroom. Jesus never refers to the redeemed community as bride, but rather as wedding guests, as in Mt. 22:2-10, 11-14; 25:1-13; Mk. 2:19a. Jesus does refer to Himself as the bridegroom in Mk. 2:19 (par. Mt. 9:15); Lk. 5:34f. In a closely related passage, John the Baptist refers to Jesus as the bridegroom and to himself as the friend of the bridegroom (Jn. 3:29).

The earliest NT reference to the Church as the bride of Christ is 2 Cor. 11:2, where Paul consciously functions as the best man: "I betrothed you to Christ to present you as a pure bride to her one husband." Since the context refers to the serpent's deception of Eve as an analogy to the possibility that the Corinthians may stray after a deviant form of the gospel, it is clear that two aspects of the OT background have influenced Paul: (1) the faithfulness/unfaithfulness aspects of nuptial imagery emphasized by Hosea, Jeremiah, and Ezekiel, and (2) the Adam-Eve typology which involves the notion of Jesus as husband (=Adam) and the Church as bride (=Eve); cf. Minear, p. 55. Paul further elaborates the Adam-Eve typology in Eph. 5:22-31, and he interprets the "mystery" of Gen. 2:24 ("the two shall become one flesh") as a reference to Christ and His Church (Eph. 5:32), thereby implying that the union of the first couple (as well as all subsequent monogamous unions) foreshadows the marriage of Christ and His Church (Chavasse, p. 75). This same typological interpretation is explicated in the early 2nd cent. in 2 Clem. 14:2. Gnostic Christianity evolved a sacrament of mystical marriage by taking such ideas to their extreme (Grant, pp. 183-194). The central ideas conveyed through Paul's use of nuptial imagery in Eph. 5:22-31 include the wife's (=Church's) role of subjection and obedience, together with the husband's (=Christ's) role of self-sacrifice and authority (Minear, p. 55).

Other marginal Pauline uses of the bride image reveal the vitality of the metaphor in his thought. In Rom. 7:1-6 he observes that a married woman is bound by the law to her husband so long as he lives. The nuptial analogy is then applied by Paul to Christians who are now free to belong to another, i.e., to Christ who has been raised from the dead. In another allusion to Gen. 2:24 Paul tells the Corinthian congregation that he who joins himself to a prostitute becomes one body with her, "but he who is united to the Lord becomes one spirit with him" (1 Cor. 6:15-17). Throughout the rest of the NT letters, only in 2 Jn. 1, 5 (cf. 1 Pet. 5:13) is feminine imagery applied to the Church, in the expression "elect lady."

The most frequent reference in the NT to the Church as the bride of Christ occurs in Revelation. John applies the image not to the redeemed community directly, but rather to the heavenly Jerusalem which descends from heaven to a transformed earth. The heavenly Jerusalem is itself a symbol for the Church (Aune, pp. 146-48). The appropriateness of the bridal imagery in the context of the eschatological consummation lies in the fact that Judaism compared the messianic age to a marriage of God and Israel (SB, I, 500ff.), as well as to a wedding feast. The fine clothing of the bride symbolizes the righteous deeds of the saints (Rev. 19:8), and the comparison of the heavenly Jerusalem with a bride adorned for her husband (alluding to Isa. 61:10) emphasizes the readiness and anxious anticipation of the Church for Christ (Rev. 21:2; 22:17).

Bibliography.–D. E. Aune, *EQ*, 38 (1966), 131-148; C. Chavasse, *The Bride of Christ: An Enquiry into the Nuptial Element in Early Christianity* (1939); R. M. Grant, *After the NT* (1967); P. Minear, *Images of the Church in the NT* (1960); SB; *TDNT*, I, *s.v.* γαμέω, γάμος (Stauffer); IV, *s.v.* νύμφη, νυμφίος (Jeremias).

D. E. AUNE

BRIDEGROOM, FRIEND OF THE [Gk. *phílos toú nymphíou*] (Jn. 3:29; cf. Jgs. 14:20, AV; 1 Macc. 9:34). The "best man" in the Eastern wedding ceremony, who also was active in arranging the marriage.

BRIDLE. *See* BIT.

BRIER. *See* THORN.

BRIGANDINE [Heb. *siryôn*] (Jer. 46:4; 51:3, AV); RSV, NEB, COAT OF MAIL. *See* WEAPONS OF WAR.

BRIGHTNESS. In He. 1:3, the AV for Gk. *apaúgasma* (*tḗs dóxēs*), "the brightness (of his glory)." The RSV takes the word in its passive sense "reflection": "He reflects the glory of God"; the NEB reads "the effulgence of God's splendour."

BRIMSTONE [Heb. *goprîṯ*; Akk. *kuprîtu*; Gk. *tó theíon*]; NEB also SULPHUR, SULPHUROUS. The combustible sulphur, known to most ancient Near Eastern peoples from mineral deposits (cf. Dt. 29:23). That the inhabitants of the land had experienced the terrors of burning sulphur is very probable. Once one of these deposits took fire it would melt and run in burning streams down the ravines spreading everywhere suffocating fumes such as come from the ordinary brimstone match. No more realistic figure could be chosen to depict terrible suffering and destruction. It is not at all unlikely that during some of the disastrous earthquakes which took place in this part of the world, the hot lava sent forth ignited not only the sulphur but also the bitumen, and added to the horrors of the earthquake the destruction caused by burning pitch and brimstone.

The term "brimstone" is used figuratively to denote divine punishment of the wicked in Dt. 29:23; Job 18:15; Ps. 11:6; Isa. 30:33; Ezk. 38:22; Lk. 17:29.

J. A. PATCH

BROAD PLACE [Heb. *merḥāḇ* (2 S. 22:20; Ps. 18:19 [MT 20]; 31:8), *raḥaḇ* (Job 36:16)]; AV LARGE PLACE; NEB OPEN PLACE, "free to range" (Ps. 31:8), etc. The Hebrew words *merḥāḇ* and *raḥaḇ*, both from the verb *rāḥaḇ*," grow wide," mean a broad, roomy place. Wherever *merḥāḇ* and *raḥaḇ* occur, a context of salvation is implied: freedom from oppression and anxiety. The same suggestion is carried in places where the translation "broad place" is not employed; e.g., Ps. 118:5, "The Lord answered me and set me free [*merḥāḇ*]." The metaphor gains its vividness from the figure of a person who understands himself to be already in the power or realm of death, imploring God that he be delivered (e.g., Ps. 30:1-3, 8-10). This does not necessarily imply any idea of a resurrection from the dead.

Dahood (*Psalms, I* [*AB*, 1966], 111) argues that *merḥāḇ* is a poetic name for the nether world, and therefore the realm *from* which one sought to be delivered rather than *to* which one should be delivered. However, his interpretation is not very convincing. Rather, in the contexts in which it occurs (except Hab. 1:6), *merḥāḇ* is more easily interpreted as referring to a place or situation that is good, safe, and unrestricted.

In Ps. 18:4f. the sufferer sees death holding him within its power. He appeals to God, and God hears his cry (v. 6) and sets him in a broad place, where he is no longer surrounded or threatened by his enemy (vv. 16-19; cf. 31:4, 7f.).

See also DISTRESS. D. P. NILES

BROAD WALL [Heb. *haḥômâ hārᵉḥāḇâ*] (Neh. 3:8; 12:38). A stretch of Jerusalem's wall between the Tower of Furnaces and the Gate of Ephraim repaired by the Jews under Nehemiah. *See* JERUSALEM.

BROIDED (1 Tim. 2:9, AV). *See* BRAIDED.

BROIDERED. *See* EMBROIDERY.

BROILED [Gk. *optós*] (Lk. 24:42); NEB "which they had cooked." When Jesus appeared to His disciples after His resurrection, they gave Him "a piece of broiled fish," which He ate before them. Jn. 21:9 gives a clear example of a common method of cooking fish: "they saw a charcoal fire there, with fish lying on it, and bread."

BROKEN. *See* BREAK.

BROKENHEARTED [Heb. *šāḇar lēḇ* (Ps. 34:18; 147:3; Isa. 61:1), *nāḵeh lēḇ* (Ps. 109:16)]; AV also "of a broken heart," "broken in heart"; NEB also "whose courage is broken," "broken in spirit." The term is used with reference to people who feel their spiritual bankruptcy and helplessness, and who long for the help and salvation of God. Such people are in the right condition to be met and blessed by God. Cf. Isa. 66:2.

BRONZE [Heb. *nᵉḥōšeṯ*]; AV BRASS, STEEL, COPPER; [*ḥašmal*]; AV AMBER; NEB BRASS; [*ḥašmannîm*] (Ps. 68:31); AV PRINCESS; NEB TRIBUTE; [Gk. *chalkíōn* (Mk. 7:4), *chalkolíbanon* (Rev. 1:15; 2:18), *chalkós* (9:20; 18:12)]; AV BRASS; NEB also COPPER, BRASS. The Heb. *nᵉḥōšeṯ* is usually translated "brass" by the AV, but more correctly rendered "bronze" by the RSV, since the alloy used was copper and tin.

In Mesopotamia the Bronze Age began in the late 4th or early 3rd millennium B.C., as indicated by excavations at Jemdet Nasr, while in Egypt the use of bronze for tools and weapons occurred during the early dynasties, about 2700 B.C. Bronze was evidently of Mesopotamian origin, and the techniques for its manufacture were subsequently introduced into Egypt, probably from Sumer. At a later period the Egyptians made the alloy themselves, bringing their copper from Sinai, Cyprus, or northern Syria (*see* COPPER), and their tin from the Balkan regions or from Spain or the British Isles (*see* TIN). When the Israelites came into the Promised Land, they found the

Bronze stand from Megiddo (1050-1000 B.C.). Each side shows a worshiper or priest bringing a gift or offering homage to a seated deity. (Oriental Institute, University of Chicago)

Cast bronze door plaque from Solomon's temple. The metal plate was fastened by spikes to a wooden door. (Oriental Institute, University of Chicago)

Lamp with seven-branched candlestick (menorah) as handle, supported by Jewish symbols of the Feast of Tabernacles (4th cent. A.D.). Such bronze lamps were extremely rare at this early date. (Jewish Museum, New York, collection of M. S. Schloessing; Religious News Service)

Canaanites already skilled in the making and use of bronze instruments. This period marked the transition from the Bronze Age to the Iron Age in Palestine. Museums possessing antiquities from Bible lands have among their collections many and varied bronze objects. Among the most common are nails, lamps, hand mirrors, locks, cutting instruments, etc. Within comparatively recent times brass, an alloy of copper and zinc, has been introduced into Syria. Bronze is practically unknown in the modern native arts (*see* CRAFTS).

On *ḥašmal* (Ezk. 1:4, 27; 8:2), *see also* ELECTRUM.

On *ḥašmannîm,* cf. KoB, p. 342; BDB, p. 365.

J. A. PATCH
R. K. H.

BROOCH [Heb. *ḥāḥ*]. The term is used in the plural by the RSV (AV "bracelets"; NEB "clasps") to denote a class of jewelry brought as offerings by both men and women of Israel (Ex. 35:22). The golden pins of the wilderness period were replaced at a later time by bow-shaped ones of bronze or iron, specimens of which have been recovered from Palestine.

See also RING. R. K. H.

BROOK. *See* RIVER.

BROOK OF EGYPT [Heb. *naḥal miṣrayim*–'torrential stream (or valley) of Egypt,' best rendered by 'wadi,' which indicates both a stream and its valley]; AV RIVER OF EGYPT; NEB TORRENT OF EGYPT. The Brook of Egypt is mentioned five times in the OT (Nu. 34:5; Josh. 15:4, 47; 1 K. 8:65; Isa. 27:12), and since its correct identification is still far from clear it is necessary to distinguish certain related Hebrew terms with considerable care. The expression *y*[e]*'ôr miṣrayim,* the "river of Egypt," refers exclusively to the Nile proper, while the term *n*[e]*har miṣrayim* occurs once only (Gen. 15:18), in a passage describing the Promised Land in general terms as lying in an area between the two great rivers of the Nile and Euphrates.

The phrases *y*[e]*'ôr miṣrayim* and *n*[e]*har miṣrayim* must therefore be kept separate from the Brook of Egypt, which is more accurately the "torrent-wadi of Egypt." Whether this wadi was actually part of the Nile, or was instead a separate desert stream near the borderland of Egypt, has been a matter of considerable debate. Adherents of the former view have associated the identification of the Brook of Egypt with that of Shihor, which for some of the OT prophets formed part of the Nile. Thus Isaiah drew a parallelism between Shihor and the Nile (Isa. 23:3), while Jeremiah envisaged Shihor as the Egyptian Nile corresponding to the great Assyrian river

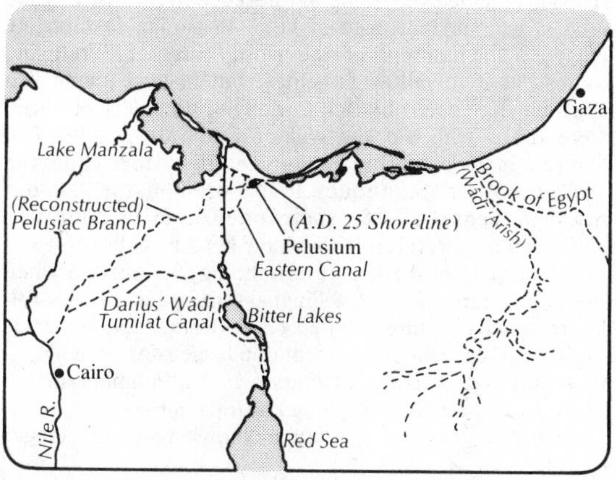

Euphrates (Jer. 2:18). According to Josh. 13:3, Shihor marked the extreme southwestern boundary of the territory to be occupied in the Promised Land, and specified it as being "before Egypt." Shihor could thus be identified with the lowest extent of the Pelusiac, the most easterly ancient branch of the Nile River, which flowed into the Mediterranean Sea just E of Pelusium (Tell Faramâ). The name Shihor (*š-ḥr*) was Egyptian in origin, and meant "Waters of Horus." Such references to it as have survived in Egyptian sources confirm the location attributed to it by OT writers insofar as they mention that Shihor produced salt and rushes for the delta capital of Tanis (Avaris), and that it was the official "river" of the fourteenth nome (province) of Lower Egypt. Arguing against the identification of the *naḥal miṣrayim* with the Shihor, the easternmost branch of the Nile, the Shihor is never designated in the OT by the Heb. *naḥal* but always by the word *y*[e]*'ôr* (which is applied on one occasion to the Tigris, Dnl. 12:5-7).

If the Brook of Egypt cannot be identified with either a portion or the whole of the Nile, the best alternative suggestion is that of the Wâdī el-'Arîsh. This wadi comes down from a plateau at the foot of the central mountain group of the Sinai Peninsula. The upper portion of the wadi is some 400 ft. (120 m.) above sea level, and its course, apart from one sharp bend to the west in the upper portion, runs almost due N along the western slope of the plateau. Its entire length of about 140 mi. (225 km.) runs through predominantly desert terrain, being situated about 90 mi. (145 km.) E of the ancient Egyptian Nile-oriented civilizations, at its northern extremity, about 50 mi. (80 km.) W of the Gaza region. Only barren desert and a little scrub can be seen lying westward toward Egypt, but this prospect is somewhat more relieved on the eastern side of the wadi, where there are some meadows and arable land of passable productivity. Most of the streams on the Sinai Peninsula are in fact dry watercourses for much of the year, and only when they are in flood do they assume the character of a torrent-wadi. Such flooding is apt to come with little or no warning when cloudbursts occur in the mountainous region drained by the particular wadi. From the above it will be apparent that the Brook of Egypt would constitute a practical southwestern boundary for the Promised Land in that it excluded the desert areas to the west and included the tolerably fertile land E of the Wâdī el-'Arîsh.

In extrabiblical texts the Brook of Egypt was mentioned in inscriptions from the time of Sargon II and Esarhaddon of Assyria. In 716 B.C. Sargon marched as far westward as the "Wadi (or Brook) of Egypt" (*naḥal muṣur*) and opened up the "sealed harbor of Egypt" for purposes of trade and commerce. The same inscription also mentioned the "border of the City of the Brook of Egypt," over which Sargon appointed an Assyrian governor. The description aligns well with the assumption that the *naḥal muṣur* was the Wâdī el-'Arîsh, and that the "City" located there (Assyr. *Arzâ*) was in fact the settlement of el-'Arîsh. Had Sargon penetrated Egyptian territory as far as the easternmost arm of the Nile, his "City" would then have been Pelusium, which seems improbable from the cuneiform evidence. The inscriptions of Esarhaddon also spoke of the "City" as *Arza*(*ni*), and again its locale corresponds better with el-'Arîsh than with Pelusium. While the Egyptians of the 19th Dynasty generally regarded the Pelusiac region as the borderline of Egypt proper, this has no necessary bearing upon Israel's concept of her own boundaries. At this time the Egyptians maintained wells along the entire coastal strip from Silē (modern Qantara), a few miles SE of the ancient Pelusiac, up to Gaza in Palestine, and for convenience defined the latter as stretching from Silē to 'Upa (Damascus). But this again says nothing about the view Israel held concerning her borders, and as far as the southern extremity is concerned has little bearing upon the problem, since the area from the el-'Arîsh to Qantara is desolate in any event, and as such would hardly be included in a catalog of fertile territory.

At present, therefore, the Wâdī el-'Arîsh seems better suited to be considered the Brook of Egypt than the Pelusiac branch of the Nile. R. K. H.

BROOM TREE [Heb. *rōtem*] (1 K. 19:4f.; Job 30:4; Ps. 120:4); AV JUNIPER; NEB also BROOM-BUSH (1 K. 19:4), lacking in Psalms ("charcoal").

The references in 1 Kings and Psalms are to the white broom, *Retama raetam* (Forsk.) Webb. and Berth., known to the Arabs as *ratam* (cf. Gk. *rathmén*, 1 K. 19:4). A beautiful shrub widely distributed in Palestine, Sinai, and Egypt, it can attain a height of 12 ft. (3.5 m.). Though its sparse leaves afford scant shade, it is often used for this purpose by desert travelers (cf. 1 K. 19:4). The wood burns vigorously, furnishing excellent charcoal (Ps. 120:4; cf. NEB).

The roots in Job 30:4 are not those of the white broom, which are nauseous and slightly poisonous. Some botanists have suggested instead the edible parasitic plant *Cynomorium coccineum*, which grows in salt marshes. Following the RV mg. and RSV, AV "their meat" should be rendered rather "to warm themselves," from a verb *ḥmm* (Ug. *ḥmm*; Akk. *emmu*). R. K. H.

BROTH [Heb. *mārāq, pārāq* (Isa. 65:4); Gk. *zōmós*]; NEB also BREW. "Broth" denotes the nutrient liquid in which meat was cooked. In sacrificial rituals it was considered part of the offering (Jgs. 6:20; cf. Isa. 65:4). In Ezk. 24:10, where the AV follows the MT with "spice it well," the RSV follows the LXX with "empty out the broth." The NEB reads similarly. R. K. H.

BROTHER [Heb. *'āḥ*; Gk. *adelphós*]. Besides the usual literal meaning, "brother" is used extensively in both the OT and NT of other relations and relationships. Abram's nephew Lot is termed "brother" (Gen. 14:14); Moses' fellow countrymen are "brethren" (Acts 3:22; cf. He. 7:5). It may indicate a member of the same tribe (2 S. 19:12); an ally (Am. 1:9); or an allied or cognate people (Nu. 20:14). It is used of common discipleship (Mt. 23:8); of moral likeness or kinship (Prov. 18:9); or friends (Job 6:15); an equal in rank or office (1 K. 9:13); one of the same faith (Acts 11:29; 1 Cor. 5:11). It is a favorite oriental metaphor used to express likeness or similarity (Job 30:29, "I am a brother to jackals"). It can indicate a fellow priest or office bearer (Ezr. 3:2). Paul called Sosthenes "brother" (1 Cor. 1:1) and Timothy his spiritual son and associate (2 Cor. 1:1). It may signify spiritual kinship (Mt. 12:50). Finally, it is a term adopted by the early disciples and Christians to express their fraternal love for each other in Christ, and universally adopted as the language of love and brotherhood in His kingdom in all subsequent time (2 Pet. 3:15; Col. 4:7, 9, 15).

Jesus made "brother" and "neighbor" in a sense equivalent terms (Mt. 7:3f.), as though to extend the love and care expected within the family unit to those with whom His people have contact. Brotherhood was to become a hallmark of the Lord's people, His Church. The rabbis distinguished between "brother" and "neighbor," applying "brother" to Israelites by blood, "neighbor" to proselytes, but allowing neither title to the Gentiles. Christ and the apostles gave the name "brother" to all Christians. Undoubtedly throughout the Christian era the exercise of brotherly affection within the body of Christ has called attention to the desirability of this fellowship and has been a powerful factor in attracting many to the faith. *See also* RELATIONSHIPS, FAMILY.

Bibliography.–*TDNT*, I, *s.v.* ἀδελφός (von Soden); *TDOT*, I, *s.v.* "'āch" (Ringgren). D. M. PRATT E. F. H.

BROTHERHOOD [Heb. *'aḥ^a^wa* (Zec. 11:14); Gk. *adelphótēs* (1 Pet. 2:17; 5:9); occurs also (RSV) for Heb. *'āḥ* (Am. 1:9) and Gk. *adelphoí* (1 Cor. 6:5)]; AV also BRETHREN, "brotherly"; NEB also KINSHIP, "brother Christian." The rare occurrence of the term in contrast with the abundant use of "brother," "brethren," seems to indicate that the sense of the vital relation naturally called for the most concrete expression: "the brethren." But in 1 Pet. 2:17 the abstract is used for the concrete. In the OT the brotherhood of all Israelites was emphasized; but in the NT the brotherhood in Christ is a relation so much deeper and stronger as to eclipse the other. *See also* BROTHER.

BROTHER-IN-LAW. *See* RELATIONSHIPS, FAMILY.

BROTHERLY LOVE [Gk. *philadelphía*] (He. 13:1); also **BROTHERLY AFFECTION** (Rom. 12:10; 2 Pet. 1:7); **LOVE OF THE BRETHREN** (1 Thess. 4:9); AV also BROTHERLY KINDNESS (2 Pet. 1:7); NEB LOVE FOR OUR BROTHERHOOD, BROTHERLY KINDNESS, "love your fellow-Christians." These terms, more than any others, set forth the distinctive character of the relationship between Christians. Whereas the term "love" (Gk. *agápē*) can be used for the attitude of believers both toward one another (Jn. 15:12) and toward society in general (1 Thess. 3:12; cf. Mt. 5:44), *philadelphía* is restricted to love of the brotherhood of believers (*adelphótēs*). This is especially apparent when the two terms occur in the same context, as in 2 Pet. 1:7. *See* LOVE III.

The insistence that all men are children of God simply by virtue of creation tends to depreciate or even obliterate the distinctiveness of *philadelphía*. All are indeed the offspring of God (Acts 17:28) and by virtue of that fact can be regarded as potential children of God, but the new birth is necessary for this to become a reality (Jn. 1:12f.).

The Mosaic law made its demand, "You shall love your neighbor as yourself" (Lev. 19:18), which was to be realized not merely in sentiment but in seeking the neighbor's good, by refusing to lie to him or bear false witness against him, and by resisting the temptation to covet his possessions. The term "neighbor" was understood to apply in a local or at most a national sense. Jesus broadened the frame of reference to include anyone who is near and in need of help. In similar fashion He enlarged the content of the word "brother," refusing to restrict it to fellow Israelites, but instead giving it a spiritual dimension by acknowledging that His brethren were those who did the will of God (Mt. 12:50). The Church is heir to this reinterpretation, for while the term "brother" continues to be used in the familiar nativistic sense it is far more often used of both men and women ("brethren") who have become believers.

A high note in the use of terminology is sounded when the NT records Jesus' willingness to speak of His followers as His brethren (Jn. 20:17; cf. Rom. 8:29; He. 2:11, 17). This is love in magnificent condescension, calculated to remove all barriers of station and attainment in the exercise of mutual love among His followers.

Apostolic teaching frankly acknowledges the danger

that brotherly love may be allowed to degenerate into a profession of word unsupported by the reality of deed (1 Jn. 3:18; cf. 1 Cor. 6:8). One's refusal to give aid to a brother in need raises a serious question as to whether God's love really dwells in him (1 Jn. 3:17). On the other hand true brotherly love produces a willingness even to sacrifice one's life for another (1 Jn. 3:16).

At times one detects a deliberate use of "brethren" in direct address when an apostle or church leader feels the need of admonishing his readers and wishes to assure them in so doing that he loves them and has their best interests at heart (e.g., 1 Cor. 1:11; Jas. 2:1, 5, 14). This serves to soften the sharpness of necessary criticism.

According to Jesus, brotherly love is the badge of true discipleship and has the potential to reflect His love for the world even to those who have not known Him or seen Him (Jn. 13:34f.). No wonder Paul challenged his converts to love one another more and more (1 Thess. 4:9f.). The manifestation of this Christian virtue amazed pagan society, as Tertullian testifies: "See, they say, how they love one another . . . how they are ready even to die for one another" (*Apol.* 39). E. F. HARRISON

BROTHERS OF THE LORD. In Mt. 12:46ff.; Mk. 3:31ff.; Lk. 8:19ff., while Jesus was in the midst of an earnest argument with scribes and Pharisees, His mother and brothers sent a message evidently intended to end the discussion. In order to indicate that no familial ties should interfere with the discharge of the duties of His messianic office, He stretched His hands toward His disciples, and said: "Whoever does the will of my Father in heaven is my brother, and sister, and mother." In Mt. 13:54ff.; Mk. 6:2ff., while He was teaching in His own town Nazareth, His neighbors, who, since they had watched His natural growth among them, could not comprehend the extraordinary claims that He was making, declared in an interrogative form that they knew all about the entire family & mother, brothers, and sisters — and they named the brothers.

In Jn. 2:12, His brothers are said to have accompanied Jesus and His mother and disciples from the wedding at Cana. In Jn. 7:3ff., they are described as unbelieving, and ridiculing His claims with bitter sarcasm. This attitude of hostility has disappeared when, at Jerusalem, after the Resurrection and Ascension (Acts 1:14), in the company of Mary and the Eleven and the faithful group of women, they "devoted themselves to prayer," awaiting the promise of the gift of the Holy Spirit. Their subsequent participation in the missionary activity of the apostolic Church appears in 1 Cor. 9:5: "Do we not have the right to be accompanied by a wife, as the other apostles and the brothers of the Lord and Cephas?"

In Gal. 1:19, James, bishop of the church at Jerusalem, is designated "the Lord's brother," thus harmonizing with Mt. 13:55, where their names are recorded as James, Joseph, Simon, and Judas. When, then, "Jude, . . . brother of James" is mentioned (Jude 1), the possibility is raised that Jude is another brother of the Lord.

In reading these passages, the natural inference is that these "brothers" were the sons of Joseph and Mary, born after Jesus, living with Mary and her daughters in the home at Nazareth, accompanying their mother on her journeys, and called the "brothers" of the Lord in a sense similar to that in which Joseph was called His father. They were brothers because of their common relationship to Mary. This impression is strengthened in that Jesus is called her *prōtótokos,* "firstborn son" (Lk. 2:7), as well as by the very decided implication of Mt. 1:25. Even though each particular, taken separately, might be explained otherwise, the force of the argument is cumulative. There are too many items to be explained away in order to establish any other inference. This view is not the most ancient. It has been traced to Tertullian, and was more fully developed by Helvidius, an obscure writer of the 4th century.

Two other views have been advocated with much learning and earnestness. The earlier, which seems to have been prevalent in the first three centuries and is supported by Origen, Eusebius, Gregory of Nyssa, and Ambrose, Epiphanius being its chief advocate, regards these "brothers" as the children of Joseph by a former marriage, and Mary as his second wife. Joseph disappears from sight when Jesus is twelve years old. We know nothing of him after the narrative of the child Jesus in the temple. That there is no allusion to him in the account of the family in Mk. 6:3 indicates that Mary had been a widow long before she stood by the cross without the support of any member of her immediate family. In the apocryphal gospels, the attempt is made to supply what the canonical Gospels omit. They report that Joseph was over eighty years of age at his second marriage, and the names of both sons and daughters by his first marriage are given. As Lightfoot (comm. on Galatians) has remarked, "they are pure fabrications." Theophylact even advanced the theory that they were the children of Joseph by a levirate marriage, with the widow of his brother Clopas. Others regard them as the nephews of Joseph whom, after the death of his brother Clopas, he had taken into his own home, and who thus became members of his family and were considered as though they were the children of Joseph and Mary. According to this view, Mary excepted, the whole family at Nazareth were no blood relatives of Jesus. It is a docetic conception in the interest of the dogma of the perpetual virginity of Mary. All its details, even that of the advanced age and decrepitude of Joseph, start from that premise.

Another view was first propounded by Jerome when a very young man, while antagonizing Helvidius, but afterward qualified by its author. This view was followed by Augustine and the Roman Catholic writers generally. At the Reformation it was accepted — though not urged — by Luther, and later by Chemnitz, Bengel, *et al.* This view understands the word "brother" in the general sense of "kinsman," and interprets it here as equivalent to "cousin." Thus these brothers would be blood relatives of Jesus, and not of Joseph. They were the children of Alphaeus, otherwise known as Clopas (Jn. 19:25), and the sister of Mary. This Mary, in Mt. 27:56, is described as "the mother of James and Joseph," and in Mk. 15:40, "the mother of James the younger and of Joses, and Salome." This theory as completely developed points to the three names, James, Judas, and Simon, found both in the list of the apostles and in that of the "brothers," and argues that it would be a remarkable coincidence if they referred to different persons, and if the two sisters, both named Mary, had found the very same names for their sons. The advocates of this theory argue also that the expression "James the younger" shows that there were only two persons of the name James in the circle of those who were closely connected with Jesus. They say, further, that after the death of Joseph Mary came to live at the home of her sister, and, with the families so combined, the presence and attendance of her nephews and nieces can be explained without much difficulty, and the words of the people at Nazareth can be understood.

But this complicated theory labors under many difficulties. The identity of Clopas and Alphaeus cannot be established, resting as it does upon obscure philological resemblances of the Aramaic form of the two names (*see* ALPHAEUS). The most that such argument affords is a mere possibility. Nor is the identity of "Mary the wife of Clopas" with the sister of Mary the mother of Jesus established beyond a doubt. Jn. 19:25, upon which it rests, can with equal correctness be interpreted as teaching that four women stood by the cross, of whom "Mary of Clopas" was one, and His mother's sister was another. The decision depends upon the question as to whether "Mary" be in apposition to "sister." If the verse be read so as to present two pairs, it would not be a construction without precedent in the NT, and would avoid the difficulty of finding two sisters with the same name — a difficulty greater yet than that of three cousins with the same name. Nor is the identity of "James the younger" with the son of Alphaeus beyond a doubt. Any argument concerning the comparative "younger" as above explained, fails when it is found that in the Greek there is no comparative, but only "James the little," the implication being probably that he was unusually short of stature. Nor is the difficulty less when it is proposed to identify three of these brothers of Jesus with apostles of the same name. For the "brothers" and the apostles are repeatedly distinguished. In Mt. 12:49, while the former stood outside, the latter are gathered around Jesus. In Jn. 2:12, we read: "his mother and his brothers and his disciples." In Acts 1:13 the Eleven are mentioned, including James the son of Alphaeus, and Simon the Zealot, and Judas the son of James, and then it is said that they were accompanied by "his brothers." But the crowning difficulty of this hypothesis of Jerome is the record of the unbelief of the brothers and of their derision of His claims in Jn. 7:3-5.

On the other hand, the arguments against regarding them as sons of Mary and Joseph are not formidable. When it is urged that their attempts to interfere with Jesus indicate a superiority which, according to Jewish custom, is inconsistent with the position of younger brothers, it may be answered that those who pursue an unjustifiable course are not models of consistency. When an argument is sought in that Jesus on the cross commended His mother to John, implying that she had no sons of her own to whom to turn in her grief and desolation, the answer need not be restricted to the consideration that unknown domestic circumstances may explain the omission of her sons. A more patent explanation is that as they did not understand their brother, they could not understand their mother, whose whole life and interests were bound up in her firstborn. And no one of the disciples understood Jesus and appreciated His work and treasured up His words as did John. A bond of fellowship had thus been established between John and Mary that was closer than her nearer blood relationship with her own sons, who up to this time had regarded the course of Jesus with disapproval, and had no sympathy with His mission. In the home of John she would find consolation for her loss, as the memories of the wonderful life of her son would be recalled, and she would converse with him who had rested on the bosom of Jesus and whom Jesus loved. Even with the conversion of these brothers within a few days into faithful confessors, provision was made for her deeper spiritual communion with her risen and ascended son through the testimony of Jesus which John treasured in his deeply contemplative spirit. There was much similarity in the characters of Mary and John. This may have had its ground in relationship, as many regard his mother Salome as the sister of the mother of Jesus.

The interpretation that they are the Lord's real brothers ennobles and glorifies family life in all its relations and duties, and sanctifies motherhood with all its cares and trials as holier than a selfish isolation from the world, in order to evade the annoyances and humiliations inseparable from fidelity to our callings. Not only Mary, but Jesus with her, knew what it was to grieve over a house divided concerning religion (Mt. 10:35ff.). But that this unbelief and indifference gave way before the clearer light of the resurrection of Jesus is shown by the presence of these brothers in the company of the disciples of Jerusalem (Acts 1:14). The reference to His postresurrection appearance to James (1 Cor. 15:7) is probably connected with this change in their attitude. 1 Cor. 9:5 shows that at least two of these brothers were active as missionaries, undoubtedly within the Holy Land and to Jews, according to the agreement into which James entered in Gal. 2 and his well-known attitude on questions pertaining to the Gentiles. Zahn regards James as an ascetic and celibate not included in 1 Cor. 9:5, which is limited then to Jude and Simon. Their marriage indicates "the absence in the Holy Family of that pseudo-asceticism which has so much confused the tradition concerning them" (Alford). *See also* JAMES.

For fuller discussions see the extensive arguments of J. Eadie (1869) and J. B. Lightfoot (1890) in their comms. on Galatians, the former in favor of the Helvidian, and the latter, with his exhaustive scholarship, of the Epiphanian views; also, on the side of the former, J. B. Mayor, *Epistle of St. James* (3rd ed. 1913); F. W. Farrar, *Early Days of Christianity* (1882); T. Zahn, *Intro. to the NT* (Eng. tr. 1909). For summarizing discussions see H-S, I, 418-425; *Zondervan Pictorial Encyclopedia of the Bible*, *s.v.* "Brothers of Jesus." H. E. JACOBS

BROTHER'S WIFE [Heb. *y^{e}ḇēmeṯ* (Dt. 25:7, 9), *'ēšeṯ 'āḥ* (Gen. 38:8f.; Lev. 18:16; 20:21); Gk. *hē gynḗ toú adelphoú* (Mk. 6:18; Lk. 3:19)]; NEB also BROTHER'S WIDOW. A brother's wife occupied a unique position in Hebrew custom and law, by virtue of the institution of the levirate. The widow had no hereditary rights in her husband's property, but was considered a part of the estate, and the surviving brother of the deceased was considered the natural heir. The right to inherit the widow soon became a duty to marry her if the deceased had left no sons, and in case there was no brother-in-law, the duty of marriage devolved on the father-in-law or the agnate who inherited, whoever this might be. The first son of the levirate marriage was regarded as the son of the deceased.

The levirate marriage undoubtedly existed as a custom before the Israelites settled in Canaan, but after this it received special significance because of the succession to the property of the first son of the marriage. This son was reckoned to the deceased and inherited from his putative rather than from his real father, thus preventing the disintegration of property and its acquirement by strangers and at the same time perpetuating the family to which it belonged. While the law limited the matrimonial duty to the brother and permitted him to decline to marry the widow, such a course was attended by public disgrace (Dt. 25:5ff.). By the law of Nu. 27:8, daughters were given the right to inherit, in order that the family estate might be preserved, and the levirate became limited to cases where the deceased had left no children at all.

See also MARRIAGE II.A. F. E. HIRSCH

BROW [Heb. *qoḏqōḏ, mēṣaḥ*; Gk. *orphrýs*]; AV also "crown of the head," FOREHEAD; NEB also HEAD. The term *qoḏqōḏ* is used in Gen. 49:26 in the sense of "crown of the head"; *mēṣaḥ* refers to the forehead. In Lk. 4:29 *ophrýs* denotes a projection of land.

BROWN. *See* COLOR V.A.

BRUISE [Heb. *šûp* (Gen. 3:15), *dāḵā'* (Isa. 53:5, 10), *mā'aḵ* (Lev. 22:24), *rāṣaṣ* (Isa. 42:3), *ḥabbûrâ* (Isa. 1:6); Gk. *syntríbō* (Mt. 12:20), *katakóptō* (Mk. 5:5)]; AV also CUT (Mk. 5:5); NEB also STRIKE AT (Gen. 3:15), TORTURE (Isa. 53:5, 10), SNAP OFF (Mt. 12:20), CUT (Mk. 5:5).

KoB suggests two meanings for Heb. *šûp*: "bruise" and "snatch" (p. 956), the second meaning more adequately describing the serpent's action toward man and the first describing man's trampling upon the serpent. The *ḥabbûrâ* in Isa. 1:6 are wounds made by stripes, the blows Judah has received as chastisement from God. The term "bruise, bruised" occurs three times in the Servant Songs. The Servant of the Lord will not crush those who are weak and oppressed, but will establish justice (Isa. 42:3); in Mt. 12:15-21 Jesus' healing of the sick and maimed is interpreted as a fulfillment of this Servant Song. The Servant will himself be crushed (*dāḵā'*, "crush, break in pieces") for the sake of sinners (Isa. 53:5, 10).   N. J. O.

BRUIT (Jer. 10:22; Nah. 3:19, AV). Archaic for "rumor" or "report."

BRUSHWOOD [Heb. *śôḵaṭ 'ēṣîm*–'branches of trees' (Jgs. 9:48), *ḥᵃmāsîm* (Isa. 64:2)]; AV BOUGH, "melting." Cut boughs of trees, decayed and dried out, useful for kindling fires.

BRUTISH. *See* STUPID.

BUBASTIS boo-bas'təs. *See* PI-BESETH.

BUCKET [Heb. *dᵉlî*]; NEB also VESSELS. The word is found only in Isa. 40:15; Nu. 24:7. The bucket was doubtless a waterskin with two crosspieces at the top to fit it for use in drawing water, like those now in use in Palestine.

BUCKLE [Gk. *pórpē*]; NEB CLASP. The buckle was used for fastening the mantle or outer robe on the shoulder or chest. As a mark of favor Jonathan Maccabeus was presented by Alexander Balas with a buckle of gold (1 Macc. 10:89), the wearing of which was restricted to rulers and their close relations or friends.

BUCKLER [Heb. *ṣinnâ, sōḥērâ, magēn*]; AV also TARGETS (2 Ch. 14:8); NEB also SHIELD. The buckler was a small rounded shield usually worn on the arm, comprising part of the defensive armor of the warrior (cf. Ps. 35:2; 91:4; Jer. 46:3; Ezk. 23:24; 38:4). *See* WEAPONS OF WAR.

BUFFET. The AV for Gk. *kolaphízō*, "beat with the fist." In Mt. 26:67; Mk. 14:65 the RSV has "strike," the NEB "strike with fists." "Buffeted" occurs in both the AV and RSV at 1 Cor. 4:11 (NEB "roughly handled"). Elsewhere the RSV has "harass" (2 Cor. 12:7; NEB "bruise") and "beaten" (1 Pet. 2:20).

BUGAEAN (Ad. Est. 12:6, NEB). *See* BOUGAEAN.

BUGLE [Gk. *sálpinx*] (1 Cor. 14:8); AV, NEB, TRUMPET. All other uses of this word are rendered "trumpet" in the RSV. *See* MUSIC II.A.

BUILD; BUILDING [Heb. *bānâ, binyān, binyâ* (Ezk. 41:13); Aram. *bᵉnâ*; Gk. *oikodoméō, kataskeuázō*]. During Iron I, from the conquest till the end of the united monarchy (1200-900), Israelite building was inferior to that of the preceding Canaanite period; and it is highly significant that Solomon had to make use of Phoenician artisans in order to effect his building program. During Iron II the art of building, as attested for example by the ruins of Ahab's palace in Samaria and the so-called Solomonic stables of Megiddo (actually from Ahab's time), rose considerably. After the Exile the economic conditions were not favorable for any intensive building activity; a definite change came with Hellenistic and Roman times, culminating in Herod's sumptuous buildings.

I. Houses.–Throughout the whole of biblical times the common man built his own house, perhaps with the help of his family and neighbors. Trenches were dug for foundations of undressed stones. These trenches seldom reached bedrock; often they cut partially through the remains of older walls. On such stone foundations walls were erected from sun-dried clay, often whitewashed in order to protect them against the rain. The roof consisted of beams on which twigs were laid, and the whole was made impermeable by a layer of clay and whitewash.

In the course of Iron II the wealthier people were not content with such simple houses. Although a light superstructure could be erected on the roof of an ordinary house (2 K. 4:10), for taller buildings stronger foundations and walls were needed. So the rich started to build the walls of their houses from stone instead of from clay, to the indignation of the prophets (Isa. 9:9; Am. 5:11).

Succession of structures, probably water tanks or storage areas, built against the Pre-pottery Neolithic stone tower (left) at Jericho (7th-6th millennia B.C.). Later inhabitants built houses upon these foundations. (A. C. Myers)

Such stones had to be dressed in regular shapes; hence they were called *gāzîṯ*. This could be done with the help of hammer and chisel; sometimes a stone saw (*m*e*gērâ*, 2 S. 12:31; 1 K. 7:9; 1 Ch. 20:3) was used. but probably most often for erecting state buildings, not private houses. The need for stronger foundations is expressed in the word for houses of at least two stories: *'armôn* ("palace"), the root of which suggests special care for foundations. Excavations have revealed foundations and a few layers of the ground floors only; but several houses show definite indications of a staircase leading to the upper story.

Doors were of wood, and thus have perished; some stone imitations show what they were like at least in Roman times. Openings in the wall for letting in air and light have not been found, so they must have been small and high. In some ivories from Samaria the face of the "goddess looking through the window" obstructs the whole opening. Tiles for covering roof first came into use in Hellenistic times (Lk. 5:19). As a rule every house had its own court surrounded by a wall; the "door of the house" is the door giving access to the courtyard (Acts 12:12-16). On one side of this courtyard the main buildings are to be found; often it is not a door but a large opening supported by columns that gives access to the main room, especially in more spacious houses where three or four column bases are no rarity. The seven columns of the house of Lady Wisdom (Prov. 9:1) show her to be a grand lady indeed. From the main room a door leads to a smaller room, the "inner chamber" (lit. "room in room") of 1 K. 20:30; 22:25; 2 Ch. 18:24, where one sleeps and should retire for prayer (Mt. 6:6).

II. Fortifications.–When it is said of someone that he "built" a town, the meaning is that he built or rebuilt the fortifications. They consist primarily of a huge wall of stones, often protected by a sloping glacis, on strong and deep foundations. Sometimes a dry moat is added. In the wall there are one or more gates, elaborate structures with defensive bulwarks on both sides, the "towers" of the OT, which were, however, only slightly higher than the walls, but by their protruding position gave opportunity of enflanking the wall. Such *migdōlîm* are known both from excavations and from Egyptian and Assyrian reliefs. Sometimes a *migdōl* was not part of a city but an independent structure erected at some strategic point, e.g., to protect trading routes. The "building" of towns, though in former times the responsibility of local authorities, was in the time of the Israelite monarchies the prerogative of kings. Joshua's building of Timnath-serah (Josh. 19:50) is an isolated case.

We do not hear of building activities by Saul, though Albright ascribed to him the fortifications of Tell el-Fûl (Gibeah). David built part of Jerusalem (1 Ch. 11:8); Solomon's building activities in Jerusalem and elsewhere are described in 1 K. 6:1–7:12; 9:15-19. Traces of his fortifications have been identified in Hazor. Fortification of towns is ascribed to Rehoboam (2 Ch. 11:5-12), Jeroboam (1 K. 12:25), and their successors, e.g., Omri (16:24) and Ahab (22:39). Hiel probably acted as an official of Ahab when he restored Jericho (16:34), just as Nehemiah rebuilt Jerusalem's walls as a governor of the Persian king (Neh. 3).

III. Other Royal Buildings.–Owing to the peculiar circumstances in Jerusalem, archeological research could not reveal anything of Solomon's temple, palace, and related buildings. The excavation of Ezion-geber, however, gives us some idea of the technique of his time. The impressive stables of Megiddo probably date not from his time but from Ahab's. The excavated parts of the royal complex in Samaria are to be ascribed to Jeroboam II. Such royal buildings were entirely of *gāzîṯ*, dressed stones. Typical are the irregular use of stretchers and layers, and the use of the so-called proto-Aeolic capitals. If one compares the findings in Egypt and Assyria, one is struck by the absence of building inscriptions in Israel. Mesha's inscription found in neighboring Moab ends with an enumeration of this king's building activities, but it is probable that Israelite kings from a sense of religious humility abstained from this self-glorifying kind of literature. Even Herod, the greatest royal builder of later times, seems to have spared his subjects' sensitivities in this regard.

Hellenistic round tower at Samaria. A series of these well-constructed fortifications reinforced the Israelite defense walls on the middle terrace. (Israel Department of Antiquities and Museums)

IV. Building Implements.–Simple buildings could be erected with the help of the carpenter's instruments. For dressing stones, hammer and chisel could be used; the stone saw was used only for elaborate buildings. For such buildings also a plumbline (Am. 7:7f.) was needed, as well as measuring rods (Ezk. 40:3, etc.) of reed and measuring lines of flax (Job 38:5). In Megiddo red ochre traces of such a line have been found. A leveling instrument is mentioned in 2 K. 21:13; Isa. 28:17. Builders made use of a model of a building they were to erect (Ex. 25:9, 40; 2 K. 16:10; Ps. 144:12). The same word (*taḇnîṯ*) in 1 Ch. 28:19 (cf. vv. 11f., 18) seems to indicate an architectural drawing.

V. Building as a Symbol.–In the OT "to build" with God as subject, often means "to give offspring" (Gen. 16:2; 2 S. 7:27; etc.; cf. Ex. 1:21); and in Dt. 25:9 a man is the subject of this verb used in the same sense. Similes are taken from the laying of foundations, especially in descriptions of creation (Ps. 24:2, etc.), and from the use of the best stones for corners (Ps. 118:22; 144:12).

A headstone as a crowning piece seems to be intended in Zec. 4:7, perhaps above the main entrance. In the NT "to build" is a metaphor for the work of God and His servants in order to establish the Church on earth. One should not look for allegoric consistency. Christ is called both the foundation (1 Cor. 3:11) and the cornerstone (Eph. 2:20-22); but elsewhere also the apostles and prophets are described as the foundation (Mt. 16:18; Eph. 2:20; cf. Rev. 21:14). There is no contradiction in this when we consider that Christ is known to us by the authoritative testimony of the apostles and prophets.

See also ARCHITECTURE; EDIFICATION; FORTIFICATION; HOUSE.

Bibliography.–*TDNT,* V, *s.v.* οἶκος (Michel); A. G. Barrois, *Manuel d'archéologie biblique*, I (1939), 100-126.

A. VAN SELMS

BUILDER [Heb. *bānâ*; Gk. *kataskeuázō, oikodoméō, technítēs*]; NEB also FOUNDER (He. 3:3f.), ARCHITECT (He. 11:10); **MASTER BUILDER** [Gk. *architéktōn*] (1 Cor. 3:10). Beyond the literal significance (*see* BUILD) are several figurative applications, notably to God as the divine Builder (1) as establishing, e.g., the nation (Ps. 69:35; 102:16; Jer. 12:16), the throne of David (Ps. 89:4), Jerusalem (147:2); (2) in restoration — rebuilding (Isa. 58:12; 61:4; 65:21; Jer. 31:4, 28; 42:10; Ezk. 36:36; Am. 9:11; cf. Acts 15:16); (3) as establishing in prosperity (Job 22:23; 1 S. 2:35; Jer. 24:6; cf. Gen. 16:2, NEB). Other figurative uses include: (4) the firm establishment of the divine attributes (Ps. 89:2); (5) divine opposition (Lam. 3:5, "He hath builded against me"); cf. Job 19:8; (6) the choosing of a corner-stone which the builders rejected (Ps. 118:22f.; quoted by Christ [MT 21:42; Mk. 12:10; Lk. 20:17]; by Peter [Acts 4:11; 1 Pet. 2:7]).

In the NT Christians are represented as being (1) built by God (1 Cor. 3:9, 16) on Christ as the one foundation (Mt. 16:18, on Jesus as the Christ; 1 Pet. 2:5f.; Acts 9:31; Rom. 15:20; 1 Cor. 3:10, 12, 14 [*epoikodoméō*]; Eph. 2:20); (2) as being continuously and progressively built up in their faith and life (Acts 20:32; 1 Cor. 8:1; 10:23; 14:4, 17; 1 Thess. 5:11; cf. Jude 20); (3) they are "builded together" (*synoikodoméō*) in Christ (Eph. 2:22; Col. 2:7 [*epoikodoméō*]; cf. 1 Cor. 3:9). In He. 3:4 God is represented as the Builder of all things, and in 11:10 as the Builder (*technítēs*) of the New Jerusalem. In 1 Cor. 3:10-14; Gal. 2:18, "building" means constructing a system of teaching; Paul speaks of himself as "a wise master builder."

Isaiah 49:17 gives a better sense if emended as in the RSV, "Your builders outstrip your destroyers" (NEB "those who are to rebuild you"), instead of the AV "Thy children shall make haste." The emendation (Heb. *bōnāyiḵ* for *bānāyiḵ* has the support of ancient versions, including 1QIsa.

W. L. WALKER

BUKKI buk'ī [Heb. *buqqî*–'proved of God'].

1. A Danite, son of the tribal prince Jogli (Nu. 34:22); he was one of the representative chiefs who assisted in the division of the land.

2. [Gk. *Bokki, Bokka* (1 Esd. 8:2)]. Son of Abishua and father of Izzi, a priest, fourth in descent from Aaron, in the line of Eleazar (1 Ch. 6:5, 51), and ancestor of Ezra (Ezr. 7:4). In 1 Esd. 8:2 the name is rendered "Boccas" by the AV and "Bocca" by the NEB. In 2 Esd. 1:2 the name appears as BORITH.

BUKKIAH bək-ī'ə [Heb. *buqqîyāhû*–'proved of God']. A Levite, son of Heman (1 Ch. 25:4, 13).

BUL bul [Heb. *bûl*]. The name of the eighth month of the Jewish year (1 K. 6:38). It is of Phoenician origin and signifies the month of rain, the beginning of the rainy season. *See* CALENDAR II.A.

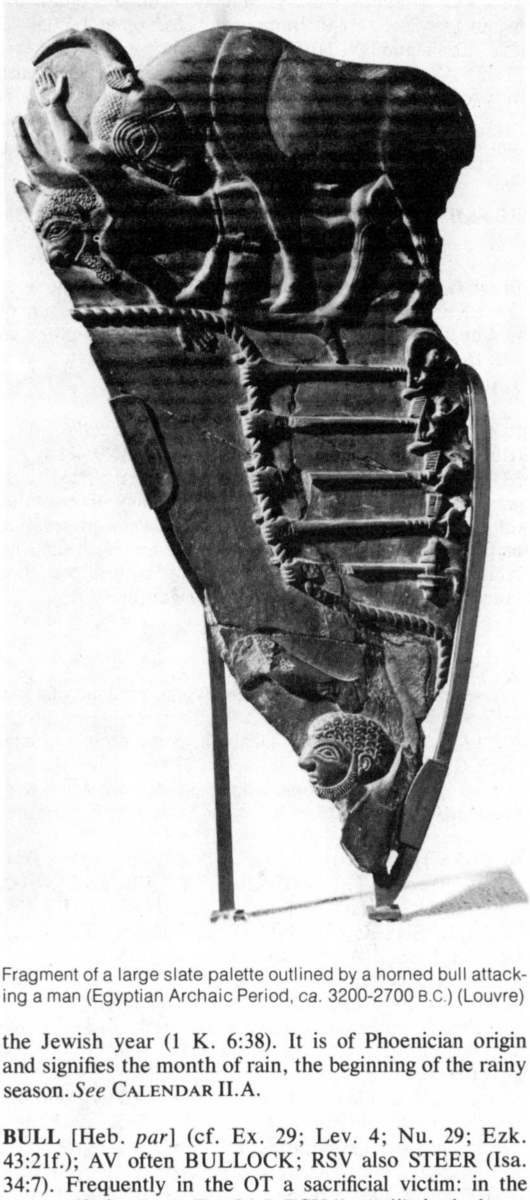

Fragment of a large slate palette outlined by a horned bull attacking a man (Egyptian Archaic Period, *ca.* 3200-2700 B.C.) (Louvre)

BULL [Heb. *par*] (cf. Ex. 29; Lev. 4; Nu. 29; Ezk. 43:21f.); AV often BULLOCK; RSV also STEER (Isa. 34:7). Frequently in the OT a sacrificial victim: in the peace offering (e.g., Ex. 24:5; RSV "oxen"), in the burnt offering (e.g., Jgs. 6:25), and in the sin offering (e.g., Ezk. 43:19). So often is it a term for a sacrificial animal that it becomes a figure for warriors killed in battle (Isa. 34:7; Ezk. 34:8) and a metaphor for praise to God (Hos. 14:2). The psalmist sees in the bull a figure for his enemies (Ps. 22:12).

See also CATTLE.

BULL, WILD. *See* ANTELOPE; CATTLE.

BULLS, JEROBOAM'S. *See* CALF, GOLDEN.

BULRUSH. *See* RUSH; PAPYRUS.

BULRUSHES, ARK OF. *See* BASKET.

BULWARK. The word represents several Hebrew terms. It occurs in the singular as a translation of *'ōz* in Ps.

8:2 (AV "strength"; NEB "mighty"); in the plural for *ḥēl* in Isa. 26:1 (NEB "ramparts"), *'ošyôṯ* in Jer. 50:15 (AV "foundations"; NEB "bastions"), *'ᵃgammîm* in Jer. 51:32 (AV "reeds"; NEB "guardtowers"). It is found only once in the NT for Gk. *hedraíōma,* where it is used figuratively of the Christian Church as "the pillar and bulwark [AV "ground"] of the truth" (1 Tim. 3:15). *See* FORTIFICATION.

BUNAH bo͞o'nə [Heb. *bûnâ*]. A son of Jerahmeel (1 Ch. 2:25).

BUNCH. The term occurs in the singular only once in the RSV for Heb. *'ᵃguddâ* in reference to a bunch of hyssop (Ex. 12:22). It occurs also once in the plural in 2 S. 16:1 of dried clusters (Heb. *ṣimmûq*) of raisins.

See also CLUSTER.

BUNDLE [Heb. *ṣᵉrôr*] (Gen. 42:35; 1 S. 25:29); [*ṣeḇeṯ*] (Ruth 2:16); AV HANDFULS; [*śôḵâ*] (Jgs. 9:48f.); AV BOUGH; [Gk. *plḗthos*] (Acts 28:3); NEB ARMFUL; [*désmē*] (Mt. 13:30). The custom of binding up precious things in bundles is the basis of the very interesting metaphor in 1 S. 25:29: "The life of my lord shall be bound in the bundle of the living in the care of the Lord your God," conveying the idea of perfect safety.

J. R. VAN PELT

BUNNI bun'i [Heb. *bunnî, bûnî, bûnnî*].

1. A postexilic Levite present when Ezra proclaimed the law (Neh. 9:4).

2. A Levite, father of Hashabiah, and a temple official (Neh. 11:15).

3. A leader of the people who sealed the covenant with Nehemiah (Neh. 10:15).

BURDEN [Heb. *massā', sēḇel, sōḇel, yᵉhāḇ, ṭōraḥ* (Isa. 1:14)]; AV also TROUBLE (*ṭōraḥ*); NEB also LOAD, HINDRANCE, TARGET (Job 7:20), FORTUNES (Ps. 55:22), LABOUR; [*nāśa'*] ("bear the burden," Ex. 18:22); [*sāḇal*]; NEB HAULIERS, "carrying loads"; [*kāḇēḏ*] ("lay heavy burdens upon," Neh. 5:15); AV "be chargeable"; [Gk. *báros, phortíon*]; NEB also LOAD, PACKS; [*katabaréō, epibaréō, katanarkáō*] ("not burden"); AV also "not be burdensome, "not be chargeable"; NEB also "not sponge."

In the OT, any kind of load was described as a burden, whether of the literal sort (Ex. 23:5; 2 K. 5:17; Jer. 17:21; etc.) or the moral figurative variety (Nu. 11:11, 17; Dt. 1:12; etc.), where *massā'* was employed. The *massā'* of prophetic responsibility was translated "burden" in the AV (cf. Isa. 15:1; 17:1) but "oracle" by the RSV and NEB (cf. Isa. 13:1; 15:1; Zec. 9:1; 12:1; Mal. 1:1). A man's iniquities could be burdensome to himself (Ps. 38:4). Nouns derived from the root *sāḇal,* "bear a load," are used to convey the idea of burden in Ps. 81:6; Isa. 10:27; 14:25, and occur in the plural in Ex. 1:11; 2:11; 5:4; etc. In Ps. 55:22, *yᵉhāḇ,* "lot," is rendered "burden" by the AV and RSV and "fortunes" by the NEB.

In the NT, *báros,* "something heavy," is used of daily burdens (Mt. 20:12), of difficult requirements (Acts 15:28; Rev. 2:24), or of one's moral infirmities (Gal. 6:2). *Phortíon,* "something to be borne," is used of the obligation which Christ imposes (Mt. 11:30) or the legal ordinances of the Pharisees (Lk. 11:46). The difference between these two terms is difficult to understand, since their use in the papyri parallels that in the NT. R. K. H.

BURDEN-BEARERS [Heb. *sabbālîm*] (2 Ch. 34:13; cf. 1 K. 5:15; Neh. 4:10). Laborers in the construction and restoration of the temple at Jerusalem, apparently engaged in transporting or clearing away building material. Those who worked on the original temple were slaves or foreign captives (cf. 1 K. 9:15; 2 Ch. 2:18).

BURGLARY. *See* CRIME.

BURIAL [Heb. *qᵉḇûrâ*; Gk. *entaphiázō*–either the act of burial (Jer. 22:19; prob. Eccl. 6:3; Isa. 14:20; and the one AV NT reference, Mt. 26:12; cf. *entaphiasmós*–'burying,' Mk. 14:8; Jn. 12:7) or the place of burial (2 Ch. 26:23)]; AV also "burying place" (Gen. 47:30), "grave" (Gen. 35:20; Ezk. 32:23f.), "sepulchre" (Dt. 34:6; 1 S. 10:2; 2 K. 9:28; 23:30); [cf. Heb. *qeḇer, šᵉ'ôl*–poetic, 'grave'].

I. Importance
II. Preparations
  A. Duties of the Family
  B. Embalming
  C. Mourners
  D. Processions
III. Interment
  A. Earthen Graves
  B. Tombs
    1. Pre-Israelite
    2. Israelite
    3. Classical
  C. Cemeteries
  D. Mourning
IV. Significance

I. Importance.–In contrast to the Greeks and the Romans, whose custom was to cremate the dead (*see* CREMATION), the Jews "bury rather than burn dead bodies" (Tacitus *Hist.* v.5). Burial constituted the biblical procedure from the days of the earliest patriarchs onward (Gen. 23:4; 25:9; Dt. 10:6; 34:6). For a corpse to remain unburied or to be exhumed subsequent to burial, and thus become food for beasts of prey, was the climax of indignity or judgment (1 K. 14:11; 16:4; 2 K. 9:37; Ps. 79:3; Jer. 7:33; 8:1; 16:4, 6; 22:19; Ezk. 29:5; Rev. 11:9). Uncovered blood cried for vengeance (Ezk. 24:8; 39:12) and brought defilement upon the whole land (Dt. 21:1-9). Even criminals were to be allowed burial (Dt. 21:22f.); and it was an obligation resting upon all to bury the dead found by the way (Tob. 1:18; 2:8); but note the exceptional denial of it to the sons of Rizpah (2 S. 21:10).

In the Orient burial takes place, if possible, within twenty-four hours after death. Moslems bury their dead on the day of death, if the death takes place in the morning; but if in the afternoon or at night, not until the following day. Haste is required because of the rapidity of decomposition, the excessive violence of grief, a reluctance to allow the dead to remain long in the houses of the living — perhaps through fear of harboring the body of one dying under divine judgment (Lev. 10:4; Acts 5:6, 10) — and the defilement to which contact with a dead body gave occasion (Nu. 19:11-16; Ezk. 43:7; Hag. 2:13; cf. Gen. 23:4, burial "out of my sight"). Even hanged corpses were not allowed to remain exposed after nightfall (Dt. 21:23); note the burial of Jesus on the day of His crucifixion (Mt. 27:57-59; Gal. 3:13).

II. Preparations.–*A. Duties of the Family.* While the ceremonies preparatory to burial must have varied somewhat from period to period, the following features appear normal. Death was announced by a shrill cry, followed by a tumult of lamentation (2 S. 1:12; 18:33; cf. Mk. 5:38). As an expression of affection, loved ones might kiss or embrace the body (Gen. 50:1). The oldest son or, failing him, the nearest of kin present would then close the eyes of the dead (cf. Gen. 46:4), perhaps symbolic of the "sleep of death" (Acts 7:60; 1 Thess. 4:13f.; Ps. 17:15). Those responsible would wash the body (Acts 9:37), anoint it with aromatic ointments (Jn. 12:7; 19:39), clothe it as in life (cf. 1 S. 28:14), swathe hands and feet in grave-bands, usually of linen (Sir. 38:16; Jn. 11:44a), and cover the face or bind it about with a napkin or handkerchief (Jn. 11:44b). Such ministries ordinarily devolved upon loving relatives and friends, mostly women (cf. Lk. 23:54–24:1).

B. Embalming. True embalming was not practiced in Israel, as evidenced by the bodily remains that have been recovered (see IV below for significance); the "sweet odors and spices" (2 Ch. 16:14) seem to have been utilized more for purification than for preservation. The quantity employed at the burial of Jesus, both by Nicodemus and by the women (Jn. 19:39; Mk. 16:1), indicate honor rather than a desire to embalm (cf. *ICC* on Jn. 19:39). Embalming (Heb. *ḥānaṭ*, "to give the color of ripeness"; cf. Cant. 2:13) is mentioned in Scripture only in the cases of Jacob and Joseph (Gen. 50:2f., 26). It was a distinctly Egyptian invention and method of preserving the bodies of men and animals (cf. the descriptions by Herodotus and Diodorus Siculus). The embalming of Jacob occupied forty days (Gen. 50:2; seventy days was also common) and was performed by Joseph's "servants the physicians" (v. 3). These notices serve primarily to demonstrate the importance of the individuals concerned, as well as to evidence their faith in the ultimate return of the Hebrew people to Palestine (Gen. 50:25; Ex. 13:19; Josh. 24:32; He. 11:22).

C. Mourners. For the pagans surrounding Israel, death was a calamity, unalleviated by hope (1 Thess. 4:13); and their corresponding acts of bitter mourning are illustrated both in Scripture (Isa. 15:2; Jer. 47:5; 48:37) and by ancient monuments. But while such excess was subject to question in both the OT and NT (2 S. 12:21-23; Mk. 5:39), it nevertheless came to be widely assimilated into Israelitish culture. Weeping, so natural in itself (Jer. 9:18), was supplemented by cries of "Alas, alas" (Am. 5:16), "Alas, my brother" (1 K. 13:30; cf. Jer. 22:18; 34:5), and similar phrases, until self-control vanished. An initial action of rending the garments (2 S. 1:11; 13:31; Job 1:20) was followed by the donning of sackcloth (Gen. 37:34; 2 S. 3:31), disheveling or tearing one's hair and beard (Jer. 7:29; Mic. 1:16), holding the hands over one's head (?) (2 S. 13:19; Jer. 2:37, as supported by archeological data), scattering dust and ashes on one's head, or wallowing in it (2 S. 13:31; Ezk. 27:30), and by fasting (2 S. 1:12), especially at times of extraordinary grief, as at the death of an only son (Jer. 6:26; Am. 8:10; Zec. 12:10); *see* GRIEF. Family members, such as wives, might mourn in separate groups (Zec. 12:12-14), while professional mourners came to occupy a prominent place (Eccl. 12:5). These latter consisted primarily of women (Jer. 9:17), "skilled in lamentation" (Am. 5:16), with dirge singers and flute players (Mt. 9:23; Mk. 5:38). The most pagan features of mourning, such as cutting the flesh (Jer. 47:5) or tearing the hair (Isa. 15:2) for the dead, were forbidden by the Mosaic law (Lev. 19:28; Dt. 14:1), though Israel's obedience appears to have been far from commendatory (Jer. 16:6). Because of the defilements involved, priests were specifically restricted in their observance of mourning (Lev. 21:1-4); and for high priests and Nazirites it was prohibited altogether (Lev. 21:10f.; Nu. 6:7).

Sarcophagus of Eshmun'azar king of Sidon (5th cent. B.C.), reflecting Egyptian style. The Phoenician inscription lists the accomplishments of the king, who was "snatched away before [his] time," and warns against tampering with his resting place. (Religious News Service)

D. Processions. When the other preparations had been made and the time came, the corpse was lifted onto a bier, or litter (Heb. *miṭṭâ*; 2 S. 3:31; cf. Lk. 7:12-14). The *miṭṭâ* seems to have rested on poles, by which it was carried by shoulder to the tomb. Chief mourners followed the bier (2 S. 3:31), accompanied by the specially robed professional lamenters (2 S. 14:2). As a particularly notable example, Gen. 50:7-11 describes in detail the funerary procession involved in the transport of Jacob's remains from Egypt to his tomb in Palestine.

III. Interment.–*A. Earthen Graves.* For groups without a settled abode, interment must have taken the form of roadside burials, marked perhaps by a tree (Gen. 38:8) or a pillar (v. 20). Coffins were not employed in ancient Israel. The only one mentioned in the Bible is the sarcophagus (Heb. *'ārôn*, "box, chest," Gen. 50:26) in which the embalmed body of Joseph was preserved in Egypt. For the majority of Israelites, without the means to afford even a simple grave marker, burial must have continued to consist simply of placing the corpse in a shallow depression. After the body had been let down into the ground, the bier, of course, was set aside; and the earth was replaced, followed by a heap of stones to preserve the dead from depredations of beasts or thieves. Achan's grave in Achor and Absalom's in the wood of Ephraim had "great heaps of stones" raised over them

(Josh. 7:26; 2 S. 18:17), in these cases, however, not for honor but for dishonor. Excavation at Canaanite sites has demonstrated the frequency of burials within houses, particularly of infants. These include both normal burials, in broken jars beneath floors, and child sacrifices, beneath foundations (cf. 1 K. 16:34). But among the Hebrews house burials appear to have been exceptional, reserved for major leaders such as Samuel (1 S. 25:1), Joab (1 K. 2:34), and the kings (see III.B.2 below); and even in these references the precincts or garden of the house may be what is intended (cf. 2 Ch. 33:20 with 2 K. 21:19 and Jn. 19:41).

B. Tombs. 1. Pre-Israelite. The earliest constructed tombs in Palestine are the dolmens or "stone tablets," found particularly in Transjordan. They consist of great slabs of stone, set on edge with a covering slab, and are relics of an otherwise unknown prehistoric nomadic people (cf. *WBA,* pp. 29f.). With the coming of the Early Bronze Age (3000-2000 B.C.), interment in natural or artificially enlarged caves predominates, those of Jericho being the most significant. The burial of Sarah (Gen. 23:19) and later of the other members of Abraham's family, in the Cave of Machpelah at Hebron (Gen. 25:9; 49:31; 50:13), follow this pattern. Excavations such as Macalister's at Gezer have revealed the inclusion of a few small food vessels in tombs of this period. Shaft tombs, hewn out of the soft limestone of Palestine and entered by a vertical well sunk to one side, characterize Middle Bronze Canaanite culture (2000-1550 B.C.). Each wealthy household would seek to possess a family tomb, prepared with stone shelves or benches to receive the bodies. Among the Canaanites of the Late Bronze Age (1550-1200 B.C.), both before and after Joshua's conquest of Palestine, chamber tombs cut from hillsides became the predominant form. Entered by a few descending steps cut into the rock, their actual doorways were sealed by heavy stones. Beneath the shelves or niches, a further cavity was customarily cut into the tomb's floor, so that when tissue disintegrated the skeletal remains could be swept into the pit and the niches reused. Many generations of a family could thus be placed in the ancestral tomb; note the biblical phrase, "gathered unto his people" (Gen. 25:8; 49:33). With the deceased, the Late Bronze Canaanites buried ornaments, weapons (e.g., swords, Ezk. 32:27), and an assortment of pottery lamps, oil jugs, and food containers. It is in opposition to such practices that Scripture prohibits offerings for the dead (Dt. 26:14). *See* Plate 8.

Philistine anthropoid sarcophagus from the northern cemetery at Beth-shan (12th-11th cents. B.C.). The terra-cotta coffin bears a crude effigy of the deceased. (University Museum, University of Pennsylvania)

2. Israelite. Under the later judges and early kingdom (Iron I, 1200-900 B.C.), Israel adopted much of the Canaanite "family tomb" procedure, though with a marked decrease in accompanying articles; note the OT notices of burials "in the sepulchre of his father" (Jgs. 8:32; 16:21; 2 S. 2:32; 17:23). Egyptian influence early in Iron I led to the utilization for a period of pottery coffins, in the well-known mummy-case pattern. Such anthropoid sarcophagi have appeared in Dibon, Beth-shan, and even in the Egyptian delta with twelfth- and eleventh-century Philistine pottery, which suggests sponsorship by this latter people (*AP*, pp. 115-17). Foreign coffins, however, were not adopted by the Hebrews. Scripture frequently refers to the Iron II (900-600 B.C.) burials of the kings of divided Israel. The southern rulers from David to Ahaz were buried in "the sepulchres of the kings of Israel" within the City of David, the old south-

Rock-cut tomb with rolling stone, from the Roman period at Heshbon. These small tombs were reused and bones from previous burials moved to small niches. (B. Van Elderen)

eastern hill of Jerusalem, presumably in two galleries, long since denuded and now partially cut away, above the Pool of Siloam (2 Ch. 28:27). The mention of King Asa's funerary "bed" (2 Ch. 16:14) is apparently in reference to his rock-cut niche "resting place" (cf. *ICC*, *in loc.*). The varied tombs of Iron III (Persian period) often came to include rich furniture (*AP,* p. 145). Special efforts were taken by the rich to prepare tombs for themselves in advance of death (Isa. 22:16; cf. Job 3:14; Mt. 27:60), with hewn stones and sometimes costly pillars set up as memorials (2 K. 23:17; Ezk. 39:15). A number of Israelite tombs have now been identified on the east side of the Kidron Valley in the village of Silwan.

3. Classical. Under Greco-Roman influence, Palestine tombs took on the exterior forms and ornamentation of classic architecture, e.g., the elaborate Tombs of the Sanhedrin or the so-called Tombs of the Kings, in Jerusalem. Exposed areas were whitewashed to obviate uncleanness through accidental contact at night (Mt. 23:27). In Roman times the entrance was often closed with a large circular stone, set up on edge and rolled in its groove to the mouth of the tomb so as to close it securely. This stone could then be further secured by a strap, or by sealing. Pilate thus directed that the tomb of Joseph of Arimathea, in which the body of Jesus was laid, should be carefully sealed and made as inviolable as possible (Mt. 27:66). Within might be excavated whole complexes of rooms, in which the former benchlike wall niches were changed into squared burial tubes, going back in directions perpendicular to the faces of the tomb walls. Such tombs might number more than a dozen per room. The monumental Silwan tombs of "Absalom," "Jehoshaphat," "Zechariah," and "St. James," on the

Hellenistic and Roman tombs of the Hezir family, in the Kidron Valley (1st cent. B.C.). They are traditionally associated with James, Zachariah, and Jehoshaphat. (A. C. Myers)

Limestone ossuary, used for secondary burials in Roman Palestine. The chest is painted red and decorated with geometric figures. (Royal Ontario Museum, Toronto)

east side of the Kidron Valley, date from approximately the 1st cent. B.C.

From the 3rd cent. B.C. onward, a further innovation was that of the bone chests or ossuaries. Patterned on Roman cremation chests, these consisted of stone boxes about 3 ft. long, with covers, in which bones were placed after a body's decomposition. Ossuaries were frequently marked with elaborate geometrical designs and with Aramaic name inscriptions, such as the famous "Simon bar Jonah" identification found on an ossuary from the early Christian cemetery under the Dominus Flevit Church on the Mt. of Olives.

C. Cemeteries. From the earliest times, community cemeteries existed outside Palestinian towns, especially in caves, as found at Jericho, Megiddo, and Tell en-Naṣbeh (Mizpah?); note the village burials in the NT (Lk. 7:12; Jn. 11:30) and the public provision made for the burial of strangers (Mt. 27:7). In the closing days of the monarchy there was a common burying ground at Jerusalem (2 K. 23:6; Jer. 26:23), probably where it is to this day between the city wall and the Kidron Valley. Thousands of Jewish and Islamic tombs on both sides of the valley bear witness today to the belief that associates the coming of the Messiah with a blessed resurrection, when He will descend upon the Mt. of Olives and pass through these graves as He enters the Holy City.

D. Mourning. Lamentation reached its peak at the tomb (Jn. 11:31). Additional rites included "a great burning" (2 Ch. 16:14; 21:19-21; Jer. 36:5), i.e., of spice and incense, not of the corpse. A seven-day fast was regularly enforced (1 S. 31:13; Gen. 50:11; Sir. 22:12), though the period might be less (Sir. 38:17) or more (cf. the thirty days of mourning observed for great leaders, Nu. 20:28f.; Dt. 10:6; 34:5-8, and the corresponding period for women captives prior to remarriage, Dt. 21:11-13). Literary laments might be composed for such occasions (2 S. 1:17-27; 2 Ch. 35:25), often in a *qînâ* or "limping" meter (*see* POETRY, HEBREW). It is disputed whether the "bread [broken] for the mourner" and the "cup of consolation" (Jer. 16:7; cf. Ezk. 24:17, 22; Hos. 9:4) were concerned with a meal served to the mourners at the conclusion of the rites, or with food brought by neighbors to the nearest of kin, prior to the interment, perhaps because of the immediate family's inability to prepare meals for themselves in a house polluted by death. There is no record of committals or other religious services at the tomb; similarly, archeological indications of funerary shrines, or of any other cult practices for the dead, are conspicuous by their absence.

IV. Significance.–As noted above, haste in Palestinian burial, as well as the subsequent sealing of tombs, was conditioned in part by the ceremonial impurity that the Mosaic law associates with death in any form (cf. Lev. 11:39; 12:2; 13:45; 15:19). Death is the result of sin, a disturbing of God's original order for man (Gen. 2:17; Rom. 3:23; 5:12); and its handiwork is therefore unnatural and to be put away (cf. Isa. 25:8; Rev. 21:4). Yet the biblical insistence upon proper burial, as well as its general opposition to cremation, bears inherent testimony to the continuing significance of the human body after death. This significance derives ultimately from the doctrine of the bodily resurrection "of those who sleep in the dust of the earth" (Dnl. 12:2; cf. 1 Cor. 15:52; Rev. 20:13). But even when this truth of resurrection had not yet been as clearly revealed as it was in the days of the eighth-century prophets (Isa. 26:19; but cf. Job 19:26, AV; He. 11:19), care for a corpse would still have been suggested by the Hebrews' knowledge of the immortality of the soul (1 S. 28:14f.; He. 11:16). Thus Jacob described his death in terms of a personal meeting, of "going to his son" Joseph (Gen. 37:35, which cannot refer to a reunion in the grave, for Joseph had supposedly been eaten by a wild beast). Similarly Abraham, Isaac, and Jacob were "gathered to their people" in life after death: for in all three instances this phrase is contrasted with, and precedes, the statement of their burial (Gen. 25:8f.; 35:29; 49:33); in the cases of Abraham and Jacob, moreover, it was spoken in lands far distant from their ancestral tombs. It is true that the Heb. *nepeš*, "soul," often signifies the whole man, body and spirit, so that even a corpse may be called a dead *nepeš* (Nu. 6:6; 23:10; it is still "somebody"). But while at death a man's body returns to dust (Gen. 3:19; Ps. 103:14), his spirit returns to the presence of God (Eccl. 12:7 [contrast that of animals, 3:21]; Phil. 1:23) and, for believers, to a conscious life in glory (Ps. 73:24; 49:14f.; Lk. 16:23; Acts 7:59). Since the term "soul" is used interchangeably with that of spirit (Isa. 26:9; Ex. 6:9; Nu. 21:4), the *nepeš* can, and does, exist in a state separate from that of the body (Gen. 35:18; Mt. 10:28; Rev. 6:9; cf. 1 K. 17:22 on the rare case of a soul's return to its body). Belief in the continuance of personal life after death is, of course, common to most men and serves to explain the Canaanite practice of spiritism (Dt. 18:11f.). Israel's pagan neighbors, however, felt that the soul of the departed continued to live in proximity to the body, underground (cf. 1 S. 28:11, the witch's statement, "Whom shall I bring *up*?"), perhaps with physical needs; hence the Canaanite grave offerings. Scripture, on the contrary, while conceiving of hell as subterranean (Job 26:5; Ps. 63:9), makes clear the heavenly abode of the spirits of the just (Prov. 15:24; 2 Cor. 12:2-4; He. 12:23). No food offerings were to be left in the grave (Dt. 26:14), a prohibition verified by archeology; for tomb vessels show a marked decrease with the Israelite occupation of Palestine. They taper off in time to but a few vases and lamps, perhaps of mere sentimental import or, at the most, as meaningless survivals of pre-Israelite customs (see *WBA*, pp. 245-47). Indeed, the only effect of the grave upon biblical teaching lies in the coloring it occasionally gives to descriptions of the state of bodily death, as "the land of darkness . . . without any order" (Job 10:21f.), or of the state of those lost in hell (Isa. 14:18f.; Ezk. 32:18-32).

Negatively, the significance of biblical burial practice lies in its opposition to the paganism surrounding Israel. Thus, despite their belief in bodily resurrection the Hebrews resisted all trends toward bodily preservation through embalming or the use of coffins. This seems to have been occasioned not simply by Israel's relative poverty and lack of resources but by its conscious antipathy to Egyptian belief and practice (cf. Ps. 114:1). Morbid otherworldliness is the antithesis of biblical faith (Isa. 38:18-20; Jn. 10:10); and, while immortality and resurrection occupy a vital place within Scripture (Ps. 17:14f.; 1 Cor. 15:14, 19), the faith of the saints lay in God's intervention, not in man's preservation of mummies within pyramids (Ps. 73:26; Phil. 3:21; cf. Dt. 11:10-12). In contrast, then, to Canaanite superstition, the OT makes clear that the dead exercise no active influence over the affairs of this world (Eccl. 9:6). Canaanite wizardry and spiritism are condemned (Lev. 19:26; 20:27), not simply as suggestive of rivalry against the only God of revelation (Isa. 47:12f.), but as frankly spurious. The dead do not possess knowledge of what goes on among the living (Job 14:21; 1 S. 28 is explicitly unique [v. 12]); they cannot draw on a treasury of merit or pray for the living (contrast 2 Macc. 15:12-15); and what is more, they do not even care (Job 21:21)! It is better for both: for the living, freed from fear of ghosts; and for the dead, freed from contact with the sin and sorrows of earth.

Scripture is particularly adamant in its opposition to any cult of the dead or worship involving the deceased (Lev. 19:28), hence the complete lack of funerary shrines at biblical Palestinian sites; the concept of prayers for the dead appears only in apocryphal writings (2 Macc. 12:44f.). The Bible insists rather that the eternal destiny of one's soul is fixed by his response to Christ in this life (Eccl. 9:4f., 10; Lk. 16:26): "It is appointed for men to die once, and after that comes judgment" (He. 9:27). But for those who follow Jesus, "Blessed are the dead who die in the Lord . . . that they may rest from their labors, for their deeds follow them!" (Rev. 14:13).

Bibliography.–J. E. Callaway, *BA*, 26 (1963), 74-91; J. P. Free, *BASOR*, 160 (Dec. 1960), esp. pp. 10-13; K. M. Kenyon, *Digging Up Jericho* (1957), pp. 233-255; F. Küchenmeister, *Die Totenbestattungen der Bibel und die Feuerbestattung* (1893); J. B. Payne, *Theology of the Older Testament* (1962), ch. 30; J. J. Simons, *Jerusalem in the OT* (1952), pp. 194-225; R. de Vaux, *Ancient Israel* (Eng. tr. 1961), pt. 2, p. 6.   J. B. PAYNE

BURIER [Heb. *qāḇar*]. The term occurs only in Ezk. 39:15, in reference to the locating of human remains for burial.

BURN [Heb. *bāʿar, qāṭar, śārap*, also *ḥāmam, ḥārâ, ḥārar, yāqaḏ, kāwâ, lāhaṭ, nāśaq, ṣûṭ*; Gk. *kaíō, kaíomai, katakaíō, emprḗthō*]; **BURNING** [Aram. *dᵉlaq, yᵉqaḏ*; Heb. *yᵉqôḏ, môqēḏ, śᵉrēpâ, rešep*, etc.; Gk. *pýrōsis, kaíomai, pýr*]. Several of these words are used metaphorically in the Bible, especially of anger (Gen. 44:18; Ex. 22:24; 32:10ff.; Josh. 7:26; Est. 1:12; Ps. 89:46; Hos. 8:5; cf. Gk. *pyróomai*, 2 Cor. 11:29, RSV "am indignant"), also for jealousy (Ps. 79:5, RSV "jealous wrath"), lust (Isa. 57:5, AV "enflaming yourselves with idols"; cf. Gk. *pyróomai*, 1 Cor. 7:9, RSV "be aflame with passion," NEB "burn with vain desire"), wickedness (Isa. 9:18), famine (Hos. 7:6), intrigue (Hos. 7:6), disease (Ps. 38:7), purification (Isa. 4:4), overwhelming emotion upon hearing the risen Christ expound the Scriptures (Lk. 24:32).

See also FIRE.   J. W. D. H.

BURNING BUSH. *See* BUSH, THE BURNING.

BURNT OFFERING. *See* SACRIFICE.

BURNT SACRIFICE. *See* SACRIFICE.

BURSTING. The AV for Heb. *mᵉḵittâ* in Isa. 30:14; the RSV and NEB have "fragments."

BUSH [Heb. *sᵉneh, śî(a)ḥ*; Gk. *bátos*]; AV also SHRUB (Gen. 21:15); NEB also wormwood" (Job 30:4), "brambles" (Lk. 6:44).

The Heb. *sᵉneh* (Ex. 3:2-4; Dt. 33:16) refers to Moses' burning bush, as does the Gk. *bátos*, in Mk. 12:26; Lk. 20:37; Acts 7:30, 35. Of several varieties of bramble (cf. Lk. 6:44) found in Palestine, *Rubus discolor* is the commonest, but is not a native. Probably the bush was one of the thorny acacias such as *A. nilotica* (L.) Forsk., the Egyptian mimosa. Some authorities have suggested that the "flame" was actually a covering of the crimson mistletoe *Loranthus acaciae* Zucc., which grows profusely on shrubs in Palestine and Sinai. Others have regarded the bush as a species of gasplant (*Dictamnus albus* L.) from which a volatile, easily ignited vapor escapes.

The Heb. *śî(a)ḥ* (Gen. 21:15; cf. 2:5; Job 30:4, 7) refers principally to the low desert bushes or scrub.

On Isa. 7:19, *see* PASTURE.

See also FLORA.   R. K. H.

BUSH, THE BURNING [Heb. *sᵉneh*; Gk. *bátos*]. The shrub at the locale of a theophany on Mt. Horeb (Ex. 3:2-4; cf. Dt. 33:16). Moses' attention was attracted by the phenomenon of a bush apparently on fire and yet not being consumed. Modern attempts at identifying the supposed species of shrub are unconvincing. The blackberry (*rubus collinus*) grown at St. Catherine's monastery was imported originally from Syria, and is not native to Sinai. Most probably the bush was some species of thorn. The divine messenger in Ex. 3:2 is a surrogate for the deity of 3:4.

The description of the whole incident is of an untechnical character, which makes an explanation in modern terms rather difficult. However, Louis Golding has described an analagous event which he witnessed in one of the wadis close to Mt. Sinai. Apparently the winds which were swirling down two or three confluent wadis met in cyclone form and sucked sand from the dry wadi bed as the column of air built up. This latter then moved across to a nearby acacia bush, and at that juncture was illumined by a burst of sunlight from behind a long bank of cloud. The effect was to make the whole hill appear to burst into flame. "The smoke of it soared in golden gusts. Every thorn was a spit of fire"; a situation which continued for several seconds until the cyclone finally passed along one of the wadis.

See L. Golding, *In the Steps of Moses the Lawgiver* (n.d.), pp. 99f.   R. K. H.

Moses and the burning bush. Wall painting from the synagogue at Dura-Europos (A.D. 244-245) (Yale University Art Gallery)

BUSHEL [Gk. *módios*]; NEB MEAL-TUB. Normally the word (< Lat. *modius*) is a dry measure nearly equal to a peck (about 8 liters), but in the NT (Mt. 5:15; Mk. 4:21; Lk. 11:33) it indicates a covering that might be used to conceal a lamp, perhaps a tub or bowl such as are used to measure grain.

BUSHY [Heb. *tāltāl*; Akk. *taltallū*; Gk. *elátai*] (Cant. 5:11); RSV WAVY; NEB "like palm-fronds." The reference is to the date panicle, and so may imply curly hair.

BUSINESS [Heb. *dāḇār, m^e lā'ḵâ, ma'^a śeh* (1 S. 25:2), *'inyān*; Gk. *emporía* (Mt. 22:5), *ergasía* (Acts 19:24f.); cf. also Jgs. 18:3, RSV, NEB; Jn. 2:14, RSV]; AV also POSSESSIONS (1 S. 25:2), TRAVAIL (Eccl. 1:13; 3:10; 4:8), MERCHANDISE (Mt. 22:5), GAIN (Acts 19:24), CRAFT (v. 25); NEB also PUBLIC DUTY (Dt. 24:5), LIVING (Ps. 107:23), EMPLOYMENT (Acts 19:24), INDUSTRY (v. 25), and cf. Est. 3:9, "officials." According to the RSV, Nabal lived in Maon, but his "business" (*ma'^a śeh*) was in Carmel." For "business" the AV has "possessions"; the NEB, however, reads simply: "There was man at Carmel in Maon." (Cf. the LXX, Gk. *tá poímnia*.)

In the NT Gk. *emporía* (Mt. 22:5) means "place of commerce," like Eng. "emporium," rather than "merchandise"; cf. Jas. 4:13; Jn. 2:16, for related words.

For AV "business" the RSV has also "work," "dealings," "matter," "service," "stores" (2 Ch. 17:13), "house" (Lk. 2:49), "duty" (Gk. *chreía*, Acts 6:3), "zeal" (*spoudḗ*, Rom. 12:11), etc. J. W. D. H.

BUSYBODY [Gk. *periergázomai, períergos*] (2 Thess. 3:11; 1 Tim. 5:13); NEB also "minding everybody's business but their own" (2 Thess. 3:11); cf. 1 Pet. 4:15, AV (*allotrioepískopos*); RSV "mischief-maker"; NEB "infringing the rights of others." If these passages are coupled with such others as Jas. 3:2-10; 4:11; Eph. 4:29, 31; Tit. 3:2, it becomes evident that sins against the eighth commandment were as common in the apostolic Church as they are today. It is this sin which is so repeatedly warned against by the apostles as in direct conflict with the ethics of Christianity, and in violation of that spirit of brotherly love and mutual trust which Christ has enjoined on His followers, and which is the very marrow of the outward revelation of the Christian faith (1 Cor. 13). H. E. DOSKER

BUT. Archaic in the AV for Heb. *kî'im* (Am. 3:7, RSV "without"). Cf. the Hebrew idiom *'im-lô'* in Gen. 24:38, and note also the AV archaism "but and if" (Gk. *eán dé*) in Mt. 24:48; Lk. 12:45; 20:6.

BUTLER [Heb. *mašqeh*]. The butler was an officer in households of kings or other dignitaries, having charge of wines and other potables. The term *maqšeh*, "one who gives drink," is rendered "butler" in Gen. 40:1-23; 41:9, "cupbearer" in 1 K. 10:5; 2 Ch. 9:4; Neh. 1:11. The office was one of considerable importance in oriental courts because of the danger to the king's life through plots of poison, etc. Nehemiah held this position to King Artaxerxes. Wealthy courts, as that of Solomon, usually had more than one such officer (1 K. 10:5); over these cupbearers or butlers was the *śar hammašqîm*, or chief butler (Gen. 40:9). E. B. POLLARD

BUTTER. *See* FOOD III.

BUTTOCKS, UNCOVERED [Heb. *ḥ^a śupay šēṯ*] (Isa. 20:4). Isaiah's symbolic act of appearing naked, a portent of the defeat of Egypt and Ethiopia, served as a warning to those who placed their hopes for deliverance from the Assyrian menace in that quarter. As the prophet walked about in shameful nudity, so Egypt and Ethiopia — and those who trusted in them — would be humiliated.

BUYING.

I. Definition
II. In the OT
  A. General Considerations
  B. Terminology
  C. Barter
  D. Sale
  E. Diffusion of Silver in Society
  F. Objects Bought and Sold
  G. Forms of Sale
III. In the NT
  A. General Considerations
  B. Terminology
  C. Objects Bought and Sold
IV. Prices
V. Buying as a Theological Metaphor

I. Definition.–The acquisition of the ownership of something (the object of sale) by one party (the buyer) from another (the seller) by the buyer's handing over to the seller some other object (the price) acceptable to the seller and agreed by both to be equal in value to the object of sale. Buying is thus but one side of a necessarily bilateral transaction that always has selling as its counterpart (cf. the term for "sale" in Roman law, Lat. *emptio venditio* [lit. "buying-selling"], and note the occurence of "buyer" and "seller" in an enumeration of necessarily paired, contrasting terms in Isa. 24:2).

Strictly speaking, buying (sale) should be distinguished from barter, as it was in Roman law, although the distinction was not normally made in biblical Hebrew, which lacked simple contrasting terms for the two activities. For a transaction to be one of sale, the price must be something recognised within that society as a money of *exchange* (although today accountancy and the use of checks often obviate the physical handling of the coins and bank notes [bills] that constitute our normal moneys of exchange). Roman law required that the price be at least partly in money (coin), to distinguish the price from the object of sale. The use of a money of *account*, specifically silver measured by weight, was customary throughout Israelite history (i.e., the value of goods and services was regularly expressed in terms of an equivalent amount of silver), but the use of a money of *exchange* was not necessarily also customary. However, before the introduction of coinage to the area, probably in the 6th cent. B.C., for which silver, gold and, later, bronze were used, silver was also used as money of exchange for true sale transactions; the use of gold in 1 Ch. 21:25 is exceptional.

Barter, the *permutatio* of Roman law, is the direct exchange of objects without the intervention of a money of exchange. Barter almost certainly played an important role in at least the ancient Israelite economy (no instance is discernible in the NT), and it must be included within the purview of this article.

II. In the OT.–*A. General Considerations.* Sale transactions were much less frequent in the simple economy of ancient Israel than in our own, especially before cities assumed an important place in the nation's life. As in any peasant society, each family (Heb. *bêṯ 'āḇ*) was largely self-sufficient for its material needs, few and simple as these were, and there was little need to acquire goods by purchase from outside. Such items as pottery or metal tools, obtained from local craftsmen, were probably as often paid for in kind, i.e., by barter, as in precious metal. Kinship ties are very strong in a patriarchal society, and a lively sense of community and mutual obligation must have existed among the members of a clan (Heb. *mišpāḥâ*) who grazed their livestock on common pasturelands and tended vineyards or tilled the soil in neighboring hereditary plots that had been worked by their fathers for generations. Because of this clan solidarity, many exchanges of goods and services that would take the form of sale or hire in modern society must have occurred as acts of simple gift-giving in ancient Israel. Such gifts would eventually be roughly reciprocated by those able to make a counter contribution, to judge from the cases of gift-exchange known to anthropologists as an integrative principle of pre-modern or non-Western economies. In the case of those unable to reciprocate — the poor, the widows, and the orphans — Israelites were expected to accept the moral obligation of helping them without thought of return (cf. Lev. 25:35; Dt. 15:7-11).

The institution of tithing was another factor that limited the frequency of sale transactions. Tithes and similar cultic dues (e.g., firstfruits, firstlings, freewill offerings) accounted for a considerable proportion of the exchange of goods and (priestly) services in Israelite society; but these exchanges bypassed the forms of sale and hire, except for the situation envisaged in Dt. 14:22-27 (this provision applied only when the offering of sacrifices was limited to the central sanctuary).

B. Terminology. The words rendered "buy" in translations of the OT may refer as much to barter as to purchase with a money of exchange. The most common verb so rendered (Heb. *qānâ*; [Aram. *qᵉnā'*, Ezr. 7:17]) means simply "become owner (of something), acquire," as in Gen. 4:1 where Eve says of Cain, "I have *gotten* a man with the help of the Lord" (it is not necessary to posit a separate verb *qānâ*, "bring into being, create," for which see KoB, p. 843), or Gen. 14:19, "God Most High, *owner* of heaven and earth" (a semantic parallel of Akk. *bēl šamê u erṣetim*), or Isa. 11:11, "the Lord will extend his hand . . . to *recover* the remnant which is left of his people"; cf. also Prov. 1:5, "acquire"; 4:5, "get." The verb *qānâ* needed to be qualified by "with silver" (Heb. *bᵉḵesep*) if the unequivocal meaning "acquire ownership by payment of silver as a money of exchange" was to be expressed; thus Jer. 32:25 (cf. v. 9); Am. 8:6.

The second most common verb rendered "buy" is Heb. *šāḇar,* but this means specifically "acquire grain" (Heb. *šeḇer*). Except for Am. 8:5 and Prov. 11:26 where the causative stem is used, meaning "sell grain," *šāḇar* is always found in contexts showing explicitly that silver was used as a money of exchange (the purchase of grain by Joseph's brothers in Egypt in Gen. 42–44, and by the Israelites from the Edomites during the wandering in the wilderness in Dt. 2:6 [cf. v. 28, causative]; those "who have no silver" are, because of God's grace, exceptionally invited to "come, *get grain,* and eat" in Isa. 55:1). But even this verb apparently does not necessarily specify the purchase of grain by means of a money of exchange; in Gen. 42–44 and Dt. 2:6, payment with a precious metal, silver, is determined more by the circumstances of the transactions — trade far from home in a distant country and travel through foreign territory, respectively — than by the nature of the transaction itself.

Nor does the verb *kārâ,* "acquire by commerce" (Dt. 2:6; Hos. 3:2) or "do business" (Job 6:27; 41:6 [MT 40:30]; RSV "bargain"; AV "dig a pit"; NEB "hurl yourselves"), necessarily imply purchase with a money of exchange. The same is true of Heb. *lāqaḥ,* "take, receive," which is occasionally rendered "buy" (e.g. Neh. 10:31 [MT 32]; Prov. 31:16); it may be noted that the antonym of this verb, *nāṯan,* "hand over, give," has the sense of "sell" in Gen. 23:4, 9 (so, regularly, the Akk. cognate *nadānu*). The normal verb "sell" is *māḵar.*

C. Barter. Unequivocal references to barter are nonetheless uncommon. Joseph paid one hundred lambs (Heb. *qᵉśîṭâ*; NEB "sheep," following LXX, Tg.; AV, RSV, "pieces of money") for a plot of land according to Gen. 33:19. Judah's arrangement to pay Tamar a kid for her services as a prostitute (Gen. 38:16f.) suggests the practice of barter, and also perhaps that silver was not the customary means of payment for small purchases of the necessaries of life for which a prostitute, often a destitute widow, probably needed her earnings. Judah's contract with Tamar, however, was properly one of hire, not sale. Although the situation described in Gen. 47:18f. was unusual (famine conditions in which the Egyptians gave the government their cattle, land, and even their own persons in return for food), there was probably nothing unusual about the barter attested there. The conditions described in Joel 3:3 (MT 4:3) are again abnormal (pillage by foreign troops), but there is no reason to think that the barter alluded to was commercially irregular. Prov. 27:26 states that "goats (will provide) the price of a field," suggesting the direct exchange of land for livestock. Taxation in kind (e.g., 1 S. 8:14-17; 1 K. 4:7, 22f., 27f.; Neh. 10:32-39), customary payments in kind (e.g., tithes), tribute in kind (e.g., Mesha of Moab paid the king of Israel an annual tribute of 100,000 lambs and the wool of 100,000 rams, 2 K. 3:4), and the direct exchange of commodities by governments (Hiram supplied Solomon with timber in return for wheat and oil, 1 K. 5:10f. [MT 24f.]) also suggest that moneys of exchange played a more limited role in the early Israelite economy than in Hellenistic-Roman times. The requirement that a Hebrew slave was not to be sent away empty-handed at his manumission — "you shall furnish him liberally out of your flock, out of your threshing floor, and out of your wine press" (Dt. 15:13f.) — again points to an economy in which payments were commonly made in kind.

The definition of a fine in terms of silver, as in Ex. 21:32, need not require payment in silver. Silver may be used in such a context simply as a money of account, to define the value of the fine, and the object actually paid may have been subject to negotiation between the wrongdoer and the injured party. The imposition of a fine is in any case not a commercial transaction, and no necessary inferences about the conditions of sale may be drawn from the amounts and means of payment fixed by tradition in such situations as the payment of fines or "bride price" (cf. Ex. 22:16f. [MT 15f.]; 1 S. 18:25).

D. Sale. Despite the practice of barter, sale transactions involving a money of exchange, normally silver, were familiar long before the introduction of coinage. Abraham, who was "very rich in cattle, in silver, and in gold" (Gen. 13:2), is explicitly said to have weighed out (Heb. *šāqal*) for the parcel of land at Machpelah four hundred shekels of silver of a kind acceptable (because of its purity?) to a merchant (Heb. *kesep 'ōḇēr lassōḥēr*, Gen. 23:16; cf. 2 K. 12:4 [MT 5]). The silver is described as "full" (*mālē'*) in v. 9, meaning that it was of full quality, without an excessive admixture of impurities (lead), or that it constituted the full quantity due (RSV, NEB, "full price"), or that the price was to be entirely in silver, not partly in silver and partly in kind (cf. 1 Ch. 21:24 for a price partly in silver, partly in kind; cf. also Hos. 3:2; Jgs. 17:10). The sons of Jacob, setting out from Canaan to buy grain in Egypt, each took as payment a package of silver, tied up and fastened (Heb. *ṣᵉrôr-kesep*, Gen. 42:25-28, 35). An imperishable treasure item like silver, a quite small quantity of which may be equivalent in value to a very large quantity of a staple commodity like grain, is obviously a highly convenient means of payment for heavy, bulky goods that must be purchased far from where they are required. The Hebrews paid with silver for the grain and water they bought from the Edomites during the trek to Canaan (Dt. 2:6). The grain was probably bought in bulk, and the payment for water permitted the Hebrews to use specific wells and watering holes for a prescribed period. David bought Araunah's threshing floor (Heb. *gōren*) and oxen for a price (*meḥîr*) of fifty shekels of silver, unless the key phrase in 2 S. 24:24 specifies only the value, not the species, of payment (1 Ch. 21:25 gives the price of the site [*māqôm*] as six hundred shekels of gold, perhaps including the value of adjacent land acquired later). Omri bought the site of Samaria for a price of two talents of silver, although again the text does not state that he actually paid the price in silver (1 K. 16:24). Like Abraham in Gen. 23, however, Jeremiah is explicitly said to have weighed out the seventeen shekels of silver that he paid for his cousin's field (Jer. 32:9).

Perhaps the best example of the use of silver as a money of exchange occurs in Dt. 14:22-27, a passage that prescribes the consumption of agricultural tithes and the firstborn of livestock at the central shrine. If the shrine was too far away for it to be reasonable to expect an Israelite to take his tithes and firstlings there, he was to convert their value into silver (Heb. *nāṯan bakkesep̱*), tie up the silver in a bag, take it to the shrine, and there spend it (*nāṯan hakkesep̱*) on whatever he wanted for the sacral meal — oxen or sheep, wine or strong drink. This provision presupposes either that a peasant farmer would have enough silver on hand to make the conversion from his own resources, or that there would be a demand for the produce and animals on the part of neighboring farmers, even though they would want to convert their own dues into silver, and that these buyers would be able to pay in silver. The passage sheds precious light on the general economic institutions of the period when the laws were drawn up.

E. Diffusion of Silver in Society. The ownership of silver, the most common precious metal in ancient Israel, was found at all social levels; there is nothing to suggest it was a "prestige commodity" restricted to people of a certain minimum social status. Saul's servant had with him a quarter-shekel of silver when his master, seeking information from Samuel regarding the whereabouts of his father's missing donkeys, wondered what gift he might offer the seer (1 S. 9:8). But it is remarkable that Saul himself, the son of a wealthy man (Heb. *gibbôr ḥayil*, v. 1), had no silver with him, and that the first thing he thought of as a gift for Samuel was not precious metal but bread (v. 7). Was it because transactions involving the transfer of silver were so uncommon in the daily life of the countryman that he would not ordinarily carry any with him?

Silver was apparently acceptable as payment in all sale transactions; there are no grounds for thinking that its use was limited to "prestige transactions" such as the purchase of land, wives, or slaves. Isa. 55:1f. (admittedly poetry) implies that silver could be used to buy water (cf. also Lam. 5:4), wine, milk, and bread.

The story of Micah the Ephraimite who purloined 1100 shekels belonging to his mother (Jgs. 17:1f.) indicates the amount of silver that a wealthy individual could amass in the early period of the settlement in Canaan. The annual salary that the same Micah offered a Levite to act as his domestic priest consisted of ten (shekels) of silver, an outfit of clothes, and his keep (v. 10; cf. also 1 S. 2:36). The compiler of 1 Kings records, with obvious hyperbole, that silver "was not considered as anything in the days of Solomon," and that this king "made silver as common in Jerusalem as stone" (1 K. 10:21, 27). Much of this wealth that entered the country via the palace must have been diffused downward through society and so entered general circulation, probably stimulating a wider use of silver as a money of exchange. 2 K. 12 shows that a little over a century later, in the reign of Jehoash of Judah, worshipers at the Jerusalem temple were in the habit of paying the priests silver, some of which was to be set aside, by royal command, for the upkeep of the temple's fabric. A chest with a hole bored in the lid was set up for the deposit of these gifts when the royal command was ignored (cf. also 2 K. 22:3-7). The story presupposes the widespread ownership of silver. In the second half of the 8th cent. B.C. when Tiglath-pileser III demanded tribute of Israel, Menahem was able to extract fifty shekels of silver from every wealthy man (Heb. *gibbôr ḥayil*) to raise the one thousand talents demanded (2 K. 15:19f.; cf. 23:35).

Nevertheless, we should beware of overestimating the extent to which silver was used as a money of exchange before the introduction of coinage. Although excavation reports often record the finding of silver coins in Hellenistic and Roman levels of Palestinian sites, rarely do they mention the discovery of silver in earlier levels, be it in strips, rings, or unwrought form. Yet silver, whatever its form, is no less resistant to oxidation when unminted than when minted, and the only good reason why little silver is found in early levels is that comparatively little was passed in the daily transactions of the masses.

F. Objects Bought and Sold. Objects of sale mentioned in the OT are land (e.g., Gen. 23; Ruth 4:3-9; Jer. 32:6-15; Prov. 31:16); houses (Lev. 25:29-33; Isa. 5:8); male and female slaves, both Hebrew (e.g., Ex. 21:2, 7; Lev. 25:39-41; cf. Am. 2:6; 8:6) and foreign (e.g., Dt. 21:14; Lev. 25:44f.); wives (Gen. 31:15); livestock (Ex. 21:35; 22:1; Dt. 14:21; Ezr. 7:17); timber and stone (2 K. 12:12; 22:6); (fire)wood (Lam. 5:4); grain (Gen. 41:56f.; Dt. 2:6; 2 K. 7:1; Neh. 10:31; Am. 8:5); flour (2 K. 7:1); sweet cane (Isa. 43:24); linen (Prov. 31:24); vegetables (2 K. 6:25; NEB "locust beans"; AV, RSV, "dove's dung"); general merchandise (Heb. *meḵer*) and food (*ṣayiḏ*), including fruit and fish (Neh. 13:15f.; cf. 10:31); water (Dt. 2:6, 28; Lam. 5:4); wine and milk (Isa. 55:1f.); oil (2 K. 4:7); and the rights of primogeniture (Gen. 25:31).

The sense of solidarity with the clan and, more vaguely, the tribe and nation set certain restrictions on what could be bought and sold. Thus there was no "free market" in land. To prevent land being alienated from the clan, a landowner who wished to sell his patrimony was required to offer it first to his "next-of-kin" (Heb. *gō'ēl*), normally a brother but sometimes, as the incident of Naomi and Boaz shows, a more distant relative (Lev. 25:25; Ruth 4). In the case of Naomi, a widow, one may wonder to what extent she held clear title to the land acquired by Boaz; note that no price or payment is mentioned, even though the terms of sale are used (Heb. *māḵar, qānâ*). If land was sold to a non-kinsman, the seller retained the right to buy it back later (Lev. 25:26f.). In any case, land had to be returned to its original owner in the year of jubilee, and the proximity or remoteness of the next such year affected the price paid by a purchaser, who in reality bought no more than the usufruct for a limited period (Lev. 25:13-16). Similar restrictions applied in varying degrees to houses and Hebrew male slaves (Lev. 25:29-33, 39-55; Ex. 21:2). But these laws may well have remained a dead letter at some periods; note that Isaiah inveighed against "those who join house to house, who add field to field, until there is no more room" (Isa. 5:8).

G. Forms of Sale. The account of Abraham's purchase of the cave of Machpelah (Gen. 23) suggests the polite but shrewd etiquette of a sale transaction in the ancient Orient, with its exaggerated assertions of generosity and indifference to personal gain (cf. also 2 S. 24:21-24). But the avowals of the parties were not to be taken at face value. " 'It is bad, it is bad,' says the buyer; but when he goes away, then he boasts" (Prov. 20:14). The laws against false weights and measures (Dt. 25:13-15) attest the practice of fraud and deception (cf. Am. 8:5).

Jeremiah 32:6-15 gives details of the conveyancing of a field. The price of seventeen shekels of silver was weighed out on a balance in the presence of witnesses. A deed of sale (Heb. *sēper miqnâ*) was drawn up (this is the only biblical reference to such a document), and the witnesses "wrote in the document," i.e., added their signatures. The deed evidently had two parts, one sealed and one open (v. 11). Verse 14 suggests that more than one copy was made, but the smoother reading of the LXX, with its reference to only one deed, is preferable. The document was apparently of a kind represented by examples from the time of Bar Cochba found in an excellent state of preservation in the Cave of Letters in the Naḥal Ḥever. In these the text was closely written on the upper half of a sheet of papyrus, which was then rolled down and tied with strings that pierced the sheet near the witnesses' signatures; the text, sometimes in abbreviated form, was then repeated on the lower half of the sheet, which was not tied up or sealed but left open for reference.

III. In the NT.–*A. General Considerations.* By the time of the Roman empire, a much more active and complex commercial life had developed than that found in OT Israel. Two developments in particular had affected the manner and frequency of buying. The first was the introduction to the Near East some time after 600 B.C. of coinage, which had become entirely commonplace by NT times (the first reference to coins in the Bible is Ezr. 2:69). The wide circulation of coins, available in several small denominations from the *statḗr* (Mt. 17:27) to the lowly *leptón* given by the widow of Mk. 12:42 (to mention only coins that occur in the NT), facilitated lively commercial intercourse. (*See also* MONEY.)

The second development that had favored a marked increase in commerce, and in particular petty sale transactions, was the rapid growth of cities, a feature of the hellenization of the Near East. The almost entirely self-sufficient life of the peasant was impossible in the city, so city dwellers acquired their daily food from commodity dealers in from the country, paying for it in coin. Barter, however, did not fall entirely into disuse, as post-NT rabbinic literature still knew of the practice (see S. Krauss, *Talmudische Archäologie*, II [1911], 351). As a result of these two developments, the sale transactions mentioned in the NT seem to us, as indeed they are, essentially no different from modern sale transactions.

B. Terminology. A standard feature of all the new cities founded under Hellenistic influence was the marketplace, the *agora,* and it is from this term that is derived the usual word for "buy" in the NT, Gk. *agorázō*. Other words meaning "buy" are *ōnéomai,* found only in Acts 7:16, and *ktáomai,* as in Acts 1:18; 8:20; 22:28 (elsewhere it retains its simple meaning "acquire"; cf. Heb. *qānâ*). The usual word for "sell" is *pōléō*. Other words with this meaning are *apodídōmi*, lit. "hand over," as in Acts 5:8 (note that *pōléō* is used in v. 1), and *pipráskō*, as in Mt. 13:46 (note that *pōléō* is used in v. 44). In Jas. 4:13 *emporeúomai* is used, meaning "trade, act as a merchant" (*émporos*).

C. Objects Bought and Sold. Things mentioned as bought or sold in the NT include fields (Mt. 13:44; 27:7; Lk. 14:18; Acts 1:18; 4:34; 5:8); houses (Acts 4:34); oxen and sheep (Lk. 14:19; Jn. 2:14); pigeons and sparrows (Jn. 2:14; Mt. 10:29; Lk. 12:6); food (Mt. 14:15; Mk. 6:36f.; Lk. 9:13; Jn. 4:8; 13:29; 1 Cor. 10:25); oil (Mt. 25:9); linen (Mk. 15:46); spices (Mk. 16:1); a pearl (Mt. 13:46); a cloak and a sword (Lk. 22:36). The small-scale retailing of fresh, cooked food, first alluded to in the Bible in Jer. 37:21, is indicated by the availability in the villages of fresh food for the casual wayfarer (Mt. 14:15; Mk. 6:37).

IV. Prices.–Prices (Heb. *m*ᵉ*ḥîr*; Gk. *timḗ*) are mentioned too infrequently in the Bible for any general statements to be made about their level, their fluctuations, and the way they were determined. However, the fact that Lev. 27:1-7, 16-18 specifies a tariff of values for the redemption of persons or land vowed to God (e.g., fifty shekels of silver, measured by the temple standard, for a male aged twenty to sixty; fifty shekels of silver, at the beginning of the jubilee cycle, for a field requiring a homer of barley for sowing) suggests that, at least in ancient Israel, values were expected to remain stable. 2 K. 6:25 shows that, as would be expected, famine boosted prices.

V. Buying as a Theological Metaphor.–Buying is used as a metaphor of God's saving activity for His people in the NT (1 Cor. 6:20; 7:23; 2 Pet. 2:1; *see also* REDEEMER, REDEMPTION), and perhaps also in some passages in the OT (e.g., Ex. 15:16; Ps. 74:2) if *qānâ* is understood as "buy" rather than simply "acquire."

See also BANK, BANKING; COMMERCE.

Bibliography.–Although not directly concerned with the Bible, several of the essays in G. Dalton, ed., *Primitive, Archaic and modern Economies: Essays of Karl Polanyi* (1968) are helpful for the study of the economic institutions of the ancient Mediterranean world.

R. F. G. SWEET

BUZ buz [Heb. *bûz*].

1. Second son of Nahor the brother of Abraham (Gen. 22:21).

2. A Gadite (1 Ch. 5:14).

BUZ buz [Heb. *bûz*]; **BUZITE** buz'īt [*bûzî*]. A location mentioned in Jer. 25:23 from which Elihu's father, "the Buzite," came (Job 32:2, 6).

BUZI bu'zī [Heb. *bûzî*]. Father of Ezekiel the prophet (Ezk. 1:3).

BUZZARD [Heb. *dā'â*] (Dt. 14:13); AV GLEDE; NEB KITE. A bird of prey, unclean to the Israelites; perhaps the kite, of which both red and black species are still common in Palestine.

BY. Archaic for "against," translating the Gk. dative *emautǭ,* in 1 Cor. 4:4, AV. "By that" in Ex. 22:36, AV, is archaic for "by the time that" or "before"; and "by the space of two years" in Acts 19:10, AV, means simply "for two years."

BY AND BY. Archaic for "immediately" as the AV translation of Gk. *exautḗs* (Mk. 6:25), of *euthýs* (Mt. 13:21), and of *euthéōs* (Lk. 17:7; 21:9).

BYBLUS bib'lus. *See* GEBAL **1.**

BYPATHS. *See* BYWAYS.

BYSTANDERS. *See* CROWD.

BYWAYS [Heb. *n*ᵉ*tîbôt*]; NEB DEVIOUS PATHS. The term is rendered "byways" by the RSV only in Jgs. 5:6. Cf. Jer. 18:15, which the RSV renders "bypaths," the NEB "byways." Elsewhere *n*ᵉ*tîbôt* is generally rendered PATH.

BYWORD [Heb. *š*ᵉ*nînâ, millâ, m*ᵉ*šōl*]; [*māšāl*]; AV also PROVERB; [*ḥerpâ*]; AV REPROACH; [*šēm*]; AV FAMOUS; [*q*ᵉ*lālâ*] ("byword of cursing," Zec. 8:13); AV CURSE; NEB "symbol of a curse"; [*š*ᵉ*mû'â*]; AV "mentioned"; NEB "hear and talk much." The term *š*ᵉ*nînâ* refers to a "sharp taunt" (Dt. 28:37; 1 K. 9:7; 2 Ch. 7:20); *millâ* to an "object of talk" (Job 30:9); *māšāl* or *m*ᵉ*šōl* to a "proverb" or "satire"; *ḥerpâ* to a "disgrace" (Dnl. 9:16; Joel 2:17); *šēm* to a "reputation," in this case a stained reputation (Ezk. 23:10); *š*ᵉ*mû'â* to "news" or "report" (Ezk. 16:56).

C

CAB kab (2 K. 6:25, AV). *See* KAB; WEIGHTS AND MEASURES.

CABBON kab'ən [Heb. *kabbôn*; Gk. *Chabra*]. A place in the Shephelah of Judah near Eglon (Josh. 15:40). Possibly it is to be identified with Hebra E of Lachish; it may be the same as MACHBENAH.

CABIN [Heb. *ḥᵃnuyyôṯ*] (Jer. 37:16, AV). Obsolete term for "cell," as it is rendered by the RSV.

CABUL kā'bəl [Heb. *kāḇûl*; Gk. B *Chōbamasomel,* A *Chabōl apó aristerṓn*].

1. A city in the territory assigned to Asher following the conquest under Joshua (Josh. 19:27). Represented by modern Kabul, the hill town is located about 10 mi. (16 km.) ENE of Mt. Carmel, overlooking the maritime plain.

2. The name given by Hiram king of Tyre to a Galilean district containing twenty cities given to him by Solomon (1 K. 9:13). Cabul may have been the governing city of the district; or by popular etymology (*kᵉḇal*, "as old, as worn out"), Hiram was complaining about Solomon's gift when compared with the 120,000 talents of gold he had sent Solomon (1 K. 9:14). Present evidence does not locate this district with certainty. R. J. HUGHES, III

CADDIS kad'is (1 Macc. 2:2, AV). *See* GADDI **2.**

CADES kā'dēz (1 Macc. 11:63, AV). *See* KEDESH **3.**

CADES-BARNE kā'dēz bär'nə; **CADESH** kā'desh; **CADESH-BARNEA** kā'desh bär'nē-ə. *See* KADESH **1.**

CAESAR sē'zər [Gk. *Kaisar*]. Originally the surname of the Julian gens (thus, Caius Julius Caesar); afterward a name borne by the Roman emperors. In the NT the name is definitely applied to Augustus (Lk. 2:1, "Caesar Augustus"), to whom it belonged by adoption, and to Tiberius (Lk. 3:1, "Tiberius Caesar"; cf. Mt. 22:17, 21). The "Caesar" to whom Paul appealed (Acts 25:11f., 21) was Nero. The form is perpetuated in "Kaiser" and "Czar."

See also ROMAN EMPIRE AND CHRISTIANITY I.

CAESAR, JULIUS jo͞o'lē-əs. *See* ROMAN EMPIRE AND CHRISTIANITY I.A.

CAESAREA ses-ə-rē'ə [Gk. *Kaisar(e)ia*]. A city on the Palestinian coast about 23 mi. (37 km.) S of Mt. Carmel and about 65 mi. (105 km.) NW of Jerusalem. The ancient name in its Arabic form is still associated with the ruined site of Qeiṣâriyeh.

Caesarea was originally a Phoenician fortification or city known as Strato's tower, and seems to have been built in the 4th cent. B.C. by a Sidonian king of that name (Josephus *Ant.* xiii.15.4). During the Maccabean war it was captured from Zoilus by Alexander Janneus *ca.* 96 B.C. (*Ant.* xiii.12.4; 15.4). The city fell to the Roman forces under Pompey in 63 B.C., and was subsequently given to Herod the Great by Augustus (*Ant.* xv.7.3). Herod then named the city Caesarea and its seaport Sebastos, in honor of the Roman emperor (*Ant.* xvi.5.1).

In a display of lavishness Herod erected sumptuous palaces and public buildings over a twelve-year period; and it was not until 10 B.C. that construction was completed and the city dedicated amid magnificent games in the amphitheater.

The harbor at Caesarea was particularly noteworthy, because the whole coastline was inhospitable to shipping. Herod constructed a huge breakwater 200 ft. (60 m.) wide and about 120 ft. (37 m.) in depth, the enormous stones of which can still be seen extending some 150 ft. (46 m.) from the shore. Elaborate buildings surrounded part of the harbor, and there were statues of the emperor at the entrance. Not all of the site has been excavated, but work there has uncovered a synagogue dating from the 4th or 5th cent. A.D.

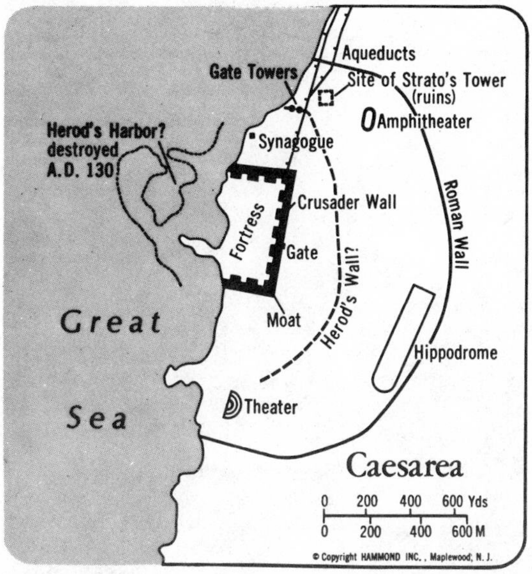

Roman amphitheater (before restoration), probably the site of Herod Agrippa's death (Acts 12:21-23). Gladiatorial contests were staged in the arena, which covers an area slightly larger than that of the Colosseum. (Consulate General of Israel in New York)

Remains of a marble statue of a Roman official. Under direct Roman rule, Caesarea was the administrative and military center of Palestine. (Consulate General of Israel in New York)

Dedication stone from the Roman theater. It bears the only inscription to name Pontius Pilate, who lived in the procurators' residence at Caesarea. (Israel Department of Antiquities and Museums)

Like most coastal communities in NT times, Caesarea had a mixed population. When Pilate was procurator of Judea he lived in the governor's residence at Caesarea. Philip preached in the city (Acts 8:40), which was also his home (Acts 21:8); and it was here that Peter was sent to minister to the Roman centurion Cornelius (10:1, 24; 11:11). Herod Agrippa resided in the city and died there (12:19, 23). Paul passed through Caesarea several times, making it his port of landing on his return from his second and third missionary journeys (18:22; 21:8). At Caesarea he made his fateful decision to visit Jerusalem (21:13), and to that city he returned under guard prior to his appearance before Felix (23:23ff.). After two years of imprisonment Paul made his defense before Festus and Agrippa II in Caesarea, and sailed from there as a prisoner when sent by Festus to Rome on his own appeal (25:11).

Josephus described the riots that broke out between Jews and Gentiles in Caesarea (*BJ* ii.13.7; 14.4f.), and recorded the atrocities practiced on the Jews under Felix and Florus. In Caesarea Titus celebrated the birthday of his brother Domitian by setting 2500 Jews to fight with beasts in the huge amphitheater. Eusebius was bishop in the city from A.D. 313 to 340. Caesarea passed into Moslem hands in 638, was held by the Christians for a time during the Crusades, and was finally overthrown by Sultan Bibars in A.D. 1265.

Bibliography.–A. Reifenberg, *IEJ*, 1 (1950/51), 20-32; S. Yeivin, *Archaeology*, 8 (1955), 122-29; L. Kadman, *Coins of Caesarea Maritima* (1957); C. T. Fritsch and I. Ben-Dor, *BA*, 24 (1960), 50-59; A. Negev, *Bible et Terre Sainte*, 41 (1961), 6-15; A. Frova, *et al.*, *Scavi di Caesarea Maritima* (1965); J. Humphrey, *BASOR*, 213 (Feb. 1974), 2-45; R. Bull, *IEJ*, 24 (1974), 187-190; L. Levine *Caesarea under Roman rule* (*Studies in Judaism in Late Antiquity*, 7, 1975); L. N. Hopfe and G. Lease, *BA*, 38 (1975), 2-10; R. Bull, L. Holland, and C. T. Fritsch, eds., *Joint Expedition to Caesarea Maritima: Studies in the History of Caesarea Maritima*, I (*BASOR Supp. Studies*, 19, 1975); A. Negev, "Caesarea," in M. Avi-Yonah, ed., *Encyclopedia of Archaeological Excavations in the Holy Land*, I (1975), 270-285.

W. EWING R. K. H.

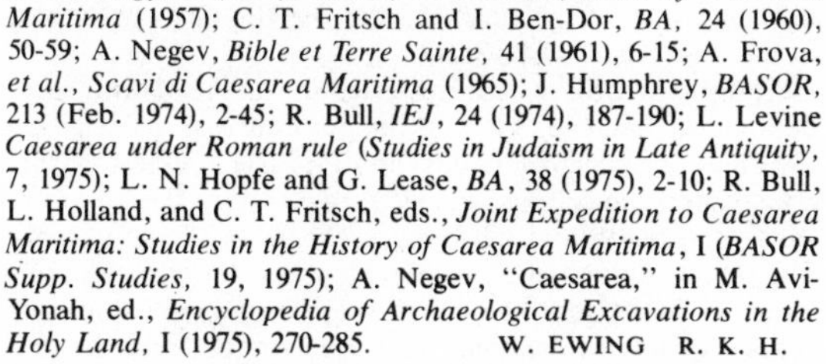

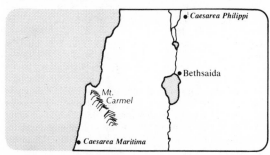

CAESAREA PHILIPPI fil'i-pī, fə-lip'ī [Gk. *Kaisareia hē Philippou*]. A city at the southwest base of Mt. Hermon on a rocky terrace 1150 ft. (350 m.) above sea level, on the main source of the Jordan River. The site was important for its strategic nature, since it guarded the fertile plain to the west. A nearby cave, from which one of the springs feeding the Jordan emerged, also housed a shrine in antiquity, which may have been dedicated to the rites of Baal-gad or Baal-hermon in OT times (cf. Josh. 11:17f.; Jgs. 3:3; 1 Ch. 5:23). Greek settlers in the area dedicated the shrine to "Pan and the Nymphs," and in NT times the name of the cave was Paneion, the surrounding territory being known as Paneas (Josephus *Ant.* xv.10.3; xvii.8.1).

In 20 B.C. the district was given by Augustus to Herod the Great, who erected at Paneas a splendid temple of white marble in honor of the emperor. After the death of

Shrine at Caesarea Philippi, possibly dedicated to Baal-gad or Baal-hermon (W. S. LaSor)

Herod in 4 B.C. the area became part of the tetrarchy of Philip, who rebuilt and beautified the town, naming it Caesarea as a compliment to the emperor Augustus. Philip added his own name in order to distinguish the city from Caesarea on the coast of Sharon (*Ant.* xviii.2.1; *BJ* ii.9.1).

Jesus and His disciples went to Caesarea Philippi from Bethsaida; on the way Peter made his celebrated confession of Christ, after which Jesus began to speak of His coming passion (Mt. 16:13ff.; 8:27ff.). Some have thought that the transfiguration of Christ occurred on an elevation near Philippi (*see* TRANSFIGURATION, MOUNT OF [4]). In the time of Christ Caesarea Philippi was a center of Greco-Roman civilization, with a largely pagan population. The environs of the city were spoken of as "the district" (Mt. 16:13) or "the villages" (Mk. 8:27).

About A.D. 50 the city formed part of the kingdom of Agrippa II, who renamed it Neronias in honor of Nero (*Ant.* xx.9.4). During the Jewish war of A.D. 66-70 Caesarea Philippi served as a stopping-place for the Roman armies under Titus and Vespasian (*BJ* iii.9.7; vii.2.1). However, the ancient name of Paneas outlived both the names Caesarea and Neronias, being preserved in the Arabic name of the village Bâniyâs, built on the same site. Most of the remains date from the time of the Crusades. W. EWING R. K. H.

CAESAR'S HOUSEHOLD [Gk. *Kaisaros oikía*] (Phil. 4:22); NEB IMPERIAL ESTABLISHMENT. These words occur in the Epistle Paul wrote from Rome near the end of his first imprisonment there, probably late A.D. 61, to the church in Philippi. They give us most interesting information in regard to the progress made in the propagation of the gospel in Rome.

I. What Does the Phrase Designate?–"Caesar's household" meant the whole of the persons, slaves and freemen alike, composing the establishment of the emperor in his palace on the Palatine Hill at Rome. The slaves of the imperial household formed a host in themselves. On the character and constitution of this household we possess more information than on perhaps any other department of social life in Rome. "In Rome itself, if we may judge by these inscriptions, the *domus Augusta* must have formed no inconsiderable fraction of the whole population; but it comprised likewise all persons in the emperor's service, whether slaves or freedmen, in Italy and even in the provinces" (J. B. Lightfoot, *in loc.*). To belong to Caesar's household would secure to even the lowest grade of slaves substantial privileges and immunities, and would give a certain social importance, which made this position a valued one. An office in the emperor's household, however mean, was thought of so highly that in the monumental inscriptions such a fact is recorded with scrupulous care.

II. How Did the Gospel Reach Caesar's Household?– There is no need to suppose that the gospel was unknown, even in the palace, previous to the arrival of Paul in Rome. For in that numerous household of the emperor there would be Jews, perhaps many of them. This was a period when the city of Rome and the court of the Caesars swarmed with Asiatics, many of whom were Jews, and many of them would be in slavery or employment in the imperial court. It cannot be forgotten that Poppaea, Nero's consort, was a proselyte to Judaism and that she continued to advocate successfully the cause of the Jews before the emperor as occasion arose.

Therefore as soon as the gospel entered Rome and was proclaimed in the many synagogues there, these members of Caesar's household could not fail to hear the story of Jesus Christ and of His cross and resurrection. This probability would be quite sufficient to account for the fact that the gospel was known in Caesar's palace.

But the propagation of the gospel received a great impetus when Paul arrived in the city. For although he was a "bound prisoner," his wrist fastened day and night to the soldier who guarded him, he was able to preach and to teach without hindrance (Acts 28:31). Immediately after his arrival in Rome he put himself in communication with "the local leaders of the Jews"— probably the rulers of the synagogues in Rome — and many of them came to him, desiring to hear his views regarding "the hope of Israel" (vv. 20-22). Naturally all the Jews in Rome would be eager to gain this information from a man of Paul's position and character; for this community had for years been permeated with messianic hopes. Indeed, successive rumors of messiahs had kept them in such a fever of excitement that on one occasion at least they had started a riot. Thus it would come about as a matter of course that the gospel would reach all the Jews in Rome, including those in Caesar's household.

But besides this, Paul's daily contact with the soldiers who guarded him could not fail to lead to the introduction of the gospel into the regiment. And as part of the praetorian guard was quartered in buildings on the Palatine Hill, attached to the emperor's palace there, here was one other channel through which the gospel would be made known to some of those who resided in the palace of Caesar.

See also PHILIPPIANS, EPISTLE TO THE II.

Bibliography.–Comms. on Philippians by J. B. Lightfoot (1878); J. J. Müller (*NIC,* 1955); F. W. Beare (*HNTC*, 2nd ed. 1969).

J. RUTHERFURD

CAGE [Heb. *sûgar*] (Ezk. 19:9); AV WARD. The context indicates that the "cage" of Ezk. 19:9 was a portable enclosure for holding a captive en route to a stationary prison. The AV and NEB have "cage" also at Jer. 5:27 (Heb. *kᵉlûḇ,* RSV BASKET), and the AV at Rev. 18:2 (Gk. *phylakē,* RSV and NEB "haunt").

The earliest known form of cage made to confine a bird, for the pleasure of its song or the beauty of its coloring, was a crude affair of willows or other pliable twigs. Later cages were made of pottery. References in the Bible make it clear that people were accustomed to confine birds in cages as pets, or to detain them for market purposes. James indicated that cages were common when he wrote (3:7): "For every kind of beasts and birds . . . is tamed, and has been tamed by humankind." In Job (41:5) we find these lines: "Will you play with him as with a bird? Or will you put him on a leash for your maidens?" The sale of sparrows as an article of food still continues in Eastern markets (Mt. 10:29); and Jesus entered the temple and overthrew "the seats of those who sold pigeons" (21:12). Cf. also Sir. 11:30, "Like a decoy partridge in a cage" (Gk. *kartállos*).

G. STRATTON-PORTER

CAIAPHAS kā'ə-fəs, kī'ə-fəs [Gk. *Kaïaphas,* some MSS also *Kaïphas*]. The name of Joseph, a son-in-law of Annas (cf. Jn. 18:13), who filled the post of high priest *ca.* A.D. 18-36, and then was deposed by Vitellius (cf. Josephus *Ant.* xviii.2.2; 4.3). He is mentioned by Luke as holding office at the time of John the Baptist's preaching in the wilderness (Lk. 3:2).

Caiaphas took a leading part in the trial and condemnation of Jesus. It was in his court or palace that the chief priests (Sadducees) and Pharisees, who together constituted the Sanhedrin, assembled "in order to arrest Jesus by stealth and kill him" (cf. Mt. 26:3f.; Jn. 11:49). The regal claims of the new Messiah and the growing fame of His works had made them dread both the vengeance of imperial Rome upon their nation, and the loss of their own personal authority and prestige (cf. Jn. 11:48). But Caiaphas pointed a way out of their dilemma: let them bide their time till the momentary enthusiasm of the populace was spent (cf. Mt. 26:5), and then by the single sacrifice of Jesus they could at once get rid of a dangerous rival and propitiate the frowns of Rome (cf. Jn. 11:49f.; 18:14).

The commentary of John upon this (Jn. 11:51f.) indicates how the death of Jesus was indeed to prove a blessing not only for Israel but also for all the children of God; but not in the manner which the cold-blooded statecraft of Caiaphas intended. The advice of the high priest was accepted by the Sanhedrin (v. 53), and they succeeded in arresting Jesus. After being led "to Annas first" (18:13), Jesus was conducted thence in bonds to Caiaphas (v. 24). According to Matthew He was led immediately upon His arrest to Caiaphas (Mt. 26:57). Mark and Luke do not refer to Caiaphas by name. The conduct of Caiaphas at this preliminary trial of Jesus (Mt. 26:57-68), its time and its procedure, were almost entirely illegal from the standpoint of the Jewish law (*see* JESUS CHRIST, ARREST AND TRIAL OF I.A.2). False witnesses were first called, and when Jesus refused to reply to their charges, Caiaphas asked of Him if He were "the Christ, the son of God" (v. 63). Upon Our Lord's answering "You have said so" (v. 64), Caiaphas "tore his robes, and said, 'He has uttered blasphemy. Why do we still need witnesses? You have now heard his blasphemy' " (v. 65). It was upon this charge that Jesus was found worthy of death (v. 66).

Caiaphas is also mentioned in Acts 4:6 as being among those who presided over the trial of Peter and John.

C. M. KERR

CAIN kān [Heb. *qayin*]. The firstborn son of Adam and Eve (Gen. 4:1). The expression of gratitude offered by his mother at his birth might imply that the name Cain was associated with a root *qānâ*, "obtain," "acquire." An alternative suggestion regards the name as related to a noun *qayin,* meaning "worker in metal," "smith" (Arab. *qayn*). The narrative, however, seems to indicate a simple play on words (cf. Gen. 2:5, 23, etc.), whereby the name Cain, whatever it may have meant to Eve under other circumstances, was linked with the verb *qānâ*. The Greek (*Kaïn*) and Latin Vulgate (*Cain*) are mere transcriptions, and thus throw no additional light on the provenance or meaning of the name.

The birth of Cain marked a fresh development in the life of Eve, who for the first time fulfilled the designation "mother of all living" (Gen. 3:20). It is significant that Eve's first child was male, and she acknowledged freely God's help in conceiving and bringing it to birth. Though now in a subordinate role to her husband, she exercised new responsibilities as a mother. After a time she bore a second child, also male, and she named him Abel.

A sedentary form of culture seems to be indicated by the narrative, since it speaks of Cain becoming a cultivator of the ground, while Abel tended flocks and herds. Religion has its place in this culture. The mention of Cain and Abel presenting offerings to God presupposes a knowledge of divine worship and its significance. It also gives clear indications of a rudimentary sacrificial schedule.

Both brothers made an offering to God from the fruits of their labor at some specific period, perhaps one that was prescribed, since they presented their offerings together. Whereas Abel's sacrifice pleased God, Cain's did not, and in consequence Cain was very annoyed and depressed. God challenged him about his attitude, pointing out that if he were following a proper way of life he would have no occasion to be indignant at God, but instead would feel uplifted spiritually. Since he was apparently not living as God desired, sin was already crouched beside him like a demon, presenting temptations that must be overcome if he desired future blessings from God (Gen. 4:5-7).

That he was not able to master the demonic impulses of temptation is seen in his continuing jealousy of his brother Abel, whom he later lured out to a piece of land, presumably one which he was cultivating. The versions have preserved a clause that has either fallen out of the MT or was included in a different type of Genesis text, from which the Samaritan Pentateuch, the LXX, and some other versions were made. Gen. 4:8 should therefore be emended to read (with the RSV and most modern English versions): "Cain said to Abel his brother, 'Let us go out to the field' " (See C. A. Simpson, *IB,* I, 519).

In mounting jealousy Cain killed Abel in the open country and presumably buried his body. This act constituted premeditated murder, and Cain was questioned subsequently about this heinous crime. He compounded his earlier offense by lying concerning Abel's whereabouts, and was told bluntly that his brother's blood was crying out to God from the very ground where he had been murdered.

Cain was cursed by being banished from his own property, and was warned that the soil would never again yield its produce to him. Instead, he would become a fugitive, wandering far from home and straying into potentially dangerous situations. Cain still seems to have been rebellious rather than contrite, for he remonstrated with God, claiming that the punishment imposed was too severe. His dread of being set upon and killed by those he might meet implies group solidarity, an indication of the existence of community life.

God forestalled Cain's death by murder, telling Cain that He was placing upon him a mark which would signify to those who met him during his wanderings in the land of Nod that he was not to be harmed. The exact nature of this mark is unknown, but it may have been some type of clan marking, or else a form of brand which some Sumerians placed upon their slaves, particularly if the slave was likely to run away. Other protective signs are referred to in Ex. 13:16; 28:36; Dt. 6:8; 11:18; Ezk. 9:4, 6.

The land of Nod (lit. "wandering") was located E of Eden, which appears to have been in the vicinity of the Babylonian plain of Shinar. The territory evidently contained settlements, from one of which Cain obtained a wife who is unnamed in the OT. They subsequently had a son, Enoch (Gen. 4:17), after whom Cain named a settlement ("city") that he established in Nod; no site answering to this modest description has been excavated to date. Enoch himself married and had a son named Irad, as recorded in the Cainite genealogy (vv. 18-24). The inclusion of such material in the Genesis narrative is paralleled by the antediluvian king lists from Sumer. If the genealogy of Cain was actually written on tablets and incorporated with similar tablet material to form the bulk of the book of Genesis, it would be natural to expect genealogical sections to occur in it, as with tablets recovered from Nuzi and other sites.

In the account of human technological developments given in Gen. 4:20-22, the mention of the use of iron is often assumed to be anachronistic. But discoveries by Russian archeologists at the northern base of Mount Ararat have revealed the existence *ca.* 2500 B.C. of some sophisticated smelters that manufactured iron ore, as well as some other metals and alloys. These discoveries demonstrate the antiquity of the tradition regarding technology as the Cainite line knew it, and place the narrative in new historical perspective.

The identity of the group from which Cain secured his wife is unknown. The setting is obviously in southern Mesopotamia and possibly the settlement involved flourished in the Ubaid period. Alternatively, Cain's wife may have come from some such group as the Rephaim or the Nephilim, both of which lived before the Flood. Certain writers have suggested the presence in southern Mesopotamia of pre-Adamic species, perhaps dating from the Neolithic period, which were subsequently drowned by the Flood, but this is speculative. Gen. 6:1 certainly conveys the impression that mankind was increasing numerically, and it may be that Cain had married a person who came into the category of the "daughters of men." While there are insufficient data upon which to base an opinion, subsequent discoveries at former Sumerian sites may aid in understanding this problem.

In the NT, Cain was stigmatized as being "of the evil one" (1 Jn. 3:12), and Christians were exhorted not to follow his example. To "walk in the way of Cain" (Jude 11) was to be wilful, rebellious, and disobedient, all of which were alien to the spirit of the new covenant, as they had been to the old. Instead, the way of life embraced by Abel was to be followed by the believer (He. 11:4).

Bibliography.–T. Jacobsen, *Sumerian King List* (1939); E. A. Speiser, *Genesis* (*AB,* 1964), pp. 29-36. R. K. HARRISON

CAIN (Josh. 15:47, AV). *See* KAIN.

CAINAN kā'nən [Gk. *Kaïnan*].

1. Greek form of KENAN (Lk. 3:37); also the AV form in the OT (except 1 Ch. 1:2).

2. A son of Arphaxad (Lk. 3:36), omitted in the MT of Gen. 10:24; 11:12.

CAKE. *See* BREAD.

CALAH kä'lə [Heb. *kālaḫ*; Gk. *Chalach,* also *Chalak, Kalach*; Assyr. *Kalḫu, Kalḫa, Kalḫi, Kalaḫ*]. One of the great cities of Nimrod (Gen. 10:11, RSV, NEB), which with Nineveh, Resen between Calah and Nineveh, and Rehoboth-Ir (probably lying more to the north) formed Assyria's great fourfold capital. The meaning of the name is unknown, but if a Sumerian etymology be accepted, some such signification as "holy gate" (*Ka-laḫ*) — a parallel to Ka-dingir-ra=*Bāb-ilī*, "gate of God" (*see* BABYLON) — is possible. In later antiquity the city was known by its present name Nimrûd.

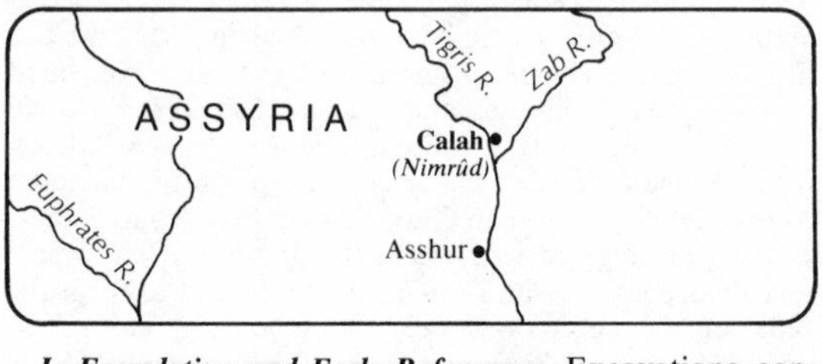

I. Foundation and Early References.–Excavations conducted from 1949 to 1963 by the British School of Archaeology in Iraq indicate that Calah was inhabited by *ca.* 2500 B.C. As Nineveh is mentioned by Hammurabi, who reigned in the 18th cent. B.C., it is clear that that city was already in his time an important place; and the passage in Gen. 10:11 implies, though it does not actually prove, that Calah was of about the same period. The Assyrian king Ashurnasirpal (*ca.* 883-859 B.C.) states that Calah was "made" by Shalmaneser (I) *ca.* 1300 B.C., but possibly this is simply an indication that he rebuilt it. Later on the site seems to have become neglected, for Ashurnasirpal states that, the city having fallen into ruin, he rebuilt it. Thereafter it became practically the capital of the country, for he not only reerected or restored its shrines and temples — the temple of Ninurta, with the god's image, the temple of "the Lady of the Land," and the temples of Sin, Gula, and Enlil — but he also received tribute there. Among his other works may be mentioned the water-channel Pati-ḫengala; the plantations, whose fruits he apparently offered to the god Ashur; and the temples of the city. It also became a favorite place of residence for the later kings of Assyria, who built palaces and restored the city's temples from time to time. The city is mentioned by Tiglath-pileser III and Sargon II as the base for their campaigns against Judah and Israel. It fell in the Median invasions of 612 B.C.

II. The Site.–Calah occupied the roughly triangular tract formed by the junction of the upper Zab with the Tigris. The ancient Tigris flowed rather closer to the western wall than it does now and seems to have separated the small town represented by Selamiyeh from the extensive ruins of Calah, which now bear the name of Nimrûd. The main ruins are situated on a large, rectangular platform on the bank of the old bed of the Tigris. The site is 22 mi. (35 km.) S of Tell Kuyunjik (Nineveh), and is surrounded by narrow mounds still having the appearance of walls. Traces of no less than 108 towers, the city's ancient defenses, are visible on the north and east, where the walls were further protected by moats. The enclosed area is about 2331 by 2095 yds. (2130 by 1915 m.), or 1000 acres (408 hectares).

III. Buildings.–The most prominent edifice was the great temple tower at the northwest corner — a step-pyramid (*ziqqurratu*) like the Babylonian towers, constructed of brick faced with stone, and rising in stages to a height of about 126 ft. (38 m.), probably with a sanctuary at the top (*see* BABEL, TOWER OF X.A). A long vault occupies the basement-stage of this structure, and caused its discoverer A. H. Layard to regard it as the probable traditional tomb of Ninus, under whose shadow the tragedy of Pyramis and Thisbe took place. Ovid (*Metamorphoses* iv.98) describes the tomb of Ninus as having been situated "at the entrance of Nineveh," and, if this be correct, Calah must have been regarded as the southern portion of that great city. On a preaching journey Nineveh may well have taken three days (Jonah 3:3) to traverse, provided Khorsabad was in reality its northern extremity.

The platform upon which the temple tower of Calah was situated measures about 700 by 400 yds. (640 by 365 m.), which left room for temples and palaces. In the center of the east side of this platform lie the remains of the palace of Ashurnasirpal. Its chambers and halls were paneled with sculptured and inscribed slabs, and the principal doorways were flanked with finely carved winged and human-headed lions and bulls. In the southeast corner are the remains of the palace of Esarhaddon, built at least in part with material taken from the palace of Tiglath-pileser IV, which was situated in the south portion of the platform. The remains of this last are, as a result of this spoliation, exceedingly meager. The southwest corner of the platform contains the remains of the last palace built on the site — a very inferior construction for Ashur-etil-ilani (*ca.* 636 B.C.). One of the temples on this platform was that dedicated to Ninurta, situated at the southwest corner of the temple tower. The left-hand entrance was flanked by man-headed lions, while the sides of the right-hand entrance were decorated with slabs showing the expulsion of the evil spirit from the temple — a spirited sculpture now in the British Museum. On the right-hand side of the entrance was an arch-headed slab with a representation of Ashurnasirpal in low relief, standing in the conventional attitude. Before it stood a stone tripod altar, implying that divine honors were paid to this king. (Both these are now in the British Museum.) The remains of another temple were found E of this, and there are traces of further buildings at other points of the platform.

The slabs from Ashurnasirpal's palace show this king's warlike expeditions, but as descriptive lettering is lacking, the campaigns cannot be identified. Notwithstanding this disadvantage, however, they are of considerable importance, for they show incidents of his various campaigns — the crossing of rivers, the march of his armies, the besieging of cities, the reception of tribute, the life of the camp, and hunting the lion and the wild bull. The reliefs from the temples, which are much larger and finer, show the king engaged in various religious ceremonies and ritual acts, and are among the most striking examples of Assyrian sculpture. The site is renowned for its many ivories, which include plaques and figurines, as well as its inlaid furniture. The Black Obelisk of Shalmaneser III (*see* JEHU) was discovered there.

Bibliography.–M. E. L. Mallowan, *Nimrud and Its Remains* (2 vols., 1966); D. Dates, *Studies in The Ancient History of Northern Iraq* (1968).

T. G. PINCHES

CALAMITY [Heb. *'êḏ, rā'â, hawwâ, behālâ* (Isa. 65:23), *'āwen* (Prov. 22:8), *massâ* (Job 9:23), *ḥᵃṯaṯ* (Job 6:21); Gk. *stenochōría* (2 Cor. 6:4; 12:10)]; AV also DESTRUC-

Alabaster relief from Ashurnasirpal's palace at Calah (Nimrûd) showing the king hunting lions, assisted by a driver and footmen (Trustees of the British Museum)

TION, EVIL, ADVERSITIES (1 S. 10:19), HURT (Ps. 35:26), MISCHIEF (Prov. 17:20; 24:16; 28:14), etc.; NEB also DOWNFALL, DISASTER, RUIN, MISFORTUNE, DOOM (Prov. 1:26f.; Ezk. 35:5), FALL (Ps. 35:26), etc.

"Calamity" denotes an unfortunate event. It is frequently used in the phrase *yôm 'êḏ,* "day of calamity" (Dt. 32:35; Jer. 18:17; etc.), which suggests not merely an event but a period of misfortune or ruin. The prophets warn of the calamity that will befall apostate Israel (Ezk. 35:5; Ob. 13) and Israel's neighbors (Jer. 46:21; 48:16). In wisdom literature calamity is frequently the deserved punishment of the wicked (Prov. 6:15; 22:8), although the righteous also suffer calamity (Job 6:21; 9:23).

E. W. CONRAD

CALAMOLALUS kal-ə-mol'ə-ləs, -mol-ā'ləs (AV, RSV mg., NEB, 1 Esd. 5:22). This name (Gk. A *Kalamōlalos,* B *Kalamōkalos)* is corrupt. It has evidently arisen through combining the two names "LOD and HADID" (RSV), which occur in the parallel lists of Ezra (2:33) and Nehemiah (7:37).

CALAMUS kal'ə-məs [Heb. *qāneh*; Gk. *kálamos*] (Cant. 4:14; Ezk. 27:19); NEB SWEET-CANE; **AROMATIC CANE** [Heb. *qᵉnēh-bōśem*; Gk. *kálamos euṓdēs*] (Ex. 30:23); AV SWEET CALAMUS; **SWEET CANE** [Heb. *qāneh* (*haṭṭôḇ*, Jer. 6:20); Gk. *thymíama* (Isa. 43:24), *kinnámomon* (Jer. 6:20)]; NEB also "fragrant spices" (Jer. 6:20).

Although some writers believe all these substances to be identical, there is at least a distinction between the sweet-tasting cane of Isaiah and the sweet-smelling substance(s) of the other passages. The former plant is perhaps the sugarcane, *Saccharum officinarum* L., while the other passages refer probably to the ginger-grass, *Andropogon aromaticus* Roxb., native to northern India and highly aromatic (see *MPB,* pp. 39-41).

R. K. H.

CALCOL kal'kol [Heb. *kalkōl*]; AV also CHALCOL (1 K. 4:31); NEB KALCOL. Mentioned in 1 K. 4:31 as one of the wise men with whom Solomon was compared. "Chalcol" is probably better orthography, since it is a genuine Canaanite name, appearing on some ivories at Megiddo, probably from the 13th cent. B.C. In 1 K. 4:31 the designation "sons of Mahol" means "members of the orchestral guild."

See *ARI* (5th ed. 1968), pp. 122f., 210 n. 97. R. K. H.

CALDRON [Heb. *qallaḥaṯ, sîr, dûḏ*]; NEB CAULDRON, STEWPOT. *Qallaḥaṯ* is found only in 1 S. 2:14; Mic. 3:3. It was a pot for cooking, of undefined size and characteristics, in the former passage for sanctuary use and in the latter for domestic. The *sîr* (Ezk. 11:3, 7, 11) was distinctly a large pot, employed both for domestic use and in the sanctuary. The *dûḏ* (2 Ch. 35:13) was also a pot for cooking.

G. R. BERRY

CALEB kā'ləb [Heb. *kālēḇ*]; **CALEBITE** [Heb. *kāliḇî*] (1 S. 25:3); **CHELUBAI** [Heb. *kᵉlûḇāy*] (1 Ch. 2:9). A personal name employed for various individuals in OT texts dealing with the occupation of Canaan, the distribution of territory, and genealogies. Comparative Semitic onomastica show "Chelubai" to be a variant of "Caleb."

These onomastica also indicate that the meaning of the name is "dog." It is used either as a name of affection that stresses the quality of faithfulness or strength (like that of a dog to his master), or as a name employed for a servant or slave either with positive emphasis on the humble and faithful relationship of the inferior to the superior, or with derogatory emphasis on the disobedient and rebellious character of the subordinate. It appears that the Masoretic pointing of this common Semitic personal name reflects an attempt to avoid the negative overtones usually associated with the dog (Heb. *keleḇ*) in the OT.

Some scholars (e.g., Noth, North) have maintained that Caleb was originally a clan name for the Calebites (cf. 1 Ch. 2:50-52 in the NEB and NAB) who helped the Judahites to take the southern part of Palestine. Later the ancestor of the Calebites was depicted as a Judean hero. Along with this view often goes the notion that the name Caleb is evidence of primitive totemism. However, the frequency with which the common Semitic personal name Caleb appears in the ancient Near East militates against the hypothesis of a clan name. In each known instance it is the name of an individual. Beltz has shown that the name Caleb does not contain any trace of totemism, and the current evidence supports the OT view that Caleb is singularly a personal name.

1. The son of Jephunneh. At Kadesh-barnea Moses chose Caleb the son of Jephunneh the Kenizzite (Nu. 32:12; Josh. 14:6, 14; cf. Gen. 15:19; 36:11) as Judah's representative to spy out the land of Canaan (Nu. 13:6). Among the twelve spies only he and Joshua returned with an encouraging report, while the others counseled not to attack Canaan (13:25–14:38). Accordingly only Caleb and Joshua were permitted to survive (14:38), because they "followed Yahweh" (Nu. 32:12; Dt. 1:36; Josh. 14:9). Some forty years later Caleb took part in the conquest of the land, and by driving out the Anakim he received Hebron as his inheritance (Josh. 14:6-15). Othniel, a younger relative of Caleb (Josh. 15:17; Jgs. 1:13; 1 Ch. 4:13), distinguished himself by capturing Debir (or Kiriath-sepher) and receiving as a reward Achsah, Caleb's daughter, who was promised to the conqueror of that city (Josh. 15:15-19; Jgs. 1:11-15). Caleb was also chosen as the "leader" (*nāśî*) and "head" (*rō'š*) of the tribe of Judah, to be in charge with other leaders in the distribution of the land (Nu. 34:18f.). The capture of Hebron and Debir with its surrounding territories (1 S. 30:14) explains how the Kenizzites came to have a portion in the tribe of Judah. Already in Jgs. 1:10f. they were reckoned as a part of the tribe of Judah, which is said to have taken both Hebron and Debir.

2. The son of Hezron. This Caleb is consistently designated as the son of Hezron of the line of Judah (1 Ch. 2:9, 18, 42). Among his descendants were Hur, Aaron's associate during Moses' absence on Mt. Sinai, and Hur's grandson Bezalel, the master craftsman who played a major role in the construction of the wilderness tabernacle and its furniture (Ex. 31:2-11; 35:30-35; 1 Ch. 2:19f.). Although attempts have been made to identify Caleb the son of Hezron with Caleb the spy, there can scarcely be any question that they were two separate individuals. Since Caleb the son of Hezron had a great-grandson Bezalel who helped to build the tabernacle at Sinai, he cannot be identical with Caleb the spy, who was only about forty years old when he was appointed as one of the twelve spies to reconnoiter the land — an event that took place in the year following the building of the tabernacle (Josh. 14:6-12). It has been held that if Caleb's daughter (or female descendant) Achsah of 1 Ch. 2:49 is the well-known daughter of Caleb the spy (Josh. 15:15-19; Jgs. 1:11-15), then Caleb the son of Jephunneh the Kennizite would be a descendant of Caleb the son of Hezron.

3. The son of Hur. According to the punctuation of some versions, 1 Ch. 2:50 refers to Caleb the son of Hur, who would be a grandson of Caleb the son of Hezron. However, more recent versions place a period after "Caleb" so as to make the beginning of v. 50 the closing phrase of the preceding pericope: "These were the descendants of Caleb" (RSV), i.e., Caleb the son of Jephunneh. The following pericope would list the family of Hur, the son of Ephratah (vv. 50-52).

Bibliography.–H. Bauer, *ZAW*, 84 (1930), 73-80; M. Noth, *ZDPV*, 55 (1932), 97-124; W. F. Albright, *BASOR*, 82 (Feb. 1941), 43-49; *GTTOT*, pp. 42-44; C. F. Jean and J. Hoftijzer, *Dictionnaire des Inscriptions Sémitiques de l'Ouest* (1965), pp. 120f.; H. B. Huffmon, *Amorite Personal Names in the Mari Texts* (1965), p. 152; W. Beltz, *Die Kaleb-Traditionen im AT* (1972); R. North, *Bibbia e Oriente*, 8 (1966), 167-171; F. Gröndahl, *Die Personennamen der Texte aus Ugarit* (1967), pp. 28, 150.

G. F. HASEL

CALEB-EPHRATAH kā'ləb-ef'rə-thə [Heb. *kālēḇ 'eprāṯâ*]. The place where Hezron died (1 Ch. 2:24, AV). However, the RSV and most scholars (including the NEB) follow the LXX: "after the death of Hezron, Caleb went in to Ephrathah, the wife of Hezron his father, and she bore him Ashhur, the father of Tekoa." To take one's father's wife was to claim his possessions. R. P. DUGAN

CALENDAR. The various methods of calendrical reckoning found in the OT and NT, and the numerous references to them, reflect the importance of the calendar at all times in Israelite and early Christian history. Without presupposing a sophisticated theory of "historical consciousness" in early Israel, the necessity of having a method by which time is organized in a more or less systematic manner is obvious. In the everyday life of the community and state the political and legal systems need some definable notion of time in order to legitimate and carry out their various functions. In the cultic sphere (often overlapping or totally subsuming the "everyday") every moment is "filled with salvation" (van der Leeuw). There arises the need to control the *tempus* and out of this need is born liturgical time, referred to in terms of calendrical notations and presupposing various organizational schemata of time.

It is impossible to speak of one normative biblical calendar. The OT reflects the use of many different calendrical systems and the precise chronological period when each system was used is nearly impossible to determine. Moreover, more than one calendrical system was often in use at the same time in ancient Israel, demonstrating that different methods of reckoning were required for different activities (cf. our fiscal, academic, church years).

An understanding of the calendar in biblical times is very important for serious biblical study. The calendar is used to organize and refer to those aspects of life that were important to the communities that used them. This is especially true of matters pertaining to the cult, more specifically worship. Moreover, an understanding of the systems by which the lives of ancient Israelites are organized introduces us more fully to the world views of the biblical period and thereby the influences that produced the Bible itself.

I. Methods of Reckoning Time in the Ancient Near East
II. Calendrical Systems in Ancient Israel
  A. Terminology
    1. Year
    2. Month
    3. Week
    4. Sabbath
    5. Day
    6. Other Terms
  B. Sequences
    1. Seasonal
    2. Cultic
    3. Regnal/Civil Years
    4. Jubilees and Qumrân
    5. Greek and Roman
    6. New Testament
    7. Intercalation
III. The Israelite New Year
IV. Historical Development of the Calendar
V. Problems of Interpretation

I. Methods of Reckoning Time in the Ancient Near East.– All calendars used in the ancient Near East are dependent in some way on the movements of extraterrestrial bodies. While an agricultural year may be defined in terms of seasons and a liturgical year in terms of festivals, the overarching system, the rationale behind the nomenclature, is invariably connected to the movements of the sun, the moon, the stars, or some combination of these. Moreover, all ancient Near Eastern calendars presuppose a cycle, with the year (see II.A.1) the most fundamental cyclical unit. Though astronomical science certainly was not as highly developed as today, keen observation assured a regularity and uniformity of calendrical reckoning in the ancient Near East.

The earliest calendars known are Egyptian in provenance. An original lunar (-stellar) cultic calendar, based in large measure on the heliacal rising of Sirius (Gk. *Sothis*) in Egyptian myth, was soon found to be inadequate and a solar civil calendar was instituted alongside the religious calendar to assure regularity in state affairs. By the middle of the 3rd millennium B.C. *both* lunar and solar calendars were used in Egypt, with the latter ultimately achieving priority to the extent that even religious festivals were fixed by the civil calendar (cf. Parker, pp. 57-60).

In Mesopotamia the distinction between civil and religious calendars was not made. The Sumerian (3rd millennium B.C.), Babylonian (2nd millennium) and Assyrian (1st millennium) calendars are best designated lunisolar calendars. As essentially religious calendars, they reflected in their broadest outlines two great mythical cycles (culminating at the equinoxes) controlled by and seen in terms of solar movements. The internal division of the solar year, however, was regulated by the moon, and the lunar months are derived therefrom. There was in Mesopotamia, therefore, a fusion of calendrical reckoning methods in *one* calendar in contrast to the juxtaposition found in Egypt.

In Syria-Palestine (Ugarit and Phoenicia in particular) the pertinent textual evidence witnesses to a year defined primarily in terms of agricultural seasons and months (see II.B.1) reflecting lunar, perhaps lunisolar, methods of calendrical reckoning. It is clear that at Ugarit the Mesopotamian calendar was "official" for state affairs, but the integration of indigenous mythical cycles certainly provided a potentially different rationale and structure for the religious year.

The earliest references to methods of calendrical reckoning in ancient Israel (e.g., Ex. 23:14-17; 34:18-26) demonstrate the influence of *both* lunar and solar phenomena. The major festivals occur at the equinoxes (solar) while the organization of the year is based on a lunar month pattern. It would be extremely tenuous to posit *direct* influence, either Egyptian or Mesopotamian, upon the calendar of ancient Israel, but a few important observations should be made. The Israelite calendar is lunisolar, thereby resembling the Mesopotamian calendar closely. On the other hand, the existence in Egypt of *two* different calendars with different purposes may be an important precedent to note when the religious and regnal years of Israel are examined.

In all societies, ancient and modern, calendrical methods of reckoning time and the resultant calendars produced are dependent upon, and reflect in their structure, cycles important in their everyday life. In ancient Israel no distinction was made between "church" and "state," "religious" and "political." The conceptions of Yahweh as a God very much associated with nature and the natural cycle as seen in the annual seasonal year (cf., e.g., Ps. 29), and as the God of the Exodus and Settlement, were not separated. Both provided important rationales and guidelines for the shape of the Israelite calendar. To the extent that this reflects a common process in ancient Near Eastern societies and that many seasonal and theological elements associated with the calendar are similar in respective myths and epics, the calendar of Israel has a heritage upon which it is dependent. To the extent that Israel's historical experiences and perception of Yahweh acting in nature and history are different and special, Israel's calendar is unique. Israel's calendar therefore reflects *both* the common and the unique — in both seasonal organization and the theological superstructure that provides its rationale.

II. Calendrical Systems In Ancient Israel.*–A. Terminology*. An examination of the various terms used to designate calendrical time in Israel reveals not simply the influence of method (cf. I above, solar and lunar phenomena), but also specific concerns in the life of the people, e.g., cultic and economic terms.

1. Year (Heb. *šānâ*). The Israelite year was the most basic unit of the calendar. The individual components of the year might fluctuate, but all of these terms were inevitably linked to the conception of an annual cycle. Sometimes the year was a part of an even larger calendrical sequence, as in the notion of a Sabbatical Year (Ex. 23:10f.; Lev. 25:3-7; 1 Macc. 6:49, 53), a seven-year cycle, or the Jubilee Year (Lev. 25:8ff.; Nu. 36:4; Ezk. 46:17; Isa. 61:2 [Lk. 4:19]), based on a forty-nine-year cycle. In general, however, the biblical calendrical terminology uses some singular form of the lunisolar year as the largest unit and calendrical references are made within this conceptual framework.

2. Month (*yeraḥ, ḥōḏeš*). The two words commonly used to designate "month" in Hebrew both have lunar referents and etymologies. *Yeraḥ* is derived from a root meaning "moon" (compare other Semitic languages where this root and its lunar referents are common). *Ḥōḏeš* may be used to refer to either the month proper (Ex. 23:15; 34:18; Dt. 16:11) or the day of the new moon (Nu. 28:11; Hos. 2:13; Am. 8:5). Textual evidence seems to indicate that both words were used as a designation for month from an early period in the history of Israel, thus reflecting the lunar nature of the calendar. Also reflective of the lunar influence upon the calendar are the "new moon" days (Nu. 28:11; etc.), which were celebrated regularly and which designated the first day of each lunar month (Gen. 38:24; Nu. 9:22; 11:20f.; Jgs. 11:37; 1 S. 6:1; Am. 4:7; etc.).

The OT uses three different systems of nomenclature in referring to months: Canaanite, numerical, and Babylonian. An etymological study of the Canaanite month names reveals that these designations are derived at least in part from the agricultural functions or phenomena associated with the particular time of the year to which each name refers. There are only four Canaanite months referred to in the OT: Abib ("fresh ear" [of grain], Ex. 13:4; 23:15; 34:18; Dt. 16:1); Ziv ("beauty" — a time of flowers[?], 1 K. 6:1, 37); Ethanim ("permanent streams[?]," 1 K. 8:2); and Bul ("rain[?]," 1 K. 6:38). It has often been noted that these four names are to be associated with the most important agricultural periods in the year, perhaps explaining their survival. It should also be noted, however, that all the activities associated with these months are cultic in character, thus providing at least partial evidence of a very early admixture of Israelite cult with Canaanite nomenclature and custom. When Canaanite month names are used, the sequence always begins in the spring.

The numerical system of referring to months is the most common one in the OT. This method of reference, which occurs in many places in the OT, also begins with the first month in the spring.

The Babylonian month names comprise the third system in use in Israel and are found in relatively late texts: Nisan (Neh. 2:1); Sivan (Est. 8:9); Elul (Neh. 6:15); Chislev (Neh. 1:1); Tebeth (Est. 2:16); Shebat (Zec. 1:7); and Adar (Ezr. 6:15). Sometimes these month names are found alone and sometimes preceded by an explanatory numerical reference (e.g., Est. 3:7; Zec. 7:1; etc.).

In each of the three systems a twelve-month schema is presupposed and the months are counted from the spring. In addition, the lunisolar character of the year and the means by which the months are calculated or reckoned are clear.

The Hebrew Months

NUMERICAL	CANAANITE	BABYLONIAN	
First	Abib	Nisan	March/April
Second	Ziv	Iyyar	April/May
Third		Sivan	May/June
Fourth		Tammuz	June/July
Fifth		Ab	July/August
Sixth		Elul	August/September
Seventh	Ethanim	Tishri	September/October
Eighth	Bul	Marheshvan	October/November
Ninth		Kislev	November/December
Tenth		Tebeth	December/January
Eleventh		Shebat	January/February
Twelfth		Adar	February/March

3. Week (*šāḇû[a]'*). The origin of the seven-day week is continually debated (cf., e.g., RSV and NEB on Gen. 29:27). While reference to the week in the OT is relatively rare and confined primarily to cultic occasions (Ex. 34:22; Lev. 12:5; Nu. 28:26; Dt. 16:9f., 16; etc.), the week appears to have been an important calendrical unit from an early period in Israel (Ex. 34:22). The most important reference to the week-system is in conjunction with the feast of weeks (*ḥag šeḇû'ōṯ*), indicating a cultic and agricultural source for its usage. Theories proposing that the week was derived originally from a lunar phase may be valid but have no supporting biblical evidence.

4. Sabbath (*šabbāṯ*). The sabbath, regardless of its origin, was a significant factor in the ancient Israelite calendrical system. Whether or however the sabbath and the week are to be related etiologically, by the time of the composition or Gen. 1, the sabbath was considered the seventh day of the week (cf. also Ex. 16:26; 20:10; 31:15; Lev. 23:3; etc.). The important point to be noted here is the use of the sabbath as a punctuation mark for various events in the Israelite cultic calendar. The sabbath could mark the end of a weekly cycle (e.g., a rest/feast day, cf. Lev. 23:3), a stopping-point from which calendrical reckoning could begin anew (Lev. 23:15), or even a numerical collection of years. In any case, the sabbath and the seven-day cycle associated with it became the most important means of calendrical reference in Israel from the monarchical period onward.

5. Day (*yôm*). The day is the smallest, most consistent unit of the Hebrew calendar. Idioms using the Hebrew word for day often indicate longer periods of time (compilations of days). Though there is evidence that in early Christian times the day was divided into hours of quite specific and regular length (Jn. 11:9; Mt. 20:1-12), in general the primary divisions are morning and evening, day (light) and night (dark). There is evidence of calculation for the beginning of the day from both the rising of the sun (Gen. 19:34) and its setting (Lev. 23:27), though the latter appears to be the most common and the later development. The morning-evening distinction and division of Heb. *yôm* was often very important for the ritual instructions with calendrical notations (e.g., Nu. 28f.; Dt. 16; etc.).

In summary, the day in the Hebrew calendar is referred to in two basic ways. On the one hand, the day, as the unit of time that was constantly and continually repeated, is symbolic of the process of time reckoning, and thus of time itself, to the ancient Israelite. On the other hand, the relative brevity of the day allows specificity of both time reckoning and those ritual requirements, *et al.*, which went with it. This notion of speciality and specificity was possible throughout the ancient Near East, but Israel developed and used the historical consciousness that went with this calendrical precision in a unique way.

6. Other Terms. In addition to the specific terminology referring to the units and subunits of the year, there are several other terms used in conjunction with calendrical concerns. The notion of "special," or "appointed," times is carried by Heb. *mô'ēḏ*. The *ḥāg*, pilgrimage feast, is one of these special times. These feasts are celebrated regularly, on a particular cycle, regulated and controlled calendrically, each year. Moreover the specific time of the year can be referred to not only by month names, but also by the agricultural activity that characterizes that period and the festival associated with it (*'āsîp*, "ingathering"; *qāṣîr*, "harvesting" [Ex. 23:16, etc.]). The notion of an annual cycle is clearly indicated by the enigmatic phrases *beṣē'ṯ haššānâ* (Ex. 23:16) and *teqûpaṯ haššānâ* (Ex. 34:22; see III below).

B. Sequences. The shape of the calendrical cycle is partially determinable by the terminology applied to it, but the sequence or order of the cycle is often dependent on factors not always immediately recognizable in the terminology. The ancient Israelite community had two different sequences for the year. Economic, political, and religious concerns combined in a variety of ways to produce these sequences. At a later period the sectarian communities devised still other calendrical sequences, and the calendars of Greece and Rome also became important in certain areas of community and national life.

1. Seasonal. The best example of a calendrical sequence shaped by seasonal concerns is the so-called Gezer Calendar. Dating from the early monarchy (10th cent. B.C.), this short text presents the sequence of the year in terms of the agricultural work done in the various months, beginning in the fall with the harvest.

His two months are (olive) harvest,
His two months are planting (grain),
His two months are late planting;
His month is hoeing up of flax
His month is harvest of barley,
His month is harvest and feasting.
His two months are vine tending,
His month is summer fruit.

(W. F. Albright, *BASOR*, 92 [Dec. 1943], 16-20; *ANET*, p. 320.)

Although there are continual debates over the precise dating of this text as well as its intended function, there is no question that it witnesses to a calendrical sequence important in the life of early Israel: the agricultural cycle beginning in the fall. It should be noted that the rationale behind this type of sequence, seasonal tasks, can be found in OT cultic texts such as Ex. 23:14-17; 34:18-26; etc., but the OT sequence begins in the spring. The cultic sequence, though very much influenced by regularly recurring seasonal phenomena, is ultimately governed by other important considerations to which we must now turn.

2. Cultic. The sequence of the Israelite cultic year is always presented as a cycle beginning in the spring (Ex. 23:14; Lev. 23; Nu. 28; Dt. 16; etc.). Both seasonal and astronomical elements seem to be important in determining the shape of the sequence. The ancient festivals are often referred to with agricultural terminology and the two most important times of the year are the spring and fall equinoxes.

The most important occasions of worship for the entire Israelite community, the major festivals, significantly influenced the shape and nature of the calendar. The year was organized around the three major pilgrimage festivals: Passover and the Feast of Unleavened Bread (March/April); Feast of Weeks (May/June); and Feast of Tabernacles/Booths (September/October). Each of these

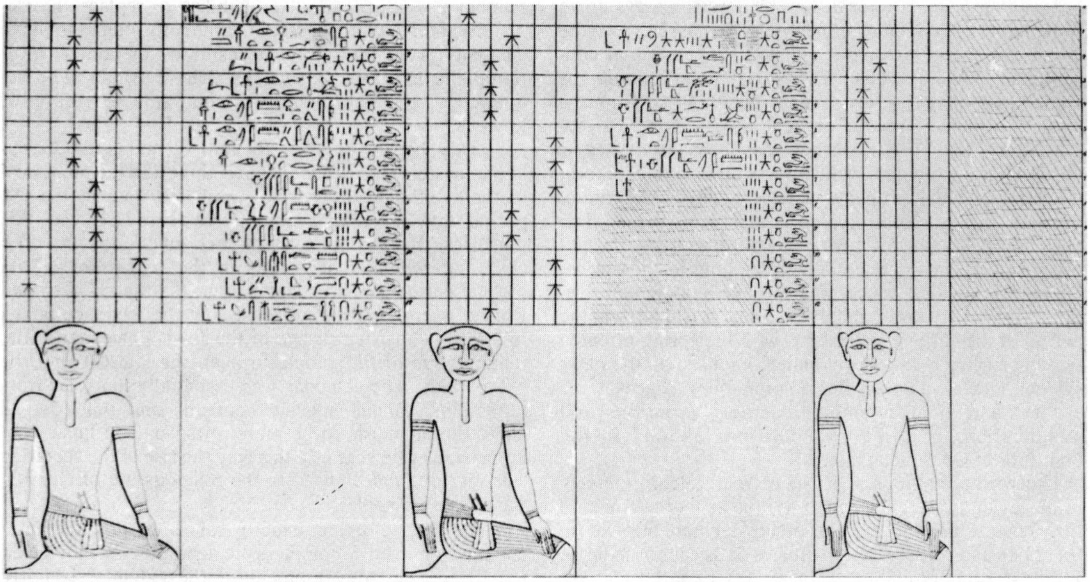

Astronomical calendar from the ceiling of Ramses VII's tomb at Thebes (1149-1142 B.C.). The seated men represent the first and sixteenth days of each month, and the coordinate net (above) depicts the positions of stars at various hours of the night. (Egyptian Museum, Cairo)

occasions has seasonal elements reflecting agricultural antecedents. In addition, ancient ritual is associated with many of these festivals pointing to early mythological conceptions behind these transformed rites (e.g., Ex. 23:18f.). In the primary OT witnesses to the festival year it is important to note the focus on worship, on obligation, on commitment, within the context of a cult-centered relationship between Israel and Yahweh. In the postexilic period the festivals of Purim and Hanukkah, each in very different ways witnessing to the diaspora nature of Judaism, were added to this cultic liturgical year.

3. Regnal/Civil Years. The sequence of the civil year, if it is possible to speak of such an entity as separate from the religious year, was dependent upon the same methods of reckoning time and used the same terminology. Often the "state" records would identify the year in question in reference to the reign of a particular monarch, but the lunisolar conception of the year and calendrical terminology remained fairly consistent whether cult or monarchy was involved. The only substantive issue concerning the regnal year is the starting point of the sequence, i.e., whether a fall or spring New Year is involved, and this will be discussed below (III).

4. Jubilees and Qumrân. In the book of Jubilees and among the texts found at Qumrân there is evidence of a calendrical system significantly different from those discussed above. The texts demonstrating this calendar may be dated to approximately 200 B.C. This calendar was definitely used by the Qumrân community, among other sectarian groups. The most noticeable characteristic of this calendar is the fixed relationship between days of the week and days of the month. Thus, e.g., a religious observation on the fifteenth of the first, fourth, seventh or tenth months would always be on a Wednesday. This was made possible by a strict 364-day solar year with four quarters of thirteen weeks each (three months, two of thirty days, one of thirty-one days; cf. Jub. 6:23-32). The year began in the fall, and its strictly solar method of organization appears to be a reaction against the lunar (actually lunisolar) months of the Babylonians and other ancient Hebrew calendrical systems (Jub. 6:36f.). The Qumrân community used the Jubilee calendar *only* for the determination of festivals in the cultic year. It is uncertain whether the antagonism of this sectarian community concerning the calendar originated from a bias against Babylonians (foreigners) or against normative Judaism.

5. Greek and Roman. Evidence of the use of the Syro-Macedonian calendar may be found in the apocryphal literature (2 Macc. 11:30, 33, 38) and Josephus (e.g., *Ant.* i.3.3; iii.10.5; etc.). No real influence of the Julian calendar is found in biblical material, though the system clearly must have played some part in Palestine during Roman occupation.

6. New Testament. Dating in the NT is by reference to the reign of particular Roman officials and to the Jewish cultic calendar. It was a common practice to refer to the regnal year as one means of dating events (Lk. 3:1, "in the fifteenth year of the reign of Tiberius Caesar"). Most such NT citations are general, providing a reference only to the reign, but not to the year, of the emperor Augustus (Lk. 2:1), the king Herod (Mt. 2:1; Lk. 1:5), the governor Quirinius (Lk. 2:2), or the proconsul Gallio (Acts 18:12). Nevertheless, the confluence of these citations and other data makes reasonably precise dating possible (cf. Finegan, pp. 215ff.). Most dating in the NT is with reference to the Jewish cultic calendar. The sabbath (cf. also "the Lord's day," Rev. 1:10), Passover (Jn. 2:13), Tabernacles (7:2), Pentecost (Acts 2:1), Unleavened Bread (20:6) are all used in referring to times and events in the life of Jesus and the early Church. *See also* CHRONOLOGY OF THE NT.

7. Intercalation. In the biblical texts there is no clear evidence of intercalation, though it must have been done in some way at all times in Israel. The Babylonian system of inserting seven intercalary lunar months in a nineteen-year cycle was probably used, though with certain local adaptations. Various other methods may have been adopted, but the texts that discuss intercalation explicitly are postbiblical.

III. The Israelite New Year.–Any conclusions about the time and function of the New Year and its celebration in Israel are subject to criticism. One must always make some kind of judgment concerning this issue, but the direct evidence is so sparse and so ambiguous that consensus is never possible. Two initial points should be made concerning the New Year in Israel. First, from the postexilic period to the present day it appears that the New Year (Rosh Hashanah) has been celebrated in the fall, in conjunction with Yom Kippur and Sukkoth, the latter of which probably was the original celebration. Second, there is good evidence that from the earliest periods of Israelite occupation and settlement the cult organized its year sequentially, beginning in the spring. Opinion is divided concerning the explanation for this. Some maintain that a fall New Year existed from the period of the earliest settlement, with the spring-oriented sequence being a later development imposed on the older system. Others maintain that a spring New Year was the earliest and most common in Israel. Variations and qualifications of these two positions abound in the literature of OT scholarship.

Those who maintain a fall New Year celebration rely primarily upon the evidence of: (1) the sequence found in the Gezer Calendar; (2) the much debated phrases in Ex. 23:16 and 34:22, which by themselves cannot indicate a fall starting point (cf. Clines); (3) hypothetical reconstructions of the nature and function of the Feast of Booths; (4) a few chronological references that may point to the reckoning of regnal years from the fall (cf. Thiele, *MNHK*). Those who maintain a spring New Year point to the sequence of the cultic year as witnessed by texts from all periods, and recently have noted the probability of a spring New Year among the Canaanites (cf. F. M. Cross), regardless of the questionable evidence of the Gezer "Calendar." It must be observed that the debates over the time and function of the Israelite New Year are motivated by far more than mere concern with chronological and calendrical knowledge of ancient Israel. For example, the fall date is often advocated as much to show that Israel was "different" as that the evidence warrants it. Moreover, one's view of the function of the festival itself is always tied quite closely to one's conception of the nature and development of Israelite religion (cf., e.g., Weiser and Mowinckel). In any case the evidence remains conflicting, though it would be fair to assess the current opinion as advocating (1) that a spring New Year at an early period in Israelite history is quite probable; (2) that the fall New Year is not necessarily operative in the monarchical period (*contra* Thiele, *et al.*) but may indeed be a reaction against Babylonian and Persian hegemony in the early postexilic period.

IV. Historical Development of the Calendar.–Possible antecedents of the calendrical systems and rationales of calendars are to be sought in Egypt, Mesopotamia, and Canaan. Egyptian influence is difficult to pinpoint, while the lunisolar calendar of Mesopotamia has clear parallels with that of early Israel. The most important antecedents, however, were the calendrical systems in use in Canaan, still only vaguely known. Calendrical reckoning in Canaan demonstrated the heavy influence of the seasonal, agricultural cycle and the mythological conceptual framework which explicated this cycle in the cultic life of the people. These influences manifest themselves both in early calendrical material (e.g., Ex. 23; 34) and in conceptual motifs and patterns used of Israel's God (Ex. 15; Jgs. 5; Isa. 51; etc.). The early Israelite calendar had an essentially cultic provenance, with nomenclature associated with both month names and religious occasions that reflected seasonal agricultural concerns (Ex. 23; 34; etc.). During the monarchy the system of referring to months by number developed, in all probability to replace the Canaanite nomenclature, which gradually came to have "pagan" associations as a result of orthodox, antipluralistic movements such as that of Elijah. The sequence of the year remained the same for the cult, however.

Shortly before or after the fall of Judah the Babylonian system was probably used alongside the numerical method, although it was not until very late in the OT period that the names actually appeared. It was this numerical Babylonian system that functioned for both civil and religious occasions in the remainder of the biblical period. Other systems, e.g., the Macedonian and Roman, were surely also in use, but the evidence points to a fairly consistent usage of the Jewish calendar in the religious life of the people through the late OT and the NT periods. The calendar was essentially lunisolar from its origins, though specific concerns and times would allow the emphasis to be more on solar than lunar phenomena, or vice versa. In this way the rise of the sectarian calendar of Jubilees used in the religious life of Qumrân is easily explainable.

While precise dating, exact parallels to show the antecedents, or even a complete "calendar," are not given us, the general development of the calendar is fairly clear. It is a growth that reflects not only a more sophisticated calendrical science, but a different and expanding conception of worship and religion.

V. Problems of Interpretation.–Since many crucial areas of biblical study are inseparably related to questions or areas concerning the calendar, it is important to recognize some basic problems that remain. First, despite many references to different calendrical systems, the biblical texts do not provide a detailed, clear "calendar" that will explain the calendrical science of ancient Israel at all times and in all places. The evidence is disparate, and any reconstruction must rely on presuppositions the validity of which are not verifiable. Another problem that arises in studying the calendar is the relationship of the calendrical systems of Israel and Judah. Much work has been done in this area, but there is not yet enough evidence and/or convincing theoretical explanation to provide consensus on the issues of regnal year reckoning, New Year, etc. Finally, the chronological overlapping of the references to particular calendrical systems and the limited pertinent textual material, biblical and extrabiblical, cause much difficulty for any study of the calendar. All of these problems, however, witness to one widely known datum: the calendar in the biblical period, as everything else, was in constant flux.

See also CHRONOLOGY OF THE OT.

Bibliography.–*Extrabiblical calendars:* S. Langdon, *Babylonian Menologies and the Semitic Calendars* (1935); R. Parker, *Calendars of Ancient Egypt* (1950). *Biblical Calendars:* F. M. Cross, *Canaanite Myth and Hebrew Epic* (1973); S. J. DeVries, *Yesterday, Today and Tomorrow* (1975); J. Finegan, *Handbook of Biblical Chronology* (1964); J. van Goudoever, *Biblical Calendars* (2nd ed. 1961); H. J. Kraus, *Worship in Israel* (1965); S. Talmon, *JAOS*, 83 (1963), 177-187; R. de Vaux, *Ancient Israel* (1961); B. Z. Wacholder, *Essays on Jewish Chronology and Chronography* (1976). *Israelite New Year:* D. J. A. Clines, *JBL*, 93 (1974), 22-40; J. C. de Moor, *New Year with Canaanites and Israelites* (1972); J. B. Segal, *Hebrew Passover* (1963); N. H. Snaith, *Jewish New Year Festival* (1947).

D. F. MORGAN

CALF [Heb. *ben-bāqār*–'son of the herd,' *'ēgel, 'eglâ* (Hos. 10:5), *pārâ* (Job 21:10)]; AV also BULLOCK (Jer. 31:18), "round" (1 K. 10:19); NEB also BULL-CALF, CALFGOD; [*yālaḏ*–'bears, brings forth'] (Jer. 14:5); [Gk. *móschos, moschopoiéō* ("make a calf," Acts 7:4)]; NEB also "make a bull-calf." *'Ēgel* is used of the golden calves and in the expression *'ēgel marbēq,* "fatted calf," or lit. "calf of the stall" (1 S. 28:24). In 1 K. 10:19 the RSV and NEB emend the vocalization of Heb. *'āgōl* ("round") to *'ēgel* in accordance with the LXX, which uses *móschos,* the Greek term for calf. *See* CATTLE.

CALF, GOLDEN [Heb. *'ēgel massēḵâ*–'molten calf,' *'ēgel zāhāḇ*–'golden calf']; NEB also BULL-CALF (Ex. 32), CALF-GOD (Hos. 10:5). A representation of a young bull, used in Israelite worship first under Aaron at Sinai and later in the northern kingdom under Jeroboam I.

I. The Term
II. Biblical Examples of Calf Worship
  A. Aaron's Golden Calf
  B. Jeroboam's Golden Calves
III. Bull Worship in Amos and Hosea

I. The term.–The term *'ēgel* is the ordinary Hebrew name for a male (or female, *'eglâ*) calf, and is as flexible as the English name, applying to any animal of the bovine family from one (Mic. 6:6) to three (Gen. 15:9; cf. Jer. 34:18f.) years old. It has been suggested that the habitual use of this diminutive term (instead of Heb. *par,* "bull") for the golden bulls Aaron and Jeroboam set up — especially as it is once made feminine (Hos. 10:5) — was a reference to their small size, expressing comtempt for them. But although this is plausible, it is by no means certain. It was not their size that made these bulls contemptible in the eyes of the prophets but rather what they had come to represent in the life and worship of Israel. By the time of Hosea and Amos calf or bull worship was obviously connected with apostasy, not only at those centers where bulls were recorded as having been erected, but quite possibly in connection with other centers such as Gilgal and Gilead (Hos. 4:15; 12:11; Am. 4:4; 5:5), Samaria (Hos. 8:6; 10:5; 13:2, 16), and Beer-sheba (Am. 5:5; 8:14).

II. Biblical Examples of Calf Worship.–*A. Aaron's Golden Calf.* Just what transpired and what meaning is to be assigned to each action in the Sinai account of the golden calf (Ex. 32) is by no means settled. Some of the words and phrases in that chapter are a verbal duplication of the narrative of Jeroboam's calf worship (cf. Ex. 32:4 with 1 K. 12:28), and there is no lack of scholars who consign most of the details of the story to a secondary reading back of the Jeroboam material (e.g., M. Noth, *Exodus* [Eng. tr. 1962], p. 246). The motivation for the story, in that case, would be to discredit further the bull worshipers of Bethel. However, it seems clearly unreasonable to suppose that a Hebrew writer at any time would so fiercely abuse his own ancestors without some firm traditional basis for his statements, merely for the sake of adding a little more reproach to his northern neighbors. Thus, even the more radical critics now accept the historicity of a core of the material, if not all the details.

Exodus 32:1 indicates that the projected gods were to function as a surrogate for Moses in his role as leader of the people rather than as a substitute for the God of Israel. If this is the case, it explains the action of Aaron (v. 5) in proclaiming a feast to Yahweh in the midst of the proceedings. It has been suggested also that the calf was merely a platform of some kind, on which the God of Israel would ride, analogous to the platform or throne concept of the ark and illustrated by the common Syrian motif of a god standing atop a lion or a bull (*ANEP,* nos. 500f.; *ANEP Supp.,* no. 830). In either case, there is no need to insist that the original intention was to introduce a cult so totally foreign as the Apis-bull of Memphis, the Mnevis-bull of Heliopolis, or even one of the less remote syncretistic bull-cults of the Delta (see E. Otto, *Beiträge zur Geschichte der Stierkulte in Aegypten* [1938]) — although the continuation of any bull-oriented worship would most certainly have led to some form of syncretism.

The actual calf of Ex. 32 was formed of molten gold and fashioned with an engraving tool (v. 4); probably, however, it was an overlay of some sort rather than pure gold, inasmuch as Moses was later able to burn it with fire and grind it to powder (v. 20) — neither of which would have been possible with pure gold. Aaron's own statement that the calf just appeared from the fire, apparently full-grown (v. 24), is usually considered to be simple fabrication; but the suggestion has been made that perhaps the calf was nothing more than a generally calf-shaped mass of molten metal which caught the imagination of the Israelites upon its emergence from the fire. Whatever the origin of the image, it was quickly identified by the people with the words, "These are your gods, O Israel, who brought you up out of the land of Egypt!" (v. 8). It is this statement, with both the noun "gods" and the verb following it in the plural, that is often considered secondary; but the context provides a natural setting in the worship of, and sacrifice to, the calf (singular). Quite possibly that statement was altered to create a verbal correspondence with the Kings passage, but this should not cause us to reject the well-attested fact that the calf was identified with Yahweh in some form. In fact, it was precisely this identification of the calf with Yahweh, possibly a result not expected by Aaron, for which the entire nation was called to account. Just what Aaron expected we cannot tell with any degree of certainty, but the tradition is relatively mild in its censure of Aaron himself when compared with its attitude toward

Bronze calf statuette of Apis, worshiped in Egypt as a fertility-god. Such foreign cults always represented a threat to Israelite religion. (Trustees of the British Museum)

the people at large. Undoubtedly a factor in the harshness with which the calf-worship was received was not only the calf itself, but the accompanying orgiastic rites (note the use of the same verb *ṣaḥaq* in Gen. 26:8, RSV "fondling"). Whatever the original intent, the matter had clearly gotten out of hand and any possibility of rescuing an element of pure Yahwistic worship was gone.

B. Jeroboam's Golden Calves. In the case of Jeroboam I (1 K. 12:28-33) it is even less plausible to hold that the two calves were intended to represent a foreign cult. Jeroboam was himself apparently a Yahwist (cf. the name of his son, Abijah, "my father is Yahweh"; but cf. also 14:31 and 2 Ch. 13:1), and the text of 1 K. 12 is full of the features of normative Yahwism and totally lacking in elements of Canaanite religion. Since his concern was to gain the allegiance of the Yahwists to whom Solomon's foreign religious adventures were offensive (1 K. 11:28-40), any major departure in favor of Canaanite religion would have been self-defeating. We are left with the conclusion that in some sense the bull symbols erected in Dan and Bethel were meant to represent Yahweh or something connected with Yahweh. A current hypothesis holds that the bulls were pedestals, like those known from Syrian sculpture as supports for the storm-god Baal-hadad (cf. J. Gray, *I & II Kings* [1964], p. 290). This is not the only possibility. The incident is clearly connected with that of Aaron's calf, and it is not impossible that both were attempts at some physical representation of Yahweh; against this hypothesis, however, is the legal proscription of images, particularly images that might serve as objects of worship (Ex. 20:4f.). Unless we are prepared to relegate the Decalogue in its entirety to a later period, we are forced to acknowledge that, even in Jeroboam's time, making an image of Yahweh would have created division, not elicited support. With evidence so plentiful for the bull-pedestal concept (see above), it would seem best to accept this solution to the problem.

What the calves were originally, and what they became eventually, are two different things. There is little doubt that as early as Hosea's time the more licentious worship of Canaanite fertility religion had been added to the official Yahwism (Hos. 10:5; 13:2). Such a development might well have been expected, for the bull-symbol had a natural affinity for the fertility element in the cult of the Canaanite Baals. That this was a gradual process and not an immediate development is clear in that Elijah, the great champion of Yahwism, seems to have been totally silent concerning this element of the religion of the north. Add to this the surprising fact that only a few years later Jehu, when viciously obliterating the cult of Baal (2 K. 10:28f.), did nothing to attack the calves, and it becomes easy to see that the calves were still identified with Yahweh and were not Baal-symbols.

III. Bull Worship in Amos and Hosea.–It is not impossible to see why Hosea might fiercely condemn a ritual that Elijah might have tolerated. Hosea lived at a time when he could trace the history of this experiment for nearly two centuries, and could see clearly that these images had not helped but greatly hindered the development of the religion of Yahweh. Even if at first recognized as symbols, these images had *become* common idols (Hos. 12:11; 13:2). "This thing became a sin" (1 K. 12:30; 13:34). As Baal worship involved associations with bulls (cf. *ANEP*, no. 490, in which the Baal wears the bull horns), and as Yahweh Himself was at times called "Baal" (meaning simply "Lord" or "Master," Isa. 54:5; Jer. 31:32 [MT 31]; Hos. 2:13 [MT 16]), this syncretistic tendency would naturally be accelerated. It is certain that by the middle of the 8th cent. the worship at Dan and Bethel had lost its uniquely Yahwistic character and become so closely affiliated with a host of heathen deities as to be practically indistinguishable from idolatry in the nations surrounding Israel. The calf was now an idol and not just a symbol (Hos. 8:5f.; 11:2; 13:2), the worship of which — evil enough in itself — was expanded to include veneration of an Asherah and the host of heaven, as well as the Tyrian Baal (2 K. 17:16f.).

Quite clearly it is this reduction of the ethical religion of Yahweh to the level of just another heathen sacrificial system that caused both Hosea and Amos to condemn even sacrifices themselves (Hos. 6:6; Am. 5:21-24). Just as it was the orgiastic rites accompanying Aaron's calf that called forth Moses' condemnation, so it was the heathen ritual associated with Jeroboam's calves that elicited prophetic rejection. In neither case could there be any pure Yahweh worship. Hosea therefore prophesied the impending destruction of the system (8:5f.), and 2 Kings records the sad fulfillment of Hosea's utterance in the removal of the ten tribes to exile (17:7-18).

Bibliography.–H. T. Obbink, *ZAW*, 47 (1929), 264-274; O. Eissfeldt, *ZAW*, 58 (1940/41), 190-215; R. de Vaux, *Ancient Israel* (Eng. tr. 1961), pp. 272, 333f.

C. M. COBERN
C. E. ARMERDING

CALITAS kal-ī'təs [Gk. *Kalitas* or *Kaleitais*] (1 Esd. 9:23, 48, AV, NEB). *See* KELITA.

CALKERS. *See* CAULKERS.

CALL; CALLING [Heb. *qārā'*; Gk. *kaléō* and cognates *klēsis, klētós*; also *légō, phōnéō, chrēmatizō*]. The word is very common in both the OT and NT, there being over seven hundred instances of the verb, noun, or adjective.

I. In the OT.–Five main uses are to be discerned in the OT. First, "to call" means "to summon or invite." Thus God called to Adam in Gen. 3:9. Moses called the elders together in Ex. 19:7. God called an assembly against Judah in Lam. 1:15. Joel issued the command to call a solemn assembly in Joel 1:14.

Second, the verb can have the sense of "calling on God." Men began to call on the name of the Lord in Gen. 4:26. All who call on the name of the Lord shall be delivered (Joel 2:32). Invocation of this kind obviously has as its purpose the summoning of divine help or protection, usually with the expectation that it will be given. In this sense "to call" has much the same force as "to pray" (cf. Ps. 31:17; 50:15; 53:4; 86:5; 102:2).

Third, "to call" is used for "to call by name," i.e., "to name." This use appears already in the creation story. God called the light day and the darkness night. He called the firmament heaven and the dry land earth (Gen. 1:5ff.). Since names are not mere identifications but also descriptions (cf. Gen. 17:19; 32:28), this calling has more than ordinary significance. Man can name as well as God; we see this very early in the naming of Eve (Gen. 2:23; cf. 22:14).

Fourth, God calls by name with a view to service. The story of Moses offers a good example. God called Moses by name out of the bush and laid upon him the task of liberating Israel from Egypt (Ex. 3:4ff.). The call of Samuel follows a similar pattern (1 S. 3:1ff.). Although the word "call" is not used for what happened to others whom God appointed (e.g., Amos, Isaiah, Jeremiah), undoubtedly one may validly speak of their prophetic calling.

Fifth, "to call" may be used in the sense of "to call one's own." Actively God calls Israel His people (Isa. 43:7; 45:4), and for this reason Israel may be described as called by the name of the Lord (Dt. 28:10; Isa. 43:1;

cf. the temple in Jer. 7:30). This calling of Israel stands closely related to its election (Isa. 45:4). It thus points to the covenant relation in which Israel is called to salvation, is given its name, has the function of a divine witness, and receives the possibility and privilege of calling on God's name with the assurance of prior response (Isa. 65:24).

II. In the NT.–All the senses found in the OT appear again in the NT. An instance of summons occurs in Acts 4:18; cf. also 24:2 and the call to the wedding in Mt. 22:3. Calling on the name of the Lord is found in the quotation from Joel in both Acts 2:21 and Rom. 10:13. Significantly, the cry for help may now be addressed to the Lord Jesus (cf. Acts 7:59; 22:16). Calling in the sense of naming has particular importance in the Infancy stories (Mt. 1:21; Lk. 1:60; 2:21); Jesus' name clearly implies service. The appointing of the disciples can be expressed in terms of calling: when Jesus saw James and John, "immediately he called them" (Mk. 1:20). Finally, Christ's people are those whom He has called and who are rightly called by His name, so that there is no shame in suffering for Christ's name, or as a Christian (1 Pet. 4:14, 16). But merely calling Jesus Lord is to no avail if His word is not also done (Lk. 6:46). On the other hand it is sinners, not the righteous, whom Jesus came to call (Mt. 9:13).

The noun "calling" takes on added significance in the NT, especially in the Pauline writings. It becomes almost a technical term for what has happened to those who through the Father's love are now called the children of God in Christ (1 Jn. 3:1). The christological reference has plainly given the term new force and depth, making possible the wealth and comprehensiveness with which the term is now employed.

One result is that the *goal* of calling now finds more specific definition. We are called to salvation, holiness, and faith (2 Thess. 2:13f.), to the kingdom and glory of God (1 Thess. 2:12), to an eternal inheritance (He. 9:15), finally to fellowship (1 Cor. 1:9), and to service (cf. Gal. 1).

The *means* of calling also is clearly stated. Calling is through grace (Gal. 1:15) and comes through the hearing of the gospel (2 Thess. 2:14; cf. 1 Thess. 1:4f.; Rom. 10:14ff.). Since God, or Christ, is the author of the call, one might also refer to the Holy Spirit as the mediator of calling through the gospel (cf. 1 Thess. 1:5).

The *ground* of calling is specifically established in 2 Tim. 1:9. Not works but the purpose and grace of God in Christ Jesus form the starting point for the divine calling.

The *nature* of God's calling is described as well. Along with God's gifts, it will not be revoked (Rom. 11:20). It is a high or upward calling (Phil. 3:14), heavenly (He. 3:1) and holy (2 Tim. 1:9), associated with hope (Eph. 4:4). Believers are exhorted to lead lives that are worthy of their calling (Eph. 4:1; cf. 2 Thess. 1:11). If not all the called are chosen, the link with election holds fast. The chosen of 2 Thess. 2:13 are the called of v. 14. Believers are exhorted to confirm their calling and election (2 Pet. 1:10). The "called and chosen and faithful" are with the Lamb in Rev. 17:14. Those whom God predestined He called, and those whom He called He justified and glorified (Rom. 8:30).

Some commentators (cf. Lietzmann) have found a distinctive use of "calling" in 1 Cor. 7:17ff., and a few even in 1 Cor. 1:26, referring the term to the state or occupation of believers, or to their condition of insignificance. This has been hotly contested, e.g., by K. L. Schmidt in *TDNT,* III, 491ff. Here as always Paul seems to be speaking of the calling to salvation and faith. This has come to people who are of little account socially (1 Cor. 1:26ff.), and it has come to them in given circumstances (slavery, marriage, circumcision, etc.) which do not have to be changed as a condition or consequence of the calling (1 Cor. 7). No basis exists in these passages for the equation of calling with status or with that which is now often designated by the term "vocation."

III. The Church.–In Christian history calling has been worked out more specifically in the two areas of calling to salvation and calling to sanctification and service. Calling to salvation, which is also calling into the divine community, is accomplished by the Holy Spirit through the administration of the word and sacraments. Within this generally accepted understanding a debate has arisen due to the fact that not all who are called are observed to be chosen. Perhaps the most common view here is that calling carries with it the possibility of response, which in some cases may be negative. In Reformed theology, as represented, e.g., by Calvin or the Westminster Confession, a different interpretation is espoused. The equation of calling and election is here upheld by a distinction between general calling, which applies to all who hear the gospel, and effectual calling, by which the God who calls, or the Holy Spirit, infallibly brings to faith those whom He has chosen. Either way salvation is by divine calling and by the ensuing human calling on the name of the Lord.

The call to service or sanctification has often been regarded as an additional call to believers either to dedicate themselves to Christian discipleship or to engage in a particular form of ministry. Sacralizing and institutionalizing tendencies have given rise to problems in this area. On the one hand we find a clericalism which insists that only ordained persons are truly called to service. On the other hand the call to dedication has been identified with a monastic vocation. Thus a false distinction between clergy and laity or religious and secular has resulted. Luther demolished these distinctions with his apparently revolutionary teaching that any sphere of work may be calling in which Christians glorify God, live dedicated lives, and engage in ministry. Unfortunately, the implied equation of calling with occupation had unforseen consequences. In a rigidly structured society it fostered the reactionary idea that people should stay in divinely ordered stations in life. In a looser societal order it led to a secularizing of the concept of calling which has all but emptied it of its true sense.

Perhaps the underlying problem in the historical outworking has been the tendency to separate what God has joined together. It seems to have been assumed too easily that there are two callings, a first to salvation and then another (or two others) to service and sanctification. Exegetical and dogmatic theology, however, have combined to bring the biblical nature of this distinction under suspicion. Thus K. L. Schmidt insists that in the NT there is just the one calling, namely, to be a Christian; and Karl Barth argues in *CD,* IV/3, that the callings in Scripture are never to salvation alone to the exclusion of sanctification and service. Certainly there may be calls to special forms of service, as one might see in the sending out of Paul and Barnabas on their first missionary journey. Nevertheless, ministry and dedication form no less an integral part of calling than does salvation. All believers are called to be God's children, disciples, and servants, whether in the state of life in which the calling comes or in new possibilities which God opens up for them. The calling itself does not change, only the form or sphere in which it is exercised.

Bibliography.–*CD,* III/4; IV/3; K. Holl, *Gesammelte Aufsätze,* III (1928); *TDNT,* III, *s.v.* καλέω κτλ. (Schmidt).

G. W. BROMILEY

CALLISTHENES kə-lis'thə-nēz [Gk. *Kallisthenēs*]. An officer of Nicanor who was charged with the burning of the sacred portals of the temple at the time of the desecration under Antiochus Epiphanes (168 B.C.). After the decisive defeat of Nicanor's army at Emmaus (165 B.C.) the Jews celebrated the victory in the city of their fathers and burned Callisthenes, who had fled into a little house with others who had set the sacred gates on fire; "so these received the proper recompense for their impiety" (2 Macc. 8:33).

CALNEH kal'ne [Heb. *kalneh, kalnê*; Akk. *kullanî, kulnia*?; Gk. *Chalannē*]; **CALNO** kal'no [Heb. *kalnô*] (Isa. 10:9). In the AV the name of the fourth city founded by Nimrod in the land of Shinar (Gen. 10:10), the three preceding ones being Babel, Erech, and Akkad; and in all English versions, a city mentioned in Am. 6:2 and Isa. 10:9. Because no city named Calneh is known from ancient Babylonia, it has been proposed that the Heb. *klnh* of Gen. 10:10 should be pointed to read *kullānâ* or "all of them," as in Gen. 42:36, a reading adopted by the RSV and NEB. This would then serve as a comprehensive designation of the cities in the plain of Shinar, which also included Ur and Nippur.

The Babylonian Talmud identified Calneh with Nippur, probably because of the antiquity of the site, which went back to *ca.* 4000 B.C. While Nippur was the undisputed cultural and religious center of Sumeria from the early 3rd millennium B.C. to the time of Hammurabi, it did not exercise political power and was never the seat of a Sumerian dynasty. In the reign of Hammurabi, Nippur yielded its cultural supremacy to Babylon but still continued as an important city down to the time of the Parthians. However, there is insufficient evidence for identifying it with Calneh, and it must be concluded that to the present the site of Calneh remains unidentified.

Some scholars locate the land of Shinar in northern Mesopotamia, and on this basis would identify Calneh with the Akkadian town named Kullanî, which was mentioned in tribute lists from Assyrian sources. Kullanî was apparently associated politically with Arpad, a city first captured by the Assyrians in 754 B.C. in their attempts to control the trading route to Hamath and Damascus. Arpad, the modern Tell Erfâd, was located about 20 mi. (32 km.) NW of Aleppo, while Kullanî has been identified with the modern Kullanköy, some 12 mi. (19 km.) SE of ancient Arpad. In Am. 6:2 Calneh was mentioned in association with Hamath and Gath, which suggests a northerly location for Calneh. If this is so, the discrepancy between the location in the plain of Shinar (if indeed the Hebrew actually refers to a city) and that contemplated by Amos may be because the Calneh known to the prophet was a northern commercial colony which derived its name from the mother city to the southwest. This practice was as familiar in antiquity as in more modern times.

If CANNEH of Ezk. 27:23 is an assimilated form of this Calneh, then its location between Haran and Eden upholds the tradition of Amos. Isaiah also mentions Calneh under the designation Calno, associating it with Carchemish (Isa. 10:9). This would seem to support a northern location also, pointing in the general direction of Aleppo. However, the LXX translators of Am. 6:2 rendered Calneh by Gk. *pántes,* "all," reflecting the Hebrew text of Gen. 42:36; 1 K. 7:37, and casting doubt on the identity of Calneh as a city.

R. K. H.

CALPHI kal'fī (1 Macc. 11:70, AV). *See* CHALPHI.

CALVARY kal'və-rē. *See* GOLGOTHA.

CALVES OF THE LIPS (Hos. 14:2, AV). *See* FRUIT.

CAMBYSES kam-bī'sēz. The second in the line of Achaemenid kings of Persia, and eldest son of Cyrus II the Great by Cassandane daughter of Pharnaspes, an Achaemenid Persian. Technically he is known as Cambyses II to distinguish him from his paternal grandfather, who was king of Anshan. He is mentioned in both the Nabonidus Chronicle and the Cyrus Cylinder as "son of Cyrus" in Babylon shortly after the conquest of the city of Cyrus in October, 539 B.C. (cf. *ANET*, pp. 306, 316).

He was formerly thought to be the "Ahasuerus" of Ezr. 4:6, but the latter is now identified as Xerxes (vv. 6-23 constituting a parenthetical history of opposition to the Jews down to Ezra's time). Thus, Cambyses does not appear in the OT except by implication in Dnl. 11:2, where he must be the first of three kings that followed Cyrus.

After turning the administration of Babylonia over to Gubaru his governor (*see* DARIUS **1**), Cyrus departed for Ecbatana toward the end of his accession year, leaving his son Cambyses as his personal representative to carry on the ritual prescribed for the king at the New Year Festival of 4 Nisan (Mar. 27), 538 B.C. In this way, Cyrus was able to receive by proxy the approval of the Babylonian god Marduk, and was able to prefix the title "king of Babylon" to his former title, "king of the lands" (cf. A. T. Olmstead, *History of the Persian Empire* [1948], p. 86).

Cambyses, however, was not permitted to use the title "king of Babylon" while Cyrus was in power. Instead, he was known simply as "the king's son." Furthermore, he did not stay in Babylon, but moved 40 mi. (60 km.) N to Sippar, where he carried on the routine duties of a crown prince. Only at New Year festivals did he appear in Babylon, and then only to act as his father's representative. The real ruler of "Babylon and the Region Beyond the River" during these years was Gubaru. Not until eight years after the fall of Babylon, when Cyrus left for his final (and fatal) campaign against nomadic peoples beyond the Jaxartes River on the far northeast frontier, was Cambyses permitted to use the formal title "king of Babylon" at the New Year Festival of Mar. 26, 530 B.C., while Cyrus retained the broader title "king of lands" (cf. W. H. Dubberstein, *AJSL,* 55 [1938], 417-19). In the autumn of the same year news reached Babylonia that Cyrus had died on the field of battle. Cambyses was now the sole ruler of the great Persian empire.

After securing his position on the throne by having his brother Smerdis (or Bardiya) murdered, Cambyses completed preparations for the long-awaited invasion of Egypt, which began in 525 B.C. The pharaoh, Amasis, had long attempted to curb the growth of the Persian empire by alliances with Croesus of Lydia, Nabonidus of Babylon, and finally with the tyrant of Samos. The commander of his Greek mercenaries betrayed his defense plans to the Persians, and six months after his death the Egyptian armies under Psamtik III were totally defeated at the Battle of Pelusium in the eastern delta (525 B.C.). Cambyses took the throne as the first king of the 27th Dynasty, and organized the land as a satrapy of the Persian empire. However, his efforts to conquer Carthage, Ethiopia, and the Oasis of Ammon in the Egyptian desert failed.

To gain favor with his new subjects, Cambyses took the Egyptian royal name and titulary, wore the royal costume, and antedated his rule in Egypt to the very beginning of his rule in Persia (cf. K. M. T. Atkinson, *JAOS,* 76 [1956], 167-177). He even prostrated himself before the goddess Neit and protected her temple at Sais from desecration by Greek mercenaries (Olmstead, p. 91). However, he considerably reduced the offerings of animals to other temples, and thus incurred the reputation of a destroyer of temples, which is reflected in the Jewish Elephantine papyri of the following century: "Now our forefathers built this temple in the fortress of Elephantine back in the days of the kingdom of Egypt, and when Cambyses came to Egypt he found it built. They knocked down all the temples of the gods of Egypt, but no one did any damage to this temple" (*ANET,* p. 492).

On his way back to Babylon in 522, Cambyses received news that one Gaumata (who claimed to be his murdered brother Smerdis) had usurped the throne and had been widely accepted in eastern provinces. He died near Mt. Carmel in Palestine, possibly by suicide, leaving no heirs. Darius Hystaspes, a Persian officer of a collateral royal line, succeeded in killing the pseudo-Smerdis within a few months, and consolidated the empire. The reign of Cambyses (530-522) fell within the period of gentile opposition to the building of the second temple (Ezr. 4:5; Hag. 1:4). J. C. WHITCOMB

CAMEL [Heb. *gāmāl*]; AV also DROMEDARY (Jer. 2:23); NEB also SHE-CAMEL (Jer. 2:23); [*beḵer*] ("young camels," Isa. 60:6); AV, NEB, DROMEDARIES; [Gk. *kámēlos*]. There are two species of camel, the Arabic or one-humped camel or dromedary, *Camelus dromedarius,* and the Bactrian or two-humped camel, *Camelus bactrianus*. The latter inhabits the temperate and cold parts of central Asia and is probably referred to in Isa. 21:7; Jth. 2:17.

The hoofs of the Arabian camel are not typical of ungulates but are rather like great claws. The toes are not completely separated and the main part of the foot applied to the ground is a large pad that underlies the proximal joints of the digits. It may be that this incomplete separation of the two toes is a sufficient explanation of the two words "do not part the hoof" in Lev. 11:4 and Dt. 14:7. Otherwise these words present a difficulty, because the hoofs are completely separated though the toes are not. The camel is a ruminant and chews the cud like a sheep or ox, but the stomach possesses only three compartments instead of four, as in other ruminants. The first two compartments contain in their walls small pouches, each of which can be closed by a sphincter muscle. The fluid retained in these pouches may account in part for the power of the camel to go for a relatively long time without drinking.

The Arabic camel furnishes hair for spinning and weaving, milk, flesh, and leather, as well as being an invaluable means of transportation in the arid desert. There are many Arabic names for the camel, the commonest of which is *jamal* (in Egypt *gamal*), the root being common to Arabic, Hebrew, and other Semitic languages. From it the names in Latin, Greek, English, and various European languages are derived. There are various breeds of camels, as there are of horses. The riding camels or dromedaries, commonly called *hajîn,* can go, even at a walk, much faster than the pack camels. Usually the males are used for carrying burdens, the females being kept with the herds. Camels are used to a surprising extent on the rough roads of the mountains, and one finds in the possession of fellahin in the mountains and on the littoral plain larger and stronger pack camels than are often found among the Bedouin.

Camels were apparently not much used by the Israelites after the time of the patriarchs. They were taken as spoil of war from the Amalekites and other tribes, but almost the only reference to their use by the later Israelites was when David was made king over all Israel at Hebron, at which time camels are mentioned among the animals used for bringing food for the celebration (1 Ch. 12:40). David had a herd of camels, but the herdsman was

Bedouin camel, invaluable for transportation and various domestic uses. The camel was domesticated by at least the 3rd millennium B.C. (W. S. LaSor)

Obil, an Ishmaelite (1 Ch. 27:30). Nearly all other Biblical references to camels are to those possessed by Abraham, Isaac, and Jacob, Ishmaelites, Amalekites, Midianites, Hagrites, and the "people of the East" (*see* East, People of the).

It is no longer necessary to regard the mention of camels in the patriarchal narratives as anachronisms, since there is ample archeological evidence for the domestication of the camel before the time of the patriarchs. Camel bones from the pre-Sargonid era (*ca.* 2400 B.C.) were excavated at Mari by Parrot, while similar remains at least a millennium older have been recovered from sites on the island of Bahrein. Camel bones dating back to the 3rd millennium B.C. have also been recovered from India and southeastern Persia, while a relief from Byblos in Phoenicia, dated in the 18th cent. B.C., depicts a camel in a kneeling position. Cylinder seals from northern Mesopotamia dating from the Middle Bronze Age show riders seated upon camels, indicating that the camel was by then a well-attested feature of Near Eastern domestic life. A. E. DAY

R. K. H.

CAMEL'S HAIR [Gk. *tríches kamḗlou*]. Hair from the back and hump of the camel was woven into a harsh material, and a softer cloth was produced from the finer hair taken from underneath the animal. The natural variations in the color of the hair could be woven into a pattern.

The garment worn by John the Baptist in his austere life in the desert was of camel's hair (Mt. 3:4; Mk. 1:6). Opinion varies about the exact nature of the garment. Alford (Alf.) suggests that it was of woven material on the ground that the skin itself would be too heavy. Others incline to the view that it was of skin, suggesting that the more expensive woven material would not be consistent with John's austerity (*ISBE* [1929]). It may be that the cloak worn by Elijah, John's forerunner, which earned for him the description of "a hairy man" (Heb. *ba'al śē'ār,* 2 K. 1:8), was similarly of camel's hair (or skin, BDB), or else of goat's hair.

The hairy garment (Heb. *'addereṯ śē'ār,* Zec. 13:4) seems to have been a distinguishing mark of a prophet. By wearing such a garment John may have indicated that he, too, was a prophet. Alternatively, G. M. Mackie (*HDB*) suggests that he was wearing merely the common and therefore inconspicuous dress of the desert folk.

G. I. EMMERSON

CAMEL'S THORN [Gk. *aspálathos*] (Sir. 24:15); AV ASPALATHUS. A sweet-smelling plant, mentioned only once in the canon and Apocrypha. The *aspálathos* is described by Pliny (*Nat. hist.* xii.24) as a white, thorny shrub used in the making of ointments and perfumes. Of the varieties that have been suggested as identifications, the camel's thorn (*Alhagi camelorum* var. *turcorum*), a spiny shrub with many branches, is most likely the one referred to here.

See *MPB*, p. 30.

CAMON kā'mən (Jgs. 10:5, AV). *See* Kamon.

CAMP. The word for camp in the OT is Heb. *maḥ^{a}neh,* which generally refers to a military encampment (*see* War).

In the NT the Gk. *parembolḗ* has an equivalent meaning but is sometimes used figuratively. In He. 13:11-13 the author writes that as the bodies of animals sacrificed for sin were burned outside the camp, so also "Jesus suffered outside the gate in order to sanctify the people through his own blood," and adds the appeal: "Therefore let us go forth to him outside the camp, bearing abuse for him." In v. 11 the reference is clearly to the Day of Atonement, when sacrificed animals were carried outside of the Israelite camp and burned. In v. 13, however, "camp" refers figuratively to the community and ordinances of Judaism, which Jesus' followers are exhorted to leave in order to follow Him.

Rectangular camp of the Roman Tenth Legion at the foot of Masada (A.D. 73). One of eight such camps under the governor Flavius Silva, it is just behind the siege walls. (W. S. LaSor)

In Rev. 20:9 the term *parembolḗ* is used of "the camp of the saints," possibly an allusion to the Israelite march through the wilderness, denoting here the body of Christian martyrs. N. J. O.

CAMPHIRE kam'fīr. *See* Henna.

CANA kā'nə [Gk. *Kana,* prob. < Heb. *qāneh*–'reed']. A town in Galilee where Jesus performed His first recorded miracle, turning water into wine (Jn. 2:1-11). It was also where He did His "second sign," the healing of the son of the official from Capernaum (4:46-54). It was the home of Nathanael (21:2). Some Greek MSS designate the disciple Simon (not Peter) as "the Cananite" (man from Cana) in Mt. 10:4; Mk. 3:18, although the preferred reading is Gk. *kananaíos*, "Cananean," which comes from an Aramaic word meaning "enthusiast, zealot." The Lukan parallel has *zēlōtḗs,* "zealot" (6:15). In all four occurrences the full name, Cana in Galilee, is used, probably to distinguish it from other places of the same name.

Apart from the mention that Jesus "went down" from Cana to Capernaum (Jn. 2:12; cf. also 4:47) there is no direct evidence for the location of Cana. Several places have been suggested:

(1) Ecclesiastical tradition has favored Kefr Kennā, a town located some 4 mi. (6.5 km.) NE of Nazareth on the road to Tiberias. The Greek and Roman churches have properties there; the Greek church displays a stone jar said to have been used in the miracle. The traditional house of Nathanael is also pointed out. This site, however,

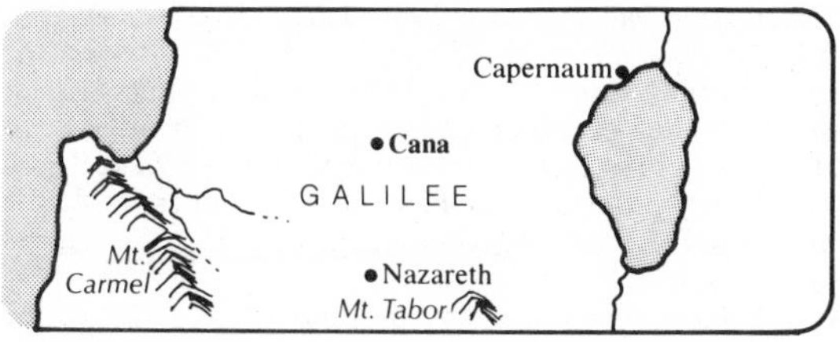

appears to have been chosen because of its accessibility for pilgrims. The doubling of the middle "n" makes it highly improbable that *kennā* was derived from *qānâ* (the probable Hebrew spelling). That there are no reeds in the area is also against the identification.

(2) Conder suggested a spot near Nazareth, 'Ain Qânā, located about 1.5 mi. (2.5 km.) from Nazareth along the road to Tabor (*PEF*, 1, p. 288). Apparently W. Sanday supported this identification (*Sacred Sites of the Gospels* [1903], p. 24 n.), but few others have followed the suggestion.

(3) The most probable site is Khirbet Qânā, an ancient ruin about 8 mi. (13 km.) NE of Nazareth. It lies on the northern edge of el-Battauf, the ancient plain of Asochis. Josephus seems to have been living here (*Vita* 41) when he wrote, ". . . my abode was in a village of Galilee, which is named Cana" (*Vita* 16). The full Arabic title for the site, Qânā el-Jelīl, is an exact equivalent of "Cana of Galilee," although this designation may have been influenced by the Gospel story. The site overlooks a marshy plain where reeds are still very much in evidence, thus explaining the name Cana, "place of reeds." The area has not yet been excavated but cisterns and the remains of buildings are visible. Nearby are tombs cut into the rocks. Some first-century coins are said to have been found on the site.

(4) Eusebius evidently identified Cana with *Kanah* in the tribe of Asher (Josh. 19:28), modern Qânah, a village 8 mi. (13 km.) SE of Tyre. Lying some 40 mi. (64 km.) N of Khirbet Qânā, this location of Cana is quite improbable.

R. H. MOUNCE

CANAAN kā'nən; **CANAANITES** [Heb. *k*^{e}*na'an*, *k*^{e}*na'*^{a}*nî*]. Canaan is an ancient name for the area that includes all of the land west of the Jordan and Syria to the level of Lebweh (see II.B below). "Canaanites" designates the occupants of that land in the period preceding the Israelite occupation, and their cultural successors; the word is also found as an appellation for merchants.

I. Name
II. Land
  A. Extrabiblical Sources
  B. Biblical Sources
III. People
IV. History
  A. Early Bronze Age
  B. Middle Bronze Age
  C. Late Bronze Age
V. Society
VI. Language
VII. Influences on Israel

I. Name.–The origin and meaning of the name Canaan has yet to be satisfactorily explained. The etymon closest at hand is the Semitic *kn'* ("be humble, bow down"; Aram., Heb. only in derived stems). The ending *-an* is quite common in Semitic names, though it remains unexplained. However, attempts to derive the name on this basis (e.g., traditional "lowlands"; cf. also M. Astour's suggestion "West" in *JNES*, 24 [1965], 346-350) have been forced to postulate unattested extensions of the root's known meaning and must remain hypothetical.

The once attractive derivation from a word for blue-colored cloth, *kinaḫḫu*, has been shown to be linguistically problematic. This word, found at Nuzi, probably represents a Hurrian version (*q[i]naǧǧu) of the culture-word found, among other languages, in Akkadian as *uqnû* and Greek as *kyános* (B. Landsberger, *JCS*, 21 [1967], 166f.). As such it has nothing to do with Canaan.

Besides the question of etymology, it would be helpful to know when and where the name originated, and whether it originally designated the land or the people. No answers to these questions are presently available, but a hint lies in an early documentation of the name in a Mari text of the Assyrian interregnum (G. Dossin, *Syria*, 50 [1973], 277-282). This text is a general's report on his activities in an unidentified area, possibly the Balîkh Valley. He mentions a group of "thieves and Canaanites" (^{lú}*ḫa-ab-ba-tum u* ^{lú}*ki-na-aḫ-nu*) with which he is "eyeball to eyeball." In parallel with "thieves," "Canaanite" might well designate an occupational class — specifically, merchants. "Merchants and thieves" is not an unlikely collocation. The earliest Egyptian reference to Canaanites, in the Memphis stele of Amenhotep II (*ANET*, pp. 245-47), presents a similar picture. In a list of captives Canaanites are found between *maryannu* (nobility associated with chariot warfare) and the children of princes. These are only hints, but it may not be far from the truth that the use of the word "Canaanite" for a merchant class is older than its use for the land and its population (cf. B. Maisler [Mazar], *BASOR*, 102 [Apr. 1946] 7-12).

If this is true, then the later biblical use of *k*^{e}*na'*^{a}*nî* for "merchant" or "trader" may have very ancient roots (Job 41:6 [MT 40:30]; Prov. 31:24; Isa. 23:8; Zec. 14:21; cf. also 11:7, 11, reading *[li]ḵ*^{e}*na'*^{a}*niyyê* for MT *[lā]ḵēn '*^{a}*niyyê*; similarly *k*^{e}*na'an* at Ezk. 16:29; 17:4; Hos. 12:7 [MT 8]; Zeph. 1:11). In any case, the name became identified with the people who were the merchants par excellence of the ancient world.

II. Land.–The name Canaan as a designation of the land was current, according to established records, only in the Late Bronze Age (*ca.* 1550-1200). By the time of the establishment of the monarchy in Israel it was clearly archaic and no longer corresponded to any political reality. Similarly, the use of the term for Phoenicia in Hellenistic texts was archaic, a nostalgic revival.

A. Extrabiblical Sources. A very early reference to the land of Canaan is found in an inscription of Idrimi king of Alalakh (15th cent.). He reports that during a period of exile, assuming the throne, he had gone to Ammia in the "land of Canaan" (*ma-at ki-in-a-nim*^{ki}). Ammia can be located near present-day Enfe, SW of Tripoli. Probably this is at or near the northern boundary of the land.

Ugarit was quite clearly not part of the land of Canaan in any period. An alphabetic cuneiform tablet (*UT* 311:7) lists a Canaanite (*kn'ny*) among other foreign merchants. An Akkadian text, unfortunately broken, describes the settlement of a dispute between some citizens of Ugarit and of Canaan (TUR.MEŠ KUR-*ki-na-ḫi*; in *Ugaritica*, 5 [1968], 112 [36:6, 8]).

The Amarna Tablets make the picture more precise. In the period represented (14th cent.) the Syro-Palestinian area was divided for Egyptian administration into three regions: the northern coastal region, including Byblos, with the administrative center at Ṣumur; the inland area from the upper Orontes south, including Damascus, with an administrative center at Kumidi; and the southern region excluding Transjordan, with its center at Gaza. To these three areas the names Amurru, Upe, and Canaan would seem to correspond (W. Helck, *Mitteilungen der deutschen Orient-Gesellschaft,* 92 [1960], 1-13); however, the evidence is not decisive. Although the king of Alašia (Cyprus) does on one occasion refer to a "province of Canaan," the word may have had a more general reference to the land under Egyptian control. This is suggested by 109 where Rib-Addi includes Amurru in Canaan. Another text (Am.Tab. 151), in which the king of Tyre responds to the pharaoh's question about Canaan by talking about the whole of upper Syria including Amurru, Danuna, Ugarit, and Kadesh, is clearly not germane to the question here. The king, who is in Canaan, is merely describing the events that impinge on his and the pharaoh's interests.

The heartland of Canaan was the coastal area from Byblos to Carmel and the Jezreel Valley. A number of Amarna references to Canaan center in this area (Am.Tab 8; 131; 137; 148; 367). Some scholars have argued that this narrower region is the original land of Canaan. That, however, goes beyond the evidence.

A most interesting Egyptian source is the satirical letter, Papyrus Anastasi I (*ANET*, pp. 475-79), which refers to the old military road from Sile to Gaza as the "end of the land of Canaan." This fixes the southern boundary of Canaan in the area of Wâdī el-'Arîsh precisely as in the biblical lists. The reference to the town of Canaan (*p-kn'n*) in the illustrated inscription of Seti I at Karnak (*ANET,* pp. 254f.) also is probably to Gaza, the first important city in Canaan.

Thus, the general picture that emerges from the scattered data is remarkably consistent. Canaan is a general name for the Asian holdings of Egypt. While in the earlier sources it may have been limited by Upe and Amurru, after the battle of Kadesh it becomes synonymous with Ḫurru, a general word for the area of Egyptian hegemony including Upe. (Amurru was by this time part of the Hittite area of influence.) The famous "Israel Stela" of Merneptah (*ANET*, pp. 376-78) uses these two terms to form an inclusion around several Palestinian place names (cf. Papyrus Anastasi IV, 16:4). At the end of the Late Bronze Age, therefore, Canaan includes all of Cisjordan from Wâdī el-'Arîsh in the south, the Mediterranean coast to the borders of Amurru in the north, and the inland area from Lebweh to Bashan.

B. Biblical Sources. The biblical descriptions of the land of Canaan correspond to the Late Bronze Age usage in a way that can be explained only by the existence of a list of the principal boundary points. The persistence of this tradition is quite remarkable in view of the fact that the territory of Israel never included the whole of Canaan.

The two principal boundary lists are Nu. 34:1-12 and Ezk. 47:15-20; 48:1-28, supplemented at various points with other materials. These lists include several sites that cannot be identified with certainty. They differ somewhat in the number and names of the sites, but the boundary lines they describe are very similar.

The southern boundary is fixed, just as in Egyptian sources, by the Brook of Egypt (Wâdī el-'Arîsh) in the west. The course of this boundary toward the east is most completely described in Josh. 15:1-4, which traces it from the southeast corner of the Dead Sea (cf. Gen. 10:19), through the Scorpion pass (exact site unknown), the wilderness of Zin, the oasis of Kadesh, to the brook of Egypt. The Sinai is not part of Canaan.

The western boundary is the Mediterranean Sea up to the southern boundary of the state of Amurru (cf. Josh. 13:4).

The northern boundary is fixed principally by the "entrance of Hamath" (Heb. *lᵉḇô' ḥᵃmāṯ*; *see* HAMATH), which is probably modern Lebweh (Egyp. *r-b-ꜣ*, *Amarna labana*; Akk. *lab'u*; cf. *LBHG*, pp. 65f.). To the west the border runs to Mt. Hor (Nu. 34:7) or Hethlon (Ezk. 47:15; 48:1), neither of which can be positively identified. To the east it runs through Zedad (Ṣadâd), NE of Lebweh on the edge of the desert, and out to Hazar-enan, probably an oasis E of Zedad (Aharoni [*LBHG*, p. 67] suggests Qaryatein).

The eastern boundary is the most difficult to define precisely. Many of the sites are unknown, but the general picture is clear. It runs S from Hazar-enan to the area of Mt. Bashan and then westward to the southeastern shore of the Sea of Galilee. There it turns S again to follow the Jordan River. The Bible clearly excludes the area E of the Jordan from the land of Canaan, a fact that lies behind Josh. 22; there the Transjordanian tribes are said to have built an altar at the Jordan because they feared later generations would say, "you have no portion in the Lord" (v. 25).

The promise that the land of Canaan would be theirs gave rise to the idea that the people of Israel had claim to all of it. Thus in Ezekiel's vision (47:13-20) the tribes are distributed across the whole territory; cf. the concept of the "land that remains" in Josh. 13:2. But this ideal was never confused with another, even more extravagant claim of all the land to the Euphrates (Dt. 1:7; contrast Gen. 15:18-20 [J] with Gen. 17:8 [P]).

See Map V; Plate 12.

III. People.–The Canaanites may best be described as the inhabitants of the land of Canaan. They should not be thought of as a race in modern terms. People in ancient times were identified by the political group to which they belonged — city, tribe, clan, or state. The land of Canaan, which was never politically unified in the historical period, contained citizens of various political groups living side by side with aliens (Heb. *gērîm*) and stateless persons called *'apiru.* The term Canaanite is a rather vague reference to these people who could be more precisely identified with their city or tribe. The use of the term in the Amarna Tablets and the records of Ugarit suggests that the scribes preferred the designation Canaanites (or kings and citizens of Canaan) when they had regional rather than local interests in mind.

With the end of Egyptian domination of the area of Canaan and the rise of nation-states like Israel and Aram in the Iron Age, the term lost its political significance and came to be applied to the people who were the cultural heirs of the Late Bronze Age civilization. This change is reflected in uses of the term "Canaan" for Phoenicia (cf. Hecateus of Miletus *Periegesis* fragment 272, in F. Jacoby, ed., *Fragmente der griechischen Historiker,* I/A [1923], 36; Eusebius *Praep. ev.* i.10; ix.17).

The Bible shows familiarity with both the L.B. and Iron Age uses of the word. The two earliest references, for example, Ex. 15:15 and Jgs. 5:19, follow the L.B. pattern. The former distinguishes between the inhabitants of Canaan and those of Transjordan and Philistia (cf. G. Steindorff, *JEA*, 25 [1939], 30-37, for an Egyptian inscription left by a "messenger of Canaan and Philistia"). The latter describes the northern coalition of kings as "kings of Canaan," much in the manner of the Amarna Tablets. These are simply generalized uses of the term without reference to more specific ethnic relationships. Particularly illustrative of this is the notation in Gen. 36:2f. (P?) that among the "Canaanite" wives of Esau is a Hittite, a Hivite (later Horite), and an Ishmaelite. Note also Ezekiel who says of Israel, "Your origin and your birth are of the land of the Canaanites; your father was an Amorite, and your mother a Hittite" (16:3).

Tablets of the palace library as discovered at Tell Mardikh (ancient Ebla). Identified by the epigrapher as "Paleo-Canaanite," these administrative texts document an extensive commercial empire. (*Biblical Archeologist*)

Early Bronze Age (3rd millennium B.C.) fortification wall with redentations, protecting the northern front at Byblos. The rampart was strengthened on the outside by a glacis. (W. S. LaSor)

A special case of the generalized use of Canaan is found in the index of political and geographical relationships in Gen. 10. Canaan is included in the Hamitic family as part of the Egyptian empire (v. 6). His sons are Sidon and Heth (the Hittites). This recalls the collocation of Ezekiel, Amorites and Hittites, and is in the same way a memory of the ethnic mixture of Semitic and non-Semitic elements that composed the Canaanite culture of the Late Bronze Age. There follows (vv. 16-18) a list of peoples, mostly of cities, in a rough order of south to north, representing the peoples of Canaan at its greatest possible extension. In its present position this list is quite probably secondary.

Alongside these general uses of the word are found frequent biblical references to the Canaanites as one people among others. These lists vary in length and complexity. The simplest have only two terms, like the Amorites and Canaanites of Dt. 1:7 (cf. Josh. 5:1), or the Canaanites and Perizzites of Gen. 34:30. The longest list (Gen. 15:19-21) specifies ten different groups. Several of the lists also indicate the area occupied by the various groups (Nu. 13:29; Dt. 1:7; Josh. 5:1; 13:3; 17:15-18; Jgs. 1:1-36). These not surprisingly locate the Canaanites in the area that was always the heartland of the culture, the coastal region including its natural extension into the Jezreel Valley and the Jordan area.

Clearly the lists contain names of very different types. Some probably were originally social classifications (e.g., the Perizzites and Rephaim), other ancient tribal groups (the Kenites, Kadmonites, and Kenizzites), still others remnants of great cultures (the Hittites and Horites). What they have in common is their antiquity at the time of the writing of the Bible.

Despite the broad diversity of the origins of the people who inhabited Canaan, one can speak of a Canaanite culture. This cultural unity extended generally to language, religion, political forms, legal institutions, architecture, and the domestic arts. Groups that arrived in Canaan with different customs, like the Philistines, were soon drawn into the dominant culture while adding to it their own special contributions.

The cultural heirs of the Bronze-Age Canaanites were the Phoenicians. While the Greeks knew them by the latter name, they apparently called themselves Canaanites (cf. Augustine *Epistolae ad Romanos inchoata expositio* 13 [*PL*, XXXV, 2096]; sources cited by Z. Harris, *Grammar of the Phoenician Language* [*American Oriental Series*, 8, 1936], p. 7). Thus the woman who in Mk. 7:26 is called a "Syro-Phoenician" (Gk. *Syrophoinikissa*) is called a "Canaanite" (*gynḗ chananaia*) in Mt. 15:22. The latter term (*Chananaios*) must be distinguished from *Kananaios*, "Zealot" (from Aram. *qan an*; cf. F. C. Burkitt, *Syriac Forms of NT Proper Names* [1912], p. 5), the designation of Simon in Mt. 10:4 (TR *Kananitēs*, "citizen of Cana") and Mk. 3:18.

*IV. **History**.*–When and how the dominant culture known as Canaanite first appeared is not directly answerable from the data now available. The most important transition points in the early history of this area are marked by the changes in the material culture that have given rise to the present, somewhat inaccurate, division of time into ages identified with specific metals — copper, bronze, and iron. Customarily the Bronze Age (*ca.* 3200-1200 B.C.) is designated as the Canaanite period, though that should not prejudice the question of when the culture known from the latest phase of this period was formed.

A. Early Bronze Age. Since only in the Late Bronze period can the political history be written with any confidence, observations about the earlier periods must be limited to general and largely hypothetical statements. The evidence is mostly archeological with occasional help from Egyptian and Mesopotamian documents. The enormous archive of Ebla holds great promise for clarifying matters for the later part of the Early Bronze Age.

The transition from the Chalcolithic Age to the Early Bronze Age was one of the most important and formative periods in the history of Canaan. Considerable disagreement still exists about the details of the transition and even about the terminology to be employed. Apparently *ca.* 3200 B.C. several groups of a distinctively new people entered Palestine and pushed out or suppressed the Ghassul-Beer-sheba culture that had preceded them. These groups, who had their origins in the north (Syria and Anatolia), are especially important because they appear to have brought with them the seeds of the first truly urban culture in Canaan. Partly for that reason some archeologists (Kenyon, Hennessy) prefer to call this period Proto-Urban (others call it E.B. I; still others Late Chal-

Remains of three Canaanite temples at Tell Kittan in the Jordan Valley. The row of stelae and the large brick wall (foreground) are from M.B. II temples; ruins of an L.B. I temple are at upper right center. (Rockefeller Museum)

colithic). The picture is not simply one of linear development, however. Along with successive population increments of divergent types (and importation of new techniques) came an increase of population density. Undoubtedly there were other now unknown factors. But, whatever the catalyst, in the early years of the 3rd millennium occurred the formation first of villages and then of fortified cities.

These were small settlements by modern standards, typically about 25 acres (10 hectares) within the walls. The fortifications were hefty, however, with walls as much as 25 ft. (8 m.) thick. Some of the towns, like Arad (cf. R. Amiran in Sanders, ed., *Near Eastern Archaeology in the Twentieth Century*, pp. 83-96), show evidence of careful planning. Houses were in one part of the city, public buildings in another; the various buildings were arranged along streets and plazas.

Why these fortifications were erected cannot be known with certainty. Egyptian interests in the area were already established and their raiding parties may have contributed to this development. Narmer of the 1st Dynasty apparently took and held Gath for a few years in the Proto-Urban period. But probably a more important factor was protection from a numerically superior non-urban population that surrounded these cities.

In view of the later pattern one might expect that these cities were small, competing city-states, needing protection from each other. Some evidence, however, suggests that these urban folk were unified on a broader basis (P. W. Lapp in Sanders, ed., p. 114). On analogy with the large commercial empire of Ebla, as well as with the movement toward unification in Egypt earlier and in Mesopotamia under Sargon, this is not unlikely.

This culture existed without major interruption for a very long time, about 700 years. It came to an end quite quickly with the destruction of the cities and a reversion to village life (*ca.* 2300). Who brought about this destruction is a matter of controversy. Egyptian raids are documented, especially for the 6th Dynasty, which overlaps this period of destruction. But this is also the time of the Amorite movements, so some have attributed these destructions primarily to them. Still others look to non-Semitic invaders from Anatolia. The question need not be decided for one of these options to the exclusion of others. What happened in Canaan is part of a large pattern of destruction which eventually enveloped every civilization of the ancient world. Many factors must have been at work, and migrations were as much the result of these destructions as the cause of them.

B. Middle Bronze Age. The first part of the Middle Bronze Age (M.B. I, *ca.* 2200-1950) is largely a continuation of the last part of the E.B. period (E.B. IV). The characteristics of this period are regionalism of the material culture, lack of fortifications, abandonment of the E.B. urban sites, and extension of occupation, at least seasonally, into fringe areas. The inhabitants of the land were primarily herdsmen, organized very likely by village and tribe. It is conventional to call this culture (or cultures) Amorite (Sum. mar-tu, Akk. *amurru[m]*), which means "Westerners." This was the designation given by the Mesopotamians to similar groups who seem to have had the same origin (the Syrian steppe) and who penetrated the Mesopotamian area in the late 3rd and early 2nd millennia. That they were a West Semitic people is clear from their names.

With the second phase of the M.B. period (M.B. IIA,

ca. 1950-1800) begins the development that led to the next great urban age in Canaan. It is owed in part to new influences, again from the north. The people who brought this new culture have been called "urbanized Amorites" (cf. Kenyon, *Amorites and Canaanites*). That expresses both the continuity and the discontinuity of this culture and the preceding phase. The newcomers were, in contrast to the people of M.B. I, city folk. Where they learned urban ways is a matter of dispute, but Kenyon's hypothesis, which centers attention on Byblos, must likely be abandoned in favor of an inland site. Once again, the materials from Ebla (Tell Mardikh) should be extremely important.

Many reflections on this period are found in Egyptian literature. Among the most important are the Tale of Sinuhe (*ANET*, pp. 18-22) and the Execration Texts (*ANET*, pp. 328f.). Although both of these sources must be used with caution, they indicate strong Egyptian interest in Asia. Numerous objects of trade and diplomacy that supplement the literary materials argue for some Egyptian hegemony during the 12th Dynasty (*ca.* 1991-1786). In fact, the commercial and diplomatic ties that link Egypt and Asia in this period are similar to those known from the Amarna period some five centuries later (cf. G. Posener, *CAH*, I/2, 532-558).

The pattern of political organization in this period appears to be a complex dimorphism of village and tribe. What little can be made out from the Execration Texts indicates that power was becoming more centralized toward the end of the period. Undoubtedly some of the more powerful centers exercised control over smaller ones, creating regional blocs. This pattern, though modified by subsequent developments, was responsible for the shape of Canaanite culture for the rest of the Bronze Age.

The remainder of the Middle Bronze Age could be considered the "golden age" of Canaanite culture. Out of the villages of the M.B. IIA period grew powerful cities, a distinctive feature of which was their fortification. Great ramparts of beaten earth were built around the city. The largest, that of the lower city of Hazor, was more than 100 ft. (30 m.) wide at the base and enclosed an area of more than 175 acres (70 hectares). This reflects the importance of Hazor, remembered in biblical times as "formerly . . . the head of all those kingdoms" (Josh. 11:10; cf. A. Malamat, *JBL*, 79 [1960], 12-19).

Toward the end of the Middle Bronze Age, Egypt came under the control of the Hyksos (Egyp. *ḥḳȝ ḫȝswt*, "foreign chiefs"). Until recently scholarship had considered them an intrusive element, responsible for fortifications in Palestine as well as disruptions in Egypt. It seems now that the fortifications must be dated independently and that the Hyksos were primarily the product of the flowering of Canaanite culture. They were Asiatics (mostly Semitic) who took advantage of the weakening of Egyptian power to take control of the Delta.

The 16th cent., in which the Middle Bronze Age ends, saw two developments of far-reaching significance. The first was the renaissance of native Egyptian power with the consequent expulsion of the Hyksos. The second was the increasing importance of a non-Semitic population in the south, mostly Hurrian (a people known from much earlier times in the north) but with rulers who possessed Indo-Aryan names. These two movements, one from the north, the other from the south, largely established the character of the subsequent centuries in Canaan.

C. Late Bronze Age (*ca.* 1550-1200). The resurgence of Egyptian power began with the campaigns of Ahmose (*ca.* 1570-1546), who, as part of his effort to rid Egypt of the hated Hyksos, ventured into Canaan. Considerable violence accompanied the change of orders and many cities were destroyed. Of more lasting importance were the campaigns of Thutmose III (*ca.* 1504-1450), detailed in a series of royal inscriptions, which extended and stabilized Egyptian rule in Canaan.

But almost from the death of Thutmose Egyptian power began to diminish, partly because Egyptian hegemony permitted the numerous small kingdoms of Canaan to continue to exist. Revolts and petty conflicts were the result. But the Egyptian decline was due mainly to the rise of a major power in the north, Hatti, and a general, though not uniform, weakening of the will or the ability of Egyptian rulers to police their holdings in Canaan.

The 14th cent. was an era of change in the Middle East. At the end of the 15th cent. there were three great powers on the periphery of Canaan: Egypt, its fortunes declining; Hatti, dormant in its Anatolian homeland, beleaguered by the Kaska; and Mitanni, a Hurrian kingdom in Upper Mesopotamia. Mitanni and Egypt were nominal allies and seem to have come to tacit agreement about holdings in Syria. But all this changed drastically in the 14th century. The Hittites, under the vigorous and ambitious Šuppiluliuma I, began a series of expansionist wars. The result was an empire that included Mitanni, the small states of southern Asia Minor, and Syria as far south as Kadesh. Egypt, in the throes of the Amarna revolution, was unable or unwilling to help.

This period in Canaan is brilliantly illumined by the Amarna correspondence. The letters, written from the vassal kings in Canaan to the pharaoh, show Canaan in turmoil. Particularly plaintive are the letters of Rib-Addi king of Byblos, who appealed for help against the encroachments of the kings of Amurru — to no avail. In the southern part of Canaan arose Lab'ayu of Shechem, much to the distress of those more loyal to Egypt. Gangs of men who had lost their citizenship (*'apiru*) roamed the land. This is, however, probably only part of the picture. Allowance must be made for the tendency of the letter writers' to overstate the case when asking for military assistance and for the fact that Canaan remained an Egyptian territory throughout this period.

Attempts to solidify the Egyptian hold on Canaan and to retake territory lost to the Hittites were made by Seti I and Ramses II. A campaign in the latter's fifth year led to a decisive confrontation with Hatti at Kadesh (*ca.* 1300). Both sides claimed victory, but the Egyptians seem fortunate to have escaped. A peace treaty followed, which established the boundary between the two great powers approximately on the line described by the northern boundary of Canaan in the biblical lists.

The battle of Kadesh was, however, the beginning of the end for both great powers' domination in the area. Soon both had a much greater problem. Already at the battle of Kadesh (and earlier) various Indo-Aryan groups of Western origin were present as mercenaries. They are a symptom of the great incursion of Western peoples that reached its peak at the end of the 13th century. These Sea-peoples, as they were known to the Egyptians, were the catalyst for a general collapse of the Bronze Age culture. Only Egypt was able to resist and throw back the invaders. As the result of that Egyptian victory, the most famous of the Sea-peoples, the Philistines, came to occupy Palestine.

In the midst of this confusing time Moses and his followers left Egypt, and Joshua with a second generation entered Canaan. They were not alone. It was a time of change, of migration, of destruction and turmoil — a dark age that ended 200 years later with the emergence of nation-states like Israel. It marked the effective end of the history of the Canaanites.

V. Society.–Direct information about the social structure is scarce from Canaan itself. The texts of Ugarit and Alalakh are very informative, however, and with due caution against too much generalizing they may be used to fill the gaps in knowledge of Canaan.

Essentially Canaanite society was in two tiers. The more fundamental of these was the society of the agricultural villages. The production of the villages was the basis for the state's economy. The villages themselves were small and organized into one or more clans, governed by the heads of the clans, the elders. In some instances the clans were organized into tribes. A leading example of the symbiosis of tribe and state can be found at Mari.

On this simple village economy was imposed the palace. In contrast to the villages, the state was highly centralized and in the case of Ugarit reached bureaucratic proportions. In theory the king was the central authority in all areas of life. In the smaller states this was probably true in practice as well, but in the larger states the actual exercise of this authority was left to his administrative personnel (Ugar. *bnš mlk*). These included a technically trained clergy, a professional army, a palace judicial system, and overseers of the various aspects of economic life.

The economy itself was largely a state monopoly. The palace regulated trade and controlled the production of artisans. At Ugarit the artisans were organized by trade. In addition, large tracts of state land were worked by tenant farmers. A military aristocracy that bore the title *maryannu* was supported in return for certain services to the state. The *maryannu* were a feature of the Hurrian Indo-Aryan overlordship that was imposed on Canaan in the middle of the 2nd millennium.

Slavery, both for debtors and prisoners of war, existed in Canaanite culture, but it seems not to have been very common. More important was the corvée imposed on the citizens and used for various state projects. The state also collected taxes. The result of this heavy state machinery was the steady alienation of persons and groups who became *'apiru,* officially stateless people who typically formed bands of freebooters and when sufficiently numerous became a danger to the state itself.

VI. Language.–The term Canaanite is used to describe the non-Aramaic group of first-millennium languages that are part of the Northwest Semitic family, principally Phoenician and Hebrew (cf. Isa. 19:18). It is also used for the postulated ancestor of these languages.

For the ancestral language the sources are chiefly Ugaritic texts (generally considered a Canaanite dialect), glosses and other peculiarities in the Amarna Tablets, and names, mostly from Egyptian sources. Another, very large, group of names culled mostly from Mesopotamian sources is classified as Amorite, a West Semitic language whose position vis-à-vis Canaanite and Aramaic is still a matter of dispute. The preliminary reports on the language of Ebla (Tell Mardikh) of the 3rd millennium indicate that it falls outside the usual classification of early Semitic languages. It exhibits important isoglosses with later Canaanite (as well as major differences) and on the strength of those similarities has been tentatively labeled as Paleo-Canaanite (G. Pettinato, *Orientalia,* N.S. 44 [1975], 361-374).

Obviously the resources for reconstructing West Semitic dialect-geography in the 2nd millennium are very meagre. It can be said, however, that some of the features that distinguish the Iron Age Canaanite dialects had begun to form at a relatively early date (e.g., *ā*>*ō*, *ca.* 1500). It is likely that some dialectic specificity characterized Canaan even earlier.

The greatest Canaanite contribution to civilization was the alphabet. The forms of writing used at that time (Egyptian hieroglyphic and Sumerian-Akkadian cuneiform) were very cumbersome, because the hundreds of signs had both ideographic and syllabic values. The simple phonetic alphabet was a great improvement, which developed into the alphabet now used in Western and Near Eastern cultures. The earliest known attempt at simplification is found in the inscriptions from Byblos, still largely undeciphered, dating to the early 2nd millennium. They use a syllabic script that has far fewer signs than the scripts of either Egypt or Mesopotamia. Far more important are a group of middle-second-millennium inscriptions that use an alphabetic script retaining some of its original pictographic features. The largest and best-known group is from Serabit el-Khadem in the Sinai. The step forward that these writings represent was probably taken under the influence of Egyptian, but it is clearly a West Semitic invention. No attempt to derive the alphabet directly from Egyptian has been successful (cf. K. A. Kitchen, in M. Liverani, ed., *La Siria nel tardo bronzo,* pp. 85-87).

Another alphabet, in cuneiform, is found at Ugarit. The cuneiform system (wedges formed by pressing a stylus into soft clay) was far better suited to the clay tablets used by Ugaritic scribes. An innovation of this alphabet is its use of three signs for the glottal stop, one for each of three principal Semitic vowels (*'a, 'i, 'u*).

VII. Influences on Israel.–The people of Israel clearly thought of themselves as separate from their Canaanite neighbors. In fact, they were repeatedly enjoined to maintain that separateness (cf. Dt. 7). But the distinctiveness of Israel was built upon a basic commonality that runs through Canaanite culture.

This can be most easily seen in language and literature. The Canaanites and Hebrews spoke a common tongue. They used, as the Ugaritic texts reveal, a common stock of literary conventions. Even the language they used in the cult — the names for sacrifices, the divine titles — are similar (cf. F. M. Cross, *Canaanite Myth and Hebrew Epic* [1973], pp. 1-75).

Canaanite influence is evident also in the structures of society. The monarchy in Israel largely follows the patterns of Canaanite kingship, especially during and after the time of Solomon. In matters of material culture, architecture, and the like, they are virtually indistinguishable.

All this does not diminish the distinctiveness of Israel. Nor can one trace a direct line of development between the cultures of Canaan and Israel. But the distinctiveness of Israel's conception of God, society, and time are most clearly seen against the backdrop the Canaanite culture in which they shared.

Bibliography.–*General:* The various chapters of *CAH* (3rd ed. 1971-1975) cover the history and archeology of this period and include extensive references. See also: W. F. Albright, "The Role of the Canaanites in the History of Civilization," in G. E. Wright, ed., *The Bible and the Ancient Near East* (1965), pp. 438-487; *Yahweh and the Gods of Canaan* (1968); F. M. Böhl, *Kanaanäer Hebräer* (1911); G. Buccellati, *Cities and Nations of Ancient Syria* (1967); I. J. Gelb, *JCS,* 15 (1961), 27-47; J. Gray, *The Canåanites* (1964); *Legacy of Canaan* (*SVT,* 5; 1957); W. Helck, *Die Beziehungen Ägyptens zu Vorderasien* (2nd ed. 1971); K. Kenyon, *Amorites and Canaanites* (1966); H. Klengel, *Geschichte Syriens im 2. Jahrtausend v.u.Z.* (3 parts, 1965-1970); M. Liverani, ed., *La Siria nel tardo bronzo* (*Orientis Antiqui Collectio,* 9, 1969); A. R. Millard, "The Canaanites," in D. J. Wiseman, ed., *Peoples of OT Times* (1973), pp. 29-52; R. de Vaux, *Early History of Israel* (Eng. tr. 1978).

Name: S. Moscati, *Studia Biblica et Orientalia,* 3 (1959), 266-69; E. A. Speiser, *Language,* 12 (1936), 121-26.

Land: *GB*; *GTTOT*; *LBHG*; G. A. Smith, *Geography of the Bible* (1894); R. de Vaux, *JAOS*, 88 (1968), 23-29.
History: A. Alt. *KS*, III; E. Anati, *Palestine Before the Hebrews* (1963); J. Bottéro, *Le problème des Ḫabiru* (*Cahiers de la Société Asiatique*, 12, 1954); E. F. Campbell, Jr., *Chronology of the Amarna Letters* (1964); E. F. Campbell, Jr., and D. N. Freedman, eds., *Biblical Archaeologist Reader*, II, III (1964, 1970); W. G. Dever, *HTR*, 64 (1971), 197-226; "The Beginning of the Middle Bronze Age in Syria-Palestine," in F. M. Cross, ed., *Magnalia Dei* (1976), pp. 3-38; R. W. Ehrich, ed., *Chronologies in Old World Archaeology* (1965); J. C. L. Gibson, *JNES*, 20 (1961), 217-238; M. Greenberg, *The Ḫab/piru* (*American Oriental Series*, 39, 1955); J. B. Hennessy, *Foreign Relations of Palestine during the Early Bronze Age* (1967); K. M. Kenyon, *Archaeology in the Holy Land* (1965); K. A. Kitchen, *Suppiluliuma and the Amarna Pharaohs* (1962); P. Lapp, *Dhahr Mirzbaneh Tombs* (1966); M. Liverani, *Storia di Ugarit nell'eta' degli archivi politici* (*Studi Semitici*, 6, 1962); B. Mazar, *IEJ*, 18 (1968), 65-97; D. B. Redford, *Orientalia*, N.S. 39 (1970), 1-51; M. B. Rowton, "The Topological Factor in the Hapiru Problem," in H. G. Güterbock and T. Jacobson, eds., *Studies in Honor of Benno Landsberger on His Seventy-fifth Birthday* (1965), pp. 375-387; J. A. Sanders, ed., *Near Eastern Archaeology in the Twentieth Century* (1970); J. Van Seters, *The Hyksos: A New Investigation* (1966); G. E. Wright, "The Archaeology of Palestine," in *BANE*, pp. 85-139.
Society: L. R. Fisher, ed., *Ras Shamra Parallels*, II (*Analecta Orientalia*, 50, 1975); H. Klengel, ed., *Beiträge zur sozialen Struktur des alten Vorderasien* (1971); M. Liverani, "La royauté syrienne de l'âge du bronze récent," in P. Garelli, ed., *Le Palais et la royauté* (1974), pp. 329-356; I. Mendelsohn, *Slavery in the Ancient Near East* (1949); *BASOR*, 83 (Oct. 1941), 36-39; 143 (Oct. 1956), 17-22; 167 (Oct. 1962), 31-35; A. F. Rainey, "Social Stratification of Ugarit" (Diss., Brandeis, 1967); M. B. Rowton, *Oriens Antiquus*, 15 (1976), 17-31 (with references to others of his articles). See generally the periodicals *Journal of the Economic and Social History of the Orient*; *Das Altertum*; and *Welt des Orients*.
Language: On the languages generally see J. H. Hospers, ed., *Basic Bibliography for the Study of the Semitic Languages* (1973). Some basic works are: W. F. Albright, *The Proto-Sinaitic Inscriptions and Their Decipherment* (*Harvard Theological Studies*, 22, 1969); E. Dhorme, *Syria*, 25 (1946-1948), 1-35; G. Garbini, *Il semitico di nord-ovest* (1960); Z. S. Harris, *Development of the Canaanite Dialects* (*American Oriental Series*, 16, 1939); W. L. Moran. "The Hebrew Language in its Northwest Semitic Background," in G. E. Wright, ed., *The Bible and the Ancient Near East* (1961), pp. 59-84; S. Moscati, *et al.*, *Intro. to the Comparative Grammar of the Semitic Language* (*Porta Linguarum Orientalium*, N.S. 6, 1969). C. G. LIBOLT

CANAANITESS [Heb. *hakkᵉnaʿᵃnîṯ*] (1 Ch. 2:3). A Canaanite woman, BATH-SHUA.

CANALS [Heb. *yᵉʾōrîm* (Ex. 7:19; 8:5), *nᵉhārôṯ* (Isa. 19:6)]; AV RIVERS; NEB STREAMS, CHANNELS. The branches of the Nile. The Heb. *yᵉʾōr* is from a common Egyptian word for the Nile, and also for the waters of Egypt in general, all of which are of the Nile, including the entire irrigation system. In Egyptian usage the plural came to mean in particular the slower-moving lesser channels, as opposed to the *nᵉhārôṯ* or "flowing streams," the main channels.

See also RIVER. M. G. KYLE

CANANEAN kā-nə-nē'ən [Gk. *ho Kananaíos*] (Mt. 10:4; Mk. 3:18); AV CANAANITE; NEB "a member of the Zealot party." A designation of the disciple Simon, distinguishing him from Simon Peter. It comes from an Aramaic word meaning "zealot," and the parallel Lk. 6:15 has Gk. *zēlṓtēs*. *See* CANA; SIMON; ZEALOT.

CANDACE kan'də-sē, kan-dā-sē [Gk. *hē Kandakē*] (Acts 8:27); NEB "the Kandake." The title of the queen-mother of ETHIOPIA. According to Bion of Soli (*Aethiopica* 1), the Ethiopians regarded the sun as the father of their kings, and gave the title Candace to the mother. Her treasurer, "a eunuch of great authority," was baptized by Philip the evangelist on his return from worshiping in Jerusalem.

CANDLE. *See* LAMP.

CANDLESTICK. *See* LAMPSTAND.

CANE. *See* CALAMUS; REED.

CANKER. *See* GANGRENE.

CANKERED (Jas. 5:3, AV). *See* RUST.

CANKER-WORM. *See* LOCUST.

CANNEH kan'ə [Heb. *kannēh*; Gk. *Chanaa*]; NEB KANNEH. A place mentioned in Ezk. 27:23 together with Haran and Eden as cities with which Tyre had commercial relations. This is the only reference to Canneh, and the site is unknown. However, its association with Haran and Eden suggests that it was located in the Mesopotamian area. Some think it is probably the same as CALNEH of Am. 6:2; Gen. 10:10, AV; and Calno of Isa. 10:9. According to the Targums, Eusebius, and Jerome, it is identical with Ctesiphon on the Tigris River, N of Babylon. Others have suggested Kulunu and Nippur.

J. F. PREWITT

CANON OF THE OT.

- I. Introduction
  - A. Concept of Canonicity
  - B. Determining Factor in the Formation of the Canon
  - C. Tripartite Division of the OT
- II. Examination of the Witnesses
  - A. The OT's Witness to Itself
  - B. Other Pre-Christian Witnesses
    1. Samaritan Pentateuch
    2. Septuagint Version
    3. Sirach
    4. 1 and 2 Maccabees
    5. Philo
  - C. The NT as a Witness
  - D. Other Witnesses from the 1st to the 5th Cent. A.D.
    1. 4 Esdras
    2. Josephus
    3. Councils of Jamnia
    4. Talmud
    5. Jewish Doubts in the 2nd Cent. A.D.
  - E. Summary and Conclusion
- III. The Canon in the Christian Church
  - A. In the Eastern Church
  - B. In the Western Church

I. Introduction.–The problem of how we came by thirty-nine books known as OT Scripture is a purely historical investigation. The question involved is not who wrote the several books, but who made them into a collection; not their origin or contents, but their history; not God's part, but man's. Our present aim, accordingly, must be to trace the process by which the various writings came together as Scripture.

A. Concept of Canonicity. The word "canon" is of Christian origin, from the Gk. *kanṓn*, which is derived from a Semitic root (Assyr. *qanû*; Heb. *qāneh*; Ugar. *qn*) borrowed from the Sum. gi-na, "reed." From this came the idea of a measuring rod, later a rule or norm of faith, and eventually a catalogue or list. In present usage it signifies a collection of religious writings divinely inspired and hence authoritative, normative, sacred, and binding. The term *kanṓn* occurs in Gal. 6:16; 2 Cor. 10:13-16; but it is first employed of the books of Scripture in the technical sense of a standard collection or body of sacred writings by the church fathers of the 4th cent.; e.g., in the fifty-ninth canon of the Council of Laodicea (A.D. 363), in the Festal Epistle of Athanasius (367), and by Amphilochius, archbishop of Iconium (395).

How the ancient Hebrews expressed the concept of canonicity is not known; but it is safe to say that the idea existed long before there was any special phrase invented to express it. In the NT the word "scriptures" conveys unquestionably the notion of sacredness (Mt. 21:42; Jn. 5:39; Acts 18:24). From the 1st cent. A.D. and following, however, according to the Talmud, the Jews employed the phrase "defile the hands." Writings which were suitable to be read in the synagogue were designated as books which "defile the hands." What this very peculiar oriental expression may have originally signified no one definitely knows. Probably Lev. 16:24 gives a hint of the true interpretation. According to this passage the high priest on the great Day of Atonement washed not only when he put on the holy garments of his office, but also when he took them off. Quite possibly, therefore, the expression "defile the hands" signified that the hands which had touched the sacred writings must first be washed before touching anything else, in order that conditions of ceremonial purity might be maintained.

Various other and somewhat fanciful explanations of it, however, have been given: e.g., to prevent profane use of worn-out synagogue rolls (Buhl); or to prevent placing consecrated grain alongside of the sacred rolls in the synagogues that it might become holy, as the grain would attract the mice and the mice would gnaw the rolls (Strack, Wildeboer, and others); or to prevent the sacred, worn-out parchments from being used as coverings for animals (Graetz); or to "declare the hands to be unclean unless previously washed" (Fürst, Green). But no one of these explanations satisfies.

The rabbis invented a special phrase to designate rolls that were worn-out or disputed. These they called *g^{e}nûzîm*, meaning "hidden away." Cemeteries filled with Hebrew manuscripts which have long been buried are frequently found today in Egypt in connection with Jewish synagogues. Such rolls might first be placed in the *g^{e}nîzâ* or rubbish chamber of the sanctuary. They were not, however, apocryphal or uncanonical in the sense of being extraneous or outside the regular collection. For such the Jews had a special term, *s^{e}p̄ārîm ḥîṣōnîm*, "books that are outside." These could not be read in the synagogues. "Hidden books" were rather worn-out parchments, or canonical rolls which might by some be temporarily disputed. *See* APOCRYPHA II.A.

B. Determining Principle in the Formation of the Canon. The idea of a norm or rule for life goes far back into Hebrew history. Specific commandments from God which were to constitute guides for holy living were given to Adam, Noah, and Abraham. These commands were enshrined in written form at an early period, and preserved in the family histories which comprise much of the book of Genesis. During the 2nd millennium B.C. collections of legislative material were promulgated by Moses, including the Book of the Covenant (Ex. 24:4ff.) and the essentials of Deuteronomy (Dt. 31:9-13).

All major world religions have treasured some indigenous literary deposit as containing authoritative norms for belief and daily living, and in the case of the Hebrews the Torah fulfilled these requirements. The legislation given through Moses was unique in binding a nation in a spiritual relationship to a living God, and setting out the terms in the manner of second-millennium B.C. suzerainty treaties. The Law thus claimed supreme authority as the revealed will of God, and from the first was regarded as normative alike for Israelite behavior and spiritual destiny. While the prophets accepted the primacy of the Law, they also believed that their own words, spoken under divine inspiration, were of equal authority with the Law, coming as they did from the same spiritual source.

Thus from an early period the Hebrews believed that God could and did reveal Himself by means of a holy book, and in practice whatever written or oral matter conformed to the spirituality of the Torah was regarded as canonical by general consent. No formal declaration of canonicity was thus needed, since from the beginning the devout believed the material to be divinely inspired, and therefore obligatory for faith and life. Each book that issued from a person acknowledged to be a prophet of God was accepted as the divine Word as soon as it appeared, because it had been written with the intention of upholding faith in God and regulating behavior in conformity with the spiritual traditions of the Torah. Thus the canon derived its authority from its consonance with the nature and will of God as revealed to man from Adam to Moses.

In the making of canonical Scripture two parties are necessarily involved — the original writers and the Church. The former wrote under divine interpretation, while the latter, whether Jewish or Christian, accepted the compositions for what they purported to be, venerating them as authoritative. Holy Scripture itself, however, must always have pride of place over any ecclesiastical or cultic judgments concerning the canon, if only because the Church necessarily stands under the judgment of the Word, written and incarnate alike.

C. Tripartite Division of the OT. The Jews early divided the OT writings into three classes: (1) the *tôrâ*, or Law; (2) the *n^{e}ḇîʾîm*, or Prophets; and (3) the *k^{e}ṯûḇîm*, or Writings, called in Greek the Hagiographa. The *tôrâ* included the five books of the Pentateuch (Genesis, Exodus, Leviticus, Numbers, Deuteronomy), which were called "the Five-fifths of the Law." The *n^{e}ḇîʾîm* embraced (a) the four so-called Former Prophets (Joshua, Judges, 1 and 2 Samuel, counted as one book, 1 and 2 Kings, also counted as one book) and (b) the four so-called Latter Prophets (Isaiah, Jeremiah, Ezekiel, the Twelve Minor Prophets, counted as one book), a total of eight books. The *k^{e}ṯûḇîm* or Writings were eleven in all, including Psalms, Proverbs, Job, the five *m^{e}gillôṯ* or Rolls (Canticles, Ruth, Lamentations, Ecclesiastes, Esther), Daniel, Ezra-Nehemiah (counted as one book), and 1 and 2 Chronicles (also counted as one book); in all twenty-four books, exactly the same as those of the Protestant canon. This was the original count of the Jews as far as we can trace it back. Later certain Jewish authorities appended Ruth to Judges, and Lamentations to Jeremiah, and thereby obtained the number twenty-two, which corresponded to the number of letters in the Hebrew alphabet; but this manner of counting was secondary and fanciful. Still others divided Samuel, Kings, Chronicles, Ezra-Nehemiah, and Jeremiah-Lamentations into two books each and thereby obtained twenty-seven books, which they fancifully regarded as equivalent to the twenty-two letters of the Hebrew alphabet plus five, the number of letters having a peculiar final form when standing at the end of a word. Jerome states that twenty-two is the correct reckoning, but he adds, "Some count both Ruth and Lamentations among the Hagiographa, and so get twenty-four." 4 Esdras, which is the oldest (A.D. 85-96) witness to the number of books in the OT, gives twenty-four.

To answer the question of how to account for the tripartite division we must investigate the whole process by which the canon actually took shape. If the process of canonization was gradual and extended over a period of time, some books would obviously be separated from others because one section of the canon would be closed before certain other books of similar character were written. If, on the other hand, the divisions were based entirely on material differences in their contents, it is difficult to see why Kings and Chronicles were not included in the same division, and especially why Daniel does not stand among the prophets. To explain this mystery, medieval Jews said that "the Prophets were inspired by the spirit of prophecy, whereas the Writings by the Holy Spirit," implying different degrees of inspiration. But this is a distinction without a difference, the Holy Spirit and the spirit of prophecy being one and the same. Modern Protestants distinguish between the *donum propheticum* and the *munus propheticum,* i.e., between the gift and the office of prophecy. They allow that Daniel possessed the gift of prophecy, but they deny that he was divinely appointed to the office of prophet. But cf. Mt. 24:15, which speaks of "Daniel the prophet," and on the other hand, Am. 7:14, in which Amos resents being considered a prophet.

The true solution probably is that the process was gradual. When all the witnesses have been examined, we shall probably discover that the Law was canonized first, the Prophets considerably later, and the Writings last of all. And it may further become evident that the two last divisions were collected synchronously, and hence that the tripartite divisions of the canon are due to material differences in their contents as well as to chronology.

II. Examination of the Witnesses.*–*A. The OT's Witness to Itself. Though the OT does not tell us anything about the processes of its own canonization, it does furnish valuable hints as to how the ancient Hebrews preserved their writings. Thus in Ex. 40:20 it is stated that the "testimony," by which is meant the two tables of the law containing the Ten Commandments, was put into the ark of the covenant for safekeeping. In Dt. 31:9, 24-26, the laws of Deuteronomy are said to have been delivered to the sons of Levi, and by them deposited "by the side of the ark . . . that it may be for a witness against you." Such language was also found in Hittite suzerainty treaties, which contained a clause requiring deposition of the text in some secure location so that in subsequent generations the treaty would be available for public reading. According to 1 K. 8:9, when Solomon brought the ark up from the city of David to the temple, the two tables were still its only contents, and they continued to be carefully preserved. According to 2 K. 11:12, when Joash was crowned king, Jehoiada the high priest is said to have given (lit. "put upon") him "the testimony," which constituted the summary of the covenant stipulations. Likewise in Prov. 25:1, it is stated that a large number of proverbs were copied out by Hezekiah's men. Now all these, and still other passages which might be summoned, witness to the preservation of certain portions of the OT. But preservation is not synonymous with canonization. A writing might easily be preserved without being made a standard of faith and conduct. Nevertheless the two ideas are closely related; for when religious writings are sedulously preserved it is natural to infer that their intrinsic value was regarded as correspondingly precious.

Two other passages of paramount importance remain to be considered. The first is 2 K. 22:8ff., which describes the finding of the "book of the law" and how Josiah the king on the basis of it instituted a religious reformation and bound the people to obey its precepts. Here is an instance in which the Law, or some portion of it (how much no one can say), is regarded as of normative authoritative character. The king and his assistants recognize at once that it is ancient and that it contains the words of Yahweh (2 K. 22:13, 18f.). Its authority is undisputed. Yet nothing is said of its "canonicity," or that it would "defile the hands"; consequently there is no real ground for speaking of it as "the beginnings of the canon," for in the same historic sense the beginnings of the canon are to be found in Ex. 24:7. The other passage of paramount importance is Neh. 8:8f., according to which Ezra is said to have "read from the book, from the law of God, clearly." Not only did Ezra read the Law; he accompanied it with an interpretation. This seems to imply, almost beyond question, that in Ezra's time (444 B.C.) the Law, i.e., the Pentateuch, was regarded as canonical Scripture. This is practically all that the OT says about itself, though other passages, such as Zec. 7:12 and Dnl. 9:2, might be brought forward to show the deep regard which the later prophets had for the writings of their predecessors. The former of these is the *locus classicus* in the OT, teaching the inspiration of the Prophets; it is the OT parallel to 2 Tim. 3:16.

B. Other Pre-Christian Witnesses. Chronologically the OT is of course our most ancient witness. It brings us down to 444 B.C. The next in order is the Samaritan Pentateuch.

1. Samaritan Pentateuch. The history of the Samaritan Pentateuch is as follows: *ca.* 432 B.C., as we know from Neh. 13:28 and Josephus (*Ant.* xi.7.2–8.4), Nehemiah expelled Manasseh, the polygamous grandson of Eliashib the high priest and son-in-law of Sanballat, from the Jewish colony in Jerusalem. Manasseh founded the schismatic community of the Samaritans, and instituted on Mt. Gerizim a rival temple-worship to that at Jerusalem. To this day there is a small Samaritan community at Nâblus that still follows the ancient traditions of worship.

From an early period the Samaritans had their own version of the Hebrew Pentateuch, and this was the only canonical material they recognized. According to Jewish tradition (2 K. 17:26ff.) it became prominent after 722 B.C. when the newly established inhabitants of Samaria asked for a deported Hebrew priest to be sent to them to instruct them in the Law. The Samaritans claim that their oldest pentateuchal manuscript goes back to the great-grandson of Aaron (cf. 1 Ch. 6:3f.), and while this is obviously exaggerated it is certainly clear that the canon of the Samaritan Pentateuch long antedated the schism under Nehemiah (*ca.* 432 B.C.). Any remaining doubts have been dispelled by the manuscript discoveries at Qumrân, which have demonstrated conclusively the antiquity of the Samaritan Pentateuch's archetype. Some have inferred from the Samaritans' acceptance of only the Pentateuch as canonical that at the time of Manasseh's expulsion the Jewish canon included only the Pentateuch. This conclusion, however, is unwarranted. The reason for the Samaritans' refusal to acknowledge other literature as canonical apparently lay in their inherent conservatism, which demanded that the text of their bible be preserved much as it was from the very beginning.

2. Septuagint Version. The LXX version in Greek is the first translation of the OT ever made. The work of

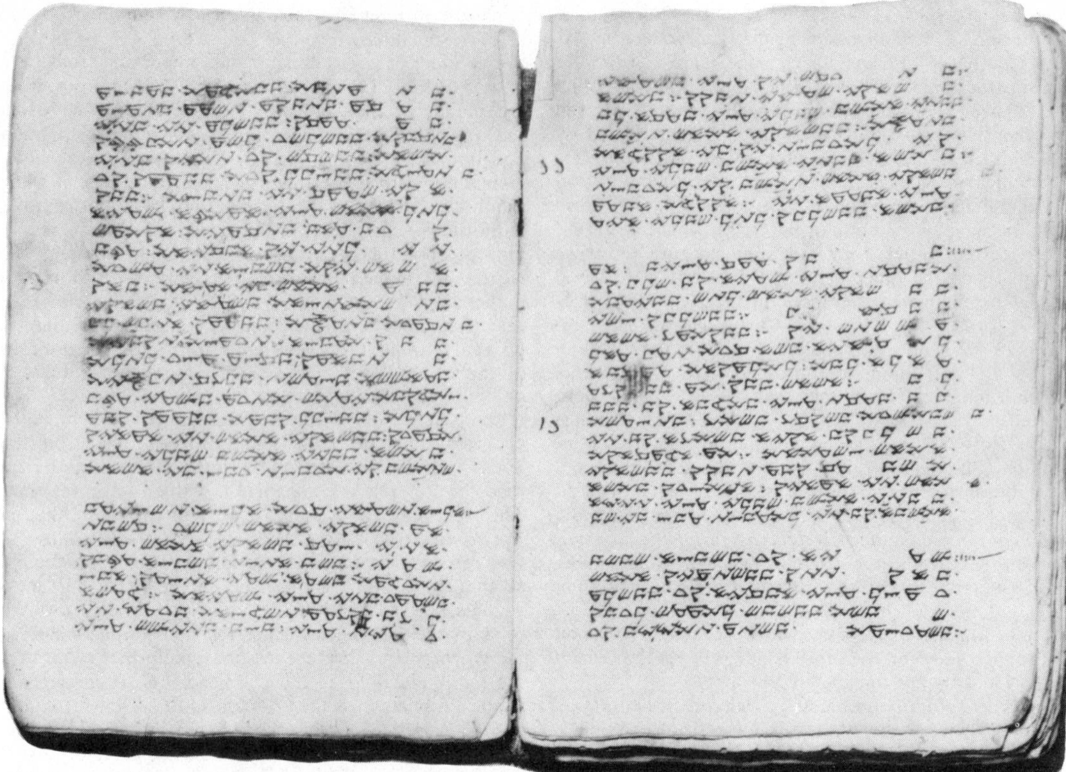

Samaritan manuscript of Deuteronomy, written on paper and bound in brown leather (*ca.* 18th cent. A.D.) (Royal Ontario Museum, Toronto)

translation was inaugurated by Ptolemy Philadelphus (285-247 B.C.), and probably continued for nearly a century (*ca.* 250-150 B.C.). Aristeas, a distinguished officer of Ptolemy, records how it came about. It appears that Ptolemy was exceedingly fond of books, and set his heart on adding to his famous collection in Alexandria a translation of the Hebrew Pentateuch. In order to obtain it, so the story goes, the king set free 198,000 Jewish slaves, and sent them with presents to Jerusalem to ask Eleazar the high priest for their Law and Jewish scholars capable to translating it. Six learned rabbis from each tribe (i.e., seventy-two in all) were sent. They were royally feasted; seventy questions were asked them to test their wisdom, and after seventy-two days of cooperation and conference they gave the world the OT in the Greek language, which is known as the LXX version. To this fabulous story, Christian tradition adds that the rabbis did the work of translating in seventy-two (some say thirty-six) separate cells on the island of Pharos, all working independently of each other, and that it was found at the expiration of their seclusion that each had produced a translation exactly word for word alike, hence supernaturally inspired. Justin Martyr of the 2nd cent. A.D. says that he was actually shown by his Alexandrian guide the ruins of these LXX cells.

The story is obviously a fable. The kernel of truth in it is probably that Ptolemy Philadelphus about the middle of the 3rd cent. B.C. succeeded in obtaining a translation of the Law. The other books were translated subsequently, perhaps for private use. The lack of unity of plan in the books outside the Law indicates that probably many different hands at different times engaged upon them. There is a subscription, moreover, at the close of the translation of Esther which states that Lysimachus, the son of Ptolemy in Jerusalem, translated it. But the whole was apparently completed before Jesus ben Sirach the younger wrote his prologue to Sirach (*ca.* 132 B.C.).

Now the LXX version, which was the Bible of the early Church, is supposed to have included originally many of the apocryphal books. Furthermore, in our present LXX, the canonical and apocryphal books stand intermingled and in an order which shows that the translators knew nothing of the tripartite division of later Judaism, or if they did they quite ignored it. The order of the books in our English OT is of course derived from the LXX through the Vulgate of St. Jerome. The books in the LXX are arranged as follows: Pentateuch, Joshua, Judges, Ruth, 1 and 2 Samuel, 1 and 2 Kings, 1 and 2 Chronicles, 1 and 2 Esdras, Nehemiah, Tobit, Judith, Esther, Job, Psalms, Proverbs, Ecclesiastes, Wisdom, Sirach, Hosea, Amos, Micah, Joel, Obadiah, Jonah, Nahum, Habakkuk, Zephaniah, Haggai, Zechariah, Malachi, Isaiah, Jeremiah, Baruch, Lamentations, Epistle of Jeremy, Ezekiel, Daniel, 1, 2, and 3 Maccabees.

On the basis of the LXX, Catholics advocate what is known as the "larger" canon of the Jews in Alexandria; Protestants, on the other hand, deny the existence of an independent canon in Alexandria in view of the "smaller" canon of the Jews in Palestine. The actual difference between the Catholic and Protestant OT is a matter of seven complete books and portions of two others, viz., Tobit, Judith, Wisdom, Sirach, Baruch, 1 and 2 Maccabees, together with certain additions to Esther (10:4–16:24) and to Daniel (3:24-90, Song of the Three Holy Children; ch. 13, Susanna; ch. 14, Bel and the Dragon). These portions Protestants reject as apocryphal because there is not sufficient evidence that they were ever reckoned

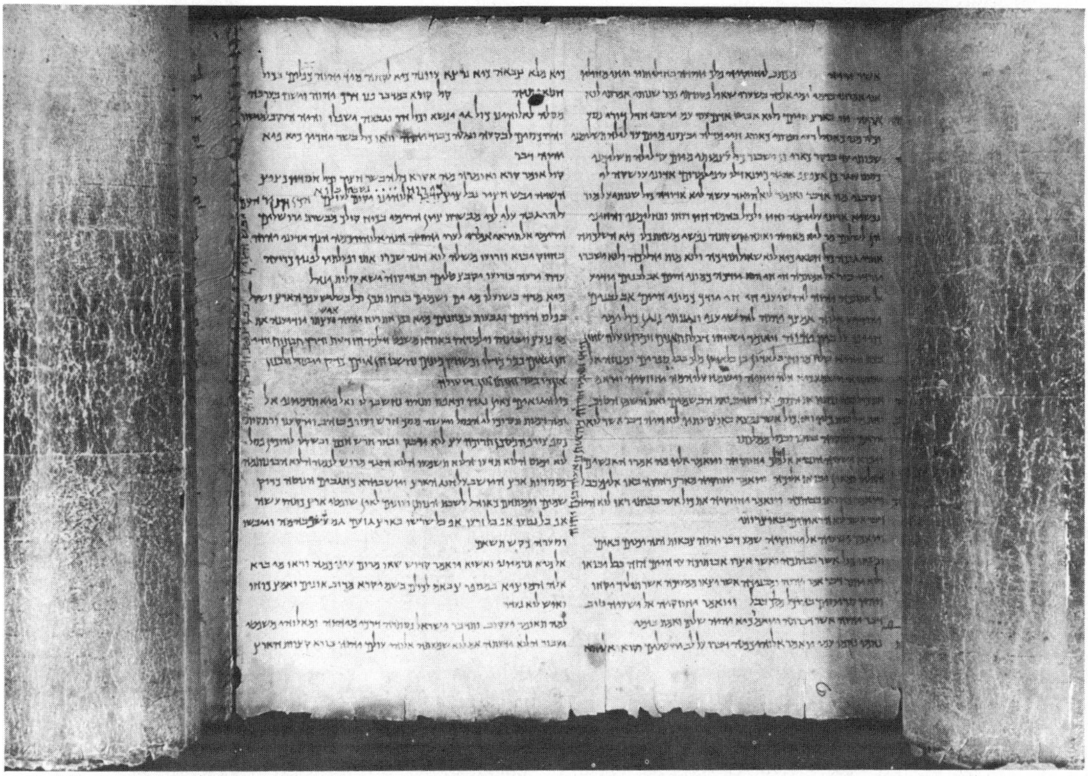

Isaiah Scroll (1QIsa^a) from Qumrân, cols. 32f. Although all OT books except Esther are represented in the Qumrân discoveries, the scrolls indicate that neither the canon nor text had been fully standardized by the 1st cent. B.C. (J. C. Trever) *See also* Plate 16.

as canonical by the Jews anywhere. The fact that the present LXX includes them is far from conclusive that the original LXX did, for the following reasons: (1) The design of the LXX was purely literary; Ptolemy and the Alexandrians were interested in building up a library. (2) All the extant MSS of the LXX are of Christian, not Jewish, origin. Between the actual translation of the LXX (250-150 B.C.) and the oldest MSS of the LXX extant (*ca.* A.D. 350) there is a chasm of fully five hundred years, during which it is highly possible that the so-called apocryphal books crept in. (3) In the various extant MSS of the LXX, the apocryphal books vary in number and name. For example, the great Vatican MS, which is probably "the truest representative which remains of the Alexandrian Bible," and which comes down to us from the 4th cent. A.D., contains no book of Maccabees whatever, but does include 1 Esdras,which St. Jerome and Catholics generally treat as apocryphal. On the other hand, the Alexandrian MS, another of the great MSS of the LXX, dating from the 5th cent. A.D., contains not only the extracanonical book of 1 Esdras, but 3 and 4 Maccabees, and in the NT 1 and 2 Clement, none of which, however, is considered canonical by Rome. Likewise the great Sinaitic MS, hardly less important than the Vatican as a witness to the LXX and like it dating from the 4th cent. A.D., omits Baruch (which Catholics consider canonical), but includes 4 Maccabees and in the NT the Epistle of Barnabas and the Shepherd of Hermas, all of which are excluded from the canon by Catholics. In other MSS, 3 Maccabees, 3 Esdras, and Prayer of Manasses are occasionally included. The problem as to how many books the original LXX version actually included is a very complicated one. It probably included none of these variants.

(4) Still another reason for thinking that there never existed in Egypt a separate or "larger" canon is the fact that during the 2nd cent. A.D. the Alexandrian Jews adopted Aquila's Greek version of the OT in lieu of their own, and it is known that Aquila's text excluded all apocryphal books. Add to all this the fact that Philo, who lived in Alexandria from *ca.* 20 B.C. till A.D. 50, never quotes from one of these apocryphal books though he often does from the canonical, and that Origen, who also resided in Alexandria (*ca.* A.D. 200), never set his *imprimatur* upon them, and it becomes reasonably convincing that there was no "larger" canon in Alexandria. The value of the evidence derived from the LXX, accordingly, is largely negative.

The MSS discovered at Qumrân make it evident that no canonical book of the OT was written later than the Persian period, a consideration that also extends to Daniel and those Psalms that were formerly regarded as Maccabean. Whatever stage the work of translation had reached in Alexandria, the Hebrew canon in Palestine was already complete in all its essentials by that period.

3. Sirach. Our next witness is Jesus ben Sirach who lived in Jerusalem (*ca.* 180 B.C.) and wrote in Hebrew. His book (Sirach or Ecclesiasticus) is a book of Wisdom resembling Proverbs; some of his precepts approach the high level of the gospel. In many respects Sirach is the most important of all the apocryphal books; theologically it is the chief monument of primitive Sadduceeism. In chs. 44–50 the author signs a "hymn to the fathers," eulogizing the mighty heroes of Israel from Enoch to Nehemiah, in fact from Adam to Simon, including the most famous men described in the OT, and making explicit mention of the Twelve Prophets. These facts would indicate that the whole or, at least, the most of the OT was known to him, and that already in his day (180 B.C.) the so-called Minor Prophets were regarded as a special group of writings by themselves.

The value of Sirach as a witness, however, depends upon the interpretation one places on 24:33, which reads: "I will again pour out teaching like prophecy and leave it to all future generations." From this it is inferred by some that he feels himself inspired and capable of adding to the canon already in existence, and that, though he knew the full prophetic canon, he did not draw any very definite line of demarcation between his own work and the inspired writings of the prophets. For example, he passes over from the patriarchs and prophets of Israel to Simon the son of Onias, who was probably the high priest in his own time, making no distinction between them. But this may have been partly due to personal conceit; cf. 39:12, "I have yet more to say, which I have thought upon, and I am filled, like the moon at the full." While in the 2nd cent. B.C. the canon was already complete, to Sirach the Law was everything. He identified it with the highest wisdom; indeed, all wisdom in his judgment was derived from a study of the Law (cf. 19:20-24; 15:1-18; 24:23; 2:16; 39:1).

The prologue or preface to Sirach was written by the grandson of Jesus ben Sirach, who bore his grandfather's name (*ca.* 132 B.C.). Jesus ben Sirach the younger translated in Egypt his grandfather's proverbs into Greek and in doing so added a preface or prologue of his own. In this prologue he thrice refers to the tripartite division of the OT. In fact, the prologue to Sirach is the oldest witness we have to the threefold division of the OT books. He says: "Whereas many great teachings have been given to us through the law and the prophets and the others that followed them . . . my grandfather Jesus, after devoting himself especially to the reading of the law and the prophets and the other books of our fathers . . . Not only this work, but even the law itself, the prophecies, and the rest of the books. . . ."

These are explicit and definite allusions to the threefold division of the OT writings, yet only the titles of the first and second divisions are the technical names usually employed; the third is especially vague because of his use of the terms, "the other books of our fathers," and "the rest of the books." However, he evidently refers to writings with religious contents; and by "the other books of our fathers" he can hardly be supposed to have meant an indefinite number, though he has not told us which they were or what was their number. From his further statement that his grandfather, having immersed himself in the law and the prophets, and other books of the fathers, felt drawn on also himself to write something for the profit of others, it may be inferred that in his time there was as yet no definite gulf fixed between canonical writings and those of other men, and that the sifting process was still going on (cf. W. R. Smith, pp. 178f.).

4. 1 and 2 Maccabees. 1 Maccabees was written originally in Hebrew, 2 Maccabees in Greek, somewhere between 134 and 70 B.C. The author of 1 Maccabees is acquainted, on the one hand, with the deeds of John Hyrcanus (134 to 105 B.C.) and knows nothing, on the other, of the conquest of Palestine by Pompey (63 B.C.). The value of this book as a witness to the history of the canon centers on his allusions to Daniel and the Psalms. In 1 Macc. 1:54 he tells how Antiochus Epiphanes "erected a desolating sacrilege" upon the altar at Jerusalem, referring most likely to Dnl. 9:24-27; and in 1 Macc. 2:59f. he speaks of Hananiah, Azariah, and Mishael, who by believing were saved from the fiery furnace, and of Daniel, who was delivered from the mouths of the lions (cf. Dnl. 1:7; 3:26; 6:23). From these allusions it would appear that the book of Daniel was at that time regarded as normative or canonical. This is supported by 1 Macc. 7:16f., which introduces a quotation from Ps. 79:2 with the solemn formula, "in accordance with the word which was written"; which would suggest that the Psalms also were already canonical, a conclusion amply supported by the Qumrân MSS.

2 Maccabees, written *ca.* 70 B.C., also contains several passages of considerable importance to this investigation. Both, however, are found in a spurious letter purporting to have been sent by the inhabitants of Judea to their fellow countrymen residing in Egypt. The first passage (2 Macc. 2:13) tells how Nehemiah "founded a library and collected the books about the kings and prophets, and the writings of David, and the letters of kings about votive offerings." These words throw no special light upon the formation of the canon, but they do connect with the name of Nehemiah the preservation of public documents and historical records of national interest, and relate how he, as a lover of books, founded a library. This is in perfect agreement with what we know of Nehemiah's character, for he compiled the genealogy in Neh. 7.

The other passage (2 Macc. 2:14) reads: "In the same way Judas also collected all the books that had been lost on account of the war which had come upon us, and they are in our possession." Though found in a letter supposed to be spurious, there is every reason for believing this statement to be true. For when Antiochus, the archenemy of the nation, sought to stamp out the religion of the Jews by destroying their books (cf. 1 Macc. 1:56f.), what would have been more natural for a true patriot like Judas than to attempt to re-collect their sacred writings? Though it yields nothing definite as to the number of the books recovered, it is obvious that the books collected were the most precious documents the nation possessed. They were doubtless religious, as was the age.

5. Philo. Philo is our next witness. He flourished in Alexandria between *ca.* 20 B.C. and A.D. 50, leaving behind him a voluminous literature. Unfortunately, he does not yield much of positive value for our present purpose. His evidence is largely negative. True, he nowhere mentions the tripartite division of the OT, which is known to have existed in his day. Nor does he quote from Ezekiel, the Five Megilloth (Canticles, Ruth, Lamentations, Ecclesiastes, Esther), Daniel, Chronicles, or from the Twelve Minor Prophets, except Hosea, Jonah, and Zechariah. Moreover, he held a loose view of inspiration. According to Philo, inspiration is by no means confined to the sacred Scriptures; all truly wise and virtuous men are inspired and capable of expressing the hidden things of God. But nowhere does he place other writers on the same level of inspiration as the writers of Scripture.

Philo's reverence for the Law is unbounded. In this respect he is typical of other Alexandrians. He quotes predominately from the Law. Moses is to him the source of all wisdom, even the wisdom of the Gentiles. Concerning the laws of Moses, he is reported by Eusebius as saying: "They have not changed so much as a single word in them. They would rather die a thousand deaths than detract anything from these laws and statutes." On the other hand, Philo never quotes any of the apocryphal books. Hence it may safely be assumed that his canon was essentially ours.

C. The NT as a Witness. The evidence furnished by

the NT is of the highest importance. When summed up, it gives the unmistakable impression that when the NT was written (*ca.* A.D. 50-100) there was a definite and fixed canon of OT Scripture, to which authoritative appeal could be made. First, it is hardly possible to exaggerate the importance of the names or titles ascribed to the OT writings by the authors of the NT: thus, "scripture" (Jn. 10:35; 19:36; 2 Pet. 1:20), "the scriptures" (Mt. 22:29; Acts 18:24), "holy scriptures" (Rom. 1:2), "sacred writings" (2 Tim. 3:15), "law" (Jn. 10:34; 12:34; 15:25; 1 Cor. 14:21), "law and prophets" (Mt. 5:17; 7:12; 22:40; Lk. 16:16; 24:44; Acts 13:15; 28:23). Such names or titles, though they do not define the limits of the canon, certainly assume the existence of a complete and sacred collection of Jewish writings that are already marked off from all other literature as separate and fixed.

One passage (Jn. 10:35) in which the term "scripture" is employed seems to refer to the OT canon as a whole: "and scripture cannot be broken." In like manner the expression "law and prophets" is often used in a generic sense referring to much more than merely the first and second divisions of the OT; it seems rather to refer to the old dispensation as a whole; but the term "the law" is the most general of all. It is frequently applied to the entire OT, and apparently held in Christ's time among the Jews a place akin to that which the term "the Bible" does with us. For example, in Jn. 10:34; 12:34; 15:25, texts from the prophets or even from the Psalms are quoted as part of "the law"; in 1 Cor. 14:21 also, Paul speaks of Isa. 28:11 as a part of "the law." These names and titles, accordingly, are exceedingly important; they are never applied by NT writers to the Apocrypha.

One passage (Lk. 24:44) furnishes clear evidence of the threefold division of the canon. Usually the NT writers mentioned the first two sections only (cf. Mt. 5:17; Lk. 16:16), but quite obviously included the Hagiographa with the prophets just as the Talmudic teachers did, due no doubt to the lack of a proper term for the Hagiographa.

Another passage (Mt. 23:35; cf. Lk. 11:51) seems to point to the final order and arrangement of the books in the OT canon. It reads: "that upon you may come all the righteous blood shed on earth, from the blood of innocent Abel to the blood of Zechariah the son of Barachiah, whom you murdered between the sanctuary and the altar." Now in order to grasp the bearing of this verse upon the matter in hand, it must be remembered that in the modern arrangement of the OT books in Hebrew, Chronicles stands last; and that the murder of Zechariah is the last recorded instance in this arrangement, being found in 2 Ch. 24:20f. But this murder took place under Joash king of Judah in the 9th cent. B.C. There is another that is chronologically later, viz., that of Uriah son of Shemaiah who was murdered in Jehoiakim's reign in the 7th cent. B.C. (Jer. 26:23). Accordingly, the argument is this: unless Chronicles already stood last in Christ's OT, why did He not say, "from the blood of Abel to the blood of Uriah"? He would then have been speaking chronologically and would have included all the martyrs whose martyrdom is recorded in the OT. But He rather says, "from the blood of innocent Abel to the blood of Zechariah," as though He were including the whole range of OT Scripture, just as we would say "from Genesis to Malachi." Hence it is inferred, with some degree of justification also, that Chronicles was in Christ's time, as it is today, in the Hebrew Bible of the Masoretes, the last book of an already closed canon. Of course, in answer to this, there is the possible objection that in those early days the Scriptures were still written by the Jews on separate rolls.

Another ground for thinking that the OT canon was closed before the NT was written is the numerous citations made in the NT from the OT. Every book is quoted except Esther, Ecclesiastes, Canticles, Ezra, Nehemiah, Obadiah, Nahum, and Zephaniah. But these exceptions are not serious. The Twelve Minor Prophets were always treated by the Jews *en bloc* as one canonical work; hence if one of the twelve was quoted all were recognized. And the fact that 2 Ch. 24:20f. is quoted in Mt. 23:35 and Lk. 11:51 presupposes also the canonicity of Ezra-Nehemiah, as originally these books were one with Chronicles, though they may possibly have already been divided in Jesus' day. As for Esther, Ecclesiastes, and Canticles, it is easy to see why they are not quoted: they probably failed to furnish NT writers material for quotation. The NT writers simply had no occasion to make citations from them. What is much more noteworthy is that they never quote from the apocryphal books, though they show an acquaintance with them.

As a matter of fact, NT writers felt free to quote from any source; for example, Paul on Mars Hill cites to the learned Athenians an astronomical work of the Stoic Aratus of Cilicia, or perhaps from a hymn to Jupiter by Cleanthes of Lycia, when he says, "For we are indeed his offspring" (Acts 17:28). And Jude 14f. almost undeniably quotes from Enoch (1:9; 60:8) — a work that is not recognized as canonical by any except the Church of Abyssinia. But in any case, the mere quoting of a book does not canonize it; nor, on the other hand, does failure to quote a book exclude it. Quotation does not necessarily imply sanction, any more than reference to contemporary literature is incompatible with strict views of the canon. Everything depends upon the manner in which the quotation is made. In no case is an apocryphal book cited by NT authors as Scripture, or as the work of the Holy Spirit. As a witness, therefore, the NT is of paramount importance. For, though it nowhere tells us the exact number of books contained in the OT canon, it gives abundant evidence of the existence already in the 1st cent. A.D. of a definite and fixed canon.

D. Other Witnesses from the 1st to the 5th Cent. A. D.

1. 4 Esdras. 4 Esdras in Latin (2 Esdras in English) is a Jewish apocalypse written originally in Greek toward the close of the 1st cent. (*ca.* A.D. 81-96). The passage of special interest to us is 14:19-48, which relates in most fabulous style how Ezra was given spiritual illumination to reproduce the Law, which had been burned; and how at the divine command he secluded himself for a period of forty days, after which he went with five skilled scribes to the open country. There a cup of water was offered him; he drank, and then dictated to his five amanuenses continuously for forty days and nights, producing ninety-four books of which seventy were kept secret and twenty-four published. The most significant section reads as follows: "And when the forty days were ended, the Most High spoke to me, saying, 'Make public the twenty-four books that you wrote first . . . but keep the seventy that were written last, in order to give them to the wise among your people'" (2 Esd. 14:45f.).

The story is obviously pure fiction. It is no wonder that a new version of it arose in the 16th cent., according to which the canon was completed not by Ezra alone, but by a company of men known as the Great Synagogue. From the legend of 4 Esdras, however, it is commonly inferred that the twenty-four books that remain after subtracting seventy from ninety-four are the canonical books of the OT. This would make it the first witness we have to the number of books contained in the OT canon. This number corresponds exactly with the usual number of sacred books according to Jewish count, as we saw above (I.C). The legend is therefore not without value. Even as legend it witnesses to a tradition that existed as early as the 1st Christian cent., to the effect that the Jews possessed twenty-four specially sacred books. It also points to Ezra as the chief factor in the making of Scripture and intimates that the OT canon has long since been virtually closed.

2. Josephus. Flavius Josephus, the celebrated Jewish historian, was born A.D. 37. He was a priest and a Pharisee. About the year 100 he wrote a controversial treatise, known as *Contra Apionem,* in defense of the Jews against their assailants. Apion, a famous grammarian who in his lifetime had been hostile to the Jews (he died some fifty years before *Contra Apionem* was written), is taken as a leading representative of these assailants. Josephus writes in Greek to Greeks. The important passage in his treatise (i.8) reads as follows: "For it is not the case with us to have vast numbers of books disagreeing and conflicting with one another. We have but twenty-two containing the history of all time, books that are justly believed in. And of these, five are the books of Moses, which comprise the laws and the earliest traditions from the creation of mankind down to the time of his [Moses'] death. This period falls short but by a little of three thousand years. From the death of Moses to the reign of Artaxerxes, king of Persia, the successor of Xerxes, the prophets who succeeded Moses wrote the history of the events that occurred in their own time, in thirteen books. The remaining four documents comprise hymns to God and practical precepts to men. From the days of Artaxerxes to our own time every event has indeed been recorded. But these recent records have not been deemed worthy of equal credit with those which preceded them, because the exact succession of the prophets ceased. But what faith we have placed in our own writings is evident by our conduct; for though so great an interval of time [i.e., since they were written] has now passed, not a soul has ventured either to add, or to remove, or to alter a syllable. But it is instinctive in all Jews at once from their very birth to regard them as commands of God, and to abide by them, and, if need be, willingly to die for them."

The value of this remarkable passage for our study is obviously very great. In the first place, Josephus fixes the number of Jewish writings that are recognized as sacred at twenty-two, probably joining Ruth to Judges and Lamentations to Jeremiah. He also classifies them according to a threefold division that is quite peculiar to himself: five of Moses, thirteen of the prophets, and four hymns and maxims for human life. The five of Moses were of course the Pentateuch; the thirteen of the prophets probably included the eight regular *n^e^bî'îm* plus Daniel, Job, Chronicles, Ezra-Nehemiah, and Esther; the "four hymns and maxims" would most naturally consist of Psalms, Proverbs, Canticles, and Ecclesiastes. There is little doubt that his twenty-two books are those of our present Hebrew canon.

Another remarkable feature of Josephus' statement is the standard he gives of canonicity, viz., antiquity; because, as he says, since Artaxerxes' age the succession of prophets had ceased. It was the uniform tradition of Josephus' time that prophetic inspiration had ceased with Malachi (*ca.* 445-432 B.C.). Hence, according to him, the canon was closed in the reign of Artaxerxes (465-425 B.C.). He does not pause to give any account of the closing of the canon; he simply assumes it. Prophecy had ceased, and the canon was accordingly closed; the fact did not require official proclamation. As remarked above, the value of Josephus as a witness is very great. But just here an important question arises: How literally must we interpret his language? Was the OT canon actually closed before 425 B.C.? Were not books and parts of books composed and added to the canon subsequent to the reign of Artaxerxes? Josephus is not always reliable in his chronology. For example, in his *Antiquities* (xi.6.13) he dates the story of Esther as occurring in the reign of Artaxerxes I (whereas it belongs to Xerxes' reign), while in the same work (xi.5.1) he puts Ezra and Nehemiah under Xerxes (whereas they belong to the time of Artaxerxes).

On the whole, it seems safer on internal grounds to regard Josephus' statements concerning the antiquity of the Jewish canon as the language not of a careful historian, but of a partisan in debate. Instead of expressing absolute fact in this case, he is reflecting the popular belief of his age. Reduced to its lowest terms, the element of real truth in what he says was simply this, that he voiced a tradition that was at that time universal and undisputed; one, however, that had required a long period, perhaps hundreds of years, to develop. Hence we conclude that the complete OT canon, numbering twenty-two books, was no new thing in A.D. 100.

3. Councils of Jamnia. According to the traditions preserved in the Mishnah, two councils of Jewish rabbis were held (A.D. 90 and 118 respectively) at Jabne, or Jamnia, not far S of Joppa, on the Mediterranean coast; at these councils the books of the OT, notably Ecclesiastes and Canticles, were discussed and their canonicity ratified. However, it is far from certain that there ever were such "councils" in the strictest sense, and very little is known about the actual occasions of meeting. While Jamnia became a center of Jewish study and learning under Rabbi Johanan ben Zakkai after A.D. 70, there is nothing to indicate that anything formal or binding was decided in connection with the OT canon, even though certain books such as Esther, Canticles, and Ecclesiastes may have been discussed in this regard.

4. Talmud. The Talmud consists of two parts: (1) The Mishnah (compiled A.D. 200), a collection of systematized tradition; and (2) the Gemara, *g^e^mārā'* (completed about A.D. 500), a "vast and desultory commentary on the Mishnah." A Baraitha', or unauthorized gloss, known as the *Baba Bathra* 14b, a talmudic tractate, relates the "order" of the various books of the OT and who "wrote" or edited them. But it says nothing of the formation of the canon. To write is not the same as to canonize, though to the later Jews the two ideas were closely akin. As a witness, therefore, this tractate is of little value, except that it confirms the tripartite division and is a good specimen of rabbinic speculation. (For the full text of the passage, see Ryle, pp. 273ff.)

5. Jewish Doubts in the 2nd Cent. A.D. During the 2nd cent. doubts arose in Jewish minds concerning four books, Proverbs, Canticles, Ecclesiastes, and Esther. In a certain talmudic tractate it is related that an attempt was made to withdraw (*gānaz,* "conceal," "hide") the book of Proverbs on account of contradictions that were found in it (cf. 26:4f.), but on deeper investigation it was not withdrawn. In another section of the Mishnah (*Yadaim* iii.5), Rabbi Akiba is represented as saying concerning Canticles: "God forbid that any man of Israel should deny that the Song of Songs defileth the hands, for the whole world is not equal to the day in which the Song of Songs was given to Israel. For all Scriptures are holy, but the Song of Songs is the holiest of the holy." Such extravagant language inclines one to feel that real doubt must have existed in the minds of some concerning the book. But the protestations were much stronger against Ecclesiastes. In *Shabbath* 30b it is stated, "The wise men desired to hide it because its language was often self-contradictory [cf. Eccl. 7:3 and 2:2; 4:2 and 9:4], but they did not hide it because the beginning and the end of it consist of words from the Torah [cf. 1:3; 12:13f.]." Likewise Esther was vigorously disputed by both the Jerusalem and Babylonian Gemaras, because the name of God was not found in it; but a Rabbi Simeon ben Lakkish (*ca*. A.D. 300) defended its canonicity, putting Esther on an equality with the Law and above the Prophets and the other Writings.

Other books, e.g., Ezekiel and Jonah, were discussed in post-talmudic writings, but no serious objections were ever raised by the Jews against either. Jonah was really never doubted until the 12th century. In the case of none of these disputed books were there serious doubts; nor did scholastic controversies affect public opinion.

E. Summary and Conclusion. This brings us to the end of our examination of the witnesses. In our survey we have discovered (1) that the OT says nothing about its canonization, but does emphasize the manner in which the Law was preserved and recognized as authoritative; (2) that the fact that the Samaritans admit of the Law alone as the true canon, does not warrant the conclusion that the Jews possessed the Law only when the renegade Manasseh was expelled by Nehemiah from Jerusalem; (3) that the LXX version as we know it from the Christian MSS extant is by no means a sufficient proof that the Alexandrians possessed a "larger" canon which included the Apocrypha; (4) that Jesus ben Sirach is a witness to the fact that the Prophets in his day (180 B.C.) were not yet acknowledged as canonical; (5) that his grandson in his prologue is the first witness to the customary tripartite division of OT writings, but does not speak of the third division as though it were already closed; (6) that the books of Maccabees seem to indicate that the Psalms and Daniel are already included in the canon of the Jews; (7) that Philo's testimony is negative, in that he witnesses against the apocryphal books as an integral part of Holy Scripture; (8) that the NT is the most explicit witness of the series, because of the names and titles it ascribes to the OT books it quotes; (9) that 4 Esdras is the first witness to the number of books in the OT canon — viz., twenty-four; (10) that Josephus also fixes the number of books, but in arguing for the antiquity of the canon speaks as an advocate, voicing popular tradition, rather than as a scientific historian; (11) that the councils of Jamnia may, with some ground, be considered an occasion on which the Jews pronounced upon the limits of their canon; but that (12) doubts existed in the 2nd cent. concerning certain books; which books, however, were not seriously questioned.

From at least the time of Samuel the Torah was considered authoritative because it contained the divine revelation to Moses, and it represented the standard by which other potentially canonical writings were to be assessed. The evidence from Qumrân shows clearly that no canonical OT composition could have been compiled later than the Persian period, regardless of when it was deemed canonical. The fact that some parts of the Hagiographa are older than certain prophecies may only mean that the second section of the canon remained "open" until much of the Hagiographa had been written. Probably the canon was essentially completed by 300 B.C.

III. The Canon in the Christian Church.–In making the transition from the Jewish to the Christian Church, we find the same canon cherished by all. Christians of all sects have always been disposed to accept without question the canon of the Jews. For centuries all branches of the Christian Church were practically agreed on the limits set by the Jews, but eventually the Western Church became divided, some alleging that Christ sanctioned the "larger" canon of Alexandria, including the Apocrypha, while others adhered, as the Jews have always done, to the canon of the Jews in Palestine.

A. In the Eastern Church. Taking the Eastern or Oriental Church first, the evidence they furnish is as follows. The Peshitta or Syriac version, dating from A.D. 150, omits Chronicles. Justin Martyr (A.D. 164) held to a canon identical with that of the Jews. The canon of Melito, bishop of Sardis, who (*ca*. 170) made a journey to Palestine in order carefully to investigate the matter, omits Esther; his list, the earliest Christian list we have, has been preserved by Eusebius in *HE* iv.26. Origen (d. 254), educated in Alexandria and one of the most learned of the Greek fathers, also set himself the task of knowing the "Hebrew verity" of the OT text. In his list (preserved by Eusebius in *HE* vi.5) he reckons the number of books as twenty-two (thus agreeing with Josephus); inadvertently he omits the Twelve Minor Prophets, but this is manifestly an oversight on the part of either a scribe or of Eusebius, as he states the number of books is twenty-two and then names but twenty-one. The so-called canon of Laodicea (*ca*. 363) included the canonical books only, rejecting the Apocrypha. Athanasius (d. 365) gives a list in which Esther is classed as among the noncanonical books, though he elsewhere admits that "Esther is considered canonical by the Hebrews"; however, he also includes Baruch and the Epistle of Jeremiah with Jeremiah. Amphilochius, bishop of Iconium (*ca*. 380), speaks of Esther as received only by some. Cyril, bishop of Jerusalem (d. 386), gives a list corresponding with the Hebrew canon, except that he includes Baruch and the Epistle of Jeremiah. Gregory of Nazianzus in Cappadocia (d. 390) omits Esther. But Anastasius, patriarch of Antioch (500), and Leontius of Byzantium (580) both held to the strict Jewish canon of twenty-two books. The Nestorians generally doubted Esther. This was due doubtless to the influence of Theodore of Mopsuestia (*ca*. A.D. 390-457), who disputed the authority of Chronicles, Ezra, Nehemiah, Esther, and Job. The oriental churches as a whole, however, never canonized the Apocrypha.

B. In the Western Church. Between A.D. 100 and 400 the NT writings became canonical, occupying in the Christian Church a place of authority and sacredness equal to those of the OT. The tendency of the period was to receive everything that had been traditionally read in the churches. But the transference of this principle to the OT writings produced great confusion. Usage and theory were often in conflict. A church father might declare that the apocryphal books were uninspired and yet quote them as Scripture, and even introduce them with the accepted formula, "As the Holy Ghost saith." Theologically they held to a strict canon, homiletically they used a larger one. But even usage was not uniform. 3 and 4 Esdras and the Book of Enoch are sometimes quoted as "Holy Writ," yet the Western Church never received these books as canonical. The criterion of usage, therefore, is too broad. The theory of the fathers was gradually forgotten, and the prevalent use of the LXX and other versions led to the obliteration of the distinction between the undisputed books of the Hebrew canon and the most popular apocryphal books; and being often publicly read in the churches, they finally received a quasi-canonization.

CANON OF THE OT

Tertullian of Carthage (*ca.* 150-230) is the first of the Latin fathers whose writings have been preserved. He gives the number of OT books as twenty-four, the same as in the Talmud. Hilary, bishop of Poitiers in France (350-368), gives a catalogue in which he speaks of "Jeremiah and his epistle," yet his list numbers only twenty-two. Rufinus of Aquileia in Italy (d. 410) likewise gives a complete list of twenty-two books. Jerome also, the learned monk of Bethlehem (d. 420), gives the number of canonical books as twenty-two, corresponding to the twenty-two letters of the Hebrew alphabet, and explains that the five double books (1 and 2 Samuel, 1 and 2 Kings, 1 and 2 Chronicles, Ezra-Nehemiah, Jeremiah-Lamentations) correspond to the five final letters of the Hebrew alphabet. In his famous *Prologus Galeatus* or "Helmed Preface" to the books of Samuel and Kings, he declares himself for the strict canon of the Jews, rejecting the authority of the deuterocanonical books in the most outspoken manner, even distinguishing carefully the apocryphal additions to Esther and to Daniel.

Contemporaneous with Jerome in Bethlehem was Augustine of North Africa (354-430). He was the bishop of Hippo, renowned as thinker, theologian, and saint. In the three great councils of Hippo (393) and Carthage (397 and 419) of which he was the leading spirit, he closed as it were the great debate of the previous generations on the subject of the extent of the canon. In his essay *De doctrina christiana* he catalogues the books of Scripture that had been transmitted by the fathers for public reading in the Church, giving their number as forty-four, with which he says "the authority of the OT is ended." These forty-four books probably correspond with the present canon of the Catholic Church. But it is not to be supposed that Augustine made no distinction between the protocanonical and deuterocanonical books. On the contrary, he limited the term "canonical" in its strict sense to the books that are inspired and received by the Jews, and denied that in the support of doctrine the books of Wisdom and Sirach were of unquestioned authority, though long custom had entitled them to respect. And when a passage from 2 Maccabees was urged by his opponents in defense of suicide, he rejected their proof by showing that the book was not received into the Hebrew canon to which Christ was witness.

At the Third Council of Carthage (397), however, a decree was ratified, probably with Augustine's approval, which in effect placed all the canonical and deuterocanonical books on the same level, and in the course of time they actually became considered by some as of equal authority (*see* APOCRYPHA). A few years later another council at Carthage (419) took the additional step of voting that their own decision concerning the canon should be confirmed by Boniface, the bishop of Rome; thereafter, the question of how large the Bible should be became a matter to be settled by authority rather than by criticism.

From the 4th to the 16th cent. A.D. the process of gradually widening the limits of the canon continued. Pope Gelasius (492-496) issued a decretal or list in which he included the OT Apocrypha. Yet even after this official act of the papacy the sentiment in the Western Church was divided. Some followed the strict canon of Jerome, while others favored the larger canon of Augustine without noting his cautions and the distinctions he made between inspired and uninspired writings. Cassiodorus (556) and Isidore of Seville (636) place the lists of Jerome and Augustine side by side without deciding between them. Two bishops of North Africa, Primasius and Junilius (*ca.* 550), reckon twenty-four books as strictly canonical and explicitly state that the others are not of the same grade. Popular usage, however, was indiscriminate. Outside of Judaism there was no sound Hebrew tradition. Accordingly, at the Council of Florence (1442), "Eugenius IV, with the approval of the Fathers of that assembly, declared all the books found in the Latin Bibles then in use to be inspired by the same Holy Spirit, without distinguishing them into two classes or categories" (cf. Gigot, p. 71). Though this bull of Eugenius IV did not deal with the canonicity of the apocryphal books, it did proclaim their *inspiration*. Nevertheless, down to the Council of Trent (1546) the apocryphal books possessed only inferior authority; and when men spoke of canonical Scripture in the strict sense, these were not included.

Luther, the great German Reformer of the 16th cent., marks an epoch in the history of the Christian OT canon. In translating the Scriptures into German, he gave the deuterocanonical books an intermediate position between the OT and the NT. The Lutheran Church, also, while it does not expressly define the limits of the canon, yet places the apocryphal writings by themselves as distinct and separate from Holy Scripture. This indeed was the attitude of all the early Reformers. In the Zürich Bible of 1529, as in the Genevan version in English of 1560, the apocryphal books were placed apart with special headings by themselves. Thus the early Reformers did not entirely reject the apocryphal writings, for it was not an easy task to do so in view of the usage and traditions of centuries.

Rome had vacillated long enough and now realized that something must be done. Accordingly the Council of Trent decreed at its fourth sitting (April 8, 1546) that the apocryphal books were equal in authority and canonical value to the other books of sacred Scripture; and to make this decree effective it added: "If, however, anyone receive not as sacred and canonical the said books entire with all their facts, and as they have been used to be read in the Catholic church, and as they are contained in the Old Latin Vulgate edition . . . let him be anathema." The Vatican Council of 1870 not only reiterated the decree but in addition canonized tradition.

Repeated endeavors were made during the 16th and 17th cents. to have the apocryphal books removed from the Scriptures. The Synod of Dort (1618-1619), Gomarus, Deodatus, and others sought to accomplish it, but failed. The only success achieved was in getting them separated from the truly canonical writings and grouped by themselves, as in the Gallican Confession of 1559, the Anglican Confession of 1563, and the Second Helvetic Confession of 1566. The Puritan Confession went farther, and declared that they were of a purely secular character. The various continental and English versions of the Bible then being made likewise placed them by themselves, apart from the acknowledged books, as a kind of appendix; e.g., the Zürich Bible of 1529, the French Bible of 1535, Coverdale's English translation of 1536, Matthew's of 1537, the second edition of the Great Bible in 1540, the Bishops' of 1568, and the AV of 1611. The first English version to omit them altogether was an edition of King James's Version published in 1629; but the custom of printing them by themselves, between the OT and the NT, continued until 1825, when the Edinburgh Committee of the British and Foreign Bible Society protested that the Society should no longer translate these apocryphal writings and send them to the heathen. The Society finally yielded and decided to exclude them (May 3, 1827).

Since 1850 in Europe the tendency has been to exclude the Apocrypha from the sacred Scriptures. The 1881 ERV included it, however, and it has since formed part of such modern translations as the RSV and the NEB.

See Plate 16.

Bibliography.–*EB*, I; *HDB*, III; Sch.-Herz., II; A. Jeffrey, *IB*, I, 32-45; J. Fürst, *Der Kanon des AT nach den Überlieferungen in Talmud und Midrash* (1868); F. Buhl, *Canon and Text of the OT* (1892); W. R. Smith, *OT in the Jewish Church* (2nd rev. ed. 1892); G. Wildeboer, *Origin of the Canon of the OT* (Eng. tr. 1895); W. H. Green, *General Intro. to the OT: The Canon* (1898); B. F. Westcott, *The Bible in the Christian Church* (1901); F. E. Gigot, *General Intro. to the Holy Scriptures* (3rd ed. 1903); H. R. Ryle, *Canon of the OT* (2nd ed. 1909); *IOTG* (rev. ed. 1914); W. F. Lofthouse, *Making of the OT* (1915); L. Ginzberg, *JBL*, 41 (1922), 115-136; W. R. Arnold, *JBL*, 42 (1923), 1-21; W. W. Christie, *JTS*, 26 (1924/25), 347-364; A. Jepsen, *TLZ*, 74 (1949), 65-74; J.-P. Audet, *JTS*, 1 (1950), 135-154; B. J. Roberts, *OT Text and Versions* (1951); C. H. Dodd, *The Bible Today* (1952); A. Richardson and W. Schweitzer, eds., *Biblical Authority for Today* (1952); J.-S. Bloch, *Mordecai Kaplan Jubilee Volume* (1953); P. Katz, *ZNW*, 47 (1956), 191-217; W. A. Irwin, *VT*, 7 (1957), 113-126; P. W. Skehan, *SVT*, Congress Volume (1957), 155-160; E. J. Young, "Canon of the OT," in C. F. H. Henry, ed., *Revelation and the Bible* (1958), pp. 153-168; G. L. Archer, *Survey of OT Intro.* (1964), pp. 59-72; R. K. Harrison, *Intro. to the OT* (1969), pp. 260-288.

G. L. ROBINSON
R. K. H.

CANON OF THE NT.

I. Introduction
II. Sources of Authority for Primitive Christianity
  A. Place of the OT
  B. The Spirit
  C. The Lord; The Word of the Lord
  D. The Apostles
III. The NT in the Early Church
  A. From the Primitive Church to A.D. 140
    1. Pauline Collection
    2. Early History of the Four Gospels
  B. From A.D. 140-180
    1. Place of Marcion
    2. Added Threat of Montanism
    3. Justin Martyr
    4. Other Christian Writers
  C. A.D. 180 and After
    1. Irenaeus
    2. Muratorian Fragment
    3. Tertullian and the African Church
    4. Egypt and Palestine
    5. Eusebius
    6. Some Final Landmarks
IV. Conclusion

I. Introduction.–The NT canon is that collection of twenty-seven early Christian writings which, together with the OT canon, is recognized by the Christian Church as its Holy Scripture, containing the final, authoritative deposit of divine revelation. These writings, as "canon," are normative for every aspect of the life of the Church, be it creed, worship, or its life in the world. (For derivation of the term "canon" *see* CANON OF THE OT I.A.) Although the development of the canon extends into the province of church history, for an adequate understanding of the nature of the Bible one must be clear as to the manner in which the canon assumed its present shape.

There is a considerable corpus of Christian literature covering the first three postapostolic centuries, which provides the source material for this historical study. However, the gaps in the material and the ambiguity of many of the witnessing passages — in short, our uneven knowledge of early church history — mean that there will always be individual variations in the selection and interpretation of the data.

It is obviously of particular importance to know *when* and *where* and *why* the NT canon came to be united with the OT canon as Holy Scripture. Why did just these twenty-seven books, out of a very extensive body of early Christian writings, come to be received as divinely authoritative — even though they generally make no claim of special inspiration for themselves? The first official recognition of the twenty-seven books of the present NT canon as being *the* NT canon of the Church did not occur until A.D. 367. Until then the whole process of collection and ultimate canonization was one that often saw a given book accepted in some churches and rejected in others, with verdicts often hanging in the balance or changing as time moved on. How did the Church come to recognize as divine unity just these twenty-seven writings, some of which had been now rejected, now accepted, now disputed, in the course of church history? As a matter of fact, one will not find a final satisfactory answer to this question within church history. Rather, it will be seen that the NT itself generates the insights that point to the final solution.

II. Sources of Authority for Primitive Christianity.–There were four focal points of authority in the earliest Church, all of which were ultimately important as factors cooperating to produce the substance of our present canon. These were the prior position of the OT canon, the "Word of the Lord," the place of the Spirit, and the authoritative position of the apostles.

A. Place of the OT. Prior to the existence of the Christian Church, Judaism, from whose bosom the earliest Church emerged, already possessed what was essentially a "canon" (*see* CANON OF THE OT I). Jesus Himself paved the way for the Church's acceptance of the "Jewish" canon by His constant appeal to the OT (*see* INSPIRATION). His basic affirmation was that of the OT Scripture as a whole and in its parts had come to fulfillment in Himself (see esp. Mt. 5:17; cf. Lk. 24:27; Jn. 5:39; Rom. 3:31). By continuing this "christological" interpretation of the OT the Church thereby proclaimed that it, and not Judaism, was the proper custodian and interpreter of the OT canon. For the apostle Paul the reading of the OT could be meaningful only in the light of the historical appearance of Jesus Christ (2 Cor. 3:6ff.; cf. 1 Cor. 10:1ff.).

B. The Spirit. It is perhaps conceivable that the earliest Church, possessing the basic certainty that it lived "in the Spirit," could have abandoned an appeal to the letter, i.e., to any kind of Scripture: "For the written code kills, but the Spirit gives life" (2 Cor. 3:6). However, the Church experienced the Spirit as "the Spirit of Christ" (2 Cor. 3:17b) — and it was to Christ that all the Scripture testified. Indeed, the Spirit gave to holy men of old the inspiration (see esp. 2 Pet. 1:21; 2 Tim. 3:16) that led to the production of the components of the OT canon. So understood, the age of the Spirit is rather to be seen as a catalyst for the production and recognition of new scriptures. If inspired men of old pointed forward to Messiah's coming, how much more could Christians filled with the Spirit use the written word to point back to Messiah's advent. If the old covenant had its book, how much more should the new have its own "spiritual" word (Harnack).

C. The Lord; The Word of the Lord. The ultimate authority for the primitive Church was the living authority of the risen Lord Himself. On a number of occasions Paul appeals directly to a "word of the Lord" (1 Thess. 4:15; 1 Cor. 7:10; 9:14; 11:23; cf. Acts 20:35). Similar direct appeal to the teaching of Jesus continued into the postapostolic age (cf., e.g., 1 Clem. 13:2; 46:8; Didache 8:2; 9:5; Ign. Smyrn. 3:2; Polyc. Phil. 2:3; 7:2; Barn. 5:9).

Even after A.D. 130, Papias bishop of Hierapolis expresses his preference for the living "word of the Lord": "For I supposed that things out of books did not profit me so much as the utterance of a voice which liveth and abideth" (Eusebius *HE* iii.39.4). His testimony is also valuable in that his actual recall of these living utterances reveals the rapid deterioration of the oral tradition by that time in Asia Minor. The Church as a whole did well to rely upon the written Gospels for its source of knowledge of the Lord's words, even in the period prior to Papias.

The exact historical background of the "words of the Lord" is given in the Gospels, and is very important in relation to any discussion of the canon. Jesus is clearly pictured as the teacher of a select group of disciples, who undoubtedly learned His sayings and other teachings and treasured them far more than the sayings of a Jewish rabbi were normally treasured by his disciples. For "No man ever spoke like this man!" (Jn. 7:46). It should be noted too that even the deeds of Jesus had a didactic thrust. As "acted parables" they would likewise be treasured.

The first elements of the canon's substance must be seen as the direct result of the conscious exercise of authority by Jesus. In calling disciples and teaching them, He further provided a vehicle for the preservation of this all-important core of the canon. Studies in the Gospels have demonstrated the very early existence of the Passion narratives, of the short stories about Jesus (pericopes) embedded in the Gospels, and of some kind of collection (probably written) of the sayings of Jesus. The very existence of these collected words of Jesus and collected stories about Jesus is already an index of the essential "canonicity" of the material for the collecting community.

D. The Apostles. The apostles constituted a fourth source of authority for the Church from its earliest days. The authority of the apostles was already granted to them by Jesus before Easter (cf. Mk. 3:14; 6:7). After Easter the apostles manifested this authority in their dual witness to the resurrection of Jesus Christ and to His work and words (cf. Acts 1:21ff.; 1 Cor. 9:1ff.). For this task they received the gift of the Spirit. Although it is true that most of our knowledge of the NT apostolate centers in the utterances of the unique apostle Paul, it is unlikely that the bearing of the other apostles was radically different. Paul compared himself with them as a group and as individuals (see esp. 1 Cor. 9:1ff.).

Studies on the canon have traditionally pointed to the occasional nature of Paul's letters and have observed that the great apostle hardly anticipated that his collected writings should someday be accepted by the whole Church as canon. True though this observation be, it is not the most profitable vantage point for viewing the apostle's work. Rather, it is important to observe the actual basis of the apostolic work in all its expressions.

The work of Paul may be positively characterized as consciously divinely authoritative. Paul's authoritative position constitutes the basis for his whole epistolary activity. Likewise, it is the necessary postulate for the churches' acceptance of Epistles that would otherwise be overbearing. This authority is general. Paul can adjure the Thessalonian community to read his letter "to all the brethren" (1 Thess. 5:27). Or he can direct that a letter be circulated to other communities beyond the original destination (Col. 4:16). This would tend to support the assumption that Paul would have deemed any given letter as generally authoritative. For he preached, as he affirmed, the same gospel to all (1 Cor. 4:17).

The depth of the Pauline authority is illustrated by his blunt demand that fellowship be withdrawn from those who refuse to obey the injunctions of his letter (2 Thess. 3:14; cf. v. 6). If his own command is secondary to the "word of the Lord" (cf., e.g., 1 Cor. 7:12ff.; 9:17ff.), it is nonetheless a command that may stand alongside the command of the risen Lord. Paul always acts as one whose apostolate is of God and unto Jesus Christ. So clearly does Paul hear the word of God and teach and write it, that rejecting his message is tantamount to rejecting Christ Himself (cf. Mk. 8:38) and can only result in damnation (Gal. 1:8.).

That is not to say, of course, that all apostolic writings *must* have been preserved (as authoritative and then as canonical). It seems that at least three of the Pauline letters did not find their way into the canon (cf. 1 Cor. 5:9; 2 Cor. 2:4; Col. 4:16). It has been argued with some force in recent years that 2 Cor. 6:14–7:1 corresponds to the letter Paul refers to in 1 Cor. 5:9 (*see* CORINTHIANS, FIRST IV.D), and that 2 Cor. 10–13 may represent the "painful" letter mentioned in 2 Cor. 2:4 (*see* CORINTHIANS, SECOND II.B). However, even though a work stood as authoritative, it is possible that it could be superseded or simply not included in a collection. It is obvious that the Evangelists in collecting their material — all of which was authoritative as an account of Jesus Christ — did not include all the tradition available to them. Indeed, John's Gospel affirms (21:25) that a "world" of material was not included.

Neither does the picture of the apostolate presented above adjudge in advance that all twenty-seven NT writings must be of immediate apostolic origin. Rather, the known apostolicity of a writing must have stood as a preferred, if not the sole, basis for inclusion in any authoritative collection. After this it would be, particularly in light of the Church's teaching on the Spirit, but a short step to acceptance of works deemed to be essentially apostolic in their teaching. Such writings could be the work of someone close to an apostle or be of such quality that their essential apostolicity was universally recognizable.

III. The NT in the Early Church.–It has long been an honored hypothesis among scholars that the early Church's belief in the imminent return of Christ naturally stood as an important bar to the production of Christian literature and the formation of a canon. There are two factors involved here that must be considered separately. First of all, eschatological convictions did not in fact stand in the way of literary activity. They were the basis for Paul's letters to the Thessalonians and, in part, to the Corinthians (cf. 1 Cor. 15). And there is no just reason to make an absolute division here between epistles and other literature of a different form.

Second, so far as the formation of canon is concerned, the evidences of early exchange and collection of the Pauline letters, as well as the wide dissemination of the Gospels, demonstrate that eschatology cannot be assumed as a barrier on abstract grounds alone. The most that could be affirmed is that eschatological convictions might have excluded a conscious movement toward a *canonical* collection. Clearly, however, even after eschatological tensions had abated, the process of canon formation continued in the same slowly evolving manner.

A. From the Primitive Church to A.D. 140. Before a large and scattered Church can have any canon, the individual components (the documents) must become known and disseminated. Even when authoritative documents have been gathered into collections, one cannot yet speak of a canon. Attainment of canonical status consists in the recognition (from internal value and apostolic origin)

Chester Beatty Papyrus ($\mathfrak{p}^{46}$), the earliest known manuscript of Paul's letters (*ca.* A.D. 200); shown are Rom. 16:23–He. 1:7 (left) and Eph. 1:1-11 (right). The order of the letters is unusual: Romans, Hebrews, 1 and 2 Corinthians, Ephesians, Galatians, Philippians, Colossians, and 1 Thessalonians. (University of Michigan Library)

and affirmation (by the Church acting officially) that only certain documents in use by the Church, perhaps a smaller number than those actually collected as authoritative, are absolutely unique and normative for the Church. However, the very presupposition for original dissemination and collection is that the documents in question are in some way authoritative.

1. Pauline Collection. The NT canon itself, and then the earliest postapostolic writings, already bear witness to collection of the documents. The letters of Paul were the first Christian writings to be collected, so far as historical evidence is available. Although such passages from the Pauline writings as Col. 4:16 may suggest the early practice of disseminating a given letter to various Christian communities, 2 Peter assumes a familiar, and perhaps considerable (cf. 3:16, "all") collection of Pauline letters. However, some have assigned 2 Peter a much later date than the bulk of the NT writings (*see* PETER, SECOND V). Marcion (see below) provides us with the first official or canonical list of the Pauline letters (*ca.* 140-150). Long before this time, near the close of the 1st cent., Clement bishop of Rome was acquainted with Paul's letter to the church at Corinth. After him, the letters of both Ignatius bishop of Antioch and Polycarp bishop of Smyrna attest the dissemination of the Pauline letters by the second decade of the 2nd century. In fact, Polycarp apparently was acquainted with all except three of the Pauline letters (1 Thessalonians, Philemon, Titus), and recognized them as authoritative. The combined testimony of the postapostolic fathers points to a general dissemination of the Pauline letters at the beginning of the 2nd century.

When and where was the collection of the Pauline letters first completed? Unfortunately, no finally clear answer exists. One may seek the answer, in the absence of clear evidence, along two lines. It may be supposed that Paul's authoritative position and the desire of the churches to acquire all possible Pauline Epistles led to an early exchange. The relative ease of communications in the Roman empire, the movement of Christians from province to province, and the increasing popularity and general availability of written matter all underline the probability that Paul's letters would soon have become known in, and then collected by, the Christian communities.

As an alternative to the theory of a gradual churchwide gathering of the Pauline corpus, some have believed that it is better to see the collecting as the work of an individual. Edgar J. Goodspeed, rejecting the Pauline authorship of Ephesians, has suggested that the author of this letter was likewise the collector and publisher of the Pauline corpus (*see* EPHESIANS II.A). John Knox has found in Onesimus (Philem. 9) the logical candidate for the completion of such a collection (*see* PHILEMON IV). The strength of the "individual" solution is that it is easy to suppose that any work of collecting must have been an individual work at some point. Even if it were accomplished by a church, an individual (a bishop?) must have been prominent in the execution of its publication. However, if this were the case, church history bears no early witness to such an act. Therefore, individualistic solutions remain speculative, and in some forms unacceptable.

2. Early History of the Four Gospels. Without doubt the most important early collection was that of the four canonical Gospels. However, the actual time and place of their union are unknown to us. Indeed, details concerning their early collection are by no means as clear as in the case of the Pauline letters.

The Gospels were originally intended for specific sectors of the Christian community. Many reasons exist for their creation. The crucial purpose they fulfilled was, of course, to provide the missionary Church with a fuller witness to the mission and teaching of Jesus. The limited group of original witnesses could not carry out the mission Christ had authorized without having recourse to every available means of promulgating the "gospel." Even the marvelous facility of the ancient memory was no decisive guarantee for the reliable preservation of the oral tradition. As already indicated, the presupposition of a gospel is that it contains tradition about Jesus Christ which is thereby authoritative tradition. Many heretical gospels arose within the Church, but they never occupied a place alongside the canonical four.

Although the Gospels were at first directed to particular Christian communities (or persons standing within them; cf. Lk. 1:1-4), there is evidence of their very early circulation. This is more remarkable than the circulation of the Pauline letters, considering the similarity of their content. Of course, any account of the Lord's mission would be eagerly sought after. Study of the structure of the Synoptic Gospels points to the dependence of Matthew and Luke upon Mark's Gospel. And the compiler of the longer ending of Mark apparently used tradition from the other three Gospels.

There are some evidences of the authoritative stature of the four Gospels in the period prior to A.D. 140. Notable are several instances where a saying of Jesus is introduced with the formula normally assigned to OT quotations in the NT. Barn. 4:14 is a probable quotation of Mt. 22:14: "As it stands written, 'Many are called, but few are chosen.' " 2 Clem. 2:4 is a clear reference to Mt. 9:13: "Another scripture says, 'I came not to call the righteous, but sinners.' " One may also note 2 Clem. 14:1, which speaks of "the Scripture which says, 'My house became a den of thieves' " (cf. Mk. 11:17). By and large it is not until the next main period that the collection of four Gospels came to be recognized as possessing full canonical stature.

B. From A.D. 140 to 180. The dates A.D. 140-180 mark off a second main period in the development of the canon. In this period a number of leading personalities in the Church provide a fuller and more concrete witness to the ongoing development of the canon. Their testimony is especially valuable because of their acquaintance with widely scattered areas of the Church in the Roman empire.

1. Place of Marcion. At the beginning of this period stands one whose role in the formation of the canon is unique. Marcion of Sinope in Pontus (Asia Minor) came to Rome in A.D. 139, and by 144 he was expelled from that church because of his gnostic-tinged heretical views. In conjunction with his rejection of the OT as the product of a God inferior to the God of Jesus (the Christian God), Marcion himself established a distinctively "Christian" canon. This is the first list or canon of exclusively Christian scriptures of which we have any knowledge. Of particular importance was the bipartite formal structure of this hyper-Paulinistic canon. Marcion himself designated the two parts as "gospel" and "apostle" (Gk. *euangélion, apóstolos*). Luke merited inclusion in this canon — the sole Gospel included — because of his association with Paul; and the apostolic section was limited to ten Pauline Epistles (the Pastorals are missing). Marcion purged from Luke's Gospel any passages incompatible with his own doctrine, and in the apostolic section he gave Galatians a leading position because of its anti-Judaizing thrust.

The work of Marcion, though heretical, is important because it represents a direct, unique attempt by an *individual* to establish a Christian canon. Many scholars (esp. Harnack) are of the opinion that it was in conscious reaction to the work of this very influential heretic (Marcionitic churches sprang up in alarming number from East to West) that the Church established the basic dimensions of the present canon. It is questionable, however, whether Marcion's role was anything more than catalytic. For the Church did not immediately counter with an orthodox canon. In fact, it is not until the Muratorian Canon (see III.C.2 below) of a half-century later that we actually find an official list produced for the Christian community. Moreover, prior to Marcion the Gospels were already accepted as Scriptures, and the letters of Paul had long since been available in collected (and for some, authoritative) form. In her struggle with Marcion, the Church, unlike Marcion, did not seek to satisfy her immediate need by sudden reduction and fixation. Rather, the recognition of many non-Pauline writings continued to remain an open question. The production of the Muratorian Canon, both as and when it appeared, is entirely conceivable had Marcion never existed. At the most, Marcion's canon may have hastened the day when the Church officially accorded the apostolic writings the same full authority as the four Gospels.

2. Added Threat of Montanism. Shortly after Marcion's removal from the Church at Rome, a new heresy sprang up in Asia Minor and worked its way westward. Montanus, a converted pagan priest, and his prophetess-disciples Prisca and Maximilla claimed to be the bearers of a new divine revelation. This tendency to expand the "canon," coupled with Marcion's narrowing of what was acceptable, immediately preceded the first efforts of the Church to fix the canon officially.

3. Justin Martyr. Justin Martyr, an orthodox contemporary of Marcion, wrote his famous *Apology* and *Dialogue with Trypho* in Rome between 150 and 160. Here, Justin reports that the Church in its Sunday worship reads "the memoirs of the apostles or the prophetic writings" (*Apol.* i.67.3). These "memoirs" are the "Gospels" (*Dial.* 66.3, the first instance in which the term "Gospel" clearly designates a book). Although Justin surely knew all four Gospels, there is no absolutely clear instance of a citation from John's Gospel in his works (but see *Apol.* i.61.4; *Dial.* 63; 88). That his pupil Tatian later compiled the famous *Diatessaron,* using all four Gospels (but only the four), is some evidence of a similar regard by Justin. While other NT writings do not appear as Scripture in Justin, he does appeal to the Apocalypse as authoritative. He also knows the letters of Paul, as well as Hebrews and Acts.

4. Other Christian Writers. Other significant testimony appears in this period. Melito of Sardis (prior to 180) speaks of the "books of the Old Covenant"; these presuppose "books of the New Covenant" (likewise authoritative) as a counterpart. Athenagoras of Athens (also prior to 180), in his treatise on the resurrection, appeals to the work of Paul (1 Cor. 15) as if it were canonical. The Scillitan Martyrs (180) in their trial prior to being sentenced to death by the Carthaginian proconsul, answered that the books they were treasuring were "the books and Epistles of Paul a just man." If it be supposed that the "books" are the OT Scriptures and the Gospels, then it would appear that the Pauline Epistles had not quite attained the full status of Scripture, at least in that locality.

C. A.D. 180 and After. From this time on there is an

entirely new situation. Lists of accepted books appear. The concreteness of the canon is such that it can become an object of theological reflection. Leading personalities from East to West attest a fuller (but not complete) and generally uniform canon.

1. Irenaeus. In his principal work, *Against Heresies,* Irenaeus gives a comprehensive picture of the situation that must have prevailed in both Rome and south Gaul from A.D. 180. If one assumes his recognition of Philemon (not cited because of its brevity), then Irenaeus cites twenty-two writings as canonical. These are the Gospels, Acts, thirteen Pauline Epistles, 1 Peter, 1 and 2 John of the Catholic Epistles, and the Apocalypse. Although he knew Hebrews, in keeping with the current practice of the Western Church he did not accord it full recognition. His citation of the Shepherd of Hermas with the formula "Scripture says" is noteworthy in that it shows that Christian writings other than our canonical twenty-seven were often accepted as Scripture during this period.

2. Muratorian Fragment. The Muratorian Fragment is named after its discoverer, the Italian historian Muratori, who published it in 1740. Written in barbarous Latin, the record is important because it contains a list of books which are for "the whole Church" (lines 55ff.) and which are deemed "apostolic" (line 80), and may therefore be "publicly read in the Church" (lines 77, 73). The Fragment also gives details concerning the author, destination, occasion, and purpose of the books listed. Although in fragmentary condition, it is clear that it listed twenty-two of the present twenty-seven canonical books, as well as the Apocalypse of Peter; the writer of the Fragment notes that many object to the public use of this book in the Church. Not included in the list are Hebrews, 1 and 2 Peter, 3 John, and James. The author's lengthy argument against the inclusion of the Shepherd of Hermas indicates that the work was in fact accorded something approximating canonical status by some (cf. Irenaeus, above). It has been suggested that Hippolytus, an antipope in Rome after 217, was the author of the Fragment. In the known writings of Hippolytus, he includes at least twenty-one books as having canonical status. Unlike the Fragment, he includes 1 and 2 Peter, but omits Philemon, 2 John, and Jude.

3. Tertullian and the African Church. Tertullian also bears witness to a rather clearly fixed canon, which he divides into an evangelical and an apostolic "instrument." For him also a writing must be by an apostle or composed under apostolic authority in order to be acceptable. His canon of twenty-two books includes the four Gospels, Acts, thirteen Pauline Epistles, 1 Peter, John, Jude, and Revelation.

4. Egypt and Palestine. Clement of Alexandria and his illustrious successor in the Alexandrian catechetical school, Origen, give the earliest extensive testimony to the progress of the canon in the Eastern area of the empire. Clement apparently knew and used all twenty-seven books of the present NT canon, as well as a number of other Christian writings which he held to be inspired in some instances. He follows the general course of the Church in according canonical status to only the four Gospels.

We can thank Origen (185-255?) for his particular concern to present the status of the canon in the many churches with which he was acquainted. His influential position meant that his findings and own evaluation of them were to influence the Church in the following generations. He notes three classes of "Scripture." The first consists of those books which are not subject to dispute or are "acknowledged." These were the four Gospels, thirteen Pauline letters, 1 Peter, 1 John, Acts, and Revelation. Those which were disputed constituted the second class: 2 Peter, 2 and 3 John, Hebrews, James, and Jude. The position of the Shepherd of Hermas, Barnabas, and the Didache was authoritative, but it is doubtful whether he recognized any of the three as possessing the full canonical status of the first class. In the third group he sets books that are "false." These were the heretical gospels still being circulated.

5. Eusebius. The great church historian Eusebius of Caesarea (*ca.* 260-340) conducted a similar investigation, and he likewise divided the books into three categories (acknowledged, disputed, heretical). His "acknowledged" category differs from Origen's in that Hebrews is included (as Pauline — though it is noted that the church at Rome does not accept it) and Revelation is set forth as a book that is not fully accepted by all. The second class is really divided into two groups, those whose canonicity is disputed, and those which are spurious. Disputed are James, Jude, 2 Peter, and 2 and 3 John. Among the spurious writings are the Didache, Barnabas, and the Shepherd of Hermas. The "acknowledged" books and the "disputed" writings of the second class actually constitute the twenty-seven books of the present canon. Heretical gospels and heretical acts made up the third class of writings.

6. Some Final Landmarks. The extant works of the fathers provide a rich store of testimony to the status of the canon in the late 3rd and 4th centuries. The various national churches, as time passed, came to occupy increasingly similar points of view. (However, the Syrian Church long constituted an exception to this general agreement.) Most significant for us is the thirty-ninth Easter letter (367) of the great Alexandrian theologian Athanasius. Here for the first time stands a list in which the twenty-seven books of the present NT canon are declared to be the canonical collection, to which nothing is to be added, from which nothing may be taken away. The decree undoubtedly was an influential instrument for fixing opinion in the Eastern Church. Jerome's translation of the Greek Scripture into Latin at the request of the Roman bishop Damasus was likewise a notable landmark; in it (the present Vulgate) are included the canonical twenty-seven books. In Africa the Third Council of Carthage (397), of which Augustine was an influential member, likewise acknowledged the present twenty-seven books as the canon. Thus, we see at approximately the same time in churches throughout the empire a unified decision fixing the limits and contents of the canon. Their common action is a testimony both to the varied history of the canonical books until that time and to the Church's recognition that it could best serve Christ through the instrument of a Word in all parts of which the whole Church could hear Christ speaking.

IV. Conclusion.–The course of church history, so far as the NT canon is concerned, seems to render problematic the belief of the Protestant Church that here in just these twenty-seven books is the final and authoritative Word of God. Indeed, the general unanimity reached at the end of the 4th cent. has been clouded time and again by collective and individual questioning of the canon. No less a person than Martin Luther relegated certain books (Hebrews, James, Jude, Revelation) to a distinctly inferior place at the end of his German translation of the NT. Voices have been raised, and are being raised, that suggest that the NT canon should be reopened for church evaluation. Is the Protestant Church to accept the (apparent) legacy of historical development or to call this history into question?

In answer, we can only point again to the christological foundation of the canon. Jesus Christ Himself chose those who should bear authoritative witness to His Word, a Word they were privileged to hear as no other generation. From the first the apostle emerges as one who makes the high claim to utter the authoritative Word of God. The earliest collections were of apostolic writings (Paul's letters). But the Gospels are most significant for our answer. Here we have what the Church clearly regarded as the apostolic testimony — and yet the Church had no qualms about attributing this testimony to Evangelists who were not themselves apostles (i.e., Mark and Luke). No doubt the primitive Church possessed a similar conviction regarding Epistles whose authorship is not always clearly discernible today.

The earliest Church has paved the way for us by adopting an elastic measure or norm of apostolicity. The apostolicity of the NT canon in its entirety cannot be historically proved. The Christian can only believe that this history, set in motion by the earthly Lord, has been superintended by the risen Lord, who will not lead His Church into error. We believe that He has built His Church upon this Scripture, and that all future development must spring from the grateful obedience exercised by a Church that may hear its Lord speak in the OT and the NT canon.

Bibliography.–W. Barclay, *Making of the Bible* (1961); F. F. Bruce, *Tradition: Old and New* (1970); H. von Campenhausen, *Tradition and Life in the Church* (1968); O. Cullmann, "The Plurality of the Gospels as a Theological Problem in Antiquity" and "The Tradition: The Exegetical, Historical and Theological Problem," Eng. tr. in A. J. B. Higgins, ed., *The Early Church* (1956); F. V. Filson, *Which Books Belong in the Bible?* (1957); B. Gerhardsson, *Tradition and Transmission in Early Christianity* (1964); E. J. Goodspeed, *Formation of the NT* (1926); A. Harnack, *Origin of the NT* (1925); C. F. D. Moule, *Birth of the NT* (1962); J. A. T. Robinson, *Can We Trust The NT?* (1977); A. Souter, *Text and Canon of the NT* (2nd rev. ed. 1960); B. F. Westcott, *General Survey of the History of the Canon of the NT* (7th ed. 1896); T. Zahn, *Geschichte des NT Kanons* (1888-1892); *Grundriss der Geschichte des NT Kanons* (2nd ed. 1904). The basic works of Westcott and Zahn are especially valuable for advanced work on the canon. The following work contains some of the important primary texts for the study of canon history: E. Preuschen, *Analecta. Kürzere Texte zur Geschichte der alten Kirche und des Kanons*, II; *Zur Kanongeschichte* (2nd ed. 1910).

R. P. MEYE

CANOPY [Heb. *sukkâ*] (2 S. 22:12; Ps. 18:11); AV PAVILION(S); [*'āḇ*] (1 K. 7:6; Ezk. 41:25); AV THICK BEAM, PLANKS; NEB CORNICE; [*ḥuppâ*] (Isa. 4:5); AV DEFENCE; NEB COVERING; [Gk. *kōnōpeíon*] (Jth. 10:21; 13:9, 15; 16:19); NEB MOSQUITO-NET, NET; **ROYAL CANOPY** [Heb. *šaprîr*] (Jer. 43:10); AV ROYAL PAVILION; NEB CANOPY. Several translation difficulties are involved in the OT passages. In 2 S. 22:12 and the closely parallel Ps. 18:11, it is clear that *sukkâ* (the plural in the MT of 2 S. 22:12 is properly emended to a singular), literally "booth," designates some kind of covering, but it is not clear whether that covering is constituted by the darkness (2 Samuel, AV, RSV) or by what follows: in the NEB of both passages, "dense vapour"; in Ps. 18, AV, "dark waters and thick clouds of the skies," RSV "thick clouds dark with water." See comms. *in loc.*

The Heb. *'āḇ* in 1 K. 7:6 describes a part of the Hall of Pillars in Solomon's palace, and *'āḇ 'ēṣ* in Ezk. 41:25 is a wooden piece in front of or over the vestibule of the nave in Ezekiel's vision of the restored temple; "cornice" is a likely translation. The *ḥuppâ* of Isa. 4:5 is a protective cover. In Jth. 10:21, etc., the Gk. *kōnōpeíon* over the bed of Holofernes may be either a mosquito net or a decorative canopy.

In Jer. 43:10 the Heb. *šaprîr*, perhaps related to an Assyrian word for "spread out," is probably a large cloth canopy, or possibly a royal carpet. J. W. D. H.

CANTICLES [Heb. *šîr haššîrîm*–'the song of songs'; Gk. *aísma asmátōn*; Lat. *canticum canticorum*]; AV, RSV, SONG OF SOLOMON; NEB SONG OF SONGS. The book that follows Ecclesiastes in the Roman Catholic and Protestant Bibles. The name Canticles comes from the Latin. The book is the first of the Five Scrolls, and is read at Passover.

I. Title
II. Methods of Interpretation
  A. Allegorical
  B. Dramatic
  C. Liturgical
  D. Lyrical
III. Canonical Status
IV. Author and Date
V. Language and Genre
VI. Theological Significance

I. Title.–The Hebrew title is "the best (or most beautiful) song which is Solomon's," the expression "Song of Songs" (Heb. *šîr haššîrîm*) being a superlative. The phrase *'ᵃšer lišlōmōh* can be translated in different ways: "of Solomon"; "by Solomon"; "to Solomon"; "for Solomon." In any event, the phrase was taken early to refer to Solomonic authorship. It is clear that the title is from a later hand, for *'ᵃšer* is used only here while the rest of the book uses the relative particle *šᵉ-*.

II. Methods of Interpretation.–As G. Fohrer has remarked, "The history of interpretation of the Song of Songs is no feather in the cap of biblical exegesis" (*Intro. to the OT* [Eng. tr. 1968], p. 300). Historically, interpretations have fallen into four categories: allegorical, liturgical, dramatic, lyrical.

A. Allegorical. The allegorical interpretation has been the dominant one in Judaism and Christianity for most of the last two millennia. The earliest possible evidence for this interpretation is 2 Esd. 5:24ff.; 7:26, in which the dove, lily, and bride as figures for the chosen people may reflect the influence of Cant. 2:9; 6:9. However, other figures that do not come from Canticles (vine, river, sheep) are used in 2 Esd. 5:24ff., and the bride figure in 7:26 need not come from Canticles. The Talmud (*Abodah Zarah* 29a) and the Targum to Canticles treat the book as an allegory that symbolically depicts the love between God and Israel. This view was held by Akiba, Saadya, Rashi, and Ibn Ezra. As Gerleman (pp. 141f.) has mentioned, all clear examples of the allegorical interpretation presuppose the canonical status of the book.

The Church took over the allegorical interpretation, substituting Christ for God, and the Church for Israel. The earliest evidence for this is in Hippolytus, but Origen wrote in more detail, even denying the validity of any other interpretation. However, the "bride" has been seen by some as other than the Church: the individual believer, the human soul, all mankind, the Virgin Mary. Luther took the bride to be symbolic of the state. The allegorical interpretation is still used by some Roman Catholic scholars, and is a teaching of their Church.

Some Scripture passages could be taken to justify allegorical interpretation. The figure of the bride is used for Israel in Hosea and Ezekiel, and for the Church in Rev. 21f. Metaphor, however, is not allegory. Neither does Canticles have to do with prophetic speech or apocalyptic. Moreover, there are the same difficulties as raised by the allegorizing of any other book of

Scripture: (1) there is no hint that Canticles understands itself as allegory; (2) allegorizing is the result either of the interpreter's failure to find what he seeks in the literal understanding of the text, or his finding elements that may be offensive or embarrassing. In the first case, the allegorical interpreter sees profound hidden spiritual truths, in the second he covers what he regards as embarrassments. Allegorizing is therefore always highly subjective, often resulting in "eisegesis."

The view that Canticles was allegorized to allow it entrance into the canon is not germane if, as seems likely, allegorizing presupposes the canonical status of the book (Gottwald, pp. 421f.).

B. Dramatic. There are marginal glosses in the Sinaiticus and Alexandrinus LXX MSS, indicating speaker and addressee. While this need not indicate that the book was understood as a drama, but merely that the identities of the speaker and addressee are sometimes unclear, there have been dramatic interpretations, which have taken two basic forms. One sees in the book two characters (Solomon and the Shulammite [6:13; LXX Shunammite]), plus a chorus, the "daughters of Jerusalem." The other view sees an additional character, the girl's lover, a shepherd. In the two-character interpretation, the loving couple, after being separated, are finally reunited. The drama praises marital love. According to the three-character view, the girl rejects Solomon's attempts to win her and remains true to her pastoral swain. Here the lesson is loyalty: love triumphs over wealth and luxury.

The difficulties with the dramatic interpretation are several: (1) there is no other evidence of drama in ancient Hebrew literature; (2) there is no movement, development, or plot in the present form of Canticles, so the parts of the book must be rearranged; (3) according to the three-character interpretation, Solomon is portrayed as the "villain," hardly conducive to acceptance by Judeans, nor to an explanation of the title. In sum, the dramatic interpretation creates more problems than it solves.

C. Liturgical. This interpretation maintains that Canticles is a survival of an old originally pre-Israelite New Year Festival liturgy. As such, it contains remnants of an old fertility myth, which depicts the male deity (*dôḏ*) and his divine consort. His disappearance and her search for him are paralleled in Mesopotamian and Canaanite mythology. The search culminates in reunion and the *hierós gámos* (sacred marriage), which ensures the life of the earth for another year. The prophetic use of the marriage metaphor to depict the relationship of Yahweh and Israel gives early evidence for the existence of this theology in an Israelite context. Although the book became secularized, it showed its cultic origins by its use in the festivals of *Maṣṣoṯ* (Unleavened Bread) and *Sukkoṯ* (Booths). Also liturgical is its use in the festivities in the vineyards on the 15th of Ab and the Day of Atonement (Mish. *Taanith* iv.8). It was this liturgical usage that provided the basis for canonization.

In favor of this interpretation is the fact that Baal, the Canaanite fertility-god, is described as a shepherd in the Râs Shamrah mythological texts, which also contain explicit erotic language, including a description of Baal's glorious appearance (L. Fisher and F. B. Knutson, *JNES*, 28 [1969], 157-167).

However, there are many problems with the liturgical interpretation: (1) it is really a type of allegorical exegesis; (2) while Israelite folk religion was undoubtedly syncretistic, there is little evidence that a Canaanite/Israelite fertility festival, complete with *hierós gámos*, ever reached a significant degree of acceptance in Israel; (3) the prophetic use of the marriage metaphor is more easily seen as coming from the sphere of the family rather than the cult, especially since its origin is found in Hosea, no friend of the Baal cult; (4) as a whole, the book gives a definite impression of secularity. Love songs can be used in the cult — the Râs Shamrah texts show that — but they do not originate there.

D. Lyrical. According to this view, Canticles is a collection of love songs and epithalamia (wedding songs praising the bride and sometimes also the groom). The first theologian to take this position was Theodore of Mopsuestia. Some anonymous medieval Jewish commentators, as well as a few men in the Reformation period, called the book secular; thus Sebastian Castellio incurred the wrath of Calvin. Herder in 1778 maintained that Canticles was folk poetry.

The lyrical interpretation is the most favored among scholars today. In the end of the 19th cent. Budde's commentary used the writings of J. G. Wetzstein (*Zeitschrift für Ethnologie,* 5 [1873], 270-302), who had observed wedding festivities of Syrian peasants. In these festivities, which last for a week, the bride and groom play the role of king and queen. The villagers sing songs before them, including the *waṣf,* a description of the physical beauty of the bride. Budde maintained that the origin of Canticles was to be found in a similar situation in Israel.

The primary problem with the wedding-cycle interpretation is that nothing in Canticles suggests the couple was married, with the exception of 3:9-11, a reference to the wedding day of Solomon. What is more likely is that love songs were used in wedding celebrations. It is possible, as some suggest, that there are genuine epithalamia in the book; but the rest of the texts are love songs. This interpretation has one great advantage — one need not contort the text; it is understood literally, i.e., as lyrical poetry.

III. Canonical Status.–There are several opinions on why Canticles was accepted into the canon. Interestingly, the raising of this issue presupposes a specific understanding of the book, i.e., it seems to be a collection of love and wedding songs, and therefore its place in the canon requires justification. Such issues never arise with regard to, e.g., Genesis or Isaiah.

One view is that the book's association with Solomon's name earned it a place in the canon. However, while this may have helped, it was insufficient in itself, for Wisdom of Solomon is not canonical. Other factors must have been involved.

Another view is that the book won acceptance on the basis of an allegorical interpretation. This assumes that the liturgical or lyrical understanding would not, in the opinion of the rabbis, warrant its inclusion in the canon. Against this is the fact that the earliest clear evidence for an allegorical interpretation is in the period after Jamnia (i.e., after *ca.* A.D. 90). Gottwald is probably correct in suggesting that canonical status preceded allegorizing.

A third position is based on the liturgical interpretation, i.e., the book was judged canonical because of its association with the feasts of *Maṣṣoṯ* and *Sukkoṯ*. Against this is the fact that it is not clear that the book was associated with these feasts in the period before Jamnia.

None of the views need be exclusive. Nor should other factors be neglected, e.g., the supposed age of the book and its popularity. The references to Solomon were likely taken as evidence of the age of the book. References to quotations from the book by the people, in different contexts, suggest its popularity (Mish. *Taanith* iv.8; Tosephta *Sanhedrin* xii.10). In the 2nd cent. the canonical status was debated, and championed by Akiba (Mish. *Yadaim* iii.5). Solomonic authorship was not universally believed (T.B. *Baba Bathra* 15a, in which Rav holds Hezekiah and his "party" to be the authors). As the discussions above suggest, the question of canonicity cannot be considered apart from that of interpretation. If, as seems likely, the lyrical interpretation was prevalent at the time of Jamnia, then several factors were significant in securing its acceptance. One was Solomonic authorship, and related to this, antiquity. Another was its popularity. Third, as Gerleman points out, the book is secular, i.e., it desacralizes sex, and thus might serve as an argument against fertility cults. Fourth, the book was perhaps also seen as a corrective to asceticism.

IV. Author and Date.–The traditional view has ascribed authorship to Solomon, based on the title. As we have seen, the title need not indicate Solomonic authorship. Apart from the title, Solomon's name occurs six times (1:5; 3:7, 9, 11; 8:11f.). Of these, 1:5 and 8:11f. are references to the wealth of Solomon. The other references are in the passage describing Solomon's procession and his "palanquin," and have little to do with the rest of the book.

Thus, besides the title, no passages in the book specifically suggest Solomonic authorship. This notion, or the dedication of the book to Solomon, may have resulted from a recognition of the units of which the book consists — songs. Songs were associated with wisdom. Gordis has drawn attention to Jer. 9:17 (MT 16), where the women who sing funeral dirges are called "wise ones" (Heb. *ḥ^{a}ḵāmôṯ*, RSV "skillful women"). He also notes 1 K. 4:31 (MT 5:11), where Solomon is said to be wiser than Ethan and Heman, who were temple singers. Also important here is 1 K. 4:32 (5:12): "He also uttered three thousand proverbs, and his songs were a thousand and five." Thus, the key to the association of the book with Solomon: the association of songs of wisdom, wisdom with Solomon, and of Solomon with songs. Here then, we have an analogy to Proverbs; probably the collecting and editing of the songs culminated in wisdom circles, which attributed the book to the patron of wisdom, Solomon.

Dating the book is more difficult. Many scholars have seen a date in the postexilic or even Hellenistic period reflected in the use of Aramaisms (1:6, 17; 2:11; 7:2; etc.) and foreign loanwords. "Nard" (1:12; 4:13f.) and "garden" (4:13, Heb. *pardēs*) are Persian, and "palanquin" (3:9, Heb. *'appiryôn*) is Greek. Another argument for lateness is the use of the relative particle *š^e*-. Others have attempted to counter this view. The Aramaisms reflect a northern dialect, not necessarily indicative of lateness. The loanwords are not Persian and Greek, but Sanskrit (Gerleman sees "palanquin" as Egyptian), i.e., coming from India (possible in Solomon's time). Gerleman suggests that use of foreign loanwords is characteristic of formal lyric poetry, and refers to Egyptian love poetry as an analogy (pp. 141f.). As for *š^e*-, the word occurs elsewhere in preexilic passages.

The arguments for lateness have greater weight. Without putting any interpretation on the Aramaisms, Persian and Greek loanwords are found in other late books in the OT, so their occurrence in Canticles should not be considered exceptional. Probably the poet(s) used these loanwords without recognizing them as such; they had become part of the Hebrew vocabulary. The relative particle *š^e*- does occur in preexilic passages; but of a total of 139 occurrences in the OT, 32 are in Canticles and 68 in Ecclesiastes; its use here represents a late development.

Another argument for an early date is the spirit expressed in the poems — a graphic appreciation of the sexual. Gerleman suggests this would be most at home in the period of "Solomonic humanism." This may be valid, but we have insufficient evidence about the Israelite world view to suggest that graphic sensual language was appreciated only in the Solomonic period. The people enjoyed it still in the time of Akiba.

Some of the songs may very well be early, but others seem to be postexilic. The songs were probably collected and edited in the Hellenistic period.

V. Language and Genre.–The language of Canticles is unique in the Hebrew Bible — the book is full of hapax legomena and rare words, including foreign loanwords, and several Aramaic words. Meek suggests that the language of Canticles represents a dialect. Even the casual reader is impressed by the striking quality of the language: sensitive, sometimes bold, sometimes subtle, sensuous, powerful. Some have seen Canticles as folk poetry: repetitious, disorderly, simple, naive, yet with "freshness and charm" (Meek). Others view the book as formal lyric poetry. Gordis sees both kinds of poetry in the book.

The book is not a unity. It is rather a collection of songs, the number of which is debated (some have seen more than thirty). Various geographical locations are mentioned, most in the north (Damascus, Lebanon, Carmel, Tirzah, etc.,), but also some in the south (Jerusalem, En-Gedi). The songs vary considerably in structure and content: speeches by each of the lovers to the other, speeches by the girl to the "daughters of Jerusalem" and their replies, speeches with no hearer indicated, a "dream narrative," a narrative poem about Solomon, etc. Some passages praise the physical appearance of the loved one, others are general observations on love: its power, its sweetness, its pain, etc. If "love song" is a genre, it is clear that there are several sub-types within this genre. Besides the "love-songs," 3:6-11 has been seen by many interpreters as an epithalamium.

On the other hand, even though the book is a collection, there are unifying factors. One is the theme — love. Another is provided by the repetition of phrases and verses: "I adjure you, O daughters of Jerusalem . . ." (2:7; 3:5; 5:8; 8:4); "whom my soul loves" (1:7; 3:1-4); "the day breathes" (2:17; 4:6); "your hair is like a flock of goats" (4:1f.; 6:5f.); "your eyes are doves" (1:15; 4:1). A third factor is the vocabulary. A number of words found rarely or not at all in the Bible outside of Canticles occur in different songs within the book, e.g., "henna" (1:14; 4:13; 7:12); "choicest" (fruits) (4:13, 16; 7:13); "locks" (of hair) (5:2, 11), etc. No doubt, some of this consistency in vocabulary is due to the subject matter. Also, the book is consistent in its use of the relative particle *š^e*-.

VI. Theological Significance.–It is noteworthy that the 20th cent. is the first one since the pre-Christian era in which the understanding of Canticles as love songs and epithalamia has gained general acceptance. The theological significance of Canticles for this period is perhaps similar to what it was in the period before canonization. In Canticles, the songs are resolutely secular — there is no place for the divinization of sex or fertility. On the other hand, the physical, sensual, even erotic element in life is neither evil nor a "lower" aspect of human beings. It is a gift of God. This book's place in the Scriptures frustrates any attempt to denigrate the sensual aspect of human life. The poems of Canticles express in artistic, colorful, joyful terms what is expressed in the creation story — "male and female he created them. . . . and it was very good."

Bibliography.–R. Gordis, *Song of Songs* (1954); L. Waterman, *Song of Songs* (1948); T. J. Meek, *IB*, V, 91-98; *IDB*, IV, *s.v.* "Song of Songs" (N. K. Gottwald); G. Gerleman, *Das Hohelied,*

II (*BKAT*, 18, 1965); M. H. Pope, *Song of Songs* (*AB*, 1977); W. H. Schoff, ed., *Song of Songs: A Symposium* (1924); H. H. Rowley, *Servant of the Lord and other Essays on the OT* (1952), pp. 187-234; R. N. Soulen, *JBL*, 86 (1967), 183-190.

F. B. KNUTSON

CAPER-BUD [Heb. *'ᵃḇiyyonâ*; Gk. *kápparis*] (Eccl. 12:5, NEB); AV, RSV, DESIRE. The greenish bud or berry of the caper, a low Mediterranean shrub (*Capparis sicula* Duham.). The general nature of the common caper accords well with a picture of human senility. The plant usually spreads itself weakly over the ground, and has large white flowers reminiscent of hoary heads. The fruit hangs down on long stalks, suggesting the drooping figure of an aged man. The berries, prized for many centuries as a condiment, excite hunger and thirst, thus stimulating the appetite, which in old age tends to diminish through degeneration of the taste buds. In antiquity the caperberry was prized as a sexual stimulant. R. K. H.

CAPERNAUM kə-pûr'nə-um [Gk. *Kapernaoum*]. The most important city on the northern shore of the Sea of Galilee. It was here that Jesus established His headquarters for the major part of His public ministry (Mt. 4:13). In Mt. 9:1 Capernaum is called "his own city." At least three of Jesus' disciples came from there. Peter and Andrew, originally from Bethsaida (Jn. 1:44), had apparently moved to Capernaum (Mk. 1:29). It was from a tax office in the same city that Matthew rose to follow Jesus (Mt. 9:9). Many miracles were performed in and around Capernaum: e.g., the paralyzed servant of the centurion was healed (Mt. 8:5-13); a paralytic, carried to Jesus by four friends and let down through the roof, picked up his bed and walked (Mk. 2:1-12); and Peter's mother-in-law was cured of a fever (Mk. 1:29-31).

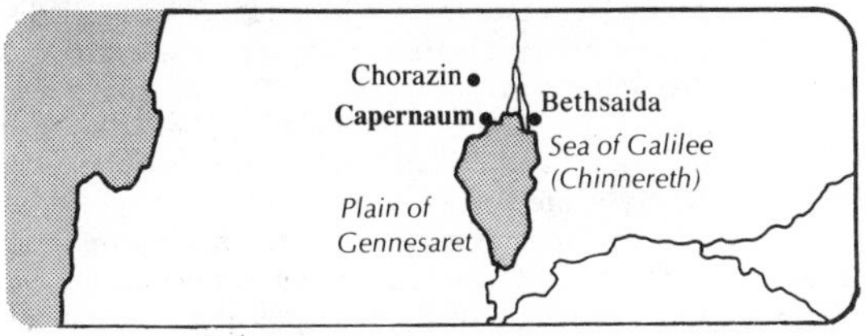

While we know Capernaum as an important place in Jesus' Galilean ministry, its larger significance is indicated by the presence of a Roman centurion and detachment of troops (Mt. 8:5-9), a customs station (Mt. 9:9), and a high officer of the king (Jn. 4:46). That Capernaum is not mentioned in the OT is no argument against its prominence at a later period, since it may have been settled after the Captivity. Its importance is reflected in Jesus' pronouncement of doom: "And you, Capernaum, will you be exalted to heaven? You shall be brought down to Hades" (Mt. 11:23).

There is no certain evidence that the name bears any relationship to the prophet Nahum, although an inscription found near the mouth of the Yarmuk refers to *Kephar Nahum,* "the village of Nahum."

The question of exact location has been a matter of prolonged discussion. Mt. 4:13 identifies the site as "Capernaum by the sea" and Jn. 6:16-24 with Mk. 6:53 places it in or near the well-known plain of Gennesaret. Only two sites can lay serious claim to the identification: Khan Minyeh 5 mi. (8 km.) W of the Jordan River on the northeast edge of the plain of Gennesaret, and Tell Ḥûm about 2.5 mi. (4 km.) NE of Khan Minyeh. Khan Minyeh lies inland along the great caravan road leading N at the junction of the eastern road heading toward Bethsaida Julias. Tell Ḥûm is immediately adjacent to the sea.

In an earlier period most scholars favored Khan Minyeh. Among the various reasons proposed were: (1) The account of the disciples and Jesus crossing the Sea of Galilee to Capernaum (Jn. 6:16-24) and coming to shore in Gennesaret (Mt. 14:34) favors Khan Minyeh. (2) Its tollhouse (Mk. 2:14) would be near the great trade route from Damascus to Egypt so as to collect revenue from the passing caravans. (3) Josephus tells us that the plain of Gennesaret was watered by the fountain of Capernaum (*BJ* iii.10.8), and this must surely be the fountains at eṭ-Ṭâbghah 0.5 mi. (0.8 km.) E of Khan Minyeh. Water from this source was led by an aqueduct around a rock cliff and into the plain at Minyeh. (4) Remains of an ancient city have been discovered between the site and the sea. (5) It is possible to find the name Minyeh in the designation of Christians as *Minim,* a group the Talmud associated with Capernaum.

More recently scholars have identified Capernaum with the ruins at Tell Ḥûm. Among the more important reasons are: (1) The extensive ruins at Tell Ḥûm are demonstrably ancient, with pottery from the Roman period, while the excavations at Khan Minyeh show it to be an Arab site of a much later date. (2) The name Tell Ḥûm may well be a corruption of Tankhum, a Jewish rabbi who is said to have been buried there. Less convincing is the etymology that sees *Tell* as the designation of *Kephar* after its fall, and *Ḥûm* as all that remains of the name Nahum. (3) The customs house would be appropriate at Tell Ḥûm as a place of levying taxes on the produce of the area as well as for collecting revenue from the traffic that moved eastward along the road to Bethsaida Julias. (4) Although the fountain of Capernaum was closer to Khan Minyeh, it was connected topographically to Tell Ḥûm. As each town in antiquity had its "territory," that of Capernaum would be sufficiently large to include either or both of the sites. (5) Eusebius' *Onomasticon* (a fourth-century work on biblical topography) places Chorazin 2 mi. (3 km.) from Capernaum. If Chorazin is best identified with Kerâzeh, Tell Ḥûm must be Capernaum. (6) The pilgrim Theodosius (*ca.* A.D. 530) coming from the west arrived at the spring *before* he came to Capernaum. This would be far less likely if the city were situated at Khan Minyeh.

The Franciscans procured the site at Tell Ḥûm in 1894. To prevent continuous pillaging of the ruins for building stones, they covered the area with earth. Partially excavated, it has revealed a wealth of material. One of the

Ruins of the Capernaum synagogue, a basilica with a gabled roof. On three sides of the second story were galleries for women. (Consulate General of Israel in New York)

Ornamentation of the synagogue, including grape leaves and five-pointed star (A. C. Myers)

Millstones, representative of numerous basalt implements found at Tell Ḥûm (W. S. LaSor)

more important ruins is a third- or fourth-century synagogue, which may well occupy the same site as the synagogue mentioned in Lk. 7:5. It measures 65 ft. (20 m.) in length, is two stories high, and is constructed of white limestone rather than the black basalt found in abundance in the area. The "chief seats" are along the side and are still to be seen. At the south end an ark of the law is represented in stone. The ornamentation, which includes animals and mythological figures, is not in accord with the strict interpretation of Jewish law. An Aramaic inscription reads "Alphaeus, son of Zebedee, son of John, made this column; on him be blessing."

From the middle of the 2nd cent. the region around the lake became the citadel of rabbinic Judaism. Because Christians were not tolerated in the area there was a serious break in tradition, which makes the specific identification of places such as Peter's house highly unlikely. In the 4th cent. large numbers of Christian pilgrims began visiting Capernaum. R. H. MOUNCE

CAPH. *See* KAPH.

CAPHARSALAMA kaf-ər-säl'ə-mə [Gk. *Chapharsalama*] (1 Macc. 7:31). The site of a battle between Judas Maccabeus and Nicanor, an officer of the king of Syria and governor of Judea. The location cannot be precisely fixed but it must have been in the neighborhood of Jerusalem, for Nicanor, after losing five thousand men, retired with the remainder to "the city of David" (1 Macc. 7:26-32). Khirbet Selmah near ej-Jîb has been suggested as the site (*WHAB*; *GAB*), and also Khirbet Deir Sellām NW of Jerusalem.

CAPHENATHEA kə-fen'ə-thə (1 Macc. 12:37, AV). *See* CHAPHENATHA.

CAPHIRA kə-fī'rə (1 Esd. 5:19, AV, NEB). *See* CHEPHIRAH.

CAPHTOR kaf'tôr; **CAPHTORIM** kaf'tə-rēm [Heb. *kaptôr, kaptôrîm*; Gk. *Gaphtorieím, Kaphtorieim*; LXX also *Kappadokía*].

I. Biblical Evidence.–It is clear from Am. 9:7 and Jer. 47:4 that in biblical tradition Caphtor is the country from which the Philistines came. Since Dt. 2:23 speaks of "the Caphtorim, who came from Caphtor," it would seem that "Philistines" and "Caphtorim" are synonymous terms.

On the other hand, a series of texts seems to distinguish between the Philistines and the Caphtorim. In Gen. 10:13f. (repeated in 1 Ch. 1:11) it is stated that Egypt was the source of "Casluhim (whence came the Philistines), and Caphtorim." It has generally been accepted that the phrase "whence came the Philistines" is misplaced and belongs after Caphtorim. However, Dt. 2:23 states that the Caphtorim, "who came from Caphtor," displaced the "Avvim, who lived in villages as far as Gaza." This places the Caphtorim in the same vicinity as the Philistines, yet not apparently in the identical area, since Josh. 13:3 distinguishes between the area occupied by the Avvim and that occupied by the Philistines.

Finally, one must take into account the "Negeb of the Cherethites" mentioned in 1 S. 30:14, located apparently in approximately the same area as the territory of the Avvim. The poetic parallelism of Zeph. 2:4f. and Ezk. 25:15f. strongly suggests that "Cherethites" and "Philistines" refer to either identical or very closely related peoples. No theory in our present state of knowledge adequately accounts for all the evidence, but it is clear that "Caphtorim" and "Philistines" refer, at the very least, to closely related peoples.

The word "caphtorim" is also used to describe an ornamental feature common to the golden lampstand in Ex. 25:31-36 and some part of a pillar (possibly the capital) in Am. 9:1 and Zeph. 2:14. This usage is likely due to the influence of the art and architecture of that part of the biblical world called Caphtor.

II. Location.–Although in the course of modern biblical interpretation numerous localities have been suggested as the site of biblical Caphtor, three identifications have been prominent in recent discussion: the island of Crete, the western part of Cilicia in southeastern Anatolia, and the north Syrian coast. Although the evidence does not permit a definitive solution, current scholarship points to the island of Crete (or perhaps Crete plus the Aegean Isles, which culturally belong together) as by far the most probable site. In cuneiform literature the word *Kaptara* occurs in a late geographical text referring to Sargon of Akkad and in economic texts from Mari. An Akkadian text from Ugarit speaks of a ship arriving from *Kapturi*, while the Ugaritic texts refer to the place *Kptr*. In none of these references is there any certain indication as to locality. However, Egyptian texts from the New Kingdom period refer frequently to a country known as Keftiou (*Kftyw*), a name that reflects an original form *Kaftaru* by a well-established principle of "phonetic decay" in Egyptian. It is thus generally assumed that Egyp. *Keftiou* and Sem. *Kaptara*/*Caphtor* are identical. If this identity is correct — and the evidence in its favor seems strong — the identification of Caphtor with Crete seems certain in the light of a recent topographical list from the time of Amenhotep III (*ca.* 1400 B.C.). In this text the name *Keftiou* is clearly linked with four certain localities on Crete. Hence, the evidence makes it highly probable that Caphtor refers to Crete, or Crete plus the Aegean Isles, and that "Caphtorim" and "Philistines" are synonymous terms or two closely related peoples.

The problem is further complicated, however, by the fact that little, if any, relationship between the Philistines and Crete specifically can be deduced from archeological or literary sources. It may well be that Caphtor had become a term for the general Aegean area, including Crete, by the late 2nd millennium B.C., or that Crete was not the original home of the Philistines but simply a stopover point on their migration, as Egypt was for Israel.

Bibliography.–G. Dossin, *Syria,* 20 (1939), 111-13; A. H. Gardner, *Ancient Egyptian Onomastica,* I (1947), 201*-203*; J. Vercoutter, *L'Égypte et le monde égéen préhellénique* (1956) — contains full bibliography and history of the discussion; J. Nougayrol, *Le Palais Royal d'Ugarit,* III (1955), xxviii, 107; *UT*, p. 422 § 1291; K. A. Kitchen, "The Philistines," in D. J. Wiseman, ed., *Peoples of the OT* (1973).

F. W. BUSH

CAPITAL [Heb. *kap̱tôr*] (Ex. 25:31, 33-36; Am. 9:1; etc.); AV LINTEL, KNOP; NEB also CALYX; [*kōṯereṯ*] (1 K. 7:16-20, 41f.; 2 K. 25:17; etc.); AV CHAPITER; NEB ARCHITRAVE; [*rô'š*] (Ex. 36:38; 38:17, 19, 28); AV CHAPITER; NEB "top of the posts." The ornamental top of a pillar or pillar-like object, e.g., a stem of the lampstand in the tabernacle.

Corinthian capitals from the temple of Olympian Zeus at Athens (174-164 B.C.) (W. S. LaSor)

CAPITAL PUNISHMENT. *See* PUNISHMENTS.

CAPPADOCIA kap-ə-dō'shə [Gk. *Kappadokia*]. An extensive territory in eastern Asia Minor whose natural boundaries were the Taurus Mountains on the south and the upper Euphrates on the east. At one time it extended to the lower Halys and N to the Black Sea; but the Persians made a separate satrapy of Pontus in the north, and the northwest parts were later included in Galatia.

The capital, Caesarea (Mazaca), modern Kayseri, stood at the foot of the highest mountain, the 13,000-ft. (3960-m.) Argaeus, now Erciyas Dağ. The chief river was the Halys, now Kızıl Irmak. The country consisted mostly of barren uplands with an extreme climate and little timber, but was rich in sheep and horses.

Cuneiform tablets from a colony at Kültepe (Kanish),

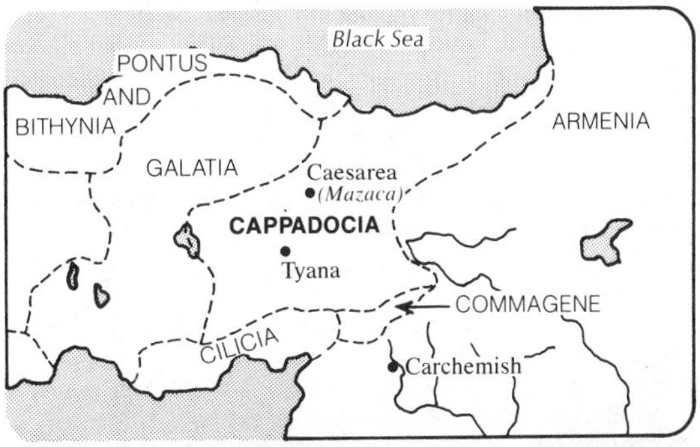

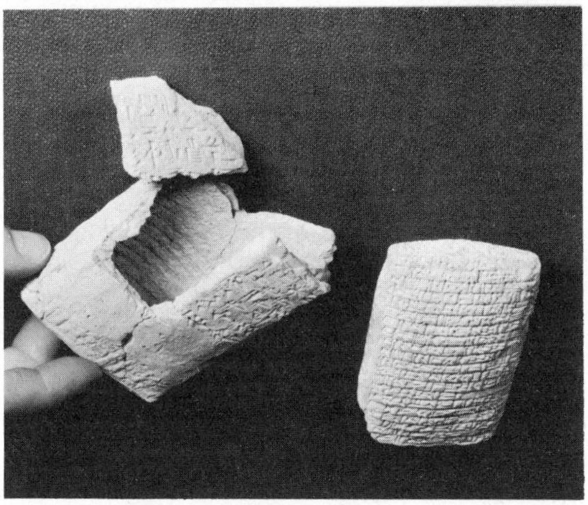

Legal document with envelope from Kültepe (ancient Kanish). An archive of more than sixteen thousand texts details the activities of an Old Assyrian merchant colony (19th cent. B.C.). (Yale University Babylonian Collection)

Byzantine churches carved in the rocky crags of Göreme (Ürgüp) in Cappadocia. Part of the holy grottoes that were the first homes of Orthodox monks in Asia Minor, their interiors are vast and highly decorated. (W. S. LaSor) *See also* Plate 21.

near Caesarea, have shown the presence of Assyrian merchants there about the 19th cent. B.C. Cappadocia was part of the empire of the Hittites, and remained under their influence until the fall of Carchemish in 717 B.C. Hittite remains have been found at many sites. The country became a Persian satrapy, and later an independent kingdom under native kings. Hellenization was slow, and the land long continued in a feudal condition under priestly domination. Comana was famous for its temple of the goddess Ma-Enyo, who had six thousand priestesses. Tiberius constituted Cappadocia a Roman province on the death of King Archelaus in A.D. 17, and Vespasian enlarged it as an important frontier bulwark after A.D. 70.

Until Roman times there were few cities apart from Caesarea and Tyana, near modern Bor; but important trade routes crossed the country, and the letter to King Ariarathes V in 1 Macc. 15:22 indicates the presence of a Jewish community by about 139 B.C.

Jews from Cappadocia were in Jerusalem at Pentecost (Acts 2:9). Christianity probably spread northward from Tarsus by the route through the Cilician Gates. Peter includes converts of the Dispersion in Cappadocia in the address of his First Epistle (1 Pet. 1:1).

Caesarea became one of the most important early centers of Christianity despite the former strength of paganism. Here Gregory the Illuminator was instructed in the faith to which he later won the formal assent of his Armenian nation. Basil, his brother Gregory of Nyssa, and Gregory of Nazianzus were from Cappadocia. The land passed with the rest of Asia Minor into the Byzantine empire, and was exposed early to the Seljuk Turks, who conquered it in 1074.

The LXX and Vulgate of Dt. 2:23 and Am. 9:7 render Caphtor as Cappadocia, and Josephus (*Ant.* i.6.1) refers Meshech (Gen. 10:2, etc.) to this land. These identifications are very doubtful.

See also GOMER; TUBAL. C. J. HEMER

CAPS [Heb. *migbā'ôt*] (Ex. 28:40; 29:9; 39:28; Lev. 8:13); AV BONNETS; NEB TALL HEAD-DRESSES. The "cap" was part of the dress of the priests, the sons of Aaron, as specified in Ex. 28:40. It was wound around the head (Lev. 8:13). The etymology of the Hebrew term suggests that it was high or hill-like. This head-dress contrasts with the TURBAN (*miṣnepeṯ*) worn by the high priest (Ex. 28:39). D. E. SMITH

CAPTAIN [Heb. *śar, raḇ, šālîš,* also *rō'š* (Nu. 14:4), *peḥâ* (2 K. 18:24 par. Isa. 36:9), *raḇ, ḥōḇēl* (Jonah 1:6); Aram. *raḇ* (Dnl. 2:14), *šallîṭ* (2:15); Gk. *stratēgós, chilíarchos, kybernḗtēs* (Acts 27:11)]; AV also LORD, PRINCE, "ruler over hundreds," SHIPMASTER; NEB also COMMANDER, CHIEF, LIEUTENANT (for *šālîš*), "outbursts of song" (2 K. 11:14 par. 2 Ch. 23:13, reading *haššārîm*; cf. LXX, Gk. *ōdoí*), "authority" (for *peḥâ*), OFFICER (of the temple police, Lk. 22:4, 52), CONTROLLER (of the temple, Acts 4:1; 5:24, 26; Gk. *stratēgós*); cf. 1 S. 22:14, where the RSV follows the LXX and Targum. The Heb. *śar,* the commonest word for "captain," can designate the chief official of any department, civil, religious, or military — cf. Gen. 40, where it is used not only for the captain of the guard but also for the chief butler and chief baker; and cf. Nu. 31:48 ("captain of thousands . . . of hundreds"); 1 K. 22:31ff. ("captains of the chariots"); 2 K. 1:9ff. ("captain of fifty"); also 2 Ch. 35:9 ("chiefs of the Levites"); 36:14; Ezr. 10:5 ("leading priests"); etc. *See also* PRINCE.

Nebuzaradan, captain of Nebuchadnezzar's bodyguard (2 K. 25:8ff.; Jer. 39:9ff.; 52:12ff.), is always called *raḇ,* as is Arioch (Dnl. 2:14), no doubt because the closely related Babylonian word was part of the title of these men. The Heb. *šālîš,* "third," meant originally the third man in the chariot, who, when the main occupant was the king or commander-in-chief, had the rank of captain (1 K. 9:22; 2 K. 7:2, 17, 19; 15:25) or lieutenant (NEB).

In 2 K. 18:24 par. Isa. 36:9 the AV and RSV have "captain" for Heb. *peḥâ,* a word of Akkadian origin elsewhere rendered "governor" (e.g., 1 K. 10:15; Jer. 51:23, 28, 57), but here denoting an Assyrian official in Sennacherib's court.

In the NT, Gk. *chilíarchos* is the Lat. *tribunus militum,* of which there were six to a legion, commanding the six cohorts of which it was composed. The literal meaning is "commander of a thousand," and it is so used in Acts (e.g., 21:31ff.; cf. Jn. 18:12), where it designates the commander of the Roman garrison in Jerusalem, consisting of a cohort (*see* TRIBUNE). It is used more vaguely in the sense of "military officer" in Mk. 6:21; Rev. 6:15; 19:18. Gk. *stratēgós* is used only by Luke in the NT, and almost exclusively of officials in charge of the temple (Lk. 22:4, 52; Acts 4:1; 5:24, 26). The captain of the temple had the superintendence of the Levites and priests who were on guard in and around the temple, and under him were *stratēgoí,* who were also captains of the temple police, although they took their instructions from him as their head. He was not only a priest but second in dignity only to the high priest himself. The exception to Luke's general usage is where the word is used of the chief authorities in civil affairs at Philippi; here "the magistrates," as the word is rendered (Acts 16:20f.), called themselves "praetors" (*stratēgoí*). They placed themselves in peril of removal from their office by ordering the beating of Paul and Silas, who were Romans and had not been condemned. *See* ARMY, ROMAN.

The AV has "captain" in a great many other passages, where the RSV has replaced it with such terms as "leader" (Heb. *nāśî*), "commander" (esp. *śar,* in historical books), "chief," "chief men," "officer," "prince," "marshal," "Carite." See separate articles.

T. NICOL
J. W. D. H.

CAPTIVE; CAPTIVITY [Heb. *šābâ, gālâ,* and derivatives; Gk. *aichmalōtízō* and derivatives]. The frequent references in the OT to taking captives, especially in the sense of deporting or removing peoples to another land, reflect the universal practice of the ancient world. The treatment of captives was sometimes barbarous (2 S. 8:2) but not always so (2 K. 6:21f.). *See* WAR.

In the AV "captivity" sometimes means "captive," e.g., Jgs. 5:12; Ps. 68:18; Hab. 1:9; Eph. 4:8.

Figurative usage of the words is mostly in the NT (but cf. Job 42:10, AV), where Paul speaks of captivity to the law and sin (Rom. 7:6, 23), and also of taking "every thought captive to obey Christ" (2 Cor. 10:5).

See also CAPTIVITY. F. K. FARR

CAPTIVITY [Heb. usually *šᵉḇî,* also *šāḇâ* (2 Ch. 6:38), *šᵉḇûṯ* (Dt. 38:41), *šiḇyâ* (Jer. 48:46), *gālâ* (Jgs. 18:30; Jer. 1:3; Ezk. 39:23), *gôlâ* (2 K. 24:15), *gālûṯ* (Jer. 52:31)]; NEB also EXILE; [Gk. *aichmalōsía*] (Rev. 13:10); NEB PRISONER. *See also* DISPERSION; EXILE.

As a cursory examination of modern translations reveals, the term "captivity" no longer receives the widespread usage found in the AV. Nevertheless, the notion of captivity is still found in the various verbal idioms used to describe this period in the history of Israel. In many ways the more modern usage of "exile" is more appropriate, since the notion of captivity can be included in this term. In addition, "captivity" does not necessarily refer to deportation to a foreign land, so much a part of the experience referred to by the Hebrew words above.

The captivity of Israel and Judah was a critical and crucial period. It evoked a variety of responses, many of them expressed in the literary activity of that time, so its impact is felt, directly or indirectly, in almost all of the OT and much of the NT. This was a period when the promises of the past and the shape of the future had to be evaluated in terms of a new experience without the traditional self-validifying structures: e.g., the monarchy and the state, the temple and the institutional cult.

I. Historical Background
  A. North (Israel)
  B. South (Judah)
II. Theological Response
III. Importance

I. Historical Background.–An introduction to the historical events is important for an understanding of this traumatic, but formative, event in the life of Israel. Unfortunately, the biblical record is incomplete concerning the actual events within the captivity itself. Much of our knowledge is based on Assyrian and Babylonian records of the time and generally known facts concerning the way of life at this time in Mesopotamia and Palestine.

A. North (Israel). It has often been noted that the success and longevity of Israel and Judah as nations were at least partially dependent upon a power vacuum in the remainder of the ancient Near East. Conversely, the periods leading up to the captivity of both Israel and Judah are characterized by the emergence of one or more superpowers. Thus the prehistory of Israel's captivity begins in the 9th cent. B.C. with the growing power and ambitions of the Assyrian nation.

With initial military successes under Aššur-dân II (935-913 B.C.), Assyria had clearly reemerged as a military power to be reckoned with by lesser and vulnerable nations in Palestine and northern Syria. It was Ashurnasirpal II (884-860) who founded the Neo-Assyrian empire, and it was his methods of warfare and his conception of domination that characterized the actions of Assyria (and Babylon) in the next three and a half centuries.

Unlike their smaller rivals, the Assyrians had a standing army, which was an enormous advantage. The Assyrians were famous for their ruthlessness in dealing with adversaries — massacres and/or deportation were used both to curb resistance and rebellion and to assure obedience and the prompt payment of tribute. A distinct pattern or plan lay behind their methods of consolidation. States within the empire had various degrees of dependence. At the outer limits of the empire the requirement was initially a vow of allegiance and loyalty, with the result that tribute was given to Assyria and a vassal status to the particular state. If any resistance to these conditions was made by the state, the Assyrians would reduce it by military means into a province and appoint another vassal state to govern it. If resistance still occurred, the final step of extermination of the state and deportation took place. This pattern is important, for it helps to explain the history of Israel and its captivity.

The importance of the Syrian and Palestinian states to any power that wished to control trade routes, as well as to tap any indigenous prosperity that could provide tribute, was clear. It appears that Israel was under the influence of Assyria from the time of Shalmaneser III (859-825 B.C.), but that this king and his immediate successors were not able to maintain this sphere of influence. Instead, the history of this period is filled with struggles among the states of Israel, Judah, Damascus, and other border states (cf. 2 K. 8ff.).

With the accession of Tiglath-pileser III (745-727) the sequence of weaker Assyrian kings was broken and a strong and systematic policy of empire-building began. The states in Syria and Palestine were no real match for Assyria with its standing army and superior military technique and prowess.

From the end of the reign of Jeroboam II, the political situation in Israel was unstable. Leadership was not always characterized by a pragmatic and knowledgeable policy of action in view of Israel's difficult position vis-à-vis Assyria. Rather, futile attempts at independence brought on by nationalistic motivations, as well as contradictory attempts by other rulers to remain in Assyria's favor, created a chaotic and dangerous situation. Menahem of Israel (745-738) is reported to have paid Pul (Tiglath-pileser III) tribute, thus placing Israel under the Assyrian sphere of influence. But in 733 Pekah of Israel joined with Rezin of Damascus in an attempt to gain independence from Assyria. Ahaz of Judah refused to join this coalition, and the subsequent Syro-Ephraimite war occurred (cf. 2 K. 15:37; 16:5; Isa. 7; etc.). Assyria was quick to quell this rebellion. Israel was reduced and many of its inhabitants were deported. With the exception of Samaria and its immediate environs, the state of Israel was partitioned into three provinces (2 K. 15:29f.).

With the death of Tiglath-pileser there was another attempt in Israel to break the vassal relationship by withholding tribute. This ultimately resulted in the siege and final fall of Samaria in 722, effected most probably by Shalmaneser V. At this point Assyria deported vast numbers of Israelites and brought into Israel many foreign peoples from other places in their empire. The upper class and those in power were deported to assure the crippling of the state. The territory of Israel was given no political status at all, and for all intents and purposes it disappeared from the scene until the postexilic period.

One footnote to this extermination of the state of Israel should be made. Although details of the actual fall of Samaria and Israel are almost nonexistent, clearly some inhabitants of the northern kingdom came into Judah. The Deuteronomic reform (see below) certainly reflects the influence of a theology and cult from Israel. Although the precise identification of this reforming element continues to be debated (Levites, prophets, etc.), its existence does not. In addition, the well-known influence of Hosea upon Jeremiah, to cite one example, also demands recognition of a circle that continued to be influenced by ideas and concerns originating in Israel.

B. South (Judah). The captivity of Judah is to be understood primarily by an examination of the political movements of the three superpowers (Assyria, Babylonia, and Egypt) and Judah's reactions to them in the last half of the 7th century. From the time of the Syro-Ephraimite war, Judah had been in a vassal relationship with Assyria. Although the ruler during most of this period (Manasseh, 687-642) was condemned soundly for his sanction of syncretistic practices (cf., however, 2 Ch. 33:10-13), his only other option was a rebellion surely doomed to failure and a complete destruction of the state. In the last years of Ashurbanipal (668-627), however, Assyria grew weaker. At this time also Babylon rose to the status of an independent power beginning with Nabopolassar (626-605), and Egypt reemerged as a power to be reckoned with (especially with the 26th Dynasty, beginning in 664).

At this time the Deuteronomic reform of Josiah (*ca.*

621) occurred. (It is now recognized that the account of the Chronicler [2 Ch. 34f.] has a sequence of actions more historically accurate than that of the "Deuteronomist" [2 K. 22f.].) Cultic reform was but a small part of a greater movement in Judah to emancipate the state from Assyrian influence. To this end, developments such as the weakening of the Assyrian state and the emergence of a strong king of Judah were requisite.

Temporary successes at both political independence and cultic reform stopped suddenly when Josiah died by the hand of Pharaoh Neco at Megiddo in 609. From 609 until 605 Egypt controlled Judah, having replaced Josiah's successor, Jehoahaz (609), with Jehoiakim (609-598), who was more amenable to Egyptian vassalage. In 605 Egypt and a remnant of the Assyrian empire were defeated at Carchemish by Babylon. This was followed by a declaration of obeisance by Jehoiakim to Nebuchadrezzar king of Babylon. Whether this action with its implications for a formal vassal status came before or after Nebuchadrezzar's defeat by the Egyptians in 601 is debated. In any case, with the death of Jehoiakim in 598 the Babylonians made a concerted effort to establish their influence permanently. Jehoiachin 598-597) was deposed and Zedekiah (Mattaniah) was placed upon the throne. The temple was plundered and the first deportation occurred. A substantial number of artisans and upper-class citizens from Jerusalem and the countryside were taken to Babylon. Foolishly, Zedekiah rebelled against Babylon. In 587, despite hopes for help from Egypt, the besieged city of Jerusalem fell, and the period of Judean captivity began. Jerusalem and much of the Judean countryside were plundered and destroyed. The temple and palace were razed, more of the populace deported, and the upper classes punished (2 K. 25:18ff.). All of the tangible institutions and powerful people were gone or crippled. The state of Judah, its long history so closely associated with Yahweh and His servant David, was no longer. In 582 a third and final deportation took place (Jer. 52:28-30).

Little is known of the life of the Judeans during the Captivity, in Palestine or Babylon. Jeremiah's account of Gedaliah's short-lived control of Judah is all the scriptural information available. Surely the conditions in Palestine were difficult (cf. Lamentations), with little or no success at establishing regular worship or other community functions. The deportees in Babylon seem to have fared better than those in Assyria. No policy separated the deportees from each other; in fact, they were placed together at the periphery of the city. Sources originating there witness to worship and other aspects of community identification and affirmation.

With the death of Nebuchadrezzar in 562 the future of Babylon as an independent power was in jeopardy. The rise of the Persian king Cyrus, and the reign of Nabonidus with all of its difficulties, spelled the end of Babylon and the beginning of Persian domination of Judah. The Persian policies for governing subject peoples were considerably different from those of Assyria and Babylonia. The Persians had no desire to erase the old order and to deport native populations. They were concerned to allow the institutions of the subject territory to control social life, especially religious life. Thus the famous edict of Cyrus in 538, only one year after the fall of Babylon, proclaimed that the temple should be rebuilt and its treasures restored (Ezr. 6:2-5). Although it is certain that the exiles were allowed to return, the precise details are unclear. Nevertheless, with this edict the historical period of the Judean captivity is usually concluded and the postexilic period begun.

II. Theological Response.–While sparse and incomplete sources limit the historical recounting of the Captivity, the great theological activity in this period is indicated by various OT books. Indeed, scholars increasingly are recognizing that much of the motivation and rationale for the formation of the OT as a whole resulted from the Captivity and the many theological responses to it.

Babylonian Chronicle for 605-594 B.C., recording the capture of Jerusalem in 597 B.C., the appointment of Zedekiah as king, and the exile of Jehoiachin and others to Babylonia (6th cent. B.C.) (Trustees of the British Museum)

The Captivity was at once the cause and the subject of necessary theological reformulation. The loss of many legitimizing institutions (the temple, the monarchy, the state) and the crippling of many others (the cult, the societal class structures, etc.) forced the Israelites to ask why, and, more importantly, to contemplate the future and its shape. Thus, it became increasingly necessary to include the phenomenon of the Captivity itself in discussing the future of Israel, for surely the changes wrought by this experience were inescapable and were to form some of the defining lines for Judaism to the present day.

The Captivity was a pluralistic age. A pluralistic age is characterized by variety and diversity, yet also by a common matrix to which all positions and stances may be related. The opposite of pluralism, orthodoxy, is characterized by at least a superficial homogeneity and also by a power base that is capable of regulating, controlling, and enforcing one perspective or position for a particular society. With the Captivity, a necessary prerequisite for orthodoxy, a power base capable of molding and controlling public opinion, no longer existed. On the other hand, the many responses to the Captivity indicate existence of a common theological matrix capable of making this period one of pluralistic creativity rather than anarchistic chaos.

The Captivity produced a variety of responses, each

with its own spheres of influence and its own hopes about the future. As in all pluralistic periods, a great deal of tension and friction existed between many of the exponents of the groups trying to comprehend the Captivity. Faced with a new situation, all of Israel drew on old patterns to describe the new situation. All of Israel necessarily spoke of a new thing that Yahweh was doing, for the special mix of old and new created a new vision. Each new vision had its own vested interests, more or less closely tied to the realities that the experience of captivity created. For some the Captivity, despite its hardships, provided the hope for a reversal of previous social and religious structures. For others it was a fall from power, and the sooner a restoration of previous status and conditions could be effected, the better.

First among those realities that would have to be dealt with was the Diaspora. New conceptions of who and what Israel was, legitimation of this identity in view of the demise of older institutions — these and many other theological questions needed to be answered because of the new nature of the people Israel. The loss of statehood, of a monarchical power base, of a central and politically (monarchically) legitimized cult — all of these realities needed to be discussed in speaking of Israel's future.

Scholars have often noted that in the period of the Captivity a fundamental change was made from a community characterized by a corporate, nationalistic focus to one more individualistically oriented. In a very real sense the Captivity, as a new and devastating event in Israel's history, was responsible for this shift with its resultant theological changes (*BHI*). On the other hand. one may also validly state that the events of the Captivity and the theological responses found there are integrally related to a long historical process that began much earlier (Noth). The pluralism of the 6th cent. in Palestine, Babylon, or Egypt was created and informed not only by the fall of Judah and its aftermath but also by the patterns and concepts that had formed and framed the Hebrew mind from the patriarchal period on. Thus, while the agenda and form of any particular theological response to the Captivity would be controlled by the vested interests of the particular person or group, the way in which that message was expressed would draw upon a continuum of theological activity stretching back into the earliest periods of Israelite history. Ultimately the new postexilic community would choose one or more theological responses as the rationale for its framework of existence, preserving the others as legitimate but inappropriate.

III. Importance.–The period of the Captivity is receiving increasing attention in biblical scholarship. No doubt some is attributable to the exemplary pluralistic religious model found in this period and a desire to learn how such a pluralism works and is maintained. But, of course, that pluralism was not maintained in Israel, as Ezra-Nehemiah demonstrates. Perhaps another reason is the analogous questions that every society must answer, questions attempting to discern God's working in circumstances that seem, at first, quite hostile to such a conception.

The primary importance of the Captivity is the effect it had upon Israel's theological development. The tension between particularism, so often associated with the hierarchical interests, and universalism, associated not simply with the exiles but also with the visionaries, became an important characteristic of Judaism and Christianity. The development of a religion of the book, and therefore more focus on "word" than on outward institutional and national signs such as temple and palace, was also an important legacy of the Captivity. The focus on the individual and his response was also a new feature and one that continued. Yet all of these important developments are seen by the various groups as ongoing actions of God, not man, developments whose roots are deep within a history of God's action to and for Israel. Perhaps this pluralistic heritage and witness, ultimately canonized, provides the greatest importance for contemporary man by its challenge to find God at work and its affirmation that in many ways and places He is indeed to be found.

Bibliography.–P. R. Ackroyd, *Exile and Restoration* (1968); *BHI* (2nd ed. 1972); W. Brueggmann, *Interp.*, 22 (1968), 387-402; W. Brueggmann and H. W. Wolff, *The Vitality of OT Traditions* (1975); F. M. Cross, Jr., *Canaanite Myth and Hebrew Epic* (1973); G. Fohrer, *History of Israelite Religions* (1972); D. N. Freedman, *Interp.*, 29 (1975), 171-186; P. Hanson, *Dawn of Apocalyptic* (1975); E. W. Nicholson, *Preaching to the Exiles* (1971); M. Noth, *Überlieferungsgeschichtliche Studien* (1943); *NHI*; G. von Rad, *Studies in Deuteronomy* (Eng. tr. 1953); J. Skinner, *Prophecy and Religion* (4th ed. 1936).

D. F. MORGAN

CAPTIVITY EPISTLES. The traditional designation of the four Epistles of Paul written while he was in prison or under house arrest, viz., Ephesians, Philippians, Colossians, and Philemon. *See* PHILEMON, EPISTLE TO III, for a general discussion.

CAR (Cant. 3:9, AV). *See* PALANQUIN.

CARABASION kar-ə-ba'zi-ən [Gk. *Karabasiōn*] (1 Esd. 9:34). One of the sons of Baani who had married foreign wives during the Captivity. The name seems to be represented by Meremoth in the list of Ezr. 10:36.

CARAVAN [Heb. *'ōrḥâ*] (Gen. 37:25; Job 6:18f.; Isa. 21:13; and, by emendation from *'ōraḥ* Jgs. 5:6); AV COMPANY, TRAVELLING COMPANY, "highway" (Jgs. 5:6), "path" (Job 6:18), "troop" (v. 19); **CARAVAN ROUTE** [Heb. *dereḵ haššeḵûnê ba'ohālîm*] (Jgs. 8:11); AV "way of them that dwelt in tents"; NEB "track used by the tent-dwellers"; cf. also Ezk. 27:25, NEB. The inhabitants of Palestine were familiar with the caravans (the goods trains of the Semitic world), for the main routes connecting Babylonia, Syria, Egypt, and Arabia passed through Canaan. Isaiah refers to "caravans of Dedanites" — a trading Arabian tribe who conveyed their wares to Babylon. Job compares his would-be friends to a deceitful brook, full in the rainy season but dry in summer, which entices caravans to turn aside from the main route in the hope of a plentiful supply of water but fails the thirsty travelers when they need it most. T. LEWIS

CARBUNCLE. *See* STONES, PRECIOUS.

CARCAS kär'kəs (Est. 1:10, AV, NEB). *See* CARKAS.

CARCASS. The term is used of the dead body of a beast, and sometimes in a contemptuous way of the dead body of a human being. (1) It occurs in Gen. 15:11 as a translation of Heb. *peger*, which is translated "dead body" in Nu. 14:29; 1 S. 17:46; Isa. 66:24; Ezk. 6:5; 43:7, 9, and "corpse" in Nah. 3:3. (2) The Heb. *neḇēlâ* is translated "carcass" in Lev. 5:2; 11:8, 11; Dt. 14:8; Jer. 16:18, but "dead body" in Dt. 28:26 ("body," Josh. 8:29; 1 K. 13:22, 29); Jer. 7:33; 16:4; 19:7. (3) In Jgs. 14:8 the Heb. *mappeleṯ* from *nāpal*, "fall," and (4) in v. 9 *gewîyâ* are also translated "carcass."

(5) In Ps. 89:10 *ḥālāl* is rendered "carcass" by the

RSV, "one that is slain" by the AV, "mortal blow" by the NEB. (6) In Ezk. 32:5 the AV follows the MT with *rāmûṯeḵā*, "thy height"; the RSV ("your carcass") and the NEB ("the worms that feed on it") emend to *rimāṯeḵa*, following the Symmachus, Syriac, and Vulgate texts. W. N. STEARNS

CARCHEMISH kär'kə-mish [Heb. *kark^{e}mîš*; Akk. usually *karkamiš, gargamiš*, but in Neo-Babylonian Chronicle *galgameš*; Gk. *Charcham(e)is, Charmeis*]. An important Syro-Hittite city on the right bank of the upper Euphrates River about 63 mi. (100 km.) NE of Aleppo. George Smith correctly identified as Carchemish the huge mound in Turkey, N of the modern Syrian border village of Jerablus. In 1879 excavations undertaken on behalf of the British Museum produced hieroglyphic Hittite inscriptions and other monuments. From 1911 to 1914 D. G. Hogarth, assisted by C. L. (later Sir Leonard) Woolley and T. E. Lawrence ("Lawrence of Arabia" of later fame), directed a second British Museum expedition which uncovered further monuments and inscriptions. Additional excavations under British Museum auspices continued until 1920.

Remains from the mound itself indicate that habitation there reaches back at least to the Chalcolithic period. Several of the eighteenth-century B.C. Mari Letters refer to Carchemish in terms that attest to its independent status in the early 2nd millennium. During the "Hyksos" period the fortifications of the city included an enormous rectangular enclosure surrounded by a beaten earth (*terre pisée*) wall, probably as a defense against the battering ram. In the 15th cent. Pharaoh Thutmose III of Egypt conquered Carchemish, presumably during his eighth Asiatic campaign in the thirty-third year of his reign. Amenhotep III in the 14th cent. and Ramses III in the 12th cent. also claim to have captured the city, but their accounts contain more of propaganda than of actual historical fact. The Hittite king Šuppiluliuma captured Carchemish after an eight-day siege *ca.* 1340 B.C. and thus turned Syria into a Hittite dependency. He installed one of his sons, Piyassilis, as king of Carchemish.

After the eclipse of Hittite power, Assyrian rulers, especially in the 9th and 8th cents., conquered and plundered Carchemish almost at will. Ashurnasirpal II received tribute from San(a)gara, the Hittite king at Carchemish, *ca.* 876 B.C. In the first year of his reign Shalmaneser III defeated the same king and in his sixth year extorted tribute from him. Tiglath-pileser III later received tribute from Pisiri(s) of Carchemish. The accession of Sargon II to the Assyrian throne *ca.* 722 was a signal for the dependent provinces to rebel. The revolt was fomented by Midas king of the Phrygian Mushki, and involved also Pisiri(s). In 717 Sargon destroyed Carchemish, deported its inhabitants, and resettled it with Assyrians. (For the Assyrian humbling of Carchemish during the second half of the 8th cent., see Isa. 10:5-11.)

The last decade of the 7th cent. B.C. witnessed the demise of both Assyrian and Egyptian imperial ambitions and influence in Syro-Palestine. The resurgent Neo-Babylonians had already dealt a fatal blow to Assyria by de-

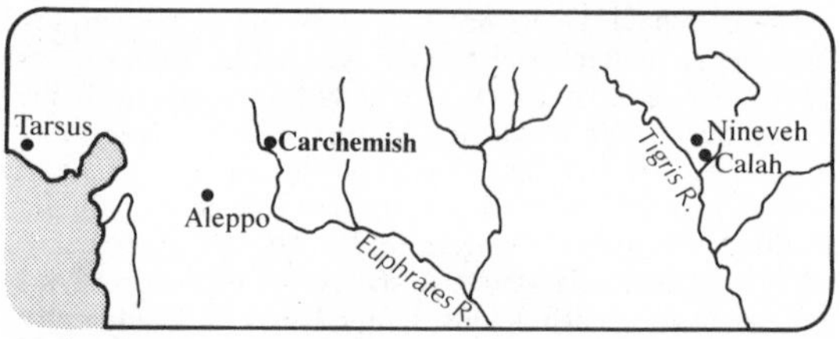

Basalt relief from the processional entry at Carchemish (9th-8th cents. B.C.), showing offering bearers with sacrificial animals (Trustees of the British Museum)

stroying her capital, Nineveh, in 612. By 609 Ashur-uballit, the last king of Assyria, had disappeared completely from the political and military scene. In that same year Pharaoh Neco II of Egypt marched northward in one last desperate attempt to help the tattered Assyrian armies stop the Neo-Babylonian juggernaut. King Josiah of Judah, perhaps preferring the Neo-Babylonian presence in Palestine to that of Assyria and Egypt, came out to block the advance of Neco (2 Ch. 35:20; 1 Esd. 1:25). The two armies joined battle in the plain of Megiddo, and Josiah was slain (2 K. 23:29f.; 2 Ch. 35:21-27). Neco then marched on to garrison Carchemish in company with the remnant of the Assyrian forces.

The year 605 B.C. was decisive in ancient Near Eastern history. Nebuchadrezzar II, crown prince of the Neo-Babylonian empire, became commander-in-chief of the Babylonian armies. His own court records detail subsequent events of that year in one of the tablets of the Neo-Babylonian Chronicle (British Museum Tablet no. 21946). In the spring he marched at the head of his assault forces up the Euphrates to Carchemish, and in May/June he engaged the Egyptians in hand-to-hand fighting within the city. There is no indication that Neco himself was with his army at the time. At any rate, the Neo-Babylonian victory was complete and marked the end of Egyptian power in Syria and Palestine. Nebuchadrezzar pursued the Egyptians to Hamath and perhaps also down the Mediterranean coast, as Jer. 46:2-12 seems to suggest. In due time Jehoiakim son of Josiah, whom Neco had installed as king of Judah, became tributary to Nebuchadrezzar (2 K. 23:34–24:1; 2 Ch. 36:4-6), who, as a result of the Battle of Carchemish, was able to march at will throughout all the Syro-Palestinian provinces.

Excavations at Tell Mardikh (ancient Ebla) in Syria indicate that CHEMOSH, the national god of Moab, was worshiped at Ebla as early as the end of the 3rd millennium B.C. He was called *Kamišu* there (a spelling that agrees with the *K* reading in Jer. 48:7, *k^{e}mîš*) and was associated with the city of Carchemish, which may now be understood provisionally to mean "City of Chemosh."

Bibliography.–D. G. Hogarth and C. L. Woolley, *Carchemish* (1914; 1921); *ANET, passim*; *CCK*; Josephus *Ant.* x.6.1.

R. F. YOUNGBLOOD

CARE. The OT uses several expressions for the various meanings of the English word "care," and the AV often translates them literally. Thus the AV has "are with me" for "are a care to me" (Gen. 33:13); "in the hand (Heb. *yāḏ*) of" for "in the care of" (Gen. 39:22f.; 1 Ch. 26:28; 29:8); "feed" (*rā'â*) for "care for" (Jer. 23:2, 4); "visitation" (*p^{e}quddâ*) for "care" (Job 10:12), and "visit" (*pāqaḏ*) for "care for" (Ps. 8:4; Zec. 11:16); also "seek" (*dāraš*, 1 Ch. 15:13; Jer. 30:14), "instruct" (*bîn*, Dt. 32:10). "Take care" is often "take heed" in the AV (e.g., *šāmar,* Josh. 22:5; cf. in the NT Gk. *proséchō*, Acts 5:35; *blépō*, 1 Cor. 3:10; 8:9; He. 3:12). In 2 S. 18:3 the Hebrew expression is literally "set the heart to" (*śûm lēḇ 'el*).

In the NT, "care for" in the sense of nurture or aid is usually expressed by Gk. *epimeléomai* (Lk. 10:34f.; 1 Tim. 3:5; cf. *epimeleías,* Acts 27:3), and also by *thálpō* (1 Thess. 2:7, AV "cherish"). For the sense "anxious concern" are used *merimnáō* (1 Cor. 12:25; *see also* ANXIETY, on 1 Cor. 7:32ff.; Phil. 2:20) and *spoudḗ* (2 Cor. 8:16). Gk. *mélō* is used in the sense of "concern" (Mk. 4:38; Lk. 10:40; Jn. 12:6), and also in the sense of partiality (Mt. 22:16 par., NEB "truckle").

The RSV has "children of their tender care" in Lam. 2:20, for Heb. *'ōl^{a}lê ṭippuḥîm*. The AV translates "children a span long," following the more common (and perhaps related) root *ṭāpaḥ* (BDB, p. 381; cf. v. 22, "dandling"); the reference is to children fully formed at birth, implying that they are born healthy (cf. KoB, pp. 355f.); thus the NEB "the children they have brought safely to birth."

J. W. D. H.

CAREAH kə-rē'ə. *See* KAREAH.

CAREFUL; CAREFULLY; CAREFULNESS. The AV often uses these words in such now obsolete senses as "anxious" or "anxiety," i.e., "full of care" (Heb. *dā'ag,* Jer. 17:8; Gk. *merimnáō,* Lk. 10:41; Phil. 4:6; cf. *amérimnos,* 1 Cor. 7:32), "fearfulness" (Heb. *d$^{e'}$āgâ,* Ezk. 12:18f.), "concerned for" (Heb. *ḥāraḏ,* 2 K. 4:13; Gk. *phronéō,* Phil. 4:10), "thinking to be necessary" (Aram. *ḥ^{a}shaḥ,* Dnl. 3:16), and "eager" (Gk. *spoudaiotérōs,* Phil. 2:28), "eagerness" (*spoudḗ,* 2 Cor. 7:11).

CARELESS. In Prov. 14:16 the participial form of the Hebrew verb *bāṭaḥ* ("trust") expresses carelessness through a false sense of security. In Mt. 12:36 the Greek adjective *argós* (AV "idle"; NEB "thoughtless") is used of the type of utterance that will bring judgment.

CAREM kā'rəm [Gk. *Karem*]. A city of Judah interpolated by the LXX (Josh. 15:59, NEB); probably BETH-HACCHEREM.

CARIA kâr'ē-ə [Gk. *Karia*]. A country in the southwest of Asia Minor extending on the north to Lydia, on the east to Phrygia, on the south to Lycia, and west to the Aegean Sea. Its borders, however, like those of most of the ancient countries of Asia Minor, were never definitely fixed; hence the difficulty presented by the study of the political divisions. The general surface of the country is rugged, consisting of mountainous ridges running across it and terminating as promontories jutting into the sea.

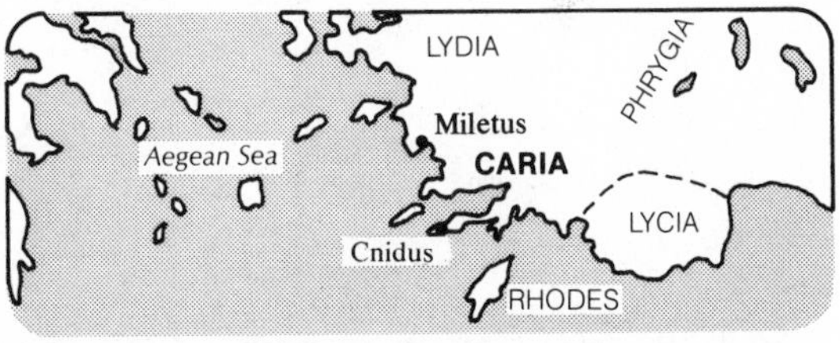

Its history consists chiefly of that of its practically independent cities, of which Miletus (Acts 20:15-20) and Cnidus (27:7) are the chief. For some time previous to 168 B.C. it had lost its independence and belonged to the island of Rhodes; but in that year Rome freed it again. According to 1 Macc. 15:23, Caria was one of several places to which the Roman senate in 139/138 B.C. sent letters in favor of the Jews, a fact showing that its population was mixed. Its coastal cities, however, were people chiefly by Greeks. In 129 B.C. Caria became a part of the Roman province of Asia, and from that date its history coincides with that of the province. Though Paul and others of the apostles traversed Caria in their missionary journeys, only its cities are mentioned by name in that connection.

Many Jewish settlements were established in Caria as elsewhere in western Asia Minor. Christianity made comparatively slow progress and in the reign of Zeno (477-491) the rebellion of Illus and Pamprepius, partly pagan-inspired, found support in the province.

Bibliography.–L. Robert, *La Carie* (1954ff.); *Monumenta Asiae Minoris antiqua* (1939, 1962), VI, VIII; Pauly-Wissowa, X/2, 1940-47.

E. J. BANKS
W. H. C. FREND

CARIATHIARIUS kâr′-ath-i-âr′ē-əs (1 Esd. 5:19, NEB). *See* KIRIATH-JEARIM.

CARITES kâr′īts [Heb. *kārî*] (2 K. 11:4, 19); AV CAPTAINS. Mercenary troops who helped guard the palace and temple at the request of Jehoiada. The people of Caria in southwest Asia Minor were noted in early times as seafarers and mercenaries. Perhaps they are the same as, or a later development of, the CHERETHITES; cf. the reading *hakkārî* in the *K* of 2 S. 20:23.

See *Enc.Brit.* (1970), IV, 901.

CARKAS kär′kəs [Heb. *karkas*]; AV, NEB, CARCAS. One of seven chamberlains ordered to summon Queen Vashti before King Ahasuerus (Est. 1:10). The Targum allegorizes the first five of the names.

CARMANIANS kär-mā′ni-ənz (2 Esd. 15:30, AV, NEB). *See* CARMONIANS.

CARME kär′mē (1 Esd. 5:25, AV). *See* HARIM **2**.

CARMEL kär′məl [Heb. *hakkarmel*–'fruit garden'; Gk. (Josephus) *ho Karmēlos, Karmēlion óros*].

1. A prominent wooded mountain range on the Mediterranean coast, stretching NW-SE for about 30 mi. (48 km.) from the south shore of the Bay of Acre to the plain of Dothan. Mt. Carmel itself reaches a height of 470 ft. (143 m.) at the promontory, and has a maximum elevation of 1742 ft. (530 m.) at Esfia.

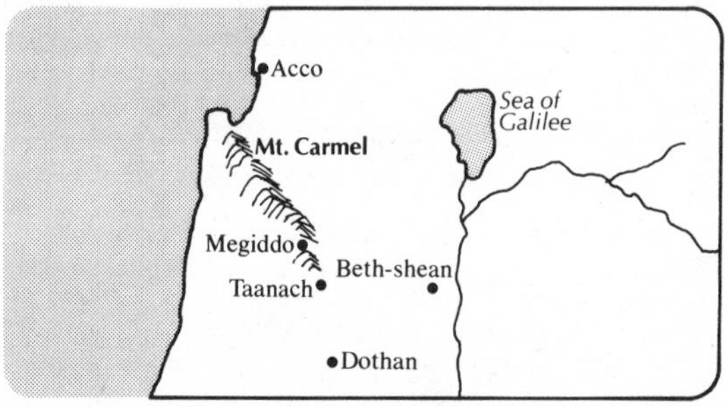

While the steep slopes on the north and east afford little scope for the growth of anything other than scrub and brushwood, the south and west of the mountain, which gives way more gradually to the coast, still justifies its fame in antiquity as the "garden with fruit trees." Although there were a few springs of water there, the cultivation of crops required the natural resources to be supplemented by means of cisterns. These, along with the oil and wine presses cut into the surface of the porous limestone rock, furnish evidence of the ancient husbandry that made Carmel famous. 2 Ch. 26:10 may refer to the viticulture of the area; elsewhere Carmel was regarded as the symbol of beauty (Cant. 7:5), fruitfulness (Isa. 35:2), majesty (Jer. 46:18), and a prosperous, happy life (Jer. 50:19). The languishing of Carmel pointed to divine vengeance on the land (Nah. 1:4), and her decay indicated complete desolation (Am. 1:2; Isa. 33:9).

Roughly triangular in form, with plains extending from its base on each of the three sides, this imposing mountain was visible from a great distance. It had little

Kebaran Caves on Mt. Carmel. A series of caverns has been discovered with deposits from the Old Stone Age (up to 9th millennium B.C.) through the Natufian or Mesolithic Age (9th-early 7th millennia). (W. S. LaSor)

strategic value in antiquity, however, since it was a wedge-shaped barrier dividing the Palestinian coastal plain into the plain of Acco to the north and the plains of Sharon and Philistia to the south. It was penetrated by two main passes, one of which emerged at Jokneam and Megiddo and the other at Taanach. In antiquity much of the commercial and military traffic traversed the range by means of these passes. Because of its isolation Mt. Carmel was sparsely occupied in historical times, though its caves and wooded glens attracted a few settlers from the Stone Age onwards.

In the lists of Thutmose III, Ramses II, and Ramses III of Egypt, a Palestinian site known as *Rosh Qidshu* or "holy peak" was mentioned, and if this is identical with Mt. Carmel it might indicate that the place was a sanctuary or a holy locale from an early period. Here stood an ancient altar of Yahweh, and probably a sanctuary of Baal also, since the worshipers of these deities chose the place as common ground for the great contest of faith (1 K. 18). On that occasion the gods of Jezebel were discredited; and since she came from Tyre the vanquished deity was almost certainly Baal Melqart, the chief Tyrian god. The site of the contest was located by tradition at el-Mahrakah, which was near to a flowing spring (1 K. 18:33ff.). From the crest of Carmel Elijah observed the coming storm, and preceded the chariot of Ahab to the gate of Jezreel (vv. 42ff.). Elijah may have used the mountain as a spiritual retreat, and Elisha was a familiar visitor to Carmel also.

Carmel was in the territory allotted to Asher, and according to Josephus (*BJ* iii.3.1) it subsequently came under the control of Tyre.

2. A town in Judah (Josh. 15:55) in the uplands near Hebron named in association with Maon and Ziph. It is identified with the present-day Kermel, about 8 mi. (13 km.) SSE of Hebron; and ruins at the site include a tower dating from the 12th cent. A.D. At Carmel Saul erected a monument after defeating the Amalekites (1 S. 15:22). From this area (*see* BUSINESS) came Nabal, the churlish alcoholic husband of Abigail, whom David married after Nabal died (1 S. 25:2-40). One of David's heroes, Hezro, also came from Carmel (2 S. 23:35).

W. EWING
R. K. H.

CARMELITE kär′mə-līt [Heb. *karm*e*lî*; Gk. *Karmēlios, Karmālítēs*]. An inhabitant of the town of Carmel in Judah. NABAL the husband of Abigail (1 S. 25:2, 4; 30:5;

2 S. 2:2; 3:3), and HEZRO, one of David's mighty men (2 S. 23:35; 1 Ch. 11:37), bear this name. In 2 S. 3:3 the LXX differs from the MT, reading *tḗs Abigaias tḗs Karmēlias,* "of Abigail the Carmelitess."

CARMELITESS kär-mə-lī'təs [Heb. *karmelîṯ*; Gk. *Karmēlia*]. A female inhabitant of Carmel in Judah. Only ABIGAIL the wife of Nabal bears this name (1 S. 27:3; 2 S. 3:3, LXX; 1 Ch. 3:1).

CARMI kär'mī [Heb. *karmî*–'fruitful'?].

1. A son of Reuben who came to Egypt with Jacob (Gen. 46:9; Ex. 6:14; 1 Ch. 5:3).

2. A Judahite (1 Ch. 2:7), son of Zabdi (according to Josh. 7:1) and father of Achan (given the name of "Achar" in 1 Ch. 2:7). In "the sons of Carmi" (1 Ch. 2:7), Carmi is probably to be taken as the son of Zimri (=Zabdi, Josh. 7:1). The Targum, however, has "Carmi who is Zimri." The LXX identifies Zimri and Zabdi.

3. In 1 Ch. 4:1 Carmi is probably an alternative form of Caleb. H. J. WOLF

CARMITES kär'mīts [Heb. *hakkarmî*] (Nu. 26:6); NEB CARMITE FAMILY. The name of a family of which CARMI (1) was head.

CARMONIANS kär-mō'ni-ənz; AV, NEB, CARMANIANS. A people from Carmania, a Persian province located along the north shore of the Persian Gulf. They are depicted in one of the visions of 2 Esdras (15:30) as a fierce and warlike nation that joins in battle with "the dragons of Arabia." The country is frequently mentioned by the ancient writers, who describe the inhabitants as closely resembling the Medes and Persians in manners and customs. J. HUTCHISON W. W. GASQUE

CARNAIM kär-nā'əm [Gk. *Karnein* (1 Macc. 5:26), *Karnain* (vv. 43f.), *tó Karnion* (2 Macc. 12:21, 26)]; AV also CARNION (2 Maccabees). One of the strong cities besieged and captured by Judas Maccabeus in his campaign E of the Jordan (1 Macc. 5:26-43). Those who fled from the city were put to death in the temple of Atargatis located here. Carnaim is apparently identical with the OT KARNAIM (modern Sheikh Sa'd). W. S. L. S.

CARNAL [Gk. *sárkinos,* var. *sarkikós*] (Rom. 7:14); NEB UNSPIRITUAL. *See* FLESH.

CARNALLY [Heb. *šiḵeḇaṯ zera'*–'lying of seed' (Lev. 19:20; Nu. 5:13), *lezāra'* (Lev. 18:20)]; NEB "have sexual intercourse." *See* ADULTERY.

CARNELIAN [Heb. *'ōḏem* (Ezk. 28:13); Gk. *sárdinos* (Rev. 4:3), *sárdinon* (21:20)]; AV SARDIUS, SARDINE STONE; NEB OT SARDIN, NT CORNELIAN. *See* STONES, PRECIOUS.

CARNION kär'nē-ən (2 Macc. 12:21, 26, AV). *See* CARNAIM.

CAROUSING [Gk. *kṓmoi*] (Gal. 5:21); AV REVELLINGS; NEB ORGIES; [*pótoi*] (1 Pet. 4:3); AV BANQUETINGS; NEB TIPPLING; [*syneuōchéō*] (2 Pet. 2:13; Jude 12); AV FEAST; NEB "sit at table," "eat and drink." The references are to gluttonous feasting, which Gentiles evidently sometimes found hard to give up after they became Christians. The *kṓmos* was originally a religious procession (cf. MM, p. 367; Bauer, p. 462), later a joyous banquet; and *pótos* is in the strict sense a drinking bout. Paul admonishes his readers that excesses in eating and drinking are unbecoming the Christian awaiting the Parousia (Rom. 13:13), and belong to one's lower nature (Gal. 5:21). J. W. D. H.

CARPENTER [Heb. *ḥārāš*; Gk. *téktōn*]; AV also "workers in timber," ARTIFICERS; NEB also WOODWORKER (Isa. 44:13). The Heb. *ḥārāš,* a general word for a graver or craftsman, is translated "carpenter" in 2 K. 22:6; 2 Ch. 24:12; 34:11; Ezr. 3:7. The same word is rendered "craftsman" in the RSV of 1 Ch. 29:5; Jer. 24:1; 29:2, and "smith" of Zec. 1:20. In 2 S. 5:11; 2 K. 12:11; 1 Ch. 14:1; 22:15; and Isa. 44:13, *ḥārāš* occurs with *'ēṣ* (wood) and is more exactly translated "carpenter" or "worker in wood." *Téktōn,* the corresponding Greek word for artificer, is translated "carpenter" in Mt. 13:55 and Mk. 6:3. *See* CARVING; CRAFTS.

CARPETS [Heb. *middîn* < *maḏ*] (Jgs. 5:10); AV JUDGMENT; NEB SADDLE-CLOTHS; [*genāzîm*] (Ezk. 27:24); AV CHESTS; NEB STORES. The Heb. *maḏ* can mean both "measure" and "cloth" or "garment" (cf. BDB, p. 551). In Jgs. 5:10 it is evidently a cloth for sitting on, either on the ground (a carpet), or covering a throne or chair, or most plausibly from the context, on the back of an ass (NEB).

The Heb. *genāzîm* in Ezk. 27:24 is even less certain. *See* CHEST.

CARPUS kär'pəs [Gk. *Karpos*] (2 Tim. 4:13). The friend with whom Paul left his cloak at Troas. From the prison in which he was confined (cf. 2 Tim. 1:8), Paul asks Timothy, among several other requests, to return the cloak to him. The incident indicates that Paul must have been well acquainted with the family of Carpus. He was presumably one of Paul's converts; and the apostle must have lodged with him and also have had considerable confidence in him, since he committed to his care not only the cloak but also his books and parchments. H. E. DOSKER

CARRIAGE [Heb. *kelî, keḇûddâ, neśû'â*; Gk. *episkeuasámenoi*]. All of these terms have been translated in the AV by "carriage" in its obsolete meaning (Jgs. 18:21; 1 S. 17:22 [twice]; Isa. 10:28; 46:1; Acts 21:15). In the RSV and NEB these are translated by more modern expressions, e.g., "goods," "baggage," "valuables."

CARRION VULTURE. [Heb. *rāḥām, rāḥāmâ*] (Lev. 11:18; Dt. 14:17); AV GIER EAGLE; NEB OSPREY. An unclean bird, perhaps the black and white Egyptian vulture. *See* BIRDS, UNCLEAN.

CARSHENA kär'shə-nə, kär-shē'nə [Heb. *karšenā'*]. The first named among the "seven princes of Persia and Media" under Ahasuerus (Est. 1:14). *See* PRINCES, THE SEVEN.

CART [Heb. *'agālâ* < *'gl*–'to be round']. Whereas Heb. *reḵeḇ* (a collective) and *merkāḇâ* (a single exemplar) denote the chariots used in war and by the highest officials in the state, *'agālâ* denotes a cart or wagon used mainly for carrying objects too heavy for beasts of burden or, in exceptional cases, for carrying women, children, and invalids.

The oldest examples of vehicles — clumsy, open wagons with four massive wheels and drawn by four asses (see the mosaic on the so-called standard-monu-

Assyrian soldiers lead away prisoners of war, with captive women seated on an ox-drawn cart with spoked wheels. Alabaster relief from Ashurbanipal's palace at Nineveh (668-633 B.C.) (Louvre)

ment in the British Museum) — are found among the Sumerians. In mountainous regions the two-wheeled cart with spokes, invented somewhat later, proved more useful. In Egypt such carts were drawn by two oxen.

It is remarkable that the Egyptian words for carts and chariots are of Semitic origin. Nevertheless the Semitic nomads immigrating into Egypt as depicted on the well-known tomb painting in Beni-hasan seem not to have had carts. Pharaoh commanded Joseph's brothers to return to their father with their beasts of burden and with "carts out of the land of Egypt" (Gen. 45:19) for carrying their invalid father and their families. The very unusual sight of the carts was proof to Jacob of the veracity of his sons' report (Gen. 45:27). In later times Assyrian reliefs depict families from conquered towns starting out into exile on small open carts drawn by two oxen.

Closed carts are mentioned in Nu. 7:3 and Isa. 66:20 (*ṣāḇ*; cf. Bab. *ṣumbu*). In the first case the sanctity of the objects carried by them is the reason for the use of this special kind of cart (Nu. 7:5-8); in the second case it is the comfort of the travelers. A closed four-wheeled wagon is known from Ashurnasirpal's obelisk (B. Meissner, *Babylonien und Assyrien,* I [1920], 249). The Philistines sent the ark to Israel on a cart drawn by two cows (1 S. 6:7, etc.). In the same way David tried to bring the ark to Jerusalem (2 S. 6:3-6; 1 Ch. 13:7-9).

Amos 2:13 mentions the use of a cart when bringing the sheaves of grain from the field to the threshing floor; in Isa. 28:27f. two words for a cartwheel are mentioned, both in connection with threshing: the cart with its oxen is driven over the ears strewed on the threshing floor. The reading "horses" in 28:28 is uncertain; some ancient versions read "(divided) hoofs," and cf. the NEB. So the rule that in Israel carts were drawn by cows may still stand. Isa. 5:18 mentions a cart rope — probably a plaited leather thong attached to the pole, forming a loop around the cow's neck. The metaphor seems to point to its strength. In Ps. 46:9 (MT 10) one should vocalize, with the LXX and Targum, *ʿ^{a}gîlôṯ*, "shields."

The "chariot" (Gk. *hárma*) of the Ethiopian minister of finances (Acts 8:28f.) must have been an open vehicle with a standing place for the driver and at least two seats; it was therefore a traveling vehicle probably drawn by horses or mules.

See also CHARIOT.

Bibliography.–A. Erman, *Aegypten und aegyptisches Leben im Altertum* (1923), II, 649-651; P. Thomsen in M. Ebert, ed., *Reallexikon der Vorgeschichte,* XIV, 231-242, esp. pp. 237f.; A. Salonen, *Die Landfahrzeuge des alten Mesopotamiens* (1951); "Notes on Wagons and Chariots in Ancient Mesopotamia," *Studia Orientalia,* 14/2 (1950).

A. VAN SELMS

CARVING [Heb. *qālaʿ, miqlaʿaṯ, ḥ^{a}rōšeṯ, pittû(a)ḥ, pāṯaḥ, ḥāqâ, ʿāśâ*; Gk. *entypóō*]; AV also GRAVING, ENGRAVEN, MADE; NEB also DECORATION, ENGRAVED. The OT references to carving are in descriptions of Solomon's temple (1 K. 6:18ff.; 2 Ch. 3:7), in Ezekiel's vision of the restored temple (Ezk. 41:17ff.), and in describing the work of the craftsmen Bezalel and Oholiab (Ex. 31:5; 35:33), who were put in charge

Ivory carving of a sphinx from Megiddo. A hoard of 383 ivory carvings dated to the period of 1350-1150 B.C. was discovered at the site. (Israel Department of Antiquities and Museums)

Stonemason carving image of Shalmaneser III (858-824 B.C.) at the source of the Tigris River. Engraving from a bronze band ornamenting the gates of a palace, provenience unknown (Trustees of the British Museum)

of the skilled work on the tabernacle and its furnishings. The use of *ḥ^{a}rōšeṯ* in the latter passages alludes to the skills of carpentry.

Carving, or engraving, was extensively used among the peoples of Bible lands. There were no materials used in the arts which were not subjected to the graver's skill. Carved objects of wood, stone, ivory, clay, bronze, gold, silver, and glass discovered today show how skilful the ancient carvers were. Carving was principally done in bas-relief, although Ex. 28:11 shows that incised lines were also used. The signets and scarabs are examples of this class of carving.

The only NT reference is to the Decalogue carved on tablets of stone (2 Cor. 3:7).

See also CRAFTS. J. A. PATCH

CASE. The archaic expression in Ex. 5:19, AV, "they were in evil case" (Heb. *b^{e}rā'*), is in the RSV "in evil plight," the NEB "in trouble."

CASEMENT (Prov. 7:6, AV); RSV, NEB, LATTICE. *See* HOUSE III.D.

CASIPHIA kə-sif'ē-ə [Heb. *kāsipyā'*]. An unidentified place in north Babylonia, near the river Ahava, to which Ezra sent for "ministers for the house of our God" (Ezr. 8:17). Some have thought the name to be connected with Heb. *kesep,* "silver" or "money." The LXX has *en argyríǭ toú tópou,* "in silver of the place," and 1 Esd. 8:45 has *en tǭ tópǭ toú gazophylakíou,* "in the place of the treasury."

CASLUHIM kas'lə-him [Heb. *kasluḥîm*–'people of Kasluḥ'; Gk. *Chasmōnieim*]; NEB CASLUHITES. A people mentioned in Gen. 10:14; 1 Ch. 1:12 as descended from Mizraim (Egypt). From them, it is said, sprang the PHILISTINES.

CASPHON kas'fon (1 Macc. 5:36, AV). *See* CHASPHO.

CASPHOR kas'fôr (1 Macc. 5:26, 36, AV, NEB). *See* CHASPHO.

CASPIN kas'pən [Gk. *Kaspein*] (2 Macc. 12:13); AV CASPIS kas'pəs. A stronghold E of the Jordan captured by Judas. There seems to be some confusion in the Greek text, and Josephus (*Ant.* xii.8.5) refers to the fortress as EPHRON (**3**). *See* CHASPHO.

CASSIA kash'-ə.

1. [Heb. *qiddâ*; Gk. *íris*] (Ex. 30:24; Ezk. 27:19). An ingredient of the holy anointing oil along with myrrh, cinnamon, calamus, and olive oil. According to Ezk. 27:19 it was one of the commodities Damascus traded with Tyre. Cassia comprised the fragrant inner bark of the *Cinnamomum cassia* Blume, a shrub native to the East Indies, imported into Palestine at a very early period. While related to the true cinnamon it is decidedly inferior in flavor and quality.

2. [Heb. *q^{e}ṣî'â*; Gk. *kasía*] (Ps. 45:8 [MT 9]); NEB "powder." Most probably the perennial *Saussurea lappa* (Decaisne) Clarke, or Indian orris. In antiquity it was widely exported from India, having reputed qualities as a medicament and an aphrodisiac. Its chief use in Palestine was as a perfume. R. K. H.

CAST. The verb is used archaically in the AV in several expressions. In Jer. 41:14 "cast about" (Heb. *sāḇaḇ*) means "turned around"; "thine olive shall cast his fruit" (Dt. 28:40, *nāšal*) means the olives will drop from the tree; "casteth her calf" (Job 21:10, *šāḵōl*; also RSV) means "miscarries" (cf. Gen. 31:38; Ex. 23:26; also, of a vine and its fruit, Mal. 3:11); "cast in her mind" (Lk. 1:29, Gk. *dialogízomai*) means "pondered." In Jer. 38:11f., AV, "cast clouts" are thrown-out rags.

Elsewhere the usual meaning of "cast" is either "throw" (esp. Heb. *šālaḵ*; Gk. *bállō*) or "form in a mold" (esp. Heb. *yāṣaq,* Ex. 25:12; 26:37; 36:36; 37:3, 13; 38:5; cf. 1 K. 7:15ff.). To be cast down is to be prostrate in grief or humility (e.g., 1 K. 18:42; Ezr. 10:1), and anguish or depression is portrayed as a cast down soul (Ps. 42:5f., 11; 43:5, Heb. *šāḥaḥ*). J. W. D. H.

CASTANETS [Heb. *m^{e}na'an'îm*]; AV CORNETS. Castanets are mentioned in 2 S. 6:5 among the musical instruments upon which David and the house of Israel played while bringing the ark from the house of Abinadab. This word is incorrectly translated "cornets" in the AV. The castanet was probably about the same kind of instrument as the Egyptian *sistrum,* a loop-shaped metal frame through which were passed loose rods with rings at the ends. The instrument was held by a long handle and was rattled during songs and dances. It was used in Egypt in religious worship or to scare away evil influences.

A. W. FORTUNE

CASTAWAY. The AV rendering of Gk. *adókimos* in 1 Cor. 9:27; the RSV has "disqualified," the NEB "rejected." The literal implication of the word is "tested and proved to be false or unacceptable."

CASTLE [Heb. *bîrâ*] (Neh. 7:2); AV PALACE; NEB CITADEL; [*'armôn*] (Prov. 18:19). *See* FORTIFICATION.

CASTOR AND POLLUX (Acts 28:11, AV, NEB). *See* TWIN BROTHERS.

CASTOR-OIL PLANT (Jonah 4:6ff., RSV mg., NEB mg.). *See* GOURD **1.**

CAT [Gk. *aílouros*]. The only mention of this animal is in Bar. 6:22, where cats are mentioned with "bats, swallows, and birds" as sitting with impunity on the images of the heathen gods which are unable to drive them off. In biblical times cats were not kept as pets in Palestine; however, they were considered sacred by the Egyptians (cf. Herodotus ii.66f.; Strabo *Geog.* xvii.1.40).

CATARACT [Heb. *ṣinnôr*; Gk. *katarráktēs*] (Ps. 42:7 [MT]); AV WATERSPOUT. The precise meaning of the word is uncertain; it may have alluded to some familiar Palestinian waterfall connected with the Jordan. In 2 S. 5:8 (AV "gutter"; RSV "water shaft"; NEB "grappling-iron") the same term may have referred either to the underground water-tunnels of Jebusite Jerusalem, or to some device for scaling the walls, such as a hook. Alternatively, a trident as part of military armor has been suggested by E. L. Sukenik. Such a weapon was recovered from Lachish at a level contemporary with David.

R. K. H.

CATECHIST; CATECHUMEN. A catechist is a teacher who instructs pupils in the elements of his or her own religion. In the OT the catechist teaches the rudiments of OT truth, in the NT the principles of the Christian faith. A catechumen is one whom the catechist instructs or catechizes, in preparation for the ceremony of baptism.

The words are derived from Gk. *katēchéō,* "give a sound," "answer," "echo," as the students echo the words of their instructor. It came to mean familiar verbal instruction, a free informal discussion between teacher and pupil. Luke informs Theophilus (Lk. 1:4) that he intends to give him a succinct and orderly account of those things which he had previously received by word of mouth (*perí hṓn katēchḗthēs*). See also Acts 18:25; 21:21, 24; Rom. 2:18; 1 Cor. 14:19; Gal. 6:6, all using *katēchéō.*

We do not find in the NT an organized catechumenate, such as existed in the 3rd and 4th centuries. The apostles preached mainly to synagogue-instructed Jews who were familiar with the Law and the Prophets and the Psalms, or to Gentiles who had learned from the Jews and had become proselytes. The purpose of the first apostolic preaching and teaching was to convince the hearers that Jesus was the promised Messiah, the Savior of the world. As believers multiplied, the contrast between them and those who rejected the teaching became more and more marked. Opposition, scorn, and persecution became bolder and more bitter. The Christians were compelled to set forth and defend their beliefs more clearly. They had to meet and answer keen and persistent objections. And so the necessity for clear, systematic teaching led more and more to an ordered catechumenate. The Apostolic Constitutions, from the latter part of the 3rd cent., show the institution in a fair state of development. A Jew, pagan, or heretic of good moral standing, upon application to the deacon, presbyter, or bishop, was admitted into the state of catechumen by the sign of the cross and the imposition of hands (Sch.-Herz.).

We find the basis for the Christian catechumenate in the Great Commission (Mt. 28:19f.), which had the aim of making disciples, i.e., believing followers, by means of baptizing and teaching. Those who have become disciples are to observe all the things that Christ has commanded. Jesus Himself at twelve years of age had become a child of the law, a catechumen. He became the great Catechist, instructing His disciples, other private individuals, and the multitudes. For an example of His catechizing, see Mt. 16:13ff. Paul was a master in the catechetical method, which appears frequently in the Epistles (see 1 Cor. 3:1f.; He. 5:11, 14; 6:1f.; 1 Pet. 2:2; 1 Jn. 2:13). Examples of his use of the pedagogical method of apperception are found in Acts 14:14ff.; 17:16ff.; 19:8f. Thus the idea of religious nurture and instruction is found throughout the NT.

Yet the catechetical method was not something new in the NT. Its roots are found throughout the OT. The narrative of God's first communication with man inside the gates of Eden, concerning commandment, law, sin, its consequences, its remedy, takes a catechetical form. The importance of systematic instruction, both public and private, is emphasized throughout the OT and NT, although it might not always take the form of catechizing in the modern pedagogical sense. In the patriarchal age the father was the prophet, the teacher, and the catechist in his house, which often included several families with their servants (see Gen. 18:19; also Ex. 12:26; Dt. 6:1-9; Josh. 4:6f.; 24:15; Ps. 34:11). In addition to their sacerdotal functions, priests and Levites were catechists (instructors) among the people (Lev. 10:11; Dt. 33:10; 2 Ch. 15:3; Ezk. 44:23). In later times the synagogues had regular instruction in the Law and the Prophets.

See EDUCATION; INSTRUCT; TEACH.

G. H. GERBERDING

CATERPILLAR [Heb. *ḥāsîl*]. A name given to a larval stage of the LOCUST, found only in 1 K. 8:37; 2 Ch. 6:28; Ps. 78:46; Isa. 33:4.

CATHOLIC EPISTLES [Gk. *hai epistolaí katholikaí*]. In distinction from the apostolic or Pauline Epistles that were addressed to individual churches or persons, the term "catholic," in the sense of universal or general, was applied by Origen and the other church fathers to the seven Epistles written by James, Peter, John, and Jude. As early as the 3rd cent. the term came to be used in the sense of "encyclical," since, as Theodoret says later, "they are not addressed to single churches, but generally [*kathólou*] to the faithful, whether to the Jews of the Dispersion, as Peter writes, or even to all who are living as Christians under the same faith." Three other explanations of the term have been given, viz., (1) that it was intended to indicate a common apostolic authorship (only a few support this view); (2) that it signifies that the seven Epistles were universally received as genuine; (3) that it refers to the catholicity of their doctrine, i.e., orthodox and authoritative *v.* heretical epistles, in harmony with Christian truth. By some misconception of the word "catholic" the Western Church interpreted it as signifying "canonical" and sometimes called these Epistles *epistolae canonicae*. That it was originally used in the sense of "general" Epistles is now commonly agreed.

This is evident from their form of address. James wrote to all Jews "of the dispersion" who had embraced the Christian faith. In his First Epistle Peter addressed the same Christians, including also gentile converts, resident in five provinces of Asia Minor; "exiles of the dispersion." His Second Epistle is to all Christians everywhere. John's first letter was evidently written to a group of churches and intended for universal use. Jude also had in mind all Christians when he wrote "to those who are called, beloved in God." The seeming exceptions are 2 and 3 John, which are addressed to individuals but included with the Catholic Epistles as properly belonging with John's First Epistle and of value to the general reader.

The character and contents of these seven Epistles are treated under their separate articles.

D. M. PRATT

CATHUA kə-thōō'ə [Gk. *Kathoua*, B *Koua*] (1 Esd. 5:30). The head of a family of temple-servants who returned from the captivity with Zerubbabel. The name corresponds to Giddel in Ezr. 2:47.

CATTLE [Heb. *bᵉhēmâ*] (Gen. 1:24-26; 2:20; 3:14; 7:14, 21; 8:1; 9:10; Ex. 11:5; 12:29; etc.); AV also BEAST; NEB also BEAST, ANIMAL, HERDS; [*miqneh*] (Gen. 4:20; 13:2, 7; 30:29; 31:9, 18; 33:17; etc.); AV also POSSESSION; NEB also HERDS(MAN), PROPERTY, LIVESTOCK, BEAST, FLOCKS, etc.; [*bāqār*] (Nu. 7:87f.; 31:33, 38, 44; 1 K. 4:23; 2 Ch. 31:6; Joel 1:18), AV also OXEN, BEEVES; NEB also BEASTS, OXEN; [*bᵉʿîr*] (Nu. 20:4, 8, 11; Ps. 78:48); AV, NEB, also BEASTS; [*'elep*] (Dt. 7:13); AV KINE; NEB HERDS; [*'allûp*] (Ps. 144:14); AV, NEB, OXEN; [*mᵉlā'ḵâ*] (Gen. 33:14); NEB LIVESTOCK; [*śeh*] (Isa. 7:25); NEB OXEN; [Gk. *thrémma*] (Jn. 4:12); [*ktḗnos*] (Rev. 18:13); AV BEASTS. The RSV emends Heb. *bāḥûr* (AV, lit. "young men") in 1 S. 8:16 to read with the LXX *bāqār*; in 2 Ch. 20:25 it emends *bāhem* (AV, lit. "among them") to read *bᵉhēmâ*.

At least ten Hebrew and three Greek terms can be referred to in English by the generic word "cattle." The English term "cattle" is in many instances far less precise than the various Hebrew and Greek terms. Cattle may refer to wild and domesticated animals, livestock, beasts of burden, and animals trained for a variety of other purposes.

- I. Biblical Terms
  - A. Hebrew Terms
  - B. Greek Terms
- II. Cattle in Biblical Life
  - A. Cattle and Economy
  - B. Cattle and Legal Practice
  - C. Cattle and Religion

I. Biblical Terms.–*A. Hebrew Terms.* The most common designation for cattle in Hebrew is the generic term *bᵉhēmâ,* which appears 185 times in the OT. In the creation account of Gen. 1, "cattle" (*bᵉhēmâ*) is a designation for the first subdivision of the created "living creatures" and is distinguished from "creeping things," or small (crawling) things, and "beasts of the earth," or animals that roam in the wilds (vv. 24-26; cf. Ps. 148:10). "Cattle" here refers to large animals that lend themselves to domestication. In Gen. 2:20 the "cattle" are a division of the animal kingdom separated from the birds of the sky and the wild animals of the earth (cf. 3:14). The distinct division of "cattle" is present also in the flood narrative as a group of animals distinguished from birds, beasts, and creeping (swarming) creatures (Gen. 7:14, 21; 8:1; 9:10).

After the creation and flood accounts the generic term *bᵉhēmâ* is employed for the first time for domesticated animals (Gen. 34:23; 36:6) of large and small kinds (Lev. 1:2), such as horses (Gen. 47:17), donkeys (asses) (47:17; Dt. 5:14), herds of bovine cattle (Gen. 47:17f.), oxen (*bāqār*; Lev. 1:2; 27:26; Dt. 5:14), and flocks of sheep (Gen. 47:17; Lev. 27:26) and goats (Lev. 1:2; 27:26). In one postexilic passage *bᵉhēmâ* designates a beast of burden (Neh. 2:12, 14). In Lev. 11:2 *bᵉhēmâ* is a subdivision of "living things" (RSV) or land "animals" (NEB, NAB) and designates the animals that are classified as clean and edible (Lev. 11:3). In four passages *bᵉhēmâ* appears in the fixed phrase "birds of the air [heaven] and beasts of the earth" (Dt. 28:26; Jer. 7:33; 19:7; 34:20); here it clearly means wild animals (cf. Dt. 32:24). Whereas the most common meaning of *bᵉhēmâ* is the domesticated animal, in a number of contexts the word carries quite different meanings.

Another generic term for "cattle" in Hebrew is *miqneh,* which appears seventy-five times in the OT. This word is employed most frequently for "possessions" of livestock either purchased or otherwise acquired. Whenever it is translated as "cattle" it has the general meaning of "livestock," a term sometimes preferred by the NEB, NAB, and NASB. *Miqneh* can be made up of flocks of goats (Gen. 31:10), of sheep and goats (30:32; 31:9f.; Ex. 12:38; Job 1:3), herds of bovine cattle and flocks of sheep and goats (Gen. 46:32, 34; Nu. 32:26; 1 S. 30:20; Eccl. 2:7), horses (Gen. 47:16f.; Ex. 9:3-7), donkeys (Gen. 47:16f.; Ex. 9:3-7; 34:19; Job 1:3), camels (Ex. 9:3-7; Job 1:3), oxen (Gen. 34:19; Job 1:3), and possibly pack animals (2 K. 3:17; KoB, p. 561; J. Gray, *I & II Kings* [2nd ed. 1970], p. 483 n. g). In one instance the term *miqneh* is used interchangeably with *bᵉhēmâ* (cf. the cultic law of Ex. 13:12 with 34:19). A clear distinction between the terms is found in the MT of 2 K. 3:17 (RSV "your cattle [*miqnêḵem*], and your beasts [*bᵉhemtᵉḵem*]"; NEB follows the Lucianic recension of the LXX with "your army and your pack-animals").

The collective term for bovine cattle is *bāqār,* a term that can include adult male or bull, Gen. 32:6; Ex. 20:17; 22:3, 8f., 29; 23:4, 12; Dt. 5:14, 21; etc.), the adult female or cow (usually *pārâ*) (Gen. 33:13; Job 1:14), the calf in the generic sense (Gen. 18:7; Ex. 29:1; Nu. 7:15; 28:11; 29:13; 1 S. 14:32), the male calf (usually *ʿēgel*), and the female calf or heifer (*ʿeglâ*). Bovine cattle (*bāqār*) could be used for pulling (2 S. 6:6), plowing (Job 1:14; Am. 6:12), as beasts of burden (1 Ch. 12:41), and as cattle to be fattened (1 K. 5:3), as well as for sacrifice (Nu. 7:88; 2 Ch. 7:5; Ps. 66:15).

The Heb. *bᵉʿîr* always has a collective meaning and is best translated as "livestock" (Gen. 45:17; Ex. 22:5 [MT 4]; Nu. 20:4, 8, 11; Ps. 78:48). The word *'elep* appears with the meaning of cattle only seven times (Dt. 7:13; 28:4, 18, 51; Ps. 8:7 [MT 8]; Prov. 14:4; Isa. 30:24). The term *'allûp* is employed once with the meaning of cattle (Ps. 144:14; cf. Sir. 38:25). The AV and RSV translate the term *mᵉlā'ḵâ* as "cattle" in Gen. 33:14, but the NEB and NAB have "livestock."

Inlaid friezes depicting a row of bulls (top) and various dairy activities (bottom), including milking and the preparation and storing of butter. Temple of Ninhursag, Tell el-Ubaid (mid-3rd millennium) (University Museum, University of Pennsylvania)

The Hebrew term for small livestock is *śeh,* which designates sheep and goats (Gen. 30:33f.; Ex. 12:5; Dt. 14:4; Isa. 7:25). In a number of passages *śeh* is contrasted with the ox (*šôr,* Ex. 34:19; Lev. 22:23; Dt. 17:1; 1 S. 14:34; etc.), with ox and donkey (*šôr* and *ḥ*ᵃ*môr,* Ex. 22:3, 8f.; Josh. 6:21; Jgs. 6:4; 1 S. 22:19), or with bull and ram (*šôr* and *'ayil,* Nu. 15:11). Sheep and goats are kept in flocks (*ṣō'n,* Gen. 12:16; 30:32), separated from the bovine cattle (*bāqār,* Nu. 22:40), and driven ahead of the latter. At times *ṣō'n* could refer to sheep only (1 S. 25:2) or merely to males among sheep and goats (Gen. 30:40).

B. Greek Terms. In the NT the hapax legomenon *thrémma* is used in Jn. 4:12 with the meaning "cattle" (RSV, NEB, NASB; NAB "flocks"). In classical and koine Greek this term is used for the domesticated animal, especially the sheep or goat. The term *ktḗnos* appears with the meaning "cattle" in Rev. 18:13, where it is contrasted with sheep (*próbatos*). 1 Cor. 15:39 employs the noun *ktḗnos* with reference to domesticated animals (RSV "beasts"), whereas in Lk. 10:34 and Acts 23:24 it refers to a riding animal. The term *boús* can mean cattle (Jn. 2:14f.) or ox (Lk. 13:15; 14:5, 19; 1 Cor. 9:9; 1 Tim. 5:18).

***II. Cattle in Biblical Life.**–A. Cattle and Economy.* The domesticated animals (Heb. *b*ᵉ*hēmâ*) were of great importance economically for biblical man, who lived under both nomadic and agricultural conditions. Livestock in the form of the flocks (*ṣō'n*) of sheep and goats and herds of bovine cattle (*bāqār*) were raised as a source of milk (Dt. 32:14; Prov. 27:27; Isa. 7:22), butter (Gen. 18:5; Dt. 32:14; Jgs. 5:25; 2 S. 17:29; Job 20:17; cf. G. Dalman, *Arbeit und Sitte* [1928-1939], V, 194; VI, 307-311), and cheese (Job 10:10; 1 S. 17:18; 2 S. 17:29). According to Gen. 9:3 the meat of animals was allowed to be a staple item in the diet of postdiluvian man, but clear distinctions were made between clean (thus, edible) animals and unclean (thus, inedible) animals (Lev. 11; Dt. 14:3ff.). It appears that meat was eaten only occasionally, except perhaps by the wealthy, who may have had it regularly. Guests were entertained to calf, kid, or lamb (Gen. 18:7; Jgs. 6:19; 2 S. 12:4). The fatted young bull was stall-fed before being slaughtered (Prov. 15:17; 1 K. 4:23; Lk. 15:23, 27, 30). Apparently the Israelites seldom, if ever, castrated their male bovine (Lev. 22:24), and since the English word "ox" or "steer" has more specific reference to a castrated male bovine, "bull" would be a better rendering in Lev. 4:10; 7:23, and similar contexts. Bovine cattle were used as draught animals for pulling wagons (Nu. 7:3; 2 S. 6:6), drawing the plow (Dt. 22:10; 1 S. 11:5; 1 K. 19:19; Job 1:14; Am. 6:12; Isa. 30:24), and dragging the threshing sled (Dt. 24:5; cf. 1 Cor. 9:9). They were used as beasts of burden (1 Cor. 12:40). Their dung could be used as fuel for cooking (Ezk. 4:15).

B. Cattle and Legal Practice. The oldest biblical sources emphasize man's position of rulership over the created creatures (Gen. 1:20-28) and stress at the same time the consciousness of the close relationship of man and animal (cf. Ps. 104: 28-30; Eccl. 3:18-21). The corresponding relationship of man and animal is reflected in legal practice. In the covenant community the cattle (*b*ᵉ*hēmâ* in Ex. 20:10; *šôr* in Ex. 23:12) are assured the sabbath rest analogous to the slave and alien (Ex. 23:12; Dt. 5:14). The threshing ox is legally assured a part in the harvest (Dt. 25:4). The wild animals may have a part of that which grows of its own accord during the sabbath year (Ex. 23:10f.; Lev. 25:7). If an ox gores a person to death, the death penalty by stoning is executed on the ox (Ex. 21:28). A number of other regulations pertinent to oxen (injuries, theft, illegal grazing, etc.) are found in Ex. 21:29–22:15 (MT 14). Man's physical cohabitation with an animal is expressly forbidden (Ex. 22:19 [MT 18]; Lev. 18:23; 20:15f.; Dt. 27:18). The interbreeding of different kinds of cattle (*b*ᵉ*hēmâ*) was legally not permitted (Lev. 19:19). The yoking together of ox and ass for plowing was prohibited (Dt. 22:10).

C. Cattle and Religion. In cultic law certain types of cattle were considered a valid substitutionary equivalent for a man who had forfeited his life through sin (Gen. 22:13; cf. Ex. 13:13; 34:20). The substitutionary and expiatory use of animals was effective both for the sin offering and the guilt offering. The "young bull" was offered as a sin offering for the unwitting sin of the "anointed priest," or high priest, whose culpabilities bring guilt upon the whole people (Lev. 4:1–5:13). A male goat could be sacrificed for the sin of a ruler (4:22-26); a female goat for the sin of a common individual (vv. 27-31); a goat or a sheep for a sin offering (4:32–5:6); a ram for a guilt offering (5:14-19). On the great Day of Atonement a bull was sacrificed as an atoning sin offering for the high priest (Lev. 16:6), two male goats as a sin offering for the congregation, and a ram for a burnt offering (v. 5). The bull was sacrificed for an individual under certain special circumstances; e.g., in Jgs. 6:25f. (Gideon), 1 S. 1:24 (Hannah), 1 K. 18:23 (Elijah), Ezr. 8:35 (returning exiles), and in Job 42:8 along with rams (Eliphaz, Bildad, and Zophar).

The bull (*šôr*) is in the OT a symbol of virility, fecundity, and strength; it is used figuratively of the virile strength of Joseph (Dt. 33:17), the enemies of the psalmist (Ps. 22:12 [MT 13]), the gentile kings (Ps. 68:30 [MT 31]), the arrogance and power of Assyria (Isa. 10:13), the rulers and leaders of Edom (Isa. 34:7) and Babylon (Jer. 50:27). Probably the rams, lambs, goats, and bulls mentioned in Ezk. 39:18 are used figuratively for the mighty.

The bull was a widespread symbol of fertility and strength in other ancient Near Eastern countries. In Cannaanite religion El, the supreme deity in the Ugaritic pantheon, is often called "the Bull El" (*Ṯor-il*), which shows him as a fertility-god. In Ugarit, Baal or Hadad, the god of storm, rain, fertility, and vegetation, is also referred to as a bull (*UT* 129:17f). Among the Babylonians, Arameans, and Hittites the bull was the symbol of — or sacred animal of — the god of fertility and of the storm, bringing fructifying rain to earth. In Egypt live bulls under the names of Apis and Mnevis were venerated as gods in Memphis and Heliopolis respectively. Various bull-cults or calf-cults linked with Horus-worship are known from the Nile Delta area (cf. Otto, *Beiträge zur Geschichte der Stierkulte in Ägypten* [1938], pp. 6-8, 32f.). Thus the Israelites, whose forefathers had "served other gods" (Josh. 24:2), were inclined to follow the pagan practice of worshiping images of young bulls or male calves at Mt. Sinai (*'ēgel,* Ex. 32) and at Bethel and Dan in the time of Jeroboam I (1 K. 12:28f.). Such practice was condemned in the Decalogue (Ex. 20:4; cf. Dt. 4:15-19) and by the prophets (Am. 4:4; 5:5f.; Hos. 8:5f.; 13:2).

Bibliography.–F. S. Bodenheimer, *Animals of Palestine* (1935); *Animal and Man in Bible Lands* (1960); H. Hilger, *Biblischer Tiergarten* (1954); J. Calvet and M. Cruppi, *Les animaux dans la littérature sacrée* (1956); M. L. Henry, *Das Tier im Bewustsein des alttestamentlichen Menschen* (1952); C. H. Wallace, "Several Animals as Symbols in the OT" (Dissertation, Basel, 1961); J. Hempel, *Apoxysmata* (*BZAW*, 81, 1961), pp. 198-229; J. Feliks, *Animal World of the Bible* (1962); W. Pangritz, *Das Tier in der Bibel* (1963); W. Nagel, *Zeitschrift für Assyriologie*, 21 (1963), 169-236; R. Pinney, *Animals of the Bible* (1964); W. Kornfeld, *Kairos*, 7 (1965), 134-147; E. Fascher, *TLZ,* 90 (1965), 561-570; W. M. Clark, *VT*, 14 (1968), 433-39; *TDOT*, II, *s.v.* "b^ehēmāh" (Botterweck); "bāqār" (Beck).

G. F. HASEL

CAUDA kô'də [Gk. *Kauda,* several MSS *Klauda*] (Acts 27:16); AV CLAUDA. An island 23 mi. (37 km.) W of Cape Matala, S of Crete. The reading "Cauda" is supported by p^{74} $\aleph^{cor}$ B etc., and by the modern name Gozzo or Gaudos.

It is a small island, and could never have supported a large population. Its elevation to the rank of bishopric in Byzantine times must have been due to its association with the voyage of Paul. The ship with Paul on board was driven under the lee of Cauda (Acts 27:16); in the calm water S of the island the crew succeeded in hauling in the boat, undergirding the ship, and slackening sail.

W. M. CALDER

CAUL. The term is found in the AV as a translation of Heb. *yōṯereṯ, s^egôr, š^eḇîsîm*. In Hos. 13:8, *s^egôr* refers literally to the inclosure or covering of the heart, or perhaps the chest as surrounding the heart. It is possible, however, that the expression should be taken in the sense of "mailcoat of the heart," i.e., hardened heart, which is shut to the influence of God's grace; so Luther and many modern translators and commentators.

See also APPENDAGE OF THE LIVER.

H. L. E. LUERING

CAULKERS; CAULKING [Heb. *maḥ^azîqê beḏeq*]; AV CALKERS; Only in Ezk. 27:9, 27 is the hiphil participle of *ḥāzaq,* "strengthen, repair," translated "caulkers" because they "repair the seams" of the ship. Most commentators regard these men more generally as "ship carpenters" whose various responsibilities are represented by "repairing the seams."

Ezekiel 27, perhaps the best description of Phoenician shipping to survive from ancient times, pictures Tyre as a mighty merchant ship to which various Phoenician cities, regions or trading partners contribute representative goods and skilled services. Thus, one may see Gebal, or Byblos, as the center of wood craftsmanship or carpentry (cf. 1 K. 5:18).

See also GEBAL **1.**

H. VAN BROEKHOVEN

CAUSE. The AV "cause" for Heb. *rîḇ* in Ex. 23:2f., 6, etc., means "legal case" or "lawsuit," as also *dāḇār* in Ex. 18:19, 26; 22:9; Dt. 1:17, etc.; *mišpāṭ* in 2 S. 15:4; Job 13:18; 23:4; Lam. 3:59; and *dîn* in Ps. 9:4; 140:12; Jer. 5:28; 22:16; 30:13. In Prov. 29:7; 31:8 the RSV has "rights" for *dîn*.

In 1 K. 12:15 par. 2 Ch. 10:15 the AV has "the cause [Heb. *sibbâ*] was from the Lord"; the RSV translates "it was a turn of affairs brought about by the Lord."

CAUSEWAY. This term occurs in the AV as a translation of Heb. *m^esillâ* (built-up road) in 1 Ch. 26:16, 18. *See* ROADS.

CAVALRY [Gk. *hippikón*] (1 Macc. 15:38; 3 Macc. 1:1; Rev. 9:16); AV HORSEMEN. In Rev. 9:16 the emphasis is more on the horses than on their riders. They are typical examples of apocalyptic animal imagery, as befits their function as instruments of divine judgment (cf. also 9:17 and 8:7-11). *See also* APOCALYPTIC LITERATURE I.E.

CAVE [Heb. *m^e'ārâ*] (Gen. 19:30; 23:9ff.; Josh. 10:16ff.; Jgs. 6:2; 1 S. 13:6; 22:1; 1 K. 18:4, 13; 19:9, 13; 1 Ch. 11:15; Ezk. 33:27; etc.); [*mir'eh*] (Nah. 2:11); AV FEEDING-PLACE; [*m^ehillâ*] (Isa. 2:19); [*ḥōr*] (Nah. 2:12); AV HOLE; NEB LAIR; [Gk. *spḗlaion*] (Jn. 11:38; Rev. 6:15); AV also DEN; [*opḗ*–'hole'] (He. 11:38); NEB HOLE; **CAVERN** [Heb. *n^eqārâ*] (Isa. 2:21); AV, NEB, CLEFT; **DEN** [Heb. *mā'ôn, m^e'ōnâ*] (Job 38:40; Ps. 104:22; Cant. 4:8; Am. 3:4; Nah. 2:11f. [MT 12f.]); AV also DWELLING (Nah. 2:11); NEB also LAIR; [*minhārâ*] (Jgs. 6:2); NEB HOLLOW PLACE; [*'ereḇ*–'hiding-place'] (Job 37:8); [*m^e'ûrâ*] (Isa. 11:8); NEB HOLE; [*m^e'ārâ*] (Isa. 32:14; Jer. 7:11); NEB "open heath," CAVE; [Aram. *gōḇ*] (Dnl. 6:7ff.); NEB PIT; [Gk. *spḗlaion*] (Mt. 21:13; Mk. 11:17; Lk. 19:46; He. 11:38); NEB CAVE. The exact meaning of *m^e'ûrâ* in Isa. 11:8 is uncertain; BDB (p. 22) suggests "light-hole," KoB (p. 489) "the young one." The AV, RSV, and NEB emend the text to *m^e'ônâ* or *m^e'ārâ*.

Rocky caves are very common in the sandstone and limestone deposits of Palestine, and in antiquity they

Tomb of the Roman Soldier, so called from the statue in the center niche, at Petra. Probably a royal tomb, the building is a cave excavated by the Nabateans (*ca.* 1st cent. A.D.). (Jordan Information Bureau, Washington)

claimed many uses, including those of sanctuaries, storage areas, burial places, and dens for animals. In limestone hills, the calcium carbonate of which the rock is mainly composed is dissolved by water trickling through crevices or underground streams. Even on more level terrain pits are formed in a similar manner, and in antiquity these holes were often used for storing such things as grain or straw (cf. Jer. 41:8). The Hebrew term most frequently translated "cave" is *m^eārâ,* rendered in the LXX by *spḗlaion.* Other Hebrew words include *sukkâ* (Ps. 10:9, RSV "covert"; NEB "lair"), *ḥāgû* (Cant. 2:14, RSV "clefts"; NEB "holes"; Jer. 49:16, RSV "clefts"; NEB "crannies").

The idea of a den is conveyed by *ma'ôn.* The lions' den (*gōḇ*) of Dnl. 6 was probably more of a cistern than a rocky cave. The imagery of a lions' den was used to describe Nineveh (Nah. 2:11f.), to depict the grandeur of divine creativity (Job 38:39f.), and to show God's provision for the natural order (Ps. 104:21f.). Mountain caves were sometimes used as lairs by robbers; hence the allusions in Jer. 7:11; Mt. 21:13; Mk. 11:17; Lk. 19:46. For a time the Israelites "made for themselves the dens which are in the mountains, and the caves and the strongholds" as places of refuge from the oppression of the Midianites (Jgs. 6:2). In He. 11:38 and Rev. 6:15 such a structure is regarded as a suitable place of hiding.

Caves were also used as tombs (e.g., for the body of Lazarus, Jn. 11:38), and as storage places — perhaps during a time of emergency — for some of the Dead Sea community's most valuable MSS. At Petra in Mt. Seir the Edomites made use of caves in the rock, while the later NABATEANS excavated whole buildings of huge dimensions out of the red sandstone cliffs.

The principal caves mentioned in the Bible are MACHPELAH, MAKKEDAH, and ADULLAM.

R. K. HARRISON

CEASE. Nu. 11:25, AV, reads "they prophesied, and did not cease" (Heb. *yāsap,* lit. "add"), which the RSV, however, renders "they prophesied. But they did so no more"; and the NEB, "they fell into a prophetic ecstasy, for the first and only time." Here the AV is simply in error.

According to Acts 12:5, AV, the church prayed for Peter "without ceasing" while he was in prison. But the Gk. *ektenṓs* (D has *en ekteneía*) may also mean "earnestly" (cf. RSV) or "fervently" (NEB). Nonetheless, both the syntax and the circumstances of the verse indicate that the prayer was continuous. J. W. D. H.

CEDAR; CEDARWOOD [Heb. *'erez*; Gk. *kédros*; also Heb. *'ezraḥ* (Ps. 37:35), *'ōren* (Isa. 44:14)]; AV also BAY TREE (Ps. 37:35), ASH (Isa. 44:14); NEB also "spreading tree" (Ps. 37:35); **CEDAR WORK** [Heb. *'arzâ*] (Zeph. 2:14); NEB omits. With few exceptions, OT references are to the stately *Cedrus libani* Loud., the most massive tree known to the Israelites, and which often attained a height of 120 ft. (36 m.). Once prolific in Palestine (1 K. 6:9f.; 10:27), cedars are now very rare. Apart from their grandeur and vigor (1 K. 4:33; Isa. 35:2; 60:13; Am. 2:9; 2 K. 14:9; Cant. 5:15), the trees were esteemed for their fragrant durable wood (2 S. 5:11; 1 Ch. 22:4), which was more highly prized than the sycamore (1 K. 10:27; Isa. 9:10). The growth of the cedar typified that of the righteous man (Ps. 92:12).

David employed Tyrian workmanship to build a house of cedar (2 S. 5:11), and obtained vast quantities of the wood for the later Solomonic temple (1 Ch. 22:4). One of Solomon's most important buildings was the "house of the forest of Lebanon" (1 K. 7:2; 10:17; 2 Ch. 9:16), named after the source of its materials. Cedar was well adapted for beams (1 K. 6:9; Cant. 1:17), boards (Cant. 8:9), pillars (1 K. 7:2), and ceilings (Jer. 22:14), as well as carved work such as idols (Isa. 44:14f.). When grown in its natural habitat cedarwood is durable, close-grained, and capable of receiving a high polish. Its resinous content (Ps. 92:14) preserves it from rot and worms. Cedar oil was used in antiquity for preserving parchments and clothing.

Cedar is twice mentioned in connection with ritual cleansing. In Lev. 14:4 it, with scarlet and hyssop, was dipped in the blood of a "clean bird," and this blood was then sprinkled over the healed lepers; while in Nu. 19:6 it was used in the sacrifice of the red heifer. The cedar employed here would not be *C. libani,* since it did not grow in the wilderness. Probably some species of juniper such as *J. lycia* L. or *J. phoenicia* L. was implied. The references in Ezk. 27:5, where a tree was used for a ship's mast, and in Ezk. 31:8, are probably to the *Pinus halepensis* or Aleppo pine.

The AV translates Heb. *'^aruzîm* in Ezk. 27:24 as "made of cedar," which the RSV renders "made secure," based on an Arabic cognate, and the NEB "rolled up."

E. W. G. MASTERMAN R. K. H.

CEDRON sē'drən (Jn. 18:1, AV). *See* KEDRON; KIDRON.

CEILAN sē'lən (1 Esd. 5:15, AV). *See* KILAN.

CEILING [Heb. *sippun*]; AV CEILING. "Ceiling" occurs only in 1 K. 6:15. It comes from the root *sāpan,* meaning "(to) cover." It has its common meaning of the upper surface of a room; there is, however, some doubt about the text, and the NEB deletes the phrase "of the ceiling." The term "ciel" or "cieled" is found in the AV in 2 Ch. 3:5 (*ḥāpâ*); Jer. 22:14 and Hag. 1:4 (*sāpan*); Ezk. 41:16 (*śāḥîp*). In none of these cases does "ceiled" refer to the upper surface of a room, but to the covering or paneling of the inner walls of a house with cedar or other costly wood, in accordance with a now obsolete use of the English word. G. R. BERRY

CELEBRATE; CELEBRATION. Several terms are translated "celebrate" by the RSV. In Neh. 12:27 the common Hebrew verb *'āśâ* ("do," "make"; AV "keep") is used in reference to celebrating the dedication of the wall of Jerusalem. In similar contexts, the verbs *hāyâ* (be) and *'āḇaḏ* (serve) are used in Ezk. 45:21 and Ezr. 6:16, respectively. In Ps. 45:17 the verb *zāḵar* is used in the phrase rendered "cause your name to be celebrated." The noun "celebration" occurs only in 2 Ch. 23:13 in the phrase *môḏî'îm lᵉhallēl,* rendered "leading in the celebration" by the RSV but "such as were taught to sing praise" by the AV. Based on the verbs *yāḏa'* and *hālal,* the phrase means literally "giving the signal to praise." The only NT occurrence of Gk. *heortázō* ("celebrate the festival") is in 1 Cor. 5:8. N. J. O.

CELESTIAL BODIES [Gk. *sṓmata epouránia*] (1 Cor. 15:40); NEB HEAVENLY BODIES. Paul's reference here is first of all to the sun, moon, and stars, which he then takes as a figure for the resurrection body, the *sṓma pneumatikón* (v. 44). Although he mentions in v. 41 the differences among the sun, moon, and stars, his primary interest is their difference from terrestrial bodies, and hence the difference of the present human body on earth from the body of man in the life to come.

Calvin (comm. *in loc.*) saw in this passage no reference to a change in substance of the resurrected body, but only to that which gives it life: now the soul (*anima*), then the Spirit. J. W. D. H.

CELIBACY. Instances of a lifelong state of celibacy are rare in Scripture. In OT times marriage was almost universal and celibacy was considered abnormal. For the Israelites as well as other ancient peoples the propagation of the family name was of supreme importance, and thus the desire for sons was the dominant factor in marriage. Moreover, marriage was commanded by God. The eunuch was not admitted into the congregation of Israel (Dt. 23:1), nor was he permitted to serve in the priesthood (Lev. 21:20f.). The institutions of marriage and family were of vital importance in the OT because in this era God used a particular race, the Hebrews, as a vehicle for carrying out His redemptive purpose. For the sake of the Kingdom, therefore, the Israelite was required to marry and have children. The author of Isa. 56, however, prophesies of a time when eunuchs will be permitted to enter the sanctuary and will receive "a monument and a name better than sons and daughters" (vv. 3-5).

In the NT we find a somewhat different attitude toward marriage from the general stance of the OT. Although marriage is still spoken of as a sacred institution — and, in fact, the imagery of bridegroom and bride is used to describe the relationship between Christ and His Church — there are indications that the institution of marriage is not as decisive for the coming of the Kingdom as it was in the OT. Here we find notable examples of celibacy: John the Baptist, the apostle Paul, and Jesus Himself. Some dispute the case of Paul, but Paul's advice to the unmarried that they remain single "as I am" (1 Cor. 7:8) makes this fairly clear, and it is not contradicted by other data.

In 1 Cor. 7 Paul specifically takes up the issue of celibacy. The apostle, as Jesus, speaks of celibacy as a "gift" (Gk. *chárisma,* v. 7) that some people have and others do not. (Cf. Jesus' teaching in Mt. 19:12, "there are eunuchs who have made themselves eunuchs for the kingdom of heaven. He who is able to receive this, let him receive it." The Church has generally understood this passage to refer to those who renounce marriage for the sake of the Kingdom; but cf. also Isa. 56:3-5.) For those who do not have this gift, Paul recommends marriage (1 Cor. 7:9). For those who can bear it, however, he recommends the unmarried state (vv. 1, 7f., 25ff.). Paul gives this advice "because of the present distress" (Gk. *diá tḗn enestṓsan anánkēn,* v. 26), and because of the "worldly troubles" (Gk. *thlípsin tę̄ sarkí,* lit. "tribulation in the flesh," v. 28) that the married will have to face. This specific counsel is based upon a general principle for conduct during the period between Pentecost and the return of Christ. The time in this period is "shortened" (Gk. *synestalménos*). As Grosheide says (p. 177), this refers to a permanent quality of time during this period: "it is compressed and that means that it should be lived intensely (cf. Mt. 24:22). . . . This period demands the end of all things and hastens toward that end. . . . For that reason our life should be free from the present time and direct itself toward life eternal (Heb. 11:13-15)." Thus the general principle is that the Christian community should be governed in conduct not by the norms of society in this present age but by the norms of the eternal Kingdom, "for the form of this world is passing away" (vv. 29-31). And Paul clearly understands marriage as belonging to the *schḗma* that is passing away. Jesus Himself stated this clearly in Mt. 22:30 (cf. Mk. 12:25): "in the resurrection they neither marry nor are given in marriage, but are like angels in heaven." For this reason Paul sees advantages in remaining single. It allows one more detachment from worldly affairs and affords the opportunity for total preoccupation with the things of God (1 Cor. 7:32-35).

Paul also states repeatedly, however, that to marry is no sin (1 Cor. 7:9, 28, 36, 38f.). Despite his adoption of the single state, he asserts his right to marry (9:5). Nowhere in the NT is marriage characterized as sinful. In 1 Tim. 4:1-3 the prohibition of marriage is labeled demonic. Such admonitions indicate that already in NT times certain heretical sects were advocating an unchristian asceticism, which focused particularly on the denigration of married life.

The elevation of celibacy, especially for the clergy, became more pronounced during the 2nd cent., due in part to a reaction against the licentiousness of the Greco-Roman world and in part to the influence of Gnostic dualism. By the 4th cent. some councils of the Western Church (Elvira, *ca.* 306) were forbidding marriage after ordination, and conjugal intercourse to those who entered the priesthood married. It was only a natural progression to prescribe celibacy for the clergy, and this gradually became the rule in the West; the attention given the subject in the canons of the Church, however, is clearly indicative of much clerical resistance and dissatisfaction. The Eastern Church, on the other hand, has maintained the position that priests and deacons may marry before ordination, though not after; absolute celibacy is required only of the bishops. This tradition goes back to the Council of Nicea (325), which rejected a proposal requiring that the clergy put away their wives.

See also ABSTINENCE III; ASCETICISM; MARRIAGE.

Bibliography.–F. W. Grosheide, Comm. on 1 Corinthians (*NIC* 1953); *ODCC, s.v.* "Celibacy of the Clergy"; P. Schaff, *History of the Christian Church,* II (1910), 392-414. N. J. O.

CELL [Heb. *ḥānûṯ*] (Jer. 37:16); AV CABIN; NEB VAULTED PIT; [Gk. *oíkēma*] (Acts 12:7); AV PRISON. In Jer. 37:16 the MT reads *'el bêṯ habbôr w^e'el-haḥ^anuyôṯ,* which the AV translates "into the dungeon, and into the cabins." The RSV has "to the dungeon cells"; the NEB "into a vaulted pit beneath the house"; and the LXX reads (44:16) *eis oikían toú lákkou kaí eis tḗn chereth.* It is possible to take the latter part of the Hebrew phrase as in apposition to the first (a common Hebraistic device; cf. Zec. 9:9), so that *haḥ^anuyôṯ* (read *haḥanûṯ*?) defines more clearly the *bêṯ habbôr.* At any rate, *ḥanûṯ* evidently designates a vaulted cell or pit (KoB, p. 315; cf. BDB, p. 333).

The Gk. *oíkēma* in Acts 12:7 is according to both MM (p. 440) and Bauer (p. 559) a euphemism for "prison."

See also PRISON. J. W. D. H.

CELLAR [Heb. *'ôṣār* (1 Ch. 27:27); Gk. *krýptē* (Lk. 11:33)]; AV NT "secret place." The *'ōṣ^erôṯ hayyayin* of 1 Ch. 27:27 are storage places for wine, no doubt wine cellars, though not necessarily below ground level. Gk. *krýptē,* occurring only in Lk. 11:33, means etymologically "a covered place," and in Classical Greek its usage includes vaults and crypts as well as cellars. It seems evident that only in the larger houses in Palestine were cellars at all common. Excavations have shown that in rebuilding a town which was in ruins the old houses were sometimes utilized as cellars for the new.

G. R. BERRY
J. W. D. H.

CELOSYRIA sē-lō-sir'ē-ə (AV Apoc.). *See* COELESYRIA.

CENCHREAE sen'krə-ē [Gk. Kenchreai]; AV CENCHREA. A seaport located 7 mi. (11 km.) SE of Corinth on the eastern side of the Isthmus of Corinth. According to Pausanius (ii.2.3) the name derives from Cenchreas, son of Poseidon and Peirene. During the NT period a temple to Aphrodite lay on one side of the harbor, and there were sanctuaries of Asklepios and Isis on the other, while a bronze image of Poseidon was located on a mole extending into the sea.

According to Acts 18:18, Paul set sail from this port for Syria after having his hair shorn in fulfillment of a vow. It was to Phoebe, a deaconess of Cenchreae, that Paul entrusted the Epistle to the Romans (Rom. 16:1f.).

Bibliography.–Pauly-Wissowa, XI/1, 165-170; W. Michaelis, *ZNW,* 25 (1926), 144-154. R. P. MEYE

CENDEBEUS sen-də-bē'əs [Gk. *Kendebaios*]; NEB KENDEBAEUS. A general of Antiochus VII who was appointed "commander-in-chief of the coastal country" of Palestine (1 Macc. 15:38ff.) after the defeat of Tryphon by Antiochus in 138 B.C. He fortified Kedron and harassed the Jews in various ways. As Simon Maccabeus was too old to attack Cendebeus in person, he sent his two eldest sons, Judas and John, who defeated him with great loss at Modin (1 Macc. 16:1-10).

CENSER [Heb. *maḥtâ, miqṭereṯ* (2 Ch. 26:19; Ezk. 8:11), *maḥ^alāp* (Ezr. 1:9); Gk. *libanōtós* (Rev. 8:3, 5)]; AV also KNIVES (Ezr. 1:9); NEB also FIREPAN, "vessels of various kinds" (Ezr. 1:9). The Heb. *maḥtâ,* from the verb *ḥāṯâ,* "rake up" (usually fire embers), was a small ladle or shovel probably made of bronze (Ex. 27:3), used for carrying live coals on which incense was burned (Nu. 16:6f.). The accounts in Lev. 10 and Nu. 16 may reflect practices that go back to the desert period of Israel's history when portable censers were used. The altar used in the temple of Solomon was the altar of perfumes, which, unlike the main altar, was inside the temple (1 K. 6:20f.; cf. LXX). The *maḥtâ* continued to be used as a portable censer, especially by the high priest, who on the Day of Atonement carried the coals, mixed with incense, from the altar of perfumes into the holy of holies (Lev. 16:12-14). Heb. *miqṭereṯ,* from the verb *qāṭar* (to "smoke"), is a term used in the postexilic period for a censer. It may have acquired this name because it carried a particular mixture of incense mentioned in priestly writings, called *q^eṭōreṯ.*

Gk. *libanōtós,* properly the gum of the frankincense tree, is taken by the translators of Rev. 8:3, 5 to mean the receptacle that carries the frankincense.

D. P. NILES

CENSUS [Heb. *rō'š, happ^equḏîm, sāpar, s^epar*; Gk. *apographḗ*]; AV SUM, NUMBERING, etc., NT TAXING; NEB also REGISTRATION, NUMBER (vb.), COUNT, etc. Use of the census as an administrative device, especially for taxation and for military purposes, is very ancient. In the history of Israel it goes back to the time of Moses, who numbered the people and levied a sanctuary tax prior to the building of the tabernacle (Ex. 30:11ff.). All those twenty years old and older were included, evidently both women and men.

At Sinai another census was made by Moses, of all the tribes except the Levites (who were later counted separately; Nu. 3:14ff.), this time only of males twenty and older who were fit for military service (Nu. 1). From each tribe was chosen a "head of the house of his fathers," i.e., head of a clan group, to assist Moses and Aaron in counting the men. The total number is given as 603,550 (v. 46), which most scholars regard as impossibly high.

After widespread apostasy to Baal of Peor, a plague is inflicted on the people, and another census is taken to determine its effects and also to distribute the land (Nu. 26). The total given here is 601,730.

David's census, related in 2 S. 24 and 1 Ch. 21, is regarded by the biblical writers as an evil deed, a result of the "anger of Yahweh" (2 S. 24) or "Satan" (1 Ch. 21) inciting David. After the census was completed, David felt guilty and repented, but the Lord sent a terrible plague upon Israel killing seventy thousand men. Why was this census evil? Perhaps the sin was purely arrogance — David conducted the census to feed his pride in the numbers of his people. Or perhaps the census included excessive taxation or forced labor. Clearly it was for David's glory rather than for the Lord's, and this no doubt was part of its sinful character. But there may well have been more involved in the incident than is now present in the biblical accounts, or more behind it than is now evident to the modern reader.

In 2 Ch. 2:17f. it is said that "Solomon took a census of all the aliens who were in the land of Israel, after [i.e., like] the census of them which David his father had taken," and put them to work on the temple. The account of this raising of forced labor in 1 K. 5:13ff. does not mention that these were aliens, but cf. 1 K. 9:20-22. David's levy referred to here is related in 1 Ch. 22:2, but not in Kings.

Later numberings include that of Ezr. 2 par. Neh. 7 par. 1 Esd. 5, after the first return from exile.

In the NT period, the emperor Augustus decreed a census of his entire empire, which touched upon the lives of Joseph and Mary right at the time she was to give birth to Jesus (Lk. 2). *See* CHRONOLOGY OF THE NT I.A.2.

See also ENROLLMENT. J. W. D. H.

CENTURION [Gk. *hekatontárchēs, hekatóntarchos,* in Mk. 15 *kenturíōn*; Lat. *centurio*]. The commander of a hundred men (a "century"), more or less, in a Roman legion. Matthew and Luke use the Greek word while Mark characteristically prefers the Latin form, since he seems to write primarily for Roman readers.

The number of centurions in a legion was always sixty, but the number in the cohort or *speíra* varied. The ordinary duties of the centurion were to drill his men, to inspect their arms, food, and clothing, and to command them in the camp and in the field. Centurions were sometimes employed on detached service, the conditions of which in the provinces are somewhat obscure. Men like Cornelius and Julius (Acts 10:1; 27:1) may have been seconded from the legion to which they properly belonged for the discharge of special duties. They and other centurions mentioned in the Gospels and Acts (Mt. 8:5; Mk. 15:39, 44f.; Lk. 23:47) are represented by the sacred writers in a favorable light. *See* ARMY, ROMAN.

T. NICOL

CEPHAS sē'fəs [Gk. *ho Kēphas* < Aram. *kêpā'*–'rock'] (Jn. 1:42, etc.). The Aramaic surname of PETER.

CERAS sē'rəs (1 Esd. 5:29, AV). *See* KEROS.

CEREAL OFFERING. *See* SACRIFICE IN THE OT, V.E.

CEREMONIAL LAW. *See* LAW IN THE OT.

CERINTHUS. *See* GNOSTICISM VIII.A.

CERTAIN; CERTAINLY; CERTAINTY [Heb. *('el-) nāḵôn*–'established, substantiated'] (Dt. 13:14 [MT 15]; 17:14); AV also "in very deed"; NEB also "it is shown that"; [Aram. *(min-) yaṣîḇ*–'established, reliable'] (Dnl. 2:8, 45); NEB SURE, "it is clear to me"; [Gk. *alēthṓs*–'truly'] (Mt. 26:73; Mk. 14:70); AV, NEB, SURELY; [*ep' alētheíās*–'in truth'] (Lk. 22:59); AV "of a truth"; NEB "of course"; [*óntōs*–'really'] (Lk. 23:47); NEB "beyond all doubt"; [*pántōs*–'by all means'] (Acts 21:22); AV "must needs"; NEB "are sure to."

These terms are also used where there is no direct Hebrew or Greek equivalent. Sometimes they express the emphasis intended by the use of a Hebrew infinitive absolute with a finite verb (Lev. 10:18; Nu. 24:11; Josh. 9:24; 1 S. 25:28; 2 S. 5:19; 1 K. 2:37, 42; Jer. 26:15; 36:29; 42:19, 22; AV also "surely," "indeed," "doubtless"; NEB omits or paraphrases). "Certainly not" (Gal. 2:17; 3:21; AV "God forbid"; NEB "no, never!") is from the Gk. *mḗ génoito* (may it not be), elsewhere translated "God forbid!" (Lk. 20:10), "Never!" (1 Cor. 6:15), or "By no means!" (Rom. 3:4, 6; 6:2, 15; 7:7, 13; 9:14; 11:1, 11). In Rom. 6:5 "certainly" is an interpretive addition by the translators.

In all other RSV uses "certain" is a term of indefinite identification meaning "one," "someone," "a man," etc.

E. W. S.

CERTIFICATE OF DIVORCE [Gk. *apostásion* (Mt. 5:31), *biblíon apostasíou* (19:7; Mk. 10:4)]; AV WRITING (Mk. 10:4, BILL) OF DIVORCEMENT; NEB NOTE OF DISMISSAL. *See* DIVORCE.

CERTIFY. As it occurs in the AV, "certify" has not the strong, specific sense "make certain," but the broader, now obsolete sense of "make to know" (cf., e.g., Gal. 1:11).

CETAB sē'tab (1 Esd. 5:30, AV), *See* KETAB.

CHABRIS kā'bris [Gk. *Abris*; Chabreis]. Son of Gothoniel, one of the three rulers of Bethulia in the time of Judith (Jth. 6:15; 8:10; 10:6).

CHADIAS kā'dē-əs. *See* CHADIASANS.

CHADIASANS kā-di-ā'səns [Gk. A *Chadiasai*]; AV "they of Chadias"; NEB CHADASIANS. A group of exiles who returned with Zerubbabel, along with the Ammidioi (1 Esd. 5:20). The name is not found in Ezra and Nehemiah. The Chadiasai have been taken for the people of Kadesh and the Ammidioi for the people of Humtah (Josh. 15:54). Possibly their city is identical with Kedesh of Josh. 15:23.

W. S. L. S.

CHAEREAS kē'rē-əs [Gk. *Chaireas*]; AV CHEREAS. Brother of Timotheus, the Ammonite leader against Judas Maccabeus (1 Macc. 5:6). He held the fortress of Gazara (the "Jazer" of 1 Macc. 5:8) to which Timotheus fled from Judas. The latter pursued him and captured the fortress after a vigorous siege. In the slaughter which followed, the two brothers, Chaereas and Timotheus, were killed (2 Macc. 10:32, 37).

CHAFF. Four OT words are translated "chaff" by the RSV. (1) Heb. *mōṣ* is found in Job 21:18; Ps. 1:4; 35:5; Isa. 17:13; 29:5; 41:15; Hos. 13:3; Zeph. 2:2. (2) Heb. *ḥ^{a}šaš* in Isa. 33:11 denotes dried grass rather than "chaff." (3) Heb. *qaš* (AV "stubble") in Job 13:25; Ps. 83:13; Jer. 13:24, was actually stubble mixed with clay. (4) Aram. *'ûr* occurs in Dnl. 2:35. In the NT, Gk. *áchyron* is found in Mt. 3:12 and Lk. 3:17.

In the process of winnowing, as it has been carried on in the East for thousands of years, the grain is tossed into the air so that the wind may cause a separation of chaff and straw. The light husks from the wheat and fine particles of straw are dispersed by the wind in the form of a fine dust; the heavier straw, which has been broken into short pieces by the threshing process, falls near at hand on the edge of the threshing floor, while the grain falls back upon the pile. In Syria and Palestine, that which falls near at hand as cut straw is called *tibn,* the same word that occurs in the Arabic translation of Mt. 3:12 and Lk. 3:17. This straw is ordinarily saved and fed as roughage to the animals. It can easily be gathered and burned, as indicated in the above-mentioned verse, while the chaff is blown away beyond recovery, providing a strong figure for depicting complete annihilation (Job 21:18; Isa. 29:5; 41:16; Hos. 13:3; Dnl. 2:35). *See* AGRICULTURE III.A.3; STRAW; WINNOWING.

J. A. PATCH

CHAIN [Heb. *šarš^{e}râ, rattûqâ* (1 K. 6:21; Isa. 40:19), *rāḇîḏ* (Gen. 41:42; Ezk. 16:11), *ziqqîm, '^{a}ziqqîm* (Jer. 40:1, 4), *n^{e}ḥōšeṯ* (Lam. 3:7), *ma'^{a}ḏannôṯ* (Job 38:31); Aram. *hamnîḵ* (Dnl. 5:7, 16, 29); Gk. *hálysis, desmós*]; AV also BONDS, "sweet influences" (Job 38:31); NEB also CHAINWORK, STUDS, FETTERS, CLUSTER (Job 38:31).

In the OT, Heb. *šarš^{e}râ* and *rattûqâ* were wreathen chains usually made of gold, though sometimes of silver (Isa. 40:19), used in the decoration of the Jerusalem temple (1 K. 7:17) and on the vestments of the high priest (Ex. 28:14, 22). Heb. *rāḇîḏ* and Aram. *hamnîḵ* refer to necklaces, usually given by a king to bestow honor on a favored person (Gen. 41:42; Dnl. 5:29). Heb. *ziqqîm* and *neḥōšeṯ* were fetters made of wood, bronze (*neḥōšeṯ*), or iron (Ps. 149:8). The RSV apparently took *maʿaḏannôṯ* (Job 38:31) to be based on the verb *ʿānaḏ,* "bind." The Pleiades is a constellation which gives the impression that the stars are bound together by chains.

In the NT, Gk. *desmós* is a general term for anything used for tying, confining, or fastening. *Hálysis* refers to chains used for securing prisoners. The Roman way of securing a prisoner was to attach one end of the chain to the prisoner and the other end to a guard; cf. Acts 12:6.

D. P. NILES

CHALCEDONY kal-sed'ə-nē, kal'sə-dō-nē. *See* STONES, PRECIOUS.

CHALCOL kal'kol (1 K. 4:31 [MT 5:11], AV). *See* CALCOL.

CHALDEA kal-dē'ə; **CHALDEANS** kal-dē'ənz; **CHALDEES** kal'dēz [Heb. *kaśdîm, 'ereṣ kaśdîm, lēḇ qāmāy* (see below); Aram. *kaśdāy*; Gk. *gḗ Chaldaíōn, Chaldai, Chaldaıoi*]; in Jer. 51:1 the RSV takes Heb. *lēḇ qāmāy* (AV "midst of them that rise up against me") as an athbash-cipher for Chaldea (so LXX, *BH*); the NEB reads "those who live in Kambul"; *see* ATHBASH. The land bordering the Persian Gulf that gave its name to the ruling dynasty and thus became a synonym for Babylonia itself.

I. Geography
II. Early References
III. Assyrian Control
IV. Merodach-baladan
V. Chaldean Dynasty
VI. Chaldeans as Learned Men

I. Geography.–The tribal territory covering the southern marshes and coastal plains of ancient Iraq bordering the Persian Gulf was called by outsiders "Chaldean land" (*māt Kaldu*) after the name of the tribes inhabiting the area. This Assyrian-Babylonian name was followed by the Greek, while the Hebrew, with the common variant of *ś* for *l*, probably follows an old dialect form *kašdu*. The name has no proven connection with Chesed (Heb. *keśeḏ*, Gen. 22:22).

The origin of the Chaldeans is uncertain but may well be in the west, or else branches of the family may have moved there (cf. Job 1:17). The general name for the area in the earliest period is unknown, since it was part of Sumer (*see* SHINAR); so it cannot be argued that the qualification of Abraham's home city UR as "of the Chaldeans" (Gen. 11:28, 31; 15:7; as later Neh. 9:7; cf. Acts 7:4) is necessarily a later insertion in the text. Such a description may well have been needed to distinguish the city from other places with a similar name, Urʿ. In the 2nd millennium the area was designated "the Sea-Lands" (*māt tâmtim*) and was described as adjacent to Elam on the east, the "west land" (Amorite or western desert) to the west, and Dilmun, the islands and coastal regions of Bahrain, to the south. First-millennium texts name the tribes of the Kaldu under chiefs: Bīt ("House of")-Dakkūri, Bīt-Adini, Bīt-Amukkani, with its major city of Sapia; Bīt-Sa'alli, Bīt-Šilani, and Bīt-Yakin, which lay on the Persian Gulf itself. Assyrian kings claimed the capture of at least seventy-five walled towns or villages and 420 hamlets from these tribes.

II. Early References.–The later rulers of the 1st Dynasty of Babylon (*ca.* 1740-1590 B.C.) referred to the "Sea-Land" as ruled by independent chiefs, of whom Gulkišar was the most renowned. Another, Ea-gāmil, was the contemporary of Samsu-ditana of Babylon (1625-1595), while the later Babylonian king list A records a second Sea-Land dynasty of three kings who reigned over most of Babylonia for twenty years and three months, *ca.* 1010-980 B.C. It is likely that these were "Chaldeans," though not so named in these texts, since Ashurnasirpal II in his annals for the year 860 mentions the Kaldu as strong in this same area.

III. Assyrian Control.–The expansionist aims of the Sargonid Assyrian kings brought them into direct clash with the independent tribes of the south in their need to control the trade routes to Elam and the Gulf. Shalmaneser III in 851 sacked the town of Baqāni, which then belonged to Adini of the Dakkūru tribe. When his capital Enzudi fell Adini paid the Assyrian tribute, as did Mušallim-Marduk of Amukkani and Bīt-Yakin; the latter is called "of the land of the Sea," thus identifying the earlier description of "Sea-Lands" with the now more frequently used "land of the Chaldeans." Adadnirari III (805) lists the Amukkani and Bīt-Yakin among his Chaldean vassals.

IV. Merodach-baladan.–In 734 the Amukkani seized Babylon, on the death of Nabû-nāṣir. Tiglath-pileser III immediately responded by sending his Assyrian army, who plundered Amukkani, Šilani, and Sa'alli while the Chaldean chief Ukīn-zēr was engaged at Sapia. His rivals Balassu of Dakkūru and Marduk-apla-iddina (the biblical Merodach-baladan) of Bīt-Yakin made a treaty with the Assyrians, and their lands were spared; Merodach-baladan even dominated Babylon itself from 721 to 710 B.C.

Sargon II of Assyria set out to win over the Li'tau and various Aramean groups. He sealed the border with Elam from which the rebels were supplied, eventually regaining control of Babylon. Marduk-apla-iddina II withdrew to Yatburu in Elam; and though the Assyrians captured Dūr-Yakin, his main city, he retained the chieftainship. However, on Sargon's death in 705 Merodach-baladan took the title "king of Babylon" (so Isa. 20:12) following the disappearance of the little-known Marduk-zākir-šumi II. It is probably at this time, rather than at the earlier rule in Babylon, that Merodach-baladan sent his embassy to Hezekiah of Judah to enlist his support against the expected Assyrian countermeasures (Isa. 39; 2 K. 20:12-19). Thus here too, "Chaldean" is rightly used as synonymous with "Babylonian" (Isa. 13:19; 47:1, 5; 48:14, 20).

For a while another Chaldean, Šūzubu (Mušēzib-Marduk), gained power when Merodach-baladan withdrew on the approach of Sennacherib's army. Sennacherib, who defeated the Chaldean tribesmen at Kish, gave Babylon into the hands of his nominee Bēl-ibni. Resistance continued for a time under a son of Merodach-baladan, who was betrayed by the Elamites. Merodach-baladan himself died in exile before Sennacherib in 695 could mount an amphibious operation to punish the supporting elements living across the gulf. When Ashurbanipal raided the south *ca.* 652 B.C. he captured Merodach-baladan's grandson Palia. This act forced the Chaldean tribes to side with Šamaš-šum-ukīn of Babylon, and their combined hostility was the prime cause of the sack of that city by the Assyrians in 648. Mannu-kī-Babili of the Dakkūri and Ea-šum-iqīša of the Amukkani were punished for their complicity, and Nabû-bēl-šumāti, another grandson of the renowned chief of the Bīt-Yakin, committed suicide when betrayed by the Elamites to whom he, like his grandfather Merodach-baladan, had fled.

V. Chaldean Dynasty.–After Ashurbanipal's death and the increasing weakness of his regime the Chaldeans rose in revolt and recaptured Babylon, putting their leader

Babylon (*ca.* 604-561 B.C.), with the Euphrates, Esagila (left), and the Marduk temple (right) in the foreground (Painting by M. Bardin, following E. Unger's reconstruction) (Oriental Institute, University of Chicago)

Nabopolassar on the throne there in 627. He inaugurated a period of remarkable political and economic recovery, allying with the Medes to sack Asshur (614) and Nineveh (612). His son Nebuchadrezzar II (605-562), while crown prince, confronted the Egyptians, defeating them at Carchemish in 605 B.C. before campaigning in Syria and Palestine (2 K. 24:7; Josephus *Ant.* x.6.86). The Babylonian Chronicle for this reign records his operations resulting in Jehoiakim's submission to the Chaldean king (2 K. 24:1; Jer. 25:1) and his defection three years later when the Chaldeans had been routed by the Egyptians in 601 (Jer. 26:1-11). In revenge the Babylonians captured Jerusalem, March 16, 597 B.C.; and when their nominee Mattaniah-Zedekiah broke his vassal's oath, they sacked the city and took the Judeans into exile (587).

Nebuchadrezzar much embellished Babylon and strengthened its defenses (Dnl. 4:30). His son Amēl-Marduk (Evil-merodach of 2 K. 25:27-30) showed compassion on the exiled Jews, but under his successors Neriglissar (560-558) and Labāši-Marduk (557), their lot deteriorated with the mounting pressure on Babylon by the powerful Medes. Nabonidus (556-539) set up a provincial administration in the Jewish diaspora area of Teimā in north Arabia, leaving his son and co-regent Bēl-šar-uṣur

(Belshazzar, "king of the Chaldeans," Dnl. 5:30) to withstand the final assault of the Persians under Cyrus in October 539. Nabonidus himself died in exile, and with the fall of Babylon the Chaldean Dynasty ended.

VI. Chaldeans as Learned Men.–The Chaldeans maintained the traditional Babylonian schools at Babylon, Borsippa, Sippar, Uruk, and Ur. Here the "learning of the Chaldeans" (Dnl. 1:4; 2:2; 4:7; 5:7, 11) comprised the study of Sumerian, Akkadian, Aramaic (formerly called "Chaldee"), and other languages, as well as the extensive literature written in them. Historiography as well as the sciences of astronomy, mathematics, and medicine formed a large part of the specialist work. Associated religious texts, both omina and astrology (horoscopes were not introduced until the 4th cent. B.C.) played a large part. (*See* BABYLON VI-IX.)

In one sense Daniel uses "Chaldean" as a synonym for "Babylonian" as elsewhere is the case in the OT. With the increasing introduction of Aramaic, "Chaldean" became a term for "magicians, enchanters, and soothsayers," since these aspects of Babylonian religious texts were the longest to survive in the popular imagination (as *ca.* 450 B.C. Herodotus i.181-83).

See Map X.

Bibliography.–*CCK*; H. W. F. Saggs, *The Greatness that was Babylon* (1962), pp. 102-153; J. A. Brinkman, in *Studies presented to A. L. Oppenheim* (1964), pp. 6-53. D. J. WISEMAN

CHALDEES (Neh. 9:7). *See* UR.

CHALKSTONE [Heb. *'aḇnê-gir*–'stones of chalk,' 'lime'] (Isa. 27:9); NEB CHALK. *'Aḇnê-gir* is compounded of *'eḇen,* "stone," which occurs in many passages, and *gir* or *gîr*, "lime" (cf. Arab. *jîr*, "gypsum" or "quicklime"), which occurs only here and in Dnl. 5:5: "wrote on the plaster [*gîr*] of the wall of the king's palace."

Nearly all the rock of Palestine is limestone. When limestone is burned, it is converted into lime, which is easily broken into pieces, and, if allowed to remain open to the air, becomes slaked by the moisture of the atmosphere and crumbles into dust. The reference is to the destruction of the altar. It may mean that the altar will be burned so that the stones will become lime, or, more probably, that the stones of the altar will be broken as chalkstones (i.e., lumps of quicklime) are broken. There is no doubt that lime was known to the Egyptians, Assyrians, and Hebrews. *See* LIME. A. E. DAY

CHALLENGE. Obsolete term for "claim," found only in Ex. 22:9, AV.

CHALPHI kal'fī [Gk. *Chalphi*]; AV CALPHI. Father of Judas, who, along with Mattathias, steadily supported Jonathan at the battle of Gennesaret when the hosts of Demetrius' princes were routed (1 Macc. 11:70).

CHAMBER [Heb. *ḥeḏer, 'ᵃlîyâ, liškâ, niškâ* (Neh. 3:30; 12:44; 13:7f.), *ḥuppâ* (Ps. 19:5), *pᵉnîm* (Ps. 45:13), *gaḇ* (Ezk. 16:24, 31, 39), *ṣēlā'* (1 K. 6:5; 7:3; Ezk. 41:5-9, 11), *ma'ᵃlôṯ* (Am. 9:6); Aram. *'illîṯ* (Dnl. 6:10); Gk. *hyperṓon* (Acts 20:8)]; AV also PARLOUR, LOFT (1 K. 17:19), "going up" (Neh. 3:31f.), "south" (Job 37:9), "within" (Dt. 32:25; Ps. 45:13), PLACE (Ezk. 16:24, 31, 39), BEAMS (1 K. 7:3), STORIES (Am. 9:6); NEB also ROOM, COUCH, ARCADE, BEAMS, STAIR (Am. 9:6), RECESS, etc. The RSV follows the LXX in Cant. 8:2, where the AV (following the MT) has "who would instruct me."

These terms identify the rooms of a building. *Ḥeḏer* is the common word for room; *liškâ* and *niškâ* are associated with the temple; *'ᵃlîyâ* is an upper-story room; *ṣēlā'* is a side room; *ḥuppâ* is the nuptial chamber.

Israelite homes were characterized by a flat roof. Often the roof was used for living rooms or guest rooms, while the lower story was used for storage and the housing of livestock. Eglon's summer parlor was probably an enclosed rooftop balcony (Jgs. 3:20-25) with windows on all sides (perhaps even containing a lavatory; cf. Jgs. 3:24). Elijah's room was on the rooftop (1 K. 17:19, 23), indicating that guests evidently had the privilege of the roof chamber (cf. 2 K. 4:10f.). The rooftops were also used for idolatry (2 K. 23:12; cf. Jer 19:13; 32:29; Zeph. 1:5).

Ḥeḏer bᵉḥāḏer (1 K. 20:30; 22:25; 2 K. 9:2) was a remote inner or private room, not an "underground cellar" (Josephus *Ant.* viii.14.4).

The side rooms (*ṣᵉlā'ôṯ,* from *ṣēlā',* which means "rib" or "side") in Ezekiel's temple (41:5-11) were similar to those of Solomon's temple (1 K. 6:5-10). They were probably storerooms. The priest's chambers (Ezk. 42:1-14) were in the templeyard, not the temple proper (as the side rooms are).

J. P. Brown (*VT,* 19 [1969], 151-53) suggests that *liškâ* (Gk. *léschē,* "drinking hall") may be associated with drinking (cf. Jer. 35:2-5 and 1 S. 9:22, where *liškâ* is a dining hall connected with a "high place").

J. T. DENNISON, JR.

CHAMBERING (Rom. 13:13, AV). *See* DEBAUCHERY.

CHAMBERLAIN [Heb. *sārîs*; Gk. *eunoúchos,* NT *ho epí toú koitṓnos* (*toú basiléōs*) (Acts 12:20)]; NEB OT EUNUCH. A court attendant whose main duty was to wait on the king's bedchamber. Heb. *sārîs* is usually rendered "eunuch," but in 2 K. 21:11, AV and RSV, Nathan-melech is called a chamberlain; cf. Est. 1:10, and in the AV 1:12, 15; 2:3, 14f.; etc. *See also* EUNUCH.

In the NT (Acts 12:20) Blastus had the position of *praefectus cubiculo,* or chief *valet de chambre* to the royal person, in the court of Herod. It was an honored position that involved much intimacy with the king.

On Rom. 16:23, *see* TREASURER. E. B. POLLARD

CHAMBERS OF IMAGERY (Ezk. 8:12, AV). *See* PICTURES, ROOM OF.

CHAMBERS OF THE SOUTH. *See* ASTRONOMY II.C.

CHAMELEON. *See* LIZARD.

CHAMOIS sham'ē, sham-wä'. *See* MOUNTAIN-SHEEP.

CHAMPAIGN [Heb. *'ᵃrāḇâ*]. *See* ARABAH I.

CHAMPION [Heb. *'îš-habbēnayim*] (1 S. 17:4, 23); [*gibbôr*] (v. 51); NEB HERO. In 1 S. 17:4, 23 this unusual expression occurs in the description of Goliath. It means literally "the man of the two spaces," and describes the warrior who fought another warrior in hand-to-hand combat in the no-man's-land between the opposing armies.

CHANAAN kā'nən; **CHANAANITE** -īt. AV Apoc. (Jth. 5:3, 16) and NT (Acts 7:11; 13:19) for CANAAN; CANAANITE.

CHANCE [Heb. *qārā'* (Dt. 22:6; 2 S. 1:6; 18:9), *miqreh* (Dt. 23:10; 1 S. 6:9), *pega'* (Eccl. 9:11); Gk. *synkyría* (Lk. 10:31), *paratynchánō* (Acts 17:17), *eípōs*–'if perhaps' (Acts 27:12), *tópos* (He. 12:17)]; AV also PLACE (He. 12:17), etc.; NEB also HAPPEN (Lk. 9:11), WAY OPEN (He. 12:17), etc.

The concept of chance as something entirely fortuitous in human experience was completely foreign to Hebrew thought. Consistently throughout the OT God is revealed as the Creator of the cosmos (cf. Ps. 104:5ff.; Isa. 40:28; Am. 4:13) and the one who sustains its operation by the rule of law (cf. Ps. 104:9, 19). The process by which the world was formulated resulted in the end product being described as "good" (Gen. 1:4, 12, 18, etc.), and the laws by which it has been subsequently governed reflect the essence of the divine personality in terms of power, orderliness, and consistency (cf. Rom. 1:20). Thus the universe did not issue from a chance agglomeration of atomic quanta, as some ancient Greek speculators imagined, but instead was ordered by a sole creative mind. The consistently monistic emphasis of the OT writers relates all phenomena in the world and all activity in human experience to the one true God who is Creator and Lord of the cosmos (Isa. 45:5-7), and for whom there can be no fortuitous happenings (cf. Mt. 10:29).

Israelite belief on the matter of chance is summed up in the aphorism: "The lot is cast into the lap, but the decision is wholly from the Lord" (Prov. 16:33). Probably the closest the OT comes to reflecting the concept of chance as something fortuitous is in the remarks of the Philistines (1 S. 6:9) to the effect that if their scheme for ascertaining the cause of their misfortunes turned out in a certain way, they would regard these misfortunes as being caused by "chance." However, even here the idea seems to be one of "accident" or perhaps "bad luck" rather than the fortuitous negative disposition of events, i.e., something without rhyme or reason.

The view that life operates rather mechanistically under the control of "time and chance" is expressed in Eccl. 9:11, where *pega'* simply means "occurrence," "happening." In Dt. 22:6; 2 S. 1:6; 18:9 the verb *qārā'* emphasizes the unintentional or accidental nature of the event, as does also the noun *miqreh* in Dt. 23:10.

In the NT the concept of coincidence is expressed by *synkyría* in Lk. 10:31, while the rare term *paratynchánō* (Acts 17:17) means "those who had occasion to be there" (cf. AV "that met with him"). Possibility rather than chance seems indicated in Acts 27:12, and opportunity in He. 12:17 (cf. AV mg. "way to change his mind").

In the LXX *týchē,* "chance," occurs only twice: (1) in Gen. 30:11, where Jacob's first wife named one of their children *gaḏ* ("fortune"; LXX *en týchę̄,* "with fortune"), reflecting her heathen upbringing; and (2) in Isa. 65:11, where the MT *m^e^nî* is represented by the Gk. *týchē*. The prophet Isaiah rebuked the rebellious Israelites for worshiping the heathen gods of fortune (*gaḏ,* a designation which occurs in inscriptions and personal names) and destiny or fate (*m^e^nî*), reminding his idolatrous countrymen in subtle wordplay of the fate awaiting those who forsook God.

M. S. SEALE

CHANGE. In Lev. 27:33, AV "the change thereof" (Heb. *t^e^mûrâ*) means "that for which it is exchanged" (RSV). Job 10:17, AV, "changes and war are against me," is emended in the RSV ("thou dost bring fresh hosts against me") and NEB ("bringest fresh forces to the attack"), following the LXX, reading *w^e^ṯaḥ^a^lip* or the like for the MT *ḥ^a^lîpôṯ* (but see KoB, p. 302, "hardship after hardship"). AV "change" in Job 14:14 (*ḥ^a^lîpâ*) is interpreted as "release" in the RSV, and as "relief" in the NEB, meaning relief from military duty (figuratively). In Ps. 55:19 the AV has "because they have no changes" (*ḥ^a^lîpôṯ*), the RSV "because they keep no law," the NEB "who have no respect for an oath." KoB suggests "mutual liabilities." The simplest explanation is that suggested by BDB, p. 323, that the phrase refers to the incessant evil of the psalmist's enemies.

"Changed the ordinance" in Isa. 24:5, AV (*ḥālap*), means as in the RSV "violated the statutes" (NEB "disobeyed").

The RSV follows the LXX at Prov. 24:21, which in the AV reads "meddle not with them that are given to change" (*šônîm*), RSV "do not disobey either of them"; the NEB has "have nothing to do with men of rank." The LXX (and RSV) is based evidently on a Heb. *š^e^nêhem.*

J. W. D. H.

CHANGER (Jn. 2:14f.). *See* MONEY-CHANGER.

CHANNEL. *See* RIVER.

CHANNUNEUS kə-nun'ē-əs (1 Esd. 8:48, AV). *See* HANANIAH **15.**

CHANT [Heb. polel of *qîn*] (Ezk. 32:16); AV LAMENT; NEB DIRGE; [*t^e^nâ*] (Ps. 8:1 [MT 2]); AV "hast set"; NEB PRAISED. The *qînâ* is a dirge or formal LAMENT (cf. the book of LAMENTATIONS). In Ezk. 32:16 (RSV "lamentation") what is described is a funeral song for the land of Egypt. The word *t^e^nâ* is very difficult (for a summary of the problems cf. Perowne, pp. 132f.). As it stands in the MT, *t^e^nâ* appears to be an imperative of *nāṯan* ("put" or "place"). However, Delitzsch suggested that it is an irregular infinitive, and would read, "thou, the setting of whose glory is above the heavens." Other commentators have suggested several alternative emendations of the MT. Morgenstern proposes *tunnâ* from similar usage in Jgs. 5:11; 11:40; the sense would then be a memorializing of God in songs of praise. Similarly, Weiser suggests reading *tānâ* from the parallel Ugaritic word meaning "to be repeated in antiphonal song"; the sense would then be praise of God by celestial beings as in Isa. 6:3.

Bibliography.–J. Morgenstern, *HUCA,* 19 (1945/46), 491ff.; J. J. S. Perowne, *Book of Psalms,* I (1908); A. Weiser, *Psalms* (*OTL*, 1962), *in loc.*

J. T. DENNISON, JR.

CHANUNAEUS kə-nun'ē-əs (1 Esd. 8:48, NEB). *See* HANANIAH **15.**

CHAOS [Heb. *lō' s^e^ḏārîm* (Job 10:22), *tōhû* (Isa. 24:10; 34:11; 45:18f.)]; AV also CONFUSION, VAIN, "without any order"; NEB also EMPTY VOID, "a place of disorder" (mg. Job 10:22). The state of formlessness, of utter disorder and confusion.

The Heb. *tōhû* is frequently used in the OT to describe the condition of emptiness, unreality, and desolation (BDB, p. 1062), when combined with the word *bōhû* (void), there is a heightened sense of chaotic, meaningless existence: "without form and void" (Gen. 1:2); "waste and void" (Jer. 4:23). In the creation account, Heb. *tohû wāḇohû* (Gen. 1:2) denotes a void or empty space, suggesting Gk. *cháos*, the misty darkness before creation.

G. von Rad speaks of chaos as "a reality that once existed in a preprimeval period but also . . . a possibility that always exists. Man has always suspected that behind all creation lies the abyss of formlessness; that all creation is always ready to sink into the abyss of the formless; that the chaos, therefore, signifies simply the threat to everything created" (pp. 48f.). Hence, Isaiah's "city of chaos" (Isa. 24:10) is a town so morally polluted (v. 5) that it has lost its reason to exist; it has become a purposeless mass of confusion and disorder. The judgment Isaiah utters against Edom (34:11) also threatens her with a return to the original state of things before the creative word of God brought order out of disorder (Gen. 1:2). The "line" and "plummet" were ordinarily used to build; here, they are to be used in the reverse procedure, to reduce to "chaos." Edom will then be a "No Kingdom There" (Isa. 34:12), i.e., a desert waste. And this is precisely what God did not create the earth to be: "he did not create it a chaos, he formed it to be inhabited!" (Isa. 45:18). The orderliness of the world and its fitness for human habitation are the express product of the Creator's purpose.

Nor does God communicate with His people in a disorderly fashion: "I did not say to the offspring of Jacob, 'Seek me in chaos.' I the Lord speak the truth, I declare what is right" (45:19). This is probably a warning against occult means of divining God's will (North, p. 159). After all, the occult is no more than conceited unreality (*tōhû*).

When Job describes the realm of the dead, he declares it "the land of gloom and chaos, where light is as darkness" (Job 10:22). Over against the chaos in the world, there stands the creative and sustaining Word of God that caused the universe to emerge from the preprimeval *tōhû* (Gen. 1:1ff., NEB), and that Word continues to give order and meaning to all history (cf. Jn. 1:1-5).

See also ABYSS; DEEP; VOID.

Bibliography.–B. Anderson, *Creation Versus Chaos* (1967); C. North, *Second Isaiah* (1964); *ILC,* I-II, 456f.; 471ff.; G. von Rad, *Genesis* (Eng. tr., *OTL,* 1961).

K. H. MAAHS

CHAPEL (Am. 7:13, AV). *See* SANCTUARY.

CHAPHENATHA kə-fen'ə-thə [Gk. *Chaphenatha*] (1 Macc. 12:37); AV CAPHENATHA. A name apparently given to part of the eastern wall of Jerusalem, or possibly a fort in that neighborhood, which was repaired by Jonathan Maccabeus. The place cannot now be identified.

CHAPITER (AV). *See* CAPITAL.

CHAPMAN. An obsolete term for "trader," used once in the AV (2 Ch. 9:14). *See* TRADE.

CHAPT. This archaic spelling of "chapped" or "cracked open" is found in Jer. 14:4, AV. The RSV renders the Hebrew term (*ḥāṯaṯ*) in its other sense of "dismayed."

CHARAATHALAR kar-ə-ath'ə-lär [Gk. *Charaathalan*] (1 Esd. 5:36, AV, NEB). Most probably a corruption of the text. The names "Cherub, Addan, and Immer" in the lists of Ezr. 2:59 and Neh. 7:61 are presented in the AV as "Charaathalar leading them, and Allar."

CHARACA kar'ə-kə (2 Macc. 12:17, AV). *See* CHARAX.

CHARACTER [Gk. *dokimḗ*] (Rom. 5:4); AV EXPERIENCE; NEB "proof that we have stood the test," "this proof." The Greek noun *dokimḗ* is derived from the adjective *dókimos,* "approved," "tried and true," "genuine," and thus connotes successful endurance of testing. In Rom. 5:4 *dokimḗ* is an intermediate step in a process of development. The renderings "approvedness" (RV) and "proof" (NEB), though basically sound, tend to obscure the flow of thought. Also, the verbal idea (*katergázetai,* "work out," "effect," v. 3) is probably best represented by the Eng. "develops" or "builds," so either "experience" or "character" seems more appropriate with the idea of the verb. Their use in this context complies with current usage, for persons with character or experience are reliable and trustworthy, having stood the test.

See *TDNT,* II, *s.v.* δόκιμος κτλ. (Grundmann).

G. E. MONTGOMERY

CHARACTERS, COMMON [Heb. *ḥereṭ ʾenôš*–'a man's stylus'] (Isa. 8:1). A common type of writing, devoid of conscious artistry, which could be easily read.

CHARASHIM kar'ə-shim (1 Ch. 4:14, AV). *See* GE-HARASHIM.

CHARAX kâr'ax [Gk. *Charax*]; AV CHARACA. A place mentioned only in 2 Macc. 12:17. Situated E of the Jordan, it belonged to the Auranitis, a district in Syria NE of Gilead, which included Jebel Haurân itself and the strip of territory running W toward Batanea, between the Trachonitis and Arabia. This district is also called Tob (1 Macc. 5:9, 13; 2 Macc. 12:17), the land to which Jephthah fled (Jgs. 11:3, 5) and from which the Ammonites secured twelve thousand mercenaries to help defend against King David (2 S. 10:6). It has also been conjectured that Charax may be modern el-Kerak in southern Moab.

D. B. PECOTA

CHARCHEMISH kär'kə-mish. *See* CARCHEMISH.

CHARCHUS kär'kəs (1 Esd. 5:32, AV). *See* BARKOS.

CHARCOAL (Prov. 26:21; Jn. 18:18; 21:9). *See* COAL.

CHAREA kar'ē-ə [Gk. *Charea*]. Head of a family of temple-servants (1 Esd. 5:32); called HARSHA in Ezr. 2:52; Neh. 7:54.

CHARGE [Heb. *ṣawâ, mišmereṯ, ʿeḏûṯ* (Ex. 19:23), *šāmar, māšal* (Gen. 24:2), *śār* (Gen. 47:6), *ʿûḏ* (1 K. 21:10, 13), *pāqaḏ, šāḇaʿ* (1 S. 14:27f.), *mišpāṭ* (1 K. 4:28), *rāḏâ* (1 K. 9:23), *nāṯan* (Job 1:22), *ʿāraḵ* (Ps. 50:21), *šālaḥ* (1 K. 14:6), *rîḇ* (Neh. 5:7), *śîm* (Job 4:18), *šāqaq* (Prov. 28:15), *maʿaleh* (Nah. 3:3), *nāgāḥ* (Dnl. 8:4), *dāḇar* (Dt. 19:15), *dāḇar šeqer* ("false charge," Ex. 23:7), *ʿalîlōṯ deḇārîm* (Dt. 22:14, 17), *nāṯan beyaḏ* (Gen. 30:35; 39:4; 2 S. 10:10; 1 Ch. 19:11), *beyaḏ* (Gen. 39:6), *ʿal-yāḏ* (1 S. 17:22; Ezr. 1:8; Est. 3:9), *ʿal-, nāṣab ʿal* (Ruth 2:5f.), *ʿāmaḏ ʿal* (Dnl. 12:1); Gk. *aitía, aitíōma* (Acts 25:7), *entéllomai* (Mt. 4:6; Lk. 4:10), *entolḗ* (Jn. 10:18), *katēgoréō, katēgoría* (1 Tim. 5:19; Tit. 1:6), *epí* (Acts 8:27), *parangelía* (Acts 16:24; 1 Tim. 1:5, 18), *parangéllō, synepitíthemai* (Acts 24:9), *enkaléō* (Rom. 8:33; Acts 19:38, 40), *énklēma* (Acts 23:29; 25:16), *exousía* (Mk. 13:34), *adápanos* (1 Cor. 9:18), *diamartýromai* (1 Tim. 5:21; 2 Tim. 2:14; 4:1), *klḗros* (1 Pet. 5:3), *embrimáomai* (Mt. 9:30; Mk. 1:43), *epitimáō* (Mt. 16:20; Mk. 8:30; Lk. 9:21), *diastéllomai, proaitiáomai* (Rom. 3:9), *martyréō* (1 Thess. 2:11), *logízomai* (2 Tim. 4:16), *diabállō* (Lk. 16:1), *phḗmi* (Rom. 3:8), *rhḗma* (2 Cor. 13:1), *ellogéō* (Philem. 18)]; AV also COMMAND, RULED, ORDINANCE (Lev. 18:30; 22:9), KEEP(ER), WATCH (2 Ch. 23:6), REBUKE, ACCUSE, ACCUSATION, etc.; NEB also WARN, KEEP (Nu. 1:53; Job 34:13), COMMISSION (Ex. 6:13; Dt. 3:28), DUTIES, RULES, ORDERS, ACCUSATION, ENJOIN, COMPLAINT, etc.

The Hebrew and Greek words have the following variety of meanings: (1) to command, in a strict or solemn manner (*ṣawâ, embrimáomai, epitimáō, diastéllomai*); occasionally used of a dying man's last commands (Gen. 49:29; cf. 50:12, 16; Dt. 31:23, 25); (2) to exercise oversight, supervision, or care (forms containing *yāḏ* and *ʿal-*); (3) to be given a special duty or particular responsibility (*mišmereṯ*), such as the charge which the various groups of Levites had for the sanctuary (cf. Nu. 3:25; 4:27; 9:19; 2 Ch. 23:6; Ezk. 40:45f.); (4) to accuse formally of a crime (*aitía*); (5) to reckon or impute

(Philem. 18); (6) to set a price (1 S. 13:21; cf. 1 Cor. 9:18); (7) to rush against or attack (Prov. 28:15; Dnl. 8:4; Nah. 3:3).

The AV uses "chargeable" in several passages (cf. 2 S. 13:25; Neh. 5:15; 2 Cor. 11:9; 1 Thess. 2:9; 2 Thess. 3:8) with the obsolete meaning of being "burdensome."

J. T. DENNISON, JR.

CHARGER. An archaic word in the AV for a flat dish or platter. *See* PLATE (Nu. 7); PLATTER (Mt. 14:8, 11 par.); BASIN (Ezr. 1:9).

In Nah. 2:3, RSV, "chargers" (i.e., cavalry horses) replaces AV "fir trees," reading Heb. *happārāšîm* for *habbᵉrōšîm* (cf. NEB "squadrons of horse").

CHARGES. The AV of Acts 21:24, "be at charges with them" (Gk. *dapanáō*), means, as in the RSV, "pay their expenses," with reference to the sacrificial expenses of the poorer NAZIRITES.

CHARIOT [Heb. *reḵeḇ, merkāḇâ,* also *rᵉḵûḇ* (Ps. 104:3), *ʿᵃgālâ* (Ps. 46:9), *hōṣen* (Ezk. 23:24); Gk. *hárma, rhédē*]; NEB also CARRIAGE (Acts 8), SHIELD (Ps. 46:9); AV also "way" (Heb. *dereḵ,* Hos. 10:13), emended to "chariot" in the RSV and NEB, following the LXX; and AV "thy paths" in Ps. 65:11 (*maʿgāl*) is in the RSV "track of thy chariot," the NEB "palm-trees"; **CHARIOT DRIVER** [Heb. *rakkāḇ*] (1 K. 22:34; 2 Ch. 18:33); **CHARIOTEER** [*rāḵaḇ*] (Jer. 51:21); AV, NEB, RIDER.

The earliest wheeled vehicles known were used in Mesopotamia at Kish and Ur prior to 3000 B.C. These were heavy, clumsy carts equipped with four solid wheels, drawn by asses or oxen. The two-wheeled chariot followed a little later and with subsequent modifications became a war machine of great importance in the history of the ancient world.

I. Chariots of Egypt.–It is to the chariots of ancient Egypt that reference is first made in Scripture. Joseph was honored by being made to ride in the second chariot of Pharaoh (Gen. 41:43). Joseph paid honor to his father on his arrival in Goshen by meeting him in his chariot (46:29). In the state ceremonial with which the remains of Jacob were escorted to Canaan, chariots and horsemen were conspicuous (50:9). In the narrative of the departure of the Israelites from Egypt and of Pharaoh's futile attempts to detain them the chariots and horsemen of Pharaoh figure largely (Ex. 14:17f., 23, 25; 15:4, 19). It was with the Hyksos invasion, some centuries before the Exodus, that the horse, and subsequently the chariot, were introduced for purposes of war into Egypt; and it may have been the possession of chariots that enabled those hated shepherd warriors to overpower the native Egyptians.

The Egyptian chariot was distinguished by its lightweight construction. It was so reduced in weight that it was possible for a man to carry his chariot on his shoulders without fatigue. The ordinary chariot was made of wood and leather and had only two occupants, the fighting man and his shield-bearer. The royal chariots were ornamented with gold and silver; and in the battle of Megiddo, Thutmose III is represented as standing in his chariot of electrum like the god of war, brandishing his lance. In the battle the victorious Egyptians captured 2041 horses and 924 chariots from the Syrian allies.

II. Canaanite Chariot.–The Canaanites had long possessed horses and chariots when Joshua hamstrung their horses and burned their chariots with fire at the waters of Merom (Josh. 11:6, 9). The chariots of iron which the Canaanites could maneuver in the plains and valleys proved a formidable obstacle to the complete conquest of the land (Jgs. 1:19). Jabin had 900 chariots of iron, and with them he was able to oppress the Israelites twenty years (Jgs. 4:3). The Philistines of the low country and the maritime plain, of whom we read in Judges and Samuel, were a warlike people, disciplined and well armed; and their possession of chariots gave them a great advantage over the Israelites. In the war of Michmash they put into the field the incredible number of 30,000 chariots and 6000 horsemen, only in the end to suffer a grievous defeat (1 S. 13:5; 14:20). In the battle of Gilboa, however, the chariots and horsemen of the Philistines bore down all opposition, and proved to be the destruction of Saul and his house.

Of these chariots there have come down to us no detailed description and no representation. But we cannot be far wrong in turning to the chariot of the Hittites as a type of the Canaanite and Philistine chariot. It is not from the monuments of the Hittites themselves, however, but from the Egyptian monuments depicting their conflicts with the Hittites, that we know what their chariots were like. Their chariotry was their chief arm of offense. The Hittites also used chariots for hunting; but a heavier wagon with paneled sides was employed for war. The Egyptian monuments represent three Hittites in each car, a practice which differed from that of Egypt and attracted attention. Of the three, one guided the chariot, another did the fighting with sword and lance, and the third was the shield-bearer.

III. Solomon and Later Kings.–The Israelites, living in a mountainous country, were tardy in adopting the chariot for purposes of war. David hamstrung all the chariot horses of Hadadezer king of Zobah, and "left enough for a hundred chariots" (2 S. 8:4); and Adonijah prepared for himself chariots and horsemen with a view to contesting the throne of his father (1 K. 1:5). But Solomon was the first in Israel to acquire chariots and horses on a national scale, and to build cities for their accommodation (1 K. 9:19). According to the MT of 1 K. 10:28f., Solomon had agents who received droves of horses from Egypt, "and a chariot came up and went out of Egypt for 600 shekels of silver, and a horse for 150; and so for all the kings of the Hittites, and for the kings of Syria, did they bring them out by their means." On the strength of a warrantable emendation of the text it is now proposed to read v. 28: "And Solomon's import of horses was from Egypt and from Kue; the king's traders received them from Kue at a price" — Kue being Cilicia. It was from Egypt that the nation was forbidden by the Deuteronomic law to acquire horses (Dt. 17:16); but according to Ezk. 27:14, Israel obtained horses, chargers, and mules from Togarmah — north Syria and Asia Minor. From Solomon's time onward chariots were in use in both kingdoms.

Zimri, who slew Elah, son of Baasha and king of Israel, was captain of half his chariots (1 K. 16:9). It was when sitting in his chariot in disguise beside the driver that Ahab received his fatal wound at Ramoth-gilead (22:34). The floor of the royal chariot was a pool of blood, and "they washed the chariot by the pool of Samaria" (vv. 35, 38). It was in his war-chariot that his servants carried Josiah dead from the fatal field of Megiddo (2 K. 23:30).

The chief pieces of the Hebrew chariot were (1) the pole to which the two horses were yoked, (2) the axle — resting upon two wheels with six or eight spokes (1 K. 7:33) — into which the pole was fixed, (3) a frame or body open behind, standing upon the axle and fitted by a leather band to the pole. The chariots of iron of which we read (Jgs. 4:3) were of wood strengthened or

Tiglath-pileser III (745-727 B.C.) standing in his war chariot with a driver and a "third man" or "captain" who holds an umbrella. Eight-spoked chariot wheels were introduced under Ashurnasirpal II (885-860 B.C.) and characterized Assyrian chariots until the Persian period. Gypsum relief from Nimrûd (Trustees of the British Museum)

Gold model of a Persian chariot with nine-spoked, knobbed wheels. The high chariot, with wheels approximately a man's height, was developed by Sennacherib (705-669 B.C.). (Trustees of the British Museum)

studded with iron. Like that of the Hittite, the Hebrew chariot probably carried three men, although in the chariot of Ahab (1 K. 22:34) and in that of Jehu (2 K. 9:24f.) we read of only two.

IV. Assyrians.–In the later days when the Assyrians overran the lands of the West, the Israelites had to face the chariots and the hosts of Sennacherib and of the kings (2 K. 19:23); and they faced them with chariots of their own. An inscription of Shalmaneser II of Assyria tells how in the Battle of Qarqar (854 B.C.) Ahab of the land of Israel had put into the field 2000 chariots and 10,000 soldiers. But the Assyrian chariotry was too numerous and powerful for Israel. The Assyrian chariot was larger and heavier than the Egyptian or the Hebrew: it had usually three and sometimes four occupants. When we read in Nahum's prophecy of "chariots flashing with steel," "rushing to and fro in the broad ways" (Nah. 2:3f.), it is the Assyrian chariots that we are to imagine being hastily gathered for the defense of Nineveh.

V. Chaldeans, Persians, and Greeks.–In early Babylonian inscriptions of the 3rd millennium before Christ there is evidence of the use of Babylonian war-chariots, and Nebuchadrezzar in his campaigns to the west had chariots as part of his victorious host (Jer. 47:3). It was the Persians who first employed scythed chariots in war; and we find Antiochus Eupator in the Seleucid period equipping a Greek force against Judea which had 300 chariots armed with scythes (2 Macc. 13:2).

VI. In the NT.–In the NT the chariot is seldom mentioned. Besides the chariot in which the Ethiopian eunuch was traveling (Acts 8:28f., 38), there is mention of the din of war-chariots to which the onrush of locusts is compared in apocalyptic vision (Rev. 9:9); and cf. Rev. 18:13.

VII. Figurative Use.–The chariot has a place in the figurative language of Scripture. It is a tribute to the powerful influence of Elijah and Elisha that they are separately called "the chariots of Israel and the horsemen thereof" (2 K. 2:12; 13:14). The angelic hosts are declared to be God's chariots, twice ten thousand, thousands upon thousands (Ps. 68:17). But chariots and horses themselves are a poor substitute for the might of God (Ps. 20:7). God Himself is represented as riding upon His chariots of salvation for the defense of His people (Hab. 3:8). In Zechariah, the four chariots with their horses of various colors have an apocalyptic significance (Zec. 6).

See also CHARIOTS OF THE SUN.

Bibliography.–Y. Yadin, *Art of Warfare in Biblical Lands* (1963), pp. 4f.; W. F. Albright, *AfO*, 6 (1930/31), 217-221; A. Salonen, "Notes on Wagons and Chariots in Ancient Mesopotamia," *Studia Orientalia* 14/2 (1950).

T. NICOL

CHARIOTS OF THE SUN [Heb. *mark^{e}ḇôṯ haššemeš*]. These, together with "horses of the sun," are mentioned in 2 K. 23:11. They are said to have stood in the temple, a gift of the kings of Judah. Josiah removed the horses from the precincts of the temple and burned the chariots. Among the Greeks, Helios was endowed with horses and chariots; thus the course of the sun as he sped across the skies was understood by the mythological mind of antiquity. The Babylonian god Shamash (=Heb. *šemeš*) likewise had his chariot and horses as well as his charioteer. The cult of the sun and other heavenly bodies, which was particularly in vogue during the latter days of the Judean monarchy (cf. 2 K. 23:5; Ezk. 8:16f.; Dt. 17:3; Jer. 8:2), seems to have constituted an element of the Canaanitish religion (cf. the names of localities like Beth-šemeš and the like). The chariots of the sun are also referred to in En. 72:5, 37; 75:4; and 3 Bar. 6.

M. L. MARGOLIS

CHARITABLY. The AV for Gk. *katá agápēn,* RSV "in love," in Rom. 14:15.

CHARITY. The AV rendering of Gk. *agápē* in 1 Cor. 8:1 and twenty-six times thereafter, including "feasts of charity" in Jude 12. *See* LOVE III.A.; AGAPE I.

CHARM; CHARMER [Heb. *lāḥaš* (Ps. 58:5; Eccl. 10:11a; Isa. 3:3; Jer. 8:17), *ḥāḇar ḥeḇer* (Dt. 18:11), *ba'al lāšôn* (Eccl. 10:11b), *kešep* (Neh. 3:4)]; AV also ENCHANTMENT (Eccl. 10:11a), BABBLER (v. 11b), ORATOR (Isa. 3:3), WITCHCRAFT (Nah. 3:4); NEB also "one who casts spells" (Dt. 18:11), ENCHANTER (Isa. 3:3), SORCERY (Nah. 3:4). The word "charm" is derived from Lat. *carmen,* "a song," and denotes strictly what is sung; then it comes to mean a magical formula chanted or recited with a view to certain desired results. A charm is to be distinguished from an AMULET, which is a material object having a magical potency, though it is frequently an inscribed formula on it that gives this object its power. The word "charm" stands primarily for the incantation, though it is often applied to an inscribed amulet.

A charm may be regarded as having a positive or a negative effect. In the first case it is supposed to secure some desired object or result. In the second, it is conceived as having the power of warding off evils, as the evil eye, the inflictions of evil spirits, and the like. In its negative meaning the word "countercharm" is commonly used.

(1) We have examples of written charms in the phylacteries and the *m*^{e}*zûzâ* (*see* AMULET). In Acts 19:13-20 we read of written charms used by the Ephesians, such as are elsewhere called "Ephesian writings" (*ephésia grámmata*). Such magical formulas were written generally on leather, though sometimes on papyrus, on lead, and even on gold. Those mentioned in the above passage must have been inscribed on some very valuable material, gold perhaps, or they could not have cost 50,000 pieces of silver. Charms of this kind have been dug up from the ruins of Ephesus.

In modern Egypt drinking-bowls are used, inscribed with passages from the Koran, and it is considered very good to drink from such a "lucky bowl," as it is called. Parts of the Koran and often complete miniature copies are worn by Egyptians and especially by Egyptian soldiers during war. These are buried with the dead bodies just as the ancient Egyptians interred with their dead certain portions of the Book of the Dead or even the whole book, and as the early Abyssinians buried with dead bodies certain magical texts. Josephus (*Ant.* viii.2.5) says that Solomon composed incantations by which demons were exorcised and diseases healed.

(2) Spoken charms are at least as widespread as those inscribed. Much importance was attached by the ancients (Egyptians, Babylonians, etc.) to the manner in which the incantations were recited, as well as to the substance of the formulas. If beautifully uttered, and with sufficient frequency, such incantations possessed unlimited power. The stress laid on the mode of reciting magical charms necessitated the existence of a priestly class and did much to increase the power of such a class. The binding force of the uttered word is implied in many parts of the OT (see Josh. 9:20). Though the princes of Israel had promised under false pretenses to make a covenant on behalf of Israel with the Gibeonites, they refused to break their promise because the word had been given. The words of blessing and curse were believed to have in themselves the power of self-realization. Therefore a curse was a means of destruction (see Nu. 22–24, Balaam's curses; Jgs. 5:23; Job 31). In a similar way the word of blessing was believed to ensure its own realization. In Gen. 48:8-22 the greatness of Ephraim and Manasseh is ascribed to the blessing of Jacob upon them (see further Ex. 12:32; Jgs. 17:2; 2 S. 21:3). It is no doubt to be understood that the witch of Endor called up Samuel from the dead by the recitation of some magical formula (1 S. 28:7ff.).

The uttering of the tetragrammaton *yhwh* was at a very early time (at the latest 300 B.C.) believed to be magically potent, and hence its ordinary use was forbidden, so that instead of "Yahweh," the Jews of the time, when the earliest part of the LXX was translated, used for this divine name the appellative *'*^{a}*ḏōnay,* "Lord." In a similar way among the Jews of postbiblical and perhaps even of biblical times, the pronunciation of the Aaronic blessing (Nu. 6:24-26) was supposed to possess great efficacy and to be a means of certain good to the person or persons involved. Evil spirits were exorcised by Jews of Paul's day through the use of the name of the Lord Jesus (Acts 19:13).

See also MAGIC. T. W. DAVIES

CHARME kar'mē (1 Esd. 5:25, NEB). *See* HARIM **2.**

CHARMIS kär'mis [Gk. *Charmeis,* A *Chalmeis*]. The son of Melchiel, one of the three elders or rulers of the town of Bethulia (Jth. 6:15; 8:10; 10:6).

CHARRAN kar'ən (Acts 7:2, 4, AV). *See* HARAN.

CHASEBA kas'ə-bə (1 Esd. 5:31, AV, NEB). *See* CHEZIB **2.**

CHASM. *See* GULF.

CHASPHO kas'fō [Gk. *Chasphō, Chasphōn, Chasphōth, Kasphōr*] (1 Macc. 5:26, 36); AV CHASPHON kas'fon, CHASPHOR kas'fôr; NEB CASPHOR. A city in Gilead captured by Judas Maccabeus (1 Macc. 5:36), probably to be identified with Caspin of 2 Macc. 12:13. It was a fortress of great strength, with a lake near it, which has led some to think it may be represented by el-Muzērīb on the Yarmuk (an important station on the pilgrim route to Mecca). Others would identify it with Khisfin, E of the Sea of Galilee. The ancient name of this city, however, has not been discovered. W. S. L. S.

CHASTE; CHASTITY. *See* MARRIAGE VI; SEX; VIRGIN.

CHASTENING; CHASTISEMENT [Heb. *yāsar, mûsār, yāḵaḥ, tôḵēḥâ, tôḵaḥaṯ, ʿāwôn* (Lam. 4:6); Gk. *paideúō, paideía*]; AV also CORRECT, PUNISH, REBUKE, INSTRUCTION; NEB also PUNISH, DISCIPLINE, INSTRUCT, CORRECT, REBUKE, TRAIN (Jer. 31:18), "take captive" (Hos. 7:12), FLOGGING (Lk. 23:16, 22). The Heb. terms *yāsar* and *mûsār* are the primary OT words for education (though they can only rarely be translated in that general sense), just as Gk. *paideúō* and *paideía* are the central terms for education in the NT, as indeed in Greek culture generally. Among the many Hebrew words associated with the Israelite notion of education are the cognates *tôḵēḥâ* and *tôḵaḥaṯ,* translated "reproof" or "correction," and frequently found as synonyms of *mûsār* (Prov. 3:11; 5:12; 6:23; 12:1; 15:10). Similarly, the Gk. *paideía* and *paideúō* are frequently associated in the NT with other terms that are virtual synonyms. In Eph. 6:4, the author speaks of "discipline and instruction" (*paideía kaì nouthesía*); *nouthesía* is elsewhere rendered "warning" (1 Cor. 10:11) and "admonishing" (Tit. 3:10), while the cognate verb *noutheteō* is variously translated "admonish" (Acts 20:31; 1 Cor. 4:14; Col. 3:16; 1 Thess. 5:12, 14), "warn" (Col. 1:28) and "instruct" (Rom. 15:14). In Rev. 3:19 the related words "reprove and chasten" (*eléncho kaì paideúō*) occur; elsewhere in the NT *eléncho* is translated "reprove" (Lk. 3:19), "rebuke" (1 Tim. 5:20; 2 Tim. 4:2), and "punish" (He. 12:5). A passage of central importance for the NT idea of discipline states that Scripture is "profitable for teaching (*didaskalía*), for reproof (*elegmós*), for correction (*epanórthōsis*), and for training (*paideía*) in righteousness" (2 Tim. 3:16). This cluster of educational terms does not consist of words with distinct nuances of meaning; but of synonyms that the author has piled up for rhetorical effect.

As an important constituent of the Israelite notion of education, the Hebrew words have three major connotations: (1) training and instruction (Ps. 6:7; Prov. 31:1; Job 4:3; Isa. 28:26; Hos. 7:15), (2) verbal correction or warning (Ps. 2:10; Prov. 9:7; Isa. 8:11; Jer. 6:8), and (3) corporal chastisement or punishment (Dt. 22:18; 1 K. 12:11, 14; 2 Ch. 10:11, 14; Prov. 22:15; 23:13; Ezk. 5:15). Education and discipline or chastening were inextricably intertwined in ancient Israelite thought, even though one or the other might be emphasized in a particular context. This interrelationship is clearly expressed in the synonymous couplet from Ps. 94:12: "Blessed is the man whom thou dost *chasten,* O Lord, and whom thou dost *teach* out of thy law." The traditional Greek conception of education, on the other hand, thoroughly ruled out the pedagogical value of corporal chastisement or punishment. Outside the NT (where the conception of education is dominated more by Israelite than by Greek ideals), only one Greek text is known in which *paideúō* may appropriately be translated "chastisement" (*TDNT,* V, 600). The Greek perspective on education is clearly expressed in a general essay on education from the 2nd cent. A.D. by Pseudo-Plutarch, *De liberis educandis* 9f. (12): "Children should be taught by encouragement and reasoning, not by beatings and maltreatment." In the Israelite view, however, education cannot dispense with corporal punishment (cf. Prov. 29:19; cf. also 13:24; 22:15; 23:12-14; 29:15, 17).

The entire biblical narrative of Israel's history may accurately be regarded as a description of God's moral and religious education of Israel. The stipulations of the Sinai covenant may be regarded as the subject matter or curriculum. Departures from the normative behavior demanded by this covenant are met with various forms of remedial discipline and chastisement (cf. Lev. 26:23, 28; Hos. 7:12). Consequently, the OT displays an intimate relation between Torah, or law, and discipline (cf. Dt. 4:36). Discipline is *always* remedial, whether for the individual or for the nation. (Cf. Dt. 8:5, which also reveals the OT penchant to conceive of the relationship between God and His people as that of a father to his son: just as a father attempts to educate and train his child through discipline and chastisement, so God tries to educate His people Israel in the ways of Torah. Similarly, He will guide the nation's leaders [2 S. 7:14].) This positive role of discipline is a frequent theme in OT wisdom traditions (cf. Prov. 6:23; 5:23). Discipline is also necessary so that the people of Israel may avoid the fate of national extinction (Jer. 30:11; 46:28), the "death" spoken of in Dt. 8:1-20.

In the NT, the conceptions of education and discipline or chastisement are as closely related as in the OT. The Gk. terms *paideúō* and *paideía* have three closely related connotations: (1) education or training (cf. Acts 7:22; 22:3), (2) corrective guidance (cf. 2 Tim. 2:25; Tit. 2:12), and (3) discipline in the sense of corrective punishment in human relationships (Lk. 23:16, 22; cf. He. 12:7, 10) and in relationships between God and man (1 Cor. 11:32; Rev. 3:19). In He. 12:3-11, a focal NT passage on the subject, external persecution is regarded as a guarantee that those to whom this letter was originally addressed were in fact legitimate sons of God (12:6f.). The analogy of a father's method of training his son is used in conceptualizing God's program of education for His people, in strong continuity with OT notions. Christians experience chastening or discipline so that they will not have to undergo a final eschatological chastening or judgment (1 Cor. 11:32; cf. 1 Tim. 1:20; 2 Tim. 2:25). As in the OT, divine discipline is always viewed as positive in its intention.

See also DISCIPLINE.

Bibliography.–W. Jaeger, *Paideia: The Ideals of Greek Culture* (3 vols., 1939-1944); *TDNT,* V, *s.v.* παιδεύω κτλ. (G. Bertram).

D. E. AUNE

CHATTER [Gk. *kenophōnía*]; AV BABBLINGS. In 1 Tim. 6:20; 2 Tim. 2:16 the rare NT term *kenophōnía* means "empty talk," and is qualified by the adjective "godless," i.e., unhallowed or profane.

CHEBAR kē'bär [Heb. *k^e^bār*; Gk. *Chobar*]; NEB KEBAR. The river by the side of which Ezekiel received his vision recorded in Ezk. 1:1. It is described as in "the land of the Chaldeans" and is probably to be identified with the canal (*nâru*) *kabari* mentioned in Babylonian records. This navigable canal flows SE from above Babylon to E of Nippur, rejoining the Euphrates near Erech. Hilprict identified this canal with the modern Shaṭṭ en-Nîl. Chebar should not be confused with Habor (Khabur).

W. EWING

CHECK. An obsolete term for "censure," occurring only in Job 20:3, AV.

CHECKER WORK [Heb. *ś^e^ḇāḵâ*] (1 K. 7:17); NEB CHAINWORK; [*tašbēṣ*] (Ex. 28:4); AV BROIDERED; NEB CHEQUERED; [*šāḇaṣ*] (Ex. 28:39); AV EMBROIDER; NEB CHEQUERED. The "checker work" of 1 K. 7:17 was a kind of ornamentation used on the tops of the pillars of JACHIN AND BOAZ before the porch of the temple, probably incorporating a crisscross design. In Ex. 28:4, 39 it apparently referred to a checked pattern of various colors which formed part of the weaving of the tunic worn by the high priest.

See also EMBROIDERY; WEAVING.

CHEDORLAOMER ked-ər-lā-ō'mər, ked-ər-lā'ō-mər [Heb. *k^e^ḏorlā'ōmer*; Gk. *Chodollogomor* (see below)]; NEB KEDORLAOMER. A king of ancient Elam who led a coalition including Amraphel of Shinar, Tidal king of nations, and Arioch king of Ellasar against the resurgent rulers of Sodom and Gomorrah (Gen. 14:1ff.). The latter had evidently been vassals of Chedorlaomer for some twelve years, but in the thirteenth year they had rebelled. Reprisals from Mesopotamia occurred the following year with the attack of the Elamite coalition, and the resistance offered by Sodom and Gomorrah was crushed. Lot, the nephew of Abram and an inhabitant of Sodom, was captured along with others and a good deal of booty. A raiding party was hurriedly assembled by Abram to rescue Lot, and after pursuing the visitors northward, doubtless along the King's Highway, he defeated Chedorlaomer and drove him N of Damascus.

In harmony with the Masoretic tradition (Gen. 14:5, 9, 17) 1QapGen and the pseudepigraphal Book of Jubilees (13:22) agree in naming Chedorlaomer as the leader of the Mesopotamian coalition that invaded southern Palestine, but neither work throws any light on the identity of this militant Elamite. Despite extensive study of this period of ancient Near Eastern history, the names of a number of the founders of Elamite dynastic power, including that of Chedorlaomer, are still not attested in extrabiblical sources.

The LXX form of the name is *Chodollogomor,* which implies a vocalization rather different from that of the MT, indicating the assimilation of *r* with *l* and the pronunciation of *'o* as *go*, making Heb. *Koḏollagomer.* Written in cuneiform, the Elamite version would most probably have been a combination of *Kutir* (or *Kudur*), meaning "servant," and the word *Lagamar,* which appears in several Elamite texts as a divine name. The element *Kutir* or *Kudur* was common in Elamite, and occurred regularly in proper names, as in Kutir-Naḫḫunte. *Kutir-* (or *Kudur-*) *Lagamar* would thus constitute a genuine Elamite construction meaning "servant of (the god) Lagamar," a title that could quite legitimately be borne by a ruler. A Babylonian deity, Lagamal, which was worshiped at Dilmun, may possibly be the same as the Elamite Lagamar; but this cannot be stated with certainty, even though they are frequently identified. The name of the deity Lagamal, which in any event is Semitic in form, occurred frequently as an element in personal names of the Old Babylonian period during the time of Hammurabi, and among the Amorites of the Mari age the deity Lagamar was venerated as "king of Mari." It has sometimes been argued from the possible identification of the two names that such a situation pointed to the presence of Elamite officials on the political scene at Mari somewhat prior to the time of Hammurabi. Since, however, this was a period of Amorite ascendancy in any event, it seems difficult to justify the identification on this ground, or on the supposition that the political history of the period included a coalition between Elamites and Akkadians. Again, it must be remembered that the name Lagamar is unquestionably Elamite in character, and should neither be confused with Semitic origins nor given a Semitic etymology.

To the present, no individual bearing the specific name Kutir- (or Kudur-) Lagamar has been recognized from extrabiblical records of any kind. Cuneiform texts have yielded the name of an Elamite monarch Kudur-KU.MAL, which is now read as Kutir-Naḫḫunti (the Sumerian Ku-mal being the equivalent of the Babylonian *nâḫu*), and speak of him as the conqueror of Babylon. Presumably, therefore, he is to be equated with Kutir-Naḫḫunte I of Elam, who ruled *ca.* 1625 B.C. Some scholars identified him with Chedorlaomer of Elam, who was actively campaigning in southern Palestine in the days of Abraham; but this view involves certain philological difficulties, and from a purely historical standpoint requires an extremely late date for Abraham and the patriarchal period. It is possible to argue philologically that the form *Naḫḫundi* is the equivalent of the West Semitic word *La'mr* (*La'nd*), but the latter with its alternative suggests the probability of confusion between the final *r* and *d* in the ancient Hebrew script. In the last resort, the absence of proper control data from Elamite cuneiform sources makes such an approach somewhat precarious. Suggestions by earlier Assyriologists to the effect that Chedorlaomer could well be identified with a person named Kudur-laḫ(gu)mal, who was mentioned in several late Babylonian legends, were based in part on the assumption that the Tudḫul(a) named in one of the sources was in fact "Tidal king of nations." While the name Tid'al can almost certainly be identified with the Hittite name Tudḫalias, it is as impossible to be sure that the "nations" over which Tidal ruled were in fact Hittite or even Luwian peoples as it is to identify Tidal himself with any degree of certainty, or to place him within a particular chronological period.

Whoever Chedorlaomer may have been, his interests in the area S of the Dead Sea were most probably related to its agricultural and mineral resources. The terrain was rich in salt, bitumen, potash, and magnesium; in antiquity the region was amply watered by springs and streams from Edomite territory, thus making for unusually good pasturage and the growth of crops such as emmer-wheat and barley.

The "King's Highway" up which Chedorlaomer most probably withdrew northward was an ancient road linking the Gulf of Aqabah with Damascus. Archeological excavations have shown the presence of numerous Bronze Age fortresses beside the road, the first of which were apparently destroyed by Chedorlaomer and his allies.

See M. C. Astour, in A. Altman, ed., *Biblical Motifs* (1966), pp. 65-112. R. K. HARRISON

CHEEK [Heb. *leḥî*] (1 K. 22:24 par.; Job 16:10; etc.); AV also CHEEK BONE (Ps. 3:7); NEB also FACE; [*raqqâ*] (Cant. 4:3; 6:7); AV TEMPLES; NEB PARTED LIPS; [Gk. *siagṓn*]. The Heb. *leḥî* has the connotation originally of freshness and rounded softness of the cheek, a sign of beauty in youth and maiden (Cant. 1:10; 5:13). The Oriental guards his cheek carefully from touch or defilement; a stroke on the cheek was, and is to this day, regarded as an act of extreme rudeness, a deadly affront. Our Savior, however, teaches us in Mt. 5:39 and Lk. 6:29 that even this insult is to be ignored and pardoned.

In Cant. 4:3; 6:7, Heb. *raqqâ* probably refers to the temples or cheekbones, as in its only other occurrences, Jgs. 4:21f.; 5:26, with reference to Sisera's temples (NEB "skull") through which Jael drove a tent peg. Here the NEB "lips" is based on the presumed root *rqq*, "be thin" (cf. BDB, p. 956). H. L. E. LUERING

CHEEK TEETH. *See* FANGS.

CHEESE. *See* FOOD III; MILK.

CHELAL kē'lal [Heb. *kelāl*]; NEB KELAL. One of the sons of Pahath-moab who had married foreign women during the Exile (Ezr. 10:30).

CHELCIAS kel'sē-əs (AV Bar. 1:1, 7; Sus. 2, 29, 63). *See* HILKIAH **7, 8.**

CHELLEANS kel'ē-ənz [Gk. *Chelleoi*]; AV CHELLIANS; NEB CHELEANS. The people of CHELOUS (Jth. 2:23).

CHELLUH kel'ə (Ezr. 10:35, AV). *See* CHELUHI.

CHELLUS kel'əs (Jth. 1:9, AV). *See* CHELOUS.

CHELOD kē'lod [Gk. *Cheleoud, Cheleoul*]. A name occurring only in Jth. 1:6, AV, where it is said that "many nations of the sons of Chelod assembled themselves to the battle." They are mentioned as obeying the summons of Nebuchadnezzar to his war against Arphaxad. The RSV translates "Chaldeans," but the NEB has "Chelodites." W. S. L. S.

CHELOUS kel'əs [Gk. *Chelous*] (Jth. 1:9); AV CHELLUS; NEB CHELUS. A place W of the Jordan to which Nebuchadnezzar sent his summons. It was located on one of the roads leading from Jerusalem to Egypt, and on another caravan route between Edom and Gaza. It is possibly to be identified with Alusa (*ḥlwṣh*), an ancient place in Idumea mentioned in the Targums. W. S. L. S.

CHELUB kē'lub [Heb. *kelûḇ*]; NEB KELUB.

1. The father of Mehir (1 Ch. 4:11). The name is probably a variation of Caleb.

2. The father of Ezri (1 Ch. 27:26), one of the officers of David.

CHELUBAI kə-lōō'bī [Heb. *kelûḇāy*] (1 Ch. 2:9); NEB CALEB. The brother of Jerahmeel and descendant of Hezron, elsewhere called CALEB.

CHELUHI kel'oo-hī [Heb. *k^elûhû, K k^elûhî*]; AV CHELLUH; NEB KELUHI. A son of Bani, listed among those who married foreign women (Ezr. 10:35).

CHELUS kel'əs (Jth. 1:9, NEB). *See* CHELOUS.

CHEMARIMS kem'ə-rims. This word appears once in the AV, in Zeph. 1:4; however, the Hebrew term *k^emārîm* (priests) also occurs in 2 K. 23:5 (AV "idolatrous priests") and Hos. 10:5 (AV "priests"). The RSV consistently translates the term "idolatrous priests," while the NEB has "heathen priests" or "priestlings." The word, which is of Aramaic origin, is used in the MT only in an unfavorable sense, its origin and associations naturally suggesting Syriac affinities.

See also PRIESTS AND LEVITES. J. R. VAN PELT

CHEMOSH kē'mosh [Heb. *k^emôš*; Gk. *Chamōs*]; NEB KEMOSH. The national God of the Moabites. In an old Hebrew song the Moabites are apostrophized as the "people of Chemosh" (Nu. 21:29). Jeremiah in his oracle of doom upon Moab has recourse to this song (Jer. 48:45f.). The impotence of the god to deliver his people is described by the prophet in figures representing him as going into captivity with them, his priests and princes together; and Moab is to be ashamed of him as Israel was of Bethel, which did not avail to save the northern kingdom from the conquering Assyrian power (48:7, 13, etc.).

I. Chemosh in Israel.–For Chemosh "the abomination of Moab," as for Moloch "the abomination of the Ammonites," Solomon, under the influence of his idolatrous wives, built a high place in the mountain before Jerusalem (1 K. 11:7). It was natural that these aliens should still desire to worship the gods of their native land; but although the effect of all this was seen in the moral and spiritual deterioration of Solomon himself, there is no indication that the immoralities and cruelties associated with such worship were then practiced in Jerusalem as they were in the days of Ahaz and Manasseh, and even as early as the days of Abijam of Judah (1 K. 15:12f.).

Josiah found these abominations of alien worship, which had been introduced by Solomon and added to by Ahaz and Manasseh, flourishing when he came to the throne. Moved by the prohibitions of the Book of the Law (Dt. 12:29-31; 18:10), Josiah pulled down and defiled the high places and the altars; and in order to make a clean sweep of the idolatrous figures, "he broke in pieces the pillars," or obelisks, "and cut down the Asherim," or sacred poles, "and filled their places with the bones of men" (2 K. 23:1-20).

II. Chemosh and the Ammonites.–There is one passage where Chemosh is designated the god of the Ammonites (Jgs. 11:24). Jephthah is disputing the right of the Ammonites to invade territory which belongs to Israel because the Lord has given it to them by conquest; and he asks: "Will you not possess what Chemesh your god gives you to possess? And all that the Lord our God has dispossessed before us, we will possess." It may be that he is called here the god of the Ammonites by a mere oversight of the historian; or, Moab and Ammon being kindred nations descended from a common ancestor Lot, Chemosh may in a sense belong to both. We notice, however, that Jephthah's argument in meeting the claim preferred by the king of Ammon passes on to Israel's relation to the Moabites and mentions only well-known Moabite cities. Chemosh is accordingly named because of his association with Moab, the cities of which are being spoken of, although strictly and literally Moloch should have been named in an appeal addressed as a whole to the Ammonites (vv. 12-28; cf. Moore, *ICC, in loc.*).

III. Moabite Stone.–The discovery of the Moabite Stone in 1868 at Dibon has thrown light upon Chemosh and the relations of Moab to its national god. The monument, which is now in the Louvre in Paris, bears an inscription which is among the oldest specimens of Semitic alphabetic writing extant, commemorating the successful effort made *ca.* 860 or 850 B.C. by Mesha king of Moab to throw off the yoke of Israel. We know from the OT record that Moab had been reduced to subjection by David (2 S. 8:2); that it paid a heavy tribute to Ahab king of Israel (2 K. 3:4); and that, on the death of Ahab, Mesha its king rebelled against Israelite rule (3:5). Not till the reign of Jehoram was any effort made to recover the lost dominion. The king of Israel then allied himself with the kings of Judah and Edom, and marching against Moab by way of the Red Sea, inflicted upon Mesha a defeat so decisive that the wrath of his god Chemosh could be appeased only by the sacrifice of his son (vv. 6ff.).

The historical situation described in the OT narrative is confirmed by Mesha's inscription. There are, however, divergences in detail. In 2 Kings the revolt of Mesha is said to have taken place after the death of Ahab. The inscription implies that it must have taken place by the middle of Ahab's reign. The inscription implies that the subjection of Moab to Israel had not been continuous from the time of David and says that Omri, the father of Ahab, had reasserted the power of Israel and had occupied at least a part of the land.

It is with what the inscription says of Chemosh that we are chiefly concerned. On the monument the name appears twelve times. Mesha is himself the son of Chemosh, and it was for Chemosh that he built the high place upon which the monument was found. He built it, among other reasons, because Chemosh had enabled him to overthrow his enemies. It was because Chemosh was angry with his land that Omri afflicted Moab for so long. Omri had taken possession of the land of Medeba, and Israel dwelt in it during his reign and half his son's reign, but Chemosh restored it in Mesha's time. Mesha took the "Ataroth" which the king of Israel had built for himself, slew all the people of the city, and made them a spectacle to Chemosh and to Moab. Mesha took the altar-hearth of Dodo, and dragged it before Chemosh in Kerioth. By command of Chemosh, Mesha attacked Nebo and fought against Israel; and after a fierce struggle he took the place, slaying the inhabitants en masse, seven thousand men and women and maidservants, devoting the city to Ashtar-Chemosh and dragging the altar vessels of the Lord before Chemosh. Out of Jahaz, too, which the king of Israel had built, Chemosh drove him before Mesha. At the instigation of Chemosh, Mesha fought against Horonaim, and, although the text is defective in the closing paragraph, we may surmise that Chemosh did not fail him but restored it to his dominions. *See also* MOABITE STONE.

IV. Chemosh and Yahweh.–Naturally enough there is considerable obscurity in local and personal allusions. Dodo may have been a local god worshiped by the Israelites E of the Jordan. Ashtar-Chemosh may be a compound divinity of a kind not unknown to Semitic mythology, Ashtar representing possibly the Phoenician Ashtoreth. What is of importance is the recurrence of so many phrases and expressions applied to Chemosh which are used of Yahweh in the OT narratives. The religious conceptions of the Moabites reflected in the inscription are so strikingly like those of the Israelites that if only the name of Yahweh were substituted for that of Chemosh we might think we were reading a chapter of the books of Kings. It is not in the inscriptions, however, but in the OT narrative that we find a reference to the demand of Chemosh for human sacrifice. "He took his eldest son," says the Hebrew annalist, "who was to reign in his stead, and offered him for a burnt offering upon the wall. And there became great wrath upon Israel: and they withdrew from him and returned to their own land" (2 K. 3:27). This appears to indicate that the Israelites had to give up their purpose to fasten the yoke of bondage again upon Mesha and that they returned empty-handed to their own land. But this fortunate result for Moab was due to the favor of Chemosh, and in particular to the human sacrifice by which he was propitiated.

If we find in these representations of Chemosh in the OT narrative and in Mesha's inscription a striking similarity to the Hebrew conception of Yahweh, we cannot fail to notice the lack of the higher moral and spiritual elements of the religion of Israel from Moses and Abraham downward, and especially in the prophets. The OT religion condemns human sacrifice from the beginning; and the OT God is a God of forgiveness, longsuffering, desiring obedience and a pure heart more than sacrifice.

T. NICOL

The name Kemiš appears in the Eblaic texts discovered at Tell Mardikh in 1975 and is almost certainly the same deity. The form agrees with the *kethibh* of Jer. 48:7 (*kmyš*; *Q* *k^e^môš*). This suggests that Carchemish was the "city of (*qar*) Chemosh (Kemiš)," and that Chemosh/Kemish was a deity of a territory larger than Moab and Ammon.

See also RELIGIONS OF THE BIBLICAL WORLD: CANAANITE RELIGION.

W. S. L. S.

CHENAANAH kə-nā'ə-nə [*k^e^na'^a^nâ*–'from Canaan'?]; NEB KENAANAH.

1. The fourth-named of the seven sons of Bilhan, son of Jediael, of the tribe of Benjamin, a leading warrior in the time of David (1 Ch. 7:10).

2. Father of the false prophet Zedekiah, who encouraged Ahab against Micaiah (1 K. 22:11, 24; 2 Ch. 18:10, 23).

CHENANI ke-nā'nī [Heb. *k^e^nānî*]; NEB KENANI. A Levite mentioned in Neh. 9:4 as one of those present when Ezra read the law in public.

CHENANIAH ken-ə-nī'ə [Heb. *k^e^nanyāhû, k^e^nanyâ*–'established by God']; NEB KENANIAH. Chief of the Levites who was the leader of the music (1 Ch. 15:22, 27); in 26:29 he is mentioned as an official who was appointed for certain duties outside the temple (cf. Neh. 11:16).

CHEPHAR-AMMONI kē-fär-am'ə-nī [Heb. *k^e^par hā'ammônî*–'village of the Ammonites'; Gk. A *Kaphērammin*, B *Kepheira kaí Monei*]; AV CHEPHAR-HAAMMONAI; NEB KEPHAR-AMMONI. A place in the territory of Benjamin (Josh. 18:24).

CHEPHAR-HAAMMONAI kē-fär-hā-am'ə-nī (AV Josh. 18:24). *See* CHEPHAR-AMMONI.

CHEPHIRAH ke-fī'rə [Heb. *hakk^e^pîrâ*; Gk. *Kapheira, Chepheira, kaí Pheira*]; AV and NEB Apoc. CAPHIRA; NEB OT KEPHIRAH. One of the cities of the Hivites, who by trickery made alliance with Israel (Josh. 9:17). It was in the lot of Benjamin (18:26), and was reoccupied after the return from Babylon (Ezr. 2:25; Neh. 7:29). Its inhabitants returned with Zerubbabel (1 Esd. 5:19). Represented by the modern Tell Kefireh 5 mi. (8 km.) SW of el-Jîb (ancient Gibeon), it stands on high ground and has many ancient remains.

W. S. L. S.

CHERAN kē'rən [Heb. *k^e^rān*]. A Horite clan-name occurring in the genealogy of Seir the Horite (Gen. 36:26) and in the parallel list in 1 Ch. 1:41.

CHERETHITES ker'ə-thīts [Heb. *k^e^rēṯîm*, sing. *hakk^e^rēṯî*; Gk. *Cherethi, Chelethi* (2 S. 8:18), *Cholthi* (1 S. 30:14), *Chetti* (2 S. 15:18), *Krētes* (Ezk. 25:16; cf. 30:5; Zeph. 2:5, cf. v. 6)]; NEB KERETHITES. Evidently, a Philistine clan whose territory was adjacent to southern Judah. 1 S. 30:14 mentions the Negeb of the Cherethites along with those parts of the south belonging to Judah and Caleb. As in Ezk. 25:16 and Zeph. 2:5 the Cherethites are mentioned in parallelism to the Philistines, we may assume that in 1 S. 30:14 that part of the Negeb is meant which fell under Philistine suzerainty, one of the towns of which was Ziklag. The name is related to the name of Crete, from which island at least part of the Philistines had come, and has nothing to do with the Hebrew verb *kāraṯ*, though Ezk. 25:16 has a wordplay with this verb.

Mercenaries from the Philistines (cf. 2 S. 15:18-22) formed a bodyguard of David, called the Cherethites and Pelethites (both sing. in Heb., 2 S. 8:18; 15:18; 20:7, 23; 1 K. 1:38, 44; 1 Ch. 18:17); Benaiah was their commander. In later times CARITES formed the bodyguard.

Bibliography.–J. A. Montgomery and H. S. Gehman, Comm. on Kings (*ICC*, 1951), pp. 85f.; R. de Vaux, *Ancient Israel* (1961).

A. VAN SELMS

CHERISH. In the AV, "cherish" translates Heb. *sāḵan* in 1 K. 1:2, 4, referring to Abishag's care of David. The RSV has "be his nurse," the NEB "take care of." The only other AV occurrences are for Gk. *thálpō* in Eph. 5:29 (so RSV) and 1 Thess. 2:7 (RSV "take care of").

Besides Eph. 5:29, RSV usage of "cherish" is limited to the OT, and all in negative contexts, as "cherish anger" (Job 36:13), "enmity" (Ps. 55:3; Ezk. 35:5), "iniquity" (Ps. 66:18), and "harlotry" (Hos. 4:10). In these texts it has the sense "nurture," "cultivate," or in the last, "hold dear."

J. W. D. H.

CHERITH ke'rith, **THE BROOK** [Heb. *naḥal k^e^rîṯ*]; NEB RAVINE OF KERITH. A stream or brook E of the Jordan, where Elijah sought refuge during the drought in Israel (1 K. 17:2-7). Traditionally this place is identified with Wâdī Qelt, which is above Jericho on the west side of the Jordan; but this location is flatly contradicted by the biblical description in 17:3, "the brook Cherith, that is east of (*'al-p^e^nê*) the Jordan." The identification with Wâdī Qelt was made in the Middle Ages.

Elijah is described as "the Tishbite, of Tishbe in Gilead" (17:1); hence one of the numerous wadis in Gilead, possibly in the region of the modern village of Lisdip, is indicated. Abel (*GP*, I, 484f.) suggests that Wâdī Yâbis fits the qualifications, but this is hardly more than careful speculation.

W. S. L. S.

CHERUB ke'rub [Heb. *k^e^rûḇ*; Gk. *Charaath*]; NEB KERUB; AV and NEB Apoc. CHARAATHALAR [Gk. *Charaathalan*, combining *Charaath* with following *Alan*]. A place in Babylonia (Ezr. 2:59; Neh. 7:61). Since none of the places listed in these verses can be identified, it is probable that they were poor settlements rather than established cities. The people of Cherub were among those returning from exile whose genealogies had fallen into confusion.

In 1 Esd. 5:36, RSV, likely through a misunderstanding of the passages cited above, Cherub has become a personal name. A. J. HOERTH

CHERUBIM cher'ə-bim, cher'oo-bim [Heb. *k^e rûḇîm* (sing. *k^e rûḇ*), perhaps related to Akk. *karūbu*–'intercessor']; AV CHERUBIMS. Winged creatures of a suprahuman variety, occasionally mentioned in the OT. They appear as guardians of the tree of life (Gen. 3:24) and as the vehicle by which God traversed the heavens (2 S. 22:11; Ps. 18:10 [MT 11]). In the latter references, however, the writer parallels the image of "cherub" by that of the "wings of the wind," perhaps merely a poetic description of swift passage in which the storm-winds have been personified in terms of familiar Mesopotamian and Canaanite iconography.

The ark of the covenant had a gold cherub of beaten work placed at each end in such a manner that their outstretched wings covered the mercy seat (NEB "cover") as they faced one another (Ex. 25:18-20; 37:6-9). When Moses entered the tent of meeting to commune with God, the divine message came from between the two cherubim (Nu. 7:89). Cherubim were also woven into the fabric of the tabernacle and the veil (Ex. 26:1, 31; 36:8, 35).

In a highly complex vision experienced by Ezekiel (1:4-28), four winged living creatures were accompanied everywhere by wheels that were "full of eyes all round" (NEB Ezk. 1:18). Although the text nowhere states that these creatures were actually cherubim, this has been inferred from a comparable vision in 10:1-22, where most translations follow the LXX as against the MT in reading a plural form of the term cherub. In the first vision these agents' only divine service was reflecting God's glorious presence, but in the second they were stationed at the right side of the temple entrance, filling the inner court and its precincts with the sound of their beating wings. These beings also were attended by wheels, and when the divine glory moved the cherubim accompanied it, ultimately halting at the east gateway of the temple (10:19). Their functions, particularly in divine worship, seemed less direct than those of the SERAPHIM of Isaiah's vision (cf. Isa. 6:1-8). The cherubim of Ex. 25:18-22 appear to have provided with their wings a visible pedestal for God's invisible throne (cf. 1 S. 4:4; 2 S. 6:2; Ps. 80:1; etc.). Such activity was apparently implicit in Ezekiel's vision, in which the throne of God that was upheld by the cherubim became highly mobile. The duties of cherubim as guardians were again reflected in the ode on the fall of the king of Tyre (Ezk. 28:11-23), where the parallel with man's decline from pristine grace is evident.

North Syrian iconic practice was amply reflected in the decor of Solomon's temple, which was constructed along contemporary lines by Phoenician craftsmen. Cherubim were prominent in a decorative frieze which was carved around the walls, while the inner sanctuary was dominated by two huge cherubim made from olivewood and plated with gold leaf (1 K. 6:23-29; 2 Ch. 3:10-14; 5:7-9). Their height and wingspan were both about 15 ft. (4.5 m.), and when assembled they covered one whole wall. Cherubim also formed part of the decorative motif on the bronze basins that were used for ritual ablutions (1 K. 7:27-39). The extent to which the Solomonic temple was indebted to Phoenician religious theory and practice has been made evident by archeological discoveries. Excavations have revealed that in Canaanite temples a winged sphinx was a popular iconic element, and the Hebrew cherubim as fashioned by Phoenician (i.e., Canaanite) craftsmen may well have been intended to represent such creatures rather than the cherubim of the tabernacle period.

Artistic representations of cherubim have been recovered from several Near Eastern sites including Taanach, Carchemish, Tell Halâf, and Aleppo. Particularly fine examples came from Nimrûd, where an ivory panel depicted two winged, sphinx-like creatures standing back to back, and also from Samaria, where cherubim were represented in considerable detail on ivory panels. These showed a figure with a human face, a four-legged animal body, and two large wings. At Gebal (Byblos) excavators recovered a carving of two cherubim sup-

Cherubim, standing back-to-back with their wings touching. One of them advances toward a sacred tree. Part of an ivory panel from Nimrûd (8th cent. B.C.) (Trustees of the British Museum)

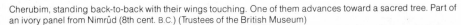

porting the throne of King Hiram of Gebal (*ca.* 1200 B.C.) and presumably guarding the monarch from danger. Symbolic winged beings were a regular feature of Near Eastern mythology and architecture alike. Statues of winged bulls (Akk. *šēdu*) and lions were stationed at the entrances of important public buildings in Assyria and Babylonia to afford magical protection for the structures and their contents. Among the Hittites the griffin was a popular mythological creature, an amalgam of lion, eagle, and sphinx.

Ezekiel's visions appear to reflect primarily the reactions of a mystic personality to the Babylonian statuary and, despite the complex descriptions, furnish little understanding of the nature and appearance of cherubim. More difficult to comprehend are the suprahuman beings of Gen. 3:24, since that material issues from a background of Sumerian historiography. Although winged creatures were represented in Sumerian literature, as in the vision of the pious Gudea of Lagash, they were not portrayed artistically in the Assyrian fashion.

The most that can be said with certainty is that in Scripture the cherubim were celestial beings whose duty in the heavenly hierarchy apparently was to guard and protect. Although they were closely associated with the personage and will of God, there is no indication that they were in any sense ethical or moral beings or that they performed functions analagous to those of the seraphim.

Bibliography.–F. Stier, *Gott und Sein Engel im AT* (1934); M. Haran, *Eretz Israel,* 5 (1958), 83-89; *IEJ,* 9 (1959), 30-38; S. N. Kramer, *The Sumerians* (1963), pp. 137f.

R. K. HARRISON

CHESALON kes'ə-lon [Heb. *kesālôn*; Gk. *Chaslon, Chasalōn*]; NEB KESALON. A city on the northern boundary of Judah (Josh. 15:10). It is now identified with Keslā, about 9 mi. (14 km.) W of Jerusalem.

CHESED kē'sed, kes'ed [Heb. *keśed*; Gk. *Chaszad*]; NEB KESED. One of the sons of Nahor and Milcah (Gen. 22:22); he was probably the ancestor of the *Kaśdîm.* The early Babylonian form *kašdu* appears in Assyrian as Kaldu or Kaldû. The RSV follows the Assyrian and Greek style of writing the name and uses Chaldees or Chaldeans instead of Casdim.

The Chaldeans dwelt in the lower valley of the Euphrates, at the head of the Persian Gulf. Abram came from Ur of the Chaldees (Gen. 11:28, 31; 15:7; Neh. 9:7). In Job 1:17 the *Kaśdîm* are described as invading the land of Uz, the eldest brother of Chesed (Gen. 22:21f.). In the days of Nebuchadrezzar the *kaśdîm* overran Syria and Palestine and carried the people of Judah in successive deportations into captivity (2 K. 24:1f., 10ff.; 25:1ff.). In Dnl. 2:2, 5 the *Kaśdîm* are named with the magicians and astrologers as a learned class, skilled in interpretations. *Kaśdîym* (or *Kaśdîmâ*) is sometimes used in Hebrew for the land of Chaldea (Ezk. 23:15f.; 11:24).

J. R. SAMPEY

CHESIL kē'səl, kes'il [Heb. *kesîl*; Gk. *Chaseir*]; NEB KESIL. A town in the extreme south of Judah named with Eltolad, Hormah, and Ziklag (Josh. 15:30). The name does not occur again. In Josh. 19:4 it is replaced by Bethul (Gk. *Baithēl*), and in 1 Ch. 4:30 by Bethuel.

CHEST [Heb. *'ārôn*] (2 K. 12:9f.; 2 Ch. 24:8, 10f.). Heb. *'ārôn* is cognate to Akk. *arānu,* Ugar. *'arn,* Phoen. *'rn,* Aram. *'rn'*. The word means "box, chest, coffin" (the latter especially in the Phoenician inscriptions and in rabbinic Hebrew; cf. Gen. 50:26). The "chest" in 2 K. 12 and 2 Ch. 24:8 was probably of wood (the "ark of the covenant" was made of acacia wood [Ex. 25:10]). In 2 K. 12:19 the LXX has Gk. *kibōtón,* "wooden box, chest," while in 2 Ch. 24:8 it renders Heb. *'ārôn eḥād,* "one chest," with *glōssókomon,* "case, container" (cf. Jn. 12:6; 13:29, "money box").

In 2 K. 12:9f., at the request of King Jehoash that temple repairs be undertaken, Jehoiada the priest took "one chest," bored a hole in its lid, and placed it "beside the altar on the right side as one entered the house of the Lord." This probably refers to the incense altar inside the temple. The parallel account in 2 Ch. 24:8f. differs slightly. There, at the command of the king, a chest is made and set "outside the gate of the house of the Lord." In both passages the money collected in the chest was used for temple repairs.

In Ezk. 27:24 the AV renders Heb. *beginzê berōmîm* "in chests of rich apparel." The RSV has "in carpets [cf. KoB, p. 190] of colored stuff," the NEB "in stores of coloured fabric." The AV and NEB translations are based on Heb. *genāzîm,* meaning "store, treasury" (cf. Est. 3:9; 4:7). The AV probably uses "chest" because it takes Heb. *'āruzîm* as "cedar": "in chests of rich apparel, bound with cords, and made of cedar. . . ." However, Heb. *beginzê* should be translated "garments, fabric" (Tg. Est. 1:3; W. Zimmerli, *Ezekiel,* II [*BKAT*, XIII, 1969], 625), and *'āruzîm,* a hapax legomenon, as an adjective modifying "ropes" ("tightened, firm"), thus giving "in bicolored garments, bound and tightened with cords," or the like.

F. B. KNUTSON

CHESTNUT; CHESTNUT TREE. *See* PLANE TREE.

CHESULLOTH kə-sul'oth [Heb. *hakkesûlôṯ*; Gk. B *Chasalōth,* A *Achaselōth*]; NEB KESULLOTH. A town assigned to Issachar following the conquest of Canaan under Joshua (Josh. 19:18). Called Chisloth-tabor ("slopes of Tabor") in Josh. 19:12, the city was on the border between Zebulun and Issachar. Modern Iksâl, 3 mi. (5 km.) SE of Nazareth, on the northern border of the plain of Esdraelon at the foot of the hills, approximates the site of the ancient city.

R. J. HUGHES, III

CHEWING THE CUD [Heb. *gērâ*–'cud,' *gārar gērâ*–'ruminate,' *ma'aleh haggērâ*–'bringing up the cud']. One of the marks of cleanliness in a quadruped, given in Lev. 11:3 and Dt. 14:6. Among the animals considered fit for food are therefore included the ox, the sheep, the goat, the hart, the gazelle, the roebuck, the wild goat, the ibex, the antelope, and the mountain-sheep (Dt. 14:5). Several of the forbidden animals are expressly named, e.g., the camel, the rock badger, the hare, and the swine (Ex. 11:4-7). *See* CLEAN AND UNCLEAN II.A; IV.B.3.

CHEZIB kē'zib [Gk. *Chaseba*]; AV, NEB, CHASEBA. The name of a family of temple servants in the list of those who returned from Babylon (1 Esd. 5:31). The name is not given in the parallel passages in Ezra and Nehemiah.

CHEZIB [Heb. *kezîḇ*] (Gen. 38:5); NEB mg. KEZIB. The town in which Shua bore Judah a son Shelah (*see* ACHZIB **1**). Where the RSV reads "she was in Chezib," the NEB emends the text to read "she ceased to bear children."

CHICKEN. There is no reference to chickens in the OT sufficiently clear to specify our common domestic bird. The many references to "fatted fowl" in these older records, in accordance with the text and the history of the other nations, were to pigeons, guineas, ducks, geese, and swans. The importation of peafowl by Solomon is mentioned in 1 K. 10:22 par. Chickens are distinctive birds and would have been equally a marvel worth recording had they been introduced at that time.

From the history of the bird in other countries it is safe to estimate that they entered Palestine at about the 6th cent. B.C. That would allow sufficient time for them to increase and become common enough to be used as illustrations by Jesus. He mentions the hen (Gk. *órnis*) and her brood (*nossíon,* Luke *nossiá*) in a moving image of divine concern for the Jews who rejected Him (Mt. 23:37; Lk. 13:34).

See also COCK; FOWL. G. STRATTON-PORTER

CHIDE [Heb. *rîḇ*]; NEB "be the accuser." The RSV translates the term *rîḇ* as "chide" only once, in Ps. 103:9, where it is used in the sense of conducting a legal case or a suit against someone.

CHIDON kī'dən, **THRESHING FLOOR OF** [Heb. *gōren kîḏōn*; Gk. B omits; A *Cheilō*]; NEB KIDON. The place where Uzzah perished because he touched the ark (1 Ch. 13:9). In 2 S. 6:6 it is called the threshing floor of Nacon. No name resembling either Chidon or Nacon has been discovered.

CHIEF; CHIEF MAN [Heb. *rō'š*–'head,' *śar, 'allûp,* also *nāśî', 'aḇîr, 'êlîm, 'aṣîlîm, gibbôr, ḥayil* ("army chief," Est. 1:3), *seḡānîm, pinnâ, qāṣîn, raḇ*; Aram. *raḇ*; Gk. *prṓtos, archi-, hēgoúmenos* (Acts 14:12)]; AV also HEAD, PRINCE, DUKE (*'allûp*), CAPTAIN, RULERS (*seḡānîm,* Ezr. 9:2), FIRST, MASTER, MIGHTY MEN, GUIDE (Prov. 6:7), CHIEFEST, NOBLES (*'aṣîlîm,* Ex. 24:11), POWER (Est. 1:3); NEB also LEADERS, FOREMOST MEN, OVERSEER, MAGISTRATES (Ezr. 9:2), MASTER, COMMANDER, HEAD, "strongest" (1 S. 21:7), etc.; **CHIEF OFFICER** [Heb. *nagîḏ, pāqîḏ nāgîḏ* (Jer. 20:1), *raḇ, śārê hanniṣṣāḇîm* (pl.)]; AV RULER, PRINCE, CHIEF GOVERNOR, CHIEF OF THE OFFICERS; NEB also FOREMAN, OFFICER IN CHARGE, OVERSEER, PRINCIPAL OFFICER, etc.; **CHIEF OFFICIAL** [Heb. *ri'šôn*] (1 Ch. 18:17); AV CHIEF; NEB "in attendance"; **CHIEF PRINCE** [Heb. *rō'š* (. . . *lenāgîḏ*), *neśî' rō'š, śar ri'šôn*]; AV also "chief, to be ruler" (2 Ch. 11:22); NEB also CROWN PRINCE (2 Ch. 11:22), "prince of Rosh" (Ezk. 38:2f.; 39:1); **CHIEFTAIN** [Heb. *nāśî'*] (1 Ch. 5:6); AV, NEB, PRINCE.

Heads of clan groups ("fathers' houses") in the time of Moses (e.g., Nu. 31:26; 36:1), tribal leaders after the settlement in Canaan (e.g., 1 Ch. 5:7, 12), heads of warrior units large and small in David's time (1 Ch. 11:10ff.; 12:3; etc.), leaders among the returned exiles (e.g., Neh. 10:14; 11:3), and many other kinds of leaders are called in the OT *rō'š*. The *śar* could be the chief official of a civil, religious, or military department (*see* CAPTAIN; PRINCE), such as the chief butler (Gen. 40:2), chief of the Levites (1 Ch. 15; 2 Ch. 35:9), the "chiefs of the service" who helped David organize the temple worship (1 Ch. 25:1), and the chief of the eunuchs in the court of Nebuchadrezzar (Dnl. 1:7ff.).

The Heb. *'allûp* in Gen. 36:15ff.; Ex. 15:15; 1 Ch. 1:51-54, translated "duke" in the AV, designates Edomite tribal leaders; the derivation from *'elep,* "a thousand," would indicate the original use for leaders over a thousand men (but the LXX has Gk. *hēgemṓn,* not *chilíarchos*). The word may relate to an Edomite title, though we know nothing of that language.

In Ex. 24:11 the seventy elders who represented the people at the covenant ratification are called "chief men" (*'aṣîlîm*). The homonymous Hebrew word in Isa. 41:9, however, is not "chief men" as in the AV, but "farthest corners" (RSV, NEB).

The RSV has "chief" for Heb. *qāṣîn* in Josh. 10:24 ("chief of the men of war") and Prov. 6:7; its Semitic cognates mean "judge," "decision-maker." In Ezr. 9:2 certain Jewish leaders are called *seḡānîm,* "chief men" — a word no doubt brought back from Babylon (cf. Akk. *šakun,* "perfect").

The *'êlîm* (sing. *'ayil*) of 2 K. 24:15 (*Q*); Ezk. 17:13, the "chief men of the land," are probably the landowners or noblemen of Israel; the literal meaning is "rams." Several MSS read the word also at Ezk. 32:21.

The Heb. *nāśî',* "one lifted up," is translated "chief" by the RSV in Nu. 3:22; Josh. 22:14, 30, 32, and "chieftain" (Beerah, leader of a "family" of the Reubenites) in 1 Ch. 5:6. The word has a variety of applications (see BDB, p. 672); in Nu. 3:24, 30, 35 (AV, NEB, "chief"; RSV "head") it refers to heads of fathers' houses (*see* FATHER'S HOUSE); in v. 32, Eleazar son of Aaron is to be "chief over the leaders of the Levites" (*neśî' neśî'ê hallewî*); in 4:34, 46, it designates the Israelite leaders directly under Moses and Aaron (also 7:2, etc.; *see* LEADER); and in Josh. 22 the word again denotes heads of fathers' houses, "among the clans (*'alāpîm*) of Israel." (In 22:14 the *nāśî'* is called *rō'š*.)

The "chief officers" mentioned in the RSV include Pashhur, head of the temple police, who beat Jeremiah and put him in stocks (Jer. 20:1ff.); Shebuel, in charge of all the keepers of the temple treasuries (1 Ch. 26:24); Conaniah, in charge of the overseers of temple contributions under Hezekiah (2 Ch. 31:12); and Azariah (v. 13; cf. 1 Ch. 9:11), Hilkiah, Zechariah, and Jehiel (2 Ch. 35:8), the "chief officers of the house of God," in charge of all those involved in the administration of the temple. All these are called *nāgîḏ*. In 1 K. 5:16; 9:23; etc., are mentioned *śārê hanniṣṣāḇîm,* superintendents under Solomon "who exercised authority over the people." The "chief officers" of Nebuchadrezzar are called *raḇ* (Jer. 39:13), no doubt influenced by Babylonian usage of the cognate term (cf. 41:1).

For "chief prince," and NEB "prince of Rosh," *see* PRINCE. *See also* ELDER IN THE OT; RULER; TEMPLE; TRIBE; etc.

Bibliography.–M. Noth, *System der zwölf Stämme Israels* (1930); C. U. Wolf, *JBL,* 65 (1946), 45ff.; *NHI* and other histories of Israel. J. W. D. H.

CHIEF HOUSE. *See* FATHER'S HOUSE.

CHIEF MUSICIAN. *See* ASAPH **2**.

CHIEF OF ASIA (Acts 19:31, AV). *See* ASIARCH.

CHIEF OFFICERS (Ezr. 4:9, NEB). *See* APHARSITES. On other references *see* CHIEF.

CHIEF PRIEST. *See* PRIEST, HIGH.

CHIEF SEATS (AV Mt. 23:6; etc.). *See* BEST SEAT.

CHILD; BABE; INFANT; SUCKLING; etc. [Heb. *bēn, yeleḏ, na'ar, ṭap, 'ôlēl, yānaq,* also *'ûl, 'awîl, ṣā'îr, zera'* (Lev. 22:13), *yāḥîḏ* ("only child," Jgs. 11:34), etc.; Gk. *paidíon, téknon, tekníon, bréphos, nḗpios, huiós, paîs,* also *thēlázōn* (Mt. 21:16), *nēpiázō* (1 Cor. 14:20), *monogenḗs* ("only child," Lk. 9:38)].

I. Terminology.–The Heb. *bēn* is the usual word for sons, children in general, or descendants, and occurs repeatedly in the phrase "children of Israel," i.e., Israelites, and in similar expressions (e.g., Ammonites, Gen. 19:38). It is used also of animals ("young," Lev. 1:14; 22:28), of members of a class or guild ("sons of the prophets," 1 K. 20:35; priests, 1 Ch. 9:30; gatekeepers, Ezr. 2:42), or other groups (soldiers, 2 Ch. 25:13; exiles, Ezr. 4:1; see also Nu. 17:25; 1 S. 14:52; 2 S. 3:34; 2 K. 14:14). *See* SON.

The Heb. *yeleḏ,* from *yālaḏ,* "bear" or "beget," is another general term for offspring, usually sons (Gen. 21; Ex. 1:17f.; 2 S. 12; Jer. 31:20), but also descendants (Isa. 29:23), "children of transgression" (57:4), and animals (Job 38:41; 39:3; Isa. 11:7). It is also used of young men (Gen. 4:23; 1 K. 12:8ff. par.).

A lad or young man is usually called *na'ar,* a word of uncertain origin (Gen. 14:24; 21:12, 17ff.; 44:30ff.; 1 S. 20; 2 K. 4:29ff.; Ps. 148:12). In Ex. 2:6; 1 S. 1:22; 4:21; Isa. 8:4, however, it is used of infants; and cf. Jgs. 13:5ff.

A collective noun for little children is *ṭap,* normally derived from *ṭāpap,* "take quick little steps" (BDB, p. 381). It is not likely related to *ṭōpaḥ,* "handbreadth" (cf. *ṭippuḥîm,* "children fully formed," Lam. 2:20). It occurs regularly in the phrase "men, women, and children" (Dt. 3:6; Jer. 43:6) or "women and children" (Jgs. 21:10; cf. Nu. 14:3; Ezk. 9:6; etc.), especially in classifying populations, distinguishing the fighters from the helpless. It is most often translated "little ones." When children are killed en masse or taken captive, the word most often used is the collective *ṭap* (Gen. 34:29; Dt. 2:34; 3:6; Est. 8:11; Ezk. 9:6). The NEB usually translates "dependants."

Other OT words include *'ôlēl* (or *'ôlāl*), the plural of which is often used like *ṭap* (1 S. 22:19; 2 K. 8:12; Isa. 13:16; Lam. 1:5); *'ûl* and *yānaq,* "suckling infant" (Isa. 49:15; Nu. 11:12; 1 S. 22:19; Ps. 8:2; Lam. 4:4); and *zera',* "seed."

In the LXX, with several exceptions, *bēn* is translated by Gk. *huiós, yeleḏ* by *paidíon, na'ar* by *paidárion* or *paidíon, ṭap* by *paidía* or *aposkeuḗ* ("baggage"), *'ôlēl* by *nḗpios* or *téknos,* and *yānaq* by *thēlázōn.*

The NT uses Gk. *huiós* much as it is used in the LXX, and also *paidíon,* diminutive of *país,* from *paideúō,* "bring up," "educate." Occurring very frequently for "child" is *téknon,* from *tíktō,* "bear," "bring forth" (Mt. 2:18; 3:9; 7:11; 10:21; Jn. 8:39; Acts 2:39; Rom. 8:16f.; Gal. 4:25, 27f.; Eph. 2:3; Col. 3:20; 1 Jn. 3:10; etc.). The context of this word is usually one of relationship with parents. The diminutive *teknίon* is used by John (Jn. 13:33) especially in his First Epistle (1 Jn. 2:1, 12, 28; 3:7, 18; 4:4; 5:21; but *paidía* in 2:13, 18, for stylistic variation).

A word for "infant" is Gk. *bréphos* (Lk. 18:15; Acts 7:19; 1 Pet. 2:2; etc.); in Lk. 1:41, 44 it is used of the unborn John the Baptist. A child viewed as innocent, immature, or not adult is called *nḗpios* (Mt. 11:25 par.; 21:16; 1 Cor. 3:1; 13:11; Gal. 4:1, 3; He. 5:13; etc.); the verb *nēpiázō* means "be like an innocent baby" (1 Cor. 14:20).

The designation *país* can mean "child" (Mt. 2:16; 17:18; 21:15; Acts 20:12), but also "servant" (Mt. 12:18; 14:2; Acts 3:13, 26; 4:27, 30). *See* SERVANT.

See *TDNT,* IV, *s.v.* νήπιος (Bertram); V, *s.v.* παῖς κτλ. (Oepke), and παῖς θεοῦ (Zimmerli, Jeremias).

J. W. D. H.

II. Children in Bible Times.–*A. Importance.* The Hebrews regarded the presence of children in the family as a mark of divine favor and greatly to be desired (Gen. 15:2; 30:1; 1 S. 1:11, 20; Ps. 127:3; Lk. 1:7, 28). The birth of a male child was especially a cause for rejoicing (Ps. 128:3): more men, more defenders for the tribe. If there were no sons born to a household, that family or branch became lost. If the wife proved childless, another wife or wives might be added to the family (Gen. 16f.). Further, each Jewish mother, at least in later times, hoped that her son might prove to be the Messiah. The custom of levirate marriage, which was not limited to the Hebrew people, rested on the principle that if a man died childless his brother should marry his widow, the children of such union being considered as belonging to the brother, whose name and line were thus preserved from extinction (Dt. 25:5; Gen. 38:26; Mt. 22:24).

B. Ceremony. Children were sometimes dedicated to God, even before their birth (1 S. 1:11). Names often were significant: Moses (Ex. 2:10); Samuel (1 S. 1:20); Ichabod (4:21; cf. Gen. 30) (*see* NAMES, PROPER). The firstborn son belonged to God, and had to be "redeemed" by a payment of five shekels (Nu. 3:44-51; cf. 1 Pet. 1:18). *See* FIRSTBORN.

Other stages in the life of the child were celebrated with fitting ceremonies. In Palestine, in the fourth year, on the second day of the Passover occurred the ceremony of the first cutting of the boy's hair, the friends sharing the privilege. Sometimes, as in the case of the wealthy, the weight of the child in currency was given as a donation to the poor. In common with the custom of other eastern peoples, male children were circumcised (Gen. 17:12), the rite being performed on the eighth day.

C. Education. Early education was cared for in the home, the children growing up more or less with the mother (Prov. 6:20; 31:1; 2 Tim. 1:5; 3:14f.), and the girl continuing with her mother until her marriage. In wealthier families tutors were employed (1 Ch. 27:32). Schools for children are first mentioned by Josephus (*Ant.* xv.10.5). Children were taught to read and write even in families of moderate means, these skills being widely diffused as early as 600 B.C., if not earlier (Isa. 8:1; 10:19). Great stress was laid on the Torah, i.e., the law of Moses. Boys were trained also in farming, the tending of cattle, and in the trades. The religious training of the boy began in his fourth year, as soon as he could speak distinctly. The religious life of the girl also began early. In later times at least, children took part in the sabbath and Passover festivals and boys attended synagogue and school regularly.

D. In the Family. Children were subject to the father (Neh. 5:5 marks the extreme), who in turn was bound to protect them though he himself had the power of life and death (Lev. 18:21; 20:2ff.). Respect for and obedience to parents were stoutly upheld by public opinion (Ex. 20:12; Dt. 5:16; cf. Prov. 6:20; Mic. 7:6; Dt. 21:18-21; Ex. 21:15).

Both the OT and NT afford abundant evidence of the the strength of the bond that bound the Hebrew family together (Gen. 21:16; 2 S. 18:33; 1 K. 3:23ff.; 2 K. 4:19; Isa. 8:4; Job 29:5; Mt. 19:13; 20:20; Mk. 9:24; Lk. 2:48; Jn. 4:47; He. 2:13; 11:23). The gift of a son from the Lord was the height of joy; the loss of a child marked the depth of woe. A hint occurs in the custom of naming a man as the father of his firstborn son, or even the use of the father's name as a surname (Bar-jonah, Bartimaeus), and this practice continues in the Middle East at the present day. This idea is further instanced in the use, in both OT and NT, of the terms to express the relation between God and men (Ex. 4:22; Dt. 14:1; 32:6; Jer. 3:4; Zec. 12:10; Mal. 1:6).

W. N. STEARNS

E. Jesus and the Child. A characteristic feature of the ministry of Jesus is the importance that He attaches to the child and to children. When children were brought to be touched by Him and the disciples tried to keep them back, Jesus was indignant, ordered that they be not hindered, said that to such belongs God's kingdom, and took them in His arms and blessed them (Mk. 10:13-16). In reply to the disciples' question about the greatest in the Kingdom, He put a child in the midst and spoke of the need to turn and become like children even to enter the Kingdom, adding that to receive a child in His name is to receive Him, but to cause a child to sin is a terrible offense (Mt. 18:1ff.). Against those who objected to the acclamation of children on the triumphant entry, He referred to Ps. 8:2 (Mt. 21:15f.). On the return of the seventy He thanked the Father that "these things" are hidden from the wise and revealed to babes (Lk. 10:21). According to one rendering Jesus Himself is called God's child in Peter's address in Acts 3:12-26 and in the prayer of the church in 4:24-30 (cf. Gk. *país* and RSV mg. in 3:13; 4:25, 27).

See also RELATIONSHIPS, FAMILY; BOY; DAUGHTER; GIRL; SON; YOUTH. G. W. B.

III. Figurative Usage.–Jesus addressed His disciples as children (Mk. 10:24). Paul referred to Timothy as his child (1 Tim. 1:2), and also to Onesimus (Philem. 10). John also designated the disciples to whom he was writing as his children (2 Jn. 4). The same use of "children" or "sons" is common in the OT (see 1 K. 20:35; 2 K. 2:3, 5, 7; 4:38). As a term of special endearment, disciples are sometimes called "little children" (*teknía*). Jesus thus addressed His disciples when He was speaking about His departure (Jn. 13:33). Paul thus addressed the Galatians (Gal. 4:19), and it was a favorite expression with John (see 1 Jn. 2:1; 4:4; 5:21). A term used similarly is *paidía* (Jn. 21:5; 1 Jn. 2:13, 18). "Children of God" is a common expression in both the OT and NT. It is based on the relation between parents and children, and in general describes God's affection for His own, their dependence upon Him, and moral likeness to Him. The term is sometimes used of those who are disloyal to God, who are designated "rebellious children" (see Isa. 30:1). *See* CHILDREN OF GOD. Those who are like the devil in thought and action are designated as "children of the devil" (1 Jn. 3:10).

"Child" is used also to express one's relation to something to which he belongs, or by which he is dominated in his affection for it. Thus we have (1) the children of a city or country (see Jer. 2:16; Mt. 23:37), meaning those who belong to that particular city or country; (2) children of wisdom (Mt. 11:19, AV; Lk. 7:35), i.e., those whose lives are dominated by wisdom; (3) children of obedience (1 Pet. 1:14), those who are eager to obey; (4) children of light (Eph. 5:8), those whose souls are illumined by the light.

Other expressions include children of cursing, or those who are exposed to cursing (2 Pet. 2:14), and children of wrath, or those who are exposed to wrath (Eph. 2:3). "Children of Abraham" (Jn. 8:39; Acts 13:26; cf. Jas. 2:21) can mean spiritual kinship as well as actual. "Babes in Christ" (1 Cor. 3:1; cf. Eph. 4:14; He. 5:13) are men of little spiritual growth, still living on the carnal level rather than the spiritual. A. W. FORTUNE

CHILD-BEARING; WITH CHILD; GIVE BIRTH; etc. [Heb. *yālaḏ, hārâ,* also *bānâ, m^elē'â* (Eccl. 11:5); Gk. *tíktō, teknogonía, énkyos* (Lk. 2:5), *échō en gastrí*]. *See also* BEAR; CONCEIVE; TRAVAIL.

The interpretation and translation of 1 Tim. 2:15 has proved difficult. The RSV reads, "Yet woman will be saved through bearing children [Gk. *diá tḗs teknogonías*], if she continues in faith and love and holiness, with modesty." The NEB has "she will be saved through motherhood," and provides in the margin two other possible readings: "saved through the Birth of the Child, *or* brought safely through childbirth."

While the first, normally accepted reading may be hardest to accept culturally, it best fits the context, which teaches male dominance and female submissiveness (2:8-15), arguing from the man's prior creation and Eve's having first sinned. Woman must be content with her maternal role in life, Paul says; the extra pain and hardship of child-bearing and child-rearing are necessary for her salvation because of her naturally lower status and because of her responsibility in the fall of man.

Calvin (*in loc.*) defends this understanding of the passage, but with the warning that "Since the apostle is not dealing here with the cause of salvation, his words cannot and should not be used to infer the merit of works. All he is concerned to do is to point out the way by which God leads us to the salvation He has by His grace appointed for us." More modern commentators have found it harder to accept this reading without modification. See, e.g., D. Guthrie (*Tyndale,* 1957), *in loc.*; but also J. N. D. Kelly (*HNTC,* 1963).

See also WOMAN. J. W. D. H.

CHILDHOOD, GOSPELS OF THE. *See* APOCRYPHAL GOSPELS II.

CHILDREN OF GOD; SONS OF GOD [Heb. *b^enê '^elōhîm*; Gk. *tékna theoú, huioí theoú*]. These phrases denote the relation in which men are conceived to stand to God, either as deriving their being from Him and depending upon Him, or as standing in that personal relation of intimate trust and love toward Him which constitutes the psychological fact of sonship. The exact significance of the expressions depends upon the conception of God, and particularly of His Fatherhood, to which they correspond. The concept therefore attains to its full significance only in the NT, and its meaning in the OT differs considerably, even though it marks stages of development up to the NT idea.

I. OT Teaching
  A. Mythological Survivals
  B. Created Sonship
  C. Israel's Collective Covenant Sonship
  D. Individual and Personal Relation
  E. Universalizing the Idea
II. NT Teaching
  A. Disappearance of Physical and Limited Sonship
  B. As Religious Experience, or Psychological Fact
    1. Filial Consciousness of Jesus
    2. Communicated to Men
  C. As Moral Condition, or Ethical Fact
  D. As State of Being, or Ontological Fact
    1. Essence of Christ's Sonship
    2. Men's Sonship
  E. As Relation to God, or Theological Fact
    1. Eternal Generation
    2. Work of Grace

I. OT Teaching.–*A. Mythological Survivals.* The most primitive form of the idea appears in Gen. 6:1-4, where the sons of God (NEB "sons of the gods") by marrying the fair daughters of men become the fathers of the giants. These sons of God were a subordinate order of divine beings or demigods, and the title here may mean no more, although it was probably a survival of an earlier idea of the actual descent of these gods from a higher God. The idea of a heavenly court where the sons of God come to present themselves before the Lord is found quite late (Job. 1:6; 2:1; 38:7; Ps. 29:1; 89:6). In all these cases the phrase implies a certain kinship with God and dependence upon Him on the part of the divine society around Him. But there is no evidence to show whether the idea of descent of gods from God survived to any extent, nor is there any indication of a very close personal relationship. A more reasonable interpretation of the phrases, "sons of God" and "daughters of men," is that they mean "the godly and the ungodly." The mingling of the good and the bad results in an immediate apparent improvement which later becomes a deterioration.

B. Created Sonship. The idea of creation has taken the place of that of procreation in the OT, but without losing the sense of sonship. "Thus says the Lord, the Holy One of Israel, and his Maker: 'Will you question me about my children, or command me concerning the work of my hands?'" (Isa. 45:11). Israel acknowledges the absolute sovereignty of God as her Father and Maker (64:8). Israel's Maker is also her Husband, and by inference the Father of her children (54:5). Since all Israel has one Father, and one God created her, the tribes owe brotherly conduct to one another (Mal. 2:10). The Lord upbraids His sons and daughters whom He as their Father bought, made, and established. "He forsook God who made him, and scoffed at the Rock of his salvation. . . . You were unmindful of the Rock that begot you, and you forgot the God who gave you birth" (Dt. 32:6, 15, 18ff.). These passages reveal the transition from the idea of original creation to that of making and establishing Israel as a nation. All things might be described as children of God if creation alone brought it to pass, but Israel stands in a unique relation to God.

C. Israel's Collective Covenant Sonship. The covenant relation of God with Israel as a nation is the chief form in which man's sonship and God's Fatherhood appear in the OT. "Israel is my firstborn son" (Ex. 4:22); "When Israel was a child, I loved him, and out of Egypt I called my son" (Hos. 11:1). And to be children of God involves the obligation to be a holy people (Dt. 14:1f.). But Israel has proved unworthy of her status: "Sons have I . . . brought up, but they have rebelled against me" (Isa. 1:2, 4; 30:1, 9). Yet He will have pity upon them: "for I am a father to Israel, and Ephraim is my first-born" (Jer. 31:9, 20). Israel's unworthiness does not abolish the relation on God's side; she can therefore return to Him again and submit to His will (Isa. 63:16; 64:8); and His pity exceeds a mother's love (49:15). The filial relation of Israel to God is summed up and symbolized in a special way in the Davidic king: "I will be his father, and he shall be my son" (2 S. 7:14 par. 1 Ch. 17:13; cf. 1 Ch. 22:10; 28:6; Ps. 2:7).

D. Individual and Personal Relation. God's Fatherhood to collective Israel necessarily tends to develop into a *personal relation* of father and son between Him and individual members of the nation. The children of Israel, whatever their number, shall be called "Sons of the living God" (Hos. 1:10). The Lord's marriage relation with Israel as a nation made individual Israelites His children (Hos. 2:19f.; Jer. 3:14, 22; cf. Isa. 50:1; Ezk. 16:20f.; 23:37), and God's ownership of His children, the individual members of the nation, is asserted (cf. Ps. 127:3). Chastisement and pity alike God deals forth as Father to His children (Dt. 1:31; 8:5; Ps. 103:13), and these are intimate personal relations which can obtain only between individuals.

E. Universalizing the Idea. In another direction the idea of God as the Father of Israel tends to be modified by the inclusion of the Gentiles. The word "first-born" (in Ex. 4:22 and Jer. 31:9, 20) may be only an emphatic form of expressing sonship, or it may already suggest the possibility of the adoption of the Gentiles. If that idea is not present in words, it is an easy and legitimate inference from several passages, that Gentiles would be admitted some day into this among the rest of Israel's privileges (Isa. 19:25; 65:1; Zec. 14:16).

II. NT Teaching.–*A. Disappearance of Physical and Limited Sonship.* As the doctrine of divine fatherhood attains its full spiritual and moral significance in the NT, so does the experience and idea of sonship. All traces of physical descent have disappeared. Paul's quotation from a heathen poet, "For we are indeed his offspring" (Acts 17:28), whatever its original significance, is introduced by the apostle for the purpose of enforcing the idea of the spiritual kinship of God and men. The phrase "Son of God" applied to Christ by the Roman centurion (Mt. 27:54; Mk. 15:39) may or may not, in his mind, have involved the idea of physical descent, but its utterance was the effect of an impression of similarity to the gods, produced by the exhibition of power attending His death. The idea of creation is assumed in the NT, but generally it is not prominent in the idea of sonship. The Virgin Birth of Jesus, however, may be understood as implying either the creative activity of the Holy Spirit, or the communication of a preexistent divine being to form a new human personality, but the latter idea also would involve creative activity in the physical realm (cf. Lk. 3:38: "Adam, the son of God"). The limitations of the OT conception of sonship as national and collective disappear altogether in the NT; through Christ men and women of all races and nations may now be the children of God.

B. As Religious Experience, or Psychological Fact. 1. Filial Consciousness of Jesus. Divine sonship was first realized and made manifest in the consciousness of Jesus (Mt. 11:27). For Him it meant unbroken personal knowledge of God and communion with Him, and the sense of His love for Him and of His satisfaction and delight in Him (Mt. 3:17; 17:5; Mk. 1:11; 9:7; Lk. 3:22; 9:35). Whether the "voice from heaven, saying, 'This is my beloved Son, in whom I am well pleased'" was objective or not, its message always dwelt in the filial consciousness of Jesus. The Father's love was to Him a source of knowledge and power (Jn. 5:20), the reward of His self-sacrifice (10:17), and the inspiration of His love for men (15:9).

Sonship meant for Him His messianic mission (Mt. 16:16f.). It involved His dependence on the Father and His obedience to Him (Jn. 5:19, 30; 8:29), and a resulting confidence in His mission (5:36; 10:36f.). It filled Him with a sense of dignity, power, and glory which the Father gave Him, and would yet give in larger measure (Mt. 26:63f.; 16:27; Jn. 17:5).

2. Communicated to Men. Jesus communicated His own experience of God to men (Jn. 14:9) that they also might know the Father's love and dwell in it (17:26). Through Him and through Him alone can they become children of God in fact and in experience (1:12; 14:6; Mt. 11:27). It is therefore a distinctively Christian experience and always involves a relation of faith in Christ and moral harmony with Him. It differs from His experience in one essential fact. It involves an inner change, a change of feeling and motive, of ideal and attitude, that may be described as a new birth (Jn. 3:3). Man must turn and return from disobedience and alienation through repentance to childlike submission (Lk. 15:18-20).

It is not the submission of slaves, but the submission of sons, in which they have liberty and confidence before God, and a heritage from Him for their possession (Gal. 4:6f.; Rom. 8:17). It is the liberty of self-realization. As sons they recognize their kinship with God, and share His mind and purpose, so that His commands become their pleasure: "For this is the love of God, that we keep his commandments. And his commandments are not burdensome" (1 Jn. 5:3). They have boldness and access to God (Eph. 2:18; 3:12). With this free union of love with God there comes a sense of power, of independence of circumstances, of mastery over the world, and of the possession of all things necessary that befit the heirs of God (Mt. 6:26, 32; 7:11). "For whatever is born of God overcomes the world" (1 Jn. 5:4). They learn that the whole course and destiny of creation is for the "revealing of the sons of God" (Rom. 8:19, 21).

C. As Moral Condition, or Ethical Fact. Christ's sonship involved His moral harmony with the Father: "I have kept my Father's commandments and abide in his love" (Jn. 15:10; 8:53). He accomplished the work that the Father gave Him to do (17:4; 5:19), becoming "obedient unto death, even death on a cross" (Phil. 2:8). And sonship makes the same demand upon men. The peacemakers and those who forgive like God are His children (Mt. 5:9, 45; Lk. 6:35). "For all who are led by the Spirit of God are sons of God" (Rom. 8:14). God will be Father to the holy (2 Cor. 6:18). The test and mark of the children of God is that they do righteousness and love the brethren (1 Jn. 3:10). They are blameless and harmless, without blemish, in the midst of a crooked and perverse generation (Phil. 2:15). Therefore their ideal of life is to be "imitators of God" and to walk in love even as Christ did (Eph. 5:1). Sonship grows to its consummation as the life grows in the likeness of Christ, and the final destiny of all sons is to be ever like Him (1 Jn. 3:2).

D. As State of Being, or Ontological Fact. Sonship is properly and primarily a relation, but it may so dominate and transform the whole of a man's life, thought, and conduct as to become his essential being, the most comprehensive category under which all that he is may be summed up.

1. Essence of Christ's Sonship. It is thus that the NT comprehends the person of Christ. Everything that He did, He did as God's son, so that He is *the* Son, always and ever Son. In the beginning, in the bosom of the Father, He is the ONLY BEGOTTEN SON (Jn. 1:1, 18). He is born a Son of God (Lk. 1:35). He begins life in the things of His Father (Lk. 2:49). His whole life is that of the beloved Son (Mt. 3:17; 17:5). As Son of God He dies (Mt. 26:63; Lk. 22:70; Mt. 27:40,43; cf. Jn. 5:18). In His resurrection He was declared to be the Son of God with power (Rom. 1:4); as Jesus the Son of God He is our great high priest in heaven (He. 4:14), and in the glory of His Father He will come to judge in the last day (Mt. 16:27).

2. Men's Sonship. Unlike Him, men's moral sonship is neither eternal nor universal. Are they therefore sons in any sense always and everywhere? All children are heirs of the kingdom of God and objects of the Father's care (Lk. 18:16; Mt. 18:10). But men may turn away from the Father and become unworthy to be called His sons (Lk. 15:13,19). They may become children of the devil (1 Jn. 3:10; Jn. 8:44), and children of wrath (Eph. 2:3). Then they lose the actuality, but not the potentiality, of sonship. They have not the experience or character of sons, but they are still moral and rational beings made in the image of God, open to the appeal and influence of His love, and able to "rise and go to their Father." They are objects of God's love (Jn. 15:13; Rom. 5:8) and of His gracious search and seeking (Lk. 15:4; Jn. 11:52). But they are actual sons only when they are led by the Spirit of God (Rom. 8:14); and even so their sonship will be consummated only in the resurrection (Rom. 8:23; Lk. 20:36).

E. As Relation to God, or Theological Fact. In the relation of father and son, fatherhood is original and creative. That does not necessarily mean priority in time.

1. Eternal Generation. Origen's doctrine of the eternal generation of Christ, by which is meant that God and Christ always stood in the relation of Father and Son to one another, is a just interpretation of the NT idea that the Son "was in the beginning with God" (*prós tón theón*). But Jesus was conscious of His dependence upon the Father and that His sonship was derived from Him (Jn. 5:19,36). Still more manifest is it that men derive their sonship from God. He made them for Himself, and whatever in human nature qualifies men to become sons of God is the free gift of God. But men in their sin and disobedience could not come to a knowledge of the Father, had He not "sent forth his Son . . . that we might receive adoption of sons" (Gal. 4:4f.); "See what love the Father has given us, that we should be called children of God" (1 Jn. 3:1); "God so loved the world that he gave his only Son" who gave "to all . . . who believed in his name . . . power to become children of God" (Jn. 3:16; 1:12). It is not the children of the flesh but the children of the promise who are children of God (Rom. 9:4). The mere act of birth does not constitute men into children of God, but His covenant of free grace must be added. God being essentially Father made men and the universe, sent His Son and His Spirit, "for the revealing of the sons of God." But they can know the Father, and realize their sonship only when they respond to His manifestation of fatherly love, by faith in God and obedience to Him. T. REES

2. Work of Grace. The question whether sonship is natural and universal, or conditional upon grace working through faith, does not admit of a categorical answer. The alternatives are not strict antitheses. God as Father graciously created man in His own image. One might thus say that He created him for sonship. In fallen man, however, there is nothing left that can have the reality or bear the name of son. To use the word son of mere creaturehood is to give it a different sense from that which it has in NT usage. God in His grace has fulfilled His original purpose by sending His own Son so that in Him fallen men and women might be newly created in His image and thus adopted, or rejuvenated, as the children of God. They grow as such as they grow in faith and in the knowledge of the Son of God (Eph. 4:13). But it is in Christ alone, and by faith in Him, that God's purpose is worked out in them and they have their sonship.

See also ADOPTION; SONS OF GOD. G. W. B.

CHILDREN OF ISRAEL [Heb. *bᵉnê yiśrā'ēl*]. A biblical term referring to the Israelites as the descendants of a common ancestor, Jacob, whose name was changed to Israel (see Gen. 32:24-32). It was customary to designate the members of the various tribes as the children of the one from whom the tribe originated (see Nu. 1:20-43; Ezr. 2:3-61), and it was natural that the people who boasted of Israel as their ancestor should be designated as his children. The first reference to the descendants of Jacob is found in the account of the changing of Jacob's name to Israel, and the purpose is to connect them with the experience in Jacob's life which led to the change in his name (Gen. 32:32). In 2 K. 17:34 they are called "the children of Jacob," and this occurs in connection with the account of the changing of Jacob's name to Israel and is intended to connect them closely with their father Jacob, who was favored of God.

After a time, it is quite likely that the term "children of Israel" lost its peculiar significance and was simply one of the popular terms designating the inhabitants of Palestine but at first it was intended to connect these people with their ancestor Jacob whose name was changed to Israel. The Jews of the NT times connected themselves with Abraham rather than with Jacob (see Jn. 8:39; Rom. 9:7; Gal. 3:7, *tékna,* or *huioí Abraham*).

A. W. FORTUNE

CHILDREN OF THE BRIDECHAMBER. *See* BRIDEGROOM, FRIEND OF THE.

CHILDREN OF THE EAST. *See* EAST, PEOPLE OF THE.

CHILEAB kil'ē-ab [Heb. *kil'āḇ*; Gk. *Dalouia*–'restraint of father']. A son of David, born to him at Hebron. His mother was Abigail, whom David married after the death of her husband Nabal, the Carmelite (2 S. 3:3). In the corresponding account (1 Ch. 3:1) he is called "Daniel," the meaning of which name ("God is my judge") points to its having been given in order to commemorate God's judgment upon Nabal (1 S. 25:39; cf. Gen. 30:6). Some suppose that he bore both names, but the LXX reading here *Dalouiá* (1 Ch. 3:1, *Damniḗl*), and the identity of the last three letters of the Hebrew word "Chileab" with the first three of the following word, seems to indicate that the text of Samuel is corrupt.

H. J. WOLF

CHILION kil'ē-on [Heb. *kilyôn*]. One of the two sons of Elimelech and Naomi, "Mahlon and Chilion . . . Ephrathites from Bethlehem in Judah" (Ruth 1:2). With his mother and brother he came into Moab and there both married Moabite women, Orpah being the name of Chilion's wife and Ruth that of the wife of Mahlon (4:9f.). Both brothers died early, and Orpah remained in Moab while Ruth accompanied Naomi back to Bethlehem. When Boaz married Ruth he "bought from the hand of Naomi all that belonged to Elimelech and all that belonged to Chilion and to Mahlon" (4:9).

W. L. WALKER

CHILMAD kil'mad [Heb. *kilmad*; Gk. *Charman*]; NEB ALL MEDIA (*kl mdy*). A city or district mentioned after Sheba and Asshur as supplying merchandise to Tyre (Ezk. 27:23). Working on the mistaken assumption that *m* and *w* are interchangeable in Assyrian/Babylonian, scholars have sometimes identified Chilmad as Kalwada near Baghdad (G. Smith, Delitzsch), but this is improbable. The LXX *Charman* and Vulgate *Chelmad* take it as the name of a country. The Targum substitutes *maḏay*, "Media," which supplies a basis for the emendation behind the NEB rendering. The absence of the conjunction *w-* ("and") has suggested other emendations, e.g., *kᵉlimmāḏ*, resulting in the rendering "Asshur was *as the apprentice* of your trading" (Kimchi, Hitzig, Cornill). Suggesting that *r* has been lost by haplography, Astour emends to *klmd(r) rkltk* and reads Kalmadara, a city of the kingdom of Unqi. Following up this emendation, Astour makes a possible identification of the site with Tell Jindara (Gindaros), with the astute suggestion that a Hurrian element *kulma* ("fertile place"?) has been replaced by Aram. *gin-*, "garden" (*IDB* Supplement). However appealing the suggestion, we must recognize that it results from an emendation, an unsupported site-identification, and a hypothetical change of place name.

W. S. L. S.

CHIMHAM kim'ham [Heb. *kimhām* (2 S. 19:37f.) or *kimhān* (2 S. 19:40) or *kᵉmôhem* (Jer. 41:17 *K*)]; NEB KIMHAM. One of the sons of Barzillai the Gileadite, who supported David while the latter was in exile in Mahanaim (2 S. 19:37). After the death of Absalom, Barzillai was invited to spend the remainder of his life with the king; but he refused, and sent his son Chimham in his stead. From the reference in Jer. 41:17 it has been inferred that Chimham received a grant of land from David's patrimony at Bethlehem, which retained his name for at least four centuries.

H. J. WOLF

CHIMNEY. *See* HOUSE IV. B.

CHINNERETH kin'ə-reth [Heb. *kinnereṯ*] (Nu. 34:11; Dt. 3:17; Josh. 13:27); **CHINNEROTH** kin'ə-roth [*kinᵃrôṯ*] (Josh. 11:2; 12:3; 1 K. 15:20); [cf. *kinnāreṯ* (Josh. 19:35); Gk. *Chenara* (Nu. 34:11), *Machanareth* (Dt. 3:17), *Kenerōth* (Josh. 11:2), *Chenereth* (Josh. 12:3; 13:27; Josh. 19:35, LXX A), *Kenereth* (Josh. 19:35, B), *Chezrath* (1 K. 15:20)]; AV also CINNERETH (1 K. 15:20); NEB KINNERETH.

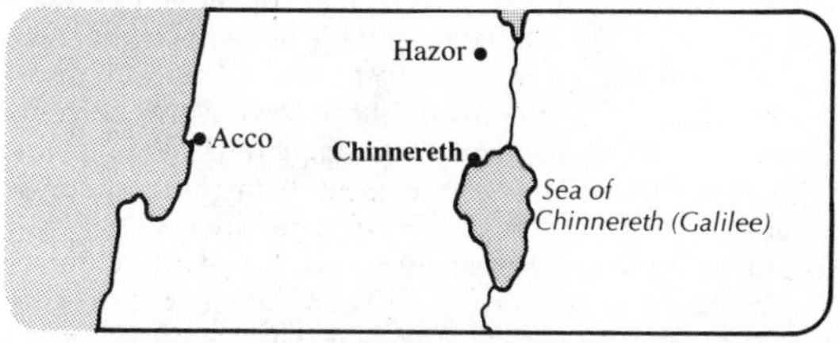

1. A fortified city controlling the fertile plain on the northwest shore of the Sea of Galilee in the territory assigned to Naphtali after the conquest under Joshua (Josh. 19:35). Excavations at modern Tell el-'Oreimeh indicate that the city was occupied when Abraham traveled to Canaan, and was abandoned soon after Ben-hadad's conquest.

2. An early name, Sea of Chinnereth, of the Sea of Galilee, used as a landmark when giving locations in the northern Jordan River (Arabah) region (Nu. 34:11; Josh. 12:3; 13:27).

3. The area included in Ben-hadad's conquest in response to Asa's plea for help against Baasha (1 K. 15:20).

R. J. HUGHES, III

CHIOS kī'os, kē'os [Gk. *Chios*]. An island belonging to Greece in the Aegean Sea, 12 mi. (19 km.) W of Izmir (ancient Smyrna) and 5 mi. (8 km.) from the mainland of Asia Minor. Paul's ship passed it on his last voyage to Jerusalem (Acts 20:15). From Luke's expression, "we came the following day over against Chios," it has been conjectured that they were becalmed; more probably it simply means that, according to the island-hopping practice of the times, they dropped anchor for the night opposite the island; ships normally did not sail at night along the island-cluttered shores of the Aegean.

Chios is shaped like a bow aimed at the Asia Minor coast and stretches 32 mi. (51 km.) North and South and 8-18 mi.

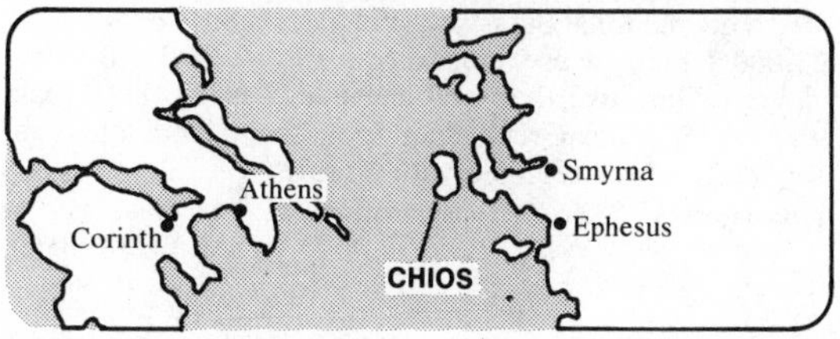

(13-29 km.) East and West. While the north end of the island is mountainous (highest altitude 4255 ft. [1296 m.]) with steep coasts, there are four plains (mostly in the south) with very fertile soil. Even though there is no real watercourse on the island, luxuriant vegetation is made possible by numerous springs. The place was renowned in antiquity for its wine, figs, wheat, and gum mastic. The last was obtained from the lentiscus tree by making incisions in the branches from which a sort of resin would flow and form a gum. This still constitutes an important element of the economy of the place.

Chios was especially noted in antiquity for its claim to be the birthplace of Homer, for its school of epic poets, and its sculptors. To Glaucus of Chios was ascribed the invention of iron-welding early in the 7th cent. B.C. The chief city, located in the southeastern part of the island and bearing the same name as the island, was founded on the finest harbor of the eastern seaboard of the Aegean; eighty ships could anchor in her roadstead. The place where Homer is said to have collected his pupils around him is still pointed out to the traveler at the foot of Mt. Epos, 6 mi. (10 km.) N of the capital. In reality it is a sanctuary of the mother goddess Cybele, with altar and figure of the goddess accompanied by two lions carved in the native rock.

The oldest inhabitants of the island were Leleges, Cretans, and Carians; they were conquered by the Ionians, who made Chios one of the most flourishing states in Ionia. Incorporated in the Persian empire under Cyrus in 546, Chios fought heroically against her overlord during the Ionian revolt forty-six years later. Crushing the revolt, the Persians burned the cities and temples of the island and carried off her most beautiful girls. During the 5th cent. B.C. Chios joined the Delian League (Athenian Alliance) and remained loyal until 413. For her insurrection she suffered terribly at the hands of the Athenians, who ultimately recaptured the entire island. During the 4th cent. Chios joined the Second Athenian Alliance and revolted successfully only a few years before conquest by Alexander the Great. Independent during the early Hellenistic era, she allied with Rome during the 2nd cent. and was virtually depopulated by the sack of 86 B.C., carried out by Mithridates in his temporarily successful contest with Rome.

The Roman general Sulla restored the Chians to their homes and bestowed on them the rights of a free city, which implied local autonomy and in certain respects the privilege of being governed according to native law, while many of their neighboring cities in the province of Asia were governed according to Roman law. Chian efforts to regain prosperity were interrupted by a violent earthquake during the reign of Tiberius. The Roman emperor helped in the rehabilitation, and a reasonable degree of prosperity had been attained by the time Paul sailed by.

Subsequently Chios remained part of the continuing Roman empire, with its capital at Byzantium. In 1307 Turkish pirates subjugated and laid waste the island; the Turks took over the island in 1566. In the war of the Greek revolution, the Chians joined the Greeks (Feb. 1821) but were overpowered by the Turks. The Pasha decreed that the island should be utterly devastated: 23,000 Chians were massacred and 47,000 sold into slavery. Only five thousand escaped. During the Balkan war of 1912 the Greek fleet took the island and subsequently it was reunited with Greece.

Bibliography.–*SPT*; G. Giustiniani, *History of Chios* (1943).

J. E. HARRY
H. F. VOS

CHIRP [Heb. *ṣāpap*] (Isa. 8:19; 10:14); AV PEEP; NEB also SQUEAK. In Isa. 8:19 the term is used as a description of the sounds made by wizards and mediums as they enunciated their oracles.

CHISLEV kis'lev [Heb. *kislēw*; Gk. *Chaseēlou, Chaseleu*]; AV CHISLEU; NEB KISLEV. The ninth month of the Hebrew calendar (Nov.-Dec.).

CHISLON kis'lon [Heb. *kislôn*–'strength'] (Nu. 34:21); NEB KISLON. A prince of Benjamin, and father of Elidad.

CHISLOTH-TABOR kis-loth-tā'bor [Heb. *kislōṯ tāḇōr*–'slopes of Tabor']; NEB KISLOTH-TABOR. *See* CHESULLOTH.

CHITLISH kit'lish [Heb. *kiṯlîš*–'separation'] (Josh. 15:40); AV, NEB, KITHLISH. An unidentified town named with Lahmam and Gederoth in the Shephelah of Judah, possibly Khirbet el-Maghāz, 7.5 km. (5 mi.) SW of Lachish.

CHITTIM. *See* KITTIM.

CHIUN kī'ən (Am. 5:26, AV). *See* KAIWAN.

CHLOE klō'ē [Gk. *Chloē*–'tender shoot']. A woman, presumably a Christian, mentioned only in 1 Cor. 1:11. She was a resident either of Corinth or of Ephesus. Paul had been informed by some of her household (RSV and NEB "Chloe's people"), probably Christian slaves, of the dissensions in the church at Corinth. Nothing more is known of her.

CHOBA kō'bə [Gk. *Chōba, Chōbai*]; AV also CHOBAI kō'bī (Jth. 15). A place named along with Jericho, Aesora, the valley of Salem, and Damascus in Jth. 4:4; 15:4. The Exact location is unknown but it may be identical with el-Mekhubbi about 11 mi. (18 km.) from Beth-shan and about 3 mi. (5 km.) from Thebez, on the important trade road leading from Beth-shan to Samaria. Some authorities have suggested that it might be the same as Hobah in Gen. 14:15.

J. F. PREWITT

CHOICE. *See* CHOOSE.

CHOKE [Gk. *pnígō, apopnígō, sympnígō*]. The AV has "choked" in Lk. 8:33 where the other versions have "drowned." The same word, *apopnígō*, is used here and in 8:7; Mt. 13:7, where thorns choke off the sower's young sprouts. Technically, drowning is a form of asphyxiation; but "choked" is unnecessarily literal in Lk. 8:33.

CHOLA (Jth. 15:4, NEB). *See* KOLA.

CHOOSE; CHOSEN [Heb. *bāḥar, qāḇal, bārā', bārâ*; Gk. *eklégō, hairéō*].

I. In the OT.–The Heb. *bāḥar* and its derivatives are used of men choosing wives (Gen. 6:2); Lot choosing the cities of the valley (Gen. 13:11); often of kings and generals choosing soldiers for their prowess (e.g., Ex. 17:9; Josh. 8:3; 1 S. 13:2; 2 S. 10:9; 17:1). The word *bāḥûr* is often used for "young men," as being choice, in the prime of manhood (e.g., Dt. 32:25; Isa. 62:5). The most important uses of *bāḥar* are these: of Israel choosing a king (1 S. 8:18; 12:13); of moral and religious choice: choosing the Lord as God (Josh. 24:15, 22), or other gods (Jgs. 5:8; 10:14); the way of truth (Ps. 119:30); to refuse the evil and choose the good (Isa. 7:15f.); cf.

David's choice of evils (2 S. 24:12). A leading idea is that of God choosing Moses as leader (Nu. 16:5, 7; 17:5), the Levites to the priesthood (1 S. 2:28; 2 Ch. 29:11), Saul as king (1 S. 10:24), David (2 S. 6:21; 1 K. 11:34), Solomon (1 Ch. 28:5). All this follows from the theocratic idea that God rules personally over Israel as His chosen people. A more important, but still subsidiary, idea is that of the Lord choosing Jerusalem as the place of His habitation and worship (Dt. 12:5, and twenty other times; Josh. 9:27; 1 K. 8:44, 48; Ps. 132:13; Zec. 1:17; 2:12; 3:2). This was the ruling idea of Josiah's reformation, which was instrumental in putting down polytheistic ideas and idolatrous practices in Israel, and was therefore an important factor in the development of Hebrew monotheism; but it was an idea that Hebrew monotheism had to transcend and reject to attain its full growth. "The hour is coming when neither on this mountain nor in Jerusalem will you worship the Father" (Jn. 4:21).

But the fundamental idea of choosing, which governs all others in the OT, is that of God choosing Israel to be His peculiar people. He chose Abraham, and made a covenant with him, to give him the land of Canaan (cf. Neh. 9:7ff.): "For you are a people holy to the Lord your God; the Lord your God has chosen you to be a people for his own possession, out of all the peoples that are on the face of the earth . . . because the Lord loves you, and is keeping the oath which he swore to your fathers" (Dt. 7:6-8). Historically this idea originated in the old conception of Yahweh as the tribal God of Israel, bound to them by natural and indissoluble ties (*see* God II.C). But as their conception of Yahweh became more moral, and the idea of His righteousness predominated, it was recognized that there was no natural and necessary relation and harmony between Israel and the Lord that accounted for the favor of a righteous God toward her, for Israel was no better than her neighbors (Am. 1f.). Why then was Yahweh Israel's God, and Israel His people? It was by an act of free choice and sovereign grace on God's part. "You only have I known of all the families of the earth" (Am. 3:2).

In Hosea the relation is described under the figure of a marriage tie. Yahweh is Israel's husband; and to realize the force of the figure, it is necessary to recall what ancient and oriental marriage customs were. Choice and favor were almost entirely made by the husband. The idea of the covenant which the Lord out of His free grace made with Israel comes to the forefront in Deuteronomy and Jeremiah. Because He loved her, and for no other reason, He chose Israel to be His peculiar people.

In Isa. 40–66 the idea is carried farther in two directions: (1) The Lord's gracious choice of Israel rests ultimately on His absolute sovereignty: "O Jacob my servant, Israel, whom I have chosen! Thus says the Lord who made you, who formed you from the womb" (44:1f.; cf. Isa. 29:16; Jer. 18:6; Isa. 64:8). For Israel's deliverance Cyrus and his world empire are in the Lord's hands as clay in the potter's hands (Isa. 45:9f.). (2) "Israel is elect for the sake of mankind." This is the moral interpretation of a choice that otherwise appears arbitrary and irrational. God's purpose and call of salvation are unto all mankind. "Turn to me and be saved, all the ends of the earth! For I am God, and there is no other" (Isa. 45:22). And Israel is His servant, chosen, the messenger He sends to "bring forth justice to the nations" (42:1, 19; 43:10, 12). The idea is further developed in the conception of the Servant of the Lord as the faithful few (or one) formed "from the womb to be his servant, to bring Jacob back to him," "as a light to the nations," God's salvation for the "end of the earth" (49:1-6; 52:13–53:12) (cf. Isaiah's doctrine of the Remnant: Shear-jashub; also, the righteous, the godly, the meek, in Psalms; and see Skinner, comm. on Isaiah [*CBSC*, 1915-17], II, xxxff.). As the conception of personality and of individual relation and responsibility to God developed from Ezekiel, together with the resulting doctrine of personal immortality, the conditions were prepared for the application of the idea of election to individuals (cf. Ps. 65:4).

Along with the idea of God choosing Israel runs the complementary idea that Israel should prove faithful to the covenant, and worthy of the choice. God has chosen her, not for any merit in her, but of His free grace, and according to His purpose of salvation; but if Israel fails to respond by faithful conduct, fitting her to be His servant and messenger, He may and will cast her off, or such portion of her as proves unworthy. See Oehler, *OT Theology* (Eng. tr. 1883), I, 256ff., 287f.

Three other Hebrew words expressing choice in minor matters are: *qāḇal,* for David's choice of evils (1 Ch. 21:11); *bārā',* to mark out a place (Ezk. 21:19), to select singers and porters for the temple (1 Ch. 9:22; 16:41); *bārâ,* to choose a man to represent Israel against Goliath (1 S. 17:8).

II. In the NT.–The whole conception of God, of His relation to Israel, and of His action in history indicated above, constituted the religious heritage of Jesus Christ and His disciples. The national consciousness had to a considerable extent given place to that of the individual; and salvation extended beyond the present life into a state of blessedness in a future world. But the central ideas remain, and are only modified in the NT in so far as Jesus Christ becomes the Mediator and Agent of God's sovereign grace. Gk. *eklégō* and its derivatives are the words that generally express the idea in the NT. They are used (1) of the general idea of selecting one out of many (Lk. 14:7); (2) of choosing men for a particular purpose, e.g., of the church choosing the Seven (Acts 6:5); of the choice of delegates from the Council of Jerusalem (Acts 15:22, 25; cf. 2 Cor. 8:19), *cheirotonéō*; choose by vote (cf. Acts 10:41), *procheirotonéō*; (3) of moral choice (Mk. 13:20): "Mary has chosen the good portion" (Lk. 10:42); (4) of Christ as the chosen Messiah of God (Lk. 23:35; 1 Pet. 2:4); (5) of Christ choosing His apostles (Lk. 6:13; Jn. 6:70; 13:18; 15:16, 19; Acts 1:2, 24); Paul (Acts 9:15; cf. 22:14, AV), *procheirízomai*; Rufus (Rom. 16:13); and Paul choosing Silas (Acts 15:40), *epilégō*; (6) of God choosing Israel (Acts 13:17; cf. Rom. 9:11), choosing the Christian Church as the new Israel (1 Pet. 2:9, AV), choosing the members of the Church from among the poor (Jas. 2:5), the foolish, weak, and despised (1 Cor. 1:27f.), choosing into His favor and salvation a few out of many: "Many are called, but few are chosen" (Mt. 20:16, AV; 22:14); God shortens the days of the destruction of Jerusalem "for the sake of the elect, whom he chose" (Mk. 13:20).

In Eph. 1:4-6 every phrase tells a different phase of the conception: (1) God chose (and foreordained) the saints in Christ before the foundation of the world; (2) according to the purpose of His will; (3) to be adopted as His sons through Jesus Christ; (4) to be holy and blameless before Him in love; (5) to the praise of His glorious grace; (6) which He freely bestowed on them in the Beloved. And in Rev. 17:14, the triumphant Church in heaven is described as "called and chosen and faithful." God's sovereign choice governs the experience and testing of the saints at every point from beginning to end.

Thus in the NT as in the OT (1) God's covenant of

grace is free and unconditional. It is for all men, now as individuals rather than nations, and without distinction of race or class. It is no less free and sovereign, because it is a father's grace. (2) Israel is still a chosen race for a special purpose. (3) The Church and the saints that constitute it are chosen to the full experience and privileges of sonship. (4) God's purpose of grace is fully revealed and realized through Jesus Christ.

This doctrine raises certain theological and metaphysical difficulties that have never yet been satisfactorily solved. (1) How can God be free if all His acts are preordained from eternity? This is an antinomy which indeed lies at the root of all personality. It is of the essence of the idea of personality that a person should freely determine himself and yet act in conformity with his own character. Every person in practice and experience solves this antinomy continually, though he may have no intellectual category that can coordinate these two apparently contradictory principles in all personality. (2) How can God be just, if a few are chosen and many are left? And (3) How can man be free if his moral character proceeds out of God's sovereign grace? It is certain that if God chose all or left all He would be neither just nor gracious, nor would man have any vestige of freedom. The doctrine describes accurately the moral fact that some accept salvation and others reject it, and the religious fact that God's sovereign and unconditional love is the beginning and cause of salvation. The meeting-point of the action of grace, and of man's liberty as a moral and responsible being, it does not define. Nor has the category as yet been discovered wherewith to construe and coordinate these two facts of religious experience together, although it is a fact known in every Christian experience that where God is most sovereign, man is most free.

See also ELECTION. T. REES

CHOP [Heb. *pāraś*]. This word, meaning to "cut in pieces," "distribute," often translated "spread," is rendered "chop" in Mic. 3:3: they "chop them up like meat," indicating the destruction of God's people through the cruel exactions of their rulers.

CHORASHAN kôr-ash'ən. *See* BOR-ASHAN.

CHORAZIN kō-rā'zin [Gk. *Chorazin*]. A city N of the Sea of Galilee, which along with Bethsaida and Capernaum was reproached by Jesus for failing to repent in spite of the many mighty works done there (Mt. 11:20-24; Lk. 10:13-15). This is the only NT reference to the city. It is not mentioned in the OT or in Josephus; however, it may be the place mentioned in the Babylonian Talmud (*Menahoth* 85a) as famous for its wheat.

Eusebius, in the 4th cent., said it was 2 Roman mi. from Capernaum; and the ruins at Kerâzeh, about 2.5 mi. (4 km.) N of the modern Tell Ḥûm, are generally accepted as the site. A less likely suggestion is Khersa on the east shore of the lake.

Extensive ruins at Khirbet Kerâzeh indicate a city of some importance. Traces can be seen of a Roman road connecting Chorazin with the great caravan route leading past the lake on its way to Damascus. As a city (Gk. *pólis*; cf. Mt. 11:20f.) it would have a synagogue, and the remains of an early synagogue constructed of black volcanic rock have been found. Of special interest is the *cathedra Mosis,* a carved seat with an Aramaic inscription (cf. Mt. 23:2) uncovered at Kerâzeh. Apparently there was once a tradition that the antichrist would come from Chorazin, and the severe words spoken to the city by Jesus may be related to this tradition (E. Nestle, *Expos.T.,* 15 [1904], 524). R. H. MOUNCE

Ruins of the fourth-century A.D. synagogue at Chorazin. The ornamentation is similar to that of the synagogue at nearby Tell Ḥûm (Capernaum). (Consulate General of Israel in New York)

CHORBE kôr'bē [Gk. *Chorbe*]; AV CORBE. The head of a family which returned with Zerubbabel (1 Esd. 5:12). The name apparently corresponds to Zaccai in Ezr. 2:9 and Neh. 7:14.

CHOSAMAEUS kos-ə-mē'əs [Gk. A *Simōn Chosamaios,* B *Chosamaos*]; NEB CHOSOMAEUS. The name occurs in 1 Esd. 9:32 as one of the sons of Annas. But in the parallel passage (Ezr. 10:31) the name is simply "Simeon," followed by "Benjamin, Malluch, Shemariah," which are omitted in 1 Esdras. The LXX of Ezr. 10:31 has *Semeōn,* followed by the three omitted names. The difference may have arisen from a mistake of a copyist, or from the use of an imperfect MS.

CHOSEN. *See* CHOOSE.

CHOZEBA kō-zē'bə. *See* ACHZIB **1.**

CHRIST AS KING, PRIEST, PROPHET. *See* CHRIST, OFFICES OF.

CHRIST, EXALTATION OF. *See* EXALTATION OF CHRIST.

CHRIST, HUMANITY OF. *See* PERSON OF CHRIST.

CHRIST, INTERCESSION OF. *See* INTERCESSION OF CHRIST.

CHRIST JESUS. *See* JESUS CHRIST.

CHRIST, OFFICES OF.

I. Introduction
II. Prophet
III. Priest
IV. King

I. Introduction.–The work of Christ in the history of the world has many sides or facets. As the personal Word of God He created, sustains, and governs the universe (Jn. 1:1ff.). Thus He manifests God in His sovereign work both by His origination of all things and by His rule over them. He is, at the same time, the Redeemer of creation from the curse and disaster of sin which have come upon it through the disobedience of man. Thus His activity extends to every part of human history and activity.

At the same time one must always beware of the danger of dividing the work of Christ into separate compartments. His work as Creator and His sustentation and rule over creation are closely bound together, for if He were Creator only, and did not also maintain His providential activity, the continued existence of creation would depend upon some other agency, which would mean that He did not possess creation and so could not rule over it. At the same time, one must take care not to separate creation and providence from redemption, for His overcoming of sin could be truly redemptive only because, as Creator and Ruler over creation, He graciously saved man from his antagonism to, and rebellion against, the One who in truth was and is creation's Lord. No one of lesser authority and power could have achieved such a victory over sin.

Although Christians have very often centered the exposition of Christ's redemptive work on His death and resurrection, these two unique events form but the core and the climax of the plan and work of salvation. In order that man might understand, a long time of preparation preceded these events, and a period of explanation and interpretation came after them. Moreover, both before and after His historical redemptive acts, it was He who brought men to faith in Himself, whether as the One who would come in the future or as the One who had accomplished redemption in the past. Throughout history He has in this way made effective His redemptive work in His elect people. To understand what this has meant and what He has accomplished, one needs to see His work as a whole and in a systematic manner. Out of this need has come the formulation theologians have called Christ's threefold office of prophet, priest, and king.

The man who originally set forth this interpretation of Christ's work was Eusebius bishop of Caesarea (d. 340). In so doing, however, he did not invent a handy formula for giving a scientific statement of Christ's work, but actually derived it from the Scriptures (cf. Dt. 18:15; Ps. 110:4; Zec. 6:13). His formulation has thus been generally accepted as genuinely biblical, and as truly setting forth Christ's redemptive work.

II. Prophet.–The biblical teaching concerning the office of a prophet is that the prophet is the mouthpiece of God speaking to man (Dt. 18:18; Jer. 1:9; Gal. 1:11f.; 1 Cor. 15:1-4). The prophet thus reveals to man the word of God, which may be a statement and explanation of that which was past, is present, or will come in the future (Dt. 34:10f.; Jgs. 2:1-5; 3:9-11; Jer. 15:1). Prediction, therefore, while usually a part of the prophetic message, did not constitute its sum total, but was made only as God spoke to men of the ultimate redemption He had prepared for them. The revelation of God's saving purpose was the primary responsibility of the prophet (Jn. 5:39; 1 Pet. 1:11). This office Christ fulfilled as the source of, and the greatest of, all the prophets.

In the opening statements of the Fourth Gospel, the writer makes the claim that Jesus Christ is the Word of God. This would seem to mean that as the second person of the triune Godhead He performs the function of revealing God. Christ revealed God first of all as Creator, and still does as Sustainer and Ruler over the universe (Jn. 1:3; Col. 1:15f.). The works of His hands manifest the divine power and Godhead to all men so that none may avoid or escape from the fact that a God of power and glory rules over all things (Ps. 19:1-6; Rom. 1:20f.). This general revelation of God, given to all men, came to man as soon as he appeared upon this earth; and it still speaks to him, so that he may never escape from the responsibility of worshiping and serving the sovereign God.

From the beginning, however, God set before man even more clearly his obligations to his Creator, by revealing directly to man through the Word that he is to act as God's vicegerent upon earth, using that which the earth produces for his own welfare, ruling over and subduing it. At the same time, he must constantly acknowledge that God is ultimately the Lord who provides all things, even the very life of man (Gen. 1:28; 2:16ff.). In his state of innocence man lived in true fellowship with God through His Word by whom God spoke to him. This would seem to be the meaning of Gen. 2:8, which refers to "the voice of God" walking in the Garden.

Despite such close communion between creature and Creator, however, man desired to set himself up as independent of God, and by so doing he declared that he possessed the power of interpreting and understanding the universe by his own wisdom (Gen. 3:1-7; Rom. 1:19ff.). Refusing to recognize God's revelation either in nature or by word, he lost even the knowledge he originally possessed. At the same time, because of his utterly false interpretation and view of everything, he also lost his fellowship with God, so that instead of enjoying God's favor he came under God's rejection and condemnation (Gen. 3:16ff.; Rom. 1:26ff.).

One aspect of God's judgment on man was that God gave him up to the delusion of his own mind so that he could no longer comprehend the meaning of God's self-revelation. Claiming to have attained wisdom, in reality he became ignorant (Rom. 1:22ff.). For this reason, if God would have further communication with man He must speak to him more directly and more clearly than before. To this end, therefore, He chose one people through whom He spoke to man, the descendants of Shem, Abraham, Isaac, and Jacob, to whom He came by way of covenant (Gen. 17; 28; 35). To this people, Israel, God gave His oracles that they might transmit them to the world, in order that men as a whole might know of the way of forgiveness which God had provided for them (Ex. 4:22; Jer. 31:9; Hos. 11:1; Rom. 9:4).

God's methods of revelation to Israel were essentially three in number: theophany, prophecy, and miracle. In theophany God appeared to man as man or as angel (Gen. 18; Ex. 3:2; 13:21f.; 14:24; Josh. 5:14), and in all these various appearances the preincarnate Son of God was the one who made His presence known (Jn. 8:56). He also performed the miracles that took place at the hands of the OT prophets, priests, and kings (Jn. 6:32). But most important of all the preincarnate Son of God spoke through the prophets as they both explained the meaning of these divine manifestations and pointed forward to that divine redemptive plan that would surely come to pass (1 Pet. 1:10f.). In this way Christ fulfilled His office of prophet in the OT dispensation.

In speaking the word of God, the prophets pointed forward to the One who would be the prophet of God par excellence. Moses in particular set forth that one would come who would more fully reveal the will of God (Dt. 18:15-19). As the woman at the well of Sychar stated, He would "tell us all things" (Jn. 4:25). Such prophetic proclamation would form part of the work of the Messiah, who would come to redeem the people of God from their bondage under sin (Isa. 61:1; Lk. 4:21; Jn. 4:25). Thus throughout the OT one finds in various places promises that God would send One who would reveal Him more fully and more completely than ever before.

This anticipation found its fulfillment in the incarnation of the Son of God, the Word of God in the flesh, Immanuel: "God with us" (Mt. 1:23; Jn. 1:2ff.). For this reason one may say that God now spoke directly to man even as He had spoken to Moses of old (Nu. 12:8). As one studies Christ's discourses one finds that He did not follow the example of other rabbis of the day, who continually looked for their authority either to the OT prophets or to the rabbis of earlier times. Instead He spoke with autonomous authority, for He spoke as the Prophet, as the very Word of God Himself (Mt. 7:29; Mk. 1:22). Moreover, He took upon Himself the right to correct earlier erroneous interpretations of the law and to reject rabbinical additions (Mt. 5:21ff.; Mk. 7:4f.). By these means He displayed His claim to be the prophet foretold by Moses, who spoke with the authority of God Himself (Jn. 3:34; 6:45ff.; Jn. 7:16ff.). In this way He fulfilled the messianic office of prophet.

The content of Christ's revelation also differed from that of the OT prophets. They had pointed forward to one who would come to establish the kingdom of God, but Christ came as the Redeemer-King who would fulfil their prophecies by establishing His rule (Mk. 1:15; Mt. 4:12ff.; Jn. 3:35; 18:36f.; Eph. 1:20ff.). Consequently He spoke not in terms of anticipation, but in terms of accomplishment. Moreover, as the Son of God He spoke concerning God in more intimate and accurate terms than could the OT prophets (Jn. 8:14ff.; 10:29ff.; 14:7ff.). Even through His human person He revealed God to men; and by His setting forth of the being and nature of God, Christ also revealed more clearly and more directly the nature and destiny of man and the world. The OT prophets had done this proleptically in the terms of their own environments, but Christ set forth these matters more universally and more fully than ever before (cf. Mt. 5–7; 25; Jn. 6; 8; 10; 14–17). And this in turn involved a definitive explanation of His own messianic work as the Priest and the King who would suffer on behalf of His people but who would rise triumphant over death, bringing redemption to His own (Jn. 6:35ff.; Mt. 16:13ff.; Mt. 26:26ff.; 1 Cor. 11:23ff.). Thus His teaching fulfilled, extended, and clarified that of the OT prophetic order. It formed the culmination of their order and the transition to that of the apostles.

His methods of revelation were various, although they followed generally the pattern already established in the OT. His very presence provided a theophany through which God made Himself visible to man. Furthermore, He taught men by means of His miraculous works (Jn. 3:2; 10:37ff.). In these He demonstrated the sovereignty of God over all creation and the divine ability to heal and save from death those who had fallen victims to its power (11:2-43). Both His incarnation and His miracles He also interpreted by word of mouth, in didactic utterances such as one finds in the Sermon on the Mount and other discourses, particularly as recorded in the Gospel of John. In these He employed various methods of teaching. He uttered simple statements of fact, or proverbial sayings as in the Beatitudes. On the other hand, He told parabolic stories that indirectly indicated what He wished men to understand. Finally, He specifically reinterpreted the OT law, showing how the traditional Jewish teachers had failed to understand its true meaning. By these various means He revealed to men the will of God for their salvation.

Christ's ascension did not bring His prophetic activity to a close. He continued to speak to His people through the prophets and the apostles. Paul says on a number of occasions that the Church rests on the foundation of these two orders (Eph. 2:20; 3:11; 4:5). In the book of Acts prophets such as Agabus appear from time to time (21:11), but Christ revealed to the Church the meaning of His work as the incarnate Redeemer even more fully through the apostles, especially Paul (Gal. 1–2). Moreover, by His Spirit He brought into existence the canon of the NT, and by the same Spirit today He enables His people to understand what He would say to them in the word which He has spoken as the Prophet and which comes to them in the Scriptures of the OT and NT (1 Cor. 2; 2 Tim. 3:16f.).

III. Priest.–The office of priest differs from that of prophet in that instead of representing God to man, the priest represents man to God. His purpose is to restore men to fellowship with God who is justly angered at man for his rebellion and his rejection of the truth. This the priest does by the sacrifice of a substitute for man whereby he makes atonement, and by intercession on man's behalf. A careful examination of the Mosaic law makes the work of the priest very clear (Ex. 29; Lev. 1–7; 16:1-34). As the one who made atonement for Israel the priest stood between the sinner and God, symbolically bringing the two together in reconciliation.

As the Word of God speaking to the prophets, Christ taught men that since the fall man could approach God only by way of vicarious, sacrificial atonement signified by the offering of animals, birds, or other produce, the immolation of which pointed to a life given in the place of man's (Gen. 4:22ff.; 8:20, 22; Rev. 13:8). This symbolism dominates the thought of the OT, for sanctification and acceptance by God could come only by cleansing through such substitution (He. 9:22). Thus Christ established symbolic sacrifice among the OT people of God as a type of what He would accomplish in the fulness of time (Gal. 4:4; He. 9).

Sacrifice, however, could not be performed by everyone, since man could not save himself. Consequently, in the organization of the Israelites as a nation on their deliverance from Egypt, at the very center of the whole religio-political structure God placed the tribe of Levi, which held the position of a priesthood for the whole people. Up to this time the head of the family had always acted as the priest. From Sinai on, the Levitical priesthood, consecrated to the service of God, had the responsibility of standing between God and man (Nu. 1:47-53; 3:21-27; Ex. 28:1). In this way they symbolically foreshadowed the coming of One who would effectively fulfil all their functions as the great High Priest (He. 8–10).

In His incarnation Christ fulfilled totally the work of the priest; but as the writer of Hebrews points out (ch. 10), He did so by the offering not of an animal but of Himself as the atoning sacrifice. By both His active and His passive obedience, in all His perfection, as the God-man He bore the penalty of sin for His people. In this way He fulfilled the Covenant of Grace on behalf of man, providing a way of entry for man into the presence of God. And by virtue of this sacrifice He makes continual intercession for His people that they may, despite all their sins and transgressions, ever have free access to the throne of the Majesty on high (He. 7:24.).

That this is the point of view of the Synoptic Gospels is abundantly clear right from the beginning. The announcements made to Joseph (Mt. 1:20f.) and to Mary (Lk. 1:31) prior to Christ's birth set forth the view that He would save His people from their sins. Although this aspect of His work does not receive much prominence in the early parts of the Gospels, even these sections have little meaning unless His priestly work is constantly kept in mind. From the time of Peter's confession at Caesarea Philippi and the Transfiguration, however, Christ spoke very plainly to the disciples of His coming death (Mt. 16:21ff.; Mk. 8:31ff.; Lk. 9:22ff.). Although the dis-

Statue of youthful Christ as the Good Shepherd, by a third-century Christian artist. The shepherd as a symbol of royalty is attested throughout the ancient world. (Lateran Museum, Rome) (*Biblical Archeologist*)

ciples did not grasp the meaning of His statements, the whole tone of the Gospels thereafter is permeated with this thought. The culmination of Christ's teaching concerning this matter came with the institution of the Lord's Supper. At this time Christ taught explicitly the purpose of His coming into the world, namely, to redeem His people by His own death. Every aspect of the symbolism pointed to His fulfillment of the typology of the OT (Mt. 26:26ff.; Mk. 14:22ff.; Lk. 22:19ff.). After His resurrection His teaching was the same, although at this time He could speak even more plainly, since He had now accomplished His work of redemption (cf. Lk. 24).

It is apparent from the book of Acts that the core of the NT Church's witness consisted primarily in the proclamation of Christ's priestly, redemptive work. Peter's sermon on Pentecost (Acts 2:14ff.) and his defense before the Sanhedrin (4:8ff.) after the healing of the lame man provide good examples. The apostle Paul, however, set this matter forth even more explicitly and systematically, if that is possible. Apart from his various sermons and speeches in Acts one finds the doctrine stated in Rom. 4–6; 1 Cor. 15; Gal. 3–4; Col. 1–2; and various other places. In so doing he receives direct support from the apostles Peter (1 Pet. 1:18ff.), while the same doctrine lies at the base of all the other apostolic writings.

Perhaps the most explicit exposition of Christ's priestly work appears in He. 8–10. There the writer presents a detailed explanation of Christ's work as the fulfillment of the whole of the OT sacrificial system. Christ the eternal High Priest has offered up Himself as a sacrifice, that men might receive forgiveness and pardon for their sins.

The latest of the NT writings, those of the apostle John, indicate that under the teaching of the Spirit the Church had by the end of the apostolic age come to see with great clarity the nature of Christ's priestly work. This theme underlies his Gospel, but appears most clearly in chs. 6; 8; 10; 14–16. 1 Jn. 1–2 sets forth the same doctrine more didactically, while Revelation states it in pictorial terms (chs. 5; 12; 14; 19; 21; 22).

That the Church came to an understanding of this only gradually is evident from the information furnished by the book of Acts. Chapters 11 and 15 indicate that many of the early Christians did not understand that the Lord had fulfilled, and therefore abolished, the ceremonial law of the OT. Peter first and then Paul found it necessary to devote considerable attention to this matter in order that the Church might have a proper appreciation of Christ's priestly work.

Yet one must also remember that Christ's priestly work did not end with His resurrection. He has once and for all time met the requirements of the law of God, paying the penalty for the sins of His people (Rom. 8:1; Gal. 3:27ff.; Col. 1:20f.; 2:14f.; He. 9:24ff.). Therefore, by His very presence before God the Father He always intercedes on His people's behalf (He. 7:25). As one reads His great high-priestly prayer in Jn. 17, one can perhaps understand a little more clearly what this means. Since Christians have an advocate before the throne of grace, they have no further need of human priests, intercessors, or sacrifices, for Christ continuously performs the work of a priest on their behalf (1 Jn. 2:1ff.).

One must never, however, separate His priestly office from His other two offices. Men come to know of His priestly work and what He has accomplished by it because He as a prophet sets forth the will of God for their salvation. Moreover, men come to faith in Christ only as He by virtue of His kingly office sovereignly brings them to faith and obedience. His priestly office is central to His redemptive work, but man would neither know nor believe were it not for the other two offices that he fulfils.

IV. King.–The work of a king consists primarily in ruling over a kingdom. His first responsibility is to maintain peace within his kingdom's borders by governing his own subjects effectively and justly. With regard to those outside his kingdom he has the responsibility of protecting his subjects from attack, and if such attack should take place he must be prepared to oppose the enemy and subdue him so that he will cease troubling the kingdom. Although in most countries today these functions come under the control of some other authority, whether democratic or dictatorial, in biblical times the king held the supreme political government of a nation, so that Christ is frequently referred to and described as a king, since He is an absolute sovereign.

Christ's kingship arises out of His sovereignty over the whole of creation by virtue of His creative and providential activities. He is Lord of the worlds because He made them and sustains them from moment to moment, and His rule involves not merely inanimate beings, but even man (Mt. 10:29; Job 33:44; 38–41; Ps. 33:6; Isa. 45). Christ from the beginning made plain as prophet that He was the ultimate authority over man, when He forbade him to eat of the Tree of the Knowledge of Good and Evil (Gen. 2:16f.). Only by reason of His lordship over man could He have laid down such a precept. Yet man rejected this order and in so doing denied the divine sovereignty, setting up in its stead his own or another creature's sovereignty which he obeyed. Sin thus crystallized itself in the denial of God's sovereignty, which meant the rejection of Christ as Lord and King (Gen. 3:1ff.; Rom. 1:25).

The only way God could in both justice and grace bring man back to his proper relationship to Him was the establishment of a truly redemptive kingdom, over which He would rule as king with man His willing subject. Such a kingdom, of necessity because of man's rebellion, would center in the fact of salvation by divine grace alone. Thus, immediately after the fall the redemptive principle was introduced into history on the divine initiative (Gen. 3:14ff.), and following this throughout Genesis the gradual establishment of the kingdom took place in the families of Seth, Noah, Abraham, Isaac, and Jacob. After the Exodus it came to full expression in the giving of the law at Sinai. There Israel appeared clearly for the first time as a redemptive kingdom centered upon the tabernacle, with the service and worship of God as the core of its very existence (cf. Ex. 20).

In this kingdom the preincarnate Christ ruled as king, for from the earliest days it existed by virtue of a covenant that God made with His chosen people, and Christ as the mediator of the covenant ruled over and governed them. In this way Christ ruled over all of Israel's life. The Mosaic law included matters relating not only to religious ordinances, but to every aspect of individual and national activity. Thus, Israel should have continued as God's covenant people under His direct rule; but they refused. When they had lived for many years in Palestine under judges, they desired a human king, forgetting that most of their difficulties since their entry into the land had resulted from their own disobedience to God. Despite the sinfulness of their desire, God acquiesced in their demand and they obtained a human ruler (1 S. 8). Yet although this represented a rejection of Yahweh's royal claim, He still ruled over the nation both in the choosing of their king and in His continuing to punish or prosper them as they obeyed His law and walked in faith toward Him (cf. Isa. 45; Hos. 1–2; Hag. 2).

The human kingship by no means met Israel's needs. Although some kings such as David, Hezekiah, Joash, and others sought to serve God and to lead the people in this service, many went their own way without regard to the covenantal character of the kingdom. The outcome of this was that the very reason for which Israel demanded a king, a desire for unity and visible leadership, ultimately led to the destruction of both her unity and nationality. Under Rehoboam, Solomon's son, the kingdom divided (1 K. 12:10), the northern ten tribes setting themselves up under the kingship of Jeroboam, who endeavored to turn them away from the worship of Yahweh at Jerusalem (vv. 25ff.). Although the two southern tribes, who remained loyal to the house of David, also continued for a time faithful to the covenant, they too eventually lapsed from the faith. In both cases unfaithfulness to Yahweh led to conquest by pagan nations; and although restoration later took place, the kingdom never was reestablished and Israel eventually fell under the domination of Rome.

Throughout the history of the two kingdoms Yahweh continually sent prophets to Israel and Judah to rebuke the people for their sins and at the same time to point forward to the reestablishment of the kingdom, this time on a spiritual and universal basis under a descendant of David possessed of divine power and authority (Isa. 9:6ff.; 11; 40:9ff.; 60; Jer. 23:5ff.; 31:22ff.; Hos. 3; Zec. 14:4ff.; Mic. 5:2). Against this background one must place the activity of John the Baptist, who came preaching the kingdom of God. The central fact he set forth was that Yahweh had come to establish His kingdom (Mt. 3:11f.), and this theme the angel declared in the annunciation to Mary (Lk. 1:31f.), as did also Christ Himself when He commenced His ministry (Mk. 1:15f.). During Christ's early ministry this continued to form the core of His preaching, but the disciples He gathered around Himself thought in terms of a political kingdom. Even when He pointed out to them that as priest He must die for men's sins, they did not believe (Mt. 16:21ff.), and eventually they attempted to make Him king (21:4ff.). After His resurrection they still thought in the same terms (Acts 1:6f.). They recognized Him as the covenant God of the OT who they believed would now reestablish literally David's kingdom. He explained, however, that His kingdom was not of this world (Jn. 18:35ff.; Acts 1:6ff.).

After the Lord's ascension the disciples gradually came to understand the spiritual nature of Christ's kingship. Through His Spirit, Christ led the apostolic Church to perceive it by bringing the Gentiles into the Church. James at the Council of Jerusalem set forth this new understanding of the Kingdom explicitly (Acts 15:13ff.), and the apostolic writers followed his example. The apostle Paul in various places speaks of Christ's exaltation and kingship over all things for the Church (Eph. 1:20ff.; Phil. 2:9ff.; Col. 2:13; 1 Tim. 6:15) as a result of His having fulfilled His work as the Redeemer, the great High Priest. The greatest statement comes, however, in Revelation, where Christ is pictured as "Lord of lords and King of kings" (Rev. 17:14; 19:11f.). By the end of the apostolic age the true nature of Christ's kingship had been fully stated by the Church.

In some ways the Church and the Kingdom are coextensive and in other ways they differ. The Church consists of those who have received and accepted the covenant promises, its primary work being that of proclaiming the gospel to men. The Kingdom, on the other hand, embraces the whole sphere of obedience to Christ's rule, including the Church. Men enter His kingdom by faith and live in it by obeying Him in every aspect of life. Such would seem to be the point of many of Christ's parables concerning the Kingdom. Yet men who live in His Kingdom do so, not because physically conquered, but by the inward compulsion of their faith, which they have received through the Holy Spirit as Christ's royal gift (1 Cor. 12:3; Eph. 2:5ff.). The consequence is that when

Christians seek to serve their King in all things, in the providence of God they also influence those around them who do not believe, so that the mediatorial kingship of Christ exercises its influence upon even those who are not Christians. Thus Christ's universal sovereignty as Creator and upholder of all things unites with His mediatorial kingship. He is truly "head over all things for the church" (Eph. 1:22).

The final demonstration of the ultimate unity of Christ's kingship both over creation and over His redeemed people will come when He returns in glory as judge of the earth (Mt. 25; Jn. 5:28f.; 1 Thess. 4:16; 2 Thess. 1:6ff.). He will at that time manifest His kingship, not only over His Church, but over all men and creation. Those in rebellion against Him He will cast into utter darkness, while those whom He has redeemed He will usher into the fulness of His kingdom, which will include a regenerated heaven and earth (Mt. 25; Rom. 8:18ff.; 2 Pet. 3:10ff.; Rev. 21). At that time Christ's mediatorial kingship shall cease, for the triune God shall be all in all (1 Cor. 15:24ff.).

See also KING, CHRIST AS.

Bibliography.–Calvin *Inst.* ii.15.1-6; C. Hodge, *Systematic Theology* (1893), II, chs. 5f., 10; Barth, *CD,* IV/1-3. W. S. REID

CHRIST, PERSON OF. *See* PERSON OF CHRIST.

CHRIST, TEMPTATION OF. *See* TEMPTATION OF CHRIST.

CHRISTIAN [Gk. *Christianós*].

I. Origin of the Term.–The word "Christian" occurs only three times in the NT (Acts 11:26; 26:28; 1 Pet. 4:16). The first passage, Acts 11:26, gives the origin of the term: "In Antioch the disciples were for the first time called Christians." The older generation of critical scholars disputed the historicity of this statement. It was argued that, had the term originated so early, it must have been found far more frequently in the records of early Christianity; sometimes also that the termination *-ianos* points to a Latin origin. But there is general agreement now that these objections are groundless. The historicity of the Lukan account was upheld not only by Harnack, but by the more radical Knopf in J. Weiss, ed., *Die Schriften des NT* (1906-1907). In early imperial times, the adjectival termination *-ianos* was widely diffused throughout the whole empire. Originally applied to the slaves belonging to the great households, it had passed into regular use to denote the adherents of an individual or a party. A Christian is thus simply an adherent of Christ. The name belongs, as Ramsay stated, to the popular slang, as indeed sect and party names generally do. It is only after a considerable interval, and very often under protest, that such names are accepted as self-designations.

The name, then, did not originate with the Christians themselves. Nor would the Jews have applied it to the followers of Jesus, whose claim to be the Christ they opposed so passionately. They spoke of the Christians as "the sect of the Nazarenes" (Acts 24:5); perhaps also as "Galileans," a term which the emperor Julian later attempted vainly to revive. The word must have been coined by the unconverted population of Antioch, as the Church emerged from the synagogue and a Christianity predominantly gentile took its place among the religions of the world.

II. Christian Attitude to the Name.–Perhaps the earliest occurrence of "Christian" as a self-designation is in Didache 12:4. In the Apologists and Ignatius, on the other hand, the word is in regular use. 1 Peter simply takes it over from the anti-Christian judicial procedure of the law courts, without in any way implying that the Christians used it among themselves. There is every probability, however, that the very element of danger that thus began at an early date to attach to the name was what commended it to the Christians themselves as a title of honor. Deissmann (Deiss.*LAE*) suggests that Christian means "slave of Christ," as Caesarian means "slave of Caesar." But the word can scarcely have had that fulness of meaning until the Christians themselves had come to be proud of it.

According to tradition, Luke himself was from Antioch. (Cf. Codex Bezae of Acts 11:27f., "when we had assembled.") If the historian was not only an Antiochene, but a member of the original gentile Christian Church, we have the explanation alike of his interest in the origin of the name Christian and of the detailed precision of his information.

III. Was "Christian" the Original Form?–In all three NT passages the uncorrected Codex Sinaiticus reads *Chrēstianoi*. We know from many sources that this variant was widely current in the 2nd century. Blass in his edition of Acts not only consistently reads "Chrestian," but conjectures that "Chrestian" is the correct reading in Tacitus (*Ann.* xv.44), the earliest extrabiblical testimony to the word. The Tacitus MS has since been published in facsimile. This has shown, according to A. von Harnack (*Mission and Expansion of Christianity in the First Three Centuries,* I [repr. 1962], 413f.), that "Chrestian" actually was the original reading, though the name "Christ" is correctly given. Harnack accordingly thought the Latin historian intended to correct the popular appellation of *ca.* A.D. 64, in the light of his own more accurate knowledge. "The common people used to call them 'Chrestians,' but the real name of their founder was Christ." Be this as it may, a confusion between "Christos" and the familiar Greek slave name "Chrestos" is more intelligible at an early date than later, when Christianity was better known. There must have been a strong tendency to conform the earlier witnesses to the later, familiar, and etymologically correct usage. It is all the more remarkable, therefore, that א retains "Chrestian." On the whole it seems probable that this designation, though bestowed in error, was the original one.

IV. Other Christian Self-Designations.–The Christians originally called themselves "disciples," a term afterward restricted to personal hearers of the Lord, and regarded as a title of high distinction. The ordinary self-designations of the apostolic age are "believers" (Acts 5:14; 1 Tim. 4:12), "saints" (Acts 9:13, 32, 41; Rom. 1:7), "brethren" (Acts 6:3; 10:23; etc.), "the elect" (Col. 3:12; 2 Tim. 2:10), "the church of the Lord [mg. God]" (Acts 20:28), "servants (slaves) to God" (Rom. 6:22; 1 Pet. 2:16). The apostolic authors refer to themselves as "servants (slaves) of Christ Jesus" (Phil. 1:1). Other expressions are occasionally met with, of which perhaps the most significant is: those "that call upon the name of the Lord" (Acts 9:14; Rom. 10:12f.; 1 Cor. 1:2). Cf. Pliny's report to Trajan (*Ep.* x.97): "They affirmed that . . . they had been wont to assemble and address a hymn to Christ as to a god."

Bibliography.–H. J. Cadbury, *BC,* V, 383-86; E. Haenchen, *Acts of the Apostles* (Eng. tr. 1971), pp. 367f. n. 3, 689.

J. DICKIE

CHRISTIANITY [Ignatius, Gk. *Christianismós*].

I. In Principle and Essence
  A. Early Use of the Term
  B. NT Implications
  C. Revelation
  D. Reconciliation

E. Resurrection
F. The Estimate of Unbelief
G. The Response of Faith
H. Christianity Is Christ
II. In History and Theology
A. Christianity and Religion
B. Uniqueness
C. Universality
D. Expansion
1. Early Church
2. Succeeding Period
3. Modern Missions
E. Theological Development
1. Early Period
2. Medieval Period
3. Modern Period

I. In Principle and Essence.–A. *Early Use of the Term.* Unlike "Christian," which occurs three times in the NT, the term "Christianity" is not used in the Bible. In its Greek form it is parallel to "Judaism" (the Jews' religion; cf. Gal. 1:13f.; 2 Macc. 2:21). It seems to have been used first by Christians themselves. Our earliest authority is Ignatius of Antioch, who says that the glory of the Christian is "to live according to Christianism" (Magn. 10). For Christians it is a title of honor. (Cf. also Ign. Rom. 3; Philad. 6.)

B. NT Implications. While the word is not used in the NT, it obviously arises from the biblical account of the person, life, and work of Jesus as the Christ. Christianity rests on the fact that Jesus is, and claims to be, the promised Messiah. Those who accept this fact and this claim are followers or adherents of Christ (Christians), and it is natural that their faith should be called Christianism or Christianity. Implied in Christianity as the fulfillment of the OT is the supreme revelation of God in Jesus Christ, the accomplishment of divine reconciliation through His life and work, and the confirmation of His messiahship and Sonship by His resurrection the third day from the dead. Along these lines the apostles have left some of the simplest and yet the most profound definitions of Christianity, e.g., in Jn. 3:16; Rom. 6; 2 Cor. 5:18ff.; He. 1:1ff.

C. Revelation. The completion of God's revelation in Jesus is bound up with His being the Word of God (Jn. 1:1). As Christ, in whom OT prophecy is fulfilled, He is not only a chosen and anointed man; He is also the Lord from heaven, very Man and very God. Whereas the prophets spoke of God and spoke in His name, He is God Himself speaking directly in word and act. To see Him is to see the Father (Jn. 14:9). His glory is as the glory of the only-begotten of the Father, full of grace and truth (1:14).

To suppose that He was a good and gifted man who simply advanced religious truth by His insights is to miss the whole nature of the divine self-revelation in Him. To argue that His disciples or their successors conferred on Him a title of divine dignity, misunderstanding His true mission, is to miss the very center of Christianity. Indeed, there is no evidence for such a reconstruction. Nor is there any evidence for the theory that Jesus was struggling for a self-awareness which finally culminated in the claim to be not only the Messiah, but in a unique sense the Son of the heavenly Father. In teaching and works, in attitude and conduct, Jesus both is and claims to be the one in whom God Himself is directly present, the incarnate Word. There is no possibility of genuinely following Jesus without confessing Him as the supreme revelation of God in this sense, for His teaching would involve concealment rather than revelation if its central reality and claim were rejected as untrue. Conversely, there is no true knowledge of God apart from knowledge of Him in whom God has given an express revelation of Himself (He. 1:1ff.). This is a necessary implication of Christianity, not as an upward stage in human religion, but as the crown of the divine self-revelation.

D. Reconciliation. The supreme revelation of the Word in fulfillment of the OT necessarily carries with it the accomplishment of reconciliation between God and man. For man's ignorance of God is part of his total estrangement, and the need for revelation is part of the need for reconciliation. Hence the Christ is the reconciler as well as the revealer. If He comes to teach, He also comes to act; if He shows God in His own person, He shows God at work. Nor is His work only an example or demonstration. If His work is also revelation, as His word is reconciliation, it is revelation because it does something. He works for others; in love He enters human life, bearing its griefs, carrying its sorrows, bringing it renewal. By His life, death, and resurrection, the sin of man is propitiated, the penalty executed, the guilt removed. He carries the old life of man to its end on the cross, and inaugurates the new life in His rising from the grave. Again, there can be no doubt that this is Jesus' own understanding of His task according to the solid testimony of the NT and in fulfillment of the prophetic testimony of the OT. More recent biblical study has shown that there can be no separating of a religious and ethical Jesus from the soteriological Christ. The baptism in the Jordan, the acceptance of the servant mission, the prophetic intimation of death and rising again, the orientation to the cross, the giving of the bread and wine at the Last Supper, the taking of the cup in Gethsemane — all point to the reconciling ministry of Jesus as His own strange but proper work. True Christianity demands commitment to this fact.

E. Resurrection. The Resurrection belongs to the reconciliation and to the revelation, as the fulfillment of both. It fulfils reconciliation as the introduction of the new and eternal life of righteousness that replaces the old, sinful, condemned life put to death for us in the crucifixion of Jesus Christ. Already in the risen Lord, the firstfruits of the coming harvest, the new life, is secured. By the life-giving work of the Holy Spirit we enter into it in faith, work it out in love, and look to its consummation in hope. Yet revelation also is fulfilled in the Resurrection. Here Jesus is declared to be the Son of God with power (Rom. 1:4). Put to death in weakness, He is manifested in glory, so that even in His incarnation and crucifixion God is self-evidently revealed to have been present and active. Indeed, by the operation of the Holy Spirit the risen Lord now continues His ministry of revelation, opening the blinded eyes of sinners to see Him as the Son of God come down for us men and our salvation, and thus bringing reconciliation itself to its subjective fulfillment. What might appear ludicrous in itself, namely, that God is revealed in Jesus of Nazareth and has reconciled us to Himself in Him, is luminous in the light of the Resurrection. To dismiss the Resurrection is to overthrow Christianity, for it is also to deny revelation and to negate reconciliation. A gospel without the Resurrection is no gospel. Christianity has nothing distinctive to offer if Christ is not risen and there is no new life in Him; it has nothing to claim if Christ is a dead teacher. It may have difficulty in giving absolute historical proof to those who are unwilling to believe; but it need not be ashamed of the facts of the empty tomb and the resurrection appearances. Its only shame would be to present its message apart from strong and convincing testimony to the supreme fact in which both revelation and reconciliation are fulfilled, to deny its own true nature by not believing that Jesus Christ, the revealer and the reconciler, is also the resurrected, and therefore by not proclaiming Him as such and not trusting Him to make Himself known.

F. The Estimate of Unbelief. In face of Christianity, in face of the revelation and reconciliation of God in Him, and in face of His resurrection from the dead, a radical decision has obviously to be made. On the one hand it is possible to resist the Christian message, to dismiss it as untrue or to reinterpret it along more acceptable lines, regarding Jesus as other than the gospel proclaims Him to be. This may be the vote of sheer unbelief or the vote of indifference. It may reflect a qualified recognition which sees in Jesus only the teacher, the example, the genius of religion. In each case, however, it is presumed that the self-witness of Jesus, the apostolic testimony to Him, the record of this testimony, and the historic confession of the Church are all mistaken. Sometimes an attempt is made to produce objective data in support of this assumption. Often recourse is had to hostile hypercriticism of the Christian data, as though the raising of this or that difficulty of detail were sufficient to invalidate the whole testimony. Yet in fact this attitude does not rest on superior data, or on the convincing demolition of the Christian witness, but on general assumptions which the Christian sympathetically sees to be the assumptions of sinful man alienated from God (cf. Rom. 1:21; Eph. 4:17f.). The decision is not just academic or historical. This is why it cannot be reversed simply by academic or historical argument. It is a theological decision, and it must be reversed by the divine self-revelation itself proclaimed in the power of the Spirit.

G. The Response of Faith. The response of faith that this evokes is very different from the decision of unbelief. It means accepting Jesus as the Christ, finding the revelation of God in Him, entering into the reconciliation with God that He has effected, knowing Him in His resurrection from the dead. This is, of course, the sum and substance of Christianity. It implies committal to what Jesus is and does. This committal is true decision, resting on rational and historical data, and demanding the highest level of emotional and volitional involvement. Nevertheless, it is more than decision. For this decision is one that man cannot make of himself (Jn. 6:65; 10:27; 12:32; Mt. 16:17). Of himself, sinful man will see in Jesus at best a prophet and at worst an impostor or a mythical figure. Faith is the response evoked by the self-witness of Jesus through the Holy Spirit. It is not the product of argumentation, nor is it the creation of religious inwardness. It is not a pretense that things are other than they seem, or an aesthetic adorning of ordinary facts with imaginative significance. Faith is the gift of the Holy Spirit through the biblical testimony. It deals with realities, but realities that are finally theological, because they involve the action of God Himself in the human story. Behind faith stands the operation of the risen Lord Himself giving true perceptions to the senses, true logic to the reason, true wisdom to the understanding, true direction and depth to the emotions, true freedom to the will. This response of faith is the one thing needed to be a Christian, and in turn it then makes it reasonable and natural to be a Christian.

H. Christianity Is Christ. From what has been said, it will be seen that Christianity takes its substance as well as its name from Jesus Christ. It is not a construct of human philosophy, though it points to true wisdom. It is not a system of theological dogmas, though dogmatic truths are involved. It is not just an inward and subjective experience, though it entails a personal relationship with God. It is no mere code of ethics, though it carries with it a way of life. In fact, it is not to be understood or explained in any anthropological terms except insofar as Jesus Himself is true man. It is supremely christological: Christ is the beginning, center, and end. Christianity is Christ, for to proclaim it is to proclaim Him. He is the revelation; He is the reconciliation; He is the Resurrection. To be sure, the whole trinity is involved, Father, Son, and Holy Spirit. But there is no competition between the Son on the one side and the Father and the Holy Spirit on the other; for to say Christ is to say God. Thus, seeing that the purpose of God is worked out in Christ, one can rightly say that Christianity is Christ. Christianity also involves us: the revelation is to us; the reconciliation is for us; the Resurrection implies our own. But the light that comes is still His light; His is the death and His the Resurrection. The Holy Spirit bears witness, not to us, but to Him, and to us only as we are in Him. Christ is the great theme of Scripture and of Christian proclamation. In Him we see God; in Him we are quickened by the Spirit; knowing Him, we know God. In other words, we have no independent status. By Him we are justified and with Him we are heirs of new and eternal life.

II. In History and Theology.–*A. Christianity and Religion.* Intrinsic to all modern scholarship is the empirical and historical method. Applied to Christianity, this has entailed the study of comparative religion. Christianity has been investigated from the outside as a phenomenon of human life, and it has been classified as one of the great world religions. As such it has been compared and contrasted with other religions, and evaluated accordingly. It has been given a place on the evolutionary ladder of religion, and given a status psychologically as an expression of religion itself, of the religious impulse as part of the constitution of man. There is, of course, a measure of justification for this approach. The great principle of the word and work of God declared in Christianity is that of incarnation. God invades the human sphere. He acts historically. He Himself, in the person of the Word, is made flesh and dwells among us. This means that God's work, and the results of God's work, are phenomena that are open to investigation as such. If Jesus Christ is very man, then Christianity is a religion. If the teaching and work of Jesus have a place among the historical achievements of the race, Christianity may be studied from the human standpoint. In fact, Christianity has been a dominant factor in the shaping of human history, more particularly in the West. In addition to the religious legacy it has bequeathed, it has also contributed to the intellectual, artistic, economic, political, and social life of humanity. Its story has been inextricably interwoven into the general story of man. To try to argue to the contrary would be a futile Docetism.

Nevertheless, it should be noted that the historical or comparative study of Christianity, if abstracted from an awareness of its other aspect, can lead to very unsatisfactory developments. Lessing initiated a whole line of theorizing by postulating a distinction between the religion of Christ and the Christian religion (*Works*, X, 242ff.). His assumption was that doctrinal Christianity has distorted the simple teaching and practice of Jesus. The task of the historian is to disentangle the one from the other, and to show how the false development could take place. Perhaps the main outworking of Lessing's postulate is to be found within the framework of the Hegelian triad, namely, in the assumption that Christianity as we know it is the resolution of a conflict, the synthesis of a thesis and antithesis, with Jesus or Peter on the one side and Paul or the postapostolic Church on the other. Increasingly in the 19th cent. attempts were then made to isolate the original message. Harnack's *What Is Christianity?* is perhaps the final and most characteristic effort of this kind. Distinguishing between the kernel and the husk, it sums up the essence of the Christian message in terms of divine Fatherhood, human brotherhood, the kingdom of God, and the infinite worth of the human soul.

The empirical approach could also lend itself to hazardous apologetical developments. Herder in the late 18th cent. argued that Christianity is itself not merely a religion among others, but *the* religion in the sense of the quintessence of religion. This point was taken up with a new intensity and thrust in Schleiermacher's *Reden* and *Glaubenslehre*. The justification of religion is that it expresses a valid psychological aspect of man, the feeling of absolute dependence. The justification of Christianity as compared with other religions, which also have relative validity, is that it expresses this human element in the purest and truest form. Religion is an inalienable part of life. Its presence is its vindication. From the standpoint of empirical study, however, it is properly to be classified in the psychological rather than the historical sphere. It can best be defended not by arguing its historical validity or ethical superiority, but by relating it to the given factors of the emotional or psychical life. If this gives relative validity to all religions, it gives highest validity to that religion which corresponds most fully and adequately to the religious element in man.

It is obvious that this apologetic involves the relativization of Christianity, the adoption of a comparative approach that denies its uniqueness, and the opening up of the counterclaim of other faiths that they really express religion just as well or even better. Attention is necessarily drawn to the similarities between Christianity and the religions. The Bible is compared with other sacred books, Jesus Christ with other religious leaders, the gospel stories with legends, and the Virgin Birth with parallels elsewhere. Christianity is, in fact, explained solely from within the human context. This does not necessarily lead to its rejection. Its grandeur may be fully recognized. But the criterion of its superiority is religious man, not self-revealing God. Hence its superiority is relative. To put it christologically, Docetism is avoided only at the expense of a far-reaching Ebionitism.

B. Uniqueness. The point is that, while Christianity is a religion and can be studied as such, it is much more. Only on the surface can it be brought exclusively under ordinary religious categories. In its true essence it can neither be regarded as a purely historical phenomenon, nor be explained in purely psychological terms. As Christ Himself is true God as well as true man, so Christianity is God's action as well as one of many historical and religious developments. A truly objective study of Jesus Christ demands that He be expounded not in abstraction from His deity, but as He is, i.e., in His divine humanity. Similarly, a truly objective study of Christianity demands that it be expounded not in abstraction from its "divine" aspect, but as it is, i.e., as attestation to, and the product of, the divine humanity of Christ. At this point the empirical approach is involved in a dilemma to which it is not equal. If it accepts the deity of Christ and the consequent uniqueness of Christianity, it denies its own fundamental principle, namely, that phenomena are to be studied solely in terms of their creaturely context. On the other hand, if it refuses to accept the deity of Christ and the consequent uniqueness of Christianity, it is false to the very basis of objectivity, namely, that things are to be studied as they are, not as we presume them to be. This is why a genuinely objective study of Christianity is possible only on the basis of faith.

The uniqueness of Christianity is true uniqueness — it is not relative superiority. It is not the uniqueness of one man or movement in distinction from others, nor the uniqueness of a higher order of genius or merit. It is the uniqueness of the work of the one God in and upon the human story. Again, it is not just the uniqueness of a higher instance of God's providential superintendence of all human events, nor of the common grace of God which might be discerned in all human achievements. It is the uniqueness of a special action, a special intervention, of the one God. God Himself is uniquely at work in Christ and in Christians. He is at work here as He is not at work elsewhere. This work takes a form which entails integration in the common story and which thus carries with it the possibility of assessment at the common level. In its true nature, however, it is without parallel. This means that Christianity, for all the similarities, cannot be classified with the other religions. Its reality is not to be known by comparative study. Apologetic based on its correspondence to the inner essence of religion is falsely based.

Indeed, one might go so far as to say that to make Christianity a religion (in abstraction) is an act of heresy or even unbelief (cf. Barth, *CD,* I/2). It requires no faith to say that Jesus is a great religious teacher but ignore His deity. It involves no faith to see in Him the personification of human religious aspiration rather than the incarnation of the Word. Hence, to construe Christianity as a development in human religion is to miss the very thing that is intrinsic to it, and is thus a serious error even though the resultant estimate be favorable. Insofar as it takes human shape Christianity may indeed be viewed as a religion. Insofar as it is also a historical phenomenon, it may be assessed historically. But Christianity, as it truly is, transcends all such study or assessment. It is genuinely unique.

C. Universality. The universality and absoluteness of Christianity are closely linked to this uniqueness. From the very first the gospel was designed for the nations. The promise to Abraham was that in him and his seed all nations should be blessed (Gen. 22:18). The servant was to be "a light to the Gentiles, my salvation to the ends of the earth" (Isa. 49:6). Christ Himself stated plainly that He had come as light into the world (Jn. 12:46; cf. 1:4ff.), and He commissioned His disciples to teach all nations (Mt. 28:19). The gospel is universal not because it best fulfils the religious aspirations of man, nor because its manifest superiority commends it as preferable to all other religions. Its universality is based on its uniqueness. The gospel is God's word to man. It is God's word to all men. Directed to all, it is to be addressed to all and it may be received by all. The human need that it meets is that alienation from God which man does not even know of himself, and which he certainly cannot remedy. The message it brings is not simply the best that man can do toward solving the riddles of creation and destiny. It is God's revealing, reconciling, and regenerating word, which solves all such riddles from God's side. It is the only revealing, reconciling, and regenerating word, and it is addressed and comes to all men equally, irrespective of their nature, history, or background, with revealing, reconciling, and regenerative force.

The universality of the gospel implies its absoluteness. The gospel is addressed to all men, because all men need it. They can have no comparable message of their own. This absoluteness is total. "All who came before me are thieves and robbers," says Jesus (Jn. 10:8). "There is no other name under heaven given among men," says Peter (Acts 4:12). "He who has the Son has life; he who has not the Son of God has not life" (1 Jn. 5:12; cf. Jn. 3:36). If this were the claim of a purely human religion it would be intolerable pretension. Some religions and philosophies advance this kind of claim; they are guilty of the kind of fanaticism and arrogance of which some Christians have also been guilty when they have forgotten that the absoluteness is only that of God and not of the human manifestations of the faith. Christianity can be so exclusive and yet remain a gospel of humility and of loving outreach only because the exclusiveness is that of God's word, not man's. It is the exclusiveness of facts, not of opinions. There is no arrogance in asserting with a certain absoluteness that two and two make four, because the fact itself is absolute. Similarly, God's word is the one truth in comparison with which all human thinking to the contrary is erroneous. This truth of God does not mean, of course, that there may not be truths or partial truths in human systems of religion or philosophy. It does not mean that one human system is alone true and that all others are false. It means that all human attempts to know God and to be in fellowship with Him are without exception fragmentary and incomplete, and that God Himself has given His one word which is addressed with equal love to all and which is to be received with equal humility by all. That God has chosen some, and constantly chooses others, to be the instruments of proclamation of this word confers on them no superiority of their own. They are to proclaim it as the absolute word, for this is what it is. But they are to do so in love, not in superiority. They are to do so with humility, realizing that of themselves they could no more attain to the truth than others. They are to do so with anxious concern, aware that their very presentation may easily be fallible and faulty. They are to do so with generosity, genuinely desiring that others may share the light they have, the power that makes all things new. They are to do so with reverence and dignity, conscious always that the absoluteness is not that of a supreme human achievement, but of God Himself in His gracious and reconciling self-revelation.

D. Expansion. Because of its universality and absoluteness, Christianity has been committed from the very first to evangelistic and missionary expansion. The history of the Church is in the last analysis the history of expansion. To be sure, the Church has been involved in many other things as well. It has not always pursued its chief and proper task. It has even undertaken expansion with the wrong motives, e.g., that of ecclesiastical imperialism. It has had its own vigorous history as a human institution or group of institutions, as a potent factor in the general story of the race. It can be studied from different angles, in terms of its political affiliations, its social effects, its music, art, literature, or liturgy. But its true history is the history of its fulfillment of the task for which it has been left in the world. And if it has had failures, if it has never discharged its task as it should, and has gone through periods of lethargy and retreat, by the grace of God it has also had its astonishing measure of success.

1. Early Church. Already in the apostolic age the gospel spread throughout the Roman empire. Apart from the witness of the NT, Tacitus and Pliny the Younger speak of the considerable numbers of Christians (Tacitus *Ann.* xv.44; Pliny *Ep,* x.96). This expansion continued throughout the patristic period. Tertullian in his *Apologeticum* (37.4-8) could taunt pagans that "all that we have left to you is the temples." If he exaggerated, he did so on the surge of an evangelistic movement which only increased in the later 3rd cent. (cf. Harnack, *Expansion of Christianity* [Eng. tr. 1904-1905], II, 455). Nor was the spread confined to the shores of the Mediterranean. Britain on the outer edge of the empire received the gospel. There was a movement through Egypt and Ethiopia. Eastward an early expansion to India is recorded, and Nestorianism in particular pioneered the way through Iran to China. An offshoot of Arianism was the preaching of Christianity to the Goths, though this was to have some unfortunate repercussions during the barbarian invasions that so quickly followed. *See* Map XXIII.

2. Succeeding Period. The collapse of the Roman empire in the West and the rise of Islam in the East put a stop to the more vigorous outgoing of the faith and even led to some contraction and loss in areas already covered. The new task facing the Church was that of reevangelization in territories that came under barbarian occupation; and so well was this work carried out under Celtic and Roman leadership that not only was there renewed expansion in northern Italy, Gaul, and Britain, but Christianity spread in a new way to Germany, Central Europe, and Scandinavia as well. Less success was enjoyed in North Africa and Syria, and the Byzantine Church failed to maintain itself in Asia Minor against increasing Moslem pressure; but the spread of Christianity to Russia was a notable achievement. By the Middle Ages, when Western Europe had finally been brought under Christian influence, horizons were beginning to widen again, and little companies of friars were attempting, with some success, to penetrate with the gospel to North Africa and Asia. But not until the world was opened up by the great oceanic explorations of the Renaissance period did global missionary expansion begin again on any scale.

3. Modern Missions. The Roman Catholic powers were the first to open up Africa, America, and Asia; and it is not surprising that the first wave of missionary advance should also be Roman Catholic. The Franciscans, Dominicans, and Jesuits in particular took up with enthusiasm the task of spreading the Christian message, and already at the end of the 16th cent. work had been started in Central and South America, along the coasts of Africa, at settlements in India, and in Southeast and Far Asia. Protestant churches were comparatively lethargic, partly due to lack of opportunity and partly to domestic preoccupation; and even when Holland and England challenged Spain, Portugal, and France as maritime and mercantile powers there was no immediate surge of missionary enthusiasm. But eventually, under strong Pietist influence, the great period of Protestant missions began during the 18th cent.; and today there is hardly a state or territory in the world without some larger or smaller Christian community.

Statistics are of little value, of course, in assessing either the range of the gospel or the response to it, for it is finally the Holy Spirit who adds to the Church (Acts 2:47). But statistically Christianity has in fact become the largest and most widespread of all religious groups. Many of those counted as Christians, however, are only the most nominal of adherents. Even when all are counted, the total is still small in comparison with the rapidly increasing population of the world. In many countries the number of Christians is pitiably small and weak, and the Asian representation especially discloses a notable and unhealthy imbalance. Political developments and resurgent religions have helped to make the modern prospect relatively much less favorable from the human standpoint, and Christianity itself is undoubtedly weakened from within by uncertainty, disunity, and theological division. If great steps have been taken toward the fulfillment of the Church's task, even greater steps remain to be taken in the future, and there is need for increased awareness that real expansion can only be in and of the Holy Spirit.

E. Theological Development. The gospel is a given message which has received normative form in Holy Scripture and which the preacher has no authority to change. On the other hand, the task of proclaiming the message is entrusted to men, and this task has to be discharged against a shifting background of human language and thought. This poses the special task of theology. Theology is biblical; it has to work at the correct translation and exposition of Scripture. Theology is dogmatic; it has to bring out the correct implications in relation to the pressure of contemporary thought forms. Theology is practical; it has to make the right application of the gospel to the individual and corporate life and ministry of the Church in the world. Theology is historical; it has to weigh what is to be thought and said and done in the present against what has been thought and said and done in the past. In all its aspects theology is, of course, evangelistic. Its concern is for the gospel and its ministry. It is not an academic department of Christianity remote from ordinary Christian life and work. It serves the ministry by checking the preaching and teaching of the Church, by giving it contemporary form, by helping it to maintain its integrity and purity, by submitting it constantly to the given norm of Scripture.

To give even a reasonably full outline of theological development is obviously impossible here. All that can be given are a few indications of some of the more important trends in the three main periods: the early, the medieval, and the modern.

1. Early Period. The first centuries were dominated by the struggle for the great essentials of Christian faith as the gospel went out into the world of current thought and religion. Out of conflict with Gnosticism came the great affirmation of God as Creator, the unity of the OT and NT, and the reality of the Incarnation and the Resurrection. Out of the trinitarian and christological controversies came the insistence on God's triunity and the unity of the person of Christ in His deity and humanity. Out of the Pelagian controversy came the further emphasis on sin and grace which, if not always in full Augustinian form, has constantly been seen to be essential to the evangelical message. The early Church was not remarkable for linguistic scholarship, but it had the advantage of speaking the language of the LXX and NT, and except for an early trend toward allegorical exegesis (Origen *De prin.* iv.2.4) its exposition was good if not always inwardly self-consistent. A serious weakness of the early Church was in relation to some aspects of practical theology. Basically loyal to the precepts of Scripture, it did not work out a sound theological basis for its practice. Thus many customs, ceremonies, disciplinary measures, and even modes of operation were adopted that carried implicitly the possibilities of theological falsification. The problem of postbaptismal sin and forgiveness is to be noted particularly in this respect, as is also the related tendency to conceive of the gospel as the new law.

2. Medieval Period. The medieval period is often the subject of facile generalization, whether in extravagant adulation or undiscerning condemnation. In fact, so many different forces are at work that any general statements can be made only with reservations. Thus the fourfold scheme of exegesis tended to prevail, not without unhappy consequences; but there were also genuine movements toward literal interpretation. Again, if sacramentalism established itself, it has also to be remembered that the doctrine of the atonement received classical formulation in Anselm's *Cur deus homo?* Aquinas, wrestling with the problems of revelation and philosophy, may have struck a doubtful balance with his principle that grace perfects nature, but Anselm in his *Proslogion* made a stand for the better theological principle of faith-seeking-understanding as the norm of the relation between reason and revelation. Radbert certainly initiated the development that was to lead to transubstantiation, but already Ratramnus and his successors provided the essentials of the Reformation answer. If a generalization may be hazarded, it is that the Middle Ages added a magnificent but confused and distorted superstructure on the genuine foundation of the gospel. The sphere of practice was again a fruitful source of error. If masses, relics, pilgrimages, and so forth were partly the results of poor theology, they were also in part the causes in a vicious circle of reciprocal interaction.

3. Modern Period. The modern period was initiated by the Reformation, with its rediscovery of the great doctrines of the authority of Scripture and justification by faith, and with its renewed attention to Scripture as the norm of true theology. In reply to the Reformation the Roman Catholic world engaged in an extensive codification of its teaching at the Council of Trent, thus enslaving itself in a rigid ecclesiastical orthodoxy from which it has only recently begun to liberate itself with the rise of the biblical movement and the discussions of the Second Vatican Council.

Within the Protestant world the understanding of the Lord's Supper led to an unfortunate rift between the Lutherans and Reformed which broadened and deepened in the century of orthodoxy (the 17th). In addition, Arminianism raised an issue that cut right across the general alignment, and its success under Laud in England created a High Church party which severed the previous close contacts between Anglican and Reformed theology, more particularly, when Puritanism displayed an intransigent extremism in the opposite direction. The Anabaptist movement also carried deep theological implications, not merely in the sphere of the sacraments, but also in the whole understanding of the Church, of the Bible, and of the nature of sin and grace. Far more important, however, has been the presentation of the liberal challenge from the 18th cent. onward, for much Protestant theology had tended to collapse in face of the new demand that Christianity must be restated to conform to the dicta of rationalism or empiricism.

The 20th cent. has been a period of peculiar interest from the theological standpoint. In both Protestantism and Roman Catholicism, the final result of increased biblical study has been to bring at least the beginnings of true theological renewal and the more solid hope of theological rapprochement. The running of the tide against missionary work has also demanded serious reflection on its theological basis, and the erosion of traditional modes of Christian belief and action has brought the issue of Christianity and Christian theology sharply into focus. There are those, of course, who cry for a radical restatement to fit a scientific age. But there are also those who see that the real choice is between gospel and no gospel, between Christianity as it truly is and a mere human shadow or substitute. To be sure, the wording of the message has to be reshaped today as it has always been. But this reshaping must take place under an intensive exegetical and dogmatic study which will ensure that the message itself remains. Only thus can theology serve the mission of Christianity.

It is to be noted that the modern debate carries three positive implications of great importance for the future. First, the Protestant and Roman Catholic worlds are willy-nilly involved together in the modern situation, not only in biblical study but also, for example, in the theology of ecumenism or the confrontation of modern issues. Secondly, the combination of the problems of communication and missionary outreach has provided at least the opportunity for a theological reestablishment of the whole message and mission of the Church, and of a discharge of its mission. Third, since mission is of the very essence of the Church's task, this involves the possibility of a genuine revival of pastoral theology that will bring all the life and activity of Christians under the control of theological criteria. This is of supreme importance, for history shows that practice is often the Achilles' heel of theology; and should the intensive discussion of the present age finally reduce its autonomy, this will be of incalculable benefit to Christian thought and work, i.e., to the reformation of Christianity in accordance with its true and underlying nature.

Bibliography.–The works dealing with Christianity are, of course, coextensive with Christian literature as such. In general cf. *ERE, RGG,* Sch.-Herz., etc. On I cf. esp. the NT theologies. On II cf. A. Harnack, *What Is Christianity?* (1957); Barth, *CD,* I/2; the church histories, esp. K. S. Latourette (1953); the histories of dogma, esp. Harnack (7 vols.; Eng. tr. 1958) and Seeberg (Eng. tr. 1952).

J. ORR
G. W. BROMILEY

CHRISTOLOGY.

- I. Patristic
  - A. Docetism and Adoptionism
  - B. Modalism and Subordinationism
  - C. Arianism and Nicea
  - D. Apollinarianism
  - E. Nestorianism
  - F. Eutychianism and Chalcedon
  - G. Monophysitism and Monothelitism
- II. Medieval
- III. Reformation
  - A. Lutheran
  - B. Reformed
  - C. Anabaptist
- IV. Modern
  - A. Schleiermacher
  - B. Kenoticism
  - C. Ritschl
  - D. Orthodoxy

For the biblical aspects of Christology *see* PERSON OF CHRIST. The present concern is exclusively with the development of the doctrine through the various historical periods.

I. Patristic.–*A. Docetism and Adoptionism.* The early patristic period is one of intrinsically correct but undeveloped thinking which allows of some looseness of statement. Two main errors are perceived and avoided: the Docetic, which would make of Christ's humanity a mere appearance, and the Ebionite or Adoptionist, which would see in Christ a man adopted into the Godhead by the descent of the Spirit. In the Apologists (Justin) there is a tendency to equate Christ rather generally with the *lógos* or reason operative in all men, and also to subordinate the Son to the Father. But in Ignatius, 2 Clement, and Melito of Sardis the true deity and humanity of Christ are both recognized as necessary to the biblical doctrine of His person and work.

B. Modalism and Subordinationism. A further step toward understanding is taken in the great writers of the late 2nd and early 3rd centuries. Irenaeus emphasizes the strong interconnection between Christ's person and work as expressed in the phrase, "He became what we are in order that He might make us what He is." Tertullian specifically refutes the Gnostic errors and also Monarchianism in its Modalistic or Sabellian form, which teaches an economic but not an essential trinity, i.e., the one God assuming three different forms or modes for different purposes. Logically, this involved the so-called patripassian deduction that we might just as well speak of the crucifixion of the Father as the Son; and, since the patripassian Praxeas was also an opponent of Montanism, Tertullian was led to his famous condemnation: "He put to flight the Paraclete and crucified the Father." Origen was a more speculative thinker, and his Christology is marked by a distinct subordinationism of the Son to the Father. Yet he also made a positive contribution with his thought of the eternal generation of the Son, and introduced the term *homooúsios,* "of one substance."

C. Arianism and Nicea. Christology became the predominant issue in the 4th cent. with the emergence of Arianism. For Arius, Christ was virtually an intermediary being. Though preexistent, He was a creature ("There was when the Son was not"). By Him as the firstborn creature the world was made. Not having a human soul, He could not be regarded as true man any more than as true God. Under the inspiration of Athanasius, the Council of Nicea (325) insisted on both the full deity and the full humanity of Christ, which Athanasius saw to be essential to His mediatorial work and therefore to salvation. The word *homooúsion* was adopted to rule

Byzantine triumphal arch at Nicea (modern Iznik, Turkey). The first Council of Nicea (A.D. 325) debated the Arian controversy, resolving that Christ was "begotten, not made," "of one essence with the Father." (B. K. Condit)

out Arian sophistries, and although opposition to this term and ecclesiastical intrigues led to long semi-Arian controversies, the Athanasian position was secured at Constantinople (381).

D. Apollinarianism. The problem of the interrelationship of deity and humanity still remained, and during the next two centuries this gave rise to a complicated movement of exaggeration and counterexaggeration. Apollinaris initiated the process by creating unity at the expense of full humanity. In body and irrational soul Christ was fully man, but in Him the rational soul was displaced by the Logos. Against this Gregory of Nazianzus brought the crushing Athanasian rejoinder that "the unassumed is the unhealed." Apollinaris was condemned at Constantinople in 381.

E. Nestorianism. Nestorius went to the opposite extreme, not by denying or diminishing the deity, but by apparently separating the humanity and deity to such a degree that there was no real unity. The term *theótokos* as applied to the Virgin brought his teaching into focus, for he did not think that Mary ought to be described as the mother of God, or indeed that the incarnate child Jesus should be worshiped as God. On the former point, something might be said on his behalf. For while the term is logically unimpeachable, it is still better to speak of Mary as the mother of the incarnate Word or of the Son in virtue of His incarnation, rather than of God more generally. How far Nestorius held the division of the persons popularly attributed to him is a matter of dispute. There can be no doubt, however, that he used incautious expressions which seemed to imply a separation of persons and not just a distinction of natures.

F. Eutychianism. After the condemnation of Nestorius at Ephesus (431) the opposite extreme was again reached in Eutyches of Alexandria, who pressed the unity of Christ to the point of a unity of nature rather than of person, thus absorbing the human nature into the divine. In answer to this new Docetism, and to the whole problem of divine and human natures in one person, the Council of Chalcedon (451) finally achieved the balanced statement that in Christ two natures are united in one person or hypostasis, without confusion, conversion, division, or separation. In explanation of the possibility of true humanity without an independent hypostasis (*anhypostatic*), as Cyril of Alexandria has already urged against Nestorius, it was taught by Leontius of Byzantium that the human nature of Christ is *enhypostatic,* i.e., that it has its substance in and through the *lógos*.

G. Monophysitism and Monothelitism. The Eutychian position still commanded support, however, and the two centuries after Chalcedon were marked by the attempts of the Monophysites and Monothelites to locate a center of unity either more generally in the nature or more specifically in the will of Christ. Progress was made in Alexandria and Rome toward a compromise that would preserve the two natures but posit a single divine human energy, and Honorius of Rome was even prepared to accept the single will in Christ. The Western Church in general, however, asserted the two wills, and this position was maintained at Constantinople (680), although a subordination of the human will to the divine was conceded. Failure to accept this reaffirmation of Chalcedon led the Syrian Jacobite and Coptic churches into schism.

II. Medieval.–Not without reason, Christology emerged as the dominant issue in early theology; and, if it led to long and tiresome controversies, it also produced a christological orthodoxy that enabled theologians to concentrate on other issues. In the Middle Ages, therefore, we find no basic contribution to the doctrine. Discussion consisted, for the most part, of an exposition of the Chalcedonian teaching. The only notable point in this respect is the general tendency to conceive and present Christ in an abstract and exalted form in which His humanity is verbally maintained but materially forfeited.

This trend in more specialized discussion is perhaps more than compensated for, however, by the firm linking of Christology to soteriology. This had always been a concern of the fathers. Athanasius, for example, had rightly perceived that the mediatorial and reconciling work of Christ is closely bound up with His person. Augustine in the West had given a particular emphasis to this aspect, underlining also Christ's exemplary humility as man and our mystical relationship with Him. These were the strains that influenced medieval thinking, whether we think of the warm attachment of St. Bernard to the person of Christ or the famous treatise of Anselm *Cur deus homo*?, which brings out the soteriological necessity or rationale of the Incarnation as understood in the orthodox sense.

III. Reformation.–*A. Lutheran.* The soteriological implication of Christology was naturally the first interest of Luther in his championing of Chalcedonian orthodoxy. Luther had indeed no great time for christological abstraction. He claimed that we should keep to the historical person of Jesus and His saving office and work. The well-known patristic conception of an exchange played a great part in his thinking. The Son had taken our human nature that we might partake of the divine nature. He had identified Himself with us that He might take our sin and His righteousness might be ours. Along these lines Luther maintained the scholastic emphasis, but with a new force and richness according to his evangelical understanding of justification.

In the context of eucharistic doctrine, however, Luther developed a particular nuance. Already in the *Tome* of Leo that underlay Chalcedon, it had been laid down that there is a communication of the attributes (*communicatio idiomatum*) of the two natures. Luther took this to mean that the attributes of each nature are transferred to and may thus be predicated of the other, the result being an interpenetration very close to the intermingling condemned at Chalcedon. This does, of course, prevent the constant artificial question whether this or that nature is at work in a given situation. Yet it raises certain difficulties of its own, e.g., How far does the human nature enjoy or exercise the divine attributes? Furthermore, it produces strange results with respect to the eucharist by justifying a real presence of Christ's body and blood in terms of Christ's ubiquity as God (Ubiquitarianism). It is hard to determine whether Luther's prior concern for a real presence helped to produce this particular emphasis, whether the emphasis contributed to the eucharistic doctrine, or whether the two simply worked hand in hand in the young Luther and early Lutheranism. It seems fairly clear, however, that Luther's dogmatic stand on the presence must have had no little influence on at least the outworking of the *communicatio idiomatum*.

B. Reformed. Reformed theology had no similar eucharistic concern, since it quickly came to see that between the Ascension and the Return the presence and action of Jesus Christ are in and by the Holy Spirit. It could thus maintain Chalcedonian orthodoxy without any undue stress on the *communicatio idiomatum*. Indeed, Calvin felt that there was a dangerous Eutychian tendency in Lutheran Christology, and he was anxious to maintain the distinction, though not of course the separation, of the natures. This concern underlay his conception of the *lógos ásarkos,* i.e., the divine Son maintaining His being and activity as the second person of the trinity *extra carnem* (outside the flesh). Lutheranism suspected a certain Nestorianism in this emphasis, although in fact the unity of Christ's person was upheld in terms of the *enhypostasis* doctrine of the early fathers. Certainly, this teaching precluded the possibility of a Kenotic theology.

The Reformed did not dispute the *communicatio idiomatum* as such. They did not argue that the divine attributes belonged only to the *lógos* and the human to the incarnate Jesus. They recognized that in the unity of Christ's person the one nature is necessarily implicated in the activities and events of the other, so that the human no less than the divine nature may be spoken of as the material and not merely the instrumental cause of salvation. Nevertheless, they did not think in terms of the assuming of the human nature into the divine, but of its assuming into the one person of the Son. Again, they emphasized the fact that the *communicatio* is an active communication of operations (*communicatio operationum*) rather than a static interpenetration, thus concentrating on the soteriological rather than the theoretical aspect. Any application to the eucharist they regarded as both unnecessary and misleading inasmuch as the concern here is specifically with the office and work of the Holy Spirit.

C. Anabaptist. Brief note may be taken of the strange christological contribution of Menno Simons among the sixteenth-century Anabaptists. Simons argued that Christ did not take flesh from the Virgin, but introduced the new and spiritual flesh of the new creation. In this way he tried to avoid the implication of the incarnate Son in sinful humanity, but at the expense of breaking the true identity of Christ with us which had always been thought necessary to His mediatorial work. The Docetic or Apollinarian strain thus reappeared at this point in new guise. How far Simons' views were followed by others has been much disputed, but in some circles at least, e.g., in England, the denial that Christ took flesh of the Virgin was commonly regarded as an Anabaptist tenet.

IV. Modern.–*A. Schleiermacher.* In the modern period the Lutheran emphasis seems on the whole to have proved more vulnerable to liberal tendencies, in spite of its original emphasis on the deity of Christ. Two factors may have contributed to this. First, a full exercise of the attributes of deity by the incarnate Son is obviously ruled out, and therefore some form of Kenoticizing is demanded. Second, Lutheranism also stresses the historical Jesus; and when attention shifts back to the human Jesus there is always the possibility that this Kenoticism will take the form of an adaptation of the divine attributes to the human, with no counterbalancing doctrine of the *lógos ásarkos* to prevent a final replacement of true deity by a vague human divinity. Something of this is to be seen in the Christology of Schleiermacher. For Schleiermacher the Chalcedon approach is completely alien because it seems to bear too little relation to the human Jesus of the Gospels. As he sees it, to understand the person of Christ we must begin with His human consciousness. In Jesus the basic dependence on God finds supreme and archetypal expression in the sense of sonship. The divinity of Jesus is thus bound up with His full humanity. The basic attributes of deity are no longer communicated. They cannot be, because the limitation of humanity and the divine immutability are thought to constitute a permanent obstacle. They thus yield before a new and generalized divinity which is ultimately true of all men.

B. Kenoticism. A similar process may be seen in the nineteenth-century Kenoticism, which found wide acceptance in Lutheran circles. Already in the Kenotic controversy of the 17th cent. a basic decision had been reached that the man Jesus genuinely, and not merely in appearance, abstained from a full exercise of the majesty imparted to Him. The reconstructed Kenoticism of Thomasius in the 19th cent., however, introduced a new factor with the distinction between the so-called essential or moral attributes (e.g., love or righteousness), which were retained, and the external attributes (e.g., omnipotence or omniscience), which were set aside. In this way it was hoped to preserve a true deity of Jesus, without the problem of limitation, and inseparable from a truly human existence. Approaching the question in this way, Kenoticism failed to see that the immutability of the living God does not prevent Him from exercising all His attributes in the form of humanity, nor force Him into the violent mutation of a self-deprivation of His attributes, which can leave only partial deity, and therefore no true deity at all, in the incarnate Son. In Kenoticism the communication of attributes ceased to be a genuinely reciprocal process, the attempt to find an interpenetration of the human nature by the divine leading finally to an adaptation of the divine to the human. A modified form of Kenoticism was adopted by the *Lux Mundi* group of Anglo-Catholics and more recently by the so-called Liberal Evangelical movement in England.

C. Ritschl. Another variation on the same theme is to be found in Ritschl. Starting with the historical Jesus, Ritschl, too, was prepared to recognize the ethical attributes of divinity, but he had no patience with the traditional formulations. As he saw it, Jesus has for us the value of God in virtue of the perfection of His divine and human moral nature. The radical obtuseness of the Kenotics is thus reproduced in Ritschl. Taking humanity as his norm, he allows a communication only of such divine attributes as he assumes to be compatible with it. In the last resort, therefore, he can base the divinity of Christ only on His subjective significance, i.e., His value for us. Naturally, this is poles apart from Luther. Yet it is a possible consequence of the Lutheran outworking of the union in a distorted form. Liberals of all kinds can accept the strictness of the union. But their concentration on humanity, and their abstract notions of the Godhead, inevitably lead them to a weakened Christology in which Jesus is finally divine only to the degree that divinity is possible for man, His full and proper deity as the eternal Son being partially or totally surrendered.

D. Orthodoxy. In spite of the liberal movement, orthodoxy has naturally maintained itself in both Reformed and Lutheran circles, not to speak of Anglican, Roman Catholic, and Eastern Orthodox. Indeed, the present century has witnessed a new and welcome interest in the Chalcedonian definition, not as a metaphysical formulation, but as a basic and almost doxological confession. Four points in particular have claimed attention. First, the mystery of the Incarnation is that of a unique relationship of grace. Second, this relationship is set up in a human person and work, and is thus to be closely connected with the gospel presentation, with no dichotomy on either side between the Jesus of history and the Christ of faith. Third, the mystery of the Incarnation does not pose an abstract problem of thought, but is to be seen in relation to the atonement and therefore to the fulfillment of the election of grace in Christ incarnate, crucified, and risen. Finally, the humanity of Christ is not a limiting factor which demands either a restriction or a spasmodic and paradoxical manifestation of the divine attributes, but a specific form in which the true and living God can and does bring all His attributes to expression, achieving a unity of person, a communion of natures, and a communication of attributes, graces, and operations, without any distortion of humanity on the one side, or on the other any forfeiture of deity, whether within the Godhead or in the human form.

Bibliography.–D. M. Baillie, *God Was in Christ* (1955); Barth, *CD*, IV/1, 2; J. F. Bethune-Baker, *Intro. to the Early History of Christian Doctrine* (1903); J. N. D. Kelly, *Early Christian Doctrines* (1959); H. R. Mackintosh, *Doctrine of the Person of Jesus Christ* (1942); *RGG*. G. W. BROMILEY

CHRISTS, FALSE [Gk. *pseudóchristoi*] (Mt. 24:24 par. Mk. 13:22); NEB "impostors . . . claiming to be messiahs." In Jesus' discourse on the last things, spoken on Tuesday of the week of His Passion, He solemnly forewarned His disciples that many would come in His name saying "I am the Christ," and that they would deceive many; that there would arise false Christs and false prophets who would show great signs and wonders in order to lead astray, if possible, even the elect; and that, therefore, if any man said to them "Lo, here is the Christ!" or "There he is!" they were not to believe it (Mt. 24:5, 11, 23-25; Mk. 13:6, 21-23; Lk. 21:8).

I. Early Notices.–Christ's warning was needed. Some commentators have, indeed, pointed out that there is no historical record of anyone expressly claiming to be the Christ prior to the destruction of Jerusalem. This, however, is probably only in appearance (cf. Lange, comm. on Mt. 24:3). Edersheim remarks: "Though in the multitude of impostors, who, in the troubled time between the rule of Pilate and the destruction of Jerusalem, promised messianic deliverance to Israel, few names and claims of this kind have been specially recorded, yet the hints in the New Testament, and the references, however guarded, in the Jewish historian, imply the appearance of many such seducers" (*LTJM,* II, 446). The revolts in this period were generally connected with religious pretensions in the leaders (Josephus *BJ* ii.13.4 — "deceived and deluded the people under pretence of divine inspiration"), and in the fevered state of messianic expectation can hardly have lacked, in some instances, a messianic character. Judas of Galilee (Acts 5:37; Josephus *Ant.* xviii.1.6; *BJ* ii.8.1) founded a numerous sect (the Gaulonites), and according to Origen (*In Luc. Hom.* 25) he was regarded by many of them as the Messiah. The Theudas of Acts 5:36, "giving himself out to be somebody," may or may not be the same as the Theudas of Josephus (*Ant.* xx.5.1), but the latter, at least, made prophetic claims and deluded many; e.g., he promised to divide the river Jordan by a word. Another instance is the "Egyptian" for whom Paul was mistaken, who had stirred up a "revolt" (Acts 21:38) — one of a multitude of "imposters and deceivers," Josephus tells us, who persuaded multitudes to follow them into the wilderness, pretending that they would exhibit wonders and signs (*Ant.* xx.8.6). This Egyptian was to show them that at his command the walls of Jerusalem would fall down (*BJ* ii.13.5). Of another class was the Samaritan Dositheus, with whom Simon Magus was said to be connected. He is alleged to have been regarded as "the prophet like unto Moses," whom God was to raise up.

II. Bar Cochba.–The most celebrated case of a false Christ is that of Bar Cochba, the leader of the great insurrection under Hadrian in A.D. 132 (Eusebius *HE* iv.6; for Jewish and other authorities, see the full account in Schürer, *HJP*², I, 534-557). The insurrection was on a scale such that it required the whole force of the Roman empire to put it down (cf. Schürer). The leader's name was Simon, but the title Bar Cochba ("son of a star") was given him with reference to the prophecy in Nu. 24:17 of the star that would come out of Jacob. Rabbi Akiba, the most celebrated doctor of his time, applied this prophecy, with that in Hag. 2:6f., to Simon, and announced him as the Messiah. He is commonly known in Jewish literature (and in letters from a cave near EN-GEDI) as Bar Coziba, probably from his birthplace. Immense multitudes flocked to his standard, and Christians in Palestine were severely persecuted. Coins were issued in his name. After tremendous efforts the rebellion was crushed and Jerusalem was converted into a Roman colony (*Aelia Capitolina*) that Jews were forbidden to enter.

III. Jewish Pseudo-Messiahs.–Among the Jews themselves, in later times, many pseudo-messiahs have arisen. An interesting account of some of these is given by Elkan Adler in his Introduction to *Aspects of the Hebrew Genius* (1910). "Such there had been," this writer says, "from time to time ever since the destruction of the Temple." In the 16th and 17th cents., however, the belief in pseudo-messiahs took new and remarkable shapes. Among the names mentioned is that of David Reubeni, or David of the tribe of Reuben (1524), who ultimately fell a martyr to the Inquisition. Under his influence a Portuguese royal secretary, Diego Pires, adopted the Jewish faith, changed his name to Solomon Molko, and finally proclaimed himself the Messiah. In 1529 he published some of his addresses under the title of *The Book of Wonder*. He was burned at the stake at Mantua.

"Other Kabbalists, such as Isaac Luria and Chajim Vital and Abraham Shalom, proclaimed themselves to be Messiahs or forerunners of the Messiah, and their works and manuscripts are still piously studied by many oriental Jews." The chief of all these false messiahs was Sabbatai Zevi, born at Smyrna in 1626. "His adventures," says Adler, "created a tremendous stir in western Europe." He ultimately became an apostate to Islam; nonetheless he had a line of successors, in whom the sect of Donmeh, in Salonica, continue to believe. Another mentioned is Jacob Frank, of Podolia, who revealed himself in 1755 as the Holy Lord, in whom there dwelt the same Messiah-soul that had dwelt in David, Elijah, Jesus, Muhammad, Sabbatai Zevi, and his followers. Jewish literature in the 18th cent. is full of controversial writing connected with Sabbatianism. Cf. G. Scholem, *Major Trends in Jewish Mysticism* (repr. 1961). J. ORR

CHRONICLES, BOOKS OF.

I. Name
II. Relationship to Ezra-Nehemiah
III. Place in the Canon
IV. Text
V. Sources
  A. Canonical Sources
  B. Noncanonical Sources
  C. Use of Sources
VI. Historical Reliability
VII. Literary Genre
VIII. Content and Purpose
IX. Date and Authorship
X. Theology

I. Name.–This work formed at first one book with the Hebrew title *dibrê hayyāmîm,* literally "the events of the days," used in the sense of a chronicle of events, much like a book of daily records (cf. 1 Ch. 27:24). Jerome suggested in *Prologus Galaetus* (*PL,* XXVIII, 554) that a more representative title would be *chronicon totius divinae historiae,* or "Chronicle of the whole divine history." Luther took from Jerome the title Chronicles, and henceforth this has always been used in Protestant Bibles. The LXX calls it *Paraleipómena,* i.e., "things passed over" or "things omitted," implying, as Theodoret explains, that the author of Chronicles put together "whatever the compiler of 1-2 Kings has passed over." The LXX divides it into two books, a division which was taken over in other versions and has since 1448 come also into Hebrew MSS.

II. Relationship to Ezra-Nehemiah.–It is common to speak today of the Chronicler who produced a historical work comparable to the so-called Deuteronomic history. It is rather widely accepted in current scholarship that Ezra-Nehemiah forms a continuation of Chronicles. In support of the unity of these books is the fact that 2 Chronicles closes with the decree of Cyrus with which Ezra begins (2 Ch. 36:22f. = Ezr. 1:1f.). This repetition is the connecting link between the two sections of the Chronicler's work and can be removed neither from 2 Chronicles, for it forms the needed completion of 2 Ch. 32:21, nor from Ezra, for this would render the following verses meaningless. The vocabulary, syntax, and usage of prepositions support common authorship, as does the method by which quotations from the Pentateuch are employed. The way in which canonical and noncanonical sources are used is also strikingly similar. The position and work of the Levites are depicted in the same style and with virtually the same words and the same diligence, and both books are equally interested in genealogies and other lists. Both works manifest a central emphasis on Jerusalem and its cult, on God's law, on the "all Israel" concept, and on the theocracy.

There are scholars who emphasize certain differences between Chronicles and Ezra-Nehemiah or certain sections in each (so, recently, Freedman, Japhet) which they believe preclude common authorship. While certain differences are to be expected, the overwhelming amount of similarity between these works in linguistic peculiarities, literary mannerism, historical outlook, and theological emphasis supports the conclusion that the Chronicler is responsible for both works and that they form an essential unity (see IX below).

III. Place in Canon.–The work of the Chronicler stands last in the third division or Kethubhim (Writings) of the Hebrew canon. In the present Hebrew canonical order Ezra-Nehemiah appears before 1 Chronicles. It has been suggested that the separation of Ezra-Nehemiah from Chronicles may have resulted from using Ezra-Nehemiah as a supplement to the story that ends in 2 Kings (cf. Denter, Pfeiffer, Katz, Myers). The LXX has Chronicles followed by both 1 Esdras (apocryphal) and 2 Esdras (or Ezra-Nehemiah). Both Jerome and Luther adopted the LXX order, which has been preserved in the English versions with the exclusion of the apocryphal 1 Esdras. Since the LXX preserved the natural sequence of Chronicles before Ezra-Nehemiah, it has been suggested that the Chronicler's history was accepted as a whole into the canon as known in Alexandria, perhaps even before Jerusalem accepted a part of it (North, comm., p. 404; cf. Sundberg, pp. 51-79). But there is no certainty on this matter.

IV. Text.–On the basis of the MS evidence from an earlier period of research, the traditional critical opinion of the Chronicler's respect for the text of his *Vorlage* (source document) is provided by R. H. Pfeiffer: "In general the Chronicler modified our canonical sources with complete freedom to suit his ideas" (*IDB,* I, 578). It was assumed that the text of the Chronicler's canonical *Vorlage* was identical with that of our present MT. As a result of the study of the synoptic parallels between Chronicles and 1 Samuel–2 Kings the Chronicler was credited with tampering with the text of his *Vorlage.* "The Chronicler rewrote, edited, shortened, expanded, and arbitrarily changed the passages [of his *Vorlage*] . . ." (*IDB,* I, 579) in order to suit his theological purposes and tendentious aims. The study of MSS discovered at Qumrân, however, has demonstrated that these conclusions are now in need of wholesale revision. The following discussion will indicate the present state of research.

The first nine chapters of 1 Chronicles are known to rely heavily on the Pentateuch. Whereas it was earlier assumed that the parallels between 1 Ch. 1–9 and the Pentateuch reflected a proto-MT from which the Chronicler diverged at will, it has now been demonstrated that there is a marked resemblance and correspondence in linguistic features (names, use of *waw,* syndetic construction, *plene* spellings, "pseudo-cohortative" forms, preference for *'el* against *'al,* change of collective forms into plural, Aramaizing tendencies), actual composition, arrangement of material, and form of narrative between 1 Ch. 1–9 and the Samaritan Pentateuch and respective Greek MSS, both of which belong to the Palestinian text-type (Cross, pp. 292-97; cf. *IEJ,* 16 [1966], 81-95; Waltke, pp. 232-34). This evidence indicates that the bulk of the textual differences between 1 Ch. 1–9 and the parallels of the Masoretic Pentateuch is due to the *Vorlage* utilized by the Chronicler, which belongs to the Palestinian text family. Thus, the Chronicler did not rewrite, edit, shorten, expand, and arbitrarily change the text of his *Vorlage,* but rather followed quite faithfully the text-type upon which he relied, one that already contained these peculiar features.

It is known that from 1 Ch. 10 onward there are extensive synoptic parallels between the Chronicler's work and Samuel-Kings. Studies of these synoptic parallels have in the past led scholars to credit the Chronicler with many tendentious or theologically motivated deviations, whenever the two histories diverge from each other (cf. Noth, pp. 110-180; Brunet, *RB*; Botterweck, *Theologische Quartalschrift,* 136 [1956], 402-432). The DSS indicate the necessity for a drastic revision of these views also.

The respective passages in Chronicles that are synoptic with Samuel have been investigated in the light of all MSS from Qumrân and especially the important Samuel scrolls (4QSam^{a}, 4QSam^{b}, 4QSam^{c}) and the pertinent LXX texts. These studies have demonstrated clearly that the scrolls are widely at variance with the MT and belong to a Palestinian text family to which Chronicles bears close resemblance (Cross, pp. 292f.). On this basis it has been shown that the Chronicler's textual *Vorlage* was not a proto-MT but rather a Palestinian textual recension (Lemke) on which the Old Greek also is based (Klein, Allen, Shenkel). The archaic Samuel MS (4QSam^{a}) proves that where Chronicles corresponds to 1 S. 1:1–2 S. 11:1, the text of Chronicles agrees with the Palestinian text-type and not with the MT. The implications of this evidence have a direct bearing both on the Chronicler's handling of his canonical sources and on the date of the composition of Chronicles (see IX below).

These developments in modern research objectively establish that the Chronicler can no longer be charged with violent and wilful distortion of his canonical sources. They prove that the present text of Chronicles is not the result of a deliberate attempt at modernization, nor does it reflect tendentious and theologically motivated changes in the bulk of the synoptic parallels, but it reflects as faithfully as textual history can expect the text-type of its *Vorlage.* It must be noted that this new situation also has a direct bearing on the evaluation of the Chronicler's history and theology.

V. Sources.–There is sufficient evidence to demonstrate that the Chronicler used both canonical and noncanonical sources in the writing of his history.

A. Canonical Sources. The Chronicler never refers explicitly to canonical sources under titles known to us. But on the basis of comparative studies it has been estimated that about half of Chronicles consists of either quotations of, or clear references to, other canonical accounts (Curtis and Madsen, pp. 17-19). New evidence from the Qumrân scrolls indicates that the Chronicler was very faithful in his usage of these canonical sources (see IV above). It seems certain that he made use of the completed Pentateuch (Sundberg, p. 38 n. 27) and the books of Samuel–Kings. The book of Judges is used in 2 Ch. 15:2ff. (Rudolph, p. xii). The description of the fall of Jerusalem (2 Ch. 36) is dependent on Jeremiah. A quotation of Isa. 7:9 appears in 2 Ch. 20:20; one from Zec. 4:10 in 2 Ch. 16:9. There are references to various prophetic words in 2 Ch. 15:5-7. 2 Ch. 6:41f. quotes Ps. 132:8ff. and a combination of Psalms appears in 1 Ch. 16:8-36. A reference to Lamentations appears in 2 Ch. 35:35. 1 Ch. 2:9-17 uses the genealogy from Ruth 4:18-22.

B. Noncanonical Sources. The Chronicler refers explicitly to a great number of other sources, which are reliable in all essentials (Bea, pp. 46-58).

The *official records* of kings are referred to: "The Book of the Kings of Israel and Judah" (2 Ch. 27:7; 25:27; 36:8; cf. 1 Ch. 9:1); "The Book of the Kings of Judah and Israel" (2 Ch. 16:11; 25:26; 28:26; 32:32); "The Chronicles of King David" (1 Ch. 27:24); "The Book of the Kings of Israel" (1 Ch. 9:1; 2 Ch. 20:34); "The Chronicles of the Kings of Israel" (2 Ch. 33:18); "The Commentary [midrash] on the Book of the Kings" (2 Ch. 24:27); "The Directions of David King of Israel and the Directions of Solomon His Son" (2 Ch. 35:4). It is widely but not universally assumed that these titles refer to the same single work. However, since all the notices of sources that occur in the Kings parallels refer to a single title, the "Chronicle of the Acts of the Kings of Judah" (1 K. 14:29; 15:7, 23; 22:45; 2 K. 14:18; 15:6, 36; 16:19; 20:20; 21:17; 23:28; 24:5), the variety of titles in the records enumerated above seems to suggest a variety of sources.

There are also *official genealogies*. A number of them are expressly noted (1 Ch. 4:33; 5:17; 7:9, 40; 9:1, 22; 2 Ch. 12:15). The Chronicler was doubtless in possession of these genealogical lists and records, and took most of them (1 Ch. 1–9) from the Pentateuch.

The Chronicler also made use of a whole series of *prophetic records*. Those referred to by name are from "Samuel the seer," "Nathan the prophet" and "Gad the seer" (1 Ch. 29:29), "Ahijah the Shilonite" (2 Ch. 9:29), "Iddo the seer" (2 Ch. 9:29; 12:15; 13:22), "Shemaiah the prophet" (12:15), and "Jehu ben Hanani" (20:34). For Manasseh there were the records of the seers of Hozai (2 Ch. 33:19). In addition, there are two references to Isaiah (26:22; 32:32). These records were undoubtedly written documents. "The language of the author is too definite to assume otherwise" (Myers, p. xlvii). Thus the Chronicler had access to royal annals, temple records, lists, genealogies, and liturgical materials as well as documents drawn up by men holding the prophetic office.

C. Use of Sources. Extraordinary divergence of opinion exists among scholars with regard to the use of sources by the Chronicler. The hypothesis of a common source used by both Samuel–Kings and Chronicles (Rothstein and Hänel, Goettsberger, Rehm) may be safely disregarded on the basis of the new understanding of textual families (see IV). There is an increasing amount of evidence suggesting that the Chronicler had a deep reverence for the sources upon which he drew. It is now certain that the TR of Samuel–Kings that we have in our Hebrew Bible is not identical with the source the Chronicler used. It has been shown that in the 12 chapters of 1 Chronicles (chs. 10–21) that have synoptic parallels in 1 Samuel, there are nearly a hundred instances in which the LXX of 1 Samuel agrees with 1 Chronicles against the MT of 1 Samuel (Lemke). Furthermore, the Chronicler is invariably supported by the LXX in those passages paralleled in 4QSam[a] where he deviates from the MT. Moreover, sources for which there is presently no extrabiblical literary evidence, such as were drawn from the temple archives, can be shown to be authentic on the basis of archeological discoveries and topographical studies (Richardson, Ehrlich, Myers). It is safe to suppose, therefore, that the Chronicler made careful use of his sources.

VI. Historical Reliability.–The question of the historical accuracy, reliability, and value of Chronicles, or the total work of the Chronicler (1 Chronicles–Nehemiah), has been answered in many contradictory ways. Some scholars have supposed that the Chronicler was a writer with a clear disregard for historical accuracy, displaying vivid imagination and graphic convictions by composing freely, without any guidance (*PIOT,* pp. 805f.; *IDB,* I, 579). The material of Chronicles not derived from Samuel–Kings, they claim, "was all freely composed" (Torrey, p. 231) and "is not to be trusted" (T. H. Robinson, *History of Israel* [1932], p. 424 n. 2). These assessments of the Chronicler's historical reliability are in need of drastic revision (see IV above).

The historical reliability of the Chronicler in those passages for which there are no parallels in Samuel–Kings can be assessed on the basis of archeological finds and related studies. A number of personal names, place names, geographical names from 1 Ch. 1–9 find their historical support from Egyptian inscriptions (Mazar, *SVT*, 4 [1957], 65f.) and other epigraphic materials. The emphasis on the Levites and their functions in 1 Ch. 15f. have the ring of historical authenticity (*ARI,* pp. 119-125). Ahijah's war with Israel is historical (Noth, p. 142). Pharaoh Shishak's campaign to Palestine, reported in 2 Ch. 12:2-16, is supported by his own inscriptions (*ANET,* pp. 242f., 263f.; Mazar, *SVT,* 4 [1957], 57-65) and by the archeological evidence of destruction levels in Megiddo, Shechem, Debir, Beth-shan, Beth-shemesh, Lachish, Arad, and other sites. King Asa's victory over Cushite and Bedouin forces (2 Ch. 14:9-15) reflects the actual circumstances of the times (*ARI,* pp. 152-56). Jehoshaphat's building activity in the Judean Buqe'ah is amply demonstrated by archeological discoveries (Cross and Milik, *BASOR*, 142 [Apr. 1956], 5-17). The conflict between the Judeans and the combined Moabite-Ammonite forces described in 2 Ch. 20:23 is historically sound (Noth, *ZDPV*, 67 [1944/45], 45-71; Rudolph, pp. 258f.). The mass of information of 2 Ch. 24 not found in Kings is amply supported by archeology (R. de Vaux, *RB*, 63 [1956], 535f.; Aharoni, *IEJ*, 8 [1958], 10f; Cross, *BASOR,* 205 [Feb. 1972], 36-42). The Babylonian Chronicle and the excavations of Megiddo support the historical reliability of 2 Ch. 35:20ff. (cf. *CCK,* pp. 18ff.).

On the basis of these and other examples the respect for the historical reliability and accuracy of the Chronicler has been notably enhanced. Myers assesses the situation as follows: "Within the limits of its purpose, the Chronicler's story is accurate wherever it can be checked" (comm., p. lxiii). If the reports of the Chronicler are from ancient and reliable biblical and extrabiblical sources, which are supported in their accuracy wherever they can be checked, then there is every likelihood that the remaining reports are similarly derived, and that the contrary must not be assumed but requires proof, which is not forthcoming.

A special problem relates to the unusually high numbers found in Chronicles, which have made the Chronicler's work suspect. At times the Chronicler has the smaller number. 2 Ch. 9:25 reads "4,000" stalls while 1 K. 4:26 reads "40,000." Often such differences can be explained on the basis of various types of textual corruption (Driver, *Textus,* 1 [1960], 125ff.; 4 [1964], 82f.; Wenham, pp. 21-24). The census of David showed that there were in Israel 800,000 that drew sword and in Judah 500,000 men (2 S. 24:9). The parallel in 1 Ch. 21:5 gives the figures as 1,100,000 and 470,000 respectively. The lower total in 2 S. leaves 1,300,000 men of military age, which would imply a population of about five million for Palestine, or nearly double the population per square mile of the most densely populated countries of modern Europe. It is to be noted that the difference between 2 Samuel and 1 Chronicles is in one case 300,000 and in the other 30,000. Wenham (presupposing a different form of notation used as some time before Masoretic standardization) has suggested that a coalescing of two figures is here evident and that in transcription extra zeros have been added. It has thus been postulated that Israel numbered 80,000 + 30 *'allûpim* and Judah 40,000 + 70 *'allûpîm* (Wenham, p. 33), accounting for the MT of both 2 Samuel and 1 Chronicles. Much depends on the meaning of the word *'elep*, which is traditionally translated "thousand." It is important to note that most of the very large numbers that cause difficulty are in thousands. It has been suggested that aside from its numerical meaning of 1000 this word can mean a social unit, such as "family," "clan," "tent group," or a military unit, such as a "company" (Mendenhall, *JBL*, 77 [1958], 52-66), or that it has individual meanings such as "chieftain" (1 Ch. 1:51-54), captain over a 1000 troops, commander of a company, professional soldier, and officer (cf. R. E. D. Clark, *Journal of the Transactions of the Victoria Institute,* 87 [1955], 82ff.; Wenham, pp. 19-53). The problem of large numbers is not confined to Chronicles, but seems characteristic of Hebrew historiography. Recent studies have provided important new insights that aid in solving the vexing problem of numbers in the OT.

VII. Literary Genre.–A common procedure in analyzing the nature of the Chronicler's type of literature is to investigate how he selects from, omits, modifies, and adds to, the canonical sources (Brunet, Rehm, Noth, etc.). On this basis it has been claimed that the Chronicler tampered with his canonical sources through conscious suppression, deliberate change, and unwarranted addition in order to make the stories conform with his views, purposes, and aims. It has therefore become customary among some scholars to follow Wellhausen's negative assessment and to designate the work of the Chronicler as a midrash. But since the Chronicler relied upon a text-type different from the MT, the customary criteria no longer warrant such a definition of the literary genre. The vast majority of some 177 points of contact between Samuel–Kings and Chronicles are now to be ruled out for this kind of evaluation (Lemke).

The literary work of the Chronicler is to be classified as history. This is evident from those sections where the Chronicler has additional historical information (see V and VI above). His history is essentially trustworthy and seeks to supplement Samuel–Kings. Of course, the Chronicler's history must be understood in the context of the OT and the ancient Near East, and cannot be studied within the canons of classical historiography (Herodotus, Thucydides), much less those of the modern historian as laid down by von Ranke, Mommsen, etc. Today's historians are becoming aware that ultimately no history is conceived or valued as an expression of naked facts, but rather as an expression of the total reality of fact and meaning. What the reader of the history of the Chronicler needs is sensitivity to the method of writing history in biblical times together with some knowledge of the milieu in which the work came into existence, the need which it was intended to fill, and the audience to which it was addressed. The Chronicler's historical work — like the other historical books of the OT — is written with the intention of showing God's action in the history of His people from Adam to Cyrus' decree ending the Exile. This work was not written to convey all aspects of Israel's historical past, but rather to emphasize those points of past history that needed special attention in view of the religious, political, and social situation of the Chronicler's time, in order to maintain and further the theocracy and to encourage and foster faith.

VIII. Content and Purpose.–The book of Chronicles, which is the only book in Scripture covering a span of time from Adam to the returned exiles, is naturally divided into four parts. The first part (1 Ch. 1–9) is made up of various genealogies and lists that set the stage for the appearance of David and his dynasty. It legitimizes the Israelites as the lineal descendants of the chosen people of God and indicates that they are the center of God's plan of salvation for the world with other peoples or tribes being grafted into those chosen by God. Judah and his descendants come first in the genealogical history (2:3–4:23; cf. 5:1f.). Special attention is also given to Levi (ch. 6).

The second part (1 Ch. 10–29) opens with a short account of Saul's death (ch. 10) and deals with the central figure of the Chronicler's history, David, the ideal ruler of God's people (chs. 11–29). After David's capture of Jerusalem and the building up of his army (chs. 11f.) comes the detailed report of the bringing of the ark to Jerusalem (chs. 13–16). David is depicted as the organizer of elaborate temple services and staff (chs. 21–28). This is followed by a brief evaluation of David's reign (ch. 29).

The third part is devoted to the activities of Solomon (2 Ch. 1–9). Though his reign was more magnificent than his father's, he finished what his father had started and thus stands in the shadow of David. He prayed for special wisdom (ch. 1) and proceeded to prepare for the building of the temple (ch. 2). The plans for the temple (ch. 3), provisions for its equipment (ch. 4), and the dedication follow (chs. 5f.), with a divine admonition (ch. 7). The remainder of this part (chs. 8f.) deals with the various activities of Solomon. Solomon reflects wisdom and piety in his own right, though he carried out the directions of his father David. The unusual emphasis on temple, cult, and its functionaries clearly indicates the theocratic interest of the Chronicler, which was to have a significant role in postexilic times.

The last part (2 Ch. 10–36) gives a description of the division of the kingdom (ch. 10), which is followed by an account of the reigns of the kings, almost exclusively of Judah (11:1–36:22). The reports about Jehoshaphat (17:1–21:1), Hezekiah (chs. 29–32), and Josiah (chs. 34f.) receive much more attention than in the parallel accounts of Kings, because of the religious reforms of these kings. The reigns of the other kings are passed over quickly. 2 Chronicles ends with the destruction of Jerusalem (586 B.C.), but closes with the hopeful note (36:22f.)

of the release of the captive Jews in Babylon by the benevolent Cyrus (*ca.* 537 B.C.).

Undoubtedly the Chronicler had in view a purpose that grew out of the new historical situation of the postexilic community; the earlier canonical histories of his people did not speak to this situation. The intent and purpose of the Chronicler was not to write a comprehensive history of God's people by gathering together what his predecessors had not covered. He was selective in the material chosen and utilized that which best met the needs of his times and future generations. It is obvious that the Chronicler accepted the Deuteronomic theology of history, in which the doctrine of retribution has a variety of expressions. The genealogies (1 Ch. 1–9) list the families of David and Judah before those of the tribes that made up the rebellious northern kingdom. This indicates that the Chronicler was supremely interested in the realization of the theocracy among God's people. When they heeded the divine word, they prospered; when they neglected it, they met disaster (1 Ch. 10:13; 2 Ch. 14:5f.). The words of Jehoshaphat express this conviction: "Believe in the Lord your God, and you will be established; believe his prophets, and you will succeed" (2 Ch. 20:20). The fact that of 822 verses in 2 Chronicles, 480 deal with four pious kings (Solomon, chs. 1–9; Jehoshaphat, chs. 17–21; Hezekiah, chs. 29–32; Josiah, chs. 34f.) and 342 with seventeen others, shows that the emphasis is placed on those characteristics that bring God's blessing. Obedience to God's will and law was the duty of His people and the prerequisite for prosperity; disobedience could be expected to lead to disaster and ruin. An essential part of the people's faithfulness to God was manifested in their worship at the central sanctuary in Jerusalem, which was God's unique dwelling place. In line with his theocratic ideals, the Chronicler placed great emphasis on religious activities.

Whereas the Davidic dynasty and the temple were major features of the Chronicler's purpose, it had to be recognized that the people of God could engage in proper worship only if they had repented of their sins and found forgiveness from their merciful God (2 Ch. 7:14; 33:11-13). The Chronicler attempted to call his people to a wholehearted return to God, so that they could experience the happiness and peace that would come through the favor of God. Their God would give peace and relief from war (1 Ch. 22:8; 2 Ch. 14:6); if they were attacked, He would protect them (2 Ch. 20:1-30). The Chronicler's ideal for his people was peace. As his people turned to their God and as other nations followed, peace would reign among them.

It is evident that the Chronicler's stress of certain motifs is aimed at guiding the Israelite community of his day. He focuses on major leaders, events, and institutions of the past to draw lessons to guide God's true people in their decisions in the present and the future.

IX. Date and Authorship.–There is ample internal evidence to support the thesis that the Chronicler was responsible for both Chronicles and Ezra-Nehemiah (see II above). Thus in the matter of the date we must keep all four books in focus. This discussion, however, will stress only those matters that concern more directly the date of Chronicles. There has been sharp disagreement among scholars about the date of this work. Many have placed it in the Greek period either after 160 B.C. or *ca.* 200 B.C. (Pfeiffer, Torrey, Goettsberger, Noordtzij, Noth, Cazelles, etc.). A date near 300 B.C. or slightly earlier is asserted by others (R. Kittel, Curtis, de Vaux, van den Born, Herbert, Galling, Michaeli, etc.) on the basis that a later date is impossible because of the complete silence about the hellenizing of Judaism after Alexander the Great. Arguments for the late dating of Chronicles (and Ezra-Nehemiah) have been undermined by linguistic, archeological, and textual-critical evidence. Arguments for a late date based on so-called Greek loanwords (Torrey) had to be discarded, because it was shown that they were of Persian origin (Albright). The Aramaic of the Elephantine papyri, the ritual texts from Persepolis, and other finds have proven that the Aramaic sections of the Chronicler's work belong to Imperial (Official) Aramaic in vogue in the Persian period, and thus do not require a date later than *ca.* 400 B.C. Aramaic influence on the Hebrew of Chronicles can be expected in the Persian period and does not serve as a proof for a late origin of these books (Kropat, Rehm, Myers, etc.). The MS evidence of Qumrân has led scholars to a date for Chronicles of *ca.* 400 B.C. (Cross, Waltke, etc.). The unusually early date of *ca.* 515 B.C. (Freedman) for the basic work of the Chronicler, starting with 1 Ch. 10, is unacceptable on textual-critical and other grounds. If the Chronicler makes use of the distinctive Palestinian text family, one must allow some time to elapse before the Palestinian and Babylonian text families could branch off the Old Palestinian text-type, which is itself dated to the 5th cent. B.C.

A date of *ca.* 400 B.C. is supported by the Davidic genealogy of 1 Ch. 3:10-24, which is traced down through the successive generations from Jehoiachin's son Pediah to Anani son of Elioenai. The Jehoiachin Tablets (Weidner texts) indicate that Pediah must have been born *ca.* 595 B.C. (*ANET*, p. 308; *DOTT*, p. 85); and allowing for each generation an average of twenty-five years (Albright, Myers), we come down to *ca.* 405 B.C. for the birth of Anani. A certain Anani living in Jerusalem is mentioned in one of the Elephantine papyri dated to the last decade of the 5th cent. B.C. (*ANET,* p. 492). That this genealogy ends with Anani is a strong indication that the material was written down by the Chronicler at about that time. Thus an increasing number of scholars rightly favor a date for Chronicles in the later Persian period, or *ca.* 400 B.C. (Albright, Rothstein, van Selms, Rudolph, Myers, Ellison, Francisco, Fritsch, etc.). A traditional objection against an early date was based on the mention in 1 Ch. 29:7 of the "daric," which was earlier identified with the Greek "drachma." Recent archeological evidence has shown that during the reign of Darius I (522-486 B.C.) Persian gold coins, called "darics," were circulating throughout the Persian empire (Weingreen, *DOTT,* p. 232). This again supports a date in the later Persian period. According to all indications the most reasonable date of composition is *ca.* 400 B.C.

The identity of the Chronicler can be established primarily on the basis of internal evidence. It is reasonably certain that a single individual, rather than a circle or school, was responsible for authoring the Chronicles (cf. Noth, p. 111). This is evident from the literary mannerisms that characterize the narrative of Chronicles and Ezra-Nehemiah (see II above), and from the fact that while the Nehemiah memoirs show a marked stylistic individuality, the Ezra memoirs contain the same kind of literary mannerisms and linguistic peculiarities that are manifested in the remainder of the Chronicler's work. They also share the same ideological and theological emphasis, with the possible exception of the messianism. A number of studies have shown that, on the basis of the first person singular (Ezr. 7:28; 8:15-17, 21-29; 9:1-5) and the first person plural in passages that include travel companions (7:27; 8:17f., 21-23, 31f.), the Ezra memoirs are from Ezra himself. While one cannot prove conclusively that the Chronicler was indeed Ezra, the evidence definitely points in this direction, and an increasing number of scholars have made this identification (so Albright, Rothstein, van Selms, Myers, Fritsch, etc.). There is also a great amount of Jewish and non-Jewish tradition that identifies Ezra with the Chronicler (cf. Brunet, *DBSup.*, VI, 1228). Nevertheless, the internal evidence, corroborated by our increased understanding of the external history, provides the most cogent support for considering Ezra the best candidate for the authorship of these works.

X. Theology.–The Chronicler has provided us with a major historical work covering a span of time from Adam to the postexilic community of *ca.* 400 B.C. It is certain that this history rests on older reports and is written from the perspective of the postexilic community. That the historical situation out of which it arose was different from those of the earlier histories is reflected in the Chronicler's choice of materials and in his theological emphases. Therefore, Chronicles makes its own special contribution to the various witnesses that make up OT theology.

The Chronicler's picture of God is strictly monotheistic, an emphasis consistent with that of the other historical writings of the OT. The only God known is Yahweh, who is all-knowing (2 Ch. 16:9), all-powerful (1 Ch. 29:12; 2 Ch. 20:6), and universally present (2 Ch. 2:6). He is the world's supreme Ruler who "has power to help or to cast down" (2 Ch. 25:8). His reign is grounded in absolute knowledge, because He "understands every plan and thought" (1 Ch. 20:9). As the God of the patriarchs (2 Ch. 13:18), Yahweh shows His determined interest in His people Israel (1 Ch. 29:20; 2 Ch. 13:18; 15:12; 19:4; etc.). He is a God of love (2 Ch. 2:11; 9:8), and His "steadfast love" (Heb. *ḥesed̲*, used fifteen times in in Chronicles) is manifested in His having bound Himself by covenant to Israel. Thus He keeps His promises and shows Himself a helper in times of need, while at the same time He remains judge over both Israel and the nations (1 Ch. 16:33; 2 Ch. 4:23).

The election (Heb. *bāḥar*) motif also plays an important role in the theology of Chronicles. The Hebrew term appears twenty-one times in Chronicles, and of all OT writings appears more often only in Deuteronomy (thirty-one times). In all but four instances (1 Ch. 19:10; 2 Ch. 11:1; 13:3; 25:5) the election motif is a distinctly theological concept in which Yahweh is the subject. In Chronicles election through Yahweh never refers directly to the patriarchs, the beginnings of Israel at the Exodus, or the taking of Canaan, but is uniquely restricted to the choice of David for leadership (1 Ch. 28:4; 2 Ch. 6:6) and of his son Solomon (1 Ch. 28:6; 29:1) for the building of a house (temple) for Yahweh (1 Ch. 28:10; 29:1; cf. 2 Ch. 7:12, 16). Likewise, the election of Jerusalem as God's chosen city has great prominence (2 Ch. 6:5, 34, 38; 7:12, 16; 12:13; 33:7). The Chronicler links together the election of king, city, and temple with its cult personnel (1 Ch. 15:2; 29:1). The election of king and city seems subsumed under the election of the temple. A theocratic emphasis is apparent here. The community that worships at the Jerusalem sanctuary is Yahweh's people, and not those who worship at the sanctuary on Mt. Gerizim or the one on the Elephantine island, etc. Thus, the true Israel is not an ethnical people but those who worship together at God's chosen place with its legitimate sanctuary.

The pregnant term "covenant" (Heb. *b^erît̲*) appears a total of thirty times in Chronicles and indicates a prominent place for covenant theology. The covenant made with Abraham, Isaac, and Jacob was an "everlasting covenant to Israel" (1 Ch. 16:16f.). The covenant made at Sinai is not mentioned, but Israel is considered God's covenant people and is called by Yahweh "my people" (1 Ch. 11:2). The Chronicler records that David made a covenant with Israel at Hebron (1 Ch. 11:3) and that Jehoiada, Hezekiah, and Josiah renewed the covenant between Yahweh and people or king (2 Ch. 23:16; 29:10; 34:30-32). The "ark of Yahweh/God" is known as the "ark of the covenant of Yahweh/God" (1 Ch. 15:15, 26, 29; 16:6, 17; 17:1; 28:2, 18; 2 Ch. 5:2, 7). Josiah's reform was strengthened when the temple yielded "the book of the covenant" (=Dt.), which was read before the people (2 Ch. 34:30). God not only elected David (1 Ch. 28:4) but also entered into a covenant with him (2 Ch. 21:7) which is not renounced even though his offspring walked in wicked ways (vv. 6f.). The covenant promise to David that his royal throne will continue for ever (1 Ch. 22:10; cf. 17:17) seems unconditional (2 Ch. 13:5; 21:7), but is in reality conditioned by the fidelity of his offspring (6:16; 7:17-22). The Chronicler's aim was hardly to vindicate the Davidic covenant over that of Sinai, but to link the second temple with the first and to legitimize the true Israel as the one worshiping at the right place, namely, God's chosen city Jerusalem.

The promise to grant David continual progeny, to establish his lineage forever, and to have a temple built (1 Ch. 17) is a correlate of the Chronicler's covenant theology. The division of the united kingdom in 931 B.C., the exile of the northern kingdom in 722 B.C. and of the southern kingdom in 586 B.C., conjunction with the political, social, and religious situation of the Chronicler's own time, appear to have frustrated God's great promises. With fervency the Chronicler unmasks what provoked such regressions. The fall of the chosen city Jerusalem came as a result of abominable acts committed by the kings and the people (2 Ch. 36:5ff.). The political and religious leaders of Israel, and the people themselves, engaged in rebellion against their God until His anger was so inflamed that there was no other remedy (v. 16). Yet there is hope, says the Chronicler, because the God who punishes wickedness blesses right-doing (2 Ch. 12:1f.; 13:4ff.; 14:11ff.; 16:9; 19:2; 20:37; 21:10; 22:4ff.; etc.). The postexilic community is therefore challenged to be faithful to Yahweh. The word "unfaithful" is a key word in the Chronicler's theology (Koch, *TLZ*, 90 [1965], 663). The keeping of the Torah with all the moral and cultic injunctions assures faithfulness to Yahweh. While cultic-ritualistic matters are stressed, it would be wrong to depict the Chronicler as either a narrow ritualist or a narrow legalist. What is at stake is the life or death of the postexilic community, which can exist only as a theocratic community. Genuine worship, which involves body, soul, and spirit, is the concern of Hezekiah's prayer: "The good Lord pardons every one who sets his heart to seek God . . ., even though not according to the sanctuary's rules of cleanness" (2 Ch. 30:18f.). What counts is pure heart-religion in place of cold legalism.

Another major element of the theology of Chronicles is the concept of retribution. In retrospective vision the Chronicler shows the inner connections between evil and doom and between good and prosperity. That retribution is neither purely automatic nor simply mechanical is shown by the fact that the long reign of wicked Manasseh is explained on the basis that he humbled himself and repented (2 Ch. 33:10ff.). Retribution comes as punishment from the time of Saul (1 Ch. 10:13f.) to the fall of Jerusalem (2 Ch. 36:13ff.), and as reward in the promises given to David (1 Ch. 12f.) and Hezekiah (2 Ch.

30:8f.). It invariably comes in a short-term manner (2 Ch. 21:1ff.; 16:7ff.; 26:16ff.; 33:1ff.) and thereby signifies that each generation, and each individual in it, must face God, respond to His revealed will, stand responsible for its choice and acts. While God's love and justice demand that He punish wrongdoing, yet "his mercy is very great" (1 Ch. 21:13) and He is ever ready to forgive (2 Ch. 30:9). Indeed, God will listen to the prayers of men (2 Ch. 30:9; 32:24; 33:6, 12f.). Only He can bestow a heart that can live in harmony with His will (1 Ch. 29:19; 2 Ch. 30:12).

The Chronicler's special interest in cult and worship is evident everywhere. It has been noted already that he recognizes only one true sanctuary, the one planned by David (1 Ch. 22:1–28:19) and built by Solomon (2 Ch. 2:1–5:1). David is also the one who established the orders of cultic functionaries for the temple services. It is clear that the priesthood of the second temple is legitimized by establishing its continuity with that of the first temple. Since the postexilic community worshiped at the temple and not at a tent tabernacle, there was less need to look to Moses as the founder of the sanctuary and its priesthood, though Moses is by no means slighted or ignored (1 Ch. 5:27-41; 6:33f.; 2 Ch. 8:12-14; 23:17f.; 30:16; 34:4, 6, 12-15). David's plan or pattern for the temple is integrated with the work of Moses (Ex. 25:9, 40; 1 Ch. 28:11f., 18f.; 29:3f.). In a sense David is another Moses. Cultic unity is emphasized repeatedly by mentioning that Yahweh's temple is in Jerusalem (2 Ch. 3:1; 6:6; 30:1; 33:4, 7, 15; 36:14, 23), the only legitimate place of worship, chosen for this purpose by Yahweh Himself (2 Ch. 6:6; 7:12; cf. Dt. 12:5ff.; 14:23-25; 15:20; 16:2ff.; etc.). No other sanctuary is recognized or even mentioned. Of equal importance is cultic purity (2 Ch. 13:10; 23:16ff.; etc.). God's abiding presence in the midst of the postexilic community, its survival and prosperity, would depend on its maintaining cultic unity and cultic purity in the tradition of David's legitimation of the Jerusalem temple with its cultic functionaries as the center of the only true worship of Yahweh.

The messianism of the Chronicler's theology cannot be considered to consist of purely royal messianic hopes. The Chronicler's rendering of the famous Nathan oracle (cf. 2 S. 7:8-16) has a unique aspect. Yahweh promises: "I will confirm him [David] in my house and in my kingdom forever" (1 Ch. 17:14; cf. 2 S. 7:16). The kingdom is clearly Yahweh's and the promise seems unconditional. The word of Yahweh that later comes to Solomon through David is clearly related to the Nathan oracle: "I will establish his [Solomon's] royal throne in Israel forever" (1 Ch. 22:10). This royal throne is "the throne of the kingdom of the Lord over Israel" (28:5). The last two statements have no counterpart in Samuel–Kings and express the same idea as 29:23: "Then Solomon sat on the throne of the Lord as king" (cf. 1 K. 2:12). 2 Ch. 9:8 reflects a heightening of the messianic motif when the Queen of Sheba confesses that Yahweh set "you [Solomon] on his throne as king for the Lord your God" (cf. 1 K. 10:9). Both throne and kingdom are Yahweh's, but He has given them "in the hands of the sons of David" (2 Ch. 13:8). The unconditional nature of the promise (1 Ch. 17:14; 22:10; 2 Ch. 13:5) is in tension with the condition that both temple and royal lineage are dependent upon loyalty to the covenant (2 Ch. 7:17ff.; cf. 1 K. 9:1ff.).

It should be noted that the integration of the tasks of the prophet Moses with that of king David has a direct bearing on the Chronicler's messianism. Like Moses, David had the "pattern" (Heb. *tabnîṯ*) for the sanctuary/temple ready (Ex. 25:9, 40; 1 Ch. 28:11f., 18f.). David's call for a freewill offering again follows the custom of Moses (Ex. 25:1-9; 35:4-29; 1 Ch. 29:3f.). This pronounced confluence of motifs indicates that the future David would combine in his person both royal *and* priestly offices. The Chronicler's royal-priestly messianism is underscored by a quotation from a messianic Psalm (2 Ch. 6:42; cf. Ps. 132:9f.). The conditional aspect (2 Ch. 7:17ff.) of Yahweh's covenant with David (2 Ch. 21:7; 1 Ch. 17:3-16) had led to the end of the temporal rule of the Davidic dynasty through prolonged disloyalty and persistent unfaithfulness (2 Ch. 36:13-17); the unconditional aspect, on the other hand, remained in force and applied to the future rule of the royal-priestly Messiah. The motif of the throne and kingdom as Yahweh's indicates that He Himself would provide this royal-priestly Messiah in the future, as he had provided David in the past.

***Bibliography.**–Commentaries:* P. R. Ackroyd (*Torch,* 1973); I. Benzinger (*Kurzer Hand-Commentar zum AT,* 1901); A van den Born (*De Boeken van het OT,* 1960); H. Cazelles, *Les Livres des Chroniques* (2nd ed. 1961); R. J. Coggins (*CBC,* 1976); E. Curtis and A. Madsen (*ICC,* 1910); H. L. Ellison (*NBC,* 1970); W. A. L. Elmslie (*IB,* 1954); C. T. Francisco (*Broadman Biblical Comm.,* 1970); C. T. Fritsch (*Interpreter's One-Volume Comm.,* 1971); K. Galling (*ATD,* 1954); J. Goettsberger (*Die Heilige Schrift des AT,* 1939); A. S. Herbert (*Peake's Comm.,* 1962); R. Kittel (*Handkommentar zum AT,* 1902); F. Michaeli (*Comm. de l'AT,* 1967); J. Mulcahy (*New Catholic Comm.,* 1969); J. M. Myers (*AB,* 1965); A. Noordtzij (*Korte Verklaring,* 2 vols., 1957); R. North (*Jerome Biblical Comm.,* 1968); M. Rehm (*EB,* 1949); J. W. Rothstein and J. Hänel (*Kommentar zum AT,* 2 vols., 1927); W. Rudolph (*HAT,* 1955); A. van Selms (*TU,* 1939, 1947); I. W. Slotki (*Smith Bible Dictionary,* 1952).

Books: P. R. Ackroyd, *Age of the Chronicler* (1970); L. C. Allen, *The Greek Chronicles* (*SVT,* 25; 1974); W. Bayer, *Die Memoiren des Statthalters Nehemia* (1937); H. van der Bussche, *Het Probleem van Kronieken* (1950); R. le Déaut and J. Robert, *Targum des Chroniques* (2 vols., 1971); T. Denter, *Die Stellung der Bücher Esdras im Kanon des AT* (1962); G. Gerlemann, *Synoptic Studies in the OT* (1948); A. S. Kapelrud, *Question of Authorship in the Ezra-Narrative* (1944); A. Kropat, *Die Syntax des Authors der Chronik verglichen mit der seiner Quellen* (1909); W. E. Lemke, "Synoptic Studies in the Chronicler's History" (Dissertation, Harvard, 1964); R. Mosis, *Untersuchungen zur Theologie des chronistischen Geschichtswerkes* (1973); M. Noth *Überlieferungsgeschichtliche Studien* (1947); R. M. Polzin, *Late Biblical Hebrew: Toward An Historical Typology of Biblical Hebrew Prose* (1976); G. von Rad, *Das Geschichtsbild des chronistischen Werkes* (1930); M. Rehm, *Textkritische Untersuchungen zu den Parallelstellen der Samuel-Königsbücher und der Chronik* (1937); A. C. Sundberg, *OT of the Early Church* (1964); C. C. Torrey, *Ezra Studies* (1910); *Chronicler's History of Israel* (1954); A. C. Welch, *Work of the Chronicler. Its Purpose and Date* (1939); P. Welten, *Geschichte und Geschichtsdarstellung in den Chronikbüchern* (*WMANT,* 42, 1973); T. Willi, *Die Chronik als Auslegung* (*FRLANT,* 106, 1972).

Articles: P. R. Ackroyd, *Concordia Theological Monthly,* 38 (1967), 501-515; *Lexington Theological Quarterly,* 8 (1973), 101-116; W. F. Albright, *JBL,* 40 (1921), 104-124; L. C. Allen, *HTR,* 61 (1968), 483-491; A. Bea, *Bibl.,* 22 (1941), 46-58; G. J. Botterweck, *Theologische Quarterschrift,* 136 (1956), 402-452; R. L. Braun, *Concordia Theological Monthly,* 42 (1971), 502-514; A. M. Brunet, *RB,* 60 (1953), 481-508; 61 (1954), 349-386; *Sacra Pagina,* 1 (1959), 384-397; A. Caquot, *Revue de théologie et de philosophie,* 99 (1966), 110-120; F. M. Cross, Jr., *HTR,* 57 (1964), 281-299; *JBL,* 94 (1975), 4-18; *DBSup.,* VI, *s.v.* "Paralipomènes" (A. M. Brunet); E. L. Ehrlich, *Theologische Zeitschrift,* 21 (1965), 281-86; D. N. Freedman, *CBQ,* 23 (1961), 436-442; *IDB,* I, *s.v.* "Canon of the OT" and "Chronicles I and II" (R. H. Pfeiffer); S. Japhet, *VT,* 18 (1968), 330-371; P. Katz, *ZNW,* 47 (1956), 191-217; R. W. Klein, *HTR,* 60 (1967), 93-105; 61 (1968), 492-95; W. E. Lemke, *HTR,* 58 (1965), 349-365; F. L. Moriarty, *CBQ,* 27 (1965), 399-406; S. Mowinckel, *TLZ,* 85 (1960), 1-8; J. M. Myers, *Interp.,* 20 (1966), 259-273; R. North, *JBL,* 82 (1963), 369-381; *CBQ,* 28 (1966), 519-524; L. Randellini, *Revista Biblica,* 10 (1962), 136-155;

H. N. Richardson, *JBR*, 26 (1958), 9-12; J. D. Shenkel, *HTR*, 62 (1969), 63-85; W. F. Stinespring, *JBL*, 80 (1961), 209-219; B. K. Waltke, "The Samaritan Pentateuch and the Text of the OT," in J. B. Payne, ed., *New Perspectives on the OT* (1970), pp. 212-239; J. W. Wenham, *Tyndale Bulletin*, 18 (1967), 19-53.

G. F. HASEL

CHRONOLOGY OF THE OT.

I. Introduction.–A. Issues. The field of OT chronology has benefited from a wealth of discoveries and investigations during the past fifty years. Many points that were obscure and that scholars had despaired of ever fully understanding have been clarified to the satisfaction of the great majority. Where previously certain questions could be answered only on the basis of philosophical a prioris and conjectures, there is now a mass of factual data from which an answer may be fortified. This is not to say, however, that no difficulties remain. The new evidence has raised several new questions, and, while making it possible to give more informed answers to the original questions, has by no means settled every issue. If nothing else, it has multiplied several fold the complexity of the subject.

Several difficulties are inherent in the subject itself. By definition, a chronology attempts to relate certain events on an absolute temporal scale. The key questions are quantitative: how much, how long, etc. The Bible, on the other hand, is interested in qualitative questions. Much more important than how long a man lived is how well he lived. The purpose is to make plain the inner meaning of history as opposed to a listing of all events that took place. Thus, giving a well-rounded summary of the political history of the Levant, or even of Palestine, is no part of the Bible's concern. It wishes to detail the relation of a people to its God and to show the inevitable effect *in history* of the character of that relationship. Therefore, those who would construct a chronology of the OT must continually remember that by and large OT writers had only a secondary interest in chronology.

Does this mean that — as maintained by Wellhausen and his followers — the chronological information given in Scripture is worthless? Is it simply window dressing to enhance the verisimilitude of the historical vehicle that the Hebrews chose to express their faith? It does not mean this, and for two reasons. The first is a logical one. That chronology was a secondary interest for the writers of Scripture does not necessarily imply that they gave no concern to the accuracy of the data they did use. It only means that they may have used the data differently from those for whom it was of interest. The very claim of the Hebrews that they had met God in history would suggest that they took a very careful attitude toward historical data.

The second reason why the chronological data of Scripture should be considered valuable, when rightly interpreted, is the continuing scientific evidence of this value. Again and again during the past fifty years the accuracy of scriptural information has been verified. The most impressive example of this is seen in the work of E. R. Thiele on the records of the kings of Israel and Judah. These numbers had long defied any kind of harmonization, both among themselves and with extra-biblical literature. This fact had been adduced as evidence of the fictionalized nature of the accounts. But Thiele, by a process described below, has shown that this harmonization is possible. More importantly, it is possible only because of the uncanny accuracy of the recorded figures.

Thiele's work has demonstrated another principle that is often only reluctantly granted in the study of Scripture. This is that the statements of Scripture shall — until proven otherwise — be regarded as correct and as being capable of harmonization with the data from other spheres of investigation. This assumption will result in work like Thiele's, which will undertake, not to *prove* Scripture, but to understand the ways in which it corresponds to truth in other areas. K. A. Kitchen has shown that this is the approach scholars of the ancient Near East ordinarily take toward their texts. Ironically, in part because of the destructive criticism of the 19th and 20th cents., the opposite tendency is manifested in biblical studies, where a skeptical attitude is taken toward every scriptural statement until it is rigorously proven to be correct. This means that the energies of many scholars are spent in the direction of proving their assumption, with the result that much scholarship continues to fragment and reconstruct the Bible. Since the assumption in large part determines the approach, it is imperative that the student of OT chronology hold the appropriate assumption.

B. Methodology. Thus the correct methodology for OT chronology is twofold.

(1) It is first of all to seek the biblical key to the interpretation of each piece of data. Modern attitudes toward chronology and chronological data will not always suffice. Whereas one number in the biblical record may be literally exact, as in the case of the royal annals, another may be a general term, as in the use of the numbers 40, 7, etc. Even when the numbers are literal, it may take an understanding of the rationale by which records are kept (as it did for Thiele) before they can be organized into a consistent scheme.

The key to interpretation varies according to the type of data that are being examined. There are three types of chronological data in the OT, all somewhat interrelated. First is genealogical information. Typically the material gives lines of descent (cf. Gen. 10; 1 Ch. 1:1–9:21; etc.). However, at certain points — and especially in the patriarchal accounts — chronological information is included in the genealogy. This will often include the father's age at the birth of his firstborn son, as well as his age at death.

Two factors have become increasingly clear for the interpretation of genealogies. First is the fact that commonly all persons in a given lineage are not included. The classic example of this is found in the first chapter of Matthew, where Jesus' genealogy is given as three successions of fourteen generations. The first section (Abraham to David) corresponds to 1 Ch. 2:3-16. However, the second section (David to the fall of Jerusalem) leaves out four generations: the three generations relating to Jezebel's daughter Athaliah, and one generation at the end, which makes Josiah the father of Jehoiachin instead

CHRONOLOGY OF THE OT

of grandfather (1 Ch. 3:10-16). An example of this phenomenon is found in the OT when four generations from Levi to Moses are said to cover the entire Egyptian sojourn, which was apparently some three hundred to four hundred years in duration (1 Ch. 6:1-3) (see III.A below). It is evident that in ancient Near Eastern parlance, speaking of someone as father of someone else meant only that he was ancestor of that person. Thus, David speaks of both Saul and Jonathan as being the father of Mephibosheth (2 S. 9:7). This means that one cannot hope to achieve a reliable chronology simply by picking a certain number of years per generation and multiplying that number by the number of generations in a given genealogy.

The second factor to be borne in mind when interpreting genealogical lists is the secondary character of any numbers attached to the list. It is clear that the primary function of genealogy in the Near East has always been to establish a person's or family's identity. With regard to this purpose chronology has no importance. This can be seen in the genealogies of 1 Chronicles, where the returnees from Babylon were attempting to recover their legitimate positions in the history of their people. No chronological references are found. Another indication of the secondary nature of chronology is the fact that no use is made of references when they occur. They are not totaled or otherwise used for establishing chronological relationships. This is not to say that the numbers are of random choice and thus of no significance; but it is to say that they perhaps do not have exact numerical significance as demanded by the modern West.

The same observation applies to a second class of data: random chronological statements, e.g., the statement in Gen. 15:13 concerning the duration of the Egyptian sojourn, or that in 1 K. 6:1 covering the time elapsed between the Exodus and the building of Solomon's temple. While there is no warrant for disregarding such statements, neither is it necessary to assume that they are precise chronological computations. In the premonarchical society especially, long-term chronological records are highly unlikely because of their lack of importance. Rather, approximations arrived at in various ways can be expected, and the use of round numbers, particularly, would suggest some degree of approximation. It is the significance of these numbers for the biblical writers that the interpreter must understand before he attempts to build an absolute chronology upon them.

The third class of chronological data is the numbers found in connection with royal annals or chronicles. This was one of the common methods by which a relative chronology for the dating of business and administrative documents could be achieved. All events during a given ruler's reign were dated from his first, or accession, year. The significance of these numbers then was primary and there is every reason, *prima facie,* to believe that they would have been kept with a high degree of exactness. Thiele's work, as mentioned above, supplies clear confirmation of this.

(2) The student of OT chronology must also avail himself of extrabiblical materials if he wishes to establish the dating of biblical events on an absolute scale with reference to the birth of Christ. One may learn the relative relations among, e.g., Rehoboam, Ahab, and Jehu from study of Scripture alone. However, that study cannot clearly establish their dates since their relative chronology is not keyed to any event, astronomical or terrestrial, which can be placed on the present absolute scale. What must be done, then, is to locate synchronisms with neighboring cultures whose events can be dated absolutely.

Larsa king list, which summarizes the dates of the Larsa Dynasty (1932-1763 B.C.) by totaling the date formulas of each king. It is dated from the 39th year of Hammurabi. (Trustees of the British Museum; photo W. S. LaSor)

Fortunately there are a number of such synchronisms with Mesopotamia during the 1st millennium B.C., which make it possible to give an absolute date at least as far back as the death of Solomon in 931 B.C. In the 2nd millennium only one extrabiblical reference is known, and it is, indeed, the first extant reference to Israel outside of the Bible. This is a reference to a defeat of Israel by Merneptah, pharaoh of Egypt, in 1224. Since the Bible mentions no such defeat, the reference is not helpful for establishing an absolute date earlier than that of Solomon. This means that prior to the kingdom period all biblical dating must be computed from within Scripture, without specific external evidence against which to check results. This counsels a caution that is often lacking among scholars of all theological leanings.

A word is in order concerning the methods used to establish an absolute date for events among Israel's neighbors and the reliability of these methods. Normally this is based on some datable astronomical event that is clearly located in that people's (Egypt's or Mesopotamia's) relative chronology. Thus, if a lunar eclipse is reported in the fourth year of a certain king, it is possible to discover in what year B.C. such an eclipse would have occurred in that area of the world and thus to give an absolute date to that king's fourth year. In addition, since the annals of both Egypt and Mesopotamia are complete for a considerable length of time, it is possible to apply the absolute dating backwards and forwards over many years. By the use of these methods and

CHRONOLOGY OF THE OT

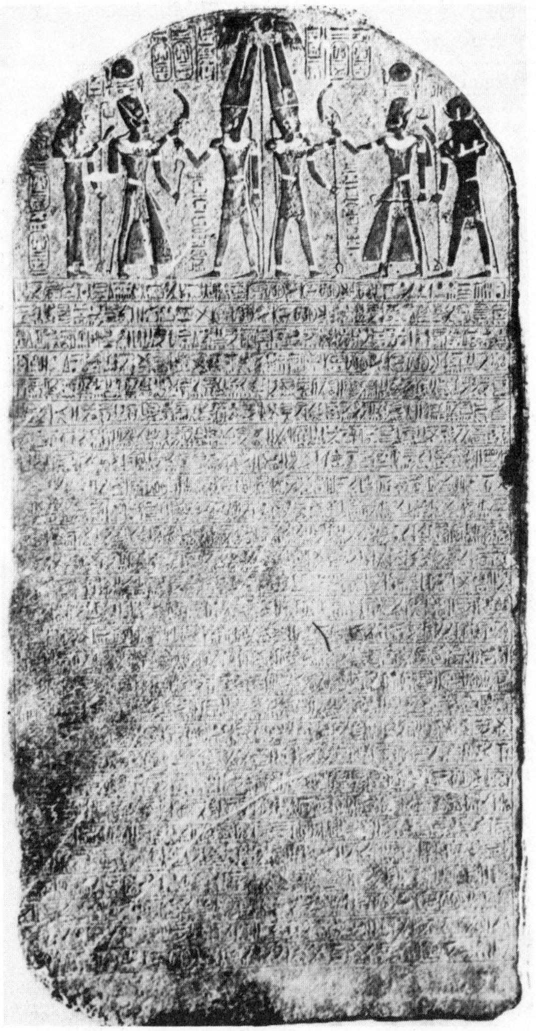

Victory stele of Merneptah with a hymn (or series of hymns) commemorating the pharaoh's defeat of the Libyans and Asiatic peoples. The boast that "Israel is laid waste and has no seed" (line 27) is the only mention of the name Israel in all ancient Egyptian writing. (Oriental Institute, University of Chicago)

with the occurrence of synchronisms between the two areas, it is generally agreed that it is possible to give an absolute date, plus or minus five years, for the major extrabiblical rulers and events into the latter half of the 2nd millennium B.C.

II. Adam to Abraham.–The date of creation is fraught with numerous problems. The first date to be widely accepted was 4004 B.C., which Archbishop Ussher advocated in his *Annales Veteris et Novi Testamenti,* and which was printed in the margins of many editions of the AV. Ussher arrived at this date through addition of the various numbers given in the Bible, especially those in the genealogies. This position is still held, although with some modification, by significant numbers of Christians. However, there are serious weaknesses in Ussher's argument. While his date of *ca.* 2000 B.C. for Abraham is within the range of probability, the dates prior to Abraham become increasingly difficult. Though it is perhaps not impossible that the high cultures of Mesopotamia and Egypt could have appeared within 1000 years of Creation (*ca.* 3500 and 3200 B.C., respectively), it is well-nigh impossible for the Flood to have occurred in 2348, as Ussher claimed. This would have been during the Akkadian empire in Mesopotamia and the Old Kingdom in Egypt. No such cataclysm as the Flood is even mentioned. This suggests that however the genealogies and their accompanying numbers are to be handled, they are not to be taken as a literal, lineal chain without breaks.

As noted above, it would be surprising if the genealogies were complete. Clear evidence of at least one such gap is found in Gen. 11:13, where Cainan is excluded from the MT, but included in the LXX between Arpachshad and Shelah. The LXX version of the genealogy is quoted by Luke (3:36), lending weight to its authenticity. Once it is admitted that there are gaps in the genealogy, there is no way to ascertain the amount of time that elapsed between Adam and Abraham, especially in view of the extraordinary longevity that is ascribed to the ANTEDILUVIAN PATRIARCHS.

It has been noted on numerous occasions that an interesting parallel to Gen. 5:3ff. exists in the Sumerian king list (cf. *ANET*, pp. 265f.), where reigns of fantastic length (tens of thousands of years) are recorded before "the flood" and reigns of reduced length afterward. Albright suggested that the same principle was operative in both cultures. Possessed of a royal or genealogical list that supposedly reached to the beginning of time and yet contained only a relatively few names, each culture — instead of supplying fictitious names to fill the gaps — lengthened the lives of those whose names they had, thus giving a more satisfactory length of time. He attributed the much higher Mesopotamian figures to the fact that the evidences of many previous cultures caused the Mesopotamians to posit creation much farther back in time. The Hebrews, lacking such evidence, were satisfied with smaller figures. Whether or not Albright's suggestion is correct, it does appear that the list of ancestors has been made to conform to an artificial scheme. With the insertion of Cainan in Gen. 11:13 there are ten names on each side of the Flood. This is reminiscent of the genealogy of Jesus in Matthew with its three groups of fourteen names.

In addition to the above considerations, the variations in the numbers in Gen. 5 and 11 as found in the MT, LXX, and Sam. Pent., indicate that extreme caution should be exercised in the use of these numbers. The total years from Adam to Abraham differ in each case, with the MT giving 1948, the Sam. Pent. 2249, and the LXX 3314. As can be seen by reference to Table 1, the variations are largely accounted for by the fact that the LXX, with few exceptions, adds a hundred years to the MT version of a man's age when his successor is born. The Sam. Pent. does this after the Flood, but not before. Numerous other, less schematic variations occur; e.g., on Lamech all the figures differ. While it appears that the MT contains the original numeration, the very fact that such sweeping extrapolations could occur in the LXX and Sam. Pent. traditions speaks of the secondary character of the numbers.

Recent archeological studies in the Near East suggest that the first indications of sedentary life in that area are to be dated between 9000 and 7000 B.C. In addition, the oldest known city, Jericho, is dated to this period. These computations are based on nuclear techniques whose uncorroborated results beyond 3000 or 4000 B.C. must be used with some caution. However, if these dates are approximately correct, then the developments of Gen. 4:17-22 would span the years 9000-5000 B.C. (assuming v. 22 to refer to the rudiments of metalworking). Generally it seems clear that the antediluvian society fits best into this timespan, which arche-

TABLE 1
AGES OF THE PATRIARCHS

Name	Age at Son's Birth			Remainder of Life			Age at Death		
	MT	LXX	SAM.	MT	LXX	SAM.	MT	LXX	SAM.
Adam	130	230	130	800	700	800	930	930	930
Seth	105	205	105	807	707	807	912	912	912
Enosh	90	190	90	815	715	815	905	905	905
Kenan	70	170	70	840	740	840	910	910	910
Mahalel	65	165	65	830	730	830	895	895	895
Jared	162	162	62	800	800	785	962	962	962
Enoch	65	165	65	300	200	300	365	365	365
Methuselah	187	167	67	782	802	653	868	969	720
Lamech	182	188	53	595	565	600	777	753	653
Noah	500	500	500	450	450	450	950	950	950
Shem	100	100	100	500	500	500			600
Arpachshad	35	135	135	403	430	303			438
Cainan		130			330				
Shelah	30	130	130	403	330	303			433
Eber	34	134	134	430	370	370			404
Peleg	30	130	130	209	209	109			239
Reu	32	132	132	207	207	107			239
Serug	30	130	130	200	200	100			230
Nahor	29	79	79	119	129	69			148
Terah	70	70	70				205	205	145
(Plus 2 years, Gen. 11:10)									
Total	1948	3314	2249						

ologists designate the Neolithic and Early Chalcolithic periods. As far as the dating of the Flood is concerned, if the lists are correct in placing Noah about midway between Abraham and Adam, then perhaps the Flood should be dated in the 7th or 6th millennium B.C. However, such a date is highly conjectural, since archeological evidence for the Flood is somewhat contradictory.

III. Abraham to the Conquest.–This period contains some of the most vigorously contested dates in the OT. The major controversy involves the date of the Exodus. Secondarily, the length of the Egyptian sojourn is a matter of debate. Once satisfaction is obtained on these issues, most of the other problems can be settled with a minimum of difficulty.

Two items of information in Scripture would seem to make these problems very simple. The first appears in 1 K. 6:1 where it is said that Solomon's temple was begun 480 years after the Exodus. Since this was *ca.* 967 (see below), the Exodus would be dated *ca.* 1447. In addition, Gen. 15:15 records God's prediction to Abraham that his descendants would be slaves and sojourners in a land not their own for 400 years. Ex. 12:40 seems to confirm this when it reports that the people of Israel dwelt in Egypt 430 years. Assuming the latter to be more exact, one arrives at a date of 1877 for the descent into Egypt. Then, by adding Jacob's age at the entry into Egypt (130 years, Gen. 47:9), Isaac's age at Jacob's birth (60 years, Gen. 25:26), and Abraham's age at Issac's birth (100 years, Gen. 21:5), the sum of 2167 B.C. is reached for the date of Abraham's birth.

A. Egyptian Sojourn. These figures, however, are beset by several problems. First of all, it is interesting to note that the LXX and the Sam. Pent. agree in reading the 430 years of Ex. 12:40 as applying to the whole time span between Abraham and the Exodus. (Cf. also Gal. 3:17, where Paul accepts the LXX dating.) This would suggest a date of 1952 for Abraham's birth and about 1852 for Isaac's birth. Even further reduction of these dates has often been called for because many of the genealogies between the descent into Egypt and the Exodus contain only a few generations. Best known is that of Moses and Aaron, which contains but four generations (Ex. 6:16-20). In this respect, it is worth noting that Gen. 15:16 follows up the statement in v. 13 of a 400-year sojourn with the declaration that "they will come back here in the fourth generation."

Albright attempted to resolve the obvious difficulty by arguing that the Hebrew word *dôr* actually means "cycle," and that the meaning "generation" is secondary. Thus, "four *dôr*" could mean four lifetimes, or four centuries (cf. Akk. *dâru*, a fifty-year cycle). Whether or not this resolution is valid is a moot point. At any rate, the combination of evidence has led several scholars who also accept a late date for the Exodus to posit a fifteenth- or sixteenth-century date for Abraham. However, it is significant that the genealogies of such figures as Bezalel and Joshua have considerably more entries (seven, 1 Ch. 2:18ff.; twelve, 1 Ch. 7:23-27, respectively). If no gap occurs in these lists, they would suggest a minimum of 250-350 years. If one does not allow for gaps in the genealogy of Moses and Aaron, he is forced to discredit Chronicles. The suggestion that Chronicles supplies fictional generations to correspond to the traditional 400-year figure seems excessively skeptical at this point.

At one time it was believed that the AMRAPHEL of Gen. 14 was Hammurabi (now dated 1792-1750, *CAH*). If this were so, it would be an invaluable synchronism. It does appear that Hammurabi extended his control as far west as the Mediterranean, but there is no evidence that he campaigned in Canaan. Beyond this, there are some yet-to-be-resolved difficulties in the correspondencies between the two names.

Another question involving the length of the Egyptian sojourn deals with the period of HYKSOS control. At present the Hyksos dynasties in Egypt are dated from 1786 to 1575. It is very tempting to equate Joseph's rise to power with the early years of these Semitic "shepherd-kings." It has often been pointed out that the Egyptian political system was an open one in which men of any class could rise to the top. Nonetheless, it would be very odd for a Semite to become vizier or prime minister under a native-born Egyptian ruler. This would not be at all odd, however, if the ruler were of Semitic extraction himself. According to this hypothesis, the king "who knew not Joseph" would be Amenhotep I, the founder of the 18th Dynasty, who destroyed the last vestiges of Hyksos power in the Delta, reestablishing Egyptian control. It is logical that he would subjugate any Semites remaining in the land for fear that they would constitute a "fifth column" (Ex. 1:10). If one assumes a date of 1447 for the Exodus, this would allow a maximum of 339 years for the sojourn and would put the birth of Abraham *ca.* 2076 B.C. A late date of *ca.* 1275 for the Exodus, and a maximum of 430 years for the sojourn, would yield 1705 for the descent into Egypt and 1995 for the birth of Abraham. With the late date, only the maximum-length sojourn would place Amenhotep I after Joseph's death. Abandoning the Hyksos equation and using the LXX chronology brings Abraham's birth down to 1780 and Joseph's death (Gen. 50:26) to *ca.* 1420. Thus, it seems likely that the birth of Abraham could be placed with some degree of confidence between 2100 and 1800 B.C. Recent archeological and historical studies tend to support this conclusion.

B. Exodus. As is clear from the preceding discussion, the issues surrounding the date of the Exodus are extremely complex. Since the date is pivotal for the chronology both before and after the event, and since in recent years a great deal of archeological evidence has been brought to bear on the discussion, it has received a considerable amount of scholarly attention. At the present time there are basically two points of view, whose conclusions have been mentioned above. The early date, sometime in the last half of the 15th cent., is based almost entirely on the figure given in 1 K. 6:1. The late date, sometime in the first half of the 13th cent., is based largely upon the conclusions of archeologists.

What evidence has led archeologists to conclude that the figure of 480 years between the founding of the temple in 967 and the Exodus is too long? Essentially, the evidence is twofold. Just before World War II, Nelson Glueck did an extensive surface survey of Transjordan. He concluded that the area's population during the pre-Christian millennia had been marked by cycles of growth and decline. According to his findings, whereas the 13th cent. had seen a significant population, there were very few inhabitants during the 14th and 15th centuries. This would seem to indicate that the encounters between the Hebrews and the various Transjordanian peoples as reported in the Pentateuch could not have taken place during the earlier centuries.

The second category of evidence concerns the destruction levels that appear in the excavations of numerous Canaanite cities. The excavators commonly note that beneath these levels is an identifiable Canaanite culture, sophisticated and technically competent, while above them is a much cruder level of culture. Since many of these are cities of which the book of Joshua reports the capture (Debir, Lachish, Eglon, Bethel, Hazor, etc.), it has seemed logical to assume that these strata are those of the Israelite takeover. In each case the levels have been dated to the 13th century. At the same time, the re-excavation of Jericho has raised serious questions concerning the validity of Garstang's claim to have found evidence of a fourteenth- or fifteenth-century destruction of that city.

In addition to these claims, there is at least one piece of biblical evidence which seems to support the late date. This is the statement that Hebrew slaves helped to build the Egyptian cities of Raamses and Pithom (Ex. 1:11; cf. also Gen. 47:11). Raamses is apparently the Pi-ramses of Egyptian texts, which Seti I (1309-1291) founded and which Ramses II (1290-1224) completed. If this is correct, the Hebrews were still in Egypt in 1300 B.C. Since the Merneptah stele has Israel in the land by 1224, it would appear that the Exodus took place sometime between 1300 and 1265, assuming the tradition of the forty-year wilderness period to be substantially correct.

Against this line of reasoning stands the plain statement of 1 K. 6:1 that there were 480 years between the Exodus and the building of the temple. If the reasoning is correct, how can that figure be explained? Commonly, it is seen as a round figure, the sum of twelve generations of forty years each. The presence of the two stock numbers, twelve and forty, is enough to create some presumption in favor of this explanation. Although there is no direction in the text that the number should be interpreted as an approximation, neither is there any evidence that the Hebrew people during the judges period had any need for, or any inclination to keep, an exact overall chronology. What the figure may well represent is a schematization based upon an estimate of the number of years involved in the work of the various judges.

On the other hand, is there evidence that argues for a literal interpretation? It is not enough to claim that any other interpretation destroys biblical authority, for interpreting the genealogies as other than literal does not destroy the integrity of Scripture. Yet many who would demand a literal interpretation of this number are strong adherents of "gap" genealogy. There is some significant evidence, as collected by L. T. Wood. Within the Bible an independent witness appears in Jgs. 11:26, where Jephthah says to the Ammonite king that Israel has the right of adverse possession to the Ammonite territory since it has dwelt in that land unmolested for 300 years. Since Jephthah was yet to be succeeded by several judges (see below), this figure would seem to agree well with a 480-year period. Again, however, it may be asked whether this is not a round figure perhaps consciously exaggerated in support of Jephthah's claims.

With reference to Ex. 1:11 it has been argued that the cities the Hebrews helped to build have not yet been positively identified. It is possible to contend that the cities were actually built long before Ramses' time and only renamed by him in honor of himself. That this was Ramses' practice is certainly true. In that case the more recent names have been added by a later editor.

Several important questions have been raised concerning the archeological evidence. The first has to do with the accuracy of the late Prof. Glueck's interpretations. Excavations at Amman by G. L. Harding appear to have shown sedentary occupation there during the Hyksos period. While it may be said that this is only one site, nonetheless it demonstrates the need for confirmation of Glueck's conclusions through excavation and re-evaluation before other, more far-reaching conclusions are made dependent upon them.

Secondly, the evidence for Israelite destruction of the Canaanite cities in the 13th cent. is not as overwhelming as it has sometimes been made to seem. In the first place, only two of the cities are conclusively identified: Lachish and Hazor. While the majority of scholars still accept Albright's identification of Tell Beit Mirsim with DEBIR, it has come under increasing question recently. Whether Tell el-Ḥesī is identical with Eglon is more questionable, and the situation concerning BETHEL is fraught with a number of difficulties,

Table 2
Abraham to the Conquest

	Exodus at Early Date: MT	Exodus at Early Date: LXX	Exodus at Late Date: MT	Exodus at Late Date: LXX	Contemporary Events
	Abraham born 2167				
2100					Ur III period 2110-2000
	Isaac born 2067				
2000	Jacob born 2007		Abraham born 1995		Isin-Larsa period 2000-1800
		Abraham born 1952			Middle Kingdom 2000-1780
1900	Descent 1877		Isaac born 1895		
		Isaac born 1852	Jacob born 1835		
1800	Slavery (?) 1786	Jacob born 1792			Hammurabi 1792-1750
				Abraham born 1780	Hyksos in Delta 1780
1700			Descent 1705		
		Descent 1662		Isaac born 1680	
1600				Jacob born 1620	
	Beginning of Slavery (?) 1575		Slavery (?) 1575		Hyksos expelled 1575
1500				Descent 1490	Thutmose 1490-1436
	Exodus 1447				
1400	Conquest 1407				
					Akhenaten 1367-1350
1300	Judges period				Raamses and Pithom (?) Ramses II 1290-1224
			Exodus 1280 (?) Conquest 1240 (?)		
1200					

one of which is the assumption that this was the city destroyed when the Bible speaks of Ai (Josh. 7:1–8:29).

Beyond this, a careful examination of the biblical records may suggest other solutions. Hazor was twice destroyed, first by fire sometime in the 15th cent. B.C. (Josh. 11:11?), and second without fire in the 13th cent. (Josh. 4:1, 17?). After the latter, Hazor was of little significance for several centuries. If this was Joshua's destruction, whence came Jabin of Jgs. 4:2? Added to this is the fact that Joshua's destruction specifically involved fire, which this second one did not. In contrast to this, it appears that Joshua did not burn Debir and Lachish (Josh. 10:31f., 38f.). This impression is strengthened by Josh. 11:13, which, while referring primarily to the northern campaign, may well indicate that Joshua's normal policy was not to burn captured cities unless they

CHRONOLOGY OF THE OT

had taken specific offensive action against him. In any case, both Debir and Lachish were burned in the 13th century. If it is true that Joshua did not burn these cities, then these destructions may be laid to the upheavals of the judges period.

The question still unanswered in these discussions is the weight of evidence that Canaanite culture continued undisturbed on these sites until the 13th cent., when it was replaced by Israelite culture. If this conclusion be judged correct, and a fifteenth-century conquest is still maintained, then serious thought must be given to the interpretation of the standard statement (e.g., Josh. 11:32) that the Hebrews destroyed every inhabitant of the cities which they captured.

As far as Egyptian history is concerned, either date is a possibility. It would seem that the late date might find more support, but this is far from conclusive. If the Exodus occurred in 1447, the great conqueror of Palestine, Thutmose III, would have been the pharaoh of the Exodus and Amenhotep II would have been ruling at the time of the conquest. At one time the heresy of Akhenaten and the Habiru incursions in Palestine were urged in support of the early date. Akhenaten's movement was seen as the result of Moses' monotheism and the Habiru were identified with the biblical Hebrews. However, there is now evidence to indicate that Akhenaten was the result of a long development within Egypt, and HABIRU, instead of being an ethnic title, has been shown to be a class appellation which was used throughout the Near East. In opposition to the early date, it has been pointed out that only during the 19th Dynasty was the capital in the north (in Memphis), where the Exodus narrative seems to place it. In addition, it is odd that Ramses II, who claims to have made several campaigns in Syro-Palestine and lists extensively the peoples he encountered and attacked, makes no mention of Israel if they had been established in the land for some two hundred years. If the late date be assumed, then Ramses was pharaoh of both the Exodus and the Conquest. In this case it is understandable that he would not have mentioned a people whose God had defeated him so soundly in his own land. Only his successor, Merneptah (who seems not to have been Ramses' firstborn son), was enough removed from the actual events to make the first extrabiblical mention of Israel.

In the light of the above discussion, it can be seen that a dogmatic stance on either date is inappropriate at this time. The case for the late date is perhaps slightly stronger, but not as strong as it is sometimes made to seem, and until some of the questions raised above have been answered, caution is dictated. Table 2 presents in graphic form the alternatives discussed in this section.

IV. Conquest to the Division of the Kingdom.–The dates of the latter part of this period, particularly the reigns of David and Solomon, are reasonably secure because the date of Shishak's raid — which took place five years after Solomon's death — can be fixed rather closely. However, the early part is confused because of the uncertainty surrounding the date of the Conquest. Depending on that decision, the period extends from *ca.* 1407 or *ca.* 1240 to 931 B.C., either 476 years or 310 years in length.

A. Judges. The major issue is the extent of overlapping in the terms of the various judges. As Table 3 shows, it is impossible in either case simply to add the numbers of years, as if the terms were consecutive. Even a minimal period of twenty years of Joshua and the elders (Jgs. 2:7) and ten years for Saul would push the total over 580. This means that adherents of the early date must reduce the total by about 125 years, while those who advocate the late date must divide it nearly in half.

TABLE 3
TERMS OF THE JUDGES AND THE OPPRESSORS

Judges	Oppressors	Terms	
Joshua and the elders, Jgs. 2:7		a	
	Cushan-Rishathaim, 3:8	8	
Othniel (Caleb), 3:11		40	(LXX 50)
	Eglon, 3:14	18	
Ehud (Benjamin), 3:30		80	
Shamgar (Judah or Naphtali?), 3:31		b	
	Jabin and Sisera, 4:3	20	
Deborah and Barak (Ephraim), 5:31 (Troops from Zebulun and Naphtali)		40	
	Midianites, 6:1	7	
Gideon (Manasseh), 8:28 (Troops from Manasseh, Asher, Zebulun, and Naphtali)		40	
	(Abimelech, 9:22)	3	
Tola (Issachar), 10:2		23	
Jair (Gilead), 10:3		22	
	Philistines and Ammonites, 10:8	18	
Jephthah (Gilead), 12:7		6	
Ibzan (Judah), 12:9		7	
Elon (Zebulun), 12:11		10	
Abdon (Ephraim?), 12:14		8	
	Philistines, 13:1	40	
Samson (Dan), 16:31		20	
Eli (Levi [shiloh]), 1 S. 4:8		40	(LXX 20)
Samuel (Ephraim), 7:2, 15		20?	
Saul, 13:1; Acts 13:21		c	
David, 1 K. 2:11		40	
Solomon, 11:42		40	
		Total 550 (plus a, b, & c)	

However, the kinds of reduction mentioned above are not as difficult as they seem. First, there are many round figures, usually multiples or fractions of forty, used in the list. No less than eleven of these are found, totalling 420 years. Obviously, these numbers may be compressed. In addition to this, it may be that 1 S. 7:2 intends to convey the total number of years between the depositing of the ark at Abinadab's house and David's removal of it to Jerusalem. This would subtract nearly fifty years from the total and compress Saul's reign to ten or twelve years. Normally the verse has been taken to indicate the time span between the return of the ark and Samuel's gathering the people at Mizpah.

Second, examination of the geographical areas in which the various judges operated shows that they were often active in localized territories within the land. Thus, Othniel and Shamgar seem to have been in the south, while Ehud was operating in the central highlands. Deborah, Barak, Gideon, and Tola moved in Ephraim and the north, Jair and Zephthah made their bases in the Transjordan, whereas Ibzan, Elon, Abdon, and Samson rather completely quartered the west side of the Jordan. Thus, judges who are listed consecutively could well have been active contemporaneously.

Further evidence is probably found in the treatment of Shamgar (3:31), who apparently operated during Ehud's judgeship, and Abimelech (9:22), whose abortive kingship may have overlapped with Tola (10:1). In addition, Jgs. 10:7 probably points to an overlapping of the Philistine and Ammonite oppressions (cf. 13:1).

Tables 4 and 5 indicate the kinds of overlapping that are necessary for the judges' terms to agree with the early and late dates, respectively. Round numbers are left as reported in the Scriptures, since there is no controlled

TABLE 4
THE JUDGES PERIOD FROM 1407 TO 1056
(Early Date of the Exodus)

Joshua and the elders	1407 - 1375
Cushan-Rishathaim	1375 - 1367
Othniel	1367 - 1327
Eglon	1327 - 1309
Ehud	1309 - 1229
Jabin	1229 - 1209
Deborah	1209 - 1169
Midian	1169 - 1162
Gideon	1162 - 1122
Abimelech	1122 - 1119
Tola and Jair	1119 - 1096
Eli	1116 - 1076
Ammonites	1096 - 1078
Jephthah	1078 - 1072
Ibzan, Elon, Abdon	1072 - 1062
Philistines	1096 - 1056
Samson and Samuel	1076 - 1056

methodology with which to compress them. Had such compression been possible, the degree of overlapping would be somewhat lessened. Comparison of the two tables will show that the main difference is in the treatment of Ehud and Othniel, the late date making them contemporaries of Deborah and Barak instead of their predecessors. Table 5 makes Samson a predecessor of Samuel, but the men could have been contemporaries as Table 4 shows them. Whether the period of Philistine oppression mentioned in Jgs. 13:1 should be considered as prior to Samson is a moot point. It appears that they continued to exercise hegemony over the Hebrews until the battle of Mizpah (1 S. 7:12-14) and intermittently after that until the time of David.

B. United Monarchy. The length of Saul's reign is highly conjectural, since the MT of 1 S. 13:1 is defective. (The LXX omits the verse entirely.) There is a blank where the king's age at accession is announced, and he is said to have reigned only two years. It has been

TABLE 5
THE JUDGES PERIOD FROM 1240 TO 1040
(Late Date of the Exodus)

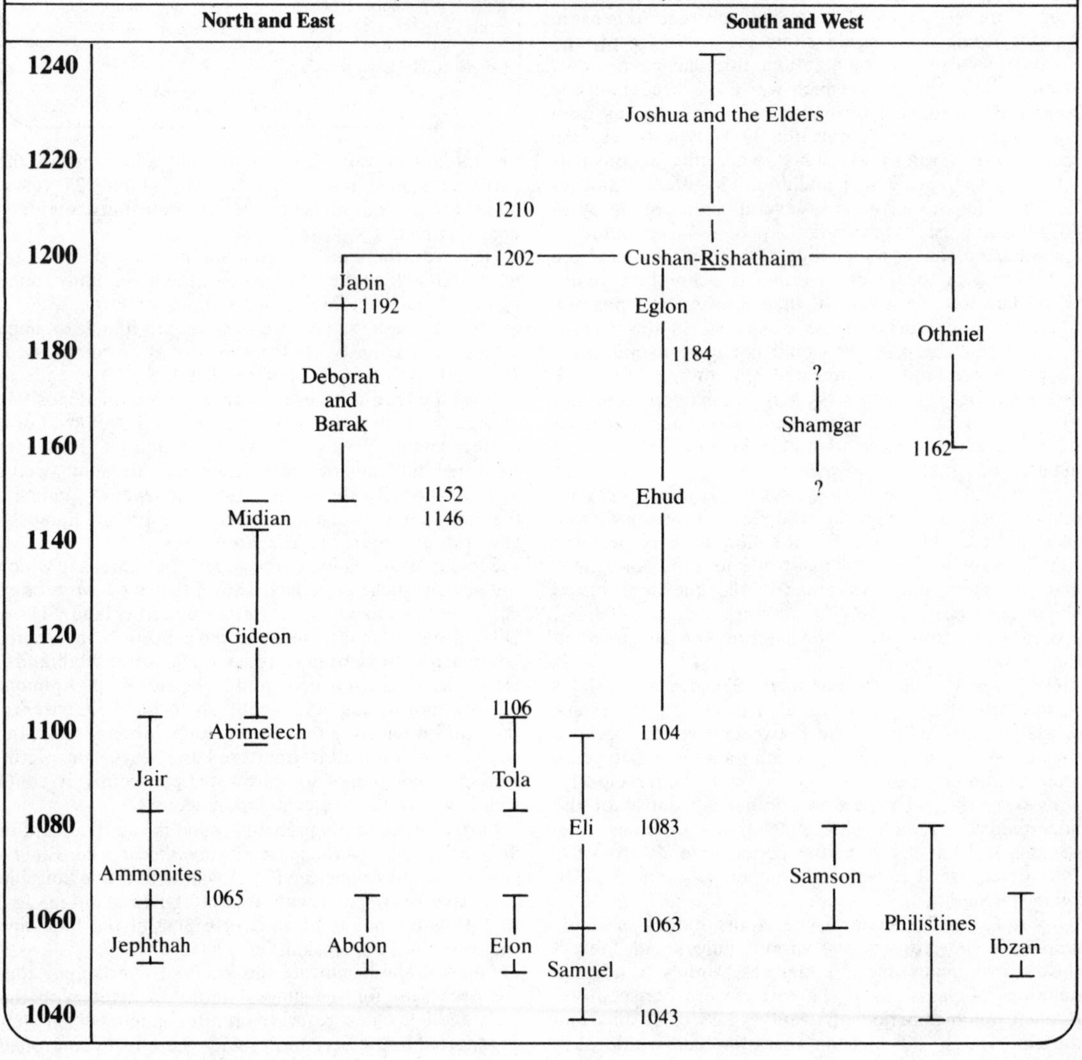

conjectured the original source might have used numerals instead of words at this point, and that, through scribal error, ב (=2) had replaced original כ (=20). Since the signs are alike only in the block script (not in the paleo-Hebrew), and since it is quite possible that paleo-Hebrew was in use until the Exile, the scribal error would have occurred quite late in transmission — a remote possibility for such a substantive error. Acts 13:21 gives Saul a reign of forty years, but this is highly dubious. Since both David and Solomon are said to have reigned forty years (1 K. 2:11; 11:42), it would be very easy to schematize the first reign of the united kingdom, making it forty years as well. As noted above, it is not impossible that the reign was as short as ten or twelve years.

With the beginning of the highly organized kingdom under David and especially Solomon, there is more reason to accept the literal accuracy of the statements concerning the length of their reigns. While the forty-year figure again gives every evidence of a scheme, it is likely that it is very close to the actual figure in each case. On this basis, David's reign over Judah would have begun *ca.* 1010 and Solomon over all Israel *ca.* 970.

The key date for the establishment of these figures is that of Shishak's invasion, which is reported to have occurred in the fifth year of Solomon's successor Rehoboam (1 K. 14:25). Because Shishak also reports this event in his annals it is possible to bring the Egyptian chronology to bear upon Israel at this point. The Egyptian system has approximately a ten-year margin of error at this time, so some flexibility results. Albright argued for the later date of 917, but this was based on his conclusions concerning an ambiguous mention in the Egyptian documents of a lunar eclipse. These conclusions are being increasingly questioned, especially since Thiele's computations concerning the Hebrew kings correspond better with the earlier date of 926. In view of these developments, the earlier date seems the more likely.

***V. Divided Monarchy.**–A. Methodology.* As mentioned above, this period is marked by a great increase in chronological information. The years of the kings of both Judah and Israel are reported in detail, as well as various congruencies with other cultures of the ancient Near East. However, this plethora of material has been an embarrassment when attempts have been made to coordinate the figures with an absolute system. As previously noted, prior to Thiele the two sets of figures could not be made to agree with one another, nor could either be made to agree with the Mesopotamian chronology, short of emendation. So, for instance, the total number of regnal years reported between Jehu's accession and the destruction of Samaria is 143, whereas the total reported from the accession of Athaliah to the sixth year of Hezekiah (when Samaria's fall occurred) is 166 years, twenty-three years more for what should be the same period. Yet both are longer than the Assyrian chronology, which gives 120 years for the period.

Thiele has shown that three factors must be taken into account before simple addition of regnal years is undertaken. First of all, there were in the ancient Near East two systems of counting the first year of a king's reign. The Mesopotamian system began the counting with the first full calendar year after the year in which the king had been crowned. This is called the post-accession dating system. On the other hand, the Egyptian system counted the year in which the coronation took place as a full year of rule. This is called the antedating system. Thus, two kings who were crowned on the same day could be recorded as having begun their reigns a year apart. It now appears that Judah used the postdating system throughout the period with one brief exception, while Israel at first used the antedating system but changed to postdating *ca.* 800 B.C.

The second factor which must be taken into account is the existence of two different calendars in the ancient Near East. One began the new year in the spring with the month of Nisan; the other in the fall, as the Jews do today, with Tishri. This introduced a further complication. If kings A and B were both crowned on June 21 according to the present calendar, and if A's reign were antedated to Tishri, while B's were postdated to Nisan, A would be (as Table 6 illustrates) in his second official year of reign when B began his first. Study has shown that Judah used a Tishri year for the duration of its history, while Israel used the Nisan year.

TABLE 6
POSSIBLE DISCREPANCIES IN OFFICIAL REGNAL YEARS

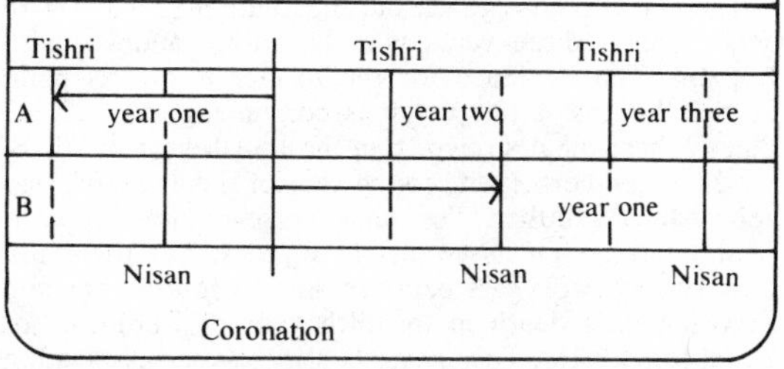

Added to such difficulties as these is the fact that when a synchronism between a Judean king and an Israelite king is reported by a scribe from the Judean realm, the Israelite's date is computed according to the Judean system. The reverse is true when a synchronism of this sort is reported by an Israelite scribe.

The final consideration is the matter of co-regencies. A case in point is that of Jotham and Uzziah (Azariah) reported in 2 K. 15:1-7, 32f. According to these verses, Uzziah reigned fifty-two years (v. 2), while his successor, Jotham, reigned sixteen (v. 33). This would give a total of sixty-eight years between the accession of Uzziah and the death of Jotham. However, v. 5 shows that Uzziah was shut up in his palace with leprosy for a part of his reign while Jotham was acting king. When did Jotham's reign begin — at his assuming the co-regency, or when he became king in his own right? Study of the synchronisms with Israel shows that his reign began with the co-regency, thus shortening the total to sixty years. Thiele's work suggests that co-regency was very common in Judah and somewhat less so in Israel.

Bearing all these factors in mind, it is possible to achieve a satisfactory reconstruction of the period between Solomon and the fall of Jerusalem with only a minimum of questions still unanswered. Table 7 illustrates this reconstruction.

B. Division of the Kingdom to the Invasion of Sennacherib. No serious difficulty appears in the chronology until the reigns of Baasha and Asa. Here the accounts in 1 K. 16 seem to disagree with 2 Ch. 15f. 1 K. 16:8 has Baasha dying in Asa's twenty-sixth year, yet 2 Ch. 16:1 has him fortifying Ramah in Asa's thirty-sixth year. The two books agree as to the length of Asa's reign: forty-one years (1 K. 15:10; 2 Ch. 16:13). Since the northern kingdom was of no interest to the Chronicler, the length of Baasha's reign is not recorded in his work. Albright used 2 Ch. 16:1 in his argument for the

CHRONOLOGY OF THE OT

later date of Solomon's death (922). While he moved the Israelite kings down the requisite nine years, he subtracted ten years from the Judean reigns. He did so on the warrant of this verse, which seems to have Baasha alive ten years longer than does Kings. However, Thiele has shown that Albright's system must destroy nearly all of the synchronisms between Israel and Judah as reported in Kings. In turn, Thiele has proposed a less radical solution which preserves those synchronisms. Zerah of Ethiopia attacked Judah in the fifteenth year of Asa and was defeated (2 Ch. 14:9-15; 15:9-11). This would be the thirty-fifth year since the division of the kingdom, or 896/5 (cf. 2 Ch. 15:19, MT "There was no war. . . ."). The celebration in honor of this victory attracted many from the north (15:9). This attraction could have supplied the motive for Baasha's work at Ramah: an attempt to seal the border against his own subjects. This could have taken place during the year following the celebration, in Asa's sixteenth year, or the thirty-sixth year since the disruption. This solution seems to fit the facts well and to require the least emendation.

The first two co-regencies in Judah are associated with Jehoshaphat: three years with his father and six with his son. The evidence for the former is not as plain as that for the latter, yet it is convincing. 1 K. 22:42 dates Jehoshaphat's reign from the fourth year of Ahab, which would correspond to the year of the death of Asa, Jehoshaphat's father. The same verse reports Jehoshaphat's total reign as twenty-five years. Yet there are only twenty-two years between Ahab's fourth year and Jehoshaphat's death in the fifth year of J(eh)oram of Israel (1 K. 8:16). This suggests a three-year association of Jehoshaphat with his father or a three-year gap between Ahab and Joram. The former is much more likely. The reason for such a co-regency is perhaps found in 2 Ch. 16:12, where Asa is said to have become seriously ill in his thirty-ninth year.

The existence of the second co-regency becomes plain upon comparison of 2 K. 1:7 with 3:1. In the former passage it is said that Joram, second son of Ahab, acceded to the throne of Israel in the second year of Jehoram king of Judah. Yet the second reference reports that this event occurred in the eighteenth year of Jehoshaphat, father of Jehoram. The co-regency is confirmed by 2 K. 8:16, which places Jehoram's accession to the Judean throne in the fifth year of Joram of Israel. Thus, it is evident that Jehoshaphat lived five official years (four actual) after the change of monarchs in Israel, but that his son had been associated with him on the throne for seven official years prior to his death.

Although the Battle of Qarqar is not mentioned in the Scripture, it is nevertheless an important anchor-point for biblical chronology. This battle, which can be dated to 853 B.C. on the basis of Assyrian records, was fought between the Assyrian Shalmaneser III and a coalition of Syro-Palestinian kings who sought to stop the westward expansion of Assyrian power. They met on the Orontes River in Syria and evidently fought to a draw, although Shalmaneser claimed a victory in his annals. More importantly, he recorded the names of those kings who dared to oppose him. Prominent among these is Ahab king of Israel, who supplied two thousand chariots and ten thousand soldiers. Ahab's death evidentally occurred that same year at the hands of his recent allies, the Syrians (1 K. 22:3, 34f.). This is fixed by the next important synchronism, which has Jehu paying tribute to Shalmaneser twelve years after Qarqar in 841. Since there were twelve years between Ahab's death and Jehu's accession (Ahaziah, one actual year, 1 K. 22:52; Joram, eleven actual years, 2 K. 3:1), 853 and 841 are the only possible dates for the respective events.

Israel's increasing dominance over Judah in the wake of Jezebel and Ahab is apparently reflected in Judah's change from postdating to antedating, effective between 848 and 797 B.C. According to 2 K. 8:17 and 2 Ch. 21:5, Ahaziah ruled for one year before being killed by Jehu, which event (as has been shown) is definitely fixed in 841. If Judah were still using the postdating system, Ahaziah would actually have begun his reign in 842, with the year of his death being counted as his first year. Ahaziah's father, Jehoram, was said to have reigned eight years (2 K. 8:17; 2 Ch. 21:5, 20). If he died during his eighth year, 842, according to the postdating system he would have begun to rule alone in 850. However, as noted above, 2 K. 8:16 records his coronation as having occurred in the fifth year of Joram of Israel. Since Joram ruled twelve official years (eleven actual) before his death in 841, he must have come to the throne in 852, making his fifth year, according to Judah's former postdating, 847. This results in a discrepancy of three years. The problem is resolved if it is understood that Ahaziah's accession year was 841 and that it was counted as his first year. This would then mean that Jehoram's eighth year was 841 and that he ruled seven actual years, 848 being the year of his coronation but also being counted as his first year. The year 848 would also be the Israelite Joram's fifth year according to the antedating system.

Confirmation of the change is found in apparently contradictory datings of Ahaziah's first year. 2 K. 9:29 places it in the eleventh year of Joram of Israel, while 2 K. 8:25 places it in the twelfth. There is no contradiction if it is understood that the former scribe was using the old system of postdating while the latter had accepted the newer system. Interestingly, when Judah returned to postdating in 798/797, Israel changed over also. It has been conjectured that Jeroboam I introduced antedating in Israel because of Egyptian influence. If that is correct, this rejection of that system may indicate the final collapse of Egyptian influence in Syro-Palestine in the face of the increasing Mesopotamian dominance under Assyria.

The chronology of Judah and Israel in the 8th cent. B.C. is exceedingly complex because of several co-regencies and the upheaval attendant upon Israel's final collapse. In Judah the first co-regency, that of Amaziah and Uzziah, was one of necessity; for Amaziah, in a burst of false confidence, challenged Israel under Jehoash and was taken captive (2 K. 14:13; 2 Ch. 25:23). That this event took place in 792 and that Uzziah became co-regent in that year is evident from a study of five apparently conflicting references. 2 K. 14:17 makes it plain that Amaziah died fifteen years after Jehoash of Israel. Since Jehoash' death (and the accession of Jeroboam II?) can be fixed in 782/781, Amaziah died in 768/767. In accord with this, 14:23 reports the coronation of Jeroboam II in Amaziah's fifteenth year, or 782. This would mean that Uzziah, Amaziah's successor, should have come to the throne in the fifteenth or sixteenth year of Jeroboam II. Yet 15:1 records Uzziah's accession in Jeroboam's twenty-seventh year. The best resolution of this difficulty sees Jeroboam II as having become co-regent with his father in 793 just before the war with Judah. Since Jeroboam ruled forty-one years (14:23), he died in 753/752 and was succeeded by Zechariah. However, 15:8 demonstrates that Zechariah began to reign in the thirty-eighth year of Uzziah. If Uzziah's reign is dated from 768, then Zechariah's accession is pushed down to 730, at least twenty-three years too late. On the other hand, if 753

TABLE 7a
CHRONOLOGY OF THE DIVIDED MONARCHY

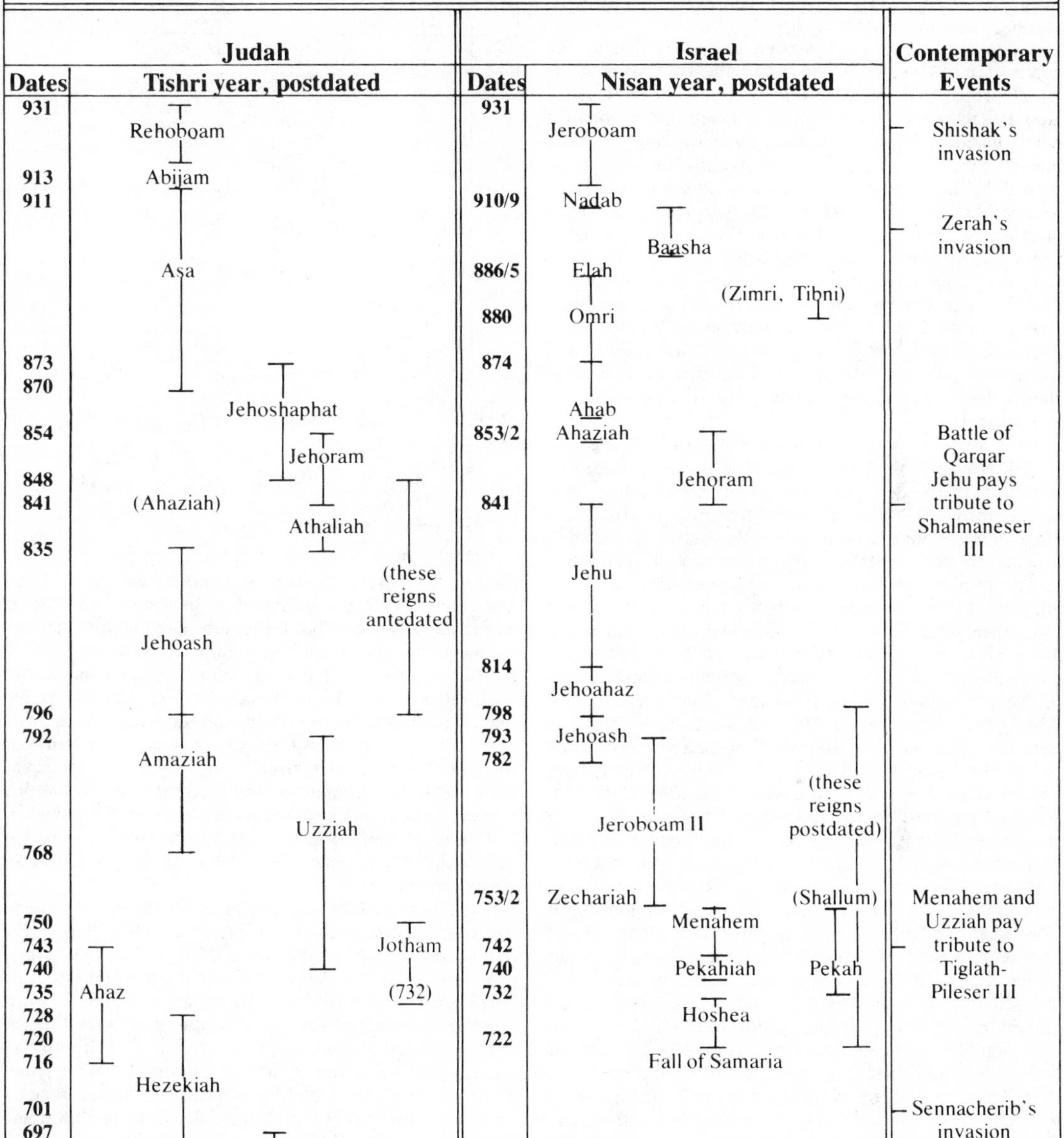
Judah
Israel
Contemporary Events
Dates
Tishri year, postdated
Dates
Nisan year, postdated
931
Rehoboam
931
Jeroboam
Shishak's invasion
913
Abijam
911
910/9
Nadab
Baasha
Zerah's invasion
Asa
886/5
Elah
(Zimri, Tibni)
880
Omri
873
874
870
Jehoshaphat
Ahab
854
853/2
Ahaziah
Battle of Qarqar
Jehoram
848
Jehoram
Jehu pays tribute to Shalmaneser III
841
(Ahaziah)
841
Athaliah
835
(these reigns antedated)
Jehu
Jehoash
814
Jehoahaz
796
798
792
793
Jehoash
Amaziah
782
(these reigns postdated)
Uzziah
Jeroboam II
768
753/2
Zechariah
(Shallum)
Menahem and Uzziah pay tribute to Tiglath-Pileser III
750
Menahem
743
Jotham
742
740
740
Pekahiah
Pekah
735
Ahaz
(732)
732
728
Hoshea
720
722
716
Fall of Samaria
Hezekiah
701
Sennacherib's invasion
697
687
Manasseh

is correct, then thirty-eight years prior to date results in a figure of 792/791 for the capture of Amaziah and the beginning of Uzziah's total reign.

The period between 753 and 701 is, if anything, even more complex than the previous fifty-year period. A twelve-year excess in Judah's total is so troublesome that Thiele is forced to abandon his own working hypothesis and suggest that an error has crept in. However, the methodology that Thiele himself applied to earlier problems suggests a solution that does not require emendation. The first problem concerns the number of regnal years that 2 K. 15:8-27 and 17:1 assign to Israel between the accession of Zechariah in 753 and the fall of Samaria in 722. Addition of these figures gives a total of forty-two years, whereas the well-established terminal dates allow a maximum of but thirty or thirty-one. That the figures from Shallum through Pekahiah are correct is shown by the fact that their addition will place the assassination of Pekahiah in the fifty-second year of Uzziah, which corresponds to the statement of 2 K. 15:25-27. Since Hoshea's nine-year reign is verifiable (see below), the difficulty occurs in Pekah's enumeration. 2 K. 15:32 records the beginning of Jotham's reign in the second year of Pekah; but if Pekah's succession occurred in 741/740, then Jotham did not come to the throne until two years after his father's death. However, as was

 CHRONOLOGY OF THE OT

shown above (V.A), Jotham had actually been co-regent with his father since 750. This suggests that Pekah had begun to reign in 752. If so, his twenty-year reign would have ended in 732, which coincides exactly with the beginning of Hoshea's reign.

In the light of this, it has been suggested that at the death of Jeroboam II Gilead may have split away from Israel proper and made Pekah its king. Thirteen years later Pekah was able to insinuate himself into a position where he could dispose of the reigning monarch and make himself king of all Israel. If this hypothesis is correct, then 2 K. 15:27 records the date of Pekah's accession to the kingship of all Israel, but lists the total years of reign over any part of the land. David's total of forty years was attained in the same fashion.

The second difficulty centers on the duration of Jotham's reign. On the one hand it is said to have been sixteen years (2 K. 15:33), yet only a few verses prior to this reference Hoshea's accession is dated in Jotham's twentieth year (v. 30). Since Hoshea's accession is clearly fixed in 732, nine years prior to Samaria's destruction in 723/722, this does correspond with the twentieth year from the beginning of Jotham's co-regency with Uzziah in 750. (As co-regent he had no accession-year.) Is 15:33, then, in error when it limits his reign to sixteen years? When the year formulae of Ahaz and Hezekiah are added, it seems so. It was in Hezekiah's fourteenth year that Sennacherib attacked Jerusalem (2 K. 18:13). This event is almost unassailably fixed in 701 B.C. This would place Hezekiah's accession in 716/715. His father, Ahaz, is reported to have reigned sixteen years. Thus, his accession would have occurred in 733/732. However, 2 K. 17:1 puts the accession of Hoshea (732) in Ahaz' twelfth year, not his first. This would place Ahaz' accession-year in 743. Yet another difficulty is posed by 16:1, which places Ahaz' coronation in Pekah's seventeenth year, 735. Thus three different dates for the beginning of Ahaz' reign are suggested: 743, 735, 732. It will be noted, first of all, that 735 corresponds to Jotham's sixteenth year. Thus, it has been suggested that Jotham was deposed — but not killed — in that year by a pro-Assyrian faction in Judah. His son Ahaz was made king, but his regnal years were not counted until 732, when his father died in his twentieth year. Thiele refused to credit 17:1; however, there is every reason to see it as an indication that Ahaz was associated with his father as co-regent in 743. He would have been eleven or twelve years of age at the time (cf. 16:2). The one difficulty with this hypothesis is that in 743 Jotham himself was still co-regent with Uzziah, his father. However, Uzziah was aged and probably largely incapacitated with leprosy, so Jotham's co-regency was in name only. Beyond this, Ahaz may have already been a tool of the pro-Assyrian faction and may have been forced upon Jotham in the light of Assyria's renewed aggressive activity under Tiglath-pileser III. It is interesting that just at this time Tiglath-pileser records having received tribute from both Judah and Israel.

The final chronological problem of the 8th cent. involves Hezekiah. As noted above, 2 K. 18:13 makes it plain that Hezekiah's regnal years began to be counted from 716/715. However, 18:1 lists his accession as having occurred in Hoshea's third year, or 728. This is confirmed by 18:9, which records Shalmanezer V's siege of Samaria as having begun in Hezekiah's fourth and Hoshea's seventh years. The siege was finally successful in the third calendar year, Hezekiah's sixth and Hoshea's ninth. Although there is some uncertainty as to whether Samaria fell to Shalmaneser (18:10) or to his successor

TABLE 7b
CHRONOLOGY OF THE DIVIDED MONARCHY
(700-586)

	Judah		Contemporary Events
697	Hezekiah	Manasseh	
687			
678			Manasseh travels to Nineveh with tribute for Esarhaddon
667			Manasseh submits to Ashurbanipal
643	Amon		
641			
	Josiah		
609		(Jehoahaz)	Neco at Harran
605	Jehoiakim		Battle of Carchemish and accession of Nebuchadrezzar
597		(Jehoiachin)	
	Zedekiah		
586	Destruction of Jerusalem		

Sargon II, there is reason to discount Sargon's claims and thus to take the earlier date in accord with 18:10. These facts indicate that Hezekiah, like his predecessors for more than a century before him, was a co-regent with his father. In fact, if one discounts 18:1,9f. and denies a co-regency for Hezekiah, as does Thiele, one is left with what would be an unusual circumstance. That 2 Ch. 29f. tells of an embassy Hezekiah sent to the north in his first year with an invitation to participate in the Passover is no argument against a co-regency. Assuredly, this could have taken place more easily in 716 than 728, but it is entirely likely that the reference is to his first year of sole reign rather than to the first year of the co-regency.

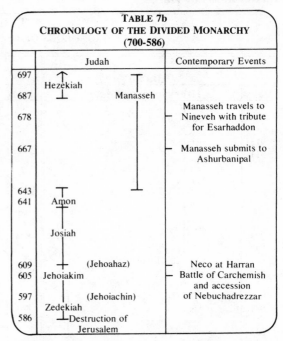

C. Sennacherib's Invasion to the Fall of Jerusalem. Between Sennacherib's invasion in 701 B.C. and the fall of Jerusalem in 587/586 B.C. there are few major problems. This may be due in part to the fact that synchronisms with Israel are no longer present to draw attention to such problems. One can only move to the next fixed date, compute the interval and attempt to arrange the recorded regnal years within that period. The first such date is 597, which the Babylonian records show was the year in which Jerusalem was captured and Jehoiakin's reign brought to an end. Since Hezekiah reigned twenty-nine years from 716/715 (2 K. 18:2), he died in 687. However, addition of the regnal years from Manasseh to Jehoiachin yields ten years and some months excess: ninety-nine years instead of eighty-nine. This suggests one or more co-regencies. Josiah, Jehoahaz, and Jehoiakim were all put on the throne through unusual circumstances that would militate against co-regencies for any of them (2 K. 21:23f.; 23:30, 34). Even if Amon's two-year reign had included time as co-regent, such time would be negligible. The same would apply to Jehoiachin (24:6-17). This leaves only Manasseh, whose very long reign and early age at accession (twelve years old, 21:1) would easily allow for a co-regency of ten or eleven years. Hezekiah's sickness (20:1), which apparently occurred about 700, may have frightened him into associating his son with him as soon as the boy reached the age of accountability. If these conjectures are correct, this event would have occurred in 698/697.

Albright and others have argued that there must have been two invasions by Sennacherib that the Scripture has conflated into the one account contained in 2 K. 18:13–19:37. Primarily, their argument rests on two biblical references: the first to Tirhakah (19:9), who did not begin to rule until 690 and who appeared from Egyptian sources to have been too young to have led an army in 701; and the second (19:37), which seems to imply that Sennacherib died immediately after his return from Jerusalem in 700, when in fact he did not die until twenty years later in 681. However, recent studies have shown that Tirhakah could have been as old as twenty-two years in 701, while the inclusion of Sennacherib's death in 19:37 only rounds out the story of God's total judgment upon Sennacherib's *hýbris*.

The closing years of the Judean monarchy are at first clear, but then somewhat difficult. It is certain that Josiah died in 609 and that Nebuchadrezzar's victory at Carchemish occurred in 605. This was followed by a victory tour through the now-defenseless West, the impact of which is reported in Dnl. 1:1 (Jehoiakim's third year — Tishri year) and Jer. 46:2 (fourth year — Nisan year). Likewise, the date when Nebuchadrezzar's punitive expedition against Jerusalem captured the city is clearly fixed in March, 597. Zedekiah's first official year began, then, in Tishri, 597. It was formerly thought that the fixing of Josiah's death in 609 would bring Jehoiakim's eleven-year reign to a close in 598. If, however, as seems entirely likely, Neco placed Jehoiakim on the throne in Tishri, 609 (Neco was at Harran from Tammuz to Elul, which would correspond to the three months of Jehoahaz' reign, and was free to return to Jerusalem in the following month, Tishri), then Jehoiakim's first official year would not have begun until Tishri, 608. According to 2 K. 24:18 Zedekiah's reign was also eleven years in duration. This would fix the final year of his rule between Tishri, 587, and Tishri, 586. 2 K. 25:1 and Ezk. 24:1f. agree that the siege began on the tenth day of the tenth month of Zedekiah's ninth year, or Jan. 15, 588 (months numbered from Nisan). The breaching of the wall came on the ninth day of the fourth month of the eleventh year, or July 19, 586 (2 K. 25:3f.; Jer. 39:2; 52:6f.).

Two factors have caused some scholars to date the destruction in 587, thus pushing all the computations back one year. Ezk. 33:21 and 40:1, which refer to the destruction of the temple in terms of Jehoiachin's regnal years, seem to require the earlier date. However, Thiele has shown that Ezekiel was using a Nisan year, and this understanding removes the difficulty. The second factor is less easily explained. This is the dating of the three deportations in Nebuchadrezzar's seventh, eighteenth, and twenty-third years (Jer. 52:28-30). The seventh year would end in Adar, 597, the month in which Jerusalem was captured first, but the eighteenth year would end in Adar, 586, four months before the breaching of the walls. However, since Jer. 52:12f. definitely places Nebuzaradan's entry into Jerusalem and the burning of the temple in Nebuchadrezzar's nineteenth year, whatever is intended by 52:29 is not sufficient reason to place the destruction of the city in Nebuchadrezzar's eighteenth year, 587.

VI. Exile and Return.–There is little biblical information for this period, and it presents but one major chronological problem: the relationship of Ezra and Nehemiah. The other dates are very clear. Cyrus' edict of *ca.* 538 set the machinery in motion for the first return under Sheshbazzar (Ezr. 1:1). This presumably occurred before 535 and perhaps as early as 538. The second temple was begun in the second year of the return (3:8). The work was suspended, however, and not resumed until the second year of Darius I, 520 (4:24). It was completed in 515, Darius' sixth year (6:15). There are then no more data until the time of Ezra and Nehemiah in the middle of the following century.

The traditional dates of Ezra and Nehemiah have been arrived at by means of synchronisms with reigning Persian monarchs. According to Ezr. 7:7, Ezra and the second group of returnees reached Jerusalem in the seventh year of Artaxerxes, whereas Nehemiah came to Jerusalem in the twentieth year of Artaxerxes. It has been assumed that this is Artaxerxes I, in which case the respective dates would be 458 and 445. However, many scholars have become convinced that conditions described in the book of Ezra relate to a period after Nehemiah's work. Thus, the hypothesis is advanced that Ezra came to Jerusalem in the seventh year of Artaxerxes II, or 398. This theory, however, denies the statements of Neh. 8f. that Ezra was a contemporary of Nehemiah. In response to this, another theory has suggested that perhaps Ezr. 7:7 originally read "*thirty*-seventh year," which would put Ezra's return in 428 B.C. Since both numbers begin with the same Hebrew letter, it is suggested that the thirty was dropped through scribal error. There is, however, no textual support for the conjecture.

Of the evidence that supposedly demands placing Ezra after Nehemiah, only one aspect constitutes a serious objection to the traditional dating. This is found in Ezr. 10:6, where Ezra is made a contemporary of Johanan (RSV "Jehohanan"), the son of Eliashib. The difficulty appears when one reads that the high priest at the time of Nehemiah was named Eliashib (Neh. 3:1, 20f.; 13:4) and that this Eliashib had a grandson named Johanan (13:22f.) who was, according to the Elephantine papyri, high priest in 408. If the Johanan of Ezr. 10 was the Johanan who was high priest in 408, then only the second theory is possible; however, this theory, as was pointed out above, does violence to the text of Nehemiah. In view of this, and especially since Johanan is not said to be high priest in Ezra, there is not sufficient reason to abandon the traditional view for theories that have problems at least as great.

Bibliography.–*General Treatments:* D. N. Freedman and E. F. Campbell, "Chronology of Israel and the Ancient Near East," in *BANE*; W. F. Albright, *Biblical Period from Abraham to Ezra* (1963); K. A. Kitchen, *Ancient Orient and OT* (1966), pp. 33-78; K. Stenring, *Enclosed Garden* (1966); R. K. Harrison, *Intro. to the OT* (1969), pp. 147-198; *CAH*.

Early Chronology: H. H. Rowley, *From Joseph to Joshua* (1950); W. F. Albright, *BASOR*, 163 (Oct. 1961), 36-54; H. Hoehner, *Bibliotheca Sacra*, 126 (1969), 306-316; L. T. Wood, *Survey of Israel's History* (1970), pp. 30-38, 83-109.

Kingdom Period: MNHK; *VT*, 16 (1966), 83-107. Other sources are: J. Begrich, *Die Chronologie der Könige von Israel und Juda* (1929); S. Mowinckel, *Acta Orientalia*, 9 (1931), 161-277; W. F. Albright, *BASOR*, 100 (Dec. 1945), 16-22; 130 (Apr. 1953), 4-11; 141 (Feb. 1956), 23-27; J. McHugh, *VT*, 14 (1964), 446-453; H. Stigers, *Bulletin of the Evangelical Theological Society*, 9 (1966), 81-89; J. M. Miller, *JBL*, 88 (1967), 276-288; J. Shenkel, *Chronology and Rescensional Development in the Greek Text of Kings* (1968); A. Jepsen, *VT*, 18 (1968), 31-46; K. T. Anderson, *ST*, 23 (1969), 69-114; J. B. Payne, *Bibliotheca Sacra*, 126 (1969), 40-52.

Later Chronology: J. S. Wright, *Building of the Second Temple* (1958); *Date of Ezra's Coming to Jerusalem* (2nd ed. 1958); *BHI* (2nd ed. 1972), pp. 296-308, 392-403; J. A. Emerton, *JTS*, N.S. 17 (1966), 1-19.

Extrabiblical Chronology: R. A. Parker and W. H. Dubberstein, *Babylonian Chronology 626 B.C. — A.D. 75* (1956); *CCK* (1956); A. Gardiner, *Egypt of the Pharaohs* (1961). J. N. OSWALT

CHRONOLOGY OF THE NT. In the reckoning of time, the ancient world used the same units that we use today: days, months, years, and eras. The day usually began at sunrise, sunset, or midnight. The month began originally at the new moon, and was alternately twenty-nine and thirty days long. The year usually began in relation to a certain position of the sun (solstice or equinox), and had twelve months. The discrepancy between twelve lunar months and one solar year was rectified with greater or less precision by intercalation of additional days or months, or by alteration of the length of months. The era, in turn, was a sequence of years reckoned from a definite point called the epoch.

In the NT period the calendars chiefly in use were the Egyptian with the year beginning on Thoth 1 = Aug. 29; the Syro-Macedonian with the year beginning on Hyperberetaios 1 = Oct. 1; the Julian with the year beginning on Jan. 1; and the Jewish with the year beginning on Tishri (Sept./Oct.) 1, or on Nisan (Mar./Apr.) 1. Eras used were the Seleucid, which began in the older form of the Macedonian calendar on Dios 1 = Oct. 7, 312 B.C., and in the Babylonian calendar on Nisanu 1 = Apr. 3, 311 B.C.; the Greek era of the Olympiads, which began July 1, 776 B.C.; and the Roman era, which reckoned from the founding of the city of Rome (Lat. *ab urbe condita*). The Roman antiquarian Varro gives a date equivalent to Apr. 21, 753 B.C., for the founding of Rome, but in practice the year was reckoned from Jan. 1 (Lietzmann, *Zeitrechnung,* p. 12); accordingly A.U.C. 753 = 1 B.C. and A.U.C. 754 = A.D. 1.

The Christian era is reckoned from the birth of Jesus and based upon the calculations of Dionysius Exiguus, who, in preparing Easter tables in A.D. 525, said: "We have chosen to note the years from the incarnation of our Lord Jesus Christ." The date established was at least four years too late, however, for by this reckoning Herod the Great, under whom Jesus was born, died in 4 B.C. In the discussion of the chronology of the life of Jesus, the Varronian era will be used coordinately with the Dionysian.

- I. Chronology of the Life of Jesus
  - A. Birth of Jesus
    - 1. Death of Herod
    - 2. Census of Quirinius
    - 3. Star of the Magi
    - 4. Course of Abijah
    - 5. Day and Month
    - 6. Summary
  - B. Baptism of Jesus
  - C. First Passover
  - D. Death of John the Baptist
  - E. Length of Jesus' Ministry
  - F. Death of Jesus
  - G. Summary of Dates
- II. Chronology of the Apostolic Age
  - A. Paul's Conversion
  - B. Death of Herod Agrippa I
  - C. Famine under Claudius
  - D. Sergius Paulus
  - E. Edict of Claudius
  - F. Gallio
  - G. Festus
  - H. Relative Chronology of Acts
  - I. Pauline Epistles
  - J. Release and Death of Paul
  - K. Death of Peter
  - L. Death of James the Just
  - M. The Synoptic Gospels
  - N. Death of John
  - O. Summary of Dates

Manger in the grotto beneath the Church of the Nativity at Bethlehem. The birth of Jesus may be assigned to the period 7 B.C. to 4 B.C. (W. S. LaSor)

I. Chronology of the Life of Jesus.*–A. Birth of Jesus.* Jesus was born before the death of Herod the Great (Mt. 2:1ff.), at the time of a census or enrollment made in the territory of Herod in accordance with a decree of Augustus, during the governorship of Quirinius (RSV; AV Cyrenius) in the Roman province of Syria (Lk. 2:1f.). At the time of Jesus' birth a star led the Magi of the East to seek in Jerusalem the infant whom they subsequently found in Bethlehem (Mt. 2:1ff.). John the Baptist was born six months before Jesus (Lk. 1:36), also in the days of Herod (Lk. 1:5; cf. 2:1), after his father Zechariah, of the priestly course of Abijah, had been performing the functions of his office in the temple.

1. Death of Herod. The death of Herod the Great occurred in the spring of 750/4. (These alternative numbers signify A.U.C. or A.D., 750 A.U.C. = 4 B.C., etc.) He ruled from his appointment in Rome 714/40 (Josephus *Ant.* xiv.14.4f.; in the consulship of Caius Domitius Calvinus and Caius Asinius Pollio) thirty-seven years, and from his accession in Jerusalem after the capture of the city 717/37 (*Ant.* xiv.16.1-3; *BJ* i.17.9; 18.1-3; Dio Cassius *Hist.* xlix.22; cf. Schürer, *HJP*^{2}, I, 284 n.11) thirty-four years (*Ant.* xvii.18.1; *BJ* i.33.7f.; cf. *HJP*^{2}, I, 326 n.165, where it is shown that Josephus reckons a year too much, probably counting from Nisan 1 and including partial years). Just before Herod's death there was an eclipse of the moon (*Ant.* xvii.6.4). According to astronomical calculations an eclipse was visible in Palestine on Mar. 23 and Sept. 15, 749/5; Mar. 12, 750/4; and Jan. 9, 753/1. Of these the most probable is that of Mar. 12, 750/4. Soon after the eclipse Herod put to death his son Antipater and died five days later (*Ant.* xvii.7; *BJ* i.33.7). Shortly after Herod's death the Passover was near at hand (*Ant.* xvii.6.4–9.3). In this year Nisan 14 fell on April 11; and as Archelaus had observed seven days of mourning for his father before this, Herod's death would fall between Mar. 17 and Apr. 4. But as the thirty-seventh (thirty-fourth) year of his reign was probably reckoned from Nisan 1 or Mar. 29, his death may be dated between Mar. 29 and Apr. 4, 750/4.

This date for Herod's death is confirmed by the evidence for the duration of the reigns of his three sons. Archelaus was deposed in 759/6 (Dio Cassius *Hist.* lv.27; in the consulship of Aemilius Lepidus and Lucius Arruntius) in the tenth year of his reign (*Ant.* xvii.13.2; cf. *BJ* ii.7.3, which gives the year as the 9th). Antipas was deposed most probably in the summer of 792/39 (*Ant.* xviii.7.1f.; cf. 6.11; xix.8.2; *BJ* ii.9.6; *HJP*^{2}, I, 352 n. 42, and 327 n.165). There are coins of Antipas from his forty-third year (F. W. Madden, *Coins of the Jews* [1881], pp. 121ff.). The genuineness of a coin from the forty-fourth year is questioned by Schürer but accepted by Madden. The coin from the forty-fifth year is probably spurious (*HJP*², I, 327 n. 165). Philip died after reigning thirty-seven years, in the twentieth year of Tiberius—Aug. 19, 786/33–787/34 (*Ant.* xviii.4.6). There is also a coin of Philip from his thirty-seventh year (Madden, p. 126). Thus Archelaus, Antipas, and Philip began to reign in 750/4. The death of Herod in 4 B.C. has been questioned by W. E. Filmer in *JTS*, N.S. 17 (1966), 283-298, but decisively reaffirmed by T. D. Barnes in *JTS*, N.S. 19 (1968), 204-209.

2. Census of Quirinius. The census or enrollment, which according to Lk. 2:1f. was the occasion of the journey of Joseph and Mary to Bethlehem where Jesus was born, is connected with a decree of Augustus embracing the Greco-Roman world. This decree must have been carried out in Palestine by Herod and probably in accordance with the Jewish method — each going to his own city — rather than the Roman. Certainly there is no intimation of an insurrection such as characterized a later census (Acts 5:37; *Ant.* xviii.1.1; *BJ* ii.17.7; cf. Tacitus *Ann.* vi.41; Livy *Epit.* cxxxviii-cxxxix; Dessau, no. 212, col. 2, line 36), and this may have been due in no small measure to a difference in method. Both Josephus and Luke mention the later census made by Quirinius on the deposition of Archelaus, together with the insurrection of Judas that accompanied it. But while Josephus does not mention the Herodian census — although there may be some intimation of it in *Ant.* xvi.9.3 and xvii.2.4 (cf. Wm. M. Ramsay, *Was Christ Born at Bethlehem?* [3rd ed. 1905], pp. 178ff.) — Luke carefully distinguishes the two, characterizing the census at the time of Jesus' birth as "first," i.e., first in a series of enrollments connected either with Qurinius or with the imperial policy inaugurated by the decree of Augustus.

The Greco-Roman writers of the time do not mention this decree, and later writers (Cassiodorus, Isidorus, and Suidas) cannot be relied upon with certainty as independent witnesses. Yet the geographical work of Agrippa and the preparation of a *breviarium totius imperii* by Augustus (Tacitus *Ann.* i.11; Dio Cassius *Hist.* liii.30; lvi.33; cf. T. Mommsen, *Römisches Staatsrecht* [1887-1888], II, 1025 n. 3), together with the interest of the emperor in the organization and finances of the empire and the attention he gave to the provinces (J. Marquardt, *Römische Staatsverwaltung* [2nd ed. 1881], II, 211f., cf. 217), are indirectly corroborative of Luke's statement. Augustus himself conducted a census in Italy in 726/28, 746/8, 767/14 and in Gaul in 727/27 (Dio Cassius liii.22.5; Livy *Epit.* cxxxiv), and had a census taken in other provinces (Pauly-Wissowa, III/2, 1918f.; Marquardt, II, 213). For Egypt there is evidence of a regular periodic census every fourteen years extending back to 773/20 (Ramsay, pp. 131ff.; B. Grenfell and A. Hunt, *Oxyrhyncus Papyri*, II [1898], 207ff.; U. Wilcken, *Griechische Ostraka* [1899], I, 444ff.), and it is not improbable that this procedure was introduced by Augustus (*HJP*², I, 404 n. 17). The inference from Egypt to similar conditions in other provinces must indeed be made cautiously (Wilcken, p. 449; Marquardt, p. 441); yet in Syria the regular *tributum capitis* seems to imply some such preliminary work (Marquardt, II, 200 n. 2; Ramsay, p. 154).

The time of the decree is stated only in general terms by Luke, and it may have been as early as 727/27 (Marquardt, II, 212) or as late as 746/8 (Ramsay, pp. 158ff.), its execution in different provinces and subject kingdoms being carried out at different times. Hence Luke dates the census in the kingdom of Herod specifically by connecting it with the administrative functions of Quirinius in Syria. But as P. Quintilius Varus was the legate of Syria just before and after the death of Herod from 748/6 to 750/4 (*Ant.* xvii.5.2; 9.3; 10.1, 9; 11.1; Tacitus *Hist.* v.9; and coins in J. Eckhel, *Doctrina numorum veterum* [1792-1798], III, 275) and his predecessor was C. Sentius Saturninus from 745/9 to 748/6 (*Ant.* xvi.9.1; 10:8; xi.3; xvii.1.1; 2.1; 3.2), there seems to be no place for Quirinius during the closing years of Herod's reign. Tertullian indeed speaks of Saturninus as legate at the time of Jesus' birth (*Adv. Marc.* iv.9). The interpretation of Luke's statement as indicating a date for the census before Quirinius was legate (C. G. Wieseler, *Chronologische Synopse* [1843], p. 116; M. J. Lagrange, *RB*, 20 [1911], 80-84) is inadmissible. It is possible that the connection of the census with Quirinius may be due to his having brought to completion what was begun by one of his predecessors; or Quirinius may have been commissioned especially by the emperor as *legatus ad census accipiendos* to conduct a census in Syria, and this commission may have been connected temporally with his campaign against the Homonadenses in Cilicia (Tacitus *Ann.* iii.48; cf. E. Noris, *Cenotaphia Pisana* [1681], pp. 320ff.; Ramsay, p. 238). It has also been suggested by R. Bour (*L'Inscription de Quirinius* [1897], pp. 48ff.) that Quirinius may have been an imperial procurator specially charged with authority in the matter of the Herodian census. The titulus Tiburtinus (*CIL*, XIV, 3613; Dessau, no. 918), if rightly assigned to him — and there seems to be no sufficient reason for questioning the conclusiveness of Mommsen's defense of this attribution (cf. W. Liebenam, *Forschungen zur Verwaltungsgeschichte* [1888], p. 365) — proves that he was twice legate of Syria, and the titulus Venetus (*CIL*, III, 6687; Dessau, no. 2683) gives evidence of a census conducted by him in Syria. His administration is dated by Ramsay (p. 243) in 747/7; by Mommsen in the end of 750/4 or the beginning of 751/3 (pp. 172ff.). The synchronism of the second census of Quirinius with the periodic year of the Egyptian census is probably only a coincidence, for it was occasioned by the deposition of Archelaus; but its extension to Syria may be indicative of its connection with the imperial policy inaugurated by Augustus (Tacitus *Ann.* vi.41; Ramsay, pp. 161f.). Stauffer (pp. 25f.) suggests that in Syria the *prima descriptio Romana* was a long process: what Luke describes is the *apographa,* a systematic listing of all taxable persons and property for which everyone had to appear personally; what Josephus reports is the *apotimesis,* the official assessment of taxes. Quirinius, he thinks (pp. 30f.), was Roman commander-in-chief of the Orient from 12 B.C. to A.D. 16; he began the *apographa* in Palestine in 7 B.C., completed the *apotimesis* in A.D. 7. J. Vardaman in an unpublished paper (" Lysanias and Quirinius: A New Solution through Micrographics" [1975]) adduces evidence that, while Saturninus and Varus were indeed legates of Syria, the supreme authority in Syria and other eastern territories was Quirinius, who served continuously as proconsul of Syria and Cilcia from 11 B.C. until at least 3 B.C. (therefore until after the death of Herod the Great) and at the same time was also procurator of numerous provinces, including Judea.

3. Star of the Magi. The identification of the star of the Magi (Mt. 2:2; cf. 2:7, 9, 16; Macrobius *Saturnalia* II, 4; Ramsay, pp. 215ff.) and the determination of the time of its appearance cannot be made with certainty, although it has been associated with a conjunction in 747/7 and 748/6 of Saturn and Jupiter in the sign of Pisces — a constellation that was thought to stand in close relation to the Jewish nation (C. L. Ideler, *Handbuch der mathematischen und technischen Chronologie*

[1825], II, 400ff.). This vey conjunction was in fact recorded at this time in Babylonia (P. Schnabel in *Zeitschrift für Assyriologie,* 36 [1925], 66-70). When the Magi came to Jerusalem, however, Herod was present in the city; and this must have been at least several months before his death, for during that time he was sick and absent from Jerusalem (*Ant.* xvii.6.1ff.; *BJ* i.33.1ff.).

Another possibility (and perhaps a complementary one, if the conjunction may be taken as a preliminary sign) is to connect the star with celestial observations recorded in Chinese sources. Here a comet or nova is reported in March, 5 B.C., and in April, 4 B.C. (K. Lundmark in *Actes du VIIe Congrès International d'Histoire des Sciences* [1953], pp. 436-39; H. W. Montefiore, *Nov.Test.,* 4 [1960], 143f.).

4. Course of Abijah. Chronological calculations of the time of the service of the priestly course of Abijah in the temple have been made by reckoning back from the time of the course of Jehoiarib, which, according to Jewish tradition, was serving at the time of the destruction of Jerusalem by Titus. These calculations have been held to be uncertain (*GJV,* II, 337 n. 3; briefer in *HJP,* II/1, 274 n. 211; cf. T. Lewin, *Fasti Sacri* [1865], p. 836), but a six-year almanac from Qumrân also gives the number, name, and order of the priestly courses and confirms Tishri 1 as the beginning point of their rotation, leading together with other evidence to a possible fixing of the Annunciation to Mary in the spring of the year and of the birth of Jesus around the time of the winter solstice (R. T. Beckwith, *RQ,* 33 [1977], 73-94).

5. Day and Month. As to the day and month of Jesus' birth, Dec. 25 was celebrated by the Church in the West as early as the 2nd cent., if the date determined by Hippolytus be genuine (cf. A. Ehrhard, *Altchristliche Literature* [1900], p. 383); but Jan. 6 was celebrated in the East as the anniversary both of the birth and of the baptism. Since these are both ancient recorded datings for the winter solstice, this fact may have contributed to the choice of the exact dates, understandably if there were already a historical tradition that Jesus had been born around that time of the year. That shepherds were keeping watch over their flocks at night when Jesus was born (Lk. 2:8) does not make it impossible that the season of the year was winter. (See R. T. Beckwith, *RQ,* 33 [1977], 73-94.)

6. Summary. The birth of Jesus may therefore be assigned to the period 747/7 to 750/4, before the death of Herod, at the time of a census made by Herod in accordance with a decree of Augustus and when Quirinius was exercising extraordinary authority in Syria—Saturninus or Varus being the regular legate of the province, i.e., probably in 747/7–748/6, or perhaps in 749/5–750/4.

B. Baptism of Jesus. The Synoptic Gospels begin their description of the public ministry of Jesus with an account of the ministry of John the Baptist (Mt. 3:1ff.; Mk. 1:1ff.; Lk. 3:1ff.; cf. Jn. 1:19ff.; 4:24; Josephus *Ant.* xviii.3.3), and Luke definitely dates the baptism of Jesus by John in the fifteenth year of Tiberius. Luke also designates this event as the beginning of Jesus' ministry, and by stating Jesus' age approximately brings it into connection with the date of His birth. If Luke reckoned the reign of Tiberius from the death of Augustus, Aug. 19, 767/14, the fifteenth year would extend from Aug. 19, 781/28 to Aug. 18, 782/29. This indeed was one of the common modes of reckoning the imperial reigns. The mode of reckoning from the assumption of the tribunician power or from the designation as imperator is altogether unlikely in Luke's case and intrinsically improbable, since for Tiberius the one began in 748/6 and the other in 745/9 (Dio Cassius lv.9; liv.33; Velleius ii.99; Suetonius *Tiberius* 9). But if, as seems likely, the method of reckoning by imperial years rather than by the yearly consuls was not definitely fixed when Luke wrote, it is possible that he may have counted the years of Tiberius from his appointment in 764/11 or 765/12 to equal authority with Augustus in the provinces (Velleius ii.121; Suetonius *Tiberius* 20; Tacitus *Ann.* i.3). This method seems not to have been employed elsewhere (Lewin, pp. 1143f.; cf. Ramsay, pp. 202f.). The coins of Antioch in which it is found are regarded as spurious (Eckhel, III, 276), the genuine coins reckoning the reign of Tiberius from the death of Augustus (III, 278). If Luke reckoned the reign of Tiberius from 764/11 or 765/12, the fifteenth year would fall in 778/25 or 779/26, probably the latter. At all events, Luke's "about thirty" for Jesus' age at the time is only approximate.

C. First Passover. At the time of the first Passover in Jesus' ministry the Herodian temple had been under construction for forty-six years (Jn. 2:20). Herod began the temple in the eighteenth year of his reign (*Ant.* xv.11.1, which probably corrects the statement in *BJ* i.21.1 that it was the fifteenth year; cf. *HJP*², I, 292 n. 12). As Josephus reckons from the accession of Herod in 717/37, the eighteenth year would be 734/20 to 735/19 and forty-six years later would be 780/27 to 781/28. It is possible, however, that *Ant.* xv.11.1 means that Herod had passed through his eighteenth year, i.e., was already in his nineteenth year, which would be 735/19 to 736/18, and then forty-six years later would be 781/28 to 782/29. This would then agree with the Lukan dating of the baptism in the year from Aug. 19, 781/28 to Aug. 18, 782/29.

D. Death of John the Baptist. The imprisonment of John the Baptist, which began before Jesus started His Galilean work (cf. Mt. 11:2-19; Lk. 7:18-35), was terminated by beheading at the order of Herod Antipas. Announcement of the death was made to Jesus when He was in the midst of His Galilean ministry (Mt. 14:3-12; Mk. 6:14-29; Lk. 9:7-9). Josephus reports that the defeat of Antipas by Aretas, in the summer of 789/36, was popularly regarded as a divine punishment for the murder of John (*Ant.* xviii.5.2). But although Josephus mentions the divorce of Aretas' daughter by Antipas as one of the causes of hostilities, no inference can be drawn from this or from the popular interpretation of Antipas' defeat, by which the interval between John's death and this defeat can be fixed (cf. H. W. Hoehner, *Herod Antipas* [1972], p. 125).

E. Length of Jesus' Ministry. The Synoptic Gospels mention the Passion Passover at which Jesus' ministry was terminated, but they contain no data by which the interval between the imprisonment of John the Baptist and this Passover can be fixed with certainty. Yet indications are not wanting that the interval consisted of at least two years. The sabbath controversy broke out in Galilee when the grain was still standing in the fields (Mt. 12:1; Mk. 2:23; Lk. 6:1), and the condition of the grass when the five thousand were fed (Mt. 14:15; Mk. 6:39; Lk. 9:12) points to the springtime, the Passion Passover marking the return of still another springtime (cf. also Lk. 13:7; Mt. 23:37). But the Gospel of John mentions explicitly three Passovers (2:13; 6:4; 11:55) and probably implies a fourth (5:1), thus necessitating a ministry of at least two years and making probable a ministry of three years after the first Passover. The Passover of Jn. 6:4 cannot be eliminated on textual grounds, for the documentary evidence is conclusive in its favor and the argument against it based on the statements of certain patristic writers is unconvincing (cf. Turner, *HDB,* I, 407f.; T. Zahn, *Kommentar zum NT* [1903], IV, 708ff.). The indications of time from 6:4 — the Passover when the five thousand were fed in Galilee — to

11:55 — the Passion Passover — are definite and clear (7:2; 10:22). But the interval between the first Passover (2:23) and the Galilean Passover (6:4) must have been one and may have been two years. The following considerations favor the latter view: Jesus was present in Jerusalem at a feast (5:1) which is not named but is called simply "a" or "the" feast of the Jews. The best authorities for the text are divided, some supporting the insertion, others the omission of the definite article before "feast." If the article formed part of the original text, the feast may have been either Tabernacles — from the Jewish point of view — or Passover — from the Christian point of view. If the article was wanting in the original text, the identification of the feast must be made on contextual and other grounds. But the note of time in 4:35 indicates the lapse of about nine months since the Passover of 2:23, and it is not likely that the Galilean ministry that preceded the feeding of the five thousand lasted only about three months. In fact, this is rendered impossible by the condition of the grain in the fields at the time of the sabbath controversy. The identification of the feast of Jn. 5:1 with Purim, even if the article be not genuine, is extremely improbable; and if so, a Passover must have intervened between 2:23 and 6:4, making the ministry of Jesus extend over a period of three years and the months that preceded the Passover of 2:23. While the identification cannot be made with certainty it seems likely that the feast was Passover; for in this case the subject of the controversy with the Jews in Jerusalem, as well as the season of the year, would harmonize with the Synoptic account of the sabbath controversy in Galilee that probably followed this Passover (cf. the variant reading in Lk. 6:1). Stauffer (p. 6) adds an additional year to the interpretation of the data in John: 1:29 assumes the Passover season at the baptism; 2:13ff. the (second) Passover and the cleansing of the temple; 4:35 winter, then the third Passover unmentioned, and in 5:1 autumn with the feast of Tabernacles; 6:4 the fourth Passover is at hand; 11:55, etc., the fifth and final Passover.

F. Death of Jesus. Jesus was put to death in Jerusalem at the time of the Passover when Pontius Pilate was procurator of Judea (Mt. 27:2ff.; Mk. 15:1ff.; Lk. 23:1ff.; Jn. 18:29ff.; 19:1ff.; Acts 3:13; 4:27; 13:28; 1 Tim. 6:13; Tacitus *Ann*. xv.44), Caiaphas being the high priest (Mt. 26:3, 57; Jn. 11:49; 18:13ff.) and Herod Antipas the tetrarch of Galilee and Perea (Lk. 23:7ff.). Pilate was procurator from 779/26 to 789/36 (*Ant*. xviii.4.3; 5.3; cf. *HJP*², I, 382 n. 130), Caiaphas was high priest from 771/18 to 789/36 (*Ant*. xviii.2.2; 4.3; cf. *HJP*, II/1, 199), and Antipas was tetrarch from 750/4 to 792/39. If the first Passover of Jesus' ministry was in 780/27, the fourth would fall in 783/30. If the first Passover was in 782/29 and if we take a minimal interpretation of the Synoptic Gospels as supposing a ministry of only somewhat over one year, the death Passover was that of the following spring, 783/30; if we take a maximal interpretation of the Fourth Gospel as supposing a ministry that included five Passovers, the fifth would be in 786/33 (Stauffer, p. 8, makes the dates extend from A.D. 28 to 32).

The Gospels name the day before the sabbath (Friday) as the day of the crucifixion (Mt. 27:62; Mk. 15:42; Lk. 23:54; Jn. 19:14, 31, 42), and the Synoptic Gospels represent this Friday as Nisan 15 — the day following (or according to Jewish reckoning from sunset to sunset, the same day as) the day on which the paschal supper was eaten (Mt. 26:17ff.; Mk. 14:12ff.; Lk. 22:7ff.). But the Fourth Gospel is thought by many to represent the paschal meal as still uneaten when Jesus suffered (18:28; cf. 13:29); and it is held that the Synoptic Gospels also contain traces of this view (Mt. 26:5; Mk. 14:2; 15:21; Lk. 23:26). Astronomical calculations show that Nisan 14 could have fallen on Friday in 783/30 and again in 786/33 (H. von Soden, *EB*, I, 806; cf. B. W. Bacon, *JBL*, 28 [1909], 130-148; J. K. Fotheringham, *JTS*, 11 [1910], 120ff.; R. A. Parker and W. H. Dubberstein, *Babylonian Chronology 626 B.C.–A.D. 75* [1956]), but the empirical character of the Jewish calendar renders the result of such calculations uncertain (*HJP*², I, 590f.). In the year 783/30 Friday, Nisan 14, would fall on Apr. 7; in 786/33 Friday, Nisan 14, would fall on Apr. 3. An attempt has also been made (Jaubert) to interpret the data of the Passion week in relation to the Jewish calendar that seems to be reflected in the books of Jubilees and 1 Enoch and to have been in use at Qumrân, in accordance with which the Passover supper would have been eaten already on the preceding Tuesday evening; but this interposes a greater length of time between the supper and the crucifixion than appears to be indicated by the Gospels. There is an early patristic tradition that dates the death of Jesus in the year 782/29, in the consulship of the Gemini (C. H. Turner, *HDB*, I, 413f.), but its origin and trustworthy character are problematical. For A.D. 30 as the most likely date see Bruce, *NT History*, p. 201 n. 20.

G. Summary of Dates. The death of Herod was in the spring of 4 B.C., and the birth of Jesus was prior to that, perhaps as much as two years (Mt. 2:16), and probably when Saturninus was legate of Syria (9-6 B.C.) and Quirinius was in supreme authority in the East; therefore the birth was probably in 6/7 B.C. The baptism of Jesus was in the fifteenth year of Tiberius (Aug. 19, 28 to Aug. 18, 29), probably in the fall of 28. the Fourth Gospel explicitly mentions three Passovers (2:13; 6:4; 11:55) but the first of these, with the cleansing of the temple, must be the same as that which the Synoptic Gospels place at the end (J. Marsh, *Gospel of St. John* [Pelican, 1968], p. 163). Therefore we have in fact to reckon with two Passovers: that of the spring of 29 and that of the spring of 30. The date of the crucifixion is probably Friday, Apr. 7, A.D. 30.

***II. Chronology of the Apostolic Age.**–A. Paul's Conversion*. The chronology of the apostolic age must be based on the data in Acts and the epistolary literature of the NT which afford contacts with persons or events of the Greco-Roman world. From the fixed points thus secured, a general outline of the relative chronology may be established with reasonable probability.

The conversion of Paul followed the stoning of Stephen (Acts 7–9), an event that may probably be assigned to the time of permissiveness in the Roman administration of Palestine that began in A.D. 36 when Vitellius, imperial legate in Syria (35-37), deposed Pilate and sent Marcellus as his representative to Caesarea, and also replaced Caiaphas with Jonathan as high priest. If Paul's conversion ensued thereafter in A.D. 36, his visits to Jerusalem "after three years" and "after fourteen years" (Gal. 1:18; 2:1), each probably counted inclusively from that momentous event, were in A.D. 38 and 49 respectively, and the latter date was presumably also that of the Apostolic Council (Acts 15) in Jerusalem (B. Reicke, *NT Era*, pp. 191-99).

Paul was converted near Damascus (Acts 9:3ff.; 22:5ff.; 26:12ff.; Gal. 1:17). After a brief stay in that city (Acts 9:19ff.) he went to Arabia and then came again to Damascus (Gal. 1:17). When he left Damascus the second time, he returned to Jerusalem after an absence of three years (Gal. 1:18). The flight of Paul from Damascus (Acts 9:24) probably terminated his second visit to the city. At that time the ethnarch Aretas (i.e., Aretas IV, who reigned as king of the Nabateans from *ca*. 9 B.C. until

CHRONOLOGY OF THE NT

ca. A.D. 40), acting with the resident Jews (Acts 9:23f.), guarded the city in order to seize him (2 Cor. 11:32).

Damascus had been taken by the Romans in 62 B.C. and probably continued under their control until the death of Tiberius (March A.D. 37). Roman coins of Damascus have been found from the time of Augustus, Tiberius, and Nero, although there are no such coins from the time of Caligula and Claudius (*HJP*², I, 582; *HJP*, II/1, 97f.). Moreover, the relations of Aretas with Augustus and Tiberius make it extremely improbable that he held Damascus during their reign as part of his kingdom, or that he acquired it by conquest. The best explanation is probably that Damascus was given to Aretas by Caligula, the change in the imperial attitude being due perhaps to the influence primarily of Agrippa and possibly also of Vitellius (Steinmann, *Aretas IV* [1909], pp. 34ff.; S. Perowne, *Journeys of St. Paul* [1973], p. 18). Caligula began to reign on Mar. 18, 37 and Aretas IV probably sent his governor to Damascus soon afterward so this was probably the situation when Paul made his escape three years after his conversion, i.e., in A.D. 38.

B. Death of Herod Agrippa I. Herod Agrippa I died in Caesarea shortly after a Passover season (Acts 12:23; cf. 12:3, 19). Caligula had given him the tetrarchy of Philip and of Lysanias in A.D. 37 — the latter either at this time or later — with the title of king (*Ant.* xviii.6.10; *BJ* ii.9.6), and this was increased in A.D. 40 by the tetrarchy of Antipas (*Ant.* viii.7.1f.; *BJ* ii.9.6). Claudius became emperor on Jan. 25, 41 and "forthwith" gave him also Judea and Samaria (*Ant.* xix.5.1; *BJ* ii.11.5), thus making his territory even more extensive than that of his grandfather, Herod the Great. Agrippa reigned over "all Judea" for three years under Claudius (*Ant.* xix.8.2; *BJ* ii.11.6), his death falling in the spring of A.D. 44 in the seventh year of his reign. The games mentioned by Josephus in this connection are probably those that were celebrated in honor of the return of Claudius from Britain in A.D. 44 (*HJP*², I, 452 n. 43). There are coins of Agrippa from his sixth year, but the attribution to him of coins from other years is questioned (*HJP*², I, 451 n. 40; Madden, p. 132). In order to show his sympathy with the Jewish priestly authorities Agrippa probably acted against the Christian leaders shortly after his arrival to rule in Judea, so the execution of James and imprisonment and subsequent departure of Peter (Acts 12:1-4, 17) are to be put at Passover time in A.D. 41.

C. Famine under Claudius. The prophecy of a famine and its fulfillment under Claudius (Acts 11:28) are associated in Acts with the death of Herod Agrippa I (11:30; 12:23). Famines in Rome during the reign of Claudius are mentioned by Suetonius (*Claudius* 18), Dio Cassius (lx.11), Tacitus (*Ann.* xii.43), and Orosius (*Historiae* vii.6). Josephus narrates in the time of Fadus the generosity of Helena during a famine in Palestine (*Ant.* xx.2.5), but subsequently dates the famine generally in the time of Fadus and Alexander. The famine in Palestine would fall therefore at some time between 44 and 48 (*HJP*², I, 457 n.8).

D. Sergius Paulus. When Paul visited Cyprus with Barnabas the island was administered by Sergius Paulus (Acts 13:7ff.), a propraetor with the title proconsul (Marquardt, I, 391). There is an inscription from Cyprus (R. Cagnat, *Inscriptiones Graecae ad res Romanas pertinentes* [906], III, 930), dating from the 1st cent., and probably from the year 53 (T. Zahn, *Neue Kirchliche Zeitschrift,* 15 [1904], 194) in which an incident in the career of a certain Apollonius is dated in the proconsulship of Paulus (*epí Paulou* [*anth*]-*ypátou*). From another inscription (*CIG,* 2632), dated in the twelfth year of Claudius, it appears that L. Annius Bassus was proconsul in 52. If the Julius Cordus mentioned by Bassus was his immediate predecessor, the proconsulship of Sergius Paulus may be dated at some time before 51.

Bema at Corinth, where Paul was brought before Gallio and the tribunal (Acts 18:12-17). The date of Gallio's proconsulship is important in establishing the chronology of Paul's journeys. (W. S. LaSor)

E. Edict of Claudius. When Paul came to Corinth for the first time, he met Aquila and Priscilla, who had left Rome because of an edict of Claudius expelling the Jews from the city (Acts 18:2). Suetonius mentions an expulsion of the Jews from Rome by Claudius but gives no date (*Claudius* 25; cf. Dio Cassius lx.6). Orosius, however, dates the edict in the ninth year of Claudius or A.D. 49 (*Historiae* vii.6.15); and although Josephus, from whom he quotes, does not mention this edict but records the favor shown by Claudius to the Jews and to Herod Agrippa I (*Ant.* xix.5.1-3; cf. Dio Cassius lx.6.6, 9f.; 8.2), it is not improbable that the date is approximately accurate (*HJP,* II/2, 237 n. 69).

F. Gallio. During Paul's first sojourn in Corinth the apostle was brought before the proconsul Gallio (Acts 18:12). This could not have been earlier than the year 44, when Claudius gave Achaia back to the Senate and the province was administered by a propraetor with the title proconsul (Dio Cassius lx.24; Marquardt, I, 331f.; W. M. Ramsay, *Expos.,* 5th series, 5 [1897], 207). Moreover, the career of Seneca makes it improbable that his brother would be advanced to this position before 49 or 50 (A. von Harnack, *Die Zeit . . . und die Chronologie* [1878], I, 237; C. G. Wieseler, *Chronologie des apostolischen Zeitalters* [1848], p. 119). There is a fragmentary inscription from Delphi containing a letter from the emperor Claudius in which mention is made of Gallio (E. Groag, *Die römischen Reichsbeamten von Achaia bis auf Diokletian* [1939], pp. 32-35). The inscription is dated by the title of the emperor, which contains the number 26. This is referred naturally to the *acclammatio* as *"imperator"* and dated in the year 52 before August, after which time the number 27 occurs in the title of Claudian inscriptions. Gallio may therefore have been proconsul for the year beginning in the spring or summer of A.D. 51 or 52. The latter date is supported by some (Hennequin, *DBSup.,* II, 355-373), but the former seems more probable. If Paul was brought before Gallio in the summer of 51 soon after the new proconsul arrived and had already been in Corinth one year and six months (Acts 18:11), he must have arrived in midwinter 49/50, perhaps in December, A.D. 49 or January, A.D. 50 (H. Lietzmann, *Zeitschrift für wissenschaftliche Theologie,* 54 [1911], 345-354; Deissmann, *Paul,* p. 272; P. Lemerle, *Philippes et la Macedoine orientale* [1945], p. 18f.).

G. Festus. When Paul had been for two years a prisoner in Caesarea, Felix was succeeded by Festus as procurator of Judea (Acts 24:27). Suetonius (*Claudius* 28) says that Claudius gave Felix command of Judea, and Josephus (*Ant.* xx.7.1) tells of the same appointment and immediately afterward mentions the completion by Claudius of his twelfth year of reign. Therefore the appointment of Felix was probably in the twelfth year of Claudius, A.D. 52. The accession of Festus, which is placed by Eusebius in his church history in the reign of Nero (*HE* ii.22.1), is dated in the *Chronicon* in the version of Jerome to the second year of Nero, A.D. 56, and in the Armenian version to the fourteenth year of Claudius, A.D. 54. The excerpts from the *Chronicon*-Syncellus apparently follow the text underlying the version of Jerome, but state simply that Festus was sent as successor of Felix by Nero (A. K. I. Schoene, ed., *Eusebi Chronicorum* [1866-1875], II, 154). After his removal from office Felix was tried in Rome, but escaped punishment through the influence of his brother Pallas, who, according to Josephus, was in favor with Nero at that time (*Ant.* xx.8.9). Pallas was removed from office before Feb. 13, A.D. 55 (Tacitus *Ann.* xiii.14.1; cf. 15.1), but apparently continued to have influence with the emperor, for he fixed the terms of his removal and was permitted to enjoy his fortune for several years (*Ann.* xiii.14.1f.; 23.1-3). His death occurred in A.D. 62 (*Ann.* xiv.65.1). The trial of Felix must therefore have occurred before 62; but it is impossible to place it before the removal of Pallas, for this would necessitate the removal of Felix in 54, and this is excluded by the fact that the first summer of Nero's reign fell in A.D. 55. Dates proposed for the succession of Festus to Felix run therefore from A.D. 55 (Knox, p. 66) to 60 (Armstrong, *ISBE* [1929], I, 649). According to new "micrographic" evidence discovered by J. Vardaman, however, the date can be fixed in A.D. 56. On a coin of Nero's fifth year are the names of the consuls of the year 58 and the notation that this was the third year of Festus. Therefore the first year of Festus was 56.

H. Relative Chronology of Acts. Of the foregoing data the most precisely defined points seem to be the proconsulate of Gallio in Corinth with the consequent conclusion that Paul arrived there in approximately December, 49 or January, 50, and the succession of Festus to Felix in A.D. 56 with the consequent conclusion that this was the date of the termination of the imprisonment of Paul in Caesarea and the beginning of his "shipwreck journey" to Rome. In agreement with these dates and within the limits indicated by the other data discussed above, the following conclusions appear probable. Paul's "first missionary journey" (Acts 13–14) was in A.D. 47-48 prior to the Apostolic Council (Gal. 2:1; Acts 15) in A.D. 49. The "second missionary journey" (Acts 15:40–18:22) was in A.D. 49-51, with Paul's appearance before Gallio in the spring A.D. 51 and his return soon thereafter. Departure on the "third missionary journey" (Acts 18:23–21:16) was in the fall A.D. 51, with two years and three months in Ephesus (Acts 19:8, 10; called three years in 20:31) and arrival in Jerusalem about Pentecost (Acts 20:46) in A.D. 54. Two years of imprisonment in Caesarea were from the summer of 54 to the summer of 56, ending soon after the arrival of Festus in the spring of 56. The "shipwreck journey" began then in the fall of 56; and after three months (Acts 28:11) on Malta in the winter of 56/57, arrival in Rome was in the spring of 57; and the two subsequent years in Rome with which Acts closes (28:30f.) extended to the spring of A.D. 59.

I. Pauline Epistles. Ten of the thirteen Pauline Epistles were written during a period of about ten years between Paul's arrival in Corinth and the close of his first Roman imprisonment. These Epistles fall into three groups, each possessing certain distinctive characteristics; and although each reflects the difference in time and occasion of its production, they all reveal an essential continuity of thought and a similarity of style which evidences unity of authorship. The earliest group consists of the Thessalonian Epistles, both of which were written from Corinth on the second missionary journey *ca.* A.D. 50, while Silas (Silvanus) was still in Paul's company and shortly after Paul's visit to Athens (1 Thess. 1:1; 3:1f., 6; 2 Thess. 1:1). The major Epistles belong to the third missionary journey. 1 Corinthians was written from Ephesus *ca.* 52-53; Galatians probably from Ephesus, either before or after 1 Corinthians, for Paul had been twice in Galatia (Gal. 4:13); 2 Corinthians from Macedonia *ca.* 54; and Romans from Corinth in early 54. The imprisonment Epistles were written from Rome; Colossians, Ephesians, and Philemon *ca.* 58, and Philippians *ca.* 59.

J. Release and Death of Paul. When Paul wrote to Philemon (Philem. 22) and to the Philippians (Phil. 2:24; cf. 1:25), he expected a favorable outcome of his trial in Rome and was looking forward to another visit to the East. Before his arrest he had planned a journey to Spain by way of Rome (Rom. 15:28), and when he bade farewell to the Ephesian elders at Miletus (Acts 20:25) he must have had in mind not only the dangers of his journey to Jerusalem, but also his determination to enter another field of labor. 1 Clem. 5, the Muratorian Canon, and the Apocryphal Acts of Peter witness to the Spanish journey, and the Pastoral Epistles to a journey to the East and to another imprisonment in Rome. The two lines of evidence for Paul's release are independent and neither can be explained as derived merely from the statement of Paul's intention in Romans and in Philemon and Philippians. The historical situation implied in the Pastoral Epistles can be charged with artificiality only on the hypothesis that Paul was not released from his first Roman imprisonment. The data of these Epistles cannot be fitted into any period of Paul's life previous to his imprisonment. But these data are embodied in just those parts of the Pastoral Epistles which are admitted to be Pauline by those who regard the Epistles as containing only fragments genuinely from Paul but assign the Epistles in their present form to a later writer. On any hypothesis of authorship, however, the tradition these Epistles contain cannot be much later than the first quarter of the 2nd century. It is highly probable, therefore, that Paul was released from his first Roman imprisonment; that he visited Spain and the East; and that he was imprisoned a second time in Rome, where he met his death under Nero. Since Clement of Rome describes the death of both Paul and Peter in connection with the martyrdom of a "vast multitude" who suffered "among us," and since Tacitus (*Ann.* xv.44) describes the persecution by Nero of a "vast multitude" in connection with the fire at Rome in the summer of 64, it is possible that this is the date of the death of the two apostles. Jerome (*De vir. ill.* 1, 5), however, puts the two martyrdoms in the fourteenth year of Nero (A.D. 67/68), while in the *Chronicon* of Eusebius the date is 67 in the Armenian version, 68 in the version of Jerome, and these dates are often cited. According to early tradition Paul suffered martyrdom by beheading with the sword (Tertullian *De praescr. haer.* 36). This was the manner of execution for a Roman citizen, which Paul was (Acts 16:37; 22:27-29; 23:27), and probably presupposes a legal proceeding eventuating in the death sentence. Sulpicius Severus (*Chronicorum* ii.29) connects the deaths of the apostles with the promulgation of laws by Nero making it unlawful to be a Christian. All of this must have taken time and may make the date of A.D. 67/68 probable for the death of Paul, perhaps most likely A.D. 67.

K. Death of Peter. In addition to what is recorded of Peter in the NT there is a tradition of his bishopric of 20 or 25 years in Rome (cf. A. von Harnack, *Geschichte der altchristlichen Litteratur* [1893-1904], II; *Chronologie*, I, 243f.). 1 Peter was probably written from Rome (5:13; cf. Eusebius *HE* ii.15.2), and the testimony to Peter's martyrdom (implied in Jn. 21:18f.) under Nero in Rome by crucifixion (Tertullian *De praescr. haer.* 36; cf. 1 Clem. 5:1ff.) is early and probably trustworthy. Tradition also associates Peter and Paul in their Roman labors and martyrdom (Dionysius in Eusebius *HE* ii.25.8; Irenaeus *Adv. haer.* iii.1.2; iii.3.1). The mention of the Vatican as the place of Peter's interment (Caius in Eusebius *HE* ii.25.6f.) may also indicate a connection of his martyrdom with the Neronian persecution following the fire in the summer of A.D. 64. The record of the fire and the persecution by Tacitus (*Ann.* xv.38-44) recounts a rather long series of events and makes it probable that the persecution followed some time after the fire itself, probably later in 64 or even in 65, and this may be taken as the probable date of the death of Peter (A.D. 64/65), perhaps most likely A.D. 65. If Peter departed from Jerusalem (Acts 12:17) and went to Rome in A.D. 41 his death in 65 would have been 25 years (counted inclusively) later, during which time he could have been considered the head of the Roman church although surely not remaining there continuously for all that time. (The arguments against the Roman sojourn and martyrdom of Peter are stated fully by Schmiedel in *EB, s.v.* "Simon Peter," esp. cols. 458ff.; on the other hand, cf. T. Zahn, *Intro. to the NT* [Eng. tr. 1909], II, 158ff.).

L. Death of James the Just. James the Just, the brother of the Lord, was prominent in the church of Jerusalem at the time of the Apostolic Council (Acts 15:13ff.; Gal. 2:9; cf. 1:19; 2:12), and later when Paul was arrested he seems still to have occupied this position (Acts 21:18ff.), laboring with impressive devotion for the Jewish people until his martyrdom *ca.* 62 (Josephus *Ant.* xx.9.1; Eusebius, *HE* ii.23.3ff.; Reicke, *NT Era*, p. 215). The Epistle of James contains numerous indications of its early origin and equally clear evidence that it was not written during the period when the questions discussed in the major Epistles of Paul were agitating the Church. It is possibly the earliest book of the NT, written before the Apostolic Council.

M. The Synoptic Gospels. In the decade just preceding the fall of Jerusalem, the tradition of the life and teaching of Jesus was committed to writing in the Synoptic Gospels. Early tradition dates the composition of Matthew's Gospel in the lifetime of Peter and Paul (Irenaeus *Adv. haer.* iii.1.1; Eusebius *HE* v.8.2ff.), and that of the Gospel of Mark either just before or just after Peter's death (Clement in Eusebius *HE* vi.14.7; cf. ii.15; and Irenaeus *Adv. haer.* iii.11.1; Presbyter of Papias in Eusebius *HE* iii.39.15; cf. also 2 Pet. 1:15). The Lukan writings — both the Gospel and Acts — are also held by some to fall in this period, on the basis of the argument that the Gospel contains no intimation that Jesus' prophecy of the destruction of Jerusalem had been fulfilled (cf. Lk. 21:21; Acts 11:28), and that the silence of Acts about the issue of Paul's trial is best explained on the hypothesis of an early date (Jerome *De vir. ill.* 7; Harnack, *Neue Untersuchungen zur Apostelgeschichte* [1911]; cf. also Lk. 10:7; 1 Tim. 5:18). To this period belong also the Epistle of Jude and the Epistle to the Hebrews (if addressed to Jewish Christians of Palestine; but later *ca.* A.D. 80, if addressed to Jewish Christians of Rome), the former being used in 2 Peter and the latter in 1 Clement.

N. Death of John. Early tradition connects John with Ephesus and mentions his continuing in life until the time of Trajan (Irenaeus *Adv. haer.* ii.22.5 [Eusebius *HE* v.24]; iii.1.1; v.30.3; v.33.4; Clement in Eusebius *HE* iii.23.5-19; Polycrates in Eusebius *HE* iii.31.3; v.24.3; Justin *Dial.* lxxxi; cf. Rev. 1:1, 4, 9; 22:8; Jn. 21:22-24; 19:35). He died probably about the end of the 1st century. There is another but less well-attested tradition of early martyrdom based chiefly on the De Boor fragment of Papias (*TU,* 1888), a Syriac martyrology of the 4th cent. (Wright, *Journal of Sacred Literature,* 8 [1865/66], the Codex Coislinianus 305 of Georgius Hamartolus). This tradition, it is thought by some, finds confirmation in Mk. 10:35-40; Mt. 20:20-23 (cf. Bousset, *TR,* 9 [1905], 225ff., 277ff.), but more probably owes its origin to a confusion with John the Baptist who did experience martyrdom. It is often supposed that it was during the closing years of his long life that John wrote Revelation, the Fourth Gospel, and the three Epistles, but there are serious grounds for considering that all of these as well as all the other writings of the canonical NT are prior in date to A.D. 70 (J. A. T. Robinson, *Redating the NT* [1976]).

O. Summary of Dates.

Conversion of Paul	36
Death of James son of Zebedee	41
Death of Herod Agrippa I	44
Famine Under Claudius	44–48
Epistle of James	before 50
First missionary journey	47–48
Apostolic Council	49
Edict of Claudius	49
Proconsulship of Sergius Paulus	before 51
Second missionary journey	49–51
1 and 2 Thessalonians from Corinth	50
Proconsulship of Gallio	51/52
Third missionary journey	51–54
Paul in Ephesus	52–53
1 Corinthians and Galatians from Ephesus	52–53
2 Corinthians from Macedonia	early 54
Romans from Corinth	early 54
Arrest of Paul in Jerusalem	54
Accession of Festus	56
First Roman imprisonment of Paul	57–59
Colossians, Ephesians, Philemon, from Rome	58
Philippians from Rome	59
Release of Paul and journeys in East and West	59–67
Death of James the Just	62
1 Timothy and Titus from Macedonia	62–63
1 and 2 Peter from Rome	before 64
Death of Peter in Rome	65
2 Timothy from Rome	67
Death of Paul in Rome	67
Synoptic Gospels, Acts, Jude, and Hebrews	before 70
Fourth Gospel, Revelation, Epistles of John from Ephesus	before 70
Death of John	98–100

Bibliography.–R. Anger, *De temporum in Actis Apostolorum ratione* (1833); J. B. Lightfoot, *Biblical Essays* (1893); H. Lietzmann, *Petrus und Paulus in Rom* (2nd ed. 1927); G. A. Deissmann, *Paul* (2nd ed.; Eng. tr. 1927); U. Holzmeister, *Chronologia Vitae Christi* (1933); H. Lietzmann, *Zeitrechnung* (1934); G. Ogg, *Chronology of the Public Ministry of Jesus* (1940); J. Knox, *Chapters in a Life of Paul* (1950); Lazzarato, *Chronologia Christi seu discordantium fontium concordantia ad juris norman* (1952); L. Fendt, *TLZ,* 78 (1953), 1-10; O. Cullmann, *Peter* (Eng. tr. 1953); H. J. Cadbury, *Book of Acts in History* (1955); R. Williams, *Acts of the Apostles* (1957); A. Jaubert, *La Date de la cène* (1957); J. Blinzler, *ZNW,* 49 (1958), 238-251; N. Walker, *Nov.Test.,* 3 (1959), 317-320; A. Jaubert, *NTS,* 7 (1960), 1-30; E. Stauffer, *Jesus and His Story* (1960); K. G. Kuhn, *ZNW,* 52 (1961), 65-73; J. Finegan, *Handbook of Biblical Chronology* (1964); E. J. Bicker-

man, *Chronology of the Ancient World* (1968); B. I. Reicke, *NT Era* (1968); G. Ogg, *Chronology of the Life of Paul* (1968); S. Dockx, *Nov.Test.*, 13 (1971), 261-304; F. F. Bruce, *NT History* (1972); S. Dockx, *Recherches de science religieuse*, 62 (1974), 221-241.
W. P. ARMSTRONG J. FINEGAN

CHRYSOLITE. *See* STONES, PRECIOUS.

CHRYSOPRASE. *See* STONES, PRECIOUS.

CHUB [Heb. *kûḇ*]. *See* LIBYA.

CHUN [Heb. *kûn*]. *See* CUN.

CHURCH [Gk. *kyriakós*–'belonging to the Lord'; NT *ekklēsía*–'gathering'; Lat. *ecclesia*].

I. Pre-Christian History of the Term
II. The Church and the Teaching of Jesus
III. The Church in Acts
IV. Pauline Doctrine of the Church
V. Notes of the Church
VI. Distinctions of the Church
VII. Order of the Church

I. Pre-Christian History of the Term.–Although Gk. *ekklēsía* became a distinctively Christian word, it has both a Greek and an OT history. In the Greek world it was used of a public assembly summoned by a herald (< *ek*, "out," and *kaleín*, "to call"; cf. Acts 19:32, 39f.). In the LXX it was used for the Heb. *qāhāl*, which denotes the congregation or people of Israel, especially as gathered before the Lord (cf. Acts 7:38). It is of interest that behind the NT term stand both Greek democracy and Hebrew theocracy, the two being brought together in a theocratic democracy or democratic theocracy.

II. The Church and the Teaching of Jesus.–In the teaching of Jesus Himself there is little mention of the Church. The only two references in the Gospels are both in Matthew (16:18: "On this rock I will build my church," and 18:17: "Tell it to the church"). In the second of these the reference might be to the Jewish synagogue, though the general context of Mt. 18 seems to suggest the emergent Christian community. Apart from the critical questions raised by some scholars, these verses give rise to many problems. For example, do they denote the intention of Jesus to found a Church? If so, or even if He only foresees its creation, what is the relation of this Church to the older congregation of the Lord? Is the new to continue the old, to supersede it, or to be quite different and perhaps parallel? Again, what is the relationship between the Church and the kingdom of God or of heaven which is the main theme of the teaching of Jesus? Are the two completely different? Are they synonymous? Or is the Church as the present sphere of Christ's rule a provisional or partial form of the kingdom?

These questions are easier to ask than to answer, and it is probably in terms of a qualified comprehensiveness that true solutions are to be sought. Thus the Church of Jesus is a new body, yet there is a continuity of fulfillment in relation to the OT congregation. Again, the kingdom is quite evidently not the Church, for we could hardly proclaim the Church as the first apostles proclaimed the kingdom (Acts 8:12). On the other hand, we certainly cannot say that the Church is an alternative after the rejection of the kingdom. To the extent that the Church is a fellowship of those who have accepted the kingdom, submitted to its rule, and become its heirs, we may rather believe that it is a creation and instrument and therefore a form and manifestation of the kingdom prior to its final establishment in glory.

III. The Church in Acts.–While the kingdom is still the theme of apostolic preaching, the word "church" is regularly used in Acts to denote the company of believers, more especially in the local sense. Thus we read of churches in Jerusalem (5:11), Antioch (13:1), and Caesarea (18:22), a similar usage being found in the seven letters of Revelation. The same word can also be used, however, for the sum of local churches or the totality of believers (9:31), though with no suggestion of an organized external structure. The same twofold usage occurs in the Pauline Epistles. Each individual group may be addressed as the church, e.g., "the church of God which is at Corinth" (1 Cor. 1:2). Indeed, the word is perhaps further localized in respect of the household group within the local church, though this is unusual (Rom. 16:5; 1 Cor. 16:19). On the other hand, the comparison between Jews and Greeks on the one side and the Church on the other (1 Cor. 10:32) shows that there is also the more general sense in Paul (cf. 1 Cor. 12:28), this being, of course, the basis of the Pauline doctrine of the Church.

IV. Pauline Doctrine of the Church.–Theologically, there is only one Church, for Christians are now fellow citizens of the saints and of the household of God, built upon the foundation of the apostles and prophets. If there is a distinction, it is that of fulfillment as compared with promise, but not of a different purpose, covenant, basis, consecration, or goal. This Church is not a human organization; it is God's workmanship (Eph. 2:10), created in accordance with His eternal purpose in Christ (Eph. 1:4f.) that in it He might show the exceeding riches of His grace (Eph. 2:7). It may thus be described in several pregnant phrases, of which the following are to be noted.

(a) The Church is the people or Israel of God (Eph. 2:12; cf. 1 Pet. 2:10), in whom there is fulfillment of the ancient covenant promise: "I will be your God, and you shall be my people."

(b) It is the household or family of God (Eph. 2:19; 3:15; 4:6), consisting of those who are adopted by God as sons and heirs in Christ.

(c) It is the planting of God to bring forth fruit to His glory (1 Cor. 3:10; cf. Jn. 15:1f.).

(d) It is the temple of God, built by God Himself in Christ to be His dwelling and therefore to be the center of true holiness and worship (Eph. 2:21f.; cf. Jn. 2:19f.; 1 Cor. 3:9; 1 Pet. 2:4f.).

(e) It is the bride of Christ for which the Bridegroom gave Himself that it might be presented, cleansed, sanctified, and pure at the eternal marriage feast (Eph. 5:25.).

(f) It is the body of Christ, the fulness of Him that fills all in all, Christ Himself being the head (Eph. 4:15f.) and yet also in a true sense the totality (1 Cor. 12:12), with each Christian being a member in particular (1 Cor. 12:27).

These descriptions obviously open up great themes which we cannot pursue in the present restricted context. The following points, however, may be observed.

(1) We are neither to isolate nor to oppose the various descriptions, nor to make any one a ruling principle, but rather to accept the rich and varied contributions that they all make toward a comprehensive view.

(2) While the descriptions naturally have a symbolical character, they are not to be referred to an ideal or mystical or nebulous church, but are to be seen as descriptions of the reality of the Church in contrast to present but passing aspects.

(3) It is to be emphasized that this reality of the Church is in Christ and not in itself. Thus the Church is the Israel

of God in Jesus Christ the true Israelite. It is the family of God in Christ the true Son. It is the planting of God in Christ the true vine or grain of wheat. It is the temple of God in Christ whose incarnate body is the dwelling place of God and therefore the foundation, cornerstone, and temple. It is the bride as the chosen and sanctified bride of this Bridegroom. It is the body, not as an independent or supplementary organism, but as He Himself is both body and head, and as it finds all its being and life and order and power in Him.

The third point obviously underlies the other two. Christ can never be exhausted by any one description and therefore there is room for a wealth of varied imagery. Christ is true reality, and therefore it is in Him rather than in its faltering and passing manifestation that the true reality of the Church is to be found.

V. Notes of the Church.–In addition to the descriptions of the Church, the NT also brings before us certain features or characteristics usually referred to as the notes of the Church. These may be classified in various ways, but we do well, perhaps, to follow the traditional grouping of the creeds in terms of unity, sanctity, catholicity, and apostolicity.

(1) The Church is one. Naturally, this is no mere unity of organization. Nor is it a necessary uniformity of practice. It is a theological unity grounded in the one body, etc., of Eph. 4:4f. It is a given indestructible unity which no external separation or schism can nullify or overthrow. Yet it is a unity that is not just invisible or vaguely spiritual. Already in the churches of the NT we see a conscious sense of unity and therefore a resistance to schism (cf. esp. 1 Cor. 1:11ff.). The fact that the Church is Christ's body is given very practical application (1 Cor. 12:12ff.). Nor is this merely a unity of the local church. From the very first there are close relations among the churches (Acts 11:22; 15:2). A conference can be held at Jerusalem that is of more than local concern (15:6ff.). Paul and Barnabas are given the right hand of fellowship by the older apostles (Gal. 2:9). Paul in his collection is concerned to forge a practical bond among the churches (2 Cor. 8f.). Everywhere there is a visible unity in the NT Church. The inward reality seeks and should be given practical expression, not only on the local scene, but also in the wider interrelations of the universal Church.

(2) The Church is holy. It is a holy nation (1 Pet. 2:9). It is the fellowship of the saints or the sanctified (1 Cor. 1:2). Here again we do not begin with externals. This is not merely a formal sanctification. It is the holiness given to the Church as the people that in Jesus Christ is called out, cleansed, and consecrated to divine service. Nor is it a merely future holiness. For all the glaring faults and failures of the Church, its holiness is its reality inasmuch as it is Christ's Church. On the other hand, the Bible certainly does not speak merely of an invisible or mystical or ideal holiness. The holiness of the Church is to find expression in sanctified life and consecrated service. Christians are commanded to be holy (2 Cor. 7:1; 1 Thess. 4:3). They are to be wholly yielded up to God (Rom. 12:1; 1 Cor. 6:19f.). Their life and work are to be brought into conformity with their true being in Christ. Prayer is made for their sanctification (1 Thess. 5:23). They are also empowered by the Holy Spirit both to achieve practical sanctification (Rom. 8:1ff.; Gal. 5:16f.; Eph. 5:9) and to discharge the ministry of preaching and praise to which they are consecrated (Acts 1:8; 1 Thess. 1:5).

(3) The Church is catholic. This does not mean that it constitutes a single worldwide organization. It means that Jesus Christ died for all classes without distinction, so that in His Church there are no external qualifications of age, sex, generation, descent, or status. In Him these distinctions have no reality. They still exist, and legitimately or illegitimately they are reflected in the life and work of the Church. But the Church is not to be ordered by them. It is catholic in its true reality. In Christ there is neither Greek nor Jew, circumcision nor uncircumcision, Barbarian, Scythian, bond nor free (Col. 3:11), male nor female (Gal. 3:28). The Church is not to be identified with any human grouping, culture, or structure. Its boundaries cannot be drawn in terms of any human differentiations. Despite the need for external manifestations of unity, it is not identical exclusively with any one ecclesiastical construct. Its catholicity is rooted in the representative action of Jesus Christ, the one for the many in whom the many are one.

(4) The Church is apostolic. This implies rather more than genealogical descent of organization or ministry from the apostles. It means that the apostles, with the prophets, are the foundation of the Church (Eph. 2:20). They are the first and authentic witnesses of Jesus Christ (Acts 1:8). It is through them that the record and message of the gospel come. They are raised up for this purpose. They are thus the criterion of true proclamation and teaching. The true Church may be recognized by its fidelity to apostolic testimony and doctrine. It believes and proclaims what it has received (1 Cor. 12:23; 15:1f.; 2 Thess. 2:15; 2 Tim. 1:13; 2:2). Nor does this apostolic tradition lie in the sphere of fallible human memory. By the Holy Spirit it has been committed to writing in order that the apostolicity of the Church might be safeguarded (Lk. 1:1ff.; Jn. 20:21; 21:24). To the prophetic testimony of the OT there has thus been added the apostolic testimony of the NT (cf. 1 Cor. 15:2). In other words, apostolicity means the preservation and honoring of Holy Scripture. Where Scripture is read and preached as the basis of evangelism and edification and the supreme rule of faith and practice, there is the apostolic Church (1 Tim. 3:15ff.).

VI. Distinctions of the Church.–From an early period it has been recognized that, while the Church is one and catholic, it presents different aspects or forms which call for differentiation in reference. Thus already in the Bible itself there is distinction between the OT Church and the NT Church. It would be wrong to deduce from this a complete dichotomy, as though the NT Church were something quite different which began only at some point in the NT story, e.g., at Pentecost. On the other hand, it would be pointless to deny that there are valid differences between the OT Church and the NT Church. A legitimate distinction may thus be drawn.

Again, the fact that many brethren are now "asleep" (1 Thess. 4:13ff.) suggests a distinction between the Church as already with the Lord and the Church still engaged in pilgrimage and conflict, i.e., the so-called Church triumphant and Church militant. Insofar as there is here a real though not an ultimate difference, a distinction may be validly made; and the terms triumphant and militant have a good scriptural basis even if they are not applied to the Church in this way. There is no justification for introducing a third category comprising the Church in purgatory.

What are we to say concerning the common Reformation distinction between the Church visible and the Church invisible? Here again there seems to be a legitimate basis, even though there is no corresponding biblical usage. Thus the true being of the Church in Christ is not seen. Believers are hid with Christ in God (Col. 3:3). We walk by faith and not by sight (2 Cor. 5:7). Faith is the evidence of things not seen (He. 11:1). There are hidden things which are yet to be brought to light (1 Cor. 4:5). These verses imply first that the visible aspect of the Church does not yet display its invisible reality, thus leading to the tension between what Christians are in themselves and what they are in Christ, and to the so-called scandal of the Church. But they also imply that the external membership of the Church is not necessarily coincident with its internal constitution. "For not all who are descended from Israel belong to Israel" (Rom. 9:6). There are tares in the field as well as wheat (Mt. 13:38). The apostolic band can contain a Judas and the early Church an Ananias and Sapphira. On the other hand, we are not to harden this distinction into a human judgment concerning the true Church and the purely nominal, as though we could know the secrets of the heart and thus anticipate the last judgment. It is striking that in the NT those who confess Christ are addressed as believers and brethren irrespective of the ultimate sincerity of their profession and sometimes in defiance of the evidence of their conduct and beliefs (cf. the Corinthians). The Reformers normally maintained this biblical usage by defining the visible Church as the company of believers in which the Word is faithfully preached and the sacraments are duly administered, but by refraining from any corresponding or counterbalancing pronouncements on the invisible Church.

In addition to these valid distinctions, brief reference may be made to two that are quite invalid. The first is between saints and ordinary Christians, saints being those who have maintained their postbaptismal righteousness and the rest being those who have incurred temporal guilt which must be finally absolved in purgatory. The second is between the clergy and the laity of the Church, the former being a special class of rulers and teachers and the latter the regular members. It may be noted that in the Bible the relevant terms "saints," "heritage" (1 Pet. 5:3; pl. of Gk. *klḗros,* whence clergy), and people (*laós,* whence laity) are all used of the whole Church, so that doctrinal misunderstanding is introduced if they are misapplied in terms of these distinctions.

VII. Order of the Church.–The Church does not exist for itself but for the discharge of a commission. Taking its place and fulfilling its task in the world, it has need of order. Even in the exercise of the free gifts of the Spirit, Paul can still plead for order (1 Cor. 14:40). Even within the one people of God, those who labor and are over you in the Lord are to be esteemed very highly for their work's sake (1 Thess. 5:12f.). Even though there is neither male nor female, the interrelations of man and woman are still to be in terms of order (Eph. 5:22ff.). If there is no rigid or hierarchical organization, the Church is an organism and therefore there is still differentiation of function (1 Cor. 12) with a view to integrated growth and effective activity.

Jesus Himself, of course, made little contribution to the establishment of an orderly pattern of life and ministry, leaving this work to the Holy Spirit as the administrator of spiritual gifts. Yet Jesus left us the basic elements, calling out the Twelve, giving the great commission, instituting the two sacraments, and constituting service the principle of rule and mutual forbearance the principle of conduct.

In Acts the worship of the Church is still linked with the temple, but household meetings are also held for prayer, exhortation, and table fellowship; and a distinctive ministry of word and sacraments is exercised by the disciples and others. The need to supervise the daily ministration leads to the election of the Seven, in whom the later diaconate probably has its origin, though it is noteworthy that two at least of the Seven (Stephen and Philip) seem to display more evangelistic initiative at this stage than the apostles. The deacons are the first instance of popular appointment, the Eleven having been appointed directly by the Lord and the mode of replacing Judas by Matthias being a little obscure.

Five further points are to be noted in relation to Acts. (1) The apostleship can denote a wider body than the Twelve, Paul in particular being directly called to this work by the risen Lord. (2) James, the Lord's brother, seems to emerge as acknowledged leader of the church in Jerusalem (cf. Acts 15:14). (3) Elders are appointed by Paul and Barnabas (not, so far as we are told, by popular election) in the new missionary communities (Acts 14:23), probably after the pattern of the Jewish synagogue (cf. 15:2). (4) These elders may also be called bishops (Acts 20:28), though it is argued by some that, while all bishops are elders, not all elders are necessarily bishops. (5) There are also prophets and teachers in the local churches (Acts 13:1), who may have exercised a more itinerant ministry (cf. 21:10) and among whom we are also to number prophetesses (21:9).

As regards the life and worship of the Church, we do not learn much from Acts. It may be noted, however, that during the period spent by Paul at Troas the disciples came together on the first day of the week to break bread, presumably in the evening (Acts 20:6ff.), although on Jewish reckoning the reference might be to the preceding evening and early morning.

In the Epistles there is obviously a ministry of spiritual gifts in connection with the orderly administration of elders and deacons. Itinerant ministry is still exercised by the apostles, prophets, and teachers, partly for evangelism and partly for instruction and exhortation. There are also special gifts of tongues, interpretations, prophecy, healing, miracles, etc., for the exercise of which opportunity seems to be given in the gatherings of the community, although Paul insists that things must be done in orderly fashion and that women must keep silence in the church (1 Cor. 12–14). The Bible does not tell us, as some suppose, that these special ministries are only for the apostolic age, although obviously there can be no continuation of apostles in the strict sense. On the other hand, these are genuine gifts of the Spirit and cannot, therefore, be made a stereotyped feature of the Church's ministry. Incidentally, the apostles on occasion seem to appoint delegates for particular purposes, e.g., Paul in the case of Timothy and Titus. But here we are in the sphere of a developing missionary situation and there can be no question of the establishment of a permanent feature of organization.

The more regular ministry of bishops and deacons or elders and deacons is, however, a normative element in the Church as we find it in Philippians, the Pastoral Epistles, 1 Peter, James, and possibly the Epistles of John. If the common exercise of ministry in Acts gives guidance for an evangelistic and missionary situation, or for the possible discharge of extraordinary ministries, here we have the pattern for regular pastoral administration within the established community. The work of bishops and elders seems to be primarily spiritual (Acts 20:17, 28, 35; 1 Tim. 3:2-5; Jas. 5:14; 1 Pet. 5:2). The deacons are more concerned with practical matters, especially the administration of help to the sick, poor, and needy (1 Tim. 5:8-11), which is probably the main financial operation of the early Church. It is also likely that in the Pastorals we have reference to deaconesses (cf. Rom. 16:1), though there is no evidence of commanded appointment as in the case of elders (cf. Tit. 1:5). The appointment of elders still seems to be from above (i.e., by the apostles or their delegates), though there is nothing to show that this function of the apostles was transmitted to others apart from the elders themselves (cf. 2 Tim. 2:2). Thus, on the modern mission field the missionary may well institute the local ministry but does not on this account appoint permanent successors to himself for the continuation or control of this ministry.

There can be no disputing the fact that the apostles and their associates exercise a special and primary ministry and take initial order for the Church. Yet this does not allow us to deduce either (1) that they appoint successors in this function or (2) that these successors are the later bishops, or some of the more outstanding of the later bishops. If there is any continuation of the apostolic ministry, it is probably to be found rather in those who pursue the same special function of evangelism and missionary outreach. Yet even here there is only a secondary and derivative form of apostolate. The apostles themselves as the first evangelists and witnesses, appointed by the Lord Himself and specially endowed for their distinctive task, are obviously unique. Not even delegates like Timothy and Titus can properly be described as their successors. The later bishops are the successors only of the first bishops or elders, who were appointed as such, and not as apostles, to provide for orderly and continuous pastoral ministry in the local congregations.

Bibliography.–Barth, *CD*, IV/1-3; Bauer; G. C. Berkouwer, *The Church* (Eng. tr. 1976); D. Bonhoeffer, *Sanctorum communio* (1954); G. W. Bromiley, *Unity and Disunity of the Church* (1958); *Christian Ministry* (1959); E. Brunner, *Misunderstanding of the Church* (Eng. tr. 1953); Calvin *Inst.* iv.1ff.; C. T. Craig, *The One Church* (1951); J. Denney, *Studies in Theology* (1894), ch. 8; *EB*; A. M. Fairbairn, *Place of Christ in Modern Theology* (1893), pp. 513-534; R. N. Flew, *Jesus and His Church* (1956); H. M. Gwatkin, *Early Church History to AD 313* (2nd ed. 1909); F. J. A. Hort, *Christian Ecclesia* (1897); G. Johnston, *Doctrine of the Church in the NT* (1943); J. Knox, *Early Church and the Coming Great Church* (1955); T. M. Lindsay, *Church and the Ministry in the Early Centuries* (1903), lectures 1-5; A. Nygren, *Christ and His Church* (1956); A. Schlatter, *Church in the NT Period* (1955); *TDNT*, III, *s.v.* ἐκκλησία (Schmidt); W. A. Visser 't Hooft, *Kingship of Christ* (1948); *Renewal of the Church* (1956).

G. W. BROMILEY

CHURCH GOVERNMENT.

I. Introduction
  A. General Sense
  B. Local Sense
II. Internal Order
  A. Subjects of Admission
  B. Definite Organizations
  C. Ministers
  D. Ecclesiastical Functions
III. External Authority
IV. Cooperative Relations

I. Introduction.–To discover in definite detail what kind of church government is mirrored in the NT is, no doubt, quite impossible. Certain general features, however, may clearly be seen.

The subject is best approached through the Gk. *ekklēsía*, translated "church." Passing by the history of this word, and its connection with the Heb. *ʿēḏâ* and *qāhāl* (which the LXX sometimes renders by *ekklēsía*), we come at once to the NT usage. Two perfectly distinct senses are found, viz., a general and a local.

A. General Sense. Christ is "head over all things for the church, which is his body . . ." (Eph. 1:22); "the assembly of the firstborn who are enrolled in heaven" (He. 12:23). Here we have "church" in the broadest sense, including all the redeemed in earth and heaven, and in all ages (see also Eph. 3:10; 5:22-27; Col. 1:24).

B. Local Sense. Here the Scripture passages are very numerous. In some cases the word is used in the singular, and in others the plural; in some it is used with reference to a specified church, and in others without such specification. In all cases the sense is local. In Acts 11:26, it is said that Paul and Barnabas "met with the church," where the church at Antioch is meant. In Acts 14:23, Paul and Barnabas are said to have "appointed elders for them in every church," i.e., in churches they had planted. In Rev. 2f. the seven churches of Asia Minor are addressed. In Acts 16:5 we are told that the churches "were strengthened in the faith." On the local sense see further Acts 8:1; 15:4; 16:5; 20:17; Rom. 16:4; 1 Cor. 1:2; 6:4; 11:16; Gal. 1:2, 22, and many other places.

A few passages do not seem exactly to fit into either of the above categories. Such, e.g., are Mt. 18:17 and 1 Cor. 12:28, where it seems best to understand a generic sense. Such, also, are passages like Acts 9:31 and 1 Cor. 10:32, where a collective sense best suits the cases.

Church government in the NT applies only to the local bodies.

II. Internal Order.–With respect to the constitution and life of these NT churches, several points may be made out beyond reasonable doubt.

A. Subjects of Admission. They were composed of persons who professed faith in Christ, and who were believed to have been regenerated, and who had been baptized. See Acts 2:41, 44, 47; 8:12; Rom. 1:8; 6:4; 10:9f.; 1 Cor. 1:2; Col. 1:2, 4; 1 Tim. 6:12, and others, where they are called "saints," "sons of God," "faithful brethren," "sanctified in Christ Jesus."

B. Definite Organizations. They were definitely and permanently organized bodies, and not temporary and loose aggregations of individuals. It is quite impossible, for example, to regard the church at Antioch as a loose aggregation of people for a passing purpose. The letters of Paul to the churches at Rome, Corinth, Philippi, Thessalonica, cannot be regarded as addressed to other than permanent and definitely organized bodies.

C. Ministers. They were served by two classes of ministers — one general, the other local.

1. General. At the head of these is the "apostle" (1 Cor. 12:28; Eph. 4:11). His official relation to the churches was general. He did not necessarily belong to the group of the original Eleven. Besides Matthias (Acts 1:26), Paul and Barnabas (1 Cor. 9:5f.), James, the Lord's brother (Gal. 1:19), Andronicus, and Junias (Rom. 16:7) are reckoned as "apostles." The one invariable and necessary qualification of an apostle was that he should have seen the Lord after the Resurrection (Acts 1:22; 1 Cor. 9:1). Another qualification was to have wrought "the signs of an apostle" (2 Cor. 12:12; cf. 1 Cor. 9:2). He was to bear witness to what he had seen and heard, to preach the gospel of the kingdom (Acts 1:8; 1 Cor. 1:17), to found churches and have a general care of them (2 Cor. 11:28). From the nature of his chief qualification, his office was temporary.

Next comes the "prophet." His relation to the churches, also, was general. It was not necessary that he should have seen the Lord, but it appertained to his spiritual function that he should have revelations (Eph. 3:5). There is no indication that his office was in any sense administrative.

After the "prophet" come the "evangelist" and "teacher," the first a traveling preacher, the second, one who had special aptitude for giving instruction.

After the "teacher" and "evangelist" follow a group with special gifts: "healers, helpers, administrators, speakers in various kinds of tongues." It may be that "helpers" and "administrators" are to be identified with "deacons" and "bishops," to be spoken of later. The other items in this part of Paul's list seem to refer to those who had special *charísmata*.

2. Local. There were two clearly distinct offices of a local and permanent kind in the NT churches. Paul (Phil. 1:1) addresses "all the saints in Christ Jesus who are at Philippi, with the bishops and deacons." *See* BISHOP; DEACON.

The most common designation of the first of these officers is "elder" (*presbýteros*). In one passage (Eph. 4:11) he is called "pastor" (*poimḗn*). In Acts 20:17-28, it becomes clear that the office of elder, bishop, and pastor was one; for there the apostle charges the elders of the church at Ephesus to feed (pastor) the church in which the Holy Spirit has made them bishops (cf. Tit. 1:5, 7; 1 Pet. 5:1f.).

The function of the elders was, in general, spiritual, but involved an oversight of all the affairs of the church (1 Tim. 3:2; 5:17).

As to the second of the local church officers, little is given us in the NT. That the office of deacon originated with the appointment of the Seven in Acts 6 is not certain. If we compare the qualifications there given by the apostles with those given by Paul in 1 Tim. 3:8-13, it seems quite probable that the necessity which arose at Jerusalem, and which led to the appointment of the Seven, was really the occasion for originating the office of deacon in the churches. The task assigned the Seven was secular, that is to say, the "service of tables." They were to relieve the apostles of that part of the work. A similar relation to the work of the elders seems to have been borne by that of the deacons.

D. Ecclesiastical Functions. Again, the churches exercised the highest ecclesiastical functions. (1) They exercised discipline. In Mt. 18:17 the final determination of disciplinary matters is in the hands of the church (although it is possible that the reference here may be to the synagogue, and just conceivable that it could be to the Church at large). More clearly, the Corinthian church is urged by Paul to settle its own disputes and to maintain internal discipline (1 Cor. 5:5; 2 Cor. 2:2). It is to be noted, however, that a special binding and loosing is committed to the apostles, that a function of rule appertains to individuals within the churches, and that the local church may finally be construed as the sum of congregations in a city or locality rather than as each particular congregation.

(2) The churches had some responsibility in the election of their ministers. This is a difficult subject. The Seven were plainly selected by the Church (Acts 6:3-13), and the special delegations of Acts 15:22 and 1 Cor. 16:3 (cf. also Phil. 2:25) are to some degree chosen by the congregations. On the other hand, when we turn to more regular ministries of preaching and discipline, we find that apostles were chosen directly by the Lord (but cf. Matthias), that the first elders were appointed or instituted by Paul and Barnabas, that Timothy had hands laid on him by Paul (2 Tim. 1:6) and by the presbytery (1 Tim. 4:14), and that Titus was to appoint elders in every city (Tit. 1:5). We cannot infer from this that there was an arbitrary imposition of ministers from above. On the other hand, we can hardly deny that oversight, especially in ordination, was exercised first by the apostles and then probably by the existing elders or bishops.

(3) The churches were responsible for their own order, e.g., in the administration of the Lord's Supper (1 Cor. 11:20-34) and the management of such matters as the collection or general poor relief. Here again we have an ultimate responsibility of each church primarily discharged through the elders or deacons or other representatives. There is no evidence that apostolic successors are created to supervise whole groups of churches. At the same time, the local church is not to be equated too easily with the individual congregation, as though a presbyterian or episcopal form of order were in essential or necessary contradiction with the NT pattern. It is also to be remembered that a measure of common responsibility cannot be evaded in view of the basic unity of the whole Church, the order or scandal of one local church being of common concern to all. Thus, while there would be no government of groups of churches either by another prominent church or by a confederation, there seems to be good reason for the summoning of larger synods for the settlement, or at least the discussion, of fundamental issues of order, life, and doctrine (cf. the gathering at Jerusalem in Acts 15).

III. External Authority.–As we have seen, the biblical evidence gives us no warrant for a single ecclesiastical organization under hierarchical government, and even less for the spectacle of denominational federations. The tendency toward an extension and centralization of control after the pattern of political government, whether autocratic, oligarchical, or bureaucratic, is one that must be constantly resisted in the Church. Nevertheless, the evidence for pure congregationalism is not quite so strong as might appear. For one thing, there is in the NT a secured interconnection of ministry through the apostles; and, while the apostles themselves can have no successors, it cannot be assumed too lightly that this interconnection should vanish with them. Again, the local church might well become much broader than a single congregation, so that there is no apparent breach of NT order in, for example, the maintenance of a united church of Geneva at the time of the Reformation. Where the local unit is expanded to become a state or nation, there is, of course, a dangerous pressure away from the NT pattern, though it is interesting that Paul can naturally enough address a single epistle to a group of churches (the Galatians) that geographically or politically constitutes a kind of unit of its own. Again, there is obvious interchange and even common decision on matters of more than local concern, the local church being constantly reminded that it cannot advance any abstract claim to individualistic autonomy. In sum, the church order of the NT demands a development of order that is not dominated by political concepts but can allow of apparently contradictory factors through the basic orientation on the principle of common edification and service. In practice, the church unity will obviously be the local congregational or territorial unity. But if the larger interconnection that may be legitimate and necessary should not be allowed to harden into enforced and authoritarian government, neither should the local or territorial independence be exalted as an abstract principle or perverted into self-assertive autonomy.

In the NT there is, of course, no interference of the civil authorities in church matters apart from attempts to silence or suppress. Christians are to be good citizens of the states in which they live (Rom. 13:1-7; 1 Pet. 2:13, 16), observing the law insofar as this impinges on their individual or corporate life. If they may sometimes be called to resist the state because of a demand that conflicts with the law of God, they are obviously not to seek to establish themselves as an *imperium in imperio,* and may rightly avail themselves of their rights as citizens as occasion requires (Acts 16:37). At the same time, they are not to take their differences into temporal, or at least non-Christian, courts (1 Cor.

6:1f.). They do finally belong to another kingdom, though it is not of this world (Jn. 18:36). They recognize that temporal rule, while it is of God, is also of the world, so that there are areas of life in which their peculiarity as citizens or colonists of heaven must transcend and even replace their civil attachment.

More complicated problems arise when rulers or judges themselves become Christians and thus seek to bring the institutions of the state into conformity with Christian standards. In these circumstances might not the judicial system become a Christian court which Christians may use without transgression of Paul's advice in 1 Corinthians? Indeed, does not the whole situation approximate more closely to that of the OT than to that of the NT? This was the conclusion that underlay a good deal of the interrelationship of church and state in the period after Constantine, and also the thinking and practice of the Reformers regarding the godly prince and the state church. At the same time, the more perspicacious Reformers perceived the dangers either of a domination of the state by the church on the one side or an interference of the state in the church on the other; and even in situations where a national church has been maintained there has been a progressive trend away from the OT theocratic conception, a conception that inspired many Separatists in their attempted communities as well as the main Reformers. It is true enough that in any circumstances there are bound to be points at which the state and the church overlap, e.g., in terms of association or the laws of property. It is also true that where leaders of state are themselves Christian the practical relationship may be much closer. Nevertheless, it seems advisable that a clear distinction should always be seen and maintained between the two, the church advising the state and the state facilitating the cause of the church without any equation of the two or subordination of the one to the other.

IV. Cooperative Relations.–Whether the churches are territorial or congregational in the NT, and irrespective of their precise relationship to the NT apostolate, there can be no doubt that in the NT we find cooperation for various purposes, e.g., in evangelism, in the settlement of questions of general interest, in common edification, and in mutual aid. The great expansion of the Church from primitive times has undoubtedly increased rather than diminished both the area of cooperative action and the need for it. Again, the rise of denominationalism in its various forms has posed a demand for joint planning and integration among the denominations, e.g., in evangelistic and missionary work, as also for a common platform on many issues of common Christian concern. It must be emphasized that there should be a measure of freedom in these cooperative ventures. But this will be the freedom of the gospel, which finds its fulfillment and impulsion in the constraint of obedience and service.

See also BISHOP; DEACON; GOVERNMENT; MINISTRY; PRESBYTER.

Bibliography.–Calvin *Inst.* iv.3ff.; *CRE*; H. Cremer, *Biblico-Theological Lexicon of NT Greek* (repr. 1954), *s.v.* ἐκκλησία, συναγωγή; R. W. Dale, *Manual of Congregational Principles* (1884); H. M. Dexter, *Congregationalism* (1880); J. J. I. Döllinger, *The Church and the Churches* (1862); S. R. Driver, *Intro. to the Literature of the OT* (1913); C. Hodge, *Discussions in Church Polity* (1878); R. Hooker, *Ecclesiastical Polity* (1594-1662); F. J. A. Hort, *The Christian Ecclesia* (1897); G. A. Jacob, *Ecclesiastical Polity of the NT* (1871); K. E. Kirk, ed., *The Apostolic Ministry* (1946); G. T. Ladd, *Principles of Church Polity* (1882); J. B. Lightfoot, "The Christian Ministry," in his comm. on Philippians (1896); T. W. Manson, *The Church's Ministry* (1948); J. Moffatt, *The Presbyterian Churches* (1928); A. P. Stanley, *Lectures on the History of the Eastern Church* (1883); B. H. Streeter, *The Primitive Church* (1929); H. B. Swete, ed., *Essays on the Early History of the Church and Ministry* (1918).

E. J. FORRESTER
G. W. BROMILEY

CHURCHES, ROBBERS OF. *See* SACRILEGE, SACRILEGIOUS.

CHURCHES, SEVEN. *See* ANGELS OF THE SEVEN CHURCHES.

CHURL [Heb. *kîlay, kēlay*] (Isa. 32:5, 7, AV); **CHURLISH** [Heb. *qāšeh*]; NEB SURLY. The term "churl," rendered "knave" by the RSV and "villain" by the NEB, is an obsolete term for KNAVE. Among the Anglo-Saxons the churl was regarded as the lowest order of freemen. In 1 S. 25:3 "churlish," meaning "hard" or difficult," is used to describe the uncouth, ill-mannered Nabal.

CHUSHAN-RISHATHAIM (Jgs. 3:8, 10, AV). *See* CUSHAN-RISHATHAIM.

CHUSI kū'sī [Gk. *Chous*]; NEB CHUS. A place named in Jth. 7:18, where it is said to be near Ekrebel on the brook Machmur. It was located about 5 mi. (8 km.) S of Nablus and just W of the Ramallah-Nablus highway at the modern village of Quza.

J. F. PREWITT

CHUZA kū'zə [Gk. *Chouzas*] (Lk. 8:3). The steward of Herod Antipas. His wife JOANNA, "and Susanna, and many others," ministered to Christ and His disciples.

CICCAR sik'är [Heb. *kikkār*–'circle']. *See* CITIES OF THE VALLEY.

CIELED; CIELING. *See* CEILING.

CILICIA si-lish'yə [Gk. *hē Kilikia*]. A large region in southeast Asia Minor divided geographically into two parts. "Flat" Cilicia (Gk. *Pedias*; Lat. *Campestris*) to the east is a wedge of plains about 100 mi. (160 km.) long in the angle formed by the Taurus (with Anti-Taurus) and Amanus ranges, along the north shore of the extreme northeast corner of the Mediterranean. Along its northwest side it is dominated by the Taurus, which rises over 10,000 ft. (3000 m.) blocking almost all access to the great hinterland plateau of Anatolia. Through a formidable gorge called the Cilician Gates, a single major route leads to Lycaonia and the west. The same mountains supply the three main rivers, called in antiquity the Cydnus, the Sarus, and the Pyramus, which have built up the lower alluvial levels and maintain their prosperity. On the southeast side a narrow coastal strip is similarly divided from the plains of Syria, which open out to the Euphrates, by the Amanus, where again there is a strategic pass, the Syrian Gates, carrying the road to Antioch.

Thus Cilicia Pedias, with its twin "gates," dominated the main land route from Asia Minor to Syria and Mesopotamia. The ruins of a number of castles attest

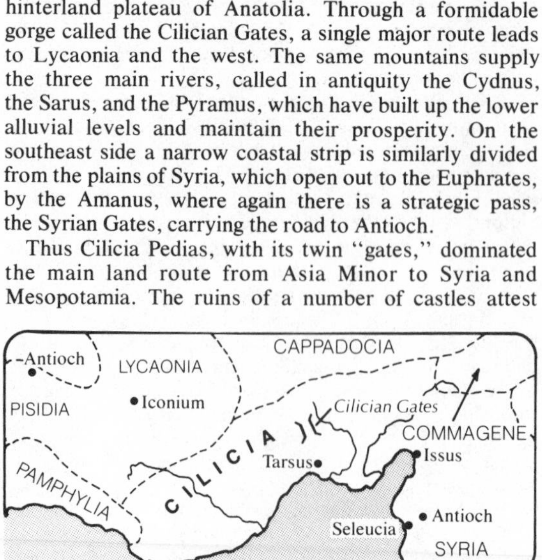

its importance in the Middle Ages as Greek control contracted toward Byzantium. Fifteen hundred years before, in the 4th cent. B.C., it had opened the way for the two great eastward expeditions of the Greeks: the fatal revolt of the younger Cyrus against the Persians (described by Xenophon), and Alexander's triumphant progress. In Cilicia, at Issus, Alexander won the victory that threw Asia open to the Hellenistic age. Greeks had in fact already long settled in these particular plains (local tradition held that they had come in the scattering of peoples after the Trojan War). Under the Seleucid successors of Alexander, there was now a thorough hellenization. By the time the Romans assumed control in the 1st cent. B.C., Cilicia Pedias was apparently divided entirely into the territories of seventeen republican cities, a mark of its intensely concentrated development. Of these Tarsus was the most eminent, and at the time, as Strabo shows, the rival of Athens and Alexandria as an international center of education (*Geog.* xiv.5.13). Rich agricultural (wheat, rice) and orchard (dates, figs, wine) industries flourished in Pedias, and the flax crop was the basis of an important linen export trade (with which Paul's family was connected? cf. Acts 18:3).

"Rugged" Cilicia (Gk. *Tracheia*; Lat. *Aspera*) to the west is the massive bastion that the Taurus thrusts down into the Mediterranean toward Cyprus, cutting Pedias off from the similar plains region to the west, Pamphylia. In spite of the string of Greek states along its seaboard, the importance of Tracheia lay in two strategic commodities of the hill country, manpower (the "Isaurians" were still famous soldiers in Byzantine times) and timber. The latter product, vital to their naval policy, had attracted the attention of the Ptolemies of Egypt, who controlled Tracheia although it was geographically part of the Seleucid domains. With the decline of Ptolemaic power and the weakening of the Seleucids and the naval republic of Rhodes by Roman intervention, Tracheia became the base of the pirates who in the 2nd cent. B.C. terrorized the eastern Mediterranean and, through the great market of Delos (which Strabo says could handle 10,000 slaves a day [*Geog.* xiv.5.2]), exported a constant flow of victims into slavery at Rome.

Eventually, in 102 B.C., the Romans set up a provincial command to police such activities; but it was not until the brilliant campaign of Pompey in 67 B.C. that piracy was exterminated and regular Roman control established for Pedias at least. There was still little question of the Romans tackling Tracheia, which was left to satellite rulers. In the NT period it was part of the kingdom of Antiochus IV of Commagene. Pedias seems to have been administered with one of the Roman provinces to either side, Cappadocia or Syria, until the two parts of Cilicia were combined as a province in their own right in A.D. 72. (Cf. *RRAM,* pp. 1419f., on this complex matter.) The coupling of Cilicia with Syria (Gal. 1:21; Acts 15:23, 41) reflects the administrative arrangements at the time, though Acts 23:34 speaks of Cilicia as a distinct province.

Although no details of the churches of Cilicia are given in the NT, they were no doubt important. There was a considerable Jewish settlement, for the Cilicians gave their name to a synagogue in Jerusalem (Acts 6:9), to which Paul (21:39; 22:3) would have belonged. He himself returned to Tarsus for some years after his conversion (9:30; 11:25), and the letter from the Jerusalem Council was addressed to Cilcia among others (15:23). Paul visited Cilician churches (15:41), subsequently passing through the Cilician Gates into Lycaonia, a journey he repeated later (18:23).

Bibliography.–Strabo *Geog.* xiv.5.1-21; M. V. Seton-Williams, *Anatolian Studies*, 4 (1954), 121-174; G. E. Beau, T. B. Milford, *Anatolion Studies*, 12 (1962), 185-217; *RRAM*; *CERP*, pp. 191-214.

E. A. JUDGE

Narrow pass of the Cilician Gates, leading south through the Taurus Mountains. Dominating the main thoroughfare to the north and east, the pass could be effectively blocked to form a closed border. (B. Van Elderen)

CIMMERIANS si-mer'ē-ənz. *See* GOMER.

CINNAMON [Heb. *qinnāmôn*; Gk. *kinnámōmon*]. In Ex. 30:23 one ingredient of the holy anointing oil; in Prov. 7:17 a perfume for a bed; in Cant. 4:14 a precious spice; in Rev. 18:13 part of the merchandise of "Babylon the great." All references are to the *Cinnamomum zeylanicum* Nees, a low tree with a smooth ashen bark, wide-spreading branches, and white flowers. A fragrant oil is extracted from the ripe fruit. Commercial cinnamon is obtained from the inner bark of the young branches, and is far superior to cassia bark, with which it is sometimes adulterated.

On Cant. 2:17, NEB, *see* MALOBATHRON.

R. K. H.

CINNEROTH sin'ə-roth (1 K. 15:20, AV). *See* CHINNERETH.

CIRAMA si-rā'mə (1 Esd. 5:20, AV). *See* RAMAH **1.**

CIRCLE [Heb. *ḥûg, sāḇaḇ*]; AV also COMPASS; NEB HORIZON, GIRDLE, "vaulted roof," "continue." The Heb. *ḥûg* is used both as a noun and as a verb. It is employed in Job 26:10 and Prov. 8:27 of God circumscribing the waters, and in Isa. 40:22 of divine transcendence. The Heb. verb *sāḇaḇ,* "encircle," is rendered "circled" in Josh. 15:10.

"Mortuary priests" using flint knives to perform the rite of circumcision on a group of boys. Relief from the tomb of Ankhmahor at Saqqarâh (6th Dynasty, 2350-2000 B.C.) (Egyptian Museum, Cairo)

CIRCUIT. The word is used to represent several OT terms in various senses, as Samuel's visiting (Heb. *sāḇaḇ*) of communities (1 S. 7:16), the construction of Zion around (*sāḇîḇ*) the Millo (1 Ch. 11:8), the territory (*kikkār*) around Jerusalem (Neh. 12:28), the sun's orbit (*t^eqûpâ*) in Ps. 19:6; and in the NT the direction taken (Gk. *perielthóntes*) from Syracuse to Rhegium (Acts 28:13). R. K. H.

CIRCUMCISION [Heb. *mûl, mālal* (Gen. 17:11), *mûlôṯ* (Ex. 4:26); Gk. *peritémnō, peritomḗ*]; also "without being circumcised" [Gk. *di' akrobystías*] (Rom. 4:11). The custom of cutting off the foreskin (prepuce) of the male genital organ, usually as a religious rite, but today often simply hygienic.

Circumcision is practiced by many peoples in different parts of the world. In biblical times it was a custom among the West Semites (Hebrews, Moabites, Ammonites, Edomites) but was unknown among the Eastern Semitic peoples of Mesopotamia. In Egypt, as indeed generally in the ancient world, circumcision was a rite performed either at puberty or in preparation for marriage (cf. *ANET*, p. 326). Among the people of Canaan the Philistines were exceptional in their nonadherence to the practice, and of them alone is the term "uncircumcised" customarily used. An additional example of uncircumcised Canaanites is given in Gen. 34:13-17, but there is the possibility that the Shechemites also were of non-Canaanite or non-Semitic descent.

In biblical times the rite of circumcision was a precondition of the enjoyment of certain political and religious privileges (Ex. 12:48; Ezk. 44:9), and was performed on the child of eight days. Various theories have been advanced with regard to its origin and original significance, but before consideration of these it would be well to consider the principal references to the rite in the OT.

I. Circumcision in the OT.–Gen. 17 outlines the origin of circumcision in Israel. In view of the widespread adherence to the custom by neighboring peoples, it is best to see in this chapter a description not of the custom's general origin but of its special meaning and perhaps restructuring for the Hebrews. Circumcision on the eighth day seems to have been an innovation, and certainly the significance assigned to the rite as a mark of God's covenant with the family of Abraham is unique. Included in the number treated were Abraham (age 99), Ishmael (age 13), and every male member of the household, whether slave or free; and the record gives no indication that any of the number had previously undergone the operation. Of course, if Gen. 17 is, as many affirm, nothing more than a late (P) etiological narrative, tying the ubiquitous custom of circumcision to Israel's salvation-history, then there is no need to search the chapter for evidence of circumcision's origin among the Hebrews. Abraham then becomes representative of all Hebrews, Ishmael pictures the Arabs, and the assorted slaves and retainers represent the Canaanite nations around. However, so much of the chapter reflects a very old tradition (e.g., the covenant concept is known to issue from the 2nd millennium; and the custom of circumcision itself, as set in a Canaanite milieu, certainly fits the period in question) that it seems unlikely that this account does not reflect something of the true beginning of the practice. As we have said, there is no reason to affirm that circumcision arrived in Israel in a vacuum, but neither is there reason to deny its application to Abraham and his posterity in the form outlined by the text. The editor of the Genesis account has no interest in the ultimate origin of circumcision; he is, rather, concerned with its subsequent application and significance in Israel. Such an obvious concern does not render his account untrustworthy.

Exodus 4:24ff. is usually considered the oldest biblical witness to the practice of circumcision. In this account, so full of strange and obscure elements, Zipporah apparently redeems Moses from the power of Yahweh (considered by many scholars to represent an original pre-Yahwistic demon of the night) by performing the rite on her son. Just why Yahweh attacked Moses and why the foreskin ritual with respect to the boy had vicarious value is not clear. The element of dedication of the son to the service of God was probably not absent; it is, however, the apparent deliverance from death by means of the symbolic act and the phrase "You are a blood-bridegroom to me" that form the core of the narrative. It is difficult to escape the conclusion that the narrative is thus somehow connecting the Israelite custom of circumcising an infant with the original and widely practiced custom of circumcising adults as a puberty or marriage rite (cf. B. Childs, *Myth and Reality in the OT* [1962], pp. 59-65). Not only does the shedding of the infant's blood indicate his dedication to God, but its application to Moses' feet (probably a euphemism for the male organ) made him ceremonially clean in a manner formerly achieved by adult circumcision. Such a connection between marriage and circumcision in Israel is further attested by the word-group from the root *ḥtn* (*ḥāṯān*, "bridegroom"; *ḥōṯēn*, "father-in-law"), a root which in Arabic means both "circumcise" and "marry."

One further account must be discussed. Josh. 5:2-9 tells of the circumcision of the Israelites born in the wilderness at a place called "hill of the foreskins," an act that removed from them the "reproach of Egypt." Taking the narrative at face value, we find that those Israelites who had been resident in Egypt had been circumcised, but the custom had not been kept up during the wilderness wanderings. Consequently, the narrative may not be seen as explaining the origin of the rite. The phrase "reproach of Egypt" has been the subject of varying explanations, the most probable being that the Egyptians, themselves a circumcised people (cf. Ezk. 32:19), would have considered the Hebrews with contempt apart from performance of the rite, and this act of Joshua's removed the stigma. For Israel, of course, it had another meaning, as the Passover was about to be celebrated (Josh. 5:10) and apart from circumcision an adult male was debarred from participation (Ex. 12:48).

II. Theories of Origin.–We have already considered the biblical evidence for the origin of circumcision in Israel; but the custom is manifestly older than its application in Israel, and some understanding of its significance to the Hebrews may result from a study of its original intent. Theories as to its origin may be arranged under four heads:

(1) Herodotus (ii.37), in dealing with circumcision among the Egyptians, suggests that it was a sanitary operation, a thought echoed by Philo and others. While there may be merit in the suggestion, and circumcision may well have facilitated marital intercourse or lessened the possibility of disease, we can hardly agree that the ancient world would have separated the religious from the secular to the extent that the custom would have been devoid of sacred significance, or even that it might have originated with the secular primarily in view. More to the point is the argument that circumcision was originally a rite celebrating a person's coming of age, a concomitant of which was the right to marry and enjoy full civic privileges.

(2) It was a kind of tribal mark which enabled one member of the tribe to recognize another and thus avoid injuring or slaying a fellow-tribesman. Since such a mark was usually hidden, this suggestion does not seem to be valid, although the custom of stripping for combat may have been practiced. (Such was not, however, normal in historical times; cf. various battle scenes from *ANEP*.) If, however, one thinks of circumcision more as an initiatory rite, whether into the tribal group or into a state of full manhood, it becomes easier to see how the concept of a tribal mark might function. For the Hebrews the initiation, connected as it was with the covenant, took place in infancy and, although normally the effect of the rite was unseen, its presence or absence provided the basic identification for every Hebrew man.

(3) It was a vestigial remnant of human sacrifice. As sacrifice of the child began to be done away with, the sacrifice of the most easily removed portion of the anatomy provided a vicarious offering. However, among the Hebrews circumcision was not performed by priests, nor was the act performed in a sacrificial context. Perhaps even more telling, circumcision was most certainly in origin a puberty rite rather than an infant rite, and what evidence we have for human sacrifice among the Semites involves infants rather than adults.

(4) It was a sacramental operation. The "shedding of blood" was necessary to the validity of any covenant between tribes or individuals. An alliance based on blood-relationship was inviolable, and the rite of blood established this relationship between the contracting parties. In the same way the tribal god was supposed to share in the blood of the sacrificed animal, and a sacred bond was established between him and the tribe. It is not quite obvious why circumcision should be necessary in connection with such a ceremony, though if it were related to the human sacrifice idea (3) such a concept is not impossible. However, in the Gen. 17 account, wherein circumcision is tied to the covenant, there is no emphasis whatever on the bloody aspect of the operation.

III. Spiritual Significance.–Though we cannot with certainty discover the original significance of the rite, we can affirm without doubt that circumcision was originally a religious act. Its value as a tribal mark has certainly come through in the application of the rite within Israel, wherein it becomes the mark par excellence of God's covenant with the descendants of Abraham. It is in this sense, as a mark given by God to indicate membership in the covenant, that the major spiritual emphasis is drawn. As early as the time of the Deuteronomist, membership in the covenant community is seen as a spiritual thing, dependent on a mark that is not outward but a matter of the heart (Dt. 10:16). Jeremiah echoes this figurative use of the term, and calls for a membership based on ethical commitment (4:4) rather than physical mutilation, although it must be recognized that there is no rejection of the outward sign either in Deuteronomy or Jeremiah. Jeremiah goes on to tell his countrymen that they are no better than Egyptians, Edomites, Moabites, and Ammonites (9:25) — peoples who are circumcised, yet uncircumcised. The Judeans, though circumcised outwardly, are uncircumcised in heart. Paul uses the term "mutilation" (AV "concision") to describe this outward circumcision unaccompanied by any spiritual change (Phil. 3:2).

The idea that spiritual rather than physical circumcision was the goal of God's people occasioned a protracted strife among the early Christians. While no one in the early Church questioned the ethical commitment involved in a truly circumcised life, there were not wanting Jews who, when the first gentile believers were added, required a commitment to the physical rite as well. Eventually the question became a touchstone for proceeding to the fundamental problem of the relationship of Judaism to the infant Christian community. The great conference in Jerusalem was called upon presentation of this very challenge in Antioch (Acts 15:1), the result of which seems to have been an agreement to allow a difference in practice between Jewish and gentile believers (15:19-21). Paul himself consented to the circumcision of Timothy (16:3), a convert from a partially Jewish family (though Luke gives the reason as "because of the Jews"); but when a principle was at stake, and in most of his Epistles, he refused to grant even a measure of compromise to the Judaizers (Gal. 2:3). That there is no more distinction between Jew and Gentile is a foundational element in Pauline teaching (Gal. 3:28). It is not a matter of circumcision or uncircumcision, but of keeping the commandments of God (1 Cor. 7:19; cf. Col. 2:11ff.).

IV. Figurative Uses.–In addition to the "spiritual circumcision" already noted, there are several passages in which we find a figurative use of the term. For three years after the settlement in Canaan the "fruit of the land" was to be considered as "uncircumcised" (lit. "you shall reject as profane its foreskin, the fruit of it; three years it shall be to you as uncircumcised," Lev. 19:23). Inasmuch as the fourth year's fruit was dedicated in praise to Yahweh, this prohibition regarding the first three years may have had sacrificial significance also.

In another passage (Ex. 6:30), Moses with characteristic humility describes himself as a man of "uncircumcised lips." Jeremiah likewise charges his contemporaries with having their ears uncircumcised (Jer. 6:10) and also their heart (9:26). In both instances the meaning seems to be that the organ so described is closed to hearing and consequently to obeying God's command.

Bibliography.–*ANEP*, nos. 332, 629; W. Eichrodt, *Theology of the OT*, I (Eng. tr. 1961), 138f.; R. de Vaux, *Ancient Israel* (Eng. tr. 1961), pp. 46ff.; *TDNT*, VI, *s.v.* περιτέμνω (Meyer).

T. LEWIS C. E. ARMERDING

CIS sis (Acts 13:21, AV). *See* KISH 1.

CISAI si'sī (Ad. Est. 11:2, AV). *See* KISH 1.

CISJORDAN. The land area W of the Jordan river, as distinguished from Transjordan.

CISTERN [Heb. *bôr, bō'r, geḇe', gēḇ*]; AV, NEB, often PIT, DUNGEON, or WELL. Any of various artificial reservoirs for storing water.

I. Necessity.–The efforts made to supplement the natural water supply, both in agricultural and in populated areas, are clearly seen in the innumerable cisterns, wells, and pools throughout Palestine. The rainy season, upon which the various storage systems depend, begins in late October and ends about the beginning of May. Records kept since 1859 indicate an average rainfall in Jerusalem of 26 in. (66 cm.), in Jericho of only 5.5 in. (14 cm.). Toward the end of the summer, springs and wells, where they have not actually dried up, diminish greatly, and cisterns and open reservoirs become at times the only sources of supply. The problems of scant rainfall and a long dry season are aggravated by the rain's falling in heavy showers, often running off in destructive flash floods when the water is not channeled into reservoirs. The town of Ma'ân in southern Jordan, in what is normally a dry area, had many of its homes destroyed by a cloudburst and flood in March 1966. In this climate cisterns and collecting pools, or reservoirs, are a necessity.

Nelson Glueck describes the Iron Age settlements in the Negeb as depending on channels, terracing of fields, damming of stream beds to hold the water in the soil, and thousands of strategically located cisterns. He comments that "no Iron II fortress or village could have existed in the Negeb without these cisterns of various types, the digging of which is biblically attested." He cites 2 Ch. 26:10 (*BASOR*, 155 [1959], 4; see also 142 [1956], 5-14 for accounts by Cross and Milik of similar cisterns and irrigation systems at Iron Age sites in Judea W of Qumrân).

II. Wells and Cisterns.–Wells and cisterns are treated similarly in the OT in some respects. Both were holes or pits, and as such required covers to prevent animals or men from falling in (cf. Ps. 7:15; Ex. 21:33f. [see Josephus *Ant.* iv.8.37], with *bōr*, "cistern" or "pit," and Gen. 14:10; 29:2f., with *b^{e}'ēr*, "well" or "pit"). Both were used to water flocks and herds, as well as to supply human needs (cf. 2 Ch. 26:10, with *bōr,* and Gen. 24:19f.; 29:2f.; Ex. 2:16, with *b^{e}'ēr*). Distinctions are also apparent, however. Cisterns, or reservoirs for the storage of water, were filled by drainage from roofs, streets, or the surface of a slope, or by water channeled from some other source. Wells, on the other hand, might be fed directly from underground springs. Jer. 2:13 contrasts cisterns, which when unbroken should be able to hold water, with "the fountain of living water." The terms "living water" and "spring" are used in connection with wells in the Bible, but not in connection with cisterns. Isaac's servants, digging in the valley of Gerar, opened a "well of living water" (RSV "springing water"; Gen. 26:19; cf. also Cant. 4:15). Prov. 5:15 speaks of water from a cistern, but of "running waters" (RSV "flowing water") from a well. Israel's song to the well calls upon it to "spring up" (Nu. 21:17). Hagar's well, and the well where Abraham's servant met Rebekah, are called both "wells" and "springs" in the biblical accounts (Gen. 16:7-14; 24:11-49), indicating a "living" source. Similarly in the NT the word for "spring" and the word for "well" are both applied to Jacob's well (Jn. 4:6, 11f.). Wells reaching groundwater levels are known also from excavations. A shaft 30 ft. (9 m.) long at Etam and one 60 ft. (18 m.) long at Beth-shemesh were sunk to groundwater, rather than to any known spring (cf. H. Donner and E. Kutsch, *ZDPV,* 79 [1963], 113-16).

III. Private Cisterns.–Many modern buildings in Jerusalem are like those of biblical times in having private cisterns, filled by rainwater from the roof. The OT speaks of ordinary citizens enjoying the water of their own cisterns (2 K. 18:31), and thousands of small cisterns have been found on the sites of ancient cities (e.g., Gezer, Beth-shemesh, Debir, and Tell en-Naṣbeh, as well as Jerusalem). In any city not adequately supplied by a natural spring or water source, such cisterns were essential. Petra has inadequate springs and scant rain, but many cisterns, with channels leading to them, are cut into the cliffs surrounding the city, as well as attached to the rock-cut houses and sanctuaries. At least six pools and cisterns at Qumrân held water channeled from Wâdī Qumrân for the community there, in an area with even less rainfall. King Mesha of Moab, the contemporary of Ahab of Israel in the 9th cent. B.C., reflects a concern and a practice common to Israelites and Moabites in his inscription, "And there was no cistern inside the town at Qarhoh, so I said to all the people, 'Let each of you make a cistern for himself in his own house.'"

Cisterns were made in various shapes, often irregular, but many were somewhat bottle- or bell-like, rounding out toward the bottom. When not in use as a cistern, a rock-cut hole such as this, its only opening at the top, made a convenient prison (Jer. 38:7-13; cf. Gen.

37:24; 40:15; and the guard room and prison or cistern that have been excavated under the Church of St. Peter *en Gallicante* in Jerusalem). Often a sump, or depression in the bottom, is provided for dipping up the last of the liquid before cleaning or replastering. The many potsherds, coins, bits of jewelry, and occasional bones or even entire skeletons found in cisterns indicate somewhat long intervals between cleanings, however. Sometimes, as in Macalister's example from Gezer, a smaller catch-pit, with its overflow channel leading to the main cistern, provides a means of purification for the water coming in. The use of lime plaster to cement and waterproof the cisterns seems to date from the beginning of the Iron Age (*ca.* 1200 B.C.); it also seems to be responsible for the great number of cisterns in use in this period in Palestine (N. Glueck, *BASOR,* 138 [1955], 16f.).

IV. Public Cisterns.–Besides private cisterns, there were many public cisterns within city walls. The great water caverns under the temple area in Jerusalem show a most extensive system of water storage, involving at least thirty-seven cisterns. One immense, rock-cut cavern, 43 ft. (13 m.) deep, has a capacity of over two million gals. (7.5 million l.); it has numerous manholes in its partly natural-rock, partly masonry roof. These cisterns are supplied to some extent by rainwater, but also, at least from the Roman period, by an aqueduct bringing water a distance of about 10 mi. (16 km.) from "Solomon's Pools" near Bethlehem (cf. J. J. Simons, *Jerusalem in the OT* [1952], pp. 347ff.). Large public cisterns were often supplemented by pools, also serving as reservoirs, and sometimes also within the city walls (cf. Siloam in Jerusalem). *See also* POOL.

Other ancient water systems involve rock-cut stairwell tunnels, leading to cisterns or reservoirs for spring water. At Gezer a cave providing a natural reservoir for spring water is reached by a great rock-cut staircase

Interior of a Late Bronze Age cistern with a stairway at Jerusalem (Israel Department of Antiquities and Museums)

Rectangular (left) and circular (right) cisterns at Khirbet Qumrân. Approximately forty such pools or reservoirs, possibly used for water storage or ceremonial washing, have been discovered in the vicinity. (B. Van Elderen)

which descends 94.5 ft. (28.8 m.) from the surface and is 23 ft. (7 m.) high and 12.8 ft. (3.9 m.) wide at its largest point (see R. A. S. Macalister *PEQ*, April, 1908, pp. 96-111). A rock-cut cistern supplements this water supply (Macalister, *Excavations*, I, 256-268). At Megiddo an almost horizontal tunnel brings water from the spring to the foot of a rock-cut staircase leading to the street level of the city, a distance of approximately 64 ft. (19.5 m.) vertically and 214 ft. (65.2 m.) horizontally. Other staircase tunnel and reservoir systems, designed to make water from a spring available within the city's defense walls, have been found in Jerusalem, Ibleam, Taanach, and Gibeon.

V. Figurative Use.–Good wives are described as cisterns that hold water (Prov. 5:15-20), while idols and other objects that drew Israel away from trust in God are "broken cisterns, that can hold no water," according to Jer. 2:13.

Bibliography.–N. Glueck, *Rivers in the Desert* (1959), esp. pp. 94-97; *BASOR*, 131 (Oct. 1953), 6-15; 138 (Apr. 1955), 16f.; 142 (Apr. 1956), 29f.; 149 (Feb. 1958), 10-14; 152 (Dec. 1958), 24,33,36; 155 (Oct. 1959), 4,12f.; R. W. Funk, *BASOR*, 150 (Apr. 1958), 17-19; J. P. Free, *BASOR*, 152 (Dec. 1958), 11,17; R. S. Lamon, *The Megiddo Water System* (1935); R. A. S. Macalister, *Excavations at Gezer* (1912), I, III; J. B. Pritchard, *BA*, 19 (1956), 66-75.

A. C. DICKIE
D. W. HARVEY

CITADEL. *See* FORTIFICATION.

CITHERN sith'ərn [Gk. *kithára*] (1 Macc. 4:54, AV); RSV, NEB HARPS. *See* MUSIC II.B.

CITIES, LEVITICAL. *See* LEVITICAL CITIES.

CITIES OF REFUGE. *See* REFUGE, CITIES OF.

CITIES OF THE VALLEY [Heb. *'ārê hakkikkār*] (Gen. 13:12; 19:29); AV, NEB, CITIES OF THE PLAIN. Principally Sodom, Gomorrah, Admah, Zeboiim, and Bela (Zoar), mentioned in Gen. 14:2. The locality was first described in Gen. 13:10, where Lot was said to have observed all the "plain" (AV, RV, NEB, JB; RSV "valley") of the Jordan, which prior to the destruction of Sodom and Gomorrah was well watered, and comparable to the irrigated terrain of Egypt. The word for "plain" or "valley" is actually the old Canaanite term for "circle" (*kikkār*), and the Hebrew of Gen. 13:10f.; 1 K. 7:46 par. preserves the geographical designation "Circle of the Jordan."

Some nineteenth-century geographers and biblical scholars saw this "Circle" in terms of the area N of the Dead Sea where the Jordan Valley broadens out into the "plain" of the Jordan (cf. Dt. 34:3). They maintained that the cities of this area were visible from the heights of Bethel (Gen. 13:10), unlike any at the southern end of the Dead Sea, which would be too distant for observation. Further, they urged that Zoar was said to be in the range of Moses' vision from the top of Pisgah (Dt. 34:1-3), whereas the south end of the Dead Sea cannot be seen from that point owing to intervening mountains. And by identifying Hazezon-tamar with Engedi, it was possible to assume that the kings of the Mesopotamian coalition, in moving to attack those petty Palestinian rulers who had rejected their suzerainty after twelve years, were conducting their campaign to the north rather than to the south of the Dead Sea. Finally, it was urged that the latter terrain could hardly be described as "the garden of the Lord."

It is true, of course, that the "plain" of the Jordan, an area more properly described as the Ghor terrace, contained on its eastern side a number of thriving communities in the Middle Bronze Age (1950-1550 B.C.), remains of which have been uncovered by archeologists. But this fact does not preclude other valleys near the Dead Sea from being inhabited, particularly at the southern and southeastern end, where in antiquity the land was well watered by means of a number of streams and rivers. To attempt to isolate one particular "Pisgah" is hazardous, for the term simply means "elevation," "height," and its invariable use in Hebrew with the article indicates that it is a common noun. If present conditions are any indication it is hardly possible to describe the region around the north end of the Dead Sea as the "garden of the Lord," although conditions there may well have changed, as they appear to have at the southern end of the Dead Sea.

Gen. 13:10 makes it clear that Lot was attracted not by the urban facilities of the Jordan Valley but by the good pasturage of the district. Furthermore, there are grounds for believing that the Circle of the Jordan once had a southern extension which was situated in the now flooded area S of the Dead Sea promontory known as el-Lisan ("the Tongue"). In this area was doubtless situated the valley of Siddim (*see* SIDDIM, VALLEY OF), originally a fertile plain watered by the five streams that now flow E and SE into the Dead Sea.

While all traces of the cities have disappeared, modern scholarship locates them under the waters of the southern part of the Dead Sea. Archeological investigation has shown that *ca.* 2000 B.C. a devastating natural catastrophe occurred there, which denuded the area of sedentary occupation for over a half a millennium. Among numerous reasons for locating the cities in this region is that the maximum depth of the water in the southernmost part of the Dead Sea is about 16 ft. (5 m.), whereas N of the peninsula of el-Lisan a depth of over 1200 ft. (365 m.) has been measured by soundings. On balance a southern location seems preferable for these cities.

Bibliography.–H. B. Tristram, *Land of Moab* (1912), pp. 330ff.; *HGHL*, pp. 505f.; W. F. Albright, *BASOR*, 13 (Feb. 1924), 5ff.; G. E. Wright, *BASOR*, 71 (Oct. 1938), 27ff.; J. P. Harland, *BA*, 5 (1942), 17ff.; 6 (1943), 41ff.

R. K. HARRISON

CITIMS sit'imz (1 Macc. 8:5, AV). *See* KITTIM.

CITIZEN [Heb. *ba'al*] (Jgs. 9:2, 6, 18, 20); AV MAN; [Gk. *polítēs* (Lk. 15:15; 19:14; Acts 21:39), *sympolítēs* (Eph. 2:19); in addition, *polítēs* is implied (cf. RSV, NEB) but not expressed (AV) in Acts 16:37f.; 22:25-29; 23:27, where instead simply *Rhōmaíos*–'Roman,' appears]; **CITIZENSHIP** [Gk. *politeía*] (Acts 22:28); AV FREEDOM. The "citizens of Shechem" in Jgs. 9 are citizens by virtue of their being landowners. The NT words come from Gk. *pólis,* "city," and indicate variously the inhabitants of a country (Lk. 15:15), the subjects of a feudal lord (19:14), legal rights of citizenship (Acts), and figuratively, "members of God's household" (Eph. 2:19). In He. 8:11 *polítēs* means "fellow-citizen" (AV, NEB; RSV "fellow"). A few MSS have *plēsíon*, "neighbor." In the Apocrypha cf. 2 Macc. 4:50; 5:6; 9:19.

Roman citizenship is of special interest to the Bible student because of the apostle Paul's relation to it. It was one of his qualifications as the apostle to the Gentiles. Luke shows him in Acts as a Roman citizen, who, though a Jew and a Christian, receives for the most part justice and courtesy from the Roman officials, and more than once successfully claims the privileges of his citizenship.

Paul himself declared that he was a citizen of Tarsus

(Acts 21:39). He was not only born in that city but had a citizen's rights in it (*See* PAUL THE APOSTLE VII.A; TARSUS). But this citizenship in Tarsus did not of itself confer upon Paul the higher dignity of Roman citizenship. Had it done so, Claudius Lysias would not have ordered him to be scourged, as he did, after having learned that he was a citizen of Tarsus (Acts 21:39; cf. 22:25). So, over and above this Tarsian citizenship was the Roman one, which availed for him not in one city only, but throughout the Roman world, and secured for him everywhere certain great immunities and rights. Precisely what all of these were we are not certain; but we know that, by the Valerian and Porcian laws, exemption from shameful punishments, such as scourging with rods or whips, and especially crucifixion, was secured to every Roman citizen; also the right of appeal to the emperor, with certain limitations. This sanctity of person had become almost a part of their religion, so that any violation was esteemed a sacrilege. Cicero's oration against Verres indicates the almost fanatical extreme to which this feeling had been carried. Yet Paul was thrice beaten with rods, and five times received from the Jews forty lashes save one (2 Cor. 11:24f.). Perhaps it was as at Philippi before he made known his citizenship (Acts 16:22f.), or the Jews had the right to whip those who came before their own tribunals. Roman citizenship included also the right of appeal to the emperor in all cases, after sentence had been passed, and no needless impediment must be interposed against a trial. Furthermore, the citizen had the right to be sent to Rome for trial before the emperor himself, when charged with capital offenses (Acts 16:37; 22:25-29; 25:11).

How then had Paul, a Jew, acquired this valued dignity? He himself tells us. In contrast to the *parvenu* citizenship of the chief captain, who seems to have thought that Paul also must have purchased it, though apparently too poor, Paul quietly says, "But I was born (a citizen)" (Acts 22:28). Thus either Paul's father or some other ancestor had acquired the right and had transmitted it to the son.

What more natural than that Paul should sometimes use this civic privilege to illustrate spiritual truths? He does so a number of times. Before the Sanhedrin he says, in the words of our English versions, "I have lived before God in all good conscience" (Acts 23:1). But this translation does not fully bring out the sense. Paul uses a noticeable word, *politeúō,* "to live as a citizen." He adds, "to God" (*tǭ theǭ*). That is to say, he had lived conscientiously as God's citizen, as a member of God's commonwealth. The day before, by appealing to his Roman citizenship, he had saved himself from ignominious whipping, and now what more natural than that he should declare that he had been true to his citizenship in a higher state? What was this higher commonwealth in which he has enjoyed the rights and performed the duties of a citizen? What but the theocracy of his fathers, the ancient Church, of which the Sanhedrin was still the ostensible representative, but which was really continued in the kingdom of Christ without the national restrictions of the older one? Thus Paul does not mean to say simply, "I have lived conscientiously before God," but "I have lived as a citizen to God, of the body of which He is the immediate Sovereign." He had lived theocratically as a faithful member of the Jewish church, from which his enemies claimed he was an apostate. Thus Paul's conception was a kind of blending of two ideas or feelings, one of which came from the old theocracy, and the other from his Roman citizenship.

Later, writing from Rome itself to the Philippians, who were proud of their own citizenship as members of a *colonia,* a reproduction on a small scale of the parent commonwealth, where he had once successfully maintained his own Roman rights, Paul forcibly brings out the idea that Christians are citizens of a heavenly commonwealth, urging them to live worthy of such honor (Phil. 1:27, RV mg.).

A similar thought is brought out when he says, "But our commonwealth [*politeúma*] is in heaven" (Phil. 3:20; cf. NEB, "for we are citizens of heaven"). The state to which we belong is heaven. Though absent in body from the heavenly commonwealth, as was Paul from Rome when he asserted his rights, believers still enjoy its civic privileges and protections; sojourners upon earth, citizens of heaven. The OT conception, as in Isa. 60–62, would easily lend itself to this idea, which appears in He. 11:10, 16; 12:22-24; 13:14; Gal. 4:26, and possibly in Rev. 21.

G. H. TREVER

CITRUS-TREES (Lev. 23:40, NEB). *See* GOODLY.

CITY [Heb. *'îr, qiryâ, qereṯ*; Aram. *qiryâ, qiryā'*; Gk. *pólis*]. No apparent distinctions are implied in the use of the various terms. Ancient cities exhibited considerable differences, and terminological distinctions on the basis of size, character, or function, if they did occur, were entirely subjective. Usage is further complicated by the nature of the biblical record, which refers to cities throughout the ancient world and throughout a long span of time.

I. Definition
II. Ancient Near East
III. Syria and Palestine
IV. Greek and Roman Cities

I. Definition.–Determination of when a residential community may be classified as a city is difficult and open to debate. The ancient languages themselves are often vague in differentiating "city," "town," and "village" (cf. *TDNT*, VI, 530 [Strathmann]). In biblical usage the primary characteristic distinguishing the city from the village (Heb. *ḥāṣēr*; Gk. *kṓmē*) was a wall or other form of enclosure such as a ring of adjoining houses (cf. Lev. 25:31). But this might indicate any fortified place (BDB, p. 745), and other social, economic, and political or administrative factors must be noted. Size, either of territory or of population, may have been a consideration, but was not in itself a determinant of city status. Implicit was a level of technological and social development sufficient to support a population that was dense enough, and sustained by enough different food resources, to permit a variety of nonagricultural specialists, including a literate group to record economic activities. One such technological development, irrigation, was not always a physical requirement, but did demonstrate a sophisticated level of community organization. The city might serve as a religious or cultural center, an economic center for the collection or distribution of goods, or the base for a political or military power exerting influence or control beyond the area necessary for the community's self-sufficiency. Kinship had been supplanted by social and economic distinctions as the organizational pattern, and ideology had replaced blood ties as a means of reinforcing community solidarity.

Ancient settlements demonstrating marked advancements in the transition to an economy based on plant cultivation and animal domestication include Palestinian Jericho (Tell es-Sulṭan), *ca.* 7800 B.C., and Jarmo, E of Kirkûk in the foothills bordering the Tigris-Euphrates plain, *ca.* 6750 B.C. Nevertheless, the various criteria for city status do not appear to have been met until *ca.* 3500 B.C. when numerous walled cities, often so closely situated as to be within view of each other, emerged throughout the lower

The mound of Jericho, oldest walled town in Palestine. In one area seventeen successive stages in town walls can be identified. (Trans World Airlines) *See also* Plate 20.

Tigris-Euphrates plain. (Caution must be taken to avoid the suggestion of a rigid evolutionary schedule of subsistence patterns and community forms leading to this "urban revolution.")

II. Ancient Near East.–The Sumerian city, upon which the later Babylonian and Assyrian cities were patterned, was generally rectangular and divided into three parts. The "inner city" (cf. Akk. *ina libbi āli*) or walled area contained the temple or other holy places and the royal palace, themselves within walled zones, and boroughs or quarters comprised of private residences; these sectors had their respective city gates, around which wide areas served as marketplaces and legal or administrative centers. The suburbs or "outer city" (Sum. uru-bar-ra), outside the city wall, included houses and agricultural lands providing the community's sustenance; at least in later times this district was protected by secondary walls. The harbor section (Sum. kar; Akk. *kāru*) was an economically and politically autonomous commercial sector housing merchants, scribes, and taverners.

Availability of space seems to have been the primary concern in Mesopotamian city planning. Monumental structures such as palaces and temples were generally symmetrical, but arranged with little regard for adjacent buildings. They consisted of elongated narrow rooms in single or multiple rows around courtyards (e.g., the sacred precinct of Ur, *ca.* 2100 B.C. and the Neo-Babylonian temples at Babylon and Borsippa). Residences followed this pattern on a smaller scale (Tepe Gawra, Mari), but simply grew outward in whatever direction possible, making streets irregular. The only consistency was a tendency for buildings to face the northwest, source of the most pleasant wind.

Mesopotamian cities covered relatively large areas by ancient standards. In the 1st millennium Babylon encompassed 2500 acres (1012 hectares); Nineveh, 1850 acres (750 hectares); Uruk (biblical Erech, modern Warka), 1100 acres (450 hectares); and Calah (Nimrûd), 800 acres (325 hectares). Athens in the 5th cent. B.C. was considered unusually large at 550 acres (225 hectares). Population figures, at least for the earliest periods, appear quite small by contrast. At its peak the population of the walled city of Ur was 34,000; counting the suburbs, harbor, and dependent areas it may have numbered nearly 100,000.

Authority in the earliest Sumerian cities appears to have been distributed among the temple, which controlled the agricultural lands (the property of the gods) and their produce; private families engaged in commerce; and the lord or ruler (Sum. en), who oversaw the civil operations. An assembly of the citizens operating on mutual agreement met to deal with crises and to select a war leader, a temporary post that eventually became the permanent claim of the en. By the early 3rd millennium some cities began to dominate others, transforming the originally autonomous cities into a territorial or national state with the dominant city as capital. Under the various Mesopotamian states the ruler increasingly demanded of the populace taxes and services, both military and corvée. Because of special religious or political status some cities, such as Nippur, Babylon, and Asshur, were "free" or "under the aegis of the *kidinnu*," a standard or symbol indicating the release of their native citizens from such assessments and their immunity from fines or imprisonment. Such cities might, however, face other restrictions, like the prohibition of weapons within Nineveh during the reign of Esarhaddon.

Literary sources, themselves urban products reflecting the life and attitudes of more privileged and stable elements, present a somewhat slanted view of urban life

Fragment of a clay tablet with a map of Nippur showing temples, walls, gates, and canals. As the center for the worship of Enlil, Nippur was the holiest of Sumerian cities. (University Museum, University of Pennsylvania)

and its acceptance by the masses. A. L. Oppenheim has noted the constant anti-urban bias of rural elements, partly because they were frequently enlisted to populate the sites of periodic royal building ventures (cf. *ANET,* p. 559; also pp. 164f., 290, 307). This displacement was intended to expand the base of taxation, increase general productivity, and balance the urban-rural population ratio. Discontent with the demands of urban life underlies the need for frequent expeditions into the open country to apprehend those who had fled the cities to avoid debts or military and corvée service. Poverty and vagrancy are the subject of Sumerian proverbs, and a seamy image of urban life is suggested because military forces drafted to protect the city were sometimes not to be trusted within the walls (A. Falkenstein, *Baghdader Mitteilungen,* 2 [1963], 59f.).

Efforts at colonization beyond Mesopotamia in the Old Assyrian period (19th cent.) included the establishment at various locations of a merchant colony (*kāru*). One such community was Kaniš (Kültepe, near Kayseri in modern Turkey), strategically located between Mt. Argaeus and the Halys River where it controlled the major Anatolian trade routes. Living in multilevel clusters of houses, the Assyrian merchants were permitted to own property and to govern themselves.

The indigenous Anatolian cities, isolated and sternly independent, were designed primarily for defense. Ḫattusa (modern Boghazköy) owed its selection as a royal residence and capital of the Hittite empire to the rugged terrain and its suitability for fortification rather than to agricultural or commercial considerations. The city was surrounded by a massive double wall with rectangular towers, all atop a stone-lined rampart through which a tunnel had been made for surprise attacks. Ḫattusa contained five great temples, each of which apparently was enclosed in a sacred precinct or *temenos*. The Hittite cities' lack of concern for the development of natural resources or for ideological contributions marked the region as a relatively uncultured backwater.

Cities in Egypt developed along the Nile River and in the delta region in the later 3rd millennium. Remains are sparse because the mud and twigs used in construction were perishable and the sites were covered by the Nile alluvium. Although surviving texts name cities, few available documents record the details of their everyday life. Periodic fluctuation between unification under a central power and fragmented regionalism, as well as the frequent relocation of the capital under the various pharaohs, prevented the growth of substantial cities. Also, the great temples and other monumental structures, which required a strong central power dominating considerable human and economic resources, took precedence over city planing. Concerned primarily with religious, funerary, or administrative functions, an Egyptian city was designed around one or more walled sacred precinct and a palace; the more mundane residential and commerical sectors were not clearly defined. Processional ways, often flanked by stone sphinxes (Luxor, Karnak), were added in later periods. Unique to Egypt was the pyramid city of the Old and Middle Kingdoms, created by royal charter to house construction workers and subsequently priests for the royal funerary services. These and the necessary agricultural and maintenance personnel were exempt from taxation and conscription.

III. Syria and Palestine.–Palestine experienced extensive urbanization in the Early Bronze Age (3rd millennium B.C.), with heavily fortified settlements dominating the entire region from Kadesh in the north to Arad in the south, and particularly in the lowlands through which passed the coastal trade route connecting Egypt and Mesopotamia. Although small by Mesopotamian standards, their size (generally 10 to 20 acres [4 to 8 hectares]) is not disproportionate to that of later Palestinian cities. Planning is evident in some cities such as Arad, with a basic division into public and residential quarters. Its buildings were fairly uniform in design, and its streets and plazas generally orderly. Many of the sites suggest a continuity with the earlier unwalled communities (Jericho, Tell el-Fâr'ah [Tirzah]), but the transition was probably not a linear evolution. Rather, urbanization appears to have been imposed upon the indigenous village peoples by an influx of groups from Syria and Anatolia. Despite some rivalries the cities demonstrate a general unification against a common external foe, predynastic Egypt.

By the latter part of the Early Bronze Age Ebla (Tell Mardikh) in northwestern Syria had become a city-state of 260,000 people, with lesser "vassal" cities forming a far-reaching empire. It was the center of a vast commercial network, and records of its enterprises contain the earliest mention of such biblical cities as Salim, Megiddo, Gaza, Hazor, Lachish, and Joppa. An indication of the city's sophisticated planning is the audience court of the royal palace, which both architecturally and functionally mediates the space between the quarters with private residences and those with administrative offices.

Sudden and violent destruction occurred throughout much of the ancient world *ca.* 2300-2100 B.C. Palestinian civilization returned to the village level, with many E.B. sites abandoned and others left unfortified, a situation that continued through the early stages of the Middle Bronze period (until *ca.* 1950 B.C.). While many factors may have been involved, especially significant were Egyptian raids and mass population movements, at the center of which were the Amorites. The influx of urban-oriented peoples in M.B. IIA (*ca.* 1950-1800) reintroduced city life and formed the basis of the "Canaanite" period. Major centers formed along the two primary trade routes, overland (Damascus, Alalakh) and coastal (Byblos, Ugarit, Tyre, Sidon). Attacks on many coastal cities *ca.* 1800 B.C. left them temporarily defenseless; inland towns such as Shechem, Gezer, and Jericho apparently had not been severely tested and thus had remained unfortified (cf. W. G. Dever, in Cross, Lemke, and Miller, eds. *Magnalia Dei*, p. 9). An intense period of building and fortification took place after 1650 (M.B. IIC), as attested at Tell Beit Mirsim and Shechem. Vertical walls of fairly small stones laid in rough courses were constructed, with additional fortification provided by high and massive ramparts several meters thick. These were of mud brick or unworked stones and often reinforced by earthen embankments (Tell el-Fâr'ah) or secondary walls immediately adjacent to the main wall (Jericho). A subsequent development in the rampart, formerly attributed to the Hyksos rulers of Egypt (1900-1500), was the use of beaten earth (*terre pisée*), often covered with a plastered surface; this was presumably intended as a defense against the battering ram. At Hazor the rampart was 100 ft. (30 m.) wide; that at Shechem was 80 ft. (24 m.) wide and 20 ft. (6 m.) high. Massive semicircular towers were incorporated into the walls (Ai, Arad, Jericho; Byblos had square towers), and a moat was occasionally added. The M.B. city was rather densely built up, with little open space. Houses often included upper-story living quarters, with stables, storerooms, and workshops on the lower level. As a result of the various population movements throughout the Bronze Age and the frequent settlement of peoples along the commercial routes, the cities' ethnic composition was mixed (cf. the reference to Jerusalem's ancestry in Ezk. 16:3, 45).

Despite the recurrent assertion of Egyptian control, the Canaanite cities continued to gain in strength, leading to the formation of a vast chain of city-states. These were for the most part powerful enough to engage in inter-city conflicts but neither strong enough nor wealthy enough to expand their territorial influence. Their relationships to each other and to the greater powers are documented in the extensive Amarna correspondence of the 14th century. Although Egyptian strength declined after the death of Thutmose III (1450), Canaan was still an Egyptian territory, and some cities were claimed as the property of the pharaoh, including Gaza and Joppa (Thutmose III), Simyra and Kumidi (Ramses II), and Ashkelon (later Ramessides).

The individual cities were dominated by the king and, especially in the larger cities, a small inner circle of landed nobility; the masses of people were peasants or tenant farmers, bound to the aristocracy in a feudal relationship. Underlying this social structure was an ideology based on sheer power and greed, whose benefits were reaped exclusively by the monarchy while the masses earned little more than constant demands for taxation and labor.

Large segments of the Canaanite population became increasingly discontented and renounced their allegiance to the city-states. Inspired by the Israelites who had escaped their own oppression in Egypt, many joined them in forming settlements in the highlands and later in overthrowing the Canaanite cities themselves. (For a summary and evaluation of studies on the conquest, cf. M. Weippert, *Settlement of the Israelite Tribes in Palestine* [1971].) Adopting the lime-plastered cistern and employing iron tools for extensive deforestation, the Israelites established cities in an area the Canaanites had been unable to inhabit. The new cities were small and poorly fortified, and Israelite occupations of previously Canaanite cities covered only fractionally the area of those Bronze Age sites. Nevertheless, these early settlements became the foundation of what might be regarded the "typical" Israelite city, that of Iron Age Palestine.

Although communities varied as a result of political and economic fortunes, a primary concern of the biblical city continued to be adequate FORTIFICATION, namely "high walls, gates, and bars" (Dt. 3:5; 2 Ch. 8:5; Neh. 3:3). In the Early Iron Age (1200-1000 B.C.) the Israelites adopted the casemate wall, which the Hittites had introduced during the Late Bronze Age in Syria and Anatolia. Two concentric walls ringed the city, generally 5 to 7 ft.

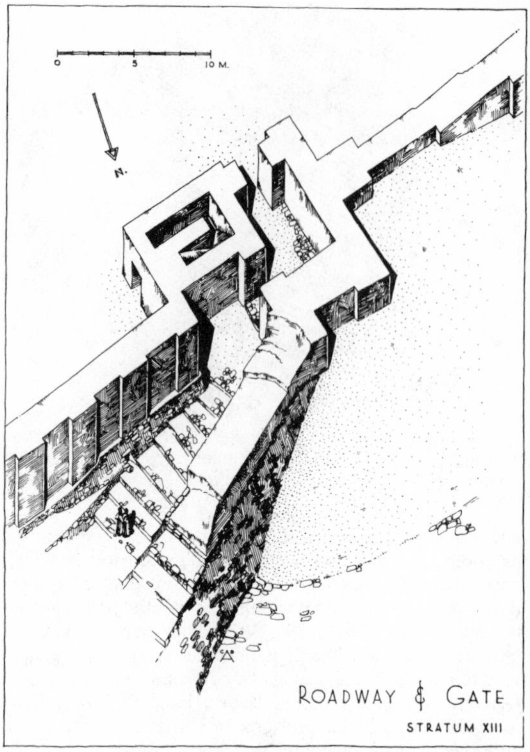

Suggested restoration of a single-chamber gate at Megiddo (Middle Bronze Age, 1800-1750 B.C.). The ninety-degree turn at the entrance offered considerable defensive advantage. (Oriental Institute, University of Chicago)

(1.5 to 2 m.) apart, joined at intervals by perpendicular walls. The fortifications were then strengthened by filling with rubble the rooms thus formed; some of these spaces, however, may have been used as residences (cf. Josh. 2:15, which suggests that the walls thus may have contained windows). The casemate wall was used most extensively at Samaria, capital of the northern kingdom. Solomon strengthened the casemate style at Megiddo and Gezer with carefully fitted cut stones on the wall faces. Other forms of Iron Age walls included massive ("cyclopean") constructions made of huge boulders, often designed with salients and recesses ("offsets and insets"; 10th-9th cents.), Rehoboam's sun-dried mud brick wall at Lachish, 20 ft. (6 m.) thick (*ca.* 900 B.C.), and the roughly contemporary rubble installation at Tell en-Naṣbeh, 20 ft. (6 m.) thick, later reinforced to 26 ft. (8 m.), covered with a thick plaster, and surrounded in sections by a sloping glacis (an elaborate construction comprising an earthen embankment and a brick wall, with earth and stone piled against the wall) and a dry moat.

City gates were important not only for defense but also as civic and commercial centers. While Bronze Age cities had only one or two gates, later cities had several. The gates generally consisted of two and sometimes even three or four sets of piers, and jutted out from the walls, forming deep recesses. A ramp provided access from the outside. Swinging wooden doors suspended from vertical timbers and rotating in stone sockets closed the main entrance, located in the outer set of piers. The doors were secured by a wooden or metal bar that could slide into a slot in one of the piers when the doors were opened. The main opening was about 14 ft. (4 m.) wide, permitting chariots to enter; a smaller second opening without doors was used for pedestrians and animals. An indirect access gate of three piers (similar to the modern Damascus and Jaffa gates in the Old City of Jerusalem) was used at many sites, including Megiddo, Shechem, and Gezer. Because of the potential for unauthorized entry into the city, gates were fortified by towers (Jgs. 9:51ff.; 2 Ch. 26:9; 32:5), sometimes with a room above the gate (Tell Beit Mirsim, Tell en-Naṣbeh; cf. 2 S. 18:24, 33). As one of the busiest points in the city, the gate and open square within served as the marketplace (2 K. 7:1), and was the seat for the administration of justice before the elders (Dt. 21:19; Josh. 20:4; Ruth 4); the heavy traffic assured a ready supply of witnesses. The gates of Jerusalem were named according to geographical orientation (Ephraim, 2 K. 14:13; Valley, 2 Ch. 26:9) or the function of their respective quarters (Sheep, Neh. 3:1, 32; Dung, v. 14; Water, v. 26; Horse, v. 28).

The citadel, a fortress or stronghold within the city, provided the last line of defense. In combination with the palace and temple or other important public buildings, it formed a walled acropolis. At Megiddo the fortified hilltop was a citadel including adminstrative buildings and the purported stables. Israelite border cities such as Bethel, Dan, and Arad converted former "high places" into sanctuaries within the royal citadels. As with the governor's palace at Megiddo, the citadel walls were often of a style, borrowed from the Phoenicians, in which massive piers of finely hewn stone were placed at 4-ft. (1.2-m.) intervals with a filling of irregularly layered rubble. In addition to the highest point, the northwest corner of the city was again a preferred location because of the breeze. The impressive Omride palace was on the northwest side of the Samaritan summit; the Megiddo palace was on the northwest side, but at a lower point in the city. Another favorable location was immediately inside the gate, as shown by the governor's palace at Beer-sheba. Ramat Rahel (7th-6th cents.) contained both an upper palace citadel and a lower stronghold.

Considerable care was taken to obtain and store water. Huge catch basins were used to collect water running off the mountains at Late Iron Age Lachish (*ca.* 600 B.C.), as it had been at E.B. Arad. The plastered CISTERN permitted Israelites to maintain an adequate supply during the long dry summers; most residences had their own cisterns, some large enough to support many households in emergencies. Wells and springs were generally located outside or even beneath the cramped cities, and wells were often dug at great length through solid rock (144 ft. [44 m.] at Lachish; cf. Beth-shemesh, Tell Beit Mirsim). Elaborate provisions were frequently made to guarantee access to water supplies during times of siege. Continuing earlier Jebusite efforts, Hezekiah built a conduit from the spring Gihon to a new pool within Jerusalem by tunneling through the rock (2 K. 20:20; Sir. 48:17), assuring safe use by residents while denying access to enemies. At Taanach a water system consisting of a square shaft and lower chamber cut beneath the city was a prototype for other Late Bronze and Iron Age installations including those at Gezer, Gibeon, and Megiddo. Most impressive is the early ninth-century system at Hazor, consisting of a vertical shaft along which was fashioned a staircase 1 ft. (30 cm.) wide, connected to the subterranean water pool by a sloping stepped tunnel. Access to the system, which reaches a depth of 138 ft. (42 m.), was by ramps in an entrance building within the city. A secondary system outside Megiddo's defenses most likely was used in peacetime, the larger underground arrangement being intended for times of siege. One of Gibeon's two systems included an enormous cylindrical shaft 37 ft. (11.3 m.) in diameter and 35 ft. (10.7 m.) deep, continued by a corkscrew tunnel to the reservoir 45 ft. (14 m.) below.

Although still comparatively small, Israelite cities reached their greatest size by the 8th cent. B.C. Tell Beit Mirsim's 7.5 acres (3 hectares) included 150 to 200 houses and a population of 2000 to 3000. Beth-shemesh was approximately the same size. Lachish had 18 acres (7.3 hectares) and 6000 to 7500 people; Megiddo, 13 acres (5.3 hectares), and 3500 to 5000 people. Immediately before the Exile Jerusalem numbered perhaps 50,000; but at the time of the return it had dropped to 12,000, and residents had to be drafted from among the neighboring populace (Neh. 11:1f.; cf. the Greek practice of *synoikísmos,* lit. "settling together"). Excavations have supported Assyrian records, which list forty-six captured Judean towns with a total of 200,000 people.

Despite their size, the cities were densely inhabited, with houses cramped together irregularly in any available space and sometimes even placed outside the walls. At Megiddo the residents were housed in the lower city and protected by a secondary wall. Houses at Tell Beit Mirsim and other sites often used the city wall as one side of the structure; these were separated by a road from the central district, where irregular dwellings were massed. Other cities, such as Tell en-Naṣbeh, separated houses from the wall by a buffer zone of cisterns and storage pits. Any attempted planning was generally restricted by the site's terrain, and extensive urban clutter contributed to the architectural jumble. Although materials were often reused, the accumulation of debris from burned houses was considerable, and compacted stones and sherds raised the level of the otherwise unpaved streets.

In addition to the area within the walls, cities maintained jurisdiction over various outlying territories (Nu. 32:33; cf. 1 S. 9:27). Included were agricultural areas such as fields (Lev. 14:53; 1 Ch. 6:56; etc.), pasture lands (Nu. 35:5,34; Josh. 21:22; 1 Ch. 6:55; etc.), and villages (Josh. 13:28; etc.), whose people tended the lands. Other extramural sites might include shrines or high places (regarded as pagan, 1 S. 9:25) or unclean areas (Lev. 14:40f., 45), such as cemeteries or refuse dumps. Villages relied on the cities as markets for produce and also for protection. Building close to or even against the walls, the villagers might seek refuge within the walls during siege, and residents might be enlisted in the city's defense. (The muddled text of Hab. 3:14 may refer to *pᵉrāzîm,* lit. "hamlet dwellers," who rush forth to meet an attacker.) Few legal distinctions are recorded; city houses that had been sold or otherwise alienated might be redeemed for the original owner by payment only within a year, while those of villages were to be returned to the seller in the Jubilee Year (Lev. 25:29-31). Kinship terminology was often used to express either relationships between cities and their villages or covenants and treaties with other cities. Beth-maacah is called "mother" (2 S. 20:19), indicating a city with dependent villages (Heb. *bānôṯ,* lit. "daughters"; Nu. 21:25, 32; Jgs. 11:26; the Philistine cities Ekron, Ashdod, and Gaza have both "daughters" and "villages" [*ḥᵃṣērîm*; Josh. 15:45-47], suggesting different degrees of dependency). After defeat in war, a city might become vassal to another (Lam. 1:1), receiving the designation *'almānâ* (lit. "widow"; Isa. 47:8f.; 54:4; cf. MT Jer. 51:5). Changes in alliances or the result of the growth and subsequent independence of villages may be reflected in variant relationships recorded in the genealogies of 1 Ch. 1–9, which lists persons, groups, and territories (cf. the Edomite cities Korah and Shammah [1 Ch. 1:35, 37]; Ephah [1:33]; note also the conflicting designations within the Perez line for Caleb, Hur, and Hezron [2:19, 50; 4:1]).

Some cities had specialized functions. Such were fortress cities (Ramath Rahel or Beth-haccherem), storage centers for grain (2 Ch. 17:12; Tell el-Kheleifeh; cf. Tell Jemmeh), chariot cities (Hazor, Lower Beth-Horon, Baalath) or bases for horsemen (Megiddo), caravan cities (Gaza, Beth-shean, Tyre), and seaports (Ezion-geber, Joppa, Sidon). Solomon's extensive building program established many of these specialized cities (1 K. 9:19). The capital of a territory or state was designated a "royal city" (1 S. 27:5; 2 S. 12:26). *See also* CITIES, LEVITICAL; CITIES OF REFUGE.

David's selection of JERUSALEM as capital was an act of political genius and of historical significance, both real and symbolical, uniting on the site of the former Jebusite stronghold the diverse and potentially separative northern and southern tribes. Because he had captured the city he regarded it as his personal possession ("city of David"). It was accordingly a neutral territory and an independent power base, strengthened by adoption of the Jerusalem Canaanite dialect as the official "Hebrew" tongue, and by the relocation there of the ark of the covenant, making the capital also the cultic center of the kingdom, a "holy city" (Isa. 48:2; 52:1; 64:10).

Under the monarchy the Israelite city, and particularly Jerusalem, showed signs of increased secularization and reflected a movement away from the original ideals of the covenant with Yahweh. The early Hebrew communities had enjoyed an ideological solidarity, despite their diverse components. This was lost through increased complacency and the influx of non-Israelite elements (including foreign artisans and merchants, as well as diplomatically arranged royal marriages and alliances). The acceptance of Jerusalem as the "city of David" was contrary to Yahweh's idealized ownership of all the land. Increased conscription for the massive building projects and heavy taxation to support the expensive and ostentatious palace, temple, and attendant bureaucracy marked a trend toward the conditions of Late Bronze Age Canaan. No longer a classless society, the city reflected clear social stratification. (Cf. Tell el-Fâr'ah, where the uniformly appointed tenth-century houses were supplanted by a wealthy section of large, well-built houses separated by a wall from crowded and relatively crude dwellings.) The contrast between the Yahwistic principles of early Israel and the later character of the Israelite city is underscored by the outspoken complaints of the prophets, representing the views of their outlying villages (by nature conservative) against the blatant hypocrisy and overt decadence of the urban centers (Micah 6:9-16; cf. Amos 3–4).

IV. Greek and Roman Cities.–Following the Exile the Palestinian city was in decline, both in size and in style. Thus the imperialist activities of Alexander the Great and his successors made significant impact on sites throughout the region, as they had in Asia Minor. To solidify their conquests and to advance Greek influence in those territories, they ambitiously constructed cities throughout the Levant, introducing the form if not so much the spirit of the Greek city, and mingling Greek and Near Eastern cultures. Many of these cities were new settlements, but others were rebuildings of existing towns. A number of Greeks settled there, some by choice and others by assignment, so the Greek cultural influence was strong; nevertheless, the stubborn independence of native elements maintained the oriental texture.

Greek *pólis* originally designated a fortified settlement, and the NT uses the term to differentiate the city, as an enclosed place of human residence, from the villages and countryside. The NT city, particularly as depicted in Acts and the Epistles, was the descendant of the classical Greek *pólis*. This city-state, which developed in scattered, isolated pockets, was thus independent, self-reliant, and strongly provincial. This spirit was reflected in the nature of the community, whose ideals were mutual responsibility and concern for general well-being through which the individual could develop to the fullest potential culturally, physically, and spiritually. Expressions of such concerns in the Greek city were such common elements as the gymnasium, stadium, and theater.

The Greek spirit also appears in the Hellenistic policy permitting communities throughout the empire to retain their respective cultures and to experience, within bounds, political autonomy. Antioch on the Orontes, founded by Seleucus in 300 B.C., was a mixture of Macedonian Greeks and Syrians, plus a colony of Jewish veterans of the Seleucid army. As provincial capital of Syria the city was considered so politically and commercially important as to warrant appointed officials. Nevertheless, it retained considerable self-government by a civic-minded aristocracy and the popular assembly. Hellenism was less successful in Jerusalem. As requested by Antiochus IV Epiphanes and in exchange for a substantial payment, the city was transformed in 175 B.C. from a temple state (*katoikía*) into the *pólis* Antioch-in-Judea (2 Macc. 4:9-14). Enfranchised citizens were designated, the local council became the *boulḗ*, and the temple priests were named magistrates. But the hellenized elements became the object of pro-Ptolemaic resistance and religious dissent, and social and economic tensions between the urban rich and agricultural peasantry forced Antiochus to take strong measures against the city (169 or 168). He rededicated the temple to Olympian Zeus and halted the observance of Judaism by suspending the city's constitution, the Mosaic law (2 Macc. 6:1-6).

Relatively little evidence of Hellenistic occupation has been preserved in Palestine proper. Marisa (OT Mareshah, Tell Sandaḥannah), Jerash (Gerasa), and Amman (Philadelphia) represent a characteristic Greek city plan attributed to Hippodamos of Miletus (5th cent.). Although adapted to the local terrain, this was a fairly rigid orthogonal plan, oriented to the four points of the compass. The cities consisted of houses in blocks formed by perpendicular streets, and a rectangular central area for public buildings.

Plan of Marisa (Tell Sandaḥanna), a typical Hellenistic city, almost square, with streets intersecting at right angles and buildings surrounding an open court in each block (F. J. Bliss and R. A. S. Macalister)

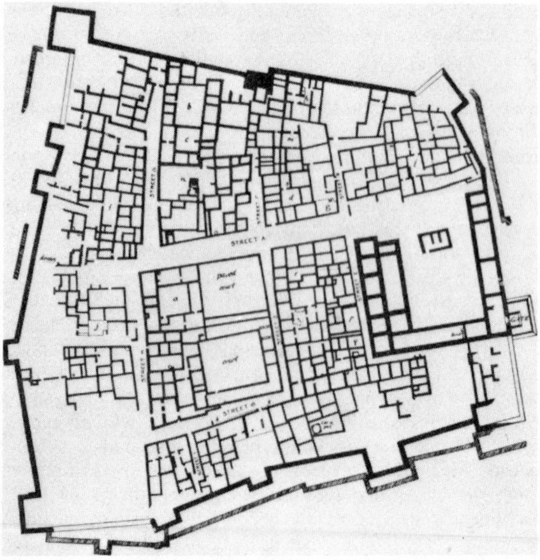

Ruins of the Asclepium on the southwest outskirts of Pergamum. Adjoining a broad courtyard flanked by colonnades (center) were a theater (foreground), library, temple of Zeus Asclepius, and the treatment center. (B. K. Condit)

Pergamum in Asia Minor (Rev. 2:12-17) was less faithful to the orthogonal form, but still a unified settlement with terraced buildings around the citadel, a central residential area, and a main street flanked by various public buildings.

Most significant of the Hellenistic innovations was the *agorá*. Combining the functions of marketplace and civic center, the agora replaced the typical Palestinian city gate as the focus of activity. Ephesus, established by Alexander's general Lysimachus, was characteristic. The rectangular agora, 300 ft. (90 m.) on each side and surrounded by pillars, focused on the shrine of Hera Boulaia with its perpetually burning sacred hearth, symbol of the city's well-being. The civic center also contained an assembly hall for the city council, offices of various officials, and a basilica, the business and legal center. Statues and inscriptions abounded, glorifying both subject and donor. No street passed through the agora, although it was adjacent to a main thoroughfare. Immediately outside the district were shops, temples, and a library.

The Romans imitated the Hellenistic city plan, using a rectilinear design characterized by north-south (*cardo*) and east-west (*decamus*) streets, which had gates at each end and intersected at right angles near the center of the city. The forum, of which there might be several, was a large, open square which was surrounded by shops and through which streets ran; it was successor to the agora as a depository for monuments and plaques. That Roman architecture was largely monumental is perhaps most apparent in the primarily ornamental city walls and triumphal arches.

Missing was the open spirit of the Greek city. Accorded different degrees of political status and thus of administrative autonomy, the cities were generally left to themselves. In Palestine the Herodians, despite their outward appearance as enlightened philhellene monarchs, were extremely wary of any threat to their highly centralized administrative system, and local autonomy was severely curtailed. Some cities (Marisa) were suppressed, while others (Joppa, Azotus [Ashdod]) were reduced to capitals of toparchies, administrative districts comprised of several villages (cf. Josephus *BJ* iii.3.5 [§§ 54f.]). Although Sebaste (Samaria) was granted additional territory to accomodate peoples relocated there, that land apparently was not considered part of the city's sphere of influence. The care taken to guarantee the privileges of Roman citizens throughout the empire led to rigid social stratification within the cities (Roman, non-Roman, free, slave). Taxes and other financial burdens, legally or illegally imposed by Roman officials, also heightened economic distinctions (landowner, merchant, agriculturalist, laborer).

Most of the Roman building activity in the Near East was done by Herod the Great (37-4 B.C.), who cultivated his reputation as a great city-builder by rebuilding and expanding many sites and renaming them for his political superiors. Thus the Phoenician fortified city of Strato's Tower became Caesarea, Samaria was named Sebaste

(Gk. for Augusta, after Caesar Augustus), and the great tower in Jerusalem was enlarged and named Antonia after his patron Mark Antony. (The practice was common in the Greek and Roman periods; Acco was called Ptolemais after Ptolemy II Philadelphus, and the Greek settlement of Panea on the slope of Mt. Hermon was named by Herod's successor Philip as Caesarea Philippi after Tiberius Caesar and himself.)

Samaria (Sebaste) displays evidence of some of the more extraordinary Herodian building. Both for sentimental reasons (the city had been loyal during his struggles with Antigonus [Josephus *Ant.* xiv.15.3], and there he married Mariamne [*Ant.* xiv.15.14]) and as a means of solidifying his political advantage, Herod restored the city to its earlier prominence, settling six thousand war veterans there and engaging in extensive building. He refortified the city with a new wall 2 mi. (3.2 km.) in circumference and 0.6 mi. (1 km.) in diameter, strengthened at intervals by gateways with towers. Most outstanding of the Herodian edifices was a temple honoring Augustus, 225 ft. (69 m.) on each side. Located on a platform 14 ft. (4.3 m.) high, it was approached by a monumental staircase from a large forecourt extending over the edge of the mound. Other Roman additions within the city walls included a roofed stadium with a track of Olympic proportions.

Magnificently built at great expense over twelve years' time (25-13 B.C.), Caesarea featured artificial harbor installations extending 0.25 mi. (0.4 km.) from shore and a stone breakwater 200 ft. (60 m.) wide and standing in 120 ft. (37 m.) of water. Josephus considered it at least the rival of Athens (*Ant.* xv.9.6; *BJ* i.21.5-8). Enclosed within a semicircular wall, the main part of the city included a forum, an oval amphitheater for gladiatorial competition measuring 300 ft. (90 m.) by 200 ft. (60 m.) — slightly larger than the Roman Colosseum — and a stadium where games were held every fifth year. A high aqueduct brought the city's water supply from the foothills of Mt. Carmel by a 3 ft. (1 m.) tunnel 6 mi. (10 km.) through the rock and another 6 mi. on arched supports. A hippodrome for equine competition (2nd cent. A.D.) seated more than 30,000 people, and a theater overlooking the coast seated 4500. Later additions included baths, tetrapylons, and colonnaded streets. As official seat of the Roman procurators and capital of Palestine (A.D. 6-66), the city was the scene of Paul's trial before Agrippa (Acts 25:23–26:32). Its Hellenistic spirit made it offensive to the pious Jew, and tensions between Jewish and gentile elements led to the riots that began the Jewish revolt against Rome in A.D. 66 (Josephus *Ant.* xx.8.7-9; *BJ* ii.13.7; ii.14.4f.).

By NT times, Jerusalem also had experienced considerable change. The city's topography had been altered over the years. The Tyropoeon Valley between the eastern and western portions of the city had been partially filled by centuries' accumulation of debris. Also, the Maccabees had constructed a powerful fortress on the site of the former lower city (the Herodian Acra), reducing the hill and filling the valley between it and the temple. To enclose urban sprawl to the north of the old city, two new walls were constructed in Hellenistic-Hasmonean times. Another wall was begun in A.D. 42 by Herod Agrippa to enclose suburban Bezetha, but it was not completed until the first Jewish revolt in A.D. 66.

Herod the Great reinforced the existing fortifications at Jerusalem by construction of a strongly fortified citadel in the northwest corner of the city near the present Jaffa Gate. Strengthened by three huge towers, the entire palace was constructed on an elevated platform and covered an area 985 ft. (300 m.) by 330 ft. (100 m.). A Maccabean fortress at the juncture of the second city wall with the temple enclosure was rebuilt and named the Tower of Antonia. The tallest of its four towers (105 ft. [32 m.]) faced the temple courts and was intended to police the worshipers, perhaps by a Roman cohort garrisoned there (cf. Acts 21:31-37). Paved with limestone blocks, the court of the fortress may be the "Pavement" of Jn. 19:13. Here Paul disputed with Jewish leaders and was confined for protection during investigation by the tribunal (Acts 21:27–22:29). Here also Jesus may have been questioned by Pilate.

Most impressive in Herod's rebuilding of Jerusalem were his efforts involving the temple area proper. Begun by Herod in 20 B.C. partly as a means of endearing himself to the Jewish populace, the program included construction of four massive retaining walls intended to support the enlarged courtyard, one of the largest such areas in the ancient world at 35 acres (14 hectares). The extensive system of vaults and columns supporting the platform is traditionally called "Solomon's Stables." Portions of the retaining walls have survived, including the Western (or Wailing) Wall. Although the general plan of the temple was fixed by sacred tradition, Herod was able to enhance it by making it higher and by providing elaborate ornamentation. A royal portico inside the temple mount courtyard was built in basilical style and apparently served as a commercial center, a likely location for money changing.

Apparently the economic status of many of Jerusalem's residents increased during this period. Residences of the wealthy included multistory structures arranged around a central court under which were cisterns and ritual bathing facilities. Ornamentation included mosaic floors and plastered walls with frescoes. Suggesting heightened cultural and recreational interests, a theater and stadium are also said to have been among Herod's additions to Jerusalem. The Herodian city was levelled by Titus' army in A.D. 70.

Herod's other activities in Palestine included enclosures for the tombs of the Jewish patriarchs at Hebron and Abraham's Oak at Mamre. Herodian public buildings were erected at Ashkelon, Jericho, and Qarn Sartabeh (Alexandria, N of Jericho). He also built a series of fortresses in the Judean wilderness and in the region around the Dead Sea, including Masada and his castle and tomb at Herodium SE of Bethlehem.

Outside Palestine, typical Roman building of biblical interest can be illustrated by CORINTH. As other cities in the western Roman empire, Corinth attempted to copy Rome, and its distinctly Roman character is important for understanding Paul's work there. The Romans, who refounded the city in 44 B.C., apparently located the forum on a different site from the earlier Greek agora. Surrounded by shops, basilicas, and monuments, the marketplace was divided into northern and southern sections by a long row of central shops. Near the center was the *bēma* ("tribunal"; cf. Lat. *rostrum*; Acts 18:12-17), a platform for public speaking with capacity for a sizable crowd. In addition, the forum contained the typical Roman gymnasium with two stoas, a theater, and underground baths. On the city's north side, adjacent to the wall and near the spring Lerna, was the sanctuary of Asclepius, god of healing; it contained facilities for votive offerings of those seeking healing, and chambers for cultic meals (cf. 1 Cor. 8, 10). North of the city on the east side of the Corinthian isthmus was the sanctuary of Poseidon, site of the Isthmian games, survivals of which continued in Roman times.

Among the last Roman efforts in Palestine were Hadrian's rebuilding of Jerusalem *ca.* A.D. 132 as the thoroughly pagan Aelia Capitolina, from which Jews were excluded under penalty of death. This Roman provincial city covered 70 acres (28 hectares), with 10,000-18,000 Roman colonists, and contained well-planned streets and the usual Roman public buildings. Included were the temple of Jupiter Capitolinus on the former Jewish sacred precinct and a temple of Venus on the approximate location of the later Church of the Holy Sepulchre. To the north, Samaria-Sebaste was reestablished as the colony Lucia Septimia Severus. Extremely prosperous from *ca.* A.D. 180 to 230, the city included architecturally uniform buidings such as a summit temple and temple of Kore, a small theater, a rectangular forum surrounded by pillars, and a large basilica.

Bibliography.*–*General: M. Hammond, *The City in the Ancient World* (1972; comprehensive annotated bibliography); C. H. Kraeling and R. M. Adams, eds., *City Invincible* (1960); I. M. Lapidus, *Middle Eastern Cities* (1969); C. B. Moore, ed., *Reconstructing Complex Societies* (*BASOR Supp. Studies,* 20, 1974).

Ancient Near East: R. J. Braidwood and G. R. Willey, eds., *Courses Toward Urban Life* (1962); R. Harris, *Ancient Sippar: A Demographic Study of an Old Babylonian City (1894-1595 B.C.)* (1975); P. Lampl, *Cities and Planning in the Ancient Near East* (1968; many pictures and diagrams); A. L. Oppenheim, *Ancient Mesopotamia* (1964), pp. 109-142.

Syria and Palestine: E. Anati, *Palestine Before the Hebrews* (1963); Archaeological Institute of America, compiler, *Archaeological Discoveries in the Holy Land* (1967); G. Buccellati, *Cities and Nations of Ancient Syria* (*Studi Semitici,* 26, 1967); F. M. Cross, W. E. Lemke, and P. D. Miller, eds., *Magnalia Dei: The Mighty Acts of God* (1976), pp. 3-54, 132-151; F. S. Frick, *City in Ancient Israel* (1977); K. M. Kenyon, *Archaeology in the Holy Land* (1960); J. A. Sanders, ed., *Near Eastern Archaeology in the Twentieth Century* (1970), pp. 83-163, 232-253; *WBA*.

Greek and Roman: V. Ehrenberg, *The Greek State* (Eng. tr. 1960), pp. 28-102; *CERP* (2nd ed. 1971); J. B. Ward-Perkins, *Cities of Ancient Greece and Italy: Planning in Classical Antiquity* (1974).

A. C. MYERS

CITY, BIBLICAL THEOLOGY OF. From Genesis to the Revelation of John, the biblical canon conveys a rich, consistent "theology of the city," which illumines not merely the city itself but also the broader sweep of God's judgment and grace in relation to man and his works. Probably the best way to summarize this message of God about the city is to consider first the stream of revelation that begins with Cain's city and culminates with the final end of Babylon, the great city, under the judgment of God; second, God's gracious action, which culminates in the eschatological city, New Jerusalem; finally, a few observations about the relationship of the two cities in human history and the problem of an urban ethics.

I. From the City of Cain to Babylon.–The origins of the city, in biblical revelation, are not to be found in Eden, nor can they be rooted satisfactorily in the mandate to Adam and Eve. Rather, the first city is built by Cain the murderer, the rejector of the word and presence of the Lord (Gen. 4). Instead of wandering under the protection of God, Cain chooses to settle in the land of Nod and build a city. The city becomes a sign of fallen man's quest for security apart from God. It is important to note that Genesis does not present the conflict as "country versus city"; rather, the city is accessory and symbolizes Cain's quest for autonomy and security.

Cain is followed by the sons of Ham, the impure and cursed son of Noah, as the next city-builders (Gen. 10). The Canaanite cities, above all Sodom and Gomorrah, were to become notorious centers of moral corruption, idolatry, and enmity against God. Mizraim (Egypt) was the place where enslaved Israel built the storage cities and is also linked to the early Philistines. Above all, Nimrod the son of Cush, is noted as the builder and conqueror of cities, most notably Babel/Babylon and Nineveh. Nimrod is called a "mighty one in the earth" and a "mighty hunter/plunderer." To Cain's city as security apart from God is added the indictment of the city as the place of moral corruption, idolatry, outright enmity against God, slavery for the people of God, and the spirit of power and war.

The Babel episode (Gen. 11) is paradigmatic for the theological understanding of the city. The pride and lust for power that motivate this work of fallen man are obvious: "Let us build for ourselves"; "let us make a name for ourselves." Providentially, God intervenes by confusing language and communication, thus bringing the work to a halt. The sad irony of this situation is that this providential restriction of the possibilities of power and pride is accomplished through a new hazard characteristic of the city: difficulty of true communication and understanding.

Sodom and Gomorrah are the next cities to receive substantial attention in Scripture (Gen. 18–19). The righteous sojourner Abraham pleads with the Lord for the preservation of the corrupt cities because of the possibility of a faithful remnant within. God accepts the terms of the bargain, but not even ten righteous can be found. The few righteous must flee the city to avoid God's judgment on these archetypes of urban moral corruption.

Israel's relationship to the city is at first peripheral, since the patriarchs are nomadic shepherds. After the death of Joseph, however, the cities of Egypt become the place of slavery. Specifically, the children of Israel must build the storage cities Pithom and Raamses (Ex. 1). The conquest of Canaan brought the people of God into direct conflict with the cities of that region. In fact, Israel's commission to conquer, or even destroy, the Canaanite cities was based largely on the divine judgment against the wickedness and idolatry which they harbored. Jericho typified the very worst of these conditions; a curse was pronounced on anyone who would try to rebuild it (Josh. 6:26).

Despite the fact that the people of God were occasionally directed to use, or even to build, some cities (above all, Jerusalem), such activity easily lapsed into the pattern of Cain and his followers, with dire results. Solomon, the first great building king in Israel, is remembered chiefly for building the temple. However, it was his building of the Millo and the many storage cities through forced labor that led to Jeroboam's revolt (1 K. 9, 11). Solomon's apostate acceptance of foreign gods opened the floodgates, so that the prophet Jeremiah later wailed "your gods are as many as your cities, O Judah!" (Jer. 11:13). The Chronicles, in particular, recount this pattern of construction of cities by kings, with its correlate of corruption and idolatry, and then separation from God. The prophets inveigh against the cities not out of a nostalgia for a rural past but because of the corruption and wickedness associated with them.

Babylon in particular becomes "the city." Built on bloodshed and slavery, filled with idols, wealth, luxury, and the wisdom of man, carrying away captive the people of God, mocking the Creator, Babylon's spirit was voiced best by King Nebuchadrezzar: "Is this not Babylon the great, which I myself have built . . . by the might of my power and for the glory of my majesty?" (Dnl. 4:30). In the oracle of Isaiah, Babylon was "the beauty of kingdoms, the glory of the Chaldeans' pride" (Isa. 13:19). It was *the* great city of Cain. Its end would be destruction by God.

Jesus' relationship to the city evidenced great compassion on His part while at the same time continuing the general attitude seen in the OT. The lament over Jerusalem is particularly instructive in regard both to Jesus' attitude and to the hardness of the city in response (Lk. 13:34f.). The cities often showed themselves at enmity with the gospel. The gospel must be proclaimed in all the cities and villages, but woe to those that reject it (Lk. 10:8-16)! It was in the city that political functionaries, religious leaders, and an urban mob rejected, sentenced, and crucified Jesus Christ.

The Apostolic Church spread from city to city gaining a foothold nearly everywhere and yet suffering much the same consequences that Jesus encountered. Finally, the Apocalypse rounds out the description and pronounces the final judgment on this city of Cain: "Fallen, fallen is Babylon the Great" (Rev. 18:2). Rev. 18 summarizes the judgment: she has become a dwelling place of demons; her sins are piled as high as the heavens. She is guilty of gross immorality, horrible violence, piling up wealth and luxury at the expense of human lives. She has rejected and slain the prophets and saints and exulted in her own power. The great city is the apotheosis of sin and evil.

II. From Salem to New Jerusalem.–From Genesis to Revelation, then, the city is under judgment and a curse. It originated in the strivings of fallen men and women for security, power, carnal satisfaction, and glory, apart from God. Separated from God it became the place of violence, moral corruption, economic oppression, slavery, idolatry, the absence of communication, the reduction of individuals to members of the crowd — in sum, the institutional incarnation of evil.

However, even in the case of the city, the grace and election of God triumphed over the works of fallen man. This is the remarkable theological counterpoint to the condemnation of the city repeatedly encountered in Scripture. Man descends to new lows. Yet God reaches down to fallen man, meets him, and redeems him at that level. The history of God's dealings with the city is analogous to His relationship to kingship (1 S. 8, 12.). God warned Israel not to seek a king like the other nations. They insisted, yet God did not reject them. Rather, He helped them choose their king. Finally, God is revealed in biblical eschatology as the true King of Kings. Similarly, the city does not appear as God's intention for human life, yet He does not reject urban man but begins to redeem him and his city. The choice of Jerusalem in the OT, with its temple of God's presence, and the eschatological vision in terms of New Jerusalem, the City of God, completes the picture.

Some of Israel is given permission to build "cities for our little ones" just before the conquest (Nu. 32:16ff.), and in dividing up the land, the tribes of Israel are assigned various Canaanite cities. These, of course, were to be purged of their idols and, thereby, their religious significance as places of rebellion against the true God. More significant yet is the choice of certain cities as "cities of refuge" (Nu. 35). Here are cities chosen by God for life, a promise of things to come, a promise of what God intends for this work of man.

Even without a conquest and purification, it is possible for the people of God to live in the cities of Cain and remain faithful to God. Short of the extreme case of Sodom, where the only remaining option was to flee, it may be possible to participate in the city while refusing to join in its evil and idolatry. "Seek the welfare of the city where I have sent you into exile, and pray to the Lord on its behalf; for in its welfare you will have welfare" (Jer. 29:7). Esther in the OT, Erastus the city treasurer in the NT (Rom. 16:23), and many others indicate the possibilities of participation in the cities of Cain by the pilgrim people of God. Jonah, of course, indicates the extreme possibility of a Nineveh repenting en masse before God.

The main counterpoint to Babylon, however, is Jerusalem. Babel has its tower to the greatness and pride of man; Jerusalem is elected by God to have the temple of God's presence within its walls. Jerusalem is to be the city under the word of God. The roots of Jerusalem go back to the Jebusite descendants of Canaan, the cursed son of Ham. Yet, in a most significant brief episode, Melchizedek, king of Salem (Jerusalem?) and "priest of the God Most High," suddenly appears with a gift of bread and wine and a blessing for Abraham (Gen. 14). Ps. 110:4 and the Letter to the Hebrews indicate that this priest-king was a type of the coming Messiah.

During the period of the conquest and the judges, Jerusalem remained "Jebus" under the control of the Jebusites. David, however, conquered the city (also called Zion) and soon after brought the ark of the Lord to Jerusalem (2 S. 5f.). A city, Jerusalem, was now the "Holy City," the city where God's presence and witness were to be centered and maintained (Isa. 52). Under Solomon, the temple was erected to symbolize even more visibly this presence of God.

The millennium that followed the period of David and Solomon was filled with the drama of Israel's apostasy and revival. Jerusalem was sacked, its temple destroyed, and its people carried away captive to Babylon, only to be rebuilt later under God's leadership. Finally, Jerusalem's status as holy city was ended with the arrival, crucifixion, and resurrection of Jesus Christ, and the destruction of the temple in Jerusalem. The earthly temple is destroyed and replaced by the body of Christ as the resurrected "temple of God" (Jn. 2:19; 1 Pet. 2). Jesus' death and resurrection are the desacralization of the earthly Jerusalem and the "sacralization" of the people of God.

Yet that is by no means the end of the city. The coming eschatological reality is described in terms of the New Jerusalem (Rev. 21). In this city there is no temple "for its temple is the Lord God the Almighty and the Lamb" (Rev. 21:22). Babylon has been destroyed completely; all things are new and the New Jerusalem is all in all. The old Jerusalem takes its place in history as a witness and pointer to the new.

III. The Two Cities.–Babylon, the city of Cain, has occasionally been so totally in dominion over particular cities that God has intervened in judgment in human history. This was the case with Babel, Sodom, Jericho, Babylon, Nineveh, and Jerusalem, for example. New Jerusalem, the city of God, has never been fully present on earth, and cannot be until Babylon is finally destroyed by God. Nevertheless, there are hints and foreshadowings of that future City of God that comes into our history. By faith we know that God is at work in our history, using the works of man (even rebellious man) toward the final end in ways that we cannot see now with total clarity.

The coming city of God is defined by the presence of God, who is all in all. Thus, in the present context, the role of the "body of Christ" is to exemplify the coming city of God even now. This should be our primary "urban identity," implying that we reside as pilgrims and aliens in the other cities of the world. Our task is to be the "city set on a hill" and the "light of the world" (Mt. 5:14). The OT saints followed Abraham in living as pilgrims, looking for the "city which has foundations, whose architect and builder is God" (He. 11:10). In Jesus Christ, however, we have "come to Mount Zion and to the city of the living God, the heavenly Jerusalem" (He. 12:22f.).

Beyond this primary task of "being present" as the

coming city of God in our present lives, we have the task of proclamation of the Gospel to the cities, in the footsteps of Jesus. And we have the task of praying for the city and seeking the welfare of the city wherein we reside as aliens and pilgrims (Jer. 29:7). The city of Cain must see within its borders and in its activities the visible indications of the coming triumph of the New Jerusalem.

Bibliography.–J. Ellul, *The Meaning of the City* (Eng. tr. 1970); J. Comblin, *Théologie de la Ville* (1968); H. Cox, *The Secular City* (1965); *Commonweal*, 94 (1971), 351-57. D. W. GILL

CITY AUTHORITIES [Gk. *politárchai*] (Acts 17:6, 8); AV RULERS OF THE CITY; NEB MAGISTRATES. Men before whom Jason and the other Christians were dragged by the mob. The term distinguishes the magistrates of a free Greek city from the ordinary Roman officials. It primarily denotes "rulers of the citizens," and hence was used only of magistrates of free cities. The term seems to have been confined largely to Macedonia, although there have been found a few inscriptions elsewhere in which it is used.

The use of this term well illustrates the accuracy of the author of Acts, for while *politárchai* is not found in classical authors, this form is attested by a number of Macedonian inscriptions, of which at least five belong to Thessalonica. See MM, p. 525; also J. H. Moulton and G. Milligan, *Expos.*, 7th series, 10 (1910), 567f.

A. W. FORTUNE

CITY, GOLDEN (Isa. 14:4, AV). *See* INSOLENCE.

CITY OF CHAOS [Heb. *qiryaṯ-tōhû*] (Isa. 24:10); AV CITY OF CONFUSION. A name applied to Jerusalem.

CITY OF DAVID. *See* ZION.

CITY OF DESTRUCTION. *See* CITY OF THE SUN.

CITY OF MOAB [Heb. *'îr mô'āḇ*; Gk. *pólis Mōab* (Nu. 22:36)]; NEB AR OF MOAB. The city to which Balak went to meet Balaam. If Heb. *'ār* (Nu. 21:28; AV, RSV, NEB, "Ar of Moab") means "city," the place was probably AR; but some scholars prefer to read "the region of Moab." *See* KIR OF MOAB; KIRHARESETH.

CITY OF PALM TREES [Heb. *'îr hatt^{e}mārîm*; Gk. *pólis phoiníkōn*]; NEB VALE OF PALM TREES. A place synonymous with or part of ancient Jericho (Dt. 34:3; Jgs. 1:16; 3:13; 2 Ch. 28:15), located at Tell *eṣ-Sulṭân* 15 mi. (24 km.) NE of Jerusalem. The area was famous for its groves of palm and balsam trees.

CITY OF SALT [Heb. *'îr hammelaḥ*; Gk. *hai póleis halṓn*]; NEB IR-MELACH. One of six frontier posts mentioned (Josh. 15:62) as located in the Wilderness of Judea. They were situated in the tribal territory of Judah, between Nibshan and En-gedi. The site of the "City of Salt" has yet to be identified with certainty, but it appears to have been S of Middin, Secacah, and Nibshan, and N of En-gedi. On the basis of excavations of Buqei'ah Iron Age II settlements at Khirbet Abū Ṭabaq and Khirbet eṣ-Samrah, it is now possible to identify Nibshan with a site in the Valley of Achor, SW of Jericho, known as Khirbet el-Maqârī.

The suggested identification of the City of Salt with Khirbet Qumrân has been confirmed by the discovery of Iron Age II (900-600 B.C.) buildings beneath the ruined Qumrân community settlement. Large numbers of iron sherds compare favorably with those found at the other Buqei'ah fortresses, to which Wâdī Qumrân may have been connected by an Iron Age II road. R. K. H.

CITY OF THE SUN [Heb. *'îr haḥeres*] (some Heb. MSS, Symm., Vulg., RSV, NEB); or **CITY OF DESTRUCTION** [Heb. *'îr haheres*; Gk. *Polis-asedek*] (MT, Aq., Th., LXX, AV). A city of Egypt (Isa. 19:18). Jewish quarrels concerning the temple that Onias built in Egypt may have been responsible for the altering of the texts of some of the early MSS, and it is now hardly possible to determine absolutely which have been altered and which accord with the original.

The context of the reference is an oracle of Isaiah concerning Egypt, occupying all of Isa. 19. In vv. 1-15, the prophet foretells divine punishments on Egypt: civil war, subjection to "a fierce king" (v. 4), and low Niles; and he castigates contemporary Egyptian rulers. Then come five parallel prophecies, each beginning with "In that day," i.e., the general period of civil confusion, oppression, and natural catastrophe of vv. 1-10, 15 (11-14 referring to the then present time). In the first prophecy God's hand of judgment and the land of Judah (His instrument?) will terrify Egypt; in the second are foreseen five cities in Egypt that speak the tongue of Canaan and swear to Yahweh, one to be called the City of the Sun (or destruction); in the third is envisaged an altar to Yahweh in Egypt and a pillar to Him at its border, as a sign; thus the Egyptians under disciplinary oppression will find Yahweh as their savior and turn to serve Him; the fourth prophesies that there will be free intercourse between, and common worship by, Egypt and Assyria; fifth, Israel will be "third" with Egypt and Assyria, and all blessed of God.

The full scope of these prophecies is not easily narrowed down; the period covered by "that day" could have begun even during the age of Isaiah's ministry (*ca.* 750-690 B.C.). Egypt knew internal conflict in the early 25th Dynasty, *ca.* 720-715 B.C., when Piankhi and Shabaka of Ethiopia (Cush) successively overcame the Saite princes Tefnakht and Bakenranef and their allies. The oppressors of Egypt could range from Assyrian and Persian emperors to Roman ones, and deliverers from the 26th Dynasty, Alexander, and the Christian era. Jewish proselytism and then the spread of Christianity in Egypt (down to modern missions) could successively contribute to fulfilling vv. 21f. Other verses may yet await fulfillment.

The five cities speaking Hebrew and worshiping Yahweh must refer to five Jewish settlements in Egypt. At various periods quite a number of such settlements are known. Thus, Jeremiah (44:1) mentions Jews at Migdol, Tahpanhes, and Memphis, plus those in Upper Egypt (Pathros). In Upper Egypt, in the Persian period (5th cent. B.C.), a Jewish military colony existed at Elephantine (Aswan), known to us from its Aramaic papyri. According to Josephus (*Ant.* xii.9.7; xiii.3; *BJ* i.9.4; vii.10), at Leontopolis in the Delta among a similar colony the fugitive priest Onias IV established a smaller temple on the Jerusalem model (*ca.* 162 B.C.). And in the Greco-Roman period (*ca.* 300 B.C. onward), there was always an important Jewish community in Alexandria; the Arabic names of various ruins in the Delta (like Tell el-Yehūdîyeh, "mound of the Jewess") may reflect the memory of still other settlements in late antiquity. The "altar" of v. 19 was perhaps first fulfilled in the building of the Jewish temple at Elephantine and later by that of Onias IV.

If the reading "city of destruction" be adopted (a purely descriptive epithet and not a proper name), there is no real clue to the identification of the city concerned, unless *heres*, "destruction," be considered as a veiled pun on *ḥeres*, "sun." In this case, or if the reading "city of the sun" be adopted, then there might be an allusion to an Egyptian name. Egyptian sources suggest two possibilities. The "city of the sun" par excellence was Heliopolis (Egyp. *'Iwnw*, Heb. *'Ôn*), near which was a Jewish community in the 1st cent. A.D. (Bell, p. 35). Otherwise there was the settlement at Tell el-Yehūdîyeh about 10 mi. (16 km.) N of Heliopolis. A Greco-Roman Jewish cemetery was found here, and the Leontopolis of Onias IV's temple was probably somewhere here (not at the Leontopolis of Tell Mokdam). However, the name of Tell el-Yehūdîyeh in Pharaonic times was not Per-Re or Pi-Re as often stated (e.g., by Naville and Montet), "house of the sun-god," but rather Nayu-Ta-Hat-Ramses ("dependency of the mansion [funerary temple] of Ramses [III]") in the domain (Egyp. *per*, lit. "house") of Re on the north of Heliopolis, later abbreviated to Natho. The allusion to "sun" is still applicable, but less direct. The whole question is still best left open.

See also ON.

Bibliography.–In general, see standard comms. on Isaiah *in loc.* On Jewish settlements in Egypt, see H. I. Bell, *Cults and Creeds in Graeco-Roman Egypt* (1953), pp. 25-49; E. G. Kraeling, *Brooklyn Museum Aramaic Papyri* (1953), Introduction. On Leontopolis, see A. H. Gardiner, *Papyrus Wilbour: II. Comm.* (1948), pp. 136f.; and his *Ancient Egyptian Onomastica* (1947), II, 146*-48*; also P. Montet, *Géographie de l'Égypte ancienne*, I (1957), 168f. On Tell el-Yehūdîyeh and Onias, E. Naville, *Mound of the Jew and the City of Onias* (1890), pp. 11-21; W. M. F. Petrie, *Hyksos and Israelite Cities* (1906), pp. 2, 19-27; and critique by T. E. Peet, *Egypt and the OT* (1922), pp. 209-227.

K. A. KITCHEN

CITY OF WATERS [Heb. *'îr hammayim*] (2 S. 12:27); NEB "pool." *See* RABBAH.

CITY, ROYAL [Heb. *'îr hammᵉlûḵâ*] (2 S. 12:26); NEB "King's Pool." *See* RABBAH.

CLAMPS. *See* BINDERS.

CLAN [Heb. *'allûp*] (Gen. 36:30; Zec. 9:7; 12:5f.); AV DUKE, GOVERNOR; [*'elep*] (Nu. 1:16; Josh. 22:14; Jgs. 6:15; Isa. 60:22; Mic. 5:2); AV THOUSAND, FAMILY; NEB also TEN THOUSAND; [*pᵉlaggâ*] (Jgs. 5:15f.); AV DIVISION; NEB FACTION; [*mišpāḥâ*] (Jgs. 9:1); AV FAMILY; [*ḥûṣ*–'outside'] ("outside his clan," Jgs. 12:9); AV "abroad"; NEB "away." A tribal unit of a nomadic or semi-nomadic society more extensive than the family. The boundaries of the group referred to are not always clearly distinct in Hebrew. The clans of Israel were united generally by a blood relationship, although other factors tending to cause union in some cases might have been: families sharing the same geographical region, the assimilation of the weaker families by the stronger, and the cooperation of several weaker families to form a strong front. Each clan was governed by the heads of the families, i.e., the "elders." In the event of war each clan theoretically provided a thousand (Heb. *'elep*) soldiers, commanded by a leader. Several of these clans formed a tribe, and twelve tribes formed the federation of Israel.

G. WYPER

CLAP [Heb. *tāqa'*, *māḥā'*, *sāpaq*, *nāḵâ*]; AV also SMITE; NEB also "snap (fingers)," BEAT. The term "clap" is used to express various emotions, e.g., of joy, "They clapped their hands [*nāḵâ*], and said, 'Long live the king'" (2 K. 11:12); "Clap your hands [*tāqa'*], all peoples" (Ps. 47:1 [MT 2]); or exultation (*sāpaq*, Lam. 2:15; *māḥā'*, Ezk. 25:6; *tāqa'*, Nah. 3:19); or repudiation (*śāpaq*, Job 27:23; *sāpaq*, 34:37).

The term is also used figuratively to denote nature's "sympathy" with God's people. "Let the floods clap [*māḥā'*] their hands" (Ps. 98:8); "All the trees of the field shall clap their hands" (Isa. 55:12).

CLAROMONTANUS. *See* TEXTS AND MSS OF THE NT.

CLASPS [Heb. *qeres*]; AV TACHES; NEB FASTENERS. The word occurs eight times in Ex. 26 and 36, which record the specifications for the erection of the TABERNACLE and their subsequent carrying out. Fifty clasps or taches of gold were ordered to be used in connecting the two sets of inner tapestry curtains (ten in number) of the tabernacle (Ex. 26:6), and fifty clasps of bronze were similarly to be used in joining the two sets of goats-hair curtains (eleven in number) which formed the outer covering (26:11). As to the nature of the clasp itself, it seems to have belonged to a double set of loops, opposite to each other, to one of which in each set (required to be of blue cord) a gold or bronze button or pin was attached which, being inserted into the loop opposite, kept the curtain in position (26:4-6). The veil separating the most holy place from the rest of the tabernacle was also suspended from clasps (Ex. 26:33).

W. S. CALDECOTT

CLAUDA klô'də (Acts 27:16, AV). *See* CAUDA.

CLAUDIA klô'dē-ə [Gk. *Klaudia*]. A member of the Christian congregation at Rome, who with other members of that church sent her greetings through Paul to Timothy (2 Tim. 4:21). More than this concerning her cannot be said with certainty. The Apos. Const. (vii.21) name her as the mother of Linus, mentioned subsequently by Irenaeus and Eusebius as bishop of Rome.

An ingenious theory has been proposed, upon the basis of the mention of Claudia and Pudens as husband and wife in an epigram of Martial, that they are identical with the persons of the same name here mentioned. A passage in the *Agricola* of Tacitus and an inscription found in Chichester, England, have been used in favor of the further statement that this Claudia was a daughter of a British king, Cogidubnus. (See argument in the Prolegomena to 2 Timothy in Alf.) It is an example of how a very few data may be used to construct a plausible theory. If it be true, the contrast between their two friends, the apostle Paul on the one hand and the licentious poet Martial on the other, is certainly unusual. If in 2 Tim. 4:21 Pudens and Claudia are husband and wife, it is difficult to explain how Linus is named between them.

H. E. JACOBS

CLAUDIUS klô'dē-əs [Gk. *Klaudios*]. The fourth Roman emperor. He reigned for over thirteen years (A.D. 41-54), having succeeded Gaius Caesar (Caligula).

Caligula had seriously altered the conciliatory policy of his predecessors regarding the Jews and, considering himself a real and corporeal god, had deeply offended the Jews by ordering a statue of himself to be placed in the temple of Jerusalem, as Antiochus Epiphanes had done with the statue of Zeus in the days of the Maccabees (2 Macc. 6:2). Claudius reverted to the policy of Augustus and Tiberius and marked the opening year of his reign by issuing edicts in favor of the Jews (Josephus *Ant.* xix.5), who were permitted in all parts of the empire to observe their laws and customs in a free and peaceable manner. Special consideration was

Tiberius Claudius Nero Germanicus, Roman emperor who, despite acts favorable to Jews in his early reign, later forbade their assembly in Rome (Trustees of the British Museum)

given to the Jews of Alexandria, who were to enjoy without molestation all their ancient rights and privileges. The Jews of Rome, however, who had become very numerous, were not allowed to assemble there (Dio Cassius *Hist.* lx.6.6), an enactment in full correspondence with the general policy of Augustus regarding Judaism in the West.

The edicts mentioned were largely due to the intimacy of Claudius with Herod Agrippa, grandson of Herod the Great, who had been living in Rome and had been in some measure instrumental in securing the succession for Claudius. As a reward for this service, the Holy Land had a king once more. Judea was added to the tetrarchies of Philip and Antipas; and Herod Agrippa I was made ruler over the wide territory which had been governed by his grandfather.

Whatever concessions to the Jews Claudius may have been induced out of friendship for Herod Agrippa to make at the beginning of his reign, Suetonius records Claudius' expulsion of Jews instigated by "Chrestus" who were continually causing an uproar (*Claudius* 25), an event assigned by some to A.D. 50, though others suppose it to have taken place somewhat later. Among the Jews thus banished from Rome were Aquila and Priscilla, with whom Paul became associated at Corinth (Acts 18:2). With the reign of Claudius is also associated the famine foretold by Agabus (Acts 11:28).

Classical writers report that the reign of Claudius was, from bad harvest or other causes, a period of general distress and scarcity over the whole world (Dio Cassius lx.11; Suetonius *Claudius* 18; Tacitus *Ann.* xi.4; xiii.43).

J. HUTCHISON

CLAUDIUS LYSIAS klô-dē-əs lis′ē-əs [Gk. *Klaudios Lysias*]. A tribune who intervened when the Jews sought to do violence to Paul at Jerusalem (Acts 21:31; 24:22).

Lysias, who was probably a Greek by birth (cf. 21:37), and who had probably assumed the Roman forename Claudius (23:26) when he purchased citizenship (22:28), was a military tribune or chiliarch (i.e., leader of 1000 men) in command of the garrison stationed in the castle overlooking the temple at Jerusalem. Upon learning of the riot instigated by the Asiatic Jews, he hastened down with his soldiers, and succeeded in rescuing Paul from the hands of the mob. As Paul was the apparent malefactor, Lysias bound him with two chains, and demanded to know who he was and what was the cause of the disturbance. Failing amid the general tumult to get any satisfactory reply, he conducted Paul to the castle, and there questioned him as to whether he was the "Egyptian," an impostor that had lately been defeated by Felix (Josephus *BJ* ii.13.5; *Ant.* xx.8.6). Upon receiving the answer of Paul that he was a "Jew of Tarsus," he gave him permission to address the people from the stairs which connected the castle and the temple. As the speech of Paul had no pacifying effect, Lysias intended to examine him by scourging; but on learning that his prisoner was a Roman citizen, he desisted from the attempt and released him from his bonds. The meeting of the Sanhedrin which Lysias then summoned also ended in an uproar, and having rescued Paul with difficulty he conducted him back to the castle.

The news of the plot against the life of one whom he knew to be a Roman citizen decided for Lysias that he could not hope to cope alone with so grave a situation. He therefore dispatched Paul under the protection of a bodyguard to Felix at Caesarea, along with a letter explaining the circumstances (23:26-30; the genuineness of this letter has been questioned by some, but without sufficient reason). In this letter he took care to safeguard his own conduct, and to shield his hastiness in binding Paul. There is evidence (cf. Acts 24:22) that Lysias was also summoned to Caesarea at a later date to give his testimony, but no mention is made of his arrival there. It is probable, however, that he was among the chief captains who attended the trial of Paul before King Agrippa and Festus (cf. 25:22).

See also TERTULLUS.

C. M. KERR

CLAWS [Aram. *ṭ*ᵉ*par*]. The term occurs only in Dnl. 7:19, there being no equivalent in the text of Dnl. 4:33. The Hebrew term *parsâ* is rendered "claw" by the AV but "hoof" by the RSV (Dt. 14:6; Zeph. 11:16).

CLAY. True clay, which is a highly aluminous soil often mixed with impurities, is found in various locations in the Near East. The Hebrews distinguished between wet and dry clay in a manner not found in the English versions. For dry clay, which had no specific Hebrew equivalent, the OT used *'āpār*, or "dust," in Job 10:9; *'ᵃdāmâ*, "ground," in Gen. 2:19; and *'ereṣ*, "ground," in Ps. 12:6 (AV "earth"; NEB "gold"). The name for unworked wet clay was *ṭîṭ* (Isa. 41:25; Nah. 3:14), whereas the common

Unbaked brick made of Nile mud and chopped straw stamped with the name and title of Ramses II (*ca.* 1330 B.C.) (Trustees of the British Museum)

designation for any kind of worked clay was *ḥōmer* (Job 33:6; Isa. 29:16; 41:25; etc.).

The image in Daniel's vision (2:33ff.) was made partly of clay (Aram. *ḥasap̱*, a term occurring only in that book). The inferior grade of worked clay was usually made into bricks (cf. Ex. 1:14), to which amounts of chopped vegetable matter were frequently added during the mixing process. Modern experiments in colloid chemistry have shown that the organic compounds produced when the vegetable matter decayed increased the strength and plasticity of the clay threefold. Finer quality worked clay was made into a wide variety of ceramic articles. The NT *pēlós* signified either the clay used by the potter (Rom. 9:21) or the muddy mixture of Jn. 9:6, 11, 14f.

R. K. H.

CLEAN AND UNCLEAN. Seeking to prevent famine and disease, Israel's neighbors focused the full power of their cults on securing fertility. These communities also desired to insure themselves against angering the gods and thus being destroyed. Consequently, rigorous standards of correct procedure for conducting the worship of the deity were established, some of which related to ritual purity. Their content reflected each community's comprehension of the deity. In other words, there was continuity between a community, its theology, and its pattern of cultic worship. The general idea of clean and unclean is in no way unique to Israel, nor are particular expressions of it, but Israel's overall system is unique because it is built on her view of Yahweh.

- I. Language
  - A. OT
  - B. LXX and NT
- II. Laws of Uncleanness
  - A. Food
  - B. Bodily Emissions
  - C. Various Kinds of Leprosy
  - D. Death
  - E. Places
  - F. Miscellaneous
- III. Purification
- IV. Theology Behind Ritual Purity
  - A. Relationship of Sin and Holiness to Ritual Purity
  - B. Possible Reasons Behind Specific Classes of Laws Regarding Ritual Purity
    - 1. Sexual Regulations
    - 2. Death
    - 3. Food
    - 4. Hygiene
  - C. Cleanness and Morality
  - D. Cleanness as Applied to the New Age
- V. NT Understanding of Clean and Unclean
  - A. Unclean
  - B. Clean

***I. Language.–A.** OT.* (1) The terms for "be clean" or "become clean" are Heb. *ṭāhēr, zāḵâ, zāḵaḵ* (Job 15:15); the AV also has "be pure"; NEB "be innocent."

(2) The terms for "cleanse" include the piel of *ṭāhēr*, piel of *ḥāṭā'* (Zec. 13:1), hiphil of *bārar* (Jer. 4:11), hiphil of *zāḵaḵ* (Job 9:30), hiphil of *dû(a)ḥ* (Isa. 4:4), *māraq* (Prov. 20:30), pual of *rāḥaṣ* (Prov. 30:12), *meš'î* (Ezk. 16:4), hiphil of *lāḇēn* (Dnl. 11:35); the AV also has "purge," "purify (oneself)," "supple" (Ezk. 16:4), "make white" (Dnl. 11:35), etc.; NEB also "purify," "rubbing" (Ezk. 16:4), etc. For the piel of *zāḵâ* ("make" or "keep clean") the NEB also renders "steer an honest (course)" (Ps. 119:9) and "have a clear (conscience)" (Prov. 20:9). For *lāqaḥ*, "cleaning (wheat)" (2 S. 4:6), the AV renders (lit.) "would have fetched"; NEB "sifting." Whereas the AV renders "cleanse" for the piel of *nāqâ*, the RSV emends to "avenge" and "clear the guilty."

(3) The terms for "cleanness" are *niqqāyôn* (Am. 4:6) and *bōr*; those for "cleansing" are *ṭohºrâ* and the piel infinitive of *ḥāṭā'* (Lev. 14:49); the AV also has "pureness," etc.; NEB also "kept teeth idle" (Am. 4:6), "get rid of impurity" (Lev. 14:49), etc.

(4) The terms for "clean" are *ṭāhôr, nāqî* (Ps. 24:4), *bar* (Job 11:4), *zaḵ* (Job 33:9); the AV also has "pure," "fair" (Zec. 3:5); NEB also "spotless," "innocent" (Job 33:9). The RSV also uses "clean" in the sense of "completely" in Ezk. 37:11 ("clean cut off," Heb. *gāzar*). The AV does this extensively, particularly in rendering the infinitive absolute preceding the verb (Isa. 24:19; Joel 1:7; Zec. 11:17; cf. also Lev. 23:22; Josh. 3:17; 4:1, 11; Ps. 77:8 [MT 9]).

(5) The terms for "be unclean" or "become unclean" are *ṭāmē'*, the pual of *gā'al* (Ezr. 2:62 par. Neh. 7:64), piel of *ṭāmē'* ("pronounce" or "hold unclean"), hiphil of *ṭāmē'* ("make [oneself] unclean"); the AV also renders "pollute," "be polluted"; NEB also "defile (oneself)."

(6) The terms for "uncleanness" are *ṭum'â* and *niddâ*; the AV also renders "filthiness"; NEB also "impurity," "forbidden," "polluted" (Ezr. 9:11), "lewdness," "period," "filth," "foul and disgusting" (*ṭum'aṯ hanniddâ* Ezk. 36:17).

(7) The terms for "unclean" are *ṭāmē'* (cf. *ṭemē'aṯ hanniddâ,* Ezk. 22:10), *niddâ* (Ezr. 9:11), *dāweh* (Isa. 30:22); the AV also renders "defiled," "menstruous" (Isa. 30:22); NEB also "forbidden," "heathen" (Am. 7:17), "foul discharge" (Isa. 30:22).

B. LXX and NT. (1) The LXX uses Gk. *katharós* for Heb. *ṭāhôr* and infrequently for other words such as *bōr* and *nāqî*; Gk. *katharismós* for Heb. *ṭohºrâ*; Gk. *katharízō* for Heb. *ṭāhēr, nāqâ*, and the piel of *ḥāṭā'*; Gk. *akáthartos* for Heb. *ṭāmē'*; Gk. *akatharsía* for Heb. *niddâ*.

(2) The NT terms for "make clean," "cleanse" are Gk. *katharízō, rhantízō* ("sprinkled clean," He. 10:22), *katharismós* ("cleansing" [Mk. 1:44; Lk. 5:14], "cleansed" [2 Pet. 1:9]), *katharós* ("clean"); the AV also gives "purge," "purify," "sprinkled" (He. 10:22); NEB also "count clean," "cure," "heal."

(3) The NT terms for "uncleanness" are *akatharsía, akáthartos* ("unclean," frequently with "spirit" to mean "demon"; cf. Mt. 10:1), *koínos*; the AV also renders "filthiness," "anything that defileth" (*koínos,* Rev. 21:27); NEB also "impurity," "indecency," "vileness," "base motive" (1 Thess. 2:3), "foul desires" (Eph. 4:19), etc.

***II. Laws of Uncleanness.–A.** Food.* The Bible pictures man as initially a vegetarian (Gen. 2:16). Eating of animals was not permitted until after the Flood. Even then animals were distinguished as clean or unclean (Gen. 7:2f., 8f.); although whether solely for sacrificial use or for dietary rules is not said. Later under the covenant the cultic laws fully distinguished between forbidden meats and those that could be eaten (Lev. 11; Dt. 14:3-20). Among quadrupeds those that have a cloven hoof and chew the cud are considered clean (Lev. 11:3-8; Dt. 14:3-8). Thus the camel, the rock rabbit, the hare, and the pig are specifically mentioned as excluded. Animals that walk on flat paws and all four feet are unclean, including dogs and cats (Lev. 11:27). Swarming creatures such as rodents and reptiles are unclean (Lev. 11:29f., 41f.), as are creatures that move on the belly, go on all fours, or have many feet (Lev. 11:41). Fish without fins and scales may not be eaten, e.g., lobsters, crabs, shrimp and other shellfish (Lev. 11:9-12; Dt. 14:9f.). Unclean birds (*see* ABOMINATION, BIRDS OF) include vultures, the ossifrage, the osprey, the buzzard, the kite, falcons, ravens, the ostrich, hawks, the sea gull, the owl, the cormorant, the ibis, the water hen, the pelican, the stork, herons, the hoopoe, and the bat (Lev. 11:13-19; Dt. 14:11-18). Although not categorized, most of these are carnivorous or live in swamps and marshes. All manner of insects are prohibited except those whose legs are jointed for leaping; certain locusts, grasshoppers, and crickets are acceptable as food (Lev. 11:20-23; Dt. 14:19f.). The unclean animals produce uncleanness when touched or eaten (Lev. 11:8, 27f., 31).

In addition, the eating of blood in any form was strictly prohibited (Lev. 17:11ff.; Dt. 12:23). At no time could one eat the flesh with its blood (Gen. 9:3f.). All clean animals had to be properly slaughtered; no animal that died naturally (Dt. 14:21) nor one that was torn by beasts (Ex. 22:31 [MT 30]; Lev. 17:15; 22:8) was to be eaten. Because the internal fat or suet of an animal belonged to God in sacrifice, it was forbidden to man (Lev. 7:23ff.). The law that one "shall not boil a kid in its mother's milk" has increasingly influenced dietary regulations in Judaism (Ex. 23:19; 34:26; Dt. 14:21), so that today all *kosher* meals must separate meat from milk and its products. Also, based upon the narrative that describes Jacob's wrestling match with the angel, the ischiatic nerve of an animal is forbidden (Gen. 32:25ff.).

B. Bodily Emissions. Bodily emissions, especially sexual discharges, were unclean (Lev. 15:2f.). A man who had an emission of semen was unclean until the evening, as was anything the semen touched. Any garments affected were to be washed and considered unclean until evening (Lev. 15:17). A woman participant was also unclean (Lev. 15:16ff.). She had to bathe but remained unclean until evening. A woman was unclean during her menstrual cycle for seven days (Lev. 15:19). Whatever she lay or sat on was considered unclean, as was anyone who touched these things (Lev. 15:20-23). A man who lay with her also became unclean for seven days (Lev. 15:24).

Whoever had a continuous discharge which was considered unclean remained ritually unclean (Lev. 15:2-12; 25-28). All beds, chairs, saddles, and vessels used by such a person were unclean, and anyone who touched him or such an object became unclean until sunset. After the discharge ceased the person remained unclean for seven days. A man washed his clothes, bathed in running water, and was considered clean, but a woman merely waited seven days. On the eighth day one had to bring either two turtledoves or two young pigeons to be offered by the priest as a sin offering and a burnt offering; thus the priest made atonement for whomever had had the discharge (Lev. 15:13ff.).

C. Various Kinds of Leprosy. When a swelling, eruption, spot, boil, or itch appeared, the person had to appear before the priest (Lev. 13), who quarantined him and periodically examined him. The general title applied to this condition was leprosy, but various diseases apparently were involved, probably including the disease labeled leprosy today (*elephantiasis graecorum*). Also, when the body had a burn and the skin was raw the person was pronounced unclean (Lev. 13:24f.). Baldness was acceptable, but not abnormal loss of hair (vv. 40-44). The leper was continuously unclean until cured (vv. 10ff.). He had to wear torn clothes, leave his hair unkempt, cover his upper lip, cry "unclean, unclean," and live alone outside the camp (vv. 45f.).

The cleansing for a leper was quite involved (Lev. 14:1-32). After examination revealed him to be healed, he presented two living birds with cedarwood, scarlet stuff, and hyssop. From the blood of one bird sacrificed in an earthen vessel over running water he was sprinkled seven times and pronounced clean. The living bird was released to the open fields. When the person had washed his clothes, shaved off all his hair, and bathed, he might enter the camp, but not his tent. After seven days he again shaved his hair, including beard and eyebrows, washed his clothes, and bathed. On the eighth day he presented two male lambs without blemish and one ewe lamb a year old without blemish, a cereal offering, and a log of oil; a poor man had lesser requirements. One male lamb was offered as a guilt offering. The priest placed some of the blood on the right earlobe, right thumb, and right big toe. Then the same places were anointed with oil; the remaining oil was put on his head. Next the priest offered a sin offering followed by a burnt offering and a cereal offering. Thereby the priest made atonement for the healed leper.

Garments or houses that were attacked by a leprous growth were examined and pronounced clean or unclean (Lev. 13:47-59; 14:33-47). A garment affected was burned, but one in which the growth was deterred was washed twice to become clean (13:56-58). A house that could not be cured was torn down and its materials carried outside the city to an unclean place (14:45), but a house in which the disease did not spread became clean when atonement was made (14:48-53). A small bird was slain, and with another dipped in the blood and in running water the priest sprinkled the house seven times, after which the living bird was released.

D. Death. Anyone who touched a corpse became unclean for seven days (Nu. 19:11). If someone died in a tent, all who were in the tent became unclean for seven days (Nu. 19:14); all open vessels became unclean (v. 15). The same period of uncleanness was sustained by coming into contact in an open field with one slain by a sword, a dead body, a human bone, or a grave (v. 16). For purification the unclean cleansed himself with specially prepared ashes from the sacrifice of a red heifer along with running water in a vessel. On the third and seventh days a clean person sprinkled him, as well as the tent and its furnishings (vv. 12, 17ff.); the one who did the sprinkling became unclean until evening. On the seventh day the person washed his clothes and bathed; at evening he became clean. If he failed to seek cleansing, he was forever cut off from his people, for he defiled the tabernacle (vv. 13, 20).

Touching or carrying the carcass of a clean or unclean animal made one unclean (Lev. 11:39f.). The defiled person washed his clothes and remained unclean until evening (Lev. 11:24-28, 39f.). Anything on which the carcass of a swarming animal fell became unclean — an earthen vessel or stove thus defiled was broken; articles of wood or of skin were put in water and declared clean at evening; food or drink in these vessels became unclean; a spring, cistern with water, or seed for sowing (unless watered) remained clean (Lev. 11:32-38).

The priests could allow themselves to become defiled by a corpse only for one who was next of kin: mother, father, son, daughter, brother, or virgin sister (Lev. 21:1-4). The high priest was not allowed to defile himself by coming near any dead body, even that of a parent (vv. 10ff.). Neither was he to mourn by letting his hair hang loose or rending his garments.

E. Places. A place could be considered clean or unclean. The area inside the camp was clean; that outside was unclean, yet there appear to have been certain areas set aside outside the camp that were considered clean (e.g., Lev. 4:12). Palestine came to be considered the Holy Land (Zec. 2:12 [MT 16]; cf. Ps. 78:54), its cities holy (Isa. 64:10 [MT 9]), and Jerusalem the Holy City (Isa. 48:2; Joel 3:17 [MT 4:17]; Ob. 17). But a clean land could become defiled when its inhabitants violated the basic moral standards, especially through sexual abuse (Lev. 18:19-30; Ezk. 36:17f.). These perversions were often combined with idolatry (cf. Jer. 2:7, 23). Leaving a person hanging on a tree overnight (Dt. 21:23), pursuing the occult (Lev. 19:31), and unavenged murder (Nu. 35:30-34; Dt. 21:1-9) also defiled the land. The sanctuary was particularly defiled by placing foreign cultic objects in or near it and by sacrificing children to foreign gods (Lev. 20:3; Jer. 7:30f.; Ezk. 20:31; 23:38f.; Ps. 106:37ff.). Thus every major reform required the elimination of foreign worship from the land and the cleansing of the temple by priests who were ritually clean (2 Ch. 29:12-19; 34:3-18). Often Passover celebrated the climax of the cleansing of the land and the sanctuary. Because many at the time of King Hezekiah had not purified themselves to celebrate the feast, adjustments were made in the sanctuary rules of cleanness, e.g., the Levites killed the Passover lamb. Then Hezekiah interceded for the pardon of these people (2 Ch. 30:13-22). This incident reflects the idea that the laws of ritual purity are secondary to moral zeal in serving Yahweh and could be partially suspended under significant circumstances.

Continuous defilement of the land ended the right of its occupants to inhabit it. The prophets accused Israel of polluting the land by forsaking Yahweh and pursuing pagan practices (Isa. 24:4f.; Hos. 4:3). Accordingly, they informed Israel that she was subject to being taken into captivity, the greatest punishment for violating the Sinai covenant (Lev. 26:27-39). The fact that the people would have to live in an unclean land and thereby be perpetually unclean only added to its intensity (Hos. 9:3; Am. 7:17). Such a law would prevent the people from setting up in a foreign land any type of sacrificial worship similar to the Jerusalem temple, for any sacrifices would have been always ritually unclean. Although such a temptation probably was strong among the exiles, it was fraught with the danger of syncretism that would destroy Yahwism, as the shrines at Samaria and Elephantine bear witness.

F. Miscellaneous. God is so pure that in comparison neither the heavens (Job 15:15) nor the stars (25:5) are clean in His sight. The fear of the Lord is considered clean (Ps. 19:9). "Clean" may also be used in the sense of free from dirt, as a clean turban (Zec. 3:5), and a clean linen shroud used for burying Jesus (Mt. 27:59).

III. Purification.–The various means of purification included the mere passing of time, cleansing agents, and various atoning sacrifices, depending on the intensity of the uncleanness. One who unknowingly became unclean had to offer a guilt offering upon becoming aware of his error (Lev. 5:2-6). Almost always some type of washing was connected with the purification rites. Thus the phrase "clean hands" symbolized that one had properly carried out all the rites for purification and was obedient to Yahweh (2 S. 22:21; Job 17:9).

Another means of cleansing was by fire (cf. Mal. 3:2f.). Any articles taken in war that could stand the test of fire were so cleansed, followed by purification with the water of impurity; less durable objects were purified by water alone (Nu. 31:21-24). When Isaiah encountered the presence of the holy God he confessed that he was a man of unclean lips and he dwelt among people of unclean lips (Isa. 6:5). A burning coal was then taken from the divine altar and was touched to his mouth; thus his sin was forgiven (Heb. *kipper*; vv. 6f.). In another passage Isaiah anticipated that in the Last Days the filth of the daughters of Zion will be washed and the bloodstains of Jerusalem will be cleansed "by a spirit of judgment and by a spirit of burning" (4:4).

IV. Theology Behind Ritual Purity.–*A. Relationship of Sin and Holiness to Ritual Purity.* The standard of ritual purity in Israel is built on the view of God's holiness and of man's alienation from God because of his sin. With man's sin also came alienation between the world and man. The result of this alienation is death and the ultimate destruction of the world (cf. Gen. 2:17; 6:5-8). In contrast is the possibility of new life that may overcome the alienation by participating in a covenant with God. Under the Sinai covenant God provided Israel the cultic apparatus to maintain the covenant and to approach him. The instruments used as a part of the cult had to be sanctified so that they could endure the presence of the holy God, and they had to be atoned for every year (Lev. 16:16, 19, 32f.). Man too had to be sure that he was morally and ritually clean before entering the precincts of the tent of meeting or the temple.

The key verse in the cultic legislation regarding ritual purity states to the priesthood, "You are to distinguish between the holy and the common, and between the unclean and the clean" (Lev. 10:10). Clean and holy, although not synonymous, are closely associated. The clean is not necessarily holy, but the holy is always clean. Cleanness has to do with fidelity to the cultic laws, rather than physical washing, which may, however, constitute a small part of it. Cleanness is a condition of being obedient to the statutes and ordinances of the law, which allows one to encounter the holy without danger. It is crucial to realize that cleanness must be attained by each person and is nontransferable. Uncleanness, on the other hand, is readily transmitted (cf. Hag. 2:12ff.). There is no harm, however, in becoming unclean. Uncleanness neither harms or destroys. Destruction comes from the holy when uncleanness is brought into its presence. Holiness is dynamically cleansing all the time. Hence uncleanness in its presence is judged, resulting in purification or destruction. The danger lies in mixing holiness and uncleanness.

Because man participates in the world of life and death, employing the essential means of preserving life, eventually he will become unclean. Man is made aware that maintaining his very existence has profound implications in his relationship to God. Thus the laws regarding ritual purity fundamentally deal with sustaining life and confronting death and build on the motif of sin and death. Since this world is cursed, it is impossible for one to live a life of constant ritual purity. Of course, all sin renders one ritually unclean. There is no sin, however, in becoming unclean so long as one does not intentionally perpetuate his uncleanness.

Since through becoming unclean one has come into contact with the curse of alienation and death, usually atonement must be made for further participation in the cult. For example, a woman by giving birth remains unclean for seven days for a boy and fourteen days for a girl, followed by a period of exclusion from the holy lasting 33 days and 66 days respectively (Lev. 12:2-5). Several reasons have been advanced to explain why the birth of a girl renders the mother unclean twice as long as the birth of a boy. Keil argues that people at that time believed the discharges following the birth of a girl were longer. Another suggestion is that the female child is a future source of menstrual uncleanness. Such a belief no doubt is traced back to the original curse and woman's role in it, both as one who was seduced and as one who provides hope by giving birth to Him who will overcome man's enemy (Gen. 3:6, 14ff.). In giving birth she encounters the pain of the curse and counters the curse by bringing life into the world to overcome the curse on behalf of the human race. Therefore atonement must

CLEAN AND UNCLEAN

be made for the woman who, in giving birth, has challenged the curse of death. And yet the child she produces lies under the curse of alienation from God if he does not fulfil the covenant.

In conclusion, the rationale behind all cultic ritual is that the participant is made aware of his basic alienation from God, and he knows that he must prepare himself to take advantage of the opportunities to approach God. In so responding he demonstrates his obedience to God and discovers the meaning of the confession that Yahweh is the Holy One of Israel.

B. Possible Reasons Behind Specific Classes of Laws Regarding Ritual Purity. Although there is no moral problem in becoming ritually unclean, there is the inherent danger of bringing uncleanness into the proximity of the tabernacle and thereby defiling it (Lev. 15:31). Thus there are proper ways of approaching Yahweh and there are other things that belong to this life which, even though they possess value, can never serve as a medium for worship. The laws of uncleanness prevented false approaches to the true God. Yahwism saw its greatest danger in syncretism, whereby the devotee might claim to worship Yahweh, not realizing that by his confusing of Yahwism and other beliefs he had broken the covenant and was subject to its curses, even though the name of Yahweh was on his lips. The regulations regarding uncleanness sought to eliminate this possibility (cf. Lev. 20:22-26) by distinguishing between what may be sanctified for worship and what must always remain a part of the common or profane.

1. Sexual Regulations. Yahweh sought interaction with His people solely by the word and sacrifice; therefore all other ways of worship were eliminated. No sexual act was permitted as a means of worshiping Yahweh. All such activity in this regard, therefore, rendered one unclean. Sex was viewed as a part of man's mundane existence, not a means of his interaction with the Divine. Becoming unclean through sex did not connote the idea that sex was sinful or without value, but that it could not be used as a means of worship or be given greater sanction by being conducted in the temple area. This belief embodied a strong polemic against paganism, which constantly associated sexual intercourse at the cultic center with guaranteed fertility (cf. Hos. 4:12ff.). In contrast, Israel's fields and flocks were productive as a result of the gracious blessing of God upon the people in response to their covenant faithfulness (cf. Lev. 26:3-13).

2. Death. Paganism also stressed the veneration of the dead. Perhaps the greatest monuments to such overemphasis on the dead are the pyramids. Ancestral worship and magical rites, including seances with the dead (cf. Isa. 65:2-5), are perversions of the reality of death as the curse on man's disobedience. In Israel the dead received their proper honor, but in no way were they given undue veneration nor did they become objects of worship. Thus the high priest was not to become involved in any connection with the dead. Again, the cultic laws created a strong barrier between Yahwism and paganism.

3. Foods. The origins of the regulations about clean and unclean animals are difficult to assess. Reasons given for classifying certain animals as unclean include their role in foreign cults, their loathsome appearance, or their repulsive habits. But all such arguments have limitations; e.g., the pig, used especially in the occult, was forbidden (cf. Isa. 65:3ff.; 66:17), but the bull, although worshiped throughout the Near East and having found its way into Israel as the golden calf (Ex. 32) and later as the two calves erected at Dan and Bethel (1 K. 12:28, 33), was accepted as a supreme sacrifice (Lev. 4:2f., 13ff.). W. Kornfeld argues that animals were classified as unclean because they were carnivorous, eaters of carrion, or inhabitants of desert places and ruins and thereby associated with beings of the underworld. For later Israel he asserts that the unclean animals were so designated because they were considered unpleasing to Yahweh. Regarding the list of unclean birds, M. Douglas suggests that "those species are unclean which are imperfect members of their class or whose class itself confounds the general scheme of the world" (*Purity in Danger* [1966], p. 55). These classifications, in her opinion, give the oneness, purity, and completeness of God a physical expression in every encounter with animals, in the field or at meals (p. 57).

Further fellowship at the festivals of pagan neighbors, which would include banqueting, was impossible for an Israelite, because their food was unclean. Thus food regulations erected a strong barrier against social intercourse with Israel's neighbors. Consequently, reasons that both symbolize the meaning of holiness and erect barriers against magic and the occult appear to be the most significant in dividing animals into clean and unclean.

The prohibition against blood may be explained on this same basis. Blood was used by Israel's neighbors to participate intimately in the life of the deity and to induce ecstatic encounters. Since in Israel blood was the basis for atonement, it belonged exclusively to Yahweh. Its exclusion as food indicated that there was no possibility of partaking of Yahweh through blood sanctified at the altar. Similarly the Canaanites made a special rite out of seething a kid in its mother's milk. For this reason, and maybe out of humanitarian concern, such a practice was forbidden.

4. Hygiene. In Yahwism all of life came under God's concern and was to be lived before Him. Thus Israel was to take care that life be healthy as well as moral. Latrines were to be properly cared for (Dt. 23:12ff.). Certain diseases were contained by a quarantine regulated by the priesthood. Although they did not understand contagious disease with the accuracy of contemporary medicine, they must have known that some diseases could be conveyed from one to another. These concerns, and also the realization that care regarding the cleanness of hands and bodies made for a healthier society, may be an implicit reason behind the legislation of ritual purity.

C. Cleanness and Morality. In "P" and "H" (*see* CRITICISM II; PENTATEUCH) the basic idea of morality is connected with the concept of the holy God (Lev. 19:2). Frequently, the reason for various regulations, especially moral standards, is that "I am Yahweh" or "I am Yahweh your God" (e.g., Lev. 19:10f.). But the idea of cleanness, more directly, means the correct ordering of one's daily routine so that he may approach the holy God without danger. Cleanness has to do more with the proper course of a truly moral life than with defining morality. The Psalms and the prophets, however, no doubt building on the intent of cultic legislation, clearly join together at the point of motive outward cleanness and moral integrity. Ps. 24 asks those approaching the temple mount: "Who shall ascend the hill of the Lord? And who shall stand in his holy place?" (v. 3), with the response "He who has clean hands and a pure heart, who does not lift up his soul to what is false, and does not swear deceitfully" (v. 4; cf. 2 Ch. 23:19). This is supported by Ps. 15, where other ideas joined to ritual purity include not uttering slander, swearing to one's own harm and holding to it, and not taking bribes. The emphasis is on pure inner motivation and integrity of life style. Job understands this interconnection by claiming, according to Elihu, "I am clean, without transgression; I am pure, and there is no iniquity in me" (Job 33:9). The author of Ps. 51 earnestly desires to go beyond ritual purity to a radical change in his innermost being. He petitions God: "Cleanse me from my sin" and "create in me a clean heart" (51:2, 10 [MT 4, 12]; cf. 7 [MT 9]).

Isaiah tried to convince Israel that in God's sight clean hands were insufficient. God claimed through him, "When you spread forth your hands, I will hide my eyes from you; even though you make many prayers, I will not listen; your hands are full of blood. Wash yourselves; make yourselves clean; remove the evil of your doings from before my eyes; cease to do evil" (1:14ff.). Of course, clean hands outstretched in prayer were inadequate when the heart was defiled. Thus Isaiah exhorted the people to transform the entire person and to have their scarlet sins washed so that they would be white as snow (1:18).

D. Cleanness as Applied to the New Age. For the prophets moral cleanness becomes the criterion for participation in the blessings of the new age. Zechariah foresees a fount available in Jerusalem to cleanse from sin and uncleanness (Zec. 13:1). Ezekiel placed a portion of the blame for the defilement of the land, which led to the captivity, on the priesthood, which failed to teach the distinction between the holy and the common, the clean and the unclean (Ezk. 22:24f.); he pictures the transformation of Israel in preparation for the new age in ritualistic terms: "I [Yahweh] will sprinkle clean water upon you, and you shall be clean from all your uncleannesses, and from all your idols I will cleanse you" (Ezk. 36:25; cf. Jer. 33:8). The people of God will receive a new heart and a new spirit (Ezk. 36:26). Then they will again inhabit cities and build palaces (36:33). The cleansing will be so complete that never again will the people or the land become defiled (37:23). There will be also a new sanctuary properly sanctified and a new priesthood that rightly carries out its functions (43:18-27; 44:15-31); they will correctly teach about the clean and the unclean (44:23). In that time the unclean shall not travel the highway of holiness that figuratively leads from captivity to Zion (Isa. 35:8), nor shall they enter Jerusalem (52:1). Revelation resumes this theme in regard to the new Jerusalem, stating that "nothing unclean shall enter it" (21:27). In both testaments the new age focuses on the city of God, which shall be inhabited by his people who live morally clean lives.

V. NT Understanding of Clean and Unclean.–*A. Unclean.* The word "unclean" in the NT is most frequently joined to "spirit" to connote a demon. Uncleanness is not a ritual term, but a moral one denoting man's wayward behavior that keeps him from fellowship with God. Included are licentiousness, covetousness, and sexual abuses (Eph. 4:19; 5:3; Rom. 1:24). Uncleanness is classified as one of the works of the flesh that prohibits following the Spirit's leadership (Gal. 5:17ff.). From these defilements the believer must cleanse himself to live a separate and unique life (2 Cor. 7:1).

B. Clean. The question of ritual purity was quite prominent among various sects of Jews at the time of Jesus, e.g., the Essenes bathed three times a day to ensure their compliance with the law. Jesus and His disciples often found themselves in conflict with the Pharisees over this question; for instance, the disciples were criticized for eating with unwashed hands (Mk. 7:1-7) and Jesus for dining with sinners (Lk. 15:1f.; 19:1-10). Jesus, in contrast, accused the Pharisees of having forgotten the weightier matter of justice in their zeal to follow the law (Mt. 23:23ff.); He compared them to whitened sepulchers, full of dead men's bones (Mt. 23:27). In light of the laws regarding ritual purity and death, Jesus could scarcely have used a more pungent reproach. In anticipation of the new covenant, Jesus went further in deliberately setting aside the whole question of ritual purity. He taught that it is words flowing from a corrupt heart that defile a man, not food, which merely enters the mouth on the way to the stomach (Mk. 7:14-23). The early Church appealed to this teaching to affirm that Jesus Himself had declared all foods clean (Mk. 7:19). Jesus desires a moral life style flowing from a pure heart, which He Himself sanctifies by the Holy Spirit (Jn. 14:20f., 23; 17:17).

The NT emphasizes that the one who confesses his sins and walks in the light is cleansed from all sin and unrighteousness (Jn. 1:7, 9). Every believer, Jew or Gentile, is clean, for God purifies the heart by faith (Acts 15:9; cf. 10:9-16, 34f.). This idea is radical, for it declares that the Jewish believer in no way is defiled by the Gentile believer and the Gentile, truly purified, also has full access to God. To show the new position of the believer before God, He. 10:22 draws on the double imagery of sprinkling with ashes of a red heifer one defiled through contact with a corpse (Nu. 19) and of the bathing of the high priests's body before serving on the Day of Atonement (Lev. 16:4); that is, the Christian, cleansed from the curse of death for sin and freed from an evil conscience, has boldness to enter the presence of God as a priestly intercessor.

The Word also plays a crucial role in the cleansing, for it is the obedient response to its proclamation that transforms the inner man (Jn. 15:3; cf. Eph. 5:26). The only rite of washing to symbolize the transformation is baptism, which is administered a single time. Thus purity of heart becomes the uncompromising demand and the possibility of the NT (Mt. 5:8; 1 Pet. 1:22; 1 Tim. 1:5; 2 Tim. 2:22). A pure heart produces the inner confidence to pursue earnestly the demands of God (1 Tim. 3:9; 2 Tim. 1:3; He. 10:22).

The goal of the believer's life is still holiness (e.g., 1 Pet. 1:14ff.). He is to pursue purity in all aspects of his life (cf. Jas. 4:7f.). He is not regulated by a set of laws, but by a liberty under his own responsible character directed by the Holy Spirit. As Paul exhorts, "Since we have these promises, beloved, let us cleanse ourselves from every defilement of body and spirit, and make holiness perfect in the fear of God" (2 Cor. 7:1). The principle which Paul lays down in Rom. 14:14, "that nothing is unclean in itself; but it is unclean for anyone who thinks it unclean," clearly shows that the Christian is entrusted with critical facilities to discern the proper use of his Father's world.

Cultic purity is no longer necessary under the new covenant because the atoning work of Christ as its foundation has proleptically secured the restoration of harmony between man and nature (cf. Rom. 8:19-23). A redeemed nature no longer defiles and hinders man's approach to God. Jesus emphasized His lordship over nature by performing various miracles; He particularly healed lepers. The word most often used is "cleansed"; it means that the leper is fully restored physically and cultically (Mt. 8:2ff.; 10:8; cf. 2 K. 5:10-14 where "cleanse" also means "heal"). These miracles point to the total healing that His redemptive work will bring. Further, just as the dedication of the first-born and the first-fruits according to the OT released the rest of the flock and the crops to God's people (Ex. 22:29; 23:19;

34:26; Nu. 18:15), so the death of God's first-born released the world back to man for its proper enjoyment as originally intended. Although this redemption is not finalized, the NT believer has been given a foretaste of the complete redemption by being freed from the tremendous burden of maintaining the standards of ritual purity.

See also ABLUTION; ABOMINATION; COMMON; DEFILE; HOLY; POLLUTION; PURITY.

Bibliography.–W. Eichrodt, *Theology of the OT*, I (1961), 133-172; T. Gaster, *The Holy and the Profane* (1955); W. H. Gispen, *OTS*, 5 (1948), 190-96; *ILC*, I-II, 474-496; III-IV, 264-295, 447-465; Y. Kaufmann, *Religion of Israel* (1956), pp. 101-121; W. Kornfeld, *Wissenschaft im Dienste des Glaubens* (1965), pp. 11-27; J. Moyer, *Concept of Ritual Purity Among the Hittites* (1969); W. R. Smith, *Religion of the Semites* (repr. 1972); N. Snaith, *Leviticus and Numbers* (1967); *TDNT*, III, *s.v.* καθαρός (R. Meyer, F. Hauck); R. de Vaux, *Ancient Israel* (1965), II; *BZAW*, 77 (1958), 250-265.

J. E. HARTLEY

CLEAVE [Heb. *dāḇaq*]; AV also "keep to" (Nu. 36:7, 9), JOINED (Job 41:23), STUCK (Ps. 119:31); NEB also UNITED (Gen. 2:24), RETAIN (Nu. 36:7, 9), "hold fast to" (Dt. 10:20; 11:22; 13:4; 30:20; Josh. 22:5; 23:8; Ps. 119:31), CLING (Dt. 28:60; Ps. 137:6), "stick to" (Job 31:7; Ps. 22:15), HAUNT (Dt. 28:21), "be found in (your) possession" (Dt. 13:17), "stick out through" (Job 19:20), "close knit" (Job 41:23), "I will have none of it" (Ps. 101:3), HANGS (Ps. 102:5), FASTEN (Ezk. 3:26), "held his tongue" (Job 29:10), "lie prone" (Ps. 44:25; 119:25); [*bāqa'*] (Ps. 74:15; 78:15; 141:7; Isa. 48:21; Mic. 1:4; Hab. 3:9); NEB also OPEN (Ps. 74:15), "splinters (of wood)" (Ps. 141:7); [niphal of *sāpāḥ*] (Isa. 14:1); NEB ATTACH; [piel of *pālag*] (Job. 38:25); [*ḥāšaq*] (Ps. 91:14); AV, NEB, "set (his love) (up)on."

The term "cleave" is used in two opposite senses: *dāḇaq, sāpāḥ,* and *ḥāšaq* mean "cling to," usually with great affection; *bāqa'* and *pillag* mean "divide" or "separate" by splitting, as in cutting wood for a fire (cf. Gen. 22:3) or cutting a channel through rock.

J. T. DENNISON, JR.

CLEFT [Heb. *niqārâ*] (Ex. 33:22); NEB CREVICE; [*sā'îp*] (Jgs. 15:8, 11; Isa. 2:21; 57:5); AV also TOP; NEB also CAVE, CRANNIES; [*nāqîq*] (Isa. 7:19; Jer. 13:4; 16:16); AV HOLE; NEB also CREVICE; [*ḥāgû*] (Cant. 2:14; Jer. 49:16; Ob. 3); NEB HOLES, CRANNIES; **CLIFF** [*madrēgâ*] (Cant. 2:14; Ezk. 38:20); AV STAIRS, "steep places"; NEB "high ledges," "terraced hills"; [*sela'*] (Isa. 2:21); AV "ragged rocks."

These terms indicate various characteristics of rocky or mountainous terrain: fissures or faults, caves, crevices, ledges, and precipices. The cleft ("cave"[?]; cf. 1 K. 19:9, 13) where God covered Moses (Ex. 33:22) on Mt. Sinai was still thought to exist a century ago (cf. KD for a discussion of the traditions). Samson fled from the Philistines to a fissure called Etam (not to be confused with the Etam SW of Bethlehem, 2 Ch. 9:6) in the hill country E of Timnah. The cleft above Wâdī Isma'in 2.5 mi. (4 km.) SE of Zorah has been suggested as the most likely identification.

In Canticles the poet desires a hiding place or refuge for his beloved; the association of cliffs with the dove (pigeon) in Cant. 2:14 is appropriate, since the rock dove is known to build its nest in remote, rocky crags (cf. Jer. 48:28).

The prophecies in Jer. 49:16 and Ob 3 are parallel; both deal with God's judgment upon Edom. Rocky gorges and cliff-top fortresses made the capital city, Sela (later Petra), virtually impregnable. In fact, the phrase *b^eḥagwê hassela'* (Jer. 49:16; Ob. 3), "in the clefts of the rock," may actually refer to the "cliffs of Sela."

For 2 Ch. 20:16, AV, *see* ASCENT; Job 30:6, AV, "clefts of the valleys" is RSV "gullies of the torrents."

Bibliography.–A. E. Cundall, *Judges* (1968), p. 170; KD, *in loc.*; C. F. Pfeiffer, ed., *Biblical World* (1964), pp. 443-46.

J. T. DENNISON, JR.

CLEMENCY. The AV for Gk. *epieíkeia* in Acts 24:4, translated "kindness" in the RSV. The NEB reads, "I crave your indulgence."

CLEMENT klem'ənt [*Gk. Klēmēs*–'mild'].

1. A fellow worker with Paul at Philippi, mentioned with special commendation in Phil. 4:3.

2. One of the APOSTOLIC FATHERS, usually identified with the third bishop of Rome. His identity with **1**, though supposed by Origen, Eusebius, Epiphanius, and Jerome, is highly unlikely given the remoteness of the two in time and place.

CLEOPAS klē'ə-pəs [Gk. *Kleopas*–'renowned father']. One of the two disciples whom Jesus met on the way to Emmaus (Lk. 24:18). The name is a contraction of Cleopatros, not identical with Clopas (an Aramaic name) of Jn. 19:25.

CLEOPATRA klē-ə-pā'trə [Gk. *Kleopatra*–'from a famous father']. The name of several Egyptian queens and princesses. One, probably the wife of PTOLEMY VI PHILOMETOR, is mentioned in Ad. Est. 11:1. According to Josephus (*Ant.* xii.9.7; xiii.3.1-3), Ptolemy and Cleopatra permitted Onias, the expatriate son of a high priest who cited Isa. 29:19 in his request, to build a temple for Jews in Heliopolis.

Their daughter is probably the Cleopatra mentioned in 1 Maccabees. Her father first gave her in marriage to Alexander Balas (1 Macc. 10:58; Josephus *Ant.* xiii.4.1), then took her from Alexander and gave her to DEMETRIUS II NICATOR (1 Macc. 11:9-12; *Ant.* xiii.4.7). Later, while Demetrius was in captivity in Parthia, Cleopatra married his brother ANTIOCHUS VII SIDETES.

J. HUTCHISON
E. W. S.

CLEOPHAS klē'ə-fəs (Jn. 19:25, AV). *See* CLOPAS.

CLERK. *See* TOWN CLERK.

CLIFF; CLIFT. *See* CLEFT.

CLOAK [Heb. *k^esuṯ*] (Dt. 22:12); AV VESTURE; [*śalmâ*] (24:13); AV RAIMENT; [*miṭpaḥaṯ*] (Isa. 3:22); AV WIMPLE; [*beged*] (Jer. 43:12); AV GARMENT; NEB CLOTHES; [Gk. *himátion*] (Mt. 5:40; Lk. 6:29); NEB COAT; AV CLOKE; [*phailónēs* (2 Tim. 4:13), *próphasis* (fig., 1 Thess. 2:5)]; AV CLOKE; **PURPLE CLOAK** [*porphýra*] (Mk. 15:17, 20); AV, NEB, PURPLE. A variety of outer garments is designated in these references; the exact type is often unclear. *See* GARMENTS.

The cloak of Dt. 22:12 had "four corners" (*see* TASSEL) and was wrapped around the body like a blanket. The *śalmâ* (more correctly *śamlâ*) of Dt. 24:13 was wrapped about the body at night for sleeping; cf. Ex. 22:26f.; also Gen. 9:23; Dt. 22:17; etc. In the list of feminine articles of dress and accessories in Isa. 3:18-24 occurs the word *miṭpaḥaṯ*; in the only other occurrence, Ruth 3:15, it designates the garment worn by Ruth (RSV "mantle"), which was loose enough to carry "six measures of barley." The cloak of the shepherd is called *beged* in Jer. 43:12, a general word used for many kinds of garments and coverings, both costly and poor.

In Mt. 5:40 and Lk. 6:29 the Gk. *himátion* is used for an outer garment, worn over the *chitṓn,* a tunic (NEB "shirt"). (For an explanation of the different order in the two passages see Bauer, p. 377.) The cloak Paul asks to be sent from Troas he calls *phailónēs* (in some MSS *phainólēs*), related, probably as a loanword, to Lat. *paenula,* a raincoat or traveling garment. The word *porphýra,* "purple," is used in Mk. 15 for the royal garments mockingly put on Jesus.

Figuratively, *próphasis* is translated "cloak" in 1 Thess. 2:5; the meaning is "pretense," as in Mk. 12:40; Lk. 20:47; Acts 27:30; Phil. 1:18.

See also MANTLE; ROBE. J. W. D. H.

CLOD [Heb. *regeḇ*] (Job 21:33; 38:38); NEB also DUST; [*megrāpâ*] (Joel 1:17); NEB SOIL. *Regeḇ* refers to a "piece of clay" or "soft lump of earth." *Megrāpâ* refers to a "furrow," or "something thrown off by the spade."

CLOGGING. In Ex. 14:25 the RSV and NEB follow the Samaritan Pentateuch, LXX (Gk. *synedḗsen*), and Syriac translations, reading Heb. *'āsar,* "bind," rather than MT *sûr,* "remove."

CLOPAS klō'pəs [Gk. *Klōpas*] (Jn. 19:25); AV CLEOPHAS. The husband of one of the women who stood by the cross of Christ. Upon the philological ground of a variety of pronunciations of the Hebrew root, he is sometimes identified with ALPHAEUS, the father of James the Less. He is said by tradition to have been the brother of Joseph the husband of Mary; *see* BROTHERS OF THE LORD.

CLOSE; CLOSED [Heb. *sāgar, 'āṭar, 'āṣar, 'āṭam, šā'â, 'ālam, ṣāpan, šîṯ, sāḇaḇ, nāqap, kāsâ, ṣûp, 'ārēl*]; AV also SHUT, STOP, HIDE, COMPASS, etc.; NEB also SHUT, ENGULF, STOP, BLOCK, etc.; [Gk. *kleíō, kammýō, ptýssō, syntéleia*]; AV also SHUT, END; NEB also ROLLED UP, SHUTS UP, END.

Some of the Hebrew verbs used in the sense of "close," "shut" are *sāgar, 'āṭar* (Ps. 69:15), *'āṣar* (Gen. 20:18), *'āṭam* (Prov. 17:28; 21:13), and *šā'â* ("be stuck shut," Isa. 32:3). In Lam. 3:56 *'ālam* means "hide," "cover" (NEB "turn a deaf ear"), and in Job 17:4 *ṣāpan* means "keep (something) away from." In Gen. 46:4, the clause rendered "Joseph's hand will close your eyes" by the RSV is translated more literally by the AV: "Joseph shall put [*šîṯ*] his hand upon thine eyes." *Nāqap* (Job 19:6; Ps. 88:17) and *sāḇaḇ* (Jonah 2:5) carry the meaning of "surround" or "encircle," while *kāsâ* (Nu. 16:33) means "cut down" and *ṣûp* (Lam. 3:54) means "flood" or "rise up." The adjective *'ārēl* means literally "uncircumsized"; in Jer. 6:10, "Behold their ears are closed," the term is used in the sense of ears that are unfit for hearing.

In the NT the Greek verbs *kleíō* (1 Jn. 3:17), *kammýō* (Mt. 13:15; Acts 28:27), and *ptýssō* (Lk. 4:20) mean "close" or "roll up." The noun *syntéleia,* used in the phrase "the close of the age" (Mt. 13:39f., 49; 24:3; 28:20), refers to the "end" or "consummation" of the age. N. J. O.

CLOSE; CLOSELY. The terms "close" and "closely" are sometimes a direct translation of an adjective or adverb; e.g., Heb. *'ummâ* (Ex. 25:27; 37:14; Lev. 3:9), *kāḇēḏ* (Jgs. 20:34, AV "sore"; NEB "heavy"), *'allûp* ("familiar," AV "chief"), *qārôḇ* (Job 19:14, AV "familiar"; NEB "intimates"; Isa. 13:22, AV, NEB, "near"), *ṣar* (Job 41:15, NEB "enclosed in"); also Gk. *engýs* (Jn. 19:42, AV "nigh"; NEB "near"), *anankaíos* (Acts 10:24, AV "near"), *ásson* (27:13, NEB "hugging"), *akribṓs* (Lk. 1:3, NEB "in detail"; Acts 23:20, AV "perfectly"; NEB "precise").

In other instances "close" or "closely" is used in translating a verb or participle based on a verb; e.g., Heb. *rāḏap* ("followed closely," Gen. 31:23), *nāga'* ("was close," Jgs. 20:41), *dāḇaq* ("keep close," Ruth 2:8, 21, 23; "were close," 2 S. 1:6), *bîn* ("looked at closely" 1 K. 3:21; AV "considered").

In Acts 11:6 the Gk. *katanoéō* is rendered "looking closely" by the RSV, "looked intently" by the NEB, and "considered" by the AV. The term connotes contemplation as well as perception. In Rom. 7:21 Paul uses *parákeimai* (RSV "lies close") to express the idea that whenever he desires to do right he finds only sin at his disposal. The author of Hebrews exhorts his readers (12:1) to lay aside the sin "which clings so closely" in order to run the race before them. The allusion to a race suggests that *euperístatos* (AV "easily besetting"; NEB "to which we cling") may be related to *euperíspaston,* "diverting from the course." N. J. O.

CLOSET. The term is used only once by the RSV, in Jgs. 3:24, to translate Heb. *ḥeḏer,* an indoor washroom. Its use in the AV for Gk. *tameíon* (Mt. 6:6; Lk. 12:3) is obsolete for "room."

See also HOUSE.

CLOTH; CLOTHING. *See* GARMENTS.

CLOTHE; CLOTHED [Heb. *lāḇēš, lāḇaš, kāsâ* (1 Ch. 21:16; Isa. 37:2), *krbl* (1 Ch. 15:27), *qāḏar* (Ezk. 31:15), idiomatic use of the prepositions *min* (Nah. 2:3) and *'al* (Job 37:22); Gk. *endýō, periDállō, amphiénnymi, enkombóomai* (1 Pet. 5:5), *ependýomai* (2 Cor. 5:2, 4)]; AV also WRAP, ARRAY; NEB also COVER, WEAR. To put on or wear as a garment or other covering, often used figuratively.

The Hebrew verbs metaphorically depict endowment with a power or quality such as righteousness (Job 29:14; Ps. 132:9), glory and splendor (Job 40:10), salvation (2 Ch. 6:41; Ps. 132:16; Isa. 61:10), shame, and dishonor (Job 8:22; Ps. 35:26; 109:29; 132:18). They describe acquisition of such characteristics as gloom (Heb. *qāḏar* [Ezk. 31:15]; AV "caused to mourn"; NEB "put in mourning"), strength (Job 39:19), cursing (Ps. 109:18), and trembling (Ezk. 26:16). God is clothed with honor and majesty (Ps. 104:1; Job 37:22 [Heb. *'al-'ᵉlō(a)h*]; cf. Ps. 93:1; Isa. 59:17; Lam. 3:43).

The metaphorical range includes several types of covering. Job's skin is clothed with worms (7:5; NEB "infested"). The victorious Nebuchadrezzar will array himself with the land of Egypt (AV Jer. 43:12; RSV "clean"). The spirit of the Lord so completely envelops a person as to gain control (Heb. *lāḇēš,* Jgs. 6:34; 1 Ch. 12:18 [MT 19]; 2 Ch. 24:20).

Various attributes are portrayed as garments or clothing (Heb. *lᵉḇûš*), including strength and dignity (Prov. 31:25), garments (Heb. *beḡeḏ*) of salvation (Isa. 59:17; 61:10), and garments (Heb. *tilbōšeṯ*) of vengeance (Isa. 59:17). Clouds are the garment of the sea (Job 38:9). Covering appears "as a garment," as when God covers the earth with the deep (Ps. 104:6) and changes earth and heaven "like raiment" (Ps. 102:26 [MT 27]; AV "vesture"; NEB "cloak"). Heb. *me'îl* ("robe, mantle") occurs in the phrase "as a mantle," referring to fury (Isa. 59:17), justice (Job 29:14), and shame (Ps. 109:29); cf. "robe of righteousness" (Isa. 61:10) and "robe of light" (Ps. 104:2).

In the AV divorce is described as "covering violence with one's garment" (Mal. 2:16).

Other Hebrew verbs that figuratively indicate clothing are *'āṭâ* ("cover" in Ps. 89:45 and 104:2 [NEB "wrap"]; "wrap" in Isa. 59:17; "array" in Jer. 43:12, AV [RSV "clean"; NEB "scour"]); *yā'aṭ* ("cover" in Isa. 61:10 [NEB "wrapped"]); *ṣārar* ("bind" in Job 26:8 [NEB "keeps penned in"]; "wrapped" in Prov. 30:4 [AV "gathered"; NEB "bound up"]; Hos. 4:19 [AV "bound up"]); *sāḵaḵ* ("wrapped" in Lam. 3:43f. [NEB "hidden"]).

Figurative occurrences in the NT include acquiring such characteristics as power (Lk. 24:49), humility (1 Pet. 5:5), and compassion, kindness, lowliness, meekness, and patience (Col. 3:12). God clothes the grass (Mt. 6:30; Lk. 12:28). Rome is a city clothed in fine linens and other riches of trade (Rev. 18:16); in another vision a woman is clothed with the sun (12:1).

Spiritual rebirth or the acceptance of Christ is depicted as having "put on Christ" (Rom. 13:14; Gal. 3:27), a new nature (Eph. 4:24; Col. 3:10), a heavenly dwelling (2 Cor. 5:2), and the imperishable and immortality (1 Cor. 15:53f.). Paul suggests an enswathement of the physical mortal body with the new life (Gk. *ependýomai*; RSV "further clothe"; NEB "put on over"). Viewed by contemporary philosophers as a covering of the soul, the body was to be simultaneously clothed and transformed by the superimposed heavenly body. Cf. Gk. *ependýtēs* (an outer garment, Jn. 21:7), frequently used in the LXX for Heb. *me'îl*, an upper garment or robe.

Metaphorical garments in the NT include the armor of light (Rom. 13:12), the whole armor of God (Eph. 6:11), and the breastplate of faith and love (1 Thess. 5:8).

See also COVER, COVERING; GARMENTS; MANTLE; ROBE.

A. C. M.

CLOTHES. *See* GARMENTS.

CLOTHES, RENDING OF. Among Eastern peoples a means of showing deep sorrow or remorse. Upon the death of a relative or important personage, or when there was a great calamity, it was customary for the Hebrews to tear their garments. Reuben rent his clothes when he found that Joseph had been taken from the pit (Gen. 37:29). The sons of Jacob rent their clothes when the cup was found in Benjamin's sack (44:13). A messenger came to Eli with his clothes rent to tell of the taking of the ark of God and of the death of his two sons (1 S. 4:12). David rent his garment when he heard that Absalom had slain his brothers (2 S. 13:31). See also 2 S. 15:32; 2 K. 18:37; Isa. 36:22; Jer. 41:5.

Rending of clothes was evidently an expression of other strong emotions as well. The high priest rent his garment when Jesus spoke what he thought was blasphemy (Mt. 26:65).

A. W. FORTUNE

CLOUD [Heb. *'ānān, 'āḇ, šaḥaq,* also *nāśî', ḥāzîz* (Zec. 10:1), *'arîpîm* (Isa. 5:30); Gk. *nephélē,* also *néphos* (fig., He. 12:1)]; AV also HEAVENS, VAPOUR; NEB also HILL-TOPS (Isa. 5:30), MIST, etc.; the RSV has "clouds" also for the difficult Heb. *ṭuḥôṯ,* Job 38:36 (AV "inward parts"; NEB "depths of darkness"); for *'arāḇôṯ,* Ps. 68:4 (AV "heavens"; NEB "desert plains") probably following the Ugar. *rkb 'rpt*; for *'aḇōṯîm,* reading *'āḇôṯ* with LXX, Ezk. 31:3, 10, 14 (AV "thick boughs"; NEB "foliage"); also "cloud [*maś'ēṯ*] of smoke," Jgs. 20:38, and "clouds of locusts" (*gôḇ*), Nah. 3:17.

I. Clouds in Palestine.–In the Bible few references are found to particular clouds or to clouds in connection with the phenomena of the weather conditions. The weather in Palestine is more even and has less variety than that in most other lands. It is a long, narrow country with sea on the west and desert on the east. The wind coming from the west is always moist and brings clouds with it. If the temperature over the land is low enough the clouds will be condensed and rain will fall, but if the temperature is high, as in the five months of summer, there can be no rain even though clouds are seen. As a whole the winter is cloudy and the summer clear.

In the autumn rain storms often arise suddenly from the sea and what seems to be a mere haze, "as small as a man's hand," such as Gehazi saw (1 K. 18:44) over the sea, within a few hours becomes the black storm cloud pouring down torrents of rain (v. 45). Fog is almost unknown and there is very seldom an overcast, gloomy day. The west and southwest winds bring rain (Lk. 12:54).

In the months of April, May, and September a hot east wind sometimes rises from the desert and brings with it a cloud of dust which fills the air and penetrates everything. In the summer afternoons, especially in August, on the seacoast there is apt to blow up from the south a considerable number of low cirro-stratus clouds which seem to fill the air with dampness, making more oppressive the dead heat of summer. These are doubtless the detested "clouds without water" mentioned in Jude 12, and "heat by the shade of a cloud" (Isa. 25:5).

II. Figurative Uses.–The metaphoric and symbolic uses of clouds are many, and furnish some of the most powerful figures of Scripture. In the OT, the Lord's presence is made manifest and His glory shown forth in a cloud. The cloud is usually spoken of as bright and shining, and it could not be fathomed by man: "Thou hast wrapped thyself with a cloud so that no prayer can pass through" (Lam. 3:44). The Lord Himself was present in the cloud (Ex. 19:9; 24:16; 34:5) and His glory filled the places where the cloud was (16:10; 40:38; Nu. 10:34); "a cloud filled the house of the Lord" (1 K. 8:10). In the NT we often have "the Son of man coming on (with) clouds" (Mt. 24:30; 26:64; Mk. 13:26; 14:62; Lk. 21:27) and received up by clouds (Acts 1:9). The glory of the Second Coming is indicated in Rev. 1:7, "he is coming with the clouds" and "we who are alive . . . shall be caught up together with them in the clouds to meet the Lord" and dwell with Him (1 Thess. 4:17).

The pillar of cloud was a symbol of God's guidance and presence to the children of Israel in their journeys to the Promised Land. The Lord appeared in a pillar of cloud and forsook them not (Ex. 33:9f.; cf. Ps. 78:14; 99:7; Neh. 9:12, 19; etc.). *See* PILLAR OF CLOUD AND FIRE.

As the black cloud covers the sky and sweeps the sun from sight, so the Lord promises to sweep away the sins of Israel (Isa. 44:22); Egypt also shall be conquered: "She shall be covered by a cloud" (Ezk. 30:18; cf. Lam. 2:1).

There is usually a wide difference in temperature between day and night in Palestine. The days are warm and clouds coming from the sea are often completely dissolved in the warm atmosphere over the land. As the temperature falls, the moisture again condenses into dew and mist over the hills and valleys. As the sun rises the "morning cloud" (Hos. 6:4) is quickly dispelled and disappears entirely. Job compares the passing of his prosperity to the passing clouds (Job 30:15).

God "binds up the waters in his thick clouds" (Job 26:8) and the "clouds are the dust of his feet" (Nah.

1:3). The Lord will "command the clouds that they rain no rain" (Isa. 5:6), but as for man, "who can number the clouds . . . ?" (Job 38:37); "Can any one understand the spreading of the clouds?" (36:29); "Do you know the balancings of the clouds, the wondrous works of him who is perfect in knowledge . . . ?" (37:16). "He who regards the clouds will not reap" (Eccl. 11:4), for it is God who controls the clouds and man cannot fathom His wisdom. "Thick clouds enwrap him" (Job 22:14).

Clouds are a central figure in many visions. Ezekiel beheld "a stormy wind . . . out of the north, and a great cloud" (Ezk. 1:4), and John saw "a white cloud, and seated on the cloud one like a son of man" (Rev. 14:14). See also Dnl. 7:13; Rev. 10:1; 11:12.

The cloud is also the symbol of the terrible and of destruction. The day of the Lord's reckoning is called the "day of clouds" (Ezk. 30:3) and a day of "clouds and thick darkness" (Zeph. 1:15). The invader is expected to "come up like clouds" (Jer. 4:13). Joel (2:2) foretells the coming of locusts as "a day of clouds and thick darkness," which is both literal and figurative. Misfortune and old age are compared to "a day of clouds and thick darkness" (Ezk. 34:12) and "the clouds returning after rain" (Eccl. 12:2).

Clouds are used in connection with various other figures: rapidity of motion, "these that fly like a cloud" (Isa. 60:8); swaddling clothes of the newborn earth (Job 38:9); great height (Job 20:6), figuratively, Isa. 14:14, "I will ascend above the heights of the clouds," portraying the self-esteem of Babylon. "A cloudless morning" is the symbol of righteousness and justice (2 S. 23:4); and clouds are a figure of partial knowledge and hidden glory (Lev. 16:2; Acts 1:9; Rev. 1:7).

A. H. JOY

CLOUD, PILLAR OF. *See* PILLAR OF CLOUD AND FIRE.

CLOUDBURST [Heb. *nepeṣ*] (Isa. 30:30); AV SCATTERING. The literal meaning of the Hebrew is "shattering," "scattering," or "dispensing"; here the context indicates that "clouds" is the implied object.

CLOUT. An archaic word in the AV for a patch or piece of cloth, leather, or the like — a rag, a shred, or fragment: old "cast clouts [Heb. *hassᵉḥāḇôṯ*] and old rotten rags" (Jer. 38:11f.). As a verb it means to "bandage," "patch," or mend with a clout: "old shoes and clouted [*ṭālā'*, RSV "patched"] upon their feet" (Josh. 9:5); cf. Shakespeare, *Cymbeline,* IV, 2: "I thought he slept, And put my *clouted* brogues from off my feet"; Milton, *Comus*: "And the dull swain treads on it daily with his *clouted* shoon."

CLOVE (Sus. 54, NEB). *See* MASTIC.

CLOVEN. The term occurs in Dt. 14:6f.; Lev. 3:3, 7, 26 for a participial form of Heb. *šāsa'*, to "split," and is applied to beasts with divided hooves. Ruminant beasts with hooves completely bifurcated were allowed to the Israelites as food. *See* CHEWING THE CUD.

CLUB [Heb. *tôṯāḥ*] (Job 41:29); AV DART; [*mēpîṣ*, emended to *mappēṣ*] (Prov. 25:18); AV MAUL; [Gk. *xýlon*] (Mt. 26:47, 55 par.); AV STAFF; NEB CUDGEL. Philologically, little is known about Heb. *tôṯāḥ*, which occurs only in Job 41:29. A presumed Semitic cognate verb means "beat with a club," and the LXX has Gk. *sphýra*, "hammer, mallet." In Prov. 25:18 the LXX reads *rhópalon*, "war club," which is the equivalent of Heb. *mappēṣ*.

The Gk. *xýlon* means basically "wood," but is used also to designate various wooden objects. Jesus was arrested by a crowd carrying swords and *xýla*, weapons of wood, perhaps shepherd staves but more likely clubs.

See also WEAPONS OF WAR.

CLUSTER; BUNCH [Heb. *'eškōl, 'ᵃguddâ, ṣimmûqîm*; Gk. *bótrys*]. The common word for a cluster of grapes is Heb. *'eškōl* (Gen. 40:10; Nu. 13:23; Isa. 65:8; Cant. 7:8; etc.). The same word is used with henna flowers (Cant. 1:14) and dates (7:7). *See also* ESHCOL.

The Heb. *ṣimmûqîm* refers to raisin cakes (1 S. 25:18; 30:12; 2 S. 16:1; 1 Ch. 12:40). Heb. *'ᵃguddâ* occurs only in Ex. 12:22, "a bunch of hyssop" (NEB "marjoram").

In Rev. 14:18 Gk. *bótrys* is used of the "clusters of the vine of the earth."

The AV has "bunches" in Isa. 30:6 for the "humps" (Heb. *dabbešeṯ*) of the camel. R. K. H.

CNIDUS nī'dəs [Gk. *Knidos*]. A Greek colony on the southwestern tip of Caria, Asia Minor. It is mentioned in Acts 27:7 with the simple statement that Paul and his companions on their journey to Rome "arrived with difficulty off Cnidus." As early as the 6th cent. B.C. Cnidus, which had been colonized by Dorians, was an important trade center, with connections to Rome and to Egypt. In the Hellenistic period, according to Strabo (*Geog.* xiv.2.15 [col. 656]), Cnidus had two harbors "one of which can be closed," and was a naval station for twenty ships. The peculiar geographical location, on a promontory about 40 mi. (65 km.) from W to E, lying between the islands of Cos and Rhodes and surrounded by other islands of the Sporades, not only gave it the two harbors, but also made it dangerous to sail past when the wind was blowing from the north. The captain of Paul's ship was forced to go with the wind and head for Crete.

Cnidus was explored in the 19th century. The ruins of a well-planned city with seawalls, piers, and many sanctuaries can be traced. Here were discovered the statue of Demeter, now in the British Museum, and the justly famous Aphrodite of Praxiteles (4th cent. B.C.). The city was a cult center of Aphrodite, and a portion of the ruins of the temple to that goddess can still be seen. Cnidus held the rank of a free city, and a colony of Jews was located here as early as the 2nd cent. B.C.

See MAP XXI. W. S. L. S.

COA. kō'ə (1 K. 10:28; 2 Ch. 1:16, NEB). *See* KUE.

COAL [Heb. *gaḥeleṯ*]; NEB also EMBER; [*peḥām*] (Isa. 44:12; 54:16; Ps. 11:6 emended); AV also SNARE (Ps. 11:6, for MT *paḥ*); [*reṣep*] (Isa. 6:6); [Gk. *ánthrax*] (Rom. 12:20); **CHARCOAL** [Heb. *peḥām* (Prov. 26:21); Gk. *anthrakiá* (Jn. 18:18; 21:9)]; AV COALS; cf. NEB at Prov. 26:21, "Like bellows for the coal"; the AV has "coal" also for Heb. *reṣep*, 1 K. 19:6 (RSV, NEB, "hot stone"), *rešep*, Cant. 8:6 (RSV "flash"; NEB "blaze"), Hab. 3:5 (RSV, NEB, "plague") and *šᵉḥôr*, Lam. 4:8 (RSV, NEB, "soot").

There is no reference to mineral coal in the Bible. Coal, or more properly lignite, of inferior quality, is found in thin beds (not exceeding 3 ft. [1 m.]) in the Nubian sandstone formations, but there is no evidence of its use in ancient times. Charcoal is manufactured in a primitive fashion which does not permit the conservation of any by-products. A flat, circular place (Arab. *beidar*, same name as for a threshing floor) 10 to 15 ft. (3 to 5 m.) in diameter is prepared in, or conveniently near to, the forest. On this the wood to be converted into charcoal is carefully stacked in a dome-shaped structure, leaving an open space in the middle for fine kindlings. All except the center is covered first with leaves and then with earth. The kindlings in the center are then fired and afterward covered in the same manner as the rest. While it is burning or smoldering it is carefully watched, and earth is immediately placed upon any holes that may be formed in the covering by the burning of the wood below. In several days, more or less according to the size of the pile, the wood is converted into charcoal and the heap is opened. The charcoal floor is also called in Arab. *mašḥarah,* from *šaḥḥār,* "soot"; cf. Heb. *šᵉḥôr*. The characteristic odor of the *mašḥarah* clings for months to the spot.

In Ps. 120:4 there is mention of "coals of the broom tree." This is doubtless the Arab. *retem, Retama roetam,* Forsk., a kind of broom which is abundant in Judea and Moab. Charcoal from oak wood, especially *Quercus coccifera,* L., Arab *sindyān,* is much preferred to other kinds, and draws a higher price.

In most of the passages where English versions have "coal," the reference is not necessarily to charcoal, but may be to coals of burning wood. *Peḥām* in Prov. 26:21, however, seems to stand for charcoal:

"As charcoal to hot embers and wood to fire,
so is a quarrelsome man for kindling strife."

The same may be true of *peḥām* in Isa. 44:12 and 54:16; also of *šᵉḥôr* in Lam. 4:8. A. E. DAY

COARSE MEAL [Heb. *'ᵃrîsâ*] (Nu. 15:20f.; Neh. 10:37; Ezk. 44:30); AV, NEB, DOUGH. Perhaps a kind of barley paste, or the first stage of dough-making, used in the offering of firstfruits.

COAST; COASTLAND; COASTLINE [Heb. *'î*] (Gen. 10:5; Est. 10:1; Ps. 97:1; Isa. 11:11; etc.); AV ISLE, ISLAND, COUNTRY (Jer. 47:4); NEB also SEA-COAST (Isa. 23:2, 6), ISLAND; [*gᵉḇûl*] (Nu. 34:6; Josh. 15:12, 47); AV also BORDER; NEB SEABOARD (Nu. 34:6), "land adjacent"; [*ḥôp*] (Josh. 9:1; Jgs. 5:17); AV, NEB, also SEA-SHORE (Jgs. 5:17); [Gk. *katá tḗn Asian*] (Acts 27:2); NEB PROVINCE.

In general, the term *'î* means "coast" or "shore," although "island" is required in Jer. 47:4 (cf. Egyp. *'w* or *'iw,* "island"); thus, any land — island or mainland — contiguous with the waters of the Mediterranean Sea. The Phoenicians were "inhabitants of the coast" (Isa. 23:2, 6) and their commercial ventures extended to the distant lands of the Mediterranean (Ezk. 27:3, 15, 35). The "shores of Kittim [Cyprus]" (Jer. 2:10; Ezk. 27:6) refers not to the entire island but to the territory on Cyprus occupied by the Phoenicians (cf. Isa. 23:1f.). These Mediterranean colonies of Phoenicia were, together with Tyre and Sidon, the objects of God's judgment (Jer. 25:22); a prophecy was fulfilled in Tyre's submission to Babylonian suzerainty in 574 B.C., after a thirteen-year siege. The place name "Elishah" in Ezk. 27:7 ("Alashia" in the El-Amarna Tablets) refers to a city (Enkomi?) on the island of Cyprus. In Isa. 40–66; Jer. 31:10; and Ezk. 26:15, *'î* refers to distant, heathen nations. Dnl. 11:18 predicts the seizure of the *'îyyîm* of Asia Minor and the Aegean during the campaign of Antiochus III against Greece, 197-191 B.C.

Hebrew *ḥôp* (Ugar. *ḫp*; Egyp. *ha-pú*) designates the shore or coastal plain of the Mediterranean (cf. Gen. 49:13; Dt. 1:7; Jer. 47:7; Ezk. 25:16). For *gᵉḇûl, see* BORDER.

In Acts 27:2, *katá* replaces a genitive and refers to water along the coasts of Cilicia and Pamphylia (cf. Acts 27:5). Paul's ship was sailing from Caesarea and going home to Adramytium in Mysia; at Myra, Paul transferred to an Alexandrian ship bound for Rome.

Bibliography.–W. F. Albright, *JBL,* 63 (1944), 231; R. Dussaud, *Anatolian Studies,* 6 (1956), 63-65; A. Schwarzenbach, *Die geographische Terminologie im Hebräischen des AT* (1954), pp. 77f.; *GTTOT.* J. T. DENNISON, JR.

COAT [Heb. *kuttōneṯ*]; AV also GARMENT; NEB also TUNIC, SHIRT, DRESS, MANTLE; [*maḏ*] (Ps. 109:18); AV, NEB, GARMENT; [Gk. *chiton*]; NEB also TUNIC, SHIRT. Apparently a long, shirtlike tunic worn next to the skin. Worn by men (Lev. 10:5; 2 S. 15:32; Job 30:18) and women (Cant. 5:3), the "coat" was the basic garment over which other apparel might be added. Jesus instructs his followers to give robbers not only the cloak (Gk. *himátion*; NEB "coat") but also the coat (Gk. *chitṓn*), which was worn underneath (Lk. 6:29; cf. Mt. 5:40; Bauer, p. 377). It was apparently worn beneath the priests' blue robe of the ephod (Ex. 29:5). The privileged may have worn two such tunics (Lk. 3:11; also Mt. 10:10 par., AV, NEB; RSV "tunics"). (*See* CLOTHE, CLOTHED.) This garment was removed at bedtime (Cant. 5:3). In time of turmoil, it was torn to display anguish (2 S. 15:32; *see* CLOTHES, RENDING OF).

The coat was usually linen, although other materials such as skins (cf. Gen. 3:21, AV; RSV "garments"; NEB "tunics") were used. In the cognate languages from which the Hebrew and Greek terms were derived (Sum. gad, gada; Akk. *kitû, kitinnu*; Ugar., Phoenician *ktn*) the same word meant both "linen" and "(linen) tunic." In Hebrew linen was designated by both *baḏ* (Lev. 16:4; originally "piece [of cloth]"; KoB, p. 108) and *šēš* (Ex. 28:39; RSV, AV, "fine linen"), high-quality Egyptian material (cf. Gk. *býssos*; KoB, p. 1013). In some instances the garment was seamless (Jn. 19:23, AV; RSV, NEB, "tunic"). The coat was sometimes decorated by embroidery (Ex. 28:4, 39, AV; RSV "checker work"; NEB "checkered tunic"). Among tribute paid by kings of Syria and Palestine, Tiglath-pileser III (744-727) lists "linen garments with multi-colored trimmings" (*ANET,* p. 282). The AV renders the Hebrew term for Joseph's garment (*kᵉṯōneṯ passîm*; Gen. 37:3, 23, 31f.) as "coat of many colors" (LXX Gk. *chitōna poikilon*; RSV "long robe with sleeves"); it was probably a robe or tunic of variegated pieces (cf. Heb. *pas,* "piece"; KoB, p. 768).

In the wall reliefs from Sennacherib's palace at Nineveh, men of Lachish are shown wearing long garments with sleeves of varying length. The garments appear to have closely-fitted collars (cf. Job 30:18, AV; RSV "tunic"; NEB "shirt"). No sashes are worn, but cf. Ex. 28:39; Mk. 1:6; Josephus *Ant.* iii.7.2.

Frequently designated as a priestly garment (Ex. 28:4, 39f.; Lev. 10:5; Ezr. 2:69; Neh. 7:70, 72 [MT 69, 71]), the coat was among the vestments bestowed in the consecration service (Ex. 29:5, 8; 39:27; 40:14; Lev. 8:7, 13). Aaron was commanded to wear the "holy linen coat" when entering the holy of holies on the Day of Atonement (Lev. 16:4).

For "coat of mail" *see* WEAPONS OF WAR.

See also CLOAK; GARMENTS; MANTLE; ROBE; TUNIC.

Bibliography.–M. Dietrich and D. Loretz, *Welt des Orients,* 3 (1966), pp. 224-26; E. Masson, *Recherches sur les plus anciens emprunts sémitiques en Grec* (1967), pp. 27-29; *WBA,* p. 192.

A. C. M.

COAT OF MAIL [Heb. *širyôn, širyān*] (1 S. 17:5, 38; 2 Ch. 26:14; Neh. 4:16 [MT 10]); AV also HABERGEON;

[*siryôn*] (Jer. 46:4; 51:3); AV BRIGANDINE; [*kepel siryôn*] (Job 41:13 [MT 5]). *See* WEAPONS OF WAR.

COCK [Gk. *aléktōr*] (Mt. 26:34, 74f. par.); **STRUTTING COCK** [Heb. *zarzîr moṯnayim*; Gk. *aléktōr emperipatṓn*] (Prov. 30:31); AV GREYHOUND. The Hebrew of Prov. 30:31 may be read "girt in the loins," a possible reference to the greyhound or horse. Or *zarzîr* could be related to the Arab. *zarzūr*, "starling"; in later Hebrew *zarzîr* refers to a starling or raven (cf. BDB, p. 267; KoB, p. 266). If so, then *moṯnayim* makes no sense; Bewer (*JBL*, 67 [1948], 61) proposed emending to *miṯnaśśē'*, "lifting itself up." The RSV and NEB follow the LXX and Vulgate (Lat. *gallus*), which are presumed to be based on a better Hebrew text here. The cock was introduced into Judea probably only with the Roman conquest (*see* CHICKEN), but Babylonian influence could explain the reference in Proverbs. J. W. D. H.

The cock is several times mentioned in the NT, always with reference to its habit of crowing with clocklike regularity. The first full salute comes almost to the minute at half-past eleven, the second at half-past one, and the third at dawn. So uniformly do the cocks keep time and proclaim these three periods of night that we find cock-crowing mentioned as a regular division of time: "Watch therefore — for you do not know when the master of the house will come, in the evening, or at midnight, or in the morning" (Mk. 13:35).

Jesus had these same periods of night in mind when he warned Peter that he would betray Him. Mt. 26:34; Lk. 22:34; Jn. 13:38, give almost identical wording of the warning. But in all his writing Mark was more explicit, more given to exact detail. Remembering the divisions of night as the cocks kept them, his record reads: "And Jesus said to him, 'Truly, I say to you, this very night, before the cock crows twice, you will deny me three times'" (Mk. 14:30). It is hardly necessary to add that the cocks crow at irregular intervals as well as at the times indicated, according to the time of the year and the phase of the moon (being more likely to crow during the night if the moon is at the full), or if a storm threatens, or there is any disturbance in their neighborhood.

G. STRATTON-PORTER

COCKATRICE kok'ə-trəs. *See* SERPENT.

COCKCROW [Gk. *alektorophōnía*] (Mk. 13:35); AV COCKCROWING. An hour of the night between midnight and morning, referred to by all the Evangelists in their account of Peter's denial (Mt. 26:34, 74 par.). *See* COCK.

COCKLE [Heb. *bo'šâ*; Gk. *bátos*] (Job 31:40, AV); AV mg. "noisome weeds"; RSV FOUL WEEDS; NEB WEEDS. A malodorous plant identified by some with the hoary nightshade, *Solanum incanum* L., whose berries are bitterly narcotic. Other authorities have suggested the corn-cockle, *Agrostemma githago* L., an attractive, vigorous weed bearing purple or white campion-like flowers, which grows often in cornfields. R. K. H.

CODE OF HAMMURABI. *See* HAMMURABI.

CODE, WRITTEN [Gk. *grámma*] (Rom. 2:27; 7:6; 2 Cor. 3:6); AV LETTER; NEB also WRITTEN DOCUMENT, WRITTEN LAW (2 Cor. 3:6). The references are to the spelled-out laws of the old covenant, which are contrasted to the spiritual transformation in Christ that changes ethics from legalism to a matter of the heart. In Christ man is enabled "to serve God in a new way, the way of the spirit, in contrast to the old way, the way of a written code" (Rom. 7:6, NEB). *See* LAW IN THE OT; COMMANDMENT, THE NEW.

COELESYRIA sē'lə-sir'ē-ə [Gk. *Koilē Syria*–'hollow Syria']; AV CELOSYRIA. The region between the Lebanon and the Anti-Lebanon mountain ranges. The term is variously used to designate other areas or larger areas, extending from the Euphrates River to the border of Egypt. The OT name *biq'aṯ hallᵉḇānôn*, "the valley of the Lebanon" (Josh. 11:17), refers to the portion of the Rift Valley which lies N of the Upper Jordan Valley, and is generally equated with Coelesyria. The modern Arabic name *Beqa'* is given to the same region (cf. Baalbek, "the Baal of the *Beqa'*"). *See* LEBANON.

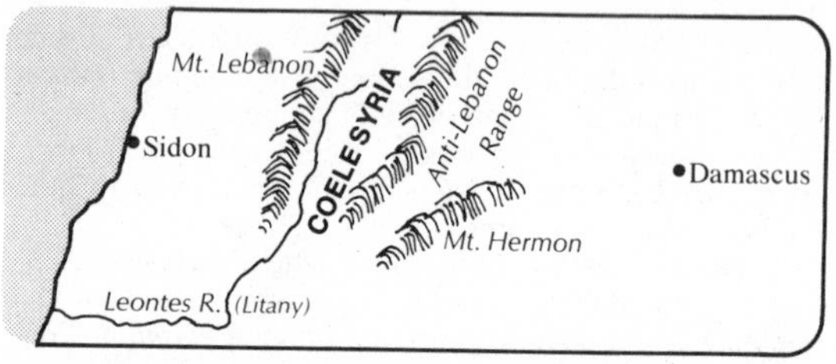

In the days of the Ptolemies and the Seleucids, the area composed of Palestine and Phoenicia was considered to be a single province, possibly the equivalent of the Persian province of Trans-Euphrates ("Beyond the River"; cf. Ezr. 8:36; Neh. 2:7; etc.). Jerusalem was one of its cities. Yet while Phoenicia was included in the province, we should note that it was not included in the term Coelesyria, for Apollonius of Tarsus is referred to as "governor of Coelesyria and Phoenicia" (2 Macc. 3:5-8; cf. 1 Macc. 10:69; etc.).

Josephus on the one hand speaks of "Coelesyria as far as the river Euphrates and Egypt" (*Ant.* xiv.4.5). On the other hand, when Josephus reports that "Herod was made general of Coelesyria and Samaria" (*BJ* i.10.8), he uses the term with reference to northern Transjordan, including Scythopolis (Beisan) in Cisjordan, and extending even to Damascus. Strabo (*Geog.* xvi.2.2-22) uses the term Coelesyria to include also the fertile area between the Anti-Lebanon and the desert, with Damascus as the principal city. Hence there is no precise meaning of the term.

Bibliography.–*GP*, I, 311; II, 129-133; *HGHL*, p. 539 (1966 paperback ed. p. 346); *GAB*, pp. 105f., maps 29, 31.

W. S. L. S.

COFFER [Heb. *'argaz*] (1 S. 6:8, 11, 15, AV); RSV BOX; NEB CASKET. A small box in which the Philistines placed their golden rats and other offerings when they returned the ark.

COFFIN. *See* BIER; BURIAL III; CHEST.

COHORT [Gk. *speíra*] (Acts 10:1; 21:31; 27:1); AV BAND. The tenth part of a legion, ordinarily about six hundred men. In Jn. 18:3, 12 the Greek word seems to be used loosely of a smaller body of soldiers, a detachment, detail; and in Mt. 27:27 par. the RSV renders it "battalion." *See* ARMY, ROMAN I.B.

COINS. *See* MONEY.

COLA kō'lə (Jth. 15:4, AV). *See* KOLA.

COLD [Heb. *qōr* (Gen. 8:22), *qeraḥ* (31:40), *qārâ, qār, ṣinnâ* (Prov. 25:13); Gk. *psychrós, psýchos*]; AV also FROST, CLEAR (Zec. 14:6); NEB also FROST, COOLNESS, COOL; [*psýchō*] ("grow cold," Mt. 24:12); AV WAX COLD. Palestine is essentially a land of sunshine and warmth, where the extreme cold of northern latitudes is unknown. January is the coldest month, but the degree of cold in a particular place depends largely on the altitude above the sea. On the seacoast and plain snow never falls, and the temperature reaches freezing-point perhaps once in thirty years. In Jerusalem, at 2500 ft. (750 m.) above the sea, the mean temperature in January is about 45° F. (7° C.), but the minimum may be as low as 25° F. (-4° C.). Snow occasionally falls, but lasts only a short time. On Mt. Hermon and on the Lebanons snow may be found the whole year, and the cold is intense, even in the summer. In Jericho and around the Dead Sea, 1292 ft. (394 m.) below sea level, it is correspondingly hotter and cold is not known.

Because cold weather in Palestine is of such short duration, little provision is made for the heating of private homes apart from portable appliances. In the biblical period the charcoal brazier was a popular source of heat in winter (cf. Jn. 18:18). Peasants and nomadic peoples often maintained camp fires in the open air in cold weather (cf. Acts 28:2) to avoid the more severe effects of winter (cf. Ps. 147:17). Extreme deprivation was described under the image of nakedness in the cold (Job 24:7).

In the burning heat of summer the shadow of a rock or the cool of the evening is a welcome boon, as is a cup of cold water to the parched traveler (Prov. 25:25). The "cold of snow" (Prov. 25:13) may perhaps refer to chips of ice used for cooling beverages in summer. Figurative usages of cold occur in Mt. 24:12; Rev. 3:15f.

A. H. JOY
R. K. H.

COLHOZEH kol-hō'zə [Heb. *kol-ḥōzeh*–'all seeing'; LXX omits]. A man whose son Shallum rebuilt the fountain gate of Jerusalem in the days of Nehemiah (Neh. 3:15; 11:5).

COLIUS kō'lē-əs (1 Esd. 9:23, AV, NEB); RSV KELAIAH. *See* KELITA.

COLLAR.

(1) [Heb. *barzel*]. An instrument used in restraint of a prisoner; literally, "iron," or a tool or weapon made of iron (Ps. 105:18).

(2) [Heb. *'anāq*]; AV, NEB, CHAINS. An ornament for the necks of camels; literally, "neck" or "necklace" (Jgs. 8:26).

(3) [Heb. *peh*]; AV also SKIRTS. Literally "mouth," also "opening, orifice"; here it is used of the opening of a tunic (Job 30:18) or of Aaron's robes (Ps. 133:2).

(4) [Heb. *ṣînōq*]; AV STOCKS; NEB PILLORY. An instrument used in the restraint of a madman (Jer. 29:26).

J. R. PRICE

COLLECTED SAYINGS [Heb. *ba'alê 'asuppôṯ*–'masters of collections'] (Eccl. 12:11); AV "masters of assemblies"; NEB "assembled people." If the RSV is correct, the phrase refers to a phenomenon common in the ancient Near East, viz., the creating or collecting of wise sayings by classes of scribes under priestly or royal patronage. The OT has both Solomon (1 K. 4:29-34) and Hezekiah (Prov. 25:1) making such collections. To the Israelite, God was the ultimate source of the wisdom reflected in the sayings of wise men like Qoheleth.

COLLECTION. *See* CONTRIBUTION (1 Cor. 16:1f.); TAX (2 Ch. 24:6, 9).

COLLEGE. This is the rendering of the AV for Heb. *mišneh* (2 K. 22:14; 2 Ch. 34:22; cf. Zeph. 1:10). It is found in the Targum of Jonathan on 2 K. 22:14 and rests on a faulty combination with Mishnah, the well-known code of laws of the 2nd cent. A.D. The RSV and NEB render "second quarter (of Jerusalem)."

COLONY [Gk. *kolōnía,* from Lat. *colonia*] (Acts 16:12). The word occurs but once, in reference to Philippi in Macedonia. Roman colonies were of three kinds and of three periods: (1) Those of the early republic, in which the colonists, established in conquered towns to serve the state as guardians of the frontier, were exempt from ordinary military service. They were distinguished as (a) *coloniae civium Romanorum,* wherein the colonists retained Roman citizenship, also called *coloniae maritimae* because they were situated on the coast, and (b) *coloniae Latinae,* situated inland among the allies (*socii*), wherein the colonists possessed the *ius Latinum,* entitling them to invoke the Roman law of property (*commercium*) but not that of the family (*connubium*), and received Roman citizenship only when elected to magistracies. (2) The colonies of the Gracchan period, established in pursuance of the scheme of agrarian reforms, to provide land for the poorer citizens. (3) Colonies founded in Italy by the republic after the time of Sulla as a device for granting lands to retiring veterans, who of course retained citizenship. This privilege was appropriated by Caesar and the emperors, who employed it to establish military colonies, chiefly in the provinces, with various rights and internal organizations. To this class belonged Philippi. Partly organized after the great battle of 42 B.C. fought in the neighboring plain by Brutus and Cassius, the champions of the fated republic, and Antonius and Octavian, it was fully established as a colony by Octavian (afterward styled Augustus) after the battle of Actium (31 B.C.), under the name Colonia Augusta Iulia Philippi, or Philippensis. It received the *ius Italicum,* whereby provincial cities acquired the same status as Italian cities, permitting them to possess municipal self-government and exemption from poll and land taxes.

See CITIZEN; PHILIPPI II. W. A. HEIDEL

COLOR; COLORS.

I. Hebrew and Greek Terms
II. Color Awareness among the Ancient Hebrews
III. Biblical References to Color
  A. Eyes, Hair, Skin, and Teeth
  B. Textiles
  C. Pottery
  D. Wall Painting
  E. Cosmetics
IV. Colors in Symbolism
V. Color Terms Most Widely Used
  A. Black
  B. Blue
  C. Crimson
  D. Gray
  E. Green
  F. Purple
  G. Red
  H. Scarlet
  I. White
  J. Others

I. Hebrew and Greek Terms.–The word translated "color" in the AV most frequently is Heb. *'ayin,* which literally means "eye" or "appearance" and is usually so translated in the RSV. In the NT the Gk. *próphasis* has the meaning of pretense or show (AV Acts 27:30; cf. Rev. 17:4). The references to Joseph's coat "of many colors" (AV Gen. 37:3, 23, 32) and to garments "of divers colors" (2 S. 13:18f.) probably do not mean the color of the garment at all; Heb. *passîm* more likely indicates that it had long sleeves, as suggested by the RSV and NEB. In Jgs. 5:30 the word for "dip" or "dye," Heb. *ṣeḇa'*, appears in the MT and has been so translated by the RSV (*see* DYE). In 1 Ch. 29:2 Heb. *riqmâ*, meaning "variegated," hence "varicolored," occurs. In Isa. 54:11 *pûḵ* is used. This name was applied to the sulphide of antimony used for painting the eyes; thus the RSV rendering "antimony" instead of "fair colors" (*see* PAINT).

II. Color Awareness Among the Ancient Hebrews.– Although the ancient Hebrews had no specific words for "color," "paint," or "painter," we know that they constantly met with displays of the art of coloring among the Assyrians, Babylonians (Ezk. 23:14), Egyptians, and the inhabitants of Palestine. Pottery, glazed bricks, glassware, tomb walls, sarcophagi, wood, and fabrics were submitted to the skill of the colorist. Babylonian and Assyrian ziggurat towers, e.g., were made of glazed enamel bricks, each story of a different color. The dominant colors in Assyrian wall paintings were bright blue (*lapis lazuli*) and red, with black and white as secondary colors. The Egyptian tomb frescoes of the New Kingdom (1580-1375 B.C.) show mainly red, yellow, and brown, but also whitewash, blue, and black. The Greek term for Phoenicia (*Phoinikē*) means "land of the red-purple"; the dye is extracted from the murex shellfish taken in waters off the coastline. This industry was still widespread in NT times (Acts 16:19).

Two reasons may be given for the indefiniteness of many of the biblical references to color. (1) The origin of the Hebrew people: they had been wandering tribes or slaves with no occasion to develop a color language. (2) Their religious laws: these forbade expression in color in the form of graven images (Ex. 20:4). Yielding to the attractions of gorgeous display was discouraged by such prophets as Ezekiel, who had sickened of the abominations of the Chaldeans (Ezk. 23:14-16): "and I said to them, Cast away the detestable things your eyes feast on" (Ezk. 20:7).

III. Biblical References to Color.–*A. Eyes, Hair, Skin, and Teeth.* Biblical references do not specify color of eyes, though presumably different darker hues were known and appreciated. David had "beautiful" eyes according to 1 S. 16:12 (lit. "health"; AV "countenance"). In Cant. 1:15; 4:1 the whites of the woman's eyes are associated with the color of doves or pigeons; in 5:12 the comparison is applied to the white of the beloved man's eyes. "Redness" of eyes (Prov. 23:29; lit. "dull") means bloodshot. Leah's "tender" (AV), "weak" (RSV), dull, pale, lackluster, or bleary eyes are contrasted with (the eyes of) her sister Rachel, described as "beautiful" (or healthy) and "lovely" (Gen. 29:17). Ideally a woman's eyes were glowing and lively. Eyes could be "like flaming torches" (Dnl. 10:6; Rev. 1:14; 2:18; 19:12), "lustful" (1 Jn. 2:16), "wanton" (Isa. 3:16), and either "disturbing" (Cant. 6:5), or "like the eyelids of the dawn" (Job 41:18). Hair color is normally shiny black-brown as of goats' hair (Cant. 4:1; 6:5); when diseased, white or yellow (Lev. 13:10, 30). With age, hair turns gray (Gen. 42:38; Ps. 71:18; Prov. 20:29; Isa. 46:4).

Skin tones seen in Palestine covered a wide range of colors with darker shades predominating. The biblical references accent the noteworthy extremes, such as brown-black from over-exposure to the sun (Job 30:28, 30), black (associated with the "sons of Ham," including Libyans, Egyptians, and Ethiopians [Am. 9:7; Jer. 13:23, where J. Bright translates Ethiopians as "Negro"]) and white (Lev. 13:10; lit. "white as milk," i.e., diseased or abnormal). Healthy skin is "fresh" (Heb. *ruṭᵃpaš*) as a child's (Job 33:25; lit. "fat") or "fair" (*ṭôḇ, yāp̄eh*, etc., Gen. 24:16; 26:7; Est. 1:11; Job 42:14; Cant. 1:8; 2:10, 13; 5:9; 6:10; Hos. 10:11; Am. 8:13; Jer. 15:2; Ps. 45:2). The term "fair" is normally used of women, but also of David (1 S. 17:42) and Absalom (2 S. 13:1); it is associated with "ruddy" (*'āḏam, 'aḏmônî*), which literally meant tinted with red ochre, "more ruddy than coral" (Lam. 4:7). Fair skin could be artificially produced with cosmetics (hithpael of *yāp̄â*, Jer. 4:30; RSV "beautify") (see III.E). Skin should "shine" (*qāran*, Ex. 34:29f., 35), sending out rays of light. Understandable was an association of skin color with bronze (*nāḥûš, nᵉḥōšeṯ*), as in Ezk. 40:3; Job 6:12. Teeth could be white as milk (*lāḇān*, Gen. 49:12) or as newly washed sheep (Cant. 4:2; 6:6).

B. Textiles. The extensive manufacture and use of textiles for tents, sacking, basketry, clothing, curtains, and decorations added a wide range of colors to the biblical culture. The natural colors of the fabrics varied. The wool of goats naturally came in dark colors from brown to black, while that of sheep came in lighter colors from brownish to off-white, and that of camels (for cheapest clothing and heavy tents) varied from brown to tan. Linen and "fine linen" (i.e., "silky") made from flax was yellow-tan to white. Cotton was always white. Sackcloth, a rough cloth which was at times woven of hair and usually dark in color (Isa. 50:3; Rev. 6:12), was used for sacks and for mourning garments (Est. 4:1-4; Job 16:15; Isa. 20:2). Haircloth (2 K. 1:8) was a recognized costume of a prophet (Zec. 13:4; Mt. 3:4).

The threads, not the woven cloth, were dyed. A principal dye from the *murex* shellfish was a deep crimson. Used in combination with other dyes, this expensive "royal purple" could produce various shades from red to blue. By bleaching (*see* FULLER) additional shades were possible. Israelite bleaching, dyeing, and weaving on an industrial scale is known archeologically from Tell Beit Mirsim (Debir?), Tell Jezer, Beth-shemesh, Tell en-Naṣbeh (Mizpah?), and Khirbet eṭ-Ṭubeiqah. "The families of the house of them that wrought fine linen" (1 Ch. 4:21) has been interpreted (*WBA*) as indicating that artisans skilled in dyeing and weaving were at times organized into recognized guilds.

Embroidery, the interweaving of threads of various colors into specific patterns, was an art for which the Israelites were famed (Prov. 31:22; Jgs. 5:30). Oholiab, a Danite, did such work for the tabernacle (Ex. 35:34f.). Israelite workers wove "purple, crimson and blue fabrics" and "fine linen" for the temple veil (2 Ch. 2:7; 3:14). Carpets, spreads, and coverings were richly colored (Ezk. 27:23; Prov. 7:16; Jgs. 5:10), while pillows were woven of black-brown goats' hair (1 S. 19:13, 16).

Extrabiblical sources illustrate colorful textiles made and worn by Semites. In the 8th cent. B.C., lists of booty taken by Tiglath-pileser III from the kings of the west — including those of Samaria and Judah — mention "linen garments with multicolored trimmings, garments of their native (industries) (being made of) dark purple wool" (*ANET*, p. 282.). A wall painting by an Egyptian artist in a tomb at Beni-hasan (*ca.* 1890 B.C.) gives a visual representation of a visiting group of "Asiatics," men, women, and children. Their clothing is decorated with colored fringes and with red, blue, and brown designs against a white background (*ANEP*, no. 3 and notes, p. 249; Avi-Yonah, pp. 42-44).

C. Pottery. Natural Palestinian clays contain varying amounts of iron, giving colors ranging from reddish brown to tan. These colors are minimized or intensified by the firing process. While glazing was not developed, but was known from imported pots, burnishing was used. Decoration with color by slip, banding, or wash was employed, but these were more widely used at some periods than others. Palestinian local wares were most highly decorated and colorful in the Late Bronze period (*ca.* 1500-1200 B.C.); the colors generally used were buff, cream, gray, red, brown, and dark brown together with combinations such as brown with gray or green; red with black, pink, or yellow; black with pink, gray, or red; green with buff or brown; yellow with red, gray, or white. Blue and purple shades were rare. Such colors and combinations of colors were more or less typical of pottery decoration throughout the history of Palestine in Bible times.

In the NT period "pompeian red" *siglata* ware was imported. Imported pottery was also seen in OT Palestine. Especially striking were Philistine types with horizontal bands, geometric designs, metopes, and pictures in black line drawing on white or buff backgrounds, highlighted with color, especially reddish purple. Imported pottery (except Egyptian) was more elaborate, colorful, and of higher quality than the local ware. From earliest Israelite times pottery was known from Greece, Cyprus, Phoenicia, and Crete in forms characteristic of these lands. Hellenistic decorated ware used varying shades of black, brown, or red in glazes, paints, slips, and washes.

D. Wall Painting. Except for slight evidence in early levels at Megiddo and Jericho, archeologists have not discovered much evidence of wall painting in OT Palestine. In Neolithic Teleilât el-Ghassûl (*ca.* 3500 B.C.) geometric patterns and pictures, such as an eight-ray star and a realistically drawn bird, appear with the colors red, yellow, black, white, and dark red. The Hellenistic tombs of Marisa (3rd cent. B.C.) had wall designs and pictures of wildlife in extraordinarily bright colors, as well as the sort of painted "imitation marble" to be seen in Herod's palace at Masada (1st cent. A.D.). The walls of Herod's palace at NT Jericho and the palace at Khirbet al Majar (8th cent. A.D.) were decorated with carved and painted stucco. The walls of the Dura Europos synagogue (built A.D. 250) were covered with richly painted scenes of OT history and include also painted "imitation marble." Note the "ivory" palace of Ahab (1 K. 22:39) and the palace of Jehoiakim, known for extensive use of vermilion paint (Jer. 22:14); Ezekiel's references to the animals and idols painted (?) on the walls of a secret place in the temple (8:10) and to a Chaldean bas-relief "portrayed in vermilion" (23:14); the Babylonian "red" shields borne by soldiers "clothed in scarlet" (Nah. 2:3). Such an accumulation of evidence goes far to suggest that Israelites were familiar with the techniques of alfresco painting with colors.

E. Cosmetics. "Adorning" herself, Jezebel "painted her eyes" (2 K. 9:30). Other references (Jer. 4:30; Ezk. 23:40) are to prostitutes who "beautify" themselves by outlining the eyes with black galena or stibnite to make them appear larger. Egyptian women customarily used black above the eye and green (occasionally yellow and more rarely red) below. Red ochre was used to decorate lips, cheeks, palms, fingernails, soles of the feet, and hair. The OT shows no trace of the magical and superstitious significance of cosmetics which appears to have been commonly accepted in Egypt and Mesopotamia.

IV. Colors in Symbolism.–Color terms have general symbolic significance: white for purity (Mk. 1:6) and joy (Eccl. 9:8); black for decay (Job 30:30) and judgment (Mic. 3:6); red (not frequent) for life-blood (2 K. 3:22f.), and also for sins (Isa. 1:18); blue, the sky-color, frequently used with white or purple in contexts of royalty, but more often (by association with the tabernacle, temple fabrics, and sacred tassels) considered the "Yahweh" color (Nu. 15:38; Ps. 11:4); red-purple for luxury and elegance (Jgs. 8:26; Est. 8:15; Lk. 16:19).

In apocalyptic symbolism, color terms are adopted, adapted, and sometimes altered. Thus the symbolism in apocalyptic writings: white for conquest or victory, either temporary or eternal (Dnl. 7:9; Zec. 6:3; Rev. 1:14; 7:13f.); black for scarcity of food, or famine (Zec. 6:6; Rev. 6:5); red for slaughter in strife, usually of war (Zec. 6:2; Rev. 6:4); "pale," or literally "greenish-gray" (the color of a corpse), for death (Rev. 6:8) (cf. "dappled gray," Zec. 6:3, 6); purple for royalty, or often for pretended royalty (Dnl. 5:7; in Rev. 17:14; 18:12, 16 joined with scarlet); rainbow, as total color, for omnipotence (Rev. 4:3; 10:1).

V. Color Terms Most Widely Used.–In Hebrew, "a language of the senses" (G. A. Smith), color terms are not abstractions but distinctions of shade by visual association with concrete sense perceptions. Thus, OT people did not think, "the color of blood is red," but, "red is the color seen in blood" (cf. 2 K. 3:22); not, "the color of vegetation is green," but, "green is the color seen in vegetation" (cf. Ps. 23:2; Jer. 11:16). As was usual in the languages of the ancient world, the Hebrew color vocabulary was simple and undeveloped. An added factor for Hebrew was the religious prohibition against image-making (Ex. 20:4; Dt. 5:8), which was understood to include the painting of pictures. With this understanding, certain observations can be made regarding the most widely used color terms:

A. Black. Different words have been translated "black," with various meanings such as "dusky," "swarthy," "dark." "Black" is applied to hair (Lev. 13:31; Cant. 5:11; Mt. 5:36), to mourning (Job 30:28, 30; Jer. 14:2), to horses (Zec. 6:2, 6; Rev. 6:5), to the heavens (1 K. 18:45; Job 3:5; Prov. 7:9; Jer. 4:28; Mic. 3:6), to the sun (Rev. 6:12), to the skin (Cant. 1:5f.), to flocks (Gen. 30:32ff., AV "brown").

B. Blue. Heb. *t^e^ḵēleṯ* is applied only to fabrics dyed with a special blue dye obtained from a shellfish, frequently in association with purple. "Blue" is applied to fringes, the veil, vestments, and embroideries in the descriptions of the tabernacle (Ex. 25; Nu. 4:6; 15:38); also to workers in blue (2 Ch. 2:7, 14; 3:14), palace adornments (Est. 1:6), and royal apparel (Est. 8:15; Jer. 10:9; Ezk. 23:6; 27:7, 24).

C. Crimson. Three words are translated "crimson": Heb. *šānî*, the dye (2 S. 1:14; Jer. 4:30); *tôlā'*, cloth dyed with *šānî* (Lev. 14:4; Isa. 1:18); and *karmîl*, a late synonym for *tôlā'* (2 Ch. 2:7, 14; 3:14). "Crimson" is applied to clothing (2 S. 1:24; Lev. 14:4), also to sins (Isa. 1:18).

D. Gray. The Heb. *śêḇ* means "be old," and hence refers to the color of the hair in old age (Gen. 42:38; 44:29, 31; Dt. 32:25; 1 S. 12:2; Job 15:10; Ps. 71:18; Prov. 20:29; Isa. 46:4; Hos. 7:9). *Śêḇ* is rendered "hoar" or "hoary" applying to hair in Lev. 19:32; Job 41:32; Prov. 16:31 (AV also in 1 K. 2:6, 9; Isa. 46:4). The RSV renders "dappled gray" for the difficult Heb. *b^e^ruddîm 'ᵃmuṣṣîm* (AV "grisled and bay") in Zec. 6:3.

E. Green. This word refers almost without exception to vegetation. The Heb. *yārāq*, literally "pale," is considered one of the three definite color words used in the OT (the others being red and white). The Greek equivalent is *chlōrós*. *Yārāq* occurs in Gen. 1:30; 9:3; Ex. 10:15; Ps. 37:2; Job 39:8, and *chlōrós* in Mk. 6:39; Rev. 8:7; 9:4. Heb. *ra'ănān,* closely allied in meaning to *yārāq,* is used to describe the color of trees in Dt. 12:2; Ex. 10:15; 1 K. 14:23; 2 K. 16:24; 17:10; 2 Ch. 28:4; Job 15:32; Ps. 52:8; etc. Elsewhere the Hebrew equivalents denote the condition of being full of sap, fresh, or unripe, as in Jgs. 16:7f.; Ps. 92:14; Ezk. 17:24; 20:47; Lk. 23:31. "Greenish" is used to describe leprous spots (Lev. 13:49; 14:37) and gold in Ps. 68:13 (RSV "green"; AV, NEB, "yellow").

F. Purple. The Heb. *'argāmān* is a loanword; the Greek word is *porphýreos*. The latter word refers to the source of the dye, a shellfish found on the shores of the Mediterranean. This color, which varied widely according to the kind of shellfish used and the method of dyeing, was utilized in the adornment of the tabernacle (Ex. 25–27; Nu. 4:13). There were workers in purple called to help in beautifying the temple (2 Ch. 2:7, 14; 3:14). Purple was much used for royal garments and furnishings (Jgs. 8:26; Est. 1:6; 8:15; Cant. 3:10; 7:5; Dnl. 5:7, 16, 29; Mk. 15:17, 20; Jn. 19:2, 5); it was typical of gorgeous apparel (Prov. 31:22; Jer. 10:9; Ezk. 23:6; 27:7, 16; Lam. 4:5; Mk. 15:17, 20; Lk. 16:19; Jn. 19:2, 5; Acts 16:14; Rev. 17:4; 18:12, 16).

G. Red. The Heb. *'āḏōm* is from *dām,* "blood," and hence it means "bloodlike." One of the three distinct color words mentioned in the OT, it is used in most of the references to red. *Ḥaḵlîlî* probably means "fiery" (Gen. 49:12; Prov. 23:29), and Gk. *pyrrós* means "fire-colored" (Mt. 16:2f.; Rev. 6:4; 12:3). "Red" is applied to dyed skins (Ex. 25:5; 26:24; 35:7, 23; 36:19; 39:34), to the color of animals (Nu. 19:2; Zec. 1:8; 6:2; Rev. 6:4; 12:3), to the human skin (as "ruddy" in Gen. 25:25; 1 S. 16:12; 17:42; Cant. 5:10; Lam. 4:7), to the eyes (Gen. 49:12; Job 16:16; Prov. 23:29), to sores (Lev. 13), to wine (Prov. 23:31), to water (2 K. 3:22), to pottage (Gen. 25:30), to apparel (Isa. 63:2; Rev. 9:17), to the sky (Mt. 16:2f.), to sins (Isa. 1:18), to shields (Nah. 2:3) (*see also* RED SEA).

H. Scarlet. Scarlet and crimson colors were probably from the same source. Heb. *tôlā'* and derivatives have been translated by both "scarlet" and "crimson" (Gk. *kókkinos*). "Scarlet" is applied to fabrics or yarns used (1) in the equipment of the tabernacle (Ex. 2:5ff.; Nu. 4:8); (2) in rites in cleansing lepers (Lev. 14); (3) in the ceremony of purification (Nu. 19:6); (4) in association with royal or gorgeous apparel (2 S. 1:24; Prov. 31:21; Lam. 4:5; Jer. 4:30; Nah. 2:3; Mt. 27:28; Rev. 17:4; 18:12, 16); (5) for marking-thread (Gen. 38:28, 30; Josh. 2:18, 21). It is also used of lips (Cant. 4:3), sins (Isa. 1:18), beasts (Rev. 17:3), and wool (He. 9:19).

I. White. The principal word for whiteness in Hebrew is *lāḇān,* a distinctive color word, associated with the color of snow (Isa. 1:18), milk (Gen. 49:12), wool (Ezk. 27:18; Rev. 1:14), and general cleanness (Eccl. 9:8; Dnl. 11:35; 12:10). "White" is applied to goats (Gen. 30:35), teeth (Gen. 49:12), leprous hairs and spots (Lev. 13; Nu. 12:10), garments (Eccl. 9:8; Isa. 19:9; Dnl. 7:9), horses (Zec. 1:8; 6:3, 6), tree branches (Gen. 30:37; Joel 1:7), coriander seed (Ex. 16:31). The corresponding Greek word *leukós* is applied to hair (Mt. 5:36; Rev. 1:14), to raiment (Mt. 17:2; 28:3; Mk. 9:3; 16:5; Lk. 9:29; Jn. 20:12; Acts 1:10; Rev. 3:4f., 18; 4:4; 6:11; 7:9, 13f.; 19:14), a harvest (Jn. 4:35), horses (Rev. 6:2; 19:11, 14), a throne (20:11), a stone (2:17), a cloud (14:14). Besides *lāḇān,* three other Hebrew words have been translated "white": (1) *ḥōrî* or *ḥûr,* meaning "bleached," as of flour (Gen. 40:16), linen (Est. 1:6; 8:15; Isa. 19:9), or a human face (Isa. 29:22, RSV "pale"); (2) *ṣaḥ* or *ṣāḥōr,* literally "whiteness," is applied to yellowish-red asses, translated "tawny" (Jgs. 5:10), to human appearance, translated "radiant" (RSV Cant. 5:10), to wool (Ezk. 27:18); (3) *dar,* occurring only in Est. 1:6, is used of a pearl-like stone floor.

J. Others. Less widely used terms include "yellow," Heb. *ṣāhōḇ,* used of leprous hair in Lev. 13; and "vermilion," Heb. *šāšar,* a deep red paint, probably an oxide of iron (Jer. 22:14; Ezk. 23:14).

See also Plate 9.

Bibliography.–R. Amiran, *Ancient Pottery of the Holy Land* (1970); M. Avi-Yonah, *History of the Holy Land* (1969); J. Bright, *Jeremiah* (*AB,* 1965); G. Contenau, *Everyday Life in Babylonia and Assyria* (1954); R. J. Forbes, *Studies in Ancient Technology* (1964), III, 205-231; H. Frankfort, *Art and Architecture of the Ancient Orient* (1959); A. Guillaume, in I. Meyerson, ed., *Problèmes de la couleur* (1957), pp. 339-348; H. Janssen, *Annuaire de l'Institut de Philologie et d'Histoire Orientales et Slaves,* 14 (1954-1957), 145-171; J. P. Love, *Layman's Bible Comm.,* XXV (1960); A. Lucas, *Ancient Egyptian Materials and Industries* (4th rev. ed. 1962), pp. 172-77; A. Mekhitarian, *Egyptian Painting* (1954); *ANET,* p. 164; C. Singer, *et al., History of Technology,* I (1954), 238-250; IV (1958), 139-143; *WBA,* pp. 190-94.

P. L. GARBER

COLOSSAE kə-los'ē [Gk. *Kolossai*] (Col. 1:2); AV COLOSSE. A city of Phrygia on the Lycus River, one of the branches of the Maeander, and 3 mi. (5 km.) from Honaz Dağ (Mt. Cadmus), 8435 ft. (2570 m.) high. It stood at the head of a gorge where the two streams unite, and on the great highway traversing the country from Ephesus to the Euphrates Valley, 13 mi. (21 km.) from Hierapolis and 12 mi. (19 km.) from Laodicea. Its history is chiefly associated with that of these two cities.

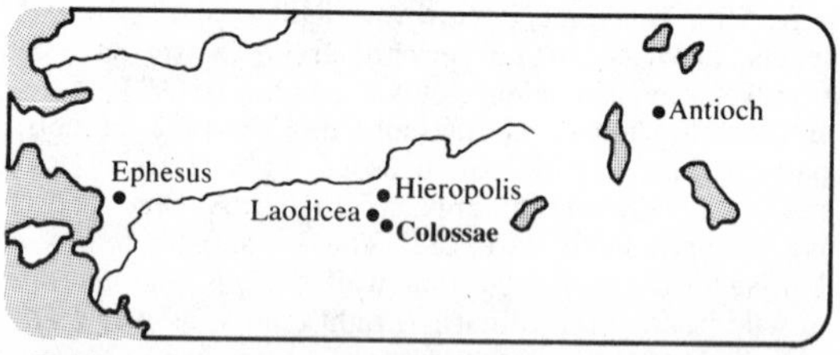

Early, according to both Herodotus and Xenophon, Colossae was a place of great importance. There Xerxes stopped 481 B.C. (Herodotus vii.30) and Cyrus the Younger marched 401 B.C. (Xenophon *Anabasis* i.2.6). From Col. 2:1 it appears unlikely that Paul visited there in person, but its Christianization was due to the efforts of Epaphras and Timothy (1:1, 7); it was the home of Philemon and Epaphras. That a church was established there early is evident from 4:12f.; Rev. 1:11; 3:14. As the neighboring cities Hierapolis and Laodicea increased in importance, Colossae declined. There were many Jews living there, and a chief article of commerce, for which the place was renowned, was the *colossinus,* a peculiar wool, probably of a purple color. In religion the people were especially lax, worshiping angels (cf. Col. 2:18). Of them Michael was the chief, and the protecting saint of the city. It is said that he once appeared to the people, saving the city in time of a flood.

During the 7th and 8th cents. the place was overrun by the Saracens; in the 12th cent. the church was destroyed by the Turks and the city disappeared. The hollow cavity and a few stones of a large theater, fragments of columns and traces of a hall, and a necropolis with stones of a peculiar shape are still to be seen. The site is 3 mi. (5 km.) NW of the modern Honaz, about 0.5 mi. (1 km.) from the modern road from Denizli to Eskişehir.

Bibliography.–*CBP*, pp. 208-213; *RRAM*, pp. 126f., 985f.

E. J. BANKS

Site of ancient Colossae. Originally at a junction of the main route from Ephesus to the Euphrates, the city lost its commercial role to Laodicea when the road to Pergamum was moved to the west. (W. S. LaSor)

COLOSSIANS, EPISTLE TO THE kə-losh'ənz. One of three or four letters that were written by Paul around the same time and sent to various churches in the Roman province of Asia by his friends Tychicus and Onesimus. The others were the Epistles to the Ephesians and to Philemon, and perhaps the enigmatic "epistle from Laodicea" mentioned in Col. 4:16.

I. Date and Occasion
II. The Colossian Heresy
III. Paul's Reply
IV. Ethical Injunctions
V. Authenticity
VI. Analysis

I. Date and Occasion.–When Paul wrote these letters he was a prisoner (they belong, that is to say, to his "Captivity Epistles"; *see* PHILEMON, EPISTLE TO). While arguments have been advanced for the view that they were written from Caesarea (so E. Lohmeyer) or Ephesus (G. S. Duncan), it is more probable that they were written from Rome during the two years Paul spent in custody there (*ca.* A.D. 60-62; cf. Acts 28:30).

The theology of Colossians and Ephesians suggests a later date for these Epistles than for Paul's other letters to churches. In particular, his presentation of the Church as the body of Christ in Colossians and Ephesians marks a later and more advanced stage of his thought on this subject than the stage represented by 1 Corinthians (*ca.* A.D. 55) and Romans (*ca.* A.D. 57). It is only in Colossians and Ephesians that the idea emerges of Christ as the head of the body. In 1 Cor. 12:12ff., where the common life of Christians is first compared to the interdependence of the various parts of the body, the head is one "member" among others; a member of the Church may be thought of as the head or as part of the head. This becomes impossible with the more advanced conception found in Colossians and Ephesians—a conception that may well reflect Paul's vigorous reaction to news reaching him from Colossae.

Some years previously (*ca.* A.D. 52-55), from his headquarters in Ephesus, Paul and his colleagues had evangelized the province of Asia (Acts 19:10). The valley of the river Lycus, in which Colossae lay (with the neighboring cities of Laodicea and Hierapolis mentioned in Col 4:13), was one of the districts evangelized at that time — not, it appears, by Paul in person, but by his lieutenant Epaphras. This Epaphras had paid Paul a visit in Rome and told him of the state of the churches in the Lycus Valley. Much of his news was encouraging, but there was one disquieting feature: at Colossae Christians were strongly inclined to accept an attractive line of teaching calculated (although they did not suspect it) to subvert the pure gospel that they had believed and to bring them into spiritual bondage.

II. The Colossian Heresy.–We have no formal exposition of the "Colossian heresy"; its features have to be inferred from Paul's references to it in the course of the Epistle and from the particular aspects of Christian truth he emphasizes in order to provide his readers with an antidote against it.

Basically the heresy was Jewish. This seems obvious from the part played in it by legal ordinances, circumcision, food regulations, the sabbath, new moon, and other prescriptions of the Jewish calendar.

But it was not the same as the straightforward form of Judaism against which the churches of Galatia had to be put on their guard at an earlier date — a form probably introduced to the Galatian churches by emissaries from Judea. This was rather a development of Phrygian Judaism, which had undergone a fusion with a philosophy of non-Jewish origin — an early and simple form of Gnosticism.

When the gospel was introduced to the area, a Jewish-Hellenistic syncretism evidently found no great difficulty in expanding and modifying itself sufficiently to take some Christian elements into its system; and we may reconstruct the resultant Colossian heresy with fair accuracy from Paul's treatment of it.

In this teaching a decisive place was accorded to the angelic beings through whom the law was given. They were not only elemental spirits but dominant ones as well — principalities and powers, lords of the planetary spheres, sharers in the plenitude of the divine essence. Since they controlled the lines of communication between God and man, all revelation from God to man and all prayer and worship from man to God could reach its goal only through their mediation and by their permission. It was therefore thought wise to cultivate their good will and pay them such homage as they desired.

Moreover, since they were the agents through whom the divine law was given, keeping the law was regarded as a tribute of obedience to them, and breaking the law incurred their displeasure and brought the lawbreaker into debt and bondage to them. Hence they must be placated, not only by the regular legal observances of traditional Judaism, but by a rigorous asceticism.

All this made an undoubted appeal to a certain religious temperament, the more so as it was presented as a form of advanced teaching for the spiritual elite. Christians were urged to pursue this progressive "wisdom" (Gk. *sophía*) and "knowledge" (*gnṓsis*), to explore the hidden mysteries by a series of successive initiations until they attained perfection (*teleíōsis*). Christian baptism was only a preliminary initiation; if they would proceed farther along the path of truth, they must put off all material elements by pursuing an ascetic regimen until at last they found themselves transported from the material to the spiritual world, from the domain of darkness to the realm of light. This was the true redemption at which they ought to aim.

If we may judge by the analogy of parallel systems, Christ was probably held to have relinquished successive portions of His power to the planetary lords as He passed through their spheres, one after the other, on His way to earth. But certainly His death was believed to prove His inferiority to them, since it was they who made Him suffer. And by the same token His servant Paul, who had to endure so many afflictions in his apostolic ministry, clearly had not attained to that degree of insight into the powers of the world and of control over them which would have enabled him to avoid these sufferings.

III. Paul's Reply.–Paul's answer to this "tradition of men" is to set against it the one trustworthy tradition, the true doctrine of Christ. Christ, he says, is the very image of God, the One who embodies the plenitude of the divine essence, in which these elemental spirits have no share at all. And those who are members of Christ realize their fulness in Him; they need not seek, and they cannot find, perfection anywhere else. It is in Christ that all wisdom and knowledge are concentrated and made available to His people — not just to an elite, but to all. Christ is the one Mediator between God and man, not in the sense of one who occupies the lines of communication between them and can transmit messages passing from one side to the other, but in the sense that He combines Godhead and manhood in His single person and so brings God and man together. Christ is the one through whom and for whom all things are created, including the principalities and powers to which the Colossians were being tempted to pay tribute. But why should those who are united with the Creator of these principalities and powers think it necessary to appease them? Above all, Christ by His death is revealed as the conqueror of these principalities and powers. On the cross He fought and won the decisive battle against them. Not only did He repel their attack upon Himself and turn the cross into His triumphal chariot before which they were driven as His vanquished foes, but by that victory He liberated His people also from their power. Why then should those who through faith-union with Christ had shared His death and resurrection go on serving those beings whom He had so completely conquered? Far from being a form of advanced wisdom, this false system that they were being urged to accept, with its taboos, bore all the marks of immaturity.

Thus, in his reply to the Colossian heresy Paul develops the doctrine of the cosmic Christ more fully than he had in his earlier extant Epistles. The doctrine was not new, indeed (cf. Rom. 8:19-22; 1 Cor. 1:24; 2:6-10; 8:6); but what was hinted at here and there in some of Paul's earlier Epistles is expounded more fully in Colossians.

IV. Ethical Injunctions.–As in most of Paul's Epistles, the doctrinal part is followed by a practical part, the two being linked together logically by the conjunction *oún*, "therefore" (Col. 3:5). Because that is the doctrine, he says in effect, this is how you should live (cf. Rom. 12:1; Eph. 4:1).

The practical injunctions of Col. 3:5–4:6 are arranged according to what appears to have been a well-established catechetical method in primitive Christianity; they may be subdivided under the headings: "Put off" (3:5-11), "Put on" (3:12-17), "Be subject" (3:18–4:1), "Watch and pray" (4:2-6). The third of these, "Be subject," takes the form of directions about the mutual duties of members of a Christian household.

V. Authenticity.–The arguments that have been used against the authenticity of Colossians cannot stand up to serious examination. Some of them depend on an unwarranted restriction of "Paulinism" to the themes treated in Galatians and Romans. The type of heresy the Epistle attacks is not the developed Gnosticism that we meet in the 2nd cent., but an incipient Gnosticism such as was prone to emerge in the 1st cent. and even earlier in areas where the Judaism of the Dispersion was influenced by dominant trends of Hellenistic and oriental thought. If Paul uses terms here in a rather different sense from what they mean in his earlier Epistles, we need not be surprised; the sense he gives to a number of technical terms in Colossians may well be due to the sense in which they were employed by the heretical teachers. Some parts of Col. 1:9-23 have been singled out as especially un-Pauline in character; but in part of this section (vv. 12-17) we probably have echoes of a primitive Christian confession of faith.

The mediating theory (propounded in varying forms by H. J. Holtzmann and C. Masson), that Paul wrote a shorter letter to Colossae which some later hand expanded by the incorporation of sections from Ephesians, is condemned by its own complexity. The literary relationship of the two Epistles presents a real problem, but the solution does not lie in this direction. Most probably Paul, having completed his letter to Colossae, continued to contemplate the cosmic reconciliation effected by Christ until he was gripped by the vision that finds expression in Ephesians, and began to dictate its contents as his testament to the Asian churches in an exalted mood of inspired meditation, thanksgiving, and prayer.

Both letters (with the companion Epistle to Philemon) are present in the Pauline corpus as far back as we can trace the existence of this collection (at least as early as Marcion, *ca.* A.D. 140), and are acknowledged as canonical by our earliest witnesses to the NT canon.

VI. Analysis.

A. Salutation (1:1f.).
B. The Person and Work of Christ (1:3–2:7).
C. False Teaching and Its Antidote (2:8–3:4).
D. The Christian Life (3:5–4:6).
E. Personal Notes and Final Greeting (4:7-18).

Bibliography.–Comms. by T. K. Abbott (*ICC*, 1897); F. W. Beare (*IB*); F. F. Bruce (*NIC*, 1957); M. Dibelius (*HNT*, 1953); W. Hendriksen (1964); J. B. Lightfoot (1875); E. Lohmeyer (*KEK*, 1957); E. Lohse (*KEK*, 1968; Eng. tr., *Hermeneia*, 1971); R. P. Martin (*New Century Bible*, 1974); C. Masson (*Comm. du NT*, 1950); C. F. D. Moule (*CGT*, 1957); H. C. G. Moule (*CBSC*, 1893); A. S. Peake (*Expos.G.T.*, 1903); E. F. Scott (*MNTC*, 1930).

C. H. Dodd, *NT Studies* (1953); G. S. Duncan, *St. Paul's Ephesian Ministry* (1929); H. J. Holtzmann, *Kritik der Epheser- und Kolosserbriefe* (1878); M. D. Hooker in B. Lindars and S. S. Smalley, eds., *Christ and Spirit in the NT* (1973), pp. 315-331; J. Lähnemann, *Der Kolosserbrief* (1971); R. P. Martin, *Colossians: The Church's Lord and the Christian's Liberty* (1972); H. C. G. Moule, *Colossian Studies* (1898); E. Percy, *Die Probleme der Kolosser- und Epheserbriefe* (1946); A. T. Robertson, *Paul and the Intellectuals* (1926).

F. F. BRUCE

COLT; FOAL [Heb. *'ayir, bēn*; Gk. *pṓlos, huiós*]; NEB also YOUNG (Gen. 32:15; Zec. 9:9); The AV has "ass colt" for *'ayir* in Jgs. 10:4; 12:14 (RSV and NEB "ass"); cf. also Isa. 30:6, 24; Jn. 12:14. Since horses are seldom mentioned in the Bible, only in connection with royal equipages and armies, "colt" does not occur in its ordinary English sense. "Colt" and "foal" refer to the young of the ass everywhere in the English versions except Gen. 32:15, where "colt" is used in the AV and RSV of the camel. In most cases *'ayir* (cf. Arab. *'air*, "ass") alone means "ass's colt," but it may be joined with *bēn*, "son," as in Zec. 9:9, *'al-ḥᵃmôr wᵉ'al-'ayir ben-'ᵃṯōnôṯ*, lit. "on an ass, and on an ass's colt, the son of the she-asses"; cf. Mt. 21:5: *epí ónon kaí epí pṓlon huión hypozygíou*, "upon an ass, and upon a colt the foal of an ass." Matthew evidently understands the Hebraism literally, and mentions two animals in his story, whereas Zec. 9:9 has in mind only one; cf. Mk. 11:2ff.; Lk. 19:30ff.

The quotation in Jn. 12:15 has Gk. *epí pṓlon ónou*, while v. 14 has the diminutive *onárion*. The commonest NT word for "colt" is Gk. *pṓlos*, which is akin to Ger. *Fahle* and Eng. "foal" and "filly" (cf. Lat. *pullus*, meaning either "foal" or "chicken").

A. E. DAY J. W. D. H.

COLUMN [Heb. *'ammûḏ*] (Cant. 5:15). From the 2nd millennium B.C. onward, columns of wood or stone were used to support upper stories or balconies of Palestinian houses. The upper story of Solomon's "House of the Forest of Lebanon," e.g., rested on rows of columns. In his temple, the two bronze pillars at the entrance may have been free-standing (1 K. 7:15-22; *see* JACHIN AND BOAZ).

COLUMN (of writing) [Heb. *deleṯ*–'door'] (Jer. 36:23). Normally in OT and NT times a book consisted of a scroll inscribed in columns called "doors" because of their appearance on the roll.

COMBAT COMMANDERS [Heb. *śārê milḥāmôṯ*] (2 Ch. 32:6); AV CAPTAINS OF WAR; NEB MILITARY COMMANDERS. Men who led the people in battle, usually the heads of families or clans. Professional *śarîm*, however, also formed a permanent officer corps (2 K. 24:12, 14; Jer. 52:10; 2 Ch. 20:11). In the time of Saul and David, the king was the supreme and active commander even though one of the generals took command. The army units of thousands, hundreds, fifties, and tens harked back to nomadic days (Ex. 18:21; Dt. 1:15).

COMELY [Heb. *šeper*] (Gen. 49:21); AV GOODLY; NEB LOVELY; [*yāpeh*] (1 S. 17:42); AV FAIR; NEB BRIGHT; [*nā'weh* (Cant. 1:5, 10; 2:14; 6:4), *nāweh* (Jer. 6:2)]; NEB LOVELY; **COMELINESS** [*hāḏār*] (Isa. 53:2); NEB MAJESTY.

The connotations of the Hebrew terms are: attractive, beautiful, lovely, handsome. *Yāpeh* ("handsome") is also applied to David in 1 S. 16:12. Isa. 53:2 has been taken literally of Christ's physical appearance, but it is more likely that it refers to His whole life-style, including His most unattractive death.

The AV sometimes employs "comely" in the obsolete sense of "fitting" or "suitable," as in Ps. 33:1; 147:1; Eccl. 5:18.

J. T. DENNISON, JR.

COMFORT; CONSOLATION [Heb. *nāḥam, nᵉḥāmâ, tanḥûmôṯ, tanḥûmîm, taḥᵃnûmîm* (Jer. 3:19), *bālag* (Job 10:20); Gk. *parakaléō, paráklēsis, paramythéomai, paramythía* (1 Cor. 14:3), *parēgoría* (Col. 4:11)]; AV also SUPPLICATIONS (Jer. 31:9); NEB also CONDOLE, CONDOLENCES, ENCOURAGE (1 Cor. 14:3), RELIEF (Job 6:10), RESTORATION (Lk. 2:25), "time of happiness" (6:24), "be happy" (Job 10:20), "ease (one's) mind" (Ruth 2:13), etc. (cf. Gen. 38:12). The AV "be of good comfort" for Gk. *tharséo* (Mt. 9:22 par.) is in the RSV "take heart" (cf. Phil. 2:19, *eupsychéō*, RSV "be cheered").

An Arabic cognate of Heb. *nāḥam* refers to the heavy breathing of a horse; in its reflexive and passive forms *nāḥam* has the basic meaning "ease oneself," "find relief." An interesting occurrence is Gen. 27:42, where Esau, it is said, "comforts himself" by planning vengeance on Jacob, i.e., his plot against Jacob is the means of venting his anger. In the intensive (piel) form, *nāḥam* means "comfort" or "console," literally "give relief" or "help find release" for pent-up sorrow and emotion. The other OT words for "comfort" and "consolation" are all derived from *nāḥam*, except for *bālag* in Job 10:20 (AV, RSV), which means "brighten up" (cf. Ps. 39:14; Job 9:27; Am. 5:9).

The most important NT word is Gk. *parakaléō* (*paráklēsis*), literally "call by the side," thus "encourage" (RSV Eph. 6:22; Col. 4:8; 1 Thess. 2:11; 5:11), "exhort" (Acts 16:40; 1 Thess. 3:2), "console" (Mt. 2:18), and "comfort" (5:4; Lk. 16:25; Acts 10:12; 2 Cor. 1:4; etc.). The "consolation [*paráklēsis*] of Israel" in Lk. 2:25 is evidently a standardized expression among the Jews of this time, alluding to prophetic promises such as Isa. 40:1, and referring to the eschatological restoration of the kingdom of Israel (cf. NEB).

The other NT words are *paramythéomai*, "cheer up" (Jn. 11:19, 31; 1 Cor. 14:3; cf. 1 Thess. 2:11; 5:14, "encourage"), and *parēgoría* (Col. 4:11), "soothing comfort" (cf. Eng. "paregoric").

As with mourning customs, giving comfort or consolation is among Eastern peoples often much less inhibited and more demonstrative and vociferous than in the West.

The consoler becomes involved empathically in the sorrow or discomfort of the one needing comfort, and together they find release for the emotions.

See also ENCOURAGEMENT; EXHORT; INCENTIVE (Phil. 2:1); REFRESH; for "son of consolation" *see* BARNABAS.

J. W. D. H.

COMFORTABLY. An obsolete term used by the AV to render the Heb. *'al lēḇ,* "to the heart." The RSV renders "kindly" (2 S. 19:7), "encouragingly" (2 Ch. 30:22; 32:6), "tenderly" (Isa. 40:2; Hos. 2:14). The words *'al lēḇ* are also the ordinary Hebrew expression for wooing; e.g., Boaz spoke "to the heart" of Ruth (Ruth 2:13; AV "friendly"; RSV, NEB, "kindly"). The term has exceptional wealth of meaning in connection with God's message of grace and forgiveness to His redeemed people (cf. Isa. 40:2; Hos. 2:14). D. M. PRATT

COMFORTER (AV Jn. 14:16, 26; 15:26; 16:7). *See* ADVOCATE; COUNSELOR; PARACLETE.

COMFORTLESS (Jn. 14:18, AV). *See* DESOLATE.

COMING OF CHRIST. *See* PERSON OF CHRIST; PAROUSIA.

COMING, SECOND. *See* PAROUSIA; SECOND COMING.

COMMAND; COMMANDMENT [mainly Heb. *miṣwâ*; Gk. *entolḗ* (see below)]. A prescription or direction, usually from God; often a reference to the Decalogue.

I. Vocabulary.–The commonest OT word for "commandment" is *miṣwâ* (pl. *miṣwôṯ,* vb. *ṣāwâ*), usually considered just one of several synonyms for "law" (*tôrâ*), as also *mišpāṭ* (Zeph. 2:3; AV "judgment"; NEB "laws"), *piqqûḏîm* (Ps. 103:18), and in the AV *dāṯ* (Est. 3:14; 8:13) and *ḥōq* (Am. 2:4). Various attempts have been made, however, to show it was a technical term used specifically to denote the Decalogue (see M. G. Kyle, *Problem of the Pentateuch* [1920], Investigation I). According to this argument, *miṣwôṯ,* when used in connection with "judgments" and "statutes" as titles for groups of laws, refers always to the Decalogue (but cf. Gen. 26:5!), and is representative of the most fundamental kind of law, analogous to the Magna Carta of England or the Constitution of the United States.

Commandments are denoted in the OT also by *peh,* "mouth" (AV also "appointment," Nu. 4:27; 2 S. 13:32; "word," Nu. 4:45; 20:24; 22:18; Josh. 19:50; 22:9); by *dāḇār, ma'ᵃmār* (Est. 1:15; 9:32), *'imrâ,* and *'ōmer,* all "word," "thing spoken" (AV often "word"; cf. 1 K. 20:35; Ps. 68:11; 147:15; Jer. 35:14; etc.); by *qôl* (Jgs. 2:2, AV "voice"), and *ṣᵉḏāqâ* (Dt. 33:21; AV "justice"; NEB "what [the Lord] deemed right"); and by Aram. *ṭa'am* (Ezr. 6:14) and *millâ* (Dnl. 3:28, AV "word"). Note also Job 37:15, "lays his command upon them," Heb. *śûm* (AV "disposed").

In the NT the main word is Gk. *entolḗ*; Paul occasionally used also *epitagḗ* (NEB also "instructions," 1 Cor. 7:25; "order," 2 Cor. 8:8). The "cry of command" in 1 Thess. 4:16 translates *kéleusma* (AV "shout"). See *TDNT,* II, *s.v.* ἐντέλλομαι (Schrenk).

II. Developed NT Concept.–In the teaching of the Jewish rabbis there are 613 specific commandments (*miṣwôṯ*) in the Torah, reference to which may form the background for certain exchanges in the NT (e.g., Mt. 19:18; 22:36; Mk. 12:28). Jesus, although explicitly affirming the absolute authority of the OT law (Mt. 5:19), stressed the organic unity of the Commandments, reducing the "Ten" to two, and these to one principle, that of love (cf. Mt. 22:37-40; Mk. 12:29-31; Lk. 10:27; Rom. 13:8-10). It is this corrective, when set over against the tendency of Pharasaic Judaism toward an atomistic ethics, that gives Jesus' teaching its unique flavor. In the Fourth Gospel the "commandments" became first the commandment of the Father to the Son (Jn. 10:18; 12:49f.) and secondarily the very personal "my commandments" given by the Son to His followers (13:34; 14:15, 21; 15:10, 12). Throughout the Johannine Epistles we hear an echo of this same language in the expression "his commandments." Here, as in the Gospel of John, the first commandment is to love (1 Jn. 4:21; cf. Jn. 13:34); indeed, it is because the new life in Christ enkindles love that the life itself becomes the free expression of the commandments and of the nature of God, in which the commandments are grounded.

This emphasis on love as the fulfilling element of the law is not absent in Paul (Rom. 13:9f.), though elsewhere in the apostle's writings the "commandment" (i.e., the Mosaic law in its character as a hostile judge) is spoken of as a negative force (Rom. 7; Eph. 2:15). Nevertheless, both the law of the Decalogue and the commandments of the Lord (Jesus) are explicitly affirmed (Eph. 6:2; 1 Cor. 14:37), rendering fatuous any attempt to picture the great apostle as an antinomian.

See also TEN COMMANDMENTS. C. E. ARMERDING

COMMANDER [Heb. *śar, ḥōqeq* (Jgs. 5:9), *mᵉḥōqēq* (Jgs. 5:14), *peḥâ* (1 K. 20:24), *šālîš* (1 Ch. 11:11), *nagîḏ* (2 Ch. 28:7), *tartān* (Isa. 20:1), *mᵉṣawwēh* (Isa. 55:4), *sāgan* (Jer. 51:23, 57; Ezk. 23:6, 12, 23), *qāṣîn* (Dnl. 11:18); Aram. *bᵉ'ēl- ṭᵉ'ēm* (Ezr. 4:8f., 17)]; AV also (CHIEF) CAPTAIN, PRINCE, RULER, GOVERNOR, TARTAN (Isa. 20:1), etc.; NEB also CAPTAIN, OFFICER, COMMANDER-IN-CHIEF, MARSHAL (Jgs. 5:9, 14), INSTRUCTOR (Isa. 55:4), etc.

The terms rendered "commander" by the RSV are imprecise designations applied to military leaders of an army (1 K. 1:19) or of a unit of an army (1 S. 8:12); *see* COMBAT COMMANDERS. In nonmilitary contexts *śar* can refer to governors of towns (Jgs. 9:30), elders (8:14), heads of families (Ezr. 8:29), leaders in occupations (e.g., chief baker in Gen. 40:16), and civil officials such as the king's ministers (1 K. 4:2; Jer. 24:8) and district governors (1 K. 20:14). *See also* CHIEF. G. WYPER

COMMANDER IN CHIEF. In 1 Ch. 27:3, Jashobeam, who is in charge of the first of the king's monthly divisions of bodyguards, is said also to be "chief of all the commanders of the army for the first month," according to the RSV reading. This implies that each of the other monthly leaders held in turn the chief commander role. The NEB translates "chief officer of the temple staff," a less literal but also less grandiose reading.

On Isa. 20:1, *see* TARTAN.

COMMANDMENT, THE NEW [Gk. *entolḗ kainḗ*] (Jn. 13:34; 1 Jn. 2:7f.; 2 Jn. 5f.; cf. Jn. 15:12, etc.).

I. Christ and the Old Commandment.–In the OT the concept of "commandment" expresses the theocratic idea of morality wherein the will or law of God is imposed upon men as their law of conduct (2 K. 17:37). This idea is not repudiated in the NT, but supplemented or modified from within by making love the essence of the command. Jesus Christ, as reported in the Synoptics, came "not . . . to abolish the law and the prophets . . . but to fulfil them" (Mt. 5:17). He taught that "whoever then relaxes one of the least of these commandments and teaches men so, shall be called least in the kingdom of heaven" (5:19). He condemned the Pharisees for rejecting the commandments of God as given by Moses (Mk. 7:8-13). Thus, there is a sense in which Christ propounded no new commandment; but the new element in His teaching was the emphasis laid on the old commandment of love, and the extent and intent of its application. The great commandment is "You shall love the Lord your God . . . [and] your neighbor as yourself. On these two commandments depend all the law and the prophets" (Mt. 22:34-40; Mk. 12:28-34; cf. Dt. 6:5; Lev. 19:18).

II. The Law Internalized as Love.–When the law realizes itself in a person's heart as love for God and neighbor, it ceases to bear the aspect of a command. The force of authority and the subject's active resistance or inertia disappear; the law becomes a principle, a motive, a joyous harmony of the human will with the will of God; and in becoming internalized it becomes universal and transcends all distinctions of race or class. Even this was not an altogether new idea (cf. Jer. 31:31-34; Ps. 51); nor did Christ's contemporaries and disciples think it was. The revolutionary factor was the death of Christ wherein the love of God was exemplified and made manifest as the basis and principle of all spiritual life (Jn. 13:34). Paul therefore generalizes all pre-Christian morality as a system of law and commandments, standing in antithesis to the grace and love which are through Jesus Christ (Rom. 5–7).

Believers in Christ felt their experience and inward life to be so changed and new that it needed a special term (Gk. *agápē,* "love") to express their ideal of conduct (*see* LOVE III). Another change that grew upon the Christian consciousness, following from the resurrection and ascension of Christ, was the idea that He was the permanent source of the principle of life. This was summarized in the confession that "Jesus is Lord" (1 Cor. 12:3). Hence in the Johannine writings the principle described by the term *agápē* is associated with Christ's lordship and solemnly described as His "new commandment." "A new commandment I give to you, that you love one another; even as I have loved you, that you also love one another" (Jn. 13:34). To the Christians of the end of the 1st cent. it was already an old commandment which they had from the beginning of the Christian teaching (1 Jn. 2:7; 2 Jn. 5); but it was also a new commandment which ever came with new force to men who were passing from the darkness of hatred to the light of love (1 Jn. 2:8-11).

III. A New Revolution.–The term "new commandment" in the Gospel we may owe to the Evangelist, but it brings into relief an element in the consciousness of Jesus that the author of the Fourth Gospel had appreciated more fully than the Synoptists. Jesus was aware that He was the bearer of a special message from the Father (Jn. 12:49; Mt. 11:27), that He fulfilled His mission in His death of love and self-sacrifice (Jn. 10:18), and that the mission fulfilled gave Him authority over the lives of men, "even as I have loved you, that you also love one another." The full meaning of Christ's teaching was realized only when men had experienced and recognized the significance of His death as the cause and principle of right conduct. The Synoptists saw Christ's teaching as the development of the prophetic teaching of the OT. Paul and John felt that the love of God in Christ was a new thing: new as a revelation of God in Christ, new as a principle of life in the Church, and new as a union of believers with Christ. While it is love, it is also a commandment of Christ, calling forth the joyous obedience of believers.

See also BROTHERLY LOVE. T. REES

COMMANDMENTS, THE TEN. *See* COMMAND; TEN COMMANDMENTS.

COMMEND [Heb. *hālal* (Prov. 12:8), *šāḇaḥ* (Eccl. 8:15); Gk. *epainéō, épainos, synístēmi, synistánō, parístēmi* (1 Cor. 8:8), *paratíthēmi* (Acts 20:32), *paradídōmi* (14:26; 15:40)]; AV also PRAISE, APPROVE, RECOMMEND; NEB also APPLAUD (Lk. 16:8), PRAISE, "bring (us) into (God's) presence" (1 Cor. 8:8), "produce (our) credentials" (2 Cor. 3:1; cf. 12:11), RECOMMEND (4:2; 5:12; 6:4; 10:18), "put forward (their own) claims" (10:12). The usual meaning of the two Hebrew words and of Gk. *epainéō* (*épainos*) is "praise." The literal meaning of *synístēmi* is "stand with," as one stands with a friend to introduce or recommend him to others (Rom. 16:1). It can also be used reflexively, "commend oneself" (2 Cor. 3:1; 4:2; 6:4; 10:12).

In discussing the problem of eating food that had been offered to idols, Paul states: "Food will not commend us to God" (1 Cor. 8:8). But *parístēmi* here may be taken in its legal technical sense "bring before" (a judge), so that the statement means, "eating such food will not cause us to be brought to judgment before God." Or it may mean simply "bring before God," without necessarily the legal sense (cf. NEB; see Bauer, p. 633).

J. W. D. H.

COMMENTARIES.

I. General Scope
II. Differences in Character
III. Range
  A. Early Commentaries
    1. Origen and the Alexandrian School
    2. Chrysostom and the Antiochian School
  B. Scholastic Period
  C. Reformation and Post-Reformation Periods
    1. Luther and Calvin
    2. Beza, Grotius, etc.
    3. Later Writers
  D. 18th Century
    1. Calmet, M. Henry, etc.
    2. Patrick, Lowth, Scott
    3. Gill, Doddridge
    4. Bengel, Wettstein
  E. Modern Period
    1. Germany
      a. Liberal School
      b. Conservative School
    2. Britain and America
  F. Recent Period
    1. Germany
    2. Britain and America
    3. France

I. General Scope.–Etymologically, a commentary (from Lat. *commentor*) denotes jottings, annotations, memoranda, on a given subject or perhaps on a series of events; hence its use in the plural as a designation for a narrative or history, as the *Commentaries* of Caesar. In its application to Scripture the word designates a work devoted to the explanation, elucidation, illustration, sometimes the homiletic expansion and edifying utilization, of the text of some book or portion of Scripture. The primary function of a good comm. is to furnish an exact interpretation of the meaning of the passage under consideration; it should also show the connection of ideas, the steps of argument, and the scope and design of the whole, in the writing in question. This can be successfully accomplished only with a knowledge of the original language of the writing and of the historical setting of the particular passage; by careful study of the context and of the author's general usages of thought and speech; and by comparison of parallel or related texts. Aid may also be obtained from external sources, e.g., information concerning the history, archeology, topography, chronology, and manners and customs of the lands, peoples, and times referred to; or, as in A. Deissmann's discoveries, from the light thrown on peculiarities of language by papyri or other ancient remains (see Deiss.*LAE*).

II. Differences in Character.–It is obvious that comments will vary greatly in character in accordance with their purpose. Some are more *scholarly,* technical, and critical; these enter, e.g., into philological discussions, and tabulate and remark upon the various views held as to the meaning. Others are more *popular,* aiming only at bringing out the general sense and conveying it to the mind of the reader in attractive and edifying form. When the practical motive predominates and the treatment is greatly enlarged by illustration, application, and the enforcement of lessons, the work loses the character of comm. proper, and takes on more of the character of homily or discourse.

III. Range.–No book in the world has been made the subject of so much commenting and exposition as the Bible. Theological libraries are full of comms. of all descriptions and all grades of worth. Some are on the original Hebrew or Greek texts, some on the English or other versions. Modern comms. are usually accompanied with some measure of introduction to the books commented upon; the more learned works have commonly also some indication of the *data* for the determination of the textual readings (*see* CRITICISM I). Few writers are equal to the task of commenting with profit on the Bible as a whole, and with the growth of knowledge this task is now seldom attempted. Frequently, however, one writer contributes many valuable works, and sometimes by the cooperation of like-minded scholars, comms. on the whole Bible are produced. It is obvious that only a very slight survey can be taken in a brief article on the work of commenting and on the literature to which it has given rise; the attempt can be made only to follow the lines most helpful to those seeking aid from this class of books. On the use and abuse of comms. by the preacher, see C. H. Spurgeon's spicy remarks in his book *Commenting and Commentaries* (1876).

A. Early Commentaries. Rabbinical interpretations and paraphrases of the OT may here be left out of account (*see* COMMENTARIES, HEBREW; *also* TARGUM; TALMUD). Comms. on the NT could not begin until the NT books themselves were written and had acquired some degree of authority as sacred writings (*see* CANON OF THE NT). The earliest comms. we hear of are from the heretical circles of the Gnostics. Heracleon, a Valentinian (*ca.* A.D. 175), wrote a comm. on the Gospel of John (fragments in Origen) and on parts, at least, of the Gospel of Luke. Tatian, a disciple of Justin Martyr, compiled at about the same time his *Diatessaron,* or *Harmony of the Four Gospels,* on which, at a later time, comms. were written. Ephraem Syrus (4th cent.) wrote such a comm., of which an Armenian translation has now been recovered. The church father Hippolytus (beginning of the 3rd cent.) wrote several comms. on the OT (Exodus, Psalms, Proverbs, Ecclesiastes, Daniel, Zechariah, etc.), and on Matthew, Luke, and Revelation.

1. Origen and the Alexandrian School. The strongest impulse to the work of commenting and exposition of Holy Scripture, however, undoubtedly proceeded from the school of Alexandria — especially from Origen (A.D. 203-254). Clement, Origen's predecessor, had written a treatise called *Hypotypōseis,* or "Outlines," a survey of the contents of Holy Scripture. Origen himself wrote comms. on the books of the OT (Ruth, Esther, and Ecclesiastes alone excepted) and on most of the books of the NT (Mark, 1 and 2 Corinthians, 1 and 2 Peter, 1, 2, and 3 John, James, Jude, Revelation excepted). In addition he furnished *scholia,* or notes on difficult passages, and delivered homilies, or discourses, the records of which fill three folio volumes. "By his *Tetrapla* and *Hexapla,*" says Farrar, "he became the founder of all textual criticism; by his Homilies he fixed the type of a popular exposition; his *Scholia* were the earliest specimens of marginal explanations; his Commentaries furnished the Church with her first continuous exegesis" (*History of Interpretation* [1886], p. 188). Unfortunately the Alexandrian school adopted a principle of allegorical interpretation which led it frequently into the most extravagant fancies. Assuming a threefold sense in Scripture — literal, moral, and spiritual — it gave rein to caprice in foisting imaginary meanings on the simplest historical statements (Farrar, pp. 189ff.). Some of Origen's comms., however, are much freer from allegory than others, and all possess high value (cf. Lightfoot, *Galatians* [repr. 1957], p. 217). The later teachers of the Alexandrian school continued the exegetical work of Origen. Pamphilus of Caesarea, the friend of Eusebius, is said to have written OT commentaries.

2. Chrysostom and the Antiochian School. At the opposite pole from the allegorizing Alexandrian school of interpretation was the Antiochian, marked by a sober, literal, and grammatical style of exegesis. Its reputed founder was Lucian (martyred A.D. 312); but its real heads were Diodorus of Tarsus (d. *ca.* 394) and Theodore of Mopsuestia (d. *ca.* 428); and its most distinguished representative was John Chrysostom (b. *ca.* 347). Chrysostom wrote continuous comms. on Isaiah (only 1:1–8:10 extant) and on Galatians; but his chief contributions were his *Homilies,* covering almost the whole of the OT and NT. Of those over six hundred remain, chiefly on the NT. They are unequal in character, those on Acts being reputed the feeblest; others, as those on Matthew, Romans, and Corinthians, are splendid examples of expository teaching. Schaff speaks of Chrysostom as "the prince of commentators among the Fathers" (*History of the Christian Church,* II [repr. 1973], 816). Thomas Aquinas is reported to have said that he would rather possess Chrysostom's homilies on Matthew than be master of all Paris. In the West, Ambrose of Milan (*ca.* 339-397) wrote expositions of OT histories and of Luke (allegorical and typical), and Jerome (*ca.* 346-420) wrote numerous comms. on OT and NT books, largely, however, compilations from others.

B. Scholastic Period. The medieval and scholastic period offers little for our purpose. There was diligence in copying MSS and producing *catenae* of the opinions of the fathers; in the case of the schoolmen, in building up elaborate systems of theology; but the Scriptures were thrown into the background. Yet all was not darkness. Such pioneers as Hugo (*ca.* 1096-1141) and his pupil Andrew (d. 1175), an ardent Hebraist, possessed a large measure of exegetical sanity, and with their emphasis on the literal sense they anticipated to a remarkable degree modern approaches to biblical interpretation.

The 14th cent. produced one commentator of real eminence — Nicholas of Lyra (*ca.* 1270-1349). Nicholas was a Franciscan monk, well versed in Hebrew and rabbinical learning. While recognizing the usual distinctions of the various senses of Scripture, he built practically on the literal, and exhibited great sobriety and skill in his interpretations. His work, which bears the name

Postillae perpetuae in universa Biblia, was much esteemed by Luther, who acknowledged his indebtedness to it. Hence the jest of his opponents, *Si Lyra non lyrasset, Lutherus non saltasset*.

C. Reformation and Post-Reformation Periods. The Reformation brought men's minds back to the Scriptures and opened a new era in biblical exposition and commentary. It became the custom to expound the Scriptures on Sundays and weekdays in all the pulpits of the Protestant churches. Luther's custom was to preach series of sermons on the OT and NT. The Reformation began at Zürich with a series of discourses by Zwingli on the Gospel of Matthew. The same was true of Calvin, Beza, Knox, and all associated with them. The production of comms. or expository homilies was the result.

1. Luther and Calvin. Outstanding examples of comms. written in this period are Luther's *Comm. on Galatians* and the comms. of Calvin. Not all by any means, but very many of the comms. of Calvin were the fruit of pulpit prelections (e.g., the expositions of Job, the Minor Prophets, Jeremiah, Daniel). Others, such as the comms. on Romans and the Psalms (reputed his best), were prepared with great care. Calvin's supreme excellence as a commentator is disputed by no one. His expositions of Scripture display breadth, moderation, and fairness in exhibiting the inward genius of Holy Writ.

2. Beza, Grotius, etc. Lutheranism had its distinguished exegetes (Brenz, d. 1570), who wrote able comms. on the OT, and in both the Calvinistic and Arminian branches of the Reformed Church the production of comms. held a chief place. Beza, Calvin's successor, is acknowledged to have possessed many of the best exegetical qualities that characterized his master. Grotius, in Holland (d. 1645), occupied the foremost place among the expositors in that century on the Arminian side. His exegetical works, if not marked by much spirituality, shows sagacity and learning, and are enriched by parallels from classical literature. The school of Cocceius (d. 1669) developed the doctrine of the covenants, and revelled in typology. Cocceius wrote comms. on nearly all the books of Scripture. His pupil Vitringa (d. 1722) gained renown by his expositions of Isaiah and Revelation.

3. Later Writers. Partly fostered by the habit of basing commentary on pulpit exposition, the tendency to undue prolixity set in early, and spread. The comms. of Peter Martyr (Swiss Reformer, d. 1562) on Judges and Romans occupy a folio each; N. Byfield (Puritan, d. 1622) fills a folio on Colossians; Caryl (Independent, d. 1673) on Job extends to two folios; Durham (d. 1658) on Isa. 53 consists of seventy-two sermons; Venema (Holland, d. 1787) on Jeremiah fills two quartos, and on the Psalms no less than six quartos. These are only samples of a large class. H. Hammond's *Paraphrase and Annotations on the NT, from an Arminian Standpoint* also belongs to this period (1675). Another work that long took high rank is M. Poole's elaborate *Synopsis criticorum aliorumgue Sacrae Scripturae . . .* (5 vols., folio, 1669-1676) — a summary of the opinions of 150 biblical critics; with which must be taken his *English Annotations of the Holy Bible*, only completed up to Isa. 58 at the time of his death (1679). The work was continued by his friends.

D. 18th Century. 1. Calmet, M. Henry, etc. The 18th cent. is marked by greater sobriety in exegesis. It is prolific in comms., but only a few attain to high distinction. Calmet (d. 1757), a learned Benedictine, produced his *Comm. littéral sur tous les livres de l'Ancien et du Nouveau Testament*, in twenty-three quarto volumes — a work of immense erudition, though now superseded in its information. On the Protestant side, Matthew Henry's celebrated *Exposition of the Old and New Testament* (1708-1710) easily holds the first place among devotional comms. for its blending of good sense, original and felicitous remark, and genuine insight into the meaning of the sacred writers. It is, of course, not a critical work in the modern sense, and often is unduly diffuse. M. Henry's work extends only to the end of Acts; the remaining books were done by various writers after his death (1714). Le Clerc (d. 1736) may be named as precursor of the critical views now obtaining on the composition and authorship of the Pentateuch. His comms. began with Genesis in 1693 and were not completed till 1731. Other commentators of note with Arminian views were Daniel Whitby (d. 1726; converted to Arianism), and, later, Adam Clarke, a Wesleyan (1762-1832), whose work extended into the next century. Clarke's *Comm. on the Holy Scriptures* (1810-1826), still held by many in high esteem, is marred to some extent by eccentricities of opinion.

2. Patrick, Lowth, Scott. In the Anglican Church the names of chief distinction in this century are Bishop Patrick, Bishop Lowth, and later Thomas Scott. Patrick, usually classed with the Cambridge Platonists (d. 1707), contributed paraphrases and comms. on the OT from Genesis to Canticles, while Lowth (d. 1787) acquired lasting fame by his *Prelections on Hebrew Poetry*, and *A New Translation, with Notes on Isaiah*. He was among the first to treat the poetical and prophetic writings really as literature. The comms. of Patrick and Lowth were subsequently combined with those of Whitby and other divines (e.g., Arnold) to form a complete *Critical Comm*. (1809), which went through many editions. The well-known comm. of Thomas Scott (1747-1821), representing a moderate Calvinism, is a solid and "judicious" piece of work, inspired by an earnest, believing spirit, though not presenting any marked originality or brilliance. Brilliance is not the characteristic of many commentators of this age.

3. Gill, Doddridge. Two other English writers deserving notice are John Gill (d. 1771; Calvinistic Baptist), who wrote *Expositions on the OT and the NT* and a separate *Exposition of the Song of Solomon* — learned, but ponderous and controversial; and Philip Doddridge (d. 1751), whose *Family Expositor*, embracing the entire NT, with a harmony of the Gospels and paraphrases of the meaning, is marked by excellent judgment, and obtained wide acceptance.

4. Bengel, Wettstein. Meanwhile a new period had been preluded in Germany by the appearance in 1742 of the *Gnomon Novi Testamenti* of J. A. Bengel (d. 1752), a work following upon his critical edition of the NT issued in 1734. Though belonging to the 18th cent., Bengel's critical and expository labors really herald and anticipate the best work in these departments of the 19th century. His scholarship was exact, his judgment sound, his critical skill remarkable in a field in which he was a pioneer; his notes on the text, though brief, were pregnant with significance and were informed by a spirit of warm and living piety.

Bengel's fame is shared by Johann J. Wettstein, whose amazing collection of classical and rabbinic parallels, *Novum Testamentum Graecum* (2 vols., 1751-1752; repr. 1962), remains a treasure trove for commentators.

E. Modern Period. The modern period to which Bengel belongs in spirit, if not in date, is marked by great changes in the style and character of commentaries. The critical temper is now strong; great advances have been made in the textual criticism of both the OT and NT (*see* CRITICISM I); the work of the higher criticism had begun in the OT; in Germany the spirit of humanism, inherited from Lessing, Herder, and Goethe, had found its way into literature; knowledge of the sciences, of oriental civilizations, of other peoples and religions, was constantly on the increase; scholarship was more precise and thorough; a higher ideal of what commentary meant had taken possession of the mind. Learning, too, had enlarged its borders, and books on all subjects poured from the press in such numbers that it was difficult to cope with them. This applies to comms. as to other departments of theological study. Comms. in the 19th cent., and in our own, are legion. Only the most prominent landmarks can be noted.

1. Germany. a. Liberal School. In Germany, as was to be anticipated, the rise of the critical spirit and the profound influence exercised by it are reflected in most of the comms. produced in the first half of the 19th century. On the liberal side, the rationalistic temper is shown in the rejection of miracle, the denial of prediction in prophecy, and the lowering of the idea of inspiration generally. The scholarship, however, is frequently of a very high order. This temper is seen in De Wette (d. 1849), whose comms. on the NT, written when his views had become more positive, show grace and feeling; in Gesenius (d. 1842), who produced an epoch-making comm. on Isaiah; in Knobel (d. 1863), pronouncedly rationalistic, but with keen critical sense, as evinced in his comms. on the Pentateuch and Joshua, Ecclesiastes, and Isaiah; in Hupfeld (d. 1866) in his *Comm. on the Psalms* (4 vols.); in Hitzig (d. 1875), penetrating but arbitrary, who wrote on the Psalms and most of the Prophets; above all, in Ewald (d. 1875), a master in the interpretation of the poetical and prophetical books, but who commented also on the first three Gospels, on the writings of John, and on Paul's Epistles. *The Exegetical Handbook (Kurzgefasstes exegetisches Handbuch)* embraced compendious annotations by Knobel, Hitzig, Bertheau (school of Ewald), etc., but also by Olshausen (d. 1839; wrote likewise on the NT), on all the books of the OT.

b. Conservative School. On the conservative side a multitude of comms. on the OT and NT were produced from a variety of standpoints — evangelical, critical, mediating, confessional. The extremely conservative position in criticism was defended by Hengstenberg (d. 1869; on Psalms, Ecclesiastes, Ezekiel, John, Revelation), by Keil (d. 1888) in the well-known Keil and Delitzsch series (Genesis to Esther, Jeremiah, Ezekiel, Daniel, Minor Prophets; also NT comms.), and by Havernick (d. 1845, Daniel, Ezekiel). Delitzsch (d. 1890) wrote valued comms. on Genesis, Job, Psalms, Proverbs, Canticles, Ecclesiastes, Isaiah, and also on Hebrews. After the rise of the Wellhausen school, he considerably modified his views in the newer critical direction. His *New Comm. on Genesis* (1887) shows this change, but with his other works is still written in a strongly believing spirit. On the other hand, the critical position (older, not newer) is frankly represented by A. Dillmann (d. 1894) in his comms. on the books of the Pentateuch and Joshua.

The mediating school, largely penetrated by the influence of Schleiermacher, had many distinguished representatives. Among the most conspicuous may be named Lücke (d. 1855), who wrote on John; Bleek, the OT and NT critical scholar (d. 1859), who has a work on the first three Gospels, and lectures on Ephesians, Colossians, Philemon, Hebrews, and Revelation (his *Comm. on Hebrews* is the best known), and Tholuck (d. 1877), whose expositions and comms. on Psalms, John, Romans, and Hebrews with his *Comm. on the Sermon on the Mount* are fine pieces of exegetical work.

A special place must be given to two names of high distinction in the present connection. One is J. P. Lange (d. 1884), the projector and editor of the great *Bibelwerk* (theological and homiletical) in twenty-two volumes, to which he himself contributed the comms. on Genesis to Numbers, Haggai, Zechariah, Malachi, Matthew, Mark, John, Romans, Revelation, with introductions and homiletic hints. The other is H. A. W. Meyer (d. 1873), whose *Critical and Exegetical Comm. on the NT* from Matthew to Philippians (the remaining books being done by other scholars, Lünemann, Huther, etc.) is an essential part of every NT scholar's equipment.

With the more positive and confessional theologians may be ranked R. E. Stier (d. 1862), whose *Words of the Lord Jesus* (Eng. tr. in 8 vols.; biblical, mystical, with a tendency to prolixity), with comms. on seventy selected Psalms, Proverbs, Deutero-Isaiah, Ephesians, Hebrews, James and Jude, found much acceptance. A. von Harless (d. 1879) wrote a *Comm. on Ephesians* praised by Tholuck as one of the finest extant. Philippi (d. 1882), of Jewish extraction, best known by his *Comm. on Romans,* was strictly Lutheran. One of the ablest of the Lutheran Confessionalists was Luthardt (d. 1892), whose works include a *Comm. on St. John's Gospel*, Ebrard (d. 1888), as stoutly confessional on the Reformed side, has an esteemed *Comm. on Hebrews*. An eminent continental theologian who cannot be overlooked is the Swiss F. L. Godet (d. 1900), whose admirable *Comm. on St. John's Gospel*, and comms. on Romans and Corinthians are highly appreciated.

2. Britain and America. Meanwhile the English-speaking countries were pursuing their own paths in the production of comms. either in continuing their old traditions or in striking out on new lines, under the foreign influences that from the beginning of the century had begun to play upon them. In England Bishop Blomfield (d. 1857) published *Lectures on John and Acts*. In the USA there appeared from the pen of J. A. Alexander of Princeton (d. 1860) a noteworthy *Comm. on Isaiah*, fully abreast of the modern learning but staunchly conservative, and also a *Comm. on Psalms*. From the seminary proceeded the massive comms. of Charles Hodge (Calvinistic) on Romans, Ephesians, and Corinthians. Adapted for popular use and greatly in demand for Sunday-school purposes were the *Notes, Critical, Explanatory, and Practical* of Albert Barnes (d. 1870; New School Presbyterian). These *Notes*, the fruit of the use of the early morning hours in a busy pastoral life, covered the whole of the NT, with several books of the OT (Job, Psalms, Isaiah, Daniel). Sensible and informatory rather than original or profound, they have proved helpful to many. Of similar aim, though less widely known, were the *Notes* of M. W. Jacobus (d. 1876; on the NT, Genesis, and Exodus).

A new era was opened in critical commentary in England by the publication of the *Greek Testament* (1849-1860) of Dean Alford (d. 1871), followed by his *NT for English Readers* (1868). These works presented a thoroughly critical treatment of the texts, with a full display of the critical apparatus, accompanied by philological and exegetical notes and learned introductions, on all the books of the NT. About the same time appeared the solid — if more theological and homiletical — comms. of the Scottish scholar J. Eadie (d. 1876) on Galatians, Ephesians, Philippians, 1 and 2 Thessalonians. Anglican scholarship produced its ripest fruits in this line in the classical *Critical and Grammatical Comms.* of Bishop Ellicott (d. 1905) on Galatians, Ephesians, Philippians, Colossians, Philemon, Thessalonians, Pastoral Epistles, and the yet more remarkable series of comms. by Bishop J. B. Lightfoot (d. 1889), massive in learning and wider in outlook than Ellicott's, on Galatians, Philippians, Colossians, and Philemon. A large part of the value of Lightfoot's works consists in the special essays or dissertations on important subjects (e.g., "St. Paul and the Three," "The Christian Ministry," "The Colossian Heresy," etc.). With these names should be associated that of Bishop Westcott, Lightfoot's successor in the see of Durham (d. 1901), whose comms. on the Gospel and Epistles of St. John, and on Hebrews take a place among the foremost. Bishop Moule, who in turn succeeded Westcott, has also written comms., simpler in character, on Romans, Ephesians, Philippians, and Colossians, in the *Cambridge Bible Series,* and on Romans in the *Expositor's Bible*. In OT exposition mention should be made of Bishop Perowne's valuable work on the *Book of Psalms* (2nd rev. ed. 1870), with his contributions to the *Cambridge Bible* (see below).

The critical and theological liberalism of Germany made its influence felt in England in the rise of a Broad Church party, of which the best products in commentary were Dean Stanley's (d. 1881) graphic and interesting *Comm. on 1 and 2 Corinthians* (1855) and B. Jowett's *Epistles of St. Paul to the Thessalonians, Galatians, and Romans, with Critical Notes and Dissertations* (1855). The new spirit culminated in the appearance of the famous *Essays and Reviews* (1860), and in the works of Bishop Colenso on the Pentateuch and Joshua (1862-1879). Colenso had already published a translation of Romans with commentary (1861).

Besides works by individual authors, there appeared during this period several general comms. to which many writers contributed. *The Speaker's Comm.* (10 vols., 1871-1882), general ed. Canon F. C. Cook (d. 1889), was initiated because of the agitation over Colenso. Cook himself wrote introductions to Exodus, Psalms, and Acts, and contributed the entire comms. on Job, Habakkuk, Mark, Luke, 1 Peter, with parts of comms. on Exodus, Psalms, and Matthew. The work is of unequal value. A serviceable series is the *Cambridge Bible for Schools and Colleges*, ed. Perowne, with the *Smaller Cambridge Bible for Schools,* and the *Cambridge Greek Testament* (1881-1933). Perowne (d. 1904) himself contributed to the first-named the comms. on Obadiah, Jonah, Haggai, Zechariah, Malachi, and Galatians. Many valuable contributions appear in this series, e.g., A. F. Kirkpatrick on 1 and 2 Samuel and Psalms, A. B. Davidson on Job and Ezekiel, Driver on Daniel, G. G. Findlay on Thessalonians, etc. Next, under the editorship of Bishop Ellicott, were produced (1877-1884) a *NT Comm. for English Readers* (3 vols.), and an *OT Comm. for English Readers* (5 vols.), which contained some valuable work (Genesis by R. Payne Smith, Exodus by Canon G. Rawlinson, etc.). Akin to this in character was the *Popular Comm. on the NT* (4 vols., 1879-1883), ed. W. Schaff. This embraced, with other excellent matter, comms. on Thessalonians by Marcus Dods, and on 1 and 2 Peter by S. D. F. Salmond. The *Pulpit Comm.* (49 vols.), ed. J. S. Exell and Canon H. D. M. Spence has expositions of good scholars and an abundance of homiletical material by a great variety of authors. The series of *Handbooks for Bible Classes* has a number of valuable comms., e.g., that of A. B. Davidson on Hebrews.

F. Recent Period. The turn of the 20th cent. and succeeding decades featured the production of many new commentary series as well as comms. by individual writers, spanning the whole range of the critical spectrum.

1. Germany. In Germany, in addition to the *Kurzgefasstes exegetisches Handbuch* of older standing (see III.E.1 above), may be mentioned three works that offer painstakingly detailed philology: W. Nowack, *Göttinger Handkommentar zum AT* (1892ff.), which includes H. Gunkel's work on Genesis and Psalms and C. Steuernagel's comments on Deuteronomy and Joshua; *Kommentar zum AT* (*KZAT*), ed. E. Sellin, *et al.* (1913-1939), with O. Procksch on Genesis, R. Kittel on Psalms, and P. Volz on Jeremiah; and *Biblischer Kommentar: AT,* ed. M. Noth, *et al.* (*BKAT*), which was launched with the first *Lieferung* of W. Zimmerli's comments on Ezekiel (1955), and includes Hans-Joachim Kraus on Psalms (1960) and H. W. Wolff on Hosea (1961), Joel, and Amos (1969). *BKAT* aims at philological accuracy combined with practical theological concerns.Less technical are K. Marti, *Kurzer Hand-Commentar zum AT* (21 vols., 1897-1906), to which Marti contributed the volumes on Isaiah, Deuteronomy, and the Minor Prophets; and Strack-Zöckler, *Kurzgefasster Kommentar* (OT and NT; critical but moderate). In the latter work Strack wrote the volumes on Genesis to Numbers (Oettli contributed Deuteronomy, Joshua, and Judges). Much less critical in spirit are the comms. of H. C. von Orelli (Basel) on Isaiah, Jeremiah, Ezekiel, and the Minor Prophets. More widely known is Otto Eissfeldt, ed., *Handbuch zum Alten Testament* (*HAT,* 1934ff.), which includes K. Galling's *Biblisches Reallexikon* (2 vol.), Joshua by Noth, and Jeremiah by W. Rudolph. *Das Alte Testament Deutsch: Neues Göttinger Bibelwerk* (*ATD*), ed. V. Herntrich and A. Weiser, began to appear in 1949; translations of some of the volumes are available in the *Old Testament Library* (*OTL*), ed. G. E. Wright, *et al.* (1961ff.), which also includes fresh treatments, such as J. Gray on 1 and 2 Kings, and B. S. Childs — who subordinates the "prehistory" of the text to interpretation of its canonical form — on Exodus (1974). The series is designed for popular use, but enjoys high prestige because of a rare combination of brief, though informed, comment on the text with a profound theological concern. Weiser himself interprets Job and Psalms, and G. von Rad offers knowledgeable comment on Genesis.

The standard NT series in German has long been "Meyer's" *Kritisch-exegetischer Kommentar über das Neue Testament* (*KEK*), begun by H. W. Meyer (1829). Some of the more recent editions (1956ff.) include E. Lohmeyer on Matthew (ed. W. Schmauch), Mark, Philippians; E. Lohse on Colossians and Philemon; R. Bultmann on John and 1-3 John; E. Haenchen on Acts; O. Michel on Romans and Hebrews; H. Conzelmann on 1 Corinthians; H. Schlier on Galatians; M. Dibelius on James (ed. H. Greeven). T. Zahn, ed., *Kommentar zum Neuen Testament* (*KZNT,* 1909-1930) is equally impressive for the broad learning exhibited by the various contributors, but is more restrained than Meyer in its critical expression. From Roman Catholic quarters comes *Herders Theologischer Kommentar zum NT* (*HTK*), ed. A. Wikenhauser (1953ff.), with contributions that include H. Schürmann on Luke (vol. I, 1969) and R. Schnackenburg on John (vol. I, 1965). The *Handbuch zum NT* (*HNT,* 1906ff.), founded by H. Lietzmann and continued by G. Bornkamm, was until the advent of E. Käsemann on Romans (1973) less ponderous than *KEK*; in addition to comms. by leading scholars, this series includes L. Radermacher, *Neutestamentliche Grammatik* (2nd ed. 1925); W. Bousset, *Die Religion des Judentums im späthellenistischen Zeitalter* (3rd ed. rev. H. Gressman, 1926; repr. with rev. bibliography [E. Lohse], 1966); and four comms. on the Apostolic Fathers. The *Theologischer Handkommentar zum NT mit Text und Paraphrase* was begun in 1928 and included F. Hauck on Mark and Luke and F. Büchsel on the Epistles of John. The series was never completed, and a new beginning was made under E. Fascher with a second edition of A. Oepke's work on Galatians (1957); W. Grundmann produced a thorough revision of the comm. on Mark (1959) and Luke (1961), and a fresh treatment of Hauck's unpublished comm. on Matthew (1968). In a more popular vein again is the counterpart to the *ATD*, *Das Neue Testament Deutsch* (*NTD*), which has gone through many revisions.

Following paths first traversed by J. Lightfoot, *Horae Hebraicae et Talmudicae* (1658-1674), P. Billerbeck explored talmudic and midrashic literature for parallels that would provide enlightenment of the NT, and H. Strack lent his editorial assistance to its publication in *Kommentar zum NT aus Talmud und Midrasch* (SB, 5 vols., 1922-1928); a sixth volume (1961), compiled largely by K. Adolph, includes a rabbinic index to the more than nine hundred biblical scholars cited, and an explanatory geographical register. In a work of related genre H. Braun, *Qumran und das NT* (2 vols., 1966), illuminates the NT seriatim at the hand of the Qumrân texts; comparative historico-theological discussion of various subjects comprises the second volume. A. Schlatter's comms. on Matthew (1929), John (1930), and Romans (1935) have in their many editions put rabbinic source material at the service of respected theological discernment.

2. Britain and America. Variations in critical approaches comparable to those in Germany find display in British and American scholarship. The leading commentary series in English on the entire Bible has been the *International Critical Comm. on the Holy Scriptures of the Old and New Testament* (*ICC*), begun by C. Briggs, S. Driver, and A. Plummer in 1895 with Driver's volume on Deuteronomy, followed among others by J. Skinner on Genesis, G. Gray on Numbers (one of the best on this book), G. F. Moore on Judges, A. Montgomery and H. Gehman on 1 and 2 Kings, C. Toy on Proverbs, G. Barton on Ecclesiastes, W. Allen on Matthew, W. Sanday and A. Headlam on Romans, A. Robertson and A. Plummer on 1 Corinthians, Plummer and F. Brown on 2 Corinthians, De Witt Burton on Galatians, J. Frame on 1 and 2 Thessalonians, W. Lock on the Pastorals, and R. Charles on Revelation. This series now may well be overtaken by *Hermeneia,* a remarkable project that incorporates the highest standards of the printer's craft with the use of Hebrew and Greek font and includes in its scope translations of distinguished comms. published in languages other than English as well as fresh contributions; the series began with a translation of E. Lohse's work on Colossians and Philemon (1971); a translation of H. W. Wolff's comm. on Hosea (1974) initiated the OT section. The *Westminster Comms.* (*WC*) is a series designed for clergymen and educated laypersons and includes such notable works as S. Driver on Genesis, W. Oesterley on Proverbs, S. Brown on Hosea, J. Wand on 2 Peter and Jude; unfortunately the series was never completed. Leading scholars also contributed to the *Century Bible,* whose popular appeal found encouragement in such volumes as W. H. Bennett on Genesis and on "General Epistles," A. R. S. Kennedy on 1 and 2 Samuel, Skinner on 1 and 2 Kings, A. S. Peake on Job and on Hebrews, and Driver on a group of the Minor Prophets. The *New Century Bible*, edited by H. H. Rowley and R. E. Clements (OT) and M. Black (NT), is based on the RSV and presents in semipopular form mid-twentieth-century exegetical developments.

Written for a similar clientele is the *Interpreter's Bible* (*IB*). Contemporary developments in exegetical inquiry expose the thinness of much of the exposition, and the introductory and supplementary articles are often more valuable than the comm., but outstanding treatments in this series are G. E. Wright on Deuteronomy, S. Terrien on Job, W. Taylor and W. McCullough on Psalms, R. Scott on Isaiah, and H. May on Ezekiel. More meaty in general is the *Anchor Bible* (*AB*), "a project of international and interfaith scope . . . aimed at the general reader," who is gradually, however, being forgotten as the series moves on. Begun in 1964 under the editorship of W. F. Albright and D. N. Freedman, this series accents fresh translation of the biblical text, with comment of varying degrees of quality and thoroughness; M. Dahood's treatment of Psalms (1966-1968) is especially noteworthy for its use of Ugaritic material; J. M. Myers' discussion of 1 and 2 Esdras (1974) reflects increasing interest in the intertestamental literature and encourages the nonspecialist to develop acquaintance with basic resources for understanding canonical documents that enjoy broader recognition; R. Brown displays a firm grasp of the critical problems relating to John (2 vols., 1966-1970); and M. Barth accepts Pauline authorship of Ephesians, emphasizing the social aspects of reconciliation (2 vols., 1974). The *New International Comm. on the OT,* under the editorship of R. K. Harrison, is more accessible to the general reader; it includes comms. on Deuteronomy by P. C. Craigie (1976), and Joel, Obadiah, Jonah, and Micah by L. C. Allen (1976). The *Layman's Bible Comm.,* begun in 1959, lives up to its title and balances informative exposition with edifying comment. With a similar reading public in mind, the *Concordia Comm.* began to appear in 1968 under the editorship of A. J. Glock (OT) and W. J. Bartling (NT), but only five volumes (1 and 2 Samuel, Jeremiah and Lamentations, Romans, Acts, and Pastorals with Philemon) were published under the original plan; a sixth, *Jesus and the New Age According to St. Luke,* by F. W. Danker, was issued by a different publisher (1972), followed by W. Wifall, *The Court History of Israel: A Comm. on First and Second Kings* (1975). Publication of the NEB encouraged fresh directions for two older series. A. Argyle piloted the *Cambridge Bible Comm. on the NEB* with his comments on Matthew (1963), in the NT portion (*CBCNT*); P. R. Ackroyd initiated the OT portion (*CBCOT*) with 1 Samuel (1971); the comm. on Job (1975), by N. Habel, is one of the more notable contributions in this series. The *New Clarendon Bible,* begun with C. K. Barrett's comm. on the Pastorals (1963), under the general editorship of H. F. D. Sparks, also uses the NEB as its base and terminates the *Clarendon Bible,* which was based on the RV.

For the exposition of the NT only, students have relied for many years on the *Expositor's Greek Testament,* ed. W. Nicoll (5 vols., 1897-1910), which was designed to supersede H. Alford's work. Although the series is largely obsolete in the light of contemporary developments in literary criticism, profit is still to be gained especially from R. Knowling on Acts and H. Kennedy on Philippians. C. F. D. Moule piloted in 1957 a new format for the old *Cambridge Greek Testament* with a comm. on Colossians and Philemon; the new series is entitled *Cambridge Greek Testament Commentary.* C. K. Barrett's comm. on Romans (1957) spearheads *Harper's NT Comms.* (*HNTC*), under the general editorship of H. Chadwick. For Greekless readers the *Moffatt NT Comm.* (1926-1950) still offers substantial fare, including C. H. Dodd on the Johannine Letters and M. Kiddle, assisted by M. Ross, on Revelation. A similar but less ambitious work is the *Torch Bible Comms.,* ed. J. Marsh, D. Paton, and A. Richardson. More reflective of contemporary biblical research is the *Pelican NT Comm.,* begun under the editorship of D. E. Nineham and based on the RSV; J. C. Fenton on Matthew (1963) and Nineham on Mark (1963) are especially instructive for the lay reader.

More traditionally oriented is the *New International Comm. on the NT* (ed. N. B. Stonehouse, beginning in 1951) and its contemporary The *Tyndale NT Comms.,* ed.

R. Tasker. The former reproduces the gist of the original in thought units and handles linguistic and special problems in footnotes, thus making comment available also to the Greekless reader. The Tyndale series follows the traditional verse by verse exposition. The frequent citations of the Greek text are transliterated and always accompanied by a clear indication of their meaning, thus making the entire comm. available to the Greekless user. In both these series, as well as in *HNTC*, editorial policies have given the advantage of space to the comms. on the Epistles.

A number of one-volume comms. have enjoyed popularity. *A New Comm. on Holy Scripture Including the Apocrypha*, ed. C. Gore, H. Goudge, and A. Guillaume (1928) is noted for its breadth and thoroughness of critical treatment, but has given way to a fresh edition of A. Peake and A. Grieve, eds., *Comm. on the Bible* (1924) under the title *Peake's Comm. on the Bible*, eds. M. Black and H. H. Rowley (1962) with the assistance of an international corps of scholars. Of comparable calibre are the *Jerome Biblical Comm.*, eds. R. Brown, J. Fitzmyer, and R. Murphy (1968) and its British cousin, *New Catholic Comm. on Holy Scripture*, eds. R. C. Fuller, L. Johnston, and C. Kearns (1969), which replaces *Catholic Comm. on Holy Scripture* (1953) and at the same time documents a fundamental change in direction of Roman Catholic biblical scholarship. Smaller-scale works range from *Comm. on the Holy Bible*, ed. J. R. Dummelow (1908), to the *New Bible Comm.*, ed. F. Davidson (1953; rev. ed. 1970 [D. Guthrie, *et al.*]). The latter introduces fewer modern critical conclusions.

Outstanding comms. published since 1900 by individual writers still commanding widespread attention are G. A. Smith on Jeremiah (4th ed. 1929) and on the Minor Prophets (rev. ed. 1929); R. S. Cripps on Amos (2nd ed. 1955); A. H. McNeile on Matthew (1915); V. Taylor on Mark (2nd ed. 1966), superseding H. Swete (3rd ed. 1909); J. M. Creed on Luke (1930); B. F. Westcott on John (2 vols., 1908); F. J. F. Jackson and K. Lake on Acts (5 vols., 1920-1933); W. M. Ramsay on Galatians (1900); J. Robinson on Ephesians (2nd ed. 1909); J. Mayor on James (3rd ed. 1913); E. Selwyn on 1 Peter (1955); J. Mayor on Jude and 2 Peter (1907). Many of the older comms., long out of print, are being republished, but the original date of publication is not always noted. The accompanying bibliography will assist the student in identifying the real age of the advertised product.

In view of their pivotal importance for interpretation of the NT books with which they are intimately associated, the following special studies in English and German deserve inclusion here: G. Bornkamm, G. Barth, and H. J. Held, *Tradition and Interpretation in Matthew* (Eng. tr. 1963); J. D. Kingsbury, *Matthew: Structure, Christology, Kingdom* (1975); on Mark, W. Wrede, *The Messianic Secret* (1901; Eng. tr. 1971); K. L. Schmidt, *Der Rahmen der Geschichte Jesu* (1919); W. Marxsen, *Mark the Evangelist: Studies on the Redaction History of the Gospel* (Eng. tr. 1969); on Luke, H. J. Cadbury, *Making of Luke-Acts* (1927); H. Conzelmann, *Theology of St. Luke* (Eng. tr. 1960); J. Jervell, *Luke and the People of God: A New Look at Luke-Acts* (1972); on Acts, besides the special studies in Jackson-Lake (above), M. Dibelius, *Studies in the Acts of the Apostles* (Eng. tr. 1956); on 1 and 2 Corinthians, W. Schmithals, *Gnosticism in Corinth* (Eng. tr. 1971); U. Wilckens, *Weisheit und Torheit* (1959); on Ephesians and Colossians, E. Percy, *Die Probleme der Kolosser- und Epheserbriefe* (1946); P. N. Harrison, *Problem of the Pastorals* (1921); on 1 Peter, J. H. Elliot, *The Elect and the Holy* (1966).

3. France. The Protestant theological faculty of the Université de Strasbourg introduced *Commentaire de l'Ancien Testament* with S. Terrien on Job (1963). Their *Commentaire du Nouveau Testament* was begun in 1949 with Jean Héring on 1 Corinthians (Eng. tr. 1962). Still valued is the series on the NT, *Études Bibliques*, begun by M.-J. Lagrange in 1903; his comms. on each of the Synoptics and on Romans set a standard that stimulated such notable publications as E. B. Allo on 1 Corinthians (1934), 2 Corinthians (1936), and Revelation (1921, 3rd ed. 1933); B. Rigaux on 1 and 2 Thessalonians (1956); and C. Spicq on Hebrews (1947) and the Pastorals (1947); most of the works in this series have gone through a number of editions or revisions. *La Sainte Bible* (43 vols., 1948-1954) was prepared under the direction of the École Biblique de Jérusalem and includes a scholarly French translation, with helpful annotations. An abridged one-volume edition appeared in 1956.

Bibliography.–Much generally inaccessible information on comms. together with a selected list of the most widely recognized comms. on each book of the Bible is included in F. W. Danker, *Multipurpose Tools for Bible Study* (3rd ed. rev. 1970), pp. 239-273; bibliography p. 240 n. 1. In addition, for older works see F. Bleek, *Intro. to the OT*, and J. Moffatt, *Intro. to the NT*. For special literature on the individual books of the Bible see the standard books on introduction, literature cited in the most recent scientific comms., and the bibliographies appended to the articles in this encyclopedia.

J. ORR F. W. DANKER

COMMENTARIES, HEBREW.

I. Philo Judaeus
II. Targum
III. Midrash
IV. Talmud
V. Karaites
VI. Middle Ages
VII. Modern Times
VIII. Dead Sea Scrolls
IX. Exegetical Methods of a Typical Midrash

Jewish comms., like their Christian counterparts, have used different exegetical approaches to Scripture through the centuries. These will be surveyed in chronological order.

I. Philo Judaeus.–A Hellenistic Jew of Alexandria, Egypt, born about 20 B.C., died after A.D. 40. By his allegorical method of exegesis (a method learned from the Stoics), Philo exercised a far-reaching influence not only on Jewish thought, but even more so on the Christian Church, particularly on Origen and other Alexandrian Christian writers. His purpose in employing his allegorical method was mainly to reconcile Greek philosophy with the OT. *See* PHILO JUDAEUS.

II. Targum.–The Aramaic translation of the OT. Literally, the word designates a translation in general; its use, however, has been restricted to the Aramaic version of the OT, as contrasted with the Hebrew text, which was called *miqrā'*. The Targum includes all the books of the OT except Daniel and Ezra-Nehemiah, which are written in part in Aramaic. Its inception dates back to the time of the second temple. One might consider it a comm., the first before the time of Jesus, for the Targum is not a mere translation, but a combination of translation and commentary, resulting in a paraphrase, or an interpretative translation, with its origin in exegesis. The language of this paraphrase is the vernacular tongue of Syria, which began to reassert itself throughout Palestine as the language of common discourse and trade, as soon as a familiar knowledge of the Hebrew tongue came to be lost. The Targums are:

(1) To the Pentateuch:

(a) Targum *Onkelos* or Babylonian Targum (the accepted and official);

COMMENTARIES, HEBREW

(b) Targum *Yerushalmi* or Palestinian Targum ("Pseudo-Jonathan"; aside from this [complete] Targum there are fragments of T.P. termed "Fragment Targum").

(2) To the Prophets:

(a) Targum Jonathan ben Uzziel (the official one; originated in Palestine and was then adapted to the vernacular of Babylonia);

(b) A Palestinian Targum called *Targum Yerushalmi* (Palestinian in origin; ed. P. de Lagarde, *Prophetae Chaldaice* [1872]).

Other Targums (not officially recognized): To the Psalms and Job; to Proverbs; to the Five Rolls; to Chronicles — all Palestinian. See TARGUM.

III. Midrash.–Apparently the practice of commenting upon and explaining the meaning of the Scriptures originated in the synagogues (in the time of Ezra), from the necessity of an exposition of the Law to a congregation many of whom did not or might not understand the language in which it was read. Such comms., however, were oral and extempore and were not until much later crystallized into a definite form. When they assumed a definite and, still later, written shape, the name Midrash (meaning "investigation," "interpretation," from *dāraš,* "to investigate" a scriptural passage) was given. The word occurs in 2 Ch. 13:22 where the RV translates "commentary" and the Jerusalem Bible, "Midrash." From this fact some have drawn the inference that such midrashim were recognized and extant before the time of the Chronicler. They are: Midrash *Rabbah* on the Pentateuch and the Five Rolls (the one on Genesis occupies a first position among the various exegetical midrashim, on account of both its age and importance). Next is that on Lamentations. (L. Zunz pointed out that the Midrash *Rabbah* consists of ten entirely different midrashim.) On the same ten books there is a similar collection called *ha-Midrash ha-gadol* (the "Great Midrash"), a collection of quotations from several works including the Midrash *Rabbah.* Other midrashim are: The Midrash *Tanhuma* on the Pentateuch; the *Mekilta* on Exodus (this has been [1909] translated into German by J. Winter and A. Wuensche; the latter also published, under the main title *Bibliotheca Rabbinica,* a collection of the old midrashim in a German translation with introductions and notes). Others include *Siphra* on Leviticus; *Siphra* on Numbers and Deuteronomy; and *Pesikta*, which comments on sections taken from the entire range of Scriptures for various festivals. There are also extant separate midrashim on the Psalms, Proverbs, and other books.

In this connection should be mentioned the *Yalkut Shimeoni*, a haggadic compilation attributed to the 11th or, according to Zunz, the 13th century. The *Yalkut* extends over the whole of the OT and is arranged according to the sequence of those portions of the Bible to which reference is made. Further, the *Yalkut ha-Makiri* is a work similar in contents to the *Yalkut Shimeoni*, ed. L. Grünhut (1902).

IV. Talmud.–This term is used here to designate the entire body of literature exclusive of the Midrash. Ample exegetical material abounds in the Talmud as it does in the midrashim. The critical notes on the Bible by some Talmudists are very characteristic of their intellectual temper. Some of them were extremely radical and expressed freely their opinions on important problems of Bible criticism, such as on the integrity of the text, or doubtful authorship. An Amora of the 3rd cent. A.D. held the opinion that the story of Job is purely fictitious as to both the name of the hero and his fate. The Talmudists also generalized and set up critical canons.

ערבי פסחים פרק עשירי פסחים קח ע"ב

והוא דאשתי רובא דכסא מיתיבי ארבע כוסות הללו צריך שיהא בהן כדי רביעי' אחד חי ואחד מזוג אחד חדש ואחד ישן ר' יהודה אומר צריך שיהא בו טעם ומרא' יין קהני מיהת כדי רביעית ואת אמרת כוס יפה אמרי אידי ואידי חד שיעורא הוא דמאי כדי מזיגת כוס יפה דקאמר לכל חד וחד דהוי להו כולהו רביעי' ר' יהודה אומר צריך שיהא בו טעם ומראה אמר רבא מ"ט דר' יהודה דכתיב אל תרא יין כי יתאדם ת"ר הכל חייבין בד' כוסות הללו אחד אנשי' ואחד נשי' ואחד תינוקות א"ר יהודה וכי מה תועלת יש לתינוקות ביין אלא מחלקין להן קליות

Section of the Babylonian Talmud (T. B. *Pesahim* 108b) concerning reclining and the drinking of wine during the Passover meal (Seder). Included are the Mishnah or oral laws (center) and the Gemara (periphery), a commentary on the Mishnah by later sages. (Rebecca Bennet Publications)

The "Baraitha of the Thirty-two Rules" is the oldest work on biblical hermeneutics (Philo's hermeneutical rules being rather fanciful) and contains exegetical notices that are still valid. Although hermeneutics is not exegesis proper, but the theory of exegesis, one results from the other. This Baraitha calls attention, for instance, to the fact that words occur in the OT in an abbreviated form — a view now generally accepted. See TALMUD.

V. Karaites.–"Followers of the Bible." Sometimes referred to as the "Protestants of the Jews," they profess to follow the OT to the exclusion of the rabbinical tradition. The founder of this Jewish sect was an eighth-century Babylonian Jew, Anan ben David; hence they were first called Ananites. The principal Karaite commentators of the 9th, 10th, and 11th cents. are: Benjamin Al-Nahawendi (the first to use the term "Karaites," Heb. *ba'alē miqrā'*), Solomon ben Jeroham. Sahl ibn Mazliah, Yusul al-Basir, Yafith ibn Ali (considered the greatest of this period), and Abu al-Faraij Harum. Of a later date were Aaron ben Joseph and Aaron ben Elijah (14th cent.).

The struggle between the Rabbinites and the Karaites undoubtedly gave the impetus to the great exegetical activity among the Jews in Arabic-speaking countries during the 10th and 11th centuries. The extant fragments of Saadia's comm. on the Pentateuch (not less than his polemical writings proper) are full of polemics against the Karaite interpretation. The same circumstance aroused Karaites to like efforts.

VI. Middle Ages.–Medieval Jewish exegetes established a fourfold form of interpretation comprising the *p^e^šāṭ* or obvious literal sense of the passage, the *remes* or allegorical significance, the *d^e^raš* or ethico-homiletical interpretation, and the *sôḏ* or mystical meaning of the text. These were subsequently designated by the acrostic PaRDeS and occurred in numerous variations and combinations.

Saadia ben Joseph (892-942), the severest antagonist of the Karaites, translated the OT into Arabic with notes. The parts published were: Pentateuch, Isaiah, Proverbs and Job.

Moses ha-Darshan (the Preacher) of Narbonne, France, and *Tobiah ben Eliezer* in Castoria, Bulgaria (11th cent.), are the most prominent representatives of midrashic-symbolic Bible exegesis. The former's work is known only by quotations and contained theological conceptions similar to those held by Christians; the latter is the author of *Lekah Tob* or *Pesikta Zutarta* on the Pentateuch and the five Megilloth.

Rashi (Solomon ben Isaac of Troyes; 1040-1105) wrote a very popular comm., which extends over the whole of the OT with the exception of Chronicles, Ezra-Nehemiah, and the last part of Job. He strove for the *p^e^šāṭ,* i.e., for a sober, natural, and rational interpretation of the Bible. His is still a comm. for both the novice and the master among the Jews. Christian exegetes of the Middle Ages as well as of modern times made use of his Bible commentary. Nicholas of Lyra followed Rashi closely, and it is known that Luther's translation of the Bible is dependent upon Nicholas. Rashi's comm. has called forth numerous expositions on his work.

An independent and important exegete was *Joseph Kara* (*ca.* 1100). He edited and partly completed Rashi's comm., particularly the part on the Pentateuch.

Abraham ibn Ezra's (1092-1168) scholarly comm. on the Pentateuch, like Rashi's works, has prompted many expositions. He was the first to maintain that Isaiah contains the work of two authors, and his doubts respecting the authorship of the Pentateuch were noticed by B. Spinoza.

The grammarians and the lexicographers were not merely exegetical expounders of words, but many of them were likewise authors of actual commentaries. Such were the *Kimḥī's,* Joseph and his sons Moses and David, and especially the latter. The Kimchis were the most brilliant contributors to Bible exegesis and Hebrew philology (like ibn Ezra) in medieval times.

Maimonides' (1135-1204) work, like Philo's, uses the allegorical method for the purpose of reconciling Plato with the OT. To Maimonides Aristotle was the representative of natural knowledge and the Bible of supernatural — and he sought for a reconciliation between the two in his religious philosophy. Exegesis proper was the one field, however, to which this great genius made no contribution of first-class importance.

His followers were the *Maimunists,* exegetes of a philosophical turn, including: Joseph ibn Aknin, Samuel ibn Tibbon, his son Moses, and his son-in-law, Jacob ben Abba Mari Anatolio, whose *Malmad ha-Talmidim* was the most important work of philosophical exegesis in that period.

Joseph ibn Kaṣpi, chiefly known as a philosopher of the Maimunist type, was an exegete of the first quality. His exposition of Isa. 53 might be the work of the most modern scholar. He refers the prophecy to Israel, not to an individual, and in this his theory is far superior to that of some other famous Jewish expositors who interpret the chapter as referring to Hezekiah.

The principal commentators with a *Kabbalistic* tendency include Naḥmanides (1194-1270?), whose great work was his comm. on the Pentateuch, and Immanuel of Rome (1270?-1330?), who, however, did not disregard the literal meaning of the Scriptures. Bahya ben Asher (d. 1340), who formulated the four methods of exegesis of PaRDeS referred to above, took Naḥmanides as his model; many super-comms. were written on his comm. on the Pentateuch. L. Gersonides (1288-1334), a maternal grandson of Naḥmanides, saw symbols in many biblical passages; on account of some of his heretical ideas expressed in his philosophy, some rabbis forbade the study of his commentaries.

The *Zohar*, the "Bible of the Kabbalists," dominated the thinking and feeling of the Jews for almost five hundred years and was in favor with many Christian scholars. This pseudepigraphic work, written partly in Aramaic and partly in Hebrew, first appeared in Spain in the 13th cent. and was made known through Moses de Leon, to whom many historians attribute it.

Mention must also be made of *Isaac ben Moses Arama* (1430-1494), whose *Akedat Yitzhak,* a comm. on the Pentateuch (homiletical in style), was the standard book for the Jewish pulpit for centuries, much esteemed by the Christian world, and is still much read by Jews, particularly in Eastern Europe.

VII. Modern Times.–Isaac Abravanel (or Abarbanel; 1437-1508) was a statesman and scholar who came nearest to the modern idea of a Bible commentator by considering not only the literary elements of the Bible but the political and social life of the people as well. He wrote a general introduction to each book of the Bible, setting forth its character; and he was the first to make use of Christian comms., which he quotes without prejudice. Moses Alshech (second half of 16th cent.) wrote comms., all of which are of a homiletical character. In the main the Jewish exegesis of the 16th and 17th cents. branched out into homiletics.

The Biurists were a school of exegetes which had its origin with Mendelssohn's (1729-1786) literal German translation of the Bible, at a time when Christian biblical studies of a modern nature had made some progress, and under whose influence the Biurists wrote. They include S. M. Dubnow, N. M. Wesseley, A. Jaroslav, H. Homberg, and J. Euchel. They laid a foundation for a critico-historical study of the Bible among modern Jews. It bore its fruit in the 19th cent. in the writings of L. Philippson, S. Munk, J. Fuerst, and others. The same century produced Zunz's (1794-1886) *Gottesdienstliche Vortraege der Juden,* the book of "Jewish science." It also produced three Jewish exegetes, S. D. Luzzatto in Italy, M. L. Malbim and A. B. Ehrlich in Russia. The last after 1878 resided in New York; he published in Hebrew a comm. on the OT, entitled *Mikra ki-Peshutah* (3 vols., 1899-1901), and, in German, *Randglossen zur hebräischen Bibel,* two scholarly works written from the conservative standpoint (begun in 1908). Malbim was highly esteemed by the Christian commentators F. Delitzsch and J. Muehlau, who studied under him. Others are Joseph Halévy, a French Jew, a most original Bible investigator, and D. Hoffmann (the last two named are adversaries of "higher criticism") and D. H. Mueller. M. Heilprin wrote a collection of *Bibelkritische Notizen* (1893), containing comparisons of various biblical passages, and *Historical Poetry of the Ancient Hebrews* (2 vols., 1879-1880). The American rabbi B. Szold published a *Comm. on Job* (1886), written in classical Hebrew and applying accurate scholarship to take full account of the work of the Masoretes. A new Hebrew comm. on the whole of the OT,

Qumrân commentary on Habakkuk (1QpHab), which interprets Hab. 1–2 in terms of the sect's history and orientation. (W. S. LaSor) *See also* Plate 16.

Has-s^e^pārîm Haḥîṣônîm, was begun in 1903 under the editorship of A. Kahana. This was the first attempt since Mendelssohn's *Biur* to approach the Bible from the Jewish viewpoint with the latest philological and archeological equipment. Among the authors are Kahana on Genesis and Jonah, S. Krauss on Isaiah, Z. H. Chajes on Psalms and Amos, Wynkoop on Hosea and Joel, G. Lambert on Daniel.

The aim of M. M. Kalisch (1828-1885) to publish a critical comm. on the entire OT remained largely unfulfilled. Of his *Historical and Critical Comm. on the OT, with a New Translation,* only the following parts were published: *Exodus* (1855); *Genesis* (1858); *Leviticus* (pts. 1-2, 1867-1872). They contain a resume of all that Jewish and Christian learning had accumulated on the subject up to the dates of their publication. His *Leviticus* anticipated J. Wellhausen to a large extent.

The works of A. Geiger, H. Graetz, and K. Kohler reflect nineteenth-century liberal thought, a trend continued by many Jewish commentators of the 20th century. The more notable conservative Jewish scholars include J. H. Hertz, chief rabbi of the British Commonwealth, whose comm. on the Pentateuch, originally published in five volumes, was an outstanding scholarly production. The *Soncino Books of the Bible* series also contained comms. by authorities such as A. Cohen, I. Epstein, H. Freedman, I. W. Slotki, and others. An important thirty-five-volume edition of the Talmud was also edited by Epstein. The most outstanding modern comm. in Hebrew, which was intended to encompass the whole OT, was begun by U. Cassuto, but he was able to complete only part of the Pentateuch.

Bibliography.–M. Steinschneider, *Jewish Literature* (1857); L. Zunz, *Gottesdienstliche Vortraege der Juden* (2nd ed. 1892); *Jew.Enc.* (articles by W. Bacher and L. Ginzbert); *Catholic Encyclopedia, s.v.* "Commentaries"; W. Rosenau, *Jewish Biblical Commentators* (1906) (popular); J. Winter and A. Wuensche, *Geschichte der Juedischen Literatur* (3 vols., 1892-1895) (the best existing anthology of Jewish literature in a modern language; it contains very valuable introductions). A. S. OKO

VIII. Dead Sea Scrolls.–*A. Sources.* Commentaries among the Dead Sea literature are now sparse and fragmentary, though adequate to show manner, tendency, and viewpoint, and to suggest that originally they were voluminous.

Qumrân Cave 1 produced the largest single item, the comm. on Hab. 1–2 (1QpHab), together with fragments on Micah (1QpMic) and Psalms (1QpPs). Splendid Hebrew transliterations and photographs of 1QpHab are available in Burrows, I, and of the fragments in Barthélemy and Milik, I (1955). (For translations, annotated and otherwise, see the Bibliography.)

Cave 4 has yielded a considerable portion of a comm. on Nahum (4QpNah) and parts of various comms. on Isaiah (4QpIsa^a,b,c,d^) and on Ps. 37. Two of its further documents, 4Q Florilegium (4QFlor) and 4Q Testimonia (4QTestim), are of special interest. They indicate not only messianic expectations — from the Jewish, not the Christian standpoint — but also the existence of a testimony book of OT proof texts for the Messiah, such as postulated by scholars to account for certain peculiarities of citation, referring to Jesus, in the NT.

B. Interpretation. The arrangement of these comms. is fairly uniform. A passage of the basic Scripture is quoted, followed by the Aramaic word *pšr* or *pšrw,* "(its) interpretation is. . . ." The Hebrew phrase in Gen. 40:12, 18, *zeh piṯrōnô,* referring to the interpretation of the dreams of Pharaoh's butler and baker, is approximately equivalent, and *pšrw* is familiar in the Targums and other Aramaic sources. It never denotes ordinary scientific exegesis. For the Qumrân community, the sacred volume was a repository of symbolism, representing the circumstances of their present, the operations of their minds, or their ultimate hopes — terms that might be rewritten as fulfilled prophecy, mysticism, and eschatology — restricted to the schismatic minority, convinced that it was the true Israel, the saved remnant. The OT had become for them something like a fortuneteller's crystal, in the mysterious depths of which they pondered their own destiny and that of their foes. To cite two vague and rather generalized examples, the grim words of Mic. 6:14-16 are eschatologically applied to the last mortal generation, and the comparable sentiments of Zeph. 1:18–2:2 to the inhabitants of Judah.

Many passages in the Qumrân literature clearly refer to historical personages and events, though modern commentators may quarrel over identity. Two of the less disputed examples may be cited. 1QpHab abounds with references to the Kittim (*hkty'ym*). These were almost certainly the Romans; and commentators see references to provincial commanders and military methods in col. 4, lines 5-9; to the Roman senate in the "house of guilt" (*byt 'šm'*) in line 11; to the soldier cult of battle standards in col. 6, line 4; and to the extortions of the fiscal taxes in lines 6-8. The suffering Lebanon of Hab. 2:17 is identified with the inner council of the Qumrân community itself (col. 12, lines 3f.; Lebanon is found as a name for the temple in the Midrash; cf. Midr. *Mekilta,* ed. J. Z. Lauterbach, II, 151). This is made explicit in the text. Many other identities are suggested by translators, some of them conjectural.

A small piece of verbal exegesis, reminiscent of rabbinic methodology, occurs in 1QpHab. col. 2, line 1. The *ḇaggôyim* (*bgwym*) of Hab. 1:5 (AV "among the heathen") is read as *bwgdym,* "the rebels" (cf. LXX *hoi kataphronētaí*), which suits the commentator's purpose. The official standing of the priest as scriptural exegete is affirmed in col. 2, line 8. The writer of the comm., almost certainly himself a priest, seems to circumscribe the reach of prophecy in col. 7, lines 1f., 7f. God, he says, revealed to Habakkuk the course of the mortal generations to their end, but did not make known to him the consummation of the end time (line 2). The intervening generations have exceeded prophetic expectation (lines 7f.). This links with certain NT sayings about the Second Coming.

The total literature so far available is a meager dozen or fifteen pages of Hebrew, making evaluations rather tentative. Certainly this is not biblical commentary in the contemporary sense. It is serenely indifferent to what the rabbis call the *p^ešāṭ,* the literal, historical meaning of Scripture. Yet it is no less commentary than the allegorical exegesis of Philo, which it partially resembles, though its aim is more immediate and practical.

IX. Exegetical Methods of a Typical Midrash.–The Rabbah group, covering the Pentateuch and Megilloth, is the best-known of the midrashim or rabbinic comms. on books of the OT. (It is extensively cited in R. A. Stewart, *Rabbinic Theology* [1961].) As there is distinctive family likeness throughout the literature, examples are drawn from the early and typical Midrash *Mekilta* on portions of Exodus. This document has the usual rabbinic admixture of Halakic (legal) and Haggadic (homiletical) material.

Mekilta frequently bases its Halakic decisions from Scripture on the "Hermeneutical Rules," particularly the "Thirteen" of Rabbi Ishmael, which were an amplification of Hillel's seven rules. (See *Jew.Enc., s.v.* "Rules of Hillel"; "Rules of Ishmael"; "Talmud Hermeneutics.") Two examples may suffice here. Ishmael Rule Two, *gzyrh šwh,* "an equivalent law," states that if two pentateuchal enactments contain words of similar or identical meanings, both laws are subject to the same application. (Cf. *Mekilta* i.41: Nu. 9:2, referring to Passover, and Nu. 28:2, referring to Tamid, or the daily whole-offering, have in common the phrase *b^emô ʻ^aḏô,* "in its due season." Thus, Passover and Tamid take precedence over sabbath restrictions.) Ishmael Rule Four, *kll wprṭ,* "general and particular," is stated and its definition completed in *Mekilta* i.117, *'yn bkll 'l' mh šb prt,* "there is nothing in general beyond what is contained in the particular." (Cf. Nu. 19:2, "[a] This is the ordinance of the law . . . [b] that they bring thee a red heifer without spot." In the context, [b] limits and defines [a]; cf. also Ex. 12:43.) If the order is reversed (cf. Ex. 19:6), Ishmael Rule Five is applied, "Particular and General." Like Aristotelian logic, they have their value and their weaknesses, and are liable to dialectical abuse.

In contrast to this legalistic exegesis are allegorical interpretations of Scripture, in slighter echo of Philo. Job 8:11 is taken to signify Israel's need for Torah (*Mekilta* ii.135). The slave of Ex. 21:6 is interpreted to have his ear bored because he was a thief, whose ear had heard the commandment "Thou shalt not steal" (iii.16). Similarly, there are various embellishments of the Bible stories of Moses, Joseph, Pharaoh, Jonah, and others, together with numerous parabolic and allegorical interpretations of the Torah. Parables also are found. A brief and pregnant one: the Torah, given in fire — impertinent proximity and irreligious avoidance bring parallel punishments (ii.220f.; cf. also i.211, 224f., 228; i.205f.).

The midrashim in general quote Scripture with considerable accuracy, acknowledging its canonical authority and respecting its literal meaning (*p^ešāṭ*). Several stock formulas of introduction occur: *ktyb, k^eṯîḇ* ("written"), *šene '^emar* ("as is said"), and others more elaborate. By the sheer bulk of quotation, these writings provide an important corroborative source for the text of the OT. Passages are sometimes shortened, as indicated by *wgwl* (i.e., *wgwmr,* "etc."), which refers the reader to the MT.

The Qumranic exegesis of Hab. 1:5 (1 QpHab) by variant reading has numerous parallels in *Mekilta.* Sometimes the MT remains unaltered, as in Ex. 21:6; 22:8, 23, where *'^elōhîm* may be read as "God" or "judges," making good sense either way (iii.151). However, the MT readings are often repointed. In Ps. 68:27 (MT 28), Benjamin is described as *rōḏēm,* "having rule over them"; but *rōḏām* would be the usual form. *Mekilta* i.232 proposes to read *rd ym* — Benjamin went down first of all the tribes, *daring* the Red Sea. This is ingenious, but the expected form, pointed, would be *rōḏeh hayyām.*

Bibliography.–*Qumrân Scrolls:* J. M. Allegro, *PEQ* (1954), pp. 69-75; *JBL,* 75 (1956), 89-95; 77 (1958), 215-221, 350-54; D. Barthélemy and J. T. Milik, *Discoveries in the Judaean Desert,* I (1955), 77-82; M. Burrows, *DSS of St. Marks Monastery* (1950), I, plates LV-LXI; M. Delcor, *Le Midrash d'Habacuc* (1952); T. H. Gaster, *Scriptures of the Dead Sea Sect* (1957); G. Vermes, *DSS in English* (1962). *See also* DEAD SEA SCROLLS; ESSENES.

Midrash: SB, I, viii-ix; *Jew.Enc.,* VIII, 548-580; *Midrash Haggadol,* ed. S. Fisch (1940); *Midrash Mekilta,* ed. J. Z. Lauterbach (3 vols., 1933-1935) (bilingual); *Midrash Rabbah* (Soncino; 1939); *Midrash Sifre on Numbers* (1926).

R. A. STEWART

COMMENTARY [Heb. *miḏrāš*] (2 Ch. 24:27); AV, NEB, STORY (cf. 13:22). These are the only two OT uses of the Hebrew term, each indicating one of the Chronicler's sources (*see* CHRONICLES, BOOKS OF, V.B.), probably didactic elaborations of more strictly historical accounts.

COMMERCE. The acquisition, distribution, and exchange of merchandise. Commerce developed in antiquity whenever the basic unit of society, the household, be it of peasant or of king (the palace), was unable to provide commodities regarded as necessary for life or desired for its enhancement. Extensive interchange of goods had occurred in the ancient Near East since long before the settlement of Canaan by the Israelites.

Israel was ideally situated geographically to participate in the important commerce that passed between Egypt and Syria, and between Arabia and the Mediterranean. But the major natural trade routes skirted Israel rather than passed through it, except for the East-West routes from the Jordan Valley to the Mediterranean through the Valley of Jezreel and the Plain of Esdraelon, and from Syria to the sea through Galilee. Israel therefore played a major role in international commerce only when its merchants chose to move out from their highland fastness.

I. In the OT
  A. Long-Distance Trade
  B. Local Trade
  C. Time and Place of Commerce
  D. Terms for "Merchant"
II. In the NT
  A. Background and General Considerations
  B. Long-Distance Trade
  C. Local Trade
  D. Terms for "Merchant"
III. Biblical Attitude to Commerce

***I. In the OT.**–A. Long-Distance Trade.* In Israel, as elsewhere in the ancient Near East, the palace appears as the organizer of long-distance trade. As the Egyptian government at Thebes sent Wen-Amon to Byblos to obtain timber for ship building (*ca.* 1100 B.C.; see *ANET*, pp. 25-29), so Solomon sent envoys to Tyre for timber, dealing directly with Hiram the king and paying with grain, oil, and land (1 K. 5:10f.; 9:11). The state took the initiative in commerce when Solomon constructed a fleet of ships at Ezion-geber on the Gulf of Aqabah. The expeditions that he mounted "once every three years" brought back gold from Ophir, and also silver, ivory, apes, and monkeys (1 K. 9:26-28; 10:22; 2 Ch. 8:17; cf. also 1 K. 10:11). A state-sponsored attempt to restore this enterprise a century later, in the days of Jehoshaphat king of Judah, met with disaster (1 K. 22:48f.; 2 Ch. 20:35-37). Another royal commercial venture is alluded to in 1 K. 10:28f. par. 2 Ch. 1:16f., although textual difficulties make the details uncertain. (The "king's merchants" obtained horses for Solomon from Muṣur [see J. A. Fitzmyer, *Aramaic Treaties of Sefire* (1967), pp. 29-31] — or Egypt [RSV, NEB; cf. Dt. 17:16] — and Kue [Que] in Cilicia and exported them to Syria with chariots obtained from Egypt.) The involvement of the palace in commerce is again clear when Ben-hadad, in his hour of defeat, conceded to Ahab the right to establish street stalls (*ḥûṣôṯ*, lit. "streets," RSV "bazaars") in Damascus, just as Israel had earlier granted trading privileges to the Syrian crown in Samaria (1 K. 20:34). Kings also

Skin-covered boat as commonly used to transport materials on the Tigris and Euphrates; relief from Sennacherib's palace at Nineveh (704-681 B.C.). (Trustees of the British Museum)

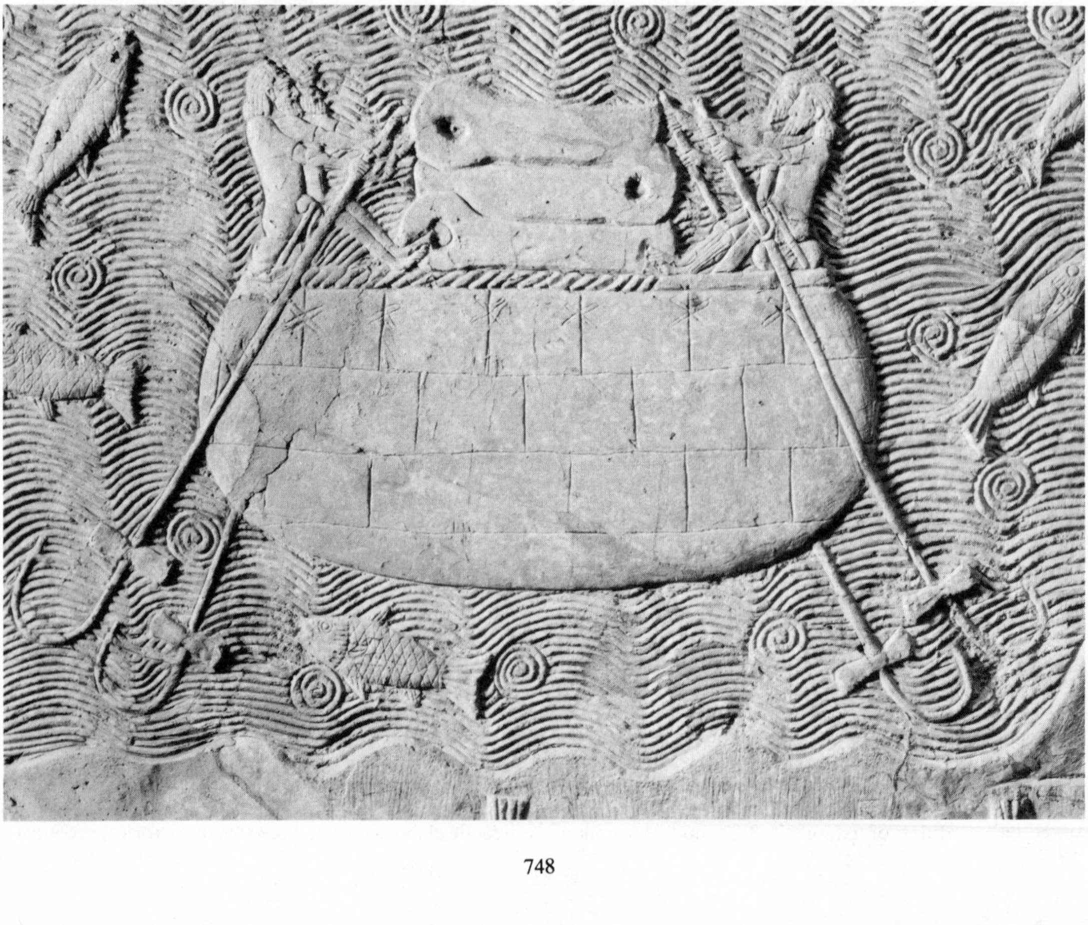

controlled trade by exacting transit tolls from merchants passing through their territory (cf. 1 K. 10:15; "all the kings of Arabia" [RV with MT "mingled people"] were not tributaries of Solomon; cf. also Ezr. 4:13, 20). The palace appears as the destination of commercial expeditions arriving from abroad. The "very great retinue" of the Queen of Sheba, in south Arabia, whose camels carried "spices, and very much gold, and precious stones," made for Solomon's palace (1 K. 10:1-10). It was a palace official who purchased Joseph from the Midianite traders ("Ishmaelites"), whose camels carried gum, balm, and myrrh to Egypt (Gen. 37:25-28; 39:1). The king's role in trade is again suggested by Solomon's construction of "store-cities" (1 K. 9:19). Exotic wares and precious metals presumably found their way out of the palace and down through the various strata of society as gifts to retainers and through exchange.

The role of the private entrepreneur in long-distance trade must not be wholly excluded, however. It is suggested by the householder who goes on a long journey with a bundle of silver (*ṣᵉrôr-hakkesep*) in his hand and is not expected back until the full moon (Prov. 7:19f.; but the passage may be no earlier than the 4th century).

Merchandise was carried overland by caravan (*'ōraḥ*, *'ōrᵉḥâ*, *hᵃlîḵâ*; e.g., Job 6:18f.; Isa. 21:13; Jgs. 5:6). In Gen. 37:25 and 1 K. 10:2 the beasts of burden are camels, but asses were also used, as in Gen. 42:26 and Isa. 30:6.

The lament over Tyre in Ezk. 27 indicates the geographical extent and the range of commodities (here uniquely termed *ma'ᵃrāḇ*) of international trade in the OT period. The reference to Asshur in vv. 23f. as an exporter of "choice garments" recalls the "beautiful mantle from Shinar" (Mesopotamia) found by Achan among the spoils of Ai (Josh. 7:21). Cappadocia imported "Akkadian garments" (*ṣubātū ša akkadî*) from Assyria already in the 19th cent. B.C. Assyrian trade with Palestine after 721 B.C. is documented by Assyrian pottery at several sites (see R. Amiran, *Ancient Pottery of the Holy Land* [1970], p. 291). Sheba is mentioned in Ezk. 7:22 as a source of "all kinds of spices, and all precious stones, and gold." The high value placed on aromatics in the ancient world is illustrated by the appearance of spices and "precious oil" together with silver and gold as the contents of Hezekiah's treasure house (2 K. 20:13).

The "industrial installations" excavated at such Palestinian sites as Tell Beit Mirsim (dye vats) and Tell el-Kheleifeh, ancient Ezion-geber (foundries), seem to have served only domestic needs. The only known exports of OT Israel are agricultural (Gen. 43:11; 1 K. 5:11; Ezk. 27:17). But Prov. 31:13, 19, 22, 24 are noteworthy as suggesting the role of women in a "cottage industry" which served more than local needs ("she delivers girdles to the merchant [*kᵉna'ᵃnî*]," v. 24).

B. Local Trade. The presence of a religious shrine favored the development of a city as a center of local commerce. This is clear from Dt. 14:22-27, which permitted an Israelite who lived far from the sanctuary to sell his agricultural tithes locally and buy an equivalent amount of commodities at the cult center for consumption there by himself and his household. The legislation presupposes the presence of retailers of livestock and produce in the city where the shrine was located, which was not always Jerusalem. The pilgrimage festivals (Passover and Unleavened Bread, Weeks, and Booths), when worshipers flocked to the sanctuary from outlying districts, were doubtless occasions for commercial fairs (for Shiloh, cf. 1 S. 1; Jgs. 21:19).

C. Time and Place of Commerce. Market days were probably held at fixed intervals. The "day of assembly" (*yôm hakkᵉnîsâ*), a term used in the Mishnah (*ca.* A.D. 200) for the second and fifth days of the week (*Megillah* i.1; *Ketuboth* i.1), may well have been a market day as well as a day when the courts sat (see S. Krauss, *Talmudische Archäologie*, II [1911], 358, 690). The custom of holding "assembly days" twice a week may go back to OT times. Trade was regarded as an unsuitable activity for the sabbath and the new moon festival (Neh. 13:16-21; Am. 8:5).

Exchange, be it barter or true sale (*see* BUYING), took place in the streets where tradesmen had their workshops, as in a modern Arab *sūq* (such presumably was "the bakers' street" of Jer. 37:21), or at the city gate (2 K. 7:1), the customary place for doing public business (cf. Dt. 21:19; Ruth 4:1-4; Prov. 8:2f.; 31:23). The city gate was probably where nonresident traders displayed their wares; such were the local peasants (*'ammê hā'āreṣ*) of Neh. 10:31 (MT 32), with their agricultural produce, and traders from distant parts (but note that Neh. 13:16 refers to Tyrian importers of [salt] fish and other merchandise as resident in Jerusalem [cf.1 K. 20:34], presumably near the Fish Gate of Neh. 3:3; 12:39). There was no large open space within an ancient Palestinian city to serve as a market place like the *agora* of a Hellenistic city; at best the street was unusually wide near the gate (cf. Neh. 8:1; Tell Beit Mirsim and Tell en-Naṣbeh provide examples).

D. Terms for "Merchant." The Hebrew terms for "merchant, trader" are *sōḥēr*, *rōḵēl*, *kᵉna'an*/*kᵉna'anî*, and (only in 1 K. 10:15 par. 2 Ch. 9:14) *tār*. Since *tār* elsewhere means "explorer, spy," it should perhaps here be emended to *taggār*, the usual rendering of both *sōḥēr* and *rōḵēl* in the Targums. The use (always late) of *kᵉna'ᵃn(î)*, lit. "Canaan(ite)," reflects the role of the Phoenicians as the merchants *par excellence* in the Mediterranean at the time of the Hebrew monarchy. The distinction between *sōḥēr* and *rōḵēl* is not clear (the LXX normally renders both by *émporos*, "merchant," or a form of the cognate verb *emporeúomai*, to "trade"). But the meaning "slander(er)" borne by the word *rāḵîl*, which is related to *rōḵēl*, suggests that the *rōḵēl* was held in low esteem, like the *kápēlos*, "petty trader," of the Greek world, who was commonly regarded as a cheat. (In Isa. 1:22 the agents of the dishonest dilution of wine with water, unspecified in the MT, are identified as *kápēloi* in the LXX; and according to Sir. 26:29, the *kápēlos* will not be justified of his sin.) The nuance of itinerant merchant has been suggested for *sōḥēr* on the basis of Akk. *saḥāru*, "go around, turn," but not without challenge (see E. A. Speiser, *BASOR*, 164 [Dec. 1961], 23-28; B. Landsberger, *SVT*, 16 [1967], 187-190). The related verb *sāḥar* is rendered "trade in (a place)" in the RSV, but "move about in (a place)" in NJV (e.g., Gen. 34:21; 42:34; cf. NEB).

II. In the NT.–*A. Background and General Considerations.* The principal events of the NT, from the public ministry of Jesus to the martyrdom of Paul, fall within the last four decades of a century of almost unbroken peace that prevailed in Palestine from the beginning of Herod the Great's rule as king of Judea (37 B.C.) until the outbreak of the First Jewish Revolt (A.D. 66). Commerce flourishes best in time of peace, and the events of the NT took place in a setting of commercial prosperity. This peace brought relief from the almost three centuries of conflict that had afflicted Palestine after the arrival of Alexander the Great in the Near East (331 B.C.), as Antigonids, Ptolemies, Seleucids, and Hasmoneans struggled for supremacy. But even in these troubled times, fortunes could be made by those with power to exploit the weak (even by Jews; cf. Josephus *Ant.* xii.4.7). The nature of Palestinian commerce *ca.* 260 B.C. is well illustrated by the archives of the Egyptian official Zeno (see V. Tcherikover, *Hellenistic Civilization and the Jews* [1959], pp. 60-73). The constant interchange of men, goods, and ideas throughout the Mediterranean lands resulting from Greek colonization, the progressive adoption of coinage in a world flooded with the squandered treasuries of plundered oriental monarchies, and the eventual unification of the known world under Roman arms stimulated intense commercial activity. Commerce principally affected the cities, especially the new (or rebuilt) Hellenistic cities along the major trade routes, such as Gaza, Ascalon, Joppa, Caesarea (earlier Strato's Tower), Ptolemais (Acre), Sepphoris, Tiberias, Sebaste (Samaria), Jericho ('Alâyiq) and the cities of the Decapolis. The North-South line of cities E of the Jordan indicates the importance at this period of the desert route from the Red Sea and the Hejaz through Nabatean Petra to Damascus. But commerce probably brought little benefit to the peasants, whose heavy taxes made possible the luxuries of the city-dwelling magnates (1 Macc. 10:29-45 indicates how heavy taxes were *ca.* 150 B.C.; for the time of Herod the Great, see Josephus, *Ant.* xvii.11.2). And as Josephus observes in a striking passage, the Jews of Palestine in the 1st cent. A.D. were still predominantly an agrarian people (*CAp.* i.12).

The opportunities for better material rewards led many Jews to try their fortunes in the wider world outside Judea (e.g., Aquila the tentmaker of Acts 18:2f.), and by the time of Jesus more Jews resided in the Diaspora, especially in Babylonia, Egypt, and Asia Minor, than in Palestine (for estimates of their number, see Tcherikover, pp. 292-95). But the Jews of the Diaspora maintained close links with Judea; each paid an annual half-shekel tax to the temple (Mt. 17:24), and many traveled to Jerusalem for the pilgrimage feasts. This constant coming and going between Jerusalem and the most diverse parts of the Greco-Roman world (cf. Acts 2:8-11) cannot have failed to make the city a center of wealth and commerce. It also facilitated the rapid spread of Christianity.

B. Long-Distance Trade. The booming prosperity of the period is indicated by the grandiose building programs undertaken in Palestine, especially by Herod the Great. At least some of the more highly skilled artisans employed for these undertakings must have come from abroad, and foreign artisans, like foreign troops (as were the Roman legionaries), are invariably accompanied by foreign traders. Evidence for the import of foreign materials for the most ambitious Palestinian structure of this period, the Jerusalem temple, is given by Josephus, who reports the use of Lebanese timber for rafters (*BJ* v.1.5) and Corinthian bronze for the gates (*BJ* v.5.3). Goods moving through ports and other toll points were subject to the imperial harbor-tax (see M. I. Finley, *Ancient Economy* [1973], p. 159), and the tax collector (*telṓnēs*) is a familiar figure in the Gospels (cf. Mt. 9:9). Josephus mentions taxes on public purchases and sales (*Ant.* xvii.8.4).

Asphalt was exported from the Dead Sea (Diodorus ii.48.6; xix.99.3) and dates and balsam from Jericho (so one may infer from Josephus *Ant.* xiv.4.1; xv.4.2). Galilee was able to export olive oil (*BJ* ii.21.2), and the export of pickled fish may be inferred from the fact that they were prepared at Taricheae (probably Magadan [Magdala] of Mt. 15:39; Taricheae means "pickling places") by the Sea of Galilee (Strabo *Geog.* xvi.2.45; cf. Mt. 4:18).

Merchandise was transported by ship whenever possible. Despite the excellence of Roman roads (introduced to Palestine by Hadrian; see *HGHL,* p. 697), it cost more to transport a wagonload of grain 75 mi. (120 km.) overland than to carry it the length of the Mediterranean by ship (see Finley, p. 126). Merchant ships, which were out of commission in the winter (cf. Acts 27:9-12), are mentioned a number of times in Acts as Paul's means of transportation on his missionary journeys (cargoes are mentioned in 21:3 and 27:10, 18, 38 [wheat]). The kinds of merchandise carried in these vessels are indicated by the list of wares of the merchants who lament the fall of Babylon (Rome) in Rev. 18:11-19 (with allusions to Ezk. 27). Roman arms had made the seas safe for commerce, but brigandage on the roads was a constant threat to traders (cf. Lk. 10:30; Josephus *Ant.* xiv. 9.2; 15.4).

Jas. 4:13 indicates the mobility of traders in the Greco-Roman world, undoubtedly with the practice of Jewish traders particularly in mind. They would "go into such and such a town and spend a year there and trade and get gain," presumably then moving on to another town. It is little wonder that Jews were to be found in all cities, as claimed by Strabo (quoted in Josephus *Ant.* xiv.7.1).

C. Local Trade. The only place on whose local trade the NT provides some information is Jerusalem. Jerusalem was never in the first rank of the commercial capitals of antiquity because it was not situated on a major natural trade route. But the presence of the temple assured the city importance as a center of at least local commerce. Even the regular daily sacrifices and the special private offerings must have required quite considerable quantities of materials. But the demand made on local suppliers must have been enormously heavy at the pilgrimage feasts, when thousands of Jews came to Jerusalem from far and wide (for Passover, see Mk. 14:1f.; Lk. 2:41-44; for Pentecost, see Acts 2:1-11; 21:27; cf. 20:16). The visitors required food, accommodation (cf. Mk. 14:14), and sacrificial animals (Jn. 2:14), especially at Passover. Coins acceptable as temple dues were obtained from money changers who did business in the temple precincts (Mt. 21:12; Mk. 11:15; Jn. 2:14).

The commercial district of Jerusalem can be identified as situated on the western hill (the traditional Mt. Zion) because Josephus calls this "the upper market" (*hē ánō agorá, BJ* v.4.1), although the city is not known to have had a large open space typical of a Hellenistic *agora.* Josephus also mentions "the wool-shops, the braziers' smithies and the clothes-market" (*BJ* v.8.1) and the "timber market" (*BJ* ii.19.1).

The parable of the talents shows that a man with the means to set himself up in business could hope to make a profit, but the nature of the business is not specified (Mt. 25:16f.; RSV "traded" is simply *ergázomai* "to work").

D. Terms for "Merchant." Only one word for "merchant" occurs in the NT. This is *émporos*, found only in Mt. 13:45 ("a merchant in search of fine pearls") and Rev. 18:3, 11, 15, 23 (of traders who lament the fall of Babylon). The absence from the NT of the term *naúklēros*, used for a seafaring merchant who outfits his own ship, occasions no surprise since the Jews were not a maritime nation (Ps. 107:23 need not refer to Israelites). The term for a petty trader or hawker, *kápēlos*, might have been expected, however, particularly since Mt. 14:15 and Mk. 6:37 show that travelers could buy cooked food (bread; perhaps also other items) in the villages. But there is no evidence of a middleman between producer and consumer in local commerce (cf. Finley, p. 144).

III. Biblical Attitude to Commerce.–Commerce was not viewed as an unmixed blessing by the biblical writers.

The riches that came from foreign trade were coveted for the glory of a restored Israel (Isa. 60:4-9, 13), but it was recognized that with foreign goods came foreign cults and customs that threatened the purity of Israel's religion (e.g., 2 K. 23:13; Isa. 2:6-8). Jesus seems to have avoided the Hellenistic cities during His ministry (although it was in the cities of the empire that the infant Church was later to become most firmly established), and He warned of the dangers of riches (Mk. 10:23-25). Whereas in Rev. 18 the saints rejoice at the fall of Babylon (v. 20), the merchants of the earth weep and mourn (v. 11); and it is by controlling buying and selling that the beast of Rev. 13:17 oppresses the saints.

See also BUYING.

Bibliography.–A. L. Oppenheim, *Fifth International Congress of Economic History, Leningrad . . . 1970* (for the background of OT commerce); *EB*, IV, *s.v.* "Trade and Commerce" (G. A. Smith) — still very valuable; V. Tcherikover, *Hellenistic Civilization and the Jews* (1959), II.A; F. C. Grant "Economic Background of the NT," in W. D. Davies and D. Daube, eds., *Background of the NT and Its Eschatology* (1956), pp. 96-114 — contains a useful survey of literature on the economic history of the Hellenistic and Roman periods; M. I. Finley, *Ancient Economy* (1973), II.B; P. Lapp, *Palestinian Ceramic Chronology 200 B.C.-A.D. 70* (1961) — Appendix A (Economic and Cultural Implications) and Appendix B (Historical Implications) are useful; J. Jeremias, *Jerusalem in the Time of Jesus* (Eng. tr. 1969) — valuable for its use of early rabbinic sources.

R. F. G. SWEET

COMMISSION; COMMISSIONED [Heb. *ṣawâ*] (Nu. 27:19, 23; Dt. 31:14, 23); AV CHARGE; [*dāṯ*] (Ezr. 8:36); [Gk. *epitropḗ*] (Acts 26:12); [*cháris*–'grace, favor'] (1 Cor. 3:10); AV, NEB, GRACE; [*oikonomía*] (1 Cor. 9:17); AV DISPENSATION; NEB "discharging a trust"; [*chríō*] (2 Cor. 1:21); AV, NEB, ANOINTED; [*hōs ek theoú*] ("commissioned by God," 2 Cor. 2:17); AV "as of God"; "as from God." Authority given to one to act in the place of (e.g., Joshua for Moses) or on behalf of (e.g., Paul as Christ's apostle) another.

COMMISSION, GREAT. *See* JESUS CHRIST IV.

COMMISSIONERS (Ezr. 4:9, NEB). *See* APHARSATHCHITES.

COMMIT [Heb. *gālal, pāqaḏ, nāṯan,* also *śîm* (Job 5:8), *'āzaḇ* (Ps. 10:14); Gk. *paradídōmi, paratíthēmi,* also *dídōmi* (Rev. 20:4)]; AV also DELIVER, TRUST (Ps. 22:8; "committed his cause"), REVEAL (Jer. 11:20, MT *gālâ*), OPEN (20:12, MT *gālâ*), SET BEFORE (Ezk. 27:24), COMMEND (Lk. 23:46; Acts 14:23), GIVE (Rev. 20:4); NEB also PUT IN CHARGE, LEAVE (WITH) (Lev. 6:4), ENTRUST, LAY (BEFORE) (Job 5:8), "threw himself on . . . for rescue" (Ps. 22:8), HAND OVER (Isa. 22:21), GIVE (Ezk. 27:24), SEND (Acts 8:3), MAKE SUBJECT (Rom. 6:17), LAY (UPON) (1 Tim. 1:18), CONSIGN (2 Pet. 2:4). In these references "commit" is used in the sense "entrust," "give in charge," and once possibly "pledge" or "bind" (Rom. 6:17). Elsewhere "commit" is used in the sense "do," "perform," as "commit adultery," "commit iniquity."

The last of the seven "words" of Jesus on the cross is in Lk. 23:46, "Father, into thy hands I commit (*paratíthēmi*) my spirit!" quoting Ps. 31:5 (MT 30:6) (*pāqaḏ*). The meaning here is "put in the care of."

In Rom. 6:17 the significance of *paradídōmi* is uncertain. It may have the technical sense "hand down," as of tradition, reading as in the AV, "that form of doctrine which was delivered you." See *TDNT*, II, *s.v.* παραδίδωμι 6 (Büchsel). The RSV, however, has "the standard of teaching to which you were committed," and the NEB "the pattern of teaching to which you were made subject" (but cf. mg.). Bauer (p. 620) suggests "the form of teaching, for the learning of which you were given over." The form of the verb used, *paradóthēte* (2nd person pl.), makes the AV reading unlikely. J. W. D. H.

COMMON. In the OT "common" as opposed to "holy" is called Heb. *ḥōl,* as "common bread" (1 S. 21:4; NEB "ordinary bread"), i.e., other than the showbread or bread of the Presence; "common journey" (v. 5, AV "common manner"; NEB "ordinary campaign"), i.e., other than a military expedition, for which David and his men would have had to be consecrated; cf. also Lev. 10:10 (AV "unholy"; NEB "profane"); Ezk. 22:26 (AV "profane"); 42:20; 44:23 (AV, NEB, "profane").

In Lev. 4:27 the "common people" (*'am hā'āreṣ,* lit. "people of the land") are distinguished from the rulers or men "of standing" (v. 22, NEB; Heb. *nāśî'*). Cemeteries for the common people (*bᵉnê hā'ām*) are mentioned in 2 K. 23:6 (AV "graves of the children of the people"; NEB "common burial-ground") and Jer. 26:23.

The "common land" (Heb. *migrāš,* AV "suburbs") mentioned in Lev. 25:34; 1 Ch. 11:14; 31:19 (elsewhere RSV "pasture land"; *see* PASTURE) is land around Palestinian towns used in common by shepherds and herdsmen for grazing sheep and cattle.

The Hebrew expression "of a man" sometimes means "common," as in the "common cubit" (*'îš*) of Dt. 3:11; the "common characters" (*'ᵉnôš*) of Isa. 8:1 (AV "a man's pen"); or the "man of the common sort" (*rōḇ 'āḏām*) mentioned in Ezk. 23:42; see also Nu. 16:29, the "common death of all men," and in the NT 1 Cor. 10:13 (Gk. *anthrṓpinos*).

In the NT the usual word is Gk. *koinós,* or the verb *koinóō,* indicating what is public, general, universal, as contrasted with *ídios,* what is peculiar, individual, not shared with others. Thus, "common faith" (Tit. 1:4) and "common salvation" (Jude 3) refer to that in which the experience of all Christians unites and is identical: "common," because there is but one faith and one salvation (Eph. 4:4-6). From this comes the derived meaning of what is ordinary and, therefore, to be disesteemed, as contrasted with what pertains to a class, and is to be prized, because rare. This naturally coincides with OT exclusivism, particularity, and separation. Its religion was that of a separated people, with a separated class as its ministers, and with minute directions as to distinctions of meat, drink, times, places, rites, vessels, etc. Whatever was common or ordinary, it avoided (*see* DEFILE). The NT, on the other hand, with its universalism of scope and its spirituality of sphere, rose above all such externals. The salvation it brought was directed to the redemption of nature as well as of man, sanctifying the creature and pervading all parts of man's being and all relations of life. The antithesis is forcibly illustrated in Acts 10:14f., where Peter says: "I have never eaten anything that is common or unclean," and the reply is: "What God has cleansed, you must not call common."

Other NT words include *dēmósios* in Acts 5:18, for the "common prison" into which the apostles were put (the NEB has "official custody," and F. F. Bruce, *in loc.,* has "public ward"); and *idiṓtēs* in 4:13, "common men," NEB "laymen." Peter and John, though without formal theological training, could argue intelligently before the Sanhedrin.

See also COMMUNITY OF GOODS; SACRED.

H. E. JACOBS J. W. D. H.

COMMON LIFE. Though not occurring specifically in the OT or NT, this phrase (based on Gk. *koínos* and cognates) appears frequently throughout history as a summary designation of the unique relationships that obtain among Christians.

The common life is established by baptism (in the true sense of Gal. 3:27; cf. 1 Pet. 3:21), and expresses a very intimate two-dimensional relationship. Believers share together vertically in and with Christ (e.g., 1 Cor. 1:9; Eph. 2:19-22; He. 3:14; 1 Jn. 1:3), and this has implications for the horizontal relationship (e.g., Jn. 13:14; 1 Jn. 1:7). Union with Christ transcends all other distinctions and ineluctably creates a new kind of loving fellowship (Gal. 3:27-29). While the vertical originates the horizontal, the vitality of the former is demonstrated by the latter (cf. Jn. 13:12ff., 34; Phil. 2:1-13).

The common life's double dimension appears most dramatically when Paul argues for helping the poor saints in Jerusalem (Rom. 15:25-28; 1 Cor. 16:1f.; 2 Cor. 8f.). The sharing of spiritual blessings necessitates outward expression (Rom. 15:27). Giving materially is, for Paul, not "charity" but a practical and tangible demonstration of organic unity. The intended recipients are not "the poor," but the Christian community in Jerusalem from which the gospel had been generated. Paul does not use Gk. *logeía* (the technical term for collecting money), but *koinonía* itself, when referring to the collection (RSV "contribution") for Jerusalem (Rom. 15:26; 2 Cor. 9:13). Likewise, Paul's passionate plea for a money offering provides the imagery for one of his most eloquent descriptions of Christ (2 Cor. 8:9). This twofold relationship is also evident in another concrete manifestation of the common life, the Lord's Supper (e.g., 1 Cor. 10:17, and possibly 11:29).

See also COMMON; COMMUNION; COMMUNITY OF GOODS.

C. G. CHRISTIANS

COMMONWEALTH [Gk. *politeía*] (Eph. 2:12); NEB COMMUNITY; [*políteuma*] (Phil. 3:20); AV CONVERSATION; NEB "(we are) citizens (of)." The "commonwealth of Israel" mentioned in Eph. 2:12 is "the Jews" as a nation, as opposed to the Gentiles, who before Christ came were separated from that chosen community. Cf. 2 Macc. 13:14.

On Phil. 3:20 *see* CITIZEN.

COMMUNE. The RSV replaces most AV uses of "commune" with "talk," "speak," "say," "discuss," "confer," "converse," translating Heb. *dāḇar* (Gen. 18:33; 23:8; 34:6, 8; Eccl. 1:16; Zec. 1:14; etc.), *sāpar* (Ps. 64:5); Gk. *dialaléō* (Lk. 6:11), *syllaléō* (22:4), *homiléo* (24:15; Acts 24:26); but retains it for Heb. *'āmar* in Ps. 4:4, where "commune with the heart" means "meditate," "engage in quiet introspection." In Ps. 77:6, the AV "I call to remembrance my song" becomes in the RSV "I commune with my heart," following the LXX and Syriac, while AV "I commune with mine own heart" in the next line is in the RSV "I meditate" (Heb. *śî[a]ḥ*).

J. W. D. H.

COMMUNICATE. In the RSV this word occurs only in Ezk. 44:19; 46:20, for Heb. *qādēš*, "communicate holiness"; the AV has "sanctify," the NEB "transmit sacred influence." The garments worn by the priests in the inner court of the sanctuary had to be taken off before the priests came back out, lest the people be too near the holy, which was the prerogative only of the Lord and His priests. Here the "holy" is not far from the "taboo" of primitive religions. *See* SACRED.

The AV has "communicate" in Gal. 2:2 for Gk. *anatíthemai* (RSV "I laid before them"); in 6:6 for *koinōnéō*, Phil. 4:14 for *synkoinōnéō*, and He. 13:16 for *koinōnía* (RSV "share"); in Phil. 4:15 for *koinōnéō* (RSV "entered into partnership"); and "willing to communicate" in 1 Tim. 6:18 for *koinōnikós* (RSV "generous").

J. W. D. H.

COMMUNICATION. Normally used in the AV of speaking (2 S. 3:17; 2 K. 9:11 [Heb. *śî(a)ḥ*; RSV "his talk"; NEB "the way his thoughts run"]; Mt. 5:37; Lk. 24:17; Eph. 4:29), but also for Gk. *koinōnía* in Philem. 6 (RSV "sharing"), and archaically for *homilía* in 1 Cor. 15:33 (RSV "company").

COMMUNION; FELLOWSHIP. The association of believers in the experience of their common salvation, or in the various consequences, expressions, and benefits of salvation. Although the idea is most explicit in the NT, it is adumbrated in the OT where the people of God share a common calling and inheritance as joint beneficiaries of the covenant made with them by God; they consequently share in the land and its fruits, in common worship and law, and are required on the one hand to share their material prosperity with their poor neighbors and on the other hand to abstain from common life with peoples outside the commonwealth of Israel (cf. Rom. 9:4f.). Some NT descriptions of "communion" clearly allude to this OT adumbration, e.g., Col. 1:12.

In the NT the fellowship of believers is chiefly designated by the Gk. verb *koinōnéō* and its cognate forms, but the verbs *metéchō* and *merízō*, with their cognate forms, are also important (the three nouns *koinōnía*, *metochḗ*, and *merís* occur in parallel in 2 Cor. 6:14f.), together with a number of words having a *syn-* prefix, and a number of images (e.g., the body) expressing the idea of common participation. Even so, "fellowship" is by no means confined to passages where these words or images are employed (see C. H. Dodd, *Johannine Epistles* [*MNTC*, 1946], pp. 6ff.).

For *koinōnía*, Hauck (*TDNT*, III, 798) distinguishes three senses: "1. 'participation,' 2. 'impartation,' 3. 'fellowship.' " For an analysis of "communion" along these lines, see *NBD*, *s.v.*

I. Acts 2:42.–Luke's only use of the noun *koinōnía* (he does not use the verb) occurs in a passage of singular interest. The three thousand converts at Pentecost "devoted themselves to the apostles' teaching and fellowship, to the breaking of bread and the prayers." "Fellowship" here has its own definite article, and the phrase "to the fellowship" should stand as a separate object of "devoted themselves," coordinate with "to the apostles' teaching." While the precise meaning here of "the fellowship" has been much discussed, it probably is at least close to being a term for the Jerusalem church seen as an "association." The verb *proskarteréō* ("devote oneself") generally means "attend regularly" or "actively engage in," which suggests that "the fellowship" was a visible activity, not merely a sense of spiritual affinity. Thus the NEB renders: "they met constantly to hear the apostles teach, and to share the common life." C. Anderson Scott suggested that *hē koinōnía* here represented the Aramaic term *ḥ^{a}ḇûrâ*, which "was in current use to describe a group of companions or partners, sharers in a common life (e.g., students at a college)," and that its use may have gone back to the days when Jesus was still on earth, as a designation for His circle of disciples (*Christianity According to St. Paul* [1927], pp. 159f.).

However that may be (for a criticism, see R. N. Flew,

Jesus and His Church [1938], pp. 111f.), the term *koinōnía* had recognized connotations in contemporary Hellenistic society. "Whatever the original Jerusalem group may have thought about the character of their society . . . , the person who wrote up its affairs a generation later for the information of a Hellenistic public presented it in terms that could not fail to identify it as a religious association of the kind familiar to them" (E. A. Judge, *Social Pattern of Christian Groups in the 1st Cent.* [1960], p. 45; see also B. Reicke, *Diakonie, Festfreude und Zelos in Verbindung mit Altchristlichen Agapenfeier* [1951]). This does not mean that *hē koinōnía* was a current title for the Christian Church, but rather that the group of Jerusalem believers had the character of a society whose most obvious feature was "association" in certain common activities. (Similarly, the term *ekklēsía,* which finally came to be a designation of Christians as a permanent society, was probably in the first place a description of the central *function* of believers, viz., "assembly.") Luke apparently means us to identify, as the activities involved in *hē koinōnía,* "the breaking of bread and the prayers," as well as the community of goods which occurred when need arose (Acts 2:44f. and 4:32; in both cases note the use of the cognate adjective *koiná,* "all things in *common*").

Although Acts 2:42 is describing the external rather than the internal character of the believers' common life, this is perhaps the only place in the NT where *koinōnía* is used as a term for this COMMON LIFE in general. Elsewhere, *koinōnía* is used with reference either to the association of *particular groups* among believers (especially the association of Gentiles with Jews), or else to *particular benefits* that believers share in common.

II. Communion Between Particular Groups.–The most remarkable instance of "communion" in the NT is that which brought Jew and Gentile into common enjoyment of the same spiritual benefits (although the similar "communion" of male and female, bond and free, was little less remarkable). The Gentile, says Paul, is joint shareholder (*synkoinōnós*) with Jews in the rich root of the olive tree (Rom. 11:17). More particularly, the gentile believers (of Macedonia and Greece) have come to share (*koinōnéō*) the spiritual benefits of the saints at Jerusalem (Rom. 15:27). The securing of this communion is a central benefit of the gospel (see esp. Eph. 2:11-21), though many problems were encountered in the attempt to give practical expression to fellowship at table and in other aspects of common life (Acts 15; Gal. 2; Rom. 14). The references to "common faith" (Tit. 1:4) and "our common salvation" (Jude 3) may well refer to the writers' being Jews and their readers Gentiles (cf. 2 Pet. 1:1, "to those who have obtained a faith of equal standing with ours"; and Acts 15:9).

This *koinōnía* in spiritual things, for which the Jews must give and the Gentiles receive, leads in turn to a *koinōnía* in material goods, for which the Gentiles must give and the poor of the saints in Jerusalem receive (Rom. 12:13; 15:26; 2 Cor. 8:4; 9:13). A similar *koinōnía,* with reciprocal giving and receiving of both spiritual and material benefits, exists between "him who is taught the word" and "him who teaches" (Gal. 6:6). An extension of such fellowship is the support of an apostle in his further labors by a church that he has founded. Paul thanks the Philippians for such support ("partnership in the gospel," Phil. 1:5), but regrets that other churches have not had fellowship with him in this way (Phil. 4:15). Although in contexts such as these *koinōnía* comes nearly to mean "give" or "receive" a share, Paul's insistence on the principle of equality (*isótēs*) of participation shows that the basic idea of *koinōnía* remains the common sharing, rather than the incidental giving or receiving that may be necessary to secure such fellowship (2 Cor. 8:14).

III. Communion in Christ and the Spirit.–In 1 Cor. 1:9ff. the common sharing of Christ is set over against a party spirit that absurdly implies that Christ is the peculiar possession of a segment of the Church. "'I am of Christ.' Has Christ been apportioned [i.e., given as the exclusive portion of one section]?" No, the whole people of God shares together in Christ, as the type in 1 Cor. 10:4 indicates. Cf. He. 3:14: "We share in Christ." A corollary of this is the fellowship of believers in Christ's sufferings (Phil. 3:10; 1 Pet. 4:13), although the *koinōnía* here is strictly a sharing in suffering by both Christ and the believers.

Likewise believers partake together of the Holy Spirit (He. 6:4). This is probably the meaning of "the fellowship of the Spirit" in Phil. 2:1 and 2 Cor. 13:14 (see *NBD, loc. cit.*). The corporate reception of the Spirit by believers (Gal. 3:2, 5; Acts 1:5; 2:4) is obviously related. Compare 1 Cor. 12:13 with 10:4 implying an identity between drinking of Christ and drinking of the Spirit. OT types and promises lie behind these ideas, as also behind the pictures of fellowship in "calling" and "inheritance" in He. 3:1 and Col. 1:12.

IV. Communion in the Body and Blood of Christ.–Any common meal is a form of *koinōnía* inasmuch as a number of persons share together in a reality external to them all. Where a meal is associated with a religious object, there is inevitably a deeper *koinōnía* in the object that the meal represents. When Israelites joined together in a sacrificial meal, they were really united in the altar whence the meal came and whence it derived its meaning. Likewise, those who joined in feasts in idol temples were actually united in the idols, or rather in the demons that were the reality beyond the idols. So, argues Paul in 1 Cor. 10:14ff., those who sit and partake together of the cup of blessing and of the broken bread in Christian assembly must know that they are associated together in the blood of Christ and in the body of Christ, i.e., in Christ crucified, since the whole purpose of eating the bread and drinking the cup is to remember Christ in relation to His death (11:23-26). Thus, while Paul does not actually designate the Lord's supper by the title of "communion," he asserts that to share together in it is a fellowship or communion with one another in the death of Christ. It weakens the force of this passage to restrict the meaning of *koinōnía* in 1 Cor. 10:16 to "partaking" merely; the full sense of "communion" is intended. There is an objective reality, the death of Christ; and the unity of believers springs from their all being joined together in that death.

V. 1 John 1:1-7.–"Fellowship" has two aspects here: first, the sharing in divine revelation by the apostles and those whom he addresses, as a result of apostolic testimony (v. 3a; cf. II above); second, an advanced fellowship stated explicitly only here in the NT: "Our fellowship is with the Father." The idea of a common life with the Father is striking, but it is not developed (cf. 2 Pet. 1:4). Possibly John speaks this way because he considers "light" to be the bond of unity between the Father and believers. Our fellowship with Him (and consequently with each other) depends on our walking "in the light" as He is "in the light."

Bibliography.–*TDNT*, III, *s.v.* κοίνος κτλ. (Hauck); A. R. George, *Communion with God in the NT* (1955); J. Y. Campbell, "ΚΟΙΝΩΝΙΑ and its Cognates in the NT," in *Three NT Studies* (1965), pp. 1-28 (= *JBL*, 51 [1932], 352-380).

D. W. B. ROBINSON

COMMUNITY OF GOODS. In Acts 2:44 it is said that in the infant church at Jerusalem "all who believed were together and had all things in common" (Gk. *eíchon hápanta koiná*)," and (4:34f.) "as many as were possessors of lands or houses sold them, and brought the proceeds of what was sold and laid it at the apostles' feet." The inference from this, that there was an absolute disposal of all the property of all the members of the church, and that its proceeds were contributed to a common fund, has been disputed upon the ground that the example of Barnabas in selling "a field" for this purpose (4:37) would not have been mentioned if this had been the universal rule. The thought conveyed is that all believers in that church held their property as a trust from the Lord, for the benefit of the entire brotherhood, and, as there was need, did as Barnabas.

No commandment of which record has been preserved prescribed any such course. It came from the spontaneous impulse of the sense of brotherhood in Christ, when the band of disciples was still small, making them in a sense one family, and under the external constraint of extreme want and persecution. Under such conditions they had so much in common already that they were ready to extend this to all things. It was, in a sense, a continuance of the practice of a common purse in the band of Jesus' immediate followers during His ministry. The penalty inflicted on Ananias and Sapphira was not for any failure to comply fully with this custom, but because the freedom of ownership which was theirs (Acts 5:4) they falsely claimed to have renounced, thus receiving in the estimation of their brethren a credit that was not their due.

This custom did not last long. It was possible only within a limited circle, and under very peculiar circumstances. Specialized revivals of it may be seen in monasticism and in various Christian communities such as the Hutterites. H. E. JACOBS

COMPACT [Heb. *b^e^rîṯ*] (2 Ch. 23:1); AV COVENANT; NEB AGREEMENT. The word here used of the alliance made by Jehoiada the priest with the military commanders, in plotting against Athaliah, is the same word used for "covenant" throughout the OT, indicating that these men made a solemn contract.

COMPACT. An archaic rendering of Heb. *ḥāḇar* in Ps. 122:3; AV "Jerusalem . . . is compact together." The RSV has "bound firmly together," the NEB "where people come together in unity." The NEB rendering is to be preferred, since it better fits the context. It is based on a slight emendation of the MT, and a different understanding of *ḥāḇar,* following the LXX (Gk. *hḗs hē metochḗ autḗs epí tó autó*), Vulgate, and other ancient versions.

COMPACTED. The AV for Gk. *symbibázō* in Eph. 4:16. The RSV and NEB read "knit together." *See* BODY.

COMPANION; COMPANIONSHIP [Heb. *qārôḇ*] (Ex. 32:27); AV, NEB, NEIGHBOUR; [*rā'â*] (Prov. 13:20; 28:7); NEB "mix with," COMPANY; [*rē'â*] (Jgs. 11:37f.); AV also FELLOW; [*rē(a)'*] (Job 30:29; Ps. 38:11; 45:14; 122:8); AV, NEB, also FRIEND; [*m^e^yuddā'*] (Ps. 88:8, 18); AV ACQUAINTANCE; NEB also FRIEND; [*mērē(a)'*] (Jgs. 14:11, 20; 15:2, 6); NEB ESCORT, GROOMSMAN; [*'allûp*] (Ps. 55:13); AV, NEB, COMPANY; [*'aḥ*] (Jer. 41:8); AV BRETHREN; NEB "the others"; [*ḥāḇēr*] (Ps. 119:63; Cant. 1:7; 8:13; Prov. 28:24; Isa. 1:23); NEB COMPANY, FRIEND, "confederate with"; "no better than" (Prov. 28:24); [*ḥ^a^ḇereṯ*] (Mal. 2:14); NEB PARTNER; [Aram. *ḥ^a^ḇar*] (Dnl. 2:13, 17f.); AV FELLOW; [Gk. *synékdēmos*] (Acts 19:29); NEB TRAVELLING-COMPANIONS. The Hebrew terms denote relationships of varying degrees of closeness. The verb *rā'â*, on which several terms are based, means to "have dealings with," while the verb *ḥāḇar* means to "be joined." The companions of Jgs. 14:20 and Ps. 45:14 performed the specific duties, respectively, of best man and bridesmaids. G. WYPER

COMPANY [Heb. *'ēḏâ, qāhāl, ṣāḇā', maḥ^a^neh, rōš,* sôḏ, also *ḥeḇrâ* (Job 34:8), *lah^a^qâ* (1 S. 19:20), *'^a^ṣereṯ* (Jer. 9:2), *šip'â* (2 K. 9:17), verbs *ḥēleq* ("keep company," Ps. 50:18), *rā'â* ("keep company," Prov. 29:3), *zā'aq* ("come with a company," Jgs. 18:23), also "companies which gave thanks" (*tôḏôṯ,* Neh. 12:31, 40, sing. v. 38), and cf. Ps. 78:49; Gk. *sympósion* (Mk. 6:39), *klisía* (Lk. 9:14), *synodía* (2:44), *óchlos* (5:29; Acts 1:15), *plḗthos* (Lk. 23:1; Acts 4:32; 14:1), *hikanós (óchlos)* (Acts 11:24, 26; 19:26), *homilía* (1 Cor. 15:33), also *hoí perí* . . . (Acts 13:13), *(ex) hēmṓn* (Lk. 24:22), *hymṓn* (Rom. 15:24), *hymī́n* (15:32)]; AV also ARMY, HOST, ASSEMBLY, MULTITUDE, CONGREGATION, BAND, DROVE (Gen. 33:8), "be partaker" (Ps. 50:18), MUCH (PEOPLE), NUMBER (Acts 1:15), COMMUNICATIONS (1 Cor. 15:33), etc.; NEB also HOST, TRIBAL HOST (*ṣāḇā'*), COLUMN (1 S. 11:11), PARTY, RETINUE (2 K. 5:15), TROOP (9:17), CHOIR (Neh. 12), BAND, "one and all" (Job 15:34), FELLOWS (16:7), "common cause" (50:18), MOB (Jer. 9:2), GANG (15:17), GROUP (Mk. 6:39; Lk. 9:14), ASSEMBLY (Lk. 23:1), BODY (Acts 4:32; 14:1), NUMBERS (11:24, 26), COMPANIONS (13:13), CROWDS (19:26).

The "companies" (*ṣ^e^ḇā'ôṯ*) of Nu. 1:3, 52; 2:3, 9f.; 10:14; etc. are military units into which the tribes were grouped, when they were numbered and also when they left Mt. Sinai. In general *ṣāḇā'* indicates an army, a host of warriors.

Other important OT words are *maḥ^a^neh,* normally an encampment, but occasionally extended to mean "group" in general, as in Gen. 32:7-10; 50:9 (Jacob's funeral party); 2 K. 5:15; *qāhāl,* a "gathering" of peoples (Gen. 28:3; 35:11; 48:4; 49:6; Ps. 26:5; Jer. 31:8; 50:9; Ezk. 17:17; 27:27; 32:22f.; 38:4), usually indicating large numbers; *'ēḏâ*, a group with common purpose or relation (Nu. 16:5ff.; 26:9f.; 27:3; Job 15:34; 16:7; Ps. 22:16; 106:17f.), most often translated CONGREGATION; and *rō'š,* "head," a small military unit (Jgs. 7:16, 20; 9:34ff.; 1 S. 11:11; 13:17f.; Job 1:17).

In Mark's account of the miraculous feeding of the five thousand, he says Jesus commanded the people to sit down *sympósia sympósia* (6:39), and that they sat down *prasiaí prasiaí* (lit. "garden beds," v. 40), group by group, "by hundreds and by fifties." In Luke's parallel account they are told to sit down in *klisíai* of "about fifty each" (9:14). The Gk. *sympósion* normally meant "banquet," and *klisía* means "people reclining" as at a banquet; here they refer to the less formal groups of people eating on the grass beside the Sea of Galilee. This grouping may have been for efficient distribution of the food, and possibly also to promote more intimate fellowship. Or could there lie behind this division into groups a cultural revulsion to eating in a disordered throng?

In Lk. 2:44 occurs the Gk. *synodía,* referring to the group returning from the Passover. This must have been a large caravan, for they had gone a day's journey before Jesus' parents realized that their son had remained in Jerusalem.

Paul warns against "bad company" in 1 Cor. 15:33, using Gk. *homilíai*, "associations."

Large crowds or gatherings of people are designated also in the NT by *óchlos, plḗthos,* and *hikanós* ("sufficient"). J. W. D. H.

COMPASS [Heb. *mᵉḥûgâ, sāḇaḇ*]; NEB also "make the circuit" (*sāḇaḇ*). The term "compass" occurs only twice in the RSV; in Isa. 44:13 the noun *mᵉḥûgâ* describes a pair of compasses (NEB "callipers") used in woodwork. The term *sāḇaḇ,* often rendered "compass" or "fetch a compass" by the AV, is rendered "compass" in the obsolete sense of this term only once by the RSV, in Josh. 6:11, with reference to marching around Jericho with the ark of the covenant.

COMPASSION [Heb. *rāḥam, rāḥᵃmîm, ḥāmal, nāḥam, niḥûmîm* (Hos. 11:8), *nōḥam* (13:14), *ḥēn* (Zec. 12:10); Gk. *splanchnízomai* (Gospels), *oikteírō* (Rom. 9:15), *splánchna oiktirmoú* (Col. 3:12), *sympathéō* (He. 10:34)]; AV also MERCY, (TENDER) MERCIES, "repent oneself for" (for RSV "have compassion on," Heb. *nāḥam*), REPENTINGS (Hos. 11:8), REPENTANCE (13:14), TENDER LOVE (Dnl. 1:9), GRACE (Zec. 12:10), BOWELS OF MERCIES (Col. 3:12); NEB also REMORSE, PITY, MERCY, MERCIES, TENDER CARE, TENDERNESS, (TENDER) AFFECTION, (TENDER) LOVE, GOODWILL, "his heart went out to them" (Mt. 14:14 par.; cf. Lk. 15:20), "feel sorry" (Mt. 15:32 par.), "share the sufferings of" (He. 10:34), etc.; **COMPASSIONATE** [Heb. *ḥannûn*] (Ex. 22:27); AV GRACIOUS; NEB FULL OF COMPASSION; [*raḥûm*] (Ps. 78:38); AV FULL OF COMPASSION; NEB NATURAL AFFECTION; [*raḥmānî*] (Lam. 4:10); AV PITIFUL; NEB TENDER-HEARTED; [Gk. *polýsplanchnos*] (Jas. 5:11); AV PITIFUL; NEB FULL OF PITY; **CORDS OF COMPASSION** in Hos. 11:4, RSV, is an inference, not following literally the MT or LXX, which read as AV "cords of a man"; cf. NEB "leading-strings," mg. "cords of leather," reading *'āḏōm* for *'āḏām*

Both *rāḥam* and *splanchnízomai* are examples of the physical origin of spiritual terms, the bowels being regarded as the seat of the warm, tender emotions or feelings. But, while *rāḥam* applied to the lower viscera as well as the higher, *splánchnon* denoted chiefly the higher viscera, the heart, lungs, liver.

Compassion, literally a feeling with and for others, is a fundamental and distinctive quality of the biblical conception of God, and to its prominence the world owes more than words can express. Along with it goes mercy, which in the OT translates much the same vocabulary. (1) It lay at the foundation of Israel's faith in Yahweh. For it was out of His compassion that He, by a marvelous act of power, delivered them from bondage and called them to be His own people. Nothing, therefore, is more prominent in the OT than the ascription of compassion, pity, mercy, etc., to God; the people may be said to have gloried in it. It is summed up in such sayings as that of the great declaration in Ex. 34:6 (NEB): "The Lord . . . compassionate and gracious" (cf. Ps. 78:38). And, because this was the character of their God, the prophets declared that compassion or kindness was an essential requirement of members of the community (Mic. 6:8; cf. Prov. 19:17). (2) In Jesus Christ, in whom God was "manifest in the flesh," compassion was an outstanding feature (Mt. 9:36; 14:14; etc.), and He taught that it ought to be extended, not to friends and neighbors only, but to all without exception, even to enemies (Mt. 5:43-48; Lk. 10:30-37).

The God of the NT, the Father of men, is most clearly revealed as "a God full of compassion." His compassion extends to the whole human race, for which He effected not merely a temporal, but a spiritual and eternal deliverance, giving up His own Son to the death of the cross in order to save us from the worst bondage of sin with its consequences; seeking thereby to gain a new, wider people for Himself, still more devoted, more filled with and expressive of His own Spirit. Therefore all who know the God and Father of Christ, and who call themselves His children, must necessarily cultivate compassion and show mercy, "even as he is merciful." Hence the many apostolic injunctions to that effect (Eph. 4:32; Col. 3:12; Jas. 1:27; 1 Jn. 3:17; etc.). Christianity may be said to be distinctively the religion of compassion.

See also MERCY; STEADFAST LOVE. W. L. WALKER

COMPEL. In the AV "compel" does not always have the strong significance it has today; cf. 1 S. 28:23 (Heb. *pāraṣ*), where the RSV replaces it with "urge," and Acts 26:11, where AV "compelled" (Gk. *ēnánkazon*) is in the RSV "tried to make" (so also NEB), and perhaps 2 Ch. 21:11; Lk. 14:23. *See also* COURIER.

COMPETE [Heb. hithpael of *ḥārâ*] (Jer. 12:5; 22:15); AV CONTEND, CLOSE; NEB VIE, "be more splendid"; [Gk. *tréchō*–'run'] (1 Cor. 9:24); AV, NEB, RUN; [*athléō*] (2 Tim. 2:5); AV STRIVE. Competition is used figuratively by Jeremiah to warn Israel and by Paul to characterize the life of a Christian.

COMPILE. The RSV rendering of the rather rare Gk. *anatáxasthai* in Lk. 1:1. Other possible renderings are "arrange," "set in order," "draw up." Luke is referring to various narratives which had been produced prior to his own attempt at Gospel writing. These were based on the reports of those who were eyewitnesses of Jesus' ministry. With the rise of numerous congregations in Palestine and beyond, such compilations were needed for instructing the saints concerning the words and deeds of Jesus. Luke's use of "narrative" is not congenial to the form-critical notion that the Gospels were pieced together from small, detached fragments of information.

E. F. H.

COMPLACENCE [Heb. *šalwâ*–'ease'] (Prov. 1:32); AV PROSPERITY; **COMPLACENT** [*bōṭᵉḥôṯ*–'careless'] (Isa. 32:9-11); AV CARELESS; NEB "that live at ease," "who have no cares." The ease of unrighteousness in the face of God's judgment is mere complacence before destruction. The peace that issues from obedience to His will is "quietness and trust forever."

COMPLAIN; COMPLAINT [Heb. *śî(a)ḥ, rîḇ* (Jgs. 21:22; Job 31:13; Jer. 2:29; 12:1), *'ānan* (Nu. 11:1; Lam. 3:39), *yāḵaḥ* (Gen. 21:25), *tôḵaḥaṯ* (Hab. 2:1); Aram. *šᵉḵaḥ* (Dnl. 6:4f.); Gk. *momphḗ* (Col. 3:13), *lógos* (Acts 19:38), *légō* (Phil. 4:11)]; AV also REPROVE (Gen. 21:25; Hab. 2:1), PLEAD (Jer. 2:29; 12:1), PRAY (Ps. 55:17), PRAYER (Ps. 64:1), CONTEND (Job 31:13), BABBLINGS (Prov. 23:29), SPEAK (Phil. 4:11), MATTER (Acts 19:38), QUARREL (Col. 3:13), etc.; NEB also GRIEF (Job 9:27; 10:1), THOUGHTS (Job 21:4; 23:2), ANXIETY (Prov. 23:29), LAMENT (Ps. 64:1), DISPUTE (Jer. 12:1), CHALLENGE (Hab. 2:1), ARGUE (Jer. 2:29), WOES (Ps. 55:17), CASE (Acts 19:38), "alluding to" (Phil. 4:11), etc.

To complain is to express one's pain, grief, or discontent. Job complains to Yahweh about his suffering (Job 7:11) even to the point of loathing his own life (10:1). The Israelites murmur in the wilderness and complain to Yahweh of their misfortunes (Nu. 11:1). The psalmist brings his complaint before Yahweh in the temple and is confident that Yahweh will hear him and save him from his trouble (Ps. 55:16f.; 142:2, 6f.).

One also makes a complaint when his legal rights have been violated (Acts 19:38; Job 31:13). Abraham complains to Abimelech when Abimelech's servants seize his well (Gen. 21:25). Israel (Jer. 2:29) and the prophet (12:1) make a case before Yahweh when they are convinced of unjust treatment. E. W. CONRAD

COMPLETE. *See* FULFIL; PERFECT.

COMPOSITION [Heb. *maṯkōmeṯ*–'measure']; NEB PRESCRIPTION; **COMPOUND** [Heb. *rāqaḥ*–'make perfume']. These terms are used of the sacred anointing oil (Ex. 30:25, 32f.) and of the holy perfume (vv. 37f.) which were to be reserved for religious usage.

COMPREHEND [Heb. *yāḏa'* (Job 37:5), *bîn* (38:18), *šāmē(a)'* (Isa. 33:19); Gk. *ginṓskō* (1 Cor. 2:11), *katalambánō* (Eph. 3:18)]; AV also PERCEIVE, KNOW; NEB also "(that pass our) knowledge" (Job 37:5), CATCH (Isa. 33:19), KNOW, GRASP. *See* KNOW.

In the AV "comprehend" has certain archaic uses. In Isa. 40:12 it translates Heb. *kûl,* which means as in the RSV "enclose" (NEB "hold"). In the NT it is used for Gk. *anakephalaióō* (Rom. 13:9), meaning "sum up" (RSV, NEB) under one head. And in Jn. 1:5 it translates *katalambánō*, "the darkness comprehended it not." The RSV reads "the darkness has not overcome it," NEB "has never mastered it." *See* OVERCOME. J. W. D. H.

COMPUTE [Heb. *ḥāšaḇ*] (Lev. 27:18, 23); AV RECKON; NEB ESTIMATE. An Israelite who had dedicated himself or part of his possessions to the Lord's service could be released from that vow by substituting a monetary payment. (The exceptions were animals suitable for sacrifice.) The amount to be rendered for one's possession was to be computed by the priest according to the time the vow was made in relation to the Year of Jubilee, when land would resort to its original owner.

G. WYPER

CONANIAH kon-ə-nī'ə [Heb. *kônanyāhû*–'Yahweh has founded' or 'Yahweh sustains'].

1. AV CONONIAH. A Levite appointed, with his brother Shimei, by Hezekiah the king and Azariah the ruler of the house of God, to be overseer of the oblations and tithes and the dedicated things (2 Ch. 31:12f.).

2. One of the chiefs of the Levites mentioned in connection with the Passover celebration in Josiah's reign (2 Ch. 35:9).

CONCEAL. The Bible is God's revelation, and He is a God who reveals Himself, through Christ; yet, "It is the glory of God to conceal things" (Prov. 25:2), and His hiddenness is proclaimed in such passages as Ps. 97:2; 1 Tim. 6:16. Moreover, on the other side of Jesus' *apokálypsis* (revelation) was the element of *parákalypsis* (concealment), as in Lk. 9:45, "it was concealed from them, that they should not perceive it," and Mk. 4:12, "so that they may indeed see but not perceive, and may indeed hear but not understand." *See* PARABLE; MYSTERY; HIDE.

CONCEIT. The phrase "wise in his own conceit" occurs in the AV at Prov. 26:5, 12, 16; 28:11, where the RSV translates more literally, "wise in his own eyes" (Heb. *'ayin*), and in Rom. 11:25; 12:16. The RSV retains it only at Rom. 11:25 ("wise in your own conceits," Gk. *heautoís phrónimoi*), translating the similar phrase at 12:16 "conceited." But in Job 37:24, where the AV has "wise of heart," the RSV renders "wise in their own conceit" (Heb. *lēḇ*).

Other words for "conceit" are Gk. *physiṓseis* (2 Cor. 12:20, AV "swellings"; NEB "arrogance"), *kenodoxía* (Phil. 2:3, AV "vainglory"; NEB "personal vanity"), and *typhóomai,* "puffed up with conceit" (1 Tim. 3:6, AV "lifted up with pride"; 6:4, AV "proud"; NEB "pompous"), "swollen with conceit" (2 Tim. 3:4, AV "highminded"; NEB "swollen with self-importance").

See HUMBLE; PRIDE. J. W. D. H.

CONCEIVE [Heb. *hārâ*, also *zāra'* (Nu. 5:28; Lev. 12:2), *yāḥam* (Ps. 51:5); Gk. *syllambánō*, also *gennáō* (Mt. 1:20), *en gastrí échō* (1:23), *échō koítēn* (Rom. 9:10), *eis katabolḗn* ("conceive," He. 11:11)]; AV also BE WITH CHILD (Mt. 1:23); Cant. 8:2, RSV, is based on the LXX and Syriac; **CONCEPTION** [Heb. *hērāyôn*] (Ruth 4:13; Hos. 9:11); the RSV "the heart of man [has not] conceived" in 1 Cor. 2:9 translates the Gk. *epí kardían anthrṓpou ouk anébē*; today we might say, "It never entered his mind" (cf. NEB "beyond our imagining"). Throughout the OT, but especially in Genesis, the phrase occurs, "she conceived and bore a son." The beginning of new life in the mother's womb was considered so important that it was mentioned as part of the birth announcement. "Conceive" is used figuratively in Job 15:35; Ps. 7:14; 35:20; Isa. 33:11; 59:4, 13; Jas. 1:15.

J. W. D. H.

CONCEPTION, IMMACULATE. *See* MARY.

CONCESSION [Gk. *syngnṓmē*] (1 Cor. 7:6); AV PERMISSION. The Greek term is used only once in the NT and rarely in the LXX. Both the RSV and the NEB have "by way of concession." Edwards convincingly argues against "pardon" as a possible translation for this word since it is not antithetical to "command." Another common translation, "by permission" (AV), is ruled out by Robertson and Plummer on the ground that it is ambiguous. Commentators (e.g., Robertson and Plummer, Edwards, Grosheide) generally agree on "concession" as the best translation.

There has been much dispute over what is being conceded. Barnes thinks Paul refers to v. 5. Rosenmüller says it speaks of what follows. However, the stronger arguments are advanced by scholars who hold that it refers to "all the Apostle has said on the subject of marriage" (Edwards), or "to the leading direction given in ver. 2, from which vv. 3-5 digressed" (Findlay). Paul is telling the Corinthians that under certain circumstances they should marry, but God has given no command that they must do so.

Bibliography.–Comms. on 1 Corinthians by T. C. Edwards (1897); A. Robertson and A. Plummer (*ICC*, 1911); F. W. Grosheide (*NIC*, 1954); A. Barnes (3rd ed. 1857); G. G. Findlay (*Expos.G.T.*, 1901); G. C. Morgan (1946). G. H. HOVEE

CONCISION. *See* MUTILATION; CIRCUMCISION.

CONCLUDE. Used archaically in the AV for Gk. *synkleíō* in Rom. 11:32; Gal. 3:22 (RSV "consign"; NEB "make prisoners," "declare to be prisoners").

CONCORDANCES. A biblical concordance is an alphabetically arranged list of words from the text of the Bible. After each word the book, chapter, and verse in which that particular word occurs is given. Each reference generally includes a context of several words. F. W. Danker writes, "In a lexicon a word is like a friend in a coffin. A concordance restores him to life."

There are three principal uses for a concordance: (1) a text can be located by looking under words known to occur in the passage; (2) similar content in other passages can be located by checking every occurrence of a particular word; (3) various shades of meaning of a word can be determined by checking its use in other contexts. For the latter two uses especially, it is very helpful for a concordance to provide a sufficient context in order to illustrate well the word under consideration. It can do this by showing the word in its grammatical construction and the words with which it is normally associated. Another use similar to (2) is for study of particular phrases, not simply single words.

The oldest known concordance was based on the work of Cardinal Hugo of St. Caro, who, with the help of hundreds of Dominican monks at St. James Convent in Paris, completed a word-index of the Vulgate in the year 1230. In 1250-1252 other Dominicans added contexts for each word, thereby making this relatively short work a real concordance. Of the concordances to the Bible that have been compiled since then, three basic kinds are pertinent to the English reader: original-language concordances, bilingual concordances, and concordances to English translations. In addition, several miscellaneous types of concordances will be briefly discussed.

I. Original-Language Concordances.–The first concordance to the Hebrew OT was produced by Rabbi Isaac Nathan in the year 1448. It was not published, however, until 1523 in Venice. There has been much work on the Hebrew concordance since that time, and currently there are two that are of great value to most OT scholars. Solomon Mandelkern produced the *Veteris Testamenti Concordantiae Hebraicae atque Chaldaicae,* originally published in 1900 and revised in 1955 and 1967. The most recent concordance to the Hebrew OT, produced by Gerhard Lisowsky in 1958, is entitled *Konkordanz zum Hebräischen AT*. Each of these concordances is exhaustive and indispensable for any study of OT texts in the original language.

The first concordance to the LXX was produced by Conrad Kircher in 1607 at Frankfort, Germany. The definitive concordance current today is *Concordance to the LXX and the Other Greek Versions of the OT*, edited by Edwin Hatch and Henry A. Redpath, originally done in 1897, most recently revised in 1954. It is an exhaustive concordance to the LXX including the Greek text of the Apocryphal books and the remains of the other versions that formed part of Origen's Hexapla, and generally gives a good context. The basic texts used were the MSS A, B, and א, and the Sixtine Edition of 1587. A supplement of some 272 pages, published in 1906, includes an index of Greek proper names and an index of Hebrew words.

The first concordance to the Greek NT was produced by Sixtus Birken, librarian at the city library in Augsburg, in 1546. The second was published in 1594 by Henry Stephens, who used the verse divisions that had been devised by his father some years before. The third, but first really good work, was produced by Erasmus Schmid at Wittenberg in 1638. The most definitive concordance of the Greek text available today is the work of W. F. Moulton and A. S. Geden, *Concordance to the Greek NT* (1897; 4th ed. [rev. H. K. Moulton] 1963). Basically it is predicated on the texts of Westcott and Hort, Tischendorf, and the English revisers. It is valuable because it is exhaustive and provides a good context for most words. Under a given word it often organizes some of the references by means of numbers indicating special uses of the term being treated. A somwhat abbreviated Greek concordance, *Handkonkordanz zum griechischen NT,* was produced by Alfred Schmoller. The 14th edition (1968), an abridged work based on the 15th and 16th editions of the Nestle text, organizes the references and gives symbols where the concordance is not complete.

The newest concordance in this field is the *Vollständige Konkordanz zum griechischen NT*, compiled under the direction of Kurt Aland. By 1976 two fascicles were in print (A-γραφω). This concordance is based on the Nestle-Aland 26th edition but includes variants from all major editions appearing in the previous hundred years. It includes every occurrence of every Greek word. The longer lists are organized and a good context for each word is provided. A list of prepositions attached to a particular verb is given at the beginning of the entry for that verb.

II. Bilingual Concordances.–Bilingual concordances have been produced to help those who are not well versed in the Greek language. The *Englishman's Greek Concordance of the NT*, produced by George V. Wigram (1839), has passed through several editions. If one is able to look up the Greek word (which is also transliterated) alphabetically, he can use this volume to find every occurrence of the translations of that Greek word. The English word that translates the Greek is always in italics. Adequate context in English is given, and the work is fairly exhaustive.

J. B. Smith's *Greek-English Concordance to the NT* (1955) is based on the TR (the Stephanus text of 1550) and the AV. A special feature is the listing of the number of times a given Greek word occurs in each NT book, in addition to the references. An index lists alphabetically all of the English words together with the various Greek words (transliterated) that are so translated, and the number of times each occurs. By the use of serial numbers the reader is referred to the concordance, where the individual Greek words are listed with all their NT occurrences.

The *Greek-English Analytical Concordance of the Greek-English NT*, produced by J. Stegena (1963), also is based on the TR and the AV. It is analytical in that it lists all forms and identifies them grammatically, and in fact also gives roots for the various Greek words.

In 1972 the *New Englishman's Greek Concordance of the NT* appeared, published by the William Carey Library of South Pasadena, California, in the preface of which the reader is advised of the advance over the old format. A new numbering system, based on the system found in *Strong*, enables the reader to find the Greek original and also the other passages in which that Greek original occurs.

III. English Translation Concordances.–Many English concordances have been produced since the first one by Thomas Gybson in London (1535). There are still three widely used concordances of the AV. The most popular is Alexander Cruden's exhaustive *Complete Concordance to the Holy Scriptures* (1737). More recent editions use an asterisk to indicate where the RV differs from the AV. References to some words are divided; e.g., "soul" has been divided into references to "my soul," "our soul," "own soul," etc. It is an abridged concordance with a supplementary list of proper names seldom mentioned in Scripture and not in the text of the concordance itself. James Strong's *Exhaustive Concordance of the Bible* (1890) has an additional comparative concordance listing all words in the American RV that are not in the AV, and gives all references to these. It is generally complete, but this comparative concordance gives no contexts. The main concordance is, as its title claims, exhaustive. It lists forty-seven unimportant words like "a," "an," "and," by reference only in an appendix. It has generally good context for each of its listings and uses special symbols to alert the user that a later translation uses different words. The supplements include a Hebrew and Chaldee dictionary listing 8674 words with transliteration and a brief definition. It also has a Greek dictionary of the NT containing 5624 words with Greek transliterations, pronunciation, and brief definitions. Robert Young's *Analytical Concordance to the Bible* (1873) also gives alternate translations and lists each word according to its Hebrew or Greek original, with transliteration. Sufficient context is supplied. The supplements in this concordance include an "index-lexicon," in which the transliterated Hebrew and Greek words are listed alphabetically, with their translations (and the number of uses of each translation) in the AV. By astute use of this concordance one can do fairly accurate word studies without a great knowledge of the original languages.

There is only one concordance to the American RV that approximates completeness, the *Complete Concordance to the American Standard Version of the Holy Bible* (1922) by M. C. Hazard, which does omit certain prepositions, pronouns, and conjunctions. The concordance often gives the definition of the word, especially of Hebrew names, and it does divide some references. For example, the reference "pleasure" is divided into "good pleasure," "his pleasure," "no pleasure," "take pleasure," etc. It has no supplements.

Nelson's Complete Concordance of the Revised Standard Bible (1957) is complete, aside from the omission of some prepositions, pronouns, and conjunctions. Fifty-nine percent of the text of the Bible is listed. This concordance also gives good context and references. There are no supplements.

New translations into English have appeared rapidly, but concordances for them are much slower in production. W. J. Gant edited *Concordance of the Bible in the Moffatt Translation* (1950), which is somewhat abridged and gives a fairly short context for each word. The *New English Bible NT Concordance* (1964) does not aim to be complete. It is simply a concordance of words not in, or not in the same verses as, the AV. Generally, however, sufficient context is given to provide the setting for each occurrence. A concordance to the *New American Standard Bible* has been issued by the Lockman Foundation, La Habra, California (1972). The *Complete Concordance to the Bible Douay Version* (1957) includes the Apocrypha, divides references to some of the words, and lists by Scripture reference all cardinal and ordinal numbers. It is basically complete and provides good context.

IV. Miscellaneous.–In addition, there are some special types of concordances, such as that for the very peculiar MS Codex Bezae, produced by James Yoder to facilitate the study of the Western text, particularly in the book of Acts. Concordances to Ugaritic literature and Aramaic inscriptions have also been compiled because of their value to OT and NT studies. C. R. Joy compiled *Harper's Topical Concordance* (rev. ed. 1962), which helps one to study topically from the standpoint of the English language. The *Zondervan Expanded Concordance* (1968) gives the key words from several translations, including the AV, Amplified, Berkeley, RV, NEB, Phillips, RSV, and the New Scofield Bible. It does divide long sections, e.g., the word "Lord" is divided into applications to men and to God. It also repeats verses with different translations of the same words, e.g., "love" and "charity."

The *Computer Bible,* published by Biblical Research Associates, composed of fascicles of individual groups of smaller books, is an attempt to aid literary-critical and linguistic-grammatical studies especially. In the NT volumes, the forward key-word-in-context concordance and the reverse key-word-in-context concordance enable the student to locate easily identical phrases and grammatical forms or uncover a series of hitherto unknown but significant phrases. There will be great difficulty in analyzing material from the complete NT because there are so many separate volumes. It is printed in transliterated computer forms. The OT volumes lack the unity of form of citation that the NT volumes have. These volumes are useful only for study of the particular books covered and not for comparative analysis of several books.

Bibliography.–*RGG*, I, *s.v.* *"Bibelkonkordanz"* (F. Hesse); *Catholic Encyclopedia*, IV, *s.v.* "Concordances of the Bible" (J. F. Fenlon); F. W. Danker, *Multipurpose Tools for Bible Study* (3rd ed. 1970). P. R. McREYNOLDS

CONCOURSE. The AV for Heb. *hāmâ* in Prov. 1:21 ("in the chief place of concourse," Heb. *bᵉrō'š hōmîyôṯ*) and for Gk. *systrophḗ* in Acts 19:40. In the OT passage the NEB has "at the top of the busy street." The RSV, following the LXX, emends to *ḥōmôṯ,* "walls," and reads "on the top of the walls." In Acts 19:40 the RSV has "commotion," the NEB "uproar." See also Jth. 10:18, AV (Gk. *syndromḗ*, RSV "excitement").

CONCUBINE [Heb. *pîlegeš*, *pilegeš*, *šiddâ* (Eccl. 2:8)]; AV also "musical instruments"; [Aram. *lᵉḥēnâ* (Dnl. 5:2f., 23)]; NEB COURTESANS. A female slave regarded as part of the Israelite family, generally designated as bearing children. She might be taken in debt or purchased from a poor Israelite family or taken captive in war (2 S. 5:13). Heb. *pîlegeš* is a non-Semitic loanword, perhaps related to Gk. *pállax,* "young girl."

Certain status was accorded concubines, who are listed among members of the family and court (2 S. 19:5; 1 K. 11:3; 2 Ch. 11:21; Cant. 6:8f.; Dnl. 5:2f., 23). Succession could be traced through concubines, hence their place in genealogies (Gen. 22:24; 36:12; 2 S. 5:13f.; 1 Ch. 1:32; 2:46, 48; 3:9; 7:14). Sons of concubines could also be equals in inheritance and succession and thus a threat to the sons of wives (Gen. 25:6; cf. 21:10). A man was regarded as a concubine's husband (Jgs. 20:4). Harm to a concubine was regarded as a crime worthy of vengeance (Jgs. 19:29).

Concubines are mentioned almost exclusively in the patriarchal period and early monarchy and, in the latter, only in relation to kings. Kings might have numerous concubines (1 K. 11:3; 2 Ch. 11:21), access to whom was regarded as a claim to the throne (2 S. 3:7; 16:21f.; 1 K. 2:22-25). For this reason, they were guarded, often by eunuchs (2 S. 20:3; Est. 2:14).

In addition to providing offspring and sexual activity (Eccl. 2:8), concubines were responsible for care of the house (2 S. 15:16; 16:21; 20:3; NEB "in charge of the palace").

Although the concubine was a slave, it is not clear whether a woman's maidservant, given to a man to provide male offspring (Gen. 16:1f., 4f.; 30:3; 31:9), was regarded as a concubine. A. C. M.

CONCUPISCENCE. The AV for Gk. *epithymía* in Rom. 7:8 (RSV "covetousness"); Col. 3:5 (RSV "desire"); and 1 Thess. 4:5 (*páthos epithymías,* AV "lust of concupiscence"; RSV "passion of lust"). *See* COVET.

CONDEMN; CONDEMNED; CONDEMNATION [Heb. *rāša', šāpaṭ, šᵉpāṭîm* (Prov. 19:29), *'āšēm* (Ps. 34:21f.); Gk. *krínō, katakrínō, kríma, krísis, katakríma, katákrisis, katadikázō, kataginṓskō, apṓleia* (2 Pet. 2:3)]; AV also JUDGE, JUDGMENTS (Prov. 19:29, DAMNED, DAMNATION, WICKED (Job 9:29), DESOLATE (Ps. 34:21f.), BLAMED (Gal. 2:11); NEB also "declare to be in the wrong" (Ex. 22:9), "accounted guilty" (Job 9:29), DISPARAGE (34:17), "put in the wrong" (40:8; He. 11:7), "brought to ruin" (Ps. 34:21f.), "a rod (in pickle)" (Prov. 19:29), SENTENCE, JUDGE, JUDGMENT, "pass judgement" (Rom. 2:27; 8:3), GUILTY (14:23), BLAME (2 Cor. 7:3), "in the wrong" (Gal. 2:11), DOOM (Jude 4), etc.; **SELF-CONDEMNED** [Gk. *autokatákritos*] (Tit. 3:11). The Heb. *šāpaṭ* and Gk. *krínō* usually mean "judge," and *kríma* and *krísis* "judgment"; condemnation — a negative judgment — is explicit in Heb. *rāša'* and in the Greek terms beginning with *kata-* ("down," "against"). Gk. *apṓleia* normally means "destruction" or "perdition." *See* JUDGING. On Am. 2:8 *see* FINES.

J. W. D. H.

CONDESCEND. Archaic in Rom. 12:16, AV, for Gk. *synapágomai,* meaning as in the RSV "associate with" (NEB "go about with").

CONDESCENSION OF CHRIST. *See* KENOSIS.

CONDUCT. *See* ETHICS.

CONDUIT [Heb. *tᵉ'ālâ*–'watercourse']. Water channel or tunnel. Hezekiah built an aqueduct from the reservoir of the spring Gihon to a pool inside the southeast wall of Jerusalem (2 K. 20:20; *see* SILOAM). An earlier channel of the Upper Pool existed, where, on the road leading to the Fuller's Field, Isaiah met Ahaz (Isa. 7:3) and officials of Sennacherib and Hezekiah conferred (2 K. 18:17; Isa. 36:2). *See* CISTERN.

CONEY. *See* ROCK BADGER.

CONFECTION; CONFECTIONARY. Obsolete AV terms for "perfume" (Ex. 30:35) and "perfumer," (1 S. 8:13). *See* PERFUMES.

CONFEDERATES. The RSV and NEB rendering of Heb. *'anšê ḇᵉrîṯeḵā,* "men of your covenant," in Ob. 7 (AV "men that were at peace with thee").

CONFESS; CONFESSION [Heb. *yāḏâ, tôḏâ* (Ezr. 10:11), also *nāgaḏ* (Ps. 38:18), *zāḵar* (Isa. 48:1), *sāpar* (Ezk. 12:16); Gk. *homologéō, exomologéō, homología*]; AV also DECLARE (Ps. 38:18; Ezk. 12:16), "make mention of" (Isa. 48:1), ACKNOWLEDGE (1 Jn. 2:23), PROFESSION, "without controversy" (for *homologouménōs,* 1 Tim. 3:16, RSV "we confess"); NEB also "make no secret of" (Ps. 38:18), "boast in" (Isa. 48:1), "tell the whole story of" (Ezk. 12:16), ACKNOWLEDGE, "beyond all question" (1 Tim. 3:16), "the religion we profess" (He. 3:1; 4:14). The Heb. *yāḏâ* can indicate both confession and praise or thanksgiving, the latter especially in the Psalms (e.g., 44:8; 54:6; 75:1; 92:1; 100:4; 105:1; 145:10). To praise God's name is to confess Him. Also, to declare (*nāgaḏ, sāpar*) one's sin is to confess it. The Gk. *homologéō* means "say the same thing," hence "agree." Confession of faith implies joining one's voice harmoniously to the voices of others, in common affirmation of belief. See *TDNT*, V, *s.v.* ὁμολογέω (Michel).

When a man is said to confess or make confession, the contents of the confession are variously distinguished. All, however, may be grouped under two heads, confession of faith and confession of sin. Confessions of faith are public acknowledgments of fidelity to God, and to the truth through which God is revealed, as 1 K. 8:33, AV; cf. RSV. They are declarations of unqualified confidence in Christ, and of surrender to His service; cf. Mt. 10:32, AV: "Whosoever . . . shall confess me before men" (cf. RSV). In Phil. 2:11, however, confession includes not only voluntary but also involuntary acknowledgment of the sovereignty of Jesus. The word stands also for everything contained in the Christian religion — "the faith" used in the objective and widest sense, in He. 3:1; 4:14 (cf. NEB). In both these passages, the allusion is to the writings of the NT.

See also CREEDS AND CONFESSIONS.

Confessions of sin are also of various classes: (1) To God alone. Wherever there is true repentance for sin, the penitent freely confesses his guilt to Him against whom he has sinned. This is described in Ps. 32:3-6; cf. 1 Jn. 1:9; Prov. 28:13. Such confession may be made either silently or, as in Dnl. 9:19, orally; it may be general, as in Ps. 51, or particular, as when some special sin is recognized; it may even extend to that which has not been discovered, but is believed to exist because of recognized inner depravity (Ps. 19:12), and thus include the state as well as the acts of sin (Rom. 7:18).

(2) To one's neighbor, when he has been wronged (Lk. 17:4): "If he sins against you seven times in the day, and turns to you seven times, and says, 'I repent,' you must forgive him." It is to this form of confession that James refers (5:16): "Confess your sins to one another"; cf. Mt. 5:23f.

(3) To a spiritual adviser or minister of the word, such as the confession of David to Nathan (2 S. 12:13), of the multitudes to John in the wilderness (Mt. 3:6), of the Ephesians to Paul (Acts 19:18). This confession is a general acknowledgment of sinfulness, and enters into an enumeration of details only when the conscience is particularly burdened.

(4) To the entire church, where some crime has created public scandal. As "secret sins are to be rebuked secretly, and public sins publicly," in the apostolic age, where there was genuine penitence for a notorious offense, the acknowledgment was as public as the deed itself. An illustration of this is found in the well-known case at Corinth (cf. 1 Cor. 5:3ff. with 2 Cor. 2:6f.).

For auricular confession in the sense of the medieval and Roman Church there is no authority in Holy Scripture. It is traceable to the practice of examining those who were about to make a public confession of some notorious offense, and of giving advice concerning how far the circumstances of the sin were to be announced — an expedient that was found advisable, since as much injury could be wrought by injudicious publishing of details in the confession as by the sin itself. The practice once introduced for particular cases was in time extended to all cases; and the private confession of sin was demanded by the Church as a condition of the absolution, and made an element of penitence, which was analyzed into contrition, confession, and satisfaction. See the *Examen Concilii Tridentini* (1st ed. 1565) of Martin Chemnitz, superintendent of Brunswick, for a thorough exegetical and historical discussion of this entire subject.

On the historical side see also H. C. Lea, *History of Auricular Confession and Indulgences in the Latin Church* (3 vols., 1896). H. E. JACOBS

CONFESSION OF FAITH. *See* CREEDS AND CONFESSIONS.

CONFIDENCE; CONFIDENT [Heb. *bāṭaḥ, biṭṭāḥôn, mibṭāḥ, kesel, kislâ,* also *sāmak* (2 Ch. 32:8), *'āman* (Job 29:24), *sôd* (Prov. 3:32); Gk. *parrhēsía, peíthō, tharrhéō, pepoíthēsis, pisteúō, hypóstasis*]; AV also BOLDNESS, BOLDLY, TRUST, HOPE, BELIEVE, FREELY (Acts 2:29), "rest oneself upon" (2 Ch. 32:8), "be secure" (Job 11:18), "folly" (Ps. 49:13, RSV "foolish confidence"), "secret" (Prov. 3:32), "boldness of speech" (2 Cor. 7:4); NEB also TRUST, BOLD(LY), ALLEGIANCE (Jgs. 9:26), "be buoyed up by" (2 Ch. 32:8), COMFORT (Job 4:6), "take heart" (29:24), "at one's ease" (40:23), UNDISMAYED (Ps. 27:3), "foolish (men)" (49:13), "at one's side" (Prov. 3:26), PLAINLY (Acts 2:29), FULL RELIANCE (2 Cor. 3:4), "perfectly frank" (7:4), CONVINCED (10:7), BRAGGING (11:17, RSV "boastful confidence"), "right to speak openly" (1 Tim. 3:13), FEARLESS (He. 3:6), "take courage" (13:6).

If it is possible to distinguish shades of meaning among the OT words, *bāṭaḥ* and derivatives express a reliance based on (presumed) strength (Jgs. 9:26; 2 K. 18:19; Job 6:20; 11:18; 31:24; 40:23; Ps. 62:10; Prov. 14:26; etc.), *'āman* is firmly based trust, *sāmak* means "find support," and *kesel* is often a naive trust, even a "foolish confidence" (Ps. 49:13; cf. Job 8:14). Confidence in the sense of "intimacy" is expressed by *sôd* (Prov. 3:32, "the upright are in his confidence," i.e., He is willing to confide in them). In Jer. 2:37, AV, "thy confidences" (*mibṭāḥ*) means "those in whom you trust" (RSV).

In the OT confidence is most often a private trusting, especially confidence in God; but in the NT, outside the shelter of an exclusivist religion, Christian faith is a public matter, and there is an emphasis on "speaking boldly" in the face of possible public ridicule or persecution. Here the commonest word for confidence is Gk. *parrhēsía*, "speaking out" (e.g., He. 3:6; 4:16; 10:19, 35; 1 Jn. 2:28; 3:21; 4:17; 5:14).

Another important NT emphasis is on Christian faith as "being persuaded"; and Gk. *peíthō*, "persuade," "convince," means in the 2nd perfect and pluperfect "be confident," "trust" (e.g., 2 Cor. 10:7; Gal. 5:10; Phil. 3:3f.; 2 Thess. 3:4), and *pepoíthēsis* is "confidence" (2 Cor. 3:4; 8:22; 10:2; Eph. 3:12; Phil. 3:4). Other NT words for confidence are *tharrhéō*, "be bold" (2 Cor. 7:16; He. 13:6), *pisteúō*, "believe" (1 Pet. 1:21), and *hypóstasis*, that which stands under one (2 Cor. 11:17; He. 3:14).

When the Bible speaks of having confidence, it nearly always mentions an object of confidence, whether the material objects of false confidence (Job 8:13-15; 31:24; Phil. 3:3f.) or the divine object and foundation of true Christian confidence (Prov. 14:26; Phil. 1:14; 2 Thess. 3:4; 1 Tim. 3:13; 1 Pet. 1:21; 1 Jn. 5:14). J. W. D. H.

CONFIRM [Heb. *qûm, 'āman, 'āmad, ḥāzaq, mālē'* (1 K. 1:14); Gk. *bebaióō, bébaion poiéō* (2 Pet. 1:10), *hístēmi* (Mt. 18:16)]; AV also ESTABLISH, STABLISH, PERFORM, VERIFY, SETTLE (1 Ch. 17:14), ACCOMPLISH (Jer. 44:25), MAKE SURE (2 Pet. 1:10); NEB also "give its full effect" (Lev. 26:9), FULFIL, PERFORM, "tell the whole story" (1 K. 1:14, RSV "confirm your words"), STRENGTHEN (2 K. 15:19), "bind oneself" (1 Ch. 16:17; Ps. 105:10; 119:106), "give a sure place" (1 Ch. 17:14), "make come true" (Isa. 44:26), HELP (Dnl. 11:1), DULY ESTABLISH (Mt. 18:16), MAKE GOOD (Rom. 15:8), CLINCH (2 Pet. 1:10), etc.; **CONFIRMATION** [Gk. *bebaíōsis*] (Phil. 1:7; He. 6:16); NEB also "to vouch for the truth" (Phil. 1:7). In the Bible, words (promise, covenant, vow, oath, statute) are confirmed by deeds (e.g., Lev. 26:9; Dt. 8:18; 9:5; 27:26; 2 S. 7:25, "do as thou hast spoken"; Jer. 44:25 — all Heb. *qûm*; 1 K. 8:26 par., *'āman*; Rom. 15:8, Gk. *bebaióō*; cf. the figurative deed-confirmation in Ruth 4:7). Thus in most instances "confirm" means "fulfil," "bring to reality."

See also ESTABLISH; FULFIL. J. W. D. H.

CONFISCATION. *See* PUNISHMENTS IV; FINES.

CONFLICT. In Dnl. 10:1, RSV, Heb. *ṣāḇā'* is translated "conflict"; the AV has "time appointed," and the NEB reads "it cost him much toil," joining this with the next phrase, "to understand it." The larger context here, and the normal military usage of *ṣāḇā'*, point to the RSV reading as most likely.

The "conflict" of Phil. 1:30 (Gk. *agṓn*, NEB "contest") is the struggle of the new Church against unbelief — both in the realm of ideology and in the arena of physical suffering.

CONFORMED [Gk. *sýmmorphos* (Rom. 8:29), *syschēmatízō* (12:2; 1 Pet. 1:14)]; AV also "fashioning yourselves according to" (1 Pet. 1:14); NEB SHAPED (Rom. 8:29), "adapt yourselves . . . to the pattern of" (12:2), "let your characters be shaped . . . by" (1 Pet. 1:14); see also Phil. 3:10, 21. These references illustrate the difference between Gk. *morphḗ*, form reflecting inner nature, and *schḗma*, the merely outward fashion. Note especially Rom. 12:2: "Be not conformed [*mḗ syschēmatízesthe*] to this age, but be transformed [*metamorphoústhe*] by the renewal of your mind."

CONFOUND [Heb. *bôš*]; AV also BE ASHAMED; NEB BE ASHAMED, HUMILIATED, IN CONFUSION, etc.; [*ḥāpēr*]; AV also BE ASHAMED; NEB HIDE ITS FACE IN SHAME, BE EATEN AWAY; [*kālam*]; NEB BE PUT TO SHAME, DISAPPOINTED, etc.; [*bāla'*] (Isa. 19:3); AV DESTROY; NEB THROW INTO CONFUSION; [Gk. *synchýnō*] (Acts 9:22); NEB SILENCED. As active verbs, these terms mean confuse (*bôš*, Ps. 14:6; 35:4; *synchýnō*, Acts 9:22) or put to rout (*bôš*, Zec. 10:5; AV "be confounded"); in the passive, be put to shame or discomfitted (*bôš*, 2 K. 19:26; Isa. 37:27; Jer. 49:23; Zec. 9:5; *ḥāpēr*, Ps. 35:4; Isa. 24:23; 33:9; *kālam*, Isa. 41:11; 54:4; Jer. 14:3; 22:22).

The AV so translates Heb. *bālal* (lit. "mix," Gen. 11:7, 9; RSV "confuse"; NEB also "made a babble"); *ḥāṯaṯ* (lit. "be shattered," Jer. 1:17; RSV "dismay"; NEB "break"); and *kataischýnō* (1 Cor. 1:27; RSV, NEB, "shame"; 1 Pet. 2:6; RSV, NEB "be put to shame"). The AV often reads "confound," in the archaic sense "put to shame" (*bôš*, Ps. 71:13; Jer. 17:18; *ḥāpēr*, Ps. 35:4; Mic. 3:7) or "be ashamed, disgraced" (*bôš*, Jer. 48:1, 20; 50:2; Ezk. 16:52; Mic. 7:16). *See* SHAME. A. C. M.

CONFUSION. Often in the AV archaic for "dishonor," "disgrace," "humiliation," "shame." *See* SHAME.

CONFUSION OF TONGUES. *See* BABEL, TOWER OF.

CONGREGATION [Heb. *'ēḏâ, qāhāl* (2 Ch. 7:8; 24:6; Ezr. 10:8; Ps. 22:22, 25; 35:18; 40:9f.; etc.), *maqhēlîm* (Ps. 26:12), *maqhēlōṯ* (Ps. 68:26); Gk. *ekklēsía* (Acts 7:38;

He. 2:12), *plḗthos* (Acts 15:30; 19:9)]; AV also PEOPLE (Lev. 10:6), ASSEMBLY (Nu. 10:2; 20:8), COMPANY (Nu. 14:7), CHURCH (Acts 7:38; He. 2:12), MULTITUDE (Acts 15:30; 19:9); NEB also COMMUNITY, COMPANY (Nu. 16:19, 21), CROWD (Nu. 25:7), PEOPLE (Josh. 9:18), ASSEMBLY.

Heb. *'ēḏâ* (from the root *y'd,* "appoint") and *qāhāl* (related to *qôl,* "voice"; thus, "call" or "summon") are virtually synonymous (cf. Lev. 4:13; Nu. 14:5). The RV consistently translates the former "congregation," the latter "assembly." A slight distinction between the nouns may lie in the fact that *'ēḏâ* suggests the group or community, whether gathered or not, while *qāhāl* suggests the gathered assembly. *'Ēḏâ* occurs more frequently in Exodus–Judges, whereas later books of the OT show a preference for *qāhāl.* In the LXX *qāhāl* is frequently, though not exclusively, translated by *ekklēsía.* This is the case in Deuteronomy (except 5:22), Joshua, Judges, Samuel, Kings, Chronicles, Ezra, and Nehemiah; in the remainder of the Pentateuch *qāhāl* is rendered *synagōgḗ.* *'Ēḏâ* is usually rendered *synagōgḗ,* never *ekklēsía.*

The nature of the gathered assembly is defined by the biblical context. The great *qāhāl* of the OT is the assembly of Israel at Mt. Sinai (cf. Dt. 5:22). Here the covenant of Yahweh was ratified (note the similarities between *'ēḏâ* and the root *y'd* in Thompson's article); the Exodus was climaxed and Israel was formally constituted the people of God. As a covenant assembly (*'ēḏâ*), Israel was a people called into a relationship of fellowship with the Lord. The Hebrew terms for "congregation" are particularly conspicuous in the Pentateuch because the constitutive history of the theocracy is contained there. Consequently, any attempt to determine the meaning of *qāhāl* from its Greek counterpart (i.e., the purely secular sense of *ekklēsía,* "an assembly") must be adjudged theologically inadequate. In both the LXX and the NT, *qāhāl* determines the meaning of *ekklēsía,* not vice versa. This point is bolstered by the way the NT writers quote the OT. The image projected by the apostolic and early Christian community in He. 2:12 and Acts 7:38 is certainly one with theological significance. The Christian *ekklēsía* is variously designated as the people of the new Exodus, the people assembled at the mount of God (cf. esp. He. 12:18-24), the people of the new covenant under a better Mediator, a pilgrim (wilderness) people, a people sustained by the living manna and living water, a people destined for an everlasting inheritance. The principle that the OT is fulfilled in the NT emphasizes that the NT congregation is an assembly in personal relationship with God through Jesus Christ, i.e., a (new) covenant community.

Plḗthos can mean either (1) a crowd or multitude (cf. Acts 2:6; 14:1; 17:4; 28:3), or (2) a full Christian assembly or congregation (cf. Acts 4:32; 6:2, 5; 15:12, 30; 19:9). The Greek word is a translation of the Heb. *rabbîm* ("the many"), which is common in the Qumrân Scrolls for the "assembly of believers."

Bibliography.–W. F. Albright, *Recent Discoveries in Bible Lands* (1955), pp. 134f.; G. W. Anderson, "Israel: Amphictyony: 'AM; QĀHĀL; 'ĒḎÂH," in H. T. Frank and W. L. Reed, eds., *Translating and Understanding the OT* (1970), pp. 135-151; J. Y. Campbell, *JTS*, 49 (1948), 130-142; *RTWB*, *s.v.* "Church" (R. H. Fuller); E. Schweizer, *Theology Today*, 13 (1957), 471-483; J. A. Thompson, *JSS*, 10 (1965), 222-240; *TDNT*, VI, *s.v.* πλῆθος (G. Delling).

J. T. DENNISON, JR.

CONGREGATION, MOUNT OF. *See* ASSEMBLY, MOUNT OF.

CONIAH kō-nī'ə [Heb. *konyāhû*]. A form of the name JEHOIACHIN, found in Jer. 22:24, 28; 37:1.

CONJUGAL RIGHTS (1 Cor. 7:3). *See* MARITAL RIGHTS.

CONONIAH (2 Ch. 31:12f., AV). *See* CONANIAH **1.**

CONQUER; CONQUEROR. In the OT the conqueror is the bearer of sorrow, the one who brings God's judgment. The usual OT word is Heb. *nāḵâ* (1 K. 15:20; 2 K. 3:19, 25; 2 Ch. 16:4; Ezk. 40:1), for which the AV has "smite"; the NEB has "attack" (1 K. 15:20; 2 Ch. 16:4), "raze to the ground" (2 K. 3:19, 25), "destruction" (Ezk. 40:1). Heb. *lāḥam,* "consume," occurs at 2 K. 16:5 (AV "overcome"; but NEB "bring to battle") and Isa. 7:1 (AV "prevail against"; NEB "force a battle"), and *bāqa'* in Isa. 7:6 (AV "make a breach"; NEB "make [her] join [with us]"). The participle of *yāraš* is rendered in the AV "them that shall inherit" in Jer. 8:10 and "heir" in Mic. 1:15; but the word can also mean "possess" in a more forceful sense, and the RSV translates "conqueror(s)" in both places (NEB "new owners," "others to take your place"). The Micah passage is a play on the name Mareshah.

In Isa. 18:2, 7 occurs the Heb. *mᵉḇûsâ,* translated "conquering" in the RSV and "proud" in the NEB. The AV has a different understanding altogether of this passage, and takes the word in a passive sense, "trodden down." *See* METE.

In the NT the usual word is Gk. *nikáō* (all in Revelation), and once *katagōnízomai* (He. 11:33). In Rom. 8:37, Paul uses the word *hypernikáō,* which the AV and RSV translate: "we are more than conquerors"; cf. the NEB, "overwhelming victory is ours," a more accurate if less memorable rendering of the sense of the prefix.

J. W. D. H.

CONSCIENCE [Heb. *lēḇ*] (1 S. 25:31); AV HEART; NEB COURAGE; [Gk. *syneídēsis*] (Acts 23:1; 24:16; Rom. 2:15; 9:1; 13:5; 1 Cor. 8:7, 10, 12; 10:25, 27-29; 2 Cor. 1:12; 4:2; 5:11; 1 Tim. 1:5, 19; 3:9; 4:2; 2 Tim. 1:3; Tit. 1:15; He. 9:9, 14; 10:22; 13:18; 1 Pet. 3:16, 21); NEB also HEART OF HEARTS (2 Cor. 5:11), INTENTION (2 Tim. 1:3), INWARD PERFECTION (He. 9:9), GUILTY HEART (He. 10:22); **CONSCIOUSNESS OF SIN** [Gk. *syneídēsis hamartiṓn*] (He. 10:2); AV CONSCIENCE OF SINS; NEB SENSE OF SIN.

An inner witness that testifies on the rightness or wrongness of one's actions or motives and, on the basis of them, pronounces judgment concerning the worth of the person.

- I. Terminology
  - A. Occurrence
  - B. Origin
  - C. Literal Meaning
  - D. Relation to Self-consciousness
- II. Usage
  - A. Secular Greek
  - B. NT
- III. Biblical Theological Interpretation
  - A. Why No OT Term?
  - B. Whose Voice is the Conscience?
  - C. Does the Conscience Speak Only Negatively?
  - D. Does the Conscience Speak Only in Relation to Past Acts?
  - E. How Reliable is the Conscience?
  - F. Can Conscience Be Trained?
  - G. How Does Conversion Affect Conscience?

I. Terminology.–*A. Occurrence.* In the RSV the term

"conscience" appears only once in the OT and twenty-eight times in the NT.

In the NT the same Greek noun *syneídēsis* lies behind all twenty-eight occurrences of "conscience" and the occurrence of "consciousness of sin" (He. 10:2) as well. Thus a study of the biblical references to conscience is for all practical purposes a study of the background and usage of *syneídēsis*.

In the NT, Paul's use of *syneídēsis* is by far the most frequent. Including the two occurrences in the book of Acts (23:1; 24:16) where Paul's dialogue is reported, he uses the term twenty of the twenty-eight times it appears. He also uses it in a larger variety of contexts than any other NT writer. Thus, Paul's usage provides the primary source of insight.

B. Origin. Many NT terms are understood only against the background of the OT Hebrew term that shaped the thinking of the writer; but this is not the case with *syneídēsis*. All but one of the RSV occurrences of "conscience" are from the NT because there simply is no close equivalent to *syneídēsis* in OT Hebrew. The Heb. *lēḇ*, translated "conscience" in 1 S. 25:31, is actually a much broader term. It is commonly translated "heart" and carries a range of meaning that includes understanding, feeling, and will, rather than the more precise inner witness indicated by *syneídēsis*.

If the background for the NT meaning of *syneídēsis* is not to be found in some OT concept, it must be found in the Greek world. Paul and other NT writers did not invent the term; they appropriated it as an existing part of the Greek language of their time. But how it entered the Greek language is a question of some importance, because the background of the term will shed light on its meaning.

On the basis of a few references to *syneídēsis* in the writings of certain Stoic philosophers, some scholars have concluded that the term was the invention of the Stoics. If so, then the term should be seen against the background of a Stoic view of the human personality. But a Stoic origin for the term is unlikely. First, the material supporting a link between *syneídēsis* and the Stoics is meager and even disputable. At best only three quotations are available, and the most vital of these, attributed to Epictetus, is of doubtful authenticity. Second, the Stoics, with their negative attitudes toward feelings and emotions, would be among those least likely to need a precise term for the inner testimony of conscience.

Stronger evidence indicates that the noun *syneídēsis* simply developed in everyday use from forms of the verb *sýnoida*. In Greek writings the noun forms *syneídēsis* and the related *syneidós* rarely appear before the 1st cent. B.C., and when they do appear the content of the terms is often unclear. But the verb forms of *sýnoida* appear frequently in a great variety of Greek writings, popular as well as technical, dating back to the 6th cent. B.C. It appears that by the 1st cent. B.C. the verb form describing an action had developed into a noun form designating the agent in the human makeup that performs the action. Thus *sýnoida* gave birth to *syneídēsis*. By Paul's time *syneídēsis* had a content so clearly established in the language that he could use the term without defining it, assuming that his readers would know what he meant.

C. Literal Meaning. Literally the verb *sýnoida* means "know in common with." It may mean simply "be conscious" or "be aware" of something. It is important to note that the verb appears in both nonreflexive and reflexive forms.

In its nonreflexive form *sýnoida* appears as *sýnoida tíni tí* or *sýnoida tínos tí* or *sýnoida perí tínos* and literally means "have knowledge of something with another person (as an eyewitness)." Its general use is to indicate knowing about another person, as a witness for or against him.

The reflexive form of the verb, *sýnoida emautǭ́*, literally, "I know with myself," moves closer to the meaning of the noun. Here the person who knows and the one who shares the knowledge or bears witness to it are the same person.

Something important happened when the verb form *sýnoida* shifted to the noun form *syneídēsis*. Literally, *syneídēsis* is "the self that knows with itself." It is significant, however, that *syneídēsis* is not merely another action performed by the self; it is now an agent within the self. The development of the noun form signaled the recognition of an alter ego, another self within the self that observes the self and then testifies as to what it sees.

D. Relation to Self-consciousness. While the tendency is to see the sole function of conscience as the making of moral judgments, the term *syneídēsis* actually has a broader meaning than that of a moral witness. As observed above, *syneídēsis* literally means the self knowing with or observing itself. It should be noted that the basic factor here is not morality but self-awareness. While self-awareness usually has moral dimensions, this is not necessarily or invariably the case. Self-awareness may cover more than awareness of one's moral status. Literally the term can include all that belongs to the self engaged in the act of reflecting upon itself.

II. Usage.–A. *Secular Greek.* Usage in secular Greek is especially important in the case of *syneídēsis*, since there is no OT background of meaning on which to draw. Whatever the NT writers did with the concept, they started not with a Hebrew concept to be translated but rather with a term that gained its meaning in the Greek culture. Since, as indicated above, the noun form *syneídēsis* appears to have developed from the reflexive verb form *sýnoida emautǭ́*, the usage of that verb form deserves some attention.

The form occurs twice in the trial of Socrates. Socrates uses the expression in his own defense when he explains that his questioning method arises from his being "aware within myself" of his complete ignorance. Alcibiades uses the same expression in declaring that he is "aware within myself" that he is helpless to resist Socrates while listening to him. In both instances there is self-awareness: Socrates is aware of his own ignorance, Alcibiades of his own helplessness. However, moral self-awareness does not seem to be involved in either instance, demonstrating that not morality but self-awareness is the more basic ingredient in the concept.

The noun form *syneídēsis* also may reflect only self-awareness in the broader sense rather than something necessarily moral. Chrysippus, a Stoic philosopher, is cited by Diogenes Laertius (*Vitae Philosophorum* vii.85) as saying, "It is suitable for every living thing to be aware of its own structure and of itself." Here *syneídēsis* plainly refers to self-consciousness but appears to have no clear moral content.

Nevertheless, in secular Greek most appearances of the reflexive verb form *sýnoida emautǭ́* and the noun form *syneídēsis* involve some definite moral self-awareness. Many instances show a keen grasp of the inner pain and damage that can be inflicted upon the self by the moral disapproval of the conscience. For example, Socrates refers to the bad conscience of those who bore false witness against him (Xenophon *Apologia Socratis* 24).

Orestes, the matricide, identifies conscience as the sickness that has destroyed him (Euripides *Orestes* 396). Democritus (297) writes of those who suffer greatly because of awareness of their evil-doing. Plutarch gives a vivid description of the conscience that reminds people of their sins and evokes the torments of hell (*De tranquillitate animi* 476-477a). In each of these instances conscience appears as an accuser within, bearing a moral witness regarding the evil behavior of the person and inflicting inward pain by an attack on his moral worth.

It should not be concluded, however, that the Greek culture saw the moral function of conscience as simply that of inflicting pain. In a passage sometimes attributed to the Stoic philosopher Epictetus there is a striking insight into the Greek view of conscience. "When we were children our parents handed us over to a nursery slave who should watch over us everywhere lest harm befall us. But when we were grown up, God hands us over to the conscience implanted in us, to protect us. Let us not in any way despise its protection for should we do so we shall be both ill-pleasing to God and have our own conscience as an enemy" (Pierce, p. 41). Whatever its true authorship may have been, the view of conscience appearing in the passage is illuminating. The conscience, like the nursery slave, is a kind of substitute parent. Its inner voice is not by nature the voice of an enemy, not just an instrument producing pain. The conscience, until alienated, is seen as having a positive and protective purpose. It is advisable and possible to stay on good terms with this inner voice.

In summary, secular Greek usage does not always give conscience a moral meaning, for conscience includes self-awareness in the broader sense. Nevertheless there was a highly developed awareness of the capacity of the conscience to inflict intense inward pain upon those who reject its testimony. Conscience is basically, however, a positive rather than a negative ingredient, and one is well-advised to live in such a way as to be on good terms with one's conscience.

B. NT. The term *syneídēsis* does not occur in any of the four Gospels, probably reflecting the Hebraic orientation of the writers. It was the apostle Paul, familiar with Greek culture, who first used the term and whose usage is by far the most extensive among the biblical writers.

Nowhere does he give a definition of conscience. Perhaps he comes closest in Rom. 2:15f. as he writes of the Gentiles, the law, and their conscience: "They show that what the law requires is written on their hearts, while their conscience also bears witness and their conflicting thoughts accuse or perhaps excuse them on that day when, according to my gospel, God judges the secrets of men by Christ Jesus." Here the conscience is seen as an inner witness in all human beings, even the Gentiles who "have not the law." This witness evaluates and may either excuse or accuse, approve or disapprove.

When the view of conscience expressed here is compared with that found in secular Greek usage, there appears to be nothing new in the concept itself. The inner witness as described by Paul was well known to the Greeks. What is new is the way Paul relates the inner witness of conscience to the law of God written in every human heart and to God's judgment of all mankind in Christ Jesus. What Paul appears to have done is to recognize the inner agent known to the Greeks as conscience, but to give his own version of the content of its testimony.

One group of Paul's references to conscience relates to the issue of meats offered to idols. These passages include 1 Cor. 8:7, 10, 12 and 10:25, 27-29, and provide important insight into the meaning of conscience as Paul sees it.

In relation to meats offered to idols the conscience of some is weak. Its testimony may be uncertain, confused, or in error. Paul recognizes that the conscience of some testifies that eating meats offered to idols is wrong in itself. Paul does not agree with the judgment of their conscience. He declares that "an idol has no real existence" and "there is no God but one." Nevertheless, even the weak or mistaken conscience should not be defiled (1 Cor. 8:7). One should not be pressured or encouraged to act in defiance of his conscience, because the offended conscience has great destructive power (8:11). Therefore those whose consciences are strong need to respect the consciences of the weak. One whose conscience is strong need not be bound by the conscience of the weak. There is a liberty of conscience that is not overruled by another man's scruples. One may "eat whatever is sold in the meat market without raising any question on the ground of conscience, for the earth is the Lord's and everything in it." But this liberty must be exercised in a way that shows caring concern for the problem of the weak. To tempt the weak to violate his conscience, and thus expose him to the destructive power of the violated conscience, is a sin against Christ (8:12).

The same concerns for the scruples of the weak are voiced in Rom. 14, although the term *syneídēsis* does not appear there. In v.1 Paul refers to those who are weak in faith (*pístis*) rather than weak in conscience (*syneídēsis*). The fact that Paul makes the same point in these two ways suggests the close relationship in Paul's mind between faith and conscience. For Paul, weakness of conscience is weakness of faith, and to do harm to a brother's relationship with his conscience is to do harm to his faith.

Elsewhere Paul also draws an intimate connection between faith and conscience. 1 Tim. 1:18f. refers to waging the good warfare, "holding faith and a good conscience." In the same reference he goes on to declare: "By rejecting conscience, certain persons have made shipwreck of their faith." He affirms the same importance of a good conscience in 1 Tim. 3:9 where he declares that deacons "must hold the mystery of the faith with a clear conscience."

Paul also testifies of his own good conscience: "I thank God whom I serve with a clear conscience" (2 Tim. 1:3). "I have lived before God in all good conscience up to this day" (Acts 23:1). "So I always take pains to have a clear conscience toward God and toward men" (Acts 24:16).

There are five occurrences of *syneídēsis* in the Epistle to the Hebrews. He. 9:9 speaks of perfecting the conscience of the worshiper, which cannot be accomplished by gifts and sacrifices. He. 9:14 affirms that the blood of Christ will "purify your conscience from dead works to serve the living God." He. 10:2, where "consciousness of sin" appears instead of "conscience," is part of a passage pointing out the need for repetition in the sacrificial system because of the inability of the sacrifices to make perfect those who draw near. If the worshipers had once been cleansed, there would no longer be any "consciousness of sin." He. 10:22 contains an exhortation to "draw near . . . with our hearts sprinkled clean from an evil conscience." He. 13:18 says "pray for us, for we are sure that we have a clear conscience."

In these passages the writer of Hebrews does not define or develop the function of conscience, but sees conscience as that which is defiled and in need of purification or cleansing, a cleansing that cannot be achieved by anything less than the sacrifice of Christ. In common with Paul, the writer of Hebrews sees the change from a bad conscience to a good or clear conscience as being essential to salvation.

1 Peter contains two references to "conscience." (The other use of *syneídēsis,* in 2:19, seems to mean "consciousness, awareness.") 1 Pet. 3:16 exhorts, "Keep your conscience clear, so that when you are abused, those who revile your good behavior in Christ may be put to shame." 1 Pet. 3:21 speaks of baptism "not as a removal of dirt from the body but as an appeal to God for a clear conscience."

Both references convey insight. The first shows that a clear conscience enables one to endure persecution. Battles without can be handled if there is no battle going on within. The second relates baptism to the conscience as an appeal for cleansing. As with Paul and the writer of Hebrews, Peter sees the clear conscience as being very important to the Christian life.

III. Biblical Theological Interpretation.–*A. Why No OT Term?* If the conscience, and especially the clear conscience, is so important to salvation, why does not the conscience receive more attention in the OT? Is this a deficiency in the OT?

It is more than likely that the differences between the Hebrew and Greek minds account for the lack of a term for conscience in the OT. While the Hebrew mind tended to focus outside of man, on God and His law as revealed, the Greek mind was more introspective and had more tendency to examine the inner workings of man's psychology. While the OT did not possess any terminology that sharply identified the conscience, it did stress the importance of righteousness in relation to both God and fellow man and the deep healing and peace signified by *šālôm.*

B. Whose Voice is the Conscience? If the conscience is recognized as an alter ego, an inner voice that bears witness to the self, the question inevitably arises: Where does that inner voice come from and whose voice is it that speaks? Textual and linguistic evidence does not immediately settle this question, and views have differed widely.

One view tends to see the conscience as the voice of God Himself speaking within. Conscience is then regarded as speaking with divine authority, and the validity of its testimony can never be challenged. Duty to one's conscience then is simple obedience.

Another view sees that inner voice as merely another element in the human makeup. On this basis the testimony of conscience is regarded as only a subjective judgment. Like other subjective judgments it can be freely challenged or even lightly dismissed. It speaks with no authority, for it has no objective reference.

Neither of the above views, at least when so simply stated, fits the biblical data on conscience. Paul makes clear that the conscience is not to be treated simply as the voice of God, for the conscience can be weak, or mistaken, and does involve subjective judgment (1 Cor. 8). However, the conscience is also not to be lightly dismissed or treated with disrespect, for a clear conscience is very important to one's faith. One cannot defile the conscience without serious spiritual consequences.

The Greek word *syneídēsis* itself provides some basis for understanding whose voice conscience is. Conscience is literally "the self that knows with itself." It is, in other words, the self looking at itself from the viewpoint of another person. Conscience is the internalized voice of those whose judgment of a person counts with him. It is the inner voice that testifies for the moral authorities that we recognize.

Some voice of conscience speaks to all (Rom. 2:15). but the content of that voice varies according to the authorities and values that we consciously or unconsciously recognize. For some the voice of conscience may reflect merely the voices of family, friends, and society. But a sensitive Christian conscience speaks in behalf of the values of the Christian fellowship, and, beyond these, is responsive to God as He reveals Himself in the Scriptures, in His law, and in the person of Christ.

C. Does the Conscience Speak Only Negatively? C. A. Pierce, in a very detailed study of conscience in the NT, concludes that conscience is always and only a negative or disapproving voice. He maintains that the numerous references to a "good" conscience in the words of Paul and other NT writers means only the absence of the voice of conscience. The good conscience is the silent conscience. Whenever the conscience speaks, as he sees it, it speaks disapprovingly and inflicts pain. This conclusion is defended after a detailed examination of all the NT materials on conscience.

That analysis appears to fail to do justice to the "excusing" conscience of Rom. 2:15 and to the positive testimony of the good conscience (e.g., 2 Cor. 1:12), which is more than mere silence. However, more than the interpretation of a few passages is at stake. At stake is the nature of conscience itself. If the voice of conscience is, as observed above, the internalized voice of all the authorities that we recognize, the question is whether those authorities speak only negatively in people's lives. While it is undeniable that both external authorities and the internalized voice of conscience speak more negatively than positively, this is not because that is the only way they can speak.

D. Does the Conscience Speak Only in Relation to Past Acts? This question is related to the previous one. Those who hold the narrower view that the conscience speaks only negatively tend also to hold that the conscience speaks only after the act. However, if the voice of conscience, as indicated above, is the internalized voice of all the authorities that we recognize, then there is an antecedent conscience, a voice that urges the right, as well as a subsequent conscience, the voice that protests the wrong. Once again, the conscience of a particular individual may tend to speak only negatively and after the fact, but this is not required by the nature of conscience.

E. How Reliable Is the Conscience? The inner voice of conscience is not always accurate in its testimony. It bears witness to the standards and values of the authorities that we recognize, but as with any witness, its testimony may be inaccurate. 1 Cor. 8 shows that the conscience can be in error in judging the eating of certain meats as sinful, when nothing is objectively wrong in eating the meat. The internalized voice may inadequately represent the standards from which it speaks. This can be true whether what is being voiced is the mores of society, the values of the parent, or the Word of God. The voice of conscience, as any other part of the human condition, is fallible and needs correction.

Nevertheless, it should be remembered that Paul warns that even the weak conscience must be taken seriously (1 Cor. 8; 10). It is wrong to violate the conscience, whether the conscience is strong or weak. Violating the conscience touches off a war within that is very damaging to the person and destructive of faith.

F. Can the Conscience Be Trained? As the internalized voice of the recognized authorities, the conscience is not a static thing. It is capable of growth and is, in fact, in a continual process of being shaped by social influences. The consciences of all are shaped by the standards of the company they keep and the groups in which they share. The Christian conscience is in a lifelong process of being shaped by the Word of God in the fellowship of believers. One of the purposes of the communion of the saints and the admonition of the Church is the shaping of the moral discernment of the individual in order that he grow up into mature discernment (cf. Eph. 4:13).

G. How Does Conversion Affect Conscience? As observed earlier, in his usage Paul draws an intimate connection between faith and the conscience. A good conscience is very important to the life of faith. However, this intimate connection may tempt some to make easy generalizations about the relation between conversion and the conscience. Generalizations about conscience and conversion or conscience and faith should be examined in the light of the NT materials.

Conversion should not be construed in such a way that the awareness of conscience appears as a product of conversion, as if apart from conversion the conscience is necessarily dull, or seared, or silent. In Rom. 2:15 Paul speaks of the witness of conscience in the Gentiles, reflecting his awareness that the testimony of conscience is a broadly human experience. Moreover, Paul came to that observation using the terminology of the Greek mind. As shown earlier, awareness of the testimony of conscience actually arose not in the OT materials, nor in the Hebrew mind, but in the secular Greek culture preceding the time of Paul. Awareness of the testimony of conscience cannot be tied to Christian conversion, for that awareness entered the stream of biblical content from a secular Greek source.

On the other hand, it also will not do to say that apart from conversion all live in an agonized relationship with their consciences. It will not do to picture everyone apart from conversion as harried and guilt-burdened because of the relentless attacks of conscience; nor to conclude that anyone who commits a crime such as murder will necessarily suffer severe pangs of conscience. The conscience may indeed torment the individual who violates the standards with which he identifies. But if he thoroughly identifies with a group that for its own purposes sanctions murder (such as an underworld organization), his inner voice may testify only to the moral code of the group, and he may suffer no pangs of conscience. Also, when one acts in conflict with conscience, that inner voice may be deadened or "seared" (1 Tim. 4:2) by repeated violations until it has become feeble and scarcely heard. Thus it cannot be assumed that apart from conversion all live in an agonized relationship with their consciences.

Nevertheless, conversion, understood as a conscious turning to faith in Christ and obedience to Him, inescapably involves the conscience. In the NT materials the change in life's focal point involves new orientations for the conscience.

This reorientation of conscience appears to have more than one dimension. The conscience undergoes change of authority focus. A conscience that has previously emphasized the standards of parents and social groups begins to witness to the will of Christ and to find its focus there (cf. 1 Cor. 4:3f.).

There appears also to be a change of sensitivity for the previously dull or insensitive conscience. The conscience that may have been insensitive may be awakened to new and possibly agonizing awareness of the conflict between Christ's standards and one's own performance (cf. Rom. 3:20; 7:19).

There is also evidence of a change from an accusing conscience to a clear or good conscience. A conscience that in its accusations attacked the worth of the individual (Rom. 7:18) becomes a conscience assured and at peace (Rom. 8:1). As observed above, the good conscience is not merely an accuser turned silent, but is a positive witness to one's moral worth and standing (cf. Acts 23:1).

Bibliography.–*IDB*, *s.v.* (Davies); MM; C. A. Pierce, *Conscience in the NT* (*SBT*, 15, 1955); H. R. Niebuhr, *Journal of Philosophy*, 42 (1945), 352-59; *TDNT*, VII, *s.v.* σύνοιδα, συνείδησις (Maurer).

R. OPPERWALL

CONSECRATE; CONSECRATED [Heb. *qāḏaš, qōḏeš, millē' yaḏ, nāzar*; Gk. *hagiázō*]; AV also SANCTIFY (usually), HALLOW, HOLY (Ex. 22:31), OF SEPARATION (Nu. 6:18), SAINTS (Dt. 33:3), DEDICATE (Jgs. 17:3), SEPARATED (Hos. 9:10), BID (Zeph. 1:7); NEB also HALLOW, DEDICATE, HOLY, KEEP HOLY, INSTALL (Lev. 16:32), "give with open hands" (2 Ch. 29:31), "belongs to God" (1 Cor. 7:14); **CONSECRATION** [Heb. *millu'îm* (Lev. 7:37), *nēzer* (21:12; Nu. 6:19)]; AV also CROWN (Lev. 21:12); NEB also INSTALLATION (Lev. 7:37), "which had been dedicated" (Nu. 6:19). The expression *millē' yaḏ,* "fill the hand," is used for the installation of a priest into his office, and the noun *millu'îm* for the installation-offerings, which evidently were put into the priest's hands to symbolize his admission into office (cf. Lev. 7:37; 16:32; 21:10; 1 K. 13:33; but also Ezk. 43:26).

See also HOLY; SANCTIFICATION; NAZIRITE.

T. REES

CONSENT. The AV expression "with one consent" is in the RSV "with one accord" at Ps. 83:5 (Heb. *lēḇ*; NEB "with one mind") and Zeph. 3:9 (*šᵉḵem 'eḥāḏ,* "shoulder to shoulder"), and "as one man" at 1 S. 11:7 (*'îš*; NEB "to a man"). However, in Hos. 6:9 *šeḵmâ* is not as in the AV "by consent" but as in the RSV and NEB "to Shechem." In Ps. 50:18 *rāṣâ*, AV "consented," is in the RSV "be a friend," NEB "choose as a friend." Elsewhere in the OT, "consent" translates Heb. *'āḇâ* (Jgs. 11:17; 1 K. 20:8; Prov. 1:10) and *'ôṯ* (Gen. 34:15).

The main NT word is Gk. *syneudokéō,* used in Lk. 11:48; 1 Cor. 7:12f.; and also Acts 8:1, where Saul was said to be "consenting" to the murder of Stephen. The word implies a positive consent, meaning "share a favorable opinion," literally "think well of along with," and in Acts 22:20 the same word reflecting on the same incident is in the RSV "approving." Other NT words are *aphíēmi* (Mt. 3:15), *synkatatíthēmi* (Lk. 23:51), and *gnṓmē* (Philem. 14, AV "mind").

See also AGREE. J. W. D. H.

CONSIDERATE. This word does not directly translate a Greek term in either of its two occurrences in the RSV: 1 Pet. 3:7 (AV "according to knowledge"; NEB "with understanding") and 1 Cor. 10:28 (AV "for his sake"). The Gk. *katá gnṓsin* in 1 Pet. 3:7 literally means "according to knowledge"; it would seem to indicate an awareness of the wife's needs. Both 1 Cor. 10:28 and Acts 16:3 (NEB "consideration"; AV, RSV, "because of") have the Greek preposition *diá* with the accusative case, expressing "on account of" or "because of."

G. H. HOVEE

CONSIST. Archaic in Col. 1:17, AV, for Gk. *synístēmi,* RSV "hold together," NEB "are held together." Christ gives *system* — and thus, to the Greek mind, meaning — to the entire universe.

CONSOLATION. *See* COMFORT.

CONSOLATION, SON OF. *See* BARNABAS.

CONSORT. "Consort with" is archaic in Acts 17:4, AV, for Gk. *prosklēróō*; RSV and NEB "join."

CONSPIRACY [Heb. *qešer*; Gk. *synōmosía* (Acts 23:13)]; **CONSPIRE** [Heb. *qāšar, nākal* (Gen. 37:18)]; NEB also PLOTTED; [*rāgaš*] (Ps. 2:1); AV "rage"; NEB "[be] in turmoil"; [*yā'aṣ*] (Ps. 83:5 [MT 6]); AV CONSULTED TOGETHER; NEB AGREED TOGETHER. Secret agreement to do wrong against a person or state. These terms may indicate formation of an agreement to commit wrong (Gen. 37:18; 2 Ch. 24:21; Ps. 83:5 [MT 6; Heb. *yā'aṣ*; cf. v. 3 (MT 4)]; Acts 23:13), the act of violence (1 K. 16:20; 2 K. 10:9; 15:15), or the perpetrators (2 S. 15:12; cf. 2 Ch. 24:26; 33:25). In combination, the noun and verb mean "make a conspiracy," indicating both the joining together and the resolution (2 K. 12:20 [MT 21]; 14:19 [par. 2 Ch. 25:27]; 15:30).

Although the basic sense is to do wrong against another (Gen. 37:18; Acts 23:13), conspiracy is most often an attempt to gain royal power (1 S. 22:8, 13; 2 S. 15:12, 31), usually involving assassination (1 K. 15:27; 2 K. 12:20 [MT 21]; 14:19 [par. 2 Ch. 25:27]; 15:25). When an individual claims the deed (1 K. 16:9, 16, 20, AV "treason"; cf. 15:15, 30), the sense may be "plot." Amos is accused of threatening Jeroboam's power (Amos 7:10).

A conspiracy may be a political alliance (Ps. 2:1; Isa. 28:12; AV "confederacy"; NEB "say 'too hard'"; cf. AV in 2 K. 17:4 [RSV "treachery"; NEB "was being disloyal"]; Neh. 4:8 [RSV "plotted together"; NEB "banded together"]).

The AV translates *qešer* in Jer. 11:9 as "conspiracy," indicating religious or moral decay, thus a plot against the Covenant and its ideals. In Ezk. 22:25, the AV "conspiracy of her prophets" follows the MT (Heb. *qešer n^e^bî'e[y]hā*); the RSV emends the text to read "her princes" (Heb. *'^a^šer n^e^śî'e[y]hā*), following the LXX (Gk. *hoi aphēgoúmenoi*).

See also REVOLT. A. C. M.

CONSTANT. Archaic in 1 Ch. 28:7, AV, for Heb. *ḥāzaq*, RSV "continue resolute," NEB "steadfastly (obeys)."

CONSTANTLY. "Affirm constantly" is archaic in Acts 12:15, AV, for Gk. *diischyrízomai* (cf. Lk. 22:59), and in Tit. 3:8, AV, for *diabebaióomai*; the RSV translates "insist." Prov. 21:28, AV, "the man that heareth speaketh constantly" (Heb. *neṣaḥ*), is in the RSV "the word of a man who hears will endure"; cf. the NEB, "he whose words ring true will leave children behind him." The MT is corrupt or obscure.

CONSTELLATIONS. *See* ASTRONOMY II.C.

CONSTRAIN. In Job 32:18 the AV and RSV render Heb. *ṣûq* "constrain," whereas the NEB gives the later meaning "gripe": "a bellyfull of wind [*rû(a)ḥ*, AV and RSV "spirit"] gripes me."

Jesus in Lk. 12:50, looking ahead to His crucifixion, says, "I have a baptism to be baptized with; and how I am constrained [Gk. *synéchō*; AV "straitened"] until it is accomplished." The verb can mean "occupied" with something, as in Acts 18:5, or "controlled," as in 2 Cor. 5:14, but here most likely means "tormented" (cf. Mt. 4:24; Lk. 4:38; also Phil. 1:23). This torment was due not only to Jesus' human fear of suffering and death, but also to His divine impatience to accomplish salvation, and divine sorrow over the divisions that He was to cause. In 1 Pet. 5:2 "by constraint" (Gk. *anankastṓs*) means "by compulsion," "as if forced."

J. W. D. H.

CONSTRUCTION. *See* BUILD.

CONSUL [Gk. *hýpatos*] (1 Macc. 15:16). One of two chief military and political magistrates of senatorial rank in the Roman republic. The identification of the consul in 1 Macc. 15:16 and the authenticity of his letter to Ptolemy are matters of debate.

CONSULT [Heb. *dāraš*]; AV also ENQUIRE, SEEK, SEEK UNTO; NEB also RESORT TO, SEEK GUIDANCE; [*yā'aṣ*]; AV also TAKE COUNSEL; NEB also CONFER, CONSPIRE, WHISPER; [*'āmaḏ*]; AV STAND UP; [*šā'al*]; AV also ASK COUNSEL, ENQUIRE; NEB also MAKE INQUIRY, RESORT TO.

Heb. *dāraš* means "resort to" or "seek"; it is used for inquiring of levitical priests and the judge (Dt. 17:9), mediums and wizards (Isa. 8:19), also idols and sorcerers (Isa. 19:3), or the Lord (Isa. 31:1). *Šā'al*, meaning "ask," is rendered "consult" when used for inquiring of an oracle of God (2 S. 16:23) or of a medium (1 Ch. 10:13); or of a method of divination, consulting the teraphim (Ezk. 21:21). *'Āmaḏ*, meaning literally "stand" or "arise," is used in Ezr. 2:63 of a priest's referring to Urim and Thummim. *Yā'aṣ* has the more usual meaning of exchanging counsel. It is used of an action taken by enemies (Ps. 71:10; 83:3) and by David (1 Ch. 13:1), also rhetorically of the Lord (Isa. 40:14). J. R. PRICE

CONSUME. The main OT words are Heb. *'āḵal* ("eat"), *kālâ* ("put an end to"), and *tāmam* ("be complete"). In Ps. 119:20, "My soul is consumed with longing for thy ordinances," the verb is *gāras* (AV "breaketh"). Other words include *bāla'* (Eccl. 10:12, AV "swallow up"), *bā'ar, śārap* ("burn"), *'āsap, ḥāsal, kārat* (Nu. 11:33, AV "chewed"), *māsâ, sāpâ, ṣāmaṯ, rā'a'*, and Aram. *š^e^maḏ* (Dnl. 7:26). In Job 20:26 the RSV "will be consumed" reads *yērō(a)'* (niphal impf.) for *yēra'*. In Ps. 49:14, AV, "consume" means "waste away" (RSV).

In the NT occur Gk. *kataphágō* ("eat up"), *analískō* (Lk. 9:54; Gal. 5:15), *katanalískō* (He. 12:29), *aphanízō* (Mt. 6:19f., AV "corrupt"), *ekkaíō* (Rom. 1:27, AV "burned"), and *esthíō* (He. 10:27). J. W. D. H.

CONSUMPTION [Heb. *šaḥepeṯ*–'wasting away']; NEB "wasting disease." One of the punishments that was to follow neglect or breach of the law. It may mean pulmonary consumption, which occurs frequently in Palestine; but from its association with fever in Lev. 26:16; Dt. 28:22, it is probably the much more common condition of wasting and emaciation from prolonged or often recurring attacks of malarial fever.

CONTAIN. The AV for Gk. *enkrateúomai* in 1 Cor. 7:9, RSV "exercise self-control," NEB "control themselves." The usual context of this word in Greek literature is one of abstinence and asceticism.

CONTEND; CONTENDER; CONTENTION; CONTENTIOUS. In the OT "contend" usually translates Heb. *rîḇ*, "dispute" or "quarrel" (AV also "plead," "strive," "debate," "chide"; NEB also "dispute," "defy," "fight," "accuse," etc.), sometimes with the formal sense of "engage in a lawsuit." In Mic. 6:2 *yākah* refers to arguing a case in a court of law. Among other OT terms, Heb. *'āśaq* (Gen. 26:20) and *nāṣâ* (Nu. 26:9) mean "quarrel," and *gārâ* (as used in Dt. 2:5, 9, 19, 24) includes the possibility of battle (AV also "meddle"; NEB "provoke"). The word in Dnl. 10:21 is a form of *ḥāzaq*, "be strong," "take courage." Isa. 41:12 uses a noun, *maṣṣûṯ*, "your adversaries," whence the RSV "those who contend with you." Terms used in the NT are: Gk. *diamáchomai* (Acts 23:9, NEB "take sides"); *éstin . . . pálē* (Eph. 6:12, AV "wrestle") and *epagonízomai* (Jude 3), both athletic imagery; and *diakríno* (Jude 9), "dispute." "Contention" in Prov. 15:18 and Hos. 4:4 translates Heb. *rîḇ*, which in Jer. 15:10 and Hab. 1:13 is rendered "strife" while "contention" is used for *māḏôn*. In Acts 15:39 the term is Gk. *paroxysmós*, here used in the unfavorable sense "irritation," "sharp disagreement" (Bauer). "Contentious" translates the Heb. *miḏyānîm* (cf. *māḏôn* above) in Prov. 21:9, 19; 25:24; 27:15, and Gk. *philóneikos* (lit. "fond of victory") in 1 Cor. 11:16. "Contenders" in Prov. 18:18 is supplied by the translators to render the sense of "powerful [persons]."

See also DISPUTE. E. W. S.

CONTENT; CONTENTMENT. The Heb. *yā'al* is used in the somewhat stylized expression "content to dwell" in Ex. 2:21; Josh. 7:7; Jgs. 17:11, where it means little more than "be willing," "agree," "be (so) disposed." In Lev. 10:20, "content" translates *yāṭaḇ bᵉ'ênê*, "be good in the eyes"; the NEB has "he deemed it right." The RSV uses "content" in 2 K. 14:10 and Ezk. 16:47 not to translate a specific Hebrew word but to draw out the sense of the original.

In the NT the main word is Gk. *arkéō* (Lk. 3:14; 1 Tim. 6:8; He. 13:5; 3 Jn. 10), "be satisfied," or even "make do," as Lk. 3:14, NEB. In 2 Cor. 12:10 the word is *eudokéō*, "think well of," for which the AV has "take pleasure in," the NEB "am well content."

The familiar passage Phil. 4:11, "I have learned, in whatever state I am, to be content" (*autárkēs*), has a different interpretation in the NEB: "I have learned to find resources in myself whatever my circumstances." This reading emphasizes the Stoic aspect of self-sufficiency present in the word; yet Paul is quick to state the ultimate source of his self-sufficiency: "him who empowers me" (v. 13). The substantive *autárkeia*, "contentment," occurs in 1 Tim. 6:6, where again the NEB renders, "the man whose resources are within him." See also 2 Cor. 9:8.

See *TDNT*, I, *s.v.* ἀρκέω (Kittel). J. W. D. H.

CONTINENCE. *See* SELF-CONTROL.

CONTRADICT [Gk. *anteípon*] (Lk. 21:15); AV GAINSAY; NEB REFUTE; [*antilégō*] (Acts 13:45; Tit. 1:9); AV also "gainsayers"; NEB also "objectors" (Tit. 1:9); [*anantírrhētos*] ("cannot be contradicted," Acts 19:36); AV "cannot be spoken against"; NEB "are beyond dispute"; **CONTRADICTIONS** [*antithéseis*] (1 Tim. 6:20); AV OPPOSITIONS. The AV "contradiction" for Gk. *antilogía* is in the RSV "(beyond) dispute" (He. 7:7) and "hostility" (12:3).

The NT words for "contradict," which mean "speak in opposition," can have the sense "oppose" or "deny" (cf. Rom. 10:21; Lk. 20:27), or "dispute"; it is not clear whether they are ever used to mean "say the opposite."

The *antithéseis* of 1 Tim. 6:20 are Gnostic teachings "antithetical" to Christian belief. J. W. D. H.

CONTRARY. The AV and RSV expression "walk contrary to," which occurs throughout Lev. 26:21-41 (Heb. *hālaḵ qerî*), means as in the NEB "defy."

CONTRIBUTION [Heb. *tᵉrûmâ*, *mᵉnāṯ* (2 Ch. 31:3); Gk. *koinōnía* (Rom. 15:26; 2 Cor. 9:13), *logía* or *logeía* (1 Cor. 16:1f.)]; AV also OFFERING, PORTION (2 Ch. 31:3), OBLATIONS (31:14), COLLECTION (1 Cor. 16:1), GATHERINGS (16:2), DISTRIBUTION (2 Cor. 9:13); NEB also SHARE (2 Ch. 31:3), COMMON FUND (Rom. 15:26), COLLECTION (1 Cor. 16:1), COLLECTING (16:2).

According to 2 Ch. 31, King Hezekiah arranged for full support of the priests and Levites by means of contributions of produce from the people of Israel. This was so successful that special rooms had to be set aside to contain the contributions (31:11), and several men assigned to oversee and distribute them (vv. 12ff.). These contributions and their chambers are mentioned in Neh. 10:35-39; 12:44, 47; 13:5; and in 13:10-13 the practice is restored by Nehemiah, after a lapse while he was away visiting the court of Artaxerxes.

Acts 11:29f. tells of the contribution made by the church in Antioch, "every one according to his ability," for the relief of Jerusalem Christians suffering from famine. The relief was sent by the hand of Paul and Barnabas, evidently on the visit related by Paul in Gal. 2:1ff. (cf. v. 10, "they would have us remember the poor").

Another contribution for the Jerusalem poor is described in Rom. 15:25-27; 1 Cor. 16:1-4; 2 Cor. 8f. In these passages, Paul three times used the terms *koinōnía* and *diakonía* (*diakonéō*) in conjunction — at Rom. 15:25f.; 2 Cor. 8:4; 9:13. The *diakonía* refers to the "service" element of the contribution, and the *koinōnía* to the "fellowship" or "sharing" aspect (cf. He. 13:16). The fellowship of believers in Christ — in this case of gentile Christians with Jewish Christians—enabled them to share of their possessions, to have their goods in common as in Acts 4:32ff. (*see* COMMUNITY OF GOODS).

Of this second series of contributions we learn that they were made in Galatia, Corinth, Macedonia, and Achaia. At least in Galatia and Corinth they were made the first day of every week, from each "as he may prosper" (1 Cor. 16:2); and they were entirely voluntary in each church (2 Cor. 8:3f.). In spite of their poverty the Macedonians gave abundantly (8:2); Paul urged the relatively more wealthy Corinthian church to give to the poor "as a matter of equality" (v. 14). In the case of Corinth, Paul sent Titus and two others as an advance party to arrange for their gift (2 Cor. 8:16–9:5), to avoid "humiliation" in case some Macedonians happened to be with Paul when he came there, and to avoid the appearance of personal pressure by Paul. Paul planned to deliver the contributions to Jerusalem himself, along with others carefully chosen (Rom. 15:25; 1 Cor. 16:3f.); but he had the option of sending accredited delegates in his place, which it seems likely he did, since Acts nowhere mentions his delivering these gifts (but cf. Acts 24:17f.).

On giving to the poor without love, see 1 Cor. 13:3.

J. W. D. H.

CONTRITE [Heb. *dakkā'*–'bruised'] (Ps. 51:17; Isa. 57:15); NEB BROKEN; [*nāḵēh*] (Isa. 66:2); NEB DISTRESSED. A contrite heart or spirit is one in which the natural pride and self-sufficiency have been completely humbled by the consciousness of guilt. The theological term "contrition" designates more than is found in these passages. It refers to the grief experienced as a consequence of the revelation of sin made by the preaching of the law

(Jer. 23:29). The Augsburg Confession (Art. XII) analyzes repentance into two parts, "contrition and faith," the one the fruit of the preaching of the law, the other of the gospel. While contrition has its degrees and is not equal in all persons, the promise of forgiveness is not dependent upon the degree of contrition but solely upon the merit of Christ. It is not simply a precondition of faith, but as hatred of sin combined with the purpose, by God's aid, to overcome it, it grows with faith.

H. E. JACOBS

CONTROVERSY [Heb. *rîḇ*; Gk. *zḗtēma, zḗtēsis*]; AV (NT) QUESTIONS; NEB DISPUTE (Ezk. 44:24), CHARGE (Hos. 4:1), CASE (Mic. 6:2), DISPUTES (Acts 26:3), "mere verbal questions" (1 Tim. 6:4), SPECULATIONS (2 Tim. 2:23; Tit. 3:9). The OT references are to legal disputes, literal in Ezekiel and figurative, of Yahweh, in Hosea and Micah.

The "controversies" of the Jews which Paul mentions in Acts 26:3 are the many "questions of their law" (23:29), the casuistic disputes, which were well known to Agrippa. See also 18:15; 25:19f.

In his letters to Timothy and Titus, Paul finds it necessary to speak out against "stupid controversies," disputes over minor details of the faith, quarrels over the law, "speculations" (*ekzētḗseis,* 1 Tim. 1:4), and the like. These warnings testify to the many problems and disruptions in the early Church caused by "false teachers" and heretics of various persuasions, in this situation including evidently Judaizers of Crete and Ephesus. *See* PASTORAL EPISTLES III.B.3.

The Gk. *zḗtēsis* (*zḗtēma*) used in all these NT passages comes from *zētéō,* "seek," "search out," and is used of various kinds of investigations, usually controversial. Cf. Jn. 3:25; Acts 15:2, 7.

"Without controversy" in 1 Tim. 3:16, AV (Gk. *homologouménōs*), RSV "we confess," means "beyond all doubt," "indisputably," "as all agree."

J. W. D. H.

CONVENIENT. Archaic in the AV for "fitting," "proper," "necessary," "suitable," etc. In Prov. 30:8 it translates Heb. *ḥōq* (RSV "needful"), and in Jer. 40:4f. *yāšār* ("right"). "Convenient day" in Mk. 6:21 and "convenient season" in Acts 24:25 translate Gk. *kairós,* RSV "opportunity"; cf. Mk. 14:11 (*eukaírōs*); 1 Cor. 16:12 (*eukairéō*). In Rom. 1:28, AV, "those things which are not convenient" (*tá mḗ kathḗkonta*) means as in the RSV "improper" conduct. The other occurrences are for Gk. *anḗkō* in Eph. 5:4 ("fitting") and Philem. 8 ("required").

J. W. D. H.

CONVERSANT. The Hebrew verb *hālaḵ* is rendered by the obsolete term "conversant" (AV Josh. 8:35; 1 S. 25:15), meaning "go along with (them)."

CONVERSATION. In the AV this word never has its modern significance, but means "behavior" or "conduct." It occurs twice in the OT, for Heb. *dereḵ,* "way" (Ps. 37:14; 50:23), several times in the NT for Gk. *anastrophḗ* or *anastréphō,* and also for *politeúō* (Phil. 1:27, RSV "manner of life"), *políteuma* (3:20, RSV "commonwealth"; *see* CITIZEN), and *trópos* (He. 13:5).

CONVERSION [Gk. *epistrophḗ*] (Acts 15:3); **CONVERT** (noun) [Gk. *aparchḗ*] ("first convert[s]" Rom. 16:5; 1 Cor. 16:15); AV FIRSTFRUITS; [*prosḗlytos*] (Acts 13:43); AV PROSELYTE; NEB "gentile worshipper"; [*neóphytos*] (1 Tim. 3:6, "recent convert"); AV NOVICE. The verb "convert" occurs several times in the AV, but in the RSV and NEB is replaced by "turn," "turn again," "return," etc.

I. Biblical Usage.–Of the Hebrew terms used for this concept, the most frequent is *šûḇ*. Others are *pānâ*, *hāpaḵ*, and *sāḇaḇ*, in hiphil. They can be used in the literal sense, e.g., in Gen. 14:7; Dt. 17:16; Ps. 56:9 (MT 10); Isa. 38:8. In the later prophetical writings *šûḇ,* in both qal and hiphil, refers to the return from captivity (Isa. 1:27; Jer. 29:14; 30:3; Ezk. 16:53; Zeph. 2:7). In the figurative sense the reference is to turning (back) to God (e.g., 1 S. 7:3; 1 K. 8:33; Isa. 19:22; Joel 2:12; Am. 4:6ff.; Hos. 6:1; 7:10) or (less often) from God (e.g., Nu. 14:43; 1 S. 15:11; 1 K. 9:6).

The terms used in the LXX and the NT are *stréphō* and its cognates, especially *epistréphō* (see *TDNT*, VII, *s.v.* [Bertram]; Bauer, p. 301). Besides its literal uses, *epistréphō* is used of turning from the wrong to the right in Mt. 13:15; Mk. 4:12; Lk. 1:16f.; 22:32; Acts 9:35; 11:21; 14:15; 15:19; 26:18; 28:17; 2 Cor. 3:16; 1 Thess. 1:9; Jas. 5:19f.; 1 Pet. 2:25 (from right to wrong cf. Gal. 4:9; *hypostréphō* in 2 Pet. 2:21). It is used in connection with *metanoéō* ("repent") in Acts 3:19; 26:20. The root word *stréphō* is used in this sense in Mt. 18:3; Jn. 12:40.

II. General Modern Usage.–The term "conversion" is often used in "a very general way to stand for the whole series of manifestations just preceding, accompanying, and immediately following the apparent sudden changes of character involved" (Starbuck, p. 21). " 'To be converted', 'to be regenerated', 'to receive grace', 'to experience religion', 'to gain an assurance', are so many phrases which denote the process, gradual or sudden, by which a self, hitherto divided and consciously wrong, inferior and unhappy, becomes unified and consciously right, superior and happy in consequence of its hold upon religious realities. That at least is what conversion signifies in general terms" (James, p. 189). In this general, imprecise way the term is used not only by psychologists, but also by theological writers and in common religious parlance. A converted person is a Christian, a believer, a person who "has religion," who has experienced regeneration.

J. L. NUELSEN

III. Theological Usage.–*A. Varied Meaning.* The biblical words for "turn" can have a very broad range of theological meaning. In relation to God they can denote God's turning to His people, His turning from them, His turning of them, and even perhaps His preventing of their turning to Him. In relation to man the terms have similar range. People turn from God, turn (back) to idols, turn (again) from idols, turn (back) to God, return to their land, turn others to God, turn people to one another, turn back those in error, or even turn the gospel into its opposite.

B. Inner and Positive Focus. In the theological development of the concept of conversion two important concentrations take place in relation to this almost bewilderingly complex usage. First, inner rather than outer turning becomes the center of attention. This aspect is significant already in the OT, where many of the references have to do with the inner relation between God and Israel. It takes on increasing importance in the NT, for, while the words can still carry a spatial reference, they bear a transferred sense in a high proportion of the instances. Second, the emphasis comes to be placed increasingly on the positive, not the negative side. This, too, is the clear tendency in the NT. The sense of turning away is still present in 2 Pet. 2:21, but most of the references have to do with turning to God or to the Lord. This is reinforced by the connection made between conversion on the one side and faith or repentance on the other. Theologically conversion emerges as the word for an inner turning (or turning back) to God.

C. Divine Side. While conversion has a decisive inner aspect, it cannot be understood simply as a human act. Thus it would not be wholly true to think of it theologically as the human side of regeneration. Throughout Scripture conversion as a human act has its ground in conversion as a divine act. God turns back Israel. He turns His people to Himself. This is not just a consequence but also a condition of His people's turning to Him. Some fifteen times in the OT God is said to convert man, and while the NT does not say so specifically it leaves no doubt that the ministry of the Holy Spirit is what makes possible the turning of sinners to God (cf. Jn. 16:18; 1 Cor. 2:4f.). In this sense God's converting stands closely related to His renewing (Eph. 2:11f.) and regenerating (Jn. 3). God accomplishes this work of His through those who proclaim His word. Thus the Baptist, filled with the Spirit, will turn many Israelites to the Lord their God (Lk. 1:16). Similarly the brethren can convert a sinner from the error of his way (Jas. 5:19f.).

D. Human Side. The relating of conversion to repentance and faith points to the human side. Freed to do so by God's converting power, sinners are converted, or convert, in a twofold movement. First, they turn from idols or Satan in the authentic repentance that means renunciation. Second, and as part of the same act, they turn to God in the true faith that means commitment. In most instances what is in view is this first turning whereby unbelievers become Christians, as in Acts 3:19 or 1 Thess. 1:9. Yet a restoration of believers, involving a renewal of renunciation and commitment, can also be intended, as in the saying of Jesus to Peter in Lk. 22:32, where Peter can hardly be coming to faith for the first time.

E. Conversion as Act. Theologically conversion must be defined as an act and not just an emotional experience. Since this act takes place in human life it can be studied and evaluated psychologically (see V). Scripture itself, however, shows no evidence of psychological interest. It portrays God at work and records the act of conversion which takes place as a result. Elements of will, intellect, and emotion go into it and yet it takes concrete form as an actual turning from sin, confession of faith, and renewing of life in conformity, not now with the world, but with God.

F. Mode of Conversion. The act of conversion need not follow a set pattern. It can often be sudden. The conversions of Paul (Acts 9) and the Philippian jailer (Acts 16) serve as examples. In other instances, although the act takes place in a moment, a period of preparation is suggested. The accounts of the Ethiopian eunuch (Acts 8) and the centurion Cornelius (Acts 10) may be quoted in support. The phrase used about Lydia in Acts 16:14, "The Lord opened her heart to give heed to what was said by Paul," points to a quiet if brief process which has nothing dramatic about it but is none the less authentic on that account. The NT has no specific accounts of children growing slowly in or to conversion, just as it has no records of the sudden conversions of Christians' children. Nevertheless, the exhortation to bring up children "in the discipline and instruction of the Lord" (Eph. 6:4) and the succession in faith of Lois, Eunice, and Timothy (2 Tim. 1:5) offer a strong indication that, while conversion always means act, an instantaneous conversion at a specific moment need not be the exclusive rule.

***IV. Historical Usage.**–A. Early Church.* The graphic nature of conversion found expression in the baptisms of pagan converts. By the early 3rd cent. the baptismal service took place on the eve of Easter or Pentecost. Exorcisms had been introduced. The candidates, in response to questions, renounced evil and professed faith in Christ and obedience to Him. The giving of new garments and sometimes of milk and honey symbolized the beginning of a new life. The church fathers saw in these conversions the work of both God and man, although not always in the same order. Chrysostom, as one might expect from a preacher, regarded conversion as a work of human choice and volition which God completes. Augustine, with his emphatic doctrine of grace, put predestination first. As we recognize in our prayers for unbelievers, God takes the initiative with His prevenient grace and only then may conversion follow.

B. The Middle Ages. In medieval theology adult conversions ceased to be the rule. In relation to infants, emphasis on the priority of God's work led to the view that conversion takes place ontologically at baptism. The new principle of being imparted in this way works itself out in a new life of instantaneous or gradual conversion through external graces. This includes living to God and acceptance of Christ through faith informed by love. Conversion in this sense extends to all life and not to its beginning alone.

C. The Reformation. The reformers did not totally dissent from the medieval interpretation. For them, too, conversion was predominantly God's act worked out over the whole life. They placed less emphasis, however, on a mysterious change effected at baptism and shifted attention to the ministry of the Holy Spirit through the Word as in the doctrine of calling. In so doing they linked conversion — a term not greatly used by theologians like Calvin — very closely to repentance and faith. When Calvin does use the word, he equates it not merely with the start of the Christian life but with the lifelong repentance of mortification and renewal, i.e., the total turning about of life that Paul describes in Rom. 12:1f. For Calvin the will "is converted by the Lord's power alone."

D. Evangelicalism. With the Pietist movement and the evangelical awakenings, a new call for individual conversion or regeneration went out which did not exclude sanctification but in some circles introduced a sharper differentiation from it. Where Arminian theology took hold, the element of personal decision acquired greater prominence and accompanying manifestations gave rise to a new psychological interest and an increasing concern for experience. Conversions could even be viewed at times as the human side of regeneration. Indeed, in extreme cases regeneration itself could be equated terminologically with the conversion experience (see II). Nevertheless, evangelical theology, especially in its Reformation components, has continued to recognize the hand of God in conversion and to find in it a life-affecting act and not just an emotional experience.

E. Roman Catholicism. In contrast to more extreme forms of emotionalizing, Roman Catholic theology has always contended for the divine introduction of a new principle of life at the entitative level. Conversion derives from this as the new life of conformity to God in which, enabled by the divine initiative of grace, believers turn to God in contrition and faith. Pre-conversion grace plays an important role by way of preparation. While conversion in the full sense is to Jesus Christ, or to faith in Him, Roman Catholic theologians speak of two other conversions as well, a moral conversion to goodness and a confessional conversion to the Roman Catholic Church.

F. Karl Barth. Trying to avoid a subjectivizing of conversion without falling victim to its sacramentalizing, Barth points to the objective ground of individual conversion in God's turning of the world to Himself in the life, death, and resurrection of Jesus Christ. On the basis of the conversion, or turning around, accomplished in this vicarious work, believers are awakened by the Holy Spirit to personal conversion, which may well be datable, as an entry into Christ, or identification with Him, in repentance, faith, and sanctification. The true deity and humanity of Christ mean for Barth that He is both the converting God and also, representatively, converted man. This does not make our conversion superfluous. On the contrary, it makes it possible by providing its objective ground. In support of this understanding Barth adduces the primary sense of conversion as "turning around" (Ger. *Umkehren*) in distinction from the common sense of conversion experience (Ger. *Bekehrung*), which has for him an anthropocentric overtone. In the last analysis our turning is not only *to* God; it is also *in* God and *by* God. G. W. BROMILEY

V. Psychological Usage.–The early psychologists of religion (e.g., Starbuck and W. James) distinguished between "gradual" and "sudden" conversions. While these distinctions are helpful, the situation is far more complex, as noted above. In fact, the underlying processes may be the same in both of these types. As Salzman and others have noted, there is probably a long period of unrest, incubation, and struggle that precedes even the sudden conversions. These processes may be conscious or unconscious. Even the Greeks whom Paul addressed on Mars Hill were prepared by long periods of interest and study.

W. James, among others such as Kildahl, feels that there are distinct personality differences that predispose persons toward one or the other type of conversion. James' "healthy-minded" persons who block out sadness and evil are inclined toward gradual conversions because they always feel that God cares about them and have faith in the goodness of life. "Sick-minded" persons are inclined to see evil in themselves and the world around them. For them conversion is usually a radical, sudden, dramatic event, since it takes an extreme experience to wrest them from their pessimism.

Much further study has been done on the conversion process (cf. Scroggs and Douglas). A number of the yet unresolved issues are these: Is there an optimal age for conversion? (Most of the literature up to this point suggests adolescence is the most *common* time; cf. Starbuck.) Are certain persons more susceptible to conversion than others? Are certain personality types immune to conversion? Do religious and secular conversions follow the same processes? Can one achieve conversion by striving, or does it happen spontaneously? Can conversion be manipulated? Finally, is conversion an experience that involves thoughts, feelings, intentions, and actions together, or need it consist of only one or more of these processes?

Although these are psychological questions they cannot be divorced from their theological implications. The crucial issue is, of course, the relationship between the action of God and the response of human beings. Faith must continue to affirm the power of God, while all that psychology can do is describe the reactions.

See also REPENTANCE; REGENERATION.

Bibliography.–*CD*, IV/2, § 66, 4; IV/3, § 71; Calvin *Inst.* ii.3.6; iii.3.5ff.; W. James, *Varieties of Religious Experience* (1902); J. P. Kildahl, *Pastoral Psychology*, 16 (1965), 37-44; H. N. Malony, ed., *Current Perspectives in the Psychology of Religion* (1977), pp. 249-265; *New Catholic Encyclopedia, s.v.*; L. Salzman, *Pastoral Psychology*, 17 (1966), 8-20; J. R. Scroggs and W. G. T. Douglas, *Journal of Religion and Health*, 6 (1967), 204-216; E. D. Starbuck, *Psychology of Religion* (1899). H. N. MALONY

CONVICT [Gk. *elénchō, exelénchō* (Jude 15)]; AV CONVINCE; NEB also "prove in the wrong" (Jn. 8:46, RSV "convict of sin"), "bring conviction" (1 Cor. 14:24); the RSV "convicts himself" in 2 S. 14:13 is a paraphrase of the Hebrew, which is literally "(he speaks) as guilty" (*k^e'āšēm*), AV "as one which is faulty," NEB "you condemn yourself." The basic meaning of *elénchō* is "show" or "demonstrate"; the further legal sense "prove guilty" is evident from the context in Jn. 8:46; Jas. 2:9; Jude 15; cf. Jn. 16:8; and cf. "confute" in Tit. 1:9, where again there is the idea of successfully demonstrating the truth of a charge. In 1 Cor. 14:24 the meaning is less obviously "convicted"; it could just as well be "exposed," as in Jn. 3:20; Eph. 5:11, 13.

See also CONVINCE. J. W. D. H.

CONVICTION [Gk. *plērophoría, élenchos*]; AV ASSURANCE (1 Thess. 1:5), EVIDENCE (He. 11:1); NEB also "makes us certain" (He. 11:1). As in 1 Cor. 2:4, so in 1 Thess. 1:5 Paul says that the gospel comes not as mere words but also "in power and in the Holy Spirit," and here he adds *plērophoría pollḗ,* "with complete certainty." Built into the gospel message is the power to convince completely, through the Holy Spirit.

In its classic definition in He. 11:1, faith is called the *élenchos* of things not seen. The AV rendering "evidence" best shows the paradox of faith: a "demonstration" of what cannot be demonstrated. *See* FAITH.

J. W. D. H.

CONVINCE. Archaic in the AV for "convict" (Gk. *elénchō,* Jn. 8:46; 1 Cor. 14:24; Tit. 1:9; Jas. 2:9; *exelénchō*, Jude 15) and for "confute" (Heb. *yākaḥ*, Job 32:12; Gk. *diakatelénchomai,* Acts 18:28). In the RSV the archaic usage seems to be retained in Jn. 16:8 (*elénchō*; AV "reprove"; NEB "confute," v. 9 "convict").

Elsewhere in the RSV, "convince" translates Gk. *peíthō* in Lk. 16:31; 20:6; Acts 28:23 (AV "persuade"), v. 24 (AV "believe"); Phil. 1:25 (AV "having this confidence"); *dokéo* in Acts 26:9 (AV "I verily thought"); *plērophoréō* in Rom. 4:21; 14:5 (AV "persuaded"); *krínō* in 2 Cor. 5:14 (AV "judge"); and *elénchō* again in 2 Tim. 4:2 (AV "reprove") and Jude 22. In this last passage most ancient MSS read *eleáte,* "have compassion" (AV; cf. NEB "who need your pity"); and there are several other textual and translational difficulties as well in the last few verses of Jude. In He. 6:17 "more convincingly" renders Gk. *perissóteron* (AV "abundantly").

J. W. D. H.

CONVOCATION. Used by the AV and RSV to render Heb. *miqrā'* in the frequent "holy convocation" (NEB "sacred assembly"). On a holy convocation no work could be done. The phrase differs from "solemn assembly," which in the Pentateuch is applied only to the concluding festivals at the end of Passover and Tabernacles, while "holy convocation" is used of the sabbath and all the great holy days of the Mosaic legislation.

CONVULSE [Heb. *rā'am*] (Ezk. 27:35); AV TROUBLED; NEB "horror is written on (their faces)"; [Gk. *sparássō*]; AV TEAR, REND; NEB "throw into convulsions," RACK. The OT reference is to the expression on the faces of the kings of the coastlands, struck with horror at the sudden downfall of Tyre. The RSV "convulsed" may be a bit strong; a better suggestion is "tremble" or "quiver" with fear.

All the NT references are to the actions of demons on their victims: Mk. 1:26; 9:20, 26; Lk. 9:39, 42. *See* DEMONOLOGY.

COOK (noun) [Heb. *ṭabbāḥ*–'butcher, cook' (1 S. 9:23f.), *ṭabbāḥâ*–'female cook (of meat)' (8:13)]. Normally in

Israel the women of the family were the cooks, although men took a hand in it at times (Jgs. 6:19). Often a cook had to butcher the meat as well as boil it. The cooks mentioned in 1 S. 8f. were professionals.

COOK; COOKING. *See* FOOD.

COOL SPIRIT. In Prov. 17:27 the RSV "cool spirit" and NEB "cool head" are based on the reading of the *kethibh*, Heb. *w^egar-rû(a)ḥ*, whereas the AV "excellent spirit" reads with the *qere*, *y^egar-ru(a)ḥ*. Although "hot" is used in the OT of anger or displeasure, nowhere else in the OT does "cold" or "cool" have an abstract sense. But if the *kethibh* is read here, a "cool spirit" probably means "calm."

COOS. *See* COS.

COPING. Traditional conjectural translation of the otherwise unattested architectural term *ṭ^epāḥôṯ* in 1 K. 7:9.

COPPER [Heb. *n^eḥōšeṯ* and cognates; Gk. *chalkós* and cognates, *leptón*]. The RSV and NEB usually render these by "bronze," though the Hebrew may imply either copper or bronze. The AV uses "copper" only in Ezr. 8:27 (RSV "bronze"; NEB "red copper"). Copper was one of the earliest metals to be known and utilized in alloy, but copper, as a single metal, was probably little used. The remains of spears, balances, arms, vases, mirrors, statues, cooking utensils, implements of all kinds, etc. from Bible times are principally of an alloy of copper hardened with tin known today as BRONZE. In such passages as Dt. 8:9, where reference is made to the native metal or ores, "copper" is the proper term. This is true also of coins (*chalkós*) in Mt. 10:9.

Our modern English word "copper" is derived from an old name pertaining to the island of Cyprus. Copper was known to the ancients as Cyprian metal, probably because that island was one of the chief sources for this metal. The Sinai Peninsula and the mountains of northern Syria also contributed to the ancient world's supply. Copper artifacts dating from the late Chalcolithic period have been recovered from various sites in Palestine.

See also METAL; MINING. J. A. PATCH
R. K. H.

Copper model of two-wheeled chariot with driver, drawn by four asses (restored, below). From the Shara temple at Tell Agrab (1st half of the 3rd millennium B.C.) (Oriental Institute, University of Chicago)

Bowl with an offset disk base, hammered from a single piece of copper (Tepe Gawra, middle 3rd millennium B.C.) (University Museum, University of Pennsylvania)

COPPERSMITH [Gk. *chalkeús*]. The vocation of the heretical Alexander of 2 Tim. 4:14 (cf. 1 Tim. 1:20). He probably worked with other metals besides copper, for the Greek word is not so specific as the English versions render it.

COPTIC VERSIONS. *See* VERSIONS.

COPY [Aram. *paršegen*] (Ezr. 4:11); NEB TEXT; [Heb. *paṯšegen*] (Est. 3:14); [*taḇnîṯ*–'image'] (Josh. 22:28); AV PATTERN; [Gk. *hypodeígma*] (He. 8:5); AV EXAMPLE; [*antítypos*] (9:24); AV FIGURE; NEB SYMBOL. In Ezra the reference is to a copy of a letter to the king; in Esther to the copies of the king's decree. Josh. 22:28 describes a duplicate of the altar of the Lord that was to be a witness to the Reubenites, Gadites, and half the tribe of Manasseh that they were a part of the people of God. The burden of the book of Hebrews is that the sanctuary of Moses' day was a mere shadow of the heavenly original (Gk. *týpos*) (cf. Ex. 25:40), into which Christ Himself has now entered.

See also TYPE. G. WYPER

COR kōr [Heb. *kōr*; Sum. GUR] (Ezk. 45:14); NEB KOR. A large liquid and dry measure. *See* WEIGHTS AND MEASURES.

CORAL [Heb. *rā'môṯ*] (Job 28:18; Ezk. 27:16); NEB BLACK CORAL; [*p^enînîm*] (Lam. 4:7); AV RUBIES;

NEB BRANCHING CORAL. The red coral or precious coral, *Corallium rubrum,* is confined to the Mediterranean and Adriatic seas. It is the calcareous axis of a branching colony of polyps. It does not form reefs, but occurs in small masses 40-100 fathoms (75-180 m.) below the surface. It differs totally in structure from the white corals which form coral reefs, belonging to the order of Octactinia or Eight-rayed Polyps, while the reef-building corals belong to the Hexactinia or Six-rayed Polyps.

Rā'môṯ occurs in Job 28:18 along with crystal in a description of wisdom. In this passage the LXX and Vulgate understand the Hebrew as a participal form. In Ezk. 27:16 *rā'môṯ* (LXX B *lamōṯ*) was traded with emeralds and cloth between Tyre and Edom. In Lam. 4:7, *peninîm* seems to indicate a red substance of a branch-like structure, but the same word in Job 28:18 is rendered "pearls" in the RSV (NEB "red coral"; AV "rubies"; LXX *líthos*).

See also STONES, PRECIOUS. A. E. DAY R. K. H.

CORBAN kôr'ban [Heb. *qorbān*, transliterated Gk. *korban* in Mk. 7:11, and translated Gk. *dṓron*–'gift' in the LXX and Mt. 15:5 as well as Mk. 7:11]. In Jewish tradition, a word used to declare something dedicated to God. In the Gospel story Jesus castigates the Jews for their practice, justified in their legal tradition, of pronouncing their property "corban" and thus rendering it unable lawfully to be used for the material support of aged parents, even though it did not then need actually to be offered to God but could be retained for personal use.

Pertinent rabbinic passages, cited by Rengstorf (*TDNT*, III, *s.v.*), include *Nedarim* i.3; viii.7; ix.1, 4-6. For a discussion of this practice *see* TALMUD IV. It is mentioned by Josephus in *Ant.* iv.4.4 and *CAp* i.22 (167).

Jesus singled out this particular bit of sophistry to show how the letter of Jewish tradition could sometimes be hostile to the spirit of the law, in this case the fifth commandment. J. W. D. H.

CORBE kôr'bē (1 Esd. 5:12, AV). *See* CHORBE.

CORD. (1) [Heb. *gaḇluṯ*]; AV WREATHEN WORK; NEB ROPE. Literally "cords of twisting," i.e., tightly twisted cords, made of gold and used on the breastpiece (Ex. 28:22). See also (5) and (8) below.

(2) [Heb. *ḥeḇel*]; AV also BAND, SORROW; NEB also BAND, BOND, CHAIN, LEADING-STRING, NOOSE, ROPE, TETHER. Bindings, used for securing hanging curtains (Est. 1:6) or carpets (Ezk. 27:24); used figuratively of an innocent man being secured by Sheol (2 S. 22:6; Ps. 18:5), or by death (Ps. 18:4), or by affliction (Job 36:8), or by the wicked (Ps. 119:61) and arrogant (Ps. 140:5), or by falsehood (Isa. 5:18); also used figuratively of compassion (Hos. 11:4); used to secure the immovable tent of the heavenly Jerusalem (Isa. 33:20); used in fishing for Leviathan (Job 41:1); and used also to secure the lamp which goes out to signal the end of time (Eccl. 12:6).

(3) [Heb. *ḥûṭ*]; AV also "line of thread"; NEB also "strand of cord." A thread or line used as a signal by Rahab (Josh. 2:18; see also (10) below). A threefold thread is unbreakable (Eccl. 4:12).

(4) [Heb. *yeṯer*]. A tent-string or bow-string; which is meant is unclear in the context (Job 30:11; cf. 4:21). What is clear is that Job is no longer held in respect by men who had previously respected him.

(5) [Heb. *migbālôṯ*]; AV WREATHEN WORK; NEB ROPE. Literally "the twisted"; hence the twisted golden chains of the ephod (Ex. 28:14).

(6) [Heb. *mêṯār*]; NEB also ROPE, TENT-ROPE. Strings used in the erection and securing of the tabernacle and its courts (Ex. 35:18), its screens (Ex. 39:40; Nu. 3:26; 4:26) and pillars (Nu. 3:37; 4:32), and tents (Isa. 54:2; Jer. 10:20).

(7) [Heb. *mōšeḵoṯ*]; AV BAND. The cords of Orion, probably a mythological allusion (Job 38:31).

(8) [Heb. *'aḇōṯ*]; AV also BAND, WREATHEN CHAIN, WREATHEN WORK; NEB also BOND, CHAIN, ROPE. Wound or twisted rope, made of gold and used on the breastpiece (Ex. 28:24; 39:15, 17) and ephod (Ex. 28:25; 39:18); restraints or bonds (Ps. 2:3), which restrict movement (Ezk. 3:25; 4:8). The Lord reveals His righteousness by cutting the righteous loose from the wicked (Ps. 129:4).

(9) [Heb. *pāṯîl*]; AV BRACELET, RIBBAND; NEB also THREAD. Decorative thread on a garment (Nu. 15:38); or a holding seal, used as part of Judah's pledge to Tamar (Gen. 38:18, 25).

(10) [Heb. *tiqwâ*]; AV LINE; NEB STRAND OF CORD. Scarlet material used as signal by Rahab (Josh. 2:21).

(11) [Gk. *schoiníon*]; AV SMALL CORDS. Rope made of rushes, used by Jesus to make a whip for clearing the temple (Jn. 2:15). J. R. PRICE

CORE kō'rə [Gk. *Kore*] (Jude 11, AV). A variant of Korah. *See* KORAH **3.**

CORIANDER kôr-ē-an'dər [Heb. *gād*; Gk. *kórian*] (Ex. 16:31; Nu. 11:7). The common coriander, *C. sativum* L., an annual herb with round dichotomous stems and fragrant leaves. The grayish aromatic fruits were used as stomachics and carminatives, and were also prized as a condiment. R. K. H.

CORINTH kôr'inth [Gk. *Korinthos*]. A famous city 1½ mi. (2½ km.) S of the narrow isthmus that joins the Peloponnesus to the rest of Greece. Paul's choice of this city as a strategic center in which to plant the gospel was justified by the control that its location gave the city over trade and travel E and W by sea, as well as N and S by land. Corinth had two good harbors, being connected by two continuous walls to Lechaeum on the Gulf of Corinth to the west, and by a series of forts to Cenchreae on the Saronic Gulf to the east. Due to the great risks encountered in a voyage around Cape Malea, the southernmost tip of Achaia, shipowners preferred to have the cargoes of larger vessels unloaded and transported the less than 5 mi. (8 km.) across the isthmus to be reloaded into other ships; smaller ships were dragged across by means of specially built devices. Her control over trade made Corinth very prosperous although located in an unfertile plain.

Corinth was one of the first parts of Greece to be inhabited. Signs of habitation date from the 4th millennium B.C. Overrun by invaders in 2000 B.C., the city remained uninhabited until 1350. Growth in military and commercial strength came to Corinth in the 8th century. While ruled by the family of Bacchiads, she established colonies in Sicily and on the western shore of the Adriatic. The prosperity and glory of Corinth continued to rise during the rule of the tyrant Cypselus (*ca.* 657-629 B.C.), and reached its high point under his son Periander (*ca.* 629-585 B.C.).

Shortly thereafter, kingship collapsed. Rivalry with Athens contributed to the decline of Corinth, so it is not surprising that she sided against Athens in the power struggle between Athens and Sparta. Corinth was made the center of a new Hellenic League by Alexander

Ruins of shops and monuments lining the Agora at Corinth. Larger than the Forum in Rome, it was the glory of Roman Corinth. (A. C. Myers)

as he made preparations for war with Persia. Her history as a Greek city terminated in 146 B.C. when the Roman General Lucius Mummius in reprisal for an anti-Roman uprising destroyed the city, exterminated the male population, and sold the women and children into slavery.

Julius Caesar rebuilt Corinth in 46 B.C. as a Roman colony with the name *Colonia Laus Julia Corinthiensis,* and settled many Roman freemen there. Latin was established as the official language, and the Roman character of the city is reflected by the many Latin names in the NT (Acts 18:7f.; Rom. 16:21-23; 1 Cor. 16:17); nevertheless, the majority of the population were Greeks, and Greek was likely the language of the common people. That many Jews resided in the city is shown by the presence of a synagogue. Augustus made Corinth the capital of Achaia, and her beauty was enhanced by the many public works of Hadrian.

The most conspicuous landmark at Corinth was the Acrocorinth, a mountain to the south of the city. Reaching a height of 1886 ft. (575 m.), it was an ideal situation for a fortress that could control all the trade routes into the Peloponnesus. The temple of Aphrodite, the goddess of love and beauty, stood on its highest peak. The thousand female prostitutes who served there contributed to Corinth's reputation for immorality. In fact, it is to this evil trade carried on in the name of religion that Strabo, the geographer, ascribed the prosperity of the city. The degree to which Corinth was given over to vice is apparent as early as the time of Aristophanes by the coining of the word *korinthiázomai* (lit. "Corinthianize"), meaning "practice immorality"; similarly "Corinthian girl" (Gk. *Korinthia kórē*) designated a prostitute. That the situation continued into Paul's day is evidenced by the evils he attacks in his Corinthian letters.

The road from Lechaeum is the best preserved of the ancient roads of Corinth. It was built of hard limestone blocks, with a raised walk on each side. As this road drew near the agora it was flanked on both sides by small shops that opened either on the street or on a courtyard. An inscription found in this area contains the term *macellum,* "market" (cf. 1 Cor. 10:25). This passage

Corinth Canal, connecting the Ionian Sea and the Aegean, a distance of 3.5 mi. (5.6 km.). Constructed in 1881-1893, it follows the route planned and begun by Nero in A.D. 66. (B. Van Elderen)

Doric columns of the archaic Temple of Apollo (6th cent. B.C.). Seven of the original thirty-eight columns survive, 24 ft. (7 m.) tall and 6 ft. (2 m.) in diameter. (W. S. LaSor)

is brought to mind also by a doorstep inscribed "Lucius the Butcher" found in a shop in the agora. A basilica, a large columned hall used by the Romans for commercial and judicial purposes, stood on the west side just before the road entered the agora. The Peribolos of Apollo was situated directly across from this basilica. This was a large paved court surrounded by columns and containing a large statue of Apollo. Corinth's most important reservoir, the Fountain of Peirene, was constructed between the Peribolos of Apollo and the agora. This reservoir had a capacity of over 81,000 gal. (306,500 l.) and was fed by subterranean waters led in by many tunnels from the east and west.

The road from Lechaeum entered the agora from the north through the Propylaea, or entrance, a staircase surmounted by a magnificent gateway. Though it comes from a later century, the discovery by archeologists in this area of a piece of white marble with the inscription "Synagogue of the Hebrews" suggests that the synagogue may have been located somewhere in the vicinity. The north and west sides of the agora were bounded by shops. A long stoa (500 ft.; 150 m.), or colonnaded pavilion, stood on the south. To the rear of this were many small shops equipped with pits cooled by water brought from the Fountain of Peirene through underground channels. These may have been restaurants or wine shops. Leading out from the middle of this stoa was the road to Cenchreae, the harbor where Paul departed from Corinth. The Bouleuterion, meeting place of the Council, was on the west side of this road and another basilica was on the east. On the eastern edge of the agora was a large building which has been called the "Julian Basilica" but whose use is unknown. The large open plaza of the agora was divided by a row of shops running E and W. In the center of these was the *bēma,* an ornate structure covered with sculptured marble, where public officials would address the populace. There were benches for the dignitaries and rooms for those waiting to present their cases to the magistrate. This is likely the place where Paul was brought before the governor Gallio (Acts 18:12-17), for the Gk. *bēma* found in Acts 18:12 and translated JUDGMENT SEAT (AV) is the equivalent of *rostra,* the Latin term found in an inscription near this structure and no doubt referring to it.

Another road led from the agora NW to Sicyon. To the east of this road and just N of the agora was the site of the temple of Apollo. Seven massive Doric columns from this structure which are still standing are the most striking remains of ancient Corinth. Alongside a temple on the west of this road was the Fountain of Glauke, an important princess in Corinthian mythology.

The temple of Asclepius the god of healing was built on the north edge of the ancient city. A number of buildings for the patients surrounded this temple. An elaborate system of water storage and supply indicates the importance of water in effecting the cures.

The Odeion, or music hall, and a large theater were located in the northwestern sector of the city. A reused paving block found near the theater bears the name of an Erastus who was Commissioner of Public Works. It has been suggested that this was none other than the associate of Paul mentioned in Acts 19:22 and Rom. 16:23. Corinth's location near the scene of the Isthmian Games is significant in the light of Paul's frequent reference to athletics in his Corinthian letters.

Bibliography.–O. Broneer, *BA,* 14 (1951), 78-96; H. J. Cadbury, *The Book of Acts in History* (1955); *LAP;* W. A. McDonald, *BA,* 5 (1942), 36-48; *SPT; WBA.*

D. H. MADVIG

CORINTHIANS, FIRST EPISTLE TO THE.

I. Authenticity
  A. External Evidence
  B. Internal Evidence
II. Integrity
III. The Corinthians

CORINTHIANS, FIRST EPISTLE TO THE

- IV. Paul's Relations with the Corinthians
  - A. Experiences Elsewhere in Greece
  - B. Founding of the Church
  - C. Visit of Apollos
  - D. The "Previous" Letter
  - E. Paul's Authority Questioned
- V. Purpose
- VI. Date and Place of Origin
- VII. Teaching
  - A. Divisions
  - B. Wisdom
  - C. Moral Laxity
  - D. Marriage
  - E. Sacrifices to Idols
  - F. Public Worship
  - G. The Resurrection

By common consent the two Epistles to the Corinthians together with those to the Romans and the Galatians form a most important block of Pauline teaching. In these writings we see Paul at the height of his ability as a writer of epistles. He is dealing with great themes and dealing with them at his magnificent best. This is the period of his controversy with the Judaizers, and he is particularly concerned to make clear the nature of the way of salvation and the implications of justification by faith.

I. Authenticity.–*A. External Evidence.* The authenticity of this Epistle, like that of the others in this group, has rarely been seriously denied. If anything bears the authentic Pauline stamp, these writings do. Even the Tübingen school accepted 1 Corinthians; and though the Dutch school of W. C. van Manen rejected it, their view has attracted scant following. It is difficult to imagine any more convincing reasons for holding this letter to be Pauline than those that are actually found. The external attestation is extremely good. The Epistle is quoted in 1 Clement, the oldest noncanonical Christian writing extant, dating from the late 1st century. 1 Corinthians accordingly is the first NT writing to be cited with the name of its author. Ignatius and Polycarp early in the 2nd cent. quote from it, and from their time onward there are many references to it. In fact, there are more references to this Epistle than to any of the other Pauline writings. In a number of early lists of books held to be canonical (e.g., the Muratorian Fragment) this Epistle heads the list of the Pauline writings. It is uncertain why it should be accorded this prominence, but the fact that it does hold it shows something of the esteem in which it was held. It is also worth noting that in all the multiplicity of references to this Epistle there is no dissentient voice. We have no record of any writer from antiquity who doubted that this was a genuine letter of Paul. The very fact of the letter's preservation by the Corinthians also indicates authenticity. The letter contains many severe rebukes, and it is not the kind of thing that one can imagine a church treasuring if it were not a genuine writing of the great apostle.

B. Internal Evidence. Questions of style and language are always to some extent subjective, but no one has produced arguments to show that 1 Corinthians is non-Pauline in either respect. Moreover, the letter accords with what little we know of the situation at Corinth. It is the kind of letter we would expect from Paul as he sought to deal with a difficult situation.

Both external and internal evidence then point us strongly in the direction of authenticity. There is much in favor and little or nothing against. We need have no hesitation in regarding 1 Corinthians as a genuine product of the great apostle.

II. Integrity.–The integrity of 1 Corinthians is beyond serious dispute. The writer deals with a number of unconnected topics, but this means no more than that this is a genuine letter. It is not a systematic theological treatise, but a genuine attempt to deal with a concrete living situation, a situation calling for an apostolic pronouncement on more than one topic. So Paul goes naturally from one subject to another, sometimes with little connecting material.

Some scholars (e.g., J. Weiss) have suggested that a number of writings have been put together to form this Epistle. But the reasons have not been found convincing. Once rid of the idea that a letter ought to read like a systematic treatise, one can find little reason for denying that this is a real letter, and one without substantial interpolation.

III. The Corinthians.–CORINTH by virtue of its geographical position was an important center of commerce. It was totally destroyed by the Romans in 146 B.C., but was later refounded as a Roman colony, and thus had a substantial Roman element in its population (the NT links many Latin names with Corinth, as Lucius, Gaius, Tertius, Erastus, Quartus, all in Rom. 16:21ff.; Fortunatus, Achaicus, 1 Cor. 16:17; Crispus, Titius Justus, Acts 18:7f.). But there were also many other lands represented. Being a seaport town it attracted men from far and wide. There were evidently enough Jews there to have a synagogue (Acts 18:4). The cosmopolitan nature of Corinth did nothing to raise moral standards; and immorality was further encouraged by a debased religion, the worship of Aphrodite, whose priestess-prostitutes at one time numbered a thousand. Corinth in the 1st cent. was characterized by the utmost in vice and evil living.

Corinth was the capital of the Roman province of Achaia. It was thus a busy and populous as well as an evil city, a place where men might be expected to develop their own interests, whether those interests lay along the lines of business, lust, sport (the biennial Isthmian Games had worldwide popularity), or culture. Corinth offered wide variety. But in that variety little place was found for the deep things of the spirit. It may be significant that Corinth never produced a writer of really great literature.

Thus the preaching of the gospel in this city was attended by enormous difficulties. Indeed some have thought that the difficulties themselves were the reason for Paul's choice of Corinth as a preaching place. This seems unlikely, and it is more probable that he was influenced by the city's strategic importance. If the gospel were well and truly planted at Corinth, from this center it would emanate in every direction throughout Achaia.

IV. Paul's Relations with the Corinthians.–*A. Experiences Elsewhere in Greece.* Paul tells us that when he first came to the city he came "in weakness and in much fear and trembling" (1 Cor. 2:3). If we consider what had happened to him in the weeks immediately preceding, this is not surprising. At Philippi, at Thessalonica, and at Beroea he had preached at first with considerable success. Then in each case his work had apparently been wrecked by the opposition of fanatics. The Jews, opposing him bitterly, had rioted against him and compelled his departure from each of these cities in turn. At Athens the situation was different, but Paul seems to have had little success in this proud, academic city. A few converts were won but nothing in Acts leads us to think that Paul was very pleased with his stay there. It is not surprising, accordingly, that he was feeling rather low when he first came to

Corinth. He was probably alone, for his companions on this particular journey, Silas and Timothy, appear to have been occupied in Macedonia at the time.

B. Founding of the Church. While he was in Corinth Paul lodged with Aquila and Priscilla (Acts 18:2f.). These were people with whom he was to have a good deal of contact in later years, and it is clear that they became beloved co-workers. They came from Rome, having been expelled by a decree of the emperor Claudius. It may be that Paul's reason for joining them in the first place was that they and he were alike tentmakers.

It was not long before Silas and Timothy rejoined Paul. When they did they brought most encouraging news from Thessalonica. They were able to assure Paul that his converts there were standing firm despite all the opposition they were meeting. Paul could discern from this news that, though he was opposed on every hand, yet God was really blessing his work. Fanatics might rage against him, but if God was with him then the work that he was doing would certainly stand. Luke tells us that he "was occupied with preaching, testifying to the Jews that the Christ was Jesus" (Acts 18:5). This seems to mean that Paul gave himself to the task with renewed vigor. He was heartened by the good news he had received and threw himself energetically into the task of evangelism in Corinth.

But his way here was not to be easy either. As in other cities, he found strong Jewish opposition. It was his custom to begin preaching in a new city in the synagogue. This gave him a preaching place, and it brought him into contact with those who might be expected to be interested in his message: Jews with their love of the OT, and pagans who were so dissatisfied with their paganism that they had gone as far as to attend the Jewish house of worship. But it was not long before Paul was compelled to leave this vantage point in Corinth. Jewish opposition came early and compelled him to leave the synagogue. He found in the house of a man called Justus a new center of activities, and as this was next door to the synagogue he could keep his contacts with interested Jews. We do not ever read of very many Jewish converts at Corinth, though among them was a man named Crispus, called "the ruler of the synagogue" (Acts 18:8). 1 Corinthians supports Acts in this, because there are very few Jewish names mentioned here (nor are there many in 2 Corinthians). However, many Corinthians believed, and Paul remained in the city for about eighteen months.

These months cannot have been easy. In addition to being expelled from the synagogue Paul was accused before the proconsul, a man called Gallio, of teaching men to worship "contrary to the law" (Acts 18:13). Gallio took little notice of the accusation, but its having been made shows that Paul's opponents were vigorous and active. It is almost certain that the letters to Thessalonica were written from this city, and they indicate that he was being opposed at the time of writing (1 Thess. 2:15f.; 2 Thess. 3:1f.).

Nevertheless Paul was instrumental in bringing into being a strong church. From 1 Cor. 1:26ff. it seems likely that the bulk of the converts were taken from the lower strata of society. Not all, for some of the converts were certainly eminent people. Thus in Rom. 16:23 (Romans was almost certainly written from Corinth) Gaius is called "host to me and to the whole church," and Erastus is spoken of as "the city treasurer." Such people were men of consequence. Chloe, who is mentioned in 1 Cor. 1:11, is likely to have been a wealthy lady with business interests in both Corinth and Ephesus. If she was a Corinthian this would indicate that at least one convert was wealthy. But it may well be that she came from Ephesus. 1 Corinthians has references to people engaging in law suits and to others attending private banquets, and these again are not commonly activities of the lowest classes. Nevertheless all the evidence indicates that most of the converts were men and women of humble origin. 1 Cor. 1:26ff. draws attention to the lowly status of many of the believers, and we have no reason for thinking that the church as a whole was composed of any other.

C. Visit of Apollos. Eventually Paul left Corinth, and in due course the church was visited by Apollos. We read of this man in Acts 18:24ff., where we find that he was an Alexandrian, an eloquent man, and that he came into Christianity by way of the teachings of John the Baptist. Indeed he was preaching Christ while still baptized only with John's baptism. But Aquila and Priscilla explained to him "the way of God more accurately" and evidently brought him into the fellowship of the Christian Church. Apollos went on in the Christian faith and employed his gifts of eloquence in preaching the gospel, for he "powerfully confuted the Jews" (Acts 18:28), and he did this in Achaia, which almost certainly means in Corinth, the capital city.

We know little else about Apollos. It is sometimes said that he was fond of the allegorical method of interpreting Scripture. This is not at all impossible, but the only evidence we have is that he came from Alexandria, a city known in later years as a center of allegorical interpretation. This is a very slight foundation for the theory. From the way Paul speaks of him we may be sure that there was no difference in the essential message proclaimed, whatever may have been different in the way Apollos presented it. However, the difference, of whatever sort it was, was enough to enable the Corinthians to take sides, some espousing Paul and others Apollos. Another group claimed Peter as their leader, and it is possible that this apostle too paid a visit to Corinth, though if he did we know nothing about it.

D. The "Previous" Letter. The next information we have is that Paul wrote a letter to the Corinthians. This letter has perished (for the hypothesis that some of it is preserved in 2 Cor. 6:14–7:1 *see* CORINTHIANS, SECOND V). All we know is that Paul in this letter told the Corinthians "not to associate with immoral men" (1 Cor. 5:9). Paul introduces the reference to this letter in order to clear up a misunderstanding. We need not be greatly surprised, therefore, that the letter has perished. If it was capable of being misconstrued, and if the correct teaching was given more fully in a letter we now have, there was no point in preserving the former letter.

E. Paul's Authority Questioned. Something went wrong in the Corinthian church. In some way Paul's authority was questioned. It is curious that though we have two fairly long letters to the Corinthians, yet we cannot find out from them or from the Acts or from any other sources the exact nature of the trouble. Obviously it was serious, and it involved calling in question Paul's authority. Whatever it was, Paul determined to send Timothy to attend to the matter on his behalf (1 Cor. 4:17; 16:10f.). It is not really certain that Timothy reached Corinth, and if he did he could not have paid a very long visit, for he was away from Corinth when 1 Corinthians was written. Clearly Timothy was unable to do anything very effective.

Paul now made contact with certain members of the church of Corinth. He picked up news from some representative of the house of Chloe (1 Cor. 1:11), which appears to mean that some of Chloe's slaves had been in Corinth and had come to Ephesus bringing news of what

CORINTHIANS, FIRST EPISTLE TO THE

they had seen and heard in the Corinthian church. Paul evidently took no action immediately, but he bore the information in mind. The opportunity to make use of it occurred when he received from the Corinthian church a letter, which appears to have been brought to him by Stephanas, Fortunatus, and Achaicus (1 Cor. 7:1; 16:17). This gave Paul a very good reason for writing to the Corinthian church, and the resultant letter is that which we know as 1 Corinthians.

V. Purpose.–The immediate purpose of the Epistle was obviously to answer the letter Paul had received from the Corinthian church. But that this was not primarily in his mind is seen in that not until 1 Cor. 7 does he turn his attention to the letter he had received. Much more important to Paul were certain matters that the Corinthians had not mentioned. He wrote to set things right. His primary concern was with the divisions in the church and the spirit of factiousness that these divisions proclaimed to all. So he took a good deal of time to make clear that such divisions are completely unworthy of a body of Christians, and to urge the brethren to return to a godly unity.

He was also concerned with the lax moral standards of which he was hearing. There was a case of incest, an easy attitude toward fornication, and a tendency to indulge in litigation before pagan judges. All these things Paul saw as incompatible with the Christian profession, and he wrote to say so plainly.

He also had in mind the questions asked by the Corinthians, and in due course he turned his attention to them. These questions included among other things marriage, complicated as it sometimes was by the conversion of one of a pagan pair. Did the standard for Christian marriage apply to this pagan union? Some evidently had a high regard for celibacy, and Paul wrote to help them on such points. There were other questions. Some pertained to the right conduct with respect to meals in idol temples and to meat offered in sacrifice. Some concerned Christian worship, including such difficult matters as the place of women and the proper estimation of speaking in "tongues." There was a question about the resurrection of the body, and Paul gives us his most important treatment of the subject in reply. Finally, the Corinthians had inquired about the collection Paul was making for the poor in Jerusalem. Paul's purpose, then, was first to deal with grave irregularities he perceived in the Corinthian church, and second to clear up certain difficulties that the Corinthians had encountered and on which they sought his guidance.

VI. Date and Place of Origin.–It is difficult to date this Epistle with precision. It is plain from 1 Cor. 16:8 that it was written from Ephesus, but it is not certain which stay in Ephesus is meant, nor at what time in his stay Paul wrote it. We know that Paul went to Ephesus immediately after his original mission at Corinth (Acts 18:18-21). But it is impossible to think that 1 Corinthians was written at this time. It was clearly a short stay, and it took time for the situation to develop to the point at which 1 Corinthians became necessary. So it is more probable that the letter was written during the visit mentioned in Acts 19, a visit that lasted for three years (Acts 20:31). If 1 Cor. 16:8 means that Paul left Ephesus at Pentecost subsequent to the writing of the Epistle, then 1 Corinthians must have been written during the last of his three years at Ephesus.

Another line of approach starts from the reference to Gallio in Acts 18:12. This is a most important statement, for it enables us to arrive at one of the few fixed points in the chronology of the NT. An inscription at Delphi gives us the reply of the emperor Claudius to a question asked by Gallio, and the date of the inscription seems to show that Gallio began his term of office in Corinth during the early summer of A.D. 51. Some of Paul's eighteen months in Corinth elapsed after this, and we must also allow for subsequent events up till his third year in Ephesus.

It is disappointing that all this does not enable us to fix the date of the Epistle with precision. It must be some time after A.D. 51, but how long after is not certain. Somewhere about the mid 50's seems as close as we can estimate.

VII. Teaching.–*A. Divisions.* Paul's first major topic is that of division in the church. He draws attention to the fact of division, for some of the believers were claiming to belong to Paul, others to Apollos, others to Cephas, and yet others to Christ. How this state of affairs came about is not known, but the fact is clear. Emphatically Paul disclaims responsibility for the situation, and he engages in a vigorous argument to show its sinfulness and folly. He points out that God does not act in the way human wisdom might suppose. He saves men by the "foolishness" of the cross, and not by anything that would be flattering to human pride. Paul discounts human greatness by reminding the Corinthians that most of their number were lowly folk. Their salvation was a demonstration not of human excellence but of God's power. The message Paul preached was not a message originating in profound human thought, but a message given by the Holy Spirit Himself. And it would be recognized as such by those who had spiritual discernment.

B. Wisdom. But the current state of affairs in Corinth showed a gross misunderstanding of the essential truth of the gospel. In all this Paul is concerned to set the wisdom of the world over against the true wisdom, the wisdom that rests on divine revelation. It is always salutary to remember that the gospel is not called upon to give account of itself before the bar of human approval. It is not and never can be merely a wise human device. It is God's answer to the problem of man's sin and must be reckoned as such, though this is something that the "natural" man cannot receive. Paul goes on to show that the Corinthians had the wrong attitude regarding the preachers, and that by this they demonstrated that they were but babes in Christ. Paul and Apollos were not in competition with each other. They were partners in the work of God, each doing his part, but depending on God for the results. Paul has an important passage about the building and the foundation (3:10-16) wherein he makes it plain that there can be but one foundation for the Christian life, namely, Jesus Christ. But each man builds on this foundation, and he may build something valuable or something worthless. The day of judgment will reveal it all. This is of relevance to the work of all preachers and indeed to that of all Christian people. Men are saved by Christ, and there is no other basis for salvation. But that does not mean that what men do is unimportant. We are building on the foundation and we must be careful how and what we build. From this Paul returns to the thought that the preachers are mere servants, and he goes on to make an appeal to the Corinthians to act on what he has written.

C. Moral Laxity. In ch. 5 Paul turns his attention to the grave moral laxity of which he had heard. He reminds the believers that incest is a crime reprobated even by the Gentiles. Yet the Corinthians had done nothing to show their detestation of such an evil in their midst. Paul urges them to clear out the evil. Then

CORINTHIANS, FIRST EPISTLE TO THE

he goes on to castigate them for a factious spirit, manifested in their taking part in lawsuits before heathen judges. Nothing could have been more unfortunate in a body of men supposedly trying to proclaim the gospel of love. The apostle goes on to deliver some important teaching on the nature of the body and on sexual relations. Fornication cannot be held to be an indifferent matter. Believers have been bought by Christ. The body is a temple of the Holy Spirit, and Christians must glorify God in their bodies.

D. Marriage. When he comes to deal with the questions the Corinthians had asked, Paul begins with marriage. This part of his teaching is commonly misunderstood today; it should be noted that he clearly views marriage as the normal rule, and although he has much to say in praise of celibacy he never belittles the married state. On the contrary, he inserts little sayings to show that, even in situations where he is counseling celibacy, there is no sin in marrying (7:9, 28, 36, 39). He has advice for various classes of people, the single, widows, Christians married to Christians, Christians married to pagans, etc. His general theme is that men should lead the kind of life that God assigns them. There is some special crisis at Corinth (7:26), and in view of this it is better that men should remain as they are. What this crisis was we do not know. Some suggest that it was the imminence of Christ's return, but this is unlikely. Nowhere in his extant Epistles does Paul link this kind of exhortation to teaching about the Second Coming. Paul's view is that there is a definite value in celibacy, for the unmarried are free to serve the Lord without the cares that are inseparable from marriage (7:32-35). But even so he refuses to discountenance marriage (7:2), and recognizes the indispensable place of the sex act within marriage (7:4f.). Some should marry and some should not. No rule can be laid down that applies to all (7:7).

E. Sacrifices to Idols. To us it seems axiomatic that the believer can have nothing to do with idol worship. But in the 1st cent. practically all social life involved some contact with idolatry. Celebrations calling for men to eat a communal meal, whether public or private, would be the very kind of occasion when the offering of a sacrifice seemed most appropriate. Christians who claimed to be mature reasoned that an idol means nothing. "What harm can it possibly do," they apparently asked, "to eat one's meat in front of a block of wood or stone? What if the heathen do think of it as a god? We know better, and know that bringing meat before a piece of wood cannot defile it." The question was wider than idol feasts, for much of the meat sold in shops and eaten in private homes was surplus from the temples. So some of the believers were puzzled and put their question to Paul. They found it difficult to eat in idol temples, or to eat meat that had been offered to an idol, without some twinge of conscience. Paul deals with the whole matter on a high plane. He reminds the strong of their responsibility toward the weak. While an idol is nothing, yet to eat in idol temples is to encourage others to do the same, who may not be able to do so with a good conscience. Such actions are harmful to the weak and may do them irreparable spiritual injury.

Paul then vigorously points out that he practices the principle he is here preaching. He has certain rights and privileges as an apostle. He has the right to be maintained by those to whom he preaches the gospel. But he has not availed himself of that right. He is always ready to waive his rights that thereby he might win men for Christ. Then he tries another tack. He shows how the Israelites, despite their high privileges, had suffered grievously in the wilderness and many of them had died when they dallied with idolatry. This leads to a recognition that the very fact of participation in the holy communion is a reminder that they ought to have nothing to do with idols, for one cannot share in the Lord's table and at the same time in the table of demons (10:21).

Paul takes a common-sense attitude to meat sold in the shops or served in homes. Since "the earth is the Lord's, and the fulness thereof" (10:26, AV), the believer ought not to ask fussy questions, but should eat whatever is set before him. He knows there are no "gods" and that therefore he may safely eat even though the meat may in fact have been offered to an idol. But if someone were to say, "This was offered in sacrifice," then the believer should not eat. It is not that the meat has become contaminated, but that to eat now is to countenance idolatry and to embolden the weak to eat to their detriment. The believer must always act in a spirit of love. This lesson is relevant to our very different circumstances. It is a chief value of this Epistle that in it we see how the great Christian principles apply to the everyday situation of the believer, whatever that situation may be.

F. Public Worship. The Corinthians were giving offense by some of the things they did in public worship. Contrary to the accepted conventions in polite society, women were attending public worship with uncovered heads, and Paul deprecates the practice. He deals with the conduct of the Lord's Supper, rebuking the Corinthians' irreverence and urging proper self-examination. It would seem that some of the Corinthians were very proud of their ability to speak in tongues, and Paul devotes his attention to the subject. A very notable part of his treatment of this subject is his great section on love (ch. 13), which has become the classic Christian treatment of the theme. He does not forbid speaking in tongues, but he shows that it is more important that believers act in a spirit of Christian love than that they acquire a reputation for wisdom, eloquence, or piety. It is a lesson that is not yet out of date. From this Paul passes to the conduct of public worship and insists that "all things be done for edification" (14:26).

G. The Resurrection. Some of the Corinthians denied the resurrection of the body, evidently holding to some such idea as the Greek concept of the immortality of the soul. To many today it seems of small consequence which of these two ideas one holds. But Paul is very clear on the importance of holding the right doctrine. Step by step he unfolds the consequence of this apparently minor aberration. He shows that when it is thought through, this error strikes at the heart of the Christian faith. It means that Christ did not rise, and this in turn that He did not deal effectively with sin. Paul goes on to deal with objections to the idea of resurrection, with the nature of the resurrection body, and with the final triumph of Christ when He returns in glory. Chapter 15 is the most important Christian treatment of resurrection.

From this mighty theme Paul turns to the collection for the poor saints at Jerusalem. He gives directions as to how it is to be taken up, and how it is to be sent to Jerusalem. He has a few terse exhortations and some greetings, and so brings the letter to a close.

From all this it is plain that there is no Epistle of the great apostle that sticks more stubbornly to local affairs. Paul never sets out to deliver a theological discourse. There is no place in the whole Epistle where he attempts to set forth in systematic form the Christian teaching on any subject. Right through he takes his starting-point in some specific practice of the Corinthian church or some specific question the Corinthians had asked him. But, though he is occupied all the time with local problems, he deals with them all in the light of great eternal principles. And because he thus brings the basic principles of the Christian faith to bear on the small problems of an individual church, he brings out for all time the way central Christian truth is related to everyday needs.

Bibliography.–Comms. by E. B. Allo (2nd ed. 1956); C. K. Barrett (*HNTC*, 1968); H. Conzelmann (*Hermeneia*, 1975); F. Godet (1887); F. W. Grosheide (*NIC*, 1953); J. Héring (*Comm. du NT*, 1949); L. Morris (*Tyndale*, 1958); J. Moffatt (*MNTC*, 1938); A. Robertson and A. Plummer (*ICC*, 1911). L. MORRIS

CORINTHIANS, SECOND EPISTLE TO THE.

- I. Authenticity
- II. Paul's Relations with the Corinthian Church
  - A. The "Painful" Visit
  - B. The Severe Letter
  - C. Reconciliation
- III. Purpose
- IV. Date and Place of Origin
- V. Integrity
- VI. Teaching
  - A. Reconciliation with the Corinthians
  - B. Implications of the Gospel
  - C. The Collection
  - D. Paul's Defense of Himself

This Epistle comes from the same period as 1 Corinthians, being written indeed at no great interval after the first letter. It arises out of a further development of the same situation.

I. Authenticity.–Like the First Epistle to the Corinthian church this one is almost universally accepted as Pauline. Only W. C. van Manen and those who agreed with him that there are no genuine Pauline Epistles have denied that this is a genuine letter of the great apostle. The external evidence is not quite as good as that for 1 Corinthians, but it is still adequate. The Epistle is first quoted by Polycarp. (It is a little puzzling that Clement of Rome does not use it; it seems as though it would have given his case quite strong support. Possibly this Epistle was somewhat slower in getting into general circulation than was 1 Corinthians.) It is also cited in the letter to Diognetus. From the time of Irenaeus it is frequently quoted.

The internal testimony is also convincing. Characteristically Pauline words and phrases abound, and the style is Pauline throughout. Indeed the letter may be said to be more Pauline than any of the others, for we see the man Paul in this Epistle as we see him nowhere else. The writer was clearly troubled about the condition of the Corinthian church, and he writes out of a deep pastoral concern. Here, better than anywhere else, we see what it meant to Paul to have resting upon him "the care of all the churches" (2 Cor. 11:28, AV). There is no real reason for doubting that this letter is a genuine Pauline writing.

II. Paul's Relations with the Corinthian Church.–*A. The "Painful" Visit.* In the article on 1 Corinthians we noticed that trouble was developing between Paul and the Corinthian church when that Epistle was written. Whatever the nature of the trouble, it grew worse with the passage of time. In 1 Corinthians we see the church looking to Paul for authoritative answers to questions, but later his authority was challenged. The exact order of events is not easy to untangle, but it seems tolerably clear that some time after the writing of 1 Corinthians Paul paid a further visit to Corinth. We know that he was planning to spend the winter with the Corinthians (1 Cor. 16:5-7), and this shortly after the writing of 1 Corinthians (1 Cor. 4:19). However, for some reason his plans had to be revised; but the new plan still provided for a visit to Corinth, in fact for two visits. Instead of going to Corinth from Macedonia Paul now proposed to go first to Corinth, then to Macedonia, then back to Corinth (2 Cor. 1:15f.). From the way he mentions it, this plan evidently was not carried through; but the point is that with all his changes of mind there was a firm and consistent determination to visit Corinth. And it seems plain that this visit did take place, even though we cannot be sure exactly when. Twice Paul speaks of visiting the Corinthians for "the third time" (12:14; 13:1). This certainly indicates that before writing 2 Corinthians he had paid a visit to Corinth other than the visit when the church was founded.

Moreover, this second visit was an exceedingly unpleasant one. Paul tells them that he had made up his mind "not to make you another painful visit" (2:1). The second visit accordingly had been painful to the apostle, and presumably also to the Corinthian church. From all this it appears that when the trouble worsened Paul determined on a personal visit to Corinth. But the visit fell far short of his expectations. Reading between the lines it appears that Paul's opponent or opponents at Corinth withstood him vigorously and that the attitude of the church as a whole was at least an equivocal one. It may have been worse. At any rate Paul did not secure the support that he felt he was entitled to. The visit was a failure, serving only to worsen the situation.

B. The Severe Letter. After leaving Corinth, Paul determined to make a further appeal by letter. This letter evidently cost him a good deal to write, and was couched in very severe terms. He tells us that he wrote it "out of much affliction and anguish of heart and with many tears" (2 Cor. 2:4). So strong was the letter that for a time Paul regretted ever having written it (7:8). This severe letter has been lost entirely (but see V below on chs. 10–13). But we can gather something about it from references in 2 Corinthians. Paul must have written it in such blunt and forthright terms that if it had not been received in the right way it could have permanently damaged his relations with the Corinthians. However, the Corinthians reacted to it in the way the apostle had hoped. It seems likely that, among other things, Paul had suggested that the principal offender should be suitably disciplined by the church, and that the Corinthians accepted the suggestion. Indeed they accepted it so wholeheartedly that Paul wondered whether they might not be going too far (2:5ff.).

C. Reconciliation. Evidently the severe letter was taken to Corinth by Titus, and the arrangement was that he should return to Paul by way of Macedonia and Troas. But Paul was too deeply concerned about the Corinthians and too worried about how his letter was being received to remain where he was until Titus returned. So he went to Troas; "but my mind could not rest because I did not find my brother Titus there" (2 Cor. 2:13). Accordingly he went across to Macedonia and here at last met Titus, who was bringing him the glad news of the way the Corinthians had received the letter (2:14ff.; 7:6ff.). 2 Corinthians is the result. This letter appears to have been written almost immediately, and is the expression of Paul's deep sense of thankfulness that all had turned out so well. He looked forward now to being able to visit Corinth. Apparently he did so, and he may even have spent the whole winter there (Acts 20:2f.; Rom. 15:25-27; 16:23).

CORINTHIANS, SECOND EPISTLE TO THE

III. Purpose.–As we have seen, this letter was written out of Paul's deep thankfulness for the favorable turn in his relations with the Corinthians. He wrote the letter partly to assure the Corinthians of his deep satisfaction, and partly to prepare the way for the visit that he hoped soon to accomplish. Paul was a realist. He knew that the worst of the trouble was over, but that did not mean there was no further cause for concern. Therefore, throughout his letter there are passages designed to prevent the recurrence of the trouble, as well as passages expressing his sense of fellowship with the Corinthians and his gratitude to God for what had happened. These warning passages are especially prominent toward the end of the Epistle, but we should not forget that they are to be found in the early part as well (cf. 2 Cor. 3:1; 4:3f.; 6:1; etc.). Paul speaks of taking severe measures against offenders (13:2, 10). He was clearly determined to stamp out the trouble. He was also deeply concerned with the collection for the saints at Jerusalem, and he wanted the Corinthians to have this completed before he came (9:3ff.). So he writes to ensure that there will be no failure on their part.

IV. Date and Place of Origin.–The date of this Epistle can be determined only approximately, and with reference to that of 1 Corinthians. There is nothing outside the Epistle to assist us in estimating the date. We can say only that the situation apparent in 1 Corinthians had developed to such an extent that a lapse of some months seems required. However, it is the same situation that is developing, and therefore we must not allow too great a length of time. To say that 2 Corinthians was written within about a year of 1 Corinthians seems as close as we can get.

The place of writing is determined by Paul's statement about Titus (2 Cor. 2:12ff.). From this it is clear that he met Titus in Macedonia, and that he wrote the letter immediately. We can say then that the letter was written from the province of Macedonia, most likely from Philippi.

V. Integrity.–Though few would be found who deny that this Epistle is genuine, it is otherwise with its homogeneity. Many think that the letter as we have it has been compiled from fragments of other Pauline letters. The principal passages called in question are 2:14–7:4; 6:14–7:1; ch. 9; and chs. 10–13.

Concerning the first and third of these little need be said. The supposition that the lengthy passage 2:14–7:4 is a fragment from another letter appears to rest on no surer foundation than that 7:5 would read very naturally if it followed immediately after 2:13. It is thought that there is an urgency in the narrative up to 2:13 which is lacking in the following section but which is resumed again at 7:5. But it is at least as reasonable to contend that the section in question is a typical example of Paul's habit of making sudden digressions. He is certainly far from being the systematic kind of writer who says all that he has on one particular subject and then quietly proceeds to another, never to return to the first. In many places he can be shown to digress from his main subject, only to return to it again at a later time. In this particular case it is not surprising, as he recalls the stress through which he has gone, that he also recalls with gratitude the sustaining grace of God, that this leads on to other thoughts, and that only considerably later does he return to the thought of stress.

Chapter 9 (AV) begins, "For as touching the ministering to the saints. . . ." This is thought by some to indicate the introduction of a new subject, and not to be a continuation of the subject already treated in ch. 8. Therefore it must come from a separate letter. This, however, seems to be unwarranted. Paul, as we have seen, does not always conform to the canons of systematic writing that we may feel inclined to lay down. But the overwhelming reason for rejecting this hypothesis is the unity of theme that binds chs. 8 and 9. Chapter 9 is really the necessary continuation of ch. 8, and it is hypercriticism to doubt this.

These two hypothesis have little support. But it is otherwise with the other two passages. There are many who are ready to suggest that 6:14–7:1 originally formed no part of this letter, but was part of the "previous" letter. It is pointed out that this passage as it stands interrupts the sequence of thought, for 7:2 follows very naturally after 6:13. Further, it not only interrupts the argument, but it is said to introduce ideas that are out of keeping with it. Moreover, from 1 Cor. 5:9 we learn that the lost letter was concerned with sexual sin, and it is urged that this present passage would fit in very well with such a letter.

Against this we must urge the consideration already noticed, namely, that Paul is far from being a consistent and systematic writer. Again and again he breaks off his theme and introduces a digression. There seems no real reason why he should not have done this here. That 7:2 follows naturally on from 6:13 may mean no more than that, having left his subject for a brief space, when Paul returns to it he connects it up in thoroughgoing fashion. It must not be forgotten also that 2 Corinthians was written at a time when Paul was in a state of great emotional upheaval. He had been terribly worried about the Corinthians, and he wrote out of a feeling of overwhelming relief. But this does not mean that he was unmindful of the dangers still lurking in the situation. Unless he and they were careful the Corinthians might well slip back again into the perilous position from which they had so lately emerged. So Paul's letter is not simply one unmitigated paean of praise and thankfulness. He includes many notes of warning. It is not at all out of character for such a man as Paul in such a situation as that in which 2 Corinthians was written to pass from the exhortation in 6:11-13 that the Corinthians open their hearts, to the further exhortation in 6:14ff. that they avoid entanglement with unbelievers. There is also the small point that "I said before" (7:3) is more natural if Paul is conscious of having made a digression since 6:11-13 than if these words immediately precede the expression.

But the passage that is most confidently claimed as no part of the original 2 Corinthians is the concluding section, chs. 10–13. There is certainly a change of tone in this part of the Epistle. Whereas before Paul has been expressing his thankfulness that the crisis is over, in these chapters he seems rather to be defending himself and urging the Corinthians to the right line of action. It seems incredible to many critics that Paul could have written chs. 10–13 *after* 1–9. They therefore suggest that these last chapters form part of the severe letter. They suggest that the bulk of this letter has perished but that this section was preserved.

At first sight this looks rather impressive. There is no denying that there is a change of tone with the beginning of ch. 10. And it is comforting to feel that we have not completely lost the severe letter but that we have part, at any rate, of Paul's passionate pleading which wrought such a change of heart among the Corinthians. Yet closer examination throws doubt on this. In the first place we should notice that these chapters do not tally with such description as we have of the painful letter. That letter, Paul tells us, was written "with many tears" (2:4). He tells us that he regretted ever having written

CORINTHIANS, SECOND EPISTLE TO THE

it (7:8). It is difficult to see anything in chs. 10–13 to which this applies. The argument, it is true, is vigorous, and Paul's defense of himself is far from being halfhearted. But it is more than difficult to point to anything in these four chapters that fairly meets the description Paul has given us of the lost letter. There is also the point that the opening words of ch. 10 — "I, Paul, myself entreat you, by the meekness and gentleness of Christ" — do seem to suggest a deliberate change of tone. The man who wrote these words was about to embark on something different from what he had already written.

It is also to be borne in mind that some such strictures as are contained in chs. 10–13 seem to have been necessary. Many writers assume that after the severe letter everything was completely satisfactory in the Corinthian church. We have no reason for thinking that this was indeed the case. The immediate crisis was over. The offender had been disciplined. The church had declared for Paul, and against his opponents. But this did not mean that opposition was crushed to such an extent that there was no possibility of its ever reviving again. The possibility was there, and Paul did not mean to give it the opportunity of developing. So, having expressed his satisfaction at the good progress thus far made, he finishes his letter with some forthright exhortation, designed to deal with the last remnants of opposition. It is also worth bearing in mind that though there is a change of tone in these chapters the extent of this change ought not to be exaggerated. The whole of chs. 1–9 is not sweetness and light. Here and there even in these chapters we have traces of argumentativeness, indications that all was not completely well. It need not surprise us accordingly that Paul decides to finish off the matter with a thoroughgoing exposition of his position.

Against all such hypotheses as those we have been examining, it can also be urged that there is difficulty in envisaging the process whereby the originals broke up and the complete letter came into being. It is not easy to think that letters would have been broken up into fragments of varying sizes, fragments moreover that conveniently have rather neat beginnings and endings. It is even more difficult to think of the passages in question as selections purposely inserted by editorial work. The editors of antiquity were surely as aware as modern critics of the sense of a passage, and of how they would be disturbing it by, say, inserting 6:14–7:1 between 6:13 and 7:2. We need a convincing account of how and why the hypothetical editors carried out their work as well as the assertion that the passages in question would read better without the intervening matter. It is also worth noting that there is no MS known to us that gives any trace of the postulated divisions. It is difficult to imagine that, had the history of the Epistle been such as we are asked to accept, there should be no trace at all in the textual tradition.

VI. Teaching.–This letter reveals Paul the pastor as none other of his writings does. It is a letter difficult to analyze, because, like any true letter, again and again it goes off into side issues. All the more is this the case in the present instance because of Paul's deep emotional involvement. He was at once concerned for his converts, relieved at their present attitude, and watchful for their future. This does not make for orderly, systematic writing.

A. Reconciliation with the Corinthians. Paul begins with praise for the way God continually gives His servants the strength they need. Adversity has its place in the life of the Christian. It fits him to serve other people. Paul refers to some great trouble that befell him in the province of Asia (1:8). We know nothing about this incident except what Paul tells us of it here, but clearly he had been in grave danger. Such dangers help the believers to help others. Paul then turns his attention to the charge of fickleness arising from the various changes in his plans. He makes it clear that there had been no wavering in his steadfast determination to serve God, or in his affection for the Corinthians. The reason he had not paid the expected visit to Corinth was "to spare you" (1:23). He reminds them that he had written a letter that made them sorry, and he had no wish to add to that. There had evidently been a ringleader in opposition to Paul, and part of the process of reconciliation involved the disciplining of this man by the Corinthian church. The Corinthians had now taken the necessary action, but Paul wonders whether they may not perhaps be inclined to go too far. He himself is ready to forgive the man (2:10).

B. Implications of the Gospel. From this point to 6:10 Paul is concerned in one way or another to bring out the implications of the gospel. He tells the Corinthians of the tremendous relief it had been to him to meet Titus with his good news, and this leads him immediately into a characteristic outpouring of praise for the triumph of the gospel (2:14-16). Paul protests his sincerity and then goes on to point out that the Corinthians are the outstanding proof of the power of the gospel he has preached. Other people might use letters of commendation, but the Corinthians themselves were all the letter Paul needed. They were the living proof that he was an apostle of God. So he passes on to a meditation on the surpassing excellence of the gospel, contrasting it particularly with Judaism. He sees the old dispensation that was to pass away as glorious, and thinks of the new that was to remain as even more glorious (3:11).

Paul's great idea that the gospel is of God and not of man comes out in the thought that the treasure of which he is writing is "in earthen vessels" (4:7). The messengers are not important. It is the message, and it alone, that matters. It is of little significance that they should be held in small esteem or persecuted. What matters is that the life that Christ brings should be made manifest (4:11). The servant of God can look for nothing but difficulty as he labors. He looks to God who raised up Jesus and will raise up believers (4:12-14). It is important to have our sense of values right, and Paul proceeds to contrast the sufferings of the here and now with the glory that awaits us (4:16-18). Chapter 5 brings the thought that the important thing is the life after the resurrection and not the difficulties of our present life. Our relationship to Christ dominates all our living.

This leads to a very important treatment of the nature of the Christian ministry and the nature of the Christian message. Paul tells us that it is "the fear of the Lord" that impels the preachers to preach (5:11), and this may be otherwise expressed by speaking of the constraint exercised by "the love of Christ" (5:14). The death of Christ transforms men's lives. Because He died, those who live in Him no longer live for their own purposes but for His (5:15). They have been created anew. Paul goes on to a memorable interpretation of the atoning work of Christ as a reconciliation. This was not brought about by man, but "God was in Christ reconciling the world to himself" (5:19). Reconciliation was effected by not reckoning unto men their trespasses. The consequence of it is that God has committed to preachers the word of reconciliation. They are ambassadors for Christ. They plead on His behalf.

Paul returns to the atoning death of Christ with the reminder that "for our sake, he made him to be sin who knew no sin." These mysterious words refer the readers to that bearing of sin (He. 9:28), that being made "a curse" (Gal. 3:13), wherein Christ took the place of sinners. He died that men might live.

Paul then appeals to his friends. He reminds them of what he and other preachers have suffered for them and of the depths of the affection he has for them. Their wrong attitude was a constriction of their feelings. He urges them to know the abundant life of real affection. This leads to an appeal to break off all connection with worldly things. Christ has nothing in common with Belial. Characteristically Paul quotes from Scripture to show that believers must have nothing at all to do with anything that is unclean.

Paul turns now to the joy that had been his when he learned of the change of heart of the Corinthians. He looks back to the time when he had waited so anxiously for the result of his severe letter. He had had other troubles. He does not tell us what they were but they were "at every turn — fighting without and fear within" (7:5). But the situation was transformed when Titus came to him, and Paul dwells on the comfort and joy that the happy outcome meant for him.

C. The Collection. In ch. 8 Paul turns to the collection for the saints at Jerusalem. He reminds the Corinthians of the good example set by the churches of Macedonia, who had evidently supported Paul very well. Tactfully he praises the many graces of the Corinthians (8:7), and then urges them to excel in this act of Christian charity. Paul was anxious that there should be no occasion for reproach in the manner either of the collection or of the disposal of the money. He gives information about the way in which the arrangements were to be made. Paul is concerned not only that things should be done rightly before God, who looks on the heart, but rightly before men, who look on that which is outward (8:21). This is an important principle in the conduct of Christian affairs. The opening of ch. 9 shows that Paul expected the money to be ready when he arrived. He goes on to the general principle of the way Christians should give. For the believer, giving is the expression of what is in the heart, not the grudging adherence to an external standard (9:7). God gives His children all they need (9:8ff.) and Paul looks to see the gentile churches behave in such a way that the Jerusalem churches will be able to glorify God for what they do. Characteristically he closes this section with the reminder of the great gift that God has given men (9:15).

D. Paul's Defense of Himself. In the concluding section of the Epistle Paul vigorously defends himself. Some of the Corinthians had evidently taken the line that he could be a terrible man when it came to writing letters but he was very insignificant in person (10:10). Paul points out that the Christian does not proceed by carnal methods (10:4). Paul's own aim is to make all his thinking subject to Christ (10:5). He is not concerned with the outward appearance. He has a real authority that the Lord has given him, but he does not wish to use it in overbearing fashion (10:8f.). If compelled he can make his position when present just what it seems in his letters. But Paul dislikes this whole matter of boasting, and concludes that it is the Lord's commendation that matters (10:18).

Paul is very anxious for the welfare of his converts (11:3), and this leads him into a reluctant commendation of his own ministry. If he were discredited, that would be no help to them, so he has to say that he came behind no apostle (11:5f.). He embarks on a list of his works and difficulties as the most effective way of refuting those who claimed eminence but were not able to measure up to him. He deals with his preeminence as a Jew (11:21f.) and the sufferings he had endured for Christ's sake (11:23-27). In ch. 12 he goes on to speak of revelations, but comes back to the thought of his own weakness. God's power is shown in its perfection in human weakness (12:9). Paul brings this section to a close by reminding them that they ought to have been the ones to commend him (12:11), for truly they had seen "the signs of a true apostle" when Paul had worked among them (12:12).

Paul is about to pay his third visit to Corinth, and he will keep to his previous practice and not be a burden to them (12:14f.). All that he does is for the profit of his Corinthian friends. He does not want them to show such evil qualities as will demand stern action from him (12:19-21), for when he comes he will not spare (13:2). He reminds them that Christ's crucifixion, though apparently evidence of weakness, was really evidence of the mighty power of God (13:4). This leads to an exhortation that his friends should examine themselves, and set right what was in need of reform. The letter concludes with salutations and the grace, the grace in this Epistle being the only one in the Pauline correspondence that includes all three members of the trinity.

Bibliography.–Comms. by E. B. Allo (2nd ed. 1956); C. K. Barrett (*HNTC*, 1973); J. Héring (*Comm. du NT*, 1958); P. E. Hughes (*NIC*, 1962); A. Menzies (1912); A. Plummer (*ICC*, 1915); R. H. Strachan (1935); R. V. G. Tasker (*Tyndale*, 1958).

L. MORRIS

CORINTHIANS, THIRD EPISTLE TO THE. *See* APOCRYPHAL EPISTLES I.

CORINTHUS kə-rin′thəs. The Latin form of CORINTH, in the note at the end of Romans, which appears in the AV.

CORMORANT kôr′mə-rant [Heb. *šālāḵ*; Gk. *kataráktēs*; Lat. *Corvus marinus*]; NEB FISHER-OWL. A large seafowl belonging to the genus *Phalactrocorax* and well described by the Hebrew word used to designate it, which means a "plunging bird." The bird appears as large as a goose when in full feather, but when plucked the body is much smaller. The adult birds are glossy black with bronze tints, touched with white on the cheeks and sides as a festal dress at mating season, and adorned with filamentary feathers on the head and bright yellow gape.

If taken young and carefully trained, these birds can be sent into the water from boats and can bring to their masters large quantities of good-sized fish; they are commonly so used in China. The nest is built mostly of seaweed. The eggs are small for the size of the birds, having a rough, thick, but rather soft shell of a bluish white which soon becomes soiled — along with the nest and its immediate surroundings — due to the habits of the birds. The young are at first leathery black, later becoming covered with soft down of brownish black above and white beneath, and taking on the full black of the grown bird at about three years. If taken in the squab state the young are said to be delicious food, resembling baked hare in flavor. The grown birds are mentioned among the abominations for food (Lev. 11:17; Dt. 14:17). Their flesh is dark, tough, and quite unfit to eat on account of their diet of fish.

G. STRATTON-PORTER

CORN. *See* GRAIN; *see also* PROVENDER (Job 24:6); THRESHING FLOOR (Dt. 16:13).

CORNELIAN (Rev. 4:3; 21:20, NEB). *See* STONES, PRECIOUS.

CORNELIUS kôr-nēl'yəs [Gk. *Kornēlios* (Latin)]. A Roman centurion converted by Peter after both had seen divine visions (Acts 10:1–11:18), the first Gentile known to become a Christian.

The name is Roman and belonged to distinguished families in the imperial city, such as the Scipios and Sulla. Thus he was probably an Italian of Roman blood. Julian the Apostate reckons him as one of the few persons of distinction who became a Christian. He was evidently a man of importance in Caesarea and well known to the Jews (Acts 10:22). He was a centurion in the Italian COHORT, at Caesarea, the residence of the Roman procurator and headquarters of the Roman garrison in Palestine. (*See* ARMY, ROMAN.)

He is described as devout and God-fearing, the latter term often indicating a non-Jew who nonetheless embraced the monotheism of the Jews, read the Scriptures, and practiced more or less the Jewish rites. He was well reported of by the Jews, and his religion showed itself in prayer at the regular hours, and in alms to the people (of Israel). Moreover, he seems to have made his house a sort of church, for his relatives and friends were in sympathy with him, and among the soldiers who closely attended him were some devout ones (Acts 10:24, 27).

The story of his conversion and admission into the Christian Church is told in some detail in Acts 10. Nothing further is known of Cornelius, though one tradition asserts that he founded the church in Caesarea, and another legend that he became the bishop of Scamandros.

The exact importance of the incident depends upon the position of Cornelius before it occurred. Certainly he was not a proselyte of the sanctuary, circumcised, under the law, a member of the Jewish communion. This is abundantly evident from Acts 10:28, 34, 45; 11:3, 18; 15:7, 14. But was he not an inferior form of proselyte, later called "proselytes of the gate"? This question has been much debated and is still under discussion. Ramsay (*SPT,* p. 43) says that the expression "God-fearing" is always used in Acts with reference to this kind of proselyte. Such were bound to observe certain regulations of purity, probably those, this author thinks, mentioned in Acts 15:29, and which stand in close relation to the principles laid down in Lev. 17f. for the conduct of strangers dwelling among Israel. Renan, on the other hand, says that Cornelius was not a proselyte at all, but simply a devout Gentile who adopted some of the Jewish ideas and religious customs which did not involve a special profession.

The importance of the whole transaction to the development of the Church seems to depend on the circumstance that Cornelius was probably not a proselyte at all. Thus we regard Cornelius as literally the firstfruits of the Gentiles. The step here taken by Peter was therefore one of tremendous importance to the whole development of the Church. The significance of the incident consists exactly in this, that under divine direction the first Gentile, not at all belonging to the old theocracy, becomes a Spirit-filled Christian, entering through the front door of the Christian Church without first going through the narrow gate of Judaism. The incident settled forever the great fundamental question as to the relations of Jew and Gentile in the Church. The difficulties in the way of the complete triumph of Peter's view of the equality of Jews and Gentiles in the kingdom of Christ were enormous. It would have been indeed little short of miraculous if the multitude of Christian Pharisees had not raised the question again and again. Did they not dog Paul's steps after the Council? Certainly Ramsay is wrong in saying that the case of Cornelius was passed over or condoned as exceptional, for it was used as precedent by both Peter and James (Acts 15:7, 14).

As for Peter's subsequent conduct at Antioch, no one who knows Peter need be surprised at it. The very accusation that Paul hurled at him was that for the moment he was carried into inconsistency with his principles (*hypókrisis*). Of course, this incident of Cornelius was only the first step in a long development; but the principle was forever settled. The rest in due time and proper order was sure to follow. By this tremendous innovation it was settled that Christianity was to be freed from the swaddling bands of Judaism and that the Christian Church was not to be an appendix to the synagogue. The noble character of Cornelius was just fitted to abate, as far as possible, the prejudices of the Jewish Christians against what must have seemed to them a dangerous, if not awful, innovation. G. H. TREVER

CORNER. The RSV renders "corner" for variety of OT and NT terms. In the OT it most frequently translates Heb. *pinnâ*, which is used of the name of a gate in Jerusalem (2 K. 14:13; 2 Ch. 25:23; 26:9; Jer. 31:38, 40; Zec. 14:10), a corner of Jerusalem (2 Ch. 28:24), a corner of a wall (Neh. 3:25, 31f.), the keystone of a building (Ps. 118:22; Jer. 51:26), a street corner as the primary hangout of loose women (Prov. 7:8, 12), the corner of a housetop as a refuge from a nagging wife (Prov. 21:9; 25:24), the corners of the altar as the location for the horns on which sacrificial blood is sprinkled (Ex. 27:2; 38:2; Ezk. 43:20; 45:19), the corners of stands for lavers (1 K. 7:34), the corners of city walls as the locations for protective weapons (2 Ch. 26:15), and the corners of a house which collapse in the wind (Job. 1:19).

Heb. *'ᵃṣîle(y)hā* (lit. "its most distant parts") is used of the "farthest corners" of the earth in Isa. 41:9. The Heb. *'āṣîl* can also mean "noble"; hence the AV rendering "chief men." *Kānāp* means literally "wing" or "extremity"; thus it refers to the corner of garments (Nu. 15:38), of a cloak (Dt. 22:12), of the earth (Job 37:3; Isa. 11:12), of the land (Ezk. 7:2). *See also* EARTH, CORNERS OF THE. *Kaṯēp* (lit. "shoulder," "side") is used in 1 K. 7:39 and 2 Ch. 4:10 to designate the location of the sea in Solomon's temple (AV renders "side"). *Pē'â* means literally "part cut off," hence side or corner of a couch (Am. 3:12), or table (Ex. 25:26; 37:13), or land (Neh. 9:22). Jeremiah identifies some peoples as those who cut their hair along the temples (Jer. 9:26; 25:23; 49:32).

Heb. *miqṣô(a)'* (lit. "angle") is used of the corner-buttress for the court (Ezk. 46:21), the altar (Ezk. 41:22; 46:22), and the tabernacle (Ex. 26:23f.; 36:28f.). Another structural term, *zāwîyôṯ,* compares daughters to decorative corner pillars in a palace (Ps. 144:12), and also refers to the location of the altar in the temple (Zec. 9:15). *Qāṣâ* (lit. "end," "border") is used of the bronze grating on the altar (Ex. 27:4; 38:5) (AV and NEB render "ends"). *Pa'am* literally means "beat" or "foot-beat," hence "foot"; it denotes the foot of the ark as the location of gold carrying-rings (Ex. 37:3) or of the stands for supporting the lavers (1 K. 7:30). The NEB also gives "flanges" and "handles."

In the NT, Gk. *gōnía* is used in a variety of contexts: of the keystone (originally of a building) of God's plan for the world (Mt. 21:42; Mk. 12:10; Lk. 20:17; Acts 4:11; 1 Pet. 2:7; cf. Ps. 118:22), of a corner as a site of clandestine activities (Acts 26:26), of a street corner as a public place to assure notice of one's prayers (Mt. 6:5), and of the corners of the earth (Rev. 7:1; 20:8). *Archḗ* (lit. "beginning") denotes the corners of the sheet in Peter's vision (Acts 10:11; 11:5).

See also CORNERSTONE. J. R. PRICE

CORNER GATE. *See* JERUSALEM.

CORNER, UPPER CHAMBER OF [Heb. *ᵃliyyaṯ happinnâ*] (Neh. 3:31); AV "going up of the corner"; NEB "roof-chamber at the corner." This northeast corner of Jerusalem was the last item in Nehemiah's description of the restoration of the city walls. The AV assumes a reading of *ᵃlôṯ* instead of *ᵃliyyaṯ*. The RSV and NEB correctly translate the latter.

CORNERS OF THE EARTH. *See* EARTH, CORNERS OF THE.

CORNERSTONE. Ordinarily the term "cornerstone" is used in the Bible in a figurative or symbolical sense. No doubt the original meaning was some important stone, which was laid at the foundation of a building. With the Canaanites, who preceded Israel in the possession of Palestine, cornerstone-laying seems to have been a most sacred and impressive ceremony. Under this important stone of temples or other great structures bodies of children or older persons would be laid, consecrating the building by such human sacrifice (*see* SACRIFICE, HUMAN). This was one of many rites and practices that Israel was to extirpate. It may throw light on the curse pronounced upon the building of Jericho (Josh. 6:26).

In every OT occurrence of this idea the Hebrew term *pinnâ* ("corner") is used, ordinarily with *'eḇen* ("stone"; e.g., Job 38:6; Isa. 28:16), though it could also be used alone to represent the whole phrase-idea (Zec. 10:4; AV "corner"). While all the passages indicate the stone at the corner, there appear to be two conceptions: (1) the foundation stone upon which the structure rested (Job 38:6; Isa. 28:16; Jer. 51:26 [RSV, AV, "corner"; NEB "corner-stone"]); or (2) the topmost or capstone, which linked the last tier together (Ps. 118:22). In both cases it is an important stone and figurative of the Messiah, who is "the First and the Last." In Job 38:6 it beautifully expresses in figures the stability of the earth, which Yahweh created. In Zec. 10:4 the leader or ruler in the messianic age is represented by the cornerstone. The ancient tradition of the one missing stone, when the temple was being built, is reflected in or has been suggested by Ps. 118:22, where the Hebrew reads *rō'š* ("head") *pinnâ*; the AV and RSV render "head (stone) of the corner"; the NEB gives "corner-stone."

Ps. 118:22 is quoted and interpreted as fulfilled in Jesus Christ in a number of NT passages: Mt. 21:42; Mk. 12:10; Lk. 20:17; Acts 4:11; 1 Pet. 2:7, the Greek being *kephalḗ gōnías,* literally "head of the corner," and so rendered by the AV and RSV; the NEB gives "corner-stone." Ps. 118:22 is also the evident basis for Eph. 2:20 (*akrogōniaíos,* "lying at the extreme corner"). Isa. 28:16 is quoted twice in the NT: in Rom. 9:33, from the LXX combined with the words of Isa. 8:14, and in 1 Pet. 2:6 (*akrogōniaíos*), which is quoted with some variation from the LXX. The OT passages were understood by the rabbis to be messianic, and were probably so applied by the NT writers.

See also HOUSE. E. MACK

Limestone pivot stone, perhaps the "cornerstone" of ancient temples. Valuables and records were deposited beneath such stones, which bore words of dedication or exorcism. Gimilsin temple at Ur, 20th cent. B.C. (Oriental Institute, University of Chicago)

CORNET. The AV rendering of Heb. *mᵉnaʿanʿîm* in 2 S. 6:5 (RSV "castanets"), of *šôpar* in 1 Ch. 15:28; 2 Ch. 15:14; Ps. 98:6; Hos. 5:8; and of Aram. *qeren* in Dnl. 3 (RSV "horn"). *See* MUSIC II.

CORNFLOOR (Hos. 9:1, AV). *See* THRESHING FLOOR.

CORONATION [Gk. *prōtoklisía*]. The term occurs in 2 Macc. 4:21 (AV, NEB, "enthronement") where Apollonius was sent into Egypt for the coronation of Ptolemy Philometor as king. The Gk. *prōtoklisia* occurs nowhere else, and its meaning is uncertain.

CORPSE [Heb. *nᵉḇēlâ* (2 K. 9:37; Isa. 5:25), *peger* (Isa. 34:3; Nah. 3:3), *gᵉwîyâ* (Ps. 110:6); Gk. *nekrós* (Mk. 9:26)]; AV CARCASE, DEAD BODIES, ONE DEAD; NEB also BODIES. The English term "corpse" comes from the Lat. *corpus,* "body." In the OT the dead were considered ceremonially unclean, and priests were forbidden to touch them, except for near relatives (Lev. 21:1-3). The high priest and Nazirites were expressly prohibited from contact with the dead (21:11; Nu. 6:6ff.) in an attempt to safeguard the symbolic purity of their vocations. The Semites were scrupulous about the burial of corpses, and considered it a calamity for the body to remain unburied after death (cf. Dt. 28:26; 2 S. 21:10; 1 Ch. 10:11f.; etc.). The bodies of executed persons were required to be buried before nightfall, so as to maintain the purity of the land (Dt. 21:23).

H. L. E. LUERING
R. K. H.

CORRECT [Heb. *yāsar* (Prov. 9:7; Jer. 10:24), *'āšar* (Isa. 1:17); Gk. *paideúō* (2 Tim. 2:5)]; AV also REPROVE (Prov. 4:7), RELIEVE (Isa. 1:17), INSTRUCT (2 Tim. 2:25); NEB also CHAMPION (Isa. 1:17), DISCIPLINE (2 Tim. 2:25); **CORRECTOR** [Gk. *paideutḗs*] (Rom. 2:20); AV INSTRUCTOR; NEB "to train"; **CORRECTION** [Heb. *šēḇeṭ* (Job 37:13), *mûsār*; Gk. *epanórthōsis* (2 Tim. 3:16)]; AV also INSTRUCTION (Zeph. 3:7); NEB, LESSON (Jer. 2:30), LEARN (RSV "take correction," Jer. 5:3), REBUKE (Zeph. 3), "reformation of manners" (2 Tim. 3:16), omits Job 37:13.

In the Hebrew mind "correction" and "instruction" are closely related; both can be indicated by the Heb. *mûsār* (vb. *yāsar*), which means "discipline" or "chastening." The literal meaning of *šēḇeṭ* is "rod." In Isa. 1:17, *'āšar* may be taken to mean "set right," as in the AV or RSV, or "advance the cause of," as the NEB.

The Gk. *paideúō* is like Heb. *yāsar* in that it can mean either "educate" (Acts 7:22) or "chastise" (Lk. 23:16). In 2 Tim. 2:25 the meaning is between the two extremes, as is true also of *paideutḗs* in Rom. 2:20. The Gk. *epanórthōsis,* which occurs only in 2 Tim. 3:16, comes from *orthóō,* "set upright." The literal significance is a setting back upright of what has fallen, but it is used further of making something or someone conform to a standard. J. W. D. H.

CORRECTIONS OF THE SCRIBES. [Heb. *neqûḏôṯ*; Lat. *puncta extraordinaria*]. Dots placed over letters or words in the Hebrew OT in fifteen instances to show the doubts of the scribes about their authenticity. These are probably the earliest occurrences of scribal influence on the text.

CORRESPOND (Gal. 4:25; 1 Pet. 3:21). *See* TYPE.

CORRUPT [Heb. *šāḥaṯ*] (Gen. 6:11f.; Ex. 32:7; etc.); NEB also VILE, EVIL, VICIOUS, etc.; [*'ālaḥ*] (Job 15:16; Ps. 14:3); AV FILTHY; NEB ROTTEN; [*'ānuš*] (Jer. 17:9); AV WICKED; NEB SICK; [*'āḇaḏ*] (Eccl. 7:7); AV DESTROYETH; NEB "break (the spirit)"; [Gk. *phtheírō*]; NEB DELUDED, RUINED; [*kataphtheírō*] ("corrupted [mind]," 2 Tim. 3:8); NEB "lost the power to reason"; [*miaínō*] (Tit. 1:15); AV DEFILED; NEB TAINTED; **CORRUPTION** [Heb. *mašḥîṯ*] ("[mount of] corruption," 2 K. 23:13); NEB MOUNT OF OLIVES; [*'āwôn*] (Hos. 7:1); AV INIQUITY; NEB GUILT; [Gk. *phthorá*] (Gal. 6:8; 2 Pet. 1:4; 2:19); [*diaphthorá*] (Acts 2:27, 31; 13:34-37).

The term generally refers to decay, whether of an organic or moral nature. *'Ālaḥ* refers specifically to moral corruption, while *'ānuš* means "incurable," and the verb *'āḇaḏ,* when used with *lēḇ,* means "deprive of the understanding." The reference in Hosea employs *'āwôn,* a common word for "sin," "perverseness," "guilt"; but the Hebrew term used most often is *šāḥaṯ,* "spoil," "become corrupt." On 2 K. 23:13, *see* CORRUPTION, MOUNT OF.

The NT references to "corruption" are generally a rendering of *phthorá,* "rottenness," "decay," "perishableness," or one of its cognates. In 2 Pet. 1:4; 2:19 it refers to moral corruption. The degeneration of the physical body is referred to in Acts 2:27, 31; 13:34ff., reflecting the use of the word *diaphthorá* in the LXX of Ps. 16:10 (RSV "the Pit"; NEB "Sheol"); the Greek term also has a broader meaning, however (cf. Lk. 12:33, where the AV gives "corrupt" in its obsolete sense of "destroy"). *Miaínō,* which means literally "stain" or "pollute," refers to moral defilement in Tit. 1:15.

R. K. H.

CORRUPTIBLE. An obsolete rendering of Gk. *phthartós* in the AV (e.g., Rom. 1:23; 1 Cor. 9:25; 15:23f.), rendered "mortal" or "perishable" in the RSV.

CORRUPTION, MOUNT OF [Heb. *har-hammašḥîṯ*; Gk. *tó óros toú Mosoath*] (2 K. 23:13); NEB MOUNT OF OLIVES. A hill "before" (i.e., E of) Jerusalem, "on the right" of which (i.e., toward the south) Solomon built high places for Ashtoreth, Chemosh, and Milcom, deities of the Sidonians, Moabites, and Ammonites, respectively (1 K. 11:7). The high places were destroyed by Josiah (2 K. 23:13). Jeremiah prophesied against a "destroying mountain" (Jer. 51:25), which in Hebrew has the same name, *har-hammašḥîṯ*. The Vulgate of 2 K. 23:13 gives *Mons Offensionis* (Mt. of Offense); this name and another Latin name, *Mons Scandali* (Mt. of Scandal), are both used in modern times.

The identification of the site is not entirely certain. There is no other geographical reference to *har hammašḥîṯ*. In the Talmud the name *har hammišḥâ* (Mt. of the Ointment) is used for the Mt. of Olives, and the term may have been already old. The Jewish scholar Rashi (11th cent.) suggested that the name was changed from *har hammišḥâ* to the similar *har hammašḥîṯ* as a reproach because of the idolaters who worshiped there. If Jeremiah was referring to the same location — which is entirely possible, since the high places were destroyed by Josiah who was a contemporary of Jeremiah — the pejorative name may be from that time or even earlier.

Early Christians identified the site with the southern knoll of the ridge which is properly known as the Mt. of Olives, although in popular terminology this name is usually applied only to the northern portion of that ridge. The southern portion is known by the Arab. *Jebel bāṭn el-Hawā*, "the ridge of the wind," and is separated from what is popularly called the Mt. of Olives by a slight depression through which runs the road to Jericho. The village of Silwān lies on the western flank, and to its southwest the Kidron and Hinnom valleys join to form Wâdī en-Nâr, the deep ravine which separates the Mt. of Olives from the Mt. of Evil Counsel, S of Jerusalem across the Hinnom Valley.

In 2 Ch. 28:3 the location of the idolatries of King Ahaz is given as the Valley of Hinnom. Since the specific abominable practice mentioned is the burning of his own sons as an offering, and since this was part of the worship of Chemosh, who is mentioned in 2 K. 23:13, there are some who suggest that the location of Solomon's high places should be sought on the Mt. of Evil Counsel. This theory, without good biblical support, is sometimes offered to tourists to Jerusalem, and is at times associated with the fact that the headquarters of United Nations is nearby.

Bibliography.–Z. Vilnay, *yerûšālayim, hā'îr hā'attîqā* (1962), pp. 209-214; *GTTOT,* p. 184. W. S. LASOR

COS kôs, kōs [Gk. *Kōs*–'summit']; AV COOS. An island off the coast of Caria, Asia Minor, one of the Sporades, under Greek control since 1948. The island is mentioned in connection with Paul's third missionary journey in Acts 21:1, and in its relations with the Jews in 1 Macc. 15:23; Josephus *Ant.* xiv.7.2; 10.15.

Cos is a long, narrow island oriented E-W. About 23 mi. (37 km.) long, it has a circumference of 65 mi. (105 km.) and consists of an area of 111 sq. mi. (287 sq. km.). It is divided into three parts or regions: an abrupt limestone ridge along the eastern half of the southern coast, a rugged peninsula at the west end, and along the northern coast a central lowland of fertile soil which produces an excellent quality of grapes. The harbor is at the eastern end of the island. Mt. Oromedon, a landmark for navigators, rises in the middle of the island to a height of 2500 ft. (762 m.).

Cos was settled by Greeks as early as the 15th cent. B.C. During the 5th cent. the city-state joined the Delian League and suffered considerable destruction during the Peloponnesian War (431-404). A member of the Second Athenian Alliance, it revolted successfully against Athens in 354. Coming under the control of Alexander, Cos subsequently oscillated between Macedon, Syria, and

Egypt to find its greatest glory as a literary center under the protection of the Ptolemies, when it was the home of such great figures as the poet Philetas. In the 2nd cent. Cos was loyal to Rome even before it became a part of the province of Asia. Herod the Great was one of the benefactors of the people of Cos. Claudius, influenced by his Coan physician Xenophon, made Cos a free city and conferred immunity from taxation upon it in A.D. 53.

One of the most beautiful ports of the ancient world, Cos not doubt was most famous as a health resort. It was the site of the first school of scientific medicine and the sanctuary of Asclepius (Esculapius). The island had a healthful climate and hot ferrous and sulfurous springs, which the great Hippocrates (*ca.* 460-377 B.C.), the father of medicine, first used to cure his patients.

The sanctuary of Asclepius (the god of healing) was excavated by Rudolf Herzog of Tübingen University, 1898-1907. He uncovered a sanctuary on three terraces set in a sacred grove of cypresses about 2 mi. (3 km.) from the town. The topmost terrace had a Doric temple built of white island marble, surrounded on three sides by a U-shaped portico with its open side facing the lower terraces, and dating *ca.* 160 B.C. The middle terrace dated *ca.* 280 B.C. and supported a great altar faced by a small temple and other structures. The lowest terrace had a U-shaped portico with its open side facing the one on the top level. Dated *ca.* 350-250 B.C., this portico contained rooms where the patients slept.

When an earthquake nearly devastated the city of Cos in 1933, the Italians, who then controlled the island, availed themselves of the opportunity to excavate the ancient city. They found a planned Hellenistic town with main cross streets, a stadium, and a surrounding wall; and they found evidence of occupation at the site as early as Mycenaean times. At the lower level of the sanctuary the excavators uncovered Roman baths which utilized the healing waters of the island's springs and which (by inscriptions) dated to Nero's reign — and thus to the time of Paul's ministry.

See MAP XXI. H. F. VOS

COSAM kō'səm [Gk. *Kōsam*]. In Luke's genealogy, an ancestor of Jesus in the fifth generation before Zerubbabel (Lk. 3:28).

COSMETICS. Numerous concoctions were employed in the ancient Near East to enhance beauty, to provide pleasant aromas, and to soothe the skin dried by the hot climate. Ointments and perfumes were the most common. Archeological excavations have recovered many cosmetic containers and applicators, but such find scant mention in the OT.

See OIL III.B; PAINT; PERFUME; Plate 9.

COSMOGONY; COSMOLOGY. *See* CREATION; WORLD.

COSTLINESS. The AV for Gk. *timiótēs* in Rev. 18:19; RSV and NEB "wealth."

COTES. *See* FOLD; SHEEP III.F.

COTTAGE. The AV rendering of words translated BOOTH (Isa. 1:8), HUT (Isa. 24:20), and MEADOW (Zeph. 2:6) in the RSV.

COTTON [Heb. *karpas*; Sanskrit *karpāsa*; Gk. *kárpasos*] (Est. 1:6); AV GREEN; NEB omits; [Heb. *ḥôrāy;* Gk. *býssos*] (Isa. 19:9); AV NETWORKS; NEB "shall grow pale." From a remote period the fruit fibers of the *Gossypium herbaceum* L. have been spun into thread from which cloth has been made. The plant seems to have originated in India, but is now cultivated in many lands. The reference in Est. 1:6 is to the cotton hangings in the royal palace at Susa, while *ḥôrāy* in Isa. 19:9 is a rare word probably meaning "pale," "white."

R. K. H.

COUCH (noun). *See* BED.

COUCH (verb) [Heb. *rāḇaṣ*] (Gen. 49:9, 25; Dt. 33:13; Ezk. 19:2); AV also LIE, LAY DOWN; NEB CROUCH, "made her lair"; [*kāra'*] (Nu. 24:9); [*šāḵēn*] (Dt. 33:20); AV DWELL. The term "couch" is used by the RSV with reference to a lion crouching in readiness to spring on its prey (e.g., Dt. 33:20) or a recumbent lion or lioness (e.g., Gen. 49:9). On the "deep that couches beneath" (Gen. 49:25; Dt. 33:13), *see* ABYSS; DEEP.

COUCHING-PLACE. *See* FOLD.

COULTER. *See* PLOW.

COUNCIL [Heb. *sôḏ*]; AV SECRET (Gen. 49:6; Job 15:8), ASSEMBLY (Ps. 89:7; Ezk. 13:9), COUNSEL (Jer. 23:18, 22); NEB also SECRET COUNCIL (Job 15:8), "assembled" (Ps. 89:7), COUNSELS (Ezk. 13:9); [*rō'ê pānîm*–'seeing the face']; AV PRESENCE (2 K. 25:19), PERSON (Jer. 52:25); NEB "(those with) right of access (to the king)"; [*yāšaḇ*] (2 K. 9:5, "in council"); AV SITTING TOGETHER; [*'ēḏâ*] (Ps. 82:1); AV CONGRE-

Ivory cosmetic container or ointment spoon with handle in the form of a woman. The hole between the shoulders is for insertion of the doweled head of the figure. (Megiddo, 1350-1150 B.C.) (Oriental Institute, University of Chicago)

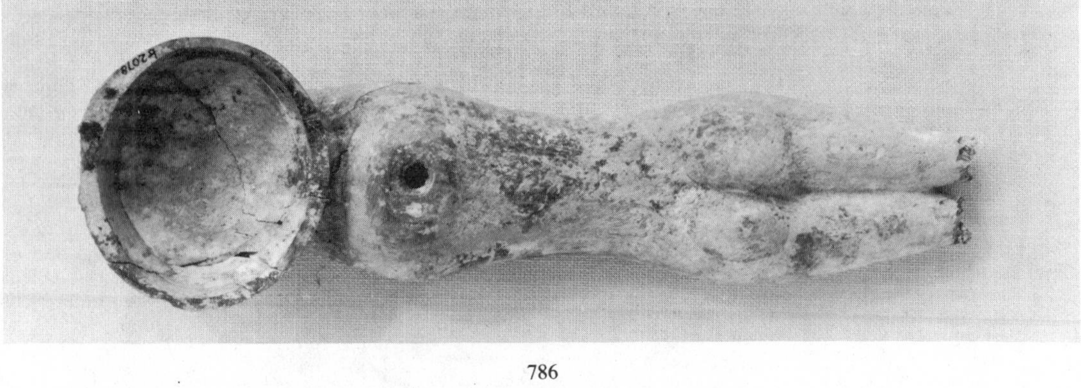

GATION; NEB COURT; [Gk. *synédrion*]; NEB also COURT, SANHEDRIN; [*symboúlion*] (Acts 25:12); NEB ADVISERS; **MEMBER OF THE COUNCIL** [*bouleutḗs*] (Mk. 15:43; Lk. 23:50); AV COUNSELLOR. The Heb. *sôḏ* can refer both to intimate or confidential speaking and to those involved in such speaking, or to a gathering of intimates. In the NT Gk. *synédrion* normally refers to the SANHEDRIN, the Jewish supreme court, but in Mt. 10:17; Mk. 13:9 and perhaps Mt. 5:22 it refers to local courts. The *symboúlion* of Acts 25:12 is a less formal group of advisers. Joseph of Arimathea is called a *bouleutḗs* in Mk. 15:43 par., which means he was a member of the Sanhedrin, or possibly of the Arimathean village council. J. W. D. H.

COUNCIL OF JERUSALEM. *See* APOSTOLIC COUNCIL.

COUNSEL; ASK COUNSEL; TAKE COUNSEL [Heb. *yā'aṣ, 'ēṣâ, mô'ēṣôṯ, 'ûṣ* (Jgs. 19:30), *'ûṣ 'ēṣâ* (Isa. 8:10), also *dāḇar* (Nu. 31:16; Est. 5:14), *yāsaḏ* (Ps. 2:2), *mālaḵ* (Neh. 5:7), *sôḏ* (Prov. 15:22), *šā'al* (2 S. 20:18), *šā'al peh* (Isa. 30:2), *taḥbulôṯ* (Prov. 12:5); Aram. *m^{e}laḵ* (Dnl. 4:27); Gk. *boulḗ, bouleúomai* (Lk. 14:31), *symboúlion, symbouleúō*]; AV also CONSULT, ADVICE, ADVISEMENT (1 Ch. 12:19), GUIDE (Ps. 32:8), WILL (Acts 13:36), THING (Est. 5:14), "ask at (my) mouth" (Isa. 30:2), "hold a council" (Mt. 12:14), "counsellor" (Nah. 1:11); NEB also ADVICE, ADVISE, PLAN(S), PURPOSE(S), DESIGN(S), CONSULT, DEPARTURE (Nu. 31:16), "give thought to the matter" (1 K. 12:28), "hold a conference" (2 K. 6:8), AGREE (2 Ch. 30:2), "I mastered my feelings" (Neh. 5:7; RSV "I took counsel with myself"), "talk the matter over" (6:7), FIRMNESS (Job 12:13), OPINION (29:21), GUIDE (Ps. 1:1), CONSPIRE (2:2), FORCE (Prov. 8:14; cf. Isa. 11:2 mg.), PLOT, CONFER, "meet in conference" (Mt. 27:1), CONSIDER (Lk. 14:31), etc. The NEB here, as with other words elsewhere, shows the wide variety of meaning in these words, which the translation "counsel" often fails to bring out clearly.

See also COUNSELOR; PLAN; PREDESTINATION; PURPOSE. J. W. D. H.

COUNSELOR [Heb. *yā'aṣ*, also *'îš 'ēṣâ* (Ps. 119:24; Isa. 40:13); Aram. *y^e'aṭ* (Ezr. 7:14f.), *'^{a}ḏargāzar* (Dnl. 3:2f.), *haddāḇar* (3:24, 27; 4:36 [MT 33]; 6:7 [MT 8]); Gk. *paráklētos* (Jn. 14:16, 26; 15:26; 16:7), *sýmboulos* (Rom. 11:34)]; AV, NEB, COUNSELLOR; AV also JUDGE (Dnl. 3:2f.), "of the counsel" (2 Ch. 25:16), COMFORTER (*paráklētos*); NEB also "official at court" (Ezr. 4:5), MINISTER (Job 3:14), COUNSEL (Ps. 119:24), "planning" (Prov. 11:14; 24:6), "in purpose" (Isa. 9:6), COURTIER (*haddāḇar*), ADVOCATE (Isa. 41:28; Jn. 14–16). King David employed certain men as advisers in his court, including Ahithophel, who was succeeded by Jehoiada son of Benaiah, and Jonathan, David's uncle, who was educated and a "scribe" (1 Ch. 27:32). The important role such advisers often played is illustrated in 2 Ch. 22:3ff.; and the esteem in which counselors were held is seen in Job 3:14, "kings and counselors." Proverbs considers it wise to employ an "abundance of counselors," both for a nation's defense (11:14) and to plan offensive strategy (24:6). That counselors occupied a regular place in ancient administrations is clear from Ezr. 4:5; 7:14f., 28; 8:25; Isa. 3:3; 19:11; etc.

In Daniel, the two Aramaic words translated "counselor" in the NEB and RSV are of Persian origin; according to F. Rosenthal (*Grammar of Biblical Aramaic* [2nd ed. 1963]) Aram. *'^{a}ḏargāzar* (Dnl. 3:2f.) probably means "counselor," and *haddāḇar* (3:24, etc.) means "companion" (cf. NEB "courtier," and cf. "king's friend" in 1 Ch. 27:33).

Various renderings have been suggested for Isa. 9:6; the name of the son is read as six names (Vulgate), five (AV), four (RSV, NEB, JB, etc.), or a single sentence (Amer. Tr.). The consensus today is that four names are here given, one of which is Heb. *pele' yô'ēṣ*, "Wonderful Counselor" (RSV, JB), or "in purpose wonderful" (NEB). See E. J. Young, *Intro. to the OT* (repr. 1963), for a discussion.

On the Gk. *paráklētos* in Jn. 14–16 *see* PARACLETE. J. W. D. H.

COUNTENANCE. The noun is the translation of a variety of Hebrew and Greek expressions, Heb. *pānîm* being the most frequent. Besides this are found *mar'eh*, "appearance," "shape," "comeliness," "visage" (Jgs. 13:6), *'ap*, "nose," "anger" (Ps. 10:4); and Gk. *stygnázō*, "be sad" (Mk. 10:22), *prósōpon*, "face," "presence," "aspect" (Lk. 9:29).

To the Oriental the countenance is particularly indicative of a person's inner feelings, reflecting such emotions as anger (Gen. 4:5f.), severity (Dt. 28:50, NEB "grim aspect"), sadness (Job 9:27, NEB "show a cheerful face"; Eccl. 7:3, NEB "sad face"), dismay (Mk. 10:22), and pride (Ps. 10:4, NEB "arrogant"). The idea of favor or presence is rendered by the phrase "light of (thy) countenance" (Nu. 6:26; Ps. 4:6; 90:8; etc.).

See FACE. R. K. H.

COUNTERFEIT. In 2 Tim. 3:8 Gk. *adókimos* is used to describe a reprobate person: "men of corrupt mind and counterfeit faith" (AV "reprobate concerning the faith"; NEB "cannot pass the tests of faith"). In Wisd. 15:9 *kíbdēlos*, "mixed with dross," is rendered "counterfeits" by the RSV and NEB, "counterfeit things" by the AV. "Counterfeit" in the obsolete sense of representation occurs in Wisd. 14:17, AV, as a translation of *anatypóō*, "make a likeness."

COUNTERVAIL [Heb. *šāwâ*–'equalize']. An archaic term for "equal" (RSV "be compared with") found in Est. 7:4, AV.

COUNTRY [Heb. *'ereṣ, śāḏeh, g^{e}ḇûl*, also *'^{a}ḏāmâ* (Jonah 4:2), *māqôm* (Gen. 29:26; Jgs. 11:19), *migrāš* (Ezk. 48:15), *merḥāq* ("far country," Zec. 10:9); Gk. *chṓra, períchōros, agrós, patrís*, vb. *apodēméō* ("go into a far country"), also *érēmos tópos* (Mk. 1:45), *méros* (Acts 19:1)]; AV also LAND, FIELD, BORDERS, COASTS, PLACE (Jgs. 11:19), SUBURBS (*migrāš*), DESERT PLACE (Mk. 1:45), REGION; NEB also LAND, COUNTRY-SIDE, TERRITORY, NATIONS, REGION, REALM (Mal. 1:4), WORLD (1 Ch. 29:30), "parts of the earth" (Isa. 8:9), "foreign lands" (Ezk. 6:8), COMMON LAND (*migrāš*), "abroad" (RSV "to another country"), HOME TOWN (Mt. 13:54, 57 par.; but "country" in Lk. 4:24; Jn. 4:44; all Gk. *patrís*; see Bauer, p. 642), FARMS (Mk. 6:36; Lk. 9:12), FARMSTEADS (Mk. 6:56), NEIGHBOURHOOD (Lk. 7:17), DISTRICT (8:37), etc.; for Heb. *śāḏeh* the RSV and NEB often have "open country," the AV "field" (e.g., Jgs. 20:31; 1 S. 30:11; Mic. 1:6; 4:10); the RSV of 2 K. 25:23 is an addition based on Jer. 40:7; and in Zec. 6:6 the RSV and NEB emend the MT; **COUNTRYMEN** [Heb. *b^{e}nê 'ammî*] (Jgs. 14:16f.); AV "children of my people"; NEB KINSFOLK; [Gk. *symphylétai*] (1 Thess. 2:14); **COUNTRYSIDE** [Heb. *migrāš* (Ezk. 27:28); AV SUBURBS; NEB "troubled waters."

Several Hebrew and Greek terms translated by the English "country" refer to a specific territory (Heb. *g^eḇûl*; lit. "boundary," thus "enclosed territory"; Ex. 8:2; 10:4; *'ereṣ*; Jgs. 11:21; Est. 8:17), often suggesting a political entity (Heb. *śāḏeh*; Gen. 14:7; 36:35; 1 Ch. 1:46; *g^eḇûl*; Ex. 10:19; Gk. *chṓra*; Mt. 8:28). Foreign nations are designated "the countries" (Heb. *'ărāṣôṯ*; Ezk. 6:8) or "the kingdoms of the countries" (*maml^eḵôṯ hā'^ărāṣôṯ*; 1 Ch. 29:30; 2 Ch. 12:8; 20:29; cf. the similar phrase *maml^eḵôṯ hā'āreṣ*, "kingdoms of the earth" in Dt. 28:25; 2 K. 19:15; Isa. 37:20; Jer. 25:26). The concept is frequently that of fatherland or homeland (*'ereṣ*; Gen. 12:1; 30:25; 1 K. 22:36; *g^eḇûl*; Jer. 31:17; *maqôm*; Gen. 29:26; Jgs. 11:19; *'aḏāmâ*; Jonah 4:2; Gk. *patrís*; Mt. 13:54, 57; Mk. 6:4 par; Lk. 4:23f.). In He. 11:16 Gk. *kreíttōn* implies that a heavenly homeland is a more desirable country than an earthly territory.

"Open country" refers to fields or pasture lands outside the walled cities (Heb. *migrāš*; Ezk. 48:15; cf. 27:28; *śāḏeh*; Dt. 21:1; Jgs. 20:31; 1 S. 30:11; 2 K. 25:23; Gk. *agrós*; Mk. 15:21; *períchōros*; Lk. 7:17; 8:37; *érēmos tópos*; Mk. 1:45). This land may be adjacent to the cities and subject to their control (Mk. 6:36; Lk. 9:12) or a completely distinct entity (1 Ch. 27:25; Mk. 6:56). In some instances the term designates rural towns (1 S. 27:5).

Implicit in some uses is a topographical or geographical reference. Gk. *méros* designates the "upper country" (thus "inland regions" or "the interior"; Acts 19:1; cf. Bauer, p. 507; *see also* HILL). Distant lands are called "far countries" (Heb. *merḥāq*; Zec. 10:9; *'ereṣ*; Isa. 8:9). Directional modifiers specify regions or nations as NORTH COUNTRY (Heb. *'ereṣ ṣāpôn*; Jer. 6:22; 10:22; 16:15; 23:8), EAST COUNTRY (*'ereṣ qeḏem*; Gen. 25:6), south country (*'ereṣ hattêmān*; Zec. 6:6), and west country (RSV reads *'el-'aḥ^arê hayyām*; Zec. 6:6).

In some instances "country" may refer to the inhabitants rather than the territory (2 S. 15:23; cf. Mal. 1:4).

See also HILL. J. W. D. H. A. C. M.

COUPLE; COUPLED [Heb. *ḥāḇar*]; NEB JOIN, JOINED. In the RSV the verb "couple" and the participle "coupled" translate the Hebrew verb *ḥāḇar* ("touch, be joined") and the participle based on it. It refers to the place where the curtains of the tabernacle are joined together (Ex. 26:3ff.; 36:10ff.).

COURAGE; COURAGEOUS. In the OT the main words for "be courageous," "be of good courage," etc., are Heb. *ḥāzaq* and *'āmaṣ*, both of which have the basic meaning "be strong (firm, hard)." For *ḥāzaq* the AV has "encouraged themselves" (Jgs. 20:22), "be strong" (1 S. 4:9; 2 Ch. 15:7; Dnl. 10:19; Hag. 2:4), "strengthened himself" (2 Ch. 23:1; 25:11), and "was strengthened" (Ezr. 7:28). For *'āmaṣ* the NEB has "be resolute" (e.g., Dt. 31:6f.; Josh. 1:6, 9, 18; 1 Ch. 22:13); *ḥāzaq* is rendered "take heart" (2 Ch. 25:11; Hag. 2:4), and "felt himself strong enough" (2 Ch. 23:1). OT words for "courage" include *lēḇ* or *lēḇāḇ* ("heart," 2 S. 7:27; Jer. 4:9; Ezk. 22:14; Dnl. 11:25), *nepeš* ("soul," Ps. 107:26; Lam. 1:16), *rû(a)ḥ* ("spirit," Josh. 2:11), and *yāḏôṯ* ("hands," 2 S. 4:1); the AV translates most of these terms literally. In 2 Ch. 17:6 "courageous" translates *gāḇah* (AV "lifted up"; NEB "he took pride").

In the NT "take courage" and "be of good courage" translate Gk. *tharrhéō* (2 Cor. 5:6, 8, AV and NEB "confident"), *tharséō* (Acts 23:11, AV "be of good cheer"), and *tolmáō* (Mk. 15:43, AV "boldly"; NEB "bravely"). In 1 Cor. 16:13 "be courageous" renders *andrízomai* (AV "quit you like men"; NEB "be valiant"). Other words are *thársos* (Acts 28:15), *parrhēsía* (Phil. 1:20, AV "boldness"; NEB "boldly"), and *parrhēsiázomai* (1 Thess. 2:2, AV "were bold"; NEB "frankly and fearlessly"). "Lose courage" in He. 12:5 renders *eklýō* (AV "faint"; NEB "lose heart").

In Wisd. 8:7 courage (Gk. *andreía*, NEB "fortitude") is one of the four cardinal virtues; and cowardice ranks as one of the mortal sins (Rev. 21:8; cf. Sir. 2:12f.).

See also BOLD; CONFIDENCE. J. W. D. H.

COURIER [Heb. *rāṣ*] (2 Ch. 30:6, 10; Est. 3:13, 15; 8:10, 14); AV POST (also in Job 9:25; Jer. 51:31, RSV and NEB "runner"). Members of the royal guard who carried royal letters and dispatches throughout the kingdom, on foot or, as in the Persian empire, on swift horses (Est. 8:10, 14; cf. Xenophon *Cyropaedia* viii.6.17; Herodotus viii.98).

The word for "force" in Mt. 5:41 and "compel" in Mk. 15:21 par. is Gk. *angareúō*, a Persian loanword, formerly used in connection with the right of couriers to command the service of men or their animals to help them deliver important messages. J. W. D. H.

COURSE. The courses or layers (AV "rows") of stones and of beams mentioned in descriptions of the Jerusalem temple and palace are called Heb. *ṭûr* in 1 K. 6:36; 7:12, and Aram. *niḏbāḵ* in Ezr. 6:4. The latter is an Akkadian loanword, occurring here in the text of a scroll from Ecbatana (6:2). The "courses" of priests and Levites in Ezr. 6:18 (Aram. *maḥl^eqâ*) are the divisions described in 1 Ch. 23:6ff., etc. (Heb. *maḥ^alōqeṯ*); cf. Lk. 1:5, 8, AV (Gk. *ephēmería*).

On Jgs. 5:20, "the stars in their courses" (Heb. *m^esillâ*), *see* ASTROLOGY; ASTRONOMY II.C. "Out of course" in Ps. 82:5, AV (Heb. *môṭ*), is poetic for "shaken" (RSV) or "giving way" (NEB).

The Gk. *drómos* is used to designate the earthly life of a servant of God in Acts 13:25 (John the Baptist); 20:24; 2 Tim. 4:7 (Paul). It is usually rendered "course," but "race" in Acts 20:24, NEB, and 2 Tim. 4:7, RSV. The use of such a term to designate one's life span shows utmost zeal for the Lord's work. For "course" of life in a bad sense cf. Jer. 8:6; 23:10 (Heb. *m^erûṣâ*).

See also RELAYS (1 K. 5:14); CYCLE OF NATURE (Jas. 3:6).
J. W. D. H.

COURT OF THE GENTILES. *See* TEMPLE (HEROD'S).

COURT OF THE GUARD. *See* GUARD.

COURT OF THE SANCTUARY. *See* TABERNACLE; TEMPLE.

COURTESY. *See* GENTLENESS.

COURTS, JUDICIAL. The judicial courts of the ancient Near East and of Israel are not to be understood in the modern sense of the word. There was no appointed session of the court, with a public accuser and an advocate in criminal cases, or advocates on both sides in civil cases. The judicial courts came into operation only when a case was presented, and only with a judge (or judges) and witnesses.

I. Judicial Practice in the Ancient Near East.–The judicial practice depended on the way of life of the people in the ancient Near East. The legal practice of nomads or seminomads was understandably different from that of an agrarian or civilized society. The nomad had freedom of movement and was bound only by legal rules arising from custom. Nomadic society consisted of families and clans; and jurisprudence was pronounced by a prominent judge, who might be a military leader and great orator of the clan, or by the elders in the clan (cf. J. Henninger, *L'antico societa Beduina* [1959], pp. 82f.). In Arabic nomadic societies today, people will travel scores of miles to consult a famous sage or to get a judgment on a certain difficult case. This kind of judicial practice existed probably in all the nomadic societies of the ancient Near East, as is shown by various sources.

As soon as certain nomadic or seminomadic tribes settled down in a civilized country, the old judicial institutions were gradually replaced by fixed institutions of judges and officials under supervision of the king. In Mesopotamian society the king got his judicial rights from Šamaš, the supreme judge under the gods, the judge of gods and men; the king in turn delegated this authority to his official and judges. On the law code of Hammurabi, the king is represented with lifted arms in adoration before the sun-god Šamaš. In the prologue of the law codes of both Ur-Nammu and Hammurabi, UTU (Sumerian) or Šamaš is represented as the protector of the widow, the orphan, and the poor; this implies that the king also must protect the weak, which was one of the common ideals of the ancient Near East.

The judicial procedure in Near Eastern courts is amply illustrated by discovered documents. No actual distinction was made between criminal and civil offenses. In every case the injury done to a person was the important point, and the usual fine was compensation. The case was stated before a judge, and witnesses were called in to assist the parties. After all the witnesses and opposing parties had been heard, a final judgment was given. Sometimes a contract between parties was presented to strengthen a case.

II. Judicial Practice in Israel.–Israelite judicial practices were mainly instituted on the same principles as those of the ancient Near East. Judicial practices were reorganized by Moses during the wandering in the desert (cf. Ex. 18). This organization was made for a seminomadic society with Moses as the leader and judge of the people and a great number of minor judges or elders to assist him. The jurisprudence during these years was normally pronounced in the presence of all the members of the covenantal tribes (cf., e.g., Nu. 15:33). With the conquest of Palestine the same procedure continued for a while. The judges in the book of Judges were nothing more than military leaders and famous sages who gave decisions on difficult problems. Some of them were local leaders; others may have had intertribal authority.

With the establishment of the Israelite kingdom the situation changed. The king was now the judge, and the elders or priests in the various cities and towns were minor judges. Law was codified and definite rules were laid down. The situation was rather fluid in the time of Saul. According to the tradition in 1 Ch. 26:29-32, David appointed judges from the ranks of the Levites. This was a reorganization of judicial activities. It is not clear from Chronicles exactly how far this reorganization was carried through.

After a century or more Jehoshaphat (873-849 B.C.) was compelled to reorganize the judicial activities after a period of decay. According to 2 Ch. 17:7-9 and 19:5-11, his reorganization was carried through extensively, and has a good parallel in the reorganization of the judicial activities of Haremheb during the New Kingdom of Egypt (cf. Albright). The practice now was that minor offenses were put under the jurisdiction of elders and priests, but major offenses were directly referred to the king. This policy continued until the Exile.

A very important point to remember is that the Supreme Judge of all men (kings included) was Yahweh. He was regarded as the protector of the weak. All earthly power is delegated to man by God. Every judge must remember that his jurisprudence is under the continuous supervision of the Lord (cf. 2 Ch. 19:6).

The question may be asked: Were all the different laws given in the OT regarded as the law of the land and actually applied? It is a difficult question to answer because of the lack of evidence. We know, for example, that great parts of these laws were disregarded by the community and judges in times of decay, making necessary a reorganization and reinstitution of legal practices. It is, therefore, difficult to ascertain to what extent all the laws were executed. We must keep in mind that the laws described in the OT were formed over a long period and that certain laws were adapted to changing conditions.

Legal procedures in ancient Israel were similar to those in the rest of the Near East. No distinction was made between criminal and civil offenses. Witnesses were summoned to give evidence in a case. The verdict of the judge was usually final. There is some evidence that an appeal could be made to the king if one of the parties was not satisfied with the decision of the clan or judge (cf. 2 S. 14:5ff.). Cases were tried at the city gate, sometimes in the presence of the whole community; and these occasions called for great oratorical skill. Difficult cases were heard by the king himself (e.g., 1 K. 3:16ff.).

III. Judicial Practice in NT Times.–The supreme legislative and judicial body in NT times was the Sanhedrin. Its authority was exercised to such an extent that it could also administer criminal cases. It had an independent police force (cf. Mt. 26:47; Acts 4:3; etc.). In cases that did not involve capital punishment, its judgments were final and irrevocable (cf. Acts 4:2-23; etc.). Only for capital offenses must the consent of the procurator be secured (cf. Jn. 18:31). The procurator was free to grant or refuse it on principle of either Roman or Jewish law.

The smaller court of the Sanhedrin consisted of twenty-three members of pure Jewish lineage and the higher one of seventy-one or seventy. They gathered in Jerusalem, and the local sessions were held on the second and fifth day of the week (Monday and Thursday). No meetings were held on feast days or the sabbath.

Bibliography.–M. San Nicolò, *Beiträge zur Rechtsgeschichte im Bereiche der Keilschriftlichen Rechtsquellen* (1931); J. G. Lautner, *Die richterliche Entscheidung und die Streitbeendigung im altbabylonischen Prozessrechte* (1922); A. Walther, *Das altbabylonische Gerichtswesen* (1917); E. Cuq, *Études sur le droit Babylonien, les lois Assyriennes et les lois Hittites* (1929); H. Cazelles, *Étude sur le code de l'alliance* (1946); A. Jirku, *Das weltliche Recht im AT* (1927); A. Menes, *Die vorexilischen Gesetze Israels* (1928); G. E. Mendenhall, *Law and Covenant in Israel and the Ancient Near East* (1955); M. Noth, *The Laws in the Pentateuch* (Eng. tr. 1966); W. F. Albright, "The Judicial Reform of Jehoshaphat," in *Alexander Marx Jubilee Volume* (1950); J. Jeremias, *Jerusalem in the Time of Jesus* (Eng. tr. 1969); H. J. Boecker, *Redeformen des Rechtslebens im AT* (1964); L. Köhler, *Hebrew Man* (Eng. tr. 1956). F. C. FENSHAM

COURTYARD [Heb. *ḥāṣēr* (e.g., 2 S. 17:18; Ex. 8:13); Gk. *aulḗ* (Mt. 26:58)]. An enclosure, open to the sky, found in private houses, gardens, the palace, the tabernacle, or the temple at Jerusalem. The inner court

(Heb. *happ^e^nîmîṯ,* "the inner") described, e.g., in Ezk. 8:3 may be an interpretation taken from 1 K. 7:12.

COUSIN [Heb. *ben-dôḏ*] (Lev. 25:49; Jer. 32:8f., 12); AV UNCLE'S SON; [Gk. *anepsiós*] (Col. 4:10); AV SISTER'S SON. The OT references are examples of the importance of kinship as a legal consideration in the ancient world (as still today). As Hanamel's cousin, Jeremiah was exercising the right, set forth in Lev. 25:25-28, of buying family property to keep it from reverting to a creditor or going to an outsider.

That Mark was related to Barnabas ("cousin" is correct) is known only from Col. 4:10, but information sheds significant light on Acts 15:36ff., where Barnabas and Paul disagree over whether Mark should accompany them on the second missionary journey.

The AV has "cousin" for Gk. *syngenḗs* in Lk. 1:36, 58; but here a broader relationship than "cousin" now denotes is intended, and so the RSV has "kinsman" and "kinsfolk" (NEB "relatives" in v. 58). J. W. D. H.

COUTHA ko͞o'thə (1 Esd. 5:32, AV, NEB). *See* CUTHA.

COVENANT (OT) [Heb. *b^e^rîṯ*; Gk. *diathḗkē*, also *synthḗkē, entolḗ*]; AV also LEAGUE (Josh. 9:6-16; Jgs. 2:2; 2 S. 3:12f., 21; 5:3); NEB also TREATY (e.g., Josh. 9), COMPACT (2 Ch. 23:3), SOLEMN COMPACT (1 S. 18:3), "come to terms" (RSV "make a covenant," 2 S. 3:12f.; Job 31:1), AGREEMENT (2 K. 11:4; Job 41:4), "pledge ourselves" (Ezr. 10:3), PROMISED WORD (Ps. 55:20), LEAGUE (83:5; Dnl. 9:27), TIES (Am. 1:9), LIGHT (Isa. 42:6), "thy creatures" (Ps. 74:20, emended).

I. General Meaning and Etymology
II. Covenants Between Men in the Ancient World
III. Covenants Between Men in the OT
  A. Examples
  B. Distinctive Language
IV. Covenants Between God and Man
  A. Religious Metaphor
  B. Language of Covenant
  C. Examples
  D. The New Covenant
V. History of the Covenant Idea

I. General Meaning and Etymology.–The etymology of Heb. *b^e^rîṯ* is by no means clear. Various roots have been suggested, but two have found wide acceptance, namely, Heb. *bārâ,* "eat bread with," and the Akk. noun *birītu,* "fetter," or perhaps the prepositional phrase *ina beri,* or the preposition *birit,* "between." Whatever the etymology, the OT term *b^e^rîṯ* came to mean that which bound two parties together. It was used, however, for many different types of "bond," both between man and man and between man and God. It has a common use where both parties were men, and a distinctively religious use where the covenant was between God and man. The religious use was really a metaphor based on the common use but with a deeper connotation.

II. Covenants Between Men in the Ancient World.–There exist today many ancient documents that show how wide was the range of agreements between men. Fundamentally, most if not all of them had religious sanctions of some kind. The contracting parties took an oath in the name of the gods, who both witnessed their solemn agreement and would act as its guarantors. Such solemn agreements were made between individuals, tribes, states, or nations. The most complex of these were international treaties between great powers like the Hittites and the Egyptians. But in all cases the solemn engagement of one party to another and the promise of fidelity were

Letter from Suwardata prince of Hebron (Am.Tab. 282) appealing to his suzerain Akhenaten for emergency military assistance (Trustees of the British Museum)

fundamental. Many of the OT covenants are paralleled in the ancient Near East. Of main interest are the alliances and treaties between city-states and neighboring tribal groups, between tribal groups in the areas of influence of more powerful states, between states and nations, and in particular between vassal states and their overlords. The records of the Hittites from Asia Minor, of the people of Ugarit on the Mediterranean seacoast, of the people of Mari on the middle Euphrates, and of the Assyrians, all provide useful source material for study.

The Mari documents from the 18th cent. B.C. have produced a number of significant phrases. In several of these a sacrificial ass was slain, and the phrase "to kill an ass" is almost the equivalent of "to make a covenant." Again, when an agreement had been reached between parties, reference was made to "peace between X and Y" (cf. Jgs. 4:17; 1 S. 7:14; 1 K. 5:12 [MT 26]). Another phrase, "to kill an ass of peace," is reminiscent of the Hebrew "to make a covenant of peace" (Ezk. 34:25; 37:26).

In international treaties, of which the most famous was that between Hattusilis III the Hittite King and Ramses II of Egypt, the two parties drew up by mutual consent a set of obligations, which were then written down on a treaty document set out according to a standard pattern. The basic elements were (1) a preamble giving the names and titles of the parties, (2) a historical prologue setting out the previous relations of the parties, (3) the stipulations, (4) a list of divine witnesses, (5) a statement of curses and blessings. Such a treaty was a "parity" treaty. A similar pattern was followed for the "suzerainty" or "vassal" treaty between the Hittite overlords and their vassals. The historical prologue here set out to define the past benefits bestowed by the Hittite king on the subject nation, benefits that put the vassal under perpetual obligation. Generally, provisions for depositing the treaty document in the temple and for a periodic public reading of it were written into the treaty tablet. In theory the Hittite suzerain drew up the stipulations that constituted

COVENANT (OT)

Widiya governor of Ashkelon informs the king that he is fulfilling his covenantal duties by guarding his cities and giving provisions and tribute (Am.Tab. 325). (Trustees of the British Museum)

the essence of the bond (*riksu*), and the vassal accepted the bond on oath (*mamitu*), so that the whole treaty was defined as "the oath and bond" (*riksu u mamitu*). In international treaties there were two bonds and two oaths, since each party drew up its own interpretation of the agreement and presented it to the other party to be accepted under oath of the gods. The presence of the gods guaranteed the fulfillment of the obligation, and in the case of a breach of the treaty ensured that the curses would operate. In the vassal treaties blessings were promised to the one who honored his obligations, and curses to him who transgressed the treaty. In every case, however, the "bond" between the parties was wider then the mere treaty obligations, although in Hittite documents the term *riksu* often seems to mean little more than the stipulations of the treaty. But there were intangible links as well, such as the sense of obligation in the vassal in many cases, the binding power of the oath, and the sanctions of the gods.

The later Assyrians used the term *adē* as the equivalent for *riksu,* which largely, though not completely, dropped out of use. The *adē* were the sworn obligations and represented the essence of the treaty, although here too the bond between the parties must have been regarded as something more than a list of stipulations.

Religious ceremonies involving the slaughter of a beast were associated with each treaty, and customs similar to those at Mari are attested among the people of Syria in the 18th cent. B.C. as well as among the Assyrians and the later Arameans of Syria at least down to the 8th cent. B.C. (cf. Gen. 15:9f.; Jer. 34:18). A common element in the cursing formula in some treaties is: "Just as this [beast] is cut up, so may X be cut up." The recitation of such a formula was probably in the nature of a self-imprecation. The man who recited it thus declared his expectation of the fate that would befall him if he broke his treaty obligations.

It is against this wider Near Eastern background that the covenants of the OT should be studied in the first instance. In that way comparisons and contrasts may be made and the uniqueness of the OT picture may be understood.

III. Covenants Between Men in the OT.*–*A. Examples. The term *b^erîṯ* is used for a wide variety of agreements between men in the OT. In translating the word it may be helpful to use different terms such as agreement, alliance, league, or treaty, according to the sense, and to preserve the term "covenant" for the *b^erîṯ* between God and man.

The following examples may be noted in the OT: (1) a mutual commitment of an intensely personal kind, as with Jonathan and David (1 S. 18:3; 20:8; 22:8; 23:18); (2) a personal agreement with political ends, as with David and Abner (2 S. 3:12f.); (3) an alliance between heads of tribes, as between Abraham and his confederates (Gen. 14:13), between Abraham and Abimelech (Gen. 21:22-32), between Isaac and Abimelech (Gen. 26:26-31), and between Jacob and Laban (Gen. 31:44-54); (4) an arrangement between an individual and tribal representatives, as for Rahab and the Israelite spies (Josh. 2); (5) an agreement between the king and an individual, as with Solomon and Shimei (1 K. 2:42-46); (6) an agreement between the king and the nation or elements of the nation, as with David and Israel (2 S. 5:1; 1 Ch. 11:3), Joash and Judah (2 K. 11:17), and Zedekiah and Judah (Jer. 34:8); (7) treaties between the king of Israel and his vassals, as with David (2 S. 8) or Solomon (1 K. 4:21); (8) treaties between states or tribes, whether a weaker state asks for an alliance — as the Gibeonites asked Israel (Josh. 9:6, 11, 15f.), the Israelites asked Nahash the Ammonite (1 S. 11:1f.), and Ben-hadad asked Ahab (1 K. 20:34) — or whether the stronger imposed a treaty, as Assyria on Israel (Hos. 12:1) and Nebuchadrezzar on Judah (Ezk. 17:13), or whether approximately equal parties arranged the treaty, as Solomon with Hiram (1 K. 5:12), and the kings of Judah and Israel with Ben-hadad (1 K. 15:19); (9) a solemn undertaking between the men of Judah to keep the law of Moses (2 K. 23:3; Jer. 34:8; Ezr. 10:3; Neh. 9:38; 10:29); (10) the marriage alliance (Mal. 2:14); (11) metaphorical covenants with things (Hos. 2:18; Jer. 33:20, 25; Isa. 28:15, 18; Zec. 11:10; Job 5:23; 31:1; 41:4).

B. Distinctive Language. In most of these OT passages elements of the Near Eastern pattern can be observed. There are references to stipulations or commandments (*miṣwôṯ*), the oath (*š^eḇû'â*), the act of swearing (*nišbā'*), the blessings (*b^erāḵâ*), and the curse (*'ālâ*). There is naturally no mention of calling on the gods as witnesses, since God is Himself the witness; but external "witnesses" (*'ēḏ*) in the form of a pillar or a heap of stones (Gen. 31:52) are known, and at times the people themselves act as their own witnesses (Josh. 24:22). The technical phrase *kāraṯ b^erîṯ,* literally "cut a covenant," is generally used for "making a covenant." The origin of this expression appears to lie in the ancient practice of slaying and cutting up sacrificial beasts at such covenant ceremonies. The covenant was made "with" (*'im* or *'ēṯ*), "between" (*bēn*), or "for the benefit of" (*l^e*) the party or parties concerned. It was to be "kept" or "guarded," and at least in intention was immutable. Very often, however, one party "despised the oath and broke the covenant" (Ezk. 17:15f., 18f.).

IV. Covenants Between God and Man.*–*A. Religious Metaphor. The Near Eastern treaty pattern provided a beautiful metaphor for the relation between God and Israel. More particularly the suzerainty treaty provided a monarchical picture in which God became Israel's sovereign and Israel became his servant. The literary pattern of the Near Eastern treaty is clearly discernible in the OT narratives at many points. Thus in the Sinai story (Ex. 19–24) there is a recital of God's acts prior to the making of the covenant (19:4), followed by the call to enter into a covenant and to obey. The stipulations in the form of the Decalogue are given in Ex. 20 and supplemented by other laws in Ex. 21–23. There is a reference to the oath that Israel took (Ex. 19:8; 24:3) and to the religious ceremony at which the covenant was ratified (Ex. 24:4-8). Curses and blessings are contained in the Decalogue (Ex. 20:1-17) and there is mention of the covenant document (Ex. 24:7). Similar patterns may be shown to exist in many passages in the OT but notably in Dt. 29–30; Josh. 23–24, and in Deuteronomy as a whole.

B. Language of Covenant. The standard Hebrew phrase *kāraṯ bᵉrîṯ* is used of God's covenant with man (Gen. 15:18; Ex. 24:8; Dt. 4:23; 5:2; 2 K. 17:15; Jer. 11:10; Ezk. 34:25), but stress is laid on the initiative of God by the use of the verbs "establish" (*hēqîm*) in Gen. 6:18; 9:11; 17:7; etc., "grant" (*nāṯan*) in Gen. 9:12; 17:2; Nu. 25:12, "set down" (*śîm*) in 2 S. 23:5, "command" (*ṣiwwâ*) in Josh. 7:11; 23:16; 1 K. 11:11. All these verbs at times have as their objects the noun *bᵉrîṯ*. Further, there are numerous references to God's having "commanded" and given Israel a "law," "statutes," "commandments," "judgments," etc. Israel on her part was expected to "obey" God's word of command, to "keep" His covenant, to "remember" it, to "do" it, and to "walk in" it. Her history shows that she "forgot" the covenant, "broke" it, "sinned against" it, "rejected" it, "transgressed" it, and "profaned" it. Hence she experienced the curses of the broken covenant in the form of natural calamities, war, sickness, exile, and death, whereas had she kept the covenant she might have enjoyed the blessings of the covenant instead (Lev. 26; Dt. 27–28).

C. Examples. While in a sense there is but one covenant between God and men through which God in sovereign fashion dispenses His grace to men and fulfils His promises to them, a variety of occasions is mentioned in the OT, and the precise character of the grace bestowed and of the promise given differs according to the circumstances. In a few cases the word *bᵉrîṯ* is used with reference to God's creative and providential activity where He showed Himself to be utterly faithful (Jer. 33:20, 25; cf. Gen. 8:22).

Apart from these the following covenants may be distinguished: (1) God's covenant with Noah (Gen. 9:9-17). This arose from God's own initiative. It was universal in scope, unconditional, and everlasting. The promise was that never again would there be a deluge; the rainbow was the sign. (2) God's covenant with Abraham (Gen. 15:8-18; 17:1-14). In this covenant God promised a land and descendants to Abraham, who was commanded to "keep" the covenant (Gen. 17:9f., 14) and was given circumcision as the sign. The obedience of Abraham was not a condition of the covenant but rather his response inside a religious relationship. There could be no blessings and no fellowship without obedience. (3) God's covenant with the nation at Sinai (Horeb). Following the recital of divine acts and the call to obey, God constituted Israel a "peculiar treasure," a "kingdom of priests," and a "holy nation," and gave them the stipulations that would guarantee the continuance of fellowship between them and their God. The covenant was ratified by a covenant sacrifice and the sprinkling of blood (Ex. 24:4-8). (4) Various covenant renewals. From time to time in Israel's history the covenant was renewed. The most important renewals were those on the plains of Moab (Dt. 29), at Shechem in the days of Joshua (Josh. 24), in the days when Jehoiada was able to restore the Davidic line of kings under Joash (2 K. 11), in the days of Hezekiah (2 Ch. 29:10), and in the days of Josiah (2 K. 23:3). (5) The Davidic covenant. God gave a promise to David that his descendants should have an everlasting kingdom and be known as his sons (2 S. 7:12-17; Ps. 89:3f., 26f., 34; Ps. 132:11f.; 2 S. 23:5; cf. Isa. 55:3f.).

D. The New Covenant. Several passages in the prophets, but most explicitly in Jeremiah, speak of a new covenant in the messianic age (Isa. 42:6; 49:6-8; 55:3; 59:21; 61:8; Jer. 31:31, 33; 32:40; 50:5; Ezk. 16:60, 62; 34:25; 37:26; Hos. 2:18). If God's promises were eternal, then even if historic Israel failed and suffered the curses of the broken covenant, the promise of God could not fail. There would be a remnant in whom, by way of judgment and repentance, God would honor His promises. He would make a new covenant, not new in essence, but new in fulfillment. His law would be written on hearts of flesh. In that day the throne of David would be occupied by one of David's line and the people would enjoy an everlasting covenant of peace (Isa. 55:3; Jer. 23:5f.; 32:37-40; Ezk. 34:23; 37:25f.), in which the nations would also share (Isa. 42:6; 49:6; 55:3-5; cf. Zec. 2:11; 8:20-23; 14:16; etc.). In those days worship would be purified (Ezk. 40–48), true theocratic government would be established, and peace would be universal. It is very evident that in this picture the original Near Eastern metaphor has been completely transformed.

V. History of the Covenant Idea.–Recent studies suggest that there is no serious ground for rejecting the biblical statements that the covenant idea was pre-Mosaic. The covenant pattern was known in lower Mesopotamia in the days of the Sumerians, in the 3rd millennium B.C. There is abundant material from the 2nd and 1st millennia B.C. to show how widespread both in area and in time this pattern was. Evidence of another kind comes from the recognition that tribal groups at an early age in the ancient Near East owned a particular god as "father" of their tribe and regarded each member of the tribe as united to the tribal head by close ties. In this conception lay the elements of the covenant idea also. The "secular" covenants in Genesis are certainly consistent with what we know of the contemporary Near East, and the idea that tribes were united by the closest ties to their God, with whom the tribal leader had particular contract, finds a parallel in the cases of Abraham, Isaac, and Jacob.

It appears that it was Moses who gave the suzerain-vassal shape to the covenant of God with Israel. The narrative in Ex. 19–24 has, as we have seen, many links with the Near Eastern covenant pattern. Post-Mosaic portions of the OT make constant reference to the covenant at Sinai and regard it as having been established at a particular time and place. It was indeed an actual historical event. Prophets, historians, and psalmists alike were aware of the significance of that event (Jgs. 5:4f.; 6:13; 11:16; 1 S. 2:27; 4:8; 10:18; 15:6; Dt. 4:10-14; 5; etc.; 33:2; Hag. 2:5; Neh. 9:13; Ps. 105:8-12, 42-45; 106:45; etc.).

Israel's covenant relationship with God became the basis of interpreting her history. The argument of Jgs. 2 and 2 K. 17 may be discerned in many places in the OT, namely, that when the covenant people transgressed the covenant, failed to hearken to God's voice, and turned aside, national calamity fell upon them. It was the operation of the curse. The only hope of deliverance was repentance and faith. But when they turned from their evil and sought the Lord, He forgave them in His mercy and restored them to the fellowship of the covenant relationship. Such a theology of history lay behind the books of Kings and Chronicles, but it is clearly evident also in the preaching of the prophets.

At times prophets like Hosea and Jeremiah made use of the metaphor of the husband-wife relationship to describe the covenant. The father-son metaphor was also used (Hos. 11). But the most significant metaphor was finally that of the suzerain and vassal or of the Lord and servant.

The failure of Israel to live loyally as the covenant people led to the development of eschatological hopes in the prophets. Preexilic prophets like Isaiah and Jeremiah saw not only impending judgment and exile, but also looked ahead to days of restoration. When the Exile came, Ezekiel pointed to the eternal character of God's covenant and spoke of restoration and renewal. With the end of the Exile and the return of the Jews to their land, new disappointments were experienced. The new age did not seem to dawn the way the people expected, but rather there was famine, opposition, and frustration on every hand. Once more it was the prophetic voice that gave hope. Haggai, Zechariah, and Malachi taught that restoration of full covenant fellowship with its attendant blessings was only delayed because of the sin of the people (Hag. 2; Zec. 2). God's covenant was eternal, and the people would yet witness the breaking in of the age of that everlasting covenant of peace.

These hopes continued through the centuries. The darker the hour, the brighter the hope. The discovery of the Qumrân Scrolls shows clearly that during the 1st cent. B.C. pious Jews in days of apostasy retired to the Dead Sea area to await the coming of Messiah and the dawn of the new age (Ezk. 47). These men constituted themselves into a covenant community and lived by the law of Moses, daily expecting the fulfillment of God's promise of an everlasting covenant of peace. The true nature of that new age and of the new covenant had to await the fuller revelation that came with the Lord Jesus Christ.

Bibliography.–*ANET,* pp. 199-266, 529-541; K. Baltzer, *The Covenant Formulary* (Eng. tr. 1971); J. Begrich, *ZAW,* 60 (1944), 1-11; W. Eichrodt, *Theology of the OT,* I (Eng. tr. 1961); D. R. Hillers, *Covenant: The History of a Biblical Idea* (1969); *Treaty Curses and the OT Prophets* (*Biblica et Orientalia,* 16, 1964); M. G. Kline, *Treaty of the Great King* (1963); D. J. McCarthy, *Treaty and Covenant* (*Analecta Biblica,* 21, 1963); G. E. Mendenhall, *Law and Covenant in Israel and the Ancient Near East* (1955); J. Murray, *Covenant of Grace* (1954); *TDNT,* II, *s.v.* διαθήκη (Quell); *TDOT,* II, *s.v.* "bᵉrîth" (Weinfeld); D. J. Wiseman, *Vassal Treaties of Esarhaddon* (1958).

J. ARTHUR THOMPSON

COVENANT (NT) [Gk. *diathḗkē*]; AV also TESTAMENT (Mt. 26:28 par.; 1 Cor. 11:25; 2 Cor. 3:6, 14; He. 7:22; 9:15ff.; Rev. 11:19); cf. NEB at Gal. 3:17; He. 9:15. The choice of Gk. *diathḗkē* in the LXX to render Heb. *bᵉrîṯ* seems to have been occasioned by a recognition that the covenant which God makes with men is not fully mutual as would be implied in *synthḗkē,* the word commonly used for covenant (although not a NT word), while at the same time the rarity of wills among the Jews made the common sense of *diathḗkē* relatively unfamiliar. The apocryphal writers also frequently use the same word in the same sense and no other.

In the NT *diathḗkē* is used some thirty times in a way that makes it plain it should be translated "covenant." In Gal. 3:15 and He. 9:15-17 it is held by many that the sense of covenant must be set aside in favor of will or testament. But in the former passage it can be taken in the sense of a disposition of affairs or arrangement made by God, a conception in substantial harmony with its regular NT use and with the sense of *bᵉrîṯ*. In the passage in Hebrews the interpretation is more difficult, but as it is acknowledged on all hands that the passage loses all argumentative force if the meaning "testament" is accepted, it seems best to retain the meaning "covenant" if possible. To do this it is only necessary to hold that the death spoken of is the death of the animal that was sometimes, if not indeed commonly, slain in connection with the making of a covenant. In the mind of the author this death symbolized the death of the contracting parties in the sense that thereafter, in the matter involved, they would no more change their minds than can the dead. If this view is taken, this passage falls in line with the otherwise invariable use of the word *diathḗkē* by Jewish Hellenists.

See also COVENANT, THE NEW; TESTAMENT.

D. F. ESTES

COVENANT, ARK OF THE. *See* ARK OF THE COVENANT.

COVENANT, BOOK OF THE [Heb. *sēp̱er habbᵉrîṯ*]. This name of the Hebrew code occurs in Ex. 24:7, where it is said that Moses read from "the book of the covenant." There are differences of opinion about the limits of this book. Some think that it comprises Ex. 20–23. The commonly accepted view today is that it runs from 20:22 to 23:33.

I. Form Analysis.–One of the milestones in the study of the form of the Covenant Code is the work of A. Alt, *Die Ursprünge des israelitischen Rechts* (1934). By using form analysis based on the form-historical method Alt reached the following conclusion: There are two kinds of laws in the Covenant Code, namely, apodictic and casuistic laws. These groups are distinguishable from each other by style. The apodictic laws occur in three different styles: the "Thou shalt not" type with the 2nd person singular and a negative command, the participial type, and the curse formulas. The casuistic laws are stated in the "if" style, with the transgression placed in the protasis and the penalty in the apodosis. Besides the differences in style, there is also a difference in origin. The apodictic laws are concerned with the sacred sphere of Yahweh. It is thus possible that these laws are of Israelite origin and can even be carried back to the time of Moses. The casuistic group on the other hand is in the common style of the ancient Near East and reflects a more advanced agricultural background, for these laws were borrowed from the Canaanites after the settlement in Palestine. In the early Israelite period the two different types of law were fused together.

Alt's views are criticized by various scholars. B. Landsberger is not at all convinced that two types of law are present. The change in type might be ascribed to a rapid change in sermon style. Other scholars, like T. Meek, point out that the apodictic style is not peculiar to Israelite legal material but occurs throughout Near Eastern jurisprudence. E. Gerstenberger has held that the origin of apodictic material must be sought in the larger family unit, the "clan" (*Sippe*; Heb. *mišpāḥâ*), while W. Richter has pointed out the importance of the school as a possible origin. Another onslaught was made on Alt's contention that the causuistic material was borrowed from the Canaanites. Both W. F. Albright and G. Mendenhall emphasized that Canaanite society was differently stratified and organized from Israelite society. It is especially on this point that the weakness of Alt's views is revealed. It seems impossible that the Israelites and even their forebears could have been without casuistic laws until they had reached Palestine, because they shared in the culture of the ancient Near East, where casuistic laws were an integral part of jurisprudence.

II. Mosaic Background.–The reliable OT tradition ascribes the Covenant Code to the legal activities of Moses. There is nothing in the laws that throws any doubt on the Mosaic origin. According to the critical standpoint of the Wellhausen tradition, these laws are regarded as the most ancient part of Hebrew legislation. They are assigned either to J or to E. Everyone will admit that it is difficult to determine when the Code was written down. Several things point, however, to a date in the time of Moses or earlier. The Covenant Code formed an integral part of the covenant that was made at Sinai. In a comparative study of Hittite vassal treaties and the OT covenant form, Mendenhall shows that a close relation between these two existed. The Hittite vassal treaties are to be dated in the 14th and 13th cents. B.C. This is roughly contemporaneous with Moses, and is thus a proof of the antiquity of the covenant idea of the OT and also of the laws of the Covenant Code. Certain laws, however, were added later as demanded by changed circumstances.

Certain scholars emphasize that an agricultural background implied by the Code makes it impossible that it could have been used during the wandering in the desert. This view is open to serious questioning. Studies by Nelson Glueck have shown that agricultural activities in seminomadic society were not an exception. Extensive agricultural activities took place in the Negeb during the time of Abraham. Almost every law of the Code can now be explained in terms of Glueck's studies. Nothing in the laws is incompatible with the organization of a seminomadic society. On the other hand, it must be remembered that some of the laws given to the Israelites at Sinai might be traditional laws from the times of the patriarchs, which were transmitted from family to family. These laws were reinstituted at Sinai as the common law of all the tribes and sanctioned by the Lord. The covenant was made between the Lord and the people. In this covenant were inserted certain stipulations according to which Israel must live. She was bound to observe the stipulations by the terms of the covenant and by the major party of the covenant, namely, Yahweh.

III. The Covenant Code and Near Eastern Codes.–After the discovery of the Code of Hammurabi in 1901-1902 at the ancient site of Susa, an enormous number of studies were produced which had the aim of comparing this code with Hebrew legal material. Some of these studies sought to establish that the Hebrew laws were dependent on the Babylonian laws. Our knowledge advanced meanwhile with the discovery of various other codes of the Near East, like the Sumerian laws published by Lutz and Langdon and finally by Steele, the Hittite by Hrozný, the Middle Assyrian by Scheil, the laws of Eshnunna by Goetze, and the Code of Ur-Nammu by Kramer. All these laws are from the 2nd and even 3rd millennium B.C. The oldest of them all is the Code of Ur-Nammu, from *ca.* 2050 B.C., although early reports of the discoveries at Tell Mardikh (Ebla) indicate that codified law may have been known by 2350 B.C. or even earlier.

There are many parallels between these laws and the Hebrew laws; indeed among laws in general there are many commonly recurring elements. All these laws, with a few exceptions in the Middle Assyrian group, are couched in the casuistic style, so that there is also a parallel trend in style with parts of the Covenant Code (the *mišpāṭîm*). It is very difficult to ascertain whether borrowing took place or not. The laws are separated by a long span of time and originated even in different countries. The parallels might be explained by noting that casuistic laws always have something in common because the same kind of problem arises in every community. On the other hand, to say that a common legal policy existed in the Near East gives a satisfactory explanation of certain parallel trends. One basic difference must be borne in mind: the different stratifications of the societies for which the laws were made. The Covenant Code was composed for a seminomadic society, the laws of Hammurabi for a highly developed community. Nearest to the Covenant Code stand the laws of the city Eshnunna, which provide important parallels to Hebrew law. All Mesopotamian codes are bound to the sun-god Utu (Sumerian) or Šamaš (Akkadian). The Covenant Code is regarded in the OT as the direct word of God (Ex. 24:3-8).

IV. Nature of the Laws.–We encounter in the Covenant Code, in contrast to legal material in the ancient Near East, a strong humane element. There is still present some degree of blood-revenge, the so-called *lex talionis* (e.g., Ex. 21:22-25), but the humane trend predominates. The widow and orphan must be protected, and even the enemy's ox or ass must be assisted in case of need (e.g., Ex. 22:22-24; 23:4f.). There is a high ethical standard in these laws which can be ascribed only to the ethical religion of Yahweh. A direct responsibility to the Lord is postulated, and this responsibility reaches down to human relations. Any kind of damage done to a person must be compensated by giving in kind or in silver. All these laws are scanctioned by God and made into a common policy of the Yahwistic religion.

Bibliography.–A. Alt, "The Origins of Israelite Law," in *OT History and Religion* (Eng. tr. 1967); B. Baentsch, *Das Bundesbuch* (1892); H. Cazelles, *Étude sur le code de l'alliance* (1946); G. R. Driver and J. Miles, *The Assyrian Laws* (1935); *The Babylonian Laws* (1952-1955, 2nd ed. 1957ff.), I-II; J. Friedrich, *Die hethitischen Gesetze* (1959); A. Goetze, *Laws of Eshnunna* (*AASOR*, 31, 1956); H.-J. Kraus, *Die prophetische Verkündigung des Rechts in Israel* (1957); G. Mendenhall, *Law and Covenant in Israel and the Near East* (1955); M. Noth, *The Laws in the Pentateuch* (Eng. tr. 1967), pp. 1-107; *ZDPV*, 73 (1957), 188f.; K. Baltzer, *The Covenant Formulary* (Eng. tr. 1971); E. Gerstenberger, *Wesen und Herkunft des "apodiktischen Rechts"* (1965); W. Richter, *Recht und Ethos* (1966); H. Schultz, *Das Todesrecht im AT* (1969); S. N. Paul, *Studies in the Book of the Covenant in the Light of Cuneiform and Biblical Law* (1970); A. Phillips, *Ancient Israel's Criminal Law* (1970); J. Liedke, *Gestalt und Bezeichnung alttestamentlicher Rechtssätze* (1971); F. C. Fensham, *VT*, 26 (1976), 262-274.

F. C. FENSHAM

COVENANT OF SALT [Heb. *b*[e]*rîṯ melaḥ*; Gk. *diathḗkē halós*]. As salt was regarded as a necessary ingredient of the daily food, and so of all sacrifices offered to Yahweh (Lev. 2:13), it became an easy step to the very close connection between salt and covenant-making. When men ate together they became friends. Cf. the Arabic expressions, "There is salt between us"; "He has eaten of my salt," which means partaking of hospitality which cemented friendship; cf. "eat the salt of the palace" (Ezr. 4:14). Covenants were generally confirmed by sacrificial meals and salt was always present. Since, too, salt is a preservative, it would easily become symbolic of an enduring covenant. So offerings to Yahweh were to be by a statute forever, "a covenant of salt for ever before the Lord" (Nu. 18:19). David received his kingdom forever from the Lord by a "covenant of salt" (2 Ch. 13:5). In the light of these conceptions the remark of Our Lord becomes the more significant: "Have salt in yourselves, and be at peace with one another" (Mk. 9:50).

E. B. POLLARD

COVENANT, THE NEW [Heb. *b^e^rîṯ ḥ^a^dāšâ* (Jer. 31:31); Gk. *diathḗkē kainḗ* (1 Cor. 11:25; 2 Cor. 3:6; He. 8:8; etc.), or *néa* (He. 12:24) (*kainḗ* normally meaning new in reference to quality, *néa* in reference to time)]; AV also NEW TESTAMENT; cf. He. 9:15, NEB.

I. Terminology
II. Christ's Use at the Last Supper
III. Use in Hebrews
  A. The Shed Blood
  B. The Mediator
  C. "Inheritance" and "Will"
  D. Relation to Jer. 31:31-34
  E. Relation to Ezekiel
IV. Paul's Contrast of the Old and New

I. Terminology.–The term "new covenant" necessarily implies an "old covenant," and we are reminded that God's dealings with His people in the various dispensations of the world's history have been in terms of covenant. The divisions of the Holy Scriptures keep this thought before us, the Old and the New Testaments or Covenants — the writings produced within the Jewish "church" being the writings or Scriptures of the old covenant, those within the Christian Church the Scriptures of the new covenant. The alternative name "Testament" — adopted into our English description through the Latin, as the equivalent of Heb. *b^e^rîṯ* and Gk. *diathḗkē*, which both mean a solemn disposition, compact, or contract — suggests the disposition of property in a last will or testament; but although *diathḗkē* may bear that meaning, *b^e^rîṯ* does not; and as the Greek usage in the NT seems especially governed by the OT usage, and the thought moves in a similar plane, it is better to keep to the term "covenant."

The one passage which seems to favor the "testament" idea is He. 9:16f. (the RV, which changed the AV "testament" into "covenant" in every other place, has left it in these two verses), but it is questionable whether even here the better rendering would not be "covenant." Certainly in the immediate context "covenant" is the correct translation, and "testament," if allowed to stand, is an application by transition from the original thought of a solemn compact to the secondary one of testamentary disposition (see III below, and *see* TESTAMENT).

The theological terms "Covenant of Works" and "Covenant of Grace" do not occur in Scripture, though the ideas covered by the terms, or at least the latter, may easily be found there. The "new covenant" here spoken of is practically equivalent to the Covenant of Grace established between God and His redeemed people, that again resting, as some think, upon the eternal Covenant of Redemption made between the Father and the Son, though there is no express reference to this in Scripture.

II. Christ's Use at the Last Supper.–While textual evidence seems to show that the word "new" in the Synoptic accounts of the Last Supper is not original, it definitely occurs in the words of institution as recorded by Paul (1 Cor. 11:25); and there need be little doubt that Jesus used it. The old covenant was so well known to these Jewish disciples that to speak of *the* covenant in this emphatic way, referring manifestly to something other than the old Mosaic covenant, was in effect to call it a "new" covenant. The expression, in any case, looks back to the old and points the contrast; but in the contrast there are points of resemblance.

It is most significant that Christ here connects the "new" covenant with His "blood." We at once think, as doubtless the disciples thought, of the transaction described in Ex. 24:7, when Moses "took the book of the covenant, and read it in the hearing of the people," indicating God's undertaking on behalf of His people and what He required of them; "and they said, 'All that the Lord has spoken will we do, and we will be obedient,'" thus taking up their part of the contract. Then comes the ratification. "Moses took the blood [half of which had already been thrown on the altar] and threw it upon the people, and said, 'Behold the blood of the covenant which the Lord has made with you in accordance with all these words'" (v. 8). The blood was sacrificial blood, the blood of the animals sacrificed as burnt offerings and peace offerings (vv. 5f.). The one half of the blood thrown on the altar tells of the sacrifice offered to God, the other half thrown on the people, of the virtue of the same sacrifice applied to the people; and so the covenant relation is fully brought about. Christ, by speaking of His blood in this connection, plainly indicates that His death was a sacrifice, and that through that sacrifice His people would be brought into a new covenant relationship with God. His sacrifice is acceptable to God and the virtue of it is to be applied to believers — so all the blessings of the new covenant are secured to them; the blood "is poured out for you" (Lk. 22:20). He specifically mentions one great blessing of the new covenant, the forgiveness of sins — "which is poured out for many for the forgiveness of sins" (Mt. 26:28).

III. Use in Hebrews.–*A. The Shed Blood.* This great thought is taken up in Hebrews and fully expounded. The writer draws out fully the contrast between the new covenant and the old by laying stress upon the perfection of Christ's atonement in contrast to the material and typical sacrifices (He. 9:11-23). He was "a high priest of the good things that have come," connected with "the greater and more perfect tent." He entered the heavenly holy place, "taking his own blood," not that of "goats and calves," and by that perfect offering He has secured "eternal redemption" in contrast to the temporal deliverance of the old dispensation. The blood of those typical offerings procured ceremonial cleansing; much more, therefore, shall the blood of Christ avail to cleanse the conscience "from dead works to serve the living God" — that blood which is so superior in value to the blood of the temporal sacrifices, yet resembles it in being sacrificial blood. It is the blood of Him "who through the eternal Spirit offered himself without blemish to God" (v. 14).

According to certain points of view, it is not the blood of Christ but His spirit of self-sacrifice for others that invests the cross with its saving power; and this last verse is sometimes cited to show that the virtue lies in the surrender of the perfect will, the shedding of the blood being a mere accident. But this is not the view of the NT writers. The blood-shedding is to them a necessity. Of course, it is not the natural, material blood, nor the mere act of shedding it, that saves. The blood is the life. The blood is the symbol of life; the blood shed is the symbol of life outpoured — of the penalty borne; and while great emphasis must be laid, as in this verse it is laid, upon Christ's perfect surrender of His holy will to God, yet the essence of the matter is found in the fact that He willingly endured the dread consequences of sin, and as a veritable expiatory sacrifice shed His precious blood for the remission of sins.

B. The Mediator. On the ground of that shed blood, as the writer goes on to assert, "Therefore he is the mediator of a new covenant, so that those who are called may receive the promised eternal inheritance, since a death has occurred which redeems them from the transgressions under the first covenant" (v. 15). Thus Christ fulfils the type in a twofold way: He is the sacrifice upon which the covenant is based, whose blood ratifies it, and he is also, like Moses, the mediator of the covenant. The death of Christ not only secures the forgiveness of those who are brought under the new covenant, but it was also for the redemption of the transgressions under the first covenant, implying that all the sacrifices gained their value by being types of Christ, and the forgiveness enjoyed by the people of God in former days was bestowed in virtue of the great Sacrifice to be offered in the fulness of time.

C. "Inheritance" and "Will." Not only does the blessing of perfect forgiveness come through the new covenant, but also the promise of the "eternal inheritance" in contrast to the earthly inheritance which, under the old covenant, Israel obtained. The mention of the inheritance is held to justify taking the word in the next verse as "will" (RSV) or "testament" (AV), the writer passing to the thought of a testamentary disposition, which is only of force after the death of the testator. Undoubtedly there is good ground for the analogy, and all the blessings of salvation which come to the believer may be considered as bequeathed by the Savior in His death, and accruing to us because He has died. It has, in that sense, tacitly to be assumed that the testator lives again to be His own executor and to put us in possession of the blessings. Still, we think there is much to be said in favor of keeping to the sense of "covenant" even here, and taking the clause which, rendered literally, is: "a covenant is of force [or firm] over the dead," as meaning that the covenant is established on the ground of sacrifice, that sacrifice representing the death of the maker of the covenant. The allusion may be further explained by a reference to Gen. 15:9f., 17, which has generally been considered as illustrating the ancient Semitic method of making a covenant: the sacrificial animals are divided, and the parties pass between the pieces, implying that they deserve death if they broke the engagement. The technical Hebrew phrase for making a covenant is "cut a covenant." *See* COVENANT (OT) III.B.

Whatever the particular application of the word in v. 17, the central idea in the passage is that death, blood-shedding, is necessary to the establishment of the covenant; and so the writer affirms that the first covenant was not dedicated without blood, quoting in proof the passage already cited from Ex. 24, and concludes that "without the shedding of blood there is no forgiveness of sins" (v. 22).

D. Relation to Jer. 31:31-34. This new covenant established by Christ was foreshadowed by the prophet Jeremiah, who uses the very word "new covenant" in describing it; and very likely Christ had that description in mind when He used the term, and meant His disciples to understand that the prophetic interpretation would in Him be realized. There is no doubt that the author of Hebrews had the passage in mind, for he leads up to the previous statement by quoting the whole statement of Jer. 31:31-34. He had in ch. 7 spoken of the contrast between Christ's priesthood "after the order of Melchizedek" (v. 11) and the imperfect Aaronic priesthood, and he designates Jesus as "the surety of a better covenant" (v. 22). Then in ch. 8, emphasizing the thought of the superiority of Christ's heavenly high-priesthood, he declares that Christ mediates a "better" covenant, "since it is enacted on better promises" (v. 6). The first covenant, he says, was not faultless, otherwise there would have been no need for a second; but the fault was not in the covenant but in the people who failed to keep it, though perhaps there is also the suggestion that the external imposition of laws could not suffice to secure true obedience. "For he finds fault with them when he says: 'The days will come, says the Lord, when I will establish a new covenant with the house of Israel and with the house of Judah.'" The whole passage (chs. 8–12) would repay careful study, but we need only note that not only is there prominence given to the great blessings of the covenant, perfect forgiveness and fulness of knowledge, but, as the very essence of the covenant — that which serves to distinguish it from the old covenant and at once to show its superiority and guarantee its permanence — there is this wonderful provision: "I will put my laws into their minds, and write them on their hearts, and I will be their God, and they shall be my people" (v. 10). This at once shows the spirituality of the new covenant. Its requirements are not simply given in the form of external rules, but the living Spirit possesses the heart; the law becomes an internal dominating principle, and so true obedience is secured.

E. Relation to Ezekiel. Ezekiel had spoken to the same effect, though the word "new covenant" is not used in the passage, in ch. 36:27: "I will put my spirit within you, and cause you to walk in my statutes and be careful to observe my ordinances." In ch. 37 Ezekiel again speaks of the great blessings to be enjoyed by the people of God, including cleansing, walking in God's statutes, recognition as God's people; and he distinctly says of this era of blessing: "I will make a covenant of peace with them; it shall be an everlasting covenant with them" (v. 26). Other important foreshadowings of the new covenant are found in Isa. 54:10; 55:3; 59:21; 61:8; Hos. 2:18-23; Mal. 3:1-4. We may well marvel at the spiritual insight of these prophets, and it is impossible to attribute their forecasts to natural genius; they can be accounted for only by divine inspiration.

The writer to the Hebrews returns again and again to this theme of the "new covenant"; in 10:16f. he cites the words of Jeremiah already quoted about writing the law on their minds, and remembering their sins no more. In 12:24, he speaks of "Jesus, the mediator of a new covenant," and "the sprinkled blood," again connecting the "blood" with the "covenant"; and finally, in 13:20, he prays for the perfection of the saints through the "blood of the eternal covenant."

IV. Paul's Contrast of the Old and New.–In 2 Cor. 3 Paul has an interesting and instructive contrast between the old covenant and the new. He begins by saying that "our sufficiency is from God, who has qualified us to be ministers of a new covenant, not in a written code but in the Spirit; for the written code kills, but the Spirit gives life" (vv. 5f.). The "written code" is the letter of the law, of the old covenant which could only bring condemnation; but the Spirit which characterizes the new covenant gives life, writes the law upon the heart. He goes on to speak of the old as that "dispensation of death" which nevertheless "came with such splendor" (v. 7), and he refers especially to the law; but the new covenant is "the dispensation of the Spirit," the "dispensation fo righteousness" (vv. 8f.), and has a far greater glory than the old. The message of this "new covenant" is "the gospel of Christ."

The glory of the new covenant is focused in Christ; it shines forth from Him. The glory of the old dispensation was reflected upon the face of Moses, but that glory was transitory and so was the physical manifestation (v. 13). The sight of the shining face of Moses awed the people of Israel and they revered him as a leader specially favored of God (vv. 7-13). When he had delivered his message he veiled his face, and thus the people could not see that the glow did not last. Every time he went into the divine presence he took off the veil, and afresh his face was lit up with glory; coming out with the traces of that glory lingering on his countenance he delivered his message to the people and again veiled his face (cf. Ex. 34:29-35), and thus the transitoriness and obscurity of the old dispensation were symbolized. In glorious contrast to that symbolical obscurity, the ministers of the gospel, of the new covenant, use great boldness of speech; the veil is done away in Christ (vv. 12ff.). The glory which comes through Him is perpetual, and fears no vanishing away. A. MCCAIG

COVER; COVERING. The RSV so translates thirty-seven Hebrew and Greek words. Most frequent is Heb. *kāsâ*; the Greek forms are *kalýptō* and derivative verbs. The AV also translates "fill," "overlay," "hide," etc.; NEB also "conceal," "wrap around," "clothe," "veil," "cancel," "uncover" (Heb. *ḥāpâ*, 2 S. 15:30; Est. 6:12), etc.

The basic meaning is to place something on, over, or in front of a person or object to shield or protect it. Yahweh's wings give protection (Heb. *sāḵaḵ*, Ps. 91:4; cf. noun *sēṯer*, Ps. 27:5 [AV "secret"]; noun *māsāḵ*, Isa. 22:8); with his hand He shields Moses from His fiery glory (Heb. *śāḵaḵ*, Ex. 33:22). The tabernacle and its contents are guarded by ram- and goatskin (NEB "porpoise-hide") coverings (Heb. *miḵseh*, Ex. 26:14; 35:11; 36:19; 39:34; 40:19; Nu. 3:25; also *kāsûy*, Nu. 4:5ff.; *ṣippûy*, Nu. 16:38f. [MT 17:3f.]; cf. Noah's ark, Gen. 8:13). The cloud, representing Yahweh's presence in the wilderness wanderings, gives protection (Nu. 16:42 [MT 17:7]; noun *māsāḵ*, Ps. 105:39).

Clothing covers a person (Gen. 9:23; Dt. 22:12; Jgs. 4:19; 2 K. 19:1f.; Isa. 37:1f.; Ezk. 16:10; 18:7, 16) or an object (Ezk. 16:18). In building activity, the meaning is "overlay," referring to the pitch applied to Noah's ark (Heb. *kāpar*, Gen. 6:14) and the ornamentation of the temple (1 K. 7:18, 41f.: 2 Ch. 4:12f.; *ṣāpâ*, 1 K. 6:15; AV, NEB, "carve"; *sapan*, 7:3). Figuratively, wealthy Tyre is decorated with precious stones (Heb. noun *mᵉsukkâ*, Ezk. 28:13).

Cover also means ensheathe or enwrap. Fat covers the entrails of the sacrificial animal (Ex. 29:13, 22; Lev. 3:3, 9, 14) and disease spreads over one's body (Lev. 13:12f.). Darkness envelops man (Heb. *šûp*, Ps. 139:11) and waters swell the sea (Hab. 2:14; cf. Heb. *mālē'*, 2 K. 3:25). Yahweh's glory covers the heavens (Hab. 3:3). He is depicted as surrounded by the seraphim's wings (Isa. 6:2) and with light (Heb. *'āṭâ*, Ps. 104:2); His hands are ensheathed with lightning (Job 36:32). Yahweh covers the dry bones with skin (Heb. *qāram*, Ezk. 37:6, 8). The various plagues blanket Egypt (Ex. 8:6 [MT 2]; 10:5, 15; 14:28; 15:5, 10), and masses of people (Nu. 22:11; Ps. 80:10 [MT 11]; Ezk. 38:9, 16) and animals (Isa. 60:6) swarm over a land.

Numerous qualities cover a person, implying pervasiveness: dishonor (Jer. 3:25; 51:51), shame (Ps. 44:15 [MT 16]; 69:7 [MT 8]; Ob. 10; Mic. 7:10; Heb. *'āṭâ*, Ps. 89:45 [MT 46]), scorn (Heb. *'āṭâ*, Ps. 71:13), cruelty (Mal. 2:16), violence (Heb. *'āṭap*, Ps. 73:6), horror (Ezk. 7:18), guile (Prov. 26:26), favor (Heb. *'āṭar*, Ps. 5:12 [MT 13]), and integrity (Heb. *'āṭâ*, Isa. 61:10).

Cover also means hide or conceal. The cause may be disease (Lev. 13:45) or mourning (2 S. 15:30; Est. 6:12 [NEB "uncover"]; Heb. *'āṭâ*, Ezk. 24:17). A woman veils herself in another's presence (Gen. 24:65), although a prostitute does not (38:15). Veiling is referred to in 1 Cor. 11:2-16 in the use of the Gk. terms *katá kephalḗs échō* (v. 4), *katakalýptō* (v. 7; also used for "to veil," "wear a veil" in v. 6), and *peribólaion* (usually, as in He. 1:12, an article of clothing) for the hair as "covering" in v. 15. (For the meaning of this difficult passage see the comms.) Covering the lips indicates silence at the lack of an oracle (Mic. 3:7). A cloud of incense screens the mercy seat (Lev. 16:13), as the olivewood cherubim the ark (2 Ch. 5:8; Heb. noun *sāḵaḵ*, 1 K. 8:7). Yahweh conceals the moon (Heb. *'āḥaz*, Job 26:9), but darkness is His covering (Heb. *sēṯer*, Ps. 18:11 [MT 12]; AV "pavilion"; NEB "hiding-place"). Figuratively, peoples are hidden by clouds (Ezk. 30:18) or waves (Jer. 51:42) in defeat; Samaria begs the mountains to conceal her from Yahweh's punishment (Hos. 10:8; cf. Lk. 23:30). Floodwaters prevent God's seeing Job (Job 22:11) and judges are blindfolded from the truth (9:24). Covering with blood (Job 16:18) or darkness (Ps. 44:19 [MT 20]) represents the obscurity of death. In the parable, one is not to hide a lamp with a vessel (Gk. *katakalýptō*, Lk. 8:16).

Similarly, to cover may indicate forgiveness (Ps. 32:1; Job 14:17; Rom. 4:7; cf. Neh. 4:5 [MT 3:37]). The RSV also translates Heb. *kāsâ* as "pardon" (Ps. 85:2 [MT 3]), "conceal" (Job 31:33; AV "cover"), and "forgive" (Prov. 17:9). Love covers a multitude of sins (Prov. 10:12; 1 Pet. 4:8; cf. Jas. 5:20). Heb. *kāpar*, "cover," indicates forgiveness (RSV, AV, "make atonement"; NEB "make expiation"; RSV also "forgive" Dt. 21:8; Ps. 78:38; 79:9; Ezk. 16:63), "pardon" (2 Ch. 30:18).

The nouns often have the simple meaning lid or top for a pit or well (Ex. 21:33; Heb. noun *māsāḵ*, 2 S. 17:19) or a utensil (Heb. noun *ṣāmîḏ*, Nu. 19:15; AV for Heb. *qaśwâ*, *qaśâ*, Ex. 25:29; 37:16; Nu. 4:7; RSV, NEB, "flagons"). A covering (Heb. *marḇēḏ*) is a fabric good, such as a bedspread (Prov. 7:16) or clothing (31:22).

A. C. M.

COVERED WAY [Heb. *mēṣāḵ*–'a covered walk']; AV CONCERT; NEB STRUCTURE. The "covered way" for the sabbath is mentioned in 2 K. 16:18 as a gallery belonging to the temple, concerning the purpose of which opinions differ. Some consider it to have been the place where the king stood or sat during the sabbath services; others, a public place for teaching; others, the way by which the priest entered the sanctuary on the sabbath.

COVERLET [Heb. *maḵbēr*] (2 K. 8:15); AV "thick cloth"; NEB BLANKET. A hapax legomenon of uncertain meaning, probably cloth that is either interlaced (cf. the cognates in Am. 9:9, "sieve"; Ex. 27:4, "grating"), or increased in some way; hence the suggestions of either netted cloth or thick cloth, blanket.

COVERT [Heb. *sukkâ*–'thicket' (Job 38:40; Ps. 10:9), *sēṯer*–'refuge,' 'secrecy' (Job 40:21; Ps. 31:20; Cant. 2:14; Isa. 32:2), *sōḵ*–'thicket' (Jer. 25:38)]; AV also SECRET PLACES, DEN; NEB also COVER, HIDDEN, CRANNIES, SHELTER, LAIR. The term "covert" is used only in the OT and denotes a hiding place or shelter.

COVET; COVETOUSNESS [Heb. *ḥāmaḏ*, also *'āwâ* (Prov. 21:26), *'āhēḇ* (Ps. 34:12), *beṣa'* (Isa. 57:17); Gk. *pleonexía, pleonéktēs* (Eph. 5:5), *epithymía, epithyméō, zēlóō* (Jas. 4:2)]; AV also DESIRE (Dt. 5:21; 7:25), DESIRE TO HAVE (Jas. 4:2), LOVE (Ps. 34:12), LUST (Rom. 7:7), CONCUPISCENCE (v. 8); NEB also DESIRE (Ps. 34:12), CRAVINGS (Prov. 21:26), "for a time" (Isa. 57:17, with LXX), RUTHLESS GREED (Mk. 7:22; Eph. 5:3; Col. 3:5), GREED (Lk. 12:15; Eph. 5:5), WANT (Acts 20:33), RAPACITY (Rom. 1:29), WRONG DESIRES (7:8), BE ENVIOUS (Jas. 4:2). (On Jer. 51:13, AV, *see* THREAD.) Both Heb. *ḥāmaḏ* and Gk. *epithymía* indicate strong desire; the bad sense of evil desire is present only in certain contexts. While the AV sometimes uses "covet" in a good sense (1 Cor. 12:31; 14:39), the RSV restricts its use to the unfavorable meanings. Gk. *pleonexía* always has the bad sense "greed," "avarice." For Heb. *beṣaʿ see* GAIN. *See also* DESIRE; GREED.

In the OT, covetousness is forbidden in the Decalogue; in the NT it is catalogued among the very gravest sins (Mk. 7:22; Eph. 5:3). Coveting is a basic and pervasive evil, for it is the very root of so many forms of sin: "Those who desire to be rich fall into temptation, into a snare, into many senseless and hurtful desires that plunge men into ruin and destruction" (1 Tim. 6:9). It lies behind biblical examples of theft (Josh. 7:21), lying (2 K. 5:20ff.), domestic trouble (Prov. 15:27), even murder (Ezk. 22:12). In Col. 3:5 it is termed "nothing less than idolatry" (NEB).

Covetousness has always been a very serious menace to mankind. It was one of the first sins that broke out after Israel had entered into the Promised Land (Achan, Josh. 7), and also in the early Christian Church immediately after its founding (Ananias and Sapphira, Acts 5); hence the many warnings against it. A careful reading of the OT will show that a very great part of the Jewish law — such as its enactments and regulations regarding duties toward the poor, toward servants, concerning gleaning, usury, pledges, gold and silver taken during war — was introduced and intended to counteract the spirit of covetousness.

Eerdmans maintains (*Expos*. [July 1909]) that the commandment, "You shall not covet your neighbor's house" (Ex. 20:17), meant to the Israelite that he should not take anything of his neighbor's possessions that were momentarily unprotected by their owner. Cf. Ex. 34:23ff. Thus it refers to a category of acts that is not covered by the commandment "You shall not steal." It is an oriental habit of mind from of old that when anyone sees abandoned goods which he thinks desirable, there is not the least objection to taking them. Ex. 20:17b is probably an explanation of what is to be understood by "house" in v. 17a.

Other examples of covetousness include Saul (1 S. 15:9, 19), Judas (Mt. 26:14f.), and Balaam (2 Pet. 2:15; Jude 11).

W. EVANS

COW [Heb. *pārâ*] (Gen. 32:14; 41:2ff.; Job 21:10; Am. 4:1; etc.); AV usually KINE; [*šôr*] (Ex. 34:19; Lev. 22:28); AV also OX; NEB also CATTLE; [*bāqār*] (Ezk. 4:15); [*ʿeglaṯ bāqār*] (Isa. 7:21); [*pārôṯ ʿālôṯ*] (1 S. 6:7, 10). The reproductive processes of the cow are mentioned in Lev. 22:27f.; Dt. 7:13; Job 21:10; etc., and the feeding of calves in 1 S. 6:7. Forty cows were part of Jacob's gift to Esau (Gen. 32:15), while Pharaoh's vision of seven fat and seven lean cows occurs in Gen. 41:1-36. In a figurative sense the term was used derogatively of Samaritan women in Am. 4:1. Similarly, in modern Israel "cow" is one of the most offensive terms that can be applied to a woman. As a general rule cows do not seem to have been sacrificed, and hence the circumstances of 1 S. 6:14 were evidently caused by the unusual conditions prevailing at the time.

See also CATTLE.

R. K. H.

Cow being milked, with calf tethered to her leg. Limestone relief from the sarcophagus of Princess Kawit at Deir el-Baḥri (11th Dynasty, 2135-2000 B.C.) (Egyptian Museum, Cairo)

COZ koz. *See* KOZ.

COZBI koz'bi [Heb. *kozbî*]. A Midianite woman, daughter of Zur, a chief of Midian. Zimri, a Simeonite, took her to his family's house against the orders of Moses. Both were killed by Phinehas at Shittim in a successful attempt to avert God's punishment of all Israel for this type of sin (Nu. 25:6-18).

COZEBA kō-zē'bə (1 Ch. 4:22). *See* ACHZIB **1.**

CRACKNEL. *See* BREAD V.

CRAFTINESS. *See* CRAFTY.

CRAFTS.

I. Sources of Our Knowledge.–The landscape of the Near East today displays impressive ruins of ancient architectural achievements. A multitude of small finds have also been unearthed, revealing the variety of crafts engaged in and the level of sophistication reached at different periods.

When the Royal Cemetery at Ur was excavated, dozens of gold objects (e.g., vessels, a helmet, daggers) and finely detailed jewelry in silver and filigree gold were found. These pieces are of a standard that has seldom been surpassed since, and they demonstrate what a skilled metalworker could do in 2500 B.C. — some five hundred years before Abraham's appearance at Ur. Similarly, when Abraham visited Egypt, the pyramids of Giza, the sole survivors of the Seven Wonders of the Ancient World, were even then centuries old. It is thus obviously a mistake to view early biblical personages such as Abraham as in a totally rustic or precivilized setting.

In addition to the small finds and architectural remains there are ancient reliefs, paintings, and models depicting various crafts and craftsmen at work. Egypt supplies the most information of this sort. Scenes of Egyptian shipwrights or masons at work provide insights into the techniques of that day as well as illustrations of the tools used.

Written records also bring us into closer touch with the early artisans. For example, two Mesopotamian texts precisely describe tanning methods and preparations in that country. There are also cuneiform texts in which Mesopotamian perfumers and glassblowers pass on their methods. Admittedly, written records sometimes allow our knowledge to proceed only so far. Thus, in spite of the wealth of technical terms pertaining to weaving in Mesopotamia, almost nothing has been deduced as to the type of loom used or the way it functioned.

II. Hebrew Craftsmen.–The Hebrews engaged in spinning and weaving (Ex. 35:25). They were able to draw from their own ranks craftsmen capable of building the tabernacle (Ex. 35:30-35). On the whole, however, the few references there are give the impression that before the Israelites came into contact with the people of Canaan and Phoenicia they had not developed any considerable technical skill. In fact, the decline in pottery and architecture that befell Palestine in the latter half of the 2nd millennium has been blamed on the coming of the Hebrews.

When David built his house he used carpenters and masons from Phoenicia (1 Ch. 14:1). David reminded Solomon of the large number of craftsmen, and the variety of their skills, on hand to construct the temple (1 Ch. 22:15f.). Solomon added to this number by importing additional workers from Phoenicia (2 Ch. 2:7, 13f.; 1 K. 5:18). By the time Nebuchadrezzar was pillaging Jerusalem one thousand craftsmen were available for deporting to Babylon (2 K. 24:16). There is an indication that when Jerusalem was rebuilt men of a like trade were grouped together (Neh. 3:8, 31f.). In spite of these hints that a body of Israelite craftsmen did develop — at least by the 6th cent. B.C. — it is usually held that the Hebrews never became greatly interested or especially creative in the arts. Certainly the Mosaic injunction against graven images must have created apathy toward at least some of the arts.

In any event it has been largely impossible to identify examples of Hebrew craftsmanship. In pottery, at least, this results from the absence of an Israelite ceramic tradition which could guide the Hebrew craftsman. Therefore the Israelite pots were copies of local Canaanite forms. The same consequence is probably true for most other crafts the Hebrews engaged in and would explain why, in the material things of life, their culture was little distinguishable from that of the other inhabitants of Palestine. Only in one field, gem cutting, has it been suggested that the Israelite craftsman attained a high degree of proficiency. Very skillfully graven seals with Hebrew inscriptions have indeed been found; but even here it is doubtful how many are really the work of this people.

III. Internationalism in the Crafts.–David's and Solomon's importation of foreign workers was not unique in the ancient Near East. For example, the Hittite King Ḫattusilis III borrowed a sculptor from the faraway Kassites. (A letter is preserved in which he requests a second sculptor.) As the craftsmen moved they took with them their technological knowledge and peculiar artistic motifs. Although their hosts might not be interested in the foreigner's language or religion, they did not hesitate to adopt his techniques and styles. Consequently, much of the Solomonic temple is "Phoenician." So widespread was the artistic borrowing that some cultures never originated a style of their own.

At times a feeling of cosmopolitanism existed in the Near East. Egyptians welcomed Aegean gifts and Canaanites coveted ornaments "made in Egypt." There are groups of objects made in obvious imitation of foreign originals. Mesopotamian lists of Syro-Palestinian booty refer to their superior multicolored garments as often as to gold and silver.

Despite this intensity of intercourse it is possible to speak of specific schools. Although the Hittites borrowed sculptors from Mesopotamia, their art shows that an original and competent school existed in Anatolia in the 14th and 13th centuries. In the glyptic art of the Near East there is a wholesale mixing of motifs and styles. But even here individual Akkadian, Assyrian, and other schools can be identified.

IV. Crafts Directly or Indirectly Mentioned in the Bible.– Only a list of the crafts need be given. For a fuller treatment see under the separate articles.

Brickmaking (*see* BRICK).
Carpentering (*see* TOOLS; CARPENTER).
CARVING.
Ceramics (*see* POTTER).
Dyeing (*see* COLOR; DYE; FULLER).
Embroidering (*see* EMBROIDERY).
Glassmaking (*see* GLASS).
Masonry (*see* MASON).
Metalworking (*see* METAL).

Scenes of arts and trades, from the tomb of the nome chieftain Amenemhat at Beni-hasan (12th Dynasty, 1971-1928 B.C.). Pictured are (from top): (1) production of flint knives, sandals; (2) bows, barrels, arrows, chairs, boxes; 3) goldsmiths; 4) potters; and 5) flax cultivation and linen manufacture. (Egypt Exploration Society)

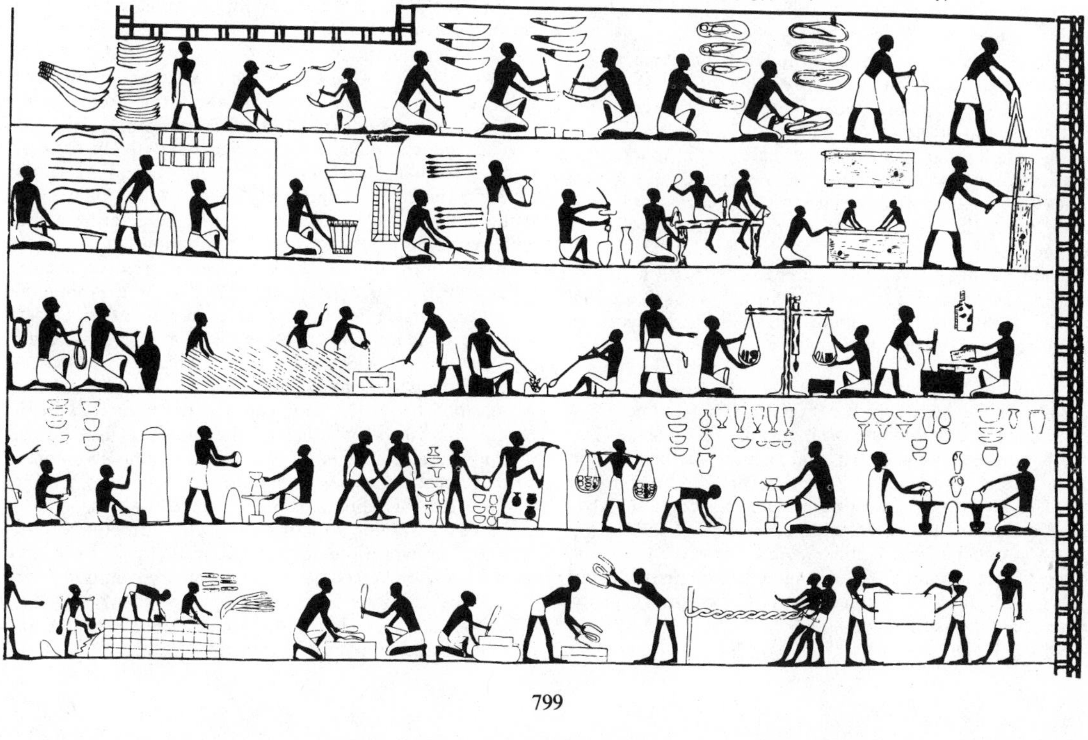

Perfumery (*see* PERFUME).
Plastering (*see* PLASTER).
Spinning (*see* SPINDLE; WEAVING).
TANNING (*see* TANNER).
Tentmaking (*see* TENT).

Bibliography.–M. Burrows, *What Mean These Stones?* (1941); R. J. Forbes, *Studies in Ancient Technology* (1964); H. Frankfort, *Art and Architecture of the Ancient Orient* (1959); A. Lucas, *Ancient Egyptian Materials and Industries* (4th ed. 1962).

A. J. HOERTH

CRAFTY [Heb. *ḥāḵām*] (2 S. 13:3); AV SUBTIL; NEB SHREWD; [*ʿārōm, ʿārûm*] (Job 5:12; 15:5; Ps. 83:3); NEB also DECEIT (Job 15:5), CUNNING (Ps. 83:3); [Gk. *panoúrgos*] (2 Cor. 12:16); NEB UNSCRUPULOUS; **CRAFTINESS** [Heb. *ʿōrem* (Job 5:13); Gk. *panourgía*]; NEB also TRICK (Lk. 20:23), CUNNING (1 Cor. 3:19); **DEAL CRAFTILY** [Heb. *nāḵal* (Ps. 105:25); Gk. *katasophízomai* (Acts 7:19)]; AV DEAL SUBTILLY; NEB DOUBLE-DEALING (OT), "make a crafty attack (on)" (NT). The basic meaning of Heb. *ḥāḵām* is "wise"; in the broader senses it can mean "skillful," "prudent," "cunning"; in 2 S. 13:3 the word is applied to Jonadab, who devised an evil plan to enable Amnon to rape Tamar. In Proverbs *ʿārûm* has the good connotation "sensible" or "prudent" (NEB "clever") (e.g., 12:16, 23; 13:16; 22:3), but elsewhere it means "shrewd" in a bad sense (like the related forms *ʿārōm*, *ʿōrēm*). In Ps. 105:25 *nāḵal* means acting in a cleverly deceitful manner.

The Gk. *panourgía* means literally "doing everything," with the usual bad implication "stopping at nothing," hence "unscrupulous." Paul's use in 2 Cor. 12:16 is ironic, thus the RSV and NEB add "you say."

J. W. D. H.

CRAG [Heb. *ṣûr* (Jer. 18:14), *selaʿ* (51:25)]; AV ROCK; NEB "rocky (slope)" (18:14), TERRACE; **ROCKY CRAG** [Heb. *šēn hasselaʿ* (1 S. 14:4), *šēn-selaʿ* (Job 39:28)]; AV also SHARP ROCK (1 S. 14:4), "forefront" (for *šēn,* v. 5); NEB "sharp column of rock" (14:4), "crevice in the rock" (Job 39:28). In mountainous country composed of sedimentary rocks, cliffs are formed on a slope where hard strata cover softer strata. The soft strata wear away more rapidly, undermining the hard strata, which project for a time but finally break off; the fragments roll down to form the talus slope at the foot of the cliff. Since the breaking off of the hard strata occurs irregularly, sometimes projecting crags are left at the top of the cliff and at times lower down.

Two such crags, named Bozez and Seneh, marked the scene of the exploit of Jonathan described in 1 S. 14. These crags also formed secure resting places for predatory birds; the eagle is said to perch there to discern its prey (Job 39:27-29).

The RSV uses "crag" to render two words for "rock" in Jer. 18:14 and 51:25. In the former passage AV "field" is emended to "Sirion," so the passage becomes a reference to crags on Mt. Hermon.

A. E. DAY
K. G. JUNG

CRANE [Heb. *ʿāḡûr*]; NEB WRYNECK. The RSV mentions the crane twice; once because of its noise (Isa. 38:14; omitted by the NEB), and again in the description of migrating birds (Jer. 8:7). However, the meaning of the Hebrew term is uncertain, and the cognate Akk. *igirū* does not help the identification specifically. If it was a member of the family *Gruidae,* it was one of the largest Palestinian birds, along with the ostrich and pelican. G. R. Driver opted for a species of the genus *Jynx,* but this also is uncertain.

See G. R. Driver, *PEQ,* 87 (1955), 132. R. K. H.

CRASH; CRASHING [Heb. *šeḇer*] (Job 41:25 [MT 17]; Isa. 30:13; Zeph. 1:10); AV also BREAKING; NEB also "lashings of his tail" (Job 41:25); [*šāʾâ, šôʾâ*] (Job 30:14; Isa. 37:26); AV DESOLATION, "lay waste"; NEB also "tumble down"; [*qôl*] (Ps. 77:18); AV VOICE; NEB SOUND; [*rē(a)ʿ*] (Job 36:33); AV NOISE; NEB THUNDER. *Šeḇer,* from the verb *šāḇar,* "break," denotes a breaking or crushing. In the hiphil form (as in Isa. 37:26) *šāʾâ* means lay waste. *Rē(a)ʿ* literally signifies "shouting," while *qôl* simply means "voice." In most of these passages the RSV uses "crash" or "crashing" to describe the cosmic manifestations of divine power. In Job 41:25 the Lord is referring to His power as manifest in the fearsomeness of the Leviathan. N. J. O.

CRATES krā'tēz [Gk. *Kratēs*]. Governor of the Cyprians, left as deputy of Sostratus when the latter, who was governor of Jerusalem, was summoned to Antioch by Antiochus Epiphanes as the result of a dispute with Menelaus (2 Macc. 4:29). As Cyprus was not at the time in the possession of Antiochus, the words generally have been taken to mean Crates "who had formerly been, or afterward was, governor of the Cyprians." The Vulgate translates the Greek into *Sostratus autem praelatus est Cypriis*.

CRAWLING THINGS [Heb. *zōḥ^{a}lê*] (Dt. 32:24; Mic. 7:17); AV SERPENTS, WORMS; NEB "creatures that crawl"; [*remeś*] (Hab. 1:14); AV CREEPING THINGS; NEB GLIDING CREATURES. Deuteronomy refers to poisonous snakes; Micah, to reptiles in general; Habakkuk, to water animals, excluding fish, caught in a net.

CREATION [Heb. verb *bārāʾ* (Gen. 2:3), noun *yeṣer* (Hab. 2:18); Gk. *ktísis*].

I. Theistic Creation Versus Other Views
II. Creation in the Bible
III. Creation a Free, Personal Act
IV. Creation and Time
V. Source of Creation
VI. Purpose of Creation

I. Theistic Creation Versus Other Views.–Much negative ground has to be cleared away for any modern discussion of the doctrine of creation. No idea of creation can now be taken as complete which does not include, besides the world as at first constituted, all that to this day is in and of creation. For God does not create being that can exist independently of Him; rather, His preserving agency is inseparably connected with His creative power. We have long ceased to think of God's creation as a machine left, completely made, to its own automatic working. With such a doctrine of creation a theistic evolution would be quite incompatible.

Just as little do we think of God's creative agency as merely that of a first cause, linked to the universe from the outside by innumerable sequences of causes and effects. Nature in its entirety is as much His creation today as it ever was. The dynamic ubiquity of God, as efficient energy, is to be affirmed. God is still All and in all, but this in a way sharply distinguished from pantheistic views, whether of the universe as God, or of God as the universe. Of His own freedom He creates, so that gnostic theories of natural and necessary emanation are left far behind. Not only have the "carpenter" and the "gardener" theories — with, of course, the architect or world-builder theory of Plato — been dismissed; not only has the conception of evolution been proved harmonious with creative end, plan, purpose, ordering, guidance; but evolutionary science is thought by some to have given the thought of theistic evolution

Fragments of the third tablet of *Enuma Elish* ("When on high"), the Assyrian creation epic recounting the struggle between cosmic order and chaos. These copies from Ashurbanipal's library at Nineveh are similar to older Babylonian versions, which in part may be traced to Sumerian originals of the 3rd millennium B.C. (Trustees of the British Museum)

its best base or grounding. The theistic conception is that the world — that all cosmic existences, substances, events — depend upon God.

The doctrine of creation — of the origin and persistence of all finite existences — as the work of God, is a necessary postulation of the religious consciousness. Such consciousness is marked by deeper insight than belongs to science. The underlying truth is the antipantheistic one, that the energy and wisdom by which the creation came into being are different in kind from their product. For science can only trace the continuity of sequences in all nature, while in creation, in its primary sense, this law of continuity must be transcended, and the world viewed solely as product of divine intelligence, immanent in its evolution. For God is the Absolute Reason, always immanent in the developing universe. Apart from the cosmogonic attempts at the beginning of Genesis, which are clearly religious and ethical in scope and character, the OT furnishes no theoretic account of the manner and order in which the creative process is carried on.

II. Creation in the Bible.–The early chapters of Genesis were, of course, not given to reveal the truths of physical science, but they recognize creation as marked by order, continuity, law, adaptable power of productiveness in the different kingdoms, unity of the world, and progressive advance. The Genesis cosmogony teaches a process of becoming as well as a creation (*see* EVOLUTION). That cosmogony has been recognized by Haeckel as meritoriously marked by the two great ideas of separation or differentiation, and of progressive development or perfecting of the originally simple matter. The OT presents the conception of time-worlds or successive ages, but its real emphasis is on the energy of the divine word, bringing into being things that did not exist.

The OT and the NT, in their doctrine of creation, recognize no eternal matter before creation. We cannot say that the origin of matter is excluded from the Genesis account of creation, and this quite apart from the use of *bārā'* as admitting of material and means in creation. But it seems unwise to build such an interpretation upon passages of Genesis that can afford only an exegetically insecure basis. The NT seems to favor the derivation of matter from the nonexistent — that is to say, the time-worlds were due to the effluent divine word or originative will, rather than to being built out of God's own invisible essence. So the best exegesis interprets He. 11:3.

In OT books such as Psalms, Proverbs, and Jeremiah, creation is expressly declared to be the work of wisdom — a wisdom not disjoined from goodness, as is yet more fully brought out in Job. The heavens declare the glory of God, the world manifests or reveals Him to our experience, as taken up and interpreted by the religious consciousness. The primary fact of the beginning of the time-worlds — the basic fact that the worlds came into being by the word of God — is something apprehensible only by the power of religious faith, as the only principle applicable to the case (He. 11:3). Such intuitive faith is really an application of first principles in the highest sense — and a truly rational one (*see* LOGOS). In creation, God is but expressing or acting out the conscious Godhood that is in Him. In it the thought of His absolute wisdom is realized by the action of His perfect love. It is philosophically necessary to maintain that God, as the Absolute Being, must find the end of creation in Himself. If the end were external to and independent of Him, then He would be conditioned by it.

III. Creation a Free, Personal Act.–What the religious consciousness is concerned to maintain is the absolute freedom of God in the production of the universe, and that He is so much greater than the universe that existence has been by Him bestowed on all things that do exist. This truth permeates the Scriptures, from first to last. Neither Kant nor Spencer, from data of self-consciousness or sense-perception, can rise to the conception of creation, for they both fail to reach the idea of divine personality. The inconceivability of creation has been pressed by Spencer, the idea of a self-existent Creator, through whose agency it has been made, being to him unthinkable. As if it were not a transparent sophism, which Spencer's own scientific practice refuted, that a hypothesis may not have philosophical or scientific value because it is what we call unthinkable or inconceivable. As if a true and sufficient cause were not enough, or a divine act of will were not a *vera causa*. Dependent existence inevitably leads thought to demand existence that is not dependent.

IV. Creation and Time.–Creation is certainly not disproved by evolution, which does not explain the origin of the homogeneous stuff itself, and does not account for the beginning of motion within it. Of the original creative action, lying beyond mortal ken or human observation, science — as concerned only with the manner of the process — is obviously in no position to speak. Creation may, in an important sense, be said not to have taken place in time, since time cannot be posited prior to the existence of the world. The difficulties of the ordinary hypothesis of a creation in time can never be surmounted, so long as we continue to make eternity mean simply indefinitely prolonged time. Augustine was no doubt right when, from the human standpoint, he declared that the world was not made in time, but with time. Time is itself a creation simultaneous with, and conditioned by, world-creation and movement. To say, in the ordinary fashion, that God created in time, is apt to make time appear independent of God, or God dependent upon time. Yet the time-forms enter into all our psychological experience, and a concrete beginning is unthinkable to us.

The time-conditions can be transcended only by some deeper intuition than mere logical insight can supply — by such intuitive endeavor, in fact, as is realized in the necessary belief in the self-existent God. If such an eternal Being acts or creates, He may be said to act or create in eternity; and it is legitimate enough, in such wise, to speak of His creative act as eternal. Clearly did Aquinas perceive that we cannot affirm an eternal creation impossible, the creative act not falling within our categories of time and space. The question is purely one of God's free volition, in which — and not in "nothing" — the Source of the world is found.

V. Source of Creation.–This brings us to notice the frequently pressed objection that creation cannot be out of nothing, since out of nothing comes nothing. This would mean that matter is eternal. But the eternity of matter, as something other than God, means its independence of God, and its power to limit or condition Him. We have, of course, no direct knowledge of the origin of matter, and the conception of its necessary self-existence is fraught with hopeless difficulties and absurdities. The axiom that out of nothing nothing comes, is not contradicted in the case of creation. The universe comes from God; it does not come from nothing. Besides, the axiom does not really apply to the world's creation, but only to the succession of its phenomena. Entity does not spring from non-entity. But there is an opposite and positive truth, that something presupposes something, in this case rather someone.

It is enough to know that God has in Himself the powers and resources adequate for creating, without being able to define the ways in which creation is effected by Him. It is a sheer necessity of rational faith or spiritual reason that the something which conditions the world is neither *hýlē* (Gk.) nor elemental matter, but personal spirit or originative will. We have no right to suppose the world made out of nothing, and then to identify, as Erigena did, this "nothing" with God's own essence. What we have a right to maintain is that what God creates or calls into being owes its existence to nothing save His will alone, ground of all actualities. Preexistent personality is the ground and the condition of the world's beginning.

In this sense, its beginning may be said to be relative rather than absolute. God is always antecedent to the universe — its *prius,* cause, and creator. It remains an effect, and sustains a relation of causal dependence upon Him. If we say, like Cousin, that God of necessity creates eternally, we run the risk of falling into Spinozistic pantheism, identifying God, in excluding from Him absolute freedom in creation, with the impersonal and unconscious substance of the universe. Or if, with Schelling, we posit in God something which is not God — a dark, irrational background, which original ground is also the ground of the divine existence — we may try to find a basis for the matter of the universe, but we are in danger of being merged — by conceptions tinged with corporeity — in that form of pantheism for which God is but the soul of the universe.

The universe, we feel sure, has been caused; its existence must have some ground; even if we held a philosophy so idealistic as to make the scheme of created things one grand illusion, an illusion so vast would still call for some explanatory cause. Even if we are not content with the conception of a first cause, acting on the world from without and antecedently in time, we are not yet freed from the necessity of asserting a cause. An underlying and determining cause of the universe would still need to be postulated as its ground.

Even a universe held to be eternal would need to be accounted for — we should still have to ask how such a universe came to be. Its endless movement must have direction and character imparted to it from some immanent ground to underlying cause. Such a self-existent and eternal world-ground or first cause is, by an inexorable law of thought, the necessary correlate of the finitude, or contingent character of the world. God and the world are not to be taken simply as cause and effect, for modern metaphysical thought is not content with such a mere *ens extra-mundanum* for the ground of all possible experience. God, self-existent cause of the ever-present world and its phenomena, is the ultimate ground of the possibility of all that is.

VI. Purpose of Creation.–Such a deity, as *causa sui,* creatively bringing forth the world out of His own potence, cannot be allowed to be an arbitrary resting place, but must be a truly rational ground of thought. Nor can His creation be an aimless and mechanical universe: it is fully imbued with end or purpose that tends to reflect the glory of the eternal and personal God, who is its Creator in a full and real sense. But the divine action is not dramatic: of His working we can truly say, with Isa. 45:15, "Truly, thou art a God who hidest thyself." As creation becomes progressively disclosed to us, its glory, as revealing God, ought to excite within us an always deeper sense of the sentiment of Ps. 8:1, 9, "O Lord, our Lord, how majestic is thy name in all the earth!"

See also CREATOR; ANTHROPOLOGY III; WORLD.

Bibliography.–K. Barth, *CD*, III/1f.; R. Bultmann, *Theology of the NT* (Eng. tr., 2 vols., 1951, 1955); W. Eichrodt, *Theology of the OT,* II (*OTL,* Eng. tr. 1967); L. Gilkey, *Maker of Heaven and Earth* (1959, 1965); E. Jacob, *Theology of the OT* (Eng. tr. 1958); P. Prenter, *Creation and Redemption* (Eng. tr. 1955, 1967); E. Stauffer, *Theology of the NT* (Eng. tr. 1955); G. von Rad, *Theology of the OT* (Eng. tr. 1962); *TDNT*, III, *s.v.* κτίζω κτλ. (Foerster); *TDOT*, II, *s.v.* "bārā'" (Bernhardt, Botterweck, and Ringgren).

J. LINDSAY

CREATOR [Heb. *bôrē'*; Gk. *ho ktísas*, *ktistḗs*].

I. God the Creator.–The clear teaching of Holy Scripture is that God is the Creator of the world. Significantly, the Bible does not begin with the Creator in general and then move on more narrowly to the God of Israel. Its affirmation from the very first is that Yahweh is the Creator. He has created all things, heaven and earth and all that is in them.

This witness is taken up again in the NT, with additional specification. It is by the Word that the world was made; without Him was not anything made that was made (Jn. 1:3). The Son is the one of whom it is said that the heavens are the works of His hands (He. 1:10). By Jesus Christ all things were created (Col. 1:16). The full extent of creation is brought out in the clearest possible way in the NT. When it is said that all things are created (Eph. 3:9), this includes heaven and earth and sea and all that is in them (Rev. 10:6; Acts 4:24; Col. 1:16). The triune God, as Creator, is marked off from all else, which is creature.

II. Creator "ex nihilo."–It must be stressed that the biblical creation is true creation. Although various words are used, some of them denoting no more than fashioning or making, creation in the Bible is more than manufacture or artistic arrangement on the assumption of existing material. God is not just an architect or builder who works with what is at hand. Nor is creation an emanation from God. Nor is it a natural product in the sense that a child is procreated by its parents. There is no organic connection between God and the cosmos. God is the Creator in the strict sense, i.e., He creates out of nothing (*ex nihilo*). In the OT this finds expression in God's transcendence (Ps. 139:15, etc.) and in His being able to destroy as well as create (Ps. 102:26-28). It is more explicitly formulated in Gen. 1:1 and Isa. 44:6, particularly in the contrast between the eternity of God and the fact that the world comes into being. In the NT the variants of "from the beginning (or "foundation") of the world" (Mk. 10:6; Rom. 1:20; 2 Pet. 3:4) indicate plainly that the world as a totality had a beginning. They leave no place for preexistent matter, and the stress on God's positive action leaves no place for emanation. Also to be considered are statements like Rom. 4:17 and He. 11:3.

III. Creator by the Word.–The agent of creation is the word. Already in Gen. 1 we read that God spoke and it was done (v. 3, etc.). It is by God's word that the heavens were made (Ps. 33:8). God summons what is not into existence, and from its very origin creation is set in a relation of obedience to command. The creative word of God is not understood as a magical incantation that carries intrinsic potency irrespective of its meaning. God is no magician; His word is a meaningful command to which there is obedience. A personal element enters here. God is the loving as well as the commanding God. He cannot be viewed abstractly as a mere first cause. He exercises an initiative of gracious power, and the world of His creating is an organic world; it is not an effect, nor a sum of secondary causes and effects. The same truth is brought out with even greater clarity in the NT. The word by which the world of heaven and earth was made is the Word which was with God and which is God (Jn. 1:1ff.). It is the Word that became flesh (Jn. 1:14). In and by this Word, God calls into being things that are not — a paradox that throws the element of true creation into all the greater relief. As creator, God is the Lord of heaven and earth (Mt. 11:25f.). His will is to be done by all His creatures (Mt. 6:10). He is worthy to receive glory and honor and power because He has created all things (Rev. 4:11).

IV. Good Creator.–The Creator is the Almighty. His creative word is a word of power and wisdom (Jer. 10:12; Prov. 3:19; 8:27; etc.). He is the God of glory and majesty who sits on the throne from which proceed lightnings and thunderings and voices (Rev. 4:1ff.). But this powerful Creator is good. "He saw every thing he had made, and, behold, it was very good" (Gen. 1:31). He can be compared to precious stones, for in Him, and in His work, there is no flaw (Rev. 4:3, 6). He is the Father in heaven who so loves man that He sends sun and rain on both the just and the unjust, i.e., irrespective of whether they bring Him anything in return (Mt. 5:45). If the combination of God's power and goodness raises a serious problem of theodicy in view of manifest evils in creation, it should be noted that creation as we know it is in a real sense fallen creation and that the Creator is at work to bring it back to perfection.

V. Creator and Purpose.–This leads us to the further biblical truth that the Creator has a purpose. He does not create out of any outer necessity. He is not Himself a blind process. There is no eternal creating coextensive with the life of the Creator. God is free and sovereign. He resolves to create (Gen. 1:3, 6, 9, 11, 14, 20, 24, 26). Nor does He do so as an act of mere caprice. Creation itself gives evidence of planning (Gen. 1). Man is given a task in relation to creation (Gen. 1:26). God wills a free response of obedience to His own will (Mt. 6:10). He has created all things unto Christ (Col. 1:16). Creation moves toward a consummation of all things, when all things will be subject to the Son, the second man, and the Son Himself will be subject to the Father, that God may be in all (1 Cor. 15:28). God has created all things for His own pleasure (Rev. 4:11), not in the sense of selfish gratification, but in the sense of purposeful and meaningful activity. Even the fall cannot arrest the divine purpose. God brings it to fulfillment in the new creation in Christ. Christians already belong to this new creation; they are a new creation by the Word (2 Cor. 5:17; Gal. 6:15).

VI. Doctrine of God the Creator.–The doctrine of God the Creator finds credal expression in the phrase: "I believe in God the Father Almighty, Creator of heaven and earth." Since the witness of the OT and NT is plain in this matter, the clause relating to creation might seem to be superfluous. It was probably included in witness against the varied errors that threatened from the side of Gnosticism, namely, distinction between the creator of this world and the true God, the description of this creator as a mere demiurge, the belief that the world of matter is evil rather than good, and also the excessive prominence of the idea of emanation in relation to the true God.

VII. Creator As Redeemer.–Philosophical intrusion has been responsible for the attempt to separate the doctrine of creation from the special revelation of God and to make it a basic constituent of natural theology. On this view God may be known generally as Creator even though He is not known as the God of Israel or as the God incarnate in Jesus Christ. Indeed, His existence may be metaphysically demonstrated in terms of a first cause or ontological necessity. In support of this view, appeal is sometimes made to Paul's statement in Acts 17:24, though it is conveniently overlooked that Paul is here declaring the God of revelation who is merely the great Unknown for his audience. In fact, the Bible itself does not take the path of a demonstration of God as Creator followed by His specific revelation as Redeemer. God ought to be known in and through His creation, but in fact He is not (Rom. 1:20f.) and for sinful man to try to force open again this door which he himself has closed can only result in confusion. For one thing, the logical demonstration will always be insecure. For another, it can just as easily lead to a mere first cause or static abstraction as to the true and living God. Even if it does lead to God, this might well be the God of deism, or pantheism, or general theism, and a gulf has still to be bridged to the true God. Along the whole path is a battery of philosophical problems regarding the relation of this God to the world, e.g., to causality, to time and space, to finitude. At the end, even if things turn out well, what emerges is still only man's concept of God, and not God Himself in His dynamic personal being as Father and Savior.

In contrast, the biblical presentation is a presentation of God Himself. This does not mean that it is experience instead of thought. It means that God declares Himself. God steps forth in His living reality. God reveals Himself, the First and the Last; the God of Abraham, Isaac, and Jacob; Yahweh, the God of Israel; the God and Father of the Lord Jesus Christ; the Alpha and Omega; the Almighty. This God, the God of history, the God of salvation, is also the Creator, the Lord of heaven and earth. It is from Him, from His revelation, that we are to learn about the Creator, for He is the Creator. It is from Him that we learn about the relation of the creature to Him. It is from Him that we are to know the Creator, i.e., God Himself as Creator, Jesus Christ as the Word of creation, and to enter into the fulfillment of His creative purpose for us.

See also CREATION.

Bibliography.–*ERE*; *TDNT*, III, *s.v.* κτίζω (Foerster); *BDTh*; *CD*, III/1; J. N. D. Kelley, *Early Christian Creeds* (2nd ed. 1960).

G. W. BROMILEY

CREATURE. The word "creature," as it occurs in the NT, often translates the Gk. *ktísis* or *ktísma,* from the verb *ktīzō*, "create." In the book of Revelation "creature" generally renders *zṓon* (*see* CREATURE, LIVING). In the OT it stands for words that have in the original no reference to creation, but come from other roots. Heb. *nepeš ḥayyâ* (lit. "a breathing creature") occurs in the accounts of the Creation and the Flood and at the close of the lists of clean and unclean animals in Lev. 11:46; while *ḥay* (lit. "a living thing") occurs thirteen times in Ezk. 1, 3, and 10 (*see* CREATURE, LIVING). *Rāmaś* and *remeś* occur frequently in Genesis, generally translated "CREEPING THING." *'Ōḥîm*, HOWLING CREATURES, occurs once only in Isa. 13:21. *See also* CREATION.

CREATURE, LIVING [Heb. usually *ḥayyâ* or *nepeš ḥayyâ*; Gk. *zṓon*, also *ktísma* (Rev. 8:9)]; AV also THING LIVING, BEAST; NEB also LIVING THING, CREATURE. Heb. *ḥayyâ* is a feminine adjective based on the root *ḥyh*, "to live." These Hebrew and Greek terms denote water or land animals and celestial beings.

I. Living Creatures as Animals.–In the creation narrative of Gen. 1 the term *ḥayyâ* is translated "living creature," referring collectively to water creatures (1:20f.; cf. Ezk. 47:9) in contrast to birds of the sky (Ps. 104:25), and to land animals (Gen. 1:28) in contrast to birds and fishes (Gen. 8:19; Lev. 11:2). The meaning of every "living creature" in Gen. 2:19 (here expressly *nepeš ḥayyâ*) includes cattle, birds, and beasts of the field (v. 20). In the flood story Yahweh vows not to destroy again "every living creature as I have done" (Gen. 8:21), which make up all land animals and birds (8:19; 9:10). These are again included in the "living creatures" of the covenant made with Noah (9:12, 15f.). *Ḥayyâ* can also refer in a more restricted sense to wild, untamed animals (RSV "beasts") in contrast to "cattle" (*behēmâ*) which can be domesticated (Gen. 8:1; Ps. 148:10; Job 37:8; Ezk. 14:15; 33:27; Zeph. 2:15). In the law concerning clean and unclean animals, "living creatures" refers to all clean animals on earth (Lev. 11:2f., *ḥayyâ*) which are edible (v. 47) as well as those that are unclean and inedible (v. 47), and even the water creatures other than the aquatic "swarming creatures" (vv. 10, 46; cf. Gen. 1:20f.). In an exceptional case we find *ḥayyâ* used once each to designate domesticated animals in the form of livestock (Lev. 35:3, NEB "livestock"; RSV "beasts") and a beast of burden or pack animal (Isa. 46:1). In Rev. 8:9 the "living creatures" (*ktísmata,* pl. of *ktísma*) are created "living creatures" in the water (cf. Rev. 5:13; 1 Tim. 4:4).

II. Living Creatures as Celestial Beings.–*A. In the OT.* The "living creatures" of the throne vision of Ezekiel reflect ancient Near Eastern symbolism in depicting the transcendence of the Ruler of the World who sits enthroned in inaccessible holiness above the clouds of heaven (1:5-21). These four "living creatures" were celestial beings that supported the throne of God (1:26; 10:20); they had the appearance or form of human beings, but each with four faces and four wings, straight legs and hooves like that of a calf, and human hands under their wings (1:6-8); they made rumbling noises with their wings (3:13; 10:5). They are identified as "cherubim" (10:15). The description of the celestial "living beings" in Ezekiel symbolizes the plenitude of offices, capabilities, and adaptabilities.

Symbolic winged creatures were a prominent feature of both mythology and architecture in the ancient Near East. Archeological discoveries in Palestine have brought to light some ancient representations of cherubim-like beings. As supporters of the divine throne and guardians of the sacred ark, winged figures support the throne of King Hiram of Byblos (ancient Gebal), who reigned *ca.* 1200 B.C., and similar creatures are found on incense altars discovered at Taanach, Hamath, and Megiddo. At Samaria some ivory panels depict a composite creature with human face and animal body of four legs and two elaborate wings. Representations of such beings, dating mostly from the 9th cent. B.C., have been found also at Carchemish, Nimrûd, Aleppo, and Tell Halaf (*ANEP*, nos. 649-655). In Mesopotamia winged bulls and lions and colossi were customarily placed at the entrance of Babylonian and Assyrian palaces and temples.

B. In the NT. The "four living creatures" of Rev. 4:6-9, which remind us of the *zṓa* (LXX) in Ezk. 1:5-22, did not support the throne but were "on each side of the throne" (4:6; cf. 7:17) and had six wings (4:8) like seraphim (Isa. 6:2) instead of four each. They had each only one face, one like that "of a man" (Rev. 4:7), in contrast to the four faces of the celestial beings in Ezekiel. The first creature resembled a lion, the second an ox, the third had a human face, the fourth looked like a flying eagle (4:7). Each had eyes all over, inside and out (v. 8), and gave glory, honor, and praise unceasingly to the Deity seated on the throne (vv. 8f.). In the vision of the opening of the seals each of the "living creatures" cried "Come forward!" as the first four seals were broken (6:1-7). They gave to the angels the seven golden bowls containing the last plagues (15:7). Otherwise they worshiped God (7:11; 14:3; 19:4).

Bibliography.–W. F. Albright, *BA*, 1 (1938), 1-3, reprinted in *Biblical Archaeologist Reader*, I (1961), 95-97; *TDNT*, II, *s.v.* ζῷον (R. Bultmann); *IDB*, I, *s.v.* "Angels" (T. H. Gaster); *THAT*, I, *s.v.* חיה (Gerleman).

G. F. HASEL

CREDIT. "Credit" occurs as a verb only in Lev. 7:18, where Heb. *ḥāšaḇ* means "reckon" or "attribute" (AV "imputed"; NEB "counted to his credit"). In the NT the noun is used in the general sense of approbation, as Gk. *kléos* (1 Pet. 2:20; AV "glory") and *cháris* (Lk. 6:32-34; AV "thank"), which is close in meaning to "reward"

(Bauer, p. 885). Phil. 4:17 has a figurative use of a commercial term, for *eis lógon* here means "in settlement (of an account)" (Bauer, p. 479).

CREDITOR. *See* DEBT.

CREEDS AND CONFESSIONS.

I. Terminology
   A. Creed
   B. Confession
   C. Symbol
   D. Rule of Faith
   E. Other Terms
II. Scriptural Basis
III. Purpose and Use of Creeds
   A. Catechetical
   B. Commendatory
   C. Doctrinal
   D. Liturgical
   E. Experiential
IV. Historic Forms
   A. Apostles' Creed
   B. Nicene Creed
   C. Athanasian Creed
   D. Reformation Confessions
      1. Augsburg Confession (1530)
      2. Waldensian Declaration of Faith (1532)
      3. First Helvetic Confession (1536)
      4. Geneva Confession (1549)
      5. Gallican Confession (1559)
      6. Thirty-nine Articles (1571)
      7. Canons of Dort (1619)
      8. Westminster Confession (1647)

I. Terminology.–*A. Creed.* The Oxford English Dictionary definition of "creed" is "a brief formal summary of the Christian faith." But both the derivation of the term and the nature of the definitive creeds indicate that the element of personal trust in God is prominent. A creed is thus something more than a symposium of accepted belief or even an epitome of divinely revealed truth. It involves the existential commitment of the confessor to God.

The English substantive "creed" stems from the Lat. verb *credo,* which is the opening word in the Latin versions of both the Apostles' Creed and Nicene Creed. Its original significance was "I place confidence in," "I rely upon." It thus corresponds to the NT Gk. verb *pisteúō*; and as the latter is frequently enforced by *eis* when the object is either God the Father or Christ the Son (cf. Bauer, p. 667), so *credo* is strengthened by *in. Credo in unum Deum* implies more than a bare recognition that only one true God exists; it brings the worshiper into a faith-relationship with Him that is expressed in the total unqualified surrender of the self. As Jungmann points out, the earlier fathers of the Church do not seem to have drawn particular attention to this factor. Nevertheless, since the time of Augustine the phrase has been interpreted as including both an intellectual adherence to God and a loving endeavor to attain to Him (J. A. Jungmann, *The Early Liturgy* [1959], pp. 95f.).

A further elucidation of significance is supplied by etymology. Although "creed" shares the same root as both "credit" and "credulity," its affinities are with the former rather than with the latter. "Rightly understood as an act of worship," explains P. T. Fuhrmann, "the use of a creed is related more to 'credit' than to 'credulity,' setting forth affirmations in order to give credit to God rather than to express credulity or unexamined statements of belief. In this sense, creeds are the declaration of confession and gratitude to the glory of God" (p. 9).

B. Confession. "Confession" comes from Lat. *confiteor* as found in the Vulgate and patristic literature. The intention of Augustine's classic *Confessiones* was not only to acknowledge former transgressions but even more to thank and bless God openly for what He had done for his soul — "the confession of him who praises," as he himself describes it, as well as "the confession of him who sighs" (*Enarrationes* iii, on Ps. 95 [Ps. 94, Vulg.], 4). The confession is usually longer than a creed. It is more detailed and systematic. It is designed not so much for recital as for reference.

C. Symbol. "Symbol" was first used in a credal context in the 3rd cent., in the correspondence between Cyprian and Firmilian. The latter refers to the baptismal formula as the "symbol of the Trinity" (*PL,* III, 1143). In the letter from the Synod of Milan to Siricius (A.D. 390) the term is specifically applied to the Apostles' Creed (*PL,* XVI, 1213). Gk. *sýmbolon* (Lat. *symbolum* or *signum*) is derived from the Gk. verb *symbállein,* "put together." It was originally a secret password used as a token of recognition among religious groups and elsewhere. In early Christianity, however, it came to signify "a compendium of the fundamental facts or truths of faith that a candidate had to recite or to confirm as an evidence of his faith before being baptized and accepted as a member of the church" (Fuhrmann, p. 12).

D. Rule of Faith. Regula fidei (or *veritatis*) is the Latin form of the Eastern *kánōn tḗs alētheías* or *ekklēsías* (cf. Origen, comm. on John, xxxii.16). According to Cyril of Jerusalem, catechumens were supplied with a considerable body of Christian doctrine on such subjects as the being and unity of God, creation, the Incarnation, Christ the Second Adam, His birth, the Cross, the Resurrection, the Ascension, the future judgment, the Holy Spirit, the Church, the Christian doctrine of man, his soul and body, his free will, his resurrection, the canon of Scripture, the sacraments, together with some simple practical guidance on Christian living in a heathen world (*Catecheses* 4). This instruction constituted the Apostolical Tradition or Rule of Faith (cf. Bindley, pp. 4f.). It was closely related to the incipient Apostles' Creed, and some scholars have actually made the identification (e.g., Harnack, Zahn). It would appear improbable, however, that these were interchangeable expressions (cf. A. J. Mason in H. B. Swete, ed., *Essays on the Early History of the Church and the Ministry* [1918], p. 51).

E. Other Terms. Other incidental terms may be noted in passing. Clement of Alexandria speaks of "the faith" (*Paed.* i.38; *Misc.* vii.10.56), and Probst claims a reference to the creed, although the allusion is uncertain. Origen describes the Latin translation by Rufinus as an "abbreviated word" (comm. on Romans, ix.25). Tertullian talks about the "words of the oath," which may relate to the baptismal confession (*Ad martyres* 3).

II. Scriptural Basis.–A recognition that the sacred Scriptures constitute a unity would make us expect to find the germs of credal confession in the OT, and this is in fact the case. Brief, spontaneous utterances of faith occur, such as those recorded in Ps. 7:1 and 63:1. In the Decalogue (Ex. 20:1-17; Dt. 5:6-21) are found the rudiments of credal formulation, and in the Shema (constructed from Dt. 6:4-9; 11:13-21; Nu. 15:37-41) we reach what may legitimately be regarded as the symbol of OT faith and the earliest attempt to enunciate a doctrine (cf. *HJP*, II/2, 77-79, 83-85). N. W. Porteous does not hesitate to describe this as a "credal statement," and H. W. Robinson speaks of it as "the primary Jewish confession of a monotheistic faith," although he prefers the third RV mg. rendering, "The Lord is our God, the Lord alone," which mitigates the strictness of the assumed monotheism and thus prepares the way for trinitarian disclosures (H. W. Robinson, ed., *Record and Revelation* [1938], pp. 242, 308).

A later passage in Dt. 26:5-9 is actually designated by recent scholars as "the little Credo," although its emphasis is less upon the nature of God than on His mighty saving acts (cf. *OTMS,* p. 89).

It is in the NT that one finds the fullest scriptural anticipations of the creeds. Immediately one is conscious of entering a realm in which the confessional declarations of the Church had their birth. "It is impossible to overlook the emphasis on the transmission of authoritative doctrine which is to be found everywhere in the New Testament," affirms J. N. D. Kelly, who has written so exhaustively on this subject that we can do no better than to summarize his evidence at this stage (*Early Christian Creeds* [2nd ed. 1960], p. 8).

Certainly in the later NT strata the references to an inherited body of doctrine are sufficiently clear. In Jude 3, for instance, we read of "the faith which was once for all delivered to the saints"; and later in v. 20 the inspired author speaks of "your most holy faith" in the same sense. Likewise in the Pastorals such expressions as "the pattern of the sound words" (2 Tim. 1:13), "sound teaching" (2 Tim. 4:3), "sound doctrine" (Tit. 1:9), "what has been entrusted to you" (1 Tim. 6:20), and "the truth that has been entrusted to you" (2 Tim. 1:14); the "faith" in its concrete acceptation (1 Tim. 1:19; Tit. 1:13); and the "good doctrine" (1 Tim. 4:6) recur repeatedly. The writer of Hebrews often refers to "the confession" (AV "profession"; Gk. *tḗs homologías*) that believers are urged to hold fast (3:1; 4:14; 10:23).

It is equally apparent that at a much earlier stage this process of formulation was at work. Paul reminds the Galatians that before their very eyes Jesus Christ had been "publicly portrayed as crucified" (3:1). In 2 Thess. 2:15 he exhorts his readers to "hold to the traditions" they had been taught, and in Rom. 6:17 he alludes explicitly to "the standard of teaching" to which they were committed (cf. also 1 Cor. 11:23; 15:3). Other recurring expressions include "the faith" (Col. 2:7; Gal. 1:23; Eph. 4:5), "the word of God" or "the word of the Lord" (1 Thess. 1:6; 2 Thess. 3:1; 1 Cor. 14:36; Gal. 6:6; Phil. 1:14), "the gospel" (Gal. 2:2; Rom. 1:16; 16:25; 1 Cor. 15:1) or "the preaching" (Rom. 16:25; 1 Cor. 1:21). This latter, of course, is reflected in the actual instances in Acts from which C. H. Dodd has compiled his reconstruction (cf. *Apostolic Preaching and Its Developments* [2nd ed. 1954], p. 17; though this is criticized by R. Mounce, *Essential Nature of NT Preaching* [1960]).

This deposit must not be accepted in isolation, for it represents only one strand among several. It needs to be supplemented from the pastoral and liturgical aspects of NT church life. It is in this realm, nevertheless, that one can begin to appreciate the manner in which the rudiments of credal statement were first established.

The evidence carries us further than this, however. As Canon Kelly observes, "The reader of the NT is continually coming across creedlike slogans and tags, catchwords which at the time of writing were being consecrated by popular usage. In addition he lights upon longer passages which, while still fluid in their phrasing, betray by their context, rhythm and general pattern, as well as by their content, that they derive from community tradition rather than from the writer's untrammelled invention. To explain them as excerpts from or echoes of an official ecclesiastical formula, as used to be fashionable, is unnecessary and misleading. Since the very existence of a creed in the precise sense implied is pure hypothesis, and unlikely hypothesis at that, it is more natural to treat them as independent units and examine them on their merits" (*Creeds*, p. 13).

Most frequent are the single-clause Christologies which recur so consistently throughout the NT. The centrality of the Son is a feature of the creeds. "Proclamation of Christ," according to Cullmann, "is the starting-point of every Christian confession" (p. 39), and this is true both historically and theologically.

These Christologies are so profuse as to outnumber all other forms. The most elementary are the titles ascribed to Jesus of Nazareth. "Son of man" was never regarded as a confession, even though it was introduced by Jesus Himself; but "Christ" (Jn. 1:41; 9:35; 1 Jn. 2:22), "Son of God" (Acts 8:37; Mt. 16:16), and "Lord" (Rom. 10:9; 1 Cor. 12:3; Phil. 2:11) soon passed into use. New titles were added, in particular the divine predication *theós*. This was initially applied to Christ in connection with liturgical formulas. In Rom. 9:5 a doxology to God is employed as a doxology to Christ. In Tit. 2:13f. a doxology to God is changed into a doxology to Christ. As Stauffer comments, "After John 20:28 in the story of the creeds of the primitive Church there was no stopping the attribution of the word God to Christ" (*NT Theology* [Eng. tr. 1955], p. 324 n. 803).

The most familiar of all the incipient credal declarations of the NT is the slogan *kýrios Iēsous* ("Jesus is Lord"). Paul insists that "no one can say 'Jesus is Lord' except by the Holy Spirit" (1 Cor. 12:3). And again, "If you confess with your lips that Jesus is Lord and believe in your heart that God raised him from the dead, you will be saved" (Rom. 10:9). The precise context of these sayings is not indicated by the apostle, but the fact that the first is contrasted with the alternative of anathematizing Our Lord would suggest that some time of testing, perhaps by persecution, is envisaged. The verse from Romans is generally associated with the sacrament of baptism. The reiterated description of the rite as being "in the name of the Lord Jesus" (Acts 8:16; 19:5; 1 Cor. 6:11) seems to indicate that the formula was included. The expression recurs in Phil. 2:11 and Col. 2:6 (cf. E. von Dobschütz, *ZNW*, 30 [1931], 97-123; *TDNT*, III, *s.v.* κύριος [Quell, Foerster]).

Thus far we have been concerned with creeds in miniature. But the NT also affords samples of fuller and more detailed confessions. In 1 Cor. 15:3-7 Paul supplies a fourfold summary worked out in the manner of the doxological formulas in the Petrine speeches of Acts. It is described as "in what terms I preached to you the gospel, which you received, in which you stand" (v. 1). It is not something he has invented but something he has received and handed on. With this we must associate the more deliberate doctrinal statement of Rom. 1:3f. and the abbreviated excerpts in Rom. 8:34 and 2 Tim. 2:8. A similar passage occurs in 1 Pet. 3:18-20.

In addition to these more elaborate multiple Christologies, we also meet instances in the NT of distinctly bipartite confessions in which the Father and Son are included together, although the approach is consistently christological. One of the most significant of such passages is 1 Cor. 8:6, "yet for us there is one God, the Father, from whom are all things and for whom we exist, and one Lord, Jesus Christ, through whom are all things and through whom we exist." Here the unity of the Godhead is maintained in contrast to the "many 'gods' and many 'lords' " (v. 5) of encircling heathendom, and the earliest allusion is made in the NT to the agency of Christ in creation. 1 Tim. 2:5f. is equally relevant, laying emphasis as it does upon the mediatorial sacrifice of Our Lord. As Lietzmann shows, these formulas, especially the former, became the basis of all confessions containing more than a single article (*ZNW*, 22 [1923], 268-273).

A fuller expression is located in 1 Tim. 6:13f. "In the presence of God who gives life to all things, and of Christ Jesus who in his testimony before Pontius Pilate made the good confession, I charge you to keep the commandment unstained and free from reproach until the appearing of our Lord Jesus Christ." The *termini a quo* and *ad quem* of the familiar credal statements are made evident here. The reference to the Parousia may be supplemented by 2 Tim. 4:1. A rather different bipartite formula appears in Rom. 4:24.

Nor is the fully trinitarian note altogether absent. The specific examples may be rarer, but the incidental references must also be taken into account. Mt. 28:19 from the first claimed a place in the rite of Christian baptism and, as Stauffer points out, on that basis came to determine the entire credal development of the primitive Church. The threefold benediction in 2 Cor. 13:14 is another explicit case. But other less obvious yet equally impressive passages must be considered, including 1 Cor. 6:11; 12:4-6; 2 Cor. 1:21f.; 1 Thess. 5:18f.; 1 Pet. 1:2. It is clear that the conception of a threefold manifestation of the Godhead was deeply embedded in Christian thought from the start. Because of this scriptural rootage, the trinitarian pattern was generally recognized as the foundation of doctrine (cf. Vincent of Lérins, *Commonitorium* [1895], p. 23; Bindley, p. 1).

We must beware, however, lest the significance of this evidence from the NT be exaggerated. "It cannot be too often repeated that, in the proper sense of the terms, no creed, confession or formula of faith can be discovered in the New Testament, with the possible exception of such curt slogans as *Kurios Iesous*." At this stage a set body of doctrine was forming, and certain patterns of expressing that doctrine were beginning to emerge. "Generally, though the underlying structure was hardening, the language still remained fairly fluid" (Kelly, *Creeds*, pp. 23f.).

III. Purpose and Use of Creeds.–Before examining some of the major credal definitions of the Church, we must pause to consider the intended use of creeds. O. C. Quick, borrowing a term from modern pedagogics, aptly described them as "the expression-work of the early Church" (*Doctrines of the Creed* [1938], p. 8). Their aim and usage may be conveniently summarized in the following categories.

A. Catechetical. A creed was designed as a basis for the instruction of candidates. When the ordinance of baptism was observed, the catechumen was required to repeat the confession. According to Rufinus, in the church of Rome "an ancient custom prevails that those who are about to receive the grace of baptism should recite the creed publicly: that is, so as to be heard by the congregation of the faithful; and of a truth the ears of those who precede them in the faith tolerate no addition of whatever kind to the words" (*De fide et symbolo* 3).

B. Commendatory. A creed was regarded as a test of church membership. This is related to the conception of the symbol as a token of identification. In primitive times, when a man sent a neighbor to a distant friend, he would take an oyster shell and break it into two pieces, forwarding one half to his friend and entrusting the other to his neighbor. When the neighbor arrived at his destination, he would present his portion as a sign of identification. If it fitted, his identity was substantiated. *Tessera* were similarly employed, and the white stone of Rev. 2:17 may well have been of this nature. But more often in the early Church the recital of a creed was accepted as proof of identity.

C. Doctrinal. A creed was intended as a compendious statement of Christian truth and a criterion by which error could be exposed. Indeed, the creeds were as much directed against heresy as concerned with the positive declaration of the faith. It was the prevalence of falsehood that determined the presentation of truth. "This is only to say that, while the truths were undoubtedly held from the beginning," writes Bindley, "they were often latent in the Christian consciousness rather than verbally expressed, until the denial of them obliged the Church to ponder upon her Faith, and to put it into reasoned words" (p. 1).

D. Liturgical. The creeds were eventually incorporated into the worship services of the Church. From the baptismal liturgy they gained entrance into that of the eucharist. The Nicene Creed was inserted in the 11th cent. at Rome, but earlier elsewhere. The Spanish churches were the first to introduce it in the West. In the East the custom already existed and in 586 Justinian made it legal. The Gallican churches sang it after the Gospel at the end of the catechumens' service, and this also is the place accorded to it in the Roman use. The Apostles' Creed has been recognized in the Anglican order from the beginning, but the date of its first liturgical adoption in the Western churches is uncertain.

E. Experiential. A creed is also in a sense a personal confession of faith and thus at once reflects and ministers to Christian experience. Cullman emphasizes that the declarations of the historic creeds are in the present tense and relate to the "now" of grace. "Christian faith does not reduce to an affirmation about the past alone: this would lead straight to a 'historism' which impaired the Biblical conception of linear time. Neither does it reduce to an affirmation about the future alone: this would lead straight to an apocalyptic which, in contrast to the Biblical eschatology, tended to separate hope and faith. Christianity is true to its origin in ascribing first-rank importance in its strictly Christological plan of salvation to the present as a time of grace" (p. 64). It is this continuing contemporaneity that imparts an existential quality to the affirmations of the traditional creeds and demands or even evokes a commensurate experience.

IV. The Historic Forms.–We can supply only a cursory survey of the principal historic forms that have gained acceptance in the Christian Church in the process of credal development.

A. Apostles' Creed. "The present Apostles' Creed," wrote H. B. Swete, "is a document of composite origin with a long and complicated history" (*Apostles' Creed,* p. 15). Into the ramifications of that provenance we cannot here enter. The title *symbolum apostolorum* first occurs, as we have already seen, in the communication from the Synod of Milan in 390, probably drafted by Ambrose.

The name originated from a widely prevalent legend that the creed was composed by the twelve apostles under the direct inspiration of the Holy Spirit. Indeed, ingenious, though forced, attempts have been made to divide the symbol into twelve parts and to claim that a separate disciple was responsible for each successive clause. In Western churches of medieval date it is not uncommon to see portraits of the apostles, under each of which is transcribed the article of the creed thus assigned.

This apocryphal account can be traced back to the 6th cent. (cf. Pseudo-Augustine, *PL,* XXXIX, 2189). It was adumbrated in a sermon attributed to Ambrose in which it is explained that the creed was "pieced together by twelve separate workmen" (*PL*, XVI, 671), and also in the Apostolic Constitutions (6:14). Rufinus provides a detailed genesis. He clearly regards it as the cooperative effort of the apostles and implies that the conference that produced it coincided with Pentecost. He furthermore explains that "they for many reasons decided that this rule of faith should be called the Symbol" (*PL*, XXI, 337). The apostolic authorship of the creed is confirmed by such writers as Maximus of Turin, John Cassian, and Isidore of Seville, whereas Priminius supports the further item of allotting each clause to a different source.

This version persisted until the 15th century. It was first seriously questioned at Ferrara in 1438 at an ecumenical council convened with a view to the reunion of East and West. At the outset Cardinal Julian Cesarini, the Latin spokesman, appealed to the authority of the Apostles' Creed. The Greeks, however, refused to recognize it, and Marcus Eugenicus, Metropolitan of Ephesus, objected that in the East they did not possess nor had they ever seen such a symbol (H. Justiniani, *Acta Concilii Florenti*, IX, 842f.).

Soon the apostolic origin was challenged by the noted humanist Lorenzo Valla, when he interrupted a Franciscan monk who was explaining the traditional story to a group of children in a church at Naples. The cudgels were taken up with additional scholarly arguments by Reginald Pecock in England. In the 17th cent. Gerhard Vos and James Ussher resumed the debate and inaugurated the modern era of credal investigation (see Ghellinck).

The 19th cent., however, saw the launching of a critical onslaught upon the creeds comparable with that simultaneously directed against the Scriptures, and doubts were seriously expressed as to whether any collected body of doctrine, much less one attributable to the apostles themselves, could have existed in the NT period. This undermining of the biblical and apostolic origin of the creed paved the way for an attack upon its contents, with the consequence that violent attempts were made to thrust out some of the fundamental tenets of the Christian faith.

It is generally recognized today that, although the primitive Church did not possess an official textually determined confession of faith, incipient creeds of a more flexible nature, anticipating the later formularies, began to emerge at a comparatively early date (cf. Kelly, *Creeds*, p. 7). The evidence from the NT itself has already been examined. It is clear that an apostolic tradition was latent from the start.

The lineal predecessor of the Apostles' Creed was the Old Roman Creed, dating from *ca.* 150. The primary source for the Latin text is the treatise of Rufinus mentioned above. Rufinus compared the creed of Aquileia, his own church, with that of Rome, which he believed to be the rule of faith composed by the apostles themselves. The Greek text is taken from the apologia of Marcellus of Ancyra delivered to Julius bishop of Rome, *ca.* 340. The latter reads: "I believe in God almighty [Rufinus has "the Father almighty"]; and in Christ Jesus His only Son our Lord, Who was born from the Holy Spirit and the Virgin Mary, Who under Pontius Pilate was crucified and buried, and the third day rose again from the dead, Who ascended into heaven and sits at the right hand of the Father, whence He will come to judge the living and the dead; and in the Holy Spirit, the holy Church, the remission of sins, the resurrection of the flesh, the life everlasting" (Rufinus omits the last clause) (from Epiphanius, *PG*, XLII, 385). F. J. Badcock has questioned the hypothesis that Rufinus and Marcellus have in fact preserved the Old Roman Creed, but his objections have not succeeded in overthrowing the theory.

It is recognized, however, that the Old Roman Creed was itself derivative and is a descendant of a more primitive form. The earliest outline is thought to have taken this shape: "I believe in God the Father almighty and in Jesus Christ, His only-begotten Son, our Lord, and in the Holy Spirit, the Holy Church, the resurrection of the flesh" (so Lietzmann; cf. Cullmann, p. 46). Two extant fragments support such a reconstruction. The first is from *Epistula Apostolorum*, which its editor, C. Schmidt, assigns to Asia Minor *ca.* 180, but which has one leaf in Latin, indicating a wider general distribution. We have to depend on Coptic and Ethiopic translations, suggesting that the work was familiar in Egypt, if indeed it did not originate there. Concerning the five loaves in the feeding miracle of the Gospels the treatise states: "They are the symbol of our faith in the Lord of the Christians, even in the Father the Lord Almighty, and in Jesus Christ our redeemer, in the Holy Spirit the comforter, in the holy church, and in the remission of sins" (*Epistula Apostolorum* 5.16, *ANT*; cf. H-S, I, 194).

The second fragment is from the Dêr Balizeh papyrus discovered by Flinders Petrie and W. E. Crum in 1907 and now housed in the Bodleian Library, Oxford. Toward the end of what is evidently an ancient Egyptian eucharistic liturgy this simple creed is recorded: "I believe in God the Father Almighty, and in His only-begotten Son, our Lord Jesus Christ, and in the Holy Spirit, and in the resurrection of the flesh, and the holy catholic Church" (C. H. Roberts and Dom B. Capelle, *An Early Euchologium: the Dêr Balizeh Papyrus* [rev. ed. 1949]). Its date may be late 2nd century.

At a later period, probably in the second half of the 2nd cent. and the beginning of the 3rd, this simple three-article formula was expanded by the inclusion of a more fully developed Christology. Certainly such an insertion is reflected in the baptismal catechesis contained in the *Apostolic Tradition* of Hippolytus (*ca.* 215 according to G. Dix [rev. ed. 1968]).

The *textus receptus* of the Apostles' Creed as we now know it is first extant in the tract *De Singulis libris canonicis Scarapsus* by Priminius, abbot-founder of the famous monastery at Reichenau (*ca.* 710-724). Despite the arguments of G. L. Hahn and A. E. Burn, its Roman origin can hardly be sustained. A Hispano-Gallic source is now widely accepted. Southern Gaul is agreed upon, possibly Burgundy, or more probably the region called in ancient times Septimania. This suggestion finds powerful support in that Caesarius of Arles quotes a strikingly similar creed in the 6th century. Its canonization as the sole baptismal formula of the Western Church and subsequent reception into the Roman eucharistic rite was due in part to the liturgical preoccupation of the Carolingian renaissance. Nor was it used exclusively in public worship. The recital of the *symbolum*, together with the Lord's Prayer, formed the beginning of every Christian's morning devotions and the conclusion of those in the evening. "Say it daily," advised Augustine. "When you rise, when you go to bed, say your symbol; say it before the Lord; call it to mind, and do not tire of repeating it" (*Sermones* 58.11).

Such is still its position today. "As the Lord's Prayer is the Prayer of prayers, the Decalogue the Law of laws, so the Apostles' Creed is the Creed of creeds," declared Philip Schaff. "It contains all the fundamental articles of the Christian faith necessary to salvation, in the form of facts, in simple scriptural language, and in the

CREEDS AND CONFESSIONS

most natural order — the order of revelation — from God and the creation down to the resurrection and life everlasting" (I, 14f.).

"Christian truth," declared Luther, "could not possibly be put into a shorter and clearer statement"; and Calvin agreed that "it gives, in clear and succinct order, a full statement of our faith, and in everything which it contains is sanctioned by the sure testimony of Scripture" (cf. *Luther's Works,* ed. Lehmann and Pelikan, XXXVII, 360ff.; Calvin *Inst.* ii.16.18). To this we may add the verdict of T. Zahn: "Judging from its contents our Creed has a full right to the title apostolical. It does not contain one sentence which cannot be well derived from the history and teaching of Jesus, and the explanatory and illustrative teaching and preaching of the apostles" (p. 213).

B. Nicene Creed. In its present form what is commonly called the Nicene Creed should be more exactly distinguished as Niceno-Constantinopolitan or Niceno-Chalcedonian. The text of the original creed approved at the Council of Nicea in the year 325 (sometimes referred to as the creed of the 318 from the number of bishops reputed to have been present) can be consulted in a letter from Eusebius of Caesarea to his flock. This is extant in four recensions (Bindley, p. 27).

According to Athanasius, Ossius of Cordoba, at whose instigation the council was convened, played a prominent part in formulating the statement. It was he who conveyed the imperial communication from Constantine to Alexander, bishop of Alexandria, and Arius the heretic, in which the emperor betrayed his imperfect grasp of the issues involved by suggesting that the trinitarian controversy was little more than a tempest in an ecclesiastical teapot. When this letter not surprisingly failed to effect a settlement, the emperor summoned a general council of bishops to decide these matters of faith, along with the Paschal question and the Meletian schism. It is probable that Ossius presided after the formal opening by Constantine himself (cf. Hefele-Leclerq, *Histoire des conciles* [1907-1952] I, 447).

In the course of the conference, it was agreed that a dogmatic standard of faith should be adopted. After an Arian creed proposed by Eusebius of Nicomedia had been summarily rejected, Eusebius of Caesarea produced his local diocesan creed which, according to his own account, was accepted as orthodox and approved (Socrates Scholasticus *HE* i.8). This was held to have formed a basis, with significant additions more specifically directed against the errors of Arianism (so Harnack, Holl, Hort, Burn, Gibson, *et al.*) It is now considered more likely, however, that the Nicene Creed represents a conflation of sources either from Jerusalem or Antioch. It is noteworthy that the formulation of a symbol was preceded by a careful searching of the Scriptures, the chief passages adduced being Prov. 8:22; Mt. 19:17; 20:23; Mk. 13:32; Lk. 2:52; Jn. 5:19; 10:30; 14:28; Acts 2:36; 1 Cor. 15:28; Phil. 2:7; Col. 1:15; He. 1:3.

The debate turned upon the nature of the Son and His relation to the Father. The term *homooúsios* ("of one substance with") became the keyword of the logomachy. The Arians rejected it outright, while the Sabellians contended for the modification *homoioúsios* ("of like substance"). The majority, however, finally endorsed the former expression as best defining the orthodox view of the relation between Father and Son. Although the term was later pressed to imply numerical identity of substance, it is doubtful whether this was in the mind of those who framed the creed, for prior to Nicea *homooúsios* had borne a primarily generic sense (cf. G. L. Prestige, *God in Patristic Thought* [1936], pp. 197ff.). It would appear that the word was originally intended to make implicit the conviction that the Son was fully God in that He shared the same divine nature as His Father. Its further implication as expressing substantial identity was more fully worked out by Athanasius.

What is now designated the Nicene Creed, expanding the affirmation of Nicea, was recognized as an official formula at the Council of Chalcedon in 451. It was proclaimed as the faith of the 150 fathers at the Council of Constantinople in 381. The text is in Epiphanius (*Ancoratus* 118), extracted from the *Catecheses* of Cyril of Jerusalem.

The traditional ascription to Constantinople has been seriously questioned, and it is now widely held that what was approved at Chalcedon was in fact based on a baptismal confession of Palestinian origin. The Council of Constantinople certainly did not invent it, although the fathers may have touched it up here and there. In 553 the Second Council of Constantinople received it as a revised edition of the Nicene Creed.

The principal additions included clauses incorporated from the Apostles' Creed relative to the Incarnation, together with the phrase "whose kingdom shall have no end" directed against Marcellus of Ancyra, who denied the extension of Christ's reign beyond the Day of Judgment; and certain statements affirming the personality and deity of the Holy Spirit as against the Pneumatomachi, who regarded Him as a mere created being.

In 589 the Council of Toledo recognized the addition of the *filioque*, which is a feature of the Western version. Cyril of Alexandria taught that the Spirit proceeds from the Father through the Son, and this interpretation became current in the Eastern Church. But Augustine preferred to say that the Spirit proceeds from the Father and from the son (*filioque*), and this has set the pattern for the West. As early as 447 the insertion occurs in Spanish confessions. This doctrinal difference was one of the causes for the ultimate separation of the Greek and Latin churches in 1054.

C. Athanasian Creed. What is known as the Athanasian Creed is often cited as *Quicunque Vult* from its opening words. In the earliest extant MS copy it is designated as *Fides Catholica.*

The first certain allusion is in the *Acta* of the Synod of Autun in Eastern Gaul, when Leger was bishop (i.e., between 659 and 670). Several canons were approved, one of which read: "If a cleric does not know exactly either the Apostolic Symbol or the Attestation of Faith of Saint Athanasius especially, let him be condemned by his Bishop." The context makes it clear that *Quicunque Vult* was intended. Further evidence of its use is contained in a capitulary of Charlemagne requiring priests to learn this creed and a similar promulgation *ca.* A.D. 800 by Haito of Basel.

The symbol is said to have been composed by Athanasius himself during his exile in the West. It occurs only in Latin, and according to the papal envoys visiting the Eastern Church in 1233 after the conquest of Constantinople, it was quite unknown there. This ascription, however, is strongly disputed, and it appears in fact that, as F. F. Bruce points out, "What is traditionally called the Athanasian Creed is not really a creed at all, and is not the work of Athanasius. It is a theological exposition in the form of a canticle, composed in the West towards the end of the Fourth Century" (*Light in the West* [1952], p. 27).

The Athanasian authorship was first challenged by Gerhard Vos in 1644. Since that time many ingenious conjectures have been propounded. Antelmius in the 17th cent. suggested Vincent of Lérins, while Waterland preferred Hilary of Arles. Other nominations include Ambrose (Brewer and Badcock), Honoratus of Arles (Burn and Kattenbusch), Caesarius of Arles (Morin and Turmel), Fulgentius of Ruspe (Stiglmayr), Vitricius of Ravenna (Harvey), and Venantius Fortunatus (Muratori). A provenance from Southern Gaul seems probable.

At one time the so-called Athanasian Creed was considered to be a forgery of the same genre as the infamous decretals and the Donation of Constantine (so Swainson and Ffoulkes). A late origin was claimed on the basis of a letter in which Alcuin thanks Paulinus for having sent him a *libellus* containing a digest of the Christian faith which might be circulated and committed to memory as *symbolum fidei*. But Alcuin's further reference to the prevailing errors refuted in this compendium reveal that it could hardly be equated with *Quicunque Vult*. Fuhrmann dates it somewhere between 434 and 670 (p. 58).

Whereas previous creeds were concerned largely with safeguarding the faith against error, *Quicunque Vult* seeks to present the trinitarian revelation in sharper focus. After its solemn introduction, declaring that eternal salvation depends upon holding fast the catholic faith, the creed asserts that this consists in worshiping one God "in Trinity, and the Trinity in Unity." We are here confronted with a most remarkable affirmation. Whereas the Apostles' Creed and Nicene Creed proclaimed first the Father, then the Son, and finally the Holy Spirit, and assigned an article to each of the three persons seriatim, the Athanasian represents the trinity as a unit. "The Father is God, the Son is God, and the Holy Ghost is God. And yet there are not three Gods: but one God."

"Of the ancient creeds of Christendom," writes Canon Leonard Hodgson in an authoritative volume, "the so-called Athanasian Creed, the *Quicunque Vult,* is the only one which explicitly and unequivocally states the full Christian doctrine of God" (*Doctrine of the Trinity* [1944], p. 102). *Quicunque Vult* reflects the fullest stage of credal development. If the Apostles' Creed determined the nature of God and the Niceno-Chalcedonian that of the relation between Son and Spirit, this may be regarded as establishing the doctrine of the trinity.

A further feature of *Quicunque Vult* is the inclusion of the monitory clauses both at the beginning and ending. "Which faith except every one do keep whole and undefiledly without doubt he shall perish everlastingly." "This is the Catholic faith: which except a man believe faithfully, he cannot be saved." Jeremy Taylor misconstrued their purpose when he complained that "it seems very hard to put uncharitableness into a creed and so to make it become an article of faith" (quoted in Schaff, I, 40). If this creed is magisterially solemn in its admonitions, we must remember that even more so are the Scriptures themselves, and in particular the sayings of Our Lord.

The Athanasian Creed has scarcely enjoyed the reputation achieved by its two major predecessors; but its stock is rising today, and we are in a better position to appreciate the enthusiasm of Luther, which led him to describe it as the most important and praiseworthy composition since the days of the apostles.

With the adoption of the Athanasian Symbol, the creed-making of the early and medieval Church virtually ceased. Of the three reviewed, only one, the Nicene, is in the broadest sense catholic. Neither the Apostles' Creed nor the Athanasian Creed is recognized by the Greek or Eastern Church, which remained loyal to the statement of faith approved at Nicea and Constantinople. The Niceno-Chalcedonian formula is in fact the one truly ecumenical creed, accepted and recited by all confessional communions.

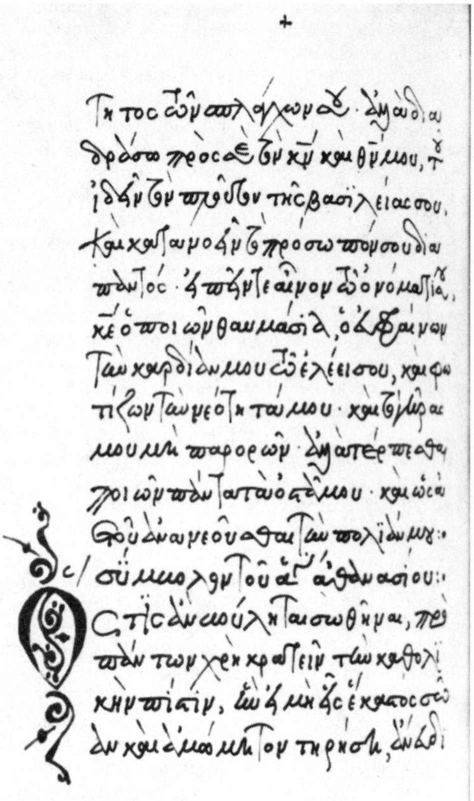

Greek manuscript (*ca.* A.D. 1500) of the creed traditionally attributed to Athanasius, establishing the doctrine of the trinity (Yale University, Beinecke Library)

D. Reformation Confessions. With the Reformation began a new and creative era in the history of credal development. The following are some of the chief confessions of Protestantism.

1. Augsburg Confession (1530). The first great Protestant symbol was the Augsburg Confession of 1530. It arose from the Marburg Colloquy, an abortive attempt by Philip of Hesse to renconcile the doctrinal positions of Luther and Zwingli. Luther subsequently drew up fifteen items to be used as a basis of further discussion with a view to agreement. With the addition of two more clauses, these appeared as the pacificatory Articles of Schwabach. When the emperor summoned the Diet of Augsburg, the Wittenberg theologians, convened by John of Saxony, agreed on a further set of propositions, derived from the previous draft and named the Torgau Articles after the place of meeting.

On arrival in Augsburg, however, the deputation discovered that Dr. John Eck had circulated a book containing some four hundred statements culled from the Reformers' writings alleged to be heretical. It was evident that the Torgau Articles in themselves were insufficient to match this new and serious challenge. The Confession was composed by Melanchthon with the approval of Luther (who was still under the ban) and signed by seven princes. It was read in German before the Diet on June 25, 1530, by Christian Beyer, vice-chancellor of Saxony. The Augsburg Confession was aimed primarily at demonstrating the orthodoxy of Protestantism and is

CREEDS AND CONFESSIONS

couched in moderate and restrained terms, although it closed by exposing certain Roman deviations from the Christian tradition.

The Confession is in two parts, the first containing twenty-one articles of faith and the second detailing the seven chief abuses requiring reform. The original document was lodged in the imperial archives in Brussels, but in 1569 Philip II had it brought to Spain "so that such a pernicious work be destroyed for ever" (C. F. Rosenstiehl, *La Confession d'Augsburg 1530* [1949], p. 11). Some fifty MS copies, however, still exist. As Fuhrmann observes, "It is a rather lengthy document and it may not create such an impact as do the shorter and more concise creeds of former times. But as Calvin, on becoming a pastor in Strassburg, endorsed this document, it should be of interest to all Protestants to know its essence" (p. 88).

"This Confession of our preachers and of ourselves shows how we have thus far taught in our territories the doctrine founded on the Holy Scripture and the pure Word of God." So runs the Preface (para. 8), indicating the unambiguously biblical foundation of the Confession. The first section culminates in the affirmation that "they wished to transmit to posterity no other teaching except that which is conforming to the pure Word of God" (Art. 21). The Augustana, as it is commonly called, was incorporated into the Book of Concord in 1580 and is thus still authoritative for the Lutheran communion.

The assessment of W. A. Curtis is worth recording, that the Confession of Augsburg "is the classical statement of Lutheran doctrine, and has remained to the present day the bond between all Lutheran Churches. Its dignified simplicity, its temperate tone, and its Christian spirit have endeared it to successive generations, and have made it the model as well as the mother of later Confessions. . . . Its profound loyalty to the best traditions of the Catholic Church and the great Fathers, its faithfulness to Scripture, none the less impressive because it is unlaboured and unobtrusive, and its deep note of evangelical experience, have secured for it a sacred place, perhaps beyond all other Confessions, in the living faith of its ministers and people" (pp. 42f.).

2. *Waldensian Declaration of Faith* (1532). In 1532 the Waldenses summoned a general convention at Cianforan and received three Reformed delegates from beyond the Alps, one of whom was William Farel. For six days the principles of the Reformation were discussed. Eventually a Declaration of Faith was adopted, running to seventeen articles and affirming the basic tenets of Protestantism (S. Morland, *History of the Evangelical Churches of Piedmont* [1658], pp. 39-41).

3. *First Helvetic Confession* (1536). The first Reformed creed of national authority was the Helvetic Confession of 1536, composed at Basel. It originated from the peacemaking overtures of the Strasbourg theologians Bucer and Capito and was adopted as the Swiss Confession. It consists of twenty-seven short paragraphs, the first five of which affirm in unequivocal language the authority and sufficiency of Scripture.

4. *Geneva Confession* (1537). A further Reformed confession emanated from Geneva in 1537. It has been attributed to Farel, but there can be little doubt that John Calvin was involved in compiling and editing it, if not in its actual composition (cf. A. Rilliet and T. Dufour, *Le Catéchisme français de Calvin* [1878]; E. Doumergue, *Jean Calvin* [1899-1928], II, 237-39). It consisted of twenty-one articles based on the *Institutes*. It was approved by the council, and the citizens were required to swear to its tenets. "Probably the first instance," claims Schaff, "of a formal pledge to a symbolical book in the history of the Reformed Church" (p. 468).

5. *Gallican Confession* (1559). A Confession of Faith was adopted by the Reformed Church of France in 1559. Two years previously, Calvin had cooperated with the Parisian pastors in drawing up a statement. In 1559 a general assembly was summoned to the capital to draft a constitution. In the strictest secrecy some twenty delegates, representing seventy-two churches, met for four days and, among other things, prepared the first French confession. Calvin's thirty-five articles were increased to forty, but his regulative affirmation concerning the supremacy of the Word was unfortunately excised. As Léonard remarks, no passage in Calvin is finer and more replete with significance. "Since the foundation of belief, as St. Paul says, is the Word of God, we believe that the living God is manifest in His law and through His prophets, and finally in the Gospel; and that He has there given testimony to His will insofar as it is expedient for the salvation of men. Further, we hold the books of sacred Scripture in the Old and New Testaments as the sum of the sole infallible truth proceeding from God, which is not to be contradicted" (E. G. Léonard, *Histoire générale du Protestantisme* [1961], II, 102). The Scripture is nevertheless set forth as the only rule of faith and source of authority, self-evident and therefore independent of man; and the three historical creeds are accepted as conforming to the Word of God. The Confessio Gallicana was confirmed at the Seventh Reformed Synod at La Rochelle in 1571.

6. *Thirty-nine Articles* (1571). The Thirty-nine Articles of the Church of England, ratified by Convocation in 1571, represent the outcome of a long process of evolution from Henry VIII's Ten Articles in 1536, which Foxe described as intended for "weaklings newly weaned from their mother's milk of Rome," and more clearly from the Thirteen Articles of 1538 promulgated by joint conferences of Anglican and Lutheran divines at Wittenberg and Lambeth. The purpose of the Articles is admirably expressed by Bishop Pearson, who insisted that they were not intended to represent "a complete body of divinity, or a comprehension and explanation of all Christian doctrines necessary to be taught: but an enumeration of some truths, which upon and since the Reformation have been denied by some persons: who upon denial are thought unfit to have any cure of souls in this Church or realm; because they might by their opinions either infect their flock with error or else disturb the Church with schism or the realm with sedition" (cf. C. Hardwick, *A History of the Articles of Religion* [1895], p. 158).

Much controversy has surrounded the proper interpretation of the Thirty-nine Articles, and it has even been urged that they are to be viewed in the light of essentially Catholic principles. The history and nature of the Articles themselves, let alone their content, are sufficient to dispose of such an account. More precisely, it must be conceded that the Articles are predominantly Calvinist in tone, though not polemically so. "These Articles are not developed, much less exaggerated Calvinism. They are not Calvinistic in any partisan sense. But with Calvinistic doctrine, as already formulated, they are in unmistakeable sympathy" (Curtis, p. 177).

7. *Canons of Dort* (1619). The Canons of the Synod of Dort (1619) constitute the final answer of orthodox Calvinism to the Arminian Remonstrants. Distinguished visitors from almost every Reformed country were present at the invitation of the Dutch States General. It has been claimed that no more learned or respectable synod was ever convened and no body more representative of the Protestant world ever met. Along with the Belgic

Confession and the Heidelberg Catechism, reaffirmed by the Synod, the Canons of Dort have remained the formal standard of the Dutch Reformed Church to the present day.

8. Westminster Confession (1647). The Westminster Confession of 1647 stands as the doctrinal norm of English-speaking Presbyterians. It arose from the Westminster Assembly, called in 1643 by the Long Parliament to revise the Thirty-nine Articles. It has been said that four major principles govern its content: the authority of Scripture, the sovereignty of God, the validity of conscience, and the independence of the Church. According to W. A. Curtis it "marks the maturest and most deliberate formulation of the scheme of Biblical revelation as it has appeared to the most cultured and most devout Puritan minds. It was the last great Creed-utterance of Calvinism and intellectually and theologically it is a worthy child of the *Institutes,* a stately and noble standard for Bible loving men" (p. 275).

The foregoing survey will have sufficed to indicate the relationship between creeds and confessions. Both are doctrinal affirmations of belief. Both are attempts to conserve the truth of revelation. Both have been employed as a criterion by which orthodoxy may be distinguished from heresy. But creeds are much more restricted in scope and confine themselves to short and simple declarations, whereas confessions range over a broader field. Creeds are properly used in public worship, whereas confessions exist primarily for reference. Yet despite these obvious differences, it would be misleading to adopt the view of R. C. Moberly that, whereas the creed is a necessary feature of spiritual reality, the confession is an unfortunate consequence of spiritual failure (*Problems and Principles* [1904], p. 379). Both are part of the Church's positive witness to the faith once delivered to the saints.

Bibliography.–*Creeds:* A. Hahn, *Bibliothek der Symbole und Glaubensregeln der Alten Kirche* (3rd ed. 1897); P. Schaff, *Creeds of Christendom* (3 vols., 1877); E. C. S. Gibson, *The Three Creeds* (1908); W. A. Curtis, *History of the Creeds and Confessions of Faith* (1911); F. J. Badcock, *History of the Creeds* (1930); H. Lietzmann, *Symbole der Alten Kirche* (1931); O. Cullmann, *Earliest Christian Confessions* (Eng. tr. 1949); J. N. D. Kelly, *Early Christian Creeds* (3rd ed. 1972); P. T. Fuhrmann, *Intro. to the Great Creeds of the Church* (1960); T. H. Bindley, ed., *Ecumenical Documents of the Faith* (4th ed. 1950).

Apostles' Creed: H. B. Swete, *Apostles' Creed* (1894); F. Kattenbusch, *Das Apostolische Symbol* (2 vols., 1894, 1900); T. Zahn, *Apostles' Creed* (Eng. tr. 1899); E. von Dobschütz, *Das Apostolicum in biblisch-theologischer Beleuchtung* (1932); J. de Ghellinck, *Recherches sur les origines du Symbole des Apôtres* (rev. ed. 1949); J. N. D. Kelly, *Rufinus: A Comm. on the Apostles' Creed* (1955); O. S. Barr, *From the Apostles' Faith to the Apostles' Creed* (1964).

Nicene Creed: F. J. A. Hort, *Two Dissertations* (1876); A. E. Burn, *Nicene Creed* (1909); J. Kunze, *Das nicänischkonstantinopolitanische Symbol* (1898); F. Loofs, "Das Nicänum" in *Festgabe von Fachgenossen und Freunden Karl Müller* (1922); I. Ortiz de Urbina, *El símbolo niceno* (1947); M. Lods, "Le Symbole de Nicée," in *Paris Protestant School of Theology Bulletin*, no. 50 (1955).

Athanasian Creed: D. Waterland, *Critical History of the Athanasian Creed* (1723); G. D. W. Ommanney, *Early History of the Athanasian Creed* (1880); *Critical Dissertation on the Athanasian Creed* (1897); H. Brewer, *Das sogennante Athanasianische Glaubensbekenntnis* (1909); A. E. Burn, *Athanasian Creed* (1912); M. Lods, "Le Symbole d'Athanase," in *Paris Protestant School of Theology Bulletin*, no. 52 (1955); J. N. D. Kelly, *Athanasian Creed* (1964).

Confessions: P. Hall, *Harmony of Protestant Confessions* (1842); G. B. Winer, *Comparative View of the Doctrines and Confessions of the Various Communities of Christendom* (1873); E. F. Karl Müller, *Bekenntnisschriften der Reformierten Kirche* (1907); W. H. Griffith Thomas, *Principles of Theology: An Intro. to the Thirty-Nine Articles* (1930); G. S. Hendry, *Westminster Confession for Today* (1960); E. Routley, *Creeds and Confessions* (1963); A. C. Cochrane, ed., *Reformed Confessions of the Sixteenth Century* (1966).

A. S. WOOD

CREEK (Acts 27:39, AV). *See* BAY.

CREEPING THINGS [Heb. *remeś*] (Gen. 1:24, 26; 6:7, 20; 7:14, 23; 8:17, 19; Ps. 148:10; Ezk. 8:10; 38:20; Hos. 2:18); NEB also REPTILES, "things that creep on the earth" (Hos. 2:18); **THING THAT CREEPS** [*rāmaś*] (Gen. 1:25f., 30; 7:8, 14; 8:17; 9:2; Dt. 4:18; Ps. 104:20; Ezk. 38:20); NEB REPTILE, THING THAT CRAWLS, THING THAT MOVES; [*šereṣ*] (Lev. 22:5); NEB VERMIN.

Remeś is a collective noun embracing a large class of animals, so designated because they appear to move close to the ground. The noun is derived from the verb *rāmaś*, meaning "move or glide about with light, smooth motions." The term frequently refers to terrestrial creatures ("every creeping thing that creeps upon the ground") and is distinguished from cattle (Gen. 1:24f.; 7:14; Ps. 148:10), animals in general (Gen. 6:20; 7:8; 8:17, 19), man (Gen. 6:7; 7:23), birds (Gen. 6:7; 7:8; etc.; Dt. 4:17f.; Ezk. 38:20; Ps. 148:10), and fish (Dt. 4:18; Ezk. 38:20).

Although commentators limit *remeś* to the reptiles, the term seems to be used more comprehensively. For instance, it apparently designates all living terrestrial forms (cf. the Hebrew of Gen. 1:28; 7:21; 9:3), fish (Ps. 69:34; 104:25; Hab. 1:14), the beasts of the forest (Ps. 104:20); and even the swarming creatures (*šereṣ*) are called *hārōmēś* (Lev. 11:44, 46). In the final instance, *šereṣ* refers to weasels, mice, lizards, and crocodiles (cf. Lev. 11:29f.). (For *šereṣ hā'ôp* [Lev. 11:20f.; Dt. 14:19] *see* INSECTS.)

Consequently, restriction of the term *remeś* to reptiles alone is too narrow. It is a general term signifying the smaller animals which, to the eye of the observer, appear to creep or crawl along the ground.

J. T. DENNISON, JR.

CREMATION. The term refers to the practice of disposing of the deceased by means of burning (Heb. *śārap*; Gk. *kaíō*). It takes two forms: (1) the ancient practice of burning all but the bones, which are later interred, and (2) the practice of complete cremation.

In the Mediterranean area cremation was avoided by the Egyptians, who embalmed their dead, the dryness of the climate facilitating this practice. The Persians, following Zoroastrian belief, exposed the corpses — a practice still followed by the Parsees, especially in and near Bombay. Among the ancient Greeks burial was the normal custom; but later cremation became widely practiced, particularly during a plague, or after a battle, in order to prevent enemies from disinterring the dead. Among the Romans likewise, especially the aristocracy, the practice of cremation largely was later than that of burial. Today memorials along the Appian Way testify to its prevalence prior to the rise of Christianity.

Among the early Hebrews cremation was the exception. It was regarded as appropriate only for serious offenders, such as Achan (Josh. 7:15, 25; cf. Lev. 20:14; 21:9; Isa. 30:33). The burning of the bodies of King Saul and his sons by the men of Jabesh-gilead is disputed (1 S. 31:11f.); it is an isolated incident and is omitted in the account given in 1 Ch. 10:11f. Tacitus noted that the Jews bury their dead rather than burn them (*Hist.* v.5). Some rabbis considered the burning of the corpse consistent only with idolatry (*Abodah Zarah* i.3). Many rabbis concluded that burial is positively commanded in the Pentateuch (cf. Dt. 21:23). The main reasons for the Jewish preference for burial appear to be their belief that God intended the soul and body to be compatible and their belief (especially in later Judaism) in the resurrection of the body. Other factors that may have contributed are the relative scarcity of fuel in the land of Israel and the availability of caves, whether natural or artificial, for burial. Exposure without burial was regarded as a calamity among the Hebrews (1 K. 14:11; Jer. 7:32; Ezk. 29:5; Ps. 79:3; 2 S. 21:10). The burial of the dead was a duty even to strangers (Tob. 1:17–2:8).

The Christians followed the precedent of the Jews with respect to disposal of the dead. The early Christians, following the example of Jesus (e.g., Mt. 9:24; Jn. 11:11), spoke of the deceased as being "asleep" (cf. 1 Cor. 15:6, 20). Early memorials referred to the deceased as "asleep in Jesus." A church in Jerusalem today bears the title the "Dormition of the Virgin Mary" ("dormition" meaning "sleep"). It seemed quite inappropriate to incinerate the body referred to as being "asleep." The early Christian expectations of the Lord's early return and NT examples of the dead being raised (e.g., Acts 9:40) contributed to their reluctance to cremate the deceased, since the Parousia might occur very soon after burial. In this respect the Christians, like the Jews, differed from many of their contemporaries, as noted by Tacitus. Unlike the Greeks, who regarded the body as a prison of the soul, both Hebrews and Christians saw it as the integration of human personality. Furthermore, the Christian emphasis upon the body as the temple of the Holy Spirit increased their disinclination toward cremation (1 Cor. 3:16f.; 6:19).

Christian apologists also approved the preference for burial (Minucius Felix *Octavius* 34 [*PL* III, 362]). Although martyrs were sometimes burned with the intent of lessening the Christians' confidence of resurrection, it did not deprive them of this hope. If possible, they would gather the ashes or bones of the martyrs and bury them (M. Polyc. 18). They were confident, however, in the affirmation that the manner of death and disposition of the corpse would not affect the resurrection, because of God's omnipotence. This has been the position of the Church — especially the Greek Orthodox Church and the Roman Catholic Church — throughout the centuries.

Bibliography.–*Jew. Enc.*, IV, *s.v.* (R. Guttheil); *New Catholic Encyclopedia* (1967), IV, *s.v.* (A. Closs); A. W. Argyle, *HibJ*, 52 (1953/54), 67ff.; C. J. Polsol, *et al.*, *Disposal of the Dead* (1953); R. W. Habenstein and W. M. Lamers, *Funeral Customs the World Over* (1963).

G. A. TURNER

CRESCENS kres'ənz [Gk. *Krēskēs*–'increasing']. An assistant of Paul, mentioned in 2 Tim. 4:10 as having gone to Galatia. That he was one of the Seventy, and that he founded the church in Vienna in Gaul, are traditions without any trustworthy basis.

CRESCENTS [Heb. *śahᵃrōnîm*] (Jgs. 8:21, 26; Isa. 3:18); AV ORNAMENTS, "round tires like the moon" (Isa. 3:18). Moon-shaped necklaces, usually worn as pendants, made of silver, gold, or bronze. Specimens have been recovered from various Palestinian sites.

CRETANS krē'tənz [Gk. *Krētes*] (Acts 2:11; Tit. 1:12). *See* CRETE.

CRETE krēt [Gk. *Krētē*]. A large island in the Mediterranean Sea. Lying SE of the Greek mainland, it forms the southern boundary of the Aegean Sea, together with Cythera on the northwest and Carpathos and Rhodes on the northeast. It is some 156 mi. (250 km.) long from west to east and varies from approximately 8 to 35 mi. (13 to 56 km.) in breadth. The island is mountainous, with three ranges: Dikte in the east, Ida in the center, and the White Mountains in the west. The last two ranges have peaks slightly in excess of 8000 ft. (2440 m.). On the south coast the mountains tend to drop sheer into the sea, so most of the cultivable areas and the best harbors are on the north side. This is nicely illustrated by the difficulties Paul encountered along the southern coast on his voyage to Rome (recounted in Acts 27). The Cretan mountains consist basically of limestone, which, exposed by the severe deforestation, has weathered to form steep ravines, fissures, crevasses and numerous caves, the source of many legendary and historical episodes throughout Crete's long history. The land is marked by the number of upland plains, with the main areas suitable for cultivation and settlement being in the east. The soil is mostly rocky with little alluvium. The main and most disastrous change since antiquity has been the deforestation of the island, which, now virtually complete, has transformed it from one of the most fertile and prosperous locations in the Mediterranean to one of the most rocky and barren.

The name Crete does not occur in the OT, but it is possible, and usually assumed, that the CHERETHITES of David's bodyguard were Cretans, because of similarity of name and their close geographic association with the Philistines. The place name CAPHTOR and the gentilic term Caphtorim, as origins of the PHILISTINES, are generally taken to refer to Crete and its inhabitants.

In the NT Cretans are named as present at the Feast of Pentecost (Acts 2:11), and the island plays a significant and unfortunate role in the shipwreck that occurred in the course of Paul's journey to Rome (Acts 27:7-44). It is possible that Paul revisited Crete upon release from prison in Rome, for he left Titus there to organize the work (Tit. 1:5). In 1:12 he quotes the Cretan poet Epimenides to the effect that Cretans were men of low repute in the ancient world.

Although the island had little significance in the classical world, such was not the case in the earlier periods. Crete was first settled by Neolithic farmers in the 4th and 3rd millennia B.C., but it was in the Bronze Age, beginning *ca.* 3000 B.C., that Crete developed a powerful civilization that frequently played a dominant role in the

Mural from the Middle Minoan palace at Knossos (*ca.* 1750 B.C.). Bull-leaping performances, such as those presented by Theseus and the Athenians for King Minos and his daughter Ariadne, probably had religious significance. (Embassy of Greece, Washington)

Remains of the Minoan palace at Phaestos. Built entirely on terraces, the palace was a self-contained community, strikingly similar in plan and architectural detail to the palaces at Knossos and Mallia. (W. S. LaSor)

Aegean, and that lasted for nearly two thousand years. This civilization has been termed Minoan by Sir Arthur Evans after king Minos, known from the Homeric epics. Minos, according to legend, ruled at Knossos, a site that Evans excavated over many years at the turn of the century. Evans divided Minoan chronology into three periods, Early, Middle, and late Minoan, which roughly correspond to the Early Bronze (3150-2200 B.C.), Middle Bronze (2200-1550 B.C.), and Late Bronze (1550-1200 B.C.) periods of Palestinian archeology.

The golden age of Minoan civilization was reached in the Middle Minoan Period, *ca.* 2000-1500 B.C. In this period colossal, almost labyrinthine, palaces were constructed. Four have now been found at Knossos, Phaestos, Mallia and Zakro. Writing was in use, initially pictographic, but developing by *ca.* 1700 B.C. into a linear script, syllabic in type, that was in use until the fall of the Palace civilization shortly after 1500 B.C. Interpretation of this script is still in its infancy, although C. H. Gordon has plausibly interpreted a few inscriptions as a dialect of West Semitic.

All the known Minoan palaces were violently destroyed, presumably by earthquake, about 1700 B.C. They were very quickly rebuilt on an even grander scale, and Minoan civilization reached its zenith during the two and a half centuries from 1700 to 1450 B.C. The general level of attainment of the arts and crafts in this period matched the grandeur and splendor of the palaces. Metalworking, pottery, and especially the carving of ivory and stone and the production of jewelry reached heights not to be rivaled before the classical age of Greek civilization in the first millennium. During the latter part of this period Minoan civilization spread overseas and colonies were established on Thera, Melos, and Rhodes, at Miletus on the Anatolian coast, and possibly even on the Greek mainland itself. Certainly the mainland was deeply influenced by Cretan culture and fashions.

This grandeur was, however, short-lived. Soon after the great volcanic eruption that destroyed Thera, *ca.* 1500 B.C., the Cretan centers were violently destroyed. Since this destruction included fire, it is probable that it was caused by an invading force rather than earthquake. Whatever the cause, none of the palaces except Knossos was occupied thereafter, and Knossos itself was taken over by foreigners. Changes in pottery style and palace architecture make it very likely that the conquerors were Mycenaean Greeks from the mainland. Strong evidence in the same direction is the fact that a new script termed Linear B, apparently an adaptation of the older Linear A, came into use in this period at Knossos, as well as at Pylos, Mycenae, and other sites on the mainland. In 1952 M. Ventris succeeded in interpreting this script as an early form of archaic Greek, although the interpretation is not without its problems or its critics.

Shortly after 1400 B.C. the last palace at Knossos was destroyed and the grandeur of Bronze Age Crete came to an end, although it apparently remained under Mycenaean domination during the next two centuries. At the end of this period Dorian Greeks invaded the island and Crete sank into relative oblivion during the Iron Age.

Crete played a minor role in the Aegean during the classical age, being noted as a source of mercenary soldiers and traders. In 67 B.C. it fell under Roman hegemony and was organized into the province of Cyrenaica, linked with territory in Libya on the North African coast.

Bibliograhpy.–Archeology and history of Neolithic and Bronze Age Crete: J. D. S. Pendlebury, *Archeology of Crete* (1939); S. Hood, *The Minoans* (1971); R. Higgins, *Archaeology of Minoan Crete* (1973); R. W. Hutchinson, *Prehistoric Crete* (1961). Excellent photographic documentation: S. Marinatos and M. Hirmer, *Crete and Mycenae* (1960). Divergent interpretation of the end of the Minoan age: L. R. Palmer, *Mycenaeans and Minoans* (1963). Decipherment: J. Chadwick, *Decipherment of Linear B* (1958); for Linear A: C. H. Gordon, *JNES*, 17 (1958), 245-255; *Orientalia*, 32 (1963), 292-97. Dorian arrival until Roman conquest: R. F. Willetts, *Ancient Crete* (1965). F. W. BUSH

CRIB [Heb. *'ēḇûs*]; NEB STALL. "Crib" (Job 39:9; Isa. 1:3) translates the Heb. *'ēḇûs* (from *'aḇas*, "to feed") exactly, as it denotes a barred receptacle for fodder used in cowsheds and foldyards; also in fields, for beasts lying out in the winter.

CRICKET [Heb. *ḥargōl*]; AV BEETLE; NEB GREEN LOCUST. A term occurring only in Lev. 11:22, doubtless referring to some kind of locust or grasshopper. *See* LOCUST; INSECTS.

CRIME; CRIMES [Heb. *'āwōn*] (Dt. 19:15); AV INIQUITY; [*ḥēṭ*] (21:22); AV SIN; NEB OFFENCE; [*rā'â*] (Jgs. 9:56); AV WICKEDNESS; [*neḇālâ*] (20:10); AV FOLLY; NEB OUTRAGE; [*'āwen*] (Ps. 56:7 [MT 8]); AV INIQUITY; NEB emends; [*'ôlōṭ*] (64:6 [MT 7]); AV INIQUITIES; NEB omits; [Gk. *aítion*] (Lk. 23:4, 22); AV FAULT; NEB "case . . . to answer"; [*rhadioúrgēma*] (Acts 18:14); AV LEWDNESS; NEB MISDEMEANOUR.

Words for "crime" and "crimes" do not appear very frequently in the original languages of Scripture nor in the English versions. The AV and RV translate no word "crime" in the OT, although with the RSV they render Heb. *mišpaṭ* in Ezk. 7:23 as "crimes." The AV, RV, and RSV all render Heb. *zimmâ* (Job 31:11) as "a heinous crime." The AV has "crimes" for Gk. *aitías* in Acts 25:27, while the RV, RSV, and NEB have "charges" (see Jn. 18:38; 19:4, 6). The AV has "crime" for Gk. *enklḗmatos* in Acts 25:16, while the RV has "matter," the RSV and NEB "charge."

A crime is a transgression against the public right, a serious offense against the law, or a base weakness or iniquity, all of which are regarded as obnoxious to the Creator. Specific forms of crime, many treated in separate articles, are the following:

ADULTERY

Bestiality. Sexual relations with a beast. This form of vice was considered loathsome and abhorrent, partly because of its associations with certain pagan rites and mythology; it called for extreme language in its description and rigorous measures in its punishment. Both the beast and the guilty human were to be put to death (Ex. 22:19; Lev. 18:23; 20:15f.; Dt. 27:21).

BLASPHEMY

Breach of Covenant. Heb. *pārar 'eṯ-habberîṯ*. According to Poucher (*HDB, s.v.* "crimes"), this term included: (1) failure to observe the Day of Atonement (Lev. 23:29); work on that day (Lev. 23:28); (2) sacrifice of children to Molech (Lev. 20:3); (3) neglect of circumcision (Gen. 17:14; Ex. 4:26); (4) unauthorized manufacture of the holy oil (Ex. 30:33); (5) anointing an alien therewith (Ex. 30:33); (6) neglect of the Passover (Nu. 9:13). Note also the following: Gen. 17:14; Lev. 26:15-44; Dt. 29:25; 31:16, 20. Paul (Rom. 1:31) speaks of *asýnthetoi*, "covenant-breakers."

Breach of Ritual. A term not found in the Scriptures, but covering a number of acts prohibited by the ceremonial law. They have been exhaustively enumerated by Poucher: (1) eating blood, whether of fowl or beast (Lev. 7:27; 17:14); (2) eating fat of the beast of sacrifice (Lev. 7:25); (3) eating leavened bread during the Passover (Ex. 12:15, 19); (4) failure to bring an offering when an animal is slaughtered for food (Lev. 17:4); (5) offering sacrifice while the worshiper is under the ban of uncleanness (Lev. 7:20f.; 22:3f., 9); (6) making holy ointment for private use (Ex. 30:32f.); (7) using the same for perfume (Ex. 30:38); (8) neglect of purification in general (Nu. 19:13, 20); (9) slaughtering an animal for food away from the door of the tabernacle (Lev. 17:4, 9; even the alien must comply, so that the introduction of worship at other places might be avoided); (10) touching holy things illegally (Nu. 4:16-20). The punishment for the nonobservance of these prohibitions was the "cutting off" of the transgressor from his people (Heb. *nikraṯ miqqereḇ*, "cut off from among," i.e., excommunicate, etc.).

Breach of Trust. *See* TRUST, BREACH OF.

BRIBERY

Burglary. This term does not occur in the main English versions. The corresponding act is defined as "thievery accompanied by breaking in," and it places the offender beyond protection from violence (Ex. 22:2). The crime might be committed in various degrees, and to burglarize the "devoted things" was punishable by death (Josh. 7:25), as was also man-stealing (Ex. 21:16; Dt. 24:7).

DEBT

Deception. *See* DECEIT.

DISOBEDIENCE

DIVINATION

DRUNKENNESS

Evil Speaking (Slander). See "Speaking Evil," below.

Falsehood. Heb. *ma'al*, "treachery," "sin," "trespass" (Job 31:34), and *šeqer*, "a sham," "deceit," "lying" (2 S. 18:13; Ps. 7:14; 119:118; 144:8, 11; Isa. 28:15; 57:4; 59:13; Jer. 10:14; 13:25; Hos. 7:1; Mic. 2:11). In every case wilful perversion of the truth or preference for untruth is at least presupposed. Hence falsehood always marks an evil disposition, enmity against truth, and thus against God. Consequently it is criminal. *See also* LIE.

False Swearing. "Swearing to a lie or falsehood" (Heb. *šeqer*) is mentioned in Lev. 6:3, 5; 19:12; Jer. 5:2; 7:9; Hos. 10:4; Zec. 5:4. From these passages and their context it appears that this crime was considered in the twofold sense of a wrong against the neighbor and against God, for the oath was an appeal to God to witness to the truthfulness of the statement; hence to swear falsely was to represent God as supporting a false statement. It is condemned also in 1 Tim. 1:10 (Gk. *epíorkoi*, "perjurers").

False Witnessing. Heb. idiom *'ēḏ šeqer*, "witness of a falsehood," "lie" (Ex. 20:16; Dt. 19:16, 18; Prov. 6:19; 14:5, 25; 19:5, 9); Gk. *pseudomartyréō*, "bring false testimony" (Mk. 10:19; 14:56f.); *pseudomartyría*, "false testimony" (Mt. 15:19; 26:59). In order that the innocent might be protected against the lying accuser, a criminal was to be convicted only on the testimony of at least two or three witnesses, testifying to the same facts (Nu. 35:30). If one was found testifying falsely, he was to be punished by suffering the penalty that would have been inflicted on the one against whom he testified, had he been convicted (Dt. 19:16-19).

Fornication. Heb. *taznûṯ* (Ezk. 16:29) and *zānâ* refer to committing fornication figuratively, by idolatry (Isa. 23:17; Ezk. 16:26), or causing to commit such (2 Ch. 21:11). The Greek counterparts, *porneía* (33 times) and *porneúō* (7 times), are much more frequent, which indicates the greater abhorrence of fornication or whoredom in the NT (although here again, some usages are figurative, referring to idolatry). The intensive Gk. *ekporneúō* is found in Jude 7, "be utterly unchaste.".

Forswear. Found only in Mt. 5:33 in the sense of committing perjury (Gk. *epiorkéō*).

Harlotry. The avocational or at least habitual, notorious practice of unchastity. In most instances the ordinary term for unchaste living (Heb. *zānâ*) is employed (Gen. 34:31; 38:15, 24; Lev. 21:14; Josh. 2:1; Jgs. 11:1; 16:1; 1 K. 3:16; Prov. 7:10; 29:3; Jer. 5:7; Am. 7:17). For the publicly known woman of the street and the professional devotee in pagan temple worship, the Heb. *qᵉḏēšâ* was employed (Gen. 38:21f., AV; Hos. 4:14). The Gk. *pórnē* occurs in Mt. 21:31f.; Lk. 15:30; 1 Cor. 6:15f.; He. 11:31; Jas. 2:25. Often it was used metaphorically of idolatry or any defection from the divine covenant, and applied particularly to Jerusalem (Isa. 1:21); the Jewish nation (Jer. 2:20; 3:1, 6ff.; often in Ezk. 16 and 23; Mic. 1:7); Israel (Hos. 4:15); Nineveh (Nah. 3:4); Tyre, with reference to the various arts employed to renew her commerce (Isa. 23:16) and to her restored traffic (v. 17); and to anti-Christian "Babylon" (Rev. 17:5, 15; 19:2). See also "Fornication," above.

HOMICIDE

Homosexual Relations. Often called sodomy, from reference to it in Gen. 19:5-7 (cf. Gen. 13:13; Isa. 3:9; Lam. 4:6; 2 Pet. 2:6f.; Jude 7). In Lev. 18:22 it is referred to as an "abomination," and according to 20:13 both parties "shall be put to death." In the OT reference is made only to men lying with men, not to the same practice among women — although in another "unnatural" sin, bestiality, the prohibition is for women as well (Lev. 18:23). When Paul in Rom. 1:26f. speaks of men who are consumed with passion for one another" (NEB), he refers also to "women" who have "exchanged natural relations for unnatural." The term "sodomite" (Heb. *qāḏēš*, a [quasi-] sacred person) is generally used in the OT, however, in connection with apostasy and licentious idolatry (Dt. 23:17; 1 K. 14:24; 15:12; 22:46; 2 K. 23:7). Cf. 1 Tim. 1:10; 1 Cor. 6:9.

IDOLATRY

Ill-treatment of Parents (Ex. 21:15, 17; Lev. 20:9; Dt. 21:18ff.). See "Parents, Crimes Against," below.

Incest. Heb. *zimmâ*, "vice," "wickedness," "refined immorality" (Lev. 18:17; 20:14); also "unnatural vice" (Heb. *teḇel*, the same word that is used to designate the unnatural commingling with beasts). Amnon's deed is designated as *ḥeseḏ*, indicating the degradation of the tenderness natural between brothers and sisters into an immoral intimacy (2 S. 13). The crime is that of sexual relation between persons within the degrees of relationship forbidden by the Levitical law, as that of Lot's daughters with their father (Gen. 19:33); the son with his father's concubines, as Reuben (Gen. 35:22), and Absalom (2 S. 16:22; cf. 1 Cor. 5:1); that of the father-in-law with his daughter-in-law (Gen. 38:15ff.; cf. Ezk. 22:11); of the brother with the sister or half-sister, as Amnon (2 S. 13:14); of the brother-in-law with the sister-in-law (Mt. 14:3); or with both a woman and her daughter or granddaughter (Lev. 20:14; 18:17). Illicit relation with the brother's widow is designated (Lev. 20:21) as a disgraceful act, literally "uncleanness" (excepting the levirate marriage). Such acts were forbidden on the ground that the Jews were to avoid the evil practices of the Canaanites and the Egyptians in regard to marriage within the specified limits, because this would naturally result in breaking down the sanctity of the bonds connecting near relatives, and in throwing open the floodgates of immorality among them. Then, too, such provisions would secure higher results in discipline and in mentally and physically healthy children.

Infanticide. This crime seems to have been quite foreign to the minds of the Hebrews, for they had too lofty a conception of the value of human life; besides, children were considered a blessing, and their absence in the home a curse (cf. Ex. 1:17, 21; Pss. 127, 128). For this reason, there was no reason to prohibit it by law, except as the Israelites might be influenced to sacrifice their children to MOLECH when following the religious customs of the Canaanites.

Injuries to the Person (cf. Ex. 21:18ff.; Lev. 24:19f.; Dt. 25:11).

Irreverence. Lack of respect for God or His natural representatives, the parents or governmental officers. See "Parents, Crimes Against," below; *see also* BLASPHEMY.

Kidnapping (Man-Stealing). No word for this is found in that OT, but in Ex. 21:16 it is said that "whoever steals a man" is to be "put to death" (see Dt. 24:7). Such a word, Gk. *andrapodistḗs*, does appear once in the NT (1 Tim. 1:10), AV and RV "menstealers," RSV "kidnapers," NEB "kidnappers." While it is a rather frequent crime in our 20th cent., even where the death penalty obtains, no instance of it appears among the Hebrews.

Lying. *See* LIE.

MALICE

Manslaughter. *See* MANSLAYER.

MURDER

OATH

Parents, Crimes Against. The law enjoined upon the child reverence toward his parents, especially the father. That the mother was to share this reverence practically on equal terms with the father is seen in that each is mentioned separately whenever obedience and reverence are enjoined upon the child (Dt. 5:16). Deliberate disobedience and stubbornness was a serious crime (Dt. 21:18). Both the father and the mother are directed to lay hands upon such a child and bring him to the elders for punishment. How greatly such conduct was held in horror is seen in many of the Proverbs, especially 30:17. Everything that would lower a parent's dignity and influence or violate his sense of just recognition must be carefully avoided (Gen. 9:20-27).

Perjury. See "False Swearing"; "Forswear," above.

Prophesying, False. By reason of his position as the recognized mouthpiece of Yahweh, the prophet's word was weighty in influence; hence to prophesy falsely was equivalent to practicing fraud publicly. Jeremiah described the condition that made such things possible as "wonderful and horrible" (5:30f.). See also Jer. 23:32; 29:8f.; Ezk. 21:23; Zec. 10:2; Mt. 7:15; 24:11, 24; Mk. 13:22; Lk. 6:26; Acts 13:6 (Bar-Jesus); 2 Pet. 2:1; 1 Jn. 4:1; Rev. 16:13; 19:20; 20:10. *See also* PROPHECY.

Prostitution. Hebrew and Christian morality never condoned this practice, although the Bible recognizes its existence even among God's people. The Hebrew father was forbidden (Lev. 19:29) to give his daughter over to a life of shame (Heb. *ḥālal*, "profane a person, place, or thing," "pollute"). See also "Fornication" and "Harlotry" above; "Whoredom," below.

Rape. Heb. *ḥāzaq*, "seize, "force," "ravish." The punishment for this crime was greater when the act was committed against a bethrothed woman (Dt. 22:25-29). See "Seduction," below.

Removing Landmarks (Dt. 19:14). *See* LANDMARKS.

Reviling (Ex. 22:28). See "Irreverence," above; *see also* REVILE.

Robbery. Heb. *gāzal*, "pluck off," "strip," "rob,"

"take away by force or violence." It was forbidden in the law and frequently referred to as despicable (Lev. 19:13; 26:22; 1 S. 23:1; Prov. 22:22; Isa. 10:2, 13; 17:14; Ezk. 33:15; 39:10; Mal. 3:8f.).

Sabbath-breaking. As the Hebrew sabbath was regarded as a day of rest, all acts absolutely unnecessary were considered a violation, a "breaking" of the sabbath, which appears sufficiently from the commandment (Ex. 20:8-11); and the head of the household was held responsible for the keeping of this commandment by all sojourners under his roof. *See also* SABBATH.

Seduction. Heb. *tā'â, ṭā'â*, "dissemble," seduce"; Gk. *apoplanáō*, "lead astray"; *planáō*, "go astray," "deceive," "err," "seduce"; *góēs*, "a wizard," "impostor," "seducer." In all the passages in which the idea of seduction is expressed in the English, the term is used not in the modern sense of sexual entrapment but in the more figurative sense of leading into sin generally (2 K. 21:9; Prov. 12:26, AV; Isa. 19:13, AV; Ezk. 13:10; Mk. 13:22, AV; 2 Tim. 3:13, AV; 1 Jn. 2:26, AV; Rev. 2:20). However, the modern English idea of the word is expressed in the law in Ex. 22:16f.

SLANDER

Sodomy. See "Homosexual Relations," above.

Sorcery. Divining, etc., by help of evil spirits; witchcraft. Heb. *kāšap*, "use sorcery" (Ex. 7:11; Dnl. 2:2; Mal. 3:5); Gk. *pharmakeía*, "enchantment with drugs" (Rev. 9:21; 18:23); other Hebrew and Greek words also appear. Sorcery was not a crime in the Mosaic law, but in Mal. 3:1-5 sorcerers are classed with adulterers and others whom God will judge when His "messenger" (Christ) will appear (see Gal. 5:20; Rev. 9:21; 18:23; 21:8; 22:15). *See also* MAGIC.

Speaking Evil. In the OT "bring an evil [Heb. *rā'*] name upon" (Dt. 19:15; 1 K. 22:23; Ps. 34:13; 41:5; 50:19; 109:20; 140:11; Prov. 15:28; 16:30). Evil speaking is considered a crime because it is simply the expression of the evil intents of the heart. This is brought out more clearly in the NT (Mt. 7:17f.; 12:34f.; Mk. 9:39; Lk. 6:45). As such, evil speaking (Gk. *blasphēmía*) is represented as entirely unworthy a Christian character (Eph. 4:31; 1 Pet. 4:4, 14; 2 Pet. 2:2, 10, 12; Jude 10; also Gk. *katalaléō*, "babble against," "gossip," Jas. 4:11). It will be noticed from the above that evil speaking against those in authority is designated with the same word (blasphemy) as raillery against God, since they are considered God's representatives on earth (Rom. 13). *See also* SLANDER.

Stealing. Heb. *gānaḇ*, "thieve" (lit. or fig.); by implication, "deceive," "carry away," "secretly bring," "steal away" (lit. Gen. 44:8; Ex. 20:15; 21:16; 22:1; Prov. 6:30; Zec. 5:3; fig. Gen. 31:20; 2 S. 15:6; 19:3; Job 27:20; Prov. 9:17 ["Stolen waters are sweet," i.e., the forbidden is attractive; cf. Rom. 7:7]); Gk. *kléptō*, "filch," "steal" (Mt. 6:19f.; 19:18; Jn. 10:10; Rom. 2:21; 13:9; Eph. 4:28). See also "Theft," below.

Suicide. No special law is found against this crime, for it is included in the prohibition against killing. Contrary to the practice and the philosophy of paganism, the act was held in deep abhorrence by the Hebrews. Only the remorse of the damned could drive one to it, as witness Saul (1 S. 31:4) and Judas (Mt. 27:5).

Theft. Heb. *g^{e}nēḇâ*, "stealing," "theft," "something stolen" (Ex. 22:3f.). It is mentioned in connection with other wickedness (Gk. *klopḗ*) in Mt. 15:19; Mk. 7:21; and (Gk. *klémma*) in Rev. 9:21. All three words are used abstractly for the act and concretely for the thing stolen. See also "Stealing," above.

Unchastity. No other form of sin is mentioned more often with disapproval and threats than the various forms of carnal vice, for no other sin is more natural or widespread. *See* LEWD; MARRIAGE; SEX; VIRGIN.

USURY

Whoredom. Heb. *zānâ*, "commit adultery," "fornicate," designates illicit incontinence of any kind; *taznûṯ*, "fornication," "harlotry," "whoredom"; Gk. *porneúō*, *porneía*. The following passages will reveal the estimate in which such uncleanness was held, and will show that both men and women given to it were held in equal abhorrence and designated by the same terms: Gen. 38:24; Lev. 19:29; Nu. 14:33; 25:1; Ezk. 16; 23:3, 7f., 11, 27, 29, 43; 43:7, 9; Hos. 1:2; 2:4; 4:11f.; 6:10; Nah. 3:4; Mt. 5:32; Rom. 1:26f; 1 Cor. 5:1; 7:2; 10:8; Jude 7; Rev. 2:14, 20f.; 18:9; 19:2. Because of the infidelity involved in such acts both to one's spouse and to right living, the practice became symbolical of infidelity to God and His law, and thus served as a frequent figure of speech for Israel's error and apostasy. See "Harlotry," above; *see also* HARLOT.

F. E. HIRSCH
J. K. GRIDER

CRIMSON. *See* COLOR V.C.

CRIPPLE [Heb. *nēḵeh*] (Ps. 35:15); AV ABJECT; NEB RUFFIAN; [Gk. *asthenḗs*] (Acts 4:9); AV IMPOTENT MAN; NEB SICK MAN; [*chōlós*] (14:8); NEB LAME; **CRIPPLED** [Heb. *nāḵēh*] (2 S. 4:4; 9:3); AV LAME; NEB also "a cripple, lame"; [*šāḇar*] (Ezk. 34:4, 16); AV BROKEN; NEB HURT. For Ps. 35:15, *BH* and KoB (p. 616) suggest emending to Heb. *k^{e}nāḵ^{e}rîm*, "like strangers." As it stands, *nēḵeh* means literally "smitten ones"; and in 2 S. 4:4; 9:3, *nāḵēh* means "smitten (here "in the feet"), thus clearly "crippled." *See* LAME.

CRISPING PINS (Isa. 3:22, AV). Pins for crisping, or curling, the hair. The RSV reads more correctly "handbags." *See* BAG.

CRISPUS kris'pəs [Gk. *Krispos*]. One of the small number baptized by Paul among the Corinthian Christians (1 Cor. 1:14). He had been ruler of the Jewish synagogue, but he "believed in the Lord with all his house," and, following Paul, withdrew from the synagogue (Acts 18:7f.). He seems to have been succeeded by Sosthenes (v. 17). According to tradition he became bishop of Aegina.

CRITICISM [Gk. *hē kritikḗ téchnē*–'the discriminatory art']. A comprehensive term embodying a number of techniques employed in the study of (among other things) written documents in order to establish as far as possible their original text, the literary categories to which they are to be assigned, their sources, mode of composition, date, style, authorship, purpose, and so forth. The techniques applicable to literature in general are of great service in the study of the Bible; this article is concerned with *biblical* criticism. Biblical criticism embraces various critical disciplines, notably textual criticism, literary and historical criticism, and form criticism.

I. Textual Criticism
II. Literary and Historical Criticism
  A. Higher Criticism
  B. Source Criticism
  C. Criteria for Dating
  D. OT Criticism
    1. Early Period
    2. Old Documentary Hypothesis
    3. Fragmentary Hypothesis
    4. Supplementary Hypothesis
    5. Development Hypothesis
    6. Since Wellhausen

I. Textual Criticism.–The function of textual criticism is the restoration of the original wording of a document when alterations have been introduced (deliberately or inadvertently) in the course of copying and recopying. Before the invention of printing, when each copy of a document had to be written out separately by hand, scribal errors were especially apt to occur. If the autograph or original document survives, scribal errors can be corrected by reference to it. But if it has long since disappeared (as has happened with all the original exemplars of biblical books), and the surviving copies differ from one another here and there, the original wording can be determined only by careful comparative study of these copies. The scribal habits of individual copyists, and the remoteness or proximity of individual MSS to the original (which is not simply a question of their relative dates), must be investigated. The main types of scribal error must be classified — those arising in copying by sight being quite different from those which arise in copying by dictation. Expertness in textual criticism comes only by long study and practice, although some scholars do seem to be gifted with a rare instinct for divining the original text even when the available copies are almost hopelessly corrupt.

Textual criticism plays a very important part in biblical study, and is an indispensable handmaid to biblical theology, for biblical theology must depend on sound exegesis, and sound exegesis in turn must be based on a reliable text. Because of this basic character of textual criticism it was formerly called "lower criticism," since it represents the lower, foundational courses in the structure of critical study. (For further details *see* TEXT AND MANUSCRIPTS OF THE NT; TEXT AND MANUSCRIPTS OF THE OT.)

II. Literary and Historical Criticism.–*A. Higher Criticism*. If textual criticism represents the lower courses of the critical structure, the upper courses consist of those critical studies that can best be pursued when a trustworthy text is established — those which used to be lumped together under the designation "higher criticism." This designation appears to have been first used in the context of biblical study by J. G. Eichhorn, in the preface to the 2nd edition of his OT introduction (1787): "I have been obliged to bestow the greatest amount of labour on a hitherto entirely unworked field, the investigation of the inner constitution of the individual books of the Old Testament by the aid of the higher criticism — a new name to no humanist." By the "inner constitution" he meant the structure of a book, including a study of the sources on which the author drew and the way in which he used or combined them. This last aspect of the study is commonly called "source criticism."

The structure of a biblical book is sometimes illuminated by internal evidence. From the narrative of Jer. 36, for example, we learn of the first edition of the collected oracles of Jeremiah, dictated to his secretary Baruch in 604 B.C., containing his spoken ministry of the past twenty-three years. This edition, which consisted of a single copy, was almost immediately destroyed by King Jehoiakim, but it was quickly followed by a second and enlarged edition (Jer. 36:32). Even the second edition was by no means the final one, for Jeremiah continued to prophesy for nearly twenty years after that. We have two extant editions of the posthumous collection of his oracles, together with some biographical and other historical material — a longer one preserved in the MT and a shorter one in the LXX. Fragmentary Hebrew copies have been found at Qumrân representing both the longer and the shorter editions.

The structure of many other books of the Bible is not so apparent from the record, and a greater measure of conjecture is necessary for reconstructing the history of their composition.

It is plain, too, from the book of Jeremiah that the author or editor of a prophetical book need not be the prophet himself; in this case the oracles are Jeremiah's but it is to Baruch, who committed them to writing, that we should probably ascribe the authorship of the narrative sections of the book and the publication of the whole.

When a book actually claims to be written by a specific person, that is substantial prima-facie evidence for its authorship. In some categories of literature, however, such as wisdom books and apocalypses, a name may sometimes (but not invariably) be employed for dramatic purposes or the like: a good canonical example is Ecclesiastes, a postexilic series of meditations put into the mouth of Solomon. (Two examples in the Apocrypha are Wisdom of Solomon and the apocalyptic 2 Esdras, ascribed respectively to Solomon and Ezra.) Again, in Jewish schools a disciple was apt to ascribe his dicta to his master, on the ground that "whosoever says a thing in the name of him who said it brings salvation to the world" (Mish. *Pirke Aboth* vi.6). It is noteworthy that a number of the most important books of the Bible are, strictly speaking, anonymous; this is so, for example, with the four Gospels and Acts. Their authorship has to be determined as far as possible by a consideration of relevant internal and external evidence.

B. Source Criticism. Source criticism can be pursued most confidently when a documentary source has survived alongside the later work that has drawn upon it. In the OT the most obvious example of this is seen in the books of Chronicles. The books of Samuel and Kings were the Chronicler's principal sources, and as they have survived we can make rather definite statements about his use of them. (It is specially interesting that an early MS of Samuel found at Qumrân, 4QSam^a, exhibits a type of text closer to that which the Chronicler appears to have used than to the MT.) In the NT the Gospel of Mark is generally recognized to have been a major source of the other two Synoptic Gospels, and since the source survives alongside the works that drew upon it we can without difficulty study the use Matthew and Luke made of Mark.

Where, on the other hand, the sources do not survive, source criticism is a much more uncertain and speculative business. In the 2nd cent. A.D. Tatian unstitched the contents of our four Gospels and rewove them (with minor additions from another document) into one continuous narrative, the *Diatessaron*. If the four separate Gospels had disappeared completely and only the *Diatessaron* survived, it would be impossible to reconstruct the four in anything like their original form. It would be clear that the *Diatessaron* was a composite work, and it would be relatively easy to isolate most of the Johannine element in it, but to disentangle the three Synoptic records would defy the keenest critical skill, not least because of the large amount of material common to the three. It might be possible in some degree to distinguish Matthaean from Lukan material, but the very existence of Mark's record would probably be unsuspected. Exponents of the four-document analysis of the Pentateuch have at times aptly compared their task of distinguishing these four lost documents to the hypothetical task of reconstituting the four Gospels on the basis of the *Diatessaron*.

C. Criteria for Dating. Structure, date, and authorship are the three principal concerns of the "higher criticism." The criteria for dating an ancient work are partly external and partly internal. If a work is quoted or alluded to in a reliably dated document, we conclude that it is earlier than that document. The work may mention persons or events whose date is clearly indicated by other documents; thus some parts of the OT can be dated from their reference to people or incidents mentioned in Mesopotamian or Egyptian historical records. Contemporary Assyrian records enable us to date the oracles of Isaiah at various points within the forty years or so preceding 701 B.C., the year of Sennacherib's invasion of Judah.

A work may date itself; thus some prophetical books of the OT name the actual years in which successive oracles were uttered or the reign or reigns within which certain prophets prophesied (cf. Isa. 1:1; Hos. 1:1; Am. 1:1; Mic. 1:1; Zeph. 1:1; Hag. 1:1, etc.; Zec. 1:1, etc.). As the history of the ancient Near East is reconstructed in ever more precise detail, it becomes increasingly possible to put the various books of the OT into their appropriate historical settings.

The predictive element in biblical prophecy necessitates special dating criteria for the prophetical oracles. To interpret all fulfilled predictions as prophecies made after the event is a completely uncritical procedure. A genuine piece of predictive prophecy will be dated before the events it predicts but after those which it records or presupposes as having taken place. Thus, if Nahum's oracle is a prediction of the fall of Nineveh (as seems probable) and not simply an outburst of exultation over its fall, it will be dated before the destruction of the city in 612 B.C. but after the fall of Thebes in 663 B.C., to which it refers as a past event (Nah. 3:8f.). Again, the oracles of Jeremiah and Ezekiel must be dated to the years preceding, during, and immediately following the Chaldean siege of Jerusalem in 588-587 B.C., since they record the happenings of those years as historical events, but before the return from exile and reconstitution of the Jewish commonwealth (537 B.C. and the years following), which they definitely predict.

D. OT Criticism. The central issue in OT criticism is that of the structure of the Pentateuch.

1. Early Period. Discussions of the authorship of the Pentateuch took place among the Jewish rabbis, but the main question debated by them was whether the account of Moses' death (Dt. 34:5-12) was written by Moses himself, which was the opinion of Rabbi Simeon ("Moses wrote with tears"), or by Joshua — a view ascribed to Rabbi Judah or, according to others, Rabbi Nehemiah (cf. T.B. *Baba Bathra* 15a; *Menahoth* 30a). An interesting anticipation of a phase of later pentateuchal criticism is the remark ascribed to Ben Azzai that where sacrifices are mentioned in the Pentateuch God is always called Yahweh (Midrash *Siphre on Numbers*, 293).

Later Jewish scholars made further critical observations. Isaac ben Yasos (Yiṣḥaqi) of Toledo (d. 1057) pointed out that the list of kings of Edom in Gen. 36:31ff. must be later than the rise of the Hebrew monarchy, and dated it not earlier than Jehoshaphat's reign; he identified Hadad of Gen. 36:35 with Hadad of 1 K. 11:14.

Abraham ibn Ezra (d. 1167), commenting on Dt. 1:1, where Moses is said to have spoken to Israel "beyond the Jordan," adds that his readers will learn the truth if they understand "the mystery of the twelve [probably the twelve verses of Dt. 34], 'and Moses wrote' [Ex. 24:4; Nu. 33:2; Dt. 31:9, 22], 'and the Canaanite was then in the land' [Gen. 12:6, a verse that he says "contains a mystery, concerning which the prudent man will hold his peace"], 'in the mount of the LORD it shall be seen' [Gen. 22:14], 'and his [Og's] bed was a bedstead of iron' [Dt. 3:11]." What he is hinting at is that these passages are later than Moses.

Isaac Abrabanel (d. 1509) adumbrated the theory that the books as they stand were later compilations out of earlier archives.

Christian scholars were making similar observations throughout these centuries. Jerome (d. 420) discerned that the law book discovered in the Jerusalem temple in Josiah's day (2 K. 22:8) was Deuteronomy (comm. on Ezk. 1:1). Commenting on the phrase "unto this day" (Gen. 35:20; Dt. 34:6) he says: "We must certainly take 'this day' to refer to the time when the history was composed; whether you take it as said by Moses, the author of the Pentateuch, or by Ezra, the restorer of Moses' work, I have no objection" (*Against Helvidius* 7). But he vigorously defended the authenticity of Daniel against Porphyry the Neoplatonist who, mainly on the evidence of ch. 11, dated it in the time of Antiochus Epiphanes (a dating revived in 1726 by Anthony Collins in his *Literal Scheme of Prophecy Considered*).

Hugh of St. Victor (1096-1141) thought that the list of kings of Edom in Gen. 36:21ff. was inserted by Ezra, "for it seems frivolous to say that Moses narrated it by the spirit of prophecy" (*PL*, CLXXV, 36 d).

Luther drew similar inferences from Gen. 36:31. His contemporary Andreas Bodenstein von Carlstadt (1480-1541) said that no sane person would suppose that Moses recorded his own death, and since the style of Dt. 34 was that of the Pentateuch generally, the Pentateuch in its completed form was not the work of Moses, but was earlier than Josiah's time.

Other biblical scholars of the 16th and 17th cents., both Roman and Reformed, made further contributions to the question, as did also Thomas Hobbes in England (*Leviathan* [1650]) and Benedict Spinoza in the Netherlands (*Tractatus Theologicopoliticus* [1671]). But thus far pentateuchal criticism was concerned with detecting the presence of post-Mosaic elements in the Pentateuch, the conclusion being that the tradition of Mosaic authorship could not be maintained without qualification.

2. Old Documentary Hypothesis. R. Simon, priest of the Oratory, argued in *Histoire critique de l'AT* (1682) that the duplication of certain narratives in the Pentateuch (e.g., the Creation and Flood narratives), accompanied by diversity of style, pointed to diversity of authorship.

H. B. Witter (*Iura Israelitarum in Palaestina* [1711]) pointed out that the duplicate accounts of the Creation were marked by the use of two different divine names, 'Elohim and Yahweh. This last point was taken up by the French court physician Jean Astruc, who used it as a criterion to distinguish two sources (A and B) throughout Genesis — pre-Mosaic sources on which Moses drew (*Conjectures sur les mémoires originaux dont il paroît que Moyse s'est servi pour composer le livre du Genèse* [1753]).

Astruc's work was epoch-making, and marks the beginning of the continuous history of modern pentateuchal criticism. His criterion was a limited one, which could not be applied to the whole Pentateuch, since it fails after Ex. 6. The real question raised by the use of the divine names in Gen. 1–Ex. 6 was later seen to be the question of *when* the name Yahweh is represented as first coming into use — whether in primeval times (Gen. 4:26) or in the days of Moses (Ex. 3:14f.; 6:2f.). But Astruc introduced on this basis the rudiments of a documentary analysis of the Pentateuch whose influence remains to this day. His general results were adopted by J. G. Eichhorn (*Einleitung in das AT* [1780]), who continued Simon's investigation into stylistic diversities in Genesis and found that they corresponded largely to Astruc's analysis.

K. D. Ilgen, in *Die Urkunden des jerusalemischen Tempelarchivs in ihrer Urgestalt* (1798), wrote out the documents from which he believed Genesis was compiled, and distinguished two unrelated documents that used the divine name 'Elohim.

3. Fragmentary Hypothesis. The fragmentary hypothesis, propounded by a Scots Roman Catholic priest, Alexander Geddes (*Biblia Sacra* [1792-1797]; *Critical Remarks* [1800]), envisaged a much greater number of sources. The Pentateuch, he argued, was not in its present form the work of Moses; together with Joshua, it was written, probably at Jerusalem, not before David nor after Hezekiah but preferably under Solomon, and it was compiled from a large number of short documents or fragments. There is an obvious similarity between Geddes' hypothesis and F. A. Wolf's contemporary view about the composition of the Homeric epics (*Prolegomena ad Homerum* [1795]). Geddes' hypothesis was introduced into Germany by J. S. Vater in his three-volume commentary on the Pentateuch (1802-1805).

Vater's work greatly influenced W. M. L. de Wette. In his *Beiträge zur Einl. in das AT* (1806-1807), de Wette accepted Vater's views, except that he envisaged one fundamental Elohist document in Genesis which was expanded by the addition of other "fragments." This fundamental document was continued in the middle books of the Pentateuch — "the epos of the Hebrew theocracy," into which collections of laws, etc., were inserted from time to time.

4. Supplementary Hypothesis. De Wette thus marks the transition from the fragmentary to the supplementary hypothesis — so called because it postulates one main document supplemented by others. But his chief importance in biblical criticism lies in his work on Deuteronomy. At the age of twenty-five he published his *Dissertatio qua Deuteronomium a prioribus Pentateuchi libris diversum alius cuiusdam recentioris auctoris opus esse demonstratur* (1805), in which, accepting Jerome's identification of Josiah's law book (2 K. 22:8ff.) with Deuteronomy, he went on to date the composition of the book in that period (7th cent. B.C.).

The chief name associated with the supplementary hypothesis is that of Heinrich Ewald. In his *History of Israel* (Eng. tr. 1867-1883) Ewald identified the foundation document (*Grundschrift*) with the "Book of Origins," so called because it was marked by the recurring formula "These are the origins" (Heb. *tôlᵉḏôṯ*, RV "generations"). Into this, he held, other (later) documents were fitted.

The foundation-document was also characterized (in Genesis and the early chapters of Exodus) by the use of 'Elohim for the divine name. But exactly a century after Astruc's work, Herman Hupfeld, in *Die Quellen der Genesis und die Art ihrer Zusammensetzung* (1857), distinguished two documents in Genesis that used the name 'Elohim. One of these was the primary "Book of Origins," which formed the framework of the whole Pentateuch; the other he called "the later Elohist." In addition two other documents had already been isolated in the Pentateuch — the Yahwist (so called from the use of the name Yahweh) and the Deuteronomist. These four were placed in that order, and indicated by the letters E^1 E^2 J D. The four-document analysis thus propounded by Hupfeld has been widely adopted in pentateuchal criticism ever since.

5. Development Hypothesis. Thus far the analysis of the Pentateuch was conducted in terms of literary criticism alone. A new stage now appears in which literary criticism was supplemented by historical (especially religious-historical) criticism. This stage saw the emergence of the development hypothesis, in which the laws and institutions of the Pentateuch, classified in three distinct codes, are correlated with three distinct periods of Israel's religious development.

The development hypothesis took over the four-document hypothesis, but treated the fundamental document (E^1) as the latest, not the earliest, of the four. Indeed, this had been done as early as 1834 by E. G. Reuss in lectures at Strasbourg, although he did not publish his views until 1879, in *L'Histoire sainte et la loi.* In 1835 W. Vatke (*Die Religion des AT nach den kanonischen Büchern entwickelt*) and J. F. L. George (*Die älteren jüdischen Feste mit einer Kritik der Gesetzgebung des Pentateuchs*) argued that Israel's religious development was gradual and that the Levitical legislation (i.e., the laws of Leviticus and kindred sections of Exodus and Numbers) was not only post-Mosaic but later than Deuteronomy, belonging, in fact, to the exilic period. Vatke and George were both greatly influenced by Hegel's philosophy of history, with its pattern of thesis, antithesis, and synthesis; Vatke in turn exercised considerable influence on Julius Wellhausen.

K. H. Graf, in *Die geschichtlichen Bücher des AT* (1866), dated much of the Levitical legislation to the age of Ezra (5th cent. B.C.). He ascribed the greater part of Lev. 17–26 to Ezekiel, thus largely anticipating August Klostermann ("Beiträge zur Entstehungsgeschichte des Pentateuchs: Ezechiel und das Heiligkeitsgesetz," *Zeitschrift für Lutherische Theologie und Kirche*, 38 [1877], 401ff.), who marked off these chapters as a separate law code, the "Law of Holiness" (H). It was objected to Graf's late dating of the Levitical legislation that, on literary-critical grounds, this legislation could not be divorced from the narrative of the foundation-document (E^1), and must therefore be dated early. Graf replied that since the Levitical legislation was later than anything else in the Pentateuch, therefore the whole of E^1 must be dated late. E^1, as containing the "priestly" legislation, came later to be known as P, and E^2 accordingly was thenceforth designated simply as E.

Graf's thesis was strengthened by the Dutch scholar Abraham Kuenen (*Religion of Israel* [Eng. tr. 1874-1875]; *Historisch-critisch Onderzoek naar het Ontstaan en de Verzameling van de Boeken des Ouden Verbonds* [2nd ed. 1885], pt. 1 of which appeared in English as *An Historico-Critical Enquiry into the Origin and Composition of the Hexateuch* [1886]).

But the long regnancy of the development hypothesis is due mainly to Julius Wellhausen. He related the order JE–D–P to the religious history of Israel, paying special attention to the laws regarding sanctuary and sacrifice. "I differ from Graf chiefly in this," he wrote, "that I always go back to the centralisation of the cultus, and deduce from it the particular divergences" (*History of Israel* [Eng. tr. 1885], p. 368). Following Vatke's Hegelian pattern, he distinguished the following stages in the history of Israelite worship:

(1) *Thesis*. JE corresponds to the period of the settlement and early monarchy, when there were many local sanctuaries at which sacrifice was offered by local priesthoods or chosen members of local families.

(2) *Antithesis*. The eighth-century prophets attacked the whole institution of sanctuary and sacrifice as an obstacle in the path of true ethical religion.

(3) *Synthesis* of "cultic" and "prophetic" positions.

(a) *Preexilic*. The Deuteronomic law code prescribed the concentration of national worship at one sanctuary only; the Levitical priests who served the local sanctuaries (suppressed in Josiah's reformation, 621 B.C.) were to be attached to the staff of the central sanctuary.

(b) *Postexilic*. The Priestly law code, which takes for granted a single central sanctuary, makes much more elaborate cultic regulations. The priesthood is restricted to the family of Aaron; the supremacy of the high priest reflects the postexilic situation in which he was head of the Judean temple-state. The Levitical priests of the older local sanctuaries are depressed to the status of temple servants (Levites) with no sacerdotal functions.

The Graf-Wellhausen development hypothesis speedily attained a dominant position because of the apparent success with which it correlated the main strata of the Pentateuch with successive phases of Israel's religious history. But it was constructed on the basis of an excessively doctrinaire philosophy of history, and at a time when hardly any external evidence for the historical setting of the religion of Israel and her neighbors before the 9th cent. B.C. was available.

The increasing evidence brought to light by archeological research, and most of all the discovery and decipherment from 1929 onward of the Ugaritic texts, with their wealth of information about Canaanite myth and ritual, have revolutionized the situation. While Wellhausen's documentary analysis of the Pentateuch and his relative order of the documents (JE–D–P) are still widely adopted as a convenient framework, his reconstruction of the religious history of Israel has gone by the board, and many would agree with H. H. Rowley: "A mere concentration on the acknowledged difficulties of the Graf-Wellhausen view, and then on a selection of points that may seem to give support to a rival view, will not do. For none of the rival views can accommodate so many of the facts, or can escape far more difficulties than the view it seeks to replace. Yet having said this, it remains true that the Graf-Wellhausen view is only a working hypothesis, which can be abandoned with alacrity when a more satisfying view is found, but cannot with profit be abandoned until then" (*Growth of the OT* [1950], p. 46).

6. Since Wellhausen. Many others, however, reject the Graf-Wellhausen scheme even as a working hypothesis. Even in its heyday there were some who refused it completely and maintained the substantial Mosaicity of the Pentateuch, like W. H. Green (*Higher Criticism of the Pentateuch* [1895]), J. Orr (*Problem of the OT* [1900]), and A. H. Finn (*Unity of the Pentateuch* [1917]); more recently, similar positions have been defended by O. T. Allis (*The Five Books of Moses* [1943]), E. J. Young (*Intro. to the OT* [repr. 1963]), and G. C. Aalders (*A Short Intro. to the Pentateuch* [1949]). Of these three Aalders allows a larger post-Mosaic element than the others do; he looks on David's capture of Jerusalem in the seventh year of his reign as the *terminus ad quem* for the final redaction of the Pentateuch.

Others have moved in the opposite direction and posited further documentary sources, subdividing J (e.g., O. Eissfeldt, *Hexateuchsynopse* [1922]; J. Morgenstern, *HUCA*, 4 [1927], 1ff.; R. H. Pfeiffer, *ZAW*, 48 [1930], 66ff.) or P (e.g., G. von Rad, *Die Priesterschrift im Hexateuch* [1934]). The seventh-century date of the Deuteronomic Code, the linchpin of the Graf-Wellhausen scheme, has been called in question — some making it postexilic, like G. Hölscher (*ZAW*, 40 [1920], 161ff.), R. H. Kennett (*Deuteronomy and the Decalogue* [1920]), and J. N. Schofield (*Studies in History and Religion*, ed. E. A. Payne [1942], pp. 44ff.), while others such as T. Oestreicher (*Das deuteronomische Grundgesetz* [1923]) and A. C. Welch (*The Code of Deuteronomy* [1924]) have pushed it back to the early monarchy; and E. Robertson (*The OT Problem* [1950]) dates it in Samuel's time. The very existence of one or another of the four documents has been doubted: M. Löhr (*Untersuchungen zum Hexateuchproblem* [1924]) denied that there was ever an independent source P, and P. Volz and W. Rudolph (*Der Elohist als Erzähler* [1933]) have argued that the hypothesis of a separate E narrative represented a false turning in pentateuchal criticism.

Unaided documentary analysis has plainly reached the limit of its powers. Other critical approaches have been made in recent years to supplement the limitations of source criticism. The cultic and liturgical influence on the grouping of the material has been emphasized; e.g., Gen. 1:1–2:4a has been looked upon as a liturgical text for the Hebrew New Year's Festival (cf. S. H. Hooke, *In the Beginning* [1947], p. 36); the whole complex of Ex. 1–15 has been regarded as a liturgical text or "cult legend" of the Passover, which has not been compiled out of originally distinct documents but has been modified and added to in the course of time (*ILC*, III-IV, 726ff.).

The "traditio-historical" school of Uppsala has presented a radical challenge of a different kind to the basic principles of classical OT criticism; it lays great emphasis on the part played by oral tradition, and on the great reliability of such tradition. The leading exponent of this "traditio-historical" criticism, I. Engell, distinguishes in the Torah and the Former Prophets two collections — the Tetrateuch (Genesis–Numbers) and the Deuteronomic history (Deuteronomy–2 Kings) — which originally had no connection with one another (*Gamla Testamentet: En traditionshistorisk inledning* [1945], I).

The reconstruction of the early history of Israel, based on an evaluation of the OT texts in the light of archeological research, has made its impact on criticism. Among the pioneers in this field are: A. Alt (*Essays on OT History and Religion* [Eng. tr. 1966]), M. Noth (*History of Israel* [Eng. tr., 2nd ed. 1960]; *Laws in the Pentateuch and Other Studies* [Eng. tr. 1966]; *OT World* [Eng. tr. 1966]); and the versatile genius of W. F. Albright, whose influence has been exercised not only in his written works (e.g., *From the Stone Age to Christianity* [1940]; *Archaeology and the Religion of Israel* [1942]; *Yahweh and the Gods of Canaan* [1968]), but also through his brilliant disciples (e.g., John Bright, *History of Israel* [2nd ed. 1972]). But the radical differences between the historical conclusions reached by them has emphasized the need for more stringent methodological controls.

The situation in OT criticism is thus completely fluid, and a new school has yet to appear whose findings will command acceptance as a fresh "regnant hypothesis."

E. NT Criticism. 1. Paul and the NT. In the NT the Pauline collection of letters constitutes the critical pivot that Deuteronomy has long provided in OT criticism. A new and vitally important phase of NT criticism was launched in 1831 when F. C. Baur contributed his paper "Die Christuspartei in der korinthischen Gemeinde" to the *Tübinger Zeitschrift* (4 [1831], 61ff.). Baur, whose theological position in Tübingen University caused the movement he unconsciously started to be called the "Tübingen school," tended increasingly, as time went on, to interpret NT history as Vatke and others interpreted OT history. The thesis and antithesis in NT history were represented on the one hand by Paul, with his liberal policy of the free admission of gentile believers into the Church, and on the other by the reactionary disciples in Jerusalem, headed by James the Just and the apostles Peter and John, with their insistence that only by accepting circumcision and other obligations of the Jewish law could Gentiles be admitted to the new Israel. The conflict between the two parties he saw most clearly in 1 and 2 Corinthians, Galatians, and Romans, which were, in the Tübingen view, the only authentic writings of Paul and moreover the oldest books of the NT. The only other pre-A.D. 70 NT book was Revelation, the one surviving document representing the opposite position. The remaining NT books reflected the outlook of a later generation, after A.D. 70, when the old conflict was not so sharp and the heirs of the two opposed parties tended to close their ranks in the face of imperial persecution and Gnostic deviations. The crowning literary manifestation of this later "synthesis" is Acts, in which Paul and the Jerusalem leaders are portrayed as maintaining harmonious relations throughout, and which was accordingly dated about the middle of the 2nd century.

Brilliant as the Tübingen reconstruction of NT history was, it was too vulnerable to endure in its pristine form. The historical and textual research of J. B. Lightfoot, A. Harnack, W. M. Ramsay, and others undermined its case for the late dating of the Gospels and Acts, and the antithesis that it postulated between the church of Jerusalem as a whole and the Pauline mission proved to be much exaggerated; in particular, the idea of a Judaizing Peter was little more than a figment of the imagination. But NT criticism has never ceased to be influenced by the work of the Tübingen school; witness the protest against its continuing influence by J. Munck in *Paul and the Salvation of Mankind* (Eng. tr. 1959). Indeed, it has enjoyed a substantial and vigorous revival at the hands of S. G. F. Brandon (*The Fall of Jerusalem and the Christian Church* [1951]), with arguments that, if not acceptable, demand a freshly reasoned confutation.

Even more radical than the Tübingen criticism was that of the Dutch scholar W. C. van Manen, who treated all the Pauline Epistles as pseudepigraphs. His views were popularized in the English-speaking world through his contributions to *EB*, but retain little more than curiosity value.

2. Gospel Criticism. Some rudimentary Gospel criticism was practiced in the patristic age. The difficulty of harmonizing the order of events in the Synoptic and Johannine Gospels was discussed by Eusebius, who, in reply to arguments that the Evangelists disagree with one another, points out that the events in the earlier chapters of John antedate the imprisonment of John the Baptist (Jn. 3:24), whereas the Synoptists record that phase of Jesus' ministry which began after the Baptist's imprisonment (*HE* iii.24.8-13). Augustine (*De consensu evangelistarum*) deals in detail with the relations between the Gospels; on the most frequently quoted remark in this work (i.4), that "Mark followed Matthew as his lackey and abbreviator, so to speak," B. H. Streeter observed that if only Augustine had had a synopsis of the Gospels in parallel columns before him, he would have seen at a glance that, where Matthew and Mark have material in common, it is not Mark who abridges it.

The Synoptic Gospels were so designated by J. J. Griesbach in 1774, because they have so much material in common that they lend themselves to a "synoptic" arrangement where the three can be studied side by side. Some 606 out of Mark's 661 verses reappear in somewhat condensed form in Matthew; some 350 of Mark's verses are paralleled in Luke. Matthew and Luke, again, have about 250 verses in common that are not paralleled in Mark. The approximate number of verses in each Gospel not paralleled in another is 31 in Mark, 300 in Matthew, and 550 in Luke. The interpretation of this distribution of common and special material in the three Gospels has been the principal task of Synoptic criticism for nearly two centuries. An epoch-making contribution to this study was made in 1835 by C. Lachmann in *Studien und Kritiken,* when he argued that Mark was the earliest Gospel and was a principal source of Matthew and Luke. His main argument, that Mark's order is the common order of the three, is not so conclusive as has often been supposed; but his thesis has been supported by other and weightier arguments, and enjoys general, almost universal, acceptance. It is also fairly generally agreed — though here the area of dissent is wider — that the common non-Markan material of Matthew and Luke was derived by these two from another documentary source, a compilation of sayings of Jesus, called Q about the beginning of the 20th cent. independently by J. Armitage Robinson and J. Wellhausen. Whether the special material in Matthew and Luke is derived from earlier documentary sources must remain very doubtful, although we have the assurance of Luke himself that, at the time when he wrote, many had taken in hand to draw up a narrative of the gospel events.

Source criticism in the Fourth Gospel (cf. R. Bultmann, *The Gospel of John* [Eng. tr. 1971]) has never been carried out convincingly; the criticism of this Gospel has centered round its historical character, purpose, theology, date, and authorship. *See* articles on the individual Gospels, and *see* GOSPELS, SYNOPTIC.

III. Form Criticism.–Form criticism (Ger. *Formgeschichte,* "form history") represents an endeavor to determine the oral prehistory of written documents or sources, and to classify the material according to the various "forms" or categories of narrative, discourse, and so forth.

A. In the OT. This approach has proved particularly fruitful in the study of the Psalms; their classification according to their principal types (Ger. *Gattungen*), where each type is related to a characteristic life-setting — e.g., Psalms of lament and thanksgiving, both individual and communal; royal Psalms; liturgical Psalms; etc. — has done more for the understanding of the Psalter than almost anything else in the 20th century.

H. Gunkel also applied form critical methods to the creation narratives and to the apocalyptic symbolism that later drew upon the ancient cosmogonic imagery (compare the overthrow of the primeval dragon of chaos in Ps. 74:13f. and Isa. 51:9 with the downfall of the great red dragon of Rev. 12:3, 7-9).

More recently form criticism has illuminated the OT law codes. Albrecht Alt pointed out in *Die Ursprünge des israelitischen Rechts* (1934) that the pentateuchal laws fall mainly into two categories — case law (beginning with a phrase like "If a man do so-and-so . . .") and apodictic law ("Thou shalt . . . ," "Thou shalt not . . . ," or "He that doeth so-and-so shall surely be put to death"). The case-law category reproduces the form known from the other ancient Near Eastern law codes; the apodictic category is not found in these. Apodictic law does, however, resemble in form the conditions embodied in interstate treaties of the ancient Near East, especially treaties between an imperial power and its vassal states. Since such treaties are essentially covenants, concluded in the names of the deities of the high contracting parties, it is evident that the apodictic laws of the OT (among which the Ten Commandments are the most prominent) represent Israel's distinctive covenant law, imposed on the nation by Yahweh. *See also* COVENANT, BOOK OF THE.

B. In the NT. Form criticism has been intensively applied to the Gospels from 1919 onward. The pioneer in this study is usually reckoned to have been Martin Dibelius, whose *Die Formgeschichte des Evangeliums* appeared in 1919 (Eng. tr. *From Tradition to Gospel*), followed in 1921 by Rudolf Bultmann's *Geschichte der synoptischen Tradition* (Eng. tr. *HST*). But several important aspects of this form-critical approach had been anticipated as early as 1902 by Allan Menzies in *The Earliest Gospel* (a comm. on Mark).

1. Classification. The main division in form classification of the Gospel material is that between narratives about Jesus and sayings of Jesus. Narratives have been subdivided into (1) pronouncement stories, (2) miracle stories, and (3) "legends"; sayings into (1) wisdom sayings, (2) prophetic and apocalyptic sayings, (3) law pronouncements and community rules, (4) "I"-sayings, and (5) parables.

Pronouncement stories (which is Vincent Taylor's name for them; Dibelius called them "paradigms") partake of the character of both narratives and sayings. In them a situation develops that elicits from Jesus a pithy saying (an "apophthegm," in Bultmann's terminology), which constitutes the point of the story. Frequently the situation is a controversial one; some action or utterance of Jesus or His disciples arouses criticism, and Jesus replies to the criticism with a decisive pronouncement, e.g., "Those who are well have no need of a physician, but those who are sick; I came not to call the righteous, but sinners" (Mk. 2:17).

A narrative may be assignable to more than one "form"; thus the incident of the paralyzed man (Mk. 2:1-12) is a pronouncement story because the criticism that breaks out when Jesus forgives the man's sins is silenced by Jesus' pronouncement that "the Son of man has authority on earth to forgive sins" (Mk. 2:10); but it can also be classified as a miracle story, more specifically a healing story. Healing stories are readily recognizable; all over the world from early times to the present day they follow a well-established form which emphasizes the interactability of the disease, the despair of the patient, the completeness of the cure, and sometimes the impression produced on the bystanders. But that a healing story conforms to this pattern tells us nothing conclusive about its historical truth.

"Legends," as Dibelius calls them, are such stories about Jesus as the baptism, temptation, transfiguration, and resurrection narratives. Bultmann, who calls them "myths," says that they are not "historical in character [but] are religious and edifying" (*HST*, p. 244). But this is not a form critical judgment; form criticism as such makes judgments about form, not substance.

Similarly, the classification of the sayings of Jesus according to form can throw but little light on the authenticity of individual sayings. Sometimes, when what is substantially the same saying or discourse has been preserved in two different "forms," it may be possible to penetrate behind both to an earlier "unformed" stage of the tradition of what He said. At other times, however, the probability is that the form in which His words have been preserved is the form He Himself gave them. Much of His recorded teaching reproduces the well-known forms of OT poetry, as found, for example, in many of the prophetic oracles. Since Jesus was recognized by His contemporaries as a prophet, it is reasonable to conclude that here we have something approaching His *ipsissima verba*.

T. W. Manson, who himself operated very fruitfully in *The Teaching of Jesus* (1931) with a classification of the sayings of Jesus based on the different kinds of audience addressed, remarked in characteristically down-to-earth language that "if Form-criticism had stuck to its proper business, it would not have made any real stir. We should have taken it as we take the forms of Hebrew poetry or the forms of musical composition. But," he went on, "Form-criticism got mixed up with two other things. One was K. L. Schmidt's full-scale attack on the Marcan framework; the other was the doctrine of the *Sitz im Leben*" (*Studies in the Gospels and Epistles* [1962], p. 5).

2. Framework. Many form critics, and outstandingly K. L. Schmidt (*RGJ*), have envisaged the Synoptic, and primarily the Markan, tradition as consisting of originally unrelated units of narrative or discourse, joined together into a continuous narrative by means of connecting editorial summaries devoid of independent historical value. (It is conceded that the Passion narrative existed as a continuous record from early days.) An impressive answer to this argument was made in 1932 by C. H. Dodd (repr. in his *NT Studies* [1953], pp. 1ff.), who argued that the "editorial summaries" in Mark, when put together by themselves, constitute a coherent outline of the ministry of Jesus, comparable to those outlines of the early apostolic preaching which can be recovered from the speeches in Acts and various passages in the Epistles. Moreover, the general Markan picture of the ministry suggests a sequence and development too spontaneous to be artificial and too logical to be accidental.

3. Life-Setting. It has become common practice among form critics to explain the various elements in the Gospels as called forth by some "life-setting" (Ger. *Sitz im Leben*) in the early Church. For example, the mission charge in Mt. 10 has been held to reflect the methods used by Jewish Christians who evangelized Palestine between A.D. 30 and 66; likewise the controversial discussions that end with some authoritative pronouncement of Jesus are said to reflect disputes in the same period between Jewish Christians and other Jews, or between legalist and libertarian groups within the Christian community. An extreme example in this last respect is the argument that the warning in Mt. 5:19 about the man who "relaxes one of the least of these commandments and teaches men so" is a covert attack by stricter Jewish Christians on Paul.

But one might ask why this practice was not carried on more widely and helpfully. The circumcision question, for example, was a live issue in Christian debate in the quarter century between A.D. 45 and 70; why has it not left a more distinct mark in the Gospels?

Early Christians, in fact, probably made a clearer distinction between their own views on disputed points and the teaching of Jesus than they are sometimes given credit for. Paul, for instance, in answering questions about marriage and divorce, distinguishes sharply between those matters on which he can quote an authoritative saying of Jesus and those on which he can express only his own judgment (1 Cor. 7:10, 12, 25).

It must not be forgotten that during the period A.D. 30-70

many people could remember what Jesus had said, and attempts to claim His authority for things that He had not in fact said could not have been so successful as is often thought. The presence of eyewitnesses would certainly place a check on the free creation of the early Church in the manner presupposed by many form critics. If the evidence of Acts can be accepted, the appeal to public recollection of the ministry of Jesus is a recurring feature of early apostolic preaching (Acts 2:29; 10:36; 26:26).

A life-setting in the early Church — in preaching, in worship, in debate, in the training of catechists — will certainly explain why many Gospel incidents and sayings were preserved and recorded. When a question arose about divorce, or fasting, or sabbath observance, or the payment of the temple tax, it was natural to remember what Jesus had said on the subject. But such a setting in the life of the early Church does not account for the *origin* of the saying; its origin must be sought in a setting in the life of Jesus.

4. Conclusion. The sweeping claims that have been made by some form critics for the value of their discipline must be subjected to a heavy discount. It cannot of itself, no matter what is said to the contrary, lead to conclusions about the historical genuineness of the material. Even the modest claim of J. Jeremias that it helps us to remove a later Hellenistic layer which has overlaid an earlier Palestinian layer, and so to move back from a setting in the life of the early Church to a setting in the life of Jesus, must be treated with caution (*Expos.T.*, 69 [1957/58], 337), if only because Palestine itself was not free of Hellenistic influences, and there were Hellenists in the primitive Jerusalem church, if not indeed in the entourage of Jesus Himself.

Form criticism does, however, make one more aware of the influence of early Christian life and witness on the shaping of the Gospel tradition. It underlines the inadequacy of documentary hypotheses alone to account for the composition of the four Gospels, and provides a fresh classification of their material which sometimes, when comparative study is possible, helps one to penetrate behind written sources to the oral stage of the tradition. It then becomes clearer than ever that no discernible stratum of Gospel tradition, written or oral, knows any Jesus but the one whom the NT presents as Messiah and Son of God.

A particular variety of form criticism relates to the study of the structure of the NT epistles. An impetus to this approach was given by Paul Schubert in his *Form and Function of the Pauline Thanksgiving* (1939). Until this work appeared, it was widely supposed that, apart from the conventional salutation and thanksgiving at the beginning and the greetings at the end, Paul's letters were unstructured for the most part; study since then has brought to light fairly well-defined structures in the main body of the letters. It is precarious, however, to use this recognition of structural forms as a means of removing as unauthentic passages which do not fit these structures easily; the structural forms are Paul's servants, not his masters.

IV. Redaction Criticism.–What is called redaction criticism has been pressed into service more recently to do more justice to the authors and redactors of biblical documents than they received in the heyday of source criticism and form criticism. This discipline has been applied to various parts of the OT, as for example to the Chronicler's use of the material which he inherited — much of it still extant in earlier OT writings — so as to present his distinctive understanding of Israel's history. But it has proved particularly fruitful in Gospel study, with reference to the way in which the individual evangelists shaped and presented, in accordance with their distinctive perspectives, the "tradition" which was delivered to them.

Thus, the First Evangelist, perhaps the spokesman of a school or other Christian community in a specific area, is well described as a "scribe . . . trained for the kingdom of heaven . . . who brings out of his treasure what is new and what is old" (Mt. 13:52); he arranges the teaching of Jesus according to its subject matter in composite discourses which might serve, among other things, as a manual of instruction for catechists and catechumens. He is clearly interested in the Church as a fellowship in which the teaching of Jesus is to be embodied and handed down from His resurrection to the end of the age. Mark not only writes to encourage Christians suffering for their faith (in Rome and elsewhere) to think of this as taking up their cross in the way of Jesus; he also gives prominence to the "messianic secret" — the veiling of the true nature of Jesus' person and ministry even from His disciples until it is divulged in His death, as is symbolically indicated by the rending of the temple veil and by the centurion's confession, "Truly this man was the Son of God!" (Mk. 15:38f.). Luke views the ministry of Jesus at the midpoint of time as the continuation and consummation of the mighty works and prophetic words in which God revealed Himself in OT times and also as being itself continued and amplified in the apostolic witness. John restates the essential gospel without changing its essence; its permanent and universal validity is brought out by its portrayal of Jesus as the eternal Logos or self-expression of God, incarnated in a real human life, active now in the new, spiritual creation as earlier in the old, material creation. Here, in the ministry and supremely in the death of Jesus, the glory of God is manifested to all who are given the power of seeing it.

V. Criticism and Christology.–In all this we have dealt with criticism as it affects the external features of the biblical record, rather than its revelational essence. But, since the biblical revelation is so closely interwoven with the historical record, historical criticism in particular can become extremely relevant to the heart of the biblical message. Above all, when we consider the biblical presentation of Christ's incarnation, earthly ministry, death, and resurrection as the midpoint of history, historical criticism, when it sets to work on the gospel story, may affect our understanding of the gospel itself. This is no reason for telling historical criticism to approach thus far and no farther; on the contrary, we must be grateful for historical criticism and all the help it can give in showing the historical Jesus in His own times. "It would seem that the only healthy attitude for conservatives is to welcome criticism and be willing to join in it. No view of Scripture can indefinitely be sustained if it runs counter to the facts. That the Bible claims inspiration is patent. The problem is to define the nature of that inspiration in the light of the phenomena contained therein" (E. F. Harrison, in C. F. H. Henry, ed., *Revelation and the Bible* [1958], p. 239).

Historical critics are not free from the influence of their intellectual milieu, and it is not to be greatly wondered at if Jesus, who a couple of generations ago was portrayed as the ideal of nineteenth-century liberalism, tends to be pictured today as a twentieth-century existentialist or as a social revolutionary. It takes a bold and independent spirit like that of Albert Schweitzer to break loose from contemporary influences in this regard as in others; but even boldness and independence are no guarantee of truth, and Schweitzer's portrayal of Jesus as an apocalyptic visionary (cf. *QHJ*) has inadequacies of its own.

The tone and thrust of biblical criticism cannot remain unaffected by the critic's own attitude; it will in the end make some difference whether or not he adopts a theistic viewpoint in harmony with that which informs the biblical record. And when the critical issue relates to the Jesus of history it will in the end make a considerable difference whether the critic is content to know Christ "after the flesh" or shares the estimate of Him reflected in the apostolic witness.

Criticism can carry us so far in bringing us face to face with the Jesus of history; but when it has brought us there, it brings us up against the christological question: "Who then is this?" The various critical presentations or reconstructions of the Jesus of history have been deeply influenced by the critics' Christology, realized or unrealized, false or true. That is why Lives of Jesus so often tell us more about their authors than they do about their subject; as T. W. Manson put it, "By their Lives of Jesus ye shall know them" (C. W. Dugmore, ed., *Interpretation of the Bible* [1944], p. 92). If the Jesus of history is the Christ of the Bible, when we are brought to Him we are brought to the very vantage point from which history must be reviewed if it is to be understood aright. Criticism has then done its perfect work, and Christology takes over.

See also JESUS CHRIST; QUOTATIONS IN THE NT; PETER, FIRST EPISTLE OF.

Bibliography.–K. Aland, *et al.*, *The Gospels Reconsidered* (1960); G. W. Anderson, *Critical Intro. to the OT* (1959); ed., *Tradition and Interpretation* (1977); D. M. Baillie, *God Was in Christ* (1947); J. A. Baird, *Audience Criticism and the Historical Jesus* (1969); A. Bentzen, *Intro. to the OT* (1948); T. K. Cheyne, *Founders of OT Criticism* (1893); Eissfeldt, *The OT: An Intro.* (Eng. tr. 1965); I. Engnell, "Methodological aspects of OT study," in *SVT*, 7 (1960), 13-30; W. B. Glover, *Evangelical Nonconformists and Higher Criticism in the 19th Cent.* (1954); F. C. Grant, ed., *Form Criticism* (1934); H. Harris, *The Tübingen School* (1975); R. K. Harrison, *Intro. to the OT* (1969); E. C. Hoskyns and F. N. Davey, *Riddle of the NT* (1931); M. Jones, *NT in the 20th Cent.* (3rd ed. 1934); F. G. Kenyon, *Text of the Greek Bible* (2nd ed. 1949); J. Knox, *Criticism and Faith* (1953); K. Koch, *Growth of the Biblical Tradition* (1969); I. H. Marshall, ed., *NT Interpretation* (1977); W. J. Martin, *Stylistic Criteria and the Analysis of the Pentateuch* (1955); A. H. McNeile, *Intro. to the Study of the NT* (2nd ed. 1953); C. F. D. Moule, *Birth of the NT* (1962); D. E. Nineham, ed., *Studies in the Gospels* (1955); *Church's Use of the Bible Past and Present* (1963); N. Perrin, *Rediscovering the Teaching of Jesus* (1967); *What is Redaction Criticism?* (1970); E. B. Redlich, *Form Criticism* (1939); B. J. Roberts, *OT Text and Versions* (1951); J. M. Robinson, *New Quest of the Historical Jesus* (1959); J. Rohde, *Rediscovering the Teaching of the Evangelists* (1968); *OTMS*; *QHJ*; W. R. Smith, *OT in the Jewish Church* (2nd ed. 1892); B. H. Streeter, *The Four Gospels* (1924); V. Taylor, *Formation of the Gospel Tradition* (1933); R. J. Thompson, *Moses and the Law in a Century of Criticism since Graf* (1970).

F. F. BRUCE

CROCODILE. *See* LEVIATHAN; DRAGON.

CROCODILE, LAND. *See* LIZARD.

CROCUS [Heb. *ḥ^{a}ḇaṣeleṯ* (Isa. 35:1); Akk. *ḫabaṣillatu*]; AV ROSE; NEB ASPHODEL. Identification of this flower is uncertain. The Akkadian cognate implies a meadow saffron. Moldenke (*MPB*, pp. 146ff.) identifies it with the polyanthus narcissus.

CROOK-BACKT (Lev. 21:20, AV). *See* HUNCHBACK.

CROOKED [Heb. *'iqqēš, 'iqq^{e}šûṯ*] (2 S. 22:27; Ps. 18:26; Prov. 2:15; 4:24; 6:12; 8:8; 17:20); AV also FROWARD, PERVERSE; NEB also PERVERSE; [*p^{e}ṯaltōl*] (Dt. 32:5); [*^{a}qalqāl*–'twisted'] (Ps. 125:5); [*h^{a}pak̲pak̲*] (Prov. 21:8); AV FORWARD; NEB TORTUOUS; [*'āwaṯ*–'make crooked'] (Eccl. 1:15; 7:13); [piel of *'āwâ*–'twist'] (Lam. 3:9); NEB "tangled up"; [*'āqaš*] (Isa. 59:8); [Gk. *skoliós*] (Lk. 3:5; Acts 2:40; Phil. 2:15); AV also UNTOWARD; NEB also CORNERS (Lk. 3:5), WARPED; [*diastréphō*] (Acts 13:10); AV PERVERT; NEB FALSIFY; **CROOKEDNESS** [Heb. *selep*] (Prov. 11:3); AV PERVERSENESS; NEB PERVERSITY.

In each passage the term is used figuratively, usually to denote a course of action or way of life which deviates from what is right, especially deceit, guile, and hypocrisy (e.g., Dt. 32:5; 2 S. 22:27; Ps. 125:5; Prov. 4:24; 11:3; 21:8; Isa. 59:8; Acts 2:40; 13:10; Phil. 2:15). A second meaning is trials sent by God; in Eccl. 1:15; 7:13 the "Preacher" complains that all things are ordained by God, and what He has made "crooked" no one can make straight. In Lam. 3:9 the poet complains that Yahweh has led him on bypaths that lead to destruction rather than on the straight path that leads to salvation (cf. v. 11). In Lk. 3:15 the "crooked" refers to uneven ground which shall be made level (cf. Isa. 40:4).

N. J. O.

CROOKED SERPENT. *See* SERPENT.

CROP [Heb. *t^{e}ḇû'â*] (Lev. 25:15f., 20; Prov. 14:4); AV INCREASE, FRUIT; [*mur'â*] (Lev. 1:16); [*m^{e}lē'â*] (Dt. 22:9); AV FRUIT; NEB YIELD; [*y^{e}ḇûl*] (Ps. 78:46); AV INCREASE; NEB HARVEST; [Gk. *karpós*] (Lk. 12:17; 2 Tim. 2:6); AV FRUIT; NEB PRODUCE. Lev. 1:16 speaks of the crop of a bird, especially a dove or a pigeon, which had to be removed before the bird could be sacrificed. *T^{e}ḇû'â* (gain, increase), *m^{e}lē'â* (full yield), and *y^{e}ḇûl* (produce) are all used to describe the harvest.

In Neh. 10:31 (MT 32) the RSV and NEB supply "crops" in the phrase "forego the crops," rendering Heb. *nāṭaš* (AV "leave"). The term "crops" is also supplied in 1 Cor. 9:10.

N. J. O.

CROSS; CRUCIFY [Gk. *staurós*, vb. *stauróō*]. No word has become more universally known than this, because the history of the world since the death of Christ has been decisively shaped by that epoch-making event. The principal content of the Christian religion is symbolized in this one word.

I. Meaning
II. Forms
III. Discovery Legend
IV. Symbolic Uses
V. Theology of the Cross
VI. Crucifixion

I. Meaning.–Originally Gk. *staurós* designated a pointed, vertical wooden stake firmly fixed in the ground. Such stakes were commonly used in two ways. They were positioned side by side in rows to form fencing or defensive palisades around settlements, or singly they were set up as instruments of torture on which serious offenders of law were publicly suspended to die (or, if already killed, to have their corpses thoroughly dishonored). The same duality of meaning may be seen in the verb *stauróō*, "put up posts, protect by a stockade," and its compound *anastauróō*, "fence around, enclose." Both have the secondary meaning "crucify" (*TDNT*, VII, 581-84). The emergence of the solitary cross as a mode of punishment may be traced back to the ancient practice of making public display of the corpses (or heads; cf. Jth. 14:1, 11) of rebels, resisters, traitors, enemies, etc., on the pointed stakes of the palisade. It is then only a

Impaled inhabitants of an unnamed Syrian town under siege. Such public display of corpses was common Assyrian practice. Engraved bronze band from gate of Shalmaneser III, provenience unknown (Trustees of the British Museum)

small step to the setting up of solitary stakes for more prominent display of miscreants in any convenient public area (e.g., impalement, as in Assyria; cf. *ANEP*, nos. 362, 368, 373; *ANET*, p. 295 [ii]).

II. Forms.–In addition to this earliest form as a simple vertical stake (Gk. *staurós* or *skólops*; Lat. *crux simplex*), four variations became prominent. (1) The form usually seen in pictures, the *crux immissa* (Latin cross ✝), is that in which the upright beam projects above the shorter crosspiece. From the mention of an inscription nailed above the head of Jesus it may safely be inferred that this was the form of the cross on which He died. (2) The *crux commissa* differs only in that the cross-beam is at the top of the vertical stake, forming the Greek letter *tau* (**T**). This has also been called St. Anthony's cross, probably because it resembles the crutch with which this noteworthy hermit is usually depicted. (3) The so-called Greek cross (+) of later date has vertical and horizontal beams of the same length. (4) The *crux decussata,* or St. Andrew's cross, took the shape of the letter **X**. The initial variation in form of the primitive cross was apparently the addition of the cross-beam. This development, in the Roman world at least, may be related to the carrying of the *patibulum* (a yoke-like instrument of punishment fastened to the neck) by convicted slaves. By the Imperial period crucifixion had become the "slaves' punishment" (*servile supplicium*; cf. Hengel, pp. 51ff.), and it had become customary for the condemned person to carry the cross-beam to the place of execution (*TDNT*, VII, 572f.).

III. Discovery Legend.–The early church historians Socrates (*HE* i.17), Sozomenus (*HE* ii.1), Theodoret (*HE* i.18), and others mention the tradition of the discovery of Jesus' cross. (It is significant, however, that Eusebius [*Vita Constantini* iii.26–28], who carries more weight than all the others, wholly omits it.) According to this tradition, Helena, the mother of Constantine the Great, in A.D. 325 when she was seventy-nine years old, discovered the true cross of Jesus by an excavation she caused to be made on the traditional site of His grave. A miracle of healing, wrought upon a crippled woman by stretching her on the true cross, revealed its identity. Along with the true cross were found the two crosses of the malefactors crucified with Jesus. The true cross was intact when found, including even the superscription and the nails. The exact number of nails used in Jesus' crucifixion has been the subject of considerable speculation. In the earliest depictions of the crucifixion Jesus' feet are shown separately nailed, but in later ones they are crossed and affixed to the upright with one nail. The number of nails used in Jesus' crucifixion is usually understood to have been four (but see VI.B below). In the Helena legend the four nails are said to have been disposed thus: one was cast into the sea to still a storm, a second was beaten into the iron ring of the crown of Lombardy, and the other two were placed as relics at Milan and Trier.

The main part of the cross was deposited by Helena in a church erected over the spot. Of the remainder, one portion was sent to Byzantium and inserted into the head of a statue of Constantine, and another was placed in a new church in Rome, specially erected and named for it, Santa Croce ("Holy Cross"). Small fragments of the wood of the true cross were sold, encrusted with gold and jewels; and since many of the wealthy believers wanted to have such priceless relics, the miracle of the "multiplication of the cross" was devised so that the relic suffered no diminution (*et quasi intacta maneret*, "and, as it were, remained intact" [Paulinus *Epistula 11 ad Serverum*]). Fragments of the true cross are thus to be found in many Roman Catholic churches of many countries.

The finding (Lat. *inventio*) of the holy cross by Helena is commemorated by a festival on May 3, called the Invention of the Holy Cross, celebrated in the Western Church since the time of Gregory the Great in the 6th century. Another festival of the holy cross, observed on

September 14, is called the Exaltation of the Holy Cross. This observance seems to have originated in the mid-4th cent. in the East in connection with new churches built at the site of the crucifixion and holy sepulchre, and from there passed to Constantinople and thence to Rome, where it apparently was introduced in the 7th century.

The legend was widely accepted as true, but the discovery and publication of the apocryphal Doctrina Addai (cf. H-S, I, 438) has made it evident that the entire legend of Helena's discovery is but a version of the old Edessa legend. This tells of an identical discovery of the cross, under the very same circumstances, during the reign of Tiberius, by Protonice (wife of Claudius who became emperor), who had been converted to Christianity by the preaching of Peter.

***IV. Symbolic Uses.**–A. Nonbiblical.* In various shapes and designs the cross appears as both decorative ornament and religious symbol on objects of art almost everywhere in the ancient world from the most remote pre-Christian ages. This has much to do, no doubt, with its striking simplicity of form and variability of design. India, Syria, Persia, Europe, and Egypt in particular have yielded numerous specimens dating from the late Stone Age to the Christian era. The Tau cross was common enough in Egyptian symbolism that it has sometimes also been called the Egyptian cross. Among the Egyptians it is said to have been the symbol of divinity and eternal life. The Spanish conquistadores found the cross to be well known as a symbol by the Incas and Aztecs, perhaps signifying the four elements, the four seasons, or the four points of the compass.

With the death of Jesus on a cross a new significance was attached to the figure. It became the primary symbol of the Christian religion and has been elaborated in a profuse variety of forms in Christian art. It was not, however, until the time of Constantine that the cross could be used without restriction as the public symbol of Christian faith. Constantine's sanction was doubtless the result of his vision of A.D. 317 in which he claimed to have seen a flaming cross in the sky with the accompanying words *en toútǭ níka*, "by this [sign] conquer" (Eusebius *Vita Constantini* i.28), and of the story of the discovery of the true cross by his mother.

Tertullian (*De corona* 3) reveals the extent to which the sign of the cross was employed among the faithful as a gesture by the late 2nd cent.: "At each journey and progress, at each coming in and going out, . . . at meals, . . . at bedtime, . . . we mark the brow with the sign of the cross." Such pervasive use of the sign of the cross by the pious believers in everyday life suggests that it was also employed ceremonially in the public worship with great frequency.

See Plate 20.

B. Biblical. The suffering implied in crucifixion naturally made the cross a symbol of pain, distress, and burden-bearing. Thus Jesus used it Himself, requiring that those who would be His disciples deny themselves, take up their crosses, and follow Him. Set in different contexts, this saying appears five times in the Synoptic Gospels (Mk. 8:34 par. Mt. 16:24 par. Lk. 9:23; Mt. 10:38; Lk. 14:27). While a variety of explanations of such cross-bearing have been proffered (cf. *TDNT*, VII, 578f.), it would seem that the basis of the metaphor is the Roman custom requiring a condemned man to carry a part of his own cross to the place of execution. It is uncertain, however, to what extent, prior to Jesus' crucifixion, His listeners would have caught this allusion. At any rate it conveyed to the disciples the awareness that the expectation of suffering applied as fully to the Messiah and His followers as it did in earlier times to God's spokesmen, the prophets (e.g., Mk. 8:31; 9:13). It is a vivid metaphor for self-surrender, a way of life which might ultimately result in the surrender of life itself.

In the Pauline literature the cross stands for the preaching of the atonement (1 Cor. 1:18ff.; Col. 1:20; 2:14), expresses the bond of unity between Jew and Gentile (Eph. 2:16), the believer and Christ, and even symbolizes sanctification (Gal. 5:24). The cross is, in a profound manner, the center and circumference of the preaching of the apostles and of the life of the NT church, and already in NT thought has begun to represent the whole of the Christ-event. H. E. DOSKER D. G. BURKE

***V. Theology of the Cross.**–*In the NT Paul elaborates a "theology of the cross." The organizing principle of 1 Corinthians is this theology of the cross — not a system of doctrinal statements but simply proclamation of the cross as the act of salvation. The "foolishness" of the cross, in fact, represents the destruction of every attempt to make a doctrinal system the way of salvation. As it is actualized in the preached word, Paul discovered this "foolishness" to be the very wisdom of God (1 Cor. 1:21). For him, then, the "word of the cross" (1 Cor. 1:18), suffices as a terse summary statement of the gospel. Mere human wisdom or philosophy cannot substitute for this "preaching" because they cannot convey the saving significance of the cross. In this preaching, form corresponds to content — not impressive words of wisdom, but, with allowance for human weakness, a demonstration of spirit and power (1 Cor. 2:3f.).

A theology that focuses disproportionately on the resurrection or exaltation of Christ too easily becomes a "theology of glory" in which knowledge becomes more important than love, lofty self-perfection than lowly self-giving. Instead, for Paul it is the crucified Christ who is the very power and wisdom of God (1 Cor. 1:23f., 30), and He comes to his exaltation only as the *crucified* Christ. In the Christ hymn of Phil. 2 the obedient death on the cross of the One who "took on the form of a slave" (*morphḗn doúlou labṓn*) is the absolute nadir of His humiliation, but also the completion of His obedience and of redemption, and simultaneously the first stage of His exaltation as Lord.

Conventional and widespread use of the cross as a common Christian symbol makes it difficult for contemporary readers to sense the harsh reality that underlies this theology of the cross and the cross sayings in the NT. When Paul preached the "crucified Christ" (1 Cor. 1:23; 2:2; Gal. 3:1) any audience in the Greek-speaking world would have known immediately that this Christ had suffered an especially agonizing and humiliating death, the sort usually reserved for rebellious slaves, political rebels, or criminals. The harsh reality of this grim fact imposed a particular burden on the early preaching — the cross was no mere symbol, but the gruesome instrument of Christ's atoning death. The Corinthians' penchant for religious enthusiasm may have been a reaction against the offensiveness of this "word of the cross."

Roman historians and literary figures contemporary with the beginning of the Christian era (e.g., Tacitus, Suetonius, Pliny the Younger) were unimpressed by the Christian persistence of belief in a "dead God." Suetonius (*Nero* 16.3) is perhaps representative when he dismisses the Christian persuasion as "a new and pernicious superstition" (*superstitio nova et malefica*). A common theme in the early anti-Christian polemic, preserved by Minucius Felix (one of the earliest Latin apologists) in his dialogue *Octavius* (29.2), was that Christians worship "a criminal and his cross" (*hominem noxium et crucem eius*). The scattered comments of Justin in his *Apologia* reveal that the extreme dishonor associated with death by crucifixion was one of the most common objections to the Christian claim that Jesus was Son of God; e.g., "They say that our madness [*manía*] consists in the fact that we put a crucified man in second place after the unchangeable and eternal God, the Creator of the world" (i.13.4; cf. 22.3f.; 55.1; also Hengel, pp. 1ff., for further documentation). This kind of contemptuous response to the theology of the cross should not have been surprising, for the "word of the cross" could not have been more incompatible with Roman political thought and the whole ethic of contemporary religion.

Not only Paul's Greek-speaking audiences would find this "word of the cross" offensive, however. Jews were all too familiar with the Roman crosses that had been erected throughout Palestine and could hardly have viewed crucifixions other than in the light of the Deuteronomic curse on anyone "hanged on a tree" (Dt. 21:23). The idea of a crucified savior was thus not only foolish to Greeks, but contradictory and offensive to Jews as well. Given his background, Paul would have been painfully aware that Jesus was "accursed" by being hung on a tree (Dt. 21:23), but it was his insight that Jesus willingly took upon Himself the law's curse, to transform it, and thus became Himself the means of freeing people from its curse (Gal. 3:13). The cross, a "stumbling block for Jews," became for this erstwhile Pharisee "the power and wisdom of God" (1 Cor. 1:23f.).

For Paul the cross of Christ is especially the mark of God's reconciliation of humankind (and of all creation; cf. Col. 1:20; 2:14) and a sign of the impotence of all barriers between persons. Christ's death on the cross was for all people and thus negated such human distinctions as Jew and Gentile, making all one new creation, and with His own body reconciling them to each other and to God by the cross (Eph. 2:14-16). In Gal. 6:14 Paul is willing to boast only in the cross, for "by means of his cross the world is crucified to me and I am crucified to the world." (The use of the perfect tense of the verb in particular indicates a state of identification with Christ.) The cross of Christ constitutes a radical "No" to the world. Paul discovers that the cross is precisely where his link with the world is severed, since he has come to share in that fundamental salvation-event himself by baptism into Christ (Rom. 6:3-11).

The ethical dimension of the baptized life is delineated in Gal. 5:24 in terms of the imagery of crucifixion: to be baptized into Christ is to be a new creature, to speak a radical "No" to sin (Rom. 6). Indeed, in Gal. 2:20 Paul can say "I have been crucified with Christ." Through baptism and lived faith he has been so identified with Christ in His suffering, death, and resurrection, that "it is no longer I who live, but Christ who lives in me" (note again the use of the perfect tense of the verb "crucify," signifying a state of identification). The "enemies of the cross" whom Paul denounces in Phil. 3:8 are not those who deny saving power to the cross, but rather those who see no implication in the cross of Christ for the shaping of their own ethical life-style.

***VI. Crucifixion.**–A. Historical Survey.* From the numerous references to crucifixion in Herodotus (i.128.2; iii.125.3, 132.2, 159.1; iv.43.2, 7; vi.30.1; vii.194.1f.; cf. Thucydides i.110.3) handbooks tend to credit the Persians with the first use of crucifixion (e.g., *TDNT,* VII, 573). Other classical sources (many of little historical value) regard crucifixion as essentially barbaric — a form of execution used by barbarians (cf. Hengel, pp. 23f.). Both Greek and Roman historians found it more palatable to mention barbarian crucifixions and overlook the use of this cruel practice by their own people.

A predecessor of crucifixion in the ancient Near East was impalement (forcing the living human body down onto a pointed stake), used by the Assyrians as a mode of executing deserters, captured enemies, rebels, and the like (cf. *ANEP,* nos. 362, 368, 373). It should be noted that the ancient texts are not always precise with respect to detail, so the descriptions cause difficulty in distinguishing impalement from crucifixion (or the crucifixion of a live person from the public display of a corpse). In any case, the process subjected the victim to the greatest possible humiliation, with the victim (whether dead or alive) either nailed or bound to a stake (Gk. *staurós* or *skólops*; it is is uncertain exactly when the cross-arm came into common use). In general, Herodotus distinguished the living victim from the dead by using the verb *anaskolopízō* for the living and *anastauróō* for corpses. After Herodotus, however, the two verbs became interchangeable.

Crucifixion was later adopted by the Greeks (though it was not a typical Greek penalty; see Hengel, pp. 69ff.). It was used frequently by Alexander the Great (e.g., after the siege of Tyre was broken, "two thousand . . . hung fixed to crosses over a huge stretch of shore" [Curtius Rufus *Historia Alexandri* iv.4.17]), by the Diadochi (cf. Diodorus xvi.61.2), the Carthaginians (Polybius i.24), and in turn by the Romans, from whom we have the term *crux*. In both Greek and Roman civilizations crucifixion was, with few exceptions, not applicable to the freeborn or to citizens (cf. Cicero *In Verrem* i.5.66). It was significant to the Roman upper classes that crucifixion was the *servile supplicium*, "the slaves' punishment." The Roman citizen's abhorrence for crucifixion is typified in a line from Cicero (*Pro Rabiro* 5): "Let the very name of the cross be far away not only from the body of a Roman citizen, but even from his thoughts." In the provinces, autocratic governors were known to bend the law as this penalty became more and more useful to the preservation of law and order. Thus Quintilian (*Declamationes minores* 274 [ed. Ritter, p. 124] finds crucifixion to be an effective deterrent for crime and sedition as well as a source of satisfaction to the victim of the crime, so he advocates erection of crosses at the busiest intersections.

In Roman times crucifixion was already the punishment of slaves as early as the Republic. Plautus (*ca.* 250-184 B.C.), the first writer to describe Roman crucifixions, considers slaves to have been crucified "from time immemorial" (Hengel, p. 52), usually for rebellion, but often at caprice (Juvenal *Satires* vi.219-223). This penalty was soon extended to include foreigners and "robbers" (Gk. *lēstaí*; cf. the Gospel accounts of the crucifixion of Jesus together with the two robbers; for other examples of the crucifixion of robbers see Josephus *BJ passim*; Petronius *Satyricon* 111.5; Apuleius *Metamorphoses* i.14.2, 15.4, etc.; Aesop *Fabulae* 152), and was applied most extensively in the provinces. The connection between slaves and robbers was natural since it was from the ranks of runaway slaves that bandit gangs most commonly replenished their numbers. Josephus, who witnessed many gruesome crucifixions in connection with the siege of Jerusalem (cf. *BJ* v.11.1 [449-451]), characterized it as "the most wretched of deaths" (*thanátōn tón oíktiston*, *BJ* vii.6.4 [202f.]). Throughout his writings there is a consistent picture of the excessive use of crucifixion for the "pacification" of seditious provincials (cf. *BJ* ii.5.2 [75], 12.6 [241], 13.2 [253], 14.9 [306, 308]; iii.7.33 [321]; v.7.5 [289]; vii.10.1 [418]; *Ant.* xvii.10.10 [295]; xx.6.2 [129]).

There was a very old Roman punishment — hanging on the "barren tree" (*arbor infelix*) — which could be applied even to Roman citizens for cases of high treason or serious crime. With very few exceptions (e.g., deserters crucified by Scipio in the Second Punic war, Gavius by

Byzantine miniature depicting Constantine's vision of the cross (top), his response in the Battle of Milvian Bridge (center), and Helena's discovery of the true cross (bottom). Detail of manuscript illumination from the *Homilies* of Gregory of Nazianzus (Bibliothèque Nationale, Paris)

Verres for spying, a guardian by Galba in Spain), this penalty was never imposed and was always considered extraordinary by citizens (cf. Hengel pp. 39f.). The Roman jurist Julius Paulus (*ca.* A.D. 200), in the *Sententiae* compiled from his works toward A.D. 300, lists *crux* as the foremost of the three *summa supplicia,* "supreme penalties" (the others are *crematio,* "burning," and usually *decollatio* "decapitation"), revealing that this was applicable in such cases as desertion, betrayal of secrets, incitement to rebellion, murder, etc. In Palestine it was particularly applied for the suppression of sedition and banditry.

Jewish law prescribed that idolaters and blasphemers, after execution by stoning, were to be hanged on a tree to demonstrate that they were accursed by God (Dt. 21:23). Such corpses, however, were not allowed to remain on the tree overnight. This rule was generally applied to those crucified as well. The excessive Roman use of crucifixion in the pacification of Judea made it unacceptable as a Jewish death penalty, but there is evidence (cf. Yadin, *IEJ*, 21; Wilcox, pp. 88f.) that crucifixion had been borrowed from the gentile world and used in cases of high treason during the Hellenistic-Hasmonean period. This would account for the crucifixion of eight hundred Pharisees by Alexander Jannaeus after he had captured the rebellious town of Bethome (Josephus *BJ* i.4.6. [97f.]; *Ant.* xiii.14.2f. [380ff.]). That no crucifixions are known to be attributable to Herod the Great may indicate his deliberate dissociation of himself from the Hasmoneans.

Crucifixion continued to be a political-military punishment, and a consistent example of class justice, until the time of Constantine when it was abolished as an insult to Christianity. After Constantine the "holy" word *crux*, "cross," is replaced in legal writings by *furca,* "gallows." This "hanging on the gallows" was also considered a more humane form of punishment in that it allowed for immediate death in contrast to crucifixion, the essence of which was slow torture.

B. Procedure. Some form of torture prior to the crucifixion was customary among the Carthaginians and, in the form of flogging, was the normal procedure of the Romans. Whatever else may have been done to the victim prior to crucifixion, there was at the least a flogging to the point of making blood flow. In actuality this hastened death and thus reduced the extreme agonies that intensified as long as the victim endured on the cross. As the next step in the process the victim carried his own cross-beam (if this form of cross was used) to the place of execution, where the upright stake had already been erected. Then on the ground he was fastened to the beam with arms outspread, usually by ropes, less commonly by nails (cf. Hewitt). The beam and body were then lifted into place on the upright. A small wooden block (*sedicula*) or a wooden peg positioned midway on the upright supported the body weight as the buttocks rested on it. This feature was extremely important in cases of nailing since it prevented the weight from tearing open the wounds. Once the condemned was thus immobilized he was left alone, unable to attend to bodily functions, unprotected from inclement weather or flies, and, because the place of execution was usually some public street or prominent place, subjected to abusive words and mockery from passersby. Often the body was left to putrify on the cross and become the prey of carrion birds to complete the utter humiliation. It could be claimed for burial, however (cf. Jn. 19:39). The extreme dishonor that lack of burial represented, especially in Jewish circles, can hardly be exaggerated (cf. Tob. 1:18ff.; 12:13). It was not unusual for a tablet identifying the crime to be hung on the condemned as he went to the execution site, then attached to his cross for all to see.

The first skeletal remains identifiable as those of a person crucified, discovered in Jerusalem in 1968, appear to raise as many questions as they answer with regard to the details of the methods of crucifixion. Ossuary remains from a first-century A.D. tomb unearthed at Giv'at ha-Mivtar in Jerusalem surprisingly included the two heel bones of a crucifixion victim still fastened together by a single iron nail (cf. Haas, pp. 49, 55f., and 56 fig. 6; Yadin, *IEJ*, 23, pp. 20-22).

The nail, 5.5 in. (14 cm.) long and bent over at the point to a length of 0.8 in. (2 cm.), also carried fragments of a plaque of acacia or pistacia wood, 0.6-0.8 in. (1.5-2 cm.) thick, between the nail and the heel bones. On the bent point of the nail minute pieces of olive wood were detected. It appears certain from this evidence that the feet in this case were not fastened to the upright post of the cross, because: (1) the gnarled wood of the olive tree would hardly be used for a cross upright; (2) the length of the nail suffices for joining two heels but leaves nothing for attaching them to the cross; (3) assuming that the point of the nail could have been driven into the cross upright, a nail of its thickness could hardly have been bent by a knot in the olivewood. It is likely, then, that the heels were joined between an acacia and an olive wood plaque with the nail deliberately bent over the bottom plaque to hold them securely. Depending on how one reconstructs the exact conjuncture of the heel bones, the victim's legs would have been in either an "adjacent" position (*IEJ*, 20, figure 24.B) or an "open" position (*IEJ*, 20, figure 24.A). The strong likelihood that the feet could not have been affixed to the cross favors the open position for this case.

In either posture a *sedicula* would have been necessary. It should be noted also that the ancient records do not mention footrests (*TDNT*, VII, 573). The evidence of heels joined in this manner admits of one other posture for the victim — an upside-down one. With the heels firmly joined by the wood plaques and the nail, the legs would have been looped over the top of the vertical shaft, thus suspending the body in place while the backs of the knees rested on the cross-beam (see further Yadin, *IEJ*, 23, p. 21).

The evidence from the other bones of this man in the ossuary is inconclusive. The bones of the lower legs clearly reveal that one was severed and the other splintered by a violent blow from a sharp tool like an axe. This undoubtedly represents a postmortem amputation of the feet — either the coup de grace familiar from Jn. 19:31-36 or the means of removal from the cross if it was an upside-down crucifixion. Since the nail was so firmly fixed in the bones as to have been buried with them, severing the feet may have been the simplest means of removal of an upside-down corpse. The "scratch" on the forearm bone (while the wrist bones appear undamaged) is inconclusive as proof that the arms of this victim had been nailed to a cross-bar. Finally, the puzzling name on the ossuary, *h'qwl* (the reading proposed by Yadin, *IEJ*, 23, pp. 18-20), admits a meaning "the one hanged with knees apart" (the verb *'ql* in Mishnaic Hebrew has this meaning; cf. Yadin, *IEJ*, 23, p. 19; Naveh, p. 35).

The suffering of death by crucifixion was intense. In addition to exposure to the weather and insects (and sometimes animals), the body suffered from the intensifying damage of the wounds and from the stretching caused by the strained position. Some think that headache and convulsions added to the agony. The ultimate cause of death has been debated; generally it is considered the result of gradual suffocation brought about by fatigue. The length of this agony was wholly determined by the constitution of the victim and the extent of the prior flogging, but death was rarely seen before thirty-six hours had passed. Instances are on record of victims of the cross who survived their ordeal when taken down after many hours of suspension (Josephus *Vita* 75). Death was sometimes hastened by breaking the legs of the victims; *crura fracta* ("broken legs") was a Roman expression for crucifixion (Cicero *Philippicae* xiii.12 [27]).

C. Crucifixion of Jesus. Since He had been charged with sedition, a serious crime, the prior flogging would have been extensive. It is thought that this flogging so weakened Him from loss of blood that He was unable to carry the beam to the execution site and required help. This is perhaps also the likely explanation of His relatively quick death, which was a matter of astonishment to Pilate (Mk. 15:44).

The actual crucifixion of Jesus is described in all the Gospel accounts with absolute brevity. The procedure in general followed Roman custom, though there were a few less common features. The mockery of Jesus was perhaps excessive (due to his claims) and the stripping and division of his clothes by the executioners, while not an unknown practice, was not common. There are also some significant Jewish features: the stupefying drink of wine mixed with myrrh (Mk. 15:23), intended to reduce the threshhold of pain, and the removal of the body on Friday evening (Jn. 19:31; cf. Dt. 21:22f.).

All the Gospels mention the two robbers, one crucified on each side of Jesus. Although binding was more common, Jesus was nailed to His cross (Lk. 24:39; Jn. 20:25). Only the Fourth Gospel (Jn. 3:14; 8:28; 12:32-34) ascribes theological significance to the fact that Jesus was "lifted up" on the cross — His obedient death being the first step in His exaltation and the crucifixion being a visual symbol of that lifting up. Only John also records the symbolic spear incident (Jn. 19:34; *see* BLOOD AND WATER). Some have claimed that this points to death by rupture of the heart, independent of the cross. But many authorities dispute such a view, attributing death to aortic aneurysm or acute dilation of the stomach. Regarding the question of responsibility for the crucifixion, none of the Gospels attempts to excuse the Roman authorities of criminal complicity in the death of Jesus, and none attempts to conceal the fact that this was a Roman crucifixion. The Gospels also assert the involvement of certain Jewish leaders in Jerusalem in bringing this about, but there is no question of any indictment of the entire Jewish nation of Jesus' time, nor of any subsequent time.

Bibliography.–N. Haas, *IEJ*, 20 (1970), 38-59; M. Hengel, *Crucifixion* (Eng. tr. 1977); J. W. Hewitt, *HTR*, 25 (1932), 29-46; J. Naveh, *IEJ*, 20 (1970), 33-37; *TDNT*, VII, *s.v.* σταυρός κτλ. (Schneider); V. Tzaferis, *IEJ*, 20 (1970), 18-32; H.-R. Weber, *The Cross* (1978); M. Wilcox, *JBL*, 96 (1977), 85-99; Y. Yadin, *IEJ*, 21 (1971), 1-12; 23 (1973), 18-22.

D. G. BURKE

CROWD. The term appears many times in the RSV but is limited to the Gospels and Acts. It is usually a translation of Gk. *óchlos, plḗthos*, or *laós*. The usual equivalent in the AV is "multitude." On many occasions the RSV also translates these Greek terms as "multitude" or "people," following the pattern set by the AV. All of these terms deal with a largely undefined group of people who apparently attached themselves to Jesus.

From the very beginning of Jesus' ministry the Gospel writers characterize Him as drawing great crowds. To a large extent these crowds were made up of the curious, who came not only to hear Jesus' teaching but also to see His miracles (Jn. 6:26). Lk. 12:1, 13, and the passages describing the feeding of the multitudes picture these crowds as being in the thousands. They came from as far away as Transjordan, Idumea, Tyre, and Sidon (Mk. 3:7f.). In general, the crowds may be characterized as desirous of healing (Lk. 6:17-19; etc.), astonished at Jesus' teaching (Mt. 7:29; Mk. 11:18), and unable to understand that teaching (Mt. 13:10-15 par.). T. W. Manson believed that "the crowds are curious and to a certain extent interested in this new teacher; but their interest is apt to be focused on wonderful cures of bodily ailments rather than on the things of the spirit."

J. Arthur Baird, on the other hand, would claim that this neutrality of the multitudes is not implied. Rather, the text usually shows that the multitudes are either sympathetic to Jesus and thus generally to be classed as his disciples, or they are hostile to him and thus a part of Jesus' opposition. The character of the audience determined the attitude with which Jesus addressed it. The Gospels reflect an increasingly critical attitude toward the Pharisees, Sadducees, and the crowds connected with them (e.g., Lk. 12:54-56, where the multitudes are called "hypocrites"). In John these hostile groups are often called "the Jews." On other occasions Jesus addressed the multitudes with the same attitude He used when He instructed His disciples in private (cf. Mt. 5:1f. at the beginning of the Sermon on the Mount). The attitude of Jesus to His hearers is an important consideration in the interpretation of His teaching. A study of the way the various Gospel writers preserved the audience relationships shows that the reaction of the audience was needed for the correct, meaningful reproduction of Jesus' teaching.

Often the Evangelists built passages on the basis of a multi-layered audience. The Sermon on the Mount begins with Jesus drawing His disciples to Himself and then speaking both to them and to the multitudes a bit further away. On other occasions the author reports one form of teaching as addressed to a group as a whole and then another form of teaching — usually explanatory in nature — as addressed to the disciples privately. (Note the roles of the disciples and the multitudes in the parabolic discourses and their interpretation, esp. Mk. 4:11.) On other occasions the Evangelists seem to gather together material on a certain subject and then divide the materials according to Jesus' audience. In Mk. 7:1-13 Jesus has a sharp exchange with the Pharisees over the way they have used their oral tradition to nullify the commands of God. In vv. 14f. He gives the people a general saying concerning the way things coming from within a man are what really defile him. Then in the remaining part of the section (vv. 17-23) He addresses His disciples privately to provide them the correct interpretation of that saying. On many of these occasions Jesus seems to be more sympathetic to the crowd than to His own disciples. The crowd did not have the real opportunity to learn what the disciples should have understood (Mk. 7:18).

The role of the crowd became increasingly important, for it was from the crowd that Jesus built the group of disciples that became the nucleus of the Church. The crowd became attached to Jesus in such a way that the Jewish leadership feared its power. Thus, the rumors that some of the crowd believed Jesus to be the Christ spurred the religious leaders into action against Him (Jn. 7). Caiaphas noted that if Jesus were not checked all of the people would become His followers (Jn. 11:47-53). Mk. 12:12 indicates that during the last week of Jesus' life the sentiment of the crowd in Jesus' favor was so strong that the rulers of the Jews did not dare to arrest Him publicly. Yet this multitude was easily swayed. The same crowds are pictured as being carried away by the Jewish religious leaders, so that they cried "Crucify him, crucify him!" along with the rest (Jn. 19:15).

Yet a part of the crowd remained faithful to Jesus. They undoubtedly became the basic element of the early Christian community in Jerusalem which Acts 1:15 numbers at about 120. They provided the nucleus of Peter's audience in the early chapters of Acts and the basis of the early Church until it had grown to the point where it was itself described as a multitude (Acts 6:1f., 5).

In accounts of the ministry of Paul the multitudes are mobs in opposition to him. In Philippi the crowd joined the owners of the girl who had been cured in raising such a tumult that Paul and Silas were imprisoned and beaten (Acts 16:19-24). In Thessalonica the Jews recruited such a crowd that they threw the whole city into an uproar, and Paul was forced to leave (Acts 17:5-9). In Ephesus the crowd became such an unruly mob that the town clerk quieted them with the observation that the Romans might take action against them for riot (Acts 19:28-41). When Paul was arrested in the temple, it was because a crowd had become a riotous mob and the Roman officer feared for the apostle's life (Acts 21:27-35). Such tumults characterized the role of the crowd in the ministry of Paul.

Several other words are used in the Gospels to refer to groups of people. The people standing in the courtyard before whom Peter denied his Lord are called "bystanders" (Mt. 26:73, Gk. *hoi hestṓtes*; Mk. 14:69f., *hoi parestṓtes*). The terms are used in a neutral sense with no connotation of opposition to or favor toward Jesus. The same terms are used in the crucifixion account for the bystanders who interpreted Jesus' call to God as a call to Elijah for help (Mt. 27:47; Mk. 15:35).

Another term for a group or crowd is the English "number" (Gk. *arithmós*). While this term may be used for a group of indefinite size, e.g., in the description of the growth of the Church (Acts 6:7; 11:21), it generally designates a specific number of people (cf. Lk. 22:3; Jn. 6:10; Acts 4:4; 5:36).

See also MULTITUDE; NUMBER IV.

Bibliography.–J. A. Baird, *Audience Criticism and the Historical Jesus* (1969); T. W. Manson, *The Teaching of Jesus* (2nd ed. 1935), pp. 17-21.

D. W. WEAD

CROWN [Heb. *ʿaṭārâ, nēzer, keṯer, kōṯereṯ* (1 K. 7:31); Gk. *stéphanos*]; AV also CHAPITER (1 K. 7:31), HELP (Ps. 89:19, for MT *ʿezer*); NEB also "symbol of (holy) dedication" (*nēzer*, Ex. 29:6; 39:30; Lev. 8:9), GARLAND (*ʿaṭārâ*, Isa. 28:1, 3, 5; Lam. 5:16), CORONET (Ezk. 16:12), "endow with princely gifts" (for "set a crown upon," Ps. 89:19); [vbs. Heb. *ʿāṭar, kāṯar*; Gk. *stephanóō*]. The Heb. *nēzer*, "set apart" (cf. Nazirite), designates in Ex. 29:6; 39:30; Lev. 8:9 a headpiece used in the ordination of high priests as a symbol of their consecration. Elsewhere it can indicate the royal crown of the king's consecration (2 S. 1:10; 2 K. 11:12; 2 Ch. 23:11; cf. Ps. 89:39; 132:18; etc.). "Crown" in the usual sense is otherwise *ʿaṭārâ* or *keṯer*, both from roots meaning "surround," and Gk. *stéphanos*, ordinarily a headwreath (1 Cor. 9:25) woven of palm or other branches (*see* CROWN OF THORNS), but a "golden" crown in Rev. 4:4; 14:14; etc.

Uses of crowns in the Bible include the following:

(1) Consecration. The *nēzer* had a twofold use as the crown of consecration: (a) It was placed as a frontlet on the turban of the high priest, and was tied with a blue lace (Ex. 39:30). The priestly crown was a flat piece of pure gold, bearing the inscription, "Holy to the Lord," signifying the consecration of the priest as the representative of the people (29:6; Lev. 8:9). (b) Likewise the Hebrew king (2 K. 11:12) was set apart by God in wearing on his head a royal *nēzer*, whether of silk or gold we do not know. It was set with jewels (Zec. 9:16) and was light enough to be taken into battle (2 S. 1:10).

(2) Coronation. Three kinds of royal crowns were used in coronation services: (a) The *nēzer* or consecration crown referred to above was the only one used in crowning Hebrew kings. What seems to be an exception is in the case of Joshua, who represented both priest and king (Zec. 6:11). (b) The *ʿaṭārâ* and (c) the *keṯer* were used in crowning foreign monarchs. No king but a Hebrew could wear a *nēzer* — a "Holy to the Lord" crown. It is recorded that David presumed to put on his own head the *ʿaṭārâ* of King Milcom (2 S. 12:30, RSV mg., NEB). The *keṯer* or jeweled turban was the crown of the Persian king and queen (Est. 1:11; 2:17; 6:8).

(3) Exaltation. The *stéphanos* was the usual crown of exaltation for victors of games, achievement in war, and places of honor at feasts (AV 1 Cor. 9:25; RSV, NEB, "wreath"). The *ʿaṭārâ* was worn at banquets (Cant. 3:11; Isa. 28:1, 3), probably taking the form of a wreath of flowers; also as a crown of honor and victory (Ezk. 16:12; 21:26; 23:42). The *stéphanos* is the crown of exaltation bestowed upon Christ (Rev. 6:2; 14:14; He. 2:9). "Exaltation was the logical result of Christ's humiliation" (Vincent). The apocalyptic woman and locusts receive this emblem of exaltation (Rev. 12:1; 9:7). The symbolic dragon and beast are elevated, wearing *diadḗmata* (Rev. 12:3; 13:1). The conquering Christ has "upon his head . . . many diadems" (Rev. 19:12).

See further Tertullian *De corona*; and *see* DIADEM.

(4) Reward. Paul, witnessing the races and games, caught the vision of wreath-crowned victors flush with the reward of earnest endeavor. (*See* GAMES.) He also saw the persistent, faithful Christian at the end of his hard-won race wearing the symbolic *stéphanos* of rejoicing (1 Thess. 2:19, AV), of righteousness (2 Tim. 4:8), of glory (1 Pet. 5:4), of life (Jas. 1:12; Rev. 2:10). Paul's fellow Christians were his joy and *stéphanos* (Phil. 4:1), "of which Paul might justly make his boast" (Ellicott). Long before Paul, his Hebrew ancestors saw the *'ᵃṭarâ* of glory (Prov. 4:9) and the *'ᵃṭarâ* of a good wife, children's children, riches, and a peaceful old age (Prov. 12:4; 14:24; 16:31; 17:6). See Macc. 10:29; 11:35; 13:39.

See also CROWN OF THE HEAD; DIADEM; MOLDING.

W. E. RAFFETY

CROWN OF THE HEAD [Heb. *qoḏqōḏ*] (Dt. 28:35; 33:16, 20; 2 S. 14:25; Job 2:7; Ps. 68:21; Jer. 2:16; 48:45); AV also SCALP, TOP OF THE HEAD; NEB also BROW, SCALP, etc. This term, equivalent to the Akk. *qaqqādu* and the Ugar. *qdqd*, means properly "vertex," and so in the AV and RSV is usually rendered "crown" or "crown of the head" (otherwise "brow" [Gen. 49:26], "head" [Isa. 3:17], "pate" [Ps. 7:16]).

CROWN OF THORNS [Gk. *akánthinos stéphanos*]. Three of the four Evangelists mention the crown of thorns with which the Roman soldiers derided the captive Christ (Mt. 27:29; Mk. 15:17; Jn. 19:2). All speak of the akanthine (Acanthus) crown, but there is no certainty about the peculiar plant from whose branches this crown of cruel mockery was plaited. *See* THORN.

CRUCIBLE [Heb. *maṣrēp*–'melting pot'] (Prov. 17:3; 27:21); AV FINING POT; NEB MELTING POT. A melting utensil, probably made of pottery, used in refining silver. In the Proverbs passages the word becomes a metaphor for the testing of men.

CRUCIFIXION. *See* CROSS.

CRUEL; CRUELTY [Heb. *'aḵzār*] (Dt. 32:33; Job 30:21; Prov. 11:17; 12:10; etc.); NEB also "without mercy"; [*qāšâ, qāšeh*] (Gen. 49:7; Ex. 6:9; Cant. 8:6); NEB also RUTHLESS; [*ḥōmēṣ*] (Ps. 71:4); [*ra'*] (Ps. 144:11 [AV, NEB, 10]); AV HURTFUL; [*raḇ*] (Prov. 28:16); AV GREAT; NEB GRASPING; [*rāṣaṣ*] ("inflict cruelties upon," 2 Ch. 16:10); AV OPPRESS; NEB "treat with great brutality."

Recent English versions (RSV, NEB) tend to substitute for "cruelty" alternate terms which reflect the root meaning of *'aḵzār*, "violence" (cf. Gen. 49:5; Jgs. 9:24; Ps. 27:12; 74:20). The only Israelites of whom the word *'aḵzār* is used are Asa (2 Ch. 16:10) and "the daughter of my people" (Lam. 4:3); elsewhere (Ex. 6:9; Jgs. 4:3; Prov. 28:16; Jer. 6:23; 50:42) *'aḵzār* characterizes an alien oppressor such as the Egyptians in the Exodus and the Canaanites of Hazor. The word is linked with wrath in Gen. 49:7; Prov. 27:4; Isa. 13:9. Isaiah (13:9) associates cruelty with the Day of the Lord. Job states that God, like a persecutor, has "turned cruel to me" (30:21). The cruel man is a wicked man (Prov. 12:10); the righteous man is kind (Prov. 11:17; 12:10). "A cruel messenger" (Prov. 17:11) denotes some violent disaster to come on one who rebels against the king. In the natural realm "the venom of asps" (Dt. 32:33) and the ostrich (Job 39:16) are cruel.

The verb *qāšâ* means literally "be hard, severe." It is used in Gen. 49:7 of the warlike wrath of Simeon and Levi, to which is apparently attributed their near disappearance among the tribes of Israel. It is used also of the Egyptian bondage (Ex. 6:9) and jealous love (Cant. 8:6). Used figuratively, the sword is cruel (*ra'*, Ps. 144:10).

P. L. GARBER

CRUSE [Heb. *ṣappaḥaṯ*]; NEB FLASK. A small elongated earthen vessel or flask about 6 in. (15 cm.) in height, generally used for holding liquids such as oil. The term is used to describe the container mentioned in the visit of Elijah to the Zarephath widow (1 K. 17:12, 14, 16).

CRY; CRYING. Words in the OT usually denoting a distressful cry are Heb. *zᵉ'āqâ* and the older form *ṣᵉ'āqâ* (e.g., Gen. 27:34; Ex. 3:7, 9; Neh. 9:9; Prov. 21:13), and *ṣᵉwāḥâ* (Ps. 144:14; Jer. 14:2; 46:12). A cry for help is *šû(a)'* (Job 30:24; 36:19) or *šaw'â* (Ex. 2:23; 1 S. 5:12; Ps. 18:6; Jer. 8:19; etc.). In 1 K. 8:28; Ps. 17:1; 61:1; Jer. 7:16; 14:2; etc., *rinnâ* is used of a crying out to the Lord in supplication (cf. 1 K. 22:36, where the word means the "proclamation" of a herald, as in the AV); the related *rᵉnānâ* in Job 3:7 is a "joyful cry" (cf. *rinnâ* in Isa. 43:14, a cry of triumph [NEB]). In 1 S. 17:20, "war cry" is *milḥāmâ*; *tᵉrû'â* is a "battle cry" in Jer. 49:2; Zeph. 1:16. An "empty cry" is *šāw'* (Job 35:13; AV "vanity"). Other words are *qôl* ("voice") in Ps. 86:6; Prov. 8:4; etc., and by emendation (following the LXX), *ṣaraḥ* in Ezk. 21:22 (AV "in the slaughter").

The NT uses Gk. *boḗ, kraugḗ, kéleusma* ("cry of command," 1 Thess. 4:16), and *phōnḗ* (Lk. 23:23; AV "voices").

The most important verbs include Heb. *zā'aq*, *ṣā'aq*, *qārā'*, and *šāwa'*; and Gk. *boáō*, *krázō*, and *phōnéō*.

J. W. D. H.

CRYSTAL [Heb. *gāḇîš* (Job 28:18), *qeraḥ* (Ezk. 1:22); Gk. *krýstallos* (Rev. 4:6; 22:1), *krystallízo* (Rev. 21:11)]; AV also PEARLS (Job 28:18); NEB also ALABASTER, "sheet of ice." Crystal is an almost transparent quartz rock. In the NT *krýstallos* is used to describe the glassy sea (Rev. 4:6) and the river of life (22:1), while the cognate verb was used of the beauty of the New Jerusalem (21:11).

See also STONES, PRECIOUS.

CUBIT [Heb. usually *'ammâ*; Gk. *pḗchys*]. The standard for measures of length among the Hebrews, and mentioned over a hundred times in Scripture. Israel followed the example of other Near Eastern nations in using the distance from the elbow to the end of the middle finger as a means of measurement. Cubits differed somewhat throughout the ancient world, however, and Egyptian cubit measuring-sticks recovered from the 12th Dynasty (*ca.* 1570-1310 B.C.) varied by as much as an inch (2.5 cm.) in length. Whereas the average Egyptian cubit was about 20.5 in. (52 cm.), the Mesopotamian average was only about 19.5 in. (49.5 cm.). Small differences also existed between Sumerian and later Babylonian cubits. In Israel, too, there were differences in cubits, that of Dt. 3:11 being the "common" cubit, whereas in Ezk. 40:5 the "long" cubit, which added a handbreadth to the forearm measurement, was implied (cf. Ezk. 43:12). Perhaps Ezekiel's cubit was the long Egyptian measure of 20.5 in. (52 cm.). The Siloam Inscription (*ca.* 701 B.C.) gave the length of Hezekiah's conduit as 1200 cubits, which on a strictly lineal basis would make the Hebrew cubit equivalent to 17.5 in. (44.5 cm.). Since 1200 is a round number, however, the length of the cubit in the 8th cent. B.C. must remain in doubt. The

cubit of Jgs. 3:16 is a Heb. *gōmeḏ* (LXX *spithamḗs*; NEB "only fifteen inches long"), a word not found elsewhere and thus indeterminate in meaning. In the NT, *pḗchys* occurs in Mt. 6:27; Lk. 12:25; Jn. 21:8; Rev. 21:17.
See also WEIGHTS AND MEASURES. R. K. H.

CUCKOO; CUCKOW (Lev. 11:16; Dt. 14:15, AV). *See* SEA GULL.

CUCUMBER [Heb. *qiššu'â*; Gk. *sikýa*, B *síkyos*] (Nu. 11:5); **CUCUMBER FIELD** [Heb. *miqšâ*; Gk. (Isaiah) *sikyḗratos*] (Isa. 1:8; Jer. 10:5); AV "garden of cucumbers" (Isa. 1:8), "upright" (Jer. 10:5); NEB also "plot of cucumbers" (Jer. 10:5). In Nu. 11:5 cucumbers are an article of Egyptian diet longed for by the wandering Israelites. Widely grown in the ancient world, two varieties, *Cucumis chate* L. and *C. sativus* L., were popular in Palestine. The former was grown under irrigation in Egypt and had a delicate flavor. Cucumbers were widely eaten by the poor in the summer months.

The "garden of cucumbers" (Isa. 1:8, AV) refers to a forcing bed made from rough boards and supported on stumps or poles. When abandoned for the season it presents a dreary spectacle of untidiness and decay.

Most modern scholars consider Heb. *miqšâ* in Jer. 10:5 to be the same word as in Isa. 1:8 (BDB; KoB; RSV, NEB; etc.); some, however, have thought it to be the *miqšâ* of Ex. 25:18, 31, etc., "beaten work," "hammered work," "the work of the turning-lathe" (KD). R. K. H.

CUD [Heb. *gērâ*]. *See* CHEWING THE CUD.

CULOM ko͞o'lom [Gk. *koulon*]. A town of Judah listed only in Josh. 15:59, NEB, following the LXX (v. 59a).

CULT PROSTITUTE [Heb. *qᵉḏēšâ*]; AV WHORE (Dt. 23:17a), HARLOT (Hos. 4:14); NEB TEMPLE-PROSTITUTE; [*qāḏēš*] (Dt. 23:37b; 1 K. 14:24; etc.); AV SODOMITE; NEB MALE PROSTITUTE. *See* HARLOT.

CULTIVATE [Heb. *'āḇaḏ*] (Ps. 104:14; Eccl. 5:9); AV SERVICE, SERVE; NEB "those who toil," TILL; [Gk. *geōrgéomai*] (He. 6:7); AV DRESS. *See* AGRICULTURE III.

CULTIVATED OLIVE TREE [Gk. *kalliélaios*] (Rom. 11:24); AV "good olive tree." *See* OLIVE TREE.

CUMBER. Archaic in Lk. 13:7, AV, for Gk. *katargéō*, RSV and NEB "use up."

CUMBERED. Archaic in Lk. 10:40, AV, for Gk. *perispáō*, RSV and NEB "distracted."

CUMBRANCE. Archaic in Dt. 1:12, AV, for Heb. *ṭōrah*, RSV "weight."

CUMI. *See* TALITHA CUMI.

CUMMIN kum'ən [Heb. *kammōn*; Gk. *kýminon*] (Isa. 28:25, 27; Mt. 23:23). The common annual, *Cuminum cyminum* L., a small plant bearing aromatic seeds which were used as a condiment and carminative. The usual spelling today is "cumin." In antiquity the best cummin grew in Ethiopia. The Maltese reportedly still grow cummin and thresh it in the manner mentioned by Isaiah. In NT times the Jews paid tithes of cummin. R. K. H.

CUN kun [Heb. *kûn*; LXX Gk. *ek tṓn eklektṓn póleōn*] (1 Ch. 18:8); AV CHUN; NEB KUN. One of the "cities of Hadadezer" king of Syria pillaged by David. In the parallel 2 S. 8:8 its place is taken by BEROTHAI. The modern site of Cun is usually given as Râs Ba'albek, SW of Ribleh, and about 30 mi. (48 km.) NE of ancient Berothai. In view of the LXX translation, however, it may be questioned whether the word is indeed a place name. A derived form of the verb *kûn*, "be, establish," could render a translation such as "even from the established cities of Hadadezer." W. S. L. S.

CUNEIFORM kū-nē'ə-fôrm [from Lat. *cuneus*–'wedge'; hence 'wedge-shaped']. A system of writing employing wedge-shaped impressions made by a stylus in plastic clay or cut with a chisel in stone or metal. Cuneiform is a very early (perhaps the earliest) and certainly the most widespread system of "writing" found in the ancient Middle East prior to the spread of the Phoenician alphabet.

Cuneiform writing is found first in lower Mesopotamia. Clay tablets from Uruk (Warka), Jemdet Nasr, and other sites are dated by various scholars to 3400 or 3200 B.C. Since these tablets are written in a Sumerian dialect, the Sumerians are generally credited with the invention of this system of writing. (The system of writing does not, however, seem to be well adapted to the phonemic structure of Sumerian; but no convincing alternate theory suggests itself.)

When the Akkadian-speaking people — Semites — entered southern Mesopotamia in the middle of the 3rd millennium, they borrowed this system of writing, making some necessary adaptations. Thus it spread through the so-called Akkadian languages, namely, the various dialects of Babylonian and Assyrian. Following the trade routes, cuneiform writing (principally for bills, receipts, etc.) spread into Persia (Elamite, Old Persian), Asia Minor (Hittite, Hurrian, Khaldian or Vannic), Syria (Tell Mardikh [ancient Ebla], Alalakh, the Amarna Letters from Syria-Palestine), and elsewhere. In the Amarna period of Egyptian history (14th cent. B.C.), diplomatic correspondence between the Egyptians, the Hittites in Asia Minor, the Kassites in Babylon, the Assyrians, the Mitanni, and an unnamed king in Cyprus, as well as with the vassal states in Syria and Palestine, was written in cuneiform (*see* AMARNA TABLETS). In the Persian period, when ARAMAIC (written in a Phoenician alphabetic script) had become the international language of diplomacy, cuneiform writing was still used by the Persians (e.g., the Behistun inscription), and Late-Babylonian documents have been dated down to the 1st cent. A.D.

At first, cuneiform writing — which could not truly be called "cuneiform" at that time — was pictographic, i.e., each sign or character was an approximate pictorial representation scratched with a stylus in soft clay. Such a system is seriously limited to concrete objects, and is, needless to say, very cumbersome. Closely related to the pictograms are "evocative" symbols which call up an idea. (Thureau-Dangin termed them *évocatrice*, and used the illustration of a sign composed of a pictogram of an egg alongside the pictogram of a bird to evoke the idea "beget, bear.")

The system quickly underwent development, at first on the rebus principle. (Using English for our example, we might draw the picture of an *eye* to suggest "I" and the picture of a *well* to suggest "in good health.") Since Sumerian was largely monosyllabic, each sign (or phonogram) could be used to represent the sound associated with it. These phonograms could then be added to pictograms to indicate morphological alterations, etc.

Predynastic Sumerian tablets, inscribed with linear characters immediately derived from pictographs (Jemdet Nasr, *ca.* 3100 B.C.). They contain accounts of fields, crops, and commodities. (Trustees of the British Museum)

When the Akkadian-speaking Semites borrowed the system of writing, additional modifications were made. For one thing, the polysyllabic nature of Akkadian led to the use of phonograms as syllabograms; in other words, signs were used to represent the sounds of syllables comprising the words. Sumerian signs, for example, having the values "a," "na," and "ku," could be combined to read a-na-ku or *anāku*, "I."

There were many complications, however. For example, the Sumerian sign for "heaven," pronounced "an," also was used to represent the word "god," pronounced "dingir." The Akkadians used this sign for the syllable "an," and they used it to represent the Akkadian word for "god," *ilum*. This proliferation of values expanded until it was possible to read five or ten different values from the same sign. The student who is puzzled to find the same deity called sometimes Enlil and sometimes Illil, or to find an official variously called an *ensi* or a pa-te-si, can attribute these minor difficulties to the extensive polyphony of cuneiform writing.

The Akkadians, moreover, kept certain signs as logograms, or symbols representing words. Of course they usually assigned Akkadian values to such signs. Thus the Sumerian signs kù-babbar, "metal-sun" = "silver," were used to represent the Akkadian word *kaspum*, "silver." Since Akkadian is an inflecting language, with number and case endings, a phonetic complement (or morphogram) was sometimes added to indicate number or case. KÙ.BABBAR-*im* could be used to represent the singular genitive form *kaspim*, "of silver." Likewise, ideograms (signs representing ideas) were sometimes used, but apparently not pronounced, when it was considered desirable to indicate the category of a word or expression. Thus the Sumerian uru (= Akk. *âlum*), "city," was added before names of cities or villages; Sum. giš (= Akk. *iṣum*), "wood, tree," was added before items made of wood; Sum. ki, "land, place" (Akk. value not definitely determined) was added after the name of a place (whether a city or a country); Sum. meš (Akk. value not determined) was added after a word to indicate the plural; etc. In transliterated Assyrian or Babylonian, superscript letters are used to indicate these determinatives (e.g., ^{uru}KA.DINGIR.RA^{ki} or ^{al}*babilum*^{ki} = "(city) Babylon (place).")

Alongside this complicated development of cuneiform writing, another had taken place. The signs, we have said, were at first linear, drawn with a stylus in soft clay. Gradually these became stylized, so that the pictographic character was partially or completely lost. With the invention of the three-cornered stylus and its use to press rather than draw the characters on soft clay, cuneiform proper came into being. Conventions of direction and position of the wedges to form the conventionalized signs developed. These were not exactly the same in all areas, so a Babylonian convention became distinct from an Assyrian convention.

The wedges were usually made of one of four different forms: vertical (Y), horizontal (▷—), sloping downward to the right (◺), and a large angle, generally called by the German term *Winkelhaken* (the Sumerians called it giguru) (∢). In some characters, a fifth form is found, sloping upward to the right (⩗). The form of the wedge was determined by the angle of the wrist and/or fingers at the time of impressing with the stylus.

Signs were made of combinations of these wedges, using one or more strokes. In complicated signs, twenty or more strokes are found. As syllabograms, the signs could represent any of the following: a single vowel (V), a consonant followed by a vowel (CV), a vowel followed by a consonant (VC), or a closed syllable (CVC). Closed syllables were more often written by a combination of CV-VC (e.g., *be-el* = *bel*), without implying any lengthening of the vowel. Sumerian had a number of polysyllabic signs (CVCVC, CVCCVC, VCV, VCCVC, etc.).

The complexity of such a system of writing is obvious. About 600 signs are used in Akkadian. W. von Soden,

Clay conical nail of Entemena, recording in Sumerian cuneiform script the building of the temple of Dumuzi (Tammuz) and Inanna (Ishtar) at Badtibra (*ca.* 3000 B.C.) (Royal Ontario Museum, Toronto)

Das akkadische Syllabar (1948), lists 325 in fairly common use; F. Thureau-Dangin, *Le Syllabaire accadien* (1926), lists only 285; A. Deimel, however, lists 598 (plus numerous variants) in *Šumerisches Lexikon*, Part 2, Vol. 4 (1933), and 972 in Part 1 (1947), many of which have Akkadian values. About 100 syllabograms (V, CV, and VC) are in common use in Akkadian, to which the student must add a score or more CVC-type syllabograms and perhaps 200 logograms (word-signs) and ideograms (determinatives), for reading the texts of any given area and period.

A change in the direction of writing also took place. It is of course impossible to determine how a clay tablet was held. But inscriptions such as Hammurabi's Code of Laws, where the form of the stele with the carved figures at the top determines the direction of the writing, indicate that writing was from top to bottom. At an undetermined date the individual characters, as well as the entire lines, were rotated 90°, and the writing was read from left to right. The original pictographic nature of some of the signs can still be recognized when they are rotated to their original position.

The decipherment of cuneiform was a long process, extending through most of the 19th cent., and the names of Georg Friedrich Grotefend (1802) and Henry Rawlinson (1846) are generally prominent in accounts of the task. Grotefend, working on Old Persian texts, managed to identify the words for "king," "son," and some of the kings' names. Rawlinson, working on the Behistun trilingual inscription (Babylonian, Old Persian, and Elamite), was able to decipher the Old Persian. Later he succeeded in deciphering the Babylonian, with the help of the Irish scholar Edward Hincks and the French scholar Félicien de Saulcy. Many refinements to the earlier efforts have been through the discoveries of bilingual lexical texts. Some of these not only list the Sumerian and Akkadian equivalents, but also give syllabic transliterations of the Sumerian signs. The fruits of studies in lexical texts can be seen in Deimel's *Šumerisches Lexikon* and in the *Assyrian Dictionary* currently being published by the Oriental Institute of the University of Chicago (*CAD*).

Cuneiform writing is three-dimensional. Publication of cuneiform inscriptions, however, is limited to two-dimensional representation. The copying of a cuneiform inscription, whether freehand or by inking over a photograph and bleaching away the background, is a laborious and painstaking process, known as transcription. The representation of the cuneiform symbols by a standardized system using Latin characters, known as transliteration, is much more economical for publication, and is therefore the most common method of publishing cuneiform texts. In the most widely used system of transliteration, diacritical marks and subscript numbers are used to distinguish sounds that are represented by different cuneiform symbols. Thus *tu* is used to represent the Sum. tu; *tú* = Sum. ud or utu; *tù* = Sum. gub or du; tu_4 = Sum. tum; etc. No difference in pronunciation or tone is indicated by those diacritical marks. The scholar, however, must always check a transliteration against the original inscription or a careful transcription thereof.

Of special note is the cuneiform writing of Ugaritic, discovered at Râs Shamrah in Syria since 1929. Although Assyrian texts have been found at Râs Shamrah alongside the Ugaritic texts, and although Ugaritic is written in cuneiform characters on clay tablets, it is important that we note that Ugaritic is written in an entirely different, specifically an alphabetic, system. There are thirty signs, each representing a consonant. The consonant *'aleph*, however, is found in three forms which represent the soundless glottal stop plus each of the three vocalizations; I have called these signs *'aleph*, *'ileph*, and *'uleph*. These alphabetic symbols are made by wedge-shaped writing on clay tablets, but they are not related in form or phonetic value to Mesopotamian cuneiform.

No.	Ugaritic character	Phonetic value	Transliteration
1	𐎀	'a, 'â (1)	*a*
2	𐎛	'i, 'ī, 'ê (1)	*i*
3	𐎜	'u, 'û, 'ô (1)	*u*
4	𐎁	b	*b*
5	𐎂	g	*g*
6	𐎄	d	*d*

No.	Ugaritic character	Phonetic value	Transliteration
7	𐎏 [1]	d	*ḏ*
8	𐎅	h	*h*
9	𐎆	w	*w*
10	𐎇	z	*z*
11	𐎈	ḥ (ح)	*ḥ*
12	𐎃	ḫ (خ)	*ḫ*
13	𐎉	ṭ	*ṭ*
14	𐎑	ẓ (ظ) [1]	*ẓ*
15	𐎊	y	*y*
16	𐎋	k	*k*
17	𐎍	l	*l*
18	𐎎	m	*m*
19	𐎐	n	*n*
20	𐎒	s	*s*
21	𐎝	s	*ś*
22	𐎓	ʿ	ʿ
23	𐎙 [1]	ǵ (غ)	*ǵ*
24	𐎔	p	*p*
25	𐎕	ṣ	*ṣ*
26	𐎖	q	*q*
27	𐎗	r	*r*
28	𐎌	š	*š*
29	𐎚	t	*t*
30	𐎘	ṯ	*ṯ*

Ugaritic alphabet, showing cuneiform signs, their phonetic value, and transliteration. From *UT*, I, 13-15 (Biblical Institute Press, Rome)

The invention of the alphabet, and its representations in linear form that could be written on papyrus or leather (or any flat surface), and its wide dissemination by the Phoenicians in the 1st millennium B.C., made cuneiform writing obsolete. After all, why learn to write with six hundred cumbersome signs when twenty-two, or twenty-six, or at most some forty or fifty, will represent any combination of sounds that you may wish to use in any language?

Bibliography.–I. J. Gelb, *A Study of Writing* (1952); D. Diringer, *The Alphabet* (1947); G. R. Driver, *Semitic Writing from Pictograph to Alphabet* (2nd ed. 1954); J. Friedrich, *Extinct Languages* (1957); L. W. King and R. C. Thompson, *Sculptures and Inscriptions of Darius the Great on the Rock of Behistun* (1907).

See also Plate 5. W. S. LASOR

CUNNING [Heb. *ḥāḇar*]; AV "never so wisely"; NEB SKILFUL; [*ḥēpeś*–'plot'] (Ps. 64:6); AV DILIGENT; [*'oqbâ*] (2 K. 10:19); AV SUBTILTY; NEB OUTWITTED; [*'āram*] (1 S. 23:22); AV SUBTILLY; NEB CRAFTY; [*'ormâ*] (Josh. 9:4); AV WILILY; NEB RUSE; [*śeḵel*]; AV POLICY; NEB "very active"; [*tārmâ*–'deceitfulness'] (Ps. 119:118); AV DECEIT; NEB TALK; [Gk. *kybeía*]; AV SLEIGHT; NEB CRAFTY; [*panourgía*]; AV CRAFTINESS, SUBTILTY.

In Ps. 58:5 *ḥāḇar* originally means "unite," then "tie a magic knot or spell"; hence the meaning "charm," of serpents who lead astray. The "cunning" of Dnl. 8:25 (*śeḵel*) is derived from prudence and insight. Gk. *kybeía* originally referred to dice-playing; hence its meaning of craftiness or trickery in Eph. 4:14. In 2 Cor. 4:2; 11:3 *panourgía* is used to denote an evil sort of cleverness, in contrast to an open statement of the truth. In the AV "cunning" does not have these evil connotations, but simply means "wise" or "skilful." J. R. PRICE

CUP [Heb. *kôs, gaḇî(a)'*, also *sap̱* (1 K. 7:50; Zec. 12:2), *qaśwâ* (1 Ch. 28:17), *'aggān* (Isa. 22:24); Gk. *potḗrion*]; AV also BOWL (*gaḇî(a)'*, Ex. 25:31-34; 37:17-20; *sap*, 1 K. 7:50); NEB also GOBLET (Gen. 44), and cf. Zec. 12:2; "cups of mixed wine" in Isa. 65:11, RSV (NEB "bowls of spiced wine"; AV "drink offering") translates Heb. *mimsaḵ*; Gen. 44:4, RSV, NEB, follows the LXX; Mk. 7:8b, AV, follows a late gloss.

The word "cup," referring either to the vessel or its contents, is often used figuratively in the Bible for that which is portioned out, and of which one is to partake. Thus it can mean God's judgments, His wrath, afflictions (Ps. 11:6; 75:8; Isa. 51:17; Rev. 14:10); and Christ used the figure for His sufferings (Mt. 26:39; shared by His followers, 20:22f.). In the OT it applies also to the blessedness and joy of the children of God, and the full provision made for their wants (Ps. 16:5; 23:5; 116:13; cf. Jer. 16:7). These passages refer not only to the experience of an allotted joy and sorrow, but also to the sharing in this experience by all the community.

"The cup of the Lord" (1 Cor. 10:21) is so called because it is the Lord who makes the feast and tenders the cup, just as "the cup of demons" with which it is contrasted refers to what they offer and communicate. In 1 Cor. 11:25 the cup is called "the new covenant in my blood"; i.e., it is a pledge and seal and means of imparting the blessings of the new covenant (He. 10:16f.) — a covenant established by the shedding of the blood of Christ. The use of the word "cup" for the sacrament shows how prominent was the part the cup had in the Lord's Supper in apostolic times. Not only were all told to drink of the wine (Mt. 26:27), but the very irregularities in the Corinthian church point to the universal use (1 Cor. 11:27). *See also* BLESSING, CUP OF.

Persian libation cup (rhyton) in the shape of an animal's horn. Silver, partially covered with gold foil; 5th cent. B.C., from Erzincan in northeastern Turkey (Trustees of the British Museum)

The reference to the use of cups for divination (Gen. 44:5) is to a superstitious practice derived from heathen peoples. *See* DIVINATION. H. E. JACOBS

CUPBEARER [Heb. *mašqeh*–'one giving drink'] (1 K. 10:5; 2 Ch. 9:4; Neh. 1:11). An officer of high rank at ancient oriental courts, whose duty it was to serve the wine at the king's table. On account of the constant fear of plots and intrigues, a person must be regarded as thoroughly trustworthy to hold this position. He must guard against poison in the king's cup, and was sometimes required to swallow some of the wine before serving it. His confidential relations with the king often endeared him to his sovereign and also gave him a position of great influence.

This officer is first mentioned in Scripture in Gen. 40:1ff., where the Hebrew word elsewhere translated "cupbearer" is rendered "butler." The phrase "chief butler" (v. 2) accords with the fact that there were often a number of such officials under one as chief (cf. Xenophon *Hellenica* vii.1.38). Nehemiah (cf. 1:11) was cupbearer to Artaxerxes Longimanus and was held in high esteem by him, as the record shows. His financial ability (Neh. 5:8, 10, 14, 17) would indicate that the office was a lucrative one. Cupbearers are mentioned further in 1 K. 10:5; 2 Ch. 9:4, where among other evidences of royal splendor they are stated to have impressed the queen of Sheba with Solomon's glory.

The RABSHAKEH of 2 K. 18:17ff.; Isa. 36:2, a highly placed Assyrian official, may have occupied this or a similar position, since Assyrian palace reliefs show how important the office of cupbearer was in relation to that of other court functionaries. See further on cupbearers in Herodotus iii.34; Xenophon *Cyropaedeia* i.3, 8f.; Josephus *Ant.* xvi.8.1; Tob. 1:22. B. R. DOWNER
R. K. H.

CURDLE [Heb. *qāpā'*–'congeal,' 'harden,' 'curdle']. Occurs in Job 10:10, "Didst thou not . . . curdle me like cheese?" i.e., make him take solid form. The formation of the embryo is a mystery about which the ancient Hebrew felt a reverential awe; cf. Ps. 139:13-16. These similes are often met with in the Koran and oriental poetry.

CURDS [Heb. *ḥem'â*] (Gen. 18:8; Dt. 32:14; Jgs. 5:25; etc.); AV BUTTER. A fermented milk product. The modern equivalent, leban, similar to yoghurt, is prepared by churning fresh milk in a goatskin holding a small remainder of a previous quantity. It is considered a delicacy, and is frequently served with honey and wine.

See also FOOD III.

CURE. *See* HEAL.

CURIOUS. The AV uses this term in the obsolete sense of "skilfully made" for Heb. *maḥᵃšeḇeṯ* in Ex. 35:32 and for Gk. *períergos* in Acts 19:19. In Ps. 139:15, AV, "curiously wrought" translates Heb. *rāqam*, "embroidered."

CURRENT MONEY. *See* MONEY, CURRENT.

CURSE [Heb. *'ālâ* (Nu. 5:21, 23; Dt. 29:20f.; 30:7; Jgs. 17:2; 2 Ch. 34:24; Neh. 10:29; Job 31:30; etc.), *ḥērem* (Zec. 14:11; Mal. 4:6), *mᵉ'ērâ* (Dt. 28:20; Prov. 3:33; 28:27; Mal. 2:2; 3:9), *qᵉlālâ* (Gen. 27:12f.; Dt. 11:26, 28f.; 23:5; 27:13; 28:15, 45; 29:27; 30:1, 19; Josh. 8:34; etc.), *qālal* (Gen. 8:21; 12:3; Ex. 21:17; Lev. 19:14; 20:9; 24:11, 14f., 23; etc.), *'ārar* (Gen. 3:14, 17; 4:11; 5:29; 9:25; 12:3; 27:29; 49:7; Ex. 22:28; Nu. 5:18ff.; 22:6, 12; 23:7; etc.), *šāḇa'* (Ps. 102:8; Isa. 65:15), *ta'ᵃlâ* (Lam. 3:65), *bāraḵ* (1 K. 21:10, 13; Job 1:5, 11; 2:5, 9; Ps. 10:3), *nāqaḇ* (Nu. 23:8, 25; Job 3:8; 5:3; Prov. 11:26; 24:24), *qāḇaḇ* (Nu. 22:11, 17; 23:8, 11, 13, 27; 24:10); Gk. *ará* (Rom. 3:14), *katára* (Gal. 3:10, 13; He. 6:8; Jas. 3:10), *kataráomai* (Mt. 25:41; Mk. 11:21; Lk. 6:28; Jas. 3:9), *epikatáratos* (Gal. 3:10, 13), *anáthema* (1 Cor. 12:3), *anathematízō* (Mk. 14:71), *katanathematízō* (Mt. 26:74), *blasphēméō* (Rev. 16:9, 11, 21)]; AV also SWEAR (Ps. 102:8; Jer. 23:10), UTTER DESTRUCTION (Zec. 14:11), BLASPHEME (1 K. 21:10, 13; Rev. 16:9, 11, 21), ACCURSED (1 Cor. 12:3), BLESS (Ps. 10:3); NEB also EXECRATE, "treat with contempt" (Lev. 19:14), "(brings out) the truth" (Nu. 5:18f., 22, 24, 27; etc.), ADJURATION, DENOUNCE, REVILE, DENUNCIATION, SCORN, etc.

This word as noun and verb renders different Hebrew words, some of them more or less synonymous, differing only in degree of strength. It is often used in contrast with "bless" or "blessing" (Dt. 11:29). In Zec. 14:11; Mal. 4:6 "curse" (Heb. *ḥērem*, RSV mg. "ban of utter destruction") refers to a ban which was sometimes placed on a captured city, which meant that everything in the city was consecrated to the deity and offered as a holocaust (cf. Josh. 6:17-19, 24). *See* DEVOTE. In some passages *bāraḵ* (which normally means "bless") is used as a euphemism for *'ārar*, "curse."

When a curse is pronounced against any person, we are not to understand this as a mere wish, however violent, that disaster should overtake the person in question, any more than we are to understand that a corresponding "blessing" conveys simply a wish that prosperity should be the lot of the person on whom the blessing is invoked. A curse was considered to possess an inherent power of carrying itself into effect. This can be illustrated by the nineteenth-century B.C. Egyptian Execration Texts, which recorded the names of the enemies of Egypt upon pottery bowls and figurines. These objects were then cursed magically and smashed, in the belief — typical of sympathetic magic — that the destruction of the nation's enemies would follow that of the pottery objects. When it was not possible to commit such curses to writing so that they would find their mark (cf. Zec. 5:1-3), it was frequently deemed sufficient to utter them aloud. Generally the name of some deity was coupled with such imprecations, as Goliath cursed David by his gods (1 S. 17:43). Such curses, once uttered, possessed the power of self-realization. It was customary for heads of families in their declining years to bless their children, such a blessing being not simply a paternal wish that their children should prosper in life but a potent factor in determining their welfare (Gen. 9:25). In this case Jacob seeks his father's blessing, which was more than his father's good wishes for his future career. The bestowal of patriarchal blessings in Genesis has been paralleled in texts recovered from Nuzi, in which it is evident that such pronouncements constituted the last will and testament of the dying man. By contrast, a series of curses directed toward the enemy quite possibly signalled the start of many a battle in the Orient. The penalty for cursing God was death (Job 2:9).

Archeological discoveries at Boghazköy in central Turkey have shown that stated curses were integral to vassal or suzerainty treaties in the 2nd millennium B.C. These were listed as part of the overall agreement, the intention being that if the vassal broke the terms of the treaty, the curses would fall upon him, aided by the sanction of those deities which had been invoked as witnesses to the particular covenant. The provisions of the Sinaitic agreement between God and Israel included similar curses as the penalties for disobedience. When the Promised Land had been occupied, the curses were to be placed symbolically on Mt. Ebal (Dt. 11:29; 27:12f.) to remind Israel of the penalties which disobedience would bring upon the nation.

In the Near East a tomb was sometimes protected by having a curse formally imposed upon anyone who might attempt to break in and pillage it. The person who would be so foolish as to try to rebuild ruined Jericho was placed under a curse (Josh. 6:26), while at a different level past, present (Ps. 35:4ff.; 40:15f.; Jer. 11:20; etc.), or future (2 S. 18:32; Job 27:7) enemies were also accorded this treatment. The serpent was cursed for tempting Eve (Gen. 3:14), as also were murderers (Gen. 4:11; 49:7; etc.) and sexual deviates (Gen. 9:25ff.; 49:4). A person sometimes took a curse upon himself so as to guarantee the truth of some of his affirmations (Nu. 5:19ff.; Job 31:7f.; Ps. 7:4ff.; 137:5f.). *See* OATH.

Whereas curses by ordinary persons were considered more or less efficacious — some god being always only too glad to speed them on their way to their destination — yet special persons ("holy" persons), in virtue of their special relation to divine beings, possessed special powers of pronouncing effectual curses. Balaam, according to the narrative in Nu. 22f., was an expert in the art. Balak was convinced that Balaam's curse would bring about the defeat of the Israelites.

The term — and the thing signified — plays an important part in Paul's interpretation of the cross. In the light of the law all men are guilty. There is no acquittal through appeal to a law that commands and never forgives, prohibits and never relents. The violator of the law is under a curse. His doom has been pronounced. Escape is impossible. But on the cross Jesus Christ endured the curse — for "cursed be every one who hangs on a tree" (Gal. 3:10, 13) — and a curse that has overtaken its victim is a spent force.

Jesus commands His disciples, "Bless those who curse you" (Lk. 6:28; cf. Rom. 12:14). He Himself cursed the fruitless fig tree (Mk. 11:21) — a symbol of the doom of a fruitless people.

T. LEWIS
R. K. HARRISON

CURTAIN [Heb. *yᵉrî'â* (Ex. 26; 36; Nu. 4:25; etc.), *ḥûr* (Est. 1:6), *dōq* (Isa. 40:22); Gk. *katapétasma* (Mk. 15:38 par.; He. 6:19; 9:3; 10:20)]; AV also VEIL, HANGINGS (Est. 1:6); NEB HANGING (Ex. 26; 36), TENT-CURTAINS (Cant. 1:5), TENT-HANGINGS (Jer. 49:29), COVERINGS (Jer. 4:20), VEIL (He. 6:19). For Heb. *yᵉrî'â* the RSV and NEB occasionally have "tent" (2 S. 7:2; 1 Ch. 17:1; Ps. 104:2); the AV uses "curtain" once for Heb. *māsāḵ* (Nu. 3:26; RSV, NEB, "screen").

"Curtain" frequently appears parallel to and is synonymous with "tent" (e.g., Isa. 54:2; Jer. 4:20; Hab. 3:7); hence those passages where the RSV and NEB so render *yᵉrî'â*. Figuratively, the heavens are also a tent of curtains spread out by their Creator (Ps. 104:2; Isa. 40:22). All pentateuchal references are in the Priestly Code, where they refer to the curtains of the tabernacle which housed the ark. Ten curtains made of fine linen with blue, purple, and scarlet ornamentation formed the tabernacle; decorated with depictions of cherubim, each curtain was 4 cubits by 28 (Ex. 26:1f.). Much later, the Jerusalem temple used two curtains to shield the holy of holies and its contents from the outer world. The first, and theologically most important, was between the holy of holies and the holy place; the second separated the temple proper from the outer porch. It is the former which the NT says was torn from top to bottom at the moment of Jesus' death (Mk. 15:38 par.). *See also* HANGINGS; TABERNACLE; TENT; VEIL.

Similarly, the book of Hebrews speaks of the true sanctuary above with its curtain guarding the heavenly holy of holies (6:19; 9:3). This curtain Jesus has opened to His followers through the curtain of His own breached flesh (10:20).

See *TDNT*, III, *s.v.* καταπέτασμα (Schneider).

K. H. MAAHS

CUSH koosh [Heb. *kûš*]. A geographical name referring to (1) a region in Africa, identified with Nubia or Ethiopia, and (2) a region in Mesopotamia, identified with the Kassites. The Hebrew term possibly has other references in certain texts, but there is no agreement on the identification (cf. 2 Ch. 14:9-15 [MT 8-14]; 21:16).

According to the Table of Nations, Cush, the first son of Ham, was the ancestor of Seba, Havilah, Sabtah, Raamah, and Sabteca (Gen. 10:7), and he "became the father of Nimrod" (v. 8). The spread of the geographical location of these names confirms the problems of identifying the geographical limits of the term Cush. Further complicating the problem is the statement in Gen. 2:13 that the GIHON, one of the four rivers issuing from the river that flowed out of EDEN, "flows around the whole land of Cush."

Cush most frequently refers to an African region, and has often been identified as ETHIOPIA; *kûš* is often so translated in English versions. This leads to at least two erroneous interpretations: first that modern Ethiopia (Abyssinia) is meant, and second that a negroid people is intended. The second error can be corrected quite simply. There is no evidence, either in the Bible or in extrabiblical material, to support the view that Ham or any of his descendants was negroid. The Greek term *Aithíops* does indeed mean "burnt face," and was doubtless applied to peoples to the south of Egypt because of their dark complexion. However, both the Ethiopians and the Nubians lack the physical characteristics, other than skin pigmentation, that are used anthropologically to define the negroid peoples. Of the identifiable descendants of Ham named in Gen. 10 all are caucasoid. The first reference to the Negroes is found in late Egyptian records.

According to Ezk. 29:10 the southern border of Egypt was its common boundary with Cush (RSV "Ethiopia"), hence there can be no doubt that Nubia, and not Abyssinia, is meant. This was located by Ezekiel at Syene (modern Aswan), at the First Cataract. Isa. 18:1 also indicates that Cush (RSV "Ethiopia") was on the Nile. The Egyptian name for Nubia was *K3š*, later *Kš*. The limits of Nubia in antiquity were not clearly fixed. At times, the region extended from the First to the Fourth Cataracts, at other times from the Second to the Fourth, and still at other times from the Second Cataract to the junction of the White and the Blue Niles at Khartoum. In fact, the northern boundary of Nubia serves as an indication of the strength of Upper Egypt, for whenever Egypt was unable to defend its southern territory, the Nubians pushed northward. It is therefore understandable why the Egyptians looked upon the Nubians as an ancient enemy. Likewise, Est. 1:1, referring to the extent of the Persian empire, places its limits at Cush (RSV "Ethiopia"), i.e., the southern boundary of Egypt.

During the Egyptian New Kingdom (*ca.* 1575-1087 B.C.), the time when the Israelites were coming into existence as a federation of tribes, Nubia was part of the Egyptian nation, and Nubian mercenaries (RSV "Ethiopians") are mentioned in the armies of Shishak (2 Ch. 12:3) and Zerah (14:9; etc.). The 25th Dynasty (*ca.* 751-656) is often referred to as "Ethiopian." Piankhy, the Nubian who conquered Egypt, had his capital at Napata, near the Fourth Cataract. His son Tirhakah (Tarhaqa) is mentioned in Isa. 37:9 (par. 2 K. 19:9). Tirhakah's intrigues were at least partly responsible for the Assyrian reaction, which led to the retreat of the Nubians and the removal of their capital further south to Meroë. Something of Nubia's fate, as well as that of Egypt, is hinted at in the prophecies of Jeremiah (46:9) and Ezekiel (30:4f., 9).

The Egyptians called the inhabitants of Cush *Nḥsy* ("Nehesyu" in *CAH*³ I/2 [1971], 508). Several writers have suggested that this word, or a related word, plus the Egyptian definite article (*p-nḥs*) underlies the name of Aaron's grandson Phinehas (*pînᵉḥās*; Ex. 6:25). A markedly similar name occurs in an Egyptian document from late in the reign of Ramses XI (1114-1087 B.C.), viz., Pinḥasi (A. Gardiner, *Egypt of the Pharaohs* [1961], p. 302). If this etymology is sustained, the name would be an additional datum to support the biblical account of Israel in Egypt.

The identification of Cush with the Kassites or some other Mesopotamian people depends largely on the references in Gen. 2:13; 10:8. Since the identification of the river Gihon is largely a matter of speculation, and since the geographical location of the Garden of Eden depends almost entirely on the mention of the Tigris and the Euphrates — an argument largely nullified by the statement that all four rivers, including the Pishon and the Gihon, originated from the one river of Eden (2:10), and by the obvious conclusion that the region's geography was greatly changed by the Flood — these references add little to our knowledge of a Mesopotamian Cush. The remaining reference, namely to Nimrod (10:8), seems clearly to tie the location of Nimrod and his descendants to Babylonia and Assyria (10:10-12).

But to assume that this identifies Cush with the Kassites, who ruled Babylonia for about four hundred years (*ca.* 1530-1151 B.C.), is certainly to assume more than the data will bear. True, the biblical word *kûš* superficially resembles the Akkadian *kašî* or *kaššû* (Kassites), but similar comparisons can be made with words from other areas. The period of Kassite domination (*see* KASSITES) does not fit well with any period proposed for the composition of the early chapters of Genesis, whether this material is considered pre-Mosaic (and possibly patriarchal), Mosaic (bearing in mind that Moses lived far from Mesopotamia), or from the time of the Israelite monarchy (the traditional date of "J").

The link between Nilotic Cush, South Arabia, and Babylonia, nevertheless, remains, and the biblical student is faced with the problem of understanding and possibly explaining it. The identifiable names of the sons of Cush (Gen. 10:7) are generally associated with locations in South Arabia. The links between South Arabia and Abyssinia are rather firmly established. The Semitic origin of the Babylonians, together with linguistic evidence (cf. W. S. LaSor, "Semitic Phonemes" [Ph.D. diss., Dropsie, 1949]), indicates that there are also links that bind the Babylonians or their ancestors to South Arabia. It is therefore tempting to speculate that the descendants of Cush spread in two directions, i.e., both toward lower Mesopotamia and across the Bab el-Mandeb into Africa, thence to Abyssinia and thence by the valleys of the Atbara and the Blue Nile to Nubia. This, however, is at present only speculation. W. S. LASOR

CUSH koosh [Heb. *kûš*] (Ps. 7 title). A Benjaminite, perhaps the person whose opposition to David prompted the composition of Ps. 7.

CUSHAN koo'shan [Heb. *kûšān* (Hab. 3:7); LXX Gk. *Aithiopōn*–'Ethiopians,' apparently reading *kûšîm*]. The name of a place or people, which appears as Midian in the parallel strophe in Hab. 3:7. There is possibly a connection with the Egyptian term *Kushu* (cf. W. F. Albright, *BASOR*, 83 [Oct. 1941], 34 n. 8), and perhaps also with the "Cushite" woman of Nu. 12:1.

W. S. L. S.

CUSHAN-RISHATHAIM koo-shan-rish-ə-thā'əm [Heb. *kûšan riš'āṯayim*–interpreted as 'Cushite of the double crime'(?); LXX *Chousarsathaim*] (Jgs. 3:8, 10); AV CHUSHAN-RISHATHAIM. A king of Mesopotamia who was chosen by God as His tool to chastise the Israelites for their idolatry. He opposed the apostate Israelites for eight years, after which Othniel, the son of Caleb's younger brother Kenaz, was raised up by God as the first of the charismatic leaders known as judges, to deliver Israel.

The identity of Cushan-Rishathaim is uncertain. He has been thought to be an Edomite chieftain, a fourteenth-century B.C. Mitanni king, or a Syrian ruler. The most probable suggestion is that he was a king named Irsu from the Upper Euphrates region who fought with the Egyptians about 1200 B.C.

Bibliography.–R. T. O'Callaghan, *Aram Naharaim* (1948), pp. 122f., 139ff.; *ARI*, pp. 110f.; A. Malamat, *JNES*, 13 (1954), 231ff.

R. K. H.

CUSHI koosh'ī [Heb. *kûšî*].

1. (2 S. 18:21ff., AV). *See* CUSHITE.

2. The great-grandfather of Jehudi, a contemporary of Jeremiah (Jer. 36:14).

3. The father of Zephaniah the prophet (Zeph. 1:1).

CUSHION [Gk. *proskephálaion*] (Mk. 4:38); AV PILLOW. The word means literally a cushion for the head, but was also used of one for sitting or reclining, e.g., a rower's cushion. The definite article in this passage suggests that it was one of the customary furnishings of the boat.

CUSHITE koosh'īt [Heb. *kûšî*] (2 S. 18:21ff.); AV CUSHI. The designation of the man who brought David the news of Absalom's death. It appears with the article seven times out of eight, indicating that the person was of the Cushite (Ethiopian) people, and precluding the use as a proper name. That the Cushite messenger to David was a stranger, and doubtless an Ethiopian, is shown by his ignorance of the shorter path taken by Ahimaaz, his unfamiliarity with the watchman, and his lack of knowledge — by comparison with Ahimaaz — of the feelings and reactions of David, whom he knew only as a king, not as a man. R. K. H.

CUSHITE WOMAN [Heb. *hakkušîṯ*]. Moses' wife is thus referred to by Miriam and Aaron (Nu. 12:1) in a derogatory manner as they protest his marriage to a non-Israelite. As a Cushite, she would be a descendant of Cush, the eldest son of Ham, grandson of Noah (Gen. 10:6) and father of Nimrod (v. 8). The habitat of this tribe was Ethiopia or Nubia.

Obviously the brother and sister of Moses resented the fact that he had married a woman outside the tribes of Israel. Mingled with this was resentment also against Moses' leadership — "Has the Lord indeed spoken only through Moses? Has he not spoken through us also?" (Nu. 12:2). Whether the source of their resentment was primarily the Cushite woman or the monopoly of Moses on divine revelation is not clear from the text. In the light of the Lord's reaction (vv. 2-15), the implication is that the real issue was their secondary status in the hierarchy and that they used the marriage as the ostensible reason for their protest.

The identity of this "Cushite woman" is far from clear. It could be a reference to Zipporah (Ex. 2:21; 4:25; 18:2) the Midianite, but here called "Cushite" because of her dark complexion. She could be a woman of Ethiopian origin, perhaps one of the "mixed multitude" (Ex. 12:38), whom Moses married either after the death of Zipporah or as an additional wife. Some scholars think that the words "because of the Cushite woman whom he had married; for he had married a Cushite woman" were inserted into the text by a later editor; it seems more probable, however, that she was Moses' second wife, an Ethiopian woman. G. A. TURNER

CUSTODIAN [Gk. *paidagōgós*] (Gal. 3:24f.); AV SCHOOLMASTER; NEB (KIND OF) TUTOR. In ancient Greek and Roman families a slave was frequently placed in charge of the lads until the age of maturity (about sixteen). Contrary to some translations, this slave was not an educator as such (cf. the meaning of "pedagogue" today). Rather, he was primarily responsible for his charges' conduct and behavior, which he often controlled by shaming and punishment (cf. 1 Cor. 4:14f.). Consequently, his position and methods did not endear him with his charges. By comparing the law with the "custodian," Paul illustrates the law's role and its temporary character. The law's role is to keep one under control by regulating one's conduct. It was a temporary measure, in force until the "age of maturity," i.e., the coming of Jesus Christ and the placing of one's faith in Him. Resubmission to the law as a way of life would be like a young man returning to his "custodian," relinquishing the freedom, rights, and privileges which had come to him through his coming of age (cf. Gal. 4:1-7).

See also GUIDE (1 Cor. 4:15). R. GUELICH

CUSTODY [Heb. *mišmār*] (Gen. 40:3f., 7; 41:10; Lev. 24:12; Nu. 15:34); AV WARD; NEB also IMPRISONED, "wait on"; [*'el-yaḏ*] (Est. 2:3, 8, 14); NEB "committed to the care," "entrusted to," "under the care"; [Gk. *tḗrēsis*] (Acts 4:3); AV HOLD; NEB PRISON; [*tēréō*] (Acts 24:23; 25:21); AV KEEP, RESERVED; NEB also "open arrest."

The word signifies being placed under official care, either in prison or under supervision. *Mišmār* comes from the verb *šāmar*, meaning "keep" or "guard." In Ezk. 19:9 the AV, RSV, and NEB emend the MT to read *yᵉḇi'uhû* (hiphil of *bô'*, plus suffix) *bammaṣṣōreṯ*, "brought him into custody" (RSV; AV "brought him into holds"; NEB "flung him into prison"). *Tēréō* means "keep in view" or "watch over." J. T. DENNISON, JR.

CUSTOM [Aram. *hᵃlāḵ*] (Ezr. 4:13, 20; 7:24); NEB POLL-TAX. *See* TAX.

CUSTOM [Heb. *ḥōq*, *huqqôṯ* (pl.), *mišpāṭ*; Gk. *éthos*, vbs. *eiōtha* (*éthō*), *ethízō*, also *synḗtheia* (Jn. 18:39)]; AV also MANNER, STATUTES (2 K. 17:8, 19), "was wont" (Mk. 10:1; Lk. 22:39); NEB also INSTITUTIONS, PRACTICE(S), TRADITION, "carved images" (Jer. 10:3), "as usual," "regularly," WAY OF LIFE. In the OT such passages as Jgs. 11:39; 1 S. 2:13; 2 K. 11:14; 17:19; Jer. 32:11; Ezr. 3:4, show the difficulty of deciding upon an English equivalent of Heb. *ḥōq* or *mišpāṭ* in cases where "custom" might become "statute," "usage" establish itself as "law." In Lev. 18:30; Jer. 10:3 the reference is to heathen religious practices.

In the NT Lk. 1:9; 2:42; Jn. 19:40; Acts 6:14; 15:1; 16:21; 21:21; 26:3; 28:17 (Gk. *éthos*); and Lk. 2:27 (*ethízō*) refer to definitely established *religious* practices, in every case except Acts 16:21 to those of the Jewish law. In Jn. 18:39 "custom" translates *synḗtheia*, in the sense of "usage" rather than law. Cf. also Acts 25:16. F. K. FARR

CUT; CUT OFF [Heb. *kāraṯ*, *kāḥaḏ*, *gāḏa'*, *nāṯah*, *qāṣaṣ*, also *gāzaz*, *mûl* (Ps. 118:10-12), *nāṯaḥ* (Ex. 29:17; Lev. 1:6, 12; 8:20), *gāḏaḏ* (Dt. 14:1; 1 K. 18:28; Jer. 16:6), *dāmam* (2 S. 2:9; Jer. 48:2; 51:6), *gāzar* (Ps. 90:10; Isa. 53:8); Gk. *kóptō*, *apokóptō*, *ekkóptō*, also *aphairéō* (Mt. 26:51; Mk. 14:47; Lk. 22:50), *keírō* (Acts 18:18; 1 Cor. 11:6), *katanýssomai* (Acts 2:37), *anáthema* (Rom. 9:3)]; AV also CUT ASUNDER, HEW, HEW DOWN, DESTROY (Ps. 118:10-12; Heb. *mûl*), etc.; NEB also "drive them away," LOOSE, MASSACRE (2 S. 11:11), DESTROY, BRING DISASTER (1 K. 14:10), BLOT OUT, EXTERMINATE, etc. For Job 33:17 "cut off pride" (RSV; AV "hide pride"; NEB "check the pride"), the original Hebrew reading (consigned to footnote in the RSV) *kāsah*, "hide," "cover," should be *kāsaḥ*, "cut down," hence "destroy," "cancel"; cf. also Isa. 33:12 and Ps. 80:16, *kāsaḥ*.

By far the most common Hebrew word for "cut," "cut off," is *kāraṯ*, and the most common Greek term is *kóptō*. The primary meaning is of course the physical act of severing, removing, or dividing one thing from another. "Command that the cedars of Lebanon be cut for me" (1 K. 5:6); "break their pillars and cut down their Asherim" (Ex. 34:13); "he cut his hair" (Acts 18:18).

The derivative or extended use of the term is just as prevalent in the biblical material. It often carries the connotation of destroying, rooting out, eliminating, extinguishing. Frequently the cutting off or separation is an act of divine judgment upon a person, group, or nation, carried out either indirectly by Yahweh's representatives or by Yahweh Himself. "If anyone eats what is leavened, that person shall be cut off from the congregation of Israel" (Ex. 12:19). This alienation from the people of Israel is frequently the punishment enjoined by the Levitical laws (Lev. 7:20ff.; 17:4ff.; 18:29; 19:8; 20:3ff.). With reference to large groups, cf. Dt. 19:1, "the Lord your God cuts off the nations. . . ." This usage is carried over into the NT. Speaking to Gentiles, Paul sounds the note of judgment to those who do not realize they are within the sphere of God's lovingkindness only through grace. "Put away your pride. . . . Observe the kindness and the severity of God . . . otherwise you too will be cut off" (Rom. 11:20-22, NEB; cf. also v. 24).

In Rom. 9:3 Paul expresses the depth of his concern for the original bearers of the covenant, the Israelites. "I could wish that I myself were accursed and cut off from Christ" (RSV; NEB "be outcast from Christ"). "Accursed and cut off" is the translation of Gk. *anáthema*. Accursed is the primary meaning of the word, but it carries the additional implication of separation from Christ; cf. also 1 Cor. 16:22; Gal. 1:6.

The Heb. verb *qāṣaṣ* is generally used of cutting off a member of the body, such as hands (Dt. 25:12), hands and feet (2 S. 4:12), thumbs and great toes (Jgs. 1:6f.), corners of the hair (Jer. 9:26). Gk. *apokóptō* in Mk. 9:43, 45 also refers to the cutting off of parts of the body. This self-mutilation is intended to eliminate the sinful influence of wayward bodily members lest eternal punishment be the result of their presence. Stählin would not take this radical self-punishment literally but sees it as the exhortation to weaken the sinful influence of such bodily members (*TDNT*, III, 853; cf. also W. Lane, Comm. on Mark [*NIC*, 1974], p. 347f.). In Mt. 5:30 and 18:8 *ekkóptō*, "cut off," is used synonymously with the *apokóptō* of Mk. 9:43, 45.

Again in the parable of the barren fruit tree (Mt. 7:19; Lk. 13:7, 9; also Mt. 3:10; Lk. 3:9) the note of judgment is sounded by *ekkóptō*. Hewing down the unfruitful tree is symbolic of the separation of unproductive and unrighteous men from life in the kingdom of God.

The Heb. verb *kāraṯ* is also used in the idiomatic formula for establishing a COVENANT, *kāraṯ bᵉrîṯ*, "cut a covenant" (e.g., Gen. 15:18; 21:27; Isa. 55:3). This expression is derived from the manner in which the covenant was sealed. For instance, in Gen. 15:9-18 Yahweh in the form of a fire pot and torch passed between the pieces of the animals that Abram had cut in two. In this way Yahweh was taking a self-maledictory oath, assuring thereby the perpetuity of the promise; cf. also Jer. 34:18-20.

Bibliography.–E. Kutsch, *Alter Orient und AT*, 18 (1973), 121-27; S. E. Lowenstamm, *VT*, 18 (1968), 500-506; J. A. Soggin, *VT*, 18 (1968), 210-15.

B. L. BANDSTRA

CUTH. *See* CUTHAH.

CUTHA koo'thə [Gk. *koutha*] (1 Esd. 5:32); AV, NEB, COUTHA. Head of a family of temple servants who returned with Zerubbabel from Babylon; not mentioned in the canonical lists.

CUTHAH kooth'ə [Heb. *kûṯâ*; Bab. *kûtû*; Sum. gu-du-a; Gk. *Chountha*] (2 K. 17:24); **CUTH** kooth [Heb. *kûṯ*; Gk. *Choua*] (v. 30). One of the cities from which Sargon of Assyria brought colonists to replace the Israelites he deported from Samaria in 722 B.C. Probably in consequence of their predominating numbers, the inhabitants of Samaria in general were then called *kûṯîyîm*, or Cutheans.

The site was identified with Tell Ibrâhîm by Hormuzd Rassam, in 1881/82. It lies NE of Babylon, and was one of the most important cities of the Babylonian empire. The explorer describes the ruins as being about 3000 ft. (915 m.) in circumference and 280 ft. (85 m.) high, and adjoining them on the west lies a smaller mound, crowned with a sanctuary dedicated to Abraham (Ibrahîm). From the nature of the ruins, Rassam came to the conclusion that the city was much more densely populated after the fall of Babylon than in earlier times. A portion of the ruins was in a very perfect state, and suggested an unfinished building.

The great temple of the city was called *Ê-mešlam*, and was dedicated to Nergal (cf. 2 K. 17:30), god of the underworld. Both city and temple would seem to have been old Sumerian foundations, as the name *Gudua* and its later Semitic form *Kutû* imply.

T. G. PINCHES

CUTHEAN koo'thē-ən; **CUTHITE** kooth'īt. *See* CUTHAH; SAMARITANS.

CUTTER [Heb. *gāzām*] (Joel 2:25); AV PALMERWORM; NEB LOCUST. Perhaps one of the stages of the maturing locust. The "palmerworm" is to be rejected because of its exclusive connection with developing moths. On account of the fearful devastation caused by plagues of locusts, the symbol in Joel is an apt one for the invasion of a powerful enemy.

CUTTINGS IN THE FLESH [Heb. *śereṭ*, *śāreṭeṯ*–'incision,' 'tattoo'] (Lev. 19:28; 21:5); NEB GASH (THE BODY); [cf. Akk. *šarātu*–'cut or tear to pieces']. Physical self-laceration or self-mutilation inflicted as a sign of mourning or to seek the favor of a deity. *See also* GASH.

The custom of self-laceration of cheeks or chest and cuts on hands, arms, and backs was widely practiced as a part of mourning rites among the ancients (cf. Jer. 47:5; 48:37; 49:3). An Ugaritic epic describes how Baal, the god of fertility, vegetation, and rain, was mourned at his death by El, the supreme god of the Ugaritic pantheon: El descended from his throne and sat on the ground, where he "lacerated himself" (Ugar. *ytlṯ*), making cuts on his face, his arms, his chest, and his back (*DOTT*, p. 130; *ANET*, p. 139; Gaster, pp. 213-15). The prohibition of such "cuttings in the flesh" among the Israelites (Lev. 19:28; 21:5; Dt. 14:1) rests in (1) the rejection of pagan (Canaanite) practices and beliefs in which ritual laceration was thought to hand over man to the realm of the dead; (2) the affirmation of the uniqueness of the Israelites as "the sons of Yahweh" (Dt. 14:1), the covenant God who revealed Himself as the "I AM WHO I AM" (Ex. 3:13); (3) the emphasis on Israel as a "people holy to Yahweh" (Dt. 14:2), which finds its basis in Yahweh's election of Israel; and (4) the concept of the sanctity of life and health. The deprivation of the sacral quality of death and the grave in Israelite religion was a great achievement. Despite this prohibition, self-inflicted laceration was practiced among the Israelites of the 6th cent. B.C. as a sign of grief and mourning (cf. Jer. 16:6; 41:5).

The Baal prophets "cut themselves after their custom with swords and lances, until the blood gushed out upon them" (1 K. 18:28) in their contest on Mt. Carmel with Elijah, the prophet of Yahweh, during the reign of Ahab. The self-laceration of the Baal prophets with its blood-letting was in all likelihood a Canaanite rite of imitative magic to cause the release of the vital rain upon which life depended, i.e., it was a rite intended to rouse Baal to bring rain (cf. Apuleius *Metamorphoses* viii.27; J. Garstang and H. A. Strong, *Syrian Goddess* [1913], p. 84). The pagan self-laceration rite of the Baal cult, apparently intended to induce rain for the crops, was practiced in the time of Hosea and condemned by him (Hos. 7:14). The reference in Zec. 13:2-6 to the abolition of debased prophecy in the messianic age shows that self-inflicted wounding on their chests was practiced by prophets during certain periods.

Bibliography.–H. J. Elhorts, *Die Israelitischen Trauerriten* (1914); P. Heinisch, *Die Trauergebräuche bei den Israeliten* (1931); H. Cazelles, *RB*, 55 (1948), 52-71; T. Canaan, *ZDPV*, 75 (1959), 97-115; R. de Vaux, *Ancient Israel: Its Life and Institutions* (1961), pp. 58-61; T. H. Gaster, *Thespis* (3rd ed. 1966), pp. 213-15; *BhHW*, III, *s.v.* "Ritzen" (Rissi).

G. F. HASEL

CYAMON sī'ə-mən [Gk. *Kyamōn*] (Jth. 7:3). Probably identical with JOKNEAM.

CYCLE OF NATURE [Gk. *trochós tḗs genéseōs*] (Jas. 3:6); AV COURSE OF NATURE; NEB WHEEL OF OUR EXISTENCE; cf. JB "wheel of creation." The AV "course" accents *tróchos* rather than *trochós*, "wheel." But either way, and whatever the origin of the phrase (it occurs in the Orphic mysteries), in this context it clearly means the whole of our existence, from beginning to end. The use of this phrase does not commit James to any particular view of history or concept of time.

CYMBAL [Heb. *m^{e}ṣiltayim* (dual), *ṣelṣ^{e}lim* (pl.); Gk. *kýmbalon* (1 Cor. 13:1)]. *See* MUSIC. II.D.

CYPRESS [Heb. *b^{e}rôš*; Gk. *kypárissos* and variously] (1 K. 5:8, 10, etc.; 2 K. 19:23; 2 Ch. 2:8; 3:5; Isa. 14:8; 37:24; etc.; Hos. 14:8; Zec. 11:2); AV FIR; NEB PINE. The uncertainty surrounding the identification of a great many trees mentioned in the OT suggests that "cypress" should be restricted to translating *t^e'aššûr* (Ugar. *tšrm*), indicating the slender *Cupressus sempervirens* L. (Isa. 41:19; 60:13; Ezk. 27:6). Elsewhere the RSV "cypress" probably refers to one of the juniper species, several of which produce wood valuable for building purposes.

See also FIR TREE; HOLM TREE; GOPHER WOOD.

CYPRIANS [Gk. *Kyprioi*] (2 Macc. 4:29). AV for mercenary troops supporting Sostrates, captain of the Jerusalem citadel during the reign of Antiochus IV Epiphanes (RSV "Cyprian troops"; NEB "Cypriots"). Ordinarily a gentilic (Bauer, p. 458; cf. Acts 4:36; 11:20; 21:16), the RSV apparently takes the Greek as a technical term. According to the NEB (2 Macc. 12:2) Nicanor was "chief of the Cyprian mercenaries" under Antiochus V Eupator (AV, RSV "governor of Cyprus"; Gk. *Kypriárchēs*; cf. JB). *See* CRATES; CYPRUS.

CYPRUS sī'prəs. An island situated near the northeast corner of the Mediterranean Sea, in an angle formed by the coasts of Cilicia (modern Turkey) and Syria. In the OT it is called KITTIM; cf. the name of its Phoenician capital Kition.

I. Geography
II. Products
III. Early History

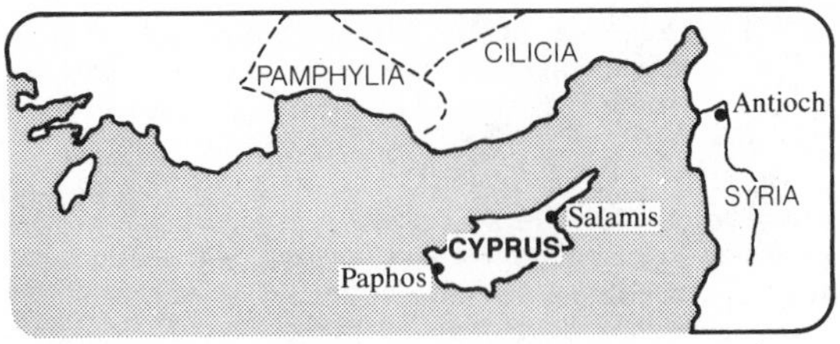

IV. Greek and Roman Periods
V. Cyprus and the Jews
VI. The Church in Cyprus
VII. Later History

I. Geography.–The island is the third largest in the Mediterranean after Sardinia and Sicily, with an area of about 3584 sq. mi. (9282 sq. km.). It lies only 46 mi. (74 km.) from the nearest point of the Cilician coast and 60 mi. (97 km.) from the Syrian. Thus from the northern shore of the island the mainland of Asia Minor is clearly visible, and Mt. Lebanon can be seen from eastern Cyprus. This close proximity to the Cilician and Syrian coasts, as well as its position on the route between Asia Minor and Egypt, proved of great importance for the history and civilization of the island. Its greatest length, including the northeast promontory, is about 140 mi. (225 km.), and its greatest breadth 60 mi. (97 km.).

The southwest portion of Cyprus is formed by a mountain complex, whose highest peak is 6403 ft. (1951 m.). To the northeast of this complex lies the great plain of the Messaoria, nearly 60 mi. (97 km.) in length and 10 to 20 (16 to 32 km.) in breadth, in which lies the modern capital Nicosia. The plain is bounded on the north by a mountain range (the Kyrenia), which is continued to the east-northeast in the long, narrow promontory of the Karpass, terminating in Cape Andrea, the ancient Dinaretum. Its two highest peaks are just over 3100 ft. (945 m.). The shore-plain to the north of these hills is narrow, but remarkably fertile.

II. Products.–Cyprus is richly endowed by nature. Its fruits and flowers were famous in antiquity. Strabo speaks of it as producing wine and oil in abundance and corn sufficient for the needs of its inhabitants. The elder Pliny refers to Cyprian salt, alum, gypsum, mica, unguents, laudanum, storax, resin, and precious stones. The chief source of the island's wealth, however, lay in its mines and forests. Silver is mentioned by Strabo; copper, which was called by the Greeks after the name of the island, was extensively mined there from the earliest period down to the Middle Ages; iron too was found in considerable quantities from the 9th cent. until Roman times. Scarcely less important were the forests, which at an early date are said to have covered almost the whole island. The cypress seems to have been the principal tree, and the island supplied timber for shipbuilding to many successive powers.

III. Early History.–The original inhabitants of Cyprus appear to have been a race akin to the peoples of Asia Minor. The island's vast resources in copper and timber gained for it a considerable importance and wide commercial relations at a very remote period. Its wealth attracted the attention of Babylonia and Egypt, and there is reason to believe that it was conquered by Sargon I king of Akkad, and about a millennium later by Thutmose III of the 18th Dynasty (1501-1447 B.C.).

But the influences that molded its civilization came from other quarters also. Excavation has shown that in Cyprus there were several seats of Minoan culture, and there can be little doubt that it was deeply influenced

Ancient harbor at Paphos, center of Roman rule on Cyprus. Paul, Barnabas, and John Mark visited the city on the first missionary journey. (W. S. LaSor)

by Crete. Phoenician influences too were at work, and the Phoenician settlements of Citium, Amathus, Paphos, and others go back to a very early date. The breakup of the Minoan civilization was followed by a "dark age"; but later the island received a number of Greek settlers from Arcadia and other Hellenic states, to judge not only from Greek tradition but from the evidence of the Cyprian dialect, which is closely related to the Arcadian.

In 709 B.C. Sargon II of Assyria made himself master of Cyprus, and tribute was paid by its seven princes to him and to his grandson Esarhaddon (681-667). The overthrow of the Assyrian empire probably brought with it the independence of Cyprus, but it was conquered anew by Aahmes (Amasis) of Egypt (Herodotus ii.182), who retained it till his death in 526 B.C. However, in the following year the defeat of his son and successor by Cambyses brought the island under Persian dominion (Herodotus iii.19, 91).

IV. Greek and Roman Periods.–In 501 the Greek inhabitants rose in revolt against the Persians, but were decisively beaten (Herodotus v.104ff.), and in 480 there were 150 Cyprian ships in the navy with which Xerxes attacked Greece (Herodotus vii.90). In 411 Euagoras ascended the throne of Salamis and set to work to assert Hellenic influence and to champion Hellenic civilization. He joined with Pharnabazus the Persian satrap and Conon the Athenian to overthrow the naval power of Sparta at the battle of Cnidus in 394, and in 387 revolted from the Persians.

Cyprus seems later to have fallen once again under Persian rule, but after the battle of Issus (333 B.C.) it voluntarily gave its submission to Alexander the Great and rendered him valuable aid at the siege of Tyre. On his death (323) it fell to the share of Ptolemy of Egypt. It was, however, seized by Demetrius Poliorcetes, who defeated Ptolemy in a hotly contested battle off Salamis in 306. Eleven years later it came into the hands of the Ptolemies and remained a province of Egypt or a separate but dependent kingdom until the intervention of Rome (cf. 2 Macc. 10:13).

In 58 B.C. the Romans resolved to incorporate Cyprus into their empire, and Marcus Porcius Cato was entrusted with the task of its annexation. The reigning prince, a brother of Ptolemy Auletes of Egypt, received the offer of an honorable retirement as high priest of Aphrodite at Paphos, but he preferred to end his life by poison, and the island passed into Roman hands and was attached to the province of Cilicia. In the partition of the Roman empire between senate and emperor, Cyprus was at first (27-22 B.C.) an imperial province. In 22 B.C., however, it was handed over to the senate together with southern Gaul in exchange for Dalmatia (Dio Cassius *Hist.* liii.12; liv.4) and was subsequently governed by ex-praetors bearing the honorary title of proconsul and residing at Paphos. Among them was Sergius Paulus, who was proconsul at the time of Paul's visit to Paphos. The title applied to him in Acts 13:7 is strictly accurate.

V. Cyprus and the Jews.–The proximity of Cyprus to the Syrian coast rendered it easy of access from Palestine, and Jews had probably begun to settle there even before the time of Alexander the Great. Certainly the number of Jewish residents under the Ptolemies was considerable (1 Macc. 15:23; 2 Macc. 12:2), and it must have been increased later when the copper mines of the island were farmed to Herod the Great (Josephus *Ant.* xvi.4.5; xix.26.28). We shall not be surprised, therefore, to find that at Salamis there was more than one synagogue at the time of Paul's visit (Acts 13:5).

In A.D. 116 the Jews of Cyprus rose in revolt and massacred no fewer than 240,000 Gentiles. Hadrian crushed the rising with great severity and drove all the Jews from the island. Henceforth no Jew might set foot upon it, even under stress of shipwreck, on pain of death (Dio Cassius lxviii.32).

VI. The Church in Cyprus.–In the life of the early Church Cyprus played an important part. Among the Christians who fled from Judea in consequence of the persecution that followed Stephen's death were some who "traveled as far as Phoenicia and Cyprus" (Acts 11:19) preaching to the Jews only. Certain natives of Cyprus and Cyrene took a further momentous step in preaching at Antioch to the Greeks also (Acts 11:20).

Even before this time Joseph Barnabas, a Levite born in Cyprus (Acts 4:36), was prominent in the early Christian community at Jerusalem, and it was in his native island that he and Paul, accompanied by John Mark, began their first missionary journey (Acts 13:4). After landing at Salamis they passed "through the whole island as far as Paphos" (Acts 13:6), probably visiting the Jewish synagogues in its cities. Whether the "early disciple," Mnason of Cyprus, was one of the converts made at this time or had previously embraced Christianity we cannot determine (Acts 21:16). Barnabas and Mark revisited Cyprus later (Acts 15:39); but Paul did not again land on the island, though he sighted it when, on his last journey to Jerusalem, he sailed S of it on his way from Patara in Lycia to Tyre (Acts 21:3), and again when on his journey to Rome he sailed "under the lee of Cyprus," that is, along its northern coast, on the way from Sidon to Myra in Lycia (Acts 27:4).

In 401 the Council of Cyprus was convened, chiefly in consequence of the efforts of Theophilus of Alexandria, the inveterate opponent of Origenism, and took measures to check the reading of Origen's works. The island, which was divided into thirteen bishoprics, was declared autonomous in the 5th cent., after the alleged discovery of Matthew's Gospel in the tomb of Barnabas at Salamis. The bishop of Salamis was made metropolitan by the emperor Zeno with the title "archbishop of all Cyprus"; and his successor, who now occupies the see of Nicosia, still enjoys the privilege of signing his name in red ink and is primate over the three other bishops of the island, all of whom are of metropolitan rank.

VII. Later History.–Cyprus remained in the possession of the Roman and then of the Byzantine emperors, though twice overrun and temporarily occupied by the Saracens, until 1184, when its ruler Isaac Comnenus broke away from Constantinople and declared himself an independent emperor. From him the rule was seized in 1191 by the Crusaders under Richard I of England, who bestowed it on Guy de Lusignan, the titular king of Jerusalem, and his descendants. In 1489 it was ceded to the Venetians by Catherine Cornaro, widow of James II, the last of the Lusignan kings, and remained in their hands until it was captured by the Ottoman Turks under Sultan Selim II, who invaded and subjugated the island in 1570 and laid siege to Famagusta, which, after a heroic defense, capitulated on August 1, 1571.

The ensuing three centuries of Turkish rule were marked in general by laxness on the part of the rulers of Cyprus. Minor revolts were frequent, and there were serious revolts in 1764 and 1823. The population declined; the copper mines ceased to be worked; in the latter part of the 18th cent. cotton, the chief crop, dropped to an average annual crop of about 4000 bales from an average crop of about 8000 bales in the earlier part of that century (and from a crop of as much as 30,000 bales during the earlier Venetian period). In 1878 Britain and Turkey made a defensive alliance in view of the encroachments of Russia toward the south. As a part of this arrangement, Cyprus was occupied and administered by Britain, though nominally remaining a part of the Ottoman empire. When Turkey entered World War I against the Allies, Cyprus was annexed to the British empire, and in 1925 became a crown colony.

In recent years Cyprus has again been a land of tension. A small but powerful minority began agitating for *henosis*, i.e., union with Greece. The first open demonstrations occurred in 1931. Turkey, however, will not permit Cyprus to become a part of Greece, insisting that the island is more properly an extension of the Anatolian mainland. Though it is true that the larger part of the population of Cyprus (four-fifths) is Greek-speaking, largely through the influence of the Greek Orthodox Church, the natural and historical ties with Greece are not strong. Early in 1959 an agreement was reached among Britain, Greece, and Turkey that provided for setting up the Republic of Cyprus. Britain indicated her willingness to give up her sovereignty over the island providing she could maintain her military bases; Greece gave up the claim to *henosis*; Turkey gave up its insistence on partition. This agreement seemed to give promise of a lasting settlement, but it soon broke down, and Turkey invaded and occupied much of the island. Throughout its long checkered history the control of Cyprus has been regarded as essential for the control of the eastern Mediterranean. The continuing recognition of its strategic importance seems to destine Cyprus to a future of tension and struggle.

Bibliography.–An exhaustive bibliography is in C. D. Cobham, *An Attempt at a Bibliography of Cyprus* (4th ed. 1900). See also G. Home, *Cyprus Then and Now* (1960); P. Newman, *A Short History of Cyprus* (1940).

M. N. TOD
R. A. GWINN

CYRENE sī-rē'nē [Gk. *Kyrēnē*]. A city in North Africa, capital of the Roman province of Cyrenaica (ancient and modern Libya). The city, modern Shakhāt, is located on the "hump" of Libya, E of the Gulf of Sirte (Syrtis), about 100 mi. (160 km.) ENE of Benghazi. It lies on a plateau at an altitude of about 1600 ft. (490 m.), approximately 6 mi. (10 km.) from the sea, 8 mi. (13 km.) SW of Apollonia (modern Marsa Susah), which was its seaport, and lying against Jebel al-Akhdar, which rises to an elevation of 2894 ft. (882 m.), S of Cyrene. The plateau slopes downward to the south, and because of its location, it enjoys excellent climate and fertility of soil. Herodotus reports that Cyrene, "which is the highest part of the Libya that the nomads inhabit, has the marvel of three harvest seasons" (iv.199).

Cyrene was founded by Dorian Greeks from the island of Thera (Santorin). The first expedition set out *ca.* 630 B.C., but landed on the island Platea on the Gulf of Bomba. According to Herodotus (iv.150-54), the expedition had been instigated by the oracle at Delphi, so a second request was made of the oracle, and the second expedition landed on the mainland and was

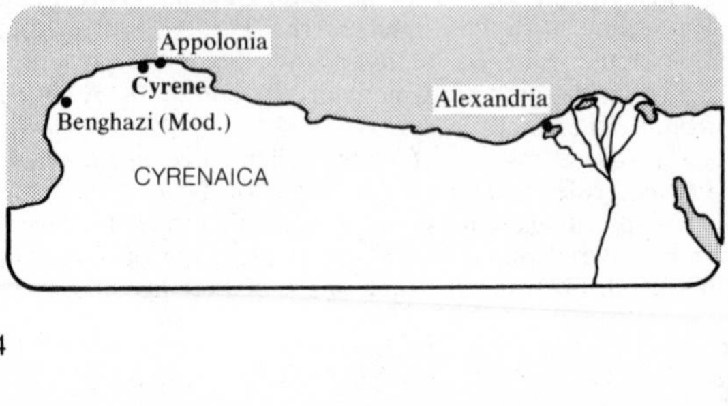

brought to the site of Cyrene by friendly Libyans. The founder was named Battus, which, according to Herodotus tells us that Cyrene was important enough for Amasis by the Delphic oracle before the expedition set sail, in fact before Battus was born. The dynasty of the Battiadae consisted of eight kings, alternately named Battus and Arcesilaus, and continued until *ca.* 440 B.C. A perennial spring nearby was named for the nature-goddess Cyrene (Kyrana) (in later Greek mythology said to be the bride of Apollo), which accounts for the city's name.

Because of its agricultural wealth, particularly in grain, stock-breeding, and the spice silphium (which was much used in Greek cooking and also had medicinal uses), Cyrene became a very important Greek colony. Herodotus tells us that Cyrene was important enough for Amasis pharaoh of Egypt (570-526 B.C.) to take a wife from there, possibly a daughter of Battus II (ii.181) — but Herodotus contains a mixture of factual and nonfactual legends. When the dynasty collapsed, a republic was established, and this passed into Ptolemaic Egypt in 322 B.C. Ptolemy I gave a constitution to Cyrene, a copy of which can be seen in the museum at Cyrene. During this period, Cyrene was one of the intellectual centers of the classical world. Its medical school was famous. Carneades (214-129 B.C.) was one of the heads of the Platonic Academy (Greek Academy), and the Cyrenaics, a Greek school of philosophers, were so called because the center of their activities was at Cyrene. Two well-known natives of Cyrene were Eratosthenes (276-194[?] B.C.), the geographer of Alexandria who calculated the circumference of the earth possibly within 50 mi. (80 km.) of the presently accepted figure, and Callimachus (*ca.* 310-240 B.C.), the poet who so strongly influenced the Latin poets, particularly Catullus and Ovid.

By the provisions of the will of Ptolemy Apion, Cyrenaica passed to the Romans in 96 B.C., and Crete was united with it in 67 B.C. to form the Senatorial Province of Cyrenaica, with Cyrene as the provincial capital. In a large Jewish revolt in A.D. 115 there was widespread destruction and, according to Dio Cassius (*Hist. Epit.* lxviii.32), 220,000 inhabitants were killed. Hadrian restored the city and left inscriptions on many of its buildings. But the city declined and the supply of silphium was exhausted. A disastrous earthquake in A.D. 365 contributed to the decline, and with the Arab conquest in 642 the city came to an end.

Simon of Cyrene bearing the cross for Jesus, reredos in relief from the fifth station of the cross on the Via Dolorosa, Jerusalem. The site follows a tradition dating to Crusader times. (W. S. LaSor)

Cyrene is significant for biblical studies because of its Jewish inhabitants. According to Josephus (*CAp* ii.4), Ptolemy I transported Jews to a number of Libyan cities, including Cyrene. From the magnitude of the disturbance in A.D. 115, mentioned above, it may be inferred that there was a sizable Jewish community there, and Jews who returned to Jerusalem from Cyrene were sufficiently numerous to have a synagogue "of the Cyrenians" (Acts 6:9). This doubtless accounts for the fact that a Cyrenian named Simon was present and could be compelled by the Romans to carry the cross of Jesus (Mt. 27:32; Mk. 15:21; Lk. 23:26). Worshipers from Cyrene are mentioned among those who witnessed the glossolalic preaching of the gospel by the disciples at Pentecost (Acts 2:10). Cyrenians not only disputed with Stephen (6:9), and possibly were also involved in his stoning, but some of them were also converted to Christianity and were spread by the subsequent persecution to become instrumental in the proclamation of the gospel to Gentiles at Antioch (11:19f.). Lucius of Cyrene was one of the prophets and teachers in the church at Antioch (13:1). We may assume that some of the Cyrenian pilgrims took the gospel back to Cyrene, for the Christian Church was established there at an early date. Two fine churches still existed in the days of Justinian (527-565). Synesius, who became bishop of Ptolemais *ca.* 409, was a native of Cyrene, boasting of royal descent, but we have no details of how or where he became a Christian.

Archeology of Cyrene, conducted by Italians between World Wars I and II, and since World War II by the Libyan government aided by British and Italians, has uncovered or restored numerous sites in the fountain area, in the upper city, and in the Roman town. These include the Greek agora, a theater (not yet fully excavated), a forum, the temple of Isis, part of the Sacred Way, a temple of Apollo, and a Greek theater. A sixth-century (B.C.) Spartan *kylix* (wine cup) provides an excellent graphic representation of the silphium trade, showing the spice being weighed and loaded in the presence of King Arcesilaus (original in Bibliothèque Nationale, Paris). Coins of Cyrene also bear the representation of the silphium plant.

In the Apocrypha see 1 Macc. 15:23; 2 Macc. 2:23.

Bibliography.–*CERP*; F. Chamoux, *Cyrène sous la monarchie des Battiades* (1953); *Enc.Brit.*, VI, *s.v.*; Herodotus iv.150-164; P. Romanelli, *La Cirenaica romana* (1943); A. Rowe, *History of Ancient Cyrenaica* (1948).

W. S. LASOR

CYRENIANS sī-rē′nē-ənz [Gk. *Kyrēnaioi*] (Acts 6:9). People of CYRENE.

CYRENIUS sī-rē′nē-əs (Lk. 2:2, AV). *See* QUIRINIUS.

CYRUS sī′rəs [Heb. *kōreš*; Old Pers. *Kuruš*]. Properly Cyrus II, the Great, founder of the Persian empire. He reigned from 559 to 530 B.C., and his empire flourished until its conquest by Alexander the Great (331 B.C.).

I. Birth and Family
II. Early Conquests
III. Conquest of Babylon
IV. Policy toward the Jews
V. Cyrus in Isaiah
VI. Final Conquests and Death

I. Birth and Family.–Cyrus was the son of Cambyses I, ruler of Anshan, a region in the uplands of eastern Elam and part of the lands of the Persian tribes. Cambyses had inherited his rule from his father Cyrus I, to whom the western parts of the Persian lands had been allotted by his father and predecessor Teispes, the eastern portion being granted to Ariaramnes, brother of Cyrus I. Cyrus

II himself has left a text (the Cyrus Cylinder) affirming his genealogy: "I am Cyrus, king of the world, great king, legitimate king, king of Babylon, king of Sumer and Akkad, king of the four rims (of the earth), son of Cambyses, great king, king of Anshan, grandson of Cyrus, great king, king of Anshan, of a family (which) always (exercised) kingship" (*ANET*, p. 316).

Various stories concerning the birth and early history of this famous figure were of course in circulation in the ancient Near East, and some may contain genuine historical information. According to the best-known of them, as told by Herodotus (i.108-122), Cyrus was the offspring of the marriage of Cambyses, the Persian vassal of the Median king Astyages, and Mandane, daughter of Astyages. Astyages was warned in a dream that the child would grow up to slay him, and so gave orders that he should be put to death. The official entrusted with this task, Harpagus, instead gave the young Cyrus to a shepherd to bring up. Although Cyrus at the age of ten came to the attention of Astyages, once again his life was spared when the royal counselors persuaded the king to let the child live. Astyages' dream, however, came true, for when Cyrus became king of the Persians he revolted against Astyages, captured him in battle, and made himself master of the Median kingdom.

This legend has affinities with several other ancient tales concerning the founder of a dynasty, including those about Sargon of Akkad (24th cent. B.C.) and later Iranian rulers like Ardashir, founder of the Sasanian dynasty (3rd to 7th cent. A.D.). Herodotus' mention (i.122) that Cyrus' foster mother was named Spako, the Median word for dog, is further reminiscent of the tale of Romulus and Remus, the legendary founders of Rome, who were supposedly suckled by a wolf or dog. The more military aspects of the legend, e.g., Cyrus' revolt against Astyages, are much more likely to be historical.

A different story was told by the historian Ctesias, a court physician to the later Persian king Artaxerxes II (404-358 B.C.). According to his account, Cyrus was the son of a Persian bandit and a shepherdess; he rose to a place of honor in the Median court and eventually led a successful revolt against Astyages. The story of Cyrus given by the Greek historian Xenophon in his *Education of Cyrus* (*Cyropaedeia*) contains many factual details, but it is essentially a historical romance, portraying the ideal education of the ideal young prince. Within a century or two after his death Cyrus had become a legendary figure.

II. Early Conquests.–By his conquest of the Median empire (550 B.C.) Cyrus had in the first place welded Medes and Persians into a unified nation. Because Cyrus remained respectful of Median culture, made Median Ecbatana one of his royal residences, and often appointed Medes to high positions in his provincial government, his kingdom became known as that of the "Medes and Persians" (cf., e.g., Dnl. 5:28; 6:8, 15; Est. 10:2). But secondly, his conquest over Media had given him rule over its former provinces of Assyria, Mesopotamia, Syria, Armenia, and Cappadocia.

To the west of the Median realm lay the powerful empire of the fabulously wealthy Croesus of Lydia. Croesus' attempts, after the downfall of the Median empire, to acquire some of the Median dependencies for himself were quickly frustrated by Cyrus. In 547 B.C. Cyrus launched an attack upon the Lydian empire, forcing Croesus, who had crossed the river Halys, his traditional eastern boundary, back to his capital city Sardis. After a short siege, the acropolis of Sardis was taken, and Croesus, rather than suffer the usual indignities meted out to a conquered ruler, had himself burned upon a pyre. The Nabonidus Chronicle from Babylon reports laconically (though restoration of certain passages is somewhat doubtful): "In May [547 B.C.] he [Cyrus] marched to the land of Lydia. He killed its king. He took its booty. He placed in it his own garrison. Afterward his garrison and the king were in it" (ii.16-18). Although Herodotus reports that Cyrus treated Croesus in a friendly manner, this may reflect the legend of Cyrus' clemency toward his conquered enemies rather than the facts.

This expedition against Croesus had taken Cyrus far into Asia Minor and had brought him into contact with the Greek cities of the Ionian coast. This was the first of many disastrous conflicts between Persians and Greeks that were to play such a dominant role in Greek history especially for a century thereafter. One by one the Greek city-states, previously under nominal Lydian rule, were picked off by Cyrus and reorganized into Persian provinces. Greek tradition holds that the general who was responsible for the subjugation of the Greek states and who became satrap of the newly formed Persian province was the same Harpagus who had saved the young Cyrus' life by his disloyalty to Astyages.

Cyrus then turned his attention to the as yet unconquered Iranian tribes in the east. Parthia, in the hands of Hystaspes, grandson of Ariaramnes and thus cousin of Cyrus, soon became a Persian satrapy, Hystaspes exchanging his role as petty king for the no less exalted title of satrap of the Persian empire. Following the course of the Oxus river from high up on the Iranian plateau, Cyrus made himself master first of the land of Sogdia, introducing Persian systems of irrigation into that region, and then of Bactria. From there he pressed on finally into India, to the region known to the Iranians as Paruparaesanna, and to its inhabitants as Gandara, on the slopes of the Hindu Kush. Cyrus had, in no more than a decade, made himself ruler of a vast territory extending from the Aegean Sea to India, and had simultaneously established the structures of provincial government that were to serve his empire so well for many generations.

III. Conquest of Babylon.–Babylon, the next goal for Cyrus' ambitions, was ripe for change. Nabonidus, the last of the Neo-Babylonian kings, had absented himself from the capital for fourteen years to pursue his own antiquarian and religious hobbies at Teimā in northern Arabia. His continued failure to take part in the New Year festival at Babylon, the chief religious ceremony of the Babylonian cult, had alienated the powerful priesthood of the city-god Marduk, as had also his bestowal of favors upon the worship of Sin, the moon deity of Haran. The government of Babylon and of the empire was in the hands of his son Belshazzar, undoubtedly one of the less capable Neo-Babylonian rulers.

Nabonidus, sensing no doubt that Cyrus' success spelled severe danger for his own empire, returned to Babylon in the spring of 539 B.C. and began to bring into the city the statues of other Babylonian city-gods in order to afford greater protection to Babylon. Though New Year's day was celebrated in proper form on Apr. 4, 539 B.C., by late summer it was clear that nothing could hold back Cyrus. In early October Cyrus defeated a Babylonian force at Opis on the Tigris, and on Oct. 10 Sippar fell without a battle. Nabonidus hastily left Babylon, and on Oct. 12 Cyrus' troops under Gobryas (Ugbaru) governor of Gutium, a former general of Nebuchadrezzar who had defected to the Persians, entered the city. That night, according to Dnl. 5:30, Belshazzar king of the Chaldeans (Neo-Babylonians) was slain. When Nabonidus returned to Babylon he was made prisoner.

Cyrus Cylinder (538 B.C.) recording the Persian king's bloodless capture of Babylon and his program of religious tolerance, including the release of the Jewish exiles and restoration of the temple (Trustees of the British Museum)

Cyrus himself entered the city on Oct. 29, and presented himself to the citizens as its liberator.

According to Herodotus, the Persians used the following stratagem to enter the city: "drawing off the river by a canal into the lake, which was till now a marsh, he [Cyrus] made the stream to sink till its former channel could be forded. When this happened, the Persians who were posted with this intent made their way into Babylon by the channel of the Euphrates, which had now sunk to about the height of the middle of a man's thigh" (i.191). A similar story is told by Xenophon (*Cyropaedeia* vii.5.7-34), though no cuneiform evidence supports this course of events.

Although the chief evidence for Cyrus' reception comes from sources obviously very favorable to Cyrus, there is little reason to doubt that his presence was welcomed. According to the "Nabonidus Chronicle," "in the month of Arahshamnu, the 3rd day, Cyrus entered Babylon, green twigs were spread in front of him — the state of 'Peace' was imposed upon the city. Cyrus sent greetings to all Babylon" (*ANET*, p. 306). The Cyrus Cylinder, apparently composed by a Babylonian temple official, reports that "all the inhabitants of Babylon as well as of the entire country of Sumer and Akkad, princes and governors (included), bowed to him (Cyrus) and kissed his feet, jubilant that he (had received) the kingship, and with shining faces" (*ANET*, p. 316).

The whole outcome of the city's conquest was officially explained to its citizens as the doing of its city-god Marduk: "[Marduk] scanned and looked (through) all the countries, searching for a righteous ruler willing to lead him (in the annual procession). (Then) he pronounced the name of Cyrus, king of Anshan, declared him to be(come) the ruler of all the world . . . Marduk, the great lord, a protector of his people/worshipers, beheld with pleasure his (i.e. Cyrus') good deeds and his upright mind (and therefore) ordered him to march against his city Babylon. He made him set out on the road to Babylon going at his side like a real friend . . . Without any battle, he made him enter his town Babylon, sparing Babylon any calamity" (Cyrus Cylinder; *ANET*, p. 315).

The events of October 539 B.C. were of more than passing importance. They marked the transition in the Babylonian and Assyrian world from Semitic to Aryan rule, a state of affairs that was to continue for a thousand years, and they made of Cyrus a world emperor, since he now became heir to the Neo-Babylonian empire, great in its heyday under Nebuchadrezzar (605-562 B.C.), and even in its decay still impressive. Cyrus was eager to make as little break in the continuity of Babylonian life as possible, so he proclaimed himself to the citizens according to ancient Semitic formularies and in the Akkadian language, to be "Cyrus, king of the world, legitimate king, king of Babylon, king of Sumer and Akkad, king of the four rims (of the earth) . . . whose rule Bel and Nebo [the Babylonian deities] love, whom they want as king to please their hearts" (Cyrus Cylinder; *ANET*, p. 316).

IV. Policy toward the Jews.–Part of Cyrus' conciliatory policy toward subject peoples was to resettle them in their homelands and to undertake the restoration of their places of worship. Cyrus' massive program of resettlement concerned more than the cities from which in recent months Nabonidus had brought the divine statues into Babylon; he wrote: "(As to the region) . . . as far as Ashur and Susa, Agade, Eshnunna, the towns of Zamban, Me-Turnu, Der as well as the region of the Gutians, I returned to (these) sacred cities on the other side of the Tigris, the sanctuaries of which have been in ruins for a long time, the images which (used) to live therein and established for them permanent sanctuaries. I (also) gathered all their (former) inhabitants and returned (to them) their habitations. Furthermore, I resettled upon the command of Marduk, the great lord, all the gods of Sumer and Akkad whom Nabonidus has brought into Babylon to the anger of the lord of the gods, unharmed, in their (former) chapels, the places which make them happy" (Cyrus Cylinder; *ANET*, p. 316). The purpose behind these acts of repatriation was that a chorus of prayer from the various gods of the empire might ascend daily to Bel, i.e. Marduk, and Nebo, whom Cyrus recognized at Babylon as the highest gods: "May all the gods whom

I have resettled in their sacred cities ask daily Bel and Nebo for a long life for me and may they recommend me (to him)" (Cyrus Cylinder; *ANET*, p. 316).

The repatriation of the Jews, reversing the deportation policies of the Assyrians and Babylonians, was in accordance with Cyrus' general policy. According to the Chronicler, generally recognized as author of the first chapters of Ezra, Cyrus' permission for the Jews' return was given in his "first year" (Ezr. 1:1), obviously not his first year as ruler (559-58 B.C.) nor yet his accession year (October 539–April 538 B.C.) in Babylon but his first full regnal year as king of Babylon commencing in April 538 B.C. Of course only after he had become king of Babylon did he come into contact with the Jews, so naturally they reckoned his reign from that time. The proclamation for the return was made both orally and in writing: he "made a proclamation throughout all his kingdom" (1:1) by dispatching a herald who after the public announcement of the royal edict would post a copy. Though Jewish exiles had settled mainly in Babylonia, the edict would apply equally to Jews elsewhere in his kingdom. This edict, preserved in Hebrew and no doubt drawn up in that language by some Jewish official in the Persian court, bears a strong Jewish coloring, especially in the phrases "Yahweh," "each survivor," "sojourns," "freewill offerings"; a shorter form of the edict, free of most of these distinctively Jewish phrases, is preserved in 2 Ch. 36:23.

The permission for the return reads as much like a royal command as the requirement to rebuild the temple. But although about fifty thousand Jews responded to the royal decree (cf. Ezr. 2:64f.), many exiles remained in Babylonia (cf. Ezr. 7:6f.). Therefore, this part of the edict must have been construed simply as permission; the command form is used because that is the only mode of speech suitable for an autocrat! Though the Jewish exiles had, unlike other deportees, no images to carry back with them, Cyrus said, "May their God be with them" as they return, a phrase that would not have been offensive to the Jews. In place of restored images, Cyrus offered as a contribution to the reestablishment of the Jerusalem temple the sacred temple vessels that had been dedicated as a war trophy in Esagila, Marduk's temple in Babylon, by Nebuchadrezzar after his capture of Jerusalem and plundering of the temple in 587 B.C. (2 K. 24:13; 25:13-16; Ezr. 1:7). These precious vessels of gold and silver, numbering between two thousand and five thousand (the text of Ezr. 1:9-11 is uncertain) were given into the charge of Sheshbazzar by the temple treasurer Mithredath.

Two further features of the royal edict of Ezr. 1 call for special comment. First, Cyrus professes himself to have been given all the kingdoms of the earth by Yahweh, the God of heaven. This does not mean that he himself was a worshiper of Yahweh; he was probably a Zoroastrian and worshiper of Ahura-Mazda, but obviously a feature of his imperial policy was to acknowledge with gratitude his blessings from the other high gods of his realm. Thus at Babylon it is Marduk, the city-god, who chooses him and declares him to be world ruler, while at Ur, it is Sin, the moon-god worshiped there, who gives him victory.

Second, Ezr. 1:4 stipulates that non-Jewish subjects of the king were to help provide for the returning exiles money, food, and transport, together with offerings for the Jewish temple. This remarkable command reflects Cyrus' determination to restore regional cults, which of course required the presence of a body of worshipers in order to maintain them.

Another edict of Cyrus relating to the rebuilding of the temple is found in Ezr. 6:2-5. Because it does not mention the repatriation of the Jews but only the restoration of the temple, some have questioned the authenticity of the decree of Ezr. 1. But the two decrees have quite different functions: that of Ezr. 1 is a proclamation in Hebrew to the Jewish people, while that of Ezr. 6 is a document in Aramaic, the official language of the Persian empire, filed in the financial archives of the Persian administration at Ecbatana, one of the three imperial capitals. This records the stipulations made at the time of the grant from the royal treasury for the rebuilding of the Jerusalem temple. Thus the permitted dimensions of the temple are noted (the length is by some accident omitted), and the building materials (three courses of stone and one of timber alternating) are specified. This decree of Cyrus was confirmed and extended by Darius (522-486 B.C.) in the following verses (6:6-12).

V. Cyrus in Isaiah.–Cyrus is alluded to or referred to a number of times in the prophecies of Isaiah 40–55. He is the one from the east whom Yahweh has "stirred up" (cf. Ezr. 1:1) and whom victory meets at every step (Isa. 41:2-4); he is likewise the one from the north and from the east who will trample on rulers as on mortar (41:25). Explicitly of Cyrus God says through the prophet: "He is my shepherd, and he shall fulfil all my purpose" (44:28); he is called Yahweh's anointed one whose hand Yahweh has grasped and whom He will grant victories (45:1-4), the man of God's counsel (46:11), the one whom Yahweh loves and who will perform Yahweh's purpose against Babylon (48:14f.).

In spite of the warmth with which the prophet refers to Cyrus and the dignity accorded the king by Yahweh, apparently the prophet does not expect Cyrus to be converted to the Jewish faith; he is a pagan summoned to do God's bidding though he does not know Yahweh (45:4). The one place which, by prophesying that Cyrus will "call on my name" (41:25), suggests that he will become a worshiper of Yahweh is textually uncertain and may in any case be adequately fulfilled in Cyrus' ascription of his victories to Yahweh (cf. Ezr. 1:2). Even though Cyrus is Yahweh's shepherd, anointed one, the one whom He loves (i.e., has chosen), Cyrus is nothing more than an instrument of God's plans. Although the service he will render will be an indispensable one, his significance in the prophecies should not be exaggerated, for God and the people of Israel, not Cyrus, stand at their center.

While Isa. 44:28 and 45:13 suggest that Cyrus was to be responsible not only for the rebuilding of the temple but also for the reconstruction of the city, actually his successors Darius (522-486 B.C.) and Artaxerxes I (465-423 B.C.) saw these tasks through to completion. Still, Cyrus' policies toward his subjects in general and toward the Jews in particular provided the basis on which the later favorable decrees of Darius, *ca.* 520 B.C. (Ezr. 6:6-12), and Artaxerxes I, in 445 B.C. (Neh. 2:1-8), could be issued. And in fact the rebuilding of the temple was begun in Cyrus' reign (Ezr. 3:8-11), as was also possibly some rebuilding of the city in order to house those working on the temple reconstruction.

Whether Cyrus was aware in any way of the prophecies of Isa. 40–55 remains uncertain. Josephus indeed says that Cyrus came to know of his destiny with respect to the Jewish people "by his reading the book which Isaiah left behind him of his prophecies; for this prophet said that God had spoken thus to him in a secret vision: — 'My will is, that Cyrus, whom I have appointed to be king over many and great nations, send back my people to their own land, and build my temple.' Accordingly, when

Tomb of Cyrus outside Pasargadae (modern Murghab), which he founded as his capital after defeating Astyages there in 550 B.C. (W. S. LaSor)

Cyrus read this, and admired the divine power, an earnest desire and ambition seized upon him to fulfil what was so written" (*Ant.* xi.1.2). It is not implausible that a highly placed Jewish official, such as the book of Daniel represents Daniel to have been, could have drawn the emperor's attention to these prophecies, but without further supporting evidence this cannot be certain.

VI. Final Conquests and Death.–At the end of his accession year (539-38 B.C.) Cyrus had left Babylon for his capital Ecbatana, leaving his son Cambyses, who was resident in Sippar, to represent him at the Babylonian New Year Festival. Of Cyrus' activities during the final decade of his career little is documented. The sources become abundant again only concerning the occasion of his death, which occurred *ca.* 530 B.C. when Cyrus was dealing with the nomadic Massagetae on his northeastern frontier. Possibly the protection of that frontier had been his major preoccupation during that decade. According to Herodotus (i.205-215), Cyrus was at first successful against the Massagetae, capturing one of the sons of their queen Tomyris. But after the son had committed suicide in captivity Cyrus was defeated and killed in a further battle with that tribe. He was succeeded on the Persian throne by Cambyses, whom he had appointed as his successor shortly before setting out on the expedition.

The tomb of Cyrus that stands at Pasargadae is plain but impressive. A simple gabled edifice built of limestone blocks cramped together with iron bands and resting on a stone platform six courses high, it contains a windowless chamber 10.5 by 7.5 ft. (3.2 by 2.3 m.) in area and 8 ft. (2.4 m.) high. On it, according to Strabo (*Geog.* xv.3.7), was inscribed the following, in old Persian characters (Arrian *Anabasis* vi. 25): "O man, I am Cyrus, who gained the empire for the Persians, and was king of Asia. Do not begrudge me this memorial!" According to Plutarch (*Alex.* 69) the inscription read, "O man, whosoever you are, and whencesoever you come, for I know that you will come! I am Cyrus, who won for the Persians their empire. Do not begrudge me this little earth that covers my corpse!"

Cyrus had been not only one of the greatest conquerors of history, but by the tradition of his clemency to those he had defeated, and his policy of religious toleration, he had also left an example to mankind that, had it been followed, would have saved the world immeasurable suffering (Weissbach, col. 1166).

See Map XII.

Bibliography.–*Commémoration Cyrus. Hommage universel, Acta Iranica,* 1-3 (1974); R. Drews, *JNES,* 33 (1974), 387-393; R. N. Frye, *Heritage of Persia* (1963), pp. 78-87; E. Jenni, *Theologische Zeitschrift,* 10 (1954), 241-256; K. Koch, *ZAW,* 84 (1972), 352-56; A. T. E. Olmstead, *History of the Persian Empire* (1948), pp. 34-58; F. H. Weissbach, "Kyros," Pauly-Wissowa, Supp. IV, 1129-1166.

D. J. A. CLINES

D (Codex Bezae). *See* TEXTS AND MSS OF THE NT.

D (Deuteronomic Source). *See* CRITICISM II.

DABAREH dab'ə-rə (Josh. 21:28, AV); **DABERAH** (NEB). *See* DABERATH.

DABBESHETH dab'ə-sheth [Heb. *dabbešeṯ*–'hump']; AV DABBASHETH. A town on the boundary of the territory allotted to Zebulun (Josh. 19:11). It may be modern Tell esh-Shammana E of Jokneam. The name may indicate that the town was built on a hill.

D. H. MADVIG

DABERATH dab'ə-rath [Heb. *dāḇeraṯ*–'pasture']; AV also DABAREH (Josh. 21:28), NEB DABERAH. A town in that part of Galilee which Joshua allotted to the tribe of Issachar. It was given to the Gershonites of the tribe of Levi (Josh. 21:28; 1 Ch. 6:72) and is named in defining the eastern boundary of Zebulun (Josh. 19:13). In NT times it was known as Dabarittha, and it has been identified with modern Dabûriyeh at the foot of Mt. Tabor on the northwest. Perhaps Daberath is the town called Rabbith in Josh. 19:20. D. H. MADVIG

DABRIA da'brē-ə [Lat. *Dabria*]. One of the five who wrote down the visions of Esdras, described (2 Esd. 14:24) as "trained to write rapidly."

DACUBI da-ku'bī (1 Esd. 5:28, NEB); AV DACOBI. *See* AKKUB **2.**

DADDEUS da-dē'əs (1 Esd. 8:46, AV). *See* IDDO **1.**

DAGGER. *See* WEAPONS OF WAR.

DAGON dā'gon [Heb. *dāgôn*–(see below)]. One of the gods of the Philistines. It was to Dagon that they offered thanks at Gaza when Samson fell into their hands (Jgs. 16:23), and to his temple (Heb. *bêṯ-dāgôn*) in Ashdod that they brought the ark after capturing it at Aphek (1 S. 5:1f.). The ark was left in the temple for two nights, but Dagon was found lying on his face each morning, the second time with head and hands severed (1 S. 5:3-5).

There was also a temple of Dagon at Beth-shan, where the Philistines fastened the head of Saul after the battle of Gilboa (1 Ch. 10:10; cf. 1 S. 31:10). During the excavations at Beth-shan, two temples were discovered in level V, which the excavator suggested might have been those of Dagon and Ashtaroth mentioned in these passages.

The god Dagon is probably to be identified with the Dagan of the ancient inscriptions. He was a grain god and the principal deity of the middle Euphrates region, as is shown in the Mari archives of the 18th cent. B.C., where the name Dagan occurs frequently, not only of the deity but also as an element in compound personal names and as the name of a month. The excavations at Mari have uncovered a temple to him. His cult was already known in southern Mesopotamia in the 3rd millennium B.C., where its center was at Puzuriash-Dagan, modern Drehem. Sargon, Naram-Sin, and Hammurabi attribute their conquests in the middle Euphrates area to his support. His importance in Babylonia may account for the substitution of Gk. *Dagōn* by the LXX for Heb. *bēl* in Isa. 46:1, probably referring to Marduk the principal god of Babylon. He is attested in the West in the fourteenth-century documents from Ugarit (Râs Shamrah), and a temple dedicated to him was found in the excavations there.

The original meaning of the name is unknown; the theories, found already in the writings of Jerome, that it derives from either Heb. *dāg*, "fish," or *dāgān*, "grain," are unsubstantiated. It is more probable that the noun *dāgān*, which occurs also in the sense of "grain" in Ugaritic and Phoenician, was derived from the name of the god.

Bibliography.–E. Dhorme and R. Dussaud, *Les anciennes religions orientales*, II (1949), 165-67, 173, 364f.; E. Dhorme, "Les Avatars du dieu Dagon," *Académie des Inscriptions et des Belles Lettres* (Apr./June, 1950), pp. 186-195; *ARI*, pp. 74, 106; G. R. Driver, *The Babylonian Laws*, II (1955), 140.

T. C. MITCHELL

DAILY. The Heb. *yôm beyôm* means "all day long" rather than "daily" (AV) in such passages as Ps. 42:10; 56:1f.; 72:15; 74:22; 86:3; 88:17; Jer. 20:7f.; also *yômām*, Ps. 13:2.

DAILY BREAD. The meaning of Gk. *epioúsios* in Mt. 6:11; Lk. 11:3 (the Lord's Prayer) has been subject to a variety of interpretation and conjecture. The English versions render "daily," with the marginal suggestion in both the RSV and the NEB "for the morrow." The RV mg. suggests "for the coming day" or "needful." In the Syriac versions the meaning is "continual." Many writers see in the phrase an eschatological significance, referring to the coming kingdom and its feast (see Bauer, p. 297).

None of these interpretations can be said to have a certain linguistic basis. But as Foerster argues in *TDNT*, II, *s.v.*, those meanings referring to time either are redundant or do not fit the immediate or larger NT context, whereas interpretations such as "needful," or "daily" in the sense of "sufficient for the day's needs," are much more appropriate to the spirit of Jesus' teachings, and are linguistically quite possible. J. W. D. H.

DAINTIES; DAINTY FOOD [Heb. *ma'ᵃḏān*] (Gen. 49:20; Lam. 4:5); AV also "[feed] delicately"; NEB DISHES, "[fed] delicately"; [*man'ammîm*] (Ps. 141:4); NEB DELIGHTS; [*ta'ᵃwâ*] (Job 33:20); AV DAINTY FOOD; NEB CHOICEST MEATS; [Gk. *liparós*] (Rev. 18:14); NEB GLITTER. The items referred to in Scripture as "dainties" were luxury-foods and costly commodities which by nature were foreign to the spartan existence of the Hebrew semi nomad. Under sedentary conditions only the very prosperous could afford certain of the luxurious items that formed part of the diet of upper and middle classes in most nations outside Israel. The sternness of traditional Hebrew life precluded luxuries for the most part except for persons such as the king and the members of his court (cf. 1 K. 4:22f.; 10:5, 21), and found characteristic expression in Amos' denunciation of extravagant living in the northern kingdom (Am. 6:4ff.). The life of the pleasure-loving individual was uniformly condemned in Scripture as alien to the godly, simple life of the wise man (cf. Prov. 23:1ff.), since it weakened the standards of spirituality associated with rigorous covenantal living and gave the self-indulgent a wholly incorrect perspective on existence. R. K. H.

DAISAN dā'sən (1 Esd. 5:31, AV). *See* REZIN.

DALAIAH də-lā'yə (1 Ch. 3:24, AV). *See* DELAIAH **1**.

DALE, KING'S (Gen. 14:17; 2 S. 18:18). *See* KING'S VALLEY.

DALETH dä'ləth (דּ, ד). The fourth letter of the Hebrew alphabet, and as such used in Ps. 119 to designate the fourth section; in *ISBE* transliterated with the *dagesh* as *d*, and without as *ḏ* (sometimes pronounced as *th* in *the*). It came also to be used for the number four, and with the diaeresis for four thousand. *See* WRITING.

DALMANUTHA dal-mə-noo'thə [Gk. *Dalmanoutha*]. A district visited by Jesus according to the more likely readings of Mk. 8:10, called in some MSS and in the parallel Mt. 15:39 MAGADAN.

DALMATIA dal-mā'shə [Gk. *Dalmatia*]. A district of the Roman empire on the Adriatic coast of the Balkan peninsula. In 2 Tim. 4:10 there is reference to the departure of Titus to Dalmatia. Nothing further is known of this journey.

Dalmatia was the southern part of the Roman province of ILLYRICUM. The name comes from the Dalmatae or Delmatae, an Illyrian tribe conquered by the Romans after a series of wars beginning in 229 B.C. Their capital Delminium fell in 155 B.C., but sporadic revolts continued until A.D. 9. The best-known city of modern Dalmatia is Dubrovnik, in Yugoslavia. W. S. L. S.

DALPHON dal'fon [Heb. *dalpôn*–'crafty']. The second of the ten sons of Haman, slain by the Jews (Est. 9:7).

DAM [Heb. *'ēm*–'mother']; NEB MOTHER. Hebrew law prohibited the sacrifice of a young sheep or ox before it had spend seven days with its mother ("dam," Ex. 22:30). This was done in an attempt to ensure that the animal would constitute a proper viable offering to God, and not be a weakling from the flock which could easily be dispensed with by being offered as a sacrifice (cf. Mal. 1:8).

DAMAGE [Aram. *ḥᵃḇālā'*]. This term occurs in the RSV only in Ezr. 4:22, where it denotes any form of loss or injury.

DAMARIS dam'ə-ris [Gk. *Damaris*]. A female Christian of Athens, converted by Paul's preaching (Acts 17:34). That she is mentioned in this passage together with Dionysius the Areopagite has led some, most probably in error, to regard her as his wife. The singling out of her name with that of Dionysius may indicate some personal or social distinction. Cf. 17:12.

DAMASCENES dam'ə-sēnz [Gk. *Damaskēnoi*]. The people of DAMASCUS (2 Cor. 11:32, AV).

DAMASCUS də-mas'kəs [Heb. *dammeśeq*; Aram. *darmeśeq* (1 Ch. 18:5; 2 Ch. 28:5); Gk. *Damaskos*; Akk. *Dimišqi, Dimas/šqi*; Am.Tab. *Dimašqa, Dumašqa*; Egyp. *Timašgi*; Arab. *Dimashq* (*ash-Sham*)]. A city of Syria (Aram). The capital of modern Syria, Damascus has survived continuously from at least 2000 B.C.

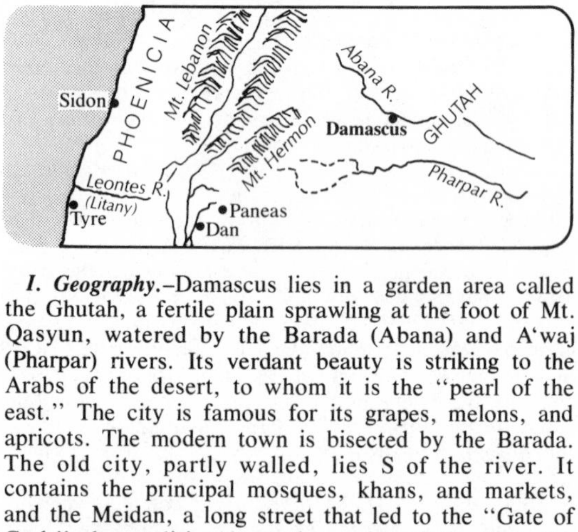

I. Geography.–Damascus lies in a garden area called the Ghutah, a fertile plain sprawling at the foot of Mt. Qasyun, watered by the Barada (Abana) and A'waj (Pharpar) rivers. Its verdant beauty is striking to the Arabs of the desert, to whom it is the "pearl of the east." The city is famous for its grapes, melons, and apricots. The modern town is bisected by the Barada. The old city, partly walled, lies S of the river. It contains the principal mosques, khans, and markets, and the Meidan, a long street that led to the "Gate of God," the traditional starting point of the Haj, the annual pilgrimage to Mecca. N of the river the city spread out during the period 1940-1960 with the appearance of modern buildings, hotels, and residential areas.

II. Antiquities.–The most imposing edifice in the city is the Great Mosque, Jami al Umawi, built within the sacred area where once stood the ancient temple of Adad (Hadad-Rimmon, the storm-god) and where later was erected the Church of St. John the Baptist, built by Theodosius I in A.D. 379. The mosque, dating from the 8th cent., was restored in the 11th, 15th, and 19th centuries. The citadel in the northwest part of the old city dates from very early times, possibly Roman. The Azam palace, built in 1749 for the governor of Damascus, now houses an institution for the study of Islamic art and architecture. The Damascus Museum beside the beautiful Tagiah Mosque in the western sector of the city contains fine archeological treasures, notably finds from

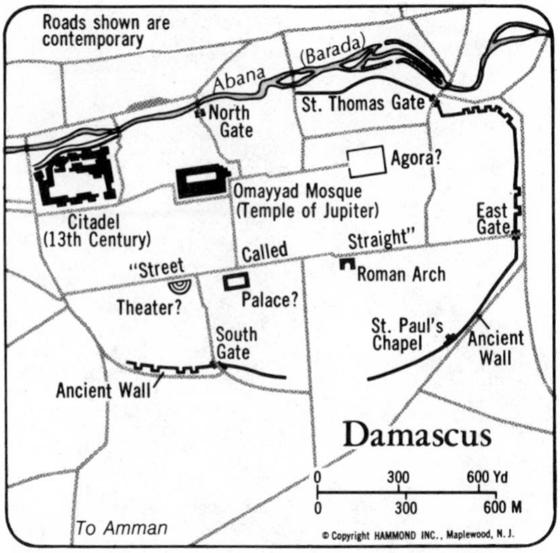

Mari, Ugarit, Arpad, and Palmyra. Little scientific excavation has been done in the city itself because of its continuous occupation through the centuries.

III. History.–Archeological research in recent years has greatly added to the knowledge of the ancient site, especially of the period before its fall to Assyria in 732 B.C. Practically all that was formerly known of the city was what appeared in the OT.

A. Patriarchal Period (*ca.* 2000 B.C.). The Bible mentions Damascus as the hometown of Abraham's steward Eliezer (Gen. 15:2f.; cf. 14:15). The Egyptian Execration Texts, dating *ca.* 1850-1825 B.C., present the earliest mention of the district of Damascus, called *Apum*, meaning "a forest of canebrake," a singularly apt designation of the lush meadowland of the eastern Damascus area. The name *Apum* is also confirmed some three generations later by the Mari Letters recovered in 1936 from Tell el-Hariri on the Middle Euphrates.

B. Under Egyptian Control (*ca.* 1475). The mention of the actual city first occurs outside the OT in the list of the conquests of Pharaoh Thutmose III (1490-1436), in the enumeration preserved in the temple of the sun-god Amon at Thebes (Karnak).

C. Amarna Period (*ca.* 1375). Before the discovery of the Execration Texts and the Mari Letters, the land of *Upi* (earlier *Apum*) had been well known as the region of Damascus from the Amarna Letters, discovered in 1886. These documents outline an uprising against Egypt in Palestine-Syria. In one of these letters King Akizzi of Qatna, a city-state N of Damascus, protests his loyalty to Pharaoh Amenhotep IV (*ca.* 1375-1370 B.C. with these words: "O Sire, as Damascus (*^{al}Timašgi*) in the land of Upe (*ina ^{māt}Upe*) is faithful to the pharaoh, so Qatna is likewise loyal" (Am.Tab. 53:63-65). Another letter mentions an official named Biriawaza as the representative of the Egyptian government in Upe and Damascus. He is said to have used mercenary troops (Habiru) to maintain Egypt's authority in the Damascus area (Am.Tab. 195:27ff.).

D. The Hittites (*ca.* 1350). Under Šuppiluliuma (*ca.* 1380-1346) the Hittites invaded Syria, and claimed they ravaged the territory of Ariwana, king of the land of Apina. This reference is clearly to be identified with Upe, the land of Damascus, of the Amarna Letters (E. F. Weidner, *Boghazkoï-Studien*, 8 [1923], 14). The Hittites, however, withdrew. Damascus must again have reverted to the sphere of Egyptian influence under the strong pharaohs Seti I (1319-1301) and Ramses II (1301-1234). Ramses concluded a treaty of peace with the Hittites giving Egypt control of the territory S of Hamath, including Upe and Damascus.

E. Hebrew Domination (*ca.* 1000-930). In the intervening period (1350-1000) the Arameans invaded Syria, settling Damascus and contiguous regions. David (*ca.* 1000) conquered the Aramean kingdoms of Zobah, Abel-beth-maacah, Tob, and Geshur; and in the Davidic-Solomonic era Damascus became a part of the Hebrew kingdom. In the declining years of Solomon, Rezon, a former official of Hadadezer of Zobah, established a strong Aramean state in Damascus (1 K. 11:24). Even under Solomon he was emboldened to flout Hebrew domination, and with the breakup of the Hebrew kingdom was furnished a golden opportunity to become a dominant power in Syria.

F. A Powerful Aramean State (*ca.* 930-801). Rezon was evidently not the first king of Damascus, unless he is to be identified with Hezion the father of Tabrimmon, the father of the famous Ben-hadad I (cf. 1 K. 15:18). The Ben-hadad stele discovered in 1940 in north Syria confirms this dynastic list preserved in 1 K. 15:18. (See *BASOR*, 87 [Oct. 1942], 23-29; 90 (April 1943), 30-32; M. Dunand, *Bulletin du Musée de Beyrouth*, 3 [1941], 65-76.) Hezion and Tabrimmon bequeathed a kingdom to Ben-hadad I (*ca.* 883-843) strong enough to challenge all foes, including Baasha (*ca.* 900-877), Omri (*ca.* 876-869), and Ahab (*ca.* 869-850). Ahab, however, defeated Ben-hadad twice (*ca.* 855 and 854 B.C.; cf. 1 K. 20:1-34).

Due to Assyrian advance, mutual foes were forced into artificial friendship, and so Ben-hadad and Ahab joined in a coalition against Shalmaneser III in 853 in the famous Battle of Qarqar, recorded on the Monolith Inscription in the British Museum. Ahab's attempt to recover Ramoth in Gilead from the perfidious Ben-hadad provoked him into an attack on the Syrians that resulted in his own death (1 K. 22:29-39).

Under Hazael (843-801), the usurper, whom the Assyrians called "son of nobody," Damascus became master of Israel. Jehu (*ca.* 842-815), who wiped out the house of Omri and the Baal Melqart cult in Israel, won Hazael's implacable hatred when he refused to ally with Syria against the invasion by Shalmaneser III in 841 and 837. Damascus was compelled to face the Assyrian colossus alone, while Jehu, as pictured on the Black Obelisk, prostrated himself before and humbly paid tribute to the Assyrian conqueror (*ARAB*, I, 590).

From 837-801, when Assyria was not a threat to the West, Hazael mercilessly overran Israel (2 K. 10:32f.) under Jehu and reduced Jehu's son Jehoahaz (815-801) to the status of a menial vassal (2 K. 13:1-9).

G. Period of Decline (801-746). Ben-hadad II succeeded Hazael after Damascus had been weakened by Assyrian conquests in northern Syria, including Adadnirari's successful campaign against Damascus (805-802). As a result Joash of Israel (*ca.* 801-786) was able to recoup Israel's fortunes (2 K. 13:25), although Damascus could still maintain leadership in northern and central Syria. The Zakir stele discovered in 1903 names "Barhadad (Ben-hadad II), son of Hazael, King of Aram" as heading a sizable north Syrian confederacy against the city-state of Hamath (*ca.* 780).

Joash's son Jeroboam II (*ca.* 786-746) continued to expand a revitalized Israelite state. He not only regained all territory Israel had lost to Aram, but "recovered Damascus and Hamath . . . for Israel" (2 K. 14:28), restoring the frontier of Israel "from the pass of Hamath"

Street called Straight, Damascus, location of the house where Ananias greeted Paul (B. K. Condit)

(between Kadesh and Riblah) "as far as the sea of Arabah" (14:25). This can only mean that Israel became master of Aram, as in the days of David and Solomon.

H. Fall to Assyria (746-732). Rezin (*ca.* 750?-732), the last king of Damascus, was able to restore Aram's fortunes before the final crushing blow from Assyria fell in 732. His name occurs as *Raṣunnu* in the Assyrian records of Tiglath-pileser III (745-727). He allied himself with Pekah of Israel against Ahaz of Judah in the Syro-Ephraimite war (*ca.* 735). Ahaz bribed Tiglath-pileser with heavy tribute to attack Aram and Israel (2 K. 16:5; Isa. 7:1-3). The Assyrian invaded northern Israel (2 K. 15:29) and then besieged and destroyed Damascus as an Aramean kingdom in 732, killing Rezin (2 K. 16:9). Assyrian records tell of 591 towns of the "16 districts of Aram" destroyed "like mounds left by a flood" (*ARAB*, I § 777).

I. Later OT Times (732-739 B.C.). After it fell to Assyria Damascus was incorporated into the Assyrian empire in the form of four new provinces: *Ṣubutu* in the north, *Dimašqu*, *Qarninu*, and *Haurina* to the south. A last intrepid attempt at revolt in 720 is known from the records of Sargon II. But it was quickly quelled, and the city entered a long period of political unimportance successively under Assyrian, Babylonian, and Persian rule. All the while, however, it was a wealthy trading emporium. Not until Antioch was founded by the Seleucids did Damascus lose its position as the chief city of Syria. In 85 B.C. Damascus became the capital of an independent Nabatean kingdom. After the Roman conquest of Syria in 65 B.C. a Nabatean governor was placed over the city.

J. NT Times (9 B.C.-A.D. 40). The city appears prominently in connection with Paul's conversion (Acts 9:1-8). At that time it was a free city, coining its own money. Some scholars think the emperor Caligula (A.D. 37-40) gave the city to Aretas IV (9 B.C.-A.D. 40), since "the governor of King Aretas" was guarding Damascus when Paul escaped (2 Cor. 11:32). Others deny that Aretas held the city, and assume that his governor (sheikh) was merely waiting outside the walls to apprehend Paul (cf. H. J. Cadbury, *Book of Acts in History* [1955], pp. 19-21).

K. Under Christianity and Islam (A.D. 40 to the present). Its connection with Paul's conversion was a factor in the city's becoming a center of Christianity till the rise of Islam in the 7th cent. A.D. Centuries of Moslem domination have left their impress upon Damascus. As capital of modern Syria it is a tourist center, its old quarters being thoroughly oriental and attractive to travelers.

Bibliography.–S. Schiffer, *Die Aramäer* (1911); E. Kraeling, *Aram and Israel* (1918); C. Watzinger and K. Wulzinger, *Damaskus die antike Stadt und die islamische Stadt* (2 vols., 1921-1924); J. Sauvaget, *Les Monuments historiques de Damas* (1932); A. Jepsen, *AfO*, 14 (1942), 141-161; M. F. Unger, *Israel and the Aramaeans of Damascus* (1957).

M. F. UNGER

DAMASCUS, COVENANT OF. A common designation of the sectarian Jewish community that produced documents the remains of which are usually called the "Zadokite Fragments." Although commonly associated with the Essenes at the time of Christ, they display significant differences from that sect, e.g., a literal practice of animal sacrifice as against a spiritualizing interpretation of the system of offerings found among the Essenes. They refer to themselves in their writings as the "New Covenant in the Land of Damascus." *See* DEAD SEA SCROLLS.

G. WYPER

DAMN; DAMNABLE; DAMNATION. The words occur in the AV with the older, weaker sense "condemn," etc., as well as the stronger meaning of eternal judgment. They do not occur in the RSV (or RV). *See* CONDEMN; JUDGING.

DAMSEL. The AV for various Hebrew words, especially *na'ᵃrâ*, and for Gk. *korásion*, *paidíon*, and *paidískē*, all denoting young girls or young women. The RSV never uses the word, but has instead "maiden," "young woman" (Dt. 22:15-29), "girl," "child" (*paidíon*, Mk. 5:39-41), "maid," and "slave girl" (Acts 16:16). *See* GIRL; MAID; YOUNG WOMAN.

DAN dan [Heb. *dān*–'judge']. The fifth of Jacob's sons, the first born to him by Bilhah, Rachel's maid; and the tribe named for him. According to the account in Gen. 30:6, his name was given him by Rachel, to whom he legally belonged, saying: " 'God has judged me . . . and given me a son'; therefore she called his name Dan."

In Jacob's blessing he is mentioned as the seventh, immediately after Leah's sons and the first among the sons of the maids (Gen. 49:16-18). In Moses' blessing the tribes of the maids are mentioned after all those of the wives (the sons of Leah and the sons of Rachel), and this time the first of them is the tribe of Gad and Dan is in the second place (Dt. 33:22). In Deborah's song (Jgs. 5:17) the tribe of Dan is again mentioned second among the tribes of the maids after Gilead (here instead of Gad). The standard of the camp of Dan in the desert march, with which were Asher and Naphtali, was on the north side of the tabernacle (Nu. 2:25; 10:25). The prince of the tribe was Ahiezer (Nu. 1:12). The tribe was the second largest on leaving Egypt, furnishing 62,700 men of war (Nu. 1:39); and at the second census they numbered 64,400 (Nu. 25:43). Here, too, the tribe is in second place. According to the genealogical list Dan had only one son, Hushim (Gen. 46:23), or Shuham (Nu. 26:42), from whom the family of the Shuhamites were descended. The prince of Dan at the time of the division of the land was Bukki the son of Jogli (Nu. 34:22).

At first Dan settled in the northern coastal plain in the boundary area of Ephraim, Benjamin, and Judah. There is no clear description of the boundaries of the tribe's territory in the book of Joshua (19:40-48). In this passage two lists have been combined; one is the list of boundaries of the territory, the other is a list of towns within this territory. It is difficult to separate these two lists (except the western part of the northern boundary, Josh. 19:46), but by comparing the list of towns inside the territory with the list of the boundaries of Judah, Ephraim, and Benjamin, one can describe the territory approximately. It included the western slopes of the central mountain area from the Valley of Sorek in the south to the Kaneh Valley in the north. It is mainly the territory of the Canaanite city of Gezer, with parts of the territories of the city-states of Jaffa and Lod. Because of its situation on the western slopes of the hills of Ephraim, and the relationship of the tribe's name with that of Dinah, Leah's daughter, and because Dan is a descendant of one of the tribes of the maids, it is possible that this tribe was a union of Hivite elements around the city of Shechem and the sons of Jacob. This fact is reflected in the story of Dinah and Hamor the son of Shechem (Gen. 34). Later the sons of Joseph pushed the sons of Dinah-Dan from the center of the mountains to their western slopes. The new territory was less secure because of the strong Canaanite cities, which possessed iron chariots (Jgs. 1:13), and which, therefore, could not be subdued by the sons of Dan. This is the reason we do not find in the list of the cities of Dan the names of Gezer and Jaffa, although the list describes their surrounding territory.

When the Philistines also settled on the coastal plain they began to push the Amorites from the south northward, and the Amorites in turn pushed Dan back to the mountains (Jgs. 1:43). But the Danites did not give up easily. During almost the entire period of the judges they fought against the Amorites. When the Philistines at last subdued the Amorites (1 S. 7:14), and approached the territory of Dan, the Danites tried to hold them back. But they were unable to resist them alone in the open field, and for this reason the book of Judges does not mention a judge who rescued the tribe of Dan from the Philistines but describes a desperate guerrilla war between the two. The hero of this fight was Samson (Jgs. 13–16). At the end of the period of the judges, however, the remnant of the tribe of Dan had to leave their territory. They went northward to conquer a new territory (Jgs. 18). Here they took the city of Laish, a Phoenician city at the north end of the Jordan Valley, and named it after their tribe (Jgs. 18:27).

We can trace the time of this event not only from its place in the book of Judges, but also by comparing quotations in other books. In Deborah's song there is the question: ". . . and Dan, why did he abide with the ships?" (Jgs. 5:17). From this reference we learn that the tribe was still in its old territory, which, as we saw earlier, was near the seashore. In Jacob's blessing the bitter fight between the Danites and their enemies is reflected in the words: "a serpent in the way, an adder in the path" (Gen. 49:17f.). Some scholars think that this is a prayer for the tribe's survival, and that it describes the Danites' way of fighting. Others think that this passage shows the Danites' way of living, namely, robbing the caravans that crossed their territory.

Only the Blessing of Moses (Dt. 33), which most scholars date at the beginning of the kingdom period, describes the tribe of Dan in its northern territory: " '. . . a lion's whelp, that leaps forth from Bashan' " (Dt. 32:22). This passage contains a hint of the boundaries of this territory. Although the number of Danites that settled in the north was small (Jgs. 18:11), they succeeded in conquering in a short time a large territory which contained the Huleh Valley and at least part of western Bashan.

Meanwhile, in the old territory, the remnants of the Danites still fought against the Philistines (1 Ch. 7:21), this time with the help of the tribes of Ephraim, Benjamin, and Judah, until the time of David, when this area became purely Israelite. Most of it belonged to Ephraim (1 Ch. 6:54) and part of it to Judah (1 Ch. 6:44).

Dan was conquered by Ben-hadad king of Syria (1 K. 15:20; 2 Ch. 16:4), but the territory remained Israelite (Jgs. 18:30). It was regained by Jeroboam II (2 K. 14:25), but it shared the general fate of the country at the hands of Tiglath-pileser III (2 K. 15:29), who made it an Assyrian province.

See DAMASCUS Map.

Bibliography.–E. Meyer, *Die Israeliten und ihre Nachbarstämme* (1906); J. Garstang, *Joshua, Judges* (1931), pp. 245-47, 324-343; A. Fernandez, *Bibl.*, 15 (1934), 237-264; W. F. Albright, *BASOR*, 62 (Oct. 1936), 27; M. Noth, *Das Buch Josua* (1938), pp. 93f.; *GP*, II, 52f., 302; A. Alt, *PJ*, 35 (1939), 38f.; H. H. Rowley, *Expos.T.*, 51 (1940), 466-471; *From Moses to Joshua* (1950), pp. 79, 81ff., 103.

A. A. SAARISALO

DAN dan [Heb. *dān*]. A city near the southern foot of Mt. Hermon to which the Danites migrated (Jgs. 18). It was the northernmost limit of ancient Israel, as indicated in the common phrase "from Dan to Beersheba" (Jgs. 20:1; 1 S. 3:20). Its ancient name was Laish or Leshem (Jgs. 18:7, 29; Josh. 19:47). That it had some connection with Sidon on the coast is clear (Jgs. 18:7). The inhabitants, pursuing the ends of peaceful traders, were defenseless against the onset of the Danite raiders. These burned the city and then rebuilt it, giving it the name of their tribal ancestor (Jgs. 18:29). It lay in the valley near Beth-rehob (Jgs. 18:28). Josephus places it near Mt. Lebanon and the fountain of the lesser Jordan, a day's journey from Sidon (*Ant.* v.3.1; viii.8.4; *BJ* iv.1.1). Eusebius (*Onom.*) says it lay 4 Roman mi. (3.7 mi., 5.9 km.) from Paneas on the way to Tyre, at the source of the Jordan. This points decisively to Tell el-Qâḍī ("mound of the judges"), in the plain W of Paneas (Bâniyâs). Nahr el-Leddan, one of the four principal sources of the Jordan River, rises at the base of this mound and flows southward for 4 mi. (6.5 km.) to join the Bâniyâs and eventually the Nahr Ḥasbânī. The mound overlooks the Huleh Valley, and the area is lush and green even in the summer.

A long-term and extensive excavation of Tel Dan was begun in 1966 under the direction of A. Biran and a team of Israeli and American archeologists. Excavations have penetrated several areas. In the northern part of the mound a high place was found dating to the 10th cent. B.C. In the southern part a sequence of occupational levels has been excavated dating to the 11th century. In the eastern section ashes, bricks, and many sherds dating to the Early and Middle Bronze Ages were unearthed, as well as the Israelite city gate and a section of wall (A. Biran, *IEJ*, 24 [1974], 262-64). An Israelite horned altar was found in the area of the high place similar to one found by Y. Aharoni at Beersheba in 1973 (Biran, *BA*, 37 [1974], 106f.; cf. Y. Aharoni, pp. 2-6). These similar artifacts from the two extremes of the land give an added dimension to the expression "from Dan to Beersheba." See also A. Biran, *BA*, 37 (1974), 26-51; Y. Aharoni, *IEJ*, 24 (1974), 13-16; B. Mazar, *et al.*, ed., *Encyclopedia of Archaeological Excavations in the Holy Land* (1970), I, 313-321.

When the Danites settled here, they set up a graven image. The sanctuary and ritual established by them persisted as long as the house of God was in Shiloh (Jgs. 18:30f.). Upon the division of the kingdom, Jeroboam declared Bethel and Dan as centers of worship to replace Jerusalem, which was in the southern kingdom. He made two golden calves and placed one at Bethel and the other at Dan, declaring, "Behold thy God, O Israel" (1 K. 12:27-29). The idolatrous shrine and ritual established at Dan continued till the conquest by Tiglath-pileser (2 K. 15:29). The calf, according to Jewish tradition, was taken away by Tiglath-pileser. Dan fell before Ben-hadad king of Syria, in the 9th cent. B.C. (1 K. 15:20; 2 Ch. 16:4). It was regained by Jeroboam II (2 K. 14:25). It shared the country's fate at the hands of Tiglath-pileser (2 K. 15:29).

In modern times, the Israeli kibbutz established near the site bears the ancient name.

See also DAN-JAAN; MAPS II, V-IX.

W. EWING
J. F. PREWITT

DAN AND JAVAN (Ezk. 27:19, AV). The AV here follows the difficult MT, *wᵉḏān wᵉyāwān mᵉʾûzzāl,* "Dan also and Javan going to and fro." The RSV translation "and wine from Uzal" is the result of the following reconstruction: (1) omission of the first word with LXX B; (2) following the LXX in understanding the second word as a possible variant spelling of *wᵉyayin,* "and wine"; (3) following thirteen Hebrew MSS, with LXX, and the Syriac in reading the third word with a different pointing, *mēʾûzāl,* "from Uzal." The NEB reconstruction, "and casks of wine from Izalla," is similar, except that *dan* is not omitted but understood as equivalent to Akk. *dannu,* a large vessel for storage of wine (cf. A. R. Millard, *JSS,* 7 [1962], 201-203); Izalla was an Anatolian district noted for quality wines.

DANCE; DANCER [Heb. *ḥûl*–'whirl, turn'] (Jgs. 21:21, 23; Ps. 87:7); AV also "players on instruments" (Ps. 87:7); [*māḥôl*] (Ps. 30:11 [MT 12]; 149:3; 150:4; Jer. 31:4, 13; Lam. 5:15); [*mᵉḥōlâ*] (Ex. 15:20; 32:19; Jgs. 11:34; 21:21; 1 S. 18:6; 21:11 [MT 12]; 29:5; Cant. 6:13 [MT 7:1]); AV also COMPANY (Cant. 6:13); [*rāqaḏ*] (1 Ch. 15:29; Job 21:11; Eccl. 3:4; Isa. 13:21); NEB also GAMBOL; [*kārar*] (2 S. 6:14, 16); NEB also CAPER; [*ḥāgag*] (1 S. 30:16); NEB CELEBRATE; [*dûṣ*–'bound, exult'] (Job 41:22 [MT 14]); AV "is turned into joy"; [Gk. *orchéomai*] (Mt. 11:17; 14:6; Mk. 6:22; Lk. 7:32); [*chorós*] (Lk. 15:25); [*paízō*–'play'] (1 Cor. 10:7); AV PLAY; NEB REVEL. Rhythmical body movement, especially of the limbs, often to musical accompaniment.

Descriptions of dancing in the Bible most often occur in the context of communal religious celebrations, and dance may therefore be classified as a cultic activity. Much of what we consider everyday life was so bound to sacral concerns in biblical times that the cultic/secular dichotomy is not as useful in classifying dance as the occasions on which it was performed.

Celebration of Hebrew feasts provided the occasion for much dancing. At the yearly feast of Yahweh at Shiloh (Jgs. 21:16-24) the Benjaminites sought wives from among the virgins dancing in the vineyards. The form of this celebration is echoed in the Talmudic account of the Days of Joy of the 15th of Ab, and the Day of Atonement, when young women danced in borrowed white dresses: "The daughters of Jerusalem came out and danced in the vineyards exclaiming at the same time, Young man, lift up thine eyes and see what thou choosest for thyself" (T.B. *Taanith* 26b; cf. figurative use, Jer. 31:4). Several specific calls to praise God with music and dance (Ps. 87:7; 149:3; 150:4) suggest that music may have invoked dancing at other times when only the music is mentioned (e.g., Ps. 42:4 [MT 5]; 47:5-7 [MT 6-8]; 98). Music and dancing by men on festal occasions are attested by the Talmudic description of the water-drawing at the Feast of Tabernacles (T.B. *Sukkah* 51a-b): "Men of piety and good deeds used to dance before them with lighted torches in their hands, and sing songs and praises. And Levites without number with harps, lyres, cymbals and trumpets and other musical instruments were there upon the fifteen steps leading down from the court of the Israelites to the court of the women, corresponding to the fifteen songs of ascents in the Psalms" (Pss. 120–134).

Unlike their Egyptian neighbors, the Hebrews apparently did not use dance in mourning or burial rites. There is no mention of dance in funerary situations; in fact, the OT uses mourning and dancing as opposites (cf. Ps. 30:8-12 [MT 9-13]; also Eccl. 3:4; Jer. 31:13; Lam. 5:15; 3 Macc. 6:32, 35). The children's taunt in Mt. 11:17 and Lk. 7:32 also employs the contrast between dance and mourning.

The Hebrew employs *ḥûl* and its derivatives *māḥôl* and *m*ᵉ*ḥōlâ* in all the OT passages discussed to this point (except Eccl. 3:4) to denote turning, twisting, whirling; hence the general interpretation of round dances is given to these instances. The same root is used of dancing in idolatrous celebration. To mark the creation of the golden calf at Sinai, Aaron proclaimed a feast to Yahweh at which the people offered sacrifices, ate, drank, and played (Ex. 32:5f.) with singing and dancing (*m*ᵉ*ḥōlâ*, v. 19). The RSV translates Gk. *paízein* ("play") in the NT reference to this scene (1 Cor. 10:7) as "dance" in light of Ex. 32:19; the LXX uses *paízein* in 32:6 for the more neutral activity of playing, making merry (so for most other occurrences of *paízein*), while reserving a more specific term for dance (*chorós*) in 32:19. Elsewhere in the OT "play" (Heb. *ṣāḥaq*) may have a sexual connotation (Gen. 26:8; 39:14); the people's "breaking loose" (Ex. 32:25) suggests that the dancing was highly sensual in this case also.

When he brought the Ark of the Covenant to Jerusalem, David held a similar but legitimate celebration of sacrifices, dancing, shouting, music, and feasting (2 S. 6:12-19). David's movements in leading the procession are described by several verbs: dancing "with all his might" (6:14, from *kārar* [pilpel], "whirl"), "leaping" (6:16, *pāzaz*), "making merry" (1 Ch. 15:29, *ṣāḥaq*). In a rare mention of a dancer's clothing, David is said to have worn a linen ephod (2 S. 6:14; in 1 Ch. 15:27 a linen robe), whose briefness roused Michal's contempt.

Although the term "dance" is nowhere used specifically to describe prophetic activity, it is hard to imagine the music and ecstasy of prophetic bands without rhythmic movement (cf. 1 S. 10:1-13; 19:18-24, for Saul's encounter with prophets). Prophets of Baal in the contest with Elijah on Mt. Carmel "limped," or hobbled (1 K. 18:26, *pāsaḥ*; cf. 18:21) around the altar crying and lacerating themselves to gain Baal's attention. (Baal Marqad, "Baal of the Dance," was one of that deity's forms in Lebanon.) Circling the altar was also practiced at the Jerusalem temple (Ps. 26:6f., *sāḇaḇ*). An awkward gait and circumambulation characterized the prescribed ritual for circling the Kaaba in Mecca at a later period, when pilgrims were required to make the first circuit "moving the shoulders as if walking in sand" (R. F. Burton, *Pilgrimage to Al-Madinah and Meccah* [1907], pp. 393f.).

The dancing most often mentioned in the OT occurred when a procession of women celebrated a military victory with music, song, and dance, led by a prominent woman (e.g., Miriam, Jephthah's daughter, Judith), in praise of God (Ex. 15:20; Jgs. 15:12f.) and in honor of returning warriors (Jgs. 11:34; 1 S. 18:6; 21:11; 29:5; Jth. 3:7; all from *ḥûl*). Although men in battle gear might join the homecoming procession (Jth. 15:13), an army could

Girls dancing to music made by the seated women; banquet scene from the Egyptian New Kingdom. Two women at left are either clapping or performing a static hand dance. Wall painting from tomb of Nebamen at Thebes (12th Dynasty, 1500-1314 B.C.) (Trustees of the British Museum)

also mark its victory in the field (1 S. 30:16, *ḥāgag*). *Ḥāgag* usually means "keep a feast," "celebrate" (Ex. 23:14; Lev. 23:39); the translations of 1 S. 30:16 ("dance") and Ps. 107:27 ("reel . . . like drunken men") emphasize elements of festive behavior.

Families as well as larger religious communities celebrated in dance. Job 21:11 complains that one sign of the prosperity of the wicked is their children's dancing (*rāqaḏ*). *Rāqaḏ* (in piel) is used often in OT prophetic oracles and poetry with a figurative meaning of "bound," "skip," or "leap." Job 41:22 and Isa. 13:21 share this sense, rather than indicating a particular dance step or occasion. The family feast for the return of the prodigal son featured music and dancing (Lk. 15:25, Gk. *chorós*). NT passages mentioning wedding celebrations (Mt. 22:1-14; 25:1-13; Lk. 14:7-11; Jn. 2:1-11) lack accounts of the bridal procession (cf. Ps. 45:15 [MT 16]; 1 Macc. 9:37-39), but Talmudic literature of the time recounts the enthusiasm of the rabbis, dancing before the bride and waving or juggling myrtle twigs (T.B. *Ketuboth* 17a). The difficult passage of Cant. 6:13 has been interpreted as referring to the two circling choruses (armies) of a wedding procession.

The universal importance of dance as part of the induction of new adherents into the mystery cults of the Greco-Roman period (cf. Lucian *De saltatione* 15) made dancing highly suspect for Christian worship. Church fathers writing to justify dance in Christian celebration often contrasted the dancing of David with that of Herodias' daughter, known to tradition as Salome (Mt. 14:6; Mk. 6:22): "But even if you wish to dance in devotion at this happy ceremony and festival, then dance, but not the shameless dance of the daughter of Herod [*sic*], which accompanied the execution of the Baptist, but the dance of David to the true refreshment of the Ark, which I consider to be the approach to God, the swift encircling steps in the manner of the mysteries" (Gregory of Nazianzus *Oratio v: contra Julianum*; the mysteries here are Christian ones). Dancing for after-dinner entertainment, although known among the Egyptians, developed more directly from the Greek *symposium*, at which professional dancers were featured in artistic performances (Xenophon *Symposium* 2-9); in later phases scantily clad courtesans, professional male dancers, and dwarfs provided lewd and flamboyant spectacles. The most popular dance entertainment in the first centuries A.D. was the *pantomimus*, a solo enactment of a popular story theme in stylized mimicry, often with dramatic and sensual movements and postures. It has been suggested that Salome's dance for Herod's birthday guests was in this tradition.

Bibliography.–E. L. Backman, *Religious Dances in the Christian Church and in Popular Medicine* (1952); E. Brunner-Traut, *Der Tanz im Alten Ägypten* (*Ägyptologische Forschungen*, 6, 1958); *Les Danses sacrés* (*Sources Orientales*, 6, 1963); R. G. Kraus, *History of the Dance in Art and Education* (1969); L. B. Lawler, *The Dance in Ancient Greece* (1964); C. Sachs, *World History of the Dance* (1937); A. Sendrey, *Music in Ancient Israel* (1969), pp. 441-476.

E. B. JOHNSTON

DANDLE [Heb. *šā'ᵉšaʿ*] (Isa. 66:12); [*ṭāpaḥ*–'rear a healthy child'] (Lam. 2:22); AV SWADDLE, NEB "brought safely to birth." In Isa. 66:12 the root *šāʿaʿ* in the pulpel form means "be fondled," as with children in play, and is the only OT use in that sense. The reference in Lam. 2:22 is to the process of nurturing a healthy child from birth.

DANGER. The AV translates Gk. *énochos* as "in danger" in both Mt. 5:21f. and Mk. 3:29. In the former passage the RSV has "liable," the NEB "must be brought" (to judgment) and "must answer." In Mk. 3:29 the RSV and NEB both translate "is guilty," another possible rendering of *énochos*. This is certainly preferable to the AV, especially if *hamártēma* is rendered as RSV and NEB "sin" rather than AV "damnation."

The word in 2 Cor. 11:26 is Gk. *kíndynos* (AV "peril"), and in Acts 19:27, 40, *kindyneúō*, "be in danger."

DANIEL dan'yəl [Heb. *dānîyēl, dāni'ēl*–'God is my judge'; Gk. *Daniēl*].

1. One of the sons of David (1 Ch. 3:1). Although he was older than either Absalom or Adonijah, he remained unmentioned in any connection, which suggests that he died at an early age.

2. A Levite of the family of Ithamar (Ezr. 8:2; Neh. 10:6), who was signatory to the covenant.

3. A person of great wisdom and righteousness, associated with Noah and Job in Ezk. 14:14, 20; 28:3, where the NEB reads "Danel." This latter vocalization of the MT has been influenced by the Ugaritic Legend of Aqht, which dealt with the activities of a Phoenician ruler named *Dnil*, which can be vocalized either as *Danel* or *Daniel*. This king dispensed justice among his contemporaries, although the legend did not actually speak of him as being wise. The NEB has assumed that the person referred to in Ezk. 14:14, 20 was the *Dnil* of the Ugaritic narrative. This seems improbable in view of the fact that a Hebrew writer would hardly associate a pagan ruler, of legendary nature at best, with historic Hebrew patriarchal figures of outstanding spirituality, in a relationship of moral equality. In Ezk. 28:3 it is possible that the prophet was using the figure of the legendary Phoenician-Canaanite *Dan'el* in a sarcastic manner to show the Tyrians how they had been deceived by their own superstitions, but even this is far from certain.

4. A prophet of the time of Nebuchadnezzar and Cyrus, the hero and author of the book of Daniel.

I. Early Life.–We know nothing of the early life of Daniel, except what is recorded in the book bearing his name. Here it is said that he was one of the youths of royal or noble seed who were carried captive by Nebuchadnezzar in the third year of Jehoiakim king of Judah. These youths were without blemish, handsome, skilful in all wisdom, endowed with knowledge, understanding science, and competent to serve in the king's palace. The king commanded that they be taught the letters and language of the Chaldeans, and assigned for them a daily portion of the king's food and wine. After being educated and nourished for three years, they were to stand before the king. Ashpenaz, the master or chief of the eunuchs into whose hands they had been entrusted, following a custom of the time, gave to each of these youths a new Babylonian name. To Daniel he gave the name Belteshazzar. In Babylonian this name was probably *Balaṭsu-uṣur* ("protect his life"), a common Babylonian form in which the name of the deity being invoked was omitted. (For changes of names, cf. Joseph changed to Zaphenath-paneah [Gen. 41:45]; Eliakim to Jehoiakim [2 K. 23:34]; Mattaniah to Zedekiah [2 K. 24:17]; and the two names of the high priest Johanan's brother in the Sachau Papyri, i.e., Ostan and Anani.)

Having determined not to pollute himself with the food and drink of the king, Daniel requested of Ashpenaz permission to eat vegetables and drink water. Through the favor of God, this request was granted, despite the fears of Ashpenaz that the attenuated physical appearance of the young Hebrews after living on such a diet would cost him his life. However, after a trial period of ten days, the result was so promising that Daniel and his companions were permitted to dispense with the rich food of the royal court in favor of a diet of vegetables and water. Then God bestowed on the young men knowledge and skill in all learning and wisdom, and to Daniel understanding in all visions and dreams; so that at the end of the three years when the king communed with them, he found them much superior to all the magicians and enchanters in every matter of wisdom and understanding.

II. Interpreter of Dreams, Signs, and Visions.–Daniel's public activities were in harmony with his education. His first appearance was as an interpreter of the dream recorded in Dnl. 2. Nebuchadnezzar has seen in his dream a vision of a great image, excellent in brightness and terrible in appearance, its head of fine gold, its breast and arms of silver, its belly and thighs of brass, its legs of iron, its feet partly of iron and partly of clay. Next he saw a stone cut out without hands smiting the image and breaking it in pieces, until the image became like chaff and was carried away by the wind, while the stone that smote it became a great mountain and filled the whole earth. When the king awoke from his troubled sleep, he had apparently forgotten the dream, and summoned the wise men, who having said that they could not tell the dream, nor interpret it as long as it was untold, were threatened with death. Daniel (who seems not to have been present when the other wise men were before the king), when he was informed that preparations were being made to slay all of the wise men of Babylon, himself and his three companions included, boldly went in to the king and requested that the latter appoint a time for him to appear in order to show the interpretation. Then he went to his house, and he and his companions prayed; and the dream and its interpretation were made known to Daniel. At the appointed time the dream was explained, and the four Hebrews were loaded with wealth and given high positions in the service of the king. In the fourth chapter, we have recorded Daniel's interpretation of the dream of Nebuchadnezzar about the great tree that was hewn at the command of an angel, thus prefiguring the insanity of the king.

Daniel's third great appearance in the book is in ch. 5, where he is called upon to explain the extraordinary writing upon the wall of Belshazzar's palace, which foretold the end of the Babylonian empire and the incoming of the Medes and Persians. For this service Daniel was clothed with purple, a chain of gold was put around his neck, and he was made the third ruler in the kingdom.

Daniel, however, was not merely an interpreter of other men's visions. In the last six chapters we have recorded four or five of his own visions, all of which are taken up with revelations concerning the future history of the great world empires — especially in their relation to the people of God — and predictions of the final triumph of the Messiah's kingdom.

III. Official of the Kings.–In addition to his duties as seer and as interpreter of signs and dreams, Daniel also stood high in the governmental service of Nebuchadnezzaar, Belshazzar, Darius the Mede, and perhaps also of Cyrus. The book of Daniel, our only reliable source of information on this subject, does not tell us much about his civil duties and performances. It does say, however, that he was chief of the wise men, that he was in the gate of the king, and that he was governor over the whole province of Babylon under Nebuchadnezzar; that Belshazzar made him the third ruler in his kingdom; that Darius made him one of the three presidents to whom his hundred and twenty satraps were to give account; and that he even thought to set him over his whole kingdom. In all of these positions he seems to have conducted himself with faithfulness and judgment.

While in the service of Darius the Mede he aroused the antipathy of the other presidents and the satraps. Unable to find any fault with his official acts, they induced the king to make a decree, apparently general in form and purpose but really aimed at Daniel alone. They saw that they could find no valid accusation against him unless they found it in connection with something concerning the law of his God. They therefore caused the king to make a decree that no one should make a request of anyone for a space of thirty days, save of the king. Daniel, having publicly prayed three times a day according to his habit, was caught in the act, accused, and on account of the irrevocability of a law of the Medes and Persians was condemned to be cast into a den of lions. The king was much troubled at this, but was unable to withhold the punishment. However, he expressed to Daniel his belief that his God would deliver him; and so indeed it happened. For in the morning, when the king came near to the mouth of the den and called to him, Daniel said that God had sent His angel and shut the mouths of the lions. So Daniel was taken up unharmed, and at the command of the king his accusers were cast into the den, where they were destroyed.

The sentence of death by being cast to lions was the Persian equivalent of the earlier Babylonian form of death by fire (cf. Dnl. 3:19ff.), since fire was sacred to the Persians and thus an unsuitable instrument for inflicting capital punishment. The last recorded vision of Daniel occurred on the banks of the river Tigris in the third year of Cyrus (536 B.C.), when the Hebrew sage was very advanced in years — probably being well over eighty when he died. By tradition Daniel was buried at Susa, though this is very difficult to substantiate. He left behind an outstanding reputation for persistent faith in God regardless of the circumstances, and his popularity in later periods is demonstrated by the number of legends which accrued to him in the intertestamentary period.

R. D. WILSON
R. K. HARRISON

DANIEL, BOOK OF.

I. Name
II. Place in the Canon
III. Divisions
IV. Languages
V. Purpose
VI. Date
VII. Unity
VIII. Objections to Traditional Authorship
A. Prophecy
B. Historical Matters
C. Language
IX. Interpretations
X. Doctrines
XI. Apocryphal Additions

I. Name.–The book of Daniel was named after its principal figure, who in Jewish tradition was uniformly regarded as the attributive author. His name, Heb. *dānîyē'l* or *dāni'ēl*, means "God is my judge"; he was evidently a Hebrew personage of noble descent whom Nebuchadrezzar carried captive to Babylon in 605 B.C., the third year of Jehoiakim's rule, after the Babylonians had defeated the Egyptians at Carchemish.

II. Place in the Canon.–In the English Bible, Daniel is placed among the Major Prophets immediately after

Ezekiel, thus following the order of the Septuagint and of the Vulgate. In the Hebrew Bible, however, it is placed in the third division of the canon, called the Kethubhim or "writings" by the Hebrews, and the hagiographa or "holy writings" by the LXX. It has been claimed that Daniel was placed by the Jews in the third part of the canon either because they thought the inspiration of its author to be of a lower kind than that of the other prophets or because the book was written after the second or prophetical part of the canon had been closed. It is more probable, however, that the book was placed in this part of the Hebrew canon because Daniel is not called a *nāḇî'* ("prophet"), but rather a *ḥōzeh* ("seer") and a *ḥāḵām* ("wise man"). None but the works of the *nᵉḇî'îm* were put in the second part of the Jewish canon, the third being reserved for the heterogeneous works of seers, wise men, and priests, or for those that do not mention the name or work of a prophet, or that are poetical in form.

In the OT economy the Law comprised the writings attributed to Moses, the human founder of the theocracy; the prophetical books, including both Former and Latter Prophets, were written by men who were prophets of God. The books known as Former Prophets were written to interpret God's dealings with Israel, while those which bear the names of the "writing prophets" were the work of the persons concerned. The third division of the canon is composed of works written by men who were inspired of God and yet did not themselves occupy the office of prophet. In ancient Israel the prophet was primarily a mediator between God and the nation, speaking to the people on behalf of God. He was in effect a spokesman for the Lord. Daniel did not occupy such a position, since his training prepared him for service as a statesman at a heathen court, a capacity in which he served throughout his long life. While, however, he did not occupy the technical office of a prophet of Israel, his outlook manifested many elements consistent with the highest aspirations of normative prophecy; and for that reason the NT speaks of him as a prophet (cf. Mt. 24:15). Quite clearly, then, the book belongs properly in the third division of the Hebrew canon.

III. Divisions.–According to its subject matter the book falls naturally into two great divisions, each consisting of six chapters. The first portion contains the historical sections and the second the apocalyptic — or predictive — portions, although the former is not devoid of predictions nor the latter of historical statements. More specifically, the first chapter is introductory to the whole book; chs. 2–6 describe some marvelous events in the history of Daniel and his three companions in their relations with the rulers of Babylon; and chs. 7–12 narrate some visions of Daniel concerning the great world-empires, especially in relation to the kingdom of God.

In the ancient Near East it was not uncommon for lengthy literary works to be compiled and circulated in two distinct though related halves. Bifid compositions of this sort were thus afforded much wider circulation than would have been the case if an entire bulky MS had to be passed from hand to hand each time before a reader could peruse it. The two related halves enabled the person who obtained possession of one of them to gain an overall impression of the author's message without necessarily reading the corresponding half. In the biblical field this was obviously an advantage for lengthy compositions such as the book of Isaiah, which has been shown by the large Qumrân Isaiah scroll (1QIsa[a]) to have been in bifid form. Other similar bipartite OT compositions include Joshua, Ezekiel, and Zechariah; the literary practice is attested by Josephus (*Ant.* x.5.1; 11.7).

IV. Languages.–Daniel is written in two languages, Hebrew (1:1–2:4a; 8:1–12:13) and Aramaic (2:4b–7:28). The Hebrew is very similar in character to that of Ezekiel, and is used when the author deals with God's people and their destiny in subsequent centuries. By contrast, Aramaic is employed chiefly for the description of great world empires. Hebrew terms such as *malḵûṯ* ("royal power," "reign"), which were once regarded as evidence of late linguistic usage (Driver, p. 508), were actually used in all periods of the Hebrew language, and represent a noun pattern found in Akkadian as early as the 18th cent. B.C. Again, the expression *'āmar lᵉ* ("command to"), which was formerly thought a late literary form, occurs in Dt. 9:25; Josh. 22:33; 1 S. 30:6 and elsewhere, as well as in the postexilic works (Neh. 9:15, 22). There is therefore nothing in the Hebrew that would have been foreign to the linguistic experience of a sixth-century B.C. person such as Daniel, who knew both Hebrew and Aramaic. The influence of the latter language can be seen clearly in the use of the phrase *'ᵃšer lāmmâ* to mean "least" (Dnl. 1:10).

The linguistic evidence once offered by nineteenth-century scholars for the late composition of Daniel has undergone sobering modification as the result of archeological discoveries in the Near East, and not least in relation to the development of Aramaic as a language. It is now known that "Aramaic" is a rather general term for a group of Semitic dialects related closely to Hebrew and even more so to one another. They have been classified by philologists into four groups: Old Aramaic, Official Aramaic, Levantine Aramaic, and Eastern Aramaic. Old Aramaic occurred in North Syrian inscriptions from the 10th to the 8th cent. B.C., while Official Aramaic was employed increasingly by Assyrian government officials between 1100 and 600 B.C., becoming the language of diplomacy in the Persian period, even though royal inscriptions were still being inscribed in Old Persian at that time. Aramaic in written and spoken form, however, goes back much further than Old Aramaic, being represented in the Ugaritic texts of the Amarna Age and the linguistic traditions of the Middle Bronze Age (cf. Gen. 31:47).

When the Aramaic vocabulary of Daniel is examined, nine-tenths of it can be attested immediately from West Semitic inscriptions, or papyri from the 5th cent. B.C. or earlier. The remaining words have been found in sources such as Nabatean or Palmyrene Aramaic, which are later than the 5th cent. B.C. While it is at least theoretically possible that this small balance of vocabulary suddenly originated after the 5th cent. B.C., it is equally possible to argue from a fifth-century B.C. written form to an earlier oral one. By far the most probable explanation, however, is that the missing tenth represents nothing more serious than a gap in our current knowledge of the linguistic situation, which we may confidently expect to be filled in process of time.

The spelling of certain Aramaic words in Daniel differs somewhat from the usage in Old Aramaic (10th to 8th cent. B.C.) and Official Aramaic as found in the 6th to 4th cent. B.C.). Where the latter have *z, š, q,* and *ṣ*, Daniel (and Ezra) reads *d, t,* ', and *ṭ* respectively. Because these variations in Daniel (and Ezra) also occur in the later Palmyrene and Nabatean Aramaic, as well as in the Targums, it might be thought possible on orthographic grounds to place Daniel's Aramaic somewhat between the Elephantine papyri (5th cent. B.C.) and the second-century B.C. Aramaic dialects. This supposition rests on the assumption that the consonantal Aramaic of Daniel underwent no changes in spelling whatever after it was first written, a position which would be extremely

DANIEL, BOOK OF

difficult to justify in the light of what is now known about the development of the various Aramaic dialects. Not only have definite orthographic changes been demonstrated from incriptions and papyri, but scholars have now become aware of the fact that Aramaic orthography and phonetics are apt to be at variance with one another on specific occasions, as sometimes happens in English and other languages. Thus in the Elephantine papyri, while the letter *z* was substituted for *ḏ*, the actual pronunciation was *d*, as in the Aramaic of Daniel and Ezra. Again, in fifth-century B.C. Egypt, a foreign name such as that of Darius was written in a way which substituted the traditional hieroglyphic sign "t" for the "d" to produce *Trwš*. These and other shifts in spelling and pronunciation should be sufficient to suggest caution in assuming that there was uniformity or constancy in the transmission of the Aramaic portions of Daniel. (*See also* ARAMAIC.)

The presence of Akkadian loanwords (F. Rosenthal, *Grammar of Biblical Aramaic* [1961], pp. 57ff.) is, of course, unexceptional in a work such as Daniel, considering the cultural milieu from which it emerged. The same is true of the nineteen or so words of Persian origin, some of which are attested in the Targums. About half of the Persian loan words occur in Official Aramaic, and in general can be found in sixth- to fifth-century B.C. literary sources. It is worth noting that all such Persian terms are Old Persian in nature, i.e., earlier than *ca.* 300 B.C., a fact which would be consistent with the linguistic situation of pre-Hellenistic Aramaic.

In the light of Dnl. 1:4 it is also a distinct possibility that Daniel both spoke and wrote in Neo-Babylonian. Since the third-person form is characteristic of the first seven chapters of the book, it may be that at least some sections were originally transcribed in Neo-Babylonian, particularly the interviews with Nebuchadrezzar. This may be even more likely if the individual chapters were in the nature of memoirs compiled by Daniel shortly after the events and visions took place, a procedure that would be thoroughly consistent with ancient annalistic practices. Ch. 4 may indicate the manner in which a first-person narrative written in cuneiform was modified when rendered into Aramaic. Perhaps 4:19 (MT 16) originally read "Then Belteshazzar was dismayed for a long time, and his thoughts alarmed him. I [i.e., the king] said, Belteshazzar, let not the dream. . . ." Similarly, as a first-person description, 4:28 (MT 25) may have begun originally: "All this came upon me. At the end of twelve months I was walking. . . ." If this was the case with some of the material in the first seven chapters, it would help to explain why, when the passages were translated into Aramaic and put into the 3rd person, it was necessary for glosses such as those in 2:26; 4:19 (MT 16); 5:12; and 8:15 to have been inserted. If this supposition is correct, it will indicate that Daniel was based upon genuine literary sources, not the garbled tales and legends posited by those scholars who have advocated a Maccabean date for the book. Neo-Babylonian would certainly have been appropriate for recording contemporary historical events, since it was the court language of Nebuchadrezzar, and aside from material involving the king himself it could also have been used for transmitting such matters as the vision of ch. 7, which occurred rather unexpectedly and was quite probably jotted down immediately after it had taken place. At the same time there are certain other materials, such as prayers, that would probably have been written down in Hebrew or Aramaic.

V. Purpose.–The book is not intended to give an account of the life of Daniel. It gives neither his lineage nor his age, and recounts but a few of the events of his long career. Nor is it meant to give a record of the history of Israel during the Exile, nor even of the captivity in Babylon. Its purpose is to show how by His providential guidance, His miraculous interventions, His foreknowledge and almighty power, the God of heaven controls and directs the forces of nature and the history of nations, the lives of Hebrew captives and of the mightiest of the kings of the earth, for the accomplishment of His divine and beneficent plans for His servants and people.

Those who have argued that the work was a product of the Maccabean era have seen it as a "tract for the times," intended to stimulate Jewish opposition to the hellenizing attempts of Antiochus Epiphanes IV. The alleged purpose of the author was to show the persecuted Jews how to combat their heathen rulers by exhibiting Daniel as a behavioral example of spiritual probity in a pagan environment. Quite aside from whether or not such a procedure would furnish an apt parallel for embattled Maccabean Jews, a date for Daniel in the 2nd cent. B.C. is absolutely precluded by the evidence from Qumrân, as indicated below.

VI. Date.–Although *Baba Bathra* 15a seems to suggest some sort of editorial work on the part of the "Men of the Great Synagogue," Hebrew and Christian tradition consistently ascribed the work to Daniel, who was held to have composed the book in the 6th cent. B.C. Only in the 3rd cent. A.D. was this position challenged by Porphyry, a Neoplatonist thinker who inveighed vigorously against Christian belief in a fifteen-volume work which has not survived. However, Jerome preserved his comments on Daniel, the main feature of which was his statement that the book was written in the Maccabean age so as to encourage the Jewish people who were persecuted by Antiochus Epiphanes IV. Porphyry arrived at this conclusion from the a priori position that prediction in prophecy was impossible. In addition, he seems to have thought that Greek was the original language of the book.

All subsequent rationalistic thought about Daniel has repeated quite uncritically most if not all of Porphyry's arguments, some of which will be considered in subsequent sections. However, the dating of Daniel can now be settled at least negatively as a result of MS discoveries from the Dead Sea caves from 1947 onwards. Fragments from 1Q, along with some complete scrolls of Daniel from other caves, have testified to the popularity of the work at Qumrân. A florilegium recovered from 4Q spoke, like Mt. 24:15, of "Daniel the prophet," furnishing eloquent second-century B.C. testimony to the way in which the book was revered and cited as Scripture. Since all the Qumrân fragments and scrolls are copies, the autograph of Daniel and other OT canonical works must of necessity be advanced well before the Maccabean period if the proper minimum of time is allowed for the book to be circulated and accepted as Scripture. Precisely how much earlier than the Maccabean period is, of course, the point at issue. Here again the Qumrân material provides invaluable assistance. When 1Q was excavated, two of the three fragments of Daniel recovered from the site proved to be related paleographically to the large Isaiah MS (1QIsa[a]). Since the book of Isaiah comes from a time several centuries prior to the earliest date to which 1QIsa[a] can be assigned on any grounds, it follows that the autograph of Daniel also must be several centuries in advance of the Maccabean period. From Cave 4 was also recovered a fragmentary second-century B.C. copy of the Psalter (4QpPs 37), and this document showed that the collection of canonical psalms had already been fixed by the Maccabean period. On the basis of this evidence alone, scholars have now assigned to the Persian period psalms which were once confidently acclaimed as unquestionably Maccabean in origin.

It is now clear from the Qumrân MSS that no part of the OT canonical literature was composed later than the 4th cent. B.C. This means that Daniel must of necessity be assigned to some point in the Neo-Babylonian era (626-539 B.C.), or a somewhat later period. If, following Near Eastern annalistic practices, the events and visions were recorded shortly after their occurrence, the book may well have been written progressively over a lengthy period of time, being finally collated by Daniel in the closing phases of his life, and perhaps being rounded out then or a little later by such final verses as 1:21; 6:28; and possibly 7:28b. However, at the latest the book of Daniel seems to have been in its extant form — whether from the hand of the author or a slightly later editor — not later than 450 B.C. There can no longer be any possible reason for considering the book as a Maccabean product.

VII. Unity.–The unity of the book was first denied by Spinoza, who suggested that the first part was taken from the chronological works of the Chaldeans, basing his supposition upon the difference of language between the former and latter parts. Newton followed Spinoza in suggesting two parts, but began his second division with ch. 7, where the narrative passes over from the 3rd to the 1st person. Kohler followed Newton, claiming, however, that the visions were written by the Daniel of the Exile but that the first six chapters were composed by a later writer who also redacted the whole work. Von Orelli held that certain prophecies of Daniel were enlarged and interpolated by a Jew living in the time of Antiochus Epiphanes, in order to show his contemporaries the bearing of the predictions of the book upon those times of oppression. Zöckler and Lange held to the unity of the book in general; but the former thought that 11:5-45 is an interpolation, and the latter that 10:1–11:44 and 12:5-13 had been inserted in the original work. Meinhold held that the Aramaic portions existed as early as the times of Alexander the Great — a view to which Strack also inclined. Eichhorn held that the book consisted of ten different original sections, which were bound together merely by the circumstance that they are all concerned with Daniel and his three friends. De Lagarde, believing that the fourth kingdom was the Roman, held that ch. 7 was written about A.D. 69. The unity of Daniel was defended among others by Von Gall, Pusey, and Cornill; but in the closing years of the 19th cent. Barton advanced the theory of multiple authorship again, and was followed by Dalman, Torrey, Eissfeldt, and others. Hölscher assigned the first six chapters to the 3rd cent. B.C., the seventh to a somewhat later period, and the remainder to the Maccabean era, being followed in varying degrees by Meinhold, Gressman, Albright, Welch, Eerdmans, and Weiser. Scholars who have defended the unity of Daniel include S. R. Driver, Bewer, Charles, Wilson, Rowley, R. H. Pfeiffer, and E. J. Young.

There has always been a wide diversity of opinion about the whole question of integrity of authorship, and the fact that this has traversed the traditional distinctions between liberal and conservative scholarship tends to make the situation rather self-defeating in nature. However, in the light of what is now known about Near Eastern literary forms, it is possible to refute conclusively the arguments for diversity of authorship posited on the ground that the book contains two languages. The device whereby the main corpus of a literary composition was enclosed within a contrasting linguistic form so as to heighten the effect was commonly used in constructing single, integrated Mesopotamian compositions such as the Code of Hammurabi. Daniel, therefore, should be understood as a consciously composed literary unit involving Hebrew and Aramaic components. Further sophistication was added to the book by the fact that it was compiled in bifid form, as observed above.

VIII. Objections to Traditional Authorship.–*A. Prophecy*. Following Porphyry, many scholars have denied the possibility of a predictive element in prophecy, especially the sort of detailed narration found in Dnl. 8 and 11. However, a casual perusal of the OT literary prophets makes it abundantly clear that they were able on many occasions to predict the future, whether in general (cf. Dt. 18:9f.; Joel 2:28; Am. 9:11ff.; etc.) or more specific (cf. 1 K. 13:2; 2 K. 6:12; Mic. 5:2; etc.) terms. There is therefore no need to assume that the author was attempting to deceive his readers by a *vaticinium ex eventu*, and particularly where a gifted seer such as Daniel is concerned. The book makes it clear that the future destiny of the remnant was a matter of specific divine revelation to Daniel, much of which seemed to puzzle him at the time and leave him rather confused. If the work is actually a retrojection from Maccabean times, as has been claimed by many critics, it is not easy to see how the beleaguered Jews could have been encouraged by a narration of past history made to look like prophecy, as in ch. 8 and 11. Furthermore, since some of the apocalyptic sections were apparently beyond even the understanding of Daniel himself, it is hard to imagine that Maccabean Jews would have had any greater degree of insight or enlightenment, and consequent encouragement, since so many of the allusions are so cryptic as to defy precise explanation or identification, particularly in 11:30-45. Fortunately it is unnecessary to rationalize such issues, partly because OT prophecy as a phenomenon always contains futuristic elements, but also because the evidence from Qumrân absolutely precludes a Maccabean dating for any canonical OT literature, including the book of Daniel.

B. Historical Matters. Liberal scholars have commonly assumed Daniel to be replete with historical blunders, one of which is an anachronistic reference in Dnl. 1:1, as compared to the "true" historical situation represented by Jer. 25:1. Dnl. 1:1 refers to the third year of Jehoiakim, whereas Jeremiah speaks of the fourth year of Jehoiakim in such a way as to show that Nebuchadrezzar had not yet attacked Jerusalem (cf. Jer. 25:1; 46:2). From Jer. 25:1 it appears that the fourth year of Jehoiakim was the first year of Nebuchadrezzar. A closer examination will show that there is in fact no error in Daniel. Some have thought that the numeral in Daniel should be "six" instead of "three" (G. C. Aalders, *EQ*, 2 [1930], 244). Another suggested solution is to translate the verb "he set out," so that the verb would merely show that in the third year of Jehoiakim Nebuchadrezzar set out for Jerusalem. While this may be possible gramatically, cuneiform documents relating to this period indicate that in each year about this time Nebuchadrezzar actually made an expedition to the west. The correct answer is to be found in the realization that Daniel was using the Babylonian method of reckoning, whereby the first year of a king's reign was known as the year of his accession, the "second" year as his first, the "third" year as his second, and so on. If this were the case, when Daniel spoke of the third year of Jehioakim he would be referring to the same year as that which Jeremiah designated as the fourth year. It should also be noted that Daniel (cf. 9:2) had been studying the prophecy of Jeremiah concerning the end of the Exile (i.e., ch. 25). Consequently it would be strange if he had not paid attention to Jeremiah's designation of the fourth year. Daniel's mention of the third year must therefore be regarded as an incidental touch of authenticity.

Some scholars have thought that Dnl. 6:8 purported to place Darius I (522-486 B.C.) before Cyrus (539-530 B.C.) and make Xerxes the father of Darius I (cf. 9:1), a mistake which could be expected of a Maccabean author. This view ignores the fact that Daniel was speaking of Darius the Mede, a contemporary of Cyrus, who bore the same name as the later Persian ruler. Even if Daniel had been written in the Maccabean period, no learned Jewish scribe could possibly have committed so gross an error, particularly when a source such as Ezr. 4:5f. was available. Exception has also been taken to Daniel's designation of Nebuchadrezzar as king, when in actual fact he was then only crown prince. The term, however, is employed proleptically, as we today may speak of the childhood of President Washington.

Certain critics have also alleged that the mention of Belshazzar as king instead of Nabonidus was clear evidence of historical error, understandable in a Maccabean author but not if the book had been written in the 6th cent. B.C. The name Belshazzar has long been known from cuneiform sources, but instead of describing him as king the texts spoke of him predominantly as *mar šarri* (i.e., son of the king, crown prince), since Nabonidus was the actual king of Babylon. Nevertheless, one document, the so-called "Persian Verse" account of Nabonidus, does in fact state that Nabonidus had entrusted the kingship to his son Belshazzar, and that he himself made his dwelling in Teimā in Arabia. The cuneiform evidence also supports the view that Belshazzar did exercise regal functions. Oaths were taken in the name of both Nabonidus and Belshazzar; Belshazzar granted leases and issued commands. Both the names of Belshazzar and Nabonidus are mentioned in connection with the payment of the royal tribute. It should be noted further that the Aramaic word *malkā'* need not have the connotation of "monarch". In the ancient Near East, as attested by the Hittite documents, for example, there was a great king (*lu-gal-gal*) as well as kings of lesser stature (*lu-gal*). In the Assyrian inscriptions the king often spoke of rulers who were in subjection to him as "kings." This usage is fairly common, so that no legitimate objection can thereby be adduced against Daniel's designation. Technically, Belshazzar occupied a position in the kingdom subordinate to that of Nabonidus, but inasmuch as he was the person in regal status with whom the Jews had to deal, Daniel spoke of him quite properly as "king." This situation explains why Daniel ruled as a member of a governing triad (7:29), since the absentee Nabonidus was nowhere mentioned in the Daniel narratives.

It should be noted in passing that in ch. 8, where Nebuchadrezzar is designated the "father" of Belshazzar (who was actually the son of Nabonidus, as noted above), the term "father" is being used in the common oriental manner to describe an ancestor. The author displays his accurate knowledge of the 6th cent. B.C. almost coincidentally by depicting Nebuchadrezzar as an absolute monarch, able to make and change Babylonian law (2:12f., 46), whereas Darius the Mede was powerless to modify the laws of the Medes and Persians (6:8f.). He also reflected accurately the fact that capital punishment by fire under the Babylonians (ch. 3) was replaced by an alternative form under the Persians, who worshiped fire as a deity.

Perhaps the principal example of alleged historical inaccuracy in Daniel has been seen in the mention of "Darius the Mede." Thus, H. H. Rowley interpreted the reference to this man in terms of a thoroughly unhistorical conglomerate of several personages, including Gubaru, Gobryas, and Gaubaruva. Unfortunately his conclusions depended upon unreliable secondary sources; and had he perused carefully Sidney Smith's translation of the Nabonidus Chronicle, he would have been able to make an accurate distinction between two persons of similar name, Ugbaru and Gubaru. The former, the governor of Gutium, was the Gobryas mentioned by Xenophon, who apparently died shortly after Babylon was captured in 539 B.C., perhaps from wounds sustained in the attack. Gubaru later became governor of southern Babylonia under Cyrus, and seems to have held this position for fourteen years. Whitcomb has suggested very plausibly that Gubaru was the person mentioned in Daniel under the name of Darius the Mede. To date, however, there is no specific evidence which would show that he was a Mede, a descendant of Ahasuerus, or a man who was about sixty years of age. An alternative view, held by D. J. Wiseman, is that Darius is to be identified with Cyrus himself, who was related to the Medes. He was evidently about sixty-two years of age when he became king of Babylon, and according to inscriptions he appointed many subordinate governors. On this view it would be necessary to translate Dnl. 6:28, "in the reign of Darius, even in the reign of Cyrus the Persian." The title "Darius the Mede" thus becomes an alternative name for Cyrus the Persian, just as James VI of Scotland was also known regnally as James I of England. The weakness in this view is that Cyrus was not spoken of as the son of Ahasuerus in inscriptions. However, if that title was actually a designation of royalty rather than being a strict genealogical reference, it would be possible for either Gubaru or Cyrus to be regarded as Darius the Mede. In any case, it is known that in the tenth year of Nabonidus (546 B.C.), a cuneiform text at Harran referred specifically to the "king of the Medes," thus making it very clear that "Darius the Mede" was a real historical personage, whatever his true identity. *See also* CYRUS.

The account of Nebuchadrezzar's disease has also been urged as an instance of historical inaccuracy, since Neo-Babylonian sources did not refer to it. This latter situation is understandable, if only because of the fear that ancient Near Eastern peoples generally had of insanity. According to their superstitious beliefs, mental derangement was the result of demon possession, and the only way to deal with the condition was to deprive the sufferer of all normal contact with society. For such an affliction to overtake a Babylonian monarch was as unthinkable as it was unmentionable, and when the impossible actually occurred it was desirable for the matter to be mentioned only in the vaguest way some three centuries later by a Babylonian priest named Berossus, who preserved a tradition that Nebuchadrezzar became ill towards the end of his reign. A century later a writer named Abydenus concurred in this opinion, and the matter was also mentioned by Josephus (*CAp*. i.20). By contrast, the description in ch. 4 of Daniel is an objective account of a psychotic condition called *boanthropy*, which though rare does still occur. Persons afflicted in this way imagine themselves to be bulls or cows, and if not restrained will go on all fours eating grass and drinking water from pools or puddles. Since the Hebrews in Babylonia were under no obligation to remain silent about such an embarrassing situation as the madness of the king, there is little reason to doubt that the account was not merely factually accurate, but also contemporary in nature — especially if the chapter as a whole was a personal memoir of Nebuchadrezzar, originally written in Neo-Babylonian.

From the fourth Qumrân cave came a small papyrus document containing the Prayer of Nabonidus, which preserved a petition allegedly uttered by Nabonidus, who, when residing in exile from Babylon at an oasis named Teimā, "was smitten with a serious inflammation by command of the most high God." When he confessed his sin, a Jewish priest from the exiles in Babylonia furnished him with a partial understanding of the affliction. Liberal scholars have understood this material as having preserved an "older" tradition (i.e., older than the Maccabean period when, in their view, Daniel was supposed to have been written) in which Nabonidus rather than Nebuchadrezzar was the victim of an incapacitating disease. According to these scholars, the name of Nebuchadrezzar was substituted for Nabonidus long after the original story had been brought to Palestine, where the former was better known than Nabonidus.

This view bristles with difficulties. In the first instance, it is impossible to explain why the author of Daniel should have employed the material found in 4Q as the basis for ch. 4, and then have changed the entire nature of the disease as well as altering the names and the locale. Secondly, Palestinians were already familiar with the brutal way in which Nabonidus had established himself at Teimā, and were in no danger of confusing him at any time with Nebuchadrezzar. While Nabonidus had a reputation among Arab tribes for cruelty, there was never any tradition that he was mentally infirm. Finally, the Prayer of Nabonidus contains pathological aspects which even liberal scholars concede are unfamiliar to modern scientific medicine, whereas the Daniel account of Nebuchadrezzar's madness is a well-attested psychotic condition. Quite obviously two different traditions are involved here. The Daniel narrative describes concisely and objectively a recognizable clinical state, and forms part of a larger tradition that attributed madness to Nebuchadrezzar II. The Qumrân material seems to preserve an account of some ailment that overtook Nabonidus at Teimā, but because of certain unrealistic items in the narrative it can be regarded at the best as only folklore or legend, originating in the region of Teimā. The material is very closely related in form and content to the Prayer of Manasses, written between 250 and 150 B.C., and should be properly be regarded as yet another hitherto unknown part of the apocryphal material that accrued to Daniel. The Prayer of Nabonidus may well have been compiled by the Qumrân sectaries themselves, and could have been written as late as 100 B.C. Since this material has no connection, historical or otherwise, with Dnl. 4, it is extremely difficult to see how the Qumrân fragment could possibly underlie the Daniel account in any sense, even if both had originated in the Maccabean period.

Archeological excavations have gone far towards explaining why Nebuchadrezzar erected an image in the plain of Dura and compelled the people to worship before it. Apparently this procedure was part of a thoroughgoing reformation of religious calendars and cultic rites that Nebuchadrezzar instituted. Excavations at the ziggurat of Ur have shown that these reforms were aimed at making the rituals less priestly and esoteric by bringing them within physical range of public participation by the assembled worshippers. In particular the king, rather than the priests, was the representative of the god in congregational worship, and everybody was able to participate publicly in the ceremonies, regardless of rank or status. This was very meaningful for sixth-century B.C. Babylonia, but would have had no significance whatever for Maccabean Palestine. The foregoing and other answers to alleged inaccuracies merely serve to show that Maccabean Jews would never have accepted Daniel as Scripture had they been able to challenge successfully any part of its content on historical grounds; they would have rejected it as unworthy of inclusion in the canon, as they did with 1 Maccabees.

A different kind of objection is that the term "Chaldean" appears in Daniel in an ethnic and also a more restricted sense, this not being found elsewhere in the OT or in inscriptions. However, Herodotus (*ca.* 450 B.C.) in his *Persian Wars* consistently spoke of the Chaldeans in an ethnic manner, referred to them as priests, and accepted some of their traditions as going back to the early days of Cyrus. Furthermore, from the 10th cent. B.C., Assyrian annals used the term *Kaldu* to describe the "Sea-land" of earlier inscriptions and the people inhabiting that area. The latter were also mentioned in inscriptions from Ashurbanipal II (883-859 B.C.) and Adadnirari III (811-783 B.C.), as well as being referred to by Isaiah (23:13; 43:14). The usage of "Chaldean" in Daniel thus conforms with normal Near Eastern practices in this respect.

External evidence for a Maccabean origin of Daniel has been adduced from the absence of Daniel's name from the list of notables in Sir. 44:1ff. Since this material was in existence about 180 B.C., it has been suggested that Ben Sira knew nothing of Daniel or his book. This argument is curious, to say the least, in view of critical theories which aver that at that same time the sagas of Daniel were about to be written and received enthusiastically by the embattled Palestinian Jews. Furthermore, Ben Sira excluded not only Daniel from his list, but also Job, Ezra, Mordecai, Asa, Jehoshaphat, and others who were equally well known. Finally, the popularity of Daniel at Qumrân as shown by the MSS deposits there demonstrates the shallowness of such an objection.

C. Language. Another alleged impediment to traditional authorship is the presence in Daniel of names said to be those of Greek musical instruments, which would presumably indicate an origin in the Hellenistic period at the earliest. The terms concerned occur in Dnl. 3:5, 7, 10, 15, and are the harp (RSV "lyre"; NEB "zither"), the sakbut (RSV "trigon"; NEB "triangle") and the psaltery (RSV "harp"; NEB "dulcimer"). The first of these can be identified without difficulty with one of the numerous Near Eastern precursors of the Greek *kithára*, such as the elaborate harp uncovered by Sir Leonard Woolley at Ur. The sakbut was another variety of chordophone similar to or derived from the *sabitu* or seven-stringed lyre of the Akkadians. The "psaltery" was the Persian-Arabic *santir,* an early variety of dulcimer represented on first-millennium B.C. Assyrian reliefs and elsewhere. The term *sûmpōnyā',* formerly rendered "dulcimer" (RSV "bagpipe"; NEB "music") apparently is not an instrument at all, but a musical notation having the meaning of "in ensemble" or its general equivalent. Despite the fact that the instruments superficially appear to have Greek names, they are all in fact of specific Mesopotamian origin. It is possible, of course, that the designations of the above instruments as found in Daniel were modernizations of older names that had become obsolete, and as such were the work of later revising hands rather than of the original author. In the light of our present knowledge, this must be regarded at best as rather conjectural. What is evident, however, is that the Near Eastern peoples had enjoyed a prolonged tradition of music and singing for many centuries before the Greeks began to influence life in that area from the 7th cent. B.C. onward, and that the various genuine musical instruments in Daniel had already claimed familiar precursors long before that period.

In the Aramaic of Daniel there are apparently twenty loanwords of Persian origin, nearly half of which have been attested, mostly from Aramaic sources, as current between the 6th and 5th cents. B.C. It is now known from a variety of literary sources that Old Persian had a considerable effect upon Official Aramaic, and this resulted in the borrowing of a wide range of technical terms in the realms of civil and military administration, law, commerce, and the like, and their ultimate absorption and usage at a much more popular level. As observed above, all the Persian loanwords in Daniel are specifically Old Persian (which is found on inscriptions from the 6th and 5th cents. B.C.), indicating that the Aramaic of Daniel in this area is certainly pre-Hellenistic rather than Maccabean. This would hardly be surprising if the Aramaic came from the 6th or 5th cents. B.C., as the traditional view of authorship requires, but very much more difficult to explain if a later date of composition were contemplated.

IX. Interpretations.–Daniel contains revelations for the benefit of God's people and relates their future destiny to that of the great world powers. The theme is introduced in ch. 2, where Nebuchadrezzar has a dream in which he sees a great image. This colossus represents the four world powers that will be destroyed when the God of heaven erects a kingdom to occupy the entire world. In ch. 7 the same theme is reintroduced under the figure of beasts that arise from the sea. By means of judgment they are destroyed, and an eternal kingdom is erected, which belongs to a heavenly figure, "one like a son of man" (7:13). Although there are many interpretations of this symbolism, three call for particular mention. The four empires are identified as: (1) Babylon, Medo-Persia, Greece, and the Diadochi; or (2) Babylon, Media, Persia, and Greece; or (3) Babylon, Medo-Persia. Greece, and Rome. The second view has been held by those who challenged the essential trustworthiness of the book and assumed that the author committed a series of historical errors. The third view probably has the most to commend it, for it fits most harmoniously not only with the evidence presented in Daniel itself, but also with the remainder of Scripture. Around this scheme of the four world empires the rest of the book is constructed. Ch. 1 is an introduction, while chs. 3–5 deal with events that occurred while the first empire was in existence. Ch. 8 has to do with the second and third empires, and ch. 9 with the fourth. In ch. 9 there occurs the messianic prophecy of the seventy weeks (9:24-27). The final three chapters describe in some detail the vicissitudes of the people of God under the third kingdom.

Two main interpretative approaches have been adopted by conservative scholars. The first is to see the prophecies concerning the statue (2:31-49), the four beasts (7:2-27), and the seventy weeks (9:24-27) as culminating in the incarnation of Christ and the fulfilment of God's promise to Israel in the New Covenant, implemented in the blood of Christ. On this basis the reference in 9:27 would be to the destruction of Jerusalem in A.D. 70. The second view understands the prophecies as finding fulfilment in the second coming of Christ. On this interpretation the age of grace is dominated by some form of continuation of the Roman empire, culminating in the contemporaneous reign of ten kings (2:41-44; cf. Rev. 17:12) who are destroyed at Christ's second coming. At that time Christ will found His divine kingdom on earth (cf. Rev. 20:1-6), which will dominate the terrestrial scene (cf. Dnl. 2:35). The "other horn" of Dnl. 7:24ff. is identified with the antichrist whose power was derived from the four kingdoms and the ten kings, and this antichrist is destroyed by one "like unto a son of man" (Dnl. 7:13). In order for the seventy weeks to extend from the decree in 444 B.C. to rebuild Jerusalem to the time of the millennial kingdom it is necessary to assume an interval between the end of the sixty-ninth week and the beginning of the seventieth week.

Whatever interpretation of Daniel is adopted, the message of the book is that, though earthly kingdoms are but temporal and local, God will establish a regime which will be both universal and eternal, and will be implemented by the work of the Messiah (cf. Lk. 17:21).

X. Doctrines.–Daniel's theological perspective is similar to that of Ezekiel in many respects. With the eighth- and seventh-century B.C. prophets he was concerned with the divine lordship over both individuals and nations; he envisaged a destiny for Israel as God's elect; he looked for a decisive phase in the history of the chosen people in the coming of the Messiah, and held that the termination of the age was to be God's work rather than man's.

The angelology of Daniel closely resembles that of Ezekiel, for in both works there is an advance upon earlier ideas of impersonal divine agents. While both men would obviously have been aware of Babylonian beliefs about good and evil spirits as the agents of deities, there is no trace in either Ezekiel or Daniel of the specific mythological elements associated with the Babylonian figures. However, the description of angelic beings is occasionally vague in Daniel (cf. 8:15; 10:18), and certainly far removed from the elaborate speculations occurring in later Jewish apocalyptic works such as 1 Enoch. The visions in Daniel have often been described as "apocalyptic," and have been thought by some to have been influenced by Zoroastrianism. This latter is a characteristically dualistic religion in which two opposing cosmic powers, God and the evil one, battle for supremacy, resulting in God's ultimate overthrow of the evil one and supreme reign in an eternal age. While this view has certain elements in common with OT eschatology, the latter quite clearly placed the redemption of the elect in this world, while precluding by its consistent monism the very possibility of a religious or metaphysical dualism. Furthermore, the later Jewish apocalyptic writings were so passive ethically that they pronounced no divine judgment upon the people, thus standing in sharp contrast to the periodic denunciations by the canonical prophets generally. Daniel's apocalypticism is therefore characteristic of neither that attributed to Zoroastrianism nor that of later Judaism, and in consequence should be distinguished carefully from both. *See* APOCALYPTIC LITERATURE.

While his doctrine of resurrection was more developed than in the eschatology of the earlier prophets, Daniel still thought of the coming kingdom largely in material terms. In contrast to earlier expectations that Israel would be resurrected corporately (Hos. 6:1f.; Ezk. 37:11ff.), Daniel maintained that wicked and good alike would be raised (12:2). The materials for his doctrine can be found in Isa. 26:14, 21; 66:24; Ezk. 37:1-14; Job 14:12; 19:25; Hos. 6:2, as well as correlative ideas in 2 K. 4; 8:1-5; Isa. 26:19; Ps. 76:6 (MT 7); 127:2; Jer. 20:11; 23:40; etc. His thought, however, is by no means as advanced as that of the NT.

XI. Apocryphal Additions.–In the Greek translations of Daniel three or four pieces are added that are not found in the original Hebrew or Aramaic text as it has come down to us. These are the Prayer of Azariah, the Song of the Three Young Men, Susanna, and Bel and the Dragon. These additions have all been rejected from the canon by the Protestant churches because they are not contained in the Hebrew canon. In the Church of England they are "read for example of life and instruction of manners." The SONG OF THE THREE YOUNG MEN was "ordered in the rubric of the first Prayer Book of Edward VI (A.D. 1549) to be used in Lent as a responsory to the OT Lesson at the Morning Prayer." It contains the Prayer of Azariah from the midst of the fiery furnace and the song of praise by the three children for their deliverance, the latter being couched largely in phrases borrowed from Ps. 148. SUSANNA presents the story of a virtuous woman's resistance of the seductive attempts of two judges of the elders of the people, whose machinations were exposed through the wisdom of Daniel. Daniel convicted them of false witness by the evidence of their own mouths, so that they were put to death according to the law of Moses, and from that day Daniel was held in great reputation in the sight of the people. BEL AND THE DRAGON contains three stories. The first relates how Daniel destroyed the image of Bel that Nebuchadrezzar worshiped, showing by means of ashes strewn on the floor of the temple that the offerings to Bel were devoured by the priests who came secretly into the temple by night. The second tells how Daniel killed a dragon by throwing lumps of mingled pitch, fat, and hair into his mouth, causing the dragon to burst asunder. The third gives a detailed account of the lions' den, stating that there were seven lions and that Daniel lived in the den six days, being sustained by broken bread and pottage delivered to him by a prophet Habakkuk, who was carried there by the hair of his head by an angel of the Lord.

Bibliography.–Comms. by M. Stuart (1850); K. A. Auberlen (1854); T. Kliefoth (1868); C. F. Keil (1877); A. A. Bevan (1892); G. Behrmann (1894); S. R. Driver (*CBSC*, 1922); J. A. Montgomery (*ICC*, 1927); R. H. Charles (1929); E. J. Young (1949); H. C. Leupold (1949); A. Bentzen (2nd ed. 1952); E. W. Heaton (1956); N. W. Porteous (1962).

E. W. Hengstenberg, *Authenticity of Daniel and the Integrity of Zechariah* (1848); E. B. Pusey, *Daniel the Prophet* (1891); S. R. Driver, *Intro. to the Literature of the OT* (1913); R. D. Wilson, *Studies in the Book of Daniel*, I (1917), II (1938); C. Boutflower, *In and Around the Book of Daniel* (1923); R. P. Dougherty, *Nabonidus and Belshazzar* (1929); H. H. Rowley, *Darius the Mede and the Four World Empires in the Book of Daniel* (1935); P. Mauro, *The Seventy Weeks and the Great Tribulation* (1944); O. T. Allis, *Prophecy and the Church* (1945); C. Lattey, *Book of Daniel* (1948); H. L. Ginsberg, *Studies in the Book of Daniel* (1948); E. J. Young, *Book of Daniel* (1949); S. B. Frost, *OT Apocalyptic* (1952); E. J. Young, *Messianic Prophecies of Daniel* (1954); R. D. Culver, *Daniel and the Latter Days* (1954); J. T. Milik, *RB*, 63 (1956), 407; D. J. Wiseman, *Chronicles of the Chaldean Kings* (1956); D. N. Freedman, *BASOR*, 145 (Feb. 1957), 31f.; E. J. Young, *Daniel's Vision of the Son of Man* (1958); J. C. Whitcomb, *Darius the Mede* (1959); D. J. Wiseman, *et al., Notes on Some Problems in the Book of Daniel* (1956); R. K. Harrison, *Intro. to the OT* (1969).

R. K. HARRISON

DANITES dan'īts [Heb. *haddānî*, *bᵉnê-ḏān*]; AV also "the children of Dan"; NEB also "the tribe of Dan." Term for those belonging to the tribe of Dan in Josh. 19:47; Jgs. 1:34; 13:2; 18:1ff.; 1 Ch. 12:35.

DAN-JAAN dan-jā'ən [Heb. *dān ya'an*; Gk. *Danidan kaí Oudan*] (2 S. 24:6, AV); RSV "to Dan and from Dan"; NEB "Dan and Iyyon." A place name listed in the itinerary of Joab and the commanders of the army as they carried out David's orders to take a census of the people of Israel. It was identified by Keil and Delitzsch as a city named Dan SW of Damascus, mentioned in Gen. 14:14. More recently two other suggestions have been favored, each of which involves emending the text. The suggestion of Klostermann that it be read "toward Dan and Ijon" (cf. 1 K. 15:20) has been followed by the NEB. From the fact that the LXX includes the name "Dan" more than once S. R. Driver suggested "to Dan and from Dan," a reading that has been adopted by the RSV and others.

Bibliography.–Comms. on 2 Samuel by A. Klostermann (1887); KD; S. R. Driver (2nd rev. ed. 1913).

D. H. MADVIG

DANNAH dan'ə [Heb. *dannâ*; Gk. *Renna*]. A city in the hill country of Judah (Josh. 15:49) between Socoh and Kiriath-sepher (Debir). Its location is uncertain but it is probably to be identified with Idhna — the Iedna of Eusebius *Onom*. — about midway between Hebron and Beit Jibrîn.

J. F. PREWITT

DAPHNE daf'nē [Gk. *Daphnē*–'bay-tree'] (2 Macc. 4:33). A suburb of Antioch on the Orontes, about 5 mi. (8 km.) SW of the city, now a part of Turkey. Here were the famous groves and sanctuary of Apollo, which owed their origin to Seleucus Nicator (306-280 B.C.). It was a place of great natural beauty, and the Seleucid kings spared no outlay in adding to its attractions.

In this part of Syria the limestone is fissured, containing underground caverns and reservoirs in which the water collects that falls during the winter rainy season. Faults in the limestone produce springs which flow all year, as was especially true of the plateau of Daphne. This plateau, roughly square in shape and measuring about 2000 yds. (1830 m.) on a side, averaged in altitude about 300 ft. (90 m.) above the level of the city. As a result, water from its springs could easily be carried by gravity through aqueducts to the city. In ancient times, five springs served the double function of watering the surface of the Daphne plateau and supplying water for Antioch.

The pleasure garden of Daphne was 10 mi. (16 km.) in circumference. It was famous for its laurel trees, old cypresses, flowing and gushing waters, its shining temple of Apollo, and its magnificent festival of the tenth of August. At the center of Daphne stood an agora with baths and temples. The streets were laid out on a regular grid plan and were lined with spacious houses. At the south edge of the suburb gushed ever-flowing springs; the temple of Apollo stood at the foot of the springs. Nearby was the Olympic stadium.

Daphne gained an evil repute for immorality, as witnessed by the proverbial "Daphnic morals." Juvenal, a Roman satirical poet writing in the 2nd cent. A.D., scored his society for its decadent morals and complained:

> Obscene Orontes, diving underground
> Conveys his wealth to Tiber's hungry shores
> And fattens Italy with foreign whores.

The precincts enjoyed the right of asylum. Hither fled Onias the high priest (171 B.C.) from the wrath of Menelaus whom he had offended by plain speech. To the disgust and indignation of Jew and Gentile alike, he was lured from the sanctuary by Andronicus and basely put to death (2 Macc. 4:33-38).

The decline of Daphne dates from the days of Christian ascendency. The place is still luxuriant with wild vegetation, but nothing now remains to suggest its former splendor. Engineers have even tapped the water supply of the area in such a way as to stop the surface flow of the springs and the beautiful waterfalls.

W. EWING   H. F. VOS

DAPPLED [Heb. *bārōḏ*] (Zec. 6:3, 6); AV GRISLED. The horses pulling the fourth chariot in Zechariah's vision were apparently dappled or spotted in their coloring; cf. Gen. 31:10, 12, where the RSV renders "mottled."

DARA. *See* DARDA.

DARDA där'də [Heb. *darda'*] (1 K. 4:31); **DARA** dâr'ə [Heb. *dāra'*] (1 Ch. 2:6, where some Hebrew MSS also read *darda'*); NEB DARDA. One of the wise men to whom Solomon was compared. He was one of the sons of Zerah son of Judah, and as a musician was included in the orchestral guild ("sons of Mahol").

See W. F. Albright, *ARI*, pp. 127f., 210.

DARIC dar'ik [Heb. *darkᵉmôn*, *'aḏarkôn*; Gk. *dareikós*]; AV DRAM; NEB also DRACHMA. A Persian gold coin, the first to be mentioned in the Bible. The first form of the word occurs in 1 Ch. 29:7; Ezr. 2:69; Neh. 7:70ff., the second in Ezr. 8:27. The name was supposedly a shortened form of the name of the Persian ruler Darius I Hystaspes (521-486 B.C.), who was thought to have introduced the gold coin into Persia after the wars against Lydia. However, the name may go back to an ancient Assyrian unit of weight *darag mana*, one sixtieth of a mina. Since coinage had not been invented in David's time, the reference in 1 Ch. 29:7 is to an equivalent in use at the time the Chronicler was compiling his work.

See also MONEY.

DARIUS də-rī'əs [Heb. and Aram. *dārᵉyāweš*; Old Pers. *darayavahuš*]. The name of three rulers mentioned in the OT.

1. Darius "the Mede." A ruler of this name is said in Dnl. 5:30 to have taken control of the Neo-Babylonian empire ("the realm of the Chaldeans," Dnl. 9:1) immediately after the death of Belshazzar. It was this Darius who, according to Dnl. 6, had Daniel thrown into the den of lions (vv. 7-18) and who ultimately issued a decree that all in his kingdom should "tremble and fear before the God of Daniel" (vv. 25-27).

Many have denied the existence of such a ruler, believing his name to have been created by the author of Daniel under the mistaken impression that an independent Median kingdom intervened between the Neo-Babylonian and the Persian empires. Cuneiform inscriptions show that Cyrus II ("the Great") was the immediate successor of Nabonidus and Belshazzar, the last of the Neo-Babylonian rulers.

This skepticism is unnecessary, however, since two alternative explanations of the identity of Darius the Mede have recently been offered. The first (see Whitcomb) is that he was in fact Gubaru, the governor of Babylon and the region Beyond the River (Abar-nahara), exercising virtually royal powers in Babylon and hence not improperly called "king" (Dnl. 6). (This Gubaru is not to be confused with Ugbaru [Gobryas], the governor of Gutium who captured Babylon for Cyrus but died three weeks later.) The second explanation (see Wiseman, Bulman) is that "Darius the Mede" was merely an alternative title for Cyrus the Persian. Dnl. 6:28 must then be translated, as is legitimate: "So this Daniel prospered during the reign of Darius, namely the reign of Cyrus the Persian."

2. Darius I Hystaspes (521-486 B.C.), the Great. Darius' autobiography, the text of which is carved in the rock at Behistun and known also to the Greek historian Herodotus (iii.30f., 61ff.), told the story of his rise to power thus: while Cambyses, son and successor of Cyrus the Great, was conquering Egypt, a usurper named Gaumata arose in Media, claiming to be Bardiya, Cambyses' brother, who had in fact been murdered by Cambyses. In July 522 B.C. Gaumata took the throne for himself, but on Sept. 29 of that year Darius led a conspiracy that overthrew Gaumata and seized the throne for himself. He omits to mention that he had no real title to the kingship, being only the cousin of Cambyses, but stresses that he came from a long line of royal ancestors.

Much of Darius' reign was spent in conquests and in quelling revolts in various parts of his empire. During his early years as emperor he had to deal with revolts in Persia, Media, Babylonia, and the East. He claimed that during the first two years of his reign he defeated nine kings in nineteen battles. Lengthier campaigns in-

Impression of agate cylinder seal, showing Darius I hunting. The inscription gives his name and title ("Great King") in Old Persian, Elamite, and Babylonian (Thebes, 521-486 B.C.) (Trustees of the British Museum)

Achaemenean dynasty tombs at Naqsh-i-Rustum: (from left) Darius I, Artaxerxes I, and Darius II (Oriental Institute, University of Chicago)

cluded that against the Scythians (*ca.* 512 B.C.), which involved him in the capture of Thrace and Macedonia. Of even greater importance were his conflicts with the Greeks. After the revolt of the Greek cities of the Ionian coast (*ca.* 500 B.C.) and their final subjugation (494 B.C.), Darius embarked upon a punitive campaign against the states of mainland Greece who had aided the Ionians. His first expedition (492 B.C.) was turned back by a storm, but on his second expedition he came within 20 mi. (32 km.) of Athens, where however he was decisively defeated by the Athenians at the battle of Marathon (490 B.C.). The third Persian expedition against Greece was undertaken by his son and successor Xerxes I.

Darius' most significant contact with the Jews occurred, according to the biblical account (Ezr. 5–6), in connection with the rebuilding of the Jerusalem temple. In 520 B.C., Darius' second year, the Jews, inspired by the prophets Haggai and Zechariah, resumed work on the still unfinished temple. The provincial governor Tattenai (Ezr. 5:3), suspicious that the temple work might prove to be a military fortification, reported the matter to Darius, along with the Jews' claim that the rebuilding had been authorized by Cyrus (v.13). Darius had the relevant decree of Cyrus located in the Ecbatana archives (6:2), reissued it with his own authority, and appended to it generous provisions for the maintenance of the temple worship (vv. 6-12). With both prophetic and royal encouragement, the temple builders increased their efforts, and the work was completed in Darius' sixth year (March, 515 B.C.).

Darius' achievements made him a worthy successor to Cyrus the Great. His organization of the satrapal system of imperial government remained definitive, and his rebuilding projects at Persepolis and elsewhere, some of which still remain, left behind him a worthy monument.

See Map XII; Plates 1, 5.

3. Darius "the Persian." A king of this name is mentioned in Neh. 12:22, in a chapter that contains a collection of lists of priests and Levites from various periods in postexilic times. If the reign of Darius is intended to be contemporaneous with the high-priesthood of the last-mentioned priest, Jaddua, the simplest identification of the king is Darius III Codomannus (336-331 B.C.), for Josephus reports that Jaddua was the high priest at the time of Alexander the Great (332 B.C.) (*Ant.* xi.8.4f.). This identification is complicated by the possibility that there may have been two high priests named Jaddua in the 5th and 4th cents. B.C., in which case the king may have been Darius II Nothus (423-404 B.C.). There is some evidence that the lists of this chapter have been brought up to date at various points, so it is difficult to decide which Darius is intended. Some scholars, believing the word translated "until" (*'al*) to be a slight scribal error for "from" (*mē'al*), have even thought the Darius in question to be Darius I.

Bibliography.–*Darius the Mede:* H. H. Rowley, *Darius the Mede and the Four World Empires in the Book of Daniel* (1953); J. C. Whitcomb, *Darius the Mede: A Study in Historical Identification* (1959); D. J. Wiseman, *et al., Notes on Some Problems in the Book of Daniel* (1965), pp. 9-16; J. M. Bulman, *WTJ,* 35 (1973), 247-267.

Darius I: A. T. Olmstead, *History of the Persian Empire* (1948), pp. 107-150, 162-213; *AJSL,* 51 (1935), 247-49; R. N. Frye, *Heritage of Persia* (1966), pp. 113-143. D. J. A. CLINES

DARK; DARKNESS [Heb. *ḥōšeḵ* (vb. *ḥāšaḵ*), *maḥšāḵ* ("dark place" in Ps. 74:20), *ḥ[a]šēḵâ*, *'ōpel*, *'[a]pēlâ*, *ma'[a]pēl* (Josh. 24:7), *ma'pēlyâ* (Jer. 2:31), *'[a]rāpel* ("thick [deep] darkness"), *ṣalmāweṯ* ("deep darkness"), *'[a]lāṭâ* (Gen. 15:17; Ezk. 12:6f., 12), *'êpâ* (Am. 4:13; Job 11:17, emended), *šāḥōr* (Cant. 1:5), vbs. *qāḏar*, *ṣālal* (Neh. 13:19); Aram. *ḥ[a]šôḵ* (Dnl. 2:22); Gk. *skotía*, *skótos*, *skoteinós*, *skotízomai*, *skotóomai* (Rev. 16:10), *auchmērós* (2 Pet. 1:19)]; AV also SHADOW OF DEATH (*ṣalmāweṯ*), TWILIGHT (Ezk. 12:6f., 12), NIGHT (Job 26:10), BLACKISH (6:16), BLACK (Cant. 1:5), "privily" (*b[e]mô 'ōpel*, Ps. 11:2), "thou shalt shine forth" (Job 11:17, *tā'upâ*), and cf. Job 24:14; Ps. 139:12; NEB also DUSK (*'[a]lāṭâ*) and other occasional variants from RSV (e.g., "dark as death" in Isa. 9:2, "darkness of death" in Ps. 44:19 [MT 20], for *ṣalmāweṯ*).

In the Bible the main use of darkness is in contrast to light (*see* DAY AND NIGHT). Light is the symbol of God's purity, wisdom, and glory. Darkness is the opposite.

Miraculous occurrence of darkness in the land of Egypt for three days is recorded in Ex. 10:21f., and there was darkness at the death of Christ (Mt. 27:45). *See* PLAGUES OF EGYPT.

The figurative uses of darkness are many and various. It is used as a symbol (a) of moral depravity and its punishment: the wicked walk and work in darkness (Ps. 82:5; Prov. 2:13; Jn. 3:19; Rom. 13:12), and their reward is to "sit in darkness" (Ps. 107:10) or to be "cast forth into the outer darkness" (Mt. 8:12); (b) of things mysterious or inexplicable (1 K. 8:12; Ps. 97:2); (c) of trouble and affliction (2 S. 22:29; Job 5:14; Prov. 20:20; Isa. 9:2; cf. Gen. 15:12); (d) of punishment (Lam. 3:2; Ezk. 32:8; Zeph. 1:15); (e) of death (1 S. 2:9; Job 10:21f.; Eccl. 11:8); (f) of nothingness (Job 3:4-6); (g) of human ignorance (Job 19:8; 1 Jn. 2:11).

"A dark place" in 2 Pet. 1:19 refers especially to the state of things described in ch. 2.

See also GLOOM. A. H. JOY

DARK SAYINGS [Heb. *ḥîḏôṯ*] (Ps. 78:2); NEB RIDDLE. The Hebrew term is elsewhere rendered "dark speech" (Nu. 12:8), "riddle," or "proverb" by the RSV; but the AV renders "dark sayings" also in Ps. 49:4 (MT 5); Prov. 1:6; Dnl. 8:23.

In the heading to the canonical book of Proverbs, the general term "proverbs" is made to include a PROVERB (Heb. *māšāl*), a figure (or, an interpretation, Heb. *m^elîṣâ*), the words (Heb. sing. *dāḇār*) of the wise, and their dark sayings or riddles. The words "proverb," "figure," "dark saying," and "riddle" are frequently interchangeable with only slight variations of meaning. The proverb is either a saying current among the people (cf. 1 S. 10:12; "the proverb of the ancients," 24:13) or a sentence of ethical wisdom composed by the order of wise men (Heb. *ḥ^akāmîm*). Of the latter kind are the maxims of the wisdom literature (chiefly Proverbs but also Job, Ecclesiastes, and among the uncanonical writings, Ecclesiasticus). This kind of wise saying was in vogue among the neighbors of Israel, in Edom, and among other people. Wise men existed in Israel at a very early period, and we find the prophets alluding to them. But the Hebrew proverb was often of a more elaborate character, corresponding to our parables; frequently a vein of taunt ran through them, and they played an important part in compositions directed against other nations (cf. Nu. 21:27). The prophets were fond of employing this kind of literary production; with them the proverb became a figure or allegorical discourse (cf. Ezk. 21:5ff.).

The proverb in the sense of a didactic poem occurs in the Psalms (49 and 78). Here wisdom, parable, and dark saying are all used interchangeably. The dark saying may be said to be the popular riddle (cf. Jgs. 14) raised to the dignity of elaborate production. It is an allegorical sentence requiring interpretation, and both prophets and psalmists used this form. The word of God came to the prophet in the form of a vision (cf. the visions of Amos or Jeremiah), i.e., the truth presented itself to them in the form of a simile. To a prophet such as Moses the revelation came directly as clear truth without the mediation of figures of speech or obscure utterances which require interpretation: "mouth to mouth, clearly, and not in dark speech" (Nu. 12:8; cf. Jer. 23:28). Paul distinguishes between the childish manner of speaking of spiritual things and the manner of a man: "For now we see through a glass, darkly [Gk. *en ainígmati,* "in a riddle"]; but then face to face" (1 Cor. 13:12, AV).

The use of riddle was very widespread among ancient peoples, and we know that Orientals especially were fond of this form. It was a literary device involving a matching of wits. The art of propounding riddles was a highly esteemed practice in the OT (Jgs. 14:12; Ezk. 17:2; 1 K. 10:1). The classical biblical example of the riddle is the one spoken by Samson in Jgs. 14, and its setting may be typical. At his wedding feast, as a game with stakes, Samson proposes his riddle (v. 14): "out of the eater came something to eat, out of the strong came something sweet." So unusual was Samson's find of honey in the carcass of a lion that his guests could not answer until Samson's wife divulged the secret of the riddle. However, the riddle was used not merely as a game but often as a test of wisdom. Solomon's renown rested largely upon his skill in solving riddles. "Now when the queen of Sheba heard of the fame of Solomon . . . she came to test him with hard questions [lit. "riddles"] . . . and Solomon answered all her questions" (1 K. 10:1-5; 2 Ch. 9:1-14). We read in Prov. 1:5f. that it is the wise who deal in riddles, and the skill in understanding them is wisdom (cf. Ps. 49:1-4). Riddles became a deposit of tradition and lore, "dark sayings from of old . . . that our fathers have told us" (Ps. 78:1-4). The riddle was one of the media by which God was thought to reveal Himself. Of Daniel it was said (Dnl. 5:12): "an excellent spirit, knowledge, and understanding to interpret dreams, explain riddles and solve problems were found in this Daniel."

L. HUNT

DARKLY (1 Cor. 13:12, AV). *See* DARK SAYINGS; DIM.

DARKON där'kon [Heb. *darqôn*–'carrier']. Ancestor of a subdivision of "Solomon's servants," so called in postexilic times (Ezr. 2:56; Neh. 7:58; called Lozon in 1 Esd. 5:33).

DARLING [Heb. *ša'^ašû'îm*] (Jer. 31:20); AV PLEASANT; NEB "in whom I delight"; [*'aḥaṯ*] (Cant. 6:9); AV "only one"; NEB "only child." The term "darling" is used by the RSV for Heb. *ša'^ašû'îm* (lit. "pleasure," "delight") and *aḥaṯ* (lit. "only") in a poetic sense as an object of love and affection. In Ps. 22:20 (MT 21); 35:17 the AV uses "darling" to render Heb. *yāḥîḏ* (lit. "only"), more correctly rendered "life" by the RSV and "precious life" by the NEB.

DART (noun) [Heb. *šēḇeṭ*] (2 S. 18:14); NEB "stout stick"; [*massā'*] (Job 41:26); NEB DAGGER; [Gk. *bélos*] (Eph. 6:16); NEB ARROWS. *Šēḇeṭ*, with the usual meaning of "staff" or "rod," is used of a weapon in 2 S. 18:14. *Massā'*, a rare word still unexplained, probably designated some sort of hand weapon. The Greek term *bélos* was used metaphorically of a missile aimed at a Christian.

See also WEAPONS OF WAR.

DASH [Heb. *šāḇar* (Dt. 7:5; 12:3), *rāṭaš* (2 K. 8:12; Isa. 13:16; Hos. 10:14; 13:16; Nah. 3:10), *nāpaṣ* (Ps. 2:9; 137:9; Jer. 13:14), *nāgap* (Ps. 91:12), *bāqa'* (2 Ch. 25:12), pilpel of *pāṣaṣ* (Job 16:12); Gk. *rhḗgnymi* (Mk. 9:18), *edaphízō* (Lk. 19:44)]; AV also BREAK, BREAK DOWN, TEAR, SHAKE (Job 16:12), LAY EVEN (Lk. 19:44); NEB also BREAK, SHATTER, STRIKE, WORRY (Job 16:12), "bring to the ground" (Lk. 19:44). The term "dash" usually has the idea of "throw violently" or "strike" with purpose of causing destruction. However, in Ps. 91:12 it means "strike against accidentally" (cf. Mt. 4:6; Lk. 4:11). "Dash" is often connected with the inflicting of punishment, which is usually expressed by *rāṭaš* ("dash to the ground"), *nāpaṣ* ("smash"), or *šāḇar* ("break"). The Gk. *edaphízō* is used in Lk. 19:44 with the meaning of "dash to the ground," while *rhḗgnymi* means "tear to pieces."

DATES. *See* PALM TREE.

DATHAN dā'thən [Heb. *dāṯān*; cf. Akk. *datnu*–'strong']. The son of Eliab the son of Pallu the son of Reuben (Nu. 26:5ff.; Dt. 11:6; Ps. 106:17). He and his brother Abiram, with others, followed Korah the Levite in disputing the authority of Moses and Aaron in the wilderness (Nu. 16f.; 26; Dt. 11:6; Ps. 106:17). Other followers of Korah perished by fire before the tent of meeting, but Dathan and Abiram, with their families and their goods, were swallowed up by the earth at their tents. *See* KORAH. W. J. BEECHER

DATHEMA dath'ə-mə [Gk. *Dathema*] (1 Macc. 5:9; cf. v. 29). A fortress in Gilead to which the Jews fled for refuge from the Gentiles. The ensuing siege was broken by Judas Maccabeus and Jonathan his brother. It was within a night's march from Bosora. *GAB* suggests Tell Hamad as a possible site, E of Carnaim. Because of the easy confusion of the letter *daleth* for *resh*, the suggestion of Tell er-Ramet must also be considered (*Macmillan Bible Atlas*, map 189; cf. *HGHL*, p. 616). W. S. L. S.

DAUB [Heb. *ṭû(a)ḥ* (Ezk. 13:10f.; 22:28), *ḥāmar* (Ex. 2:3)]. NEB also PLASTER (Ezk. 13:12), "make watertight" (Ex. 2:3). "To daub" always has the meaning "to cover," "to smear with" in the Scriptures. Ezekiel compares the flatteries of the false prophets to a slight wall covered with whitewash (lit. "spittle").

DAUGHTER [Heb. *baṯ*; Gk. *thygátēr*, also *thygátrion* ("little daughter," Mk. 5:23; 7:25)]; NEB also GIRL (Gen. 34:8, 17; Ex. 1:16, 22), WOMAN (Gen. 36:39; Ex. 2:1; Nu. 36:8; Hos. 1:3), YOUNG WOMAN (Dnl. 11:17), PEOPLE (Isa. 23:10; Jer. 49:4; Lam. 2:11), CITY (Isa. 23:12), SUPPLICANTS (Zeph. 3:10), NATIVE PEOPLE (Jer. 46:19), NATIVES (Jer. 48:18), VILLAGES (Jer. 49:3), CHILD (Jer. 31:22; Mk. 7:30).

Baṯ is also variously translated in the RSV "granddaughter" (2 K. 8:26; 2 Ch. 2:3), "princess" (Ps. 45:13 [MT 14]; Jer. 43:6), "maiden(s)" (Cant. 7:1 [MT 2]; Lam. 3:51), "women" (Gen. 27:46; 28:1, 8; 30:13), "inhabitant(s)" (Jer. 46:19; 48:18), "villages" (Jer. 49:2). Contrary to the AV, the RSV and NEB construe *baṯ* as part of the proper name "Bathshua" in 1 Ch. 2:3. Similarly, the NEB translates "Bath-gallim" in Isa. 10:30. The RSV translates *baṯ-bᵉlîyā'al* (1 S. 1:16) as "base woman," while the AV renders "daughter of Belial." In 1 S. 18:28 the RSV follows the LXX reading *pas Israēl* ("all Israel"), while the AV and NEB retain the meaning of the MT *mîḵal baṯ-šā'ûl* ("Michal the daughter of Saul"). The difficult *baṯ gᵉḏûḏ* (Mic. 5:1 [MT 4:14]) is translated literally "daughter of troops" by the AV, while the RSV and NEB use the LXX noun *phragmós* ("wall"), translating respectively "you are walled about with a wall" and "you people of a walled city." The AV "daughters" (*tékna*) of 1 Pet. 3:6 is rendered more literally "children" by the RSV. In a number of cases the NEB simply omits the word *baṯ* from its translation (e.g., Gen. 38:12; 2 Ch. 11:21; Ps. 137:8; Isa. 1:8; Jer. 8:11, 19, 21f.; Lam. 3:48; Zec. 2:7 [MT 11]).

In the great majority of cases, "daughter(s)" is used in the Bible in a context of immediate familial relationship. This may occur in genealogical listings (e.g., Gen. 5; 11; 2 S. 3:3), narratives (e.g., Gen. 29; 34; 1 S. 18; Mt. 14:6; Lk. 8:42), and direct discourse (e.g., Gen. 20:12; Ruth 3; Mt. 9:18; Acts 7:21). A frequent secondary usage of the term is generic. This occurs predominantly in texts with a legal character (e.g., Ex. 20:10; 21:7, 31; Lev. 18; Dt. 13:6; cf. Ezk. 44:25), but also in prophetic speech (e.g., Ezk. 14:20; 16:45; Mic. 7:6; Joel 2:28; cf. Acts 2:17), proverbial material (Prov. 30:13; cf. Ez. 16:44), and psalms (Ps. 45:9f. [MT 10f.]; 106:38).

The plural "daughters" may be used figuratively as a "personification of a city, a land, or a people, etc." (BDB, p. 123). This usage has the sense of all the (female) residents of a particular region. W. F. Stinespring (*Encounter,* 26 [1965], 133-141) has shown that the singular "daughter" is also used as an appositional genitive with certain nouns (most frequently "Zion," less often "my people," "Chaldeans," "Jerusalem," "Edom," "Babylon," "Judah," "Tyre"). Such a personification should be given translations such as "maiden Zion" or "my darling people," instead of "daughter of Zion" (cf. RSV, Isa. 10:32; 16:1; Jer. 4:31; Lam. 1:6; Mic. 1:11; Zec. 2:10; Jn. 12:15; etc.) or "daughter of my people" (e.g., Jer. 6:26; 14:17). Stinespring points out that only Moffatt's translation employs this understanding; his rendering of Isa. 47:5 is a classic example: "Sit silent in the dark, lady Chaldaea! Never again shall you be queen, a mistress over realms." *See also* DAUGHTER OF ZION.

The sociological and economic situations of daughters in ancient Israel are summarized in *TDOT*, II, *s.v.* "bath," II (H. Haag). C. MABEE

DAUGHTER OF ZION [Heb. *baṯ ṣîyôn* (2 K. 19:21; Ps. 9:14 [MT 15]; Cant. 3:11; Isa. 3:17; 16:1; 52:2; Jer. 4:31; 6:2, 23; Lam. 2:1ff.; Mic. 4:8, 10, 13; Zeph. 3:14; Zec. 2:10 [MT 14]; 9:9; etc.); Gk. *thygátēr Siōn* (Mt. 21:5; Jn. 12:15)]. A phrase that occurs frequently in the OT as a synonym for Jerusalem and its people, since Jerusalem was built on Mt. Zion. The phrase was sometimes used only of the women, but it could also refer to the whole population of the city. The people were regarded as belonging to the city as children belong to their parents. Cf. "daughters of Judah" (Ps. 97:8) and "daughters of the Philistines" (Ezk. 16:27).

See also DAUGHTER.

DAUGHTER-IN-LAW. *See* RELATIONSHIPS, FAMILY.

DAVID dā'vid [Heb. *dāwiḏ*; Gk. *Dauid, Daueid, Dad,* NT *Dabid*]. The second and greatest king of Israel, whose dynasty ruled in Judah for over four hundred years.

I. Background and Youth
   A. Name
   B. Genealogy
   C. His Youth
   D. His Anointing
   E. Meets Saul
   F. Defeats Goliath
   G. At Saul's Court
   H. Flees from the Court
   I. As a Fugitive
   J. As a Philistine Vassal
II. Reign
   A. King in Hebron
   B. Defeats the Philistines
   C. Capture of Jerusalem
   D. Jerusalem as Capital
   E. Consolidation and Expansion
   F. David and Bathsheba
   G. David's Sons
   H. Amnon and Absalom
   I. Absalom's Rebellion

J. Absalom's Defeat and Death
K. Sheba's Revolt
L. Famine and Plague
III. Last Years
A. The Succession Question
B. David's Death
C. Duration of Reign
IV. Administration and Character
A. Administrative Measures
B. Ability and Character

I. Background and Youth.–*A. Name.* The name "David" would appear to be connected with the Hebrew verbal root *d-w-d*, "to love." "David," then, would mean "beloved," presumably by Yahweh. Indeed, the name may well be an abbreviated form of Heb. *dōḏāwāhû* (cf. 2 Ch. 20:37) or of *dōḏîyāhû* (unattested). The Mari texts present a form *dawidum* (if the reading is correct, which is not certain), which would probably indicate a troop commander or brigand chief; the parallel with David's erstwhile position and activities, when based on the cave of Adullam, needs no emphasizing.

It is quite possible that "David" was a throne name. The king's personal name, in that case, may well have been Elhanan, who in 2 S. 21:19 is credited with killing Goliath. However, the parallel passage in 1 Ch. 20:5 credits Elhanan with the death of Goliath's brother. Both texts are corrupt, but the phrase in 2 Samuel can plausibly be emended to read "Elhanan the son of Jesse the Bethlehemite." A. M. Honeyman argues thus, and proposes to equate Elhanan ("God has been gracious") with Baal-hanan ("Baal [or "the lord"] has been gracious"), the king of Edom mentioned in Gen. 36:38f. (par. 1 Ch. 1:49f.). It is tempting, to be sure, to equate Samlah of the preceding verses with Samuel, and Shaul with Saul (the latter two names are identical in Hebrew), while Baal-hanan's successor Hadad (1 Ch. 1:50; Hadar in Gen. 36:39) is very probably the Edomite prince who caused Solomon some trouble (1 K. 11:14). But the names of Baal-hanan's father (Achbor) and of Shaul's city (Rehoboth by the Euphrates) seriously conflict with Honeyman's theory.

B. Genealogy. David was the youngest of the eight sons of Jesse the Bethlehemite. Their tribe was Judah, and the genealogy given in Ruth 4:18-22 traces their ancestry to Perez, Judah's son by Tamar (Gen. 38). Ruth herself was David's great-grandmother; she was a Moabitess. David's sisters Zeruiah and Abigail (1 Ch. 2:16) are said to be the daughters of Nahash in 2 S. 17:25. This permits three possibilities: Nahash was another name for Jesse; Nahash was their mother's name, and therefore David's mother too; or Nahash died, and his widow then married Jesse and became David's mother. The third seems the most likely; we may note that 1 Ch. 2:13-16 states that Jesse was the father of David and his brothers, but Zeruiah and Abigail are not specifically said to be Jesse's daughters. At any rate, David's mother's name is unknown, if it was not Nahash.

C. His Youth. The young David was obviously an outstanding youth, red-haired and handsome (1 S. 16:12), and strong and courageous, to judge from his remarks to Saul (17:34ff.). He was also endowed with musical skill (16:18). He was the shepherd of the family, and it was while pursuing this occupation that he proved his physical prowess in dealing effectively with bears and lions that sought to prey on the flocks.

D. His Anointing. David was actually in the field with his flock when Samuel arrived, divinely guided to find and anoint the successor to Saul as king of Israel. Jesse paraded his elder sons before the prophet; but

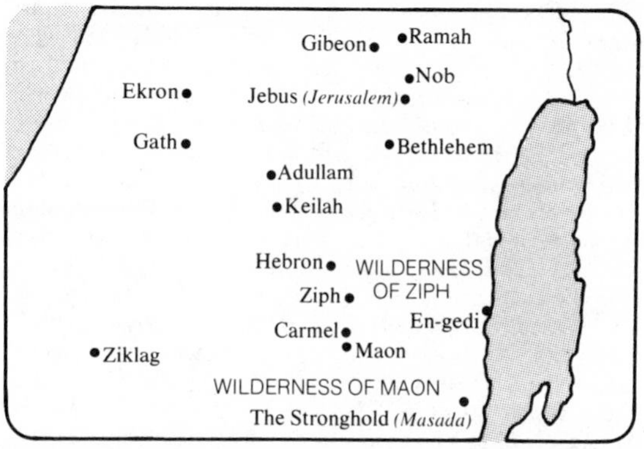

Samuel was not content with any of them, and pressed Jesse, who then sent for David. Samuel anointed David in front of his brothers, but we have no way of telling how widely publicized the anointing was. Certainly Saul's suspicions of David were quick to arise, so perhaps he did hear of Samuel's action. David continued as a shepherd in Bethlehem for some time after this ceremony; but we are told that from now on he began to display charismatic qualities, that is, he was influenced by the "Spirit of Yahweh" (1 S. 16:13), like the "judges" and Saul before him. These qualities of ecstatic utterance and action marked him out as a divinely appointed leader.

E. Meets Saul. David's introduction to Saul and his court is said to have been in the capacity of a musician. Saul began to be subject to fits of melancholia, and music alone seemed to help him. David's skill with the harp was mentioned to Saul, and the king sent for him at once (1 S. 16:14ff.). David's charm, as well as his skill, soon won over the king, who made the young man his armor bearer. But if this is the true story, what are we to make of 1 S. 17:55-58, where Saul apparently does not know David or his antecedents? Here it seems that David was unknown to Saul until his encounter with Goliath. However, the contradiction may be more apparent than real. When David came to the court as a harpist, Saul could not have been very concerned about his parentage, although Jesse's name was mentioned (16:18); but the prospect of David's becoming a soldier of note, and the possibility that he would win the hand of the king's daughter (cf. 17:25), might well lead Saul to inquire more closely into his family's standing. At any rate, in the second account Saul does not ask David what his own name is. We may then accept both accounts. On the other hand, a simple expedient is to follow the LXX B text of 1 S. 17, a shorter version, which omits most of the material that seems to contradict the details of the previous chapter.

F. Defeats Goliath. It seems that David's duties at court did not occupy his time fully, and he was still able to help with his father's sheep at Bethlehem (1 S. 17:15). This state of affairs continued until Saul engaged in warfare with the Philistines in the Vale of Elah. A huge Philistine warrior, Goliath of Gath, challenged and defied the Israelite army, in which three of David's brothers were fighting. Jesse now dispatched David with provisions for his soldier brothers; reaching the camp, David soon learned what the situation was, and offered to take on Goliath's challenge. The result needs no retelling: disdaining armor, the young man, armed with only a sling and five stones, advanced to meet the giant warrior, and brought him down with a well-aimed stone. He then used the giant's own sword to decapitate him, whereupon the Israelites took heart and routed the Philistines.

It seems unnecessary to challenge the historicity of this story. If Elhanan (2 S. 21:19) is not to be equated with David, then it is possible that his feat was credited to David at a later stage. But without doubt David's early fame rested on some adequate foundation, and it is more likely that the name Goliath was misapplied to some anonymous warrior defeated by David. The name occurs twice only (vv. 4, 23) in the account of 1 S. 17, and could be a late addition to the narrative. However, Elhanan may have killed Goliath's brother, as the parallel in Chronicles has it (1 Ch. 20:5), in which case there is no obstacle in the way of accepting that David himself killed Goliath. And if Elhanan was David's personal name (see above), no difficulty remains.

G. At Saul's Court. The victory thus created by David caused great joy in Israel, and David immediately became a popular hero (1 S. 18:6f.). He returned to the court of Saul in a very different position, honored by the king, made an army commander, and rapidly becoming a close friend of Saul's son and heir, Jonathan. But at this point Saul began to be jealous of the young hero. Perhaps he realized David's ambitions — and clearly David must have been ambitious, since Samuel had anointed him. So Saul began to desire David's death, and in a fit of mad rage twice threw a spear at him (18:10f.). He promised to give his daughter Merab as wife to David if he would only achieve a few more military exploits; but the king's hopes that thereby David would die in battle were doomed to disappointment. Saul broke his promise about Merab, marrying her to another man; but he now offered David his daughter Michal, on yet another very difficult condition. David continued to prosper nonetheless, and married Michal; and his consistent military success merely added to his prestige and made Saul the more jealous (18:27-30).

H. Flees from the Court. Saul's hostility at last became overt, and although Jonathan managed to restrain him for a time, he determined to kill David. To escape, David was obliged to flee from the court, with the aid of Michal, who was able to trick the would-be assassins sent by Saul (1 S. 19:11-17). David's chief regret was his enforced separation from Jonathan, who felt strong ties of loyalty both to his father and to his friend. The story of their parting is told in considerable detail and with great pathos in 1 S. 20. David remained in the south of his homeland for some time, but he was relentlessly pursued by Saul, who did not even hesitate to massacre priests who had innocently aided the fugitive (22:9-19). After brief interludes at Naioth and Nob, David in despair entered hostile Philistine territory. He might well have lost his life at the hands of Achish king of Gath, but escaped yet again by resorting to another trick: this time he feigned madness (21:10-15).

I. As a Fugitive. Leaving Gath, David returned to Judah, and set about establishing himself in the remote wilderness parts. Hitherto he had been a lone fugitive; now he banded together a group of malcontents and the like, four hundred strong, with the cave of Adullam as his headquarters (1 S. 22:2). His brothers and other kin joined him; and David placed his parents in the care of the king of Moab, in case Saul's anger should extend to them (22:3f.). A priest (Abiathar) and a prophet (Gad) also attached themselves to David's company. The guerrillas had, of course, to find an occupation and a livelihood, and their first effort in this direction was a raid on the Philistines, who were attacking the town of Keilah in the lowlands of Judah (23:1-5). The success of the raid saved Keilah, and no doubt won David some popular support, while it brought his men booty and provisions; but at the same time it rendered him liable to Philistine attacks, without in any way lessening Saul's hostility. So his position was, if anything, weaker as a result. Presently he had to rely on money and provisions from wealthy Judean farmers; this was exacted as toll for his protection (cf. 25:5-8). Presumably this payment was given reluctantly (cf. 25:9-12), but he sought to counteract any latent hostility by marrying into two influential families (25:42f.). Thus we see that David, unlike Saul, started the harem principle, even before he came to the throne; but in the process he lost Michal, at least temporarily (25:44).

J. As a Philistine Vassal. David's position was precarious, then; and Saul for his part could not be expected to tolerate such a center of disaffection, so he redoubled his efforts to exterminate the nuisance. The result was that David had one or two narrow escapes. Twice, it seems, Saul came close to capturing David, and twice David, in hiding, could have taken the opportunity to assassinate his persecutor (1 S. 24; 26). However, David had a great regard for the king's person, and restrained his men from killing "Yahweh's anointed." In each case he had a brief interview with Saul, who, mentally unstable as he was, expressed his shame and regret; but such emotion was of short duration. These two accounts have a number of similarities but also a number of wide divergences of detail, so it is not easy to decide whether or not we have here two different accounts of the same incident.

Realizing that he could not escape Saul indefinitely, David at last decided to return to Philistia, not now as an unaccompanied exile, but as a military captain with some six hundred men behind him. On this occasion Achish of Gath welcomed him, happy to see the Israelite forces thus split. David spent over a year as the vassal of Achish, with his headquarters in the frontier town of Ziklag. From here he raided the bedouin of the Negeb, at the same time persuading his overlord that he was in fact harassing the Israelites (27:5-12). The major battle with Israel now loomed ahead, and Achish wanted to integrate David's force with the Philistine armies at the battle of Gilboa. David appeared willing, but fortunately for him many of the Philistines doubted his loyalty to them, and prevailed on Achish to send him back to the south of Philistia (ch. 29). Returning to Ziklag, David and his men found that the Amalekites, foes of Philistines and Israelites alike, had raided the town, burning it down, and had taken captive all the women and children; David's two wives were among the captives. Thus it came about that while in the north the Philistines were routing the Israelites at Mt. Gilboa, David in the south pursued the Amalekite raiders and decimated them, recovering the captives and the spoil taken from Ziklag (ch. 30).

II. Reign.*–*A. King in Hebron. The defeat and death of Saul and Jonathan was a real disaster for Israel, as David himself fully realized. His elegy (2 S. 1:19-27) not only indicates his real sorrow at Jonathan's death, but also his awareness that Israel once again lay helpless before the Philistines, who indeed seem to have controlled the whole country west of the Jordan afresh. One of Saul's sons, Eshbaal (or Ish-bosheth), set up a kingdom of sorts in Transjordan with the support of Abner, hitherto Saul's commander in chief (2 S. 2:8f.). But W of the Jordan there remained only one Israelite with any power or influence, and that was David. He had skillfully avoided offending his fellow tribesmen, and he was now, at Hebron, acclaimed king over Judah (2:3f., 11). There can scarcely be any doubt that this step was taken with Philistine cognizance; probably David at first pretended

Site of the City of David, the earliest stages of Jerusalem located on two ridges S of the present Old City. David made the city his capital to unite the potentially separative northern and southern tribes that had chosen him king. (A. C. Myers)

to be the vassal of Achish still. No doubt it suited the Philistines well at this stage to support a rival to the house of Saul. But as it happened, the situation changed entirely two years later. Eshbaal had not the influence or ability of his father, and indeed he made little or no effort to do battle with the Philistines. His sole measure of power really lay in the hands of Abner. Northern Israel W of the Jordan meanwhile chafed under the domination of the enemy, whereas in Judah David had what amounted to a free hand. Eshbaal's rule lasted a mere two years; by then Abner had deserted him on the pretext that Eshbaal had insulted him, and came over to David's side with a considerable following. This was the end of Eshbaal's influence, and he was shortly afterward assassinated by two of his officers. David now had no rival, and all Israel acclaimed him king at Hebron (5:1-3). He acted very circumspectly, seeking throughout to cause no offense to Saul's supporters. He demanded the return of his wife Michal, Saul's daughter (3:12-15), to strengthen his links with the dead king's house; and he persuaded Israel that he was innocent of Eshbaal's blood, by executing the latter's assassins. Earlier, David had further strengthened his position by new advantageous marriages (3:2-5).

B. Defeats the Philistines. The Philistines suddenly found that their erstwhile vassal was now king of a united Israel. They could not tolerate this situation, and they opened hostilities (2 S. 5:17). But David's experienced standing army was altogether stronger than Saul's hurriedly assembled tribal levies had been, and twice in quick succession the Philistine inroads were repulsed (5:19-25); these defeats meant that the Philistines lost permanently their hold on the hill country. But David was not content to leave the matter there; he later switched from defense to attack, and eventually took Gath and rendered the whole of Philistia tributary. Of these campaigns we have no details, so it is impossible to say how or when these victories were won. The facts are certain however (cf. 2 S. 8:11f.; 1 Ch. 18:1). Before long, David's personal bodyguard was largely drawn from Philistine ranks (2 S. 15:18).

C. Capture of Jerusalem. David's capital was Hebron for seven years in all. During this period he dealt effectively with the Philistine threat, but it is probable that his capture of Jerusalem preceded his attacks on Philistia itself. Indeed, it is quite likely that the attack on Jerusalem was his first aggressive action. Until David's reign, numerous cities in Palestine remained in Canaanite hands, and many of them were in alliance with the Philistines. David was determined to put an end to this state of affairs and he now moved on Jerusalem, a city of great strategic importance, which was almost impregnable. It was held by a Canaanite people, the Jebusites. The details of its capture are difficult to follow, since the text of 2 S. 5:6-9 is corrupt, while 1 Ch. 11:4-8 helps little. If we can take a detail of each uncorroborated by the other passage, it seems that Joab (1 Ch. 11:6), David's commander in chief, led a party of troops up a water shaft (2 S. 5:8). It is clear, at any rate, that the inhabitants were taken by surprise in some way.

D. Jerusalem as Capital. David refortified the city, and made it his own property (2 S. 5:9). Its advantages as a capital were several. It was very important militarily. Also, it was for the Israelites a neutral city, i.e., not in Judah or in any other tribe's territory; thus it served to alleviate some of the jealousies that so readily sprang up between north and south. David saw, too, that Saul had been foolish to neglect the cultus; and he set about making Jerusalem the most important sanctuary in Israel by fetching the long-neglected ark of the covenant and installing it with great pomp and ceremony in a shrine at Jerusalem (2 S. 6). It was left to Solomon to erect a permanent building to house the ark, but the initial steps were certainly David's.

Jerusalem became, then, the administrative and religious capital of Israel; here David set up court in regal fashion, with a considerable harem (cf. 5:13), and surrounded by his personal troops. He appointed a number of administrative officers (8:15-18). There were two leading priests at the Jerusalem shrine, Abiathar and Zadok. The king himself took some part in the cultic ritual (6:17ff.), and showed great interest in the worship, enriching and embellishing it in various ways, especially musical (1 Ch. 16:4ff.). The tradition that he himself composed numerous Psalms is firmly established. Finally, he closely associated his own position with the worship of Yahweh, so that within a generation or two the line of David and the Jerusalem temple were the two visible signs of Yahweh's presence and favor. Judah never knew a non-Davidic king for over four hundred years.

E. Consolidation and Expansion. No doubt the capture of Jerusalem was part of a pattern. David could not allow the Canaanite cities to retain their independence, remaining potential centers of disaffection. We have no details of their capture; probably there was little or no real opposition to David. Thus consolidating his own realm, David next meant to subdue Israel's ancient foes. Philistia was presumably the first to capitulate; Moab and Edom soon followed (2 S. 8:2, 13f.). If 10:1f. is to be believed, David had no aggressive intentions toward Ammon; but the king of Ammon, Hanun, feared Israel's growing power, and insulted David's envoys in a very ill-advised fashion. David could not overlook this, and warfare resulted, Hanun hastily forming alliances with some Aramaean states to the north of Ammon. David was victorious, and finally captured Hanun's capital, Rabbah (Rabbath Ammon, the modern Amman) (12:26ff.). It must have been subsequent to this that David made most of Syria tributary (8:3-12); the allies of Ammon had to be pursued and punished. David was now at the pinnacle of success, master of a considerable empire. His victories were due largely to his own abilities, although Joab must also have been a very able soldier. The weakness of Egypt and the Mesopotamian states during this period also contributed to David's success.

F. David and Bathsheba. Hitherto David had shown himself ruthless in battle and as cunning as his ancestor Jacob at times; but his loyalty to his friends and supporters had been conspicuous. He had even spared Saul's life; and out of loyalty to the memory of Jonathan, he had given Jonathan's son Mephibosheth an honored place at court (2 S. 9), despite the possibility that Mephibosheth might have had designs on the throne. But David now went right beyond the pale of morality; while the siege of Rabbah was taking place, he desired a married woman in Jerusalem, Bathsheba, and committed adultery with her (11:2-5). When she became pregnant, David tried to cover up his guilt by fetching her husband Uriah home from the battle. Uriah refused to sleep with his wife, however, since he was consecrated for battle (cf. 1 S. 21:4f.); so David found himself obliged to conceal his immoral actions by other means, and he sent Joab instructions to engineer the death of Uriah in battle. Uriah's subsequent death, therefore, was at the hands of the Ammonites, but David was solely responsible.

With Uriah out of the way, David permitted Bathsheba to observe the proprieties of mourning, and then made her his wife quite openly (2 S. 11:26f.). But this gross immorality did not go unheeded, and the prophet Nathan came to remonstrate with the king (ch. 12). By telling the parable of the ewe lamb, he skillfully led David to condemn his own actions; David thereupon expressed his deep repentance, but the misdeed could not be undone, and in a sense this incident proved to be the turning point in his life. Nathan warned him that his own household would in future know constant distress and bereavement (v. 11); and so it turned out. The first loss was the son born of the adultery, who fell sick and died while very young.

G. David's Sons. Bathsheba soon gave birth to another son, Solomon, who was to succeed his father as king of Israel. But he was by no means the eldest son of David. The eldest was Amnon, then came Chileab (of whose life we have no details recorded), Absalom, and Adonijah, all born of different mothers (2 S. 3:2-5). These four, and two others, were born before David made Jerusalem his capital, whereas Solomon and a number of other sons were born in Jerusalem (5:13-16). David had not the same ability to rule his own house that he showed in the administration of his realm; his indulgent treatment of Adonijah, at least, is explicitly mentioned (1 K. 1:6). Moreover, there was no precedent to follow as regards the heir to the throne of Israel, so not unnaturally these half brothers maneuvered for position, each hoping to win the throne eventually. Amnon's claim was very strong, as the eldest; but Solomon seems to have been his father's favorite from the first, possibly because Bathsheba was a wife of David's own choice, whereas most of the other marriages had been political moves. Had Michal had a son, he would have had a good claim to the throne as Saul's grandson and David's son by his first wife. But Michal was estranged from David and never bore a child (2 S. 6:20-23).

H. Amnon and Absalom. Amnon's selfish and wanton nature stands out clearly in the story of his raping his half sister Tamar (2 S. 13:1-19). Apparently the king did nothing whatever to punish the miscreant, and it is no wonder that the girl's full brother Absalom determined to avenge his humiliated sister. For two years he was content to wait his chance, and then he murdered Amnon. Fearful of his father's reprisal, he fled from the court to spend three years in exile (13:37f.). David missed his wayward son (14:1), however, so Joab eventually took a hand in the matter and succeeded in persuading the king to allow Absalom to return to Jerusalem but David obstinately refused to let the young man have a place at court (14:21-24). This was an ill-advised way to punish Absalom, who was evidently given to harboring grudges. Again he bided his time for two full years, and then he arrogantly used Joab to secure him a place in the palace again (14:28-33).

I. Absalom's Rebellion. David took no further action to punish or restrain Absalom, who in turn could not forgive his father for the years of humiliation. He thus determined to oust David. Amnon was no obstacle now, and we may well presume that Chileab was either dead by this time or else lacking in ambition. Absalom saw that the crown could be his, and he took steps to detract from David's popularity and to win popular support for himself. His most effective method was to underline the faults in the existing judicial system, persuading the populace that he himself was passionately interested in justice (2 S. 15:1-4). For four years he pursued tactics of this sort, until he judged that the time was ripe for raising the standard of revolt. He then resorted to yet another subterfuge to go to Hebron with a large following, and once at Hebron proclaimed himself king (15:7-12). Evidently there was a measure of discontent with David's regime, but it seems that on the whole it was a struggle between the popularity of father and son.

They were rather evenly balanced, although speed and surprise at first gave Absalom the advantage. David had to flee from his capital (15:14-16), and Absalom was able to enter Jerusalem (v. 37). But there were several friends of the king still in the city, notably Hushai, one of David's counselors, and the two priests of the sanctuary, Zadok and Abiathar. Hushai posed as Absalom's friend, taking care to give him poor advice, while the priests undertook to pass on to David news of Absalom's plans. In a prolonged struggle, the decisive factor was bound to be the loyalty of the royal troops and of Joab, David's able general; Absalom's only hope was to pursue his father while the latter's forces were still disorganized. Absalom's wisest counselor, Ahithophel, fully realized this, but he was overruled after the cunning Hushai had listed specious arguments for delay (17:1-14).

J. Absalom's Defeat and Death. The pause gave David time to recoup at Mahanaim, E of the Jordan; and when battle was at last joined the greater experience of his men told. Absalom's band was cut to pieces, and the pretender was forced to flee. He was as much hampered by the unfamiliar terrain as his army had been (2 S. 18:8), with the result that he was swept off his mount and left dangling from a tree by his hair (v. 9). The king had issued strict orders that Absalom was not to be killed, but the experienced Joab, aware that the treacherous youth would always endanger David's position, disregarded these orders and killed the helpless rebel (v. 14). The news of his son's death desolated the king, whose excessive grief overshadowed his men's delight in their victory. Joab had no patience with the king's emotions, and upbraided him severely. So at length David made his way back to the capital, victorious but grief-stricken. Joab was primarily responsible for the sorrow as well as the victory, and David found it hard to forgive. He was more ready to forgive Absalom's supporters. Ahithophel had committed suicide (17:23), but Amasa, the commander of Absalom's army, was elevated to the same position in David's army, over Joab's head.

K. Sheba's Revolt. Fresh trouble broke out almost at once. Surprisingly enough, much of Absalom's support had come from Judah, which was now anxious to placate David in every way possible. The king accepted the overtures handsomely, but in so doing he somewhat offended the northern tribes, whose support had so recently turned the scales in his favor (2 S. 19:40-43). The quarrel illustrates clearly how brittle was the union between north and south. In this partial estrangement, a certain Benjamite named Sheba thought he saw an opportunity to wrest the northern tribes from David's control. He himself probably represented the Saulite faction. Thus a fresh revolt broke out (20:1f.) before David had time even to reach his capital again. The new commander in chief, Amasa, was sent to deal with the situation; but he took too long to muster the army, and David was forced to rely on Joab once more. Joab took the personal troops of the king northward and soon overtook Amasa, whom he assassinated, and so resumed command of the whole army (20:4-10). Meanwhile Sheba's supporters fell away, and the rebel leader could not match David's troops. He took refuge in Abel of Beth-maacah, in the territory of Naphtali, hoping to be able to withstand a siege (20:14f.); but the citizens were wise enough to dissociate themselves from him, and they assassinated him and presented his head to Joab (vv. 16-22). With that the revolt collapsed.

L. Famine and Plague. Two other events that troubled the nation are recorded in 2 S. 21 and 24. These chapters do not follow in chronological order. The famine (ch. 21) must have taken place quite early in David's reign, long before the two rebellions. After three years of famine, the king sought to find a religious reason for the national distress and learned that bloodguilt by Saul was the cause. Saul had on some unrecorded occasion killed some Gibeonites, who now demanded revenge on the dead king's family. David handed over seven of Saul's sons, but took care to save Mephibosheth, Jonathan's son.

The second disaster was a plague, and again a religious reason was sought and found. David was to blame, it seems, for conducting a census (24:1). It is not absolutely certain where the sin lay; it may have been connected with the taxation and forced labor which would follow the census, and which were, of course, never popular (these same two factors eventually split the kingdom after Solomon's death). Or perhaps the sin lay in some pride of achievement on David's part. At any rate, the plague was brought to an end when David confessed his sin, and raised an altar and made sacrifice (24:17-25).

***III. Last Years.**–A. The Succession Question.* As David's reign drew to a close a fresh palace intrigue broke out, though without rebellion this time. The eldest surviving son was Adonijah, who determined to thwart David's purpose to make Solomon his successor. He managed to win the allegiance of Joab and Abiathar (1 K. 1:7), and went just out of Jerusalem to hold a coronation ceremony and feast (v. 9), taking care not to invite his rival and the opposing faction. No doubt he hoped by his unpublicized actions and strong support to present Israel, and the aged king, with a *fait accompli*. But Solomon was not inactive; as soon as his rival had left the city he enlisted the aid of his mother to persuade David to proclaim him king. He too had strong support, in Nathan the prophet, Zadok the priest, and Benaiah, who commanded the royal bodyguard. David was roused from his lethargy and took steps to prevent Adonijah's coronation and to further that of Solomon. David's support must have been decisive, and so was that of the troops Benaiah had in readiness. Joab evidently had no ready troops with which to back up Adonijah's cause (1 K. 1).

B. David's Death. Solomon thus became king before his father's death. David had acted very leniently and mercifully with his own enemies, but he now counseled Solomon differently (1 K. 2:1-9). Some historians doubt the truth of this about-face, but in his age and infirmity — this was his last recorded act — his nature may well have soured, to some extent. In any case, he may well have wished his son to be spared the hostility and revolts he had himself faced. Solomon took his

Mameluke building housing the traditional tomb of David on the Western hill of Jerusalem. The monument, a large Crusader sarcophagus, is located below the Coenaculum, traditional site of the Last Supper. (A. C. Myers)

father's advice, and had a less troubled reign than did David, who died (2:10) at the age of about seventy.

C. Duration of Reign. David is thought to have become king *ca.* 1000 B.C. (perhaps as early as 1010). He reigned two years as king of Judah, and a further five as king of the united nation, in Hebron; for the remainder of his reign Jerusalem was his capital. He is credited with a forty-years' reign altogether (2 S. 5:4), and whereas this figure may well be a round number, it must be approximately correct. W. F. Albright suggests the year 961 B.C. for Solomon's accession, but it may have taken place ten years earlier.

IV. Administration and Character.–*A. Administrative Measures.* David began his reign as vassal ruler of a small, disunited people, and ended it as the master of a considerable empire, with not a few vassals of his own. It is self-evident that he must have made many changes in the administration to cope with his growing, changing realm. We know little about them, apart from his change of capital. There are two lists of his officials, however, which yield some information (2 S. 8:15-18; 20:23-26). The only political officers, apparently, were the recorder (Heb. *mazkîr*) and secretary (Heb. *sôpēr*) in the early part of his reign, and later a chief of corvée was added to them. (Probably most of David's forced labor came from subject peoples, and not from free born Israelites.) The king himself, of course, was head of the machinery of state; and he was also in sole charge of the legal administration.

In the field he had two military commanders, one leading the Israelite levies (Joab, who was also commander in chief), the other commanding the mercenary troops. But David himself often led the armies into battle; 2 S. 18:1-4 makes it clear that he superintended operations and often went to the battlefield in person. David also imposed his will and played no small part in religious matters. He had a golden chance to do so when he selected Jerusalem as chief shrine, for he could appoint what priests he wished and could even undertake some priestly functions himself (2 S. 6:17f.), as did also his sons (8:18). The tradition that he embellished the Jerusalem cultic ritual is by no means improbable. While the detailed information of the Chronicler (1 Ch. 15; 23–26) is sometimes to be regarded as an idealization, since the cultus must have undergone considerable development down to the Chronicler's time and beyond, there is no good reason to doubt that David took a great part in the institution of the Jerusalem cultus and arrangements. He was absolute head of the political and military machine, and had a remarkably free hand in the administration of the religious ritual too.

B. Ability and Character. It is clear that David was well able to fulfil these functions. If he was not wholly successful in his legal administration (to judge from 2 S. 15:2-4), he was supremely able in the military and political spheres. He took a defeated nation and made it practically unassailable. Admittedly, the problem of the traditional jealousies between Ephraim and Judah was not finally solved, but so great was his own personal popularity and achievement that no real trouble broke out till after his son's long reign had ended.

His successes were a tribute to his personal courage, and to his ability as soldier and statesman. He could not only win battles and organize his territory efficiently, but he could win over even those who were at first hostile to him. His tact and charm are evidenced by the devotion he inspired in Jonathan, who could have become his jealous rival but instead was his staunchest friend. David's loyalty to his friends is plainly shown in his generous treatment of Jonathan's son Mephibosheth, who again could so easily have been a bitter opponent of David. Revenge was foreign to his nature; time and again he treated former enemies leniently and even generously. The chief flaws one can discern in his character are his deceitfulness (which was, however, a common trait, and probably thought to be more of a virtue than a failing by his contemporaries), his indulgence toward his sons, and of course his actions where Bathsheba was concerned. While his adultery and murder cannot be condoned, with this glaring exception he was in every way the ideal ruler. When we remember also his contribution to the temple, the cultus, and the Psalter, it is no wonder that his reign was regarded as a golden age, and that Scripture consistently viewed him as the prototype of the Messiah, who was to be "great David's greater Son."

See also KING, KINGDOM; SAMUEL, BOOKS OF; Maps VII, XXIV.

Bibliography.–Comms. on 1 and 2 Samuel; B. W. Anderson, *Understanding the OT* (2nd ed. 1966); *BHI*; *NHI*.

D. F. PAYNE

DAVID, CITY OF. *See* ZION.

DAVID, ROOT OF [Gk. *hē rhíza Daueid*] (Rev. 5:5; 22:16); NEB SCION OF DAVID. Root here means stock, family, descendant; hence "the Root of David" is that which descended from David, not that from which David descended. Jesus Christ in His human nature and family connections was a descendant of David, a member of his family.

DAVID, TOWER OF. *See* JERUSALEM.

DAWN; DAWNING [Heb. *šaḥar*, *nešep*, *ʿālâ*–'go up' (Gen. 19:15; Josh. 6:15), *bōqer* (Zeph. 3:5), *nōgah*–'shining' (Prov. 4:18), *zāraḥ*–'shine' (Dt. 33:2), *zāraʿ*–'sow' (Ps. 97:11), *ʾôr* (Mic. 2:1); Gk. *epiphṓskō* (Mt. 28:1), *anatolḗ* (Lk. 1:78), *anatéllō*–'rise' (Mt. 4:16), *bathéōs* (Lk. 24:1), *gínomai*–'become,' 'arise' (Acts 27:33), *diaugázō* (2 Pet. 1:19)]; AV also DAY, MORNING, TWILIGHT, DAYSPRING, AROSE, etc.; NEB also DAYBREAK, TWILIGHT, MORNING, etc. In Ps. 97:11 the RSV emends the MT to read *zāraḥ*.

In the OT the term *šaḥar* is usually rendered "dawn" (cf., however, Gen. 19:15, RSV "morning"; 32:24 [MT 25], RSV, NEB, "daybreak"; 32:26 [MT 27]; Josh. 6:15, RSV "morning"). The Hebrew term actually denotes that brief moment before dawn in which a reddish light appears (L. Köhler, *ZAW*, 44 [1926], 56-59). The AV renders this term "dayspring" in Job 38:12: "Hast thou . . . caused the dayspring to know his place?" The place of the dayspring is the particular point of the horizon at which the sun comes up at any given day. This slowly changes day by day through the year. The term also occurs once in the NT (Lk. 1:78, AV) for Gk. *anatolḗ* (see below).

Isa. 14:12 uses the term *šaḥar* in a name — *Hêlēl*, son of Dawn (*hêlēl ben-šaḥar*). In Ugaritic literature the god *Šaḥar* is a son of El, born of a seduced woman, and has a twin brother *Šalem* (C. Gordon, *Ugaritic Textbook* [1965], nos. 52f.; G. R. Driver, *Canaanite Myths and Legends* [1956], pp. 22f.). It has been suggested therefore that Isa. 14:12ff. is a Canaanite dirge quoted in the book of Isaiah (W. F. Albright, *JPOS*, 12 [1932], 192 n. 22; *Yahweh*, pp. 187, 232). A Mesopotamian text from Asshur (Staatliche Museen, Berlin; Vorderasiatische Abteilung, Thontafelsammlung 10173, v, 1-6) lists the god Šeru (i.e., Šaḫru) behind such celestial figures as Rainbow (^{d}TIR.AN.NA) and Ornament of Heaven (^{d}ME.TE.AN.NA). The name of this god appears in personal names from the period of Hammurabi and in Phoenician and neo-Punic texts (Gaster, p. 411). In the Râs Shamrah texts Šaḥar is the Venus star at dawn. Venus was regarded by the Arabs as *zahra*, "the bright shining one."

It is doubtful that Isa. 14:12ff. reflects direct dependence on Ugaritic material, though there is a terminological relationship. The poet of Isa. 14:12 employs *šaḥar* as an attributive term in order to indicate by this "extended figure of speech" (Childs, p. 72) *Hêlēl's* former fame and present shame, caused by his fall (vv. 15-20). He has done so without adopting the various aspects of polytheistic, pagan mythology. The references to "dawn" (*šaḥar*) in Job 3:9; 41:11 (MT 10); Ps. 57:8 (MT 9); 108:2 (MT 3) are at times considered to be originally mythical. But this is very doubtful, since there is no conclusive evidence for this. These poetic passages seem rather to be personifications. The enigmatic phrase "to the hind of the dawn" in Ps. 22:1 (MT 2) does not refer to the Ugaritic god *Šaḥar*, because the latter is the god of dawn and not the sun-god represented as a horned male deer from Alaca Hüyük, Anatolia (so Jirku, p. 85).

The term *nešep* is rendered at times as "dawn" (Job 3:9; 7:4, AV "dawning"; Ps. 119:147, AV "dawning") whereas most often it is translated with "twilight," viz., the dusk after sunset (2 K. 7:5; Job 24:15; Prov. 7:9; Isa. 5:11; 59:10) and the twilight just before sunrise (1 S. 30:17; 2 K. 7:5, 7; Job 3:9; 7:4). In Jer. 13:16 it means general darkness (*CHAL*, p. 248).

In the NT the word "dawn" appears in Mt. 28:1 (cf. G. F. Moore, *JAOS*, 26 [1905], 323-29; P. Gardner-Smith, *JTS*, 27 [1926], 179-181; M. Black, *An Aramaic Approach to the Gospels* [3rd ed. 1967], pp. 99f.), where it translates *epiphōskoúsē* and refers to dawn rather than dusk. But in Lk. 23:54 another form of this same verb refers to the "dawning" of the sabbath, which is sundown on Friday. In Lk. 24:1 the term *bathéōs* is rendered as "dawn" by the RSV. The term "dawn" (*anatolḗ*, AV "dayspring"; NEB "morning sun") in Lk. 1:78 is used figuratively of the first coming of the Messiah (Schlier, Vielhauer, Gnilka, Hahn). In 2 Pet. 1:19 the phrase "until the day dawns" (*diaugázō*) is a figure of speech for the second coming of the Lord Jesus Christ (v. 16).

***Bibliography*.**–L. Köhler, *ZAW*, 44 (1926), 56-59; H. G. May, *ZAW*, 55 (1937), 269-281; J. Gray, *JNES*, 8 (1949), 72-83; A. Jirku, *ZAW*, 65 (1953), 85f.; B. S. Childs, *Myth and Reality in the OT* (2nd ed. 1962), pp. 69-72; T. H. Gaster, *Thespis* (3rd ed. 1966), pp. 409-417; W. F. Albright, *Yahweh and the Gods of Canaan* (1968), pp. 187, 232f.; *TDNT*, I, *s.v.* ἀνατολή (Schlier); P. Vielhauer, *ZTK*, 49 (1952), 255-272; J. Gnilka, *BZ*, 6 (1962), 215-238; F. Hahn, *Titles of Jesus in Christology* (Eng. tr. 1969), pp. 365-67; J. J. M. Roberts, *Earliest Semitic Pantheon* (1972).

G. F. HASEL

DAY. The usual Hebrew term for day is *yôm*, which derives from a common Semitic root *yawm*. The usual Greek term is *hēméra*. The basic meaning of "day" expresses a division of the solar unit of time, but its use in a great variety of biblical contexts reveals a wide semantic range.

***I. Beginning of the Day*.**–The basic solar unit of time is the day. The astronomical day was reckoned by the Hebrews from evening to evening (Gen. 1; Ex. 12:18; Lev. 23:27, 32); i.e., the day began at sunset and ended at sunset (cf. Lev. 22:6f.; Dt. 16:16; Neh. 13:19; Ps. 55:17 [MT 18]; Est. 4:16; Isa. 34:10; Jer. 27:3; Mt. 28:1; Lk. 23:54; Mk. 16:1f.; Acts 20:7; 2 Cor. 11:25) or in the evening (cf. von Rad, W. H. Schmidt, Stroes, etc., against de Vaux). In the creation account of Gen. 1 appears the repeated phrase "and there was evening and there was morning, . . . day" (vv. 5, 8, 13, 19, 23, 31). This formula indicates (1) that "evening and morning" should be understood alike in all six days, (2) that the day begins with evening, (3) that each day is a real twenty-four-hour day, and (4) that thus the daily rhythm of time has its beginning. The creation day is understood as a normal twenty-four-hour day in Ex. 20:8-11; 31:15, 17 (cf. Stroes, Schmidt). The Hebrew compound "evening-morning" (*'ereḇ bôqer*) in Dnl. 8:14 is a circumlocution for "day." It is the equivalent of the expression "there was evening and there was morning" — and emphasizes again that evening or sunset is the beginning of the twenty-four-hour calendar day in the OT and NT (cf. Mk. 4:27; Lk. 2:37; Acts 20:31; 26:7). In antiquity the Babylonians began the day likewise with sunset, but the Egyptians with sunrise. The custom of beginning the day at midnight derives from the Romans.

***II. Divisions of the Day*.**–The astronomical or calendar day of twenty-four hours is divided into the dark part, i.e., night, and the light part, i.e., day (Est. 4:16; Ps. 55:18; Isa. 34:10; Jer. 27:3; 1 K. 8:29 par. 2 Ch. 6:20; cf. Dt. 28:66f.; 1 S. 30:12; Isa. 28:19; Jer. 33:20; etc.). The time of daylight is called *yôm*, "day," just as the twenty-four-hour day, but the former is contrasted to night (Heb. *laylâ*) in the above passages. A threefold division for a twenty-four-hour day appears in Ps. 55:17 (MT 18) with evening, morning, and noon. Although in Mesopotamia the astronomical day was divided into twelve two-hour periods (*bēru*), the OT does not seem to reflect a division of the day into hours, which is later found in the NT.

In postexilic and NT times the day was divided into twelve hours (Jn. 9:11; cf. Mt. 20:1-12) between approximately sunrise and sunset, or dawn and dusk. Thus the sixth hour was at noon. The length of the hour was different in summer and winter depending on the sunrise and sunset. In Neh. 9:3 there is a division of a day into "fourths." The night is divided into three watches (Ex. 14:24; Jgs. 7:19; 1 S. 11:11; Lam. 2:19). By NT times the Roman (and Egyptian) custom of four night watches had been adopted (Mt. 14:25; Mk. 13:35). "Midday" (Neh. 8:3), "broad daylight" (Am. 8:9), "full day" (Prov. 4:18), "heat of the day" (Gen. 18:1; 1 S. 11:11; 2 S. 4:5), and "high day" (Gen. 29:7) all refer to noon. The "cool of the day" (Gen. 3:8; Cant. 2:17) is the time of the westerly afternoon wind.

In the OT the days had no names, except the "seventh day" (Gen. 2:2f.; Ex. 12:15f.; 13:6; 16:26-30; 20:8-11; etc.), which is the sabbath (Ex. 16:26-30; 20:8-11; etc.; cf. 2:2f.). Otherwise the days are just numbered "first day," etc., usually with reference to the days of the month (Nu. 7:12-78, "first" to "twelfth" day; 29:17-35, "second" to "eighth" day). Some days of the week (e.g., *yôm šēnî*) are found in Gen. 1.

***III. Extended and Figurative Descriptions*.**–In many cases the term "day" is employed loosely and becomes an extended term for "time" or "point of time." Thus "in the day that" (Gen. 2:4, 17; Isa. 11:16; Jer. 7:22; Ezk. 20:5; Am. 3:14; etc.) means "when." The term "day" is used in circumlocutions for important events of salvation history: creation (Dt. 4:32), Exodus (Dt. 9:7; 1 K. 8:16 par. 2 Ch. 6:5; 2 K. 21:15; Jer. 7:25; 1 Ch. 17:5), giving of the law (Nu. 15:23; Dt. 4:10), entry into the Promised Land (Dt. 27:2), appointment of judges (2 S. 7:11), building or capture of Jerusalem (Jer. 32:31; 38:28), laying of the temple's foundation (Hag. 2:18), eschatological intervention of Yahweh (Mal. 3:17, 21; cf. Jn. 8:56), "day of salvation" (2 Cor. 6:12), and "day of God's wrath" (Job 20:28). As meteorological descriptions appear "day of rain" (Ezk. 1:28; Prov. 27:15), "day of snow" (2 S. 23:20 par. 1 Ch. 11:22), "day of the east wind" (Isa. 27:8), and "day of cold" (Nah. 3:17; Prov. 25:20). Aside from many other usages, there are references to special historical events: "day of the plague" (Nu. 25:18), "day of the assembly" at the giving of the law (Dt. 9:10; 10:4; 18:16), "day when you came out of the land of Egypt" (Dt. 16:3), "day of small things" at the rebuilding of the temple (Zec. 4:10), "day of Midian" (Isa. 9:3; cf. Jgs. 7:9ff.), "day of Massa" (Ps. 95:8; cf. Ex. 17; Nu. 20), "day of Jerusalem" (Ps. 137:7), etc.

The phrase "his day," in which the pronoun does not indicate its meaning, can stand for birthday (Job 3:1) as well as day of death (1 S. 26:10; Job 15:32; 18:20; Ps. 37:13), or for the day of one's turn (Job. 1:4), or one's "lifetime" (Job 14:6; cf. 30:15; Gen. 26:1; He. 5:7). The phrase "on that day" in contrast to "in this day" refers to a distant point of time in the past (e.g., Gen. 15:18; 30:35) or in the future (e.g., Ex. 13:8; Lev. 27:23) and has the meaning of "then." The distant past is designated also by "days of old" (Isa. 37:26 par. 2 K. 19:25; Isa. 23:7; 51:9; Jer. 46:26; Mic. 7:20; Ps. 44:2 [MT 3]; Lam. 1:7; 2:17; Isa. 63:9, 11; Mic. 5:1; 7:14; Mal. 3:4), while the past in general is referred to by "days that are past" (Dt. 4:32; Eccl. 7:10; Zec. 8:11). The future is designated also with "the days to come" (Eccl. 2:16) and "behold, days are coming" (1 S. 2:31; 2 K. 20:17; Isa. 39:6; Jer. 7:32; 9:24; 16:14; etc.; Am. 4:2; 8:11; 9:13). The formula "until this day" refers to the present, i.e., the time of the person speaking, and confirms a received tradition (Gen. 26:33; 32:33; 47:26; Josh. 4:9; 5:9; 6:25; 7:26; Jgs. 1:21, 26; 6:24; 1 S. 5:5; etc.).

The manifold usage of the term "day" indicates that it not only serves to designate an important division of time, but that it also develops into the most important key term for expressing points of time and epochs of time. The day stands, as does everything in this world, under the rulership of God, because He has created it (Gen. 1:5, 14). "Thine is the day, thine also the night; thou hast established the luminaries and the sun" (Ps. 74:16). A strongly theological usage appears in Gen. 8:22, where it is promised that "day and night shall not cease." An eschatological passage, however, promises a "continuous day . . . not day and not night" (Zec. 14:7). For the rich terminology of eschatology, such as "in that day" (cf. Isa. 4:2; 5:30; 10:20; etc.), "in the latter days" (Gen. 49:1; Isa. 2:2; Jer. 20:23; Ezk. 38:16; Dnl. 2:28; 10:14; etc.), and "day of the Lord" (Isa. 13:6, 9, Ezk. 13:5; Joel 1:15; 2:1, 11; 3:4; 4:14; Am. 5:18, 20; Ob. 15; Zeph. 1:7; 14:14; Mal. 3:23), *see* DAY OF THE LORD. In the NT the term "day" often means the eschatological time of judgment and salvation that will dawn with the second coming of Jesus (Mt. 24:38, 42; 26:29; Lk. 17:30; 1 Cor. 3:13; 1:8; Phil. 1:6, 10; 1 Thess. 5:2, 5; 2 Thess. 2:2; etc.).

Bibliography.–R. de Vaux, *Ancient Israel: Its Life and Institutions* (1961), pp. 180-83; B. S. Childs, *JBL*, 82 (1963), 279-292; *TDNT*, II, *s.v.* ἡμέρα (von Rad, Delling); C. Westermann, *Forschung am Alten Testament* (1964), pp. 43-47; H. R. Stroes, *VT*, 16 (1966), 460-475; W. H. Schmidt, *Die Schöpfungsgeschichte der Priesterschrift* (2nd ed. 1967), pp. 68f.; B. O. Long, *Problem of Etiological Narrative* (1968); *THAT*, I, *s.v.* יום (Jenni); S. J. DeVries, *Yesterday, Today and Tomorrow* (1975).

G. F. HASEL

DAY AND NIGHT [Heb. *yômām*–'by day,' *yôm*–'day'; *laylâ*–'night'; Gk. *hēméra*–'day'; *nýx*–'night']. An expression that encompasses the period of twenty-four hours of the astronomical day.

The phrase "day and night" (1 Ch. 9:33; 2 Ch. 6:20; Neh. 1:6; 4:3 [MT 9]; Isa. 60:11; 62:6; Eccl. 8:16; Lk. 18:7; Rev. 4:8; 7:15; 12:10; 14:11; 20:10), with the term "day" before the term "night," expresses the idea of not only by day but even at night. That is to say, it emphasizes the continuity of activity that has begun in the hours of day through the night. Since the Israelite-Jewish day began with sunset and ended with sunset (Gen. 1:5; Lev. 11:24; 15:5; 23:32; Dt. 23:11; Ps. 55:18 [MT 19]; Isa. 34:10; Jer. 27:3), one finds the expression "night and day" (1 S. 25:16; 1 K. 8:29; Isa. 27:3; 34:10; Est. 4:16; cf. Dt. 1:33; 1 S. 15:16; Jer. 14:17; 1 Thess. 2:9; 3:10; 2 Thess. 3:8; 1 Tim. 5:5; 2 Tim. 1:3; cf. Mk. 5:5), where the term "night" precedes the term "day," to be the regular expression for the complete astronomical calendar day. The day in Mesopotamia began with sunset. The Romans introduced the reckoning of the day from midnight to midnight. (*See also* DAY.)

The sunset marked the transition from one day to the next. The "evening" (Heb. *'ereḇ*) is the time of the going down of the sun (Prov. 7:9) and the declining of the day (Jgs. 19:8f.) as well as the sunset itself (Gen. 1:5). The sunset is followed by a short period of "twilight" or "dusk" (*nešep*, 2 K. 7:5; Job 24:15; Prov. 7:9; Isa. 5:11; 59:10). Then follows the "night," i.e., the dark part of the astronomical day, which was divided into three watches: the first watch (Lam. 2:19), the midnight watch (Jgs. 7:19), and the morning watch (Ex. 14:24; 1 S. 11:11). By NT times the Egyptian and Roman custom of four night watches was adopted: dusk, midnight, cockcrowing, and early dawn (Mk. 13:35; Mt. 14:25). The sunrise, which is preceded by the reddish light of the DAWN, marks the beginning of the daylight part of the calendar day. Since the length of the daylight part of the day depends on the season, the daylight at the latitude of Palestine could extend from ten to fourteen hours (Dalman). The OT does not reveal any terminology for the hours of the day as they are known from Egypt (twelve hours of daytime, twelve hours of nighttime) and Mesopotamia (twelve two-hour periods called *bēru*). But the Israelites had ways of telling the hours of the day, as an Egyptian sundial from the 13th cent. B.C. found at Gezer indicates. A "sundial" appears to be referred to in Isa. 38:8 par. 2 K. 20:9-11 (see DIAL OF AHAZ). In the time of Jesus the daylight period of the day was divided into twelve hours from about 6 a.m. to 6 p.m. (Mt. 20:1ff.; Mk. 15:33; Jn. 1:39; 4:52; 11:9; Acts 2:15). Customary designations for various times of the daylight part of the astronomical day were "morning," "noon" or "midday," and "evening" (Gen. 3:8; 18:1; 1 S. 11:11; Neh. 8:3). The "broad daylight" (Am. 8:9) is noon as well as the "heat of the day" (2 S. 4:5).

At times "day" and "night" are employed in Scripture as religious symbols. The believer is admonished to do the works of the One who sent Christ "while it is day" because the "night is coming" (Jn. 9:4). The antithesis of day-night (cf. Jn. 11:9f.; 1 Thess. 5:1-8) contrasts here the span of human activity on earth with the time when no such activity is possible. The old and the new aeons are in antithesis to each other as the "night" to the "day" (Rom. 13:11f.). The figurative terms of night-day correspond to darkness-light. The believers are "sons of the day" (Rom. 13:13) casting off the works of darkness. The OT and NT expect the inbreaking of the new day in which there is no night (Zec. 14:7; Rev. 21:25; 22:5).

Bibliography.–G. Dalman, *Arbeit und Sitte in Palästina* (1928), I, 2; A. Strobel, *ZNW*, 49 (1958), 157-196; S. Talmon, *Scripta Hierosolymitana*, 4 (1958), 162-199; G. Mensching, *RGG* (3rd ed. 1960), IV, cols. 1293f.; R. de Vaux, *Ancient Israel: Its Life and Institutions* (1961); pp. 180-83; *TDNT*, II, *s.v.* ἡμέρα (von

Rad, Delling); IV, *s.v.* νύξ (Delling); *BhHW,* II, *s.v.* "Nacht und Tag" (Rordorf). G. F. HASEL

DAY BEFORE THE SABBATH. *See* DAY OF PREPARATION.

DAY, BREAK OF. *See* DAWN.

DAY, JOSHUA'S LONG. *See* BETH-HORON, BATTLE OF.

DAY, LAST [Gk. *hē eschátē hēméra*]. An expression repeatedly used by Jesus in John (6:39f., 44, 54; 11:24; 12:48) for the day of resurrection and judgment (*see* ESCHATOLOGY). Cf. the usage in the OT of "latter days" (Isa. 2:2; Mic. 4:1) and in the NT (Acts 2:17; 2 Tim. 3:1; 1 Pet. 1:5; 2 Pet. 3:3; 1 Jn. 2:18; Jude 18) of "last days" and "last time" to denote the messianic age.

In Jn. 7:37 "the last day of the feast," the great day refers to the eighth day of the Feast of Tabernacles. This closing day was observed as a sabbath (Lev. 23:36). On it the libation of water made on other days was not made; hence the allusion of Jesus to Himself as the giver of the living water. J. ORR

DAY, LORD'S. *See* LORD'S DAY.

DAY OF ATONEMENT. *See* ATONEMENT, DAY OF.

DAY OF CHRIST. *See* DAY OF THE LORD.

DAY OF JUDGMENT. *See* JUDGMENT, LAST.

DAY OF PREPARATION [Gk. *hē paraskeuḗ*–'preparation']; AV also THE PREPARATION; NEB FRIDAY, PREPARATION-DAY, "eve [of Passover]," "eve of the Sabbath." The day before the sabbath was considered a day of preparation, in accordance with Ex. 16:23, both before the regular sabbath and before a feast sabbath (Mt. 27:62; Mk. 15:42; Lk. 23:54; Jn. 19:14, 31, 42). At 3 p.m., the Hebrews began to prepare their food for the next day and to perform all the necessary labors that were forbidden on the sabbath. They bathed and purified themselves, dressed in festive apparel, set their tables, and lighted their lamps. On the day before Passover, the Hebrews of the later period made it their chief business to remove all leaven from the house (cf. 1 Cor. 5:7). This custom of converting at least a portion of the day before the sabbath into a holy day was recognized by the Romans to such an extent that, according to a rescript of Augustus, Jews need not appear in court after 3 p.m. on such days. Criminal cases were not brought before court on this day, and journeys exceeding 12 Roman mi. (11 mi., 17.8 km.) were prohibited. The signal for the preparations was given by the priests by means of trumphets blown six times at intervals.

See *TDNT*, VII, *s.v.* σάββατον, παρασκευή (Lohse). F. E. HIRSCH

DAY OF THE LORD [Heb. *yôm YHWH*; Gk. *hē hēméra toú Kyriou*]. In the OT, the future consummation of the kingdom of God and the absolute cessation of all attacks upon it (Isa. 2:12; 13:6, 9; 34:8; Ezk. 13:5; 30:3; Joel 1:15; 2:11; Am. 5:18; Zeph. 1:14; Zec. 14:1). It is a "day of visitation" (Isa. 10:3), a day "of the wrath of the Lord" (Ezk. 7:19), a "great day of the Lord" (Zeph. 1:14). The entire conception in the OT is dark and foreboding.

On the other hand the NT idea is pervaded with the elements of hope and joy and victory. In the NT it is eminently the day of Christ, the day of His coming in the glory of His Father. The very conception of Him as the "Son of man" points to this day; e.g., Jn. 5:27 says that the Father "has given him authority to execute judgment, because he is the Son of man" (cf. Mt. 24:27, 30; Lk. 12:8). In the NT also, however, there is a dark background to the bright picture, for it still remains a "day of wrath" (Rom. 2:5f.), a "great day" (Rev. 6:17; Jude 6), a "day of God" (2 Pet. 3:12), a "day of judgment" (Mt. 10:15; 2 Pet. 3:7; Rom. 2:16).

Sometimes it is called "that day" (Mt. 7:22; 1 Thess. 5:4; 2 Tim. 4:8), and again it is called "the day" without any qualification whatever, as if it were the only day worth counting in all the history of the world and of the race (1 Cor. 3:13). To the unbeliever, the NT depicts it as a day of terror; to the believer, as a day of joy. For on that day Christ will raise the dead, especially His own dead, the bodies of those that believed in Him — "that of all that which he hath given me I should lose nothing, but should raise it up at the last day" (Jn. 6:39). In that day He comes to His own (Mt. 16:27), and therefore it is called "the day of our Lord Jesus" (2 Cor. 1:14), "the day of Jesus Christ" or "of Christ" (Phil. 1:6, 10), the day when there "shall appear the sign of the Son of man in heaven" (Mt. 24:30). All Pauline literature is especially suffused with this longing for the Parousia, the day of Christ's glorious manifestation. The entire conception of that day centers therefore in Christ and points to the everlasting establishment of the kingdom of heaven, from which sin will be forever eliminated.

See also ESCHATOLOGY. H. E. DOSKER

DAY STAR [Heb. *hêlîl*] (Isa. 14:12); AV LUCIFER; NEB MORNING STAR; **MORNING STAR** [Gk. *phōsphóros*] (2 Pet. 1:19); AV DAY STAR; [*astḗr prōinós*] (Rev. 2:28); NEB STAR OF DAWN. The morning "star" is actually the planet Venus, which, when in its orbital swing to the west of the sun, rises before dawn as the herald of a new day. Thus it is a fitting description of the person of Christ Jesus.

In the poetic passage Isa. 14:12 this same figure is applied to "Lucifer, son of the morning" (AV), who, in attempting to usurp God's exalted state is "felled to the earth" (NEB).

See also ASTRONOMY II.C. N. GREEN

DAY, THAT (THE). *See* DAY OF THE LORD.

DAY'S JOURNEY [Heb. *dereḵ yôm* (Gen. 30:36; Ex. 3:18; 5:3; 8:27; Nu. 10:33; 11:31; 33:8; Dt. 1:2; 1 K. 19:4), *mahᵃlaḵ yôm* (Jonah 3:3f.); Gk. *hēméras hodós* (Lk. 2:44), *sabbátou hodós* (Acts 1:12)]; NEB also "marched for [three] days," "journey takes [eleven] days," etc. The common way of estimating distances in the East was by hours and days. This is natural in a country where roads are mere bridle paths or are nonexistent, as in the desert. The distance traveled must of course differ largely according to the difficulties of the way, and it is more important to know where night will overtake the traveler than the actual distance accomplished. The rate of travel with a loaded mule is now commonly reckoned at 3 mi. (about 5 km.) per hour, and a day's journey is generally eight hours. Hence a day's journey is about 24 mi. (40 km.) and this may be taken as a fair estimate for Bible times. An alternative reckoning is by the distance between towns or caravansaries on a road — which is usually between 25 and 30 mi. (40 and 48 km.).

H. PORTER

DAYSMAN (Job 9:33, AV). *See* UMPIRE.

DAYSPRING. An archaic word in the AV for "dawn" (RSV), in Job 38:12 (Heb. *šaḥar*; NEB "morning") and Lk. 1:78 (Gk. *anatolḗ*; NEB "morning sun"). *See* DAWN.

DEACON; DEACONESS [Gk. *diákonos*, *hypērétēs*, *doúlos*, and their cognates]. In general the words denote the service of slaves, underlings, and helpers. They are used to emphasize that all Christians are ministers and all Christian life is a ministry. In addition, however, the word "deacon" has acquired a specialized meaning, being used both in the NT and in Christian history for one of the regular church officers.

The origin of the diaconate has been sought in the appointment of the Seven in Acts 6. These men were selected primarily to serve tables (*diakoneín trapézais*), thus freeing the Twelve for prayer and the ministry (*diakonía*) of the word. They were not given the title of deacons, and there can certainly be no implication of the institution of an order, or of the restriction of diaconate to the Seven. Nevertheless, they are given a function of practical administration for which the words diaconate and deacon are peculiarly apt. For the rest, it may be noted that at least Stephen and Philip also undertook a wider ministry of the word.

An even looser usage is probably to be seen in the description of Phoebe as a "deaconess" in Rom. 16:1. Some have argued that this denotes official appointment. This is, however, neither a necessary nor a likely conclusion. A diaconate was fairly certainly fulfilled by some women, either along the lines of the ministry of the women to Jesus or more especially in the visitation of other women. Yet we do not read of any formal selection or institution as in the case of the Seven.

The reference to bishops and deacons in Phil. 1:1 carries more of the suggestion of formal office for the fulfilment of the diaconate. Yet we are not told anything of the qualifications or functions, and therefore we cannot press the reference too strongly. In 1 Tim. 3:8-12 the picture becomes clearer. Deacons are to be "serious, not double-tongued, not addicted to much wine, not greedy for gain." They are first to be proved. Women in like manner (their wives, or deaconesses?) must be "serious, no slanderers, but temperate, faithful in all things." Deacons are to be husbands of one wife (possibly in the sense of not remarried after divorce), and must rule their children and houses well. Their main task seems to be practical administration in the primary form of dispensing alms.

W. A. HEIDEL
G. W. B.

ANGLICAN VIEW

In Anglican churches the diaconate is one of the three traditional orders of ministry. It has survived, however, only in a truncated form, serving for the most part only as a first step to the presbyterate.

In keeping with the provisions of the Pastoral Epistles, the deacon is to be of sufficient age and to furnish evidence of godly conversation, learning being also a requirement. The passage 1 Tim. 3:8ff. is read in the course of his ordination, as is also Acts 6:2ff.

Contact is made with the historical diaconate in the delineation of duties. The deacon is to assist at divine service, to read the Scriptures and homilies, to instruct in the catechism, to baptize and to preach if permitted, to seek out the poor, sick, and infirm, and to help solicit and distribute alms. It may be noted, however, that there is greater stress on assistance in spiritual ministry than on the original function.

The archdeacon furnishes an even greater departure from the original order, for, in keeping with later medieval usage, much resisted at first, he is a presbyter. Yet paradoxically he perhaps fulfils more of the function of diaconate, especially in the proper maintenance of churches and property. He also supervises the examination and presentation of candidates for the diaconate.

With the truncation of the original diaconate, the Anglican Church naturally tended to develop a kind of substitute in the churchwardens, sidesmen, vestries, and later Parochial Councils, who are vested with practical and financial responsibility for the churches. In this regard, it is interesting that the wardens are each year admitted (though not ordained) by the archdeacon, although a certain confusion is caused by the inclusion of disciplinary powers that also attach to the archdeacon. Today these are very seldom exercised.

In the 19th cent. an order of deaconesses was introduced into the Anglican Church. It did not develop to any great extent and full ordination, as in the case of the deacon, was not presupposed. Many Anglican communions now ordain women as deacons and in some places their diaconate may be a stage to the priesthood.

REFORMED VIEW

Various attempts were made early in the Reformation period to restore the place of the deacon as a distinctive office in the Church, e.g., at Hesse in 1526, and at Basel in 1529 (see Sch.-Herz.).

Calvin held that the distinctiveness of this office had been obscured in the practice of the Roman Church, where it was merely a step to the priesthood, nothing more being demanded of its holder than that he should assist at the altar, chant the gospel, and "goodness knows what other trifles" (*Inst.* iv.15.5). Calvin believed that the office originated in the election of the Seven (Acts 6:1-6), and was referred to by Paul in the latter half of Rom. 12:8. The office especially involves care for the poor and the distribution of alms (*Inst.* iv.3.9; 4.1). Women also can exercise a similar diaconate (cf. 1 Tim. 5:9f.), for the term *diakonía* has a wide application. Calvin also believed that in the early Church the bishops delegated this office to the deacons, who rendered account of their stewardship to the bishop. Calvin himself gave a place to the deacon as an assistant in the celebration of the Lord's supper, in giving the cup to the people and in uttering words encouraging the people to communicate. In the *Institutes* and in the Reformed confessions the deacons are usually mentioned along with the elders as officers of a local congregation, the elders being charged with the supervision of discipline, the deacons with the care of the poor (cf. Gallic Confession 29; Belgic Confession 30f.).

In the Reformed Church of Scotland the elders undertook the care of the poor and any other function the deacons may have had, and the office tended to disappear. Indeed there has been a strong theological tradition in some branches of the Reformed Church that the Presbyterian elder is himself the closest thing possible to the NT deacon, and this position was restated in a report to the General Assembly of the Church of Scotland by its Panel on Doctrine (1964). In other branches of the Reformed Church, however, the tradition of the deacon as an officer distinct from the elder reappeared. In the Free Church of Scotland (1843), e.g., deacons other than elders were ordained to administer, along with the Kirk Session, the "temporal" affairs of the congregation. In the Churches of the Secessions which later formed the United Presbyterian Church of Scotland, a court of "managers" under a "preses" was set up in each congregation for such affairs. The United Presbyterian Church in the U.S.A. defines deacons as "distinct officers of the Church," whose business is the care of the poor, but to whom "may be properly committed" the management of the temporal affairs of the church. Deacons, as distinct from elders, are here given the duty of developing the grace of liberality and of receiving and administering the offerings of the people. Deacons are sometimes ordained to office for life. They may also be appointed, whether for life or for a limited period.

In some Reformed communions the attempt to find a distinctive place for the ministry of women in the church has led to appearance of the woman deaconess, often set apart for full-time service, and (e.g., in the Church of Scotland) sometimes licensed to preach the word of God. It is not always clear whether such deaconesses belong to a separate order of women, or hold a distinct office within the church. R. S. WALLACE

DEAD. *See* DEATH.

DEAD, ABODE OF THE. *See* DEATH III.

DEAD, BAPTISM FOR THE. *See* BAPTISM FOR THE DEAD.

DEAD BODY. *See* CORPSE.

DEAD SEA. The large salt lake between Jordan and Palestine at the mouth of the Jordan River, known variously in the OT as the Salt Sea (Heb. *yām hammelaḥ*, Gen. 14:3; Nu. 34:3, 12; Dt. 3:17; Josh. 3:16; 12:3; 15:2, 5; 18:19), the Sea of the Arabah (*yām ha'ᵃrāḇâ*, AV "son of the plain," Dt. 3:17; 4:49; Josh. 3:16; 12:3), and the Eastern Sea (*yām haqqadmônî*, AV "east sea," Ezk. 47:18; Joel 2:20; "former sea," Zec. 14:8). Josephus called it Lake Asphaltitis; the Arabic name is Baḥr Lûṭ, "Sea of Lot." The name "Dead Sea" (which the NEB uses in place of "Salt Sea") is probably postbiblical.

I. Geological History
II. Present Characteristics
III. Biblical Period
IV. Waters of the Dead Sea
V. Historical Importance

I. Geological History.–The area of the Dead Sea seems to have been continuously covered by salt water from the Cambrian era on, though its form and extent have changed many times. From the mid-Pleistocene, however, the Palestinian rift valley took on approximately its present form. In the mid-Pleistocene a period of very heavy rain set in which created a salt lake stretching from the Sea of Galilee southward to 'Ain Ḥoṣob (Oboth?), some 15 mi. (24 km.) S of its present limits. The rift valley has retained its present appearance for about the past fifty thousand years. (For detailed information see L. Picard, *Structure and Evolution of Palestine* [1943], and in outline *GB,* ch. 2.)

The Dead Sea began as a portion of the Cambrian "Tethys Sea," a saltwater body. In addition the presence of Jebel Usdum (now Har Sedom), the salt mountain at its southwest extremity, must have greatly increased its salinity, even without the effects of evaporation, which are normally overstressed. In other words there is no basis for the popular theory that the high salinity is primarily due to the phenomena connected with the destruction of the cities of the valley. Many of the more extreme travelers' tales, e.g., that no bird could fly over the sea and live, were really based on the concept that the existence of the sea was the result of God's judgment. Raised beaches testify to changing levels in its waters through the centuries, but care must be taken to distinguish them from deposits from pre-Pleistocene times, which have also been found.

II. Present Characteristics.–The surface of the Dead Sea is about 1294 ft. (394 m.) below sea level, and its deepest point more than 1300 ft. (396 m.) lower. It is thus the lowest point on the earth's surface. The sea is about 50 mi. (80 km.) long, with a maximum width of about 10 mi. (16 km.) and a surface area of about 395 sq. mi. (1020 sq. km.). The area is divided into two uneven portions by the promontory known as el-Lisan ("the tongue"), which projects about halfway across the lake from the eastern shore, about 15 mi. (24 km.) up from the southern end of the lake.

The main northern basin is fairly uniform in depth, largely because of the heavy deposits of salt from the salt-saturated water, except at the northern end, where there has been much silting from the Jordan; silting occurs also, to a smaller degree, by the mouths of the other streams that flow into the sea. The descent on the eastern side is very rapid, but the depth increases more gradually on the western side. The lower basin, which forms about 27 percent of the total area of the lake, is never more than 30 ft. (9 m.) deep.

Apart from the Jordan, the Dead Sea receives water from the Wâdī Kerak, Zerqā-Mā'în, Arnon, and Zered, as well as from winter torrents and springs, e.g., Callirhoë, En-gedi, 'Ain Feshkha (Qumrân). In spite of this large volume of water, the seasonal variation in the surface level is no more than 10-15 ft. (3-4.5 m.). Owing to the physical formation of the rift valley the sea lies in a rain shadow, and so the rainfall seldom exceeds 2 in. (5 cm.) per year.

III. Biblical Period.–More than thirty shore terraces have been traced along the sides of the Dead Sea. While most of them belong to the pre-Quaternary, it remains clear that the water level has fluctuated ever since the appearance of man. Though there is no evidence for any major change in Palestinian climatic conditions since the time of Abraham, it has been established that the rainfall has tended to vary in quantity in gradual cyclic periods. In addition the amount of forest cover, irrigation, and agricultural methods generally will have influenced the amount of water flowing into the sea. Early in this century the surface level had risen some 30 ft. (9 m.) above the height established in the first half of last century. Now it has fallen again. The rise was probably due mainly to the somewhat increased rainfall reported early this century; the decrease will be due as much to increasing afforestation and irrigation as to declining rainfall. The surface level may be expected to fall even more with the increasing irrigation on both sides of the Jordan.

This should be a warning to us not to take for granted that the surface level in the biblical period was the same as now. As noted, there is strong evidence for much silting where the Jordan flows in, and this is true in less measure of the other rivers. The description of Judah's northern boundary (Josh. 15:5f.) strongly suggests that it ran due W from "the bay of the sea at the mouth of the Jordan." With the present topography it would have to run N before it could reach Beth-hoglah and then turn W. The same impression is created by the description of the southern boundary of Benjamin (Josh. 18:19), where no suggestion of a change of direction from E to S can be found. If this inference is correct, it means that the sea stretched some distance further N at the time, and this silting in itself must have raised the level considerably. When we further consider the greater degree of tree cover and irrigation in the biblical period, we have solid grounds for postulating a considerably lower level for the surface of the Dead Sea. It would not need any very drastic lowering of the present level for the southern basin to be separated from the main body of water, in which case it would very soon dry out; there are various strands of evidence that this was the case in the biblical period.

Josephus' estimate of the length and breadth of the sea (*BJ* iv.8.4), though manifestly incorrect, is likely to be approximately true of their ratio to one another; in that case it would apply much better to the northern basin than to the sea as it now is. There are traces of a Roman road across the el-Lisan peninsula joining Transjordan and Judea; it is unlikely that when it was first made its users had either to ford the shallow waters or use a ferry. If the area S of el-Lisan was the Valley of Salt (2 S. 8:13; 1 Ch. 18:12; Ps. 60 title; 2 K. 14:7; 2 Ch. 25:11), it would have furnished a better site for David's and Amaziah's victories than the marshy plain at present S of the Dead Sea (though with the southern basin dry it may have been less marshy) or some valley S of Beer-sheba. The account in 2 Ch. 20:2 is easier to understand if the Ammonites and Moabites did not have to go around the southern end of the Dead Sea at its present extent. Had they done so, it is improbable that they would have reached En-gedi before their presence was reported in Jerusalem. In any case, it is improbable that they would have chosen such a difficult invasion route. The same impression is given by the (admittedly defective) Madeba Map, dating from *ca.* A.D. 560.

There was an increase in rainfall in the 7th cent. A.D. In addition, the Arab conquest of Palestine in 636 led to the destruction or cessation of much of the irrigation. As a result the level of the sea should have risen steadily until the southern basin was once again flooded, as it is to this day.

If this view is correct, it gives the fortress of Masada a much more strategic position. It would no longer have been mainly a stronghold to which one could retreat in time of need; it would have been in a highly strategic position to control the sensitive area S of the Dead Sea. The same would be true to a smaller degree of the fortress of Machaerus E of the sea. The implications of the "circuitous march of seven days" (2 K. 3:9) are too vague for anything to be built on them. The interpretation of the route of the four Mesopotamian kings (Gen. 14:5-8) depends mainly on our location of the cities of the valley, and so cannot be used as evidence. There is no suggestion at all that their site was covered by the waters of the sea after the catastrophe. We cannot tell whether the Valley of Siddim (Gen. 14:8, 10) should be identified with the Valley of Salt. While bitumen is found from time to time floating on the water or thrown up on the shore, today there are no traces of anything that could be called "bitumen pits."

IV. Waters of the Dead Sea.–Though there is unanimous agreement that the Dead Sea, with an approximate 25 to 30 percent salinity, is the most saline natural body of water of any size in the world, there are varying estimates of its mineral content. This is largely due to the varying depth and location from which specimens of water have been taken.

The actual water conditions of the sea have been established only in comparatively recent times. Because of the shallowness of the southern basin, its rate of evaporation is greater than in the northern basin, and this in turn somewhat increases its salinity compared with the surface waters of the northern basin. In the latter there is a sharp division in the water at a depth of about 130 ft. (40 m.). In the upper layer the salinity is about 300 grams per liter, whereas in the lower layer the salinity increases rapidly to reach about 332 grams per liter, when the water represents a saturated solution. In the lower levels much of the sodium chloride has been precipitated, forming a deep layer on the floor of the sea wherever the depth is

Moon-like formations along the mineral-filled Dead Sea shore. The sea and its environs display an abundance of geological and mineralogical phenomena. (Consulate General of Israel in New York)

more than 130 ft. (40 m.). As a result there is a far higher precentage of magnesium, potassium, and bromide salts in the lower than in the surface waters. The general view is that we are dealing with "fossil" water, which has been in its present state for many millennia. It has been sealed off from the atmosphere by the less dense upper water, which has covered it in times of rising water level. The precipitation of salts on the sea bed is made up by replacement from the upper layers. There is no likelihood of the water's becoming homogeneous unless the surface level falls very considerably.

Various estimates of the commercial value of the Dead Sea salts are offered from time to time. They are normally impressively high, but they almost invariably neglect the cost of extraction and transport, and the demands of the world market. The potash extraction is the most important. Both in primitive form down the centuries and by scientific methods today, first at Kallia at the north end of the sea and now at Sedom at the south end, the salts have been won by turning the water into shallow evaporation pans.

V. Historical Importance.–While rough tracks have led from the north end of the sea to Qumrân and from the south end to En-gedi, it is only very recently that a road has been driven over the headland between them. There has never been a road along the east bank. Shipping has been used on the sea at various times in its history, but this has almost invariably been when one power controlled both shores. Sudden storms militate against its popularity. As a result, the sea has served as an almost impregnable defense for the eastern boundary of Judea, the more so as it is flanked by Jeshimon, or the Wilderness of Judea, which is almost impregnable to any large body of soldiers. Near as Qumrân was to Jericho, its site guaranteed its almost complete isolation except for those who had business there.

See also CITIES OF THE VALLEY; SIDDIM, VALLEY OF.

Bibliography.–*HGHL* (with references to much of the earlier literature); Baly, *GB*; N. Glueck, *River Jordan* (rev. ed. 1968); D. Neev & K. O. Emery, *Science Journal*, 2/12 (Dec. 1966).

H. L. ELLISON

DEAD SEA SCROLLS. The name generally given to the manuscripts and fragments of manuscripts discovered in caves near the northwestern end of the Dead Sea in the period between 1946 and 1956. They are also called by several other terms, such as the 'Ain Feshka Scrolls, the Scrolls from the Judean Desert, and — probably best of all — the Qumrân Library (QL). The name Dead Sea Scrolls (DSS), however, has become firmly attached in English, and likewise its equivalent in several other languages, in spite of its imprecision. According to many experts, this is one of the greatest recent archeological discoveries, and for biblical studies certainly one of the greatest manuscript discoveries of all times.

I. Discoveries
  A. Original Finds
  B. Subsequent MS Discoveries
  C. The "Monastery" of Qumrân
II. The Qumrân Community
  A. MS Evidence
  B. Origin of the Community
  C. Names for the Community
  D. Organization
  E. Daily Life
  F. Doctrine of God
  G. Doctrine of Man
  H. Eschatology
  I. Teacher of Righteousness
III. Significance of the Scrolls
  A. Text and Canon
  B. Developments in Early Judaism
  C. Relationship to the NT
  D. Uniqueness of Christ

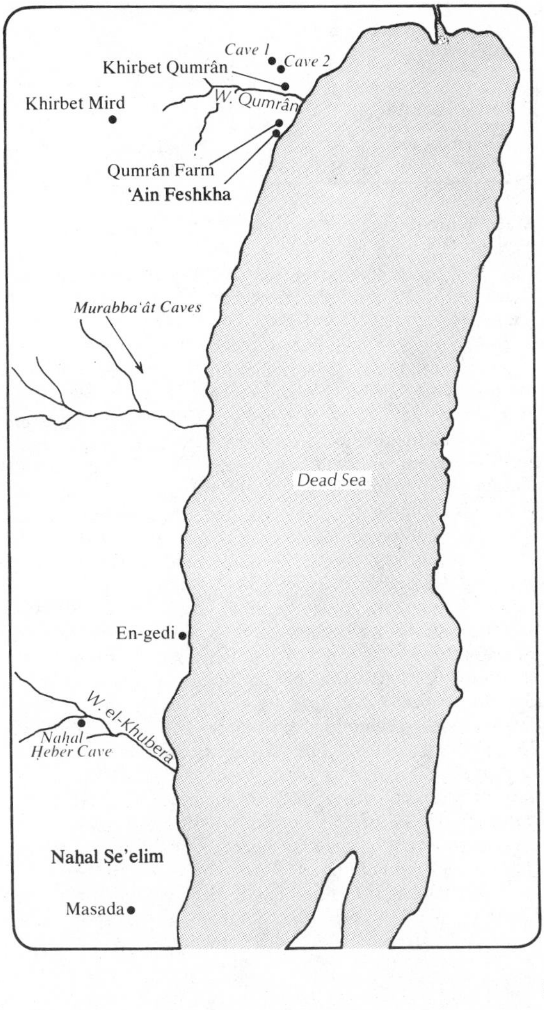

I. Discoveries.–A. Original Finds. The story of the "discovery" of the DSS has been told many times, and with some significant variations. Probably the best accounts are given by J. C. Trever (*The Dead Sea Scrolls: A Personal Account* [rev. ed. 1978]) and Y. Yadin (*Message of the Scrolls* [1957]). For an exhaustive bibliography of early reports, see W. S. LaSor, *Bibliography of the Dead Sea Scrolls 1948-1957* (1958), pp. 19-39.

As reconstructed by Trever, the first "discovery" was made by three bedouin of the Ta'amireh tribe, Muhammed Ahmed el-Hamed (known as "edh-Dhib"), Jum'a Muhammed Khalib, and Khalil Musa, who by chance came upon what later was to be known as Cave 1 and discovered a number of jars, some containing manuscripts. The date is not known, but it was probably toward the end of 1946 or early 1947. In March 1947 the scrolls were offered to an antiquities dealer in Bethlehem, but he did not buy them. In April, the scrolls were taken to Khalil Eskander Shahin ("Kando"), a shoemaker and antiquities dealer in Bethlehem, who became an intermediary in numerous sales of the materials. Meanwhile George Isha'ya Shamoun, a Syrian Orthodox merchant who often visited Bethlehem, was taken to Cave 1 by bedouin, and later he and Khalil Musa secured four scrolls. Isha'ya had in the meantime (about April 1947) informed St. Mark's Monastery of the find, and the Metropolitan, Mar Athanasius Yeshue Samuel, offered to buy them. Four scrolls were taken to the monastery about July 5 by Jum'a Muhammed, Khalil Musa, and George Isha'ya, but they were mistakenly turned away at the gate. About July 19, Kando purchased scrolls from the bedouin and sold them to St. Mark's Monastery for twenty-four Palestinian pounds ($97.20). That same month, Fr. S. Marmardji of École Biblique was consulted about the scrolls, and he and Fr. J. van der Ploeg went to the monastery to see them. Van der Ploeg recalls with some embarrassment that he mistakenly identified the scrolls as medieval. Other scholars also examined the scrolls, but none recognized their great value.

In addition to the four scrolls that were sold by Kando, three others were sold by Jum'a and Khalil to Faidi Salahi, also an antiquities dealer. He paid seven Palestinian pounds ($28.35) for the scrolls and twenty piasters (about 80 cents) each for two jars. These were the first MSS to come into the possession of recognized scholars, for two of them were purchased by E. L. Sukenik of Hebrew University on Nov. 29 and the third on Dec. 22, 1947. The MSS were later identified as the *Hebrew University Isaiah Scroll* (1QIsa^b), the *Order of Warfare,* or the *War of the Sons of Light Against the Sons of Darkness,* later called the *War Scroll* (1QM), and the *Thanksgiving Hymns* (1QH). (For details of the negotiations, see Yadin [Sukenik's son], *Message of the Scrolls.*)

Sukenik had heard about the other scrolls in the possession of St. Mark's Monastery, was permitted to examine them, and offered to buy them. Fr. Butrus Sowmy, librarian of the monastery, contacted the American School of Oriental Research in Jerusalem on Feb. 18, 1948, seeking to get a better idea of the value of the scrolls, and he and his brother Ibrahim took four scrolls to the school on the following day. They were examined by J. Trever, a postdoctoral fellow at the school. Excited by the Hebrew paleography, Trever managed to secure permission to visit the monastery, and then was given permission to photograph the scrolls. On Feb. 21 and 22 and again on March 6-11, he photographed three of the scrolls, column by column, and his photographs became the basis for the *editio princeps* of these scrolls, later identified as the *Isaiah Scroll* (1QIsa[a]), the *Habakkuk Commentary* (1QpHab), and the *Manual of Discipline* (1QS). The fourth scroll could not be opened. From a fragment, it was named the "Lamech Scroll," and later, when opened by J. Biberkraut, an expert in unrolling delicate MSS (cf. *BA,* 19/1 [1956], 22-24), it was renamed the *Genesis Apocryphon* (1QapGen).

To understand the confusion that is found in various reports, one must bear in mind that the British Mandate was nearing its end, and sporadic fighting between Arabs and Jews was taking place. On Nov. 29, 1947, the day that Sukenik purchased the first of the scrolls, the United Nations voted to partition Palestine and establish an independent nation of the Jews, and on May 14-15, 1948, the Mandate ended, the State of Israel came into being, and warfare broke out on a large scale. For obvious reasons, Fr. Sowmy took the scrolls in his possession to Beirut for safekeeping (March 25, 1948); he returned to Jerusalem and was later killed in the bombing that damaged St. Mark's Monastery. Athanasius Samuel took the four scrolls from Beirut to New York in January 1949. Efforts were made by several institutions to purchase the scrolls, but the Metropolitan was asking a huge sum, reportedly a million dollars, for them. In February 1955 the Prime Minister of Israel revealed that Yadin had secretly purchased the scrolls on July 1, 1954, for $250,000, and that the scrolls were in a vault in the Prime Minister's office. Subsequently they were moved to a building that had been built for them near the University, known as the Shrine of the Book. All the scrolls of the original discoveries in Cave 1 were now in Israel.

It was impossible for qualified scholars to visit and explore the cave where the scrolls allegedly had been found, so there was much distrust of the story told by the bedouin and repeated by many others. There were unauthorized visits to the cave in the summer and again in the fall of 1948, and many additional fragments of scrolls and other items were recovered. It became obvious that some controlled exploration should be undertaken.

In September 1948 the first articles on the scrolls were published, along with photographs, both by the American Schools of Oriental Research and by Hebrew University, and "the Battle of the Scrolls" had begun. For many months there was considerable discussion of the date and authenticity of the discoveries. It is probably correct to state that never in history had so many scholars from so many different nations become involved in the problems associated with a single discovery.

Capt. P. Lippens, a Belgian army officer serving as observer for the United Nations, was able to interest Major General Lash, British commander of the Arab Legion, Colonel Ashton, archeological advisor to the Legion, and G. L. Harding, Director General of the Department of Antiquities of the Hashemite Kingdom of the Jordan. An expedition and a detachment of the Arab Legion under Captain A. ez-Zeben located Cave 1, only to find that it had been almost completely looted. Systematic excavation was undertaken by Harding and Père R. de Vaux, director of École Biblique, between Feb. 8 and March 5, 1949, and thousands of MS fragments, together with jar fragments, pottery remains, and fragments of the cloth that had wrapped the scrolls, were recovered. (For an inventory, cf. Trever, pp. 149f.) It seemed certain, although hotly disputed by some, that the cave of the original finds had indeed been discovered, and that the bedouin story was basically correct. The cave was located by Harding at coordinates 1934.1287 of the Palestine Survey

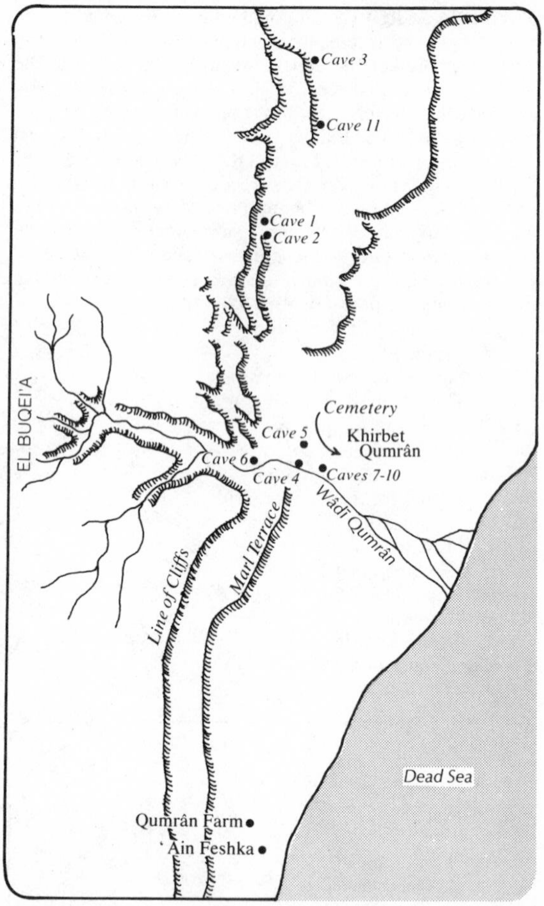

Map, which is about 6.8 mi. (11 km.) S of Jericho, 2.2 mi. (3.5 km.) N of 'Ain Feshkha, in the marly cliffs about 1.2 mi. (2 km.) from the northwestern shore of the Dead Sea and about 1000 ft. (305 m.) above the surface of the sea (which is 1292 ft. [394 m.] below sea level).

B. Subsequent MS Discoveries. Materials that were obviously related to the original finds were turning up in the hands of various antiquities dealers. Caves in Wâdī Murabba'ât as well as in Khirbet Mird were discovered by bedouin. Meanwhile, expeditions led by École Biblique and the American Schools were exploring the region and finding other caves. Between March 10 and 29, teams explored the region for 5 mi. (8 km.) N and S of Wâdī Qumrân, discovering 230 caves, of which twenty-six contained pottery similar to that found in Cave 1, but only one (Cave 3) contained MS fragments.

It is important, to assure that scholarly control was maintained, to note that Cave 3 was discovered by an expedition, Cave 4 (which had been discovered by bedouin) was excavated by a scholarly expedition, who also discovered Cave 5, and Caves 7, 8, 9, and 10 were discovered by archeologists working at Khirbet Qumrân. The marked relationship of the discoveries from the various Qumrân caves (with the possible exception of the copper scroll from Cave 3) makes it clear that the materials in all of the caves, whether discovered by bedouin or archeological expeditions, are of common origin. (The caves were numbered in the order in which they were discovered.) On the other hand, the discoveries in the caves in Wâdī Murabba'ât, Khirbet Mird, and Naḥal

Ḥeber belong to different categories, and should not be confused with the Dead Sea Scrolls. Caves 4, 5, 7, 8, 9, and 10 were located in the terrace around Khirbet Qumrân, while Caves 1, 2, 3, 6, and 11 were in the cliff that extends north and south, to the west of the Jordan Valley and the Dead Sea. The most significant cave yields were from Caves 1, 4, and 11, which will be discussed more fully. Cave 3 yielded the "Copper Scroll" (3QInv or 3Q*15*); Cave 6 provided a quantity of papyrus fragments and significant fragments of the "Damascus Document" (6QD; CD is exemplar from Cairo); Caves 2, 5, and 7 through 10 yielded smaller quantities of MS fragments.

The most extensive MSS were found in Cave 1 (mentioned above) and Cave 11, which yielded at least seven MSS, including a Targum of Job (11QtgJob), a portion of Leviticus in Paleo-Hebrew script (11QpaleoLev), a scroll of Ezekiel (11QEzek) in bad condition, and three partial scrolls of Psalms (11QPs^{a,b,c}). The large Psalms scroll (11QPs^{a}) contains thirty-six canonical Psalms, the Hebrew text of Ps. 151 (previously known only from Greek, Syriac, and Old Latin texts), and eight Psalms not otherwise known. It is possible that the "Temple Scroll" (seized by Israelis in 1967 from a Jerusalem antiquities dealer, provisionally identified as 11QTemple) also came from Cave 11.

In addition to the more extensive MSS or portions of MSS, great quantities of fragments of MSS were recovered, the importance of which is at least equal to that of the MSS that suffered lesser damage. From Cave 1 came fragments that were at first thought to be part of the *Manual of Discipline* (1QS), namely the *Order of the Congregation* (1QSa or 1Q*28a*) and the *Benedictions* (1QSb or 1Q*28b*). There were also fragments of commentaries on Micah, Ps. 37, and Ps. 68, as well as fragments of the *Book of Mysteries* (1QMyst or 1Q*27*), the *Sayings of Moses* (1QDM or 1Q*22*), and a portion of Daniel including 2:4, where the language changes from Hebrew to Aramaic (1QDan^{a}). Cave 4 yielded about 40,000 fragments, representing about 382 different MSS, of which more than 100 are biblical. An international team of eight scholars worked for several years putting together the pieces of this gigantic jigsaw puzzle, and the result included portions of every book of the Hebrew Bible except Esther, fragments of apocryphal works not previously known in Hebrew, and many extrabiblical works, most of which had not previously been known. Among the more significant discoveries are: a *Florilegium* or collection of messianic promises (4QFlor); a portion of Gen. 49 with commentary, known as the *Patriarchal Blessings* (4QBless); a document that sheds some light on the messianic beliefs of the Community, known as the *Testimonia* (4QTestim); a commentary on Ps. 37 (4QpPs 37); fragments of seven MSS of the *Damascus Document* (4QD^{a-g}); fragments of the *War Scroll* (4QM); and portions of Daniel where the language changes from Aramaic to Hebrew (Dnl. 7:28–8:1, 4QDan^{a,b}).

A full inventory of the published materials from these caves can be found in J. A. Fitzmyer, *The Dead Sea Scrolls: Major Publications and Tools for Study* (1975), pp. 11-39. Fitzmyer also lists the published discoveries from Masada, Wâdī Murabba'ât, Naḥal Ḥeber (Wâdī Ḥabra), Naḥal Ṣe'elim (Wâdī Seiyal), Naḥal Mishmar (Wâdī Mahras), Khirbet Mird, and pertinent texts from the Cairo Genizah (pp. 40-53), as well as lists that contain some of the unpublished materials (p. 65). There is no published inventory of all the items discovered at Qumrân.

C. The "Monastery" of Qumrân. The region above the cliffs that flank the northwestern shore of the Dead Sea is a shallow depression known as el-Buqei'a. It is cut by a seasonal river or wadi that bears several names,

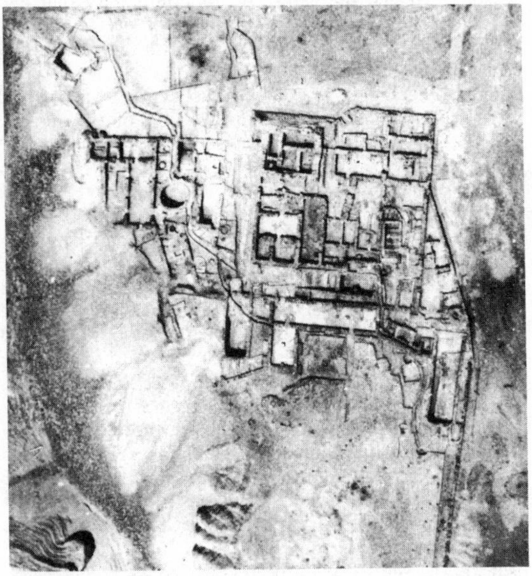

Air view of Qumrân community ruins after five seasons of excavation. The library and scriptorium are at the center of the complex. (Israel Department of Antiquities and Museums)

but where it cuts down through the cliff it is best known as Wâdī Qumrân. At the base of the cliff is a plateau or terrace formed by the detritus from the cliff, presumably when it was eroded by an unusual amount of water during the last Pluvial Age. Wâdī Qumrân has since cut its way through this plateau that rises about 330 ft. (100 m.) above the surrounding littoral. The cliff is cut by a number of similar wadis, of which three others might be mentioned S of Wâdī Qumrân is Wâdī Nâr, which issues from the confluence of the Kidron and Hinnom Valleys SE of Jerusalem. S of Wâdī Nâr is Wâdī Murabba'ât. Considerably further S are En-gedi, Naḥal Ḥeber, Naḥal Ṣe'elim, and Masada. About 6 mi. (10 km.) W of Qumrân on Wâdī Nâr is Khirbet Mird. Our present interest, however, focuses on the ruins located on the plateau at Wâdī Qumrân, known by the Arabic name Khirbet Qumrân ("the ruins of Qumrân").

The ruins had long been known, but never excavated. In 1873 the French orientalist Canon Clermont-Ganneau noted and described a ruin near Qumrân. A. Vincent had visited the ruins in 1906 and G. Dalman in 1914. Dalman had identified the site — not incorrectly — as a Roman fort. When the official examination of Cave 1 was being conducted (1949) the ruins were explored, but it was concluded that there was no relationship between the ruins and the Scrolls' cave. But when more discoveries were made in the vicinity it was decided to make a thorough archeological excavation of the ruins. This was conducted in five campaigns from 1951 to 1955. Excavations were also made in the area between Wâdī Qumrân and 'Ain Feshkha in a sixth campaign during 1958. Harding and de Vaux were in charge of the excavations. (The definitive account is given by de Vaux in *Archaeology*.)

The first season (1951) yielded coins and pottery that appeared to link the buildings to the same period that was indicated by the jars from the caves and by the paleography of the scrolls, namely Early Roman. After the exciting discoveries of 1952 that included five Qumrân caves and four Murabba'ât caves, the archeologists returned to Khirbet Qumrân with a new zeal. The second and third seasons revealed the nature of the community that had occupied the ruins, and, in the light of the *Manual of Discipline* (1QS), linked it definitely with the community of the scrolls.

The archeologist, of course, must work from the top downward, whereas his reconstruction of the history must be just the reverse. On the surface of the terrace a complex of buildings and a water system cover an area of approximately 345 ft. (105 m.) N-S and 250 ft. (76 m.) E-W. The walls are built on a grid that runs NNE-SSW. The principal distinguishing points for identifying corresponding areas of the different levels are: (1) a circular cistern about 20 ft. (6 m.) in diameter toward the western side of the complex; (2) the noticeably heavier walls and height of a tower about 39 by 42 ft. (12 by 13 m.) in the north-central part of the complex; and (3) a rectangular complex about 114 by 98 ft. (35 by 30 m.) joined to the tower, with the tower at its northwestern corner.

The earliest construction, identified by pottery sherds of Israelite style (including a jar handle bearing a stamp reading *lmlk* and some ostraca), comprised the circular cistern and the rectangular complex. This was identified by de Vaux as probably not earlier than the 8th cent. B.C., on the basis of the pottery and the writing on the ostraca. The site has often been identified as *ʿÎr-hammelaḥ* ("City of Salt"; Josh. 15:62). At any rate, it has no connection with the DSS, for it suffered violent destruction centuries earlier.

Level IA, on the other hand, was clearly the work of new inhabitants. At this time the southern wall of the rectangular area was extended, a north-south wall was joined to it (bringing the circular cistern into this building complex), and a number of small rooms were added N of the round cistern and W of the tower. Two rectangular cisterns, an aqueduct, and a common settling basin were dug, one N and one E of the round cistern. A potter's shop was added at the southeastern corner of the compound. Coins found in this level suggested that it was occupied during the time of Alexander Janneus (103-76 B.C.), and was possibly constructed in the days of John Hyrcanus (135-104 B.C.) or one of his predecessors.

The complex came much closer to completion in Period IB (Level IB). Workshops and storerooms were added W of the circular cistern. A large hall — the largest in the entire compound (72 by 15 ft. [22 by 4.5 m.]) — with a smaller adjoining room, was added S of the main building complex, workshops were built at the southeastern part of the area, and a complicated water system was installed.

An aqueduct brought the water from Wâdī Qumrân, where it cut through the cliffs, to the northwestern corner of the community area. Here it encountered piles of stones, which broke the current, and entered a large settling basin, near which was a bath. From the basin a channel led to the round cistern and the newer rectangular cisterns. Thence a channel led to another settling basin, which fed a very large rectangular cistern, 39 by 16 ft. (12 by 5 m.) SW of the main complex, and a second large rectangular cistern, 59 by 10 ft. (18 by 3 m.), which was dug between the main building and the new large hall. A branch channel led to a small, square basin, and from there the channel branched to feed a cistern E of the main building and another complex of cisterns at the southeastern part of the area, the largest of which was 56 by 23 ft. (17 by 7 m.). Some of these cisterns and basins seem clearly to have been associated with the potter's shop and other workshops in that area. The large- and medium-size cisterns had steps leading down into them. All were plastered with clay that is impervious to water. When some of the clay was removed, it was apparent that the cisterns had been lined with masonry and then plastered over. Altogether there were seven (possibly eight) cisterns, six decantation or settling basins, two smaller cisterns described as baths, and a tank for tempering potter's clay. There is only one round cistern, which is also the deepest of all the cisterns, and while it comes from the Israelite period (Iron II), it had been thoroughly cleaned by the later occupants, for no Israelite remains were found in it. The entire water system strongly suggests that this was not a complex of individual residences but a commune of some sort. The number of cisterns that cannot be explained as serving for water storage or for industrial purposes, specifically those with steps leading down into them and particularly those where the steps are divided to suggest one-way traffic, suggest that some kind of ritual bathing was a practice of the community.

The one large hall, S of the main building and separated from it by a large cistern with divided stairway, and the smaller room that adjoins the hall lend support to this tentative conclusion. The smaller room, 23 by 26 ft. (7 by 8 m.) contained 210 plates, 708 bowls in piles of twelve, 75 drinking vessels, 38 pots, 11 pitchers, and 21 small jars. The contents identified the room as a pantry, and the adjacent structure as a combination assembly hall and dining room.

The area W of the main building contained what appeared to be workshops and storage rooms, and at its southern end what de Vaux described as possibly a stable for beasts of burden. The area E of the main building contained also workshops and a pottery industry, described by de Vaux as "the most complete and best preserved in Palestine" (*RB*, 61 [1954], 567).

Between the western shop area and the large settling basin were found a number of containers with bones of animals which obviously had been butchered and boiled or roasted. Upon examination they proved to be from sheep, goats, and bovines. It is not clear, however, why the bones were carefully preserved. A likely suggestion is that the bones were the remains of sacred meals and were considered to be too holy to be simply thrown away.

Coins recovered from level IB included three of the time of Antiochus VII that could be precisely dated, 132/131, 131/130, and 130/129 B.C., and altogether eleven Seleucid coins. After the Seleucid era Jewish coinage was used, including 143 coins of Alexander Janneus (103-76 B.C.), one of Salome Alexandria and Hyrcanus II (76-67 B.C.), five of Hyrcanus II (67 and 63-40 B.C.), four of Antigonus Mattathias (40-37 B.C.), and one of the third year of Herod the Great (35 B.C.).

A severe earthquake left its evidence in a cleft that runs the full length of the compound, just E of the eastern wall of the main building, dropping the eastern side of the cleft 20 in. (50 cm.) lower than the rest of the complex. The cisterns E of the main building were destroyed and later abandoned. Evidence of fire is also found. The date of this earthquake can be established from the writings of Josephus, for he records that it occurred in the seventh year of Herod, at the time of the battle between Octavius Caesar and Antony at Actium, i.e., in the spring of A.D. 31 (*Ant*. xv.5.2 § 121; *BJ* i.19.3 § 370).

Level II clearly indicated occupation by much the same group as Level I. The buildings had been cleaned, with the result that evidence of Period IB was removed. This debris had been placed in a dump N of the complex, and a trench made by the archeologists recovered a quantity of remains, including coins, from Period IB. Repairs were made where earthquake damage occurred. The cisterns E of the main building were abandoned and the water

Scriptorium of the Qumrân monastery, where the scrolls were produced. In the background is Wâdī Qumrân. (J. C. Trever)

channel blocked. The most important alteration was the covering over of a court alongside the rooms by the western wall of the main building, and reconstruction of a second floor area above it. When this subsequently collapsed (at the time of the destruction that ended Period II, no doubt), the debris found by the excavators gave evidence of much importance. A number of pieces of burned brick covered with plaster were recovered, which, when reconstructed in the museum, formed a long, low table, 16.4 by 1.3 ft. (5 m. by 40 cm.), and 19.6 in. (50 cm.) high, along with fragments of a bench. Also found in the debris were two inkwells, one bronze and one pottery, from the Early Roman period. The upper room was identified as a "scriptorium," where the manuscripts of the community were produced.

East of the tower was the kitchen area with five fireplaces, basins, and other items. A mill for grinding grain was found in another area, and there was a well-designed area for latrines.

Pottery remains, coins, etc., from Period II were plentiful, suggesting that the end had come suddenly. This was confirmed by the widespread destruction to the buildings, and a layer of ash that contained iron arrowheads. All evidence suggests a military action. The testimony of the coins, eighty-three of which were year 2 of the First Revolt, and five of year 3 — the latest coins of Level II — dates the destruction A.D. 68/69. An early report that a coin or coins surcharged with "X" of the Roman Tenth Legion had been found has been retracted by de Vaux (*Archeology*, p. 40, n. 1). The account in Josephus is not easy to follow, but it seems certain that the Tenth Legion, or a detachment of it under Trajan, was garrisoned at Jericho and from there moved on Jerusalem (*BJ* v.1.6 § 42). We may assume that part of this legion moved through Qumrân and on to Jerusalem via Wâdī Nâr or another route, devastating the Qumrân community on the way.

Level III adds little to this study. Evidence indicates that it was occupied for a brief period as a Roman outpost and then again, probably by Jewish rebels, at the time of the Second Revolt. The complex of buildings was not restored to the usage of Periods I and II.

East of the buildings, and separated from the complex by more than 165 ft. (50 m.), was a cemetery with more than 1100 graves, arranged neatly in rows and sections, the bodies placed on their backs, lying N-S with the head to the south, and the arms crossed over the pelvis or placed alongside the bodies. At the eastern edge of the terrace was another group of graves, less regular. Among the six bodies that were examined here were four women and a child.

The excavations of the region between the ruins and 'Ain Feshkha, 2 mi. (3 km.) S, indicated that this was also used by the same community. Farm buildings, stables, tool sheds, an irrigation system, and rooms that gave evidence of being used for tanning leather were identified. The water that flows abundantly from the springs at 'Ain Feshkha is drunk by animals, but it appears to be too brackish for the cultivation of cereals, although it is suitable for date palms. We may assume that the community grew the barley or wheat that it used in el-Buqei'a above the edge of the cliffs.

From the number of graves, the number of dishes and bowls in the pantry, and the period of time that Levels I and II were occupied, the size of the community at any given time can be estimated at about two hundred persons. The presence of skeletons of females and a child and the provision for admission of women and children to the community suggest that this was not strictly a

Reconstructed jars in which scrolls were preserved in Cave 1. Pottery types indicate that the caves and monastery belong together. (J. C. Trever)

monastery, but the rigors of life there and the fact that all of the exhumed skeletons in the main part of the cemetery were males suggest that most of the members were men.

The relevance of the excavation of Khirbet Qumrân to the dating and interpretation of the DSS will become apparent upon examination of the Scrolls in detail.

***II. The Qumrân Community.**–A. MS Evidence.* From the caves at Qumrân came the remains of hundreds of MSS that could be categorized as follows: canonical scriptures, i.e., copies of the books of the Hebrew Bible (with the exception of Esther); deuterocanonical scriptures, i.e., those in the Apocrypha; extracanonical scriptures, sometimes classified as pseudepigraphical; and sectarian documents, i.e., those which appear to be the product of the community and which relate specifically to its life and beliefs. Since some of the works not previously known seem to be more in the category of apocryphal or pseudepigraphical writings, the lines are not too firmly drawn, but that should present no serious problems for this study, which will deal principally with the sectarian literature.

The MSS that pertain uniquely to the sect are: the Manual of Discipline (1QS), the Damascus Document (CD), the Thanksgiving Hymns or *Hôdāyôt* (1QH), the War Scroll (1QM), the Order of the Congregation (1QSa or 1Q*28a*), the Benedictions (1QSb or 1Q*28b*), the *p*[e]*šārîm* or comms. on portions of Scripture such as the Habakkuk Commentary (1QpHab), and several other more fragmentary works. The Temple Scroll (11QTemple), not yet published at this writing, also should be included. Possibly its choice of extracanonical documents would tell something of the sect, but that approach is rather subjective. *See* Plate 16.

The introduction of the Damascus Document into this list must be justified. As soon as the Manual of Discipline (1QS) was published, scholars began to point out its similarity to what was known as the Zadokite Fragments or the Damascus Document. A quantity of MSS had been discovered in the Genizah of the Ezra Synagogue in Old Cairo in 1897 and taken to the library of Cambridge University. S. Schechter, president of Jewish Theological Seminary, New York, identified a number of fragments as similar in character and content, and published them (*Fragments of a Zadokite Work* [1910]). The work drew the attention of many scholars, and the bibliography from 1910 to 1946 (the year before the DSS came to the attention of scholars) is voluminous (see L. Rost, *Die Damaskusschrift* [1933]; H. H. Rowley, *Zadokite Fragments and the Dead Sea Scrolls* [1952]). Since the provenance of these fragments was Cairo, the *siglum* CD (for Cairo, Damascus) was assigned to the work. In spite of striking parallels between 1QS and CD, many scholars resisted the conclusion that CD was a product of the Qumrân community, until fragments of the Damascus Document were recovered from Cave 5 (5QD = CD 9:7-10), Cave 6 (6QD = CD 4:19-21; 5:13f.; 5:18–6:2; 6:20–7:1; and a fragment not in CD), and fragments of five (or seven?) different MSS from Cave 4 (4QD^{a-e}). The questions of how the document got to Cairo and how two MSS of it came to be produced in the 10th and 11th cents. have not yet been satisfactorily answered.

But can the MSS be connected with the buildings at Khirbet Qumrân and 'Ain Feshkha? This is a crucial question, for unless it is established beyond reasonable doubt that the documents and the building complex belong to the same community, the one cannot be used to interpret the other. (De Vaux has taken this up in detail in

Archeology, pp. 91-138.) The evidence may be summarized as follows. The MSS are ancient. From paleographic, linguistic, textual, and physico-chemical studies, they must be dated between the 3rd cent. B.C. and the Second Revolt. The MSS were found in the caves in the immediate vicinity of Khirbet Qumrân, in some cases in caves that were in the steep-sloping sides of the plateau on which the buildings were located. The MSS had been deposited in the caves in antiquity, as evidenced by dust and other material that had covered them, and the pottery that was found in the same level in the caves was of the same type as the pottery in the ruins. In some cases (such as Cave 4), there was clear evidence that the caves had been dug and the MSS placed on the fresh ground in great haste, with no signs of previous or later occupation. Further, the evidence of the nature of the Qumrân community as described in the MSS is in agreement with the archeological discoveries of the Khirbet, and the coins, pottery, and carbon-14 testing of material found with the MSS fit precisely the dates established for the MSS by the means mentioned above. No other theory suggested for the MSS has any support other than the ingenuity of the theorizers, and no other explanation of the ruins can be supported by other evidence. The MSS explain the Khirbet, and the ruins explain the presence and contents of the MSS.

B. Origin of the Community. There can be no doubt that the Qumrân community was a Jewish sect, using the term "sect" in much the same way it is used by Josephus and in Acts. The great quantity of Jewish scriptures, and the stress on the Torah in the sectarian documents, make this irrefutable. The community members thought of themselves as a Jewish remnant, living in the "end-time of the ages," penitents whose God had remembered them and raised up for them a "teacher of righteousness" (or a "righteous teacher" — the annexion of the words [construct] can indicate either an objective genitive [what the teacher teaches] or a descriptive genitive [the character of the teacher]). If the figures in CD 1:3-13 are pressed literally, God's "visitation" occurred 390 years after the fall of Jerusalem to Nebuchadrezzar, which could be 208/207 B.C. (from 597 B.C.) or 197/196 (from 586 B.C.), and twenty years later God raised up the teacher of righteousness (i.e., 189/188 or 178/177 B.C.). It should be noted that nowhere is the teacher presented as the founder of the sect. It should also be noted that such mathematical and chronological precision should not be demanded.

The dates thus inferred point to a time of crisis in Jerusalem. Antiochus III the Great (223-187 B.C.) had defeated the Egyptian forces at Paneas (Caesarea Philippi) in 198 B.C., and had taken Palestine from the Ptolemies. His son Antiochus IV Epiphanes (175-164 B.C.) plundered Jerusalem, exacted a large tribute from the Jews, and in 167 B.C. erected a pagan altar at the temple where the sacred altar had stood. Meanwhile, there was a strong movement among the Jews to end the separation of Jews and Gentiles, to erase the marks of Judaism, and become Greek. The story is told in great detail in 1 Maccabees. Onias III, high priest 185-174 B.C., was a pious man, but he was deposed by his brother Jason who sought to complete the hellenization of the Jews (2 Macc. 4:7-26). Such was the background of the revolt led by Mattathias of the Hasmonean line, who was joined by the Hasideans (*ḥᵃsîḏîm*, "faithful/pious ones"). This is not the place to give the details of the period that followed, but simply to note that it is in the time of John Hyrcanus (134-104) that Josephus first mentions the Pharisees and Sadducees. The Pharisees (*pᵉrûšîyim*, "separated ones") are perhaps the successors of the Hasidim, for when the Hasmoneans (Macabbees) took over the political power, the Hasidim separated themselves from the Hasmoneans. The name "Sadducees" is the source of much discussion. The best etymology seems to be *ṣᵉḏôqîyim* or *bᵉnê ṣāḏôq*; in other words, they claimed descent from Zadok (cf. 2 S. 8:17; Ezk. 40:46; 44:15; etc.) to support their claim to the priesthood. (See R. North, *CBQ*, 17 [1955], 173.) A good case can be made for the division of the Hasidim (or the Pharisees) into several groups, one of which was the Essenes. It is therefore reasonable to assume that the original of which Qumrân was a direct descendant (or one of several descendants) came into existence in the period of the struggle against the hellenizers. Attempts to identify the teacher of righteousness or the "wicked priest" of Qumrân literature with historical persons, however, have not been convincing (discussed more fully in LaSor, "A Preliminary Reconstruction of Judaism in the Time of the Second Temple in the Light of the Published Qumran Materials" [Th.D. diss., University of Southern California, 1956]).

Against this brief historical background, some of the statements in the DSS take on a richer meaning. The Qumrânians were "the Penitents of Israel who go out from the Land of Judah," to "dwell in the land of Damascus" (CD 6:5f.). Whether Damascus is to be understood literally or, as some hold, to be taken as a reference to Qumrân is not clear. The community took the reference to the "sons of Zadok" in Ezk. 44:15 as applying to itself (CD 3:21–4:2). It expressed contempt for the "priests of Jerusalem" (1QpHab 9:4f.), particularly for "the wicked priest" who "did works of abominations and defiled the temple of God" (12:7-9). Possibly the same wicked priest is referred to as "the man of the lie" (2:11f.) and "the preacher of the lie" (10:9).

C. Names for the Community. The most common term, used more than a hundred times, is "the Community" (*hayyaḥaḏ*), often combined with another term such as "the Counsel of the Community" or "the men of the Community." Another common term is "the Counsel" (*hā'ēṣâ*). The word also means "advice," and is used in this sense, but terms such as "the Counsel of the Community," "the Counsel of the Torah," and "the Counsel of the Fellowship of Israel" indicate that it is also a proper noun. The term "the Congregation" (*hā'ēḏâ*) is used in compound terms, both for Qumrân and for those outside. Compare the terms "the Congregation of Israel," "the Holy Congregation," and "the Congregation of God" with the terms "the Congregation of Belial," "the Congregation of Men of Unrighteousness," and the Congregation of Nothing." Another term, also translated "congregation," but preferably "the Assembly," is *qāhāl*. This occurs alone, "the Assembly," and in compounds, "the Assembly of God," and it is also used for those outside: "the Assembly of the Wicked" and "the Assembly of Gentiles." A very difficult term to translate is *sôḏ*, "council," or "secret (council)." (For an excellent study, see H. Muszyński, *Fundament, Bild und Metapher in den Handschriften aus Qumran* [1975].) It occurs in compounds, "the Council of the Community," "the Council of Truth and Understanding," and "the Sons of an Eternal Council." It, too, is used of those outside: "the Council of Violence," and "the Council of Nothing and the Congregation of Belial." The names give some idea of their self-image and of their attitude toward those who were not members of the community.

The use of the terms "Israel and Aaron" (CD 1:7) and "Aaron and Israel" (1QS 9:11) seems to be simply a reference to the community. There are indications, however, that a distinction between the priests (Aaron) and the laymen (Israel) was intended. The community is described as consisting of priests, Levites, and "all the people" (1QS 2:19-21), or "Israel and Levi and Aaron" (1QM 5:1), or priests, Levites, sons of Israel, and proselytes (CD 14:3-6). Such expressions seem to rule out the idea that the community considered itself a community of priests.

A particularly troublesome term is *hārabbîm*, which can mean "the many" (i.e., either the entire community or the majority of the community) or "the great ones, the chiefs" (i.e., a hierarchy in the community). The word occurs about fifty-six times in the DSS, about thirty-four times in cols. 6-8 of 1QS, and with significant use in cols. 13-15 of CD. Each occurrence must be studied carefully in context, for the word is used in every possible way.

D. Organization. Authority was committed to the priests, the "sons of Zadok" (or "the sons of Aaron"), but one priest seems to stand above the others, possibly the one called "Chief Priest" (1QM 2:1f.). In CD 14:6-8 is a description of "the priest," followed by one of "the examiner" (*m^ebaqqēr*), which suggests a hierarchy of the offices. The examiner (or it may be translated "supervisor," "superintendent," "overseer," "visitor," etc.) was obviously of considerable importance. The word occurs fifteen times in CD, always in passages where the "many" are under discussion. His duties included the admitting of new members, instructing the Many in the works of God, restoring the wandering ones, hearing witnesses, arbitrating disputes, advising the priest in case of disease in the camp, and taking the oath of the covenant.

"Twelve men and three priests" (1QS 8:1) have important responsibilities, but it is not fully clear whether the "counsel of the community" mentioned immediately before this term is the name of this group or the name of the entire community. The language seems to mean that fifteen persons are intended, but some scholars make the "three" a sort of "inner circle" of the twelve and find a point of comparison with the disciples of Jesus. The "judges of the congregation" (CD 10:4) resemble the Twelve and Three, and one group may have developed from the other. In each case the laymen outnumber the priests: in the case of the judges, four were from the tribe of Levi and Aaron and six from Israel, or "up to ten men selected from the Congregation." In 1QM, fifty-two "fathers of the congregation" are mentioned (2:1), and twenty-six "heads of the courses," i.e., priests who rotate in the service (2:2, 4). Their duties are described in relation to the eschatological battle.

"The Prince of all the Congregation" is mentioned in connection with the star-and-scepter prophecy (Nu. 24:17) and identified with the scepter (CD 7:20f.). The same title is found on the shield(?) of a person in the eschatological battle (1QM 5:1) and in the Benedictions (1QSb 5:20). It is not established that this person was then alive; rather, he appears to belong to the future and may be the messiah.

The order of precedence of the community is a point that recurs in various expressions, and "position" or "turn" was closely adhered to. The membership was mustered every year, and a member was advanced or set back in rank according to his deeds or his perversity (1QS 5:20-25). Members were listed by rank ("written by their names," CD 14:3-6), and everyone knew the place of his standing and was expected to stay in that place (1QS 2:22f.). Even in the smallest meeting of a *minyan* (ten men), they were to speak in order, "each according to his position" (6:3f.). It seems clear that this rank was based on spiritual and moral behavior, and was not a matter of heredity — which may have been a protest against the aristocracy of the Sadducees.

Details of admission to the sect are spelled out in 1QS and 1QSa. There was a year of testing, sometimes likened to postulancy, when one seeking admission was carefully examined. This was followed by a second year, likened to the novitiate, at which stage the person seeking admission became a member of the community but was not entitled to all its privileges. His wealth and his work were handed over to the Examiner, but were not to be used by the community until the novice had successfully completed his second year. At that time he was mustered "according to the mouth of the Many," and, if the lot fell for him to "draw near to the Community," he was written in the order of his position (1QS 6:13-33). The provisions in 1QSa 1:19-21; 2:3-9 add other details, but these may apply to a smaller group within the community.

E. Daily Life. That Qumrân was a sectarian community that separated itself from Jerusalem Judaism cannot be disputed. Its relationship to other sects or "camps" is not so clearly defined. Specifically, the precise relationship of Qumrân to the Essenes is not known, so this description of life at Qumrân is limited to the DSS.

The members of the community "passed over" into the covenant and were not to turn back (1QS 1:16-18). They were to do good, truth, and justice, to walk before God perfectly, "to love all the sons of light . . . and to hate all the sons of darkness" (1:2-11).

The knowledge, strength, and wealth of each member was to be brought into the community (1:11-13; cf. 6:17, 22), and this communalism extended to much of the daily life, including common meals and common counseling (6:2f.). The occurrence of the term "poor" (*'ebyôn*) in a number of texts has led some scholars to conclude that the vows of poverty and celibacy were part of this "monastic" sect, but this conclusion gets little support from the texts. We may nevertheless infer that life at Qumrân was devoid of luxuries and was probably little above the level of poverty. On the matter of celibacy, there is likewise conflicting evidence. The texts state that women and children could be admitted to the community; cf. 1QSa 1:4-12, where provision is made for their "entering," and CD 7:6-9, where provision is made for marrying women and begetting sons. Nevertheless, the remains found in the cemetery and the rigorous life demanded by the location suggest that few women did in fact enter the community. If it was not a monastery *de jure* it seems likely that Qumrân was monastic *de facto*.

The community had gone to the wilderness to prepare the way of *Hû'hā'* (a surrogate for the divine name, possibly an abbreviation of *hû' hā'^elôhîm*, "He is God"), which was to be done by the study of the Law (1QS 8:13-16). In CD 6:4, the Law is associated with the very origin of the sect. But what precisely is meant by the term "Law"? An examination of the DSS will show that the positive virtues of the Mosaic law are stressed: truth, righteousness, kindness (*ḥesed*), justice, chastity, honesty, humility, and the like. The most concentrated expression of these virtues can be found in the description of the conflicting "two spirits" (1QS 3:13–4:26). It is also possible to draw from the DSS a body of texts that will define works of the law as a legalism not greatly different from that of the Pharisees (cf. CD 9–16; 10:14–11:18 goes into great detail concerning the keeping of the sabbath).

The attitude of Qumrân toward the Mosaic sacrificial system is not clear. There is reference to sacrifices in 1QM 2:1-6, and reference to "the altar of burnt offering" in CD 12:8f. Nothing that appears to be an altar has been excavated at Qumran, however. (H. Steckoll announced the discovery of an altar at Qumrân in *Madda'*, Jan. 1956, pp. 246ff., but de Vaux denied that the stone was an altar in *RB*, 75 [1968], 204f.) There is no mention of sacrifices in 1QS and some scholars are inclined to date CD from an earlier, pre-Qumrân period. In fact, one passage in 1QS seems to put "the offering of the lips" and "perfection of way" in place of animal sacrifices "to make atonement for the guilt of rebellion and the infidelity of sin" (1QS 9:3-5). This would be in keeping with some of the attitudes toward sacrifices expressed by the prophets (cf. Isa. 1:12-20; Mic. 6:6-8; etc.); and it certainly must be recognized that diaspora Judaism had substituted prayer and good deeds (*miṣwôṯ*) for animal sacrifices even before the destruction of the Temple in A.D. 70.

The systems of aqueducts and cisterns at Khirbet Qumrân promptly led scholars to discuss whether this was a baptist sect. The use of the term "baptist" needs careful definition, for there were several contemporary types of baptist movements. (See J. Thomas, *Le mouvement baptiste en Palestine et Syrie (150 av. J.-C. — 300 ap. J.-C.)* [1935].) Unfortunately, the texts of Qumrân do not spell out the details of their ritual washing, necessitating conclusions drawn only from negative statements. The bathing was a means of purification (CD 10:10-13), yet it did not have in itself the power of cleansing unless the sinner had repented of his wickedness (1QS 3:1-6). If "the Purity" refers to the water (cf. 1QS 5:13f.), no postulant or novice could touch it (6:16f., 20f.), but it is possible that the term applies to some part of a sacred meal. At any rate, we may safely conclude that baptism at Qumrân was not an initiatory rite (such as the baptism of John), but rather a ritual for purification reserved for members of the community who had the proper attitude toward the statutes of God (cf. 3:6-9).

The community observed the Jewish holy days, and the Day of Atonement was important in the history of the sect (1QpHab 11:7). Qumrân observed a different calendar from that of Jerusalem Judaism, or, more accurately, used both a lunar calendar of 354 days (like the "Jewish" calendar today) and a solar calendar of 365 days, similar to that of the book of Jubilees. The statement in 1QpHab 11:4-7 makes no sense unless the Day of Atonement was observed by the "wicked priest" on a different day from that which Qumrân observed. Considerable literature has appeared on the subject, some of which involves the problem of the date of the Last Supper in the Synoptics and in the Fourth Gospel. (For discussion and bibliography, see Fitzmyer, *Dead Sea Scrolls*, pp. 131-37.)

Certain texts indicate an annual examination of the members of the community in connection with the Feast of Weeks (cf. 1QS 5:24) or the Day of Atonement, at which time the promotions and demotions took place. Possibly at the same time the postulants and novices were examined (6:13-23). A detailed list of punishments and fines for offenses against the community is given (6:24–7:25), and for more serious offenses banishment (or excommunication) was a possibility (7:19-21), either for two years, or, in the case of one who had been a member for more than ten years, permanently (7:24f.).

F. Doctrine of God. Since Qumrân was a Jewish sect with its roots in the Hebrew Scriptures, its doctrine of God is essentially that of Judaism. God is the God of Israel (1QS 10:8-11), the Lord of creation (1QM 10:11-15), the God of history (11:1-4), and in particular the God of the Qumrân covenanters (11:9-15; see also 1QH 1:6-20). Much has been written on "Qumrân dualism," some of it with confusion of terminology. There is matter-spirit dualism, good-evil dualism of a personal, ethical nature, and cosmological dualism of two opposing deities in the universe, to mention only three categories. The Hebrew Bible knows nothing of philosophical matter-spirit dualism. Ethical dualism, on the other hand, is thoroughly scriptural (cf. Prov. 2:13-15; Jn. 1:5; etc.). Ethical dualism is found in the DSS, and can be summarized in the terms "sons of light" and "sons of darkness." (For an extended passage, see 1QS 4:2-8.) But the doctrine of the two spirits (1QS 3:17-21), with its Angel of Darkness (3:21–4:1), together with the prominence given to Belial and Mastema in the DSS have led some to see a cosmological dualism in Qumrân, which is sometimes traced to Zoroastrianism. (For early discussions, see LaSor, *Bibliography*, nos. 3130-3211.) It must be kept clearly in view, however, that true cosmological dualism starts with two coeval opposing deities, whereas the OT presents its God as the only God, the creator of everything and everyone else, including evil (cf. Isa. 43:10-13; 44:6-8, 24-28; 45:1-7; 46:8f.). Even Satan is presented as operating only with God's permission (cf. Job 1:6-12; 2:1-6). Likewise in the DSS, God is the only God. He created the two spirits (1QS 3:17, 25), and He has decreed their times and their works (4:25f.). God is ruler over all angels and spirits, including Belial and Mastema (which seems to be another name for Belial; cf. 1QM 13:9-13).

G. Doctrine of Man. Although the last and highest being created, man was tempted and disobeyed God's command. Thus the Hebrew Bible tells of God's redemptive activity on behalf of sinful mankind, a concept that certainly underlies Qumrân anthropology. Like the canonical Psalmist, however, the Qumrânian was burdened by a sense of unworthiness and wickedness (1QS 11:9-15; 1QH 10:3-8, 12; 4:29-37; 9:14-18; 13:13-21; 18:21-29).

The Qumrân doctrine, however, seems to develop a more rigid concept of election, amounting almost to a "double predestination," according to which God created the righteous from the womb for agelong salvation, but the wicked He created for the time of His anger (1QM 15:14-19; cf. 1QS 3:13–4:26). Possibly this is simply a rhetorical way of stressing the doctrine that man's righteousness comes from God (1QH 4:30-33), for man's responsibility to do good works is likewise emphasized (cf. 1QS 5:11f.). In fact, any legalistic system (such as found at Qumrân) would have difficulty developing in a strongly predestinarian theology.

The emphasis on "knowledge," "mysteries," "truth," and similar terms in the DSS has led some to see a kind of Gnosticism in Qumrânian beliefs. This has been beset by a marked imprecision in the use of the terms "gnosis" and "Gnosticism" (discussed at some length in LaSor, *Amazing Dead Sea Scrolls* [rev. ed. 1962], pp. 139-150). There is no philosophical dualism in the DSS, no demiurge or series of emanations, such as are a necessary part of classical Gnosticism. But the question of gnosis or secret knowledge of the "mysteries" of the system deserves careful study. The secret knowledge of Qumrân, revealed by God to the covenanters (1QS 8:11f.; 9:17f.; 1QH 1:21; 2:17f.), concerns the community's salvation in the end time (1Q27 5-8; 1QpHab 7:1-8; 1QS 4:18f.; 1QH 11:3f., 11f.). For fuller study cf. H. W. Huppenbauer, *Der Mensch zwischen zwei Welten, Der dualismus der Texte von Qumran (Hohle I) und der Damaskusfragmente* (1959).

H. Eschatology. The community believed it was the last generation, living at the end of the age (1QSa 1:1f.; CD 1:10-13). The War Scroll (1QM) is a description of the final war, with the destruction of the gentile nations and the triumph of the people of the new covenant (i.e., Qumrân). In keeping with the eschatology of the Hebrew Bible, the community looked for a "day of vengeance" (1QS 10:19), a "day of slaughter" (1QH 15:17), a "day of judgment" (1QpHab 13:2f.), by which God would be glorified (1QH 2:24). There would be suffering and distress for Israel, but destruction for the wicked (1QM 15:1f.; cf. 1QH 6:29f.). The language is graphic (cf. 1QS 2:5-9; 4:11-14; 1QH 3:29-36). Following the judgment would be a time of peace and blessing (1QM 17:7), of purification (1QS 4:19-34), and salvation (1QM 1:5). The people of God would live a thousand generations (CD 7:6), forming an eternal house (4QFlor [4Q*174*] 1:2-7).

The Qumrânian concept of the Messiah has been much discussed (see Fitzmyer, *Dead Sea Scrolls*, pp. 114-18; LaSor, *Dead Sea Scrolls and the NT* [1972], pp. 98-105). To carry on the discussion with some degree of precision, the term "Messiah" should be limited to the "son of David" who is to come at some future time to establish once again the kingdom of Israel and to usher in an age of righteousness and peace. This is the meaning of the term as used in "normative" Judaism. In Christianity the term "Christ," taken from the Greek equivalent of "Messiah," has become much more complex by incorporating the Suffering Servant and the apocalyptic Son of Man into the figure. Sectarian Judaism sought to avoid some of the complexities by adding a suffering "Messiah son of Joseph," a Messiah from the tribe of Levi, and an apocalyptic heavenly being. How much of this expansion is found in Qumrân theology?

The "Messiah of Israel" is mentioned in 1QSa 2:14, 27, and "Messiah" in 1QSa 2:12. In the Patriarchal Blessings, the "Messiah of righteousness, the sprout of David" is mentioned (4QPBless 2-5) and in the Florilegium, the Davidic descent of the one who shall arise in the latter days is stated (4QFlor 1:11-13). There can be no doubt that the community looked for the Davidic Messiah. The more difficult question to answer concerns another messianic figure, or other such figures.

When the Damascus Document was first published a number of scholars suggested that the formula "the Messiah of Aaron and Israel" (CD 8:24 par 20:1; 12:23–13:1; 14:19) should be emended to read "the Messiahs of Aaron and Israel." The expression "the Messiahs [or anointed ones] of the Holy One" is found in CD 6:12. When the Manual of Discipline was published, it was quickly noted that 1QS 9:11 reads "the Messiahs [in plural!] of Aaron and Israel," which was taken as confirmation of the proposed emendations in CD. However, to take *mᵉšîḥê 'āhᵃrôn wᵉyiśrā'ēl* to mean one Messiah from Aaron (a priestly messiah) and a second Messiah from Israel (a lay Messiah) raises serious grammatical questions (LaSor, *VT*, 6 [1956], 425-29). Moreover, the expression in CD 8:24 (par. 20:1) reads *māšî(a)ḥ mē'āhᵃrôn ûmîyiśrā'ēl*, "an anointed one from Aaron and from Israel"; in no way can this be made plural by simply emending a construct singular to construct plural. The evidence from 4QD^b = CD 14:19 supports the reading *in the singular*, thereby denying the possibility of textual emendation of CD in the Middle Ages. The simple expression "the Messiah of Aaron" is never found in the DSS. For these reasons, a Messiah of Aaron *per se* cannot be found in Qumrân eschatology. A curious passage in the Order of the Congregation, however, refers to what has been called "the messianic banquet" (1QSa 2:11-23). Everything about the event seems to raise some question, particularly the words that prescribe the ritual for every assembly where ten men are present (1QSa 2:21f.), and, except for the fact that the "Messiah" is present (1QSa 2:12, 14 [broken text], 20), it could hardly be called a "messianic banquet." The most important point to be noted is that "the priest" or "the chief [priest]" at the ritual takes precedence over "the Messiah." The concept of a priestly person of eschatological significance therefore cannot be entirely dismissed. (For the full text in translation with all restorations of the broken text indicated, see LaSor, *Dead Sea Scrolls and the NT,* p. 101.)

It is of primary significance that the apocalyptic "Son of Man" does not appear in the DSS. Eleven different MSS of Enoch are represented in the fragments from the Qumrân caves, representing all parts of Enoch except Book II (the Similitudes or Parables). Only in Book II does the figure of the Son of Man appear, and its absence from the DSS suggests either that it was composed at a later time or that it was deliberately excluded by Qumrân. Since apocalyptic elements are usually associated with sectarian Judaism (and indeed are absent from "normative" Judaism), and since such elements are supposed to have come into Judaism as a result of contact with the Zoroastrian religion, the absence of these elements from Qumrân eschatology becomes doubly significant. A number of theories about apocalyptic in general and about supposed Zoroastrian origins of Qumrân eschatology in particular need to be reexamined.

Attempts to identify other eschatological figures, such as "the seeker" (or commander or law-giver), the "prince of the congregation," and especially the (or a) "Teacher of Righteousness" (see below), have found no general agreement.

1. Teacher of Righteousness. The term *môrê haṣṣeḏeq* "teacher of righteousness" or "righteous teacher" occurs seven times in the Habakkuk Commentary (1QpHab 1:12; 2:2; 5:10; 7:4; 8:3; 9:9f.; 11:4f.), once in 1QpMic 16, and once (partially restored) in what was formerly identified as 4QpPs 37. The Damascus Document has several slightly different terms, namely, *môrê ṣeḏeq,* "a righteous teacher" (CD 1:11; 8:55); *yôrê haṣṣeḏeq,* "teacher of [or the one teaching] righteousness" (6:10f.); *môrê hayyaḥaḏ,* "the teacher of the community" (8:23f.); *yôrê hayyaḥaḏ,* "the one teaching the community" (8:36f.); *môrê,* "a teacher" (8:51); and *yôrêhem,* "their teacher" (3:7f.). In some of these passages the context indicates that the reference is not to the one generally identified as "the Teacher of Righteousness," but to a future teacher, or in one instance (3:7f.) to God Himself.

From these texts the following points can be established beyond reasonable doubt. In former times, men did not listen to their Teacher (probably meaning God) (3:7f.). He punished them, but brought into being the community of penitents; after twenty years He raised up for them a teacher of righteousness (1:11). This teacher was a priest who was given understanding in order to interpret the words of the prophets (1QpHab 2:6-9; 7:4f.), which would result in deliverance from judgment for the doers of the Law (1QpHab 8:1-3). The men of the community heeded his words (CD 20:27f., 31f.). He was, however, opposed and persecuted, pursued and probably "swallowed up" by the Wicked Priest (1QpHab 11:4-8; 1:12), for which God allowed the latter to be humbled (9:9f.). The "house of Absolam" (interpretation uncertain) did not help the teacher (5:9-12). The teacher of the community was "gathered in," probably meaning that he died (CD 19:33–20:1, 13-15). The covenanters looked for "the rising of one teaching righteousness in the last days" (6:10f.).

From this body of material, passages in the Hymns (1QH) that are believed to be autobiographical, numerous statements or beliefs about Jesus, and good imaginations, scholars have built up a composite picture of the Teacher of Righteousness that fills many volumes. This, however, is not to reject scholarly efforts to sift probabilities and possibilities from the DSS. It is not established that the Teacher of Righteousness was the author of any of the Thanksgiving Hymns (1QH). The Teacher is not mentioned in a single psalm, nor is he elsewhere identified as a "psalmist" or by any equivalent terms. On the other hand, the Teacher is recognized as one whom God caused to know the mysteries of the words of the prophets (1QpHab 7:4f.) and one who was the target of abuse and persecution by the Wicked Priest (11:4-8; 5:9-12). The Teacher was not the founder of the movement (he was raised up twenty years after its beginning; CD 1:8-11), but he was appointed by God to build the congregation of His elect (4QpPs 37). Therefore the Teacher must be recognized as one of the significant leaders in the community, probably the most significant of its spiritual leaders in its earlier days, and possibly the only spiritual leader of any stature in the entire history of the sect. It is entirely reasonable to assume that some, if not all, of the *Hôdāyôt* were either composed by the Teacher or inspired by him ("inspired" in its common and not its specialized theological sense).

The task, then, is to apply critical methods to the fantastic claims made by certain writers, and to separate what is clearly false from what is reasonably possible. This may be summarized in a simple statement that needs to be amplified by careful scholarship: any element in the reconstructed life of the Teacher that can be traced to NT statements about Jesus, but which has no textual support from the DSS (such as the virgin birth, the atoning death, the crucifixion, the resurrection, and the second coming of the Teacher of Righteousness), must be suspect and is probably to be rejected. (Such a textual study of the major problem areas has been attempted in LaSor, *Dead Sea Scrolls and the NT*, pp. 106-130. See also H. H. Rowley, *The Dead Sea Scrolls and the NT* [1957]; *BJRL*, 44 [1961/62], 119-156; 40 [1957/58], 114-146; 49 [1966/67], 203-232.)

III. Significance of the Scrolls.–Assessment of the values of the Qumrân discoveries must be limited in this article to the areas relevant to biblical studies. These may be grouped as: text and canon of the OT; developments in early ("intertestamental") Judaism; and relationship to the NT.

A. Text and Canon. Prior to the discovery of the DSS, witnesses to the OT text and canon were principally the following: (1) the so-called Masoretic Text of the Hebrew Bible, which could more accurately be designated the received consonantal text and the text with vocalization and other pointing by the Masorites (MT) — they should not be confused, for the consonantal text is several centuries older than the MT; and (2) translations, such as the Septuagint (LXX) and Jerome's Vulgate. Other witnesses of significance included the Old Latin, the Syriac, the Samaritan, and other versions. The oldest extant Hebrew text was no earlier than the 10th cent. A.D., but the versions give evidence that goes back to the 5th cent. A.D. (the time of Jerome's work) and to the 2nd or 3rd cent. B.C. (the time of the LXX). With the discovery of the DSS there is primary evidence, not merely that of translations, that goes back to the 1st and 2nd (and possibly even the 3rd) cents. B.C.

The text of the biblical MSS from Qumrân may be divided into two main categories. In one group are those portions that agree within reasonable limits with the consonantal text. (Since the DSS texts are not vocalized, they cannot be compared with the MT.) By "reasonable limits" is intended the inclusion of orthographic differences (such as *hw'h* for *hw'*, *lw'* for *l'*, etc.) that do not present any significant difference in the text. The second category includes those readings that clearly are not in agreement with the consonantal text. This second group could be further subdivided into readings that agree with LXX but differ from the consonantal text, and those that differ from both. Published studies indicate that certain OT books, such as Genesis, Deuteronomy, and Isaiah, are textually much closer to the consonantal text than others, such as Exodus and Samuel. The evidence leads to the conclusion that there were in existence in the first cents. B.C. and A.D. at least three Hebrew text-types: the received text that formed the basis of the consonantal, the text that was used for the Greek translation, and a text that differs from both of these.

This conclusion should cause no surprise, for it was already indicated by at least two lines of evidence. The witness of NT quotations of OT passages indicates that some quotations can be traced to the Hebrew Bible (received text), some to the Greek version, and some to neither of these (the third text). It has sometimes been the practice to consider this third group of NT quotations as "loose dealing" with the OT text, but it is open to question whether a writer seeking scriptural authority for his statement would be allowed to handle the biblical passages with such abandon. The second line of evidence comes from Jewish tradition, where the formation of the "received text," often but questionably traced to the Council of Jamnia (sometime after A.D. 90), is described as taking the reading of two witnesses against one (*Taanith* iv.2; *Sopherim* vi.4; *Siphre* 356), in other words, working from three texts or text recensions that were in existence at the time.

This should lead, once and for all, to the rejection of the view that "only the MT" is inspired and to be considered the authoritative reading. While it is true that in most cases the reading of the MT is to be preferred, it is also true that each reading must be studied in the light of the available witnesses to the text.

A much more difficult problem exists with regard to canon. The presence of a certain writing in the DSS is certainly no indication that the community considered that writing canonical. The evidence of the *pᵉšārîm* ("commentaries") indicates that only the books of the Hebrew Bible—and not all of them, by any means — were studied and commented upon. Arguments in support of the "Protestant" canon have at times included the claim that only those books written in Hebrew are canonical. But the discoveries at Qumrân call into question the validity of this argument, for fragments of a Hebrew text of at least one of the deuterocanonical books (4QTob hebr[a]) have been found.

As a matter of fact, it can be seriously questioned whether we can dismiss so summarily the noncanonicity of books in the Qumrân Library. Since it was the library of a sectarian group, and not a public lending library or a resource library for scholarly research, we must ask why certain works were found there and why others were not. Perhaps a strict definition of "canon" cannot be insisted upon for Qumrân. We may have to accept the simple fact that these were the books that the community considered significant for them. The canonicity of Esther is not called into question by its absence from a sectarian library, nor is canonicity established for a work like Jubilees (of which more MSS were present in the DSS than of some biblical books). There is a subjective element in canonicity, for the term means "those books which are considered by a group to be authoritative." There is also an objective element, for divine origin alone is the basis for divine authority. Qumrân obviously recognized the divine authority of the Law, and the members set themselves to study it and put it into practice. Likewise, they recognized divine authority, or at least divine mysteries, and believed that special knowledge had been given by God to the Teacher to interpret these mysteries. There are

End view of the Genesis Apocryphon (1QapGen) before unrolling. Nine layers of the white interleaving leather can be detected. (J. C. Trever)

interpretations of Psalms as well as of a number of the Prophets in the DSS. The adherence at Qumrân to the calendar of Jubilees, plus the presence of a considerable number of MSS of Jubilees, brings into focus the question of whether we can objectively establish canonicity for that group, or for any other group. "The inner testimony of the Spirit" may well be the principal basis for canonicity.

B. Developments in Early Judaism. The relevance of the rise of Judaism to biblical studies may not be readily understood, but just a few facts should clarify the matter. By any but the most extreme critical positions, the OT was completed at least two centuries before the writing of the earliest NT book, and more probably three or four centuries before. Much can happen in that period of time. For example, the word "Messiah" as a term denoting the coming eschatological son of David does not occur in the OT. (In Dnl. 9:25f., the word lacks the definite article and simply means "an anointed one.") Yet by the time of Jesus' birth, the term was widely used by Jews and had a fairly well defined meaning, so that both John the Baptist and Jesus could be asked, "Are you the Messiah?" (cf. Mt. 26:63; the question is implied by John's answer in Jn. 1:20, cf. v. 25). The concept of the Messiah, though rooted in the OT, took its NT form in the intertestamental period.

At the change of the eras, the 1st cents. B.C. and A.D., the Jews were not a homogeneous people, ethnically, socially, or religiously. The Dispersion was already several centuries old, and Jews were scattered far and wide. Some were strongly hellenized. Synagogues existed even in Jerusalem — by tradition, 480 of them (T.P. *Megillah* 73d). There were several Jewish sects, including the Pharisees, Sadducees, Essenes, Christians, Ebionites, and others. Epiphanius (*ca.* A.D. 375) listed seven Jewish sects, and R. H. Pfeiffer adds four Samaritan sects. The sects were marked by differences; their common Judaic tenets were what identified them as Jews. The NT mentions only the Pharisees and Sadducees (the Zealots were a political movement, rather than a religious sect). With the discovery of the DSS, some scholars identified the community as Essenes, naively viewing that as the only alternative to their being Pharisees or Sadducees.

Practically all that is known about the Pharisees and the Sadducees comes from two sources: Josephus and the NT. All that is known about the Essenes comes from Philo, Josephus, and Pliny the Elder. (Hippolytus of Rome drew from Josephus.) The relationship of the Essenes to early

Genesis Apocryphon scroll and small fragments. The document is an Aramaic midrash (paraphrase) on portions of the patriarchal narratives of Genesis. (J. C. Trever)

Christianity has been discussed at various times. A fairly full treatment, including a study of the suggested etymologies of the name "Essene," can be found in J. B. Lightfoot, *St. Paul's Epistles to the Colossians and to Philemon* (1875), pp. 82-95, 114-179. All the relevant texts from Philo, Josephus, and Pliny can be found in Dupont-Sommer, *Essene Writings from Qumran,* pp. 21-38.

That there are many points of similarity between the Essenes and the Qumrân community is beyond question. There are also serious points of difference. The differences could be explained by saying that the DSS are the primary sources for knowledge of the Essenes, whereas the other writings are only secondary material and that Philo, Josephus, and Pliny therefore must be corrected by the statements in the DSS. But this method is flagrantly circular reasoning, for it assumes what it sets out to prove, namely that the Qumrânians were Essenes. Another way of explaining the differences is to introduce elements of time and geography. Josephus writes that he was determined to know the three Jewish sects at first hand, and therefore planned to join each in turn. He joined the Essenes when he was sixteen, but since he was already a Pharisee at nineteen, it is certain that he had time only to meet the entrance requirements of the Qumrân group. It is known that Qumrân was only one of several "camps" of the covenanters (CD 14:3, 7-11), and some possibly did not live in camps (cf. 7:6-9). Also it is known that the Essenes left the cities and dwelt in towns and villages (Philo *Quod omnis probus liber sit* 75, cf. *Apologia* 11.1; Josephus *BJ* ii.8.4 § 124). Since Josephus was born in A.D. 37, he was sixteen in A.D. 52/53, and the writing of his account was decades later. It is therefore highly probable that he belonged to an Essene group other than that located at Qumrân (if indeed Qumrân was Essene), and he certainly was separated by at least several decades from the time when CD and 1QS were first formulated. We therefore must reckon with the possibility of developments in Essenism. It is also possible that the Essenes and the Qumrânians were separate groups or sects that split from a common source sometime in the 2nd cent. B.C. (see LaSor, *Dead Sea Scrolls and the NT*, pp. 131-141). But whether the Essenes and Qumrânians were of the same sect or divergent sects from a common origin is of little import for the present discussion. What is important is to note that Judaism was a house divided, and that Jerusalem Judaism was severely criticized not only by Jesus but also by the Qumrânians. G. F. Moore distinguished "normative Judaism" from "sectarian Judaism" (*Judaism,* I [1927], 3). Some modern Jewish scholars object to this distinction; S. Sandmel prefers to speak of "Synagogue Judaism" as distinguished from "Temple Judaism" (*Judaism and Christian Beginnings* [1978], pp. xvii, 10f.). Whatever terms are used, Judaism cannot be treated as a monolithic structure, and interpretation of parts of the NT requires a more careful study of the various forces that were at work in early Judaism. Some of the concepts in Paul's writings, for example, which have long been held to be reactions against a second-century Greek type of Gnosticism, may now be viewed as possibly having their origins in Jewish sectarian movements.

Especially in the area of Jewish eschatological or messianic thought and in the development of apocalyptic concepts do NT students need to study Jewish materials, both rabbinic and sectarian. Here the Qumrân documents are helpful. There were Jews living in the 1st cent. B.C. who were looking for the Messiah; the Qumrânians believed that they were in the last generation. The rise and sudden acceptance of John the Baptist is not at all incredible, when seen against this background. The attribution to Jesus of messianic terms, although He made no such claims in His early public ministry, and forbade men to say that He was the Messiah, must likewise be viewed against this eschatological fervor. Again, the expectation of Jesus' disciples that He was about to restore the kingdom to Israel is part of the spirit of the times that is also found at Qumrân. The DSS in no way undermine the uniqueness of Jesus Christ, but they do help define more precisely wherein that uniqueness lies.

C. Relationship to the NT. A question often asked is, "Why were there no NT writings among the DSS?" Some NT fragments were found at Khirbet Mird, when the general search for caves took place following the Qumrân discoveries, but these clearly belonged to a later period (5th to 8th cent. A.D.) and came from the ruins of a Christian (Byzantine) monastery. It is unfortunate that they were ever connected with the Qumrân discoveries in written accounts. There was also the claim that fragments of the NT had been found in Cave 7. (See J. O'Callaghan, *Biblica,* 53 [1972], 91-100; there has been no marked scholarly acceptance of his claims. For bibliography, see Fitzmyer, *Dead Sea Scrolls,* 119-123.) Given the dates of Qumrân (*ca.* 140 B.C.-A.D. 68), the dates of the earliest NT writings, and the places to which they were addressed (those written before A.D. 68 are probably 1 and 2 Thessalonians, Galatians, Romans, 1 and 2 Corinthians, James, Paul's prison Epistles, and possibly the sources of the Synoptics), there is little reason to suppose that any of them would have reached Qumrân. Moreover, this was an exclusivist sect, according to its own words, and would have had little or no interest in another Jewish sect.

The claim has sometimes been made that John the Baptist received his training at Qumrân. This may be supported by two lines of reasoning, first, that John was brought up in the Wilderness of Judea until he began his ministry (cf. Lk. 1:80), and second, that John's ministry, with its denunciation of sinners, its call to repentance, its quoting of Isaiah, and the central place of baptism, seems to have some relationship with Qumrân. These points may be refuted. John's parents were part of the Jerusalem religious group against which the Qumrânians hurled invectives; Zacharias was a priest. Would he and Elizabeth entrust their only son, for whom they had waited so many years, to such a hostile group? John's ministry was indeed a fiery one, but could that not have been influenced by the OT prophets rather than by Qumrân? John's baptism was clearly initiatory: it was administered at once to anyone who repented. Qumrân baptism was certainly not that, but was rather a cleansing rite reserved to members who were scrupulous in their observance of the Law. John's attitude was open and sinners were invited, even urged, to repent. The Qumrânians proclaimed a curse on anyone who made the truth known to the "sons of darkness."

The claim has likewise been made that Jesus studied at Qumrân. A long list of similarities between His teaching and the writings from Qumrân can be compiled, and many scholars have contributed to such a list. It can be said as a general rule that these points can all be traced to the OT or to early Judaism. In no single case does Jesus seem to show clear-cut dependence on Qumrân. Moreover, the suggestion that He studied at Qumrân is highly improbable. Some of the same objections set forth against identifying John with Qumrân can be used in the case of Jesus. In addition, there is the psychological objection that the people of Nazareth were caught completely by surprise at the beginning of His ministry, for they knew Him and they knew His family. As for the extravagant claims that Jesus "appears in many respects as an astonishing reincarnation of the Teacher of Righteousness" (A. Dupont-Sommer, *Dead Sea Scrolls* [1952], p. 99), and the labored efforts to show that every major fact in Jesus' life can be traced to a similar point in the life of the Teacher of Righteousness, these have been refuted by careful scholars many times. (See LaSor, *Dead Sea Scrolls and the NT,* pp. 117-130, 206-236, and footnotes. See especially Rowley's works, mentioned above, and his exhaustive bibliographical references.)

Several studies have been published in which certain Pauline ideas have been compared to statements in the DSS. Some of the parallels have been made by scholars who would deny Pauline authorship on critical grounds to the very works that they quote, namely, Ephesians, Colossians, and the Pastorals. Such scholarship does not commend itself. There are, however, several points at which the Qumrân writings help scholars understand the development of ideas in early Judaism, and see that some of these ideas could lie behind some of Paul's statements. Paul is a curious mixture of what Sandmel calls "Temple Judaism" and "Synagogue Judaism," being both a strict Pharisee and also a native of the Hellenistic world. To see Paul as only a Hellenist Jew, and to fail to see the complexities in Judaism, is to take a somewhat distorted view of both. (For fuller discussion, see articles on the subject in K. Stendahl, ed., *The Scrolls and the NT,* [1957], notably those by W. D. Davies and K. G. Kuhn; see also J. Murphy-O'Connor, ed., *Paul and Qumrân: Studies in NT Exegesis* [1968].)

An important study of the Epistle to the Hebrews and the DSS was published by Y. Yadin (C. Rabin and Y. Yadin, eds., *Aspects of the Dead Sea Scrolls* [1958], pp. 36-55). While many points need careful study, the article does not appear to have evoked any strong reception. The treatment of Melchizedek is particularly noteworthy, since a "Melchizedek Scroll" (11QMelch) has been found at Qumrân. (See M. de Jonge and A. S. van der Woude, *NTS,* 12 [1965-66], 301-326; J. A. Fitzmyer, *JBL,* 86 [1967], 25-41.)

In the area of Johannine writings and the DSS significant studies have been published. The concept of "dualism" has been discussed, especially in the light of John's use of contrasting categories (light–darkness, truth–error, of the world–not of the world, etc.). One point that has been the focus of attention concerns the date of the Last Supper in the Fourth Gospel and the Qumrân calendar. It has long been recognized that the date of the Last Supper in the Fourth Gospel does not appear to agree with that in the Synoptics, and some writers on the subject have seen a possible solution to the problem in the Qumrân calendar. While the entire problem deserves full study, a serious obstacle seems to be that it is John who is seen to have the most in common with Qumrân, but it is the Synoptic date of the Last Supper that would fit the Qumrân calendar — just the opposite to what would be expected. (For bibliography on John and the DSS, see Fitzmyer, *Dead Sea Scrolls,* pp. 129f. Note particularly H. Braun, *Qumran und das NT* [1966], I, 96-138, 290-326; II, 118-144; and R. E. Brown, "Qumrân Scrolls and the Johannine Gospel and Epistles," in Stendahl, ed., pp. 183-207.)

Burrows considered the "church idea" to be more important, when comparing Qumrân and Christianity, than some of the other comparisons that had been suggested (see Burrows, *Dead Sea Scrolls* [1955], p. 332). By this term he meant the "concept of a spiritual group, the true people of God, distinct from the Jewish nation as such." Stendahl pointed out much the same fact when he observed that the Pharisees and Sadducees are "parties" within Judaism, whereas the Essenes and Christianity are "sects" (pp. 7-10). It is clear from the Qumrân texts that the community repudiated the Jerusalem priesthood and considered itself the faithful remnant (CD 1:4f.; 1QM 13:7), preserved by God from the judgment that was about to fall. It is also clear in Acts that the Church had a somewhat similar view. Salvation was possible through Jesus Christ alone, and the Church was the fellowship of those who believed in Him. This basic concept has undergone considerable elaboration, with some scholars calling attention to similarities of organization (the twelve laymen and three priests in Qumrân and the twelve apostles and three "pillars" in the Church; the *m^e^baqqēr* ["overseer"] in Qumrân and the *epískopos* ["overseer," "bishop"] in the Church; etc.) and of ritual (the sacred meal in Qumrân, the Lord's Supper in the Church). Some have compared the community of goods in Qumrân with the same concept in Acts (4:32–5:11). Careful scholars have examined the points of similarity. In no case is the similarity such that the dependence of the Church on Qumrân is required as an explanation, but rather, the ideas can be traced back to the OT. The concept of the remnant in the latter days is drawn from the prophets. The sacred meal developed from the Passover. The concept of twelve apostles is clearly tied to the twelve tribes of Israel. The community of goods was an enforced obligation of any who wished to enter the Qumrân community, but was entirely voluntary in the Church (Acts 4:5). (See L. Mowry, *The Dead Sea Scrolls and the Early Church* [1962]; and B. Reicke, "Constitution of the Primitive Church," in Stendahl, ed., pp. 143-156.)

D. Uniqueness of Christ. According to some writers on the subject, and in the mind of many who have read only the more sensational books on the DSS, this discovery destroys or brings into serious question the uniqueness of Jesus Christ. Two points must be noted. First, many of the NT doctrines on which the uniqueness of Christ is established have been "found" at Qumrân by the process of reading them back into the DSS from the NT. If, for example, the virgin birth, the crucifixion, and the resurrection of Jesus were not known at all, either from the NT or from the writings of the Church Fathers, the ideas would never have occurred to anyone reading the DSS. By no acceptable method of exegesis can these ideas be found in any of the Qumrân texts. This is the conclusion of scholars of widely different personal religious convictions, including M. Burrows, J. Carmignac, H. Gaster, and the author.

But another observation must be made, for which purpose a penetrating question must be asked: in what does the uniqueness of Christ consist? If a doctrine of His uniqueness is built on the basis that He said things never said before, established rituals never used before, laid the groundwork for an organization unlike any that had previously existed, was put to death in a manner never known before, or even had a name never used before, there will be many rude shocks. He was an Israelite named "Joshua" (Jesus is the Greek form), and He was brought up in the religious system of the Jews of His day. Some of the things He said sounded strange, and His followers searched the Jewish Scriptures. They followed Him not because He was different, but because what He said and did could be justified by the testimony of the Scriptures. His uniqueness is to be found in His divine origin and in His atoning death, and these are witnessed to by God in the Resurrection (Rom. 1:4; 1 Cor. 15:17).

See also ESSENES; QUMRÂN; Plates 13, 15, 16, 17.

Bibliography.–Bibliographical Works: W. S. LaSor, *Bibliography of the Dead Sea Scrolls 1948-1957* (1958); B. Jongeling, *Classified Bibliography of the Finds in the Desert of Judah, 1958-1969* (1971) (these two works are arranged by topic); J. A. Fitzmyer, *The Dead Sea Scrolls: Major Publications and Tools for Study* (1975); C. Burchard, *Bibliographie zu den Handschriften vom Toten Meer* (*BZAW*, 76, 1957); II (*BZAW*, 89, 1965); "Bibliographie," in *RQ* (since 1958).

Discoveries: M. Burrows, *The Dead Sea Scrolls* (1955); *More Light on the Dead Sea Scrolls* (1958); J. C. Trever, *The Dead Sea Scrolls: A Personal Account* (rev. ed. 1978); R. de Vaux, *Archaeology and the Dead Sea Scrolls* (Eng. tr. 1973); J. T. Milik, *Ten Years of Discovery in the Wilderness of Judaea* (*SBT*, 26; 1959); F. M. Cross, *The Ancient Library of Qumran and Modern Biblical Studies* (1958); G. Vermès, *Discovery in the Judean Desert* (1956); for the first announcements and reports as they appeared see LaSor, *Bibliography,* nos. 1000-1533, especially those marked with asterisks.

Texts: Lists: Fitzmyer, *Dead Sea Scrolls,* pp. 9-58; Burchard, *Bibliographie,* II, 313-359; J. A. Sanders, *JJS*, 24 (1973), 74-83; H. Stegemann, *ZDPV,* 83 (1967), 95-100 (supplements Burchard).

Texts: D. Barthélemy and J. T. Milik, *Discoveries in the Judaean Desert I, Qumran Cave I* (1955); M. Burrows, ed., *The Dead Sea Scrolls of St. Mark's Monastery,* I (1950) (1QIsa[a] and

1QpHab in Hebrew transcription with photographic plates); II, fascicle 2 (1951) (1QS, transcription and plates; fascicle 1 was never published); F. M. Cross, *et al.*, eds., *Scrolls from Qumran Cave I: The Great Isaiah Scroll, The Order of the Community, the Pesher to Habakkuk* (1972); E. L. Sukenik (posthumously edited by M. Avigad and Y. Yadin), *The Dead Sea Scrolls of the Hebrew University* (1955); N. Avigad and Y. Yadin, eds., *Genesis Apocryphon* (1956); A. M. Habermann, *m^egillôṯ midbar y^ehûdâ: The Scrolls from the Judaean Desert* (1959) (1QpHab, 1QSa, 1QS, 1QSb, CD, 1QM, 1QH, 1QPBless, 4QFlor, and several other fragments in vocalized Hebrew, with concordance); M. Baillet, J. T. Milik, and R. de Vaux, eds., *Les "Petites Grottes" de Qumran: Exploration de la falaise, les grottes 2Q, 3Q, 5Q, 6Q, 7Q, à 10Q, le rouleau de cuivre* (1962); J. M. Allegro, *Treasure of the Copper Scroll* (1960) (an unauthorized publication); J. A. Sanders, *Psalms Scroll of Qumran Cave 11 (11QPs^a)* (1965); J. P. M. van der Ploeg and A. S. van der Woude, *Le targum de Job de la grotte XI de Qumran* (1971); J. M. Allegro, *Qumran Cave 4: I (4Q158-186)* (1968); C. Rabin, *Zadokite Documents* (1954) (text and translation of CD); E. Lohse, ed., *Die Texte aus Qumran* (2nd ed. 1971).

Concordance: K. G. Kuhn, *et al.*, *Konkordanz zu den Qumrantexten* (1960); supplement in *RQ*, 4 (1963/64), 163-234.

Translations and Commentaries: Burrows, *Dead Sea Scrolls*, I, 348-415 (excellent translations); J. Carmignac, P. Guilbert, and E. Cothenet, *Les textes de Qumrân traduits et annotés* (2 vols., 1961, 1963); Y. Yadin, *Scroll of the Sons of Light against the Sons of Darkness* (Eng. tr. 1962) (1QM with commentary); R. G. Jongeling, *Le rouleau de la guerre* (1959); G. Vermès, *Dead Sea Scrolls in English Translation* (1956); P. Wernberg-Møller, *Manual of Discipline* (1957); Avigad and Yadin, *Genesis Apocryphon* (tr. of 1QapGen); J. A. Fitzmyer, *Genesis Apocryphon of Qumran Cave I: A Commentary* (2nd ed. 1971); J. Licht, *Thanksgiving Scroll* (1957) (text and translation of 1QH and commentary; Hebrew with English summary); A. Dupont-Sommer, *Essene Writings from Qumran* (Eng. tr. 1961) (translations often seriously distorted by Dupont-Sommer's assumptions).

Other Discussions: General: G. Vermès, *Discovery in the Judean Desert* (1956); W. S. LaSor, *Amazing Dead Sea Scrolls* (rev. ed. 1962; republished as *Dead Sea Scrolls and the Christian Faith*, 1972); F. F. Bruce, *Second Thoughts on the Dead Sea Scrolls* (1956).

Archeology: G. M. Crowfoot, *PEQ*, 83 (1951), 5-31; O. R. Sellers, *BASOR*, 123 (Oct. 1951), 24-26; R. de Vaux, *RB*, 60 (1953), 83-106; 60 (1953), 540-561, plates xx-xxiv; 61 (1954), 193-236; 63 (1956), 533-577; 66 (1959), 225-255; J. T. Milik, "Le travail d'édition des manuscrits du Désert de Juda," in *SVT*, 4 (1957), 17-26; H. W. Baker, "Notes on the Opening of the Copper Scrolls from Qumran," in Baillet, Milik, and de Vaux, pp. 203-210.

Textual Studies: H. H. Rowley, *Zadokite Fragments and the Dead Sea Scrolls* (1952); S. A. Birnbaum, *Qumran (Dead Sea) Scrolls and Palaeography* (*BASOR Supp. Studies* Nos. 13-14, 1952); F. M. Cross, "The Development of the Jewish Scripts," in *BANE*, pp. 170-264; D. N. Freedman, *Textus*, 2 (1962), 87-102; H. M. Orlinsky, "The Textual Criticism of the OT," in *BANE*, pp. 140-169.

DSS and OT: F. F. Bruce, *Biblical Exegesis in the Qumran Texts* (1959); J. A. Fitzmyer, "The Use of Explicit OT Quotations in Qumran Literature and in the NT," in *Essays on the Semitic Background of the NT* (1974), pp. 3-58; J. de Waard, *Comparative Study of the OT Text in the Dead Sea Scrolls and in the NT* (1965); W. H. Brownlee, *Meaning of the Qumrân Scrolls for the Bible* (1964).

Theology: H. Ringgren, *Faith of Qumran: Theology of the Dead Sea Scrolls* (1963); F. Nötscher, *Zur theologischen Terminologie der Qumran-Texte* (1956); J. Jeremias, *Die theologische Bedeutung der Funde am Toten Meer* (1962); K. Schubert, *The Dead Sea Community* (1959); F. Nötscher, *Gotteswege and Menschenwege in der Bible und in Qumran* (1958); P. von der Osten-Sacken, *Gott und Belial: Traditionsgeschichtliche Untersuchungen zum Dualismus in den Texten aus Qumran* (1969).

Teacher of Righteousness: A. Michel, *Le Maître de Justice* (1954); G. Jeremias, *Der Lehrer der Gerechtigkeit* (1963); J. Carmignac, *Christ and the Teacher of Righteousness* (Eng. tr. 1962); R. E. Brown, "The Teacher of Righteousness and the Messiah(s)," in M. Black, ed., *The Scrolls and Christianity* (1969), pp. 37-44, 109-112; F. F. Bruce, *Teacher of Righteousness in the Qumran Texts* (1957).

Messianic Idea: K. G. Kuhn, "Two Messiahs of Aaron and Israel," in K. Stendahl, ed., *Scrolls and the NT* (1957), pp. 54-64; M. Burrows, *ATR*, 34 (1952), 202-206; W. S. LaSor, *VT*, 6 (1956), 425-29; "The Messianic Idea in Qumran," in M. Ben-Horin, *et al.*, eds., *Studies Presented to A. A. Neuman* (1962), pp. 343-361; R. B. Laurin, *RQ*, 4 (1963/64), 39-52; H. H. Rowley, *Jewish Apocalyptic and the Dead Sea Scrolls* (1957).

Calendar: A. Jaubert, *VT*, 3 (1955), 250-264; S. Talmon, "The Calendar Reckoning of the Sect from the Judaean Desert," in *Aspects of the Dead Sea Scrolls* (1958), pp. 162-199; J. T. Milik, *SVT*, 4, 24f. (see Archeology above); E. Vogt, *Bibl.*, 39 (1958), 72-77; P. W. Skehan, *CBQ*, 20 (1958), 192-99.

History: J. Murphy-O'Connor, *RB*, 81 (1974), 215-244; H. H. Rowley, *BJRL*, 49 (1966/67), 203-232.

Qumran and Christianity: J. van der Ploeg, ed., *La secte de Qumrân et les origines du Christianisme* (1959); E. Stauffer, *Jesus und die Wüstengemeinde am Toten Meer* (2nd ed. 1960); M. Black, *The Scrolls and Christian Origins* (1961); ed., *The Scrolls and Christianity* (1969).

DSS and NT: H. Braun, *Qumran und das NT* (2 vols., 1966); J. Daniélou, *The Dead Sea Scrolls and Primitive Christianity* (2nd. ed. 1963); J. A. Fitzmyer, *Essays on the Semitic Background of the NT* (1971), pp. 3-89, 127-160, 187-354, 435-480; J. H. Charlesworth, ed., *John and Qumran* (1972); R. E. Brown, "John and Qumran," in *Gospel According to John* (*AB*, 1966), lxii-lxvi; J. Roloff, *NTS*, 15 (1968/69), 129-151; J. Murphy-O'Connor, ed., *Paul and Qumran* (1968); J. A. Sanders, *JR*, 39 (1959), 232-244; J. E. Wood, *Expos.T.*, 78 (1966/67), 308-310.

W. S. LASOR

DEAD, STATE OF THE. *See* DEATH III.

DEAF [Heb. *ḥērēš, ḥāraš* (Ps. 28:1; Mic. 7:6)]; AV also SILENT (Ps. 28:1); [Gk. *kāphós*] (Mt. 11:5; Mk. 7:32, 37; 9:25; Lk. 7:22). Used either in the physical sense, or figuratively as expressing unwillingness to hear the divine message (Ps. 58:4), or incapacity to understand it for want of spirituality (Ps. 38:13). The prophetic utterances were sufficiently forcible to compel even such to hear (Isa. 42:18; 43:8) and thereby to receive the divine mercy (Isa. 29:18; 35:5).

The expression "deaf adder that stops its ear" (Ps. 58:4) alludes to a curious notion that the adder, to avoid hearing the voice of the charmer, laid its head with one ear on the ground and stopped the other with the tip of its tail (*Diary of John Manninghan* [1602]). The erroneous idea probably arose from the absence of external ears.

Physical deafness was regarded as a judgment from God (Ex. 4:11; Mic. 7:16), and it was consequently impious to curse the deaf (Lev. 19:14). In NT times deafness and kindred defects were attributed to evil spirits (Mk. 9:18ff.). *See also* DUMB.

A. MACALISTER

DEAL. "Deal" does not occur as a noun in the RSV; it occurs frequently as a verb, however, translating such OT and NT terms as Heb. *'āśâ*–"do" (Gen. 24:49; Ex. 5:15; Dt. 7:5; etc.), *šāqar*–"deal falsely with" (Gen. 21:23; Lev. 19:11; Isa. 63:8), *gāmal*–"confer benefit on" (Ps. 13:6 [MT 7]; 116:7; 119:17; etc.); Gk. *chráomai*–"use" (1 Cor. 7:31), *metriopathéō*–"treat gently" (He. 5:2), *chōrís*–"without," "apart from" (He. 9:28), etc. In Jn. 4:4 the Gk. *synchráomai* conveys the idea that the Jews use no vessels or utensils in common with the Samaritans.

The AV also uses "deal" in sense of "apportion," "distribute" in 2 S. 6:19; 1 Ch. 16:3; Isa. 58:7; Rom. 12:3.

DEALER [Heb. *sōḥēr*] (Ezk. 27:21); AV "occupy"; NEB "source of commerce"; [*'āraḇ*–'barter'] (27:27); AV OCCUPIER; NEB MERCHANT; [Gk. *pōlṓn* (from *pōléō*)] (Mt. 25:9); AV "them that sell"; NEB "shop." Traveling peddlers, transporting their merchandise on camels, mules, oxen, donkeys, or by slaves, were common in biblical times. They were especially fond of setting up their stalls near religious shrines, to which many pilgrims went. *See also* COMMERCE; MERCHANDISE.

DEAR. In Col. 1:13, AV and NEB "of his dear Son" translates Gk. *toú huioú tḗs agápēs autoú*, lit. "of his Son of love," or as RV "of the Son of his love." The RSV has "of his beloved Son."

DEARTH. Archaic in the AV for FAMINE.

DEATH (substantives) [Heb. usually *māweṯ, mûṯ*]; [*dām*–'blood'] (Ps. 30:9 [MT 10]; 94:21); AV BLOOD; [*nepeš*] (Ps. 109:31); AV "soul"; NEB "adversaries"; [*bôr*] (Prov. 28:17); AV THE PIT; NEB "well"; [*māmôṯ*] (Ezk. 28:8; cf. Jer. 16:4, "deadly"); [Gk. usually *thánatos*]; [*hádēs*] (Mt. 2:15; var. Acts 2:24 and 1 Cor. 15:55); AV also HELL; [*teleutḗ*–'end'] (Mt. 2:15); [*anaíresis*] (Acts 8:1); NEB MURDER; [*nekrós*] (Rom. 6:13; He. 9:17); NEB DEAD; [*nékrōsis*] (2 Cor. 4:10); AV DYING; **DEAD** (usually a complement of a verb for "to be") [Heb. *mûṯ, gāwa'* (Nu. 20:29), *šāḏaḏ*–'fall dead' (Jgs. 5:27)]; NEB also DIED, DONE TO DEATH; [Gk. *nekrós, nekróō, apothnḗskō, thnḗskō*]; (also a substantive) [Heb. *mûṯ* (Gen. 23 *passim*; Isa. 26:19; etc.); Gk. *nekrós* (Lk. 9:60)]; (a collective noun) [Heb. *mûṯ, nepeš, repā'îm*; Gk. *nekrós*]; (an adjective) [Heb. *mûṯ, māweṯ* (Eccl. 10:1), *nepeš* (Nu. 6:11; 9:6f., 10), *peger, neḇēlâ, g^{e}wîyâ* (Nah. 3:3); Gk. *nekrós, ptṓma, teleutáō* (Jn. 11:39)]; AV also CORPSE (Nah. 3:3); NEB also YOU SHALL DIE (Gen. 20:3), CORPSE (Nu. 9:6f., 10); [*hēmithanḗs*] ("half dead," Lk. 10:30); **DIE** [Heb. usually *mûṯ*, also *gāwa'* (Gen. 6:17; 7:21; Nu. 20:3; Job 13:19; etc.), nouns *māweṯ, neḇēlâ* ("dies of itself," Lev. 7:24; 17:15; 22:8; Dt. 14:21; Ezk. 4:14; 44:31); Gk. usually *apothnḗskō*, also *teleutáō, thnḗskō* (Lk. 7:12; Jn. 8:21), *synapothnḗskō* (Mk. 14:31; 2 Cor. 7:3; 2 Tim. 2:11), *koimáō*–'sleep, fall asleep' (1 Cor. 7:39; 11:30), *ekpsýchō* (Acts 5:5; 10; 12:23), *nekrós* (Rev. 1:18; 2:8), *apogínomai* (1 Pet. 2:24), *thánatos*–'death' (Rom. 1:32; Phil. 2:30), *thanatóō*–'put to death' (1 Pet. 3:18)]; AV also DECEASED (Mt. 22:25), "give up the ghost" (Job 13:19; Acts 5:5; 12:23), "sleep" (1 Cor. 7:39), "being put to death" (1 Pet. 3:18), etc.; NEB also PERISH (Gen. 6:17; 7:21), FAIL (Ps. 104:29), DEATH PENALTY (Dt. 19:6), "has died a natural death" (Dt. 14:21), SUFFER DEATH (Mt. 15:4), "ended his days" (Acts 7:15), etc.

I. Vocabulary
 A. Death
 B. Dead
 C. Die
II. End of Earthly Existence
III. State of the Dead
 A. Estrangement
 B. Abode of the Dead
 C. Shades
IV. Death as Penalty
V. Release from Death

I. Vocabulary.–*A. Death.* The Heb. verb *mûṯ*, "die," is translated "death" in many expressions, such as "guilty of death" (Nu. 35:31; NEB "guilty of a capital offense"), "at the point of death" (2 K. 20:1 par.; AV "sick unto death"; NEB "dangerously ill"), "stone to death" (Nu. 15:36; 1 K. 12:18; etc.; AV "that he died"). In the hiphil the verb means "put to death" (AV also "slay," "kill") and in the hophal, "be put to death" (AV also "be slain," "die"). In Job 33:22 the hiphil participle is rendered "those who bring death" (AV "destroyers"; NEB "ministers of death").

Other OT expressions are "be put to death" for *nāḵâ* (2 Ch. 25:16; AV "be smitten"; NEB "risk your life"), "caused the death" for *nāpaḥ nepeš* (Job 31:39; lit. "cause to breathe out life"; AV "cause to lose their life"; NEB "disappointed"), "close to death" for *gāwa'* (Ps. 88:15 [MT 16]; AV "ready to die"; NEB "near to death"), "be put to death" for *rāṣaḥ* (Nu. 35:30), and "occasioned the death of" for the euphemistic *sāḇaḇ* (1 S. 22:22; lit. "bring about"; NEB "gambled with [the lives]"). In 2 S. 19:28 "men doomed to death" is read for Heb. *'anšê-māweṯ*, for which the AV has simply "dead men" (NEB "deserved to die"). The construction *b^{e}nê ṯ^{e}mûṯâ* is rendered "those doomed to die" (Ps. 79:11; 102:20 [MT 21]; AV "those that are appointed to die"; NEB "death's prisoners," "men under sentence of death"). The construct of *māweṯ* has intensive force (Ps. 13:3 [MT 4] "sleep of death," meaning a profound sleep simulating death), and the infinitive construct of *mûṯ* indicates an extreme degree, as "vexed to death" (Jgs. 16:16). In Ps. 23:4 the compound *ṣalmāweṯ* means "shadow of death" (elsewhere "deep darkness").

In Ps. 55:15 [MT 16] the RSV follows the *Q yaššî māweṯ*, "let death come" (AV "let death seize"; NEB "may death strike"); the RSV mg. follows the *K y^{e}šîmôṯ*, "desolations"). According to the AV of Prov. 14:32, "the righteous hath hope in his death" (*b^{e}môṯô*); following the LXX (Gk. *hosiótēs*) and Syriac the RSV reads "integrity," the NEB "honesty" (emending the MT to *b^{e}ṯummô*). In Ps. 73:4 the AV reads "there are no bands in their death," rendering Heb. *'ên ḥarṣubbôṯ l^{e}môṯām*; the RSV has "they have no pangs," ending the line with *lāmô* and reading *tām*, "sound," with the next line (NEB "no pain, no suffering").

The RSV renders as "put to death" the Gk. verbs *thanatóō, apokteínō, anairéō, apóllymi* (Mt. 21:41; AV "destroy"; NEB "bring to a bad end"), *apágō* (Acts 12:19; NEB "ordered their execution"), *paradídōmi* (Rom. 4:25; AV "delivered"; NEB "given up to death"), and *nekróō* (Col. 3:5; AV "mortify").

The expression "at [on] the point of death" occurs with the verb *apothnḗskō* in Jn. 4:47; Rev. 3:2 (NEB "which must otherwise die"), and with *teleutáō* (Lk. 7:2; NEB "near to death"); in Mk. 5:23 it translates *eschátōs échō* (NEB "at death's door"). The archaic "in deaths oft" as rendered by the AV in 2 Cor. 11:23 means "often near death" (*en thanátois pollákis*; NEB "many a time face to face with death"). In 1 Cor. 4:9 *epithanátios* means "sentenced to death" (AV "appointed"; NEB "condemned").

See also MORTAL (1 Jn. 5:16f.); PESTILENCE (*māweṯ*, Jer. 43:11; *thánatos*, Rev. 6:8; 18:8). J. W. D. H.

B. Dead. Following the Syriac and Targum the RSV and NEB emend Heb. *n^{e}ḇēlāṯî* in Isa. 26:19 (AV "my dead body") to read "their bodies." The RSV renders "that he was dead" in Mk. 15:45, drawing upon *apothnḗskō* in v. 44, and "he has been dead four days" in Jn. 11:39 (lit. "it is four days"). In Rev. 2:23 the RSV and NEB translate Gk. *apoktenṓ en thanátō* as "strike dead" (lit. "kill with death"). Gk. *egeírō*, "raise," is translated "raised from the dead" in Rom. 8:34, adding *ek nekrṓn* on the basis of the versions. (*See also* CORPSE.)

C. Die. In Mt. 15:4 *thanátō teleutáō* is translated "surely die" (AV "die the death"; NEB "suffer death").

II. End of Earthly Existence.–Although variously interpreted throughout the OT and NT, death is basically understood as the termination of life on earth. Most frequently it indicates the end of an individual's existence (e.g., "the death of Abraham," Gen. 25:11; etc.), often suggesting a predetermined date (Gen. 27:2; etc.;

cf. Ps. 90:9). "Death" might be equated with the means of one's demise (Jn. 18:32), as plague (Ex. 10:17), poison (2 K. 4:40), or disease (Job 18:13). Death is described as the falling and shattering of a lamp or the breaking of a water pitcher or well (Eccl. 12:6); the body returns to dust (Gen. 3:19; Eccl. 3:20) and the spirit (Heb. *rû[a]ḥ*) to God (Eccl. 12:7; Bar. 2:17). The soul or "essence" that characterizes life (*nepeš*) departs at death (Gen. 35:18; 1 K. 12:21; cf. Mt. 10:28; *see* SOUL).

Concern was shown for the circumstances surrounding one's death. Ideally it came only after a long life (Jgs. 8:32; 1 Ch. 29:28; Job 5:26; 6:5; cf. Eccl. 7:17; Wisd. 4:7). A person would prefer the "death of the righteous" (Nu. 23:10) rather than to "die as a fool" (2 S. 3:33; NEB "so base a death") or to suffer the ignoble "death of the slain" or "the uncircumcised" (Ezk. 28:8, 10; NEB "a death of disgrace," "die strengthless"). A person might also wish to die "in [his] own city" (2 S. 19:37).

Constantly confronted by the disease and warfare of the ancient world, people were well aware of the inevitability of death (2 S. 14:14; Sir. 14:17; cf. Gen. 3:19), the "fate of all men" (Nu. 16:29; cf. Josh. 23:14; 1 K. 2:2). They were highly conscious of the imminence of death, viewing disease, "the first-born of death" (Job 18:13), as a foretaste of their fate. The weakness and decay of advanced age made one "as good as dead" (Rom. 4:19; He. 11:12; AV "now dead"). Peril was "but a step between me and death" (1 S. 20:3). Beaten by robbers, a man was left "half dead" (Gk. *hēmithanḗs*, Lk. 10:30). The Egyptians, reeling under a series of plagues, were "dead men" (Ex. 12:33).

The inescapable human fate was described as greedy (Hab. 2:5), with waves that encompassed mankind (2 S. 22:5), or a trap with cords or snares (Ps. 18:4f. [MT 5f.]; 116:3; Prov. 13:14; 21:6). It was also represented as a city that detained one within its gates (Job 38:17; Ps. 9:13 [MT 14]; 107:18). Elsewhere death is personified, often in mythological terms (cf. Jer. 9:21) reminiscent of Canaanite and Mesopotamian paired deities (Job 28:22; Rev. 1:8; 20:13f.). It is portrayed as a royal figure, the shepherd (Ps. 49:14 [MT 15]), and as one of the four horsemen (Rev. 6:8). In political metaphor one might enter a covenant with Death (Isa. 28:15, 18). It was, however, a lesser power that, like the mythological serpent, might be "swallowed up" and deprived of its "sting" (Isa. 25:8; Hos. 13:14; 1 Cor. 15:55).

Figuratively, aspects of life may be viewed as "death." To live without love is to experience death (1 Jn. 3:14); even faith in Christ is lifeless unless expressed in works of love (Jas. 2:17, 26). Derogatorily labelled "the dead" (Mt. 8:22 par.), those outside the Christian community are given the gospel (1 Pet. 4:6) and enjoined to cease from "dead works" (He. 6:1; 9:14). The common ancient Near Eastern pejorative "dog" was compounded in references to a "dead dog" (1 S. 24:14; 2 S. 9:8; 16:9), but a "living dog" was better than a "dead lion" (Eccl. 9:4).

III. State of the Dead.*–*A. Estrangement. Death is significantly distinct from all aspects of human life, an alien form of existence (2 S. 15:21; Jer. 21:8) or nonexistence (cf. Job. 7:21; Ps. 39:13 [MT 14]). It is viewed as separation (Ruth 1:17), euphemistically termed "departure." Cloaked in mystery, this condition was thought to be marked by bitterness (1 S. 15:32), terror (Ps. 55:4 [MT 5]), and pain (Acts 2:24) and was thus the object of fear (He. 2:14; Sir. 40:5).

When differentiated from living creatures by death, both humans and animals became unclean and were to be avoided. Hebrew law forbade contact with the carcass of an animal that died "of itself" (Lev. 7:24; 11:39; 17:15) or was killed (22:8). Touching a dead body could render a person unclean (Nu. 9:6f.; 19:11, 16, 18). For this reason burial took place immediately (Jn. 11:17-39; Acts 5:6-10; *see* BURIAL).

Several passages refer to observation of the transition from life to death. "Mourning for the dead" had apparently become a standardized seven-day period (Gen. 50:10; Jth. 16:24; Sir. 22:12). Priests were restricted from participation in mourning rites except for the nearest of kin (Lev. 21:2f.). Specifically proscribed were heathen practices such as shaving and mutilating one's body by incisions or tatooing "on account of the dead" (Lev. 19:28; 21:5; Dt. 14:1). Offering food or drink to the dead, a common ancient Near Eastern custom, was prohibited (Dt. 26:14; cf. Tob. 4:17; Sir. 30:18), as was placing bodies before idols (Ezk. 6:5; 43:7, 9 may refer to royal cults). The Hebrews were not to seek oracles from the spirits of the dead (1 S. 28:9; 2 K. 21:6; Isa. 8:19; *see* DIVINATION; MEDIUM).

Jackal-headed Anubis weighing the hearts of the deceased in the judgment hall of Osiris. Ani papyrus, one of the papyri of the Egyptian Book of the Dead (*ca.* 1300 B.C.) (Trustees of the British Museum)

See also MOURNING; BAPTISM FOR THE DEAD (1 Cor. 15:29).

B. Abode of the Dead. The Hebrews, like other ancient Near Eastern peoples, pictured the dead as inhabitants of a realm totally detached from earthly existence. Early references indicate only that the deceased had departed to join their ancestors (Gen. 15:15; 35:29; etc.). Later accounts show all who die descending to a subterranean region (Prov. 2:18; 5:15; Jonah 2:6; cf. Job 7:21) where they abide in ambiguous oblivion. Described as a house (Job 30:23; cf. Prov. 7:27) or a walled city with gates (Isa. 38:10; cf. Job 38:17; Wisd. 16:13; Mt. 16:18 mg.), the abode of the dead was conceived as a void or empty space (as Gk. *cháos*; Job 10:21). It was a dusty area (Job 17:16; 21:26; Ps. 7:5 [MT 6]; cf. Gen. 3:19), characterized by a deep silence (Ps. 94:17; 115:17) and shadowy darkness (Job 11:21f.; Ps. 23:4; 143:3; Lam. 3:6; Sir. 22:11). As such, many viewed it as a welcome contrast to their earthly burdens and a release from torment (Job 3:21; Jonah 4:3; Sir. 41:2), a place of quiet rest (Jer. 51:39, 57; Job 3:17; Wisd. 4:7; Sir. 22:11; Jn. 11:11).

Of the various OT names for this region, the most frequent is Sheol (Heb. *šeʾôl*). Although the precise meaning of the term is debated, it appears to have been derived from Heb. *šāʾal*, "ask" or "inquire" (cf. Akk. *šaʾālu*), suggesting the practice of necromancy (cf. Isa. 8:19). Sheol is frequently personified with gaping jaws and an insatiable throat (Prov. 1:12; Isa. 5:14; Hab. 2:5), a figure reminiscent of the Canaanite god of the nether world, Mot (*ANET*, p. 135). Other terms for the region are technical applications of common nouns, often with Mesopotamian parallels. They include *ʾereṣ*, "earth" (Ex. 15:12; cf. Ps. 72:20; Akk. *erṣetu*; Ugar. *ʾrṣ*) and the related expression *ʾereṣ taḥtîṯ* "nether world" (Ezk. 31:14; Akk. *erṣetu šaplītu*), also *ʾaḇaddôn* "[place of] destruction" or "perdition" (Job 26:6; Ps. 88:11 [MT 12]; Prov. 15:11; cf. Rev. 9:11), *bôr* "pit" (Ps. 28:1; 88:4, 6 [MT 5, 7]; Isa. 14:15; Ezk. 32:18; Akk. *būru*), *mûṯ* "[the realm of] death" (Job 28:22; 30:23; 38:17; Ps. 6:5 [MT 6]; 9:13 [MT 14]; Prov. 7:27; cf. Akk. *bīt mūti*), and *šaḥaṯ* "pit," "grave" (Job 33:18; Ps. 16:10; 30:9 [MT 10]; Isa. 38:17; 51:14; Jonah 2:6 [MT 7]; Akk. *šuttu*).

Although the NT description of the abode of the dead (Gk. *hádēs*) differs little from the OT, the destinies of the righteous and the unrighteous are more closely distinguished (Mt. 7:13f.; 11:23 par.; Lk. 22:43; Phil. 1:23; cf. 2 Esd. 7:36). The introduction of Iranian thought into Palestine during the Hellenistic period certainly influenced the concept of a separate place of fiery torment for the wicked (Isa. 66:24; 2 Esd. 7:36; Jth. 16:17; Mk. 9:44, 46, 48; *see* GEHENNA). Having first experienced physical death (He. 9:27), the dead were to be judged, after which Death and Hades would be thrown into the lake of fire, the spiritual or "second" death (Rev. 2:11; 20:6, 13f.; 21:8; *see* LAKE OF FIRE; DEATH, SECOND). Christ Himself has the keys of Death and Hades (Rev. 1:18).

See also GLOOM; HADES; HEAVEN; NETHER WORLD; PIT; SHEOL.

C. Shades. Inhabitants of this region are called "shades" (Heb. *repāʾîm*; AV also "deceased" [Isa. 26:14], "dead things" [Job 26:5]; NEB also "ancient dead" [Isa. 14:9], "those long in their graves" [Isa. 26:14] or "long dead" [v. 19]; elsewhere RSV "the dead" [Prov. 9:18; 21:16]). Similar uses of the term are found in Phoenician (*rpʾm*) and Ugaritic (*rpʾum*; *UT*, 485; also "deities," suggesting the royal cult). Collectively the "assembly of the dead" (Prov. 21:16), i.e., residents of Sheol, the "land of the shades" (Isa. 26:19), lead a soporific existence Dt. 31:16; Ps. 13:3 [MT 4]; Acts 7:60), devoid of luxury (Ps. 49:17 [MT 18]; Sir. 14:16) or reward (Eccl. 9:5) and marked by trembling (Job 26:5; Mt. 28:4) and weeping (Jth. 16:17). Their consciousness numbed, they can remember neither their previous existence nor God (Ps. 6:5 [MT 6]; 88:12 [MT 13]; Eccl. 9:5) and thus are no longer capable of praising Him (Ps. 115:17; Bar. 2:17; Sir. 17:27f.; cf. Ps. 30:9 [MT 10]). Apparently distinctions were maintained on the basis of earthly status (Isa. 14:9f.; Ezk. 32:21-25).

See also GHOST; SPIRIT.

IV. Death as Penalty.–As in many societies, death was imposed as a sanction against behavior deemed contrary to the best interests of the community. For Israel this was particularly true of actions that might jeopardize the people's relationship to God. Under penalty of death ("lest you die," Lev. 8:35; 10:6f.; etc.), the Hebrews were to obey God's instructions (Gen. 2:17; 3:3) and the stipulations of the covenant. The caution taken to avoid looking at God and thus dying from contact with His manifest power (Ex. 10:28; Jgs. 13:22; etc.) was extended to ensure proper respect toward the holy shrines (Lev. 8:35; 10:6f., 9; 16:2, 13; Nu. 4:15, 19f.; etc.). Capital punishment was prescribed for murder and various other crimes (Ezr. 7:26; Jer. 26:11, 16; cf. Dt. 22:26; *see* PUNISHMENTS); offenders were regarded as "guilty of death" (Nu. 35:31) and "doomed to death" (Ps. 79:11; 102:30; etc.; cf. Gen. 20:3). Knowing the penalty for such actions, one could "choose" death by pursuing evil (Dt. 30:15; Prov. 11:19; etc.); those who did so "deserved" death (1 K. 2:26; Ezk. 13:19; Mk. 14:64). The law held that each person was responsible for his own actions and could not be executed for another's crime (Dt. 24:16; 2 K. 14:6; 2 Ch. 25:4; Jer. 31:30; Ezk. 18:4, 20); this had not always been the practice (Ex. 20:5; Dt. 5:9; cf. 1 K. 21:21f.).

The ultimate experience of death as penalty is its occurrence as the consequence of sin (Rom. 6:16, 21, 23; Jas. 1:15). On account of sin, death came into the world and became the common fate of mankind (Gen. 2:17; 3:17-19; Rom. 5:12-14), even Jesus of Nazareth (Rom. 6:10). Mankind exhibits a tendency toward evil, marked by human concerns (Rom. 8:6), and is therefore worthy of death (cf. 4 Esd. 7:21ff., 46, 68; 8:31, 35). Those who participate in trespasses and sins are already under the power of death (Eph. 2:1f., 5; Col. 2:13; 1 Tim. 5:6); Christians are urged to assist the sinner's repentance and thus "save his soul from death" (Jas. 5:20). Although reluctant to permit death (Ezk. 18:23, 32; 33:11; cf. Ps. 116:15), God uses it to punish those who turn aside from His way.

Paul contends that Jewish law — the entire system of religious thought and practice as based upon rabbinic interpretation of God's word — had become a tool of sin and, consequently, death (Rom. 8:2). Through the law mankind became conscious of sin and fell prey to its influence (Rom. 7:5, 7-13). Human nature thereby came under the dominion of death (v. 24).

V. Release from Death.–Although many had regarded death as a condition from which there is no escape (2 S. 12:23; Job 7:9f.; 10:21; 14:12), hope abounded that God's power might enable mankind to conquer it (Isa. 25:8; cf. Dnl. 12:2). Numerous pleas were issued for Yahweh's intervention in the lives of His people to deliver them from such manifestations of death as political oppression (Isa. 26:19; Sir. 51:9) and illness (Job 5:20; Ps. 9:13 [MT 14]).

From this faith in God's ability to "swallow up death forever" emerged a new understanding of future life.

In the OT life after death had been envisioned as establishing one's name in posterity through heirs (Gen. 30:1; Lev. 20:20; Mt. 22:24) who would maintain his inheritance in the land (Ruth 4:5, 10). Restoration of the dead had been evidenced throughout the OT and NT (1 K. 17:22; 2 K. 4:32-37; Mt. 10:8; 11:5; 14:2; 17:9; Lk. 7:11-17; 20:34-38 par.; Jn. 11:1-44; Acts 9:36-43; He. 11:35). However, the ultimate victory over death was won through Christ's death and resurrection (Rom. 6:9; 1 Cor. 15:26, 54f.; 2 Tim. 1:10). Because Jesus took human form to overcome the powers of death (He. 2:14f.), all of mankind has been enabled to pass "from death to life" (Jn. 5:24) by believing in Him (Jn. 11:25f.; cf. 8:24), participating in His death and resurrection (Rom. 6:3-5; 2 Cor. 4:10-12), and proclaiming His victory (1 Cor. 11:26). Just as Christ "died to sin" (Rom. 6:10), through Him His followers may also dissolve the claim and control of sin and the law (Rom. 6:11; 7:4-6; Gal. 2:19; cf. Rom. 8:2) and overcome the weaknesses of the flesh (lit. "put to death"; AV "mortify"; Rom. 8:13; Col. 3:5). By suffering death, Christ has overcome it, giving it new meaning and depriving it of its sting (Phil. 1:21; Jn. 12:24; 1 Cor. 15:36). A. C. M.

DEATH, BODY OF. *See* BODY OF DEATH.

DEATH PENALTY (Acts 28:18; cf. OT, e.g., Lev. 20:9ff.; 24:16ff.; Dt. 21:22). *See* PUNISHMENTS.

DEATH, SECOND [Gk. *ho deúteros thánatos*] (Rev. 2:11; 20:6, 14; 21:8). The final penalty of the unrighteous. The first death is the physical end of one's life on earth; the second death is spiritual, cutting off the soul (Mt. 10:28). In Rev. 20:14f.; 21:8, those who die the second death are said to be thrown into "the lake of fire." *See* LAKE OF FIRE; GEHENNA; and cf. 1 En. 10:12f., etc.

DEBATE [*zḗtēsis*] (Acts 15:2, 7); AV DISPUTE; NEB also CONTROVERSY; **DEBATER** [Gk. *syzētētḗs*] (1 Cor. 1:20); AV DISPUTER. The term "debate" occurs only twice in the RSV, each time rendering a common Greek term denoting "searching," "questioning," "enquiry," and hence "debate." *See also* DISCUSSION. In Rom. 1:29 (RSV "strife") and 2 Cor. 12:20 (RSV "quarreling") the AV renders "debate" in the obsolete sense of "fighting" or "contending." *See also* DISPUTE.

DEBAUCHERY [Gk. *koítai*] (Rom. 13:13); AV CHAMBERING; [*asōtía*] (Eph. 5:18); AV EXCESS; NEB DISSIPATION. The first word, literally "beds," refers to sexual incontinence; the second denotes a lack of self-control or self-discipline, resulting in wild living (cf. the use in Tit. 1:6; 1 Pet. 4:4, "profligacy").

DEBIR də-bēr′ [Heb. *d^{e}ḇîr, d^{e}ḇir*–'oracle']; King of Eglon, one of the five Amorite kings whose confederation against Israel was overcome and who were killed by Joshua (Josh. 10:3).

DEBIR də-bēr′ [Heb. *d^{e}ḇîr*].

1. A town in the Judean hill country S of Hebron; originally a Canaanite city called Kiriath-sepher, (Heb. *qiryaṯ-sēper*), "house of the book," which the LXX renders *pólis grammátōn*, "city of books" (Josh. 15:15; Jgs. 1:11). The correct geographical location of this city is fixed by its place in the roster of Judah's towns (Josh. 15:49), where it is said to be situated in the southernmost district of the Judean hill country; it appears

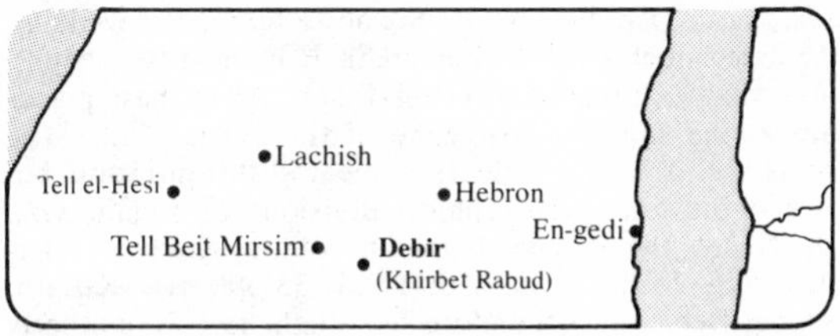

here as "Kiriath-sannah (that is, Debir)." M. Noth insisted that KIRIATH-SANNAH was the original name here (*lectio difficilior*), and the equation with Debir was only a later gloss that should be excised. H. Orlinsky decisively demonstrated that Noth's view violated the sound rules of textual criticism and showed that the LXX, which reads *pólis grammátōn hautē (estin) Dabir* ("city of books, which [is] Debir") is a reliable witness to the text of Josh. 15:49. Therefore, the original Hebrew of this passage was undoubtedly *qiryaṯ-sēper*(!) *hîʾ d^{e}ḇîr*, "Kiriath-sepher(!), which is Debir."

I. The Biblical Evidence
II. The Quest for the Site
III. Recent Discovery and Excavation
 A. Survey
 B. Excavation
IV. Concluding Arguments

I. The Biblical Evidence.–From the eleven occurrences of "Debir" in Scripture, the principal details of its history can be gleaned. Debir was one of the pre-Israelite cities occupied by the ANAKIM, along with Hebron and Anab in "the hill country of Judah" (Josh. 11:21). The conquest of southern Canaan under Joshua included Makkedah, Libnah, and Lachish in the Shephelah, followed by Hebron and Debir in the hill country (10:28-41). Debir was ruled by a king, i.e., it was a Canaanite city-state (10:39; 12:13).

Othniel the son of Kenaz is credited with the conquest of Debir (Josh. 15:15-19; Jgs. 1:11-15) for which he was given Achsah, daughter of Caleb, as his wife. As in the account in Josh. 10:28-41, the seizure of Debir follows directly on that of Hebron (by Caleb; Josh. 15:13f.; Jgs. 1:20; cf. 1:10f.). The Othniel-Achsah affair supplied further details on the nature of the terrain around Debir and the problem of its water. Debir was obviously located in a zone topographically like the Negeb and the city evidently lacked its own sufficient water sources. So Achsah requested and was granted *gullōṯ ʿillî(yō)ṯ* and *gullōṯ taḥtî(yō)ṯ*, "upper springs" and "lower springs" (Josh. 15:19; Jgs. 1:15; the plural form of the adjectives is preserved only in Joshua). The term *gullōṯ*, literally "basin(s)," was defined by W. F. Albright as "subterranean pockets and basins of water under some of the wadis," to which access was gained by cutting a well shaft through the rock in the dry creek beds (*AASOR*, 17 [1936/37], 4). The various ancient versions gave differing interpretations of this word, none of them satisfactory (e.g., LXX *Golathmain* [Josh. 15:19] or *lýtrōsin*, "redemption" [presupposing Heb. *g^{e}ʾullâ*, Jgs. 1:15]; Symm. *ardeía*, "watering"; Vulg. *irrigua*; Tg. and Pesh. *bēṯ šaqyāʾ*, "place of watering"). Recent investigation (see below) has confirmed Albright's interpretation. These "upper" and "lower" water sources must have been outside the natural territorial limits of Debir, but close enough to be transferred to its jurisdiction.

Within the description of Judah's inheritance, Kiriath-sepher (corrected according to the LXX, see above) = Debir is located in the first hill country district of the list (Josh. 15:49) in association with ten other towns, at least five of which have positive identifications based on the Arabic names and suitable archeological remains, viz., Jattir (Khirbet 'Attir), Socoh (Khirbet Shuweikeh), Anab (Khirbet 'Anâb eẓ-Ẓeghīreh), Eshtemoh (es-Semû'), and Anim (Khirbet Ghuwein et-Taḥtā). All of these places are in the southernmost zone of the Judean hills. The roster as a whole reflects a clear differentiation between the four topographical divisions of Judah, viz., the Negeb, the Shephelah, the hill country and the wilderness (cf. Josh. 10:40 with 15:21, 33, 48, 61). Kiriath-sepher/Debir must therefore be sought in this southerly hill region.

Finally, Debir was assigned to the sons of Aaron from the families of the Kohathites (Josh. 21:15; 1 Ch. 6:58 [MT 43]) for an inheritance. Therefore, one would expect Debir to be an important city during the period of the monarchy.

In the postexilic period the southern hill country was outside the province of Yehud (of which Nehemiah was the most famous governor), since the southernmost outpost of the latter was Beth-zur (Neh. 3:16). There were some recognized Judean communities outside of Yehud, but Hebron is the only one in the hill country, the others being in the Negeb or the Shephelah (Neh. 11:25-30). By NT times, the entire zone from Hebron south was occupied by Idumeans (Edomites), who probably had penetrated into this area in 587 B.C., shortly after the fall of Jerusalem. Neither Josephus nor the church fathers make any attempt to locate Debir.

II. The Quest for the Site.–C. R. Conder, taking the biblical data seriously, identified Debir with the village of Ẓâharîyeh (edh-Dhâherîyeh), the most important town S of Hebron (on the road to Beer-sheba). The hypothetical semantic link between its name and Debir had no solid basis of fact, since local tradition derives the present name from that of the Mamluk Sultan al-Malik aẓ-Ẓâhir Baybars (A.D. 1260-1277). But because the town's location seemed to satisfy the clear meaning of the biblical texts and no rival sites were known, Condêr's proposal held the field until it became clear that there were no appropriate archeological remains at Ẓâharîyeh.

It became an accepted dogma among archeologists that there were no settlements in the hill country S of Hebron. No one had found a site with substantial remains of city fortifications or with ceramic material typical of a Canaanite center. Therefore Albright turned his attention to the southwest, to three tells not in the hill country, but in the valley that marks the eastern boundary of the Shephelah. Of these candidates, Albright (mistakenly) thought that Tell 'Aiṭûn did not have Late Bronze remains. (Investigation since 1967 has shown that Tell 'Aiṭûn was the largest Canaanite city in that valley; thus M. Noth's proposal to equate it with Eglon is considerably strengthened.) The southernmost of the three, Tell el-Khuweilfeh, was too small. This left Tell Beit Mirsim (Tel Mirsham on Israeli maps), which Albright excavated in four campaigns (1926, 1928, 1930, 1932).

Albright argued for the following reasons that Tell Beit Mirsim was the only likely candidate for Debir: (1) the absence of any other Canaanite city in the area S of Hebron; (2) the presence of underground basins in the bedrock tapped by well shafts to the north and south of Tell Beit Mirsim; (3) according to Josh. 10f., Debir ought to be S of the road connecting Eglon with Hebron (an assumption predicated on his own identification of Eglon with Tell el-Ḥeṣî, commonly accepted, though nearby Tell 'Aiṭun is now a serious competitor); (4) the archeological finds at Tell Beit Mirsim correspond in a remarkable way to the history of Debir as reflected in the written sources. This latter argument is purely circumstantial; a site anywhere in Palestine might have material remains from the same periods in which Debir received mention in the sources. Once a serious alternative in the hill country presents itself (having the requisite material remains), the case for Tell Beit Mirsim collapses completely. The clear inference of Scripture, that Debir was located in the hill country, led European scholars — particularly from Germany—to deny the value of the archeological evidence, both the "negative" (absence of L.B. in the hills) and the "positive" (impressive finds from Tell Beit Mirsim). K. Elliger had suggested Khirbet Zānûtā in 1934, and M. Noth advocated Khirbet Tarrâmā in 1935. Finally K. Galling proposed to identify Debir with Khirbet Rabûd in 1954. Lacking ceramic evidence, Galling argued from the geographical location and its suitability according to the written sources. M. Noth came to accept this new site (Khirbet Ṭarrâmā has nothing earlier than the Roman period), albeit with some reservations. In 1965 H. Donner reported that abundant Iron Age sherds and one wishbone handle from a Cypriot milk bowl (a vessel well known in L.B.!) had been found at Khirbet Rabûd.

III. Recent Discovery and Excavation.–*A. Survey.* In October 1967 M. Kochavi began a systematic survey of the Judean hill country. A rich L.B. and Iron Age cemetery was found beside Khirbet Rabûd on a hill called 'Ušš eṣ-Ṣaḳrah, and Khirbet Rabûd itself was shown to have ample ceramic evidence from both the L.B. and Iron Ages. The ancient site, occupied by a small modern village called Rabûd, stands on a high, rocky hill nestled in a sweeping loop of the Hebron Valley (Wâdī el-Khalîl; but here called Wâdī el-Ḥamâm on the north and Wâdî en-Nâr on the south of Khirbet Rabûd) and thus is isolated from the surrounding hills on three sides by this imposing gorge. Only to the southeast is it connected by a narrow saddle to the adjacent hill. Almost completely barren of soil on the top, the site has a small Roman fort perched in the center of a broad expanse of naked bedrock. At the point where the adjoining saddle carries a roadway up toward the summit, a marked indentation in the contour of the rock forms a sort of amphitheater. Large wall segments converge here at an angle strongly reminiscent of a gate area; from the heights above one can visualize an ancient approach ramp that would have ascended across the saddle up to the city walls. Many Bronze and especially Iron Age sherds have been found above and below these impressive wall remains and between the adjacent dwellings. The city wall can be traced around the hill on all sides. In some places, especially on the west and northwest, the original courses are preserved to a height of 2 yds. (1.8 m.) or more. Although Khirbet Rabûd is badly eroded on the top (like many hill country sites), the terraces on the northwest and north slopes still preserve layers of ancient debris, largely because impressive segments of the city wall have remained intact.

Further down the slope on the northwest side is a second "terrace," which might have been the line of the Canaanite city wall. On a lower shelf projecting out from the northwest slope of Khirbet Rabûd stands an unwalled "suburb," a surface ruin called Khirbet Rabdeh by the villagers.

B. Excavation. Because the site had been looted by antiquity hunters, an emergency excavation was ordered. M. Kochavi led brief expeditions in 1968 and 1969, following up the results of his 1967 survey.

Although the looters had not left one tomb intact, some good ceramic materials were obtained from the loose soil dumped outside the cemetery, and a few burial caves had some sherds *in situ*. Sherds were found from the E.B., some fragments from the M.B. I (more properly the Intermediate Bronze), and a wide selection from the L.B., including imports from Cyprus and the Aegean. The cemetery was used for only a very short period in the Iron Age, viz., during the 10th-9th cents. B.C.

At the tell itself, two trenches were opened on the western slope. Trench A ran from above the upper wall down to and beyond the line of the lower wall. Trench B was confined to an area inside the upper wall. On the terrace below the upper wall, in the lower half of Trench A, four L.B. occupation levels were discerned, consisting of beaten earth floors and one stone pavement, with associated walls. The lower "terrace" wall was found to be a rebuilt older wall that followed the same line, which must have been the Canaanite city wall. The various levels showed a continuous tradition of architectural orientation. The pottery, combined with contemporary materials from the tombs, indicated that the city was founded at least by the beginning of the 14th cent. B.C., if not slightly before; it seems to have enjoyed a continuous existence throughout the 14th and 13th cents. B.C.

A floor of beaten earth that sealed off the last L.B. stratum produced sherds from the 12th cent. B.C., i.e., Iron I. A cavern in the rock under the Israelite wall on the higher terrace (see below) was found to be a deep cistern lined with plaster, yielding pottery from the 10th cent. B.C. This was the only locus discovered from the united monarchy, although similar pottery was found in the cemetery. During the united monarchy (Iron I) the city was apparently surrounded by a wall built on the line of the former Canaanite fortifications. Both the E.B. Canaanite city wall and the Iron I rebuild (as well as the Iron II wall; see below) must have had a circumference of nearly 1000 yds. (914 m.)!

From the upper terrace, both trenches A and B produce ample evidence that the impressive stone wall, about 4 yds. (3.7 m.) thick and built with occasional salients and recesses, was from the period of the divided monarchy. One stratum, datable to the 9th cent. B.C., was cut by the foundation trench of this massive upper wall. Artifacts typical of the 8th cent. B.C., including a rich horde of vessels, one royal (*lmlk*) and two private seal impressions, and a pair of figurines, all came from a stratum having signs of destruction by fire; this level most likely represents a city conquered by Sennacherib in 701 B.C. When the fortifications were rebuilt after that calamity, a tower was added inside the solid wall, increasing its width at this point to about 7 yds. (6.5 m.). Occupation resumed in the 7th-6th cents. until Judah fell to Nebuchadrezzar in 587 B.C. It was during that last century of the Judean monarchy that Khirbet Rabdeh, the unwalled "suburb" on the rocky platform below the city to the northwest, was settled. One locus near the surface in Trench A showed an occupation in the 5th cent. B.C. (the postexilic period), but a house wall angled across the foundation of the former city wall indicates that the settlement was then unfortified. A refuse pit in Trench B produced Hellenistic ware, but its associated stratum had been eroded away long ago. The small Roman fort — actually more a watch tower — crowning the bare summit of the hill, marks the last stage of occupation until modern times.

The results of excavation on such a limited scale have been singularly impressive. In spite of a heavily eroded and disturbed site, four clearly defined phases of L.B. occupation and four equally distinct levels of the Iron Age were identified. The artifactual evidence discovered leaves no doubt that Khirbet Rabûd was one of Judah's major cities. The surface contours and the circumference of the fortification walls during the L.B. and Iron Age periods reveal a city of about 15 acres (6 hectares) in the Canaanite and united monarchy periods, and about 12 acres (5 hectares) in the divided monarchy period. Khirbet Rabûd is thus in a class with such famous sites as Lachish (18 acres [7.3 hectares]) and Megiddo (13 acres [5.3 hectares]); Tell Beit Mirsim was only 7½ acres (3 hectares). Since the written sources know of only one important city-state S of Hebron during the Canaanite period, and since the intensive survey of all other likely candidates in the area has not produced another L.B. site, the identification of Khirbet Rabûd with Kiriath-sepher/Debir is unavoidable.

IV. Concluding Arguments.–Albright continued to oppose the new identification for Debir. His main objections were: (1) Tell Beit Mirsim is the only large Canaanite tell in the area S of Hebron. As mentioned above, however, it is now known that even Tell ʿAiṭûn, its closest neighbor, is larger and also had Bronze Age remains, (2) Khirbet Rabûd is too close to Dumah (Khirbet Dômeh ed-Deir), which is only 2 mi. (3 km.) to the west and belongs to another district (Josh. 15:52). But Conder had discerned that the central watershed runs just about along the line of the Hebron-Beersheba highway; and Cross and Wright had suggested in 1956 that the watershed served as a boundary line for three other districts from Josh. 15, but they failed to see that the same must apply to the southern district with Debir. In fact, the watershed separates Khirbet Dômeh ed-Deir from Khirbet Rabûd, and Kokhavi has discovered that all the towns in the southern hill country are grouped into three districts according to the drainage basins in which they are located. Thus, a watershed marks the boundary between each one, and the close proximity of Dumah is no argument. (3) There were no suitable underground basins with well shafts in the hill country, but only in the Shephelah. One of the most striking results of the recent survey was Kokhavi's discovery of two such subterranean chambers, fed by underground sources and tapped by well shafts through the bedrock, located just a bit less than 2 mi. (3 km.) NNW of Khirbet Rabûd. One is farther up the valley than the other and on the maps is called Bîr el-ʿAlaqah el-Fōqâni, "The Upper Well of the Leech," while its counterpart below is Bîr el-ʿAlaqah et-Taḥtâni, "The Lower Well of the Leech." So two water sources of a type corresponding exactly to Albright's definition of the Heb. *gullōṯ*, and bearing the designations "Upper" and "Lower," are found in a valley not far from Khirbet Rabûd. To be sure, there are no such wells or springs in the immediate vicinity of Khirbet Rabûd; but this only makes the location of these Upper and Lower Springs even more significant. The account of Caleb's granting such additional water sources to Achsah (Josh. 15:19; Jgs. 1:15) makes sense only if the wells in question were being assigned to Kiriath-sepher/Debir even though they would not normally have been reckoned to its territory!

The identification of Khirbet Rabûd with Debir is further enhanced by its agricultural regime. Kokhavi has noted that agriculture in this southern region of the hill country consists mainly of small plots marked off by dikes in the bottom of the stream beds. Only here can the rich alluvial deposits coming down from the higher region around Hebron be held in place and cultivated; such soil is far superior to the local rendzina on the surrounding hills. Furthermore, the minimal annual precipitation is marginal — only about 4-8 in. (10-20 cm.). This means that the agricultural regime here is identical to that in the true Negeb farther south. Achsah's description of Debir's region as "land of the Negeb" is, therefore, correct. On the other hand, it is obvious that this zone is distinctly a hill region in contrast to the lower alluvial basin directly to the south of it that forms the eastern half of the biblical Negeb. Josh. 15 clearly makes this distinction, placing Debir and its neighboring towns in the hill country and not in the Negeb proper.

Bibliography.–C. R. Conder, *PEQ*, 7 (1875), 48-56; *SWP*, III, 402, 406ff.; W. F. Albright, *BASOR*, 15 (Oct. 1924), 2-11; 23 (Oct. 1926), 2-14; 31 (Oct. 1928), 1-11; *ZAW*, 47 (1929), 1-18; *BASOR*, 39 (Oct. 1930), 1-10; J. Garstang, *Joshua and Judges* (1931), pp. 210-14, 370-72; W. F. Albright, *BASOR*, 47 (Oct. 1932), 3-17; *Archaeology of Palestine and the Bible* (1932), pp. 63-126; *The Excavation of Tell Beit Mirsim, I: The Pottery of the First Three Campaigns* (*AASOR*, 12, 1932); *I A: The Bronze Age Pottery of the Fourth Campaign* (*AASOR*, 13, 1933); K. Elliger, *PJ*, 30 (1934), 47-71; M. G. Kyle, *Excavating Kirjath-sepher's Ten Cities* (1934); W. F. Albright, *BASOR*, 58 (Apr. 1935), 10-18; M. Noth, *JPOS*, 15 (1935), 44-50; W. F. Albright, *The Excavation of Tell Beit Mirsim, II: The Bronze Age* (*AASOR*, 17, 1938); *GP*, II, 303f., 421f.; W. F. Albright, *BASOR*, 74 (Apr. 1939), 11-23; H. M. Orlinsky, *JBL*, 58 (1939), 225-261; W. F. Albright and W. F. Kelso, *The Excavation of Tell Beit Mirsim, III: The Iron Age* (*AASOR*, 21-22, 1943); K. Galling, *ZDPV*, 70 (1954), 135-141; M. Noth, *ZDPV*, 72 (1956), 35f.; F. M. Cross and G. E. Wright, *JBL*, 75 (1956), 202-226; H. Donner, *ZDPV*, 81 (1965), 24f.; W. F. Albright, "Debir," in D. W. Thomas, ed., *Archaeology and Old Testament Study* (1967), pp. 207-220; [M. Kochavi], *Hadashot Arkhe'ologiot*, 26 (Apr. 1968), 29-35; W. F. Albright, "Tell Beit Mirsim," in B. Mazar, *et al.*, eds., *Encyclopedia of Archaeological Excavations in the Holy Land* (1970), II, 567-573; M. Kochavi, *Tel-Aviv*, 1 (1974), 1-33.

A. F. RAINEY

2. A place on the northern boundary of Judah with Benjamin (Josh. 15:7), identified by *WHAB* with Thoghret ed-Debr 8 mi. (13 km.) ENE of Jerusalem.

3. [Heb. *liḏᵉḇir*; Gk. *Dabir*] (Josh. 13:26); NEB LO-DEBAR. A place on the border of Gad, near Mahanaim, probably identical with LO-DEBAR of 2 S. 9:4f.; 17:27.

DEBORAH deb'ər-ə [Heb. *dᵉḇôrâ*–'bee'].

1. The nurse of Rebekah who died at or near Bethel and was buried in the vicinity, in the shade of an oak tree later known as the Weeping Oak (Gen. 35:8).

2. The prophetess and judge (Jgs. 4–5), who belonged to the tribe of Issachar (5:15), and directed the affairs of the tribes from a spot between Ramah and Bethel, later known as Tomer Deborah, i.e., the palm tree of Deborah (4:5). It has been conjectured that her house may have been at Doberath of Issachar, at the western foot of Mt. Tabor (Josh. 21:28) (G. F. Moore, *ICC* on Judges [1895], pp. 113f.).

There are two accounts of her story, one in prose and the other in poetry. Some have argued that we have here a combination of two traditions: Jabin king of Hazor, who figures in the prose version, is not mentioned in the poem, in which Sisera seems to be the king and the head of a confederacy of Canaanite vassal rulers (Jgs. 5:19). But the sacred writer sees the war with Sisera as only a part of the struggle with the king of Hazor. Recent investigations have shown that Hazor, once a mighty kingdom (Josh. 11:10), had retained during the Israelite conquests at least a vestige of its former greatness (A. Malamet, *JBL*, 79 [1960], 12-19). Another supposed disagreement is the manner of Sisera's death: in the poem it looks as if he was killed while standing and drinking, while in the prose account he is killed in his sleep. But this sort of criticism makes no allowance for poetic description and reiteration, which are so different from matter-of-fact prose.

The oppressor at that time was Sisera, who had nine hundred war chariots of iron against the Israelites' meager supply of arrows (Jgs. 5:8). Deborah, together with Barak, whom she summoned to take action in the name of God, raised a force of ten thousand men from Zebulun and Naphtali (4:10). They mustered their forces on Mt. Tabor, NE of the great plain of Esdraelon; Sisera's forces took up positions on the Kishon on the way to "Taanach by the waters of Megiddo" (5:19). Directed by the prophetess, Barak's army rushed down the mountain and attacked and routed Sisera's army in the plain. God's hand was discernible in a tremendous storm that burst over the plain at the time, turning the shallow waters of the river into a raging torrent which played havoc with the chariots (Jgs. 5:20f.; also Josephus *Ant.* v.5.4). Sisera, who escaped on foot, met his death at the hands of Jael, a bedouin chieftainess, who first received him and then when he fell into a stupor, killed him by driving a tent peg into his temple.

The song of Deborah is now recognized as an eyewitness account, and therefore of the highest value as a historical document. It begins by extolling the God revealed in all His might at Sinai. After describing the plight of the Israelite tribes, it eulogizes first Deborah and Barak, the heroine and hero who came to the rescue (Jgs. 5:7, 9, 12, 15), and then the brave people of Zebulun and Naphtali (5:18). They fought and won because God was on their side: "The stars in their courses fought against Sisera" (5:20). After execrating the malingerers who stayed away from the battle (5:23), it blesses Jael, who killed the oppressor, and then depicts Sisera's mother looking out and waiting for Sisera and the spoil. "So perish all thine enemies, O Lord!" concludes the song, "But thy friends be like the sun as he rises in his might."

See also DEBORAH, SONG OF. M. S. SEALE

3. [Gk. *Debbōra*] (Tob. 1:8); AV DEBORA. The grandmother of Tobit; or according to the NEB, which follows Sinaiticus, his great-grandmother. (In 1:8 of Sinaiticus, Hananiel is said to be "our father," but it is clear from 1:1 that he was Tobit's grandfather.)

DEBORAH, SONG OF. The Song of Deborah (Jgs. 5:2-31a) is generally regarded by biblical scholars as one of the earliest examples of Hebrew poetry. Composed in the latter half of the 12th cent. B.C., it preserves ancient poetic patterns and contains several examples of archaic Hebrew grammatical usage. Thus it is viewed as an authoritative historical account and is a valuable tool in the study of Hebrew language and literature.

The Song describes the defeat of a coalition of Canaanite kings headed by Sisera, probably the leader of Indo-European sea peoples. This battle, at Taanach, "by the waters of Megiddo" (v. 19), climaxed the Hebrew conquest of central and northern Palestine, subduing the final Canaanite uprising against the Israelites and marking the end of Canaan as a political unit.

Several insights are provided into the historical and geographical circumstances of twelfth-century Israel. The role of charismatic leaders (judges) is depicted (vv. 2, 9), and the marshalling of representative troops from the tribes (v. 2) recalls the form of military muster employed at Mari. The song reflects a growing awareness of the tribes' need to act together. Nevertheless, not all of Israel participated (vv. 16f., 23). The poem depicts the arrangement and interaction of the ten northern tribes, but no mention is made of the southern tribes Judah and Simeon, or of Levi. The description of Reuben and Gilead (vv. 15f.) suggests their instability. Many from the tribe of Dan, which attempted unsuccessfully to settle next to the Philistine territory, apparently served aboard the ships of the sea peoples (v. 17). Issachar's active role would fit a twelfth-century date. The report varies from other lists as to the names and order of the tribes (cf. Gen. 49; Dt. 33). The song is marked by the religious ideology that Yahweh was king over Israel, the focus of the Israelite covenant in the period of the Judges and the core of the nation's existence.

Grammatically the poem reflects the early stages of the Hebrew language, showing its development as a Canaanite dialect, and the frequent repetition of poetic parallelism indicates stylistic influence by Ugaritic poetry. The many early Hebrew forms include older forms of personal pronouns (v. 3) and pronominal indicators (v. 7), archaic use of the demonstrative pronoun (v. 5), energic *nun* (v. 26), and plural endings (v. 10), application of the adverb *'āz* similar to Ugaritic usage (vv. 8, 11, 13, 19, 22), and pronominal suffixes reflecting Phoenician forms (vv. 13, 15). Some scholars believe that the poem may reflect an early Northern dialect.

The literary genre is the victory hymn, also common in Egypt and Assyria in the 15th-12th centuries B.C. Similarities can be seen in the Egyptian "Hymn of Victory of Thut-mose III" (*ANET*, pp. 373-75) and "Hymn of Victory of Mer-ne-Ptah" (*ANET*, pp. 376-78) and the Assyrian Tukulti-Ninurta epic (R. C. Thompson, *Archaeologia*, N.S. 29 [1926], 128 ff.; *Annals of Archaeology and Anthropology*, 20 [1930], 116ff.; W. G. Lambert, *AfO*, 18 [1957], 38-51). The song reflects many ancient Near Eastern literary forms adapted by the Hebrews to their own purposes. One image is the march of Yahweh and His attendants from the southern wilderness into Canaan (vv. 4-6; cf. Dt. 32:3f.; Ps. 68:7f. [MT 8f.]; cf. also Hab. 3:3-6). Natural elements also participate (vv. 20-23); the cloudburst and subsequent flood of the river Kishon (Nahr el-Muqaṭṭa') cause Sisera's defeat, a phenomenon supported by similar occurrences at that site throughout history. Thus Yahweh and the Israelite troops together brought about the Canaanite demise, illustrating the dominant OT theme of Yahweh's acting in His people's history.

Occurrence of the archaic second person singular in v. 7 indicates that the song was composed in response to Deborah's actions rather than by the prophetess herself. She is called "mother" in v. 7, an honorific title parallelling the use of "father" to depict the oracular function of priests and prophets (Jgs. 17:10; 18:19; 2 K. 6:21; 8:9; 13:14). Deborah's accurate prophecy contrasts with the wrong answer given Sisera's mother by the "wisest" women (vv. 28-30). Her active military role as prophetess or charismatic judge reflects yet surpasses the ancient Near Eastern function of women and priestesses in providing inspiration for battle (v. 12).

This poetic account is generally believed to have been composed in direct response to the historical events, in contrast with the prose version in Jgs. 4. The latter apparently conflates these events with another story about Jabin, inaccurately labelled "king of Canaan," to whom Sisera is shown as a subordinate, commander of the army (4:2). The Song does not mention Jabin, and the locus is Taanach rather than Mt. Tabor. The two accounts provide differing versions of Sisera's death (4:17-22; 5:21, 24-27). From Jgs. 4:6 it would appear that only Zebulun and Naphtali participated in the battle; at least six tribes took part according to ch. 5, although Zebulun and Naphtali receive particular recognition (v. 18).

Composed in immediate response to the Israelite victory, the poem is a carefully constructed unit that suggests repetition and transmission by oral poets or minstrels (cf. vv. 10f.). It was probably later used in the cult, celebrating the renewal of the Israelite tribal covenant.

Bibliography.–G. W. Ahlström, *JNES*, 36 (1977), 287f.; W. F. Albright, *BASOR*, 62 (Apr. 1936), 26-31; R. G. Boling, *Judges* (*AB*, 1975), pp. 101-120; P. C. Craigie, *JBL*, 88 (1969), 253-265; D. N. Freedman in H. Goedicke and J. J. M. Roberts, eds., *Unity and Diversity* (1975), pp. 3-35; A. Globe, *JBL*, 93 (1974), 493-512.

A. C. M.

DEBT [Heb. *n^ešî*] (2 K. 4:7); NEB "boys who are being taken as pledges"; [*maššā'â*] (Prov. 22:26); NEB SURETY; [*yāḏ*] (Neh. 10:31 [MT 32]); [Gk. *opheilḗ*] (Mt. 18:32); [*opheílēma*] (Mt. 6:12); NEB "wrong"; [*dáneion*] (Mt. 18:27); [*opheílō*, part.] (Mt. 18:30, 34); AV "that was due"; **DEBTOR; IN DEBT** [Heb. *nāšā'*, part.] (1 S. 22:2; Isa. 24:2); AV TAKER OF USURY; [*nāšaḵ*, part.] (lit. "bite," so AV Hab. 2:7); NEB CREDITORS [*ḥôḇ*] (Ezk. 18:7); [Gk. *opheilétēs*] (Mt. 6:12; Rom. 8:12; 15:27); NEB OBLIGATION, "who have wronged us," etc.; [*chreopheilétēs*] (Lk. 7:41; 16:5); NEB "in debt"; **CREDITOR** [Heb. *nāšâ*, part.] (Ex. 22:25 [MT 24]; Dt. 15:2; 2 K. 4:1; Ps. 109:11; Isa. 24:2; 50:1); AV also USURER, GIVER OF USURY, EXTORTIONER; NEB MONEY-LENDER; [*ba'al maššēh yāḏô*] (Dt. 15:2); NEB "anyone who holds a pledge"; [Gk. *daneistḗs*] (Lk. 7:41); NEB MONEY-LENDER.

The economic legislation preserved in the Pentateuch, especially in Deuteronomy, was designed to prevent poverty (Dt. 15:4). Whoever loaned money to a fellow Israelite was not to exact interest (Ex. 22:25 [MT 24]; Lev. 25:35-38). This law is in marked contrast to the customs of nations surrounding Israel where interest exacted ranged from 20 percent to 50 percent. A higher rate was charged on grains than on precious metal; e.g., in the Old Babylonian era the interest on barley was 33⅓ and on silver 20 percent (Saggs, p. 290). Such practices insured the increasing wealth of the established upper class. A Hebrew creditor could, however, charge a foreigner interest (Dt. 15:3). The Israelite law is addressed to an agricultural society in which BANKING was at best very primitive. There were apparently few or no loans for commercial enterprise; rather, loans were to avert hunger and loss of what little the poor had to sustain life. Loans were frequently against future crops.

Two words, *nešeḵ* and *tarbîṯ*, suggest different ways of assessing interest. Although the exact form of collecting interest is uncertain, it is suggested that "interest" (*nešeḵ*) was taken from the principal of the loan and "increase" (*tarbîṯ* or *marbîṯ*) was the amount added to the value of the loan on its payment and possibly any add-on charges.

A pledge was usually taken as security for the payment of a loan. The creditor was not allowed to enter a debtor's house to secure a pledge; rather he had to wait outside for the debtor to bring him a pledge (Dt. 24:10f.). Any object that helped one support his family, such as a millstone, could not be taken for a pledge (Dt. 24:6). A garment accepted as security had to be returned to the debtor by nightfall (Ex. 22:26f. [MT 25f.]; Dt. 24:12f.). A person could also become "surety" (*'āraḇ*) for another; he guaranteed the creditor payment of the loan in case the debtor defaulted. The wisdom school offered some sound advice against becoming surety for debts: "Be not one of those who give pledges, who become surety for debts" (Prov. 22:26; cf. 6:1ff.; 11:15; 17:18).

Every seventh year was a time of releasing the debtor from his obligation to a creditor (Dt. 15:1ff.). It is questioned whether the creditor cancelled the loan or merely forgave interest during the seventh year. Whether the time of release was the sabbatical year or the seventh anniversary of the debt is also debated. Very probably "the year of release" is another way of referring to the sabbatical year. It is most likely that the possible loan potential was established with the idea that the pledge would be available for service only until the sabbatical year. A larger indebtedness that involved servitude or the sale of land in unwalled villages was corrected in the jubilee year; then a slave was freed and land reverted to its original owner (Lev. 25:8-17, 25-46).

However, the legislation of the Pentateuch regarding debts apparently was not followed during much of Israel's history. David organized a group of men displaced by reason of debt and other grievances into a powerful band (1 S. 22:2); this group enabled him to resist Saul and supported his efforts to secure the throne. The prophets frequently denounced the sin of luxury and affluence at the expense of the poor (cf. Am. 2:6-8; 4:1ff.; 6:4ff.). Some specific crimes included keeping garments taken in pledge and selling the poor into slavery for the smallest of debts (Am. 2:6-8). Habakkuk pronounced a woe on those who borrow money for capital to increase their wealth (2:6f.). He declared that a day was coming when the creditor would exact his due and thereby destroy the speculator. In the northern kingdom under King Jehoram, a woman recently widowed was threatened by her creditor with the enslavement of her two sons. Elisha performed a miracle, filling numerous vessels with oil, which he bade her to sell in order to pay the debt (2 K. 4:1-7). Debt-related problems continued in postexilic Jerusalem. Many people were so far in debt that they used their children for pledges in order to get money for food (Neh. 5:1-5). To correct these economic abuses Nehemiah had the officials swear to return the people's property and the interest paid on debts. Then Nehemiah and his servants lent money and grain without interest. Later the people covenanted to keep the sabbatical year, including the release of debts (Neh. 10:30f. [MT 31f.]; the language clearly points to Dt. 15:2).

As the result of the harsh circumstances resulting from debts, the moneylender held a despised and hated occupation. One psalmist prayed that all the possessions of his wicked oppressor would be seized by the latter's creditor (Ps. 109:11). Here the creditor is paralleled by strangers (*zar*), i.e., a hated foreigner who comes only to raid a settlement. Jeremiah, too, compared the strife he encountered only to the people's hatred for the creditor (Jer. 15:10).

By NT times the Pharisees had built a solid fence around the laws of the Pentateuch to insure observance of the laws. But in any legal system there exist loopholes, and the Pharisaic rabbis, sensing the difficulties of the regulations, worked out various compromises. The Pharisees, by taking advantage of these legal tricks, accumulated wealth and interpreted it as God's blessing on their piety. Jesus, however, tried to make them realize that they were "lovers of money" (Lk. 16:14f.); and He accused them and the scribes of "devouring widows' houses" (Mt. 23:14). Their riches were accumulating at the expense of the unfortunate, a practice that violated the intent of the OT legislation.

The words for debt also have metaphorical application with regard to morals. In a prophetic lawsuit, Isaiah compares Israel's captivity with being divorced or sold to a creditor (50:1). Since Israel belonged to God, it appeared that He had become impoverished. Of course, God has no creditors. Rather, Israel sold herself by means of her iniquities. This passage is moving in the direction of the use of words regarding economic indebtedness for moral guilt which was made by late Judaism and in some NT references. Jesus taught His disciples to pray, "Forgive us our debts, as we also have forgiven our debtors" (Mt. 6:12). "Debts" here clearly means "sins" (cf. Mt. 6:14f.; Lk. 11:4). Jesus taught that to be forgiven, one must forgive (Mt. 18:23-35). Jesus defended the sinful woman who anointed Him by relating a parable concerning debtors (Lk. 7:36-50), in which the debtor who had been forgiven the largest debt would respond with the greatest love. Thereby He praised that woman's demonstration of love and declared to the woman that her sins were forgiven.

By the time of the NT, banking had become very complex. The NT does not continue to reinforce the injunctions about extending a loan at interest in the same manner as did the OT. The teachings of Jesus went behind the laws of usury to the principles on which they were founded. The believer is apparently to follow just business practices within the existing economic system. He is to conduct his business as a steward to God Himself and is never to violate the principles of industry, mercy, and generosity. The parable of the unjust steward, who discounted loans in order to have mercy extended to him by his creditors upon dismissal from his office, teaches that all money may be placed in service to God (Lk. 16:1-9). The Pharisees had argued that money gained by any type of oppression was tainted and could not be offered to God (Derret, p. 218). But Jesus declared that all money could rightly be used in deeds of mercy. The wise person uses his resources to meet human need; then he becomes rich in friends (Lk. 16:9). Although the believer is free from the technicalities of OT laws regarding debt, he is now under obligation to the greater principle of mercy.

The NT words for debt also carry the meaning of obligation. The Pharisees taught that to swear by the temple was nothing, but "whosoever shall swear by the gold of the temple . . . is a debtor" (Mt. 23:16, AV; RSV "is bound by his oath"). The object by which one swore obligated him to fulfil his oath. Jesus showed how the Pharisees had consequently placed precious metals above the temple in value. Paul speaks about being under moral and spiritual obligation. In Gal. 5:3 he argues that he who becomes circumcised to follow Jesus is then bound to keep the entire law. The reward rendered to one who works is then out of debt, not out of grace (Rom. 4:4, AV). In Rom. 8, Paul describes the tremendous freedom possessed by the one who lives for Christ by faith. Such a believer no longer has any obligation to all the laws pertaining to the flesh; rather he is now led by the Spirit (Rom. 8:12f.). In his own inner life, Paul possessed a very strong obligation to proclaim the gospel to the Greeks and to the barbarians (Rom. 1:14). No doubt he is defining his divine commission as an apostle to the Gentiles as a spiritual obligation he feels compelled to fulfil (cf. 1 Cor. 9:16f.). Further spiritual indebtedness may be expressed in material generosity. The believers of Macedonia and Achaia supplied gifts for the relief of the poor at Jerusalem. Paul says that they were in debt to the saints of Jerusalem, since the Jerusalem church was the foundation of the spiritual blessings the Gentiles had come to share (Rom. 15:26f.).

See also EXTORTION; INTEREST; LEND; PLEDGE.

Bibliography.–J. Derrett, *NTS*, 7 (1960/61), 198-219, 364-380; S. R. Driver, *Deuteronomy* (*ICC*, 1902), pp. 174-180; E. Neufeld, *HUCA*, 26 (1955), 355-412; G. von Rad, *Deuteronomy* (Eng. tr., *OTL*, 1966), pp. 105ff.; H. Daniel-Rops, *Daily Life in Palestine at the Time of Christ* (1962), pp. 138-149, 357f., 390, 473; H. W. F. Saggs, *The Greatness that was Babylon* (1962), pp. 209, 289ff., 296f.; *TDNT*, V, *s.v.* ὀφείλω κτλ. (F. Hauck); R. de Vaux, *Ancient Israel* (1965), I, 164-177; J. H. Yoder, *The Politics of Jesus* (1972).

J. E. HARTLEY

DECALOGUE. *See* TEN COMMANDMENTS.

DECAPOLIS de-kap'ə-lis [Gk. *Dekapolis*–'ten-city (area, confederation, etc.)']. A loose confederation of ten essentially independent Hellenistic cities; or the region in which they were located, S and E of the Sea of Galilee.

The historical background of the Decapolis is somewhat elusive, as the historical sources regarding the time of its creation and the contingencies that brought it into being are meager. This much is clear, however: as early as the 3rd cent. B.C., Greek Hellenists migrated to Palestine and its environs, where they either established new cities for settlement or reestablished older cities in which they became the dominant power.

The century that followed (2nd cent. B.C.) was a period of rising nationalism among the Jews in Palestine. One thing they refused to tolerate was the presence of non-Jews on their eastern border. Hostilities between the Jews and Hellenists multiplied, with the result that violent fighting sometimes erupted. For example, the famous Hasmonean leader Alexander Janneus (103-76 B.C.) successfully led troops against these cities and managed to conquer some of them.

In 63 B.C., when the Roman leader Pompey brought Jewish independence to an end, he liberated Hippos, Scythopolis, and Pella from the Jews and attached them to the province of Syria. In 30 B.C. Augustus gave Herod the cities of Gadara and Hippos. Later, Canatha and Rephana came under the control of Agrippa II.

The first to enumerate the cities of the Decapolis was Pliny (*Nat. hist.* v.16 [74]), who identifies them as: (1) Scythopolis, 25 mi. (40 mi.) S of the Sea of Galilee, the only one W of the Jordan; (2) Pella, 7 mi. (11 km.) SE of Scythopolis; (3) Hippos, on the slopes of the southern end of the eastern shore of the Sea of Galilee; (4) Gadara, 8 mi. (13 km.) SE of the Sea of Galilee; (5) Rephana, exact location uncertain; (6) Dion, near the Yarmuk River, E of the Sea of Galilee; (7) Gerasa, the second-most southerly city and the best preserved; (8) Canatha, near the edge of the Syrian desert; (9) Damascus, the northern

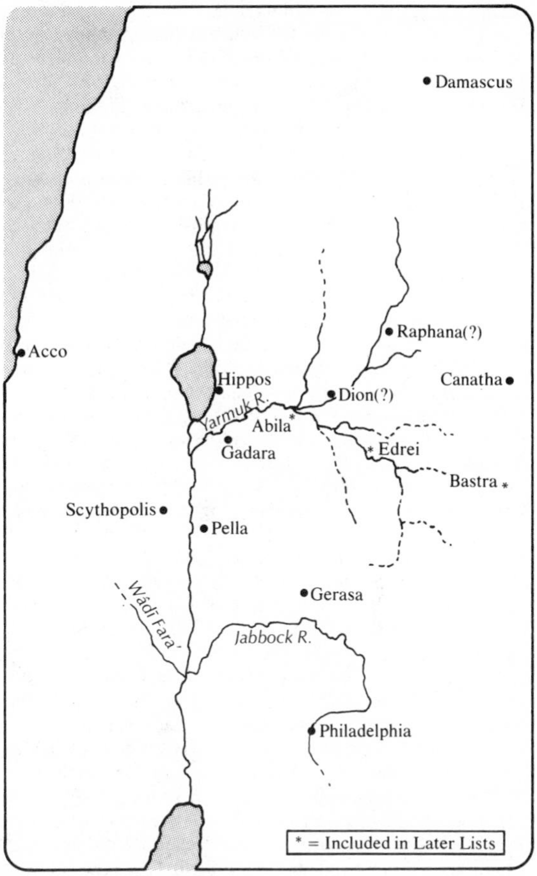

Gerasa (modern Jerash), second city of the Decapolis. A prime example of a rich Greco-Roman city, it included a circular colonnaded forum (center) and three theaters, the largest seating four thousand people (restored, foreground). (Jordan Information Bureau, Washington)

boundary; (10) Philadelphia, the southern boundary, known as Rabbah in the OT and now as Amman, capital of the Hashemite Kingdom of Jordan. As many as eighteen cities are listed in later enumerations of the Decapolis, including that of the geographer Ptolemy, who also replaced Rephana with Abila, S of the Yarmuk.

Besides their basically Greco-Roman tradition and spirit, these cities had in common the fact that they were thriving centers of trade, for they were situated on the three roads that connected Damascus with southern Arabia. They were subject only to the general administration of the Roman legate of Syria, and each exercised a degree of autonomy in its own immediate territory. Several possible reasons for their establishment of reciprocal relationships in a confederation have been suggested: (1) to form a barrier against Arab/Syrian desert marauders, because of the potentially vulnerable position of the cities on the fringes of the desert; (2) to protect member cities against Jewish aggression of the sort led by Janneus; (3) to serve as a Roman security ring around part of Palestine (possibly only after the death of Herod the Great in 4 B.C.), counterbalancing Jewish nationalism.

In any case, the Decapolis seems to have been well established by the time of the earliest extant references to it in the 1st cent. A.D. These include Pliny's enumeration and Josephus' mention of *hai déka póleis* (*Vita* 65 [341]; but *Decapolis* in 74 [410], *BJ* iii.9.7 [446]), as well as the three references in the NT.

In Mt. 4:25 it is referred to, along with Galilee, Jerusalem, Judea, and Transjordan, as one of the areas from which people followed Jesus. A demoniac from "the country of the Gadarenes" (Mk. 5:1ff.) who was healed by Jesus testified "in the Decapolis" to his deliverance (v. 20). The presence in this story of swine, anathema to the Jews, suggests a predominately gentile population. Finally, Mk. 7:31 informs us that Jesus toured the area of Decapolis on a trip from Phoenician Tyre and Sidon to Galilee, surely the "long way around." It was an area infrequently visited by Jesus; but this is not surprising, since He Himself said, "I was sent only to the lost sheep of the house of Israel" (Mt. 15:24).

See S. Parker, *JBL*, 94 (1975), 437-441. V. P. HAMILTON

DECAY [Gk. *phthorá*]; AV CORRUPTION; NEB MORTALITY. The English term is used only once in the RSV (Rom. 8:21) to describe the innate tendency toward deterioration possessed by terrestrial creation.

DECEASE. *See* DEATH.

DECEIT; DECEITFUL; DECEIVE; DECEPTION; etc. [Heb. *mirmâ, remîyâ, šeqer, tarmît, kāzāḇ* (Prov. 23:3), *'āqōḇ* (Jer. 17:9), *tāpēl* (Lam. 2:14), *'aḵzāḇ* (Jer. 15:18; Mic. 1:14), vbs. *rāmâ, nāšā', pāṯâ, 'āšaq* (Lev. 6:2), *šālâ* (2 K. 4:28), *šāgâ, šāgag* (Job 12:16), *hāṯal* (13:9), *tā'â* (15:31), *sûṯ* (Jer. 38:22), *kāḥaš* (Zec. 13:4); Gk. *apátē, dólos, plánē, dólios, plános, phrenapátēs* (Tit. 1:10), vbs. *apatáō, exapatáō, dolióō* (Rom. 3:13), *planáō, planáomai* (Jas. 1:16), *paralogízomai* (1:22), *phrenapatáō* (Gal. 6:3)]; AV also GUILE, FALSEHOOD, CRAFT, SUBTILTY, LIE, LYING, LIAR, FOOLISH, FEIGNED, SEDUCING, SEDUCE, BEGUILE, MOCK (*hāṯal*), ENTICE (*pāṯâ*), SET ON (*sûṯ*), ERR (Jas. 1:16), DECEIVABLENESS (2 Thess. 2:10, RSV "deception"); NEB also TREACHERY, LIES, FRAUD, SLANDER, FALSEHOOD, "deluding fancies" (Jer. 23:26), "crafty designs" (Dnl. 8:25), WILES (He. 3:13), "painted shams" (*tāpēl*), "not what they seem" (*kāzāḇ*), DELUSION (Prov. 31:30), TRAITOR (Ps. 5:6), LIAR (43:1), SCANDAL-MONGER (101:7), SLANDEROUS (52:4; 120:3), FALSE (36:3), DISHONEST (Gen. 34:13), "not to be trusted" (Jer. 15:18), FRAUDULENT (Dnl. 11:23; Am. 8:5), SWINDLER (Acts 13:10), CROOKED (2 Cor. 11:13), DELUSIVE (Col. 2:8), DELUDE, LEAD ASTRAY, MISLEAD, SEDUCE, "play a trick on" (Josh. 9:22; 1 S. 19:17), TRICK (Jer. 20:10), DUPE (20:7), BREAK FAITH (Lam. 1:19), MISREPRESENT (Prov. 24:28), "be taken in" (2 K. 18:29), QUIBBLE (*hāṯal*, Job 13:9), "raise my hopes and then dash them" (2 K. 4:28), "allege what is false" (Job 13:7, RSV "speak deceitfully"), "commit perjury" (Ps. 24:4, RSV "swear deceitfully"), DISAPPOINT (*'aḵzāḇ*, Mic. 1:14), "make no mistake" for "be not deceived" (usually Gk. *mḗ planásthe*, 1 Cor. 3:18; 6:9; 15:33; Gal. 6:7; Jas. 1:16), etc.

The Heb. *rāmâ* and its derivatives *mirmâ, remîyâ*, and *tarmîṯ* connote a betrayal of trust and confidence. The word *šeqer* indicates something false, or deliberately misleading. In the NT the idea of leading astray is conveyed in the Gk. *planáō* and cognates; *apátē* and related words often imply seduction (Rom. 7:11), or deceiving by words (Rom. 16:18; Eph. 5:6; Jas. 1:26). The normal meaning of *dólos* and cognates is cunning or guile (Mk. 7:22; Rom. 1:29; 3:13).

In Mic. 1:14 the play on words ("Achzib shall be *'aḵzāḇ*" [RSV "a deceitful thing"]) is one of a series of puns in vv. 10ff., as the prophet names the places to be destroyed.

See LIE. J. W. D. H.

DECENTLY [Gk. *euschēmónōs*] (1 Cor. 14:40). This word occurs in the last verse of that remarkable chapter on the proper use of spiritual gifts in the church and the proper conduct of public worship. It does not refer here to absence of impurity or obscenity. It refers rather to good order in the conduct of public worship. All things that are done and said in public worship are to be in harmony with the becoming and reverent spirit and tone that befit the true worshipers of God. Cf. also Rom. 13:13 ("becomingly"); 1 Thess. 4:12.

DECISION [Heb. *mišpāṭ*] (Dt. 17:8f., 11; Prov. 16:33; Zeph. 3:8); AV JUDGMENT, DISPOSING, DETERMINATION; NEB LAWSUIT, SENTENCE, INSTRUCTION, ISSUE, "mine it is" (Zeph. 3:8); [*dāḇār, dāḇar*] (Dt. 17:9; 2 S. 14:13); AV SENTENCE, "speak"; NEB SENTENCE, "out of your own mouth"; [*tôrâ*] (Ex. 18:16, 20); AV, NEB, LAW; [*qesem*] (Prov. 16:10); AV, NEB, SENTENCE; [Aram. *še'ēlā'*] (Dnl. 4:17); AV DEMAND; NEB SENTENCE; [Gk. *phaínō*] (Mk. 14:64); AV "think"; NEB OPINION; [*dógma*] (Acts 16:4); AV DECREE; [*diágnōsis*] (Acts 25:21); AV HEARING.

In the RSV this term is used to describe judgments relating to specific matters. The Heb. *mišpāṭ* denoted a rule established by formal authority or ancient custom while *dāḇār* ("word," "statement") was also used to signify a decision. *Tôrâ* ("instruction," "teaching") described a body of divine law in Ex. 18:16, 20. In the NT the noun "decision" was used by the RSV in Mk. 14:64 to render the sense of the verb *phaínō*, "appear." The words *dógma* ("opinion," "decree," "ordinance") and *diágnōsis* were also employed in this manner.

Perplexing questions were many times decided by the casting of lots (*see* DIVINATION), for the people believed that God would direct them to the right decision in this way (cf., e.g., Prov. 16:33; Josh. 7:10-21; 14:2; 1 S. 10:20f.; 14:41f.; Jonah 1:7). The apostles cast lots to decide which of the two men they had selected should take the place of Judas (Acts 1:21-26). A. W. FORTUNE

DECISION, VALLEY OF. *See* JEHOSHAPHAT, VALLEY OF.

DECK [Heb. *qereš*] (Ezk. 27:6); AV BENCHES. The term is supplied in the RSV of Gen. 6:16 to render Heb. *taḥtîyim šᵉnîyim ušᵉlišîm,* "lower, second, and third [decks]"; the AV supplies "stories," while the NEB also supplies "decks." The meaning of *qereš* in Ezk. 27:6 is not certain; cf. its use in the account of the building of the tabernacle (Ex. 26; 35:11; 36; etc.), where it is rendered by the AV "board"; RSV "frame"; NEB "plank." Only the context of Ezk. 27:1-9 supports the meaning "deck." KoB (p. 858) suggests "prow."

DECK (verb). Most uses (Job 40:10; Jer. 4:30; Ezk. 16:11, 13; 23:40; Hos. 2:13) are Heb. *'āḏâ,* "adorn" (so translated in Isa. 61:10; Jer. 31:4; *see* ADORN). In Isa. 61:10 "deck" translates Heb. *yᵉḵahēn,* which has been understood (BDB) as a form of *kāhan,* "act as a priest"; but some prefer to read it as *yāḵîn,* a hiphil form of *kûn,* "prepare." "Deck" has been supplied interpretatively by translators in Ezk. 16:16 (for *ṭᵉlu'ôṯ,* "colored padding") and Ps. 45:13. Other terms are Heb. *yāpâ,* "become beautiful" (Jer. 10:4; cf. 31:4), *'āṭap,* "wrap" (Ps. 65:13), and *rāḇaḏ,* "prepare" (Prov. 7:16).

DECLARATION; DECLARE. "Declaration" occurs only once in the RSV, translating Heb. *'aḥwâ* (Job 13:17, NEB "exposition"). "Declare" is used to translate a variety of terms in the OT and NT, appearing to bear uniformly the meaning "make known" or "set forth." These terms include: *dāḇar,* "speak" (Lev. 23:44; etc.); hiphil of *yāḏa',* "make known" (Job 26:3; 40:7; etc.); *nāgaḏ,* "declare" (Job 38:18; Isa. 42:9; 48:6; etc.); *sāpar,* "recount" (Job 12:8; Ps. 119:13; etc.); *šāma',* "cause to hear" (Isa. 41:22, 26; 45:21; etc.); Gk. *anangéllō,* "recount" (Acts 15:4; 20:27; etc.); *diēgéomai,* "relate" (Acts 9:27; etc.). In Dt. 1:5; Eccl. 9:1; Mt. 13:36; 15:15, the AV renders "declare" with the obsolete sense of "explain."

N. J. O.

DECLINE [Heb. *yāraḏ*] (2 K. 20:11; Isa. 38:8); AV GO DOWN; NEB ADVANCE DOWN, GO DOWN; [*pānâ*] (Jer. 6:4); AV GO AWAY; [*nāṭâ* (*yôm*)] (Jgs. 19:8); AV "afternoon"; NEB "late afternoon"; [Gk. *ouk epineúō*] (Acts 18:20); AV "consent not." In Jgs. 19:8 *nāṭâ* is used of the daylight waning; *pānâ* (lit. "turn the face") and *yāraḏ* are used in the same sense. In Acts 18:20, however, "decline" denotes the refusal of an invitation, *epineúō* (lit. "nod in consent") being a rare word found nowhere else in the NT. In the AV "decline" occurs nine times in its original but now obsolete sense of "turn aside" or "depart" (cf. Ex. 23:2; Dt. 17:11; 2 Ch. 34:2; Job 23:11; Ps. 44:18; 119:51, 157; Prov. 4:5; 7:25).

N. J. O.

DECREE [Heb. *dāṯ*] (Est. 3:14f.; 4:3, 8; 8:13f.; 9:14); AV also COMMANDMENT; NEB also EDICT; [*piṯgām* (Est. 1:20), *gāzar* (2:1)]; NEB also EDICT; [*ḥoq, ḥēqeq, ḥāqaq*] (Lev. 6:18, 22; Job 28:26; Ps. 2:7; Prov. 8:15; 31:5; Isa. 10:1); AV also STATUTE, LAW; NEB also DUE, RULE, LIMIT, LAW, RIGHTS; [*'ēḏûṯ* (Ps. 81:5; 122:4), *'ēḏâ* (93:5)]; AV TESTIMONY; NEB CHARGE, DUTY, LAW; [*ḥāraṣ*] (Isa. 10:22f.; 28:22; Dnl. 9:26f.); AV DETERMINED; NEB also FINAL, INEVITABLE; [*dāḇar*] (2 Ch. 30:5; Ps. 58:1; Jer. 19:5); AV also SPEAK; NEB RESOLVE, JUDGEMENT, SPEAK; [*kāṯaḇ*] (Est. 3:9); AV "be written"; NEB "an order be made in writing"; [*ṭa'am*] (Jonah 3:7); [*'ēmer*] (Job 20:29); AV, NEB, APPOINT; [*ḥāṯaḵ*] (Dnl. 9:24); AV DETERMINED; NEB "marked out"; [*ṣᵉḏāqâ*] (Dt. 33:21); AV JUSTICE; NEB "what (the Lord) deemed right"; [Aram. *ṭᵉ'ēm, śîm, ṭᵉ'ēm*] (Ezr. 4:19, 21; 5:3, 9, 13, 17; 6:1, 3, 8, 11f., 14; 7:13, 21; Dnl. 3:10, 29; 4:6; 6:26); AV also COMMAND, COMMANDMENT; NEB also ORDER; [*gᵉzērâ*] (Dnl. 4:17); NEB DETERMINE; [*dāṯ*] (Dnl. 2:13, 15); [Gk. *dógma*] (Lk. 2:1; Acts 17:7); NEB also LAW; [*dikaíōma*] (Rom. 1:32); AV JUDGEMENT; [*proorízō*] (1 Cor. 2:7); AV ORDAINED; NEB FRAMED; **EDICT** [Heb. *ṭᵉ'ēm* (Ezr. 6:11), *dāṯ* (Est. 2:8)]; AV, NEB also, DECREE; [*kᵉṯāḇ*] (Est. 8:8f.); AV WRITING; NEB WRIT, ORDER; [Gk. *diatágma*]; AV COMMANDMENT.

Both "decree and "edict" have the force of a public pronouncement of law given by a king or ruling body; a decree can refer also to a judicial decision or religious ordinance. These public, written proclamations were widely used by the Persian emperors, and thus the terms occur most frequently in those books that reflect life under the Persian empire. What distinguished the laws of the Medes and the Persians was the fact that they could not be revoked or altered (cf. Ezr. 6:11; Est. 8:8f.; Dnl. 6:8).

N. J. O.

DECRETUM GELASIANUM. *See* APOCRYPHA II.E.

DEDAN dē'dən; **DEDANITES** dē'dən-īts [Heb. *dᵉḏān, dᵉḏānîm*]. An Arabian people or peoples. According to Gen. 10:7, Dedan was descended from Ham through Cush and Raamah and was the brother of Sheba. The identifiable names in the immediate context are generally located in the southern part of the Arabian peninsula. According to Gen. 25:1-3, Dedan was descended from Abraham and Keturah through Jokshan, and was the brother of Sheba. It is possible to look upon these two accounts as resulting from the confusion of two traditions, the one ascribing a Hamitic and the other a Semitic origin for the same Dedan. It is equally possible to assume that certain personal and tribal names were well known long before the time of Abraham (as, indeed, the Eblaic materials now indicate), and that the Abrahamic Dedanites had no other relationship with the south Arabian peoples. 1 Ch. 1:9 preserves the tradition of Gen. 10:2 while 1 Ch. 1:32 preserves the tradition of Gen. 25:2. Isaiah refers to "caravans of Dedanites" (Isa. 21:13). In his account of the fall of Tyre, Ezekiel mentions the mercantile characteristic of Dedan (Ezk. 27:20), and in the immediate context (v. 22) includes "the traders of Sheba and Raamah." In both Isaiah and Ezekiel the references to Dedan could be to either north or south Arabian tribes, but are more likely to the latter. The reference to Dedan in Ezk. 27:15 is generally emended to read "Rhodes" following the LXX, which requires simply the substitution of resh (ר) for daledh (ד). The "inhabitants of Dedan," mentioned in Jer. 49:8, seems to refer to a north Arabian tribe living in or near Edom.

See TABLE OF NATIONS Map. W. S. LASOR

DEDICATE [Heb. *qāḏaš, ḥānaḵ, nûp* (Ex. 35:22), *šālēm* (Isa. 42:19), *nāṯan* (2 K. 23:11)]; AV also HALLOW, SANCTIFY, CONSECRATE, HOLINESS, (Isa. 23:18), OFFER (Ex. 35:22), PERFECT (Isa. 42:19), GIVE (2 K. 23:11); NEB also HALLOW, CONSECRATE, SACRED (GIFTS), DONOR (Lev. 27:15), DEVOTE (2 Ch. 24:7), PRESENT (Ex. 35:22), "[one] who holds my commission" (Isa. 42:19), "set up in honor" (2 K. 23:11). The term "dedicate" generally means to set apart and consecrate to a deity or to a sacred purpose.

The Hebrew root *qdš* has the idea of being set apart

for sacred use. Something or someone withheld from ordinary use and given to God for His exclusive use is *qōḏeš* (1 K. 7:51). No English word fully approximates this concept found in other ancient Near Eastern societies and modern primitive societies. But in the hiphil *qāḏaš* is probably best translated "dedicate," implying that whatever is referred to is transferred into God's possession for His exclusive use. Practically anything can be dedicated to God: house (Lev. 27:14), field (v. 16), temple (2 Ch. 2:4), articles of silver, gold, and bronze (2 S. 8:10f.), vessels (1 K. 7:51), spoil won in battle (1 Ch. 26:27). If one adds the occurrences of the Hebrew noun *ḥ^{a}nukkâ*, "dedication," then the altar (Nu. 7:10), the wall of Jerusalem (Neh. 12:27), and an image (Dnl. 3:2) can be added, though the latter is for pagan use.

In 2 K. 23:11, the reference is to the Assyrian practice of dedicating (*nāṯan*, "give") horses to the sun. In Ex. 35:22 the verb *nûp* probably means only "offer," though originally it referred to the waving of the offering by the priest. Isa. 42:19 is a difficult passage. It is translated "my dedicated one," but probably has nothing to do with dedication. The Heb. *m^{e}šullām* is passive and suggests "the one who has been brought into peace (friendly relations)." J. C. MOYER

DEDICATION, FEAST OF [Gk. *tá enkaínia* (Jn. 10:22)]. A feast (NEB "festival") held by the Jews throughout Palestine for eight days, commencing on the 25th of Chislev (Nov.-Dec.), in commemoration of the cleansing of the temple and the dedication of the altar by Judas Maccabeus after their desecration by Antiochus Epiphanes (1 Macc. 4:52-59; cf. 2 Macc. 5:10; cf. Bauer, p. 214, "festival of Rededication"). Jewish sources call it the "Feast of the Maccabees."

The feast was to be kept "with mirth and gladness." 2 Macc. 10:6f. says it was kept like the Feast of Tabernacles, with the carrying of palm and other branches, and the singing of psalms (cf. 2 Macc. 1:9; Ps. 30:1). Josephus calls it "Lights" (*Ant.* xii.7.7) and the T.B. the "Festival of Illumination," following the tradition that Judas Maccabeus had discovered in the temple a cruse of oil sufficient for one day, which miraculously lasted for eight.

The Hebrew name of the festival, Hanukkah (Heb. *ḥ^{a}nukkâ*), was commonly applied to celebrations of dedication, including those of the altar (Nu. 7:10; 2 Ch. 7:9) and the wall of Jerusalem (Neh. 12:27). The Aramaic form was applied to the dedication of a pagan image (Dnl. 3:2).

At this feast Jesus delivered in the temple at Jerusalem the discourse recorded in Jn. 10:24ff. J. ORR

DEED [Heb. *sēper*–'book'] (Jer. 32:10ff.); AV EVIDENCE. In the account of Jeremiah's purchase of a field at Anathoth from his cousin Hanamel, the transaction is described in detail. A deed of purchase was signed by Jeremiah and by witnesses. A sealed copy, and also an unsealed copy for reference, were put in an earthen jar. The Heb. *sēper* here indicates a papyrus scroll.

DEEP; DEEPS; DEPTHS [Heb. *t^{e}hôm, m^{e}ṣûlâ, m^{e}ṣôlâ, ṣûlâ* (Isa. 44:27), *ma'^{a}maqqîm, 'āmōq* ("dwell in the depths," Jer. 49:8, 30), *'ēmeq* (Prov. 9:18), *taḥtî, merḥāq* (MT *meḥqār*, Ps. 95:4), *yar^{e}ḵa* (Isa. 14:15); Gk. *báthos* (Lk. 5:4)]; AV also BOTTOM (Ex. 15:5); for *taḥtî*: LOW (Lam. 3:55), LOWEST (Dt. 32:22; Ps. 86:13; 88:6 [MT 7]), LOWER PARTS (Ps. 63:9 [MT 10]; Isa. 44:23), LOWEST PARTS (Ps. 139:15); also SIDES (Isa. 14:15), "fields of offerings" (2 S. 1:21; RSV "upsurging of the deep" [emended]), DEEP PLACES (Ps. 95:4; 135:6); NEB also ABYSS (*t^{e}hôm*, Gen. 1:2; 7:11; 8:2; Ps. 36:6 [MT 7]; Isa. 51:10; Am. 7:4; *m^{e}ṣûlâ*, Ps. 69:15 [MT 16); for *t^{e}hôm* also OCEAN, PRIMEVAL OCEAN (Ezk. 26:19), GREAT RIVER (Job 41:32), SEA (Ps. 78:15), DEEP SEA (Hab. 3:10), UNDERGROUND WATERS (Ezk. 31:4); also "showers on the uplands" (2 S. 1:21 [emended]), LOWEST (*taḥtî*, Ps. 88:6 [MT 7]), FARTHEST PLACES (Ps. 95:14), DEEP WATERS (*ṣûlâ*), "take refuge in remote places" (*'āmaq*), DEEP WATER (Lk. 5:4); the RSV emendation of 2 S. 1:21, from *ś^{e}ḏê t^{e}rûmōṯ* to *š^{e}rê' t^{e}hômōṯ*, is suggested by the Ugaritic passage 1 Aqhat 45 (*ANET*, p. 153).

The etymological background of Heb. *t^{e}hôm* in ancient Near Eastern mythology (cf. Tiamat in the Babylonian epic *Enuma Elish*) does not mean that every Bible passage using the word is mythological (cf. our word "ocean," originating in the Greek myth of Oceanus). In certain contexts, however, it cannot be denied that literary allusion, at least, is made to the ancient myths of cosmogony. The extent to which these cosmogonies were accepted by the Hebrew authors is disputed.

In the Babylonian epic, Tiamat is a dragon, slain by Marduk (cf. Isa. 51:9). Little personification of *t^{e}hôm* is discernible in Genesis in the accounts of creation and the Flood; but in the Blessing of Jacob at Gen. 49:25, and also in Moses' blessing at Dt. 33:13, it is said that *t^{e}hôm* "couches beneath." The verb used is *rāḇaṣ*, NEB "lurks," in Gen. 49:9 used of a lion. In Job 28:14 *t^{e}hôm* speaks, as in Hab. 3:10, where also "it lifted its hands on high." In Ps. 77:16 (MT 17) *t^{e}hôm* trembles at the sight of God. In 148:7 the *t^{e}hōmôṯ* are mentioned along with the "sea monsters" (*tannînîm*; NEB "waterspouts"; *see* DRAGON I). The creation account in Ps. 104 resembles *Enuma Elish* more than do the Genesis accounts: "At thy rebuke they [i.e., the waters of *t^{e}hôm*] fled; at the sound of thy thunder they took to flight" (v. 7). *See also* LEVIATHAN; RAHAB. But all these passages are poetic; by no means do they imply a literal belief in the myths to which they allude.

Similar poetic expression is sometimes used of the waters crossed in the Exodus, as in Ex. 15:8; Ps. 109:9; Isa. 51:10; cf. 63:13. In Ezekiel's lament over Tyre he says that *t^{e}hôm* will be brought up over the ruined city (26:19). Elsewhere in the Prophets see Ezk. 31:4, 15; Am. 7:4; Jonah 2:5.

In the biblical poetic view, then, *t^{e}hôm*, the primeval water deep that seemed to surround the earth, and which was believed by ancient man to be under the earth, existed from the beginning of creation (Gen. 1:2), was in the process of creation subdued by God, but burst forth again in the Deluge (7:11) before it was again restrained (8:2). This restrained monster nonetheless lurks beneath the earth and behind his bounds, needing to be overcome at the Exodus, in the rescue of Jonah, and in God's judgment envisioned by Amos (Am. 7:4).

See also ABYSS; WATERS. J. W. D. H.

DEEP SLEEP. *See* SLEEP, DEEP.

DEEP THINGS [Heb. *ḥēqer*] (Job 11:7); AV "by searching"; NEB MYSTERY; [Aram. *'^{a}mîq*] (Dnl. 2:22); [Gk. *bathýs*] (Rev. 2:24); AV DEPTHS; NEB DEEP SECRETS; **DEEPS** [Heb. *'āmōq*] (Job 12:22); AV DEEP THINGS; NEB MYSTERIES (DEEP); **DEPTHS** [Gk. *báthos*] (1 Cor. 2:10); AV DEEP THINGS. The "deep things of God" are those mysteries of His being that man can never fathom (Job 11:7). Certain mysteries, however, He reveals to man (12:22; Dnl. 2:22); but the revelation is apparent only to spiritual man: "For the Spirit searches everything, even the depths of God" (1 Cor. 2:10).

In Rev. 2:24 the expression "deep things of Satan" is an ironic twist mocking the perverse beliefs of heretics in Thyatira, evidently the followers of the prophetess "Jezebel." J. W. D. H.

DEER. Cloven-hoofed ruminants distinguished by antlers rather than horns. Of the numerous members of the deer family (*Cervidae*), three species are known to have occupied Palestine in Bible times and later.

The Heb. *'ayyāl* occurs twenty-two times. In the AV and RSV it is translated "hart" (NEB "buck") or "STAG." The feminine forms *'ayyalâ* and *'ayyeleṯ* are translated "hind" (NEB also "doe," "goddess" [Canticles], "terebinth" [2 S. 22:34; cf. the change of AV "hind" to "oak," a similar Hebrew word, in Ps. 29:9, RSV]). The usual identification with the European-Asian red deer (*Cervus elaphus*) has been challenged (A. E. Day) because its usual habitat is N of Palestine. This does not mean, however, that it was not in Palestine in the time of Solomon (1 K. 4:23). In prehistoric times it was present in the Middle East, as bones discovered in caves in Carmel and the mountains of Lebanon testify. A similar genus, the *Cervus Capreolus* or roe deer, may be the biblical "hart." The hart, the male of the species, may weigh as much as three hundred pounds and has six-pronged antlers. Unlike the gazelle it cannot thrive in arid countries; hence the appropriateness of the psalmist's simile, "As the hart pants for the water-brooks . . ." (Ps. 42:1). This beautiful beast (30 in. [75 cm.] high) was last seen in Palestine during World War I.

The *ṣᵉḇî* ("gazelle" in RSV, NEB; AV "roe," "roebuck," "fallow deer" [Dt. 14:5; 1 K. 4:23]) is mentioned sixteen times in the Bible. The horns of the gazelle differ from the antlers of the deer in that they are hollow and not branched. These small antelopes abound in the dry areas of North Africa, Arabia, and Palestine and Syria. Of the three score varieties of gazelles, there are two species in Israel today: the *Gazella gazella* (27.5 in. [70 cm.] high) is found in the hill country while the smaller *Gazella dorcas* (23.5 in. [60 cm.] high) is now found in the Negeb. The gazelle is mentioned along with the "hart" in seven passages (Dt. 12:15, 22; 14:5; 15:22; 1 K. 4:23; Cant. 2:9, 17). Ashael was said to be "as swift of foot as a wild gazelle" (2 S. 2:18; cf. 1 Ch. 12:8). Their grace and beauty were greatly admired; some men likened their daughters to gazelles.

The roebuck (*yaḥmûr*) is mentioned only twice in the Bible, in a list with other ruminants considered edible (Dt. 14:5; 1 K. 4:23). The sequence is the same in both passages: *'ayyāl, ṣᵉḇî,* and *yaḥmûr*, or "hart," "gazelle," and "roebuck" as in the late versions. The "roebuck" seems to be the *Cervus dama* familiar in North Africa and countries around the Mediterranean, and was known popularly as the "fallow deer." The latter term is now applied to the smaller deer found in central Europe, while the "roebuck" is found in south Europe, North Africa, and — until the 20th cent. — in Palestine. Since this species is mentioned only twice, it appears to have been less common than either the *'ayyāl* or the *ṣᵉḇî*. This animal stood about 35 in. (90 cm.) high and was pictured in hunting scenes (as in the mosaics at Beit Guvrin and near Jericho) as having antlers with five branches.

The RSV renders Heb. *'ōper* as "fawn" in Cant. 4:5; 7:3 (MT 4; AV "young roe"), but elsewhere as "young stag" (Cant. 2:9, 17; 8:14; AV "young hart"; NEB "young wild goat"). In Gen. 49:21 the RSV emends Heb. *'imrê* to read "comely fawns" (AV "goodly words"; NEB "lovely boughs").

In most of the passages alluded to, these animals are compared to human beings in highly poetic fashion (e.g., Cant. 2:7, 9, 17; 3:5; 8:14). The lame will "leap like the hart" (Isa. 35:6). Naphtali was "like a hind let loose" (Gen. 49:21).

For "doe" (Prov. 5:19; AV "roe"; NEB "hind") *see* GOAT.

Bibliography.–*Enc.Brit.*, *s.v.*; J. Feliks, *Animal World of the Bible* (1962), pp. 10-12; H. B. Tristram, *Natural History* (10th ed. 1911), pp. 127-130. G. A. TURNER

DEFAME [Gk. *blasphēméō*] (1 Tim. 6:1); AV BLASPHEME; NEB BRING INTO DISREPUTE. *See* BLASPHEME; *see also* SLANDER (1 Cor. 4:13).

DEFECT. In Lev. 21:20, Heb. *tᵉḇallul* may indicate a white spot in the eye (KoB, p. 1018), or a discharge (NEB) or some other eye defect. The word is probably derived from *bālal*, "mingle, confuse," also "overflow" (hence NEB?); cf. Arab. *balal*, "moisten."

See also BLEMISH.

Red deer stag, attacked by lion. Panel from the Black Obelisk of Shalmaneser III (858-824 B.C.) (Trustees of the British Museum)

DEFEND; DEFENSE. *See* COURTS, JUDICIAL; FORTIFICATION.

DEFERENCE [Heb. *marpē'*] (Eccl. 10:4); AV YIELDING; NEB SUBMISSION. The word is derived from *rāpâ*, "droop," "be passive"; the meaning is "remaining passive," perhaps more with the idea of composure than of compromise (cf. Prov. 14:30; 15:4).

DEFILE; DEFILEMENT [Heb. *ṭāmē, ḥālal, gā'al*, also *gā'al* (2 S. 1:21), *gō'el* (Neh. 13:29), *'ānâ* (Ezk. 22:11), *ṭum'â* (44:26, emended from MT *ṭohºrâ*); Gk. *koinóō*–'make common,' *koinós* (Mk. 7:2, 5), *miaínō*–'stain,' *molýnō* (1 Cor. 8:7; Rev. 14:4), *molysmós* (2 Cor. 7:1), *miasmós* ("defiling passion," 2 Pet. 2:10), *míasma* (2:20)]; AV also POLLUTE, PROFANE (*ḥālal*, Lev. 21:7, 14; Ps. 89:39), STAIN (Isa. 23:9), HUMBLE (*'ānâ*), "vilely cast away" (*gā'al*), FILTHINESS (2 Cor. 7:1), UNCLEAN (He. 9:13), UNCLEANNESS (2 Pet. 2:10), POLLUTIONS (2:20), CLEANSED (Ezk. 44:26, with MT), UNWASHEN (Mk. 7:5, var. *ániptos*); NEB also "make (render, become) unclean," "make ritually unclean" (Nu. 6:9), POLLUTE, POLLUTION, "who has lost her virginity" (*ḥālal*, Lev. 21:7, 14), "lie tarnished" (2 S. 1:21), DESECRATE (2 K. 23:8, 10, 13), PRICK (Isa. 23:9), "reject as unclean" (30:22), STAINED (59:3; Lam. 4:14), DISHONOUR (Ezk. 18:6, 11, 15), RAVISH (*'ānâ*), "lay in the dust" (Ezk. 28:7), CONTAMINATE (Dnl. 1:8), FOUL (Zeph. 3:1), PROFANE (Acts 21:28), POISON (He. 12:15), ABOMINABLE (2 Pet. 2:10), PURIFICATION (Ezk. 44:26, with MT).

I. Ceremonial Defilement.–Persons and objects could, in priestly tradition, become ritually defiled, i.e., disqualified for religious service or worship, and capable of communicating the disqualification. (a) Persons were defiled by contact with carcasses of unclean animals (Lev. 11:24); or with any carcass (17:15); by eating a carcass (22:8); by contact with issues from the body, one's own or another's, e.g., abnormal issues from the genitals, male or female (15:2, 25); by menstruation (15:19); by contact with anyone thus unclean (15:24); copulation (15:16-18); uncleanness after childbirth (12:2-5); by contact with unclean persons (5:3), or unclean things (22:6), or with leprosy (esp. defiling, 13:14), or with the dead (Nu. 6:12), or with one unclean by such contact (19:22); by funeral rites (Lev. 21:1); by contact with creeping things (22:5), or with unclean animals (11:26).

(b) Holy objects were ceremonially defiled by the contact, entrance, or approach of the defiled (Lev. 15:31; Nu. 19:13); by the presence of dead bodies, or any remains of the dead (Ezk. 9:7; 2 K. 23:16, Josiah's defilement of heathen altars by the ashes of the priests); by the entrance of foreigners (Ps. 79:1; see Acts 21:28); by forbidden treatment, as the altar by being tooled (Ex. 20:25); objects in general by contact with the unclean. Ceremonial defilement, strictly considered, implied not sin but ritual unfitness.

II. Ethical or Religious Defilement.–The land might be defiled by bloodshed (Nu. 35:33), especially of the just or innocent; by adultery (Jer. 3:1); by idolatry and idolatrous practices, like sacrificing children to idols (Lev. 20:3; Ps. 106:39). The temple altar was polluted or profaned by disrespect (Mal. 1:7, 12); by offering the unclean (Hag. 2:14); by any sort of unrighteousness (Ezk. 36:17); by the presence of idols or idolatrous paraphernalia (Jer. 7:30). The nation was defiled by unfaithfulness to God (Hos. 5:3; 6:10). Persons were defiled by illicit intercourse (Lev. 18:20), murder (Isa. 59:3), and other transgressions (Ezk. 37:23). Ethical defilement involved one's relationship with the Lord as covenant God and God of righteousness.

III. Defilement in the NT.–The scope of defilement in its various degrees (direct, or primary, as from the person or thing defiled; indirect, or secondary, tertiary, or even further, by contact with the defiled) had been greatly widened by rabbinism into a complex and burdensome system whose shadow falls over the whole NT life.

Ceremonial defilement is mentioned in the NT, but not approved: by eating with unwashed, "common," not ceremonially cleansed hands (Mk. 7:2, 5); by eating unclean, "common" food (Acts 10:14, Peter's vision); by intimate association with Gentiles, such as eating with them (not expressly forbidden in Mosaic law, Acts 11:3), or entering into their houses (Jn. 18:28, the Pharisees refusing to enter the praetorium); by the presence of Gentiles in the temple (Acts 21:28).

But with Christ's decisive and revolutionary dictum (Mk. 7:19: "Thus he declared all foods clean," etc.), and with the command in Peter's vision ("What God has cleansed, you must not call common," Acts 10:15), and with Paul's bold and consistent teaching ("Everything is indeed clean," Rom. 14:20, etc.), the idea of ceremonial or ritual defilement, having accomplished its educative purpose, passed. Defilement in the NT teaching, therefore, is uniformly ethical or spiritual: "But what comes out of the mouth proceeds from the heart, and this defiles a man" (Mt. 15:18); "conscience . . . is defiled" (by concession to idolatry, Cor. 8:7); "that no 'root of bitterness' spring up and cause trouble, and by it the many become defiled" (He. 12:15).

Whatever use God may have made of ideas and feelings common among many nations in some form, the divine purpose was clearly to impress deeply and indelibly on the Israelites the ideas of holiness and sacredness in general, and of the Lord's holiness, and their own required holiness and separateness in particular, thus preparing for the deep NT teachings of sin, and of spiritual consecration and sanctification.

See also CLEAN AND UNCLEAN; HOLY.

P. W. CRANNELL

DEFY [Heb. *ḥārap* (1 S. 17:10, 25f.), *'āmar* (Ps. 139:20), *mārâ* (Isa. 3:8)]; AV also SPEAK AGAINST, PROVOKE; NEB also PROVOKE, REBEL (Isa. 3:8). In the narrative of David's encounter with Goliath the term is used in its most familiar sense of "taunt" or "challenge to combat." In Isa. 3:8 *mārâ* ("quarrel," "resist") is used in the sense of defying.

DEGENERATE [Heb. *sûr*]; NEB DEBASED. This English term occurs only in Jer. 2:21, where Judah is compared to a "choice vine" which "turned degenerate and became a wild one." It represents Heb. *sûrîm*, "stray" or "degenerate [shoots]," from *sûr*, "turn aside," especially to turn aside from the right path.

DEGREE. The RSV uses this term twice as a general expression of rank or status. In Lk. 1:52 it translates Gk. *tapeínos* ("low degree"), rendered "humble" by the NEB. In 1 Cor. 3:18 the RSV supplies "degree" to translate the Gk. *apó dóxēs eis dóxan*. In the AV this term is also used in the obsolete sense of "step" in 2 K. 20:9-11; Isa. 38:8, and in the obsolete sense of "standing" or "position" in 1 Tim. 3:13.

DEGREES, SONGS OF. *See* ASCENTS, SONG OF.

DEHAVITES. A people listed in the AV of Ezr. 4:9 (RV "Dehaites"), for the MT *dehāwē'*. The RSV ("that is") and NEB, following LXX B, vocalize *dî-hû'*. This accords with Susa's being then in Elam.

DEHORT. An obsolete English term used by the AV in 1 Macc. 9:9 to translate Gk. *apostréphō*; the opposite of "exhort." It means to "dissuade," "forbid," "restrain from."

DEITY [Gk. *tó theíon*] (Acts 17:29); AV GODHEAD; [*theiótēs*] (Rom. 1:20); AV GODHEAD; [*theótēs*] (Col. 2:9); AV, NEB GODHEAD. These three closely related Greek terms are descriptive of the basic nature of God. They seem to vary but slightly in connotation.

I. Greek Terms.–*A. Tó Theíon. Tó theíon*, "the divine thing," is derived from the adjective *theíos*, meaning "pertaining to God," "divine" (2 Pet. 1:3f.). It signifies "God" in an impersonal sense. In Acts 17:29, in Paul's speech to Greek intellectuals on Mars Hill, the term *tó theíon* draws attention to the qualitative aspect of God. Paul demonstrates the Greeks' shallow conception of God, seeking to heighten their receptivity to the revealed truth of the gospel of Christ. The term *tó theíon* was common in their discussions, being used to designate the deity apart from any reference to a particular god. Paul focuses attention upon that quality of "the divine" which distinguishes God from all else. English terms based on the word "divine," however, are used too commonly and are therefore inadequate to set forth the connotation of *tó theíon* (see II.A, B below). The idea is more adequately represented by "the Deity," so that an appropriate translation of Acts 17:29 might be: "It is inconceivable that 'the Deity' can be appropriately represented by the artistic talents of men working with mere earthly elements."

B. Theiótēs. The term *theiótēs* is an abstract noun closely related to *tó theíon*, derived from the same adjective, *theíos*. It is commonly understood as a summary term for the attributes of deity. However, the term merely "defines" with regard to essence, signifying "the quality of the divine," that character which makes God God, and sets Him apart as worthy of worship. The Greeks used the term of their deities. Later it was applied to men by the Roman imperial cult as a term for the divinity of imperial majesty. It is rarely used in later Jewish works and occurs in biblical literature only in Wisd. 18:9 and Rom. 1:20. The term is not as impersonal as *tó theíon*, but its abstractness does not lend a readily discernible distinction. Its meaning is approximated by "deity," perhaps "divineness."

In Rom. 1:20 *theiótēs* is used of that nature of the Creator discernible to the mind by observation of the existing worlds. Verse 19 states, "For what can be known about God is plain to them, because he has shown it to them." Verse 20 affirms that man's mind is able to form a concept of the invisible nature of God by visual perception of the universe. The discernible features of His transcendent being ("his invisible nature") are specifically His "eternal power" and "deity." The universe displays the eternal power it took to bring the universe into existence; in addition it displays the divine character of the one who created it, i.e., His deity. Specific attributes are not in view in the term *theiótēs*, simply His quality of "Godness," which depicts Him as worthy of worship. But men suppressed this truth in unrighteousness (v. 18), and are without excuse, subject to the wrath of God revealed from heaven (v. 20). They did not acknowledge "his deity" as it is discernible in the things He has created.

C. Theótēs. Theótēs is a kindred term, but is distinctive in that it is derived from the word "God" (*theós*). On this basis it is the most personal of the three terms, and is nearly a name. Whereas *tó theíon* marks "the quality of deity," and *theiótēs* connotes "that which makes God God," *theótēs* signifies "the being of God." *Theótēs* apparently denotes the utmost idea of God. On heathen lips it could do no more than designate their highest concept of God, "The Supreme Being."

In Col. 2:9 Paul uses *theótēs* in declaring that "the whole fulness of deity dwells bodily" in Christ. Although it conveys the idea of a "being," the use of "Divine Being" here would impersonalize the total expression, "the whole fulness of the Divine Being." The term "deity," or even "the Deity," is likewise impersonal; furthermore, the connotation "being" is lacking. A term that better preserves the personal and qualitative aspect of *theótēs* is "godhead" (see III below). The total expression "the whole fulness of the Godhead," then, signifies the sum of all that enters into the conception of "Godhead," God in nature, character, and being. All this dwells in Christ "bodily," i.e., in such a manner as to be shown in a bodily organism. Cf. Jn. 14:9, where Philip's request that Jesus show them the Father was met by the Lord's response, "He who has seen me has seen the Father."

II. English Terms.–In English the words most representative of these three Greek terms are "deity," "divinity," and "godhead."

A. Deity. "Deity" means "divine character" or "nature" and is used of false gods as well as of the persons of the trinity. "Deity" is qualitative in its import. The expression "the deity of Christ" is much stronger than "the divinity of Christ," probably because "divinity" is commonly applied to men and things. When used with the article, the resultant term "the Deity" becomes a designation of God the Supreme Being, although it can also be used of specific lesser deities. Hence, the term "deity," when used with the article, is qualitative and somewhat personal in connotation.

B. Divinity. The term "divinity" is much like "deity" in that it refers to divine character or nature. But although it is used in connection with the persons of the trinity, it lacks the force of "deity." These Latin derivatives bring into English the basic distinction created by the Latin fathers. Before the controversy about the deity of Christ, Latin had only the general term *divinitas*. The Latin fathers coined the term *deitas* as a distinctive rendering of the Gk. *theótēs*, and employed it to express the "deity" of the persons of the trinity. They, as well as the Greek fathers, needed unique terms to combat the attempt to ascribe to the Son and the Spirit a reduced "divinity." This distinctiveness is largely preserved in English, although there is a tendency for "divinity" and "deity" to merge in meaning.

C. Godhead. The English term "godhead" was originally a synonym for "godhead," a word that has all but passed out of use. As manhood is that quality which makes a man a man, so godhead is that which makes God God. This significance, however, is not readily discernible in the term today. It is presently a somewhat neutral term for the essential being of God as unique. By prefixing the article, the term becomes an abstract way of saying "God." In fact, the article prefixed to any of these terms, "the Deity," "the Divinity," or "the Godhead," draws attention to the constitutive qualities that make God the kind of being we call "God." In strength of affirmation, or personalizing force, "godhead" seems most substantial, with "deity" nearly as strong and "divinity" weakest in this regard. All are abstract terms, nearly synonymous in meaning, yet the context will often decide the choice of one word over another.

III. Summary.–Since the context of Col. 2:9 deals with the person of Christ, Paul apparently chose a term distinctive in that respect, *theótēs*. The contexts of Acts

17:29 and Rom. 1:20 emphasize the character rather than the person of God. The terms used are impersonal in connotation. Because of these differences in context and word derivation it is preferable to use distinctive English terms. "Deity" seems appropriate for the concept of *tó theíon* in Acts 17:29 and for *theiótēs* in Rom. 1:20, but inadequate for *theótēs* in Col. 2:9. "Godhead" more adequately portrays the truth that all that constitutes God in person, character and being dwells in Christ the Son. Speaking of God in respect to His "Godness" the term "deity" is sufficient, but in reference to His person and/or being a designation with the word "god" seems preferable.

Bibliography.–Comms. on Romans by F. L. Godet (1969); C. Hodge (1950); J. Murray (*NIC*, 1960); W. Sanday and A. C. Headlam (*ICC*, 5th ed. 1902); comms. on Colossians by J. B. Lightfoot (1879); F. F. Bruce (*NIC*, 1957); Bauer, pp. 354, 359; *TDNT*, III, *s.v.* θεότης (Stauffer), θεῖος, θειότης (Kleinknecht); H. S. Nash, *JBL*, 18 (1899), 1-34. G. E. MONTGOMERY

DEKAR. *See* BEN-DEKER.

DELAIAH də-lā'yə [Heb. *d^elāyâ*–'God has raised'].

1. AV, NEB, DALAIAH. A descendant of David (1 Ch. 3:24).

2. One of David's priests and leader of the twenty-third course (1 Ch. 24:18).

3. One of the princes who pleaded with Jehoiakim not to destroy the roll containing the prophecies of Jeremiah (Jer. 36:12, 25).

4. [Gk. Apoc. *Dalan*]; AV Apoc. LADAN; NEB Apoc. DALAN. The ancestor of a postexilic family whose genealogy was lost (Ezr. 2:60; Neh. 7:62; 1 Esd. 5:37).

5. The father of timorous Shemaiah (Neh. 6:10).

DELAY. In Ex. 22:29, "You shall not delay to offer" is better translated in the NEB "Do not hold back" (Heb. *'āḥar*), the idea being not procrastination but discontinuation of a custom. The verb used in Ex. 32:1 of Moses' delay on Mt. Sinai is the polel of *bôš*, "be ashamed"; the implication is that the people suspected Moses had failed in his mission, which better explains their subsequent idolatry. A. L. BRESLICH

DELECTABLE [Heb. *ta'^anûg*] (Cant. 7:6); AV "for delights"; NEB "of delights." The MT indicates an object of pleasure or gratification which could be sexual in nature. The RSV, however, avoids so narrow an interpretation.

DELIBERATE SIN [Gk. *hekousíōs hamartánō*–'sin deliberately'] (He. 10:26); AV "sin wilfully"; NEB "wilfully persist in sin." This type of offense reflects the OT distinction between sins of IGNORANCE or inadvertence and sins of intent, those done with "a high hand" (Nu. 15:27-31). The latter passage is followed immediately by a narrative which illustrates the kind of sin for which no forgiveness was possible but rather death was prescribed — the case of the man who gathered sticks on the sabbath in defiance of the law of sabbath rest (15:32-36). Another instance is that of Achan (Josh. 6:18; 7:1, 25).

Apparently the OT did not recognize any classification of sins other than the two mentioned above. This raises a question concerning David's double transgression, which was certainly deliberate. The very fact that Nathan the prophet assured him he would not die (2 S. 12:13) indicates that he was worthy of death. Evidently God, who knows the heart of man, perceived that David had not acted out of rebellion against Him or His law. So mercy was allowed to triumph over judgment. Similarly, Peter's sin in denying the Lord Jesus was not involuntary, yet it was forgiveable since it was not something planned but was entirely spontaneous and was followed immediately by genuine repentance.

Returning to He. 10:26, one can see why it is that there is no sacrifice for sins if the sinner rejects the one sacrifice that put away sins for ever — the death of Jesus Christ. No further sacrifice can be made once the final sacrifice has been offered. All that is left is the option to accept or reject, with appropriate consequences.

E. F. HARRISON

DELICACIES, ABUNDANCE OF. Archaic in Rev. 18:3, AV, for Gk. *dýnamis toú strḗnous*, RSV "wealth of [her] wantonness," NEB "bloated wealth." *See also* DELICIOUSLY, LIVE.

DELICATE; DELICATELY; DELICATENESS. The Heb. *'ānōg* can mean "be delicate" or "delicately bred" (Dt. 28:54, 56; Isa. 47:1; Jer. 6:2), but also "delight in," so that the AV "delicate children" (*ta'^anûg*) in Mic. 1:16 is better translated in the RSV and NEB "children of your delight." (Cf. Cant. 7:6; Isa. 66:11.)

The AV has "delicately" for Heb. *ma'^adannōṯ* in 1 S. 15:32 and for *l^ema'^adannîm* in Lam. 4:5. In the first passage the RSV reads "cheerfully," deriving from *'āḏan*, "delight"; the NEB, following the Gk. *trémōn*, derives from *mā'aḏ* and reads "with faltering step." Another suggestion is "reluctantly," for *ma'^anaddōṯ* (KoB, p. 544). The context favors these last two, since Agag had good reason to be fearful.

In Lam. 4:5 the meaning is "on dainties" (RSV; cf. Gen. 49:20). The LXX renders *tás tryphás*; cf. Lk. 7:25, *en tryphḗ*, AV "delicately," RSV "in luxury."

J. W. D. H.

DELICATES. Archaic in Jer. 51:34, AV, for Heb. *'ēḏen*, RSV "delicacies."

DELICIOUSLY, LIVE. Archaic for Gk. *strēniáō* in Rev. 18:7, 9, AV. The RSV has "played the wanton" and "were wanton." The NEB paraphrases the two verbs in v. 7a, "voluptuous pomp," and in v. 9 renders "wallowed in her luxury."

DELIGHT; DELIGHT IN; etc. [Heb. *ḥāpēṣ, śûś, ta'^anûg* (Eccl. 2:8; Mic. 1:16), *'ōneg* (Isa. 58:13), *'ānag* (Job 22:26; 27:10; Ps. 37:4, 11; Isa. 55:2; 58:14; 66:11), *rāṣâ, rāṣôn* (Prov. 11:1, 20; 12:22; 15:8; 16:13), *šā'a', ḥāmaḏ* (Job 20:20; Prov. 1:22; Cant. 2:3; Isa. 44:9), *maḥmāḏ* (Ezk. 24:16, 21, 25), *'āḏan* (Neh. 9:25), *'ēḏen* (Ps. 36:8 [MT 9]), *ma'^aḏannîm* (Prov. 29:17), *gîl* (Prov. 2:14), *rāwâ* (Prov. 5:19), *rî(a)ḥ* (Isa. 11:3), *'ālas* (Prov. 7:18), *nā'ēm* (Prov. 24:25), *śāmaḥ* (Jer. 15:16), *ta'^awâ* (Gen. 3:6); Gk. *apátē* (Mt. 13:22; Mk. 4:19), *synḗdomai* (Rom. 7:22)]; AV also REJOICE, DESIRE, FAVOR (Ps. 44:3 [MT 4]), SATISFY (Prov. 5:19), ACCEPT (Hos. 8:13), "have pleasure in" (Ps. 5:4 [MT 5]; 35:27), SMELL (Am. 5:21), "deceitful" (Mt. 13:22; Mk. 4:19), SOLACE (Prov. 7:18), "delectable things" (Isa. 44:9), DELICATE (Mic. 1:16), PLEASANT (Gen. 3:6), etc.; NEB also PLEASING, WISH (Est. 6:6ff.), ENJOY, "trust in" (Job 27:10), "depend on" (Ps. 37:4), REVEL (Ps. 68:30 [MT 31]; Isa. 66:3), DESIRE, "set store by" (Ps. 147:10), EXULT (Prov. 2:14), HAPPINESS (Jer. 15:16), etc.

Delight is an affection of the "inmost heart" (cf. Ps. 40:8 [MT 9]). It signifies that in which one finds pleasure, i.e., the object of one's love. In Prov. 5:19 the piel form of the verb *rāwâ* (lit. "drink one's fill") is used to denote being saturated with sensual pleasure. *Rî(a)ḥ*, meaning literally "enjoy the smell of," is used metaphorically in Isa. 11:3 of delight in the fear of the Lord.

In Isa. 62:4 the prophet speaks of Yahweh's vindication and salvation of Zion (cf. vv. 1f.). The new names He gives represent the new marriage relationship between Yahweh and His people. "Hephzibah" (AV, NEB), from Heb. *ḥāpēṣ*, means "My delight is in her" (RSV, NEB mg.) (cf. 54:6-8; 60:14, 18; Jer. 33:16; Hos. 2:22f.).

J. T. DENNISON, JR.

DELILAH də-lī'lə [Heb. *d^elîlâ*; Gk. *Daleida, Dalida*]. The woman who betrayed Samson to the Philistines (Jgs. 16). She was presumably a Philistine, though that is not expressly stated, only that she belonged to the valley of Sorek. She is not spoken of as Samson's wife, though many have understood the account in that way. The text simply says that he loved her (v. 4). The Philistines paid her a very high price for her services: eleven hundred pieces of silver. The account indicates that for mental ability, self-command, and nerve, she was a remarkable woman. Unfortunately she put her gifts to an evil use by exploiting Samson's love.

See also SAMSON. W. J. BEECHER

DELIVER. The numerous Hebrew, Aramaic, and Greek words that the RSV translates "deliver" and the numerous variant renderings in the AV and NEB indicate this word has several distinct meanings.

(1) [Heb. *nāṣal, yāšaʿ, ḥālaṣ, mālaṭ, pālaṭ, šāpaṭ, pāḏâ, yāšāʾ, pāraq* (Lam. 5:8), *gāʾal* (Ps. 106:10); Aram. *šêziḇ, n^eṣal* (Dnl. 3:29); Gk. *rhýomai, exairéō* (Acts 7:34; 26:17; Gal. 1:4), *apallássō* (He. 2:15)]; AV also SAVE, REDEEM (Ps. 44:26; 106:10), BRING OUT (Ps. 107:20, 28), AVENGE (2 S. 18:19, 31), ESCAPE (Dnl. 11:41), DEFEND (Jgs. 10:1), RID (Ex. 6:6); NEB also SAVE, RESCUE, SET FREE, GO FREE (Prov. 11:21), "be a safeguard" (Prov. 10:2; 11:4), PRESERVE (2 K. 17:39; Jer. 39:17), ESCAPE (Isa. 37:11; 2 K. 19:11), GIVE VICTORY (Jgs. 7:2), CLAIM BACK (Ps. 106:10), etc.; **DELIVERER** [Heb. *m^epallēṭ* (2 S. 22:2; Ps. 18:2; 40:17; 70:5; 144:2), *môšî(a)ʿ* (Josh. 3:9; Jgs. 3:15), *y^ešûʿâ* (Ps. 140:7), *maṣṣil* (Jgs. 18:28); Gk. *lytrōtḗs* (Acts 7:35); *rhyómenos* (Rom. 11:26)]; AV also SALVATION (Ps. 140:7); NEB also "man to deliver," "one to save," CHAMPION, LIBERATOR, SALVATION, SAFETY, REFUGE; **DELIVERANCE** [*ṣ^eḏaqâ* (Ps. 22:31; Isa. 46:12; Mic. 7:9), *ṣeḏeq* (Ps. 40:9; Isa. 51:1, 5), *yāšaʿ* (Ps. 72:4), *t^ešûʿâ* (Jgs. 15:18; 1 S. 11:9, 13; Ps. 51:14; Isa. 46:13), *y^ešûʿâ* (Ps. 3:8; 9:14; 14:7; 35:3, 9; 53:6; Isa. 26:18; 51:6, 8; 56:1; Jonah 2:9), *yešaʿ* (Ps. 62:7; 65:5), *pallēṭ* (Ps. 32:7), *p^elêṭâ* (2 Ch. 12:7), *haṣṣālâ* (Est. 4:14); Gk. *sōtēría* (Acts 7:25; Phil. 1:19)]; AV also SALVATION, SAVE, HELP, RIGHTEOUSNESS; NEB also SALVATION, VICTORY, JUSTICE, RIGHTEOUSNESS, RIGHT, "what is right," SAVING POWER, ESCAPE, SUCCESS, etc. To deliver someone from peril or bondage, hence to save or rescue. "Deliverer" and "deliverance" are always so understood.

Reuben delivered Joseph from the hand of his brothers (Gen. 37:21), David the people from their enemies (2 S. 19:19; cf. 1 S. 23:5), and Moses the daughters of Reuel from the shepherds (Ex. 2:19); Darius wanted to deliver Daniel from the den of lions (Dnl. 6:14). As a shepherd David delivered a sheep from the mouth of a lion (1 S. 17:34f.), and Job delivered the poor from their plight. In wisdom literature one is delivered by his righteousness (Prov. 11:6), wisdom (Prov. 28:26), or integrity (Prov. 28:18).

The idea of rescuing from a hostile power or an immediate peril witnessed to the dominant motif of Israel's faith, i.e., that Yahweh enters into the historical situation of His people and delivers them from bondage. In this sense the word's meaning approaches "save" or "redeem." Yahweh was remembered throughout Israel's history as the God who delivered His people from slavery in Egypt (Ex. 3:8; cf. Acts 7:34; Ex. 18:9-11; Jgs. 6:9; etc.). This was only the beginning; as the psalmist says, "Many times he delivered them" (Ps. 106:43; cf. Neh. 9:8). Yahweh often delivered Israel through human deliverers, e.g., the judges of Israel (Jgs. 3:9, 15; cf. NEB "man to deliver") or Moses (Acts 7:35).

Much more frequently, Yahweh Himself was proclaimed as the Deliverer of His people (Ps. 18:2; 40:17; 140:7; etc.). Israel's faith was that only Yahweh had the power to deliver. The warrior cannot hope to deliver himself by his great strength (Ps. 33:16), nor can a man deliver his own soul from Sheol (Ps. 89:48). No god can deliver as can Yahweh. Therefore Deutero-Isaiah mocks those who pray for deliverance to idols of their own craftsmanship (Isa. 44:17). Faith in Yahweh as Deliverer is expressed repeatedly in the Psalter. There are Psalms of the individual or of the entire nation petitioning Yahweh to deliver, as well as Psalms of thanksgiving, praising and thanking Yahweh for delivering His people from many kinds of troubles: enemies (106:10; 18;17; etc.), affliction (119:53), battle (55:18), death (56:13), Sheol (86:13), lying lips (102:2), persecutors (142:6), the land of aliens (144:11), etc. The God who delivered Israel from Egypt was the God to whom Israel and the individual Israelite turned for deliverance from any difficulty.

Yahweh delivered His people because of His steadfast love for them (Ps. 44:26). Yahweh's loyalty to the covenant which He had made with Hezekiah's fathers was the basis of his faith in Yahweh's deliverance when Assyria threatened to annihilate Judah. Despite the Rabshakeh's demoralizing remarks that no god had demonstrated the power to deliver his people from the Assyrian king (2 K. 18:19ff. par. Isa. 36:4ff.; cf. 2 Ch. 32), Isaiah could speak confidently Yahweh's word of deliverance (2 K. 20:6).

Yet Israel often forgot to respond to Yahweh's deliverance with obedience to the demands of the covenant. Could Yahweh deliver a disobedient people? Jeremiah asked in his temple sermon whether his people were right to say, "We are delivered," yet continue to "steal, murder, commit adultery, swear falsely, burn incense to Baal, and go after other gods that you have not known" (Jer. 7:8-10). Those whom Jeremiah addressed learned that Yahweh punishes a disobedient people and delivers them not *from* but *into the hand of* their enemy (see 2). When the kingdom was destroyed during the Exile, Israel's faith in a God who could or would deliver His people was put to a severe test, as witnessed in the contemporary lament: "Slaves rule over us; there is none to deliver us from their hand" (Lam. 5:8). Preaching to the exiles of Babylon, Deutero-Isaiah had to summon the people back to faith in Yahweh, who had the power to deliver them (Isa. 50:2). He preached that Yahweh's deliverance (*ṣ^eḏaqâ*), which was forever (51:6, 8), was speedily drawing near again (40:31; 51:5).

Although this use occurs only infrequently in the NT, the thought permeates the background of NT thought. Jesus Himself is never referred to as the deliverer; where the word does occur it refers to Moses (Acts 7:35). But the thought of the NT is that the life, death, and resurrection of Jesus Christ make deliverance possible. Paul asks the Thessalonians to pray that he may be delivered from evil and wicked men (2 Thess. 3:2; cf. Rom. 15:31; 2 Cor. 1:10). Teaching His disciples to pray, Jesus instructed them to seek deliverance from evil (Mt. 6:13). Paul preaches that Christ's death and resurrection deliver men from the present evil age (Gal. 1:4), from the wrath to come (1 Thess. 1:10), and from the dominion of darkness into His kingdom (Col. 1:13; 1 Cor. 15:24). *See also* SALVATION; REDEEMER.

(2) [Heb. *nāṯan, sāḡar, māḡan* (Gen. 14:20; Isa. 64:7), *māḡar* (Ezk. 21:12 [MT 17]), *šālaḥ* (Job 8:4); Gk. *paradídōmi, ékdotos* (Acts 2:23)]; AV also GIVE, CAST AWAY (Job 8:4), "shut up" (Ps. 31:8), "be upon" (Ezk. 21:12), "consume" (Isa. 64:7), BETRAY; NEB also HAND OVER, HAND BACK (1 S. 30:15), GIVE, GIVE UP, GIVE INTO (Mk. 9:31), PUT, BETRAY, ABANDON, BRING, ARREST (Mk. 10:19; 13:11), COMMIT FOR TRIAL (Acts 3:13), ENSLAVE (Jer. 46:24), CONDEMN (Mt. 18:34), CONSIGN (1 Cor. 5:5; 1 Tim. 1:20), SURRENDER (Ps. 78:61), "leave" (Job 8:4), "send" (Isa. 43:8), "restore" (Gen. 42:34). To deliver into the hands of an enemy or legal authority; hence to hand over. The most frequent OT phrase here is Heb. *nāṯan b^eyāḏ* (lit. "give into the hand," i.e., "place in the power of another"). Yahweh, who delivers Israel from her enemies, also delivers them into her hand or power (Gen. 14:20; Ex. 23:31; 1 S. 17:46). But when Yahweh punishes His people as He did through the Exile, He is said to have delivered Israel into the hand of her enemies (Ps. 78:61). Thus Jeremiah tells Zedekiah that he will be delivered into the hand of Nebuchadrezzar (Jer. 34:3; 37:17), and Amos prophesies that Yahweh will deliver up the city and all within it (Am. 6:8).

The idea of delivering or handing over into the power of another is the most frequent NT use of the word (Gk. *paradídōmi*). Judas Iscariot asks the chief priests, "What will you give me if I deliver [Jesus] to you?" (Mt. 26:15). The texts record the chief priests' delivering Jesus to Pilate to be crucified (Mt. 27:18; Mk. 15:1, 10; Lk. 20:20). Jesus speaks both of His future delivery into the hands of men (Mt. 17:22; Mk. 9:31; cf. Lk. 18:32), and of the disciples to councils to be flogged and beaten (Mt. 10:17; Mk. 13:9; cf. Lk. 21:12). Paul tells how he persecuted the Way, delivering men and women into prison (Acts 22:4), and how he himself was taken prisoner from Jerusalem and delivered over to the Romans (27:1; 28:17). One who is excluded from the Church because of immorality is said to have been delivered into the hand of Satan (1 Cor. 5:5; cf. 1 Tim. 1:20).

(3) [Gk. *paradídōmi, diatagḗ* (Acts 7:53)]; AV also "by the disposition" (Acts 7:53); NEB also HAND DOWN, HAND ON, ENTRUST, GIVE (Acts 7:53). To deliver past traditions to someone; hence to hand down or hand on. In this sense Gk. *paradídōmi* was a technical word in the early Church, as it was in Judaism. Luke sees his task as passing on the traditions about Jesus just as they had been transmitted to him (Lk. 1:2). Paul handed on the traditions of the early Church to his converts (1 Cor. 11:2), delivering to the Corinthians what he had already received regarding the Last Supper (11:23) and Jesus' resurrection (15:3).

(4) [Heb. *nāṯan, māsā'* (Lev. 9:12f., 18), *šûḇ* (Lev. 26:26; 2 K. 3:4); Aram. *y^ehaḇ* (Ezr. 5:14), *š^elem* (Ezr. 7:19); Gk. *paradídōmi, anadídōmi* (Acts 23:23), *epidídōmi* (Acts 15:30), *sphragízō* (Rom. 15:28), *diakonéō* (2 Cor. 3:3)]; AV also GIVE, PRESENT, PUT (2 Ch. 34:10), RENDER (2 K. 3:4), "seal" (Rom. 15:28), "minister" (2 Cor. 3:3); NEB also GIVE, HAND, HAND OVER, HAND OUT, PUT, SUPPLY (2 K. 3:4; Prov. 31:24), PRODUCE (Ex. 5:18), DOLE OUT (Lev. 26:26), LEAVE (Mt. 25:20, 22). To deliver something to someone; hence to give or hand over. One delivers money (2 K. 12:15), vessels (Ezr. 7:19), bread (Lev. 26:26), letters (2 Cor. 3:3), etc.

(5) [Heb. *yālaḏ* (1 K. 3:18); Gk. *tíktō* (Lk. 1:57; 2:6; Rev. 12:2), *gennáō* (Jas. 16:21)]; AV also BRING FORTH (Job 39:3), TRAVAIL (Gen. 38:27); NEB also BE BORN, BRING FORTH TO BIRTH (Job 39:3), GIVE BIRTH (Ex. 1:19), etc. To deliver a child; hence to give birth.

E. W. CONRAD

DELOS dē'los [Gk. *Dēlos*] (1 Macc. 15:23); AV DELUS. An island in the Aegean Sea. It is about 3 mi. (5 km.) long and 1 mi. (1.6 km.) wide, and is known in modern times as Mikra Dili. Its high point is Mt. Cynthus (350 ft. [107 m.]). Delos is listed among the names of kings and localities to which Lucius, the Roman consul, sent letters *ca.* 138/137 B.C., declaring that the Jews were being given the protection of Rome and that no hostile action was to be taken against them (1 Macc. 15:15-24). Josephus (*Ant.* xiv.10.14) reports that all Jews in Delos were exempt from military service.

Though the smallest of the Cyclades, Delos was the most famous. Greek legend states that the island floated about until Poseidon fastened it in its present location for Leto, who there gave birth to Apollo and Artemis; therefore the island was made a sacred place for worship of these two deities. On Delos French excavators uncovered a number of temples in honor of Apollo, Artemis, and Dionysus. The most splendid was one dedicated to Apollo, to which Greeks from far and near came to worship. Delos was inhabited by Ionians from *ca.* 1000 B.C. It was here that the Ionic festival in honor of the birth of Apollo was held.

Mosaic from the House of the Dolphin at Delos (3rd-2nd cents. B.C.). Under Macedonian rule Delos flourished as a holy city and commercial center. (Embassy of Greece, Washington)

Representatives of the Greek states gathered on Delos in 478 B.C. to plan defensive measures against Persia. After the Persian War Delos was subject to Athens, but during the Macedonian ascendancy (322-166 B.C.) the island enjoyed independence. Under Roman rule in the last two centuries B.C. Delos became one of the principal ports of the Aegean and a center of trade. When the island was once again subject to Athens *ca.* 167 B.C. the inhabitants fled to Achaia, and Delos was colonized jointly by Athenians and Romans. Strabo (*Geog.* x.5.2-4) records the razing of Delos in A.D. 46. It is now uninhabited.

Bibliography.–*Enc.Brit.*; R. C. Jebb, *Journal of Hellenic Studies,* 1 (1889), 7-62.

D. H. MADVIG

DELUDE; DELUDED. *See* DELUSION.

DELUGE OF NOAH. *See* FLOOD (GENESIS).

DELUS dēl'əs (1 Macc. 15:23, AV). *See* DELOS.

DELUSION [Heb. *kāzāḇ*] (Ps. 62:9 [MT 10]); AV LIE; NEB FAITHLESS; [*'āwen*] (Isa. 41:29); AV VANITY; NEB EMPTY THINGS; [*šeqer*] (Jer. 3:23); AV "in vain"; NEB "no help"; [*ta'tu'îm*] (Jer. 10:15; 51:18); AV ERRORS; NEB MOCKERIES; [Gk. *plánē*] (2 Thess. 2:11); **DELUSIONS; DELUSIVE (VISIONS)** [Heb. *šāw'*] (Ezk. 13:7-9, 23); AV VANITY, VAIN; NEB FALSE (VISIONS); **DELUDE** [Gk. *paralogízomai*] (Col. 2:4); AV BEGUILE; NEB "talk into error"; **DELUDED** [Heb. *nāšā'* (Isa. 19:13), *tālal* (44:20)]; AV DECEIVED; NEB also DUPES (19:13). The Heb. *kāzāḇ* indicates something that falls short of expectations, or fails to live up to its promise, in this case (Ps. 62:9) man. The remaining references are to idolatry and false religions, which are wickedly deceitful, and which prove to be empty, worthless (*'āwen, šāw'*), a sham (*ta'tu'îm*), disappointing all trust (*šeqer*). J. W. D. H.

DEMAND. The peremptory, imperative sense is absent from this word in its occurrences in the AV, where it means no more than "ask," "inquire" (cf. French *demander*), e.g., in 2 S. 11:7; Mt. 2:4; Lk. 3:14; 17:20; Acts 21:33.

DEMAS dē'məs [Gk. *Dēmas*]. A "fellow worker" with Paul at Rome (Col. 4:14; Philem. 24), who eventually, "in love with this present world," forsook the apostle and left for Thessalonica (2 Tim. 4:10). No other particulars are given concerning him.

DEMETRIUS də-mē'trē-əs [Gk. *Dēmetrios*–'belonging to Demeter']. A common Greek name used of three Seleucid kings of Syria.

1. Demetrius I Soter ("savior") (186-150 B.C.), son of Seleucus IV Philopator ("Father-loving") and nephew of Antiochus IV Epiphanes.

Antiochus III was defeated at Magnesia in Asia Minor in 190 B.C. In the peace treaty at Apamea in 189 B.C. he agreed to give up most of Asia Minor, pay a heavy indemnity over a twelve-year period, and hand over twenty hostages, including his third son Antiochus IV Epiphanes, to guarantee payment (Appian *Syr.* 36-39; Polybius xx-xxxi; Livy xxxvi-xxxvii; Dan. 11:18f.; 1 Macc. 1:10; 8:6-8; Josephus *Ant.* xii.10.6). In 187 B.C. Antiochus III was killed in a rebellion and was succeeded by his second son Seleucus IV. In 175 B.C. Seleucus IV sent his son Demetrius I to Rome as a hostage to replace Seleucus IV's brother, Antiochus IV (Appian *Syr.* 45). Before Antiochus IV's arrival in Syria, Seleucus IV was assassinated by his chief minister Heliodorus, who attempted to seize the throne. However, Antiochus IV ousted Heliodorus and made himself king. Demetrius I remained in Rome as a hostage during the reign of his uncle Antiochus IV. Antiochus IV died insane in Tabae/Gabae, Persia, in spring/summer, 163 B.C., and was succeeded by his nine-year-old son Antiochus V Eupator, who was under the guardianship of Lysias, regent of the western Seleucid empire. Upon hearing of Antiochus IV's death, Demetrius I twice asked the Roman senate to be released and become the king (which was his right) in place of Antiochus V; the senate refused because they preferred a weak ruler to the energetic Demetrius I. With Polybius' help he escaped Rome in early summer, 162 B.C. (Polybius xxi.11.1–15.13; Appian *Syr.* 46-47). Upon arrival in Tripolis, Syria, he learned that Antiochus V and Lysias were not liked; with the support of the Syrian army Demetrius proclaimed himself king, removing his rivals in late summer, 162 B.C. (1 Macc. 7:1-4; 2 Macc. 14:1-2; Josephus *Ant.* xii.10.1; Appian *Syr.* 47; Livy *Epit.* xlvi). When he established himself in Syria he sent monies to Rome in an attempt to placate them (Appian *Syr.* 47; Polybius xxxi.33.5).

Demetrius I confirmed Alcimus as Jewish high priest (162 B.C.) and sent him against the Judeans with an army under his general Bacchides. The Hasidim accepted Alcimus as high priest probably because of his Aaronic descent and the Syrians' guarantee of religious freedom. Thus the Hasidim split from Judas Maccabeus' ranks but quickly returned when Alcimus broke his promise to cause them no evil and slew sixty Hasidim (1 Macc. 7:15-20; Josephus *Ant.* xii.10.2). Alcimus asked Demetrius I for more military aid against Judas and his followers, the Hasideans (2 Macc. 14:6). The king sent Nicanor who was defeated and killed at Adasa (4 mi. [6 km.] N of Jerusalem) on March 9, 161 B.C. (Adar 13, which the Jews celebrate annually as Nicanor's Day), and the army fled to Gazara (20 mi. [32 km.] W of Adasa), where it was wiped out. Alcimus fled to Syria (1 Macc. 7:26-50; Josephus *Ant.* xii.10.3-5). Judas sent for help from Rome, but before it could come, Demetrius I sent Bacchides with Alcimus to avenge Nicanor's death. Because of the might of the Syrian army many deserted Judas, who was slain in the Battle of Elasa (about 10 to 12 mi. [16 to 19 km.] N of Jerusalem; 160 B.C.). Demetrius I was also successful in quelling the insurrection in the eastern provinces led by Timarchus, governor of Babylonia (winter, 161/160 B.C.).

Demetrius I again offended the Romans (159 B.C.) by removing Ariarathes from the throne of Cappadocia and replacing him with Orophernes, one of his own supporters (Appian *Syr.* 47; Polybius iii.5.2). Furthermore, his tyrannical rule alienated his own people. As a result Alexander Balas, who posed as the son of Antiochus IV Epiphanes, captured Ptolemais (Acco) and desired to capture all of the Syrian domain (152 B.C.). Demetrius I sent a letter to Jonathan the brother of Judas Maccabeus, who was now ruling, asking for his support; in return he handed over to Jonathan Jewish hostages held in the citadel (a Syrian garrison within Jerusalem) and permitted him to raise an army. Demetrius also abandoned all fortresses except Beth-zur and the citadel (cf. 1 Macc. 10:14; 11:41). Jonathan exploited the situation, moving his headquarters from Michmash to Jerusalem (1 Macc. 10:1-14; Josephus *Ant.* xiii.2.1). Alexander Balas in turn appointed Jonathan high priest (there had been none since Alcimus' death in May 159 B.C.) and gave him the title "Friend of the King" (1 Macc. 10:15-21; Josephus *Ant.* xiii.2.2). Not to be outdone, Demetrius I offered more promises, viz., exemption from many taxes, surrender of the citadel, attachment of three Samaritan toparchies to Jerusalem, subsidy of the Jewish army and temple, and money for rebuilding the city walls (1 Macc. 10:22-44). The Jews chose to follow Alexander Balas, a strange alliance indeed — Alexander Balas, professed son of Antiochus IV Epiphanes, in league with a Maccabean! After two years of struggle Alexander Balas won. Demetrius I was killed in battle in 150 B.C. when his horse fell in a deep swamp (1 Macc. 10:48-50; Josephus *Ant.* xiii.2.1-4; Appian *Syr.* 67; Polybius iii.5.3; Justinus xxxv.1.8-11).

2. Demetrius II Nicator ("victor") (161-125 B.C.), son of Demetrius I.

Because of the threat posed by Alexander Balas, Demetrius II was sent for safety by his father to Cnidus, a harbor on Cape Krio, the southwestern tip of Asia

Minor adjacent to Rhodes and Cos (Justin xxxv.2). When Alexander Balas' popularity declined Demetrius II, only fourteen years old, arrived in Cilicia with Cretan mercenaries in spring/summer, 147 B.C., three years after his father's death. All of Syria except Judea joined him, so he appointed his general Apollonius as governor of Coele-Syria to subject Judea. However, Apollonius was defeated near Ashdod by the Maccabean Jonathan. Alexander Balas rewarded Jonathan by giving him the city of Ekron and its surrounding area (1 Macc. 10:67-89; Josephus *Ant.* xiii.4.3f.).

Meanwhile Alexander Balas married Cleopatra, daughter of Ptolemy VI. However, when Ptolemy VI discovered Alexander Balas' plot to kill him, he took his daughter Cleopatra from Alexander and gave her to Demetrius II, joining him against Alexander (1 Macc. 11:1f.; Josephus *Ant.* xiii.4.5-7; Diodorus xxxii.27.9c; Livy *Epit.* lii). The combined forces defeated Alexander Balas at the Oenoparos River near Antioch. Ptolemy VI died of wounds received in battle and Demetrius II became king of Syria in 145 B.C. (1 Macc. 11:14-19; Josephus *Ant.* xiii.4.8; Appian *Syr.* 67; Diodorus xxxii.27.9d, 10.1; Livy *Epit.* lii; Strabo xvi.2.8).

Since Demetrius II was sixteen years old and inexperienced, Jonathan took the opportunity to attack the citadel in Jerusalem where the Hellenistic Jews were still in control. Demetrius II demanded that Jonathan withdraw the siege and report to him at Ptolemais. Jonathan boldly ordered his men to continue the siege while he went to Ptolemais with many gifts for Demetrius II. Demetrius II, impressed by his audacity, made him "Friend of the King," confirmed his high priesthood, and granted Jonathan's request of annexation of three districts of Samaria to Judah and exemption from tribute. With Demetrius II weakened by the concessions and the release of his own army since there was peace, Diodotus Trypho (AV Tryphon), a general of Alexander Balas, claimed the Syrian throne for Alexander Balas' son Antiochus VI. With this new threat Demetrius II asked for Jonathan's help. Jonathan agreed to help on the condition that Demetrius II would remove the Syrian garrison in Jerusalem after the war (1 Macc. 11:20-43; Josephus *Ant.* xiii.4.9–5.2). Jonathan's aid enabled Demetrius II to regain Antioch. But Demetrius did not keep his promises to Jonathan. Thus Jonathan sided with Trypho and supported Antiochus VI's claim to the throne. Trypho made Jonathan head of civil and religious affairs and his brother Simon head of the military. However, Trypho, fearful of Jonathan's success, arranged a deceptive meeting whereby Trypho killed Jonathan in 143 B.C. (1 Macc. 11:44–13:24; Josephus *Ant.* xiii.5.3–6.6).

Simon succeeded his brother Jonathan. About a year later (142 B.C.) Trypho killed Antiochus VI and reigned in his stead (1 Macc. 13:31; Josephus *Ant.* xiii.7.1; Diodorus xxxiii.28.1; Livy *Epit.* lv; Appian *Syr.* 68; Justinus xxxv.1.7). Because of Trypho's wicked treachery against Jonathan, Simon attached himself to Demetrius II on the condition of Judea's complete independence. Demetrius II sent a letter confirming that independence. Later Demetrius II went to Media ostensibly to secure help in his war against Trypho. There he was captured and imprisoned by Arsaces VI (Mithradates I) king of Parthia in 140/139 B.C. In Demetrius II's place, his brother Antiochus VII Sidetes took over the struggle against Trypho (1 Macc. 13:33–14:3; Josephus *Ant.* xiii.5.11, 7.1; Appian *Syr.* 67; Justinus xxxvi.1.1-6; xxxviii.9.2).

After ten years of Parthian captivity Demetrius II, then married to Mithradates' sister, was released to Syria to divert his brother Antiochus VII's attack on Parthia. In 128 B.C. Antiochus VII was killed in a battle against the Parthians, and Demetrius II became the sole king for the second time (129-125) B.C. (Josephus *Ant.* xiii.8.4; Appian *Syr.* 67). Shortly thereafter he became involved in a war against Ptolemy VII Physcon of Egypt. Ptolemy VII claimed the Syrian crown for Alexander Zabinas, who was the son of either Alexander Balas or Antiochus VII. Demetrius II was defeated at Damascus and fled to Tyre where in 125 B.C. he was murdered, possibly at the instigation of his erstwhile wife Cleopatra (formerly the wife of Alexander Balas, then of Demetrius II, and later of Antiochus VII) (Josephus *Ant.* xiii.9.3; Appian *Syr.* 68; Livy *Epit.* lx). The confusion of the times is illustrated by the fact that Demetrius ousted Alexander Balas, a pretender of the Seleucid line, later was captured by the Parthians while attempting to defeat Tryphon, Alexander Balas' general and another Seleucid pretender, finally was defeated by a third Syrian pretender, Alexander Zabinas, possibly a son of Alexander Balas!

3. Demetrius III Eukairos ("the timely, prosperous") (95-88 B.C.), son of Antiochus VIII Grypos, who was the second son of Demetrius II and Cleopatra. When Antiochus VIII died in 96 B.C. he was succeeded by his eldest son Seleucus VI Epiphanes Nicator, who in turn was challenged by his cousin Antiochus X, son of Antiochus IX. Subsequently the other four sons of Antiochus VIII, viz., Antiochus XI, Philip, Demetrius III, and Antiochus XII all attempted to wrest the throne from their cousin Antiochus X. Within months after Antiochus VIII's death there were three Seleucid kings, viz., Antiochus X, Philip, and Demetrius III. Shortly thereafter Antiochus X died in battle, so Syria was held by the two brothers, Philip and Demetrius III. Demetrius III, at the encouragement of Egyptian King Ptolemy Lathyrus, left exile in Cnidus and made himself king of central Syria with Damascus as his capital. By 88/87 B.C. he controlled Antioch (Josephus *Ant.* xiii.13.4).

Demetrius III was the last Seleucid to interfere with Jewish affairs. In 94 B.C. Alexander Janneus, ruler of Judea, attacked Obedas, king of the Arabs, but suffered a severe defeat, barely escaping with his life. Upon his return to Jerusalem the people turned against him; with the help of foreign mercenaries Alexander Janneus fought six years against his people, slaying no less than fifty thousand Jews. In 88 B.C. the Pharisees finally called upon Demetrius III to help them. Wars bring strange allies, for the descendants of the Hasidim asked those of Antiochus IV Epiphanes to aid their fight against the descendants of the Maccabees! Alexander Janneus was defeated at Shechem and fled to the mountains. However, six thousand Jews, realizing that their national existence was threatened, sided with Janneus because they felt it better to side with him in a free Jewish state than to be annexed to the Syrian empire. When Alexander Janneus reestablished himself he forced Demetrius III to withdraw. He also ordered eight hundred Pharisees to be crucified and their wives and children killed before their eyes while he was feasting and carousing with his concubines. Because of these atrocities eight thousand Jews fled the country (Josephus *Ant.* xiii.13.5–14.2; *BJ* i.4.4-6).

Upon their return from Judea, war broke out between Demetrius III and his brother Philip. Philip was allied to Strato who ruled the territory of Beroea (60 mi. [97 km.] E of Antioch). Philip was in Beroea when Demetrius III laid siege to that city. Strato and Philip appealed to Aziz, an Arab chief, and to Mithradates I, governor of Parthia. The result was that they besieged the aggressor Demetrius III, who was forced to capitulate when they cut off his water supply. Demetrius III was taken prisoner by Mithradates, but was treated with honor and finally died of an illness. The dates of his reign are difficult to determine but his coins are dated from the Seleucid year 217 to 224, i.e., *ca.* 95-88 B.C. After Demetrius III's defeat his brother Philip conquered Antioch and became the king of Syria.

See also ANTIOCHUS.

Bibliography.–E. R. Bevan, *House of Seleucus,* II (1902), 115-268; E. R. Bevan, *CAH,* VIII (1930), 495-533; S. Tedesche and S. Zeitlin, *First Book of Maccabees* (1950); J. C. Dancy, *Commentary on I Maccabees* (1954); G. Downey, *History of Antioch of Syria* (1962), pp. 119-142; S. Zeitlin, *Rise and Fall of the Judaean State,* I (1962); D. S. Russell, *Jews from Alexander to Herod* (*New Clarendon Bible,* V; 1967); J. R. Bartlett, *First and Second Books of the Maccabees* (*CBC,* 1973); E. Schürer, *HJP*², I, 129-135, 164-208, 223-25.

H. W. HOEHNER

DEMETRIUS (NT).

1. A Christian disciple praised by John (3 Jn. 12).

2. A silversmith of Ephesus who manufactured little silver shrines of the goddess Diana (ARTEMIS) to sell to the visiting pilgrims (Acts 19:23-41). Because Paul's teachings were injuring their trade Demetrius instigated a riot among the silversmiths. An inscription discovered among the city's ruins mentions Demetrius, a warden of the Ephesian temple A.D. 57; some believe him to be identical with the ringleader of the rebellion. The name, however, has been most common among the Greeks of every age. For this reason also one cannot suppose that Demetrius the disciple of 3 Jn. 12 was the silversmith of Ephesus, nor that Demas of 2 Tim. 4:10, who bore the name in a contracted form, is to be identified with either.

E. J. BANKS

DEMETRIUS OF PHALERUM. *See* SEPTUAGINT.

DEMON; DEMONIAC. *See* DEMONOLOGY.

DEMON; DEMONOLOGY.

I. Terminology
II. OT
III. Intertestamental Judaism
IV. NT

I. Terminology.–In the OT, the only term translated "demon" is Heb. *šēḏ* (Dt. 32:17; Ps. 106:37; Albright, p. 240, suggests changing the Masoretic pointing of *laśśîḏ* [RSV "to lime"] in Am. 2:1 to *laššēḏ,* making the verse a very close parallel to Ps. 106:37, a very probable emendation), which is related to the Assyr. *šêdu,* "protecting spirit." The Heb. *śā'îr,* "satyr" (lit. "hairy one"), is always found in the plural (Lev. 17:7; 2 Ch. 11:15 [AV "devils," NEB "demons"]; Isa. 13:24; 34:14 [NEB "he-goats"]). Two specific demonic figures are named, *'ᵃzā'zēl,* "AZAZEL" (Lev. 16:8, 10, 26; NEB "Precipice"; AV "scapegoat"), and *lîlîṯ,* "night hag" (Isa. 34:14; NEB "nightjar"; AV "screech owl" [night birds are occasionally associated with demons]). Several other OT names for demonic figures are more conjectural: *rešep,* "plague" and *deḇer,* "pestilence," are personified as marching before and behind Yahweh (Hab. 3:5; NEB "pestilence" and "plague" respectively; AV "pestilence" and "burning coals"), *'ᵃlûqâ,* "leech" (Prov. 30:15; AV "horseleech"; *'aulaq* is an Arabic name of a vampire who may be named with her two daughters here in the OT), *māweṯ,* "death" (Isa. 28:15, 18; Jer. 9:21 [MT 20]), may also be the name of a demonic figure. Other Hebrew terms that may refer to demonic figures include *ṣiyyim,* "wild beasts" (Isa. 13:21; NEB "marmots"; 23:13; NEB "ships"; 34:14; Jer. 50:39; NEB "marmots"), and *'iyyîm,* "hyenas" (Isa. 13:22; 34:14; Jer. 50:39; NEB "jackals"; AV "wild beasts"), and the Heb. verb *rāḇaṣ,* "lie down," is used of demonic figures in Isa. 13:21 and should be considered part of the OT vocabulary of demonology since it is related to the Assyr. *rabîṣu,* the name of a Babylonian demon (Ringgren, p. 139). Several more general and less problematic terms must be considered as integral elements of the OT vocabulary of demonology. The term *'ᵉlōhîm,* "god," while normally referring to Yahweh or the god(s) of the nations, may also refer to a deceased person, as in 1 S. 28:13 it refers to the shade of Samuel. Several times the expression *rû(a)ḥ-'ᵉlōhîm ra'â,* "evil spirit from God," is found (1 S. 16:15f., 23; 18:10; 19:9; 1 K. 22:21; LXX *pneúma* [*kyríou*] *ponērón*); a related expression is *rû(a)ḥ šeqer,* "lying spirit" (1 K. 22:21-23; 2 Ch. 18:20-23). The term *mašḥîṯ,* "destroyer" (Ex. 12:23), is probably a term for a demonic figure (Ringgren, p. 187), as in the expression *mal'ᵃḵe-rā'îm,* "destroying angels" (Ps. 78:49; NEB "messengers of evil"; AV "evil angels"). Further, the term *'ᵉlîlîm,* "idols" (Ps. 96:5), is translated *daimónia,* "demons," in the LXX.

In the NT the Gk. *daimónion,* "demon," is the most common term for demonic figures, occuring sixty-three times. Surprisingly, the common Gk. term *daímōn,* "demon," is found in the NT only in Mt. 8:31. The cognate terms *daimoniṓdēs,* "devilish" (Jas. 3:15; NEB "demonic"), and *daimonízomai,* "be possessed by a demon," "[be a] demoniac" (Mt. 4:24; 8:16 par. Mk. 1:32; Mt. 8:28, 33; 9:32; 12:22; 15:22; Mk. 5:15f., 18; Lk. 8:36), also occur. The term *pneúma,* "spirit," is essentially a neutral word, but is frequently applied to evil spirits; cf. Mt. 8:16; 9:33; Lk. 9:39; 10:20; Acts 16:18; 1 Cor. 12:3; 1 Jn. 4:1-3; 1 Pet. 3:19 (this last reference may be to fallen angels as *pneúmata*). In the vast majority of instances, however, *pneúma* or *pneúmata* are qualified to refer specifically to demons: *pneúma akátharton,* "unclean spirit" (Mt. 10:1 par. Mk. 6:7; Mt. 12:43 par. Lk. 11:24; Mk. 1:23, 26f. par. Lk. 4:35; Mk. 3:11, 30; 5:2, 8 par. Lk. 8:29; Mk. 7:25; 9:25 par. Lk. 9:42; Lk. 6:18; Acts 5:16; 8:7; Rev. 16:13; 18:2), *pneúma ponērón,* "evil spirit" (Mt. 12:45 par Lk. 11:26; Lk. 7:21; 8:2; Acts 19:12f., 15f.), *pneúmata planá,* "deceitful spirits" (1 Tim. 4:1; NEB "devils"; AV "seducing spirits"), *tó pneúma tḗs plánēs,* "the spirit of error" (1 Jn. 4:6), *pneúma astheneías,* "spirit of infirmity" (Lk. 13:11; NEB "spirit that had crippled"; the demonic nature of this *pneúma* is made clear by the expression in Lk. 8:2, *pneumátōn ponērṓn kaí astheneiṓn,* "evil spirits and infirmities"), *pneúma álalon,* "dumb spirit" (Mk. 9:17; NEB "spirit which makes him speechless"; the same demon is described in Mk. 9:25 as *tó álalon kaí kōphón pneúma,* "dumb and deaf spirit"), *pneúma pýthōna,* "spirit of divinaticn" (Acts 16:16; NEB "oracular spirit"), *pneúmata daimoniōn,* "demonic spirits" (Rev. 16:14; NEB "these spirits were devils"; AV "spirits of devils"), *pneúma toú kosmoú,* "spirit of the world" (1 Cor. 2:12; cf. the expression *hó theós toú aiṓnos toútou,* "the god of this world" in 2 Cor. 4:4; NEB "the god of this passing age"), *pneúma daimoníou akathártou,* "the spirit of an unclean demon" (Lk. 4:33; NEB "a devil, an unclean spirit"; AV "a spirit of an unclean devil").

II. OT.–The Hebrew of the OT, as the other Semitic languages of the ancient Near East, had no single, comprehensive term for demonic figures as did the ancient Greeks. The variety of OT terms listed above indicates that, while demonic figures were undoubtedly an aspect of ancient Israelite religious beliefs, no consistent demonology can be found in the OT. While the existence of malevolent supernatural beings is never questioned, the ancient Israelite notion of Yahweh's sovereignty did not encourage or necessitate the development of religious thought in this area. OT angelology, in contrast to demonology, is rather highly developed, for the vast multitude of angels or spirits served God and did His bidding. In the OT, demonic figures are not evil by nature, but rather in their effect on mankind. In the history of Israel, apparently the gradual increase in concern with the problem of evil produced a more concentrated focus on the function of malevolent supernatural beings. Demonological thought in the OT is in an inchoate state, yet most of the elements that were later emphasized in intertestamental Judaism and in early Christianity appear to be present.

In the OT both good and evil were thought to come from Yahweh, the creator and sustainer of all things. "Lying spirits" did not act on their own volition but were sent by God (1 K. 22:21-23 par. 2 Ch. 18:20-23), as were the "evil spirit" that tormented Saul (1 S. 16:15f., 23) and the destroying angel that slew the Egyptian firstborn (Ex. 12:23; cf. Ps. 78:49). Even Satan (mentioned only in Job, Zechariah, and 1 Chronicles) is nowhere claimed to be inherently evil, but rather acts only under divine authority (Job 1:11-13; 2:5f.; note that Satan's tormenting of Job is viewed as a "putting forth" of God's hand). As an important OT demonic figure, Satan functions as an accuser of men before God (Job 1:9-11; 2:4f.; Zech. 3:1) and as one who tempts men to sin (in Gen. 4:7, sin is personified as a demonic figure "couching at the door"). In OT folk medicine, as in the ancient Near East and postbiblical Judaism generally, demons were thought to play an important role in the transmission of disease (2 S. 24:15-17; 2 K. 19:35; Job 2:7; cf. Albright, p. 180). In Lev. 14:2-9, skin disease is apparently thought to be caused by a demon that must be frightened away by a red heifer (R. de Vaux, *Ancient Israel* [Eng. tr. 1961], p. 463). This notion continues on into the NT era in the expression "spirit of infirmity" (Lk. 8:2; 13:11); the crippled woman whose healing is narrated in Lk. 13:10-17 is described as having been "bound by Satan" for eighteen years (v. 16). In the OT at least two probable terms for demonic figures, *rešep̱* and *deḇer* (Hab. 3:5), are closely connected with illness and disease.

Demons were closely associated with arid and unsettled regions. On the Day of Atonement one of the sacrificial goats was sent out into the wilderness to Azazel, probably a demon of the desert (Lev. 16:8, 10, 26). Similarly, demonic figures such as "satyrs," "wild beasts," and "hyenas" (Lev. 17:7; 2 Ch. 11:15; Isa. 13:21f.; 34:14; Jer. 50:39) are closely associated with the wilderness. The "night hag" of Isa. 34:14 is said to have inhabited ruins. The notion that demons are at home in arid regions is found also in the NT (Mt. 12:43), making appropriate the scene of Jesus' temptation in the wilderness (Mk. 1:12f. par. Mt. 4:1-11; Lk. 4:1-13; note that Mk. 1:13 alone mentions "wild beasts," a possible reference to demonic forces).

Finally, while ancient Israelites apparently had no widespread fear of demons and their malevolent influences, many references suggest that demonic figures were worshiped and received sacrifices (Dt. 32:17; Ps. 106:37; Lev. 17:7; 2 Ch. 11:15). This practice is reflected in the use of the Greek word for "demons" in the LXX rendition of the Hebrew term for "idols" in Ps. 96:5.

Similar practice is reflected also in early Christianity (cf. 2 Cor. 10:20).

III. Intertestamental Judaism.–In the postexilic era, foreign domination and oppression appear to have been major factors in stimulating Jewish religious thought to focus on the problem and the origin of evil. Evil began to be traced increasingly, not directly to Yahweh Himself, but rather to supernatural beings who had rebelled against God sometime in the primeval past. While the OT had tacitly assumed that God Himself had created all beings, both mortal and immortal, that view was first made explicit in the intertestamental period. Jub. 2:2 states that on the first day of creation God made "all the spirits which serve before him" in addition to the heavens above and the earth and waters beneath. According to a late mishnaic tradition God created the evil spirits [*mazziḵîm*] on Friday of the creation week (*Aboth* v.6). Two major traditions in Judaism were used to account for the existence of malevolent supernatural beings. The more popular focused on Gen. 6:1-4, which was interpreted as narrating the fall of angelic beings who through unbridled lust had mated with mortal women (Jub. 4:15-22; 1 En. 69:4; 106:13-17; 2 Bar. 56:12, CD 2:18). Though these fallen angels were thought to have been imprisoned by God until the day of judgment, their offspring, the "giants" of Gen. 1:4, were thought to be the demons or evil spirits that thereafter oppressed mankind (1 En. 15:8-10; 16:1; 19:1; cf. Athenagoras *Supplicatio* 25:1). Their malevolent role is comprehensively described in 1 En. 15:11, where they are said to "afflict, oppress, destroy, attack, do battle, and work destruction on the earth, and cause trouble" (*APOT*). In yet another intertestamental Jewish tradition, the fallen angels themselves are identified with demons and evil spirits, and their fall is frequently described as occurring prior to creation (1 En. 69:1-15). Philo of Alexandria identified the angels of Gen. 6:1-4 with "demons" (*De gigantibus* 6), noting

Inscribed bronze statue of the Babylonian demon Pazuzu. The figure has the feet and wings of an eagle, a human body with claws for hands, and a misshapen head. (Archives Photographiques)

Fragment from an amulet for the exorcism of a lion-headed demon. From the time of Nebuchadrezzar (605-562 B.C.) (Metropolitan Museum of Art)

Exorcism amulet. Each of the seven demons at the top has a different animal head. The horned, lion-headed figure in the lower center is Lamashtu, a fierce female demon. (Louvre; photo Éditions "TEL," Paris)

that the Gk. term *daímōn* can be given to both good and bad "demons" alike (*De gigantibus* 16). Generally, the precreation accounts of the revolt of the angels of God make one such being the primary cause of the rebellion. This leader is called many names, including Mastema (Jub. 10:8-10; 11:5, 11; 49:2; 17:16; 18:9, 12; 48:1-15), Satanael (2 En. 18:3; 29:4; 31:4), Satan (Jub. 10:11; Adam and Eve 9:1; Apoc. Mos. 17:1; 1 En. 40:7; 54:6), Samael (CD 16:5), Beliar/Belial (T. Dan 5:1; Mart. Isa. 1:8f.; 2:4; 3:11; Sib. Or. iii.63; CD 5:18; 1QS 2:5), and Devil (Adam and Eve 10:2; 11:1; 12:1; 13:1; Apoc. Mos. 15:3; 16:1, 5). In one account the fall of Satan is attributed to his refusing to worship Adam, the image of God, at the express command of God (Adam and Eve 12:1–16:4).

Whether demons are thought of as fallen angels or as the offspring of fallen angels and mortal women, it is they, together with their leader, to whom most of the evils experienced by mankind are attributed. Terminologically they have a variety of designations, many of which recur in the NT: "demons" (1 En. 19:1; 69:12; 99:7; Jub. 10:1; Tob. 3:8, 17; 6:7, 13-15, 17; 8:3; Bar. 4:7, 35), "spirits" (Jub. 10:5, 8; 11:5; 19:28; 1 En. 15:10-12; 16:1; 19:1; 69:12; T. Dan 6:1), "unclean/evil spirits" (1 En. 99:7; 15:8f.; Tob. 6:7). The subjection of these demonic figures to a single infernal leader or prince is indicated by such phrases as "spirits of Beliar" (T. Dan 1:7; T. Jos. 7:4; T. Benj. 3:3; T. Iss. 7:7), "angels of Satan" (T. Ash. 6:4), "Satan and his spirits" (T. Dan 6:1), and "angels of dominion of Belial" (1QM 1:15).

In postbiblical Judaism Satan was still regarded as subject to God's dominion (Jub. 10:4-13), even though he and his minions enjoyed a degree of freedom till the day of judgment. In response to the prayer of Noah in Jub. 10, God imprisoned nine-tenths of the demons plaguing mankind, yet allowed one-tenth to continue their evil work at the pleading of their leader Mastema or Satan. The function of these demons in the experience of mankind is similar to their role in the OT, except that the authors of the apocryphal and pseudepigraphal writings show a much greater preoccupation with the reality and influence of demonic beings. In intertestamental Judaism demons appear to function in four primary ways: (1) they cause and transmit disease among men (Jub. 10:10-13); (2) they accuse men who dwell on the earth (1 En. 40:7); (3) they act as agents of divine punishment (1 En. 53:3; 56:1; 62:11; 63:1); and (4) they tempt men to sin (1 En. 69:6). In the book of Tobit, which contains one of Judaism's earliest accounts of demonic affliction and exorcism, the evil demon Asmodaeus (from Pers. *aësma daëva,* "evil demon") afflicts Sarah the daughter of Raguel to the extent that each of her seven successive fiancés dies on his wedding night. On Tobias' wedding night he performs a magical ceremony of exorcism involving the burning of the heart and liver of a fish. Asmodaeus is instantly exorcized and flees to the "remotest parts of Egypt" where the angel Raphael binds him (Tob. 8:2f.). This example of exorcism in postbiblical Judaism is an instance of one way in which demonic influences on mankind were popularly thought to be eliminated.

In the literature of rabbinic Judaism, codified beginning

with the 2nd cent. A.D. though often retaining earlier traditions, a rather elaborate demonology is developed, though in a markedly unsystematic fashion. Demons are viewed primarily as enemies of mankind who inflict harm through illness and disease; only occasionally are demonic figures regarded as benevolent. The earlier rabbinic traditions codified in the Mishnah (late 2nd cent. A.D.) contain but a single (late) reference to demons in *Aboth* v.6. The legal nature of mishnaic traditions at least partially accounts for the paucity of references to rabbinic demonology. References to demons become more prominent in the Jerusalem Talmud, and even more so in the Palestinian midrashim. Demonology pervades the Babylonian Talmud, probably reflecting the influence of pagan Babylonian demonology. Corresponding to native Babylonian traditions, three classes of demons were thought to exist, the *mazziḵîm,* the *šēḏîm,* and the *rûḥoṯ*; it is difficult, however, if not impossible to differentiate these classes precisely (Blau, p. 14). The number of demons was thought to be astronomical; in *Berakoth* 6a, for example, demons are said to be so numerous that if one could see them one would be terribly frightened. They were thought to inhabit the air, various kinds of trees (especially the palm), plants, rocks, niches, and waste areas (*Berakoth* 3a). In nature, they share some attributes of angels and some of mankind (Goldin, p. 153). They were thought to be powerless on the eve of Passover (*Pesahim* 109b-110b). In general, it may be stated that the belief in demons and their effect upon mankind increased in Judaism from A.D. 150 to 450.

Demonic possession as a cause of disease appears to have been a relatively uncommon belief in Palestine during the 1st cent. A.D. (Blau, p. 23). While this judgment is based on the silence of the Mishnah and other Tannaitic traditions, it is partially confirmed by the general distinction in the NT between illness and demon possession. That demon exorcism was practiced in first-century Palestine by Jews is clear from such NT references as Mk. 9:38f.; Mt. 12:27 par. Lk. 11:19; Acts 19:13-17. The first-century Jewish historian Josephus describes the technique of a contemporary exorcist named Eleazar (*Ant.* viii.2.5). A first-century Galilean rabbi, Ḥanina ben Dosa, reportedly restrained the queen of the demons herself, Agrat bat Mahalat (SB, IV, 534f.). The texts of several Jewish exorcistic formulas have apparently been preserved in *Papyri Graecae Magicae,* IV, nos. 3007-3086 (Eitrem, pp. 15-30; Knox).

IV. NT.–In continuity with intertestamental Judaism, Jesus and early Christians regarded demons as very real and very powerful adversaries of man. In contrast to the Greek understanding of the terms *daímōn* and *daimónion* as spiritual beings, some of which were malevolent and others benevolent (Philo *De gigantibus* 6), in the NT and early Christianity generally demons are always regarded as evil spirits. This viewpoint is made clear through the frequent use of such terms as "evil spirits," "unclean spirits," and "deceitful spirits" as interchangeable with "demons." In the NT the primary function of demons is the possession and control of human beings upon whom they effect a variety of malevolent influences. In a few instances *daimónion* is applied to pagan deities venerated through images (Acts 17:18; 1 Cor. 10:20f.; Rev. 9:20). This view, also reflected in the OT (Dt. 32:17; Ps. 106:37; Lev. 17:7; 2 Ch. 11:15), was increasingly emphasized by early Christian apologists of the 2nd and 3rd cents. A.D. (Justin *Apol.* i.5; Minucius Felix *Octavius* 27; Athenagoras *Supplicatio* 26.1-5; Theophilus *Ad Autolycum* i.10; Tatian *Oratio ad Graecos* 16-19; Tertullian *Apol.* 20; *De spectaculis* 13; Origen *Contra Celsum* vii.69; Cyprian *Ad Fortunatum* 7). The gods worshiped by pagans are viewed, not as nonexistent, but rather as demons masquerading as traditional pagan divinities. Occasionally the term *daimónion* is used of evil spirits in general (Jas. 2:19).

In general, the Gospels carefully differentiate between sickness and demon possession (Eitrem, pp. 34f.). In Lk. 13:32 Jesus describes His ministry in terms of casting out demons and performing cures. In the Markan summaries of Jesus' activities, His ministry of healing the ill is carefully differentiated from His performance of exorcisms (Mk. 1:32-34 par. Mt. 8:16 par. Lk. 4:40f.; Mk. 1:39 par. Mt. 4:24; Mk. 3:10f. par. Lk. 6:17f.). In one miracle story, however, the healing of the woman with a spirit of infirmity (Lk. 13:10-17), the "spirit of infirmity" (*pneúma astheneías,* v. 11) that was the cause of the woman's curvature of the spine is more specifically described as a binding by Satan (v. 16). Here illness appears to have a demonic cause.

The Gospels contain six accounts of Jesus exorcizing demons from afflicted individuals: (1) the demoniac in the synagogue (Mk. 1:23 par. Lk. 4:33-36), (2) the Gerasene demoniac (Mk. 5:1-20 par. Mt. 8:28-34 par. Lk. 8:26-39), (3) the daughter of the Syrophoenician woman (Mk. 7:24-30 par. Mt. 15:21-28), (4) the epileptic lad (Mk. 9:14-29 par. Mt. 17:14-21 par. Lk. 9:37-43), (5) the dumb demoniac (Mt. 9:32-34), and (6) the blind and dumb demoniac (Mt. 12:22f. par. Lk. 11:15). The healing of the woman with a spirit of infirmity (Lk. 13:10-17), if considered an exorcism, may be added to this list. Further, an exorcism twice mentioned but never narrated concerns Mary Magdalene, who had been delivered from seven demons (Lk. 8:2; Mk. 16:9). Although the Gospels allude several times to the practice of demonic exorcism by Jesus' disciples (Mk. 3:14f.; Mk. 6:7 par. Mt. 10:1 par. Lk. 9:1; Lk. 10:17-20; Mk. 16:17f.; Mk. 9:18, 28 par. Mt. 17:16, 19 par. Lk. 9:40), the only specific instance of a NT exorcism not performed by Jesus is that attributed to Paul in Acts 16:16-18, in which a "spirit of divination" is cast out of a slave girl.

Based on these NT reports of demonic possession, the symptoms of demonic possession include: (1) insane raving (Mk. 1:24; 5:5; Lk. 9:39; cf. Jn. 10:20); (2) self-destructive behavior (Mk. 5:5; 9:18 par. Mt. 17:15; cf. Mk. 5:13 par. Mt. 8:32 par. Lk. 8:33); (3) the antisocial behavior of nudity (Lk. 8:35); (4) seizures (Mk. 1:26; 9:18, 20, 26 par. Mt. 17:15); (5) dumbness (Mk. 9:25, 32; 12:22 par. Lk. 11:14); (6) deafness (Mk. 9:25); (7) blindness (Mt. 12:22); and (8) performance of the involuntary function of spirit mediumship (Acts 16:16-18; cf. Mk. 1:24 par. Lk. 4:33f.; Mk. 5:7 par. Mt. 8:29 par. Lk. 8:28). In contrast to the elaborate exorcistic formulas used by Jewish and pagan magicians and exorcists, Jesus' exorcistic technique was a simple word of command, such as "Be silent and come out of him!" (Mk. 1:25), "Come out of the man, you unclean spirit" (Mk. 5:8), or "You dumb and deaf spirit, I command you, come out of him, and never enter him again" (Mk. 9:25). Jesus did not regard exorcism in itself as a sure cure unless the evil spirit was replaced with something better (Mt. 12:43-45 par. Lk. 11:24-26). Jesus' ministry of exorcism was not an end in itself, nor was it motivated solely by His compassion for the afflicted individuals whom He rescued from demonic possession. The statement in Lk. 11:20 par. Mt. 12:28 makes it clear that Jesus regarded His exorcisms as an indication that the kingdom of God was breaking into present human experience: "If it is by the finger [Mt.: "Spirit"] of God that I cast out demons, then the kingdom of God has come upon you." Considered as a whole, the ministry of Jesus was regarded in the NT as a conquest or exorcism of Satan (Lk. 10:18; Jn. 12:31; cf. 1 Jn. 3:8). The OT knew but one exorcist, David (1 S. 16:13-23), and in Jewish tradition Solomon the son of David ruled over the demons and was an expert exorcist (*Pesikta Rabbathi* 69a; Josephus *Ant.* viii.2.5). Since there is evidence that some strands of Jewish belief looked forward to the eschatological removal of the unclean spirit from man (Zec. 13:2; 1QS 4:19-21; 1QM 14:10), these traditions combine to indicate that Jesus as son of David (= Solomon) expelled demons as part of His role as Messiah (cf. L. R. Fisher, in *Jesus and the Historian*, F. T. Trotter, ed. [1968], pp. 82-97; K. Berger, *NTS*, 20 [1973/74], 3-9).

Some opponents of John the Baptist accused him of being demon-possessed (Mt. 11:18 par. Lk. 7:33), and a similar charge was leveled against Jesus (Jn. 7:20; 8:48-53; 10:20f.). Jewish religious leaders who were antagonists of Jesus even accused Him of being possessed by Beelzebul, the prince of the demons (Mk. 3:22 par. Mt. 12:24 par. Lk. 11:15). In essence, these accusations are indirect claims that Jesus was a magician or sorcerer, and that by His control of powerful supernatural forces He was enabled to perform miracles of healing and exorcism (Samain). Jesus' lingering reputation as a sorcerer in the literature of rabbinic Judaism (Klausner, pp. 18-47) and among Greco-Roman pagans (Origen *Contra Celsum* i.6, 28, 38, 68; ii.9, 14, 16, 48) confirms the historicity of His ministry of healing and exorcism. In another important passage, Mk. 6:14-16, apparently some of the common people of Jesus' time, together with Herod, thought that "Jesus was using the spirit of John brought back from the dead to perform his miracles for him" (Kraeling, p. 155). This notion apparently conforms to the Jewish and Greco-Roman notion that some demons were souls of the dead (Josephus *BJ* vii.6.3; *Sanhedrin* 109a).

While Jesus Himself used no formulas to exorcise demons from afflicted individuals, His disciples used Jesus' name to effect their exorcisms (Lk. 10:17; Acts 16:18). The name of Jesus was such an effective tool in controlling demons that Jewish exorcists not in Jesus' company began to use it as an exorcistic formula (Mk. 9:38 par. Lk. 9:49; Acts 19:13). The use of Jesus' name for this purpose even appears in pagan exorcisms (*Papyrus Graecae Magicae,* IV, 1234, 3019f.), and in the 3rd cent. A.D. Origen observes that "mean exorcists" succeed only when uttering the name of Jesus (*Contra Celsum* i.6; ii.4). During the 2nd cent. A.D. the relatively simple exorcistic and healing formula "in the name of Jesus" became elaborated into a recitation that included some of the basic elements of the life of Jesus. Exorcisms were performed "in the name of Jesus Christ, crucified under Pontius Pilate" (Justin *Dial.* 30.3; 76.6; 85.2; *Apol.* ii.6.6; Irenaeus *Adv. haer.* ii.49.3: *in nomine Christi Jesu crucifixi sub Pontio Pilato*). During the late NT era and particularly during the 2nd cent. A.D. the chief obstacle to man's salvation was thought to be the demonic powers controlled by Satan, the prince of demons. Exorcistic formulas found their way into baptismal liturgies, and those who experienced that rite were thought to have been freed from demonic powers and influence (Böcher, pp. 170-180).

Apart from the Gospels and Acts, the NT has relatively little to say about demons and their role. The term *daimónion,* which occurs sixty-three times in the NT, is found only nine times outside of the Gospels and Acts. In 1 Cor. 10:20-22, where the term occurs four times, demons are regarded as the malevolent supernatural beings to whom men sacrifice and give worship (cf. Rev. 9:20). Life prior to faith in Christ is described by Paul as bondage to the "elemental spirits of the universe" (Gal. 4:3, 9), and since Gal. 4:8 makes it clear that the Galatians had previously been worshipers of idols, he may well be referring to demonic beings. Certainly in Rom. 8:38f. the principalities and powers (cf. Eph. 6:12) appear to be demonic forces hostile to God who are unable to frustrate His redemptive purposes. Evil spirits are also thought to instigate error (Rev. 16:13f.; 1 Jn. 4:1-3), particularly through false prophets (Mk. 13:22; Mt. 24:11, 24; 1 Jn. 4:1) who lead men astray. Jude 6 and 2 Pet. 2:4 refer to the fallen angels who have been restrained until the Day of Judgment (cf. 1 Pet. 3:19f.), but these are nowhere in the NT regarded as demonic beings. In general, NT demonology presupposes those views that had developed from OT traditions during the intertestamental period.

See also EXORCISM; MEDIUM; BEELZEBUL.

Bibliography.–W. F. Albright, *Yahweh and the Gods of Canaan* (1969); L. Blau, *Das altjüdische Zauberwesen* (1898); O. Böcher, *Christus Exorcista* (1972); S. Eitrem, *Some Notes on the Demonology in the NT* (2nd ed. 1966); J. Goldin, ed., *The Fathers According to Rabbi Nathan* (1974); F. Heitmüller, *Engel und Dämonen: Eine Bibelstudie* (1948); J. Klausner, *Jesus of Nazareth* (1925); W. L. Knox, *HTR,* 31 (1938), 191-203; C. H. Kraeling, *JBL,* 59 (1940), 147-157; E. Langton, *Essentials of Demonology* (1949); *Good and Evil Spirits* (1942); *Papyri Graecae Magicae. Die griechischen Zauberpapyri,* K. Preisendanz and A. Henrichs, eds. (2 vols., 2nd ed. 1973-1974); H. Ringgren, *Israelite Religion* (1966); P. Samain, *Ephermerides theologiae Lovanienses,* 15 (1938), 449-490; M. Ziegler, *Engel und Dämon im Lichte der Bibel* (1957).

D. E. AUNE

DEMOPHON dem'ə-fon [Gk. *Dēmophōn*]. A Syrian general in Palestine under Antiochus V (Eupator) who continued to harass the Jews after covenants had been made between Lysias and Judas Maccabeus (2 Macc. 12:2).

DEN. *See* CAVE.

DENARIUS də-när'ē-əs [Gk. *dēnárion*]; AV PENNY, PENCE, PENNYWORTH; NEB "a whole day's wage," or modern equivalents at 10 denarii per British pound; at Mt. 22:19 par. the RSV has "coin," the NEB "silver piece." A Roman silver coin equal to 1/25 aureus, the aureus being the standard gold coin of the empire at the time of Augustus. The denarius was the ordinary wage of a soldier or day laborer (cf. Mt. 20:1-16). *See* MONEY.

DENOUNCE [Heb. *zā'am*] (Nu. 23:7f.); AV DEFY; [*nāgaḏ*] (Jer. 20:10); AV REPORT; [Gk. *blasphēméō*] (1 Cor. 10:30); AV "speak evil of"; NEB BLAME. Heb. *zā'am* can mean either "express indignation" or "curse," while Gk. *blasphēméō,* when used in relation to other human beings, means "defame." Heb. *nāgaḏ* generally means "tell" or "declare." In Dt. 30:18 the AV translates "denounce" in the archaic sense of "declare solemnly"; however, the RSV rendering accurately conveys the meaning "expose" or "condemn" in Jer. 20:10.

N. J. O.

DEPART [Heb. *hālaḵ*] (Ps. 39:13 [MT 14], NEB "go away"; Isa. 38:10, AV "cutting off my days"; NEB "pass away"); **DEPARTURE** [Gk. *éxodus*] (Lk. 9:31; 2 Pet. 1:15 AV "decease"; NEB "be gone"; cf. Wisd. 3:2; 7:6); [*análysis*] (2 Tim. 4:6); [*áphixis*] (Acts 20:29). Euphemistic expressions for death, indicating its sharp distinction from all aspects of earthly life. *See* DEATH III.

DEPENDENT [Gk. *échō chreían*–'have need'] (1 Thess. 4:12); AV "have lack"; NEB "be in want." The RSV understands the negative object as personal, "be dependent on nobody"; the AV as impersonal, "have lack of nothing"; while the NEB resorts to a change of idiom, "never be in want."

Though the gender of the negative object cannot be determined exactly, the meaning of the passage is the same — Paul encourages believers to work diligently and to conduct their personal affairs honestly, so that they will be seen as productive persons rather than as those dependent on others, looking for a handout.

G. E. MONTGOMERY

DEPENDENTS [Heb. *ṭap̱*] (Gen. 47:12); AV FAMILIES; NEB "all they needed." *See* RELATIONSHIPS, FAMILY.

DEPORTATION (Mt. 1:11f., 17). *See* CAPTIVITY.

DEPOSIT [Heb. *piqqāḏôn*]. Personal property placed in the care of another for safekeeping. Laws regarding such practice indicate the trust was bound by oath, with the holder financially responsible for the goods (Lev. 6:1-7 [MT 5:20-26]). In Ex. 22:7-13 (MT 6-12) the laws of trusteeship distinguish the deposit as money, goods, or animals (cf. Code of Hammurabi, *ANET*, p. 171; Josephus *Ant.* iv.8.38).

In later times orphans and widows, as well as people of rank, entrusted their property to the sanctity and inviolability of the Temple (2 Macc. 3:10-15). Such deposits may have been reserves for times of need (2 Macc. 3:10, AV; cf. Gen. 41:36).

In the NT the disciples were given the gospel as a deposit ("what has been entrusted to you"; Gk. *parakathḗkē*; *parathḗkē*; 1 Tim. 6:20; 2 Tim. 1:12, 14) for faithful proclamation and teaching (*see* ENTRUST).

Although the term "deposit" is not specified, movable property was given as security for a debt (*see* PLEDGE).

See also ENTRUST. A. C. M.

DEPRAVED [Heb. *'ālaḥ*] (Ps. 53:3 [MT 4]); AV FILTHY; NEB "rotten to the core"; cf. use in Ps. 14:3; Job 15:16; [Gk. *diaphtheírō*] (1 Tim. 6:5); AV CORRUPT; NEB ATROPHIED. A corruption of man's nature that accompanies (1) the denial of God's existence, the failure to seek God, and the complete absence of all goodness (Ps. 14:3, "corrupt"; 53:3); (2) the failure to recognize one's sin in contrast to God's holiness (Job 15:16, "corrupt"); or (3) the departure from apostolic teaching, being robbed of all truth, so that only false values, ungodliness, and constant wranglings ensue.

The OT term centers in each context, as does the NT term in 1 Tim. 6:5, upon the man whose mind is absolutely contrary to that of God. A mind so adverse to God's mind is considered destroyed, corrupt, deprived of truth apparently by a refusal to follow the teaching of the Lord. This results in a commercializing of godliness, and is accompanied by constant arguing over minor details. In contrast, godliness is described in 1 Tim. 6:11 as including righteousness, faith, love, etc. Other NT uses of the term include destruction of material by moths (Lk. 12:33); ships destroyed in judgment (Rev. 8:9); the wasting away or decay of the outer man (2 Cor. 4:16); and the final destruction of the destroyers of the earth (Rev. 11:18).

In the history of theology mankind's depravity has been interpreted as coming from Adam. Augustine, credited with formulating the concept of original sin, held that Adam's fall corrupted man, making the human race a mass of sin. Man inherited both the tendency to sin and the guilt for Adam's sin, for in him the entire race sinned. According to the Arminians Adam's sin was transmitted to humanity through the natural laws of heredity. However, man's propensity for sin does not of itself imply guilt, which results from actual sin, the product of voluntary transgression. Calvin held that Adam's sin was immediately imputed to all mankind. As the representative head of the human family, Adam, through his first sin, made all men depraved and actually guilty. By contrast, Pelagianism denied any necessary connection between Adam's sin and the subsequent character and actions of his descendants, whose depravity is the result solely of each individual's choice of sin. The Heidelberg Catechism (Question 10) makes a comprehensive statement, contending that God's punishment is directed at "our original as well as actual sins." The degree of depravity has been understood over a range from complete inability to move toward God unless divine aid is received to no depravity at all. According to the Protestant Reformers, total depravity, the effect of original sin upon mankind, implies not mankind's total evilness but the pervasive influence of the power of sin upon all aspects of mankind. The importance that regeneration is given in salvation is often related to the degree of depravity that man is viewed to have suffered.

Bibliography.–MSt, IX, *s.v.* "Sin"; *Twentieth Century Encyclopedia of Religious Knowledge* (1955), *s.v.* "Depravity" (J. Murray); "Man, Doctrine of" (E. Liggitt); *BDTh, s.v.* "Depravity, Total" (C. C. Ryrie). R. J. HUGHES, III

A. C. M.

DEPTHS. *See* DEEP.

DEPUTY [Heb. *niṣṣāḇ*] (1 K. 22:47); NEB VICEROY; [*sāgān*] (Jer. 51:28); AV RULER; NEB GOVERNOR. The literal meaning of the participle *niṣṣāḇ* is "someone set in place" or "appointed," here probably by Jehoshaphat of Judah, to whom Edom was vassal. The RSV "deputies" in Jer. 51:28 deviates from the usual rendering "commanders" in similar phrases (51:23, 57; Ezk. 23:6, 12, 23).

See also GOVERNOR; PROCONSUL.

DERBE dûr'bē [Gk. *Derbēs*]. A place mentioned in the NT in connection with Paul's missionary journeys through south-central Asia Minor. Luke reports that on his first missionary journey Paul went from Lystra to Derbe, and after preaching the gospel and making many disciples in that city he returned to Lystra (Acts 14:20f.). Luke identifies Lystra and Derbe as cities of Lycaonia (Acts 14:6). Paul revisited Derbe on his second missionary journey (16:1) and it is possible that he also passed through Derbe at the beginning of his third missionary journey (18:23). A disciple and companion of Paul from Derbe is mentioned in Acts 20:4.

It was not until about the end of the 19th cent. that a location for Derbe in the vicinity of Gudelisin was suggested by J. R. Sitlington Sterrett. Shortly after that, W. M. Ramsay (*Cities of St. Paul* [1907], pp. 393-97) advanced the theory that the mound of Gudelisin was the site of Derbe. He based this theory primarily on inferential evidence, not having any epigraphic or extensive archeological evidence. Nevertheless, this has been the accepted location for Derbe for the last fifty years.

However, recently discovered evidence, in the form of two inscriptions, has fairly positively identified the mound of Kerti Hüyük as the site of Derbe. Kerti Hüyük is about 30 mi. (50 km.) E of the area suggested by Ramsay as the territory of Derbe. It is a sizable mound located about 15 mi. (25 km.) NNE of Karaman (ancient Laranda), which is about 60 mi. (100 km.) SE of Konya (ancient Iconium).

The first inscription was discovered at Kerti Hüyük in

Mound of Kerti Hüyük, identified as ancient Derbe. Paul visited the city on his first missionary journey. (B. VanElderen)

Fourth-century A.D. inscription that was instrumental in identifying the site of Derbe. It refers to the "most beloved of God, Michael, bishop of Derbe." (B. VanElderen)

1956 by Michael Ballance (*Anatolian Studies*, 7 [1957], 147-151). It is a dedication by the council and people of Derbe and can be dated in A.D. 157. The inscription is now housed in the Museum of Classical Antiquities in Konya.

The second inscription was discovered in 1962 in the village of Suduraya, having been brought there by the natives from Kerti Hüyük. On the basis of the dateline and paleography the stone can be dated in the last quarter of the 4th century. The inscription is the tombstone of a bishop of Derbe named Michael.

In the light of the foregoing evidence, the new site for Derbe is convincingly established. Further exploration and possible excavation should increase our knowledge of this new site. This new location suggests that Acts 14:20b should be read: "On the morrow he set out with Barnabas for Derbe," since the journey would take more than a day. The second inscription also provides evidence regarding the Christian church at Derbe — there was a bishop there in the latter part of the 4th century. The names of four other bishops are also known, one of whom, Daphnus, was present at the Council of Constantinople in A.D. 381. In view of the extensive evidence of Christianity in the area of the new site for Derbe (e.g., the 1001 churches and the complex of churches and monastery at Alahan), it appears that Paul's initial work in this area bore much fruit for years to come.

See B. Van Elderen, "Some Archaeological Observations on Paul's First Missionary Journey," in W. W. Gasque and R. P. Martin, eds., *Apostolic History and the Gospel* (1970), pp. 156-161.

See Map XIX. B. VANELDEREN

DERIDE; DERISION [Heb. *lā'ag, la'ag*] (Neh. 2:19; Ps. 2:4; 44:13; 59:8; Ezk. 23:32; 36:4; Hos. 7:6); AV also SCORN, "laugh to scorn"; NEB also JEER, "laugh to scorn," MOCKERY, SCORN, DESPISE, "stammering speech" (mg. Hos. 7:16); [*ś^{e}ḥôq*] (Jer. 48:26f., 39); NEB "butt of derision"; [*qeles*] (Ps. 79:4; Jer. 20:8); NEB MOCK, MOCKERY; [*lûṣ*] (Ps. 119:51); NEB SCORN; [*ḥālal*] (Ps. 102:8); AV "be mad against"; NEB "mad with rage"; [*rāḥab*] (1 S. 2:1); AV "be enlarged"; [*m^{e}lîṣâ ḥîḏôt*] ("scoffing derision," Hab. 2:6); AV "taunting proverb"; NEB "insults and abuse"; [Gk. *blasphēméō*] (Mt. 27:39; Mk. 15:29); AV REVILE, RAIL; NEB "hurl abuse."

God's people have many times been the object of derisive laughter and scorn, sometimes due to the unbelief of those who mock (cf. Neh. 2:19; Ps. 119:51; Jer. 20:7f.; etc.), sometimes due to God's judgment upon His people for their apostasy (cf. Ezk. 23:32; Hos. 7:16); however, the wicked who have gloated over the suffering of God's chosen will also be held in derision (Ps. 2:4; 59:8; Jer. 48:26f., 39; Ezk. 36:4-7; Hab. 2:6).

In the NT those who mocked Jesus as He hung on the cross were guilty of blasphemy (*blasphēméō*) in that they were challenging His messianic claim. Matthew and Mark record that these blasphemers expressed their contempt for Him by "wagging their heads," a common gesture of scorn in the ancient Near East (cf. 2 K. 19:21; Ps. 22:7; 64:8; 109:25; Isa. 37:22; Jer. 18:16; 48:27; Lam. 2:15). GESTURE).

See also MOCK; SCORN; GESTURE.

See *TDNT*, I, *s.v.* βλασφημέω (Beyer). N. J. O.

DESCEND [Heb. *yāraḏ, nāḥaṯ* (Job 17:16; Isa. 30:30), *šālaḥ* (Lam. 1:13); Gk. *katabaínō*]; AV also REST (Job 17:16), SEND (Lam. 1:13), COME DOWN (Ps. 7:16; Isa. 34:5; Jn. 3:13), LIGHT DOWN (Isa. 30:30); NEB also COME DOWN, SEND DOWN (Lam. 1:13), GO DOWN, etc. "Descend" is used in the OT to refer to God's presence on Mt. Sinai (Ex. 19:18), the angels in Jacob's dream (Gen. 28:12), man's going down to Sheol in death (Job 17:16; Ps. 49:17; Isa. 5:14; Ezk. 26:20), and the judgment that descends upon one in life (Ps. 7:16; Isa. 34:5). In the NT it is used in reference to the Spirit's descent upon Jesus (Mt. 3:16), angels' descent from heaven (Mt. 28:2; Jn. 1:51), and Christ's descent from heaven (Jn. 3:13; 6:33; 1 Thess. 4:16; and possibly Eph. 4:9) or to the place of the dead (Rom. 10:7 and possibly Eph. 4:9).

The passage in Eph. 4:9, "he had also descended into the lower parts of the earth," has been interpreted variously as referring to (1) the Incarnation, (2) Christ's descent to the place of the dead, or (3) the descent of Christ's Spirit at Pentecost. The first and third views regard the phrase "of the earth" as an appositive genitive, so that a better translation would be "the lower regions, i.e., the earth." The second view regards the genitive as partitive, thus referring to the lower regions of (i.e., under) the earth. Linguistic considerations alone cannot decide the question, so the theological context becomes determinative of the interpretation. Although Christ's relation to the underworld, or Hades, is usually associated with His defeat of the powers of evil (Mt. 16:18; 1 Pet. 3:18-22), Ephesians envisions the heavenly realm, not a region under the earth, as the place of evil spirits (1:20f.; 2:2; 3:10; 6:12); hence the passage at hand probably refers to His descent from heaven to earth rather than from earth to the underworld. *See* DESCENT INTO HELL (HADES).

Bibliography.–G. B. Caird, *SE*, II, 535-545; H. Schlier, *Christus und die Kirche im Epheserbrief* (1930). R. L. RIBLE

DESCENT

1. [Heb. *môrad̲*] (Josh. 7:5; Jer. 48:5); AV "going down"; NEB also PASS; [Gk. *katábasis*] (Lk. 19:37). A geographical decline, in the case of Josh. 7 from Ai, some 2500 ft. (760 m.) above sea level, to Jericho, about 800 ft. (245 m.) below sea level. Cf. Mic. 1:4, AV, RSV, "steep place"; NEB "hill-side." The RSV rendering of Josh. 8:14 represents a textual emendation of the Heb. *lammô'ēd̲* ("appointed time") to read *lāmmôrad̲*. G. WYPER

2. [Heb. *zera'*–'seed,' 'offspring'] (Ezr. 2:59; Neh. 7:61); AV SEED. "Descent" here is equivalent to "origin" or "ancestry." "Those of foreign descent" in Neh. 13:3 translates Heb. *'ēreb̲*, "mixture," "mixed company" (AV "mixed multitude"; NEB "[who were of] mixed blood"). The RSV renders Gk. *nómos entolḗs sarkínēs* as "legal requirement concerning bodily descent" (AV "law of a carnal commandment"; NEB "system of earth-bound rules").

DESCENT INTO HELL (HADES). This is not a directly biblical concept but rests on the clause in the Apostles' Creed that Christ descended into hell (Hades). Even in the creed the clause did not occur in the earliest versions, e.g., the Old Roman Symbol. By the early 5th cent., however, it had a place in the Creed of Aquileia (*ca.* 404), as may be seen from the exposition of this creed by Rufinus, who refers in support to Pss. 21, 29, 68; Luke 7:10; 1 Pet. 3:18ff. It has been traced back beyond Aquileia to Constantinople in 360 and Sirmium in 359, and even if it did not find earlier creedal expression was evidently known to such early fathers as Origen in the first half of the 3rd cent. and Justin Martyr, Irenaeus, Tertullian, and Clement of Alexandria in the second half of the 2nd century.

I. NT Basis.–The brief treatment by Rufinus shows that the concept of the descent was believed to have a biblical basis. Rufinus himself refers mainly to the Psalms but in fact the NT provided the main support and impetus for it.

Thus the NT, when it speaks of Christ's resurrection, consistently describes it as His resurrection, not merely from death, but "from the dead" (Mt. 17:9; Acts 4:10; Rom. 4:24; 1 Cor. 15:20; Lk. 24:5). The comparison with Jonah in Matthew 12:38ff. points in the same direction: "So will the Son of Man be three days and three nights in the heart of the earth." Peter's quotation and application of Ps. 16:10 in his sermon in Acts 2 (vv. 25ff.) also seems to hint at the presence of Christ in Hades as well as His deliverance from it ("he was not abandoned to Hades, nor did his flesh see corruption"), although the meaning might be that He was preserved from Hades rather than out of it. Ephesians 4:9, "he had also descended into the lower parts of the earth," could be taken in a similar sense, for while many exegetes see a more general reference to the descent of Incarnation in a contrasting of the descending and ascending Christ, even on this view Hades can be regarded as the low point of the incarnational descent, followed at once by the raising from the dead and the subsequent Ascension.

Two passages in 1 Peter, even if they are not the sole basis of the belief in the descent, have always played an important role in relation to it and suggest a possible purpose. In 3:19 we read that Christ "went and preached to the spirits in prison, who formerly did not obey, when God's patience waited in the days of Noah." Then in 4:6, in the context of "giving an account to him who is ready to judge the living and the dead," reference is made to the preaching of the gospel "even to the dead, that though judged in the flesh like men, they might live in the spirit like God." Both these passages have been the subject of considerable exegetical debate. Some scholars deny any connection between the verses (or one or the other of them) and the descent, while others accept a connection but differ as to the precise nature of Christ's ministry to the dead in Hades. Rev. 1:18, "I have the keys of Death and Hades," is sometimes brought into the discussion in view of the preceding reference to death and everlasting life, but the bearing of this on the descent is at best obscure.

II. Historical Development.–*A. Introduction.* Various factors inclined the early Church to develop a doctrine of the descent out of the sparse biblical materials. Since the Resurrection took place on the third day, questions naturally arose about the second day, between the Crucifixion and the Resurrection. These questions were set in the broader context of ideas of the intermediate state in the OT and NT. An obvious answer was that with the separation of Christ's body and soul at death, the body rested in the tomb but in the soul Christ spent a brief period among the dead before being reunited as body and soul at the Resurrection. The problem of the righteous dead prior to the coming of Christ arose in this connection. How could they benefit by His saving work seeing they were already dead before its enactment and proclamation? The full reality of Christ's identification with humanity even in death offered further food for thought in the same field, for if Christ authentically "tasted death for every one" (He. 2:9), how could He not also be among the dead even if only temporarily, even if teleologically, even if in pursuit of the saving goal that those who are buried with Him might also enjoy with Him the resurrection from the dead?

B. The Early Church. In the early Church the soteriological factor, the saving purpose of the descent, commanded the greatest attention. Initially it would seem that the releasing of the righteous dead by the proclamation of His saving work was the ministry which Christ performed in Hades (cf. Hermas, Justin Martyr, and Irenaeus). The Alexandrians, sensitive like all the fathers to the charge that Christ had come too late, and that His works could not benefit the pagan dead, extended the preaching in Hades to cover pagans too, so that not just the generation of the Flood but all their spiritual counterparts should have the chance of responding to God's gracious work. The concept of triumph over the powers of sin, the devil, death, and hell easily came to be attached to this understanding. Not only did Christ Himself prove superior to Hades; by His descent He broke the power of Hades over those already dead, liberating from it the righteous or all indeed who accepted His proclamation.

C. The Middle Ages and Trent. By the time of the Council of Trent in the middle of the 16th cent. it was firmly believed that the soul of Christ, separated from the body at death, descended briefly into Hades. The alternative view of Abelard, that only His power invaded hell, had been rejected at the Council of Sens in 1241. Aquinas (*Summa Theol.* iii.52.2, 4-8) had formulated the four tasks performed by Christ in His descent: He opened heaven to the saints; He shamed unbelievers; He gave hope to those in purgatory; and He gave light to just and holy souls in the so-called limbo of the patriarchs. Trent followed Aquinas closely in its own understanding, accepting the new and not expressly biblical ideas of a purgatory for souls who had still to make good the temporal guilt of sin and of a special limbo for pre-Christian believers. The descent had predominantly a victorious aspect expressed artistically in portrayals of the harrowing of hell.

D. The Reformers. By and large the Reformers of the 16th cent. had no quarrel with the creedal affirmation of the descent but they differed in their interpretation of it. Luther could speak at times of Christ's going to hell with us in vicarious identification but he seems to have favored the concept of a victory over hell. By His descent Christ demolished the powers of evil, routed the devils, and put out infernal fire. Calvin (*Inst.* ii.16.8ff.) could see a positive side to the descent: "Christ shone upon the patriarchs by the power of His Spirit," but he found in it a primary reference to Christ's paying the full price of our redemption by "suffering in his soul the terrible torments of a condemned and forsaken man." In taking this line Calvin appealed to He. 5:7f. and quoted the early father Hilary (*De trinitate* iv.42). He was also following some medieval thinkers such as Nicholas of Cusa. He dissented strongly from the view of his fellow-reformer Martin Bucer of Strassburg, who argued that Hades is merely a metaphor for the grave. He also took issue with some minor figures, e.g., Christopher Carlisle and Walter Deloenus in London, who thought that the article had no real basis and should thus be dropped from the creed. The Lutheran and Reformed theologians of the 17th cent. adopted much the same approaches as their predecessors.

III. The Issues. The view of Bucer, which appealed also to Calvin's successor Beza, raises the crucial question whether the NT statements are not in fact to be taken in a purely metaphorical or transferred sense. Even Calvin had to concede that Scripture does in fact use Hades as an equivalent of the grave. Hence the Resurrection from the dead might simply be a way of expressing raising up from death or the tomb and even "being in the heart of the earth" could simply imply death in view of the committal of the body to the ground. The passage in Eph. 4, of course, could easily refer to the Incarnation as itself a descent to the earth. Even the obscure statements in 1 Peter might not refer to any actual ministry in Hades but only to the effects of Christ's saving work for the dead; indeed they could be no more than a vivid way of portraying the ongoing ministry of the gospel to those imprisoned by sin and death. Calvin himself, for all his apparent realism, had in view only the torment of the soul, so that the descent into Hades might be taken as a metaphor for what he calls "the invisible and incomprehensible judgment which He underwent in the sight of God."

In contrast to a purely metaphorical understanding lies the more realistic one which accepts the fact of an intermediate abode of the dead between death and resurrection, although, since this is the dwelling of the soul, quasi-physical depictions of it, and its quasi-geographical charting, cannot be taken in a literal corporeal sense. On this view Christ, after the parting of soul and body at death, came to the intermediate abode but could not be held there, since by the resurrecting power of God He was taken from it, united to the resurrected body, and exalted as the firstfruits of the dead. His going to the intermediate state constituted the final point of His identification with sinners, His taking from it represented the divine victory over sin and death, and the saving purpose of His descent meant the proclamation of freedom to those who apart from His ministry could have no hope of new and eternal life with God.

See also HADES; PRISON, THE SPIRITS IN.

Bibliography.–Calvin *Inst.* ii.16.8ff.; H. Heppe, *Reformed Dogmatics* (1950); J. A. MacCulloch, *The Harrowing of Hell* (1930); B. Reicke, *Disobedient Spirits and Christian Baptism* (1946); E. G. Selwyn, *First Epistle of Peter* (2nd ed. 1947); *TDNT*, III, *s.v.* κῆρυξ κτλ. (Friedrich), 707; H. Thielicke, *Evangelical Faith,* II (Eng. tr. 1977), 415-420.

G. W. BROMILEY

DESCRIBE; DESCRIPTION [Heb. *kāṯaḇ* (Josh. 18:4-9)]. The Heb. *kāṯaḇ* means literally "write down." Joshua ordered a written report of the survey and sevenfold division of the Promised Land to form a basis for the settlement of Israel's tribes. The RSV has "described a circle" in Job 26:10 (Heb. *ḥûg*) where the AV has "compassed with bounds" (NEB "fixed the horizon").

DESCRY (Jgs. 1:23, AV). An obsolete term meaning "explore" or "spy out" (RSV).

DESERT [Heb. *miḏbār, ʿarāḇâ, yešîmôn, ṣîyâ, ḥorbâ*; Gk. *erēmía, érēmos*]; AV also WILDERNESS (esp. for *miḏbār*), DRY PLACES (Ps. 105:41); NEB also DRY LAND, BARREN HEATH, PARCHED LAND, BARREN DESERT, "solitary places," "lonely place"; AV translates *yešîmôn* as place name Jeshimon (Nu. 21:28; 23:28; [here also NEB]); in Jer. 5:6 AV reads *ʿereḇ* ("evenings") with Syriac, Vulgate, *et al.* The primary word for desert, *miḏbār,* is found most often as "wilderness" in all translations. The roots from which these nouns derive all witness to specific characteristics associated with the desert: *dbr,* "depart," "perish," perhaps "desolate"(?); *ḥrb,* "waste, be wasted"; *yšm, šmm,* "be desolated, appalled"; *ʿrb,* "be arid"; *ṣyh,* "be parched"; *erēmóō,* "lay waste, depopulate." These designations may refer to purely geological and meteorological phenomena such as barrenness, heat, or dryness; or they may be derived from man's personal experience of the desert, such as solitude or desolation.

A perusal of the many occurrences of *miḏbār* and other words connoting desert areas in the Bible demonstrates the importance of the desert in all the biblical period. This is easily explained in light of the geography of Israel, bordered on two sides by huge deserts, the Arabian desert to the east and the Sinai wilderness to the south. Moreover, much of Israel itself, particularly the Negeb and the Transjordanian steppe, possesses many or all of the physical characteristics usually associated with deserts. An examination of Israel's history shows that the patriarchs were well acquainted with desert life, whether or not the term nomadic can be used to describe them. This observation and the close connection of Moses with the Midianites and Mount Sinai, both located in desert areas, has caused many to speak of a "desert ideal" that forms the basic framework or matrix for the subsequent development of Israelite religion (cf., however, Talmon). Surely the desert forms the basic geographical and theological background for the wilderness wandering, a complex of tradition associated not simply with the Exodus but with many subsequent periods in Israel as well. The wilderness is at once the place of murmuring and of testing, as well as an integral part of a salvation pattern (exodus-wandering-Sinai-promised land) found, in whole or in part, throughout the history of Israel (cf., e.g., Hosea, Ezekiel, Deutero-Isaiah). Any or all of these perspectives demonstrates the fact that the desert was a well-known entity for all who lived in Palestine and a formative factor for their world view. It is therefore not surprising to find the terms for desert used in a variety of ways by the biblical authors.

Often the desert refers to a particular geographical locale. Certainly *yešîmôn* in Nu. 21:20; 23:28 refers to such a locale in the SE of Israel (cf. also 1 S. 23:24; 26:1). Similar references to the area of Moab and/or the desert beyond it are quite common (Isa. 16:1, 8; Jer. 9:26; 12:12; 25:24). At one point *miḏbār* refers to the area E of Jordan and the desert stretching to the Euphrates valley (1 Ch. 5:9). *Érēmos* can refer to the Negeb itself (Acts

Bedouin encampment in the Sinai desert near Beersheba. Only rarely do favorable conditions and rainfall repay their diligent efforts at cultivation. (W. S. LaSor)

8:26). Many of the words that refer to desert are found together in synonymous parallelism (e.g., Dt. 32:10; Isa. 35:1) and are capable of referring to any of the barren wasteland areas in or near Palestine. In addition, it must be recognized that, though the primary connotation of *miḏbār* when used to refer to the wilderness wandering may often stress nongeographical elements, the Sinai-Negeb locale is implicit in that context.

More often, the terms translated "desert" do not refer primarily to a geographical locale, but to some characteristic aspect of the desert itself. The desert is a dry place, where water is rarely found (Ps. 106:9; 107:33; Isa. 35:1, 6; 50:2; 51:3; Jer. 4:11; 13:24; 50:12). Nevertheless, animals do live there (Job 24:5; Jer. 5:6; 48:6 [as LXX]; Mal. 1:3). Perhaps the most common reference to the desert attempts to characterize the effect this land has upon man. It is a barren and terrifying place, where man does not, cannot live easily (Job 38:26; Isa. 21:1; 40:3; 41:19f.; Jer. 9:2 [MT 1]; 15:33; Mk. 8:4). It is lonely, sometimes characterized by a solitude that is threatening and frightening to man (Ps. 107:4; Prov. 21:19; Jer. 17:6; Lk. 8:29; He. 11:38). It is desolate, and is often used to symbolize the desolation that has or is to come upon Israel or her enemies (Isa. 14:17; 33:9; Jer. 4:26; 22:6; 50:12; Zeph. 2:13).

Many of these nuances are present when references are made to the wilderness tradition associated with the Exodus-Sinai traditions and others. At least two themes within this complex can be seen when the desert is referred to. The desert is the general place where the wandering occurred, where guidance was needed (Ps. 105:41; Isa. 48:21). It is also the place where the people murmured against Yahweh (Ps. 78:17, 40; 106:14).

In addition to the ways in which "desert" is used above, another theological use in many of the passages already cited must be mentioned. The desert is used, often in metaphors or similes, to demonstrate God's power to transform. The desert represents aridity, solitude, desolation. Sometimes God will make things like a desert, desolate and lifeless (Isa. 50:2; Jer. 4:26; 22:6; 50:12; 51:43; Zeph. 2:13). At other times the desert itself is to be transformed positively into a place of greenery and water, of life, demonstrating God's ability to change all conditions of man and his world (Isa. 35:1, 6; 41:19; 43:19f.; 51:3). A vivid example of this latter ability to transform the desert and all it symbolizes is found in the feeding of the four thousand (Mt. 15:32-39 par. Mk. 8:1-10). There the desert represents quite clearly and explicitly a place incapable of providing food (life!) for great numbers of people. And yet, as in the OT passages cited above, God is able to make the desert a place capable of providing food and of giving life. The power of this transformation, and its use in both OT and NT, is ample witness to the importance of desert and all it symbolizes in ancient Israel and the early church.

Bibliography.–G. W. Coats, *Rebellion in the Wilderness* (1968); G. Fohrer, *History of Israelite Religion* (Eng. tr. 1972); *LBHG*; M. Noth, *OT World* (Eng. tr. 1966); S. Talmon, "The 'Desert Motif' in the Bible and in Qumran Literature," in A. Altmann, ed., *Biblical Motifs* (1966). D. F. MORGAN

DESIGN [Heb. *ma'ᵃseh ḥōšēḇ*] ("skilled design," Ex. 39:3); AV CUNNING WORK; NEB "be worked in by a seamstress"; [*maḥᵃšāḇâ*] (Ex. 31:4; 35:32; 2 Ch. 2:14); AV WORK, DEVICE; **DESIGNER** [Heb. *ḥōšēḇ*] (Ex. 35:35; 38:23); AV CUNNING WORKMAN, "them that do cunning work"; NEB also SEAMSTER. These Hebrew terms are all from the verb *ḥāšaḇ*, which means "make" or "devise" but in these passages probably refers more specifically to WEAVING. In biblical times weaving was an occupation of both men and women (Ex. 35:35; 2 K. 23:7). Beginning as a family enterprise, the craft later ministered to the needs of the whole community. G. WYPER

DESIGNATED [Heb. *yā'aḏ*] (Ex. 21:8); AV BETROTHED; NEB "had intercourse with"; [*mû'āḏâ*] (Josh. 20:9); AV, NEB, APPOINTED; [niphal of *nāqaḇ*] (2 Ch. 31:19); AV EXPRESSED; NEB NOMINATED; [Gk. *horízō*] (Rom. 1:4); AV, NEB, DECLARED; [*prosagoreúō*] (He. 5:10); AV CALLED; NEB NAMED;

[*prográphō*] (Jude 4); AV ORDAINED; NEB "marked down." The RSV and NEB also supply "designated" in rendering Heb. *b^ešēmôṯ*, literally "by names" (Ezr. 10:16; cf. AV).

In the RSV "designated" represents six different Hebrew and Greek terms with a variety of meanings. Heb. *yā'aḏ*, to which the substantive *mû'āḏâ* is related, means "appoint, arrange, designate," while *nāqaḇ* means "specify." Gk. *horízō* can mean either "appoint, install" or "designate, declare." The former sense, adopted by many modern commentators in Rom. 1:4, can be taken as supporting an "adoptionist" Christology in which Jesus *became* the Son of God only at His resurrection (see J. Knox, comm. on Romans [*IB*, 1954]). Others, however, interpret the passage as referring to Jesus' manifestation (or being "declared"; cf. AV, NEB) as the son of God. According to C. K. Barrett, the adoptionist tinge here is due to the functional (rather than essential) nature of the earliest Christologies (comm. on Romans [*HNTC*, 1957], pp. 20f.) — Jesus functioned as the Son of God in power only after the Resurrection. The author of Hebrews is more clearly concerned with function in salvation-history when he says that Jesus was "designated by God a high priest after the order of Melchizedek" (5:10). The emphasis in this passage (vv. 7-10) is upon Jesus' suffering as qualifying Him for the designation of eternal high priest.

The term represented by "designate" in Jude 4, Gk. *prográphō* (lit. "write beforehand"), refers to what was previously written ("long ago," v. 4) in another document. It may have been the prophecy of 1 Enoch (cf. Jude 14f.) or some of the apostolic material that predicted the appearance of such "ungodly persons" and the judgment awaiting them. N. J. O.

DESIRE [Heb. *ḥāpēṣ, ḥēpeṣ, ḥāmaḏ, maḥmaḏ* (Ezk. 24:16, 21, 25), *'āwâ, 'awwâ, ta'^awâ, ma'^awayyîm* (Ps. 140:8 [MT 9], *nepeš* (Jer. 34:16), *t^ešûqâ, ḥāšaq* (Dt. 21:11), *ḥēšeq, rāṣôn*, also *'^aḇiyônâ* (Eccl. 12:5), *bāḥur* (2 S. 19:38 [MT 39]), *šā'al, miš'ālâ* (Ps. 37:4), *'āmar* (Est. 2:13)]; AV also LUST (vb.), COVET, FAVOR, WISH, SOUL PLEASURE (Jer. 34:16), REQUIRE (2 S. 19:38 [MT 39]), THOUGHTS (Job 17:11); NEB also PURPOSE (Ps. 140:8 [MT 9]), CAPERBUDS (Eccl. 12:5; *see* CAPER-BUD), HEARTSTRINGS (Job 17:11); [Aram. *ṣ^eḇâ* (Dnl. 7:19)]; AV WOULD; [Gk. *thélō, thélēma* (1 Cor. 13:3; Eph. 2:3), *boúlomai, epithymía, epithyméō, zēlóō* (1 Cor. 12:31; 14:1, 39), *zētéō* (2 Cor. 13:3), *axióō* (Acts 28:22), *eudokía* (Rom. 10:1), *orégomai* (He. 11:16); also *homeíromai*–'being affectionately desirous' (1 Thess. 2:8)]; AV also WISH, LUST (vb., noun), COVET, SEEK (2 Cor. 13:3), INTEND, "be forward" (2 Cor. 8:10), CONCUPISCENCE (Col. 3:5), WILL (1 Cor. 7:37), etc.; NEB also LONGING (He. 11:16), "with yearning love" (1 Thess. 2:8); **DESIRABLE** [Heb. *ḥemdâ* (1 S. 9:20), *maḥmaḏ* (Cant. 5:16), *ḥemeḏ* (Ezk. 23:6, 12, 23)]; AV also THE DESIRE OF (1 S. 9:20), LOVELY (Cant. 5:16); NEB also WANTING (1 S. 9:20), HANDSOME (Ezk. 23:6, 12, 23). A wide variety of human wants, wishes, cravings, or appetites. The terms used carry no intrinsic moral valuation, which must be contextually derived. Human desires are God-given and God-prospered (2 S. 23:5), and a fulfilled desire is "sweet" to the soul (Prov. 13:19). Hence, not only are such bodily appetites as hunger (Dt. 12:15; Lk. 15:16) and sexual fulfillment (Ps. 45:11 [MT 12]) taken as natural, but so also are a variety of other human wants: long life (Ps. 34:12 [MT 13]), a prosperous family situation (Ps. 128), or physical health (Ps. 38).

However, the pursuit of these God-given desires can become sinful when His will is ignored. So, for instance, the wanton consumption of food (Am. 6:4), or desire for food that is linked to the return to the Egyptian bondage (Ps. 78:18, 30f.; 106:14). The desire for material wealth is evidently a special human weakness, and stern warnings are given about this (Ex. 20:17; Mic. 2:2). It creates dangerous pitfalls (1 Tim. 6:9), and can stifle the gospel message (Mk. 4:19), create discord among men (Jas. 4:1f.), and influence even the Christian ministry (Acts 20:33; 2 Cor. 12:14-18). In a similar way, sexual desire must be controlled, especially by young men (Prov. 6:23-33; 2 Tim. 2:22; 3:6). Jesus emphasized that this desire may be sinful in its contemplation, not just in the act (Mt. 5:28).

Desire can also be morally good, as in man's religious inclinations. Ultimately, these are directed to God (Isa. 26:9), to His law (Ps. 19:10 [MT 11]), or to His service (1 Tim. 3:1). Such religious yearning frequently is not satisfied by the present experience of God but longs for more complete fulfillment — even death, which leads one to Christ, may be desired (Phil. 1:23; cf. also Mt. 13:17; Lk. 17:22). That desire can be morally good is seen emphatically in that both Jesus and God Himself can be said to have desires (Lk. 22:15; Ps. 68:16 [MT 17]).

While the NT picture of desire includes most of the above features, the dominant theme is the sinfulness of desire as a revolt of the human will against God. Hence the "desire of the flesh" (*epithymía*) can appear as parallel to the "will of the flesh" (*thélēma*) (Eph. 2:3), and human desire can be placed in opposition to the will of God (1 Pet. 4:2). So also pagan sexual desires find expression that is contrary to sanctification (1 Thess. 4:5), and the Jews' refusal of Jesus' word amounted to their choice to do the desires of their "father the devil" (Jn. 8:44).

This opposition finds special expression in the conflict between the "desires of the flesh" and the "desires of the Spirit." This Pauline formulation takes its starting point from the view of "flesh" as man in his weakness, his inability to keep God's law, and his vulnerability to sin (Rom. 7:7-25). Sin works through the law by creating desire in man. Negatively, the law produces the desire to break the commandment simply by announcing it (vv. 7-9); and positively, although the law promised life and created desire for it, no power was provided whereby life could be attained, and hence deception and death resulted (7:10f.). It is only when the new life in Christ brings the power of the Spirit that the flesh can be overcome and the desire of the Spirit produced (Rom. 8:1-4; Gal. 5:16f.). The death of Christ meant crucifixion of the flesh and its desires (Gal. 5:24), and the believer is to "put to death . . . what is earthly," which includes "evil desire" (Col. 3:5). So for Paul (and elsewhere in the NT), desire is characteristic of the "former manner of life" — i.e., before becoming a believer (Eph. 2:3; 4:22; Tit. 3:3; 1 Pet. 1:14; 4:3). In addition to its association with flesh and the law, desire is also closely tied to the world and its corruption (Tit. 2:12; 2 Pet. 1:4; 1 Jn. 2:16f.). And just as desire was associated with the "former life," so also it "passes away" with the world (1 Jn. 2:17). (For the connection of desire and flesh in non-Pauline writing, cf. 1 Pet. 2:11; 2 Pet. 2:10, AV; 1 Jn. 2:16. *See also* FLESH.)

One additional passage worthy of special note is Jas. 1:14f., where desire is presented as enticing an individual, as "conceiving" and "giving birth" to sin, which in turn "brings forth death." The intent of the metaphor, evidently, is that just as there is life and growth of the fetus in the womb prior to birth, so sin has a real existence as desire prior to the sinful act.

Bibliography.–*TDNT,* III, *s.v.* θυμός (Büchsel); G. Bornkamm, *Early Christian Experience* (1969), pp. 87-104; R. Bultmann, *Theology of the NT,* I (Eng. tr. 1951), 224-26, 245f.

J. J. HERZOG

DESIRE OF ALL NATIONS. *See* TREASURES OF ALL NATIONS.

DESOLATE [Heb. *šāmēm, šᵉmamâ, šammâ* (frequent), *šô'â* (Job 30:3; 38:27), *ḥārēḇ* (Jer. 2:12; 26:9; 33:10), *ḥorbâ* (Ezk. 25:13), *kāḥaḏ* (Job 15:28), *šā'ôn* (Ps. 40:2), *bālaq* (Isa. 24:1), *ḥᵃlōp̄* (Prov. 31:8), *yāḥîḏ* (Ps. 68:6), *šāḏaḏ* (Jer. 4:30), *bûqâ* (Nah. 2:10) *ṣāḏâ* (Zeph. 3:6); Gk. *érēmos* (Mt. 23:38; Acts 1:20; Gal. 4:27), *erēmóō* (Rev. 17:16), *orphanós* (Jn. 14:18)]; AV also WASTE, HORRIBLE (Ps. 40:2), DESTRUCTION, SOLITARY (Ps. 68:6), EMPTY (Nah. 2:10), DESTROYED, COMFORTLESS (Jn. 14:18), etc.; NEB also DERELICT, DESPAIR, WASTE, RUINS, MUDDY (Ps. 40:2), "will empty the earth" (Isa. 24:1), FRIENDLESS (Ps. 68:6), PLUNDERED, LAID WASTE, DESERT, UNINHABITED (Isa. 5:9), BEREFT (Jn. 14:18), etc.; **DESOLATION** [Heb. *šāmēm* (Ezk. 30:12, 14; Ps. 69:25; Isa. 15:6), *šᵉmānâ* (Jer. 4:27; 9:11; etc.), *šammâ* (2 K. 22:19; 2 Ch. 30:7; etc.), *šōḏ* (Isa. 59:7), *horbâ* (Jer. 27:17; 44:2, 22; etc.), *mᵉḇûqâ* (Nah. 2:10), *'ᵃśēh hārattôq* ("make a desolation," Ezk. 7:23); Gk. *erēmōsis* (Lk. 21:20)]; AV also MAKE WASTE, WASTING, SPOILING, VOID, etc.; NEB also DESOLATE WASTE, DESERT, "lie derelict," "lay waste," "object of horror," DISASTER, RUIN, SCANDAL, DESTRUCTION, etc.

In the OT "desolate" renders many terms, often denoting devastation as well as abandonment. "Desolate" is most often the translation of Heb. *šāmēm, šᵉmāmâ, šammâ*. The usual meaning of the *šmm* group is "destroy, devastate," or "be devastated, appalled." In Ezk. 36:3 the NEB follows the *BH* conjecture *šāmô(a)ḥ,* "gloat." *Šô'â* expresses the high degree of impotence which characterizes the land when it cannot support those in search of food. *Ḥāreḇ* denotes "be amazed, astounded" in Jer. 2:12 (BDB, p. 351), but elsewhere signifies "depopuated." In Ezk. 25:13 "desolate" describes the land of Edom, which will be without human or animal inhabitants. *Šā'ôn* means literally "roar," as the waters of the sea (cf. Ps. 65:8), and may refer to the raging waters of the underworld (cf. Ps. 69:2, 14f.). The destruction announced by Isa. 24:1 will include all people (vv. 2, 17), the cities (vv. 12f.), the earth (vv. 19f.); it will affect even the heavenly bodies (vv. 21a, 23a). In Prov. 31:8 the conjectures of the RSV and NEB ("that oppose them") are unnecessary. The ruler is to speak forth with regard to the cause of all transitory flesh (MT *bᵉnê ḥᵃlôp,* "sons of vanishing, passing away"). The Heb. *yāḥîḏ* denotes "aloneness" without implying devastation, while *šāḏûḏ* (pass. part. *šāḏaḏ*) represents "one who is violently treated, plundered, deprived of possessions or status." In Nah. 2:2b, 10 (MT 2:3b, 11) the root *bqq* occurs four times. In 2:10 judgment is coming upon Nineveh: the plunderer becomes the plundered who experiences the devastating wrath of Yahweh (cf. 2:13). "Emptiness" (*mᵉḇûqâ*) will describe Nineveh when it will have been destroyed and its people slain (Nah. 2:10, 13). The RSV of Ezk. 7:23 is a conjecture. The AV renders the Hebrew literally "make a chain" (cf. RSV mg.; NEB conjectures "clench your fists").

Frequently the sanctuary of Jerusalem and the people of Judah are described as desolate or about to become desolate as a result of Yahweh's punishment for rebellion against His lordship (cf. Lev. 26:31; Isa. 6:11; Ezk. 6:4, 14; 14:15f.; 15:7f.). Judah and Israel are desolate because they are no longer free and populated by the chosen people (cf. Isa. 54:1, 3; 62:4, where populating the land will nullify its desolate state). This may mean, however, that the land is populated by foreigners (cf. Lev. 26:32; Isa. 1:7; Jer. 12:10f.; Lam. 1:4; 5:18; Ezk. 33:28; 36:34). For the people of Israel desolation may mean either destruction or captivity (cf. 2 Ch. 36:20f.; Isa. 5:9; Lam. 1:15-18).

The foes of Israel will also be desolate, for they will be destroyed on Israel's day of restoration. These enemies will become a "desolate mound" in which will be found neither man nor beast (cf. Jer. 49:2; 51:62; Ezk. 30:7; 32:15; 35:14f.; Joel 3:19).

"Desolate, desolation" occur nine times in Daniel, indicating either (1) abandonment, being made useless, destruction, or (2) defilement. In 8:13 the former is more prominent: "desolate" describes the sanctuary in which the continual burnt offering has been prohibited and removed (cf. v. 11). The continual burnt offering was, in part, food for the priests and their families (cf. Lev. 10:12-15; Nu. 18:8-20); thus the priests and their families would perish and those who normally would come bearing sacrifices would remain away, leaving the temple deserted. Both the cessation of worship and the destruction of Jerusalem and the sanctuary constitute the desolation prophesied for Jerusalem in 9:27. By contrast, in 11:31 and 12:11 that which desolates is "set up," presumably a reference to "the pagan altar which was on top of the altar of the Lord" (1 Macc. 1:59, NEB), on which swine were sacrificed, thereby bringing upon the sanctuary total defilement. *See* DESOLATING SACRILEGE.

Tamar was desolate in the sense of "deserted" after her brother Amnon ravished her, for she had no husband (2 S. 13:20).

In Lk. 21:20 Jesus warns that Jerusalem's desolation (*erēmōsis,* NEB "destruction") will be imminent when the city is surrounded by armies. "Desolation" is probably intended to encompass not only the desecration of the temple (cf. Mt. 24:15ff.) but also the destruction of the temple and city.

Elsewhere in the NT "desolate" usually means "abandoned" without denoting "destruction." In Jn. 14:18 *orphanós,* literally "bereft of one's parents," is used figuratively to signify "without a source of assistance." *See* ORPHAN.

J. A. HEWETT

DESOLATING SACRILEGE [Heb. *šiqqûṣîm mᵉšōmēm* (Dnl. 9:27), *haššiqqûṣ mᵉšômēm* (Dnl. 11:31), *šiqqûṣ šōmēm* (Dnl. 12:11), and perhaps *happeš' šōmēm* (Dnl. 8:13); Gk. *tó bdélygma tḗs erēmṓseōs* (Mt. 24:15; Mk. 13:14)]; AV "abomination of desolation," "abomination(s) making desolate"; NEB "the abominable thing that causes desolation" (Dnl. 11:31). A substitute name or a byname for a detestable and idolatrous action or image, usually connected with the desecration of the temple in 168 B.C. by the Seleucid ruler Antiochus IV Epiphanes.

I. The Hebrew Terms.–In the OT *šiqqûṣ,* "sacrilege" or "abomination," usually refers to something detested, an idol (Jer. 4:1; 7:30; Ezk. 5:11; 37:25; etc.). Thirty-eight times Ezekiel inserted the vowels of this word into the word *galālu,* thereby coining the term *gillûlîm,* meaning "pellets of dung," to stigmatize the idols of his time.

The other term is from the Hebrew root *šāmem,* "be desolate" or "be appalled." In the Daniel passages the participial form can be rendered either "something desolating" or "something desolated." E. Nestle was the first to suggest (*ZAW,* 4 [1884], 248) that the whole expression was probably a cacophemistic reference to the Syrian god

Baal Shamem, "Lord of Heaven" (the Greek Zeus Olympios), for whom Antiochus Epiphanes erected an altar and thus desecrated the Jerusalem temple in 168 B.C. Rather than saying Baal or "Lord," in disgust the prophet forced himself to say "that detested thing." Then he deliberately distorted *šāmayîm*, "heaven" (or perhaps the Phoenician form *šamen*) into *šōmēn*, "desolating." Certainly this is a deliberate cacophemism for its official designation.

II. The Maccabean Identification.–1 Macc. 1:54, 59 reports that "they erected a desolating sacrilege upon the altar of burnt offering. They also built altars in the surrounding cities of Judah. . . . And . . . they offered sacrifice on the altar [Gk. *bōmós*] which was upon the altar of burnt offering." Apparently an altar dedicated to Zeus was erected on Yahweh's altar (*thysiastḗrion*) of burnt offerings. According to 2 Macc. 6:2, Antiochus ordered that the Jerusalem temple be called the temple of "Olympian Zeus."

III. History of Interpretation.–Several different identifications have been suggested for the use of this phrase by Jesus. Three citations from Josephus' *Jewish War* have been used to equate this desecration with the acts of the wounded Zealots who went into the temple and defiled it with their blood (*BJ* iv.3.12; iv.6.3; vi.2.1). More commonly, it has been connected with an idol such as the one erected by Hadrian in the time of the apostate R. Elisha ben Abija, *ca.* A.D. 120 (Baur and Schlatter), or with Caligula's attempted introduction of his statue into the Jerusalem temple in A.D. 39-40 (Pfleiderer, J. Weiss).

However, the earliest and best supported identification equates this desecration with the antichrist. As early as Hippolytus and Irenaeus, 2 Thess. 2:3f. had been associated with Mk. 13:14. This adversary (1) exalts himself and opposes everything connected with God, (2) sits in the sanctuary of God, and (3) proclaims that he is God. Since Mark had used a masculine participle, *hestēkóta*, where the antecedent would normally have demanded a neuter, this connection seems secure.

Others have noted that the Lukan parallel (21:20) connects Jesus' meaning with the Roman army about to destroy Jerusalem. Pilate's desecration of the temple precincts by admitting one Roman standard there was especially odious. Frequently these ensigns had the image of the emperor affixed to them and were worshiped as part of a soldier's military duty.

IV. Daniel's Meaning.–Dnl. 9:27 foresaw a time when an unidentified "he" would make a covenant with the Jews for seven years. Halfway through this contracted time he would revoke the Jewish privilege of sacrifice and offerings "even upon *kᵉnap šiqqûṣîm mᵉšomēm*." The question is, what is meant by *kᵉnap*?

Usually it is understood to be "wing," hence the translation, "upon the wing of abominations shall come one who makes desolate." In this case, the "wing" would signify an eagle or perhaps the winged solar disk of Zeus. A. Bentzen recalled "Baal of the wing," *b'l knp* in Ugaritic literature. Less imaginatively, some thought of the wing of the temple, i.e., the desolator would appear on the pinnacle of the temple (cf. Mt. 4:5).

However, *kānap* may mean "cover over" in a destructive sense (cf. Isa. 8:8), hence "even the overspreading of the desolating sacrilege" (Dnl. 9:27, AV). This act, much like Antiochus Epiphanes' act (cf. Dnl. 8:22-25; 11:29-32). will so desecrate the temple that God and worshipers will abandon it until the consummation. The plural form of "sacrilege" here (cf. the singular form in 11:31 and 12:11) may be an abstract plural or plural of importance.

While Dnl. 11:31 uses "desolating sacrilege" to refer historically to Antiochus' declaration that all regular Mosaic ceremonies cease and the altar and/or image of Zeus Olympius (Baal Shamem) be erected in the temple, Dnl. 12:11 returns to the eschatological situation of the coming antichrist who will enact a similar abomination.

V. NT Usage.–Jesus, obviously aware of how Daniel has blended his prediction of the acts of the coming Antiochus IV Epiphanes with the acts of the coming antichrist (cf. Dnl. 11:35ff., which no doubt marks the transition from the Seleucid to the "man of sin" of 2 Thess. 2, the "little horn" of Dnl. 7 or "beast" of Rev. 13), also indicates that, as Daniel's prophecy was not emptied of its intended reference by the events of the Maccabean period, no more will it be by the events of that 1st Christian century. Rather, he sternly warns that a final act of desecration, which would exceed all other acts, is yet to come. So abominable is this act that the temple itself will be rejected as the abode of God.

Just what this act is and who will do it is suggested in the masculine participle of Mk. 13:14. The desecrator will be some concrete figure in history. The act itself is to be identified by the reader's awareness ("Let the reader understand") of the Danielic context with its immediate association with sacrifices.

This is neither an apocalypticized nor historicized secondary reinterpretation by Jesus or by the Gospel writers. On the contrary, given Daniel's careful argument, even the plural form of the noun, it carries out his intended meaning.

VI. Conclusion.–Most of these equations point to the concept of a local expression of a power at work against God. Each participates in that collective entity known as antichrist, who will make a final personal appearance just before the parousia of Jesus Christ at the end time. Thus, just as there is a collective solidarity among believers known as "seed," which can be expressed in the one Seed representative of that whole group, Christ Jesus Himself, there is also a collective solidarity witnessed in Scripture for all the forces that oppose God. These forces have their single historical representatives, just as the Man of Promise had in the persons of Abraham, Isaac, Jacob, David, *et al.* Similarly, many antichrists have already come (e.g., Antiochus Epiphanes, Caligula, and their armies; cf. 1 Jn. 2:18); but these are only weak samples of the final one who will stand in the Holy Place, desecrate again the divine things, and attempt to usurp God's place.

Bibliography.–G. R. Beasley-Murray, *Comm. on Mark 13* (1957), pp. 59-72; E. Bickermann, *Der Gott der Makkabäer* (1937), pp. 92-96; D. Daube, *NT and Rabbinic Judaism* (1956), pp. 418-437; L. Gaston, *No Stone on Another* (1970), pp. 23-29.

W. C. KAISER, JR.

DESOLATION, ABOMINATION OF. *See* DESOLATING SACRILEGE.

DESOLATOR [Heb. *šōmēm*] (Dnl. 9:27); AV DESOLATE; NEB DESOLATION. The problem in translating *šōmēm* (from the verb *šāmam,* "be desolated or horrified," thus, lit. "that which causes shock or horror") is reflected in the versions. The identity of the desolator — assuming the correctness of the RSV rendering — is also a problem and is part of a chapter that in itself is puzzling. Some have seen the desolator as being an image of the Semitic "god of heaven" or the Greek Zeus Olympios, i.e., the horror that appalls. Others refer the term to the author of the abomination, usually Antiochus Epiphanes, the Seleucid invader of Palestine (*see* ANTIOCHUS IV).

Still others find the prophecy fulfilled in the Roman Titus who led the army that destroyed Jerusalem's temple, while yet others find the desolator to be the king of the North or the antichrist at the end of the age. *See also* DESOLATING SACRILEGE. G. WYPER

DESPAIR; IN DESPAIR. Heb. *yā'aš* bears the basic meaning "desist from, give up hope" (1 S. 27:1; NEB "lose all further hope"; Job 6:26; AV "desperate"; Eccl. 2:20). As a participle it is an interjection of hopelessness (Isa. 57:10). The literal sense of *lō'-aman* is "do not confirm" (Job 24:22; AV "no man is sure"; NEB "have no firm hope"). Heb. *nûš* (*'ānûš*; KoB, p. 67; *CHAL,* p. 22) means to be "incurable" (Ps. 69:20 [MT 21]; AV "full of heaviness"; NEB "past hope"). Shame is implied by Heb. *bôš* (Isa. 19:9; NEB "hang their heads"; AV "confounded"). The condition of the princes in Ezk. 7:27 implies the vast devastation of a desolate wasteland (Heb. *š^e^māmâ*; AV "desolation"; NEB "horror"). Gk. *exaporeúomai* indicates perplexity, a condition marked by great difficulty, doubt, and embarrassment (2 Cor. 4:8; NEB "at our wits' end").

A. C. M.

DESPITE. Archaic in the AV for "contempt," as in Ezk. 25:6, 15; 36:5 (Heb. *še'āṭ*, RSV "malice," "utter contempt"); Mt. 5:44; Lk. 6:28 ("use despitefully," Gk. *epēreázō*, RSV "abuse"); Acts 14:5 ("use despitefully," *hybrízō*, RSV "molest"); Rom. 1:30 ("despiteful," *hybristḗs*, RSV "insolent"); He. 10:29 ("do despite unto," *enybrízō*, RSV "outrage").

DESSAU des'ô [Gk. Dessaou] (2 Macc. 14:16); NEB ADASA. A Judean village of uncertain identification where the Jewish forces engaged Nicanor in battle.

DESTINE [Heb. *ṣāpâ*] (Job 15:22); AV WAITED; NEB MARKED; [*'āṯaḏ*] (Job 15:28); AV "ready to become"; NEB "will soon become"; [*yāsaḏ*] (Isa. 23:13); AV FOUNDED; [*mānâ*] (Isa. 65:12); AV NUMBER; NEB DELIVER; [*šāṯal*] (Hos. 9:13); AV PLANTED; NEB EMERGE; [Gk. *proorízō*] (Eph. 1:5, 12); AV PREDESTINATED; NEB also (v. 11) DECREED; [*títhēmi*] (1 Thess. 5:9; 1 Pet. 2:8); AV APPOINTED; NEB also APPOINTED; [*prógnōsis*] (1 Pet. 1:2); AV FOREKNOWLEDGE; NEB PURPOSE; [*proginṓskō*] (1 Pet. 1:20); AV FOREORDAINED; NEB PREDESTINED.

A notable variety of ideas stands behind the RSV "destine." The Heb. *ṣāpâ* conveys a "looking out or about" in an attempt to spy out something. "Be ready" or "prepared" is the idea of *'āṯaḏ*. "Establish" or "appoint" is the sense of *yāsaḏ*. To "number" or "assign" lies behind *mānâ*. The Heb. *šāṯal* means "transplant," but the Hosea passage is very difficult; the NEB observes in a footnote that the Hebrew is "unintelligible." The RSV apparently emends to *šîṯ*.

Three of the four NT words begin with *pró-*, which indicates something primary in time or position and may be translated "before." The Gk. *proorízō* is a rather rare and late word that means "predetermine"; it grows out of a stem that deals with setting the limits of a boundary. *Títhēmi* lacks the highly descriptive connotations of the other NT terms; it simply and boldly notes divine "placement" and "appointment." Knowledge is prominent in Gk. *prógnōsis* and *proginṓskō*; the first is a noun, "advance knowledge," and the second a verb, "know beforehand." Both terms are obviously limited to God's foreknowledge and determinative will.

See also PREDESTINATION. G. H. HOVEE

DESTINY [Heb. *m^e^nî*] (Isa. 65:11); AV "that number"; NEB FORTUNE. A pagan deity, perhaps the god of luck. *See* FORTUNE.

DESTROYER [Heb. part. of *šāḏaḏ, šāḥaṯ, hāras* (Isa. 49:17); Gk. part. of *olothréuō* (1 Cor. 10:10; He. 11:28), *diaphtheírō* (Rev. 11:18)]; AV also SPOILER, "he that destroyed" (He. 11:28), "them which destroy" (Rev. 11:28); NEB also SPOILER, DESPOILER, MARAUDER, PLUNDERER (Jer. 12:12), RAIDER (Job 15:21), HORDE OF RAIDERS (Jer. 15:8), ARMED HOST (Jer. 22:7), "ones who pulled down" (Isa. 49:17), DESTROYING ANGEL (1 Cor. 10:10), "those who destroy" (Rev. 11:18). The RSV also supplies "destroyers" for *mišpāḥôṯ* in Jer. 15:3, "kinds of destroyers," (AV "kinds"; NEB "kinds of doom").

The word "destroyer" is usually used to refer to the human power which brings destruction to a nation (e.g., "destroyer of nations," Jer. 4:7; "destroyer of Moab," Jer. 48:15, 18). However, "destroyer" (Heb. *mašḥîṯ*; Gk. *olothreutḗs*) is used several times to refer to an angelic power which brings death and destruction. It is in this latter sense that the word is used in Ex. 12:23 (cf. He. 11:28). In the intertestamental period *mašḥîṯ* was sometimes used as a title for a specific angel of destruction. Paul's use of the word in 1 Cor. 10:10 is somewhat ambiguous. He may have in mind the general term for an angel of destruction, or he may be thinking of a specific angel of destruction, namely, Satan (postexilic Judaism understood Satan as God's agent of destruction; cf. Wisd. 2:24). E. W. CONRAD

DESTROYER (Joel 2:25); **DESTROYING LOCUST** (1:4) [Heb. *ḥāsîl*–'devourer']; AV CATERPILLAR; NEB GRUB. Perhaps a kind of LOCUST. The RSV elsewhere translates Heb. *ḥāsîl* as CATERPILLAR.

DESTRUCTION. ***I. OT Terms.***–The RSV translates seventeen different Hebrew roots by the Eng. "destruction." Each of these roots is variously translated by the RSV in different contexts.

A. Heb. Šeḇer. The Hebrew word most commonly translated "destruction" is *šeḇer* (NEB also "disaster," "devastation," "ruin," "wound," etc.). The focal meaning is "fracture," used of a foot or hand (Lev. 21:19), wall (Isa. 30:13), pottery (Isa. 30:14). But the field of meaning is large enough to include "depression" (cf. Isa. 65:14) on the one hand, and "death and deportation of whole segments of the population" (cf. Jer. 6:1) on the other. Such destruction is often associated with the noise of battle (Isa. 15:5; Jer. 50:22; 51:54). The common formula "devastation and destruction" (Heb. *haššoḏ w^e^haššeḇer*: Isa. 51:19; 59:7; 60:18; Jer. 48:3) may reflect an ancient battle cry (see Jer. 48:3). A cognate of *šeḇer, šiḇārôn* ("collapse"), occurs in Jer. 17:18 (NEB "destroy").

B. Heb. Šōḏ. The focal meaning of *šôḏ* (AV also "spoil," etc.; NEB also "devastation," etc.) is "violent destruction"; its field of meaning is much narrower than that of *šeḇer*. In addition to the formula *haššôḏ w^e^haššeḇer* (see above), *šôḏ* occurs in the formula "violence and destruction" (*ḥāmās wāšôḏ*, Jer. 6:7; 20:8; Ezk. 45:9; Am. 3:10). Here, too, a cry of battle may be involved (cf. Jer. 20:8: "I shout, 'Violence and destruction!' ").

Am. 5:9 presents a special problem. It is possible, though not certain, that in this instance Heb. *šôḏ* should be read *šôr* (cf. NEB "Taurus"). Several factors support this emendation: the Hebrew *d* and *r* are similar in form throughout most Hebrew scripts; Am. 5:8 mentions the constellations Pleiades and Orion; and *šôr* is the spelling for Taurus that would be expected from the principles of comparative phonetics, an expectation reinforced by the caption above the Taurus figure in the inner room of the Beth Alpha Synagogue. G. R. Driver sees Capricorn and Virgo in v. 9 as well as Taurus (*JTS*, N.S. 4 [1953], 208f.). If Driver is correct, the verse reflects God's control over the changing seasons. However, it is difficult to see both *'āz* as *'ēz* ("goat" = "Capricorn") and *mibṣār* as *mibaṣṣer* ("Virgo"?). The latter is especially difficult in the light of the Beth Alpha zodiac, where Virgo is called *beṯûlâ* as it is in rabbinic literature (see *Yalkut* Ex. 418). If one emends only *šōḏ* to *šôr* in v. 9, then the passage is saying that Taurus is under the command of God just as were the Pleiades and Orion. If one follows the MT, then he should understand the passage as drawing a parallel between God's destructive power and His ability to create and maintain the universe.

C. Heb. Šāḥaṯ. The hiphil stem of *šāḥaṯ* means "spoil," "ruin," or "wipe out." The verb *yašḥîṯ* occurs in Dnl. 8:24 with the meaning "cause destruction" (AV "destroy"; NEB "work havoc"). The infinitive *hašḥîṯ* occurs in 2 Ch. 12:12 (AV, NEB, "destroy") and 26:16 (NEB "undoing"), both contexts dealing with pride. The participle *mašḥîṯ* occurs in Ezk. 5:16 and 2 S. 24:16 for destruction in the form of pestilence (although famine and wild beasts may be meant in Ezk. 5:16). In Ps. 107:20 the MT reads *miššeḥîṯôṯām*, "from their destruction" (cf. this word with a different preposition in Lam. 4:20). However, it is possible that the text should read *miššaḥaṯ*, two words having been welded together by haplography. In this case the text should be rendered "from the pit of death," or "the pit of their lives," or better, following A. Weiser, "and saved their lives from the Pit" (*Psalms* [*OTL*, 1962], p. 684). In Ezk. 19:4 *šaḥaṯ* designates an animal trap.

D. Heb. Ḥērem. *Ḥērem* is rendered "destruction" seven times in the RSV: Josh. 6:17, 18 (twice); 7:12; 1 S. 15:21 (AV "accursed"; NEB "ban"); 1 K. 20:42 (NEB "ban"); Isa. 43:28 (AV "curse"; NEB "doom"). *Ḥērem* referred to those things that were excluded from profane use — often war booty — and dedicated solely to God (see III below). *See also* DEVOTE.

E. Heb. Šāmaḏ. The root *šmd* is rendered "destruction" in Est. 4:8 (*hašmîḏ*); Isa. 26:14 (*tašmîḏ*); Ps. 92:7 (*hiššāmēḏ*); Isa. 14:23 (*hašmēḏ*). In these cases the syntax allows, and in Isa. 14:23 it requires, that the infinitives and the finite verb be rendered as nouns. The root meaning is "exterminate."

F. Heb. 'āḇaḏ. The root *'bd* is rendered "destruction" in Nu. 24:20, 24 (*'aḏe 'ôḇēḏ*, AV "perish forever"; NEB's renderings "wind" and "storms" are more difficult unless one sees in the Hebrew a reflection of Arab. *haway*, "to blow."

G. Heb. Hawôṯ. *Hawôṯ* occurs in Ps. 5:9 (MT 10; AV "wickedness"; NEB "wind"); Ps. 52:2 (MT 3; AV "mischiefs"; NEB "wild lies"); Ps. 57:1 (MT 2; AV "calamities"; NEB "storms"). Destruction as indicated by this word is potential as opposed to having actually occurred. Sometimes it merely indicates the threat of ruin (Ps. 38:12 [MT 13]; Prov. 17:4). On this basis the AV translations are all justified, as is the NEB "wild lies." However, the NEB's renderings "wind" and "storms" are more difficult unless one sees in the Hebrew a reflection of Arab. *haway*, "to blow."

H. Other Terms. Several Hebrew roots are translated "destruction" twice in the RSV. The root *blh*, "become old" or "worn out," occurs in Isa. 10:25 and 38:17, the *t*-formative noun *taḇlîṯ* occurring only in 10:25 (NEB "spent"). In 38:17 *belî*, a common word for "without," occurs in the phrase *miššaḥaṯ belî*, "from the pit of 'nothingness'" (AV "from the pit of corruption"), which clearly refers to Sheol (see the discussion of *šaḥaṯ* above). *Ḥāḇal*, rendered "destruction" in Mic. 2:10 (NEB "mischief") and Prov. 13:13 (AV "destroyed"; NEB trouble"), means "treat badly." The nouns *killayôn* (Isa. 10:22) and *kālâ* (Isa. 28:22) are both based on the root *klh*, which means "become complete, bring to an end." *Kāraṯ*, literally "cut off" (cf. AV), occurs in Ps. 37:34 and Hos. 8:4. In the latter passage the NEB relegates the gloss containing *yikkārēṯ* to a note; however, while certainly a later addition to Hosea, the gloss *is* in the text (see J. L. Mays, *Hosea* [*OTL*, 1969], pp. 117f.). The same Hebrew root occurs in references to the legal penalty of banishment, and this may be implied in both Ps. 37:34 and Hos. 8:4 (cf. Lev. 17:3f.). *Qeṭeḇ* appears in Ps. 91:6 (NEB "plague") and Hos. 13:14 (NEB "sting"). Its only other occurrence is in Dt. 32:24, where it is associated with the arrows of the Lord (v. 23). It is also associated with arrows in Ps. 91:6; and in Hos. 13:14 the LXX renders it *kéntron*, "point" or "prick." For this reason the word is to be understood as "prick" or "sting"; however, a pricking or stinging disease is very possible.

Five words are translated "destruction" only one time in the RSV. The root of Heb. *'êḏ* in Job 30:12 is "great calamity." The NEB takes the phrase "ways of calamity" to mean the ramps laid against the wall of a city in order to breach it. The noun *meḥittâ* in Prov. 10:29 (cf. v. 14) is based on the stem *ḥtt* meaning "fill with terror." The term rendered "destruction" by the RSV in Prov. 19:18 is the hiphil infinitive of *mwt*, meaning "to bring death." The NEB's translation of the term ("death") is linguistically better than that of the RSV or AV ("crying"), but it seems to miss the point of the verse. The point is not the danger of killing a son by beating him, but rather that he will die if he is not properly disciplined. The context of Job 21:20 requires that *kîḏ*, a hapax legomenon, refer to a disaster of some kind (cf. NEB "damnation"). It has been suggested that it is a scribal error for *'êḏ* (see above) or *pîḏ*, which means "disaster" (cf. Job 30:24). Isa. 30:28 is problematic. The RSV renders "destruction" for Heb. *šāwe'*, literally "worthless," "empty," "in vain" (cf. AV "vanity"), which should possibly be read *šō'* ("ravage") instead, as in Ps. 35:17. *See also* SIEVE.

II. NT Terms.–The situation in the NT is not nearly so complex. The term occurring most frequently is Gk. *apṓleia*, a common word for "destruction" or "waste" (Mt. 7:13; Rom. 9:22; Phil. 1:28; 3:19; 1 Tim. 6:9; 2 Pet. 2:1, 3; 3:7, 16; AV also "damnation," "perdition"; NEB also "destroyed," "disaster," "doom," "perdition," "ruin"). In 1 Cor. 5:5; 1 Tim. 5:3; 2 Tim. 1:9 the Greek term is *ólethros*, "destruction" (NEB also "calamity," "ruin"), and in 2 Pet. 2:12 *phthorá*, "ruin, corruption" (AV "corruption"; NEB "perish").

III. God as Destroyer.–Along with His other attributes, Yahweh is described as a God who wages war and destroys. He decrees destruction to the people of Israel (Isa. 10:20-23), and brings destruction to Babylon (Jer. 51:54-58). His angel of destruction ravages the land from Dan to Beersheba (2 S. 24:15-17). Isaiah speaks of Yahweh as having brought destruction on all the previous rulers of his people so that they can now be ruled by Him alone (Isa. 26:13-15). Yahweh is in control of the great military forces of the world. He will turn His anger from Israel to the Assyrians (Isa. 10:24-27). He brings destruction from the north and the east; first He brings the Babylonians against what remains of the southern kingdom (Jer. 4:6; 6:1), and then the Babylonians are destroyed at the hand of Cyrus (Isa. 41:2-4; 43:14).

Yahweh's military authority is well illustrated in His requirement that booty be specially set aside for His own purposes. This holy booty, the *ḥērem*, is sometimes called "destruction." When Yahweh captures Jericho for Israel (Josh. 6:15-21), the priests proclaim that the booty thus captured is the property of Yahweh Himself, and if the people of Israel take any of it they run the risk of themselves becoming Yahweh's sacred booty. According to Isa. 43:28, Jacob is delivered as sacred booty because of the sins of his ancestors, both distant and near.

The theme of God as destroyer is continued in the NT. According to Phil. 1:28, God will destroy the opponents of the gospel. In Rom. 9:22 the conditional clause complicates interpretation. Paul seems to be contrasting the wrath of God with His mercy. He may be referring to God's previous destructive activity; but the Day of the Lord is also a day in which He brings destruction. The Hebrew phrase *k^{e}šōḏ miššadî*, "as destruction from the Almighty," is used twice with reference to the coming DAY OF THE LORD (Isa. 13:6; Joel 1:15). In Isa. 22:4-8 such a destructive day has just occurred. Such a day of destruction is part of the apocalyptic vision of those events that will usher in the next age. The very structure of the universe itself is to be destroyed, according to the account given in the Assumption of Moses (ch. 10). Paul also understands the Day of the Lord as a day of destruction that comes unpredictably and with violence (1 Thess. 5:1-6); however, God will save those who believe from the certainty of destruction. The OT also speaks of God's activity of saving persons from destruction (Ps. 107:20; Job 5:21f.).

IV. Self-destruction.–According to many biblical texts it is possible for men to bring destruction upon themselves. Pride is one cause of such destruction (2 Ch. 26:16; cf. Phil. 3:19); likewise, temptation can lead to destruction (1 Tim. 6:9). However, the committing of evil acts is the main cause that is mentioned (Ps. 37:34; 92:7; Prov. 10:29; 2 Thess. 1:9; 2 Pet. 2:1, 3; 3:7). Prov. 17:19 seems to indicate a relationship between pride and specific evil deeds. The first half of the verse clearly deals with evil deeds and their result, while the second half is a metaphor concerning pride: "He who makes his door high seeks destruction," i.e., he who erects a monumental entrance to his house invites its collapse. The NEB's rendering, "He who builds a lofty entrance invites thieves," gives an incorrect image, since Heb. *šeḇer* means "a fracture" or "a breaking down" but never "one who breaks in."

Bibliography.–R. de Vaux, *Ancient Israel* (Eng. tr. 1961), I, 260; W. Eichrodt, *Theology of the OT*, I (*OTL*, Eng. tr. 1961), 258-269; G. von Rad, *OT Theology*, II (Eng. tr. 1965), 119-125.

D. E. SMITH

DESTRUCTION, CITY OF (Isa. 19:18, AV). *See* CITY OF THE SUN.

DETAINED BEFORE THE LORD [Heb. *ne$^{'e}$ṣar lipnê Yahweh*] (1 S. 21:7 [MT 8]). The precise meaning is not certain. Doeg the Edomite was evidently in the sanctuary when David arrived, but the question is whether he was involuntarily detained until he had completed some rite of purification (cf. Lev. 13:4; Jer. 36:5) or had voluntarily entered the sacred place for consecration or fulfillment of a vow.

DETERMINE [Heb. *kālâ*] (1 S. 20:7, 9, 33; 25:17; Est. 7:7); NEB also "be set on," "be bent on," "be certain"; [*śîm*–'fix,' 'define,' 'order'] (2 S. 13:32; Job 38:5); AV also LAY; NEB "look black" (2 S. 13:32), SETTLE; [*'āśâ*–'do,' 'make'] (2 K. 19:25; Isa. 37:26); AV, NEB, DO; [*yā'aṣ*–'decide,' 'plan'] (2 Ch. 25:16); [*ḥāraṣ*] (Job 14:5; Dnl. 11:36); NEB also CHOOSE; [*ḥāšaḇ*–'plan'] (Lam. 2:8); AV PURPOSE; NEB "be minded"; [*yā'al*] (Hos. 5:11); AV "willingly"; NEB "doggedly"; [*bā' l^{e}pānay*–'come before me'] (Gen. 6:13); AV "come before me"; NEB "has become plain to me"; [hithpael of *'āmaṣ*–'prove oneself to be strong'] (Ruth 1:18); AV "be stedfastly minded"; [*mānâ*–'count'] (Ps. 147:4); AV TELL; NEB NUMBER; [*pālal*–'judge,' 'arbitrate'] (Ex. 21:22); NEB ASSESSMENT; [*yāḏa'*–'know'] (Job 34:4); AV KNOW; NEB ESTABLISH; [Gk. *horízō*–'fix,' 'define'] (Lk. 22:22; Acts 11:29; 17:26; 20:3); AV also "be about to" (Acts 20:3); NEB APPOINTED, AGREE, FIX, "be on the point of" (Acts 20:3); [*krínō*–'judge'] (1 Cor. 7:37; 10:29); AV JUDGE, DECREE; NEB "call in question," DECIDE; [*diaginṓskō*] (Acts 23:15); AV ENQUIRE; NEB INVESTIGATION.

The word "determine" has two basic meanings. The primary and most common meaning is to "resolve" or "decide" (e.g., Heb. *kālâ*, *ḥāšaḇ*; Gk. *krínō*, *diaginṓskō*). The other frequently used meaning is "decree" or "ordain" (e.g., Heb. *śîm*, *ḥāras*). Both meanings coincide when the subject is God. In 2 K. 19:25 par. Yahweh declares through His prophet Isaiah that Sennacherib has no grounds for arrogance, since it is God Himself who has ordained the fall of the cities he has conquered.

N. J. O.

DETESTABLE THINGS [Heb. *šiqquṣ*] (Dt. 29:17; Ezk. 5:11; 7:20; 11:18, 21; 20:7f., 30; 37:23; cf. Jer. 16:18; Hos. 9:10); AV also ABOMINATIONS; NEB LOATHSOME IDOLS, GODS, THINGS, WAYS, "vile . . . rites," IMAGES, PRACTICES, "thing of shame" (Hos. 9:10). Objects of worship or veneration associated with pagan cults, and so "detestable" in God's sight and that of His people who kept His covenant. Love of such idols and rites brought on the Lord's judgment.

DEUEL dōō'əl, də-ōō'əl [Heb. *d^{e}'û'ēl*–'knowledge of God']; NEB REUEL. A Gadite, the father of Eliasaph; he was the representative of the tribe of Gad in the census-taking (Nu. 1:14), in making the offering of the tribe at the dedication of the altar (7:42, 47), and as leader of the host of the tribe of the children of Gad in the wilderness (10:20). He is called REUEL in Nu. 2:14, ד (d) being confused with ר (r).

DEUTERO-CANONICAL BOOKS. *See* APOCRYPHA.

DEUTERONOMY.

I. Name and Purpose
II. Analysis
III. Basic Concepts
IV. Provenance, Authorship, and Date
V. Language and Style
VI. Influence in Israel's History
VII. Summary of Teaching

I. Name and Purpose.–In Heb. *'ēlleh hadd^{e}ḇārîm*, "these are the words"; in Gk. *Deuteronómion*, "second law"; whence the Lat. *deuteronomii*, and the Eng. Deuteronomy. The Greek title is due to a mistranslation by the LXX of the clause in Dt. 17:18 rendered, "and he shall write for himself this *repetition* of the law." The Hebrew really means "and he shall write out for himself a *copy* of this law." However, the error on which the English title rests is not serious, as Deuteronomy is in a very true sense a *repetition* of the law.

Deuteronomy is the last of the five books of the Pentateuch, or "five-fifths of the law." It possesses an individuality and impressiveness of its own. In Exodus–Numbers Yahweh is represented as speaking to Moses, whereas in Deuteronomy, Moses is represented as speaking at Yahweh's command to Israel (1:1-4; 5:1; 29:1).

The book is in effect a covenant-renewal document which expounds and expands upon the implications of the historic agreement at Sinai between God and Israel by which the latter became the chosen people. The purpose of the author was to maintain that loyalty towards God which Israel had professed when the Sinai covenant was ratified, and to ensure that the nation would never be in doubt as to the high moral and spiritual standards which the divinely revealed law demanded of its adherents. Taken as a whole the book is an exposition of the great commandment: "you shall love the Lord your God with all your heart, and with all your soul, and with all your might." It was from Deuteronomy that Jesus summarized the entire old covenant in a single sentence (Mt. 22:37; cf. Dt. 6:5), and from the same book He quoted the divine revelation as a means of conquering the Satanic tempter (Mt. 4:4, 7, 10; cf. Dt. 8:3; 6:16, 13).

II. Analysis.–Deuteronomy is composed of three discourses, followed by three short appendices: (1) 1:1–4:43, historical; a review of God's dealings with Israel, specifying in great detail where and when delivered (1:1-5), recounting in broad oratorical outlines the chief events in the nation's experience from Horeb to Moab (1:6–3:29), on which the author bases an earnest appeal to the people to be faithful and obedient, and in particular to keep clear of all possible idolatry (4:1-40). Appended to this first discourse is a brief note (vv. 41-43) concerning Moses' appointment of three cities of refuge on the eastern side of the Jordan. (2) 4:44–26:19, hortatory and legal; introduced by a superscription (4:44-49), and consisting of a resume of Israel's moral and civil statutes, testimonies, and judgments. Analysed in greater detail, this second discourse is composed of two main sections: (a) chs. 5-11, an extended exposition of the Ten Commandments on which the theocracy was based; (b) chs. 12–26, a code of special statutes concerning worship, purity, tithes, the three annual feasts, the administration of justice, kings, priests, prophets, war, and the private and social life of the people. The spirit of this discourse is mostly ethical and religious. The tone is that of a father no less than that of a legislator. A spirit of humanity pervades the entire discourse. Holiness is its ideal. (3) 27:1–31:30, predictive and minatory; the subject of this third discourse is "the blessings of obedience and the curses of disobedience." This section begins with directions to inscribe these laws on plastered stones to be set up on Mt. Ebal (27:1-10), to be ratified by an antiphonal ritual of blessings and curses from the two adjacent mountains, Gerizim and Ebal (vv. 11-26). These are followed by solemn warnings against disobedience (28:1–29:1) and fresh exhortations to accept the terms of the new covenant made in Moab and to choose between life and death (29:2–30:20). Moses' farewell charge to Israel and his formal commission of Joshua close the discourse (ch. 31). The section is filled with predictions, which were woefully verified in Israel's later history. The three appendices, spoken of above, close the book: (a) Moses' Song (ch. 32), which the great lawgiver taught the people (the law was given to the *priests*, 31:24-37); (b) Moses' Blessing (ch. 33), which forecasts the future for the various tribes (only Simeon being omitted); (c) a brief account of Moses' death and burial (ch. 34) with a noble panegyric on him as the greatest prophet Israel ever had. Thus closes this majestic and marvelously interesting and practical book. Its keyword is "possess"; its central thought is "Yahweh has chosen Israel, let Israel choose Yahweh."

III. Basic Concepts.–The great central thought of Deuteronomy is the unique relation that Yahweh as a unique God sustains to Israel as a unique people. "Hear, O Israel; the Lord our God is one Lord." The monotheism of Deuteronomy is very explicit. Following from this, as a necessary corollary almost, is the other great teaching of the book, the unity of the sanctuary. The motto of the book might be said to be, "One God, one sanctuary."

A. Yahweh, a Unique God. Yahweh is the only God. "There is no other besides him" (4:35, 39; 6:4; 32:39), He is "God of gods and Lord of lords" (10:17), "the living God" (5:26), "the faithful God, who keeps covenant and steadfast love with those who love him and keep his commandments" (7:9), who abhors graven images and every species of idolatry (7:25f.; 12:31; 13:14; 18:12; 20:18; 27:15), to whom belong the heavens and the earth (10:14), who rules over all the nations (7:19), whose relation to Israel is near and personal (28:58) — even that of a Father (32:6), whose being is spiritual (4:12, 15), and whose name is "Rock" (32:4, 15, 18, 30f.). Being such a God, He is jealous of all rivals (7:4; 29:24-26; 31:16f.), and hence all temptations to idolatry must be utterly removed from the land; the Canaanites must be completely exterminated and all their altars, pillars, Asherim, and images destroyed (7:1-5, 16; 20:16-18; 12:2f.).

B. Israel, a Unique People. The *old* Israel had become unique through the covenant which Yahweh made with them at Horeb, creating out of them "a kingdom of priests, and a holy nation" (Ex. 19:6). The *new* Israel who had been born in the desert were to inherit the blessings vouchsafed to their fathers, through the covenant just now being made in Moab (Dt. 26:16-19; 27:9; 29:1; 5:2f.). By means of it they became the heirs of all the promises given to their fathers the patriarchs (4:31; 7:12; 8:18; 29:13); they too became holy and peculiar, and especially beloved of Yahweh (7:6; 14:2,21; 26:18f.; 28:9; 4:37), disciplined, indeed, but for their own good (8:2f., 5, 16), to be established as a people, as Yahweh's peculiar lot and inheritance (32:6, 9; 4:7).

C. The Unique Relation between Yahweh and Israel. Other nations feared their deities; Israel was expected not only to fear Yahweh but to love Him and cleave to Him (4:10; 5:29; 6:5; 10:12, 20; 11:1, 13, 22; 13:3f.; 17:19; 19:9; 28:58; 30:6, 16, 20; 31:12f.). The highest privileges are theirs because they are partakers of the covenant blessings; all others are strangers and foreigners, except they be admitted into Israel by special permission (23:1-8).

IV. Provenance, Authorship, and Date.–Until the 19th cent. most Christians held that Deuteronomy was substantially Mosaic in origin, but when European liberal thinkers attacked the Mosaic authorship of the Pentateuch systematically, Deuteronomy, known by that time as the "D" document, was relegated to the 7th cent. B.C. Wellhausen crystallized earlier thought concerning Deuteronomy by asserting that it was compiled anonymously about 622 B.C. The author's aim was to reform religious practices and dispense with the various "high places," locating cultic worship solely in Jerusalem. Wellhausen further supposed that the author hid his work in the temple fabric and allowed it to be found when repairs were being made to the building in the time of Josiah (640-609 B.C.). When it was read, the book was found to pertain to the spiritual needs of the day, and in consequence provoked a series of religious reforms (2 K. 22f.). This novel explanation was at first dismissed by scholars as heresy, but when finally the Wellhausenian reconstruction of

Israelite history and religion gained many more adherents, it soon became integral to the literary-critical theory of pentateuchal origins. Thus H. H. Rowley, a lifelong adherent of the Wellhausen views, stated the situation clearly by saying that the code of Deuteronomy "is of vital importance to Pentateuchal criticism since it is primarily by relation to it that the other documents are dated" (*Growth of the OT* [1951], p. 29).

Not all the literary critics placed Deuteronomy in the 7th cent. B.C., however. Berry suggested that Deuteronomy was of postexilic origin (*JTS,* 26 [1925], 156); Kennett placed it *ca.* 520 B.C. in the time of Haggai and Zechariah (*Deuteronomy and the Decalogue* [1920], pp. 6ff.), while Pedersen and others of the Uppsala school assigned its final form to *ca.* 400 B.C. (cf. *ILC,* III-IV [1963], 750-52). Von Rad, in contrast, placed the book considerably earlier, assuming it to have arisen in what he called "circles of country Levites," and to have been completed shortly after 701 B.C. While Albright recognized that the Song of Moses was of great antiquity, his general adherence to the tenets of the Graf-Wellhausen school precluded a date much before the 7th cent. B.C. for the final form of Deuteronomy. (*See also* PENTATEUCH, PROBLEM OF; CRITICISM II.)

Part of the problem connected with the dating turned on the question of the centralization of worship in Jerusalem, which Wellhausen thought was the main point at issue in the book. Unfortunately for Wellhausen's speculations, there is no evidence whatever in Deuteronomy that Jerusalem was the place where the cultus was meant to be centralized. Dt. 12:5, 11, etc. speaks of "the place which the Lord your God will choose," but that place is never specified by name, and, as J. Skinner observed, Deuteronomy lays no emphasis whatever upon the peculiar claim of Jerusalem to be the sole place of worship (*Prophecy and Religion* [1922], p. 167), a position supported by Rowley (*Studies in OT Prophecy, presented to T. H. Robinson* [1950], p. 166). Indeed, a careful reading of Dt. 12:14 shows that Jerusalem is specifically excluded, since the "place" is to be "in one of your tribes." Jerusalem stood outside tribal jurisdiction until it was conquered by David and made his stronghold, and then it was a success as the political capital of the united kingdom only because it could claim the allegiance of all the tribes without favoring any of them. Had Jerusalem been mentioned when the land of Canaan was being allotted to the Israelite tribes, it could certainly not have enjoyed the loyalty which it experienced in later ages, or have been venerated so consistently as the center of national and religious aspirations for Israel. The cogency of this situation was recognized by von Rad, who observed that the command to build an altar on Mt. Ebal and inscribe the law on the stones there raised a "barricade" against the theory of centralization (*Deuteronomium Studien* [1947], p. 47). Actually Deuteronomy demolishes the Wellhausen position completely by prescribing what the law is supposed to prohibit, utilizing the phraseology of Ex. 20:24 which, according to Wellhausen, the Deuteronomic pronouncements were meant to revoke. Dt. 27:1-8 supports Dt. 12 in looking forward to a national cultic center but permitting divine worship at properly accredited altars elsewhere.

Thus the centralization theory of Wellhausen, so important for his general chronology, rests upon a misreading and misunderstanding of the Hebrew text. As indicated above, Jerusalem was the least likely place for focusing Hebrew worship, since from *ca.* 2000 B.C. to the time of David it had been under successive Hurrian, Hyksos, and Jebusite rulers, and being in neutral territory was not included in any list when the land of Canaan was being apportioned. Jerusalem as a proper name occurs nowhere in the Pentateuch, although it was mentioned in the fourteenth-century B.C. Amarna texts in the form *Urusalim*. Although the "Salem" of Gen. 14:18 has been regarded as an abbreviated form of "Jerusalem," this may well be an entirely gratuitous assumption; it has, in fact, been challenged ever since the time of Eusebius. Archeological excavations have demonstrated without any doubt the pre-Israelite origin and nature of the city, which had its own distinctive designations during that period. There is actually no evidence to show that Salem is connected in any way with Jerusalem, and most probably instead is to be identified with a site near Balâṭah-Shechem, or with the Salim of Jn. 3:23, the latter perhaps being the modern Umm el-'Amdân. The "centralization" indicated by Deuteronomy points clearly to a locale in central Canaan, viz., in the Ebal-Gerizim area, and as Dt. 27:1-8 shows, this was to serve as a focus for national and spiritual objectives in Israel, and not as a site for elaborate cultic worship. Quite obviously the Samaritans were more correct in their traditions than the Jews in this regard (J. Macdonald, *Theology of the Samaritans* [1964], p. 16) in insisting that Gerizim, not Jerusalem, was the "place" of Dt. 12:5.

On this basis the literary-critical claim that the aim of Deuteronomy was to abolish the "high places" must also be criticized. A reading of Dt. 12 shows that such a consideration was not particularly pressing for the author, since the *bāmôṯ* were nowhere mentioned in that chapter. Its aim, as Pedersen pointed out (*ILC,* I-II, 27), was to cement the spiritual relationship between God and Israel and to protect the latter against the Canaanite religious and social degradations. The period which the author had in mind had not become sufficiently corrupt religiously to demand the kind of outright reformation necessary in later periods of Judah's history.

Since liberal scholars have been intent upon relating the provenance and date of Deuteronomy to Josiah's reformation, it should be observed that the latter merely abolished idolatry in Judah and did not centralize cultic worship in Jerusalem, since this had already been established there in the time of Solomon. If Deuteronomy had been composed by a disciple of Isaiah, as suggested by Rowley (*Growth of the OT*, p. 31), modifying S. R. Driver (*ICC* on Deuteronomy [3rd ed. 1951], p. lv), it is curious that the whole question of centralization was raised outside the context of either the "high places" or Jerusalem itself. Such a provenance and date can be dismissed easily, however, by noting that there are no traces whatever in Deuteronomy of either the doctrinal issues or literary style of the notable eighth-century B.C. prophet. How Deuteronomy could possibly constitute a manifesto for religious reform promulgated by a follower of Isaiah during the most vehement period of the idolator Manasseh is a problem to which no literary critic has chosen to address himself.

A coincident historical problem concerning the nature of the "law scroll" discovered by Hilkiah could perhaps be considered at this juncture. From about 1800 this document was considered to have comprised the bulk of Deuteronomy, but this assumption has been challenged increasingly by more recent scholarship. From 2 K. 22:3ff. it is admittedly impossible to determine the nature of the law scroll, but since the document could be read at least twice in one day it seems very unlikely that it could comprise the whole of Deuteronomy. It may have included part of the book, however, or perhaps it was an augmented form of the Book of the Covenant. Equally possible is the suggestion that it was a *testimonium* abstracted from the covenant material contained in Exodus, and was thus analagous to a summary of Deuteronomy. In the present state of the evidence it seems virtually impossible to equate the content of the law scroll with the totality of the extant book of Deuteronomy. The earlier view that the canonical book was a "pious fraud" has now been disproved decisively by archeological discoveries (cf. *FSAC*, p. 78), so that Deuteronomy has to be taken seriously as an authentic literary composition.

As observed above, the a priori approach of the Wellhausen school, aside from being completely unscientific methodologically, raises far more problems than it solves because of its arbitrary and entirely unwarranted reconstruction of Hebrew history. In view of the surprisingly wide range of critical opinion about the provenance and date of Deuteronomy, it would seem desirable to examine the work in the light of what it claims to be, namely, a second-millennium B.C. composition emerging from a wilderness milieu and dealing in detail with the implications of the Sinaitic covenant. Even viewed superficially on this basis it is immediately apparent that Deuteronomy contains nothing which is in the slightest way incompatible with substantial authorship by Moses. The laws are primitive and strictly authoritarian in nature, and the work manifests exactly the same kind of moral, ethical, and humanitarian concerns as those characterizing the covenant relationship.

Deuteronomy has always been considered unique, even among literary critics; for whereas other pentateuchal books have been divided up piecemeal among hypothetical underlying "documents," Deuteronomy has been regarded from the beginning as comprising a "document" in itself. Furthermore, the essential unity of the great kernel of Deuteronomy (chs. 5–26) is recognized and freely allowed by nearly everyone (e.g., Kautzsch, Kuenen, Dillman, Driver). Some would even defend the unity of the whole of chs. 1–26 (Knobel, Graf, Kosters, Colenso, Kleinert). No other book of the OT, unless it be the prophecies of Ezekiel, bears such unmistakable signs of unity in aim, language, and thought. Many striking expressions characterize the style of this eloquent book of oratory; e.g., "give to possess"; "Hear O Israel"; the oft-repeated root, meaning in the qal "learn" and in the piel "teach"; "be willing"; "so you shall purge the evil from the midst of you"; "as at this day"; "that it may go well with you"; "the land which you are going over to possess"; "with all your heart and with all your soul"; and many others, all of which occur frequently in Deuteronomy and rarely elsewhere in the OT, thus binding — so far as style can — the different sections of the book into one solid unit. Barring various titles and editorial additions (1:1-5; 4:44-49; 29:1; 33:1, 7, 9, 22; 34:1) and a few archeological notes such as 2:10-12, 20-23; 3:9, 11, 14; 10:6-9, and of course the last chapter, which gives an account of Moses' death, there is every reason necessary to suppose that the book is a unit. Few writings in the entire field of literature have so clear a unity of purpose or so uniform a style of address.

Considerable light has been thrown on the provenance and date of Deuteronomy by recent studies in ancient Near Eastern treaty forms, particularly those in use among the ancient Hittites. Excavations at Boghazköy have shown that the great Hittite kings were accustomed to negotiating two types of international treaties, one of which was an agreement with an equal, the so-called parity treaty, while the other was the kind entered into with an inferior, the suzerainty or vassal treaty. The latter variety has survived in abundance, and was of obvious importance in maintaining the stability of the Hittite empire. Vassal treaties were formulated according to a well-established pattern, and contained most if not all of the following ingredients:

(a) A preamble in which the great king is identified and, as suzerain, begins to define the obligations of the vassal.

(b) A historical prologue describing the past benevolence of the suzerain towards his vassal. This material, always carefully compiled, is extremely important for a study of Hittite history; its inclusion marks the difference between second- and first-millennium B.C. international treaties.

(c) Stipulations of a basic and more detailed nature, in which the vassal binds himself by accepting the conditions laid down by the suzerain.

(d) Deposition of the treaty text in the sanctuary of the vassal, so that it would be in contact with the most sacred national cultic objects of the vassal and be afforded analagous reverence as a result.

(e) Provision for public reading of the treaty. The Hittites generally required such a document to be read between one and four times annually, irrespective of the fact that all covenants were normally renewed in each generation.

(f) A list of witnesses, this being a regular concluding element in ancient Near Eastern legal documents. In the vassal treaties the gods of both participating states were listed, so as to give proper authority to the text.

(g) A list of blessings and curses which the witnessing parties would bring upon themselves according as they kept or broke the provisions of the agreement. Peace and prosperity were obviously the greatest blessings that the vassal could expect from the treaty.

(h) The mention of a feast, which on some occasions followed the ratification ceremony.

While this analysis is somewhat schematic, it contains all the elements deemed necessary for a valid treaty. The form of the suzerainty treaty was evidently well known throughout the ancient Near East in the Late Bronze Age (*ca.* 1400-1200 B.C.), and when the structure of Deuteronomy is analyzed it will be seen to correspond strikingly to the secular covenantal forms, as follows:

(a) preamble (1:1-5; cf. Ex. 20:1; Josh. 24:2);

(b) historical prologue (1:6–3:29; cf. Ex. 20:2; Josh. 24:2-13);

(c) stipulations: basic (4–11; cf. Ex. 20:3-17, 22-26; Josh. 24:14-25); detailed (12–26; cf. Ex. 21:23; 25–31);

(d) deposit of text (31:9, 24-26; cf. Ex. 25:16; 34:1, 28f.; Josh. 24:26);

(e) provision for public reading (31:10-13);

(f) witnesses (31:16-30; 32:1-47; cf. Ex. 24:4; Josh. 24:22, 27);

(g) blessings (28:1-14; cf. Lev. 26:3-13; Josh. 24:19f.); curses (28:15-68; cf. Lev. 26:14-33).

Hittite treaties frequently mentioned the oath sworn by a vassal at a solemn ratification ceremony (cf. Ex. 24:1-11; Dt. 27), though the form of words has not survived. Second-millennium B.C. treaties also paralleled the OT procedure for action taken against a perfidious vassal, the so-called "controversy" (Heb. *riḇ*) pattern.

The character and order of the Deuteronomic covenantal elements make it clear that the book was designed to serve as a renewal of the Sinai covenant, and corresponds in structure to late second-millennium B.C. secular treaties, as observed above. The criterion for this is that whereas treaties from that period always contained a historical prologue, covenants from the first millennium B.C. always omitted it. This has been made clear by

G. E. Mendenhall (*Law and Covenant in Israel and the Ancient Near East* [1955]) and others, and has only been contested by a writer such as D. J. McCarthy (*Treaty and Covenant* [1963], pp. 7, 80ff., 171) on the basis of a misunderstanding of the situation. Therefore, any treaty which contains a historical prologue always follows the second-millennium B.C. pattern, and should be assigned quite properly to that period, since there is no evidence to date of first-millennium B.C. Hittite treaties being drawn up as though they had been written in the preceding millennium, for fairly obvious historical reasons. As M. Kline (*Treaty of the Great King* [1963], pp. 13ff.) has shown, when Deuteronomy is viewed holistically, it demonstrates on a large scale the complete covenantal formulation of the ancient Near East, a fact which points strongly to its fundamental structural unity on grounds other than those advanced previously by scholars. The importance of viewing Deuteronomy against the background of second-millennium B.C. suzerainty treaties has even been recognized by so liberal a scholar as von Rad. In his article entitled "Deuteronomy" in *IDB* (I, 831-38), he ignored the archeological evidence completely; but by 1962 he was compelled to admit that a comparison of Deuteronomy with the Hittite treaties showed so many points of contact, especially in matters of form, that there must be some connection between the treaties and the exposition of details of the covenant with Israel (*OT Theology*, I [1962], 132).

If it is correct to emphasize the structural unity of Deuteronomy against the background of Near Eastern international treaties, it can no longer be considered necessary to entertain it as the product of numerous redactions of the material that allegedly stimulated the reforms of Josiah. What were originally thought to be "two introductions" (Dt. 1–4; 5–11) cannot now be regarded as the result of two editors working over the text at different times, since in second-millennium B.C. Hittite treaties a historical prologue regularly followed the preamble and preceded the stipulations. Since form-critical data now require the recognition of the antiquity of Deuteronomy as an integer, it seems pointless for liberal writers to insist upon a "final edition" of the book in the 7th cent. B.C., or even later, since the date of composition of the material in substantially its final form is within the 2nd millennium B.C., i.e., relative to the age of Moses, the attributive author. The only adequate explanation of the provenance and date of Deuteronomy is that the Sinai covenant was instituted in the 13th cent. B.C., and also renewed at that time by Moses in the plains of Moab. This occurred at precisely the period of other Late Bronze Age covenants (*ca.* 1400-1200 B.C.), which as indicated above are reflected in detail in the structure and text of Deuteronomy. Had the book only begun to move towards literary fixity between the 9th and 6th cents. B.C., as many liberal scholars were wont to suggest, it is hard to see why obsolete second-millennium B.C. covenantal forms were employed in the composition when less complex and more commonly used first-millennium B.C. structures were studiously ignored.

The simplest and most obvious explanation of origins and date is that supplied by the book itself, viz., that Deuteronomy is actually a covenant-renewal document formulated in the 13th cent. B.C. along thoroughly familiar international treaty patterns. The hortatory utterances of Deuteronomy are represented as words placed in the mouth of Moses. His name occurs nearly forty times, mostly as the authoritative author of the subject matter. The 1st person is used frequently throughout (cf. 1:16; 3:21; 29:5; etc.), and the book depicts Moses as teaching Israel divine statutes and judgments as a preparation for sedentary occupation of Canaan (cf. 4:5, 14; 5:31; 7:1; etc.). Coupled with these are prophetic exhortations from Moses which give Deuteronomy its outstanding parenetic character. Israel is warned time and again about the dangers of being lured into grave sin through indulgence in idol-worship. The way in which Moses undertook to "explain" the law (1:5) indicates that he thought it desirable to expound what had been delivered previously, which is consistent with the nature of Deuteronomy as a covenant-renewal document.

The group of appendices (Dt. 31:1–34:12) refer specifically to Moses as a compiler of the law. This law must have been of a written character, since the term "book" (Heb. *sēper*) was never used in the ancient Near East of material transmitted orally. From Dt. 31:22 it might appear that Moses wrote down the Song before actually reciting it in public. This material is thoroughly consistent with Mosaic authorship, and its concepts and vocabulary point to the late Amarna Age for its provenance. The blessing (33:1-29), by contrast, was originally oral in nature, following the usual pattern of Near Eastern benedictions (cf. Gn. 27:27ff.). The final chapter of Deuteronomy was formerly hailed by critical scholars as evidence that Moses could not possibly be taken seriously as the author of the Pentateuch, since he could hardly have written his own obituary notice. This is an unwarranted conclusion, to say the least, since all that is implied is that the final eight verses of Deuteronomy did not proceed from Moses' hand. While the literary activity of the great Hebrew lawgiver ended with the deposit of the "book of the law" near the ark (Dt. 31:24ff.), the Mosaicity of chs. 32 to 34 is extremely difficult to dispute. As regards the obituary itself, Jewish tradition is most probably correct in assigning the final eight verses of the Torah to Joshua. Following normal Near Eastern tradition, narratives dealing with events of any importance were written down at the time of, or shortly after, the particular incidents had occurred, and this doubtless took place in connection with the death of Moses.

V. Language and Style.–Written in good classical Hebrew, the book compares well with the best models in the OT. Grammatically and linguistically it is superior to some of the later books in the Hebrew canon. It uses a standard vocabulary, but at the same time employs skilfully some words rarely found in normal prose, and the book also manifests a tendency to use certain Hebrew emphatic forms. Certain alleged Aramaisms, formerly cited in support of a seventh-century date, are today invalid as evidence in the light of linguistic evidence from the Amarna Age and earlier. Aramaic is now recognized as having had a long pre-history and as having overlaid in Palestine an older stratum of Canaanite at an early stage of its development, so that "many of the alleged Aramaisms in the Hebrew Bible, on which occasionally far-reaching critical conclusions have been based, are in fact pure Canaanitisms or common North-west Semitic" (A. M. Honeyman in *OTMS*, p. 278). The Pentateuch itself reminds the reader that Jacob had specific Aramean connections (Dt. 26:5), while Laban was described as speaking to his son-in-law in Aramaic (Gen. 31:47).

The literary style of Deuteronomy is very marked. In no other OT book is there such a sustained and palpable flow of rhetoric. The discourses are memorable for their stately periods and reflect "a prophet in whom we must acknowledge one of the most marvellous minds of original power" (H. Ewald, *Geschichte des Volkes Israel*

[1843-1855], II, 323). Resonant words combine with felicitous phrases to sweep the reader along in graceful cadences. The presentation of the subject matter is sometimes stern, sometimes tender, but always urgent and expansive, without ever becoming prolix or tedious.

VI. Influence in Israel's History.–The influence of Deuteronomy began to be felt from the very beginning of Israel's career in Canaan. Though the references to Deuteronomy in Joshua, Judges, Samuel, and Kings are comparatively few, yet they are sufficient to show that not only the principles of Deuteronomy were known and observed but also that they were known in written form as codified statutes. For example, when Jericho was taken, the city and its spoil were "devoted" (Josh. 6:17f.) in keeping with Dt. 13:15ff. (cf. Josh. 10:40; 11:12, 15 with Dt. 7:2; 20:16f.). Achan trespassed and he and his household were stoned, and afterward burned with fire (Josh. 7:25; cf. Dt. 13:10; 17:5). The fact that his sons and his daughters were put to death with him seems at first sight to contradict Dt. 24:16, but there is no proof that they suffered *for their father's sin* (*see* ACHAN; DEVOTE; besides, the Hebrews recognized the unity of the household, even that of Rahab the harlot (Josh. 6:17). Again, when Ai was taken, "only the cattle and the spoil" did Israel take as their booty (Josh. 8:27), in keeping with Dt. 20:14; also, the body of the king of Ai was taken down before nightfall from the tree on which he had been hanged (Josh. 8:29), which was in keeping with Dt. 21:23 (cf. Josh. 10:26.). As in warfare, so in worship. For instance, Joshua built an altar on Mt. Ebal (Josh. 8:30f.), "as Moses the servant of the Lord had commanded" (cf. Dt. 27:4-6), and he wrote on the stones a copy of the law (Josh. 8:32), as Moses had also enjoined (Dt. 27:3, 8). Moreover, the elders and officers and judges stood on either side of the ark of the covenant between Ebal and Gerizim (Josh. 8:33), as directed in Dt. 11:29; 27:12f., and Joshua read to all the congregation of Israel all the words of the law, the blessings and the curses (Josh. 8:34f.), in strict accord with Dt. 31:11f.

But the passage of paramount importance is the story of the two and a half tribes who, on their return to their home on the east side of the Jordan, erected a memorial at the Jordan and, when accused by their fellow tribesmen of plurality of sanctuary, emphatically disavowed it (Josh. 22:29; cf. Dt. 12:5). Obviously, therefore, Deuteronomy was known in the days of Joshua. A few instances in the history of the judges point in the same direction: e.g., the utter destruction of Zephath (Jgs. 1:17; cf. Dt. 7:2; 20:16f.); Gideon's elimination of the fearful and faint-hearted from his army (Jgs. 7:1-7; cf. Dt. 20:1-9); the author's studied concern to justify Gideon and Manoah for sacrificing at altars other than Shiloh on the ground that they acted in obedience to Yahweh's direct commands (Jgs. 6:25-27; 13:16); the case of Micah, especially, who congratulated himself that Yahweh would do him good since he had a Levite for a priest, is clear evidence that Deuteronomy was known in the days of the judges (Jgs. 17:13; cf. Dt. 10:8; 18:1-8; 33:8-11).

In 1 S. 1:1-9, 21, 24 the pious Elkanah is pictured as going yearly to worship Yahweh at Shiloh, the central sanctuary at that time. After the destruction of Shiloh, when the ark of the covenant had been captured by the Philistines, Samuel indeed sacrificed at Mizpah, Ramah, and Bethlehem (1 S. 7:7-9, 17; 16:5), but in doing so he only took advantage of the elasticity of the Deuteronomic law: "when he gives you rest from all your enemies round about, so that you dwell in safety, then to the place which the Lord your God will choose, to make his name dwell there, thither shall you bring all that I command you: your burnt offerings and your sacrifices" (Dt. 12:10f.). It was not until Solomon's time that Israel's enemies were all subdued, and even then Solomon did not observe strictly the teachings of Deuteronomy: "his wives turned away his heart," so that he did not faithfully keep Yahweh's "covenant" and "statutes" (1 K. 11:3, 11). Political disruption followed, and religion necessarily suffered. Yet Jehoiada the priest gave the youthful Joash "the crown" and "the testimony" (2 K. 11:12; cf. Dt. 17:18). King Amaziah did not slay the children of the murderers who slew his father, in conscious obedience, apparently, to the law of Deuteronomy (2 K. 14:6; cf. Dt. 24:16). Later on, Hezekiah, the cultured king of Judah, reformed the cultus of his day by removing the high places, breaking down the pillars, cutting down the Asherahs, and even breaking in pieces the brazen serpent which Moses had made (2 K. 18:4, 22). Hezekiah's reforms were unquestionably carried through under the influence of Deuteronomy.

It is equally certain that the prophets of the 8th cent. were not ignorant of this book. For example, Hosea complains of Israel's sacrificing upon the tops of the mountains and burning incense upon the hills, and warns Judah not to follow Israel's example in coming up to worship at Gilgal and Beth-aven (Hos. 4:13, 15). He also alludes to striving with priests (Hos. 4:4; cf. Dt. 17:12), removing landmarks (Hos. 5:10; cf. Dt. 19:14), returning to Egypt (Hos. 8:13; 9:3; cf. Dt. 28:68), and of Yahweh's tender dealing with Ephraim (Hos. 11:3; cf. Dt. 1:31; 32:10). The courage of Amos, the shepherd-prophet of Tekoa, can best be explained also, on the basis of a written law such as that of Deuteronomy with which he and his hearers were already more or less familiar (Am. 3:2; cf. Dt. 7:6; 4:7f.). He condemns Israel's inhumanity and adultery in the name of religion, and complains of their retaining overnight pledges wrested from the poor, which was distinctly forbidden in Deuteronomy (Am. 2:6-8; cf. Dt. 24:12-15; 23:17). Likewise, in the prophecies of Isaiah there are conscious reflections of Deuteronomy's thought and teaching. Zion is constantly pictured as the center of the nation's religion and as the Lord's secure dwelling-place (Isa. 2:2-4; 8:18; 28:16; 29:1f.; cf. Mic. 4:1-4). In short, no one of the four great prophets of the 8th cent. B.C. — Isaiah, Micah, Amos, Hosea — ever recognized "high places" as legitimate centers of worship.

VII. Summary of Teaching.–The doctrine of the book presents a lofty spirituality, setting forth important ethical truths which Moses, as the leader of God's chosen people, wished to impress upon the covenant nation before they entered the land of promise. Deuteronomy teaches a strict monotheism which precludes any "other gods" (4:24, 35, 39). The God of Israel is God alone, majestic and supreme (3:24; 6:14f.; 7:4f.; 8:19f.; 11:16f., 28; etc.). This God who revealed Himself to Israel (1:6) is a faithful and covenant-keeping deity (7:9, 12) whose love is manifested in His choice of Israel (7:6-8; 10:15; 14:2). The Israelite nation, standing in a special filial relationship to Him (1:31; 8:2f., 16, 14:2) must reciprocate this love (6:5). Therefore, Israel's worship and service must be motivated by genuine love for God (10:12; 11:1, 13, 22; 13:3f.; 19:9; 30:6, 16, 20), that she may walk before Him in holiness of life (7:6; 14:2; 18:13; 26:19). In particular, she must be kind to the needy, the poor, the orphan, the widow, the Levite, the stranger (10:18f.; 24:17-21; 26:12), to the animal creation (25:4), even to the mother bird and her young (22:6f.). The strong humanitarian emphasis of other pentateuchal writings is just as prominent in Deuteronomy. In order to ensure that the spiritual traditions of the covenant relationship will be sustained at the highest level through future generations, the Israelites are urged to bring up their children in the reverence and admonition of the Lord (4:9; 6:7, 20-25; 11:19-21; 31:13). Such obedience to the Lord will bring joy, while disobedience will result in evil (28:1ff.). Temporal rewards are promised to those who make right conduct a consistent way of living (8:18; 14:29; 15:10; 16:20; 28:8). The appeal in Deuteronomy to fear God and keep His commandments is directed to the individual as well as to the nation. Its purpose is to demonstrate that type of religious faith and practice which reaches down to the common affairs of life as well as up to the throne of God. Optimism, sustained by implicit faith in God's saving power, is the hallmark of the prophetic outlook which the author of Deuteronomy manifests.

See also Map V; Plate 14.

Bibliography.–R. Y. French, ed., *Lex Mosaica* (1894); *HDB*, I, *s.v.* "Deuteronomy" (H. E. Ryle); J. Orr, *Problem of the OT* (1906); W. L. Alexander, *Pulpit Commentary*, III (1906); G. A. Smith, *Cambridge Bible* (1918); R. H. Kennett, *Origin of the Book of Deuteronomy* (1920); G. Hölscher, *ZAW*, 40 (1922), 161-255; A. C. Welch, *Code of Deuteronomy* (1924); *Deuteronomy: The Framework to the Code* (1932); H. M. Wiener, *Das Hauptproblem des Deuteronomiums* (1924); A. H. Finn, *Unity of the Pentateuch* (1928); J. H. Hertz, *Pentateuch and the Haftorahs*, V (1936); *ILC*, III-IV (1959); R. Brinker, *Influence of Sanctuaries in Early Israel* (1946); O. T. Allis, *The Five Books of Moses* (1949); G. C. Aalders, *Short Intro. to the Pentateuch* (1949); E. Robertson, *The OT Problem* (1950); S. R. Driver, *ICC* (1951); E. J. Young, *An Intro. to the OT* (1952); G. von Rad, *Studies in Deuteronomy* (1953); G. T. Manley, *Book of the Law* (1957); K. Baltzer, *Covenant Formulary* (Eng. tr. 1971); J. N. M. Wijngaards, *The Formulas of the Deuteronomic Creed* (1963); J. A. Thompson, *Ancient Near Eastern Treaties and the OT* (1964); K. A. Kitchen, *Ancient Orient and OT* (1966); R. K. Harrison, *Intro. to the OT* (1969), pp. 635-662 (with bibliography); P. C. Craigie, *Deuteronomy* (*NICOT*, 1976; with bibliography).

D. M. EDWARDS R. K. HARRISON

DEVICE; DEVISE [Heb. *bāḏā'*] (1 K. 12:33); NEB CHOOSE; [*hāgâ*] (Prov. 24:2); AV STUDY; NEB THINK OF; [*zāmam*] (Prov. 30:32); AV THINK; NEB "be fond of"; [*zimmâ*] (Ps. 26:10; Prov. 24:9; Isa. 32:7); AV also MISCHIEF, THOUGHTS; NEB also INTRIGUE, MISCHIEF, PLAN; [*ḥāraš*] (Prov. 6:14, 18; 12:20; 14:22); AV also IMAGINE; NEB also FORGE, INTEND, INTENTIONS, PLOT; [*ḥāšaḇ*] (Ex. 31:4; 35:32; 2 S. 14:14; Est. 8:3; 9:25; Ps. 10:2; 21:11 [MT 12]; 35:4; Jer. 11:19; 18:11; Ezk. 11:2; 38:10; Dnl. 11:24f.; Hos. 7:15; Mic. 2:1, 3; Zec. 7:10; 8:17); AV also FORECAST, IMAGINE, THINK; NEB also CONTRIVE, DESIGN, HATCH PLOTS, LAY, LAY PLANS, PERFECT, etc.; [*ḥiššāḇôn*] (Eccl. 7:29); AV INVENTION; NEB SUBTLETY; [*yā'aṣ*] (Isa. 7:5; 32:7f.; Mic. 6:5; Hab. 2:10); AV also CONSULT, TAKE COUNSEL; NEB also BRING, FORM, LAY PLANS, SCHEME; [*mô'eṣâ*] (Prov. 1:31); [*m^{e}zimmâ*] (Ps. 37:7; Prov. 12:2); NEB also END, SCHEMER; [*maḥ^{a}šāḇâ*] (Est. 8:5; Job 5:12; Isa. 65:2; Jer. 6:19; Lam. 3:60f.); AV also IMAGINATIONS, THOUGHTS; NEB also PLOT, SCHEMING, WRITE; [*pā'al*] (Ps. 58:2 [MT 3]); AV WORK; [Gk. *sophízō*] (2 Pet. 1:16); NEB SPIN.

Most of the OT terms mean think, plan, or invent, usually in a bad sense, though sometimes in a good sense (e.g., Prov. 14:22). Heb. *hāgâ* originally meant "moan" or "growl," then "speak"; hence it came to mean "imagine," particularly violence. The term *ḥāraš*, originally meaning "cut in," "engrave," or "plough," came to have the broader meaning of "practice" or "devise." In Eccl. 7:29 "devices" refers to inventions which man has sought out in contradistinction to the righteousness with which God created him. Heb. *yā'aṣ* means literally "advice" or "counsel." The wicked devise wickedness, the noble nobleness (Isa. 32:7f.). Similarly, *mô'ēṣâ* denotes "counsel," "advice," or "plan."

The term "devise" occurs only once in the NT, in 2 Pet. 1:16. The verb *sophízō* means literally "make wise." Here it is used in the passive in the phrase "cleverly devised myths," apparently referring to the false wisdom of Gnostic teachings. (See *TDNT*, VII, *s.v.* σοφίζω [Wilckens].)

J. R. PRICE

DEVIL. *See* DEMONOLOGY; SATAN.

DEVOTE; DEVOTED THING [Heb. *ḥērem*, hiphil of *ḥāram*] (Lev. 27:21, 28f.; Nu. 18:14; Dt. 13:17; Josh. 6:17f.; 17:1, 11-13, 15; 22:20; 1 S. 15:21; 1 K. 20:42; 1 Ch. 2:7; Ezk. 44:29; Mic. 4:13); AV CURSED THING, ACCURSED, ACCURSED THING, APPOINT (1 K. 20:42), "things which should have been utterly destroyed" (1 S. 15:21), DEDICATED THING, CONSECRATE; NEB also "(laid, forbidden, etc.) under the ban" (Dt. 13:17; Josh. 6:17f.; 7:12; 1 S. 15:21; 1 K. 20:42), BAN, SACRED BAN, FORBIDDEN THINGS; [hiphil of *'āḇar*–'let pass through'] (Lev. 18:21); AV "let pass through (the fire)"; NEB SURRENDER.

Something "devoted" to the Lord, or "placed under the ban" (NEB), was forbidden to common use. The *ḥērem* was particularly associated with warfare. Yahweh instructed Israel that when she entered the cities of the land promised to her she was to put to death everything that breathed (Dt. 7:1f.; 20:16-18; cf. Nu. 21:2f.), so that the inhabitants would not teach Israel their abominable practices. Everything flammable was to be burned, while the precious metals were to be put into the treasury of the house of the Lord (Dt. 7:25f.; Josh. 6:24). Thus all that was in the city was to be offered as a whole burnt offering to Yahweh. Because Achan broke the ban placed on Jericho (Josh. 7:1, 20f.; cf. 6:17-21, 24), all Israel was punished with defeat at the hand of Ai, and Achan and his family and all his belongings were placed under the ban (7:11-15, 24f.). An Israelite city that turned to practicing idolatry was to be devoted to destruction in the same way as the Canaanite cities, as well as any individual who sacrificed to another god (Ex. 22:20). No devoted person or thing could be ransomed (Lev. 27:28f.). Fields and possessions that Israelites devoted to the Lord became the property of the priests (Lev. 27:21; Nu. 18:14; Ezk. 44:29).

The concept of the *ḥērem* was also used by the prophets. Isaiah prophesies that the Lord has "doomed" (RSV, Heb. *ḥāram*) the heathen nations (34:2; cf. Mic. 4:13). In the day of the Lord, however, there shall be no more curse (*ḥērem*, Zec. 14:11).

See also DEDICATE; DESTRUCTION I.D, III.

N. J. O.

DEVOTION [Heb. *rāṣâ*] (1 Ch. 29:3); AV AFFECTION; NEB DELIGHT; [*ḥeseḏ*] (Jer. 2:2); AV KINDNESS; [Gk. *eupáredros*] (1 Cor. 7:35); AV ATTEND; NEB "wait upon"; [*haplótēs*] ("sincere devotion," 2 Cor. 11:3); AV SIMPLICITY; [*ethelothrēskeía*] (Col. 2:23); AV WORSHIP; NEB PIETY. The Heb. *rāṣâ* has a general meaning of "being pleased with" something. *Ḥeseḏ*, on the other hand, denotes a demonstration of faithfulness in the context of a mutual relationship (*see* KINDNESS). Gk. *ethelothrēskeía* is apparently a term coined by Paul; it occurs only in Col. 2:23, designating religion that is "self-made" (Bauer, p. 217).

In Acts 17:23, AV, the plural term *sebásmata* is rendered "devotions," an obsolete term for "objects of worship" (RSV, NEB). N. J. O.

DEVOUT [Heb. *ḥeseḏ*] (Isa. 57:1); AV MERCIFUL; NEB "of good faith"; [Gk. *eulabḗs*] (Lk. 2:25; Acts 2:5; 8:2; 22:12); [*eusebḗs*] (Acts 10:2, 7); NEB also RELIGIOUS; [*sebómenos*] (Acts 13:43, 50; 17:4, 17); AV also RELIGIOUS; NEB WORSHIPPER, GOD-FEARING. The "devout" men of Isa. 57:1 were the God-fearing men who had been faithful to the covenant with Yahweh. On the concept of *ḥeseḏ*, *see* KINDNESS.

In the NT *eulabḗs* is used only of Jews. It always refers to one who is punctilious in his observance of the law. The participle *sebómenos* (from verb *sébomai*, "worship") and the cognate adjective *eusebḗs* are generally used in Acts to refer to a class of Gentiles who attended the synagogue and observed the Jewish laws but were not full proselytes, inasmuch as they were not circumcized. (The usage in 13:43 appears to be an exception, as *sebómenos* is used with *prosēlýtos*.) This class of *sebómenoi* was the most receptive to Paul's preaching, since circumcision was not a condition for salvation.

See also PROSELYTE. N. J. O.

DEW [Heb. *ṭal*]. Two things are necessary for the formation of dew; moisture and cold. Palestine is fortunate in being near the sea, so that the air always contains a large amount of water vapor; and because the skies are clear, the rapid radiation beginning immediately after sunset cools the land and air so that the moisture is condensed and settles on cool objects.

In Palestine it seldom rains from April to October, and if it were not for the dew in summer all vegetation would perish. Dew and rain are equally important. If there is no rain the winter grass and harvests fail; if no dew the late crops dry up and there is no fruit. Even on the edge of the great Syrian desert in Anti-Lebanon, beyond Jordan, and in Sinai, a considerable vegetation flourishes in the summer, although there is not a drop of rain for six months. The dews are so heavy that the plants and trees are literally soaked with water at night, absorbing sufficient moisture to supply more than the loss due to evaporation in the day. Yet more impressive is the sight of a flourishing vineyard practically in the desert itself. Some of the small animals of the desert, such as the jerboa, seem to have no water supply except the dew. The wetting of Gideon's fleece (Jgs. 6:38) is an indication of the amount of dew that is formed.

Drawing on the Israelites' experience of dew as a necessity for life, Yahweh says, "I will be as the dew to Israel" (Hos. 14:5). Dew and rain are spoken of together in 1 K. 17:1. Failure of either of these gifts would cause great want and hardship; the failure of both would cause famine and death. Dew was especially valued by the Israelites in the desert, for it supplied the manna for their sustenance (Ex. 16:13; Nu. 11:9).

"Dew" is used in a symbolic sense in Gen. 27:28, where Isaac in blessing Jacob asks that the "dew of heaven," i.e., those things that make for fertility and prosperity, be granted to him. Micah prophesied a restoration in which "the remnant of Jacob shall be in the midst of many peoples like dew from the Lord" (Mic. 5:7), i.e., a means of blessing to the nations. The author of the Song of Moses says, "May . . . my speech distil as the dew" (Dt. 32:2). The beloved, coming from the garden, says, "my head is wet with dew" (Cant. 5:2). In the Psalms "dew" is used as a figure for brotherly unity (133:3) and youthfulness (110:3), while Isaiah speaks of "a dew of light" (26:19) and describes Yahweh's dwelling-place as "a cloud of dew" (18:4) that refreshes the harvesters. Job describes his past prosperity as a time when "the dew [was] all night on my branches" (29:19).

In other figures dew is a symbol of stealth — of that which comes up unawares (2 S. 17:12) — and of inconstancy (Hos. 6:4; 13:3). God's knowledge covers the whole realm of natural phenomena that are mysteries to man (Job 38:28; Prov. 3:20). A. H. JOY

DIADEM. In each biblical use the diadem is a badge of royalty. In Isa. 28:5 Heb. *ṣ^epîrâ* denotes something encircling the head, while in Isa. 62:3 *ṣānîp* indicates some kind of headgear, such as a turban or cloth twisted around the forehead. In the NT, *diádēma* (Rev. 12:3; 13:1; 19:12) means "something bound around the head." The Greeks gave the name "diadem" to the band surrounding the tiara of a Persian king, and later adopted it for their own wreath-like crown. *See* CROWN.

DIAL OF AHAZ [Heb. *ma'^alôṯ*–'steps'] (2 K. 20:11; Isa. 38:8); AV also SUN DIAL OF AHAZ; NEB STAIRWAY OF AHAZ. One of the most striking instances of divine intervention in human affairs at the behest of a prophet was connected with the sign of divine healing given to the ailing Judean king Hezekiah 716/715-687/686 B.C.). The monarch was given a choice between seeing the shadow on the dial go down ten steps, or backward by the same amount. When the latter was chosen, the prayer of Isaiah was answered and the shadow returned ten steps (2 K. 20:5-11; Isa. 38:8).

This passage contains the only biblical reference to a horologe, i.e., some mechanism or device marking the passage of time. Various kinds of sundials were known to both the Mesopotamians and Egyptians. According to Herodotus (ii.109), the Babylonians had long been using a device consisting of a gnomon and dial marked in twelve-hour gradations. Excavators at Gezer uncovered a small portable sundial of Egyptian manufacture, and assigned it to the first half of the 15th cent. B.C. (cf. E. J. Pilcher, *PEQ*, 55 [1923], 85ff.). It is not impossible, therefore, that a sundial such as the foregoing was being used to measure the passing of time in the palace of Hezekiah.

However, it is unfortunate that the term *ma'^alôṯ* has been translated in both the AV and RSV by a term that describes a recognized astronomical instrument. The word means "steps of a stairway," and there is no evidence to support the view of the Targums and Vulgate that the "dial" of Ahaz was a horologe of the Babylonian variety. The stairway in question was probably connected with the covered way for the sabbath, which had been built inside the palace by Ahaz at a time when the outer royal entrance was being removed (2 K. 16:18). This stairway may have served as a replacement for the causeway made by David westward at the gate of Shallecheth (1 Ch. 26:16). Whatever the case, it appears that at certain times of the day the shadow of some projecting object fell upon the staircase, and we learn from both 2 Kings and Isaiah that this shadow had already gone down the steps, while from Isaiah we learn in addition that the sun also was going down. The miracle therefore took place in the afternoon, when the sun moves on its downward course, and when all shadows are thrown in an easterly direction. We are not told what the object was that cast the shadow, but it must have stood to the west of the staircase; and the top of the staircase must have passed into the shadow first, the foot of the staircase remaining longest in the light. The royal palace is understood to have been placed SE of the temple, and it is therefore probable that it was some part of the temple buildings that had cast its shadow down the stairway in full view of the dying king, as he lay in his chamber. If the afternoon were well advanced, the sun would be moving rapidly in altitude and but little in azimuth; or, in other words, the shadow would be advancing down the steps at its quickest rate, but be moving only slowly toward the left of those who were mounting them. It may well have been the case, therefore, that the time had come when the priests from Ophel and the officials and courtiers from the palace were going up the ascent into the house of the Lord to be present at the evening sacrifice, passing from the bright sunshine at the foot of the stairs into the shadow that had already fallen upon the upper steps. The sun would be going straight down behind the buildings and the steps already in shadow would sink into deeper shadow, not to emerge again into the light until a new day's sun had arisen.

When Hezekiah was given the choice of a sign, it would have been easy for him, as he remarked to Isaiah, to choose to hasten the decline of the shadow, since a bank of cloud behind the temple would have achieved that effect readily. But no disposition of cloud could bring the shadow back from that part of the stairway that had already passed into it and restore it to the sunshine. To see the more difficult of the two choices executed before his very eyes would be the best possible guarantee that he would in fact recover and go to the house of the Lord on the third day. The shadow returned ten steps (AV "degrees"), and in fulfillment of His promise God healed Hezekiah, adding another fifteen years to his life.

Various explanations of the phenomenon have been offered, but as it is impossible to know the astronomical conditions at the time of the incident, they must remain in the realm of conjecture. There can be no doubt as to the actuality of the stairway, since time-measuring devices employing such staircases were used in Egypt (cf. S. Iwry, *BASOR*, 147 [Oct. 1957], 30-33). Equally, it is impossible to accept the suggestion that the horologe may have had a dial-face improperly constructed so as to reverse the motion of the shadow at certain times, since such a device would have been completely useless, to say nothing of reproducing the phenomenon of retrograde motion with disconcerting and meaningless frequency. The biblical narrative makes it clear that the occurrence was not connected with any known natural law, since the dying king was given free choice and exercised it without restriction. Indeed, the very character of natural law precludes the possibility of alternative consequences resulting from its operation. Because the movement of the shadow cannot be explained by any known astronomical law, it does not seem possible to do other than assign the phenomenon to the supernatural realm and to attempt, as far as is possible, to explain known details of the general setting.

Bibliography.–E. W. Maunder, *Astronomy of the Bible* (1908); R. N. and M. L. Myall, *Sundials* (1938); J. A. Montgomery and H. S. Gehman, *Kings (ICC*, 1951), pp. 508f.

R. K. HARRISON

DIAMOND. *See* STONES, PRECIOUS.

DIANA. *See* ARTEMIS.

DIASPORA dī-as'pə-rə. *See* DISPERSION.

DIBLAIM dib'lə-im, dib-lā'əm [Heb. *diḇlayim*–'two cakes']. A native of Northern Israel and father of Gomer, the wife of Hosea (Hos. 1:3).

DIBLATH (Ezk. 6:14, AV). *See* RIBLAH.

DIBON dī'bon, dē'bon [Heb. *dîḇôn*].

1. (Neh. 11:25); also **DIMONAH** dī-mō'nə [Heb. *dîmônâ*] (Josh. 15:22). A town in the south of Judah, near the boundary of Edom. The modern urban settlement Dimonah, founded in 1955, 18 mi. (29 km.) SE of Beer-sheba, is not to be identified with the Judean town; 2 mi. (3 km.) N of it there is a group of cisterns which might indicate the location of the ancient town.

2. Also **DIBON-GAD** dī'bon-gad [Heb. *dîḇōn gāḏ*] (Nu. 33:45f.); AV, NEB, also DIMON [*dîmôn*] (Isa. 15:9). Dibon in Moab, present-day Dhībân, where the Moabite (Mesha) Stone was discovered, 11 mi. (18 km.) E of the Dead Sea, 3 mi. (5 km.) N of the river Arnon. According to the excavations by the American School, there was an Early Bronze settlement on the northern hill, while the present Arabic village occupies the southern one. After a gap during the Middle and Late Bronze ages the site was densely inhabited during Iron I, the "Moabite" period, and again successively in Nabatean, Roman, Byzantine, and early Arabic times. The excavations yielded a small fragment of a Moabite stele which might antedate the Mesha Stone by a few decades, and much pottery from the times of Mesha.

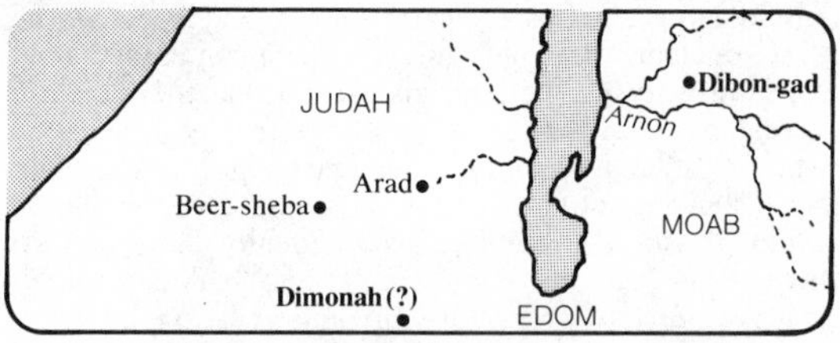

An Amorite satirical poem on the conquest of Moab N from the river Arnon by Sihon (13th cent.), quoted in Nu. 21:30, mentions Dibon. With other towns, the region was given to the tribes of Reuben and Gad (Nu. 32:3; Josh. 13:9). Gad rebuilt Dibon (Nu. 32:34), which therefore is called Dibon-gad in Nu. 33:45f. In Josh. 13:17, however, the town is allotted to Reuben. Mesha, who called himself "the Daibanite" (Moabite Stone, line 1), restored Moab's independence (*ca*. 840); one of his principal centers of power was Daibān, biblical Dibon (Moabite Stone, lines 21, 28). Isa. 15 has preserved a mocking song on a defeat of Moab; Dibon is mentioned in vv. 2 and 9, in the latter place under the form Dimon (1QIsa^{a,b} have "Dibon") making possible the pun with Heb. *dām*, "blood"; cf. Dimonah above (**1.**), and possibly Madmen in Jer. 48:2. In a new adaptation the same song appears in Jer. 48, where Dibon is mentioned in vv. 18 and 22. The original song probably referred to some bedouin raid; Isaiah's adaptation is to what happened in the days of Sennacherib, and Jeremiah's prophecy was fulfilled when Nebuchadrezzar marched against the country in his twenty-third year, 582 (Josephus *Ant*. x.9.7).

Bibliography.–A. H. van Zyl, *The Moabites* (*Pretoria Oriental Series*, 3, 1960); H. Donner and W. Röllig, *Kanaanäische und Aramäische Inschriften*, II (1964), 171; F. V. Winnet, *BASOR*, 125 (Feb. 1952), 7-20; R. E. Murphy, *ibid*., pp. 20-23; A. D. Tushingham, *BASOR*, 133 (Feb. 1954), p. 6-26; W. H. Morton, *BASOR*, 140 (Dec. 1955), pp. 5f.

A. VAN SELMS

DIBRI dib'rī [Heb. *diḇrî*]. A Danite, whose daughter Shelomith married an Egyptian. Their son was "cut off" (stoned) for blasphemy (Lev. 24:11).

DICE-PLAYING. *See* GAMES.

DICTATION (Jer. 36; 45:1). *See* SECRETARY.

DICTIONARIES. *See* BIBLE DICTIONARIES AND ENCYCLOPEDIAS.

DIDACHE did'ə-kē, di'də-kā. *See* APOSTOLIC FATHERS.

DIDYMUS did'ə-məs [Gk. *Didymos*–'twin']. The surname of THOMAS.

DIE. *See* DEATH.

DIET. Used by the AV in the obsolete sense of "allowance" in Jer. 52:34.

DIG [Heb. *ḥāṣaḇ*] (Dt. 8:9); [*ḥāpar*] (Dt. 23:13; Job 3:21; Ps. 7:15; Eccl. 10:8); NEB also SEEK; [*ḥāṯar*] (Job 24:16; Ezk. 8:8; 12:5, 12; Am. 9:2); NEB also BREAKS INTO; [*nāqar*] (Isa. 51:1); [*'āzaq*] (Isa. 5:2); AV FENCE; NEB TRENCH; [*kārâ*] (Ex. 21:33; Prov. 26:27); [Gk. *skáptō*] (Lk. 13:8; 16:3).

The several Hebrew words rendered "dig" have slightly different connotations. The verb *ḥāṣaḇ* is used in Dt. 8:9 of the mining of copper from the ore-laden terrain of southern Palestine. *Ḥāpar* ("search," "dig") is used of digging a pit (cf. Gen. 21:30; 26:15; etc., where it is used of digging for water), while *ḥāṯar* has the meaning of "dig through." The pual of *nāqar*, found in Isa. 51:1, means to "be quarried," while *'āzaq* ("till") was used of clearing land for a vineyard. The proverb "He who digs a pit will fall into it" occurs twice. In Prov. 26:27 it warns that he who seeks the ruin of someone else will be destroyed by his own schemes. In Eccl. 10:8, however, there is no indication of evil motivation; rather, Qoheleth is indicating the uncertainty of life and the hazards of each occupation. N. J. O.

DIGNITY [Heb. *g^e^ḏûlâ*–'greatness'] (Est. 6:3); [*gōḇah*–'height'] (Job 40:10); AV EXCELLENCY; [*hāḏār*] (Prov. 31:25); AV HONOUR; [*ś^e^'ēṯ*] (Hab. 1:7); NEB JUDGEMENT; **DIGNIFIED** [Gk. *kósmios*] (1 Tim. 3:2); AV "of good behavior"; NEB COURTEOUS. In Est. 6:3; Job 40:10; Hab. 1:7 the word "dignity" denotes rank or position rather than nobility or austerity of personal character. The ideal wife of Prov. 31, however, is characterized by the kind of true dignity that elevates her above pettiness and enables her to look to the future with confidence.

The Greek adjective *kósmios*, related to the noun *kósmos* (commonly meaning "order" and secondarily "adornment"), denotes a virtue that is not peculiarly Christian but was highly valued by the Greek philosophers — that of being "disciplined," "well-mannered," and "honorable." (Cf. 1 Tim. 2:9, "seemly," RSV; AV "modest"; NEB "in becoming manner").

See *TDNT*, III, *s.v.* κόσμος, κόσμιος (Sasse).

N. J. O.

DIKLAH dik'lä [Heb. *diqlâ*–'place of palms']. One of the "sons" of Joktan (Gen. 10:27; 1 Ch. 1:21). Perhaps a south-Arabian tribal or place name connected with a palm-bearing district.

DILEAN dil'i-ən [Heb. *dil^e^'ān*–'protrusion'(?)]. A town in the Shephelah of Judah named with Migdal-gad and Mizpeh (Josh. 15:38; NEB "Dilan"), which was probably N of Lachish and Eglon. It is possibly to be identified with Tell en-Najileh.

DILIGENCE; DILIGENT; DILIGENTLY [Heb. *ḥārûṣ*] (Prov. 10:4; 12:24, 27; 13:4; 21:5); NEB also BUSY, INDUSTRIOUS; [*šāḥar*] (Prov. 1:28; 8:17; 11:27; 13:24); AV also EARLY (Prov. 1:28; 8:17); BETIMES (Prov. 13:24); NEB also EAGERLY (Prov. 11:27); [hiphil of *yāṭaḇ*] (Dt. 13:14; 17:4; 19:18; Mic. 7:3); AV also EARNESTLY; NEB also THOROUGH, CAREFUL, EAGERLY; [*m^e^'ōḏ*] (Dt. 4:9; Ps. 119:4); NEB "take good care," FAITHFULLY; [piel of *šānan*] (Dt. 6:7); [*qešeḇ raḇ-qāšeḇ*] (Isa. 21:7, RSV "diligently, very diligently"); AV "with much heed"; NEB "alert, always on the alert"; [Aram. *'osparnā'*] (Ezr. 5:8; 6:12f.; 7:17, 21); AV SPEED, FAST, SPEEDILY; NEB THOROUGHLY, EXACTLY, "to the letter" (Ezr. 6:12f.); [Gk. *akribṓs*] (Mt. 2:8); NEB CAREFUL; [*epimelṓs*] (Lk. 15:8); NEB "(look) in every corner."

In some of the places where "diligently" occurs, the use of the infinitive absolute (*šāmô(a)'*, Ex. 15:26; Isa. 55:2; Zec. 6:15; *šāmôr*, Dt. 6:17; *dārōš*, Lev. 10:16; *lāmōḏ*, Jer. 12:16) serves to strengthen the idea expressed by the verb; thus, "hear diligently," "keep diligently," etc. (cf. W. Gesenius, E. Kautzsch, and A. E. Cowley, *Hebrew Grammar* [1910], § 113 l-s). In Proverbs, prosperity is a fruit of diligence (*ḥārûṣ*, lit. "the one running"), while hunger and want are the reward of carelessness or indolence. The Aramaic word *'osparnā'* is derived from an Old Persian loanword, *usprna,* which means "carefully." J. T. DENNISON, JR.

DILL [Heb. *qeṣaḥ*; Gk. *melánthion*] (Isa. 28:25, 27); AV FITCHES; [Gk. *ánēthon*] (Mt. 23:23); AV ANISE. A weedy annual umbellifer (*Anethum graveolens* L.) resembling parsley; not the true anise (*Pimpinella anisum* L.). Dill was widely grown for its seeds, which have carminative and aromatic properties. Dill seeds were also used as a condiment in cooking. R. K. H.

DIM [Heb. *kāhâ*] (Gen. 27:1; Dt. 34:7; 1 S. 3:2; Job 17:7); [*kēhâ*] (Lev. 13:6, 21, 26, 28, 56); AV DARK; NEB FADED; [*kāḇēḏ*] (Gen. 48:10); [*'āmam*] (Lam. 4:1); NEB DULLED; [*ḥāšak*] (Eccl. 12:3; Lam. 5:17); AV also DARKEN; NEB also "look no longer"; [*qûm*] (1 K. 14:4); AV SET; NEB FIXED; [*kālâ*] (Ps. 69:3 [MT 4]); AV FAIL; [*dā'aḇ*] (Ps. 88:9 [MT 10]); AV MOURN. In Lev. 13:6 a spot on the skin that had become dull during a period of quarantine was one of the indications that a person suspected of "leprosy" could be pronounced clean by the priest. A similar blemish in a "leprous" garment, however, was to be torn out (v. 56). Gen. 27:1 uses *kāhâ* to describe Isaac's loss of sight and the consequent inexpressive appearance of his eyes. Cf. the Preacher's metaphorical description of old age (Eccl. 12:3) and Paul's reference to the incompleteness of our present understanding (1 Cor. 13:12). G. WYPER

DIMINISH [Heb. *gāra'*] (Ex. 21:10; Ezk. 16:27); NEB DEPRIVE, CUT DOWN; [*mā'aṭ*] (Lev. 25:16; Ps. 107:39); AV also MINISH; NEB "the lower," "lose their strength"; [*dālal*] (Isa. 19:6); AV "be emptied"; NEB "be parched." The term *gāra'* is used twice for "withdrawing" a part of the portion of food (Ex. 21:10) or land (Ezk. 16:27) which has been allotted to someone. *Mā'aṭ*, "make small or few," is used in Lev. 25:16 of lowering the price of goods and in Ps. 107:39 of the hungry for whom God provides. The drying up of the Nile is described in Isa. 19:6 by *dālal*, "be dry."

DIMLY. The word occurs in 1 Cor. 13:12 Gk. *en ainígmati* as part of the clause "For now we see through a mirror [*ésoptron*] dimly." The literal meaning of *aínigma* is "riddle." The NEB's paraphrase captures the meaning: "Now we see only puzzling reflections in a mirror." *See* MIRROR.

DIMNAH dim'nä [Heb. *dimnâ*–'dung'; Gk. *Damna*]; NEB RIMMON. A city of the Merarite Levites in the territory of Zebulun (Josh. 21:35). The name is probably a misreading of Rimmon (Josh. 19:13; 1 Ch. 6:77), as in the NEB.

DIMON dī'mən; **DIMONAH** di-mōn'ə. *See* DIBON.

DINAH dī'nə [Heb. *dînâ*–'justice'?] (Gen. 30:20; 34; 46:15). The daughter of Jacob and Leah, full sister of Simeon and Levi. Her violation by Shechem son of Hamor caused her brothers to engage in an act of treachery which made them "odious" to the Canaanites (Gen. 34:30): after inducing the Shechemites to believe that if they would submit to circumcision Shechem would be permitted to have Dinah for a wife, the brothers, led by Simeon and Levi, went in and slew the inhabitants of Shechem. The political elements of the story (34:21-23, 30) suggest a tribal as well as a personal significance for the narrative. N. ISAACS

According to later rabbinic legend, Dinah gave birth to a daughter, who was brought up in Egypt and was the Asenath whom the pharaoh gave to Joseph as a wife.

DINAITES dī'nə-īts [Aram. *dînāyē'*]. A people mentioned in Ezr. 4:9 as settled in the city of Samaria by Osnapper (Ashurbanipal). According to the context the word is not a gentilic but a title, rendered "judges" in the RSV. The word is mentioned frequently in the Aramaic papyri of the 5th cent. B.C., where it designates "the court" (A. E. Cowley, *Aramaic Papyri of the Fifth Century* [1923], p. 282). W. S. L. S.

DINHABAH din'hə-bə [Heb. *dīnhāḇâ*]. The royal city of Bela son of Boer, king of Edom (Gen. 36:32; 1 Ch. 1:43). No acceptable identification of the site has been made.

DINNER [Heb. *mišteh*] (Est. 5:4f., 8, 14); AV, NEB, BANQUET; ['*ᵃruḥâ*] (Prov. 15:17); NEB DISH; [Gk. *áriston*] (Mt. 22:4; Lk. 11:38; Lk. 14:12); NEB FEAST, MEAL, LUNCH. In 1 Cor. 10:27 "dinner" is not represented by any term in the Greek text (cf. AV "feast"; NEB "meal"). *See* BANQUET; FEAST; DRINK.

The Heb. *mišteh* is translated "feast" throughout Esther with the exception of the passages cited above. The Hebrew is from the root *šāṯâ*, "drink." In the context of Esther the derived noun comes close to its root meaning, "a celebration involving the drinking of wine" (cf. Est. 5:6). *Mišteh* occurs often to indicate a secular celebration (e.g., Jgs. 14:12).

The *'ᵃruḥaṯ yārāq* of Prov. 15:17 is a modest meal of herbs. Such a meal shared in love is seen as better than a meal of fatted ox shared in hate. The Heb. *'ᵃruḥâ*, translated "dinner" by the RSV and AV, should be understood as a portion or serving. In other contexts (2 K. 25:30; Jer. 40:5; 52:34) the word is to be understood as an ALLOWANCE of food.

In the NT "dinner" is used to designate the noon meal. In Lk. 14:12 it is contrasted with Gk. *deípnon*, the evening meal. Originally the Gk. *áriston* was a breakfast, but by Hellenistic times its meaning was expanded to include the midday meal. In Mt. 22:4 *áriston* designates a marriage feast to which the invited guests refused to come, with the result that others were invited in their place (cf. Lk. 14:16-24). In 1 Cor. 10:27 "dinner" is supplied in order to define Gk. *kaléō*, "invite." (The tradition of adding a further definition to *kaléō* can be seen in the addition of the words *eis deípnon*, "to supper," in two ancient MSS.) D. E. SMITH

DIONYSIA. *See* DIONYSUS.

DIONYSIUS dī-ə-nish'i-əs [Gk. *Dionysios*]. One of the few Athenians converted by Paul (Acts 17:34). We know nothing further about him except that he was apparently of a high social position, for he was a member of the AREOPAGUS. According to one account he was the first bishop of the church at Athens (Eusebius *HE* iii.4.11; iv.23.3). He has also been identified with Dionysius of Paris (3rd cent.), the patron saint of France, who after migrating to Rome was sent to Paris; there he became a bishop and was later beheaded on Montmartre (Gregory of Tours *Historia Francorum* i.31).

In the Middle Ages a body of pseudonymous Dionysian writings claiming apostolic authority exerted enormous theological influence. These are now believed to have been written *ca.* 500 by a Syrian theologian. The mystic theology contained in these writings attempts to synthesize Christian and Neoplatonic thought. In the 9th cent. a translation of these writings into Latin by John Scotus, and commentaries on them by renowned theologians, enhanced their popularity and doctrinal authority, which continued into and beyond the 16th century.

See *ODCC*, pp. 401-403. N. J. O.

DIONYSUS dī-ə-nī'səs [Gk. *Dionysos*]. A Greek deity, mentioned in biblical literature only in the Apocrypha (2 Macc. 6:7; 14:33) as the object of a cult that Nicanor and Antiochus Epiphanes tried to force upon their Jewish subjects.

Dionysus was not one of the original Olympian gods, but was introduced as a foreign cult, apparently from Phrygia or Thrace. Basically he was a god of vegetation, presiding over fruit trees, the ivy, and the vine, and finding embodiment either in the bull or the goat. The Cretans, especially, practiced a form of worship in which they reenacted the mythical adventures of the god by pantomine or pageant, and then at the frenzied climax tore a live bull to pieces with their teeth and devoured his raw flesh in a rite that was supposed to invest the worshipers with superhuman energy. One account of the life of this deity related how he transformed himself into various guises in an effort to escape a band of murderous Titans sent by Hera to destroy him; it was as a bull that they finally captured him and devoured his flesh. Another legend stated that Zeus changed him into a goat in order to help elude the wrath of Hera; hence he was often represented as wearing a goatskin. In some cities in Chios, Tenedos, and Boeotia it was a human victim who was thus torn to pieces and eaten by the frenzied worshipers, in an effort to appropriate the divine potencies of their god.

The personal career of Dionysus was said to have been tragic. Hera hated him because her husband Zeus had begotten him by another mate, either Persephone, Demeter, or Semele, depending upon the local tradition (although Semele was most widely regarded as his mother); and she had him murdered by the Titans, who were subsequently executed with torture by Zeus himself. His grave was variously assigned to sites near Delphi or Thebes; the pomegranate allegedly arose from the ground where his blood was spilled by his brutal attackers. Afterward, however, according to some legends, he was raised from

Temple of Bacchus (Dionysus) at Baalbek (mid-2nd cent. B.C.). Almost entirely preserved, the Corinthian-style temple is ornately decorated with geometrical and mythological figures. (A. C. Myers)

death and ascended to join the other gods. This dying, resurrected deity may be assigned to the same class with Adonis (the Semitic Tammuz) and Attis, and the goddess Persephone as well, whose yearly death and resuscitation explained the vegetation cycle of winter and spring. Yet, unlike the others, the emphasis in the Dionysus cult was upon his triumphant vitality rather than his descent into Hades, and the element of lamentation and mourning was hardly to be found in his worship.

As the god of the vine, Bacchus, he was thought to communicate his power to his devotees through the intoxicating influence of wine, stimulating them to orgiastic excesses, wild dancing and music, and every form of ecstatic revelry. Some of the legends reported an initial resistance to this cult by Greek leaders who deplored this type of extravagance; but an enthusiasm for Bacchus spread rapidly through Hellas during the post-Homeric era, and he became one of the most zealously cultivated gods in the entire pantheon. Even Homer records (*Il.* vi. 130ff.) how a Thracian king named Lycurgus drove Dionysus and his votaries from the grove of Nyssa, and was in consequence struck with blindness and met a miserable death. The Theban king Pentheus was said to have made a futile effort to suppress worship of Bacchus on Mt. Citheron, but when he came upon their orgies he was mistaken for a wild boar by his mother and aunts, who were among the frenzied votaries, and they tore him limb from limb. There was also a legend of how Dionysus was abducted by a crew of greedy sailors from Delos, who hoped to sell him for ransom in Egypt, supposing him to be a wealthy prince. But for their pains they were transformed into a school of dolphins.

Dionysus introduced his worship into India (his conquests there became a favorite theme of artists, who pictured him astride an elephant), Persia, Phrygia (where the goddess Rhea is said to have cured him of his madness and taught him the cultivation of the vine), and many other oriental lands, as well as into Greece itself. It was in celebration of his annual festivals that the first crude farces were performed, which later developed into satyr plays and finally into the comedies of Aristophanes at Athens, performed in the theater of Dionysus. The early hymn in honor of the god, called the dithyramb, later became the inspiration for the tragic chorus, and then of tragedy as a dramatic genre, which was performed on the stages of Athens and the other leading centers of Greece. Greek drama, then owes its origin to the worship of Dionysus.

See W. F. Otto, *Dionysus: Myth and Cult* (Eng. tr. 1965).

G. L. ARCHER, JR.

DIOSCORINTHIUS dī-əs-kə-rin′thē-əs. A certain (unidentified) month (2 Macc. 11:21). It may allude to the first month named in the Macedonian calendar, but a more probable suggestion is that it corresponds to an intercalary month in that calendar which perhaps came just before April. *See* CALENDAR.

DIOTREPHES dī-o′trə-fēz [Gk. *Diotrephēs*–'nourished by Zeus']. A local church leader of Asia Minor whose domineering practice occasioned the writing of 3 John. His desire for prestige and power led him to oppose the apostolic authority of John (v. 9). The opposition took the form of empty accusations, rejection of John's messengers, and excommunication of church members who favored reception of the emissaries who came from John (v. 10).

Diotrephes' position in the church is unclear. The

possibilities are: (1) he was the bishop of the church (assuming an established monarchical episcopacy); (2) he was the dominant member of a local church board of presbyters; (3) he was an influential lay member who was able to impose his will on the congregation. Inasmuch as the time of John was somewhat early for a developed episcopacy, and since John does not refer to Diotrephes as a church official, the third possibility seems most likely.

Bibliography.–Comms. on the Johannine epistles by F. F. Bruce (1970), pp.151-54; R. Bultmann (Eng. tr. 1973), pp. 100f.; C. H. Dodd (1946), pp. 161-66; I. H. Marshall (*NICNT,* 1978), pp. 88-91.

D. W. BURDICK

DIP [Heb. *ṭāḇal*] (Gen. 37:31; Ex. 12:22; Lev. 4:6, 17; 9:9; 14:6, 16, 51; Nu. 19:18; Dt. 33:24; Josh. 3:15; Ruth 2:14; 1 S. 14:27; 2 K. 5:14; 8:15); NEB also BATHE (Dt. 33:24); [*ḥāśap̱*] (Isa. 30:14); AV TAKE; NEB SCOOP; [*śîm*] (Jer. 13:1); AV PUT; NEB "let come near"; [Gk. *báptō*] (Lk. 16:24; Jn. 13:26; Rev. 19:13); NEB also DRENCH (Rev. 19:13); [*embáptō*] (Mt. 26:23; Mk. 14:20; Jn. 13:26).

Priests when offering a sin offering were required to dip a finger into the blood of the sacrificed bull and "to sprinkle part of the blood seven times before the Lord" (cf. Lev. 4:6, etc.). See also the laws referring to the cleansing of infected houses (Lev. 14:51) and the cleansing of a leper (14:16). In all such cases "dip" is "moisten," "besprinkle," "dip in," the Heb. *ṭāḇal* or the Gk. *báptō*. *See also* CLEAN AND UNCLEAN.

The command to Jeremiah that he not put his linen waistcloth in water (13:1) meant that he was not to wash it. The waistcloth was to become filthy in order to symbolize Israel covered with the filth of its sins.

Rev. 19:13 is an uncertain passage. Some MSS use a form of the verb *rhantízō*, "sprinkle." The passage may refer to a garment that has been "dyed" in blood (Bauer, p. 132).

N. J. O.

DIPHATH dī'fath [Heb. *dipaṯ*]. A son of Gomer, son of Japheth, son of Noah (1 Ch. 1:6), called RIPHATH in the corresponding genealogy in Gen. 10:3.

DIRECT; DIRECTION [Heb. *yārâ*] (Dt. 17:10; 24:8); AV INFORM, TEACH; NEB INSTRUCTION, TELL; [hiphil of *kûn*–'prepare,' 'make firm'] (1 S. 7:3; 1 Ch. 29:18; Prov. 16:9; Jer. 10:23); AV also PREPARE; NEB also TURN, DETERMINE, GUIDE; [*šālaḥ*–'send'] (1 K. 5:9); AV, NEB, APPOINT; [*yāsar*] (1 Ch. 15:22); AV INSTRUCT; NEB "in charge of"; [hiphil of *rûm*–'lift up'] (Ps. 74:3); AV LIFT UP; NEB RESTORE; [piel of *yāšar*] (2 Ch. 32:30; Ps. 119:128); AV BRING STRAIGH ESTEEM; NEB also "find the right way"; [*'āšar*] (Prov. 23:19); AV GUIDE; NEB SET; [*nāṯan*] (Ezk. 23:25; 26:9); AV SET; NEB TURN LOOSE, LAUNCH; [*dāḇar*] (Nu. 27:23); AV COMMAND; NEB INSTRUCT; [piel of *nāṣaḥ*] (2 Ch. 34:13); AV "be overseer"; [*'āraḵ*–'put in order,' 'confront'] (Job 32:14); NEB "string together"; [piel of *tāḵan*–'put in order'] (Isa. 40:13); NEB "set limits"; [hophal of *yā'aḏ*] (Ezk. 21:16 [MT 21]); AV SET; NEB AIM; [*keṯāḇ*] (2 Ch. 35:4); AV WRITING; NEB WRITTEN INSTRUCTIONS; [*yāḏ*–'hand'] (Ex. 38:21; Nu. 7:8; 1 Ch. 25:2f., 6; 2 Ch. 23:18; 26:11; Ezr. 3:10; Jer. 5:31); AV HAND, MEANS, ORDINANCE; NEB also CHARGE, "manner prescribed" (Ezr. 3:10), "hand in hand" (Jer. 5:31), sometimes omits; [*dabberôṯ*–'words'] (Dt. 33:3); AV WORDS; NEB INSTRUCTION; [*peh*–'mouth'] (Josh. 9:14); AV COUNSEL; NEB GUIDANCE; [Gk. *kateuthýnō*–'make straight'] (1 Thess. 3:11; 2 Thess. 3:5); NEB also BRING DIRECT; [*tássō*–'assign,' 'fix'] (Mt. 28:16); AV APPOINT; NEB TELL; [*prostássō*] (Mt. 21:16); AV COMMAND; [*syntássō*] (Mt. 26:19; 27:10); AV APPOINT; [*diatássō*] (Lk. 8:55; Acts 7:44; 1 Cor. 11:34; 16:1; Tit. 1:5); AV COMMAND, APPOINT, GIVE ORDER, "set in order"; NEB also TELL, ARRANGE, PRESCRIBE; [*atenízō*–'look steadily'] ("direct his gaze," Acts 3:4); AV "fasten his eyes"; NEB "fix his eyes"; [*chrēmatízō*–'warn'] (Acts 10:22); AV WARN; [*entéllomai*] (He. 11:22); AV "give commandment"; NEB INSTRUCT; [*boúlomai*–'will'] (Jas. 3:4); AV LIST; NEB CHOOSE.

The RSV uses "direct" to translate a wide variety of Hebrew and Greek terms with a correspondingly broad range of meanings. Some of the words mean to impart something orally (e.g., *dāḇar*); others mean to turn or to point (e.g., *kateuthýnō*), while still others denote supervision, instruction, or guidance by someone who is enabling another in the accomplishing of a task. On 1 Ch. 15:22, *see also* MUSIC.

N. J. O.

DIRGE [Heb. *qînâ*] (Jer. 9:20; cf. 2 S. 1:17; 2 Ch. 35:25; Ezk. 2:10; 19:14; 32:16; Am. 8:10); AV LAMENTATION. The main feature of an Israelite funeral was the lamentation for the dead. It might be a brief cry of the name of the deceased (2 S. 19:4) or a fully developed expression of sorrow (2 S. 1:17ff.). The latter was usually composed by professional mourners according to established patterns. The prophets employed dirges to describe the bitterness of Israel arising from calamities that had befallen them; e.g., the book of LAMENTATIONS is such a dirge.

See also BURIAL II.C; LAMENT; MUSIC I.A.

DISALLOW. The AV uses this term in an archaic sense to translate Gk. *apodokimázō*, lit. "consider useless," in 1 Pet. 2:4, 7 (RSV, NEB, "reject").

DISANNUL. Archaic in the AV for ANNUL.

DISAPPOINT. This term occurs in four places in the RSV. In Job 6:20 and Ps. 22:5 (MT 6; NEB "not put to shame") the Hebrew term *bôš* ("be ashamed," "disappointed") is used, but in Job 41:9 (MT 41:1) the idea is expressed by the verb *kāzaḇ* ("be proven a lie"). In Rom. 5:5 the Greek term *kataischýnō*, the LXX equivalent of *bôš*, is used in relation to the Christian's continuing hope.

DISCERN; DISCERNING; DISCERNMENT [Heb. *bîn*] (Dt. 32:29; 1 K. 3:9, 11; Job 6:30; 38:20; Ps. 19:12 [MT 13]; 139:2; Prov. 14:8; Isa. 44:18; Hos. 14:9); AV also CONSIDER, KNOW, UNDERSTAND; NEB also "give thought to" (Dt. 32:29), DISTINGUISH, WARN, ESCORT (Job 38:20), AWARE, FIND, UNDERSTAND, "him who considers" (Hos. 14:9); [niphal of *bîn*] (1 K. 3:12; Isa. 29:14; Prov. 16:21); AV PRUDENT, UNDERSTANDING; NEB also UNDERSTANDING, WISE; [*bînâ*] (Isa. 27:11; 29:14); AV UNDERSTANDING; NEB also SENSE (Isa. 27:11); [*teḇûnâ*] (Isa. 44:19); AV UNDERSTANDING; NEB SENSE; [*šāma'*] (2 S. 14:17); NEB DECIDE; [*ṭa'am*] (2 S. 19:35; Job 12:20); AV also UNDERSTANDING; NEB TELL, JUDGMENT; [hiphil of *nāḵar*] (Job 4:16); [*Gk. anakrínō*] (1 Cor. 2:14); NEB JUDGED; [*diakrínō*] (1 Cor. 11:29); [*kritikós*] (He. 4:12); NEB SIFTS; [*aísthēsis*] (Phil. 1:9); AV JUDGMENT; NEB DISCRIMINATION. The faculty of decision-making (cf. wisdom literature) and/or moral judgment, exemplified in the divine gift to Solomon (1 K. 3:9, 11f.). In the OT these cognate terms are most frequently a translation of Heb. *bîn* or one of its cognates.

Bîn is related to *bēn*, the preposition that means

"between," thus expressing the idea of discrimination in making decisions.

In the NT "discern" and discernment" occur only four times. Three of the Greek terms are based on the root *krínō* (*kritikós, anakrínō, diakrínō*), which basically meant "sift" or "distinguish," then "select" or "divide out," and finally received the common meaning "decide" or (esp. in the NT) "judge." The adjective *kritikós*, denoting "one who has the manner of a judge, who is capable of judging, who has the right to judge, who is engaged in judging" (*TDNT*, III, 943), is used of the Word of God in He. 4:12: "For the word of God is living and active, . . . discerning the thoughts and intentions of the heart." The verb *anakrínō* generally has reference to some sort of examination or judicial investigation. The RSV renders the same verb "discern" in 1 Cor. 2:14 and "judge" in v. 15; the sense of the passage is that the man who does not possess the Spirit is not capable of properly examining and evaluating the gifts of the Spirit. *Diakrínō* was used in many different senses; in general, it tends to strengthen the meaning of *krínō*. In 1 Cor. 11:29 it has reference to distinguishing the body and blood of the Lord from ordinary food. The fourth NT term, *aísthēsis*, is unrelated to *krínō* and occurs only once in the NT. It is used here in the sense of that "moral discrimination" (*TDNT*, I, 188) which enables one to "approve what is excellent" (Phil. 1:9f.).

***Bibliography.*–*TDNT*, I, *s.v.* αἴσθησις (G. Delling); III, *s.v.* κρίνω, κριτικός, ἀνακρίνω, διακρίνω (F. Büchsel); *TDOT,* II, *s.v.* "bîn" (Ringgren). J. T. DENNISON, JR.

DISCERNINGS OF SPIRITS. *See* SPIRITUAL GIFTS.

DISCHARGE [Heb. *zôḇ*] (Lev. 15; 22:4, 22; Nu. 5:2; 2 S. 3:29); AV ISSUE. Not all the discharges mentioned in Lev. 15 would be infectious, but making a distinction between infectious and noninfectious would necessitate microscopic examination not available until modern times, so the course of treating all discharges alike was then the safest one. The Levitical laws for controlling gonorrhea, source of the main infectious discharge in view, were among the earliest recorded. Vivid descriptions of the disease are to be found also on second-millennium B.C. Assyrian tablets.

Lev. 15:19-24 refers to menstruation. G. WYPER

DISCHARGED FROM THE LAW (Rom. 7:2, 6). *See* LAW IN THE NT.

DISCIPLE [Heb. *limmuḏ*] (Isa. 8:16); NEB TEACHING; [Gk. *mathētḗs*]. The disciple, as an adherent and follower of Jesus is a prominent figure in each of the four Gospels, and is the counterpart of Jesus in His role as teacher, as well as LORD (Mt. 8:25) and MASTER (Lk. 8:24). The NT also employs a verbal form (*mathēteúein*) for the act of being a disciple or making a disciple (Mt. 13:52; 27:57; 28:19; Acts 14:21).

I. Background.–In the Greek world, *mathētḗs* variously designated an apprentice, one who companied with a teacher in order to learn from him, one who belonged to a certain school of philosophy (e.g., a disciple of Socrates), and one who adhered to the teaching of another, even though that one could be removed in time and place. Groups of disciples continued even after a teacher died. Their commitment to a master/teacher led to passing along his wisdom and sayings. In antiquity the disciple could function in the philosophic or in the cultic sphere, as in the mystery religions.

Although the vocabulary of teaching and learning is prominent in the OT, the disciple figure is virtually absent — there is only the doubtful Isa. 8:16, and Heb. *talmîd*, 1 Ch. 25:8, designating one who is a pupil. Rengstorf suggests that the reason is to be found in Israelite faith as a religion of revelation: "In the sphere of revelation there is no place for the establishment of a master-disciple relation, nor is there the possibility of setting up a human word alongside the Word of God which is proclaimed. . ." (*TDNT,* IV, 431).

In the rabbinic realm, the *talmîd* devoted himself to learning Scripture and the religious tradition, above all that tradition which is passed on through his teacher (RABBI, as in Mt. 23:7f.; Mk. 7:8, 13). A disciple was himself esteemed; he would become a teacher after the proper period of listening and learning. In this system, both teacher and disciple typically sat in an appointed room, and the teacher taught by question, and through repetition and memorization. It was expected that the disciple would render respectful service to his teacher during his apprenticeship.

II. Discipleship to Jesus.–*A. General.* Of the some 260 instances of the term disciple in the NT, about 230 appear in the four Gospels. The word generally refers to the disciples of Jesus, but there are also disciples of Moses (Jn. 9:28), of the Pharisees (Mt. 22:16; Mk. 22:18), of John the Baptist (Mk. 2:18; Lk. 11:1), and perhaps of Paul (Acts 9:25).

Although there were many similarities between discipleship to Jesus and discipleship to the rabbis, there were also significant differences. Above all, whereas rabbinic pupils could select their teacher, Jesus Himself chose and called His disciples (Mk. 1:6ff. par.). He called them to leave everything, and to follow Him (Mk. 10:28; Lk. 9:11f., 14:25f.). In the end, the disciple is even called to face martyrdom (Mk. 8:34f.). There are other formal differences. Jesus' pupils did not assemble in a classroom, but in open fields or in secluded places. The circumstances were as varied as the situations and locations of Jesus' ministry. Jesus gave to the disciples His own interpretation of the OT and His direct teaching, rather than a catena of traditions to which He simply added His own word. His word superseded all else before; a consequence was that Jesus' disciples not only often failed to understand Him, but were constantly amazed at what He said and taught (Mk. 4:10f. par.; 7:17ff. par.; 9:32 par.).

B. The Meaning of Discipleship. Understanding the role of disciples in Jesus' ministry requires a decision regarding the relationship between the Twelve (Mk. 3:13ff. par.) and disciples generally. Many descriptions of discipleship (e.g., Mk. 1:17, "I will make you become fishers of men") are addressed only to members of the circle, the Twelve (*see* APOSTLE). On the other hand, although there are instances of persons volunteering their allegiance and discipleship (Lk. 9:57ff.), this is rare; such do not become a part of the inner circle (the Twelve). Both the Gospels of Luke and John present the picture of a circle of disciples larger than the Twelve (Lk. 6:13; 10:1; Jn. 6:66). By way of contrast, there are very few indications, if any (see Mk. 4:10 par.), of a larger community of disciples beyond the Twelve in Mark's Gospel (Meye, 113-172), and Matthew describes the Twelve as "the disciples" (Mt. 10:1; 11:1; 12:1, *et al.*). There were also others who followed Jesus, such as the women who followed Him even to the cross (Mk. 15:40f. par.), but who are never called disciples; this would accord with the rabbinic practice, and is congruent with the NT picture of apostleship in the church after the death and resurrection of Jesus.

Jesus' reason or reasons for assembling a community of disciples about Him is subject to continuing discussion.

Interpretations range from those that place more emphasis upon the personal relation to Jesus sustained in discipleship as participation in salvation or life (Kittel) to those that emphasize the durative effects of the teacher-pupil relationship in the formation of a tradition (a canon) for the Church (Gerhardsson). Mark 1:17 indicates that He called them to become fishers of men. But the meaning of this expression is problematic in itself (Meye, pp. 100-109; Wuellner, *passim*). Some view the disciples as the believing remnant foreseen by Israel's prophets, who should become the New Israel; this accords well with the formation of a special circle of *Twelve*. As such, they are a group in contrast to the Old Israel; in them the full implications of the reign of God are being realized in their identification with Jesus. This view converges with the perception that Jesus formed a community of disciples or apostles as the foundation for the Church, which would attain its full reality only after His death, resurrection, and ascension. All these views have value, and should be seen as parts of a whole, rather than as mutually exclusive.

The view that Jesus did not form a historical community of Twelve disciples is unacceptable. There are impressive arguments for the historicity of the Twelve, as well as sound counterarguments against the contrary view (Meye, pp. 192-209).

Only a few of the disciples — most notably Peter, James, and John — have any marked individual significance within the Gospel narratives, or later NT narrative. The disciples had quite divergent origins (fisher, tax-collector, political activist), and were not the sort one would ordinarily choose as disciples within the Palestinian milieu. All this adds to the impresssion of uniqueness of the discipleship to Jesus.

III. Discipleship in Acts. Finally, it should be noted that the book of Acts uses the term disciple to describe the post-Easter community of faith (Acts 6:1f., 7; 9:36; 11:26; 19:1-4). However, the uniqueness of the pre-Easter community of disciples has left its imprint on the NT, with the result that the specific language of discipleship did not become the standard way of describing those who believed in Jesus after Easter.

See also FOLLOW.

Bibliography.–H. D. Betz, *Nachfolge und Nachahmung Jesu Christi im NT* (1968); N. A. Dahl, *Das Volk Gottes* (1963); B. Gerhardsson, *Memory and Manuscript* (1961); *Tradition and Transmission in Early Christianity* (1964); R. Meye, *Jesus and the Twelve* (1968); R. Schnackenburg, *The Church in the NT* (1965); A. Schulz, *Nachfolgen und Nachahmen* (1962); E. Schweizer, *Lordship and Discipleship* (1960); *TDNT*, I, *s.v.* ἀκολουθέω (G. Kittel); IV, *s.v.* μανθάνω κτλ. (K. H. Rengstorf); W. H. Wuellner, *The Meaning of "Fishers of Men"* (1967).

R. P. MEYE

DISCIPLINE [Heb. vb. *yāsar*; noun *mûsār*; Gk. vb. *paideúō*; noun *paideía*]; AV also CHASTENING (Prov. 3:11; He. 12:5ff.), CHASTISEMENT (Dt. 11:2; He. 12:8), CORRECTION (Prov. 15:10; 22:15; Jer. 7:28), INSTRUCTION (Ps. 50:17; Prov. 5:12; 6:23; 12:1), NURTURE (Eph. 6:4), BE REFORMED (Lev. 26:23); NEB also CORRECTION (Prov. 3:11; 5:12; 6:23; 12:1; 15:10; Jer. 7:28), INSTRUCTION (Dt. 4:36; Ps. 50:17; Eph. 6:4), "a good beating" (Prov. 22:15), "keep (him) in order" (Prov. 13:24).The AV translates "discipline" only in Job 36:10 (RSV "instruction"; NEB "warnings").

I. OT
II. Intertestamental Period
III. NT

I. OT.–The biblical concept of discipline combines the nuances of training, instruction, and firm guidance with those of reproof, correction, and punishment. In Hebrew culture discipline was an integral element of household life. The father's task was to make his children aware of God's claim for filial obedience, based upon His redemption of Israel in the Exodus, and to enforce with integrity the Law given at Sinai, in the knowledge that blessing from God depended upon compliance with His revealed will (cf. Ex. 12:26; 13:14; Dt. 6:7, 20ff.).

A father disciplines his child, with the rod if necessary, precisely because he loves him and desires him to experience life as approval by God (Prov. 13:24; 19:18; 22:15; 23:13f.; 29:17).

The concept of God as disciplinarian was derived from the parent-child relationship; "As a man disciplines his son, the Lord your God disciplines you" (Dt. 8:5). God is the loving Father who desires His children to experience fulfillment, but who knows that obedience to His revealed will is the condition for realizing this goal. The imposing of discipline in the life of individuals and of nations is an evidence of God's enduring love and commitment (Prov. 3:11f.; 13:24; He. 12:5-10); the absence of corrective measures would indicate rejection. The prophets interpreted Israel's experience of adversity and deprivation as disciplinary acts by God designed to call the nation to faithful and obedient sonship (Jer. 7:28; cf. Hos. 11:1-11). The rejection of divine discipline, in the form of prophetic instruction or rebuke, invited hardship and suffering as the bitter consequence of rejecting God Himself. The context for understanding the character of the divine discipline of Israel is the covenant, which binds God and His people together in a familial relationship. In reference to the other nations, it is God's sovereign control of the course of human history and the affairs of men.

The two Hebrew verbs that in the OT express the notion of discipline, with their derivative nouns, overlap considerably in meaning. Both describe the actions both of men and of God. *Yāsar* (also translated "instruct, correct, punish") and *mûsār* (also "instruction, correction, punishment") always presuppose an educational purpose. Through correction, one whose understanding or performance has been deficient is made aware of the demands upon him and of the importance of obedience. The concept of discipline is thus related to the formation of character, whether individual or national. In a comprehensive study of these terms J. A. Sanders classifies the passages in which God is the subject as follows: (a) Israel is disciplined by adversity (cf. Hos. 5:2; 10:10; Jer. 5:3); (b) Israel is disciplined by instruction or warning (e.g., Jer. 7:28; cf. 17:23); (c) an individual is disciplined by suffering (cf. Jer. 10:24; Ps. 6:1 [MT 2]); and (d) an individual is disciplined by instruction or warning (cf. Isa. 8:11; Job 33:16). These terms are never used in the OT in reference to the correction of animals or the divine discipline of foreign nations.

The term *yāḵaḥ* ("correct, reprove, punish") and its derivative noun *tûḵaṯ* are similar in meaning, but are employed with a wider range of reference. When predicated by God the terms denote: (a) divine punishment, without an explicit educational purpose, of Israel (e.g., Hos. 5:9; Ezk. 5:15), foreign nations (2 K. 19:4; 1 Ch. 16:21), and individuals (Prov. 30:6; Ps. 39:11 [MT 12]); (b) divine discipline, with an express educational purpose, of individuals (Prov. 3:12; Job 5:17); and (c) judicial judgments by God upon Israel (Isa. 1:18; RSV "reason together"; Mic. 6:2; RSV "contend"), the nations (Isa. 2:4; Mic. 4:3; RSV "decide"), and individuals (Job 13:10; 16:21; RSV "maintain the right"). In some instances it is difficult to determine whether corrective chastening or retributive punishment is the intent in reference to Israel (Hab. 1:12), the nations (Ps. 94:10), and individuals (Gen. 31:42). Punishment can be a form of instruction or an expression of divine wrath in the administration of discipline.

The translators of the LXX employed *paideúō* ("instruct, educate, discipline") and *paideía* ("instruction, education, discipline") as equivalent to *yāsar* and *mûsār,* associating the biblical tradition of discipline with the broader educational ideal of Hellenism. Originally these Greek terms placed little emphasis on chastisement. Although they could be applied to the training of children within a household, they more commonly denoted the formal education that took place through the schools. Writers who plied a literary Greek commonly distinguished between the nurture a child received in his home (*anatréphō*; *anatrophḗ*) and the formal instruction he received from school masters (*paideúō*; *paideía*); Luke twice preserves this distinction in reference to the youth of Moses (Acts 7:21f.) and of Paul (22:3). The use of *paideúō* and its derivative noun in the LXX, however, broadened the scope of the term to include the notions of reproof and chastisement.

II. Intertestamental period.–During the intertestamental period the concept of discipline was given greater precision as elements of the older biblical tradition were taken up and developed by different groups of Judaism. Four lines of development may be distinguished. (1) The notions of parental and divine discipline that are an integral element in the wisdom tradition of the book of Proverbs (cf. 3:11f.; 5:12, 23; 6:23; 12:1; 13:24; 15:10; 19:18; 22:15; 23:13f.; 29:17) continue to be emphasized in documents that stand in continuity with that tradition. Sirach, which preserves the teachings of a Jerusalem scribe, Joshua ben Sira, at the turn of the 3rd cent. B.C., demonstrates the impact of the wisdom tradition upon the scribal tradition in Palestine. On the issue of parental discipline Ben Sira writes: "Do you have children? Discipline them, and make them obedient from their youth" (Sir. 7:23). As for divine discipline, Wisdom is the source of discipline that tests the character of those who walk with God (Sir. 4:11-18, esp. v. 17). Yet Ben Sira does not hesitate to speak of discipline as the direct action of the Lord. In a passage that unravels the several strands of discipline as set forth in the OT (correction, instruction, firm guidance) he sets discipline in the context of divine compassion: "The compassion of the Lord is for all living beings. He rebukes and trains and teaches them, and turns them back, as a shepherd his flock. He has compassion on those who accept His discipline and who are eager for his judgments" (Sir. 18:13f.). The acceptance of discipline validates the fear of the Lord that is the foundation of genuine piety (Sir. 32:14). Similar emphases upon divine Wisdom as the source of discipline and upon testing as the purpose of discipline find expression in the Wisdom of Solomon (cf. 3:4-7; 11:9f.), a document that sets forth the wisdom tradition as developed in Alexandrian Judaism in the 2nd cent. B.C.

(2) Significant strands of the prophetic tradition inform the teaching on discipline in 2 Maccabees. The writer is concerned to clarify how God could permit the sufferings endured by Jews in the pogrom that followed the decree by Antiochus IV Epiphanes banning the practice of Judaism (175 B.C.). The prophets had interpreted the political and socio-economic upheavals of their day as disciplinary measures imposed by God, remedial in character, designed to call Israel back to the status of sonship. The book of Hosea, for example, finds in Israel's experience a unified record of God's love and discipline, and makes explicit use of the language of parental discipline to define God's action toward Israel (cf. Hos. 5:2; 7:12, 15; 10:10; cf. also 11:1-11). The author of 2 Maccabees draws upon this prophetic interpretation of national adversity, and develops a concept of judgment as an expression of divine mercy. Although suffering is the inevitable consequence of indifference to God and His law, its purpose is not to destroy the nation but to discipline it (2 Macc. 6:12). When disciplined by suffering, Israel is prevented from lapsing into those excesses of sin that draw down upon the gentile nations God's shattering penalties for their iniquity (2 Macc. 6:13-15). Israel's sufferings are disciplinary in character, but they express the mercy and commitment of God: "Therefore he never withdraws his mercy from us. Though he disciplines us with calamities, he does not forsake his own people" (2 Macc. 6:16; cf. 10:4).

(3) A basic component of early Pharisaism was the importance of discipline in the formation of character. One aspect upon which attention was focused was correction by the rod. The biblical roots of this strand of teaching are found in the Mosaic legislation providing for chastisement of offenders by a judge or the city elders (cf. Dt. 22:13-19; 25:1-3). By the 1st cent. the administration of discipline by the rod had been entrusted to the synagogues and the schools attached to them. In the Psalms of Solomon, a collection of early Pharisaic hymns from the first half of the 1st cent. B.C., the writer equates submission to God's yoke with the experience of the rod of chastening (Ps. Sol. 7:8). On one level, the reference is to the adversities experienced by the nation at the hands of Pompey, Antipater, and others. But on a more personal level submission to synagogue discipline is seen as a meritorious expression of submission to divine discipline: "Blessed is the man whom the Lord remembers with reproof, and whom he restrains from the way of evil with strokes, that he may be cleansed from sin, that it may not be multiplied. He who makes his back ready for strokes shall be cleansed, for the Lord is good to those who endure discipline" (Ps. Sol. 10:1f.). One of the oldest tractates of the Mishnah, *Makkoth* (lit. "Strokes"), provides legislation governing the administration of synagogue discipline.

(4) A sectarian perspective on discipline is provided by the Essene Manual of Discipline (1QS), which regulated the communal life of the Qumrân covenanters. This document reflects the priestly organization and ideals of a community devoted to the study of Torah and to life in accordance with its mandates (1QS 1:3; 8:15f.). Members of the community pledged themselves to pursue mutual love, humility, and obedience to God's will in a period marked by perversity and rebellion (2:24; 4:3; 5:23). With a high consciousness of election they dismissed as "men who have abhorred discipline" those who showed no inclination to enter the community (2:25–3:1). Conversely, the man who is qualified for admission to the council of the community is one who "desires a disciplined life" (6:13-15). Once admitted to membership, a man's energies and property were governed by community rule. Infractions of communal regulations were disciplined in accordance with specified measures, which ranged from depletion of the food allotment to exclusion from the community (6:24–7:25; 8:16–9:2). Within the sect, communal discipline expresses divine discipline, in the conviction that God is preparing for Himself a people who will experience the blessings of the new covenant and exoneration in the judgment that will fall upon the covenant-breakers in Israel.

III. NT.–In the NT the importance of parental discipline continues to be stressed in the instruction given to members of the household embracing the Christian faith. A father was not to deal harshly with his children, but to "bring them up in the discipline and instruction of the Lord" (Eph. 6:4; cf. Col. 3:21). In this context discipline has taken on a comprehensive character equivalent to the truth of God. What is demanded is training by act, example, and word. The linguistic distinction between "discipline" and "instruction" may have reference to education by means of deeds, which is to be complemented by means of words. The "discipline of the Lord" is divine discipline (subjective genitive) exercised through the father who acts for God in training his children. Submission to parental discipline found its finest expression in the life of Jesus, whose obedience to Joseph and Mary is noted by the Evangelist Luke (cf. Lk. 2:51).

The fullest NT treatment of divine discipline occurs in He. 12:5-11. The writer addresses a people who have grown apathetic in their convictions at a time when martyrdom could become a reality of Christian experience (cf. 2:3f.; 5:11-14; 10:32-39; 12:3f.). Citing Prov. 3:11f., he reminds his readers that the presence of discipline validates sonship (He. 12:5f.), and adds: "It is for discipline that you have to endure" (12:7). In this context "discipline" signifies the suffering that may have to be endured because of fidelity to God (cf. He. 10:32-34; 11:32–12:4). Its prototype was the hostility that Jesus endured from men when they crucified Him (12:2f.). Those who submit to disciplinary suffering participate in the triumph of the cross (12:7-10). The goal of discipline is Christian maturity, and ultimately participation in the holiness of God (12:10f.). Even those who attempt to humiliate the people of God through the infliction of painful sufferings cannot frustrate the divine purpose motivated by the Father's love for His children. Here the notions of parental discipline and divine discipline are joined in an exhortation to faithfulness that is strengthened by appeal to the fidelity of Jesus Christ.

See also CHASTENING, CHASTISEMENT.

Bibliography.–S. Brown, *Apostasy and Perseverance in the Theology of Luke* (1969); J. Campos, *Revista Calasancia,* 6 (1960), 47-73; L. Dürr, *Die Erziehungswesen im AT und im antiken Orient* (1932); W. Eichrodt, *Theology of the OT,* I (Eng. tr. 1961), 228-288, 457-501; II (Eng. tr. 1964), 413-495; G. Forkman, *Limits of the Religious Community* (1972); W. Jentsch, *Urchristliches Erziehungsdenken* (1951); S. Liebermann, *JBL,* 71 (1952), 199-206; J. E. Mignard, "Jewish and Christian Cultic Discipline to the Middle of the Second Century" (diss., Boston University, 1966); J. A. Sanders, *Suffering as Divine Discipline in the OT and Post-Biblical Judaism* (1955); *TDNT,* V. *s.v.* παιδεύω κτλ. (G. Bertram).

W. L. LANE

DISCOMFIT; DISCOMFITURE. These words are obsolescent. As employed by the AV, the meaning in general is "annoy," "harass," "confuse," "rout," and "destroy" (e.g., AV Josh. 10:10; Jgs. 4:15; 1 S. 7:10; 2 S. 22:15; Ps. 18:4). In the RSV "discomfit" occurs twice: in Ex. 14:24 for Heb. *hāmam*, "confound" (NEB "threw them into a panic"), and in Job 32:15 for *ḥāṯaṯ*, "be disheartened" (NEB "be confounded").

DISCOURSE [Heb. *māšāl*] (Nu. 23:7, 18; 24:3, 15, 20f., 23; Job 27:1; 29:1); AV PARABLE; NEB also ORACLE. The term *māšāl* can denote any of various types of sayings. In Nu. 23f. it refers to a prophetic word.

DISCOVER [Heb. *ḥāqar*] (Ps. 44:21 [MT 22]); AV SEARCH OUT; NEB FIND OUT; [*yāḏa'*] (1 S. 22:6); NEB SEE; [*māṣā'*] (2 K. 12:5); AV FIND; NEB FIND NECESSARY; [*bîn*] (Neh. 13:7); AV UNDERSTAND. The RSV employs "discover" in the modern sense of "get first sight or knowledge of," "ascertain," or "explore." In the AV, however, "discover" often occurs in a sense now obsolete. (Note in cases cited below that the Hebrew word is *gālâ*, except in Jer. 13:26 [*ḥāšap*, "make bare"] and Hab. 3:13 [*'ārar*, "make naked"].) (1) "Exhibit," "uncover," or "betray" (Ex. 20:26; Job 12:22; Isa. 57:8 ["discover thyself"]; Jer. 13:26; Lam. 2:14; Hos. 7:1; Nah. 3:5). (2) "Cause to be no longer a covering," "lay bare" (2 S. 22:16). (3) "Bring to light," "disclose" (1 S. 14:8, 11). (4) "Unmask" or "reveal oneself" (Prov. 18:2). (5) "Take away the covering of" (Isa. 22:8). (6) "Lay bare" (Hab. 3:13). In Ps. 29:9 the AV reads, "The voice of the Lord . . . discovereth the forests," where the RSV reads "strips the forests bare."

DISCREPANCIES. Discrepancies in the Bible are an old problem. Such other problems as alleged scientific or historical difficulties are of more recent nature, inasmuch as extensive attention to scientific matters and details of history has been a more recent phenomenon. But discrepancies have always been obvious to careful students of the Bible and the reaction of early authors to such problems is usually indicative of their attitude toward the truthfulness of the Bible.

The Jewish rabbis of the 1st cent. are reported to have considered some of the famous discrepancies and they pronounced them to be not real contradictions. They questioned whether the book of Proverbs belonged in the OT canon because it says "Answer not a fool according to his folly" and "Answer a fool according to his folly" (Prov. 26:4f.), but they concluded that Proverbs could indeed be canonical. It need not be held that Proverbs then and there became part of the canon. It is already quoted with the formula "It is written" in the Zadokite Document, portions of which are found among the Dead Sea Scrolls (*CD* 11:20).

The NT does not discuss any particular OT discrepancies. It validates the whole OT to the jot and tittle. But early Christian authors do discuss the subject of discrepancies in the Bible and positively reject the possibility of real contradictions. Justin Martyr, writing near the middle of the second century, speaks explicitly on the subject: "Since I am entirely convinced that no Scripture contradicts another, I shall admit rather that I do not understand what is recorded, and shall strive to persuade those who imagine that the Scriptures are contradictory, to be rather of the same opinion as myself" (Justin Martyr *Dial.* 65). It may be added that the Christian Church has been trying to persuade such people ever since! The Westminster Confession of Faith holds that "the consent of all the parts" is part of the proof that the Scriptures are "immediately inspired by God."

Whole books have been written on the subject of alleged contradictions. Of those mentioned in the bibliography, the present author's book takes up a number of representative examples. That of Haley is of special value because he searched the literature of criticism to discover all the significant discrepancies that have been alleged.

The contradictions can be illustrated by taking examples of different types of problems. For some problems the solution is seen by better understanding of the fact, for others a more correct text helps, for others the proper viewpoint gives an answer, and others are matters of doctrine.

The Christian religion, in contrast to most others, is a historical religion. It proclaims good news based on certain events. In accord with this, the Bible is full of the history of ancient days. But historical data are hard to establish and preserve. Some historical problems are, therefore, to be expected. It is amazing that in a book with the breadth of the Bible, the problems are as few as they are.

One problem sometimes mentioned is the discrepancy between the reigns of the kings of Judah and Israel as reported in Kings and Chronicles. For instance 2 K. 18:10 says that Samaria fell (722 B.C.) in the sixth year of Hezekiah; therefore he began to reign in 728 B.C. However, in v. 13 it says that Sennacherib attacked Judah (701 B.C.) in the fourteenth year of Hezekiah; therefore, he began to reign in 715 B.C. It is barely possible that our dates for the fall of Samaria or Sennacherib's invasion are wrong, but it is much more likely that Hezekiah began to reign as co-regent with his father in 728 and became sole ruler in 715. Such co-regencies are well witnessed for other kings of Palestine and surrounding nations. The alleged discrepancies of these kings' reigns have not been mentioned so much since the careful treatment and explanation given by E. R. Thiele (*MNHK*).

The alleged contradictions of Gen. 1 and 2 can certainly be answered, although the solution may be found both in matters of fact and viewpoint. The contradiction is said to lie in the differing orders of creation — Gen. 1 has plants, animals and man; Gen. 2 has man, plants, woman, and animals. The problem is not real. The plants mentioned after man in 2:9 are clearly plants in Eden. The animals mentioned in 2:19 had probably been created previously and were now brought to Adam for recognition. S. R. Driver declares that this verb form in Gen. 2:19 cannot be translated by a pluperfect "had formed," but he gives no evidence (*Introduction to the Literature of the OT* [ed. 1910], p. 8). In 2 Ch. 21:3 the identical form clearly refers to a pluperfect situation. Moreover, it can be argued (cf. this writer's article, *JETS*, 11 [1968], 177-79), that Gen. 2 refers exclusively to events in the Garden of Eden and not at all to the events of general creation. Therefore, a contradiction would be out of the question. In vv. 5f. the word "mist" is a mistranslation of a word borrowed from Sumerian through the Akkadian meaning "river" or "river flood." It refers to a local phenomenon — the natural irrigation of Eden — and the meaning is that God had not caused it to rain on that territory, for the river watered the whole face of the land of Eden. The verses do not refer to the whole world and say nothing about climate or rain elsewhere, or the order of creation in the world at large.

NT problems of this nature include the genealogies of Jesus in Mt. 1 and Lk. 3. For fuller treatment of this and several of the following problems cf. *Inspiration and Canonicity*, pp. 105-120. It is often alleged that the Matthaean genealogy is of Joseph and the Lukan one of Mary. But we can go further. Careful comparison of Mt. 1:12 with 1 Ch. 3:17-19 will show that the Matthaean list is not a true genealogy. It jumps from Shealtiel to Zerubbabel the son of Pedaiah who was Shealtiel's brother. This succession would not be appropriate in a genealogy, but is quite appropriate for a list of dynastic succession. Shealtiel had no children. None is listed for his next oldest brother, Malchiram. Zerubbabel as next of kin was the heir next in line for David's throne. With this example in Mt. 1:12 we can understand Mt. 1:16 better. It was important to establish the true relationship of Jesus and Joseph. Joseph was in the dynastic succession and had the title to the throne of David. Jesus, though virgin-born, was Joseph's legal son and thus was the legitimate king of the Jews. He was not the natural descendant of Jeconiah. Indeed, Jeremiah's curse on Jeconiah prevented any of his natural issue from having the throne (Jer. 22:30). Jeremiah's curse was broken by the Virgin Birth. However, Jesus' natural genealogy through his mother, probably identified in rabbinic literature as Heli's daughter, is found in Lk. 3 (cf. also Rom. 1:3).

New information helps us to understand the alleged contradiction of Mk. 15:42 and Lk. 23:42 compared with Jn. 19:14. The Synoptics say that Christ ate the Passover and was crucified the next day. John seems to say that he was crucified Friday, the day before the passover. Close study of the book of Jubilees and of the DSS shows that different sects of the Jews celebrated the Passover on different dates. Some therefore suggest that both accounts are correct; the disciples followed a different system of the feasts. A better and older treatment suggests that the phrase "preparation of the passover" in John does not mean "preparation for the passover" but rather the "preparation for the Saturday sabbath of the passover week." This use of "preparation day" for Friday afternoon is still current among Jews and is as old as the Jewish colony of Elphantine of 400 B.C. (A. Dupont-Sommer, *Sabbat et Parasceve à Elephantine* [1950], p. 3f.).

We now may turn to errors caused by miscopying of the text through the centuries. There are many very small discrepancies in parallel references to names. This is very understandable to anyone who has tried to keep a mailing list in order. Names are hard to record and preserve because they change from language to language, as, for example, Xerxes and Ahasuerus. The same man may use different names, e.g., Tiglath-Pileser and Pul. And if a letter is miscopied there is no change in the sense which will warn the next copyist of the error. Only one instance needs to be given, the parallel lists of names in Ezr. 2 and Neh. 7, which show minor differences. Most of them concern a single letter. The differences of consequence occur in only six names. Two names are quite likely dropped in Neh. 7:48 because of similar sound. Ezra has the sequence: Hagabah, Akkub, Hagab, Shamlai. Nehemiah has Hagabah, Salmai. This is obviously a case of homoioteleuton. It was an early error, for the LXX agrees with the Hebrew text. The other variants are: Bani-Binnai; Jorah-Hariph; Gibeon-Gibbar; Asna-Besai. The differences are slight and easily explainable. There are also differences of enumeration in these two lists, usually minor and probably due to confusion of letters which were used to express the numerals in early writing.

There are other cases of variant numbers which are rather clearly caused by copying and do not reflect any contradiction in the original manuscripts. An example is the age of Jehoiachin at his captivity. In 2 K. 24:8 his age is said to be eighteen years when he began to reign, and he reigned three months. The LXX agrees. The parallel in 2 Ch. 36:9 has it as eight years of age and says he reigned three months and ten days. One important LXX manuscript (Alexandrian) reads eighteen years and three months. It is clear that eighteen is correct. He had wives and children (2 K. 24:15). The numeral 10 got separated from the 8 by mistake and appears as 10 days in the Chronicles text. Careful use of textual critical principles can correct these scribal errors and remove the contradictions in these small matters.

Other discrepancies concern matters where the alleged contradiction is merely due to a varying viewpoint or mode of expression. The statements of Jesus in the Sermon on the Mount do not contradict the OT (cf. *Inspiration and Canonicity*, pp. 48-56). Christ here was, as often, opposing the Pharisees with their rabbinic traditional exegesis, which was a misunderstanding of the OT. In the last instance (Mt. 5:43) they added to the OT. In the matter of oaths they found loopholes enabling them to swear dishonestly. In the law of an eye for an eye, they were taking the rule of justice for Israel's judges and making it into an excuse for personal vengeance. And so the other examples also are contradictions of Pharisaic legalism, not of the OT.

The alleged contradictions in the Synoptic Gospels have been noted and considered by numerous scholars. Competent believing men through the ages have been convinced that no insoluble problem remains. There are problems because we have four stories giving a fourfold witness and not witnesses in collusion giving carbon copies. It must be remembered that there is no assurance that all the Gospels are in strict chronological order. Also, the Evangelists do not reproduce verbatim Jesus' long sermons. We have an inspired precis of His messages which is doubtless more valuable than verbatim snippits of the sermons taken out of context. Also, Jesus' speeches were given in Aramaic. An Aramaic expression can properly be translated into Greek by different words. There are also cases where one Evangelist will tell of two blind men or two demoniacs healed. Another will concentrate on one of them alone. According to Mt. 20:29; Mk. 10:46 Jesus performs a miracle while leaving Jericho, while according to Lk. 18:35 it happened "as he drew near to Jericho." It should be remembered that there was an ancient Jericho as well as a NT Jericho, and this may have given rise to the variant expression. But in any case the expressions are quite general.

Apparent contradictions may be caused by the different purposes of the different synoptists which result in a different selection, or a different ordering of their material. Thus Mark and Matthew mention both feedings of the multitudes. Luke and John give only the feeding of the 5000. Again, Mark probably implies that Jesus' cleansing of the temple took place on the day after the triumphal entry (Mk. 11:15). Matthew puts it right after the triumphal entry, with only the notation that "Jesus entered the temple of God" (Mt. 21:12). Since it is said that He taught daily in the temple (Lk. 19:47), the brief notations of Matthew and Luke (Lk. 19:45) may be taken to be not determinative of the day on which the event occurred. There are other possibilities of harmonization and, in particular cases it may be uncertain what is the correct view. But because of our confidence in the Spirit's work, we may believe with Justin Martyr that "no Scripture contradicts another," although sometimes we "do not understand what is recorded" (see above).

It has often been pointed out how remarkable it is that such problems in the Bible are so few. The Bible was written in foreign languages, not too well known, and in the midst of ancient and varying cultures with different designations for time, weight, money, measurement, clothes, climate, diet, etc. As tourists make odd mistakes abroad, surely we make odd mistakes in interpretation of the Bible. They concern matters of minor importance and careful study reduces these mistakes. More information would doubtless eliminate such few difficult problems that remain in our understanding of the biblical records.

Bibliography.–J. W. Haley, *Examination of the Alleged Discrepancies of the Bible* (1874); T. Engelder, *Scripture Cannot Be Broken* (1944); R. L. Harris, *Inspiration and Canonicity of the Bible* (1969); R. Manasseh ben Israel, *The Conciliator, A Reconcilement of the Apparent Contradictions in Holy Scripture* (1632; tr. E. H. Lindo repr. 1972). R. L. HARRIS

DISCRETION [Heb. *śeḵel*] (1 Ch. 22:12; 2 Ch. 2:12; Ezr. 8:18); AV also WISDOM, PRUDENCE, UNDERSTANDING; NEB also INTELLIGENCE; [*ṭa'am*] (1 S. 25:33; Prov. 11:22; 26:16; Dnl. 2:14); AV also ADVICE, WISDOM, "render a reason"; NEB also GOOD SENSE, SENSIBLY; [*m^e^zimmâ*] (Prov. 1:4; 2:11; 3:21; 5:2; 8:12; 14:17); AV also WITTY INVENTIONS, WICKED DEVICES; NEB PRUDENCE, CAREFUL THOUGHT.

Hebrew *śeḵel* comes from a verb meaning "see or understand," or "have insight," particularly the kind that can lead to success. *Ṭa'am* comes from a verb meaning "taste" and refers to good taste or judgment. *Mᵉzimmâ*, according to BDB (p. 273), is based on the verb *zāmam*, which means "purpose" or "devise." It can be used in the good sense of discrimination or shrewdness, or — when used in the plural — in the bad sense of intrigue (AV Prov. 8:12; 14:17; cf. Job 21:27; Prov. 12:2; etc.).

N. J. O.

DISCUS [Gk. *dískos*] (2 Macc. 4:14). The discus was a round stone slab or metal plate of considerable weight (a kind of quoit). The contest of throwing the discus was one of the exercises in the Greek gymnasium, being included in the pentathlon. It was introduced into Jerusalem by Jason the high priest in the time of Antiochus Epiphanes, 175-164 B.C., in the palaestra Jason had formed there in imitation of the Greek games. His conduct led to his being described in 2 Macc. 4:13f. as that "ungodly man" on account of whom even the priests forsook their duties to play at the discus. A statue of a *discobolos* (discus thrower) by Myron illustrates the game.

See also GAMES I.B. W. L. WALKER

DISCUSSION [Gk. *zḗtēsis*] (Jn. 3:25); AV QUESTION; NEB DISPUTE; [*syzētéo*] (Mk. 9:16; Lk. 24:15); AV QUESTION, REASON; NEB also ARGUMENT; [*dialogízomai*] (Mt. 16:7f.; Mk. 8:16f.; 9:33); AV REASON, DISPUTE (Mk. 9:33); NEB SAY, TALK, ARGUE; [*syllogízomai*] (Lk. 20:5); AV REASON; NEB ARGUE; [*mataiología*] (1 Tim. 1:6); AV JANGLING; NEB "wilderness of words"; [*dialégomai*] (Mk. 9:34); AV DISPUTE; [*dialaléō*] (Lk. 6:11); AV COMMUNE.

The Gk. *zḗtēsis* carries with it connotations of two sides seeking the answer to a certain question from opposite points of view. In secular usage it is often a technical term applied to a philosophical quest or search for truth. The verb *zētéō* thus is translated "investigate." This usage undoubtedly affects the NT, so that this term is applied to investigation or discussion in quest of truth, philosophical or otherwise. In Jn. 3:25 the controversy is between the disciples of Jesus and the disciples of John the Baptist over matters of purification. The discussion comes in a context of baptism. Perhaps therefore the issue under investigation is the relationship between baptism and purification. The word appears several other times in the NT (Acts 15:2, 7; 25:20; 1 Tim. 6:4; 2 Tim. 2:23; Tit. 3:9) and is translated either "debate," "question," or "controversy" (AV "question," "disputation"; NEB "controversy," "debate," "discussion," "verbal question," "speculations").

Related to this verb is Gk. *syzētéō*. This word in verb form seems to carry many of the same connotations, i.e., two sides carrying on discussion to find the answer to a question. However, it may relate more to the polarization of opinions and heated discussions. The RSV and NEB often translate it with "argue" (Mk. 8:11; 9:14) or "dispute" (Mk. 12:28; Acts 6:9; 9:29). The usual translation in the AV is "question," but "reason," "inquire," and "dispute" are used also. *See also* DISPUTE.

Gk. *dialogízomai* is the most usual term for "discuss" in the NT. This Gk. term also appears in Mk. 2:6, 8 (RSV "question"; AV "reason"; NEB "harbour thoughts"); Mk. 11:31 (RSV "argue"; AV "reason"; NEB "say"); and Lk. 1:29; 3:15; 5:21f.; 12:17; 20:14, where it is translated by either "considered," "questioned," "thought," "said to themselves" in the RSV; "cast in mind," "reasoned," "thought," or "talked it over" in the NEB. *See also* ARGUE.

The Greek term is used in three types of construction. It most properly means "discuss" when it is used with *prós allḗlous* ("to one another"). In this context the emphasis is upon intercommunication between people (Mk. 8:16; Lk. 20:14). It is also used with two constructions to indicate an internal process of contemplation or thought by which a decision is reached. The first combines the verb with *en heautoís* ("among themselves," Mt. 16:7f.; 21:25; Mk. 2:8; 11:31) and refers to a discussion taking place reflexively within a group. The other combines the verb with *en kardía* ("in heart," Mk. 2:6; Lk. 3:15; 5:22) and refers to the process which takes place within one person's mind. In such a case the process of discussion is internalized and thus becomes closely related to the thought process. When *dialogízomai* is connected with *taúta* ("these things") it means to harbor or retain certain thoughts within our minds. The noun related to this verb, *dialogismós*, comes into biblical literature meaning "thought" and is used in such important passages as Mt. 15:19 and Mk. 7:21, where Jesus says that it is out of the heart that evil thoughts proceed. As the role of thought is very important in Jesus' ethical teaching, this internal process of discussion relates to that which defiles a being. Thought precedes action and governs intent. Thus this process which God alone can see becomes a basis by which He judges us. 1 Cor. 3:20 shows that God knows that the thoughts of the wise are futile. While this noun is most often translated by the RSV as "thought" (Mt. 15:19; Mk. 7:21; Lk. 2:35; 6:8; 9:47; Rom. 1:21; 1 Cor. 3:20; Jas. 2:4), we also encounter the other synonyms we have found for "discussion": "question" (Lk. 5:22; 24:38; Phil. 2:14), "argument" (Lk. 9:46), "disputes" (Rom. 14:1), "quarreling" (1 Tim. 2:8).

Gk. *syllogízomai* (Lk. 20:5) refers to a discussion that takes place within a group. The situation here arises when Jesus poses the question to the Jewish leaders about the origin of John's baptism. Their dilemma sets them into an internal discussion for which they can find no solution without serious consequences. If they affirm that John gained from God his authority to baptize, they stand condemned for not accepting that authority. If they deny that John's authority came from God they will be stoned by the people who held John to be a prophet. Thus they can give no answer without suffering from the results.

The term *mataiología* (1 Tim. 1:6) means "empty, fruitless talk." Paul shows that it is opposed to love from a pure heart, to a good conscience, and to sincere faith. This vain discussion results from a desire to become a teacher of the law without the proper understanding of what the law really says. The admonition is that we refrain from covering our ignorance with meaningless discussions about words. The related word *mataiológos* is used in Tit. 1:10. The translations here speak of one who talks vainly, emptily, or wildly. Rom. 1:21 shows this to be one of the means by which man degrades himself, i.e., he becomes futile (*mataióō*) in his thinking (*dialogismós*). This self-degradation results in those who claim to be wise while really showing themselves to be fools. This same thought is emphasized by Paul in 1 Cor. 3:20 when he quotes Ps. 94:11: "the Lord know that the thoughts [*dialogismoús*] of the wise are futile [*mátaioi*]." The vain thought that is condemned is that thought which does not take God into account. This seems to be a preoccupation of those whom the world considers wise. It is a mark of the godly man that God is a part of his thought and of the way he considers the entire world. Thus, his thoughts are not vain.

See TDNT, II, *s.v.* διαλέγομαι, διαλογίζομαι, διαλογισμός (Schrenk), ζητέω, ζήτησις (Greeven).

D. W. WEAD

DISEASE [Heb. *ḥālâ, ḥ*ᵒ*lî, maḥ*ᵃ*leh, maḥ*ᵃ*lâ, taḥ*ᵃ*lu'îm, madeweh* (Dt. 7:15; 28:60), *baddê*–'limbs' (Job 18:13), *nega'* (Lev. 13f.); Gk. usually *nósos*, also *mástix* (Mk. 3:10), *asthéneia* (Acts 28:9)]; AV also SICK, DEATHS, "strength" (Job 18:13), PLAGUE (Lev. 13f.; Acts 28:9), INFIRMITY; **LEPROUS DISEASE** [Heb. *nega' ṣāra'at*] (Lev. 13f.); AV PLAGUE OF LEPROSY; **ITCHING DISEASE** [Heb. *nega' hanneteq* (Lev. 13:31-33), *gārāb* (Lev. 21:20)]; AV SCURVY, SCALL; **WASTING DISEASE; WASTING SICKNESS** [Heb. *rāzôn*] (Ps. 106:15; Isa. 10:16); AV LEANNESS; **SICK; SICKNESS** [Heb. usually *ḥālâ, ḥ*ᵒ*lî, maḥ*ᵃ*lâ*, also *dāweh, dawāy* (Jer. 8:18), *taḥ*ᵃ*lu'îm* (Dt. 29:22), *'ānaš* (2 S. 12:15), *'ānâ* (Ps. 107:17), *nōsēs* (Isa. 10:18); Gk. usually *asthenéō, asthenḗs*, also *árrhōstos, échō kakṓs, nósos* (Mt. 8:14), *pyréssō* (Mt. 1:30), *katechómenos* (Acts 28:8), *kámnō* (Jas. 5:15)]; AV also DISEASE, FAINT, INFIRMITY, IMPOTENT (Jn. 5:7), etc.; **ILL; ILLNESS** [Heb. *ḥālâ, ḥ*ᵒ*lî*; Gk. *asthenéō, asthéneia, árrhōstos* (1 Cor. 11:30)]; AV SICK, SICKNESS, INFIRMITY (Jn. 5:5); [*synechómenos pyretǭ́ megálǭ*] ("ill with a high fever," Lk. 4:38); AV TAKEN WITH A GREAT FEVER; **INFIRMITY** [Gk. *asthéneia, malakía*]; AV also DISEASE; **AILMENT** [Gk. *asthéneia*] (Gal. 4:13; 1 Tim. 5:23); AV INFIRMITY. *See also* AFFLICTION.

There are actually no diseases as such, but only technical and broadly descriptive names assigned to concomitant symptoms. Infecting organisms are parasitic in nature, since they can feed only on viable entities. Not all ailments arise from external sources, however. Some, such as the endocrinal disorders, come from a disturbance in body chemistry, while psychogenic disease originates within mental and emotional processes to affect the body, the mind, or both. In general, disease exhibits recognizable variations from what the individual has assumed to be — or has established as — the norm of health, and it is the pattern of such a deviation that makes diagnosis and treatment possible.

I. Antiquity of Disease
II. Disease in the Ancient Near East
  A. In the Paleolithic and Neolithic Periods
  B. In Sumer
  C. In Babylon
  D. In Egypt
III. Diseases Mentioned in the OT
  A. OT Concept of Disease
  B. Circulatory Diseases
  C. Paralysis
  D. Mental Disease
  E. Childhood Diseases
  F. Physical Deformities
  G. Eye Diseases
  H. Fever
  I. Skin Diseases
  J. Diseases of Unknown Nature or Origin
IV. Diseases Mentioned in the NT
  A. Jesus' Concept of Disease
  B. Paralysis

C. Blindness
D. Skin Diseases
E. Diseases of the Bowels
F. Psychosomatic Illnesses
G. Other Illnesses
H. Mental Afflictions
I. Demon Possession

I. Antiquity of Disease.–What appear to be the earliest manifestations of disease come from the Middle Paleozoic era, and are represented by various types of parasites, the most common being worm-infestation of corals, annelids on molluscs, and sea anemones on corals. While the invertebrate animals of that period are suspected of having sustained bacterial or viral infection, specific lesions have not been easy to establish.

The earliest vertebrates seem to have been immune to disease, and it was only at the beginning of the Mesozoic era that morbid states came into any prominence. Some conditions resulted from infection by pathogenic bacteria, but the environment also played a decided part, as is indicated by the arthritic and rheumatoid modifications of certain fossil bones from the Triassic and Jurassic periods. From the Cretacious period have come examples of dental caries, necroses, osteoma in a mosasaurus, and hemangioma of the caudal vertebrae of a dinosaur. Spondylitis deformans and Potts's disease have also been reported from the Cretacious, a period that was apparently productive of bone diseases such as osteosarcoma, alveolar osteitis, osteoperiostitis, exostoses, pachyostoses, and gigantism, the last probably indicating the termination of the phylum or class.

Viral diseases of animal species occurred from the Oligocene period, and the recovery of several varieties of tsetse fly from contemporary deposits raises, among other issues, the possibility of trypanosomiasis among the Tertiary ungulate mammals. Apart from the possibility of epidemics during and after the Tertiary period, it must be observed that the individual mortality was apparently low, especially in the case of the larger vertebrates. The marked similarity of preserved lesions in animals and man suggests that human beings contracted at least some of their earliest afflictions from the animal kingdom. If the foregoing evidence is at all reliable, it will be clear that certain specific forms of disease are considerably older than the species *homo sapiens*.

II. Disease in the Ancient Near East.–*A. In the Paleolithic and Neolithic Periods*. In Paleolithic and Neolithic times the prime concern of those involved with disease was the relief of pain, whatever the attributive causes of the pathology were imagined to be. The shaman was prominent in therapy as a priestly personage whose duty was to exorcise or placate the demon or evil force that had cast a baleful influence on the sufferer. For this purpose he used a variety of magical incantations and spells, aided by charms, drugs, and certain primitive surgical procedures.

In the Neolithic period some forms of unusual physical behavior such as epilepsy were attributed to the presence of a demon imprisoned in the head of the sufferer, and relief was sought by the shaman's making one or more apertures in the skull to facilitate the release of demonic forces. In this procedure, known as trephining (trepanning), a sharp flint was used to scrape a circular bevelled groove in the cranium, and then this was deepened to form a hole. One female skull from the Neolithic period exhibited five such apertures, suggesting that the woman may have been an epileptic. The Wellcome-Marston expedition in 1936 recovered from Lachish three eighth-century B.C. trephined skulls from a cistern, but the examination of the artifacts could not suggest the cause of the apparent intra-cranial pressure. Trephining was not popular in the ancient Near East, and only one instance of a rather dubious nature has been cited from Egypt.

B. In Sumer. The first to establish medical treatment on an empirico-rational basis were the Sumerians, although even they attributed many of their diseases to the activity of underworld demons who had entered the body through the apertures of the head. Only two medical tablets have survived from Sumer, both containing prescriptions. The largest of these came from the 3rd millennium B.C., and is the oldest extant pharmacopoeia. It divided up the various prescriptions according to mode of application, and while it presents formidable linguistic difficulties, it is clear that minerals such as oil, salt, and bitumen were used along with therapeutic agents from a wide variety of botanical sources. The willow (genus *Salix*) seems to have been either infused or decocted to produce the earliest form of aspirin (acetylsalicylic acid).

Although no deities or magical rites are mentioned in these texts, there can be little doubt that the application or ingestion of such therapeutic substances under the direction of the priest-physician (a-zu) was accompanied by the appropriate magical ceremonies. The diseases of the Sumerians are not well known, but probably included typhoid and paratyphoid fever, jaundice, cerebro-spinal meningitis, malaria, streptococcal sore throat, erysipelas, cholera, and possibly early forms of venereal disease.

C. In Babylon. The Babylonians inherited and developed Sumerian medical and therapeutic concepts, attributing the incidence of sickness to the violation of some taboo or to visitation by a demon. Such suprahuman activity required the physician-priest (*ašipu*) to enlist the aid of powerful beneficent deities, of whom Ea the water god and Marduk his son, patron of Babylon, were the most prominent. Whatever the prescription, it was administered against a background of magical ceremony, but with the passing of time the incantations became stereotyped and formal in nature.

Diseases mentioned in early Babylonian tablets are cholera, bubonic plague, dysentery, typhoid fever, smallpox, and oriental boil, while others that seem to be suggested include malignant tertian malaria, septicaemia, leprosy, syphilis, and various alimentary diseases. The code of Hammurabi (*ca*. 1792-1750 B.C.) included medical enactments that show the empirico-rational nature of contemporary surgical practice. There were operations for cataract, fractures, and abdominal disorders, and a scale of fees was established for patients in the three levels of society. *See also* BABYLONIA X.B.

D. In Egypt. Egyptian medical practice reached back at least to the beginning of the Old Kingdom period (*ca*. 2700 B.C.). As in other ancient cultures, the Egyptian physician was originally a priest; but at an early period the physician and surgeon were differentiated from the priesthood as such, and were remunerated from public funds. Nevertheless, Egyptian medicine was closely connected with religion, and gods such as Re, Isis, Horus, and Thoth were credited with healing functions.

Probably the earliest evidence for Egyptian medical practice consists of the fiber-splinted fractures found from the 5th Dynasty (*ca*. 2300 B.C.) onward, and the engraved representations of surgical procedures from a tomb near Memphis, dated *ca*. 2500 B.C. Literary sources dealing with Egyptian medicine include the Ebers papyrus on medicine and pharmacy, largely duplicated by the Hearst papyrus. A rather later document, the Greater

Berlin papyrus, was apparently compiled from even more ancient materials. A surgical casebook known as the Edwin Smith papyrus lists forty-eight surgical cases along with observations on the procedures relating to examination, diagnosis, and treatment. All of these materials draw on sources that are at least as old as the early 3rd millennium B.C. The Edwin Smith papyrus indicates that the Egyptian doctors were familiar with hemiplegia, cranial traumata, febrile states, spinal injuries, upper respiratory tract afflictions, cutaneous and alimentary diseases, and certain gynecological disorders. Obstetrics was not a branch of regular medical practice in ancient Egypt, but was assigned to the midwives. Though many medicinal compounds contained fanciful — and even revolting — ingredients, the remedies themselves were classified into sedatives, carminatives, astringents, diuretics, anthelmintics, expectorants, tonics, etc. The ancient Egyptians were pioneers in utilizing animal secretions such as blood and bile in therapeutics, and the fats of birds and mammals formed the base of some emollients and unguents. Common diseases in ancient Egypt included a variety of arthritic conditions, arteriosclerosis, tuberculosis, and possible indications of meningitis, syphilis, and smallpox.

III. Diseases Mentioned in the OT.–There is no reason to think that the environment of Palestine was any healthier than any other part of the ancient Near East. The home of the Israelites was a land-bridge, and as such its inhabitants were exposed to whatever communicable diseases were brought to the area by visitors.

A. OT Concept of Disease. What was unique, however, was the attitude adopted by the religious tradition of the Hebrews toward disease. The ethos of the Mosaic legislation repudiated entirely any magical or demonic etiology of disease. In the Pentateuch, illness is sent by God to punish the transgressor or to make clear divine displeasure (cf. Ex. 4:11; 32:39). The book of Job departs from this tradition by ascribing the incidence of disease to the activity of the adversary (2:7) or to the jealousy of other persons (5:2). Disease was thus regarded as conditioned largely by moral and spiritual factors, and the major ailments of the OT were accepted accordingly as punishment for personal iniquity or rebellion. *See also* AFFLICTION.

For this reason it is important to avoid associating Hebrew concepts of the etiology of disease with the Egyptian kind of humoral pathology. According to this theory, bodily health depended upon a balance of four vital fluids or humors, viz., blood, phlegm, yellow bile (choler), and black bile (melancholer), which were contained in internal channels and distributed throughout the body. A preponderance of black bile, e.g., would produce a melancholy disposition.

What the Hebrews did, in fact, was to assign emotional functions to the major organs of the body, excluding the brain; the heart became the locus of intelligence, purposiveness, and will; the bones typified strength of personality (cf. Job 20:11; Ps. 35:10; etc.); the kidneys expressed passions, desires, and strong feelings, including anger (cf. Job 11:27; Ps. 7:10 [MT 11]; etc.); the liver was the location of powerful affective and emotional states; while the abdomen frequently typified the seat of carnal inclination and appetite, as well as human feelings of quite a different order. This association of emotional states and physical changes was characteristic of the Hebrews; and in its assumption of the fundamental holism or unity of the human physical-metaphysical entity, it has laid an assured theoretical foundation for modern psychosomatic medical investigation.

Yet the Hebrews recognized that not all disease originated from the emotions, and that much sickness arose from the individual's relationship to his physical environment. Consequently the Hebrews, like the Egyptians, laid great stress on hygiene, and the medicine of the Mosaic era was preventive in the best sense of the term. Its basic principles were as follows: (a) sabbath observance for human beings, animals, and the land itself — the "sabbath" concept being quite different from the Babylonian *šapattu* or *šabattu* (cf. B. Landsberger, *Der Kultische Kalender der Babylonier und Assyrer* [1915], pp. 93, 131) and designed to enforce regular periods of rest (Gen. 2:3); (b) dietary regulations, which divided foodstuffs into readily recognizable categories of clean and unclean (Lev. 11); (c) circumcision, the only form of physical mutilation permitted by the Mosaic law, which carried with it religious and moral implications as well as physical benefits (Gen. 17:9; etc.); (d) laws governing sexual relationships and sexual health (Lev. 18–20; etc.), which included a list of the forbidden degrees of marital relationships; (e) provisions for individual sexual hygiene (Lev. 15); (f) cleanliness and bodily purification (Lev. 14:2; 15:2; etc.); (g) regulations for conducting camp life along sanitary and hygienic lines (cf. Dt. 22:12; Nu. 31:7ff.; etc.). The Hebrew priests, like their counterparts in other ancient Near Eastern cultures, were the responsible medical and sanitary officers, and the preventive measures they promoted undoubtedly prevented serious outbreaks of disease. The ethical view of health that the foregoing precepts enshrined was intended to show that the observance of the sanitary and hygienic regulations would of itself ensure for the Hebrews a great measure of freedom from the diseases of neighboring peoples.

Comparatively few of the ailments recorded in the OT can be diagnosed with complete confidence, due to the untechnical descriptions and the uncertain meanings of some terms in the OT, and to the general inadequacy of symptomatic descriptions. There is, however, less obscurity in the Hebrew text than in the medical writings of Sumer, Babylonia, or Egypt, and within broad limits it is possible to come to some sort of conclusion as to the pathology under consideration. It should be stressed that OT references to disease are usually incidental to other considerations, and in consequence only a few of the diseases prevalent in ancient Palestine are recorded.

B. Circulatory Diseases. Circulatory conditions, then as now, formed an important part of the pathological picture. One such instance was the cerebral hemorrhage that overtook Nabal (1 S. 25:37f.). This man was evidently a confirmed alcoholic who had arteriosclerosis and associated hypertension. The lesion was probably located in one of the atheromatous patches in the brain. The attack sent Nabal into a coma for some nine days before he died. The AV, RV, and RSV rendering "heart," following the MT, has been interpreted by some writers in terms of coronary artery disease, but most probably the term "heart" was being used in its correlative emotional sense of will, intelligence, or purposiveness to depict dramatically his comatose condition. The NEB "seizure" describes the cerebral accident more correctly in popular parlance.

Some have also seen the dramatic collapse of Uzzah (2 S. 6:6f.), when he inadvertently came into contact with the sacred ark, as an instance of apoplectic seizure; but this seems improbable since no actual paralysis was described and death occurred almost immediately. No doubt the shock of unwitting contact with Israel's most sacred cultic object precipitated Uzzah's collapse and death, which may have resulted from a coincident rupture of an aortic aneurism, or more probably from coronary thrombosis.

C. Paralysis. Paralysis is described clearly in the case of Jeroboam I (1 K. 13:4ff.), who in a furious outburst demanded the arrest of a prophet who had condemned his activities. Some medical authorities have suggested that the paresis resulted from cerebral hemorrhage or embolism in the corona radiata, which produced paralysis of the arm with immediate muscular atrophy as opposed to flaccid flexor paralysis. The restoration of the arm to its normal activities (v. 6) would follow readily in the case of embolism, once the clot was dispersed. However, the rapid succession of events makes it unlikely that the paralysis was in fact muscular atrophy consequent upon hemorrhage or embolism, since this would require a longer interval of time. Others have thought that the physical cause was a chronic cerebral abscess that ruptured and produced temporary paralysis in the process of evacuation. However, the intense anger of Jeroboam indicates that the paralysis was an instance of cataplexy, where the king's unconscious mind sought through associations of guilt to suppress his aggressive attitude towards the prophet. Once the emotional outburst was calmed by the prophet's prayer, the function of the arm was restored.

A form of paralysis, involving the complete atrophy of the arm as well as blindness in the right eye, was employed as a threat against the faithless shepherd of God's people (Zec. 11:17). Posterior spinal sclerosis (*tabes dorsalis*), marked by ataxia, patches of anesthesia, gastric, circulatory, urinary, or bronchial crises, and paralysis, form some of the symptoms of this disease, which usually originates from syphilis and may be marked by early loss of eyesight.

D. Mental Disease. King Saul represents one of the more notable cases of mental disease in the OT. While impressive in physique, Israel's first king gave early indications of personality instability. His pride and self-aggrandisement were symptoms (cf. 1 S. 11:6; 13:12; 15:9, 19; etc.), along with an ability to behave like an ecstatic prophet — a neuropathic function that immediately aroused the suspicions of those who knew him (10:11f.). A marked deterioration in personality occurred just after David was anointed his successor (16:14), and this understandable threat to his security grew more serious in his mind as David's popularity increased (18:10). Poor translations in the English Versions tend to cloud the etiology somewhat, so that the phrase "an evil spirit from God" should actually be rendered "a powerful evil spirit." The clinical picture has sometimes been described as cyclothymia or manic-depressive insanity, in which depressive phases alternate with episodes of wild excitement, separated by intervals of apparent mental balance. The attributes of fear, jealousy, insecurity, a developed sense of persecution, and patent homicidal tendencies point, however, quite decidedly to paranoid schizophrenia.

A rare mental disease reported with great accuracy in Dnl. 4 overtook Nebuchadrezzar of Babylon. His ailment was a form of monomania, in which the psychosis is restricted to a single concept or subject, and which in his case manifested itself in boanthropy, a highly unusual condition in which people imagine themselves to be cattle and behave accordingly. (One such case is described in R. K. Harrison, *Intro. to the OT* [1969], pp. 1115ff.) Nebuchadrezzar was fortunate enough to recover his mental balance, which is not common in this form of paranoia. Contemporary Babylonian records made no mention of this acutely embarrassing episode, because of the horror and superstitious dread with which insanity was viewed in the ancient world. David took advantage of this attitude to save his own life by feigning an epileptic seizure in the presence of Achish king of Gath (1 S. 21:12ff.); his discomfitted audience was quite convinced of his insanity.

E. Childhood Diseases. Although infant mortality was always high in antiquity, little indication of this is given in the OT. The death of the Shunammite woman's son (2 K. 4:18ff.) has been regarded as a genuine instance of siriasis (sunstroke), marked by high fever, acute headache, and coma. However, on purely environmental grounds this diagnosis seems less probable than that of meningococcal meningitis, an acute infectious disease of childhood, the symptoms of which include catarrh, headache, vomiting, and convulsions. To the mother, however, it could still have looked like a simple attack of sunstroke. The nature and etiology of the ailment occasioning the death of the widow's son at Zarephath (1 K. 17:17) are unknown, but it may have been of a similar character.

F. Physical Deformities. Physical disabilities of various kinds are noted in the OT, and Lev. 21:18ff. contains a list of congenital deformities disqualifying persons from the priesthood. A descendant of a family of giants is recorded as having had the congenital abnormality of extra fingers and toes (2 S. 21:20; 1 Ch. 20:6), and it was apparently from this same family that Goliath came. According to some authorities his unusual stature was caused by an anterior pituitary tumor; however, genetic factors seem to have been at work in the group of Gittite giants, suggesting that the extra fingers and toes resulted from a mutation in which certain genetic patterns had been altered dramatically. It is known that in prehistoric animals gigantism is usually an indication of impending familial dissolution through weakness of the stock, and this may have been the case with Goliath.

Mephibosheth the grandson of Saul apparently became lame due to a childhood accident (2 S. 4:4), although he may have had a congenital deformity that was made worse by his fall. The condition evidently required some care (cf. 19:24), implying that the lameness had been complicated by eczema or some kind of infection. The lameness sustained by Jacob in his struggle with the divine messenger (Gen. 32:24ff.) has been interpreted as a spasm of the adductor longus or the sartorius muscle, though this would not have produced the dislocation of the hip envisaged in the MT, unless it was an incomplete dislocation. Spontaneous fracture of the surgical neck of the femur seems precluded by the nature of the narrative.

G. Eye Diseases. Various forms of eye disease were common in antiquity. By the wilderness period, there were enough Hebrews afflicted in this way to merit special legislation on their behalf (Lev. 19:14; Dt. 27:18). The causes were generally external in nature: irritants such as dust and sand, or flies that caused infection. Flies were responsible for much of the conjunctivitis found in children, although *ophthalmia neonatorum*, a severe purulent form that results from venereal infection, probably caused a considerable amount of blindness. Apostasy merited blindness as a punishment from God (Dt. 28:28), who alone could cure the affliction (Ex. 4:11). Although blindness was not necessarily a concomitant of senility, Isaac (Gen. 27:1), Eli (1 S. 3:2; 4:15), and Ahijah the prophet (1 K. 14:4) lost their sight in old age. Leah seems to have suffered from blepharitis or mucopurulent conjunctivitis (Gen. 29:17). The condition described as "the fever that wastes the eyes" (Lev. 26:16) may have been the ophthalmia (inflammation of the eyeball) that occasionally follows malarial fever. While there is no firm OT evidence, it is highly probable that glaucoma, albugo, trachoma, pannus, iridocyclitis, and other eye diseases were an accepted part of life in ancient Israel.

The most accurate description of a specific eye disease occurs in the Apocrypha. A man named Tobit was evidently afflicted with a dense white opacity of the cornea (*leucoma*), usually caused by ophthalmia. According to the narrative, fish gall was applied to the cornea, presumably as an attempt at pigmentation, and this therapy brought healing (Tob. 11:4ff.).

See also BLINDNESS.

H. Fever. Fevers were common in the ancient Near East, and Dt. 28:21f. provides a list of febrile and inflammatory conditions that God would visit upon disobedient Hebrews. "Fever" commonly connotes a rise in body temperature, with such associated symptoms as chills, an accelerated pulse rate, lassitude, some inhibition of the secretory glands, malaise, and occasionally collapse. However, it is doubtful that the Hebrews were aware of more than the rise in temperature and general malaise. Three terms describing fever may be noted: *qaddaḥaṯ* (Lev. 26:16; Dt. 28:22), perhaps malarial fever, or possibly acute infectious hepatitis, since the LXX of Lev. 26:16 calls the disease *íkteros* (jaundice); *dalleqeṯ* (Dt. 28:22), "inflammation," probably describing the rigor and malaise of quartan malaria; and *ḥarḥur* (Dt. 28:22; LXX *erethismós*, "irritation"), perhaps indicating erysipelas or some other disease accompanied by a specific rash.

If the ailment described in Ps. 38:3ff. reflects an actual physical condition, it could perhaps be that of typhus, an acute infectious disease characterized by fever, petechial patches on the skin, macular eruptions, and profound depression. It occurs commonly where dirt, overcrowding, inadequate hygiene, and poor ventilation are in evidence. A less likely diagnosis would be confluent smallpox, which though well attested in antiquity was of uncertain dissemination in Palestine.

One of the most deadly febrile diseases was bubonic plague, described most fully in 1 S. 5–6. This dreaded infection is conveyed to man by the rat-flea (*Pulex Cheopis*). After a brief period of incubation sudden illness occurs, marked by severe malaise, chills, high fever, petechial eruptions, pneumonia, and hemorrhage from the mucous membranes. Within twenty-four hours the characteristic buboes appear in the groins, axillae, or elsewhere, and the sufferer generally dies shortly thereafter. The narrative mentions the chief symptom of buboes (5:12), and even notes the presence of dead rodents (6:5). This plague may also have ravaged the forces of Sennacherib (2 K. 19:35), though specific information on this matter is lacking.

See also FEVER; PLAGUE.

I. Skin Diseases. Skin diseases of various kinds occurred frequently in the Orient, and in Israel they were often associated with ceremonial uncleanness. The "boils of Egypt" (Dt. 28:27, 35) were apparently the result of staphylococcal infection of the tissue around a skin follicle, with the usual formation of pus and necrosis of the core. The "boils" (*'ᵃḇa'bu'ōt*) of Ex. 9:9f. (Akk. *bubu'tu*) were vesicles or perhaps pustules, and the fact that the sixth Egyptian plague affected both animals and human beings suggests that the "boil" was in fact the malignant pustule of anthrax. (*See also* BOIL.) The itching disease of Dt. 28:27 was apparently scabies, caused by the itch-mite that burrows beneath the epidermis to produce dermatitis and itching. The soft skin between fingers and toes is the commonest site of infection, and the condition may be complicated by eczema due to scratching. The disease of Lev. 13:30; 14:54 was ringworm, caused by several fungous parasites that invade the skin of the scalp and neck to produce *tinea tonsurans*, *tinea kerion*, and other related froms. (*See also* ITCH.) The "scab" of Isa. 3:17 was probably favus, a fungous disease in which small yellow crusts form over the hair follicles to give a typical honeycombed appearance. These skin afflictions, along with some others, were mentioned in Lev. 13 as differential diagnoses for leprosy.

LEPROSY, one of the scourges of antiquity, was undoubtedly a recurrent part of Hebrew life. The Heb. *ṣāra'aṯ* designates an eruptive condition that could affect houses in the manner of a mineral efflorescence (Lev. 14:44), clothing (13:47, 59) and leather (14:55), as well as persons. While the technical terms in Lev. 13 are obscure, it is clear that they provide for the diagnosis of the malignant condition known to modern authorities as Hansen's disease (clinical leprosy). Localized tissue inflammation, a crust on some small area of the epidermis, or a pinkish-red swollen spot were enough to arouse suspicions of leprosy, which was diagnosed if the local cuticular hairs became white and the condition penetrated beneath the skin. A period of quarantine decided the issue and enabled differential diagnoses to be made where appropriate. These would certainly include vitiligo, psoriasis, acne, favus, alopecia, and other conditions familiar to modern physicians. When leprosy was diagnosed, the afflicted person was normally isolated (cf. 2 Ch. 26:21) or banished from society to prevent the disease from spreading.

J. Diseases of Unknown Nature or Origin. The OT mentions several diseases of obscure nature and etiology, of which some can be noted here. Job's ailment was characterized by neurasthenia, multiple irritant ulceration, muscular debility, and depression. The chief symptom was an outbreak of boils over all parts of his body, which in view of his acute emotional distress was probably of psychosomatic character. If this is correct, the eruptions would have been the raised wheals of a typical allergic reaction. Suggestions that Job was suffering from a disease such as impetigo, Delhi boil, or framboesia fail to recognize the obvious emotional factors provoking the malady. The boil of Hezekiah (2 K. 20:7; Isa. 38:21) was evidently a simple staphylococcal infection of the skin, since the application of a fig poultice sufficed to clear up the trouble. (*See also* BOIL.)

King Asa succumbed to a disease after only two years (2 Ch. 16:12f.). The mention of his feet has led to suggestions that he might have had a circulatory dysfunction of the extremities culminating in gangrene. But since the word "feet" (Heb. *regel*) was sometimes used euphemistically of the sexual organs (cf. Jgs. 3:24, AV; Ruth 3:4; Isa. 6:2; etc.), his disease may well have been of a venereal nature, perhaps tertiary syphilis.

A true case of Hansen's disease seems to have afflicted Uzziah (2 Ch. 26:21) as a punishment for usurping priestly prerogatives (cf. Nu. 12:10), and until he died he was quarantined in a separate dwelling — this privilege doubtless being a concession to his rank.

Another Judean king, Jehoram, was afflicted by a painful bowel disease from which he died two years later (2 Ch. 21:18f.). While the cause may have been a malignant tumor of the descending colon or the rectum, the breakdown of intestinal function suggested by the text could well indicate the presence of bacillary dysentery. Caused by one species or other of the bacillus *Shigella*, it is marked by the usual symptoms of dysentery but can also exhibit a necrotic inflammation of the mucous membrane of the colon. A separation of dead intestinal tissue and sloughing off of the rectum probably marked the last agonizing moments of this unfortunate king.

Fatal diseases of unknown nature overtook Abijah in infancy (1 Kgs. 14:17), Elisha in old age (2 Kgs. 13:14), and the wife of Ezekiel, probably in middle life (Ezk. 24:16). Rachel's life was terminated by hard labor, of which the only symptom recorded was severe pain (Gen. 35:16ff.). By contrast, the precipitate labor that took the life of Phinehas' wife (1 S. 4:19) was incurred by profound shock.

***IV. Diseases Mentioned in the NT.**–A. Jesus' Concept of Disease.* By the time of Christ some of the superstitions of pagan Near Eastern life had infiltrated Judaism, with the result that magical charms and incantations were employed along with folk remedies in attempts to cure the sick. In His ministry Jesus emphasized the fundamental unity of the individual personality, as the ancient Hebrew writers had done, but He gave no support to the OT view that sickness and disease were punitive in character. He behaved as though disease was contrary to the divine order, and nowhere lent credence to the idea that illness might be God's will for the individual in order to teach patience, courage, or similar virtues. Instead, He paid close attention to the emotional and spiritual turmoil of the sufferer, thereby indicating His awareness of conflict, anxiety, hatred, fear, etc. as factors in disease. He sought to establish true healing of the personality by making faith, hope, love, and divine peace dominant. The Sermon on the Mount (Mt. 5–7) recognizes the fundamental importance of motive in all of human activity and establishes behavioral standards and patterns that promote the total health of the individual.

B. Paralysis. Organic disease of the central nervous system seems to have been the cause of several instances of paralysis healed by Christ. As indicated by Luke's clinical terminology, the centurion's servant (Lk. 7:1f.; Mt. 8:5ff.) was very ill with what was probably Landry's paralysis. This ailment begins in the legs and proceeds rapidly through the trunk to the arms and neck, usually terminating fatally within twenty-one days. Acute spinal meningitis or anterior poliomyelitis are less probable diagnoses. The paralytic at Capernaum (Mt. 9:2; Mk. 2:3; Lk. 5:18ff.) was probably a victim of paraplegia, in which the lower part of the body is paralyzed. There are several types of paraplegia, and the man may have had a congenital spastic variety resulting from a birth injury. If, however, he had tuberculous spondylitis, the paresis would have resulted from compression of the spinal cord. Luke's medical term *paralelyménos* suggests an ailment of chronic proportions involving organic changes. The man with the atrophied hand (Mt. 12:9ff.; Mk. 3:1ff.; Lk. 6:6ff.) seems to have suffered from a case of acute anterior poliomyelitis in childhood. In this disease, common in the ancient Near East, the anterior horns of the spinal cord become inflamed and paresis occurs in one or more groups of muscles. That there was marked atrophy is indicated by the medical use of *xērós*, "withered, atrophied." The chronically ill man at Beth-zatha (Jn. 5:2) was probably suffering from some slowly degenerating condition such as amyotrophic lateral sclerosis, which involves progressive muscular atrophy. Tabes dorsalis (*locomotor ataxia*) is a less probable diagnosis, since this disease usually begins in mid-life and is generally the result of earlier syphilitic infection.

The congenital cripple at one of the temple gates (Acts 3:2ff.) may have been suffering from spastic spinal paralysis, cerebral palsy, or ataxic paraplegia. The cripple at Lystra (14:8ff.) was probably disabled by infantile spastic paraplegia due to a birth injury. The chronic condition that afflicted Aeneas (9:33) may also have resulted from some form of paraplegia.

Pool of Bethesda on the grounds of St. Anne's Church in Jerusalem. Its waters were believed to have curative powers, and invalids gathered about its five porticoes to be healed. (J. N. Milidonis)

C. Blindness. BLINDNESS was just as much a scourge in Christ's time as in the OT period, and some of His miracles involved the restoration of sight. The specific cause is not mentioned in the narratives, though the congenital nature of the blindness afflicting the beggar in Jerusalem (Jn. 9:1ff.) was noted in passing. Christ's healing techniques were apparently adapted to the needs of the individuals concerned. In the above instance He made a sticky or dust paste, reminiscent of man's original constituent elements (cf. Gen. 2:7), and having placed it symbolically on the man's eyes requested him to wash it off. Another blind man at Beth-saida (Mk. 8:22ff.) was anointed with saliva and had his sight restored by stages, no doubt to offset the shock of sudden exposure to bright sunlight. The deaf-mute (7:32ff.) was also anointed with saliva and received the imposition of Christ's hands as a means of inculcating his confidence and trust before healing occurred. The beggar Bartimaeus (10:46ff.), apparently a familiar figure since his father's name is mentioned, had probably become blind as a child. Deeply disturbed by his disabled condition, he was an outstanding example of a person healed by faith in Christ's power. Ophthalmia may have been the cause of this particular instance of blindness. Another healing involved two blind beggars in the same general area (Mt. 20:29ff.), and the fact that these two incidents are quite separate, though similar in nature, indicates the prevalence of blindness in NT times. (See IV.F below.)

D. Skin Diseases. The LEPROSY Christ healed probably included specific instances of Hansen's disease, as well as other skin afflictions of the kind provided for in Lev. 13. The ten lepers (Lk. 17:12ff.) were probably victims of clinical leprosy, as suggested by their isolation from society, and had doubtless formed their own colony for mutual support. The incident was used not merely to demonstrate the healing power of Christ, but also to teach a lesson concerning gratitude. In Mt. 8:2ff.; Mk. 1:40ff.; Lk. 5:12ff. the ailment in question was probably acquired leucoderma, since the sufferer was in contact with society in a manner forbidden to one afflicted with Hansen's disease. Lk. 5:12 indicates that the disease had reached an advanced stage (*plḗrēs lépras*), which would suggest that most of the body had been affected.

E. Diseases of the Bowels. Luke's accurate use of the rare Greek compound *skōlēkóbrōtos* (Acts 12:23, RSV "eaten by worms") indicates that Herod Agrippa died from complications of human myiasis. The immediate cause of death may have been intestinal obstruction and subsequent perforation of the bowel, followed by peritonitis and death. Evidence of myiasis would probably have been voided by the bowel at death.

Luke gives what seems to have been an eyewitness account of a specific disease in his description of the FEVER and DYSENTERY of Publius' father (Acts 28:7ff.). The febrile state may have accompanied a severe form of malaria, perhaps the pernicious variety, since the plural form of the Greek word for fever (*pyretós*) indicates the acuteness of the condition. Cholera and undulant (Malta) fever are less likely diagnoses.

F. Psychosomatic Illnesses. Some of the diseases that Christ healed were evidently psychosomatic in nature, having arisen from the impact of environmental stress upon the emotions and will. Others were apparently congenital, or else the products of lesions or secondary manifestations of primary diseases.

The healing of a woman who seems literally to have buckled under the pressures of life is described in Lk. 13:11, where Luke's medical terminology indicates a case of spondylitis deformans. This is an arthritic condition in which union (ankylosis) of the discs and vertebrae produces an abnormal curvature of the spine (kyphosis). The psychosomatic relationship between arthritis and chronic anger is now well established, and the dispelling of resentment has been known to produce dramatic healings of a number of arthritic conditions. *See also* BENT OVER.

Other NT examples of psychosomatic illnesses include the aphonia and deafness of Zechariah (Lk. 1:11ff.), which resulted from shock and severe emotional conflict and disappeared only when the tensions were removed. Instances of the same phenomenon have been reported in the psychosomatic medical literature. A profound shock also precipitated the temporary amaurosis that overtook Paul on the Damascus road (Acts 9:3ff.). His sudden conversion required him to "see things differently" within an extremely short space of time, and his BLINDNESS gave psychosomatic expression to the resultant psychic conflict. Once the emotional tension was resolved and Paul was able to orient himself to his new vocation, his sight was restored. There is no evidence to suggest that the "thorn in the flesh" (2 Cor. 12:7) had anything to do with an impairment of his sight resulting from his conversion experience. Acute emotional tension with profound overtones of guilt resulted in the amaurosis experienced by Elymas (Acts 13:10f.), and also the sudden demise of Ananias and Sapphira (5:1ff.) — probably from coronary thrombosis.

G. Other Illnesses. The third Gospel (14:2) records one instance in which Jesus healed a man with DROPSY, an abnormal accumulation of watery fluid in body cavities or tissues. This condition usually indicates disease in some related area of the body; but because the Greek medical writers used *hydrōpikós* ("dropsical") with as much imprecision as it is used now, it is impossible to determine the location of the disease. Some writers have seen the cause in terms of angioneuredema, a disorder of the nerves that dilate or constrict the blood-vessels, but this is at best conjecture.

The hemorrhaging woman of Mt. 9:20ff. (par. Mk. 5:25f.; Lk. 8:43ff.) had either carcinoma cervix uteri, a uterine fibroid, or possibly menorrhagia. The uterine fibroid seems the most likely condition, since her illness was of a chronic nature and was deteriorating (Mk. 5:25). (*See also* HEMORRHAGE.) The nobleman's son (Jn. 4:46ff.) may have been suffering from meningitis, although malaria, a disease that caused high infant mortality in antiquity, should not be discounted. It is possible that Peter's mother-in-law (Mt. 8:14ff.; Mk. 1:29ff.; Lk. 4:38ff.) was ill with pernicious malaria and was exhibiting cerebral disturbances.

Diseases of an unspecified nature overtook Jairus' daughter (Mk. 5:22ff.; Lk. 8:41ff.), Lazarus (Jn. 11:11ff.), and the son of the widow at Nain (Lk. 7:11); the latter two were already dead when Christ encountered them. Tabitha (Acts 9:40f.) had succumbed to an unspecified disease before being restored to life by Peter.

H. Mental Afflictions. Mental conditions of various kinds were reflected in the NT narratives. It is sometimes possible to distinguish between functional neuroses such as neurasthenia, on the one hand, and organic conditions designated by the term "epilepsy," on the other. By the time of Christ, the long-held pagan belief that insanity was the work of demons had also become the common opinion among the Jews. Demons were said to have been cast out by others than Jesus Himself (cf. Mk. 9:38; Lk. 9:49; Acts 19:14), and this kind of exorcism had a prominent place in His ministry too. Any form of bizarre behavior or eccentric conduct might suggest demon possession, and even Christ Himself was not exempt from allegations of this nature. Turning to more specific instances, the healing of a functional neurosis seems exemplified in the case of Mary Magdalene, out of whom Christ cast "seven demons" (Lk. 8:2), an expression that presumably described a state of acute psychoneurosis. Christ's conversation with the Samaritan woman at a well (Jn. 4:7ff.) furnishes a classic instance of the application of nondirective counseling techniques to what seems to have been a resentful and generally disturbed personality.

A chronic nervous disability that Christ healed on several occasions (cf. Mt. 4:24) was EPILEPSY, attributed in one instance to the activities of a "dumb spirit" (17:14ff.; Mk. 9:17ff.; Lk. 9:37ff.). This particular case is of interest, because, while a convulsive seizure typical of severe epilepsy is described in Mk. 9:20, the disorder had taken other forms on earlier occasions (v. 22). In Mt. 17:15 the father describes his son as "moon-struck" (AV "lunatick"), referring to the popular idea of a relationship between the lunar phases and the erratic behavior of some demented people — an idea that still claims its supporters among scientists and non-scientists alike. Suprisingly little is known about the cause of epilepsy, historic though the ailment is, aside from those symptomatic forms that are obviously the result of cerebral lesions of various kinds. Certain people are subject to epileptic-like seizures as the result of shock or suggestion, and these attacks are very difficult to distinguish from hereditary epilepsy. The Markan narrative, which is apparently an eyewitness account, seems to point to a congenital condition while suggesting that deep personality derangement was also part of the clinical picture.

I. Demon Possession. Gross mental disorientation was frequently referred to in terms of demon possession, and NT cases of this include the child of the Syrophoenician woman (Mt. 15:27; Mk. 7:25), the demoniacs at Gerasa (Mt. 8:28; Mk. 5:2; Lk. 8:27) and Capernaum (Mk. 1:23; Lk. 4:33), along with a blind and dumb demoniac (Mt. 12:22; Lk. 11:14), and a girl with powers of divination (Acts 16:16). Some of the reactions described are suggestive of paranoid schizophrenia; but others indicate that the sufferer was possessed by a separate personality, or at least the sufferer's personality was so fragmented that it gave convincing indication of possession. Medical missionaries and others working in cultures dominated by demonism and superstition have reported instances of personality possession by demonic forces that closely approximate those recorded in the NT, and some have been able to exorcise the sufferers successfully. While the term "demon-possession" may be regarded as too subjective and ill-defined for modern clinical purposes, it must be remembered that the same criticisms can be levelled equally against much of the current psychiatric terminology. The fact that in both ancient and modern times the exorcism of certain "possessed" people has enabled them to live reasonably normal lives would suggest that some extraneous negative force had in fact gained control of the mind and disoriented its functioning. It has been suggested that "possession" is actually the result of a glandular dysfunction caused by emotional stress; however, while glandular dysfunction does play a part in certain psychotic conditions, it does not assume the character of a distinct personality speaking through the sufferer. The empirical terminology of antiquity enabled observers to distinguish between epilepsy and demon possession. The latter was always the more complex, with profound emotional and spiritual involvement. In addition to the feeling of possession or compulsion, some other criteria — perhaps suicidal or homicidal impulses — may have helped in establishing the diagnosis.

See also DEMONOLOGY.

Bibliography.–M. A. Ruffer, *Studies in the Palaeopathology of Egypt* (1921); R. L. Moodie, *Antiquity of Disease* (1923); A. R. Short, *The Bible and Modern Medicine* (1953); F. Dunbar, *Emotions and Bodily Changes* (1954 ed.); L. T. Swaim, *Arthritis, Medicine and the Spiritual Laws* (1962); S. N. Kramer, *The Sumerians* (1970 ed.), pp. 95ff.

R. K. HARRISON

DISEASES OF THE EYE. *See* BLINDNESS.

DISGUISE [Heb. hithpael of *ḥāpaś*] (1 S. 28:8; 1 K. 20:38; 22:30; 2 Ch. 18:29; 35:22); in 2 Ch. 35:22 the NEB omits, following the LXX; [hithpael of *šānâ*] (1 K. 14:2); [*śûm sēṯer*] (Job 24:15); NEB "his face covered with a mask"; [Gk. *metaschēmatízō*] (2 Cor. 11:13-15); AV TRANSFORM THEMSELVES; NEB MASQUERADE.

In each of the OT occurrences someone (usually the king) changes his clothes so as to obscure his identity. In 2 Cor. 11:13-15 Paul alludes to the practice of "false apostles" disguising themselves as true. In this they are following their master Satan, who habitually (present tense) portrays himself as one of God's faithful angels. *Metaschēmatízō* speaks of a more superficial change than *metamorphóō* (cf. Mt. 17:2). For this reason the RSV and NEB translations seem better here than the AV. (But cf. the use of *metaschēmatízō* in Phil. 3:21 — "who will change our lowly body to be like his glorious body" — where a deeper change is implied.)

G. A. VAN ALSTINE

DISH [Heb. *kap*] (Ex. 25:29; 37:16; Nu. 4:7; 7:14ff.; 1 K. 7:50; 2 K. 25:14; 2 Ch. 4:22; 24:14; Jer. 52:18f.); AV SPOON; NEB SAUCER; [*ṣallaḥaṯ*] (2 K. 21:13; Prov. 19:24; 26:15); AV also BOSOM; NEB also PLATE;

Philistine dishes and bowl from Gath (Late Bronze Age) (Consulate General of Israel in New York)

[Gk. *trýblion*] (Mt. 26:23; Mk. 14:20); NEB BOWL; [*pínax*] (Lk. 11:39); AV PLATTER; NEB PLATE.

The small golden cup or incense bowl used in the sanctuary was shaped like the hollow of the hand; hence the name *kap* which means "hand" or "palm of the hand." The *ṣallaḥaṯ* was a medium-sized bowl used for serving food. The sluggard in Proverbs is too lazy to withdraw his hand from the serving dish in order to feed himself.

The *trýblion* was a deep bowl used in measuring medicines; however, a "serving bowl" is indicated by its use at the Last Supper. The *pínax* was originally a wooden board; thus it came to indicate anything flat, especially a flat dish.

See J. L. Kelso, *Ceramic Vocabulary of the OT* (*BASOR, Supp. Studies*, nos. 5-6 [1948]). J. T. DENNISON, JR.

DISHAN dī'shan [Heb. *dîšān*]; **DISHON** dī'shon [*dîšōn*]. A Horite clan, mentioned as the youngest "son" and elsewhere as the "grandson" of Seir. The form "Dishon" occurs several times in the list of Horite clans, together with many similar names (Gen. 36:21-30; 1 Ch. 1:38, 41f.).

DISHONEST (GAIN) [Heb. *bāṣa'*, *beṣa'*] (Jer. 22:17; Ezk. 22:13, 27); AV also COVETOUSNESS; NEB also ILL-GOTTEN (GAINS); [*'āwel*] (Dt. 25:16); AV UNRIGHTEOUSLY; [Gk. *adikía*, *ádikos*] (Lk. 16:8, 10); AV UNJUST. A profit made unjustly, by violence, or by the destruction of others' lives. This is one of the sins for which Israel was taken into captivity; it is always spoken of as an abomination to the Lord. The NT term is formed by the negation of a root used extensively in the NT; from this root come the important terms "right," "just," "righteousness," "justice," "justification."

R. J. HUGHES, III

DISOBEDIENCE [Gk. *parakoḗ*] (Rom. 5:19; 2 Cor. 10:6; He. 2:2); NEB also MISDEED, REBELLION; [*apeítheia*] (Rom. 11:30, 32; Eph. 2:2; 5:6; He. 4:6, 11); AV also UNBELIEF; NEB also REBELLIOUS, REBEL, UNBELIEF; **DISOBEDIENT** [Heb. *mārâ*–'be obstinate'] (Neh. 9:26); NEB REBELLED; [Gk. *apeithḗs*] (Lk. 1:17; Acts 26:19; etc.); AV also NOT BELIEVE; NEB REBELLIOUS, OBSTINACY, etc.; [*apeithéō*] (Rom. 10:21; 11:30; etc.); AV also NOT BELIEVE; NEB also UNRULY, "refused to believe," UNBELIEVERS; [*anypótaktos*] (1 Tim. 1:9); NEB UNRULY; **DISOBEY** [Heb. *mārâ*] (1 K. 13:21, 26); NEB DEFY; [*'āraḇ*] (Prov. 24:21); AV "meddle not with"; NEB "nothing to do with"; [*lō' šāma'*] (Josh. 1:18; Jer. 42:13); AV "not hearken unto," "neither obey"; NEB also "fail to carry out"; [Gk. *apeithéō*] (1 Pet. 2:8); NEB DISBELIEVE; [*parérchomai*] (Lk. 15:29); AV TRANSGRESS; [*mḗ tēréō*–'not keep, observe'] (1 Jn. 2:4); AV KEEP NOT.

The NT concept "disobey" and its cognates have their roots in the OT word *šāma'* which literally means "hear." In the OT *šāma'* + b^e has the sense of "obey," the translation normally used in English versions of the Bible. The full meaning of the term is clear when it is seen that its proper context is the relationship of God and man, or more specifically of God and Israel. God has revealed Himself through His "word" or "voice" (Gen. 27:8; Ex. 19:5), making known His purposes and the action by which these purposes will be fulfilled. Man as the recipient of this revelation hears it, through God's chosen representative, responds to it in trust and faith, and then becomes involved in action obedient to that word. ("In ancient Israel the ear of a slave was pierced to emphasize his duty of obedience" [Richardson, p. 30].) Really to "hear," then, involved one in faithful obedient action prompted by a faith in the God who revealed Himself. Not to respond in this way is really not to "hear" and thus not to believe. This is called "revolt" or "rebellion" (Neh. 9:26).

The NT presupposes this OT understanding of obedience and uses the term *hypakoḗ* (from *akoúō*, "hear") in the sense of "obedience." The antithesis of this word is *parakoḗ*, which means "hearing aside," "overhearing," or "unwillingness to hear," i.e., "disobedience." "*Parakoḗ* in the NT always means "bad hearing" in consequence of unwillingness to hear, and therefore in the guilty sense of disobedience which does not and will not proceed to the action by which hearing becomes genuine hearing" (*TDNT*, I, 223). In Scripture disobedience (*parakoḗ*) is seen as "in opposition to the original goal of obedience (*hypakoḗ*) or communion with God" (Berkouwer, p. 266). Thus there is the contrast between Adam and Christ in Rom. 5:19, between *parakoḗ* and *hypakoḗ* (cf. 2 Cor. 10:6). To turn a deaf ear in disobedience is to sin, for "not-hearing and not-listening are the same as rebellion and transgression against God" (Berkouwer, p. 267). Thus *parakoḗ* and *parabásis* ("transgression") are tied up together as in He. 2:2 (cf. Rom. 5:14; Gal. 3:19), where *parábasis* is transgression of a positive command and *parakoḗ* is the neglect to obey (*Expos.G.T.*, IV, on He. 2:2).

Another NT word for disobedience is *apeítheia*, meaning "unwillingness to be persuaded." This term is used of the disobedience toward God both of Jews (Rom. 11:30) and of all men in general (v. 32). The classical example of Jewish disobedience was in the wilderness period (He. 4:6, 11), but in Ephesians the phrase "sons of disobedience," for whom opposition to the divine will is their very nature, is used to describe all the unregenerate outside of Christ (Eph. 2:2; 5:6).

The actions of disobeying and being disobedient are expressed by the Gk. *apeithéō* and *apeithḗs*. These words are found in the LXX, the verb *apeithéō* always denoting the sinful attitude of the people in being rebellious against God (Ex. 23:21; Isa. 65:2; Jer. 5:23). Isa. 65:2 is quoted by Paul in Rom. 10:21, *apeithoúnta* being translated "disobedient" in the RSV (cf. Justin Martyr *Apol.* i.35, 38, 49; *Dial.* 24, 97, 114). The Jews of the wilderness generation were especially disobedient (He. 3:18), but in He. 11:31 "those who declined to submit to the claims of Israel's God are described by the same word as are the recalcitrant Israelites themselves" (Moffatt, p. 184). Thus all men are guilty of disobedience to God, and gentile Christians are reminded of their own sin by Paul in Rom. 11:30 as he sets their former disobedience over against the present disobedience of the Jews (v. 31). For the early Christians the "supreme disobedience was a refusal to believe their gospel" (Bauer, p. 82), so "obedience" became almost a "technical expression for the acceptance of the Christian faith" (Richardson, p. 30; cf. 1 Pet. 2:7f.).

It is the function of the forerunner of the Messiah to turn the "disobedient to the wisdom of the just" (Lk. 1:17), by which is meant turning the Jews to God (Plummer, p. 15). False teachers are said to be "detestable" and "disobedient" (Tit. 1:16), while disobedience is also listed among the vices of pre-Christian mankind in Tit. 3:3. Both in Paul's day and in the last days there appear those who are "disobedient to their parents" (Rom. 1:30; 2 Tim. 3:2). A special use of *apeithḗs* is found in Acts 26:19, where the object is "the heavenly vision" to which Paul was not disobedient. The only other NT occurrence of "disobedient" is in 1 Tim. 1:9, where it renders the word *anypótaktos*, referring to those who are undisciplined and refuse to obey the law.

Bibliography.–G. C. Berkouwer, *Sin* (1971); Bauer, pp. 76, 81f., 624; *Expos.G.T.,* IV; J. Moffatt, *ICC* on *Hebrews* (1924); A. Plummer, *ICC* on *II Corinthians* (1915); A. Richardson, *Intro. to the Theology of the NT* (1958); *TDNT*, I, *s.v.* ἀκούω (Kittel); VI, *s.v.* ἀπειθέω (Bultmann). D. K. McKIM

DISORDER [Gk. *akatastasía*] (2 Cor. 12:20; Jas. 3:16); AV TUMULTS, CONFUSION; NEB also GENERAL DISORDER. The literal meaning of the Greek noun is "without order or stability." The RSV translates the same word as "confusion" in 1 Cor. 14:33 and its plural form as "tumults" in Lk. 21:9 and 2 Cor. 6:5. In the passages cited, *akatastasía* is used of political unrest (Lk. 21:9), personal distress (2 Cor. 6:5), and of confusion among the worshiping community due to an improper exercise of spiritual gifts (1 Cor. 14:33).

In 2 Cor. 12:20 and Jas. 3:16 the context clearly suggests that *akatastasía* is used of the disruption of the Christian community by worldly disputes among its members. It is worthy of note that in both of these passages "jealousy" and "selfish ambition" are listed prior to "disorder" as contributing factors.

The cognate *akatástatos* is used of an "unstable" or "fickle" person (Jas. 1:8) and of the tongue as a "restless" evil (Jas. 3:8).

See *TDNT,* III, *s.v.* καθίστημι κτλ. (Oepke).

A. J. BIRKEY

DISPATCH [Heb. *šālaḥ*–'send'] (2 K. 6:32); AV SENT; [*bārā'*–'cut down'] (Ezk. 23:47); NEB "hack to pieces"; [Gk. *syntémnō*–'cut short,' 'shorten'] (Rom. 9:28); AV "cut . . . short"; NEB "(will be) final." In Ezk. 23:47 *bārā'*, "cut down," as of a forest, is used of the punishment of immorality. The RSV translates Rom. 9:28, a passage of uncertain interpretation (see Bauer, p. 300), as "the Lord will execute his sentence . . . with rigor and dispatch," indicating that God will shorten the time, i.e., He will not continue forever in His long-suffering.

DISPENSATION [Gk. *diakonía*] (2 Cor. 3:7-9); AV MINISTRATION; NEB also DISPENSED. The term refers to the action of giving out, specifically referring to God's dealings with men. In 2 Cor. 3 Paul contrasts the brightness of Moses' face in the giving of the OT law (v. 5) which brought death (v. 7), with the "greater splendor" (v. 8) of the giving of the Spirit which brought righteousness (v. 9). In the AV of 1 Cor. 9:17; Eph. 1:10; 3:2; Col. 1:25, the Greek term *oikonomía* is rendered "dispensation" with the obsolete meaning of administration, as of a household, of a commission, or of stewardship.

D. K. McKIM

DISPERSION [Gk. *diasporá*]. The term used to designate the Jews living outside Palestine and maintaining their religious observances and customs among the Gentiles. The Gk. *diasporá* is regularly used in the LXX and extrabiblical Jewish literature, and is found in Jas. 1:1 and 1 Pet. 1:1, where it is used figuratively of the Church dispersed from its heavenly homeland. This article will be concerned with the Dispersion situation mainly in the 1st cent. and especially in the lands connected with the NT.

I. Extent.–James prefaced his judgment at the Jerusalem Council with the significant remark that "from earliest generations Moses has had in every city those who preach him" (Acts 15:21). This "every city" may seem to be an exaggeration, but it is quite modest in comparison to the statements in other literature regarding the extent of the Dispersion. The most famous is that of Philo, quoting a letter from Agrippa to Caligula:

> In this way Jerusalem became the capital, not only of Judea, but of many other lands, on account of the colonies which it sent out from time to time into the bordering districts of Egypt, Phoenicia, Syria, Coele-Syria, and into the more distant regions of Pamphylia, Cilicia, the greater part of Asia Minor as far as Bithynia, and the remotest corners of Pontus. And in like manner into Europe: into Thessaly, and Boeotia, and Macedonia, and Aetolia, and Attica and Argos, and Corinth, and into the most fertile and fairest parts of the Peloponnesus. And not only is this continent full of Jewish colonists, but also the most important islands, such as Euboea, Cyprus, and Crete. I say nothing of the countries beyond the Euphrates. All of them except a very small portion, and Babylon, and all the satrapies which contain fruitful land, have Jewish inhabitants (*De legatione ad Gaium* 36).

1 Macc. 15:22-24 records the sending of a circular letter favoring the Jews by the consul Lucius to Syria, Pergamum, Cappadocia, Parthia, Sparta, Delos, Myndos, Sicyon, Caria, Samos, Pamphylia, Lycia, Halicarnassus, Rhodes, Phaselis, Cos, Side, Aradus, Gortyna, Cnidus, Cyprus, and Cyrene. Cicero notes that Flaccus the governor of Asia confiscated Jewish money designated for the temple in Jerusalem from central collection points in Apameia, Laodicea, Adramyttium, and Pergamum (*Pro Flacco* 28 [67f.]). It is no wonder that Strabo could conclude: "This people has already made its way into every city, and it is not easy to find any place in the habitable world which has not received this nation and in which it has not made its power felt" (quoted in Josephus *Ant.* xiv.7.2).

From such literary data and from inscriptions found all over the Roman world, scholars have attempted to estimate the number of Jews who lived in the Dispersion. Juster set the figure at six to seven million in the Roman empire, Harnack at four to four-and-one-half million. Modern scholars tend toward the higher figure, concluding that the Jews represented approximately 10 percent of the population of the entire Roman empire. About four million Jews lived in the empire outside Palestine and about three million in Palestine. In addition there were about one million in the Eastern Dispersion. Such a high percentage of Jews in the population is not easy to explain, since it represents a phenomenal increase from their numbers at the end of the OT period. The reason for the increase has often been sought in that the Jews, unlike their heathen neighbors, did not practice infanticide and were also by nature more prolific than other peoples. But in the final analysis this explanation is inadequate, and the conclusion must be drawn that Jewish proselyting activities were much more successful than is usually supposed.

II. Causes.–According to the OT prophets, the *ultimate* cause for the Dispersion was that Israel had sinned (e.g., Jer. 9:16). The more proximate causes were varied. In earliest times the Jews seem to have left their homeland only under the terms of forced deportation, as after the conquest of Israel by Assyria and of Judah by Babylon. But as time passed and Palestine became the unfortunate buffer state between the Ptolemaic and Seleucid dynasties, many Jews voluntarily left the land because of greater opportunity and security elsewhere. Indeed the Seleucid kings seem to have had a policy of granting Jews extensive privileges to encourage them to settle in newly formed Greek cities in Asia Minor and Syria. They evidently considered the clannish, peace-loving Jews to be a desirable stabilizing influence. And although the Jews were not yet the outstanding merchants they became during the Middle Ages, they were not slow to react to the unlimited economic opportunities presented by the Greek cities.

III. Distribution of Dispersion Jewry.–*A. In the East.* As a result of the Babylonian Exile of Judeans after 597 B.C., a sizable Jewish Dispersion developed in the eastern regions: Babylonia, Elam, Parthia, Media, and Armenia. These lands were not part of the Roman empire and had not been substantially influenced by Hellenistic culture. Consequently the Jewish communities that flourished there were quite distinct from those of the Western Dispersion. Much of what will be said below about the political, social, and cultural situation that obtained in the West does not apply to the East. The Babylonian Jews became numerous, so that in the 1st cent. A.D. Josephus could speak of them as "innumerable myriads" (*Ant.* xi.5.2). They were highly favored by the Parthians, who ruled the area in the time of Christ. Their taxes were light and their *Resh Galutha* ("Prince of the Exile") was dignified as a vassal prince under the Parthian king. In fact, one of the Parthian princes, King Izates of Adiabene, converted to Judaism, as did his mother and other members of his family (*Ant.* xx.2, 4). The Babylonian Jews were considered of purer stock than Palestinian Jews, which led to some jealousy and pride. They remained true to the tenets of Judaism and became exceptional students of the law and oral tradition. In the 6th cent. A.D. their rabbis produced the Babylonian Talmud, the most extensive and influential piece of postbiblical Jewish literature.

B. Syria. Since it was Palestine's neighbor, Syria early received its share of Jewish immigrants. The first clear notice of Jews settling there is in the time of Seleucus I Nicator, who offered them special privileges in the Syrian cities. But Jews had probably already established colonies in the older cities. Indeed the impact between Ben-hadad and Ahab recorded in 1 K. 20:34 implies that there was a Jewish quarter in Damascus even at that time. With such a long history and with the added incentive of the political privileges granted by Seleucus, it is not surprising to find that the Jews of Syria came to comprise a greater percentage of the population than in any other area of the Dispersion (Josephus *BJ* vii.3.3). Philo testifies that the Jews lived in Syria "in large numbers in every city" (*De legatione ad Gaium* 33). In Antioch they occupied an entire quarter.

C. Egypt. The Egyptian Dispersion was established early, but its origin is not precisely understood. Some Jews were taken as prisoners by Sheshonq (the Shishak of 1 K. 14:25f.; 2 Ch. 12:2f.), the founder of the 22nd Egyptian Dynasty, who invaded Palestine in the 10th cent. B.C. Testimony to this effect exists in inscriptions on the walls of the temple of Karnak. Another inscription refers to the participation of Jewish mercenaries in the expedition of Psamtik II against Ethiopia (594-589 B.C.). But one of the most important pieces of evidence about the Egyptian Dispersion is the writing of the prophet Jeremiah. He recounts the establishing of Jewish settlements at Migdol, Tahpanhes, and Noph (Memphis) in Lower Egypt, and in the country of Pathros in Upper Egypt (Jer. 43f.). Many of these Jews succumbed to pagan worship and were assimilated by intermarriage. Others were taken prisoner to Babylon by Nebuchadrezzar during one of his later western expeditions (Josephus *Ant.* x.9.7; cf. Jer. 43:8f.). But the remainder settled in Egypt and evidently maintained their Judaism.

One of the most interesting discoveries of recent archeology is that of a series of Aramaic papyri from the island of Elephantine, near Aswan, which includes official records of a Jewish colony dwelling there. This is concrete evidence that by 500 B.C. there was a settled Jewish community in a remote region of Egypt. Among the records are papyri testifying to the existence of a distinct Hebrew court and a temple dedicated to the worship of Yahweh. That certain sacrifices were rendered in this temple indicates that the community was somewhat schismatic and unorthodox. The most likely theory of origin is that the Jews were descendants of a colony of Jewish mercenaries established to defend this hinterland military outpost. From such evidence it has become apparent, contrary to previous skepticism, that the Dispersion developed very early in Egypt. Philo and Josephus testify that by the 1st cent. A.D. it had become a strong minority force in Roman-controlled Egypt.

D. Alexandria. Jewish influence in Egypt was most strongly felt in the great Greek city Alexandria. At its founding in 332 B.C. the Jews seem to have been granted extensive privileges, and they responded by immigrating in large numbers. According to Philo, two sectors of the city were exclusively Jewish (*In Flaccum* 8).

It was once thought, based on explicit statements by Josephus (*Ant.* xiv.10.1; cf. xii.1.1; 3.1; xix.5.2; *BJ* ii.18.7) and Philo (*In Flaccum* 10.80), that the Jews as a body had been granted Alexandrian citizenship. But more recently a copy of a letter from the emperor Claudius to the people of Alexandria was discovered and published (H. I. Bell, *Jews and Christians in Egypt* [1924]). Its purpose seems to have been to settle disputes between the Jews and the Greeks of that city by defining the limits of Jewish privileges there. It would appear to be a decree subsequent to the one referred to by Josephus (*Ant.* xix.5.2). On the basis of this new datum, the trend among scholars has been to deny that the Jews of Alexandria had rights of full citizenship. Josephus evidently read more into the words of Claudius than they warranted. The Jews enjoyed great privileges, and possibly formed their own *políteuma* as they did at Berenice; but they were not Alexandrian citizens. Such, at least, is the present judgment of scholarship.

The Jewish community was undoubtedly large and influential. Philo estimates that there were a million Jews in Egypt (*In Flaccum* 43), a sizable percentage of whom

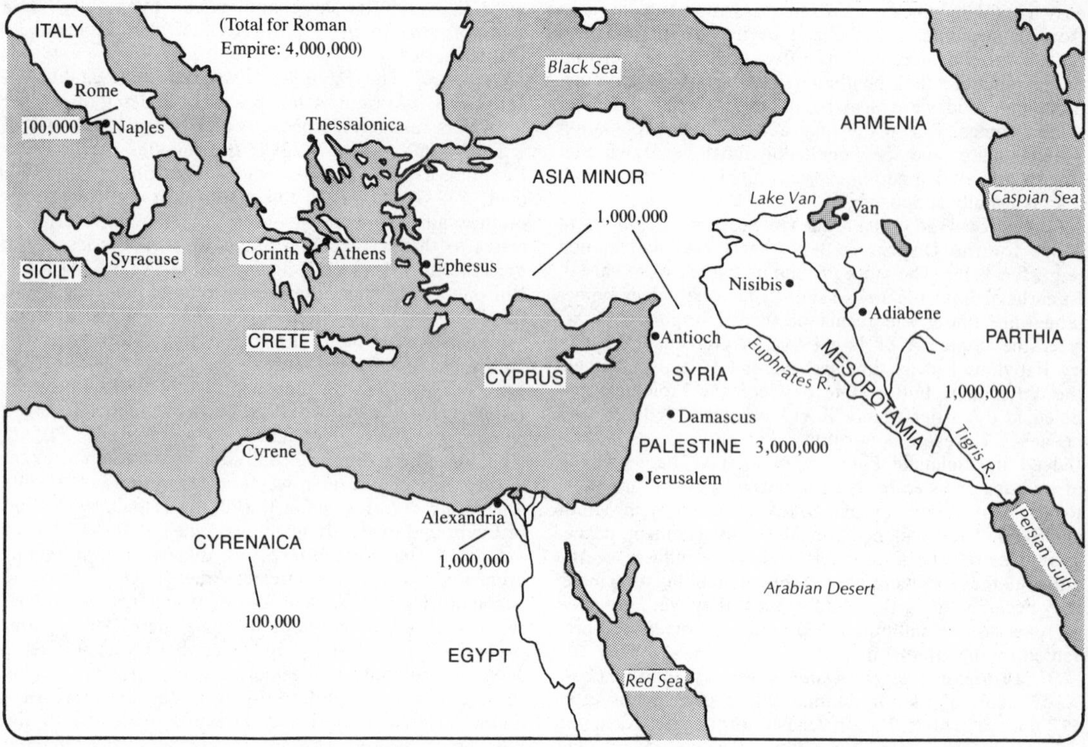

were in Alexandria. Many have been skeptical of this figure; but S. Baron, the author of the most recent authoritative work on the subject, believes that Philo's estimate is quite possible.

E. Asia Minor. The favorable Seleucid policy that helped to people the Syrian cities with Jews was used in Asia Minor as well. In one instance Antiochus III transplanted two thousand Jewish families from Mesopotamia to Lydia and Phrygia (Josephus *Ant.* xii.3.4). The tone of the letter preserved by Josephus leads to the conclusion that the Jews were valued as a stable, leavening force in these politically turbulent frontier states. It is therefore likely that this was no isolated instance but part of the regular Seleucid strategy of government. Once located in Asia Minor, the Jews quickly established themselves and adapted to their new environment. The result is that by the time Paul reached that part of the world there was a powerful Jewish settlement in all major cities and towns, even those some distance from the trade routes. Baron finds concrete evidence of thirty-one Jewish communities in Asia Minor and Cyprus. It may be safely inferred that many more have left no mark of their existence.

F. Greece and Macedonia. Jews were less numerous in the Balkan Peninsula than in Asia Minor. This was probably because there were few Roman colonies there, for the Jews most often flourished where the Roman influence predominated over the Greek. However, the NT provides evidence of Jewish communities at Philippi, Beroea, Athens, Corinth, and Thessalonica. The two last-named cities, along with the island of Cyprus, seem to have been the only large Jewish settlements in localities inhabited mainly by Greeks and Macedonians. Elsewhere few records remain. Inscriptions indicate that some Jews lived in Delphi in the 2nd cent. B.C. By that time Jewish settlements had been established at Sparta and Sicyon as well (1 Macc. 15:23).

G. Italy and the West. Outside the capital city, Rome, not many Jews lived in Italy. The only other localities where literature and inscriptions reflect the presence of Jews in biblical times are Pompeii, Puteoli, and Porto. Puteoli and Porto were seaport towns and suburbs of Rome. Pompeii was evidently a resort town and attracted many Romans, among them a few Jews. Elsewhere in western Europe direct evidence of the early establishment of Jewish communities is notably absent. But Paul's desire to reach Spain with the gospel message (Rom. 15:24) would seem to presuppose that settlements of Jews were already to be found at the western extremity of the continent, for it was Paul's missionary strategy to approach a given locality through its Jewish synagogue. Furthermore, the evidence of a rich Jewish heritage in western Europe in subsequent centuries requires the conclusion, despite the lack of direct testimony, that Jews had already become rooted there by the 1st century.

H. Rome. As early as 161 B.C. Judas Maccabeus had negotiated a treaty for mutual defense and friendship with the Roman senate. This treaty was renewed by Jonathan (144 B.C.), Simon (141 B.C.), and John Hyrcanus (129 B.C.) (1 Macc. 8:17; 12:1; 14:24). On each of these occasions an embassy from Jerusalem made its way to Rome, and it is quite likely that some of the Jews involved settled there permanently. But the major impetus toward the strengthening of the community was the return of Pompey in 63 B.C. from the conquest of Jerusalem with a large number of Jewish slaves. For reasons now unknown, most of these slaves were soon given their freedom. Meanwhile, Jewish merchants found their way to the capital city of the empire, settled there, and further enlarged the community. So by the 1st cent. A.D. a substantial body of Jews had settled in Rome.

The majority lived in the portion of the city across the river known as Trastevere, which gradually took on the characteristics of a Jewish ghetto. But others were scattered about the city, even in the best residential sections. Remarks by Cicero, Suetonius, Tacitus, and Josephus lead to the conclusion that the Jewish population in Rome at that time numbered some forty thousand. Inscriptional notations give evidence of at least seven (Baron finds evidence for thirteen) distinct synagogues within the city. Some owed their existence to the patronage of important figures (Augustus, Agrippa, Bolumnis). Some grew around certain cultural distinctives ("Synagogue of the Hebrews"). Others were oriented to the economic station of their congregations. Still others originated simply to meet a need in a given locality within the city. There is no evidence of an overall organizational structure between synagogues, but there must have been well-established unofficial lines of communication (cf. Acts 28:21). At any rate, the number of these synagogues witnesses to the size of the Jewish community at Rome, and their variety reflects a multifarious population.

The gentile population of Rome seems to have had an underlying anti-Semitism, which periodically expressed itself openly. Portions of the Jewish community were expelled from Rome in 139 B.C. (evidently for proselyting among Roman citizens), in A.D. 19 (for the action of two swindlers who pretended to be taking a collection for the temple), and in A.D. 49 (possibly because of Jewish-Christian clashes). On the other hand, Julius Caesar and his immediate successors gave the Jews extensive privileges, evidently because they were valuable political allies. When Caesar died many peoples lamented him, but "above all the Jews, who even flocked to the palace for several successive nights" (Suetonius *Caesar* 84).

IV. Characteristics.–*A. Political Relationships.* Wherever the Jews may have been dispersed they still belonged to "the Nation of the Jews." Pilgrimages to Jerusalem, the annual tax paid by the faithful to the support of the temple, traveling merchants bringing news from place to place — all these factors helped to preserve a feeling of unity among Dispersion Jews and between the Dispersion and Palestine. All the "children of Abraham" were related in the nation Israel, and at this point in her history the nation was scattered all over the world. Such was the Jew's relationship to his native land and heritage. But what of his relationship to the nation, province, or city in which he found himself? There was a sense in which he was integrated into the local political structure and a sense in which he could not be. On the one hand, certain Jews received the privileges of citizenship, both Roman and local, and could therefore hold office. On the other hand, the Jewish communities maintained some degrees of autonomy and developed their own governmental structure, under the protection of the Romans. In actual practice, the Jews found themselves in a very favorable position, enjoying the privileges of integration into the pagan governmental structure and at the same time exercising relative autonomy in their own self-government.

Roman citizenship had by the 1st cent. A.D. become less exclusive than it had been in earlier times. Many Jews were among those granted this honor as a return for favors. Some ancestor of Paul was evidently so honored (Acts 22:25-28). Other Jews received the right when they were freed from servitude to a Roman citizen (Acts 6:9; 22:28). Whatever the means of obtaining the citizenship, those Jews who did so enjoyed great advantages. At the same time they were exempted as Jews from some of the responsibility usually associated with Roman citizenship, notably from military service (because of their observance of the sabbath).

Citizenship in the Greek cities was evidently less commonly held by Jews than Roman citizenship. It has previously been suggested that, contrary to the statements of Philo and Josephus, the Jews of Alexandria did not enjoy full citizenship rights (see III.D above). But what of the other cities mentioned by these same writers as localities where Jews were citizens (Antioch, Ephesus, Sardis, Cyrene)? Some scholars suggest that these statements be discounted as exaggerations. They think that any Jew who was a citizen of a Greek city (e.g., Paul, Acts 21:39) became such in his own right, not because the entire Jewish community had attained citizenship. But Ramsay has pointed out that this is highly unlikely unless the individual Jew had apostatized from Judaism, for Greek citizenship depended upon membership in "tribes" (Gk. *phylaí*), each of which worshiped its own deity. Ramsay's own reconstruction is that Jews were admitted to citizenship as a tribe of their own, worshiping Yahweh rather than a pagan deity (*Expos.*, 5 [1902], 19-33). He finds evidence for the existence of such a Jewish tribe in Tarsus, the very city of Paul's birth. It seems, therefore, that in certain cities the Jews had as a body received the rights of citizenship. Their status in each city must be judged independently, not in the light of the peculiar Alexandrian situation.

The Jewish communities themselves had a high degree of internal organization. The center of the community was the synagogue, and the officers of the synagogue were the officers of the community. They maintained autonomous courts for civil cases involving only Jews, and they preserved records in their own archives. But these are generalizations. They should not be allowed to obscure the fact that Jewish community structure was expressed in a unique way in every locality.

B. Socioeconomic Status. The activities of Jews in the economic world were just as varied as were their political positions. Most discussions of the means of livelihood commonly pursued by Dispersion Jews err by reading the first-century situation in the light of medieval history. It is, therefore, a frequently held misconception that the Jews were as exclusively involved in mercantile activities at the time of Christ as they became in later centuries. This is an unwarranted assumption. The Syrian, not the Jew, was the proverbial merchant in the literature of the period. And out of sixty bankers mentioned in Egyptian papyri, not one has a Jewish name. This is not to deny that many urban Jews became involved in money-lending and selling. But Jews living in alien lands became farmers, artisans, tax-gatherers, actors, etc., *as well as* merchants, peddlers, and bankers.

While it is true that Jews were to be found in all classes, from the highly privileged nobility to the beggars and slaves, the distribution was, no doubt, rather heavier at the bottom of the socioeconomic scale. In Alexandria the Jews seem to have been relatively well-to-do, occupying one of the finest seaboard residential quarters and holding a number of official positions. The situation was similar in the Eastern Dispersion. But in Europe, Asia Minor, Syria, and North Africa the bulk of the Jewish population was quite poor. It would seem that in the Dispersion as a whole the Jews were more often than not of the lower middle class and below.

C. Anti-Semitism. The generally low socioeconomic status of the Jewish communities may partly explain the widespread anti-Jewish sentiment among pagan peoples. But this is at best a superficial explanation. From Rome, Horace, Juvenal, Persius, Martial, Cicero, and Tacitus all wrote in derogatory terms of the Jews. Records remain of popular uprisings against the Jews at Rome,

Alexandria, Cyrenaica, Antioch, Caesarea, and Damascus. One of the most vexing problems facing the historian concerned with this period is to determine the causes of such universal prejudice against Jews, and solutions are as numerous as scholars who deal with the question. But the answer is probably to be found in a combination of the following factors: (1) that the Jews were favored by the Romans over native peoples, thus becoming the objects of jealousy; (2) that the Jewish religion was mysterious, exclusive, and full of strange practices; (3) that the Jews were socially aloof, clannish, and proud of their inferior (to the pagan mind) heritage. In short, the Jews were *different* in every way, and they refused to conform. Nonconformity is the simplest and most common cause of antagonism in human relationships.

D. Cultural Integrity. The Jews were different, but how different were they? There are two trends of thought as to how successfully the Jews maintained their cultural integrity in the pagan world. Traditionally, the most prevalent view has been that, while Dispersion Jews adopted certain external aspects of Hellenistic culture, they remained distinctly Jews in heart and mind. These "external aspects" are such things as the Greek language, Greek names, attendance at Greek games, and the use of human and animal figures in decoration. But more recent scholars, especially E. R. Goodenough, contend that these "external aspects" really reflect an internal transformation. Goodenough points out that the animal and human figures are found in synagogues and cemeteries, the very places where they would seem to have the most religious and cultural significance. He concludes that the Jews were very deeply influenced by Hellenistic ideas and thought patterns. The consensus of scholarship, however, is that Goodenough's arguments are one-sided and that his views are, therefore, far too extreme.

It is obvious that this problem can never finally be solved, for its solution would require a knowledge of the mind of a Dispersion Jew that is impossible to attain. Some suggest that the closest approach can be made through the writings of PHILO. That Alexandrian Jewish philosopher is an enigmatic figure. He has variously been interpreted as a Greek using Jewish terminology (e.g., by Goodenough) and as a Jew seeking a point of contact with the Greek view of life (e.g., by Wolfson). There is something to be said for both explanations. Philo's use of Greek philosophy is not at all superficial — he understands it and sympathizes with it. But it is not his first love. He is at heart a Jew, secondarily a Greek. His purpose in writing is not to develop a Judeo-Hellenistic philosophical system, but to commend a Judaism to the Greek mind.

But even if it might be granted that Philo was at heart a Hellenist, nothing could be concluded from this about the mentality of Dispersion Jewry as a whole. For one thing, Alexandrian Jews are generally admitted to have been more hellenized than the Jews of other Dispersion communities. And furthermore, Philo was by his own admission more liberal than other Alexandrian Jews, for he makes allusion to the "literalists" as a considerable body of theologians opposed to his views. The truth is that the writings of Philo, even if they are rightly understood, cannot be taken as a doorway into the mind and mood of Dispersion Jewry. He was a unique figure and had an uncommon relationship with Hellenistic thought.

A common but misleading practice is to equate Palestinian with "orthodox" Judaism and Dispersion with "Hellenistic" Judaism. The facts do not warrant such a distinction. Palestinian Judaism was by this time quite "hellenized." The cities of the Decapolis were thoroughly Greek, as were those along the Mediterranean coast. Greek games had been established at Gaza, Ascalon, Caesarea, Damascus, Kanatha, Scythopolis, Gerasa, Philadelphia, Caesarea-Philippi, Tiberias, Jericho — even at Jerusalem. The Greek language had wide currency in Palestine. Rabbis taught it to their children and borrowed its phraseology for their writings. The Babylonian Talmud contains the remark, "Why speak Syrian [Aramaic] in the land of Israel? Use either the holy tongue [Hebrew] or Greek" (*Sotah* 49b).

On the other hand, there were unique forces at work in the Dispersion against the assimilation of Hellenistic elements. It is not reasonable to suppose that many Jews were able successfully to straddle the fence between the Greek and Jewish cultural heritages. The tendency would be either to fall into complete apostasy or to withdraw into an exclusive form of "Jewishness." There is therefore no basis for supposing that Dispersion Jewry was necessarily Hellenistic.

E. Religious Orthodoxy. Nor is there any evidence that the Judaism of the Dispersion was particularly heterodox. Goodenough has attempted to prove that the religion of Dispersion Jews was a syncretism of Jewish and pagan elements. He bases his case almost exclusively on a set of inscriptions found at Panticapaeum, where the Jewish title of deity *theós hýpsistos* ("God Most High") is found beside the names of Greek gods. Though mystery still surrounds these findings, it would seem that they do indeed reflect a syncretistic Jewish community. But Panticapaeum is on the north shore of the Black Sea, on the fringe of the Dispersion; and there is very little corroborative evidence from other areas of the Dispersion.

Philo's particular brand of Judaism has previously been alluded to. Some would represent his philosophical system as a kind of Jewish mystery religion. But these commentators seem to have ignored the basic apologetic bent of his writings. His purpose is rather to persuade Greeks of the truth of Judaism than to formulate the definitive statement of a new sect. In the final analysis it is impossible to be sure of the nature of Philo's personal faith, but it was apparently a brand of Judaism within the boundaries of orthodoxy.

There were, to be sure, a great number of Jewish magicians in the Roman empire of the 1st century. The mysterious oriental language, the strange practices, the unutterable name of God — these factors equipped a Jew admirably to label himself a sorcerer and capitalize on the superstitions of the pagan mind. But magicians were outside the mainstream of Judaism and were consistently denounced in the rabbinic writings. Magic cannot be called heterodoxy because it is not really religion at all. It is a degeneration of those human impulses that are naturally religious into superficial manipulation of the deity.

There is no evidence of any weight that Dispersion Judaism was anything but orthodox. The basic tenets of Judaism were maintained: monotheism, God's sovereignty and self-revelation, the elevation of the law, and a lofty ethical code. The ceremonial regulations were maintained except where distance from the temple at Jerusalem (and, after A.D. 70, its destruction) proved an insurmountable obstacle. There may have been a de-emphasis of certain specific requirements in some circles to encourage proselytism, but this was not sanctioned by the majority of Dispersion Jews. The Judaism that Paul encountered in his journeys was distinctly and consistently orthodox.

F. Proselytism. It may seem strange that a religious group so aloof, so unyielding, so much the object of prejudice and ridicule should attract large numbers of adherents from paganism. But such was the case. Proselytes are mentioned in all areas of the Dispersion. Josephus reports that "many have agreed to adopt our laws; of whom some have remained faithful, while others, lacking the necessary endurance, have again seceded" (*CAp* ii.10). Tacitus deplores the frequent conversions to Judaism, for the proselytes, "the worst rascals among other peoples," follow all the despicable rules of the Jews (*Hist.* v.5). Juvenal describes the inevitable, though gradual, proselytism of an entire family to Judaism once the father has begun to observe the sabbath (*Satires* xiv.96f.). Many of the rabbis went to considerable lengths to justify missionary activities among pagans, and the great Hillel is reported to have taught that one's duty is "loving mankind and bringing them nigh to the Law" (Mish. *Aboth* i.12). A number of the rabbis themselves are said to have been either proselytes or descendants of proselytes (e.g., Shemiah, Abtalion, Akiba, Meir).

The general impression one receives from all the literary notices bearing on the subject is that proselytes came over to Judaism in large numbers. There is no possible way of estimating what those numbers might have been. But it seems that the Jews really took seriously their mission of being "a light to the Gentiles" (Isa. 42:6; 49:1; Rom. 2:19). The hunger of pagans for spiritual reality in the degenerating Hellenistic civilization presented them with their great opportunity. The same factors that acted in favor of the spread of the Christian gospel in the 1st cent. had earlier been found advantageous to Jewish activities as well.

Proselytes came to Judaism for a variety of reasons and through several different channels. Some lonely souls were attracted by the closely knit fellowship within the Jewish communities. Some were intellectually persuaded through reading apologetic works like the Sibylline Oracles, the Letter of Aristeas, and Philo's writings. Some were won by Pharisaic Jewish missionaries (cf. Mt. 23:15). But in the final analysis, the reason so many were attracted is the one frankly given by Josephus: "The greatest miracle of all is that our Law holds no seductive bait of sensual pleasure, but has exercised this influence through its own inherent merits" (*CAp* ii.38). Judaism was a genuinely superior religion. A great variety of religions were available to the first-century seeker. The Stoics represent an appreciation of the highest ethical standards. The success of the mystery religions witnesses to a general desire for significant religious experience. Yet nowhere outside of Judaism and Christianity were the ethical and the religious successfully combined.

V. Importance to Early Church History.–*A. The LXX.* A number of factors lead to the conclusion that, whatever else the Dispersion may have been, it was a providentially ordained preparatory step for the eventual missionary activity of the Church. One of these factors is the existence and worldwide distribution of the LXX, the Greek translation of the OT dating from the 2nd cent. B.C. The LXX is intimately associated with the Dispersion. Such a translation was necessary because large numbers of Jews found themselves in lands where the dominant language, at least of commerce, was Greek. And not only did the need for a Greek OT arise first in the Dispersion, but the translation itself is a product of non-Palestinian Judaism, since it was done in Alexandria. A study of the OT passages quoted in the NT reveals that, though they knew the Hebrew OT as well, the NT writers were quite familiar with the language of the LXX. The early missionaries took advantage of the seedbed prepared throughout the Dispersion by the LXX. Long before they came to a given community the ground had been unknowingly cultivated by Jews who had distributed the translation of the OT in the common tongue.

B. Synagogues. Wherever the Jews established themselves in any numbers a synagogue quickly developed. Throughout the Dispersion the synagogue had a more prominent function in Jewish life than it could ever have in Palestine. The local synagogue became the general meetinghouse and community hub, the center of philanthropic activities, the schoolhouse, the public court and archive. And of course it continued to function as the locus of religious education, propagation, and worship. In short, it was the very heart of the Dispersion Jewish community. It was into synagogues such as this that Paul and his associates went as soon as they came upon a new town or city. Their missionary strategy was to go "to the Jew first," and the synagogue was the best place to find the most Jews. It was in such synagogues that they received a hearing and proclaimed the gospel of Jesus Christ. A more efficient method of evangelizing the world of Dispersion Jewry can hardly be conceived.

C. "God-fearers." As Paul stood to speak in a synagogue, he was faced with four more or less distinct classes of people: (1) Jews by birth, (2) proselytes, (3) curious gentile onlookers, and (4) "God-fearers" (eleven times in Acts; cf. esp. chs. 10 and 13). The last-mentioned class consists of a considerable number of Gentiles who had been deeply impressed by the tenets of Judaism and were desirous of embracing it as their own religion, but were not yet willing to take some final step that would bring them into the fold as proselytes. The stumbling block may have been circumcision, or some point of the oral law, or the general social stigma attached to Jews and Judaism.

Theirs was an unstable situation; they had become Jews in the deepest recesses of their hearts, but they lacked either the conviction or the fortitude to make a clean break with the past. It is not difficult to imagine the great opportunity these "God-fearers" offered to the early Christian missionaries. Here were people who recognized the truth of the great principles of Judaism but were not committed to the accretions to the OT religion commonly accepted by first-century Jews. The demands of Judaism most commonly hindering "God-fearers" were exactly those repudiated by Christianity. It is no wonder, therefore, that many of the early converts to the Church had previously been "God-fearers," among them Cornelius, Lydia, Titius Justus, and (probably) the Ethiopian eunuch.

D. A "Licensed Religion." Though the Jews saw Christianity as a religion alien to Judaism, the pagan world for a long time refused to view it as anything but a sect of Judaism. This is reflected in the attitude of Gallio, who decided that the conflict between the Jews and Christians at Corinth was merely a matter of "words and names and your own law" (Acts 18:15). It is also apparent in the defenses of Paul before Agrippa and Felix that he has chosen his words carefully so as to portray Christianity as part of Judaism. The reason he was so anxious to do this was that Judaism enjoyed the privilege of assembly as a "licensed religion." As long as Christian assemblies could remain in the category of "Jews" in Roman eyes they would have legal status. Otherwise their meetings for prayer and worship could be illegal. So in whatever direction the Church was extended it was preceded by Dispersion Judaism, whose status as a licensed religion was applied to the Christian community as well.

VI. Conclusion.–The Dispersion has been interpreted in several ways: (1) as viewed by the OT prophets, it was a just punishment for Israel's sin; (2) as viewed by the ancient pagan world, it was an occasion for hostility against a nonconforming people; (3) as viewed by Dispersion Jews themselves, it was a testimony to the tenacity of their faith and the durability of their heritage; (4) as viewed by the Church, it was the divinely ordained means of providing a beachhead for the spread of the gospel in alien territory. Whatever else may be said, the Jewish Dispersion was and is a phenomenon unparalleled in human history.

See also HELLENISM.

Bibliography.–*HJP*, II/2, § 31; J. Juster, *Les Juifs dans l'Empire romain* (1914); A. Bertholet, *Die Stellung der Israeliten und der Juden zu den Fremden* (1896); *Jew.Enc., s.v.* "Diaspora"; H. Wolfson, *Philo* (2 vols., 1947); V. Tcherikover, *Hellenistic Civilization and the Jews* (1959); E. R. Goodenough, *Jewish Symbols in the Greco-Roman Period* (13 vols., 1953ff.); S. Baron, *A Social and Religious History of the Jews* (1952).

G. A. VAN ALSTINE

DISPERSION OF NATIONS. *See* BABEL, TOWER OF; TABLE OF NATIONS.

DISPOSITION (Acts 7:53, AV). The AV phrase "by the disposition of" is archaic for "by directions [*diatagaí*] of."

DISPUTE [Heb. *dāḇār*] (Ex. 18:16); AV MATTER; [*rîḇ*] (Dt. 19:17; 21:5; 25:1; 2 Ch. 19:8); AV CONTROVERSY; NEB also DISPUTANTS, LAWSUITS; [*dîn*] (Eccl. 6:10); AV, NEB, CONTEND; [*miḏyānîm*] (Prov. 18:18); AV CONTENTIONS; NEB QUARREL; [Gk. *philoneikía*] (Lk. 22:24); AV STRIFE; [*zḗtēma*] (Acts 25:19); AV GREAT REASONING; NEB ARGUING; [*antilogía*] (He. 6:16; 7:7); AV CONTRADICTION, STRIFES; [*máchomai*] (Jn. 6:52), AV STROVE; [*syzētéō*] (Acts 6:9; 9:29; Mk. 12:28); AV also REASONING; NEB ARGUE, DEBATE, DISCUSSION; [*dialogismós*] (Rom. 14:1); AV DISPUTATIONS; NEB "attempting to settle"; [*dialégomai*] (Acts 24:12; Jude 9); NEB also ARGUE; [*logomachía, logomachéō*] (1 Tim. 6:4; 2 Tim. 2:14); AV STRIFE, STRIVE; NEB also QUIBBLES; **DEBATE** [Gk. *zḗtēsis*] (Acts 15:2, 7); AV DISPUTATION, DISPUTING; NEB also CONTROVERSY; **DEBATER** [Gk. *syzētḗtēs*] (1 Cor. 1:20); AV DISPUTER.

In the OT *rîḇ* is often used for problems that arose between people, either a mere quarrel (Prov. 18:18), or a matter that had to be settled by the legal processes. In the latter case the dispute was brought before a judge for his decision (Ex. 18:16; Dt. 19:17; 21:5; 25:1; 2 Ch. 19:8). Originally this judge was Moses, apparently because he was most skilled in the law of God and therefore its application. As the work load became more than one man could bear, it was passed on to priests and Levites or other heads of families so that they might determine the judgment in terms of the law of God.

The most common translation for this term in the LXX is *antilogía*. This means speaking against what someone else has to say. In the NT it is chiefly used in Hebrews (6:16; 7:7; 12:3), where it refers to the one greater in authority settling disputes, and to the sinner as he spoke against Jesus. The term also occurs in Jude 11 of the rebellion of Korah, the point being that those who enter into such disputes will come to the same end as Korah.

Greek *máchomai* means to fight or quarrel. This term may apply either to a serious dispute (Jn. 6:52) or to that into which a dispute develops, such as the fight in which Moses found his two fellow Hebrews (Acts 7:26). Such quarreling is condemned among Christians (2 Tim. 2:24). The Christian is admonished to be kindly to all. Thus also the elder is admonished to be *ámachos*, i.e., one who does not fight or quarrel.

The root idea of *logomachía* is a dispute that arises concerning the meanings of words and therefore their application. 1 Tim. 6:4 says that such disputes give rise to jealousy, quarreling, slander, base suspicions, and endless wrangles. Such are typical of those whose reasoning powers have been stifled (cf. Rom. 1:21). 2 Tim. 2:14 also points to the bad effect that such quarreling has upon those who participate and those who hear. The Christian is to avoid such disputings. (See *TDNT*, IV, p. 143.) The term *philoneikía* points to love of victory so that one is continuously contending for it, i.e., to one who is contentious. 1 Cor. 11:16 (*philóneikos*, RSV "contentious") shows that Christians are not to engage in jealous disputes, as this is against the custom known to the Church. This precept may have arisen from Jesus' condemnation of such disputes and the desire for rank. Such a dispute broke out at the Last Supper (Lk. 22:24) and was condemned by the Lord. *Dialégomai*, meaning to speak together from disagreeing points of view, is often used in the NT, usually translated in the RSV "argued" or "talked." In Acts 24:12 Paul states in his defense before Felix that he was not arguing with men in Jerusalem but minding his own business. The term also is used of Michael's dispute with Satan over the body of Moses (Jude 9). (*See also* ARGUE; CONTEND.)

Most often the term is used of Paul, describing his method of evangelism (Acts 17:2, 17; 18:4, 19; 19:8f.; 20:7, 9; 24:25). We are told in Acts 20 that this took the form of a drawn-out talk with the Christian assembly as it was gathered in Troas. In Acts 24:25 it designates the discourse of Paul before Felix as it turned to morals, clearly a monologue. In the other cases this term is used of Paul's missionary practice of entering the synagogue of the Jewish Diaspora and there contending that Jesus is the Christ. Thus he openly placed the Christian position in conflict with the Jews' religion, so that he might convert them. In Ephesus when Paul was forced to withdraw from the synagogue he went to the school of Tyrannus and continued this same disputation. This tendency to a monologue-type speech is emphasized in He. 12:5, where the word is translated "address" in the RSV and NEB. But even here there is a connotation that the persons addressed should not remain where they have been but accept the new position offered. The refutation of the persons' former position is implied and therefore this position is disputed. Such an element cannot be absent from any attempt to convict or evangelize.

Syzētéō comes from a family of words that have to do with the meaning "seek." This family has a technical usage which points to an investigation into philosophical truth. *Syzētéo* is used in this way several times in Mark (1:27; 8:11; 9:10, 14, 16; 12:28). This disputation with non-Christians is carried on by the Church, as is shown when the Greek-speaking Jews rise against Stephen (Acts 6:9) and several contend with the newly converted Paul (9:29). This conflict may also occur within a group, although this signifies that the group is further divided (cf. Acts 28:29, a passage not found in our better Greek texts). Such disputing seems to have been a part of the Greek culture as Paul notes in 1 Cor. 1:20. Socrates and later Greek philosophers practiced this method of teaching. Paul says God's wisdom is superior to such approaches and thus renders them vain. (*See also* DISCUSSION.)

The term *zḗtēma* (Acts 25:19) refers to a matter that is controversial. It is used of the case that was brought against Paul in the latter part of Acts. This case, brought by the Jewish leaders, dealt with controversial matters within Judaism itself (23:29; 26:3). Paul stated his satisfaction at appearing before Agrippa because he was expert in such matters. Gallio (18:15) did not wish to enter into such controversial matters of the Jewish religion and thus dismissed the case the Jews brought before him in Corinth. The NEB describes this as a "bickering about words and names in your Jewish law." Similarly, the term *zētēsis* is used of the clash of opinions between Paul and Barnabas and the Judaizers (15:2, 7).

Dialogismós is used in Rom. 14:1 of a discussion whether an action is correct and proper for the Christian. Paul says that a man's faith is more important than having every question answered. Thus we are to accept a weaker man's faith without attempting to settle all uncertain points, so that we may nurture such a person's faith. Such matters may be settled later, but not at the expense of a man's relation with his God. (*See also* DISCUSSION.)

See *TDNT*, II, *s.v.* ζητέω (Greeven), διαλέγομαι (Schrenk); IV, *s.v.* λογομαχέω (Kittel). D. W. WEAD

DISQUALIFY. The term is found twice in the RSV. In 1 Cor. 9:27 the Greek is *adókimos,* "not standing the test" (AV "a castaway"; NEB "rejected"). Paul expresses concern that he keep his body disciplined lest he forfeit the prize in the Christian race. He is not contradicting 3:15, where salvation itself is the issue, for his theme in 9:24-27 is not salvation *per se* but service to Christ.

A different Greek word is used in Col. 2:18, the rare verb *katabrabeúō*; but it has in it the same basic root as the term "prize" (*brabeíon*) in 1 Cor. 9:24, and therefore it may mean "rob of a prize" (the NEB joins the RSV in rendering it "disqualify"; AV "beguile . . . of your reward"). Another possibility is that the verb has the force of "condemn," an intensification of "pass judgment" in v. 16. E. F. HARRISON

DISREPUTE; DISREPUTABLE [Heb. *b^elî-šēm*–'without a name'] (Job 30:8); AV, NEB, BASE; [Gk. *apelegmós*] (Acts 19:27); AV NOUGHT; NEB DISCREDIT; [*átimos*] (1 Cor. 4:10); AV DESPISED; NEB DISGRACE, *See* REPUTE.

DISRESPECTFUL [Gk. *kataphronéō*] (1 Tim. 6:2); AV DESPISE; NEB "respect any less." *See* RESPECT.

DISSENSION [Gk. *stásis*] (Acts 15:2; 23:7, 10); NEB "fell out among themselves" (Acts 23:7); [*dichostasía*] (Rom. 16:17; Gal. 5:20); AV DIVISIONS, SEDITIONS; NEB QUARRELS; [*éris*] (1 Tim. 6:4; Tit. 3:9); AV STRIFE, DIVISIONS; NEB QUARREL; [*schísma*] (1 Cor. 1:10); AV, NEB, DIVISIONS.

The first word, *stásis*, appears originally to have meant that which continues or exists, and therefore that which stands or continues to exist (He. 9:8); however, most biblical usage involves a later meaning, strife and discord. Thus Paul is accused before Felix of causing dissension among the Jewish people with his teaching (Acts 24:5). This dissension may even go so far as to become outright rioting or revolt (Mk. 15:7; Lk. 23:17, 25; Acts 19:40). In two instances the dissension relates to differences within a group. In Acts 23 Paul capitalizes on the deep-seated disagreements between the Pharisees and Sadducees concerning the Resurrection. Their disagreement became so heated that the Roman captain, Lysius, felt a riot might develop and took Paul out of the area. The passage in Acts 15 deals with the controversy that arose within the Church over the keeping of the ceremonial law and the admission of Gentiles into membership without circumcision. This problem became so important that the first full council of the Church was called that the issue might be resolved.

The early Church sought to eliminate dissension and promote harmony among its members. This is shown not only by the discussions of Acts 15, but also by the uses of the second term, *dichostasía*. Thus, in Rom. 16:17 Paul admonishes the Romans that they should "take note of those who create dissensions and difficulties" and "avoid them." This seems to point to those who are of such a nature that they enjoy quarreling and thus create an atmosphere of unrest in the church. In Gal. 5:20 Paul includes this as one of the works of the flesh, implying that those who cause dissension in the church are led not by the Spirit but by the flesh, and shall not inherit the kingdom of God. While there will not be complete agreement at all times within the Church, the Spirit of God will lead us to a state in which there should not be dissension among Christian people.

Admonitions against dissension became quite prevalent in the writings of the early Church fathers. The Shepherd of Hermas continually warns against it. Dissension in the church at Corinth seems to have been the occasion for the First Epistle of Clement of Rome. In the first chapters he warns the Corinthian Christians that dissension caused great persecution against the Roman church (probably the Neronian persecution) and that the Corinthians should avoid it or they also will pay for their sin. At the beginning of the 2nd cent. Ignatius calls Christians to accept the authority of their bishops, thus moving to eliminate any dissension in the face of persecution.

See *TDNT*, VII, *s.v.* στάσις (Delling), σχίσμα (Maurer).
D. W. WEAD

DISSOLVE [Gk. *lýō*] (2 Pet. 3:10-12); AV also MELT; NEB DISINTEGRATE, BREAK UP, FALL APART. The verb *lýō* is most commonly translated "loose," but is also rendered "break," "destroy," "release," etc. The NEB renderings seem closer to the root meaning of *lýō*. The graphic picture Peter gives is that of the carefully ordered universe being dismantled and thrown piece by piece into fire of judgment.

See also DAY OF THE LORD. G. A. VAN ALSTINE

DISTAFF [Heb. *kîšôr*] (Prov. 31:19); AV SPINDLE. The AV takes *kîšôr* to mean "spindle" and *pelek̲* to mean "distaff," while the RSV and NEB reverse the two meanings. The context indicates that the latter is more plausible. "She puts her hands to the distaff" could mean that she was reaching to pull the prepared fibers from the stick on which they were held. *See* SPINDLE.

DISTIL [Heb. *nāzal*] (Dt. 32:2); [*nāṭap*] (Cant. 4:11; 5:13); AV, NEB, DROP; [*zāqaq*] (Job 36:27); AV POUR DOWN. In each case the term means "fall in drops," as dew or rain. It does not occur in its later technical sense, for the process we call "distillation" was not known in ancient times. In Cant. 4:11 the beloved says of his bride that her speech is like drops of nectar (cf. Prov. 16:24), while in 5:13 she says that his is like myrrh. A similar metaphor occurs in Dt. 32:2, where Moses expresses the desire that his teaching will refresh and strengthen the people as the DEW revives the land.

The term used in Job 36:27 is the 3rd person plural of the verb *zāqaq*; thus the subject is the "drops of water," rather than God. The verb means literally "strain," as with a strainer. M. H. Pope translates the verse, "He draws the waterdrops / That distill rain from the flood" (*Job* [*AB*, 1965], pp. 231, 235f.). R. K. H.

DISTINCTLY. In Isa. 32:4 stammerers are given the promise of distinct speech, the MT *ṣaḥ* indicating clarity and elegance of diction (AV "plainly"; NEB "plain").

DISTRESS; DISTRESSED [Heb. *ṣar, ṣār, ṣārâ,* qal and hiphil of *ṣārar, mēṣar* (Ps. 118:5; Lam. 1:3), hiphil of *ṣûq*–'oppress' (Dt. 28:53ff.), *māṣoq* (Isa. 22:2; Jer. 19:9), *m^eṣûqâ* (Ps. 25:17; 107:6; Zeph. 1:15), *mar* (1 S. 1:10; Prov. 31:6), *mārar* (2 K. 4:27), *k^eēḇ*–'pain, anguish' (Ps. 39:2 [MT 3]), *ṣ^ewāḥâ*–'wail' (Ps. 144:14), niphal of *'aṣaḇ* (Gen 45:5), niphal of *nagaš* (1 S. 14:24), hithpael of *ḥîl*–'be filled with anxiety' (Est. 4:4), niphal of *qašâ*–'oppressed' (Isa. 8:21); Aram. *b^e'ēš* (Dnl. 6:14 [MT 15]); Gk. *anánkē, basanízō*–'torment' (Mt. 8:6; Mk. 6:48), *stenochōría* (Rom. 2:9; 8:35), *lypéō*–'grieve' (Mt. 17:23; 18:31), *adēmonéō* (Mk. 14:33; Phil. 2:26), *synochḗ* (Lk. 21:25), *kataponéomai* (2 Pet. 2:7)]; AV also TROUBLE, AFFLICTION, STRAIT, SORROW, etc.; NEB also SUFFERING, STRAITS, BESIEGE (Dt. 28:53ff.), TROUBLE, ANGUISH, HARD PRESSED, etc.

In most cases "distress" translates Heb. *ṣar* or one of its cognates. *Ṣar* originally means "narrow" or "narrowness" (cf. Nu. 22:26); thus it connotes being under constraint or in an adverse situation: being oppressed by enemies (Jgs. 10:14; 1 S. 28:15; Ps. 31:9; 59:16; 69:17; etc.), in dire need (e.g., Isa. 8:21f.; 25:4), in difficult straits (cf. AV 2 S. 24:14; 1 Ch. 21:13; Job 36:16; Lam. 1:3; Jer. 19:9; etc.), pressed in by difficulties on all sides (e.g., Neh. 9:37; Job 15:24). Ps. 106 describes various types of distressing situations from which God delivers His people. In 1 S. 2:32 the AV follows a second meaning of *ṣar* ("enemy"). In Job 36:19 the AV reads "gold" (Heb. *beṣer*) in place of the RSV "from distress" (MT *b^eṣār*). *See also* BROAD PLACE.

Hebrew *mar* literally means "bitter, bitterness," and the cognate verb *mārar* "be bitter." Childlessness and bereavement were sources of bitter grief among women (1 S. 1:10; 2 K. 4:27; cf. Ruth 1:20f.).

The Gk. *anánkē* is used in the LXX to translate *ṣar, ṣārâ*. In the NT it is used of the sufferings of Christians who live in a time of tension between the "form of this world [which] is passing away" (1 Cor. 7:31; cf. v. 29) and the new creation in Christ (1 Cor. 7:26; 1 Thess. 3:7; cf. Rom. 8:18-23). In 1 Cor. 7:26, *tḗn enestṓsan anánkēn* is probably best translated "present distress" as in the later editions of the RSV (cf. NEB "a time of stress like the present"; JB "these present times of stress"), rather than "impending distress" (see Grosheide; *TDNT*; cf. Barrett). The same term and also *synochḗ* are used in Lk. 21:23, 25 to describe the fall of Jerusalem and the signs accompanying the coming of the Son of man. *See* ESCHATOLOGY III.B; TRIBULATION.

Paul comforts the Romans with the assurance that there is no distress that can separate them from the love of Christ (Rom. 8:35).

Bibliography.–Comms. on 1 Corinthians by C. K. Barrett (*HNTC,* 1968) and F. W. Grosheide (*NICNT,* 1953); *TDNT,* I, *s.v.* ἀναγκάζω (Grundmann).

N. J. O.

DISTRICT [Heb. *m^eḏînâ*] (1 K. 20:14ff.); AV PROVINCE; [*peleḵ*] (Neh. 3:9, 12, 14-18); AV PART; [*qōḏeš*] (Ezk. 45:1, 6f.); AV PORTION; NEB RESERVE; [*middâ*] (Ezk. 45:3); AV MEASURE; NEB AREA; [*'ereṣ*] (2 Ch. 11:23); AV COUNTRY; NEB TERRITORY; [Gk. pl. *hória*–'boundaries'] (Acts 13:50); AV COASTS; [*méris, méros*]; (Mt. 2:22; 15:21; 16:13; Mk. 8:10; Acts 16:12); AV PART, COAST; NEB also REGION, TERRITORY; [*gḗ*] (Mt. 9:26, 31); AV LAND, COUNTRY; NEB COUNTRY(-SIDE).

This term seems to be used in four distinct ways in biblical literature. First, the usage derived from the Gk. *hórion,* which strictly means "boundary," refers to a region that falls within certain limits. It may have reference to the ancient tribal boundaries (Mt. 4:13), a region within the country (Mk. 8:10), or a part of a province (Mt. 19:1). It may also refer to a part of a country as "the interior region" (Gk. *tá anōteriká mérē*) (Acts 19:1).

Second, a district may be a region around a city or the territory within which the influence of a city is felt. This usage is closely akin to the Gk. *tá períchōra* used in the LXX, meaning "region around." In ancient times the rule of a city was effective as far as its ruler could establish his dominion. Thus we have the region around Bethlehem (Mt. 2:16) and the region around Tyre (Mt. 7:24, 31). Although it was probably more clearly defined as far as its borders and rights were concerned, the region of DECAPOLIS (Mt. 15:22) would also probably fall into this category.

Third, "district" may refer to an administrative unit of a province. Thus in Acts 16:12 we have a reference to the division of the province of Macedonia into four administrative districts by Aemilius Paulus in 167 B.C. It is uncertain whether Luke means that Philippi was the leading city of the province (not the capital, as Amphipolis was) or whether the text has been corrupted by dittography and should read that Philippi was a city of the first administrative district of Macedonia.

Nehemiah divided his work force for the reconstruction of the wall around the city of Jerusalem (Neh. 3) according to administrative districts. These seem to have been the districts that were set up as part of the Neo-Babylonian administration, for the word *peleḵ* (used only here in the OT) is derived from the Akk. *pilku,* and would indicate a Neo-Babylonian origin. When the province of Judea was divided from the province of Samaria, Nehemiah undoubtedly continued the same administrative units, each of which is named for the chief town of the district. There were three double districts: Jerusalem, Beth-zur, and Keilah.

The administrative districts of the time of Ahab provided the basis upon which he chose those who led the Israelite army into battle against the Syrian king Ben-hadad (1 K. 20:14ff.). The victory of these servants of the district rulers, who seem to have gone out and fought individual conflicts with the leading warriors of the Syrians, led to the rout of the whole Syrian army.

The fourth use of "district" in the RSV is found in Ezk. 45:1-8. The Heb. *qōḏeš,* meaning "holy," is here translated "holy district" because it refers to the tract of land that is to be set aside as holy to the Lord.

Bibliography.–*BHI* (1959), pp. 365-67; F. F. Bruce, *Acts of the Apostles* (2nd ed. 1952), pp. 312-14; *NHI* (2nd ed. 1960), pp. 320, 323.

D. W. WEAD

DIVERSE [*'eḇen wā'eḇen*–'a stone and a stone'] ("diverse weights," Prov. 20:10, 23); AV DIVERS WEIGHTS; NEB "double standard in weights"; [*'êpâ w^e'êpâ*–'an ephah'] ("diverse measures," Prov. 20:10); AV DIVERS MEASURES; NEB "double standard in measures"; [Gk. *poikílos*] (He. 13:9); AV DIVERS; NEB "all sorts of"; **DIVERS** (AV Dt. 22:9; 25:13f.; Jgs. 5:30; 1 Ch. 29:2; 2 Ch. 30:11; Prov. 20:10, 23; Ezk. 17:3; Mt. 4:24; 24:7; Mk. 1:34; 8:3; 13:8; Lk. 4:40; 21:11; Acts 19:9; 2 Tim. 3:6; Tit. 3:3; He. 1:1; 2:4; 9:10; 13:9; Jas. 1:2).

The term "diverse" occurs only four times in the RSV. In Proverbs it refers to two different kinds of weights or measures. Stones were used for weighing, and thus the Hebrew may refer to two different sizes of stones (cf. LXX *méga kaí mikrón*–'large and small') which could be interchanged to cheat the buyer (cf. Prov. 11:1; 16:11; Dt. 24:13-16; *see also* WEIGHTS AND MEASURES).

In He. 13:9 *poikílos* refers to teachings "of various kinds." The term generally employed by the RSV for *poikílos* is "various." The AV frequently translates this and other OT and NT words as "divers," a term which is now obsolete. The distinction between "divers" and "diverse" in the AV seems to be that the former is the wider term, referring either to difference in kind ("various") or to difference in number ("several"), while the latter is restricted to meaning "different in kind."

N. J. O.

DIVES dī'vēz. *See* LAZARUS 1.

DIVIDE [Heb. *ḥālaq* (Gen. 14:15; 49:7, 27; Ex. 15:9; Nu. 26:53, 55f.; Josh. 13:7; 18:5; 19:51; 22:8; etc.), *bāqaʿ* (Ex. 14:16, 21; 15:9; Neh. 9:11; Ps. 78:13; Isa. 63:12), *ḥāṣâ* (Gen. 32:7; 33:1; Ex. 21:35; Nu. 31:27; Jgs. 7:16; 9:43; Job 41:6; Ezk. 37:22; Dnl. 11:4), *bāḏal* (Lev. 1:17), *nāḥal* (Nu. 34:17f., 29; Ezk. 47:13f.), *šālaš* (Dt. 19:3), *gazar* (1 K. 3:25f.; Ps. 136:13), *pārar* (Ps. 74:13), *bāzāʾ* (Isa. 18:2, 7), *hāḇar* (Isa. 47:13), *pāraḏ* (Gen. 2:10; 25:23; 2 S. 1:23), *pālag* (1 Ch. 1:19); Aram. *pᵉlag* (Dnl. 2:41), *pᵉras* (Dnl. 5:28); Gk. *merízō* (Mt. 12:25f.; Mk. 3:24-26; 6:41; Lk. 12:13; 1 Cor. 1:13; 7:34), *diamerízō* (Mt. 27:35; Mk. 15:24; Lk. 11:17f.; 12:52f.; 22:17; 23:34), *diairéō* (Lk. 15:12), *schízō* (Acts 14:4; 23:7), *diadídōmi* (Lk. 11:22)]; AV also PART, SPOIL (Isa. 18:2, 7), INHERIT, SEPARATE, etc.; NEB also SCATTER, CLEAVE, SHARE, SEVER, ASSIGN, DISTRIBUTE, etc.; **DIVIDER** [Gk. *meristḗs*] (Lk. 12:14); NEB ARBITRATE; **DIVIDING WALL** [Heb. *gᵉḏērâ*] (Ezk. 42:12); AV WALL; NEB INNER WALL; [Gk. *mesótoichon*] (Eph. 2:14); AV MIDDLE WALL.

The various OT terms have different shades of meaning. Heb. *bāqaʿ* means "cleave" and *gāzar* "cut," while the frequently used *ḥālaq* means "allot" or "split up." In Lev. 1:17 *bāḏal* means "separate" or "detach." The phrase *hōḇᵉrēw šāmayim* in Isa. 47:13 refers to those who classify the heavenly bodies, i.e., the "astrologers" (AV, NEB). The term *nāḥal* means here "apportion the land for hereditary possession."

In the NT "divide" generally renders Gk. *merízō* or *diamerízō*. The Gospel writers use the two terms interchangeably, usually meaning "divide into parts." Matthew (12:25f.), Mark (3:24-26), and Luke (11:17f.) record Jesus' answer to those who attributed His power over demons to His being in league with Satan. If He were casting out demons by Beelzebub, He says, then Satan would be undoing the work of his subordinates, and his would be a divided kingdom which cannot stand. John (19:24) sees the "parting" (RSV; Gk. *diamerízō*) of Christ's garments as being a literal fulfillment of the words of the psalmist, "they divided [Heb. *ḥālaq*] my garments among them" (Ps. 22:19 [MT 20]).

The difference between the RSV and AV translations of 1 Cor. 7:34a is due to a difference in MSS. The AV follows the Western textual tradition, in which the verb *meméristai* refers to the wife and the virgin. The RSV and NEB, on the other hand, have the stronger support of p^{15} p^{46} ℵ A B etc. However, Paul does go on to say that the married woman has the same problem with distractions as the married man.

In 1 Cor. 1:13 Paul uses *merízō* in his rhetorical question, "Is Christ divided?" (AV, RSV). According to F. W. Grosheide, "assign" is a preferable translation here since one group had claimed Christ's name and had thereby excluded others from calling themselves His followers. The apostle emphasizes that Christ is not the property of some exclusive group.

The "dividing wall of hostility" of which Paul speaks in Eph. 2:14 is probably an allusion to the wall that separated the inner court of the temple, open only to the circumcized, from the outer court, called the Court of the Gentiles. The penalty for a Gentile who entered the inner court was death. Thus, this "middle wall" (AV) separated the Gentiles not only from the Jewish people but also from fellowship with God. Through the death of Christ this barrier has been broken down and there is reconciliation between God and man, and between Jew and Gentile.

See also DIVISION.

Bibliography.–Comms. on 1 Corinthians by C. K. Barrett (*HNTC*, 968); C. T. Craig (*IB*, 1953); F. W. Grosheide, (*NIC*, 1953); comm. on Ephesians by F. W. Beare (*IB*, 1953).

N. J. O.

DIVINATION [Heb. *qesem*] (Nu. 22:7; 23:23; Dt. 18:10; 1 S. 15:23; 2 K. 17:17; Jer. 14:14; Ezk. 13:23); AV also WITCHCRAFT (1 S. 15:23); NEB also AUGURY (Nu. 22:7; 23:23); [*miqsām*] (Ezk. 12:24; 13:7); vbs.: "(practice or use) divination" [*qāsam*] (Dt. 18:10; 2 K. 17:17; Ezk. 13:9; 13:23; 21:21 [MT 26], 23 [MT 28]; Mic. 3:6); AV also DIVINE (Ezk. 13:9; Mic. 3:6); NEB also TAKE OMENS Ezk. 21:21), AUGURIES (Ezk. 21:23); [Gk. *manteúomai*] (Acts 16:16); "(learn by) divination" [Heb. *nāḥaš*] (Gen. 30:27); AV "learn by experience"; NEB "become prosperous"; **DIVINE** [Heb. *qāsam*] (1 S. 28:8); NEB TELL FORTUNES; [*nāḥaš*] (Gen. 44:5, 15); NEB DIVINATION [elsewhere the RSV translates "augur" (Dt. 18:10), "augury" (Lev. 19:26; 2 K. 21:6=2 Ch. 33:6), "omen" (1 K. 20:33), "sorcery" (2 K. 17:17); cf. noun *naḥaš*–'enchantment' (Nu. 23:23), 'omens' (Nu. 24:1)]; noun [*qesem*] (Ezk. 13:6; 21:19 [MT 34]); AV also DIVINATION (Ezk. 13:6); NEB also AUGURIES (Ezk. 21:19); **DIVINER** [Heb. *qōsēm*] (Dt. 18:14; 1 S. 6:2; Isa. 2:6; 3:2; 44:25; Jer. 27:9; 29:8; Mic. 3:7; Zec. 10:2); AV also "the prudent" (Isa. 3:2); NEB also AUGUR (Dt. 18:14), SOOTHSAYER (1 S. 6:2); [*ʿānan*] (Jgs. 9:37); AV 'Meonenim'; NEB SOOTHSAYER; *see* DIVINERS' OAK [elsewhere the RSV translates "soothsayer" or "soothsaying" (Dt. 18:10, 14; 2 K. 21:6=2 Ch. 33:6; Jer. 27:9)]. The variety of OT words used for "divination," together with the inconsistent ways in which modern versions translate these terms, indicates that the Hebrew terms are essentially synonyms and not descriptive of particular forms or aspects of the practice of divination in ancient Israel.

I. Definition
II. Divination in the Bible
III. Forms of Divination
  A. Dreams (Oneiromancy)
  B. Lots (Cleromancy)
  C. Arrows (Belomancy)
  D. Water (Hydromancy or Lecanomancy)
  E. Liver Inspection (Hepatoscopy)
  F. Staff or Rod (Rhabdomancy)
  G. Consultation with the Dead (Necromancy)
  H. Heavenly Bodies (Astromancy or Astrology)
  I. Teraphim
  J. Predetermined Signs or Omens

I. Definition.–Divination may be defined as the art or science of deducing the future or the unknown through the observation and interpretation of some facet of nature or human life, ordinarily of an unpredictable and trivial character. The first systematic treatment of divination in antiquity was Cicero's *De divinatione,* in which the

Temple of Apollo, seat of the Delphic oracle. Here the prophetess uttered sounds that the priests translated into hexameter verse, often ambiguous, which they submitted to the pious who awaited the god's answer. (H. D. Betz)

Latin concept of *divinatio* and the parallel Greek concept of *mantikḗ* are discussed at length. Following Posidonios of Apamea, he places all divinatory phenomena in one of two categories, *ars* or *natura* (Cicero *De divinatione* i.6.12). Divination dependent on *ars* (more commonly rendered as "artificial" or "inductive" divination) relies on the technical skill of the diviner to observe and interpret various signs or omens. Divination dependent on *natura* (more commonly rendered as "natural" or "intuitive" divination) receives knowledge of the future or the unknown through the direct inspiration of the diviner through trance, ecstasy, or vision. Although this twofold distinction has been extremely influential in subsequent discussion, it appears to have little heuristic value. In the OT and NT, the emphasis is placed heavily on natural or intuitive divination (*see* PROPHECY; INSPIRATION). The present discussion of divination is almost exclusively concerned with artificial or inductive divination.

II. Divination in the Bible.–The biblical attitude toward divination may be generally characterized as one of disapproval and prohibition, though certain forms of divination are either viewed neutrally or receive tacit approval (e.g., divination by lots and divination by dreams; see below). In biblical passages that prohibit various forms of divination (e.g., Lev. 19:26, 31; 20:27; Dt. 18:9-14; 2 K. 17:17) such practices are closely associated with various forms of magic and sorcery. Nevertheless, magic must be carefully distinguished from divination. While magic in its various forms attempts to influence and manipulate the future (and is frequently both illegal and antisocial), divination primarily seeks to discover or determine what the future holds. While divination is a universal phenomenon in the religions of man, it does not necessarily presuppose that the world is either controlled or influenced by a personal God or a pantheon of divinities (e.g., modern horoscopic astrology). All forms of divination, however, do presuppose a form of cosmic harmony whereby the diverse elements and aspects of the material and spiritual universe form an interrelated whole. Those few forms of divination that are tacitly accepted in the Bible are seen to be valid because of that aspect of the biblical doctrine of God that sees Him as sovereign in the affairs of men and of nature. For example, the validity of cleromancy is expressed in Prov. 16:33: "The lot is cast into the lap, but the decision is wholly from the LORD." The validity of oneiromancy is similarly accounted for (Dnl. 2:25-30). An apparently valid generalization is that the ancient Mesopotamians, Egyptians, Arabians, Greeks, and Romans sought to understand the future primarily through the practice of various techniques of divination monopolized by skilled adepts. In contrast, the central way in which the will of Yahweh was made accessible in ancient Israel and in early Christianity was through the medium of inspired prophetic spokesmen. Further, with the passage of time the Greeks and Romans apparently became preoccupied with technical means for divination and less with such intuitive forms of divination as the oracles (cf. Plutarch *De defectu oraculorum* [On the Cessation of Oracles] and *De Pythiae oraculis* [on the Pythian (Delphic) Responses]). On the other hand, apparently divination of various kinds declined in popularity in Israel (consultation with prophets became increasingly popular, but the sacred lots Urim and Thummim were apparently not used after the time of David).

III. Forms of Divination.–*A. Dreams (Oneiromancy).* The most common form of divination in the Bible is the art or science of interpreting dreams. The popularity of this form of divination in the ancient Near East is indicated by the fact that handbooks for the interpretation

Clay liver model, inscribed with omens and magical formulae for instructing students of divination. Most widely attested in Babylon, models also have been discovered at Alalakh and Hazor. (1st Dynasty of Babylon, *ca.* 1830-1530 B.C.) (Trustees of the British Museum)

of dreams were compiled in Egypt and Mesopotamia. While there is no evidence that such handbooks were compiled in ancient Israel, the supposition that they were is not improbable. Dreams and night visions were a common source of prophetic revelation (cf. Nu. 12:6; Dt. 13:1, 3, 5; Isa. 29:7; Jer. 23:25-32; *see* DREAM). Many dreams in the Bible have self-evident meanings, either because the recipient is directly addressed by God or His messenger in the dream (Gen. 20:3, 6f.; 28:12-15; 31:10-13; 1 K. 3:5-15; Mt. 1:20; 2:13, 19; Acts 16:9f.), or because of the transparent symbolism of the dream (Gen. 37:5-11; Jgs. 7:13f.). Not infrequently, revelatory dreams that are difficult to interpret use the device of the interpreting angel, who clarifies its meaning to the recipient (Dnl. 7:16f.; 8:16ff.; 9:21-26; Zec. 4:1-6:8; Rev. 1:20; 7:13-17). Strictly speaking, the technical skill of divination is required only when the meaning of a dream is elusive or unclear (cf. Eccl. 5:3, 7). Dreams that require the technical skill of divination are relatively rare in the Bible; two important biblical figures who were adepts at such dream interpretation were Joseph (Gen. 40:5-8; 41:1-8; cf. 44:5, 15) and Daniel (Dnl. 1:17; 2:1-11).

B. Lots (Cleromancy). While divination is normally dominated by specialists, divination by lot is a partial exception to that generalization (*see* LOTS). Lots were used for a variety of purposes, yet in every case the outcome was thought to be an expression of the will of God (Prov. 16:33). In the Bible the lot was used for the following purposes: (1) to identify a guilty individual (Josh. 7:14f.; 1 S. 14:41f.; Jonah 1:7); (2) to select someone for a particular task or office (1 S. 10:20f.; 1 Ch. 24:5, 7-19; 25:8; 26:13; Neh. 10:34; Lk. 1:9; Acts 1:26); (3) to divide up the land of Israel into tribal portions (Nu. 26:55f.; 33:54; 34:13; 36:2; Josh. 15:1; 16:1; 17:1, 14, 17; 18:11; 19:1, 10, 17, 24, 32); and (4) to select the goat for Azazel and the goat for Yahweh on the Day of Atonement (Lev. 16:7-10). The precise nature of the lot in the OT and the NT is not known. A specific form of the sacred lot was the URIM AND THUMMIM. These lots were used exclusively for public matters in ancient Israel and were apparently kept in a special pocket attached to the EPHOD of the high priest (Ex. 28:30). They may have been in the form of small pebbles, dice, or short sticks that were used to secure a "yes" or "no" answer on various matters (Nu. 27:21; 1 S. 23:9-12), particularly the selection of goats on the Day of Atonement (Lev. 16:7-10). No evidence appears that after the reign of David the Urim and Thummim were ever used for purposes of divination. In part their decreasing use may be accounted for by the growing practice of consultation with prophets (1 K. 22:6; 2 K. 3:11).

C. Arrows (Belomancy). In Ezk. 21:21 (MT 26) the king of Babylon is said to have used three methods of divination in tandem: the shaking of arrows, consultation of the teraphim, and examination of an animal liver. Precisely how arrows were thought to indicate the future is not known; the practice of belomancy, however, appears to have been widespread in Mesopotamia and among the ancient Arabs (cf. J. Wellhausen, *Reste arabischen Heidentums* [1897], pp. 132f.). Hos. 4:12 may be interpreted to mean that belomancy was practiced in ancient Israel. The story of David and Jonathan's encounter in 1 S. 20:18-42, in which arrows shot by Jonathan carried a message for David, may presuppose belomancy, but the present form of the story obscures this possibility. Clearer, perhaps, is the account in 2 K. 13:14ff., in which Elisha tells Joash of Israel to shoot the Lord's arrow of victory over Syria and then to strike the ground with the remaining arrows in token of the number of successes.

D. Water (Hydromancy or Lecanomancy). Gen. 44:5, 15 contains a reference to a silver cup belonging to Joseph that he used to practice divination. In this form of divination, various objects or liquids were placed or poured into water or other liquids; the resulting configurations or patterns were thought to be a source of knowledge of the future (cf. J. Vergote, *Joseph en Egypte* [1959], pp. 172-76). Hydromancy was a common form of divination in ancient Babylonia (cf. J. Hunger, *Becherwahrsagung bei den Babyloniern* [1903]).

E. Liver Inspection (Hepatoscopy). This form of divination was widespread and common in the various religions of Mesopotamia and Palestine and among the Hittites, Greeks, Romans, and later Arabs. No evidence appears, however, that hepatoscopy was practiced in ancient Israel (but cf. A. Murtonen, *VT,* 2 [1952], 170ff.). The only explicit reference to the practice is found in Ezk. 21:21 (MT 26), where it is said to have been practiced by the king of Babylon. The liver, particularly of sacrificial animals, may have been regarded as important for purposes of divination since the liver was widely regarded as the seat of the blood and therefore of life itself. While this notion is common in Mesopotamia, the OT also occasionally refers to the liver as the seat of human consciousness or the center of life (AV Lam. 2:11; Prov. 7:23). Balaam was a practicing diviner (Nu. 23:23; 24:1), and some have conjectured that the many sacrifices that he offered in an attempt to curse the Israelites for Barak (Nu. 23:1-4, 14f., 29f.) had some connection with hepatoscopy.

F. Staff or Rod (Rhabdomancy). While the use of a rod or staff for a variety of magico-religious purposes is not uncommon in the OT (cf. Ex. 4:4, 17; 17:9 [the rod of Moses]; 7:9, 19 [the rod of Aaron]), the use of the rod for purposes of divination is referred to in the OT only in Hos. 4:12: "My people inquire of a thing of wood, and their staff gives them oracles." Here the "thing of wood" may refer to the Asherah that was a cult object found in all Canaanite sanctuaries of Baal; the "staff" undoubtedly refers to the practice of rhabdomancy, though the precise technique of this form of divination is not known. It is clear, however, that Hosea condemns such practices.

G. Consultation with the Dead (Necromancy). The Heb. *'ôḇ*, always translated "medium" in the RSV (AV "a consulter with familiar spirits"), could equally well be rendered "necromancer" or "necromancy" (Lev. 19:31; 20:6, 27; Dt. 18:11; 1 S. 28:3, 7, 9; 2 K. 21:6; 23:24; 1 Ch. 10:13; 2 Ch. 33:6). Necromancy is roundly condemned wherever it is mentioned in the Bible. Consultation with the dead for purposes of divination takes two major forms. A deceased person may be summoned from the grave by a medium to answer questions (as in Saul's consultation with the dead Samuel through the offices of the witch of Endor in 1 S. 28:3-25; cf. the "voice of a ghost" mentioned in Isa. 29:4), or a spirit may speak through the voice of the medium (the apparent meaning of the chirping and muttering of the mediums referred to in Isa. 8:19; a kind of ventriloquism). Necromancy, however, has a wider connotation that includes not only the elicitation of oracles from the dead, but also the utterance of secret knowledge by evil spirits, as in the case of the slave girl with the spirit of divination who spoke involuntarily to Paul in Acts 16:16-18 (cf. the involuntary oracles of demon possessed individuals in Mk. 1:23-28; 3:11; 5:7-13). On the basis of Mk. 6:14-16, C. Kraeling has set forth the hypothesis that Jesus himself was accused of necromancy (*JBL*, 59 [1940], 147-157).

H. Observation of Heavenly Bodies (Astromancy or Astrology). ASTROLOGY, while widely practiced in Babylonia and Egypt, does not appear to have been employed in ancient Israel. References to astrologers and the astrological arts almost always refer to Babylonian practitioners and practices (Dnl. 1:20, AV; 2:27; 4:7; 5:7; Isa. 47:13). The worship of heavenly bodies, occasionally practiced in ancient Israel, is always condemned by the biblical authors (Dt. 4:19; 17:3; 2 K. 17:16; 21:3; 2 Ch. 33:5; Zeph. 1:5). In the language of poetry and apocalyptic, important or cosmic events are signaled by upheavals and signs among the heavenly bodies (Ezk. 32:7; Dnl. 8:10; Joel 2:10; Lk. 21:25; cf. Jgs. 5:20). However, such imagery cannot be taken literally and consequently does not lend support to the notion that the necessary presuppositions for the practice of astrology were present in ancient Israelite religion. The MAGI in Mt. 2:1-12 appear to have been practicing astrologers in that they were enabled to ascertain the time and general location of the birth of the Messiah. This, however, is in reality another example of the biblical notion that heavenly bodies may act as signs or portents of the will of God (cf. Acts 2:17-21; Rev. 6:12-14).

I. Teraphim. TERAPHIM appear to have been cultic images of varying size and number (the term is always found in the plural). Some were small and portable (Gen. 31:19, 34f.), others were extremely large (1 S. 19:13-16); they functioned in the premonarchical period as objects of worship in Israel (Jgs. 18:14-20) and were ultimately condemned. Divination by teraphim is mentioned in Ezk. 21:21; Zec. 10:2, but in both references the practice appears to be exclusively Babylonian.

J. Predetermined Signs or Omens. In this form of divination, the diviner or his agent agrees to follow a particular course of action or make a particular decision in the event that a predetermined (and generally trivial) action or sign occur. In 1 S. 14:8ff., Jonathan determines to attack a Philistine garrison if the enemy responds in a particular way. In Jgs. 6:36-40, Gideon determines the will of God on the basis of whether or not a fleece is wet or dry. In Jgs. 7:4-7 the particular way in which men in Gideon's army drink water determines whether or not they will be eliminated from the strike force.

Bibliography.–R. Bloch, *Les prodiges dans l'antiquité classique* (1963); A. Bouché-Leclerq, *Histoire de la divination dans l'antiquité* (4 vols., 1879-1882); A. Caquot and M. Leibovici, eds., *La divination* (2 vols., 1968); G. Contenau, *La divination chez les Assyriens et les Babyloniens* (1940); T. W. Davies, *Magic, Divination and Demonology among the Hebrews and their Neighbors* (1898); E. L. Ehrlich, *Der Traum im AT* (1953); A. Guillaume, *Prophecy and Divination among the Hebrews and Other Semites* (1938); H. A. Hoffner, *JNES*, 27 (1968), 61-68; *JBL*, 86 (1967), 385-401; *TDOT*, I, *s.v.* "'ôbh"; R. La Roche, *La Divination* (1957); E. Lipinski, *VT*, 20 (1970), 495-96; B. O. Long, *JBL*, 92 (1973), 489-497; J. Nougayrol, ed., *La divination en Mésopotamie et dans les régions voisines* (1966); A. L. Oppenheim, *Ancient Mesopotamia* (1964), pp. 206-227; *Interpretation of Dreams in the Ancient Near East* (1956); H. Tadmor and B. Landsberger, *IEJ*, 14 (1964), 201-217.

D. E. AUNE

DIVINE; DIVINER. *See* ASTROLOGY; DIVINATION.

DIVINE NAMES. *See* GOD, NAMES OF.

DIVINE VISITATION. *See* VISITATION.

DIVINERS' OAK [Heb. *'ēlôn mᵉ'ônᵉnîm*] (Jgs. 9:37); AV PLAIN of MEONENIM; NEB SOOTHSAYERS' TEREBINTH. The Heb. *mᵉ'ônᵉnîm* is probably a poel participle of the verb *'ānan,* and would therefore refer to "those who practice divination." *See also* DIVINATION. It is probably the same tree as that referred to as the "oak of Moreh" in Gen. 12:6, for in each case the neighborhood is that of Shechem. It was not doubt a sacred tree which took its name from the soothsayers who sat under it. Several times mention is made of sacred trees in the vicinity of Shechem (Gen. 35:4; Josh. 24:26; Jgs. 9:6; etc.). The exact location of the tree is not known. *See also* MOREH, OAK OF.

DIVISION [Heb. *gᵉdûḏ* (2 Ch. 26:11), *ḥēleq* (Josh. 18:6, 9), *yaḏ* (2 K. 11:7), *maḥᵃlōqeṯ* (1 Ch. 23:6; 24:1; 26:1, 12, 19; etc.), *pᵉḏûṯ* (Ex. 8:23), *rō'š* (1 Ch. 12:23), *pᵉluggâ* (Ezr. 6:18)]; AV also BAND, PART, COURSE; NEB also CENSUS (2 Ch. 26:11), PORTION, COMPANY, ROSTER, DISTINCTION, BAND, GROUP; [Gk. *apodiorízō* (Jude 19), *merismós* (He. 4:12), *diamerismós* (Lk. 12:51), *ephēmería* (Lk. 1:5, 8), *schísma* (Jn. 7:43; 9:16; 10:19; 1 Cor. 11:18)]; AV also SEPARATE, COURSE, DIVIDE ASUNDER; NEB also "draw a line" (Jude 19), "place where . . . divide" (He. 4:12), DIFFERENT SIDES, DIVIDED GROUPS, SPLIT.

Hebrew *gᵉdûḏ* and *rō'š* (lit. "head") refer to a band of armed troops, *yaḏ* (lit. "hand") to a portion of the guards. *Maḥᵃlōqeṯ* is a technical term for the organization of priests and Levites (1 Ch. 23:6; 28:13, 21; 2 Ch. 5:11; 8:14; 23:8; 31:2, 15-17; 35:10; Neh. 11:36), of the people of Israel for their responsibilities as an army during the year (1 Ch. 27:1f., 4-15), of gatekeepers (1 Ch. 26:1, 12, 19), of the sons of Aaron (1 Ch. 24:1), of servants of the king (1 Ch. 28:1). *Pᵉluggâ* is another organizational term used of the priests. *Ḥēleq,* on the other hand, denotes a tract of land. *Pᵉḏûṯ* normally refers to "ransom" or "redemption," but in Ex. 8:23 it is used of a distinction between peoples.

In Lk. 12:51 *diamerismós* is used as the opposite of *eirḗnē*, where Jesus says He came not to bring "peace" but rather "division." Jn. 7:43; 9:16; 10:19 illustrate the divisions (*schísma*) which resulted from the preaching of Christ. However, those who cause dissension and divisions within the Church are severely criticized by Jude (v. 19) and Paul (1 Cor. 11:18).

See also DIVIDE.

J. R. PRICE

DIVORCE [Heb. *kᵉrîṯûṯ*–'a cutting off' (Dt. 24:1, 3; Isa. 50:1; Jer. 3:8), *šālaḥ*–'send away' (Jer. 3:1; Mal. 2:16), *gāraš*–'drive out, banish' (Lev. 21:7, 14; 22:13; Nu. 30:9; Ezk. 44:22); Gk. *apolýō*–'dismiss, send away' (Mt. 1:19; 5:31f.; 19:3, 8f.; Mk. 10:2, 11f.; Lk. 16:18), *aphíēmi*–'send away,' 'leave' (1 Cor. 7:11-13)]; AV also DIVORCEMENT, PUT AWAY, LEAVE (1 Cor. 7:13); NEB also PUT AWAY (Jer. 3:1), "have the marriage contract set aside"; **CERTIFICATE OF DIVORCE** [Gk. *apostásion*–a technical legal term for relinquishing property, giving up one's claim] (Mt. 5:31; 19:7; Mk. 10:4); AV WRITING OF DIVORCEMENT, BILL OF DIVORCEMENT; NEB NOTE OF DISMISSAL.

IN THE OT

I. Relation to the Marriage Institution.–Divorce in the OT can be properly evaluated when the divine and original institution of marriage is taken into account. According to Gen. 1:27f. God created man male and female, and blessed them. When the woman, after having been "taken out of man," was presented to the man, he said, "This is now bone of my bones, and flesh of my flesh." For this reason an inviolable union was established which took precedence over every tie of kindred, even the tie existing between parents and children. A man and wife become "one flesh" (Gen. 2:22-24). Love is a prominent factor in this divinely ordained institution. "And he loved her (Rebekah)" is said of Isaac (Gen. 24:67); "he loved also Rachel" is written of Jacob (Gen. 29:30); and of Abraham it is recorded that at the death of his wife Sarah he "came to mourn for Sarah, and to weep for her" (Gen. 23:2).

That the divinely ordained marriage institution was regarded as inviolable in the OT itself is borne out by the initial absence of any reference to the possibility of abrogating it, and by the word of the prophet Malachi: "For I hate divorce, says the Lord the God of Israel" (2:16). It is also substantiated by Our Lord's appeal to the original institution in Mt. 19:3-8. By quoting from the original word in Genesis Jesus made it clear that His position was that of the Torah, namely, that God joined man and wife, and therefore it is not man's prerogative to break the marriage bond. "From the beginning it was not so." This teaching of Jesus must be given its full weight in dealing with the OT data. By virtue of His own authority He could add to the Mosaic record at other parts, but this He let stand both for the old economy and for the new. And yet we find that in practice the law of Israel made provision for the dissolution of the marriage bond.

II. OT Practice.–In the case of adultery the guilty spouse was punished by death: "The adulterer and the adulteress shall surely be put to death" (Lev. 20:10; cf. Dt. 22:23f.). (*See* ADULTERY.) But while adultery severs the marriage tie, it is not properly divorce as found in the biblical references.

Under certain conditions the separation of man and wife is legalized without civil or ecclesiastical penalties. Recognition of a status quo, however, does not necessarily carry with it divine approval. The crucial question is whether the practice of divorce in the OT had divine sanction. The passage that has been interpreted as lending support to an affirmative answer is Dt. 24:1-4. The phrase particularly involved is Heb. *w^{e}kāṯaḇ lāh sēper k^{e}rîṯuṯ*, translated in the AV "then let him write her a bill of divorcement," and in the RV "that he shall write her a bill of divorcement"; LXX: *kaí grápsei autḗ biblíon apostasíou*. Syntactically, the *waw* with *kāṯaḇ*, "write," does not require the jussive or the force of command. Full justice is done to the Hebrew construction if it is rendered as indicative (so RSV, NEB; cf. J. Reider, *Deuteronomy with Comm.* [1937], pp. 220f.). The intent of the legislation is to forbid the remarriage of a divorced wife to her former husband after she has married another man who has divorced her or died. The conditioning clauses in vv. 1-3 — "When a man takes a wife . . . and if she goes and becomes another man's wife . . . and the latter husband dislikes her" — constitute the protasis of which v. 4 is the apodosis or conclusion. The whole emphasis falls upon the conclusion, namely, that the divorced woman in view may not remarry her former husband, for such a practice would be an "abomination before the Lord" and would bring guilt upon the land (cf. C. F. Keil and F. Delitzsch, *Biblical Comm. on the OT* [Eng. tr. 1880], III, 416f.; S. R. Driver, *ICC* on Deuteronomy [1916], p. 269).

Thus the relevant OT data do not provide a basis for regarding divorce as mandatory, nor do they lend divine sanction to the practice. (See *LTJM,* II, 332-35.) They do recognize, however, the legal existence of the practice, provide protection for the divorced wife, and prohibit remarriage to the former husband under specified conditions. In no case does the evidence indicate that the right of divorce is taken for granted, or that the purpose of the legal formalities is to prevent the abuse of a right (J. Murray, *Divorce* [1953], pp. 7f.). In the code of Hammurabi there is also found regulatory divorce legislation without intimation of any inherent right (*ANET*, pp. 171f.). In the Hebrew theocracy, as in other ancient forms of government, evils were tolerated and regulated. The very sufferance of the practice of divorce emphasizes that it was an evil in itself, because what is inherently right does not have to be tolerated. This is the understanding Our Lord had of the OT enactments on divorce when He said: "For your hardness of heart Moses allowed you to divorce your wives, but from the beginning it was not so" (Mt. 19:8).

III. OT Regulation.–The ground of divorce under the conditions stipulated in Dt. 24:1 is that the man has found in his wife *'erwaṯ dāḇār*, "an unclean thing." The word *'erwaṯ* in Lev. 20:18f. refers to illicit sexual intercourse, and in Dt. 23:14 (MT 15) it refers to human excrement. It is used in other forms for "nakedness" in Ex. 28:42; 1 S. 20:30; Isa. 47:3; Lam. 1:8; 4:21; Ezk. 16:8, 36f., and for "shame," referring to Egypt, in Isa. 20:4. However, the words "unclean thing" in Dt. 24:1 cannot mean the adultery or sexual uncleanness of a spouse, because adultery was punishable with death. Neither can they apply to suspected adultery. For such cases there were prescribed procedures (Nu. 5:11-31; Dt. 22:13-21). Just what the phrase denotes cannot be stated with certainty, although it is clear that it is behavior that the husband finds shameful, immodest, or unclean in his wife (E. Neufeld, *Ancient Hebrew Marriage Laws* [1944], p. 179).

Even though the OT is silent concerning the woman as plaintiff in a divorce proceeding, it does not follow that there was no provision for this. In the code of Hammurabi, a woman is granted permission to leave her husband and go to her father's house, taking her dowry with her if it was proven she was not at fault (Neufeld, p. 172 § 142; cf. § 149). There is no intimation of any prior proceeding on the part of the husband.

The bill of divorcement (Heb. *sēper k^{e}rîṯuṯ*) was a legal document certifying a divorce on the grounds specified with no reflection on the wife's marital faithfulness. It thus afforded protection for the woman's reputation and guaranteed her freedom to remarry (Murray, p. 9). Other beneficial provisions for the divorced wife and her children were legalized in Bible times; thus the dowry was to be returned and arrangements were made for income for herself and children (Neufeld, p. 172 §§ 131f.).

IV. Grounds for Divorce in Nonbiblical Literature.–To get some idea of the character of the grounds for divorce that were recognized by nations contemporary with the people of Israel we may note the provision in the code of Hammurabi that a man could divorce his wife if she did not bear him children, or if she humiliated her husband by engaging in business that caused her to neglect the home (Neufeld, p. 172).

It is well known that the Talmud devotes a special tractate to the subject of divorce. Here the two schools of interpretation express their opinions. The school of Shammai granted the validity of divorce for unchastity, while the school of Hillel allowed divorce for ill fame, violation of vows made publicly, childlessness, spoiling of food, and the husband's finding another woman more beautiful (see I. Epstein, *The Babylonian Talmud, Gittin* [Eng. tr. 1936], pp. 200f., 437). The teaching of the OT cannot be inferred from the rabbis. In all the literature of the ancient Near East that bears upon divorce the OT is unique in its lofty views of the marriage bond and in its concern for the rights of the wife in the event of separation. D. FREEMAN

IN THE NT

The NT position on divorce has been much debated, and it will very likely continue to be debated, for it is indeed both an important and a complex issue. It is important because the Church has always looked — must always look — to the teaching of Jesus for moral guidance. It is also important, of course, because divorce has always been such a pressing moral issue. It is complex not because the passages are numerous (for they are not) but because it is difficult to assess how the relations of the Gospels to each other and the relation of Paul and the Gospels to Jesus' own words are properly allowed to bear on interpretation. Additional complexities are encountered with the meaning of Gk. *porneía* in Matthew's "exceptive clause" and of Paul's meaning in the "Pauline privilege."

The complexities and the significance make it imperative to say at the very beginning that, however the various questions are resolved, the NT honors marriage and shuns divorce. Whenever divorce is easy for us and unaccompanied by mourning and repentance, we follow culture rather than Scripture.

I. Rabbinic Discussion of Dt. 24:1.–The complexities and resulting disagreements are by no means new. The rabbis were undoubtedly debating the question of divorce during Jesus' lifetime. Mishnah *Gittin* ix.10 preserves something of this debate. The rabbis agreed that Dt. 24:1ff. was normative, but they disagreed about its interpretation. Hillel and Shammai disagreed particularly about the meaning of "some indecency" (RSV; Heb. *'erwaṯ dāḇār*). Hillel said the words quite plainly meant "some unseemly thing" and argued accordingly that a man is licensed to divorce his wife for any "unseemly thing," including burning the toast. Shammai's exegesis transposed the words so the he read *daḇar 'erwâ* (cf. Gk. *lógos porneías*) and argued accordingly that the only legitimate reason for divorce was adultery. Perhaps it is better to read Heb. *'erwâ* (Gk. *porneía*) as some unlawful sexual conduct, an issue to which Matthew will force a return.

II. Jesus' Saying.–Jesus surely encountered and participated in the debate concerning divorce during His lifetime. It would be interesting historically to know exactly what position He took. That is another of the complexities of this issue. The content and intention of Jesus' "very words" is a difficult issue, and even when that issue is decided, the relevance of these words may be debated. Some scholars seem to take their reconstruction of the teaching of Jesus which stands behind the scriptural texts as the genuinely normative element. But such a substitution of a historical reconstruction for the Scriptures themselves as the Church's "canon" seems to many — including this writer — to be unwarranted and dangerous. The historical reconstruction can help, however, to identify the intentions of the biblical authors themselves as they use and shape the traditional materials.

The context of the original words of Jesus was very likely an unqualified prohibition of divorce on the basis of the intention of God in creation. Such content has multiple, early, and independent attestation. Paul, the earliest of the witnesses, says explicitly that his concession, the "Pauline privilege," is not based on a saying of the Lord (1 Cor. 7:12ff.). That leaves the "exceptive clause" in Matthew the only exception. Some, however, have suggested that because Matthew's representation preserves the rabbinic character of the discussion, his account — with the "exceptive clause" — should be taken as closest to the "very words" of Jesus.

The character of the original saying is at least as important as its content. Some have insisted that the saying was a legislative interpretation of the law as it bears on conduct. This is typical of those who take Matthew's saying as original, somewhat atypical of those who take the original saying to be an absolute prohibition based on the creation account. A number of contrasts to legislation have been suggested: Jesus' absolute standard has been characterized as "principle" rather than "precept," as "prophetic" rather than "legal," as "a catechetical ideal" rather than "a casuistic absolute." The distinction most to be commended is the rabbinic one between Halakah and Haggadah (S. E. Johnson, "Jesus' Teaching on Divorce," in B. S. Easton, *et al., Five Essays on Marriage* [1946]). Halakah is commentary on the laws of the OT. It interpreted and applied the law as relevant to conduct. Haggadah is usually commentary on the OT narratives. It intended the religious and moral edification of the people, shaping character and dispositions. Jesus' original teaching on divorce, where this distinction is used in interpretation, would be Haggadah. Merely eternal observance of the law is put in crisis by Jesus' announcement of the kingdom; He shifts the focus to the whole person, to character and disposition rather than external conduct, commenting on the narrative of creation to inculcate a readiness not to divorce even when Dt. 24:1ff. would license it.

Even among those who agree that the original teaching was legislative there are complicated differences of opinion. Some insist that its rigor as legislation is due to the expectation of the imminent kingdom. One Roman Catholic moralist has argued that Jesus' saying is an "evangelical counsel" (V. Pospishil, *Divorce and Remarriage: Toward a New Catholic Teaching* [1967]). But to most who take the saying as legislative, such suggestions and the variety of categories recommended as alternatives to legislation are likely to seem attempts to avoid a costly discipleship with respect to divorce.

III. The NT Passages.–*A. Mark.* Mark is the earliest of the Gospels, but neither he nor his gentile audience were very interested in the rabbinic debates or in the rabbinic mode of moral reflection. In Mark's use of Jesus' saying on divorce Jesus brushes aside the rabbinic question about the exegesis of Dt. 24:1; indeed, He brushes aside the sacred text itself as a mere concession made by Moses. The Mosaic legislation is tried and found wanting against the standard of the original and ideal law of creation. That quite unrabbinic contrast between the "positive law" and the "natural law" would not be lost on Mark's readers — Mark has more than one other passage in which Jesus rejects the "positive law" of Moses and the traditions of the scribes for the sake of true religion and reasonable morality. That original and ideal law of creation stands against the freedom of divorce in Roman law as well as in Jewish law, and Mark's inclusion of women as well as men among the initiators of divorce action may well have the Roman law in view.

If, as suggested above, Jesus' original saying was a Haggadic commentary on the narrative of the creation of man and woman, then Mark has translated that into a Greek mode of moral reflection with the narrative passages as the key to the "natural law." The argument in Mark goes something like this: The primordial will of God, His intention in creation, was expressed in the event, "He made them male and female." The inference is that the union of marriage is also an act of the creator God — so that they are no longer two but one. The consequent "natural law" is clear and stated by Jesus Himself in the new words of institution, "What God has joined together, let not man put asunder" (Gk. *mḗ chōrisétō*, Mk. 10:9). Marriage as created and intended by God transcends and makes relatively inconsequential its human voluntary character.

It might be asked whether Mark intended this "natural law" to be directly legislative or to be continually critical of the hardness of human hearts and the ease of divorce in this age. This is another difficult question. Jesus will brook no departures from the intention of the Creator; He will permit no concessions to the hardness of human hearts. Yet human hearts remain hard, and Jesus was no visionary idealist when it came to the hardness of human hearts. His realism is shown in the following saying in Mark (10:10-12), which assumes divorce even as it proscribes remarriage. There ought to be no divorce, but if there is, there ought to be no remarriage. The point, then, seems less legislative than principial. Mark's "natural law" seems less a substitute for positive law than a principal of indiscriminate criticism of the culture's easy acceptance of divorce. But it must be quickly said, of course, that the principle is not honored by words alone. It is honored by the readiness not to divorce even when the "positive law" would allow it. So Mark preserves, in a different idiom, the meaning of the saying of Jesus.

B. Matthew. Matthew probably was written after Mark, using Mark as one of its basic sources. In contrast to Mark, however, the author and audience are very interested in the rabbinic discussions and in that mode of argument. Mt. 19:3-12 is only one example of this interest. The rabbinic background and interest of this passage have led some to prefer Matthew's presentation here as closer than Mark's to the very situation and words of Jesus. Here Jesus brushes aside neither the rabbinic exegetical discussion nor the text itself. The order of Mark is reversed: Jesus first takes up the texts of Genesis which, significantly, the Pharisees could and should have "read," and gives the Marcan conclusion, "What therefore God has joined together, let not man put asunder." At that point the Pharisees raise the issue of Dt. 24:1. Jesus responds by saying that it is a concession to the hardness of human hearts, but He does not for that reason brush it aside. On the contrary, Matthew with his so-called "concession" (except for unchastity, Gk. *mḗ epí porneíą*) represents Jesus as taking the stricter side, the side of Shammai, in the rabbinic controversy. Mt. 5:31f. has a similar phrase, linguistically even closer to the school of Shammai (Gk. *parektós lógou porneías*; cf. Heb. *dāḇār ʿerwâ*, Shammai's transposition of the text).

The specific reference of Gk. *porneía* in Matthew's "concession" is much debated. The focus of the debate is usually Matthew's intention in preferring Gk. *porneía* to the specific Greek word for adultery, *moicheía*. J. Bonsirven surveys plausible references to Gk. *porneía* and finally favors a reference to illegal marriages, marriages forbidden by Jewish law. (See, e.g., Lev. 18:6-18.) In 1 Cor. 5:1 the word does apparently refer to incest. If this were the specific reference in Matthew, Matthew would be speaking of the nullification of a marriage contract rather than divorce, and the "concession" would be properly understood as a parenthetical "of course, I am speaking of legal marriages here." Such a restricted reference for Gk. *porneía* is unusual, and in our passage makes the point almost too obvious to require special mention. It seems better to take *porneía* as unlawful sexual intercourse rather than as unlawful marriage. Even so, it may be asked what is meant by "unlawful" here. Some have taken Matthew's use of Gk. *porneía* rather than Gk. *moicheía* to indicate a specific reference to fornication or premarital sexual intercourse rather than adultery. (See, e.g., E. J. Mally, *Jerome Biblical Commentary*. Against such an interpretation see B. Malina, *Nov.Test.*, 14 [1972], 10-17.) Such an interpretation has some apparent support from Matthew's description of Joseph's plan to have the marriage contract with Mary, his betrothed, set aside when Mary is found to be pregnant (Mt. 1:19). Sometimes the fact that the OT punishment for adultery is death (e.g., Lev. 20:10; Dt. 22:22) is used in support of such an interpretation. Capital punishment for adultery would, of course, make the permission of divorce superfluous. But the death penalty for adultery was formally dismissed *ca.* A.D. 30 (T.B. *Sanhedrin* 41a) and probably had been little used for some time before. While Gk. *porneía* can mean "fornication," it has ordinarily a broader reference. It includes and sometimes explicitly refers to incest, fornication, homosexual behavior, prostitution, and adultery. (For the specific reference to adultery, see Sir. 23:22f.) On the basis of this, Matthew's preference for Gk. *porneía* seems adequately explained in terms of Shammai's *dāḇār ʿerwâ* and properly interpreted as the range of unlawful sexual conduct covered by the Heb. *ʿerwâ*, the Gk. *porneía*, or the RSV "unchastity," which include rather than exclude adultery.

The specific intention of Matthew's "concession" may also be debated. Many have observed that the sayings on divorce occur in contexts that penetrate the heart and shape character rather than provide moral rules. The interpretations of the contextual material in the Sermon on the Mount and ch. 19 (with its sayings about eunuchs and riches) have themselves long and complex histories. But on the basis of these contexts it seems plausible to suggest that even Matthew is interested not so much in directly legislating the external behavior of his community as in forming its dispositions to the intention of the Torah (given its strictest interpretation). Plausible as that may be, however, the impression here of Halakah, of legal interpretation of the precepts of Torah to govern external behavior, is unavoidable and probably correct.

Still, to call Matthew's saying a "concession" seems a misnomer. If, as suggested, neither Jesus' saying nor Mark's use of it were intended as legislation but rather as Haggadah and "natural law" respectively, then Matthew's "concession" does not concede new and previously unheard legal grounds for divorce. He does not concede a laxer legal standard, but applies the Christian stance toward divorce, with its dispositions and intentions not to divorce, to the legal question which his community continues to ask. In the light of the creation texts and Jesus' use of them, Matthew prefers the stricter interpretation of Dt. 24:1. It is not so much a legal concession as a legal application to the concrete life of his community. It is, incidentally, in terms of this Halakah on Dt. 24:1 that Matthew's often-overlooked restriction of divorce to males is to be explained and understood.

C. Luke. Luke 16:18, like Matthew, mentions nothing about a woman obtaining a divorce. The man is the agent in both Matthew and Luke. This fits traditional Jewish patterns reflected in the use of "to marry" (Gk. *gámein* [active]) for men and "to be given in marriage" (Gk. *gamízesthai* [passive]) for women (cf. Mk. 12:25; Mt. 22:30; Lk. 17:27; 20:35). This agreement between Luke and Matthew may suggest that they had an additional source besides Mark for the saying of Jesus on divorce. But Luke, like Mark, makes no mention of Gk. *lógos porneías*.

D. Paul. Like Mark, Paul can use the Genesis texts. In 1 Cor. 6:16 he uses Gen. 2:24 to insist that sexual relations, even with a prostitute, make the two persons "one flesh." In 1 Corinthians the text functions only polemically against such immorality, but in Eph. 5:31f. it is taken to refer to Christ and His church, and that union is itself explicated to fathom and elucidate the meaning of marriage. The Ephesians passage — without mentioning divorce — quite effectively shapes Christian dispositions toward divorce and invites and permits marriage partners to live marriage on the basis of the gospel.

The passage in 1 Cor. 7, in which Paul explicitly deals with divorce, seems prosaic by comparison, but it is quite illuminating. The passage is obviously a response to an inquiry from the Corinthians: "Now concerning the matters about which you wrote." There were in Corinth some who denied any future resurrection (1 Cor. 15). Paul consistently reminds these enthusiasts of the "not yet" character of our existence against the arrogance of claiming to participate already without remainder in the new age. Among the consequences of that arrogance was an encratism which forbade marriage; for if this is already without remainder the new age, then we are already like the angels. Paul begins by quoting the slogan of these encratists: "It is well for a man not to touch a woman" (7:1). He does not reject the slogan, but qualifies it by reference to the "not yet" character of our existence: "But because of the temptations to immorality, each man should have his own wife and each woman her own husband" (7:2). Voluntary celibacy is accepted, even welcomed, as a sign of the new age. There has been by the turning of the ages a radical revision of the Jewish attitude toward celibacy, and Paul acknowledges that much truth in the encratism of the Corinthians. But "that much truth" is falsely held. It is only in view of "the present distress" (v. 26), in view of the eschatological situation as "between the times," that our celibacy or our marriage is consecrated to God. *Now* we are not released from marital responsibilities and our separation — even for prayer — must be by mutual agreement (v. 5). The church's disposition toward divorce is still shaped by the Lord's saying, to which Paul directly appeals in his advice that women not be divorced (Gk. *mḗ chōristhḗnai*, RSV "not separate"; cf. Mk. 10:9; Mt. 19:6; 1 Cor. 7:15b; the form is passive here, but it is possible to take it in an active sense) and that men not divorce (Gk. *mḗ aphiénai*) their wives. Gk. *porneía* is not mentioned here, but a different problem arises, to which Paul addresses not any word of the Lord but his own judgment (v. 12). Paul's solution has been called "the Pauline privilege." The problem is not simply one of desertion but much more narrowly whether marriage to an unbeliever may be dissolved. Paul's answer is that the Christian is not to seek it (and certainly not on the basis of pretensions about being already "angelic"), but, if the initiative comes from the unbelieving partner, then divorce is allowable.

IV. Conclusion.–The NT teaching on divorce is difficult and complex. This study, while attempting to acknowledge some of the difficulties and alternatives, has made the following suggestion: Jesus' saying was Haggadic, concerned with creating among His followers a readiness not to divorce even when the law permitted it. Mark faithfully rendered Jesus' saying in a new and Greek idiom. Neither Jesus Himself nor Mark was directly legislating, but both weighed, and found wanting, an easy recourse to Jewish or Roman legislation that permitted divorce. Matthew — with dispositions formed and informed by the statement of Jesus — applied the teaching to the legal question faced by his community. And Paul did the same — quite differently — when confronted with a different sort of case.

Finally, if the question of the meanings of the NT authors then is difficult and complex, the question of how to apply them faithfully today is still more difficult and complex. Although that cannot be the focus of this article, two observations may be allowed. First, we cannot avoid the difficult task of thinking about the concrete cases presented by our communities and situations, and of trying to formulate general rules to cover them. We must address divorce cases out of the same loyalty to the risen Lord and in terms of the same invitation to live marriage on the basis of His grace that marked Matthew and Paul. But we may do injustice to Matthew, Paul, and their Lord if we simply repeat their case-applications to our own situations. Second, we must attempt to form dispositions that are ready not to divorce even when divorce is legally and culturally acceptable — even, indeed, when the rules of Matthew, Paul, or subsequent Christian communities would permit divorce. God calls us to honor marriage and shun divorce. Divorce is always, therefore, an evil; it is never something to be intended as itself the end-in-view. But divorce is sometimes permissible "between the times" for the protection and honoring of marriage itself or of one of the partners in marriage. As killing is sometimes allowable with fear and trembling, as in a just war, so divorce may sometimes be permissible with mourning and repentance.

Bibliography.–J. Bonsirven, *Le Divorce dans le NT* (1948); R. H. Charles, *The Teaching of the NT on Divorce* (1921); J. D. M. Derrett, *Law in the NT* (1970), pp. 363-388; *TDNT*, I, *s.v.* γαμέω, γάμος (E. Stauffer); VI, *s.v.* πόρνη κτλ. (F. Hauck, S. Schulz).

A. D. VERHEY

Historical Survey

In its general thinking and practice across the centuries, the Church, especially in the West, has followed the view that the NT does not permit divorce, or divorce with the possibility of remarriage.

I. Early Church.–In the first two centuries Hermas and Clement of Alexandria seem to reflect the common position. Both allowed for separation but both came out strongly against second marriage. Thus Hermas argued that one may put away a wife for adultery but must take her back if she repents (Mand. 4:1:4-8). The question was urgent for Christians in the world of pagan antiquity, since divorce was common. With increasing evangelization male converts in particular tried to maintain the right to end their marriages, but Augustine strongly championed the position of women in opposing remarriage after divorce and bringing husbands under the common rule. The Council of Carthage in 407, which also took a stand against marriage with pagans, plainly disallowed remarriage after divorce (canon 8), and thus stated what became, or continued to be, the Western position. Later the Eastern

Church took a less stringent attitude under the Justinian Code (6th cent.), although this code maintained strong control over the granting of divorces.

*II. **Medieval Church.***–New marital problems arose in the West with the conversion of the Celtic and Germanic peoples, whose laws and customs had permitted divorce. At first, concessions were made to pre-Christian practice, but the indissolubility of marriage was reaffirmed by the early 2nd millennium, especially as the Roman Church came to view marriage as one of the so-called seven sacraments, the union of husband and wife being a sign of the union of Christ and the Church (cf. Peter Lombard *Sentences*; Thomas Aquinas *Summa Contra Gentiles* iv.78[6]). Thus Pope Alexander III (1159-1181) would not allow separation, even for the sake of taking vows, unless there had been no consummation and therefore no real marriage. A marriage might be dissolved if consent had previously been given to another, but prior consent to another, like nonconsummation, would really be a ground of nullification, not of divorce. Innocent III in 1199 ruled that the Pauline privilege had to be taken very strictly and would not apply if a believing partner became a heretic and abandoned the other spouse. The Council of Florence (1438-1445) permitted "separation from bed and board," but gave no permission to contract a second marriage. Summing up the medieval teaching and carrying it over into the modern period, the Council of Trent in its 1563 session adopted the same position and retained the view that there can be no dissolution of a marriage by reason of the heresy of one of the partners. (Cf. *New Catholic Encyclopedia,* IV, *s.v.* "Divorce" [J. M. Egan].)

III. Reformation.–As may be seen from the ruling of Alexander III, nullification, which left the door open for a new marriage, could still be declared for particular causes. These included such things as bigamy and impotence as well as prior consent to another, but, unless protected by a papal dispensation, marriage within the prohibited degrees (the ground of the nullity suit of Henry VIII against Catharine of Aragon) formed perhaps the most common cause, especially when the degrees were extended to cover not only biological and legal relationships but also spiritual ones, e.g., those contracted in baptism. The loopholes which popes and canonists found allowed for comparatively easy invalidations by the 15th cent., and made marriage itself more difficult.

This stirred up a revolt on the part of the reformers, most of whom pleaded both for simpler conditions of marriage and also for a simpler possibility of dissolution. Luther in his *Babylonian Captivity* (*WA*, vi, 553f.) sharply attacked the papal control of marriage by means of legislation, dispensation, nullification, and sacramentalization. He himself would accept dissolution on the ground of impotence or ignorance of a previous marriage (*WA*, vi, 558f.). He had no liking for divorce (preferring bigamy in the famous case of Philip of Hesse [1540]), but he would permit it in the case of unchastity, with no obstacle to remarriage (*WA*, vi, 235f.). Calvin, in a similar assault on the evils of papal practice, complained that "a man who has put away an adulterous wife is not permitted to take another" (*Inst.* iv.19.37). Bucer of Strassburg was ready to extend the grounds for divorce to include cruelty and refusal of conjugal duty. Among the radical reformers, Sattler in 1527 allowed the remarriage of the innocent party in a case of adultery, though this did not go uncontested. Application of the "ban" (excommunication) could mean separation from the erring or unbelieving spouse and this could be carried to the length of divorce, although a ruling in 1571 decided against this. The Anglican reformers ran into problems with the odd matrimonial ventures of Henry VIII, although natural death, execution, and nullification on the grounds of prohibited degrees or nonconsummation made the remarriages possible. They did not, however, carry through any reform of canon law on the issue, so that as late as the 19th cent. a special act of Parliament was needed for divorces, and when this was changed a serious rift developed between civil and ecclesiastical law.

IV. Modern Period.–During the post-Reformation age few changes took place so long as the Western churches exercised a powerful influence over civil laws and mores. Nullifications might be granted in the Roman Catholic Church, but with considerable restraint. Divorces could take place in the Protestant churches, not only for adultery but also for desertion, as among the New England Puritans; yet few divorces actually took place, and when legislation to make divorce easier was passed in England, the Church, as we have noted, strongly resisted it. The 19th and 20th cents., however, introduced an increasing secularization of society which resulted in a rapid escalation of civil divorce in many Western countries. This brought problems for the Roman Catholic Church. Pius XI, in the encyclical *Casti connubii* (1930), bravely repeated the principle of Augustine that "the law of the gospel . . . abrogated all dispensations." He argued, then, that an exception "does not depend on the will of man or on any merely human power, but on divine law." Nevertheless, in answer to popular pressure, a broadening of the grounds of invalidation seriously weakened the force of this statement, since in practice dissolution and remarriage became hardly more difficult than divorce and remarriage in the Protestant churches. These churches in turn found that the wholesale adoption of secular laws and mores by their members were quickly making the exception the rule, notwithstanding the verbal insistence on marital commitment and divine conjoining.

V. Conclusion.–The situation that developed in the latter part of the 20th cent. was no new problem but simply a repetition, in one of its more acute forms, of the Church's ongoing task is to proclaim and practice biblical marriage in a world of opposing secular ideas and customs. In the past, even—and perhaps especially—in times of the most urgent conflict, as in the first centuries, the Church took up the challenge, resisting conformity to civil patterns and practicing conformity to the NT model plainly set forth by Jesus and Paul. Through every failure and distortion, and in spite of a few concessions, it thus maintained the substance of indissoluble Christian marriage, either totally excluding successive marriages during the life of the original partners, or permitting them only as an extreme exception which proves the rule (but does not itself become the rule of establish a qualifying, or competing rule).

G. W. BROMILEY

DIZAHAB dīz'ə-hab, diz'ə-hab [Heb. *dî-zāhāḇ*; Gk. *katachrýsea*–'that which has gold']. One of four names in Dt. 1:1 describing the place E of the Arabah where Moses delivered his farewell address. The location is unknown, but from the similarity of the other names to earlier wilderness stopping-places it was identified with Minet edh-Dhahab, due E of Sinai. However, this is not in the area of the known camps, nor is it suitable for such activity. Since the only probable deposits of gold in this region are in the crystalline rocks E of the Arabah, Dizahab might possibly be identified with Edh-Dheibeh E of Heshbon; but this again is an indifferent campsite. It does not appear to be the Mezahab of Gen. 36:39.

R. K. H.

DO NOT DESTROY (Heading to Pss. 57, 58, 59, 75). Probably a melody to which the Psalm was to be sung. *See* AL-TASCHITH; MUSIC III.B.

DOCTOR. In the AV of Lk. 2:46 "doctor" (Gk. *didáskalos*) is used in the sense of "eminent teacher," as is also "doctor of the law" (*nomodidáskalos*) in Lk. 5:17; Acts 5:34.

DOCTRINE [Heb. *leqaḥ*] (Job 11:4); [Gk. *didachḗ*] (Rom. 16:17; 2 Jn. 9f.); NEB also TEACHING; [*didaskalía*] (Mt. 15:9; Mk. 7:7; Eph. 4:14; Col. 2:22; 1 Tim. 1:10; 4:1, 6; Tit. 1:9; 2:1, 10); NEB also TEACHING, INSTRUCTION; [*heterodidaskaléō*] ("teach a different doctrine," 1 Tim. 1:3); [*lógos*] (He. 6:1); NEB RUDIMENT. In the OT the term occurs only once, to translate Heb. *leqaḥ*, denoting "that which is received."

The term "doctrine" is derived from the Lat. *doctrina*, based on the verb *doceo*, "teach." Both *didachḗ* and *didaskalía* can refer to "teaching" either in the active sense of "instruction" or in the passive sense of "what is taught." The use of "doctrine" for "teaching" in the former sense, now obsolete, is found in the AV (e.g., for *didachḗ*, Mk. 4:2; Acts 2:42; for *didaskalía*, 1 Tim. 4:13, 16; 5:17; 2 Tim. 3:10, 16); the RSV uses the term only in the latter sense.

The meaning of these words varied as the apostolic proclamation of the message of Christ (*kḗrygma*) and the "teaching" began to assume certain more fixed forms and to have a certain recognizable content. (1) The doctrines of the Pharisees were a fairly compact and definite body of teaching, a fixed tradition handed down from one generation of teachers to another (Mt. 16:12, AV "doctrine"; cf. Mt. 15:9; Mk. 7:7). (2) In contrast with the Pharisaic system, the teaching of Jesus was unconventional and occasional, discursive and unsystematic, so that His contemporaries were astonished at it and recognized it as a new teaching (Mt. 7:28; 22:33; Mk. 1:22, 27; Lk. 4:32). So we find it in the Synoptic Gospels, and the more systematic form given to it in the Johannine discourses is undoubtedly the work of the Evangelist, who wrote rather to interpret Christ than to record His *ipsissima verba* (Jn. 20:31).

The earliest teaching of the apostles consisted essentially of three propositions: (a) that Jesus was the Christ (Acts 3:18); (b) that He was risen from the dead (Acts 1:22; 2:24, 32); and (c) that salvation was by faith in His name (Acts 2:38; 3:16). While proclaiming these truths, it was necessary to coordinate them with OT revelation. The method of the earliest reconstruction may be gathered from the speeches of Peter and Stephen (Acts 2:14-36; 5:29-32; 7:2-53). A more thorough reconstruction of the relating of the Christian facts not only to Hebrew history but to universal history, and to a view of the world as a whole, was undertaken by Paul. The type of "doctrine" which simply related the basic truths and coordinated them with the OT is found in Paul's speech at Antioch (Acts 13:16-41), while the type which presented the events in a more general context is illustrated in his speeches at Lystra (14:15-17) and Athens (17:22-31). The ideas given in outline in these speeches are more fully developed into a doctrinal system, with its center moved from the resurrection to the death of Christ, in the Epistles, especially in Galatians, Romans, Ephesians, Philippians, and Colossians. But as yet this reconstruction is the theological system of one teacher, and there is no sign of any attempt to impose it by authority on the Church as a whole. As a matter of fact the Pauline system never was generally accepted by the early Church. (Cf. James and the Apostolic Fathers.)

In the Pastoral and General Epistles a new state of things appears. The repeated emphasis on "sound doctrine" (1 Tim. 1:10; 4:6; 6:3; 2 Tim. 1:13; 4:3; Tit. 1:9; 2:1) implies that a body of teaching has now emerged which is generally accepted, and which should serve as a standard of orthodoxy. The faith has become a body of truth "once for all delivered to the saints" (Jude 3). The content of this "sound doctrine" is nowhere formally given, but it is possible that it corresponded very nearly to the Roman formula that became known as the Apostles' Creed.

See also DOGMA.

Bibliography.–Bauer, pp. 190f.; *TDNT*, II, *s.v.* διδαχή (Rengstorf); C. H. Dodd, *Apostolic Preaching and Its Development* (2nd ed. 1954).

T. REES

DOCUMENT [Heb. *k^e^ṯāḇ* (Est. 3:14); Aram. *k^e^ṯāḇ* (Ezr. 6:1, etc.)]. The RSV rendering of a word that elsewhere it translates "writing." The term is used of a writing on any material, including the wall surface (Dnl. 5:7ff.).

DOCUS dō'kəs. *See* DOK.

DODAI dō'dī (1 Ch. 27:4). *See* DODO.

DODANIM dō'də-nēm [Heb. *dōḏānîm*] (Gen. 10:4); NEB RODANIM. A people mentioned in Gen. 10:4 among the sons of Javan, the son of Japheth. This would place the Dodanim among the Ionians. The parallel passage 1 Ch. 1:7, along with the LXX of Gen. 10:4, has RODANIM, which is probably the true reading. This identifies the people with the Rhodians (cf. on Ezk. 27:15 under DEDAN).

See TABLE OF NATIONS Map.

DODAVAHU dō-də-vä'hōō [Heb. *dôḏāwāhû*] (2 Ch. 20:37); AV DODAVAH. Father of Eliezer of Mareshah, a prophet in the days of Jehoshaphat.

DODO dō'dō; **DODAI** [Heb. *dôḏô*, *dôḏay*–'beloved'].

1. The grandfather of Tola of the tribe of Issachar, one of the judges (Jgs. 10:1).

2. "The Ahohite," father of Eleazar, one of David's heroes (2 S. 23:9; 1 Ch. 11:12), and himself the commander of one of the divisions of the army (1 Ch. 27:4).

3. The Bethlehemite, father of Elhanan, one of David's mighty men (2 S. 23:24; 1 Ch. 11:26).

DOE [Heb. *ya'^a^la*] (Prov. 5:19); AV ROE. Although traditionally translated as though it referred to a form of deer, this term is now considered to be a designation of (the female of) a form of GOAT or ibex (*CHAL*, p. 138).

DOEG dō'eg [Heb. *dô'ēg*, *dō'ēg*]. "The Edomite," a servant of Saul who watched David's encounter with the priest Ahimelech and then denounced the priest to the king. Later he executed the king's command to slay the priests at Nob. The position he held is described as that of "the chief of Saul's herdsmen" (1 S. 21:7). Rabbinical legends speak of him as the greatest scholar of his time. The traditional title of Ps. 52 associates the composition of that Psalm with the events that led to the slaying of the priests (1 S. 21:7; 22:9, 18, 22).

N. ISAACS

DOG [Heb. *keleḇ*] (Ex. 11:7; 22:31; Dt. 23:11; Jgs. 7:5; 1 S. 17:43; 24:14; etc.); [Gk. *kýōn*, *kynárion*] (Mt. 7:6; 15:26f.; Mk. 7:27f.; Lk. 16:21; Phil. 3:2; 2 Pet. 2:22; Rev. 22:15). References to the dog, both in the OT and in the NT, are usually of a contemptuous character. A dog, and especially a dead dog, is used as a figure of insignificance. Goliath says to David (1 S. 17:43): "Am I a dog, that you come to me with sticks?" David says to Saul (1 S. 24:14): "After whom do you pursue? After a dead dog! After a flea!" Mephibosheth says to David (2 S. 9:8): "What is thy servant, that you should look upon a dead dog such as I?" The same figure is found in the words of Hazael to Elisha (2 K. 8:13). The meaning, which is obscure in the AV, is brought out well in the RSV: "What is your servant, who is but a dog, that he should do this great thing?" The characteristically oriental interrogative form of these expressions should be noted.

Other passages express by inference the low esteem in which dogs are held. Nothing worse could happen to a person than that his body should be devoured by dogs (1 K. 14:11; 16:4; 21:19, 23, etc.). Job (30:1) says of the youths who deride him that he disdained to set their fathers with the dogs of his flock. In Phil. 3:2 and Rev. 22:15 dogs are coupled with evil-workers, sorcerers, etc. In Mt. 7:6 we read: "Do not give dogs what is holy; and do not throw your pearls before swine."

Job 30:1 (cited above) refers to the use of dogs to guard flocks; and the comparison of inefficient watchmen with dumb dogs (Isa. 56:10) implies that at least some dogs are useful. In the apocryphal book of Tobit, Tobias' dog is his companion on his travels (Tob. 5:16; 11:4). For the reference in Prov. 30:31, AV, to the greyhound, *see* COCK.

Precisely when the dog was domesticated is unknown, but the recovery of canine skeletal remains from the pre-pottery Neolithic levels of Jericho (Tell eṣ-Sulṭân) suggests that it occurred at a remote period of human history. In protodynastic Egypt a whippet-like breed of dog, now extinct, was used in hunting animals and game.

The pariah dogs of Syria and Palestine resemble the jackals, especially in color and in the tail, differing in their greater size and in the shape of muzzle and ears. It is fair to assume that they are much the same as existed in biblical times. They are in general meek and harmless creatures and are valuable as scavengers, but they disturb the night with their barking. Each quarter of the city has its own pack of dogs, which vigorously resents any invasion of its territory. The pariah dog is sometimes brought up to be a sheep dog, but the best shepherd dogs are great wolfish creatures, which are usually obtained from Kurdistan.

A. E. DAY
R. K. H.

DOGMA [Gk. *dógma* < *dokéo*–'think,' 'suppose,' intrans. 'seem,' 'appear']. In Greek *dógma* has two basic meanings. The first is "what seems to be right," "what is thought to be true." It yields the subdivisions (a) "opinion" and (b) "philosophical opinion, principle, or doctrine." In this sense the word may be compared with two other terms that come to play a role in theology, viz., *dóxa* (from the same root *dokéō*), which again has the primary sense of "opinion," and *haíresis*, which in addition to its primary meanings "capture" and "choice" also denotes a philosophical "sect" or "school."

The second basic meaning of dogma is "resolution," "decree." This might be either the resolution or decree made or passed by an individual or group, or an official "ordinance, edict, or decree." In the Jewish world there is perhaps a combination of both basic senses when dogma is used for the law (the Torah), since this is both teaching and also the commandment of God.

In biblical use dogma usually has the second of its two basic senses. Thus in Dnl. 6:16 the decree by which Daniel is put in the lions' den is a dogma. In the NT Joseph and Mary go to Bethlehem in obedience to a dogma of Caesar Augustus, namely, that a census should be taken for taxation purposes (Lk. 2:1). In the Epistles (Eph. 2:15; Col. 2:14) the statutes or decrees of OT law are dogmas. At issue in Acts 16:4 are the resolutions or decrees of the Apostolic Council, not doctrinal resolutions.

When we turn to the fathers the biblical usage still has a place. Thus the reference is often to imperial or ecclesiastical decrees in Eusebius *HE* (e.g., vi.3). Possibly the broader sense of divine or apostolic direction in Ign. Magn. 13:1; 1 Clem. 20:4; Did. 11; Barn. 6:1 forms a transition to the later use. Lacking any biblical basis, the sense of "opinion" makes its way only slowly into the vocabulary of the church. Primarily it carries a natural enough reference to pagan thought. Thus it is human teaching or natural law in 1 Clem. 20:1; Tatian *Oratio ad Graecos* 3.3. Athenagoras uses it for the opinions of philosophers in *Supplicatio pro Christianis* 6; cf. Clement of Alexandria *Misc.* i.118. Along the same lines Justin refers to ungodly dogmas in *Apol.* i.58.2. Even when the doctrines of the church are denoted, as in Eusebius *HE* iii.26.4, the word may be applied equally to the false opinions of heretics, as in Gelasius I *Epistula* 4.2.

Rather oddly the use for false doctrines seems to have been no less common in early writers than the use for orthodox teaching. Irenaeus has this sense in *Adv. haer.* i.31.3 and Augustine hardly seems to know any other. (The Greek word had been adopted into Latin for "philosophical tenet" as early as Cicero.) Later Vincent of Lerins condemns Arianism as a new dogma. Indeed, even in 1878 Leo XIII could refer in an encyclical to the wicked dogmas of the Socialists. He follows a common custom in attaching an uncomplimentary adjective to the word when it denotes the ideas of opponents. One recalls the "ungodly" of Justin and the "new" of Vincent; Gelasius has "nefarious" in the same connection.

For dogma as the church's own teaching Ignatius (Magn. 13:1) might be adduced as the earliest instance. This example is followed mainly by the Greek church. Thus Origen speaks of the Christian dogma of faith and morals in *De prin.* iv.1 and *Contra Celsum* i.7. Justinian has a reference to the dogma of the four synods. In contrast Latin writers such as Tertullian, Cyprian, Ambrose, Augustine, Leo, and Gregory seem not to have employed the word in this sense or even perhaps to have avoided it, possibly to avoid confusion with "philosophical opinion." Even in the Middle Ages, when the definition of doctrines was beginning to have greater force with the development of canon law, "dogma" still found no great favor even in so important a writer as Thomas Aquinas.

From the 16th cent. onward, however, the Roman Catholic Church in particular has adopted the word "dogma" to describe its own authoritative teaching. Often a qualifying adjective or genitive is added to show that orthodox teaching is intended. Thus, as distinct from the wicked dogmas of Socialists and others, we are now dealing with catholic dogmas or dogmas of the faith or the church. The definition is finally reached that dogma is immutable truth of faith or morals revealed by God, transmitted by the apostles, and defined by the church either ordinarily, i.e., by consensus, or by solemn pronouncement of a council or pope. In relation to individual dogmas many detailed distinctions may then be made. Thus the truths themselves can be revealed explicitly, implicitly, or virtually (inferentially). The dogmas may be general or special, material or formal, pure or mixed, credal or noncredal, more necessary or less. A category of facts relating to dogmas also comes into the picture, e.g., whether a given council is ecumenical or not, and some difference arises as to whether judgments on these share the authority of the dogmas themselves.

Parallel with Roman Catholic development comes a similar process in the Reformation world. The main difference arises out of the different understanding of authority. Dogmas may still be regarded as revealed truths which are also enshrined in creeds and confessions but now the confessional statement does not have the same force as the truth in its biblical form. Dogmas, then, play a less authoritative role insofar as they are understood as ecclesiastical formulations. As revealed truths they are binding; as confessional statements they are reformable and have only relative and subsidiary authority. In other words, no direct correlation is postulated between revelation and ecclesiastical definition.

In the modern understanding of dogma it is evident that something of the second basic sense of "decree" still clings to the idea of "teaching" or "opinion." Possibly this is true of the very early usage and as late as Eusebius and Athanasius. Later (e.g., in Cyril of Jerusalem *Catecheses* 4.2 and Gregory of Nyssa *Epistula* 24) this is weakened to some degree by the separation between doctrinal and ethical use, i.e., dogma as doctrine and dogma as moral commandment. Doctrinal dogma is predominantly intellectual, and while it claims assent it does not demand obedience as moral dogma does. In the medieval West, however, increasing authoritarianism gives added weight to definition. The defined dogma has to be believed on pain of eternal damnation. While some writers, e.g., Barth in *CD* I/1 § 7,1, argue that as intellectual propositions dogmas have lost their character as decrees and becomes neutral, their binding force does in fact seem to preserve something of their mandatory element.

Barth, of course, resists strongly the confusion which underlies this development. In good Reformation style he cannot allow a simple equation between revealed truths and dogmas as defined propositions. The latter have an authentic place but they must always have a tentative character as the church's attempt to state biblical truth in a particular situation. Even Roman Catholicism itself is not unaware of this. It admits that all dogmas are not yet defined, and that the substance of a dogma lies in its truth and not in its formulation. Hence a certain reformability of dogma is not precluded and the idea that ecclesiastical formulations can be dogmas in the sense of decrees undergoes some relativization.

Nevertheless, Barth himself argues firmly that a biblical understanding of dogma must entail the use of the term in the sense of "decree" even if the only dogmas in the NT are secular or ethical. This is not possible, however, if dogmas are merely ecclesiastical definitions posing as revealed truths. Barth himself, therefore, tries to work his way through the problem by making a not very perspicuous distinction between dogma in the singular and the venerable but fallible definitions of the church which may be called dogmas in the plural. On this view dogma, which is the essence of dogmas, is a relational and eschatological concept. It is relational inasmuch as it is church proclamation to the extent that this agrees with the Word of God. It is eschatological inasmuch as it does not exist as the full manifestation of this agreement but always in approximation to it. The Lutheran J. A. Quenstedt is quoted here. Dogma as Quenstedt sees it has to do, not with archetypal theology, nor with direct revelation (e.g., to the prophets and apostles), nor with man in heaven or prior to the fall, but with the ektypal theology of indirect revelation pursued by pilgrim man subsequent to the fall (*Theologia* [1685], I, ch. 1, section 1, theses 3-14).

Along these lines, however, dogma is also decree — not the decree of the church nor indeed the mere demand of teaching for assent, but the decree of God which demands obedience. Thus the search for agreement between proclamation and the Word of God is not simply an intellectual investigation by scholars but first and foremost the work of servants fulfilling the will and purpose of their master. The final and basic relation, then, is the relation between the Lord who commands and servants who obey.

Whether or not Barth or anyone else can succeed in applying the sense of "decree" to dogma today is highly questionable. The real implication of biblical usage would seem to be that there is no basis at all for the modern understanding and use of the term. Nevertheless, a point of value has been raised by Barth in respect of the work of dogmatics. As a mere science of church dogmas, dogmatics easily become an abstract and finally superfluous enterprise. When related to God's command, however, dogmatics has a responsibility to consider at every level the church's obedience with respect to the proclamation which lies at the heart of its mission and ministry. This means that the church has an obligation to pursue dogmatics, since it stands or falls by the result of the inquiry into dogma. Since an equation between dogma and the church's dogmatic formulations can never be presupposed, not only does the urgency of dogmatics come into proper focus but the church itself is jolted out of authoritarianism or complacency and the question of obedience is constantly raised.

Bibliography.–*CD* I/1 (1975), § 7,1; B. Bartmann, *Lehrbuch der Dogmatik* (1928), I, 2; *Catholic Encyclopedia, s.v.* "Dogma" (C. Coghlan); A. Deneffe, *Scholastik* (1931), pp. 381f., 505f.; F. Diekamp, *Katholische Dogmatik* (1930), I, 11; W. Lohff, "Dogma" in *LTK*; R. Rothe, *Zur Dogmatik* (1863), p. 14.

G. W. BROMILEY

DOK dōk [Gk. *Dōk, Dagōn*]; AV DOCUS. A small fortress near Jericho which was built by Ptolemy son of Abubus. Ptolemy invited Simon Maccabeus, his two sons, and some servants to the stronghold to be his guests. When they were drunk Ptolemy killed them (1 Macc. 16:11-16). Josephus (*Ant.* xii.8.1; *BJ* i.2.3) calls the place Dagon, located N of Jericho. The name persists in the modern 'Ain Dûk, known for its springs, about 2 mi. (3.2 km.) NW of Jericho. K. G. JUNG

DOLEFUL CREATURES (Isa. 13:21, AV). *See* HOWLING CREATURES.

DOLMENS dōl'menz. Boxlike burial structures made of slabs of stone. The simplest form is shaped like the Greek letter Π, and has a single chamber, but dolmens with two chambers are also found. According to one theory, they were originally covered with a mound of dirt; but this cannot be proven.

Dolmens can be found in many parts of the Old World: in Europe, Asia, and Africa. Thousands of dolmens are found in Transjordan, the largest field being located in the foothills of the Jordan Valley E of Damieh (or ADAM, where Wâdī Fâr'ah enters the Jordan). The second-largest field in Jordan is located at Tell el-Ashiar, a few miles from Irbid. Other fields are located in the foothills E of Teleilât el-Ghassûl and in the hill country near Ḥasban E of Jerash.

The dolmens are either late Neolithic or early Chalcolithic (*ca.* 4000 B.C.); but since no pottery has been found in any of them that can be certainly dated as contemporary, more precise dating of the dolmens is not yet possible.

Some scholars have suggested that references to

"mighty men that were of old" (Gen. 6:4), the Anakim, the Rephaim, etc., arose from legends that were early developed to account for the dolmens. No biblical term has been identified as meaning "dolmen."

See G. L. Harding, *Antiquities of Jordan* (1959), pp. 30, 57, 63, 81. W. S. L. S.

DOMESTIC [Gk. *oikourgós*] (occurs only in Tit. 2:5); NEB "busy at home." Some MSS have *oikouroús* (cf. AV "keepers at home"), but on the basis of superior external support and a preference for the more difficult reading textual critics favor *oikourgoús* as the proper reading here. The literal meaning of the latter term is "workers at home," and thus it is not far different in meaning from the variant. The RSV rendering covers both alternatives and conveys the essential meaning.

Paul uses this term in describing the role of young women. In addition to loving their husbands and children, being sensible, chaste, kind, and submissive to their husbands, Paul exhorts the older women to train the younger women also to be "domestic," i.e., to recognize their proper sphere of responsibility in the home. The faithful service of the active housewife is distinguished from the activity of the busybody, whose idleness and wagging tongue become a disgrace both to herself and to her household (cf. 1 Tim. 5:13).

A. J. BIRKEY

DOMINION; HAVE DOMINION OVER; etc. [Heb. *rāḏâ*] (Gen. 1:26, 28; Nu. 24:19; 1 K. 4:24; Neh. 9:28; Ps. 72:8); NEB RULE, TRAMPLE DOWN, HOLD IN SUBJECTION, HOLD SWAY; [*māšal*] (Gen. 37:8; Jgs. 14:4; Job 25:2; Ps. 8:6 [MT 7]; 19:13 [MT 14]); NEB LORD IT OVER, BE MASTER OF (OVER), AUTHORITY RESTS WITH, "get the better of"; [*mōšel*] (Dnl. 11:4; Zec. 9:10); NEB EMPIRE, RULE; [*memšālâ*] (1 K. 9:19; 2 Ch. 8:6; Ps. 103:22; 114:2; 145:13; Jer. 34:1; 51:28; Mic. 4:8); NEB also VASSAL (Jer. 34:1), REALM, SOVEREIGNTY; [*mimšāl*] (Dnl. 11:3, 5); NEB KINGDOM; [*m^e^lûḵâ*] (Ps. 22:28 [MT 29]); AV KINGDOM; NEB KINGLY POWER; [*šālaṭ*] (Ps. 119:133); NEB HAVE MASTERY; [*môṭâ*] (Ezk. 30:18); AV, NEB, YOKE(S); [Aram. *šolṭān*] (Dnl. 4:3, 22, 34 [MT 3:33; 4:19, 31]; 6:26; 7:6, 12, 14, 26f.; 11:3, 5); NEB SOVEREIGNTY, DOMAIN, SOVEREIGN POWER, KINGDOM; [Gk. *kyrieúō*] (Rom. 6:9, 14); NEB also BE MASTER; [*kyriótēs*] (Eph. 1:21; Col. 1:16); NEB also SOVEREIGNTY; [*exousía*] (Col. 1:13); AV POWER; NEB DOMAIN; [*krátos*] (1 Tim. 6:16; 1 Pet. 4:11; 5:11; Jude 25; Rev. 1:6); AV also POWER; NEB also MIGHT, POWER; [*échō basileían*] (Rev. 17:18); AV REIGN; NEB HOLD SWAY.

The biblical terms generally denote the power to rule. The OT verb *rāḏâ* has the meaning of "tread" or "trample" (cf. use in Joel 3:13 [MT 4:13] for treading in the wine press), and so "dominate" or "rule." *Māšal* is a general term for "ruling" or "having mastery over" something or someone. The noun *môṭâ* denotes in Ezk. 30:18 a bar or yoke as a symbol of oppression. In the NT the term most frequently rendered "dominion" is *krátos*, which means "power" or "might." When used of God it denotes His "sovereignty."

The OT and NT Scriptures confess that "dominion" belongs ultimately to God (Job 25:2; Ps. 22:28; 145:13; Dnl. 4:3, 34; 6:26; 7:27; 1 Tim. 6:16; 1 Pet. 4:11; 5:11; Jude 25; Rev. 1:6; etc.); however, the term is also used for man's mastery over nature (Gen. 1:26, 28; Ps. 8:6), political power over a realm (Gen. 37:8; Nu. 24:19; Jgs. 14:4; 1 K. 4:24; etc.), and sin's rule over man (Ps. 19:13; 119:133; Rom. 6:9, 14; etc.).

In Eph. 1:21 and Col. 1:16 the term *kyriótēs* appears to denote a rank or order of angels with "thrones," "authorities," "principalities," etc. that were believed to rule over the various divisions of the cosmos. In these passages Paul is combatting the heretical belief that these beings acted as mediators between Creator and creation, and that they had the power to shape the destiny of the world. Paul contends that these beings too (if they exist) owe their existence to Christ (for "all things were created through him and for him") and are subservient to Him (for God "has put all things under his feet"). Christ alone is Mediator, and in Him alone rests the full power of God; it is not distributed among a multitude of intermediary spiritual beings. *See also* ANGEL.

See *IB*, X, 634f.; XI, 166f. N. J. O.

DOMITIAN. *See* ROMAN EMPIRE AND CHRISTIANITY I.C.

DOOM [Heb. *ra'*] (Jer. 4:18; 11:15); AV WICKEDNESS, "do evil"; NEB PUNISHMENT, DISASTER; [*'^a^tiḏōṯ*–'things to come'] (Dt. 32:35); AV "things that shall come"; [*'aḥ^a^rîṯ*] (Lam. 1:9); AV LAST END; NEB FATE; [*ṣ^e^pîrâ* (cf. Akk. *ṣappāru*–'destroy')] (Ezk. 7:7, 10); AV MORNING; **DOOMED** [Heb. *ḥērem*] (Isa. 34:5); AV CURSE; [hiphil of *ḥāram*] (Isa. 34:2); AV "hath utterly destroyed"; NEB "gives (them) over to destruction." In the seventeen other occurrences of "doom, doomed" the RSV is not rendering a Hebrew or Greek word but is supplying the word to offer a more intelligible translation; e.g., in Ezk. 30:3 the RSV gives "time of doom for the nations" for Heb. *'ēṯ gôyîm*, lit. "time of (the) nations" (AV "time of the heathen"; NEB "day of reckoning for the nations"), and in 30:9 the RSV gives "in day of Egypt's doom" for Heb. *b^e^yôm miṣrayîm* (AV lit. "in day of Egypt"; NEB "in Egypt's hour"). In Ps. 92:11 (MT 12) the RSV inserts "doom" where the AV supplies "my desire" and the NEB "downfall."

In the OT "doom" most frequently spells the end (in Lam. 1:9 *'aḥ^a^rîṯ* literally means "the end"; cf. Ezk. 7:5-9) of the existence of a nation on which Yahweh's punishment or judgment has fallen. Because Israel has been unfaithful to her covenant with Yahweh and has pursued other gods (Jer. 11:1ff.), Jeremiah preaches Israel's doom (v. 15). But the prophets also speak of Israel's deliverance and announce that the nations which acted as God's agents of destruction will also face their "hour" or "day of doom" (Ezk. 30:3, 10; Dt. 32:35).

"Doomed" means destined to a particular fate. One may be doomed to destruction (Ps. 92:7 [MT 8]), to captivity (Jer. 43:11) or to death (Rev. 11:5). Those defeated in "holy war" were "devoted" (i.e., offered as spoils of battle) to Yahweh (Isa. 34:2, 5) and thus were doomed to their death. *See* ACCURSED; DEVOTE.

In Hebrew, a person or nation destined or doomed to a certain fate is spoken of in a way which suggests that the fate is already an accomplished fact. "Those who are doomed to die" (Ps. 79:11; 102:20 [MT 21]) are literally "sons of death" (*b^e^nê ṯ^e^mûṯâ*), and "men doomed to death" (2 S. 19:28) are literally "men of death" (*'anšê-maweṯ*). The RSV frequently supplies the word "doomed" to make the Hebrew concept of fate intelligible to Western man, for whom fate is a future event.

E. W. CONRAD

DOOR [Heb. *peṯaḥ*] (Gen. 4:7; Ex. 12:22; Prov. 5:8; Cant. 7:13; etc.); AV also ENTRANCE, GATE; NEB also ENTRANCE, OPENING, GATEWAY, DOORWAY, GATE, etc.; [*deleṯ*] (Gen. 19:6; Dt. 15:17; 1 K. 6:34; etc.); AV, NEB, also GATE; [*dal*] (Ps. 141:3); [*ša'ar*] (Neh. 13:19; Ezk. 40:38); AV GATE; NEB GATE, OPENING; [*t^e^ra'*] (Dnl. 3:26); AV MOUTH; [Gk. *thýra*]

(Mt. 6:6; Jn. 18:16; 1 Cor. 16:9; etc.); NEB also ENTRANCE, GATE, "great opportunity," etc.; [*pýlē*] (Lk. 13:24); AV GATE; **DOORWAY** [Heb. *peṯaḥ*] (1 K. 7:5; 2 K. 4:15); AV DOOR.

In the OT the Heb. *peṯaḥ* is used to refer to the opening or outside entrance or doorway to a dwelling, while *deleṯ* is used for the "door," or that object which is used to close the opening. In the NT the Gk. *thýra* is used with both meanings (Mt. 6:6; 27:60).

The domestic doors of the tent homes in the nomadic period were nothing more than openings in the coarse cloth which were closed by an extra flap (Gen. 18:1; Nu. 11:10). When Israel was in Canaan the doors were usually made either of hardwood studded with nails or of stone, and they were often very heavy. They always opened inwardly and had on the inside strong bars and bolts for protection against intruders (Jgs. 19:26). The locks were of wood, consisting of "a slide attached to one of the folds which entered into a hole in the doorpost and was secured there by teeth cut into it, or catches" (MSt, II, *s.v.*; cf. 2 S. 13:17). The keys too were wooden, with key holes sometimes so large that the finger could be slipped in to lift up the slide, thus making the key unnecessary.

The doorways were often highly ornamented (the only part of the outside of the house that had any architectural attractiveness), and after the conquest of Canaan the people of Israel inscribed their doorposts with sentences of Scripture in accordance with the Mosaic law (Dt. 6:4-9; 11:13-21). The doorways had three parts: the threshold or sill (often translated "door" in the AV), which was particularly sacred; the two doorposts; and the lintel, the horizontal beam above the door (Ex. 12:7ff.). "Connected to the sill and the lintel were metal pivot sockets into which were fitted hinge pivots which allowed the door to swing" (*HDB*, p. 140).

Doors were often found in city gates; the term for "opening" or "entrance" in the wall (which could be either a single or double door) is sometimes translated "gate" when it actually refers to the door. The doors of the temple in Ezekiel's vision are fully described throughout his book (Ezk. 8:7; 10:19; 41:24; etc.), as are those of Solomon's temple in 1 K. 6:31-35; 7:50. *See* HOUSE III.C.

The NT uses *thýra* both literally and figuratively. A house door is mentioned in various places (Mt. 25:10; Mk. 1:33; Lk. 13:25; etc.), as well as the outer door which opened from the street into the courtyard (Jn. 18:16; Acts 12:13) and the door of a single room like a closet (Mt. 6:6). The doors of the prison were opened when the apostles were imprisoned there (Acts 5:19); and the great stone, which was placed at the entrance of a tomb to protect its contents from robbers and wild beasts, was rolled away from the opening on the first Easter morning (Mt. 27:60; 28:2; Mk. 15:46; 16:3f.).

"Door" is used figuratively in a number of ways. "At the door" indicates nearness, as when Peter told Sapphira after Ananias' death that "the feet of those who buried your husband are at the door" (Acts 5:9), and when the risen Christ stands at the door and knocks (Rev. 3:20). "Door" is also used for the entrance into the kingdom of heaven. The door shut by the householder is said to be "narrow" in Lk. 13:24 (*pýlē*, "gate"); and as a contrast to the Pauline metaphor of God's opening the "door of faith" (Acts 14:27) by which men enter the kingdom of God, Christ's full power both to open and to shut "the door" of the kingdom is seen. He has full authority in giving both grace and judgment (Rev. 3:7).

A further use of "door" is in referring to something made possible or feasible. Paul speaks of a "wide door for effective work" (1 Cor. 16:9); a "door for the word" (Col. 4:3); and of a door that "was opened for me in the Lord" (2 Cor. 2:12; cf. Hos. 2:15, which refers to a "door of hope"). All of these speak figuratively of the opportunities provided for the spread of the gospel.

In John's Gospel, Jesus refers to himself as "the door" (Jn. 10:9), certainly meaning the door for the sheep (*see* SHEEP III.F). He is the gate to salvation who "mediates membership of the Messianic community and reception of the promised blessings of salvation" (*TDNT*, III, 180; Jn. 10:7, 9).

Colloquially, a form of the verb *synomoréō*, "border on" or "adjoin," is used in Acts 18:7 to say that the house of Titius Justus was "next door" to the synagogue.

Bibliography.–E. F. Bishop, *Expos.T.*, 71 (1959/60), 307-309; R. E. Brown, *John 1-XII* (*AB*, 1966), pp. 393-95; *DCG*, I, 490-91; *HDB*, II, 434; *TDNT*, III, *s.v.* θύρα (J. Jeremias).

D. K. MCKIM

DOORKEEPER. *See* GATEKEEPER.

DOORPOST. *See* HOUSE III.

DOPHKAH dof'kə [Heb. *dopqâ*]. A desert camp of the Israelites, their first after leaving the Wilderness of Sin (Nu. 33:12f.). *See* WANDERINGS OF ISRAEL.

DOR dôr [Heb. *dō'r*–'habitation,' 'circle'; Gk. *Dōr*; Josephus, *Dōra*]; AV Apoc. DORA. A city on the Mediterranean seacoast S of Mt. Carmel, probably the same as Naphath-Dor (Josh. 12:13; 1 K. 4:11) and Naphoth-Dor (Josh. 11:2). The modern site of Dor is a small harbor town 15 mi. (25 km.) S of Haifa, near to which excavations were conducted by the British School of Archaeology in 1923/24.

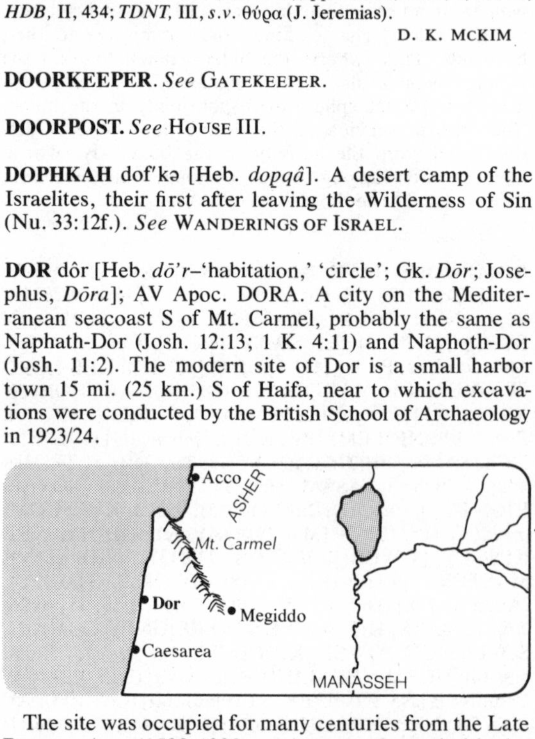

The site was occupied for many centuries from the Late Bronze Age (1500-1200 B.C.) onward, probably by Canaanites. The sea in the area furnished an abundant supply of the molluscs used in the manufacture of Tyrian purple dye, and the territory seems to have been occupied by the Phoenicians early in the Late Bronze Age. Sporadic raids were made there in the 12th cent. B.C. by an aggressive maritime group from the Aegean, whose antecedents had made periodic incursions into Palestine as early as the patriarchal period. These people, who were later known as the Philistines, raided the entire coast of Syria and penetrated as far S as the Egyptian border before being halted. Some Philistines settled in the coastal regions S of Carmel and occupied Dor. Although on the borders of Asher, Dor was given to the tribe of Manasseh, which failed to expel the native population (Jgs. 1:27; cf. 1 K. 4:11; 1 Ch. 7:29). It was governed by a king who was a member of the military coalition defeated by Joshua (Josh. 11:2), although for reasons not stated the town was not immediately occupied by the Israelites (Josh. 17:11).

In the eleventh-century B.C. story of Wen-Amon, an

Egyptian emissary sent to Phoenicia to obtain cedar wood for the sacred barge of the Egyptian god Re, Dor was described as "a town of the Ṯeker." These people probably migrated with the Philistines in the 12th cent. B.C. It was probably because the Sidonians were attempting to gain control over the rich supplies of shellfish that the Philistines, under the lead of Ashkelon, fought against Sidon in the middle of the 11th cent. B.C. Sidon was besieged by land, and its inhabitants fled to Tyre. Dor was subsequently controlled by Solomon (1 K. 4:11), and was reduced by Tiglath-pileser III. Here Trypho was besieged by Antiochus Sidetes (139-129 B.C.), but escaped to Apamea (1 Macc. 15:11, 13, 25). It was granted autonomy by Pompey in 64 B.C., and in Greco-Roman times was called Dora.

Bibliography.–G. Dahl, *Transactions of the Connecticut Academy of Arts and Sciences*, 20 (1915), 1-131; W. F. Albright, *JPOS*, 5 (1925), 31f. R. K. HARRISON

DORCAS dôr'kəs [Gk. *Dorkás*, the Greek equivalent of Aram. *ṭeḇîṯā'*–'gazelle']. The name of a Christian woman of Joppa. Dorcas is called a disciple (*mathḗtria*, Acts 9:36, the only NT use of the fem. form). She seems to have had some means and to have been a leader in the Christian community. She was beloved for the manner in which she used her position and means, for she "was full of good works and acts of charity." Among her charitable deeds was the clothing of the poor with garments she herself made (v. 39). By following her example, numerous "Dorcas societies" in the Christian Church perpetuate her memory.

The book of Acts records her restoration to life by Peter. At the time of her death Peter was in Lydda, where he had healed Aeneas. Having been sent for, he went to Joppa and, by the exercise of the supernatural powers granted him, "he presented her alive" to the mourning community. In consequence of this miracle "many believed in the Lord" (vv. 41-43).

S. F. HUNTER

DORYMENES dôr-im'ə-nēz [Gk. *Dorymênēs*]. Father of Ptolemy Macron (1 Macc. 3:38; 2 Macc. 4:45); probably the same man who fought against Antiochus the Great (Polybius v.61).

DOSITHEUS dō-sith'ē-əs [Gk. *Dosítheos*].

1. A captain of Judas Maccabeus (2 Macc. 12:19-25); along with Sosipater he captured Timothy after the battle of Carnion, but granted him his life and freedom because Timothy led them to believe that "he held the parents of most of them and the brothers of some and no consideration would be shown them" if they proceeded to put him to death.

2. A soldier in the army of Judas Maccabeus (2 Macc. 12:35). He made a special attack upon Gorgias, governor of Idumea, the opposing general, and would have taken the "accursed man" prisoner but for the interference of a Thracian horseman.

3. A Jew, son of Drimylus (3 Macc. 1:3), who rescued Ptolemy Philopator from a plot of Theodotus. He afterward proved an apostate from Judaism.

4. A Levite priest who "in the fourth year of the reign of Ptolemy and Cleopatra" carried the translation of the book of Esther to Alexandria (Ad. Est. 11:1).

J. HUTCHISON

DOSITHEUS, APOCALYPSE OF. A tractate in the Nag Hammadi library now usually known as "The Three Steles of Seth." *See* NAG HAMMADI LITERATURE.

DOT [Gk. *keraía*] (Mt. 5:18; Lk. 16:17); AV TITTLE; NEB STROKE. A minute stroke or mark. The Greek means literally "horn" or "projection" as part of a letter. It could designate a distinguishing mark, e.g., an accent, a diacritical mark, or a breathing mark; or it could denote an ornamentation. In both of the above passages, it represents something very insignificant.

DOTE [Heb. *'āgaḇ*] (Ezk. 23:5, 7, 9, 12, 16, 20); NEB BE INFATUATED, LUST; **DOTING** [Heb. *'agāḇâ* (Ezk. 23:11); AV LOVE; NEB LUST. In Ezk. 23 "dote" is employed in the sense of "desire" or "lust after." In the AV of Jer. 50:36 the same term is used in the obsolete sense of "be weakminded" or "become a fool."

DOTHAIM dō'thā-əm. Mentioned in the AV of Jth. 4:6 and frequently in connection with the invasion of Holofernes. *See* DOTHAN.

DOTHAN dō'thən [Heb. *dōṯayin, dōṯān*; Gk. *Dōthaeim*]; AV Apoc. DOTHAIM dō'thā-əm. In Gen. 37:17-28, the place where Joseph found his brothers, who were pasturing their flocks in the area. They put Joseph in a pit and later sold him to a passing caravan of Ishmaelites. The prophet Elisha lived at Dothan when the king of Syria sought to take him because he was revealing the secret movements of the Syrian army (2 K. 6:13f.).

Dothan also appears in nonbiblical literary sources: Thutmose III, king of Egypt, records the taking of tribute (*ca.* 1480 B.C.) from a place he lists as Tutayana, first identified by Maspero as biblical Dothan. Dothan is also mentioned by Eusebius (*Onom.* 76.13), and appears three times in the book of Judith (3:9; 4:6; 7:3).

The modern site of Tell Dôthā was recognized as biblical Dothan by Van de Velde in 1851 (*GP*, II, 308). By modern road it is 60 mi. (95 km.) N of Jerusalem. The mound now stands nearly 200 ft. (60 m.) above the surrounding fertile plain, with nearly 50 ft. (15 m.) of archeological stratification superimposed on an original natural hill some 150 ft. (45 m.) high. The top of the mound is about 10 acres (4 hectares) in area, and the slopes include another 15 acres (6 hectares).

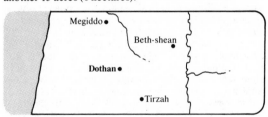

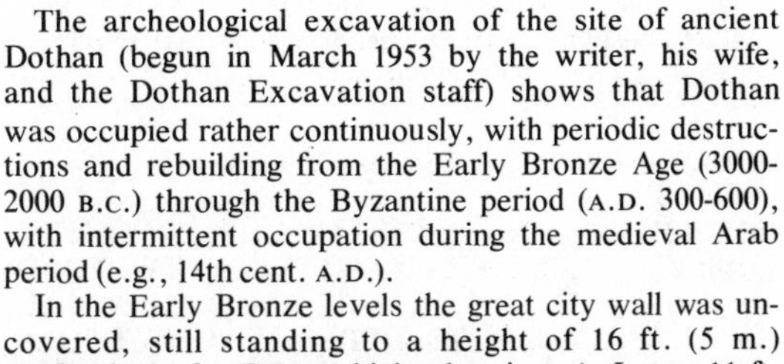

The archeological excavation of the site of ancient Dothan (begun in March 1953 by the writer, his wife, and the Dothan Excavation staff) shows that Dothan was occupied rather continuously, with periodic destructions and rebuilding from the Early Bronze Age (3000-2000 B.C.) through the Byzantine period (A.D. 300-600), with intermittent occupation during the medieval Arab period (e.g., 14th cent. A.D.).

In the Early Bronze levels the great city wall was uncovered, still standing to a height of 16 ft. (5 m.) (probably 25 ft. [7.5 m.] high when intact). It was 11 ft. (3.5 m.) thick at the base, and 9 ft. (3 m.) thick at the top.

From the Middle Bronze period (2000-1600 B.C.) there was uncovered a staircase some 13 ft. wide, of which eighteen steps were revealed before coming to the edge of the excavation property. The stairs led up to the gateway area in the city wall.

Bridging the Middle Bronze and the Late Bronze period (1600-1200 B.C.) was a citadel just inside the great city wall. Ten rooms were uncovered with walls 4 ft. (1.2 m.) thick, representing a structure built for a last-ditch defense in case an assault against the city gate succeeded.

On the west slope of the mound a tomb was discovered, which was in use from *ca.* 1300 B.C. (or a little earlier) to *ca.* 1100 B.C., bridging the end of Late Bronze (1600-1200 B.C.) and the beginning of Iron I (1200-1000 B.C.). Over 3200 pottery objects were taken from the tomb — craters, ring-flasks, "milkbowls," chalices; pyxides (small squat jugs) and lamps (nearly 600 of each); seven-spouted lamps, funnels, jewelry, beads, and a host of other objects including a bronze lamp in the shape of a pottery lamp. Several dozen bronze spear points and bronze daggers, along with bone carved objects, brought the grand total of objects in the tomb including pottery to more than 3400. It was evidently a family tomb, in use for 200 to 300 years, and was the recipient of some 600 burials during that time. It was nearly circular in shape, with an approximate diameter of about 30 ft. (9 m.).

In the Iron II period (1000-600 B.C., time of the biblical kings), a well-built administrative building of the days of Solomon (950 B.C.) was uncovered. A paved courtyard, drains, and well-squared building stones characterized the structure. One small room contained 96 storage jars, all the same size; apparently for measuring standard amounts (possibly tax payments). Evidence of the Assyrian invasion (2 K. 17:5f.) and domination, *ca.* 725 B.C., was afforded by the appearance in the excavation of Assyrian palace bowls in the level shortly before 700 B.C.

Hellenistic (300-50 B.C.), Roman (50 B.C.–A.D. 300), and Byzantine (i.e., late Roman, A.D. 300-600) levels have been uncovered on the higher part of the top of the mound, and surmounting them all, a medieval fortress-palace of the 14th cent. A.D., 25 rooms of which were uncovered, with indications of a total of 150 rooms.

It was the view of the older school of criticism (Wellhausen and successors) that the concept of a sevenfold light, ascribed to the tabernacle, was a late idea (600 B.C.), hundreds of years after the time of Moses and the tabernacle. The discovery at Dothan (and other sites) of several seven-spouted lamps has shown that this concept was not restricted to a late period, but already appeared by 1200 B.C. or earlier, fitting into the biblical implication of the concept of a sevenfold light in the days of the tabernacle.

In summary, the successive levels at Dothan have illuminated every main period of biblical history beginning with 3000 B.C. and running through the NT period.

Bibliography.–J. P. Free, *BASOR*, 131 (Oct. 1953), 16-29; 135 (Oct. 1954), 14-20; 139 (Oct. 1955), 3-9; 143 (Oct. 1956), 11-17; 152 (Dec. 1958), 18; 156 (Dec. 1959), 22-29; 160 (Dec. 1960), 6-14; *BA*, 19 (1956), 43-48; D. Ussishkin, in M. Avi-Yonah, ed., *Encyclopedia of Archaeological Excavations in the Holy Land* (1975), I, 337-39.

J. P. FREE

DOUAY VERSION. *See* ENGLISH VERSIONS IV.

DOUBLE [Heb. *mišneh*] (Gen. 43:12, 15; Isa. 61:7; Jer. 17:18; Zec. 9:12); NEB also UTTERLY, TWOFOLD; [*šnayim*] (Ex. 22:4, 7, 9; Dt. 21:17; 2 K. 2:9; Ezk. 41:23; Hos. 10:10); AV also TWO; NEB also TWO, TWOFOLD; [*kāpal*] (Ex. 26:9; 28:16; 39:9); NEB also FOLDED; [*kepel*] (Job 41:13; Isa. 40:2); NEB also DOUBLET; [Gk. *deúteros*] (2 Cor. 1:15); AV SECOND; [*diploús*] (1 Tim. 5:17; Rev. 18:6); NEB also TWICE; **DOUBLING** [Heb. *šānâ*] (Gen. 41:32); **DOUBLY** [Heb. *mišneh*] (Jer. 16:18); NEB "in full."

"Double" is used quite frequently in the OT. The Hebrew verb *šānâ*, on which the nouns *šnayim* ("two") and *mišneh* ("double," "second," "copy") are based, means "repeat." The verb *kāpal* (cf. noun *kepel*) means "fold" or "double over." Jacob ordered his sons to take double money in their hands, i.e., twice the necessary amount (Gen. 43:12, 15). If a thief was caught with a living animal he was to restore double (Ex. 22:4); if property was stolen out of the house of one to whom it was entrusted he was to restore double (Ex. 22:7, 9). The firstborn was to receive a double portion of the inheritance (Dt. 21:17). Likewise also Elisha asked for a double portion of Elijah's spirit to fall upon him (2 K. 2:9). Degrees of punishment or sufferings were also expressed by the idea of a doubling (Isa. 61:7; Jer. 16:18; 17:18; Zec. 9:12).

The use of *kepel* in Job 11:6 presents some problems in translation. The AV translates simply "double," while the RSV attempts to derive more meaning from the passage with "manifold" and the NEB with "wonderful" (perhaps emending the text to read *p^elā'îm*). M. H. Pope renders the line, "For there are two sides to wisdom," and comments, "We take the sense to be that God knows both sides of every matter, the manifest as well as the hidden, and it is the hidden side that he would reveal if he were to speak to Job's challenge" (*Job* [*AB*, 1965], pp. 80, 82).

N. J. O.

DOUBLE MIND; DOUBLE-MINDED [Heb. *sē'ēp*] (Ps. 119:113); AV VAIN THOUGHTS; NEB NOT SINGLE-MINDED; [Gk. *dípsychos*] (Jas. 1:8; 4:8); **DOUBLE HEART** [Heb. *lēḇ wālēḇ*] (Ps. 12:2 [MT 3]). A term denoting a lack of integration within the personality, characterized by doubt, hesitancy, instability, and divided loyalty. This is seen, for example, in 1 K. 18:21 where *sē'^apîm* is used in Elijah's challenge to the faltering Israelites on Mt. Carmel: "How long will you go limping with two different opinions? If the LORD is God, follow him; but if Baal, then follow him."

The Gk. *dípsychos* (lit. "double-souled") occurs only twice in the NT (Jas. 1:8; 4:8), and the fact that it is not used in secular Greek or in the LXX has led a number of NT scholars to believe that James coined the term himself. Whether or not this be the case, the term was quickly adopted by subsequent writers and occurs frequently in certain of the early church fathers (esp. Shep. Herm.). In Jas. 1:8 it has to do with wavering in prayer, a failure to turn one's whole mind toward God in single-hearted devotion and trust. As an inevitable consequence, such a man is "unstable in all his ways." In Jas. 4:8 the term is used of one who is vacillating between loyalty to God and friendship with the world (4:4). He is trying to serve two masters, an impossible pursuit (cf. Mt. 6:24). The stinging parallel between "you sinners" and "you men of double mind" in Jas. 4:8 is very explicit. In direct contrast to the sin of double-mindedness, "single-mindedness" is often the subject of commendation in the NT (e.g., Mt. 6:22; Acts 2:46; Eph. 6:5).

See also DOUBT.

In Ps. 12 the Psalmist complains about the ungodly who speak "with flattering lips and a double heart" (lit. "a heart and a heart"; *see* DIVERSE), referring to those whose speech is characterized by insincerity and deceit.

Bibliography.–*TDNT*, IX, *s.v.* ψυχή κτλ.: δίψυχος (Schweizer); J. H. Ropes, *James* (*ICC*, 1916), pp. 142-44.

A. J. BIRKEY

DOUBLE-TONGUED [Gk. *dílogos*] (1 Tim. 3:8); NEB DOUBLE TALK. The literal meaning of *dílogos* is "saying the same thing twice," but it is very unlikely that deacons would be barred from such innocent activity. The more probable meaning of this use of the term is the saying of a thing to one person and then saying it differently to another. It may be described otherwise as "talking out of both sides of one's mouth." The ever-present temptation to tailor the truth to fit the hearer confronts every believer, but is particularly devastating when practiced by the deacon who is engaged in a constant cycle of visitation. Such an insincere practice borders on hypocrisy and should find no place in the Christian community. James gives ample warning regarding the destructive potential of an unbridled tongue (1:26; 3:1-12).

A. J. BIRKEY

DOUBT [Heb. *ṭārōp̄ ṭōrap̄*] ("without doubt [torn to pieces]," Gen. 37:33); omitted in NEB; [*tālā'*] (Dt. 28:66); NEB SUSPENSE; [*'omnām*] ("no doubt," Job 12:2); [Gk. *distázō*] (Mt. 14:31; 28:17); NEB BE DOUBTFUL, HESITATE; [*diakrínō*] (Mt. 21:21; Mk. 11:23; Rom. 14:23; Jas. 1:6; Jude 22); AV also WAVER, "making a difference"; NEB also DOUBTER; [*pántōs*] ("no doubt," Acts 28:4); NEB "must be"; **DOUBTLESS** [Gk. *pántōs*] (Lk. 4:23); AV SURELY; NEB NO DOUBT; [*ei týchoi*] (1 Cor. 14:10); AV, NEB, "may be."

The NT sense of "to doubt" reflects man's dividedness of attitude when confronted with a promise of God. It occurs within the context of prayer and action, at times when God's word itself is what is being questioned.

When Peter began to sink as he walked on the water toward Jesus, Jesus asked him why he doubted (*distázō*, Mt. 14:31). The disciples were told by Jesus that if when they prayed they would "never doubt" but would "have faith," a mountain could be "taken up and cast into the sea" (Mt. 21:21; Mk. 11:23). The verb used (*diakrínō*) literally means "make a distinction" (Bauer, p. 184) and has the further sense of "judge between two" (*TDNT*, III, 946). In its NT figurative sense it is used for being divided or "at odds with oneself." In these instances the man has the word of Christ as authority, but still "thinks it impossible or at least not certain that what he says should be done" (*TDNT*, III, 947). He believes, yet somehow he does not believe. Jesus saw this attitude as the opposite of true faith.

For the people of Israel the result of disobedience to the law of God was that "your life shall hang in doubt before you" (Dt. 28:66). The term *tālā'*, "hang up," emphasizes the suspense that arises from doubt.

The AV uses "doubt" in the obsolete sense of being at a loss or greatly perplexed, to render Gk. *diaporéō* (Acts 2:12; 5:24; 10:17).

See *TDNT*, III, *s.v.* διακρίνω (Büchsel).

D. K. McKIM

DOUGH. *See* BREAD.

DOVE [Heb. *yônâ*, *tôr*–'turtledove' (Ps. 74:19); Gk. *peristerá*]; AV also TURTLEDOVE (*tôr*); NEB also PIGEON. The usual meaning of the Hebrew and Greek terms is "dove" or "(young) pigeon."

I. In Antiquity.–The wild pigeon was domesticated (*Columba domestica*) in early historic if not prehistoric times. Pictures of domesticated house pigeons appear on pre-Semitic Sumerian monuments and a terracotta dove (*ca.* 4500 B.C.) has been discovered in Mesopotamia. The "rock dove" (*Columba livia*), found throughout much of the Orient, North Africa, and Europe, is considered to be the parent of the various domesticated species. The earliest evidence for the use of the dove as food comes from the 4th Dynasty of Egypt (*ca.* 2500 B.C.). The Greeks apparently domesticated doves later than the inhabitants of the Fertile Crescent but prior to 492 B.C., when, according to Charon of Lampsacus, the white house pigeon came to Greece from the Orient from the destruction of a Persian fleet off Cape Athos (Athenaeus *Deipnosophistae* ix [394]). It is assumed that Semitic sailors were carrying the breed — closely linked to the Babylonian and Assyrian cults of Ishtar — for religious purposes, for the Persians themselves hated the dove.

From very early times the dove was a bird of the gods. First found at Knossos in Crete and Mycenae in the Peloponnesus in the 2nd millennium, the dove-goddess later appeared in Etruria, Sicily, Carthage, and Phoenicia. The Cypriote Aphrodite was portrayed as a dove-goddess on many coins. In ancient Greece the dove was a bird of the gods; coins from Phaistos, Crete, depict Zeus with a dove, and legend tells of doves at the Zeus oracle in Dodona. Male and more frequently female deities are associated with doves (Werth, pp. 273ff.).

Some scholars have attempted to connect directly the dove-goddess of Ashkelon and the legendary Assyrian queen Semiramis (*Sammu-râmat*) who was fed by doves when found by shepherds. They argue that the first element of her name, i.e., *sammu*, was a derived from an infrequently used Akkadian name for dove, *summu*, thus providing evidence for the origin of the dove attributes of the goddess Aphrodite of Ashkelon in the eastern dove cult of Ishtar-Astarte; from Ashkelon the cult moved west. The linguistic argument is questionable, and archeological evidence from Crete and Mycenae demonstrates conclusively that Aphrodite was known and worshiped as a dove-goddess in pre-Homeric times. Apparently the Phoenicians brought the dove cult west in early times, introducing it in Sicily.

A number of scholars (Gressmann, Sühling, etc.) have collected considerable material concerning the dove as a bird of the soul. Egyptian literature and reliefs depict the dove bringing the soul to man from an unknown location and carrying it back after death. Ample evidence for the dove's soul-bird aspects is also available from Greek and Roman materials. The so-called *columbaria*, caves adapted for the purpose of housing doves in cemeteries, are undoubtedly to be connected with soul-bird concepts, as are the dovecotes that were erected as monuments. Roman dovecotes are known that housed as many as five thousand birds.

In a number of literary ways ancient man has reflected intimate knowledge of the dove gained through careful observation. In both Greece and Rome the affection of the dove had become proverbial. The bringing together of the heads in courtship and the practice of one dove taking the other's beak in its own has been likened to human kissing. The cooing of the turtledove was applied to women's chit-chat and, more negatively, to the bewailing of one's misfortune (Pliny *Nat. hist.* xxviii. 68 [267]). The dove was used as a symbol of chastity in ancient Greece (Aristotle *Historia animalium* ix.6 [Academia Regia Borussica ed., p. 612]; Pliny *Nat. hist.* x.52 [104]). Various Greek terms for dove (*peristerá, phássa, pháttion, pérdix*) were employed as expressions of endearment.

II. In the OT.–Among all the birds in the Bible the dove is the most important. Although several species of doves and pigeons of a subfamily of birds (*Columbinae*) are found in Palestine, Hebrew has a distinct term for only one of these species, the "turtledove" (*tôr*) of the genus *Stretopelia turtur* (cf. Bodenheimer, pp. 171ff.). The "turtledove" appears frequently in a sacrificial or cultic role. It serves as a burnt offering (Lev. 1:14) or guilt offering (5:7, 11); it has a part in the ritual of purification for a woman after childbirth (12:6, 8), for a healed leper (14:22, 30), and for a person who has been cleansed of bodily discharge (15:14, 29). A Nazirite who has defiled himself may cleanse himself either by offering "turtledoves" (*tôr*) or "young pigeons" (*yônâ*, Nu. 6:10). The "turtledove is a migratory bird that keeps the time of return (Jer. 8:7), and its voice is the harbinger of springtime (Cant. 2:12).

The term "dove" (*yônâ*) means literally "moaner" (from Heb. *'ānâ*, "moan," Isa. 3:26; 19:8), hence the common expression to "moan like a dove [*yônâ*]" (Isa. 38:14; 59:11; Nah. 2:7 [MT 8]). The scientific generic name *Turtur* (Lat.) for the "turtledove" derives from the bird's call, perhaps through its similar Hebrew and Akkadian names (*tôr, tūrtu*). The term *yônâ* is a general designation for various species of doves and pigeons that are more or less permanent residents in the area. Certain species of the *yônâ* family nests in the clefts of the rocks and recesses of the cliffs (Cant. 2:14; Jer. 48:28; Ezk. 7:16) and may belong to the species of "rock dove" (*Columba livia*), domesticated in antiquity and used widely both as a source of food and as a message-carrier. The "dovecotes" (Heb. *'ᵃrubbâ*) of Isa. 60:8 (NEB; AV, RSV, "windows") may refer to those natural apertures in cliffs or the pigeon holes of houses in which domesticated doves were kept. The term *yônâ* is usually translated "dove," except in the sacrificial and cultic passages of the Pentateuch, where it is rendered "young pigeon" (Lev. 1:14; 5:7, 11; 12:6, 8; 14:22, 30; 15:14, 29; Nu. 6:10).

The earliest mention of "dove" (*yônâ*) in the OT is in connection with the flood story, where Noah releases three doves in seven-day intervals after he had released a raven (Gen. 8:8-12). The relationship between the biblical flood story and that of the Gilgamesh Epic has long been noted. In the Babylonian flood story the hero Utnapishtim likewise sent out birds, first a dove and then a swallow, which was followed by a raven (*ANET*, pp. 94f.; *DOTT*, p. 22). Despite striking similarities in these bird episodes, the Hebrew and the Babylonian flood stories differ decidedly in detail. Noah sent out three doves after first sending out a raven; Utnapishtim sent out only one dove and it was the first bird. The types of birds, sequence, intervals, and number of attempts find no parallel in the respective narratives. The biblical writer vividly describes the first dove's disappointing return. The second dove brings a fresh olive leaf, the symbol of new life; the dove itself is here a symbolic harbinger of renewed life. The third dove does not return, a sign that the earth is again in a habitable state.

Various aspects of the dove symbolism occur in the OT. The psalmist laments the distress caused by his enemies, wishing to escape like a dove and be at rest (Ps. 55:6 [MT 7]). He knows that the most effective defense of the "dove," or Israel, against the "vulture," or ferocious foe, is Yahweh Himself (Ps. 74:19). The iridescent silvery and golden sheen of dove feathers seems to symbolize the cloud in which Yahweh was present in the early days of Israel's existence (Ps. 68:14 [MT 13]). The prophet Hosea compares the dove's silliness and senselessness with that of the northern kingdom (7:11), which is as easily caught as the dove. The bird's homing instinct and speed is symbolic of the return to Yahweh of scattered Israel (Hos. 11:11). The return of the doves to their dovecotes symbolizes the eschatological coming of the nations to Zion (Isa. 60:8). Jeremiah counsels Moab to dwell in places hard to reach, like doves that nest out of reach (48:28), and Ezekiel speaks of Judah fleeing to the mountains like doves of the valleys (7:16). In the OT the term *yônâ* is employed as a term of endearment only in Canticles (2:14; 5:2; 6:9); twice the eyes of the beloved are called doves (Cant. 1:15; 4:1), and symbols of purity, gentleness, simplicity, and longing. In Cant. 5:12 the eyes of the lover are compared to doves, perhaps symbolizing sparkling brightness (Dalman, VII, 264) or keen alertness.

The "dove's dung" (RSV) of 2 K. 6:25 (Heb. *diḇyōnîm*) is variously translated (NEB "locust beans"; NAB "wild onion"). It may be a substitute for salt (cf. Josephus *Ant.* ix.4.4) or more likely a botanical term for some vegetable food. The Arabs know a plant called *bara' al-ḥamām* ("doves' dung"), and the analogy of Arabic *ḥarwu 'l- 'aṣāfīr* ("sparrow's dung") suggests strongly that the biblical phrase refers to some vegetable (plant) food. The term *yônâ* ("dove") in the superscription of Ps. 56 remains a problem of interpretation.

The word "dove" appears in two biblical names. The name of the prophet Jonah means "dove." Job's daughter is called Jemimah (Job 42:14), which in its Hebrew form *yᵉmîmâ* is related to the cognate Arab. *yamâmatu(n)*, "dove, pigeon" (Driver, p. 130).

III. In the NT.–Doves play a significant role at various occasions in the Gospels. Jesus' parents followed the levitical stipulation (Lev. 12:6-8) in bringing for their purification (v. 22) a sacrifice of "a pair of turtledoves, or two young pigeons" (Lk. 2:24), a specification based on the LXX; the Hebrew text reads that one could offer "two *tōrîm* or two *bᵉnê-yônâ*" (Lev. 12:8), which means more properly "two turtledoves or any other two birds of the pigeon species." Had Jesus' parents been more prosperous, they would have sacrificed a lamb for a burnt offering (Lev. 12:6). Instead they brought the offering of the poor (SB, II, 123f.).

The story of Jesus' baptism relates that the "Spirit of God" (Mt. 3:16) or "Holy Spirit" (Lk. 3:22) or simply "Spirit" (Mk. 1:10; cf. Jn. 1:32f.; Acts 10:19; 11:12; Rom. 8:16, 26f.; etc.) descended upon Jesus "in bodily form" (Lk. 3:22) "as a dove" (Gk. *hōs peristerán*, Mt. 3:16; Mk. 1:10; Lk. 3:22). In the Fourth Gospel John the Baptist is himself an eyewitness to the manifestation of the "Spirit descending as (like) a dove from heaven" (Jn. 1:32). The common suggestion that *hōs peristerán* refers to the manner of descent rather than to the Holy Spirit's form is to be rejected, as is the supposition that this was merely a visionary and not a real experience. The comparison of the Holy Spirit to a dove seems to reflect Gen. 1:2, where the Spirit of God broods over the waters. Rabbi Ben Zoma, a younger contemporary of the apostles, quotes the rabbinic tradition that "the Spirit of God was brooding on the face of the waters like a dove which broods over her young but does not touch them" (T.B. *Hagigah* 15a). The Evangelists' emphasis on the Holy Spirit's descent on Jesus in the shape or form of a dove, perhaps similar to the tongues of fire at Pentecost (Acts 2:3), marked Him out as God's unique instrument, the Messiah and the Servant of the Lord (Isa. 11:2f.), whose activity would create new life and order in the hearts and lives of men.

The dove appears as a symbol of guilelessness and innocence in the proverb of Jesus that characterizes the nature of His disciples in their mission: "be wise as serpents and innocent as doves" (Mt. 10:16). Jesus' disciples need all the wisdom proverbially attributed to serpents, but deceitful cunning and treacherous guile are to be replaced by the harmless and gentle innocence attributed to doves.

The narratives of the cleansing of the temple contain the remaining NT references to the dove. Jesus drove away the merchants among whom were those who sold doves (Mt. 21:12; Mk. 11:15; Jn. 21:14, 16), overturning their seats (Mk. 11:15). The doves (or pigeons) were needed in large quantities, for they were the poor man's sacrifice.

Bibliography.–Pauly-Wissowa, IV A/2, 2479-2500; H. Gressmann, *Archiv für Religionswissenschaft,* 20 (1920/21), 1-40, 323-359; F. Sühling, *Römische Quartalschrift, Supp.-Heft,* 24 (1930); *RGG* (2nd ed.), V, *s.v.* "Taube" (K. Galling); F. S. Bodenheimer, *Animal Life in Palestine* (1935); E. Werth, *Sitzungsberichte der Gesellschaft naturforschender Freunde zu Berlin* (1935), 273-283; G. Dalman, *Arbeit und Sitte in Palästina* (1928-1939), VII, 256-290; *RGG* (3rd ed.), V, *s.v.* "Taube" (K. Goldammer); *TDNT,* VI, *s.v.* περιστερά (H. Greeven); G. R. Driver, *PEQ,* 86 (1954), 5-20; 87 (1955), 129-140; A. Parmelee, *All the Birds of the Bible* (1959); G. Cansdale, *Animals of the Bible* (1970), pp. 169-173.

G. F. HASEL

DOWRY [Heb. *zeḇeḏ*] (Gen. 30:20); [*šillûḥîm*] (1 K. 9:16); AV PRESENT; NEB MARRIAGE GIFT; **MARRIAGE PRESENT** [Heb. *mōhar* (Gen. 34:12; Ex. 22:17; 1 S. 18:25), *māhar* (Ex. 22:16)]; AV DOWRY, ENDOW (Ex. 22-16); NEB BRIDE-PRICE. "Dowry" generally refers to the gift that a bride brought to marriage. When Leah gave birth to her sixth son she regarded herself as possessing a good dowry (Gen. 30:20). In 1 K. 9:16 the term *šillûḥîm* designates the dowry given by a father to his daughter as she was about to marry. In this instance the gift was a city, given by the pharaoh when his daughter married Solomon (cf. a similar gift of property, Josh. 15:18f. par. Jgs. 1:14f.). Sometimes the bride's father gave her servants as a dowry (Gen. 24:61; 29:24, 29).

The groom also brought a gift, the *mōhar* (AV "dowry"; RSV "marriage present"; NEB "bride-price"), which was paid to the bride's father as compensation for the loss of a daughter. This "marriage present" was very important, for it sealed the betrothal (cf. Ex. 22:17). The size of this gift was based on the social standing of the bride (cf. 1 S. 18:23). Often this exchange was the subject of negotiation, as with Shechem, who in bargaining for Dinah was prepared to pay whatever Jacob demanded (Gen. 34:12). The gift could consist of services rendered (Gen. 29:18; cf. Ex. 3:1) or deeds of valor (cf. Josh. 15:16; 1 S. 18:25) instead of money or property. Some have concluded that the *mōhar* designated the price of the bride and that marriage therefore was simply by purchase; however, among the Jews a wife was not purchased like a slave, as is indicated by the fact that she could own her own property (cf. Josh. 15:18f. par. Jgs. 1:14f.). In later Jewish history a written marriage contract specified the size and nature of the marriage present.

See also MARRIAGE. R. K. H.

DOXOLOGY [Gk. *doxología,* from *dóxa*–'praise, honor, glory' and *lógos*–'utterance']. A brief expression of praise, primarily to God or to other members of the trinity.

The basic form is the blessing formula "Blessed be the Lord" or "Blessed be the God and Father . . ." (Heb. *bārûḵ*; Gk. *eulogētós*; Gen. 24:27; Ex. 18:10; 1 Ch. 16:36; Lk. 1:68; 2 Cor. 1:3f.; Eph. 1:3; 1 Pet. 1:3; etc.), followed by a statement of the attributes motivating the utterance, primarily God's activities in the lives of His people. Variants are "Worthy is the Lamb" (Gk. *áxios,* Rev. 4:11; 5:9, 12) and "Holy, holy, holy is the Lord God Almighty" (Gk. *hágios,* Rev. 4:8). *See* BLESS.

Doxologies may begin with an imperative verb, exhorting the hearers to "ascribe to the Lord glory and strength" or "the glory of his name" (Heb. *yāhaḇ*; Ps. 29:1f. par. 96:7-9; 1 Ch. 16:28f.; cf. Bar. 2:18) or "ascribe power" (Ps. 68:34 [MT 35]), "praise the Lord" (Heb. *hālal,* (Ps. 150; cf. Gk. *ainéō,* Rev. 19:5), "worship the Lord" (hithpalel of *šāḥâ*; Ps. 29:2), or "glory in his holy name" (hithpael of *hālal*; 1 Ch. 16:10). Among the qualities thus attributed to God (frequently using only the phrase "to him be") are glory (Rom. 16:27; Gal. 1:5), honor, dominion (1 Tim. 6:16; 1 Pet. 4:11), salvation, power (Rev. 19:1), majesty, and authority (Jude 25; cf. 1 Clem. 61). Such blessings are "for ever" (Rom. 11:36) or "for ever and ever" (2 Tim. 4:18; 1 Pet. 5:11; cf. 4 Macc. 18:24). In the NT doxologies may begin with exclamations of "Hallelujah" (Rev. 19:1), "Glory to God in the highest" (Lk. 2:14), or "Hosanna to the Son of David" (Mt. 21:9, 15; Mk. 11:9f.; Jn. 12:13; *see* HOSANNA).

Although God is the primary focus of NT doxologies, other objects of praise include Christ (Mt. 21:9; Rev. 5:12) and the kingdom of God (Mk. 11:10). A frequent Christological doxology exclaims "Blessed is he [or the King] who comes in the name of the Lord" (Mt. 21:9; 23:39; Mk. 11:9; Lk. 19:38; cf. Ps. 118:26). To Him are ascribed salvation and power (Rev. 19:1), blessing and might (Rev. 5:18), glory (He. 13:21), and dominion (Rev. 1:6) "both now and to the day of eternity" (2 Pet. 3:18). Blessings are frequently offered to God "through Jesus Christ" (Rom. 16:27; He. 13:21; Jude 25; cf. 1 Clem. 61:3) or "in Christ" (Eph. 1:3; 3:21).

Only rarely are the doxologies expressed in the second person, as "Blessed art thou" and "thine" is the greatness, power, glory, victory, and majesty (1 Ch. 29:11f.). Following this prayer of David, some NT MSS and the Didache add to the Lord's Prayer the doxology "For thine is the kingdom and the power and the glory, for ever. Amen" (Mt. 6:13 mg.; Did. 8:2; 9–10. *See* LORD'S PRAYER). Cf. Pr. Man. 15, "sings thy praise"; 1 Clem. 61:3, "O Thou . . . , glory and majesty to thee."

Originally doxologies were voiced by the congregation at the conclusion of hymns and prayers (1 Ch. 16:36; Rom. 11:33-36), in connection with the response "Amen" (Mt. 6:13 mg.; Rev. 1:6; cf. Rom. 9:5; 16:27; 1 Pet. 4:11; 5:11; etc.). However, blessings do occur in the opening lines of prayers (1 Ch. 29:10-13; Dnl. 2:20-23; Lk. 1:67-79). As in Jewish ritual, they may have been uttered in response to each mention of God's name (cf. Rom. 1:25; 2 Cor. 11:31). It is generally held that doxologies were added editorially to mark the conclusion of the five sections of the Psalter (Pss. 41:13 [MT 14]; 72:18f.; 89:52 [MT 53]; 106:48; 150).

The doxology was commonly employed in the various parts of the NT epistle, including the salutation (Gal. 1:5), opening thanksgiving (2 Cor. 1:3f.; Eph. 1:3; 1 Pet. 1:3), final exhortations (1 Tim. 6:15f.; 1 Pet. 5:11; 2 Pet. 3:18), and closing (He. 13:20f.; Jude 24f.).

Doxologies of the early Christian Church reflect the various interpretations of the trinity. To the forms ascribing praise "through Christ" were added the phrases "through Christ and the Holy Spirit" (Clement of Alexandria *Quis dives salvetur?* 42.2), "through Christ in the Holy Spirit" (Origen *De oratione, passim*), and "to the Father and Son with the Holy Spirit in your holy church" (Hippolytus *Traditio apostolica* 6.4). The *Gloria Patri* or "Lesser Doxology," used as a response to the Psalms since the 4th cent., equates the three members of the trinity (cf. Basil the Great *De Spiritu sancto* 29), a reaction against the Arian heresy. Other Christian doxologies include the *Gloria in Excelsis*, the "Greater Doxology" or "Angelic Hymn," an expansion of Lk. 2:14 that begins

"Glory be to God on high." Often emphasizing a particular aspect of Christ or of the ecclesiastical calendar, doxologies were added to various hymns; perhaps most familiar is the stanza beginning "Praise God from whom all blessings flow," written by the Anglican Bishop Thomas Ken (1637-1711).

Bibliography.–L. G. Champion, *Benedictions and Doxologies in the Epistles of Paul* (1934); *Dictionnaire d'Archéologie Chrétienne et de Liturgie*, IV, 1525-1536 (G. F. Moore); *LTK*, III, 534-36 (J. M. Neilen, J. A. Jungmann); *RAC*, IV, 210-226 (A. Stuiber).

A. C. M.

DRACHMA. *See* MONEY.

DRAG (Hab. 1:15f., AV). *See* NET.

DRAGNET [Heb. *ḥērem*] (Ezk. 32:3); AV, NEB, NET. A net which is drawn along the bottom of a body of water or along the ground. Pharaoh king of Egypt, figuratively depicted as a "dragon in the seas," will be caught and hauled up in Yahweh's dragnet. *See* NET.

DRAGON [Heb. *tannîn* (Ps. 74:13; Isa. 27:1; 51:9), *tan*, pl. *tannîm* (Ezk. 29:3; 32:2); Gk. *drákōn* (Rev. 12:3ff.; 13:2, 4, 11; 16:13; 20:2)]; AV also WHALE (Ezk. 32:2); NEB also SEA-SERPENT (Ps. 74:13), MONSTER.

I. In the OT.*–*A. Tannîn. This term appears in fourteen OT passages and is also translated by the RSV as "sea monster" (Gen. 1:21; Job 7:12; Ps. 148:7), "monster" (Jer. 51:34), "serpent" (Ex. 7:9f., 12; Dt. 32:33; Ps. 91:13).

Some interpreters distinguish two layers of meaning in the respective OT passages, namely, an older stratum in which *tannîn* is a mythical chaos monster and a later one in which it is a creature among creatures (Gunkel, *Schöpfung*, p. 120). New evidence no longer supports such a twofold distinction. *Tannîn* appears only once parallel to Rahab (Isa. 51:9), and only twice parallel to Leviathan (Ps. 74:13; Isa. 27:1). Its appearance with the article (Isa. 27:1 [Ezk. 29:3; 32:2, emended]) and in plural form (Gen. 1:21; Dt. 32:33; Ps. 74:13; Ex. 7:12) suggests that it is never used as a proper noun (in poetic passages the absence of the article is no safe guide), but always as a generic term. Thus *tannîn*, unlike Rahab and Leviathan, is properly a generic term and not a personal name.

In eight of the fourteen *tannîn* passages, this term refers to an animal such as a serpent or snake (Ex. 7:9f., 12 [in 4:3 and 7:15 the "serpents" produced from Aaron's rod are *nāḥāš*, the regular OT generic word for "serpent, snake"]; Dt. 32:33, where "poison of serpents" is in synonymous parallelism to "venom of asps [*p*ᵉ*ṯānîm*]"; Ps. 91:13, where "serpent" is in synonymous parallelism to "adder [*peṯen*]"; also Ps. 58:5 [MT 6]; Prov. 23:32), crocodile, or another mighty river creature (Ezk. 29:3; 32:2; Jer. 51:34). Two *tannîn* passages are found in clearly "nonmythological" contexts. In Ps. 148:7 the *tannînîm* are created beings called to praise Yahweh, as is all creation. Gen. 1:21 speaks of the creation of the *tannînim*, here a generic designation of large aquatic creatures contrasted with the small aquatic creatures (cf. Ps. 104:25f.). The choice of the term *tannîn* in connection with the term *bārā'*, "create," which emphasizes God's effortless creation of the large aquatic creatures, exhibits a conscious polemic against the pagan battle myth with its notion of creation in terms of a struggle (cf. the Canaanite myth of Baal and Anat from Ugarit [*DOTT*, pp. 129f.; *ANET*, p. 137] and the Marduk-Tiâmat conflict of the Babylonian Tiâmat myth [*ANET*, pp. 66f.; Heidel, pp. 102-114]).

Often a special and separate tradition is seen in four texts (Job 7:12; Ps. 74:13; Isa. 27:1; 51:9) in which the generic animal designation *tannîn* is believed to take on extrabiblical mythical meanings. Significantly, there is no close ancient Near Eastern parallel to the relationship of "sea" (*yām*) and *tannîn* in Job 7:12, where *tannîn* seems to refer to a natural aquatic creature with its habitat in the sea and is as little mythical as Leviathan in 40:1–41:3 (Ruprecht, pp. 222, 230). In Isa. 51:9 *tannîn* appears parallel to Rahab, an OT poetic name (Job 9:13; 26:12; Ps. 89:10 [MT 11]; Isa. 30:7; 51:9f.) that has no extrabiblical parallel. Some scholars consider Rahab to be a mythical monster (Gunkel, *et al.*); but this is to read into it from ancient Near Eastern mythology and is difficult to maintain since Rahab is often employed as a poetic synonym for Egypt (Isa. 30:7; Ps. 87:4; 89:10 [MT 11]; Job 9:13; cf. Ezk. 29:3). It is not unlikely that *tannîn* in Isa. 51:9 is but an aquatic creature (cf. Job 26:12) used metaphorically of Egypt.

In both Isa. 27:1 and Ps. 74:13f. *tannîn* is associated with Leviathan, a name parallel to the mythical seven-headed serpent Lotan in the Râs Shamrah texts (*UT*, 'nt: iii.34-39; *DOTT*, pp. 129f.; cf. *UT*, 67:i:1-3; 9:17; 75:i:8?) and the multi-headed dragon of Mesopotamian cylinder seals (*ANEP*, nos. 691, 671). It is often assumed that Leviathan in these two texts reflects a direct indebtedness to the Canaanite myth, which refers in the same context to the personified antagonistic Dragon (*Tannîn*). However, the OT *tannîn* is neither personified nor a name in any passage. In Job 41:1 and Ps. 104:25-29 Leviathan is just another real creature, as is *tannîn* in most OT passages — a sure indication that the Israelites did not associate with these terms any clear concept of a mythical monster (G. Fohrer, *Jesaja* [2nd ed. 1967], II, 35). (In Job 41:1 [MT 40:25] the RSV mg. reads "the crocodile" for Heb. *liw*ᵉ*yāṯān*.) The context of Isa. 27:1 confirms *tannîn* and Leviathan as metaphorical and symbolic designations for real enemies of Yahweh, including such historical entities as Egypt, Assyria, and Babylon. Ps. 74:13 speaks of the "heads of the *tannînîm*," plural according to the MT and therefore not identical with the "heads of Leviathan" (v. 14); each *tannîn* apparently has only one head. This poetic metaphor refers figuratively and symbolically to the destruction of the Egyptian army in the Red Sea at the Exodus.

Although Ugaritic and Mesopotamian myths could have influenced biblical metaphors and figures of speech, the OT's conscious polemic against the pagan battle myth indicates Israel's effective resistance of that which was incompatible with its understanding of reality and its rejection of mythical implications.

Cylinder seal showing seven-headed dragon attacked by two gods. Three of the heads continue to fight, while four hang limp. (Tell Asmar, *ca.* 2360-2180 B.C.) (Oriental Institute, University of Chicago)

B. Tan. This term appears in fourteen OT passages in the plural (*tannîm*); in Ezk. 29:3 and 32:2 it is usually emended to read *tannîn*. In the AV it is rendered "dragons" (Job 30:29; Ps. 44:19 [MT 20]; Isa. 13:22; 34:13; 35:7; 43:20; Jer. 9:11 [MT 10]; 10:22; 14:6; 49:33; 51:37; Mic. 1:8; Mal. 1:3), except in Lam. 4:3, where the AV has "sea monster." The RSV translates in all these passages "jackal," while the NEB reads "wolf" (except in Ps. 44:19, "sea-serpent"; Isa. 13:22, "jackal"; Lam. 4:3, "whales"; Mal. 1:3, "lodging"). In all these passages, "jackal" suits the context better than "dragon," "sea monster," "whale," or any other term. *See* JACKAL.

II. In the NT.–The twelve NT usages of Gk. *drákōn* are restricted to Revelation (12:3f., 7, 9, 13, 16f.; 13:2, 4, 11; 16:13; 20:2). It is a distinctly figurative term, a symbol for Satan, "that ancient serpent, who is the Devil and Satan" (20:2), "the deceiver of the whole world" (12:9). The view that Revelation is borrowing from mythology (Gunkel, *et al.*) breaks down both because the symbol of the "dragon" is the key figure of speech in the whole book and not merely in ch. 12 and because of differences in the conception of Michael's role (12:7; cf. Dnl. 10:13, 21; 12:1; Jude 9; W. Foerster, *Theologische Studien und Kritiken*, 104 [1932], 280-85). A significant connection is given in the link between the "dragon" and the "serpent" (12:9; 20:2) on the one hand and the "serpent" in Gen. 3:1-7, 14f. on the other. *See* REVELATION, BOOK OF.

Bibliography.–H. Gunkel, *Schöpfung und Chaos in Urzeit und Endzeit* (1895); P. Deimel, *Orientalia*, 5 (1922), 26-42; P. Joüon, *Recherches de Science Religieuse* 17 (1927), 444-46; B. Renz, *Der orientalische Schlangendrache* (1930); H. Wallace, *BA*, 11 (1948), 61-68; A. Heidel, *Babylonian Genesis* (2nd ed. 1951); G. R. Driver, *Studia Orientalia*, 1 (1956), 234-39; *RAC*, IV, *s.v.* "Drache" (R. Merkelbach); C. F. Pfeiffer, *EQ*, 32 (1960), 208-211; *TDNT*, II, *s.v.* δράκων (W. Foerster); T. H. Gaster, *Thespis* (2nd ed. 1966); M. K. Wakeman, *God's Battle with the Monster: A Study in Biblical Imagery* (1973); E. Ruprecht, *VT*, 21 (1971), 209-231.

G. F. HASEL

DRAGON, BEL AND THE. *See* BEL AND THE DRAGON.

DRAGON WELL. (Neh. 2:13, AV). *See* JACKAL'S WELL.

DRAM. *See* MONEY; DARIC.

DRAUGHT. The term "draught" occurs twice in the RSV; in both passages it is supplied to clarify the meaning. The AV gives the literal translation in each case: "the same" for Heb. *hazzeh* in Ps. 75:8 (MT 9) and "double" for Gk. *diploús* in Rev. 18:6.

The AV uses "draught" in an obsolete sense in 2 K. 10:27; Mt. 15:17; Mk. 7:19. A more accurate rendering would be "latrine."

DRAWER OF WATER [Heb. *šō'ēḇ mayim* < *šā'aḇ*–'bail up water']. In biblical times one who had the essential task in the community of drawing water from wells. This was recognized as one of the most menial tasks, and was frequently assigned to women (Gen. 24:11, 13, 43; 1 S. 9:11; Jn. 4:7, 15), though Moses did not disdain to perform it for the daughters of Midian (Ex. 2:16-19). It was work associated with that of hewing wood (Dt. 29:11).

When the Gibeonites saved themselves by a ruse from destruction by Joshua, they were made "hewers of wood and drawers of water," a duty later connected directly with the sanctuary (Josh. 9:21, 23, 27; cf. the "Nethinim" of 1 Ch. 9:2; Ezr. 2:43, 70; Neh. 7:46, 60). In Nah. 3:14 the inhabitants of Nineveh were exhorted to draw water in preparation for the siege.

The verb is used metaphorically in Isa. 12:3, when the prophet speaks of the "wells of salvation," a figure especially meaningful to a people dependent upon wells for their very existence.

J. G. G. NORMAN

DREAM [Heb. nouns *ḥ^{a}lôm*, also *šēnâ*–'sleep' (Ps. 90:5); Aram. *ḥēlem* (Dnl. 2:4; etc.); Gk. *ónar* (Mt. 1:20; 2:12f., 19, 22; 27:19), also *enýpnion* (Acts 2:17)]; AV also A SLEEP (Ps. 90:5); NEB also BAD DREAMS (Gen. 40:5), "sensible man" (Eccl. 5:3), "wise women" (Jer. 23:32; 29:8), omits in Eccl. 5:7; [Heb. vbs. *ḥālam*, also *hôzîm*–'raving,' or *ḥôzîm*–'seeing' (Isa. 56:10); Gk. *enypniázomai* (Acts 2:17; Jude 8)]; AV also SLEEPING (Isa. 56:10), FILTHY DREAMERS (Jude 8); NEB also DREAMS (Jude 8); **DREAMER** [Heb. *ḥôlēm* (Dt. 13:1, 3, 5), *ḥ^{a}lômôṯ*–'dreams' (Jer. 27:9; 29:8)]; NEB also "wise women." "Dreamer" is also supplied by the RSV in Zec. 10:2.

I. General Character.–Dreams are a very common human phenomenon, not restricted to particular peoples, historical eras, or cultures. They have universally aroused interest and have been made the object of reflection.

The ancient Israelites noted their fleeting character, and OT writers employed them as similes for that which quickly vanishes (Job 20:8; Ps. 73:20; 90:5; Isa. 29:7). The vividness and realism of some dreams, possessing power to confuse the boundary line between dream and reality, was also noted and drawn upon by biblical writers for literary purposes (Ps. 126:1; Isa. 29:8). In two proverbs, the application of which remains unclear, the writer of Ecclesiastes associates dreams with the many (empty) words of a fool (5:3, 7). Of course, biblical writers nowhere reflect attempts to investigate dreams for the purpose of psychoanalysis.

II. Revelatory Dreams.–Of greater significance for students of the Bible are those instances in which dreams were employed as vehicles of revelation. In the time of Saul dreams were viewed as one of the regular means of receiving messages from God (1 S. 28:6, 15), and they are frequently associated with prophecy, both authentic (Nu. 12:6; Joel 2:28) and false (Dt. 13:1, 3, 5; Jer. 23:25, 27f., 32; 27:9; 29:8; Zec. 10:2).

Biblical references to revelatory dreams tend to appear in clusters, however: in the patriarchal era (Gen. 20–41), in the ministry of Daniel (chs. 1–7), and in the Nativity narratives of Matthew's Gospel (1:20; 2:12f., 19, 22). More isolated instances occur in the stories of Gideon (Jgs. 7:13, 15) and Solomon (1 K. 3:5, 15), and in Matthew's account of Jesus' trial (Mt. 27:19). Job speaks of nightmares from God that frighten him (Job 7:14; cf. 4:12ff.), and Elihu of terrifying dreams by which God warns men away from evil (Job 33:15).

In Isa. 56:10, a passage that speaks of unfaithful "watchmen" (prophets), the Hebrew text is uncertain — whether *hôzîm*, "raving," or *ḥôzîm*, "seeing" (as of a vision or a dream). The RSV renders at this point "dreaming" (without footnote), in accordance with the LXX, Symmachus, Aquila, 1QIsa, Vulgate, and some Massoretic MSS. This is likely correct, in view of the association with lying down and sleep. In this rebuke of unfaithful prophets the author is probably engaging in wordplay that evokes the common use of *ḥozeh* for "seeing a (revelatory) vision." It may be that Jude (v. 8) echoes the LXX version of this verse, when referring to the corrupt persons against whom he warns the Church (cf. "these dreamers pollute their own bodies" (NIV).

Revelatory dreams in the Bible can be classified into two basic kinds: (1) auditory — message — dreams (those experienced by King Abimelech [Gen. 20:3, 6], Laban [31:24], Solomon [1 K. 3:5, 15; see also 9:2ff.], Joseph [Mt. 1:20; 2:13, 19, 22], and the wise men [2:12]), and (2) visual — usually symbolic — dreams (those experienced by Jacob [Gen. 28:12; 31:10f.], Joseph [37:5ff.], Pharaoh's butler [40:9ff.], Pharaoh's baker [vv. 16ff.], Pharaoh himself [41:1ff., 7ff.], a soldier in the camp of Midian [Jgs. 7:13], Nebuchadrezzar [Dnl. 2:31ff.; 4:10ff.], and Daniel [Dnl. 7:1ff.; see also 8:2ff., etc.]).

Revelatory dreams sometimes occurred in pairs (to Joseph [Gen. 37:5ff., 9f.] and to Pharaoh [41:1ff., 7ff.]). This duplication was interpreted by Joseph as underscoring the certainty and imminence of the events portended (Gen. 41:32). Cf. the triple repetition in Peter's vision of the "great sheet, let down by four corners upon the earth" (Acts 10:10ff.).

Revelatory dreams (of the type that involved primarily visual experiences) were often distinguished from ordinary dreams by their psychological (usually unsettling) effect on the dreamers, which aroused in them a strong desire to seek interpretation (Gen. 40:7f.; 41:8; Jgs. 7:13; Dnl. 2:1ff.; 4:2ff.; 7:15f.). Message dreams are presented as having been self-evident.

Biblical writers appear to have made no clear distinction between a revelatory dream and a night VISION.

There are a number of passages where dreams (or night visions) are not explicitly mentioned, but seem to be implied (Gen. 26:24; Nu. 22:20; 1 S. 15:16; 2 S. 7:4; 1 K. 9:2; 1 Ch. 17:3; 2 Ch. 1:7; 7:12; Jer. 31:26; Zec. 1:8; 4:1; Acts 23:11; 27:23) — but perhaps in some instances these did not involve a sleep experience; cf. 1 S. 3:4ff.

III. Dream Interpretation.–According to biblical testimony, the royal courts of both Mesopotamia and Egypt had among their wise men and prognosticators those who professionally interpreted dreams. Extrabiblical literature recovered from both areas contains documents of instructions for these professionals. From these and related materials we learn that there was among the peoples of the ancient Near East generally a much greater preoccupation with dreams as portents of the future than appears to have been present in Israel.

In the biblical literature, revelatory dreams of the visual type all (except for those appearing to Jacob) required subsequent interpretation. The great interpreters of dreams in the biblical narratives are Joseph at the court of Pharaoh, and Daniel at the court of Nebuchadrezzar. Both succeeded after the wise men of the realms had failed, and both testified that God had sent the dreams and that He (the God of Israel) alone could give the interpretation.

In the ancient Near East, revelations from the gods were often sought by sleeping at night in a temple or holy place — a practice now technically called "incubation." References to similar incubation in the OT have been alleged by some scholars in such passages as 1 S. 28:15 (Saul); 1 K. 3:4ff. (Solomon); 1 K. 9:2ff. (Solomon); 2 K. 16:15 (Ahaz); 2 K. 19:1, 14ff. (Hezekiah); etc. But these must all remain doubtful.

Bibliography.–E. L. Ehrlich, *Der Traum im AT* (1953); A. L. Oppenheim, *Transactions of the American Philosophical Society* (1956), pp. 179-353; J. Obermann, *How Daniel Was Blessed with a Son: An Incubation Scene in Ugaritic* (1946).

J. H. STEK

DREGS [Heb. *šemārîm*] (Ps. 75:8 [MT 9]); [*māṣâ*] ("have drunk to the dregs," Isa. 51:17). In Ps. 75:8 *šemārîm* ("lees," "dregs") is used in a poetic context of the sediment left in the cup of divine wrath, which the wicked must drink to the very last drop. The same imagery is used in Isa. 51:17ff., where Yahweh tells Jerusalem that she has already "drained to the last drop" (Heb. *māṣâ*; BDB, p. 594) the cup of His wrath, and that He will now give this cup to her oppressors (vv. 22f.).

DRESS. (1) Garments, or (verb) put on garments. Heb. *šîṯ*, "garment," denotes the attire of a prostitute in Prov. 7:10. In 2 S. 19:24 the general Hebrew verb *'āśâ* means "attend to" or "care for." Removal of footwear was a sign of mourning. Heb. *lāḇaš* (Jer. 4:30) and Gk. *peribállō* (Mk. 16:5) simply mean "put on (a garment)." In Acts 12:8 a stunned Peter has to be told the stages of dressing himself: first to fasten his girdle (Gk. *zṓnnymi*; cf. AV "gird thyself"; NEB "do up your belt"), then to put on his sandals, and finally to wrap his cloak around him. *See* GARMENTS.

(2) Hew or square (stones). In 1 K. 5:17; 1 Ch. 22:2; Isa. 9:10, Heb. *gāzîṯ* refers to stones that have been cut along straight lines in preparation for building.

(3) Cultivate. To dress a vineyard (Heb. *'āḇaḏ*, "serve," Dt. 28:39) means to cultivate or till it.

(4) Slaughter and prepare for cooking. The five sheep that Abigail sent to David and his men had already been killed and cleaned (Heb. *'āśâ*, 1 S. 25:18). N. J. O.

DRESSER OF SYCAMORE TREES [Heb. *bôlēs šiqmîm*] (Am. 7:14); AV GATHERER OF SYCAMORE FRUIT; NEB DRESSER OF SYCAMORE-FIGS. The phrase probably refers to one who prunes the trees for better yields or scratches open the fruit in order to promote its ripening. In describing himself thus, Amos was claiming to belong to the ranks of the common man and not to those of the professional prophet.

DRIED GRAPES [Heb. *'anāḇîm yeḇēšîm*] (Nu. 6:3). Grapes which had been dried in the sun were forbidden to one who had taken the vow of the Nazarite. *See also* RAISINS.

DRINK [Heb. *šāḵar, šāqâ, šāṯâ, mišteh, mašqeh,* also *gāmā'* (Gen. 24:17), *māṣaṣ* (Isa. 66:11), *rāwâ* (Isa. 34:5), *šeṯîyâ* (Est. 1:8); Aram. *šeṯâ* (Dnl. 5:1-4, 23); Gk. *pínō, potízō, póma,* also *oínos* (Tit. 2:3), *pósis* (Jn. 6:55; Rom. 14:17; Col. 2:16), *sympínō* (Acts 10:41), *hydropotéō* (1 Tim. 5:23)]; AV also "milk out" (Isa. 66:11), "be bathed" (Isa. 34:5), WINE (Tit. 2:3); NEB also DRAUGHT (Mt. 27:34), "entertain" (Jgs. 19:4), FEAST (1 Cor. 10:7), "is watered" (Dt. 11:1), LAP UP (Job 15:16), "pierce" (Isa. 63:6), "share" (Mt. 20:23), SIP (Gen. 24:17), etc.; **DRINK OFFERING** [Heb. *neseḵ*, also *nāsîḵ* (Dt. 32:38); Aram. *nesaḵ* (Ezr. 7:17)]; NEB also LIBATION. *See also* DRINK, STRONG.

I. Beverages.–Beverages mentioned in Scripture include water (e.g., Ex. 15:23-25a), wine (e.g., Am. 2:8), and milk (Ezk. 25:4; Cant. 5:1). In some cases the drinking of milk is referred to in a figurative sense. In Isa. 66:10f. the people are called to rejoice in the hoped for restoration of Jerusalem, "that you may suck and be satisfied with her consoling breasts; that you may drink deeply [Heb. *māṣaṣ*] with delight from the abundance of her glory." The verb root *mṣṣ* means "quaff," thus the AV and NEB "milk out." Frequent mention is also made of "strong drink" (see below).

In addition to human beings, both animals (e.g., Nu. 20:19) and plants (usually *šāqâ* in the hiphil stem, e.g., Dt. 11:10) must imbibe water. In Gen. 2:6 the whole land is said to drink. In Nu. 23:24 Balaam depicts Israel as a lion that drinks the blood of its prey.

Giving a drink to someone in need is one of the ethical acts commended to his followers by Jesus (Mt. 25:31-46). Prov. 25:21 (cf. Rom. 12:20) calls for the giving of drink (and food) even to enemies.

II. Cultic Usage.–"Drink" has cultic significance in both the OT and the NT. The OT mentions drink offerings (Heb. *nesek*) as one form of sacrifice (*see* SACRIFICE V.E). In Dt. 32:38 the people are said to drink the wine offered as a drink offering to other gods (cf. Dt. 32:17). It is possible that such drink offerings were given to a god of Ugarit (J. Nougayrol, *Le Palais Royal d'Ugarit*, II (1957), 1:1). In 2 S. 23:13-17 David, while encamped against the Philistines, expressed a desire for water from the well at Bethlehem. When some of his men broke through the Philistine lines and returned with water from this well, David refused to drink it because the men had risked their lives (i.e., their blood) for it. David asked if this water was not the very blood of his men (cf. 1 Ch. 11:19), and he poured it out as a libation to the Lord. Lev. 17:14 stipulates the prohibition against the "eating" of blood and identifies it with life itself. In the NT the drinking of wine, as an element in the eucharist, represents participation in the blood of the resurrected Christ (1 Cor. 10:16; 11:27f.).

In Nu. 5:11-31 a test for adultery requires that the priest write curses in a book, wash them off, and give the water used in the washing to be drunk by the woman accused of adultery. If she is guilty her body will swell and be in great pain. This procedure of literally drinking the words of a curse or charm is echoed in the directions for curing a scorpion sting given at the end of an Egyptian text (*ANET*, p. 14; see also the code of Hammurabi § 132). D. E. SMITH

DRINK OFFERING. *See* DRINK II; SACRIFICE IN THE OT V.E.

DRINK, STRONG [Heb. *šēḵār* (Lev. 10:9; Nu. 6:3; etc.); Gk. *síkera* (Lk. 1:15)]; AV also STRONG WINE (Nu. 28:7); NEB also LIQUOR (Isa. 5:11; etc.), DRINK (Isa. 5:22), CUPS (Isa. 28:7). With the exception of Nu. 28:7, "strong drink" is always coupled with "wine." The two terms are commonly used as mutually exclusive, and as together exhaustive of all kinds of intoxicants.

Originally *šēḵār* seems to have been a general term for intoxicating drinks of all kinds, without reference to the material out of which they were made; and in that sense, it would include wine. Reminiscences of this older usage may be found in Nu. 28:7 (where *šēḵār* is clearly equivalent to wine, as may be seen by comparing it with v. 14, and with Ex. 29:40, where the material of the drink offering is expressly designated "wine").

When the Hebrews were living a nomadic life before their settlement in Canaan, grape wine was practically unknown to them, and there would be no need of a special term to describe it. But when they settled down to an agricultural life and came to cultivate the vine, it became necessary to distinguish it from the older kinds of intoxicants; hence the borrowed word Heb. *yayin* ("wine") was applied to the former, while the latter were classed together under the old term *šēḵār*, which then came to mean all intoxicating beverages other than wine (Lev. 10:9; Nu. 6:3; Dt. 14:26; Prov. 20:1; Isa. 24:9). The exact nature of these drinks is not clearly indicated in the Bible itself. The only fermented beverage other than grape wine specifically named is pomegranate wine (Cant. 8:2: "juice of my pomegranates"); but we may infer that other kinds of *šēḵār* besides that obtained from pomegranates were in use, such as drinks made from dates, honey, raisins, barley, apples, etc. Probably Jerome was near the mark when he wrote, "Sikera in the Hebrew tongue means every kind of drink which can intoxicate, whether made from grain or from the juice of apples, or when honeycombs are boiled down into a sweet and strange drink, or the fruit of palm oppressed into liquor, and when water is coloured and thickened from boiled herbs" (*Ep.* 52.11). Thus *šēḵār* is a comprehensive term for all kinds of fermented drinks, excluding wine.

Probably the most common sort of *šēḵār* used in Bible times was palm or date wine. This is not actually mentioned in the Bible, and we do not meet with its Hebrew name *yên t^emārîm* ("wine of dates") until the Talmudic period. But it is frequently referred to in the Assyrian-Babylonian contract tablets, and from this and other evidence we infer that it was very well known among the ancient Semites. Moreover, it is known that the palm tree flourished abundantly in Palestine, and thus it is likely that wine made of the juice of dates was a common beverage.

There can be no doubt that *šēḵār* was intoxicating. This is proved (1) from the etymology of the word, it being derived from *šāḵar*, "be or become drunk" (Gen. 9:21; Isa. 29:9; Jer. 25:27; etc.); cf. the word for drunkard (*šikkār*), and for drunkenness (*šikkārôn*) from the same root; (2) from descriptions of its effects: e.g., Isaiah graphically describes the stupefying effect of *šēḵār* on those who drink it excessively (28:7f.). Hannah defended herself against the charge of being drunk by saying, "I have drunk neither wine nor strong drink" (1 S. 1:15). The attempt made to prove that it was simply the unfermented juice of certain fruits is quite without foundation. Its immoderate use is strongly condemned (Isa. 5:11.; Prov. 20:1; *see* DRUNKENNESS). It was forbidden to ministering priests (Lev. 10:9) and to Nazirites (Nu. 6:3; Jgs. 13:4, 7, 14; cf. Lk. 1:15), but was used in the sacrificial meal as drink offering (Nu. 28:7), and could be bought with the tithe money and consumed by the worshiper in the temple (Dt. 14:26). It is commended to the weak and perishing as a means of deadening their pain, but not to princes, lest it lead them to pervert justice (Prov. 31:4-7).

See also WINE.

Bibliography.–R. J. Forbes, *Studies in Ancient Technology*, III (1955), 70-77; C. Seltman, *Wine in the Ancient World* (1957); *TDNT*, V, *s.v.* οἶνος (Seesemann). D. M. EDWARDS

DROMEDARY [Heb. *kirkārâ*] (Isa. 66:20); AV SWIFT BEAST. The Hebrew term designates a "fast-running female camel" (*CHAL*, p. 164). *See* CAMEL.

DROP; DROPPING; DROP DOWN [Heb. *nāšal*] (Dt. 28:40); AV CAST; [*'ārap*] (Dt. 32:2; 33:28); NEB also DRIP; [*nāpal*] (Jgs. 2:19; Ezk. 39:3); AV CEASE, FALL; NEB "give up," DASH; [*rāpâ*] (Neh. 6:9); AV WEAKENED; NEB RELAX; [*šālaḵ*] (2 Ch. 24:10; Job 29:17); AV CAST, PLUCK; NEB CAST, RESCUE; [*nāzal*] (Job 36:28); NEB DESCEND; [*rā'ap*] (Prov. 3:20); [*mar*] (Isa. 40:15); [*nāṭap, neṭep*] (Jgs. 5:4; Job 29:22; 36:27); NEB STREAM DOWN; [*hēleḵ*] (1 S. 14:26); NEB DRIPPING; [*'ēgel*] (Job 38:28); [*rāsîs*] (Cant. 5:2); NEB MOISTURE; [Gk. *thrómbos*] (Lk. 22:44); NEB CLOT; [*katabaínō*] (Rev. 16:21); AV, NEB, FALL.

Four OT verbs — *'ārap, rā'ap, nāzal*, and *nāṭap* (Jgs. 5:4) — are used of the falling of DEW or rain from the heavens, while in Dt. 28:10 the verb *nāšal* describes the loosening and dropping off of olives from the trees. In Jgs. 2:19 and Ezk. 39:3 the hiphil of *nāpal* is used, meaning to "leave off" or "let fall." The RSV translates literally the phrase *yirpû yedêhem*, "their hands will drop" (Neh. 6:9), a figurative expression for losing courage and strength (cf. 2 S. 4:7; 2 Ch. 15:7; Isa. 13:7; Jer. 6:24, 50:43; Ezk. 7:17; 21:7 [MT 12]; Zeph. 3:16).

"Drop" occurs only twice in the NT, once as a noun — to describe Jesus' sweat, "like great drops (Gk. *thrómboi*) of blood" (Lk. 22:44), as He prayed at the Mount of Olives — and once as a verb. The Greek vb. *katabaínō* ("come down," "descend") is used frequently in the book of Revelation in descriptions of eschatological events which begin in heaven and come down upon the earth, e.g., the hailstones in 16:21; cf. 3:12; 10:1; 13:13; 18:1; 20:9; 21:2; etc. N. J. O.

DROPSY [Gk. *hydrōpikós*–'a man afflicted with dropsy'] (Lk. 14:2). The word used by Luke is a technical term widely used by Greek physicians for "dropsy," which is not a disease in itself but the symptom of a disease of the heart, kidneys, or liver which causes water to collect in the limbs, on the surface of the body, or in the abdomen. This condition indicates that the disease is in an advanced stage, and the condition can be cured only if the disease itself is curable.

See also DISEASE IV.G.

DROSS [Heb. *sîg*] (Ps. 119:119; Prov. 25:4; Isa. 1:22, 25; Ezk. 22:18f.); NEB SCUM, IMPURITY, BASE METAL, ALLOYED; [*K sûg, Q sîg*] (Ezk. 22:18a); NEB ALLOY. The refuse left after the smelting of precious metal (Prov. 25:4); used figuratively of what is base or worthless (Isa. 1:22, 25; Ezk. 22:18f; Ps. 119:119).

DROUGHT [Heb. *ṣîyâ* (Job 24:19; Jer. 2:6; 51:43), *baṣṣōreṯ* (Jer. 14:1; 17:8), *ḥōreḇ* (Jer. 50:38; Hag. 1:11), *tal'uḇôṯ* (Hos. 13:5)]; AV also DRY; DEARTH; NEB also BARREN, DRIED UP, "sword" (Jer. 50:38), BURNING HEAT. All of these Hebrew terms refer to the dryness of a land that has received insufficient rainfall over a prolonged period of time. In Dt. 28:22 the RSV and NEB emend the MT *ḥereḇ* ("sword"; cf. AV) to read *ḥōreḇ* ("drought"); in Jer. 50:38 the NEB emends the MT to read *ḥereḇ*.

Drought was greatly feared as the most frequent cause of famine. A severe drought could make a land uninhabitable (Jer. 2:6; 51:43). *See* FAMINE; RAIN.

DROVE. [Heb. *'ēḏer*] (Gen. 30:40; 32:16, 19); AV also FLOCK; NEB also FLOCK, HERD.

DROWNING. Drowning was not a form of capital punishment among the Jews, but was practiced by the Phoenicians, Syrians, Greeks, and Romans (cf. Mt. 18:6, Gk. *katapontízomai*).

DRUNKENNESS [Heb. *šikkārôn*] (Jer. 13:13; Ezk. 23:33); NEB also "wine until they are drunk"; [*šeṯî*] (Eccl. 10:17); NEB DRUNKARDS; [Gk. *méthē*] (Lk. 21:34; Rom. 13:13; Gal. 5:21); NEB also DRINKING BOUTS; [*oinophlygía*] (1 Pet. 4:3); AV EXCESS WINE.

I. Its Prevalence.–The Bible affords ample proof that excessive drinking of intoxicants was a common vice among the Hebrews, as among other ancient peoples. This is evident not only from individual cases of intoxication, such as Noah (Gen. 9:21), Lot (19:33, 35), Nabal (1 S. 25:30), Uriah (made drunk by David, 2 S. 11:13), Amnon (13:28), Elah king of Israel (1 K. 16:9), Benhadad king of Syria and his confederates (20:16), Holofernes (Jth. 13:2), etc., but also from frequent references to drunkenness as a great social evil. Thus Amos proclaims judgment on the voluptuous and dissolute rulers of Samaria "who drink wine in bowls" (Am. 6:6), and the wealthy ladies who press their husbands to join them in carousing (4:1); he also complains that this form of self-indulgence was practiced even at the expense of the poor and under the guise of religion, at sacrificial meals (2:8; see also Isa. 5:11f., 22; 28:1-8; 56:11f.).

Its prevalence is also reflected in many passages in the NT (e.g., Mt. 24:49; Lk. 21:34; Acts 2:13, 15; Eph. 5:18; 1 Thess. 5:7). Paul complains that at Corinth even the love feast immediately preceding the celebration of the eucharist was sometimes the scene of excessive drinking (1 Cor. 11:21). It must be noted, however, that it is almost invariably the wealthy who are charged with this vice in the Bible. There is no evidence that it prevailed to any considerable extent among the common people. Intoxicants were an expensive luxury, beyond the reach of the poorer classes.

II. Its Symptoms and Effects.–These are vividly portrayed. (1) Some of its physical symptoms are mentioned in Job 12:25; Ps. 107:27; Prov. 23:29; Isa. 19:14; 28:8; 29:9; Jer. 25:16. (2) Its mental effects include exhilaration (Gen. 43:34), jollity, mirth, and forgetfulness (1 Esd. 3:20), loss of understanding and balanced judgment (Isa. 28:7; Hos. 4:11). (3) It affects man's happiness and prosperity: its immediate effect is to make one oblivious of his misery, but ultimately it "bites like a serpent, and stings like an adder," and leads to woe and sorrow (Prov. 23:29-32) and to poverty (23:21; cf. 21:17; Sir. 19:1); hence wine is called a "mocker" deceiving the unwise (Prov. 20:1). (4) In its moral and spiritual effects, it leads to a maladministration of justice (Prov. 31:5; Isa. 5:23), provokes anger and a contentious, brawling spirit (Prov. 20:1; 23:29; 1 Esd. 3:22; Sir. 31:26, 29f.), and conduces to a profligate life (Eph. 5:18). It is allied with gambling and licentiousness (Joel 3:3) and indecency (Gen. 9:21f.). Above all, it deadens the spiritual sensibilities, produces a callous indifference to religious influences, and destroys all serious thought (Isa. 5:12).

III. Biblical Teaching Regarding Drunkenness.–Although the Bible does not prescribe total abstinence as a universal rule, it does condemn all forms of intemperance. In the OT certain special cases did, however, call for total abstention from strong drink. The Nazirite under his vow (Nu. 6:3ff.; cf. Am. 2:12), the priest on duty (Lev. 10:9; Ezk. 44:21), and the nomadic Rechabites at all times (Jer. 35:6, 8, 14) were to abstain. The latter case may point to an earlier time when drunkenness, a vice of the rich urban dweller, was happily missing from the simpler society. Daniel and his friends provide another example of abstinence from strong drink, though it should be noted that they abstained from Babylonian food also (1:8-16).

In the NT drunkenness is explicitly condemned by Our Lord only once (Lk. 21:34), with reference to the need to watch for the coming of the Kingdom. The Epistles, however, give repeated warnings against drunkenness (e.g., 1 Cor. 5:11; 6:10; Eph. 5:18) and everywhere insist on temperance and sobriety (e.g., Gal. 5:23; 2 Pet. 1:6; cf. Acts 24:25). A bishop and those holding honorable positions in the church should not be addicted to wine (1 Tim. 3:2f.; Tit. 1:7f.; 2:2f.).

IV. Drunkenness in Metaphor.–Drunkenness very frequently supplies biblical writers with striking metaphors and similes. Thus, it symbolizes intellectual or spiritual perplexity (Job 12:25; Isa. 19:14; Jer. 23:9), bewilderment and helplessness under calamity (Jer. 13:13; Ezk. 23:33). It furnishes a figure for the movements of sailors on board ship in a storm (Ps. 107:27), and for the convulsions of the earth on the day of the Lord (Isa. 24:20).

Yahweh's "bowl of staggering" is a symbol of affliction, the fury of the Lord causing stupor and confusion (Isa. 51:17-23; cf. Isa. 63:6; Jer. 25:15ff.; Ezk. 23:33; Ps. 75:8). The sword and the arrow are said to be sodden with blood like a drunkard with wine (Dt. 32:42; Jer. 46:10). In the Apocalypse, Babylon (i.e., Rome) is portrayed under the figure of a "great harlot . . . with the wine of whose fornication the dwellers on earth have become drunk," and who is herself "drunk with the blood of the saints, and the blood of the martyrs of Jesus" (Rev. 17:1f., 6).

See also DRINK, STRONG.

See *TDNT*, IV, *s.v.* μέθη κτλ. (Preisker).

D. M. EDWARDS
C. E. ARMERDING

DRUSILLA drōō-sil'ə [Gk. *Drousilla*]. Wife of Felix, a Jewess, who along with her husband "heard him [Paul] speak upon faith in Christ Jesus" during Paul's detention in Caesarea (Acts 24:24).

The chief extrabiblical source of information regarding Drusilla is Josephus. He records that she was the youngest of three daughters of Herod Agrippa I, her sisters being Bernice and Mariamne (*Ant.* xviii.5.4). She was born *ca.* A.D. 38 (xix.9.1), and at the age of fourteen was given in marriage by her brother Agrippa II to Azizus king of Emesa. Shortly afterward, Felix, when he was procurator of Judea (A.D. 52-60), employed a Cyprian sorcerer named Simon to persuade her to desert her husband and marry himself. Her decision to break the Jewish law and marry Felix was also influenced by the cruelty of Azizus and the hatred of Bernice, who was jealous of her beauty. By Felix she had one son, Agrippa, who died in the eruption of Mt. Vesuvius in A.D. 79.

DUALISM. *See* PHILOSOPHY.

DUKE. The AV rendering in Gen. 36:15ff.; Ex. 15:15; and 1 Ch. 1:5ff. of Heb. *'allûp* and in Josh. 13:21 of *n^{e}sîḵim*. It occurs also as the rendering of Gk. *stratēgós* in 1 Macc. 10:65. The RSV translates "chief."

At the time the AV was made the word "duke" could still be used in England with the same general force as Latin *dux* (i.e., "leader" or "ruler"), the word employed in the Vulgate. *See* CHIEF.

DULCIMER (Dnl. 3:5, 10, 15, AV). *See* BAGPIPE.

DULLNESS (OF HEART) [Heb. *m^{e}ginnâ*–'covering'] (Lam. 3:65); AV SORROW; NEB HARD; [Gk. *pachýnō*–'thicken,' 'fatten'] (Mt. 13:15; Acts 28:27); AV, NEB, GROSS. Lam. 3:65 speaks figuratively of a hard shell covering the heart, probably denoting obstinacy or insolence. Gk. *pachýnō* is used of a people whose heart had become impervious to the prophets' calls to repentance on account of their refusal to act upon what they knew to be the will of God. Both NT passages quote Isa. 6:10. Cf. Ps. 92:6 (MT 7); 94:8; Isa. 59:1; He. 5:11. *See also* HARDEN.

See *TDNT*, V, *s.v.* παχύνω (K. L. and M. A. Schmidt).

DUMAH dōō'mə [Heb. *dûmâ*–'silence']. The name of a person and a place (or two places). Dumah is mentioned as a son of Ishmael (Gen. 25:14; 1 Ch. 1:30). Since many of the names in context are eponymous, it is generally assumed that Dumah is the ancestor of a tribe, and attempts have been made to locate such a tribe. One such identification is Dumah (Deir ed-Dômeh) in the vicinity of Hebron, mentioned in Josh. 15:52. The oracle concerning Dumah in Isa. 21:11f., however, seems better suited to a place in Arabia (unless we emend *dûmâ* to read *'^{e}dôm*, and take it as parallel with Seir), and Dûmet ej-Jendel has been suggested. This site, now known as ej-Jauf, is an oasis located in the midst of the Arabian peninsula, about halfway between the head of the Persian Gulf and the Gulf of Aqabah. Sennacherib mentions an Adummatu "situated in the desert" (*ARAB*, II, § 358), and Esarhaddon speaks of an Adumu as "the fortress of Arabia, which Sennacherib . . . destroyed" (*ARAB*, II, §§ 518a, 536), which could be references to a conjectural *ed-Duma(t)*, a likely Arabic form of the name. The use of the word *dûmâ* in Pss. 94:17 and 115:17 is probably to be taken literally, meaning "silence," and not as a place name. The same has been suggested for the oracle in Isa. 21:11f., but this seems less likely in context.

W. S. LASOR

DUMB [Heb. *'illēm, 'ālam*] (Ex. 4:11; Ps. 31:18 [MT 19]; 38:13 [MT 14]; 39:2, 9 [MT 3, 10]; Prov. 31:8; Isa. 35:6; 53:7; 56:10; Ezk. 3:26; 24:27; 33:22; Dnl. 10:15; Hab. 2:18); NEB also "unable to speak" (Ezk. 3:26); [*dûmān*] (Hab. 2:19); NEB DEAD; [Gk. *kōphós*] (Mt. 9:32f.; 12:22; 15:30f.; Lk. 1:22; 11:14); AV also SPEECHLESS; NEB also PATIENT (Mt. 9:33); [*álalos*] (Mk. 7:37; 9:17,25); NEB also SPEECHLESS; [*áphōnos*] (Acts 8:32; 1 Cor. 12:2; 2 Pet. 2:16); **BE DUMBFOUNDED** [Heb. *dāmam*] (Ps. 31:17 [MT 18]); AV BE SILENT; NEB SINK. Used either as expressing the physical incapability to speak, generally associated with deafness, or to mean the temporary inability to express oneself, such as that produced by the weight of God's judgments (Ps. 39:2-9; Dnl. 10:15) or the expression of external calamity (Ps. 38:13). As an adjective it is used to characterize inefficient teachers destitute of spirituality ("dumb dogs," Isa. 56:10). The speechlessness of Saul's companions (Acts 9:7) was due to fright; that of the man without the wedding garment was because he had no excuse to give (Mt. 22:12). Idols are called dumb, because they are helpless and voiceless (Hab. 2:18f.; 1 Cor. 12:2), i.e., lifeless. The dumbness of the sheep before the shearer is a token of submission (Isa. 53:7; Acts 8:32).

Temporary dumbness was inflicted as a sign upon Ezekiel and as a punishment for unbelief upon Zechariah (Lk. 1:22). There are several cases recorded of Our Lord's healing the dumb (Mt. 15:30; Mk. 7:37; Lk. 11:14; etc.). Dumbness was often associated with imbecility and was regarded as caused by demoniac possession (Mt. 9:32; 12:22). The Evangelists therefore describe the healing of these as effected by the casting out of demons.

A. MACALISTER

DUNG [Heb. *pereš*] (Ex. 29:14; Lev. 4:11; 8:17; 16:27; Nu. 19:5; Mal. 2:3); NEB OFFAL; [*gālal*] (1 K. 14:10); [*gēlel*] (Job 20:7; Ezk. 4:12, 15; Zeph. 1:17); [*K ḥiryyônîm, Q ḥ^{a}rēy-yônîm*] ("dove's dung," 2 K. 6:25); NEB "locustbeans"; [*dōmen*] (2 K. 9:37; Ps. 83:10 [MT 11]; Jer. 8:2; 9:22; 16:4; 25:33); [*Q ṣō'ā, K ḥ^{a}ra'îm*] (2 K. 18:27; Isa. 36:12); **DUNG GATE** [*ša'ar hā'ašpōṯ*] (Neh. 2:13; 3:13f.; 12:31); **DUNGHILL** [Aram. *n^{e}walû*] (Ezr. 6:11); NEB "forfeit"; [Gk. *kopría*] (Lk. 14:35); NEB DUNG-HEAP; **DUNG-PIT** [Heb. *maḏmēnâ*] (Isa. 25:10); AV DUNGHILL; NEB MIDDEN.

The first mention of dung is in connection with sacrificial rites. The sacred law required that the dung, along with the parts of the animal not burned on the altar, should be burned outside the camp (Ex. 29:14; Lev. 4:11; 8:17; 16:27; Nu. 19:5).

The fertilizing value of dung was appreciated by the cultivator, as is indicated by Lk. 13:8 and possibly Ps. 83:10 and Isa. 25:10.

Dung was also used as a fuel. Ezk. 4:12, 15 is better understood when it is known that the dung of animals is a common fuel throughout Palestine and Syria, where other fuel is scarce. During the summer the villagers gather the manure of their cattle, horses, or camels into a dunghill or dung pit, mix it with straw, make it into cakes, and dry it for use as fuel for cooking, especially in the winter when wood, charcoal, and straw are not procurable. Isa. 25:10 uses the figure of straw being trampled in a dung pit to describe the destiny of Moab. The fuel that results from this process burns slowly like peat and meets the needs of the kitchen. In Ezekiel's mind there was no idea of uncleanness associated with the use of animal dung as fuel, though there was with the use of human dung (Ezk. 4:12-15).

The word used to designate one of the gates of Jerusalem (*'ašpōṯ*, Neh. 2:13; etc.) is more general than the others and may mean any kind of refuse. The gate, now thought to have been located near the southwest corner of the wall, was probably so named because outside it was the general dump heap of the city.

"Dung" was frequently used figuratively to express the idea of (a) worthlessness, especially of a perishable article for which no one cared (1 K. 14:10; 2 S. 6:25; 9:37; Job 20:7; Ps. 83:10; Jer. 8:2; 9:22; 16:4; 25:33; Zeph. 1:17), (b) disgust (Isa. 36:12), (c) rebuke (Mal. 2:3). To have one's house turned into a dunghill (Ezr. 6:11; cf. Dnl. 2:5; 3:29) or to be flung upon a dunghill (Lk. 14:35) marks the extreme of ignominy.

J. A. PATCH

DUNGEON. *See* PRISON.

DURA do͞o'rə [Aram. *dûrā'*] (Dnl. 3:1). A plain in the province of Babylon.

Early identifications included Dura on the Euphrates (*see* DURA-EUROPAS), where the Habor River meets the Euphrates (Polybius v.48; Ammianus Marcellinus xxiii.5, 8; xxiv.1, 5), but that site is beyond the bounds of provincial Babylon. A second proposal, N of Babylon and E of the Tigris near Apollonia (Polybius v.52; Ammianus xxv.6,9), was in the district of Sittakene, which was in some periods part of the province, but is discounted because of its distance from the capital. More likely is Tulul Dura, a series of mounds or tells a few miles S of Babylon (J. Oppert, *Expédition scientifique en Mésopotamie*, I [1863], 238ff.). However, Akk. *dûru* ("circuit, wall, walled place"), from which the name is derived, is a common element in Mesopotamian place names. It can indicate a circular enclosure or fortress (KoB, p. 1064; cf. H. Donner and W. Röllig, *Kanaanäische und aramäische Inschriften*, II [2nd ed. 1968], 286), as implied by the LXX reading *períbolos* "enclosure." Identification of the site thus remains uncertain; the author of Daniel may have neither known nor intended a specific reference, nor may it have been significant for the narrative.

At Dura Nebuchadrezzar set up a golden image 60 cubits (90 ft. or 27 m.) high and 6 cubits (9 ft. or 2.7 m.) wide. The LXX places the event in the 18th year of his reign, when he "subdued towns and provinces and all the inhabitants of the world from India to Ethiopia" (Jer. 52:29; cf. Est. 1:1; 8:9; see also *ANET*, p. 307). A. C. M.

DURA-EUROPOS do͞o-rə-ūr-ō'pəs. Also called Dura-Nicanoris, the village of Nicanor. An ancient Assyrian city formerly known as Ṣâliḥîyeh, it is located on the Euphrates River at the northern edge of the Syrian desert about 20 mi. (32 km.) NW of Mari. Its name is derived from the Assyrian *dûr*, "palace," "fortress" and

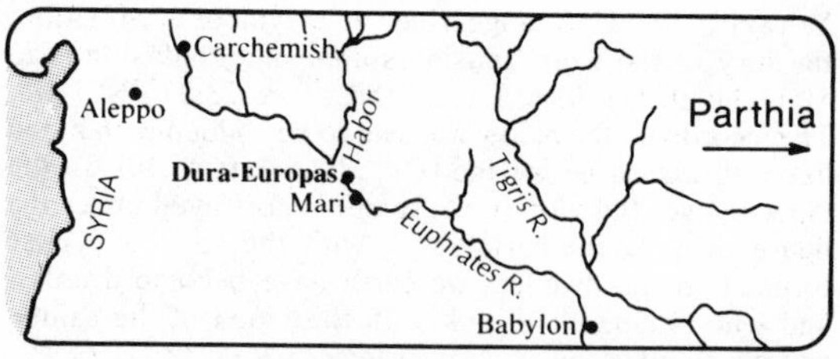

Europos, the home town of Seleucus I Nicator of Macedonia, who raised the city to prominence.

I. History.–The site of Ṣâliḥîyeh had long been known to voyagers who traveled along the Euphrates from Aleppo to Baghdad. Seleucus I (312-280 B.C.) occupied the ancient city, using it as a convenient military outpost where goods shipped along the Euphrates could be loaded and unloaded.

Because of its precarious geographical location between Roman Syria and the Parthian empire, Dura-Europos was vulnerable to attack. In 140 B.C. the Parthians gained control of the city, and it soon flourished as a trade center. In A.D. 116 Trajan took the city as he led his Roman army through Syria, but he soon allowed it to fall back into Parthian hands. A violent earthquake shook the city in 161, causing much damage to the buildings and walls. In 165, before the people could restore the broken walls, the Roman legions of Lucius Verus defeated the Parthian army and regained the city. The city continued to prosper under the Romans until almost one hundred years later when the Persian Sassanids captured it in 256. At the beginning of the 4th cent., during the time of Constantine, Dura-Europos was abandoned in ruins. Julian, while marching to Ctesiphon in 363, found at the site only "the vestiges of that which at one time had been a city."

II. Description.–The city is built regularly with right angles — the walls straight except for those following the ravine down to the Euphrates, the streets intersecting squarely, and the buildings rectangular-shaped with open courtyards for light and air. To the east the ancient wall follows the windings of a ravine that descends to the alluvial plain bordering on the Euphrates. To the west the walls facing the Syrian desert are straight with square corners. To the south the walls follow the contours of a deep ravine as far as the most prominent cliff descending down to the plain along the Euphrates.

The city was inhabited by its conquerors, the Macedonians and Romans, and by the indigenous races — Palmyrenians, Nabateans, Parthians, and Babylonians. The cultural climate tended to be oriental although the Hellenistic influence of its invaders left its mark as well.

III. Excavations.–In 1872 appeared a brief description of the site by the Austrian engineer Czernick, but not until March, 1921, was anything unearthed. During an English occupation a Captain Murphy, who was fortifying the site against continual attacks by neighboring hostile tribes, dug up some beautiful, unusually well preserved frescoes from the temple of the gods of Palmyra. J. H. Breasted, director of the Oriental Institute in Chicago who had explored the Mesopotamian basin, was only able to make preliminary observations before the British army was ordered to evacuate. F. Cumont of Belgium did the first significant excavating during 1922/23. The bulk of the work was done jointly under the leadership of M. Pillet of the French Academy of Inscriptions and M. Rostovtzeff of Yale University beginning in 1928 and continuing until 1936.

Torah shrine and western wall of the synagogue at Dura-Europos. The walls were covered with five horizontal bands of tempera *al secco* paintings, including fifty-eight biblical episodes as interpreted in the contemporary rabbinic writings (A.D. 244-245). (Yale University Art Gallery)

Baptistery of the Dura-Europos house church (A.D. 232). One room contains a rectangular basin beneath a ciborium, possibly a baptismal font. (Yale University Art Gallery)

The city is less than one-fourth excavated within the walls. A Christian church, a Jewish synagogue, and several pagan temples are the most noteworthy finds. The church is profusely decorated with frescoes commemorating OT and NT themes. A large baptistry, a chapel, a courtyard, and a large room with what appears to be a pulpit are contained within its walls.

The synagogue was found to be built on top of a smaller, earlier synagogue. It, too, was covered by wall paintings of OT scenes, but many pagan symbols and figures had been blended into the familiar biblical themes. This combination of Jewish-Hellenistic culture in art form is significant for the study of the history of religious art.

The temples were likewise filled with murals depicting the cultic rituals performed there in honor of the various gods and goddesses. One of the oldest is a gigantic figure of the god Bel.

See BUSH, THE BURNING.

Bibliography.–F. Ambrière, *Les Guides bleus: Moyen Orient* (1956), pp. 395-97; E. R. Goodenough, *IEJ*, 8 (1958), 69-79; 11 (1961), 161-170; M. I. Rostovtzeff, *et al.*, *Excavations at Dura-Europos: Final Reports*, 4-8 (1943-1959). H. E. HAHN

DURE (AV Mt. 13:21). Obsolete term for "endure."

DUST [Heb. *'āpār*] (Gen. 2:7; 3:14, 19; 13:16; 18:27; 28:14; Ex. 8:16f.; Lev. 17:13; Nu. 5:17; 23:10; Dt. 9:21; 28:24; etc.); AV also POWDER (2 K. 23:6, 15); NEB also EARTH, HOST (Nu. 23:10), etc.; [*'āḇāq*] (Ex. 9:9; Isa. 5:24; 29:5; Ezk. 26:10; Nah. 1:3), [*dāqaq*] (2 Ch. 34:4); NEB POWDER; [*galgal*] ("whirling dust," Ps. 83:13; Isa. 17:13); AV WHEEL, "rolling thing"; NEB THISTLE-DOWN; [*'ereṣ*] (Ps. 89:39 [MT 40]; Lam. 2:21); AV, NEB, GROUND; [*dakkā'*] (Ps. 90:3); AV DESTRUCTION; [*šaḥaq*] (Isa. 40:15); [Gk. *koniortós*] (Mt. 10:14; Lk. 9:5; 10:11; Acts 13:51; 22:23); [*choús*] (Mk. 6:11; Rev. 18:19); [*choïkós*] (1 Cor. 15:47-49); AV EARTHY.

In the OT "dust" usually translates Heb. *'āpār*, which occurs more than sixty times. The verb *dāqaq* literally means "crush" or "grind fine," while the verb *dāḵā'* (of which the noun *dakkā'* is a cognate) has the same general meaning but is used in poetic literature. *Galgal* literally means "wheel" but is used figuratively in Ps. 83:13 and Isa. 17:13, probably of some sort of tumbleweed. The NT term *choïkós*, "of dust," is not found previous to the Pauline literature and therefore may have been coined by Paul.

The biblical writers frequently use dust in one of several figurative senses: (1) In Dt. 28:24 ("The Lord will make the rain of your land powder and dust") it refers to the consequences of the drought Yahweh will send. In the vicinity of Judea during a sirocco the air becomes filled with sand and dust, which are blown by the wind with great violence. (2) It is used of an innumerable multitude (e.g., Gen. 13:16; 28:14; Job 27:16; Ps. 78:27). (3) Such actions as lying in the dust, licking the dust, and sprinkling dust on the head, are symbolic, expressive of deep humiliation, abasement, or grief (e.g., Job 2:12; 42:6; Ps. 72:9; Isa. 2:10; 47:1; 49:23; Lam. 2:10; 3:29; Ezk. 27:30; Mic. 7:17; Rev. 18:19). *See also* ASHES.

(4) In the NT "dust" occurs five times with reference to shaking the dust off one's feet (Mt. 10:14; Mk. 6:11; Lk. 9:5; 10:11; Acts 13:51), and act symbolic of renunciation. It was practiced by the Pharisees on passing from gentile soil, since it was a rabbinical doctrine that the dust of a heathen land defiles. (5) Along similar lines was the act of throwing dust into the air, which expressed execration. When David fled from Jerusalem, Shimei expressed his hatred not only by cursing the king but also by throwing stones at him and flinging dust (2 S. 16:13). The crowd Paul addressed at Jerusalem demonstrated their wrath against him by waving their garments and throwing dust into the air (Acts 22:23).

(6) The most significant use is with reference to the material out of which God formed man (Gen. 2:7). Here it affirms the Hebrew view of man as being a temporal creature in intimate unity with the rest of creation. It is also symbolic of man's frailty (Ps. 103:14; cf. Gen. 18:27; Job 4:19; etc.) and of his mortality (Gen. 3:19; cf. Job 34:15; Ps. 104:29; Eccl. 3:20; 12:7; etc.); hence it is used figuratively for the grave (Ps. 22:15, 29; 30:9; Dnl. 12:2). In the OT "dust," or man's temporality, does not connote sin. In later Jewish literature, however, the idea of sin enters in — especially in the Qumrân literature, where "dust" is used in parallel with "flesh" (cf. 1QH 15:21), and in Philo, whose antithesis between the earthly (*choús*) man and heavenly man was influenced by the Platonic conception of man (*TDNT*, IX, 473-77). Philo based his understanding of man on what he took to be two accounts of the creation of man: the creation of the ideal man in Gen. 1:26 and that of the material man in 2:7. Although Paul uses similar terminology in his discussion of the resurrection body (1 Cor. 15:47-49), he repudiates the Philonic interpretation. For Paul the "heavenly man" is the resurrected Christ, while the "man of dust" is everyone who has descended from the first Adam and shares in his perishable nature. At the resurrection all those who believe will exchange their perishable nature for the imperishable (15:49-54).

See *TDNT*, IX, *s.v.* χοϊκός (E. Schweizer).

D. M. EDWARDS N. J. O.

DUTY [Heb. piel of *yāḇam* (Gen. 38:8; Dt. 25:5, 7), *bô'* (2 K. 11:5, 9; etc.), *yāṣā'* (2 K. 11:7, 9; etc.), *mišmereṯ* (Nu. 3:7f.; 1 Ch. 9:27; etc.), *mᵉlā'ḵâ, mi'šmār, 'ᵃḇōḏâ, dāḇār, mišpāṭ, pᵉquddâ*]; AV also "marry her" (Gen. 38:8), "enter in," "go forth," CHARGE, WORK, OFFICE, PORTION, PART, etc.; NEB also REQUIRED, PART, ATTENDANCE, etc.; [Gk. *ephēmería*] (Lk. 1:8); AV COURSE; NEB TURN; [*opheílō*] (Lk. 17:10); [*chreía*] (Acts 6:3); AV BUSINESS; NEB MATTERS; [*taúta*] (1 Tim. 4:15; 6:2); AV (THESE) THINGS; NEB MATTERS, etc.; [*eusebéō*] (1 Tim. 5:4); AV "show piety"; [*latreía*] (He. 9:6); AV SERVICE; also, the RSV renders as "it was the duty of" the Hebrew idiom *yihyeh* (impf. of *hayâ*) *'al* or *lᵉ*, or sometimes simply the preposition (cf. 2 Ch. 5:13; Neh. 13:13; Ezk. 45:17).

The concept of a specific obligation laid upon a man is found in Judah's command to Onan to perform the "duty of a brother-in-law" to Tamar in Gen. 38:8. The underlying basis of this obligation is the custom of the levirate law (Dt. 25:5-10) whereby a man was commanded to marry and have children by his deceased brother's wife if that couple was childless. *See* MARRIAGE. "To fear God and keep his commandments" is the duty of every man (Eccl. 12:13).

The chief use of "duty" in the OT, however, is to refer to the works and services rendered in the daily care of the temple (Nu. 3:7; 18:5; etc.). This included keeping the furniture of the tabernacle safe and clean. In Jerusalem in David's time he "divided the Priests and Levites into classes, every one of which had to perform service for a week and was relieved on the Sabbath" (1 Ch. 23:2-6; cf. KD). There were twenty-four such divisions. Zechariah, father of John the Baptist, was performing his duty when the angel appeared to him (Lk. 1:5, 8, 11).

Jesus shows a man to be a debtor to God by saying that the servant who had done all that was commanded had done only his "duty," what he owed and was obliged to do (Lk. 17:10). The Seven in Acts 6:1-6 were appointed to distribute charitable provisions as a "duty" or an office in which they were to serve.

"Duty" as reverent and respectful behavior or piety toward others is the use in the Pastorals (1 Tim. 5:4), while the OT meaning of performing the rites in the service of God by those in the sacrificial ministry is found in He. 9:6.

Bibliography.–Josephus *Ant.* vii.14.7; KD *in loc.*; Bauer, p. 330.

D. K. McKIM

DWARF [Heb. *daq*–'thin, lean'] (Lev. 21:20); NEB "with mis-shapen brows." "Dwarf" is the rendering of most of the English versions in a passage listing the physical failings that forbade a man of the seed of Aaron to officiate at the altar, though he might partake of the sacrificial gifts. The precise meaning of the Hebrew word here is uncertain, as the NEB illustrates. The LXX and Vulgate suggest defective eyes; but "withered" would perhaps best express the meaning. Elsewhere in the MT the term is used of the lean kine (Gen. 41:3) and blasted ears (v. 23) of Pharaoh's dream, of the grains of manna (Ex. 16:14), of the "still small voice" (1 K. 19:12), of dust (Isa. 29:5), etc.

F. K. FARR

DWELL [Heb. *yāšaḇ, môšāb, šāḵan, gûr, dûr, zᵉḇul* (1 K. 8:13), *sāḇaḇ* (2 S. 14:24), *lûn* (Job 17:12); Gk. *oikéō, katoikéō, enoikéō, káthēmai, skēnóō, ménō*]; AV also INHABIT, ABIDE, CONTINUE, TARRY (Lev. 14:8), HAVE HABITATION (Dnl. 4:21), SITUATE (Ezk. 27:3), TURN (2 S. 14:24), SIT (2 S. 7:1), etc.; NEB also LIVE, SETTLE, TAKE REFUGE (Jer. 49:8, 30), CONTINUE, LODGE, HAVE A DWELLING (Dnl. 2:22), HAVE A RESIDENCE (2 Ch. 19:4), etc.; **DWELLER** [Heb. part. of *yāšaḇ*, part. of *šāḵan*; Gk. part. of *katoikéō*]; AV "they that dwell"; INHABITANTS; NEB MEN, "they that sleep" (Isa. 26:19), etc.; **DWELLING** [Heb. *môšāḇ, šeḇeṯ, miškan, šāḵan, māḵôn* (Isa. 18:4), *māqôm, mā'ôn, me'ônâ, nāweh, dôr* (Isa. 38:12), *mᵉnuḥâ* (Isa. 11:10); Aram. *miḏor*; Gk. *skēnḗ, oikētḗrion, katoikētḗrion*]; AV also HABITATION, TABERNACLE, REFUGE (Dt. 33:27), REST (Isa. 11:10), AGE (Isa. 38:12), HOUSE (2 Cor. 5:2), etc.; NEB also HOUSE, REFUGE, SETTLEMENT, TABERNACLE, TENT (1 Ch. 17:5), BUILDING (Jer. 51:30), "places occupied" (Nu. 16:27), RESTING PLACE (Isa. 11:10), etc.

The RSV "dwell" most often reflects Heb. *yāšaḇ*, "sit, stay, dwell," less often *šāḵan*, "settle down," usually following the AV. The NEB diverges from this frequently, often rendering *yāšaḇ* as "live" and *šāḵan* as "settle." Eng. "dwell," as the Hebrew words, has a considerable semantic range: "inhabit or settle in a location," "remain in a location, company, situation, or condition," "persist or endure in a location, situation, or condition." Although sometimes periphrastic, the NEB usually accurately conveys the meaning of the Hebrew words, and its rendering is often less wooden than that of the RSV.

Hebrew *dûr* and *zᵉḇul* are nominal forms, referring to habitations; *gûr* is a verb with the basic meaning of "sojourn"; *lûn* has the root meaning "spend the night, lodge"; and *sāḇaḇ* usually means "turn, surround."

In the LXX, Gk. *oikéō* (from *oikía*, "house") and its compounds often translate Heb. *yāšaḇ*, and mean "dwell, live" or "inhabit." Gk. *káthēmai*, literally "sit," occurs in the LXX as a translation of Heb. *yāšaḇ* and Aram. *yᵉṯiḇ*. Gk. *ménō* has the basic meaning "abide," and *skēnóō* is related to the noun *skēnḗ*, "booth, tent, tabernacle."

In the OT, in addition to the most common use of "dwell" and "dwelling" to designate habitation in a given location, the terms have numerous derivative meanings. To "dwell" with another means to be in an amicable relationship with him (Ps. 133:1; Isa. 11:16 [wolf and lamb]; Jer. 31:24). A pious individual (and/or a priest?) is said to dwell with or before Yahweh, or in the "house" of Yahweh (Isa. 23:18; Hos. 14:7; Isa. 57:15; Ps. 23:6; 27:4; 61:4; 65:4; 84:4; 140:13).

Followed by a prepositional phrase containing an abstract substantive, "dwell" can designate a physical or psychological state. "Wisdom" dwells "in prudence" (Prov. 8:22). In the Blessing of Moses, Benjamin will dwell "in safety" (Dt. 33:12). A survivor of the destruction of Jerusalem says of God, "he has made me dwell in darkness, like the dead of long ago" (Lam. 3:6; cf. in Ezekiel's prophecy against Tyre: "Then I will thrust you down with those who descend into the Pit, to the people of old, and I will make you to dwell in the nether world" [Ezk. 26:20]).

As Israel dwelt in booths (Lev. 23:42ff.), Yahweh had His dwelling in the tabernacle (Ps. 78:60), the temple/Mt. Zion (2 S. 7:2, 5; 1 K. 8:12f.; Ps. 9:11; 43:3; 68:16; 74:2; 76:2; 84:1; 132:14; Isa. 8:18; Joel 3:21; Zec. 2:13), but also "on high" (Isa. 33:5) and "in heaven" (1 K. 8:30ff.; cf. 1 Ch. 6:21ff.; Isa. 18:4). Yahweh "caused his name to dwell" in Jerusalem (Dt. 12:11ff.). From Heb. *šāḵan* comes a rabbinic name for God, *šᵉḵînâ*, "the Presence." Thus, the Targum renders those passages in which God is said to "dwell" with "He lets his *šᵉḵînâ* dwell" (1 K. 8:27; Ps. 68:17 [MT 16]). Similarly, God's glory and justice dwell in the land (Ps. 26:8; 85:9; Isa. 32:16).

According to Ezk. 37:27, part of the restoration of Israel will be the reestablishment of God's "dwelling place" with them. In the Blessing of Moses, the protection of God is stressed: "The eternal god is your dwelling place" (Dt. 33:27).

The NT also contains a number of figurative uses of "dwell" and "dwelling." In Revelation, mankind is referred to as "those who dwell upon the earth" (3:10; 6:10; 8:13); cf. "those who dwell in heaven" (12:12; 13:6). Sinners at Pergamum are said to "dwell" with Satan (2:13). Demonic possession is sometimes described as unclean spirits dwelling in a person (Mt. 12:45; Lk. 11:26). According to Paul, it is sin dwelling within a man that prevents him from doing good (Rom. 7:17f., 20). "Dwell" also describes the "possession" by Christians of the Spirit of God (Rom. 8:9, 11; 1 Cor. 3:16; Jas. 4:5), the Holy Spirit (2 Tim. 1:5), faith (2 Tim. 1:5), the "spirit of truth" (Jn. 14:17), or Christ (Eph. 3:17).

Christ, who in the prologue of John's Gospel "became flesh and dwelt among us" (1:14), is the "host" for God: "The Father dwells in me" (14:10). The "whole fulness of deity" (Col. 2:9) or the "fulness of God" (1:19) "dwells" in Christ.

In Mt. 23:21, as in the OT, God dwells in the temple; but cf. Acts 7:48 and 1 Tim. 6:16. In Rev. 13:6 heaven is referred to as God's dwelling (*skēnḗ*). Paul contrasts the heavenly "dwelling" of the future for Christians with the present "earthly tent" (*oikētḗrion,* 2 Cor. 5:2). In Eph. 3:22, members of the "household of God," the Church, comprise the "dwelling place [*katoikētḗrion*] of God in the Spirit." In the new age, according to Rev. 21:3, God's "dwelling" will again be with men.

Bibliography.–E. Lohse, *Colossians and Philemon* (*Hermeneia,* 1971); pp. 56-58; *TDNT,* III, *s.v.* κάθημαι (C. Schneider); IV, *s.v.* μένω (F. Hauck); V, *s.v.* οἶκος, οἰκέω, κατοικέω (O. Michel); VII, *s.v.* σκηνή (W. Michaelis). F. B. KNUTSON

DYE. The Israelites were already familiar with the use of dyes at the time of the Exodus. The tabernacle was hung with curtains worked in blue, purple, and scarlet thread that the women themselves had spun (Ex. 35:25) and possibly dyed. During the period of the judges, dyed fabric (Heb. *ṣeḇa'*) was highly prized as spoil taken in battle (cf. Jgs. 5:30, "dyed stuffs," "dyed work,"; AV "divers colours"). In Job 38:14 the RSV emends the MT *w^{e}yiṯyaṣṣ^{e}ḇû,* "and they take their stand" (cf. AV, NEB), to read *w^{e}ṯiṣṣāḇa',* "and it is dyed." If this emendation is correct then the reference is to the reddish hue that the dawn gives to the earth (see M. H. Pope, *Job* [*AB,* 1965], pp. 247, 252). For Ex. 26:14, AV *see* TANNED.

The Israelites may have learned the art of dyeing partly from the Egyptians, whose skill is attested by the fabrics found in their tombs, and also from the Phoenicians, who were famed for their "Tyrian purple" (cf. 2 Ch. 2:7). This red-purple and violet dye was, in fact, the most highly valued of ancient times, and was produced from the molluscs purpura and murex of the eastern Mediterranean coast. Early reference to this trade is found in the Râs Shamrah tablets (*ca.* 1500 B.C.). Tyre was the center of the industry, though molluscs may have been imported from distant countries (Ezk. 27:7, 24). In later times the dye was sold, if not manufactured, in Asia (Acts 16:14). The dye was prepared by boiling certain tissues of the mollusc in a salt solution for a period of three days.

Scarlet dye was prepared by drying and crushing the kermes insects found attached as small berry-like protuberances to the leaves and twigs of a species of oak tree (*Quercus coccifera*). Lichens and madder roots (*Rubia tinctorum*) were also used in ancient Egypt as a source of red dye.

Yellow and orange dyes were also of vegetable origin. Turmeric, saffron from the dried stigmas of flowers (*Crocus sativus*), safflower from the petals of the *Carthamus tinctorius* (which was used in Egypt to dye the linen sheets of the mummies), and ground pomegranate rinds were all sources of yellow dye, this last being in use in Palestine for dyes and inks.

Indigo plants imported from India and cultivated in Egypt and Syria and woad grown in Egypt and Mesopotamia were used to obtain blue dye. Black dyes came from oak-galls and myrtles.

The industry centered on certain towns. Tell Beit Mirsim (Kiriath-sepher) was one such center in the 7th cent. B.C. Dye vats have been excavated, consisting of stones about 3 ft. (1 m.) high and of similar diameter, flat at the top and bottom, and hollowed into a basin 1.5 ft. (.5 m.) across, with a channel at the rim to catch surplus dye and return it to the vat. Large stones about 15 in. (.4 m.) across with a hole through the center may have been used as weights to press the dye out of the cloth to conserve it (*AP,* plate 52). Variations in the shades could be produced by steeping the cloth either more or less, by varying the mordants used to fix the dye, or by using two different dyes successively.

The NT contains a number of references to dyed garments. In the story of Dives and Lazarus the rich man was "clothed in purple and fine linen" (Lk. 16:19). At the mocking of Jesus, the soldiers put on Him a purple cloak or robe (Mk. 15:17; Jn. 19:2). Lydia, who came from Thyatira and was converted at Philippi, was a "seller of purple goods" (Acts 16:14). The glorified Jesus of Revelation wore a "golden girdle" (1:13). The lament for fallen Babylon refers both to its clothing "in purple and scarlet" (18:16) and to a "cargo of . . . fine linen, purple, silk and scarlet" (18:12).

See also COLOR.

Bibliography.–C. Singer, *et al.,* eds., *A History of Technology,* I (1954); R. J. Forbes, *Studies in Ancient Technology* (6 vols., 1955ff.). G. I. EMMERSON

DYSENTERY [Gk. *dysenteríon*] (Acts 28:8); AV BLOODY FLUX. The RSV employs "dysentery" to render the medical term Luke used in designating the disease by which the father of Publius was affected in Malta at the time of Paul's shipwreck. In Malta the acute form of this disease is often attended with a high temperature; hence Luke speaks of it as "fever and dysentery" (*pyretoís kaí dysenteríǭ*). The disease is still occasionally epidemic in Malta, where it has proved to be intractable and fatal. It is due to a parasitic microbe, the *Bacillus dysenteriae,* found in the goat's milk.

In 2 Ch. 21:19 there is reference to a similar disease in the days of Jehoram. The malady, as predicted by Elisha, attacked the king and assumed a chronic form in the course of which portions of the intestine sloughed. This condition sometimes occurs in the amoebic form of dysentery.

See also DISEASE III.J; IV.E. A. MACALISTER

DYSMAS diz'məs. The name given to the penitent thief (cf. Lk. 23:39-43) in the apocryphal Acts of Pilate and other legendary literature.

Index of Color Maps

INDEX OF COLOR MAPS

INDEX OF COLOR MAPS

INDEX OF COLOR MAPS

INDEX OF COLOR MAPS

INDEX OF COLOR MAPS

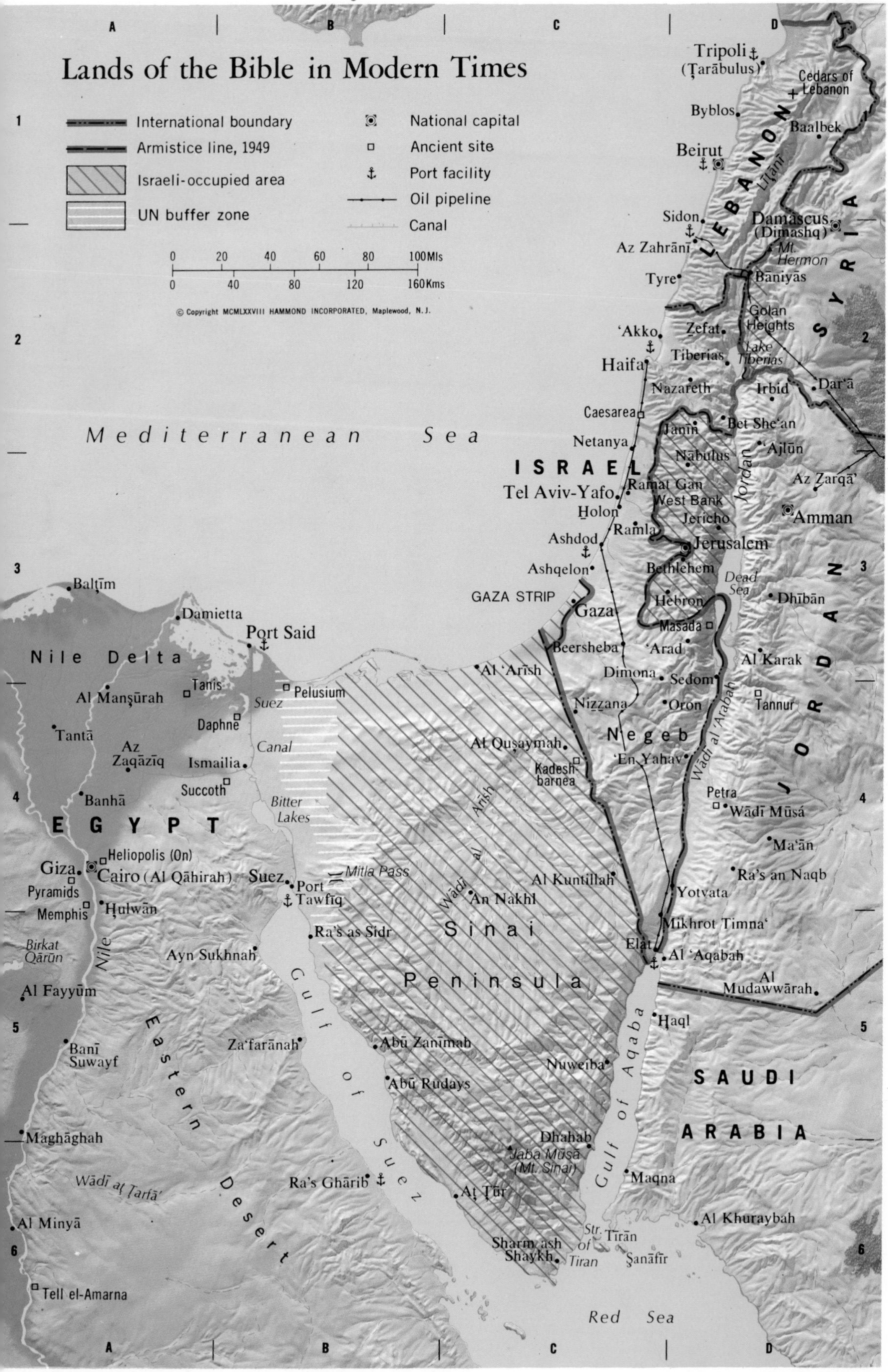
Lands of the Bible in Modern Times
International boundary
Armistice line, 1949
Israeli-occupied area
UN buffer zone
National capital
Ancient site
Port facility
Oil pipeline
Canal
0 20 40 60 80 100 Mls
0 40 80 120 160 Kms
© Copyright MCMLXXVIII HAMMOND INCORPORATED, Maplewood, N. J.
A
B
C
D
1
2
3
4
5
6
Tripoli (Ṭarābulus)
Cedars of Lebanon
Byblos
Baalbek
Beirut
LEBANON
Līṭānī
Sidon
Damascus (Dimashq)
Az Zahrānī
Mt. Hermon
Tyre
Bāniyās
SYRIA
Golan Heights
'Akko
Zefat
Lake Tiberias
Tiberias
Haifa
Nazareth
Irbid
Dar'ā
Caesarea
Janīn
Bet She'an
Mediterranean Sea
Netanya
Nābulus
'Ajlūn
ISRAEL
Jordan
Ramat Gan
Az Zarqā'
Tel Aviv-Yafo
West Bank
Ḥolon
Jericho
Amman
Ramla
Ashdod
Jerusalem
Ashqelon
Bethlehem
Dead Sea
JORDAN
GAZA STRIP
Hebron
Dhībān
Gaza
Masada
Baltīm
Damietta
Port Said
Beersheba
'Arad
Al Karak
Nile Delta
Al 'Arīsh
Dimona
Sedom
Tanis
Pelusium
Al Manṣūrah
Suez
Nizzana
Oron
Tannur
Daphne
Ṭanṭā
Canal
Al Quṣaymah
Negeb
Az Zaqāzīq
Ismailia
Kadesh-barnea
'En Yahav
Wādī al 'Arabah
Succoth
Bitter Lakes
Petra
Banhā
Wādī Mūsā
EGYPT
Wādī al 'Arīsh
Ma'ān
Heliopolis (On)
Giza
Cairo (Al Qāhirah)
Suez
Mitla Pass
Al Kuntillah
Ra's an Naqb
Pyramids
Port Tawfīq
An Nakhl
Yotvata
Memphis
Ḥulwān
Sinai
Mikhrot Timna'
Birkat Qārūn
Nile
Ra's as Sidr
Elat
Al 'Aqabah
Ayn Sukhnah
Peninsula
Al Mudawwārah
Al Fayyūm
Gulf of Suez
Ḥaql
Eastern Desert
Za'farānah
Abū Zanīmah
Banī Suwayf
Nuweiba
Gulf of Aqaba
SAUDI ARABIA
Abū Rudays
Maghāghah
Dhahab
Jabal Mūsā (Mt. Sinai)
Maqna
Wādī aṭ Ṭarfā'
Ra's Ghārib
Aṭ Ṭūr
Al Khuraybah
Al Minyā
Str. of Tiran
Tīrān
Sharm ash Shaykh
Ṣanāfīr
Tell el-Amarna
Red Sea

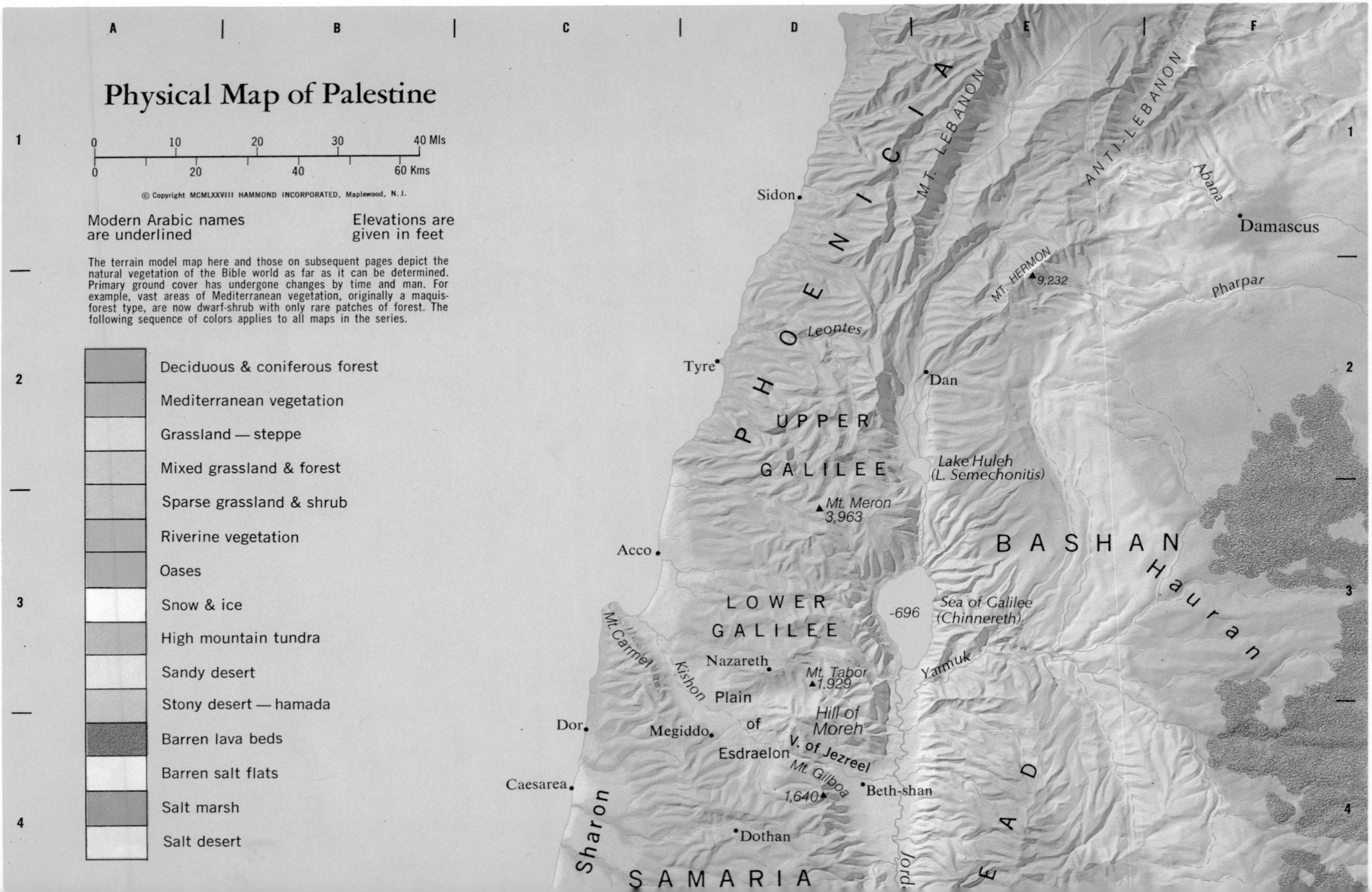
Physical Map of Palestine
0 10 20 30 40 Mls
0 20 40 60 Kms
© Copyright MCMLXXVIII HAMMOND INCORPORATED, Maplewood, N. J.
Modern Arabic names are underlined
Elevations are given in feet
The terrain model map here and those on subsequent pages depict the natural vegetation of the Bible world as far as it can be determined. Primary ground cover has undergone changes by time and man. For example, vast areas of Mediterranean vegetation, originally a maquis-forest type, are now dwarf-shrub with only rare patches of forest. The following sequence of colors applies to all maps in the series.
Deciduous & coniferous forest
Mediterranean vegetation
Grassland — steppe
Mixed grassland & forest
Sparse grassland & shrub
Riverine vegetation
Oases
Snow & ice
High mountain tundra
Sandy desert
Stony desert — hamada
Barren lava beds
Barren salt flats
Salt marsh
Salt desert
A
B
C
D
E
F
1
2
3
4
PHOENICIA
MT. LEBANON
ANTI-LEBANON
Sidon
Abana
Damascus
MT. HERMON 9,232
Pharpar
Leontes
Tyre
Dan
UPPER GALILEE
Lake Huleh (L. Semechonitis)
Mt. Meron 3,963
Acco
BASHAN
Hauran
LOWER GALILEE
Sea of Galilee (Chinnereth)
-696
Mt. Carmel
Kishon
Nazareth
Mt. Tabor 1,929
Yarmuk
Plain of Esdraelon
Hill of Moreh
Dor
Megiddo
V. of Jezreel
Mt. Gilboa
1,640
Beth-shan
Caesarea
Sharon
Dothan
SAMARIA
Jord.

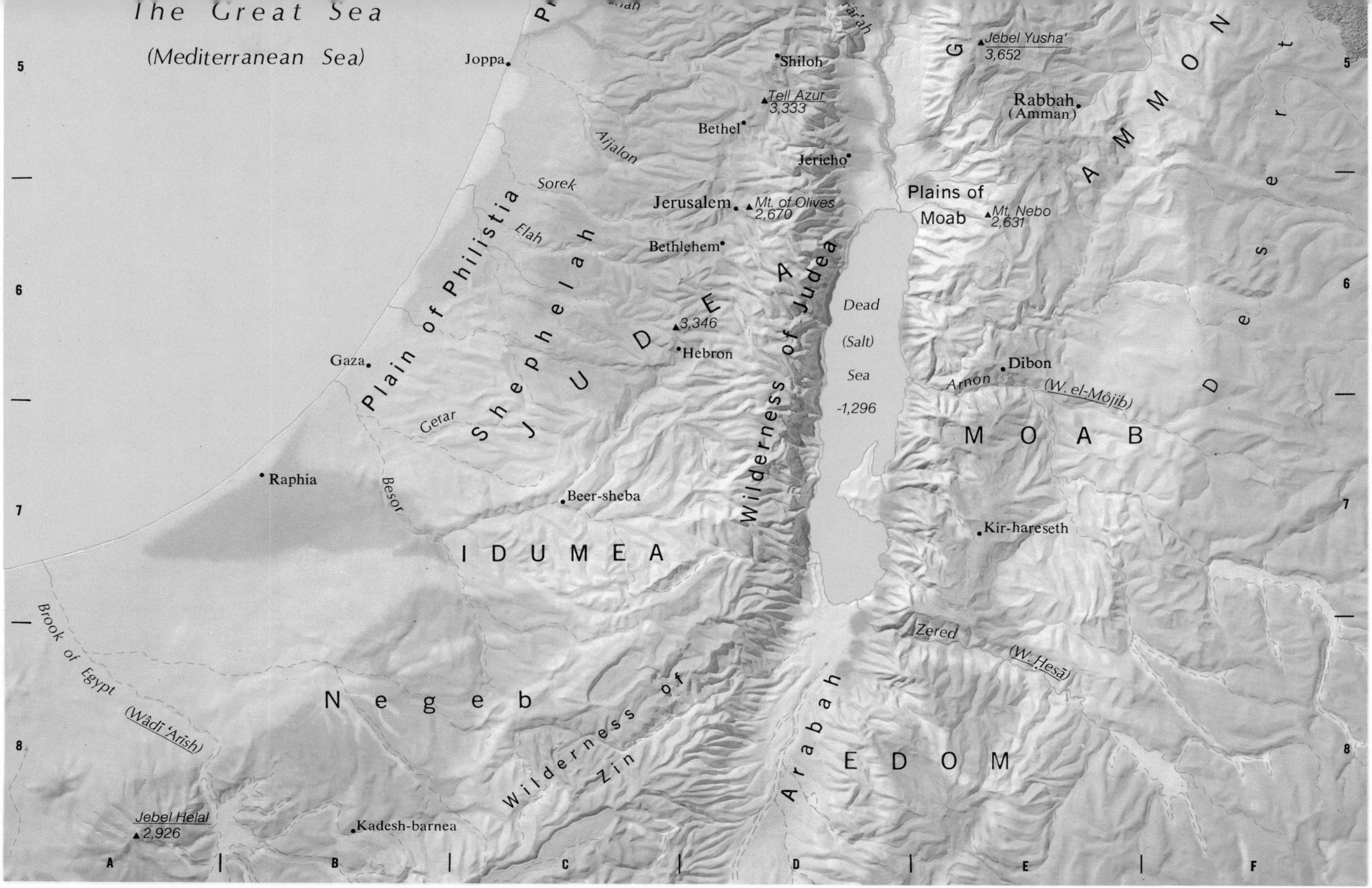

The Great Sea
(Mediterranean Sea)
Joppa
Shiloh
Tell Azur
3,333
Bethel
Jericho
Aijalon
Sorek
Elah
Jerusalem
Mt. of Olives
2,670
Bethlehem
3,346
Hebron
Gaza
Plain of Philistia
Shephelah
JUDEA
Gerar
Raphia
Besor
Beer-sheba
IDUMEA
Wilderness of Judea
Dead
(Salt)
Sea
-1,296
Jebel Yusha'
3,652
Rabbah
(Amman)
AMMON
Plains of
Moab
Mt. Nebo
2,631
Dibon
Arnon
(W. el-Môjib)
MOAB
Kir-hareseth
Zered
(W. Hesā)
EDOM
Arabah
Wilderness of
Zin
Negeb
Brook of Egypt
(Wâdī 'Arīsh)
Jebel Helal
2,926
Kadesh-barnea
A
B
C
D
E
F
5
6
7
8

The geographical setting for much of the Biblical narrative is within that half circle of arable land known as the Fertile Crescent. In the east the arc follows the alluvial plains of the Euphrates and Tigris rivers. It widens as one moves northwest through grassland and steppe, then it turns southwest at the Mediterranean coast and continues as a narrow belt through Phoenicia and Palestine. The arc ends in the green ribbon of the Nile. Rainfall, always scant and seasonal in the Middle East, has changed little since the beginning of the biblical era. Cropland and grassland areas remain much as they were in Abraham's day and the extent of desert is unchanged. Forests, however, have been slowly cut back by man so that today large expanses of mountain forest or wooded areas of the Mediterranean type are scarce.

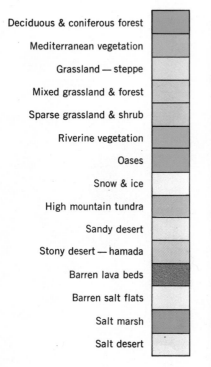

Deciduous & coniferous forest
Mediterranean vegetation
Grassland — steppe
Mixed grassland & forest
Sparse grassland & shrub
Riverine vegetation
Oases
Snow & ice
High mountain tundra
Sandy desert
Stony desert — hamada
Barren lava beds
Barren salt flats
Salt marsh
Salt desert

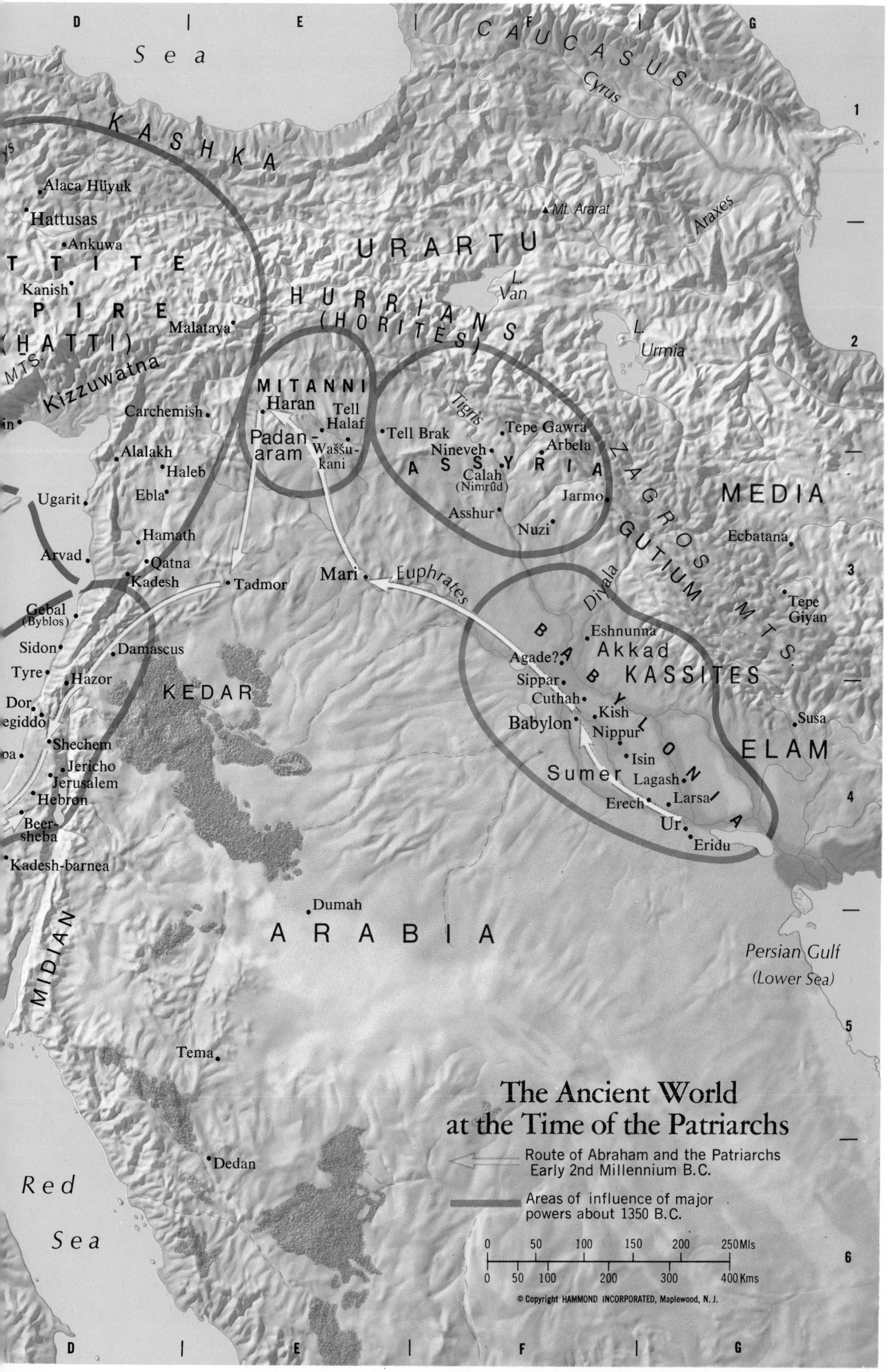
The Ancient World at the Time of the Patriarchs
Route of Abraham and the Patriarchs Early 2nd Millennium B.C.
Areas of influence of major powers about 1350 B.C.
0 50 100 150 200 250 Mls
0 50 100 200 300 400 Kms
© Copyright HAMMOND INCORPORATED, Maplewood, N. J.
D
E
F
G
1
2
3
4
5
6
Sea
CAUCASUS
Cyrus
KASHKA
Alaca Hüyük
Hattusas
Ankuwa
Kanish
(HATTI)
MTS.
Kizzuwatna
Malataya
Mt. Ararat
Araxes
URARTU
L. Van
L. Urmia
HURRIANS
(HORITES)
MITANNI
Haran
Tell Halaf
Padan-aram
Waššu-kani
Carchemish
Alalakh
Haleb
Ebla
Ugarit
Hamath
Arvad
Qatna
Kadesh
Tadmor
Mari
Euphrates
Tigris
Tell Brak
Tepe Gawra
Nineveh
Arbela
ASSYRIA
Calah (Nimrûd)
Asshur
Jarmo
Nuzi
ZAGROS
GUTIUM
MTS.
MEDIA
Ecbatana
Tepe Giyan
Diyala
Gebal (Byblos)
Sidon
Damascus
Tyre
Hazor
Dor
KEDAR
Shechem
Jericho
Jerusalem
Hebron
Beer-sheba
Kadesh-barnea
BABYLONIA
Eshnunna
Akkad
Agade?
KASSITES
Sippar
Cuthah
Kish
Babylon
Nippur
Susa
Isin
ELAM
Sumer
Lagash
Larsa
Erech
Ur
Eridu
Dumah
ARABIA
MIDIAN
Persian Gulf (Lower Sea)
Tema
Dedan
Red Sea

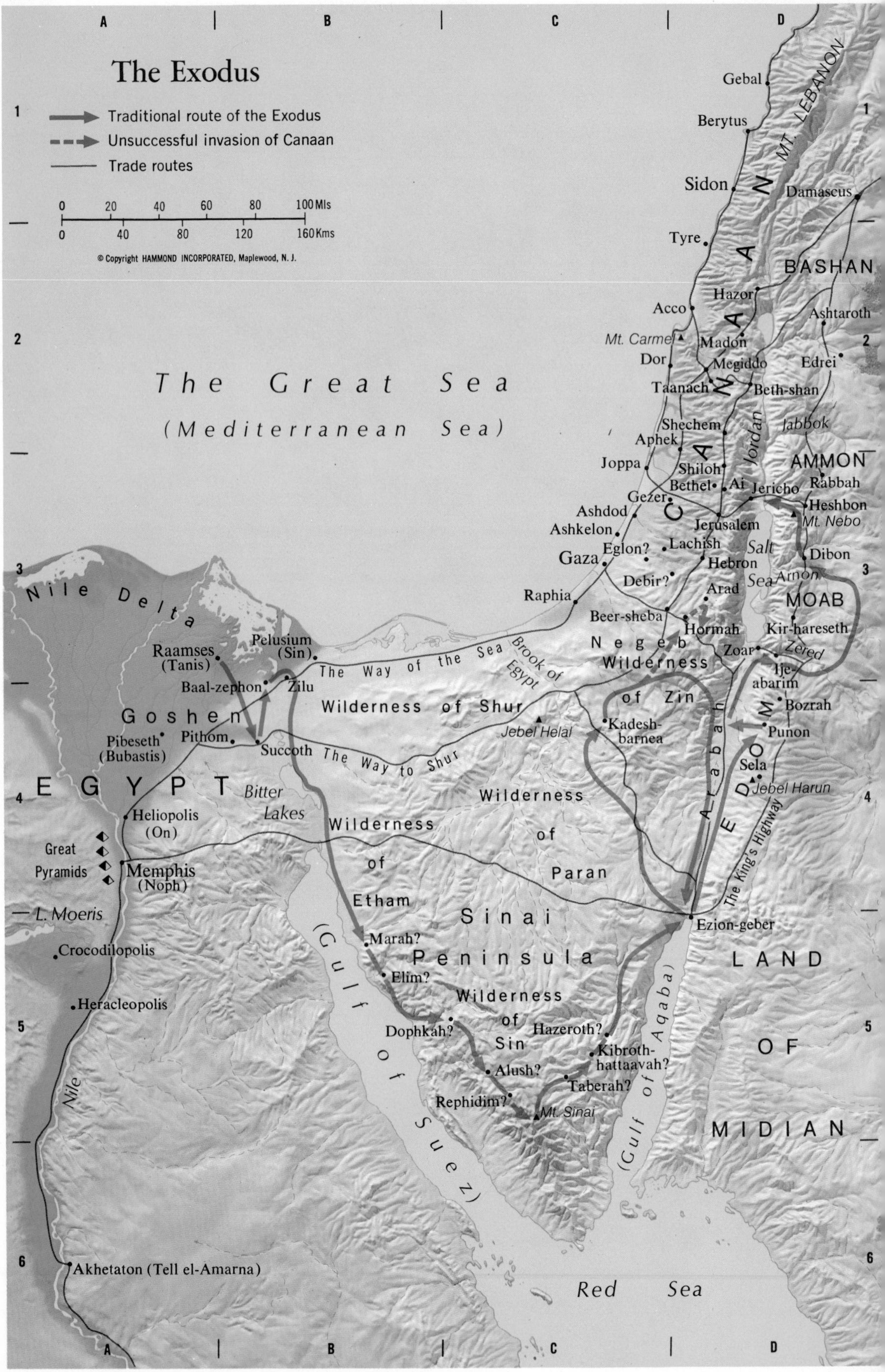
The Exodus
Traditional route of the Exodus
Unsuccessful invasion of Canaan
Trade routes
0 20 40 60 80 100 Mls
0 40 80 120 160 Kms
© Copyright HAMMOND INCORPORATED, Maplewood, N. J.
A
B
C
D
1
2
3
4
5
6
The Great Sea
(Mediterranean Sea)
Gebal
Berytus
MT. LEBANON
Sidon
Damascus
Tyre
BASHAN
Hazor
Acco
Ashtaroth
Mt. Carmel
Madon
Dor
Megiddo
Edrei
Taanach
Beth-shan
Shechem
Jabbok
Aphek
Jordan
Joppa
Shiloh
AMMON
Bethel
Ai
Jericho
Rabbah
Gezer
Heshbon
Ashdod
Mt. Nebo
Ashkelon
Jerusalem
Lachish
Salt
Gaza
Eglon?
Hebron
Dibon
Debir?
Sea
Arnon
Raphia
Arad
MOAB
Beer-sheba
Hormah
Kir-hareseth
CANAAN
Negeb
Zoar
Zered
Wilderness of Zin
Ije-abarim
Kadesh-barnea
Bozrah
Punon
Arabah
Sela
Jebel Harun
EDOM
The King's Highway
Nile Delta
Raamses (Tanis)
Pelusium (Sin)
The Way of the Sea
Brook of Egypt
Baal-zephon
Zilu
Wilderness of Shur
Goshen
Jebel Helal
Pibeseth (Bubastis)
Pithom
Succoth
The Way to Shur
EGYPT
Bitter Lakes
Wilderness of Paran
Heliopolis (On)
Wilderness of Etham
Great Pyramids
Memphis (Noph)
L. Moeris
Sinai Peninsula
Ezion-geber
Marah?
Crocodilopolis
Elim?
LAND OF MIDIAN
Heracleopolis
Wilderness of Sin
Dophkah?
Hazeroth?
Kibroth-hattaavah?
Alush?
Taberah?
Nile
Rephidim?
Mt. Sinai
(Gulf of Suez)
(Gulf of Aqaba)
Akhetaton (Tell el-Amarna)
Red Sea

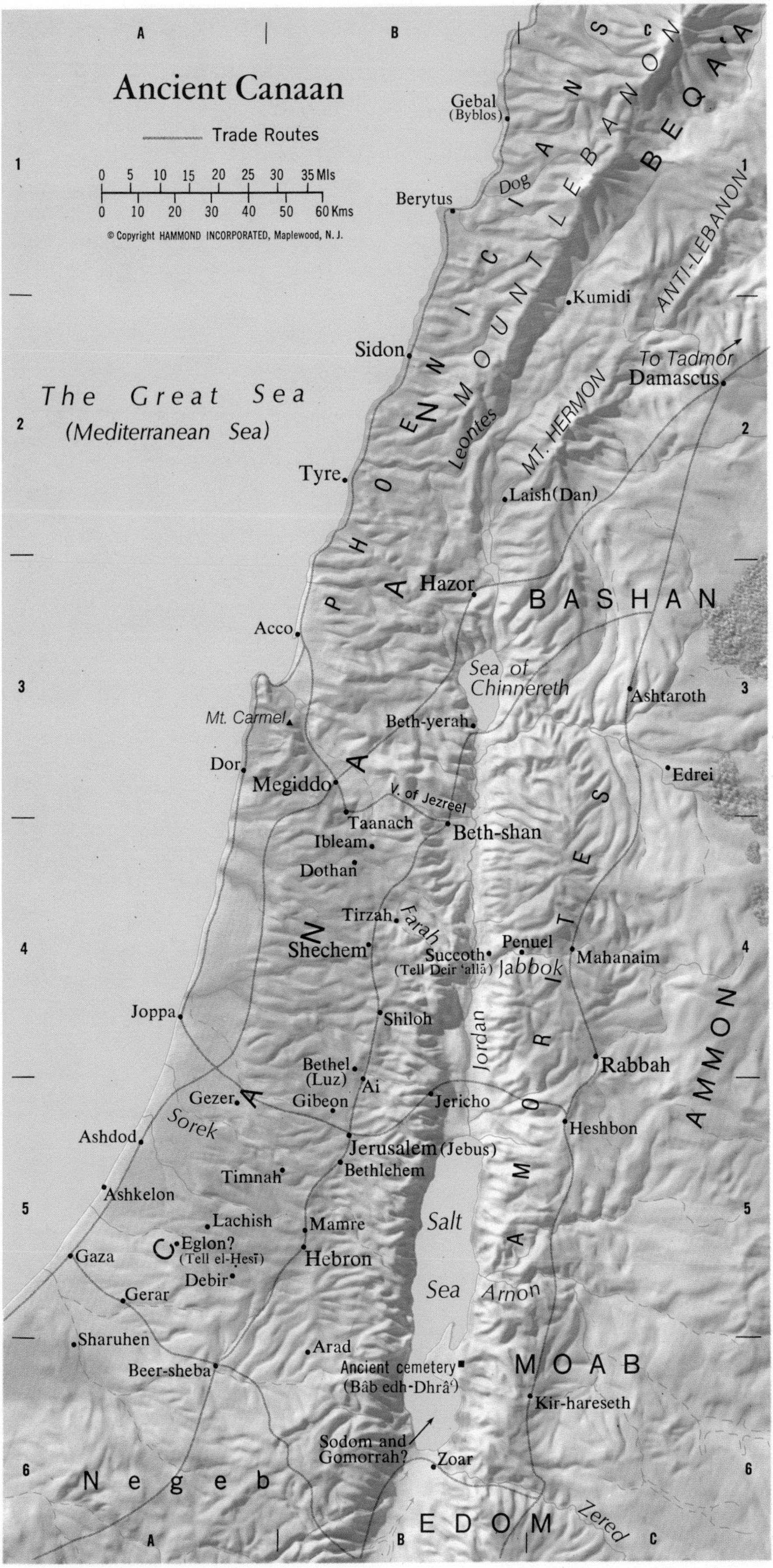
Ancient Canaan
Trade Routes
0 5 10 15 20 25 30 35 Mls
0 10 20 30 40 50 60 Kms
© Copyright HAMMOND INCORPORATED, Maplewood, N. J.
A
B
C
1
2
3
4
5
6
The Great Sea
(Mediterranean Sea)
Gebal
(Byblos)
Berytus
Dog
PHOENICIANS
MOUNT LEBANON
BEQA'A
ANTI-LEBANON
Kumidi
Sidon
To Tadmor
Damascus
Leontes
MT. HERMON
Tyre
Laish (Dan)
Hazor
BASHAN
Acco
Sea of
Chinnereth
Ashtaroth
Mt. Carmel
Beth-yerah
Dor
Megiddo
V. of Jezreel
Edrei
Taanach
Beth-shan
Ibleam
Dothan
Tirzah
Farah
CANAAN
Shechem
Succoth
(Tell Deir 'allā)
Penuel
Jabbok
Mahanaim
AMORITES
Joppa
Shiloh
Jordan
AMMON
Bethel
(Luz)
Ai
Rabbah
Gezer
Gibeon
Jericho
Sorek
Heshbon
Ashdod
Jerusalem (Jebus)
Bethlehem
Timnah
Ashkelon
Lachish
Mamre
Salt
Sea
Eglon?
(Tell el-Ḥesī)
Gaza
Hebron
Debir
Gerar
Arnon
Sharuhen
Arad
Ancient cemetery
(Bâb edh-Dhrâ')
MOAB
Beer-sheba
Kir-hareseth
Sodom and
Gomorrah?
Zoar
Negeb
EDOM
Zered

MAP VI

Early Israelite Settlement in Canaan
Area settled by Israelites
JUDAH Twelve Israelite tribes
Gezer Unconquered Canaanite city (according to Judges 1)
A
B
C
1
2
3
4
5
6
SIDONIANS
HIVITES
ARAMEANS
MT. LEBANON
MT. HERMON
Sidon
Damascus
Ahlab
Tyre
Beth-shemesh?
DAN
Dan (Laish)
Kedesh
ASHER
NAPHTALI
Achzib
Merom
Hazor
Beth-anath?
Acco
Rehob
Aphek
The Great Sea
Sea of Chinnereth
Bashan
Golan
Ashtaroth
ZEBULUN
Shimron
Mt. Tabor
Kishon
ISSACHAR
Edrei
Havvoth-jair
Dor
Megiddo
Jezreel
Ramoth-gilead
Taanach
Beth-shan
Ibleam
Jabesh-gilead
Gilead
Hepher
MANASSEH
Plain of Sharon
Tirzah
Mt. Ebal
Shechem
Mt. Gerizim
Jordan
Succoth
Jabbok
AMMON
Aphek
GAD
Joppa
Shiloh
PHILISTINES
EPHRAIM
Jazer
Rabbah
Gath
Bethel
Ai
Gilgal
Shaalbim
Gezer
BENJAMIN
Jericho
Gibeon
Sorek
Ekron
DAN
Aijalon
Heshbon
Bezer
Ashdod
Jerusalem
Mt. Nebo
Libnah
Beth-shemesh
Ashkelon
Adullam
REUBEN
Gath?
Beth-zur
Lachish
Salt Sea
Gaza
Eglon?
Hebron
Aroer
Debir?
JUDAH
Wilderness of Judah
Arnon
Gerar
Ziklag?
Arad
Beer-sheba
MOAB
Besor
Hormah
Kir-hareseth
SIMEON
Negeb
Zoar
Zered
Tamar
EDOM
0 5 10 15 20 25 30 35 Mls
0 10 20 30 40 50 60 Kms
© Copyright HAMMOND INCORPORATED, Maplewood, N. J.

The Empire of David and Solomon
Boundary of the empire at its greatest extent
Territory in the far north under economic influence of Solomon
Fortified places of Solomon
Copper mining centers
0 10 25 50 75 100 Mls
0 20 40 60 80 100 120 140 160 Kms
© Copyright HAMMOND INCORPORATED, Maplewood, N.J.
A
B
C
D
1
2
3
4
5
6
The Great Sea
(Mediterranean Sea)
KITTIM
(CYPRUS)
HITTITES
Haleb
Euphrates
Tiphsah
Ugarit
Orontes
HAMATH
Hamath
Arvad
Kadesh
Tadmor
ARAM–
ZOBAH
Zedad
Lebo-hamath
Hazar-enan
Gebal
Berothai
Berytus
PHOENICIA
MT. LEBANON
BETH-REHOB
Syrian
Desert
Sidon
ARAM–
Damascus
DAMASCUS
MT. HERMON
Tyre
Abel
Dan
Kedesh
MAACAH
Hazor
ARGOB
Acco
Cabul
Mt. Carmel
GESHUR
Ashtaroth
Dor
TOB
Edrei
Megiddo
Jezreel
Taanach
Ramoth-gilead
Salecah
Mt. Gilboa
Beth-shan
Hepher
Jordan
Mahanaim
Shechem
Succoth
Joppa
ISRAEL
Gezer
Beth-horon
Rabbah
PHILISTIA
Bethel
AMMON
Gibeah
Jericho
Ashdod
Jerusalem
Heshbon
Beth-shemesh
Ashkelon
Gath?
Medeba
Gaza
Hebron
Lachish
Salt Sea
JUDAH
Aroer
Ziklag ?
Gerar
Raphia
Beer-sheba
Arad
MOAB
Kir-hareseth
Tamar
AMALEK
Bozrah
Kadesh-barnea
Punon
River of Egypt
EDOM
Arabah
Sela
Sinai
Ezion-geber

The Kingdoms of Israel and Judah
Approximate frontiers
ISRAEL Hebrew kingdoms
AMMON Foreign kingdoms
0 10 20 30 40 Mls
0 20 40 60 Kms
© Copyright HAMMOND INCORPORATED, Maplewood, N. J.
A
B
C
D
1
2
3
4
5
6
The Great Sea
(Mediterranean Sea)
Sidon
Damascus
PHOENICIA
MT. HERMON
SYRIA
(ARAM)
Ijon
Leontes
Tyre
Abel-beth-maachah
Dan
Kedesh
Hazor
Merom
Galilee
Bashan
Acco
Cabul
Chinnereth
Sea of Chinnereth
Karnaim
Ashtaroth
Rumah
Hammath
Mt. Carmel
Aphek
Plain of Esdraelon
Mt. Tabor
Yarmuk
Kishon
Havvoth-jair
Edrei
Dor
Shunem
Megiddo
Jezreel
Mt. Gilboa
Ramoth-gilead
Taanach
Beth-shan
Ibleam
Abel-meholah
Dothan
Jabesh-gilead
Tishbe
Plain of Sharon
Socoh
ISRAEL
Tirzah
Samaria
Mt. Ebal
Gilead
Mt. Gerizim
Shechem
Succoth
Penuel
Mahanaim
Jordan
Jabbok
Kanah
Aphek
AMMON
Shiloh
Joppa
Jazer
Lod
Zemaraim
Rabbah
Gath
Bethel
Mizpah
Gilgal
Jabneel
Gezer
Geba
Gibbethon
Aijalon
Gibeon
Ramah
Jericho
Shittim?
Heshbon
Ekron
Ashdod
Zorah
Jerusalem
PHILISTIA
Beth-shemesh
Bethlehem
Mt. Nebo
Medeba
Jahaz
Ashkelon
Adullam
Judah
Tekoa
Mareshah
Beth-zur
Ataroth
Lachish
JUDAH
Salt Sea
Gaza
Dibon
Adoraim
Hebron
En-gedi
Aroer
Debir?
Ziph
Arnon
Gerar
Wilderness of Judah
Ziklag?
Raphia
Sharuhen
Arad
Ar?
Beer-sheba
MOAB
Besor
Kir-hareseth
Zoar
Tamar
Zered
Negeb
Ascent of Akrabbim
EDOM

Palestine After the Fall of the Northern Kingdom
Approximate frontiers
AMMON Independent kingdoms
DU'RU Assyrian provinces
0 10 20 30 40 Mls
0 20 40 60 Kms
© Copyright MCMLXXVIII HAMMOND INCORPORATED, Maplewood, N. J.
A
B
C
D
1
2
3
4
5
6
Sidon
Phoenicia
Leontes
Ijon
Tyre (free city)
Abel-beth-maachah
Dan
Kedesh
Hazor
Achzib
Nahariyah
Acco
DŪR-BELḪARRAN-ŠADUA
Damascus
DIMAŠQI (ĀRĀM)
MT. HERMON
ASSYRIAN EMPIRE
QARNINI
Chinnereth
Sea of Chinnereth
Karnaim
Ashtaroth
ḪAURINA
Jotbah
Mt. Carmel
MAGIDŪ
Aphek
Yarmuk
Mt. Tabor
Kishon
GAL'AZA
The Great Sea (Mediterranean Sea)
Dor
Megiddo
Shunem
Jezreel
Ramoth-gilead
Taanach
Beth-shan
DU'RU
Ibleam
Dothan
Jabesh-gilead
Gilead
SAMERINA
Tirzah
Jordan
Samaria
Mt. Ebal
Mahanaim
Shechem
Penuel
Mt. Gerizim
Succoth
Jabbok
Kanah
Aphek
Shiloh
Joppa
Bene-berak
AMMON
Beth-dagon
Jazer
Lod
Rabbah
Rimmon
Gath
Bethel
Aiath
Gilgal
Eltekeh?
Mizpah
Geba
Jabneel
Gezer
Jericho
Shittim?
Gibbethon
Aijalon
Gibeon
Ramah
Elealeh
Gibeah
Anathoth
Sibmah
Heshbon
Ashdod
Ekron
Jerusalem
Nob
Mt. Nebo
Timnah
Beth-shemesh
Bethlehem
Medeba
Jahaz
ASDUDU
Azekah
Ashkelon
Adullam
Philistia
Moresheth-gath
Tekoa
Gath?
Mareshah
Beth-zur
Ataroth
Lachish
JUDAH
Salt Sea
Dibon
Gaza
Adoraim
Hebron
Aroer
En-gedi
Ziph
Debir?
Beth-ezel
Arnon
Gerar
Ziklag?
MOAB
Raphia
Sharuhen
Arad
Ar?
Beer-sheba
EGYPT
Besor
Kir-hareseth (Kir, Kir-heres)
Zoar
Tamar
Zered
Negeb
EDOM

MAP X

The Assyrian Empire
Assyrian empire – ca.824 B.C.
Assyrian empire – ca.640 B.C.
Cyrene Greek colonies underlined in red
0 50 100 150 200 250 300 350 Mls
0 100 200 300 400 500 Kms
© Copyright HAMMOND INCORPORATED, Maplewood, N.J.
Caspian Sea
Black Sea
Upper (Western) Sea
Lower (Eastern) Sea
Red Sea
Aegean Sea
ASSYRIAN EMPIRE
CIMMERIANS (GOMER)
URARTU (ARARAT)
TUBAL
CILICIA
PHRYGIA
MESHECH
LYDIA
GREEK CITY STATES
MADAI
ELAM
BABYLONIA
CHALDEANS
ARIBI (ARABS)
KEDAR
SYRIA
PHOENICIA
AMMON
MOAB
EDOM
JUDAH trib. to Assyria
EGYPT to Assyria 671-651 B.C.
LIBYANS
Libyan Desert
Nairi
Minni
Byzantium
Chalcedon
Astacus
Tieum
Cyzicus
Abydos
Thasos
Lesbos
Chios
Samos
Euboea
Athens
Corinth
Sparta
Crete
Rhodes
Miletus
Sardis
Phaselis
Cyrene
Ancyra
Gordion
L. Tuz
TAURUS MTS.
Halys
Kanish
Tarsus
Cyprus
Arvad
Sidon
Tyre
Samaria
Elteketh
Raphia
Jerusalem
Sela
Pelusium
Bubastis
Tanis
On
Sais
Memphis
Heracleopolis
Hermopolis
Siut
Abydos
Thebes
Syene
Nile
Oasis of Siwa
Trapezus
Melitene
Sam'al
Carchemish
Arpad
Aleppo
Qarqar
Hamath
Damascus
Haran
Til-Barsip
Tadmor
Nisibis
Gozan
Habor
Anat
Euphrates
Tigris
Diyala
Nineveh
Calah (Nimrûd)
Asshur
Arbela
Dūr-Šarrukin
Turushpa
L. Van
Mt. Ararat
L. Sevan
Cyrus
Araxes
L. Urmia
Ecbatana
Susa (Šušan)
Sippar
Cuthah
Babylon
Borsippa
Nippur
Erech
Larsa
Ur
Dumah
Tema
Dedan

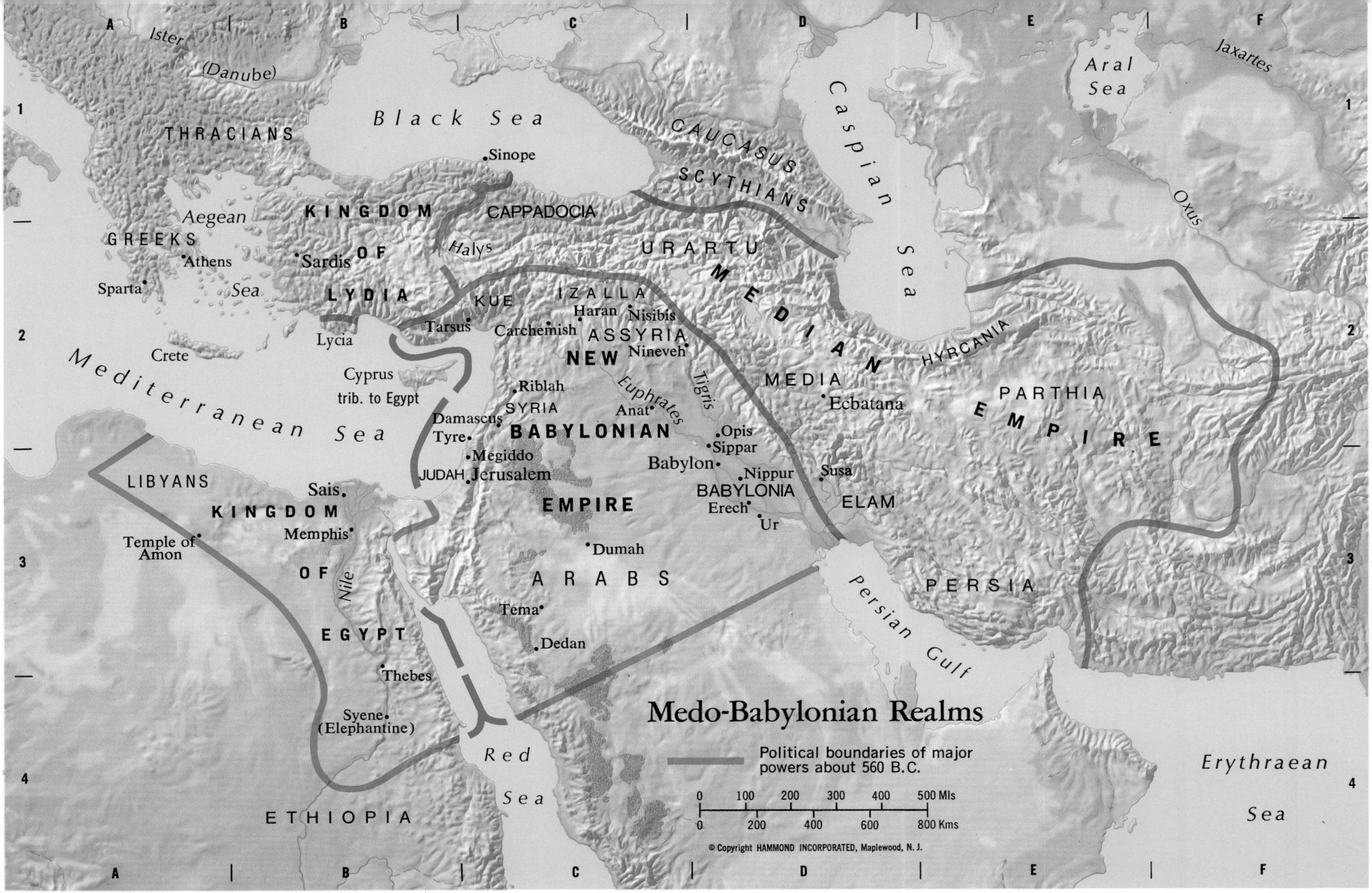
Medo-Babylonian Realms
Political boundaries of major powers about 560 B.C.
0 100 200 300 400 500 Mls
0 200 400 600 800 Kms
© Copyright HAMMOND INCORPORATED, Maplewood, N. J.
A
B
C
D
E
F
1
2
3
4
Ister
(Danube)
Black Sea
THRACIANS
Sinope
Caspian Sea
Aral Sea
Jaxartes
Oxus
CAUCASUS
SCYTHIANS
KINGDOM OF LYDIA
CAPPADOCIA
Aegean Sea
GREEKS
Athens
Sparta
Sardis
Halys
URARTU
MEDIAN EMPIRE
KUE
IZALLA
Haran
Nisibis
Tarsus
Carchemish
ASSYRIA
Nineveh
NEW BABYLONIAN EMPIRE
Lycia
Crete
Cyprus
trib. to Egypt
Mediterranean Sea
Riblah
SYRIA
Euphrates
Tigris
Anat
Damascus
Tyre
Megiddo
JUDAH
Jerusalem
Opis
Sippar
Babylon
Nippur
BABYLONIA
Erech
Ur
MEDIA
Ecbatana
HYRCANIA
PARTHIA
Susa
ELAM
PERSIA
Persian Gulf
LIBYANS
KINGDOM OF EGYPT
Sais
Memphis
Temple of Amon
Nile
Thebes
Syene
(Elephantine)
Dumah
ARABS
Tema
Dedan
Red Sea
ETHIOPIA
Erythraean Sea

MAP XII

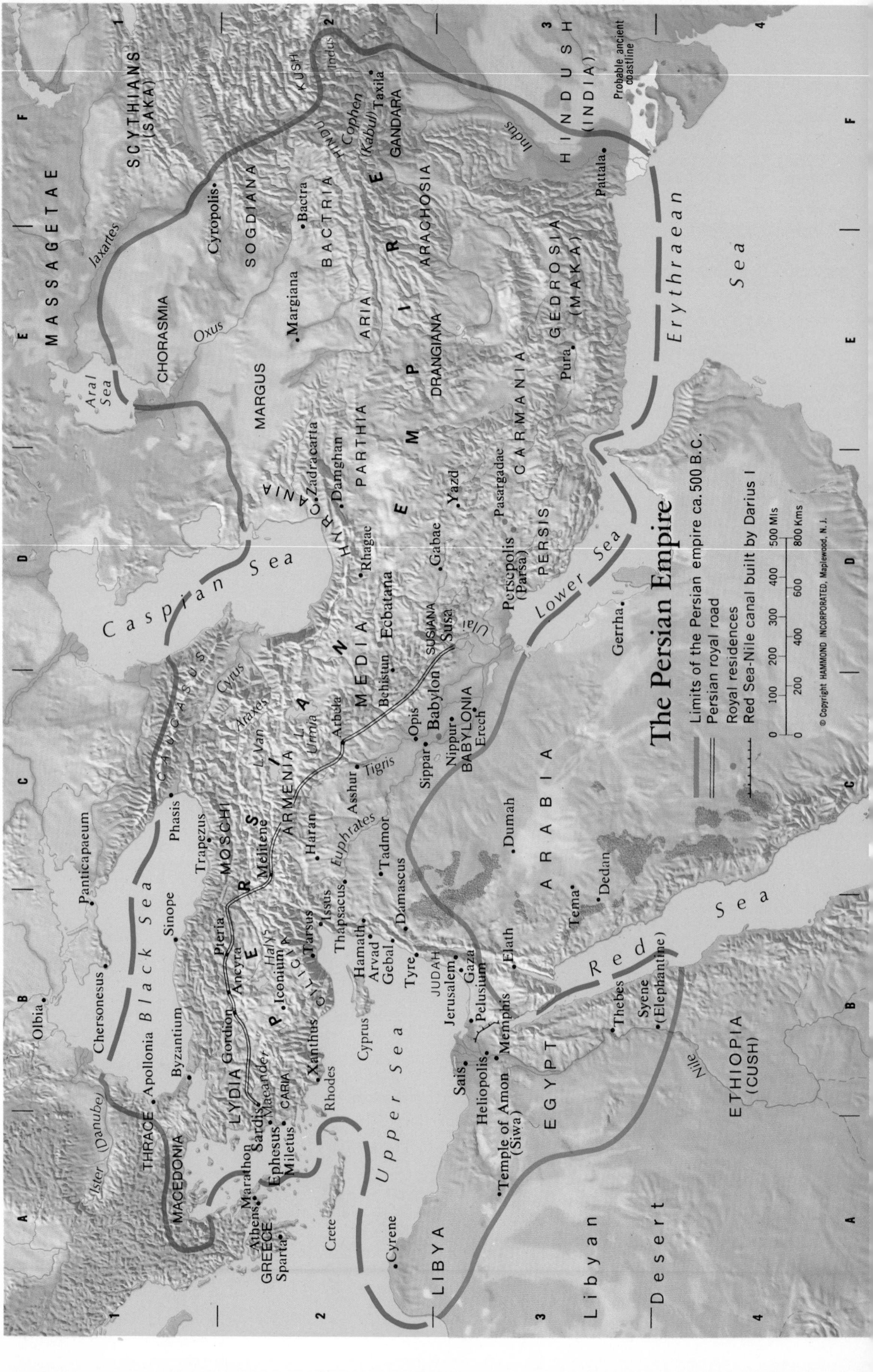
The Persian Empire
Limits of the Persian empire ca. 500 B.C.
Persian royal road
Royal residences
Red Sea-Nile canal built by Darius I
0 100 200 300 400 500 Mls
0 200 400 600 800 Kms
© Copyright HAMMOND INCORPORATED, Maplewood, N.J.
P E R S I A N E M P I R E
MASSAGETAE
SCYTHIANS (SAKA)
CHORASMIA
SOGDIANA
BACTRIA
MARGUS
Margiana
ARIA
PARTHIA
HYRCANIA
DRANGIANA
ARACHOSIA
GANDARA
HINDU KUSH
HINDUSH (INDIA)
GEDROSIA (MAKA)
CARMANIA
PERSIS
MEDIA
SUSIANA
BABYLONIA
ARMENIA
MOSCHI
CAUCASUS
LYDIA
CARIA
THRACE
MACEDONIA
GREECE
LIBYA
EGYPT
ETHIOPIA (CUSH)
ARABIA
JUDAH
Caspian Sea
Aral Sea
Black Sea
Upper Sea
Lower Sea
Red Sea
Erythraean Sea
Libyan Desert
Jaxartes
Oxus
Indus
Cophen (Kabul)
Cyrus
Araxes
L. Van
L. Urmia
Tigris
Euphrates
Halys
Maeander
Ulai
Nile
Ister (Danube)
Probable ancient coastline
Cyropolis
Bactra
Taxila
Pattala
Pura
Zadracarta
Damghan
Rhagae
Ecbatana
Behistun
Gabae
Yazd
Pasargadae
Persepolis (Parsa)
Susa
Babylon
Opis
Sippar
Nippur
Erech
Gerrha
Arbela
Asshur
Haran
Tadmor
Thapsacus
Issus
Tarsus
Melitene
Trapezus
Phasis
Panticapaeum
Sinope
Chersonesus
Olbia
Apollonia
Byzantium
Pteria
Ancyra
Gordion
Iconium
Sardis
Ephesus
Miletus
Xanthus
Rhodes
Marathon
Athens
Sparta
Crete
Cyrene
Cyprus
Hamath
Arvad
Gebal
Damascus
Tyre
Jerusalem
Gaza
Elath
Tema
Dedan
Dumah
Pelusium
Memphis
Heliopolis
Sais
Temple of Amon (Siwa)
Thebes
Syene (Elephantine)

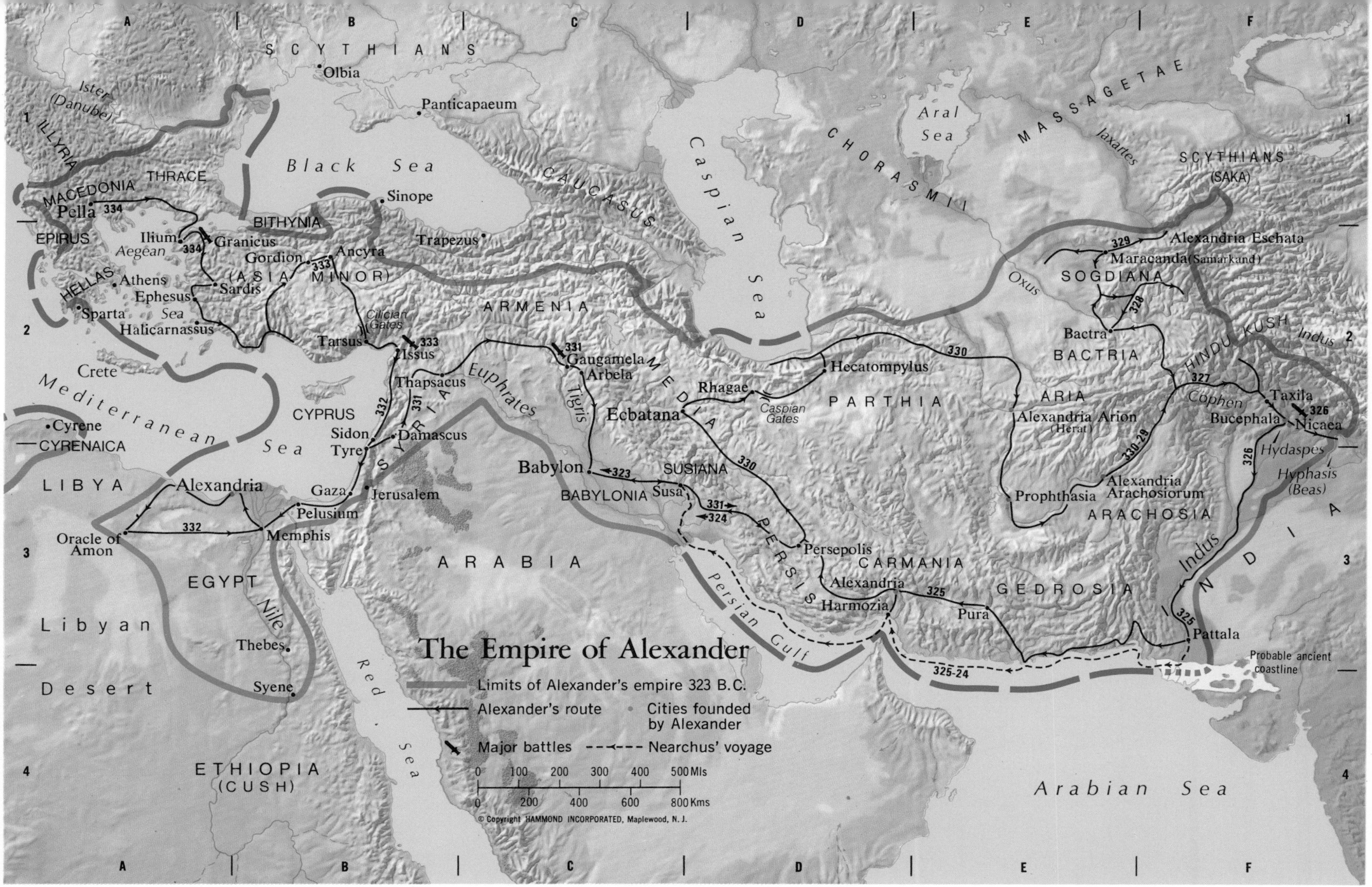
The Empire of Alexander
Limits of Alexander's empire 323 B.C.
Alexander's route
Cities founded by Alexander
Major battles
Nearchus' voyage
0 100 200 300 400 500 Mls
0 200 400 600 800 Kms
SCYTHIANS
Olbia
Panticapaeum
Ister (Danube)
ILLYRIA
THRACE
MACEDONIA
Pella
334
EPIRUS
Black Sea
Sinope
BITHYNIA
Trapezus
Ilium
Granicus
Aegean Sea
Gordion
Ancyra
333
(ASIA MINOR)
HELLAS
Athens
Sardis
Ephesus
Sparta
Halicarnassus
Cilician Gates
Tarsus
Issus
ARMENIA
CAUCASUS
Caspian Sea
CHORASMII
Aral Sea
MASSAGETAE
Jaxartes
SCYTHIANS (SAKA)
Alexandria Eschata
329
Maracanda (Samarkand)
SOGDIANA
Oxus
328
Bactra
BACTRIA
HINDU KUSH
Indus
327
Cophen
Taxila
326
Bucephala
Nicaea
Hydaspes
Hyphasis (Beas)
INDIA
Crete
Mediterranean Sea
Cyrene
CYRENAICA
CYPRUS
Sidon
Tyre
Damascus
SYRIA
Thapsacus
Euphrates
331
Gaugamela
Arbela
Tigris
MEDIA
Ecbatana
Rhagae
Caspian Gates
Hecatompylus
330
PARTHIA
ARIA
Alexandria Arion (Herat)
330-29
Alexandria Arachosiorum
Prophthasia
ARACHOSIA
332
LIBYA
Alexandria
Gaza
Jerusalem
Pelusium
Memphis
Oracle of Amon
Babylon
323
BABYLONIA
SUSIANA
Susa
324
PERSIS
Persepolis
CARMANIA
Alexandria
Harmozia
325
Pura
GEDROSIA
Pattala
325-24
Probable ancient coastline
EGYPT
Nile
Thebes
Syene
ARABIA
Persian Gulf
Red Sea
Libyan Desert
ETHIOPIA (CUSH)
Arabian Sea
A B C D E F
1 2 3 4

MAP XIV

Rival Powers ca. 192 B.C.
Major Hellenistic states
Lesser Hellenistic states
Roman domain
Carthaginian realm
0 200 400 600 Mls
0 200 400 600 800 1000 Kms
Gaul
Hispania
ROMAN DOMAIN
Massilia
Corsica
Sardinia
Carthago Nova
Tingis
MAURETANIA
NUMIDIA
Carthage
CARTHAGE
Padus (Po)
ITALY
Rome
Tarentum
Messana
Sicily
Syracuse
ILLYRIA
Ister
Dacia
(Danube)
THRACE
Pella
ANTIGONID KDM.
EPIRUS
AETOLIAN LEAGUE
ACHAEAN LEAGUE
Athens
Sparta
Crete
Rhodes
Mediterranean Sea
Cyrene
PTOLEMAIC EGYPT KINGDOM
Alexandria
Memphis
Nile
Black Sea
BITHYNIA
PONTUS
CAPPADOCIA
GALATIA
Pergamum
CYPRUS
SELEUCID KINGDOM
Antioch
SYRIA
Damascus
Tyre
Jerusalem
NABATEA
CAUCASUS
ARMENIA
Caspian Sea
PARTHIA
Tigris
Euphrates
Seleucia
Babylon
Persian Gulf
Arabia
Red Sea
A B C D E F
1 2 3
© Copyright HAMMOND INCORPORATED, Maplewood, N. J.

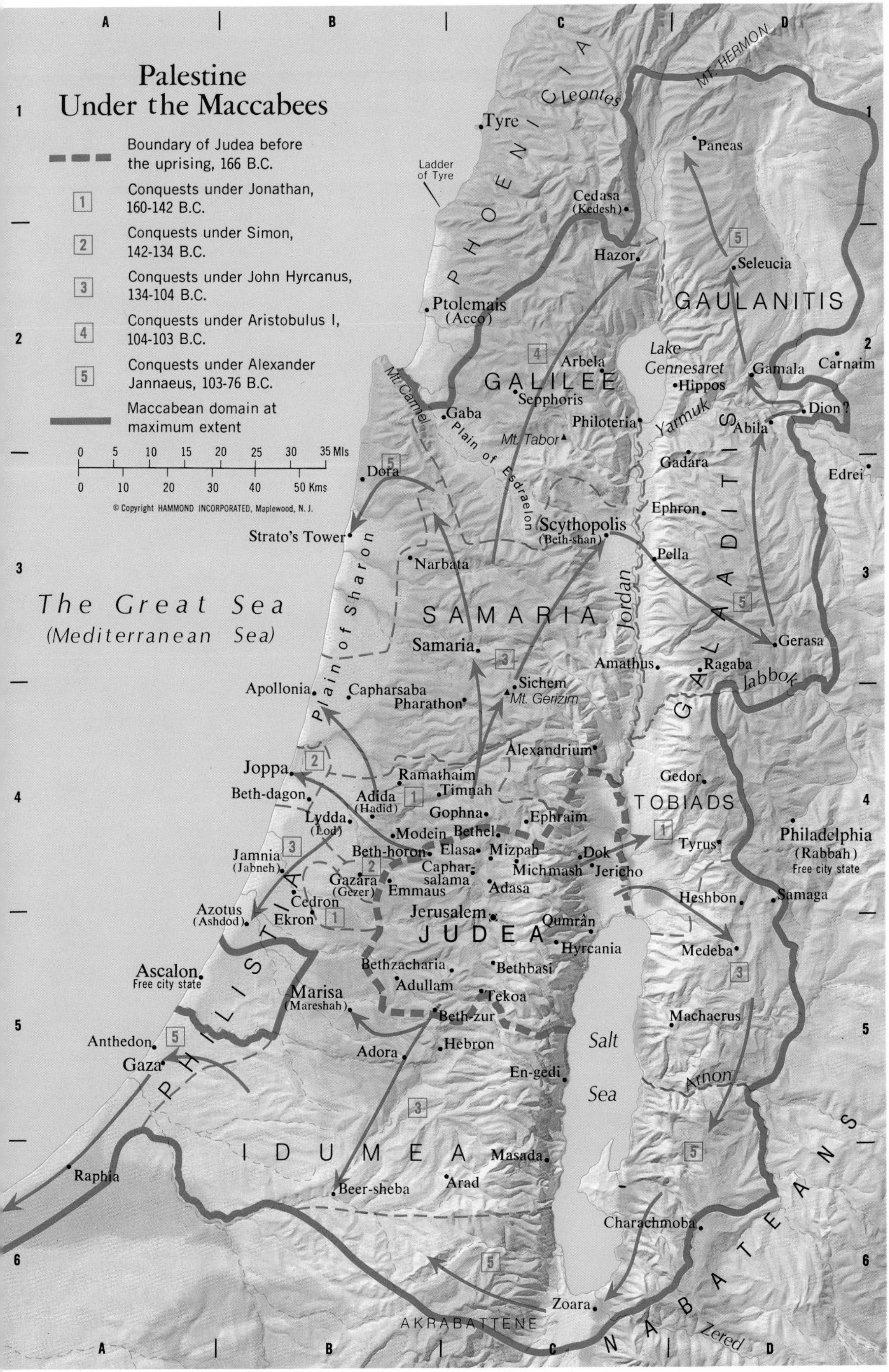
Palestine
Under the Maccabees
Boundary of Judea before the uprising, 166 B.C.
1 Conquests under Jonathan, 160-142 B.C.
2 Conquests under Simon, 142-134 B.C.
3 Conquests under John Hyrcanus, 134-104 B.C.
4 Conquests under Aristobulus I, 104-103 B.C.
5 Conquests under Alexander Jannaeus, 103-76 B.C.
Maccabean domain at maximum extent
0 5 10 15 20 25 30 35 Mls
0 10 20 30 40 50 Kms
© Copyright HAMMOND INCORPORATED, Maplewood, N. J.
A
B
C
D
1
2
3
4
5
6
PHOENICIA
Leontes
MT. HERMON
Tyre
Ladder of Tyre
Paneas
Cedasa (Kedesh)
Hazor
Seleucia
GAULANITIS
Ptolemais (Acco)
Lake Gennesaret
Arbela
GALILEE
Carnaim
Gamala
Hippos
Mt. Carmel
Sepphoris
Gaba
Plain of Esdraelon
Philoteria
Yarmuk
Dion ?
Abila
Mt. Tabor
Gadara
Edrei
Dora
Ephron
Strato's Tower
Scythopolis (Beth-shan)
Pella
GALAADITIS
Narbata
Plain of Sharon
The Great Sea (Mediterranean Sea)
SAMARIA
Jordan
Samaria
Gerasa
Amathus
Ragaba
Jabbok
Apollonia
Capharsaba
Pharathon
Sichem
Mt. Gerizim
Alexandrium
Joppa
Ramathaim
Gedor
Beth-dagon
Adida (Hadid)
Timnah
TOBIADS
Lydda (Lod)
Gophna
Ephraim
Modein
Bethel
Philadelphia (Rabbah)
Free city state
Jamnia (Jabneh)
Beth-horon
Elasa
Mizpah
Dok
Tyrus
Gazara (Gezer)
Caphar-salama
Michmash
Jericho
Emmaus
Adasa
Cedron
Heshbon
Samaga
Azotus (Ashdod)
Ekron
Jerusalem
Qumrân
JUDEA
Hyrcania
Medeba
Ascalon
Free city state
Bethzacharia
Bethbasi
PHILISTIA
Adullam
Marisa (Mareshah)
Tekoa
Beth-zur
Machaerus
Anthedon
Salt Sea
Gaza
Adora
Hebron
En-gedi
Arnon
IDUMEA
Masada
Raphia
Arad
Beer-sheba
Charachmoba
NABATEANS
Zoara
AKRABATTENE
Zered

MAP XVI

The Roman World
Limits of direct Roman rule or political influence at the birth of Christ
Provincial or state boundaries
SYRIA Roman provinces
LYCIA Client kingdoms or states
0 100 200 300 400 500 Mls
0 200 400 600 800 Kms
© Copyright HAMMOND INCORPORATED, Maplewood, N.J.
Atlantic Ocean
Britannia
LUGDUNENSIS
Lutetia
BELGICA
Gaul
AQUITANIA
Lugdunum
Burdigala
NARBONENSIS
Narbo
ALPES
Augusta Treverorum
Rhine
Lost to Rome in A.D. 9
Albis (Elbe)
Germania
Danube
RAETIA
NORICUM
ALPS
Aquileia
PANNONIA
ILLYRICUM
Salonae
TARRACONENSIS
Tarraco
Caesarea Augusta
Hispania
LUSITANIA
Emerita Augusta
BAETICA
Corduba
Tingis
MAURETANIA
Caesarea
Cirta
Carthage
CORSICA AND SARDINIA
Caralis
Rubicon
ITALY
Rome
Tarentum
Sea of Adria
SICILIA
Syracuse
Mare Internum
(Mediterranean Sea)
AFRICA
Leptis Magna
Cyrene
CYRENAICA
CRETA
Sarmatia
CARPATHIANS
Dacia
Ister (Danube)
MOESIA
THRACE
MACEDONIA
Thessalonica
Byzantium
ACHAIA
Corinth
Athens
Aegean Sea
ASIA
Pergamum
Ephesus
BITHYNIA & PONTUS
Sinope
Black Sea
BOSPORUS KDM.
Trapezus
CAPPADOCIA
Ancyra
GALATIA
LYCIA
PAMPHYLIA
CILICIA
Tarsus
COMMAGENE
Antioch
SYRIA
CYPRUS
KDM. OF HEROD
Jerusalem
NABATEA
Alexandria
Memphis
EGYPT
Nile
Thebes
Red Sea
Arabia
CAUCASUS
Colchis
Iberia
Albania
ARMENIA
Artaxata
Caspian Sea
Rha (Volga)
PARTHIAN EMPIRE
Ctesiphon
A B C D E F
1 2 3 4

Palestine in New Testament Times
Political boundaries A.D. 6-44
Cities of the Decapolis
Fortresses
0 10 20 30 40 Mls
0 20 40 60 Kms
© Copyright HAMMOND INCORPORATED, Maplewood, N. J.
A
B
C
D
1
2
3
4
5
6
Sidon
Sarepta
Tyre
Ladder of Tyre
Ecdippa
Ptolemais
Phoenicia
MT. LEBANON
MT. HERMON
Leontes
ABILENE
Abila
Ituraea
SYRIA
Damascus
Panias
Caesarea Philippi (Panias)
Ulatha
Gaulanitis
Batanea
Raphana
Cedasa
Gischala
Chorazin
Bethsaida-Julias
GALILEE
Capernaum
Cana
Magadan
Sea of Galilee
Asochis
Tiberias
Hippos
Sepphoris
Dion?
Yarmuk
Abila
Mt. Carmel
Mediterranean Sea
Nazareth
Plain of Esdraelon
Mt. Tabor
Gadara
Nain
Capitolias
Dora
Agrippina
Arbela
Caesarea
Scythopolis
DECAPOLIS
Pella
Narbata
Ginaea
Salim
Aenon
Jordan
SAMARIA
Gerasa
Sebaste (Samaria)
Plain of Sharon
Amathus
Neapolis
Mt. Ebal
Mt. Gerizim
Sychar
Jabbok
Apollonia
Antipatris
Alexandrium
Joppa
Arimathea?
Phasaelis
Gadara
PEREA
Philadelphia
Ephraim
Lydda
Gophna
Archelais
Jericho
Betharamphtha (Livias, Julias)
Jamnia
Emmaus (Nicopolis)
Cyprus
Emmaus?
Esbus
Azotus
Jerusalem
Bethany
Qumrân
Medeba
Bethlehem
Hyrcania
Ascalon
JUDEA
Herodium
Marisa
Bethsura
Callirhoe
Machaerus
Agrippias
Hebron
Gaza
Engaddi
Lake Asphaltitis (Dead Sea)
Arnon
NABATEA
Masada
IDUMEA
Areopolis
Bersabee
Malatha
Charachmoba

MAP XVIII

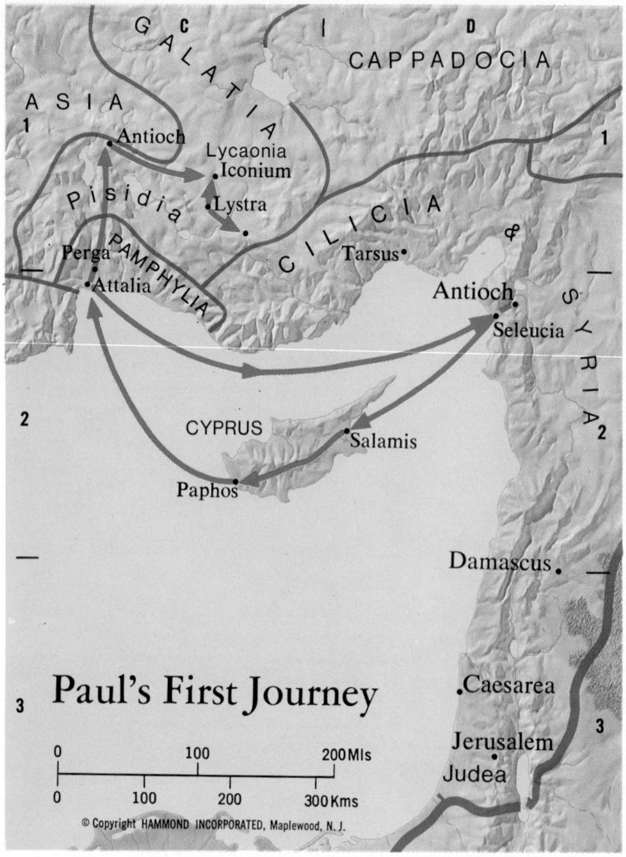

This division of Paul's travels into three round-trip journeys based in Antioch of Syria has been a convenient tradition for Bible study. There is no evidence, however, that Paul thought of his travels according to this geographical pattern. In fact, on the "second journey" Paul spent most of his time at Corinth (eighteen months), and on the "third journey" Ephesus was the base for most of his missionary activity (three years). *See* PAUL APOSTLE VII.F, G.

MAP XIX

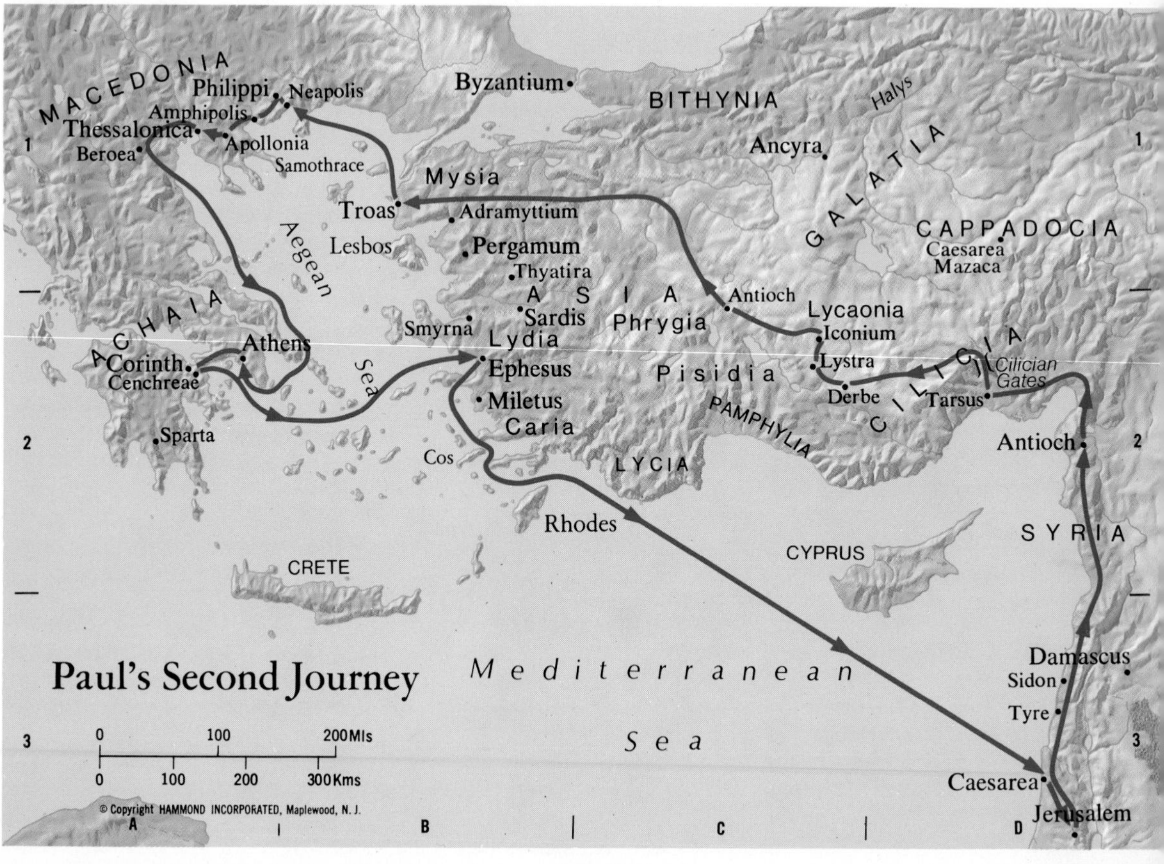

MAP XX

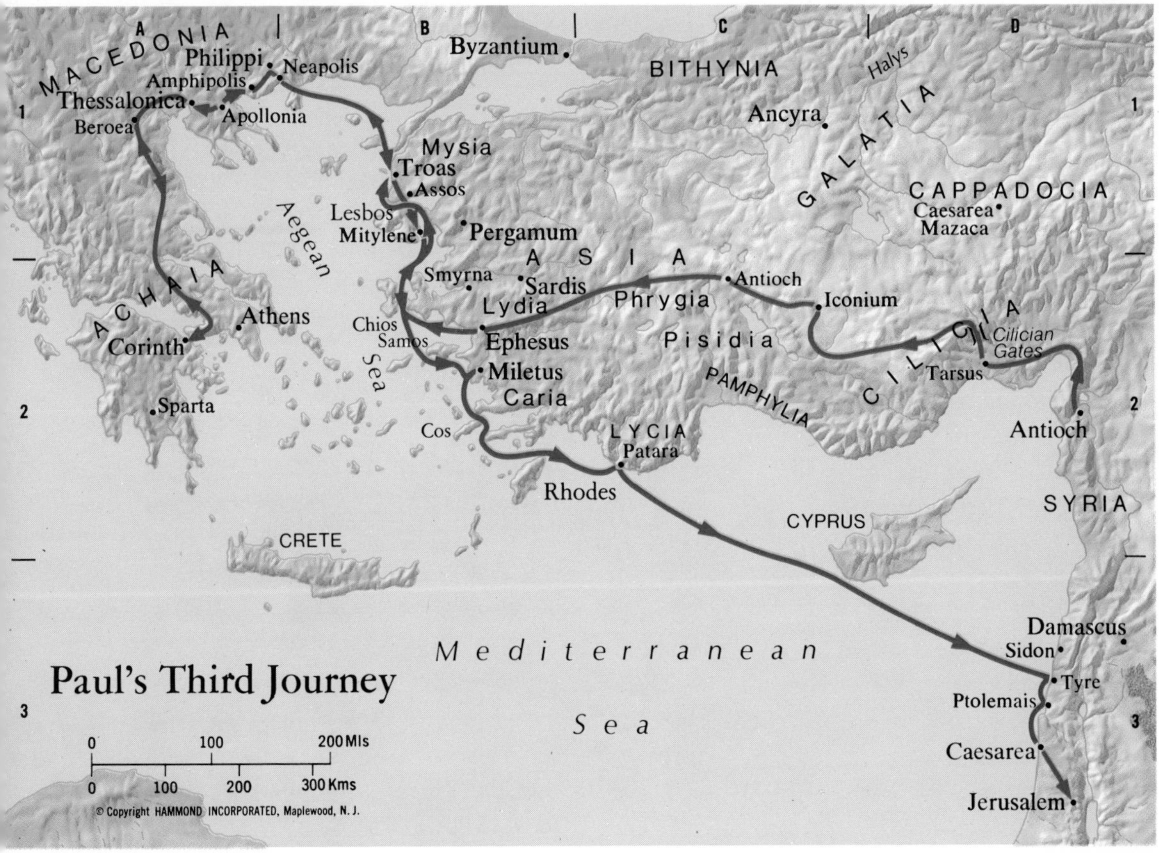

MAP XXI

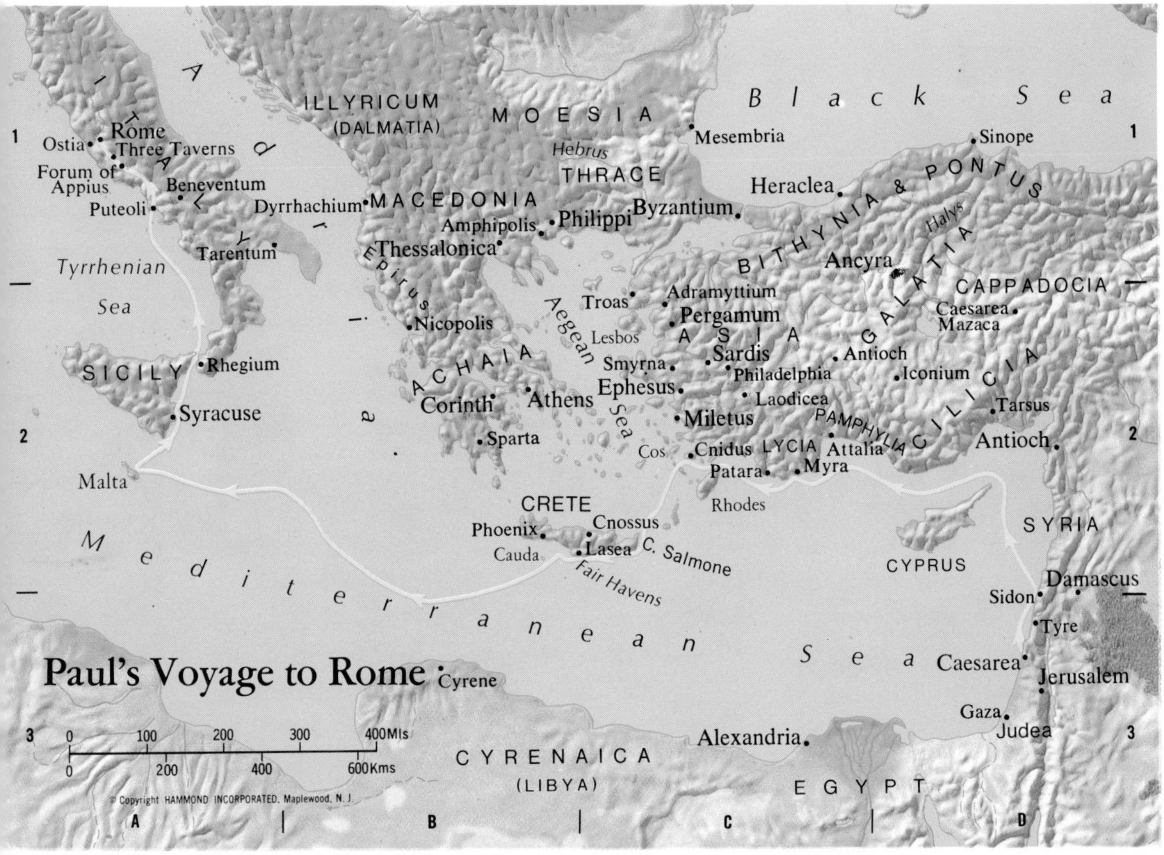

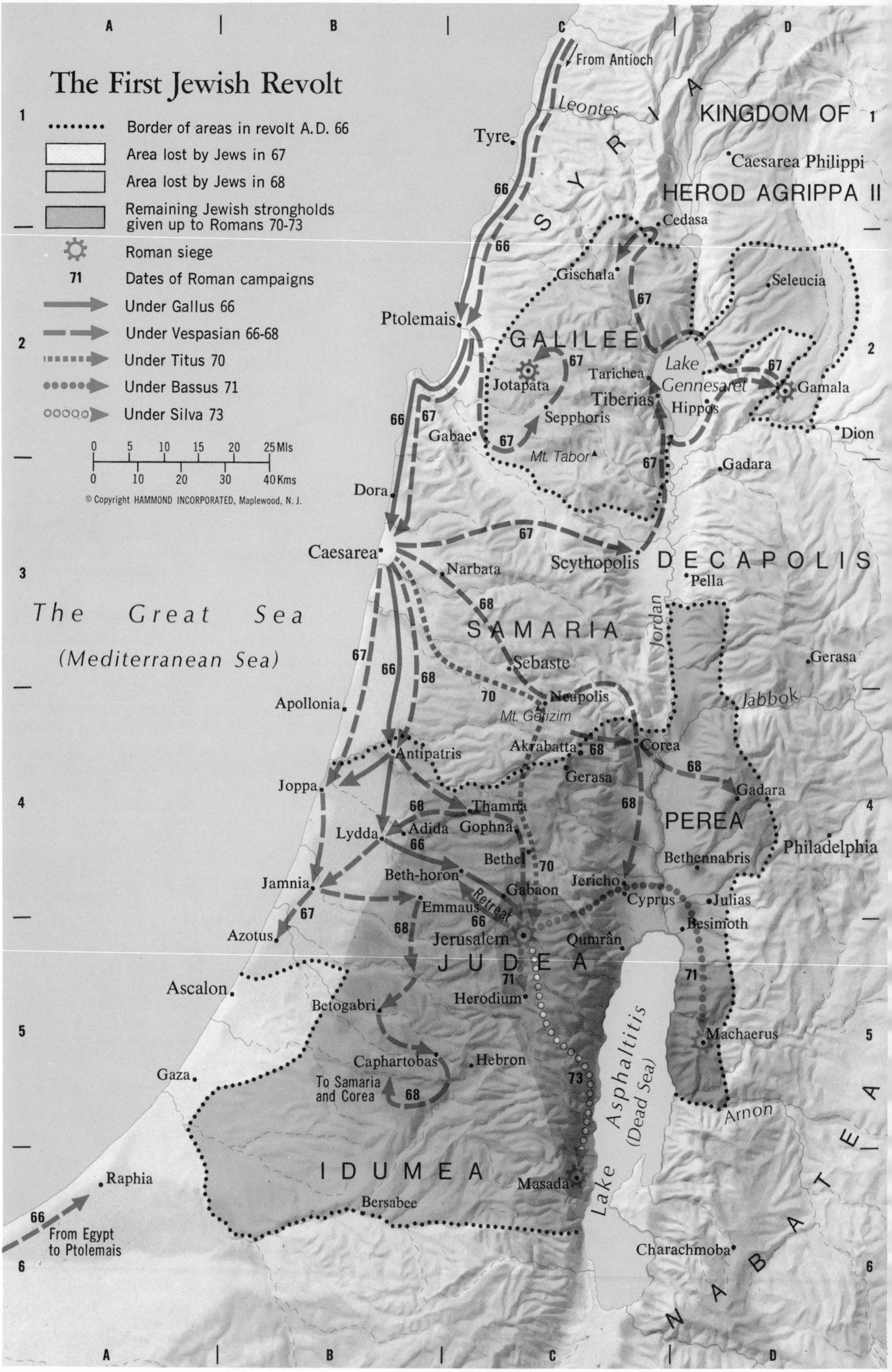
The First Jewish Revolt
Border of areas in revolt A.D. 66
Area lost by Jews in 67
Area lost by Jews in 68
Remaining Jewish strongholds given up to Romans 70-73
Roman siege
71 Dates of Roman campaigns
Under Gallus 66
Under Vespasian 66-68
Under Titus 70
Under Bassus 71
Under Silva 73
0 5 10 15 20 25 Mls
0 10 20 30 40 Kms
© Copyright HAMMOND INCORPORATED, Maplewood, N. J.
A B C D
1 2 3 4 5 6
From Antioch
Leontes
SYRIA
KINGDOM OF HEROD AGRIPPA II
Tyre
Caesarea Philippi
Cedasa
Gischala
Seleucia
Ptolemais
GALILEE
Jotapata
Sepphoris
Tarichea
Tiberias
Lake Gennesaret
Hippos
Gamala
Dion
Gabae
Mt. Tabor
Gadara
Dora
Caesarea
Narbata
Scythopolis
DECAPOLIS
Pella
Jordan
The Great Sea
(Mediterranean Sea)
SAMARIA
Sebaste
Gerasa
Apollonia
Neapolis
Mt. Gerizim
Jabbok
Antipatris
Akrabatta
Corea
Joppa
Gerasa
Gadara
Thamna
PEREA
Lydda
Adida
Gophna
Philadelphia
Bethel
Bethennabris
Jamnia
Beth-horon
Gabaon
Jericho
Emmaus
Retreat
Cyprus
Julias
Azotus
Jerusalem
Qumrân
Besimoth
JUDEA
Ascalon
Betogabri
Herodium
Asphaltitis (Dead Sea)
Machaerus
Caphartobas
Hebron
Gaza
To Samaria and Corea
Arnon
IDUMEA
Raphia
Masada
Lake
Bersabee
From Egypt to Ptolemais
Charachmoba
NABATEA
66 67 68 70 71 73

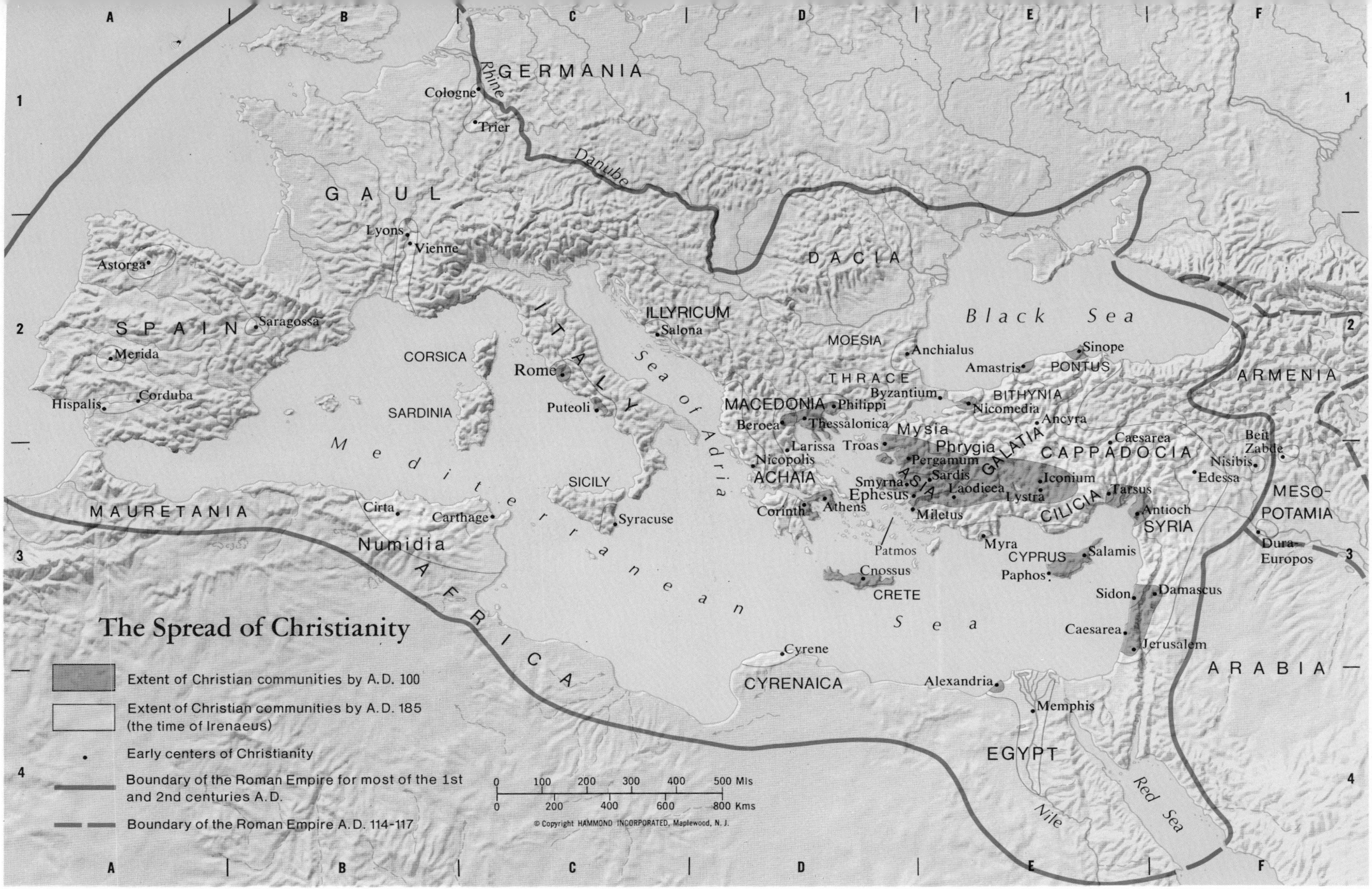
The Spread of Christianity
Extent of Christian communities by A.D. 100
Extent of Christian communities by A.D. 185 (the time of Irenaeus)
Early centers of Christianity
Boundary of the Roman Empire for most of the 1st and 2nd centuries A.D.
Boundary of the Roman Empire A.D. 114-117
0 100 200 300 400 500 Mls
0 200 400 600 800 Kms
© Copyright HAMMOND INCORPORATED, Maplewood, N. J.
GERMANIA
Rhine
Cologne
Trier
Danube
GAUL
Lyons
Vienne
Astorga
SPAIN
Saragossa
Merida
Corduba
Hispalis
CORSICA
SARDINIA
ITALY
Rome
Puteoli
SICILY
Syracuse
ILLYRICUM
Salona
Sea of Adria
DACIA
MOESIA
THRACE
MACEDONIA
Philippi
Thessalonica
Beroea
Larissa
Nicopolis
ACHAIA
Corinth
Athens
Byzantium
Anchialus
Black Sea
Amastris
Sinope
PONTUS
BITHYNIA
Nicomedia
Ancyra
Mysia
Troas
Phrygia
Pergamum
ASIA
Smyrna
Sardis
Ephesus
Miletus
Laodicea
GALATIA
CAPPADOCIA
Caesarea
Iconium
Lystra
CILICIA
Tarsus
Antioch
SYRIA
Patmos
Myra
CYPRUS
Salamis
Paphos
Cnossus
CRETE
Sidon
Damascus
Caesarea
Jerusalem
ARMENIA
Beit Zabde
Nisibis
Edessa
MESO-POTAMIA
Dura-Europos
ARABIA
MAURETANIA
Cirta
Carthage
Numidia
AFRICA
Mediterranean Sea
Cyrene
CYRENAICA
Alexandria
Memphis
EGYPT
Nile
Red Sea
A B C D E F
1 2 3 4

MAP XXIV

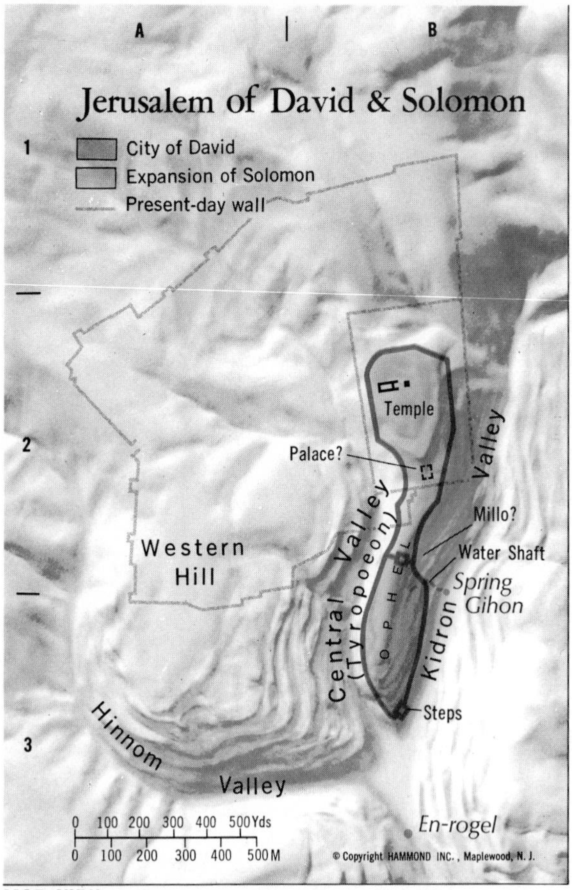

A
B
Jerusalem of David & Solomon
City of David
Expansion of Solomon
Present-day wall
1
2
3
Temple
Palace?
Valley
Millo?
Water Shaft
Western
Hill
Central Valley
(Tyropoeon)
OPHEL
Spring
Gihon
Kidron
Steps
Hinnom
Valley
0 100 200 300 400 500 Yds
0 100 200 300 400 500 M
En-rogel
© Copyright HAMMOND INC., Maplewood, N. J.

MAP XXV

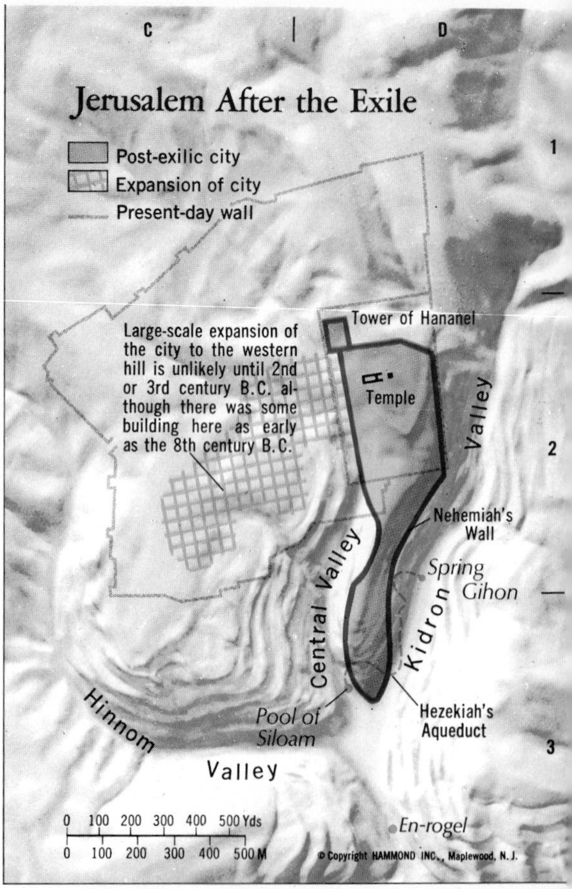

C
D
Jerusalem After the Exile
Post-exilic city
Expansion of city
Present-day wall
1
2
3
Large-scale expansion of the city to the western hill is unlikely until 2nd or 3rd century B.C. although there was some building here as early as the 8th century B.C.
Tower of Hananel
Temple
Valley
Nehemiah's Wall
Spring
Gihon
Central Valley
Kidron
Hinnom
Pool of Siloam
Hezekiah's Aqueduct
Valley
0 100 200 300 400 500 Yds
0 100 200 300 400 500 M
En-rogel
© Copyright HAMMOND INC., Maplewood, N. J.

MAP XXVI

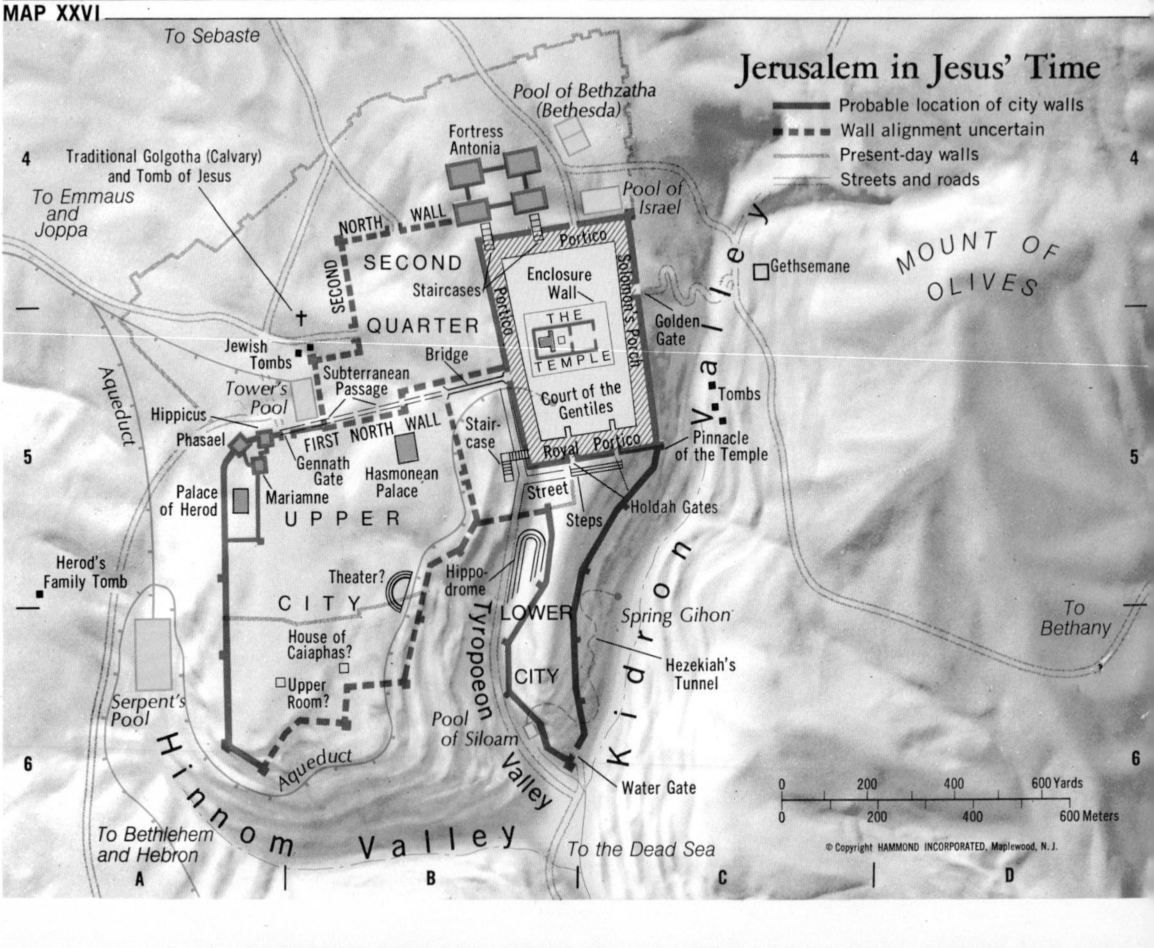

To Sebaste
Jerusalem in Jesus' Time
Probable location of city walls
Wall alignment uncertain
Present-day walls
Streets and roads
Pool of Bethzatha
(Bethesda)
Fortress
Antonia
4
5
6
Traditional Golgotha (Calvary)
and Tomb of Jesus
To Emmaus
and
Joppa
Pool of
Israel
NORTH
WALL
Portico
SECOND
SECOND
QUARTER
Staircases
Enclosure
Wall
Portico
Solomon's Porch
Gethsemane
MOUNT OF
OLIVES
Golden
Gate
THE
TEMPLE
Jewish
Tombs
Bridge
Subterranean
Passage
Court of the
Gentiles
Tombs
Aqueduct
Tower's
Pool
Hippicus
Phasael
FIRST NORTH WALL
Gennath
Gate
Hasmonean
Palace
Stair-
case
Royal
Portico
Pinnacle
of the Temple
Palace
of Herod
Mariamne
UPPER
Street
Steps
Holdah Gates
Herod's
Family Tomb
Theater?
Hippo-
drome
CITY
Tyropoeon
LOWER
Spring Gihon
To
Bethany
House of
Caiaphas?
Upper
Room?
CITY
Hezekiah's
Tunnel
Kidron
Valley
Serpent's
Pool
Pool
of Siloam
Hinnom
Aqueduct
Valley
Water Gate
0 200 400 600 Yards
0 200 400 600 Meters
To Bethlehem
and Hebron
Valley
To the Dead Sea
© Copyright HAMMOND INCORPORATED, Maplewood, N. J.
A
B
C
D